February 4–8, 2013
Rome, Italy

Association for
Computing Machinery

Advancing Computing as a Science & Profession

Proceedings of the 6th ACM International Conference on

Web Search and Data Mining

Sponsored by:

ACM SIGIR, ACM SIGMOD, ACM SIGWEB, and ACM SIGKDD

Supported by:

BiCi, Yandex, Sapienza-Università di Roma, Google, Microsoft Research, Facebook , and Yahoo! Labs,

Association for
Computing Machinery

Advancing Computing as a Science & Profession

The Association for Computing Machinery
2 Penn Plaza, Suite 701
New York, New York 10121-0701

ISBN: 978-1-4503-1869-3 (Digital)

ISBN: 978-1-4503-2088-7 (Print)

Additional copies may be ordered prepaid from:

ACM Order Department
PO Box 30777
New York, NY 10087-0777, USA

Phone: 1-800-342-6626 (USA and Canada)
+1-212-626-0500 (Global)
Fax: +1-212-944-1318
E-mail: acmhelp@acm.org
Hours of Operation: 8:30 am – 4:30 pm ET

Printed in the USA

Foreword from the WSDM'13 General Chairs

On behalf of the Organizing Committee, we would like to extend a warm welcome to the Sixth ACM International Conference on Web Search and Data Mining (WSDM 2012), held in Rome, Italy, February 4-8, 2013. WSDM (pronounced "wisdom") is one of the premier annual international ACM conference for presenting cutting edge research in the fields of web (re)search and data mining. We expect the 2013 edition to be, like previous editions, a thriving melting pot at the crossroads of academic and industrial research.

Following the successes of previous editions in Stanford, California, USA (WSDM 2008), Barcelona, Spain (WSDM 2009), New York, New York, USA (WSDM 2010), Hong Kong, The People's Republic of China (WSDM 2011), and Seattle, WA, USA, Rome, the Eternal City, was the chosen venue for 2013.

Thanks to the efforts of the program committee, with Aris Gionis and Paolo Ferragina at the helm, an excellent technical program has been assembled that unfolds across three days. The conference itself is complemented by a suite of very interesting tutorials and workshops – fourteen in total! – on timely and challenging topics, taking place during the previous two days. The doctoral consortium, a data challenge and an "unconventional" workshop on issues of gender and diversity provide the finishing touches to a very rich and interesting week of events. We owe a debt of gratitude to the colleagues who put together such a wonderful set of options.

In keeping with previous instances of WSDM, the main conference itself is three days, single track, and consists primarily of paper presentations with three keynote lectures. 33 papers will be presented in traditional, full-length plenary sessions, and 40 will be presented via shorter spotlight presentations.

Organizing a conference requires a lot of time and effort. We would like to thank all the members of the Organizing Committee for their dedication and hard work: Aris Anagnostopoulos, Ricardo Baeza-Yates, Luca Becchetti, Paolo Boldi, Flavio Chierichetti, Fabrizio Silvestri, Tamir Tassa and Sebastiano Vigna. Sabrina Giampaoletti and Gisella Penazzi provided invaluable help for a variety of issues, from financial bookkeeping to creative art design. The Steering Committee provided as usual "WSDM" and guidance.

Special thanks to the financial supporters of WSDM 2013: BiCi, Bertinoro International Center for Informatics, Facebook, Google, Microsoft Research, Sapienza, University of Rome, Yandex, and Yahoo! Research. We also thank the sponsors SIGIR, SIGKDD, SIGMOD, SIGWEB, and ACM.

Once again, we welcome you to WSDM 2013, and wish you a stimulating, productive, and fruitful experience in Rome!

Stefano Leonardi and Alessandro Panconesi
General Chairs

Welcome from the Program Chairs

We are delighted to welcome you to the sixth ACM International Conference on Web Search and Data Mining (WSDM 2013) held on February 4–8, 2013, in Rome, Italy. As in the previous years, WSDM has attracted an impressive number of submissions tackling the most recent technical challenges in Web search and data mining, with an ever-growing interest in their social aspects. Now in its sixth year, the conference has reached maturity and has become a leading forum for disseminating the latest research developments in the field. We are happy to present here the proceedings of the conference.

We received a total of 387 submissions (compared to 362 of the last year) from 36 countries and regions, out of which 73 were accepted for full paper publication in the proceedings, thus reaching an acceptance rate of 18.9% (compared to 20.7% of last year, and 22.3% of two years ago). The authors of the accepted papers are from 20 countries, spanning four continents – making this a truly international forum. Oral presentation slots were allocated to all papers. Yet, in order to maintain the single-track model that most attendees prefer, we preserved this year the format with "spotlight" type and "plenary" type presentations. Out of the 73 accepted papers, 40 were assigned a "spotlight" slot, while 33 were assigned a plenary slot. The type of slot was chosen by the Program Chairs, mostly based on whether the topic and the content of the paper were best suited for a large group presentation or for a more focused and interactive "spotlight" style of presentation.

We would like to acknowledge the tremendous work of the 187 members of the international Program Committee (representing 25 countries), of the 190 additional external reviewers, and in particular the effort of the 26 Senior PC members. They should all be credited for the high quality of the program this year. We would also like to thank the general Conference Chairs, Stefano Leonardi and Alessandro Panconesi, who were wonderful partners in getting this program together.

Finally, we are in debt to the authors and attendees, who are the ones who make this conference possible and have allowed WSDM to become a wonderful forum to advance Web research and the premier ACM conference in the field. We hope that you will find this program interesting and thought-provoking. Our goal was not only to give you the opportunity to share ideas with other researchers and practitioners from around the world, but also to foster new research and innovation in this fascinating Web era.

Paolo Ferragina
Program co-chair
University of Pisa
Pisa, Italy
http://www.di.unipi.it/~ferragin/

Aristides Gionis
Program co-chair
Yahoo! Research
Barcelona, Spain
http://research.yahoo.com/Aris_Gionis

Table of Contents

Session 3 (long): Large-scale Data and Social Networks

Keynote Address

Best Paper Award

Session 4 (long): Web and Usage Mining

Session 5 (short): Web Mining, Prediction, and Recommendation

Session 6 (long): Learning and Modeling

Keynote Address

Best Student Paper Award

Session 7 (long): Social Media

Session 8 (short): Mining of Web and Social Data

Session 9 (long): Search

Doctoral Consortium

Abstracts, Workshops, Etc.

WSDM 2013 Organization

General Chairs: Stefano Leonardi, Sapienza University of Rome, Italy
Alessandro Panconesi, Sapienza University of Rome, Italy

Program Chairs: Paolo Ferragina, University of Pisa, Italy
Aristides Gionis, Yahoo! Research, Barcelona, Spain

Local Chairs: Aris Anagnostopoulos, Sapienza University of Rome, Italy
Flavio Chierichetti, Cornell University, USA

Publicity Chair and Web Presence: Aris Anagnostopoulos, Sapienza University of Rome, Italy

Treasurer and Registration Chair: Luca Becchetti, Sapienza University of Rome, Italy

Sponsor Chair: Alessandro Panconesi, Sapienza University of Rome, Italy

Proceedings Chair: Fabrizio Silvestri, ISTI CNR, Pisa, Italy

Tutorial Chair: Paolo Boldi, University of Milan, Italy

Data Challenge Chairs: Paolo Boldi, University of Milan, Italy
Tamir Tassa, The Open University of Israel

Workshop Chair: Sebastiano Vigna, University of Milan, Italy

Doctoral Consortium Chairs: Ricardo Baeza-Yates, Yahoo! Research, Barcelona, Spain
Fabrizio Silvestri, ISTI CNR, Pisa, Italy

Steering Committee: Rakesh Agrawal, Microsoft, USA
Ricardo Baeza-Yates,Yahoo! Research, Barcelona, Spain
Ziv Bar-Yossef, Technion, Google, Israel
Soumen Chakrabarti, IIT Bombay, India
Monika Henzinger, EPFL, Google, Switzerland
Jon Kleinberg, Cornell University, USA
Marc Najork, Microsoft, USA

Senior Program Committee:

Deepak Agarwal, Yahoo! Research, USA
Aris Anagnostopoulos, Sapienza University of Rome, Italy
Arindam Banerjee, University of Minnesota, USA
Roberto Bayardo, Google, USA
Klaus Berberich, MPI fur Informatik, Germany
Soumen Chakrabarti, IIT Bombay, India
Xueqi Cheng, Chinese Academy of Sciences, China
Massimiliano Ciaramita, Google, Switzerland
Antonio Gulli, Microsoft, UK
Monika Henzinger, University of Vienna, Austria
Yehuda Koren, Yahoo! Research, Israel
Nick Koudas, University of Toronto, Canada
Silvio Lattanzi, Google, USA
Kristen Lefevre, University of Michigan, USA
Hang Li, Microsoft Research, China
Amelie Marian, Rutgers University, USA
Michael Mitzenmacher, Harvard University, USA
Kamesh Munagala, Duke University, USA
Jennifer Neville, Purdue University, USA
Rina Panigrahy, Microsoft Research, USA
Filip Radlinski, Microsoft Research, UK
Luo Si, Purdue University, USA
Sergei Vassilvitskii, Yahoo! Research, USA
Sebastiano Vigna, University of Milan, Italy
Qiang Yang, The Hong Kong University of Science and Technology
Cheng Zhai, University of Illinois at Urbana-Champaign, USA

WSDM 2013 Program Committee

Lada Adamic, University of Michigan
Eytan Adar, University of Washington
Luca Aiello, Yahoo! Research
Enrique Alfonseca, Google
James Allan, University of Massachusetts, Amherst
Ismail Sengor Altingovde, L3S Research Center
Krisztian Balog, Norwegian University of Science and Technology
Ziv Bar-Yossef, Technion - Israel Institute of Technology & Google Haifa
Hannah Bast, University of Freiburg
Luca Becchetti, Sapienza University of Rome
Behshad Behzadi, Google Inc.
Ron Bekkerman, Linked-in
Andras A. Benczur, Hungarian Academy of Sciences
Michael Bendersky, University of Massachusetts, Amherst
Paul Bennett, Microsoft Research
Elisa Bertino, Purdue University
Arnab Bhattacharya, Indian Institute of Technology, Kanpur
Mikhail Bilenko, Microsoft Research
Roi Blanco, Yahoo! Research
Francesco Bonchi, Yahoo! Research
Ilaria Bordino, Yahoo! Research
Edward Bortnikov, Yahoo! Research
Ulf Brefeld, University of Bonn
John Byers, Boston University
Michael Cafarella, University of Michigan
Jamie Callan, Carnegie Mellon University
B. Barla Cambazoglu, Yahoo! Research
Guihong Cao, Bing
Claudio Carpineto, Fondazione Ugo Bordoni
Carlos Castillo, Yahoo! Research
Augustin Chaintreau, Columbia University
Yi Chang, Yahoo! Labs
Edgar Chavez, Universidad Michoacana
Nitesh V. Chawla, University of Notre Dame
Weizhu Chen, Microsoft Research Asia
Hsin-Hsi Chen, National Taiwan University
Wei Chen, Microsoft Research Asia
Nick Craswell, Microsoft
Fabio Crestani, University of Lugano
Bruce Croft, University of Massachusetts Amherst
Gautam Das, University of Texas at Arlington, USA & QCRI, Doha, Qatar
Anish Das Sarma, Stanford University
Anirban Dasgupta, Yahoo! Research
Brian Davison, Lehigh University
Gianmarco De Francisci Morales, IMT Institute for Advanced Studies Lucca
Edleno Silva De Moura, Universidade Federal do Amazonas
Arjen De Vries, Centrum Wiskunde & Informatica
Alberto Delbimbo, University of Florence
Hongbo Deng, University of Illinois at Urbana-Champaign
Shuai Ding, Polytechnic Institue of NYU
Gideon Dror, The Academic College of Tel-Aviv-Yaffo
Susan Dumais, Microsoft Research
George Dupret, Yahoo! Research
Tina Eliassi-Rad, Rutgers University
Ariel Fuxman, Microsoft Research
Evgeniy Gabrilovich, Yahoo! Research
Fosca Giannotti, ISTI-CNR
David Gleich, Purdue University
Sharad Goel, Yahoo! Research
Nazli Goharian, Georgetown University
Sreenivas Gollapudi, Microsoft Research
Manuel Gomez Rodriguez, Stanford University / MPI for Biological Cybernetics
Marco Gori, Dipartimento di Ingegneria dell'Informazione, Universita di Siena
Gregory Grefenstette, EXALEAD
Francesco Gullo, Yahoo! Research
Dimitrios Gunopulos, University of Athens

Jiafeng Guo, Chinese Academy of Sciences
Maxim Gurevich, Google
Jiawei Han, University of Illinois at Urbana-Champaign
Djoerd Hiemstra, University of Twente
Katja Hofmann, ISLA, University of Amsterdam
Andreas Hotho, University of Wuerzburg
Vagelis Hristidis, University of California, Riverside
Jane Hsu, National Taiwan University
Samuel Ieong, Microsoft Research
Alejandro Jaimes, Yahoo! Research
Shen Jialie, Singapore Management University
Jing Jiang, Singapore Management University
Vanja Josifovski, Yahoo! Research
Jaap Kamps, University of Amsterdam
Evangelos Kanoulas, Google
Alexandros Karatzoglou, Telefonica Research
Krishnaram Kenthapadi, Microsoft Research
Irwin King, The Chinese University of Hong Kong
George Kollios, Boston University
Nitish Korula, Google Research, New York
Georgia Koutrika, HP Labs
Peer Kröger, Ludwig-Maximilians-Universität München
Ravi Kumar, Yahoo! Research
Oren Kurland, Technion, Israel Institute of Technology
Arnd Christian König, Microsoft Research
Laks Lakshmanan, University of British Columbia
Mounia Lalmas, Yahoo Research Barcelona
Theodoros Lappas, Boston University
Daniel Lemire, Université du Québec à Montréal
Ronny Lempel, Yahoo! Research
Lihong Li, Yahoo! Research
Juanzi Li, Tsinghua University
Edo Liberty, Yale University
Ee-Peng Lim, Singapore Management University
Yu-Ru Lin, Arizona State University
Yan Liu, University of Southern California
Huan Liu, Professor, Arizona State University
Bing Liu, University of Illinois at Chicago
Chao Liu, Microsoft Research
Bo Long, Yahoo! Research
Hao Ma, Microsoft Research
Yoelle Maarek, Yahoo! Research
Michael Mahoney, Stanford University
Mark Manasse, Microsoft Research
Winter Mason, Stevens Institute of Technology
Yutaka Matsuo, University of Tokyo
Edgar Meij, University of Amsterdam
Massimo Melucci, University of Padua
Donald Metzler, University of Southern California
Peter Mika, Yahoo! Research
Vahab Mirrokni, Google Research
Alan Mislove, Northeastern University
Alistair Moffat, University of Melbourne
Vanessa Murdock, Yahoo! Research
Roberto Navigli, Sapienza Universitá di Roma
Hamid Nazerzadeh, USC Marshall School of Business
Wolfgang Nejdl, L3S and University of Hannover
Raymond Ng, University of British Columbia
Iadh Ounis, University of Glasgow
Rasmus Pagh, IT University of Copenhagen
Themis Palpanas, University of Trento
Spiros Papadimitriou, IBM Research
Stelios Paparizos, Microsoft Research
Dmitry Pavlov, Yandex
Jian Pei, Simon Fraser University
Dan Pelleg, Yahoo! Research
Evaggelia Pitoura, Univ. of Ioannina
Benjamin Piwowarski, University of Glasgow
Justin Rao, Microsoft Research
Chandan K. Reddy, Wayne State University
Giuseppe Riccardi, Universit di Trento
Matthew Richardson, Microsoft Research
Tetsuya Sakai, Microsoft Research Asia
Giovanni Semeraro, University of Bari
Pavel Serdyukov, Yandex
Huawei Shen, Chinese Academy of Sciences

Milad Shokouhi, Microsoft Research
Fabrizio Silvestri, ISTI - CNR
Vikas Sindhwani, IBM Research
Yaron Singer, University of California, Berkeley
Mauro Sozio, Telecom ParisTech
Fabian M. Suchanek, INRIA Saclay
Torsten Suel, Polytechnic Institue of NYU
Idan Szpektor, Yahoo!
Domenico Talia, University of Calabria
Katsumi Tanaka, Kyoto University
Jie Tang, Tsinghua University
Evimaria Terzi, Boston University
Martin Theobald, Max Planck Institute for Informatics
Paul Thomas, CSIRO
Andrew Tomkins, Yahoo! Research
Hanghang Tong, Carnegie Mellon University
Panayiotis Tsaparas, University of Ioannina
Antti Ukkonen, Yahoo! Research
Eli Upfal, Brown University
Andrea Vattani, University of California, San Diego
Petros Venetis, Stanford University
Rossano Venturini, ISTI-CNR
Vishwa Vinay, Microsoft Research Cambridge
Haixun Wang, Microsoft Research Asia
Jun Wang, University College London
Haifeng Wang, Baidu Inc.
Ingmar Weber, QCRI, Doha, Qatar
Xing Xie, Microsoft Research Asia
Lexing Xie, Australian National University
Hui Xiong, Rutgers University
Jun Xu, Microsoft Research Aisa
Rong Yan, Facebook
Hui Yang, Georgetown University
Emine Yilmaz, Microsoft Research Cambridge
Philip Yu, UI Chicago
Cong Yu, Google Research
Yisong Yue, Carnegie Mellon University
Giorgos Zervas, Yale University
Kun Zhang, University of Tuebingen
Ben Zhao, University of California, Santa Barbara
Elena Zheleva, University of Maryland, College Park
Yu Zheng, independent
Xingquan Zhu, University of Technology, Sydney

WSDM 2013 Additional Reviewers

Mohammad Abbasi
Zeinab Abbassi
Jussara Almeida
Rajul Anand
Anastasios Arvanitis
Andrew Bagdanov
Lamberto Ballan
Nicola Barbieri
Pierpaolo Basile
Florian Bäurle
Jennifer Bayzick
Martin Becker
Richard Berendsen
Michele Berlingerio
Klessius Berlt
Ron Berman
Sebastian Blohm
Arkady Borkovsky
Leonid Boytsov
Marc Bron
Cliff Brunk
Björn Buchhold
Suratna Budalakoti
Bin Cao
Nan Cao
Annalina Caputo
Mark Carman
Marc Cartright
Diego Ceccarelli
Tony Chan
Shiwen Cheng
Zhiyong Cheng
Shouyuan Chen
Tony Chen
Yinpeng Chen
Freddy Chong Tat Chua
Michele Coscia
Lorenzo Coviello
Marco Cristo
Cheyun Dai
Gianpaolo D'Amico
Maarten de Rijke
Engin Demir
Milad Eftekhar
Dora Erdos
Lujun Fang
Stefano Faralli
Henry Feild
Zhuo Feng
David Fernandes
Barbara Furletti
Huiji Gao
Marco de Gemmis
Shima Gerani
Nico Goernitz
Behzad Golshan
Angshuman Guha
Andrey Gulin
Pritam Gundech
Ancsa Hannak
Morgan Harvey
Elmar Haußmann
Jiyin He
Dzung Hong
Liangjie Hong
Lei Hou
Yoshiyuki Inagaki
Giacomo Inches
Mohsen Jamali
Adam Jatowt
Xiaolong Jin
Rongrong Ji
Svebor Karaman
Maryam Karimzadehgan
Abhijith Kashyap
Makoto P. Kato
Enver Kayaaslan
Mostafa Keikha
Yubin Kim
Marius Kloft
Dimitrios Kotsakos
Anagha Kulkarni
Abhishek Kumar
Shamanth Kuma
John Labiak
Monica Landoni
Pei Lee
Michael Levin
Shangsong Liang
Baichuan Li
Guang Ling
Ping Li
Giuseppe Lisanti
Matteo Lissandrini
Bin Liu
Chuanren Liu
Jialu Liu
Qi Liu
Yandong Liu
Zhixing Li
Dionysios Logothetis
Daniel Lokshtanov
Pasquale Lops
Brendan Lucier
Yue Lu
Giuseppe Manco
Ilya Markov
Gaurav Misra
Anna Monreale
Andrea Moro
Fred Morstatter
Davide Mottin
Arjun Mukherjee
Cataldo Musto
Franco Maria Nardini
Fedelucio Narducci
Matti Nelimarkka
Thomas Niebler
Chikashi Nobata
Daan Odijk
Hiroaki Ohshima
Rifat Ozcan
Junfeng Pan
Luca Pappalardo
Aditya Parameswaran
Maria-Hendrike Peetz
Diego Pennacchioli
Simone Paolo Ponzetto
Meng Qu
Vineeth Rakesh
Xiang Ren
Daniel Ricketts

Matteo Riondato
Giulio Rossetti
Afshin Rostamizadeh
Natali Ruchansky
Eduardo Ruiz
Ankan Saha
Anne Schuth
Lior Seeman
Aparna Seetharaman
Lorenzo Seidenari
Lei Shi
Yue Shi
Jianfeng Si
Marc Sloan
Evgeny Stepanov
Karthik Subbian
Hongyu Su
Umar Syed
Kosetsu Tsukuda
Mikalai Tsytsarau
Shikui Tu
George Valkanas
Bo Waggoner
Chong Wang
Hongning Wang
Jingjing Wang
Xuanhui Wang
Yajun Wang
Zhigang Wang
William West
Matthew Wiley
Fei Wu
Le Wu
Guang Xiang
Min Xie
Takehiro Yamamoto
Yusuke Yamamoto
Feng Yan
Haiqin Yang
Yang Yang
Zaihan Yang
Zhepeng Yan
Mao Ye
Shuai Yuan
Xiao Yu
Morteza Zadimoghaddam
Hongyi Zhang
Weinan Zhang
Yuchen Zhang
Bo Zhao
Le Zhao
Shenglin Zhao
Xiaohan Zhao
Tom Chao Zhou
Jun Zhu

WSDM 2013 Sponsors & Supporters

Sponsors:

Supporters:

The Virtual Lab

Duncan J. Watts
Microsoft Research
102 Madison Avenue, 12th Floor
New York, NY 10016
duncan@microsoft.com

ABSTRACT

The Internet and the Web have transformed society, spawning new industries, altering social and cultural practices, and challenging long-accepted notions of individual privacy, intellectual property, and national security. In this talk, I argue that social science is also being transformed. In particular, I describe how crowd sourcing sites like Amazon's Mechanical Turk are increasingly being used by researchers to create "virtual labs" in which they can conduct behavioral experiments on a scale and speed that would have been hard to imagine just a decade ago. To illustrate the point, I describe some recent experiments that showcase the advantages of virtual over traditional physical labs, as well as some of the limitations. I then discuss how this relatively new experimental capability may unfold in the near future, along with some implications for social and behavioral science.

Categories and Subject Descriptors
H.1.2 User/Machine Systems, Human factors, Human information processing

General Terms
Economics, Experimentation, Human Factors

Keywords
Online Experimental Social Science

WSDM'13, February 4–8, 2013, Rome, Italy.
ACM 978-1-4503-1869-3/13/02.

Information-Theoretic Measures of Influence Based on Content Dynamics

Greg Ver Steeg
Information Sciences Institute
University of Southern California
Marina del Rey, California
gregv@isi.edu

Aram Galstyan
Information Sciences Institute
University of Southern California
Marina del Rey, California
galstyan@isi.edu

ABSTRACT

The fundamental building block of social influence is for one person to elicit a response in another. Researchers measuring a "response" in social media typically depend either on detailed models of human behavior or on platform-specific cues such as re-tweets, hash tags, URLs, or mentions. Most content on social networks is difficult to model because the modes and motivation of human expression are diverse and incompletely understood. We introduce *content transfer*, an information-theoretic measure with a predictive interpretation that directly quantifies the strength of the effect of one user's content on another's in a model-free way. Estimating this measure is made possible by combining recent advances in non-parametric entropy estimation with increasingly sophisticated tools for content representation. We demonstrate on Twitter data collected for thousands of users that content transfer is able to capture non-trivial, predictive relationships even for pairs of users not linked in the follower or mention graph. We suggest that this measure makes large quantities of previously under-utilized social media content accessible to rigorous statistical causal analysis.

Categories and Subject Descriptors

H.1.1 [**Systems and Information Theory**]: Information Theory; H.3.4 [**Systems and Software**]: Information networks; J.4 [**Social and Behavioral Sciences**]: Sociology

Keywords

influence; social networks; entropy; causality

1. INTRODUCTION

While the emergence of various online social networking platforms provides a steady source of data for researchers, it also provides a source of constantly evolving complexity. Most prior research has focused on analyzing static topological properties of networks induced by social communication, while discarding the content of communication. At the same time, there is a growing recognition that a more nuanced understanding of social interactions requires analyzing the semantic content of communications. For instance, it has been suggested that linguistic cues in communicative patterns, as well as the ways individuals echo and accommodate each other's linguistic styles, can be indicative of relative social status of participants [6]. Despite recent progress, however, content-based analysis of social interactions is still a challenging problem due to the lack of adequate quantitative methods for extracting useful signals from unstructured text. Another significant hurdle is that the design and usage of social networks, and thus the interpretation of various signals, are changing over time.

Here we suggest a novel, information-theoretic approach for leveraging user-generated content to characterize interactions among social media participants. Specifically, given all the content generated by a set of users (e.g., a sequence of tweets), our goal is to find meaningful edges that indicate social interactions among this set of users. Our approach is model-free in the sense that it does not presuppose a particular behavioral model of users and their interactions. Instead, we view users as producers of some arbitrarily encoded information stream. If Y's stream has an effect on X's, then access to Y's signal can, in principle, improve our prediction of X's future activity. This is what we mean by a *predictive link*. We show that this general notion of predictability can be used to identify social influence. Many declared friendship links on a network may not be useful for predicting future activity, a possibility with major implications for information diffusion. We contrast the identification of predictive links with *link prediction*, whose primary goal is to reproduce the declared friendship graph, even if those links are useless for predicting future dynamics.

The technical approach proposed here consists of two main ingredients (see Fig. 1). First, we represent user-generated content in a high-dimensional space so that a sequence of user-generated posts is mapped to a time-series in this space. Second, we apply information-theoretic measures to those time series to discover and quantify directed influence among the users. Because our method is based on information-theoretic principles, it is easy to interpret, applicable to arbitrary signals and/or platforms, and flexible with respect to the representation of content.

Our approach ultimately reduces to calculating an information-theoretic measure called *transfer entropy* between pairs of stochastic processes [34]. Intuitively, transfer entropy between processes X and Y quantifies how much better we are able to predict the target process X if we use

WSDM'13, February 4–8, 2013, Rome, Italy.

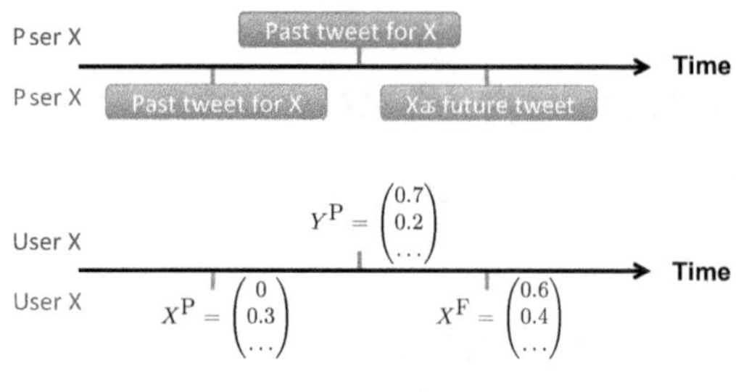

$$IT_{Y\to X} = \hat{H}(X^{\mathrm{F}} : Y^{\mathrm{P}}|X^{\mathrm{P}})$$

Figure 1: Is the content of X's future tweet, X^F, predictable from past tweets, Y^P, X^P? We answer this question by first transforming the text of tweets into vectors. Joint samples of these variables can be used to estimate information transfer, or transfer entropy, quantifying how predictive Y's tweets are of X's future tweets.

the history of the process Y and X rather than the history of X alone. By using transfer entropy as a statistical measure of the relationship between the content of Y's tweets and the content of X's subsequent tweets, we construct a graph of *predictive links*, based only on the content of users' tweets. Our results demonstrate that transfer entropy indeed reveals a variety of predictive, causal behaviors. Surprisingly, we also discover that many of the most predictive links *are not present in the social network*, through mentions nor friend links. On the other hand, we find that most of the declared friendship links do not have very high transfer entropy. The fact that most of a user's declared friends on the social network do not influence their behavior will perhaps come as little surprise to users of these networks. From a research perspective, relying on the declared friendship network to understand the spread of information can then be seen as a major shortcoming which we hope this work helps to remedy. In Sec. 4.4, we verify the meaningfulness of our measure by showing that predictive links are a statistically significant predictor of mentions on Twitter.

To summarize, our main contribution is a novel application of an information-theoretic framework to content-based social network analysis, providing a general, flexible measure of meaningful relationships in the network. This construction is made possible by two apparently novel technical insights. (1) Current state-of-the-art methods for estimating entropic measures such as mutual information continue to perform well in high-dimensional spaces as long as they are effectively low-dimensional in some sense. (2) While content representations of user activity are high-dimensional, they are effectively low dimensional in the required sense. Taken together, these two points allow us to successfully apply entropic estimators in a previously inaccessible regime.

After motivating our technical approach and defining the relevant information-theoretic quantities in Section 2, we describe how to estimate those quantities in Sec. 3, and demonstrate their use on real-world data from Twitter in Sec. 4. Finally, we give an overview of related work in Sec. 5, followed by a discussion of results in Sec. 6.

2. TECHNICAL APPROACH

Let us consider a set of users that generate a time-stamped sequence of text documents, e.g., tweets. Let X and Y be two such users. Let X^P and Y^P denote the content of tweets generated by those users up to some time, in some representation. While our approach is not limited to a particular representation, below we will use X^P and Y^P to describe topical representation of the content (e.g., obtained via Latent Dirichlet Allocation, or LDA).

Consider now the problem of predicting the content of the next tweet generated by X, denoted by X^F; see Fig. 1. Generally speaking, X^F is a random variable that can depend on a large number of factors that might not be directly observable: topical interests of user X (and her friends), exogenous events, and so on. Here, however, we are interested in the extent to which X^F is influenced by the past tweets X^P and Y^P. Namely, we would like to see how much knowing the past content generated by user Y, Y^P, helps us to better predict X^F. If knowing Y's past tweets helps us to predict X^F more accurately, then we can say that Y exerts certain influence on X.

The notion of *influence* described above is in the spirit of Granger causality [10] which demands that (1) the cause occurs before the effect; (2) the cause contains information about the effect that is unique, and is in no other variable [12]. The principle behind Granger causality was originally considered in the context of regression models, but applying these ideas in the context of information theory leads to effective tests of *causality* given simple structural assumptions [12, 15], i.e., determining that information is "in no other variable." In this paper, we only attempt to rule out the user's own recent history as an alternate causal explanation. Exogenous and long-term effects are difficult to account for but will be discussed in some interesting cases.

2.1 Transfer Entropy

We denote by $H(X)$ the entropy of a random variable, X, with some associated probability distribution, $p(\vec{x}) \equiv \Pr(X = \vec{x})$, for $\vec{x} \in \mathbb{R}^{d_x}$. In this case (differential) entropy is defined in the standard way, using the natural log,

$$H(X) = \mathbb{E}(-\log p(x)) = -\int dx\ p(x) \log p(x).$$

We sometimes speak of entropy as quantifying our "uncertainty" about X. Standard higher order entropies such as mutual information and conditional entropy can be defined in terms of differential entropy as $H(X : Y) = H(X) + H(Y) - H(X,Y)$ and $H(X|Y) = H(X,Y) - H(Y)$, respectively. Conditional information can be interpreted as the reduction of uncertainty in X from knowing Y.

Transfer entropy, or information transfer [34], can be defined as,

$$\begin{aligned} IT_{Y\to X} &= H(X^{\mathrm{F}} : Y^{\mathrm{P}}|X^{\mathrm{P}}) \qquad (1)\\ &= H(X^{\mathrm{F}}|X^{\mathrm{P}}) - H(X^{\mathrm{F}}|Y^{\mathrm{P}}, X^{\mathrm{P}}), \end{aligned}$$

where X^{F} is interpreted as information about user X's future behavior, and $X^{\mathrm{P}}, Y^{\mathrm{P}}$ as user X and Y's past behavior, respectively. The temporal indices dictate that cause should come before effect, and conditioning on X's past insures that any explanatory value from Y is not already present in X's past behavior. The first line writes this quantity succinctly as a *conditional mutual information* while the second line has the nice interpretation that we are interested in how much knowing Y^{P} reduces our uncertainty about X^{F}. This quantity is asymmetric, so in principle $IT_{Y\to X} \neq IT_{X\to Y}$. We will see examples where this is the case.

In this paper, we take $Y^{\mathrm{P}}, X^{\mathrm{P}}, X^{\mathrm{F}}$ to be random processes representing the content of tweets for users X and Y, and so we refer to this measure as *content transfer*. In particular, referring to Fig. 1, given some concrete procedure to turn an individual tweet into a vector, $\vec{x}$, we consider samples, $i = 1 \dots N$, of triples of tweets $(\vec{x}^{\mathrm{F},i}, \vec{y}^{\mathrm{P},i}, \vec{x}^{\mathrm{P},i})$ representing X's tweet, Y's most recent previous tweet, and X's most recent previous tweet. Note that we demand that Y's tweet should occur after X's previous tweet, otherwise the causal effect of Y's tweet is already being taken into account as affecting X's previous tweet . Also, Y could tweet many times in between X's tweets, but we only consider the most recent tweet for simplicity. Many possibilities exist to represent a tweet as a vector and in Sec. 4.2 we describe some of them along with the topic model approach used in this paper.

Note that we could drop the conditioning on X^P to get the mutual information between X's future and Y's past, sometimes called time-delayed or time-shifted mutual information. We will compare this simpler quantity to transfer entropy below. On the other hand, in principle, we could add even more conditioning on other variables like news stories, other users' activity, Z^{P}, or more history for users X and Y. The benefit of that course of action is that the resulting quantity can be given a rigorous causal interpretation [15]. The difficulty is in estimating these entropies from sparse data, and adding more conditions also increases the dimensionality of the problem.

3. ESTIMATING TRANSFER ENTROPY

Generally speaking, calculating entropic measures for high-dimensional random variables is problematic due to data sparsity [26]. Rather than binning data and estimating probability distributions as a prerequisite for calculating entropy, Kozachenko and Leonenko [18] introduced an entropy estimator that was asymptotically unbiased and did not require binning of data. Binless estimators were extended to higher order quantities like mutual information [19], and divergence between two distributions [39]. Below we make use of a generalization of the approach that allows binless estimation of the more nuanced transfer entropy [35].

The basic idea behind non-parametric binless entropy estimators is to average local contributions to the entropy in the neighborhood of each point, where the neighborhood size is chosen adaptively according to the point's k nearest neighbors. The neighborhood shrinks as we add more data, improving the estimate. The fundamental strength of this approach comes from the fact that it is easier to locally estimate entropy than to locally estimate a probability density; mathematically, the equivalent local density estimators are not consistent while the entropy estimators are consistent [28]. For fixed k, various entropy estimators have been shown to be asymptotically unbiased and consistent under only mild technical assumptions [39, 19, 28, 29].

Generally, suppose we have samples $i = 1, \dots, N$ of points $(\vec{x}^{(i)}, \vec{y}^{(i)})$ drawn from some unknown joint distribution. For each point, i, we construct the random variable $\epsilon_k(i)$, representing the distance to the k-th nearest neighbor in the joint x-y space according to some metric. We will use the maximum norm in all dimensions following previous work [19, 35]. For instance, the distance between points i and j in the joint space would be

$$||\vec{w}^{(i)} - \vec{w}^{(j)}||_\infty = \max_l |w_l^{(i)} - w_l^{(j)}|,$$

where $\vec{w}^{(i)} = (x_1^{(i)}, \dots, x_{d_x}^{(i)}, y_1^{(i)}, \dots, y_{d_y}^{(i)})$ and d_x, d_y are the dimensions of the x and y spaces, respectively. If we project only onto the x (or y) subspace, the number of points strictly within a distance $\epsilon_k(i)$ is defined as $n_x(i)$ (or $n_y(i)$). We can now proceed to write down the Kraskov mutual information estimator [19].

$$\hat{H}(X:Y) = \psi(k) + \frac{1}{N}\sum_{i=1}^{N}\left(\psi(N) - \psi(n_x(i)+1) - \psi(n_y(i)+1)\right) \quad (2)$$

Here, ψ is the digamma function (asymptotically similar to log). Note that this simple expression depends only on distances between samples, and does not depend on the dimension of the space.

The Kraskov estimator has been extended to conditional mutual information(CMI) [35]. Now we add a third covarying vector, $\vec{z}$, and define $\epsilon_k(i)$ as the distance to the k-th nearest neighbor in the full joint x-y-z space, while $n_{yz}(i)$, for instance, represents the number of points strictly within a distance $\epsilon_k(i)$ projecting onto the y-z subspace.

$$\hat{H}(X:Y|Z) = \psi(k) + \frac{1}{N}\sum_{i=1}^{N}\left(\psi(n_z(i)+1) - \psi(n_{xz}(i)+1) - \psi(n_{yz}(i)+1)\right) \quad (3)$$

These two estimators can interpreted as estimators of time-delayed mutual information and transfer entropy, respectively, through appropriate choice of X, Y, Z.

Note that because transfer entropy (and mutual information) estimators are an average over all samples, we can easily determine the contribution of one sample to the estimated entropy.

$$\hat{H}^{(i)}(X:Y|Z) = \psi(k) + \psi(n_z(i)+1) - \psi(n_{xz}(i)+1) - \psi(n_{yz}(i)+1) \quad (4)$$

We refer to this quantity as *local transfer entropy* and note its similarity to a previously introduced measure [21]. In principle, not only can we identify a pair of users, X, Y, so that Y has high content transfer towards X, we can also order their tweet exchanges to see which ones contribute most to that assessment. An example is shown in Table 1 in Sec. 4.3.

3.1 Empirical study of CMI estimators

Although entropy estimators have many nice theoretical properties in the asymptotic limit, for finite sample sizes we must ultimately rely on empirical results. Many papers have reported impressive empirical results from these entropy estimators already [37, 39, 12, 19], so we will explore only one unusual feature of our problem, with surprising results.

Note that the estimators in Eq. 2 and 3, do not explicitly rely on the dimension. In fact, they only rely on the vectors themselves through a distance function. Therefore, adding extra dimensions to a vector that are constant will have no effect on the distance function or the estimator. I.e., we would be transforming the vectors $\vec{x}^{(i)}$,

$$\vec{x}^{(i)\prime} = (x_1^{(i)}, \dots, x_{d_x}^{(i)}, c_1, \dots, c_{d_c}),$$

where the c_l are arbitrary constants (that is, they are the same for each point i). Clearly, the distances are unchanged, $||\vec{x}^{(i)} - \vec{x}^{(j)}|| = ||\vec{x}^{(i)\prime} - \vec{x}^{(j)\prime}||$ (similarly in the joint $\vec{x}$-$\vec{y}$-$\vec{z}$

space), and this is all that is relevant for the estimators in Eq. 2 and 3. The question we explore in Fig. 2 is the effect of adding extra dimensions which are only nearly constant. The intuition for exploring this scenario is that vectors that represent content should be high dimensional, but we expect most individual users to participate in only a small subset of the full content space (we make this intuition concrete in Fig. 3 in Sec. 4.2). Can we expect entropy estimators to work in this case?

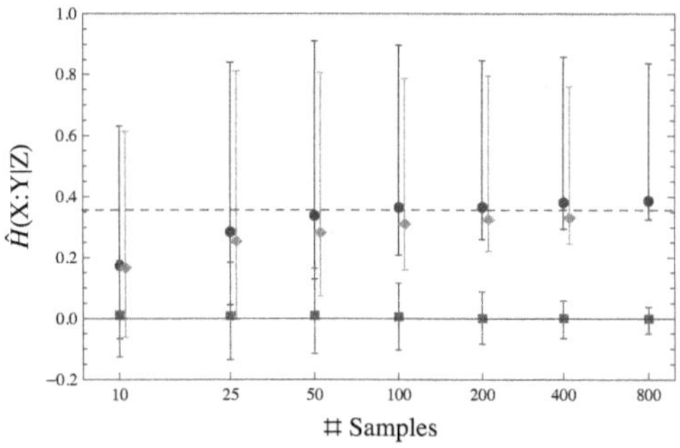

(a)

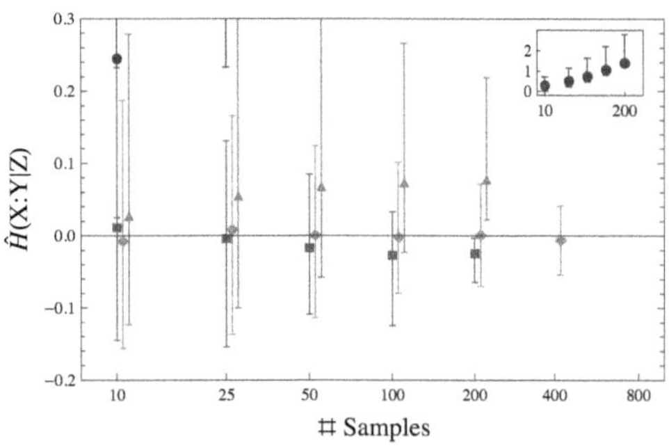

(b)

Figure 2: (a) Demonstrating convergence for the estimator in Eq. 3(circles) when the true CMI (dotted line) is known. This estimator succeeds even in the presence of many extraneous dimensions with small noise (diamonds). When labels are permuted, the estimator converges to zero (squares) (b) Comparing transfer entropy for pairs of interacting Twitter users (circles, continued in inset, and triangles) to null hypotheses (diamonds and squares). All points include 95% confidence intervals, see Sec. 3.1 for details.

We start by considering a situation in which we can calculate conditional mutual information(CMI) analytically. As an example, we consider a Gaussian where $\vec{x}, \vec{y}, \vec{z} \in \mathbb{R}^1$, and we take X and Y to be strongly correlated, while Y, Z and X, Z are weakly correlated. For illustration purposes, we consider the following covariance matrix.

$$\begin{pmatrix} x \\ y \\ z \end{pmatrix} \sim \mathcal{N}\left(\begin{pmatrix} 0 \\ 0 \\ 0 \end{pmatrix}, \begin{pmatrix} 4 & 3 & 1 \\ 3 & 4 & 1 \\ 1 & 1 & 2 \end{pmatrix}\right)$$

In this case, $H(X : Y|Z) = 0.357$, while $H(X : Y) = 0.413$.[1] Because Z is correlated with Y, conditioning on it reduces some of Y's usefulness for predicting X. In Fig. 2(a), we attempt to estimate this entropy from random samples. We show the mean of the estimator over many trials(circles), along with the 95% confidence intervals. For comparison, we apply the estimator to samples where the sample indices of the y and z components are randomly permuted and it converges quickly to zero(squares).

What happens if we now take $\vec{x}, \vec{y}, \vec{z} \in \mathbb{R}^{150}$? We will let x_1, y_1, z_1 be drawn from the same low-dimensional distribution above, but all the other components of the vector will be uncorrelated Gaussian noise with standard deviation 0.05. The MI and CMI should be unchanged. Now we are estimating CMI in a 450 dimensional space with fewer than 400 samples. Surprisingly, the estimator still works well, only slightly underestimating the true CMI. If we increase the standard deviation of the noise, eventually the signal is lost and the estimator converges to 0.

In Fig. 2(b), we look at the convergence of the estimator for examples from pairs of users on Twitter (details in the Sec. 4). First, we consider a very strong signal corresponding to the edge $kar \rightarrow spo$ discussed later (circles). The estimate increases relatively quickly so that it must be continued in the inset. We consider two null hypotheses as comparisons. First, we permute the order of tweets for kar, spo and calculate content transfer(squares). Second, we construct two Twitter streams from random tweets in our dataset, and we estimate the content transfer (diamonds). Finally, we calculate content transfer for the user pair $no \rightarrow li$ from Sec. 4.4, which represents more social behavior (triangles). Note that the estimator in this case is quite noisy, and we do not expect perfect discrimination of the signal with so little data.

3.2 Implementation details

There are several details to be considered before implementing the estimators above. First of all, we are required to find the k-nearest neighbors to each point, but how should we choose k? Smaller k reduces the bias, but larger k reduces the variance [39]. We find the results are not very sensitive to k. We use $k = 3$ as suggested by Kraskov et al. [19] and this choice is confirmed by numerical results shown in the inset of Fig. 7. To avoid situations where two points are exactly the same distance away, we also add low intensity (10^{-10}) noise to the data [19].

The most intensive part of the calculation is the search for nearest neighbors. In high dimensions, as is the case in this paper, this cannot be sped up much beyond $O(N^2)$ for N samples. This could be sped up if we only look for approximate nearest neighbors [24]. Instead, we can fix some constant N_c, and only make estimates using samples of this fixed size. Besides bounding the computational complexity, if we average over multiple samples we can also reduce the variance. For N samples of tweet exchanges, we take $2\lceil N/N_c \rceil$ random subsets of size N_c. We set $N_c = 100$ (which will be the minimum sample size we keep in our data, discussed in Sec. 4). This also insures that any bias from finite sample size will affect all edges equally.

Since we fix the number of samples to use in estimation, this contributes a constant to the complexity, which is then just linear in the number of user pairs we consider. Because

[1] Both mutual information and conditional mutual information must be non-negative, though estimators may be negative due to sampling error. For our purposes, conditioning on another variable generally reduces the mutual information, but it is possible for conditional mutual information to be larger than the associated mutual information.

we attempted to evaluate transfer entropy between all of the millions of user pairs in our dataset (only some of which had the minimum number of samples), we had to split our calculation over many processors.[2]

4. RESULTS

We will apply the entropy estimators to real world data from Twitter. After describing the dataset, we will discuss options for representing tweet text as vectors. In Sec. 4.3, we will examine the directional links with the highest content transfer on the entire dataset. Although we lack a ground truth to validate our results, in Sec. 4.4 we consider activity of a subset of users for whom mentions can be used to test the significance of content transfer.

4.1 Dataset description

We make use of data originally collected and described in [32]. All tweets are collected for a set of 2400 users over a one month period from 9/20/2010–10/20/2010. The set of users was picked by starting with a small, random initial set and constructing a snowball sample using mentions and re-tweets. The dataset was constrained to users who self-reported in their profile a location in the Middle East. The dataset also contained sampled tweets from tens of thousands of other users who mentioned users in the original set. We used those tweets to help train the topic model (giving a total of over half a million tweets after preprocessing described in the next section), but we did not consider those users when calculating content transfer for pairs of users. After eliminating users with less than 100 tweets, we considered all possible directed edges among the remaining 770 users. Note that not all ordered pairs of users had at least 100 tweet triples as defined in Sec. 2.1 in which case content transfer was not calculated.

4.2 Topic vector representation

A crucial ingredient in our attempt to apply information-theoretic measures to social media is a way to represent content as vectors. Luckily, a great deal of work has been done on mathematical representations of content, a few examples are discussed in Sec. 5. The richness of our results are ultimately limited by the quality of content representation. On the other hand, higher dimensional representations make entropy estimation more difficult.

Compounding this difficulty, social media presents some unique challenges. For instance, on Twitter, messages are very short (140 characters), providing little context to determine what a tweet is about. The use of "netspeak", emoticons, and abbreviations challenge traditional models of communication. Many languages are represented, sometimes mixed within a single tweet. Spelling mistakes and URLs multiply the number of unique tokens. On the other hand, the sheer volume of data provides an advantage that outweighs these difficulties.

Ultimately, we chose to use topic models to represent tweets because of convenient off-the-shelf implementations [30], and a growing body of work exploring their applicability to Twitter [41, 14]. Our purpose in using a topic model differs from standard aims. In particular, our ultimate goal is not to find distinct topics with clear interpretations, but to find the minimal representation that preserves relevant detail.

For our experiments, we trained an LDA topic model implemented in *gensim* [30]. For pre-processing the text, we followed most of the prescriptions in [14]. (1) We replace all URLs with the word "[url]". (2) We replace all words starting with "@" with the word "[mention]" (3) We remove all non-Latin alphabet characters and convert to lower-case. (4) We removed a standard list of English stop-words. Because we will use mentions later in our validation, step (2) is particularly important to insure that our topic model has not learned name associations. We also removed all tweets that begin "RT @" (re-tweets), since this type of information diffusion has been well-studied, as discussed in Sec. 5.

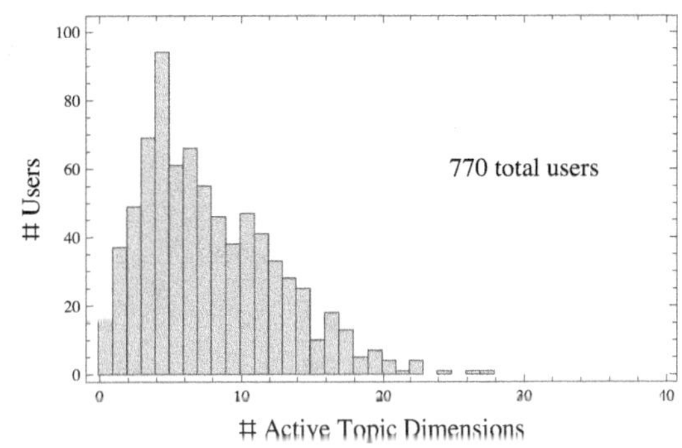

Figure 3: The effective dimension of topic vectors for most users is low. We consider all users with at least 100 tweets. For each component of the 150 dimensional topic vector, we calculate the standard deviation over all tweets from one user. If the standard deviation is greater than 0.05, we say that topic dimension is "active" for that user.

Next, we constructed a bag-of-words vector representation with the remaining words in the dataset that appeared more than once. Each component of the vector represents the frequency with which one of these words occurred in a given tweet. These vectors were transformed using the TF-IDF score.[3] Finally, we used the TF-IDF vectors to learn an LDA topic model. We tried topic models with 10, 50, 100, 125, 150, 175, and 200 topics. At first, we assumed that the lower dimensional topic models, while being worse representations of the text, would be more amenable to entropy estimators. However, larger topic models actually fared much better, despite the high dimensionality of the vectors. One reason for this surprising result is that the effective dimensionality of most Twitter users is far smaller than the dimensionality of the topic vector. To verify this, we considered all the users in our dataset with at least 100 tweets. For each component of the topic vector, we calculated the standard deviation over all tweets for one user. We define the number of "active topics" as those for which the standard deviation was over 0.05. Although this notion does not conform to a standard intuition about what should be considered an "active topic", it does describe what is relevant for entropy

[2]All results were obtained on USC's HPCC [1]. Code is available: `http://www.isi.edu/~gregv/te.py`

[3]Term frequency-inverse document frequency: we use the standard definition. If a term occurs f times it is transformed to $f \log_2 D/d$, where D represents the number of documents (tweets) and d represents the number of documents containing the term.

estimation, as discussed in Sec. 3.1. The result is shown in Fig. 3 for a topic model with 150 topics. The dynamics of most users are constrained to a handful of dimensions. The fact that the active topics may differ for different users is irrelevant for the purpose of entropy estimation.

4.3 Full graph

We begin by calculating content transfer for all ordered pairs of users with sufficient samples. Unless otherwise specified, we use $n_{topics} = 125$ in the following examples, although the high content transfer edges were insensitive to this choice. Looking at the histogram of content transfer for all edges in Fig. 4, we note that there are a few obvious outliers. We also show the network consisting of only these high content transfer edges, with account names abbreviated. Inspection of the tweets reveal that these links are all strongly predictive, we proceed to give several examples.

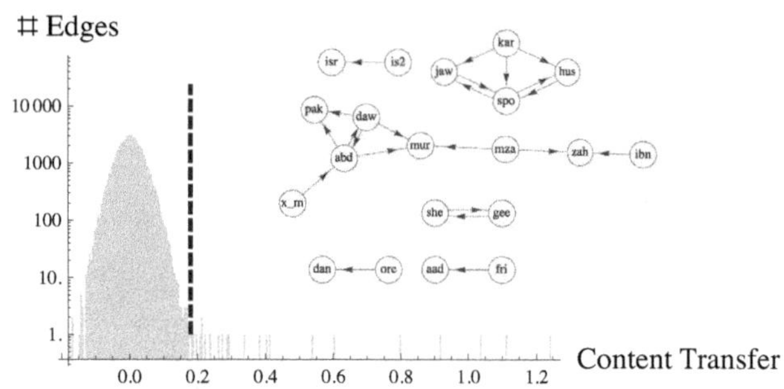

Figure 4: Histogram of content transfer for all ordered pairs of users with sufficient samples. Edges with content transfer to the right of the dotted line are shown in the inset graph. Many of these edges are not present in the follower graph or mention graph.

We start with the edge $mza \to zah$ with sample tweets shown in Table 1 and point out some things notably lacking. For these two users there are no friend links, no mentions, no retweets, no matching URLs (though the shortened URLs point to the same stories), and no matching hash tags. Nevertheless, even though the text is altered, content transfer recognizes that zah's tweets strongly predict the content in mza's tweets. We use the local transfer entropy from Eq. 4 to order the 288 tweet exchanges. We also read through all the tweet exchanges and hand labeled 228 instances in which the two users' tweets clearly referred to the same story. The probability that the local transfer entropy was higher for a pair of tweets which referred to the same story rather than unrelated topics was 0.68. We also note the asymmetry of this edge: the content transfer from $mza \to zah$ is 0.24 while in the other direction it is only 0.01. This asymmetry is often taken to suggest a causal connection [35]. Nevertheless, there remains the possibility of an external, mutual cause. The impossibility of ruling out such alternatives is one reason we emphasize the interpretation of content transfer as a measure of predictability. Of course, this is a well-known caveat regarding transfer entropy. A simple explanation in this case is that both accounts simply read and post from the same news site. However, in that case we would expect the order of tweets to sometimes be reversed, causing the transfer entropy to be more symmetric. In fact, the order of tweets is always preserved. A more nuanced alternative is that one of the users is temporally "closer" to the news source. E.g., a service like "twitterfeed.com" can automatically post news stories to your Twitter account the instant they are published. In that case, mza serves as a proxy for the true causal source which is not even present in our dataset.

As opposed to the previous example, the kar cluster contains some bi-directed edges. In this case, the users are all following each other, however, once again, no retweets or mentions are used. The tweets revolve around sports and some samples are shown in Table 2. The tweets are clearly all copies of each other. Confirming the previous intuition about temporal ordering, the bi-directed edges are duplicates that occur in arbitrary order, while the directed edge away from kar is reflected by the fact that all posts appear first on that account. In this case, we appear to have a coordinated information dissemination campaign. Although it appears that this campaign is instigated by kar, higher order transfer entropies can be used to verify structure among groups of nodes [15].

The remaining clusters in Fig. 4 have similar easy qualitative interpretations. The isr cluster users post identical Israeli news stories. The remaining edges of the largest cluster also revolve around news, mostly of stories in the Middle East. The profile of gee lists itself as the Twitter stream of a tech news site, while the profile of she lists itself as the founder of the same website. Tweets are copied in arbitrary order, leading to symmetric content transfer. The edge $aad \leftrightarrow fri$ has a similar interpretation, with aad's profile declaring himself a radio presenter for the internet radio station represented by account fri. Again, no mention or follower edges are declared.

Figure 5: Illustration of a scenario when time delayed mutual information is high while transfer entropy is low. Colors represent repetition of a particular tweet.

We also calculated the time-delayed mutual information for all pairs of users. In general, this quantity was correlated with the content transfer (see Fig. 7). However, there were several examples where mutual information was high while content transfer was low. The intuition behind this phenomena is expressed in Fig. 5. To use a concrete example from the dataset, we have user Y repeatedly tweeting the same message `#shoutout for Floods in #Pakistan #pkfloods [url]`, which we can imagine as a red line in the picture. At some point, user Y switches to repeatedly tweeting a new message `#TEAMFOLLOW 100 FREE MORE TWITTER FOLLOWERS! [url]`[4] (blue lines). Coincidentally, at nearly the same time user X switches from repeatedly tweeting `In My View: HOW TO EXPLODE RESOURCES TO EARN FOREIGN EXCHANGE [url]` (green lines) to `In My View: PAKISTAN ON THE SHOULDERS OF N.R.O BENEFICIARIES [url]`[5] (grey

[4]This tweet refers to increasingly popular services to inflate the number of followers for an account. Basically, you agree to either pay, follow people in the service, or tweet advertisements about the service in exchange for followers. This service formed a prominent signal in [36].

[5]We also estimated the mutual information $\hat{H}(X^{\mathrm{F}} : X^{\mathrm{P}})$, and this user was an example that had a high score for this

lines). From looking at the figure, you can see that a red line for user Y is quite predictive of a subsequent green line for user X, and this is reflected in the high mutual information. On the other hand, if you condition on user X's past, you can easily predict that a green line is most likely followed by another green line, and seeing a red line from user Y does not improve that prediction. Therefore, transfer entropy is low in this scenario.

LTE	User	Tweet
2.65	zah	KARACHI, Pakistan, Oct. 12 (UPI) – Intelligence agencies in Pakistan are warning of terrorist atta... http://bit.ly/bscYoX #news #Pakistan
	mza	Is Mobile Video Chat Ready for Business Use?: Matthew Latkiewicz works at Zendesk.com, creators of web-based custo... http://bit.ly/cAx3Ob
	zah	Matthew Latkiewicz works at Zendesk.com, creators of web-based customer support software. He writes for... http://bit.ly/bkuWCV #technology
2.53	zah	Man-made causes cited for Pakistan floods: ISLAMABAD, Pakistan, Oct. 14 (UPI) – Deforestation ... http://bit.ly/92afA0 #pkfloods #Pakistan
	mza	Google Shares Jump 7% on Impressive Earnings: Google has posted its latest earnings report, and early indications ... http://bit.ly/9oi4zr
	zah	Google has posted its latest earnings report, and early indications suggest that investors are more tha... http://bit.ly/cyT35p #technology
-0.33	zah	ISLAMABAD: Former adviser Sardar Latif Khosa resigned as adviser to the prime minister on Tuesday giv... http://bit.ly/bBKJ32 #news #latest
	mza	Explore Interesting, Personal Photos on Yahoo! Search: Following up on our announcement of new Yahoo! Search enhan... http://bit.ly/diR9ls
	zah	KABUL: A cargo plane crashed into mountains east of Afghanistan's capital Kabul on Tuesday, with init... http://bit.ly/9ExkjR #news #latest

Table 1: Tweet exchanges between two users with high content transfer from $mza \rightarrow zah$. Examples were picked which have high and low local transfer entropy.

kar	[url] – South Korean GP gets F1 go-ahead
hus	[url] – South Korean GP gets F1 go-ahead
jaw	[url] – South Korean GP gets F1 go-ahead
spo	[url] – South Korean GP gets F1 go-ahead
kar	The Sports Encounter – It's all about Sports – ICC cleared Oval ODI [url] via @AddThis
jaw	The Sports Encounter – It's all about Sports – ICC cleared Oval ODI [url] via @addthis
spo	The Sports Encounter – It's all about Sports – ICC cleared Oval ODI [url] via @AddThis
hus	The Sports Encounter – It's all about Sports – ICC cleared Oval ODI [url] via @AddThis

Table 2: The sports cluster in Fig. 4. User *kar* always tweets first, while the others repeat sporadically and in varied order.

4.4 High mention users

We saw that the user pairs with the highest transfer entropy, while clearly good predictors of content, did not have the typical markers associated with "influence": no mentions, no retweets, and no following. In this section we consider a subset of Twitter users with two goals. (1) Can content transfer capture more subtle social behavior? (2) Can we use some of the metadata about mentions and followers to validate the effectiveness of content transfer?

A first idea would be to consider the set of users who use "@mentions" with the intuition that if a user mentions somebody, they are responding to them somehow. Unfortunately, this intuition would often fail. A major use of mentions is to attempt to get the attention of celebrity Twitter users. E.g. one user mentioned "@justinbieber" over seven hundred times during the month of our dataset. Instead we want to find people who use mentions for conversation, which was the primary focus of Macskassy [32]. To do this, for each pair of users, we call the number of mutual mentions the minimum of the number of times X mentions Y and the number of times Y mentions X. We ranked the top 50 pairs with the highest mutual mentions. For this set of users (38 users total), we can reasonably assume that mentions are a weak proxy for online influence. The full mention graph for this set of users is shown in Fig. 6.

For this restricted set of users, we see how well content transfer corresponds to the underlying mention graph. For an evaluation metric we use area under the receiver operating characteristic curve (AUC) [11]. We rank all edges according to which have the highest content transfer. In principle, we would like the edges in the mention graph to have the highest content transfer. The AUC can be interpreted as the probability that a mention edge (X mentions Y at least once) has a higher content transfer ($IT_{Y \rightarrow X}$) than an edge without a mention. As a null hypothesis, we can imagine that content transfer scores are random. In that case the mean AUC will be 0.5. Since we have 74 mention edges and 785 non-mention edges, the standard error of the AUC under the null hypothesis is about 3.5% [11]. The best result for AUC (using $n_{topics} = 125$) in Fig. 7 is 0.648, which is over four standard deviations away from the null hypothesis. As an alternate perspective, we point out that the precision and recall for the top 100 edges were 20%, 28%, respectively, which are both about twice the baseline.

Fig. 7(a) shows the AUC for various topic models using either transfer entropy or time-delayed mutual information. Because the results are noisy and, in principle, our method does not rely on the details of any particular topic model, in Fig. 7(b), we used the average rank given by multiple topic models to predict mention edges. On average, transfer entropy slightly outperforms time-delayed mutual information. The inset of Fig. 7(b) shows the effect of trying various k (number of nearest neighbors in our entropy estimator), with $n_{topics} = 100$. We see that $k = 3$ is a good choice, but larger values of k give similar results.

In Fig. 6, we consider the full mention graph of the set users with high mutual mentions. We also highlight the top 5 edges according to content transfer for $n_{topics} = 125$ since it gave the best AUC. Four edges are true positives, with example tweets shown in Table 3. Some comments are in order about how tweet processing affected these examples. First of all, we eliminated messages that started with "RT @", but not "partial retweets", where a message was prepended to the re-tweet. Second, no language detection was done, though eliminating non-Latin characters eliminated most of the foreign text which was in Arabic and Hebrew. However, a tweet containing any Latin characters (including mentions) was still represented. Most of the topics represented English words, but a few topics contained mostly transliterated Hindu and Urdu, or Spanish. Identifying that if one user tweets in a language another user will respond in kind is a strongly predictive signal.

The discussion in Table 3 between *sh* and *ta* perhaps represents the ideal for detecting social influence. In that case we see that if one user broaches a political topic, the other will follow suit. Note that this pair of users was detected through content dynamics alone, without reference to mentions or even knowledge of follow edges. In fact, the distance is not even calculated between tweet vectors for *sh* and *ta*,

measure. Basically, the user tweets many different story titles, but repeats each one dozens of times.

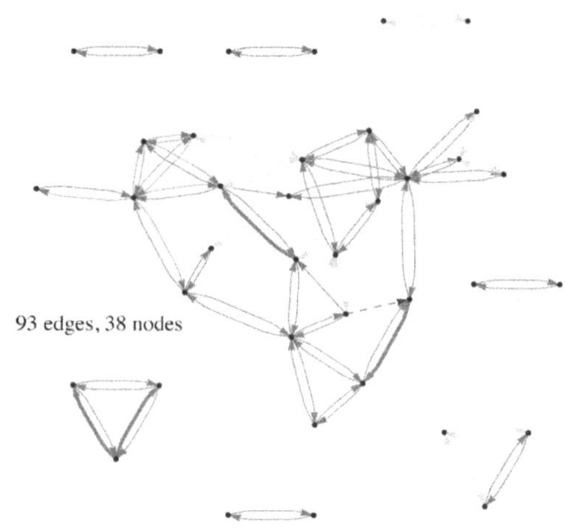

Figure 6: The mention graph for users described in Sec 4.4. The five edges with the highest transfer entropy are highlighted. True positives are thick red arrows and false positives are blue dashed arrows. The green, dotted arrows are mention edges for which content transfer was not calculated due to insufficient data.

the content transfer only looks for a predictable *co-variation* in the content of their tweets.

5. RELATED WORK

Much research has focused on characterizing and identifying influential users that can facilitate information diffusion along social links. Researchers have suggested different characterizations of influentials based on various network centrality measures [25, 16, 8]. For Twitter data, various influence measures include number of followers, mentions, retweets [4], Pagerank of follower network [20], size of the information cascades [2]. In principle, because these methods rely on the declared friendship network, which includes links that do not predict future activity, these methods could all be improved by instead considering the weighted content transfer network. More recent work has attempted to utilize temporal information through the influence–passivity score [31], and transfer entropy [36]. None of those measures, however, take content into account. More recently, several authors have suggested topic-sensitive influence measures such as TwitterRank [40], which takes into account topical similarity among the users. Topic-specific re-tweeting behavior was examined in [33].

More generally, there is an increasing trend to use communication content for inferring the nature of relationships between users [3, 7, 9]. An interesting line of research grounded in psycholinguistic theory of communication have studied the convergence of communicative behavior among Twitter users [5]. In particular, it has been suggested that conversational behavior can be indicative of relative social status of participants, and subtle language-based signals can be used to infer power relationships among the users [6]. Similar to our work, those approaches too work by projecting unstruc-

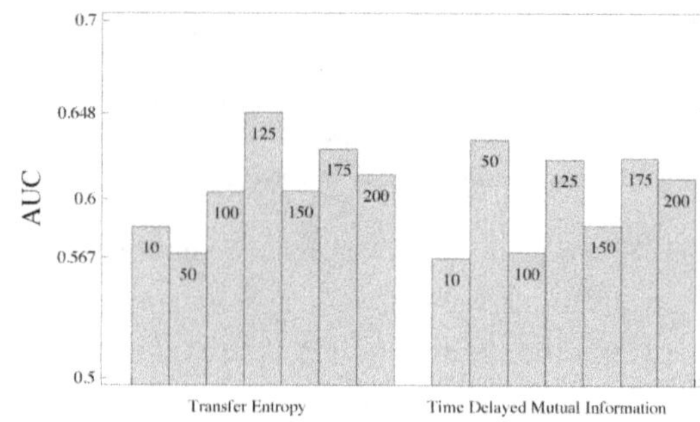

(a)

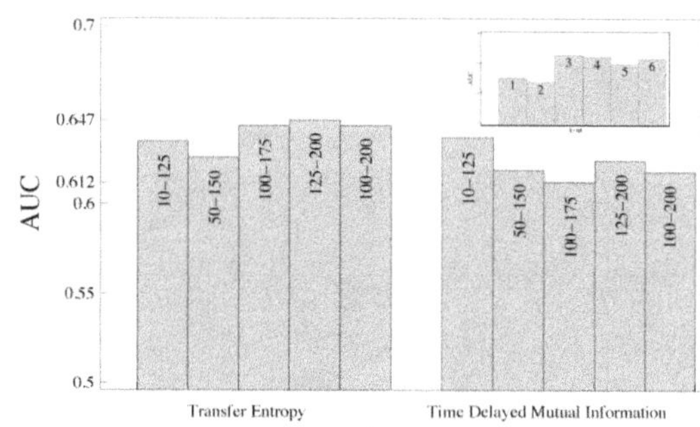

(b)

Figure 7: AUCs for reconstructing the mention graph in Sec. 4.4 for various parameters. (a) Transfer entropy and MI for various topic models, $k = 3$. (b) AUC using the average ranking for several topic models. Inset shows the effect of changing k, for a topic model with 100 topics.

User	Tweet
sh	@ta tsalk to police officers. 6 prominent policemen of Op Cleanup have been killed in last 2 yrs. Still tolerating MQM
ta	@sh I meant the "participation" of the hijacked public was a function of fear perp by Talibs. Same thing here. ppl don't want 2 die
sh	@ta what does it serve them?More pathetic f*tards snatching their mobiles and wallets? Small-crime is engrained in MQM structure
ta	@sh re: "no soul n honor"... well I think MQM zia's creation to puncture the Sindh Nationalist cause. ISI _will_ slap its b*
en	@fz oye oye Ajj MJ ke barri hai .. tm kal sa lyrics tweet ker rahe ho .. khariat hai na larki ?
fz	@EN Jo b dimagh mai ata hy krdaiti hun m not listening to him atm though
en	@fz mujhe na urdu na english songs ka lyrics kabhe yadd howa hain ...bhalla bhae tera :P
fz	@EN Lol i love memorizing songs ;)
en	NEW VERSION OF TWITTER IS HERE ...
fz	u got it? :O RT @EN NEW VERSION OF TWITTER IS HERE ..
en	@fz YEAH I THINK SO ... YOU GOT IT ??? SPLIT SCREEN VERSION ?
fz	@EN no :(m still waiting for it
re	queremos unaa fotooooo deee @celeb1 y @celeb2
li	QUIERO UNA FOTO DE @celeb1 & @celeb2
no	@celeb2 nico .. please que la segunda imagen sera de vos con @celeb1
re	duele tanto decir ALGO ?
li	@celeb2 nico porfi saca una foto con emi :(
re	@No [Hebrew characters]
no	@Li @Re [Hebrew characters]
no	@re twiitcam baby, yes o no?!
re	@No yesssss, and my brother will be theirr !! hahah , your sweet
no	@Re jaja! very good sister! :)

Table 3: Representative examples of tweet exchanges between the four pairs of users identified as being among the top 5 highest transfer entropies for all user pairs defined in Sec. 4.4. Edges were $no \to re$, $no \to li$, $en \to fz$, $ta \to sh$. User's re, no, li tweet primarily in Spanish, but all three occasionally address each other and respond in Hebrew or English.

tured user-generated text onto a multivariate time series, in their case using LIWC categories [27] rather than LDA-induced topics. However, the influence measures suggested in [5, 6] are defined in a rather *ad hoc* manner, as opposed to a more fundamental entropic measure used here. We believe that our approach based on transfer entropy provides a more principled measure of directed influence.

A crucial component of our approach is based on the ability to estimate entropic quantities for very-high-dimensional random variables. Due to data sparsity, naive methods based on *binning* are not feasible. The binless approach for entropy estimation introduced in [18] has been used for quantifying information in neural spike trains [38]. The binless approach has been extended for estimating higher order entropic quantities such as mutual information [19], divergences between two distributions [39], and transfer entropy [35]. We also note that a linear version of the transfer entropy known as Granger causality [10] has been used recently for uncovering predictive causal relationships in neuroscience [17], genetics [22], climate modeling [23] and various other applications.

6. DISCUSSION

We have seen that using content transfer as a general, statistical measure of predictivity captures a wide variety of nontrivial behavior on Twitter. Information-theoretic techniques provide powerful, flexible tools for discovering patterns in data, but typically are impractical to implement. Surprisingly, non-parametric entropy estimation was quite effective on a dataset that would be considered small by recent research standards. This is despite the fine-grain application of these entropic measures to individual user pairs. Extraordinarily, Table 1 suggests the measure may even provide a meaningful signal at the level of individual tweets.

The strongest, most predictive signals discovered in Sec. 4.3 were all characterized by some type of news dissemination. Most interesting about these results were how many of the links appeared to be purposely hidden in the explicit follower graph. If news dissemination is for the purpose of promoting your internet radio station, as in the $fri \leftrightarrow aad$ example, it may be advantageous for the accounts promoting your web site to appear as independent as possible. Indeed, Twitter terms of usage prohibit automatic re-tweets, so if you are copying content on multiple accounts, it would be a mistake to call attention to the practice by using re-tweets. Ironically, for these purposes it may be advantageous to hide the truly influential edges, while at the same time it is advantageous to accrue as many followers as possible to appear influential, even if most of these followers are dummy accounts that are not influenced at all. These false edges can be eliminated from the friendship network using content transfer, leading to a more useful network for analyzing information diffusion.

We also found a statistically significant result in Sec. 4.4 for distinguishing "social influence", i.e., one user eliciting a response in another. The evaluation task we performed is akin to hearing hundreds of people talking at once and inferring who is talking to whom, just by the content of their statements and without reference to any explicitly declared relationships. While the data were not sufficient to distinguish an arbitrary social tie, on average edges identified with mentions had a higher content transfer and this effect was over four standard deviations from the null hypothesis. One of the top examples corresponded to an intuitive notion of social influence, revolving around political discussion, but the strongest signals were for multi-lingual users. Responding in-kind to a certain language is a relatively easy signal to identify, at least within a topic model representation. We can see from Fig. 2 that to distinguish independent signals from correlated ones with transfer entropy requires either a strong signal or more data. It would be interesting to see what types of social influence are detected with even an order of magnitude more data, which is still many orders of magnitude away from the amount of data regularly processed by companies like Twitter and Facebook.

A subtle point about our measure of content transfer is that at no point are Y's tweets directly compared to X's tweets. Rather, the measure checks if X's future content varies in a predictable way based on Y's past content. While this distinction may be overly general for the purpose of discovering connections from what topics are being discussed, it may be relevant for more subtle social cues. For instance, whenever Y makes an aggressive statement, if X always responds submissively, this is a predictable, but not matching, response. To capture this type of scenario would require content representation that includes things like stance, attitude, or sentiment, as discussed in Sec. 5.

Social media is in a state of constant growth and change. Subtle changes in the mechanisms that underly social media platforms can have dramatic effects on the user behavior [13]. Results based on detailed modeling of hash tags, mentions, or re-tweets may not be relevant for the next generation of social media. On the other hand, a measure based on information-theoretic principles will remain relevant for any communication medium. By providing a model-free way to discover unexpected relationships in data, information-theoretic analysis is an effective tool for data exploration. Finally, using content dynamics to identify the predictive links leads to a more meaningful network on which to perform further analyses.

Acknowledgments

We would like to thank Sofus Macskassy for providing data and valuable comments. We also thank Kristina Lerman and Jaebong Yoo for useful discussions. GV would like to thank LARC, SMU for their hospitality while finishing this work. This research was supported by DARPA grant No. W911NF-12-1-0034 and AFOSR award FA9550-11-1-0417.

7. REFERENCES

[1] Computation for the work described in this paper was supported by the University of Southern California Center for High-Performance Computing and Communications (www.usc.edu/hpcc).

[2] E. Bakshy, J. M. Hofman, W. A. Mason, and D. J. Watts. Everyone's an influencer: quantifying influence on twitter. In *Proc. fourth ACM international conference on Web search and data mining*, WSDM '11, pages 65–74, New York, NY, USA, 2011. ACM.

[3] P. Bramsen, M. Escobar-Molano, A. Patel, and R. Alonso. Extracting social power relationships from natural language. In *Proceedings of the 49th Annual Meeting of the Association for Computational Linguistics: Human Language Technologies - Volume 1*, pages 773–782, Stroudsburg, PA, USA, 2011.

[4] M. Cha, H. Haddadi, F. Benevenuto, and K. P. Gummadi. Measuring user influence in twitter: The million follower fallacy. In *ICWSM-10: Proceedings of international AAAI Conference on Weblogs and Social*, 2010.

[5] C. Danescu-Niculescu-Mizil, M. Gamon, and S. Dumais. Mark my words!: linguistic style accommodation in social media. In *Proceedings of the 20th international conference on World wide web*, WWW '11, pages 745–754, New York, NY, USA, 2011. ACM.

[6] C. Danescu-Niculescu-Mizil, L. Lee, B. Pang, and J. Kleinberg. Echoes of power: language effects and power differences in social interaction. In *Proceedings of the 21st international conference on World Wide Web*, WWW '12, pages 699–708, New York, NY, USA, 2012. ACM.

[7] C. P. Diehl, G. Namata, and L. Getoor. Relationship identification for social network discovery. In *Proceedings of the 22nd national conference on Artificial intelligence - Volume 1*, AAAI'07, pages 546–552. AAAI Press, 2007.

[8] R. Ghosh and K. Lerman. Predicting influential users in online social networks. In *Proceedings of KDD workshop on Social Network Analysis (SNA-KDD)*, July 2010.

[9] E. Gilbert and K. Karahalios. Predicting tie strength with social media. In *Proceedings of the 27th international conference on Human factors in computing systems*, CHI '09, pages 211–220, New York, NY, USA, 2009. ACM.

[10] C. W. J. Granger. Testing for causality : A personal viewpoint. *Journal of Economic Dynamics and Control*, 2(1):329–352, May 1980.

[11] J. Hanley. The meaning and use of the area under a receiver operating characteristic (roc) curve. *Radiology*, 743:29–36, 1982.

[12] K. Hlavackovaschindler, M. Palus, M. Vejmelka, and J. Bhattacharya. Causality detection based on information-theoretic approaches in time series analysis. *Physics Reports*, 441(1):1–46, Mar. 2007.

[13] N. Hodas and K. Lerman. How visibility and divided attention constrain social contagion. *Arxiv preprint arXiv:1205.2736*, 2012.

[14] L. Hong and B. Davison. Empirical study of topic modeling in twitter. In *Proceedings of the First Workshop on Social Media Analytics*. ACM, 2010.

[15] V. P. J. K. Jakob Runge, Jobst Heitzig. Escaping the curse of dimensionality in estimating multivariate transfer entropy. *Phys. Rev. Lett.*, 108(258701), Jun 2012.

[16] G. Jeh and J. Widom. Scaling personalized web search. In *Proceedings of the 12th international conference on World Wide Web*, WWW '03, pages 271–279, New York, NY, USA, 2003. ACM.

[17] M. Kamiński, M. Ding, W. A. Truccolo, and S. L. Bressler. Evaluating causal relations in neural systems: granger causality, directed transfer function and statistical assessment of significance. *Biological cybernetics*, 85(2):145–157, Aug. 2001.

[18] L. F. Kozachenko and N. N. Leonenko. Sample estimate of the entropy of a random vector. *Probl. Peredachi Inf.*, 23(2):95–101, Nov. 1987.

[19] A. Kraskov, H. Stögbauer, and P. Grassberger. Estimating mutual information. *Phys. Rev. E*, 69:066138, Jun 2004.

[20] H. Kwak, C. Lee, H. Park, and S. Moon. What is twitter, a social network or a news media? In *Proceedings of the 19th international conference on World wide web*, WWW '10, pages 591–600, New York, NY, USA, 2010. ACM.

[21] J. Lizier, M. Prokopenko, and A. Zomaya. Local information transfer as a spatiotemporal filter for complex systems. *Phys. Rev. E*, 77(2):026110, 2008.

[22] A. C. Lozano, N. Abe, Y. Liu, and S. Rosset. Grouped graphical granger modeling for gene expression regulatory networks discovery. *Bioinformatics*, 25(12):i110–i118, 2009.

[23] A. C. Lozano, H. Li, A. Niculescu-Mizil, Y. Liu, C. Perlich, J. Hosking, and N. Abe. Spatial-temporal causal modeling for climate change attribution. In *Proceedings of the 15th ACM SIGKDD*, KDD '09, New York, NY, USA, 2009. ACM.

[24] M. Muja and D. Lowe. Fast approximate nearest neighbors with automatic algorithm configuration. In *International Conference on Computer Vision Theory and Applications (VISSAPPÕ09)*, pages 331–340, 2009.

[25] L. Page, S. Brin, R. Motwani, and T. Winograd. The PageRank Citation Ranking: Bringing Order to the Web. Technical report, Stanford Digital Library Technologies Project, 1998.

[26] S. Panzeri, R. Senatore, M. A. Montemurro, and R. S. Petersen. Correcting for the sampling bias problem in spike train information measures. *Journal of Neurophysiology*, 98(3):1064–1072, 2007.

[27] J. W. Pennebaker and M. E. Francis. Linguistic inquiry and word count: A computerized text analysis program, 2007.

[28] F. Pérez-Cruz. Estimation of information theoretic measures for continuous random variables. In *Proceedings of NIPS-08*, pages 1257–1264, 2008.

[29] B. Póczos and J. Schneider. Nonparametric estimation of conditional information and divergences. 2012.

[30] R. Řehůřek and P. Sojka. Software Framework for Topic Modelling with Large Corpora. In *Proceedings of the LREC 2010 Workshop on New Challenges for NLP Frameworks*, pages 45–50, Valletta, Malta, May 2010. ELRA. `http://is.muni.cz/publication/884893/en`.

[31] D. Romero, W. Galuba, S. Asur, and B. Huberman. Influence and passivity in social media. *Machine Learning and Knowledge Discovery in Databases*, pages 18–33, 2011.

[32] S.A. Macskassy. On the study of social interactions in twitter. In *Sixth International AAAI Conference on Weblogs and Social Media. ICWSM*, 2012.

[33] S.A. Macskassy and M. Michelson. Why do people retweet? Anti-Homophily wins the day! In *Proceedings of the Fifth International Conference on Weblogs and Social Media*, Menlo Park, CA, USA, 2011. AAAI.

[34] T. Schreiber. Measuring information transfer. *Phys. Rev. Lett.*, 85(2):461–464, Jul 2000.

[35] M. Vejmelka and M. Paluš. Inferring the directionality of coupling with conditional mutual information. *Physical Review E*, 77(2):026214, 2008.

[36] G. Ver Steeg and A. Galstyan. Information transfer in social media. In *Proc of. World Wide Web Conference*, 2012.

[37] J. Victor. Binless strategies for estimation of information from neural data. *Physical Review E*, 66(5):051903, 2002.

[38] J. D. Victor. Approaches to information-theoretic analysis of neural activity. *Biological Theory*, 1(3):302–316, 2006.

[39] Q. Wang, S. R. Kulkarni, and S. Verdú. Divergence estimation for multidimensional densities via k-nearest-neighbor distances. *IEEE Trans. Inf. Theor.*, 55:2392–2405, May 2009.

[40] J. Weng, E.-P. Lim, J. Jiang, and Q. He. Twitterrank: finding topic-sensitive influential twitterers. In *Proceedings of the third ACM international conference on Web search and data mining*, WSDM '10, pages 261–270, New York, NY, USA, 2010. ACM.

[41] W. Zhao, J. Jiang, J. Weng, J. He, E. Lim, H. Yan, and X. Li. Comparing twitter and traditional media using topic models. *Advances in Information Retrieval*, pages 338–349, 2011.

Characterizing and Curating Conversation Threads: Expansion, Focus, Volume, Re-entry

Lars Backstrom
Facebook
lars@fb.com

Jon Kleinberg
Cornell University
kleinber@cs.cornell.edu

Lillian Lee
Cornell University
llee@cs.cornell.edu

Cristian Danescu-Niculescu-Mizil
Stanford/Max Planck Institute SWS
cristiand@cs.stanford.edu

ABSTRACT

Discussion threads form a central part of the experience on many Web sites, including social networking sites such as Facebook and Google Plus and knowledge creation sites such as Wikipedia. To help users manage the challenge of allocating their attention among the discussions that are relevant to them, there has been a growing need for the algorithmic curation of on-line conversations — the development of automated methods to select a subset of discussions to present to a user.

Here we consider two key sub-problems inherent in conversational curation: length prediction — predicting the number of comments a discussion thread will receive — and the novel task of re-entry prediction — predicting whether a user who has participated in a thread will later contribute another comment to it. The first of these sub-problems arises in estimating how interesting a thread is, in the sense of generating a lot of conversation; the second can help determine whether users should be kept notified of the progress of a thread to which they have already contributed. We develop and evaluate a range of approaches for these tasks, based on an analysis of the network structure and arrival pattern among the participants, as well as a novel dichotomy in the structure of long threads. We find that for both tasks, learning-based approaches using these sources of information yield improvements for all the performance metrics we used.

Categories and Subject Descriptors: H.2.8: Data Mining

General Terms: Measurement; Experimentation; Theory

Keywords: user-generated content, comment threads, threads, Facebook, Wikipedia, conversations, likes, feed ranking, recommendation, on-line communities, social networks, discussions

1. INTRODUCTION

Many Web sites are organized around a continuously evolving set of discussion threads. This style of interaction is a key component of on-line groups and message boards, social networking sites such as Facebook and Google Plus, and the workflow of collaborative projects such as Wikipedia and open-source development. In all these cases, a user must continuously decide how to allocate his or her attention to a range of relevant discussions, and this can be a challenging task when content arrives at a rapid rate.

A growing number of sites are helping users address this challenge through the algorithmic *curation* of discussion threads, automatically selecting which threads to bring to a user's attention at any given point in time. A canonical example is Facebook's News Feed — for users with a sufficient number of active friends on the site, an unfiltered stream of all stories generated by friends is generally much less valuable to the user than a ranked and filtered version of the stream that attempts to highlight the stories estimated to be most engaging to the user.

The problem of curating discussion threads is thus a wide-ranging one in the context of applications, but it is one which for the most part has not been systematized in prior research. Our goal in this paper is to facilitate such a systematization, by identifying and formalizing two important sub-problems in conversational curation, and then developing and evaluating techniques to address them. For our evaluation, we use discussion threads from two sites where such threads form a core part of the experience: discussions among users on Facebook and discussions among editors on Wikipedia. As on many other sites, threads on Facebook and Wikipedia can be conceptualized as an initial *post* and a subsequent sequence of *comments*; we will use this terminology in what follows.

The present work: Two problems in conversational curation. We now describe the two problems that we study, together with their motivation as components of conversational curation.

1. *Length prediction*: given the initial portion of a thread (a post and the first few comments following it), how well can we predict the eventual length of the thread? We use this length prediction problem as a concretely formulated proxy for the general issue of estimating the level of interest a thread will generate, based on observation of its early stages.

2. *Re-entry prediction*: given the initial portion of a thread and the identity of one of the commenters, how well can we predict whether this commenter will contribute another comment later in the thread? This is a key issue in determining whether to keep a user notified of the progress on a thread once he or she has contributed to it — some threads have the structure of a conversation where users are motivated to return repeatedly, while others involve each user contributing once (for example, to offer congratulations or condolences) but then not returning.

Taken together, these two problems cover a set of central issues in conversational curation: identifying threads that will generate sustained interest, so as to be able to highlight them to users, and

WSDM'13, February 4–8, 2013, Rome, Italy.

recognizing whether a thread is something that a contributing user will want to continue to follow as it evolves.

We develop techniques for these problems by first analyzing the structure of threads, and then formulating a set of properties that we in turn use for the prediction tasks.

We begin by investigating the following issue, on data described in **§2**. Intuitively, one feels from experience that there are two distinct types of long threads: those that become long because a small group of people engage in an extensive conversation via the comments, and those that become long because many users each contribute a single comment. A canonical example of the latter would begin with a post in which a user announces a major life event, and then many friends contribute congratulations in the comments as in a wedding guestbook. We refer to the first type of thread as *focused*, and the second type as *expansionary*.

But is this notion of two types simply one's perception of two extremes of a broad distribution, or is there quantitative evidence for it? We find (**§3**) in fact that threads genuinely exhibit this two-type effect: for long threads, the distribution of the number of distinct commenters is bimodal, with threads either dominated by a very small number of distinct users, or by a sequence of commenters who generally do not return to the thread after commenting once. In addition to providing what is, to our knowledge, the first evidence for this basic dichotomy, this finding helps reinforce the importance of our second problem — re-entry prediction — by establishing that active discussion threads can vary considerably in the extent to which participants are interested in returning after their initial contribution.

In order to build a framework for approaching our two basic problems, we begin by studying (**§4**) a range of related thread properties. One of the most useful of these is the thread's *arrival pattern* — the ordering by which new entrants into the thread are interleaved with returning participants. Formalizing this notion allows us to work with relaxed versions of the two extremes of focused and expansionary threads discussed above, and to explore the region that interpolates between them. We also study network and temporal structure: whether the first few commenters are linked within a social network, and how quickly after the post do they arrive in real-time; both convey information about the future trajectory of the thread.

We incorporate these properties into a machine learning approach for predicting length (**§5**) and re-entry (**§6**). Evaluating the prediction performance enables us to identify the features that are most effective for our two problems. At a high level, we find that the structure of the arrival pattern is the most useful for re-entry prediction, while temporal properties together with the arrival pattern give the strongest performance for length prediction.

Next, in **§7**, we explore a probabilistic model of participant re-entry related to the dichotomy between focused threads and expansionary ones. Clearly some styles of post tend to lead to one type of thread or the other, but for other kinds of posts, one sees both types of threads emerge; for example, the same shared link to a news story can generate a focused thread when it is shared among one set of users and an expansionary thread when it is shared among a different set. It is therefore natural to ask whether a type of symmetry-breaking can arise directly from the dynamics of a discussion itself — that is, whether there is a simple probabilistic generative model capable of producing both focused and expansionary threads over different realizations of its random trajectory. We show how to construct such a model from plausible assumptions about turn-taking and new entrants in discussion threads; the model exposes interesting connections between discussion threads and nonlinear urn processes.

In **§8**, we review related work on the dynamics of on-line discussions. For now, we note that the general issue of thread length has been studied, using different techniques, in contexts distinct from ours — primarily for comments on blog and news sites, where essentially all threads are expansionary, with many participants who typically contribute only once or very few times each [14, 23, 25, 26]. In contrast, our approach incorporating the notion that there can be multiple structurally distinct types of long threads is suited to settings where the participants maintain long-running relationships with one another. These structural distinctions also provide a core part of the motivation for re-entry prediction, which is a key issue for organizing conversations in these settings; the problem of re-entry prediction has not, to our knowledge, been formulated or studied previously.

2. DATA AND BASIC DEFINITIONS

We use data from Facebook and Wikipedia to construct three distinct populations of users whose discussion threads we study. We choose Facebook as perhaps the most well-known example of a post-plus-comments interface for socially-oriented conversations. Conversations among Wikipedia editors form a contrasting case that has also received research attention [7, 13, 17]: the discussions are task-oriented, as opposed to socially-oriented, and there is no formal structure imposed on conversations by the interface; nonetheless, they can still be naturally treated as instances of comment threads.

For completeness, we briefly describe the structure of these discussion threads at a general level. On Facebook, we study instances in which a user posts a status update, and then other users with permission to comment on the status update contribute comments to it. On Wikipedia, editors interact on *talk-pages* to discuss issues concerning articles, projects or Wikipedia policies. Each editor has the option of hosting a talk-page, and most active users do.

On both Facebook and Wikipedia, we will refer to the status update or initiating text as the *post*; the sequence of comments that follows the post will be called the *comment thread*, and the post together with all the comments will be called the *full thread*. The poster together with the commenters in a full thread will be called the full thread's *participants*. The number of items in the thread (including the post in the case of a full thread, but not in a comment thread) will be called its *length* or its *volume*; we use these two terms synonymously.

From Facebook, we first selected 100,000 users uniformly at random from the population of US Facebook users. We will refer to this set $\mathcal{U}$ in our analysis as the *uniform* Facebook population. Also, out of all US Facebook users who posted beween 200 and 300 status updates over an 80-day period, we randomly selected 100,000 of these heavily engaged users. We will refer to this set $\mathcal{A}$ as the *high-activity* Facebook population. For both $\mathcal{U}$ and $\mathcal{A}$, we study the comment threads associated with all their posts during the same 80-day period. All Facebook data was used anonymously, and all analysis was done in aggregate.

Our Wikipedia data is derived from the corpus of Danescu-Niculescu-Mizil et al. [7]. We used 118,447 conversation threads of length at least 1 (to discard posts made by automated bots, which never attract responses) which took place asynchronously on the talk-pages hosted by 6,555 highly active editors; posts average 2.12 comments. We also use the content of the talk-pages to assess the existence of an interactional link between a given pair of Wikipedia editors: we say that two editors are linked if at least one of them added a post or comment on the other's editor talk page. Our Wikipedia data will be available at
`http://www.mpi-sws.org/~cristian/Echoes_of_power.html`.

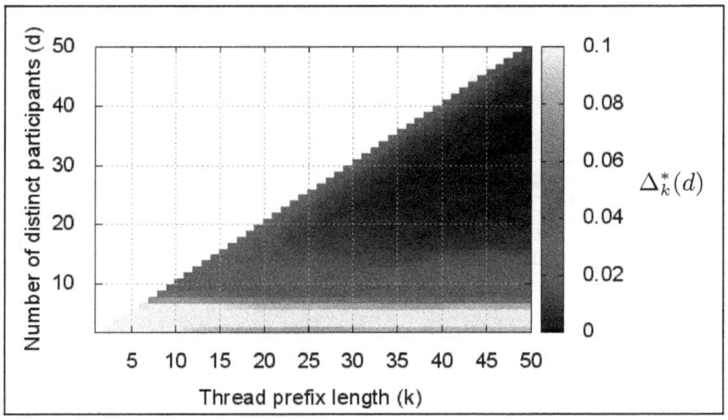

Figure 1: Heat map (best viewed in color) of the density functions on distinct commenters, uniform Facebook population. For each thread prefix length k, there is a peak in density (lighter color) at a small number and a second peak approximately at the maximum number of distinct participants d.

3. FOCUSED VS. EXPANSIONARY THREADS

If a post leads to a long comment thread, then it is one that attracts a great deal of attention and so is likely of interest; thus, the thread-length prediction problem is crucial to the curating of conversations. In thinking about how to bring long threads to users' attention, though, a natural question is whether there are sub-classes of such conversations that should be treated differently.

This question leads us to conjecture that there is a dichotomy between *expansionary* high-activity threads, created by the one-time actions of many different "drive-by" commenters, versus *focused* high-activity threads, reflecting a high-level of repeated engagement among relatively few people. In this section, we provide supporting evidence for this conjecture and discuss its consequences.

Distinct Participants: Two Local Maxima. To investigate the validity of our conjecture, we consider how the number of distinct participants in a thread is distributed. To do so, we must account for two issues. First, we do not want the idiosyncratic actions of any one high-volume user to dominate the quantities involved, so we work with a macro-averaged function.[1] Second, the possible number of distinct participants in a thread depends on the thread's length, and so we need to parametrize by it.

Thus, formally, for a population of users $\mathcal{P}$, let $\mathcal{P}_k$ be the set of users who authored at least one post having comment thread length at least k. For each user $u \in \mathcal{P}_k$, we take all full threads associated with a post by u that produced at least k comments, and we truncate each of these threads to the prefix consisting of just the post and the first k comments. Let $\delta_u(k)$ be the average number of distinct participants in all these prefixes of full threads initiated by u. (For a given such prefix, the number can range from 1 — the original poster contributed all of the comments as well — to $k+1$ — all commenters are distinct, and the original poster didn't comment.) We then define $\Delta_k^*(d)$ to be the fraction of users $u \in \mathcal{P}_k$ for whom $\lfloor \delta_u(k) \rfloor = d$. Note that Δ_k^* is a density function. In what follows, for brevity we will sometimes refer to it simply as an average or an expectation, with the understanding that this refers in fact to a macro-averaged quantity.

In these terms, our conjecture can be expressed as follows: for threads of sufficient length k, the density function $\Delta_k^*(d)$ should have (at least) two local maxima: one at a small value of d, i.e., $d \ll k$, and one at a large value of d, i.e., $d \approx k+1$.

In Figure 1, we show the family of density functions Δ_k^* for $k \in 1, 2, ..., 50$ on our uniform Facebook population $\mathcal{U}$. The densities are drawn as a heat map, with column k representing the density function Δ_k^*. We see that as k increases, $\Delta_k^*(d)$ is first maximized at $d = 4$, reflecting the dominant role of the focused effect; but then, a second local maximum emerges at a value of d very close to k. For the population $\mathcal{A}$ of high-activity Facebook users, we see essentially the same effect, including the two local maxima at $d = 4$ and d close to k (figure omitted for space).

Although the smaller data volume makes it more difficult to discern the effect on Wikipedia, when we group together the possible values of d into contiguous intervals, we find significant evidence of two local maxima there too. To quantify the effect on Wikipedia, we compare quantiles of Δ_k^*, defining $f_k(p,q) = \sum_{pk \le d \le qk} \Delta_k^*(d)$. We find that as k increases (in particular, considering $k \geq 15$), we have $f_k(0, \frac{1}{4}) > f_k(\frac{1}{4}, \frac{1}{2})$ and $f_k(\frac{3}{4}, 1) > f_k(\frac{1}{2}, \frac{3}{4})$. This inequality is consistent with Figure 1, where the density function is larger at the two extremes than in comparably-sized intervals in between.

Consequences: Predict Both Length and Re-entry. As argued earlier, conversational-curation systems should contain a thread-length prediction component. But our new observation about the distinction between expansionary and focused threads shows that long threads can differ significantly in the extent to which a commenter will want to return to contribute a second time. This heterogeneity in long threads motivates the formulation of our second task, *re-entry prediction*: determining whether a given participant in the thread is likely to contribute again. To our knowledge, re-entry in on-line conversations is a problem that has not been previously formalized or studied.

Length and re-entry are important, and distinct, issues in the task of conversational curation. Length prediction, since it provides information about the amount of attention a thread is likely to receive, helps in assessing whether a user should be made aware of the thread at all. Re-entry prediction, on the other hand, provides information about how to keep a user informed of the evolution of the thread once he or she has already contributed to it: a high re-entry probability indicates that the user may well want to know about subsequent comments, so that he or she can contribute in response to them.

Predicting a particular user's re-entry is different from predicting whether the thread itself will be focused or expansionary. While very few users re-enter an expansionary thread by definition, it is easily possible for a user u to contribute to a thread that later becomes dominated by a back-and-forth discussion among a small set of other participants; in this case, the thread is focused, but user u's re-entry probability might be low. Predicting re-entry provides a concrete recommendation with respect to a given user, in a way that predicting whether a thread will be focused or expansionary does not.

We note that re-entry prediction is focused on a user's *production* of comments — specifically, whether the user will write another comment in the future. An interesting open question is to consider the analogous prediction task for a user's *consumption* of comments. In particular, a user might be interested in continuing to read comments on a thread as they come in, despite having no intention of contributing again. (Consider a string of congratulatory messages on a life event that include interesting side information, such as personal reminiscences or clever quips.)

[1]The results turn out to be similar for the micro-averaged analog.

4. EARLY PARTICIPANTS: SOCIAL, SEQUENTIAL, AND TEMPORAL STRUCTURES

In this section, we show how properties of the initial participants in a thread can provide information about the thread's later dynamics, thus laying the groundwork for the features in our subsequent prediction experiments. First (§4.1), we show that the presence or absence of social links among the initial participants in a thread turns out to provide useful information, though in interestingly different ways for different settings. Second (§4.2), inspired by our expansionary vs. focused analysis in §3, which introduces the importance of re-entry, we develop a novel representation for the sequence of participant contributions. Third (§4.3), we demonstrate that how fast the initial commenters arrive provides important information about the eventual number of comments, though its connection with re-entry probability is less clear.

4.1 Links Among the Initial Participants

We first consider comment threads in our Facebook High-Activity population (outcomes are analogous for the Uniform set), focusing on threads with at least two comments and where the first two commenters are distinct from each other and from the post's author. The tension between the focused and the expansionary effects has a natural reflection in the relationship between these first two commenters. If they are friends, then interest in the post might be limited to a particular portion of the poster's social neighborhood. That is, interest in such a post could have limited *reach*, which could restrict thread length. At the same time, though, there might also be increased potential for an extended conversation to ensue as friends interact, which would lead to a longer thread.

The top-left plot in Figure 2 shows that in fact, these Facebook threads are significantly longer when the first two commenters are friends.

We can further validate this hypothesized effect of conversational interaction by examining a related mechanism in which the role of interaction is much more limited. The Facebook "like" feature is very useful for this purpose. Users can respond to a post not just by commenting on it but also by clicking the *like* (thumbs-up) button, which provides a one-bit endorsement of the content. Thus, likes are a light-weight communication alternative to comments, and we can consider "like threads" — the sequence of likes arriving on a post — as the corresponding analog of comment threads. But there is a crucial difference: in like threads, there is no analog to the back-and-forth interaction that characterizes conversational interaction.

When the first two likers in a like thread are distinct, how is the eventual length of the like thread affected by whether these two users are friends? The top-middle plot of Figure 2(b) shows that, in the absence of repeated interactions to offset its consequences, a limited-reach effect is clear: the like thread is shorter when the first two likers are linked.[2]

Applying the same analysis to Facebook thread prefixes of length $k = 3, 4$, and 5 yields very similar results. For space reasons, we only depict the case $k = 3$ (bottom-left and bottom-middle plots in Figure 2), but the results are that expected length of comment threads continues to increase almost perfectly monotonically in the number of edges among the first k commenters when they are all distinct. Also, we find completely analogous results for re-entry in Facebook threads: the re-entry of the first participant increases

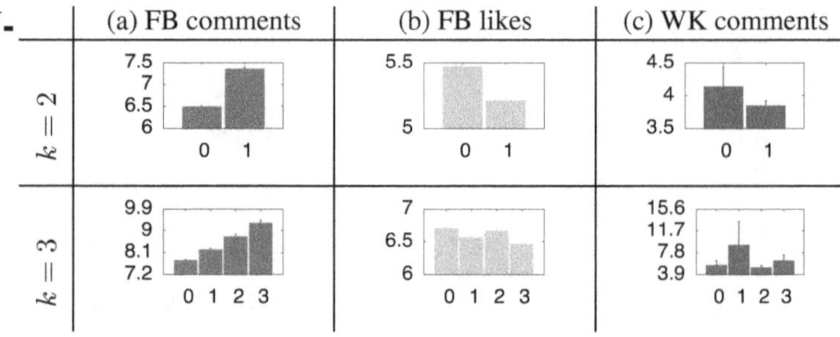

Figure 2: Thread length vs. number of connections between the first k commenters when they are distinct. More-connected commenters make for longer Facebook (FB) comment threads but shorter "like threads" and Wikipedia (WK) discussion threads. (Y-axes not aligned to heighten trend visibility.)

strongly with the number of edges among the first k commenters when they are all distinct.

What about Wikipedia comment threads? As depicted in the rightmost column of Figure 2, in this domain, it is *not* the case that more connections between the first participants leads to longer threads, although the available data here is quite sparse. We conjecture that the root cause for the striking contrast to Facebook may be the task-oriented nature of the setting, in which conversations may be less discursive, and editors who have interacted in the past may be more conversationally efficient in reaching a conclusion.

It is interesting to note that earlier work of Ugander et al. considered the level of connectedness among the set of users who appear in an invitation to join Facebook [24]; invitations that displayed users who were not linked to each other had higher overall conversion rates than invitations that displayed linked users. While invitations and comment threads are clearly different in nature, they both involve opportunities to engage a user in the activity of the site; whether there is a deeper relationship between the connectedness of commenters here and the connectedness of inviters in that setting is an interesting open question.

4.2 Arrival Patterns

Having looked at the *number* of distinct commenters, and at the *graph structure* on the first few participants in the case when they are distinct, we now develop a general method for representing the precise *sequence* of arrivals of the first few participants, and show that these sequences have the potential to be very useful features in our prediction tasks.

For a comment thread t, let t_i (for $i = 1, 2, ...$) denote the identity of author of the ith comment in the thread. We now define the following encoding $\gamma(t)$ of comment thread t. $\gamma(t)$ is a sequence of non-negative integers; the ith entry in the sequence, denoted $\gamma(t)_i$, is equal to 0 if t_i is the author of the post that started the thread (returning to the thread in this case as the ith commenter), and otherwise $\gamma(t)_i$ is equal to the value of j such that t_i is the jth distinct commenter to take part in t. In what follows, we refer to $\gamma(t)_i$ as the *ID code* of commenter t_i. We will also use the term *arrival pattern* to refer generically to any prefix of $\gamma(t)$ (including the full sequence). Figure 3 illustrates these concepts via two sample discussions, exemplifying that focused threads should have arrival patterns in which some back-and-forth between two participants is evident, whereas expansionary threads should have arrival patterns in which all ID codes occur very few times, mostly just once.

Can early (i.e., short) arrival patterns serve as useful features for our prediction tasks? Before describing our full experiments (detailed in the next sections), it is useful to show some preliminary evidence of these patterns' potential utility.

[2]We note that measuring the number of *distinct* commenters shows the same limited-reach effect: although the comment thread is longer when the first two commenters are linked, the total number of distinct commenters is smaller.

Facebook High-Activity, Length-5 arrival patterns		
pattern	1 re-enters	% of occ.
1,0,1,0,1	55.2%	19.2
1,0,1,0,0	47.5%	2.8
1,0,1,0,2	26.7%	4.9
1,0,1,2,0	26.1%	4.1
1,0,2,0,2	16.5%	4.6
1,2,0,2,0	14.6%	3.1
1,0,2,3,0	12.5%	1.9
1,2,0,3,0	11.5%	2.0
1,0,2,0,3	10.9%	2.6
1,2,3,4,5	5.6%	3.6
		sum: 48.8

Wikipedia, Length-5 arrival patterns		
pattern	1 re-enters	% of occ.
1,0,1,1,0	60.2%	2.4
1,1,0,1,0	58.6%	2.8
1,0,1,0,0	55.3%	4.8
1,0,0,1,0	52.2%	5.5
1,1,1,1,1	47.5%	2.3
1,0,1,2,1	46.0%	3.2
1,0,1,0,2	45.8%	2.7
1,2,1,2,1	41.1%	5.1
1,0,1,0,1	38.8%	27.0
1,2,3,4,5	7.2%	1.7
		sum: 57.5

Facebook High-Activity, length-9 arrival patterns		
pattern bins	1 re-enters	% of occ.
#0:3, #1:6	67.7%	1.7
#0:4, #1:5	66.9%	12.1
#0:5, #1:4	65.5%	4.0
#0:3, #1:4, #2:2	56.8%	2.1
#0:3, #1:3, #2:3	50.9%	1.7
#0:4, #1:4, #2:1	47.6%	5.2
#0:4, #1:3, #2:2	38.5%	3.5
#0:4, #1:3, #2:1, #3:1	28.2%	2.0
#0:4, #1:2, #2:3	22.3%	2.8
#0:4, #1:1, #2:4	9.6%	2.7
		sum: 37.8

Table 1: *Left* and *middle*: the most common length-5 arrival patterns on Facebook, accounting for 48.6% of the occurrences of all possible such arrival patterns, and on Wikipedia, accounting for 57.5% of all occurrences of all possible such patterns. The patterns are sorted by the percentage of corresponding threads in which the user with ID code 1 returns to the thread to comment again. "% of occ.": percentage of threads of length ≥ 5 prefixed by that pattern. *Right*: The same for the most common length-9 arrival patterns, except that patterns have been binned by counts of ID codes since there are many possible length-9 patterns. For example, "#0:3, #1:6" = the set of length-9 patterns where ID code 0 occurs 3 times and ID code 1 occurs 6 times, in any order. (Some populations omitted for brevity or due to data sparseness.)

focused thread		*expansionary thread*	
Mary:	Anyone there	James:	we're engaged!
Mary:	?	Dina:	congrats!
Don:	me	Fred:	congrats!
Pat:	not me	Mia:	great!!!
Don:	v funny	Moe:	great!
Pat:	i know	James:	Thanks guys :)
...	...	...	...
Length-2 arrival pattern: 0,1		*Length-2 arrival pattern: 1,2*	
Length-5 arrival pattern: 0,1,2,1,2		*Length-5 arrival pattern: 1,2,3,4,0*	

Figure 3: Example conversations demonstrating our arrival-pattern coding scheme for the comment portion of threads.

First, we see whether different (early) arrival patterns tend to correspond to different thread lengths. Figure 4 shows, for each of our three populations, the (macro-averaged) length of threads whose length-two prefixes correspond to each of the five possible length-two patterns; the fact that the mean thread lengths fall in mostly disjoint confidence intervals indicates that the patterns do have predictive value.[3]

Second, we see whether different arrival patterns tend to correspond to differing re-entry probabilities, focusing on the chance that the user with ID code 1 (i.e., the first commenter who isn't the original poster) subsequently re-joins the thread by adding another comment. Table 1 demonstrates that arrival patterns carry significant information about ID code 1's re-entry probability. In all the populations shown, it appears that guestbook-style patterns containing many distinct ID codes tend to results in noticeably lower re-entry probabilities. For Facebook, we also see a strong positive correlation between the number of times ID code 1 appears in an arrival pattern and the likelihood that ID code 1 will subsequently appear again.

4.3 Timing effects

Our analysis thus far has considered the sequence of commenters without any information about the speed at which they arrive in real time. We now show some basic results establishing that this type of temporal structure contains important information about the length and re-entry properties of threads; in the next section, we use this information as part of our prediction methods.

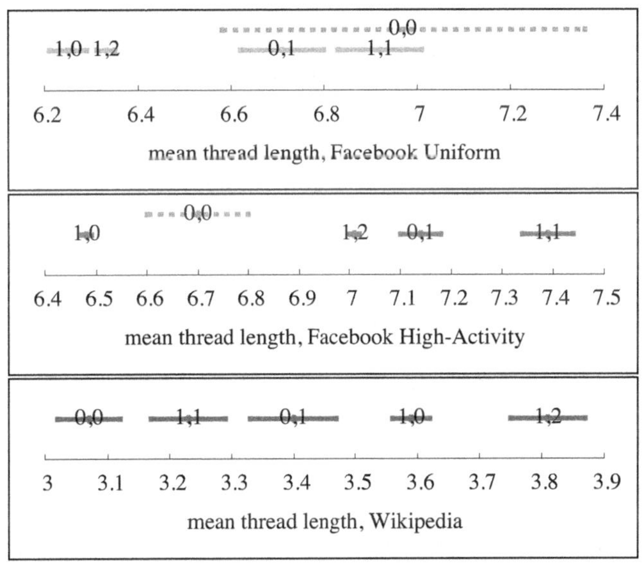

Figure 4: In all populations, the 95%-confidence-intervals for mean thread length for the five possible length-2 arrival patterns — indicated as labels on the intervals — are almost all disjoint. Grey/dashed intervals indicate rare arrival patterns (at most 1% of threads), so the long interval involved in the single overlap (0,0 in Facebook Uniform) is for a sparse situation.

In Figure 5, we see (black curve) that the longer it takes for the first comment to arrive on an initial post, the shorter the thread, presumably because "late" first comments correspond to less overall activity around the post. But note that timing isn't everything: beyond a certain point, the probability that the first commenter re-enters a thread (green curve) becomes approximately independent of the first-comment arrival time lag.

5. PREDICTING THREAD LENGTH

We now engage in the two main prediction tasks of this paper. Recall that the first task, which we describe in this section, is to

[3]We note that the two most frequent arrival patterns in all three populations are (1,0) and (1,2), which is interesting because (1,0) corresponds to the canonical turn-taking structure in a pairwise conversation, while (1, 2) is the canonical sequence of successive new arrivals — a further reflection of our focused/expansionary dichotomy.

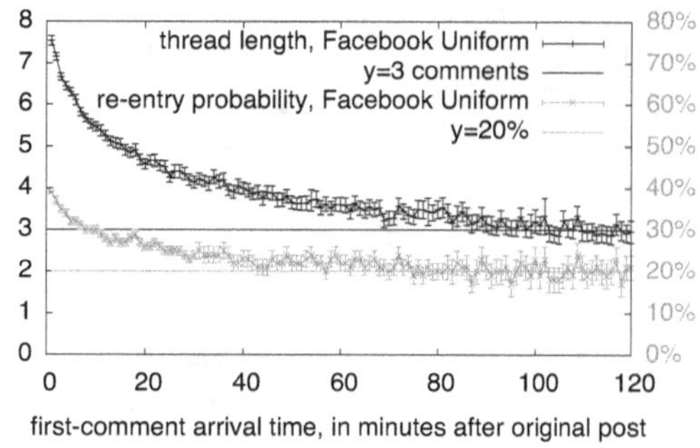

Figure 5: Black (left axis, top curve): the longer it takes for the original post to attract its first comment, the lower the expected thread length. Green (right axis, bottom curve): in contrast, the probability that the first commenter re-enters the thread is eventually independent of the first comment's arrival time. The $y = 3$ and $y = 20\%$ lines are included to allow for visual comparison of the real data curves with theoretical curves in which the arrival lag has no effect.

predict thread length, as an indication of how much interest a post will eventually generate, given the state of the thread at a certain early point. For example, we ask, given a thread initiated by a Facebook user posting a status update to their friends that has already accumulated 5 comments, how well can we predict the final length of the thread?[4] The results of the second task, to predict whether a user that has already participated in a thread will later re-enter that same thread, are described in Section 6.

For thread-length prediction, we formulate two concrete tasks on the Wikipedia and Facebook High-Activity datasets (the results on the Facebook Uniform dataset are similar, but with larger error bars). From the set of all posts made by the active Facebook users, we selected the subset of posts that received at least 5 comments, and randomly reserved 50% of them for evaluation, using the other 50% for feature exploration. This gave us a test data set of 1,996,624 posts. Out of these, we chose a threshold of 8 comments to create an approximately balanced binary prediction problem: given the state of the thread after five posts, will the thread eventually receive at least 8 comments? (55.25% of the posts are in the positive class.) Similarly, for Wikipedia, we look at all talk-page posts that have received at least two comments, and ask, will they receive a third one? In this case, our data is smaller, with only 44,732 items in the test set (54.55% of which are in the positive class).

5.1 Features (used here and in §6)

The features we employed are summarized in Table 2. The first three sets are based on our discussion above of links between participants (§4.1), arrival patterns (§4.2), and timing effects (§4.3). We describe the other two sets now.

An important question is whether the textual features of the original post are more or less effective for this task than the non-textual features we have already described. To investigate this issue, we elected to gather a small, presumably general set of such "Original post terms" features via text regression, which has previously been employed for blog comment-volume prediction [26]. Specifically, we used J. M. White's TextRegression R package, which employs linear regression with elastic-net regularization [9], run on a set of posts disjoint from the training and test data used for

[4]Naturally, for this task, we use only features that can be derived from the state of the thread when it had 5 comments.

LINKS	
$edges\_prev[i]^*$	Number of links from commenter to previous commenters
$mutual\_poster[i]^*$	Number of links from commenter to users linked to the original poster
ARRIVAL PATTERNS	
$id\_code[i]$	commenter ID code as described in §4.2
$uniq\_comm[i]$	Unique commenters through comment i
TIME	
$time[i]$	Time taken for the first i comments to arrive
TEXT REGRESSION FEATURES	
$Orig\_post\_terms$	"comment", "agree", etc.: see §5.1
MISC	
$num\_words[i]$	Number of words in comment i
$num\_chars[i]$	Number of characters in comment i
$question[i]^*$	Comment i has a '?'
$exclaim[i]^*$	Comment i has a '!'
$likes[i]^*$	Num likes on original post before comment i is made
$comment\_likes[i]^*$	Num likes on comments before comment i

Table 2: Features used in our prediction experiments. For each indexed feature, we also build a comparable feature for the original post when it makes sense (the *id_code* for the original post is always 0 and so is omitted but, for example, the length of the original post in words or characters is meaningful). Features marked with * were applied only for Facebook data.

classification. 50 terms were selected for the Facebook data — among them were "comment" and "anybody" (positive coefficient for thread length), and "re-post" and URLs (negative coefficient). Among the 30 selected terms for Wikipedia were "agree" (positive) and "thank" (negative).

Also, preliminary pilot studies revealed a set of fairly intuitive miscellaneous features, listed in the last section of Table 2, that are potentially correlated with thread length. For instance, one might expect that on average, posts containing a question mark pose questions that prompt comments as responses.

5.2 Performance Results

Our testing methodology was: for a given set of features and train/test set, create bagged decision trees with 60 trees trained on independent samples of the training data; then, apply the bagged decision trees on the disjoint test set.

Our main method was to use all the features described in Table 2. We compared its performance against the following two **baselines**. The *positive-percentage bias baseline* chooses an item's label randomly with bias equal to the percentage of test items in the positive class (55.52% in the Facebook case, 54.55% in the Wikipedia case). The *text-regression baseline* uses only the $Orig\_post\_terms$ features chosen via text regression as described in §5.1.

The performance of our method versus the two baselines is shown in Table 3. Clearly, the combined use of participant-link, arrival-pattern, timing, and other information yields the best results for all five of our performance metrics. The small set of text-regression features extracted from the original post sometimes did worse that the positive-percentage bias baseline.[5]

[5]This is consonant with De Choudhury et al. [8], who remark that

		ACC	AUC	RMSE	APR	CXE
FB	Pos.-% bias baseline	.552	.500	.497	.550	.992
	Text baseline	.537	.529	.503	.568	1.01
	All our features	**.672**	**.729**	**.457**	**.758**	**.872**
Wiki	Pos.-% bias baseline	.548	.500	.498	.549	.993
	Text baseline	.488	.505	.517	.550	1.06
	All our features	**.595**	**.627**	**.486**	**.661**	**.958**

Table 3: Main thread-length prediction results. Bold = best performance per dataset, under various metrics: ACC: accuracy (for FB active: after 5 comments, predicting whether the thread achieves length ≥ 8; for Wiki: after 2 comments, predicting whether an additional comment will occur). AUC: area under the ROC curve. RMSE: root mean square error. APR: mean average precision. CXE: cross-entropy.

Key Facebook Features. To better understand the individual factors contributing to the length of a comment thread, we perform stepwise forward feature selection. In iteration j of this algorithm, we create working feature set F_j by finding the best single feature to add to the set F_{j-1} to maximize our objective function, area under the ROC curve (AUC). Because it only selects a single feature at a time, this method prevents us from adding more than a single copy of highly correlated features, and the order that the features are installed gives us some insight into the nature of these comment threads.

Table 4 shows the features selected by this process for the Facebook dataset. There are three things worth noting from these results. The first is that a relatively small set of features contributes almost all of the predictive value. In particular, the amount of time it takes for the first five comments to arrive (the TIME:$time[5]$ feature) is highly indicative of whether or not the thread will eventually reach 8 comments. Second, most of the key features come from the fifth comment. Thus, when predicting whether or not the thread will continue, one should focus on the most recent activity of the thread. We highlight this in Figure 6, where we show the prediction performance when using only the subsets of features derived from a single message in the thread, ranging from the original post ($x = 0$) to the fifth comment. The third item of note is the fact that the link-based features do not have much effect. We believe this is because they are low-recall, in the sense that we only showed in §4.1 that they are useful when all the early commenters in the thread are distinct.

Given the strength of the time feature, it is interesting to ask what would be the effect of its removal. The combination of the other features is unable to make up for the loss of temporal information: removing that key feature, the AUC drops from 0.729 to 0.588. With or without that feature, and even if we slice the data to predicting only for a fixed TIME:$time[5] \in [15m, 20m)$, the relative ordering of the other features remains more or less unchanged.

Key Wikipedia Features. In the case of Wikipedia, we see a somewhat similar ordering to the features. Again, the features regarding the most recent comment (here, the second one) are the most predictive of future comments. Here, however, we find that the *length* of the second comment is the most important feature, followed by the time to the second comment, and the ID code of the second and first commenters. Beyond these first four features, the relatively small size of the dataset makes the predictive power of other features unclear.

"textual analyses ... alone are not adequate to capture conversational interestingness because [they] do not consider the dialogue structure between users".

Feature added	AUC
TIME:$time[5]$	0.6954
+ARRIVAL PATTERN:$uniq\_comm[5]$	0.7053
+MISC:$num\_words[5]$	0.7138
+TIME:$time[3]$	0.7214
+MISC:$question[5]$	0.7256
+ARRIVAL PATTERN:*id_code*[5]	0.7258
+ARRIVAL PATTERN:$uniq\_comm[4]$	0.7260

Table 4: Results of stepwise forward feature selection on Facebook. Each row represents performance for all features listed in that row and above.

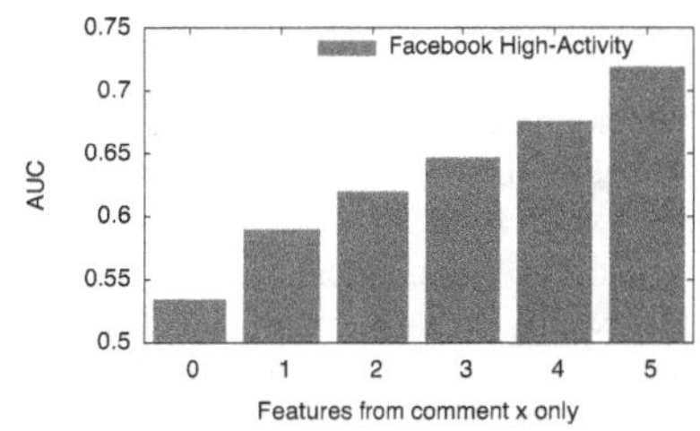

Figure 6: Performance when predicting using only the features derived from a *single* comment (or original post for $x = 0$). The later the comment, the more informative.

6. PREDICTING THREAD RE-ENTRY

Here we examine our second, and novel, prediction task: given the initial portion of a thread and the identity of one of the commenters, how well can we predict whether that commenter will contribute another comment later in the thread? As noted earlier, the idea here is to determine whether to keep a user notified of the progress on a thread after they have commented on it already — there are some threads for which the user might want to actively return to the discussion. For space reasons, we can only provide an overview of results here, omitting detailed feature analysis.

For simplicity, we focus on the following two (related) questions. Recall that we use ID code 0 for the original poster of a thread, and ID code 1 for the first commenter other than the original poster, assuming there is such a commenter. (a) Assuming that ID code 1 occurs in the length-5 arrival-pattern prefix, does that user ever appear again? (The value 5 was used in our thread-length prediction problem as well.) (b) The same, but for the first 9 comments. We use the same features as in the previous task; see §5.1 and Table 2.

Using cross-validation, we find (Table 5) that the performance on the full feature set for Facebook is an AUC of 0.855 for the 9 comment version, and 0.808 for the 5 comment version of the task. Using the same feature selection methodology described above, we find that the most important features are the identities of the individuals posting the comments (*id_code*[i]), and especially the identities of the most recent few commenters. The time between the two most recent comments also plays an important role, as the longer it takes, the slower the conversation is moving, and the more likely it is to come to an end.

7. MODELING THREAD RE-ENTRY

Having gained some empirical understanding of thread re-entry, including relatively good performance at predicting it, we now seek

		AUC (x-val)
FB (after 5 comments)	Pos.-% bias baseline	.500
	Text baseline	.520
	Our features	**.808**
FB (after 9 comments)	Pos.-% bias baseline	.500
	Text baseline	.525
	Our features	**.855**
Wiki (after 5 comments)	Pos.-% bias baseline	.500
	Text baseline	.494
	Our features	**.644**

Table 5: Main thread-re-entry prediction cross-validation results. Bold marks the best performance per dataset.

to develop further theoretical understanding of re-entry by formulating a set of probabilistic generative models that produce arrival patterns of a given fixed length. We then study which of these models produce the qualitative phenomena we observe in real threads — particularly bimodality in the number of distinct commenters.

The first class of models $\mathcal{F}$ we consider has the following basic structure for choosing who makes the jth comment, reminiscent of the Chinese Restaurant Process [1]. With some fixed probability $p_j \geq 0$, we introduce a new participant; with probability $1 - p_j$ we select, according to some underlying probabilistic rule, a participant who has already appeared in the thread. (We refer to such participants as *re-entrants*). The re-entrant selection rule is assumed to be a randomized algorithm θ that takes a thread prefix as input and produces the name of an existing participant in the thread. This is a very general definition; depending on the choice of the function θ, we can define arbitrary rules, that, for example, pick a re-entrant uniformly, or according to "rich-get-richer" principles that favor people who have commented more in the past [15], or according to recency principles so that an individual's selection probability decreases in the time since they last commented. Each model $\Omega(k, \theta, \mathbf{p})$ in this class $\mathcal{F}$ is described by a thread length k, selection rule θ, and sequence of probabilities $\mathbf{p} = p_1, p_2, p_3, \ldots, p_k$, $p_i \in (0, 1]$.

A Negative Result. Although $\mathcal{F}$ initially seems reasonable and covers a large space, it turns out to be a poor fit to reality, because *none* of its members can yield the expansionary vs. focused bimodality that we found empirically in §3.

THEOREM 1. *Let $\Omega(k, \theta, \mathbf{p})$ be an arbitrary model in the class $\mathcal{F}$, and let X be a random variable equal to the number of distinct participants in a length-k thread t generated by $\Omega(k, \theta, \mathbf{p})$ (counting the initial poster). Then X has a unimodal density function: there is a number d^* such that $\Pr[X = d]$ is monotonically increasing for $d \leq d^*$ and monotonically decreasing for $d \geq d^*$.*

We omit the proof due to lack of space, but it consists essentially of projecting the arrival pattern onto a binary sequence that records only whether each participant is a re-entrant or not.

Models Exhibiting Bimodality. In view of this negative result, we seek an alternate class of models capable of generating arrival patterns that exhibit bimodality in the number of distinct commenters.

Arguably the simplest approach is to consider mixture models that have bimodality "built in": We need only suppose that there are two distinct types of posts, one which concentrates the number of distinct participants on a small value, and the other which concentrates it on a large value, and that threads are constructed by drawing one of the first type with fixed probability $\pi > 0$ or one of the second with probability $1 - \pi$.

While this mixture principle is presumably an important reason why we see bimodality in the real data, it is not the whole story. Indeed, we ran the following experiment to see whether the same type of post can lead both to focused and expansionary threads. As it turns out, the CNN link that was most shared among a large sample of Facebook users in the first quarter of 2012 was a report of Whitney Houston's death. Although the set of threads spawned just by shares of this link is small by the standards of Figure 1, it is large in an absolute sense, and we observed in this controlled-content case the same sort of bimodality exhibited by threads overall: sometimes, the news provoked a series of "drive-by" comments when it was shared by a user, and other times, the same news prompted extended small-group discussion.

This finding motivates us to construct models of arrival patterns that produce the expansion/focus bimodality as a byproduct without assuming post type as its cause. To do this, we posit a type of internal symmetry-breaking during thread generation, taking inspiration from the theory of nonlinear urn processes [2]. In this new class of models, the probability that a new participant enters at step j depends on the identities of the participants in the first $j-1$ steps. Intuitively, when there are many distinct participants, the process should make re-entry less likely, thereby producing momentum in the expansionary direction; when a few participants have each interacted multiple times, the process should make it harder for new participants to break in, thereby building up momentum in the conversational direction.

The class is parametrized by $\alpha \geq 1$ and $\beta \geq 0$. For each participant c already in the thread (including the original poster, 0), and each length $j \leq k$, each such existing participant will have a *weight* $w_j(c)$ after step j of the thread that controls their probability of providing the next comment. The fixed weight $\beta > 0$ controls the probability that a new participant arrives in the next step. We also impose the constraint that the same person never appears twice in a row.[6]

Generating the arrival pattern $\gamma = \gamma_1 \cdots \gamma_k$ proceeds as follows. The first commenter will be labeled 1 (since we do not have the poster, labeled 0, provide the first comment too); so we initialize by setting $\gamma_1 = 1, w_1(0) = w_1(1) = 1$, and following this initialization we are positioned to determine the author of the second comment. In general, consider an arbitrary step $j < k$, and let c_j be the commenter in that step. We proceed as follows.

(i) *Choose commenter* $j + 1$. We choose a participant (different from c_j) with probability proportional to the weights. Specifically: pre-existing participant $c \neq c_j$ is chosen with probability $w_j(c)/(\beta + \sum_{c' \neq c_j} w_j(c'))$, and a new participant is introduced into the thread with probability $\beta/(\beta + \sum_{c' \neq c_j} w_j(c'))$. We use c_{j+1} to denote the participant chosen for step $j + 1$.

(ii) *Update weights.* If the participant c_{j+1} in step $j + 1$ is a re-entrant, we define $w_{j+1}(c_{j+1}) = \alpha w_j(c_{j+1})$, and leave all other weights unchanged. If instead c_{j+1} is new, we define $w_{j+1}(c_{j+1}) = 1$ and for all other pre-existing participants $c \neq c_{j+1}$ we reduce their weights by setting $w_{j+1}(c) = w_j(c)/\alpha$.

The key point is the weight update rule in part (ii). A new arrival suppresses the weight of all existing participants, making it less likely they will comment again and paving the way for further new

[6]This is essentially without loss of generality, since on the real threads we can also build a comparable representation where we collapse out consecutive occurrences of the same participant.

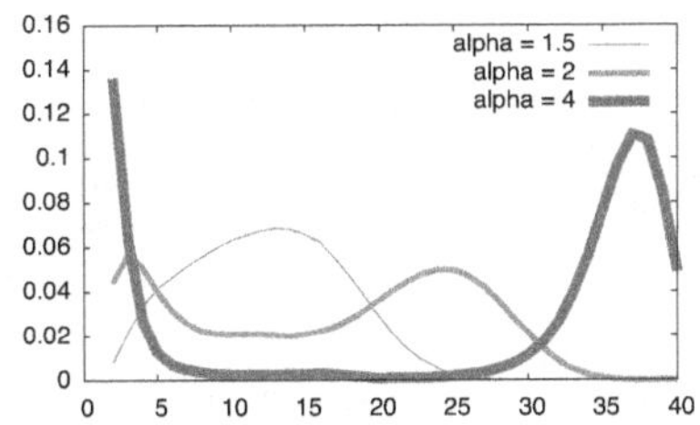

Figure 7: Density function of distinct participants in threads produced by our proposed family of processes with $\alpha = 1.5$, 2, and 4 ($\beta = 1$ and $k = 40$).

arrivals. On the other hand, when an existing participant provides the next comment, their increase in weight makes it more likely they will return, thereby promoting back-and-forth interaction.

We show via simulation that bimodality emerges naturally in this model. To paraphrase Langston Hughes, the number of distinct participants can dry up like a raisin in the sun, or it can explode. Figure 7 shows the empirical density function obtained through simulation for the number of distinct participants under multiple settings of the model parameters: we fix the length $k = 40$ and $\beta = 1$, and then we simulate the process with $\alpha = 1.5$, 2, and 4. As we see there, bimodality emerges as α increases, which accords with intuition — larger values of α are more aggressive in amplifying both the focused and expansionary effects, and hence serve to bifurcate the process into its two modes more strongly.

The model appears to be quite challenging to analyze rigorously, and it is an interesting open question to prove that it produces bimodality, as well as to characterize the transition from unimodality to bimodality as we increase α. The model shares some properties with nonlinear urn processes [2], but also has ingredients that lie beyond what is usually needed for the analysis of such processes.

8. RELATED WORK

To our knowledge, there has not been prior consideration in the literature of the overall problem of algorithmic conversation curation — an emerging key component in enhancing user experience in current forms of on-line social interaction. This problem involves many issues, including those investigated in this paper: **(a)** determining which posts are interesting enough to bring to a user's attention; **(b)** among discussions a user already has knowledge of, choosing which the user should continue to be updated about; and, indirectly, **(c)** understanding the structure of discussions, both to aid in the two issues just described and potentially for implications in user-interface design. Of course, there has been much valuable work on the first and last issue individually, which we now describe. (Our attention to **(b)** appears to be novel.) On **(a)**, we point out De-Choudhury et al.'s research [8] on the interestingness of Youtube comment threads, as measured by interestingness of topic and participants (not length), and Shmueli et al.'s work [8] on predicting which stories a particular user is most likely to comment on. Prior work on comment-volume prediction [3, 14, 23, 25, 26] is of course also quite relevant. How fast a piece of information spreads or diffuses [3, 4, 16, 18, 21] is another important aspect of interestingness. Quality of posts or comments, as determined by ratings, is potentially also relevant; see for example Siersdorfer et al. [22]. On **(c)**, there is intriguing work [12, 15] on structural characterizations of discussions when viewed as trees (not an approach we have taken in this paper, and arguably less natural as a model for discussions on sites like Facebook that have post-and-comment-interfaces). Different perspectives are taken by researchers looking at characterizations of agreement and/or sentiment among comments [5, 11, 19, 20], and by sociological analyses of turn-taking in group conversations [10].

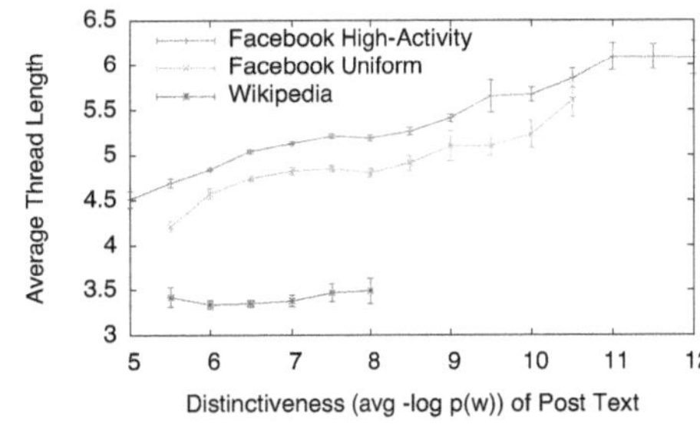

Figure 8: Considering only 8+-word posts that generated responses, for Facebook, the more distinctive the text of the original post, the more comments it garners, but for Wikipedia, which is more task-oriented, there is no such effect.

9. FUTURE WORK: DISTINCTIVENESS

We see many exciting future directions to pursue. Here, we briefly highlight two preliminary explorations into *distinctiveness features* that we believe hold promise, although we have not yet identified a way of applying them in their current form to improve prediction performance. The main idea is that the likelihood of a post's text or early commenters should be informative.

Distinctiveness of Text. A basic property of a piece of text is its *likelihood* — whether its word choices look typical when compared to a reference collection, or whether its word choices are less likely and hence more *distinctive*. In recent work, measures of distinctiveness were shown to help in recognizing movie quotes that were deemed "memorable" in the sense of cultural penetration [6]. In our case, the question is the following: When a post contains unusual text, what should this lead us to estimate about the length of the resulting comment thread? There are intuitive arguments in both directions: some low-probability posts might generate discussion because they are provocative and unexpected, but others might simply be hard to understand and thus be mainly ignored.

We built a unigram language model from 3.5 million Facebook posts by authors whose posts weren't in our main dataset; for each word w, the model provides a probability $p(w)$. We define a post's *distinctiveness* to be the average over its tokens w of $\log(1/p(w))$; lower distinctiveness means a more likely post. Figure 8 shows the macro-averaged post length as a function of text distinctiveness, considering *only* posts containing at least 8 words[7] and that received at least one comment in the case of Facebook or at least two for Wikipedia. For these particular subsets, our two Facebook populations exhibit a clear positive effect of the distinctiveness of the text, whereas for Wikipedia there seems to be no effect at all (which perhaps stems from the task-oriented nature of Wikipedian discussions). We note, however, that the effects become less clear if we include posts that turned out to generate no comments (or at most one on Wikipedia).

Distinctiveness of First Commenter. For a user u who posts regularly, a set of frequent commenters on u's threads often emerges — the people who generally weigh in when u says something. Thus, shifting from the likelihood of words to the likelihood of

[7]At 8 words and beyond, post distinctiveness becomes empirically almost independent of post length, disentangling the two features.

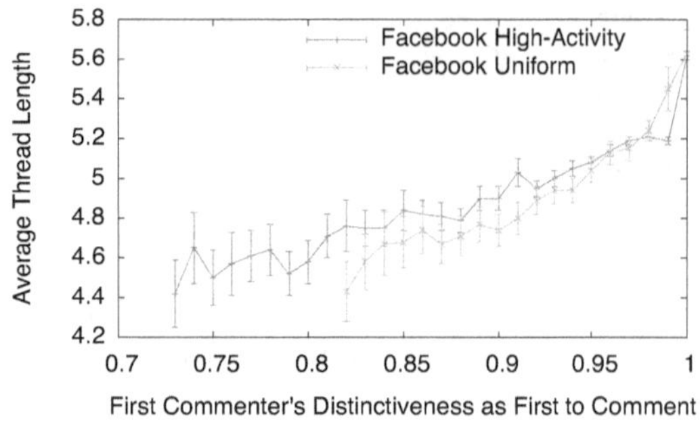

Figure 9: In Facebook, the more distinctive the first commenter is (in terms of not often being first to respond to the original poster), the longer the thread. Wikipedia is not depicted due to sparseness, but the overall trend is the opposite.

users, it makes sense to ask about the effect on thread length of the first commenter's distinctiveness — the extent to which this commenter is usually or rarely first in one of u's threads. Again, there are intuitive arguments each way: if the first commenter v is someone who's often a first commenter on u's posts, then v is presumably familiar to both u and the audience for u's comments, which could make it easier for the thread to grow; but it may also be socially easier to let v's comment pass by without much activity.

In Figure 9 we show for Facebook the expected thread length as a function of the fraction of times the first commenter was *not* the first to respond to the original poster's posts[8]. We see a clear upward trend: when someone you rarely hear from first is in fact the first to comment on your post, on average it foreshadows a longer thread, perhaps because this indicates that the post has greater reach.

We note that Wikipedia appears to exhibit the opposite behavior. We do not depict the Wikipedia results due to sparseness of recurring first commenters, but when restricting to users with at least 10 posts and binning the distinctiveness values, we see a significant decreasing trend.

10. CONCLUSIONS

Motivated by the growing role of automated mechanisms to manage users' interactions with on-line discussions, we have identified and studied two key problems in the curation of such discussions. The first of these, length prediction, is related to earlier studies of comment volume on blog and news sites, but it acquires additional complexity in our context due to the heterogeneity we find in long threads, which can either be focused on a few participants or expand to reach many. The second problem, re-entry prediction, has to our knowledge not been formulated previously; it is a crucial issue in applications that must decide when to notify users about updates to discussions in which they have participated.

We see these two problems as helping to define the contours of the problem of conversational curation more broadly, and as such the results here suggest a range of further open questions. Among these are a deeper understanding of the features that can help predict the trajectory of an on-line discussion from its early stages, and the integration of these techniques into systems that deliver discussion-oriented content to users in on-line applications.

Acknowledgments We thank Tom Lento and the anonymous reviewers for their helpful comments. Supported in part by NSF grant IIS-0910664. This work was done while the last author was at Cornell University.

[8]For the uniform population, the plot only consider users with at least ten posts, although different threshold values do not greatly affect the resulting trends.

References

[1] D. J. Aldous. Exchangeability and related topics. *École d'Été de Probabilités de Saint-Flour XIII (Lec. Notes. Math. vol 1117)*, 1985.
[2] W. B. Arthur. Competing technologies, increasing returns, and lock-in by historical events. *The Economic Journal*, 1989.
[3] Y. Artzi, P. Pantel, M. Gamon. Predicting responses to microblog posts. *NAACL (short paper)*, 2012.
[4] E. Bakshy, J. M. Hofman, W. A. Mason, D. J. Watts. Everyone's an influencer: Quantifying influence on Twitter. *WSDM*, 2011.
[5] A. Chmiel, J. Sienkiewicz, M. Thelwall, G. Paltoglou, K. Buckley, A. Kappas, J. A. Hołyst. Collective emotions online and their influence on community life. *PLoS One*, 2011.
[6] C. Danescu-Niculescu-Mizil, J. Cheng, J. Kleinberg, L. Lee. You had me at hello: How phrasing affects memorability. *ACL*, 2012.
[7] C. Danescu-Niculescu-Mizil, L. Lee, B. Pang, J. Kleinberg. Echoes of power: Language effects and power differences in social interaction. *WWW*, 2012.
[8] M. De Choudhury, H. Sundaram, A. John, D. D. Seligmann. What makes conversations interesting?: Themes, participants and consequences of conversations in online social media. *WWW*, 2009.
[9] J. Friedman, T. Hastie, R. Tibshirani. Regularization paths for generalized linear models via coordinate descent. *J. Statistical Software*, 2010.
[10] D. R. Gibson. Marking the turn: Obligation, engagement, and alienation in group discussions. *Social Psychology Quarterly*, 2010.
[11] E. Gilbert, T. Bergstrom, K. Karahalios. Blogs are Echo Chambers: Blogs are Echo Chambers. *HICSS*, 2009.
[12] V. Gómez, A. Kaltenbrunner, V. López. Statistical analysis of the social network and discussion threads in Slashdot. *WWW*, 2008.
[13] V. Gómez, H. J. Kappen, A. Kaltenbrunner. Modeling the structure and evolution of discussion cascades. *Hypertext*, 2011.
[14] M. Guerini, C. Strapparava, G. Özbal. Exploring text virality in social networks. *ICWSM (poster)*, 2011.
[15] R. Kumar, M. Mahdian, M. McGlohon. Dynamics of conversations. *KDD*, 2010.
[16] H. Kwak, C. Lee, H. Park, S. Moon. What is Twitter, a social network or a news media? *WWW*, 2010.
[17] D. Laniado, R. Tasso, Y. Volkovich, A. Kaltenbrunner. When the Wikipedians talk: Network and tree structure of Wikipedia discussion pages. *ICWSM*, 2011.
[18] K. Lerman, R. Ghosh. Information contagion: An empirical study of the spread of news on Digg and Twitter social networks. *ICWSM*, 2010.
[19] G. Mishne, N. Glance. Leave a reply: An analysis of weblog comments. *Wksp. on the Weblogging ecosystem*, 2006.
[20] S. Park, M. Ko, J. Kim, Y. Liu, J. Song. The politics of comments: predicting political orientation of news stories with commenters' sentiment patterns. *CSCW*, 2011.
[21] D. M. Romero, B. Meeder, J. Kleinberg. Differences in the mechanics of information diffusion across topics: Idioms, political hashtags, and complex contagion on Twitter. *WWW*, 2011.
[22] S. Siersdorfer, S. Chelaru, W. Nejdl, J. San Pedro. How useful are your comments?: Analyzing and predicting YouTube comments and comment ratings. *WWW*, 2010.
[23] M. Tsagkias, W. Weerkamp, M. Rijke. Predicting the volume of comments on online news stories. *CIKM*, 2009.
[24] J. Ugander, L. Backstrom, C. Marlow, J. Kleinberg. Structural diversity in social contagion. *PNAS*, 2012.
[25] C. Wang, M. Ye, B. A. Huberman. From user comments to on-line conversations. *KDD*, 2012.
[26] T. Yano, N. A. Smith. What's worthy of comment? Content and comment volume in political blogs. *ICWSM*, 2010.

Structure and Dynamics of Information Pathways in Online Media

Manuel Gomez-Rodriguez
MPI for Intelligent Systems
Stanford University
manuelgr@stanford.edu

Jure Leskovec
Stanford University
jure@cs.stanford.edu

Bernhard Schölkopf
MPI for Intelligent Systems
bs@tuebingen.mpg.de

ABSTRACT

Diffusion of information, spread of rumors and infectious diseases are all instances of stochastic processes that occur over the edges of an underlying network. Many times networks over which contagions spread are unobserved, and such networks are often dynamic and change over time. In this paper, we investigate the problem of inferring dynamic networks based on information diffusion data. We assume there is an unobserved dynamic network that changes over time, while we observe the results of a dynamic process spreading over the edges of the network. The task then is to infer the edges and the dynamics of the underlying network.

We develop an on-line algorithm that relies on stochastic convex optimization to efficiently solve the dynamic network inference problem. We apply our algorithm to information diffusion among 3.3 million mainstream media and blog sites and experiment with more than 179 million different pieces of information spreading over the network in a one year period. We study the evolution of information pathways in the online media space and find interesting insights. Information pathways for general recurrent topics are more stable across time than for on-going news events. Clusters of news media sites and blogs often emerge and vanish in matter of days for on-going news events. Major social movements and events involving civil population, such as the Libyan's civil war or Syria's uprise, lead to an increased amount of information pathways among blogs as well as in the overall increase in the network centrality of blogs and social media sites.

Categories and Subject Descriptors: H.2.8 **[Database Management]**: Database applications—*Data mining*

General Terms: Algorithms; Experimentation.

Keywords: Networks of diffusion, Information cascades, Blogs, News media, Meme-tracking, Social networks.

1. INTRODUCTION

Networks represent a fundamental medium for spreading and diffusion of various types of behavior, information, rumors and diseases [27]. A *contagion* appears at some node of a network and then spreads like an epidemic from node to node over the edges of the underlying network. For example, in case of information diffusion, the contagion represents a piece of information [16, 18] and infection events correspond to times when nodes mention or copy the information from one of their neighbors in the network. Similarly, we can think about the spread of a new type of behavior or an action, e.g., purchasing a new cellphone [15], or the propagation of a contagious disease over the edges of the underlying social network [6].

In the context of network diffusion, we often observe the temporal traces of diffusion while the pathways over which contagion spreads remain hidden. In other words, we observe the times when each node gets infected by the contagion, but the edges of the network that gave rise to the diffusion remain unobservable. For example, we can often measure and observe the time when people decide to adopt a new behavior while we do not explicitly observe which neighbor in the social network influenced them to do so. In case of information diffusion, we often observe people (or media sites) talking about a new piece of information without explicitly observing the path it took in the information diffusion network to reach the particular node of interest. And, epidemiologists often observe when a person gets sick but usually cannot tell who infected her. In all these examples, one can observe the infection events themselves while not knowing over which edges of the network the contagions spread. Therefore, one of the fundamental research problems in the context of network diffusion is inferring the structure of networks over which various types of contagions spread [10]. Moreover, many times networks over which contagions diffuse are not static but change over time. Depending on the type of contagion, the time of the day, or death of the existing and birth of new nodes, the underlying network may dynamically change and shift over time.

In recent years, several network inference algorithms have been developed [9, 10, 12, 20, 24, 30]. Some approaches infer only the network structure [10, 30], while others infer not only the network structure but also the *strength* or the average latency of every edge in the network [9, 20]. However, to the best of our knowledge, previous work has always assumed networks to be static and contagion pathways to be constant over time. However, in most cases, networks are dynamic, and contagion pathways change over time, depending upon the contagions that propagate through them [22, 28]. For example, a blog can increase its popularity abruptly after one of its posts turns *viral*, this may create new edges in the information transmission network and so the content the blog produces in the future will likely spread to larger parts of the network. Similarly, at any given time a particular unexpected event may occur and a topic or piece of news may become very popular for a limited period of time. This again will lead to different emerging and vanishing information pathways, and thus to a time-varying underlying

WSDM'13, February 4–8, 2013, Rome, Italy.

Model	Edge $(\mathbf{j},\mathbf{i})$ transmission likelihood $\mathbf{f}(\mathbf{t_i}\|\mathbf{t_j};\alpha_{\mathbf{j,i}})$
EXPonential	$\begin{cases} \alpha_{j,i} \cdot e^{-\alpha_{j,i}(t_i-t_j)} & \text{if } t_j < t_i \\ 0 & \text{otherwise} \end{cases}$
POWer law	$\begin{cases} \frac{\alpha_{j,i}}{\delta}\left(\frac{t_i-t_j}{\delta}\right)^{-1-\alpha_{j,i}} & \text{if } t_j+\delta < t_i \\ 0 & \text{otherwise} \end{cases}$
RAYleigh	$\begin{cases} \alpha_{j,i}(t_i-t_j)e^{-\frac{1}{2}\alpha_{j,i}(t_i-t_j)^2} & \text{if } t_j < t_i \\ 0 & \text{otherwise} \end{cases}$

Table 1: Various models of edge transmission likelihood.

network. In order to better understand these temporal changes, one needs to reconstruct the time-varying structure and underlying temporal dynamics of these networks and then study the information pathways of real-world events, topics or content.

Our approach to time-varying network inference. In this paper we investigate the problem of inferring dynamic networks based on information diffusion data. We assume there is an unobserved dynamic network that changes over time, while we observe the node infection times of many different contagions spreading over the edges of the network. The task then is to infer the edges and the dynamics of the underlying network. We develop an efficient on-line dynamic network inference algorithm, INFOPATH, that allows us to infer daily networks of information diffusion between online media sites over a one year period using more than 179 million different contagions diffusing over the underlying media network.

We model diffusion processes as discrete networks of fully continuous temporal processes occurring at different rates building on our previous work [9, 11]. Our model allows information to propagate at different rates across different edges by adopting a data-driven approach, where only the recorded temporal diffusion events are used. The model considers the information which propagates through the network due only to diffusion, while ignoring any external sources [22]. However, our original diffusion model considered only static networks [9]. Here, we generalize the model and develop a new inference method to support dynamic networks. Our time-varying network inference algorithm, INFOPATH, uses stochastic gradient [26] to provide estimates of the time-varying structure and temporal dynamics of the inferred network. The framework enables us to study the temporal evolution of information pathways in the online media space.

We apply the INFOPATH algorithm to synthetic as well as real Web information propagation data. We study 179 million different information cascades spreading among 3.3 million blog and news media sites over a one year period, from March 2011 till February 2012.[1] Results on synthetic data show INFOPATH is able to track changes in the topology of dynamic networks and provides accurate on-line estimates of the time-varying transmission rates of the edges of the network. INFOPATH is also robust across network topologies, and temporal trends of edge transmission dynamics.

Experiments on large-scale real news and social media data lead to interesting insights and findings. For example, we find that the information pathways over which general recurrent topics propagate remain more stable over time, while unexpected events lead to dramatically changing information pathways. Clusters of mainstream news and blogs often emerge and vanish in a matter of days, and our on-line algorithm is able to uncover such structures. News events that involve large-scale social movements, as the Libyan civil war, Egypt's revolution or Syria's uprise, result in a greater increase in information transfer among blogs than among mainstream media. Perhaps surprisingly, the amount of mainstream media and blogs among the most influential nodes for most topics or news events are comparable. However, we find that growing numbers of influential blogs on some topics or news events are often temporally correlated with large-scale social movements (*e.g.*, the Occupy Wall Street movement in Sept-Nov 2011).

Further related work. Previous methods for inferring diffusion networks [9, 10, 12, 20] also use a generative probabilistic model for modeling cascading processes over networks. NETINF [10] and MULTITREE [12] infer the network connectivity using submodular optimization. NETRATE [9] and CONNIE [20] infer not only the network connectivity but also transmission rates of infection or prior probabilities of infection using convex optimization. Moreover, there have been also attempts to model information diffusion without assuming the existence of an underlying network [33, 32].

However, to the best of our knowledge, all previous approaches to network inference assume the network and the underlying dynamics of the edges to be constant, *i.e.*, the network structure and the transmission rates of each edge do not change over time. Therefore, they consider the pathways over which information propagates to be time-invariant. The main contribution of this paper is to combine stochastic gradient and the diffusion model introduced in [9] to develop an efficient on-line network inference algorithm that provides time-varying estimates of the edges of a network and the transmission rates of each edge. This allows us to detect how information pathways emerge and vanish over time, and identify when nodes produce highly viral content.

The remainder of the paper is organized as follows: in Sec. 2, we revisit the model of diffusion and state the dynamic network inference problem. Section 3 describes the proposed time-varying network inference method, called INFOPATH. Section 4 evaluates INFOPATH quantitatively and qualitatively using synthetic and real diffusion data. We conclude with a discussion of results in Section 5.

2. PROBLEM FORMULATION

In this section, we build on our fully continuous time model of diffusion [9, 11]. We start by briefly describing the generative model for the observed data. We then revisit how to compute the likelihood of a cascade using the model and state the continuous time network inference problem for both static and dynamic networks. Across the section, we explicitly point out which assumptions of the original model need to be extended in order to support dynamic networks.

Observed data. For now let's consider a single static directed network. Over the edges of the network multiple contagions propagate. As the contagion spreads from infected to non-infected nodes over the edges of the network the contagion creates a *cascade*. For each contagion c, we observe a cascade $\mathbf{t}^c$, which is simply a record of observed node infection times during a time window of length T^c. In an information propagation setting, each cascade corresponds to a different piece of information and the infection time of a node is simply the time when the node first mentioned the piece of information c.

Cascade is a N-dimensional vector $\mathbf{t}^c := (t_1^c, \ldots, t_N^c)$ recording the times when each of N nodes got infected by the contagion c: $t_k^c \in [t_0, t_0 + T^c] \cup \{\infty\}$, where t_0 is the infection time of the first node. Generally contagions do not infect all the nodes of the network, symbol ∞ is used for nodes that were not infected by the contagion c during the observation window $[t_0, t_0 + T^c]$. Contagions often propagate simultaneously [21, 25] over the same net-

[1]All data, code and additional results are available at the supporting website [1]: `http://snap.stanford.edu/infopath`.

Model	Log survival function $\log S(t_i\|t_j;\alpha_{j,i})$	Hazard function $H(t_i\|t_j;\alpha_{j,i})$	Cascade gradient for uninfected $\nabla_{\alpha_{j,i}} L_c(\mathbf{A})$	Cascade gradient for infected $\nabla_{\alpha_{j,i}} L_c(\mathbf{A})$
EXP	$-\alpha_{j,i}(t_i - t_j)$	$\alpha_{j,i}$	$T - t_j^c$	$(t_i^c - t_j^c) - \frac{1}{\sum_{k:t_k^c<t_i^c} \alpha_{k,i}}$
POW	$-\alpha_{j,i}\log\left(\frac{t_i-t_j}{\delta}\right)$	$\alpha_{j,i}\cdot\frac{1}{t_i-t_j}$	$\log\left(\frac{T-t_j^c}{\delta}\right)$	$\log\left(\frac{t_i^c-t_j^c}{\delta}\right) - \frac{(t_i^c-t_j^c)^{-1}}{\sum_{k:t_k^c<t_i^c}\alpha_{k,i}(t_i^c-t_k^c)^{-1}}$
RAY	$-\alpha_{j,i}\frac{(t_i-t_j)^2}{2}$	$\alpha_{j,i}\cdot(t_i-t_j)$	$\frac{(T-t_j^c)^2}{2}$	$\frac{(t_i^c-t_j^c)^2}{2} - \frac{t_i^c-t_j^c}{\sum_{k:t_k^c<t_i^c}\alpha_{k,i}(t_i^c-t_k^c)}$

Table 2: Contagion transmission models for the three edge transmission likelihoods: Exponential, Power-law and Rayleigh.

work but we assume each contagion to propagate independently of each other.

Given a set of node infection times of many different contagions, our goal is to infer the underlying dynamic network over which contagions propagated. We apply the Maximum Likelihood principle in order to infer the network that most likely generated the observed data. We proceed by assuming a static network and describe the generative model of information diffusion. We then generalize the model to dynamic networks.

Pairwise transmission likelihood. The first step in modeling diffusion dynamics is to consider pairwise node interaction. For every pair of nodes (j,i), we define a pairwise transmission rate $\alpha_{j,i}$ which models how frequently information spreads from node j to node i; the *strength* of an edge (j,i). We pay attention to the rather general case of heterogeneous pairwise transmission rates, *i.e.*, infections can occur at different transmission rates over different edges of the network. As $\alpha_{j,i} \to 0$ the expected transmission time from node j to node i becomes arbitrarily long. In contrast with the original model [9], we will later allow transmission rates $\alpha_{j,i}$ to change over time. In particular, we will allow the transmission rates $\alpha_{j,i}$ to change across cascades but not within a cascade. Allowing edge transmission rates to dynamically increase and decay over time will enable us to infer time-varying diffusion networks.

Next, we define $f(t_i|t_j;\alpha_{j,i})$ to be the conditional likelihood of transmission between node j and node i and assume it depends on the infection times (t_j,t_i) and the edge transmission rate $\alpha_{j,i}$. We allow information to only propagate forward in time, i.e., node j that has been infected at time t_j may infect node i at time t_i only if $t_j < t_i$, otherwise $f(t_i|t_j,\alpha_{j,i}) = 0$. The shape of the conditional likelihood of transmission may depend on the particular setting (information, influence, diseases, etc.) in which propagation takes place. In some scenarios, it may be possible to estimate a non-parametric likelihood while in others, expert knowledge may be used to decide upon a parametric model. For simplicity, we consider three well-known parametric models of edge transmission rates: exponential, power-law, and Rayleigh, defined in Table 1. Exponential and power-law likelihoods have been used in modeling information propagation in social and information networks [9, 10, 11, 12, 20], while Rayleigh has been used in previous work in disease spread in epidemiology [31]. In all three models, as $\alpha_{j,i} \to 0$, the likelihood of infection tends to zero.

We recall some additional standard notation [14] that we will use in the remainder of the section. Given some node j, infected at time t_j, we define the *survival function* of edge $j \to i$ as $S(t_i|t_j;\alpha_{j,i}) = 1 - F(t_i|t_j;\alpha_{j,i})$ where $F(t_i|t_j;\alpha_{j,i}) = \int_{t_j}^{t_i} f(t|t_j;\alpha_{j,i})\,dt$ is the cumulative transmission density function, computed from the transmission likelihood. Finally, the *hazard function*, or instantaneous infection rate, of edge $j \to i$ is the ratio $H(t_i|t_j;\alpha_{j,i}) = f(t_i|t_j;\alpha_{j,i})/S(t_i|t_j;\alpha_{j,i})$. We derive the log survival and hazard functions for the three edge transmission models in Table 2.

Likelihood of a cascade. Consider some node i in a directed network. Node i can get infected by any of its parents (i.e., nodes pointing to i). Once infected, node i can then also spread the contagion to its children (i.e., nodes i points to). As in the independent cascade model [13], we assume that node gets infected once the *first* parent infects it (i.e., a node can get infected only once). Then, the likelihood of infection of node i at time t_i given a collection of previously infected nodes $(t_1,\ldots,t_N|t_k \le t_i)$ results from summing over the likelihoods of the mutually disjoint events that each node is the first parent that generated the infection event of our node i:

$$f(t_i|t_1,\ldots,t_N\setminus t_i;\mathbf{A}) = \sum_{j:t_j<t_i} f(t_i|t_j;\alpha_{j,i}) \times \prod_{j:j\neq k,t_k<t_i} S(t_i|t_k;\alpha_{k,i}), \quad (1)$$

where $\mathbf{A} := \{\alpha_{j,i}\,|\,i,j = 1,\ldots,n, i \neq j\}$. If we assume that infections are conditionally independent given the parents of the infected nodes, the likelihood of the infections in a cascade is:

$$f(\mathbf{t}^{\le T^c};\mathbf{A}) = \prod_{t_i\le T}\sum_{j:t_j<t_i} f(t_i|t_j;\alpha_{j,i}) \times \prod_{j:j\neq k,t_k<t_i} S(t_i|t_k;\alpha_{k,i}), \quad (2)$$

where $\mathbf{t}^{\le T^c}$ denotes the vector of infected nodes in the cascade up to T^c. Removing the condition $k \neq j$ makes the product independent of j,

$$f(\mathbf{t}^{\le T^c};\mathbf{A}) = \prod_{t_i\le T}\prod_{k:t_k<t_i} S(t_i|t_k;\alpha_{k,i}) \times \sum_{j:t_j<t_i} \frac{f(t_i|t_j;\alpha_{j,i})}{S(t_i|t_j;\alpha_{j,i})}. \quad (3)$$

The fact that some nodes are *not* infected during the observation window is also informative. We therefore add multiplicative survival terms to Eq. 3 and rearrange with hazard functions:

$$f(\mathbf{t};\mathbf{A}) = \prod_{i:t_i\le T}\prod_{m:t_m>T} S(T|t_i;\alpha_{i,m}) \times \quad (4)$$

$$\prod_{k:t_k<t_i} S(t_i|t_k;\alpha_{k,i}) \left(\sum_{j:t_j<t_i} H(t_i|t_j;\alpha_{j,i})\right). \quad (5)$$

Perhaps surprisingly, our continuous time model of diffusion is a particular case of Aalen's additive regression model, frequently used in survival theory analysis [3]. In Aalen's model, the hazard function, or instantaneous infection rate, of node i is parametrized as $\alpha_{i,0}(t) + \alpha(t)_i^T \mathbf{s}_i(t)$, where $\alpha(t)$ is a vector that accounts for the effect of a collection of observable covariates $\mathbf{s}(t)$ and $\alpha_{i,0}(t)$ is a baseline. It is easy to show that the hazard function of node i at time t_i for the three pairwise transmission models: exponential, power-law and Rayleigh, has the following form:

$$H(t_i|t_1,\ldots,t_N\setminus t_i;\mathbf{A}) = \alpha_i^T \mathbf{s}_i(t_i;t_1,\ldots,t_N\setminus t_i), \quad (6)$$

Algorithm 1 INFOPATH: the dynamic network inference algorithm

Require: C, t, K, T, ρ
  while $k < K$ **do**
    $c_k \leftarrow$ cascade-sampling(C, t, T);
    for all $(j,i) : t_j^{c_k} < t_i^{c_k}$ **do**
      $\alpha_{j,i}^k = \left(\alpha_{j,i}^{k-1} - \gamma_k \nabla_{\alpha_{j,i}} L_{c_k}(\mathbf{A}^{k-1})\right)^+$;
    for all $(j,i) : \alpha_{j,i}^{k-1} > 0, t_j^{c_k} \to \infty$ **do**
      $\alpha_{j,i}^k = \rho \alpha_{j,i}^{k-1}$;
    k = k+1;
  $\mathbf{A}^* \leftarrow \mathbf{A}^{K-1}$;
  return $\mathbf{A}^*$;

where $\alpha_i = (\alpha_{1,i}, \ldots, \alpha_{N,i})$ accounts for the effect of a collection of observable covariates $\mathbf{s}_i(t_i; t_1, \ldots, t_N \setminus t_i)$, the covariates depend on the pairwise transmission model (exponential, power-law or Rayleigh) and the previously infected nodes, and the baseline is zero.

Dynamic network inference problem. Given a static network with constant edge transmission rates $\alpha_{j,i}$, the network inference problem reduces to solving a maximum likelihood problem over set of recorded cascades C [9]:

$$\begin{array}{ll} \text{maximize}_{\mathbf{A}} & \sum_{c \in C} \log f(\mathbf{t}^c; \mathbf{A}) \\ \text{subject to} & \alpha_{j,i} \geq 0, i, j = 1, \ldots, N, i \neq j, \end{array} \tag{7}$$

where $\mathbf{A} := \{\alpha_{j,i} \,|\, i, j = 1, \ldots, n, i \neq j\}$ are the edge transmission rates we aim to infer. The edges of the network are those pairs of nodes with transmission rates $\alpha_{j,i} > 0$.

Now we generalize the network inference problem to dynamic networks with edge transmission rates $\alpha_{j,i}(t)$ that may change over time. To this aim, at any given time t, we solve a maximum weighted likelihood problem over the set of recorded cascades by time t, $C_t = \{\mathbf{t}^1, \ldots, \mathbf{t}^{|C_t|}\}$:

$$\begin{array}{ll} \text{maximize}_{\mathbf{A}(t)} & \sum_{c \in C_t} w_c(t) \log f(\mathbf{t}^c; \mathbf{A}(t)) \\ \text{subject to} & \alpha_{j,i}(t) \geq 0, i, j = 1, \ldots, N, i \neq j, \end{array} \tag{8}$$

where $w_c(t) \geq 0$ is a weight that penalizes the importance of cascade c based on how old it is at time t and $\mathbf{A}(t) := \{\alpha_{j,i}(t) \,|\, i, j = 1, \ldots, n, i \neq j\}$ are the variables. The intuition here is that diffusion network smoothly changes over time and that recent cascades have higher importance in determining current network structure than old cascades. Thus, at any point in time, we can solve the above optimization problem to obtain the structure of the diffusion network at that particular time. Next, we show how to efficiently solve the above optimization problem for all time points t.

3. THE INFOPATH ALGORITHM

The problem defined by equation Eq. 8 is convex for the three transmission models we consider. Therefore we can aim to find the unique optimal solution at any given time point t:

THEOREM 1 ([9]). *Given log-concave survival functions and concave hazard functions in the parameter(s) of the pairwise transmission likelihoods, the network inference problem defined by equation Eq. 8 is convex in* $\mathbf{A}$.

Stochastic gradient (SG) methods have been shown to be extremely successful for taking advantage of the structure exhibited by the optimization problem stated in Eq. 8. They have received increasing attention in the machine learning literature [4, 5, 7, 8, 29]. Although many optimization methods based on stochastic gradient descent have been proposed, we have found that in practice the basic projected stochastic gradient method [26] works well for our problem. Other more sophisticated methods, like the stochastic average gradient [29] or incremental average gradient [7] do not offer a significant advantage. Therefore, we proceed with the basic stochastic gradient method in the remainder of the paper.

Projected Stochastic Gradient. The projected stochastic gradient method [26] uses iterations of the form:

$$\alpha_{j,i}^k(t) = \left(\alpha_{j,i}^{k-1}(t) - \gamma_k \nabla_{\alpha_{j,i}} L_{c_k}(\mathbf{A}^{k-1}(t))\right)^+, \tag{9}$$

where $\nabla_{\alpha_{j,i}} L_{c_k}(\cdot)$ is the gradient of the log-likelihood $L_c(\cdot)$ with respect to the edge transmission rate $\alpha_{j,i}$, γ_k is a step-size, $(z)^+ = \max(0, z)$, and cascade c_k is sampled (with replacement) from C_t. The gradients for all three edge transmission models are given in Table 2.

Note that instead of using all historic data and then explicitly penalizing each cascade by a different weighting factor $w_c(t)$, we use a different, more scalable approach. We sample cascades with replacement, where the probability of a cascade being sampled decays with the age of the cascade. This way recent cascades get sampled more often and thus implicitly hold higher importance when inferring the network. In practice, we achieve a significant speed up by using this approach. Moreover, in our dynamic network inference problem, the edge transmission rates usually vary smoothly. This means that stochastic gradient descent is a perfect method as we can use the inferred network from the previous time step as initialization for the inference procedure in the current time step. We find that setting the starting point $\alpha_{j,i}^0$ of each edge transmission rate $\alpha_{j,i}$ to the last outputted estimate of the transmission rate allows us to further speed up the algorithm.

Importantly, in each iteration k of the projected stochastic gradient method, we only need to compute the gradients $\nabla_{\alpha_{j,i}} L_{c_k}(\mathbf{A}^k)$ for edges (j,i) such that node j has been infected in cascade c_k, and the iteration cost and convergence rate are independent of $|C|$ [5, 23]. Rigorous theoretical analysis of convergence turns out to be a challenging problem which we leave for future work. However, we point out that standard analyses [26] typically assume the gradients $\nabla_{\mathbf{A}} L_c(\mathbf{A}^k)$ to be either bounded above by a constant M, where $||\nabla_{\mathbf{A}} L_c(\mathbf{A})|| \leq M$, or Lipschitz-continuous with constant L, $||\nabla_{\mathbf{A}} L_c(\mathbf{A}_2) - \nabla_{\mathbf{A}} L_c(\mathbf{A}_1)|| \leq L||\mathbf{A}_2 - \mathbf{A}_1||$. In our case, these conditions are violated if at any iteration k, there is a node i infected in cascade c_k such that $H(t_i^{c_k} | t_j^{c_k}; \alpha_{j,i}^{k-1}) = 0 \; \forall j : t_j^{c_k} < t_i^{c_k}$, *i.e.*, node i has no parents that *explain* the infection at $t_i^{c_k}$, and the objective function is positively unbounded. In practice, we obtain a good performance and avoid such scenario by bounding below each *feasible* transmission rate, $\alpha_{j,i} \geq \varepsilon$. An edge transmission rate $\alpha_{j,i}$ is *feasible* if there is at least one cascade in which both node j and i get infected. When outputting the final solution, we simply omit edges with transmission rates ε.

Aging edges. Suppose we solve the dynamic network inference problem for a given time t using the projected SG method. In each iteration k, we only update edge transmission rate $\alpha_{j,i}^k$ if node j has been infected in cascade c_k. Now, suppose a few edge transmission rates $\alpha_{j,i}^0$ are greater than zero for a given node j, *i.e.*, their last outputted estimates before t have been positive. Then, if node j turns to be infected in many sampled cascades at time t but it never transmits information to any of its neighbors i in the future, the edge transmission rates $\alpha_{j,i}^k$ will eventually converge to zero for large k. However, if node j is never infected for any of the future cascades, then none of edge transmission rates $\alpha_{j,i}$ will be updated, and they will remain positive. So, if node j is never infected in subsequent future cascades, the transmission rates $\alpha_{j,i}$ will remain positive for-

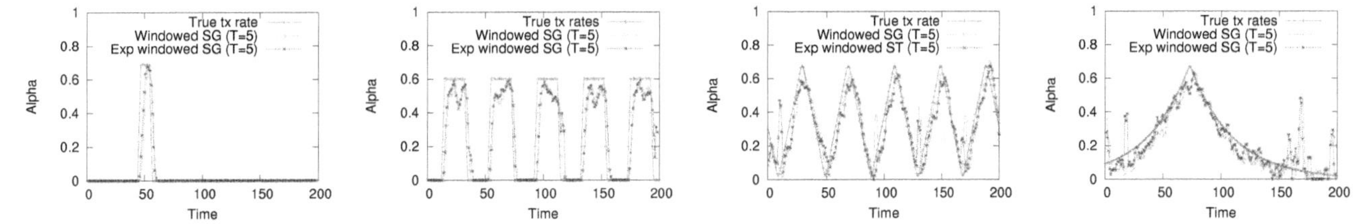

(a) Slab (b) Square (c) Chainsaw (d) Hump

Figure 1: True and inferred edge transmission rates for edges with different 4 transmission rate evolution patterns: (a) Slab, (b) Square, (c) Chainsaw, (d) Hump. Results are for the Kronecker core-periphery with exponential edge transmission model for 200 time units with 1,000 cascades per time unit. Our INFOPATH method is able to track the evolving edge transmission rates over time. INFOPATH works better for continuously evolving edge transmission rates (c, d).

ever. However, we would like these *unused* edges (j,i) to decay and eventually vanish, or equivalently the transmission rates $\alpha_{j,i}$ to converge to zero. To achieve this, we multiply transmission rates of *unused* edges by *aging* factor ρ every time we solve the dynamic network inference problem. We use $\rho = 0.95$ in all experiments.

Cascade sampling. In Eq. 9, instead of sampling cascades uniformly at random and explicitly penalizing each cascade by a different weighting factor $w_c(t)$, we achieve a significant speed up by sampling cascades using a sampling procedure that penalizes old cascades and considers $w_c(t) = 1$ for all cascades. There are many possible sampling schemes. In practice, and for simplicity, we use windowed uniform sampling or windowed exponential sampling. Windowed means that when solving the network inference problem for time t, we only sample (uniformly or exponentially) cascades that have started in a sampling time window $(t-T,T)$. Here, we find an an important tradeoff. The shorter is the sampling time window T in the stochastic gradient descend, the quicker our algorithm is tracking changes in the edge transmission rates. However, short sampling time window results in less reliable estimates because of sampling from a smaller universe of distinct cascades. Therefore, in order to be able to track changes quickly, we would need to observe many cascades over time.

4. EXPERIMENTAL EVALUATION

We evaluate the performance of INFOPATH on time-varying synthetic networks that mimic the structure of real networks as well as on a dataset of more than 179 million information cascades extracted from 300 million blogs and news articles from 3.3 million media sites over a period of one year, from March 2011 till February 2012. All the data, code and additional results are available at the supporting website [1].

4.1 Experiments on synthetic data

The goal of the experiments with synthetic data is to understand how temporal changes in a network affect the performance of our algorithm. We aim to detect not only when an edge appears (*i.e.*, its transmission rate becomes > 0) or disappears (*i.e.*, its transmission rate becomes 0) but also provide instantaneous transmission rate estimates that track the true edge transmission rates over time.

Experimental setup. First, we generate synthetic networks using Kronecker graph models of directed real-world networks [17]. For all our experiments, we consider two different Kronecker networks, both with 1,024 nodes and 2,048 edges: A *core-periphery* Kronecker network with parameter matrix [0.9, 0.5; 0.5, 0.3]) and a *hierarchical* Kronecker network with parameters [0.9, 0.1; 0.1, 0.9].

The next step is to make each edge to follow a particular edge transmission rate evolution pattern. Our goal later will be to recover the network as well as the evolution of the transmission rate of each individual edge.

We consider five edge evolution patterns: Slab, Square, Chainsaw, Hump and constant (see Figure 1). Slab and Hump patterns model outgoing connections of sites that become popular for a short period of time. Square and Chainsaw patterns model incoming connections to sites that perform updates periodically at specific times of the day or days of the week. Constant pattern represents connections between sites that interact at any time and during a long period of time, usually large media sites. We consider Chainsaw, Hump and Continuous to be examples of *Type I* pattern, without discontinuities, and Slab and Square to be examples of Type II patterm, with discontinuities.

We assign to each edge in the network an evolution pattern chosen uniformly at random from the set of the above 5 patterns. Then, we generate transmission rate values $\alpha^*_{j,i}(t)$ for each edge according to its chosen evolution pattern. The evolving edge transmission rate $\alpha^*_{j,i}(t)$ models how quickly information spreads from one node to another. Finally, we generate 1,000 information cascades per time step. For each cascade we randomly pick the cascade initiator node.

Given the node infection times from the recorded cascades, our goal then is to find the true edges of the network and for each edge discover its transmission rate evolution pattern. In other words, inferring how each edge transmission rate $\alpha(t)$ evolves over time. Figure 1 shows the true and inferred edge transmission rates for four different edges, each with a different evolution pattern: Slab, Square, Chainsaw and Hump. Observe that INFOPATH is able to track the evolving edge transmission rates over time for all evolution patterns. INFOPATH gives near perfect performance when edge transmission rate evolves continuously (Chainsaw, Hump). Interestingly, even when the edge transmission rate evolves discontinuously (Slab, Square), INFOPATH manages to track it.

Accuracy of INFOPATH. We evaluate the INFOPATH method quantitatively by computing four different measures for every time step: Precision, Recall and Accuracy of inferred edges as well as the Mean Squared Error (MSE) in the edge transmission rate. Precision at time t is the fraction of edges in the inferred network $\hat{G}(t)$ present in the true network $G^*(t)$. Recall at time t is the fraction of edges of the true network $G^*(t)$ present in the inferred network $\hat{G}(t)$. And accuracy at time t is defined as

$$1 - \frac{\sum_{i,j} |I(\alpha^*_{i,j}(t)) - I(\hat{\alpha}_{i,j}(t))|}{\sum_{i,j} I(\alpha^*_{i,j}(t)) + I(\hat{\alpha}_{i,j}(t))},$$

where $\alpha^*(t)$ is the true transmission rate at time t, $\hat{\alpha}(t)$ is the estimated transmission rate at time t, and $I(\alpha(t)) = 1$ if $\alpha(t) > 0$ and $I(\alpha(t)) = 0$ otherwise. Inferred networks with no edges or only false edges would have zero accuracy. Last, Mean Squared Error

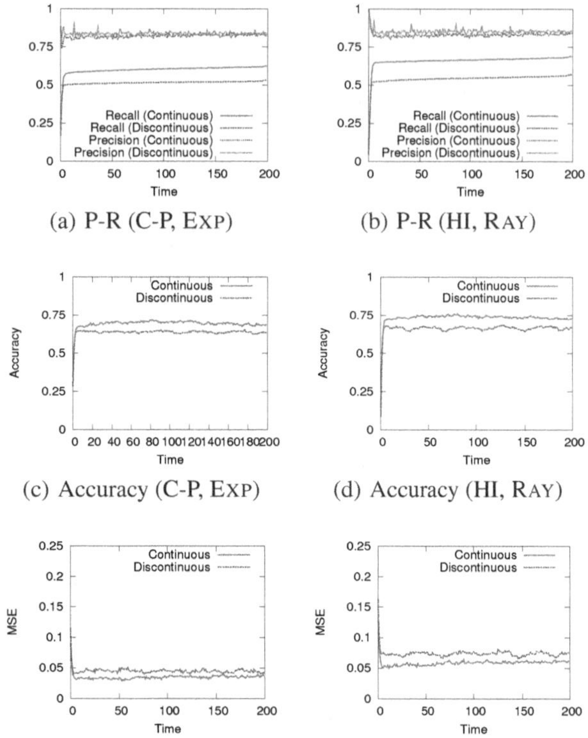

(a) P-R (C-P, EXP) (b) P-R (HI, RAY)

(c) Accuracy (C-P, EXP) (d) Accuracy (HI, RAY)

(e) MSE (C-P, EXP) (f) MSE (HI., RAY)

Figure 2: Precision and Recall (P-R), Accuracy and Mean Squared Error (MSE) of our INFOPATH method against time. (a,c,e): Core-periphery (C-P) Kronecker network with exponential edge transmission model (b, d, f), and Hierarchical (HI) Kronecker network with Rayleigh edge transmission model. Performance on Type I (Chainsaw, Hump) and Type II (Slab, Square) edge transmission rate evolution patterns is plotted.

(MSE) at time t is defined as $E\left[||\alpha^*(t) - \hat{\alpha}(t)||^2\right]$, where $\alpha^*(t)$ is the true edge transmission rate at time t and $\hat{\alpha}(t)$ is the estimated transmission rate.

Figure 2 shows Precision, Recall, Accuracy, and MSE over time for the time-varying core-periphery Kronecker network with exponential edge transmission model, and hierarchical Kronecker network with Rayleigh edge transmission model. Observe that the performance of our method is stable across time, and as mentioned before, continuous evolution patterns are easier to track and estimate than discontinuous ones.

Accuracy vs. running time in static networks. Our stochastic gradient descend based method, INFOPATH, can be also used to speed-up inference of static networks. In such scenario, stochastic gradient descend processes cascades in a random round-robin fashion. Here, we compare INFOPATH to the state of the art methods for inference of static networks: NETINF [10] and NETRATE [9]. First, we compare the methods by computing the accuracy against running time. Second, we compare INFOPATH to NETRATE in terms of mean squared error of the estimated transmission rates against the running time. We omit NETINF from this last comparison since it only infers the network structure (and no edge transmission rates). For the sake of fairness in the running time comparison we implemented all methods in C++. Our C++ implementation of NETRATE is much faster than the public Matlab implementation.

Figure 3 compares Accuracy and MSE against running time for the three network inference methods for a static core-periphery

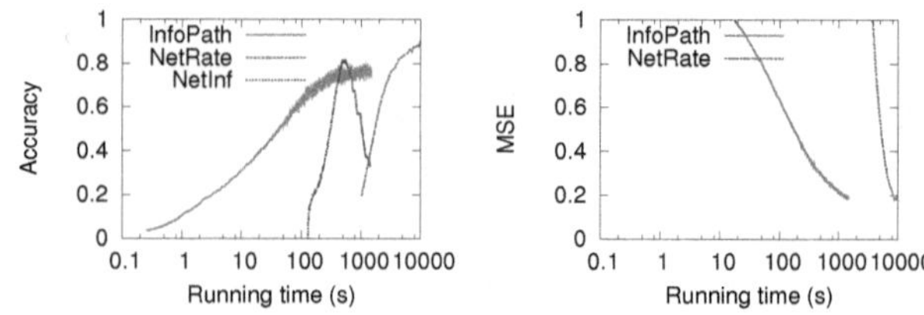

(a) Accuracy (b) MSE

Figure 3: Accuracy and Mean Squared Error (MSE) against running time for a 1,024 node, 2,048 edge time-invariant core-periphery Kronecker network with power-law edge transmission model and 5,000 cascades. Longer running times mean the algorithms run for more iterations. INFOPATH and NETRATE improve accuracy until convergence. However, INFOPATH achieves the same level of performance 10-100 times faster.

Kronecker network. INFOPATH is about 10 to 100 times faster than NETRATE and as fast as NETINF, while achieving the same accuracy as NETRATE. Importantly, INFOPATH and NETRATE always improve accuracy with the running time, until convergence. In terms of MSE, INFOPATH achieves lower MSE values much quicker than NETRATE.

4.2 Experiments on real data

The emergence of specific information pathways often depends on the information content of the news that is propagating [22, 28]. For example, a real world event may occur for a limited period of time and thus news related to the event spread quicker and to larger parts of the network around such time period. At any given time, there are many different real world events, topics, and content that propagates through the Web, leading to different emerging and vanishing information pathways, and thus an underlying time-varying network. In order to better understand these temporal changes, we aim to reconstruct time-varying networks and the information pathways for particular real world events and topics.

Dataset description. We experiment with more than 300 million blog posts and news articles collected from 3.3 million websites over a period of one year, from March 2011 till February 2012. We trace the flow of information using *memes* [16]. *Memes* are a short textual phrases (like, "lipstick on a pig") that travel through the Web. We consider each meme m as a separate information cascade c_m. Since all documents which contain memes are time-stamped, a cascade c_m is simply a record of times when sites first mentioned meme m. We extracted more than 179 million memes, longer than four words. Out of these, 34 million distinct memes appeared at least twice, resulting in 34 million different information cascades.

Experimental setup. Our aim is to consider sites that actively spread memes over the Web. We achieve this by selecting top 5,000 sites in terms of the number of memes they mentioned. Moreover, we are interested in inferring dynamic networks related to particular topics or events. So, we assume we are also given a keyword query Q related to the event/topic of interest. When inferring a network for a given query Q, we only consider documents (and the memes they mention) that include keywords Q. Then, we build information cascades using only those memes and apply the INFOPATH algorithm to infer the edges and evolving edge transmission rates. The edge transmission rates explain the propagation of information related to a given topic or real world event Q. For each query Q we infer one network per day. Table 3 summarizes

Topic or news event (Q)	# sites	# memes
Amy Winehouse	1,207	109,650
Fukushima	1,666	383,745
Gaddafi	1,358	440,646
Kate Middleton	1,427	191,777
NBA	2,087	1,543,630
Occupy	1,875	655,183
Strauss-Kahn	1,263	204,238
Syria	1,565	615,176

Table 3: Topic and news event statistics.

the number of sites and meme cascades for several topics and real world events.[2].

Implementation and scalability. We developed an efficient distributed implementation of our INFOPATH algorithm in C++ based on the network analysis library SNAP [2]. We deployed the implementation in a cluster with 1,000 CPU cores and 6 TB of RAM. With this setup, we considered 38 different topics/events Q. For each topic, we inferred a time-varying network with a daily temporal resolution for a period of one year, from March 2011 to February 2012. Each network has thousands of nodes and is based on hundreds of thousands of cascades. Inferring 38 different time-varying networks took less than 4 hours on our cluster. Note that this is equivalent to solving Eq. 8 more than 13,000 times (38 x 365) for millions of pairwise transmission rates. We also tested our algorithm on larger datasets. For example, for "Occupy Wall Street movement", we were able to infer a 43,415-node time-varying network over a period of 18 months, from January 2011 to June 2012, using 1,381,793 information cascades.

Visualizing the information pathways. Figure 4 plots diffusion networks for three different 2011 world events: Fukushima nuclear disaster, UK royal wedding, and civil uprise in Syria. Each network is shown at three different time points. Red nodes represent mainstream media sites, and blue nodes represent blogs [16].

Based on the figure, we draw several interesting observations. Most often, information propagates through a core-periphery network structure. Such structure emerges by few central media sites and blogs driving the adoption of memes across the Web [10]. However, the network structure often changes dramatically over time, and we find clusters that emerge and vanish in short periods of time. For example, the information networks for Syria's uprise illustrated in Figures 4(g-h), do not have any clear clustering structure. However, on December 2, 2011 (Figure 4(i)) a cluster suddenly emerges in the network. Further investigation reveals that the cluster is composed of UK news sites and blogs that discuss recently implemented EU sanctions against Syria. Generally, it is common to observe sudden formation of clusters of sites from specific geographical areas. This is specially noticeable in the information network for Fukushima's disaster, in Figures 4(a-c). Such clusters often form due to language boundaries, since such boundaries prevent memes to flow across countries or continents. Moreover, we often observe that such clusters are caused by a common external event [22], like in the case of UK discussion on EU sanctions against Syria. Inferred dynamic networks can thus be used to investigate the flow of information as well as to detect external events that cause sudden perturbations to the diffusion network structure.

[2]Additional time-varying diffusion networks for other topics and news events are available at the supporting website [1]

Evolution of edge transmission rates. Next, we aim to study the evolution of links among different types of sites. We label the nodes in our network as mainstream media and blog, and compute the number of links between different types of sites over time. Figure 5 gives the results for several inferred diffusion networks for different topics and world events. We note several interesting patterns.

The connectivity changes tend to reflect the amount of attention that a news event or a topic triggers over time. Unexpected news events, like the sex scandal of the director of the International Monetary Fund Strauss-Kahn on May 14, 2011 in Fig. 5(g) or the death of British singer Amy Winehouse on July 23, 2011 in Fig. 5(a), result in a dramatic increase in the number of edges over a short period of time. More general topics, like the NBA in Fig. 5(e), result in a network with more stable connectivity over time. Certain types of news are sometimes spreading earlier among blogs than mainstream media. This is especially the case for population wide events like the Fukushima nuclear disaster, civil war in Libya and civil uprise in Syria (Fig. 5(b, c, h). However, it happens more frequently that the largest amount of links are mainstream media-to-mainstream media and the fewest links point from blogs to mainstream media. These results are intuitive and consistent with previous work [10, 16] that observed most often information flows from mainstream media to blogs (and rarely the other way around). However, as we see here for population level events and social movements (like, in case of the civil unrest in the Middle East) social media plays crucial role in information dissemination and organization of civil movements.

Evolution of node centrality. Having studied the dynamics of edges in the network we now move towards investigating the network centrality of blogs and mainstream media sites over time for different topics and world events. To measure network centrality of node S in the network at time t, we first compute shortest path length from S to any other node R in the network. Then centrality of node S is defined as $\sum_R 1/d(S,R)$, where $d(S,R)$ is the shortest path length from S to R (if R is not reachable from S then $d(S,R) = \infty$). For networks with core-periphery structure, nodes with high centrality are typically located in the "central" core of the network.

Figure 6 plots the percentage of blogs among the top 100 most central sites over time for eight different topics/events of 2011. Perhaps surprisingly, we observe there is a about the same number of mainstream media and blogs in the top-100 most central nodes for most networks – the number of blogs in the top-100 does not typically decreases below 30% or increases over 70%. For some topics, mainstream media are always more *central* (*e.g.*, baseball and NBA in Figures 6(a, b)). In contrast, for other topics, blogs dominate mainstream media over a significant amounts of time (*e.g.*, Gaddafi in Fig. 6(c)). Centrality of mainstream media and blogs can be relatively constant (Fig. 6(a,b)) or more time-varying (Fig. 6(c,h)). We find that a significant rise in the number of central blogs is often temporally correlated with an increasing social unrest (*e.g.*, the Occupy Wall Street movement in Sept-Nov 2011 in Fig. 6(f)).

Accuracy on real data. So far, we have used *memes* to trace the flow of information over the Web and have made several qualitative observations about the structure and dynamics of information pathways in online media. We now proceed and attempt to also quantitatively evaluate INFOPATH on real data. In case of real data the ground-truth information diffusion network is impossible to obtain. However, we can use the temporal dynamics of hyperlinks created between news sites as a proxy for real information flow. Thus, by observing the times when sites create hyperlinks, our goal is to infer the 'targets' of the links (i.e., infer the hyperlink network from the hyperlinks times).

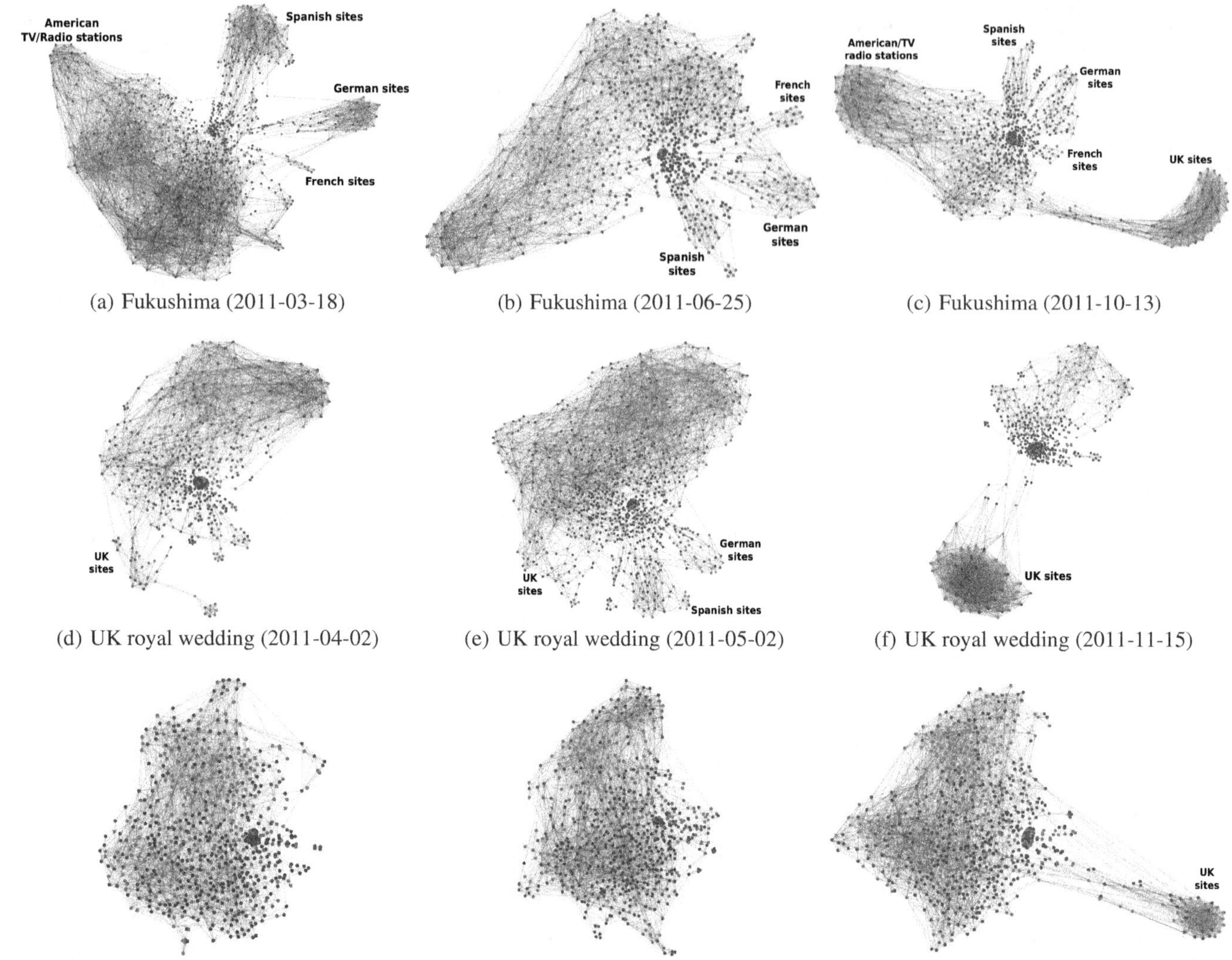

(a) Fukushima (2011-03-18) (b) Fukushima (2011-06-25) (c) Fukushima (2011-10-13)

(d) UK royal wedding (2011-04-02) (e) UK royal wedding (2011-05-02) (f) UK royal wedding (2011-11-15)

(g) Syria's uprise (2011-04-05) (h) Syria's uprise (2011-06-02) (i) Syria's uprise (2011-12-02)

Figure 4: Time-varying diffusion networks for three different major events of 2011. Red nodes are mainstream media, and blue nodes are blogs. Additional visualizations for other topics and events are available at the supporting website [1].

We proceed as follows. First, we discretize the time in days, we generate one network $G^*(t)$ per day t, in which we add an edge (u, v) if a document on a site u linked to a document on a site v within the last day. Then, we build a set of hyperlink cascades. A hyperlink cascade c_h starts when a site publishes a piece of information and then other sites use hyper-links to refer to it. Since all our documents/posts are time stamped, we can trace the hyperlinks in the reverse direction and obtain information cascades. We extracted almost 0.5 million hyperlink cascades from 3.3 million websites from July 2011 till December 2012. Our aim is to use the hyperlink cascades to infer the time-varying network $G^*(t)$. We then evaluate how many edges INFOPATH estimates correctly by computing Accuracy, Precision and Recall for each day.

Figure 7 shows Precision, Recall, and Accuracy over time for a time-varying hyperlink network with 11,461 nodes and 19,915 edges created over time, using 495,655 hyperlink cascades from July 2011 to December 2011. We assume an exponential edge transmission model. We observe weekly periodicity and the overall encouraging performance of around 0.4 to 0.5 for all three performance metrics.

5. CONCLUSION

All previous network inference algorithms have assumed diffusion networks to be static. Therefore, they have considered the pathways over which information propagates to be static over time. In contrast, we developed an algorithm for time-varying network inference, INFOPATH. Our algorithm provides on-line time-varying estimates of the edges of the network as well as the dynamic edge transmission rates, which allows us to detect how information pathways emerge and vanish over time.

We evaluated our algorithm on synthetic data and demonstrated that INFOPATH successfully tracks changes in the topology of dynamic networks, provides accurate on-line estimates of the time-varying edge transmission rates and is also robust across network topologies, edge transmission models and patterns of evolution of edge transmission rates.

We also run INFOPATH on real data and investigated how real networks and information pathways evolve over time. We found that information pathways over which general recurrent topics propagate remain relatively stable across time. In contrast, major real-world events lead to dramatic changes and shifts in the information pathways. We observed that clusters of mainstream news and

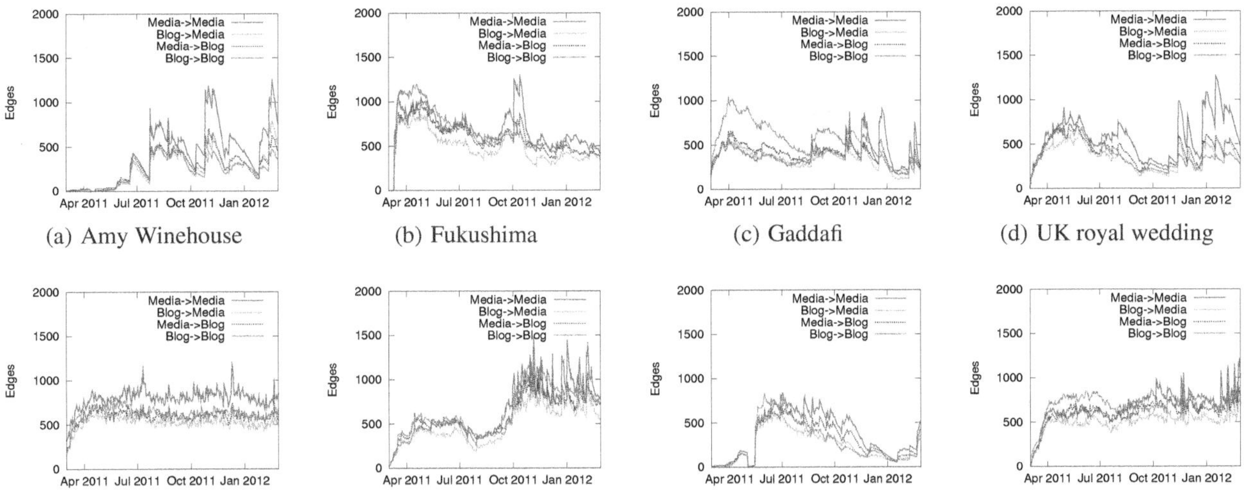

(a) Amy Winehouse (b) Fukushima (c) Gaddafi (d) UK royal wedding

(e) NBA (f) Occupy (g) Strauss-Kahn (h) Syria

Figure 5: The number of links that point between different types of sites over time for eight different inferred diffusion networks. We split the sites into mainstream media and blogs and count the links among these two node types.

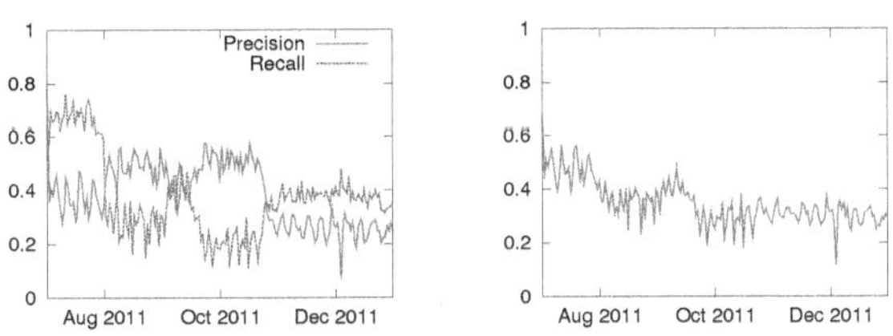

(a) Precision-Recall (b) Accuracy

Figure 7: Precision, Recall, and Accuracy of INFOPATH for a time-varying hyperlink network with 11,461 nodes and 19,915 edges over time, using 495,655 hyperlink cascades from July 2011 to December 2011.

blogs often emergence and vanish in matter of days. We discovered that there is an early greater increase in information transfer among blogs than among mainstream media for news involving general population and social unrest, such as the Libyan civil war, Egyptian revolution, Syria's uprise and the Occupy Wall Street movement.

Our work also opens various venues for future work. For example, rigorous theoretical analysis of the convergence of our stochastic gradient descent method would provide further insights for its performance. Moreover, we notice that many times the changes in the inferred network structure could be attributed to sudden external real-world events. This opens two interesting questions. How can diffusion network inference be combined with methods for detecting external influence in networks [22]? And also, how can dynamic network inference be extended for detecting unexpected real-world events based on a stream of documents? Last, many times not only information but also sentiment attached to a piece of information spreads through the network [19]. It would be interesting to think about inference of signed networks, where a positive/negative valence of an edge models sentiment relationship between a pair of nodes. Overall, such methods would allow us to improve our understanding of the current landscape of news coverage, the role that news media plays in framing the discussion of important topics, and the evolving ecosystem that news media occupies.

Acknowledgements. This research has been supported in part by NSF IIS-1016909, CNS-1010921, IIS-1159679, IIS-1149837, DARPA SMISC, ARO MURI, Brown Institute for Media Innovation, Albert Yu & Mary Bechmann Foundation, Allyes, Boeing, Docomo, Intel, Samsung, Alfred P. Sloan Fellowship, the Microsoft Faculty Fellowship, and Barrie de la Maza Graduate Fellowship.

6. REFERENCES

[1] INFOPATH supporting website: `http://snap.stanford.edu/infopath`.

[2] SNAP: Stanford Network Analysis Platform. `http://snap.stanford.edu`.

[3] O. Aalen, Ø. Borgan, and H. Gjessing. *Survival and event history analysis: a process point of view*. Springer, 2008.

[4] A. Agarwal and J. Duchi. Distributed delayed stochastic optimization. 2011.

[5] F. Bach, E. Moulines, et al. Non-asymptotic analysis of stochastic approximation algorithms for machine learning. In *Advances in Neural Information Processing*, 2011.

[6] N. T. J. Bailey. *The Mathematical Theory of Infectious Diseases and its Applications*. Hafner Press, 1975.

[7] D. Blatt, A. Hero, and H. Gauchman. A convergent incremental gradient method with a constant step size. *SIAM Journal on Optimization*, 18(1):29–51, 2008.

[8] J. Duchi, A. Agarwal, M. Johansson, and M. Jordan. Ergodic subgradient descent. In *Allerton '11: Proc. of the 50th Annual Allerton Conference on Communication, Control, and Computing*, 2011.

[9] M. Gomez-Rodriguez, D. Balduzzi, and B. Schölkopf. Uncovering the Temporal Dynamics of Diffusion Networks. In *ICML '11: Proc. of the 28th International Conference on Machine Learning*, 2011.

[10] M. Gomez-Rodriguez, J. Leskovec, and A. Krause. Inferring Networks of Diffusion and Influence. In *KDD '10: Proc. of the 16th ACM SIGKDD International Conference on Knowledge Discovery in Data Mining*, 2010.

[11] M. Gomez-Rodriguez and B. Schölkopf. Influence Maximization in Continuous Time Diffusion Networks. In *ICML '12: Proc. of the 29th International Conference on Machine Learning*, 2012.

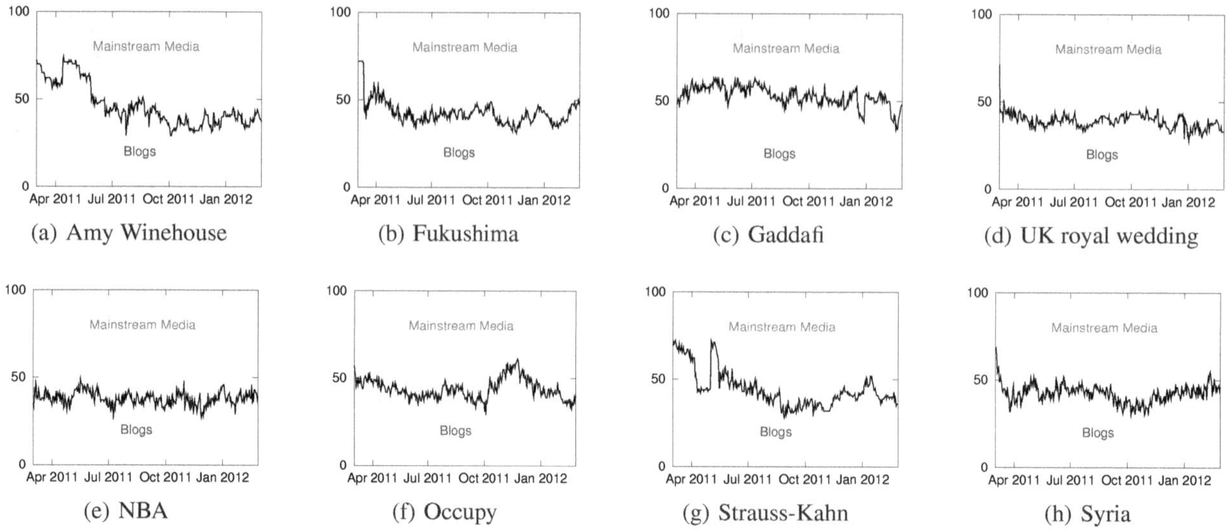

Figure 6: Percentage of blogs and mainstream media in top-100 most *central* sites for eight different inferred diffusion networks. Mainstream media are represented in red, and blogs in blue.

[12] M. Gomez-Rodriguez and B. Schölkopf. Submodular Inference of Diffusion Networks from Multiple Trees. In *ICML '12: Proc. of the 29th International Conference on Machine Learning*, 2012.

[13] D. Kempe, J. M. Kleinberg, and E. Tardos. Maximizing the spread of influence through a social network. In *KDD '03: Proc. of the 9th ACM SIGKDD International Conference on Knowledge Discovery and Data Mining*, 2003.

[14] J. Lawless. *Statistical models and methods for lifetime data.* Wiley New York, 1982.

[15] J. Leskovec, L. A. Adamic, and B. A. Huberman. The dynamics of viral marketing. In *EC '06: Proc. of the 7th ACM conference on Electronic commerce*, 2006.

[16] J. Leskovec, L. Backstrom, and J. Kleinberg. Meme-tracking and the dynamics of the news cycle. In *KDD '09: Proc. of the 15th ACM SIGKDD International Conference on Knowledge Discovery and Data Mining*, 2009.

[17] J. Leskovec, D. Chakrabarti, J. Kleinberg, C. Faloutsos, and Z. Ghahramani. Kronecker graphs: An approach to modeling networks. *The Journal of Machine Learning Research*, 11:985–1042, 2010.

[18] D. Liben-Nowell and J. Kleinberg. Tracing the flow of information on a global scale using Internet chain-letter data. *Proc. of the National Academy of Sciences*, 105(12):4633–4638, 2008.

[19] M. Miller, C. Sathi, D. Wiesenthal, J. Leskovec, and C. Potts. Sentiment flow through hyperlink networks. In *ICWSM '11: Proc. of the AAAI International Conference on Weblogs and Social Media*, 2011.

[20] S. Myers and J. Leskovec. On the Convexity of Latent Social Network Inference. In *NIPS '10: Advances in Neural Information Processing Systems*, 2010.

[21] S. Myers and J. Leskovec. Clash of the contagions: Cooperation and competition in information diffusion. In *ICDM '12: Proc. of the 12th IEEE International Conference on Data Mining*, 2012.

[22] S. Myers, C. Zhu, and J. Leskovec. Information diffusion and external influence in networks. In *KDD '12: Proc. of the 18th ACM SIGKDD international conference on Knowledge discovery and data mining*, 2012.

[23] A. Nemirovski, A. Juditsky, G. Lan, and A. Shapiro. Robust stochastic approximation approach to stochastic programming. *SIAM Journal on Optimization*, 19(4):1574, 2009.

[24] P. Netrapalli and S. Sanghavi. Finding the graph of epidemic cascades. In *Proc. of the 12th ACM SIGMETRICS/Performance*, 2012.

[25] B. Prakash, A. Beutel, R. Rosenfeld, and C. Faloutsos. Winner takes all: competing viruses or ideas on fair-play networks. In *Proc. of the 21st International Conference on World Wide Web*, pages 1037–1046, 2012.

[26] H. Robbins and S. Monro. A stochastic approximation method. *The Annals of Mathematical Statistics*, pages 400–407, 1951.

[27] E. M. Rogers. *Diffusion of Innovations*. Free Press, New York, fourth edition, 1995.

[28] D. M. Romero, B. Meeder, and J. Kleinberg. Differences in the mechanics of information diffusion across topics: idioms, political hashtags, and complex contagion on twitter. In *WWW '11: Proc. of the 20th International Conference on World Wide Web*, 2011.

[29] N. Roux, M. Schmidt, and F. Bach. A stochastic gradient method with an exponential convergence rate for strongly-convex optimization with finite training sets. *Advances in Neural Information Processing*, 2012.

[30] T. Snowsill, N. Fyson, T. De Bie, and N. Cristianini. Refining causality: who copied from whom? In *KDD '11: Proc. of the 17th ACM SIGKDD international conference on Knowledge discovery and data mining*, 2011.

[31] J. Wallinga and P. Teunis. Different epidemic curves for severe acute respiratory syndrome reveal similar impacts of control measures. *American Journal of Epidemiology*, 160(6):509–516, 2004.

[32] J. Yang and J. Leskovec. Modeling information diffusion in implicit networks. In *ICDM '10: Proc. of the IEEE International Conference on Data Mining*, 2010.

[33] J. Yang and J. Leskovec. Patterns of Temporal Variation in Online Media. In *WSDM '11: ACM International Conference on Web Search and Data Mining*, 2011.

Cascade-based Community Detection

Nicola Barbieri
Yahoo! Research
Barcelona, Spain
barbieri@yahoo-inc.com

Francesco Bonchi
Yahoo! Research
Barcelona, Spain
bonchi@yahoo-inc.com

Giuseppe Manco
ICAR-CNR
Rende, Italy
manco@icar.cnr.it

ABSTRACT

Given a directed social graph and a set of past information cascades observed over the graph, we study the novel problem of detecting modules of the graph (communities of nodes), *that also explain the cascades.* Our key observation is that both information propagation and social ties formation in a social network can be explained according to the same latent factor, which ultimately guide a user behavior within the network. Based on this observation, we propose the Community-Cascade Network (CCN) model, a stochastic mixture membership generative model that can fit, at the same time, the social graph and the observed set of cascades. Our model produces overlapping communities and for each node, its level of authority and passive interest in each community it belongs.

For learning the parameters of the CCN model, we devise a Generalized Expectation Maximization procedure. We then apply our model to real-world social networks and information cascades: the results witness the validity of the proposed CCN model, providing useful insights on its significance for analyzing social behavior.

Categories and Subject Descriptors

H.2.8 [**Database Applications**]: Data Mining

Keywords

Social networks, Community Detection, Information Cascades

1. INTRODUCTION

Understanding how the adoption of new practices, ideas, beliefs, technologies and products can spread trough a population driven by *social influence*, is a central issue for the whole of social sciences. Taking into account the modular structure of the underlying social network provides further important insight in the phenomena known as *social contagion* or *information cascades.* In particular, individuals tend to adopt the behavior of their social peers, so that cascades happen first locally, within close-knit communities, and become global "viral" phenomena only when they are able cross the boundaries of these densely connected clusters of people. Therefore, the study of social contagion is intrinsically connected to the problem of understanding the modular structure of networks (known as *community detection*), and together form the central core of network science.

Recently with the explosion of on-line social platforms such as Twitter and Facebook, the interest in these topics has exploded accordingly. Researchers have investigated how to exploit social influence for "word-of-mouth" driven viral marketing applications [17, 44, 28, 10], studying person-to-person recommendation for purchasing books and videos [36, 35] or telecommunications services [27] finding conditions under which such recommendations are successful. Others have focussed on the important problems of how to measure social influence [47, 50, 24, 53] and how to distinguishing real social influence from "homophily" and other external factors of correlation [3, 16, 4, 20]. Finally, a growing effort has been devoted to the analysis of influence-driven information cascades in Twitter [14, 52, 5, 45].

At the same time a large effort has been devoted to develop community detection algorithms (surveyed later in Section 1.2), but quite surprisingly there has not been much effort to explain the modular structure of social networks and the phenomenon of social contagion, *jointly.* We say that the lack of research in the intersection of these two themes is surprising because, as discussed above, they are intrinsically connected. This is expressed nicely by Easley and Kleinberg in their book [18, page 577]:

> *"cascades and clusters truly are natural opposites: clusters block the spread of cascades, and whenever a cascade comes to a stop, there's a cluster that can be used to explain why."*

If a cluster can explain why a cascade comes to a stop, then observing past cascades we can find out something about the existence of clusters. Inspired by this observation, we propose to take benefit of an available set of traces of past information cascades, in order to better determine the community structure of the underlying social network.

1.1 Our proposal

Given a graph and a set of cascades, we tackle the community detection task by fitting a unique stochastic generative model to the observed social graph and cascades.

Since we deal with information propagation, it is natural to consider a *directed* social graph $G = (N, A)$ where an arc $(u, v) \in A$ indicates that v is a follower of u, i.e., v is notified about u's activity. In other terms, information can propagate from u to v. For instance, in `Twitter` v can see something posted by u and re-tweet so that the information becomes available to her own followers, thus propagating further in the network. A cascade of an item i is a sequence of pairs $(user, timestamp)$ recording which nodes adopt i (e.g., re-tweeting it, in the `Twitter` example) and at which time. We are given a set of such propagations.

In our CCN model we assume that each observation is the result of a stochastic process where a given user u acts in the network according to a set of topics/communities which also represent her interests. Given a community c, the degree of involvement of user u to that community is governed by two parameters, namely $\pi_u^{c,s}$ and $\pi_u^{c,d}$. Specifically, $\pi_u^{c,s}$ measures the degree of "active involvement" of u in c, while $\pi_u^{c,d}$ measures the degree of "passive involvement" of u in c.

Let us use the `Twitter` example again and let us consider an hypothetical user u which uses the microblogging platform for three specific interests: (*i*) network science and data mining, (*ii*) the city of Barcelona, and (*iii*) the rock legend Bruce Springsteen. While on the first topic u is actively posting, using the platform for communicating with other researchers, in the other two topics u is just passively listening: for sake of information needs, u follows users which are good information sources for events happening in Barcelona and users which are authorities for whatever concerns Bruce Springsteen. These users which are good sources of information usually have a large number of followers and are, in some sense, "influential". In the second and third community u might re-tweet some pieces of information, but it is quite unlikely that u would produce some original information.

Going back to our parameters we can expect u to have both high $\pi_u^{c,s}$ and $\pi_u^{c,d}$ in the first community. Instead, in the other two communities we can expect u to have a low $\pi_u^{c,s}$ and a high $\pi_u^{c,d}$. Not surprisingly u has many followers in the first community and almost no followers in the other two communities.

Indeed, this is the key observation behind our model: the likelihood of u posting something on a topic, the likelihood of this information being further propagated, and the likelihood of u having followers interested in that topic, are all strongly correlated. In our model they are jointly represented by the parameter $\pi_u^{c,s}$. Similarly, we model the likelihood of having an incoming arc in a community and the likelihood of being influenced by other users in that community with the parameter $\pi_u^{c,d}$. This is how we achieve the jointly modeling of the social graph and the set of cascades.

Another important observation is in place. As seen in the `Twitter` example one user can belong to more than one community, but a link is usually explainable because of a unique topic. In graph terminology this translates in the fact that the communities of nodes are *overlapping* and induced by a *partitioning of the links*. In our model information starts in a community, propagates trough the links of that community, and can jump in another community only thanks to users which are in the overlap of the two communities.

1.2 Related work

Communities have a long history in social sciences, but it was in 2002 that the seminal paper by Girvan and Newman [23] triggered a lot of interest on the problem of *community detection*, which has since then been extensively studied, mainly in the physics and in the computer science literature. Until recently most of such literature[1], has focussed on finding disjoint communities in simple undirected graphs. That is to say that (*i*) nodes can belong to one and only one cluster, (*ii*) the relation between the nodes is symmetric, and (*iii*) no additional information is considered beyond the graph structure. In the following we review various proposals that have dropped one or more of these assumptions.

Overlapping communities. Nowadays is widely understood and accepted that people in social networks rarely belong to only one community: for instance the same individual usually has family, friends, colleagues and several interest-based affiliations. This idea has also been explicitly implemented in `Google+` "circles" or `Facebook` "smart lists".

A recent survey by Xie et al. [54] categorizes algorithms for overlapping community detection in various classes: methods based on *clique percolation* [41, 42, 30]; methods that extend the idea of *label propagation* [43] to produce overlapping communities [25, 56, 55]; agent-based and particles-based models [15, 12]; methods based on local expansion and optimization [7, 31, 32, 40]. But the two classes more relevant for our proposal are *link partitioning* methods and *stochastic generative* models, discussed next.

Link partitioning has recently gained popularity [1, 19]. Clustering links instead of nodes is a very appealing approach to obtain overlapping communities: it is simple, more understandable and realistic than simply having a soft (or fuzzy) assignment of nodes to communities. In fact, as highlighted before, while for nodes is natural to belong to more than a community, links are usually explainable by a co-affiliation to some topic/community (as in the famous *affiliation networks* [33] model). Evans and Lambiotte [19] use the idea of applying normal node partitioning to the *line graph* of the given network, in order to obtain a link partitioning in the original network. Ahn et al. [1] use a simple hierarchical clustering of the links, where the similarity among two links incident in the same node is defined based on the Jaccard coefficient of the neighborhoods of the other two nodes. Kim and Jeong [29] extend the *Infomap* method to the line graph which encodes the path of the random walk on the line network under MDL.

While these methods are based on heuristic quality function, in recent years approaches based on fitting a generative model to the data have emerged. Airoldi et al. [2] introduce *mixed membership block model*: this technique factorizes the adjacency matrix in a low dimensional space expressing patterns of directed social relationships between blocks of vertices. According to the generative process, for each pair of nodes group membership is sampled for both for the source and the destination: the link is generated by sampling from the binomial distribution which encodes the probability of observing a directed connection between the considered groups. Since membership assignment are drawn independently for each possible link, users can belong to multiple groups.

A different generative model is proposed by Ball et al. [6]. The basic assumption is the existence of $n \times k$ parameters, where n is the number of nodes and k the number of communities, which specify the propensity of each vertex to have links of each possible label. The number of links of label z between two vertices is then assumed to be distributed

[1]See Fortunato [21] for a comprehensive survey.

according to a Poisson distribution parameterized by the product of the two vertex-label components.

Despite their elegant formulation, both [6, 2] suffer from a main drawback: their parameter estimation phase requires to estimate the link probability between any pair of vertices and this might be unsuitable for large networks.

Communities in directed graphs. Regardless the wide availability of directed networks (e.g., `Twitter` or the WWW itself), methods for community detection in directed networks are relatively new: for many years the most common practice to deal with directed networks has been to ignore directionality and apply the methods developed for undirected networks. In our setting, as we want to study communities and information propagation jointly, ignoring directionality would be an unacceptable loss of relevant information.

One of the first proposal is by Guimerà et al. [26] consider a bipartite graph with *actors* on one side and *teams* on the other, and they propose to optimize a measure of *bipartite modularity*, which adapts modularity to the bipartite case. Another recent modularity optimization approach is by Leicht and Newman [34]. Neither of the two approaches above consider overlapping communities. Palla et al. [42] extend the method of *clique percolation* [41] to deal with directed networks by considering *directed k-cliques*, which are complete sub-graphs of size k in which an ordering can be made such that between any pair of nodes there is a directed link from the higher order node towards the lower one. This work and [2] are among the few methods we are aware of, that can produce overlapping communities from directed networks.

When additional information is available. Most of the literature on community detection focuses on finding (either disjoint or overlapping) groups of nodes from a given (either undirected or directed) graph. However, in online social networking sites, richer data is available. Beyond the mere link information, users might be annotated with, e.g., demographical information, shopping behavior, interests, tags and so on. Also the links might be labeled with a relationship type: e.g., family, friend, colleague and so on. Similarly nodes and links in biological networks are typically labeled with additional information. Recently researchers (mainly in the data mining community) have started proposing method to discover communities in nodes-attributed graphs [22, 37, 57, 49] and in edge-labeled graphs [11].

The two papers which are probably the most related to ours are [46, 51]. Sachan al. [46] use topic-detection methods over the content of exchanged messages for discovering overlapping communities of nodes. The main distinction with our proposal is that we focus on the structure of the propagations without modelling the content. Wang et al. [51] study the *influence maximization* problem [28] for finding the Top-K influential nodes in *mobile* social networks. In order to speed-up the costly influence maximization process, they propose to first detect communities and then assume that the influence of a user is limited to her community. Therefore they propose an algorithm based on label propagation [43] where the propagation follows the *independent cascade* model [28]. In other terms, they modify label propagation to deal with a directed graph whose links have associated an *influence probability*. This is different from modeling a social graph and a set of cascades jointly, as we do in this paper. Another difference is that [51] produces disjoint communities.

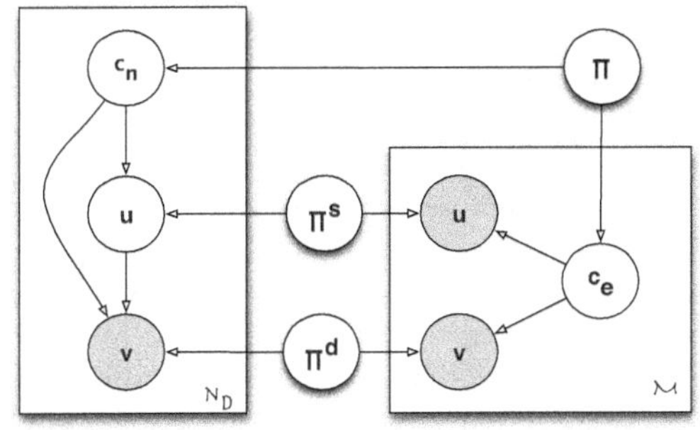

Figure 1: The CCN generative model.

2. THE CCN MODEL

We are given a directed graph $G = (N, A)$, where N is the set of the nodes and a link $(u, v) \in A$ indicates that v is a follower of u, i.e., v is notified about u's activities. Let n and m be the cardinality of N and A respectively.

We are also given a log $\mathbb{L}$ of past information cascades defined on a set of items $\mathcal{I}$ and on the nodes of the network. A tuple $(i, u, t) \in \mathbb{L}$ represents the fact that user u adopted i at time t. Let $t_i(u)$ be the activation timestamp for the user u on i; we assume that no user adopts the same item more than once and $t_i(u) = \infty$ if u does not adopt i in $\mathbb{L}$. We also denote by $D_i(t)$ the set of users that become active on i at time t, and $C_i(t)$ will denote the set of user who are active on i by time t, i.e $C_i(t) = \bigcup_{t' \leq t} D_i(t')$.

When a node u adopts i, we can think of this as information flowing from u's neighbors that have adopted i before. We assume that only users that adopted i *recently* (i.e., within an *influence window* represented by a threshold Δ) can influence their neighbors. Let t represent the current timestamp. We define the set $\mathcal{F}_i(t)$ of the nodes that can propagate i at the current time:

$$\mathcal{F}_i(t) = \{u \in N | t - t_i(u) \leq \Delta\}.$$

We also define the set of u's neighbors, $\mathcal{F}_{i,u}(t)$ that potentially can have influenced u in the selection of i at time t:

$$\mathcal{F}_{i,u} = \{v \in N | (v, u) \in A \wedge 0 \leq t_i(u) - t_i(v) \leq \Delta\}.$$

Since we are interested in modeling only activation which are likely to be triggered by some influencer (as the others represent autonomous activations), we will focus on the subset $\mathbb{D}$ of $\mathbb{L}$ defined as $\mathbb{D} = \{(i, v, t) \in \mathbb{L} : \mathcal{F}_{i,v} \neq \emptyset\}$. Let n_d denote the cardinality of $\mathbb{D}$.

As justified in Section 1.1 we assume that each observation is the result of a stochastic process where a given user u acts in the network according to a set of topics/communities which also represent her interests. Given a community c, the degree of involvement of user u to that community is governed by two parameters, namely $\pi_u^{c,s}$ and $\pi_u^{c,d}$. Specifically, $\pi_u^{c,s}$ measures the degree of "active involvement" of u in c, while $\pi_u^{k,d}$ measures the degree of "passive involvement" of u in c.

Figure 1 provides a description of the dependencies in the generative process. There are 3 prior components representing, respectively:

- the probability (Π) to observe a phenomenon in a certain topic/community,
- the level of activeΠ ^{s} and passiveΠ ^{d} interest of each user in each community.

Each phenomenon in the social network can be explained according to the above priors:

- a link (u, v) can only be observed if, by picking a latent topic/community c, u has a high degree of activeness and v have a high degree of passive interest in c.
- Analogously, a user v can only perform an action i if there is a latent topic/community k that likely enables an influencer u, and v can be influenced by u according to their degrees of activeness and subordination.

An interesting perspective is as follows. The action log $\mathbb{D}$ can be interpreted as a weighted bipartite graph, where links are only possible between the set of items $\mathcal{I}$ and the set of users N. The weight for a link is given by the timestamp $t_i(u)$. Under this perspective, a link (u, v) in G is only possible if a latent factor k makes it possible that u is the source and v is the destination. Analogously, a link (i, v) in $\mathbb{D}$ is only possible if there are *two* latent factors: namely, a community k and an influencer u, such that u has a high influence ratio, and v a high subordination ratio.

Based on these premises, a social network graph G and the set of observed diffusions $\mathbb{D}$ are drawn according to the following generative model:

For each link $\ell = (u, v) \in A$:

- sample a community $c_\ell \sim \mathit{Discrete}(\Pi)$
- sample a source $u \sim \mathit{Discrete}(\vec{\vartheta}^{c_\ell})$
- sample a destination $v \sim \mathit{Discrete}(\vec{\varphi}^{c_\ell})$

For each item $i \in \mathcal{I}$ and timestamp t

- Sample the number of activations $a_{i,t}$
- for each activation a where $1 \leq a \leq a_{i,t}$
  - Sample a community $c_a \sim \mathit{Discrete}\,(\Pi)$
  - pick an influencer $u_a \sim \mathit{Discrete}\left(\vec{\theta}_u^{c_a,a}\right)$
  - sample activation $v_a \sim \mathit{Discrete}\left(\vec{\phi}_u^{c_a,a}\right)$

The scheme assumes that there are two independent processes, regarding respectively the generation of the directed links and of the activations. For the first process, source and destination of a link are based on two multinomial distributions $\vec{\vartheta}^k$ and $\vec{\varphi}^k$. In our modeling we assume that both these parameters are defined in terms of the prior parameters $\vec{\pi}^{k,s}$ and $\vec{\pi}^{k,d}$, as follows:

$$\vartheta_u^k = \frac{\exp\left\{\pi_u^{k,s}\right\}}{\sum_{\overline{u}\in N} \exp\left\{\pi_{\overline{u}}^{k,s}\right\}} \quad (1)$$

$$\varphi_u^k = \frac{\exp\left\{\pi_u^{k,d}\right\}}{\sum_{\overline{u}\in N} \exp\left\{\pi_{\overline{u}}^{k,d}\right\}} \quad (2)$$

There is an interesting correlation between the above formulas and the traditional *Preferential Attachment* model: if we interpret the terms $\exp\left\{\pi_u^{k,s}\right\} / \exp\left\{\pi_u^{k,d}\right\}$ as the in-degree/outdegree of node u, then the likelihood of u to be connected is compatible with the above mentioned model, in a community-based fashion.

The second process takes a pair item/timestamp, and delves into a sequence of activations. In practice, at each timestamp, we sample the activations for the item under consideration. Since an activation a involves both an influencer and an influenced, we pick them from two multinomial distributions $\vec{\theta}^{k,a}$ and $\vec{\phi}_u^{c_a,a}$. With an abuse of notation, we associate with each activation a a timestamp t_a and an action i_a (besides the active user v_a and the latent influencer u_a). Then, we can define the multinomials as follows:

$$\theta_u^{k,a} = \frac{\exp\left\{\pi_u^{k,s}\right\}}{\sum_{u'\in\mathcal{F}_{i_a}(t_a)} \exp\left\{\pi_{u'}^{k,s}\right\}} \quad (3)$$

$$\phi_{u,v}^{k,a} = \frac{\exp\left\{\pi_v^{k,d}\right\}}{\sum_{v':(u,v')\in A, v'\notin C_{i_a}(t_a-1)} \exp\left\{\pi_{v'}^{k,d}\right\}} \quad (4)$$

Notice that an influencer u is chosen among those users who can propagate i, that is, $u \in \mathcal{F}_{i_a}(t_a)$. Analogously, a node v can only be influenced to adopt i_a if it is connected to the influencer, and if it is still inactive: $(u, v) \in A$ and $v \notin C_{i_a}(t_a - 1)$. Again, by looking at the interpretation of the action log as a bipartite graph, a new link connects i to a user v, according to a markovian process that selects an influencer u among those who already expressed a links with i in the past, and then by choosing v among those connected to u.

The above multinomials are both conditioned to the hyperparametersΠ ^{s} andΠ ^{d}, whereΠ $^s = \{\vec{\pi}^{1,s}, \ldots, \vec{\pi}^{K,s}\}$ and $\Pi^d = \{\vec{\pi}^{1,d}, \ldots, \vec{\pi}^{K,d}\}$, which associate to each user its degree of active and passive interest within a given community. Finally, Π= $\{\pi_1, \ldots, \pi_K\}$ represents the prior multinomial distribution of the K communities involved in the process.

3. LEARNING

Given the social graph G, the propagations log $\mathbb{D}$ and a positive integer K, our aim is to detect and estimate a set of K overlapping communities, which are specified by the parameter set Θ= $\{\Pi, \Pi^s, \Pi^d\}$. Assuming links and propagation traces independent, the likelihood of the data given the model parameters Θ, can be expressed as:

$$P(G, \mathbb{D}|\Theta) = \prod_{(u,v)\in A} P(u, v|\Theta) \cdot \prod_{a\in\mathbb{D}} P(a|\Theta) \quad (7)$$

where

$$P(u, v|\Theta) = \sum_k \vartheta_u^k \varphi_v^k \pi_k$$

and

$$P(a|\Theta) = \sum_k \sum_{u\in\mathcal{F}_{i_a,v_a}} \pi_k \theta_u^{k,a} \phi_{u,v_a}^{k,a}$$

The above likelihood is difficult to maximize, due to the presence of three latent variables modeling respectively the community assignments and the latent influencer. Making these variables explicit through binary assignments z_ℓ^k, z_a^k and w_a^u, yields:

$$P(G, \mathbb{D}, Z_G, Z_{\mathbb{D}}, W_{\mathbb{D}}|\Theta) = \prod_{\ell\equiv(u,v)\in A} \prod_k \left(\vartheta_u^k \varphi_v^k \pi_k\right)^{z_\ell^k} \cdot \prod_{a\in\mathbb{D}} \prod_k \prod_{u\in\mathcal{F}_{i_a,v_a}} \left(\pi_k \theta_u^{k,a} \phi_{u,v_a}^{k,a}\right)^{z_a^k w_a^u} \quad (8)$$

$$\delta_{\bar{u}}^k = \log \left\{ \frac{\sum_{v:(\bar{u},v)\in A} \gamma_{\bar{u},v,k} + \sum_{a\in\mathbb{D}:\bar{u}\in\mathcal{F}_{i_a,v_a}} \eta_{\bar{u},a,k}}{\vartheta_{\bar{u}}^k \sum_{(u,v)\in A} \gamma_{u,v,k} + \sum_{a\in\mathbb{D}:\bar{u}\in\mathcal{F}_{i_a}(t_a)} \theta_{\bar{u}}^{k,a} \sum_{u\in\mathcal{F}_{i_a,v_a}} \eta_{u,a,k}} \right\} \tag{5}$$

$$\lambda_{\bar{v}}^k = \log \left\{ \frac{\sum_{u:(u,\bar{v})\in A} \gamma_{u,\bar{v},k} + \sum_{a:v_a=\bar{v}} \sum_{u\in\mathcal{F}_{i_a,\bar{v}}} \eta_{u,a,k}}{\varphi_{\bar{v}}^k \sum_{(u,v)\in A} \gamma_{u,v,k} + \sum_{a:\bar{v}\notin C_{i_a}(t_a-1)} \sum_{u\in\mathcal{F}_{i_a,v_a}:(u,\bar{v})\in A} \eta_{u,a,k}\phi_{u,\bar{v}}^{k,a}} \right\} \tag{6}$$

Figure 2: Update formulas for the GEM procedure.

As a consequence, the expected complete-data log-likelihood can be defined as:

$$Q(\Theta, \Theta') = \sum_{(u,v)\in A} \sum_{k} \gamma_{u,v,k}(\Theta') \left[\log \pi_k + \log \vartheta_u^k + \log \varphi_v^k\right]$$
$$+ \sum_{a\in\mathbb{D}} \sum_{k} \sum_{u\in\mathcal{F}_{i_a,v_a}} \eta_{u,a,k}(\Theta') \left(\log \pi_k + \log \theta_u^{k,a} + \log \phi_{u,v_a}^{k,a}\right)$$

where

$$\gamma_{u,v,k}(\Theta) = P(z_\ell^k | \ell \equiv (u,v) \in A, \Theta) = \frac{\vartheta_u^k \varphi_v^k \pi_k}{\sum_{k'} \vartheta_u^{k'} \varphi_v^{k'} \pi_{k'}} \tag{9}$$

and

$$\eta_{u,a,k}(\Theta) = P(z_a^k, w_a^u | a \in \mathbb{D}, \Theta) = \frac{P(a \in \mathbb{D} | w_a^u, z_a^k, \Theta) P(w_a^u | z_a^k, \Theta) P(z_a^k | \Theta)}{P(a \in \mathbb{D} | \Theta)} = \frac{\phi_{u,v_a}^{k,a} \theta_u^{k,a} \pi_k}{\sum_{k'} \sum_{u'\in\mathcal{F}_{i_a,v_a}} \phi_{u',v_a}^{k',a} \theta_{u'}^{k',a} \pi_{k'}} \tag{10}$$

The standard EM approach expects that, given a previous valueΘ^{old}, $Q(\Theta, \Theta^{old})$ can be optimized with respect to Θ. An optimal solutions for Π is straightforward:

$$\pi_k = \frac{\sum_{(u,v)\in A} \gamma_{u,v,k} + \sum_{a\in\mathbb{D}} \sum_{u\in\mathcal{F}_{i_a,v_a}} \eta_{u,a,k}}{m + \sum_{a\in\mathbb{D}} \sum_k \sum_{u\in\mathcal{F}_{i_a,v_a}} \eta_{u,a,k}} \tag{11}$$

The remaining parameters cannot be solved in a closed form, due essentially to the non-linearity of the multinomial parameters. We overcome this limitation by resorting to a slight modification of the EM approach, which combines the *Improved Iterative Scaling* algorithm in the *Generalized Expectation-Maximization (GEM)* procedure [38]. Rather than maximizing $Q(\Theta, \Theta^{old})$, we look for an upgrade Γ of Θ^{old} that guarantees

$$Q(\Theta^{old} + \Gamma, \Theta^{old}) \geq Q(\Theta^{old}, \Theta^{old})$$

We introduce for each $\pi_u^{k,s}$ an upgrade δ_u^k, and for each $\pi_v^{k,d}$ an upgrade λ_u^k. By algebraic manipulations, the above inequality yields the updates 5 and 6 in Figure 2. It is worth noticing how both the updates add two main contributions, coming respectively from the links in the graph and the propagations log.

The general scheme of the parameter estimation is given in Algorithm 1. The initialization can be accomplished in several different ways, for instance: (*i*) randomly, enforcing the constraint $\sum_k \pi_k = 1$ and with $\pi_u^s, \pi_u^d \in [-\pi_{MIN}, \pi_{MAX}]$ (e.g., $[-2, 2]$); (ii) by fitting a simpler model (e.g., considering only the social graph structure). Also, the estimation of the number of communities K is accomplished through

Algorithm 1: CCN model parameters estimation

Input : Graph $G = (N, A)$, propagation log $\mathbb{D}$, and $K \in \mathbb{N}^+$.
Output: The set of all parameters, $\Theta = \{\Pi, \Pi^s, \Pi^d\}$.

init(Π, Π^s, Π^d); //Initialization of parameters
repeat
  E-step:
  forall the $k \in \{1, \ldots K\}$ **do**
    forall the $\ell \equiv (u, v) \in A$ **do**
      compute $\gamma_{u,v,k}$ according to eq. 9
    end
    forall the $a \equiv (i_a, v_a, t_a) \in \mathbb{D}$ **do**
      forall the $u \in N$ **do**
        compute $\eta_{u,a,k}$ according to eq. 10
      end
    end
  end
  M-step:
  forall the $k \in \{1, \ldots K\}$ **do**
    compute π_k according to equation 11
    forall the $u \in N$ **do**
      compute δ_u^k and λ_u^k according to eqs. 5-6
      $\pi_u^{k,s(new)} \leftarrow \pi_u^{k,s} + \delta_u^k$
      $\pi_u^{k,d(new)} \leftarrow \pi_u^{k,d} + \lambda_u^k$
    end
  end
until convergence;

model selection, by resorting to the standard BIC criterion [48] which penalizes the log likelihood in a way proportional to the complexity of the model:

$$BIC(\Theta) = -2 \log P(G, \mathbb{D} | \Theta) + C \log(m + n_d) \tag{12}$$

where C represents the number of free parameters, that is, $C = |\Pi| - 1 + |\Pi^s| + |\Pi^d| = K(2n + 1) - 1$.

4. EXPERIMENTAL EVALUATION

The joint modeling of the incidence matrix and the propagation logs, provides a powerful framework to detect and understand different patterns within the data. In this section we analyze the application of the proposed technique to real networks and propagation logs. More specifically, we are interested in:

- investigating whether the CCN method is actually capable of detecting communities within data;
- assessing the adequacy of the model to fit real data;
- unveiling the complex and hidden relationships between groups and influence propagation;
- charactering the discovered community structures.

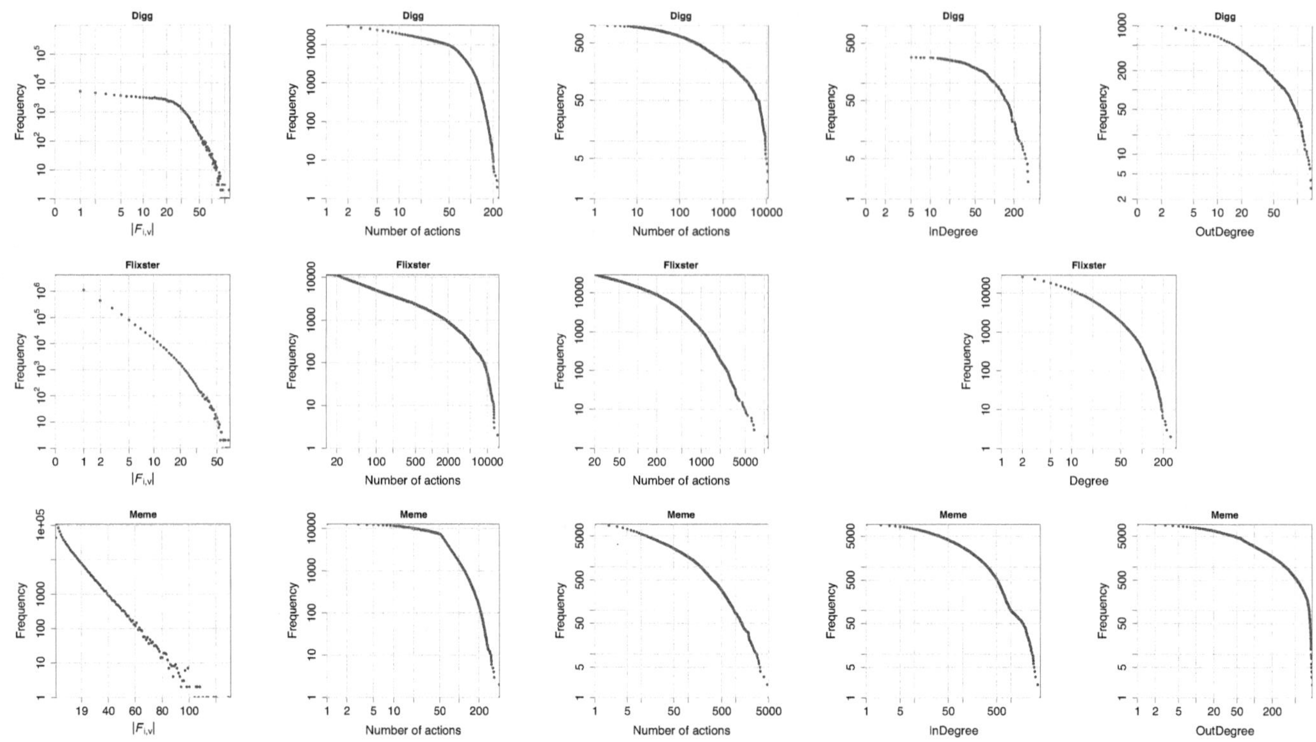

Figure 3: Cumulative distribution of $\mathcal{F}_{i,v}$ (col. 1); cumulative distribution of actions per item (col. 2); cumulative distribution of actions per user (col. 3); cumulative InDegree (col. 4); cumulative OutDegree (col. 5).

Datasets. We use three real-world datasets, each of them containing both a social graph G and a log $\mathbb{D}$ of past activations relative to a given time interval. These datasets come from Digg[2] (`www.digg.com`), Flixster [3] (`www.flixster.com`) and Yahoo! Meme (`http://meme.yahoo.com`). Digg is a social news website, where users vote stories. In this case the activation log contains information about which user voted which story (item) at which time. If we have user v vote a story about the new iPhone, and shortly later v's friend u does the same, we consider the story as having propagated from v to u, and v as a potential influencer for u. Flixster is one of the main players in the mobile and social movie consumption business. Here, an item is a movie, and the action of the user is rating the movie; an item propagates from v to u, if the v's activation on the item is followed shortly enough by u's activation. Meme is a (discontinued, as of today) microblogging service which allows users to share snippets of text, images, sounds or videos with their social connections. Here the propagations are by means of re-posting information "memes". The *propagation window* Δ is set to 1 month for all the three datasets.

Table 1 and Figure 3 report the main characteristics of the datasets. It is worth noticing how the three datasets exhibits different features. For instance, the first column of Figure 3 reports the distribution of $\mathcal{F}_{i,v}$, that is, for each pair item-user (i, v) the number of possible influencers: we can see that this number is quite low in Digg and high in both Flixster and Meme. Also, the social graph in Flixster is undirected, allowing us to investigate how the CCN technique adapts to undirected graphs.

[2]`www.isi.edu/~lerman/downloads/digg2009.html`

[3]`http://www.cs.sfu.ca/~sja25/personal/datasets/`

	Digg	Flixster	Meme
Users	1,000	29,357	9,385
Social Relationships	24,842	425,228	1,144,932
Bidirectional	N	Y	N
Items	31,911	11,659	12,760
Overall Activations($\lvert\mathbb{L}\rvert$)	1,086,065	6,529,011	726,809
Influence Episodes ($\lvert\mathbb{D}\rvert$)	315,377	2,239,744	684,368

Table 1: Summary of the propagation and link data.

Model assessment. There are a number of measurements which can be used to asses the performance of the CCN model. First, the study of the likelihood provides insight on how the models fit the data. Table 2 shows both the penalized log-likelihood of eq. 12 and the *likelihood ratio*. The latter is the ratio between the hypothesized model and an alternative model [13]. In our case, it is the ratio between a given model and the previous model: i.e., 2 communities are compared to 1 community, 4 are compared to 2 and so on. A large value of the ratio denotes that there is a better fitting of the hypothesized model with respect to the previous model. It has been shown that the likelihood ratio approximates the χ^2 distribution for large values of the sample size. Hence, this value gives us an insight of the statistical significance of the model, compared to simpler models.

In a preliminary measurement (not reported here), we found that the ratio between models $K > 1$ and the null model,where $K = 1$, passes the test with 95% significance. This is a clear sign of the presence of community structures in the data. Notably, the test exhibits high positive values on all the cells. The significance of such values can be measured by resorting to the χ^2 test, as mentioned before. What is worth observing here is that both the likelihood ratio and the penalized log-likelihood agree on the optimal number of communities, which is assessed to 8 communities for Digg, and 16 for Flixster and Meme.

		# Communities				
		2	4	8	16	32
Likelihood Ratio	Digg	5.06E+04	1.50E+05	2.28E+04	2.28E+03	1.82E+03
	Flixster	1.85E+06	2.11E+06	1.65E+06	3.40E+06	4.19E+06
	Meme	1.48E+05	1.80E+05	3.91E+05	1.51E+06	1E+06
Penalized LogLikelihood	Digg	-4.54E+06	-4.41E+06	**-4.40E+06**	-4.45E+06	-4.54E+06
	Flixster	-5.37E+07	-5.21E+07	-5.15E+07	**-5.02E+07**	-5.02E+07
	Meme	-5.08E+07	-5.07E+07	-5.06E+07	**-4.97E+07**	-4.99E+07
Learning Time(Hours)	Digg	1.191	1.87	3.15	6.064	10.81
	Flixster	15.90	20.04	28.73	32.05	59.27
	Meme	15.10	23.89	40.98	74.69	129.73
$\mathcal{Q}_G$/ $\mathcal{Q}_{\mathbb{D}}$	Digg	4.31E-08/2.60E-02	5.11E-08/2.95E-02	6.56E-08/2.98E-02	7.00E-08/3.75E-02	8.16E-08/3.97E-02
	Flixster	7.34E-13/1.72E-03	1.61E-12/1.90E-03	4.35E-12/1.96E-03	7.55E-12/2.00E-03	1.67E-11/2.63E-03
	Meme	5.42E-11/1.22E-03	9.22E-10/1.26E-03	1.30E-09/1.30E-03	1.49E-09/1.36E-03	1.87E-09/1.67E-03

Table 2: Summary of the quality measures.

For the learning time, the table highlights a main issue with the CCN model: a slow (albeit linear) convergence, due mainly to two reasons: (i) the extreme computational burden of the update equations $\delta_{\bar{u}}^k$ and $\lambda_{\bar{v}}^k$, and (ii) the fact that the M step is an improvement, rather than an optimization step. The GEM procedure typically exhibits a slower convergence rate than the standard EM procedure: the result is that the learning phase requires more iterations, and each iteration is extremely heavy.

Regarding the first issue mentioned above, it is worth noticing that the main overhead is intrinsic in the exploration of the set of active neighbors who may have potentially triggered the considered activation, in order to determine the most likely influencer. This phase is generally recognized as extremely computing-intensive, and it is a common problem in several method for the estimation of the influence probabilities in a network.

Next, inspired by the well-known *modularity* measure [39], we define two quality measures (for the graph and the propagations log respectively) suitable for our context. In the original formulation, the modularity compares the structure of the graph to that resulting from a random graph, representing a null model. It can be loosely interpreted as follows: for each pair u, v of nodes, the modularity measures whether an actual edge is likely in the hypothesized model. A non-positive weight is associated with unlikely edges, as well as to prospective edges not actually appearing in the graph. Conversely, actual edges which fit the model get a positive weight. We adopt an alternative formulation suitable for our context, but based on a similar principle: actual edges get a positive weight only if they are likely in the model, whereas prospective edges which do not appear in the graph and are likely in the model get a negative weight. The weight is proportional to the probability to observe the edge in the random graph model:

$$\mathcal{Q}_G = \frac{1}{n(n-1)} \sum_{c=1}^{K} P(c) \sum_{u,v \in V} \left[A_{u,v} - P(u,v)\right] r_{uvc} \quad (13)$$

In the above equation, $A_{u,v}$ is the cell of the adjacency matrix corresponding to the pair (u, v), and $P(u, v) = k_u^{out} k_v^{in}/m^2$ represents the probability of observing the link (u, v) in the null (random graph) model. Also, r_{uvc} is the likelihood of observing the link (u, v) in the community c ($r_{uvc} = \vartheta_u^c \cdot \varphi_v^c$ in the CCN model) and $P(c) = \pi_c$.

A similar formulation can be established for the $\mathcal{Q}_{\mathbb{D}}$ measure relative to the action log $\mathbb{D}$. Following the interpretation of $\mathbb{D}$ as a bipartite graph, the null model is again a random bipartite graph associating items to users. Hence, $P(i, v) = \tilde{k}_i^{out} \cdot \tilde{k}_v^{in}/n_d^2$ where $\tilde{k}_{i_n}^{out}$ is the outdegree of i_n in $\mathbb{D}$, and $\tilde{k}_{v_n}^{in}$ the indegree of v_n. Computing $\mathcal{Q}_{\mathbb{D}}$ for action logs involving a large number of items and users is unpractical, as it requires considering all the possible triplets (i, v, t). A simplified formulation can only consider the actions actually occurring in $\mathbb{D}$:

$$\mathcal{Q}_{\mathbb{D}} = \frac{1}{n_d} \sum_{c} P(c) \sum_{a \in \mathbb{D}} (1 - P(a))\, \tilde{r}_{ac} \quad (14)$$

where again $\tilde{r}_{ac}$ represents the probability of observing $a = (i, v, t_i(v))$ in c (encoded as $\sum_{u \in \mathcal{F}_{i,v}} \theta_u^{c,a} \cdot \phi_{v,u}^{c,a}$ in the CCN model). Notice that, since we only concentrate on true actions, $\mathcal{Q}_{\mathbb{D}}$ is non-negative and its value increases with the numbers of communities, although we can expect to observe a saturation point.

The values for $\mathcal{Q}_G$ and $\mathcal{Q}_{\mathbb{D}}$ are shown in table 2. We can observe the following:

- the values of $\mathcal{Q}_G$ are always positive. The bias towards 0 is mainly due to the distribution of the values r_{uvc}, which we investigate in the following section.
- The values of $\mathcal{Q}_{\mathbb{D}}$ increase (as expected) with the number of communities, and in general tend to exhibit a higher value than those of $\mathcal{Q}_G$. Again, the distribution of $\tilde{r}_{ac}$ tends to bias the values towards 0.

Analysis. Here we concentrate on the three best models detected in the previous section, and analyse them. We begin with an overall glance at how the models fit the data. To this purpose, for each dataset we plot both the adjacency matrix A and the *influence* matrix I, the latter being the matrix where each pair (u, v) denotes the number of actions $a \in \mathbb{D}$ where u influenced v according to the model, i.e.

$$I_{u,v} = |\{a = (i, v, t) \in \mathbb{D} | u \in \mathcal{F}_{i,v}, u = \underset{u' \in \mathcal{F}_{i,v}, 1 \le k \le K}{\arg\max} \eta_{u,a,k}\}|$$

Rows and columns in both matrices are grouped in buckets, where a user u is associated to a bucket r computed as $r = \arg\max_k P(c_k|u) = \arg\max_k \sum_v \gamma_{u,v,k}$ for the rows and $r = \arg\max_k P(c_k|u) = \arg\max_k \sum_v \gamma_{v,u,k}$ for the columns. The expected results are matrices where both the adjacencies and the influences exhibit block structures with different densities. Indeed blocks are clearly visible in Figure 4. For the Digg dataset, which does nor provide an immediate visual perception, we also produced density plots (Figure 5), where the greyscale in each block represents the density of values within the block. In these latter plots, the structure is once again evident. A closer look at such matrices allows us to get some insights on how the communities are structured. First of all, the matrices reflect a community structure that is inferred by both the action log and the graph structure: indeed, blocks are clearly visible in both the incidence and

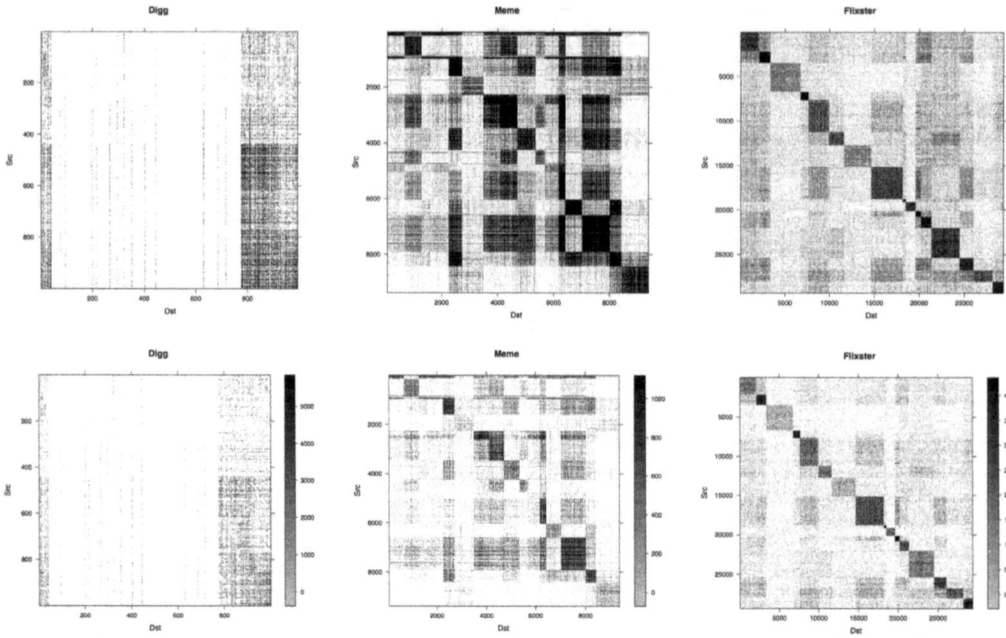

Figure 4: Density plots of the blocks within the adjacency matrix (first row), and of the influence matrix (second row).

the influence matrices. Also, the way blocks are structured is clearly different in the two matrices: for Digg, for example, Figure 5 shows two different blocks of high density: the one relative to the 5th community for the incidence matrix, and the one relative to the 7th community for the influence matrix, respectively. It is also useful to compare the incidence matrix with the one that would result by learning a model without the action log $\mathbb{D}$. Figure 6 shows the blocks that would result in the incidence matrix by running the CCN algorithm without the $\mathbb{D}$ component. A comparison of this matrix with the one in Figure 5 highlights significant differences in the way communities are structured.

For all the three datasets, the matrices exhibit a diagonal structure, a clear indication that users are generally bound to single community. Nevertheless, other blocks can be detected, and they denote the overlapping behavior of some users: since communities model links and actions, some users are likely to assume different roles in more than one community. To this purpose, it is interesting to investigate the distributions of the parameters inferred by the model. We concentrate on Digg only in the following, although similar conclusions can be drawn for the other two datasets.

Figure 7 shows such distributions. Notice that, for each community, the value corresponding to a specific user is given by a strip line, where the grey level represent the value in scale. Again, users are sorted according to a given rank, and ranks are assigned by associating each user to the community whose corresponding value is higher (for example, a user u where $\varphi_u^k \geq \varphi_u^{k'}$ is ranked by k in the plot relative to $\vec{\varphi}$).[4] Again, plots exhibit a diagonal structure, where values tend to predominate within a specific community. A similar pattern can be observed also when investigating in-

[4]The rankings in these matrices are different from the previous ones, because in this case we are interested in detecting peaks in the distributions. In principle, we expect that each community is characterized by a kernel of users whose values dominate over those of the others.

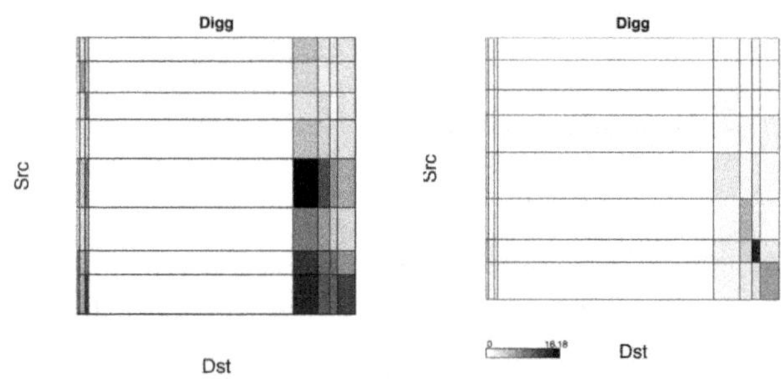

Figure 5: Density plots of the blocks within the adjacency and influence matrices for Digg.

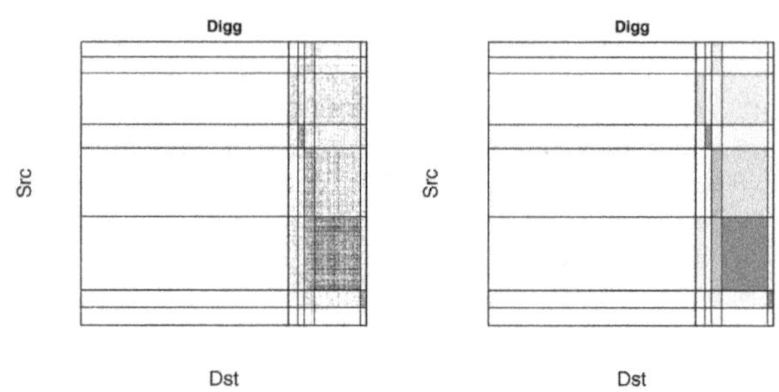

Figure 6: Blocks within the adjacency matrix, resulting by applying CCN to G only: actual values and density regions.

fluence (second row of Figure 7): the first plot shows the frequency distribution actions for influencing users, the second plot (where users are ranked according to $\vec{\vartheta}$) shows how such values distribute for each user and each community. Third and fourth plots report the same information but this time for influenced users.

Finally, Figure 8 plots some characterization of the eight communities found in the Digg dataset. The first plot reports in how many communities each user and each item participate. The histograms show that, while users tend to contribute to few communities, a similar tendency cannot be

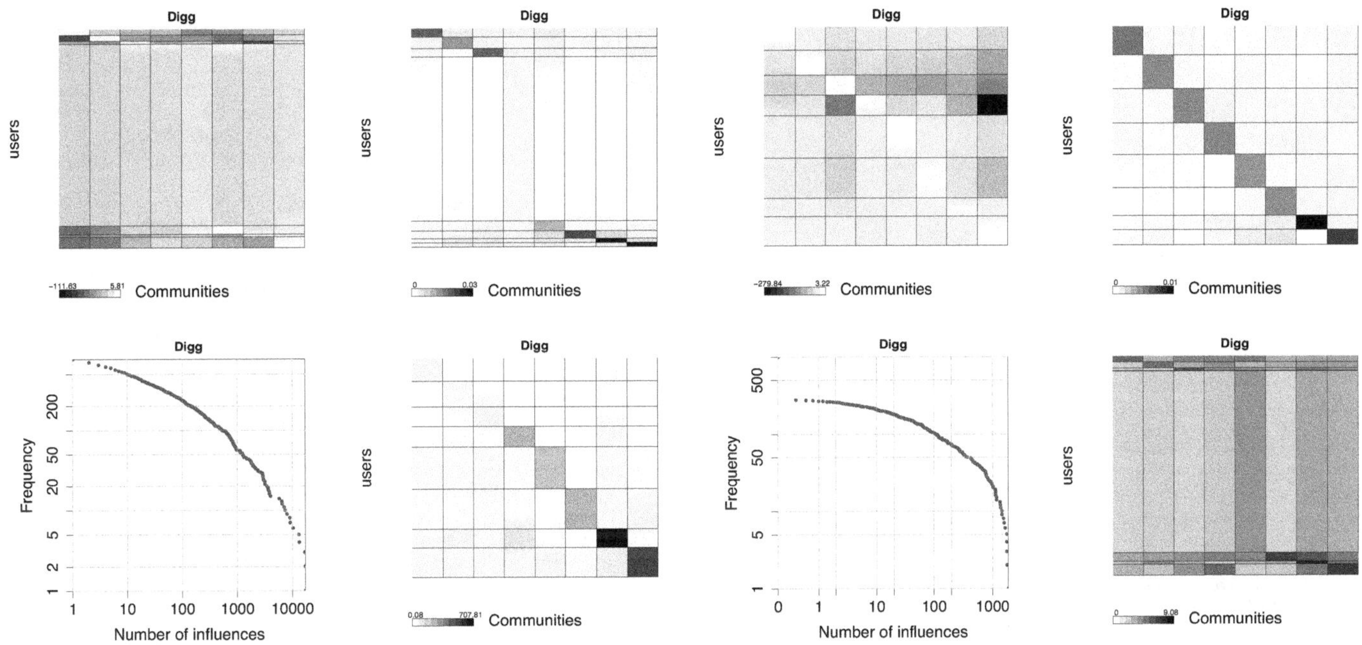

Figure 7: First Row: Distribution of the model parameters:Π^{d}, $\vec{\varphi}$, Π^{s} and $\vec{\vartheta}$. Second row: Frequency distributions for influence: influencing (first two plots) and influenced users (remaining plots).

detected for items involved in actions, which spread across different communities. The second plot shows how nodes, links, and items populate each of the eight communities. We can observe that the communities found are quite equilibrated in this respect. Note that in this histogram nodes and items can simultaneously appear in multiple communities, whereas links are associated to a single community.

5. CONCLUSIONS AND FUTURE WORK

The CCN model proposed in this paper provides a simple probabilistic framework for jointly modeling the community structure of a social network and the information cascades happening on the same social network. The key intuition is that each observed action (e.g, the creation of a follower-followed link in `Twitter`, or the re-tweeting of a meme) can be explained by the same hidden factors, namely the level of "active involvement" $\pi_u^{c,s}$ of user u in a topic/community c, and the degree of "passive involvement" $\pi_u^{c,d}$. The experimental analysis on three real-life datasets confirms our intuition.

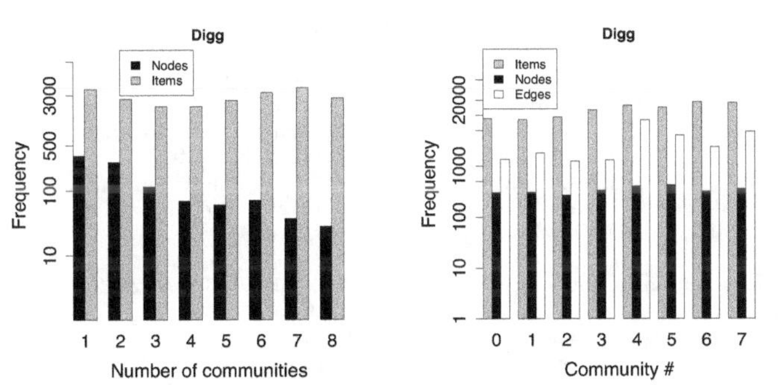

Figure 8: Distribution of the number of communities per item/node (left), nodes, links and items population for each of the eight communities (right).

We believe that, thanks to its simplicity, our CCN model has a wide range of potentialities still unexplored. By modeling communities and cascades formation jointly, CCN might be a useful tool in the analysis of both social phenomena, potentially providing interesting insights that cannot be obtained by analysing the two phenomena in isolation.

Being a stochastic generative model, CCN lends itself to a variety of predictive tasks. As a matter of fact, there are several application scenarios where it is important to predict whether a user shall adopt a given item, or whether two users are likely to be connected. For instance, predicting whether a user will be influenced and will participate in a cascade is a key step in *influence maximization* [28] for viral marketing. Predicting links formation instead can be used for user-to-user recommendation, as well as to the analysis of the evolution of the social networks. Since CCN models directly such probabilities, it is important to evaluate the accuracy of such predictions. In our previous studies [8, 9], we already showed that topic modeling improves the predictive accuracy for item adoption. We expect similar findings for CCN, and we plan to assess this in our future work.

A main drawback of the CCN model is the slowness of the learning phase. However, some of the causes of such slowness are structural and related to the general problem of estimating influence strength. Under this perspective, we plan to study how to parallelize the learning phase.

Finally, it is important to devise a extension of the CCN approach which relies on a bayesian treatment: since large graphs and action logs are sparse data, a treatment of priors can make the technique more robust, even in the presence of extreme values.

Acknowledgments. This research was partially supported by the Torres Quevedo Program of the Spanish Ministry of Science and Innovation, and partially funded by the European Union 7th Framework Programme under grant n. 270239 (ARCOMEM).

6. REFERENCES

[1] Y.-Y. Ahn, J. P. Bagrow, and S. Lehmann. Link communities reveal multiscale complexity in networks. *Nature*, 466(7307):761–764, 2010.

[2] E. M. Airoldi, D. M. Blei, S. E. Fienberg, and E. P. Xing. Mixed membership stochastic blockmodels. *Journal of Machine Learning Research*, 9:1981–2014, 2008.

[3] A. Anagnostopoulos, R. Kumar, and M. Mahdian. Influence and correlation in social networks. In *KDD*, 2008.

[4] S. Aral, L. Muchnik, and A. Sundararajan. Distinguishing influence-based contagion from homophily-driven diffusion in dynamic networks. *Proc. of the National Academy of Sciences*, 106(51):21544–21549, 2009.

[5] E. Bakshy, J. M. Hofman, W. A. Mason, and D. J. Watts. Everyone's an influencer: quantifying influence on twitter. In *WSDM*, 2011.

[6] B. Ball, B. Karrer, and M. E. J. Newman. An efficient and principled method for detecting communities in networks. *Phys. Rev. E 84, 036103*, 2011.

[7] J. Baumes, M. K. Goldberg, M. S. Krishnamoorthy, M. Magdon-Ismail, and N. Preston. Finding communities by clustering a graph into overlapping subgraphs. In *IADIS AC*, 2005.

[8] N. Barbieri, and G. Manco. An Analysis of Probabilistic Methods for Top-N Recommendation in Collaborative Filtering. In *ECML PKDD*, 2011.

[9] N. Barbieri, G. Manco, R. Ortale and E. Ritacco alancing Prediction and Recommendation Accuracy: Hierarchical Latent Factors for Preference Data. In *SDM*, 2012.

[10] F. Bonchi. Influence propagation in social networks: A data mining perspective. *IEEE Intelligent Informatics Bulletin, Vol.12 No.1: 8-16, December 2011.*

[11] F. Bonchi, A. Gionis, F. Gullo, and A. Ukkonen. Chromatic Correlation Clustering. In *KDD*, 2012.

[12] F. A. Breve, L. Zhao, M. G. Quiles, W. Pedrycz, and J. Liu. Particle competition and cooperation for uncovering network overlap community structure. In *ISNN*, 2011.

[13] G. Casella and R. Berger. *Statistical Inference.* Duxbury Press, 2001.

[14] M. Cha, H. Haddadi, F. Benevenuto, and K. P. Gummadi. Measuring user influence in twitter: The million follower fallacy. In *ICWSM*, 2010.

[15] W. Chen, Z. Liu, X. Sun, and Y. Wang. A game-theoretic framework to identify overlapping communities in social networks. *Data Min. Knowl. Discov.*, 21(2):224–240, 2010.

[16] D. J. Crandall, D. Cosley, D. P. Huttenlocher, J. M. Kleinberg, and S. Suri. Feedback effects between similarity and social influence in online communities. In *KDD*, 2008.

[17] P. Domingos and M. Richardson. Mining the network value of customers. In *KDD*, 2001.

[18] D. Easley and J. Kleinberg. *Networks, Crowds, and Markets: Reasoning About a Highly Connected World.* Cambridge University Press, 2010.

[19] T. S. Evans and R. Lambiotte. Line graphs, link partitions, and overlapping communities. *Phys. Rev. E*, 80:016105, 2009.

[20] T. L. Fond and J. Neville. Randomization tests for distinguishing social influence and homophily effects. In *WWW*, 2010.

[21] S. Fortunato. Community detection in graphs. *Physics Reports*, 486(3–5):75–174, 2010.

[22] R. Ge, M. Ester, B. J. Gao, Z. Hu, B. K. Bhattacharya, and B. Ben-Moshe. Joint cluster analysis of attribute data and relationship data: The connected *k*-center problem, algorithms and applications. *TKDD*, 2(2), 2008.

[23] M. Girvan and M. Newman. Community structure in social and biological networks. *Proceedings of the National Academy of Sciences*, 99(12):7821–7826, 2002.

[24] A. Goyal, F. Bonchi, and L. V. S. Lakshmanan. Learning influence probabilities in social networks. In *WSDM*, 2010.

[25] S. Gregory. Finding overlapping communities in networks by label propagation. *New Journal of Physics*, 12(10):103018, 2010.

[26] R. Guimerà, M. Sales-Pardo, and L. Amaral. Module identification in bipartite and directed networks. *Phys. Rev. E*, 2007.

[27] S. Hill, F. Provost, and C. Volinsky. Network-based marketing: Identifying likely adopters via consumer networks. *Statistical Science*, 21(2):256âĂŞ-276, 2006.

[28] D. Kempe, J. M. Kleinberg, and É. Tardos. Maximizing the spread of influence through a social network. In *KDD*, 2003.

[29] Y. Kim and H. Jeong. The map equation for link communities. *Phys. Rev. E 84, 026110*, 2011.

[30] J. M. Kumpula, M. Kivelä, K. Kaski, and J. Saramäki. Sequential algorithm for fast clique percolation. *Phys. Rev. E*, 78:026109, 2008.

[31] A. Lancichinetti, S. Fortunato, and J. Kertesz. Detecting the overlapping and hierarchical community structure of complex networks. *New Journal of Physics*, 11:033015, 2009.

[32] A. Lancichinetti, F. Radicchi, J. J. Ramasco, and S. Fortunato. Finding statistically significant communities in networks. *PLoS ONE*, 6(4):e18961, 04 2011.

[33] S. Lattanzi and D. Sivakumar. Affiliation networks. In *STOC*, 2009.

[34] E. Leicht and M. Newman. Community structure in directed networks. *Phys. Rev. Lett.*, 100(11), 2008.

[35] J. Leskovec, L. A. Adamic, and B. A. Huberman. The dynamics of viral marketing. *TWEB*, 1(1), 2007.

[36] J. Leskovec, A. Singh, and J. M. Kleinberg. Patterns of influence in a recommendation network. In *PAKDD*, 2006.

[37] F. Moser, R. Colak, A. Rafiey, and M. Ester. Mining cohesive patterns from graphs with feature vectors. In *SDM*, 2009.

[38] R. M. Neal and G. E. Hinton. *A view of the EM algorithm that justifies incremental, sparse, and other variants*, pages 355–368. MIT Press, Cambridge, MA, USA, 1999.

[39] M. E. J. Newman. Modularity and community structure in networks. *Proceedings of the National Academy of Sciences*, 103(23):8577–8582, 2006.

[40] A. Padrol-Sureda, G. Perarnau-Llobet, J. Pfeifle, and V. Muntés-Mulero. Overlapping community search for social networks. In *ICDE*, 2010.

[41] G. Palla, I. Derenyi, I. Farkas, and T. Vicsek. Uncovering the overlapping community structure of complex networks in nature and society. *Nature*, 435(7043), 2005.

[42] G. Palla, I. Farkas, P. Pollner, I. Derenyi, and T. Vicsek. Directed network modules. *New J. Phys.*, 9(6), 2007.

[43] U. N. Raghavan, R. Albert, and S. Kumara. Near linear time algorithm to detect community structures in large-scale networks. *Phys. Rev. E*, 76:036106, 2007.

[44] M. Richardson and P. Domingos. Mining knowledge-sharing sites for viral marketing. In *KDD*, 2002.

[45] D. M. Romero, B. Meeder, and J. M. Kleinberg. Differences in the mechanics of information diffusion across topics: idioms, political hashtags, and complex contagion on twitter. In *WWW*, 2011.

[46] M. Sachan,D. Contractor,T Faruquie, and L.V. Subramaniam Using content and interactions for discovering communities in social networks. *WWW*:331–340, 2012.

[47] K. Saito, R. Nakano, and M. Kimura. Prediction of information diffusion probabilities for independent cascade model. In *KES*, 2008.

[48] G. Schwarz. Estimating the dimension of a model. *Annals of Statistics*, 6:461–464, 1978.

[49] A. Silva, W. M. Jr., and M. J. Zaki. Mining attribute-structure correlated patterns in large attributed graphs. *PVLDB*, 5(5):466–477, 2012.

[50] J. Tang, J. Sun, C. Wang, and Z. Yang. Social influence analysis in large-scale networks. In *KDD*, 2009.

[51] Y. Wang, G. Cong, G. Song, and K. Xie. Community-based greedy algorithm for mining top-k influential nodes in mobile social networks. In *KDD*, 2010.

[52] J. Weng, E.-P. Lim, J. Jiang, and Q. He. Twitterrank: finding topic-sensitive influential twitterers. In *WSDM*, 2010.

[53] R. Xiang, J. Neville, and M. Rogati. Modeling relationship strength in online social networks. In *WWW*, 2010.

[54] J. Xie, S. Kelley, and B. Szymanski. Overlapping community detection in networks: the state of the art and comparative study. *ACM Computing Survey*, 45(4), 2013.

[55] J. Xie and B. K. Szymanski. Towards linear time overlapping community detection in social networks. In *PAKDD*, 2012.

[56] J. Xie, B. K. Szymanski, and X. Liu. Slpa: Uncovering overlapping communities in social networks via a speaker-listener interaction dynamic process. In *ICDM Workshops*, 2011.

[57] Y. Zhou, H. Cheng, and J. X. Yu. Graph clustering based on structural/attribute similarities. *PVLDB*, 2(1):718–729, 2009.

Patent Partner Recommendation in Enterprise Social Networks

Sen Wu
Department of Computer Science
Tsinghua University
Beijing 100084, China
ronaldosen@gmail.com

Jimeng Sun
IBM T. J. Watson Research Center
USA
jimeng@us.ibm.com

Jie Tang
Department of Computer Science
Tsinghua University
Beijing 100084, China
jietang@tsinghua.edu.cn

ABSTRACT

It is often challenging to incorporate users' interactions into a recommendation framework in an online model. In this paper, we propose a novel interactive learning framework to formulate the problem of recommending patent partners into a factor graph model. The framework involves three phases: 1) candidate generation, where we identify the potential set of collaborators; 2) candidate refinement, where a factor graph model is used to adjust the candidate rankings; 3) interactive learning method to efficiently update the existing recommendation model based on inventors' feedback. We evaluate our proposed model on large enterprise patent networks. Experimental results demonstrate that the recommendation accuracy of the proposed model significantly outperforms several baselines methods using content similarity, collaborative filtering and SVM-Rank. We also demonstrate the effectiveness and efficiency of the interactive learning, which performs almost as well as offline re-training, but with only 1 percent of the running time.

Categories and Subject Descriptors

J.4 [**Social and Behavioral Sciences**]: Miscellaneous; H.3.3 [**Information Search and Retrieval**]: Text Mining

General Terms

Algorithms, Experimentation

Keywords

Cross collaboration, Social network, Predictive model

1. INTRODUCTION

Collaboration exists almost everywhere, for example patent application, academic research, product development, and decision making. 98% of US patents are results of collaborations. Figure 1(a) shows a rapid increase of the co-invention relationships between inventors in the past 35 years (1975-2010). Today's patent collaborations are almost 6 times higher than that of 35 years before. In particular, the number of new collaborations has an even more rapid increase. Figure1(b) shows another interesting analysis, the changes of average number of patents by each individual and the average number of inventors for each patent over the past 35 years. We see the number of inventors for each patent has a clear increasing trend.

Indeed, collaboration is becoming so important that the Open Government Initiative has given high priority to increase the use of collaboration in the federal government[1]. In most of the industries, employees only use part of their time to create patents. Time constraint often limits their scope for choosing new collaborators. In general, collaborators should be ideally in closer proximity (i.e, within same company and geography), engaged in similar interests, and working on similar product. However, it is often challenging for researchers to establish successful collaborations. This is sometimes even more challenging within a company. IBM has 300,000 employees distributed in many different locations across the globe. How can healthcare researchers find the right data mining experts with right skills and are willing to help?

There are a few systems for patent search and analysis such as Google Patent, WikiPatent, PatentMiner, FreePatentsOnline, Patents, PatentLens, and PriorArtSearch. However, most of these systems focus on search and provide limited micro-level analytic functions. Few systems provide the function of patent partner recommendations. For research on the patent data, Tang et al. [26] propose a topic-driven patent analysis and mining method and develop a system named as PatentMiner. Jin et al. [11] propose a method to evaluate the quality of patents. Liu et al. [18] and Mann [19] study how to estimate patent quality from the perspective of court validity rulings or the number of forward citations. However, all these works focus on analyzing patent content, but ignore the collaborative relationships between inventors. In the space of data mining and web search, a number of relevant works have been conducted, such as collaborator recommendations [13, 27], friends suggestions [22], and reviewer finding [21, 29]. Kautz et al. [13] introduce a system called ReferralWeb which attempts to combine social networks for collaborative filtering. None of the above works directly target at patent collaborations, which is the focus of this paper.

[1]http://www.crosscollaborate.com

WSDM'13, February 4–8, 2013, Rome, Italy.

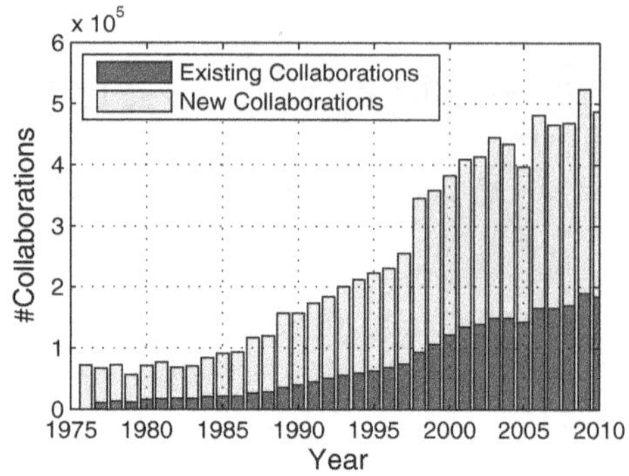

(a) #co-invention relationships

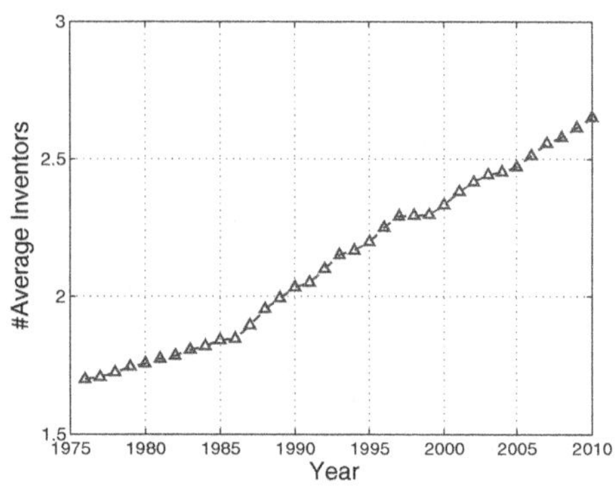

(b) #average inventors

Figure 1: Trends of co-invention relationships from 1975 to 2010.

Challenges and Contributions. In this work, we study the problem of recommending patent partners in enterprise social networks. We address three challenges: First, what are the fundamental factors that influence the formation of co-invention relationships? Will inventors with similar interests tend to collaborate, or they collaborate because they have complementary research interest, or simply due to the geographical proximity? Second, how to design an interactive mechanism so that the user can provide feedback to the system to refine the recommendations? Third, technically, how to learn the interactive recommendation framework in an online mode?

We formulate the problem and propose a ranking model to recommend patent collaborators according to the user's profile. More specifically, we propose an interactive learning framework to formulate the problem of recommending patent partners into a factor graph model. The framework involves three phases:

- **Candidate generation**, where we identify the potential set of collaborators by performing similarity retrieval on various features including homophily, referral chaining, and recency;
- **Candidate refinement**, where a factor graph model RankFG is used to adjust the candidate rankings;
- **Interactive learning**, where we propose an efficient online update algorithm RankGF+ to adjust the existing recommendation model based on inventors' feedback.

We evaluate the proposed model on large patent data sets. We show that the proposed model can significantly improve (up to 30% in terms of Precision@5) the recommendation performance of collaborations, compared with several baseline methods.

Organization. Section 2 formulates the problem; Section 3 explains the proposed model and describes the algorithm for learning the model; Section 4 introduces the data set and our observations to verify the hypotheses. Section 5 presents the results; finally, Section 6 discusses related work and Section 7 concludes this paper.

2. PROBLEM DEFINITION

The patent data set can be considered as an inventor social network $G = (V, E)$, where V is a set of $|V| = N$ inventors and $E \subseteq V \times V$ is a set of co-invention relationships between inventors. Let $\mathbf{x}_i$ be a set of attributes associated with inventor v_i. An attribute can be the inventor's interest, her employed company or the number of published patents. We use $X = \{\mathbf{x}_1, \cdots, \mathbf{x}_N\}$ to denote the attributes of all inventors. Our goal is to suggest future collaborators for a specific inventor v_q, based on her historic attributes $\mathbf{x}_q$, her existing co-invention relationships, and the idea she wants to patent. More precisely, we are concerned with the following problem:

Problem 1. **Suggesting co-invention relationships.** Let $G = (V, E, X)$ be an attribute augmented inventor network. For a particular inventor $v_q \in V$ and the topic t she wants to find co-invention relationships, the task of suggesting co-invention relationships is to find a predictive function such that we can suggest (infer) co-invention relationships between v_q and other inventors on topic t, i.e.,

$$f : (G, v_q, t) \to Y,$$

where $Y = \{y_1, \cdots, y_{|V|}\}$ is a set of inferred results between inventor v_q and all inventors in the network G; $y_k \in \{0, 1\}$ is binary score indicating whether the corresponding inventor $v_k \in V$ will have a co-invention relationship with v.

In addition, we consider how to interactively refine the learned predictive function. Specifically, the inventor can provide feedback on the recommendation list and then the technical objective is to incrementally update the prediction at a real time. The problem can be also generalized to suggest top-K collaborators (under some constraints) for any social networks. To keep things concrete, we focus on studying this problem in the inventor social network.

The problem formulation is different from existing work on patent quality analysis [11, 18, 19, 26], which has focused on mining patent content. It is also different from existing works on collaborator recommendations [13] and friends suggestions [22]. Here we mainly consider how to provide an interactive mechanism for supporting inventors to provide feedback to the recommended collaborators so as to refine the recommendations at a real time.

3. MODEL FRAMEWORK

A major motivation for our work comes from the intuition that inventors' content and social networks are both important for establishing co-invention relationships. At a high level, the proposed approach framework consists of three stages.

- **Candidate generation.** First, given a user v_q and the topic t on which she/he wants to establish co-invention relationships, we extract potential collaboration candidates through the similarity on several features.
- **Candidate refinement.** Second, the candidate list is fed to a ranking factor graph (RankFG) model to refine the ranking. The model incorporates various factors and the correlation among the collaboration candidates.
- **Interactive feedback.** Third, users can provide feedback to the suggested co-invention relationships. An interactive learning algorithm is designed to update the ranking model incrementally based on the user's feedback.

3.1 Candidate Generation

For a given user v_q and the topic t (i.e., query keywords), we consider three factors to generate the candidate list, i.e., *Homophily*, *Referral chaining*, and *Recency*.

The idea of homophily comes from the principle of "birds of a feather flock together" [20], which suggests that "connected" inventors tend to have similar characteristics (e.g., social status or interests). Regarding the homophily between inventors, we consider the following inventors' attributes: *geographical proximity* and *interest homophily*. Because of the companies' specific policies, the inventors can barely collaborate with other inventors in other companies. So we consider that geographical proximity indicates that if two inventors in one company come from the same country or geographical close places, they are more likely to collaborate. In this work, we simply consider the company and country information extracted from patents, and accordingly define the geographical proximity as a binary score (which stands for whether the two inventors in one company are from the same country or not). Interest homophily represents that significant interest overlapping between two inventors implies a higher likelihood of the two inventors to have a co-invention relationship. Formally the interest homophily is defined based on Jaccard coefficient. We did try different similarity algorithms such as cosine similarity and found that the inferring accuracy is not very sensitive to the similarity algorithms.

$$CI(v_i, v_j) = \frac{I_{v_i} \cap I_{v_j}}{I_{v_i} \cup I_{v_j}} \tag{1}$$

where I_{v_i} is a set of keywords describing inventor v_i's interests.

Regarding to *referral chaining*, the idea is that if two inventors can be connected via a short referral chain, then they are more likely to collaborate. Regarding to *Recency*, the idea is that a more recent collaboration tends to be more important. To quantify the length of a chain, we define the closeness measure of a referral link by considering the concept of recency. For any two inventors (v_i and v_j) who co-invented a set of patents S, we define the closeness of their referral link (in this case their co-inventing relationship) as:

$$R(v_i, v_j) = \sum_{d_i \in S} e^{-(\frac{t_{now} - t_{d_i}}{\lambda})} \tag{2}$$

where t_{now} is the current year; t_{d_i} is the year when patent d_i has been published; and λ is a tunable parameter. (We empirically set λ as 0.5.) This definition comes from our observation that an inventor's recent collaborator is usually closer than those of many years ago. A similar definition is also used in [22]. Based on Eq. 2, given two inventors (v_i and v_j), we first find the shortest path in terms of accumulative closeness scores on the path.

Finally, given an attribute augmented inventor network $G = (V, E, X)$, and a particular inventor v_q and the topic t, we first use the keywords contained in topic t to retrieve a list of "related" inventors using vector space model or language model [2]. We then calculate the homophily scores and the referral chaining score between inventor v_q and all inventors in the list. We combine the different scores together with the same weight and use the combination score to select top K inventors as the candidate collaborators for suggesting to inventor v_q[2].

3.2 RankFG: Ranking Factor Graph Model

After the initial retrieval of potential collaborator candidates, we now propose a ranking factor graph (RankFG) model to refine the co-invention relationships. Figure 2 shows the graphical structure of the RankFG model. For a given inventor v_q, we feed the model with the candidate list $\{v_1, v_2, v_4, v_5\}$ obtained in the initialization stage; v_3 and v_6 are two existing collaborators of v_q. The graphical model has two layers of variables: observations and latent variables. The observations are a collection of inventor pairs $\{(v_q, v_i)\}$. The corresponding latent variable y_i to each inventor pair (v_q, v_i) represents whether the two inventors have a co-invention relationship. We define two types of functions to capture the underlying factors that may influence the formation of co-invention relationships.

- **Pairwise factor function:** It captures the characteristics of the two inventors, e.g., the relationships between attributes of the two inventors. It is defined as an exponential function

$$f(v_q, v_i, y_i) = \frac{1}{Z_a} \exp\{\sum_k \alpha_k \psi_k(\mathbf{x}_q, \mathbf{x}_i, y_i)\} \tag{3}$$

  where $\psi_k(.)$ is the kth feature function defined between v_q and v_i with respect to the value of y_i; α_k is the weight of the feature; $\mathbf{x}_q$ and $\mathbf{x}_i$ are attributes associated with v_q and v_i. Z_a is a normalization factor.

- **Correlation factor function:** It captures the correlation between latent variables. It is also defined as an exponential function

$$g(y_i, y_j) = \frac{1}{Z_b} \exp\{\sum_l \beta_l \phi_l(y_i, y_j)\} \tag{4}$$

  where $\phi_l(y_i, y_j)$ is the lth feature function defined between y_i and y_j; β_l is the weight of the feature.

[2]The number of K is empirically set as 50 in the experiments. We will study how the number affects the inferring accuracy.

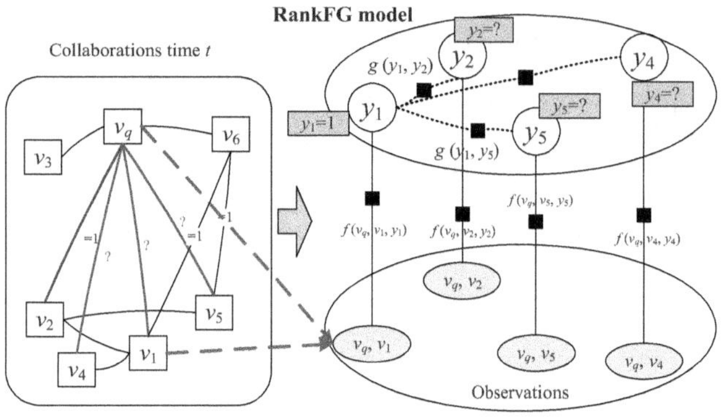

Figure 2: Graphical representation of the RankFG model. v_q is the given inventor who intends to find patent partners; $\{v_1, v_2, v_4, v_5\}$ are four candidate collaborators obtained in the initialization stage; v_3 and v_6 are two existing collaborators of v_q; $\{y_1, \cdots, y_4\}$ are latent variables defined for pairs of inventors, with each representing whether the corresponding pair of inventors will have a co-invention relationship; $f(.)$ represents a factor function defined for each pair of inventors; $g(.)$ represents a correlation factor function defined between latent variables.

In general, the pairwise factor captures the characteristics on each potential co-invention relationship and the correlation factor captures correlations between the suggested results. By integrating the defined factor functions, and also following the Markov assumption [8], we can define the following log-likelihood objective function:

$$\log P(Y|X,\theta) = \sum_{y_i \in Y} \sum_{k} \alpha_k \psi_k(\mathbf{x_q}, \mathbf{x_i}, y_i) + \sum_{v_i \sim v_j} \sum_{l} \beta_l \phi_l(y_i, y_j) - \log Z \quad (5)$$

where $Z = Z_a Z_b$ is the normalization factor; $v_i \sim v_j$ indicates that there is a (directed or indirected) correlation between v_i and v_j; $\theta = (\{\alpha\}, \{\beta\})$ are parameters to estimate.

Feature definitions. We now introduce possible ways to define the factor functions $\psi_k(\mathbf{x}_q, \mathbf{x}_i, y_i)$ and $\phi_l(y_i, y_j)$. In principle, the factor functions can be instantiated in different ways to reflect our prior knowledge (or intuitions) for different applications. It can be defined as either a binary function or a real-valued function. For example, for the pairwise factor function, we can define a binary feature function according to an attribute in X: if two inventors are from the same country and they have a co-invention relationship, then a feature $\psi(x_{qk} = x_{ik}, y_i) = 1$, where k is the attribute of country. More specifically, in total, we define nine pairwise factor functions which can be divided into four categories: Basic statistics of co-inventors, Link homophily, Interest homophily, and Correlation.

Basic statistics. We calculate a set of statistics for each potential co-inventor, the number of patents published by the inventor, the number of existing patent partners, and the number of patents published per year.

Table 1: Features defined for co-invention relationship (v_i, v_q).

Feature	Description
#Patent	Number of patents published by v_i
#Co-inventor	Number of existing co-inventors of v_i
Ratio	#Patent / #Collaborator
Experience	Difference of the years of the first patent published by v_q and v_i
CS-interest	Cosine similarity of interests between v_q and v_i
#C-interests	Number of common interests between v_q and v_i
#P-interests	Percentage of common interests between v_q and v_i
Cat-similarity	Similarity between patents' categories of v_q and v_i
#C-neighbor	Number of common co-inventors of v_q and v_i
#2-C-neighbor	Number of 2-step common co-inventors of v_i and v_j
Referral	Referral chaining length between v_q and v_i
Recency	Difference of current year and last collaborated year between v_q and v_i over the referral chaining
Correlation	Represent whether two candidates have a co-invention relationship.

Input: Query inventors $Q = \{v_q\}$ with corresponding topics $\{q\}$, $G = (V, E, X)$, and the learning rate η;
Output: learned parameters θ;
$\theta \leftarrow \mathbf{0}$;
repeat
  foreach $v_q \in Q$ *and* q **do**
    //Initialization;
    $L \leftarrow$ initialization list;
    Factor graph $FG \leftarrow BuildFactorGraph(L)$;
    // Learn the parameter θ for factor graph model;
    repeat
      foreach $v_i \in order$ **do**
        Update the messages of v_i by Eqs. 8 and 9;
      end
    until *(all messages μ do not change)*;
    foreach $\theta_i \in \theta$ **do**
      Calculate gradient ∇_i according to Eq. 7;
      Update $\theta^{new} = \theta^{old} + \eta \cdot \nabla_i$;
    end
  end
until *converge*;

Algorithm 1: Learning algorithm for RankFG.

Link homophily. This feature represents the number of common co-inventors between the candidate inventor and the query user.

Interest homophily. We use keywords appearing in patents published by each inventor as her interest. Three features are then defined as: the number of common interests, percentage of common interests between each inventor and the query inventor, cosine similarity of the interests between two inventors.

Correlation. If two candidate inventors in the initial list have a co-invention relationship, we define a correlation factor here.

In addition, we define two features based on the referral chain length and the recency. Table 1 summarizes the main features defined in the RankFG model.

Model learning. Learning the RankFG model is to find a parameter configuration $\theta = (\{\alpha\}, \{\beta\})$ from a given historic data set, such that the log-likelihood objective function $L(\theta) = \log P(Y|X, \theta)$ can be maximized,

$$\theta^\star = \arg\max_\theta \log P(Y|X,\theta) \tag{6}$$

We can use a gradient ascent algorithm (or a Newton-Raphson method) to solve the objective function $L(\theta)$. The gradient of each parameter θ wrt $L(\theta)$ is:

$$\begin{aligned} \frac{\partial L(\theta)}{\partial \theta_i} &= \sum_j f(\mathbf{x}_i, \mathbf{y}_i) - \frac{Z(\theta)'}{Z(\theta)} \\ &= \mathbb{E}[\phi(\mathbf{x}_i, \mathbf{y}_i)] - \mathbb{E}_{P(\mathbf{x}_i,\mathbf{y}_i)}[\phi(\mathbf{x}_i, \mathbf{y}_i)] \end{aligned} \tag{7}$$

Here, we use ϕ to indicate both ϕ and ψ. The first term $\mathbb{E}[\phi(\mathbf{x}_i, \mathbf{y}_i)]$ in Eq. 7 is easy to calculate. However, in the second term, it is intractable to estimate the marginal probability $P(\mathbf{x}_i, \mathbf{y}_i)$ as the graph structure may contain cycles. There are several methods to approximately solve the problem. In our work, we choose the sum product algorithm [14] (also known as Loopy Belief Propagation (LBP) [31]). To perform the sum product algorithm, we first derive a factor graph from the original graph G. The likelihood $P(Y|X)$ is a factorization of the graph and we can flexibly add factor nodes for feature functions. Then we perform the sum-product algorithm on the factor graph to compute the approximate marginal distributions. In particular, the sum-product algorithm operates according to the sum-product update rule: the message sent from variable v to factor f (or g) is the product of local function at v with all messages received at v from all factors other than f and the message sent from factor f to variable v is the sum of all factor functions associated with v, i.e.,

$$\mu_{v\to f}(x_v) = \prod_{f^*\in N(v)\backslash f} \mu_{f^*\to v}(x_v) \tag{8}$$

$$\mu_{f\to v}(x_v) = \sum_{\sim x_v} f(\mathbf{x}_f) \prod_{v^*\in N(f)\backslash\{v\}} \mu_{v^*\to f}(v^*) \tag{9}$$

where $N(v)$ are neighborhood variables of factor f and $N(f)$ are neighborhood factors of variable v; $\mathbf{x}_f$ is the set of arguments of $f(.)$; $\sum_{\sim x}$ indicates the summation over all variables except x. Algorithm 1 describes the learning process in the RankFG model. In each iteration, the messages are updated sequentially in a certain order. We randomly select a node as the root and perform breadth-first search on the factor graph to construct a tree. We update the messages from the leaves to the root, then from the root to the leaves. The process repeats updating messages until the convergence or until the number of iterations is large enough. Based on the received messages from factors, we can calculate the marginal probabilities for each variable. Then we compute the gradient according to Eq. 7 and update the parameters by $\theta_j^{new} = \theta_j^{old} + \eta \cdot \frac{\partial L(\theta)}{\partial \theta_j}$, with η the learning step.

Recommending patent partners. Given the observed value $\mathbf{x}$ and the learned parameters θ, the patent partner recommendation is to find the most likely configuration of Y_q for a given inventor v_q. This can be obtained by:

$$Y_q = \arg\max_{Y_q} P(Y_q|X,\theta) \tag{10}$$

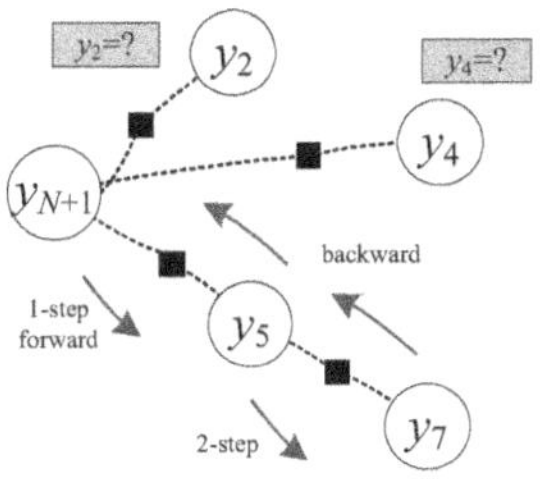

Figure 3: Illustration of the l-step message passing update.

For inference, we use the max-sum algorithm (the max version of Eqs. 8 and 9) to find the values of Y_q that maximizes the likelihood. This max-sum algorithm is similar with the sum-product algorithm, except for the message passing functions, which calculate the message according to *max* instead of *sum*.

3.3 Interactive Learning

Now, we introduce how to interactively update the ranking model based on the feedback given by the inventor. The idea is to allow the user to provide feedback to the recommended patent partners and then use an efficient algorithm to refine the ranking model by leveraging the user feedback. The algorithm supports both online interactive update and offline complete update.

For the interactive learning, the technical challenge is how to update the learned RankFG model efficiently and effectively. We design an algorithm to incrementally update the parameters. The key is still how to calculate the gradient. According to Eq. 7, for the first term, it is easy to obtain an incremental estimation, i.e.,

$$\mathbb{E}^{new}[.] = \frac{N}{N+1}\mathbb{E}^{old}[.] + \frac{1}{N+1}\sum_k \theta_k\phi_k(\mathbf{x}_{N+1}, \mathbf{y}_{N+1})$$

where $\{\theta_k\phi_k(\mathbf{x}_{N+1}, \mathbf{y}_{N+1})\}$ denotes a set of k factor functions defined for the new learning instance with the inventor's feedback ($y_{N+1} = 1$ for relevant or 0 for not). For the second term, it is again intractable to compute the marginal probabilities. Performing message passing on the complete factor graph is obviously time-consuming. We approximate this by performing a local message passing. Specifically, we first add new factor nodes (variable node and factor nodes) to the factor graph built in the model learning process. Then an l-step message passing is performed on the new factor graph starting from the new variable node y_{N+1}. More precisely, we take the new variable node y_{N+1} as the root node, begin by calculating messages $\mu_{y_{N+1}\to f}$, and then send messages to all of its neighborhood factors. We propagate the messages according to a function similar to Eqs. 8-9 up to l-depth, and then perform a backward messages passing, which propagates all messages back to the root note y_{N+1}. In this way, based on the messages sent between variables and factors, we can calculate an approximate value of the marginal probabilities of the newly added factors/variables. Accordingly, we can estimate the second term of Eq. 7.

Figure 3 illustrates the update algorithm with an l-step message passing. The interactive update is approximate and may lead to biased results. To avoid this, we perform an offline update (a complete model learning) when the number of inventors' feedback reaches a threshold.

Table 2: **Statistics of four test data: IBM and Sony have much higher numbers in both measures than Intel and Exxon. Values in parenthesis are the standard deviation**

Data	#inventors per patent	#patents per inventor
IBM	3.06(+/-1.68)	7.57(+/-0.76)
Intel	2.65(+/-1.49)	2.63(+/-0.69)
Sony	2.94(+/-1.47)	5.66(+/-0.82)
Exxon	2.42(+/-1.66)	3.00(+/-0.77)

4. DATA AND OBSERVATIONS

Before presenting the empirical results, we describe the datasets and observations on the datasets. All the datasets and codes used in this paper are publicly available.[3]

4.1 Data Collection

As patents represent intellectual properties of companies, co-invention relationships across different companies are merely impossible. Thus we mainly focus on analyzing co-invention relationships within companies. We have collected patent information from USPTO[4], which consists of 2,445,350 inventors and 3,770,411 patents with issued date from 1976 to 2010. We select four companies who own a large number of patents in our study: IBM, Intel, ExxonMobil and Sony. For each company, we select all its owned patents and extract all inventors and co-inventor relationships from the patents. More specifically, the data characteristics are:

IBM: with largest number of patents in the patent database, owns 55,967 patents published by 46,782 inventors. On average, each patent has three inventors, there are 269,333 co-invention relationships in total. It has a 8.26% average increase on the patent number and 11.9% increase on the number of co-invention relationships year over year.

Intel: one of the largest semiconductor chip maker corporations. We collect 18,264 patents for Intel, which include 54,095 co-invention relationships within Intel. Intel has a 18.8% increase on patent number and 35.5% average increase on the number of co-invention relationships.

ExxonMobil: the largest oil and gas corporation. For ExxonMobil, we have collected 8,505 patents and 31,569 co-invention relationships. Per day, ExxonMobil has a 11.7% increase on patent number and 13.0% increase on the number of co-invention relationships.

Sony: one of the largest electronics companies. For Sony, we obtain 19,174 patents and 53,671 co-invention relationships. Sony has a 10.6% average increase on the patent number and 14.7% average increase on the number of co-invention relationships.

4.2 Observations

We focus on studying the interplay between several basic factors and the co-invention relationships via the following statistics:

1. Inventor history and collaboration scale vary across companies;

[3]http://arnetminer.org/patents/

[4]Home page of the United States Patent and Trademark Office's main web site. http://www.uspto.org/

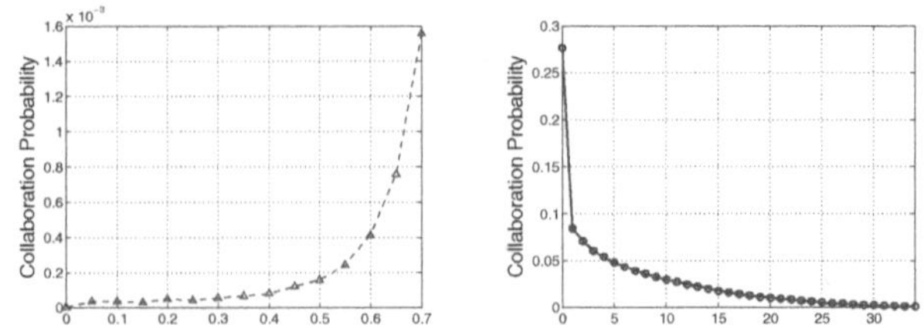

(a) Interest similarity (b) patent experience difference

Figure 4: Patent collaboration probability vs. similarity between inventors. (a) Interest similarity. X-axis: interest similarity between co-inventors; Y-axis: the collaboration likelihood of the two inventors. (b) patent experience difference: X-axis: time difference in years from the first patent published by the two inventors; Y-axis: the collaboration probability of the two inventors.

2. Probability that two inventors have similar interest, conditioned on whether or not they have a co-invention relationship;
3. Probability that two inventors have a co-invention relationship, conditioned on the referral chaining length;
4. Probability that two inventors maintain a co-invention relationship, conditioned on whether they have a co-invention relationship recently.

Inventor history and collaboration scale. We present the average number of inventors per patent and the average number of patents per inventor in Table 2. The former shows the collaboration scale, i.e., how many collaborators work together on a single patent. The latter shows the invention history, i.e., how many patents an inventor typically generates. In particular, IBM and Sony have much higher measures than Exxon and Intel. Both measures turn out to affect the recommendation performance as we will present in the next section. Intuitively, the higher these two measures are, the better the recommendation will be.

Similar inventors tend to collaborate. Figure 4 shows that, in general, similar inventors tend to have a co-invention relationship. For each inventor v, a feature vector is generated based on the frequencies of words in those patents published by the inventor. The value of each element in the vector is normalized by TFIDF [2]. Then *Interest Similarity* is computed as Cosine similarity between the two feature vectors.

Figure 4(a) shows that the collaboration probability increases dramatically as the similarity increases, which confirms the homophily feature in our model. Figure 4(b) shows how the collaboration probability changes with the difference of patent experience. We use the year from the first patent published by the inventor as the estimate of her patent experience. We show that inventors seem to like to find others of with similar patent experiences to develop patent with. The likelihood of two inventors with little difference (difference=0) to collaborate is almost 10 times more than ones with 10 year difference.

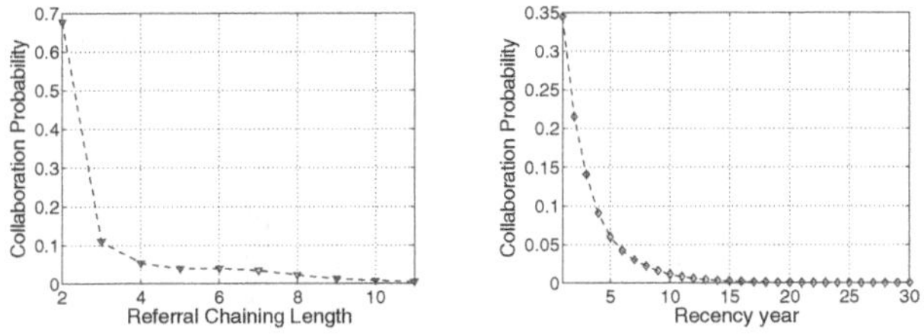

(a) Referral chaining length (b) Recency

Figure 5: (a) Patent collaboration probability vs. referral chaining length; X-axis: referral chaining length between two inventors; Y-axis: collaboration likelihood of the two inventors. (b) Patent collaboration conditioned on recency; X-axis: the difference of the current year and the last collaborated year; Y-axis: collaboration likelihood of the two inventors.

Inventors with a short referral chain tend to collaborate. We study how likely two inventors collaborate conditioned on the referral chaining length between them. Figure 5(a) gives two observations. The first one is "Your friends' friends are very likely to be your friends", which is consistent with the phenomenon of in the social balance theory [6]. The collaboration probability drops sharply with the increase of the referral chaining length. When the length increases to 4, the likelihood becomes less than $\frac{1}{10}$ of that at the length of 2. Another observation is that the analysis validates the theory of "six degrees of separation". More than 96% of pairs of inventors can be connected in less than six referral steps.

Inventors tend to continue collaborating Figure 5(b) illustrates that people tend to maintain collaborations. The likelihood of two inventors to maintain a recent co-invention relationship (in recent 2 years) is more than 10 times higher than re-establish a co-invention relationship of five years before.

5. RESULTS AND ANALYSIS

We present quantitative performance of the proposed approach with the comparison in each settings. After that, we make some analysis and discussion.

5.1 Experimental Setup

We use the data set described in §4 to evaluate the proposed model and to compare with several baseline methods. We evaluate our models RankFG and RankFG+ on the patent datasets from each of the four companies. We partition the 35 years' data into the first 25 years as training and the last 10 years as testing.

Comparison methods. We compare the following methods for suggesting co-invention relationships:

Content Similarity (Content): it calculates similarity between inventors based on patents published by the two inventors. It uses word frequencies in one's published patents as features and calculates the similarity score $Sim(v_q, v)$ between the query inventor v_q and another inventor v based on the words. The patent partner recommendation is then made based on the similarity score.

Collaborative Filtering (CF): it leverages the existing co-invention relationships to make the recommendation. The basic idea is that if an inventor A has similar patent partner as another inventor B, A is likely to collaborate with B's other patent partners. We employ a memory-based collaborative filtering algorithm [5], in which recommendations are made for a query user v_q using the following formula:

$$CF\_score(v_q, v) = \frac{1}{N} \sum_{v_i \in V^S} I(v_i, v) r(v_q, v_i)$$

where $r(v_q, v_i)$ describes one element of the pairwise similarity between inventors, which is typically measured by Pearson correlation coefficient or cosine similarity based on links; the indicator variable $I(v_i, v')$ is 1 if the inventor v_i collaborated with v' and 0 otherwise; N denotes the size of $|V^S|$.

Hybrid: it considers a linear combination of the scores from the Content and the CF methods, specifically,

$$Hybrid(v_q, v) = \mu CF\_score(v_q, v) + (1 - \mu) Sim(v_q, v)$$

where μ is a balance parameter. We empirically set it as 0.5.

SVMRank: The above three methods do not use training data. We then consider a learning approach which use the same training data as our RankFG. As for the learning model, we use SVM Light [12].

RankFG: The proposed method, which trains a RankFG model to suggesting patent partners.

RankFG+: it uses the proposed RankFG model with 1% interactive users' feedbacks.

Evaluation measures. We use the following performance metrics: Precision(P): P@5, P@10, P@15, P@20, Mean Average Precision(MAP) and Recall(R): R@100 [2].

All codes are implemented in C++ and JAVA, and all the evaluations are performed on an x64 machine with E7520 1.87GHz Intel Xeon CPU and 128GB RAM. The operation system is Microsoft Windows Server 2008 R2 Enterprise. All methods yields good performances. The training time needed for prediction by all algorithm on all data sets less than 5 minutes.

5.2 Performance Analysis

We compare the performance of all methods for suggesting co-invention relationships in the four companies. Table 3 lists the performance of comparison methods. The proposed method (RankFG) shows clearly better performance than the baseline methods. On average, RankFG achieves a +3.2-20.3% improvement compared with other methods in terms of MAP. SVM-Rank also uses training data; however, it does not consider the correlation among suggested inventors, thus performes worse than our method RankFG and RankFG+. We can also see that RankFG+ obtains a clear improvement (2-4% in terms of MAP) than RankFG, which confirms the effectiveness of interactive learning. The results also suggest that in different companies the co-inventing patterns are very different. Some interesting observations include

- Content based recommendation method *Content* performs better than network based method *CF* in the patent recommendation, due to the sparsity of the underlying network. This is very different from other social networks such as publication collaboration network, where CF often performs better than Content.

Table 3: **Performance of patent partner recommendation for different companies (%).**

Data	Method	P@5	P@10	P@15	P@20	MAP	R@100
IBM	Content	23.0	23.3	18.8	15.6	24.0	33.7
	CF	13.8	12.8	11.3	11.5	21.7	36.4
	Hybrid	13.9	12.8	11.5	11.5	21.8	36.7
	SVM-Rank	13.3	11.9	9.6	9.8	22.2	43.5
	RankFG	31.1	**27.5**	25.6	22.4	40.5	46.8
	RankFG+	**31.2**	**27.5**	**26.6**	**22.9**	**42.1**	**51.0**
Intel	Content	16.4	12.6	11.3	10.3	20.1	22.9
	CF	4.8	6.0	5.6	5.6	10.1	18.3
	Hybrid	4.9	6.2	5.9	5.7	11.4	18.3
	SVM-Rank	8.4	13.6	14.5	14.1	20.4	32.0
	RankFG	**17.3**	**14.2**	12.9	12.1	26.0	**33.0**
	RankFG+	**17.3**	**14.2**	**14.7**	**14.9**	**29.3**	**33.0**
Sony	Content	23.0	16.5	13.5	11.6	23.9	34.9
	CF	10.0	17.0	16.0	16.5	5.2	20.9
	Hybrid	9.0	7.2	6.0	6.8	14.1	20.2
	SVM-Rank	28.0	24.0	16.5	14.2	34.8	44.2
	RankFG	37.0	34.5	30.7	**26.3**	39.9	48.8
	RankFG+	**38.4**	**38.5**	**31.0**	**26.3**	**43.3**	**55.5**
Exxon	Content	25.0	20.3	18.1	16.1	23.6	16.1
	CF	3.3	5.0	5.4	5.6	8.1	12.8
	Hybrid	3.3	5.3	5.4	5.9	8.9	20.7
	SVM-Rank	25.5	**23.3**	**21.6**	21.5	28.2	29.3
	RankFG	26.6	19.2	20.0	23.9	28.5	32.3
	RankFG+	**27.1**	19.4	20.7	**24.7**	**30.4**	**34.0**

Table 4: **Performance comparison of patent partner recommendation with online interactive learning and offline complete learning for the four companies.**

Data	Algorithm	P@5	P@10	P@20	MAP	R@100
IBM	Interactive	31.2	27.5	22.9	42.1	51.0
	Complete	31.6	27.9	23.1	42.3	52.1
Intel	Interactive	17.3	14.2	14.9	29.3	33.0
	Complete	17.3	15.2	15.4	29.5	34.4
Sony	Interactive	38.4	38.5	26.3	43.3	55.5
	Complete	40.0	39.7	26.5	43.5	58.4
Exxon	Interactive	27.1	19.4	24.7	30.4	34.0
	Complete	27.2	19.4	24.7	30.4	34.5

- All methods achieve better recommendation accuracy in IBM and Sony than in Intel and Exxon. This is because IBM and Sony have higher number of inventors per patent as well as the higher number of patents per inventor. Longer patent history per inventor and more common collaborations help improve the recommendation performance.

In all cases, the proposed methods RankFG and RankFG+, because of incorporating the data correlations and the user feedback, obtain consistent better performance than all the baselines.

In Figure 6, we give a detailed comparison between the online interactive learning and the offline complete learning for the proposed RankFG model. The offline complete learning re-trains the RankFG model and the interactive learning only performs the learning on neighborhood nodes. Thus the offline complete learning can be considered as the upper bound of the interactive learning. We see that the proposed interactive learning achieves a close performance to the complete learning. Notice that the interactive learning only is usually finished in 3 seconds, 1/100 of the running time used for complete training (even on a relative small data set). Figure 6 shows the performance of interactive learning by varying the number of user feedbacks. We see that the performance of online interactive learning becomes very close to the offline complete learning when the number of feedbacks increases to 1% of the total collaborations, which confirms the effectiveness of the proposed interactive learning method.

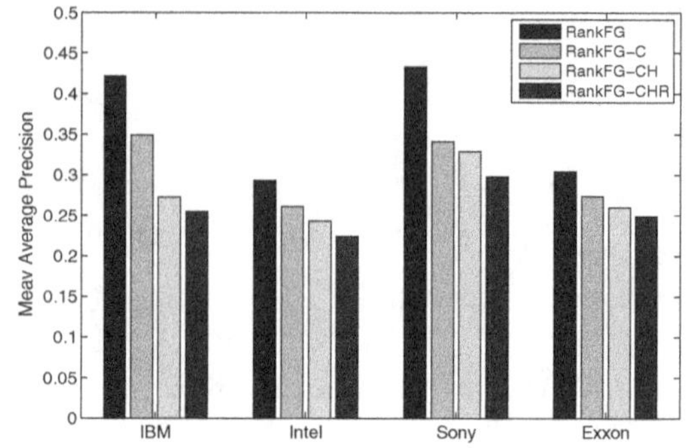

Figure 7: Factor contribution analysis: RankFG-C stands for ignoring referral chaining factor functions. RankFG-CH stands for ignoring both referral chaining and homophily. RankFG-CHR stands for further ignoring recency.

Factor contribution analysis. We now analyze how different factors can help us. In the RankFG model, we consider five major factors: homophily (H), referral chaining length (C), recency (R), basic statistics, and correlation. Here we examine the contribution of different factors defined in our RankFG model. Specifically, we take basic statistics and correlation as the basic features in the model and study the contribution of the other three factors. Figure 7 shows the Mean Average Precision score over the different data sets. In particular, RankFG-C represents that we remove referral chaining based features from our model and RankFG-CH denotes that we further remove homophily features. It can be clearly observed that the performance drops when ignoring each of the factors. We often observe that for recommending patent partners the referral chaining length is more important than others. The analysis confirms that our model works well when combining all the features together.

Convergence analysis. We conduct an experiment on the effect of the number of iterations of the loopy belief propagation. Figure 8 shows the convergence analysis results of the learning algorithm RankFG. We see on all the test cases, the learning algorithm can converge less than 10 iterations. After about 7 iterations, the performance becomes stable.

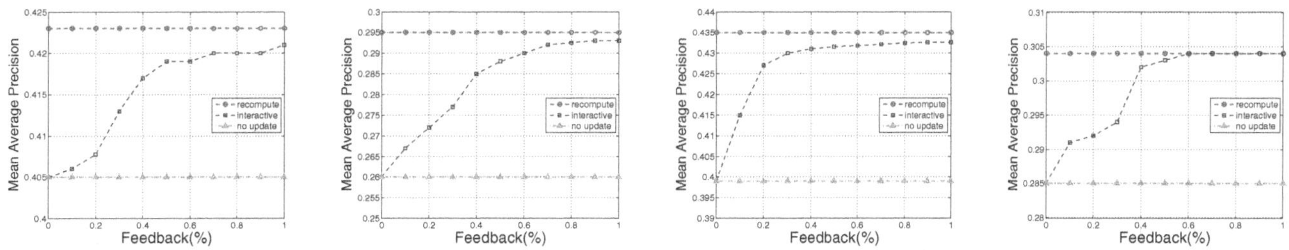

(a) IBM (b) Intel (c) Sony (d) Exxon

Figure 6: Interactive learning with different numbers of feedbacks.

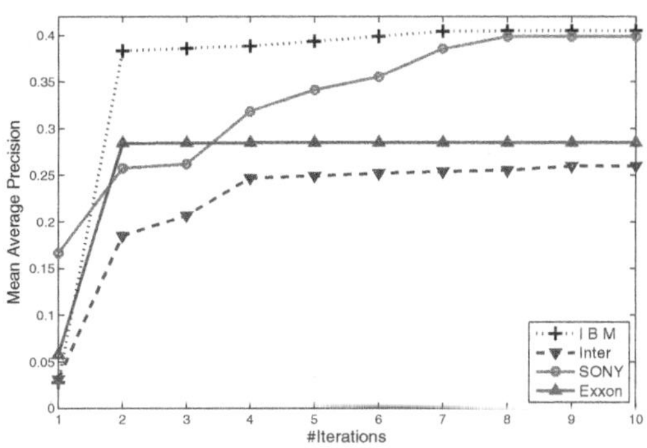

Figure 8: Convergence analysis of learning algorithm for different cross domains.

This suggests that learning algorithm is very efficient and has a good convergence property.

6. RELATED WORK

Collaboration plays an important role in social networks. While a large body of works focuses on expert finding [3, 28, 33], friends recommendations [9, 13, 22], and expertise matching [21, 29], few publications consider the problem of patenting partner recommendation. Kautz et al. [13] introduced a system called ReferralWeb which attempts to combine social networks for collaborative filtering. Roth et al. [22] leveraged the implicit social graphs that are formed by users' interactions to suggest recipients in the Google Gmail system. Shi et al. [24] introduced rank heterogeneous content to make recommendations, and Sculley et al. [23] presented a method to rank that combines regression and ranking. Quan et al. [32] considered social relations: membership, friendship to recommend top-n people. However, none consider the cross-field problem. Mimno et al. [21] and Tang et al. [29] studies the problem of paper reviewers recommendation, a subtask of expert finding. The proposed algorithms can be leveraged for collaborator recommendations. Lappas et al. [15] investigated the problem of finding a team of experts to fulfill a given task in social networks. They theoretically proved that the problem is NP-hard and propose two instantiation models to approximately solve this problem.

There are a few systems for patent search and analysis such as Google Patent, WikiPatent, PatentMiner, FreePatentsOnline, Patents, PatentLens, and PriorArtSearch. However, most of these systems focus on search and provide limited micro-level analytic functions. Few systems provide the function of patenting partner recommendations. For research on the patent data, Tang et al. [26] propose a topic-driven patent analysis and mining method. Jin et al. [11] proposed a method to evaluate the quality of patents. Liu et al. [18] and Mann [19] studied how to estimate patent quality from the perspective of court validity rulings or the number of forward citations. Tseng et al. [30] introduced a series of text mining techniques for patent analysis, including text segmentation and summary extraction. However, all these works have focused on analyzing patent content, but ignore the collaborative relationships between inventors.

Our work is also related to link prediction, which is one of the core tasks in social networks. For example, Liben-Nowell et al. [17] presented a unsupervised method for link prediction. Backstrom et al. [1] proposed a supervised random walk algorithm to estimate the strength of social links. Leskovec et al. [16] employed a logistic regression model to predict positive and negative links in online social networks. Cradall et al. [4] studied how to infer the friendship from geographic coincidence data. Hopcroft et al. [10] studied the extent to which the formation of a reciprocal relationship can be predicted in a dynamic network. Eric Gilbert et al. [7] presented a predictive model that maps social media data to tie strength. Tang et al. [25] developed a framework for classifying the type of social relationships by learning across heterogeneous networks. In this work, we focus on studying the underlying patterns that influence the formation of co-invention relationships and propose a novel rank factor graph model to incorporate the discovered patterns for recommending co-invention relationships.

7. CONCLUSION

In this paper, we study the problem of recommending patenting partners in enterprise social networks. We precisely define the problem and propose a ranking factor graph (RankFG) model for suggesting co-invention relationships. Through a careful observable investigation, we discover several interesting patterns. We incorporate the discovered patterns into the proposed RankFG model. We evaluate our proposed model on large patent data sets and the experimental results show that the proposed model can significantly improves the performance for recommending co-invention relationships compared with several alternative methods.

Finding the right patenting partner is an important step toward producing successful patents in an enterprise social network. There are many potential research topics in this direction. It would be interesting to further consider subtopics in the recommendation. The user may be not aware of the subtopics of the query topic. It would be helpful to extract subtopics and to allow the user to refine the recommendation results according to the subtopics. It is also interesting to study how the topic trend of a company influence the enterprise co-invention relationships.

Acknowledgements. The work is supported by the National Basic Research Program of China (No. 2011CB302302), Natural Science Foundation of China (No. 61222212, No. 61073073), and a fund for Fast Sharing of Science Paper in Net Era by CSTD.

8. REFERENCES

[1] L. Backstrom and J. Leskovec. Supervised random walks: predicting and recommending links in social networks. In *WSDM'11*, pages 635–644, 2011.

[2] R. Baeza-Yates and B. Ribeiro-Neto. *Modern Information Retrieval.* ACM Press, 1999.

[3] K. Balog, L. Azzopardi, and M. de Rijke. Formal models for expert finding in enterprise corpora. In *SIGIR'2006*, pages 43–55, 2006.

[4] D. J. Crandall, L. Backstrom, D. Cosley, S. Suri, D. Huttenlocher, and J. Kleinberg. Inferring social ties from geographic coincidences. *PNAS*, 107:22436–22441, Dec. 2010.

[5] A. Das, M. Datar, A. Garg, and S. Rajaram. Google news personalization: Scalable online collaborative filtering. In *WWW'07*, pages 271–280,2007.

[6] D. Easley and J. Kleinberg. *Networks, Crowds, and Markets: Reasoning about a Highly Connected World.* Cambridge University Press, 2010.

[7] E. Gilbert and K. Karahalios. Predicting tie strength with social media. In *CHI'09*, pages 211–220, 2009.

[8] J. M. Hammersley and P. Clifford. Markov field on finite graphs and lattices. *Unpublished manuscript*, 1971.

[9] P. Heymann and H. Garcia-Molina. Collaborative creation of communal hierarchical taxonomies in social tagging systems. Technical Report 2006-10, Stanford University, April 2006.

[10] J. E. Hopcroft, T. Lou, and J. Tang. Who will follow you back? reciprocal relationship prediction. In *CIKM'11*, pages 1137–1146, 2011.

[11] X. Jin, S. Spangler, Y. Chen, K. Cai, R. Ma, L. Zhang, X. Wu, and J. Han. Patent maintenance recommendation with patent information network model. In *ICDM'11*, pages 280–289, 2011.

[12] T. Joachims. *Making large-Scale SVM Learning Practical.* MIT-Press, 1999.

[13] H. Kautz, B. Selman, and M. Shah. Referral web: Combining social networks and collaborative filtering. *Communications of the ACM*, 40(3):63–65, 1997.

[14] F. R. Kschischang, B. J. Frey, and H. andrea Loeliger. Factor graphs and the sum-product algorithm. *IEEE TOIT*, 47:498–519, 2001.

[15] T. Lappas, K. Liu, and E. Terzi. Finding a team of experts in social networks. In *KDD'09*, pages 467–476, 2009.

[16] J. Leskovec, D. Huttenlocher, and J. Kleinberg. Predicting positive and negative links in online social networks. In *WWW'10*, pages 641–650, 2010.

[17] D. Liben-Nowell and J. M. Kleinberg. The link-prediction problem for social networks. *JASIST*, 58(7):1019–1031, 2007.

[18] Y. Liu, P.-y. Hseuh, R. Lawrence, S. Meliksetian, C. Perlich, and A. Veen. Latent graphical models for quantifying and predicting patent quality. In *KDD'11*, pages 1145–1153, 2011.

[19] R. Mann. A new look at patent quality. *American Law and Economics Association Annual Meetings*, 2008.

[20] M. McPherson, L. Smith-Lovin, and J. Cook. Birds of a feather: Homophily in social networks. *Annual review of sociology*, pages 415–444, 2001.

[21] D. Mimno and A. McCallum. Expertise modeling for matching papers with reviewers. In *KDD'07*, pages 500–509, 2007.

[22] M. Roth, A. Ben-David, D. Deutscher, G. Flysher, I. Horn, A. Leichtberg, N. Leiser, Y. Matias, and R. Merom. Suggesting friends using the implicit social graph. In *KDD'10*, pages 233–242, 2010.

[23] D. Sculley. Combined regression and ranking. In *KDD'10*, pages 979–988, 2010.

[24] Y. Shi, D. Ye, A. Goder, and S. Narayanan. A large scale machine learning system for recommending heterogeneous content in social networks. In *SIGIR'11*, pages 1337–1338, 2011.

[25] J. Tang, T. Lou, and J. Kleinberg. Inferring social ties across heterogenous networks. In *WSDM'12*, pages 743–752, 2012.

[26] J. Tang, B. Wang, Y. Yang, P. Hu, Y. Zhao, X. Yan, B. Gao, M. Huang, P. Xu, W. Li, and A. K. Usadi. Patentminer: topic-driven patent analysis and mining. In *KDD '12*, pages 1366–1374, 2012.

[27] J. Tang, S. Wu, J. Sun, and H. Su. Cross-domain collaboration recommendation. In *KDD'12*, pages 1285–1293, 2012.

[28] J. Tang, J. Zhang, R. Jin, Z. Yang, K. Cai, L. Zhang, and Z. Su. Topic level expertise search over heterogeneous networks. *Machine Learning Journal*, 82(2):211–237, 2011.

[29] W. Tang, J. Tang, T. Lei, C. Tan, B. Gao, and T. Li. On optimization of expertise matching with various constraints. *Neurocomputing*, 76(1):71–83, 2012.

[30] Y.-H. Tseng, C.-J. Lin, and Y.-I. Lin. Text mining techniques for patent analysis. *Inf. Process. Manage.*, 43:1216–1247, September 2007.

[31] J. S. Yedidia, W. T. Freeman, and Y. Weiss. Generalized belief propagation. In *NIPS'01*, pages 689–695, 2001.

[32] Q. Yuan, L. Chen, and S. Zhao. Factorization vs. regularization: fusing heterogeneous social relationships in top-n recommendation. In *RecSys'11*, pages 245–252, 2011.

[33] J. Zhang, J. Tang, and J. Li. Expert finding in a social network. In *DASFAA'07*, pages 1066–1069, 2007.

Exploiting Homophily Effect for Trust Prediction

Jiliang Tang, Huiji Gao, Xia Hu and Huan Liu
Computer Science and Engineering
Arizona State University
Tempe, AZ 85281
{Jiliang.Tang, Huiji.Gao, Xia.Hu, Huan.Liu}@asu.edu

ABSTRACT

Trust plays a crucial role for online users who seek reliable information. However, in reality, user-specified trust relations are very sparse, i.e., a tiny number of pairs of users with trust relations are buried in a disproportionately large number of pairs without trust relations, making trust prediction a daunting task. As an important social concept, however, trust has received growing attention and interest. Social theories are developed for understanding trust. Homophily is one of the most important theories that explain why trust relations are established. Exploiting the homophily effect for trust prediction provides challenges and opportunities. In this paper, we embark on the challenges to investigate the trust prediction problem with the homophily effect. First, we delineate how it differs from existing approaches to trust prediction in an unsupervised setting. Next, we formulate the new trust prediction problem into an optimization problem integrated with homophily, empirically evaluate our approach on two datasets from real-world product review sites, and compare with representative algorithms to gain a deep understanding of the role of homophily in trust prediction.

Categories and Subject Descriptors

H3.3 [**Information Storage and Retrieval**]: Information Search and Retrieval—*Information filtering*

General Terms

Algorithms, Design, Experimentation

Keywords

Trust Prediction, Homophily Effect, Homophily Regularization, Trust Networks, Social Correlation

1. INTRODUCTION

With the pervasive of social media, the explosion of user generated data makes the information overload problem increasingly severe. Trust, which provides information about from whom we should accept information and with whom we should share information [6], plays an important role in helping online users collect reliable information. For example, users in e-commerce are likely to gather information from their trusted users to make decisions. Hence, the trust mechanism is widely implemented by online service providers, especially e-commerce websites such as eBay[1] and product review websites like Epinions[2].

Recent years witness many trust related online applications, such as trust-aware recommendation systems [6, 12, 21], finding high-quality user generated content [11, 3] and viral marketing [19]. However, in reality, the available explicit trust relations are extremely sparse, and, online trust relations follow a power law distribution, suggesting that a small number of users specify many trust relations while a large proportion of users specify a few trust relations. Trust prediction is proposed to infer unknown trust relations, and it is important to address the problem of sparseness in user-specified trust relations.

Literature on trust prediction is rapidly growing [7, 10, 1, 17], roughly divided into two groups: unsupervised methods [7, 1] and supervised methods [10, 17]. As illustrated in Figure 1(a), after extracting features from available sources and considering the existence of trust as labels, supervised methods train a binary classifier. However, these methods have inherent limitations. The huge disproportion of pairs of users with (positive samples, labelled as 1 in Figure 1(a)) and without relations (negative samples, labelled as 0 in Figure 1(a)) makes the classification problem extremely imbalanced and the performance of these methods is sensitive to the sampled negative samples. While unsupervised methods such as trust propagation [7] are able to infer trust relations for two indirectly connected users as demonstrated in Figure 1(b.1). However, the power law distribution indicates that the available trust relations may not be enough to guarantee the success of these methods (u_5 in Figure 1(b.1)) [13, 22]. As a social concept, trust has received growing attention and there are many social theories are developed. Homophily is one of the most important theories that attempt to explain why people establish trust relations with each other [10]. The homophily effect suggests that similar users have a higher likelihood to establish trust relations. For example, people with similar tastes about items are more likely to trust each other in product review sites. Exploiting that effect provides a new perspective for trust prediction and enables us to do advanced research on trust prediction.

[1]http://www.ebay.com/
[2]http://www.epinions.com

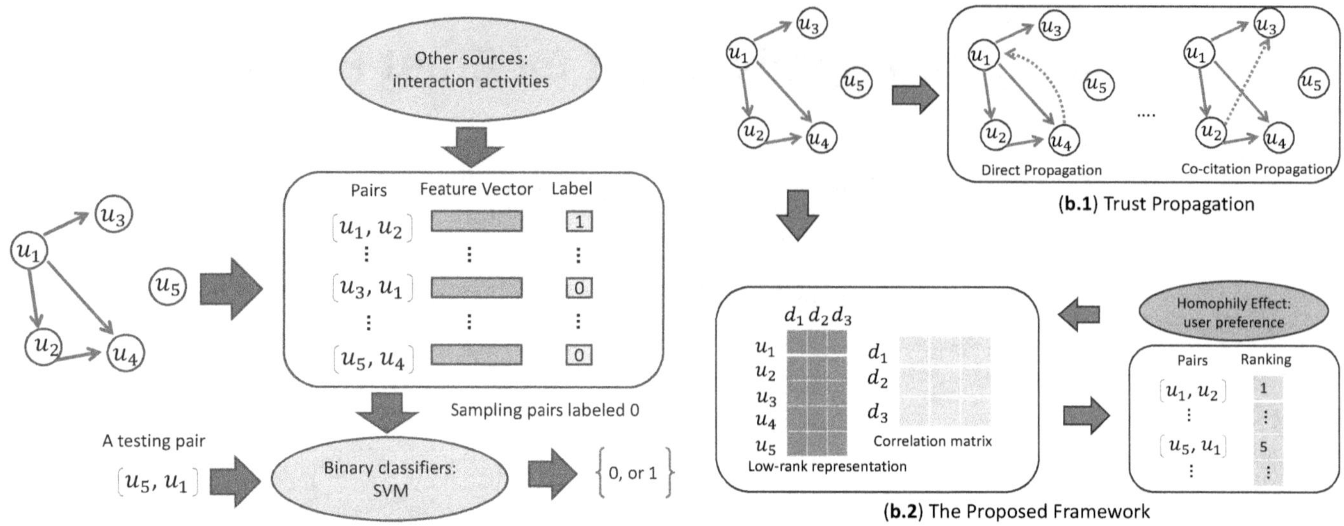

(a) Supervised Trust Prediction

(b) Unsupervised Trust Prediction

Figure 1: Supervised and Unsupervised Trust Prediction

In this paper, we study the problem of trust prediction by exploiting homophily effect. In essence, we investigate: (1) how to capture homophily effect in trust relations; and (2) how to take advantage of that effect for trust prediction. Our solutions to these two challenges result in a new framework, hTrust, for trust prediction. As demonstrated in Figure 1(b.2), hTrust does trust prediction in an unsupervised scenario by seeking low-rank representations for users and their correlations while exploiting homophily effect. Our main contributions are summarized next.

- Demonstrate the existence of homophily in trust relations: similar users are more likely to establish trust relations while trusted users are more similar;
- Provide an approach to exploit homophily effect in trust relations via homophily regularization;
- Propose an unsupervised framework, hTrust, for the problem of trust prediction, incorporating low-rank matrix factorization with homophily regularization; and
- Evaluate hTrust extensively using datasets from product review sites to understand the working of hTrust.

The rest of paper is organized as follows. Section 2 describes the datasets and verifies homophily in trust relations. Section 3 introduces how to employ the low-rank matrix factorization method for trust prediction. Section 4 introduces the details on homophily regularization and the proposed framework. Section 5 presents experimental results and our observations. Section 6 briefly reviews related work. Section 7 concludes this study with future work.

2. DATA ANALYSIS

We collect two publicly available datasets for this study, i.e., Epinions and Ciao[3]. Both sites are product review sites where users can rate items by writing reviews and establish trust networks with their like-minded users.

[3]These datasets are available from the first author webpage: http:// www.public.asu.edu/~jtang20/ datasetcode/truststudy.htm

Table 1: Statistics of the Datasets

	Epinions	Ciao
# of Users	8,527	6,262
# of items	26,552	20,416
# of Ratings	225,579	167,320
# of Trust Relations	302,177	109,524
Max # of Trustors	1,285	100
Max # of Trustees	1,805	797
Trust Network Density	0.0042	0.0028
Clustering Coefficient	0.2242	0.2254

We filter the users with less than two trustors and items with less than two ratings, aiming to obtain datasets that are large enough and have sufficient historical information for the purpose of evaluation. Some statistics of the datasets are shown in Table 1. On average, users of Epinions have 35.43 trust relations and 26.45 ratings, while users of Ciao have 17.49 trust relations and 26.72 ratings.

The distributions of trustors and trustees for each user are demonstrated in Figure 2. Most users have few trustors and trustees, while a few users have an extremely high number of trustors or trustees, suggesting a power law distribution that is typical in social networks.

Both Epinions and Ciao employ 5-star system to rate items and the rating distributions are shown in Figure 3(a) and Figure 3(b) for Epinions and Ciao, respectively. We note that the majority of ratings are scores of 4 and 5 and this observation is consistent with previous studies: users are likely to give positive ratings to items [21].

2.1 Homophily in Trust Relations

Homophily is one of the most important social correlation theories, observed in many social networks such as following relations in Twitter [24]. In this subsection, we investigate

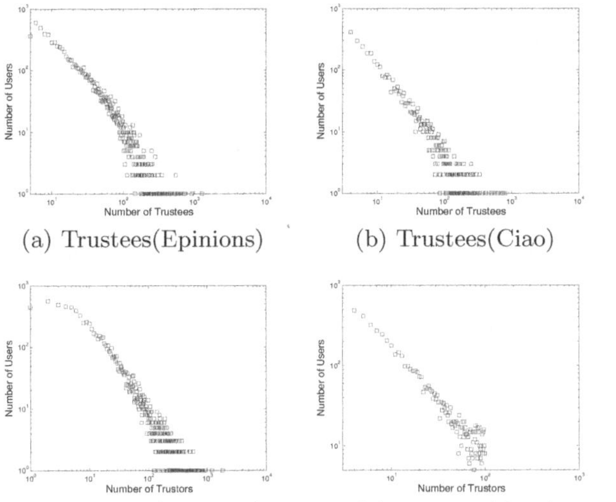

(a) Trustees(Epinions) (b) Trustees(Ciao)

(c) Trustors(Epinions) (d) Trustors(Ciao)

Figure 2: Trustors and Trustees Distributions in Epinions and Ciao

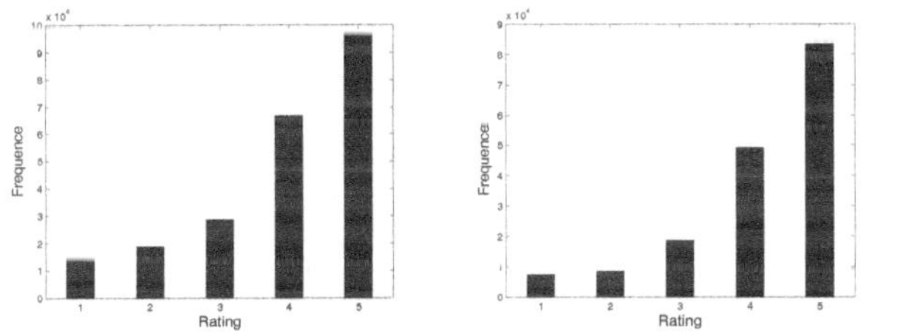

(a) Epinions (b) Ciao

Figure 3: Rating Distributions in Epinions and Ciao

homophily in trust relations via studying the correlation between trust relations and users' similarity. Specifically, in the context of product review sites, we ask two questions:

- Are users with trust relations more similar in terms of their ratings than those without?
- Are users with higher similarity more likely to establish trust relations than those with lower similarity?

To answer the **first question**, we have to define users' rating similarity. In this work, we use the cosine similarity of users' rating vectors to measure their rating similarity. With this definition, we calculate two similarities for each trust relation, i.e., trust similarity ts and random similarity rs. For example, for the trust relation $u_i \rightarrow u_j$, indicating that u_i trusts u_j, ts is the rating similarity between u_i and u_j while rs is the similarity between u_i and a randomly chosen user without trust relations. Finally we obtain two similarity vectors, $\mathbf{s}_t$ and $\mathbf{s}_r$. $\mathbf{s}_t$ is the set of all trust similarities ts while $\mathbf{s}_r$ is the set of rs.

We conduct a two-sample t-test on $\mathbf{s}_t$ and $\mathbf{s}_r$. The null hypothesis is $H_0 : \mathbf{s}_t = \mathbf{s}_r$, and the alternative hypothesis is $H_1 : \mathbf{s}_t > \mathbf{s}_r$. For both datasets, the null hypothesis is rejected at significance level $\alpha = 0.01$ with p-value of $5.12e{-18}$ and $3.76e{-21}$ in Epinions and Ciao, respectively. The evidence from t-test suggests a positive answer to the first question: *with high probability, users with trust relations have higher rating similarity than those without.*

For the **second question**, we want to investigate if users with higher similarity at time t is more likely to establish trust relations at time $t+1$ than those with lower similarity. We study this problem in Epinions since it provides temporal information when ratings are created and when trust relations are established. The earliest rating was published on Jul 05, 1999 and the latest one was on May 08, 2011. However, temporal information about the trust relations established before Jan 11, 2001 is not available from Epinions. Therefore, we split the whole dataset into 11 timestamps, i.e., $\mathbf{t} = \{t_1, \ldots, t_{11}\}$, where t_1 covers the data before Jan 11, 2001, t_{11} contains data after Jan 11, 2010 and for t_2 to t_{10}, each of them contains data for one year.

For timestamp $t_i (1 \leq i \leq 10)$, we rank all pairs of users without trust relations in terms of rating similarity in descending order and then we pick out $x\%$ pairs from the top and $x\%$ pairs from the bottom to form a higher-similarity group, denoted as $\mathcal{G}_h^i$ and a lower-similarity group, represented by $\mathcal{G}_l^i$, respectively. Finally we check whether pairs in $\mathcal{G}_h^i$ are more likely to establish trust relations at t_{i+1} than those in $\mathcal{G}_l^i$. We assume that $h_i(x)$ and $l_i(x)$ are the percentages of pairs in $\mathcal{G}_h^i$ and $\mathcal{G}_l^i$ establishing trust relations at time t_{i+1} at the ratio of $x\%$, respectively.

Since the percentage of pairs with trust relations is very small such as 0.0042 in Epinions, we vary x from 0.0001 to 0.01 with an incremental step of 0.0001. For each $x\%$, the average percentages of pairs establishing trust relations for higher-similarity groups, $\bar{h}_x$, and lower-similarity groups, $\bar{l}_x$, over timestamps from t_1 to t_{10}, are defined as follows,

$$\bar{h}_x = \frac{1}{10}\sum_{i=1}^{10} h_i(x), \quad \bar{l}_x = \frac{1}{10}\sum_{i=1}^{10} l_i(x) \tag{1}$$

Let $\mathbf{h} = [\bar{h}_{0.0001}, \ldots, \bar{h}_{0.01}]$ and $\mathbf{l} = [\bar{l}_{0.0001}, \ldots, \bar{l}_{0.01}]$. With these two vectors, we also conduct a two-sample t-test on them. The null hypothesis is $H_0 : \mathbf{h} = \mathbf{l}$, and the alternative hypothesis is $H_1 : \mathbf{h} > \mathbf{l}$. The null hypothesis is rejected at significance level $\alpha = 0.01$ with p-value of $7.59e{-59}$ in Epinions. This supports that *users with higher rating similarity are more likely to establish trust relations than those with lower similarity,* which answers the second question.

Positive answers to both questions provide evidence of the existence of homophily in trust relations. With the verification of homophily in trust relations, we next study how to exploit homophily effect for trust prediction.

3. LOW-RANK MATRIX FACTORIZATION MODEL FOR TRUST PREDICTION

Low-rank matrix factorization method is widely employed in various applications such as collective filtering [8, 21] and document clustering [26, 2]. Let $\mathbf{u} = \{u_1, u_2, \ldots, u_n\}$ be the set of users where n is the number of users. $\mathbf{G} \in \mathbb{R}^{n \times n}$ is the matrix representation of trust relations where $\mathbf{G}(i,j) = 1$ if we observe that u_i trusts u_j and $\mathbf{G}(i,j) = 0$ otherwise. A few factors can influence people to establish trust relations and a user usually establishes trust relations with a small proportion of $\mathbf{u}$, resulting in $\mathbf{G}$ very sparse and low-rank, hence users can have a more compact but accurate representation in a low-rank space. The matrix factorization model seeks a low-rank representation $\mathbf{U} \in \mathbb{R}^{n \times d}$ with $d \ll n$ for $\mathbf{u}$

via solving the following optimization problem,

$$\min_{\mathbf{U},\mathbf{V}} \quad \|\mathbf{G} - \mathbf{U}\mathbf{V}\mathbf{U}^\top\|_F^2, \tag{2}$$

where $\|\cdot\|_F$ is the Frobenius norm of a matrix and $\mathbf{V} \in \mathbb{R}^{d\times d}$ captures the correlations among their low-rank representations such as $\mathbf{G}(i,j) = \mathbf{U}(i,:)\mathbf{V}\mathbf{U}^\top(j,:)$. To avoid overfitting, we add two smoothness regularizations on $\mathbf{U}$ and $\mathbf{V}$, respectively, into Eq. (2), and then we have,

$$\min_{\mathbf{U},\mathbf{V}} \quad \|\mathbf{G} - \mathbf{U}\mathbf{V}\mathbf{U}^\top\|_F^2 + \alpha\|\mathbf{U}\|_F^2 + \beta\|\mathbf{V}\|_F^2, \tag{3}$$

where α and β are non-negative and are introduced to control the capability of $\mathbf{U}$ and $\mathbf{V}$, respectively. Non-negative constraints are always applied to $\mathbf{U}$ and $\mathbf{V}$ in Eq. (3) as,

$$\min_{\mathbf{U},\mathbf{V}} \quad \|\mathbf{G} - \mathbf{U}\mathbf{V}\mathbf{U}^\top\|_F^2 + \alpha\|\mathbf{U}\|_F^2 + \beta\|\mathbf{V}\|_F^2$$
$$s.t. \quad \mathbf{U} \geq 0, \;\; \mathbf{V} \geq 0, \tag{4}$$

if the dimensionality of the latent space d is set to the number of communities, and then the low-rank representation of users $\mathbf{U}$ can be explained as an affiliation matrix, indicating the community structure of users [20].

There are several nice properties of the matrix factorization method [4, 16]: (1) many optimization methods such as gradient based methods can be applied to find a well-worked optimal solution, scaled to thousands of users with millions of trust relations; (2) it has a nice probabilistic interpretation with Gaussian noise; (3) it is very flexible and allows us to include prior knowledge such as homophily regularization, introduced in the next section.

4. MODELING HOMOPHILY FOR TRUST PREDICTION

In this section, we study how to model homophily effect in trust prediction under the low-rank matrix factorization model. After introducing homophily regularization, we present our proposed framework with its optimization method. To verify the efficiency, we present the time complexity of our framework.

4.1 Homophily Regularization

The analysis in Section 2 suggests the existence of homophily in trust relations and homophily effect indicates that users with higher similarity are more likely to establish trust relations. We define $\zeta(i,j)$ as the *homophily coefficient* between u_i and u_j, satisfying: (1) $\zeta(i,j) \in [0,1]$; (2) $\zeta(i,j) = \zeta(j,i)$; (3) the larger $\zeta(i,j)$ is, the more likely a trust relation is established between u_i and u_j. With homophily coefficient, homophily regularization is to minimize the following term as,

$$\min \quad \sum_{i=1}^{n}\sum_{j=1}^{n} \zeta(i,j)\|\mathbf{U}(i,:) - \mathbf{U}(j,:)\|_2^2, \tag{5}$$

users close to each other in the low-rank space are more likely to establish trust relations [18] and their distances in the latent space are controlled by their homophily coefficients. For example, $\zeta(i,j)$ controls the latent distance between u_i and u_j. A larger value of $\zeta(i,j)$ indicates that u_i and u_j are more likely to establish trust relations according to the property (3) of homophily coefficient. Thus we force their latent representations should be as close as possible, while a smaller value of $\zeta(i,j)$ tells that the distance of their latent representations should be larger.

For a particular user u_i, the terms in homophily regularization related to her latent representation $\mathbf{U}(i,:)$ are,

$$\sum_{j=1}^{n} \zeta(i,j)\|\mathbf{U}(i,:) - \mathbf{U}(j,:)\|_2^2, \tag{6}$$

we can see that the latent representation for u_i is smoothed with other users, controlled by homophily coefficient, hence even for long tail users, with a few or even without any trust relations, we still can get an approximate estimate of their latent representations via homophily regularization, addressing the sparsity problem with traditional unsupervised methods.

After some derivations, we can get the matrix form of homophily regularization,

$$\begin{aligned}
&\frac{1}{2}\sum_{i=1}^{n}\sum_{j=1}^{n} \zeta(i,j)\|\mathbf{U}(i,:) - \mathbf{U}(j,:)\|_2^2 \\
&= \frac{1}{2}\sum_{i=1}^{n}\sum_{j=1}^{n}\sum_{k=1}^{d} \zeta(i,j)\big(\mathbf{U}(i,k) - \mathbf{U}(j,k)\big)^2 \\
&= \sum_{i=1}^{n}\sum_{j=1}^{n}\sum_{k=1}^{d} \zeta(i,j)\mathbf{U}^2(i,k) \\
&\qquad - \sum_{i=1}^{n}\sum_{j=1}^{n}\sum_{k=1}^{d} \zeta(i,j)\mathbf{U}(i,k)\mathbf{U}(j,k) \\
&= \sum_{k=1}^{d} \mathbf{U}^\top(:,k)(\mathbf{D} - \mathcal{Z})\mathbf{U}(:,k) \\
&= Tr(\mathbf{U}^\top \mathcal{L}\mathbf{U}),
\end{aligned} \tag{7}$$

where $\mathcal{L} = \mathbf{D} - \mathcal{Z}$ is the Laplacian matrix and $\mathbf{D}$ is a diagonal matrix with the i-th diagonal element $\mathbf{D}(i,i) = \sum_{j=1}^{n} \mathcal{Z}(j,i)$. $\mathcal{Z}$ is the homophily coefficient matrix among n instances, defined as,

$$\mathcal{Z} = \begin{pmatrix} \zeta(1,1) & \zeta(1,2) & \cdots & \zeta(1,n) \\ \zeta(2,1) & \zeta(2,2) & \cdots & \zeta(2,n) \\ \vdots & \vdots & \ddots & \vdots \\ \zeta(n,1) & \zeta(n,2) & \cdots & \zeta(n,n) \end{pmatrix}$$

Ziegler et al. pointed out that there is a strong and significant correlation between trust and user preference similarity [27]. Meanwhile, homophily effect indicates that the more similar two people are, the more likely they will establish trust relations. In the context of product view sites, user preference can be inferred from their ratings, hence homophily coefficient in this work is simply measured via rating similarity although there are other more sophisticated measures [15]. For u_i, we assume that $I(i)$ is the set of items u_i rates and R_{ij} is the rating to the j-th item from u_i. We investigate the following three widely used rating similarity measures [12] for homophily coefficient.

- *Jaccard's coefficient (JC):* Jaccard's coefficient is defined as the number of common rated items of two users divided by the total number of their unique rated items, formally stated as,

$$\zeta(i,j) = JC(u_i,u_j) = \frac{|I(i) \cap I(j)|}{|I(i) \cup I(j)|}. \tag{8}$$

- *Rating similarity (RS):* JC counts the common rated items, however, different users might rate the same item differently. For example, u_i rates the j-th item 5 stars while u_j gives 1 star to the j-th item. To capture different tastes from different users, we define rating similarity (RS) as,

$$\zeta(i,j) = RS(u_i, u_j) = \frac{\sum_k R_{ik} \cdot R_{jk}}{\sqrt{\sum_k R_{ik}^2}\sqrt{\sum_k R_{jk}^2}}, \qquad (9)$$

actually $RS(u_i, u_j)$ is the cosin similarity between the rating vectors of u_i and u_j, already discussed in above section 2.1.

- *Pearson Correlation Coefficient (PCC):* Different users may have different rating styles: some users have the propensity to give higher ratings to all items while others probably tend to rate lowly, motivating us to propose PCC,

$$\begin{aligned}\zeta(i,j) &= PCC(u_i, u_j) \\ &= \frac{\sum_{k\in I(i)\cap I(j)}(R_{ik} - \bar{R}_i)\cdot(R_{jk} - \bar{R}_j)}{\sqrt{\sum_k (R_{ik} - \bar{R}_i)^2}\sqrt{\sum_k (R_{jk} - \bar{R}_j)^2}}, \qquad (10)\end{aligned}$$

where $\bar{R}_i$ denotes the average rate of u_i and k belongs to the subset of items rated by both u_i and u_j.

From these definitions of similarity functions, $JC(u_i, u_j)$ and $RS(u_i, u_j)$ range within $[0, 1]$, however, $PCC(u_i, u_j)$ ranges from -1 to 1. According to the definition of homophily coefficient, $\zeta(i,j)$ belongs to $[0,1]$. Therefore, a mapping function $f(x) = \frac{x+1}{2}$ is applied to PCC, limiting the value of $PCC(u_i, u_j)$ within $[0, 1]$. It is easy to verify that JC, RS and PCC satisfy the three properties of homophily coefficient. Note that in this paper, we donot consider the combinations of different measures for homophily coefficient, introducing more parameters to prune and leaving it as our future work.

4.2 The Proposed Framework: hTrust

With the definition of homophily regularization, we propose a framework, hTrust, based on matrix factorization while exploiting homophily effect for trust prediction. hTrust is to solve the following optimization problem,

$$\begin{aligned}\min_{\mathbf{U},\mathbf{V}} \quad & F = \|\mathbf{G} - \mathbf{U}\mathbf{V}\mathbf{U}^\top\|_F^2 \\ & + \alpha\|\mathbf{U}\|_F^2 + \beta\|\mathbf{V}\|_F^2 + \lambda Tr(\mathbf{U}^\top \mathcal{L}\mathbf{U}) \\ s.t. \quad & \mathbf{U} \geq 0, \;\; \mathbf{V} \geq 0. \qquad (11)\end{aligned}$$

By removing constants in the objective function, Eq. (11) can be rewritten as,

$$\begin{aligned}F = & Tr(-2\mathbf{G}^\top\mathbf{U}\mathbf{V}\mathbf{U}^\top + \mathbf{U}\mathbf{V}^\top\mathbf{U}^\top\mathbf{U}\mathbf{V}\mathbf{U}^\top) \\ & + \alpha Tr(\mathbf{U}\mathbf{U}^\top) + \beta Tr(\mathbf{V}\mathbf{V}^\top) + \lambda Tr(\mathbf{U}^\top\mathcal{L}\mathbf{U}). \qquad (12)\end{aligned}$$

The coupling between $\mathbf{U}$ and $\mathbf{V}$ makes the problem in Eq. (11) difficult to find optimal solutions for both $\mathbf{U}$ and $\mathbf{V}$ simultaneously. In this work, we adopt an alternative optimization scheme [2] for Eq. (11), under which we update $\mathbf{U}$ and $\mathbf{V}$ alternatingly with the following updating rules,

$$\begin{aligned}\mathbf{U}(i,k) &\leftarrow \mathbf{U}(i,k)\sqrt{\frac{\mathbf{A}(i,k)}{\mathbf{B}(i,k)}}, \\ \mathbf{V}(i,k) &\leftarrow \mathbf{V}(i,k)\sqrt{\frac{[\mathbf{U}^\top\mathbf{G}\mathbf{U}](i,k)}{[\mathbf{U}^\top\mathbf{U}\mathbf{V}\mathbf{U}^\top\mathbf{U} + \beta\mathbf{V}](i,k)}}, \qquad (13)\end{aligned}$$

where $\mathbf{A}$ and $\mathbf{B}$ are defined as,

$$\begin{aligned}\mathbf{A} &= \mathbf{G}^\top\mathbf{U}\mathbf{V} + \mathbf{G}\mathbf{U}\mathbf{V}^\top + \lambda\mathcal{Z}\mathbf{U}, \\ \mathbf{B} &= \mathbf{U}\mathbf{V}^\top\mathbf{U}^\top\mathbf{U}\mathbf{V} + \mathbf{U}\mathbf{V}\mathbf{U}^\top\mathbf{U}\mathbf{V}^\top + \alpha\mathbf{U} + \lambda\mathbf{D}\mathbf{U}. \qquad (14)\end{aligned}$$

Next we will prove the correctness of the updating rules in Eq. (13) by showing that the final solution would satisfy the KKT condition. The Lagrangian function of Eq (11) is:

$$\begin{aligned}L_F = & Tr(-2\mathbf{G}^\top\mathbf{U}\mathbf{V}\mathbf{U}^\top + \mathbf{U}\mathbf{V}^\top\mathbf{U}^\top\mathbf{U}\mathbf{V}\mathbf{U}^\top) \\ & + \alpha Tr(\mathbf{U}\mathbf{U}^\top) + \beta Tr(\mathbf{V}\mathbf{V}^\top) + \lambda Tr(\mathbf{U}^\top\mathcal{L}\mathbf{U}) \\ & - Tr(\Lambda_1\mathbf{U}) - Tr(\Lambda_2\mathbf{V}), \qquad (15)\end{aligned}$$

where Λ_1 and Λ_2 are Lagrangian multipliers for non-negativity of $\mathbf{U}$ and $\mathbf{V}$, respectively.

Then we have,

$$\begin{aligned}\frac{\partial L_F}{\partial\mathbf{U}} &= 2(-\mathbf{G}^\top\mathbf{U}\mathbf{V} - \mathbf{G}\mathbf{U}\mathbf{V}^\top + \mathbf{U}\mathbf{V}^\top\mathbf{U}^\top\mathbf{U}\mathbf{V} \\ &\quad + \mathbf{U}\mathbf{V}\mathbf{U}^\top\mathbf{U}\mathbf{V}^\top + \alpha\mathbf{U} + \lambda\mathcal{L}\mathbf{U}) - \Lambda_1^\top, \\ \frac{\partial L_F}{\partial\mathbf{V}} &= 2(-\mathbf{U}^\top\mathbf{G}\mathbf{U} + \mathbf{U}^\top\mathbf{U}\mathbf{V}\mathbf{U}^\top\mathbf{U} + \beta\mathbf{V}) - \Lambda_2^\top. \qquad (16)\end{aligned}$$

The KKT complementary condition is,

$$\begin{aligned}&\mathbf{U}(i,k)\Lambda_1(i,k) = 0, \;\; \forall\, i \in [1,n], \; k \in [1,d] \\ &\mathbf{V}(i,k)\Lambda_2(i,k) = 0 \;\; \forall\, i, \; k \in [1,d]. \qquad (17)\end{aligned}$$

Let $\frac{\partial L_F}{\partial\mathbf{U}} = 0$ and $\frac{\partial L_F}{\partial\mathbf{V}} = 0$,

$$\begin{aligned}&-\mathbf{G}^\top\mathbf{U}\mathbf{V} - \mathbf{G}\mathbf{U}\mathbf{V}^\top + \mathbf{U}\mathbf{V}^\top\mathbf{U}^\top\mathbf{U}\mathbf{V} \\ &+ \mathbf{U}\mathbf{V}\mathbf{U}^\top\mathbf{U}\mathbf{V}^\top + \alpha\mathbf{U} + \lambda\mathcal{L}\mathbf{U} = \Lambda_1, \\ &-\mathbf{U}^\top\mathbf{G}\mathbf{U} + \mathbf{U}^\top\mathbf{U}\mathbf{V}\mathbf{U}^\top\mathbf{U} + \beta\mathbf{V} = \Lambda_2. \qquad (18)\end{aligned}$$

Using the KKT complementary condition in Eq. (17), we have,

$$\begin{aligned}&[-\mathbf{G}^\top\mathbf{U}\mathbf{V} - \mathbf{G}\mathbf{U}\mathbf{V}^\top + \mathbf{U}\mathbf{V}^\top\mathbf{U}^\top\mathbf{U}\mathbf{V} \\ &+ \mathbf{U}\mathbf{V}\mathbf{U}^\top\mathbf{U}\mathbf{V}^\top + \alpha\mathbf{U} + \lambda\mathcal{L}\mathbf{U}](i,k)\mathbf{U}(i,k) = 0, \\ &[-\mathbf{U}^\top\mathbf{G}\mathbf{U} + \mathbf{U}^\top\mathbf{U}\mathbf{V}\mathbf{U}^\top\mathbf{U} + \beta\mathbf{V}](i,k)\mathbf{V}(i,k) = 0. \qquad (19)\end{aligned}$$

It is easy to verify that the updating rules in Eq. (13) do satisfy the above KKT condition. Furthermore, since $\mathbf{G}$, $\mathcal{Z}$, $\mathbf{D}$ are nonnegative, so $\mathbf{U}$ and $\mathbf{V}$ are nonnegative during the updating process. Until now, we prove the correctness of the updating rules in Eq. (13). It can be proven that the updating rules in Eq. (13) are guaranteed to converge. Since the proof process is similar to that in [2], to save space, we omit the detailed proof of the convergence of the updating rules in Eq. (13).

4.3 The Algorithm and Time Complexity

The detailed algorithm for the proposed framework, hTrust, is shown in Algorithm 1. We construct homophily coefficient matrix in line 1. From line 4 to line 9, we alternatingly update $\mathbf{U}$ and $\mathbf{V}$ until achieving convergence. Note that in practice, Algorithm 1 will stop when reaching predefined maximal iterations or there is little change for the objective function value. After obtaining the optimal $\mathbf{U}$ and $\mathbf{V}$, $\tilde{\mathbf{G}} = \mathbf{U}\mathbf{V}\mathbf{U}^\top$ is the new low-rank representation of $\mathbf{G}$. Since $\mathbf{U}$ and $\mathbf{V}$ are non-negative, the new low-rank representation of the trust network $\tilde{\mathbf{G}}$ is non-negative. The likelihood of u_i and u_j to establish trust relation is indicated by $\tilde{\mathbf{G}}(i,j)$[4].

Algorithm 1 The Framework of Trust Prediction with Homophily Regularization

Input: $\mathbf{G}$, α, β, λ
Output: Ranking list of pairs of users

```
Construct the Homophily Coefficient Matrix Z and D
Initialize U randomly
Initialize V randomly
while Not convergent do
    Set A = GᵀUV + GUVᵀ + λZU
    Set B = UVᵀUᵀUV + UVUᵀUVᵀ + αU + λDU
    for i = 1 to n do
        for k = 1 to d do
            Update U(i,k) ← U(i,k) sqrt(A(i,k) / B(i,k))
        end for
    end for
    for i = 1 to d do
        for k = 1 to d do
            Update V(i,k) ← V(i,k) sqrt([UᵀGU](i,k) / [UᵀUVUᵀU + βV](i,k))
        end for
    end for
end while
Set G̃ = UVUᵀ
Ranking pairs of users (e.g., ⟨u_i, u_j⟩) according to G̃
    (e.g., G̃(i,j)) in a descending order.
```

At each iteration, the high cost of the updating rules for $\mathbf{U}$ and $\mathbf{V}$ may limit the applications of the proposed algorithm, so it is essential to analyze the time complexity and find an efficient implementation of Algorithm 1.

First we consider the time complexity of $\mathbf{A} = \mathbf{G}^\top\mathbf{U}\mathbf{V} + \mathbf{G}\mathbf{U}\mathbf{V}^\top + \lambda\mathcal{Z}\mathbf{U}$. The matrix representation of trust network $\mathbf{G}$ is very sparse thus $\mathbf{G}^\top\mathbf{U}\mathbf{V}$ and $\mathbf{G}\mathbf{U}\mathbf{V}^\top$ can be computed in $O(nd^2)$. In our studied datasets, $\mathcal{Z}$ is very sparse (by considering the top similar users, we also can obtain a sparse homophily coefficient matrix $\mathcal{Z}$ for other datasets). Therefore, the time complexity of $\lambda\mathcal{Z}\mathbf{U}$ is $O(nd^2)$.

For $\mathbf{B} = \mathbf{U}\mathbf{V}^\top\mathbf{U}^\top\mathbf{U}\mathbf{V} + \mathbf{U}\mathbf{V}\mathbf{U}^\top\mathbf{U}\mathbf{V}^\top + \alpha\mathbf{U} + \lambda\mathbf{D}\mathbf{U}$, we can calculate $\mathbf{U}\mathbf{V}^\top\mathbf{U}^\top\mathbf{U}\mathbf{V}$ by either,

$$(((\mathbf{U}\mathbf{V}^\top)\mathbf{U}^\top)\mathbf{U})\mathbf{V}, \quad or \quad \mathbf{U}(\mathbf{V}^\top((\mathbf{U}^\top\mathbf{U})\mathbf{V})) \tag{20}$$

The former takes $O(n^2d)$ operations, while the latter costs $O(nd^2)$. As $d \ll n$, the latter is much more efficient. Similarly, $\mathbf{U}\mathbf{V}\mathbf{U}^\top\mathbf{U}\mathbf{V}^\top$ should be calculated as

$$\mathbf{U}(\mathbf{V}((\mathbf{U}^\top\mathbf{U})\mathbf{V}^\top)). \tag{21}$$

Note that $\mathbf{U}^\top\mathbf{U}$ is only calculated once for $\mathbf{U}\mathbf{V}^\top\mathbf{U}^\top\mathbf{U}\mathbf{V}$ and $\mathbf{U}\mathbf{V}\mathbf{U}^\top\mathbf{U}\mathbf{V}^\top$. Since $\mathbf{D}$ is a diagonal matrix, the time complexity of $\mathbf{D}\mathbf{U}$ is $O(nd)$.

Due to the sparsity of $\mathbf{G}$, $\mathbf{U}^\top\mathbf{G}\mathbf{U}$ in the updating rule for $\mathbf{V}$ costs $O(nd^2)$. $\mathbf{U}^\top\mathbf{U}\mathbf{V}\mathbf{U}^\top\mathbf{U}$ should be computed as,

$$(\mathbf{U}^\top\mathbf{U})\mathbf{V}(\mathbf{U}^\top\mathbf{U}) \tag{22}$$

[4]The code is available at http://www.public.asu.edu/~jtang20/datasetcode/hTrust.m

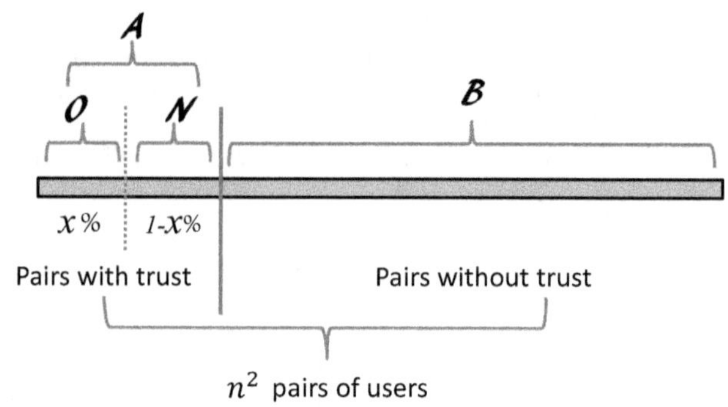

Figure 4: Separation of the dataset. $\mathcal{A}$ is the set of pairs with trust relations, sorted in chronological order, $x\%$ of which is chosen as old trust relations $\mathcal{O}$ and the remaining $1 - x\%$ as new trust relations $\mathcal{N}$ to predict, and $\mathcal{B}$ is the set of pairs without trust relations.

whose time complexity is $O(nd^2)$.

In summary, with above implementations, the overall time complexity for Algorithm 1 is $\#iterations * O(nd^2)$.

5. EXPERIMENTS

In this section, we conduct experiments to evaluate the proposed framework. After introducing the experiment settings and the evaluation metric, we compare different trust prediction methods, and then study the effect of homophily regularization and different measures of homophily coefficient on the proposed framework.

5.1 Experiment Settings

The experiment setting of the dataset is demonstrated in Figure 4. $\mathcal{A} = \{\langle u_i, u_j\rangle | \mathbf{G}(i,j) = 1\}$ is the set of pairs of users with trust relations and $\mathcal{B} = \{\langle u_i, u_j\rangle | \mathbf{G}(i,j) = 0\}$ is the set of pairs of users without trust relations. The pairs in $\mathcal{A}$ are sorted in chronological order in terms of the time when they established trust relations. We choose $x\%$ of $\mathcal{A}$ as old trust relations $\mathcal{O}$ and the remaining $1 - x\%$ as new trust relations $\mathcal{N}$ to predict. We remove trust relations in $\mathcal{N}$ by setting $\mathbf{G}(i,j) = 0$, $\forall\langle u_i, u_j\rangle \in \mathcal{N}$ and the new representation of $\mathbf{G}$ is the input of each predictor. x is varied as $\{50, 55, 60, 65, 70, 80, 90\}$.

We follow the common metric for unsupervised trust prediction in [9] to evaluate the performance of trust prediction. In details, each trust predictor ranks pairs in $\mathcal{B} \cup \mathcal{N}$ in decreasing order of confidence and we take the first $|\mathcal{N}|$ pairs as the set of predicted trust relations, denoting as $\mathcal{C}$. Then the prediction accuracy (PA) can be calculated as,

$$PA = \frac{|\mathcal{N} \cap \mathcal{C}|}{|\mathcal{N}|} \tag{23}$$

where $|\cdot|$ denotes the size of a set.

5.2 Comparison of Different Trust Predictors

In this subsection, we compare the proposed framework with various baseline methods as follows,

- *TP:* the trust relations are inferred through trust propagation. Four atomic propagations are utilized in this

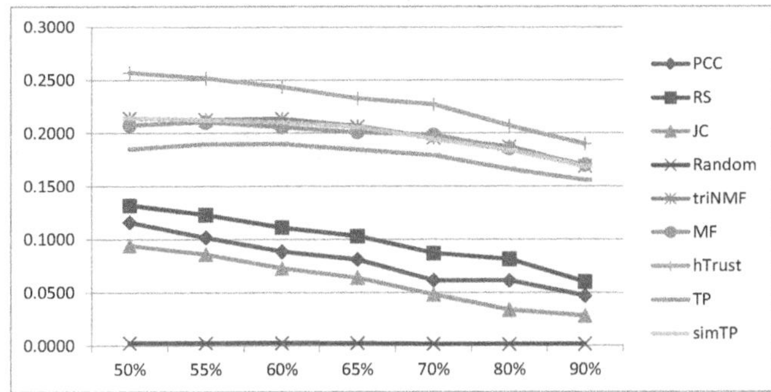

	50%	55%	60%	65%	70%	80%	90%
TP	0.1852	0.1897	0.1897	0.1845	0.1790	0.1663	0.1558
RS	0.1319	0.1230	0.1110	0.1029	0.0869	0.0813	0.0598
PCC	0.1160	0.1019	0.0884	0.0811	0.0614	0.0610	0.0469
JC	0.0940	0.0858	0.0725	0.0637	0.0480	0.0336	0.0279
simTP	0.2076	0.2105	0.2057	0.2011	0.1982	0.1857	0.1702
MF	0.2145	0.2121	0.2102	0.2057	0.1944	0.1837	0.1688
triNMF	0.2142	0.2129	0.2134	0.2064	0.1958	0.1875	0.1692
hTrust	0.2569	0.2517	0.2434	0.2326	0.2268	0.2072	0.1900
Random	0.0027	0.0026	0.0025	0.0024	0.0017	0.0015	0.0016

Figure 5: Performance Comparison for Different Trust Predictors in Epinions

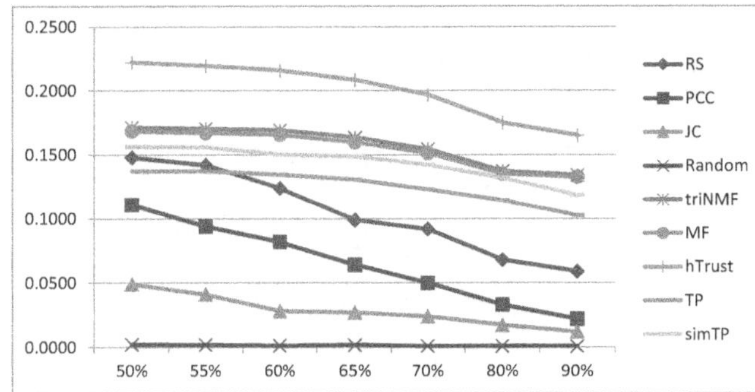

	50%	55%	60%	65%	70%	80%	90%
TP	0.1374	0.1371	0.1345	0.1306	0.1231	0.1145	0.1027
RS	0.1480	0.1420	0.1240	0.0990	0.0920	0.0680	0.0590
PCC	0.1110	0.0940	0.0820	0.0640	0.0500	0.0330	0.0220
JC	0.0490	0.0410	0.0280	0.0270	0.0240	0.0170	0.0120
simTP	0.1685	0.1671	0.1657	0.1599	0.1513	0.1351	0.1328
MF	0.1564	0.1559	0.1502	0.1489	0.1424	0.1321	0.1185
triNMF	0.1714	0.1703	0.1691	0.1635	0.1546	0.1372	0.1342
hTrust	0.2220	0.2193	0.2158	0.2082	0.1966	0.1749	0.1650
Random	0.0022	0.0020	0.0014	0.0017	0.0010	0.0009	0.0008

Figure 6: Performance Comparison for Different Trust Predictors in Ciao

predictor, i.e., direct propagation, co-citation, transpose trust and trust coupling [7].

- *RS*: RS ranks the pairs of users via their rating similarity defined in Eq. (9).
- *PCC*: PCC ranks the pairs of users through Pearson Correlation Coefficient as in Eq. (10).
- *JC*: the likelihood of a pair of users to establish a trust relation is computed by Jaccard's coefficient on their rated items shown in Eq. (8).
- *simTP*: the score of a potential trust relation is estimated via a combination of trust propagation and users' rating similarity, following the basic ideas in [5, 1]. We use *RS* to measure the rating similarity.
- *MF:* it conducts a matrix factorization on the matrix representation of trust relations [26].
- *triNMF:* triNMF is a variant of our proposed method without homophily regularization as shown in Eq. (4).

Note that we do not compare our proposed framework with the methods proposed in [10, 17, 13] because: (1) these methods need additional data sources to work such as users' interaction activities; (2) homophily regularization is easy to incorporate into these methods to improve prediction performance through graph regularization; and (3) these methods are supervised methods while our proposed framework is unsupervised learning. We would like to leave the work of exploiting homophily effect for supervised methods as future work since we focus on unsupervised trust prediction in this work.

The parameters in all methods are determined through cross validation. For hTrust, we choose RS to measure the homophily coefficient and other parameters are set as $\alpha = \beta = 0.01, \lambda = 10, d = 100$. More details about the effect of homophily regularization and measures of homophily coefficient on hTrust will be discussed in later subsections. The comparison results are demonstrated in Figure 5 and Figure 6 for Epinions and Ciao, respectively.

The first observation is that with the increase of x, the performance of all methods reduces. In general, with more old trust relations , we should obtain better performance for *the same set* of new trust relations. However, in our experiments, the sets of new trust relations are different for different x%s and the difficulty of inferring new trust relations, buried in a large amount of pairs without trust relations, increases with the increase of x, supported by the trend of the performance of randomly guessing. To clarify the confusion, we conduct a validation experiment by fixing the set of new trust relations to 10% and the experimental results are shown in Table 2. Note that we only show the results of *TP*, *MF* and *hTrust*, since other methods are independent on trust networks (e.g., JC) or are variants of selected methods (e.g., *triNMF* is a variant of *hTrust*). It is clear that with the increase of new trust relations, the performance does increase in our expectation. We also note that when x is from 90 to 50, hTrust is more stable than both *TP* and *MF*. On average, the performance of *hTrust*, *TP* and *MF* relatively reduces 5.70%, 8.71% and 8.64% in Epinions, respectively, and 7.81%, 11.28% and 11.58% in Ciao, respectively. *With homophily regularization, hTrust is more robust to the sparsity problem of trust prediction.*

We have the following observations:

- The performance of RS, PCC and JC is much better than that of randomly guessing, further demonstrating the existence of homophily in trust relations. We also note that RS and PCC obtain better performance than JC. It supports that users rating the same items might have very different preferences.
- *simTP*, combining both trust propagation and rating similarity, outperforms both *TP* and similarity-based methods (RS, PCC, JC). We believe that rating infor-

Table 2: Performance of Different Predictors when the Percentage of Testing Trust Relations is Fixed to 10%

Datasets		*TP*	*MF*	*hTrust*
Epinions	50%	0.1201	0.1291	0.1578
	55%	0.1327	0.1401	0.1689
	60%	0.1335	0.1454	0.1751
	65%	0.1437	0.1555	0.1799
	70%	0.1473	0.1611	0.1821
	80%	0.1521	0.1643	0.1872
	90%	0.1558	0.1688	0.1900
Ciao	50%	0.0831	0.0988	0.1450
	55%	0.0902	0.1025	0.1496
	60%	0.0943	0.1079	0.1537
	65%	0.0957	0.1109	0.1591
	70%	0.0983	0.1132	0.1613
	80%	0.1009	0.1163	0.1649
	90%	0.1027	0.1185	0.1650

mation provides complementary information beyond trust networks for trust prediction.

- Comparing *MF* and *triNMF* with *TP*, we note that low-rank matrix factorization methods obtain better performance than trust propagation.
- Our proposed framework obtains better performance than *triNMF*. As mentioned above, *triNMF* is a variant of the proposed framework without homophily regularization, hence, these results directly demonstrate that homophily regularization can improve the performance of trust prediction. Furthermore, it also outperforms *simTP*, which also takes advantage of both existing trust relations and rating information, suggesting the effectiveness of homophily regularization in terms of capturing rating information.

In summary, with the help of homophily regularization, the proposed framework always outperforms all the baseline methods and its variant. In the next subsection, we investigate more details about the impact of homophily regularization on the proposed framework.

5.3 Impact of Homophily Regularization

The parameter λ is introduced to control the contribution from homophily regularization for our proposed framework hTrust. Therefore we investigate the impact of homophily regularization via analyzing how the changes of λ affect the performance of hTrust in terms of the trust prediction accuracy. We vary the value of λ as $\{0, 0.01, 0.1, 0.3, 0.5, 0.7, 1, 10, 1e2\}$ and the results are shown in Figure 7(a) and Figure 7(b) for Epinions and Ciao, respectively.

In general, with the increase of λ, the performance in Epinions and Ciao shows similar patterns: first increasing, reaching its peak value and then degrading rapidly. These patterns can be used to determine the optimal value of λ for hTrust in practice. In particular, it can be observed,

- when λ is increased from 0, eliminating the impact of homophily regularization on hTrust, to 0.01, the performance improves a lot, suggesting that homophily regularization can significantly improve the performance of trust prediction.

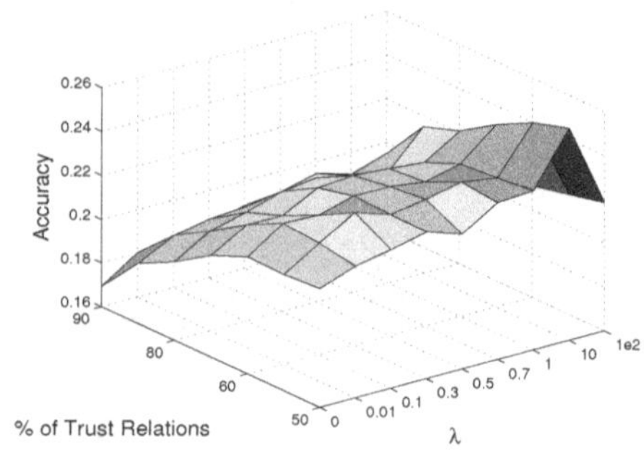

(a) Epinions

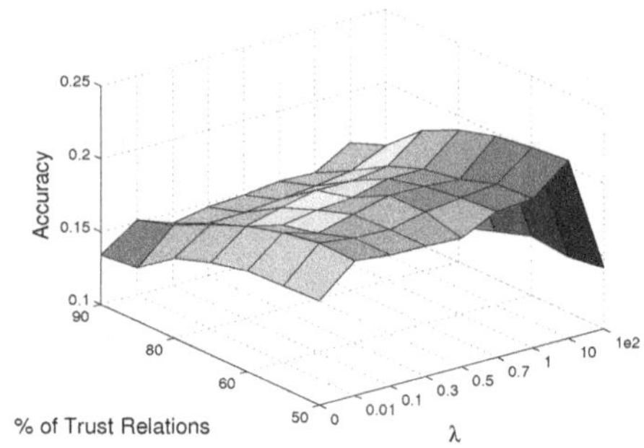

(b) Ciao

Figure 7: Effect of Homophily Regularization

- hTrust achieves its best performance when $\lambda = 10$, further demonstrating the importance of homophily regularization in hTrust.
- From $\lambda = 10$ to $\lambda = 1e2$, the performance decreases rapidly. When λ is very large, homophily regularization dominates the learning process and the learned latent presentation is inaccurate. For example, when $\lambda \to +\infty$, we will obtain a trivial solution: all $\mathbf{U}(i,:)(1 \leq i \leq n)$ are exactly the same.

In summary, an appropriate combination of matrix factorization and homophily regularization can greatly improve the performance of trust prediction.

5.4 Impact of Homophily Coefficient

Homophily coefficient $\zeta(i,j)$ controls the distance of u_i and u_j in the latent space. In this paper, we employ three widely used measures for homophily coefficient, i.e., Jaccard's coefficient, Rating Similarity and Pearson Correlation Coefficient. To investigate the impact from homophily coefficient, we try to answer the following three questions through experiments,

- Among JC, RS and PCC, which measure of homophily coefficient is more effective?
- What is the performance of our proposed framework if we discard homophily coefficients by giving equal homophily coefficients to all pairs of users?
- If we randomly assign homophily coefficients to all pairs of users, what is the performance of our proposed framework hTrust?

Table 3: Different Measures of Homophily Coefficient. Note that $\zeta(i,j) = random$ means we randomly assign homophily coefficients ,while $\zeta(i,j) = 1$ indicates that homophily coefficients for all pairs of users are set to 1

Datasets		$\zeta(i,j) = JC(i,j)$	$\zeta(i,j) = PCC(i,j)$	$\zeta(i,j) = RS(i,j)$	$\zeta(i,j) = random$	$\zeta(i,j) = 1$
Epinions	50%	0.2382	0.2415	0.2569	0.2172	0.2192
	55%	0.2301	0.2354	0.2517	0.2153	0.2208
	60%	0.2227	0.2285	0.2434	0.2027	0.2071
	65%	0.2131	0.2196	0.2326	0.1907	0.1966
	70%	0.2019	0.2073	0.2268	0.1799	0.1856
	80%	0.1871	0.1937	0.2072	0.1558	0.1697
	90%	0.1732	0.1753	0.1900	0.1433	0.1498
Ciao	50%	0.1967	0.2098	0.2220	0.1630	0.1742
	55%	0.1941	0.2041	0.2193	0.1728	0.1721
	60%	0.1865	0.2069	0.2158	0.1585	0.1627
	65%	0.1780	0.1958	0.2082	0.1591	0.1613
	70%	0.1639	0.1820	0.1966	0.1479	0.1491
	80%	0.1441	0.1618	0.1749	0.1242	0.1304
	90%	0.1319	0.1502	0.1650	0.1214	0.1268

Table 3 demonstrates the performance of the proposed framework with different measures of homophily coefficient. In the table, $\zeta(i,j) = random$ means we randomly assign homophily coefficients within $[0,1]$,while $\zeta(i,j) = 1$ indicates that homophily coefficients for all pairs of users are set to 1. From the table, we observe answers to the questions proposed at the beginning of this subsection:

- RS obtains the best performance among the three measures of homophily coefficient, i.e., JC, RS and PCC. We also note that RS and PCC always obtain better performance than JC. It suggests that different users might have different tastes to the same item.
- Compared to JC, RS and PCC, the performance degrades when we assign equal homophily coefficient, i.e.,$\zeta(i,j) = 1$. JC, RS and PCC can improve the performance of trust prediction.
- Among the measures of homophily coefficient, most of the time, random assignment of homophily coefficients obtains the worst performance. Homophily coefficient should not be a random value.

After answering the three questions, we can conclude that (1) JC, RS and PCC can help our framework obtain better performance; (2) we cannot either discard homophily coefficient from our framework or simply use some random values to denote homophily coefficients.

6. RELATED WORK

Trust plays an important role in helping online users collect reliable information and trust prediction, inferring unknown trust relations among pairs of users, attracts more and more attention in recent years [7, 5, 14, 10, 17, 13, 1]. Existing trust prediction methods can be roughly divided into two categories: unsupervised trust prediction [7, 5, 14] and supervised trust prediction [10, 17, 13].

Most existing unsupervised trust prediction methods are based on trust propagation. Several atomic propagations are proposed in [7] such as direct propagation, cocitation propagation, transpose propagation and trust coupling propagation. It also discusses the propagation of distrust and develop a formal framework of trust propagation schemes. Various properties of trust such as transitivity, composability and asymmetry are discussed by Golbeck in [5] and based on these properties, algorithms for inferring binary and continuous trust values from trust networks are proposed. The continuous trust inference algorithm, *TidalTrust*, leverages the path length from the source to sink and various properties of continuous ratings [5]. Trust propagation based methods strongly depend on existing trust relations among users and they might fail when existing trust relations are sparse. In [1], rating similarity is exploited to enrich traditional trust propagation methods. This work demonstrates that predicting trust is more successful for pairs of users that are similar to each other if we combine the topology of the trust network with rating similarity.

Supervised trust prediction methods first construct features from available sources and then train a binary classifier based on these features by considering the existence of trust relations as labels. In [10], a taxonomy is developed to systematically organize an extensive set of features for predicting trust relations. The features include user and interaction factors. User factors contain rater-related, writer-related, or commenter-related. The latter captures various interactions between the users. Viet-An Nguyen et al. [17] proposes various trust prediction models based on a well-studied Trust Antecedent Framework used in management science, capturing the three following factors: ability, benevolence and integrity. Each factor is approximated through a set of quantitative features. For example, the features for integrity are called trustworthiness, equal to the number of trust statements the user receives while ability are the features that compute the average rating given by a rater to the reviews written by a particular reviewer and the number of reviews rated by the rater. In [13] , various features based on writer-reviewer interactions are extracted and used in personalized and cluster-based classification methods. As mentioned above, these methods have inherent limitations. The huge disproportion of pairs of users with (positive samples) and without relations (negative samples) makes the classification problem extremely unbalanced and the performance of these methods are sensitive to the sampled negative samples [23]. Trust has multiple facets and people place trust differently on different people [21]. Considering heterogeneous trust relations and their evolution can improve various trust-related applications such as trust prediction and trust-aware recommendation [22].

7. CONCLUSION

In this paper, we study the problem of exploiting homophily effect for trust prediction. First we conduct experiments on datasets from real-world product review sites to demonstrate the existence of homophily in trust relations. Homophily regularization is then introduced to capture homophily effect in trust relations. An unsupervised framework is proposed, incorporating low-rank matrix factorization and homophily regularization. Extensive experiments are conducted to evaluate the proposed framework on real-world trust relation datasets and the experimental results demonstrate the effectiveness of our proposed framework as well as the role of homophily regularization for trust prediction.

There are several interesting directions for future work. In the current work, homophily regularization is utilized under an unsupervised scenario. As mentioned above, homophily regularization can be easily extended for supervised learning methods via graph regularization. Hence one direction of our future work is to examine the effect of homophily regularization on supervised trust predictors. Previous work demonstrated that homophily is widely observed in other relations such as following relations in Twitter; another direction of our future work is to generalize homophily regularization to other relations. Users might change their preferences over time, indicating their homophily coefficients might evolve. In the future, we will further study homophily regularization with temporal dynamics for trust prediction.

Acknowledgments

The work is, in part, supported by ARO (#025071) and NSF (#IIS-1217466).

8. REFERENCES

[1] P. Borzymek, M. Sydow, and A. Wierzbicki. Enriching trust prediction model in social network with user rating similarity. In *International Conference on Computational Aspects of Social Networks*, 2009.

[2] C. Ding, T. Li, and M. Jordan. Nonnegative matrix factorization for combinatorial optimization: Spectral clustering, graph matching, and clique finding. In *ICDM*, 2008.

[3] Y. Hu, A. John, F. Wang,and S. Kambhampati. ET-LDA: Joint Topic Modeling for Aligning Events and their Twitter Feedback. In *AAAI*, 2012.

[4] D. Dunlavy, T. Kolda, and E. Acar. Temporal link prediction using matrix and tensor factorizations. *TKDD*, 2011.

[5] J. Golbeck. Generating predictive movie recommendations from trust in social networks. *Trust Management*, 2006.

[6] J. Golbeck. Trust and nuanced profile similarity in online social networks. *ACM Transactions on the Web*, 3(4):1–33, 2009.

[7] R. Guha, R. Kumar, P. Raghavan, and A. Tomkins. Propagation of trust and distrust. In *WWW*, 2004.

[8] Y. Koren. Factorization meets the neighborhood: a multifaceted collaborative filtering model. In *KDD*, 2008.

[9] D. Liben-Nowell and J. Kleinberg. The link-prediction problem for social networks. *Journal of the American society for information science and technology*, 2007.

[10] H. Liu, E. Lim, H. Lauw, M. Le, A. Sun, J. Srivastava, and Y. Kim. Predicting trusts among users of online communities: an epinions case study. In *EC*, 2008.

[11] Y. Lu, P. Tsaparas, A. Ntoulas, and L. Polanyi. Exploiting social context for review quality prediction. In *WWW*, 2010.

[12] H. Ma, D. Zhou, C. Liu, M. Lyu, and I. King. Recommender systems with social regularization. In *WSDM*, 2011.

[13] N. Ma, E. Lim, V. Nguyen, A. Sun, and H. Liu. Trust relationship prediction using online product review data. In *Proceeding of the 1st ACM international workshop on Complex networks meet information & knowledge management*, pages 47–54. ACM, 2009.

[14] P. Massa and P. Avesani. Controversial users demand local trust metrics: An experimental study on epinions.com community. In *Proceedings of the National Conference on Artificial Intelligence*, 2005.

[15] M. McPherson, L. Smith-Lovin, and J. Cook. Birds of a feather: Homophily in social networks. *Annual review of sociology*, 2001.

[16] A. Menon and C. Elkan. Link prediction via matrix factorization. *Machine Learning and Knowledge Discovery in Databases*, 2011.

[17] V. Nguyen, E. Lim, J. Jiang, and A. Sun. To trust or not to trust? predicting online trusts using trust antecedent framework. In *ICDM*, 2009.

[18] S. Oyama, K. Hayashi, and H. Kashima. Cross-temporal link prediction. In *ICDM*, 2011.

[19] M. Richardson and P. Domingos. Mining knowledge-sharing sites for viral marketing. In *KDD*, 2002.

[20] J. Tang, X. Wang, and H. Liu. Integrating Social Media Data for Community Detection. In *Modeling and Mining Ubiquitous Social Media*, 2012.

[21] J. Tang, H. Gao, and H. Liu. mTrust: Discerning multi-faceted trust in a connected world. In *WSDM*, 2012.

[22] J. Tang, H. Gao, H. Liu, and A. Das Sarma. eTrust: Understanding trust evolution in an online world. In *KDD*, 2012.

[23] D. Wang, D. Pedreschi, C. Song, F. Giannotti, and A. Barabási. Human mobility, social ties, and link prediction. In *KDD*,2011.

[24] J. Weng, E. Lim, J. Jiang, and Q. He. Twitterrank: finding topic-sensitive influential twitterers. In *WSDM*, 2010.

[25] L. Peng, R. Yu, K. Selcuk, and X. Wang. Object and Combination Shedding Schemes for Adaptive Media Workflow Execution. In *TKDE*, 2010.

[26] S. Zhu, K. Yu, Y. Chi, and Y. Gong. Combining content and link for classification using matrix factorization. In *SIGIR*, 2007.

[27] C. Ziegler and J. Golbeck. Investigating interactions of trust and interest similarity. *Decision Support Systems*, 2007.

Efficient and Effective Retrieval using Selective Pruning

Nicola Tonellotto
Information Science and Technologies Institute
National Research Council
56124 Pisa, Italy
nicola.tonellotto@isti.cnr.it

Craig Macdonald, Iadh Ounis
School of Computing Science
University of Glasgow
Glasgow, G12 8QQ, UK
{craig.macdonald,iadh.ounis}@glasgow.ac.uk

ABSTRACT

Retrieval can be made more efficient by deploying dynamic pruning strategies such as WAND, which do not degrade effectiveness up to a given rank. It is possible to increase the efficiency of such techniques by pruning more 'aggressively'. However, this may reduce effectiveness. In this work, we propose a novel selective framework that determines the appropriate amount of pruning aggressiveness on a per-query basis, thereby increasing overall efficiency without significantly reducing overall effectiveness. We postulate two hypotheses about the queries that should be pruned more aggressively, which generate two approaches within our framework, based on query performance predictors and query efficiency predictors, respectively. We thoroughly experiment to ascertain the efficiency and effectiveness impacts of the proposed approaches, as part of a search engine deploying state-of-the-art learning to rank techniques. Our results on 50 million documents of the TREC ClueWeb09 collection show that by using query efficiency predictors to target inefficient queries, we observe that a 36% reduction in mean response time and a 50% reduction of the response times experienced by the slowest 10% of queries can be achieved while still ensuring effectiveness.

Categories and Subject Descriptors: H.3.3 [Information Storage & Retrieval]: Information Search & Retrieval

Keywords: Efficient & Effective Search Engines, Dynamic Pruning, Learning to Rank, Query Efficiency Prediction

1. INTRODUCTION

Web search engines and other large-scale information retrieval (IR) systems are not just concerned with the quality of search results (also known as *effectiveness*), but also with the speed with which the results are obtained (*efficiency*). These aspects form a natural tradeoff that all search engines must address, in that many approaches that increase effectiveness may have a corresponding impact on efficiency due to their complex nature [35].

Increasingly, search engines deploy learning to rank approaches, whereby a learned model combines many features into an effective approach for ranking [20]. Our work is firmly placed in a learning to rank setting, where a typical search engine consists of three phases of operation, as follows (illustrated in Figure 1):

WSDM'13, February 4–8, 2013, Rome, Italy.

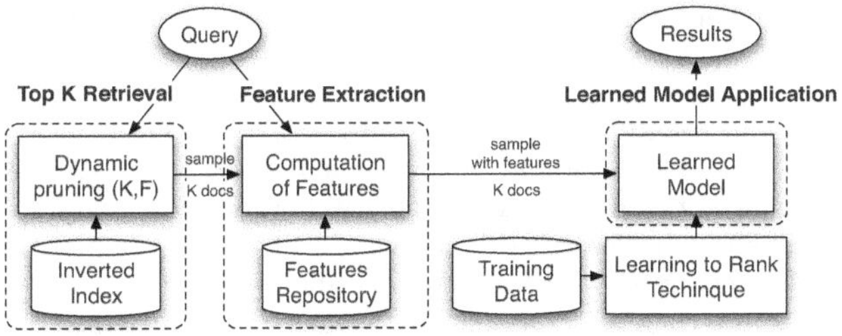

Figure 1: Phases of retrieval by a search engine.

Top K Retrieval: An initial ranking strategy selects K documents from the inverted index, identified using a single feature (often the BM25 weighting model) [7, 20]. Dynamic pruning strategies such as WAND can be applied to efficiently generate the set of K results (called the *sample* [20, 25]).

Feature Extraction: Computation of additional features for each document in the sample, such as other weighting models, including those calculated on different fields (anchor text, title, etc.) or query independent features (URL length, PageRank, etc.).

Learned Model Application: Re-ranking of the sample results by the application of a learned model, obtained by earlier learning on training data, to increase effectiveness compared to the sample [20].

The first phase of the retrieval process – where the K documents of the sample are identified – is data intensive, and hence, as we will later show, has the largest impact on efficiency. For this reason, efficient retrieval strategies such as the WAND dynamic pruning strategy can be deployed. Indeed, WAND can enhance efficiency by avoiding the scoring of documents that can never be retrieved in the top K results, without degrading the effectiveness up to rank K, known as *safe-to-rank-K*. WAND can be made more efficient by reducing the number of documents K to be retrieved. It is possible to further increase the efficiency of WAND by applying the pruning more *aggressively*, but at loss of the guaranteed safeness, with possible degradations in the effectiveness of the results. The Top K Retrieval phase also impacts overall effectiveness in two manners: (i) Decreasing K such that a smaller sample is obtained may miss relevant documents at deeper ranks, which will have no chance of being re-ranked towards the top by the learned model, hence degrading the overall effectiveness of the search engine; (ii) The pruning aggressiveness used to obtain the sample may also impact the resulting effectiveness after re-ranking by the learned model, as the sample is no longer safe-to-rank-K.

In this work, we aim to ensure effective and efficient retrieval, by selecting which queries should be pruned more aggressively. In particular, not all queries have similar effectiveness. Moreover, not all queries have equal response time, even with dynamic pruning [23] - yet search engine users are not willing to wait long for queries to be answered [33]. Hence, our work addresses the following key question: for which queries should the pruning be applied more aggressively to obtain efficient yet effective retrieval? We examine two novel approaches for selecting queries that can be aggressively pruned: those that are predicted to be easy, and hence can tolerate a lower quality sample; and those that are predicted to be particularly inefficient. We postulate that easier queries have more relevant documents highly ranked within the sample, and hence can be more aggressively pruned. On the other hand, targeting queries that will be inefficient can attain more efficiency gains, but may have more impact on effectiveness. Moreover, as the effectiveness and efficiency of a query cannot be known before retrieval commences, our approaches use pre-retrieval query performance predictors [8] and query efficiency predictors [23], to select an appropriate amount of pruning for each query.

The contributions of this work are as follows: We provide an analysis on how the parameters affecting the aggressiveness of a dynamic pruning strategy impact on the effectiveness of a learned model; Moreover, we propose a selective pruning framework for identifying the appropriate pruning setting of a dynamic pruning strategy on a per-query basis, to ensure efficient yet effective retrieval. Two methods are proposed, based on predicting the effectiveness of the query, or on predicting its efficiency. To the best of our knowledge, this is the first work on the selective application of dynamic pruning on a per-query basis. Experiments are conducted on a standard TREC Web test collection of 50 million documents, deploying learned models from two learning to rank techniques. Our results show that marked improvements in efficiency can be obtained while ensuring effectiveness, with the strongest results being obtained when the queries that are predicted to be inefficient are aggressively pruned.

The remainder of this paper is structured as follows: Section 2 provides background material on dynamic pruning for efficient retrieval; In Section 3, we review related work that examined both efficiency and effectiveness; Section 4 introduces the proposed framework for selectively determining pruning on a per-query basis; Section 5 details the experimental setup used in this paper; Section 6 analyses the efficiency and effectiveness of different pruning settings for the K and F parameters. Experiments and conclusions follow in Sections 7 & 8, respectively.

2. BACKGROUND

Even in large search engines, the matching of documents in the Top K Retrieval phase still uses the classical inverted index data structure [14], by traversing the postings lists for each query term. Moreover, due to its data intensive nature [23], we will later show that this represents the largest contribution to the time that a search engine takes to retrieve documents in response to a query.

Various techniques have been proposed that improve efficiency by pruning documents that are unlikely to be retrieved. For example, in [3], Anh & Moffat proposed a pruning strategy that uses posting lists pre-sorted by the impact of the postings. Alternatively, documents that are unlikely to be retrieved can be removed from the index [5]. Both approaches can cause possible loss of effectiveness. However, we focus on techniques that can be configured to be *safe-to-rank-K* – i.e., cannot degrade retrieval effectiveness up to a given rank K – and use docid sorted posting lists, since this is deployed by at least one major commercial search engine [14]. In particular, *dynamic pruning* strategies [6, 30, 34][1] aim to avoid the scoring of postings for documents that cannot make the top K retrieved set, thereby saving disk access, decompression and score computation costs. This is achieved by maintaining additional information during retrieval, namely: a *threshold* τ, which is the minimum score that documents must achieve to have a chance to be present in the final top K results; and, for each query term, a *term upper bound*, which is the maximal contribution of that particular term to any document score. The upper bound is usually obtained by pre-scanning the posting lists of each term at indexing time, to record the maximum score found in each posting list [21].

The WAND strategy [6] – which represents the state-of-the-art in safe dynamic pruning [16] – repeatedly calculates a *pivot term*, based on the terms that the next document must contain to exceed threshold τ. The next document containing the pivot term is the *pivot document*, which will be the next document to be fully scored. In this manner, WAND makes use of skipping [28] forward in posting lists, which reduces posting list decompression overheads, and can reduce IO, with resulting improvements in efficiency [16, 21]. Moreover, importantly for our work, the overall tradeoff between efficiency and effectiveness in WAND can be adjusted by changing parameters affecting the threshold and the size of K. A key novelty of our work is showing how these parameters can be automatically selected for each query.

3. RELATED WORK

This paper proposes a selective framework for adjusting the effectiveness and efficiency of WAND on a per-query basis. In particular, we build upon the experiments of Broder et al. [6], who examined how the efficiency and effectiveness of WAND are affected by increasing the *aggressiveness* of the pruning. In particular, two parameters were shown to affect the efficiency of WAND. Firstly, with a smaller K, the threshold τ, i.e., the current minimum score that documents must achieve to have a chance to be present in the final top K results, is higher, and hence more pruning of low-scoring documents can be achieved. Secondly, since a new document is scored only when its approximate score beats the current threshold τ, the threshold can be artificially increased by using a new threshold $\tau' = F \cdot \tau$, where $F \geq 1$ is a tunable parameter. In doing so, the dynamic pruning strategy is not guaranteed to be safe-to-rank-K anymore, but new documents are scored only if they can achieve a score F times greater than the current threshold τ, with resulting improvements in efficiency. The experiments in [6] showed that increasing F and decreasing K did increase efficiency, but that effectiveness was impacted for a sufficiently large F. However, their work predates modern IR, where machine learned models are applied directly on the ranking produced by the dynamic pruning strategy. In contrast, in our work, we not only show the impact of K and F on a Web corpus that is 30 times larger than that used in [6], but we also investigate the impact of the pruning parameters on the effectiveness of a learned model, where the lower ranks of the sample are also important. Moreover, we show how different K and F can be selected on a per-query basis to attain efficient retrieval.

[1]We omit the database-focused threshold algorithms of Fagin et al. [15], which assume lists sorted by score, while we assume docid-based sorting.

There exists some previous work on selective approaches for information retrieval. For instance, Amati et al. [2] noted that query expansion underperforms for difficult queries. By identifying such difficult queries using *query performance predictors* (QPP), they were able to selectively apply query expansion, i.e. decide whether to apply query expansion on a per-query basis. Similarly, Cronen-Townsend et al. also used query performance predictors for selective query expansion [13]. Plachouras & Ounis [31] applied different retrieval approaches for Web search on a per-query basis. Other recent work tackles the efficiency/effectiveness trade-off. In particular, Wang et al. [35] devised a tradeoff metric that measures both effectiveness and efficiency. By using this within a learning to rank technique, they could identify uni- and bi-gram query term "features" to discard within the Sequential Dependence model [26], to balance efficiency and effectiveness. However, as their work is not concerned with more common document features, it is less widely applicable.

In a work applicable to document features for learning to rank, Wang et al. [36] observed that the expense of applying a feature was related to the number of documents on which that feature was computed. As only the final top-ranked documents are required, they adapted a learning to rank technique such that it also selects how many low-ranked documents should be discarded before the application of each feature. Hence the output of applying the learned model is an effective ranking shorter than the input sample, with features calculated on a reduced number of documents. In our work, we will show that the initial Top K Retrieval is the most expensive of the three phases. While the approach of [36] places emphasis on reducing the number of documents for feature calculations, we focus on adjusting the efficiency and effectiveness of the Top K Retrieval phase.

Learned models encompassing additive regression trees, such as those obtained from the LambdaMART [37] learning to rank technique, are more complex to apply than those that are simple linear combinations of feature values (e.g. [27]). For this reason, Cambazoglu et al. [7], showed how such regression trees could be pruned at retrieval time - although effectiveness could be slightly degraded. This work is orthogonal to ours, in that it could be used to reduce the duration of the Learned Model Application phase. However, instead of pruning regression trees from the learned model, our work aims to reduce the expense in identifying the documents in the first Top K Retrieval phase.

No work from the literature has examined the full picture concerning the application of dynamic pruning within the context of a learned model, such that the interplay between effectiveness and efficiency is examined. Indeed, in the next section, we propose a framework that selects an appropriate K and F settings for WAND on a per-query basis, ensuring effective yet efficient retrieval. Differing from previous work, this framework varies the aggressiveness of the dynamic pruning strategy deployed in the Top K Retrieval phase on a per-query basis, by making use of efficiency and effectiveness predictions.

4. SELECTIVE PRUNING FRAMEWORK

Dynamic pruning techniques such as WAND permit the efficient retrieval compared to an exhaustive scoring of all documents containing occurrences of every query term. For $F = 1$, the produced ranking is safe-to-rank-K. As mentioned above, WAND can prune documents more aggressively by increasing a factor F on the current threshold τ, or by retrieving less documents (reducing K). Changes to K and F offer efficiency advantages, but can have disadvantages in terms of effectiveness. For instance, if K is decreased, the ranking up to K documents is still safe, however as the sample may have less relevant documents for the learner to identify, the learned model effectiveness can be degraded. On the other hand, while increasing F no longer guarantees that the document ranking will have the same effectiveness as for $F = 1$, Broder et al. [6] showed that the top ranked documents often remain unchanged for small values of $F > 1$ while still permitting efficiency benefits. However, as mentioned in Section 3, they did not consider the impact of pruning on the effectiveness of learned models, which often markedly re-rank documents from deep within the sample.

Our proposed selective pruning framework obtains efficiency benefits by applying aggressive pruning for queries where possible, based on appropriate selections of K and F when generating the sample. In particular, the selection is based upon two hypotheses about which queries can be more aggressively pruned without damaging overall effectiveness. For each of these hypotheses, based on a prediction for each query, a selection of the appropriate K and F values is made. The outline for the selective pruning framework is shown in Algorithm 1: steps 2-4 follow the familiar outline of the three retrieval phases from Figure 1; in step 1, instead of setting K and F uniformly for all queries, the SELECT(•) function selects appropriate values for each query, taking into account a prediction from PREDICT(q) for query q.

Algorithm 1 Selective Pruning Framework

```
    Input:   The query q
    Output:  The top K ranked documents
1: {K, F} ← SELECT(PREDICT(q))
2: Sample S ← WAND(q,K,F)
3: Features T ← EXTRACT(q,S)
4: Results A ← APPLY(T, MODEL(K,F))
```

We investigate two approaches – based on predicted effectiveness (Sections 4.1) and efficiency (Section 4.2) – for selecting the settings of pruning parameters K and F for WAND for each query. Each approach uses different instantiations of both SELECT(•) and PREDICT(q).

4.1 Pruning Effective Queries

Marginally unsafe pruning (e.g. $F = 2$ or 3) by WAND can leave the top-ranked documents unchanged [6]. Moreover, given the usual effectiveness of the weighting model used to generate the sample, relevant documents are expected to appear at high ranks in the sample. However, when the output of WAND is re-ranked as part of a learned model, the learned model may rank highly documents that were originally ranked quite low in the sample. Such lowly-ranked sample documents are more likely to be omitted by an aggressive unsafe setting of WAND, thereby possibly degrading the effectiveness of the learned model. We postulate that some queries are 'easier' than others, where the applied learned model does not have to re-rank relevant documents from deep in the document ranking. In other words, K is unnecessarily large for such queries, and their effectiveness is less likely to be affected by more aggressive pruning. However, it is impossible to know a-priori how large a sample is necessary for effective retrieval for a given query. Instead, we turn to the field of pre-retrieval query performance prediction [8], where various techniques have been developed to predict the effectiveness of a query before retrieval commences. Hence, we arrive at our first hypothesis:

Hypothesis 1. *Queries that are predicted to be easier should be more aggressively pruned to benefit response time while minimising effectiveness degradations.*

Based on this hypothesis, in Section 6, we propose a definition for $\text{SELECT}_{QPP}(\bullet)$ using the predicted effectiveness $\widehat{E}(q)$ of query q, as determined by pre-retrieval query performance predictor(s) [19] (QPP).

4.2 Pruning Inefficient Queries

While efficiency may be improved by applying WAND compared to an exhaustive scoring of all documents containing occurrences of every query term, the response time of a query q (denoted $R(q)$) can markedly differ from another query with similar surface characteristics (e.g. number of query terms, length of posting lists) [23].

Given that some queries are particularly inefficient, they should naturally be targeted for improving efficiency. The key to this intuition is being able to predict the queries that will be inefficient, and hence predict the response time of the query, denoted $\widehat{R}(q)$. Indeed, the amount of pruning possible by WAND for different queries is variable, depending on the distribution of scores among the postings of the constituent query terms [23]. Essentially, the pruning difficulty of a query is related to how quickly the threshold τ rises to exclude documents as retrieval proceeds. Queries for which the high value documents occur more towards the start of the posting lists are more likely to be easier to prune [23]. However, as there is a universe of possible queries with different constituent terms, Macdonald et al. [23] showed that an accurate model for predicting the response time of a given query can be obtained by aggregating statistics for the constituent query terms. These statistics - such as the number of postings, and the number of postings with scores within 5% of the upper bound - can be calculated at indexing time, and hence can be easily obtained as the query arrives, such that the response time for a query can be quickly and accurately predicted before retrieval commences. Hence, in this work, we obtain $\widehat{R}(q)$ from response time estimates from query efficiency predictors (QEP). The predicted response time is then used to select the K and F values before the IO-intensive dynamic pruning phase starts:[2]

Hypothesis 2. *Queries that are predicted to take longer to retrieve should be more aggressively pruned to benefit response time while minimising effectiveness degradations.*

Based on this hypothesis, in Section 6 we propose a definition for $\text{SELECT}_{QEP}(\bullet)$ using the predicted response time of a query $\widehat{R}(q)$. In the following section, we provide the experimental setup, which we use to obtain the empirical analysis, from which the definitions for $\text{SELECT}_{QPP}(\bullet)$ and $\text{SELECT}_{QEP}(\bullet)$ follow.

5. EXPERIMENTAL SETUP

In the following, we describe our experimental setup in terms of the corpus and queries used (Section 5.1), and the three retrieval phases described in Section 1: Top K Retrieval (Section 5.2), Feature Extraction (Section 5.3), and Learned Model Application (Section 5.4). We describe how efficiency is measured in Section 5.5. Finally, the setups for query effectiveness and efficiency predictors are described in Sections 5.6 & 5.7, respectively.

[2]Our experiments have found that an efficiency prediction can be made in a few milliseconds.

5.1 Documents & Queries

The experiments in the following sections are conducted using the large TREC ClueWeb09 category B corpus, which consists of 50 million Web documents. ClueWeb09 provides a larger, more realistic Web setting than other TREC Web corpora, such as GOV2. Indeed, this corpus has both TREC topics with relevance assessments, as well as a generally available query log. As we wish to measure and analyse both efficiency and effectiveness, we use two separate topics sets, for measuring each in separation.

Best practices in efficiency experiments demand a large number of queries, however the number used in the literature can vary widely, from the 50-150 TREC topics used in [35] to thousands of queries from commercial search engines used in [7]. In this work, we use a set of consecutive user queries from a generally available real search engine log, thereby measuring the mean query response time for retrieval. In particular, we select the first 1,000 queries of the MSN 2006 query log [12], without any stemming and without removing standard stopwords. This amounts to 981 queries (queries with no matching documents are discarded). This query set exhibits all of the expected properties of a query log, such as frequently repeated 'head' queries and a tail of infrequent queries. The mean query length is 2.7 terms. For training/testing, the query set is split chronologically: 500 for training, 481 for testing. Finally, we note that the LETOR learning to rank datasets [20] are not suitable for our experiments as they use a safe sample with fixed $K = 1000$.

A query set with relevance assessments is required for measuring effectiveness. For this reason, we use the 150 topics of the TREC 2009-2011 Web tracks, which form a test collection based on ClueWeb09 [10]. In particular, for the purposes of learning to rank, these topics are mixed and split into three equally sized training, validation and test sets. Effectiveness is measured using NDCG@20, an official TREC Web track measure [10].

5.2 Top K Retrieval Phase

We index ClueWeb09 using the Terrier IR platform,[3] applying no stemming, and keeping all stopwords. Term positions are recorded within the compressed inverted index, as well as terms from the URLs and titles of documents, and any incoming anchor text, as separate fields [22]. We also build skip lists for the inverted index [28], with a skip pointer every 1,000 postings. The resulting index size is 126GB.

During the Top K Retrieval phase, the WAND [6] dynamic pruning strategy is used to select K documents, where each document has been scored for each query using the parameter-free DPH Divergence from Randomness weighting model [1]. DPH is a parameter-free model that exhibits similar effectiveness to BM25 without requiring any training [1]. As an effective default setting for WAND, we use the safe $F = 1$, and $K = 1000$. The latter is the sample size used in the LETOR learning to rank v3.0 datasets [20].

5.3 Feature Extraction Phase

We deploy 33 document features in the feature extraction phase of our ranking approach, covering the most typically applied categories of query independent (encompassing URL, link analysis and content quality features) and query dependent features (including term weighting models and term dependence models). Indeed, many of these features have been shown to create effective learned models on the ClueWeb09 corpus [32]. Table 1 lists the deployed features.

[3]`http://terrier.org/`

Type	Features	Total
QD	Weighting models (DPH [1], PL2 [1], BM25, Dirichlet Language Models, Matching Query Terms [32])	21
QD	Fields-based model (PL2F [22])	1
QI	URL/link analysis features (e.g. PageRank, Outlinks)	3
QI	Quality features (e.g. spamminess [11], field lengths, fraction of stopwords, table text [4])	5
QI	Click feature (click count)	1
QD	term dependence/proximity models (MRF [26], pBiL [29])	2

Table 1: Deployed features for document ranking.

While query independent features are retained in memory, the calculation of additional query dependent features after the first phase has ended requires access to the postings of the query terms. To facilitate this, we adapt WAND such that the matched postings of any document making the top K are retained in memory; any document expelled from the top K (due to another higher scoring document) has its retained postings discarded. As the postings contain frequencies, positions and field information, additional query dependent features can be efficiently calculated.

5.4 Learned Model Phase

We create learned models for the 33 document feature using 2 different learning to rank techniques namely:

Automatic Feature Selection (AFS) [27] obtains a weight for the linear combination of the most effective feature at each iteration to the features selected in the previous iteration(s). In our implementation, we use simulated annealing to find the combination weight for each feature that maximises NDCG. The weight of a newly selected feature is obtained without retraining the weights of those features already selected. The set of feature weights with the highest performing iteration on the validation data is chosen (in this manner, the validation data is used to determine the correct number of AFS iterations, as suggested by [20]).

LambdaMART [37] deploys gradient boosted regression trees internally, while considering NDCG values within the training of the trees. We use the Jforests implementation [18].[4] A LambdaMART approach was the winning entry in the 2011 Yahoo! learning to rank challenge [9]. The model with the highest validation performance is chosen.

5.5 Measuring Efficiency

All efficiency experiments are made with a dual quad-core Intel Xeon 2.4GHz, with 32GB RAM, using a single monolithic index. Indeed, following Wang et al. [35], we did not use a distributed retrieval setting over multiple smaller indices coordinated by a broker (as might be deployed in a real-world system) as we did not wish to consider unrelated issues such as network latencies. Hence, while our query response times may be larger than would suffice for an interactive environment, this does not detract from the generality of the proposed selective pruning framework.

The mean response times (MRTs) of each of the retrieval phases for $K = 1000$ $F = 1$ are as follows: Top K Retrieval (12.9 s); Feature Extraction (18 ms); Learned Model Application (AFS: 0.71 ms; LambdaMART: 17.44 ms). Considering the fact that [35] directly uses the compression library of Terrier, our larger MRT for the first phase compared to [35] is expected as our index contains 4 additional frequencies per posting (for each field: title, body, anchor text & URL). Moreover, these response times justify our focus on the first retrieval phase to benefit efficiency, as the learned model application costs are negligible. Indeed, in applying the learned models of LambdaMART, we do not use the tree pruning

[4] `http://code.google.com/p/jforests/`

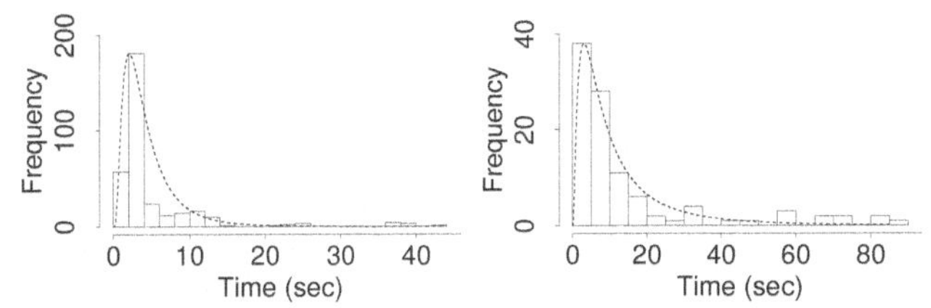

(a) 2 terms (b) 4 terms

Figure 2: Response time distributions for 2 and 4 terms queries (boxes), and fitted log-normal distributions (dashed lines).

method of Cambazoglu et al. [7], as the Feature Extraction and Learned Model Application phases have an insignificant duration compared to the initial Top K Retrieval phase.

5.6 Effectiveness Prediction

Two forms of effectiveness prediction have been proposed in the literature [8]: *pre-retrieval* predictors are calculated solely on statistics from the query, without resorting to inverted index access [19]; in contrast, *post-retrieval* predictors have more evidence, such as the scores or contents of the retrieved documents [13]. In this work, as we require to estimate the effectiveness of a query before retrieval commences such that K and F parameters can be selected, we deploy only existing well-known pre-retrieval predictors, namely: AvICTF, AvIDF, $\gamma 1$ and $\gamma 2$ [19], Similarity Collection Query (SCQ), Normalised SCQ and Maximal SCQ [38]. These seven performance predictors are combined to estimate the effectiveness $\widehat{E}(q)$ of query q, by using gradient boosted regression trees (GBRT) [17] targeting NDCG, based on the 50 training and 50 validation effectiveness queries.

5.7 Efficiency Prediction

Query efficiency prediction [23] allows the response time of a query $R(q)$ to be accurately predicted before retrieval commences, denoted $\widehat{R}(q)$. Following Macdonald et al. [23], we calculate various statistics of each term at indexing time (e.g. maximum score, number of postings, number of posting with score less than 5% from maximum score), which are then combined into features using aggregated functions such as SUM and MAX for each constituent term of a query (more details can be found in [23]). We deploy GBRT [17] to learn the accurate response time predictions, based on the 500 efficiency training queries.

6. ON PRUNING AGGRESSIVENESS

In Section 4, we postulated two hypotheses concerning how query performance and efficiency predictions can be used to select which queries should be aggressively pruned by WAND. In this section, we aim to identify suitable definitions for SELECT(•) within the selective pruning framework of Algorithm 1. To do so, instead of considering all possible values $K > 1$ and $F \geq 1$, we use a set of discrete *candidate* settings that exhibit either good effectiveness or efficiency. In the following, we identify the candidate settings of K and F that the framework can select from in response to a query – this is in line with the methodology applied in previous experiments in identifying candidates within selective approaches (e.g. [2, 31]). Finally, we use the results of this analysis to instantiate definitions for $\text{SELECT}_{QPP}(\bullet)$ and $\text{SELECT}_{QEP}(\bullet)$.

To illustrate the potential for a selective approach that tackles inefficient queries (i.e. Hypothesis 2), Figure 2 shows the distribution of response times of WAND for queries of

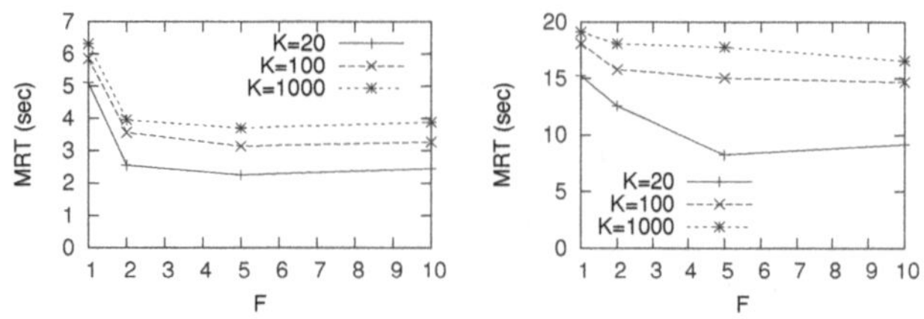

(a) 2 terms (b) 4 terms

Figure 3: Efficiency of different F and K for 2 and 4 terms queries.

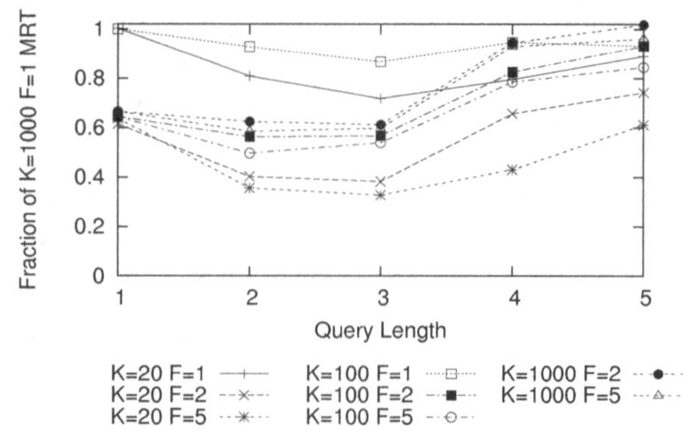

Figure 4: Efficiency improvements: Fraction of MRT exhibited by $K = 1000$, $F = 1$ achieved by various settings of K and F over 1000 queries.

two different lengths. Other query lengths produce similar, scaled distributions. From this, we can see that the response times for each query length approximately follow a log-normal distribution (shown as dashed lines), with a number of queries taking considerably longer than the most frequent response time. These are the queries that we target by the application of the selective pruning framework.

In the following, we analyse the impact of K and F on WAND efficiency (Section 6.1) and effectiveness (Section 6.2). In Section 6.3, we propose definitions for the $\text{SELECT}_{QPP}(\bullet)$ and $\text{SELECT}_{QEP}(\bullet)$ functions.

6.1 Impact on Efficiency

The K and F parameters depict the aggressiveness of pruning, and hence the resulting efficiency of WAND. Broder et al. [6] previously showed the efficiency impact of these parameters on a small corpus. In contrast, we examine these parameters on the 30 times larger ClueWeb09 corpus.

Reducing K: Reducing the K parameter of WAND for a given query causes the threshold τ to rise more quickly, with the effect of allowing pruning to occur more often. This benefits efficiency, as the number of scored postings is reduced and more skipping can be performed. Figure 3 shows the efficiency, measured by the mean response time (MRT) in seconds of the Top K Retrieval phase across the 981 real queries, for two different query lengths. The WAND strategy is used to retrieve the sample (with representative sample sizes of $K = \{20, 100, 1000\}$). From Figure 3, we can see that smaller K values have decreased mean response times.

Increasing F: Instead of reducing the number of retrieved documents to increase the threshold value, the threshold factor F can be used to directly increase the threshold. Indeed, increasing F requires that documents have to contain more query terms before they will be fully scored and admitted to the top K result set. Figure 3 also shows the benefit of different representative threshold factors ($F = \{1, 2, 5, 10\}$). Clearly, increasing F from 1 to 2 produces a marked efficiency benefit for shorter queries, however, this benefit is less marked for longer queries when K is large.

Recall that we aim to identify settings of K and F that lead to overall efficiency benefits. Figure 4 shows the reduction in MRT for various settings across various query lengths, compared to an initial, standard safe setting of $K = 1000$, $F = 1$. From the figure, we observe that increasing F from 1 to 2 has the most marked benefit on efficiency (up to 40% reduction in response time). However, $F = 5$ does not show as much benefit over $F = 2$. Thereafter, MRT improvements are only obtained for reducing K. Therefore the most efficient settings of WAND are $K = 20$ for some $F > 1$.

6.2 Impact on Effectiveness

Increasing F also results in an unsafe and possibly degraded effectiveness, as documents that should have been retrieved in the top K may be omitted. Broder et al. [6] also showed how this impacted on the retrieval effectiveness, when directly measured on the resulting set of documents. However, in our scenario employing learning to rank, the output of K documents from WAND is used as the sample for re-ranking by the learned model. Indeed, varying K also has an impact on the resulting effectiveness of the model. For instance, a sample of size $K = 20$ used as input to a learned model will usually have lower effectiveness in terms of NDCG@20 than a sample of size $K = 100$, as the larger sample is likely to have higher recall, such that more relevant documents can be re-ranked within the top 20.

Figure 5 shows the effectiveness across the test set of the TREC Web track 2009-2011 queries for various K and F values. In particular, in Figure 5 (a), the NDCG@20 for three different sample sizes is plotted as F is varied. We firstly note that the $K = 20$, $K = 100$ and $K = 1000$ samples are super-imposed, as they identically rank documents up to rank 20. However, with respect to the threshold factor, effectiveness across all K values is reduced as F increases. In general, unsafe ranking does not impact on effectiveness to rank 20 for small values of F, which is in line with the findings of earlier experiments by Broder et al. [6]. In terms of recall, Figure 5 (b) shows that both reducing K and increasing F reduces the number of relevant documents identified.

In Figures 5 (c) & (d), the performances of the resulting learned models are shown for the AFS and LambdaMART learning to rank techniques, respectively. For different settings of K and F, we created new learned models for each learner. This is motivated in that the learned models are dependent on the size of the input sample of documents being ranked, since the probability of relevance within the sample increases as the sample size decreases [25]. For example, a learned model obtained on a small sample may apply a feature such as PageRank more aggressively than a learned model obtained from a larger sample. Note that retaining multiple learned models within the search engine is not a significant overhead, as they are lightweight to store and use at querying time, while their learning is conducted offline.

On analysing Figures 5 (c) & (d), we find that, in general, models from the two learners result in markedly increased effectiveness compared to the corresponding sample of the same K and F (Figure 5 (a)). The models are also affected by the decreasing recall of the sample, either as K decreases, or as F increases. In particular, analysing the impact of F, we find that effectiveness is generally decreased for $F > 2$. However, the effectiveness of a learned model obtained

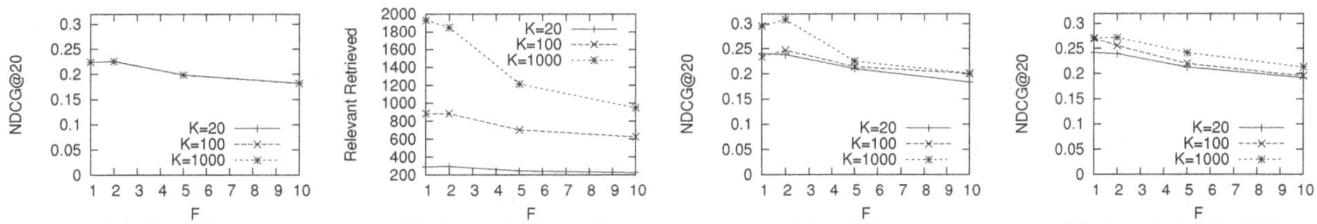

(a) Sample (b) Sample Recall (c) AFS (d) LambdaMART

Figure 5: Effectiveness of the sample and learned models for different F and K.

for $F = 2$ is often comparable (or better) than for $F = 1$. This is caused by the indeterminate nature of unsafe retrieval: unsafeness does not necessarily imply degraded effectiveness by WAND. Indeed, an irrelevant document that is pruned from the sample for $F = 2$ may cause another relevant document to be retrieved that normally would not appear in the top K [24]. When evaluating the output of WAND directly using NDCG@20 (as in Figure 5 (a)), the impact of unsafe retrieval is not marked, as it rarely affects the top 20 documents. However, the effect of unsafe retrieval is, to some extent, magnified by the application of a learned model, which by re-ranking can promote documents from very low ranks in the sample.

Finally, we analyse the impact of K in Figures 5 (c) & (d). As expected, the learned models exhibit higher performance for $K = 1000$. Reducing this to $K = 100$ has some impact, but not as marked as for $K = 20$. This shows the importance of having sufficient relevant documents in the sample for an effective learned model, necessitating using a K as large as possible. Overall, we conclude that when evaluating for high precision (such as NDCG@20), adding a learned model to the output of WAND increases overall effectiveness. However, the learned models are also more sensitive to a large degree of unsafe retrieval (i.e. $F > 2$). Decreasing the number of K sample documents considered for re-ranking by the learned model also results in degraded effectiveness.

6.3 Definitions for SELECT

A search engine can take advantage of our observation that accurate search results can still be obtained when an unsafe ranking is used as input to the learned model (Section 6.2). However, while the use of degraded unsafe samples are desirable to ensure efficiency (Section 6.1), they should be avoided to maximise overall learned model effectiveness.

To use these observations for selecting appropriate WAND settings on a per-query basis, we firstly decide on the K and F values that are appropriate for candidate settings within the definitions of SELECT(•). Based on our analysis of Figures 3 & 4, we identify $K = 20, F = 2$ as a setting that produces the highest efficiency benefit with the least aggressive pruning. However, this setting can markedly degrade the effectiveness of learned models (see Figure 5 (c) and (d)). On the other hand, the $K = 1000, F = 1$ setting is safe, effective, but inefficient. Hence, $K = 1000, F = 1$ and $K = 20, F = 2$ form our candidate settings for WAND that can be selected by definitions of SELECT(•). Next, we propose definitions for SELECT(•) for our two hypotheses.

Selecting on Predicted Effectiveness

Our first hypothesis suggests that when a query is expected to be easier, where relevant documents are likely to be ranked highly in the sample, then the effectiveness of safe retrieval is likely to be sufficiently high, that unsafe retrieval can be applied to increase efficiency without perceivable effectiveness degradation. In contrast, if the query is expected to have few relevant documents, or that these are deeply ranked within the sample, then safe retrieval should be applied to preserve effectiveness. To support this, we examined the Spearman's ρ correlation between the effectiveness of learned models created from $K = 1000$, $F = 1$ and $K = 20$, $F = 2$. Across the 50 effectiveness test queries, we observed $\rho = 0.73$ for AFS and $\rho = 0.81$ for LambdaMART, suggesting that easier queries remain effective even when aggressively pruned. To estimate the difficulty of each query, we apply a combination of 7 pre-retrieval query performance predictors, as described in Section 5.6. Hence, for a newly arrived query q, we compare the estimated effectiveness $\widehat{E}(q)$ with a threshold ϵ to select an appropriate candidate setting of K and F:

$$\text{SELECT}_{QPP}(\text{PREDICT}(q)) = \begin{cases} \{20, 2\} & \text{if } \widehat{E}(q) > \epsilon \\ \{1000, 1\} & \text{otherwise} \end{cases}$$

If the predicted effectiveness $\widehat{E}(q)$ of query q is higher than threshold ϵ, the correct results are expected to be highly ranked in the sample, and hence effective retrieval should still be obtained with aggressive pruning ($K = 20, F = 2$). Otherwise, a safe but less efficient setting is selected for WAND. $0 < \epsilon < 1$ controls the number of queries aggressively pruned, where increasing ϵ reduces the number of applications of $K = 20, F = 2$.

Selecting on Predicted Efficiency

Hypothesis 2 suggests that when a query will not take a long time to complete, safe retrieval can be applied. In contrast, if the query terms have long postings lists and the query is difficult to prune, then the safe retrieval would take a significant amount of time, and more aggressive pruning should be applied. To decide which queries should be aggressively pruned, we recall that the response time distributions in Figure 2 follow log-normal distributions for each query length. With this in mind, we fit a log-normal distribution for each query length, centred around the geometric mean G_l for a given query length l. G_l represents a time above which we consider a query to be inefficient, obtained from the 500 efficiency training queries (see Section 5.1), while inefficient queries are identified using the query efficiency predictors, as described in Section 5.7. Hence, for a newly arrived query q, if the predicted response time $\widehat{R}(q)$ of the query is above the geometric mean, we select a more aggressive candidate K and F setting to increase the efficiency of the query:

$$\text{SELECT}_{QEP}(\text{PREDICT}(q)) = \begin{cases} \{20, 2\} & \text{if } \widehat{R}(q) > c \cdot G_l \\ \{1000, 1\} & \text{otherwise} \end{cases}$$

where $0 \le c \le 1$ is a parameter for adjusting the threshold above which a query will be aggressively pruned.

In the next section, by instantiating either $\text{SELECT}_{QPP}(\bullet)$ or $\text{SELECT}_{QEP}(\bullet)$ into the selective pruning framework of Algorithm 1, we evaluate the efficiency and effectiveness impacts of the two proposed definitions for SELECT(•).

7. EXPERIMENTS

In the following, we experiment to validate Hypotheses 1 and 2 in Sections 7.1 and 7.2, respectively, using the experimental setup defined in Section 5. In particular, we compare both approaches to the efficiency and effectiveness of four *Uniform* settings of K and F. These include the candidate settings of $K = 1000, F = 1$ and $K = 20, F = 2$, as well as two other settings ($K = 1000, F = 2$; $K = 100, F = 2$) from Section 6.2 that represent good tradeoffs of efficiency and effectiveness. Indeed, effectiveness is measured by NDCG@20 on 50 TREC Web track queries, while efficiency is measured by the mean and 90th percentile response times on the 481 efficiency queries (denoted MRT and 90%tl-RT, respectively). 90%tl-RT is an indicator of the response time suffered by users for the slowest 10% of queries. Following [35], we measure the significance of improvements by a learned model over the effectiveness of the unlearned safe sample (NDCG@20 0.224 from Figure 5 (a)), thereby using a common basis for all significance tests. In general, we consider a successful approach to be one with a significant improvement over the unlearned safe sample, while minimising MRT and 90%tl-RT.

7.1 Selecting on Predicted Effectiveness

Table 2 reports the efficiency and effectiveness of the uniform settings of K and F, as well as our selective approach based on query performance prediction. From the top part of the table, we observe that while the effectiveness of the uniform settings varies, an effective AFS learned model can significantly improve over the unlearned safe sample with $p < 0.01$ (denoted **), and an effective LambdaMART model can achieve a significant improvement over the sample at the 5% level ($p < 0.05$, denoted *). Hence, successful selective approaches should achieve such effectiveness improvements as a minimum – for both learners, this cannot be achieved with MRTs lower than 10.6 seconds.

To investigate the selective approach using query performance predictors – namely $\text{SELECT}_{QPP}(\bullet)$ – Table 2 reports the effectiveness, efficiency and percentage of queries aggresively pruned for various settings of the query performance predictor threshold ϵ. Indeed, recall that increasing ϵ decreases the number of predicted easy queries that will be aggressively pruned. The query performance prediction deployed in this work is a supervised combination of pre-retrieval predictors, and hence requires training data - as detailed in Section 5.6, we use the 50 training and 50 validation queries to learn to predict the NDCG@20 of the learned model. For this reason, the reported response times for $\text{SELECT}_{QPP}(\bullet)$ differ across the learned models in Table 2.

On examining the results, we note that for $\epsilon = 0.25$ for AFS and $\epsilon = 0.2$ for LambdaMART (denoted with dashed underlines in Table 2), significant NDCG@20 improvements over the safe sample can be obtained, with marked reductions in response time compared to the uniform setting of $K = 1000, F = 2$. In particular, for AFS, by aggressively pruning 77% of the 481 efficiency queries, a response time of 9.3s can be achieved, which is comparable to $K = 100$, $F = 2$, while still achieving higher NDCG@20 on the 50 effectiveness queries. For LambdaMART, a MRT of 9.0s is achieved – again, better than $K = 100, F = 2$ while still significantly improving over the effectiveness of the unlearned sample. In general, the results across AFS and LambdaMART are similar, with LambdaMART achieving the significantly improved effectiveness over the unlearned safe sample with slightly more aggressive pruning. In terms of 90th percentile response time, $\text{SELECT}_{QPP}(\bullet)$ is unable to improve upon the uniform $K = 100, F = 2$ setting, suggesting that while the aggressive pruning of predicted easy queries can enhance efficiency without significantly degrading effectiveness, it does not directly target the particularly inefficient queries.

Overall, we conclude that although selectively applying aggressive pruning on a per-query basis by using query performance predictors can improve response times while assuring effectiveness, it does so in a conservative manner. In contrast, in the next section, we show how directly targeting the inefficient queries is a more suitable approach for selective pruning.

7.2 Selecting on Predicted Efficiency

We now report the experimental results for $\text{SELECT}_{QEP}(\bullet)$. The deployed query efficiency predictors and the estimation of G_l require training data. These are trained on the 500 efficiency training queries, and efficiency results are reported on the separate testing set of 481 queries.

Table 3 reports both the efficiency and effectiveness results of our selective framework based on query efficiency prediction for estimating response times. To examine if the accuracy of the efficiency predictors impact upon the selective pruning framework, we report results when the actual response times are assumed to be known, i.e., using a perfect response time predictor $R(q)$, in addition to estimated response time $\widehat{R}(q)$.[5] We vary the c parameter of SELECT_{QEP} to measure its impact on efficiency and effectiveness.

On examining Table 3, we note that varying the c parameter indeed affects efficiency and effectiveness, with the lowest c value providing the best response times but not attaining the significant improvements in effectiveness over the unlearned safe sample. In particular, we observe that with $c = 1$ (dashed underline in Table 3), very low response times can be achieved without aggressively pruning all queries, while still retaining high effectiveness by the learned models. For instance, for the AFS learner with the predicted response time, a MRT of 8.4s is achieved, which is close to the lower bound of 8.1s exhibited by the uniform aggressive pruning ($K = 20, F = 2$), while only aggressively pruning 35% of queries. Compared to the uniform safe setting ($K = 1000, F = 1$), this represents a 36% improvement in MRT. Moreover, we note that the 90th percentile response time drops 50% compared to the uniform safe setting of $K = 1000, F = 1$ and 24% compared to $K = 100, F = 2$ (19.3s vs. 38.3s and 24.9s, respectively). This attests that selecting K and F for each query based on predicted response time indeed targets the most inefficient queries.

Meanwhile the NDCG@20 of the AFS learned model for $c = 1$ still significantly improves over the unlearned safe sample at $p < 0.01$ - indeed, this is 21% higher than for $K = 20, F = 2$ (0.287 vs. 0.238), and 16% higher than the good uniform tradeoff setting of $K = 100, F = 2$ (viz. 0.247). For LambdaMART, similar results are observed, with the $c = 1$ setting offering a good tradeoff of effectiveness and efficiency. We note one exception for LambdaMART, where $c = 0.5$ still offers a significant improvement over the unlearned safe sample performance, but by a smaller absolute margin (9%). Finally, comparing the results using actual and predicted response times ($R(q)$ vs. $\widehat{R}(q)$), we note that using $R(q)$ only results in small improvements in

[5]Unlike in Table 2, the efficiency results of Table 3 are not dependent on the effectiveness of the learner on the training queries, thus the efficiency results are identical for both learners.

	AFS					LambdaMART				
	MRT	90%tl-RT	(%agg.)	NDCG@20	(%agg.)	MRT	90%tl-RT	(%agg.)	NDCG@20	(%agg.)
Uniform: same setting of K and F for all queries										
$K = 1000$ $F = 1$	12.9	38.3	-	0.296**		12.9	38.3	-	0.272*	-
$K = 1000$ $F = 2$	10.6	29.1	-	0.308**		10.6	29.1	-	0.273*	-
$K = 100$ $F = 2$	9.6	24.9	-	0.247*		9.6	24.9	-	0.256	-
$K = 20$ $F = 2$	8.1	17.8	-	0.238*		8.1	17.8	-	0.239	-
SELECT$_{QPP}(\widehat{E}(q))$: selective pruning framework applied using query performance predictors										
$\epsilon = 0.05$	8.6	25.2	(97%)	0.238*	(100%)	8.1	17.8	(97%)	0.239	(100%)
$\epsilon = 0.1$	9.0	26.2	(93%)	0.238	(94%)	8.6	25.2	(94%)	0.237	(96%)
$\epsilon = 0.15$	9.2	26.4	(89%)	0.246*	(91%)	8.9	26.2	(90%)	0.245	(94%)
$\epsilon = 0.2$	9.2	26.4	(85%)	0.248*	(83%)	9.0	26.2	(82%)	0.246*	(87%)
$\epsilon = 0.25$	9.3	26.4	(77%)	0.258**	(74%)	9.0	26.2	(75%)	0.241	(81%)
$\epsilon = 0.3$	9.7	27.0	(65%)	0.268*	(64%)	9.2	26.4	(69%)	0.250*	(70%)
$\epsilon = 0.35$	10.4	32.4	(48%)	0.276**	(51%)	9.3	26.4	(56%)	0.248	(60%)
$\epsilon = 0.4$	11.3	34.2	(33%)	0.293**	(38%)	9.8	26.4	(45%)	0.251*	(51%)

Table 2: Efficiency and effectiveness results of the selective pruning framework using query performance predictors. Significant improvements in effectiveness compared to the uniform application of the $K = 1000$ $F = 1$ sample (NDCG@20 0.224), as measured by the paired-t test, are denoted by * ($p < 0.05$) and ** ($p < 0.01$). The percentage of queries that experience aggressive pruning are shown in parentheses, denoted (%agg).

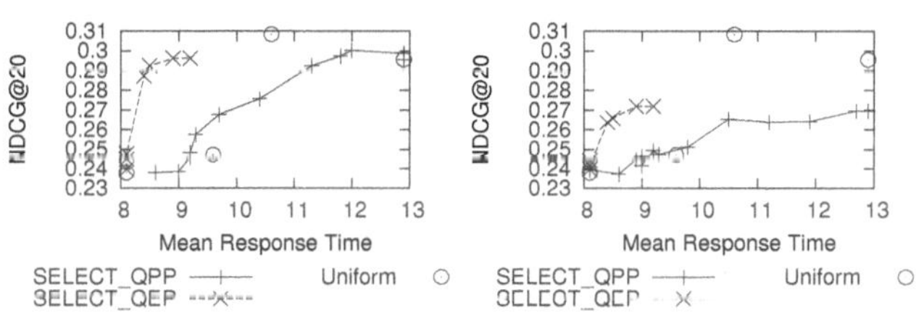

(a) AFS (b) LambdaMART

Figure 6: Comparison of efficiency and effectiveness for Hypotheses 1& 2 selective pruning approaches.

MRT, 90%tl-RT and NDCG, suggesting that our predicted response times are sufficiently accurate.

Overall, with respect to our second hypothesis, we find that the proposed approach for selective pruning based on estimated response times attains impressive efficiency benefits while still attaining high effectiveness, thereby validating Hypothesis 2. In particular, the results in this section suggest that queries that are predicted to be particularly inefficient typically represent those that can be more aggressively pruned, thereby ensuring efficiency, without damaging overall effectiveness. To aid in the comparison of our two selective approaches based on Hypotheses 1 & 2, Figure 6 shows the efficiency and effectiveness of each approach, where points nearest to the top-left are both efficient and effective. Indeed, we can see that the approach of Hypothesis 2 is markedly better for ensuring efficient yet effective retrieval on a per-query basis. In contrast, the approach of Hypothesis 1 is only slightly markedly more efficient and effective than the various used uniform settings. We posit that the success of selective pruning by query efficiency prediction can be explained in that the queries that take longer have longer posting lists (posting list length has a marked impact on efficiency [23]). Such queries may have more relevant documents, which are more likely to be found in the top-ranked sample, in contrast to more efficient queries.

8. CONCLUSIONS

This work proposed a selective pruning framework for ensuring efficient yet effective retrieval, by appropriately setting the pruning parameters of WAND on a per-query basis, before re-ranking the results using a learned model. Two alternative approaches are proposed within our selective pruning framework for selecting queries to prune, by using query performance predictors to identify easier queries, and by using query efficiency predictors to identify inefficient queries. Our experimental results showed that using the proposed selective pruning framework in conjunction with query efficiency predictors to select the queries to aggressively prune gave the best overall results. In particular, it could improve mean response time by 36% and the response time experienced by the slowest 10% of queries by 50%, while still maintaining significantly high effectiveness.

Our proposed selective pruning framework can have further applications. In particular, when the search engine is receiving a high volume of queries, pruning can be made more aggressive to ensure that a maximum allowed response time is adhered to. We will address this in future work. Moreover, we would like to investigate loss functions that permit efficiency and effectiveness to be considered within a learned approach for obtaining appropriate K and F settings on a per-query basis. A key practical challenge in this respect is the availability of large query sets with corresponding relevance assessments, to permit efficiency and effectiveness to be measured for the same queries.

9. REFERENCES

[1] G. Amati, E. Ambrosi, M. Bianchi, C. Gaibisso, G. Gambosi. FUB, IASI-CNR and Univ. of Tor Vergata at TREC 2007 Blog track. In *Proc. of TREC*, 2007.

[2] G. Amati, C. Carpineto, G. Romano. Query Difficulty, Robustness, and Selective Application of Query Expansion. In *Proc of ECIR*, 2004.

[3] V. N. Anh, A. Moffat. Pruned query evaluation using pre-computed impact scores. In *Proc. of SIGIR*, 2006.

[4] M. Bendersky, W. B. Croft, Y. Diao. Quality-biased ranking of web documents. In *Proc. of WSDM*, 2011.

[5] R. Blanco. *Index compression for information retrieval systems.* PhD thesis, Univ. of A Coruna, 2008.

[6] A. Z. Broder, D. Carmel, M. Herscovici, A. Soffer, J. Zien. Efficient query evaluation using a two-level retrieval process. In *Proc of CIKM*, 2003.

[7] B. B. Cambazoglu, H. Zaragoza, O. Chapelle, J. Chen, C. Liao, Z. Zheng, J. Degenhardt. Early exit optimizations for additive machine learned ranking systems. In *Proc. of WSDM*, 2010.

	AFS					LambdaMART				
	MRT	90%tl-RT	(%agg.)	NDCG@20	(%agg.)	MRT	90%tl-RT	(%agg.)	NDCG@20	(%agg.)
Uniform: same setting of K and F for all queries										
$K = 1000$ $F = 1$	12.9	38.3	-	0.296**	-	12.9	38.3	-	0.272*	-
$K = 1000$ $F = 2$	10.6	29.1	-	0.308**	-	10.6	29.1	-	0.273*	-
$K = 100$ $F = 2$	9.6	24.9	-	0.247*	-	9.6	24.9	-	0.256	-
$K = 20$ $F = 2$	8.1	17.8	-	0.238*	-	8.1	17.8	-	0.239	-
SELECT$_{QEP}(R(q))$: selective pruning framework applied using actual response times										
$c = 0.1$	8.1	17.8	(99%)	0.240*	(98%)	8.1	17.8	(99%)	0.240	(98%)
$c = 0.25$	8.1	17.8	(98%)	0.240*	(98%)	8.1	17.8	(98%)	0.240	(98%)
$c = 0.5$	8.1	17.8	(77%)	0.245**	(89%)	8.1	17.8	(77%)	0.244*	(89%)
$c = 0.75$	8.1	19.0	(51%)	0.248*	(68%)	8.1	19.0	(51%)	0.242	(68%)
$c = 1$	8.2	19.0	(36%)	0.290**	(32%)	8.2	19.0	(36%)	0.268*	(32%)
$c = 1.25$	8.4	19.3	(31%)	0.296**	(23%)	8.4	19.3	(31%)	0.272*	(23%)
$c = 1.5$	8.7	19.3	(25%)	0.296**	(23%)	8.7	19.3	(25%)	0.272*	(23%)
$c = 2$	9.1	21.9	(20%)	0.296**	(17%)	9.1	21.9	(20%)	0.274*	(17%)
SELECT$_{QEP}(\widehat{R}(q))$: selective pruning framework applied using predicted response times										
$c = 0.1$	8.1	17.8	(100%)	0.240*	(98%)	8.1	17.8	(100%)	0.240	(98%)
$c = 0.25$	8.1	17.8	(95%)	0.240*	(98%)	8.1	17.8	(95%)	0.240	(98%)
$c = 0.5$	8.1	18.9	(78%)	0.245**	(89%)	8.1	18.9	(78%)	0.244*	(89%)
$c = 0.75$	8.1	19.0	(53%)	0.248*	(70%)	8.1	19.0	(53%)	0.242	(70%)
$c = 1$	8.4	19.3	(35%)	0.287**	(34%)	8.4	19.3	(35%)	0.264*	(34%)
$c = 1.25$	8.5	19.3	(31%)	0.293**	(28%)	8.5	19.3	(31%)	0.266*	(28%)
$c = 1.5$	8.9	19.3	(25%)	0.296**	(21%)	8.9	19.3	(25%)	0.272*	(21%)
$c = 2$	9.2	21.0	(19%)	0.296**	(21%)	9.2	21.0	(19%)	0.272*	(21%)

Table 3: Results of the selective pruning framework using query efficiency predictors. Notation as in Table 2.

[8] D. Carmel and E. Yom-Tov. Estimating the Query Difficulty for Information Retrieval. *Synthesis Lectures on Information Concepts, Retrieval, and Services*, 2(1), 2010.

[9] O. Chapelle, Y. Chang. Yahoo! learning to rank challenge overview. *J. Machine Learning: Workshop and Conference Proceedings*, 14:1–24, 2011.

[10] C. L. A. Clarke, N. Craswell, I. Soboroff, G. V. Cormack. Overview of the TREC 2010 Web Track. In *Proc. of TREC*, 2010.

[11] G. V. Cormack, M. D. Smucker, C. L. A. Clarke. Efficient and effective spam filtering and re-ranking for large Web datasets. *Inf. Retr.*, 14(5):441–465, 2011.

[12] N. Craswell, R. Jones, G. Dupret, E.Viegas, editors. Proc. of the Web Search Click Data Workshop at WSDM 2009.

[13] S. Cronen-Townsend, Y. Zhou, W.B. Croft. A Framework for Selective Query Expansion. In *Proc. of CIKM*, 2004.

[14] J. Dean. Challenges in building large-scale information retrieval systems: invited talk. In *Proc. of WSDM*, 2009.

[15] R. Fagin, A. Lotem, M. Naor. Optimal aggregation algorithms for middleware. *J. Computer and System Sciences*, 66(4):614–656, 2003.

[16] M. Fontoura, V. Josifovski, J. Liu, S. Venkatesan, X. Zhu, J. Zien. Evaluation strategies for top-k queries over memory-resident inverted indexes. *Proc. VLDB Endowment*, 4(12):1213–1224, 2011.

[17] J. H. Friedman. Greedy function approximation: A gradient boosting machine. *Annals of Statistics*, 29:1189–1232, 2000.

[18] Y. Ganjisaffar, R. Caruana, C. Lopes. Bagging gradient-boosted trees for high precision, low variance ranking models. In *Proc. of SIGIR*, 2011.

[19] B. He, I. Ounis. Inferring query performance using pre-retrieval predictors. In *Proc. of SPIRE*, 2004.

[20] T.-Y. Liu. Learning to rank for IR. *Foundation and Trends in IR*, 3(3):225–331, 2009.

[21] C. Macdonald, I. Ounis, N. Tonellotto. Upper bound approximations for dynamic pruning. *ACM Trans. Inf. Sys.*, 29(4):1–28, 2011.

[22] C. Macdonald, V. Plachouras, B. He, C. Lioma, I. Ounis. Univ. of Glasgow at WebCLEF 2005: Experiments in per-field normlisation and language specific stemming. In *Proc. of CLEF*, 2005.

[23] C. Macdonald, N. Tonellotto, I. Ounis. Learning to predict response times for online query scheduling. In *Proc. of SIGIR*, 2012.

[24] C. Macdonald, N. Tonellotto, I. Ounis. Effect of dynamic pruning safety on learning to rank effectiveness. In *Proc. of SIGIR*, 2012.

[25] C. Macdonald, R. Santos, I. Ounis. The whens and hows of learning to rank. *Information Retrieval*, 2012.

[26] D. Metzler, W. B. Croft. A Markov random field model for term dependencies. In *Proc. of SIGIR*, 2005.

[27] D. Metzler. Automatic feature selection in the Markov random field model for information retrieval. In *Proc. of CIKM*, 2007.

[28] A. Moffat, J. Zobel. Self-indexing inverted files for fast text retrieval. *ACM Trans. Inf. Sys.*, 14(4):349–379, 1996.

[29] J. Peng, C. Macdonald, B. He, V. Plachouras, I. Ounis. Incorporating term dependency in the DFR framework. In *Proc. of SIGIR*, 2007.

[30] M. Persin. Document filtering for fast ranking. In *Proc. of SIGIR*, 1994.

[31] V. Plachouras, I. Ounis. Usefulness of hyperlink structure for query-biased topic distillation. In *Proc. of SIGIR*, 2004.

[32] R. L. T. Santos, C. Macdonald, I. Ounis. Intent-aware search result diversification. In *Proc. of SIGIR*, 2011.

[33] E. Shurman, J. Brutlag. Performance related changes and their user impacts. In *Velocity: Web Performance and Operations Conf.*, 2009.

[34] H. Turtle, J. Flood. Query evaluation: strategies and optimizations. *Inf. Proc. Mngmnt*, 31(6):831–850, 1995.

[35] L. Wang, J. Lin, D. Metzler. Learning to efficiently rank. In *Proc. of SIGIR*, 2010.

[36] L. Wang, J. Lin, D. Metzler. A cascade ranking model for efficient ranked retrieval. In *Proc. of SIGIR*, 2011.

[37] Q. Wu, C. J. C. Burges, K. M. Svore, J. Gao. Ranking, boosting, and model adaptation. Technical Report MSR-TR-2008-109, Microsoft, 2008.

[38] Y. Zhao, F. Scholer, Y. Tsegay. Effective pre-retrieval query performance prediction. In *Proc. of ECIR*, 2008.

Document Selection for Tiered Indexing in Commerce Search

Debmalya Panigrahi*
Microsoft Research
Redmond, WA 98052
depan@microsoft.com

Sreenivas Gollapudi
Search Labs, Microsoft Research
Mountain View, CA 94043
sreenig@microsoft.com

ABSTRACT

A search engine aims to return a set of relevant documents in response to a query, while minimizing the response time. This has led to the use of a tiered index, where the search engine maintains a small cache of documents that can serve a large fraction of queries. We give a novel algorithm for the selection of documents in a tiered index for commerce search (i.e. users searching for products on the web) that effectively exploits the superior structural characteristics of commerce search queries. This is in sharp contrast to previous approaches to tiered indexing that were aimed at general web search where queries are typically unstructured. We theoretically analyze our algorithms and give performance guarantees even in worst-case scenarios. We then complement and strengthen our theoretical claims by performing exhaustive experiments on real-world commerce search data, and show that our algorithm outperforms state-of-the-art tiered indexing techniques that were developed for general web search.

Categories and Subject Descriptors

H.3 [**Information Storage and Retrieval**]

General Terms

Algorithm, Performance

Keywords

Tiered Indexing, Structured Search

1. INTRODUCTION

With the astronomical growth of the internet over the last decade, *search engines* have been playing a pivotal role in guiding users to internet resources that they desire. Over the last few years, *commerce search*, i.e. users searching for products with the intention of purchasing them online, has come to occupy a prominent place in this domain. On being presented a user query, the goal of a commerce search engine is to output a set of relevant products from its online catalog. Since query response time is a key parameter in user experience, a natural approach is to use a *tiered index* where the search engine maintains a smaller index over a subset of documents (product descriptions) that can serve a large fraction of popular queries. The selection of these documents is a challenging task in general web search because of the *diversity* and *lack of structure* in user queries. However, in commerce search, queries typically comprise a list of desirable product features. Therefore, the query space, while being extremely large, is much more structured than in general web search. In this correspondence, we show that we can exploit this additional structure to design efficient algorithms for selecting the set of documents in a tiered index for commerce search with significantly better performance than the state-of-the-art in general web search. While we present our results in the context of commerce search, our techniques automatically extend to other structured search domains (e.g. travel, music, movies, etc.) as well.

As mentioned above, commerce search queries are characterized by a set of product features (we call these *attribute values* or *keywords*) that the user desires in the product she is searching for. This makes it feasible to categorize commerce search queries based on these features, and to decompose them into their constituent attribute values. For instance, it is relatively easy to identify that a query `Canon EOS black 12MP` was issued by a user searching for cameras, and that her desired attribute values are `Canon`, `EOS`, `black`, and `12MP` for attributes *manufacturer*, *model line*, *color*, and *resolution* respectively. Given that such categorizers exist (see e.g. [23]), the central question that we seek to address in this paper is the following: *can we use the structure in commerce search queries to select documents for a tiered search index aimed at faster query response?*

In response to a user query, a commerce search engine displays a set of relevant products from its online catalog. So, we need to understand how a search engine evaluates the relevance of a user query to a product. Since commerce search queries are a collection of attribute values, this boils down to finding the relevance of a document to an attribute value. For example, a `Nikon D7000` camera is likely to be more relevant to the keyword `Nikon` than to `Canon`. This is a rather straightforward assertion, but in general we might have more ambiguous scenarios: e.g. is a `blue` or a `red` camera more relevant to a user who is searching for `purple` cameras? Recently, we suggested a completely automated technique for inferring these *relevances* (or *similarities*) based on previous user behavior represented by browse trail data collected from toolbars of web browsers [19]. In this paper, we use the algorithm in [19] to obtain, for every keyword a, a list of relevance scores of a with ev-

*Part of this work was done as a graduate student supported, in part, by NSF contract CCF-1117381 at the Massachusetts Institute of Technology, Cambridge, MA 02139.

WSDM'13, February 4–8, 2013, Rome, Italy.

ery other keyword for the same attribute (e.g. between Canon and every other manufacturer). (We may note that most of these scores are 0 allowing for succinct representation.) For a product in the catalog (say a Nikon D7000 camera), its relevance score for a user-specified attribute value (say Canon) is the relevance score of its corresponding attribute value (i.e. the similarity score of Nikon with Canon). We note that such a model of similarity between attribute values allows us to extend our techniques presented in this paper to indexes where the data is probabilistic in nature and the matching score of a record to the user query is some function of these probabilities.

The next step is to infer the relevance score of a product for a query q from its relevance scores for the constituent attribute values of q. A natural strategy is to say that a product is relevant to a query if it has a high relevance score for most attribute values in the query. There are multiple functions implementing this strategy, and we discuss some of them later in the paper. Once we have decided on such a function, the problem of constructing a tiered index of size b boils down to finding the set of b products that maximizes the weighted (by query frequency) fraction of queries that have at least k relevant products in the index, k being the number of search results returned to the user. Note that these are precisely the set of queries that can be exclusively served from the cache, and therefore represent *cache hits*. We formalize this problem later, and call it the INDEX SELECTIONproblem.

Caching posting lists v/s query results. As mentioned earlier, algorithms for selecting documents in a tiered index have been proposed in the literature for general web search. Two prominent strategies are: (1) include posting lists, i.e., list of documents, for relevant popular search terms (e.g. [3]), or (2) include search results for popular queries (e.g. [1]). Both strategies suffer from serious deficiencies. While the former strategy generalizes better since it does not restrict itself to only optimizing over the training set of queries, it is unable to differentiate between documents in the same posting list. For example, the posting list for Canon would typically contain documents that are relevant to many manufacturers as well as those that are specific to Canon, and the algorithm fails to preferentially select documents of the first type over those of the second type. In addition, the strategy of copying entire posting lists leads to wastage of valuable cache space since posting lists for related but distinct keywords tend to have substantial overlap. On the other hand, selecting the contents of the tiered index based solely on a training set of queries leads to poor generalization characteristics since the query space is enormous and typical query distributions have large support. Further, the algorithm in [1] uses an exhaustive search over the entire set of training queries, which hampers efficiency and scalability of the technique. In this paper, we present a novel solution that exploits the structure of commerce search queries to overcome the deficiencies of both these techniques.

Our solution. Before describing our solution, let us first understand the structure of the query space for commerce search. As we stated earlier, a query comprises a set of attribute values. For example, a user searching for digital cameras can opt for one of several manufacturers/model lines, various different resolutions, multiple colors, price ranges, lens types, and so on, and these choices are largely independent of each other. Note that typical search queries also contain "free text", i.e. textual description that does not correspond to any particular attribute. We strip queries of such free text at the very outset, and consider queries to be composed only of the identifiable attribute values in them. Even though the number of attribute values for each such attribute is not very large (say around 20), and there are a manageable number of different attributes (there are at most 10 important attributes for most categories of products), the total number of possible queries generated by combining these attribute values is enormous. Our solution bypasses the obvious computational challenges of this large query space by using its structural characteristics to avoid exhaustive searches.

At a high level, our solution borrows (from [1]) the idea of greedily selecting documents one at a time based on the incremental query coverage they offer. However, we want to ensure that the solution generalizes well to an arbitrary query test set. To this end, we derive marginal frequencies on individual attribute values from the training data and use the structure of the query space to estimate the overall query distribution from these marginal frequencies. This would naturally suggest a greedy algorithm on the entire query distribution (rather than the one observed in the training data). However, a naïve implementation of this idea would lead to an exhaustive search over the support of the query distribution. Our main technical contribution is an efficient implementation of this greedy strategy using algorithmic sampling techniques to reduce the sample space to a sequence of marginal distributions (rather than the overall query distribution) in order to obtain estimates on the incremental query coverage of individual documents.

It is worth mentioning that our algorithms apply not only to commerce search but to any other structured search domain where queries predominantly consist of a set of attribute values for which relevance scores as described above can be computed. However, our techniques do not naturally extend to general web search. In particular, our sampling technique is based on the query space being a Cartesian product of sets of attribute values for individual attributes. Unfortunately, the query space for general web search is substantially less structured and cannot be interpreted as the Cartesian product of a small number of small sets. We leave the extension of our ideas to general web search as an interesting and independent open question.

An additional algorithmic complication arises from the *dynamic* nature of the set of documents. To ensure that the tiered index reflects changes in the catalog, one option is to discard the contents of the index periodically and re-run the algorithm to generate a new set of documents. However, this is a rather expensive solution since it involves repeated re-runs of the algorithm on the entire set of documents. We propose simple algorithmic solutions that overcome this inefficiency.

To evaluate the performance of our algorithm in practice, we perform extensive experiments on the product catalog used by a commercial online shopping portal. A query is said to have a *cache hit* if at least k of the products returned by the commercial search engine on being issued the query are indeed in the index. We vary the parameters of the algorithm such as the size of the index, the relevance threshold, the value of k, etc. and observe the resulting changes in the cache hit ratio. For these parameter ranges, we compare our performance with those of standard algorithms in the literature for tiered indexing in general web search [1, 3].

Our Contributions. The following is a brief sketch of our main contributions in this paper:

- We formalize the problem of selecting products in a tiered index for commerce search (or any other structured search domain). We call this the INDEX SELECTIONproblem.
- We propose a randomized algorithm for the INDEX SELECTIONproblem, and show that it achieves a near-optimal approximation ratio (subject to standard assumptions in complexity theory).

- To address the practical consideration of changing catalogs, we give a natural extension of our algorithm that adjusts the contents of the index in response to the arrival of new products, without having to compute the entire contents of the index from scratch.
- We complement our theoretical results by performing extensive experiments on real-world data. Our experiments confirm that our algorithm is scalable, accurate, and efficient, and outperforms the state-of-the-art techniques in tiered indexing for general web search.

2. PROBLEM DEFINITION

Recall that commerce search queries can be classified into categories (such as *digital cameras*, *cellphones*, etc.), where each category is characterized by a set of attributes (e.g. *resolution* is an attribute for *digital cameras*). Each attribute, in turn, has a set of attribute values (e.g. `Canon`, `Nikon`, etc. for attribute *manufacturer* in the category *digital cameras*). Formally, suppose there are L categories, where category j has k_j attributes. Let $A_1^{(j)}, A_2^{(j)}, \ldots, A_{k_j}^{(j)}$ denote the sets of attribute values for these attributes. Further, for every attribute value a, we estimate its relative frequency in the set of queries, and denote it by f_a. On the other hand, let D be the set of documents,[1] and let w_{ad} denote the relevance score of attribute value a for document $d \in D$.

Each query comprises attribute values for a subset of attributes in its category (recall that we assume that we have stripped the query of its free text). For example, a query `Canon EOS 12MP` has attribute values `Canon`, `EOS`, and `12MP` for attributes *manufacturer*, *model line*, and *resolution* respectively but is missing attributes such as *color*. For ease of notation, we introduce the special element ϕ in the set of attribute values $A_i^{(j)}$ for every attribute i in every category j, and denote the augmented set of attribute values by $A_i^{(j,\phi)} = A_i^{(j)} \cup \{\phi\}$. A query missing attribute i is now assumed to have the special attribute value ϕ for attribute i, and the relative frequency of ϕ for attribute i is the fraction of queries that are in category j and are missing attribute i. The set of all queries in category j is then given by

$$Q_j = A_1^{(j,\phi)} \times A_2^{(j,\phi)} \times \ldots \times A_{k_j}^{(j,\phi)}.$$

In any such query $q \in Q_j$, the attribute value for attribute i is denoted by $q(i)$ (note that $q(i)$ could be ϕ). The relative frequency of a query q in category j is defined as $f_q = \prod_{i=1}^{k_j} f_{q(i)}$.

We are implicitly assuming independence over the set of attributes for any category. While this is accurate for attributes such as color, manufacturer, product specifications, etc. that have small correlation, it does not hold for highly correlated attribute combinations such as manufacturer and model line. To overcome this problem, following [19], we treat correlated subsets of attributes as single attributes, and leave the problem of obtaining a more refined treatment of attribute correlation as future work.

Relevant documents for a Query. As mentioned in the introduction, there are multiple options for defining the set of relevant documents for a query, based on the relevance scores of the documents for individual keywords in the query. Perhaps the simplest option is to define relevance of a document for individual keywords by setting a threshold on the relevance score. The document is now defined to be relevant for a query as a whole if it is relevant for *every* keyword in the query. However, this suffers from the shortcoming that even if a document is relevant for all but one keyword in a query, it is deemed to be irrelevant for the query as a whole. A natural relaxation is to call a document relevant if it is relevant to most (e.g. at least some fixed fraction) of the keywords in the query. Noting that this strategy does not differentiate between two documents that meet the relevance threshold for an attribute value but have very different relevance scores, we finally converge on the following definition of relevance: *A document is said to be* relevant *to a query if the average of the relevance scores of the document over all the keywords in the query is at least some fixed threshold* θ. Both the previous definitions of relevance can be simulated using the new definition, and therefore our algorithm can also handle either of the previous definitions.

If a document d is relevant for a query q, then we say that q is *covered* by d. Similarly, if at least one document in a set of documents X covers a query q, then we say that q is covered by X. Let $Q(d)$ denote the set of queries that are covered by document d, and let $Q(X)$ be the set of queries that are covered by a set of documents X. Corresponding, let $f_d = \sum_{q \in Q(d)} f_q$ and $f_X = \sum_{q \in Q(X)} f_q$.

Choice of index size.[2] A key input is the size of the index denoted by b. The choice of the relevance threshold θ is dictated by the size of the index (e.g. a large value of θ and a small index size might lead to most of the index remaining unused). In turn, the size of the index is a function of external parameters such as the desired cache hit ratio and the amount of memory and indexing infrastructure available to the search engine.

Objective Function. For simplicity, we set the number of results returned by the algorithm k to 1. (We will consider general values of k later.) Then, the objective of the algorithm is to output a set X of at most b documents that maximizes the sum of relative frequencies of queries covered by X, i.e. maximizes f_X.

We call this the INDEX SELECTION problem.

3. THE GREEDY SELECTION ALGORITHM

We propose a natural, greedy algorithm for the INDEX SELECTION problem, which we call the GREEDY SELECTION algorithm (see Figure 1). The algorithm has b iterations, where in each iteration, we add the document $d \in D \setminus X$ to X that maximizes the value of the objective function f_X. The primary challenge lies in the polynomial-time implementation of this algorithm. For every document $d \in D \setminus X$, the algorithm requires to compute the increase in the objective function if d were added to the index X. This entails computation of the sum of relative frequencies of queries in $Q(d) \setminus Q(X)$ for any document $d \in D \setminus X$. In a naïve implementation, this would take time proportional to the total number of queries, which is exponential in the size of the input. Our main technical contribution is a polynomial time implementation of the GREEDY SELECTION algorithm that proves the following theorem.

THEOREM 1. *For any* $\epsilon > 0$, *there is a randomized polynomial-time*[3] *algorithm (which we call the* GREEDY SELECTION *algorithm) for the* INDEX SELECTION *problem that achieves an approximation ratio of* $1 - 1/e - \epsilon$ *with high probability.*[4]

[1]For commerce search, a document is a product.

[2]By index/cache size, we mean the number of unique documents in the index.

[3]The running time is polynomial in the input parameters as well as in $1/\epsilon$.

[4]A statement is said to hold *with high probability* (or whp) if the statement holds with probability $1 - o(1)$.

```
X ← ∅
for i from 1 to b do
    d* ← arg max_{d∈D\X} COUNT QUERY(X ∪ {d})
    X ← X ∪ {d*}
end for
return X
```

Figure 1: The GREEDY SELECTION algorithm

Since $Q(d) \setminus Q(X) = Q(X \cup \{d\}) \setminus Q(X)$, our problem boils down to estimating the sum of relative frequencies of queries covered by a given subset of documents Y (here $Y = X \cup \{d\}$), i.e. estimating f_Y. We call this the COUNT QUERY problem.

Algorithm for the COUNT QUERY problem. We now describe an algorithm for estimating the sum of frequencies of queries that are covered by Y in a single category; the overall estimate is the sum of these estimates over all categories. Our algorithm will have an error parameter $\epsilon > 0$; as a preprocessing step, we round the relevance scores w_{ad} to multiples of a small enough value η such that the error due to the rounding can be absorbed in ϵ.

A simple idea would be to sample of a set of queries uniformly at random and use the fraction of sampled queries that are covered by Y as an estimator for the fraction of queries in $Q(Y)$. Unfortunately, the size of the sample required to control the sampling error is inversely proportional to the fraction that we are trying to estimate, which in our case implies that we might need exponentially many samples. To overcome this difficulty, we use a technique called *importance sampling* that was originally proposed by Karp, Luby, and Madras [12] for counting the number of truth assignments of a DNF[5] formula. The main idea is to sample queries from a *multiset* where each query appears as many times as the number of documents in Y that cover it, and then use a pre-determined order on the documents to estimate the ratio of the number of *distinct* queries in the multiset to the size of the multiset. It is easy to show that this ratio is always at least inverse polynomial, and can therefore we estimated using a polynomial number of samples.

We order the documents in Y in an arbitrary fixed order d_1, d_2, ..., $d_{|Y|}$. Let $N_r = f_{d_r}$ and $N = \sum_{r=1}^{|Y|} N_r$, which is the size of multiset formed by combining $Q(d_r)$ for all documents $d_r \in Y$. Our algorithm has two phases. In the first phase, we estimate the values of N_r (and therefore of N), and in the second phase, we perform the sampling procedure described above.

Phase 1. The first phase of our algorithm employs a dynamic program (DP) to estimate the values of N_r. Let I_q denote the set of attributes in query q (i.e. $q(i) \neq \phi$ iff $i \in I_q$). Further, let $S(j, \ell, \gamma)$ denote the sum of relative frequencies of queries q which have exactly ℓ attribute values, all of which are among the first j attributes, and have a sum of relevance scores over these attribute values of at least γ. Let $Q(d_r, j, \ell, \gamma)$ (for $\ell \leq j$) be the set of queries that have exactly ℓ attributes, all of which are among the first j attributes, and would have been covered by document d_r if the threshold on the average relevance score were some value γ/ℓ. Let $[n] = \{1, 2, \ldots, n\}$. Formally, $Q(d_r, j, \ell, \gamma) = \{q : |I_q| = \ell, I_q \subseteq [j], \sum_{i \in I_q} w_{q(i),d_r} \geq \gamma\}$, and $S(d_r, j, \ell, \gamma) = \sum_{q:q \in Q(d_r,j,\ell,\gamma)} f_q$. Note that $Q(d_r) = \cup_{\ell=1}^{k} Q(d_r, k, \ell, \theta\ell)$. Therefore, $N_r = \sum_{\ell=1}^{k} S(d_r, k, \ell, \theta\ell)$. (Recall that k is the number of attributes in the current category.) We will compute the values of $S(d_r, k, \ell, \theta\ell)$ using a DP that we describe below, which yields the values of N_r.

We make the following observations:

- If $j = \ell = 1$, then the queries in $Q(d_r, j, \ell, \theta\ell)$ are precisely the singleton queries containing attribute values $a \in A_1$ that satisfy $w_{ad_r} \geq \gamma$.
- If $j > \ell = 1$, then the queries in $S(d_r, j, \ell, \theta\ell)$ are also singleton queries, and contain attribute values $a \in A_t$ for all $t \leq j$ that satisfy $w_{ad_r} \geq \gamma$.
- If $j = \ell > 1$, then the queries in $S(d_r, j, \ell, \theta\ell)$ must contain an attribute value for every attribute in $[j]$.
- if $j > \ell > 1$, then the queries in $S(d_r, j, \ell, \theta\ell)$ either contain an attribute value for attribute j and $\ell - 1$ attribute values for attributes in $[j-1]$, **or** contain ℓ attribute values for attributes in $[j-1]$ and ϕ for attribute j.

These observations lead to the following DP:

$$S(d_r, 1, 1, \gamma) = \sum_{a \in A_1 : w_{ad_r} \geq \gamma} f_a$$

$$S(d_r, j, 1, \gamma) = f_\phi \cdot S(d_r, j-1, 1, \gamma) + \sum_{a \in A_j : w_{ad_r} \geq \gamma} f_a \quad \text{for } j \in [k], j > 1$$

$$S(d_r, j, j, \gamma) = \sum_{a \in A_j} f_a \cdot S(d_r, j-1, j-1, \max(\gamma - w_{ad_r}, 0)) \quad \text{for } j \in [k], j > 1$$

$$S(d_r, j, \ell, \gamma) = f_\phi \cdot S(d_r, j-1, \ell, \gamma) + \sum_{a \in A_j} f_a \cdot S(j-1, \ell-1, \max(\gamma - w_{ad_r}, 0)) \quad \text{for } j \in [k], j > 1, \ell \in [j-1]$$

Since the relevance scores are in multiples of η, which is polynomial in the error parameter ϵ, the running time of the this DP is polynomial.

Phase 2. In the second phase of the COUNT QUERY algorithm, we draw a set of n sample queries $q_1, q_2, \ldots, q_n$ (the value of n will be determined later). Each query $q_j \in cup_{r=1}^{|Y|} Q(d_r)$ is drawn i.i.d. using the following procedure: First, we sample a document d_r with probability $\frac{N_r}{N}$. Next, we sample the number of attributes ℓ in q_j with probability $\frac{S(k,\ell,\theta\ell)}{N_r}$. This restricts the set of queries to $Q(k, \ell, \theta\ell)$. Finally, we sample a query in $Q(k, \ell, \theta\ell)$ using a DP like the one in phase 1, the details of which are given in Figure 2. (In Figure 2, $q(-j)$ denotes $(q(1), q(2), \ldots, q(j-1))$ and f_Φ is the product of f_ϕ over all attributes $k < j$.)

Next, we need to define the estimator for f_Y that we generate using these sampled queries. Let

$$Q'(d_s) = \{q \in Q(d_s) : \forall t < s,\ q \notin Q(d_t)\}.$$

For each $j \in [n]$, we set $x_j = 1$ if $q_j \in Q'(d_r)$; otherwise, $x_j = 0$. The estimate for f_Y returned by the algorithm is

$$X = \left(\frac{\sum_{j=1}^{n} x_j}{n} \right) N.$$

Analysis. Our main technical lemma establishes the accuracy of the above algorithm for the COUNT QUERY problem.

LEMMA 1. *There is a randomized polynomial-time[6] approximation scheme for the* COUNT QUERY *problem that has a multiplicative error of* $1 - \epsilon$ *for any fixed* $\epsilon > 0$ *with high probability.*

[5]Disjunctive Normal Form

[6]The algorithm runs in time polynomial in the input parameters and in $1/\epsilon$.

$B \leftarrow \{a \in A_j : w_{ad} \geq \gamma\}$
For each $a \in A_j$, $r_a \leftarrow \frac{f_a}{\sum_{x \in B} f_x}$
if $\ell > 1$ **then**
  For each $a \in A_j$, $p_a \leftarrow \frac{f(a) \cdot S(d,j-1,\ell-1,\max(\gamma - w_{ad},0))}{S(d,j,\ell,\gamma)}$
end if
if $j > \ell$ **then**
  $p_\phi \leftarrow \frac{f_\phi \cdot S(d,j-1,\ell,\gamma)}{S(d,j,\ell,\gamma)}$
end if
Case 1 ($j = \ell = 1$):
  For each $a \in B$ with probability r_a, $q(j) \leftarrow a$
Case 2 ($j > \ell = 1$):
  For each $a \in B$ with probability $\frac{f_a \cdot f_\Phi}{S(d,j,\ell,\gamma)}$,
  $q(j) \leftarrow a$ and $q(-j) \leftarrow (\phi, \phi, \ldots, \phi)$;
  with the remaining probability,
  $q(j) \leftarrow \phi$ and $q(-j) \leftarrow \mathbf{Sample}(d, j-1, \ell, \gamma)$
Case 3 ($j = \ell > 1$):
  For each $a \in A_j$ with probability p_a, $q(j) \leftarrow a$ and
  $q(-j) \leftarrow \mathbf{Sample}(d, j-1, \ell-1, \max(\gamma - w_{ad}, 0))$
Case 4 ($j > \ell > 1$):
  For each $a \in A_j \cup \{\phi\}$ with probability p_a, $q(j) \leftarrow a$.
  if $q(j) = \phi$ **then**
    $q(-j) \leftarrow \mathbf{Sample}(d, j-1, \ell, \gamma)$;
  else
    $q(-j) \leftarrow \mathbf{Sample}(d, j-1, \ell-1, \max(\gamma - w_{a,d}, 0))$.
return q

Figure 2: The subroutine $\mathbf{Sample}(d, j, \ell, \gamma)$ used in phase 2 of the algorithm for the COUNT QUERY problem

Before proving this lemma, let us show that it is sufficient to prove Theorem 1. Let us denote the COUNT QUERY algorithm by $\mathcal{O}$ (we call it an *oracle*), and the GREEDY SELECTION algorithm by $\mathcal{A}$. Recall that in each iteration of $\mathcal{A}$, the document to be added to the index X is selected as follows: for every document $d \in D \setminus X$, we use oracle $\mathcal{O}$ to estimate $f_{X \cup \{d\}}$ and add the document for which this estimate is the maximum to X.

The next lemma maps the approximation ratio of $\mathcal{A}$ to that of $\mathcal{O}$.

LEMMA 2. *For any $\delta > 0$, there is a setting of ϵ for oracle $\mathcal{O}$ such that algorithm $\mathcal{A}$ has an approximation ratio of $1 - \delta$ whp, and has running time polynomial in $1/\delta$.*

To prove this lemma, we introduce some terminology. In any call to oracle $\mathcal{O}$, we say that the oracle is *successful* if the estimate produced is $(1 \pm \epsilon)$-accurate; otherwise, we say that the oracle failed. The next lemma quantifies the impact of a successful call to $\mathcal{O}$ on algorithm $\mathcal{A}$.

LEMMA 3. *Suppose in an iteration of algorithm $\mathcal{A}$, document d is selected, and let $d^* = \arg\max_{d \in D \setminus X} f_{X \cup \{d\}}$. Further, let $Z = f_{X \cup \{d\}}$ and $W = f_{X \cup \{d^*\}}$. If all the calls to oracle $\mathcal{O}$ in this iteration (with parameter ϵ) are successful, then $Z \geq \left(\frac{1-\epsilon}{1+\epsilon}\right) W$.*

PROOF SKETCH. Let $Y = f_X$; let $\widetilde{Y}$, $\widetilde{Z}$, and $\widetilde{W}$ denote the values of Y, Z, and W as estimated by oracle $\mathcal{O}$. Let $\rho = \frac{\widetilde{Y}}{Y} - 1$. Thus, $\rho \in [-\epsilon, \epsilon]$. Then,

$$Z - Y \geq \frac{\widetilde{Z}}{1+\epsilon} - \frac{\widetilde{Y}}{1+\rho} \geq \left(\frac{1-\epsilon}{1+\epsilon}\right) W - Y.$$

(Calculation details deferred to full version.) □

We use this lemma to prove Lemma 2.[7]

PROOF OF LEMMA 2. The probability that the oracle $\mathcal{O}$ fails in at least one call is $o(1)$, and is therefore absorbed in the failure probability of algorithm $\mathcal{A}$. Hence, we only need to show that if the oracle $\mathcal{O}$ is successful in every call of $\mathcal{A}$, then the approximation ratio of $\mathcal{A}$ is at most $1 - 1/e - \delta$.

Let X_i denote the selected documents in the first i iterations. Let the sum of relative frequencies of queries covered by an optimal solution be OPT. By averaging, there is at least one document $d \in D \setminus X_i$ such that

$$f_{X_i \cup \{d\}} - f_{X_i} \geq \frac{\text{OPT} - Y_i}{b}.$$

By Lemma 3, the success of oracle $\mathcal{O}$ with parameter ϵ (we will set the value of ϵ later) in iteration $i+1$ implies that

$$f_{X_{i+1}} \geq \rho \left(\frac{\text{OPT} - f_{X_i}}{b} + f_{X_i} \right),$$

where $\rho = \frac{1-\epsilon}{1+\epsilon}$. Since $X_0 = \emptyset$, the above recurrence yields

$$\begin{aligned} f_{X_b} &= \left(\frac{\rho}{b}\right) \text{OPT} \left(\sum_{i=0}^{b-1} \rho^i \left(1 - \frac{1}{b}\right)^i \right) \\ &= \left(\frac{\rho}{1 + (1-\rho)b}\right) \text{OPT} \left(1 - \rho^b \left(1 - \frac{1}{b}\right)^b \right). \end{aligned}$$

We set $\rho = 1 - \frac{c}{b}$ for some constant c that we will determine later. Then,

$$f_{X_b} > \left(\frac{1 - c/b}{1+c}\right) \text{OPT} \left(1 - e^{-(c+1)}\right) > 1 - \frac{1}{e} - \delta,$$

where we set $\epsilon = \frac{\delta}{b}$ to ensure that

$$c = \left(1 - \frac{1-\epsilon}{1+\epsilon}\right) b > \epsilon b = \delta > \frac{\delta}{2(1-1/e)}.$$

We used $\left(1 - \frac{x}{b}\right)^b < e^{-x}$ (first step), $b \geq 1$ (second step), and $\frac{1-c}{1+c} < 1 - 2c$ and $c > 0$ (third step) in the calculation. □

We now analyze the COUNT QUERY algorithm, and prove Lemma 1. The analysis comprises two claims: that the estimator X is unbiased, and that for a large enough value of n, X has small variance. The next lemma combines these claims.

LEMMA 4. *In the algorithm for the* COUNT QUERY *problem,*

$$\mathbb{P}[X \notin (1 \pm \epsilon) f_Y] = o(1).$$

PROOF. For any sample query q_j in the above algorithm,

$$\mathbb{E}[x_j] = \sum_{r=1}^{|Y|} \left(\frac{N_r}{N}\right) \cdot \left(\frac{\sum_{q \in Q'(d_r)} f_q}{N_r}\right) = \frac{\sum_{r=1}^{|Y|} \sum_{q \in Q'(d_r)} f_q}{N}.$$

Clearly, each query in $Q(Y)$ is present in $Q'(d_r)$ for exactly one document $d_r \in Y$. Therefore, $\mathbb{E}[x_j] = \frac{f_Y}{N}$, and hence, the estimator is unbiased.

Now, we employ Chernoff bounds (see e.g. [17]) to bound the probability of deviation of the estimator. Let $\zeta = \frac{f_Y}{N}$. Then

$$\mathbb{P}[X \notin (1 \pm \epsilon) f_Y] = \mathbb{P}\left[\sum_{i=1}^{n} x_i \notin (1 \pm \epsilon)\zeta n\right] \leq e^{-\frac{\epsilon^2 \zeta n}{3}},$$

[7]The proof implicitly uses the fact that the objective function for the INDEX SELECTION problem is *submodular.*

which is $o(1)$ for $n = \omega\left(\frac{3}{\epsilon^2 \zeta}\right)$.

We now note that $\frac{1}{\zeta} = \frac{N}{f_Y}$, which in turn equals

$$\frac{\sum_{q \in Q(Y)} f_q |\{r : q \in Q(d_r)\}|}{\sum_{q \in Q(Y)} f_q} \leq \max_{q \in Q(Y)} |\{r : q \in Q(d_r)\}| \leq |Y|.$$

Hence, n is polynomial in the input parameters. □

Running Time. The overall running time of the algorithm is

$$O\left(b \cdot |D| \cdot n \cdot \max_j \left(\sum_{i=1}^{k_j} |A_i|\right) + \sum_j k_j \cdot \sum_{i=1}^{k_j} \frac{|A_i|}{\eta}\right),$$

which is markedly better than the running time of a naïve implementation of the greedy algorithm, $O(b \cdot |D| \cdot \sum_j \prod_{i=1}^{k_j} |A_i|)$. Further, we will now describe algorithmic and data structural optimization that makes our implementation of the algorithm much more efficient than that suggested by the worst-case running time above. Our first observation is that the sets of sample queries generated in various calls to the COUNT QUERY sub-routine need not be independent since we are using an union bound over the error probabilities. This leads to the first optimization: For every document $d \in D$, we use the **Sample** sub-routine to generate apriori a set of (mutually independent) sample queries from $Q(d)$ with probabilities proportional to their relative frequencies (we call the set $SQ(d)$). Whenever the COUNT QUERY algorithm requires a sample query from $Q(d)$, it is provided the first query in $SQ(d)$ that has not been used previously in the current run of the COUNT QUERY algorithm.

To improve the performance and scalability of the GREEDY SELECTION algorithm further, we design the following data structure. Let P be a max priority queue of all the documents $d \in D$ ordered according to $f_d \cdot (1 - g_d)$, where f_d is the sum of frequencies of all queries covered by d, and g_d is the fraction of queries in $SQ(d)$ that are already covered by the current index X. Clearly, the document at the front of this priority queue is the next document that should be inserted in X. However, this data structure presents two challenges:

- Every time a document is inserted in X, we incur the huge overhead of having to update the values of g_d for every document d in P.
- Since the set of documents D is enormous, it would take a large amount of memory space to store the query samples corresponding to all the documents in P.

We overcome these challenges by adopting a *lazy policy*: For every document d in P, we maintain a counter c_d indicating the last index in X for which the value of g_d has been updated for document d. Initially, $c_d = 0$ and $g_d = 1$ for every document $d \in D$. Further, no sample query is generated for any document at the outset. Every step of the algorithm now comprises the following operations: We dequeue the document at the front of the priority queue P; let this document be d. If $c_d = 0$, then we generate the set of sample queries $SQ(d)$. Now, we check if $c_d < |X|$; if so, then we update the value of g_d for the current contents of X, set c_d to $|X|$, and re-insert document d in P. (Note that d may no longer be at the front of the queue since the value of g_d might have increased). On the other hand, if $c_d = |X|$, then we add d to X. Clearly, in this case, even though some of the documents in P have stale (i.e. smaller than actual) values of g, document d is indeed the one that maximizes $f \cdot (1 - g)$. Note that this solves both problems: we are now updating the values of c and g only when required, and also generating sample queries only for documents that show up at the front of P. In fact, we observe that most documents have small values of f and therefore never appear at the front of P.

If we are required to handle multiple coverages (see the first extension in the next section), we keep a counter $n(q, d)$ for every sample query $q \in SQ(d)$ (rather than g_d for document d) that indicates the number of documents in $X_{c(d)}$ that cover document d. (Recall that X_i is the prefix of X containing the first i inserted documents.) The priority queue P is now ordered on $\sum_{q \in SQ(d)} \rho^{n(q,d)+1} f_q$. When document d appears at the front of P, we increase the counters $n(q, d)$ by the number of documents in $X \setminus X_{c(d)}$ that cover query q.

4. EXTENSIONS

In this section, we describe various extensions to the GREEDY SELECTION algorithm.

Multiple Coverage. As mentioned in the introduction, $k > 1$ in most applications, e.g. a search engine returns multiple results in response to a user query. We generalize the INDEX SELECTION problem to this scenario by introducing an utility function u that maps the number of documents relevant to a query to their aggregate benefit. The objective function now becomes $\sum_{j=1}^{L} \sum_{q \in Q_j} f_q \cdot u(N(X, q))$, where $N(X, q)$ is the number of documents in X that are relevant to query q.

Note that the GREEDY SELECTION algorithm should logically prefer a document that covers queries that already have a significant coverage in the index to a document that covers queries having low coverage. This follows from the fact that the index is useful for a query only if has at least k relevant documents. To reflect this bias, we define the utility function as $u(i) = \min(2^i, 2^k)$ in our experiments. We may note that this choice violates the submodularity of the overall utility function, but as we show in the experiments, this leads to better results than choosing $u(i) = \min(i, k)$ (which is submodular) as in [1].

Dynamic Set of Documents. Recall that in most practical situations, the set of documents typically change over time. First, we consider the modifications to the index on the removal of a document. If the document was not present in the index, then we do not need to do anything. On the other hand, if the document was in the index, then we replace it by a new document which is chosen by running a single iteration of the GREEDY SELECTION algorithm.

Now, let us consider the modifications to the index on the addition of a document. Note that we have two decisions in this case: first, do we add the document to the index; and second, if we do, which document do we evict from the index? Further investigation of the problem reveals that the new document may cause more drastic changes of the following kind: if the new document covers all queries covered by the documents currently in the index, then inserting the new document in the index would make the current documents redundant (for $k = 1$). In this case, we have to recompute the index from scratch.

However, note that the situation described above is rather pathological. In practice, we do not expect the index to change drastically on the addition of a single document. To quantify this intuition, we impose the additional constraint that the index cannot change by more than one document for every document arrival. This has the added benefit that auxiliary data structures such as the indexing mechanisms do not need frequent drastic changes. The following simple algorithm now solves this problem efficiently: For every document $x \in X$, we estimate $f_{X,x,d} = f_{(X \setminus \{x\}) \cup \{d\}}$

using COUNT QUERY calls, where d is the new document. If $f_X \geq f_{X,x,d}$ for all $x \in X$, then we do not include the new document d in the index; otherwise, we evict $x^* = \arg\max_{x \in X} f_{X,x,d}$ from the index and replace it by d. Note that the number of calls to the COUNT QUERY sub-routine is now proportional to b rather than $|D|$.

Streaming Set of Documents. Finally, consider the scenario where the set of documents appear sequentially, and the algorithm needs to immediately decide whether to include a document or discard it on its arrival. We propose the following algorithm in this scenario: The algorithm has multiple *epochs*, where each epoch is characterized by a guessed value opt of the objective in an offline optimal solution. An epoch ends when the objective of the algorithmic solution exceeds opt, at which point we double our guess and start the next epoch. In any epoch, the algorithm includes every document that increases the objective value by at least $\frac{\text{opt}}{b_r}$, where $b_r = b - |X|$. Note that the increase in the objective can be computed by making a single call to the COUNT QUERY sub-routine. If the set of documents have some desirable properties (e.g. are drawn i.i.d. from a distribution), then this simple algorithm can be shown to have a constant approximation factor.

5. EXPERIMENTS

In this section, we evaluate the GREEDY SELECTION algorithm on real-world data. Recall that this algorithm can be used to generate a tiered index for the set of products in the index of a commerce search engine. We will begin by describing the datasets used in our experiments.

5.1 Datasets

For our experiments, we built a prototype search engine and populated it with real data from the shopping vertical of a commercial search engine. To this end, we downloaded detailed descriptions for about 30 million products from a commercial online shopping catalog. These products were categorized into around 600 leaf-level categories under 32 top-level categories such as `electronics`, `camera and optics`, `clothing and shoes`, and so on. The GREEDY SELECTION algorithm does not interact between categories, and therefore can be scaled to large indexes by processing combinations of categories in parallel. For clarity and without loss of generality, we restrict our analysis to two top-level categories in the catalog: `electronics` and `cameras and optics` with around 150,000 and 40,000 products respectively. We note that there are 74 sub-categories under electronics (such as `televisions`, `equalizers`, and `GPS Receivers`) and 49 sub-categories under cameras (such as `digital cameras`, `telescopes`, and `lenses`).

Next, we describe how we set the relevant scores w_{ad} for the products in the dataset. Consider, for example, a `sony bravia xbr tv` (with product id d). Since its product description contains attribute `brand:sony`, we set $w_{\text{sony},d} = 1.0$. Further, as mentioned in the introduction, we enrich the product with related attribute value information. For example, if `samsung` is a relevant brand for `sony` (i.e. users searching for `samsung` products previously have ended up buying `sony` products), then we set $w_{\text{samsung},d}$ to some value between 0 to 1. For a detailed description of how such similarity scores are chosen, the reader is referred to [19].

The Query Set. For our experiments, we sampled around 100,000 queries ($\mathcal{Q}$) from the query log of the same online shopping portal. We used uniform sampling over the queries in the query log (note that popular queries automatically get a bias because they appear more frequently in the query log). In order to analyze the effect of structure in the query on the performance of GREEDY SELECTION, we categorized these queries into five buckets depending on the degree of structure extracted from the query ranging from bucket 1 containing highly unstructured queries (mostly with one annotated keyword) to bucket 5 composed of many annotated tokens (sometimes as many as six). The number of queries in bucket 1 constituted around 20% of the queries in $\mathcal{Q}$. The number of queries in bucket 5 had a higher fraction of around 32%. In fact, the fraction of queries with at least 3 annotated keywords was close 70% of $\mathcal{Q}$. We note that annotation of queries is not the focus of this study. Toward this end, we used the query annotator described in [23].

In our experiments, we only considered the important attributes associated with each category. These are attributes that have a high *selectivity*, i.e. occur in a large fraction of product descriptions or user queries. We set the selectivity threshold to a conservative value of 0.5 and this yielded around six important attributes in each category, and for each selected attribute, we computed the relative frequencies of individual attribute values in a query log that spanned a six-month period.

5.2 Baseline Algorithms

We compare the performance of GREEDY SELECTION with the cache selection algorithms in Baeza-Yates *et al* [3] and Anagnostopoulos *et al* [1].

In the first algorithm, the goal is to populate the cache with a set of posting lists for important query terms. Each posting list is characterized by the frequency f of the associated term, and the size of the posting list s. The algorithm greedily selects the posting list with the minimum ratio s/f repeatedly until the entire cache is filled up. We refer to this algorithm as POSTING LISTS in our experiments.

The algorithm in [1] is also an iterative greedy algorithm, but selects, in each iteration, only the document that is relevant for the maximum number of queries not already covered by k cached documents. We refer to this algorithm as STOCHASTIC QUERY COVER in our experiments.

5.3 Experimental Results

Our experimental results can be categorized into two parts that we call *index generation* and *index serving*.

Index Generation Experiments. In the index generation experiments, we use around 10% of our query set $\mathcal{Q}$ (we call this the *training set* $\mathcal{T}$) for generating the index using all three algorithms separately. The performance of the algorithms in this step is measured by the fraction of queries in $\mathcal{T}$ covered by the index. This gives us a measure of the quality of the selection process used by the three algorithms in terms of coverage achieved on the training data itself. Note that this measure of effectiveness is extremely well-suited to STOCHASTIC QUERY COVER since it does not test the generalizability of the algorithm. Nevertheless, we show that GREEDY SELECTION has almost the same performance as STOCHASTIC QUERY COVER at small values of k and outperforms STOCHASTIC QUERY COVER for larger values of k. In addition, we show that we consistently outperform POSTING LISTS in this set of experiments.

We ran our experiments for cache sizes (or budgets) b ranging from 1% to 5% of the total index size, number of results k ranging from 6 to 14[8], and the relevance threshold θ ranging from 0.1 to 0.5. We also varied the number of samples in GREEDY SELEC-

[8]We selected this range so that the typical value of $k = 10$ falls in the middle of the range.

TION from 10 to 50, but observed that the sample size has negligible effect on the performance of the algorithm. We therefore only report the results for a sample size of 10 in all the experiments.

Fig. 3 illustrates the relative performance of GREEDY SELECTION compared to POSTING LISTS and STOCHASTIC QUERY COVER for all the aforementioned parameter values. In Fig. 3(a), all algorithms exhibit a drop in performance as k is increased since it becomes more difficult to cover a query. (Recall that a query is covered only if at least k relevant documents are present in the index.) Also, as expected, STOCHASTIC QUERY COVER performs better than GREEDY SELECTION at small values of k because (1) STOCHASTIC QUERY COVER optimizes over only the training query set whereas GREEDY SELECTION optimizes over the entire query space, and (2) STOCHASTIC QUERY COVER uses an expensive but accurate exhaustive search to make its greedy choices wheareas GREEDY SELECTION uses a much more efficient but slightly less accurate sampling technique to make its greedy choices. Interestingly, as k increases, the performance of STOCHASTIC QUERY COVER degrades rapidly. This can be attributed to the fact that STOCHASTIC QUERY COVER treats documents that cover queries already having significant cache coverage identically to documents that cover queries having no cache coverage. Clearly, the former set of documents should get precedence, and as mentioned in Section 4, GREEDY SELECTION ensures this by using an increasing utility function on coverage for making our greedy choices. Comparing with POSTING LISTS, we note that GREEDY SELECTION performs better than POSTING LISTS in the entire range of k since it is able to use cache space more judiciously by distinguishing between individual documents in a posting list based on whether they are relevant for other queries or not. In fact, GREEDY SELECTION does better than POSTING LISTS by almost 20% at the typical value of $k = 10$.

In Fig. 3(b), where we vary the relevance threshold θ, GREEDY SELECTION consistently outperforms POSTING LISTS by at least 20% and the gap in performance increases with the relevance threshold. Again, the greater selectivity of GREEDY SELECTION in terms of choosing documents gives it this advantage over POSTING LISTS. Furthermore, the performance of GREEDY SELECTION is either better than or comparable to that of STOCHASTIC QUERY COVER at all values of θ, even though the evaluation is only on the training query set.

Finally, in Fig. 3(c), we observe that POSTING LISTS has a less smooth uptick in performance than GREEDY SELECTION with increasing index size. This is because it is always forced to include entire posting lists, and therefore often cannot use residual space in the cache. Such behavior causes pockets of relatively less progress with increase in budget, which is illustrated in Fig. 3(c). On the other hand, GREEDY SELECTION, with its ability to select one document at a time, exhibits a smoother increase in query coverage as the budget is increased. Further, GREEDY SELECTION gets closer to STOCHASTIC QUERY COVER as b increases and again, does not show a significant drop in performance when compared to STOCHASTIC QUERY COVER across the whole range of budgets.

To summarize, this experiment shows us that even when we restrict ourselves to evaluation on training data, GREEDY SELECTION exhibits performance that is comparable to (and sometimes better than) STOCHASTIC QUERY COVER. Further, for various ranges of parameters, we have exhibited that GREEDY SELECTION comfortably outperforms POSTING LISTS in this set of experiments.

Index Serving Experiments. In the next set of experiments, we measured the generalization capabilities of the algorithms by defining our test query set as $\mathcal{S} = \mathcal{Q} \setminus \mathcal{T}$ and measuring the hit ratios for different parameter values. We further analyzed the effect of the extent of structure in a query on the hit ratios. As described earlier, we classified the queries into five buckets ranging from highly unstructured ($= 1$) to highly structured ($= 5$). Again, we varied k from 6 to 14 and θ from 0.1 to 0.5, whereas the budget was fixed to 3% of the total index size. In Fig. 4, we illustrate the performance of the three algorithms as a function of these parameters.

As Fig. 4(a) shows, GREEDY SELECTION results in a much better hit ratio compared to POSTING LISTS and STOCHASTIC QUERY COVER when the queries are highly structured. However, when the queries become less structured, even though GREEDY SELECTION continues to dominate POSTING LISTS in performance, STOCHASTIC QUERY COVER starts performing marginally better than GREEDY SELECTION. Unstructured queries are less specific than structured queries and therefore, are often covered by more documents in the index. STOCHASTIC QUERY COVER performs well in this regime since the lack of specificity in unstructured queries implies that they are covered by many documents that also cover queries in the training set. On the other hand, structured queries tend to be more specific and are often covered by fewer documents in the index. Such queries are often missed by a typical LRU cache and therefore, almost always, rely on a tier-one index to be served efficiently. For such queries, GREEDY SELECTION outperforms POSTING LISTS and STOCHASTIC QUERY COVER by around 30% for typical values of $k = 10$. In fact, the relative performance of GREEDY SELECTIONincreases as the value of k increases. This reflects the powerful generalizing capability of GREEDY SELECTION to queries with unseen or rare combination of attribute values.

Fig. 4(b) shows the performance of the algorithms for different values of θ. Here, we observe that while the performance of all the algorithms drops as θ increases, GREEDY SELECTIONconsistently exhibits a better hit ratio than POSTING LISTS and STOCHASTIC QUERY COVER , especially for the highly structured queries. For example, for $\theta = 0.3$, GREEDY SELECTIONalmost outperforms the other algorithms 2 to 1. This again highlights the difference in the generalizing capabilities of the algorithms. In order to explicitly measure the effectiveness of the algorithms on less frequent queries, we repeated the experiment using unique queries in $\mathcal{S}$ (by ignoring the query frequencies) and we observed a similar gap in performance between GREEDY SELECTION and the other algorithms.

Since one of the primary applications of the selected documents is for tiered indexing, we measured the quality of the resulting index built using these documents. The quality of a document is measured as its average relevance score over all attribute values. In Fig. 5, we note that GREEDY SELECTION includes more relevant documents in the index compared to POSTING LISTS. In fact, the document quality is almost 40% better when using GREEDY SELECTION (see Fig. 5(a)). This can be attributed to the fact that while POSTING LISTS does not distinguish between documents in the same posting list, GREEDY SELECTION selects one document at a time and therefore, selects only high quality documents in the cache.

6. RELATED WORK

Previous work on understanding user query distributions in terms of their relative frequencies and repetition (see e.g. [26, 6]) has observed on numerous occasions that users share many popular queries. This immediately motivates a caching infrastructure such as the one that we propose in this paper in order to improve the performance of search engines. In the context database applications, there has been extensive work on building efficient middle-

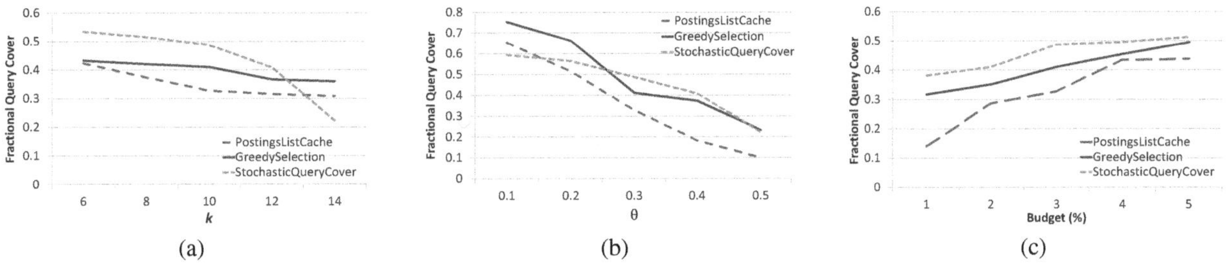

Figure 3: Performance of GREEDY SELECTION **compared to** POSTING LISTS **and** STOCHASTIC QUERY COVER **using cache hit ratio on the training set of queries for various parameter ranges: (a) Effect of number of results k needed to cover a query, with $b = 3\%$ and $\theta = 0.3$, (b) Effect of relevance threshold θ, with $b = 3\%$ and $k = 10$, and (c) Effect of index size b with $\theta = 0.3$ and $k = 10$.**

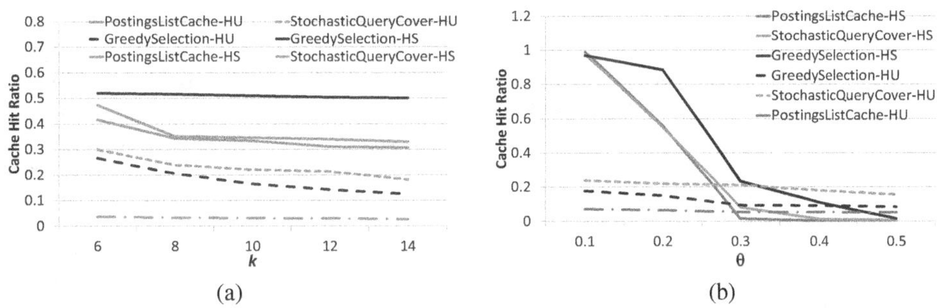

Figure 4: Performance of GREEDY SELECTION **compared to** POSTING LISTS **and** STOCHASTIC QUERY COVER **at index serve time: (a) Effect of the number of documents k needed to cover a query, with $b = 3\%$ and $\theta = 0.3$, (b) Effect of the relevance threshold θ, with $b = 3\%$ and $k = 10$. (HU = "Highly Unstructured", HS = "Highly Structured")**

tier caches [2, 5, 15]. Early work on caching and tiering techniques for search queries can be largely categorized into two broad areas — result caching [20, 3, 25, 10, 9] and tiered indexing [21, 16, 18, 25, 4, 14, 11, 1]. The basic problem behind caching is to understand the cost of serving a given query workload. For example, Raghavan and Sever [20] focused on popular queries in query logs. More recently, Gan and Suel [9] proposed a weighted caching scheme that includes the cost of processing the more frequent queries to a search engine. Risvik *et al* [21] introduced the concept of tiering in order to improve the performance of search engines. Ntoulas and Cho [18] studied term and document pruning strategies with the aim of reducing resources needed to handle a given query. Skobeltsyn *et al* [25] combined result caching with index pruning for better efficiency. Baeza-Yates *et al* [3] compared the impact of results caching and static caching of posting lists on the performance of web search engines. They concluded that static caching of posting lists outperforms all other variations of caching they considered in their study. Long and Suel [16] introduced a three-level caching architecture that includes on-disk caching of the posting lists for popular term combinations. Leung *et al* [14] studied the problem of tier selection for storing documents with the goal of minimizing the number of tier traversals for a given workload of queries. The work of Anagnostopoulos *et al* [1] is the closest to ours. They gave a greedy algorithm for document selection based on a training set to queries. In fact, we will compare the performance of our algorithm to those of [3] and [1].

Another line of work that incorporates relevance and similarity functions is on top-k queries (also referred to as k nearest neighbors (kNN))in databases [22]. More recent work focused on applying the kNN problem to searching over a database [27, 24]. Our work differs from this line of work in that we focus our work on generating a tiered index that addresses the low latency requirements often imposed in online search settings.

From a theoretical perspective, our algorithms fall in a class of well-studied combinatorial optimization problems called *covering* problems. Of particular relevance is the maximum k-coverage problem, where the goal is to select a collection of at most k sets in a universe of weighted elements such that the sum of weights of elements covered by these sets is maximized. This is a classical NP-complete problem, and it has been shown that the natural greedy algorithm for this problem is indeed optimal under standard assumptions in complexity theory [8]. Many variants and generalizations of this problem have also been studied in the literature (see e.g. [13, 7]), including ones where we have oracle access to the sets. Our problem falls in this category, and the main technical contribution of this paper is to design a suitable oracle for our setting by exploiting the structural properties of commerce search queries.

7. CONCLUSION AND FUTURE WORK

In summary, we proposed a technique for caching search results for structured search domains such as commerce search, and demonstrated the effectiveness of our proposed algorithm both theoretically and via experiments on real-world data. There are multiple important questions that this work raises. For what other search domains can such result caches be generated using our techniques? In particular, can our techniques be extended to unstructured domains such as general web search? How to handle arbitrarily correlated attributes and arbitrary relevance functions?

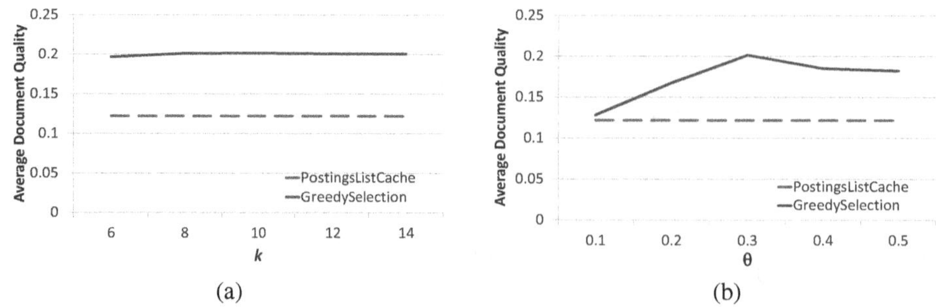

Figure 5: The quality of the index computed using GREEDY SELECTION compared to POSTING LISTS: (a) Effect of the number of documents k needed to cover a query, with $b = 3\%$ and $\theta = 0.3$, and (b) Effect of relevance threshold θ, with $b = 3\%$ and $k = 10$.

8. REFERENCES

[1] Aris Anagnostopoulos, Luca Becchetti, Stefano Leonardi, Ida Mele, and Piotr Sankowski. Stochastic query covering. In *WSDM*, pages 725–734, 2011.

[2] Jesse Anton, Lawrence Jacobs, Xiang Liu, Jordan Parker, Zheng Zeng, and Tie Zhong. Web caching for database applications with oracle web cache. In *SIGMOD Conference*, pages 594–599, 2002.

[3] Ricardo A. Baeza-Yates, Aristides Gionis, Flavio Junqueira, Vanessa Murdock, Vassilis Plachouras, and Fabrizio Silvestri. The impact of caching on search engines. In *SIGIR*, pages 183–190, 2007.

[4] Ricardo A. Baeza-Yates, Vanessa Murdock, and Claudia Hauff. Efficiency trade-offs in two-tier web search systems. In *SIGIR*, pages 163–170, 2009.

[5] Christof Bornhövd, Mehmet Altinel, Sailesh Krishnamurthy, C. Mohan, Hamid Pirahesh, and Berthold Reinwald. Dbcache: Middle-tier database caching for highly scalable e-business architectures. In *SIGMOD Conference*, page 662, 2003.

[6] Andrei Z. Broder, Marcus Fontoura, Vanja Josifovski, Ravi Kumar, Rajeev Motwani, Shubha U. Nabar, Rina Panigrahy, Andrew Tomkins, and Ying Xu. Estimating corpus size via queries. In *CIKM*, pages 594–603, 2006.

[7] Chandra Chekuri and Amit Kumar. Maximum coverage problem with group budget constraints and applications. In *APPROX-RANDOM*, pages 72–83, 2004.

[8] Uriel Feige. A threshold of *ln n* for approximating set cover. *J. ACM*, 45(4):634–652, 1998.

[9] Qingqing Gan and Torsten Suel. Improved techniques for result caching in web search engines. In *WWW*, pages 431–440, 2009.

[10] Charles Garrod, Amit Manjhi, Anastasia Ailamaki, Bruce M. Maggs, Todd C. Mowry, Christopher Olston, and Anthony Tomasic. Scalable query result caching for web applications. *PVLDB*, 1(1):550–561, 2008.

[11] Jun-Seok Heo, Junghoo Cho, and Kyu-Young Whang. The hybrid-layer index: A synergic approach to answering top-k queries in arbitrary subspaces. In *ICDE*, pages 445–448, 2010.

[12] Richard M. Karp, Michael Luby, and Neal Madras. Monte-carlo approximation algorithms for enumeration problems. *J. Algorithms*, 10(3):429–448, 1989.

[13] Samir Khuller, Anna Moss, and Joseph Naor. The budgeted maximum coverage problem. *Inf. Process. Lett.*, 70(1):39–45, 1999.

[14] Gilbert Leung, Novi Quadrianto, Alexander J. Smola, and Kostas Tsioutsiouliklis. Optimal web-scale tiering as a flow problem. In *NIPS*, pages 1333–1341, 2010.

[15] Wen-Syan Li, Daniel C. Zilio, Vishal S. Batra, Calisto Zuzarte, and Inderpal Narang. Load balancing and data placement for multi-tiered database systems. *Data Knowl. Eng.*, 62(3):523–546, 2007.

[16] Xiaohui Long and Torsten Suel. Three-level caching for efficient query processing in large web search engines. In *WWW*, pages 257–266, 2005.

[17] R. Motwani and P. Raghavan. *Randomized Algorithms*. Cambridge University Press, 1997.

[18] Alexandros Ntoulas and Junghoo Cho. Pruning policies for two-tiered inverted index with correctness guarantee. In *SIGIR*, pages 191–198, 2007.

[19] Debmalya Panigrahi and Sreenivas Gollapudi. Result enrichment in commerce search using browse trails. In *WSDM*, pages 267–276, 2011.

[20] Vijay V. Raghavan and Hayri Sever. On the reuse of past optimal queries. In *SIGIR*, pages 344–350, 1995.

[21] Knut Magne Risvik, Yngve Aasheim, and Mathias Lidal. Multi-tier architecture for web search engines. In *LA-WEB*, pages 132–143, 2003.

[22] Nick Roussopoulos, Stephen Kelley, and Frédéic Vincent. Nearest neighbor queries. In *SIGMOD Conference*, pages 71–79, 1995.

[23] Nikos Sarkas, Stelios Paparizos, and Panayiotis Tsaparas. Structured annotations of web queries. In *SIGMOD Conference*, pages 771–782, 2010.

[24] Thomas Seidl and Hans-Peter Kriegel. Optimal multi-step k-nearest neighbor search. In *SIGMOD Conference*, pages 154–165, 1998.

[25] Gleb Skobeltsyn, Flavio Junqueira, Vassilis Plachouras, and Ricardo A. Baeza-Yates. Resin: a combination of results caching and index pruning for high-performance web search engines. In *SIGIR*, pages 131–138, 2008.

[26] Yinglian Xie and David R. O'Hallaron. Locality in search engine queries and its implications for caching. In *INFOCOM*, 2002.

[27] Wenjie Zhang, Xuemin Lin, Muhammad Aamir Cheema, Ying Zhang, and Wei Wang. Quantile-based KNN over multi-valued objects. In *ICDE*, pages 16–27, 2010.

Quasi-Succinct Indices

Sebastiano Vigna
Dipartimento di Informatica, Università degli Studi di Milano, Italy

ABSTRACT

Compressed inverted indices in use today are based on the idea of gap compression: documents pointers are stored in increasing order, and the gaps between successive document pointers are stored using suitable codes which represent smaller gaps using less bits. Additional data such as counts and positions is stored using similar techniques. A large body of research has been built in the last 30 years around gap compression, including theoretical modeling of the gap distribution, specialized instantaneous codes suitable for gap encoding, and *ad hoc* document reorderings which increase the efficiency of instantaneous codes. This paper proposes to represent an index using a different architecture based on quasi-succinct representation of monotone sequences. We show that, besides being theoretically elegant and simple, the new index provides expected constant-time operations, space savings, and, in practice, significant performance improvements on conjunctive, phrasal and proximity queries.

Categories and Subject Descriptors

H.3.1 [**Information Storage and Retrieval**]: Content Analysis and Indexing—*Indexing methods*

Keywords

Compressed indices; succinct data structures

1. INTRODUCTION

An *inverted index* over a collection of documents contains, for each term of the collection, the set of documents in which the term appears and additional information such as the number of occurrences of the term within each document, and possibly their positions. Inverted indices form the backbone of all modern search engines, and the existence of large document collections (typically, the web) has made the construction of efficient inverted indices ever more important.

Compression of inverted indices saves disk space, but more importantly also reduces disk and main memory accesses [7], resulting in faster evaluation. We refer the reader to the book by Manning, Raghavan and Schütze [19] and to the very complete and recent survey by Zobel and Moffat [28] for a thorough bibliography on the subject.

Two main complementary techniques are at the basis of index compression: *instantaneous codes* provide storage for integers that is proportional to the size of the integer (e.g., smaller numbers use less bits); *gap encoding* turns lists of increasing integers (for instance, the monotonically increasing list of numbers of documents in which a term appear) into lists of small integers, the *gaps* between successive values (e.g., the difference). The two techniques, combined, make it possible to store inverted indices in highly compressed form. Instantaneous codes are also instrumental in storing in little space information such as the number of documents in which each term appears.

Since inverted indices are so important for search engines, it is not surprising that a large amount of research has studied how to maximize either the speed or the compression ratio of gap-encoded indices. Depending on the application, compression or speed may be considered more important, and different solutions propose different tradeoffs.

In this paper, we describe a new type of compressed index that does not use gaps. Rather, we carefully engineer and tailor to the needs of a search engine a well-known *quasi-succinct* representation for monotone sequences proposed by Peter Elias [12].[1] We explain how to code every part of the index by exploiting the bijection between sequence of integers and their *prefix sums*, and we provide details about the physical storage of our format.

Our new index is theoretically attractive: it guarantees to code the information in the index close to its *information-theoretical lower bound*, and provides on average constant-time access to any piece of information stored in the index, including searching for elements larger than a given value (a fundamental operation for computing list intersections quickly). This happens by means of a very simple addressing mechanism based on a linear list of forward pointers. Moreover, sequential scanning can be performed using a very small number of logical operation per element. We believe it is particularly attractive for in-memory or memory-mapped indices, in which the cost of disk access is not dominant.

To corroborate our findings, in the last part of the paper, we index the TREC GOV2 collection and a collection of 130 million page of the `.uk` web[2] with different type of encodings, such as δ and Golomb. We show that, while not able to beat gaps coded with Golomb codes, our index compresses better than γ/δ codes or variable-length byte codes.

WSDM'13, February 4–8, 2013, Rome, Italy.

[1] Incidentally, Elias also invented some of the most efficient codes for gap compression [13].

[2] We remark that TREC GOV2 is publicly available, and that the latter collection is available from the author.

We then compare a prototype Java implementation of our index against MG4J (using its high-performance indices) and Lucene, two publicly available Java engines, and Zettair, a C search engine. MG4J has been set up to use γ/δ codes, whereas Lucene and Zettair use variable-length byte codes. We get a full confirmation of the good theoretical properties of our index, with excellent timings for conjunctive, phrasal and proximity queries. We also provide some evidence that for pointer lists our index is competitive with the Kamikaze implementation of PForDelta codes [29].

The quasi-succinct indices described in this paper are the default indices used by MG4J from version 5.0.[3] All code used in this paper is available for download under the Lesser GNU GPL.[4]

2. RELATED WORK

The basis of the current compression techniques for inverted indices is *gap encoding*, developed at the start of the '90s [3]. Gap encoding made it possible to store a positional inverted index in space often *smaller* than the compressed document collection. Gaps (differences between contiguous document pointers in the posting list) have to be encoded using instantaneous codes that use shorter codewords for smaller integers, and previous research in information theory provided γ, δ [13] and Golomb [15] codes, which achieve excellent compression. Moreover, a wealth of alternative codes have been developed in the last 30 years.[5]

When speed is important, however, such codes are rather slow to decode: in practice, often implementation use the folklore *variable-length byte code* (e.g., the open-source search engine Lucene, as well as Zettair). Recent research has developed a number of *word-aligned* codes (e.g., [1]) that encode in a single machine word several integers, providing high-speed decoding and good compression. In [29], the author tailor their PForDelta code to the behavior of modern super-scalar CPUs and their caches.

More specialized techniques tackle specific problems, studying in great detail the behaviour of each part of the index: for instance, [27] studies in great detail the compression of positional information.

Another line of research studies the renumberings of the documents that generate smaller gaps. This phenomenon is known as *clustering* [20], and can be induced by choosing a suitable numbering for the documents [4, 25, 5].

As indices became larger, a form of *self-indexing* [21] became necessary to compute quickly the intersection of lists of documents, an operation that is at the basis of the computation of conjunctive Boolean queries, proximity queries and phrasal queries.

The techniques used in this paper are based on a seminal paper by Elias [12], which is a precursor of *succinct data structures* for indexed sets [23]. We do use some of the knowledge developed by the algorithmic community working on succinct data structures, albeit in practice the theoretical encodings developed there, which concentrate on attaining asymptotically optimal speed using $o(n)$ additional bits, where n is the optimal size for the data structure, have presently too high constant costs to be competitive in real applications with methods using $O(n)$ additional bits.

We remark that the literature on the subject is actually immense, and impossible to recap in this section. The references above should be considered mostly as pointers. We refer the reader again to [19, 28] for a complete historical overview.

[3] `http://mg4j.di.unimi.it/`

[4] `http://vigna.di.unimi.it/`

[5] Alternative approaches, such as *interpolative coding* [20], have been proposed to code some part of an index, but they lack the direct-access and skipping features that are necessary for fast query resolution.

3. DEFINITIONS

In this paper we discuss the indexing problem for a collection of documents. We give definitions from scratch as we will need to discuss formally the index content.

Each document is represented by a number, called *document pointer*, starting from zero. Each document d has a length ℓ, and is formed by a sequence of terms $t_0, t_1, \ldots, t_{\ell-1}$. For each document and each term, the *count* specifies how many times a term appears in the sequence forming the document. The *frequency* is the number of documents in which a term appears (i.e., the number of documents for which the count is not zero). The *occurrency* of a term is the number of occurrences of the term in the whole collection, that is, the sum of the counts of the term over all documents.

The *posting list* for a term is the (monotonically increasing) list of documents where the term appears. With each document we associate also the (nonzero) count of the term in the document, and the (monotonically increasing) list of *positions* (numbered from zero) at which the term appears in the given document.

The *unary code* associates with the natural number $n \geq 0$ the codeword 0^n1. The *negated unary code* associates with the natural number $n \geq 0$ the codeword 1^n0.

A *bit array* of length n is a sequence of bits $b_0, b_1, \ldots, b_{n-1}$. We sometime view such an array as a *stream*: we assume that there is an implicit pointer, and that I/O operations such as reading unary codes are performed by scanning the array and updating the implicit pointer accordingly.

4. QUASI-SUCCINCT REPRESENTATION OF MONOTONE SEQUENCES

In this section we give a detailed description of the *high bits/low bits* representation of a monotone sequence proposed by Elias [12] and independently by Fano [14]. We assume to have a monotonically increasing sequence of $n > 0$ natural numbers

$$0 \leq x_0 \leq x_1 \leq \cdots \leq x_{n-2} \leq x_{n-1} \leq u,$$

where $u > 0$ is any upper bound on the last value.[6] The choice $u = x_{n-1}$ is of course possible (and optimal), but storing explicitly x_{n-1} might be costly, and a suitable value for u might be known from external information, as we will see shortly. We will represent such a sequence in two bit arrays as follows:

- the lower $\ell = \max\{\, 0, \lfloor \log(u/n) \rfloor \,\}$ bits of each x_i are stored explicitly and contiguously in the *lower-bits array*;[7]
- the upper bits are stored in the *upper-bits array* as a sequence of unary-coded gaps.

In Figure 1 we show an example. Note that we code the gaps between the values of the upper bits, that is, $\lfloor x_i/2^\ell \rfloor - \lfloor x_{i-1}/2^\ell \rfloor$ (with the convention $x_{-1} = 0$).[8]

The interesting property of this representation is that it uses at most $2 + \lceil \log(u/n) \rceil$ bits per element: this can be easily seen from

[6] If $u = 0$, the list is entirely made of zeroes, and its content is just defined by n.

[7] Actually, Elias discusses just the case in which $u + 1$ and $n + 1$ are powers of two, but extending his definitions is an easy exercise.

[8] We remark that, despite a superficial similarity with the upper/lower splitting of Rice and Golomb codes, the representation above has no connection with neither code, as lower bits contain an *explicit value*, and not a *gap*.

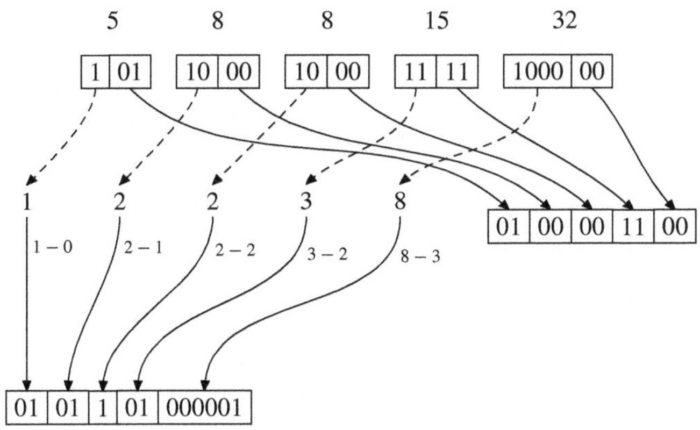

Figure 1: A simple example of the quasi-succinct encoding from [12]. We consider the list 5, 8, 8, 15, 32 with upper bound 36, so $\ell = \lfloor \log(36/5) \rfloor = 2$. On the right, the lower ℓ bits of all elements are concatenated to form the lower-bits array. On the left, the gap of the values of the upper bits are stored sequentially in unary code in the upper-bits array.

the fact that each unary code uses one stop bit, and each other written bit increases the value of the upper bits by 2^ℓ: clearly, this cannot happen more than $\lfloor x_{n-1}/2^\ell \rfloor$ times. But

$$\left\lfloor \frac{x_{n-1}}{2^\ell} \right\rfloor \le \left\lfloor \frac{u}{2^\ell} \right\rfloor \le \frac{u}{2^\ell} = \frac{u}{2^{\max\{0, \lfloor \log(u/n) \rfloor\}}} \le 2n. \qquad (1)$$

Thus, we write at most n ones and $2n$ zeroes, which implies our statement as $\lceil \log(u/n) \rceil = \lfloor \log(u/n) \rfloor + 1$ unless u/n is a power of two, but in that case (1) actually ends with $\le n$, so the statement is still true.

Since the information-theoretical lower bound for a monotone list of n elements in a universe of u element is

$$\left\lceil \log \binom{u+n}{n} \right\rceil \approx n \log\left(\frac{u+n}{n}\right)$$

we see that the representation is close to succinct: indeed, Elias proves in detail that this representation is very close to the optimal representation (less than half a bit per element away). Thus, while it does not strictly classify as a *succinct* representation, it can be safely called a *quasi-succinct* representation.[9]

To recover x_i from the representation, we perform i unary-code reads in the upper-bits array, getting to position p: the value of the upper bits of x_i is then exactly $p - i$; the lower ℓ bits can be extracted with a random access, as they are located at position $i\ell$ in the lower-bits array.

We now observe that, assuming to have a fictitious element $x_{-1} = 0$, we can equivalently see the list $x_0, x_1, \ldots, x_{n-1}$ as a list of natural numbers by computing gaps:

$$a_0 = x_0 - x_{-1}, a_1 = x_1 - x_0, \cdots, a_{n-1} = x_{n-1} - x_{n-2}.$$

Conversely, given a list $a_0, a_1, \ldots, a_{n-1}$ of natural numbers we can consider the list of *prefix sums* $s_k = \sum_{i=0}^{k-1} a_i$ for $0 \le k \le n$. The two operations give a bijective correspondence between monotone sequences[10] bounded by u and lists of natural numbers of the same length whose sum is bounded by u.[11] Thus, we can represent using the high bits/low bits presentation either monotonically increasing sequences, or generic lists of integers.[12]

The quasi-succinct representation above has a number of useful properties that make it quite advantageous over gap-encoded sequences:

- The distribution of the document gaps is irrelevant: there is no code to choose, because the lower bits are stored explicitly in a fixed-width format, and the representation of the upper bits, being made by n ones and at most $2n$ zeroes, is a perfect candidate for the unary code.
- Compression is guaranteed irrespective of gaps being well distributed (e.g., because of correlation between the content of consecutive document) or not. In particular, renumbering documents in a way that improves retrieval speed (e.g., to ease early termination) will not affect the index size.
- Scanning sequentially the list using a longword buffer requires to perform just a unary read and using few shifts for each element.
- In general, the high bits/low bits representation concentrates the difficulty of searching and skipping on a simple bit array of unary codes containing n ones and at most $2n$ zeroes. We can devise extremely fast, practical *ad hoc* techniques that exploit this information.

Actually, Elias's original paper suggests the most obvious solution for quick (on average, constant-time) reading of a sequence of unary codes: we store *forward pointers* to the positions (inside the upper-bits array) that one would reach after kq unary-code reads, $k \ge 0$, where q is a fixed *quantum* (in other words, we record the position immediately after the one of index $kq - 1$ in the bit array).

Retrieving x_i now can be done by simulating $q\lfloor i/q \rfloor$ unary reads using a forward pointer, and completing sequentially with $i \bmod q < q$ unary-code reads. On average, by (1), the sequential part will read at most $3q$ bits.[13] Smaller values of q yield less reads and use more space.

Skipping. A more interesting property, for our purposes, is that by storing *skip pointers* to positions reached after *negated* unary-code reads of the upper bits it is possible to perform *skipping*, that is, to find very quickly, given a bound b, the smallest $x_i \ge b$. This operation is fundamental in search engines as it is the base for quick list intersection.[14]

[9]Actually, the representation is one of the ingredients of sophisticated, modern succinct data structures that attain the information-theoretical bound [23].

[10]Note that sequences of prefix sums contain an additional element $s_0 = 0$ that is not part of the bijection.

[11]The same bijection is used normally to code monotone sequences using gaps, but we intend to to the opposite.

[12]Prefix sums have indeed several applications in compression, for instance to the storage of XML documents [10].

[13]This problem is essentially (i.e., modulo an off-by-one) the *selection* problem for which much more sophisticated solutions, starting with Clarke's [8], have in the last years shown that constant-time access can be obtained using $o(n)$ additional bits instead of the $O(n)$ bits proposed by Elias and Fano, but such solutions, while asymptotically optimal, have very high constant costs. Nonetheless, there is a large body of theoretical and practical knowledge that has been accumulated in the last 20 years about selection, and we will use some of the products of that research to read multiple unary codes quickly in the upper-bits array.

[14]Elias describes a slightly different analogous operation, by which he finds the largest $x_i \le b$; the operation involves moving *backwards* in the bit array, something that we prefer to avoid for efficiency. Note that this is again essentially equivalent to *predecessor search*, a basic problem in fast retrieval on sets of integers for which very strong theoretical results are known in the RAM model [22].

To see why this is possible, note that by definition in the upper-bits array the unary code corresponding to the smallest $x_i \geq b$ must terminate *after* $\lfloor b/2^\ell \rfloor$ zeroes. We could thus perform $\lfloor b/2^\ell \rfloor$ negated unary-code reads, getting to position p, and knowing that there are exactly $p - \lfloor b/2^\ell \rfloor$ ones and $\lfloor b/2^\ell \rfloor$ zeroes to our left (i.e., we are in the middle of the unary code for $x_{p-\lfloor b/2^\ell \rfloor}$). From here, we complete the search exhaustively, that is, we actually compute the values of the elements of the list (by reading unary codes and retrieving the suitable lower bits) and compare them with b, as clearly the element we are searching for cannot be represented earlier in the upper-bits array. An example is shown in Figure 2.

By setting up an array of *skip pointers* analogously to the previous case (i.e., forward pointers), the reading of negated unary-codes can be perform quickly. Note, however, that in general without further assumptions it is not possible to bound the number of bits read during the $\lfloor b/2^\ell \rfloor \bmod q$ negated unary-code reads that must be performed after following a skip pointer, as there could be few zeroes (actually, even none) in the bit array. Nonetheless, if a linear lower bound on the number of zeroes in the bit array is known, it can be used to show that skipping is performed in constant time on average.

Strictly monotone sequences. In case the sequence $x_0, x_1, \ldots, x_{n-1}$ to be represented is *strictly* monotone (or, equivalently, the a_i's are nonzero), it is possible to reduce the space usage by storing the sequence $x_i - i$ using the upper bound $u - n$. Retrieval happens in the same way—one just has to adjust the retrieved value for the i-th element by adding i. This mechanism was already noted by Elias [11] (more generally for k-spaced sequences, $k > 0$), but it is important to remark that under this representation *the algorithm for skipping will no longer work*. This happens because x_i is actually represented as $x_i - i$, so skipping $\lfloor b/2^\ell \rfloor$ negated unary codes could move us arbitrarily *after* the element we would like to reach.

5. SEQUENCES AS A RANKED CHARACTERISTIC FUNCTIONS

In some cases, the quasi-succinct representation we described is not very efficient in term of space: this happens, for instance, for very dense sequences. There is however an alternate representation for strictly monotone sequences with skipping: we simply store a list of u bits in which bit k is set if k is part of the list x_0, x_1, $\ldots$, x_{n-1}. This is equivalent to storing the list in gap-compressed form by writing in unary the gaps $x_i - x_{i-1} - 1$, and guarantees by definition that no more than u bits will be used.

Skipping in such a representation is actually trivial: given the bound b, we read a unary code starting at position b. The new position x_i is such that x_i is the smallest element satisfying $x_i \geq b$. The only problem is that at this point we will have lost track of the index i.

To solve this problem, we take a dual approach to that of the previous section and store a simple *ranking* structure: for each position kq, where q is the quantum, we store the number of ones to the left. After a skip, we simply rank the current position x_i by first reading the precomputed number of ones before $\lfloor x_i/q \rfloor$, and then then computing the number of ones in the at most q remaining bits.

6. REPRESENTING AN INVERTED INDEX

We now discuss how the quasi-succinct representation presented in the previous section can be used to represent the posting list of a term. We defer to the next section a detailed discussion of the data-storage format.

Pointers. Document pointers form a strictly monotone increasing sequence. We store them using the standard representation (i.e., not the specialized version for strictly monotone sequences), so to be able to store skip pointers, as skipping is a frequent and useful operation (e.g., during the resolution of conjunctive Boolean queries or phrasal queries), whereas random access to document pointers is not in general necessary.[15] The upper bound is the number of documents N minus one, and the number of elements of the list is f, the frequency.

We remark that the apparent loss of compression due to the necessity of using the standard representation (to make skipping possible) turns actually into an advantage: if the last pointer in the list is equal to αN, with $0 \leq \alpha < 1$, since $N \geq f$, we can write $N = df + r$ with $d > 0$ and $0 \leq r < f$, and then we have

$$\left\lfloor \frac{\alpha N}{2^\ell} \right\rfloor = \left\lfloor \frac{\alpha(df+r)}{2^{\lfloor \log((df+r)/f) \rfloor}} \right\rfloor \geq \left\lfloor \frac{\alpha(df+r)}{2^{\lfloor \log d \rfloor}} \right\rfloor \geq \alpha f. \quad (2)$$

In other words, the slight redundancy guarantees that there are at least αf zeroes in the upper-bits array: if $\alpha \approx 1$, we can thus guarantee that on average skipping can be performed in a constant number of steps, as, on average, reading a one implies reading at least a zero, too (and viceversa). Since we write forward pointers only for lists with $f \geq q$, under realistic assumptions on q in practice α is close to 1.

Finally, even in pathological cases (i.e., a every uneven distribution of the zeroes in the list), one every $2^\ell \leq N/f$ bits must necessarily be zero, as the list is strictly monotone. Thus, terms with dense posting lists must have frequent zeroes independently of the considerations above.

Note that if

$$f + \lfloor N/2^\ell \rfloor + f\ell > N$$

then the representation above uses more than N bits (in practice, this happens when $f \gtrsim N/3$). In this case, we switch to a ranked characteristic function. Since there are at most two zeroes for each one in the bitmap, it is easy to check that all operations can still be performed in average constant time.

Counts. Counts are strictly positive numbers, and can be stored using the representation for strictly monotone sequences to increase compression. In this case the upper bound is the occurrency of the term, and the number of elements is again the frequency.

Positions. The format for positions is the trickiest one. Consider, for the i-th document pointer in the inverted list for term t with count c_i, the list of positions $p_0^i, p_1^i, \ldots, p_{c_i-1}^i$. First, we turn this list into a list of strictly positive smaller integers:

$$p_0^i + 1, p_1^i - p_0^i, p_2^i - p_1^i, \ldots, p_{c_i-1}^i - p_{c_i-2}^i.$$

Consider the concatenation of all sequences above:

$$\begin{aligned} &p_0^0 + 1, p_1^0 - p_0^0, \ldots, p_{c_0-1}^0 - p_{c_0-2}^0, \\ &\qquad p_0^1 + 1, p_1^1 - p_0^1, \ldots, p_{c_1-1}^1 - p_{c_1-2}^1, \ldots, \\ &\qquad p_0^{f-1} + 1, p_1^{f-1} - p_0^{f-1}, \ldots, p_{c_{f-1}-1}^{f-1} - p_{c_{f-1}-2}^{f-1}, \end{aligned} \quad (3)$$

and store them using the representation for strictly positive numbers. In this case it is easy to check that the best upper bound is

$$f + \sum_{0 \leq i < f} p_{c_i-1}^i, \quad (4)$$

and the number of elements is the occurrency g of the term.

[15] Nothing prevents from storing both kind of pointers. The increase in size of the index would be unnoticeable.

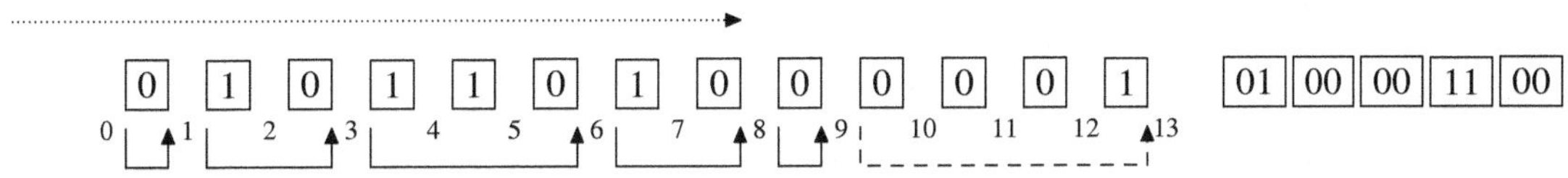

Figure 2: An example of skipping based on the sequence shown in Figure 1. On the left we have the upper-bits array, and on the right the lower-bits array. We want to skip to the first item larger than or equal to 22, so since $\ell = 2$ we have to perform $\lfloor 22/2^2 \rfloor = 5$ negated unary-code reads (the continuous arrows), getting to position 9, so we are positioned in the middle of the unary code associated with the element of index $9 - 5 = 4$. Then we perform a unary-code read (the dashed arrow), which returns 3, so we know that the upper bits of the current element (of index 4) are $3 + 5 = 8$. Since the block of lower bits of index 4 is zero, we return 32. If we had at our disposal a skip pointer for $q = 4$ (the dotted arrow), we could have skipped the first four negated unary-code reads. Note that in general more than one unary-code read might be necessary after reading the negated unary codes.

We now show how to retrieve the positions of the i-th document. Let $s_0, s_1, \ldots, s_f$ be prefix sums of the counts (e.g., $c_i = s_{i+1} - s_i$). We note that the list provides the starting and ending point of the sequence of positions associated to a document: the positions of document i occur in (3) at positions j satisfying $s_i \leq j < s_{i+1}$. Let $t_0, t_1, \ldots, t_g$ be the sequence of prefix sums of the sequence (3). It is easy to check that the positions of i-th document can be recovered as follows:

$$p^i_j = t_{s_i+j+1} - t_{s_i} - 1 \qquad 0 \leq j < c_i.$$

We remark that the nice interplay between prefix sums and lists of natural numbers is essential in making this machinery work: we need the counts c_i (e.g., to compute a content-based ranking function), but we need also their prefix sums to locate positions.

7. A QUASI-SUCCINCT BITSTREAM

We now discuss in detail the bit stream used to store the quasi-succinct representation described in Section 4—in particular, the sizing of all data involved.

Metadata pertaining the whole representation, if present, can be stored initially in a self-delimiting format. Then, the remaining data is laid out as follows: pointers, lower bits, upper bits (see Figure 3). The rationale behind this layout is that the upper-bits array is the only part whose length is in principle unknown: by positioning it at the end of the bitstream, we do not have to store pointers to the various parts of the stream. The lower-bits array will be located at position sw, where s is the number of pointers and w their width, and the upper-bits array at position $pw + n\ell$ bits after the metadata. We can thus compute without further information the starting point of each part of the stream.

We assume that the number of elements n is known, possibly from the metadata. The first issue is thus the size and the number of pointers. If the upper bound u is known, we know that the upper-bits array is $n + \lfloor u/2^\ell \rfloor$ bits long at most, so the width of the pointers is $w = \lceil \log(n + \lfloor u/2^\ell \rfloor + 1) \rceil$; otherwise, information must be stored in the metadata part so to be able to compute w.

If we are storing forward pointers for unary codes, the number of pointers will be exactly $\lfloor n/q \rfloor$; otherwise (i.e., if we are storing forward pointers for negated unary codes), they will be at most $s = \lfloor (n + \lfloor u/2^\ell \rfloor)/q \rfloor$.[16] Again, if the bound u is not known it is necessary to store information in the metadata part so to be able to compute s.

Analogously, if u is not known we need to store metadata that makes us able to compute $\ell = \lfloor \log(u/n) \rfloor$.

[16]We remark that if $u > x_{n-1}$ some of the s pointers might actually be unused. It is sufficient to set them to zero (no other pointer can be zero) and consider them as skips to the end of the list.

Finally, in the case of a ranked characteristic functions instead of pointers we store $\lfloor f/q \rfloor$ cumulative ranks of width $w = \lceil \log N \rceil$, followed by the bitmap representation of the characteristic function.

8. LAYING OUT THE INDEX STRUCTURE

We now show how to store in a compact format all metadata that are necessary to access the lists. For each index component (document pointers, counts, positions) we write a separate bit stream. We remark that for an index that provides naturally constant-time access to each element, there is no point in interleaving data, and this is another advantage of quasi-succinct encoding, as unnecessary data (e.g., counts and positions for a Boolean query) need not be examined. As usual, for each term we store three pointers locating the starting point of the information related to that term in each stream.

The bit stream for *document pointers* contains as metadata the frequency and the occurrency of the term. We write the occurrency in γ code and, if the occurrency is greater than one, the difference between occurrency and frequency, again in γ code (this ensures that hapaxes use exactly one bit). This information, together with the number of documents in the collection, is sufficient to access the quasi-succinct representation of document pointers (see Section 6).

The bit stream for *counts* contains no metadata. The occurrency and frequency can be obtained from the pointers stream, and they are sufficient to access the representation.

The bit stream for *positions* requires to store in the metadata part the parameter ℓ and the skip-pointer size w, which we write again in γ code, as the upper bound (4) is not available. Note that if the occurrency is smaller than q, there is no pointer, and in that case we omit the pointer size. Thus, the overhead for terms with a small number of occurrences is limited to the parameter ℓ.[17]

9. IMPLEMENTATION DETAILS

Implementation details are essential in a performance-critical data structure such as an inverted index. In this section we discuss the main ideas used in our implementation. While relatively simple, these ideas are essential in obtaining, besides good compression, a significant performance increase.

Longword addressing. We either load the index into memory, or access it as a memory-mapped region. Access happens always by longword, and shifts are used to extract the relevant data. The bit k of the index is represented in longword $\lfloor k/64 \rfloor$ in position k mod 64. While direct access to every point of the bitstream is possible, we keep track of the current position so that sequential reads use the

[17]Actually, it is easy to check that the overhead for hapaxes is exactly 2 bits with respect to writing the only existing position in δ code.

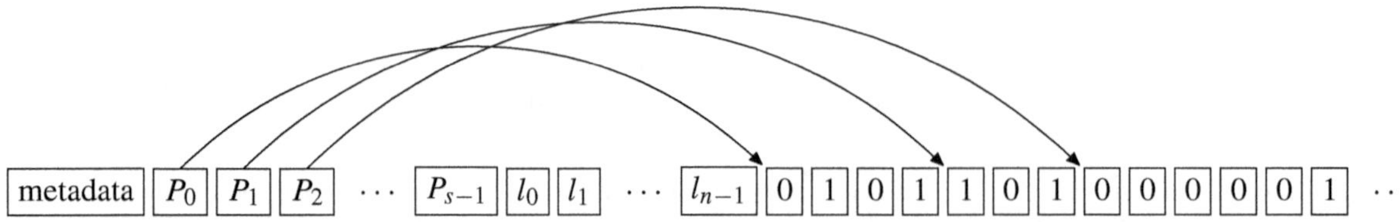

Figure 3: The bit stream of a quasi-succinct encoding for a list of n items using s forward pointers. After a self-delimiting metadata section, there are fixed-width forward pointers, the lower-bits array, and finally the upper-bits array. In this example, P_i points at the location of the upper-bits array where one would get after iq unary-code reads, with $q = 2$. Pointer P_0 is never stored explicitly.

last longword read as a bit buffer. Extraction of lower bits requires very few logical operations in most cases when ℓ is small.

Reading unary codes. Reading a unary code is equivalent to the computation of the least significant bit. We use the beautiful algorithm based on de Brujin's sequences [18], which is able to locate the least significant bit using a single multiplication and a table lookup. The lack of any test makes it a very good choice on superscalar processors, as it makes prediction and out-of-order execution possible.[18]

Both when looking up an entry and when skipping, we have, however, to perform a significant number of unary-code reads (on average, $\approx q/2$). To this purpose, we resort to a *broadword* (a.k.a. *SWAR*, i.e., "SIMD in A Register") *bit search* [26]. The idea is that of computing the number of ones in the current bit buffer using the classical algorithm for *sideways addition* [17], which involves few logical operations and a multiplication. If the number of reads we have to perform exceeds the number of ones in the current buffer, we examine the next longword, and so on. Once we locate the right longword, we can complete the search using the broadword *selection* algorithm presented in [26].

Our experiments show that broadword bit search is extremely effective, unless the number of reads is very small, as in that case computing iteratively the least significant bit becomes competitive. Indeed, when skipping a very small number of position (e.g., less then eight) we simply resort to iterating through the list.

Cache the last prefix sum. When retrieving a count or the first position of a position list, we have, in theory, to compute two associated prefix sums. During sequential scans, however, we can cache the last computed value and use it at the next call. Thus, in practice, scanning sequentially counts or positions requires just one unary-code read and one fixed-width bit extraction per item. Reading counts is however made slower by the necessity to compute the difference between the current and the previous prefix sum.

Trust the processor cache. The cost of accessing an in-memory index is largely dominated by cache misses. It is thus not surprising that using a direct access (i.e., by pointer) can be slower than actually scanning linearly the upper-bits array using a broadword bit search if our current position is close to the position to get to. The threshold depend on architectural issues and must be set experimentally. In our code we use $q = 256$ and we do not use pointers if we can skip to the desired position in less that q reads.[19] An analogous strategy is used with ranked characteristic functions: if we have to skip in the vicinity of the current position and the current index is known we simply read the bitmap, using the sideways addition algorithm to keep track of the current index.

[18] Actually, we first check whether we can compute the least significant bit using an 8-bit precomputed table, as the guaranteed high density of the upper bits makes this approach very efficient.

[19] Remember, again, that we will actually simulate such reads using a broadword bit search.

10. EXPERIMENTS

We have implemented the quasi-succinct index described in the previous section in Java, and for the part related to document pointers and count, in C++. All the code used for experiments is available at the MG4J web site. In this section, we report some experiments that compare its performance against three competitors:

- Lucene, a very popular open-source Java search engine (release 3.6.0);
- the classical high-performance indices from MG4J [6], another open-source search engine (release 5.0);
- Zettair, a search engine written in C by the Search Engine Group at RMIT University.
- The Kamikaze[20] library, implementing the PForDelta [29] sequence compression algorithm (up-to-date repository version from GitHub);
- We compare also with recent optimized C code implementing PForDelta compression document pointers and count kindly provided by Ding Shuai [24].

Zettair has been suggested by the TREC organizers as one of the baselines for the efficiency track. The comparison of a Java engine with a C or C++ engine is somewhat unfair, but we will see actually the Java engines turn out to be always significantly faster.

We use several datasets summarized in Table 1: first, the classical public TREC GOV2 dataset (about 25 million documents) and a crawl of around 130 million pages from the `.uk` domain that is available from the author. Tokens were defined by transition between alphanumerical to nonalphanumerical characters or by HTML flow-breaking tags, and they were stemmed using the Porter2 stemmer[21]. Besides an index considering the whole HTML document, we created some indices for the title text only (e.g., the content of the HTML `TITLE` element), as such indices have significantly different statistics (e.g., documents are very short).

Additionally, we created a *part-of-speech* index used within the Mímir semantic engine [9]; such indices have a very small number of terms that represent synctactic elements (nouns, verbs, etc.), very dense posting lists and a large number of positions per posting: they provide useful information about the effectiveness of compression when the structure of the index is not that of a typical web text index. For the same reason, we also index a collection of about a dozen millions tweets from Twitter.

Small differences in indexing between different search engines are hard to track: the details of segmentation, HTML parsing, and so on, might introduce discrepancies. Thus, we performed all our

[20] `http://sna-projects.com/kamikaze/`

[21] Zettair, however, supports apparently only the original Porter stemmer.

	Documents	Terms	Postings	Occurrences
TREC GOV2				
Text	25 M	35 M	5.5 G	23 G
Title	25 M	1.1 M	135 M	150 M
Web .uk				
Text	132 M	99 M	21 G	62 G
Title	132 M	3.2 M	609 M	691 M
Mímir index				
Token	1 M	49	27 M	1.2 G
Tweets				
Text	13 M	2.3 M	147 M	156 M

Table 1: Basic statistics for the datasets used in our experiments.

indexing starting from a pre-parsed stream of UTF-8 text documents. We also checked that the frequency of the terms we use in our queries is the same—a sanity check showing that the indexing process is consistent across the engines. Finally, we checked that the number of results of conjunctive and phrasal queries was consistent across the different engines, and that `bpref` scores were in line with those reported by participants to the Terabyte Track.

Using MG4J, we have created indices that use γ codes for counts, and either δ or Golomb codes for pointers and positions[22], endowed with a mild amount of skipping information using around 1% of the index size: we chose this value because the same amount of space is used by our index to store forward and skip pointers when $q = 256$. These indices (in particular, the ones based on Golomb codes) are useful to compare compression ratios: if speed is not a concern, they provide very good compression, and thus they provide a useful reference points on the compression/speed curve.[23]

We remark that we have indexed *every word* of the collections. No stopword elimination has been applied. Commercial search engines (e.g., Google) are effortlessly able to search for the phrase "Romeo and Juliet", so our engine should be able to do the same.

Compression. Table 2 reports a comparison of the compression ratios. Our quasi-succinct index compresses always better than γ/δ, but worse than Golomb codes. In practice, our index reduces the size of the γ/δ index by $\approx$ 10%, whereas Golomb codes reach $\approx$ 20%.

The compression of Lucene and Zettair on the text of web pages is not very good (a $\approx$ 15% increase w.r.t. our index). This was partially to be expected, as both Lucene and Zettair use variable-length byte codes for efficiency, and while such codes are easy to decode, they are ill-suited to compression. When the distribution of terms and positions is different, however, compression is significantly worse: for titles we have a 50% increase in size, and for the Mímir semantic index or tweets a 40% increase. This is somewhat typical: variable-length byte codes compress most positions in a single byte if the distribution of words comes from a "natural" distribution on documents of a few thousand words. Using shorter documents (e.g., titles and tweets) or a different distribution (e.g.,

[22]The Golomb modulus has been chosen separately for each document. The results we obtain seems to be within 5% of the best compression results obtained in [27], which suggest a space usage of 21 MB/query on average for an average of 20.72 millions positions per query. A more precise estimate is impossible, as results in [27] are based on 1000 unknown queries, and no results about the whole GOV2 collection are provided.

[23]We have also tried *interpolative coding* [20], but on our collections the difference in compression with Golomb codes was really marginal.

	QS	MG4J γ/δ	Golomb	Lucene	Zettair
TREC GOV2 (text)					
Pointers	7.59	8.47	6.94		
Counts	2.98	2.56	—		
Positions	10.17	11.11	8.65		
Overall	37.0 GB	40.3 GB	31.9 GB	42.1 GB	40.7 GB
TREC GOV2 (title)					
Pointers	10.29	11.44	9.54		
Counts	1.10	1.14	—		
Positions	3.84	4.63	3.05		
Overall	268 MB	308 MB	241 MB	396 MB	395 MB
Web .uk (text)					
Pointers	8.59	9.72	7.98		
Counts	2.39	2.06	—		
Positions	10.16	10.95	8.41		
Overall	108 GB	117 GB	92 GB	126 GB	
Web .uk (title)					
Pointers	11.92	13.51	11.27		
Counts	1.13	1.18	—		
Positions	4.36	5.06	3.35		
Overall	1.39 GB	1.59 GB	1.26 GB	2.00 GB	2.15 GB
Mímir token index					
Pointers	1.51	1.42	1.48		
Counts	6.42	6.28	—		
Positions	5.83	6.22	5.03		
Overall	0.96 GB	1.01 GB	0.83 GB	1.34 GB	1.36 GB
Tweets					
Pointers	10.13	10.29	9.22		
Counts	1.06	1.11	—		
Positions	4.67	5.94	3.86		
Overall	302 MB	341 MB	266 MB	423 MB	484 MB

Table 2: A comparison of index sizes. We show the overall index size, which includes skipping structures, and, if available, the number of bits per element of each component, excluding skipping structures.

a semantic index) yields very bad results. A 50% increase in size, indeed, can make a difference.

While we are not aiming at the best possible compression, but rather at high speed, it is anyway relieving to know that we are improving (as we shall see shortly) *both* compression *and* speed with respect to these engines.

Interestingly, counts are the only index component for which we obtain sometimes worse results than γ coding. This is somewhat to be expected, as we are actually storing their prefix sums. The impact of counts on the overall index, however, is quite minor, as shown by the small final index size.

Speed. Benchmarking a search engine brings up several complex issues. In general, the final answer is bound to the architecture on which the tests were run, and on the type of queries. A definite answer can be given only against a real workload.[24] Our tests were performed on a recent workstation sporting a 3.4 GHz Intel i7-3770 CPU with 8 MiB of cache and 16 GiB of RAM.

We aim at comparing speed of in-memory indices, as one of the main reasons to obtain smaller indices is to make more information fit into memory; moreover, the diffusion of solid-state disks makes this approach reasonable. Thus, in our tests we resolve each query three times before taking measurements. In this way we guarantee that the relevant parts of the index have been actually read and memory mapped (for MG4J and Lucene, or at least cached by the file system, for Zettair), and we also make sure that the Java virtual machine is warmed up and has performed inlining and other runtime optimizations. With this setup, our tests are highly repeatable and indeed the relative standard deviation over several runs is less than 3%.

We used the 150 TREC Terabyte track (2004–2006) title queries in conjunctive, phrasal and proximity form (in the latter case, the terms in the query must appear in some order within a window of 16 words). We also extracted the terms appearing in the queries and used them as queries to measure pure scanning speed: all in all, we generated 860 queries. MG4J and Lucene were set up to compute the query results without applying any ranking function. Zettair was set to Okapi BM25 ranking [16], which appeared to have the smaller impact on the query resolution time (no "no-ranking" mode is available).

All engines were set up to return a single result, so that the logic needed to keep track of a large result size would not interfere with the evaluation. The results are shown in Table 3. The first column (QS) shows the results of query resolution on a quasi-succinct index. The third column (MG4J) for a γ/δ-coded high-performance MG4J index. The fourth column for Lucene, and the last column for Zettair.

The second column (QS*) needs some explanation. Both Lucene and MG4J interleave document pointers and counts. As a consequence, resolving a pure Boolean query has a higher cost (as counts are read even if they are not necessary), but ranked queries require less memory/disk access. To simulate a similar behaviour in our setting, we modified our code so to force it to read the count of every returned document pointer. This setting is of course artificial, but it provides a good indication of the costs of iterating and applying a count-based ranking function, and it will be the based of our comparison. For phrasal and proximity queries there is no difference between QS and QS* as counts have in any case to be read to access positions.

[24]Note that in real-world search engines the queries that are actually solved are very different by those input by the user, as they undergo a number of rewritings. As a consequence, blindingly analzying queries from large query logs in disjunctive or conjunctive mode cannot give a reliable estimate the actual performance of an index.

First of all, we note that decoding a quasi-succinct index is slightly ($\approx$ 7%) faster than decoding a gap-compressed index that uses variable-byte codes. It is nonetheless important to notice that our timings for purely boolean resolution (QS) are much lower, and this can be significant in a complex query (e.g., a conjunction of disjunctively expanded terms). Zettair is much slower.

More interestingly, we have a $\approx$ 50% improvement for conjunctive queries, a $\approx$ 40% improvement for phrasal queries and a $\approx$ 60% improvement for proximity queries: being able to address in average constant time every element of the index is a real advantage. We also remind the reader that we are comparing a Java prototype with a mature implementation.

We expect the asymptotic advantage of quasi-succinct indices to be more evident as the collection size grows. To test this hypothesis, we performed further experiments using the Web `.uk` collection and 1000 multi-term queries randomly selected from a large search-engine query log. The results are shown in Table 6: now conjunctive and proximity queries are more thrice faster with respect to Lucene.

In Table 4 we show some data comparing in-memory quasi-succinct indices with PForDelta code. The data we display is constrained by some limitations: the Kamikaze library does not provide count storage; and the optimized C code we are using [24] does not provide positions. This is an important detail, as quasi-succinct indices trade some additional efforts in decoding counts (i.e., computing their prefix sums) in exchange for constant-time access to positions. Our main goal is to speed up positional access—indeed, nothing prevents using PForDelta for document pointers and storing counts and positions as described in this paper (or even using a separate PForDelta index without positions as a first-pass index).

Kamikaze turns out to be slightly slower for scanning term lists, and almost twice as slow when computing conjunctive queries. To estimate the difference in compression, we computed the space used by the document pointers of our TREC collections using Kamikaze: the result is an increase of $\approx$ 55% in space usage. While not extremely relevant for the index size (positions are responsible mostly for the size of an index), it shows that we would gain no advantage from storing pointers using PForDelta in a Java engine.[25]

The comparison of C implementations, on the other hand, is definitely in favour of PForDelta: apart from pointer enumeration our C implementation is slower, in particular when enumerating terms and their counts.

There are some important *caveats*, however: the code we have been provided for PForDelta testing [24] is a bare-bone, heavily optimised C benchmarking implementation that is able to handle only 32-bit document pointers and has a number of limitations such as hardwired constants (e.g., the code needs to be recompiled if the number of document in the collection changes). Our C++ code is a 64-bit fully usable implementation derived from a line-by-line translation of our Java prototype code that could be certainly improved by applying CPU-conscious optimizations. A more realistic comparison would require a real search engine using PForDelta to solve queries requiring positional information, it happens in Table 3.[26] Another important aspect that makes the comparison difficult is that quasi-succinct indices compute, beside the count of each document, the *cumulative* count, which is then used to access

[25]Note that storing *positions* with PForDelta codes is known to give a compression rate close to that provided by variable-byte coding [27].

[26]Such an engine is not available, to the best of the authors's knowledge. The authors of [27] have refused to make their engine available for replication of their results.

	QS	QS*	MG4J	Lucene	Zettair
Terms	4.51	7.82	10.33	8.26	19.17
And	1.29	1.79	4.90	3.90	20.92
Phrase	4.00	—	11.01	6.77	21.14
Proximity	4.76	—	12.15	12.05	—

Table 3: Timings in seconds for running the test queries from the TREC Terabyte track on GOV2 without scoring. The column QS shows the timings for resolving a query on a quasi-succinct indices, whereas the column QS* shows the timings for a modified version in which counts are forced to be read for each decoded document pointer. Measurements were taken after three executions of each query, with memory map and disk caches already filled. Note that Zettair is actually reading from disk and scoring the queries, whereas in the other cases pointers and counts are being read from a memory-mapped region and no score is being computed.

	QS	QS*	Lucene
Terms	70.9	132.1	130.6
And	27.5	36.7	108.8
Phrase	78.2	—	127.2
Proximity	106.5	—	347.6

Table 5: Timings in seconds for running 1000 randomly selected queries from a search-engine query log on the Web `.uk` collection. See also Table 3.

quickly positions. In pratice, part of the work that is necessary to access positions is moved into the count computation. While this makes the count access slower, it provide exceptional performance when positions are accessed, as our benchmarks show.

Finally, quasi-succinct indices improve by definition their relative performance as the collection gets larger: in Table 6 we report similar data for our Web `.uk` collection, and conjunctive queries are only $\approx$ 13% slower than PForDelta, instead of $\approx$ 21%.

11. CONCLUSIONS

We have presented a new inverted index based on the quasi-succinct encoding of monotone sequences introduced by Elias and Fano, and on ranked characteristic functions. The new index provides better compression than typical gap-encoded indices, with the exception of extremely compression-oriented techniques such as Golomb or interpolative coding. When compared with indices based on gap compression using variable-length byte encoding (Lucene) or γ/δ codes (MG4J), not only we provide better compression, but significant speed improvement over conjunctive, phrasal and proximity queries. In general, any search engine accessing positional information for selecting or ranking documents out of a large collection would benefit from quasi-succinct indices (an example being tagged text stored in parallel indices).

Our comparison with a C implementation of PForDelta compression for pointers and counts showed that PForDelta is slightly faster than quasi-succinct indices in computing conjunction, and significantly faster at retrieving counts, albeit in queries mixing terms with high and low frequency (benchmarks not shown here) quasi-succinct indices can be extremely faster. As the collection size grows, moreover, quasi-succinct indices becomes relatively faster.

	QS(C)	QS*(C)	PFD(C)	PFD*(C)
Terms	23.8	56.8	23.6	31.6
And	19.2	24.5	16.9	19.4

Table 6: Timings in seconds for running 1000 randomly selected queries from a search-engine query log on the Web `.uk` collection. See also Table 4.

For what matters size, PForDelta (more precisely, the Kamikaze library) use 55% more space than a quasi-succinct index to compress pointers from the GOV2 collection.

A drawback of quasi-succinct indices is that some basic statistics (in particular, frequency, occurrency and the bound (4)) must be known before the index is built. This implies that to create a quasi-succinct index from scratch it is necessary to temporary cache in turn each posting list (e.g., using a traditional gap-compressed format) and convert it to the actual encoding only when all postings have been generated. While it is easy to do such a caching offline, it could slow down index construction.

On the other hand, this is not a serious problem: in practice, large indices are built by scanning incrementally (possibly in parallel) a collection, and merges are performed periodically over the resulting *segments* (also called *barrels* or *batches*). Since during the construction of a segment it is trivial to store the pieces of information that are needed to build a quasi-succinct index, there is no need for an actual two-pass construction: segments can be compressed using gap encoding, whereas large indices can be built by merging in a quasi-succinct format.

Note that if computing selection-in-a-word and sideways addition were available in *hardware* (the latter was actually available in the SPARC architecture), the decoding speed of a quasi-succinct index would significantly increase. Moreover, faster hardware selection of the least significant bit would increase significantly the decoding speed. In Java virtual machines, this would lead a to better *intrinsification* of the method `Long.numberOfTrailingZeros()`, whereas the `gcc` compiler could provide faster versions of built-in functions such as `__builtin_ctzll()`.

All in all, we believe that quasi-succinct indices occupy a very interesting and previosuly unoccupied spot in the size/speed tradeoff curve, in particular for documents (e.g., tweets) that are different in distribution than web pages, and for queries that involve positional access. We remark that there is an obvious advantage in speed in having an index that is significantly smaller, as a larger part of the index can be cached.

An interesting area of future research would be extending the techniques described in this paper to *impact-sorted* indices, in which documents are sorted following a retrieval-based *impact order* [2], and only documents pointers with the same impact are monotonically increasing. A technique similar to that used in this paper to store positions (i.e., a different encoding for the start of each block) might provide new interesting tradeoffs between compression and efficiency.

12. ACKNOWLEDGMENTS

The author would like to thank Roi Blanco for an uncountable number of useful suggestions and for moral support.

13. REFERENCES

[1] V. N. Anh and A. Moffat. Inverted index compression using word-aligned binary codes. *Inf. Retr*, 8(1):151–166, 2005.

[2] V. N. Anh and A. Moffat. Pruned query evaluation using pre-computed impacts. In E. N. Efthimiadis, S. T. Dumais, D. Hawking, and K. Järvelin, editors, *SIGIR 2006: Proceedings of the 29th Annual International ACM SIGIR Conference on Research and Development in Information Retrieval, Seattle, Washington, USA, August 6-11, 2006*, pages 372–379. ACM, 2006.

	QS	QS*	Kamikaze	QS(C)	QS*(C)	PFD(C)	PFD*(C)
Terms	3.83	7.30	4.23	1.61	4.05	1.57	2.39
And	1.16	1.62	2.08	0.91	1.25	0.75	0.87

Table 4: Timings in seconds for running the term and conjunctive test queries from the TREC Terabyte track on GOV2 directly from RAM. Timings for quasi-succinct indices are provided both for Java and C++ 64-bit implementations. PForDelta timings have been computed both using the Kamikaze library and using optimized 32-bit C code provided by Ding Shuai [24]. Starred versions include reading counts for all returned document pointers.

[3] T. C. Bell, A. Moffat, C. Neville-Manning, I. H. Witten, and J. Zobel. Data compression in full-text retrieval systems. *Journal of the American Society for Information Science*, 44:508–531, 1993.

[4] R. Blanco and A. Barreiro. Tsp and cluster-based solutions to the reassignment of document identifiers. *Information Retrieval*, 9(4):499–517, 2006.

[5] D. K. Blandford and G. E. Blelloch. Index compression through document reordering. In *DCC*, pages 342–351. IEEE Computer Society, 2002.

[6] P. Boldi and S. Vigna. MG4J at TREC 2005. In E. M. Voorhees and L. P. Buckland, editors, *The Fourteenth Text REtrieval Conference (TREC 2005) Proceedings*, number SP 500-266 in Special Publications. NIST, 2005. `http://mg4j.di.unimi.it/`.

[7] S. Büttcher and C. L. A. Clarke. Index compression is good, especially for random access. In M. J. Silva, A. H. F. Laender, R. A. Baeza-Yates, D. L. McGuinness, B. Olstad, Ø. H. Olsen, and A. O. Falcão, editors, *Proceedings of the Sixteenth ACM Conference on Information and Knowledge Management, CIKM 2007, Lisbon, Portugal, November 6-10, 2007*, pages 761–770. ACM, 2007.

[8] D. R. Clark. *Compact Pat Trees*. PhD thesis, University of Waterloo, Waterloo, Ont., Canada, 1998.

[9] H. Cunningham, V. Tablan, I. Roberts, M. A. Greenwood, and N. Aswani. Information extraction and semantic annotation for multi-paradigm information management. In M. Lupu, K. Mayer, J. Tait, A. J. Trippe, and W. B. Croft, editors, *Current Challenges in Patent Information Retrieval*, volume 29 of *The Information Retrieval Series*, pages 307–327. Springer Berlin Heidelberg, 2011.

[10] O. Delpratt, N. Rahman, and R. Raman. Compressed prefix sums. In J. van Leeuwen, G. F. Italiano, W. van der Hoek, C. Meinel, H. Sack, and F. Plasil, editors, *Proc. SOFSEM 2007: Theory and Practice of Computer Science, 33rd Conference on Current Trends in Theory and Practice of Computer Science*, number 4362 in Lecture Notes in Computer Science, pages 235–247. Springer–Verlag, 2007.

[11] P. Elias. On binary representations of monotone sequences. In *Proc. Sixth Princeton Conference on Information Sciences and Systems*, pages 54–57, Dep. of Electrical Engineering, Princeton U., Princeton, N. J., 1972.

[12] P. Elias. Efficient storage and retrieval by content and address of static files. *J. Assoc. Comput. Mach.*, 21(2):246–260, 1974.

[13] P. Elias. Universal codeword sets and representations of the integers. *IEEE Transactions on Information Theory*, 21:194–203, 1975.

[14] R. M. Fano. On the number of bits required to implement an associative memory. Memorandum 61, Computer Structures Group, Project MAC, MIT, Cambridge, Mass., n.d., 1971.

[15] S. W. Golomb. Run-length encodings. *IEEE Trans. Inform. Theory*, IT-12:399–401, 1966.

[16] K. S. Jones, S. Walker, and S. E. Robertson. A probabilistic model of information retrieval: development and comparative experiments — part 1. *Inf. Process. Manage*, 36(6):779–808, 2000.

[17] D. E. Knuth. The Art of Computer Programming. Pre-Fascicle 1A. Draft of Section 7.1.3: Bitwise Tricks and Techniques, 2007.

[18] C. E. Leiserson, H. Prokop, and K. H. Randall. Using de Bruijn sequences to index a 1 in a computer word, 1998. Unpublished manuscript.

[19] C. D. Manning, P. Raghavan, and H. Schütze. *Introduction to information retrieval*. Cambridge University Press, 2008. Available online.

[20] A. Moffat and L. Stuiver. Exploiting clustering in inverted file compression. In J. A. Storer and M. Cohn, editors, *Proceedings of the 6th Data Compression Conference (DCC '96)*, pages 82–91. IEEE Computer Society, 1996.

[21] A. Moffat and J. Zobel. Self-indexing inverted files for fast text retrieval. *ACM Trans. Inf. Syst.*, 14(4):349–379, 1996.

[22] M. Pătraşcu and M. Thorup. Time-space trade-offs for predecessor search. In *Proceedings of the thirty-eighth annual ACM symposium on Theory of computing*, STOC '06, pages 232–240, New York, NY, USA, 2006. ACM.

[23] R. Raman, V. Raman, and S. S. Rao. Succinct indexable dictionaries with applications to encoding k-ary trees, prefix sums and multisets. *ACM Transactions on Algorithms (TALG)*, 3(4):43, 2007.

[24] D. Shuai. Personal communication.

[25] F. Silvestri, R. Perego, and S. Orlando. Assigning document identifiers to enhance compressibility of web search engines indexes. In H. Haddad, A. Omicini, R. L. Wainwright, and L. M. Liebrock, editors, *Proceedings of the 2004 ACM Symposium on Applied Computing (SAC)*, pages 600–605. ACM, 2004.

[26] S. Vigna. Broadword implementation of rank/select queries. In C. C. McGeoch, editor, *Experimental Algorithms. 7th International Workshop, WEA 2008*, number 5038 in Lecture Notes in Computer Science, pages 154–168. Springer–Verlag, 2008.

[27] H. Yan, S. Ding, and T. Suel. Compressing term positions in web indexes. In J. Allan, J. A. Aslam, M. Sanderson, C. Zhai, and J. Zobel, editors, *SIGIR 2009*, pages 147–154. ACM, 2009.

[28] J. Zobel and A. Moffat. Inverted files for text search engines. *ACM Comput. Surv.*, 38(2), 2006.

[29] M. Zukowski, S. Héman, N. Nes, and P. A. Boncz. Super-scalar RAM-CPU cache compression. In L. Liu, A. Reuter, K.-Y. Whang, and J. Zhang, editors, *Proceedings of the 22nd International Conference on Data Engineering, ICDE 2006*, page 59. IEEE Computer Society, 2006.

Identifying Users' Topical Tasks in Web Search

Wen Hua[†‡*] Yangqiu Song[‡] Haixun Wang[‡] Xiaofang Zhou[§†]
[†]Renmin University of China, Beijing, China
[‡]Microsoft Research Asia, Beijing, China
[§]University of Queensland, Brisbane, Australia
huawen@ruc.edu.cn {yangqiu.song, haixun.wang}@microsoft.com zxf@itee.uq.edu.au

ABSTRACT

A search task represents an atomic information need of a user in web search. Tasks consist of queries and their reformulations, and identifying tasks is important for search engines since they provide valuable information for determining user satisfaction with search results, predicting user search intent, and suggesting queries to the user. Traditional approaches to identifying tasks exploit either temporal or lexical features of queries. However, many query refinements are topical, which means that a query and its refinements may not be similar on the lexical level. Furthermore, multiple tasks in the same search session may interleave, which means we cannot simply order the searches by their timestamps and divide the session into multiple tasks. Thus, in order to identify tasks correctly, we need to be able to compare two queries at the semantic level. In this paper, we use a knowledgebase known as *Probase* to infer the conceptual meanings of queries, and automatically identify the topical query refinements in the tasks. Experimental results on real search log data demonstrate that *Probase* can indeed help estimate the topical affinity between queries, and thus enable us to merge queries that are topically related but dissimilar at the lexical level.

Categories and Subject Descriptors

H.3.3 [**Information Storage and Retrieval**]: Information Search and Retrieval—*Clustering, Query formulation, Search process*

General Terms

Algorithms, Design, Experimentation, Performance

Keywords

Task Identification, Probase, Conceptualization, Interleaved Task

1. INTRODUCTION

A search *task* consists of a query and its refinements for accomplishing a specific information need. A recent study [13] suggests that tasks are better information units than single queries or sessions[1] for many web search applications such as query suggestion, determination of user satisfaction with search results and prediction of user search intent, to name a few. Consider for example, query suggestion. In Web search, query suggestion uses click data to recommend queries that are co-clicked with the original query. Given a query "flight to LA", we may recommend a query "cheap US flight". However, queries such as "hotel in LA", which do not have co-clicks with the original query, are also relevant because they also belong to the task of planning a trip to Los Angeles. In order to be able to recommend such queries, we can extend single-query-based query suggestion to session-based query suggestion. That is, we leverage the co-occurrence frequency of queries in search sessions for recommendation. However, a session may contain queries with multiple user intents, so if we treat queries in a session indiscriminately, we may recommend queries that are not related to the original query. Tasks, on the contrary, represent atomic information needs, which means that queries contained in the same task are usually related. Therefore, tasks can serve as better units for query suggestions, and thus help improve user search experience.

However, task identification itself is far from simple, due to the following reasons: First, it is not trivial to decide whether two queries belong to the same task. A real task may contain queries on the same topic but have no lexical similarity, e.g., similarity on the bag-of-words level. For example, queries 4, 5, and 6 in Table 1 may belong to the same task, as "cat", "dog" and "snake" may be of the same topic ("animal"), although the three queries share little bag-of-words similarity. Therefore, we need a semantic mechanism to identify topical query refinements. Second, inferring semantics from a query or a short piece of text is a complex task. Lucchese et. al. [14] address this problem by simply mapping each word in a query to a set of Wikipedia articles that contain the word. Then, the "meaning" of a query is represented by the combination of the Wikipedia articles that correspond to each word in the query. However, we may not be able to derive topics from single words. For example, when the query "tiger woods" is split into two words, namely "tiger" and "woods", the concepts related to "animal" and "material" will then be retrieved, instead of "athlete". Additionally, many words are ambiguous. Consider for example, the word "python" in Table 1. It may refer to a snake or a programming language. Consequently, the problem of detecting topical query refinements becomes much more challenging, due to the existence of ambiguity. Third, tasks in one session may interleave (e.g., task 1 and 2 in Table 1). Previous attempts ignore this phenomenon and identify task boundaries using a Sequential Cut

*The work is done at MSRA, Beijing, China.

[1]In this paper, we use *session* to denote a sequence of queries issued within a fixed period of time, or queries issued on a particular web browser as long as the user does not close the browser.

WSDM'13, February 4–8, 2013, Rome, Italy.

algorithm. Recently, Jones and Klinkner [11] use a Graph Cut algorithm to merge every pair of similar queries into one task. This approach, which is obviously more accurate, also introduces two issues: 1) it is computationally costly; and 2) it may lead to the problem of "over-merging". For instance, consider the query "the rain song youtube" in Table 1. It contains two concepts, i.e., "song" and "video site", but its real intent is to find a "song". Similar for query "the largest dog youtube". If we calculate the similarity of each pair of queries based on their common concepts, which is the process used in Graph Cut, the two queries mentioned above will be regarded as similar and grouped together. The problem also exists in Sequential Cut, but it becomes more obvious in Graph Cut, as every pair of queries is considered. Therefore, we need to merge queries in interleaved tasks efficiently without over-merging. This requires us to detect concepts that truly reflect users' search intent.

QUERYID	QUERY	TASKID
0	the rain song youtube	0
1	cool math	1
2	the ugliest cat in the world	2
3	the cutest cat in the world	2
4	the tiniest cat in the world	2
5	the largest dog youtube	2
6	the largest snake on the earth	2
7	python wikipedia	2
8	cool math for kids	1

Table 1: An example of tasks in one session.

In this work, we build a conceptualization mechanism based on an external knowledgebase (*Probase* [17]) to infer the underlying conceptual meanings of queries and reduce query ambiguity. We also employ a Sequential Cut and Merge (SCM) algorithm to address the problem of interleaving tasks. The algorithm has higher accuracy and less computational cost, compared with state-of-the-art methods. More specifically, our contributions are three-fold:

- We employ lexical, conceptual, template and temporal features to measure query similarities, which are then used to estimate whether two queries should be clustered into one task. Particularly, we leverage Probase to build a conceptualization mechanism to infer the underlying conceptual meanings of queries. Our experimental results show that by incorporating conceptual features into our model, we can increase the accuracy of the identified tasks by 13% on average.
- We use multi-word terms, rather than single words, to identify topics contained in queries. We also intersect the concepts of topically-related terms, and thus emphasize on common concepts, which reduces query ambiguity.
- We introduce a Sequential Cut and Merge (SCM) algorithm to identify interleaving tasks. We compare it with Sequential Cut (SC) and Graph Cut (GC). Both SCM and GC can address the problem of interleaving tasks that SC cannot handle. Additionally, as SCM merge similar subtasks derived by SC rather than similar queries as in GC, it does not have the "over-merging" problem that GC has. This also enables us to greatly reduce the computational cost at the same time.

The remainder of this paper is organized as follows: in Section 2, we briefly review the related works in the context of task identification; then we divagate from the main line in Section 3 to talk about *Probase*, the knowledgebase we utilized in this work; our approaches and experiments are depicted in Section 4 and 5, respectively, followed by a brief conclusion and a discussion of future work in Section 6.

2. RELATED WORKS

The problem of identifying tasks from query logs has attracted a great deal of attention in the web search community. Existing methods fall into two categories: time-based and content-based approaches. In time-based approaches, two consecutive queries are considered to be of two different tasks if the timespan between them exceeds the pre-defined timeout threshold, thus constitute a task boundary. Catledge and Pitkow [5] claimed in 1995 that a 25.5-minute timeout exists between consecutive tasks, and many works [13, 4, 16, 18] use a 30-minute time window to bound tasks. There are also works that use varying thresholds to detect tasks. For example, He and GÃűker [9] used timeouts ranging from 1 to 50 minutes to detect task boundaries from Excite query logs. Jones and Klinkner [11] formulated the task identification problem as a supervised classification problem, and tried four different timeouts (i.e., 5, 30, 60 and 120 minutes) in their experiments. Lucchese et. al. [14] also used different timeouts, i.e., 5, 15 and 26 minutes, to detect tasks from the 2006 AOL query logs. The experimental results of these works show that the choice of different timeout thresholds does not have a huge influence on the accuracy of the detected tasks, and that these time-based features alone do not perform well for task identification. In other words, other information such as content-based features, is needed for task identification. Furthermore, as the timeout features only make sense between consecutive queries, these approaches cannot detect interleaved tasks, which are prevalent in real life query logs. In content-based approaches, queries are clustered to the same task if they are similar in content. However, current approaches [2, 6, 11] consider lexical similarity only. In other words, they treat queries, titles and snippets of clicked URLs as a bag-of-words, and use some string similarity metrics (e.g. Levenstein edit distance, n-gram jaccard, etc.) to measure the similarity between two queries. The assumption is that users often change the words just slightly when reformulating queries. For example, if a user wants to find the lyric of Justin Bieber's song "As Long As You Love Me," she may issue the following three queries in a sequence: "justin bieber", "justin bieber as long as you love me", and "justin bieber as long as you love me lyric". Given this assumption, the content-based approaches using lexical features have long been the state-of-the-art approaches for task identification.

However, a recent study by Huang and Efthimiadis [10] pointed out that many query reformulations cannot be characterized by lexical features. In their work, they manually created a taxonomy of query reformulations (e.g. substring/superstring, word substitution, word reordering, stemming, spelling correction, etc.) and built an automatic classifier to detect each type of reformulation. Their experimental results showed that 962 out of 9091 query refinements were missed by their classifiers. This phenomenon is usually referred to as the *vocabulary-mismatch problem*, that is, queries of the same task are dissimilar in their surface form. The misclassified queries are related at the topic level. For example, a user interested in cars may enter the following queries to express her information need: "honda", "nissan", and "ford". To capture this topical relatedness and thus improve the accuracy of task identification, Lucchese et. al. [14] exploit *Wikitionary* and *Wikipedia* to estimate the conceptual affinity of queries whose lexical similarities are low. However, it still lacks the power of fully quantifying semantic similarity and semantic relatedness: First, it is still a bag-of-words based approach; And second, it limits the power of disambiguating concepts by simply combining the Wikipedia articles. In our work, we build a conceptualization mechanism based on Probase – a large and general-purpose knowledgebase automatically acquired from the web corpus. Probase has more concepts for better describing short text, and our conceptualization mechanism finds meaningful conceptual features for queries, which makes the similarity calculation more accurate.

3. PROBASE

As we know, semantic knowledge can help fill the gap between the bag-of-words representation and the human understanding of queries. In this section, we briefly introduce Probase, including what knowledge is contained in Probase, and where and how we acquire these knowledge.

3.1 Knowledge Representation

Probase can be regarded as a huge semantic network [17]. The nodes are divided into three categories, i.e., entities (e.g., "Barack Obama"), concepts (e.g., "President of America") and attributes (e.g., "age", "color"), and the edges represent the relationships between nodes. Probase now mainly focuses on two relationships that can be used for conceptualization, namely the *isA* relationship and the *isAttributeOf* (also called *isPropertyOf*) relationship. The *isA* relationship exists between entities and concepts (e.g., "Barack Obama" *isA* "President of America"), while the *isAttributeOf* relationship exists between attributes and concepts (e.g., "population" *isAttributeOf* "country"). Note that a term can be categorized as an attribute or an entity at the same time. For example, "population" can be regarded as an attribute of "country", but it can also be an entity of "demographic datum". The edges in Probase are weighted with probabilistic information. For example, the probability $P(instance|concept)$ tells us how typical or popular the *instance* is in the given *concept*. Intuitively, knowing that both "poodle" and "pug" are dogs is sometimes not enough. We may also need to know that "poodle" is a much more popular dog than "pug", that is, when people talk about dogs, it is more likely that they are talking about "poodle" rather than "pug". Such information is essential for understanding the intent behind a query. Besides $P(instance|concept)$, we also obtain many other probabilistic information such as $P(concept|instance)$, $P(concept|attribute)$ and $P(attribute|concept)$.

3.2 Knowledge Acquisition

In order for a knowledgebase to be useful for conceptualization, it should be large enough, i.e., it should have a broad coverage of the concept space. Existing knowledgebases[8, 12, 3, 7, 1] are usually manually built and only contain a limited number of concepts, which severely limits their power to discover the hidden meaning of a natural language. The knowledge contained in Probase is extracted from a web corpus that contains billions of web pages, from which we achieve millions of concepts, attributes, and entities. These obviously lay the foundation for conceptualization. Specifically, Probase obtains its knowledge through an iterative information extraction process. That is, to obtain the *isA* relationships, we use Hearst patterns (e.g., *such as* patterns) and other syntactic patterns. For instance, from a sentence "...Dogs *such as* Labradoodles and Goldendoodles ...", we obtain "Labradoodle" *isA* "Dog" and "Goldendoodle" *isA* "Dog". To obtain the *isAttributeOf* relationships, we consider sentences such as "*What is* the population *of* China?", from which we can infer that "population" *isAttributeOf* "China" and that "population" *isAttributeOf* "country". The probabilistic information related with each relationship is calculated during this information extraction process, for example:

$$P(instance|concept) = \frac{n(instance, concept)}{n(concept)} \quad (1)$$

where $n(instance, concept)$ denotes the number of times *instance* and *concept* appear in the same sentence, and $n(concept)$ is the frequency of *concept*. Finally, we perform a series of sophisticated inferencing to clean and enrich the knowledge acquired from the syntactic patterns. For details of how Probase is constructed and how the probabilistic information are calculated, please refer to [17].

4. METHODOLOGY

The problem of task identification boils down to two questions: First, how to quantify the similarity or relatedness of two queries (Section 4.1); Second, how to efficiently cluster similar queries in a query session (Section 4.2). Before we present our answers to the two questions, we first formally define *task*. A task is a sequence of queries ordered by their timestamps, and each pair of queries in the same task has a similarity larger than a threshold. Formally, if we donate a session as $\{q_1, q_2, q_3 \ldots\}$, then a task in that session is:

$$task_k = \{(q_{k_1}, q_{k_2}, q_{k_3} \ldots)|\forall i, j, t(q_{k_i}) < t(q_{k_{i+1}}) \wedge sim(q_{k_i}, q_{k_j}) > \theta\}.$$

Here, $t(q_{k_i})$ is the timestamp of query q_{k_i}, $sim(q_{k_i}, q_{k_j})$ is the similarity of queries q_{k_i} and q_{k_j}, and θ is the similarity threshold. $k_1, k_2 \ldots$ might not be consecutive.

4.1 Similarity Calculation

We employ four types of features to estimate query similarity, i.e., conceptual features, lexical features, template features, and temporal features. In order to combine all these features to calculate an overall similarity, we consider a supervised machine learning process. In the following sections, we present the details of how these features are calculated, with an emphasis on the conceptual features.

4.1.1 Conceptual Features

In this part, we describe the techniques of inferring the conceptual meaning behind any short text, and how to use the conceptualization results to calculate the similarity between queries in the concept space. In our work, we merge together both the words contained in the original query and those contained in the titles of the clicked urls when conducting conceptualization. But we still use *query* to refer to the merged string, in order to simplify the description. We formulate the process of calculating the conceptual similarities between queries into three steps detailed below.

Step 1: Parsing

Given a query, we split it into a set of terms, and then use *longest cover* to map each term to an instance/attribute contained in Probase. If two instances/attributes are of the same length, we choose the one connected to more concepts. For example, for query "truck driving school pay after training", we obtain "truck driving", "driving school", "pay" and "training", which are the longest instances in Probase that appear in the query. Note that, "driving" is also an instance in Probase, but we won't use it as there are longer instances that match the example query. Similarly, for query "tiger woods", we obtain one instance "tiger woods", instead of two instances "tiger" and "woods". In this way, we can better interpret queries, compared with the bag-of-words splitting method used in [14].

Step 2: Conceptualization

After parsing, a query is mapped to a collection of instances/ attributes. We denote it as $T = (t_1, t_2, \ldots, t_L)$. We want to infer the best concepts to describe those instances/attributes. To do this, we first identify the candidate concepts for each instance/attribute ranked by $P(instance|concept)$ and $P(attribute|concept)$, which is then represented as a concept vector $\mathbf{c} = (c_1, c_2, \ldots, c_M) \in \mathcal{R}^M$, where M is the total number of concepts in Probase. As we only retrieve the top K concepts for each instance/attribute, $\mathbf{c}$ is usually a sparse vector. Then in order to detect multiple topics contained in a query, we group the instances/attributes into clusters with each cluster representing one topic. For example, from a query "alabama home insurance" we can obtain two clusters, one is "alabama" which relates to the concept "state", and the other is "home insurance" which relates to the concepts "insurance" and "benefits". We use a clustering procedure to group topically related instances/attributes together, as shown in Algorithm 1. We build a

Algorithm 1 Conceptualization by Clustering.

Input: A set of instances/attributes $T = (t_1, t_2, \ldots, t_L)$. The weight threshold θ.
Conceptualization: Conceptualize each t_i to obtain a concept vector $\mathbf{c}_i$.
Build Graph: Build a graph $G_T = (V_T, E_T)$. Compute weight w_{ij} between t_i and t_j using Eq. (2). Remove an edge between t_i and t_j if $w_{ij} < \theta$.
Retrieve Clusters: Merge all instances/attributes that are connected in G_T into a cluster.

weighted graph $G_T = (V_T, E_T)$ from T, where V_T is the set of nodes equal to T and E_T is the set of edges connecting each pair of nodes. Each edge is weighted by a cosine similarity between concept vectors of the corresponding nodes. More specifically, we define the weight w_{ij} of edge $e_{ij} = (t_i, t_j)$ as:

$$w_{ij} = cosine(\mathbf{c}_i, \mathbf{c}_j) = \frac{\mathbf{c}_i \mathbf{c}_j^T}{||\mathbf{c}_i|| \cdot ||\mathbf{c}_j||}. \tag{2}$$

We then examine each edge in the graph and remove it when its weight is smaller than a pre-defined threshold. This results in a set of connected sub-graphs whose nodes will be grouped together to form an instance/attribute cluster. We denote cluster r as $T^r = (t_1^r, t_2^r, \ldots, t_{L^r}^r)$, where L^r is the number of instances/attributes contained in cluster r.

Next, we conceptualize the instances/attributes contained in each cluster r as a concept vector $\mathbf{c}^r$. Here, we solve the query ambiguity problem mentioned in Section 1. Instead of summing up the concept vectors of all the instances/attributes contained in cluster r, which is the approach used in [14], we calculate their intersection by a Naive Bayes function, as depicted in Eq. (3).

$$P(c_k|T^r) \propto P(c_k) \prod_{l=1}^{L^r} P(t_l^r|c_k) \propto \frac{\prod_{l=1}^{L^r} P(c_k|t_l^r)}{P(c_k)^{L^r-1}} \tag{3}$$

where $P(c_k|t_l^r)$ is the k-th value in the concept vector for instance/attribute t_l^r calculated using the method in [15], and $P(c_k)$ is the popularity of concept c_k in Probase which can be derived directly from the probabilistic information stored in Probase. In this equation, we assume that the instances/attributes are independent of each other. In this way, the common concepts of the instances/attributes in cluster r will be ranked higher than the individual ones. For example, given a cluster $(microsoft, apple)$, we obtain concepts related to "company", as shown in Figure 1 (a); while given a cluster $(pear, apple)$, all the retrieved concepts are related to "fruit", as shown in Figure 1 (b). We can see that ambiguity has been eliminated in this case.

After we obtain the disambiguated concept vector for each cluster, the conceptualization result of the whole query q can be expressed as:

$$\mathbf{c}_q = \frac{\sum L_r \cdot \mathbf{c}_q^r}{L} \tag{4}$$

where L is the total number of instances/attributes extracted from query q, and L_r is the number of instances/attributes contained in cluster r of query q. From Eq. (4) we can see that the final conceptualization results of query q is a weighted combination of multiple topics, with each topic represented by a set of related concepts. For example, given the query "microsoft windows 7", our algorithm first detects that there are two instances, namely "microsoft" and "windows 7". It then groups all the instances together into one cluster, so the conceptualization result contains only one topic, i.e., concepts related to "operating system"; on the contrary, given the query "alabama home insurance", our algorithm automatically identifies two topics after clustering. As a result, we then obtain two sets of concepts, one including "state" related concepts derived from the instance "alabama", and the other including "insurance" and "benefits" related concepts derived from the instance "home insurance".

Step 3: Calculating conceptual similarity

Now we have obtained the conceptualization result of each query expressed as a concept vector $\mathbf{c}_q = (c_{q1}, c_{q2}, \ldots, c_{qM}) \in \mathcal{R}^M$. We can use the concept vectors to calculate the conceptual similarities between queries simply by a *cosine* function:

$$sim_c(q_i, q_j) = cosine(\mathbf{c}_{q_i}, \mathbf{c}_{q_j}) = \frac{\mathbf{c}_{q_i} \mathbf{c}_{q_j}^T}{||\mathbf{c}_{q_i}|| \cdot ||\mathbf{c}_{q_j}||}. \tag{5}$$

where $\mathbf{c}_{q_i}$ and $\mathbf{c}_{q_j}$ are the concept vectors of queries q_i and q_j respectively, and $\mathbf{c}_{q_i}^T$ and $\mathbf{c}_{q_j}^T$ are the transposes of concept vectors $\mathbf{c}_{q_i}$ and $\mathbf{c}_{q_j}$ respectively.

4.1.2 Lexical Features

We use two types of lexical features to formulate the bag-of-words similarities between queries: *N-word Jaccard* and *N-char Jaccard*.

For *N-word Jaccard*, we use three steps to calculate the similarity between two queries. We first divide the bag-of-words representation of a query into a collection of N-words. For example, from the query "the car james bond drive", we get a set of 2-words as {"the car", "car james", "james bond", "bond drive"}. We then calculate the N-word similarity between two queries using a modified jaccard metric on the two corresponding N-word collections with term frequencies:

$$sim_{Nwj}(q_i, q_j) = \tilde{J}(v_i, v_j) = \frac{\sum(v_{ik_i} + v_{jk_j})}{\sum_{k=1}^m v_{ik} + \sum_{k=1}^n v_{jk}} \tag{6}$$

where v_i is the N-word set of query q_i, v_{i_k} is the term-frequency of the kth N-word in set v_i, m and n are the sizes of set v_i and v_j respectively. For each common N-word in query q_i and q_j, k_i and k_j are the indexes of that N-word in set v_i and v_j respectively, and v_{ik_i} and v_{jk_j} are the term frequencies of that common N-word in set v_i and v_j respectively. We range the value of N from 1 to 5, and get five N-word Jaccard similarities for each pair of queries: sim_{1wj}, sim_{2wj}, ..., sim_{5wj}.

Analogously, for *N-char Jaccard*, we first divide the bag-of-words representation of a query into a collection of N-chars. For example, from the query "mlb trades", we get a collection of 3-chars as {"mlb", "lb ", "b t", " tr", "tra", "rad", "ade", "des"}. We then calculate the N-char similarity between two queries using a modified jaccard metric on the two corresponding N-char collections similar to Eq. (6). Here, v_i is the N-char set of query q_i, and v_{i_k} is the term-frequency of the kth N-char in set v_i. We range the value of N from 1 to 9, and get nine N-char Jaccard similarities for each pair of queries: sim_{1cj}, sim_{2cj}, ..., sim_{9cj}.

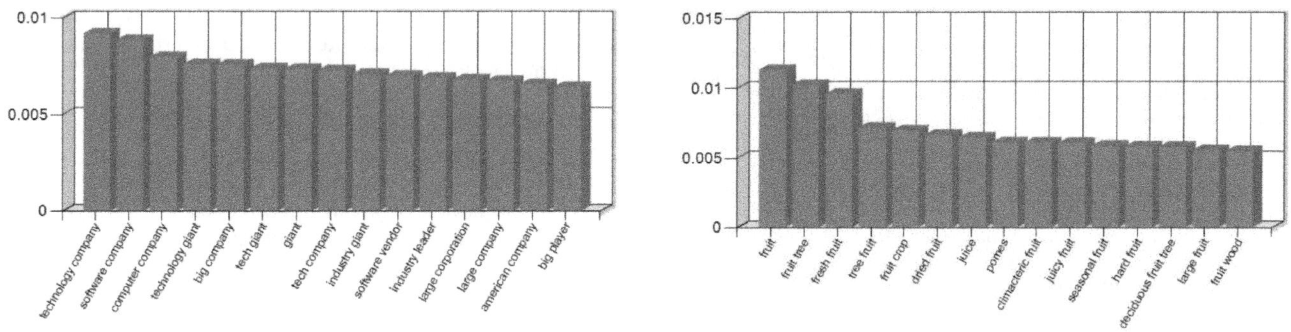

(a) Conceptualization of cluster *(microsoft, apple)*.

(b) Conceptualization of cluster *(pear, apple)*.

Figure 1: Examples of conceptualization and disambiguation.

4.1.3 Template Features

Huang et al. show that some query refinement strategies are very prevalent in the query logs [10], including substring/superstring, add/ remove words, stemming, spelling correction, acronym and abbreviation, etc. We formulate these templates of query refinements as a similarity function based on *Levenshtein edit distance*:

$$sim_{ed}(q_i, q_j) = 1 - \frac{ed(q_i, q_j) - abs(len(q_i) - len(q_j))}{max(len(q_i), len(q_j))} \tag{7}$$

Where $ed(q_i, q_j)$ is the *Levenshtein edit distance* between query q_i and q_j, and $len(q_i)$ is the length of query q_i, namely the number of characters in query q_i. We can see from Eq. (7) that when query q_i and q_j satisfy one of the refinement strategies mentioned above, the result of $ed(q_i, q_j) - abs(len(q_i) - len(q_j))$ will be close to 0, then $sim_{ed}(q_i, q_j)$ will be close to 1.

4.1.4 Temporal Features

The temporal features are only calculated between consecutive queries. We find that the time intervals between consecutive queries in the same task are usually shorter than those that cross a task boundary. Thus the more temporally close two consecutive queries are, the larger the probability of them belonging to the same task (Or the smaller the probability of them constituting a task boundary). So we define a temporal feature to capture the characteristics of time intervals between consecutive queries:

$$sim_t(q_i, q_{i+1}) = \frac{t(q_{i+1}) - t(q_i) - d(q_i)}{max_i(t(q_{i+1}) - t(q_i) - d(q_i))} \tag{8}$$

where $t(q_i)$ is the time query q_i is issued, and $d(q_i)$ is the dwelltime of query q_i, i.e., the sum of dwelltimes of clicks after query q_i.

4.2 Task Identification

Now that we have obtained the overall similarity of each query pair using a supervised machine learning process, the next thing we need to do is to merge queries with significant similarities into one task. Most previous works assume that tasks are never interleaved with each other, so they simply try to detect task boundaries between consecutive queries. More specifically, they model each session as a query chain $G_1 = (V, E_1)$, in which $V = \{q_i\}$ is the set of queries, and $E_1 = \{edge(q_i, q_{i+1})\}$ is the set of undirected edges between consecutive queries. They then examine each edge in the query chain and remove it when the similarity between the two consecutive queries connected by that edge is smaller than the similarity threshold θ. As shown in Figure 2 (a), edge $edge(q_3, q_4)$ is removed from the query chain, or in other words, a task boundary between queries q_3 and q_4 is detected after edge examination. Finally, for each pair of consecutive queries, if they are still connected in the query chain after edge examination, they will be clustered together into one task. We denote this process of task identification as **Sequential Cut (SC)**.

However, we can see from the example in Table 1 that tasks can be interleaved (e.g., task 1 and task 2 are interleaved in this example). Actually, we find in our evaluation dataset that 42.67% out of 600 randomly sampled sessions contain interleaved tasks. To detect these interleaved tasks, Jones and Klinkner [11] employ a **Graph Cut (GC)** algorithm. Particularly, they model each session as a query graph $G_2 = (V, E_2)$, in which $V = \{q_i\}$ is the set of queries, and $E_2 = \{edge(q_i, q_j) | i \neq j\}$ is the set of undirected edges between each pair of queries. They then examine each edge in the query graph and remove it when the similarity between the two queries connected by that edge is insignificant. As shown in Figure 2 (b), edges $edge(q_1, q_2)$, $edge(q_1, q_4)$, $edge(q_2, q_3)$ and $edge(q_3, q_4)$ are removed from the query graph after edge examination. Finally, the queries contained in a connected sub-graph will be clustered into one task. This approach is obviously more accurate, compared with SC.

Nevertheless, as we discussed in Section 1, GC is usually time-consuming, and sometimes may even lead to over-merging. In order to detect interleaved tasks more quickly and avoid over-merging at the same time, we propose a new algorithm for task identification, which we call **Sequential Cut and Merge (SCM)**. As depicted in Algorithm 2, SCM can be considered as a combination of SC and GC. Or more specifically, we first apply SC on the target session and refer to the tasks derived from SC as subtasks. We merge together the bag-of-words interpretations of queries contained in a subtask to form a new query, which is used to represent that subtask. We then apply GC to the set of subtasks. In other words, we build a subtask graph $G_3 = (V', E_3)$ on the derived subtasks similar to the query graph. Here, $V' = \{Q_1, Q_2, \ldots, Q_m\}$ is the set of subtasks, and E_3 is the set of edges connecting each pair of subtasks. We then examine each edge in the subtask graph and remove it when the similarity between the two subtasks (represented by the new queries) connected by that edge is smaller than the similarity threshold θ. Finally, we merge together queries contained in subtasks that are still connected in the subtask graph after edge examination. Consider the example illustrated in Figure 2 (c). In the SC process, edges $edge(q_1, q_2)$, $edge(q_2, q_3)$ and $edge(q_3, q_4)$ are removed from the query chain after edge examination, resulting in four subtasks with each subtask consisting of a single query. Then in the GC process, subtasks q_1 and q_3, q_2 and q_4 are merged together respectively, to form two tasks: $task_1 = (q_1, q_3)$ and $task_2 = (q_2, q_4)$.

Compared with GC, SCM can reduce the computational time

Algorithm 2 Sequential Cut and Merge (SCM)

Input: A session represented as a sequence of queries $S = (q_1, q_2, \ldots, q_n)$. A similarity threshold θ.
Build Query Chain: Build a query chain $G_1 = (V, E_1)$ on S.
Edge Examination: Calculate the similarity of consecutive queries q_i and q_{i+1} connected by an edge $edge(q_i, q_{i+1})$. Remove this edge if $sim(q_i, q_{i+1}) < \theta$. This results in a new query chain $G'_1 = (V, E'_1)$.
Retrieve Subtask: Merge queries that are still connected in G'_1 into a subtask. Each subtask is represented by a query Q_i, which is a union of the bag-of-words interpretations of queries contained in that subtask. This result in $S = (Q_1, Q_2, \ldots, Q_m)$.
Build Subtask Graph: Build a subtask graph $G_3 = (V', E_3)$ on S.
Edge Examination: Calculate the similarity between subtasks Q_i and Q_j connected by an edge $edge(Q_i, Q_j)$. Remove this edge if $sim(Q_i, Q_j) < \theta$. This results in a new subtask graph $G'_3 = (V', E'_3)$.
Retrieve Task: Merge queries contained in subtasks that are still connected in G'_3 into a task.

(a) Illustration of Sequential Cut in query chain.

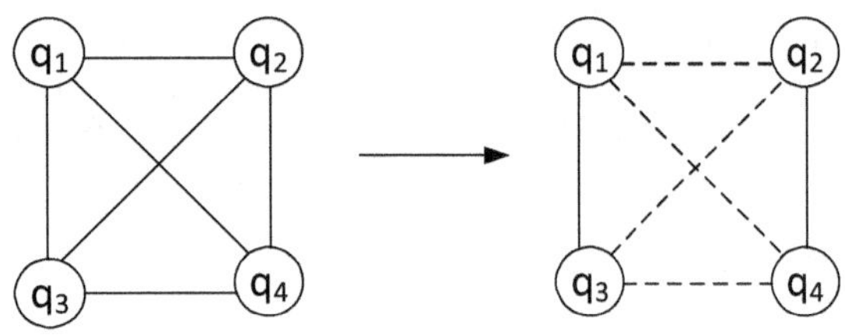

(b) Illustration of Graph Cut in query graph.

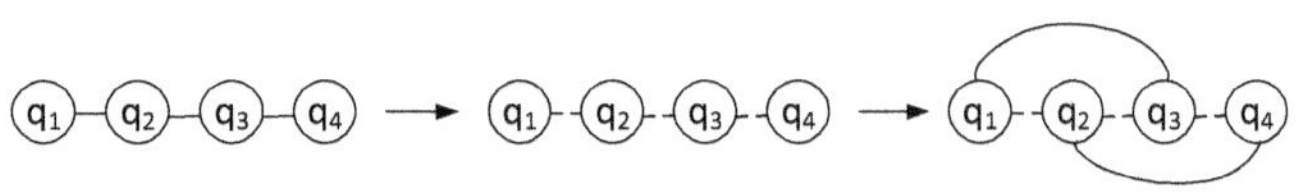

(c) Illustration of Sequential Cut and Merge.

Figure 2: Illustration of SC (a), GC (b) and SCM (c).

required. This is obvious, because GC calculates the similarities of all pairs of queries in one session. Then given the number of queries n in a specific session, the number of calculations in GC will be $\frac{n \cdot (n-1)}{2}$, or $O(n^2)$. Whereas, SC only calculates the similarity of each consecutive query pair, then the number of calculations in SC will be $n - 1$, or $O(n)$. Additionally, the *merging* process in SCM calculates the similarity of each subtask pair, so it will require $\frac{m \cdot (m-1)}{2}$ calculations where m is the average number of subtasks in a specific session. Then the total number of calculations needed for SCM will be $(n - 1) + \frac{m \cdot (m-1)}{2}$, and thus $O(n + m^2)$. Though the order of magnitude of the computational complexity hasn't changed, SCM can still tremendously reduce the computational time as long as n (namely, the number of queries in one session) is large enough, and at the same time, $m \ll n$. We will prove this analysis in our experiments. Additionally, we will also show that SCM can sometimes produce more accurate tasks than GC.

5. EXPERIMENTS

In this section, we present the experiments to demonstrate that (1) Probase can help inferring the topical meaning behind each query and reduce query ambiguity at the same time, and thus can be utilized to automatically detect topical query refinements, which in turn improves the performance of task identification; (2) SCM algorithm can significantly reduce the computational cost while preserving the task identification accuracy, compared with GC algorithm. We first present the evaluation dataset used in our experiments. Then we introduce the evaluation metrics used to measure the effectiveness of various features and algorithms. Finally we present the results and discussions.

5.1 Benchmark

We extract all the sessions one day in May, 2012 from a commercial internet browser. By *session*, we mean a sequence of queries issued in the browser without the use closing it. For simplicity and accuracy, we introduce three constraints on the dataset: (1) queries should have been entered to the "web" browser by users in the "United States"; (2) queries should have been written in "English"; (3) each session should have contained at least 10 queries. After filtering with these constraints, we obtain 45,813 sessions, from which we randomly sample 600 sessions and manually label them as our evaluation dataset.

task-unrelated statistics	
# queries	9144
# sessions	600
# queries per session	15.24
# clicks per query	0.65
dwelltime per click (seconds)	131.7
task-related statistics	
# subtasks per session	4.43
# tasks per session	3.435
# queries per task	4.437
# sessions containing interleaved tasks	256

Table 2: Statistics of evaluation dataset.

Table 2 lists some statistics of the dataset. We can see that there are an average if 3.4 tasks in each session, with each task containing 4.4 queries, which means that a typical information need can be satisfied within 4 or 5 queries. Note that, 256 out of 600 sessions (i.e., 42.67% sessions) in our evaluation dataset contain interleaved tasks.

5.2 Evaluation Metrics

In order to measure and compare the effectiveness of all the features and task identification algorithms we mentioned in Section 4, we introduce three evaluation metrics: error rate, f-measure, and jaccard index. Error rate is used to evaluate features, while f-measure and jaccard index are used to evaluate various task identification algorithms.

5.2.1 Error Rate

We formulate the process of edge examination described in Section 4 as an edge classification problem:

$$\{edge(q_i, q_j) | i \neq j\} \rightarrow \{0, 1\}.$$

Here, $edge(q_i, q_j)$ will be removed from the query chain/query graph /subtask graph, if it is mapped to 0. Then, the error rate can be defined as the misclassification rate in edge classification. Or more formally, the error rate of a classifier is defined as

$$error = \frac{|ErrorEdge|}{|TotalEdge|} \tag{9}$$

where $|ErrorEdge|$ is the number of misclassified edges in the query chain/query graph/subtask graph, and $|TotalEdge|$ is the number of edges before classification that connect each pair of (consecutive) queries/subtasks. For query chain of session $S = (q_1, q_2, \ldots, q_n)$, $|TotalEdge| = n - 1$; for query graph of session S, $|TotalEdge| = \frac{n(n-1)}{2}$; and for subtask graph of session S, $|TotalEdge| = \frac{m(m-1)}{2}$. Here m and n are the number of subtasks and queries respectively in session S.

5.2.2 F-measure

In this part, we denote *labeled tasks* as human annotated tasks, and *result tasks* as tasks identified by our algorithms. We use a three-step procedure to calculate the f-measure of a particular session S.

Step 1: For a result task $result_i$ and a labeled task $labeled_j$, we compute precision $p_{ij} = \frac{|result_i \cap labeled_j|}{|result_i|}$ and recall $r_{ij} = \frac{|result_i \cap labeled_j|}{|labeled_j|}$, where $result_i \cap labeled_j$ denotes the set of queries that belong to both $result_i$ and $labeled_j$. Then the f-measure of result task $result_i$ with respect to labeled task $labeled_j$ is defined as:

$$fmeasure_{ij} = \frac{2 \cdot p_{ij} \cdot r_{ij}}{p_{ij} + r_{ij}}$$

Step 2: We consider the problem of measuring the degree of correspondence of a result task $result_i$ and the labeled tasks as the problem of finding the best corresponding labeled task given $result_i$. To this point, the f-measure of the result task $result_i$ is defined as the largest f-measure of $result_i$ with respect to any labeled task $labeled_j$, i.e.,

$$fmeasure_i = \max_{j=1}^{J} fmeasure_{ij}$$

where J is the number of labeled tasks in session S.

Step 3: Finally, the f-measure of session S can be calculated as a weighted sum of all the f-measures of the result tasks contained in S

$$fmeasure = \sum_{i=1}^{I} \frac{|result_i|}{|S|} \cdot fmeasure_i \quad (10)$$

where $|result_i|$ and $|S|$ are the number of queries in $result_i$ and session S respectively, and I is the number of result tasks in session S.

5.2.3 Jaccard Index

In contrast to f-measure, which considers the task id of each single query, jaccard index considers the task ids of each pair of queries. We can calculate the jaccard index as follows:

$$Jaccard = \frac{n_{11}}{n_{01} + n_{10} + n_{11}} \quad (11)$$

where n_{01} = the number of query pairs that belong to different result tasks while belonging to the same labeled task; n_{10} = the number of query pairs that belong to the same result task while belonging to different labeled tasks; and n_{11} = the number of query pairs that belong to the same result task and also the same labeled task.

The above three scores are calculated for each session. In order to obtain the overall measure for the evaluation dataset, we simply use an average function over all the sessions in our evaluation dataset.

5.3 Results

We conduct two experiments to evaluate: (1) the effectiveness of different classifiers and features using *error rate*; (2) the accuracy of identified tasks by GC, SC and SCM using *f-measure* and *jaccard index.*

5.3.1 Effectiveness of Classifiers and Features

We experiment with three typical classification methods (i.e., Logistic Regression, Naive Bayes and Linear SVM (Support Vector Machine)), as well as three optimization methods (i.e., Stochastic Gradient Descent, L_BFGS (Limited-memory Broyden Fletcher Goldfarb Shanno) and SMO (Sequential Minimal Optimization)).[2] This leads to the following five classifiers:

- C1: Logistic Regression + Stochastic Gradient Descent
- C2: Logistic Regression + L_BFGS
- C3: Naive Bayes + Stochastic Gradient Descent
- C4: Linear SVM + SMO
- C5: Linear SVM + L_BFGS

For the problem of edge classification in the query chain, we consider six different combinations of the features we mentioned in Section 4 to evaluate the influence of each feature on the performance of the classifiers. The six feature sets (FSs) are as follows:

- FS1: temporal feature
- FS2: template feature
- FS3: lexical features
- FS4: conceptual feature
- FS5: template + lexical features
- FS6: template + lexical + conceptual features

We conduct a 5-fold cross validation on the 600 labeled sessions. The mean (Avg) and standard deviation (Std) of error rates for edge classification are shown in Table 3.

		FS1	FS2	FS3	FS4	FS5	FS6
C1	Avg	24.0%	22.7%	17.3%	21.5%	17.3%	15.2%
	Std	1.4%	1.5%	1.9%	1.3%	1.8%	1.0%
C2	Avg	24.2%	22.7%	17.3%	21.8%	17.3%	14.9%
	Std	1.4%	1.4%	2.0%	1.1%	2.0%	1.1%
C3	Avg	24.1%	23.4%	24.3%	25.1%	24.1%	20.6%
	Std	1.3%	1.3%	1.4%	1.7%	1.4%	1.8%
C4	Avg	24.0%	24.1%	17.4%	22.5%	17.4%	14.9%
	Std	1.4%	1.4%	1.8%	1.0%	1.8%	0.7%
C5	Avg	24.0%	24.1%	17.1%	23.0%	17.1%	15.5%
	Std	1.4%	1.4%	1.8%	1.8%	1.8%	0.8%

Table 3: Error rate of edge classification in query chain.

From Table 3, we can make the following conclusions:

First, when comparing the error rates of FS1, FS2, FS3 and FS4, we find that the lexical features (FS3) perform the best in all the classifiers except C3, in which template features are the best. This to some extent verifies the assumption exploited in the traditional content-based approaches ([2], [6] and [11]) that most users only make a small change of words when refining queries. Particularly, time-based features (FS1) are not comparable with content-based features (FS2 and FS3) in task identification. This result is also consistent with those found in [2], [6] and [11].

Second, the results using only conceptual features (F4) are usually better than time-based features (F1) and template features (F2), but not as good as lexical features (F3). However, when comparing the error rates of FS5 and FS6, we find an obvious improvement in all the five classifiers (12.14% improvement for C1, 13.87% for C2, 14.52% for C3, 14.37% for C4, and 9.36% for C5). It seems that topical query refinements are not only dominant patterns in tasks but also very prevalent in real query logs, and thus conceptual features are very significant complementary features to lexical

[2]From the internal use of Sho.NET, `http://research.microsoft.com/en-us/projects/sho/`.

ones. To further confirm the importance of conceptual features, we randomly select a real session in which the classifier using FS6 performs better than that using FS5. We list the tasks identified by Sequential Cut after edge classification using FS5 and FS6 in Table 4. The last three columns are task ids of the labeled tasks and result tasks using FS5 and FS6 respectively. We find that FS6 clusters all the queries together into one task because Probase can successfully detect that "honda", "suzuki", "mitsubishi" and "nissan" are brands of cars, which cannot be recognized by FS5.

QUERYID	QUERY	LABELED	FS5	FS6
0	honda civic	0	0	0
1	honda civic 1999	0	0	0
2	1994 suzuki katana 600	0	1	0
3	1997 mitsubishi diamante	0	2	0
4	1994 nissan sentra	0	3	0
5	1994 nissan sentra for sale	0	3	0

Table 4: Importance of conceptual features.

As for the edge classification in the query graph and subtask graph, sequentiality has been lost in these graph structures, because the edges are added between each pair of queries/subtasks that are not necessarily consecutive. This makes temporal feature meaningless. So we only consider five combinations of features (i.e., FS2, FS3, ..., FS6) for each classifier. Tables 5 and 6 list the mean (Avg) and standard deviation (Std) of error rates for edge classifications in the query graph and subtask graph respectively, using all the five feature combinations. From these two tables we also find that, when combining both content-based and conceptual features (i.e., FS6), the classification accuracy can be improved, compared with only using content-based features (i.e., FS5).

		FS2	FS3	FS4	FS5	FS6
C1	Avg	35.20%	27.71%	35.15%	27.91%	25.49%
	Std	4.02%	6.08%	5.47%	5.39%	5.08%
C2	Avg	35.54%	27.56%	35.70%	28.47%	25.50%
	Std	4.14%	5.97%	4.72%	5.25%	5.12%
C3	Avg	36.41%	35.25%	35.76%	35.20%	31.81%
	Std	4.48%	8.30%	6.03%	8.32%	6.51%
C4	Avg	35.38%	27.48%	39.07%	28.31%	24.97%
	Std	5.17%	5.80%	3.15%	5.07%	4.72%
C5	Avg	36.17%	27.97%	39.31%	28.03%	25.47%
	Std	5.44%	6.32%	2.51%	6.54%	6.59%

Table 5: Error rate of edge classification in query graph.

		FS2	FS3	FS4	FS5	FS6
C1	Avg	10.46%	5.52%	7.47%	5.36%	5.34%
	Std	3.25%	1.33%	2.75%	1.81%	1.33%
C2	Avg	10.14%	5.36%	7.14%	5.33%	5.16%
	Std	3.54%	1.30%	2.26%	1.75%	1.15%
C3	Avg	8.68%	6.00%	9.55%	7.66%	6.01%
	Std	3.84%	1.80%	3.05%	3.39%	1.77%
C4	Avg	10.46%	5.65%	6.84%	5.63%	5.44%
	Std	3.25%	1.08%	1.86%	1.35%	1.15%
C5	Avg	10.46%	5.52%	7.22%	5.52%	5.38%
	Std	3.25%	1.18%	2.32%	1.55%	1.13%

Table 6: Error rate of edge classification in subtask graph.

Furthermore, in order to verify that our approach to conceptualization using Probase can indeed reduce ambiguity, we manually pick out three queries, namely "tiger woods", "the cutest cat" and "python vs. java", and illustrate the Graph Cut results using Wikipedia ([14]) and Probase respectively in Table 7. As mentioned in Section 1, Lucchese et. al. [14] infer the conceptual meaning behind each query by combining the concept vectors (represented by TF-IDF vectors of Wikipedia articles) of all words contained in that query. Therefore, for the query "tiger woods", they will first divide it into two words, namely "tiger" and "woods", and then map the word "tiger" to a set of Wikipedia articles related to "tiger" or "animal", and the word "woods" to articles related to "material" or "plant". Finally, they add up all these articles, weighted by TF-IDF values. Similarly, the query "the cutest cat" is mapped to articles about "cat" or "animal", and the query "python vs. java" is mapped to articles about "snake" or "animal", as well as articles about "programming language". Consequently, all these three queries will be merged into one task because they all contain many concepts related to "animal". On the contrary, Probase maps the query "tiger woods" to "athlete" related concepts only, because "tiger woods", rather than "tiger" or "woods", is the longest cover found in the *Parsing* process of our approach, which will then be used to obtain the concepts about "golfer" or "athlete". Besides, we use an intersection function to emphasize common concepts of all the instances/attributes. Then "programming language", which is the common topic of "python" and "java", will be ranked higher in the conceptualization results, while "snake", which is only derived from "python", will be ranked extremely low or even disappear from the top K concepts. Consequently, all these three queries will be divided into different tasks. This indicates that our conceptualization approach using Probase can indeed reduce query ambiguity to some extent.

QUERY	Wikipedia	Probase
tiger woods	0	0
the cutest cat	0	1
python vs. java	0	2

Table 7: Disambiguation using Probase.

5.3.2 Accuracy of Algorithms

In this section, we evaluate the accuracy of tasks identified by GC, SC and SCM using f-measure and jaccard index. For GC and SC, we first pick out the best classifier built for edge classification in query graph and query chain respectively. Here by *best* classifier, we mean the classifier with the lowest error rate. We then group the queries that are still connected in the query graph/query chain after classification into one task. For SCM, we first pick out the best results from SC and define the retrieved tasks as subtasks. We then apply the "Merging" process of SCM on the resulting subtasks, to group together queries contained in similar subtasks. Table 8 shows the best f-measure and jaccard index of each algorithm. For the sake of comparison and analysis, we also build two baseline approaches: **NotMerge** and **MergeAll**. In NotMerge, all the queries in one session are classified into distinctive tasks. And in MergeAll, all the queries in one session are merged into the same task. The f-measure and jaccard index of NotMerge and MergeAll are also listed in Table 8.

		NotMerge	MergeAll	GC	SC	SCM
fmeasure	Avg	0.333	0.796	0.848	0.758	0.861
	Std	0.000	0.000	0.010	0.012	0.012
jaccard	Avg	0.053	0.345	0.393	0.267	0.443
	Std	0.000	0.000	0.024	0.073	0.027

Table 8: F-measure and jaccard index of identified tasks.

From Table 8 we can note that, SC is always worse than GC in terms of task identification (GC has a 12.03% improvement on f-measure and a 46.21% improvement on jaccard index, compared with SC). Note that, the f-measure and jaccard index of SC (0.758 and 0.267 respectively) are even worse than those of MergeAll (0.796 and 0.345 respectively), the baseline approach. This successfully verifies the prevalence of interleaved tasks in real sessions. So when we further merge together similar subtasks derived from SC, which is the procedure used in SCM, the results should be comparable with those obtained using GC. The data depicted in Table 8 is consistent with our expectation, with SCM increasing the f-measure and jaccard index by 1.49% and 12.61% respectively, over GC.

QID	QUERY	TID	GC	SC	SCM
0	the rain song youtube	0	0	0	0
1	cool math	1	1	1	1
2	the ugliest cat in the world	2	0	2	2
3	the cutest cat in the world	2	0	2	2
4	the tiniest cat in the world	2	0	2	2
5	the largest dog youtube	2	0	2	2
6	the largest snake on the earth	2	0	2	2
7	python wikipedia	2	0	2	2
8	cool math for kids	1	1	3	1

Table 9: An example of task identification results using GC (4th column), SC (5th column), and SCM (6th column) respectively.

Table 9 shows the task identification results of the session depicted in Section 1. The numbers listed in the last four columns are the task ids of all the queries with human labeling and different algorithms. It shows that SCM can perform better than SC and GC. We give two examples below to verify this.

First, in Table 9, SC cannot group the queries "cool math" and "cool math for kids" together into one task, even though they are similar from both the lexical and topical views. This is because SC only considers the similarities between consecutive queries. Thus, two queries (be they similar or not) will not be grouped together as long as there is another query between them that is similar with neither of them. However, by further applying a graph cut process on the subtask graph derived from SC, SCM can successfully merge together the interleaved parts of one task, thus improve its task identification accuracy.

Second, SCM can reduce the over-merging phenomenon of GC. This is mainly because the real user intent can be better exposed by a subtask (i.e., a collection of queries) than by a single query. In Table 9, when conceptualizing the query "the rain song youtube", we obtain two topics, i.e., "song" related concepts, as well as "video site" related concepts derived from the word "youtube". When conceptualizing query "the largest dog youtube", we also obtain two topics, i.e., "animal" related concepts derived from the word "dog" and "video site" related concepts derived from the word "youtube". Thus, these two queries will be grouped together into one task, as they both contain many concepts about "video site" that rank relatively high in the conceptualization results. Besides, queries 2 to 7 all refer to "animal"s, so they will be clustered together. Then, all these seven queries will be merged into one task in the result of GC. However, when conceptualizing queries 2 to 7 together as a subtask, as we emphasize on common topics that appear frequently in the query in our conceptualization procedure, the "animal" related concepts will be ranked higher in the conceptualization result, while the "video site" related concepts derived from the word "youtube" will be ranked extremely low, or will not be found in the top K results at all, as shown in Figure 3. This results in the better performance of SCM than GC.

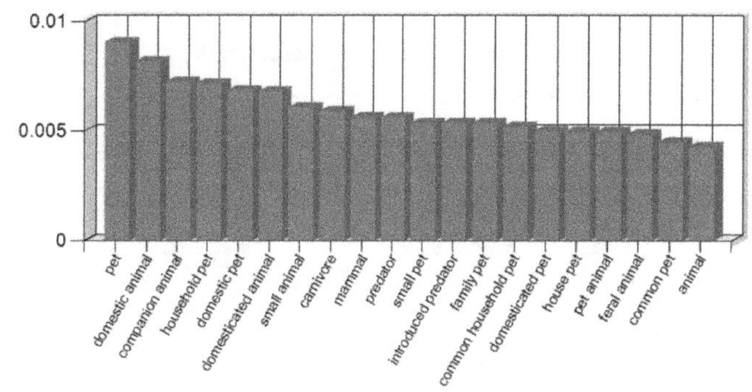

Figure 3: Conceptualization of subtask as a whole.

We mentioned in Section 4 that the computation complexity of GC is $O(n^2)$, while the computation complexity of SCM is $O(n + m^2)$. From the statistics of the evaluation dataset listed in Table 2 we can see that, there are on average 15.24 queries and 4.43 subtasks in each session. If we assume that $m = \frac{1}{3} \cdot n$ or $m = \frac{1}{4} \cdot n$, then the calculations required for SCM will be $O(\frac{n^2}{18})$ or $O(\frac{n^2}{32})$, which is about one-tenth of that required for GC. In order to confirm our analysis, we derive the *training time* and *task forming time* of GC and SCM using all the five classifiers in the above experiments. The training time of GC is the time required to train the classifiers used for edge classification in the query graph; the training time of SCM is the training time of classifiers used for edge classification in the query chain, plus the training time of classifiers used for edge classification in the subtask graph. The task forming time of GC is the time required to merge connected queries in the query graph after edge classification; and the task forming time of SCM is the time required for SC to merge connected queries in the query chain, plus the time required to merge connected subtasks in the subtask graph after edge classification. In Figure 4, we vary the number of sessions contained in the dataset from 100 to 600, differentiated using different colors. GC_i and SCM_i on the x-axis represents $classifier_i$ used for edge classification in GC and SCM respectively. And the numbers on the y-axis are the time required in seconds. We apply a *logarithmic* function on the training time in order to make the histograms increase smoothly.

From Figure 4 we can reach the following conclusions: 1) The training time and task forming time will increase with the increment of dataset size, for both GC and SCM. 2) Both the training time and task forming time required for GC are always larger than those required for SCM. Additionally, the computation time of GC rises faster than that of SCM. The most notable case is the classifier4 (Linear SVM + SMO) for GC (or edge classification in the query graph), whose training time has a tremendous increment from 10 seconds to 3500 seconds, when the number of sessions increases from 100 to 600.

6. CONCLUSIONS

In this paper, we attempt to improve the performance of task identification by capturing topical query refinements, as well as detecting interleaved tasks in each session. Queries may be ambiguous, which makes it extremely challenging to infer the real intent behind each query. We exploit Probase – an external knowledgebase extracted from web collection, to reduce query ambiguity. Previous approaches that leverage Wikitionary or Wikipedia usually map the bag-of-words expression of a query to a set of concept vectors represented as TF-IDF vectors of Wikipedia articles, and then sum up all the concept vectors to form the topical meaning of

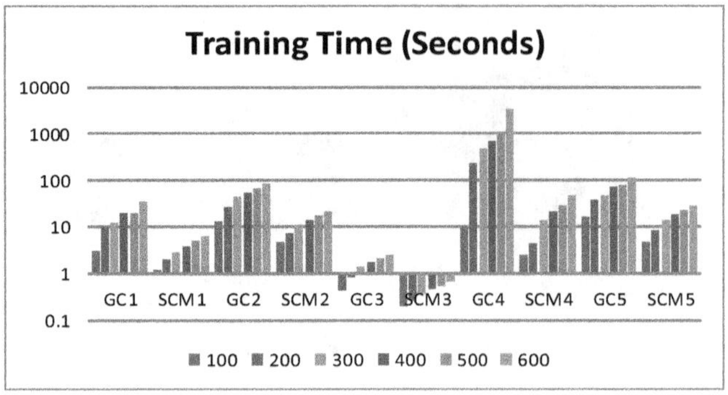

(a) training time.

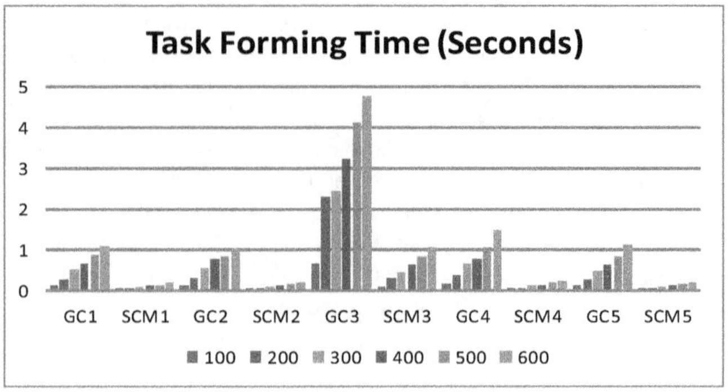

(b) task forming time.

Figure 4: Training time (left) and task forming time (right) of GC and SCM using different classifiers

the original query. In this way, many unrelated concepts will be retrieved if some words reflect multiple topics. On the contrary, we use the longest cover method to express a query as a bag-of-terms, with each term representing an instance/attribute. Our experiments show that the bag-of-terms expression can reflect the queries' topical components better than the simple bag-of-words expression. Furthermore, we use a Naive Bayes function to intersect the concept vectors of all terms, and thus emphasize on common concepts. This will to some extent reduce query ambiguity, as proved in our experiments. Additionally, tasks are often interleaved with each other. To address this, we build a Sequential Cut and Merge (SCM) algorithm, which can be considered as a combination of Sequential Cut (SC) and Graph Cut (GC). We prove that SCM can detect interleaved tasks and thus retrieve comparable or even better performance, compared with GC. Moreover, SCM can significantly reduce the computational time required by GC, as long as the session size (or the number of queries contained in that session) is large enough, and there are significantly fewer subtasks than queries in one session.

We have found that the queries contained in some tasks are related to each other, rather than similar. Take for example, queries "celtics members" and "kevin garnette". Although they are not similar in the concept space with one being an NBA team and the other being an NBA player, they should still be clustered into one task, because they are actually topically related, with the former query searching for members of an NBA team and the entity contained in the latter query being a member of that NBA team. Currently, Probase doesn't have any mechanism to calculate the relatedness score of each query pair. We leave it for future work.

7. ACKNOWLEDGMENTS

This paper is partially supported by National 863 High-tech Program (2012AA010701). We would also like to thank Weizhu Chen for his instruction and useful suggestions.

8. REFERENCES

[1] M. Banko, M. J. Cafarella, S. Soderland, M. Broadhead, and O. Etzioni. Open information extraction from the web. In *IJCAI*, pages 2670–2676, 2007.

[2] P. Boldi, F. Bonchi, C. Castillo, D. Donato, A. Gionis, and S. Vigna. The query-flow graph: model and applications. In *CIKM*, pages 609–618, 2008.

[3] K. Bollacker, C. Evans, P. Paritosh, T. Sturge, and J. Taylor. Freebase: a collaboratively created graph database for structuring human knowledge. In *SIGMOD*, 2008.

[4] H. Cao, D. Jiang, J. Pei, Q. He, Z. Liao, E. Chen, and H. Li. Context-aware query suggestion by mining click-through and session data. In *KDD*, pages 875–883, 2008.

[5] L. D. Catledge and J. E. Pitkow. Characterizing browsing strategies in the world-wide web. *Computer Networks and ISDN Systems*, 27(6):1065 – 1073, 1995. Proceedings of the Third International World-Wide Web Conference.

[6] J. Cui, H. Liu, J. Yan, L. Ji, R. Jin, J. He, Y. Gu, Z. Chen, and X. Du. Multi-view random walk framework for search task discovery from click-through log. In *CIKM*, pages 135–140, 2011.

[7] O. Etzioni, M. Cafarella, and D. Downey. Webscale information extraction in knowitall (preliminary results). In *WWW*, 2004.

[8] C. Fellbaum, editor. *WordNet: an electronic lexical database*. MIT Press, 1998.

[9] D. He and A. GÃűker. Detecting session boundaries from web user logs. In *In Proceedingsof of the BCS-IRSG 22nd Annual Colloquium on Information Retrieval Research*, pages 57–66, 2000.

[10] J. Huang and E. N. Efthimiadis. Analyzing and evaluating query reformulation strategies in web search logs. In *CIKM*, pages 77–86, 2009.

[11] R. Jones and K. L. Klinkner. Beyond the session timeout: automatic hierarchical segmentation of search topics in query logs. In *CIKM*, pages 699–708, 2008.

[12] D. B. Lenat and R. V. Guha. *Building Large Knowledge-Based Systems: Representation and Inference in the Cyc Project*. Addison-Wesley, 1989.

[13] Z. Liao, Y. Song, L.-w. He, and Y. Huang. Evaluating the effectiveness of search task trails. In *WWW*, 2012.

[14] C. Lucchese, S. Orlando, R. Perego, F. Silvestri, and G. Tolomei. Identifying task-based sessions in search engine query logs. In *WSDM*, pages 277–286, 2011.

[15] Y. Song, H. Wang, Z. Wang, H. Li, and W. Chen. Short text conceptualization using a probabilistic knowledgebase. In *IJCAI*, pages 2330–2336, 2011.

[16] R. W. White, P. N. Bennett, and S. T. Dumais. Predicting short-term interests using activity-based search context. In *CIKM*, pages 1009–1018, 2010.

[17] W. Wu, H. Li, H. Wang, and K. Q. Zhu. Probase: A probabilistic taxonomy for text understanding. In *SIGMOD*, 2012.

[18] B. Xiang, D. Jiang, J. Pei, X. Sun, E. Chen, and H. Li. Context-aware ranking in web search. In *SIGIR*, 2010.

Differences in Search Engine Evaluations Between Query Owners and Non-Owners

Alexandra Chouldechova
Stanford University
Stanford, CA 94305
achould@stanford.edu

David Mease
Google
Mountain View, CA 94043
dmease@google.com

ABSTRACT

The query-document relevance judgments used in web search engine evaluation are traditionally provided by human assessors who have no particular association with the specific queries selected for the evaluation. Most commonly, queries are randomly sampled from search logs and in turn randomly assigned to the human assessors. In this paper, we consider a very different approach in which we instead ask the human assessors to provide their own queries from their recent search experiences. Using these queries as our sample, we compare the relevance judgments from the "owners" of the queries to the relevance judgments of the non-owners.

We conduct experiments which reveal that query ownership has a substantial and beneficial impact on the accuracy of relevance judgments. In particular, we observe that owners are more consistently able to distinguish a higher quality set of search results from a lower quality set in a blind comparison. The implication for web search evaluation is that query owners provide more valuable relevance judgments than non-owners, presumably due to the background knowledge associated with their queries. We quantify the benefit of using owner assessments versus non-owner assessments in terms of sample size reduction. We also touch on some of the practical challenges associated with using query owners as assessors.

Categories and Subject Descriptors

G.3 [**Mathematics of Computing**]: Probability and Statistics—*experimental design*; H.3.3 [**Information Storage and Retrieval**]: Information Search and Retrieval

General Terms

Experimentation, Measurement

Keywords

Evaluation; experiment design; search engines; user queries

WSDM'13, February 4–8, 2013, Rome, Italy.

1. INTRODUCTION

Traditionally web search engines are evaluated based on queries sampled from the logs of the search engine. The human assessors who are employed to provide relevance judgments of documents returned for these queries may have very little subject matter background knowledge for certain queries. The assessors will usually be required to be fluent in the query language, but other than that there are often no assurances made to be certain that the assessors are familiar with the query's meaning. Conversely, the person who originally issued the query would generally have more background knowledge and additionally would often be aware of the specific information or types of web content that would best satisfy the query. In short, there is reason to believe that the person who issues a query should be a better judge of relevance than a random assessor. In this paper we design experiments to test for and measure the magnitude of this effect.

For obvious practical reasons it would be impossible to learn the identities of search engine users who issued particular queries found in the logs and ask those users to assess the relevance of documents for those queries. Thus, in this paper we take a different approach. We begin with assessors and ask these assessors to recall queries they have issued in the past for their own personal reasons. Using this approach we are able to pair queries with their "owners". We then construct two sets of 10 search results for each query, one set which is known to have better quality (on average) than the other. We ask the assessors to choose the more relevant set of 10 from the pair, and we measure the extent to which their preferences for the queries they own are more accurate than their preferences for queries which they do not own. Accuracy in this context refers to the selection of the higher quality result set.

The paper is organized as follows. Section 2 provides a review of some relevant literature. Section 3 outlines the experimental design. In particular, in that section we provide details pertaining to how queries were elicited from assessors as well as how we constructed the two sets of 10 results for each query. Sections 4 and 5 summarize the results of our data analysis. In Section 6 we describe the inference carried out in order to establish the statistical significance of the results. Section 7 outlines the implications that these results have with regard to the sample size needed for experiments using human assessors. Conclusions and discussion of the results are presented in Section 8.

2. LITERATURE REVIEW

As mentioned earlier, it is most common in web search evaluation that assessors are randomly assigned to queries. This is generally the case, for instance, with the extremely popular TREC [5] assessments.

In addition to TREC, other authors have collected relevance judgments in a variety of ways. For example, Alonso and Mizzaro [1] examined the use of crowdsourcing via Mechanical Turk as an alternative to TREC assessors, and Al-Maskari et al. [10] collected relevance judgments from participants in an interactive IR experiment they conducted. Both of these studies are similar to each other (as well as to the vast majority of the literature dealing with human assessors) in that the assessors are randomly assigned to queries, and there is no notion of query ownership. This is also generally the case with evaluation experiments carried out by commercial search engines such as the studies by Chapelle et al. [3], by Singla et al. [14], and by Huffman and Hochster [7].

While the random assignment of assessors to queries is most common, there is a fair amount of literature that examines more intelligent and sophisticated assignments. We review this literature in the following two subsections. In particular, we first consider assessor assignments in which the assessors have some expertise on the topics to which they are assigned. Secondly we consider literature involving assessments by topic "owners", which is more similar to the experiments that will be presented in this paper.

It should be noted that the literature reviewed here considers *absolute* assessments of *single* documents, while our experiments deal with *relative* measures of *sets* of documents. For this reason, it is difficult to compare our quantitative results to those in the literature; however, the general findings are very much related and relevant.

2.1 Expert Assessments

In Kinney et al. [8], the authors compared generalist assessors to assessors with domain expertise ("experts") for two specific classes of queries: computer-programming queries and biomedical queries. The authors concluded that the assessors with domain expertise were in fact providing higher quality and more in-dept relevance judgments, while the generalist assessors seemed to focus too much on query-keyword prominence.

The findings that will be presented in this paper can be thought of as a generalization of the expertise research in Kinney et al. [8] in the sense that assessors who have issued a query in the past for their own personal reasons (i.e., the owners) will generally have more domain expertise for that query than would a random assessor (i.e., a non-owner.) From this viewpoint, our research extends the work of Kinney et al. [8] beyond computer-programming queries and biomedical queries to a general sample of user-issued queries.

Law et al. [9] also compared random assessors to assessors with expertise. In that study, the expertise was discovered by allowing assessors to choose a set of queries from a given list. For each query selected, these assessors were asked to judge the relevance of five web pages. These assessors were then compared to assessors who were instead randomly assigned the same subsets of queries. The comparison revealed that the assessors who were permitted to choose queries did in fact have a higher (self-reported) degree of expertise than the assessors who were randomly assigned queries. No comparison was made in terms of the accuracy of the relevance judgments; however, the study did show that the assessors who were permitted to choose queries were less likely to make modifications to their original interpretations of the query intentions after providing their relevance judgments as compared to the randomly assigned assessors.

2.2 Owner Assessments

Next we discuss two studies which examined the impact of ownership (as opposed to merely expertise). In that regard, these two studies are more similar to ours.

The first of these is described by Voorhees [16]. In that paper, the author considers TREC data and examines the difference in relevance judgments between TREC topic authors and non-authors. She concludes that the authorship (ownership) does *not* have a substantial impact on the evaluation of the relative performance of the retrieval systems.

The second of these is described by Bailey et al. [2]. That research deals with three types of assessors labeled as "gold", "silver" and "bronze". Gold assessors are topic originators (owners). Silver assessors are non-owners but experts in the topics. Bronze assessors are neither owners nor experts. Again, the authors did not directly compare the accuracy of the relevance judgments, but did observe that the agreement between the gold and silver assessors was stronger than the agreement between the gold and bronze assessors.

2.3 Search Behavior

In addition to the research above dealing with how *evaluations* of owners are different from those of non-owners, we conclude this review of the literature by mentioning that there is also a substantial amount of work showing how *search behavior* can be quite different based on the user's familiarity with the query or topic. Most of these papers [4, 6, 17] focus generally on the differences in search behavior between experts and non-experts in the spirit of the Kinney et al. [8] paper mentioned above; however, the paper by Russell and Grimes [13] deals specifically with ownership in our sense. In particular, Russell and Grimes [13] found that study participants behaved differently when carrying out their own search tasks as opposed to experimenter assigned tasks. The behaviors found to differ included the amount of time spent completing the task as well as the number of distinct queries issued in the process. Since ownership leads to differences in search behavior, it is not suprising that it also leads to differences in search evaluation as will be demonstrated in this paper.

3. EXPERIMENTAL DESIGN

In this section we describe the design of our experiments in detail. We begin by describing the method by which we collected the queries from the assessors. Next we describe the nature of the evaluation tasks presented to the assessors in each experiment. Finally, we describe the construction of the search result sets being compared in each experiment.

3.1 Query Collection

At seven different time points over a 19 week period we contacted the members of a large pool of paid assessors in the United States to invite them to contribute queries. At each time point, any individual assessor was only permitted to contribute at most one single query. In this manner, we collected 23,530 queries, not all of which are unique.

The instructions to the assessors asked them to visit their Google query history at http://www.google.com/history and to select a single query from their history which they had issued for their own personal reasons (as opposed to a query issued as part of a previous assessment task). The assessors were told that their queries would be used in future evaluation tasks for both themselves as well as for other assessors in the pool. For this reason, they were encouraged not to include any highly personal or confidential information.

From here on, we will refer to the assessor who submitted a query as the "owner" of the query.

3.2 Task Description

Using subsets of these 23,530 queries, we conducted six evaluation experiments over a seven week period following the inital nineteen week query collection period. In each of these six experiments, two sets of 10 search results were shown side-by-side along with the query. The instructions to the assessors stated, "Please pick the side you would prefer if you were the user issuing the query." The assessors could indicate a preference for the right side, the left side or no preference.

In all six of our experiments, each assessor was always assigned any queries in the subset that he or she owned, and additionally five other queries that were randomly selected from the subset. For example, in Experiment 1 we used a subset of 5,000 queries from the set of 23,530. Thus, there were 30,000 total assessment tasks assigned, since each of the 5,000 queries was assigned to the owner plus five more random assessors from the same pool of query owners.

It is important to note that there was no indication provided to signal to the assessor whether he or she was evaluating a query he or she owned or a query that belonged to a different assessor. The only way an assessor could identify his or her own query would be from memory.

In an effort to make the comparison of the two sets of 10 search results easier, any search results which appeared on both sides of the comparison were marked accordingly. Figure 1 shows an example of the actual presentation to the assessors from the fourth of our six experiments. For all assessor tasks, the presentation of the two sides was randomized so that there was no left/right bias.

3.3 Experiment Descriptions

In this section, we describe how we constructed the two sets of 10 search results for each query. With the exception of Experiment 6, which will be discussed later, the two sets of results for each query were constructed such that one set would be known to be of higher quality (on average). In order to do this, we drew on the basic principle that Google's search results are on average ranked better than any re-ranking. For example, switching the first and second Google results will on average lead to a worse overall ranking than Google's original ranking. This type of experimentation is similar to studies such as those in [12]. In fact, our Experiment 2 is very similar to one used there.

The subsections below describe specifically how the two sets of 10 search results were constructed in Experiments 1 to 5. These are also summarized in Table 1. Some limited details regarding Experiment 6 are also provided.

Experiment 1

For Experiment 1, the higher quality search result set was constructed by taking Google's first search result for each query followed by its 12th through 20th in order. The lower quality search result set also used Google's first search result on top but then followed it with Google's 42nd to 50th results in order. Using the notation Gn to denote the nth result retrieved by Google as in Table 1, the higher quality result set for Experiment 1 is [G1, G12, G13, G14, G15, G16, G17, G18, G19, G20] and the lower quality result set is [G1, G42, G43, G44, G45, G46, G47, G48, G49, G50].

One advantage of constructing Experiment 1 in this manner is that neither of the two result sets is equivalent to Google's original search result ranking. Additionally, both result sets differ from Google's original ranking for exactly results 2 through 10. This helps eliminate any memory effect originating from previous experiences with the same queries on Google. To say this a different way, if one of the two result sets were more similar to Google's original search result ranking than the other result set, the ownership effect we are trying to measure could be confounded with a memory effect, since all owners have necessarily previously issued their queries on Google.

The queries selected for Experiment 1 were a random sample of 5,000 queries from the total set of 23,530. Experiments 2, 3 and 4 described below also use this same subset of 5000 queries.

Experiment 2

For Experiment 2, the higher quality result set is the top 10 Google search results in order, and the lower quality search result set is the same except two results between ranks 2 and 5 are randomly swapped with two results between ranks 6 and 10. This is a minor modification of the SWAP2 procedure described in [12].

Experiment 3

For Experiment 3, the higher quality result set is again the top 10 Google search results in order, and the lower quality result set is the same except Google's 11th and 12th results are inserted into the second and third positions (pushing Google's 9th and 10th results out of the set). Using Table 1 notation, the lower quality search result set is [G1, G11, G12, G2, G3, G4, G5, G6, G7, G8]. We refer to this type of change as an *insertion*.

Experiment 4

Experiment 4 is also an insertion experiment. The higher quality search result set is the same as that for Experiment 1: [G1, G12, G13, G14, G15, G16, G17, G18, G19, G20]. The lower quality search result set is obtained by inserting G21 into the fifth position of that set to produce [G1, G12, G13, G14, G21, G15, G16, G17, G18, G19]. Figure 4 shows exactly what an assessor would see for an example query ('Tyler Perry") in Experiment 4.

Experiment 5

Unlike Experiments 1-4 which used a random subset of 5,000 queries, for Experiment 5 we used all queries with five or more words. This yielded 4,870 queries from the complete set of 23,530 queries.

The higher quality search result set is once again the top

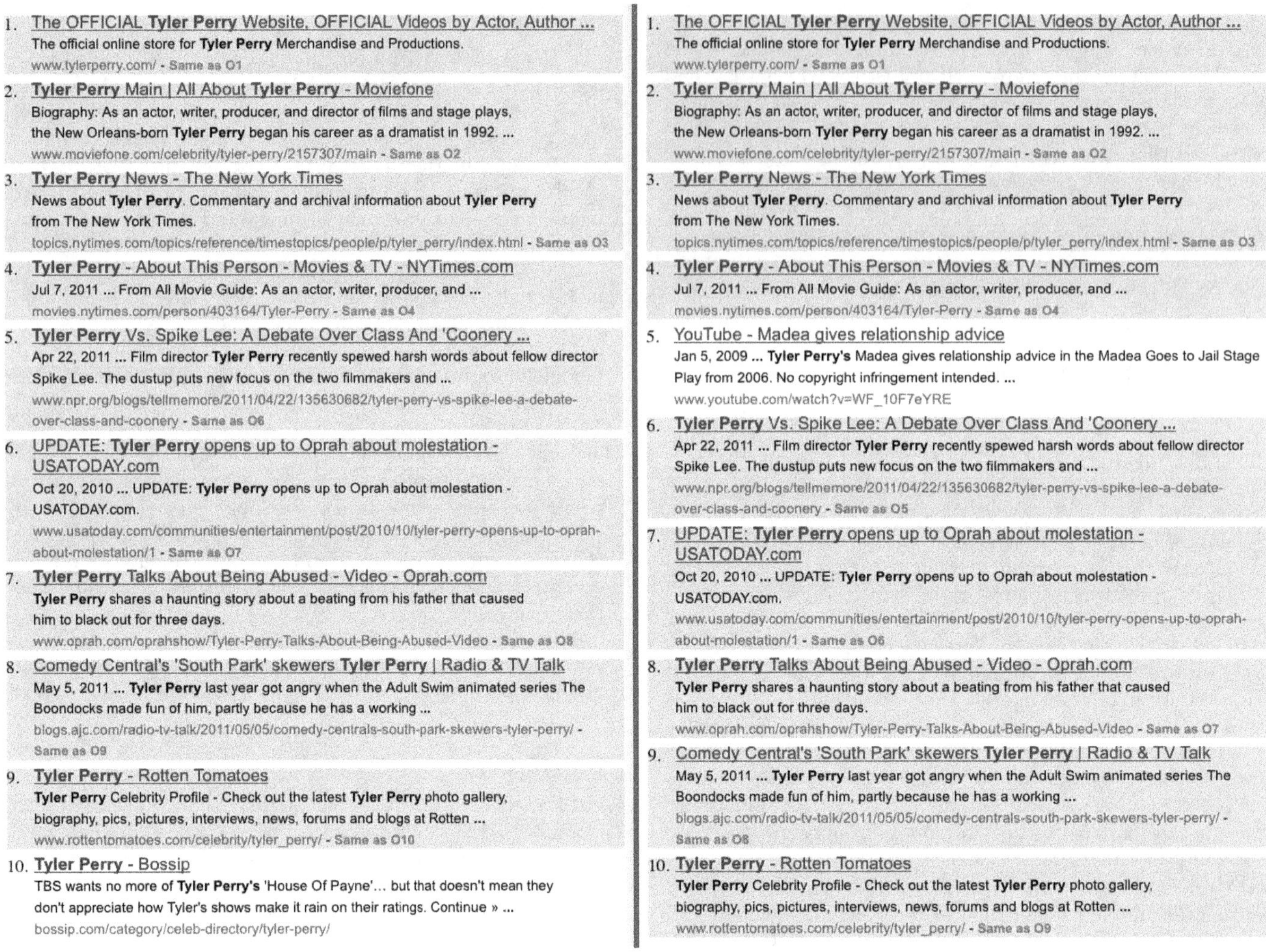

Figure 1: The two sets of 10 results as presented to the assessors in Experiment 4 for the query "Tyler Perry"

10 Google search results in order. The lower quality search result set consists of the top 10 Google search results for the query with the third word removed. For instance, the lower quality search result set for the query "Chase Freedom Mastercard double warranty" would be the top 10 Google search results for the query "Chase Freedom double warranty".

Experiment 6

Experiment 6 is unique in that instead of artificially creating higher quality and lower quality result sets, we used an actual experiment concerning a particular aspect of the Google search algorithm that was being investigated at the time of writing this paper. As a result, it is not known which set is actually of higher quality on average, and the positive/negative sign for the Experiment 6 display later in Figure 2 is arbitrary.

Unfortunately, we are not able to provide any details for either of the two result sets in Experiment 6. We are, however, able to say that the experiment was run using 4,420 of the 23,530 queries as the other queries were not impacted. Further, we will note that this experiment was of particular interest due to contradictory data from a number of various evaluation procedures that otherwise had proven to be quite consistent with one another historically across a variety of experiments.

4. RESULTS

In this section we summarize our findings concerning the effect of query ownership in our data. We begin by describing the data and scoring system used in our analysis, and then provide a discussion of the results.

4.1 Method

Due to nonresponse, many of the tasks assigned to the assessors were not completed during the study period. Our analysis is restricted to the subset of queries for which we obtained an assessment from the query owner and at least one of the five random assessors assigned. Across the six experiments the percentage of the queries we were able to keep ranged from 39% to 55%, with the variation in this number due mainly to the fact that some experiments were kept open to the participants for a longer period of time than others.

In order to carry out a quantitative analysis, we converted the assessor feedback to a numerical score of $+1$, 0 or -1 depending, respectively, on whether they preferred the higher

Experiment 1 Higher Quality Search Result Set	G1, G12, G13, G14, G15, G16, G17, G18, G19, G20
Experiment 1 Lower Quality Search Result Set	G1, G42, G43, G44, G45, G46, G47, G48, G49, G50
Experiment 2 Higher Quality Search Result Set	G1 , G2 , G3 , G4 , G5 , G6 , G7 , G8 , G9 , G10 (Google's top 10)
Experiment 2 Lower Quality Search Result Set	Google's top 10 with two results between ranks 2 and 5 randomly swapped with two results between ranks 6 and 10 - for example, G1 , G9 , G3 , G6 , G5 , G4 , G7 , G8 , G2 , G10
Experiment 3 Higher Quality Search Result Set	G1 , G2 , G3 , G4 , G5 , G6 , G7 , G8 , G9 , G10 (Google's top 10)
Experiment 3 Lower Quality Search Result Set	G1 , G11, G12, G2 , G3 , G4 , G5 , G6 , G7 , G8
Experiment 4 Higher Quality Search Result Set	G1, G12, G13, G14, G15, G16, G17, G18, G19, G20
Experiment 4 Lower Quality Search Result Set	G1, G12, G13, G14, G21, G15, G16, G17, G18, G19
Experiment 5 Higher Quality Search Result Set	G1, G2 , G3, G4, G5, G6, G7, G8 , G9 , G10 (Google's top 10)
Experiment 5 Lower Quality Search Result Set	Google's top 10 for query with 3rd word removed
Experiment 6 Higher Quality Search Result Set	(no details given)
Experiment 6 Lower Quality Search Result Set	(no details given)

Table 1: Descriptions of the search results for the six experiments (Gn denotes the nth search result returned by Google)

quality result set, had no preference, or preferred the lower quality result set. Again, for Experiment 6 this assignment was arbitrary so we just chose one of the two ranking algorithms being considered to be +1 and set the other as −1.

4.2 Discussion of Results: Experiments 1 - 5

Figure 2 shows a plot of the mean scores for owners and non-owners for each experiment. This analysis reveals that for Experiments 1-5 query owners did in fact demonstrate a stronger preference for the higher quality results than did the randomly assigned non-owners.

These results argue in favor of the idea that owners are better able to assess relevance than non-owners since they more often chose the higher quality set of results. We will examine the statistical significance of the difference between owners and non-owners in Section 6.

4.3 Discussion of Results: Experiment 6

As discussed earlier, Experiment 6 is an actual experiment concerning a particular aspect of the Google search algorithm that was being investigated at the time of writing this paper. The experiment previously had tested fairly negatively on human assessors (consistent with what is seen with the non-owner data in Figure 2) but relatively much more neutral on live traffic metrics. This discrepancy made the experiment a bit of a curiosity and raised questions about the extent to which human assessors could be trusted to represent real users for this particular type of experiment.

Since the owner assessments for Experiment 6 in Figure 2 also appeared to be quite neutral, this gave the experimenters increased confidence in the value of owner evaluations over those of non-owners. In other words, the owner data seemed to agree more with live traffic experiment data than the non-owner data.

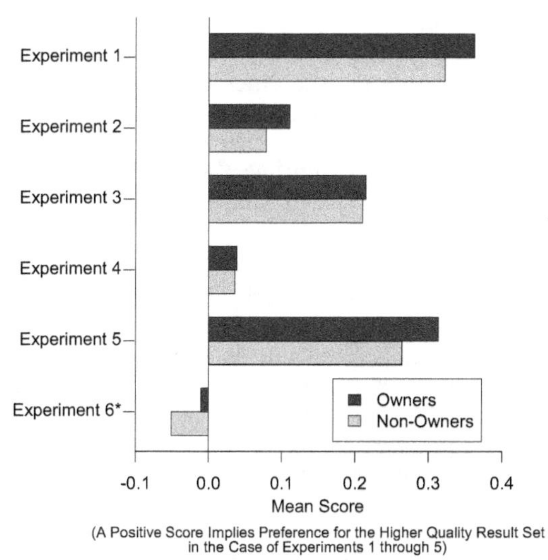

Figure 2: Comparision of owner and non-owner experiment mean scores for Experiments 1-6

Admittedly, we are not able to make this argument at all convincing to the reader since we are not revealing the details of the two search algorithms in Experiment 6 nor the accompanying live traffic experiment data. However, for the purposes of this paper, at the very least Experiment

6 represents an interesting example of how owner and non-owner evaluations can differ substantially for an experiment.

5. FURTHER ANALYSIS OF RESULTS

While it is clear in Figure 2 that the owner's scores are on average more positive than the non-owner's scores for Experiments 1 through 5, the mean alone does not tell us why this change is occurring. For example, two possible explanations are that (a) owners give roughly the same amount of -1's but fewer 0's or (b) owners give fewer -1's but roughly the same amount of 0's. These two explanations would suggest different underlying effects for query ownership.

To address this question, we analyzed histograms of the assessors -1, 0 and $+1$ scores. Interestingly, no single pattern emerged and in fact we observed slightly different trends from one experiment to the next. For example, Figure 3 shows the distribution of scores for owners and non-owners in the cases of Experiments 1 and 5. Experiment 1 seems to be an instance of (a), and Experiment 5 better matches (b).

6. STATISTICAL INFERENCE

In this section we investigate the question of the statistical significance of the owner versus non-owner differences seen in Figure 2. In other words, we examine whether the differences between owner and non-owner experiment mean scores are too large to be attributed simply to variability in human assessment. We will conclude that indeed the differences are statistically significant for Experiments 1, 2, 5 and 6 but not for Experiments 3 and 4. This would be a logical guess after looking at Figure 2, but the purpose of this section is to formally validate this.

To verify statistical significance, we will construct 95% confidence intervals for the differences in the mean scores of owners minus non-owners. By definition, if a 95% confidence interval does not include the value zero, then we have established statistical significance (at the $\alpha = .05$ level). We compute these 95% confidence intervals for each of the five experiments as

$$\text{mean of score differences} \pm 1.96 \cdot \frac{\text{s.d. of score differences}}{\sqrt{\text{number of queries}}}.$$

In this expression, the "number of queries" refers to the total number of queries in each experiment for which we have obtained an assessment from the query owner and at least one random assessor. We discard queries in the confidence interval calculation for which this is not true. The value of "score differences" is obtained by subtracting the mean of the random assessor scores for each query from the (single) owner score. Using that quantity, the values of "mean of score differences" and "s.d. of score differences" are obtained by taking the mean and standard deviation respectively.

These confidence intervals are displayed in Figure 4. We note that for Experiments 1, 2, 5 and 6 these confidence intervals do not include zero, thus establishing the statistical significance.

7. SAMPLE SIZE IMPLICATIONS

In this section we discuss some of the implications that our findings have for the number of assessors (sample size) required in human evaluation experiments of web search engine quality. We show that by collecting assessments from

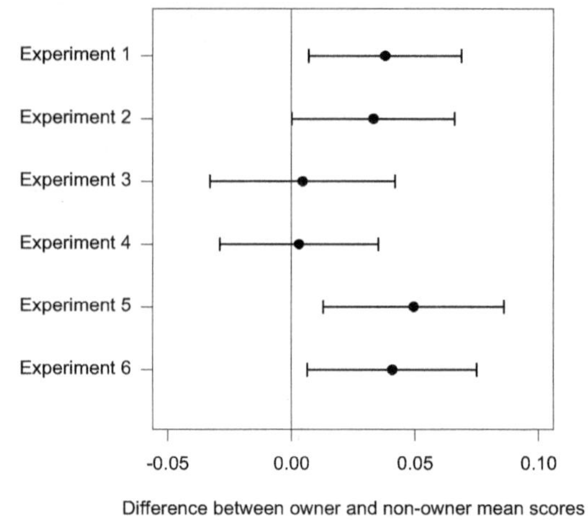

Figure 4: 95% confidence intervals for the difference between owner and non-owner mean scores

query owners instead of non-owners we are able to determine whether an experiment reflects a (statistically significant) positive or negative change to the search engine with fewer assessors than we would otherwise require. Depending on how large an effect the given experiment has on the quality of the search engine, the difference in the number of assessors required to detect it can be very large.

For the purpose of this discussion, we assume that the human evaluation experiment is conducted in an attempt to determine whether a particular change has a positive or negative mean effect on the search engine. To simplify the analysis, we will further assume from here on that we collect exactly one owner and one non-owner assessment per query. Note that the non-owner datasets for our experiments do not follow this assumption; however, it is valuable to consider this design since it turns out to be the most efficient (for a fixed budget of assessments) in addition to being the most simple to analyze.

The main question which we seek to address can be stated as follows: How many assessors (or equivalently, how many queries) are required to determine (with a fixed statistical significance level) whether a particular change to the search engine has a positive or negative effect, and how does this quantity depend on whether the assessors are query owners or non-owners?

7.1 The 5 Experiments

Before addressing this question in generality, we demonstrate how it can be answered in each of the first five experiments we conducted. For the purpose of simplifying this analysis, we downsample our dataset such that we retain exactly one owner assessment and one non-owner assessment per query.

Figure 5 shows a plot of confidence intervals for the owner and (downsampled) non-owner data for Experiments 1 to 5. These confidence intervals are computed as

$$\text{mean score} \pm 1.96 \cdot \frac{\text{s.d. of scores}}{\sqrt{\text{number of assessors}}}.$$

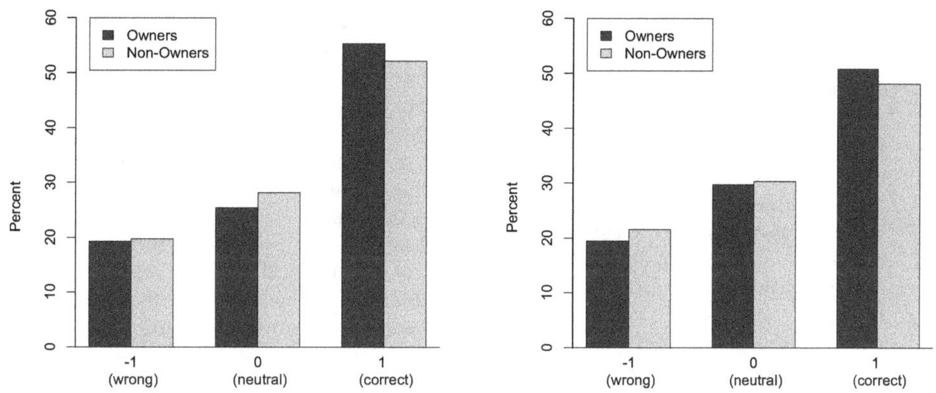

(a) Experiment 1

(b) Experiment 5

Figure 3: Histograms of scores for Experiments 1 and 5

Note that we use "number of assessors" here as opposed to "number of queries". These two counts are of course equivalent as a result of our downsampling, but we prefer to use the former in order to emphasize that the main cost is the assessment as opposed to the query sampling.

Since all 10 of the confidence intervals lie entirely above zero, each of the experiments is sufficient for us to conclude that the given change had a positive effect on the search engine regardless of whether we use owner or non-owner assessments and even in spite of the downsampling. This is a consequence of our large sample sizes for these experiments. However, for smaller sample sizes the width of the confidence intervals will widen and the sample size benefits of using owner assessments will become clear.

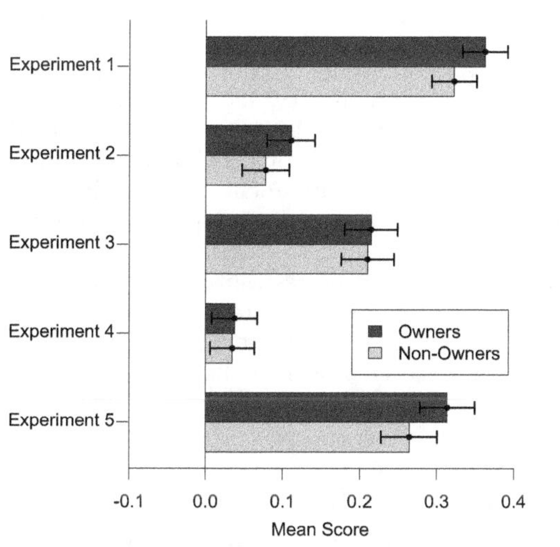

Figure 5: 95% **Confidence intervals for owner and non-owners from the downsampled data**

In particular, based on the data we collected we are able to deduce the minimal number of assessors that would be required in order to obtain statistical significance. We do

	Owners	Non-Owners	% Reduction
Experiment 1	19	24	21%
Experiment 2	191	322	41%
Experiment 3	60	60	0%
Experiment 4	1381	1545	11%
Experiment 5	24	43	44%

Table 2: The minimal number of assessors needed to establish statistical significance for Experiments 1 through 5

so by computing the mean scores and the standard deviations of the scores for the owners and non-owners in each experiment, and then determining the minimal number of assessors for which the corresponding 95% confidence interval lies above 0. The minimal number of assessors required for statistical significance for each experiment is tabulated in Table 2. We can see in Table 2 that for both Experiments 2 and 5 the sample size needed for statistical significance is reduced by more than 40% as a result of using owner assessments.

7.2 General Case

In this section we generalize our observations from the five experiments by identifying the features of the experiment which are most relevant in determining how many assessors are required to detect an effect. A common feature of confidence intervals, regardless of their construction, is that their width decreases at a rate proportional to the square root of the number of assessors used in the study. That is to say they take the form

$$\text{mean score} \pm \frac{C}{\sqrt{\text{number of assessors}}}$$

where C is some constant which typically depends on the desired confidence level and the variability of the data. In our analysis above, we took $C = 1.96 \cdot \text{s.d. of scores}$.

From this expression for the confidence interval, we can deduce that in order to detect that the given experiment had an effect, we require that

$$\text{number of assessors} > C^2/\text{mean score}^2.$$

In particular, if the experiment results in only a minor change, corresponding to a small mean score, we require a very large number of assessors.

Assuming that an experiment truly is positive (as is the case with our Experiments 1 through 5), we saw in our data that the owners consistently had higher mean scores than non-owners. Pairing that fact with the above expression for the minimal number of assessors reveals why using owners instead of non-owners in human evaluation studies requires fewer assessors in order to determine whether a given change to the search engine did in fact have a positive effect. How much fewer depends on the difference between owner and non-owner assessments for the given experiment.

In general we can state that the minimum number of assessors required to detect a change depends primarily on two quantities: the severity of the change induced by the experiment (experiment mean score) and the difference between owner and non-owner mean scores. In our Experiments 1 to 5, the experiment mean score ranged from 0.03 to 0.37, and the difference between owner and non-owner mean scores ranged from 0.003 to 0.049.

Figure 6 helps to illustrate how the minimum number of assessors required to detect a change depends on the experiment mean score for three values of owner minus non-owner mean differences within our observed range. These curves are plotted by taking C equal to 1 for simplicity so that the required sample size for the non-owners becomes $1/\text{mean score}^2$ compared to that for the owners which is $1/(\text{mean score} + \Delta)^2$ where Δ denotes the difference between the owner and non-owner mean scores. The three plots correspond to owner minus non-owner mean score differences of $\Delta = 0.005$, 0.010 and 0.040 which are within the range of our observed values (0.003 to 0.049 as mentioned above.) The x-axis in all three plots ranges from 0.03 to 0.37 which matches the range of our observed experiment mean scores. These plots show that the sample size savings from using owners' assessments can be quite substantial for small experiment mean scores. This is especially true for large values of Δ such as $\Delta = .040$ similar to what was observed in Experiments 1 and 5.

8. CONCLUDING REMARKS

The results of this paper show that in general owners provide more accurate assessments than non-owners with regard to choosing higher quality result sets. The magnitude of the difference between owners and non-owners varies depending on the experiment, and can be quite substantial in some cases. One benefit from the more accurate assessments is a reduction in the sample size needed to obtain statistical significance for experiment mean scores.

Despite the desirability of using owner assessments over non-owner assessments, there are a number of practical reasons which make this difficult. We mention three of these below.

First, as mentioned earlier, it is not possible to sample queries from the search engine logs and subsequently locate the corresponding users who issued the queries. Rather, some method of sampling users who are willing to do assessment and subsequently eliciting queries from these users must be employed. We do not pretend to have developed a good method for doing this.

Second, once a set of queries with owners is established by some means, there is the additional problem that some of the assessors will eventually drop out of any long-term study. Thus, maintaining a query set with current relevance assessments over any extended period of time becomes difficult. Either the query set will constantly decrease in size or "replacement" owners must be found for queries which have been orphaned.

Finally, when eliciting queries from assessors, it is difficult to ensure and control representativeness of the query sample. Some analysis comparing the 23,530 queries used in this paper to a random sample from Google's US query logs suggests that there are some pronounced differences between the nature of the queries in the two samples. For example, the rate of spelling errors in our 23,530 queries is roughly half of that in a random sample from the Google US query logs. (The spelling error rate here was computed using the triggering of Google's "Showing results for" spelling correction.) One possible explanation for this large difference is that when visiting http://www.google.com/history to select queries, many misspelled queries are often immediately followed in the user session by a correctly spelled query (either corrected by the user or by Google). Since the assessor selects only one query each time, it is plausible the assessors gravitated toward the correctly spelled query. Note that when sampling from query logs it is possible to programmaticly choose the first query, last query or a random query from a session; whereas, when asking assessors to volunteer queries it is somewhat difficult to control this type of selection.

While it will never be as simple to use owner assessors as it is to use non-owner assessors, we believe this is a technique that will become more popular in the future. We believe the main driving force behind this will not necessarily be the increased accuracy illustrated in this paper, but rather this increased accuracy will be a beneficial byproduct and that the use of query owners as assessors will become necessary as search engines continue to personalize results based on a user's location, query history, social graph and other data. The result sets considered in the experiments in this paper were by construction unpersonalized, and it is interesting to imagine the equivalent experiments with results personalized for the owners to better match the true user experience. For such personalized results, the difference between owner assessments and non-owner assessments would be even more substantial, perhaps to the extent that non-owner assessments become completely useless for many experiments. We note that the research on personalization techniques already follows the practice of using owner assessments. Examples include [11] and [15].

9. ACKNOWLEDGMENTS

The authors would like to thank Daniel Russell and Ya Xu for their help with the preparation of this paper.

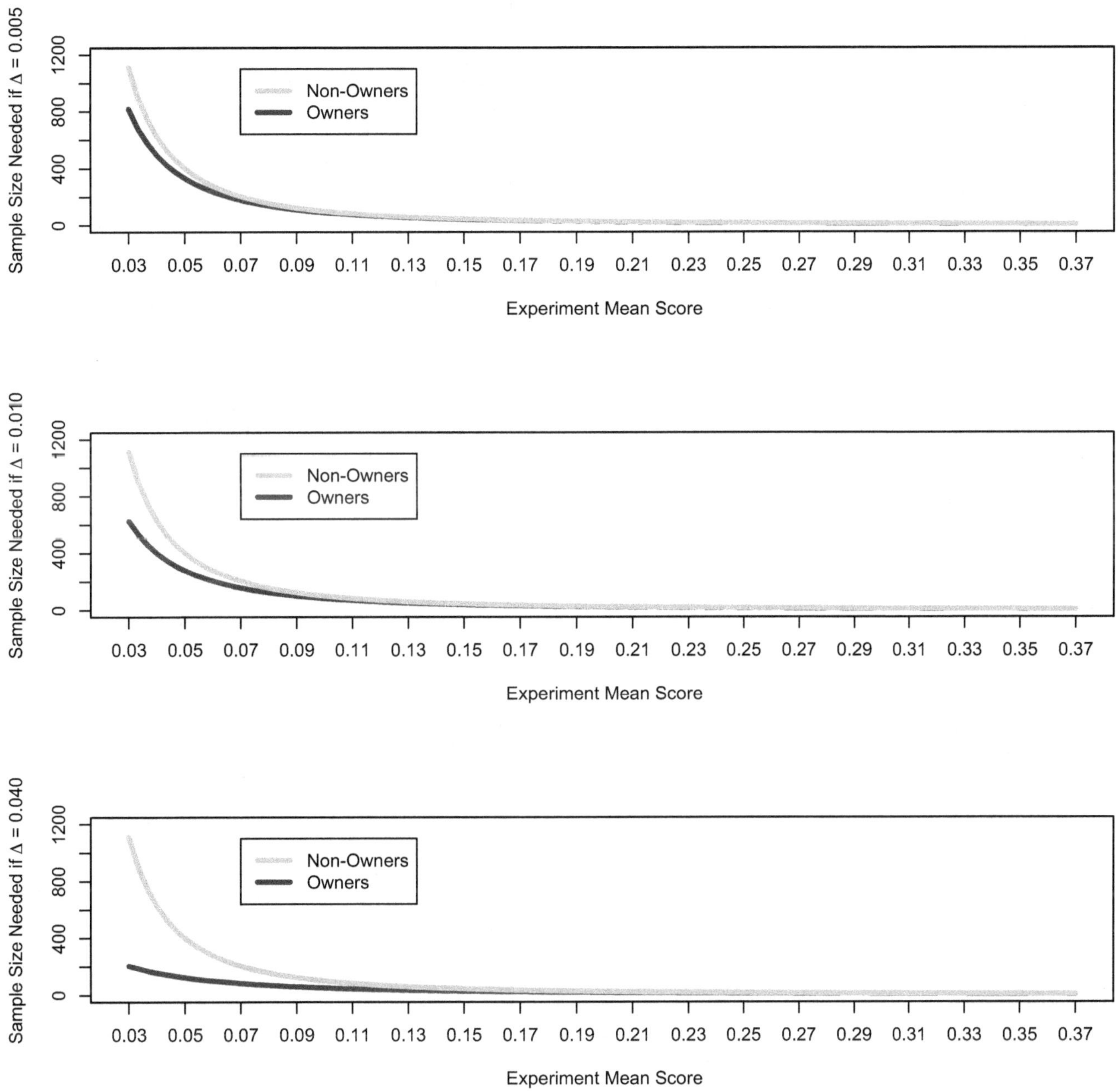

Figure 6: Comparison of the functions $1/(\text{mean score} + \Delta)^2$ and $1/(\text{mean score})^2$ for $\Delta = 0.005$, 0.010 and 0.040 respectively to illustrate the difference between owners and non-owners with respect to the minimal sample sizes required for statistical significance

10. REFERENCES

[1] O. Alonso and S. Mizzaro. Can we get rid of trec assessors? Using mechanical turk for relevance assessment. In *SIGIR '09: Workshop on The Future of IR Evaluation*, 2009.

[2] P. Bailey, N. Craswell, I. Soboroff, P. Thomas, A. P. de Vries, and E. Yilmaz. Relevance assessment: are judges exchangeable and does it matter. In *Proceedings of the 31st annual international ACM SIGIR conference on Research and development in information retrieval*, SIGIR '08, pages 667–674, New York, NY, USA, 2008. ACM.

[3] O. Chapelle, D. Metlzer, Y. Zhang, and P. Grinspan. Expected reciprocal rank for graded relevance. In *Proceedings of the 18th ACM conference on Information and knowledge management*, CIKM '09, pages 621–630, New York, NY, USA, 2009. ACM.

[4] G. B. Duggan and S. J. Payne. Knowledge in the head and on the web: using topic expertise to aid search. In *Proceedings of the twenty-sixth annual SIGCHI conference on Human factors in computing systems*, CHI '08, pages 39–48, New York, NY, USA, 2008. ACM.

[5] D. Harman. Overview of the first trec conference. In *Proceedings of the 16th annual international ACM SIGIR conference on Research and development in information retrieval*, SIGIR '93, pages 36–47, New York, NY, USA, 1993. ACM.

[6] C. Hölscher and G. Strube. Web search behavior of internet experts and newbies. *Comput. Netw.*, 33:337–346, June 2000.

[7] S. B. Huffman and M. Hochster. How well does result relevance predict session satisfaction? In *Proceedings of the 30th annual international ACM SIGIR conference on Research and development in information retrieval*, SIGIR '07, pages 567–574, New York, NY, USA, 2007. ACM.

[8] K. A. Kinney, S. B. Huffman, and J. Zhai. How evaluator domain expertise affects search result relevance judgments. In *Proceeding of the 17th ACM conference on Information and knowledge management*, CIKM '08, pages 591–598, New York, NY, USA, 2008. ACM.

[9] E. Law, P. N. Bennett, and E. Horvitz. The effects of choice in routing relevance judgments. In *Proceedings of the 34th international ACM SIGIR conference on Research and development in Information Retrieval*, SIGIR '11, pages 1127–1128, New York, NY, USA, 2011. ACM.

[10] A. A. Maskari, M. Sanderson, and P. Clough. Relevance judgments between TREC and Non-TREC assessors. In *Proceedings of the 31st annual international ACM SIGIR conference on Research and development in information retrieval*, SIGIR '08, pages 683–684, New York, NY, USA, 2008. ACM.

[11] N. Matthijs and F. Radlinski. Personalizing web search using long term browsing history. In *Proceedings of the fourth ACM international conference on Web search and data mining*, WSDM '11, pages 25–34, New York, NY, USA, 2011. ACM.

[12] F. Radlinski, M. Kurup, and T. Joachims. How does clickthrough data reflect retrieval quality? In *International Conference on Information and Knowledge Management*, pages 43–52, 2008.

[13] D. M. Russell and C. Grimes. Assigned tasks are not the same as self-chosen web search tasks. In *Proceedings of the 40th Annual Hawaii International Conference on System Sciences*, HICSS '07, page 83, Washington, DC, USA, 2007. IEEE Computer Society.

[14] A. Singla, R. White, and J. Huang. Studying trailfinding algorithms for enhanced web search. In *Proceedings of the 33rd international ACM SIGIR conference on Research and development in information retrieval*, SIGIR '10, pages 443–450, New York, NY, USA, 2010. ACM.

[15] J. Teevan, S. T. Dumais, and E. Horvitz. Personalizing search via automated analysis of interests and activities. In *Proceedings of the 28th annual international ACM SIGIR conference on Research and development in information retrieval*, SIGIR '05, pages 449–456, New York, NY, USA, 2005. ACM.

[16] E. M. Voorhees. Variations in relevance judgments and the measurement of retrieval effectiveness. *Inf. Process. Manage.*, 36:697–716, September 2000.

[17] B. M. Wildemuth. The effects of domain knowledge on search tactic formulation. *J. Am. Soc. Inf. Sci. Technol.*, 55:246–258, February 2004.

Optimizing Top-k Document Retrieval Strategies for Block-Max Indexes

Constantinos Dimopoulos
Polytechnic Institute of NYU
constantinos@cis.poly.edu

Sergey Nepomnyachiy
Polytechnic Institute of NYU
snepom01@students.poly.edu

Torsten Suel
Polytechnic Institute of NYU
suel@poly.edu

ABSTRACT

Large web search engines use significant hardware and energy resources to process hundreds of millions of queries each day, and a lot of research has focused on how to improve query processing efficiency. One general class of optimizations called early termination techniques is used in all major engines, and essentially involves computing top results without an exhaustive traversal and scoring of all potentially relevant index entries. Recent work in [9, 7] proposed several early termination algorithms for disjunctive top-k query processing, based on a new augmented index structure called Block-Max Index that enables aggressive skipping in the index.

In this paper, we build on this work by studying new algorithms and optimizations for Block-Max indexes that achieve significant performance gains over the work in [9, 7]. We start by implementing and comparing Block-Max oriented algorithms based on the well-known Maxscore and WAND approaches. Then we study how to build better Block-Max index structures and design better index-traversal strategies, resulting in new algorithms that achieve a factor of 2 speed-up over the best results in [9] with acceptable space overheads. We also describe and evaluate a hierarchical algorithm for a new recursive Block-Max index structure.

Categories and Subject Descriptors

H.3.3 [**INFORMATION STORAGE AND RETRIEVAL**]: Information Search and Retrieval

General Terms

Algorithms, Performance

Keywords

top-k query processing, early termination, block-max inverted index, docID-oriented block-max index

WSDM'13, February 4–8, 2012, Rome, Italy.

1. INTRODUCTION

Large web search engines have to answer hundreds of millions of queries per day over tens of billions of documents. To process this workload, such engines use hundreds of thousands of machines distributed over multiple data centers. In fact, query processing is responsible for a significant part of the cost of operating a large search engine, and a lot of industrial and academic research has focused on decreasing this cost. Major families of techniques that have been studied include *caching* of full or partial results or index structures at various levels of the system, *index compression* techniques that decrease both index size and access costs, and *early termination* (or pruning) techniques that, using various shortcuts, try to identify the best or most promising results without an exhaustive evaluation of all candidates. Previous work can also be divided into work that improves the efficiency of the overall distributed architecture (say through smart query routing, data partitioning, and distributed caching), and work that focuses on the throughput and response time of individual nodes in the system.

In this paper, we are interested in early termination techniques for optimizing performance within individual query processing nodes, assuming some distributed architecture has successfully partitioned the problem over many machines. More precisely, we study *safe* early termination (ET) techniques for (ranked) *disjunctive queries*. We define these terms later, but *disjunctive queries* basically means queries with a simple term-based ranking function (e.g., Cosine, BM25) that is applied to all documents containing at least one of the query terms, and *safe* means that the technique must return exactly the same results as an exhaustive evaluation [19].

While state-of-art search engines use highly complicated ranking functions based on hundreds of features, simple ranking functions as discussed above are still important for performance reasons. This is because it would be much too costly to evaluate every candidate result using the full ranking function. Instead, search engines typically first use a simple ranking function to narrow the field of candidate results, and then apply more and more complicated ranking functions in later phases [23].

In the initial phase, search engines may use either disjunctive queries, as discussed above, or conjunctive queries where only documents containing all query terms are considered (or possibly a mix of the two). Disjunctive queries are known to return higher-quality results in many scenarios; however, they are also significantly more expensive to compute than conjunctive queries that can discard any documents that are missing even a single query term.

This has motivated some amount of previous work on early termination techniques for disjunctive queries that attempts to narrow the efficiency gap, including [22, 6, 2, 20, 9, 7]. In particular, two recent papers [7, 9] independently proposed an augmented inverted index structure called *Block-Max Index* [9], and showed how it can be used for faster early termination. In a nutshell, a Block-Max Index augments the commonly used inverted index structure, where for each distinct term t we store a sorted list of the IDs of those documents where t occurs, with upper-bound values for blocks of these IDs. That is, for every say 64 IDs of documents containing a term t, we store the maximum term-wise score of any of these documents with respect to t. This then allows algorithms to quickly skip over blocks of documents that score too low to make it into the top results.

1.1 Our Contribution

In this paper, we study and evaluate new and (modifications of) existing early-termination algorithms for disjunctive queries that use such Block-Max Indexes. The previous work in [7, 9] proposes essentially the same structure, but describes different algorithms to exploit it. In particular, [9] proposes algorithms based on the WAND approach in [6], while [7] describes algorithms based on the Maxscore approach described in [22]. The algorithms achieve significant speedups over previous work, and thus motivate additional study of Block-Max Indexes and how to best exploit them.

We will start out by performing a direct experimental comparison of WAND- and Maxscore-based algorithms with and without Block-Max Indexes, which leads to some new and unexpected observations. Next, we build on these observations by designing and implementing new techniques for exploiting Block-Max Indexes, in particular docID-oriented block selection schemes, on-the-fly generation of Block-Max Indexes, and a new recursive query processing algorithm that uses a hierarchical partitioning of inverted lists into blocks. Overall, we achieve roughly a factor of two improvement in running time over the fastest previous results in [9], though we believe that additional improvements are possible by extending our techniques.

2. BACKGROUND AND RELATED WORK

In this section, we provide some technical background knowledge on inverted indexes, query processing, and early termination techniques, and discuss related work.

2.1 Inverted Indexes and Index Compression

Current search engines perform query processing using an inverted index, which is a simple and efficient data structure that allows us to find documents containing particular terms [24, 27]. Given a collection of N documents, we assume each document is identified by a unique document ID (docID) between 0 and $N-1$. An inverted index contains many inverted lists, where each inverted list L_w is a list of postings describing all places where term w occurs in the collection. More precisely, each posting contains the docID of a document that contains the term w, the number of occurrences of w in the document (called frequency), and sometimes the exact locations of these occurrences in the document or other context such as font size etc. Postings in each list are typically sorted by docID, or sometimes in some other way as described later. Thus, in the case where we store docIDs and frequencies, each posting is of the form (d_i, f_i). We focus on this case, but our techniques also apply to cases where positions, context information, or quantized impact scores are stored.

The inverted lists of common query terms may consist of many millions of postings. To allow faster access and limit the amount of memory needed, search engines use various compression techniques that significantly reduce the size of the inverted lists [27]. Compression is crucial for search engine performance and there are many compression techniques in the literature; see [26, 25, 18] for some recent work. In this paper we use a version of the PForDelta compression method [28] described in [26], but all ideas also apply to other methods.

Because lists can be very long, we often want to skip parts of the lists during query processing. To allow this, inverted lists are usually split into blocks of, say, 64 or 128 postings, such that each block can be decompressed individually. This requires an additional table that stores for each block the uncompressed maximum (or minimum) docID and the block size. The size of this extra table is small compared to the overall index. For performance reasons, we store the data in each a block as 64 or 128 docIDs followed by the corresponding frequencies.

2.2 Query Processing

The simplest form of query processing is called *Boolean query processing.* A query *apple AND orange* looking for all documents containing both *apple* and *orange* can be implemented by intersecting the docIDs in the inverted lists for *apple* and *orange.* In simple *ranked queries*, a ranking function is used to compute a score for each document passing a Boolean filter, such as the union or intersection of the query terms, and then the k top-scoring documents are returned. The ranking function should be efficiently computable from the data in the inverted lists (frequencies and maybe positions), plus maybe a limited amount of other statistics stored outside the inverted index (e.g., document lengths or global scores such as Pagerank). Many classes of simple ranking functions similar to BM25 or Cosine have been studied; see [3].A common property of many of these is that they are decomposable into term scores, i.e., a sum or other simple combination of per-term scores.

Real search engines use ranking functions based on hundreds of features. However, such functions are quite expensive to evaluate. To achieve efficiency, search engines commonly separate the ranking process into two or more phases. In the first phase, a very simple and fast ranking function such as BM25 is used to get, say, the top 100 or 1000 documents. Then in the second and further phases, increasingly more complicated ranking functions with more and more features are applied to documents that pass through the earlier phases. Thus, the later phases only examine a fairly small number of result candidates, and a significant amount of computation is still spent in the first phase. In this paper, we focus on executing such a simple first-phase function, a problem that has been extensively studied in the literature.

Recall that simple ranked queries consist of a Boolean filter followed by ranking the documents that pass this filter. The most commonly used Boolean filters are conjunctive (AND) and disjunctive (OR). Disjunctive queries return better results than conjunctive queries in many scenarios, but are much more expensive to compute as they have to evaluate many more documents. For this reason, web search engines try to use conjunctive queries as much as possible, but improvements in the speed of disjunctive queries could make these a more attractive alternative.

2.3 Early Termination

When processing simple ranked queries on large document collections, the main performance challenge is caused by the lengths of the inverted lists and the large number of candidates that pass the Boolean filter and thus need to be evaluated. Early termination is a set of techniques that addresses this problem. Following [9], we say that a query processing algorithm is *exhaustive* if it fully evaluates all documents that satisfy the Boolean filter condition. Any other algorithm uses *early termination* (ET).

We note that early termination can be achieved in many different ways, including by (1) *stopping early*, where each inverted list is arranged from most to least promising posting and traversal is stopped once enough good results are found, (2) *skipping*, where inverted lists are sorted by docIDs, and thus promising documents spread out over the lists, but we can skip over uninteresting parts of a list, or (3) *partial scoring*, where candidate documents are only partially or approximately scored. But the above definition of ET can also include techniques such as static pruning [5, 11] and index tiering [15].

In this paper we focus on *safe early termination* [19], where we get exactly the same results as an exhaustive algorithm, i.e., the same documents in the same order with the same scores. Also, we focus on main memory-based indexes as motivated in [20, 8]. Most major engines either keep the entire index in memory, or at least a large enough part of it such that any I/O bottlenecks can be hidden using fairly standard caching techniques.

2.4 Index Layout and Access

As discussed, some ET techniques may require inverted index structures to be arranged in specific ways. In particular, many techniques assume a layout such that the most promising documents appear early in the inverted lists, which can be done by either reordering the postings in a list, or partitioning the index into several layers. In general, most techniques use one of the following layouts:

- **Document-Sorted Indexes**: The standard approach for exhaustive query processing, where postings in each inverted list are sorted by docID.
- **Impact-Sorted Indexes**: Postings in each list are sorted by their impact (or term score), that is, their contribution to the document score.
- **Impact-Layered Indexes**: Each list is partitioned into several layers, such that all postings in layer i have a higher impact than those in layer $i+1$. In each layer, postings are sorted by docID.

Impact-sorted and impact-layered indexes are very popular for ET algorithms as they place the most promising postings close to the start of the lists [14, 10, 2, 1, 4, 20, 13, 22]. A problem with impact-sorted indexes is that index compression suffers when docIDs are not in sorted order. In this case, an impact-layered index that uses a small number of layers often provides a better alternative.

In contrast, in document-sorted indexes the most promising results are spread out over the inverted list, and the goal in ET is to find ways to skip most of the postings in between. Few ET algorithms use document-sorted indexes; see, e.g., [6, 22, 21, 9, 7]. However, recent work in [7, 9] showed very good results for document-sorted indexes through the use of an additional Block-Max structure, and this motivates our work here where we build on these results. Thus, unless stated otherwise, we assume document-sorted indexes throughout the paper.

One advantage of document-sorted indexes is that they allow simple and fast index traversal during query execution based on a *Document-at-a-time* (DAAT) approach. Here, each list has a pointer to a *current* posting, and all pointers move forward in parallel as a query is processed. At any point in time, all postings with docID less than some value have already been processed, while documents with larger docID are yet to be considered. In contrast, impact-sorted and impact-layered indexes employ other, often more complicated, traversal strategies.

DAAT traversal is commonly implemented using the following methods reminiscent of file system or database access: First, there are methods for opening and closing inverted lists for reading. Second, a forward-seek operation called *nextGEQ* can be used to move the read pointer in an opened list forward to the first posting with a docID at least some specified value. Finally, there is an operation for returning the term score of the posting at the current pointer position. All our algorithms perform DAAT traversal using these methods, and we report the number of nextGEQ operations and term score computations in some of our results.

2.5 Basic ET Algorithms

We now describe previous safe early termination algorithms for disjunctive queries. We focus on methods using document-sorted indexes and DAAT traversal that are closely related to our approaches, in particular the WAND algorithm in [6], the Maxscore algorithm in [22], and recent enhancements of these algorithms based on Block-Max Indexes in [7, 9].

WAND: The WAND algorithm proposed by Broder et al. in [6] maintains for each query term a pointer to the current posting in the list. It also stores for each inverted list the highest impact score of any posting in the list, called the *maxscore* of the list. Whenever the algorithm moves forward in the inverted lists, it does so in three steps, pivot selection, alignment check, and evaluation.

In the first step, the current list pointers are sorted by docID. Then a *pivot* term is selected by summing up the maxscores of the query terms in ascending order of list pointer docID, until the sum becomes larger or equal to the threshold θ that is needed to be part of the current top-k results. The term where this happens is selected as the pivot, and used to drive query processing. This is illustrated in Figure 1, where *cat* is selected as the pivot term. The crucial observation is that no docID smaller than the current docID of the pivot term can make it into the top-k results, unless it was already considered earlier.

In the second step, we try to align the terms above the pivot term with the docID of the pivot term, called the pivot ID. To do this, we take these terms one after the other (in the figure, just the list for *mouse*) and do a forward seek using nextGEQ to the pivot docID. If such a seek results in

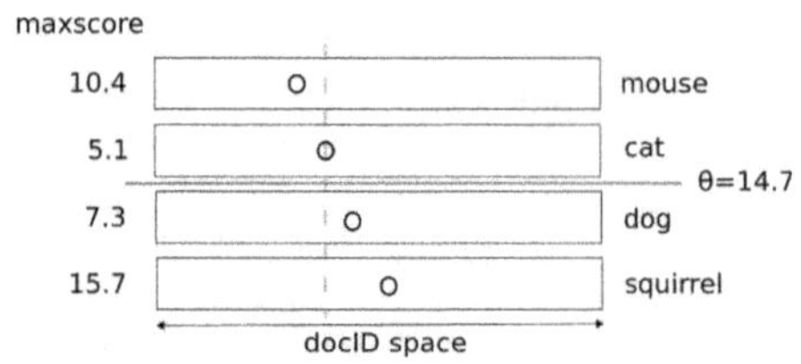

Figure 1: Pivot selection in the WAND algorithm with 4 terms, where the current threshold for the top-k results is 14.7. The list for *cat* is selected as pivot since $10.4+5.1 > 14.7$.

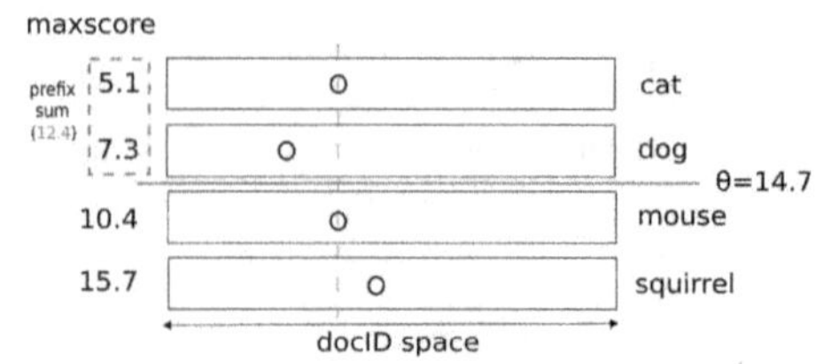

Figure 2: Selecting non-essential lists in the Maxscore algorithm. Here, the lists for *cat* and *dog* are non-essential as their maxscores sum up to $5.1 + 7.3 < 14.7$.

a docID strictly larger than the pivot docID (because the list does not have a posting for the pivot docID), then we go back to the first step and re-sort and select another pivot. If all seeks result in a posting at the pivot docID, then in the third step we fully evaluate this docID, check if it needs to be inserted into the current top-k, move all pointers forward to at least this docID plus one, and then continue.

Maxscore: This algorithm has been known for a long time but was first described in detail in [22]. There are several versions of Maxscore based on both DAAT and TAAT traversal. The version described here is similar to those presented in [21, 12]. Like WAND, this algorithm also exploits knowledge of the maxscore of a list, hence the name. However, instead of using sorting by current docID and pivot selection to dynamically partition the lists into lists above and below the pivot term, Maxscore distinguishes between essential and non-essential lists.

Suppose the lists for the query terms are sorted from top to bottom by their maxscore, as shown in Figure 2. We again have a threshold θ that a document score has to reach to make it into the current top-k results. We now select as non-essential lists a set of lists such that their maxscores sum up to less than θ, by adding lists starting from the list with the smallest maxscore. The other lists are called essential. Observe that no document can make it into the top-k results just using postings in the non-essential lists, and at least one of the essential terms has to occur in any top-k document.

Thus, we can safely execute a top-k query by essentially performing a union operation over the essential lists, and then performing lookups into the non-essential lists to get the precise document scores. In every step we select the next larger docID in the essential lists, but instead of fully scoring each such candidate in all lists, we perform partial scoring as follows. We first evaluate the scores of this docID in the essential lists. If the sum of these scores plus the maxscores of the non-essential lists is less than θ, then we can abort the evaluation. Otherwise, we score the candidate in the non-essential lists until either we have a complete score, or the maximum possible score drops below the threshold. Whenever we find a new top-k result, we also check if the resulting increase in the threshold θ means that another list can be added to the non-essential lists.

To optimize this algorithm, we need to decide how to select the non-essential lists and in which order to evaluate postings in the non-essential lists. We could select non-essential lists with the smallest maxscore (minimizing the number of essential lists), or select the longest lists (minimizing the total size of the essential lists). Not surprisingly, the longest lists are almost always the ones with the smallest maxscore in common ranking functions such as BM25, and thus selecting by maxscore usually achieves both objectives.[1] When evaluating scores in the non-essential lists, it is best to go from highest to lowest maxscore.

Block-Max Indexes and Algorithms: Two recent papers [9, 7] independently proposed an augmented inverted index structure called a *Block-Max Index* and used it to speed up the WAND [9] and Maxscore [7] approaches. The basic idea of the structure is very simple: Since inverted lists are often compressed in blocks of say 64 or 128 postings, we store for each block the maximum term score within the block, called *block maxscore*. Thus each inverted list maintains a piece-wise constant upper bound approximation of the term scores, as shown in Figure 3.

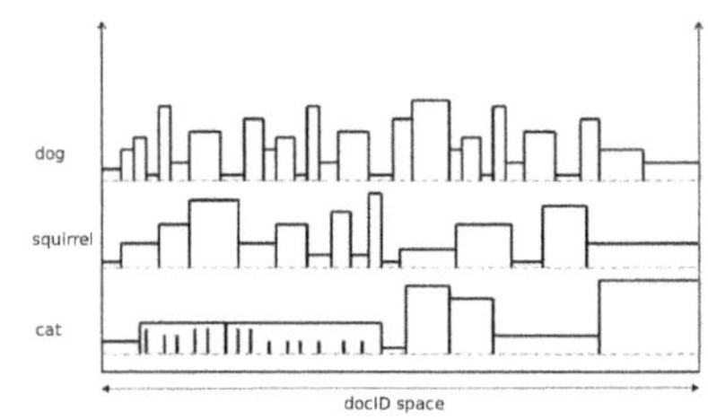

Figure 3: Three inverted lists are piecewise upper-bounded by the maximum scores in each block. As shown for one block in the bottom list, inside each block we have various values, including many zero values, that can be retrieved by evaluating the postings.

Since both WAND and Maxscore use the maxscore of a list to enable skipping, the simplest idea for using the Block-Max Index is to try to use block maxscores instead of list maxscores whenever possible. In fact, this is basically what the approaches in [9, 7] do, but there are some technical challenges that need to be overcome to make this work. These challenges are due to the fact that block maxscores are only valid within a block, and thus we have to be careful whenever we move over one or more block boundaries. Moreover, block boundaries in different lists are not aligned.

In the following, we refer to the approach in [9] as *Block-Max WAND* (BMW), and to the approach in [7] as *Block-Max Maxscore* (BMM). BMW and BMM differ in two main ways. First, BMW builds on WAND [9] while BMM builds on Maxscore. Second, BMW deals with block boundaries in an online fashion as they are encountered, while BMM uses a preprocessing step that detects and aligns block boundaries.

More precisely, BMW selects a candidate pivot using list maxscores as in WAND, but then uses block maxscores to check if this is really a viable pivot or if its score is too low to make it into the top-k results. In general, a combination

[1]We observed that this correlation between list length and maxscore value is quite strong over most of the range of lists lengths, but breaks down for lists with only a few postings.

of block maxscores and partial evaluation in selected lists is used to quickly rule out many pivots. Thus, block boundary issues are avoided by using list maxscores for pivot selection, and only using block maxscores once a pivot candidate has been selected. We refer to [9] for more details.

BMM first preprocesses the block boundaries in order to partition the docID space into intervals, such that we have an interval boundary whenever any of the participating lists has a block boundary. Then BMM runs Maxscore within each interval, selecting non-essential lists and doing partial scoring using block maxscores instead of list maxscores. More details and some additional variations of this basic idea are discussed in [7]. Also, followup work to [9, 7] in [16] shows how to deal with ranking functions that add a query-independent score such as Pagerank to the term scores.

Our work in this paper starts from the work in [9, 7] and asks how we can further improve query processing with Block-Max Indexes, by either refining the BMW or BMM approaches or designing new algorithms. It seems to us that there are a lot of additional benefits that can be obtained by using Block-Max Indexes and related structures.

3. PRELIMINARY EXPERIMENTS

In this section, we implement and evaluate a set of baseline algorithms derived from previous work. While the algorithms are not really novel, we are not aware of any previous comparison.

In our experiments, we use the TREC GOV2 dataset consisting of 25.2 million web pages with an uncompressed size of 426GB. We build inverted index structures with 64 docIDs and frequencies per block, using the version of PForDelta used in [26]. The resulting compressed index size is 8.75GB. We use 1000 queries selected at random from the TREC 2006 Efficiency track queries, and 1000 random queries from TREC 2005 as our testing sets.

All algorithms were implemented using C++ and compiled using gcc with -O3 optimization. Algorithms were carefully optimized for performance. We use BM25 as ranking function, and return top-10 results unless stated otherwise. All experiments were conducted on a single core of a 2.27Ghz Intel Xeon (E5520) CPU. All data structures are memory-resident.

3.1 Methods without Block-Max Indexes

We start by comparing the methods without Block-Max Indexes, in particular WAND, Maxscore, and the method of Strohman and Croft (SC) [20]. For SC, we use the numbers reported in [9] which were on the same data and machine. All other methods were re-implemented for this paper.

The implementation of WAND follows closely the description in [6] and the implementation in [9]. Recall that the method first selects a pivot, then aligns the lists, and then evaluates. We tried using partial scoring techniques in the evaluation phase, and interleaving alignment and scoring, but found no performance benefits in this. For Maxscore, we follow the description in Section 2.5, with careful use of partial scoring techniques.

In Table 1 we compare the performance of SC, WAND, and Maxscore on the TREC 2006 and 2005 queries. We show average times over all queries, and average times for queries with 2, 3, 4, 5, and more than 5 terms. The most important observation is that Maxscore consistently and significantly outperforms the SC and WAND algorithms, by roughly a factor of 2. This is surprising because SC and WAND were intended to be performance optimizations over the older Maxscore algorithm. Comparing WAND and Maxscore, we believe there are two main costs that slow down WAND, the pivot selection via sorting (which we carefully optimized by updating the sorted order), and the large number of calls to *nextGEQ* as part of the alignment process as shown in Table 2. We also note that Maxscore is especially strong on queries with 5 or more queries, where it outperforms the others by more than a factor of 2.

TREC 06						
Algorithm	avg	2	3	4	5	>5
SC (from [9])	64.3	12.2	36.7	75.6	117.2	226.3
WAND	75.43	20.59	42.42	88.25	146.73	240.44
Maxscore	34.17	10.67	22.76	41.71	60.32	91.05
TREC 05						
WAND	51.4	18.19	34.82	55.33	102.14	321.29
Maxscore	20.13	9.42	17.51	25.85	35.33	87.84

Table 1: Running times in ms per query for methods without Block-Max Index structure.

TREC 06			
Algorithm	Time (ms)	# evals	# nextgeq
WAND	75.43	448,209	1,211,034
Maxscore	34.17	673,862	722,867
TREC 05			
WAND	51.4	366,063	775,581
Maxscore	20.13	409,444	429,835

Table 2: Number of term score evaluations and calls to *nextGEQ* per query for methods without Block-Max Index structure.

3.2 Block Max-Based Methods

Next, we compare basic methods that use Block-Max Indexes, in particular BMW, BMM, and some modifications of these. We note that previous work [9, 7, 16] chooses block boundaries in the Block-Max Index by placing a fixed number of postings, e.g., 64, in each block. This is a natural choice for two reasons: First, since blocks are also used in index compression, it seems natural to piggy-back onto this mechanism and add another value, the block maxscore. Second, this allows easy control over the space overhead of the structure. We refer to such an approach as a Posting-Oriented Block-Max Index, and use this approach for our first experiments. However, in later sections we revisit this assumption and look at other choices of block boundaries that result in better performance.

For the experiments, we re-implemented BMW as described in [9] and re-used some code from the core compression and index access mechanisms. Our baseline in this study is the BMW algorithm in [9], which to the best of our knowledge, achieves the best reported query processing times. We also implemented a Maxscore-based method (BMM), but with some changes over the implementation described in [7]. In particular, we removed the preprocessing for aligning block boundaries and the selection of non-essential lists in each interval as described in [7], as we found this to be a performance bottleneck. We note here that while the numbers reported in [7] are higher than those in [9] and for a smaller data set, they include some disk access costs and make somewhat different architectural assumptions. Thus, it is difficult to directly compare the numbers.

In the implementation of BMM, we select the essential

lists as in Maxscore, based on list maxscores, but use a series of filters based on block maxscores to rule out most candidates. In particular, after selecting the next unprocessed posting from the essential lists, we first check if the (pre-computed) sum of the list maxscores of the non-essential lists plus the sum of the block maxscores of the essential lists is above the threshold. If yes, then we replace the list maxscores of the non-essential lists with block maxscores, and check again. Next, we get the term scores of the candidate in the essential lists, and check if the potential score is still above the threshold. If so, we then start scoring the non-essential lists until all terms have been evaluated or the candidate has been ruled out.

In case the first (or second) filter above fails, we can in fact not just skip the current posting, but move directly to the end of the shortest (or shortest essential) block. (This is similar to the GetNewCandidate() method described in [9].) We note that in many cases, we may be able to skip even beyond the end of that block, for example when the block is followed by one with a smaller block maxscore. We can exploit this by a more aggressive optimization, where we skip over block boundaries until we arrive at the next *live* block where the sum of the block-max scores of all terms is larger than θ. We note that [7] has a similar idea for skipping over dead areas. We refer to the version of BMM that uses this optimization as *Block-Max Maxscore-Next Live Block* (BMM-NLB).

Finally, initial experiments found that some methods are better for queries with few terms, and some for queries with many terms. Since all algorithms use exactly the same data structures, it is easy to call the best method for any number of query terms; this combined method is called BM-OPT. We did not see any way to implement a good Block-Max based version of SC, which takes a very different, non-DAAT based, approach from the other algorithms.

In Table 3, we report the performance of the various algorithms on the TREC 2006 and 2005 queries. We observe that BMW obtains very large gains over WAND, as reported in [9]. BMM, however, achieves only slight improvements over our optimized version of Maxscore, which already did much better than WAND. Overall, BMW now performs better than BMM. The BMM-NLB version that tried to skip additional block boundaries actually performs worse than BMM except for 2-term queries; the reason is that there are not that many dead areas for multi-term queries, so the benefit is limited while the added complexity slows down performance. We also observe that BMM outperforms BMW for queries with many terms, and for this reason BM-OPT performs slightly better on average than BMW.

Finally, Table 4 shows the average number of term score evaluations and calls to *nextGEQ* per query. We can see that BMW evaluates significantly fewer documents and makes fewer calls than all other algorithms. However, while BMM performs many more evaluations and calls, its running time was only slightly slower than BMW. This indicates that these evaluations and calls are not the only indicator of performance. In fact, it seems that BMW spends a fair amount of effort trying to avoid evaluations and calls, while BMM does not spend as much time thinking about avoiding them and instead keeps the control structure simple.

For the remainder of the paper we report the performance of our algorithms only for the TREC 06 query traces, due to space limitation.

TREC 06						
Algorithm	avg	2	3	4	5	>5
BMW	27.44	4.14	12.09	32.83	55.11	108.47
BMM	32.77	10.35	21.95	39.8	57.73	87.41
BMM-NLB	51.48	9.62	30.24	64.32	99.09	159.08
BM-OPT	25.95	4.14	12.09	32.83	55.11	87.41
TREC 05						
BMW	16.25	3	10.38	17.55	33.66	127.61
BMM	19.97	9.33	17.35	25.66	35.18	86.45
BMM-NLB	29.46	8.85	25.19	41.02	61.37	168.15
BM-OPT	13.83	3	10.38	17.55	33.66	86.4

Table 3: Running times in ms per query for basic methods with Block-Max Index Structures.

TREC 06			
Algorithm	Time (ms)	# evals	# nextgeq
BMW	27.44	27,440	431,817
BMM	32.77	661,072	667,642
BMM-NLB	51.48	573,630	581,442
TREC 05			
BMW	16.25	17,555	240,756
BMM	19.97	404,441	407,331
BMM-NLB	29.46	309,047	312,552

Table 4: Number of term score evaluations and calls to *nextGEQ* for the different algorithms.

4. A HIERARCHICAL ALGORITHM

Next, we describe a new query processing algorithm that uses a modified hierarchical Block-Max Index. The basic intuition for this is very natural; instead of using only one size of blocks, we partition inverted lists into a hierarchy of blocks and store block maxscores at all different levels. We would expect that different terms and queries lead to different optimal choices for the block size, and that even for a particular term and query, a hierarchical structure would enable large skips whenever possible while allowing us to drill into smaller block sizes if needed. As indicated before, this structure is now completely decoupled from the blocks used in index compression.

We start with a basic partitioning into fairly small blocks containing, say, 8 or 16 postings. We then build a binary tree structure on top of these blocks, where each higher-up block stores as its block maxscore and right block boundary the larger of the two childrens' block maxscores and right block boundaries, respectively. Finally, the root contains the list maxscore and has as its right boundary the value N (where all docIDs are between 0 and $N-1$. We also implicitly treat the actual postings, and the empty spaces between them, as child nodes of the basic blocks at the bottom of the tree; this is called the posting level of the tree.

Given this structure, we now design an algorithm that uses it. The basic idea is to perform a traversal of the trees for the query terms, reminiscent of branch-and-bound computations. During traversal, we maintain a value *cub* that is an upper bound on the scores of any documents in the intersection of the current blocks. For each term, we have a stack or other mechanism (say successor pointers) for efficient tree traversal. We first place the roots of the trees for the query terms on a stack, and initialize *cub* to the sum of their maxscores.

Now we repeatedly check if *cub* is above the current threshold for top-k results. If yes, there are two cases: (1) If we have reached the posting level in all lists, this means that we have completely evaluated a docID and can place it into the top-k, and then continue with the next docID by popping any blocks associated with postings (but not those representing space between postings). (2) In the other case, there is the possibility of a top-k result, but we need to go deeper into the trees to check. To do so, we select one of the lists, say the one with the farthest right boundary, pop it from the stack, and instead push its children on the stack and update *cub* as needed. Once we reach the posting level, we do not immediately place all postings in the block on the stack, but materialize them one at a time from the inverted index using *nextGEQ* and scoring of terms.

If the *cub* was below the threshold, this means that no top-k result can be in the intersection of the current nodes, and we can skip to the end of the block with the closest right boundary, by popping this block from the stack and updating *cub*. The algorithm stops when the stacks are empty. We note that this algorithm cannot easily be classified as being WAND or Maxscore based. There are also various ways to modify and optimize this algorithm, but due to space constraints we have to omit some of the details.

We show performance results for the new algorithm in Table 5. The performance of the algorithm depends on the size of the basic blocks at the bottom of the tree, and for this case we used a size of 4 postings per block for lists shorter than 1500000 postings and 8 postings per block for longer ones. Thus, the resulting hierarchical Block-Max structure is comparable to the size of the entire inverted index. Despite this size, the algorithm only outperforms the BMW algorithm by a moderate amount. The reason is that there is a fair amount of overhead for pushing and popping nodes onto the stack, and for selecting which nodes to push and pop. We will revisit the performance of this algorithm later in the context of reordered indexes.

Algorithm	avg	2	3	4	5	>5
BMW	27.44	4.14	12.09	32.83	55.11	108.47
HIER	24.47	2.14	9.06	31.03	50.40	100.75

Table 5: Running times in ms per query for BMW and for the new algorithm with a hierarchical Block-Max Index, for 2, 3, 4, 5, and more than 5 query terms.

In the following section, we describe new algorithms that move beyond the posting-oriented Block-Max Index structures used here. This means that we decouple the choice of blocks for storing block maxscores from the choice of blocks for inverted index compression.

5. DOCID-ORIENTED BLOCKS

We now go back to the non-hierarchical case and try to further improve the BMW and BMM approaches. As in the hierarchical case, we decouple the Block-Max structure from the blocks used for index compression, thus allowing us to choose block boundaries in a way that optimizes performance. In particular, we could define block boundaries based not on the number of postings in a block, but based on docID space. For example, if we choose to have one block maxscore say for every 1024 docIDs, then given the docID of a candidate, we can find the location of its corresponding block maxscore by just shifting the docID by 10 bits to the right.

We call such blocks that are based on a simple partitioning of docID space docID-oriented Block-Max structures. Their main benefit is extremely fast lookup. The main challenge is how to select the block sizes. Having one block for every 1024 docIDs might be feasible for longer lists, but would be a huge waste of space for a term with only a handful of postings, where most block maxscores would be zero. We now consider three ways to select docID-oriented block boundaries, choosing a fixed size, choosing sizes based on the expected number of postings in a block, and choosing variable block sizes. Some of the methods result in very large Block-Max structures, and we will address the space problem in the next section.

Fixed Block Size: We first consider docID-oriented Block-Max structures that split the docID space into blocks of the same fixed size for all inverted lists. We consider docID ranges that are powers of two, to achieve very fast block maxscore lookups. Figure 4 shows the running times of the BMW, BMM, and BMM-NLP algorithms from Section 3.2 as we vary the block size from 2^3 to 2^{19} docIDs. We note that the methods do not perform very well for very large or extremely small blocks. For large blocks, we get very little pruning power from block maxscores, and we would be better off just using the Maxscore algorithm. For very small blocks, we only get very small skips and have a lot of memory accesses to fetch block maxscores. However, in between, in the range from 2^6 to 2^8, we see very good performance. In particular, BMM-NLB achieves a running time of less than $13ms$ per query for blocks of size 64 docIDs.

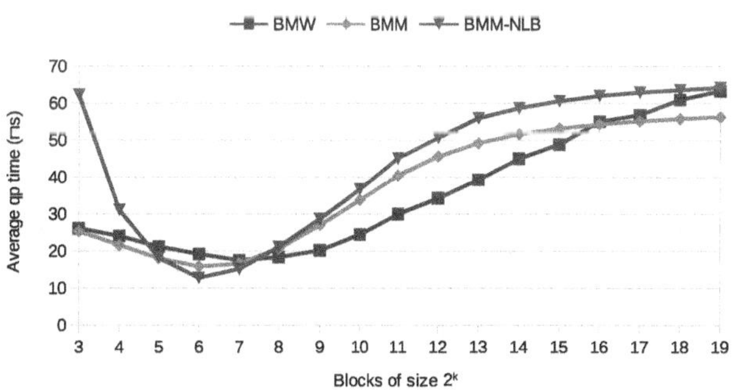

Figure 4: Times per query for fixed block sizes ranging from 2^3 to 2^{19} docIDs.

However, if we actually store one 4-byte block maxscore for every 64 docIDs in docID space, then for the GOV2 collection of 25.2 million documents this means about $1.5MB$ of data per inverted list. Since there are more than 20 million distinct terms in the collection, the space requirement would be about $35TB$.

Expected Block Size: Another natural approach would be to choose larger docID ranges for short lists, and smaller docID ranges for long lists. In particular, we could pick the docID range for each inverted list such that the expected number of postings in each block (total number of postings divided by total number of blocks) is kept constant. This gives us direct control over the total size of the structure, similar to the case of posting-oriented blocks before.

In Figure 5 we show the running time of our algorithms as we vary the expected number of postings per block from 1 to 2^{19}. More precisely, given a target b, we choose the block size as the smallest number 2^x such that the expected number of postings per block is at most b. We observe that BMW performs well for values of b up to 2^5, while BMM and BMM-NLB only do well for even smaller values of b. However, none of the methods achieves running times below $20ms$. Thus, this method limits the size of the Block-Max

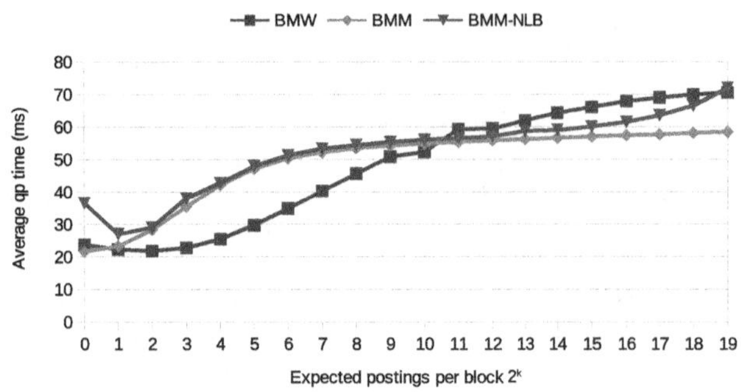

Figure 5: Times per query for expected number of postings per block ranging from 1 to 2^{19}.

Algorithm	Time (ms)	# evals	# nextgeq
BMW	18.44	2,230	369,230
BMM	16.16	45,060	443,789
BMM-NLB	12.73	45,060	57,391

Table 6: Running times for one particular variable block size setting.

structure, but performance degrades compared to the fixed block size method.

Variable Block Size: As seen, both fixing the block size and fixing the expected number of postings per block has problems. The former uses too much space, and the latter is slow. We now check if there is some way to get the same performance as in the fixed case by using (slightly) less space and a variable block size. Experiments showed that we can basically match the best running times for the fixed case, as shown in Table 6 where the best method, BMM-NLB, achieves a time of $12.73ms$.

Note that these results are meaningless without more information about the settings and space consumption. In particular, the results in Table 6 use a block size of 2^{10} docIDs for any inverted list of up to 2^{10} postings, then 2^6 up to length 2^{12}, 2^7 up to length 2^{15}, 2^8 up to length 2^{17}, 2^7 up to length 2^{18}, and 2^6 for any list longer than 2^{18}. The astute reader will notice that this still uses block sizes of at most 2^{10} docIDs for all lists, including for lists with only a few postings. Thus, this can save at most a factor of $2^4 = 16$ over the earlier setting that required more than $35TB$. In fact, this setting still requires about $2.25TB$ of space! We will show in the next section how we can reduce this by a factor of 1000 to obtain a more realistic structure, without significant increases in running time.

6. ENGINEERING THE SPACE ISSUE

In the previous section, we discovered some settings that achieve very fast running times, but at the cost of an unrealistic space consumption. In this section, we address this problem, and study two simple ways to significantly reduce the required space, thus making these settings feasible in practice.

On-The-Fly Block-Max Generation: Most of the inverted lists in a collection are very short, consisting of only a few postings. In fact, 96.95% of all distinct terms in our dataset occur in less than 128 documents. However, for such terms, it is quite feasible to create the docID-oriented Block-Max structure on-the-fly, that is, during query processing. Note that this requires three steps, initializing an array to hold the Block-Max structure, decompressing the entire inverted list and evaluating its postings, and using the uncompressed docIDs and computed scores to set the block maxscores in the array. The first step involves zeroing out an array of about 25,000 numbers in the case of block size 2^{10} docIDs on GOV2, and modern CPUs can do this in a few microseconds. The other steps depend on the list length, but we will see that this is efficient for lists of up to a few ten thousand postings.

In Table 7, we show the total space for the variable docID-oriented Block-Max index in Table 6 in the last section, which had a raw size of about $2.25TB$, and the resulting additional cost in ms per query of generating Block-Max structures on the fly. If we limit on-the-fly generation to lists of at most 2^{11} postings, we still have a space requirement of over $94GB$ for the Block-Max structure. Performing on-the-fly generation for lists up to length 2^{17} brings the size down to $8.41GB$, about the same size as the inverted index, but adds several ms to the running time of a query. However, doing on-the-fly generation for lists up to length 2^{15} brings us to a space of about $11GB$ with less than $0.5ms$ in overhead. We note that the small overhead per query is due to the speed of one-the-fly generation and the fact that not every query has a query term with a short enough list.

Method	Space (GBs)	Overhead (ms/q)
on-the-fly $\text{BMG}_{<2^{11}}$	94.53	0.02
on-the-fly $\text{BMG}_{<2^{13}}$	24.52	0.10
on-the-fly $\text{BMG}_{<2^{15}}$	11.07	0.44
on-the-fly $\text{BMG}_{<2^{17}}$	8.41	3.42
No on-the-fly BMG	2249.66	–

Table 7: Space/time trade-off for one-the-fly block-max generation.

Block-Max Score Quantization: We can further decrease the space requirements by replacing the 4-byte floating point representation of the maxscores with 1-byte unsigned chars. To do this, we need to quantize the floating point numbers to 256 distinct values. Quantization is a standard technique in information retrieval, and a number of methods have been proposed for quantizing term scores.

Our problem here is actually a little simpler since the block maxscores are only used as a rough initial filter, and not for the final ranking of the results. In this case, a simple linear quantization is good enough, where for each inverted list we choose a basic quantile z and then represent each block maxscore m by the smallest i such that $i * z \geq m$. If z is chosen by dividing the list maxscore by 255, then each i can be stored in one unsigned char. When we access a block maxscore, we simply multiply i with the (term-dependent) quantile z. The rounding-up to the next multiple of z results in slightly larger block maxscores and thus slightly less pruning, but the difference is negligible.

Experimental Results: We now present the space/time trade-off that are achieved when using both on-the-fly Block-Max generation and block maxscore quantization in our query processing algorithms, using the same block size settings as in Table 6.

We start by looking at the performance of our fastest algorithm, BMM-NLB. Table 8 shows the performance of BMM-NLB with on-the-fly generation and with and without quantization. We note that there are two factors that can increase the running time of the algorithm, the time for the on-the-fly generation, and the cost of accessing the

Method	Space (GBs)	Time (ms)
on-the-fly $BMG_{<2^{13}}$	24.52	12.83
on-the-fly $BMG_{<2^{13}}$ + BMQ	6.13	14.34
on-the-fly $BMG_{<2^{15}}$	11.07	13.17
on-the-fly $BMG_{<2^{15}}$ + BMQ	2.76	14.64
No on-the-fly BMG and, no BMQ	2249.66	12.73

Table 8: Space/time trade-off for on-the-fly block-max generation and quantization in BMM-NLB.

quantized values and multiplying them with the quantile z. We see that with on-the-fly generation only for lists shorter than 2^{13} and no quantization, we get a running time of 12.83 ms and a space requirement of $24.52GB$. At the other hand of the spectrum, we get a running time of $14.64ms$ with a space requirement of $2.76GB$, about 30% of the size of the inverted index, by using quantization and on-the-fly generation for lists up to length 2^{15}.

Algorithm	Time (ms)	# evals	# nextgeq
BMW	19.82	1,646	369,571
BMM	17.44	46,207	444,569
BMM-NLB	14.64	46,207	58,809
BM-OPT	14.32	45,905	74,027
Posting-oriented BMW	27.44	27,440	431,817

Table 9: Performance of the algorithms when both on-the-fly generation and quantization are used.

Next, in Table 9 we show the performance of all three basic algorithms when both on-the-fly generation and quantization is applied, using the setting from Table 8 that results in the smallest space requirement. We see that all algorithms are significantly faster than the state-of-the-art postings-oriented BMW. Finally, Table 10 shows the results for different numbers of query terms.

Algorithm	avg	2	3	4	5	>5
BMW	19.82	3.79	10.08	22.73	39.67	73.4
BMM	17.44	4.4	9.98	21.36	32.71	54.66
BMM-NLB	14.64	5.59	9.54	17.44	24.55	42.23
BM-OPT	14.32	3.79	9.54	17.44	24.55	42.23

Table 10: Time in ms per query (ms) for queries with 2, 3, 4, 5, and more than 5 terms.

7. ADDITIONAL RESULTS

In this section, we provide a few additional results. In particular, we look at the performance of the methods for reordered and impact-layered indexes, and at how performance changes when we need top-100 or top-1000 results rather than just the top-10. Due to space constraints, we only present some selected results.

Document ID Reordering: A lot of work over the last decade has looked at how to improve the compressibility of inverted indexes by reordering them, that is, by assigning docIDs to documents in a way that minimizes index size. In general, this is done by assigning consecutive docIDs to similar documents; one particularly simple and effective way to do this is to assign docIDs to web pages based on an alphabetic sorting of their URLs [17]. Recent work in [25] showed that this not only decreases index size, but also accelerates conjunctive query processing, and [9] extended this observation to the BMW algorithm for disjunctive queries.

Thus, we decided to check how our new methods fare under reordering, using URL-sorting as suggested in [17] and used in [9]. Table 11 shows the resulting running times for our new docID-oriented Block-Max Index structures with quantization and on-the-fly generation. Note that the best previous result for this case in [9] was $8.89ms$, for the old posting-oriented version of BMW. As we see, reordering also gives a significant boost to the new algorithms, though BMM-NLB benefits less than the other methods.

Algorithm	Time (ms)	# evals	# nextgeq
BMW	8.34	4,324	129,560
BMM	7.02	17,476	169,709
BMM-NLB	10.33	17,476	18,964

Table 11: Impact of docID reordering on the query processing time of BMW, BMM, and BMM-NLB with quantization and on-the-fly generation.

In Table 12 we show the performance of the hierarchical method from the previous sections under reordering. Somewhat surprisingly, the hierarchical method did extremely well under reordering and significantly outperformed all others. We believe that this is due to the ability of the hierarchical method to exploit the larger but also the highly variable (between different queries and different regions of the docID space) skips that are possible under document reordering. We note that it also has the largest space requirement for its hierarchical Block-Max structure, and we give results for two settings with sizes of $6GB$ and $10GB$. (These numbers can be reduced using quantization and on-the-fly generation of hierarchical Block-Max structures.)

Algorithm	Time (ms)
HIER 6GB	4.85
HIER 10GB	4.29

Table 12: Impact of docID reordering on the query processing time of the hierarchical method.

7.1 Document ID Reordering and Layering

The work in [9] also proposed a version of BMW that uses an impact-layered index structure with two layers. This means that each inverted list longer than some threshold is split into two layers, the first layer containing postings with high term scores, and the second layer containing postings with low scores. Then the resulting lists are fed into the query, which treats the two layers as two distinct inverted lists. We implemented layered versions of our BMW, BMM, and BMM-NLB algorithms with quantization and on-the-fly generation, and evaluated the results. For the non-reordered case, there were no significant improvements over the non-layered version, but in the case of reordered indexes we obtained the results in Table 13. We can see that BMW benefits significantly from layering, while BMM and BMM-NLB actually perform worse by adding layers in the index-reordered case. For comparison, the best result for this case in [9] was $7.4ms$.

Algorithm	Time (ms)	# evals	# nextgeq
BMW	5.7	2,085	72,314
BMM	12.53	58,560	287,494
BMM-NLB	21.63	58,560	69,027

Table 13: Impact of docID reordering and layering on query processing times with quantization and on-the-fly generation.

Increasing k: Finally, we look at the performance of our methods when we are interested not just in the top-10, but the top-100 or top-1000 results. Getting more than 10 results is necessary in scenarios where results are re-ranked in subsequent phases, as done in current web search engines. (We note however that even in that case, we might only need top-10 results from each of 100 query processing nodes.)

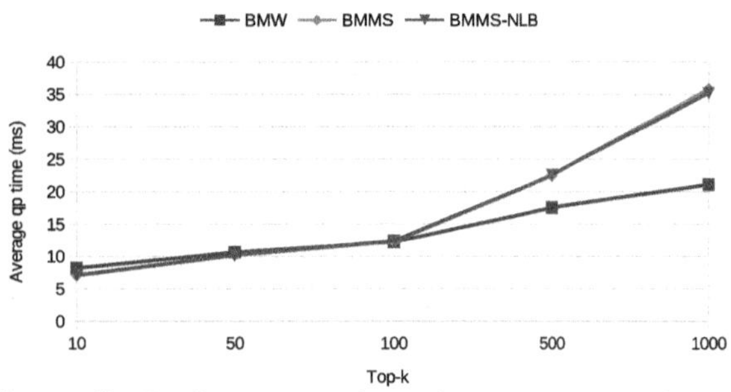

Figure 6: Performance of top-k query processing as we increase k.

We show results for the case of reordered indexes in Figure 6. We observe that while BMM and BMM-NLB show some performance degradation as we increase k, BMW fares much better, achieving around $12ms$ per query for top-100 and around $21.5ms$ per query for top-1000.

8. CONCLUSIONS AND FUTURE WORK

In this paper, we have proposed improved algorithms for safe early termination in disjunctive queries based on the recently proposed Block-Max Index structures. Our main contributions are an experimental comparison of several new and existing methods, a new hierarchical algorithm that outperforms existing methods on reordered indexes, and new and extremely fast methods using docID-based block boundaries plus techniques that make them feasible in terms of space requirements. Overall, we achieve about a factor of 2 in speed-up over the fastest previous methods for standard inverted indexes, and slightly less improvement for reordered and layered index structures.

There are still many open problems and opportunities for future research, including additional and better hierarchical algorithms, potential Block-Max structures for pairs of frequently co-occurring terms, or early termination methods that better exploit the data parallel (SSE) instructions available in current generations of processors.

Acknowledgement

This research was supported by NSF Grant IIS-1117829 "Efficient Query Processing in Large Search Engines", and by a grant from Google. Sergey Nepomnyachiy was supported by NSF Grant ITR-0904246 "The Role of Order in Search".

9. REFERENCES

[1] V. N. Anh, O. de Kretser, and A. Moffat. Vector-space ranking with effective early termination. In *Proceedings of the 24th Annual Int. ACM SIGIR Conference on Research and Development in Inf. Retrieval*, 2001.

[2] V. N. Anh and A. Moffat. Pruned query evaluation using pre-computed impacts. In *Proc. of the 29th Annual Int. ACM SIGIR Conf. on Research and Development in Information Retrieval*, 2006.

[3] R. A. Baeza-Yates and B. A. Ribeiro-Neto. *Modern Information Retrieval*. ACM Press / Addison-Wesley, 1999.

[4] H. Bast, D. Majumdar, R. Schenkel, M. Theobald, and G. Weikum. IO-Top-K: Index-access optimized top-k query processing. In *Proceedings of the 32th International Conference on Very Large Data Bases*, 2006.

[5] R. Blanco and A. Barreiro. Probabilistic static pruning of inverted files. *ACM Transactions on Information Systems*, 28(1), Jan. 2010.

[6] A. Z. Broder, D. Carmel, M. Herscovici, A. Soffer, and J. Y. Zien. Efficient query evaluation using a two-level retrieval process. In *Proc. of the 12th ACM Conf. on Information and Knowledge Management*, 2003.

[7] K. Chakrabarti, S. Chaudhuri, and V. Ganti. Interval-based pruning for top-k processing over compressed lists. In *Proc. of the 27th Int. Conf. on Data Engineering*, 2011.

[8] J. Dean. Challenges in building large-scale information retrieval systems. In *Proceedings of the Second ACM International Conference on Web Search and Data Mining*, 2009.

[9] S. Ding and T. Suel. Faster top-k document retrieval using block-max indexes. In *Proc. of the 34th Int. ACM SIGIR Conf. on Research and Development in Information Retrieval*, 2011.

[10] R. Fagin. Combining fuzzy information: an overview. *SIGMOD Record*, 31:2002, 2002.

[11] R. Fagin, D. Carmel, D. Cohen, E. Farchi, M. Herscovici, Y. Maarek, and A. Soffer. Static index pruning for information retrieval systems. In *Proceedings of the 24th Annual Int. ACM SIGIR Conference on Research and Development in Inf. Retrieval*, 2001.

[12] S. Jonassen and S. E. Bratsberg. Efficient compressed inverted index skipping for disjunctive text-queries. In *Proc. of the 33th European Conf. on Information Retrieval*, 2011.

[13] X. Long and T. Suel. Optimized query execution in large search engines with global page ordering. In *Proceedings of the 29th International Conference on Very Large Data Bases*, 2003.

[14] M. Persin, J. Zobel, and R. Sacks-davis. Filtered document retrieval with frequency-sorted indexes. *Journal of the American Society for Information Science*, 47:749–764, 1996.

[15] K. Risvik, Y. Aasheim, and M. Lidal. Multi-tier architecture for web search engines. In *1st Latin American Web Congress*, 2003.

[16] D. Shan, S. Ding, J. He, H. Yan, and X. Li. Optimized top-k processing with global page scores on block-max indexes. In *Proc. of the Fifth Int. Conf. on Web Search and Data Mining*, 2012.

[17] F. Silvestri. Sorting out the document identifier assignment problem. In *Proc. of the 29th European Conf. on Information Retrieval*, 2007.

[18] F. Silvestri and R. Venturini. Vsencoding: efficient coding and fast decoding of integer lists via dynamic programming. In *Proc. of the 19th ACM Conf. on Information and Knowledge Management*, 2010.

[19] T. Strohman. *Efficient Processing of Complex Features for Information Retrieval*. PhD thesis, University of Massachusetts Amherst, 2007.

[20] T. Strohman and W. B. Croft. Efficient document retrieval in main memory. In *Proc. of the 30th Annual Int. ACM SIGIR Conf. on Research and Development in Information Retrieval*, 2007.

[21] T. Strohman, H. R. Turtle, and W. B. Croft. Optimization strategies for complex queries. In *Proc. of the 28th Annual Int. ACM SIGIR Conf. on Research and Development in Information Retrieval*, 2005.

[22] H. R. Turtle and J. Flood. Query evaluation: Strategies and optimizations. *Inf. Processing and Management*, 31(6):831–850, 1995.

[23] L. Wang, J. J. Lin, and D. Metzler. A cascade ranking model for efficient ranked retrieval. In *Proc. of the 34th Annual Int. ACM SIGIR Conf. on Research and Development in Information Retrieval*, 2011.

[24] I. H. Witten, A. Moffat, and T. C. Bell. *Managing Gigabytes: Compressing and Indexing Documents and Images, Second Edition*. Morgan Kaufmann, 1999.

[25] H. Yan, S. Ding, and T. Suel. Inverted index compression and query processing with optimized document ordering. In *Proc. of the 18th Int. Conf. on World Wide Web*, 2009.

[26] J. Zhang, X. Long, and T. Suel. Performance of compressed inverted list caching in search engines. In *Proc. of the 17th Int. Conf. on World Wide Web*, 2008.

[27] J. Zobel and A. Moffat. Inverted files for text search engines. *ACM Comput. Surv.*, 38(2), 2006.

[28] M. Zukowski, S. Heman, N. Nes, and P. Boncz. Super-scalar RAM-CPU cache compression. In *Proceedings of the 22th Int. Conf. on Data Engineering*, 2006.

Improving the Sensitivity of Online Controlled Experiments by Utilizing Pre-Experiment Data

Alex Deng*
Microsoft
One Microsoft Way
Redmond, WA 98052
alexdeng@microsoft.com

Ya Xu*
Microsoft
1020 Enterprise Way
Sunnyvale, CA 94089
yaxu@microsoft.com

Ron Kohavi
Microsoft
One Microsoft Way
Redmond, WA 98052
ronnyk@microsoft.com

Toby Walker
Microsoft
One Microsoft Way
Redmond, WA 98052
towalker@microsoft.com

ABSTRACT

Online controlled experiments are at the heart of making data-driven decisions at a diverse set of companies, including Amazon, eBay, Facebook, Google, Microsoft, Yahoo, and Zynga. Small differences in key metrics, on the order of fractions of a percent, may have very significant business implications. At Bing it is not uncommon to see experiments that impact annual revenue by millions of dollars, even tens of millions of dollars, either positively or negatively. With thousands of experiments being run annually, improving the sensitivity of experiments allows for more precise assessment of value, or equivalently running the experiments on smaller populations (supporting more experiments) or for shorter durations (improving the feedback cycle and agility). We propose an approach (CUPED) that utilizes data from the pre-experiment period to reduce metric variability and hence achieve better sensitivity. This technique is applicable to a wide variety of key business metrics, and it is practical and easy to implement. The results on Bing's experimentation system are very successful: we can reduce variance by about 50%, effectively achieving the same statistical power with only half of the users, or half the duration.

Categories and Subject Descriptors

G.3 [**Probability and Statistics/Experiment Design**]: controlled experiments, randomized experiments, A/B testing

General Terms

Measurement, Variance, Experimentation

*Corresponding authors.

WSDM'13, February 4–8, 2013, Rome, Italy.

Keywords

Controlled experiment, Variance, A/B testing, Search quality evaluation, Pre-Experiment, Power, Sensitivity

1. INTRODUCTION

A controlled experiment is probably the oldest and the most widely accepted methodology to establish a causal relationship (Mason et al. 1989; Box et al. 2005; Keppel et al. 1992; Kohavi et al. 2009b; Manzi 2012). Now widely used and re-discovered by many companies, it is referred to as a randomized experiment, an A/B test (Wikipedia), a split test, a weblab (at Amazon), a live traffic experiment (at Google), a flight (at Microsoft), and a bucket test (at Yahoo!). This paper is focused on online controlled experiments, where experiments are conducted on live traffic to support data-driven decisions in online businesses, including e-business sites like Amazon and eBay, portal sites like Yahoo and MSN (Kohavi et al. 2009b), search engines like Microsoft Bing (Kohavi et al. 2012) and Google (Tang et al. 2010b).

Online controlled experiments are critical for businesses. Small differences in key metrics, on the order of fractions of a percent, can have very significant business implications. At Bing it is not uncommon to see experiments that impact annual revenue by millions of dollars, even tens of millions of dollars, either positively or negatively. We begin with a motivating example of an online controlled experiment run at MSN (Kohavi et al. 2009a). MSN Real Estate (`http://realestate.msn.com`) had six visual design candidates for the "Find a home" widget, as shown in Figure 1. During the experiment, users were randomly split between the 6 variants, where the control is the production version and treatment 1 through 5 are five new designs. The goal was to increase visits to the linked partner sites through the widget. Users' interactions with the widget were instrumented and key metrics such as the number of transfers to partner sites were computed. In this experiment, the winner, treatment 5, increased revenue from transfer fees by almost 10% compared to the control.

One challenge with any controlled experiment is the ability to detect the treatment effect when it indeed exists, usually referred to as "power" or "sensitivity." Improving sen-

Figure 1: Widgets tested for MSN Real Estate.

sitivity is particularly important when running online experiments at large scale. A mature online experimentation platform runs thousands of experiments a year (Kohavi et al. 2012; Manzi 2012). The benefit of any increased sensitivity is therefore amplified by economies of scale. It might seem unnecessary to emphasize sensitivity for online experiments because they tend to have very large sample sizes already (e.g. millions of users (comScore 2012)) and increasing sample size is usually the most straightforward way to improve power. In reality, even with a large amount of traffic, online experiments cannot always reach enough statistical power. Google made it very clear that they are not satisfied with the amount of traffic they have (Tang et al. 2010a, Slide 6) even with over 10 billion searches per month (comScore 2012). There are several reasons for this. First, the treatment effects we would like to detect tend to be very small. The sensitivity of controlled experiments is inversely proportional to the number of users squared, so whereas a small site may need 10,000 users to detect a 5% delta, detecting a 0.5% delta requires 100 times (10 squared) more users, or one million users. Even a 0.5% change in revenue per user equates to millions of dollars for large online sites. Second, it is crucial to get results fast. One wants to launch good features early, and more importantly, if the treatment turns out to have a negative impact on users, we need to stop it as soon as possible. Third, there are many experiments that have low triggering rates; that is, only a small fraction of the experiment's users actually experience the treatment feature. For example, in an experiment affecting only recipe-related queries, the majority of the users will not see the target feature because they didn't search for recipes during the experiment. In these cases, the effective sample size can be small and statistical analysis can suffer from low statistical power. Finally, in a data-driven culture, there is always demand to run more experiments to keep up with the rate of innovation. A good online experimentation platform should allow many experiments to run together. This also requires that we make optimal use of large but still limited traffic.

One way to improve sensitivity is through variance reduction. Kohavi et al. (2009b) provides examples where we can achieve a lower variance using a different evaluation metric or through filtering out users who are not impacted by the change. Deng et al. (2011) shows how we can use page level randomization at the design stage to reduce variance of page level metrics (Chapelle et al. 2012). However, these methods are limited in their applicability to special cases and we want a technique that is applicable to any metric as, in practice, businesses are likely to have a set of Key Performance Indicators (KPIs) that cannot be changed easily. Moreover, the technique should preferably not be based on any parametric model because model assumptions tend to be unreliable and a model that works for one metric does not necessarily work for another.

In this paper, we propose a technique, called CUPED (Controlled-experiment Using Pre-Experiment Data), which adjusts metrics using pre-experiment data for users in the control and treatment to reduce metric variability.

The key contributions of our work include:

- A theoretically sound and practical method to reduce variances for online experiments using pre-experiment data, which greatly increases experiment sensitivity.
- Extensions of approach to non-user metrics and partially missing pre-experiment data.
- Criteria for selecting the best covariates, including the empirical result that using the same metric from the pre-experiment typically gives the greatest variance reduction.
- Validation of the results on real online experiments run at Bing, demonstrating a variance reduction of about 50%, equivalent to doubling our traffic or halving the time we need to run an experiment to get the same sensitivity.
- Practical guidance on choices important to successful application of CUPED to real-world online experimentation, including factors like the best length to use for the pre-experiment period and the use of multiple covariates.

2. BACKGROUND AND RELATED WORK

2.1 Analyzing Experiments

Because of its wide applicability, we focus on the case of the two-sample t-test (Student 1908; Wasserman 2003). This is the framework most commonly used in online experiment analysis. Suppose we are interested in some metric Y (e.g. Queries per user). To apply the t-test, we assume the observed values of the metric for users in the treatment and control are independent realizations of random variables $Y^{(t)}$ and $Y^{(c)}$. The null hypothesis is that $Y^{(t)}$ and $Y^{(c)}$ have the same mean and the alternative is that they do not. The t-test is based on the t-statistic:

$$\frac{\overline{Y}^{(t)} - \overline{Y}^{(c)}}{\sqrt{\operatorname{var}\left(\overline{Y}^{(t)} - \overline{Y}^{(c)}\right)}}, \tag{1}$$

where $\Delta = \overline{Y}^{(t)} - \overline{Y}^{(c)}$ is an unbiased estimator for the shift of the mean and the t-statistic is a normalized version of that estimator. For online experiments, the sample sizes for both control and treatment are at least in thousands, hence the normality assumption on Y is usually unnecessary because of the Central Limit Theorem.

Because the samples are independent,

$$\mathrm{var}(\Delta) = \mathrm{var}\left(\overline{Y}^{(t)} - \overline{Y}^{(c)}\right) = \mathrm{var}\left(\overline{Y}^{(t)}\right) + \mathrm{var}\left(\overline{Y}^{(c)}\right).$$

In this framework, the key to variance reduction for the difference in mean lies in reducing the variance of the means themselves. As we will see in Section 3, this connects our problem to techniques used in Monte Carlo sampling to improve estimation of a mean through variance reduction.

At a very high level, our proposal for variance reduction works as follows. We conduct the experiment as usual but when analyzing the data, we compute an adjusted or corrected estimate of the delta. That adjusted estimate, Δ^*, incorporates pre-experiment information, such that

- Δ^* is still an unbiased estimator for the shift in the means (same as Δ), and
- Δ^* has a smaller variance than Δ.

Note that because of the reduced variance, the corresponding t-statistic would be larger for the same expected effect size. We therefore achieved better sensitivity.

2.2 Linear Models

We begin with a short review of related work. Variance reduction has been a longstanding challenge for analyzing randomized experiments. The most popular parametric method is based on linear modeling (Gelman and Hill 2006). A linear model for an experiment assumes that the outcome is a linear combination of a treatment effect coupled with additional covariate terms. In particular, suppose Y_i is the outcome metric, Z_i is the treatment assignment indicator and $\mathbf{X}_i$ is a vector of covariates. The linear model assumes $\mathbb{E}(Y_i|Z_i,\mathbf{X}_i) = \theta_0 + \delta Z_i + \boldsymbol{\theta}^T\mathbf{X}_i$. Under the assumptions of the model, linear regression (also called ANCOVA when covariates are categorical variables) gives a consistent estimator for the average treatment effect and reduces variance. However, the linear model makes strong assumptions that are usually not satisfied in practice, i.e., the conditional expectation of the outcome metric is linear in the treatment assignment and covariates. In addition, it also requires all residuals to have a common variance.

2.3 Semi-Parametric Models

To overcome limitations of the linear model, researchers have developed less restrictive models called semi-parametric models (Tsiatis 2006), for which Generalized Estimating Equations (GEE) are used for fitting the model. Comparing standard linear models with semi-parametric models, Yang and Tsiatis (2001) showed that linear model (ANCOVA) and GEE are asymptotically equivalent under the less restrictive semi-parametric model and both give more efficient estimates for the average treatment effect than the unadjusted t-test. Leon et al. (2003), Davidian et al. (2005) and Tsiatis et al. (2008) further refined the work using semi-parametric statistical theory (Tsiatis 2006) and gave the analytical form of a class of estimators for the average treatment effect. This class is complete in the sense that all possible RAL (regular and asymptotically linear) estimators for the average treatment effect are asymptotically equivalent to one in the class. The problem left is to find the estimator in the class with the smallest variance and they provided general guidance.

In this paper, we look at the problem from a different perspective. By connecting the variance reduction problem in randomized experiments to a similar problem in Monte Carlo simulation, we are able to derive a very powerful result. Instead of diving into abstract Hilbert spaces and functional influence curves, our argument only involves elementary probability. In particular, we propose to use the data from the pre-experiment period to reduce metric variability, which turns out to be very effective and practically applicable.

3. VARIANCE REDUCTION

Variance reduction is a common topic in Monte Carlo sampling, where the goal is usually to estimate a parameter by repeatedly simulating possible values from the underlying distribution. In Monte Carlo sampling significant efficiency gains can be had if we use sampling schemes that reduce the variance by incorporating prior information. Unlike Monte Carlo simulations, in the world of online experiments, the population is dynamic and data arrive gradually as the experiment progresses. We cannot design a sampling scheme in advance and then collect data accordingly. However, we will show that because we have pre-experiment data, we can adapt Monte Carlo variance techniques by applying them "retrospectively."

The two Monte Carlo variance reduction techniques we consider here are stratification and control variates. For each technique, we review the basic concepts and then show how it can be adapted to the online experiment setting. We devote Section 3.3 to discussing the connections between these two approaches and the implications in practice.

3.1 Stratification

Stratification is a common technique used in Monte Carlo sampling to achieve variance reduction. In this section, we show how it can be adapted to achieve the same goal in the world of online experimentation.

3.1.1 *Stratification in Simulation*

The basic idea of stratification is to divide the sampling region into strata, sample within each stratum separately and then combine results from individual strata together to give an overall estimate, which usually has a smaller variance than the estimate without stratification.

Mathematically, we want to estimate $\mathbb{E}(Y)$, the expected value of Y, where Y is the variable of interest. The standard Monte Carlo approach is to first simulate n independent samples $Y_i, i = 1,\ldots,n$, and then use the sample average $\overline{Y}$ as the estimator of $\mathbb{E}(Y)$. $\overline{Y}$ is unbiased and $\mathrm{var}(\overline{Y}) = \mathrm{var}(Y)/n$.

Let's consider a more strategic sampling scheme. Assume we can divide the sampling region of Y into K subregions (strata) with w_k the probability that Y falls into the kth stratum, $k = 1,\ldots,K$. If we fix the number of points sampled from the kth stratum to be $n_k = n \cdot w_k$, we can define a stratified average to be

$$\widehat{Y}_{strat} = \sum_{k=1}^{K} w_k \overline{Y}_k, \tag{2}$$

where $\overline{Y}_k$ is the average within the kth stratum.

The stratified average $\widehat{Y}_{strat}$ and the standard average $\overline{Y}$ have the same expected value but the former gives a smaller variance when the means are different across the strata. The intuition is that the variance of $\overline{Y}$ can be decomposed into the within-strata variance and the between-strata variance, and the latter is removed through stratification. For example, the variance of children's heights in general is large. However, if we stratify them by their age, we can get a much smaller variance within each age group. More formally,

$$\begin{aligned}\text{var}(\overline{Y}) &= \sum_{k=1}^{K} \frac{w_k}{n}\sigma_k^2 + \sum_{k=1}^{K} \frac{w_k}{n}(\mu_k - \mu)^2 \\ &\geq \sum_{k=1}^{K} \frac{w_k}{n}\sigma_k^2 = \text{var}(\widehat{Y}_{strat})\end{aligned}$$

where (μ_k, σ_k^2) denote the mean and variance for users in the kth stratum. More detailed proof can be found in standard Monte Carlo books (e.g. Asmussen and Glynn (2008)). A good stratification is the one that aligns well with the underlying clusters in the data. By explicitly identifying these clusters as strata, we essentially remove the extra variance introduced by them.

3.1.2 Stratification in Online Experimentation

In the online world, because we collect data as they arrive over time, we are usually unable to sample from strata formed ahead of time. However, we can still utilize pre-experiment variables to construct strata after all the data are collected (for theoretical justification see Asmussen and Glynn (2008, Page 153)). For example, if Y_i is the number of queries from a user i, a covariate X_i could be the browser that the user used before the experiment started. The stratified average in (2) can then be computed by grouping Y according to the value of X,

$$\widehat{Y}_{strat} = \sum_{k=1}^{K} w_k \overline{Y}_k = \sum_{k=1}^{K} w_k \left(\frac{1}{n_k} \sum_{i:X_i=k} Y_i \right).$$

Using superscripts to denote treatment and control groups, the stratified delta

$$\Delta_{strat} = \widehat{Y}_{strat}^{(t)} - \widehat{Y}_{strat}^{(c)} = \sum_{k=1}^{K} w_k(\overline{Y}_k^{(t)} - \overline{Y}_k^{(c)})$$

enjoys the same variance reduction as the stratified average in Eq. (2). It is important to note that by using only the pre-experiment information, the stratification variable X is independent of the experiment effect. This ensures that the stratified delta is unbiased.

In practice, we don't always know the appropriate weights w_k to use. In the context of online experimentation, these can usually be computed from users not in the experiment. As we will see in Section 3.3, when we formulate the same problem in the form of control variates (Section 3.2), we no longer need to estimate the weights.

3.2 Control Variates

We showed how online experimentation can benefit from the stratification technique widely used in the simulation literature. In this section we show how another variance reduction technique used in simulation, called control variates, can also be adopted in online experimentation. In Section 3.2.1, we review control variates in its original form as a variance reduction technique for simulation. We then show how the same idea can be applied in the context of online experimentation in Section 3.2.2.

3.2.1 Control Variates in Simulation

The idea of variance reduction through control variates stems from the following observation. Assume we can simulate another random variable X in addition to Y with known expectation $\mathbb{E}(X)$. In other words, we have independent pairs of $(Y_i, X_i), i = 1, \ldots, n$. Define

$$\widehat{Y}_{cv} = \overline{Y} - \theta\overline{X} + \theta\mathbb{E}X, \tag{3}$$

where θ is any constant. $\widehat{Y}_{cv}$ is an unbiased estimator of $\mathbb{E}(Y)$ since $-\theta\mathbb{E}(\overline{X}) + \theta\mathbb{E}(X) = 0$. The variance of $\widehat{Y}_{cv}$ is

$$\begin{aligned}\text{var}(\widehat{Y}_{cv}) &= \text{var}(\overline{Y} - \theta\overline{X}) = \text{var}(Y - \theta X)/n \\ &= \frac{1}{n}(\text{var}(Y) + \theta^2\text{var}(X) - 2\theta\text{cov}(Y, X)).\end{aligned}$$

Note that $\text{var}(\widehat{Y}_{cv})$ is minimized when we choose

$$\theta = \text{cov}(Y, X)/\text{var}(X) \tag{4}$$

and with this optimal choice of θ, we have

$$\text{var}(\widehat{Y}_{cv}) = \text{var}(\overline{Y})(1 - \rho^2), \tag{5}$$

where $\rho = \text{cor}(Y, X)$ is the correlation between Y and X. Compare (5) to the variance of $\overline{Y}$, the variance is reduced by a factor of ρ^2. The larger ρ, the better the variance reduction. The single control variate case can be easily generalized to include multiple variables.

It is interesting to point out the connection with linear regression. The optimal $\boldsymbol{\theta}$ turns out to be the ordinary least square (OLS) solution of regressing (centered) Y on (centered) X, which gives variance

$$\text{var}(\widehat{Y}_{cv}) = \text{var}(\overline{Y})(1 - R^2),$$

with R^2 being the proportion of variance explained coefficient from the linear regression. It is also possible to use nonlinear adjustment. i.e., instead of allowing only linear adjustment as in (3), we can minimize variance in a more general functional space. Define

$$\widehat{Y}_{cv} = \overline{Y} - \overline{f(X)} + \mathbb{E}(f(X)), \tag{6}$$

and then try to minimize the variance of (6). It can be shown that the regression function $\mathbb{E}(Y|X)$ gives the optimal $f(X)$.

3.2.2 Control Variates in Online Experimentation

Utilizing control variates to reduce variance is a very common technique. The difficulty of applying it boils down to finding a control variate X that is highly correlated with Y and at the same time has known $\mathbb{E}(X)$.

Although in general it is not easy to find control variate X with known $\mathbb{E}(X^{(t)})$ and $\mathbb{E}(X^{(c)})$, a key observation is that $\mathbb{E}(X^{(t)}) - \mathbb{E}(X^{(c)}) = 0$ in the pre-experiment period because we have not yet introduced any treatment effect. By using only information from before the launch of the experiment to construct the control variate, the randomization between treatment and control ensures that we have $\mathbb{E}X^{(t)} = \mathbb{E}X^{(c)}$.

Given $\mathbb{E}X^{(t)} - \mathbb{E}X^{(c)} = 0$, it is easy to see the delta

$$\Delta_{cv} = \widehat{Y}_{cv}^{(t)} - \widehat{Y}_{cv}^{(c)} \tag{7}$$

is an unbiased estimator of $\delta = \mathbb{E}(\Delta)$. Notice how Δ_{cv} does not depend on the unknown $\mathbb{E}(X^{(t)})$ and $\mathbb{E}(X^{(c)})$ at all as they cancel each other. With the optimal choice of θ from Eq (4), we have that Δ_{cv} reduces variance by a factor of ρ^2 compared to Δ, i.e.

$$\mathrm{var}(\Delta_{cv}) = \mathrm{var}(\Delta)(1 - \rho^2).$$

To achieve a large correlation and hence better variance reduction, an obvious approach is to choose X to be the same as Y, which naturally leads to using the same variable during pre-experiment observation window as the control variate. As we will see in the empirical results in Section 5, this indeed turns out to be the most effective choice we found for control variates.

There is a slight subtlety that's worth pointing out. The pair (Y, X) may have different distributions in treatment and control when there is an experiment effect. For Δ_{cv} to be unbiased, the same θ has to be used for both control and treatment. The simplest way to estimate it is from the pooled population of control and treatment. The impact on variance reduction will likely be negligible. In the general nonlinear control covariates case, we should use the same functional form in both $\widehat{Y}_{cv}^{(t)}$ and $\widehat{Y}_{cv}^{(c)}$.

3.3 Connection between Stratification and Control Variates

We have discussed two techniques that both utilize covariates to achieve variance reduction. The stratification approach uses the covariates to construct strata while the control variates approach uses them as regression variables. The former uses discrete (or discretized) covariates, whereas control variates seem more naturally to be continuous variables. It is, however, not surprising that these two approaches are closely related. In fact, we can show that when the covariate X is categorical (say, with discrete values $1, \ldots, K$) the two approaches produce identical estimates. Details are included in Appendix A. The basic idea is to construct an indicator variable $1_{X=k}$ for each stratum and use it as a control variate with mean being the stratum weight w_k. To this end, the control variates technique is an extension of stratification, where both continuous and discrete covariates are applicable.

While these two techniques are well connected mathematically, they provide different insights into understanding why and how to achieve variance reduction. The stratification formulation has a nice analogy with mixture models, where each stratum is one component of the mixture model. Stratification is equivalent to separating samples according to their component memberships, effectively removing the between-component variance and achieving a reduced variance. A better covariate is hence the one that can better classify the samples and align with their underlying structure. On the other hand, the control variates formulation quantifies the amount of variance reduction as a function of the correlation between the covariates and the variable itself. It is mathematically simpler and more elegant. Clearly, a better covariate should be the one with larger (absolute) correlation.

4. CUPED IN PRACTICE

A simple yet effective way to implement CUPED is to use the same variable from the pre-experiment period as the covariate. Indeed, this is essentially what we have implemented in practice for Bing's experimentation system. However, there are situations when this is not possible or practical. For example, if we want to measure user retention rate or conduct an experiment on new users, there are no pre-experiment data to work with. In fact, in most online experiments, we may not have pre-experiment information on *all* users. An additional challenge is how to use pre-experiment data for metrics whose analysis unit is not a user. This section is devoted to address practical challenges like these using Bing's experimentation system as a case study.

4.1 Selecting Covariates

The choice of covariates is critical, as it directly determines the effectiveness of variance reduction. With the choice of the right variables we can halve the variance but with the wrong choice there is little reduction in variance. To understand which pre-experiment variables worked best we evaluated a large number of possible pre-experiment variables. Across a large class of metrics, our results consistently showed that using the same variable from the pre-experiment period as the covariate tends to give the best variance reduction. In addition, the lengths of the pre-experiment and the experiment periods also play a role. Given the same pre-experiment period, extending the length of the experiment does not necessarily improve the variance reduction rate. On the other hand, a longer pre-period tends to give a higher reduction for the same experiment period. We discuss more details in the context of an empirical example in Section 5.

4.2 Handling Missing Pre-Experiment Data

In online sites, we might not have pre-experiment data on all users in the experiment. This can occur because some users are visiting for the first time, or users simply do not visit the site frequently enough to appear during the pre-experiment period. In addition, users are identified by cookies, which are unreliable and can "churn" (i.e. change due to users clearing their cookies).

This poses a challenge for using the pre-experiment information to construct covariates. For users who are in the experiment but not in the pre-experiment period, the corresponding covariates are not well-defined. One way to address this is to define another covariate that indicates whether or not a user appeared in the pre-experiment period. With this additional binary covariate, we can set the missing covariate values to be any constant we like. Intuitively, this is equivalent to first splitting users into two strata: those that appeared in the pre-experiment period and those that did not. Note that for the stratum of users with pre-experiment data, their pre-experiment covariates are well-defined so further variance reduction based on these covariates is possible. In addition, the stratification by presence in the pre-period is a further source of variance reduction.

4.3 Beyond Pre-Experiment Data

So far we only considered reducing metrics variability based on covariates constructed using the pre-experiment data. This is not only because using the same variable from the pre-period tends to give the best variance reduction, but also because the pre-experiment information is guaranteed to be independent of the experiment's effect, which is crucial to avoid biased results.

It is probably easier to demonstrate this mathematically with the control variates formulation. In Eq. (7), the delta

Δ_{cv} is computed assuming $\mathbb{E}(X^{(t)}) = \mathbb{E}(X^{(c)})$. If there is truly a difference between control and treatment in terms of X and this equality does not hold, Δ_{cv} will be biased. For example, we know a faster page load-time usually leads to more clicks on a search page (Kohavi et al. 2009b). If we use the number of clicks as the covariate in an experiment that improves page load-time, we will end up underestimating the experiment impact on the load-time because part of the improvement is "adjusted away" by the covariate. See Section 5 for a real example of biased results caused by using a covariate that violates the requirements described here.

However, this does not mean that covariates based on pre-experiment data are the only choice. All that is required is that the covariate X is not affected by the experiment's treatment. A natural extension is the class of covariates constructed using information gathered at the first time a user appears in the experiment. For instance, the day-of-week a user is first observed in the experiment is independent of the experiment itself. Such covariates can serve as an additional powerful source for variance reduction. To further extend this idea, covariates based on any information established before a user actually *triggers* the experiment feature are also valid. This can be particularly helpful if the feature to be evaluated has a low triggering rate.

4.4 Handling Non-User Metrics

As we mentioned in Section 1, in online experiments, users (cookies) are the common randomization unit. In the discussion thus far, we have assumed that the analysis unit is also "user." However, this is not always the case. For example, we may want to compute click-through-rate (CTR) as the total number of clicks divided by the total number of pages. The analysis unit here is a "page" instead of a "user." Variance estimation itself is harder when there is a mismatch between the analysis unit and the experiment unit. The most common solution is to use the delta method to produce correct estimate of variance that takes into account the correlation of pages from the same user (Deng et al. 2011; Tang et al. 2010b; Kohavi et al. 2009b). To achieve variance reduction for these non-user level metrics, we need to combine the delta method and our variance reduction techniques together. The details are provided in Appendix B. In fact, not only can the metric of interest (e.g. CTR) be at page level, we can have page-level covariates as well. This opens the door to a larger class of covariates that are based on features specific to a page that may be not specific to a user, e.g. time stamp on a page-view.

5. EMPIRICAL RESULTS

In this section, we share empirical results that show the effectiveness of CUPED for Microsoft Bing's experimentation system. First we show how CUPED can greatly improve the sensitivity for a real experiment run at Bing. Next we look deeper into a 3-week A/A test, which is a controlled experiment where treatment is identical to control and hence the treatment effect is known to be 0. Using an A/A experiment we can examine important decisions that can have a large impact of the success of variance reduction for real-world online experimentation. Finally, we show how biased estimates arise if we go past the user triggering into the experiment and choose a covariate inappropriately.

5.1 Slowdown Experiment in Bing

To show the impact of CUPED in a real experiment we examine an experiment that tested the relationship between page load-time and user engagement on Bing. Delays, on the order of hundreds of milliseconds, are known to hurt user engagement (Kohavi et al. 2009b, Section 6.1.2). In this experiment, we deliberately delayed the server response to Bing queries by 250 milliseconds. The experiment first ran for two weeks on a small fraction of Bing users, and we observed an impact to click-through-rate (CTR) that was borderline statistically significant, i.e., the p-value was just slightly below our threshold of 0.05. To confirm that the treatment effect on this metric is real and not a false positive, a much larger experiment was run, which showed that this was indeed a real effect with a p-value of 2e-13.

We applied CUPED using CTR from the 2-week pre-period as the covariate. The result is impressive: the delta was statistically significant from day 1! The top plot of Figure 2 shows the p-values over time in log scale. The black horizontal line is the 0.05 significance bar. The vanilla t-test trends slowly down and by the time the experiment was stopped in 2 weeks, it barely reached the threshold. When CUPED is applied, the entire p-value curve is below the bar. The bottom plot of Figure 2 compares the p-value curves when CUPED runs on only half the users. Even with half the users exposed to the experiment, CUPED results in a more sensitive test, allowing for more non-overlapping experiments to be run. While most experiments are not known to be negative to the user experience a-priori, it has been well documented that most experiments are flat or negative (Kohavi et al. 2009a; Manzi 2012), so being able to run

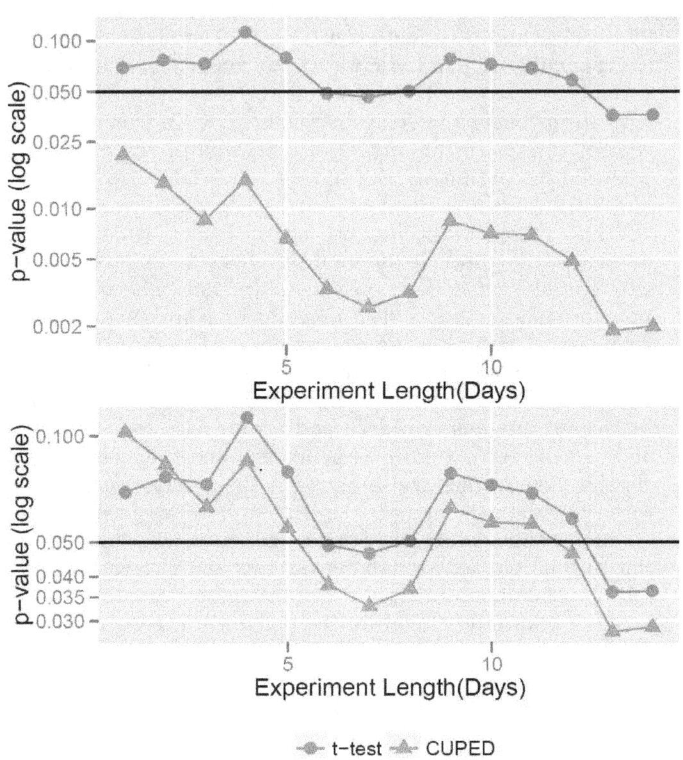

Figure 2: Slowdown experiment. Top: p-value. Bottom: p-value when using only half the users for CUPED.

experiments with the same statistical power on smaller populations of users is very important.

Applying CUPED to other experiments at Bing has resulted in similar increases to statistical power.

5.2 Factors Affecting CUPED Effectiveness

In this section we look at factors that can have a large impact on the success of using CUPED in practice. The data we use here are from a 3-week A/A experiment.

5.2.1 Covariates

Figure 3 shows CUPED's variance reduction rate for the metric queries-per-user. Two covariates are considered: (1) entry-day, which is a categorical variable indicating the first day a user appears in the experiment and (2) queries-per-user in the 1-week pre-experiment period. Note that the entry-day is not pre-experiment data, but it satisfies the condition required in Section 4.3 because the treatment has no effect on when a user will come for the first time during the experiment.

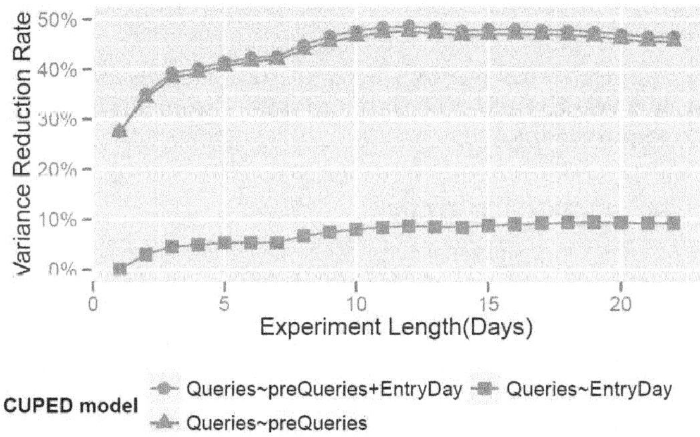

Figure 3: Variance reduction for Queries/UU using different covariates.

Note that the full experiment ran for 3 weeks, but the reduction rate is evaluated and plotted as the experiment accumulates data up until to the full 3 weeks. From the plot we can see that when only entry-day is used as the covariate, the variance reduction rate increases as the experiment runs longer and stays at about 9% to 10% after 2 weeks. On the other hand, using only the pre-experiment period queries-per-user, variance reduction rate can reach more than 45%. When we combine the two covariates together, we only gain an extra 2% to 3% more reduction compared to the pre-experiment queries-per-user alone. This suggests that the same metric computed in the pre-experiment period is a better single covariate. That is intuitive since the same metric in the experiment and pre-experiment periods should naturally have high correlation. The fact that when combining two covariates together the marginal variance reduction is small means most correlation between entry-day and queries-per-user can be "explained away" by the pre-experiment queries-per-user. More precisely, the partial correlation between entry-day and queries-per-user given pre-experiment queries-per-user is low.

5.2.2 Lengths of Experiment and Pre-Experiment

In addition to the effect of covariates, Figure 3 also provides insights on the impact of the experiment length. An interesting observation is that the variance reduction rate for the pre-experiment covariate (green/triangle) is not monotonically increasing as the experiment duration increases. It reaches the maximum at about 2 weeks and then starts to slowly decrease. To help understand the underlying reasons for this trend, we plot 4 variations of this curve with pre-period length varying from 3 days to 2 weeks. As shown in Figure 4, we see that a longer pre-period gives a higher variance reduction rate.

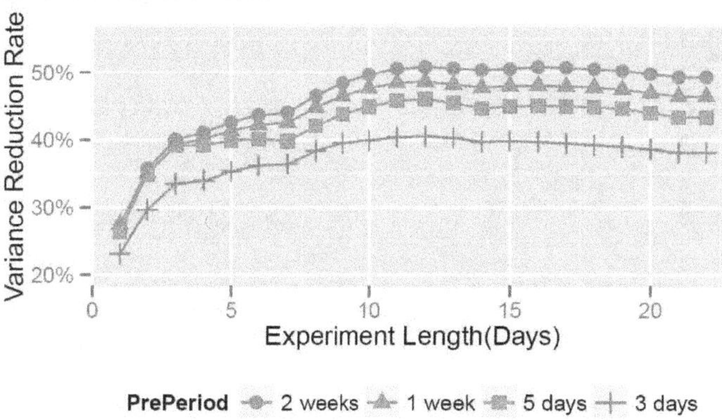

Figure 4: Impact of pre-experiment period length.

The trends in Figure 3 and 4 together reveal two conflicting factors that impact the effectiveness of CUPED.

- *Correlation.* The higher the correlation, the better the variance reduction. When we increase the pre-experiment period length or increase the experiment duration, the correlation increases for "cumulative" metrics such as queries-per-user. This is because the longer the period, the higher the signal-to-noise ratio.
- *Coverage.* Coverage is the percentage of users in the experiment that also appeared in the pre-experiment period. Coverage is determined by:
  - *Experiment Duration.* As the experiment duration increases, coverage decreases. The reason is that frequent visitors are seen early in the experiment and users seen later in the experiment are often new or "churned" users. The result is that as coverage decreases, the rate of variance reduction goes down.
  - *Pre-period Duration.* Increasing the pre-period length increases coverage because we have a better chance of matching an experiment user in the pre-period.

When pre-experiment period was chosen to be 2 weeks, the variance reduction rate is about 50% for a large range of experiment durations.

5.2.3 Metric of Interest

Besides the choice of covariates and the lengths of experiment and pre-experiment, CUPED effectiveness varies from metric to metric, depending on the correlation between the metric and its pre-experiment counterpart. We applied CUPED on a few metrics, such as clicks-per-user and visits-per-user. CUPED performed well on all these metrics with similar variance reduction curves as in Figure 3. One notable exception is revenue-per-user, where CUPED reduced the variance by less than 5% due to the low correlation of revenue-per-user between the pre-experiment and the experiment periods. We also applied CUPED on a few page level metrics (see the discussion in Section 4.4). Figure 5 shows the reduction rate for click-through-rate (CTR), using 2-week pre-experiment CTR as the CUPED covariate. Figure 6 plots the correlation curve between the two periods. Both the variance reduction rate and the correlation are similar to those of queries-per-user.

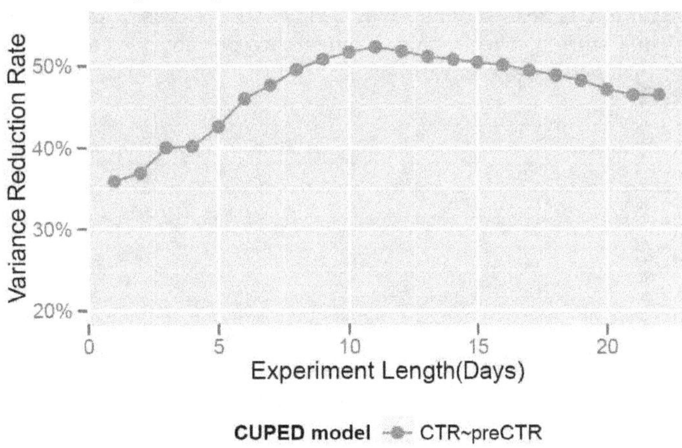

Figure 5: Variance reduction rate for CTR.

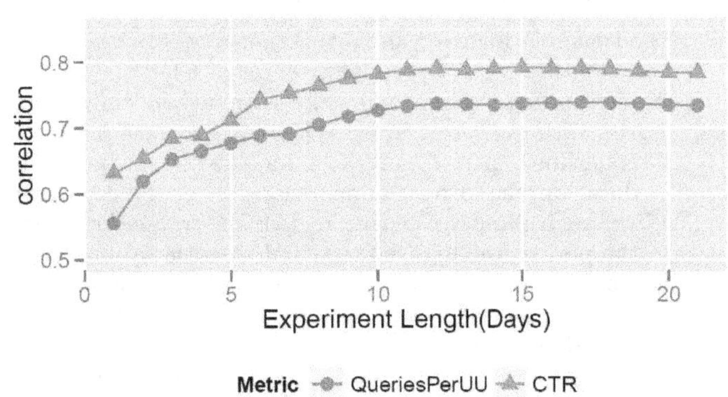

Figure 6: Correlation between the metrics of interest and their covariates within the matched users.

5.3 Warning on Using Post-Triggering Data

In Section 4, we mentioned that to guarantee unbiased results, any covariate X has to satisfy the condition $\mathbb{E}(X^{(t)}) = \mathbb{E}(X^{(c)})$. We illustrate this point in Figure 7. The data is from another Bing experiment, where queries-per-user increased statistically significantly. If we were to look for a metric with high correlation to queries-per-user, there is actually a much better candidate than the pre-experiment queries-per-user: the "in-experiment" Distinct Queries-per-user (DQ-per-user). DQ is defined as query counts for a user after consecutive duplicated queries are removed. As a result, DQ is extremely highly correlated with queries-per-user. Seemingly, DQ-per-user as covariate sounds like a good idea. However, Figure 7 shows that the CUPED estimates Δ_{CUPED} are negative and the confidence intervals are almost always below 0 (Note how narrow the confidence intervals are. DQ-per-user indeed reduced variance a lot!). This suggests the queries-per-user difference between the treatment and control is negative with 95% confidence, a result that is directionally opposite of the known effect. The contradiction is only apparent because DQ-per-user does not satisfy $\mathbb{E}(X^{(t)}) = \mathbb{E}(X^{(c)})$. In fact, since we know treatment has larger queries-per-user, it has larger DQ-per-user too. By (7), CUPED estimate Δ_{cv} can be interpreted as the in-experiment delta for the metric of interest "corrected" by the delta for the covariate. In this case the covariate delta is also positive, driving down the CUPED estimate below 0. This example illustrates the pitfall when extending CUPED beyond using pre-experiment (or pre-triggering) data.

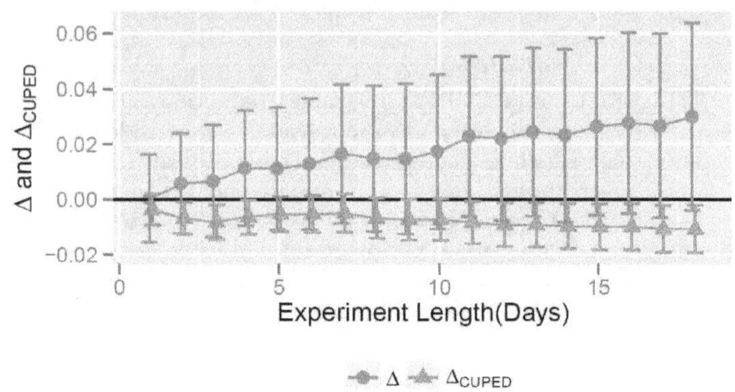

Figure 7: Example where results are directionally incorrect when covariates violate the pre-triggering requirement.

6. CONCLUSIONS

Increasing the sensitivity of online experiments allows for more precise assessment of value, or equivalently running the experiments on smaller populations (supporting more non-overlapping experiments) or for shorter durations (improving the feedback cycle and agility). We introduced CUPED, a new technique for increasing the sensitivity of controlled experiments by utilizing pre-experiment data. CUPED is currently live in Bing's online experimentation system. Three important recent experiments showed variance reductions of 45%, 52% and 49% with one week of experiment and one week of pre-experiment data. This reassures that CUPED can indeed help us effectively achieve the same statistical power with about only half the users, or half the duration.

CUPED is widely applicable to organizations running online experimentation systems because of its simplicity, ability to be added easily to existing systems, and its support for metrics commonly used in online businesses. Based on our experience applying CUPED at Bing, we can make the following recommendations for others interested in applying CUPED to their online experiments:

- Variance reduction works best for metrics where the distribution varies significantly across the user population. One common class of such metrics where the value is very different for light and heavy users. Queries-per-user is a paradigmatic example of such a metric.
- Using the metric measured in the pre-period as the covariate typically provides the best variance reduction.
- Using a pre-experiment period of 1-2 weeks works well for variance reduction. Too short a period will lead to poor matching, whereas too long a period will reduce correlation with the outcome metric during the experiment period.
- Never use covariates that could be affected by the treatment, as this could bias the results. We have

shown an example where directionally opposite conclusions could results if this requirement is violated.

While CUPED significantly improves the sensitivity of online experiments, we would like to explore improvements:

- *Optimized Covariate Selection.* Extend CUPED to optimize the selection of covariates, both for particular metrics and for particular types of experiments (e.g., a backend experiment might use data center as a covariate). We also plan to study the theory and practice to optimize selection of multiple covariates from a large library of potential covariate variables.
- *Incorporating Covariate Information into Assignment.* Rather than adjusting the data after the experiment completes, if we can make randomization aware of covariates we can potentially improve the sensitivity of our experiments even more as well as allocating traffic more efficiently to experiments.

7. ACKNOWLEDGMENTS

We wish to thank Sam Burkman, Leon Bottou, Thomas Crook, Kaustav Das, Brian Frasca, Xin Fu, Mario Garzia, Li-wei He, Greg Linden, Roger Longbotham, Carlos Gomez Uribe, Zijian Zheng and many members of the Bing Data Mining team.

References

Soren Asmussen and Peter Glynn. *Stochastic Simulation.* Springer-Verlag, 2008.

George E. P. Box, J. Stuart Hunter, and William G. Hunter. *Statistics for experimenters: design, innovation, and discovery.* Wiley, 2005.

Olivier Chapelle, Thorsten Joachims, Filip Radlinski, and Yisong Yue. Large-scale validation and analysis of interleaved search evaluation. *ACM Trans. Inf. Syst.*, 30(1): 6:1–6:41, March 2012. ISSN 1046-8188.

comScore. comscore releases june 2012 u.s. search engine rankings, June 2012. `http://www.comscore.com/Press_Events/Press_Releases/2012/6/comScore_Releases_June_2012_U.S._Search_Engine_Rankings`.

M. Davidian, A.A. Tsiatis, and S. Leon. Semiparametric estimation of treatment effect in a pretest-posttest study with missing data. *Statistical Science*, 20, 2005.

Shaojie Deng, Roger Longbotham, Toby Walker, and Ya Xu. Choice of the randomization unit in online controlled experiment. *JSM proceedings*, 2011.

Andrew Gelman and Jennifer Hill. *Data analysis using regression and multilevel/hierarchical models.* Cambridge University Press, 2006.

Geoffrey Keppel, William H. Saufley, and Howard Tokunaga. *Introduction to design and analysis: A Student's Handbook.* Worth Publishers, 1992.

Ron Kohavi, Thomas Crook, and Roger Longbotham. Online experimentation at Microsoft. *Third Workshop on Data Mining Case Studies and Practice Prize.*, 2009a. `http://www.exp-platform.com/Pages/expMicrosoft.aspx`.

Ron Kohavi, Roger Longbotham, Dan Sommerfield, and Randal M. Henne. Controlled experiments on the web: survey and practical guide. *Data Mining Knowledge Discovery*, 18:140–181, 2009b. `http://www.exp-platform.com/Pages/hippo_long.aspx`.

Ron Kohavi, Alex Deng, Brian Frasca, Roger Longbotham, Toby Walker, and Ya Xu. Trustworthy online controlled experiments: Five puzzling outcomes explained. *Proceedings of the 18th Conference on Knowledge Discovery and Data Mining*, 2012. `http://www.exp-platform.com/Pages/PuzzingOutcomesExplained.aspx`.

S. Leon, A.A. Tsiatis, and M. Davidian. Semiparametric estimation of treatment effect in a pretest-posttest study. *Biometrika*, 59, 2003.

Jim Manzi. *Uncontrolled: The Surprising Payoff of Trial-and-Error for Business, Politics, and Society.* Basic Books, 2012.

Robert L. Mason, Richard F. Gunst, and James L. Hess. *Statistical design and analysis of experiments with applications to engineering and science.* Wiley, 1989.

Student. The probable error of a mean. *Biometrika*, 6:1–25, 1908.

Diane Tang, Ashish Agarwal, Deirdre O'Brien, and Mike Meyer. Overlapping experiment infrastructure: More, better, faster experimentation (presentation). 2010a. URL `http://research.google.com/archive/papers/Overlapping_Experiment_Infrastructure_More_Be.pdf`.

Diane Tang, Ashish Agarwal, Deirdre O'Brien, and Mike Meyer. Overlapping experiment infrastructure: More, better, faster experimentation. *Proceedings of the 16th Conference on Knowledge Discovery and Data Mining*, 2010b.

Anastasios Tsiatis. *Semiparametric Theory and Missing Data.* Springer-Verlag, 2006.

Anastasios A. Tsiatis, Marie Davidian, Min Zhang, and Xiaomin Lu. Covariate adjustment for two-sample treatment comparisons in randomized clinical trials: A principled yet flexible approach. *Statistics in Medicine*, 27, 2008.

Larry Wasserman. *All of Statistics: A Concise Course in Statistical Inference.* Springer, 2003.

Wikipedia. A/b testing. `http://en.wikipedia.org/wiki/A/B_testing`.

Li Yang and Anastasios A. Tsiatis. Efficiency study of estimators for a treatment effect in a pretest-posttest trial. *The American Statistician*, 55, 2001.

APPENDIX

A. CONTROL VARIATES AS AN EXTENSION OF STRATIFICATION

Here we show that when the covariates are categorical, stratification and control variates produce identical results.

For clarity and simplicity, we assume X is binary with values 1 and 0. Let $w = \mathbb{E}(X)$. The two estimates are

$$\begin{aligned}\widehat{Y}_{strat} &= w\overline{Y}_1 + (1-w)\overline{Y}_0,\\ \widehat{Y}_{cv} &= \overline{Y} - \hat{\theta}\overline{X} + \hat{\theta}w,\end{aligned}$$

where $\overline{Y}_1$ denotes the average of Y in the $\{X = 1\}$ stratum and $\hat{\theta} = \widehat{\text{cov}}(Y, X)/\widehat{\text{var}}(X) = \overline{Y}_1 - \overline{Y}_0$. Plugging in the expression for $\hat{\theta}$, we have

$$\begin{aligned}\widehat{Y}_{cv} &= \overline{Y} - (\overline{Y}_1 - \overline{Y}_0)\overline{X} + (\overline{Y}_1 - \overline{Y}_0)w\\ &= (1-\overline{X})\overline{Y}_0 + \overline{Y}_0\overline{X} + (\overline{Y}_1 - \overline{Y}_0)w\\ &= w\overline{Y}_1 + (1-w)\overline{Y}_0 = \widehat{Y}_{strat},\end{aligned}$$

where the second equality follows from the fact that $\overline{Y} = \overline{X}\overline{Y}_1 + (1-\overline{X})\overline{Y}_0$.

To prove for the case with $K > 2$, we construct $K-1$ indicator variables as control variates. With the observation that the coefficients $\hat{\theta}_k = \overline{Y}_k - \overline{Y}_0$, the proof follows the same steps as the binary case outlined above.

B. GENERALIZATION TO OTHER ANALYSIS UNIT

As we mentioned in Section 4, to achieve variance reduction for non-user level metrics, we need to incorporate delta method. The formulation we lay out in Section 3 makes it easy to achieve this, as we will see below.

We use CTR as an example and derive for the control variates formulation since it's more general.

Let n be the number of users (non-random). Denote $Y_{i,j}$ the number of clicks on user i's jth page-view during the experiment and $X_{i,k}$ the number of clicks on user i's kth page-view during the pre-experiment period. Let N_i and M_i be the numbers of page-views from user i during the experiment and pre-experiment respectively. The estimate for CTR in Eq. (3) using $X_{i,j}$ as the control variate becomes

$$\begin{aligned}\widehat{Y}_{cv} &= \frac{\sum_{i,j} Y_{i,j}}{\sum_{i,j} 1} - \theta\frac{\sum_{i,k} X_{i,k}}{\sum_{i,k} 1} + \theta\mathbb{E}(X_{i,k})\\ &= \frac{\sum_i Y_{i,+}}{\sum_i N_i} - \theta\frac{\sum_i X_{i,+}}{\sum_i M_i} + \theta\mathbb{E}(X_{i,j}),\end{aligned}$$

where $Y_{i,+} = \sum_j Y_{i,j}$ is the total number of clicks from user i. Similar notation applies to $X_{i,+}$.

Following the same derivation as in Section 3.2.1, we know $\text{var}(\widehat{Y}_{cv})$ is minimized at

$$\begin{aligned}\theta &= \text{cov}\left(\frac{\sum_i Y_{i,+}}{\sum_i N_i}, \frac{\sum_i X_{i,+}}{\sum_i M_i}\right)/\text{var}\left(\frac{\sum_i X_{i,+}}{\sum_i M_i}\right)\\ &\doteq \text{cov}\left(\frac{\overline{Y}}{\mu_N} - \frac{\mu_Y\overline{N}}{\mu_N^2} - \frac{\mu_Y}{\mu_N}, \frac{\overline{X}}{\mu_M} - \frac{\mu_X\overline{M}}{\mu_M^2} - \frac{\mu_X}{\mu_M}\right)\\ &\quad /\text{var}\left(\frac{\overline{X}}{\mu_M} - \frac{\mu_X\overline{M}}{\mu_M^2} - \frac{\mu_X}{\mu_M}\right)\\ &= \text{cov}\left(\frac{\overline{Y}}{\mu_N} - \frac{\mu_Y\overline{N}}{\mu_N^2}, \frac{\overline{X}}{\mu_M} - \frac{\mu_X\overline{M}}{\mu_M^2}\right)/\text{var}\left(\frac{\overline{X}}{\mu_M} - \frac{\mu_X\overline{M}}{\mu_M^2}\right)\end{aligned} \qquad (8)$$

where the second equality follows from using Taylor expansion to linearize the ratios and $\overline{Y} = \frac{1}{n}\sum_i Y_{i,+}$ with $\mu_Y = \mathbb{E}(\overline{Y})$ (similarly for μ_X, μ_N and μ_M).

Because the user is the randomization unit and user level observations are i.i.d., we have

$$\sqrt{n}\,(\overline{Y}, \overline{N}, \overline{X}, \overline{M}) \Rightarrow N(\mu, \Sigma),$$

following a multivariate normal distribution with mean vector μ and covariance matrix Σ easily estimated from the i.i.d. samples.

It is now straight forward to estimate θ in Eq. 8 using

$$\theta = (\beta_1^T \Sigma \beta_2)/(\beta_2^T \Sigma \beta_2),$$

where $\beta_1 = (1/\mu_N, -\mu_Y/\mu_N^2, 0, 0)^T$ and $\beta_2 = (0, 0, 1/\mu_M, -\mu_X/\mu_M^2)^T$ are the coefficients in Eq. 8.

Note that in the example above, both the metric of interest (CTR) and the covariate metric are at page-view level. We can easily see that the derivation works generally for various combinations. The metric can be at user level while the covariate can be at page-view level, etc. This opens door to a whole new class of covariates which are based on features specific to a page not to a user. Finally, it is easy to see that the case with multiple control variates follow similarly.

Playing by the Rules: Mining Query Associations to Predict Search Performance

Youngho Kim[1*], Ahmed Hassan[2], Ryen W. White[2], Yi-Min Wang[2]
[1] 140 Governors Drive, University of Massachusetts, Amherst, MA 01003, USA
[2] One Microsoft Way, Microsoft Research, Redmond, WA 98052, USA
yhkim@cs.umass.edu, {hassanam,ryenw,ymwang}@microsoft.com

ABSTRACT

Understanding the characteristics of queries where a search engine is failing is important for improving engine performance. Previous work largely relies on user-interaction features (e.g., clickthrough statistics) to identify such underperforming queries. However, relying on interaction behavior means that searchers need to become dissatisfied and need to exhibit that in their search behavior, by which point it may be too late to help them. In this paper, we propose a method to generate underperforming query identification rules instantly using topical and lexical attributes. The method first generates query attributes using sources such as topics, concepts (entities), and keywords in queries. Then, association rules are learned by exploiting the FP-growth algorithm and decision trees using underperforming query examples. We develop a query classification model capable of accurately estimating dissatisfaction using the generated rules, and demonstrate significant performance gains over state-of-the-art query performance prediction models.

Categories and Subject Descriptors

H.3.3 [**Information Search and Retrieval**]: Search Process

General Terms

Algorithms, Experimentation

Keywords

Underperforming query analysis; User dissatisfaction.

1. INTRODUCTION

Automatic detection of underperforming queries (where search engines are failing and users are dissatisfied with their search results) has been extensively studied [1][13][18][23]. In Web-search environments large volumes of query logs are readily attainable. This makes it affordable to collect many training examples that can be used to improve classification performance.

The ability to identify underperforming queries is especially important to Web search engines. Since those systems need to cover a broad range of diverse queries and since ranking algorithms are typically trained using a single sampled data set, there will be queries on which the ranking algorithms cannot execute effectively.

Previous work on predicting underperforming queries has primarily targeted user interactions (e.g., clickthrough statistics) [18][23] and combined features from user behaviors in query logs and physical sensors [13]. Although previous systems are quite successful, they are less effective from the search engine perspective. The reason is those dissatisfaction signals are only available *a posteriori* (e.g., once search is abandoned). This means that search engines rarely have the opportunity to interfere and remedy the user dissatisfied experience. Conversely, query performance predictors [10][24], for example, are more useful for that purpose because those predictors do not require interaction behavior signals and can help recognize dissatisfaction before the search session ends.

Table 1: Sample rule and example queries. Label indicates if query leads to satisfaction (SAT) or dissatisfaction (DSAT).

Association Rule		
{Movie, Art, "Robocop remake"} ⟹ {DSAT}		
No.	**Query**	**Label**
1	Robocop remake poster	DSAT
2	pics from Robocop remake	DSAT

In this paper, we propose a method for generating underperforming query identification rules using topical and lexical attributes of queries (e.g., topic of interest, important entities (concepts) in queries). We assume that there are frequent patterns among the features of underperforming queries and the association of those frequent features with dissatisfaction is helpful for identifying user queries likely to be associated with future dissatisfaction. Table 1 shows a sample association rule and examples of matching queries. For example, the rule {Movie, Art, "Robocop remake"} ⇒ {DSAT} consists of an antecedent with a set of binary attributes: Movie, Art, and "Robocop remake" and a consequent which is in our case a query satisfaction label: DSAT. Note that each query label is obtained using a DSAT prediction model [21], which is described briefly later. Since those attributes can be identified from only query, search systems can be informed of DSAT likelihood to the queries implied by the antecedent (LHS) of this rule promptly. Moreover, we can identify that current search systems cannot handle particular classes of queries successfully, which is valuable for improving the search experience.

In our system, given DSAT and SAT query examples, we perform two sub-tasks: (1) Attribute Generation, and (2) Association Rule Mining. In the first task, we define various attributes which can effectively characterize diverse Web queries. For example, categories in the Open Directory Project (ODP, dmoz.org) (e.g., Art) can be used as a binary attribute. Wikipedia categories and named entity categories (e.g., "Robocop"→ Movie) are also useful. Besides, we consider lexical attributes (e.g., "Robocop remake") because many DSAT queries frequently share some keywords. In addition to these topical attributes, we adopt behavior attributes that can characterize user-search actions (e.g., number of issued queries, and frequency

* This work was conducted while interning at Microsoft Research

WSDM'13, February 4–8, 2013, Rome, Italy.

of viewing search result pages). We extract distinct distributions of defined search actions, and label similar distributions for an identical category (i.e., a category label indicates a behavior attribute) by employing a spectral hashing algorithm [32]. From this, we can identify how behavior attributes (typically used in previous work) are combined with our topic attributes.

Using those attributes, we mine association rules to identify DSAT queries. Among many association rule learning techniques (e.g., [2][3]), we selected the FP-growth algorithm [20] because our system needs to handle a large amount of Web queries and FP-growth can effectively work on such large datasets [20]. In mining, we apply the FP-growth algorithm to both DSAT and SAT queries using categorical attributes (e.g., ODP categories), and identify what subsets of the attributes (item-sets) frequently appear in DSAT queries. In other words, the identified item-sets (antecedent) imply DSAT queries (i.e., the consequent of the rule is {DSAT}). After generating categorical rules, we augment the antecedent of the rules with lexical attributes. Since the number of lexical attributes (i.e., keywords) extracted from all queries is prohibitively large, we adopt a two-tiered approach where we first extract categorical rules and then mine lexical rules using queries to which certain categorical rules apply.

We show the effectiveness of our rule mining system by verifying that the system is capable of generating effective DSAT segments. We also demonstrate the effectiveness of the rules by using them as features for building a DSAT prediction system and show that it achieves superior performance when compared to state-of-the-art query performance prediction baselines [10][17][25].

The remainder of this paper is structured as follows. Section 2 describes relevant related work in the areas of search satisfaction, search quality analysis, and query performance. Section 3 defines our problem and Section 4 describes the main approach. We present experimental results in Section 5 and conclude in Section 6.

2. RELATED WORK

Relevant research in a number of areas is presented: (1) satisfaction, (2) search quality, and (3) query performance prediction.

2.1 Search Satisfaction

There has been significant prior work on deriving signals related to search satisfaction and success from online behavior. Methods for doing this typically correlate users' search behavior with their in-situ self-reporting [16] or judgments of search success provided by expert judges [18][22]. Early investigations by Fox et al. [16] correlated self-reported measures of search satisfaction with interaction signals gathered implicitly from search behavior, such as search-result clicks and dwell time for clicks. They deployed an instrumented browser and showed a relationship between explicit measures of search satisfaction and implicit measures derived from search behavior. In particular, they found that short dwell times and clicks on many results for a query were both indicators of search dissatisfaction. Ageev et al. [1] propose a formalization of different types of success for informational search via a scalable game-like infrastructure for crowdsourcing search behavior studies. They show that their model can predict search success effectively on their data and on a separate set of logs comprising search engine sessions. Hassan et al. [23] developed models of user behavior to accurately estimate search success on a session level, independent of the relevance of documents retrieved by the search engine. In recent follow-up work, Hassan [21] proposed a semi-supervised approach for search satisfaction modeling via both labeled and unlabeled data.

2.2 Search Quality Analysis

Beyond studying search session satisfaction in isolation, others have investigated how the quality of search results can affect search behavior. Huffman and Hochster [26] discovered a fairly strong correlation with search session satisfaction using a linear model encompassing the relevance of the first three results returned for the first query in a search task, whether the information need was navigational, and the number of events in the session. Aula et al. [6] investigated the behavioral signals that are suggestive of a user struggling in a search task. They showed in a laboratory study and in a larger-scale remote study that when searchers have difficulty in finding relevant information, they formulate more diverse queries, they are more likely to use advanced operators (e.g., '+', '–', 'OR'), and they spend a longer time on the search result page as compared to the successful tasks. Feild et al. [13] studied the affective impact of searching and developed methods to predict search frustration from behavioral and physiological signals. They gave users difficult information seeking tasks and estimated their degree of frustration via query logs and physical sensors. One behavior that can be associated with dissatisfaction is search engine switching: the voluntary transition between different engines. Guo et al. [18] characterized the reasons that searchers switch via a browser plugin that captured an explanation at switch time. They showed that one of the primary reasons that people switched was dissatisfaction with the search results on the pre-switch engine.

2.3 Query Performance

Search engine performance for a particular query is typically measured using relevance metrics such as precision and recall. Al-Maskari et al. [4] found a reasonable correlation between many information retrieval metrics and satisfaction with result rankings. Beyond performance measurement, research on *predicting* query performance has been conducted to understand differences in the quality of search results provided by search systems for different queries. Such predictions do not require relevance judgments (at least not when the models are being applied, but perhaps during a separate training phase) and can be used to determine when to use additional computational resources or use alternative methods (e.g., specialized ranking algorithms or different interface support) to improve results for difficult queries. While it has been shown that different query representations [8] or retrieval models [9] improve search performance, it is more challenging to accurately predict which methods to use for a particular query.

Methods using Jensen-Shannon divergence [8], query clarity [10], and weighted information gain [35] have been developed to predict the retrieval performance on a query (e.g., as measured via precision) post retrieval. Rather than using post-retrieval query-document relevance scores, which can take time to compute, He and Ounis [24] proposed the use of pre-retrieval properties that can be generated prior to the retrieval process (e.g., query length, query scope). Pre-retrieval predictors are advantageous because they can be calculated during indexing, rather than waiting for the query to be received, making them more efficient. Zhao et al. [33] propose pre-retrieval predictors based on the similarity between a query and the underlying collection and the variability with which query terms occur in documents. Leskovec et al. [28] used graphical properties of the link structure of the result set to predict the quality of the set and the likelihood of subsequent query reformulation. Some research has also been conducted on predicting query performance using searcher interaction behavior. Carterette and Jones [9] used click-through behavior to evaluate the quality of search advertising results, but they did not study other user interaction features, and their focus was on search advertising not general Web search. Guo et al. [17] used behavioral features, including engine switches, to predict query performance. Their method involved the use of interaction logs for a large number of their most important prediction features. However, the reliance on log data limits the generalizability of the model, meaning that it can only be applied in commercial search engines and evaluating the model outside of those settings is potentially problematic.

Our work extends the research presented in this section in a number of ways. First, rather than simply modeling or identifying the attributes of search satisfaction, we use apply DSAT modeling to identify queries where the search engine may be underperforming. Second, the method that we propose is not dependent on interaction behavior meaning that our approach can help before users have to experience dissatisfaction with the engine. Also, by not relying on interaction behavior makes our results more reproducible by academic researchers trying make advances in query performance prediction. Third, we demonstrate through a large-scale evaluation with search queries drawn from search logs that our approach outperforms several baselines that draw on query properties, search interaction, and their combination.

3. PROBLEM FORMULATION

In this section, we formulate the task of mining DSAT association rules and predicting query performance. We start by defining terms that we will use throughout the paper.

Definition 1 (Search Session) A *search session* is a sequence of user actions that begin with a query, includes subsequent queries, URL visits, click information, and ends with a period of inactivity. We assume that a session ends if the user was idle on a page for over 30 minutes, typically used in previous work, e.g., [12].

Definition 2 (Search Goal) A *search goal* is a single information need that may result in one or more queries. Every search session could be segmented into one or more search goals. We adopt the search goal definition and the goal extraction method from [27]. Using the prediction model in [21], we label each goal to either of {DSAT, SAT} and use a search goal as an instance in mining. We assume that each instance (i.e., search goal) is represented by the first query. If we use the subsequent queries of an instance, we explicitly specify "subsequent" queries.

Definition 3 (Attribute): An *attribute* is a binary property of a query instance that describes a specific characteristic of that instance. For example, the attribute "Shopping" indicates that the query is topically related to retail.

In this work, we present solutions to the following problems:

Problem 1 (Attribute Generation): *Attribute generation* is the process of defining and generating a set of attributes to represent query instances. Given a query instance, our objective is to generate effective attributes and associate (binary) values to them. The attributes should describe different aspects of the query instance and they should be dynamic in the sense that they may be easily extendible and need minimal human intervention to define.

Problem 2 (DSAT Association Rule Mining): *DSAT association rule mining* is the process of discovering frequent patterns (subsets) of generated attributes (from Problem 1) to identify DSAT queries. Given attributes and labeled queries, we generate rules that imply DSAT. The task is formally defined as follows.

Let $A = \{a_1, a_2, ..., a_n\}$ be a set of n binary attributes and $Q = \{q_1, q_2, ..., q_m\}$ be a set of (query) instances where each instance is labeled as DSAT or SAT. Based on A, each instance can be represented by a vector of binary attributes, e.g., $q_i = \{a_1 = 1, a_2 = 0, ..., a_n = 1\}$. Then, an association rule can be formulated as $\{a_i, a_j, ...\} \Rightarrow \{\text{DSAT}\}$ where a_i and a_j in LHS are the frequent attributes of DSAT instances, and as an output, we generate multiple association rules. Since we are interested in rules whose consequent (RHS) is {DSAT}, we simply represent every rule by only its antecedent (LHS). The instances represented by a rule indicate queries implied by the antecedent of the rule. Based on mined rules, DSAT segments are formed by the queries matched to the rules.

Problem 3 (DSAT Prediction): *DSAT Prediction* is the process of predicting, at query time, whether a query will be satisfied or not. In solving this, we use the association rules defined in Problem 2.

4. MINING UNDERPERFORMING QUERY ASSOCIATIONS

We now present our methodology for generating underperforming (DSAT) query identification rules. We first describe how useful attributes are defined for rule generation, and then explain how to generate DSAT identification rules using the defined attributes.

4.1 Attribute Generation

Generally, many attributes can be used to describe query impressions including query topic, query entities, and search behavior. However, most behavior-related features (e.g., search state [1], dwelling time [23]) have been examined in previous studies, and behavior information is typically available only after the user has abandoned searches. Instead, we attempt to devise topical and lexical attributes (which can be mainly identified from query texts) and the values for these attributes are instantly computed from current queries. For this, we exploit the categories in ODP, Named Entity Recognition (NER) [30], and Wikipedia (wikipedia.org). In addition, we also generate behavior attributes from distributions of historic user search actions. Thus, given a query instance, we generate attributes described as follows.

4.1.1 ODP Attributes

Open Directory Project (ODP, dmoz.org) is a hierarchical ontology for Web pages and lists similar topic pages in the same category including smaller categories. We use each ODP category as a binary attribute, and the ODP classifier, proposed in [7], can classify queries into 219 categories from the top two levels of the ODP hierarchy (see [7] for more details, including results of a performance evaluation). Specifically, for each query instance, the classifier outputs top-5 probable categories, and among them we select the categories whose probabilities are greater than 0.5 (empirically set) as attributes. In our experiments, we allow more than one category to describe every query instance.

4.1.2 Named Entity Attributes

Named Entity Recognition (NER) is the process of identifying entities (e.g., $People$, $Locations$, $Organizations$, etc.) from text. NER systems are oftentimes domain dependent and need large amounts of labeled data for training. This makes them less suitable for Web search queries that are short in nature and not usually represented by well-formed sentences. For our purpose we need a named entity tagger that can be easily adapted to new classes, works well on short and ill-formed text, and uses available knowledge sources instead of domain-dependent human labeled training data.

We rely on Wikipedia and n-gram Language Models (LMs) to tag named entities in queries [30]. Specifically, given a sequence of words, salient entities in a domain-specific LM are identified. A

User	Q	SERP	SR	SR_long	Ad
A	4	1	1	0	0
B	2	4	2	2	0

Figure 1: Sample distributions of search action frequencies. Q, SERP, SR, SR_long, and Ad indicate a query submission, search result page, search result click, long dwell (> 30s) result click, and ad click, respectively.

domain-specific LM is generated by a domain corpus (e.g., "Movies" LM contains n-gram statistics of a movie corpus). Salient domain entities are identified by measuring statistical differences between the domain model (foreground) and general LM (background). For each word, if a word belongs to the background, or the outside-tag, the word should be generated using the background LM. On the other hand, if the word belongs to the foreground, begin-tag, or inside-tag, the word should be generated using the foreground LM that named entities are built from. Weak unsupervised signals from each domain corpus (e.g., Wikipedia titles and click counts) are used to estimate parameters in the recognition model. This approach achieves 0.51 precision and 0.48 recall [30], when applied to short and not necessarily grammatical dataset with 1,300 queries, compared to 0.35 precision and 0.43 recall from a Conditional Random Fields system [15] .

One motivation to use this NER tagger is that topics in Web queries are diverse and recognizing only basic entities (i.e., Person, Location, and Organization) is less useful for identifying effective attributes. Thus, to cover various web topics, we train the classifier using domain language models corresponding to the following domains (*Person, Location, Organization, Food, Restaurant, Local review, Wikipedia, Movie,* and *Game*). We use each domain (category) as a binary attribute, and assume that a query can contain multiple attributes if the query contains entities from multiple domains. As an example, "Caesar salad recipe in TGI Friday's" can contain the attributes $\{Food, Restaurant\}$ because "Caesar salad" is a $Food$ entity and "TGI Friday's" is a $Restaurant$ entity.

4.1.3 Wikipedia Attributes

Wikipedia is an online encyclopedia which contains four million articles (entities). We use Wikipedia entities to generate a set of descriptive and diverse attributes. Specifically, we first crawl about one million Wikipedia articles, and extract Wikipedia entities from query texts as described in the previous subsection. Then, for each extracted entity, we identify the most relevant Wikipedia article by using a surface-level exact matching. (Note that other types of matching (e.g., semantic-level) can be used further if it can perform reasonably well). Once Wikipedia articles are matched to the query entities, we extract Wikipedia topic-categories from each article. Each Wikipedia article generally contains one or more topic-categories, e.g., the article of "Ford Mustang" includes Ford Vehicle, Coupe, etc. As a result, we can link a query instance to the categories via identified entities from the query texts, and use those categories as attributes. In experiments, each query instance contains 0.9 entities on average, and 4,482 Wikipedia topic-categories are extracted and used as attributes.

4.1.4 Behavior Attributes

Here we present a method to generate behavior attributes. Since previous work proves that using behavior information is effective to predict query performance [17], we devise the attributes which recognize the characteristics of the general search behavior of users. We assume that dissatisfied users act differently in searches compared to satisfied users. For example, we observed that some dissatisfied users issue many queries, but spend less time on examining search results. To capture such behavior characteristics, we generate a distribution of search action frequencies from each query instance. Specifically, we define seven distinct search actions and identify frequent distributions that occur more than 10 times (i.e., we ignore extremely rare patterns). Figure 1 shows some examples of the distributions. Then, we group similar distributions into the same cluster (attribute) by using spectral hashing [32], which can develop a hashing function that maps similar vectors into the same bucket (i.e., hash code). Given a set of behavior distributions, we consider a distribution as an input vector and run the spectral hashing algorithm [32] with k-bits (the bit length of a hashing code). After a hash function is obtained, we use a mapped hash code as a binary attribute. In experiments, we hash 3,069 distinct distributions into 2-bit codes (i.e., four different hash values are mapped), and accordingly four behavior attributes are generated.

Table 2: Mean frequencies of search actions. Due to the space limit, the statistics of less significant actions (e.g., Ad) are omitted. In each column, a superscript indicates a significant difference at $p < 0.01$ using the Wilcoxon rank-sum test, e.g., ^{C13} denotes a significant difference from the code of 1 and 3.

Code	Q	SERP	SR	SR_long
0	5.01^{C13}	0.18	0.38	0.56
1	1.60	0.53	0.56	0.61
2	4.82^{C13}	1.18^{C01}	1.09^{C01}	1.55^{C01}
3	1.74	1.96^{C01}	1.26^{C01}	1.35^{C01}

One motivation for using spectral hashing is that a hashing-based algorithm is much faster than clustering algorithms, such as k-Nearest Neighbor, in learning patterns. Moreover, in pilot experiments, a simple clustering method failed to find a reasonable number of clusters (attributes); only a single cluster was identified. To understand the effectiveness of using the spectral hashing, we conduct pilot experiments using about 140,000 session instances randomly sampled from our dataset. From that data, we extract 237 distinct distributions of search action frequencies and generate 4-bit hash codes. Then, as shown in Table 2, we measure the mean frequency of each action among the instances mapped to each code (i.e., 0, 1, 2, and 3). First, the instances mapped to 0 and 2 include significantly more query submission (Q) while the instances belonging to 1 and 3 have fewer query submissions. Second, regarding search result actions (i.e., SERP, SR, and SR_long), the users in 2 and 3 spend more times on SERP and SR than the users in 0 and 1. To prove these, we perform a statistical significance test on each of those actions (see Table 2). In summary, we can characterize the users (instances) in each code; 0 indicates more query submission and short search result examination, 1 denotes less query submission and short search result examination (generally most DSAT users belong to this category), 2 indicates more query submission and long search result examination, and 3 indicates relatively less query submission and long search result examination (i.e., spend more time on a few search results).

4.2 DSAT Association Rule Mining

In this section, we describe our method for finding DSAT association rules using FP-growth algorithm and decision trees. Specifically, we first use the FP-growth algorithm with the "categorical" attributes (i.e., ODP, NER, Wikipedia, and Behavior) to identify categorical rules (e.g., {Movie, Art}). After this, we apply Decision Tree learning using "lexical" attributes that include n-gram keywords from the queries identified by the categorical rules, and extract lexical rules (e.g., {Movie, Art, "Robocop remake"}). We provide the details of each method in the remainder of this section.

a_1	...	...	...	a_n	*DSAT*	*SAT*
True	...	...	...	False	True	False
False	...	...	...	True	False	True
True	...	...	...	False	False	True
...	...	...	...	...	...	...

ODP NER WIKI BH

Figure 2: Input data set for FP-growth algorithm.

4.2.1 Categorical Rule Mining

Given a set of attributes, we identify subsets of attributes (item-sets) to identify DSAT instances. For this, we can utilize several well-known approaches to find frequent patterns in transactional or relational data sets that are described in the data-mining literature. A typical example of this approach is the market basket analysis problem [2]. Using a similar formulation, we formally define the DSAT association rule mining problem as follows: Let $A = \{a_1, a_2, \ldots, a_n\}$ be a set of n binary attributes containing ODP, NER, Wikipedia (WIKI), and Behavior (BH) attributes, and $Q = \{q_1, q_2, \ldots, q_m\}$ be a set of instances and each instance is labeled as DSAT or SAT. We define a new attribute set, $A' = \{a_1, a_2, \ldots, a_n\} \cup \{\text{DSAT}, \text{SAT}\}$ where the labels are included as attributes. Figure 2 illustrate an input data set, $\{I \times A'\}$. Then, a "DSAT" association rule is defined as an implication of the form $\text{X} \Rightarrow \text{Y}$ where $\text{X} \subseteq A$, $\text{Y} = \{\text{DSAT}\}$ and $\text{X} \cap \text{Y} = \emptyset$.

Among many algorithms to solve this problem (e.g., [3]), we chose to use the FP-growth algorithm [20] because it is more efficient than generate-and-test algorithms given that it adopts a divide-and-conquer strategy. The proposed approach should be able to handle millions of instances and hence efficient rule mining is necessary. Briefly, the algorithm consists of two main steps. First, it builds the FP-tree which efficiently represents information about item-set (subset of attributes) association, and in the next step, frequent patterns are mined from the FP-tree. To build the tree, the whole data set is scanned twice; in the first scan, the attributes are sorted in descending order by their frequencies, and the tree is constructed by spanning attribute nodes from more frequent attributes to less frequent ones, scanning each row in the data (see [20] for details).

Before running the algorithm, to reduce the computational complexity and obtain more effective rules, we define 3 constraints:

1) The number of attributes from a single group may not exceed a threshold l.
2) Minimum support-level needs to be reasonably small.
3) Minimum confidence-level is more than or equal to the portion of DSAT instances to the whole data set.

In our data set, originally there are four different attribute groups (i.e., ODP, NER, WIKI, BH), and the first constraint limits a mining path (from the root to a leaf node in the FP-tree) to have maximally $4l$ different attributes from those groups. In other words, a mined rule resembles any combination of {[ODP], [NER], [WIKI], [BH]} where each attribute group (bracket) contains at most l attributes from the corresponding group. Thus, we impose a constraint on the maximum depth of the tree, which can reduce the time-complexity in practice. Since the algorithm for mining the FP-tree structure is a recursive procedure during which many sub FP-trees are created, too long paths (e.g., containing more than 100 nodes (attributes)) are problematic and defining an effective length is complicated. The second and the third constraints allows more effective rules to be generated. The support (S) of an item-set (X) is defined as the proportion of instances in the data set which contain X, and the minimum support level denotes the minimum number of

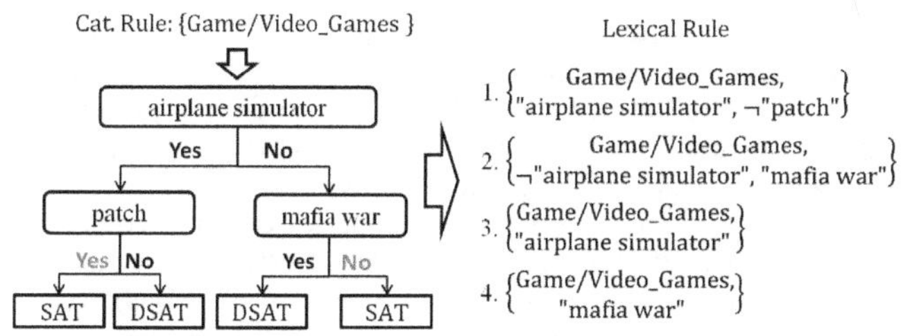

Figure 3: Decision tree-based lexical rule generation.

instances which support a generated rule. If the rule can cover many queries (instances), it may contain more SAT queries and is ineffective. Thus, targeting relatively small number of instances is more helpful to obtain effective rules, and in experiments, we have about one million instances and we set S to 20.

Based on S, the confidence (C) of a rule is defined as $C(\text{X} \Rightarrow \text{Y}) = S(\text{X} \cup \text{Y})/S(\text{X})$, an estimation of probability $\text{p}(\text{Y}|\text{X})$. By the third constraint, we can recognize effective rules which can cover relatively more DSAT queries comparing to the general proportion of DSAT instances to the whole dataset, $\text{p}(\text{DSAT}|\text{X}) \geq \text{p}(\text{DSAT})$. However, a confidence level that is too high can also mean that very few rules are extracted because generally $\text{p}(\text{DSAT})$ is low, which is also ineffective.

Next, we run the FP-growth algorithm on the augmented data set with two parameters, S and C. We use an improved-version of FP-growth implemented by [11], which can reorder and prune the input data so that more common attributes appear first and unsupported 1-item-sets are discarded. Among the extracted rules, we only select the ones whose consequent (RHS) is DSAT (i.e., Y = {DSAT}). As a result of this step, we generate multiple categorical rules that contain effective attributes for identifying DSAT queries.

4.2.2 Lexical Rule Mining

In this section, we provide the details of generating lexical rules that use DSAT query keywords as lexical attributes.

One motivation for adopting lexical rules is to identify more specific information about DSAT queries. Although categorical attributes provide general topic information of DSAT queries (e.g., search engines perform worse with queries related to the categorical attributes, Ford Vehicle and Shopping/Vehicle), identifying detailed lexical information (e.g., among Ford Vehicle and Shopping/Vehicles queries, the queries containing "lease" are not properly handled) would be much more helpful for analysis purposes. Besides, more specific rules are more likely to have higher confidence (i.e., $\text{p}(\text{DSAT}|\text{X})$) than general rules because typically $\text{p}(\text{DSAT})$ is much lower than $\text{p}(\text{SAT})$.

We generate a lexical rule by combining categorical rules with discriminative keywords in *DSAT* queries. The formal definition is given as: $\text{X} \cup \text{Z} \Rightarrow \text{Y}$ where $\text{X} \subseteq A$, $\text{Z} \subseteq K$, $\text{Y} = \{\text{DSAT}\}$, $(\text{X} \cup \text{Z}) \cap \text{Y} = \emptyset$, A is the attribute set (Section 4.1), and K is the set of keywords extracted from the DSAT queries represented by X. Since effective categorical rules (i.e., $\text{X} \Rightarrow \text{Y}$) are already extracted, we need to identify effective DSAT keywords (i.e., Z).

To solve this problem, we propose a decision tree learning-based method which extracts effective lexical attributes from DSAT query texts. If we could train a decision tree where a node corresponds to a term appearing in DSAT queries (instances) in order to determine whether a query is DSAT, a decision rule which represents DSAT examples includes a set of discriminative terms (features). In addition, to combine those key terms with categorical rules, for each categorical rule, we identify the set of queries implied by the categorical rule, and generate a decision tree using the instance set. Then, extracted keywords are effective when combined with the categorical rule. Figure 3 depicts how lexical rules are generated from a categorical rule. Since decision trees can represent negation, we originally extract the first and second lexical rules containing negated lexical attributes (e.g., ¬"patch"). However, to generalize these rules (i.e., expanding their coverage in real situations), we can ignore negation and the third and fourth rules can be formulated. Figure 4 describes the algorithm.

For the lexical rule generation, we can alternatively consider pattern mining approaches (e.g., FP-growth algorithm [20] used in Section 4.2.1) using keywords as attributes. However, in comparison with the FP-growth algorithm, decision tree learning has the following advantage: decision tree rules can imply negation whereas FP-growth algorithm mines only association rules that do not imply negation. In some circumstances, negation is important because some attributes rarely appear in DSAT queries but frequently appear in SAT queries. For example, let us consider the first lexical rule in Figure 3. This rule indicates that among the queries represented by {Game/Video_Games, "airplane simulator"}, the queries not related to "patch" are DSAT (otherwise the queries are SAT), i.e., not every query in {Game/Video_Games, "airplane simulator"} is DSAT. Moreover, if we ignore negation (e.g., the third and fourth rules in Figure 3), the mining results are almost identical to the ones identified by the FP-growth algorithm (ideally, checking the confidence of each decision tree rule can be necessary, but in our experiments, every decision rule ignoring negation had $p(\text{DSAT}|\text{X}) \geq p(\text{DSAT})$) because the FP-growth algorithm uses the confidence (the proportion of DSAT to the instances represented by the rule) to identify DSAT association rules and similarly decision-tree learning also considers the entropy of each attribute (the proportion of DSAT to the examples that contain selected attributes) in generating DSAT decision rules. In our experiments, we discovered that the rules including negation can provide more specific information. We describe some examples in Section 5.3. We use WEKA implementation of C4.5 algorithm [19] to train decision trees, query texts are stemmed by WordNet [14], and stop-words are removed.

4.3 DSAT Query Prediction Model

In this section, we describe a DSAT query prediction model that can classify a given query into DSAT or SAT. Since we generated categorical and lexical rules to be effective to identify DSAT queries (Section 4.2) we use these rules as features, and train the model using labeled examples. The formal definition is given as follows.

Suppose that $R = \{r_1, r_2, \dots, r_n\}$ is a set of n rules, $Q = \{q_1, q_2, \dots, q_m\}$ is a set of m query examples, and the label of each example $L(q_i)$ is known. For training, a feature vector of each q_i is created as $x_{q_i} = \{r_1(q_i), r_2(q_i), \dots, r_n(q_i)\}$ where $r_j(q_i)$ is a binary value; if q_i is matched to r_j then 1; otherwise, 0. Then, a set of training examples is given as $\text{X} = \{\langle x_{q_i}, L(q_i)\rangle\}_{i=1}^{m}$, and a classification function $f\colon \text{X} \mapsto \{1,0\}$ maps a feature vector associated with a query to a binary label where 1 and 0 indicate DSAT and SAT, respectively, and the model is learned to minimize a loss function defined by the disagreement between a mapped label and original label, $L(q_i)$ for every training example. For learning, we use Support Vector Machine and Logistic Regression (see Section 5.2).

ALGORITHM Lexical Rule Generation
INPUT:
- Set of labeled query instances, $Q = \{q_1, q_2, \dots, q_n\}$ where the label of q is $DSAT$ or SAT, i.e., $L(q) \in \{\text{DSAT}, \text{SAT}\}$
- Categorical rule, $C\colon \text{X} \Longrightarrow \{\text{DSAT}\}$ where X is a subset of categorical attributes (item-set)
- Boolean value, b, which indicates ignoring negation

OUTPUT: A set of lexical rules
PROCESS:
1) Initialize $R = \{\,\}$
2) Find the set of query instances implied by X, i.e., $Q' = \{q|\text{X}(q) = 1\}$ and $q \in Q$
3) If $Q' = \emptyset$ Then return $\emptyset$
4) Generate K which contains n-grams extracted from Q'
5) Train a binary decision tree, DT, which uses K as features and Q' as examples where $L(q)$ indicates a label of $q \in Q'$
6) For each $DSAT$ leaf node, l_{DSAT}
   a. Generate Z the set of nodes (features) in the path from the root to l_{DSAT} in DT
   b. If $b = 1$ Then exclude the node corresponding to negation from Z
   c. Append Z into R
7) End For
8) Return $C \times R$

Figure 2: Lexical rule generation algorithm.

5. EXPERIMENTS

In this section, we provide experimental results of our DSAT identification rule mining system. In Section 5.1, we analyze the generated rules in terms of topical cohesiveness, clickthrough rate, and DSAT correlation. Section 5.2 describes our query performance classification model that uses the mined rules to predict dissatisfaction of queries, and demonstrates its effectiveness.

5.1 Rule Analysis

5.1.1 Experimental Set-up

We obtained interaction logs (from June 2012) for 1.5 million search sessions from hundreds of thousands of consenting users using several commercial search engines through a widely-distributed Web browser toolbar. Log entries include a unique identifier for the user, a timestamp for each page view, and the URL of the Web page visited. Intranet and secure (https) URL and any personally identifiable information were removed from the logs prior to analysis.

Using the DSAT prediction model [21], we classify each instance into either of DSAT or SAT. To implement [21], we develop a semi-supervised model; we first build a supervised classifier using a small set of labeled DSAT and SAT query instances, and by this classifier, initial parameters are obtained; the membership of unlabeled data is calculated using an updated model whose parameters are re-estimated by the Expectation-Maximum algorithm. Then, we randomly split the data into two distinct equally-sized groups, non-overlapping in time: *mining* and *analysis*. We use the mining set to generate association rules (setting the support (S) to 20), and analyze rules using the analysis set (i.e., unseen data).

Table 3: Basic rule statistics. OUR includes both categorical and lexical rules. The percentile ratio indicates the reuse ratio of the generated rules in the analysis set.

Metric \ Method	TC (baseline)	OUR
# of rules generated from *mining set*	1,160	26,845
# of rules matched in *analysis set*	1,158 (*99.83%*)	5,861 (*21.83%*)
Percentage of the matched queries in the *analysis set*	0.7310	0.7520

In analysis, we use three different metrics defined as follows.

(**Cosine-Similarity**) Cosine-Similarity is measured to identify the topical similarity between the instances (queries) represented by each rule. We hypothesize that more topically cohesive segment (set of queries) would be obtained if the rule is effective. We describe each query by a vector of all unique terms in the whole data set and each dimension corresponds to the frequency of a term in the query. The similarity between two queries, q_i and q_j is given:

$$\text{similarity} = \frac{q_i \cdot q_j}{\|q_i\|\|q_j\|}$$

(**Clickthrough Rate**) Clickthrough Rate (CTR) indicates the fraction of times the query results in a click on the algorithmic results when it is issued. Given a query, CTR is computed by:

$$\text{CTR} = \frac{\text{\# of algorithmic clicks}}{\text{\# of impressions}}$$

CTR is calculated using a different and much bigger set of queries that does not overlap with our data set.

(**DSAT Correlation**) DSAT Correlation is a simple measure that estimates the correlation/dependence between a rule and dissatisfaction. Given a rule, $X \Longrightarrow \{DSAT\}$, the metric is defined as:

$$\text{DSAT Correlation} = \frac{p(X, DSAT)}{p(X)p(DSAT)} = \frac{p(DSAT|X)}{p(DSAT)}$$

$p(DSAT|X)$ is the confidence of X defined in Section 4.2.1, and $p(DSAT)$ is estimated by the proportion of DSAT instances in the data. If the value is exactly 1, X and dissatisfaction is independent, and if the value is greater than 1, X is positively correlated with dissatisfaction. Otherwise, X is negatively correlated with DSAT. Comparing with the confidence, this metric is more robust because the confidence can be misleading if the data are imbalanced, and generally much more SAT queries are recognized in query logs. In addition, we considered the confidence in rule generation.

(**Fixed Attribute Set Baseline**) Traditionally, some predefined query attributes (e.g., IsCommerce indicates the query is related "Commerce" topics) have been used to segment queries into classes. For this, text classifiers are trained using manually labeled data. We refer to those attributes as the Text Classification (TC) attributes. As a baseline, we generate association rules using these query attributes, and compare the rules generated by our system to the TC rules. In our method, we do not consider using the TC attributes because they need extensive human involvement in terms of selecting which classifiers to build and labeling training data. In addition to the need for extensive human involvement, using these attributes has two more downsides. First, they put a burden on the human building the system to decide which attributes to consider and hence which classifiers to build. Contrast this with the proposed approach where a huge number of attributes is automatically introduced using existing resources (e.g. Wikipedia). Second, these classifiers may be readily available to commercial search engines as private properties, but they are not publicly available which limits their usefulness to the research community. Instead, we use them as a baseline to validate our method which utilizes public resources. For generating TC rules, we use a set of 60 proprietary classifiers (e.g. Technology, Travel, etc.) and we apply the FP-growth algorithm to the same data set (*mining set*).

Table 4: Comparison against TC baseline. Bold indicates statistically significant difference at $p < 0.01$ from TC (using Wilcoxon rank-sum test).

Metric \ Method	TC	OUR
Avg. Cosine-Similarity	0.0133	**0.5296**
Avg. CTR	0.4509	0.4554
Avg. DSAT Correlation	1.9420	**4.0141**
Avg. # of queries	2122.44	**530.79**
Correlation Coefficient (CTR vs. DSAT Correlation)	−0.2718	−0.3204

5.1.2 Analysis Results

Table 3 shows basic statistics of rule generation using our system and the baseline. Using the mining set, we generate lexical rules with ignoring negation (Section 4.2.2) because negation can reduce the rule coverage and the rules containing negation are hard to reuse in unseen data (*analysis set*). As a result, 3,859 categorical rules and 22,986 lexical rules are generated (OUR). For TC, 1,160 rules are extracted from the same data. To identify rule coverage, we measure the number of the rules that can match any analysis instances, i.e., reusable with unseen data. Comparing with TC, our system can generate many more rules but many of them are not reusable in unseen data. That said, slightly more examples in the analysis set can be represented by the rules generated by our system, i.e., generally both systems can cover the almost same amount of new queries.

Next we provide the results using the metrics defined in Section 5.1.1. For each rule, we first identify which analysis instances can be matched (i.e., generate clusters), and calculate the average statistic of each metric in a cluster. Every rule corresponds to a query cluster which contains all queries that match this rule. Then, we report the mean of the average value of each metric over all clusters. Table 4 shows the results of each metric. First, the clusters obtained by OUR rules are more topically coherent. Since lexical rules containing keywords of DSAT queries are quite topically specific, this result is somewhat straightforward. Second, the rules generated by our system are strongly positively correlated with dissatisfaction, which means that OUR rules are more effective for identifying DSAT queries than TC rules. Third, the CTR of both systems is not significantly different. Generally, low CTR indicates dissatisfaction, but sometimes DSAT queries can include more clicks. For example, users do more clicks on search results but they immediately leave from the clicked results because those are not relevant. However, DSAT Correlation provides more direct relation between the rules and DSAT. Lastly, we calculate Kendall's τ coefficient between avg. CTR and DSAT Correlation. In both systems, DSAT Correlation is negatively correlated with CTR, which means generally low CTR indicates dissatisfaction. Besides, more salient negative relation is identified by OUR as is evidenced by a much higher DSAT Correlation in OUR.

5.2 DSAT Query Classification

5.2.1 Experimental Set-up

We conduct experiments to evaluate our system in DSAT query classification (Section 4.3). In this, a system would perform better

Table 5: Summary of Baseline Features.

Baseline	Class	Feature
Baseline 1	Query	query clarity score [10] query word length inverse web term probability [25]
Baseline 2 [17]	Query	query word length query character length
	User Interaction	# of distinct subsequent queries, # of SR, # of SERP, # of all search actions, # of clicked answers query impression count, # of long actions (dwelling time is more than 30 seconds), # of algorithmic clicks, clickthrough rate (CTR), $\text{SAT Rate} = \frac{\#\text{ of long actions}}{\#\text{ of algorithm clicks}}$

if its features (e.g., association rules in our system) are more effective to identify DSAT queries. We use the mining set to generate the rules, and exclude all behavior attributes because we are interested in predicting query performance at query time before observing any user behavior. For evaluation, a balanced data set is used, which contains 40,000 query instances (i.e., 20,000 instances are DSAT and the others are SAT); this comes from another random sampling of the queries that does not overlap with the mining set. For learning, we use a Linear Support Vector Machine (SVM) [29] and Logistic Regression (LR) [5]. We run each classifier 10 times and for each run, we perform 10-fold cross-validation using random partitioning.

5.2.2 Baselines

To develop baselines, we leverage the features from previous work on predicting query performance [10][17][25]. We compare our system to four different baselines each of which uses different features. Table 5 summarizes the features used in Baseline 1 and 2.

The first baseline is developed by using a combination of the query performance predictors presented in [10][25]. We chose to use query clarity score ([10]) because it performs as well as other models (e.g. [34]), does not require access to external resources ([34] requires the ranking results from two different search algorithms), and is not limited to any specific query types ([34] focuses on only two types of queries; named-page finding and content-based). To estimate inverse collection term frequency ([25]), we used term probabilities obtained from the Web N-Gram services [31] that provide smoothed n-gram probability. We calculate the sum, standard deviation, ratio of the maximum to the minimum, maximum, arithmetic mean, and geometric mean among the term probabilities of all query terms. While the first baseline only uses the features extracted from query texts, the work of [17] additionally considers interaction behavior (e.g., clickthrough statistics) which can largely improve prediction performance. Thus, as Baseline 2, we implement the features proposed in [17], which showed best performance in that paper. For more robust baselines, we combine the features from the Baseline 1 and 2 to form Baseline 3. In addition, we develop Baseline 4 which uses all the attributes (see Section 4.1) as features but does not use the association rules. The purpose of Baseline 4 is to verify the effectiveness of our rule mining method (Section 4.2) by comparing a system that uses the association rules as features and another that uses the original binary attributes used to mine the rules.

5.2.3 Classification Results

To perform a fair comparison, we run the methods with various settings. First, to compare with Baseline 1, we exclude behavior attributes and generate association rules (Cat+Lex(NOBH)) because Baseline 1 uses only query texts for extracting its features and in our method only behavior attributes require out-of-query information (sequence of search actions). Second, to compare with Baseline 4, we use only categorical rules (Cat) because our objective is to verify the effectiveness of the rule mining method. Third, we combine our approach with the most robust baseline (Baseline 3) to verify further enhancements when using behavioral signals. Tables 6 and 7 (overleaf) show the classification results with SVM and LR, respectively. We measure Precision, Recall, and F1 for each class. The area under the receiver operating characteristic curve (AUC) is measured to identify overall classification performance. Since we focus on DSAT query identification, the metrics related to DSAT are more important.

First, as we intended, Baseline 3 performs better than Baseline 1 and 2. In both classifiers, Baseline 3 can significantly outperform the two baselines in terms of DSAT precision, AUC and all metrics regarding SAT. Second, the rule mining method (Section 4.2.1) is effective using both classifiers. Comparing Cat with Baseline 4, the performance of Cat is significantly better in most metrics (except DSAT Recall and SAT Precision using SVM). This is because a categorical rule itself is a meta-feature, one effective subset of the features in Baseline 4 (i.e., categorical attributes). In other words, learning with the rules, the classifier can find an effective linear combination of equally associated features (i.e., the rules). Third, concerning Cat+Lex (NOBH), our system can significantly outperform Baselines 1, 2, and 3 in every DSAT metric and AUC, which means that the rules are more effective than the existing predictors [10][17][25]. This result is important because as we described in Section 1, we attempt to identify dissatisfaction without behavior information (before searches terminate), and our system excluding behavior attributes is better than the baselines using the interaction features. Moreover, Cat+Lex using all proposed attributes can outperform the baselines as well. Fourth, we combine our system (Cat+Lex) with the robust baseline (Baseline 3), and in SVM experiments (Table 6), we observed significant improvements on overall classification performance (i.e., AUC). However, using LR (Table 7), the combination performs worse than our system; especially in DSAT Recall, where a significant falloff (about a 32% drop from the performance of Cat+Lex) is observed, but in AUC the performance slightly decreases and significance is not observed. This is because in LR experiments (Table 7), when compared to Cat+Lex, Baseline 3 performs poorly in terms of DSAT Recall (though in AUC, Baseline 3 is much better than Baseline 1 and 2) and combining with it is harmful to our system which basically performs much better than the baselines. On the other hand, in SVM experiments (Table 6), comparing to Cat+Lex, Baseline 3 is competitive and the combined approach can perform significantly better in AUC. Overall, our methods (Cat+Lex and Cat+Lex (NOBH)) are more effective at identifying DSAT than existing performance predictors [10][17][25] in two statistical learning frameworks.

5.3 Further Analysis

We provide a qualitative analysis of our approach via query examples. Table shows three sample rules generated by our system and example queries represented by the rules. In the first rule, the queries (instances) related to 0 (behavior category, which indicates more query and less search result exploration) and Society/ People are dissatisfaction. In particular, the users querying for [lisa hill] reformulated the query several times but only clicked on two results with short dwell time (less than 30 seconds).

Table 6: Classification results using SVM. Cat indicates using only categorical rules, Lex indicates using lexical rules, NOBH denotes excluding behavior attributes (Section 4.1.4), and Baseline4 uses categorical attributes as features (Section 5.2.2). In each column, a significant improvement over each baseline is marked by its number, e.g., B12 indicates improvement over Baseline 1&2. A † and ‡ denote a significant improvement over Cat and Cat+Lex, respectively. The paired t-test is performed with $p < 0.01$.

Method \ Metric	DSAT Precision	DSAT Recall	DSAT F1	SAT Precision	SAT Recall	SAT F1	AUC
Baseline 1 [10][25]	0.5951	0.6614	0.6265	0.6210	0.5277	0.5706	0.6427
Baseline 2 [17]	0.5965	0.6535	0.6237	0.6189	0.5393	0.5764	0.6425
Baseline 3 [10][17][25]	0.6932 [B12]	0.6742	0.6836 [B12]	0.7248 [B12]	0.7395 [B124†‡]	0.7321 [B124†‡]	0.7710 [B124]
Baseline 4	0.6911 [B12]	0.7297 [B123]	0.7099 [B123]	0.7165 [B12]	0.6685 [B12]	0.6917 [B12]	0.7557 [B12]
Cat	0.7119 [B1234]	0.7242 [B123]	0.7180 [B1234]	0.7201 [B12]	0.7052 [B124]	0.7126 [B124]	0.7794 [B1234]
vs. Baseline 4	*+3.01%*	*−0.75%*	*+1.14%*	*+0.50%*	*+5.49%*	*+3.02%*	*+3.14%*
Cat+Lex (NOBH)	0.7081 [B1234]	0.7348 [B123]	0.7212 [B1234]	0.7253 [B12]	0.6953 [B124]	0.7100 [B124]	0.7787 [B1234]
vs. Baseline 1	*+18.99%*	*+11.10%*	*+15.12%*	*+16.80%*	*+31.76%*	*+24.44%*	*+21.16%*
vs. Baseline 2	*+18.71%*	*+12.44%*	*+15.36%*	*+17.19%*	*+28.93%*	*+23.18%*	*+21.20%*
vs. Baseline 3	*+2.15%*	*+8.99%*	*+5.51%*	*+0.07%*	*−5.98%*	*−3.02%*	*+1.00%*
Cat+Lex	0.7167 [B1234]	0.7221 [B123]	0.7194 [B1234]	0.7210 [B12]	0.7125 [B124]	0.7167 [B124]	0.7831 [B1234†]
vs. Baseline 1	*+20.43%*	*+9.18%*	*+14.83%*	*+16.10%*	*+35.02%*	*+25.62%*	*+21.85%*
vs. Baseline 2	*+20.15%*	*+10.50%*	*+15.34%*	*+16.50%*	*+32.12%*	*+24.35%*	*+21.88%*
vs. Baseline 3	*+3.39%*	*+7.10%*	*+5.24%*	*−0.52%*	*−3.65%*	*+2.10%*	*+1.57%*
Cat+Lex+Baseline3	0.7124 [B1234]	0.7261 [B123]	0.7192 [B1234]	0.7534 [B1234†‡]	0.7360 [B124†‡]	0.7446 [B1234†‡]	0.8175 [B1234†‡]
vs. Baseline 3	*+2.77%*	*+7.70%*	*+5.21%*	*+3.95%*	*−0.47%*	*+1.71%*	*+6.03%*
vs. Cat+Lex	*−0.60%*	*+0.55%*	*−0.03%*	*+4.49%*	*+3.30%*	*+3.89%*	*+4.39%*

Table 7: Classification results using LR. The same notation is used as in Table 6. The paired t-test is performed with $p < 0.01$.

Method \ Metric	DSAT Precision	DSAT Recall	DSAT F1	SAT Precision	SAT Recall	SAT F1	AUC
Baseline 1 [10][25]	0.6386	0.5257 [B3]	0.5767	0.5414	0.6537	0.5923	0.6282
Baseline 2 [17]	0.6173	0.5718 [B3]	0.5937	0.5538	0.6146	0.5826	0.6338
Baseline 3 [10][17][25]	0.6936 [B12]	0.4778	0.5658	0.6429 [B12]	0.8160 [B124†‡]	0.7192 [B124]	0.7747 [B124]
Baseline 4	0.6789 [B12]	0.7319 [B123]	0.7044 [B123]	0.7092 [B123]	0.6536	0.6803	0.7529 [B12]
Cat	0.7155 [B1234]	0.7350 [B123]	0.7251 [B1234]	0.7276 [B1234]	0.7077 [B124]	0.7175 [B124]	0.7942 [B1234]
vs. B4	*+5.39%*	*+0.42%*	*+2.94%*	*+2.59%*	*+8.28%*	*+5.48%*	*+5.49%*
Cat+Lex (NOBH)	0.7128 [B1234]	0.7408 [B1234]	0.7265 [B1234]	0.7302 [B1234]	0.7015 [B124]	0.7156 [B124]	0.7938 [B1234]
vs. Baseline 1	*+11.62%*	*+40.92%*	*+25.99%*	*+34.87%*	*+7.31%*	*+20.82%*	*+26.36%*
vs. Baseline 2	*+15.47%*	*+29.56%*	*+22.38%*	*+31.85%*	*+14.14%*	*+22.82%*	*+25.24%*
vs. Baseline 3	*+2.77%*	*+55.04%*	*+28.40%*	*+13.58%*	*−14.03%*	*−0.50%*	*+2.47%*
Cat+Lex	0.7163 [B1234]	0.7363 [B123]	0.7262 [B1234]	0.7287 [B1234]	0.7084 [B124]	0.7184 [B124]	0.7953 [B1234]
vs. Baseline 1	*+12.17%*	*+40.06%*	*+25.92%*	*+34.60%*	*+8.37%*	*+21.30%*	*+26.60%*
vs. Baseline 2	*+16.04%*	*+28.77%*	*+28.77%*	*+31.58%*	*+15.26%*	*+23.31%*	*+25.48%*
vs. Baseline 3	*+3.27%*	*+54.10%*	*+28.34%*	*+13.35%*	*−13.19%*	*−0.11%*	*+2.66%*
Cat+Lex+Baseline 3	0.7148 [B1234]	0.5036 [B3]	0.5909 [B123]	0.6504 [B123]	0.8207 [B124†‡]	0.7257 [B1234†]	0.7882 [B1234]
vs. Baseline 3	*+3.06%*	*+5.40%*	*+4.43%*	*+1.17%*	*+0.58%*	*+0.91%*	*+1.74%*
vs. Cat+Lex	*−0.21%*	*−31.60%*	*−18.63%*	*−10.75%*	*+15.85%*	*+1.01%*	*−0.89%*

Table 8: Sample rules and query examples. BH denotes Behavior attributes (Section 4.1.4), ODP denotes ODP attributes (Section 4.1.1), and WIKI denotes Wikipedia attributes (Section 4.1.3). For each rule, the consequent ({DSAT}) is omitted.

No.	Rule	Example Query	Label
1	{0[BH], Society/People[ODP]}	lisa hill	DSAT
2	{automobiles[WIKI], "warranty"}	1989 toyota mr2 warranty	DSAT
		2011 suzuki sx4 factory warranty	SAT
3	{motor vehicle company of Italy[WIKI], ¬aventador, ¬fiat, "ferrari"}	used ferrari cars scottsdale	DSAT
		certified ferrari cars phoenix	DSAT

The second rule describes a set of underperforming queries for auto warranty information. We found that sometimes the warranty information of older models (e.g., [1989 toyota mr2]) is not readily located whereas the information for newer models (e.g., [2011 suzuki sx4]) is easily found. The third rule contains negation, and shows that some users are dissatisfied with results for a group of queries related to "ferrari" and not containing "fiat" or "aventador".

6. CONCLUSION

In this paper, we proposed a framework to automatically generate association rules to identify underperforming queries. In order to build effective rules, we first generate topical attributes recognized from query text and formulate association rules that discover frequent patterns of the attributes for identifying dissatisfaction queries. Then, we apply a decision tree learning to identify discriminative keywords of dissatisfaction queries and combine the keywords with the association rules. In experiments, we verified the effectiveness of our system in the task of dissatisfaction query classification in comparison to existing query performance prediction baselines. Considering previous work on modeling user satisfaction, the advantage of our method is identifying dissatisfaction at query time and our system can provide evidence of dissatisfaction to search engines before users abandon searches. For future work, we plan to devise effective methods to improve the instances of search dissatisfaction identified by our method.

REFERENCES

[1] Ageev, M., Guo, Q., Lagun, D., and Agichtein, E. (2011). Find it if you can: a game for modeling different types of web search success using interaction data. *SIGIR*, 345–354.

[2] Agrawal, R., Imielinski, T., and Swami, A. (1993). Mining association rules between sets of items in large databases. *SIGMOD*, 207–216.

[3] Agrawal, R. and Srikant, R. (1994). Fast algorithms for mining association rules in large databases. *VLDB*, 487–499.

[4] Al-Maskari, A., Sanderson, M, and Clough, P. (2007). The relationship between IR effectiveness measures and user satisfaction. *SIGIR*, 773–774.

[5] Andrew, G. and Jianfeng, G. (2007). Scalable training of L_1-regularized log-linear models. *ICML*, 33–40.

[6] Aula, A., Khan, R.M., and Guan, Z. (2010). How does search behavior change as search becomes more difficult? *CHI*, 35–44.

[7] Bennett, P.N., Svore, K., and Dumais, S.T. (2010). Classification-enhanced ranking. *WWW*, 111–120.

[8] Carmel, D., Yom-Tov, E., Darlow, A., and Pelleg, D. (2006). What makes a query difficult? *SIGIR*, 390–397.

[9] Carterette, B. and Jones, R. (2007). Evaluating search engines by modeling the relationship between relevance and clicks. *NIPS*, 217–224.

[10] Cronen-Townsend, S., Zhou, Y., and Croft, W.B. (2002). Predicting query performance. *SIGIR*, 299–306.

[11] Coenen, F., Goulbourne, G., and Leng, P. (2004). Tree structures for mining association rules. *Data Mining and Knowledge Discovery*, 8(1): 25–51.

[12] Downey, D., Dumais, S.T., and Horvitz, E. (2007). Models of searching and browsing: languages, studies, and applications. *IJCAI*, 2740–2747.

[13] Feild, H., Allan, J., and Jones, R. (2010). Predicting searcher frustration. *SIGIR*, 34–41.

[14] Fellbaum, C. (1998). *WordNet: An Electronic Lexical Database*. Bradford Books.

[15] Finkel, J., Grenager, T., and Manning, C. (2005). Incorporating non-local information into information extraction systems by Gibbs sampling. *ACL*, 363–370.

[16] Fox, S. Karnawat, K., Mydland, M., Dumais, S., and White, T. (2005). Evaluating implicit measures to improve web search. *ACM TOIS*, 23(2): 147–168.

[17] Guo, Q., White, R.W., Dumais, S.T., Wang, J., and Anderson, B. (2010). Predicting query performance using query, result, and user interaction features. *RIAO*, 198–201.

[18] Guo, Q., White, R.W., Zhang, Y., Anderson, B., and Dumais, S.T. (2011). Why searchers switch: understanding and predicting engine switching rationales. *SIGIR*, 335–344.

[19] Hall, M., Frank, E., Holmes, G., Pfahringer, B., Reutemann, P., and Witten, I.H. (2009). The WEKA data mining software: an update. *SIGKDD Explorations*, 11(1): 10–18.

[20] Han, J., Pei, J., and Yin, Y. (2000). Mining frequent patterns without candidate generation. *SIGMOD*, 1–12.

[21] Hassan, A. (2012). A semi-supervised approach to modeling web search satisfaction. *SIGIR*, 275-284.

[22] Hassan, A., Jones, R., and Klinkner, K.L. (2010). Beyond DCG: user behavior as a predictor of a successful search. *WSDM*, 221–230.

[23] Hassan, A., Song, Y., and He, L. (2011). A task level user satisfaction model and its application on improving relevance estimation. *CIKM*, 125–134.

[24] He, B. and Ounis, I. (2004). Inferring query performance using pre-retrieval predictors. *SPIRE*, 43–54.

[25] He, B. and Ounis, I. (2006). Query performance prediction. *Information System*, Vol. 31(7), 585–594.

[26] Huffman, S. and Hochster, M. (2007). How well does result relevance predict session satisfaction? *SIGIR*, 567–574.

[27] Jones, R. and Klinkner, K. (2008). Beyond the session timeout: automatic hierarchical segmenting of search topics in query logs. *CIKM*, 699–708.

[28] Leskovec, J., Dumais, S., and Horvitz, E. (2007). Web projections: learning from contextual sub graphs of the web. *WWW*, 471–480.

[29] Shalev-Shwartz, S., Singer, Y., and Srebro, N. (2007). Pegasos: primal estimated sub-gradient solver for SVM. *ICML*, 807–814.

[30] Wang, C., Hsu, B., Chang, M., and Kiciman, E. (2012). Simple and knowledge-intensive generative model for named entity recognition. *Microsoft Research Technical Report.*

[31] Wang, K., Thrasher, C., Viegas, E., Li, X. and Hsu, P. (2010). An overview of Microsoft web n-gram corpus and applications. *NAACL HLT Demo Session*, 45–48.

[32] Weiss, Y., Torralba, A., and Fergus, R. (2008). Spectral hashing. *NIPS*, 1753–1760.

[33] Zhao, Y., Scholer, F., and Tsegay, Y. (2008). Effective pre-retrieval query performance prediction using similarity and variability evidence. *ECIR*, 52–64.

[34] Zhou, Y., and Croft, W.B. (2006). Ranking robustness: a novel framework to predict query performance. *CIKM*, 567–574.

[35] Zhou, Y. and Croft, W.B. (2007). Query performance prediction in web search environments. *SIGIR*, 543–550.

NCDawareRank: a Novel Ranking Method that Exploits the Decomposable Structure of the Web

Athanasios N. Nikolakopoulos
nikolako@ceid.upatras.gr

John D. Garofalakis
garofala@ceid.upatras.gr

Computer Engineering and Informatics Department, University of Patras
Computer Technology Institute and Press "Diophantus"
GR-26504 Patras, Greece

ABSTRACT

Research about the topological characteristics of the hyperlink graph has shown that Web possesses a nested block structure, indicative of its innate hierarchical organization. This crucial observation opens the way for new approaches that can usefully regard Web as a *Nearly Completely Decomposable*(NCD) system; In recent years, such approaches gave birth to various efficient methods and algorithms that exploit NCD from a computational point of view and manage to considerably accelerate the extraction of the *PageRank* vector. However, very little have been done towards the qualitative exploitation of NCD.

In this paper we propose *NCDawareRank*, a novel ranking method that uses the intuition behind NCD to generalize and refine PageRank. NCDawareRank considers both the link structure and the hierarchical nature of the Web in a way that preserves the mathematically attractive characteristics of PageRank and at the same time manages to successfully resolve many of its known problems, including Web Spamming Susceptibility and Biased Ranking of Newly Emerging Pages. Experimental results show that NCDawareRank is more resistant to direct manipulation, alleviates the problems caused by the sparseness of the link graph and assigns more reasonable ranking scores to newly added pages, while maintaining the ability to be easily implemented on a large-scale and in a computationally efficient manner.

Categories and Subject Descriptors

H.3.3 [**Information Search and Retrieval**]: Search process; G.1.3 [**Numerical Linear Algebra**]: Sparse Structured and Very Large Systems; G.2.2 [**Probability and Statistics**]: Markov processes

Keywords

Link Analysis; Ranking; Link Spamming; Sparsity; Near Complete Decomposability; NCDawareRank; PageRank

1. INTRODUCTION

For years now, Web searching has become an integral part of everyone's daily activities. Due to the astonishing amount of information available on the Web and because of the fact that unlike traditional text collections, Web is dynamic and its content exhibits highly variable quality, classic information retrieval methods can only be used by search engines to a small extend. This fact generates the need for an absolute measure of importance for Web pages, that can be used to improve the performance of Web search.

Link Analysis algorithms such as the celebrated *PageRank*, try to answer this need by using the link structure of the Web to assign authoritative weights to Web pages. PageRank's approach is based on the assumption that links convey human endorsement. For example, the existence of a link from page 3 to page 4 in Figure 1(a) is viewed as a testimonial of the importance of page 4. In their original paper, Page et al.[25] imagined of a *random surfer* who with probability α follows the links of a Web page uniformly at random, and with probability $1 - \alpha$ jumps to a different page according to a given distribution. Then, following this intuitive metaphor, the overall importance of a page will be equal to the fraction of time this random surfer spends on it, in the long run.

Although PageRank has proven to be a very effective paradigm for ranking Web pages and it is believed to be part of the ranking functions of most today's commercial search engines, it suffers from a number of problems. One of these problems is susceptibility to manipulation through link spamming; a form of Web spamming that involves the artificial creation of a large number of pages that carefully funnel all their rank towards a single page of interest [13, 24]. Spam Web pages represent a significant fraction of the overall pages in most domains (in some, this fraction is alarming; according to [24], about 70% of .biz domain can be characterized as spam) and if we take into account the fact that Web search is the *de facto* control point for e-commerce, the economic incentive behind high ranking immediately justifies the need for spam resistant ranking schemes.

Another problem of PageRank comes from the low density of the link graph. It is well known that the link distribution of the Web graph generally follows a power law [14]. This leads to a sparse hyperlink matrix. Furthermore, in [26] it was observed that such link distributions caused the probability values produced by PageRank to decay according to a power law, making most of the pages unable to obtain reasonable score. The latter is especially true for the newly

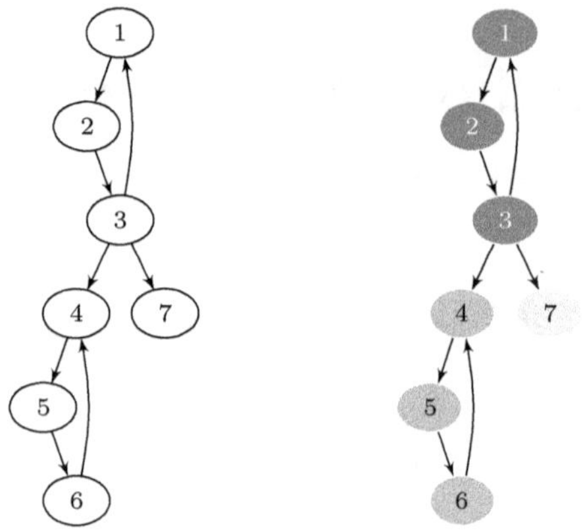

(a) "flat" web (b) NCD web

Figure 1: Tiny web graph

added pages which usually have too-few incoming links, and thus cannot receive reasonable ranking [9].

We believe that one of the main causes of the previously mentioned problems is that PageRank, as in fact most link analysis algorithms, approach Web in a "flat" way. Research about the topological structure of the Web has shown that the hyperlink graph has a nested block structure [19], with domains, hosts and websites, introducing intermediate levels of affiliation and revealing an interesting macro-structure [3, 12]. Thus, the Web just like many naturally emerging complex systems has a hierarchical nature. According to Simon [30] this is no accident; basically all viable complex systems, be they physical, social, biological, or artificial, share the property of having a *nearly completely decomposable* architecture: they are organized into hierarchical layers of blocks, sub-blocks, sub-sub-blocks and so on, in such a way that interactions among elements belonging to the same block are much stronger than interactions between elements belonging to different blocks.

The analysis of decomposable systems has been pioneered by Simon and Ando [29], who reported on state aggregation in linear models of economic systems, but the versatility of Simon's idea has permitted the theory to be used with noticeable success in many complex problems originated from evolutionary biology, social sciences, cognitive science, management, etc. The introduction of near complete decomposability (NCD) in the fields of computer science and engineering is due to Courtois [11] who achieved the full mathematical development of the theory, and applied it with great originality in a number of queueing and computer system performance problems.

In recent years, the decomposability of the Web has been exploited mainly from a computational point of view. The "mathematical fingerprint" of NCD in the PageRank problem is the special spectral structure [11, 23] of the stochastic matrix corresponding to the random walk on the Web graph. This property opens the way for the use of numerical methods like Iterative Aggregation/Disaggregation (IAD) [27] that can be used to accelerate the computation of the PageRank vector considerably. Many researchers have followed such approaches with promising results. Kamvar et al.[19] use the first two steps of the general IAD method to obtain an initial vector for subsequent Power Method iterations. Zhu et al.[33] propose a distributed PageRank computation algorithm based on IAD methods. Langville and Meyer [21] use a two-block IAD to accelerate the updating of PageRank vector, and Ipsen et al.[17] analyse its asymptotic convergence. Recently, Cevahir et al.[8] used site based partitioning techniques in order to accelerate PageRank.

However, little have been done to exploit decomposability from a qualitative point of view. Knowing that a complex system possesses the property of NCD, points the way towards a more appropriate modelling approach and a mathematical analysis, which highlights the system's endemic characteristics, gives us invaluable insight to its behaviour and consequently, provides us a theoretical framework to develop algorithms and methods that materialize this insight from a qualitative, computational as well as conceptual angle.

The main question we try to address in this work is *"How could someone incorporate the concept of NCD to the basic PageRank model in a way that refines and generalizes it while preserving its efficiency?"*. For example, if we have the information that the tiny Web graph of Figure 1(a) can be decomposed like in Figure 1(b)[1], in what way can we utilize this to achieve better ranking, without obscuring the simplicity and the clarity of PageRank's approach?

Summary of Contributions.

The main contribution of this paper is the proposal of *NCDawareRank*, a novel ranking measure which:

- provides a theoretical framework that enables the exploitation of Web's innately decomposable structure in a computationally efficient way.
- can serve as a generalization of PageRank that enhances its expressiveness while inheriting its attractive mathematical characteristics and approach.
- displays low sensitivity to the problems caused by the sparsity of the Web graph and treats newly added pages more fairly.
- exhibits resistance to direct manipulation through link spamming.

The rest of the paper is organized as follows. In Section 2, we outline the basic idea behind NCDawareRank and we briefly discuss the nature of the basic NCD blocks. In Section 3, we develop the mathematical framework of NCDawareRank. Our experimental results are presented in Section 4. Finally, Section 5 concludes this paper and outlines directions for future work.

2. EXPLOITING WEB'S DECOMPOSABILITY: THE INTUITION

2.1 From PageRank to NCDawareRank

Underlying the definition of PageRank is the assumption that the existence of a link from page u to page v testifies the importance of page v. Furthermore, the amount of importance conferred to page v is proportional to the importance of page u and inversely proportional to the number of pages u links to.

[1]same coloured nodes represent pages belonging to the same block

To formulate PageRank's basic idea with a mathematical model, we view the Web as a directed graph with Web pages as vertices and hyperlinks as edges. Given this graph, we can construct a *row-normalized hyperlink matrix* $\mathbf{H}$, whose element H_{uv} is one over the outdegree of u if there is a link from u to v, or zero otherwise.

When the graph contains *dangling nodes* (i.e nodes with no outgoing links), the corresponding rows of $\mathbf{H}$ will be entirely made of zeros, which makes $\mathbf{H}$ a substochastic matrix. A simple adjustment that fixes this problem, originally proposed by Page et al.[25], is to replace the $\mathbf{0}^\intercal$ rows with the uniform distribution over all pages, thereby transforming $\mathbf{H}$ to a stochastic matrix.

A second adjustment is needed to verify that the final matrix is irreducible and aperiodic, so that it possesses a unique positive stationary probability distribution. That is ensured by the introduction of the *damping factor* α and a *teleportation* matrix $\mathbf{E}$, usually defined by $\mathbf{E} = \mathbf{e}\mathbf{v}^\intercal$, where $\mathbf{v}$ a probability vector with non-negative elements. The resulting matrix is given by:

$$\mathbf{G} = \alpha\mathbf{H} + (1-\alpha)\mathbf{E} \tag{1}$$

PageRank vector is the unique stationary distribution of the Markov chain corresponding to matrix $\mathbf{G}$.

The choice of the damping factor α is very important and has recently received great research attention [1, 7, 22]. This parameter determines how often the Markov chain follows the hyperlink graph rather than jumping at a random page. Picking a very small damping factor ignores the link structure of the Web and thus results in uninformative ranking vectors. On the other hand, as α gets closer to 1, the Web component becomes increasingly important.

While this may seem intuitively preferable, picking an α very close to 1 results in a number of problems: From a computational point of view, the number of iterations till convergence required by the Power Method and its variants (commonly used for the extraction of the PageRank vector) grows with α and the computation of the ranking vector becomes numerically ill-conditioned [18]. Furthermore, from a qualitative prospective, various studies also indicate that damping factors close to 1 result into counterintuitive ranking vectors where the Web's core component is assigned null rank and all the PageRank gets concentrated mostly in irrelevant nodes [1, 6, 7].

Several ranking methods proposed lately try to address the damping factor issue. Boldi in [4] proposed the *TotalRank* algorithm which aims at eliminating PageRank's dependency on the arbitrarily chosen parameter α by integrating the ranking vector over the entire range of possible damping factors. Baeza-Yates et al.[2] introduce a family of link based ranking algorithms parametrised by the selection of a *damping function* that describes how rapidly the importance of paths decays as the path length increases. *HyperRank* assumes general hyperbolic damping, whereas *LinearRank* assumes a linear damping function. In a recent work, Constantine and Gleich [10, 15] generalize the standard random surfer model and propose a ranking method that considers the influence of a population of random surfers. Each surfer chooses its own teleportation parameter from a probability distribution and thus the ranking vector produced is random.

Exploiting Decomposability. Our goal is to introduce an approach that tries to address this fundamental issue by exploiting the fact that Web can be viewed as a nearly completely decomposable system. The partitioning of the Web into NCD blocks introduces new levels of abstraction, which we aim to exploit without creating coarser-level graph models that may obscure the direct link structure of the Web and hide valuable information. In the core of NCDawareRank is the idea that the existence of a link suggests *multiple levels of proximity* corresponding to the different decompositions of the underlying space. This basic idea can be used to attack the importance propagation issue from a different angle.

As explained above, quality and computational reasons force PageRank to keep the parameter α not so close to 1. This, however, leaves $1-\alpha$ of the rank spread uniformly on every page of the Web, in a hardly meaningful way. The basic idea behind our method is *a fraction of the importance of a page that is scattered throughout the Web, to be propagated instead, to the NCD blocks that contain the pages it links to.* In other words, the existence of an outgoing link, except for justifying the importance of the page it points to, "hints" about the importance of the block that contains this page. But before we explain the details behind the use of Decomposability in generalizing and refining PageRank, we must first describe the nature of the basic NCD blocks.

2.2 The basic NCD blocks

PageRank's view, while considering the direct structure of the Web, disregards the fact that Web pages are organized into Web sites, and these sites many times prove to be the real unit of interest. Bharat et al.[3] present a number of convincing arguments that make websites the appropriate level of abstraction to study Web's macro-structure. When compared to an individual page, a website can many times provide a wealth of semantic information. Pages included in a website are usually authored by the same person or group of persons and their content is often highly correlated. This fact is directly reflected to the topological properties of the Web graph; websites contain higher density of hyperlinks inside them (about 75% according to the authors in [16]) and lower density of edges in between. This is why websites have usually been used as the standard unit of partition in most NCD-based approaches to accelerate PageRank. For the same reasons, we choose to use websites as the basic blocks of the nearly completely decomposable Web.

3. NCDAWARERANK

3.1 Our Model

In order to model mathematically the basic idea of NCDawareRank, we introduce a new parameter μ and an associated *Inter-Level Proximity Matrix* $\mathbf{M}$. Before we proceed further, we need to define the parameters of our problem.

- Let $\mathcal{W}$ be the universe of Web pages and denote $n = |\mathcal{W}|$.
- Consider a Web page u in $\mathcal{W}$. We denote $\mathcal{G}_u$ to be the set of pages that can be visited in a single step from u. Clearly, $d_u \triangleq |\mathcal{G}_u|$ is the out-degree of u, i.e. the number of outgoing links of u.
- We consider a partition $\{\mathcal{A}_1, \mathcal{A}_2, \ldots, \mathcal{A}_N\}$ of $\mathcal{W}$. Each set of pages $\mathcal{A}_I$ is referred to as an *NCD block.* Obviously, it holds that for every Web page u there exists

a unique K such that $u \in \mathcal{A}_K$. We also use $\mathcal{A}_{(u)}$ to denote the unique block that includes page u.

- We define $\mathcal{X}_u$ to be the set of the *proximal* pages of u, i.e the union of the NCD blocks that contain u and the pages it links to. Formally, the set $\mathcal{X}_u$ is defined by:

$$\mathcal{X}_u \triangleq \bigcup_{w \in (u \cup \mathcal{G}_u)} \mathcal{A}_{(w)}$$

- Finally, we use N_u to denote the number of different blocks in $\mathcal{X}_u$.

The hyperlink matrix $\mathbf{H}$, as in the PageRank Model, is a row normalized version of the adjacency matrix induced by the Web graph, and its uv^{th} element is defined as follows:

$$H_{uv} \triangleq \begin{cases} \frac{1}{d_u} & \text{if } v \in \mathcal{G}_u \\ 0 & \text{otherwise} \end{cases}$$

Matrix $\mathbf{H}$ is assumed to be a row-stochastic matrix. The matter of dangling nodes is considered fixed through some sort of stochasticity adjustment.

The uv^{th} element of the Inter-Level Proximity matrix $\mathbf{M}$ is defined as follows:

$$M_{uv} \triangleq \begin{cases} \frac{1}{N_u |\mathcal{A}_{(v)}|} & \text{if } v \in \mathcal{X}_u \\ 0 & \text{otherwise} \end{cases}$$

For example, the matrix $\mathbf{M}$ that corresponds to the tiny Web graph of Figure 1(b) where we see 3 NCD blocks is:

$$\mathbf{M} = \begin{bmatrix} 1/3 & 1/3 & 1/3 & 0 & 0 & 0 & 0 \\ 1/3 & 1/3 & 1/3 & 0 & 0 & 0 & 0 \\ 1/9 & 1/9 & 1/9 & 1/9 & 1/9 & 1/9 & 1/3 \\ 0 & 0 & 0 & 1/3 & 1/3 & 1/3 & 0 \\ 0 & 0 & 0 & 1/3 & 1/3 & 1/3 & 0 \\ 0 & 0 & 0 & 1/3 & 1/3 & 1/3 & 0 \\ 0 & 0 & 0 & 0 & 0 & 0 & 1 \end{bmatrix}$$

NCDawareRank also uses a teleportation matrix $\mathbf{E}$, as a remedy to ensure that the underlying Markov chain, corresponding to the final matrix, is irreducible and aperiodic and thus has a unique positive stationary probability distribution.

One very simple and convenient way to define $\mathbf{E}$ is the following:

$$\mathbf{E} \triangleq \mathbf{e}\mathbf{v}^{\intercal}$$

where vector $\mathbf{v}^{\intercal}$ is a probability vector that first distributes the rank evenly between the ncd blocks and then in each block evenly to the included pages. Of course, as in PageRank, one can construct a *personalized* version of the teleportation matrix, using a different stochastic vector instead of $\mathbf{v}^{\intercal}$.

Finally, the resulting matrix which we denote $\mathbf{P}$ is expressed by:

$$\mathbf{P} = \eta\mathbf{H} + \mu\mathbf{M} + (1 - \eta - \mu)\mathbf{E} \tag{2}$$

Parameter η controls the fraction of importance delivered to the outgoing links and parameter μ controls the fraction of importance that will be propagated to the proximal pages. In order to ensure the irreducibility and aperiodicity of the final stochastic matrix, $\eta + \mu$ must be less than 1. This leaves $1 - \eta - \mu$ of importance scattered throughout the Web through matrix $\mathbf{E}$.

Remark 1. Notice that the standard PageRank model can be seen as a special case of our framework in two different ways: When there is only one block containing all the nodes, matrix $\mathbf{M}$ collapses into the standard teleportation matrix, and NCDawareRank becomes PageRank. The latter is also true if we have n ncd blocks, each of which contains a single node; in this case, the inter-level proximity matrix coincides with the hyperlink matrix $\mathbf{H}$.

3.2 The Algorithm: Theory and Implementation Considerations

In a world where Web counts several billions of pages, every ranking method that realistically wants to attack the problem, needs to ensure its large scale implementability.

In our case it is crucial to be able to express matrix $\mathbf{P}$ as the sum of sparse matrices in order to efficiently compute its steady state distribution. The basic difference between PageRank and NCDawareRank from a computational point of view is the introduction of matrix $\mathbf{M}$. If we want our ranking system to be applicable in realistic scenarios, we need to ensure that matrix $\mathbf{M}$ can be handled efficiently.

3.2.1 *The Inter-Level Proximity Matrix* M

Matrix $\mathbf{M}$ is by definition a sparse matrix. For realistic purposes though, it is not sparse enough! Fortunately, $\mathbf{M}$ has a very special structure that can be exploited in order to achieve efficient storage and computability as well as other advantages. The key observation is that matrix $\mathbf{M}$ can be expressed as a product of 2 extremely sparse matrices, $\mathbf{R}$ and $\mathbf{A}$, defined below:

Matrix $\mathbf{A} \in \mathbb{R}^{N \times n}$ is defined as follows:

$$\mathbf{A} \triangleq \begin{bmatrix} \mathbf{e}^{\intercal}_{|\mathcal{A}_1|} & \mathbf{0} & \mathbf{0} & \cdots & \mathbf{0} \\ \mathbf{0} & \mathbf{e}^{\intercal}_{|\mathcal{A}_2|} & \mathbf{0} & \cdots & \mathbf{0} \\ \mathbf{0} & \mathbf{0} & \mathbf{e}^{\intercal}_{|\mathcal{A}_3|} & \cdots & \mathbf{0} \\ \vdots & \vdots & \vdots & \ddots & \mathbf{0} \\ \mathbf{0} & \mathbf{0} & \mathbf{0} & \cdots & \mathbf{e}^{\intercal}_{|\mathcal{A}_N|} \end{bmatrix}$$

where $\mathbf{e}^{\intercal}_{|\mathcal{A}_k|}$ denotes a row vector in $\mathbb{R}^{|\mathcal{A}_k|}$ whose elements are all 1. In order to define the other factor of matrix $\mathbf{M}$ we first consider a vector

$$\mathbf{c} = \begin{pmatrix} 1/|\mathcal{A}_1| & 1/|\mathcal{A}_2| & \cdots & 1/|\mathcal{A}_N| \end{pmatrix}^{\intercal}$$

and a row normalized matrix $\mathbf{R}' \in \mathbb{R}^{n \times N}$ whose rows correspond to pages and columns to blocks and its ij^{th} element is equal to $\frac{1}{N_u}$ if $\mathcal{A}_j \in \mathcal{X}_u$, zero otherwise.

Now, if $\mathbf{R}'_{*\mathbf{j}}$, denotes the jth column of matrix $\mathbf{R}'$, and c_i the ith element of $\mathbf{c}$, we can define the matrix $\mathbf{R}$ as follows:

$$\mathbf{R} \triangleq \begin{bmatrix} c_1\mathbf{R}'_{*\mathbf{1}} & c_2\mathbf{R}'_{*\mathbf{2}} & \cdots & c_N\mathbf{R}'_{*\mathbf{N}} \end{bmatrix}$$

From the definition of these matrices it is clear that it holds $\mathbf{M} = \mathbf{R} \times \mathbf{A}$. For the sake of example, these matrices for the tiny Web graph of Figure 1(b) are:

$$\mathbf{R} = \begin{bmatrix} 1/3 & 0 & 0 \\ 1/3 & 0 & 0 \\ 1/9 & 1/9 & 1/3 \\ 0 & 1/3 & 0 \\ 0 & 1/3 & 0 \\ 0 & 1/3 & 0 \\ 0 & 0 & 1 \end{bmatrix} \quad \mathbf{A} = \begin{bmatrix} 1 & 1 & 1 & 0 & 0 & 0 & 0 \\ 0 & 0 & 0 & 1 & 1 & 1 & 0 \\ 0 & 0 & 0 & 0 & 0 & 0 & 1 \end{bmatrix}$$

The computational and storage gains of using matrices $\mathbf{R}$ and $\mathbf{A}$ instead of $\mathbf{M}$ are very big:

Table 1: **Storage Savings**

Dataset	# of pages	M	R + A	H
cnr-2000	325557	42.57 GB	**8.209 MB**	51.56 MB
eu-2005	862664	588.8 GB	**34.42 MB**	300.1 MB
india-2004	1382908	131.6 GB	**38.82 MB**	268.7 MB
indochina	7414866	1.095 TB	**262.3 MB**	2.947 GB
uk-2002	18520486	1.323 TB	**604.5 MB**	4.580 GB

Storage Savings. Matrix $\mathbf{A}$ has only n non zero elements, all equal to 1. Thus, it is very easy to choose a compact storage mechanism that exploits its extreme sparseness. The number of non-zero elements of matrix $\mathbf{R}$ is by definition upper bounded by the number of non-zero elements of hyperlink matrix $\mathbf{H}$, but in realistic cases matrix $\mathbf{R}$ contains much less elements. In Table 1, we see the storing requirements[2] of these matrices for some of the datasets we experimented on (details about the datasets and the experimental methodology can be found in Section 4.1). Notice that after the factorisation, the combined storage needs for matrices $\mathbf{R}$ and $\mathbf{A}$ are significantly lower even when compared to the storage requirements of hyperlink matrix $\mathbf{H}$.

Computational Advantages. The factorization of matrix $\mathbf{M}$ also leads to considerable computational savings as well. If we assume the use of the Power Method for the extraction of the ranking vector, every step involves a calculation that looks like this:

$$\begin{aligned}\hat{\pi}^\intercal &= \pi^\intercal \mathbf{P}\\ &= \eta\pi^\intercal\mathbf{H} + \mu\pi^\intercal\mathbf{M} + (1-\eta-\mu)\pi^\intercal\mathbf{E}\end{aligned}$$

The Matrix×Vector (MV) product $\pi^\intercal\mathbf{M}$ needs to be computed in each iteration. Now, if we replace matrix $\mathbf{M}$ with the product $\mathbf{RA}$ we have a significant drop to the number of floating point operations needed. In particular:

Let $\Omega_\mathbf{M}$ denote the number of floating point operations involved in the direct computation of the product $\pi^\intercal\mathbf{M}$ using matrix $\mathbf{M}$. If we make use of the factorization, we have the product $(\pi^\intercal\mathbf{R})\mathbf{A}$. First, we compute the product $\pi^\intercal\mathbf{R}$ and then, the resulting vector is multiplied with $\mathbf{A}$. If we denote $\Omega_\mathbf{R}$ and $\Omega_\mathbf{A}$ the corresponding number of operations, we get $\Omega_{\mathbf{R}\times\mathbf{A}} \triangleq \Omega_\mathbf{R} + \Omega_\mathbf{A}$ as the total number of operations for the second case.

Assuming that the number of operations of a Sparse Matrix Vector product (SpMV) is twice the number of non-zero elements of the sparse matrix involved and if we use $n_z(\cdot)$ to denote the number of non-zero elements of a matrix, we get:

$$\Omega_\mathbf{M} = 2n_z(\mathbf{M}) \text{ and } \Omega_{\mathbf{R}\times\mathbf{A}} = \Omega_\mathbf{R} + \Omega_\mathbf{A} \approx 2n_z(\mathbf{R})$$

Note that because of the special structure of matrix $\mathbf{A}$ and of the fact that it contains only zeros and ones, $\Omega_\mathbf{A}$ is computationally negligible, because it can be implemented in a way that it costs only n assignment operations. Thus, we see that

$$\Omega_\mathbf{M} = 2n_z(\mathbf{M}) \gg 2n_z(\mathbf{R}) \approx \Omega_{\mathbf{R}\times\mathbf{A}}$$

Actually, if we take into account the fact that matrices $\mathbf{A}$ and $\mathbf{R}$ are much smaller than $\mathbf{M}$ and more likely to fit into the main memory, we see that each iteration requires less disk I/Os, which by its own means, greatly accelerates the computation.

[2]The values of Table 1 assume the usage of *Harwell-Boeing* sparse matrix storage scheme.

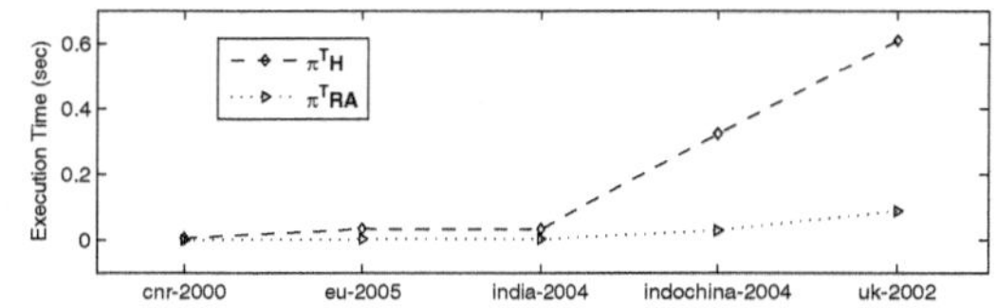

Figure 2: Execution time of the SpMV products, $\pi^\intercal\mathbf{H}$ and $(\pi^\intercal\mathbf{R})\mathbf{A}$ for a number of different datasets

Furthermore, observe that

$$\Omega_\mathbf{H} \triangleq 2n_z(\mathbf{H}) \gg 2n_z(\mathbf{R}) \approx \Omega_{\mathbf{R}\times\mathbf{A}}$$

which means that the bottleneck of each iteration is by far the computation of the SpMV product $\pi^\intercal\mathbf{H}$ (involved to the computation of PageRank as well). Figure 2 provides experimental evidence of this fact. In this simple experiment we compare the execution times per iteration of these products for the five different datasets of Table 1 and we clearly see the significant time difference.

Finally, the product $(\pi^\intercal\mathbf{R})\mathbf{A}$ of each iteration can be computed in a completely parallel or distributed fashion, with the introduction of very small communication cost. So, in the parallel case, the additional burden becomes negligible.

All these observations suggest that the computational cost induced by the inter-level proximity matrix, is practically very small and, as we will see in the following section, can be compensated by the fact that the introduction of $\mathbf{M}$ results in slightly faster convergence.

3.2.2 The Algorithm

Having defined the components of matrix $\mathbf{P}$, we are now ready to state the NCDawareRank algorithm. Because of the sparseness of the involving components and in order to be able to make direct comparisons with the standard PageRank algorithm, we suggest using the Power Method for the computation of the steady state probability distribution. The algorithm is given below:

Algorithm 1 NCDawareRank $(\mathbf{H}, \mathbf{A}, \mathbf{R}, \pi^0, \epsilon)$

1. Let the initial approximation be π^0. Set $k = 0$.
2. Compute

$$\begin{aligned}\pi^{(k+1)\intercal} &= \pi^{(k)\intercal}\mathbf{P}\\ &= \eta\pi^{(k)\intercal}\mathbf{H} + \mu\pi^{(k)\intercal}\mathbf{RA} + (1-\eta-\mu)\pi^{(k)\intercal}\mathbf{E}\end{aligned}$$

3. Normalize $\pi^{(k+1)\intercal}$ and compute

$$r = \|\pi^{(k+1)\intercal} - \pi^{(k)\intercal}\|_1$$

If $r < \epsilon$, quit with $\pi^{(k+1)\intercal}$, otherwise set $k = k+1$ and go to step 2.

It is known that the convergence rate of the Power Method applied to a stochastic matrix depends on the magnitude of the subdominant eigenvalue, $|\lambda_2|$. Precisely, the asymptotic convergence rate is the rate at which $|\lambda_2|^k \to 0$. The following theorem bounds the subdominant eigenvalue of the NCDawareRank matrix $\mathbf{P}$.

THEOREM 1. *The subdominant eigenvalue of matrix* $\mathbf{P}$ *involved in the NCDawareRank, defined by (2), is upper bounded by* $\eta + \mu$.

PROOF. We define the matrix

$$\mathbf{Z} \triangleq \frac{1}{\eta+\mu}(\eta\mathbf{H}+\mu\mathbf{M})$$

Notice that since matrices $\mathbf{H}$ and $\mathbf{M}$ are row-stochastic, matrix $\mathbf{Z}$ is also row-stochastic:

$$\begin{aligned}\mathbf{Ze} &= \frac{1}{\eta+\mu}(\eta\mathbf{H}+\mu\mathbf{M})\mathbf{e}\\ &= \frac{1}{\eta+\mu}(\eta\mathbf{He}+\mu\mathbf{Me})\\ &= \frac{1}{\eta+\mu}(\eta\mathbf{e}+\mu\mathbf{e}) = \mathbf{e}\end{aligned}$$

Now, notice that we can express matrix $\mathbf{P}$ in terms of $\mathbf{Z}$ as follows:

$$\mathbf{P} = \alpha'\mathbf{Z} + (1-\alpha')\mathbf{E}$$

where $\alpha' \triangleq \eta+\mu < 1$ and $\mathbf{E} = \mathbf{ev}^\intercal$, for some probability vector with non-zero elements $\mathbf{v}^\intercal$.

But from the celebrated Google lemma (for a proof see [22]) we know that if the spectrum of the stochastic matrix $\mathbf{S}$ is $\{1, \lambda_2, \ldots, \lambda_n\}$ then the spectrum of matrix $\mathbf{G} = \alpha\mathbf{S}+(1-\alpha)\mathbf{ev}^\intercal$, where $\mathbf{v}^\intercal$ a probability vector with positive elements, is $\{1, \alpha\lambda_2, \ldots, \alpha\lambda_n\}$.

Thus, the subdominant eigenvalue of $\mathbf{P}$ is $(\eta+\mu)\lambda_2$ where λ_2 denotes the second largest eigenvalue of the stochastic matrix $\mathbf{Z}$. However, for every eigenvalue of a stochastic matrix, $|\lambda| \leq 1$ holds (see [28]), and the bound follows. □

Table 2 shows the number of iterations till convergence and the running time of NCDawareRank against PageRank for the different datasets of Table 1. To isolate the effect of the introduction of parameters η, μ we used the same teleportation matrix for both algorithms and we took as criterion of convergence a difference in the L_1-norm, lower than 10^{-5}. From the values of Table 2 we see that the introduction of parameter μ results in reduction of the number of iterations.

To further test this effect, we run NCDawareRank introducing increasingly big values of μ while keeping the sum $\eta+\mu$ constant. The results are presented in Table 3. Even for values of μ as low as 0.005, we have a drop of the number of iterations till convergence, and this drop continues as μ increases and then stabilizes. This is true for all the datasets we experimented on. These results and the fact that we want to avoid ignoring the direct link structure, suggest that a good choice for parameter μ is a value near 0.10.

Remark 2. Of course many other methods could be used to extract the steady state distribution of $\mathbf{P}$. In fact, because of the similarity in the definitions between PageRank and NCDawareRank, almost every algorithm or approach proposed for PageRank could easily be applied to the calculation of NCDawareRank as well.

Table 3: Iterations till Convergence for Different Values of Parameter μ

$\mu =$	0.005	0.01	0.02	0.05	0.1	0.2	0.3
cnr-2000	47	45	43	41	**40**	40	41
eu-2005	42	41	40	39	**38**	40	41
india-2004	47	46	45	42	**42**	42	42
indochina-2004	46	45	44	42	**42**	42	42
uk-2002	45	44	43	42	**41**	41	41

3.3 Block-wise Ranking

The factorisation of matrix $\mathbf{M}$ has another very useful side-effect: it makes it very easy to calculate a block-level ranking. For example, when the blocks correspond to websites, we can easily compute site ranking as a by-product of NCDawareRank. Let's see how.

In order to compute the probability of being in a given block, we have to construct a $N \times N$ stochastic matrix whose ij^{th} element denotes the probability of a transition from block $\mathcal{A}_I$ to block $\mathcal{A}_J$ (see [31]). This can be done in two steps: First we replace each row of each block $\mathbf{P}_{IJ}$ of matrix $\mathbf{P}$ by the sum of its elements, $\mathbf{P}_{IJ}\mathbf{e}$, and then we reduce each column subvector $\mathbf{P}_{IJ}\mathbf{e}$ to a scalar which will represent the total probability of leaving any page of block $\mathcal{A}_I$ to enter any page of block $\mathcal{A}_J$. To determine the latter probability we need to sum the elements of $\mathbf{P}_{IJ}\mathbf{e}$, after each of these elements have been weighted by the conditional probability of being in a particular state of block $\mathcal{A}_I$ given that we are in block $\mathcal{A}_I$.

These weighting factors can be obtained easily by the steady state probability vector of matrix $\mathbf{P}$. Let's assume that we partition the steady state vector according to the NCD blocks, $\boldsymbol{\pi} = (\boldsymbol{\pi}_1, \boldsymbol{\pi}_2, \ldots, \boldsymbol{\pi}_N)$, where each subvector $\boldsymbol{\pi}_I$ is equal to :

$$\boldsymbol{\pi}_I = (\pi_{I_1}, \pi_{I_2}, \ldots, \pi_{I_{|\mathcal{A}_I|}})$$

where π_{I_k} denotes the element of the steady state vector $\boldsymbol{\pi}$ corresponding to the kth page of the Ith NCD block. Then, the ij^{th} element of the resulting matrix, which we denote $\mathbf{C}$, will be given by:

$$C_{ij} \triangleq \frac{\boldsymbol{\pi}_I^\intercal}{\boldsymbol{\pi}_I^\intercal\mathbf{e}}\mathbf{P}_{IJ}\mathbf{e} \tag{3}$$

Remark 3. The matrix defined in (3) is quite similar to the coupling matrix of the NCD literature [31], except the fact that here we use the previously calculated stationary

Table 2: Number of Iterations till Convergence and Running Time Comparisons

	cnr-2000 325557 nodes		eu-2005 862664 nodes		india-2004 1382908 nodes		indochina-2004 7414866 nodes		uk-2002 18520486 nodes	
Algorithm	iter	time(sec)	iter	time(sec)	iter	time(sec)	iter	time(sec)	iter	time(sec)
NCDawareRank ($\eta = 0.75, \mu = 0.10$)	40	0.4759	38	1.8807	42	2.5576	42	20.3740	41	42.3371
PageRank (damping factor = 0.85)	48	0.6041	42	1.9989	48	2.7251	47	22.0154	46	44.9578
NCDawareRank ($\eta = 0.85, \mu = 0.10$)	107	1.2698	111	5.5493	114	6.7577	115	55.9905	113	116.3179
PageRank (damping factor = 0.95)	141	1.7698	122	5.9013	141	8.2676	136	63.9854	133	130.4432

distribution of matrix $\mathbf{P}$ instead of the approximations obtained by the independent solution of each NCD block.

The steady state probability vector of matrix $\mathbf{C}$, i.e the block-level ranking vector, can be obtained directly from the steady state vector of matrix $\mathbf{P}$ and matrix $\mathbf{A}$, without ever needing to explicitly compute $\mathbf{C}$.

THEOREM 2. *The unique steady state probability vector* $\boldsymbol{\vartheta}$ *of matrix* $\mathbf{C}$, *is given by*

$$\boldsymbol{\vartheta} = \boldsymbol{\pi}^\intercal \mathbf{A}^\intercal$$

where $\boldsymbol{\pi}$ *is the stationary distribution of* $\mathbf{P}$, *and* $\mathbf{A}$ *is the matrix defined during the factorization of the inter-level proximity matrix* $\mathbf{M}$.

PROOF. See Appendix A □

Thus, one can get block-wise ranking as a by-product of the computation of NCDawareRank, paying just a SpMV product.

4. EXPERIMENTS

4.1 Experimental Methodology

Throughout the paper we experiment with several medium and large sized snapshots of the Web obtained from the collection [5][3]. In particular, we used the `cnr-2000`, `eu-2005`, `india-2004`, `indochina-2004` and `uk-2002` Web graphs. Tables 1 and 2 provide information about these graphs. The larger graphs have been used for the storage need tests as well as for the computational and convergence comparisons of Section 3.2, whereas the medium sized ones for the sparsity and link spamming experiments presented in the following sections. During dataset preparation, we sorted the URLs lexicographically, we extracted the lengths of NCD blocks (which in our experiments correspond to websites) and we created matrices $\mathbf{R}$ and $\mathbf{A}$.

We compare NCDawareRank (with $\eta = 0.85$ and $\mu = 0.1$) against several other state-of-the-art link analysis algorithms. In particular:

- HyperRank (Baeza-Yates et al.[2]) with $\beta = 3$
- LinearRank (Baeza-Yates et al.[2]) with $L = 10$,
- PageRank (Page et al.[25]) using the canonical value for the damping factor, $\alpha = 0.85$.
- RAPr (Constantine and Gleich [10]) with the random variable A, following the $Beta(1, 1, [0, 1])$ distribution (the default distribution used by the authors in their publicly available implementation).
- TotalRank (Boldi [4]).

[3]These dataset are available at `http://law.dsi.unimi.it/`

These were the parameters we used for our experiments, with a few specifically stated exceptions.

In our tests in Section 4.2 we make use of the Kendall's τ correlation coefficient [20]; This is an intuitive nonparametric correlation index that has been widely used lately within the Web community (for example [2, 4, 19]) for ranking comparisons. The value of τ is 1 for perfect match and -1 for reversed ordering. All the experiments were done in Matlab on a 64bit machine with 12GB RAM.

4.2 Newly Added Pages and Sparsity

To show the performance of NCDawareRank in dealing with the problems caused by the low density of the Web-graph, we conduct the following two experiments using the `cnr-2000` and the `india-2004` datasets.

Newly Added Pages.

In the first experiment, we simulate the phenomenon of newly added pages by extracting the 90% of the incoming links of a set of randomly chosen pages. The altered graph then represents an "earlier version" of the Web, where these pages were new, and thus had fewer incoming links.

First, we run all the algorithms on the complete graph. Then we randomly choose a number of n pages for several values of n and we randomly remove 90% of their incoming links. Afterwards, we rebuild matrices $\mathbf{A}$ and $\mathbf{R}$ using the new hyperlink matrix, we re-run the algorithms and we calculate how different is the ordering induced on the new graph from the original. The measure used for this purpose is Kendall's τ correlation coefficient.

We repeat the above experiment 10 times; each time for all the different values of newly added pages and we present the average results in Table 4. High value of this metric means that the new ordering is very close to the ordering on the original graph, where all the links were included. We see that NCDawareRank outperforms all other algorithms, and its advantage becomes bigger as the number of newly added pages becomes larger. Thus, even they lack sufficient number of incoming links, the newly added pages get more appropriate ranking.

This was expected and is consistent with the way NCDawareRank views the Web. In NCDawareRank the importance of a page is not exclusively determined by its incoming links as in the other ranking methods; its "neighbourhood" also matters, since the existence of a link confers a small amount of rank to the corresponding ncd block. So, because the importance of a page is correlated with the importance of the website which contains it, even with fewer incoming links, more appropriate ranking is achieved.

Sparseness.

In this experiment, following the same methodology as before, we simulate the sparseness of the link graph by randomly selecting to include 90% - 40% of the links on the

Table 4: Ranking Performance for the Newly Added Pages Bias Problem Using the cnr-2000 Graph.

# New Pages	8000	10000	12000	15000	20000	25000	30000
HyperRank	94.51 ± 0.22	93.26 ± 0.19	92.96 ± 0.21	90.37 ± 0.30	87.72 ± 0.28	84.87 ± 0.31	82.34 ± 0.30
LinearRank	93.80 ± 0.48	92.60 ± 0.24	91.23 ± 0.28	89.41 ± 0.47	86.56 ± 0.44	83.41 ± 0.53	80.69 ± 0.49
NCDawareRank	$\mathbf{96.81 \pm 1.06}$	$\mathbf{96.48 \pm 1.10}$	$\mathbf{96.64 \pm 0.42}$	$\mathbf{95.44 \pm 1.39}$	$\mathbf{94.77 \pm 0.72}$	$\mathbf{93.31 \pm 1.59}$	$\mathbf{91.49 \pm 1.42}$
PageRank	93.68 ± 0.59	92.46 ± 0.30	91.04 ± 0.37	89.19 ± 0.55	86.33 ± 0.53	83.05 ± 0.63	80.26 ± 0.57
RAPr	94.16 ± 0.37	92.96 ± 0.20	91.64 ± 0.23	89.87 ± 0.49	87.15 ± 0.41	84.08 ± 0.45	81.47 ± 0.41
TotalRank	94.15 ± 0.38	92.94 ± 0.21	91.62 ± 0.25	89.84 ± 0.51	87.12 ± 0.43	84.01 ± 0.48	81.37 ± 0.44

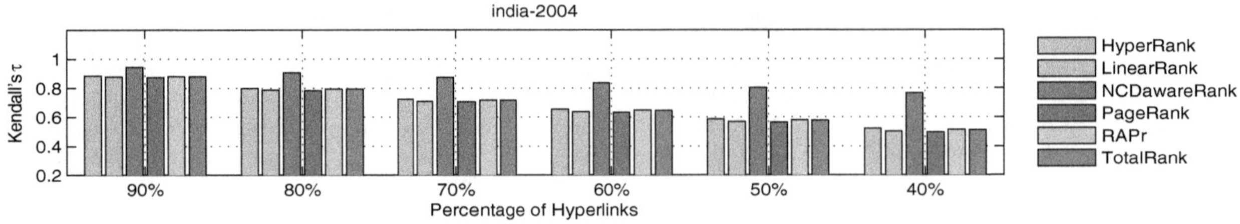

Figure 3: Testing the ranking quality on sparse versions of the india-2004 graph

altered graph and we compare the ranking results of the algorithms against their corresponding original rankings. In Figure 3 we see that NCDawareRank produces ranking that is more resistant to the effects of graph's sparseness when compared to the other ranking methods. Moreover, its advantage becomes bigger as the graph becomes sparser.

These results verify the intuition behind NCDawareRank; even though the direct link structure of the graph collapses with the exclusion of such many links, the inter level proximity captured by matrix $\mathbf{M}$ decays harder and thus preserves longer the coarser structure of the graph. This results in a ranking vector that proves less sensitive to the sparsity of the underlying space.

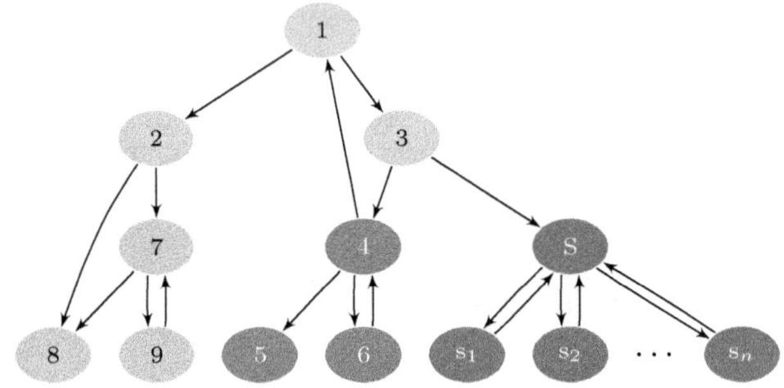

Figure 5: Example graph with spamming node S

4.3 Resistance to Manipulation

In this section we show how the intensity of manipulation affects NCDawareRank's ranking scores. The example graph of Figure 5 shows our approach to simulate the link spamming phenomenon. In this example, the spamming node S creates n nodes that funnel all their rank towards it. In fact, this is a standard technique commonly used in practice [13].

We follow the same approach in our experiments using the `cnr-2000` graph instead. In particular, we randomly pick a node with small initial ranking (from now on referred to as the "spamming node") and we add a number of n nodes that their only incoming link is from the spamming node and their only outgoing link is towards it, in the same manner as in the small example graph of Figure 5. Then, we run NCDawareRank and the other algorithms, for several values of n.

In Figure 4(a), we see the ranking score of the spamming node as a function of n, for all the different algorithms we experimented with. Notice that the anti-manipulation effect of NCDawareRank becomes immediately clear. The introduction of the matrix $\mathbf{M}$ and the ncd-based teleportation of our method, ensure that the ranking increment rate, after a small number of added nodes, becomes very small. So, in order to gain rank, a node has to have incoming links originated from other ncd blocks as well; the effect of nepotistic links is limited and thus, artificial boosting of the ranking score becomes harder.

In order to better isolate the resistance effect induced by the introduction of parameter μ and the corresponding matrix $\mathbf{M}$ alone, we run NCDawareRank using uniform teleportation, for several values of the ratio η/μ, while holding $\eta + \mu$ equal to 0.95, and we plot the results in Figure 4(b). We see that even with the introduction of a very small μ, NCDawareRank starts to exhibit positive resistance properties with the anti-manipulation effect increasing as the ratio η/μ tends to zero, as expected.

Of course as η/μ is getting more close to zero, the direct link structure of the Web values less, because the hyperlink matrix $\mathbf{H}$ gets increasingly ignored. However, the increased sensitivity of the spamming node's ranking score for small

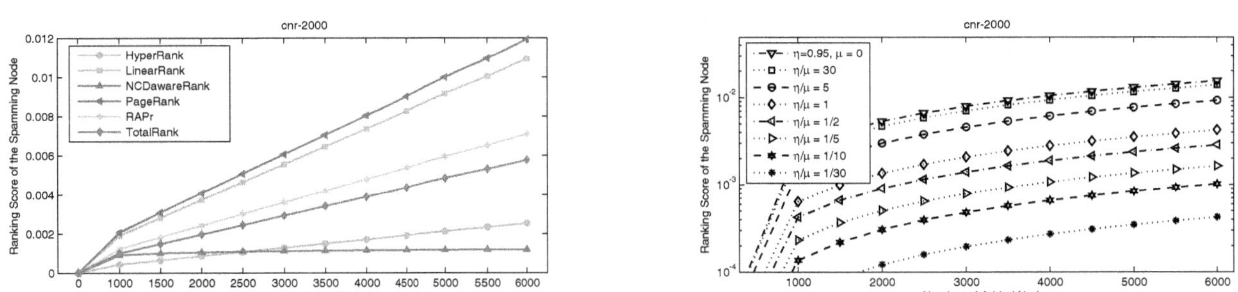

(a) Ranking of the spamming node for different algorithms

(b) NCDawareRank's sensitivity to ratio η/μ

Figure 4: Ranking of the spamming node as a function of the added nodes n, for the cnr-2000 graph

values of the ratio η/μ, could lead to interesting alternative uses of our measure. For example, this characteristic could be exploited by a machine learning framework for better spam classification. This is an interesting research direction we are currently pursuing, with the results so far being very promising.

5. CONCLUSIONS

As already stated in the introduction, the near complete decomposability of the Web has primarily been regarded as a property that could be exploited to compute PageRank faster, or in a distributed manner.

Most approaches that exploit Web's hierarchical nature for ranking, typically involve the creation of a new, coarser level Web graph, on which afterwards, standard ranking technologies are applied. HostRank and DirRank algorithms proposed by Eiron et al.[13] follow this method. Xue et al.[32] construct a multi-layer hierarchical graph and introduce a random walk model on this layered graph, which they use to calculate the importance of the coarser layer first and then distribute this importance to the page layer.

NCDawareRank differs significantly, because it builds directly on the PageRank model using the complete Webgraph, instead of aggregated versions that may hide interesting aspects of its direct link structure. Furthermore, unlike other hierarchical techniques, our framework has the flexibility to bring together heterogeneous decompositions of the underlying space on the same model. For example, one can incorporate different criteria of decomposition like the language of a Web document, the category of its content, or perhaps coarser level structural decompositions by simply introducing new interlevel proximity matrices $\mathbf{M}_1, \mathbf{M}_2, \ldots$ and associated parameters. This opens new and interesting research paths that remain to be explored.

In this paper we considered the single level decomposition case. Our experiments suggest that the introduction of the inter-level proximity matrix involved in NCDawareRank can help alleviating known problems many state-of-the-art link analysis algorithms share, including biased ranking of newly added pages, and susceptibility to direct manipulation through link spamming. Our method introduces a new approach to the Web ranking problem and presents what we believe to be a mathematically attractive and elegant generalization of the basic PageRank model; a generalization that provides an intuitively appealing and computationally efficient theoretical framework for the exploitation of Web's decomposable nature.

6. REFERENCES

[1] K. Avrachenkov, N. Litvak, and K. S. Pham. Distribution of pagerank mass among principle components of the web. In *Proceedings of the 5th international conference on Algorithms and models for the web-graph*, WAW'07, pages 16–28, Berlin, Heidelberg, 2007. Springer-Verlag.

[2] R. Baeza-Yates, P. Boldi, and C. Castillo. Generalizing pagerank: damping functions for link-based ranking algorithms. In *Proceedings of the 29th annual international ACM SIGIR conference on Research and development in information retrieval*, SIGIR '06, pages 308–315, New York, NY, USA, 2006. ACM.

[3] K. Bharat, B.-W. Chang, M. R. Henzinger, and M. Ruhl. Who links to whom: Mining linkage between web sites. In *Proceedings of the 2001 IEEE International Conference on Data Mining*, ICDM '01, pages 51–58, Washington, DC, USA, 2001. IEEE Computer Society.

[4] P. Boldi. Totalrank: ranking without damping. In *Special interest tracks and posters of the 14th international conference on World Wide Web*, WWW '05, pages 898–899, New York, NY, USA, 2005. ACM.

[5] P. Boldi, B. Codenotti, M. Santini, and S. Vigna. Ubicrawler: A scalable fully distributed web crawler. *Software: Practice & Experience*, 34(8):711–726, 2004.

[6] P. Boldi, M. Santini, and S. Vigna. A deeper investigation of pagerank as a function of the damping factor. In *Web Information Retrieval and Linear Algebra Algorithms*, 2007.

[7] P. Boldi, M. Santini, and S. Vigna. Pagerank: Functional dependencies. *ACM Trans. Inf. Syst.*, 27(4):19:1–19:23, Nov. 2009.

[8] A. Cevahir, C. Aykanat, A. Turk, and B. Cambazoglu. Site-based partitioning and repartitioning techniques for parallel pagerank computation. *Parallel and Distributed Systems, IEEE Transactions on*, 22(5):786–802, 2011.

[9] J. Cho and S. Roy. Impact of search engines on page popularity. In *Proceedings of the 13th international conference on World Wide Web*, WWW '04, pages 20–29, New York, NY, USA, 2004. ACM.

[10] P. Constantine and D. Gleich. Random alpha pagerank. *Internet Mathematics*, 6(2):189–236, 2009.

[11] P.-J. Courtois. *Decomposability: Queueing and Computer System Applications*. ACM monograph series. Academic Press, 1977.

[12] N. Eiron and K. S. McCurley. Locality, hierarchy, and bidirectionality in the web. In *In Workshop on Algorithms and Models for the Web Graph*, 2003.

[13] N. Eiron, K. S. McCurley, and J. A. Tomlin. Ranking the web frontier. In *Proceedings of the 13th international conference on World Wide Web*, WWW '04, pages 309–318, New York, NY, USA, 2004. ACM.

[14] M. Faloutsos, P. Faloutsos, and C. Faloutsos. On power-law relationships of the internet topology. *SIGCOMM Comput. Commun. Rev.*, 29(4):251–262, Aug. 1999.

[15] D. F. Gleich, P. G. Constantine, A. D. Flaxman, and A. Gunawardana. Tracking the random surfer: empirically measured teleportation parameters in pagerank. In *Proceedings of the 19th international conference on World wide web*, WWW '10, pages 381–390, New York, NY, USA, 2010. ACM.

[16] M. R. Henzinger, R. Motwani, and C. Silverstein. Challenges in web search engines. In *Proceedings of the 18th international joint conference on Artificial intelligence*, IJCAI'03, pages 1573–1579, San Francisco, CA, USA, 2003. Morgan Kaufmann Publishers Inc.

[17] I. C. F. Ipsen and S. Kirkland. Convergence analysis of a pagerank updating algorithm by Langville and Meyer. *SIAM J. Matrix Anal. Appl.*, 27(4):952–967, Dec. 2005.

[18] S. Kamvar and T. Haveliwala. The condition number of the pagerank problem. *Stanford University Technical Report*, 2003.

[19] S. D. Kamvar, T. H. Haveliwala, C. D. Manning, and G. H. Golub. Exploiting the block structure of the web for computing pagerank. In *Stanford University Technical Report*, 2003.

[20] M. Kendall and J. Gibbons. *Rank Correlation Methods*. Oxford University Press, USA, 1990.

[21] A. N. Langville and C. D. Meyer. Updating pagerank with iterative aggregation. In *Proceedings of the 13th international World Wide Web conference on Alternate track papers & posters*, WWW Alt. '04, pages 392–393, New York, NY, USA, 2004. ACM.

[22] A. N. Langville and C. D. Meyer. *Google's PageRank and Beyond: The Science of Search Engine Rankings*. Princeton University Press, Princeton, NJ, 2006.

[23] C. D. Meyer. Stochastic complementation, uncoupling markov chains, and the theory of nearly reducible systems. *SIAM Rev.*, 31(2):240–272, June 1989.

[24] A. Ntoulas, M. Najork, M. Manasse, and D. Fetterly. Detecting spam web pages through content analysis. In *Proceedings of the 15th international conference on World Wide Web*, WWW '06, pages 83–92, New York, NY, USA, 2006. ACM.

[25] L. Page, S. Brin, R. Motwani, and T. Winograd. The pagerank citation ranking: Bringing order to the web. Technical Report 1999-66, Stanford InfoLab, November 1999.

[26] G. Pandurangan, P. Raghavan, and E. Upfal. Using pagerank to characterize web structure. In O. Ibarra and L. Zhang, editors, *Computing and Combinatorics*, volume 2387 of *Lecture Notes in Computer Science*, pages 1–4. Springer Berlin / Heidelberg, 2002.

[27] I. Pultarová and I. Marek. Convergence of multi-level iterative aggregation-disaggregation methods. *J. Computational Applied Mathematics*, 236(3):354–363, 2011.

[28] E. Seneta. *Non-negative Matrices and Markov Chains*. Springer Verlag, 2006.

[29] H. Simon and A. Ando. Aggregation of variables in dynamic systems. *Econometrica: Journal of The Econometric Society*, pages 111–138, 1961.

[30] H. A. Simon. *The Sciences of the Artificial (3rd ed.)*. MIT Press, Cambridge, MA, USA, 1996.

[31] W. J. Stewart. *Probability, Markov Chains, Queues, and Simulation: The Mathematical Basis of Performance Modeling*. Princeton University Press, Princeton, NJ, USA, 2009.

[32] G.-R. Xue, Q. Yang, H.-J. Zeng, Y. Yu, and Z. Chen. Exploiting the hierarchical structure for link analysis. In *Proceedings of the 28th annual international ACM SIGIR conference on Research and development in information retrieval*, SIGIR '05, pages 186–193, New York, NY, USA, 2005. ACM.

[33] Y. Zhu, S. Ye, and X. Li. Distributed pagerank computation based on iterative aggregation-disaggregation methods. In *Proceedings of the 14th ACM international conference on Information and Knowledge Management*, CIKM '05, pages 578–585, New York, NY, USA, 2005. ACM.

APPENDIX

A. PROOF OF THEOREM 2

THEOREM 2. *The unique steady state probability vector* $\boldsymbol{\vartheta}$ *of matrix* $\mathbf{C}$*, is given by*

$$\boldsymbol{\vartheta} = \boldsymbol{\pi}^\intercal \mathbf{A}^\intercal$$

where $\boldsymbol{\pi}$ *is the stationary distribution of* $\mathbf{P}$*, and* $\mathbf{A}$ *is the matrix defined during the factorization of the inter-level proximity matrix* $\mathbf{M}$.

PROOF. It can be proven that the matrix defined by (3) is a stochastic irreducible matrix [23] and hence it possesses a unique stationary equilibrium distribution. We will show that this probability distribution is $\boldsymbol{\vartheta}$, defined above.

It suffices to verify that equations $\boldsymbol{\vartheta}\mathbf{C} = \boldsymbol{\vartheta}$ and $\boldsymbol{\vartheta}\mathbf{e} = 1$ hold. This can be seen by straightforward calculations:

$$\begin{aligned}
\boldsymbol{\vartheta}\mathbf{C} &= \boldsymbol{\pi}^\intercal \mathbf{A}^\intercal \mathbf{C} \\
&= \boldsymbol{\pi}^\intercal \mathbf{A}^\intercal \begin{bmatrix} \frac{\boldsymbol{\pi}_1^\intercal}{\boldsymbol{\pi}_1^\intercal \mathbf{e}} & \cdots & \mathbf{0} \\ \vdots & \ddots & \vdots \\ \mathbf{0} & \cdots & \frac{\boldsymbol{\pi}_N^\intercal}{\boldsymbol{\pi}_N^\intercal \mathbf{e}} \end{bmatrix} \mathbf{P} \begin{bmatrix} \mathbf{e} & \mathbf{0} & \cdots & \mathbf{0} \\ \mathbf{0} & \mathbf{e} & \cdots & \mathbf{0} \\ \vdots & \vdots & \ddots & \vdots \\ \mathbf{0} & \mathbf{0} & \cdots & \mathbf{e} \end{bmatrix} \\
&= \boldsymbol{\pi}^\intercal \mathbf{P} \mathbf{A}^\intercal = \boldsymbol{\pi}^\intercal \mathbf{A}^\intercal = \boldsymbol{\vartheta}
\end{aligned}$$

and

$$\boldsymbol{\vartheta}\mathbf{e} = \boldsymbol{\pi}^\intercal \mathbf{A}^\intercal \mathbf{e} = \boldsymbol{\pi}^\intercal \mathbf{e} = 1$$

Thus, probability vector $\boldsymbol{\vartheta}$ is the unique steady state solution of matrix $\mathbf{C}$, and the proof is complete. □

Rank Quantization

Ravi Kumar*
Google
Mountain View, CA, USA
ravi.k53@gmail.com

Ronny Lempel
Yahoo! Labs
Matam, Haifa 31905, Israel
rlempel@yahoo-inc.com

Roy Schwartz†
Technion, Israel Institute of Technology
Haifa 32000, Israel
schwartz@cs.technion.ac.il

Sergei Vassilvitskii‡
Google
New York, NY, USA
sergeiv@google.com

ABSTRACT

We study the problem of aggregating and summarizing partial orders, on a large scale. Our motivation is two-fold: to discover elements at similar preference levels and to reduce the number of bits needed to store an element's position in a full ranking. We proceed in two steps: first, we find a total order by linearizing the rankings induced by the multiple partial orders and removing potentially inconsistent pairwise preferences. Next, given a total order, we introduce and formalize the *rank quantization* problem, which intuitively aims to bucketize the total order in a manner that mostly preserves the relations appearing in the partial orders. We show an exact quadratic-time quantization algorithm, as well as a greedy 2/3-approximation algorithm whose running is substantially faster on sparse instances. As an application, we aggregate rankings of top-10 search results over millions of search engine queries, approximately reproducing and then efficiently encoding the underlying static ranks used by the engine. We evaluate the performance of our algorithms on a web dataset of 12 million ($2^{23.5}$) pages and show that we can quantize the pages' static ranks using as few as eight bits, with only a minor degradation in search quality.

Categories and Subject Descriptors

H.3.3 [**Information Systems**]: Information Search and Retrieval

*Work done while at Yahoo! Research, Sunnyvale, CA.
†Work done while interning at Yahoo! Labs, Haifa, Israel.
‡Work done while at Yahoo! Research, New York, NY.

WSDM'13, February 4–8, 2013, Rome, Italy.

Keywords

Bucketization of static ranks; Rank linearization

1. INTRODUCTION

With the proliferation of comparison data available, whether implicitly derived from movie or restaurant ratings or explicit as in the case of "top-10" lists, there is a need for aggregating and summarizing the ranking derived from the large-scale data. While the rank aggregation problem has been well studied in the past [7], the problem of accurately quantizing the ranking into a given number of buckets in order to concisely summarize the ordering has not been sufficiently addressed.

Quantizing ranks is related to the problem of discovering partial orders [18, 22] and bucket orders [9, 12]: given information on the preference relation between pairs (or higher-order subsets) of elements, the goal is to assign elements to any number of ordered buckets in a way that is most compatible with the given preferences. In addition to practical uses of this problem [10, 16], it has also been studied from a theoretical perspective [12, 23]. While the positive results known for this problem imply almost linear-time algorithms, they all assume that the input is a tournament, i.e., *every* pair of elements has a preference relation [23]. Our setting of interest, however, is fundamentally different for two main reasons. First, the number of buckets is prespecified in advance which is not the case in the bucket ordering problem. Second, and more importantly, our setting is extremely sparse as the vast majority of pairs of elements have no specified preference ranking, though through syllogism we can compare elements indirectly. These reasons make our problem also different from the rank aggregation problem [1, 17].

A running example. A concrete example that we will use throughout this work is that of quantizing static rank scores in the context of web search. It is well known that search engines make use of query independent *static scores* to quantify the inherent quality of Web pages. Such scores may be based on link-based attributes of the page (e.g., the widely used PageRank score [4]), URL-based attributes, various design and content signals, click counts, and more [6, 25]. At runtime, upon submission of a query, static scores are mixed with query-dependent page scores to rank query results. Search engines also expose static scores to users (e.g., via browser toolbars) to give them indications on the quality of pages being browsed.

As the size of the searchable Web grows to tens of billions of pages, storing fine-grained static scores requires a significant number of bits. Even storing the rank of each page, as derived from the scores, requires over 32 bits per page. Representing static scores with many bits is problematic on several counts. First, exposing fine-grained page scores via toolbars is an overkill for users and may reveal engine-internal scoring logic to competitors. Second, fine-grained scores cause the size of the index to increase. Expanding on the latter issue, we note that in order to keep query latencies low, search engines — by means of massive distribution [2] — keep their indexes (mostly) in main memory. This means fitting the lexicon, postings lists, and per-document ranking-related metadata in RAM. The fit is tight, and conserving memory for various optimizations is crucial. While the vast body of index compression literature (see [19, 24] and references therein) focuses on reducing the footprint of the postings lists, reducing the size of per-page ranking metadata is also beneficial, especially with access patterns to such data being more random and less sequential than the access patterns to postings lists.

Our contributions. In this work we describe how to quantize the ranks, encoding them with a given number of bits while preserving as much as possible the relative rankings reflected in a given set of partial orders. This allows the quantized ranks to be utilized in the original task with only minor degradation of quality. Specifically, in the Rank Quantization problem, we are given an order (static rank) over items (Web pages), a set of relative ranks $\mathcal{Q}$ (for example the relative rankings of top-t results for a set of queries), and a bit budget b. The goal is to *quantize* the total order into $k = 2^b$ buckets in a way that minimizes the number of ties in $\mathcal{Q}$ induced by the new, quantized ranking.

We formally define the problem and the objective function in Section 3, and show an optimal dynamic programming algorithm for this problem. However, as its running time is quadratic in the number of pages, it does not scale to Web sized inputs. We therefore develop a greedy approximation algorithm whose running time is substantially faster on sparse instances, and prove its near-optimality by carefully exploiting the structure of the Rank Quantization problem. We note that a typical input in the above setting is sparse.

For the formalization of the problem, we assume that the input to Rank Quantization is consistent: for every pair (i, j) of elements either i is preferred to j or vice-versa and for every triple (i, j, k) of elements, if i is preferred to j and j is preferred to k, then i is preferred to k. In practice, however, these assumptions rarely hold, and thus we begin with a pre-processing step, aggregating all of the (potentially inconsistent) rankings into a total order, which we call Rank Linearization. As this problem is NP-complete (it is equivalent to the Feedback-Arc-Set problem), we describe a number of heuristic approaches aimed at removing a minimal number of data points so that the remaining rankings are consistent.

A summary of our contributions is the following:

- We define the Rank Quantization problem, and give an exact quadratic-time algorithm and a greedy approximation algorithm whose running time is substantially faster on sparse instances. In particular, the structure of the problem allows us to prove a better approximation result than that obtained for general submodular problems.
- We show experimentally that our approximation algorithm far exceeds its guaranteed approximation ratio, and is superior to several baselines.
- We show evidence that static scores play a significant role in ranking the top results of search engine queries.
- We evaluate the approaches for Rank Linearization and Rank Quantization on a dataset collected by posing millions of queries to Bing and show that we can quantize the (approximate) static scores to just eight bits while still distinguishing the relative rankings of the vast majority, $\approx 98\%$, of pairs of pages that appear together in the search results.
- Finally, we empirically show that a very simple baseline, which is inferior to our approximately optimal quantization, can close the performance gap if it is allowed to use twice the number of rank buckets.

Organization. The rest of this paper is organized as follows. Section 2 surveys the related work. Section 3 formally defines the problem we solve. Section 4 describes the datasets used throughout our experiments. Section 5 details the algorithms we use and the results they achieve for the Rank Linearization problem. Section 6 details the same for the Rank Quantization problem. Concluding remarks are in Section 7.

2. RELATED WORK

The specific application of quantizing static scores was first addressed by Haveliwala [13]. He proposed two metrics to measure how quantized scores distort fine-grained scores. The first metric, *TDist*, is similar in spirit to the metric we use: it is a function of the number of ties induced by the quantized scores, among the results of a particular query. He proposed several instance-independent heuristic quantization schemes, and measured their empirical performance on a small set of queries. He also considered a model whereby query results are drawn from a uniform sample over the space of Web pages, and are ranked solely by the static score. For this model he proved that the best quantization partitions the space of pages uniformly so that each bucket will hold the same number of pages. In contrast, we optimize the quantization for an actual sample of query results, solving an instance-dependent problem.

Botev et al. [3] bucket static scores in an incremental indexing context, where postings lists are maintained in decreasing static score order. They relaxed the requirement of strict document ordering by static score, instead only demanding that document ordering respects a bucketized static score. In addition to experimenting with the quantization schemes proposed by [13], they experimented with buckets where the difference between the largest and smallest static score did not exceed a certain value. They show that the enterprise search engine's rank function was hardly affected by the move from fine grained scores (over 500K documents) to bucketized scores (with 64 buckets). Their work is purely experimental in the sense that they do not pose rank (or score) quantization an optimization problem but rather evaluate the performance of various heuristics.

Moffat et al. [20, 21] attempt to reduce the memory required by the index to store a different attribute of documents, namely their lengths (document lengths play a role in the scoring phase). They experiment with several heuristic quantization schemes and measure the ranking degradation on TREC datasets.

We note that the tools and techniques we use in our work touch upon many well-researched problems in theoretical computer science. For ease of presentation, we survey related work around those problems in the context of the exposition rather than in this section.

3. PRELIMINARIES

In this section we formally describe the setting of the Rank Quantization and the Rank Linearization problems.

Let $V = \{v_1, v_2, \ldots, v_n\}$ be a set of n elements and let $\mathcal{Q} = \{\sigma_1, \sigma_2, \ldots, \sigma_s\}$ be a set of s partial orders over V. In the context of this work, the partial orders in $\mathcal{Q}$ will refer to total orders over (typically very small) subsets of V. For a partial order σ, we write $u \succ_\sigma v$ if u dominates v according to σ. Any partial order σ can be represented as a directed acyclic graph $G = (V, T_\sigma)$ where T_σ are the edges of the tournament induced by σ, i.e., $(u, v) \in T_\sigma$ if and only if $u \succ_\sigma v$. Additionally, any σ can also be represented by another directed graph $H = (V, R_\sigma)$ where R_σ are the edges of a directed *path* from the highest ranking node in σ to the lowest ranking node in σ, i.e., R_σ is the longest path in the tournament T_σ.

In the concrete example we consider, V is the set of web pages and the partial orders $\mathcal{Q}$ are given by the ordering of the top t results for each query; we will use the terms query and partial order interchangeably. For a fixed query σ, let $v_1 \succ_\sigma v_2 \succ_\sigma \cdots \succ_\sigma v_t$ be the set of the top t results. The path R_σ simply has one edge from (v_i, v_{i+1}) for $1 \leq i < t$, whereas the tournament T_σ has an edge (v_i, v_j) for any pair $1 \leq i < j \leq t$.

For a given set $\mathcal{Q}$ of partial orders, we define the *query graph* as the multigraph over V whose edge set corresponds to all R_σ (keeping multiple parallel edges) and denote it by $G_\mathcal{Q}$. The closure multigraph $G_\mathcal{Q}^T$ of the query graph has an edge (u, v) any time u appeared prior to (i.e., was ranked higher than) v in some query (keeping multiple parallel edges).

Rank quantization. In the Rank Quantization problem we are given a weighted graph $G = (V, E)$ with a topological order π on the nodes and an integer $k > 0$. The solution to rank quantization is characterized by $k - 1$ topologically decreasing "break point" nodes $\{b_1, b_2, \ldots, b_{k-1}\}$ such that $B_1 = \{v : v \succ_\pi b_1\}$, for $1 < i < k$, $B_i = \{v : b_{i-1} \succeq_\pi v \succ_\pi b_i\}$ and $B_k = \{v : b_{k-1} \succeq_\pi v\}$. Each B_i is called a *bucket* and let us denote by $\mathcal{B}$ the ordered set of all k buckets. The value of the solution, denoted by cost($\mathcal{B}$), is the total weight of edges whose both endpoints are in the same bucket, i.e., an edge $(u, v) \in E$ contributes its weight to cost($\mathcal{B}$) if there exists a bucket $B \in \mathcal{B}$ s.t. $u, v \in B$. Intuitively, by both endpoints falling in the same bucket, the original order between them is obscured.

We now formally define the rank quantization problem.

PROBLEM 1 (Rank Quantization). *Given a weighted graph $G = (V, E)$, an ordering π on V, and the desired number k of buckets, find the partition of V into an ordered set $\mathcal{B}$ of k buckets that minimizes* cost($\mathcal{B}$).

Rank linearization. In practice, there is rarely a single consistent ordering π. In the example of web ranking, although a static score composes a large part of the final order, many query and user specific factors also influence the final ordering of results for a specific query. Therefore, before running the rank quantization algorithms, we must first find the most consistent order from a set of partial orders, such as those given by the individual queries.

Formally, given a collection of partial orders $\mathcal{Q}$, the Rank Linearization problem asks to find a total order π that best corresponds to $\mathcal{Q}$. This is equivalent to the minimum Feedback-Arc-Set problem: given a directed multigraph $G = (V, E)$, or equivalently a weighted directed graph where the weight of an edge (u, v) is set to the number of copies of this edge in the multigraph, find the smallest subset $F \subseteq E$ such that $(V, E \setminus F)$ is acyclic. It is known that the minimum Feedback-Arc-Set problem is NP-complete [15]. Depending on the multigraph we are working with, we define two versions of the Rank Linearization problem that differ in their objective. In the *query* version we want to remove the fewest number of edges from $G_\mathcal{Q}$, whereas in the *tournament* version we want to remove the fewest number of edges from the closure graph $G_\mathcal{Q}^T$.

4. DATASETS

This section describes the two datasets collected for our experiments. Both are based on Bing query results collected for samples of queries submitted to Yahoo! between 23–25 of August 2011. The first dataset, hereby referred to as the *random* sample, is — as its name suggests — a sample where each instance in the query log was chosen at random with a certain probability. The second dataset, hereby referred to as the *popular* sample, was generated by taking a single instance of each of the million or so most frequently submitted queries over the three days above. For each query instance in both samples, we collected the top-10 Bing results (or all results returned in those rare cases where Bing returned fewer than 10 results per query). Table 1 shows the number of queries and distinct URLs in each sample.

Since the random sample may include multiple instances of the same query string (submitted by different users and/or by the same user at different times), it can be seen as a weighted query sample, where each query is weighted by its popularity, as opposed to the unweighted popular sample.

Table 1: Statistics of the two query samples.

	Random	Popular
# query instances	2,707,972	1,002,172
# distinct URLs	12,522,552	5,901,147
size of largest component	6,891,145	3,931,689
size of second largest component	261	968

Note that Bing occasionally returned slightly different results for different instances of the same query string.

We checked several properties of the samples that relate to the construction of the multigraphs G_Q and G_Q^T. Specifically, the sizes of the two largest connected components when ignoring the directions of the edges.[1] This is a measure of the overlap between the results of different queries, as edges between nodes (pages) in G_Q^T indicate that the nodes appeared together in at least one set of top-10 query results. As shown in Table 1, both samples have a single, dominating connected component, containing over half the nodes, that is orders of magnitude larger than all other components.

Note that both algorithmic steps, linearization and rank quantization, can be done on each connected component of G_Q separately. In particular, the buckets resulting from all connected components can be trivially aggregated[2] without any loss in the objective. As the large connected component dwarfs all other components, the rest of our experiments were conducted on the large component of each sample rather than on the entire set of fragmented graphs.

5. RANK LINEARIZATION

Section 3 established the equivalence of the Rank Linearization step to solving a minimum Feedback-Arc-Set instance. This section applies known heuristics (and adaptations thereof) for approximating minimum Feedback-Arc-Set on our test collections. The results indicate that static scores play a significant role in ranking search results.

5.1 Rank Linearization: Algorithms

It is known that the minimum Feedback-Arc-Set problem is hard to approximate [11, 14]. The current best algorithm [8] achieves an approximation of $O(\log n \log\log n)$ and requires the computation of a *spreading metric* (this is in fact true for all known approximation algorithms that achieve a polylogarithmic guarantee). We will not define exactly what a spreading metric is, only mention that it is expensive to compute in practice. Thus we resort to heuristic approaches for Rank Linearization detailed below. Let $G = (V, E)$ be a weighted directed graph where $|V| = n, |E| = m$.

5.1.1 Sorting by out-degree

One way to compute a full order is to sort the nodes by their weighted out-degree: those with the highest weighted out-degree should come early in the order, while those with out-degree of 0 should come last. In the case of unweighted tournament graphs (where, for any pair of nodes u, v, either $(u, v) \in E$ or $(v, u) \in E$) this simple heuristic returns a 5-approximation to the optimum Feedback-Arc-Set [5]. Although the performance guarantees do not carry over to the more general case, this heuristic is very simple to compute in time $O(n \log n + m)$.

5.1.2 Eigenvector method

The eigenvector method [7] works by computing the stationary distribution of a random walk induced by this graph with a small teleportation probability to make sure the walk is ergodic. Let w_{ij} denote the weight of the edge from v_i to v_j in G. Let the $n \times n$ transition matrix be $M = \{m_{ij}\}$ with $m_{ij} = \max(w_{ij} - w_{ji}, 0)$. Also, we define a constant "teleportation" matrix R with $R_{i,j} = \varepsilon$, for all $1 \leq i, j \leq n$. These two matrices are incorporated together by considering the matrix $\lambda M + (1 - \lambda)R$ for some predefined constant $0 \leq \lambda \leq 1$. The algorithm proceeds by finding the eigenvector that corresponds to the largest eigenvalue of the latter matrix, and the final order orders the nodes by their value in this eigenvector.

We use the iterative power method to find the stationary distribution. The algorithm begins with a uniform distribution: $u_0 = (n^{-1/2}, \ldots, n^{-1/2})$. In the ith step, this distribution is updated as: $u_i = (\lambda M + (1 - \lambda)R)u_{i-1}$ and renormalized. The algorithm halts when the change between steps is bounded: $||u_i - u_{i-1}||_2 \leq \delta$, for some pre-specified constant $\delta > 0$. Since M is generally sparse, and has at most $m \ll n^2$ values, each iteration can be implemented in $O(n + m)$ time.

5.1.3 Generalized Quicksort

The generalized quicksort algorithm has been shown to lead to near optimal solutions for Feedback-Arc-Set in weighted tournament graphs [1, 7, 17]. This algorithm was subsequently extended to the closely related bucket ordering problem in weighted tournament graphs [23]. Here we adapt it to general graphs, preserving the intuition behind the algorithm, but losing the associated performance guarantees.

This is a recursive algorithm that at each step, chooses a pivot node from G uniformly at random and partitions the remaining nodes of G' into two sets, the *left* set and the *right* set (the algorithm then recurses on the two induced subgraphs). The total order π is obtained by placing the left set to the left of the pivot and the right set to the right of the pivot.

In the tournament version the nodes to the left (resp. right) of the pivot are those that have edges incoming to (resp. going from) the pivot. Below we describe the adaptation to general graphs where some nodes may not be directly connected to the pivot.

As before, the algorithm chooses a node $v_p \in G$ uniformly at random and labels it as the pivot. The next step is to select the *left* and *right* sets. We first consider the nodes that are directly connected to v_p and then we explore the remaining nodes.

Let v_i be a node in G such that either $(v_p, v_i) \in E$ or $(v_i, v_p) \in E$. Equivalently, v_i is such that $w_{ip} + w_{pi} > 0$, where w_{uv} is the total weight of edges from u to v as described above. Intuitively, the higher the value of w_{ip} the

[1] G_Q and G_Q^T have the same connectivity properties.

[2] The ith bucket of G_Q is simply the union of the ith buckets of all components.

higher the probability that v_i should be placed to the left of v_p. At the same time, if there are very few edges between v_i and v_p making an inconsistent choice has a low cost, and hence we skew the probability closer to 1/2.

Formally, let θ be a parameter of the algorithm. Denote by L_i the event that v_i was placed in the left set. Then, we have

$$\Pr[L_i] = \begin{cases} \frac{w_{ij}}{w_{ij}+w_{ji}} & \text{if } w_{ij}+w_{ji} \geq \theta, \\ \frac{1}{2} + \frac{w_{ij}-w_{ji}}{2\theta}, & \text{otherwise.} \end{cases}$$

In the second step we consider each remaining node one at a time and decide whether to place it to the left or to the right of the pivot, v_p. Let $\mathcal{L}$ be the nodes already placed to the left, similarly let $\mathcal{R}$ be those already placed to the right. Among the nodes that share an edge with some node in $\mathcal{L}$ or $\mathcal{R}$ the algorithm chooses a node v_i at random. (If no such nodes exist, v_i is chosen at random from all of the remaining nodes and added to $\mathcal{L}$ or $\mathcal{R}$ with equal probability.)

The algorithm again makes a probabilistic decision whether to place the node v_i in $\mathcal{L}$ or in $\mathcal{R}$. To compute the probability of placing v_i in each bucket, we consider a simple Markov Chain with one state for $\mathcal{L}$ and one for $\mathcal{R}$. For a set $S \subset V$, let $w_{iS} = \sum_{v_j \in S} w_{ij}$ be the total weight of the edges from v_i into the S, and $w_{Si} = \sum_{v_j \in S} w_{ji}$ be the total weight of edges from S to v_i.

The probability transition matrix of the Markov chain is the following:

$$P = \begin{matrix} \\ (\mathcal{L}) \\ (\mathcal{R}) \end{matrix} \begin{matrix} (\mathcal{L}) & (\mathcal{R}) \\ \end{matrix} \begin{pmatrix} \frac{w_{i\mathcal{L}}}{w_{i\mathcal{L}}+w_{\mathcal{L}i}} & \frac{w_{\mathcal{L}i}}{w_{i\mathcal{L}}+w_{\mathcal{L}i}} \\ \frac{w_{i\mathcal{R}}}{w_{i\mathcal{R}}+w_{\mathcal{R}i}} & \frac{w_{\mathcal{R}i}}{w_{i\mathcal{R}}+w_{\mathcal{R}i}} \end{pmatrix}.$$

We add the node v_i to $\mathcal{L}$ with the probability given to $\mathcal{L}$ by the stationary distribution of P:

$$\Pr[L_i] = \frac{\frac{w_{i\mathcal{R}}}{w_{\mathcal{R}i}+w_{i\mathcal{R}}}}{\frac{w_{i\mathcal{R}}}{w_{\mathcal{R}i}+w_{i\mathcal{R}}} + \frac{w_{\mathcal{L}i}}{w_{\mathcal{L}i}+w_{i\mathcal{L}}}}.$$

The above algorithm can be efficiently implemented, with each pivot round taking $O(n+m)$ time.

5.1.4 *Local search improvements*

None of the above algorithms guarantees that the final linear orders are locally optimal, therefore we perform a local search to further reduce the number of edges removed (see Section 5.2 for the specific use). Given a size parameter s, the algorithm checks whether swapping a pair of nodes within s of each other in the total order improves the cost function, and halts when no such pairs are found.

5.2 Rank Linearization: Experimental results

We executed all three linearization algorithms: sorting by out-degree (SO), the eigenvector heuristic (EG), and the generalized quicksort (GQ), for each of the two query samples (on the largest component of G_Q when viewed as an undirected graph). We also applied the local improvement heuristic (LI) on each of the orderings generated by the algorithms above. The exact settings of our executions were

Table 2: Percentage of edges in the feedback set for each linearization algorithm.

	Random	Popular
Lower Bound	3.7	4.4
SO	17.62	19.91
SO + LI	15.54	19.74
EG	17.03	19.02
EG + LI	15.07	18.86
GQ	19.53	19.16
GQ + LI	19.53	19.16

as follows. We ran EG with $\lambda = 0.85$, $\varepsilon = 1$ and $\delta = 10^{-10}$. Since the GQ algorithm is randomized, we report the average results across 32 independent runs for each setting of the parameters. The standard deviation of the results due to different random seeds and different values of θ was under 0.1%. For SO, no special parameters are needed. We chose $s = 512$ for LI.

The results are summarized in Table 2, where we measure the performance of each algorithm according to the fraction of the edges of G_Q^T that belong to the feedback set. The results in Table 2 indicate that, for both samples, we can find linear orderings that agree with the direction of over 80% of the edges in G_Q^T. Intuitively, this suggests that the static score signal plays a significant role in determining the order among the top-10 results of queries. Another interpretation is that query-dependent score factors are all quite high at the very top of the results list, and so those factors do not dominate the static score there.

Note that unlike SO and EG, the GQ algorithm did not benefit from a local improvement step, but produced qualitatively worse results. To estimate the performance of the linearization algorithms, we find that 3.7% of edges in the random graph and 4.4% of edges in the popular graph must be cut to break cycles of length 2. These cycles are formed when a pair of results appears in reverse order in two different queries.

6. RANK QUANTIZATION

Ultimately, the quality of quantized ranks is task-specific, namely determined by its impact on the application. In our case we are quantizing search engine static ranks, with the application being ranking query results. Ideally, we would want to check the performance of the search engine with the quantized scores; however, this type of evaluation is beyond our reach. We therefore use the number of ties introduced by quantization as a proxy [13], where a tie occurs when two of the top t results of a query are assigned to the same bucket. Whenever this happens, the quantized scores obscure any difference in the static ranks of these two pages. Conversely, when the quantized scores allow the engine to reconstruct the score relation between all or most pairs of top-t pages, it should be able to utilize the quantized static ranks to approximate its original query results as well. With this measure of success in mind, we present quantization algorithms and their results in the remainder of this section.

6.1 Rank Quantization: Algorithms

We present algorithms for the Rank Quantization problem. Our first algorithm shows how to solve the problem exactly, albeit in time quadratic in the total number of elements, which is untenable at Web scale. The second algorithm is an adaptation of the classical greedy set cover method to this setting and can be implemented substantially faster for sparse inputs (a typical input in our setting is indeed sparse). The added structure of the problem allows us to prove a $2/3$-approximation performance guarantee in the worst case.

Recall that in the Rank Quantization problem we are given a weighted graph $G = (V, E), |V| = n, |E| = m$ and a topological order π on the nodes. The solution to rank quantization has a compact representation. It can be characterized by $k-1$ decreasing *breakpoint* nodes $\{b_1, b_2, \ldots, b_{k-1}\}$ such that $B_1 = \{v : v \succ_\pi b_1\}$, for $1 < i < k$, $B_i = \{v : b_{i-1} \succeq_\pi v \succ_\pi b_i\}$ and $B_k = \{v : b_{k-1} \succeq_\pi v\}$. We will drop the subscript π when it is clear from the context.

6.1.1 *Exact algorithm*

We exploit the structure of the optimum solution to define a simple dynamic programming algorithm for the problem. We will maintain a table A where $A[i, j]$ for $1 \le i \le n+1, 1 \le j \le k$ stores the cost of bucketing the elements v_i through v_n into j buckets. Our goal is to compute $A[1, k]$. We proceed to fill in $A[i, j]$ in decreasing order of i. When processing element v_i we decide on the last element, v_ℓ of this bucket, and look up the cost of quantizing the subsequent elements $v_{\ell+1}, \ldots, v_n$. Formally the recursion step is:

$$A[i, j] = \min_{i \le \ell \le n} \left(A[\ell+1, j-1] + \sum_{v_i \succ v_x \succ v_y \succ v_\ell} w_{xy} \right).$$

Algorithm 1 presents all the details. With some preprocessing, we can execute the recursive step in $O(n)$ time, which leads to an $O(n^2 k)$ overall running time for the algorithm. As we stated earlier, this is prohibitive for large n.

Algorithm 1 Dynamic programming.

for $j = 1, \ldots, k$ **do**
 $A[n+1, j] \leftarrow 0$
end for
for $i = n, \ldots, 1$ **do**
 for $j = 1, \ldots, k$ **do**
  $A[i, j] \leftarrow \min_{i \le \ell \le n}(A[\ell+1, j-1]$
   $+ \sum_{v_i \succ v_x \succ v_y \succ v_\ell} w_{xy})$
 end for
end for
Output $A[1, k]$

6.1.2 *Greedy approximation*

Since the exact dynamic programming algorithm takes quadratic time, one can settle for a provable approximation that can be computed much faster. Recall the objective of the problem is to find a set of buckets that minimizes the number of edges in the subgraphs induced by each bucket:

$$\sum_{i=1}^{k} \sum_{u,v \in B_i} w_{uv}.$$

Alternatively, we can maximize the number of edges between buckets. To proceed with the analysis, we say an edge (u, v) is *cut* by a breakpoint b if $u \succ b \succeq v$. Let $C(b) = \{(x, y) \in E \mid x \succ b \succeq y\}$ be the set of edges cut by a breakpoint. Then the total weight of the cut is:

$$|C(b)| = \sum_{(x,y) \in C(b)} w_{xy}.$$

Extending this definition to multiple breakpoints, for a set $B = \{b_1, b_2, \ldots, b_\ell\}$, the set of edges cut is:

$$C(B) = \bigcup_{b \in B} C(b).$$

Similarly, the total weight is:

$$|C(B)| = \sum_{(x,y) \in C(B)} w_{xy}.$$

Therefore an equivalent formulation of the rank quantization problem is to find a set $B = \{b_1, \ldots, b_{k-1}\}$ of breakpoints that maximizes the total number (weight) of edges cut, $|C(B)|$. This can be viewed as a special case of the well studied Maximum Coverage problem [11]: given a (weighted) ground set $\mathcal{N}$, a collection $\mathcal{S} \subseteq 2^{\mathcal{N}}$ of subsets of $\mathcal{N}$, and a parameter k, find at most k subsets out of $\mathcal{S}$, say $S_1, S_2, \ldots, S_k \in \mathcal{S}$ that maximize $| \cup_{i=1}^{k} S_i|$, i.e., the weight of the elements in the union.

In this formulation each edge (u, v) defines an element of the ground set E, and each breakpoint b_i defines a set $S_i = C(b_i) \subseteq E$. Algorithm 2 shows all the details. With a careful implementation this problem can be solved in time $O(nk + m \log m)$. The greedy algorithm that iteratively selects the set that covers the highest number of yet uncovered elements yields a $1 - 1/e$ approximation for Maximum Coverage. Below we show that due to the special structure of the problem, the same greedy algorithm achieves a $2/3 > 1 - 1/e$ approximation for rank quantization. (We conjecture that the correct bound for this algorithm is $3/4$.)

Algorithm 2 Greedy algorithm.

$S \leftarrow \emptyset$
$T \leftarrow \emptyset$
while $|S| < k$ **do**
 $b \leftarrow \arg\max_{b'} |C(b') \setminus T|$
 $T \leftarrow T \cup C(b)$
 $S \leftarrow S \cup \{b\}$
end while
Output $|C(S)|$

THEOREM 2. *The greedy algorithm achieves a $2/3$-approximation to the maximization version of* Rank Quantization.

PROOF. Let g_i be the element selected in the ith round, and denote by G_i the solution computed by selecting the first i elements greedily. Thus $G_i = G_{i-1} \cup \{g_i\}$, where $G_0 = \emptyset$. Let H_i be the $k - i$ elements that optimally extend the solution G_i. We will compare the cost of the greedy solution, G_k to that of the optimal solution, H_0.

Finally, for a set S, let

$$\Delta_i(S) = |C(G_i \cup S)| - |C(G_i)|,$$

be the incremental benefit of selecting breakpoints in S, having already selected G_i. To simplify notation for singleton sets S, we will write $\Delta_i(s)$ instead of $\Delta_i(\{s\})$.

We will show that, in every step, the greedy algorithm's decision is nearly optimal.

LEMMA 3. *For* $i \geq 1$, $\Delta_{i-1}(H_{i-1}) - \Delta_i(H_i) \leq \frac{3}{2}\Delta_{i-1}(g_i)$.

Given Lemma 3, we can complete the proof of the theorem by the following argument:

$$\begin{aligned}|C(H_0)| &= \Delta_0(H_0) \\ &= \Delta_k(H_k) + \sum_{i=1}^{k}\Big(\Delta_{i-1}(H_{i-1}) - \Delta_i(H_i)\Big) \\ &\leq \frac{3}{2}\sum_{i=1}^{k}\Delta_{i-1}(g_i) \\ &= \frac{3}{2}|C(G_k)|,\end{aligned}$$

where we use Lemma 3 and the fact that $H_k = \emptyset$ to reach the first inequality. □

Now, we proceed to establish Lemma 3, which uses the specific structure of our problem.

PROOF OF LEMMA 3. To prove the lemma, given the greedy solution after $i-1$ steps, G_{i-1}, its optimal extension, H_{i-1} and the greedily selected breakpoint g_i, we exhibit a set $S \subset H_{i-1}$ with $|S| = k - i$ such that

$$\Delta_{i-1}(H_{i-1}) - \Delta_i(S) \leq \frac{3}{2}\Delta_{i-1}(g_i).$$

Since H_i is the optimal extension of G_i, $\Delta_i(H_i) \geq \Delta_i(S)$ and this establishes the proof.

Denote the elements of $H_{i-1} = \{h_1 \prec h_2 \prec \cdots \prec h_{k-(i-1)}\}$ and let $g = g_i$ be the next point selected by the greedy algorithm.

Case 1. Suppose $g \prec h_1$ (a similar argument holds for, $g \succ h_{k-i+1}$). Consider a solution $S = H_{i-1} \setminus \{h_1\}$.

By the greedy property of g, $\Delta_{i-1}(g) \geq \Delta_{i-1}(h_1)$. Furthermore, g covers no more edges from $C(S)$ than h_1 and hence we have

$$C(g) \cap C(S) \subset C(h_1) \cap C(S).$$

Therefore, $\Delta_i(S) \geq \Delta_{i-1}(S)$, and we have:

$$\Delta_i(S) + \Delta_{i-1}(g) \geq \Delta_{i-1}(S) + \Delta_{i-1}(h_1) \geq \Delta_{i-1}(H_{i-1}).$$

Case 2. Suppose $h_j \prec g \prec h_{j+1}$. To untangle the interactions between $\Delta_{i-1}(h_j), \Delta_i(g)$ and $\Delta_i(g_{j+1})$, consider subdividing the edges cut by h_j and h_{j+1} into the following five disjoint sets:

$E_1 = C(h_j) \setminus C(g) \setminus C(G_i)$,
$E_2 = C(h_j) \cap C(g) \setminus C(G_i)$,
$E_3 = C(g) \setminus (C(h_j) \cup C(h_{j+1})) \setminus C(G_i)$,
$E_4 = C(h_{j+1}) \cap C(g)| \setminus C(G_i)$, and
$E_5 = C(h_{j+1}) \setminus C(g) \setminus C(G_i)$.

Then,

$\Delta_{i-1}(h_j) = |E_1| + |E_2|$,
$\Delta_{i-1}(g) = |E_2| + |E_3| + |E_4|$, and
$\Delta_{i-1}(h_j) = |E_4| + |E_5|$.

Assume that:

$$|E_1| \leq |E_5|. \tag{1}$$

The reverse case is similar. Since g was the point maximizing $\Delta_{i-1}(g)$, we have:

$$\Delta_{i-1}(g) = |E_2| + |E_3| + |E_4| \geq |E_1| + |E_2| = \Delta_{i-1}(h_j). \tag{2}$$

And:

$$\Delta_{i-1}(g) = |E_2| + |E_3| + |E_4| \geq |E_4| + |E_5| = \Delta_{i-1}(h_{j+1}). \tag{3}$$

Let $S = H_{i-1} \setminus \{h_j\}$. Then, compared to $G_{i-1} \cup H_{i-1}$, the solution $G_{i-1} \cup S \cup \{g\}$ will cut the edges in E_3, but will no longer cut those in E_1. Hence:

$$\Delta_{i-1}(H_{i-1}) - (\Delta_i(H_i) + \Delta_{i-1}(g_i)) = |E_1| - |E_3|.$$

Summing Equations (1) and (2) we have:

$$2|E_1| \leq |E_5| + |E_3| + |E_4|.$$

Using Equation (3) we have:

$$\begin{aligned}&2|E_1| \leq |E_2| + |E_3| + |E_3| + |E_4| \\ \Longrightarrow\ &2(|E_1| \quad |E_3|) \leq |E_2| + |E_4| \\ \Longrightarrow\ &\Delta_{i-1}(H_{i-1}) - (\Delta_i(H_i) + \Delta_{i-1}(g_i)) \leq \frac{1}{2}\Delta_{i-1}(g_1).\end{aligned}$$

In both cases we bound the loss due to greedy behavior, which allows us to conclude the proof. □

6.2 Bucketing results on synthetic datasets

Recall that the dynamic programming algorithm that optimally solves the rank quantization problem is quadratic in the number of input pages (graph nodes), which is prohibitive for the sizes of our query samples. Therefore, to evaluate the performance of Greedy with respect to the optimal algorithm, and in particular to empirically check whether it exceeds the 2/3 approximation guarantee on the Maximum Coverage instances generated by Rank Quantization (see Section 6.1), we compare the two on synthetic workloads where we can afford to optimally solve the problem instances.

We generated random ordered graphs with the following parameters: $N = 2^{15}$ is the number of nodes, $Q = 2^{13}$ is the number of queries, and $k = 32$ is the number of required buckets. The nodes are ordered $1, \ldots, N$, meaning that all edges are ordered from lower-numbered nodes to higher-numbered nodes. We denoted the number of results per query by t, and experimented with $t = 8,\ 10,\ 12,\ 14$ and 16.

We considered each query as a random subset of t nodes (this is similar to the model used in [13]). We ran both algorithms on these synthetic graphs and measured the performance of the greedy approximation as compared to the optimal solution. Table 3 lists the ratio of the objective functions of the greedy approximation to the optimal solution for both the minimization and maximization versions of the problem. Each entry in the table was computed by averaging 128 independent samples of the input graph. As can be seen from the table, the greedy approximation works

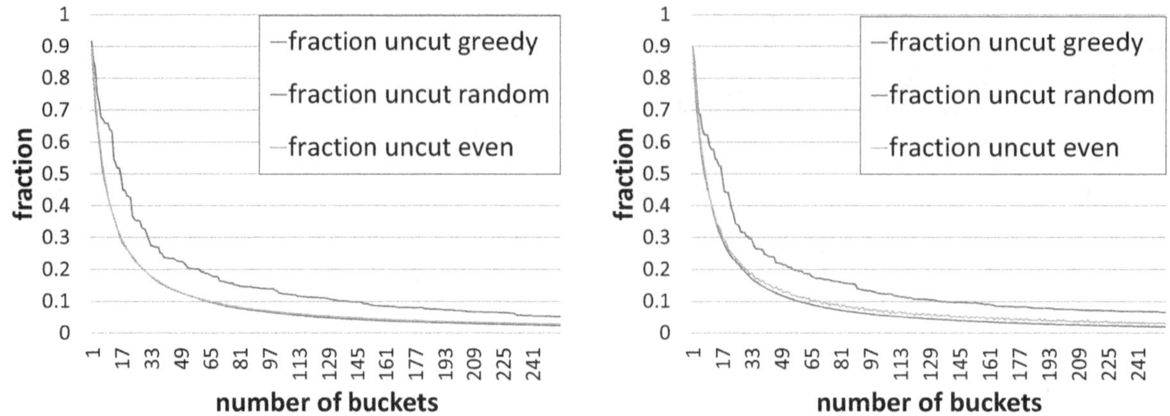

(a) Popular (b) Random

Figure 1: Fraction of edges left uncut by the different rank quantization methods in the *unweighted* (a) popular (b) random query graphs.

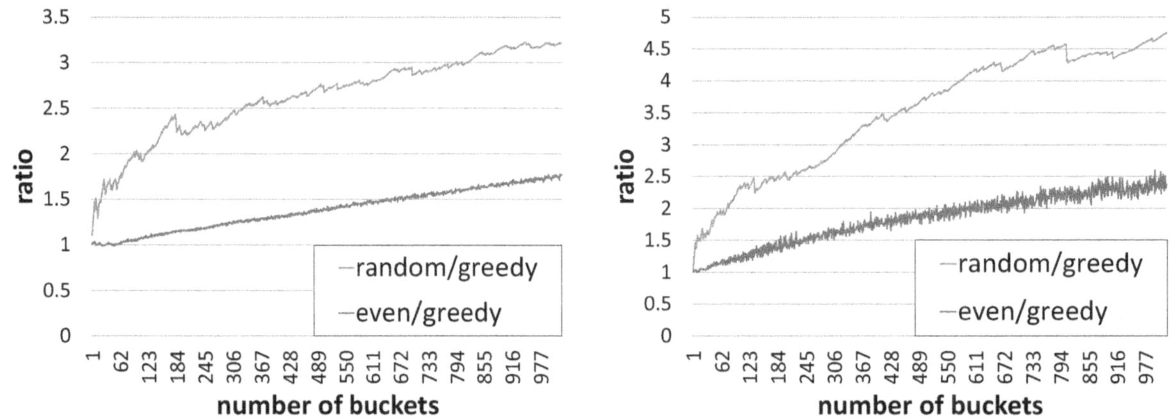

(a) Popular (b) Random

Figure 2: The relative performance of the `random` and `even` baselines as compared to the greedy approximation algorithm, in terms of uncut edges, on the *unweighted* (a) popular and (b) random query graphs.

Table 3: The approximation ratio of the greedy algorithm on synthetic random queries.

t	Minimization	Maximization
8	1.024	0.997
10	1.019	0.997
12	1.017	0.997
14	1.019	0.996
16	1.022	0.994

extremely well for both objectives, with a deviation from optimum of at most 2.5% for the minimization objective and roughly 0.5% for the maximization objective.

The synthetic graphs above have certain characteristics that are similar to the graphs induced by the real query samples. When linearizing both the random and popular samples (see Section 5.2), the average length of an edge connecting two adjacent results of the same query was approximately $n/12$. Since queries had almost exclusively 10 results, this implies that on average, in both samples, queries are well distributed throughout the linear order, and can be reasonably approximated by a random subset of 10 pages.

6.3 Bucketing results on query samples

We evaluated the performance of the greedy approximation algorithm on weighted and unweighted multigraphs induced by both the popular and random query samples.[3] For each graph we chose the best linearization (as described in Section 5.2). Since the original query results were not fully consistent with the linearized rankings, for the purposes of the quantization experiment we reordered each top-t list to be consistent with the linearized order.

When evaluating unweighted multigraphs, we assigned each (individual) edge a weight of 1. The weighted versions were constructed to account for the fact that inducing a tie be-

[3]Even in the popular sample, where queries do not repeat, edges may repeat (hence creating a multigraph) as the same pair of pages may appear in the results of multiple queries.

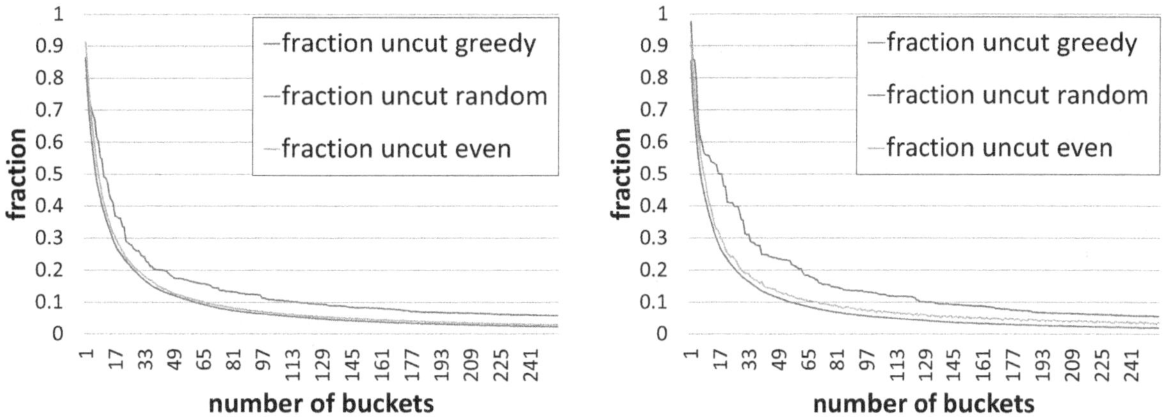

(a) Popular (b) Random

Figure 3: Fraction of edges left uncut by the different rank quantization methods in the *weighted* (a) popular (b) random query graphs.

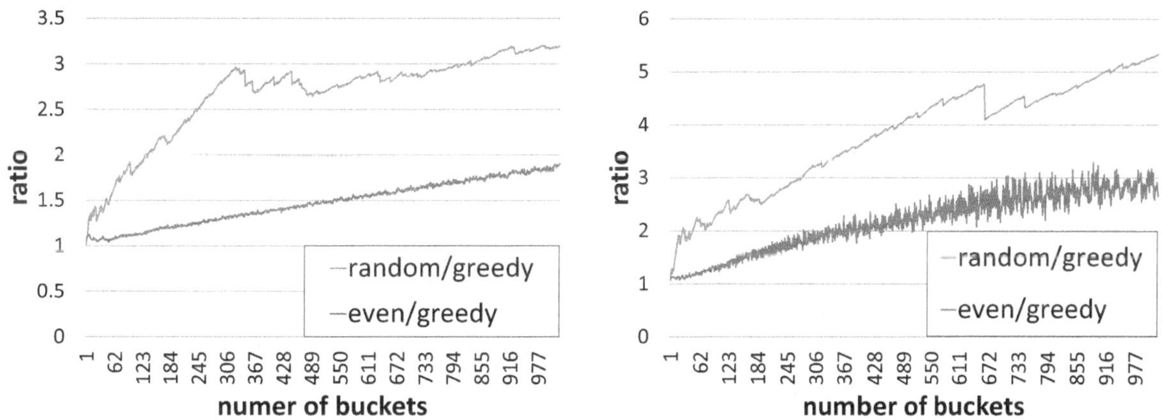

(a) Popular (b) Random

Figure 4: The relative performance of the `random` and `even` baseline, in terms of uncut edges, as compared to the greedy approximation algorithm on the *weighted* (a) popular and (b) random query graphs.

tween the static ranks of the first two results of a query causes higher potential damage than inducing a tie at the bottom of the results page (as ties may cause the engine to erroneously swap the results). Thus, in the weighted version of the problem, we assign an edge connecting results i and $i+1$ a weight of $\frac{1}{\log_2(1+i)}$ (this weighting was motivated by the position discount used in computing DCG).

To evaluate the performance of the greedy approximation algorithm, we consider two additional quantization heuristics. The first, which we call `even`, selects evenly spaced breakpoints in the total order. Given an ordering on n points, it selects points in positions $n/k, 2n/k, \ldots, n - n/k$ as the breakpoints. The second, which we call `random`, selects $k-1$ points uniformly at random as breakpoints. For all heuristics, when quantizing a total order, we measure the cost of the solution, i.e., the number of *uncut edges* — edges whose endpoints belong to the same bucket. Equivalently, this counts the number of induced static rank ties between pages co-appearing in the results of a query, i.e., pairs of results whose true rank relation has been obscured.

Figure 1 illustrates the number of uncut edges as a function of the number of buckets, in the unweighted versions of the popular and random graphs. Both the greedy approximation and the `even` heuristics perform very well, whereas `random` lags behind. For example, when the number of bits available to store the static rank is set to 8, corresponding to 256 distinct buckets, the greedy approximation leaves 1.9% of edges in the random sample uncut (and 2.3% in the popular sample). The `even` heuristic does not perform as well, leaving 3% and 2.8% of edges uncut respectively. To further illustrate the difference between the three approaches, we plot the relative performance of the two baselines as compared with the greedy algorithm (in terms of uncut edges) in Figure 2. Here, we can clearly see that the gap between the greedy algorithm and the two baselines increases with an increased number of buckets.

We repeated the same set of experiments on the weighted graphs. We again show both the absolute results in Figure 3 and the relative performance of greedy over the baseline in Figure 4. Here the difference between the greedy algorithm and the `even` heuristic is more pronounced. The effect is not surprising, since the `even` heuristic is independent of the weights, whereas the greedy algorithm selects more breakpoints near the top of the ranking and fewer near the bottom. The relative performance of `even` is about 50% worse in the weighted case: with 256 buckets on the popular graph it leaves 85% more weight uncut than the greedy algorithm (3.5% versus 1.9%); when the total number of buckets is around one thousand, the `even` heuristic is a factor of 3 worse than the greedy algorithm on the random query graph.

Despite the `even` heuristic not performing as well as the greedy algorithm and not being able to adapt to weighted edges, the loss in performance may be small in practical terms. Note that granting `even` a single extra bit for storing the quantized rank enables `even` to catch up to the performance of the greedy algorithm. In other words, `even` quantization with a bit budget of $b+1$ — using twice the number of buckets — outperforms greedy bucketization with a budget of b bits.

7. CONCLUSIONS

This work formally defined the Rank Quantization problem and presented (quadratic) exact and approximation algorithms for it. Technically, before tackling the Rank Quantization instance, we performed a Rank Linearization step for finding a full order of good agreement with many partial orders over a set of elements.

Our experimental results, over two different samples comprised of millions of queries and pages each, showed that it is possible to find a linear order of the pages that agrees with roughly 80% of the rank preferences expressed by queries. This indicates that static scores play a significant role in deciding the ranking among the top results of queries. Moreover, we find that this linear order can be effectively quantized. Perfectly preserving the ranks in the largest connected component of the graphs we consider requires 23 bits of precision for the random query graph and 22 bits for the popular query graph. However, if a small loss in precision can be tolerated, significantly fewer bits are needed. Specifically, when quantizing with just 8 bits, i.e. when using *just 256* different ranks, the relative rankings of only 2% of pairs of URLs in the top-10 results are obscured.

8. REFERENCES

[1] N. Ailon, M. Charikar, and A. Newman. Aggregating inconsistent information: Ranking and clustering. *JACM*, 55(5), 2008.

[2] L. A. Barroso, J. Dean, and U. Hölzle. Web search for a planet: The Google cluster architecture. *IEEE Micro*, 23(2):22–28, 2003.

[3] C. Botev, N. Eiron, M. Fontoura, N. Li, and E. Shekita. Static score bucketing in inverted indexes. In *CIKM*, pages 311–312, 2005.

[4] S. Brin and L. Page. The anatomy of a large-scale hypertextual web search engine. In *WWW*, pages 107–117, 1998.

[5] D. Coppersmith, L. Fleischer, and A. Rudra. Ordering by weighted number of wins gives a good ranking for weighted tournaments. *TALG*, 6(3), 2010.

[6] N. Craswell, S. Robertson, H. Zaragoza, and M. Taylor. Relevance weighting for query independent evidence. In *SIGIR*, pages 416–423, 2005.

[7] C. Dwork, R. Kumar, M. Naor, and D. Sivakumar. Rank aggregation methods for the web. In *WWW*, pages 613–622, 2001.

[8] G. Even, J. Naor, B. Schieber, and M. Sudan. Approximating minimum feedback sets and multicuts in directed graphs. *Algorithmica*, 20(2):151–174, 1998.

[9] R. Fagin, R. Kumar, M. Mahdian, D. Sivakumar, and E. Vee. Comparing partial rankings. *SIDMA*, 20(3):628–648, 2006.

[10] J. Feng, Q. Fang, and W. Ng. Discovering bucket orders from full rankings. In *SIGMOD*, pages 55–66, 2008.

[11] M. R. Garey and D. S. Johnson. *Computers and Intractability: A Guide to the Theory of NP-Completeness*. W. H. Freeman and Company, San Francisco, 1979.

[12] A. Gionis, H. Mannila, K. Puolamäki, and A. Ukkonen. Algorithms for discovering bucket orders from data. In *KDD*, pages 561–566, 2006.

[13] T. Haveliwala. Efficient encodings for document ranking vectors. In *IC*, pages 3–9, 2003.

[14] V. Kann. *On the Approximability of NP-complete Optimization Problems*. PhD thesis, Royal Institute of Technology, Stockholm, 1992.

[15] R. Karp. Reducubility among combinatorial problems. *Complexity of Computer Computations*, pages 85–104, 1972.

[16] S. Kenkre, A. Khan, and V. Pandit. On discovering bucket orders from preference data. In *SDM*, pages 872–883, 2011.

[17] C. Kenyon-Mathieu and W. Schudy. How to rank with few errors. In *STOC*, pages 95–103, 2007.

[18] H. Mannila and C. Meek. Global partial orders from sequential data. In *KDD*, pages 161–168, 2000.

[19] C. D. Manning, P. Raghavan, and H. Schütze. *Introduction to Information Retrieval*. Cambridge University Press, 2008.

[20] A. Moffat, J. Zobel, and R. Sacks-Davis. An efficient indexing technique for full-text database systems. In *VLDB*, pages 352–362, 1992.

[21] A. Moffat, J. Zobel, and R. Sacks-Davis. Memory efficient ranking. *IPM*, 30:733–744, 1994.

[22] A. Ukkonen, M. Fortelius, and H. Mannila. Finding partial orders from unordered 0-1 data. In *KDD*, pages 285–293, 2005.

[23] A. Ukkonen, K. Puolamäki, A. Gionis, and H. Mannila. A randomized approximation algorithm for computing bucket orders. *IPL*, 109:356–359, 2009.

[24] I. Witten, A. Moffat, and T. Bell. *Managing Gigabytes*. Morgan Kaufmann, 1999.

[25] J. Zobel and A. Moffat. Inverted files for text search engines. *ACM Computing Surveys*, 38, 2006.

Time-Sensitive Web Image Ranking and Retrieval via Dynamic Multi-Task Regression

Gunhee Kim
Computer Science Department
Carnegie Mellon University
Pittsburgh, PA 15213
gunhee@cs.cmu.edu

Eric P. Xing
Machine Learning Department
Carnegie Mellon University
Pittsburgh, PA 15213
epxing@cs.cmu.edu

ABSTRACT

In this paper, we investigate a time-sensitive image retrieval problem, in which given a query keyword, a query time point, and optionally user information, we retrieve the most relevant and temporally suitable images from the database. Inspired by recently emerging interests on query dynamics in information retrieval research, our time-sensitive image retrieval algorithm can infer users' implicit search intent better and provide more engaging and diverse search results according to temporal trends of Web user photos. We model observed image streams as instances of multivariate point processes represented by several different descriptors, and develop a regularized multi-task regression framework that automatically selects and learns stochastic parametric models to solve the relations between image occurrence probabilities and various temporal factors that influence them. Using Flickr datasets of more than seven million images of 30 topics, our experimental results show that the proposed algorithm is more successful in time-sensitive image retrieval than other candidate methods, including ranking SVM, a PageRank-based image ranking, and a generative temporal topic model.

Categories and Subject Descriptors

H.3.3 [**Information Search and Retrieval**]: Retrieval models

General Terms

Algorithm, Experimentation

Keywords

Web image retrieval, Point process, Multi-task regression

1. INTRODUCTION

As digital images are gaining popularity as a form of communicating information online, image search and retrieval has become an indispensable feature in our daily Web uses. Most commercial Web image search engines such as Bing, Google, and Yahoo largely rely on the text-based approach [5], in which given a query keyword, relevant pictures are retrieved and ranked by matching textual information of images such as surrounding texts, titles, or captions. Although the text-based image search has been successful as an effective and scalable image retrieval approach, it suffers from ambiguous and noisy results due to the mismatch between images and their surrounding texts. Moreover, it is still limited to correctly exploit visual contents of images and identify implicit or explicit search intent of a user.

Figure 1: Overview of time-sensitive Web image ranking and retrieval with a query example of the *cardinal*. (a)-(b) Top ten images retrieved by Google/Bing and Flickr search engines at 7/31/2012. (c) The results of our time-sensitive image retrieval for two query time points in winter and summer. (d) The result of our personalized image retrieval for a designated time and user.

In this paper, we study one additional aspect to improve image search quality: *temporal dynamics of image collections*. In other words, given Web image collections associated with keywords of interest, we aim at identifying their characteristic temporal patterns of occurrences on the Web, and leveraging them to improve search relevance at a query time. This problem is closely related to one recent emerging research in information retrieval: *exploring the temporal*

WSDM'13, February 4–8, 2013, Rome, Italy.

dynamics of Web queries to improve search relevance [6, 17, 20, 22]. Many queries are time-sensitive; the popularity of a query and its most relevant documents change over time. For example, a statistical analysis of Web query logs in [20] reported that more than 7% of queries have implicitly temporal intents (*e.g.* NBA, Olympics). This new area of research has cast a variety of interesting research questions, for example, identifying search terms that are sensitive to time, and reranking documents according to the query time. However, much of previous work has targeted at the search of text documents such as blogs and news archives by analyzing the query log data; the time-sensitive Web image retrieval has yet received little attention.

With our experiments on more than seven million Flickr images, we have found three good reasons why the discovery of *temporal* patterns in Web image collections is beneficial to existing image retrieval systems. We present them with a query example of the *cardinal* in Fig.1. *First, knowing when search takes place is useful to infer users' implicit intents.* Fig.1.(a) shows the top ten images retrieved by Google and Bing image search engines. Seemingly, they are reasonable because the *cardinal* usually refers to the red bird in America. However, the term *cardinal* is polysemous; it is also the names of popular sports teams (*e.g.* the American football and the baseball team). Therefore, some of *cardinal* queries in summer and winter are likely to be associated with the baseball and football team, respectively, according to the scheduled seasons of the sports.

Second, the timing suitability can be used as a complementary attribute to relevance. Fig.1 illustrates two such cases: One is that, as shown in Fig.1.(a), due to explosion of images shared on the Web, there are redundantly relevant images to popular queries like the *cardinal.* Timing suitability would be a good complementary ranking attribute to improve diversity or break ties between almost equally relevant images. The other case is that, in Fig.1.(b), the actual user images in the photo-sharing site Flickr are extremely diverse, and thus it is still very challenging to rank those images in any meaningful order. As shown in Fig.1.(c), the query time information can help obtain a more focused search output, which may include the images about *a cardinal bird in snowy field* in winter, but the images of *baby cardinals or eggs* in summer.

Third, temporal information is synergetic in personalized image retrieval. If a query word has a broad range of concepts, its dominant usages vary much according to users. Our experiments show that once we can identify a user's preference, image retrieval can be further specific since the term usages of individual users are relatively stationary. For example, as shown in Fig.1.(d), if a user took or searched *cardinal* pictures a lot for a basketball team last winter, he tends to do the same this winter as well.

Problem Statement: As an input, we gather a large-scale pool of unordered Web images along with metadata (*e.g.* timestamps, owners) by querying Q topic keywords from a text-based image search engine. We use raw Flickr images since our time-sensitive image retrieval is more interesting for extremely diverse general users' photos rather than sufficiently cleaned-up Google or Bing images. In this paper, our objective is two-fold: Our first goal is to automatically identify the temporal properties of each topic keyword, because every topic is not necessarily time-sensitive, and has its own characteristic temporal behaviors. The second goal is to leverage the learned temporal models to rank the images in database according to temporal suitability when a topic keyword and a query time are given. In real scenarios, the query time is usually *now* (*i.e.* the time when the search takes place), but we assume that it can be *any time even in future* for generality. We also address the *personalized* time-sensitive image ranking, which is customized image retrieval for a designated user.

Proposed method: The two objectives are accomplished by a unified statistical model: regularized multi-task regression on multivariate point process. We view an observed image stream as an instance of multivariate point process, which is a stochastic process that consists of a series of random events occurring at points in time and space [7]. Then, we automatically test what temporal models or their combinations are the best to describe the image occurrence behaviors, and formulate a regression problem to learn the historical relations between image occurrence probabilities and various temporal factors or covariates that influence them (*e.g.* seasons, dates, and other external events). From the learned models, we can easily compute the ranking scores of images for any given time point. We explore the idea of multi-task learning to incorporate multiple types of image representation for a more accurate ranking. Consequently, our algorithm offers several important advantages for large-scale image retrieval as follows: (i) *Flexibility*: We can easily build a set of parametric models to capture any number of possible temporal behaviors of image collections, and automatically choose the most statistically suitable ones (Section 4.1). We can achieve a globally optimal or approximate solution to the learning of temporal models (Section 4.4). (ii) *Scalability*: The learning is performed offline once, and the online query step is very fast. Both processes run in a linear time with most parameters such as time steps and the number of image descriptors (Section 5.3). (iii) *Retrieval accuracy*: We perform experiments on more than seven millions of Flickr images over a wide range of 30 topic keywords. We demonstrated that our image retrieval algorithm outperforms other candidate methods including Ranking SVM [14], a PageRank-based image retrieval [13, 16] and a generative author-time topic model [23] (Section 6).

1.1 Relations to Previous work

The time-sensitive image retrieval for large-scale Web photo collections remains an under-addressed topic in information retrieval literature. Our work is remotely related to following two lines of research, but is significantly different on the task, utility and methodology.

Image retrieval and reranking: Recently, image reranking has been actively studied to improve text-based image search by leveraging visual or user feedback information [5, 13, 19, 21, 29, 31]. Most image reranking methods have exploited three sources of information, which are human-labeled training data [31], user relevance feedback [5, 29], and pseudo-relevance feedback [21]. Given an image database retrieved by text-based search, the user relevance feedback approach asks a user to select a query image to clarify her search intent. The pseudo-relevance feedback approach assumes the top images retrieved by text-based search as pseudo-positive examples and bottom ranked images as pseudo-negative examples. Once the training data are obtained, almost all existing methods learn ranking models relying on the semantic meaning of a query word and the feature-wise image similarity, beyond which our approach additionally emphasizes the temporal trends and user history associated with the images. The time-sensitive retrieval can be becoming more important and anticipated, given that the majority of Web photos are now coming from hundreds of millions of general users with different experiences.

Web image dynamics: This line of research aims at modeling how the contents of large-scale Web image collections change over time [12, 15, 16, 24]. In [12] and [24], Flickr images are analyzed to infer other phenomena in user behaviors such as social trends in politics and markets [12] and spatio-temporal events [24]. In [16], the topic evolution is modeled to perform the subtopic outbreak detection and the classification of noisy web images. However, the study of Web content dynamics has not yet contributed much to solve the image ranking and retrieval, which is the main objective of this paper. Also, they did not explore any issues regarding personalization, as we do in this work. The most related work to ours may be [15], whose task is to predict future likely images in Flickr datasets. However, our work overcomes their two critical limitations to be a practical time-sensitive image retrieval method. First, their approach has no mechanism to test which queries are actually time-sensitive and to discover query-specific temporal properties, even though all submitted queries are not necessarily time-sensitive. Therefore, all topics are equally treated, which may cause degrading performance for some query classes. Second, they oversimplified the image representation by assuming that millions of images can be clearly clustered into 500 clusters. This assumption leads their approach to be an incomplete image ranking since it lacks a way of ranking the images in the same cluster.

1.2 Summary of Contributions

Departing from the literature reviewed above, the main contributions of our work can be summarized as follows:

(1) We develop an approach for time and optionally user sensitive image ranking and retrieval. To the best of our knowledge, there have been few attempts so far on such retrieval methods that leverage the temporal aspects of large-scale Web photo collections.

(2) We design our image retrieval algorithm using multi-task regression on multivariate point processes. Consequently, our algorithm can automatically select and learn stochastic temporal models while satisfying a number of key challenges of Web image ranking, including flexibility, scalability, and retrieval accuracies.

2. META-DATA OF IMAGES

We assume that each of input Flickr images is assigned to topic keywords, timestamp, and owner ID. In addition to such meta-data from Flickr, we extract two types of information modalities: image description and user description.

2.1 Image Descriptions

In this paper, we extract four different image descriptors because no single descriptor can completely capture various contents of an image, and thus leveraging multiple descriptors is a widely accepted common practice in recent computer vision research. The four descriptors that are explained below can be classified into two low-level (SIFT and HOG) and two high-level descriptors (Tiny and Scene), all of which are extracted by using publicly available codes[1].

Color SIFT (SIFT): We densely extract HSV color SIFT on a regular grid at steps of 4 pixels. We form 300 visual words by applying K-means to randomly selected SIFT descriptors. The nearest word is assigned to every SIFT, and binned using a three-level spatial pyramid.

HOG2x2 (HOG): We also use the histogram of oriented edge (HOG) feature, inspired by its recent success in object detection research [9]. We extract HOG descriptors on a regular grid at steps of 8 pixels by following the method called HOG2x2 in [30].

Tiny Image: Inspired by [27], we resize an image to a 32×32 tiny color image, and use pixel values as features. This approach not only reduces image dimensionality to be computationally feasible, but also is discriminative enough to convey high-level statistics of an image.

Scene description: Since a large portion of Web images contain scenes, the scene classifier outputs can be a meaningful high-level description of an image. SUN database [30] is an extensive dataset of 397 scene categories. As a scene descriptor, we compute the scores of linear one-vs-all SVM classifiers for 397 scene categories using Hog2x2 features, by following the classification benchmark protocol in [30].

Visual clusters: Since all the above descriptors except (Scene) are high-dimensional (*e.g.* 6,300 of (SIFT)), they are down-sampled further by the soft-assignment idea. For each descriptor type, we construct $L(=300)$ *visual clusters* by applying K-means to randomly sampled image descriptors. Then, an image I is assigned to r-nearest visual clusters for each descriptor type with the weights of an exponential function $\exp(-d^2/2\sigma^2)$, where d is the distance between the descriptor and the visual cluster and σ is a spatial scale. Finally, an image I is described by four ℓ-1 normalized vectors with only r nonzero weights. They are denoted by $\{\mathbf{h}_k(I)\}_{k=1}^4$ with dimensions of $[L_k]_{k=1}^4 = [300\ 300\ 300\ 374]$.

2.2 User Description

Clustering users and measuring similarity between users are important for personalization in collaborative filtering [8]. Its basic assumption is that similar users are likely to share common photo taking and search behaviors. We use the pLSA (Probabilistic latent semantic analysis) clustering as proposed in Google News personalization [8]. We first choose a fixed number of top users who have uploaded images most, and compute an L-dimensional histogram for each user where each bin represents the count of images belonging to the corresponding visual cluster. In pLSA, the distribution of visual cluster v in user u_i's images, $p(v|u_i)$, is given by the following generative model:

$$p(v|u_i) = \sum_{z \in \mathcal{Z}} p(v|z)p(z|u_i). \qquad (1)$$

The latent variable $z \in \mathcal{Z}$ represents the cluster of user propensity. Thus, $p(z|u_i)$ is proportional to the fractional membership of user i to cluster z. We use $p(z|u_i)$ as the descriptor of user u_i. The user clustering can be done by grouping users with the same $z^* = \text{argmax}_z\, p(z|u_i)$ or run K-means on the user descriptors $p(z|u_i)$. The user similarity is calculated by histogram intersection on user descriptors.

[1]We use following codes: (SIFT) at http://www.vlfeat.org, (HOG) at http://www.cs.brown.edu/~pff/latent, (Tiny) and (Scene) at http://people.csail.mit.edu/jxiao/SUN/.

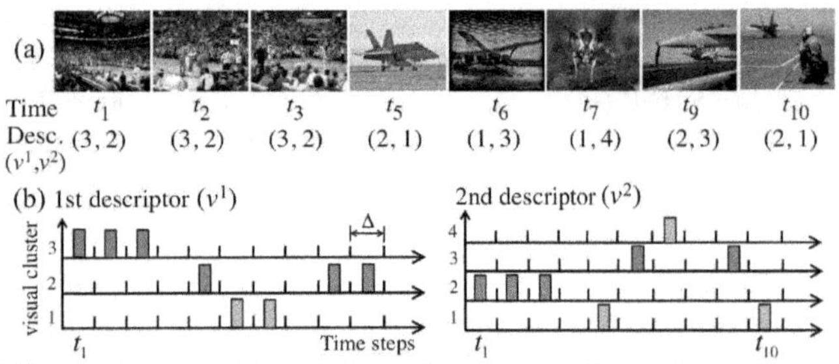

Figure 2: A multivariate point process for a short image stream of the *hornet*. (a) Each image is assigned to a timestamp and visual clusters of two different descriptors ($K = 2$, $L_1 = 3$, $L_2 = 4$). (b) The image stream is modeled by two multivariate discrete-time point processes.

3. MULTIVARIATE POINT PROCESSES

In this section, we discuss the mathematical background of multivariate point process for modeling Web photo streams. Fig.2 shows a toy example for a short image stream of the *hornet*. Suppose that we extract K image descriptors from each image, and for each descriptor, we cluster the images into L_k visual clusters (In this example, $K = 2, L_1 = 3, L_2 = 4$). Intuitively, one can easily construct K multivariate point processes as shown in Fig.2.(b). For simplicity, we first assume that the occurrence of each visual cluster is independently modeled. Hence, the point process of Fig.2 can be regarded as a single multivariate point process with $L = L_1 + L_2 = 7$. In section 4.3, we will consider an extended multi-task framework with considering correlations between different descriptors.

Intensity functions: Since the intensity function can completely define a point process [7], we first introduce its definition. Formally, a multivariate point process can be described by a counting process $\mathbf{N}(t) = (N^1(t), \cdots, N^L(t))^T$ where $N^l(t)$ is the total number of observed images assigned to visual cluster l in the interval $(0, t]$. Then, $N^l(t + \Delta) - N^l(t)$ represents the number of images in a small interval Δ. By letting $\Delta \to 0$, we obtain the *intensity function* at t, which is the infinitesimal expected occurrence rate of visual cluster l at time t [7]:

$$\lambda^l(t) = \lim_{\Delta \to 0} \frac{P[N^l(t+\Delta) - N^l(t) = 1]}{\Delta}, \; l \in \{1, \ldots, L\}. \quad (2)$$

Generalized Linear Model: We assume that the intensity function $\lambda^l(t)$ is represented by the covariates that influence the occurrence of visual cluster l. We define the the parametric form of $\lambda^l(t_i|\theta^l)$ as the exponential of a linear summation of the functions f_j^l of the covariates x_j with a parameter vector $\theta^l = (\theta_1^l, \cdots, \theta_J^l)$:

$$\log \lambda^l(t_i|\theta^l) = \sum_{j=1}^{J} \theta_j^l f_j^l(x_j), \quad l \in \{1, \ldots, L\}. \quad (3)$$

Data likelihood: Suppose that we partition the interval $(0, T]$ by a sufficiently large number M (*i.e.* $\Delta = T/M$) so that in each time bin Δ only one or zero image occurs. Then, we can denote the sequence of images up to T by $N_{1:M}^l = n_1^l \cdots n_M^l$ with $n_i^l \in \{0, 1\}$. It is shown in [28] that the likelihood of such a point process along with λ^l of Eq.(3) is identical to that of the *Poisson regression*. Therefore, the log-likelihood of an observed image sequence is

$$\ell(N_{1:M}^l|\theta^l) = \sum_{i=1}^{M} \Big(n_i \lambda^l(t_i|\theta^l) - \exp(\lambda^l(t_i|\theta^l)) - \log n_i! \Big). \quad (4)$$

L1 regularized likelihood: Although numerous factors or covariates can be plugged in Eq.(3), each visual cluster is likely to depend on only a small subset of them. Hence, it is important to detect a few strong covariates by encouraging a sparse estimator of θ^l for each visual cluster l. This approach is also practical because we usually do not know what factors are important beforehand; we safely include as many candidate factors as possible, and then choose only a few covariates for each visual cluster via MLE learning. Therefore, we introduce *Lasso* penalty [25] into the likelihood of Eq.(4) with a regularization parameter μ controlling sparsity level:

$$\ell_L(N_{1:M}^l|\theta^l) = \ell(N_{1:M}^l|\theta^l) - \mu \sum_{j=1}^{J} |\theta_i^l|. \quad (5)$$

4. TEMPORAL MODELING OF PHOTO STREAMS

Our first objective is to identify the temporal properties of a given image stream. This goal is achieved via the learning of temporal models as follows. We first represent the image stream with a multivariate point process $\{N_{1:M}^l\}_{l=1}^L$ as described in previous section. Then, we define multiple models for $\lambda^l(t_i|\theta^l)$ by enumerating all possible temporal factors that influence the image occurrences (section 4.1). Finally, for each occurrence data $N_{1:M}^l$ of visual cluster l, we select a subset of most statistically plausible models (section 4.2), and learn the parameters θ^{l*} of the models to discover which factors are actually contributing (section 4.4). Note that the whole processes above can be automatically performed.

4.1 Models of Temporal Behaviors

In this section, we enumerate a set of models for the intensity functions, each of which is designed to capture a particular temporal property. Thanks to the flexibility of our framework, one can freely add or remove such models according to the characteristics of image topics unless they contradict the definition of Eq.(3). In this paper, we construct two groups of models: *temporal attributes* and traditional *time series*.

Temporal attributes: Human time perception and photo taking and search behaviors are not only continuous on time but also temporal attribute-driven. For example, *zoo* photos may be more frequently taken in weekend rather than in weekdays, or *ski* images appear more often in January than in June. Therefore, we build a set of intensity function models for temporal attribute-driven covariates as follows.

$$\log \lambda_y^l(t_i|\alpha^l) = \alpha_0 + \sum_{y=Y_s}^{Y_t} \alpha_y I_y(t_i) \quad (6)$$

$$\log \lambda_m^l(t_i|\beta^l) = \beta_0 + \sum_{t=1}^{12} \beta_t g(t_i - t) \quad (7)$$

$$\log \lambda_d^l(t_i|\gamma^l) = \gamma_0 + \sum_{t=1}^{12} I_t(t_i) \sum_{d=1}^{31} \gamma_{m,d} I_d(t_i) \quad (8)$$

$$\log \lambda_w^l(t_i|\zeta^l) = \zeta_0 + \sum_{w \in \{M, \ldots, S\}} \zeta_w I_w(t_i) \quad (9)$$

$$\log \lambda_h^l(t_i|\eta^l) = \eta_0 + \sum_{h \in \mathcal{H}} \eta_h I_h(t_i). \quad (10)$$

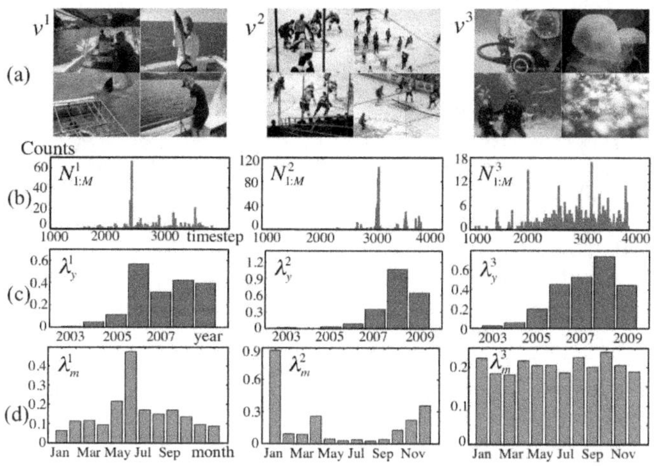

Figure 3: Examples of intensity function models of years and months for three visual clusters (VC) of the *Shark*: v^1*(sea tour)*, v^2*(ice hockey)*, v^3*(diving in aquarium)*. (a) Four images sampled from each VC. (b) Observed image occurrences. (c)-(d) Estimated intensity functions for years and months. λ_m^1 and λ_m^2 have different image occurrence rates peaked in summer and winter, respectively. λ_m^3 is stationary along the timeline.

In equations, λ_y^l, λ_m^l, λ_d^l, λ_w^l, and λ_h^l are the models of intensity functions for years, months, days, weekdays (from Monday to Sunday), and holidays[2], whose lists are denoted by $\mathcal{H}$. The parameter set to be learned comprises $\{\alpha^l, \beta^l, \gamma^l, \zeta^l, \eta^l\}$. $I_y(t_i)$ is an indicator function that is 1 if the year of t_i is y, and 0 otherwise (*e.g.* $I_y(t_i) = 1$ if $y = 2008$ and t_i= 6/3/2008). Similarly, $I_w(t_i)$ and $I_h(t_i)$ are indicators for week and holidays. For month covariates, we use Gaussian weighting $g(t_i - t) \propto \exp(-(t_i - t)^2/\sigma)$, which leads that if an image occurs in May, for example, some contributions are also given on nearby months like April and June, assuming that images smoothly change on the timeline.

Here, our models are mainly built based on calendric temporal attributes, but the models driven by other textual or social factors (*e.g.* news articles) can be supplemented.

An example: Fig.3 is a toy example of the *shark* topic to intuitively show how the intensity function models are used for fitting observed image streams. This example illustrates the intensity function models for years (λ_y^l of Eq.(6)) and months (λ_m^l of Eq.(7)), where the parameter set comprises seven $[\alpha_y^l]_{y=2003}^{2009}$ and twelve $[\beta_m^l]_{m=1}^{12}$. Fig.3.(a) shows four sampled images from three visual clusters, each of which approximately corresponds to *sea tour*, *ice hockey*, *diving in aquarium*. Fig.3.(b) presents their actual occurrence sequences. Fig.3.(c)-(d) show the learned intensity functions λ_y^l and λ_m^l. Most of intensity functions for years roughly increase every year because the number of uploaded photos in Flickr grows yearly. Interestingly, the visual clusters show different monthly behaviors in Fig.3.(d). λ_m^1 has a higher intensity value (*i.e.* more frequently occurred) in June, λ_m^2 peaks around January, and λ_m^3 is stationary all year long. This result is reasonable because sea tours are popular in summer, the ice hockey season takes place during winter, and visiting aquarium is favored regardless of season. The learned intensity functions can be used for a simple time-sensitive image retrieval. For example, if the month of the query time t_q is January, then $\lambda_m^2(t_q) \gg \lambda_m^3(t_q) > \lambda_m^1(t_q)$. Therefore, we can rank the images from v^2 as the highest.

[2]We use the lists at http://vpcalendar.net/Holiday_Dates/.

Autoregression: The other group of temporal models is based on autoregression, which is one of most popular models for the analysis of time series. We assume that the occurrence of each visual cluster is affected by its own history in Eq.(11), and the history of other visual clusters in Eq.(12). The first history model is represented by a linear autoregressive process:

$$\log \lambda_a^l(t_i|\phi^l) = \phi_0 + \sum_{p=1}^{P_d} \phi_p \Delta N_{i-dp}^l + \sum_{p=1}^{P_w} \phi_p \Delta N_{i-wp}^l + \sum_{p=1}^{P_m} \phi_p \Delta N_{i-mp}^l \quad (11)$$

where ΔN_{i-dp}^l denotes the occurrence counts of visual cluster l during $[t_i - dp, t_i)$, and d is the time window width. In Eq.(11), we use three different time windows: $d = 1$ day, and w =1 week, and $m = 1$ month. That is, λ_a^l is modeled by three different time-scaled (daily, weekly, and monthly) regressors whose orders are P_d, P_w, and P_m, respectively. The history model can capture the dynamic behavior of a visual cluster such as periodic or bursty occurrences.

The second correlation model represents the influence from the history of other visual clusters. Its mathematical form is almost identical to that of Eq.(11):

$$\log \lambda_c^l(t_i|\psi^l) = \psi_0 + \sum_{c=1,c\neq l}^{L} \left(\sum_{q=1}^{Q_d} \psi_q^{lc} \Delta N_{i-dq}^l + \sum_{q=1}^{Q_w} \psi_q^{lc} \Delta N_{i-wq}^l + \sum_{q=1}^{Q_m} \psi_q^{lc} \Delta N_{i-mq}^l \right) \quad (12)$$

The parameter set consists of $(L-1) \times (Q_d + Q_w + Q_m) + 1$ number of ψ in the full model. For fast computation, instead of using the full pairwise model, we can learn the correlations with respect to some selected most frequent visual clusters. This correlation model is useful when the existence or absence of a particular visual cluster can give a strong clue for others' occurrences.

4.2 Model Selection

In previous section, we introduce rather exhaustive seven temporal models from Eq.(6) to Eq.(12). However, the occurrence of each visual cluster does not necessarily depend on all the above models. For example, the occurrence of the *ice hockey* visual cluster v^2 of Fig.3 can be explained sufficiently well by the month intensity function model λ_m^l while other models may not be required any further. Therefore, we perform a model selection procedure, to choose a subset of temporal models by removing the ones with little or no predictive information.

Algorithm 1 summarizes the overall procedure of our model selection. It is based on the well-known *greedy forward selection* scheme, in which we keep increasing models one by one by adding at each step the one that increases the goodness-of-fit score the most, until any further addition does not increase the score. As the goodness-of-fit test, we use Kolmogorov-Smirnov (KS) test using time-rescaling theorem [2], which is one of most popular approaches for statistical model assessment in point process literature. The KS statistic is a quantitative measure for the agreement between

Algorithm 1: Model selection for each visual cluster

Input: (a) A set of intensity function models in Eq.(6)–(12): $\Lambda^l = \{\lambda_y^l, \lambda_m^l, \lambda_d^l, \lambda_w^l, \lambda_h^l, \lambda_a^l, \lambda_c^l\}$. (b) $N_{1:M}^l$: Occurrence data of visual cluster l.

Output: The best intensity function model λ^{l*} with learned parameter set θ^{l*}.

1: Let $\theta_i \leftarrow$ param_est $(\lambda_i,\ N_{1:M}^l)$ be the function that computes the MLE solution of parameters for a given λ_i and $N_{1:M}^l$. This will be discussed in section 4.4.
2: For λ_a^l and λ_c^l, decide the AR orders using AIC measure: $AIC(P) = -2\log \ell(N_{1:M}^l|\theta_t) + 2P$ where P is the total number of parameters.
foreach $\lambda_i \in \Lambda^l$. **do**
  3: Compute $\theta_i \leftarrow$ param_est $(\lambda_i,\ N_{1:M}^l)$.
  4: Compute KS static d_i by applying time rescaling theorem to the learned $\lambda_i(\theta_i)$ and $N_{1:M}^l$.
5: Sort λ_i in an increasing order. Let o to be this order. Initialize $\lambda^{l*} = \mathrm{argmin}_{\lambda_i \in \Lambda^l} d_i$ and $d^{l*} = \min d_i$.
repeat
  foreach $\lambda_i \in \Lambda^l$ *and* $\lambda_i \notin \lambda^{l*}$ *in the order of* o. **do**
    6: Set $\lambda_t = \lambda_i^{l*} \cdot \lambda_i$. $\theta_t \leftarrow$ param_est $(\lambda_t,\ N_{1:M}^l)$.
    7: Compute KS static d_t as done in step **4**.
    if $d_t < d^{l*}$ **then** $\lambda^{l*} \leftarrow \lambda_t$, $d^{l*} = d_t$, and $\theta^{l*} = \theta_t$.
until λ^{l*} *is not updated*;

Algorithm 2: Build the correlation set $\mathcal{E}$.

Input: (1) A set of images $\mathcal{I}$, each of which is assigned to the closest visual clusters of K descriptors.

Output: The correlation set $\mathcal{E}$.

1: Initialize $K(K-1)/2$ number of co-occurrence matrices $\mathcal{C}$, where $\mathbf{C}_{ab} \in \mathcal{C}$ is an $(L_a \times L_b)$ zero matrix between descriptor a and b.
foreach $I \in \mathcal{I}$. *Let visual cluster of* I *be* $(v_1, \ldots, v_K)$ **do**
  foreach $a, b \in \{1, \ldots, K\}$ *with* $a \neq b$ **do**
    2: $\mathbf{C}_{ab}(v_a, v_b) \leftarrow \mathbf{C}_{ab}(v_a, v_b) + 1$.
foreach $a, b \in \{1, \ldots, K\}$ *with* $a \neq b$ **do**
  3: $C_{ab} =$ row_normalize(C_{ab}) + column_normalize(C_{ab}).
3: Select top R highest edges (v_a, v_b) from $\mathcal{C}$. The weight of a pair is $r_{ab} \propto \mathbf{C}_{ab}(a,b)/|\mathcal{I}|$. Set $\mathcal{E} \leftarrow (v_a, v_b, r_{ab})$.

a learned intensity function and actual image occurrence data. This value is a distance metric, and thus a smaller value indicates a better model. In step 2 of Algorithm 1, the orders of the autoregressive models, λ_a^l of Eq.(11) and λ_c^l of Eq.(12), are decided by Akaike's information criterion (AIC). We choose the order parameters that lead to the smallest AIC, implying that the approximate distance between the model and the true process generating the data is the smallest. In practice, this step is important because temporal behaviors of visual clusters can operate at different time scales (*i.e.* monthly, weekly, or daily).

4.3 Regularized Multi-Task Regression

Until now, each visual cluster is independently modeled and learned without considering which description it is derived from. In order to fully take advantage of any arbitrary number of image descriptions, we introduce the idea of multi-task learning [3, 18], in which multiple related tasks are jointly learned by analyzing data from all of the tasks at the same time. This framework is powerful when the multiple tasks of interest are *different enough* to be specified by separate models, but are at the same time *similar enough* to be jointly learned.

We treat each descriptor as a *task*. Since each descriptor characterizes an image from a different perspective, it should be separately expressed. However, at the same time, it is likely that the descriptors from the same image share enough correlation that makes simultaneous learning beneficial. For example, suppose that a large portion of images of visual cluster 35 of HOG are also assigned to visual cluster 27 of Scene descriptors. It indicates that these two visual clusters are highly correlated, and thus are likely to share common covariates affecting their occurrences. Algorithm 2 discovers the set of frequently co-occurred visual cluster pairs as $\mathcal{E}$, where $e = (v_a, v_b, r_{ab}) \in \mathcal{E}$ consists of three tuples: a pair of visual clusters v_a and v_b with correlation weight $r_{ab} > 0$. We can model this dependency structure across multiple tasks (*e.g.* the correlations between the visual clusters of different image descriptors) by introducing regularization term $\Omega(\mathbf{\Theta}_E)$ to the log-likelihood:

$$\mathcal{L} = \sum_{l \in \mathcal{E}} \ell(N_{1:M}^l|\theta_k^l) - \Omega(\mathbf{\Theta}_E) \quad (13)$$

$$\Omega(\mathbf{\Theta}_E) = \mu \sum_{l \in \mathcal{E}} \|\theta_k^l\|_1 + \nu \sum_{(a,b) \in \mathcal{E}} r_{ab} \sum_{j=1}^{J} |\theta_j^a - \theta_j^b| \quad (14)$$

The regularization term $\Omega(\mathbf{\Theta}_E)$ consists of two different types of penalties, which are the *Lasso* penalty [25] and *graph-guided fusion* penalty [3]. μ and ν are regularization parameters that control sparsity and fusion levels. The overall effect of *graph-guided fusion* penalty is that each subgraph of visual clusters in $\mathcal{E}$ tends to share common relevant covariates, and the degree of commonality is proportional to the correlation strength r_{ab}.

4.4 Optimization for Parameter Learning

The goal of parameter learning is to obtain the MLE solution θ^{l*} that maximizes the likelihood with respect to an intensity function model λ^l and an observed image sequence $N_{1:M}^l$ for all $l = 1, \ldots, L$. Alternatively, if we explicitly represent the descriptor k as subscript, the set of parameters is denoted by $\mathbf{\Theta}^* = \{\mathbf{\Theta}_1^*, \ldots, \mathbf{\Theta}_K^*\}$ where $\mathbf{\Theta}_k^* = \{\theta_k^{1*}, \cdots, \theta_k^{L_k*}\}$ is the set of learned parameters for all visual clusters of descriptor k. We have introduced three likelihoods with different regularizations, which are optimized differently. First, the likelihood of Eq.(4) with no regularization term reduces to that of Poisson regression, and the globally-optimal solution can be attained by an iteratively reweighted least square algorithm [7]. Second, for the likelihood of Eq.(5) with the Lasso penalty, the globally-optimal MLE solution can be achieved by using the cyclical coordinate descent in [10]. Finally, for the likelihood of Eq.(13) with the graph-guided fusion penalty, we obtain an approximate MLE solution by modifying the *Proximal-gradient method* [3], which is a scalable first-order method (*i.e.* using only gradient) with a fast convergence rate. We extend this method that was developed for linear regressions to the regularized Poisson regressions.

5. TIME-SENSITIVE IMAGE RETRIEVAL

In this section, we discuss our second goal, which is to perform image ranking using the learned temporal models.

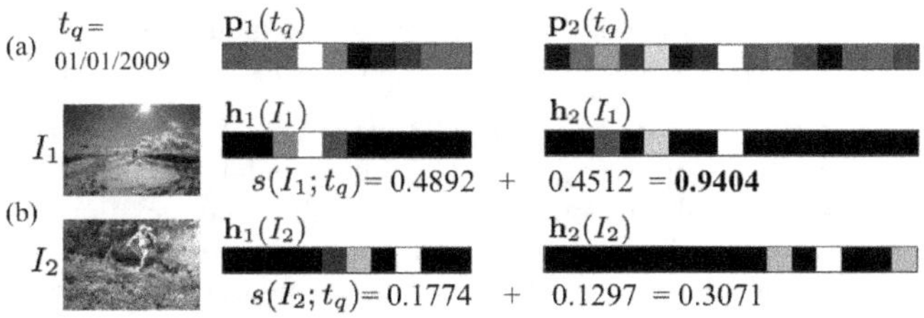

Figure 4: A toy example of computing ranking scores of two *mountain+camping* images I_1 and I_2 for t_q = (01/01/2009) with ($K = 2$, $L_1 = 10$, $L_2 = 15$). (a) Two membership vectors $\mathbf{p}_1(t_q)$ and $\mathbf{p}_2(t_q)$ are computed from the learned intensity functions. (b) Two descriptor vectors $\mathbf{h}_1$ and $\mathbf{h}_2$ are extracted from each image, and the ranking scores $s(I_1;t_q)$ and $s(I_2;t_q)$ are computed by Eq.(15).

5.1 Predictive Ranking

Computing intensity functions: As a result of optimization, we have the learned parameters of all visual clusters of all K descriptors: $\mathbf{\Theta}^* = \{\mathbf{\Theta}_1^*, \dots, \mathbf{\Theta}_K^*\}$.

In the retrieval step, given a query time t_q, we first obtain $\mathbf{\Lambda}(t_q|\mathbf{\Theta}^*) = \{\mathbf{\Lambda}_1(t_q|\mathbf{\Theta}_1^*), \dots, \mathbf{\Lambda}_K(t_q|\mathbf{\Theta}_K^*)\}$, which is the set of intensity functions of all visual clusters of all K descriptors for t_q. ($|\mathbf{\Lambda}(t_q|\mathbf{\Theta}^*)| = \sum_{k=1}^K L_k$). Each $\lambda_k^l(t_q|\theta_k^{l*}) \in \mathbf{\Lambda}_k(t_q|\mathbf{\Theta}_k^*)$ is computed by gathering covariate values for t_q, and plugging them along with learned θ_k^{l*} into Eq.(3). Here, let us remind that $\lambda_k^l(t_q|\theta_k^{l*}) \propto P(N_k^l(t_q+\Delta)-N_k^l(t_q)|N_{1:M}^l)$[3]. That is, the intensity function of a visual cluster at t_q is proportional to its occurrence probability at t_q. Therefore, for each $k \in K$, we can define a membership vector: $\mathbf{p}_k(t_q) = \mathbf{\Lambda}_k(t_q|\mathbf{\Theta}_k^*)/\|\mathbf{\Lambda}_k(t_q|\mathbf{\Theta}_k^*)\|_1 (\in \mathbb{R}^{L_k \times 1})$, where each $p^l \in \mathbf{p}_k(t_q)$ is the membership probability that an image occurred at t_q belongs to visual cluster l of descriptor k.

Ranking: The next step is to compute the ranking score of any given image I for t_q. We use the idea of continuos error-correcting output codes (ECOC) [4]. We first extract K image descriptors $\{\mathbf{h}_k(I)\}_{k=1}^K$ by the feature extraction methods in section 2.1. Then, the ranking score of image I at t_q is defined by the histogram intersection[4]

$$s(I;t_q) = \sum_{k=1}^{K} \| \min(\mathbf{h}_k(I), \mathbf{p}_k(t_q))\|_1. \tag{15}$$

Fig.4 illustrates a toy example of computing ranking scores for two images of the *mountain+camping* with $K = 2, L_1 = 10, L_2 = 15$. Fig.4.(a) shows two membership vectors $\mathbf{p}_k(t_q)$ that are computed from the learned intensity functions for t_q=(01/01/2009), and Fig.4.(b) illustrates four descriptor vectors for I_1 and I_2. The $\mathbf{p}_k(t_q)$ are more similar to the descriptors $\mathbf{h}_k(I_1)$ of image I_1 (*snowy mountain*) than $\mathbf{h}_k(I_2)$ of I_2(*tracking in woods*), and thus image I_1 is ranked higher.

The computation of our ranking score is very fast; the histogram intersection requires only element-wise min operations between K vector pairs. It is also easy to organize the descriptor vectors of images in the database by using any data structure such as trees or hashes for fast retrieval.

[3]It can be easily shown by that λ_k^l is an infinitesimal expected occurrence rate at t_q and a series of images is modeled by a sequence of conditionally independent Bernoulli trials during the derivation of the likelihood function of Eq.(4).

[4]In terms of the ECOC terminology, Eq.(15) means that the histogram intersection is chosen as the decoding metric.

5.2 Personalization

The key idea of personalization is, given a query user u_q, to assign more weights to the pictures taken by u_q and similar users to u_q during learning. In a normal setting, one image occurrence is equally counted by one for $N_{1:M}^l$ (See an example in Fig.3.(b)). However, for personalization, the images by u_q and the users in the same user cluster with u_q are weighted by larger values so that model fitting is more biased to their images. We implement the personalization by using the locally weighted learning framework [1], which is a form of lazy learning for a regression to adjust the weighting of data samples according to a query.

In order for personalization to be done offline, we apply this idea at the user cluster level. Suppose that there are Z user clusters as a result of pLSA based user clustering in section 2.2. We then compute $Z \times Z$ pairwise user similarity matrix $\mathbf{U}$ by $\mathbf{U}(x,y) = \sqrt{\exp(-(\mathbf{u}_x - \mathbf{u}_y)^2/\sigma)}$, where $\mathbf{u}_x$ and $\mathbf{u}_y$ are the user descriptors of cluster centers of U_x and U_y, respectively[5]. We learn the personalized model for each user cluster U_z, in which the weights of image occurrences are adjusted by $\mathbf{U}(z,*)$ (*i.e.* the z-th row of $\mathbf{U}$). That is, if the owner of an image I is in user cluster U_x, then I is reweighted by $\mathbf{U}(z,x)$. At the query stage, given a query user u_q, we identify the user cluster to which u_q belongs, and then use the pre-computed learned model of that cluster.

5.3 Computation time

Learning: The learning step performs only once, offline. The learning time without the graph-guided fusion penalty is $O(L|T|J)$ while that with the fusion penalty is $O(L|T|J^2)$ where $|T|$ is the number of time steps (*e.g.* discretized by day), J is the number of covariates, and $L = \sum_{k=1}^K L_k$. For a linear model, our Matlab code takes about less than one hour to learn the model for the 553K of *world+cup* images with $L = 1,050$, $|T| = 2,000$, and $J = 32$.

Querying: At the online querying stage, computing the intensity functions for a given query time t_q (and optionally a user u_q) runs in $O(LJ)$, and calculating the ranking scores of N images takes $O(LN)$. The overall querying step takes less than 0.5 second with N = 1K in the same experiment. Querying is fast enough to run online, but it can be also pre-computed offline, for example, processing queries for next one year (365 days) can be done within a couple of hours.

6. EXPERIMENTS

We evaluate the performance of our time-sensitive image retrieval algorithm using Flickr datasets.

6.1 Evaluation Setting

Datasets: Fig.5 summarizes our dataset that consists of more than seven million images of 30 topics from Flickr. We download all images that are retrieved by topic names as search keywords from Flickr without any filtering. The *date_taken* field of each image provided by Flickr is used for the timestamp.

Tasks: We first divide each image set into training and test set by time $T_T = T-$(1 year) where T is the end time point of the dataset. That is, for each topic, the test set consists of the images in the last one year of the database, and the training set $\mathcal{I}_B$ comprises the other images, which are used to learn the image occurrence patterns.

[5]We use the Gaussian kernel function for image weighting.

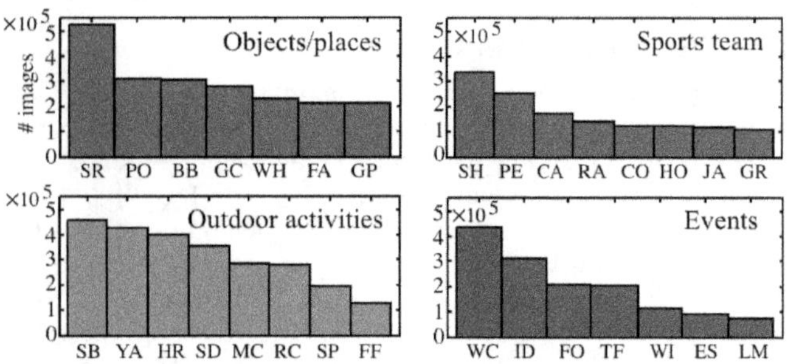

SR(spider), PO(potato), BB(blackberry), GC(grandcanyon), WH(white +house), FA(fine+art), GP(grape), SH(shark), PE(penguin), CA(cardinal), RA(raptor), CO(coyote), HO(hornet), JA(jaguar), GR (grizzly), SB(snowboarding), YA(yacht), HR(horse+riding), SD(scuba+diving), MC(mountain+camping), RC(rock+climbing), SP(safari+park), FF(fly+fishing), WC(world+cup), ID(independence+ day), FO(formula+one), TF(tour+de+france), WI(wimbledon), ES (easter+sunday), LM(london+marathon)

Figure 5: 30 topics of our Flickr dataset. The topic words are classified into four categories. The total numbers of images and users are (7,592,426, 1,434,749).

Our tasks for experiments are similar to those of other image ranking and retrieval papers [5, 19, 29] except that time suitability of retrieved images is the key performance index to be evaluated. Our image retrieval task is performed as follows; a topic name and a query time point $t_q > T_T$ are given. That is, t_q is a *future* time point with respect to training data since T_T is the time threshold that divides the training set from the test set. The images that are actually taken in t_q are the positive test set $\mathcal{I}_P$. The negative test set $\mathcal{I}_N$ is gathered by randomly selecting the same number images outside of [$t_q \pm 3$ months] from the test set. The algorithm is supposed to rank the test images $\mathcal{I}_P \cup \mathcal{I}_N$ from which average precisions are computed. The personalized retrieval is the same except that a query user u_q is specified at the test. u_q is randomly chosen from a set of users who have at least 100 images in both training and test sets. For each topic, we randomly generate 36 t_q test cases (*i.e.* three random choices per month) for normal retrieval, and 20 (t_q, u_q) test pairs on average for personalized retrieval. That is, we examine more than 1,500 test instances in total to evaluate the performance of our algorithm.

Baselines: The time-sensitive image retrieval is relatively new, and thus there are few existing methods to be compared. Hence, we select and adapt three baselines from popular image ranking methods for quantitative comparison with our algorithm. Below we summarizes the baselines, each of which is denoted by (`RSVM`) [14], (`PageR`) [13, 16], and (`Topic`) [23]. In the personalized retrieval, the locally weighted learning is also applied to all the competitors.

- Ranking SVM(`RSVM`) [14]: We obtain pseudo-relevant and pseudo-irrelevant training data by sampling images from the training set $\mathcal{I}_T$ based on their timestamps. The pseudo-relevant images are randomly sampled from Normal distributions whose mean are the same dates (m/d) of t_q in previous years. The pseudo-irrelevant images are randomly chosen from the images whose timestamps are outside [date(m/d) of $t_q \pm$ 3 months] at every year. Then, we learn the Ranking SVM using the code provided by the authors of [14].
- PageRank-based model(`PageR`) [11, 16]: Given the same training data above, we build a similarity graph between training and test data by using HOG and SIFT features, and compute ranking scores using the *random walk with restart* [26] (*i.e.* a query-specific PageRank).
- Author-Time Topic Model(`Topic`) [23]: We modify the Author-Topic model [23] to jointly model users, months, and visual clusters of images. Using the same training data above, we estimate the subtopic distribution of each month and the subtopic assignments of visual clusters, from which we compute the ranking scores of test images for t_q.

6.2 Quantitative Results

Fig.6 and Fig.7 show the quantitative comparison of normal and personalized image retrieval between our approach and three baselines, respectively. We report the mean average precision at top 40 and 80 ranked images, which are denoted by mAP@40 and mAP@80. In each figure, the leftmost bar set is the average performance of 30 topics, and the results of all 30 topics follow. Our algorithm significantly outperformed all the competitors in most topic classes for both tasks. In the average accuracy of normal retrieval, our mAP@40(80) values are higher by 5.6% (8.0%) points than the best baseline (`Topic`). In the average accuracy of personalized retrieval, our method also outperforms the best baseline (`PageR`) by 4.7% (4.2%) points for mAP@40(80). The personalized retrieval is more accurate to rank the images than the normal one, because knowing the user at query time provides a strong clue to narrow down the search space.

6.3 Qualitative Results

Fig.8 shows some examples of retrieval comparison between our method in the top row and the best baseline in the bottom row. We illustrate top eight ranked images by each method, along with the average images of top 100 images to show the mean statistics of the two output sets. In these examples, our method reports fewer false positives (*i.e.* the images with red boundaries) than the best baselines.

As another qualitative result, Fig.9 shows the predicted power of our algorithm for unseen future images. Fig.9.(a) illustrates retrieval results for the *independence+day* at four t_q from different months. In each set, the top row shows five images that are sampled out of ten highest ranked training images for t_q, and the bottom row presents their best-matched test images. The matched pairs are obtained from one-to-one correspondences by feature-wise distances. If the matched pairs are similar each other, it means that our algorithm can predict unseen future images very well. The *independence+day* is national holidays for many countries with different dates. Hence, according to four different t_q, we can observe various views of the events in different countries. For example, the second t_q (top-right) of Fig.9.(a) is near to the US independence day; the high ranked images show its common storyline: parades, parties with children, and fireworks at night. They are distinctive with the scenes in the Independence day of India (bottom-left) and an African country (bottom-right) of Fig.9.(a).

Fig.9.(b) shows examples of the importance of personalization. The *raptor* in Fig.9.(b) show the variation of the term usages including a basketball team, a fighter aircraft, an eagle, and an ice hockey team, most of which are seemingly irrelevant to its first semantic meaning as a dinosaur. Each user perceives the term *raptor* narrowly for his or her interests, which are relatively stationary and predictable once they are learned.

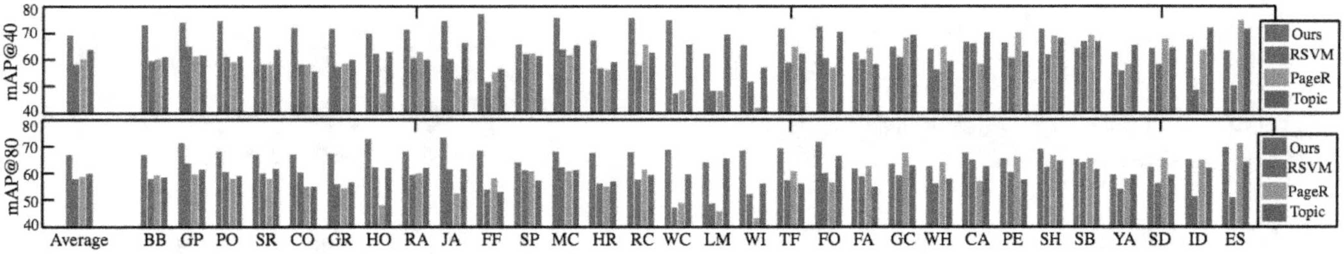

Figure 6: Quantitative comparison of image retrieval between our method and three baselines (`RSVM`, `PageR`, `Topic`) using mAP@40(top) and mAP@80(bottom) metrics. The average performances for mAP@(40,80) in the left-most bar set are ours (69.1%,66.7%), `RSVM` (58.0%,57.6%), `PageR` (60.1%,58.6%), `Topic` (63.5%,59.7%).

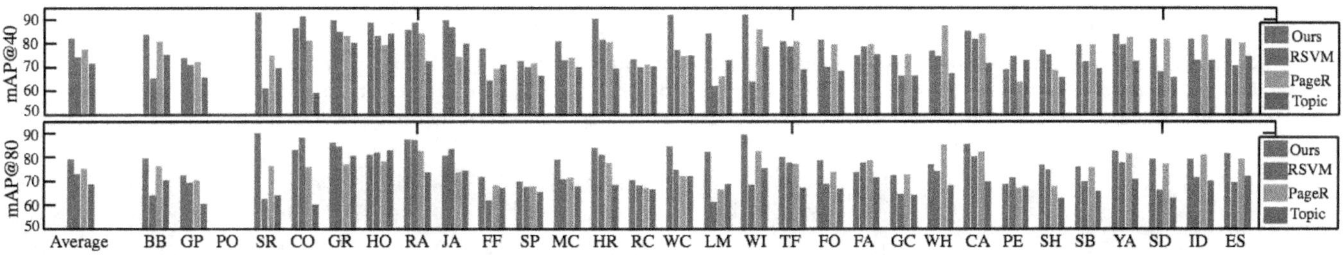

Figure 7: Quantitative comparison of personalized image retrieval between our method and three baselines using mAP@40(top) and mAP@80(bottom). The average performances for mAP@(40,80) in the left-most bar set are ours(82.1%,79.2%), `RSVM`(74.3%,72.8%), `PageR`(77.4%,75.0%), `Topic`(71.4%,68.7%).

Our experimental results conclude that some topics follow periodical patterns that are predictable, and our algorithm can enhance the image retrieval quality according to the temporal trends. Specifically, our method is successful for polysemous topics that show strong annual or periodic trends (*e.g.* sports related topics such as *shark* and *hornet*), and event topics that many people share but experience in different ways (*e.g.* outdoor activities such as *mountain+camping*). Moreover, we observe that the time-sensitive personalization is promising for image retrieval when a query keyword has a board range of concepts, which are differently recognized according to people's thoughts and interests. Although the personalized search has been studied much in text retrieval research, our results reveal that images can convey more subtle information about user preferences that are hardly captured by texts.

7. CONCLUSION

In this paper, we propose an approach for time-sensitive image ranking and retrieval that is based on multi-task regression on multivariate point processes. With experiments on more than seven millions of Flickr images for 30 topic keywords, we show the superiority of the proposed approach over other candidate method. Among future work that could further boost performance, first, we can incorporate other meta data of Flick (*e.g.* comments or favs) as covariates for the temporal models; second, it is worth exploring the joint temporal behaviors of topics along with other data modalities such as associated texts or social networks of users.

Acknowledgement: This work is supported by NSF IIS-1115313 and AFOSR FA9550010247.

8. REFERENCES

[1] C. G. Atkeson, A. W. Moore, and S. Schaal. Locally Weighted Learning. *AI Review*, 11(1):11–73, 1997.

[2] E. N. Brown, R. Barbieri, V. Ventura, R. E. Kass, and L. M. Frank. The Time-Rescaling Theorem and Its Application to Neural Spike Train Data Analysis. *Neural Computation*, 14(2):325–346, 2001.

[3] X. Chen, Q. Lin, S. Kim, J. G. Carbonell, and E. P. Xing. Smoothing Proximal Gradient Method for General Structured Sparse Learning. In *UAI*, 2011.

[4] K. Crammer and Y. Singer. On the Learnability and Design of Output Codes for Multiclass Problems. *Machine Learning*, 47:201–233, 2002.

[5] J. Cui, F. Wen, and X. Tang. Real Time Google and Live Image Search Re-ranking. In *ACM MM*, 2008.

[6] W. Dakka, L. Gravano, and P. G. Ipeirotis. Answering General Time-Sensitive Queries. In *CIKM*, 2008.

[7] D. Daley and D. Vere-Jones. *An Introduction to the Theory of Point Processes*. Springer, 2003.

[8] A. S. Das, M. Datar, , A. Garg, and S. Rajaram. Google News Personalization: Scalable Online Collaborative Filtering. In *WWW*, 2007.

[9] P. F. Felzenszwalb, R. B. Girshick, D. McAllester, and D. Ramanan. Object Detection with Discriminatively Trained Part Based Models. *IEEE PAMI*, 32(9):1627–1645, 2010.

[10] J. Friedman, T. Hastie, and R. Tibshirani. Regularization Paths for Generalized Linear Models via Coordinate Descent. *J. Statistical Software*, 33:1–22, 2010.

[11] W. H. Hsu, L. S. Kennedy, and S.-F. Chang. Video Search Reranking Through Random Walk over Document-Level Context Graph. In *ACM MM*, 2007.

[12] X. Jin, A. Gallagher, L. Cao, J. Luo, and J. Han. The Wisdom of Social Multimedia: Using Flickr for Prediction and Forecast. In *ACM MM*, 2010.

[13] Y. Jing and S. Baluja. VisualRank: Applying PageRank to Large-Scale Image Search. *IEEE PAMI*, 30:1877–1890, 2008.

[14] T. Joachims. Optimizing Search Engines Using Clickthrough Data. In *KDD*, 2002.

[15] G. Kim and E. P. Xing. Web Image Prediction Using Multivariate Point Processes . In *KDD*, 2012.

[16] G. Kim, E. P. Xing, and A. Torralba. Modeling and

Figure 8: Comparison of eight top-ranked images for normal image retrieval in (a) and (b) and for personalized image retrieval in (c) and (d), by our method in the top row and by the best baseline in bottom row. The pictures with red boundaries are false positives. We also present average image of top 100 retrieved images in the left-most of each row.

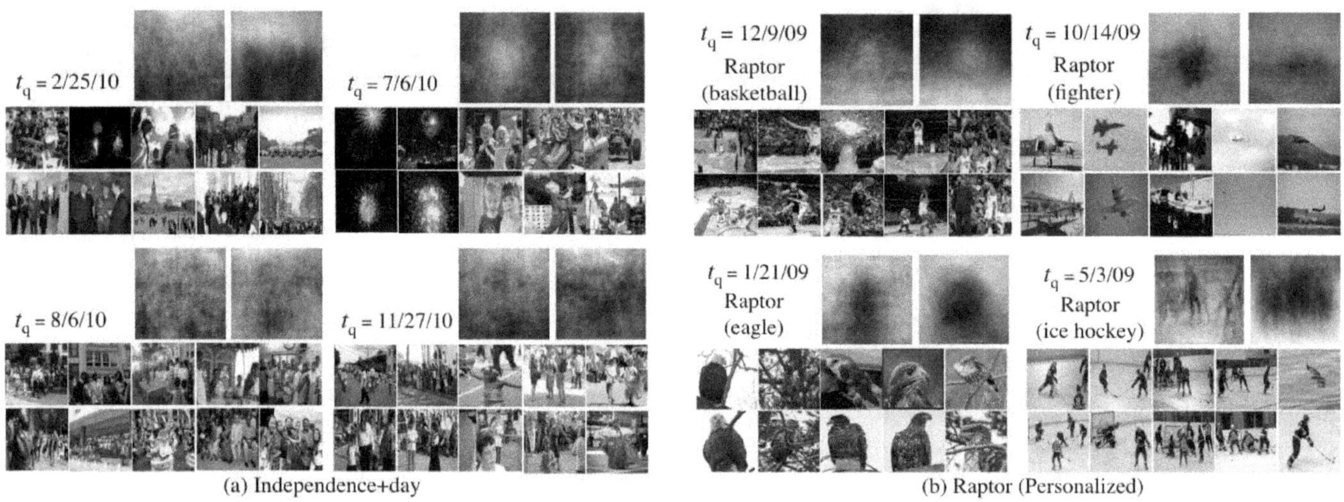

Figure 9: Image retrieval examples. (a) Normal retrieval for the *independence+day* at four t_q in different months. In each set, we show five sampled images form top 10 ranked training images in the top row, and their best-matched test images in the bottom row. We also present the average images of top 100 retrieved training images (left) and their best-matched test images (right). Independence day scenes in different countries are shown according to query time t_q. (b) Personalized retrieval for the *raptor* at four different (t_q, u_q) pairs. Even though the images are associated with the same keyword, their contents extremely vary according to users' interests.

Analysis of Dynamic Behaviors of Web Image Collections. In *ECCV*, 2010.

[17] A. Kulkarni, J. Teevan, K. M. Svore, and S. T. Dumais. Understanding Temporal Query Dynamics. In *WSDM*, 2011.

[18] H. Liu, M. Palatucci, and J. Zhang. Blockwise Coordinate Descent Procedures for the Multi-task Lasso, with Applications to Neural Semantic Basis Discovery. In *ICML*, 2009.

[19] W. Liu, Y.-G. Jiang, J. Luo, and S.-F. Chang. Noise Resistant Graph Ranking for ImprovedWeb Image Search. In *CVPR*, 2011.

[20] D. Metzler, R. Jones, F. Peng, and R. Zhang. Understanding Temporal Query Dynamics. In *SIGIR*, 2009.

[21] N. Morioka and J. Wang. Robust Visual Reranking via Sparsity and Ranking Constraints. In *ACM MM*, 2011.

[22] K. Radinsky, K. M. Svore, S. T. Dumais, J. Teevan, A. Bocharov, and E. Horvitz. Modeling and Predicting Behavioral Dynamics on the Web. In *WWW*, 2012.

[23] M. Rosen-Zvi, T. Griffiths, M. Steyvers, and P. Smyth. The Author-Topic Model for Authors and Documents. In *UAI*, 2004.

[24] V. K. Singh, M. Gao, and R. Jain. Social Pixels: Genesis and Evaluation. In *ACM MM*, 2010.

[25] R. Tibshirani. Regression Shrinkage and Selection via the Lasso. *J. Royal. Statist. Soc B.*, 58(1):267–288, 1996.

[26] H. Tong, C. Faloutsos, and J.-Y. Pan. Fast Random Walk with Restart and Its Applications. In *ICDM*, 2006.

[27] A. Torralba and W. T. F. Rob Fergus. 80 Million Tiny Images: A Large Data Set for Nonparametric Object and Scene Recognition. *IEEE PAMI*, 30:1958–1970, 2008.

[28] W. Truccolo, U. T. Eden, M. R. Fellows, J. P. Donoghue, and E. N. Brown. A Point Process Framework for Relating Neural Spiking Activity to Spiking History, Neural Ensemble, and Extrinsic Covariate Effects. *J. Neurophysiol*, 93(2):1074–1089, 2005.

[29] X. Wang, K. Liu, and X. Tang. Query-Specific Visual Semantic Spaces for Web Image Re-ranking. In *CVPR*, 2011.

[30] J. Xiao, J. Hays, K. A. Ehinger, A. Oliva, and A. Torralba. SUN Database: Large-scale Scene Recognition from Abbey to Zoo. In *CVPR*, 2010.

[31] L. Yang and A. Hanjalic. Supervised Reranking for Web Image Search. In *ACM MM*, 2010.

Absence Time and User Engagement: Evaluating Ranking Functions

Georges Dupret
Yahoo! Labs Sunnyvale
gdupret@yahoo-inc.com

Mounia Lalmas
Yahoo! Labs Barcelona
mounia@acm.org

ABSTRACT

In the online industry, user engagement is measured with various engagement metrics used to assess users' depth of engagement with a website. Widely-used metrics include clickthrough rates, page views and dwell time. Relying solely on these metrics can lead to contradictory if not erroneous conclusions regarding user engagement. In this paper, we propose the time between two user visits, or the `absence` time, to measure user engagement. Our assumption is that if users find a website interesting, engaging or useful, they will return to it sooner – a reflection of their engagement with the site – than if this is not the case. This assumption has the advantage of being simple and intuitive and applicable to a large number of settings. As a case study, we use a community Q&A website, and compare the behaviour of users exposed to six functions used to rank past answers, both in terms of traditional metrics and `absence` time. We use Survival Analysis to show the relation between `absence` time and other engagement metrics. We demonstrate that the `absence` time leads to coherent, interpretable results and helps to better understand other metrics commonly used to evaluate user engagement in search.

Categories and Subject Descriptors

H.1.2 [**User/Machine Systems**]: Human information processing

General Terms

Measurement

Keywords

User engagement, time between visits, metrics, ranking evaluation, interleaving, search engine, clickthrough data.

1. INTRODUCTION

In the online industry, *user engagement* refers to the quality of the user experience with a website. Various *engagement metrics* used to assess users' depth of engagement have been proposed. Widely-used metrics include clickthrough rates, page views, time spent on a site ("dwell time"), or more generally "activity" metrics which relate to the user behaviour during an online session. Another class of metrics, "loyalty" metrics, are concerned with how often users return to a site[1].

Dwell time has proven to be a robust measure of user engagement over the years, for example in the context of web search where it is used to improve retrieval performance [2, 3]. The same holds for clickthrough rates because they provide a clear signal that users were attracted to the content of a site or to a search result. They have been used to compute relevance scores or to personalise websites [7, 8, 16].

Relying solely on user clicks and time spent can, however, lead to contradictory if not erroneous conclusions regarding user engagement, as they do not necessarily relate to users being engaged. In particular, with the current trend of displaying rich information on web pages in special modules or inserts called "Direct Displays[2]", for instance the phone number of restaurants or weather data in search results, users do not need to click to access the information and the time spent on a website is shorter.

In this paper, we propose the time between two user visits, or the `absence` time, to measure user engagement. Our intuition is that if users find a site interesting, engaging or useful, they will return to it sooner. The `absence` time is simply the time elapsed between two sessions of a user. More precisely, it is the time between the end of a session and the start of a new session with respect to X where X is a site, a set of sites (e.g. Yahoo! network of services), but also any part of a page, for example a particular module. We use the term `absence` time instead of return time to avoid ambiguity, since a return can occur during a session of a multitasking user, for example.

The `absence` time measures the time it takes a user to decide to return to the site of interest to accomplish a new task. Taking a news site as an example, a good experience associated with quality articles might motivate the user to come back to that news site on a regular basis. On the other hand, if the user is disappointed (the articles were not interesting, the site was confusing) he or she may return less often and even switch to an alternative news provider. Another example is a visit to a community questions and answers website. If the questions of a user are well and promptly answered, the odds are that he or she will be enticed to raise

[1]In this paper, we use the terms site, website, application and service interchangeably.

[2]Also sometimes called "Answers".

new questions and return to the site soon. *In summary, we assume that engaged users come back sooner, and hence their* `absence` *times are shorter.* This assumption has the advantage of being simple and intuitive and applicable to a large number of settings.

The aim of this work is to identify observable correlations between the `absence` time and user engagement. However, since user engagement is not directly observable, we study the relation between the `absence` time and various established "activity" metrics such as clicks and page views. We show that these metrics complement each other and that the `absence` time adds significant insights to the interpretation of activity metrics.

Using `absence` time to measure use engagement has three potential issues. A user might decide to return sooner or later to a website due to reasons unrelated with the previous visits (being on holidays for example). The signal is therefore expected to be noisy, so it is important to have a large sample of interaction data to detect coherent signals and to develop methods to take systematic effects into account. Another issue is how to identify session boundaries. It is sometimes difficult to decide whether a particular user action initiates a new session or belong to a previous one, and this decision has potentially a large impact on the `absence` time estimates. Finally, changes that affect the user experience, especially visible one such as a new interface, can have a transient impact. We must wait until the "novelty" effect shades away before studying `absence` time, or we must model it. In this paper, we account for the first two issues.

As a case study, we use a community querying and answering website hosted by Yahoo! Japan. We compare the behaviour of users exposed to six functions used to rank past answers both in term of traditional metrics and of `absence` time. We organise the rest of this paper as follows. Section 2 describes related work. Section 3 presents the application chosen in this study and limitations with common measurement approaches. We show in Section 4 how Survival Analysis and the `absence` time can be used to measure engagement. Section 5 shows how the `absence` time relates to different measures of engagement and provides additional insights into user interaction with search results. We end with conclusions and plans for future work.

2. RELATED WORK

One main approach for measuring user engagement makes use of the record of users online behaviour. We alluded above to such widely used metrics: clickthrough rates, page views, time spent on a site, how often users return to a site and number of users per specified time span. Although these metrics cannot explain why users engage with a service, they have been used for many years by the web analytics community and Internet market research companies such as comScore as proxy for online user engagement. Major web sites and online services are compared on their basis.

Two of the most widely employed engagement metrics are clickthrough rates and dwell time, in particular for services where user engagement is about clicking, for example in the context of search where presumably users click on relevant results, and/or spending time on a site, for example consuming content in the context of a news portal. In search, both have been used as indicator of relevance, and together with other metrics have been exploited to infer user satisfaction with their search results [3, 5, 10, 17].

However, how to properly interpret the relations between these metrics and retrieval quality and in the long term user engagement with the search application is not straightforward. For instance, in [19], metrics such as abandonment rate, reformulation rate, and clicks per query were shown to not reflect retrieval quality in a "significant, easily interpretable, and reliable way". We reach similar conclusions in Section 3. As a consequence, alternative approaches have been sought. One is interleaving, an evaluation method that performs paired-wise comparisons of two rankings [6]. However, this approach is only applicable to search and can compare a maximum of two rankings at a time. A second one, which can be used across applications, is based on tracking mouse movement, for example on the search result page [11, 12]. The use of mouse tracking brings additional signals on how users interact with the site, but faces the same issues regarding how to interpret this signal. Our work follows another direction, through the proposal and experimentation of the `absence` time, which is shown to bring complementary insights about user behaviour with an application.

New insights are important because user engagement possesses different characteristics depending on the web application. For instance, how users engage with a mail tool or a news portal is very different. Using several metrics to evaluate user engagement can cater for the diversity of experiences as demonstrated in [15], where a large-scale study led to the identification of patterns of user engagement. These patterns were characterised by engagement metrics related to popularity (e.g. number of users or clicks per day), activity (e.g. time spent or number of clicks per visit) and loyalty (e.g. how often users return to a site). Dwell time and clickthrough rates are activity metrics whereas our proposed `absence` time relates to loyalty. Visit activity depends on the sites, e.g. search sites tend to have a significantly shorter dwell time than sites related to entertainment (e.g. games). Loyalty per application differs as well. Media (news, magazines) and communication (e.g. messenger, mail) have many users returning to them much more regularly, than sites containing information of temporary interests (e.g. buying a car). Overall, the work described in [15] showed that activity and loyalty metrics capture different aspects of engagement.

The analysis of visit frequency and the method based on `absence` time presented in this paper are related. First, the visit frequency is simply the inverse of the `absence` time if we do not distinguish `absence` time and "return" time as we are doing in this paper. This difference is nevertheless important and makes the interpretation of the results possible. Second, our proposed method is different. Survival Analysis takes a longitudinal view of the data, and we attempt to relate the experience of individual users and their activity on the site of interest to their `absence` time. In other words, our proposed method allows us to relate "activity" metrics to the `absence` time at a more fined grained level, without sacrificing the large-scale character of the analysis that is possible with the record of users online behaviour.

3. MOTIVATION AND CONTEXT

In this section, we motivate the use of the `absence` time by looking at the limitations of other widely used measures of engagement. We do this by carrying out a two-week experiment in the context of Yahoo! Answers[3], a popular service in

[3]`http://chiebukuro.yahoo.co.jp/`

Table 1: DCG with respect to hand on a set of 653 queries chosen randomly from the clickthrough data.

	emlr	attr	util	attrc	satis
DCG@1	11.93%	-0.26%	0.74%	3.35%	2.35%
DCG@5	10.73%	1.16%	1.54%	3.93%	4.39%

Japan. This service is similar to other Q&A systems available in different countries where users are given the possibility to ask questions about any topic of their interest. Other users may respond by writing an answer. In Yahoo! Answers, these answers are recorded and can be searched by any user through a standard search interface.

3.1 Ranking Functions

We compare the user interaction data for six ranking functions deployed on Yahoo! Answers. During a period of two weeks, a subset of the users were randomly distributed towards six distinct "buckets" based on their browser cookie, one for each ranking function. This paper focus is not the ranking functions themselves but a method to compare them, so their description is intentionally succinct:

- hand: a baseline function that is the result of very carefully human hand-tuning over several years,
- emlr: a state-of-the-art machine learned ranking function trained on an extensive set of editorial labels.

The remaining functions are based on the click models described in [8]:

- attr: an attractiveness based model,
- util: a utility based model,
- attrc: an attractiveness model with extra click features,
- satis: utility & attractiveness combination model with click features.

In Table 1 we report the DCG [13] of these functions relative to the baseline hand. The performance of emlr stands out, but this not surprising as this function is trained to learn the editorial labels while the click models are learned without labels. We investigate next whether emlr higher DCG performance translates into better user engagement.

3.2 Sessions

We study the actions of approximately one million users during two weeks, with "one million" being large enough to separate between noisy and non-noisy signals. A user "action" happens every time a user interacts in some way with the Yahoo! Answers site, which happens every time he or she issues a query or clicks on a link, be it a answer, an ad or a navigation button. A "view" is defined as a page of search results (SERP) served to a user. A session is a set of user actions and views that belong together. A session is defined as the set of views and actions that are the consequences of a user decision to use Yahoo! Answers to meet one or more information needs, or to be entertained. Within a session, user might leave Yahoo! Answers to for example access other sites for a limited amount of time (multitasking), as long as the activity on Yahoo! Answers remains the main one.

To draw boundaries between sessions, we simply look into how the time between actions distributes (more sophisticated methods exist [4]). We plot in Figure 1 the histogram and the empirical cumulative distribution of the time between two consecutive actions of a user. The vast majority

Table 2: Number of session per bucket for different session threshold times (in minutes).

	emlr	attr	util	attrc	satis	hand
15	418299	414416	413103	415223	417805	413129
30	390001	386448	385884	387358	390196	385641
60	365604	362457	362048	363060	366117	361845

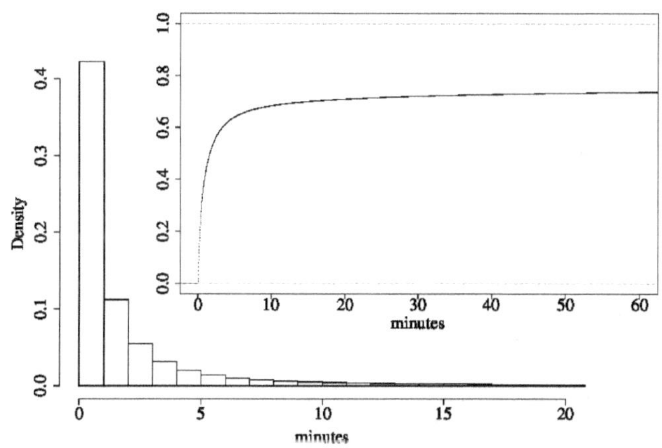

Figure 1: Histograms and cumulative distribution of time between consecutive user actions.

of actions occurs during the first 15 minutes, with only 2% happening between 15 and 30 minutes from the previous action, and 3.6% between 15 and 60 minutes.

A heuristic commonly used to separate sessions is to define a "session threshold" beyond which two user actions are assigned to two distinct sessions. A common value is 30 minutes [14], and we see that this is a reasonable choice here as well. We nevertheless use different thresholds in this work to investigate how they impact the results. When these are not significantly different – in practical, not statistical terms, we only report one of them.

Table 2 reports the number of sessions per bucket, as a function of the thresholds taken as 15, 30 and 60 minutes. Even with a threshold of only 15 minutes between user actions, some sessions contain a very large number of views and/or clicks. We considered these as outliers and we identified the browser cookies associated with sessions containing more than 30 views. Approximately 15,000 browser cookies matched this condition and were removed from our data set. This had an almost negligible effect on the data set size. The results we report from now on are based on this cleaned data set. We report in Table 3 a summary of the number of views per session as we increase the "session threshold" and in Table 4, we do the same exercise with the number of clicks per session. Finally, Table 5 describes the distribution of the number of clicks per view.

3.3 Clickthrough Rates

It is common practice to use clickthrough rate (CTR) to compare the online performance of ranking functions. It is also commonly accepted that the CTR at position 1 is deemed particularly important and is related to the ability to place in first position a "relevant" result for a given query, i.e. one that is clicked by users. This is somewhat blurred by the

Table 3: Distribution of the number of views per session for different session thresholds (in minutes). The last column is the percentage of sessions with no more than 10 views. The maximum number of views per session is 30 by design.

	Min.	1st Qu.	Median	Mean	3rd Qu.	% ≤ 10
15	1	1	2	3.545	4	93%
30	1	1	2	3.710	4	93%
60	1	1	2	3.851	5	92%

Table 4: Distribution of the number of clicks per session for different session thresholds (in minutes).

	Min.	1st Qu.	Median	Mean	3rd Qu.	Max.
15	0	0	2	3.467	4	216
30	0	0	2	3.646	4	224
60	0	0	2	3.807	5	224

Table 5: Distribution of the number of clicks per view. These numbers are identical for the 15, 30 and 60 minutes session thresholds. There is a maximum of 10 clicks because this is the maximum number of results presented on a result page.

Min.	1st Qu.	Median	Mean	3rd Qu.	Max.
0	0	0.8333	1.0310	1.5000	10

fact that users tend to click on the first result by default, even if it is not a priori very good [19]. Typically also, if the total number of clicks for two functions are similar, one function is better if clicks tend to occur at earlier positions.

In Figure 2 we plot the CTR of five of our ranking functions with respect to the reference hand (baseline) function (a carefully human hand-tuned function). According to the criteria listed above, all ranking functions but util are better than the reference. We also observe that attrc dominates attr. The comparison between emlr and both attrc and attr on the other hand is less clear cut. On one hand, emlr CTR@1 is clearly higher, but the overall CTR is lower. Also, emlr is dominated everywhere but at position 1. In view of this we can argue either that users find what they need at the first position more often with the emlr function and hence need not click further, or that attrc and attr offer more interesting results, and hence compel users into examining more results. If emlr receives less clicks than attrc and attr because users are satisfied with their first click, then we should observe more sessions with one click and less with several clicks. Table 6 reports the percentage of sessions with a given number of clicks for each ranking function[4]. We see that the data does not support this assumption. The percentage of sessions with exactly one click is quite stable across ranking functions, and, with 0.993 times the number of sessions in hand, emlr has even one of the lowest proportion of single click sessions.

This discussion illustrates the inherent ambiguity associated to interpreting clicks. CTR comparisons generally ignores that only part of the clicks are "good" clicks, leading to a good user experience. We note for example that util is a function derived from a model that attempts to identify

[4]We restricted the sessions to those with only one view and normalised by the same proportion in hand for privacy reasons.

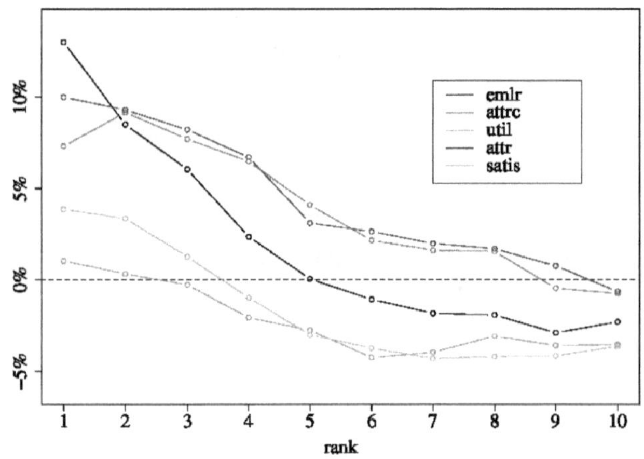

Figure 2: Clickthrough rate relative to the hand function.

Table 6: Percentage of single-view sessions with a given number of clicks for each ranking function, normalised by the same proportion for hand.

	emlr	attr	util	attrc	satis	hand
0	0.968	0.969	0.994	0.965	0.980	1.000
1	0.993	0.987	0.995	0.979	0.989	1.000
2	1.044	1.039	1.020	1.037	1.037	1.000
3	1.080	1.076	1.028	1.108	1.062	1.000
4	1.107	1.129	1.022	1.164	1.076	1.000
5	1.066	1.095	0.996	1.167	1.028	1.000
more	1.179	1.215	0.971	1.246	1.096	1.000

"bad" clicks from "good" ones. Hence we expect by design a lower CTR and we indeed observe this in Figure 2. It is also worth mentioning the sharp contrast between the DCG performance reported in Table 1 and the conclusions we draw from comparing CTR.

3.4 Query Reformulation

A higher number of query reformulations might suggest that users are not satisfied with the current search results. Therefore, if the click pattern observed with emlr (receives less clicks than for attrc and attr overall) reflects users finding sooner the answers they want (i.e. in the first position), then we should observe less query reformulation with that ranking function. In fact we observe the opposite. Table 7 contains the number of distinct queries issued by a user in the course of a given session for all six ranking functions. We see that emlr has a lower proportion of sessions with only one query than attr and attrc, suggesting that users reformulate their queries slightly more often.

3.5 Abandonment Rates

Finally, we compute the proportion of abandoned sessions, defined as sessions without a click, no matter how many views and how many reformulations the session contains. The abandonment rate is often used in evaluating search results, where a high abandonment rate suggests that poor search results were returned to users who then give up. Table 8 reports its value normalised by the abandonment rate on hand taken as the reference. Again, the conclusions are not in favour of emlr which shows a slightly higher abandon-

Table 7: Percentage of distinct queries in a session (columns add up to 100%).

	emlr	attr	util	attrc	satis	hand
1	61.76	61.90	61.68	61.95	61.69	61.54
2	18.35	18.31	18.40	18.23	18.37	18.34
3	8.41	8.30	8.45	8.42	8.44	8.47
4	4.33	4.39	4.39	4.31	4.37	4.46
5	2.49	2.45	2.47	2.45	2.47	2.54
more	4.66	4.66	4.60	4.65	4.66	4.65

Table 8: Abandonment rate relative to hand for different session time thresholds. The choice of a threshold has little impact on the conclusions.

	emlr	attr	util	attrc	satis	hand
15'	0.975	0.969	1.007	0.970	0.986	1.000
30'	0.978	0.969	1.007	0.971	0.987	1.000
60'	0.980	0.972	1.008	0.973	0.989	1.000

ment rate than attr and attrc. However, Yahoo! Answers users see part of the answers on the SERP, which makes the interpretation of abandonment rate as a sign of failure not always accurate.

In this section we showed that in a ranking context two well known metrics of user satisfaction (CTR and abandonment rate) as well as DCG, the corner stone of web search evaluation, are not clearly and unambiguously related to an interpretation of user behaviour. In the remainder of this paper, we show how our proposed absence time brings additional perspectives, not accounted for by the above metrics, and that together with them, lead to a more intuitive understanding of search quality and long term user engagement.

4. SURVIVAL ANALYSIS

We use Survival Analysis[5] [1] to study absence time. Survival Analysis has many applications, the most important one is concerned with the death of biological organisms who have received different treatments. The latter are controlled by variables that can potentially alter the death rate. An example is throat cancer treatment where patients are administered one of several drugs and the practitioner is interested in seeing how effective the different treatments are. The survival of a particular patient might be influenced by his or her smoking habits, in which case a "confounding" or "control" variable associated with smoking is created, and treatment is administered once at the beginning, i.e. at time 0.

The analogy with our analysis of Yahoo! Answers absence times is unfortunate but nevertheless useful. We associate the user exposition to one of the ranking functions as a "treatment" and his or her survival time as the absence time. In other words, a Yahoo! Answers user "dies" each time he or she visits the site, but hopefully "resuscitates" instantly as soon as his or her visit ends.

Related to Survival Analysis is the Survival curve such as shown in Figure 3 where the percentage of users (or patients)

[5]See also the Wikipedia article at http://en.wikipedia.org/wiki/Survival_analysis for a short introduction.

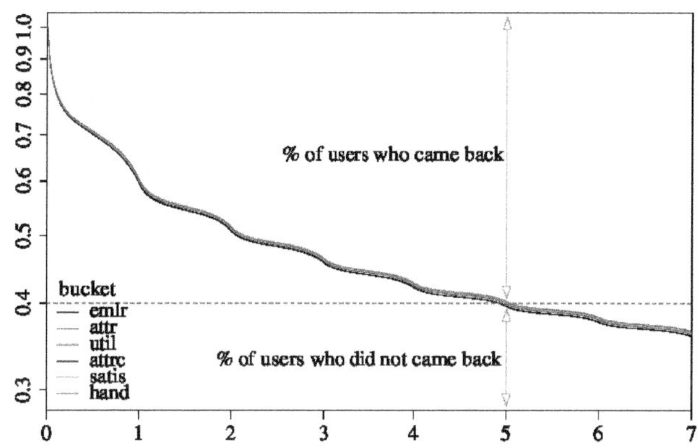

Figure 3: Proportion (log scale) of users who did not return to Yahoo! Answers after a given number of days. The absence time has been multiplied by a constant for confidentiality reasons.

still in the experiment (*y-axes*) is reported as a function of time. For example, we observe that 40% of the users return to Yahoo! Answers later than 5 days after their last visit. One such curve is drawn for each one of the six buckets. The differences are minimal, but a close look shows that the absence time of the users presented with the emlr ranking function is lower, implying that they return to Yahoo! Answers earlier. We also observe that hand is associated with a longer absence time, hinting at a lower performance (and hence associated user satisfaction with the search results).

The survival curves exhibit waves of an approximately 24 hours periodicity. This most probably reflects that user have habits regulated by whole day periods. In Section 5 we draw upon Survival Analysis to analyse the absence time in more detail and show that we can control for the 24 hour periodicity and quantify it. We also show that we can isolate different aspects such as the number of clicks, number of views, reformulations to obtain a better understanding of user engagement and to more accurately distinguish which ranking function performs best.

In the rest of this section we describe survival analysis in its classical usage, which has three main components, namely survival function, hazard rate, and Cox model. The analogy with the absence time is made in Section 5,

4.1 Survival Function and Hazard Rate

We define the survival function at time t as the percentage of users who survive past time t as $S(t)$. This is directly related to the probability $P(T \leq t)$ that a user dies at or before time t: $S(t) = 1 - P(T \leq t) = P(T > t)$. It happens that modelling the *hazard rate* rather than the survival function has several advantages. We therefore introduce the latter and describe its relation with $S(t)$.

The *hazard rate* $h(t)$ is the instant probability that a user dies at time t. Formally, this is:

$$h(t) = \lim_{\Delta t \to 0} \frac{1}{\Delta t} P(t \leq T < t + \Delta t | T \geq t). \quad (1)$$

It can be *very loosely* understood as the speed of death of a population of patients at a given moment t whereas the survival function $S(t)$ is the proportion of users who survived until t. The hazard rate and the survival function are closely related. Without demonstration:

$$h(t) = -\frac{S'(t)}{S(t)} \quad (2)$$

where $S'(t)$ is the derivative of $S(t)$, or, by integration

$$S(t) = \exp\{-\int_0^t h(s)ds\} \quad (3)$$

This relation shows that if the hazard rate of throat cancer patients administered with –say– **Drug** is higher than the hazard rate of patients under the **Placebo** treatment since the treatment was administered, then **Placebo** patients have a higher probability of surviving until time t. Nothing in the model prevents this situation to be reversed at a later time, depending on how both hazard rates evolve with time t. Overall, a higher hazard rate implies a lower survival rate.

4.2 Cox Model

The Cox model is a parametrisation of the previous model where the hazard rates under study are constrained to be proportional, thus allowing us to quantify their relations. Suppose that the **Drug** hazard rate is proportional to the **Placebo** hazard rate. We can then write:

$$h_{\texttt{Drug}}(t) = \alpha\, h_{\texttt{Placebo}}(t) \quad (4)$$

This does not entail that the hazard rates are constant.

The above (simple) Cox model can be extended by supposing that α is a function of any number of variables, as long as these variables are independent of the time t. We write $\alpha = \exp(\beta^T \mathbf{x})$ where $\mathbf{x} = (x_1, x_2, \ldots)$ is a vector of features and $\beta = (\beta_1, \beta_2, \ldots)$ are parameters or weights that control the influence of the corresponding variable. This is referred to as the Cox Model of Proportional Hazard.

Returning to our example of **Drug** and **Placebo**, we can set variable x_1 to be 0 if the observation comes from a user exposed to the **Placebo** cohort, and $x_1 = 1$ if it comes from the **Drug** cohort. The hazard rate of **Placebo** becomes:

$$h_{\texttt{Placebo}}(t) = h_0(t)\exp(\beta_1 x_1) = h_0(t)\exp(\beta_1 0) = h_0(t)$$

In this case, the baseline coincides with **Placebo**. For **Drug**, we have:

$$h_{\texttt{Drug}}(t) = h_0(t)\exp(\beta_1 x_1) = h_0(t)\exp(\beta_1 1) = h_0(t)\exp(\beta_1)$$

that is, if $\exp(\beta_1) > 1$ or, equivalently $\beta_1 > 0$, then the **Drug** hazard rate is higher than the baseline $h_0(t) = h_{\texttt{Placebo}}(t)$ and hence the **Drug** treatment is detrimental.

More generally, an arbitrary number of variables can be included in the Cox model. This is useful among other things to remove the effect of undesirable factors. For example, the number of smoking patients might be larger among the patients administered with the **Drug**. This higher number might be enough to explain the poor performance of the treatment. The multivariate equivalent of the model presented above can be rewritten:

$$\begin{aligned} h(t) &= h_0(t)\exp(\beta^T \mathbf{x}) \\ &= h_0(t)\prod_i \exp(\beta_i x_i) \\ &= \underbrace{h_0(t)}_{\text{baseline hazard}} \quad \overbrace{\exp(\beta_1 x_1)}^{\text{multiplicative effect of } x_1} \quad \exp(\beta_2 x_2)\ldots \end{aligned} \quad (5)$$

Table 9: Distribution of **absence** time per bucket with a session threshold of 15 minutes. (The results are normalised by the corresponding **hand absence** time for confidentiality reasons.)

	1st Qu.	Median	Mean	3rd Qu.	Max.
emlr	0.977	0.951	0.986	0.981	0.998
attr	0.978	0.957	0.988	0.990	1.003
util	0.996	0.989	0.997	1.002	0.997
attrc	0.969	0.970	0.992	0.989	0.999
satis	1.002	0.973	0.993	0.987	0.999

If we now set x_2 to be an indicator variable that is 1 if the patient is a smoker, then if β_2 is positive, then the effect of smoking on the hazard rate is to increase it. Another effect could be that a different estimate of β_1 can actually reverse the conclusions about which is best of **Drug** or **Placebo**. The treatment of categorical and continuous variables is similar. For example, x_2 could be redefined to represent the number of daily cigarette or the daily amount of nicotine.

Depending on whether the sign of β_i is positive or negative, a true value for x_i will contribute to, respectively, an increase or a decrease of the hazard rate and consequently will indicate whether x_i is associated with the survival of the patient to be, respectively, shorter or longer. In our case study comparing different ranking functions, a positive β_i and a large hazard rate translate into a short **absence** time and a prompter return to Yahoo! Answers, which itself can be considered as a sign of higher engagement.

5. CASE STUDY

We apply the survival analysis of the **absence** time to the six ranking functions described in Section 3. The aim of this section is to demonstrate the additional insights gained from the Cox models on specific aspects of user engagement. We use the R [18] statistical software and more specifically the Survival package [20] and the Survplot package [9] to compute the various Cox models.

We first present in Table 9 some statistics relating to the distribution of the **absence** time in the different buckets. All reported times are relative to the **hand** bucket, so for example, the median **absence** time in the **emlr** bucket is 0.951 times the **absence** median time in **hand**. We observe that **emlr** has the shortest median time while the shortest first quantile corresponds to **attrc**. This suggests that the **absence** times are spread, and that **attrc** results quality varies more than that of **emlr**. We study this further using the Cox model.

In Table 10, we show the Cox model parameter estimates associated with the 15 minutes session thresholds. The value of the β parameter for each bucket is reported together with its exponential, i.e. the coefficient that multiplies the baseline hazard $h_0(t)$. The baseline coincides with **hand**, i.e. the hand tuned ranking function. We see for example that the hazard rate of **emlr** for a 15 minutes threshold is $h_{\texttt{emlr}}(t) = \exp(0.01589)\, h_0(t) = 1.016\, h_0(t) = 1.016\, h_{\texttt{hand}}(t)$. This means that users exposed to **emlr** are returning faster to Yahoo! Answers. Moreover the *p-value* of H_0, i.e the null hypothesis $\beta = 0$, is 1.9e-8, which means that the value of β is statistically significantly different from zero. We also observe that **attr** and **attrc** are better, i.e. have a higher

Table 10: Cox model results with "bucket" as the independent variable. The baseline h_0 coincides with `hand` and is not reported

	β	exp(β)	se(β)	z	*p-value*
`emlr`	0.01589	1.016	0.00283	5.619	1.9E-08
`attr`	0.00768	1.008	0.00284	2.706	6.8E-03
`util`	-0.00147	0.999	0.00284	-0.516	6.1E-01
`attrc`	0.00779	1.008	0.00284	2.745	6.0E-03
`satis`	0.00504	1.005	0.00283	1.780	7.5E-02

hazard rate, than the baseline `hand`, and these differences are statistically significant. On the other hand, neither `util` nor `satis` are significantly different from the baseline. The se(β) column reports the standard deviation of the corresponding β and z is the value of β after transformation into a standard normal variable under H_0.

The `DCG` values reported in Table 1 also singled out `emlr` as the best performing function, but it also predicted that `attrc` was significantly superior to `attr`, which contradicts the above findings. More striking, `satis` has the second best performance in terms of `DCG` but this clearly does not translate in users returning to Yahoo! Answers as often as for `attrc` or `attr`.

Using larger threshold values does not change the conclusions substantially (we tried 30 and 60 minutes). The main difference is that most parameters cease to be significantly different from zero. The estimated β parameters on the other hand retain their sign, and their numerical values remain surprisingly stable. For example, the factors exp(β) associated with `emlr` goes from 1.016 when the threshold is 15 minutes to 1.015 when it is one hour. Similarly, `attr` goes from 1.008 to 1.006 and `util` from 0.999 to 0.998. This is a hint that the choice of a specific threshold does not impact the qualitative conclusions.

In the remainder of this section, we focus on specific insights derived from our proposed survival analysis of the `absence` time.

5.1 Taking Periodicity into Account

In Section 4, we already noted that the time of the day and the day of the week influence user behaviour. This is also apparent in Figure 3. In this section, we study this quantitatively.

For example, the next session to an evening session will probably not start within 8 hours simply because most users sleep during the night. Also, behavioural patterns change during the weekend [15] and naturally influence the `absence` time. To control for this effect we introduce a categorical variable for both the hour of the day and the day of the week. The results can be found in Table 11 for a threshold of 15 minutes. Interestingly, the coefficients associated with the buckets turn out to be remarkably similar to the previous experiment where neither time nor week day were taken into account. An `anova` analysis nevertheless shows that the model fit is significantly better (*p-value* of 2.2e-16).

In the interest of space, we do not report the numerical values associated with each of the 24 hours in a day. Instead we represent them graphically in Figure 4. They are all statistically significant and we clearly observe a daily trend.

Table 11: Cox model summary with "bucket" as the independent variable. The hour of the day at the start of the visit and the weekday of the visit are included as control variables. The coefficients associated to hours are not represented to save space. The baseline h_0 coincides with `hand` on Sunday at hour 0.

	β	exp(β)	se(β)	z	*p-value*
`emlr`	0.01561	1.016	0.00283	5.517	3.4E-08
`attr`	0.00780	1.008	0.00284	2.749	6.0E-03
`util`	-0.00191	0.998	0.00284	-0.671	5.0E-01
`attrc`	0.00795	1.008	0.00284	2.801	5.1E-03
`satis`	0.00499	1.005	0.00283	1.761	7.8E-02
hours	...	...	...	...	...
Mon	0.05349	1.055	0.00315	16.970	0.0E+00
Tue	0.08549	1.089	0.00329	25.948	0.0E+00
Wed	-0.01017	0.990	0.00302	-3.365	7.7E-04
Thu	0.04059	1.041	0.00304	13.352	0.0E+00
Fri	0.07100	1.074	0.00307	23.149	0.0E+00
Sat	0.02719	1.028	0.00308	8.823	0.0E+00

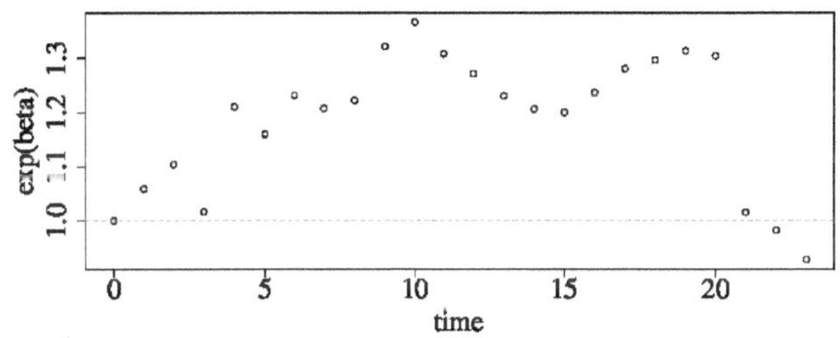

Figure 4: The influence of (GMT) time on the hazard rate as estimated by the exp(β) coefficients.

5.2 Relation between Activity & Engagement

We have explored in Section 3 several measures often used as indirect ways of assessing engagement: various guises of `CTR`, number of query reformulations and abandonment rates. In this section we add other measures and investigate how all these measures relate to the `absence` time. We show that Survival Analysis leads to a more nuanced interpretation of user interactions, as well as unifying them into a coherent framework.

5.2.1 Number of Clicks in a Session

Here, we investigate the common assumption that a higher number of click is a reflection of a higher user satisfaction and/or engagement with the search results. Table 12 shows the analysis of sessions with a single view. For ease of interpretation, we represented the number of clicks based on 10 binary variables $I_n, n = 0, \ldots, 10$ with I_n set to *true* if the sessions has more than n clicks. For example, a session with three clicks will have I_0, I_1 & I_2 set to true and $I_n, n > 2$ set to false. This has the advantage that each I_n represents the individual contribution of the nth click to the hazard rate.

Interestingly we observe that up to 5 clicks, each new click is associated with a higher hazard rate, but the contributions from the third click are weak. The contributions of the fourth and fifth clicks are not statistically significant, suggesting that the effect on `absence` time of a session with three, four or five clicks is essentially equivalent. From the sixth click, the contribution is negative ($\beta < 0$ and hence

Table 12: The impact of the number of clicks on the hazard rate of sessions with a single view.

	β	exp(β)	se(β)	z	*p-value*
`emlr`	0.02271	1.023	0.00489	4.646	3.4E-06
`attr`	0.01158	1.012	0.00491	2.356	1.8E-02
`util`	0.01105	1.011	0.00491	2.249	2.5E-02
`attrc`	0.01468	1.015	0.00490	2.995	2.7E-03
`satis`	0.01754	1.018	0.00489	3.583	3.4E-04
clicks					
> 0	0.32701	1.387	0.00339	96.413	0.0E+00
> 1	0.10594	1.112	0.00451	23.507	0.0E+00
> 2	0.01528	1.015	0.00634	2.411	1.6E-02
> 3	0.01631	1.016	0.00877	1.860	6.3E-02
> 4	0.01177	1.012	0.01227	0.959	3.4E-01
> 5	-0.05710	0.944	0.01742	-3.277	1.0E-03
> 6	-0.06359	0.938	0.02476	-2.569	1.0E-02
> 7	-0.01657	0.984	0.03542	-0.468	6.4E-01
> 8	-0.08001	0.923	0.05020	-1.594	1.1E-01
> 9	-0.15279	0.858	0.06893	-2.216	2.7E-02

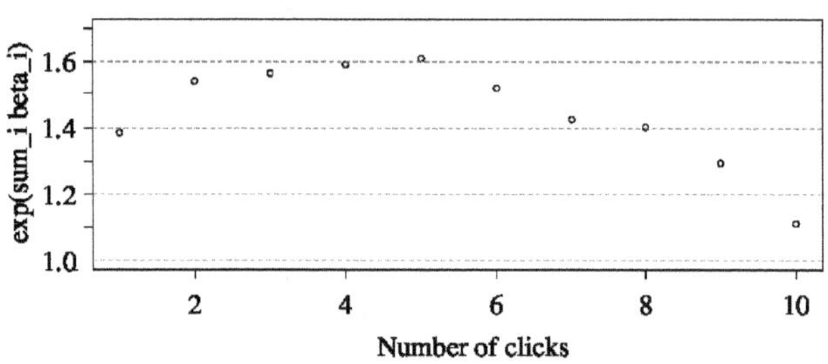

Figure 5: Influence of the number of clicks on the hazard rate, compared to no clicks (for which the value is 1.0).

exp(β) $<$ 1) and the hazard rates decreases slowly. This suggests that on average, clicks after the fifth one reflect a poorer user experience. The experience is nevertheless better than when there are no clicks at all. Indeed, in Figure 5 we present graphically the coefficient multiplying the hazard rate as a function of the number of clicks (i.e. the exponential of the cumulative sum of the β coefficients).

As for the influence of the number of views and distinct queries, the survival analysis provides additional insights. In particular, it makes clear that more clicks is not always better, which makes sense. Carrying the same analysis for sessions with more views while controlling for the number of views and distinct queries led to similar conclusions, and hence are not reported in this paper.

5.2.2 Click Position

We investigate whether the position at which a click occurs has an effect on the hazard rate. Table 13 shows the results obtained for sessions with one view and one click, where our baseline is a session with one view and one click at rank 1. Interestingly, the hazard rate is larger for ranks 2, 3 and 4, the maximum arising at rank 3. For lower ranks, the results are not statistically significant, but the trend is toward decreasing hazard. Only the click at rank 10 is statistically significant and clearly less valuable than a click at the first rank. We thus report in Table 14 the percentage of clicks at a given rank for a session with one view and one click. We

Table 13: Influence on the hazard rate of the position of the click in sessions with one view and a single click.

	β	exp(β)	se(β)	z	*p-value*
`emlr`	0.04989	1.051	0.00885	5.641	1.7E-08
`attr`	0.03586	1.037	0.00891	4.026	5.7E-05
`util`	0.03006	1.031	0.00890	3.379	7.3E-04
`attrc`	0.03765	1.038	0.00891	4.227	2.4E-05
`satis`	0.04489	1.046	0.00887	5.063	4.1E-07
hours	...				
weekdays	...				
click position					
2	0.02359	1.024	0.00712	3.314	9.2E-04
3	0.05054	1.052	0.00874	5.783	7.4E-09
4	0.03822	1.039	0.01032	3.704	2.1E-04
5	0.02012	1.020	0.01184	1.699	8.9E-02
6	0.00047	1.000	0.01355	0.035	9.7E-01
7	-0.01963	0.981	0.01506	-1.304	1.9E-01
8	0.01632	1.016	0.01641	0.994	3.2E-01
9	-0.01130	0.989	0.01693	-0.667	5.0E-01
10	-0.06625	0.936	0.01621	-4.087	4.4E-05

Table 14: Percentage of clicks at a given rank for a session with one view and one click.

rank: 1	2	3	4	5	6	7	8	9	10
44.9	18.0	10.3	7.0	5.1	3.9	3.1	2.5	2.4	2.7

observe more click at rank 10 than at ranks 8 and 9. A possible explanation is that users unhappy with the snippets at earlier ranks simply click on the last displayed result, for no apparent reason apart for it being the last one on the `SERP`.

It appears then that a click at position 3 for example is associated with a higher engagement than a click at the first position. Clicking lower in the ranking suggests a more careful choice from the user, which might be an explanation, while clicking at the bottom of the ranking might be a sign that the overall ranking is of low quality.

5.2.3 Time to the First Click

Although it would have been interesting to compare dwell time on a `SERP` and `absence` time, the dwell time of the whole search session is not available because the time when a user leaves the Yahoo! Answers site is generally not known. Instead we look at the relation between the time of the first click and the `absence` time. In other words, we want to see if the time a user takes to decide which search result to click first has an effect on the `absence` time. The results are reported in Table 15. We see that the faster the decision (shorter time between the search results of a query being displayed and the first click), the higher the hazard rate. The trend seems to reverse for time longer than 300 seconds. However, five minutes seems a very long time to select one result from a list of 10, which calls for further investigations not carried out in this paper.

5.2.4 Number of Views and Queries in a Session

We now investigate the relation between the number of views and the number of distinct queries during a session and the hazard rate. (One query can have several views if the user clicks on the next button.) The results are reported in Ta-

Table 15: Relation between time to click and hazard rate for one view sessions, one click sessions. The baseline is the **hand** bucket with a click within 5 seconds.

	β	$\exp(\beta)$	$se(\beta)$	z	*p-value*
buckets...					
$[5, 10)$	-0.20314	0.816	0.00704	-28.867	0.0E+00
$[10, 30)$	-0.39477	0.674	0.00680	-58.074	0.0E+00
$[30, 60)$	-0.65160	0.521	0.01071	-60.850	0.0E+00
$[60, 300)$	-0.67722	0.508	0.01494	-45.319	0.0E+00
> 300	-0.32264	0.724	0.02999	-10.758	0.0E+00

ble 16. We included the six ranking functions in the model and a binary variable reporting whether the number of views during the session was higher than the number of distinct queries.

The baseline is a session with a unique view (and a single query). Overall, the hazard rates associated with more views and more queries are significantly different, both in practical and statistical terms. For instance, the hazard rate of a session with two views and one query is $\exp(0.34982 + 0.05910) = 1.505$[6] times the hazard rate of a session with a unique view, while the hazard rate of a session with two views and two queries is $\exp(0.34982 + 0.11716) = 1.595$ times the baseline, all this for a given ranking function.

A similar computation can be carried out for all the combinations of number of views and number of distinct queries. We can conclude that having more views than distinct queries is associated on average with a longer **absence** times and hence a worse user experience. Without the **absence** time, it would have been harder to decide whether more page views is a sign of improved engagement or the opposite because we would have needed to understand why users decided to see more results, for example, whether they found the results interesting and wanted more of them, or browsed more because they did not find what they were looking for.

5.3 Click Value

Finally, we investigate whether a click "value" in terms of engagement depends on the bucket where it is observed (the deployed ranking function). We speculate that a click on the **SERP** of a better ranking function leads to a "better" result, and hence a shorter **absence** time.

In Table 17, we show the analysis of sessions with one view and a single click. We observe an effect of the ranking function. For example we see that a click originating on the **emlr** function is associated with a higher hazard rate when compared to the baseline (**hand**). This contradicts to some extent the "interleaving" hypothesis according to which all clicks have the same value [6]. A similar remark could have been done in Sections 5.2.1 and 5.2.2.

If we compare the values of the coefficients, we conclude that the **emlr** function is the best, followed by **attrc** and **satis**, respectively. On the other hand, if we study sessions with one view and two clicks (not reported here), we also observe a significant effect, but the functions' performances ranking is different; now **satis** turns out to be the best.

To decide which function to deploy on large-scale, it is best to compare overall performances as reported in Table 16

[6]The second term comes from the "views > queries" variable being true.

Table 16: The combined importance of the number of views and distinct queries on the hazard rate.

	β	$\exp(\beta)$	$se(\beta)$	z	*p-value*
emlr	0.01845	1.019	0.00283	6.524	6.9E-11
attr	0.00859	1.009	0.00284	3.028	2.5E-03
util	-0.00041	1.000	0.00284	-0.146	8.8E-01
attrc	0.00969	1.010	0.00284	3.417	6.3E-04
satis	0.00618	1.006	0.00283	2.181	2.9E-02
views					
2	0.34982	1.419	0.00362	96.733	0.0E+00
3	0.41630	1.516	0.00468	88.990	0.0E+00
4	0.44909	1.567	0.00541	83.076	0.0E+00
5	0.46877	1.598	0.00597	78.503	0.0E+00
> 5	0.54433	1.723	0.00566	96.166	0.0E+00
queries					
2	0.11716	1.124	0.00292	40.114	0.0E+00
3	0.13529	1.145	0.00384	35.252	0.0E+00
4	0.15573	1.169	0.00472	32.975	0.0E+00
5	0.18158	1.199	0.00573	31.702	0.0E+00
> 5	0.29641	1.345	0.00472	62.808	0.0E+00
views > queries					
TRUE	0.05910	1.061	0.00334	17.700	0.0E+00

Table 17: Influence of the originating bucket on the hazard rate of a single click session.

	β	$\exp(\beta)$	$se(\beta)$	z	*p-value*
emlr	0.02951	1.030	0.00636	4.640	3.5E-06
attr	0.01931	1.019	0.00641	3.014	2.6E-03
util	0.01410	1.014	0.00637	2.215	2.7E-02
attrc	0.01966	1.020	0.00641	3.069	2.1E-03
satis	0.02180	1.022	0.00635	3.433	6.0E-04
hours, weekdays, views, queries, etc.					

but it is nevertheless interesting to analyse the importance of clicks at this level of detail. For example, **satis** better performance when there are two clicks might reflect a better ability at showing diversified results. A possible way to verify this hypothesis would be to classify queries according to whether they would benefit from diversification and compare the performance on the two classes.

6. DISCUSSION AND FUTURE WORK

In this paper we presented new insights in measuring and interpreting user engagement. We proposed to use between-visit or "**absence**" time to measure user engagement, motivated by the fact that it is easy to interpret and often less ambiguous than the "activity" metrics commonly used. We used a community querying and answering website hosted by Yahoo! Japan to demonstrate the benefits associated with the use of "**absence**" time.

We explored the relations between **absence** time and various "activity" metrics such as abandonment rates, click-through rates, number of views, etc. We found reasonable interpretations for what we observed and were able to quantify the relation between some activity metrics and engagement. For example, we saw that while observing a click is on average better than observing no click, a click at the first position of the ranking is a weaker indicator of success than a click at the third position. While these experiments have been carried in the context of Yahoo! Answers in Japan, we believe they are representative of the results we would obtain for other ranking applications.

In addition, we compared six ranking functions deployed on Yahoo! Answers, one of them being hand tuned and the other learned either on a set of editorial labels or from clicks. In such settings, comparing the performance of these ranking functions using `DCG` is difficult because this metric is biased by construction in favour of the editorial ranking function. We showed that analysing the `absence` time and the user interaction data can lead to a more levelled comparison, making the case that some of the click learned functions [8] were in fact on par with the editorially based function.

It should be straightforward to extend this study to other web applications besides algorithmic search as long as we are confident that the `absence` time reflects user engagement. Of particular interest is the fact that the analysis can be carried out when no clicks or other record of user interaction are observed as is the case with "Direct Displays". In addition, we can also go beyond basic Survival Analysis, where only the last user experience is taken into account and instead generalise towards a complete longitudinal analysis where each interaction with a site is considered as a "treatment" of some kind that can potentially have an impact on a user engagement over time.

This research opens more questions than can be addressed in this paper regarding the relation between the user behaviour during a session and user decision to return to the site and their long term engagement, but it provides a direction on how to proceed with this challenge.

7. REFERENCES

[1] Aalen, O., Borgan, O., and Gjessing, H. *Survival and Event History Analysis: A Process Point of View.* Statistics for Biology and Health. Springer, 2008.

[2] Agichtein, E., Brill, E., and Dumais, S. Improving web search ranking by incorporating user behavior information. In *29th annual international ACM SIGIR conference on Research and development in information retrieval* (2006), pp. 19–26.

[3] Bilenko, M., and White, R. W. Mining the search trails of surfing crowds: identifying relevant websites from user activity. In *17th international conference on World Wide Web* (2008), pp. 51–60.

[4] Boldi, P., Bonchi, F., Castillo, C., Donato, D., Gionis, A., and Vigna, S. The query-flow graph: model and applications. In *Proceedings of the 17th ACM Conference on Information and Knowledge Management* (2008), pp. 609–618.

[5] Carterette, B., and Jones, R. Evaluating search engines by modeling the relationship between relevance and clicks. In *Advances in Neural Information Processing Systems 20, Proceedings of the Twenty-First Annual Conference on Neural Information Processing Systems* (2007).

[6] Chapelle, O., Joachims, T., Radlinski, F., and Yue, Y. Large-scale validation and analysis of interleaved search evaluation. *ACM Trans. Inf. Syst. 30*, 1 (2012), 6.

[7] Chapelle, O., and Zhang, Y. A dynamic bayesian network click model for web search ranking. In *Proceedings of the 18th International Conference on World Wide Web, WWW 2009, Madrid, Spain* (2009).

[8] Dupret, G., and Piwowarski, B. A user behavior model for average precision and its generalization to graded judgments. In *Proceedings of the 33st Annual International ACM SIGIR Conference on Research and Development in Information Retrieval, SIGIR* (2010), pp. 531–538.

[9] Eklund, A. *survplot: Plot survival curves with number-at-risk*, 2011. R package version 0.0.5.

[10] Hassan, A., Jones, R., and Klinkner, K. L. Beyond DCG: user behavior as a predictor of a successful search. In *Proceedings of the third ACM international conference on Web search and data mining* (2010), WSDM '10, pp. 221–230.

[11] Huang, J., White, R. W., Buscher, G., and Wang, K. Improving searcher models using mouse cursor activity. In *35th Annual International ACM SIGIR Conference on Research and Development in Information Retrieval (SIGIR)* (2012).

[12] Huang, J., White, R. W., and Dumais, S. T. No clicks, no problem: using cursor movements to understand and improve search. In *CHI Conference on Human Factors in Computing Systems* (2011), pp. 1225–1234.

[13] Järvelin, K., and Kekäläinen, J. Cumulated gain-based evaluation of ir techniques. *ACM Trans. Inf. Syst. 20*, 4 (2002), 422–446.

[14] Jones, R., and Klinkner, K. L. Beyond the session timeout: automatic hierarchical segmentation of search topics in query logs. In *17th ACM conference on Information and knowledge management* (2008), pp. 699–708.

[15] Lehmann, J., Lalmas, M., Yom-Tov, E., and Dupret, G. Models of user engagement. In *20th conference on User Modeling, Adaptation, and Personalization* (2012).

[16] Li, L., Chu, W., Langford, J., and Wang, X. Unbiased offline evaluation of contextual-bandit-based news article recommendation algorithms. In *Proceedings of the Forth International Conference on Web Search and Web Data Mining, WSDM* (2011), pp. 297–306.

[17] Liu, Y., Gao, B., Liu, T.-Y., Zhang, Y., Ma, Z., He, S., and Li, H. Browserank: letting web users vote for page importance. In *Proceedings of the 31st Annual International ACM SIGIR Conference on Research and Development in Information Retrieval* (2008), pp. 451–458.

[18] R Development Core Team. *R: A Language and Environment for Statistical Computing.* R Foundation for Statistical Computing, Vienna, Austria, 2011. ISBN 3-900051-07-0.

[19] Radlinski, F., Kurup, M., and Joachims, T. How does clickthrough data reflect retrieval quality? In *Proceeding of the 17th ACM conference on Information and knowledge management* (2008), pp. 43–52.

[20] Therneau, T., and original Splus->R port by Thomas Lumley. *survival: Survival analysis, including penalised likelihood.*, 2011. R package version 2.36-9.

Reusing Historical Interaction Data for Faster Online Learning to Rank for IR

Katja Hofmann
k.hofmann@uva.nl

Anne Schuth
a.g.schuth@uva.nl

Shimon Whiteson
s.a.whiteson@uva.nl

Maarten de Rijke
derijke@uva.nl

ISLA, University of Amsterdam

ABSTRACT

Online learning to rank for information retrieval (IR) holds promise for allowing the development of "self-learning" search engines that can automatically adjust to their users. With the large amount of e.g., click data that can be collected in web search settings, such techniques could enable highly scalable ranking optimization. However, feedback obtained from user interactions is noisy, and developing approaches that can learn from this feedback quickly and reliably is a major challenge.

In this paper we investigate whether and how previously collected (historical) interaction data can be used to speed up learning in online learning to rank for IR. We devise the first two methods that can utilize historical data (1) to make feedback available during learning more reliable and (2) to preselect candidate ranking functions to be evaluated in interactions with users of the retrieval system. We evaluate both approaches on 9 learning to rank data sets and find that historical data can speed up learning, leading to substantially and significantly higher online performance. In particular, our preselection method proves highly effective at compensating for noise in user feedback. Our results show that historical data can be used to make online learning to rank for IR much more effective than previously possible, especially when feedback is noisy.

Categories and Subject Descriptors

H.3 [**Information Storage and Retrieval**]: H.3.3 Information Search and Retrieval

Keywords

Information retrieval, Interleaved comparisons, Learning to Rank

1. INTRODUCTION

In recent years, learning to rank methods have become popular in information retrieval (IR) as a means of tuning retrieval systems to the requirements of specific search environments, groups of users, or individual users [18]. However, most current approaches work *offline*, meaning that manually annotated data needs to be collected beforehand, and that, once deployed, the system cannot continue to adjust to user needs, unless it is retrained with additional data.

WSDM'13, February 4–8, 2013, Rome, Italy.

An alternative setting is *online* learning to rank, where the system learns directly from interactions with its users [10]. These approaches are typically based on reinforcement learning (RL) techniques [25], meaning that the system tries out new ranking functions (also called rankers), and learns from feedback inferred from users' interactions with the presented rankings. In contrast to offline learning to rank approaches, online approaches do not require any initial training material, but rather automatically improve rankers while they are being used.

A main challenge that online learning to rank for IR approaches have to address is to learn as quickly as possible from the limited quality and quantity of feedback that can be inferred from user interactions. Learning speed is particularly important in terms of the number of user interactions. The better the system's performance is after a smaller number of interactions, the more likely users are to be satisfied with the system. Also, the more effective an online learning to rank algorithm is, the more feasible it is to adapt to smaller groups of users, or even individual users.[1] Furthermore, user feedback is limited because the learning algorithm should be invisible to system users, i.e., feedback is inferred from natural (noisy) user interactions.

In this paper, we address the following question: *Can previously observed (historical) interaction data be reused to speed up online learning to rank?* Current online learning to rank approaches for IR utilize each observed data sample (consisting of a query, the displayed results, and observed user clicks on the result list) only once. This was necessary because, until recently, it was not clear how feedback from previous user interactions (that were collected with different rankers) could be reused. However, a recently developed probabilistic method for inferring relative feedback [9] has been shown to allow data re-use [11] for ranker evaluation. It was found to be effective for making ranker comparisons more reliable, especially when large amounts of historical data were available. Here, we investigate whether and how this evaluation method can be integrated with online learning to rank approaches, and whether and in what way these additional (historical, and possibly noisier or biased) evaluations can lead to faster learning.

Specifically, we make the following contributions.

- We propose the first two approaches for reusing historical data in online learning to rank for IR: *reliable historical comparisons* (RHC), which uses historical data directly to make feedback more reliable, and *candidate preselection* (CPS), which uses historical data to preselect candidate rankers.
- In extensive experiments using 9 learning to rank data sets, we

[1]In this paper we focus on the effectiveness of the learning algorithm, and assume a system is used by a group of users with similar search behavior and preferences. The question of how to form user groups to which to adapt is orthogonal to this work.

investigate whether and how historical data reuse can speed up online learning to rank and lead to higher online performance. In addition to investigating our proposed methods, we analyze the effect of noise in user feedback, and the effect of bias and variance in ranker comparisons based on historical data.

We find that historical data can be effectively reused to speed up online learning to rank for IR. Particularly effective is the CPS approach, which reuses historical data to preselect candidate rankers, and can thereby compensate for noise in user feedback. Our results directly impact the effectiveness of online learning to rank approaches, especially in settings where feedback may be noisy.

We discuss related work in §2, and detail our approaches in §3. Our experimental setup and results are described in §4 and §5 respectively. We analyze our results in §6 and conclude in §7.

2. RELATED WORK

In this section we first give a brief overview of learning to rank approaches for IR, with a focus on approaches for learning in an online setting. While the reuse of previously collected data has not been investigated in this setting, the area of off-policy evaluation in RL is related, and is briefly reviewed as well.

Learning to rank for information retrieval is an active research area, and many approaches have been proposed and refined in recent years [18]. The vast majority of these learn in a supervised manner, from manually annotated data. A number of semi-supervised approaches have been proposed more recently, which can, in addition to expensive labeled data, take into account unlabeled sample data, for example as a means of regularization [26].

Both supervised and semi-supervised approaches typically work offline, meaning that labeled training data need to be collected before training (and typically, the data are assumed to be sampled i.i.d. from some underlying distribution). Collecting training data is often expensive and, because annotators may interpret queries differently from actual users, it may not accurately capture users' preferences [22]. In contrast, online methods hold the promise of allowing learning while interacting with users of the retrieval system [10, 28]. In this setting, no training data is required before deploying the system (but any existing data could be used for bootstrapping the system), and the system is expected to transparently adapt to its users' true preferences.

Online learning to rank for IR has been modeled as a contextual bandit problem (also known as *bandits with side information* or *associative RL* [15, 24]), a type of IR problem where states (i.e., queries) are independent of each other [2, 3]. A difference between typical contextual bandit formulations and online learning to rank for IR is that in IR reward cannot be observed directly. Instead, feedback for learning can be inferred from observed user interactions with the result list, e.g., clicks can be used as noisy relative preference indications, allowing probabilistic comparisons between documents [13], or between lists of documents [21].

Several methods for online learning to rank for IR have been proposed. Most of these perform listwise learning, meaning that they learn from probabilistic comparisons between pairs of candidate rankers using [28, 29]. A first such method, Dueling Bandit Gradient Descent (DBGD) was proposed in [28]. This method implements stochastic gradient descent over a large or infinite space of ranking solutions. Alternatively, algorithms based on multi-armed bandit formulations have been developed to efficiently find the best ranking solutions of a given set [29]. Besides listwise online learning to rank approaches for IR, a pairwise approach was investigated in [10]. Our work is based on the listwise DBGD algorithm (cf., Section 3).

Central to the performance of DBGD is the choice of a reliable feedback mechanism. The algorithm learns using relative feedback, typically implemented in the form of an *interleaved comparison method* (i.e., a method for inferring relative comparisons between rankers). Previously, DBGD was evaluated with a method called Balanced Interleave (BI) [10, 14, 21]. An alternative is the Team Draft (TD) method, which addresses limitations of BI and proved reliable in large-scale IR evaluation [5, 21].

Until recently, it was not clear how interleaved comparison methods could reuse historical data. However, the recently developed Probabilistic Interleave (PI) method bridges this gap [9, 11]. PI is based on a probabilistic interpretation of interleaved comparisons, which allows it to infer comparison outcomes using data from arbitrary result lists, even if they were obtained in comparisons of rankers different from the current target rankers. Our approaches for learning with historical data reuse are enabled by this evaluation approach. To the best of our knowledge they are the first approaches that integrate comparisons based on historical data with an online learning to rank for IR approach.

From an RL perspective, our work is related to *off-policy learning* [19, 25]. Off-policy learning means that an algorithm takes actions according to one policy but uses the resulting feedback to learn about another policy. The PI method that forms the basis of our approaches can be seen as a form of off-policy learning.

Work on RL approaches for information retrieval and related areas is ongoing. In particular, solutions have been proposed in the areas of news recommendation [1, 16] and ad placement [15, 24]. Other approaches for off-policy evaluation have been developed for applications related to IR, such as news recommendation. An off-policy evaluation method for news recommendation [17] uses rejection sampling to compensate for differences in how frequently specific news articles were shown to users by the behavioral policy. However, this approach cannot be easily applied to the online learning to rank for IR setting, because here the number of actions (result lists) is very large so that a similar approach would require prohibitively large amounts of data. Our methods are the first to reuse historical data for online learning to rank in a setting where feedback is available through interleaved comparison.

3. METHOD

In this section we detail our method for online learning to rank for IR with re-use of historical data. First, we describe our problem formulation (cf., §3.1), and methods for online learning (§3.2) and for inferring feedback (§3.3) on which our work is based. Finally, we detail our two methods for reusing historical data in online learning to rank for IR (§3.4 and §3.5).

3.1 Problem Formulation

Our model of online learning to rank for IR follows [10]. In it, a retrieval system repeatedly observes queries q, submitted by users of the system. The system generates a result list $\mathbf{r}$ and presents it to the user. Users interact with $\mathbf{r}$, and any clicks $\mathbf{c}$ on result documents are again observed by the system. The system can use the observed q and $\mathbf{c}$ to update its ranking function, and is ready to observe the next query. We assume that queries are independent of each other, rendering the problem a contextual bandit problem (cf., §2) [2, 3].

The objective of our learning system is to optimize online performance, formulated as discounted cumulative reward.[2] Again following [10] we adopt the following formulation:

$$C = \sum_{t=0}^{\infty} \gamma^{t-1} reward_t(\mathbf{r}_t). \quad (1)$$

[2]Note that reward is not directly observed by the system, but is only used for external system evaluation.

Here, reward of the result list $\mathbf{r}_t$ is accumulated over an infinite number of timesteps t, and weighted by a *discount factor* $\gamma \in [0, 1)$. This means that immediate rewards are weighted higher than future rewards. The discount factor can be interpreted such that there is a $1 - \gamma$ probability that interactions will end after each timestep, e.g., if users abandon the search engine. Thus, cumulative reward weights the reward at each timestep by its probability of actually occurring and online performance is highest for systems that present the best rankings after the fewest user interactions.

3.2 Dueling Bandit Gradient Descent

Our baseline learning algorithm uses stochastic gradient descent to learn a weight vector $\mathbf{w}$ for a linear combination of ranking features. Given a query q and a document collection D, the relations between the query and each document are expressed as vectors of ranking features $\mathbf{X}$. Given a weight vector $\mathbf{w}$, document scores are obtained by $\mathbf{s} = \mathbf{wX}$. A result list for the given weight vector can then be generated by simply sorting the documents by score.

Algorithm 1 Baseline algorithm, based on [28].

1: **Input**: $f(\mathbf{l}_1, \mathbf{l}_2)$, $g(\delta, \mathbf{w})$, α, δ, $\mathbf{w}_0$, λ (default: 0)
2: $\mathbf{h} \leftarrow []$
3: **for** query q_t ($t \leftarrow 1..\infty$) **do**
4: $(\mathbf{w}'_t, \mathbf{u}_t) \leftarrow g(\delta, \mathbf{w}_t)$ *// generate candidate ranker*
5: $\mathbf{l}_1 = generate\_list(\mathbf{w}_t)$; $\mathbf{l}_2 = generate\_list(\mathbf{w}'_t)$
6: $(o_L, \mathbf{r}, \mathbf{c}) \leftarrow f(\mathbf{l}_1, \mathbf{l}_2)$
7: **if** $o_L > 0$ **then**
8: $\mathbf{w}_{t+1} \leftarrow \mathbf{w}_t + \alpha \mathbf{u}_t$ *// update current best ranker*
9: **else**
10: $\mathbf{w}_{t+1} \leftarrow \mathbf{w}_t$
// maintain historical data if needed
11: **if** $\lambda > 0$ **then**
12: **if** $len(\mathbf{h}) = \lambda$ **then**
13: $remove(\mathbf{h}, \mathbf{h}[0])$
14: $append(\mathbf{h}, (\mathbf{r}, \mathbf{l}_1, \mathbf{l}_2, \mathbf{c}))$

Algorithm 2 $generate\_candidate(\cdot)$ (baseline method for generating candidate rankers, to be used as $g(\delta, \mathbf{w})$ in Algorithm 1).

Input: δ, $\mathbf{w}$
Sample unit vector $\mathbf{u}$ uniformly.
$\mathbf{w}' \leftarrow \mathbf{w} + \delta \mathbf{u}$
return $(\mathbf{w}', \mathbf{u})$

To learn weight vectors for ranking, we use DBGD [28], shown in Algorithm 1. Its first input is a comparison function $f(\mathbf{l}_1, \mathbf{l}_2)$, which compares two result lists $\mathbf{l}_1$ and $\mathbf{l}_2$ using user clicks $\mathbf{c}$ (the return value $o_L \in R$ indicates whether the quality of the two lists was inferred to be equal ($o_L = 0$), or whether the first ($o_L < 0$) or second ($o_L > 0$) list was inferred to be better; cf., 3.3). A second function, $g(\delta, \mathbf{w})$ is provided to generate candidate rankers. The remaining inputs are the step sizes α and δ, and an initial weight vector $\mathbf{w}_0$. An optional parameter λ indicates the maximum amount of most recent historic interaction data that the algorithm should keep in memory for possible reuse. This parameter is set to 0 in the baseline version.

The algorithm learns while interacting with search engine users as follows. At all times, the hypothesized best solution up to this point is maintained as $\mathbf{w}_t$. When a query q_t is observed, a new candidate weight vector $\mathbf{w}'_t$ is generated using $g(\cdot)$ (line 4). Then, the result lists generated for q_t using $\mathbf{w}_t$ and $\mathbf{w}'_t$ are compared using $f(\mathbf{l}_1, \mathbf{l}_2)$ (lines 5-6). If $\mathbf{w}'_t$ wins the comparison, $\mathbf{w}_t$ is updated using the update rule $\mathbf{w}_t \leftarrow \mathbf{w}_t + \alpha \mathbf{u}_t$ (line 8). Otherwise, $\mathbf{w}_t$ is not changed.

In the baseline version of this algorithm, $generate\_candidate(\cdot)$ is used to generate candidate weight vectors as follows (Algorithm 2). First, a vector $\mathbf{u}$ is generated by randomly sampling a unit vector. Then, $\mathbf{w}'$ is obtained by moving $\mathbf{w}$ by a step of size δ in the direction $\mathbf{u}$. An alternative method of candidate selection using historical data is presented in Section 3.5.

3.3 Probabilistic Interleave

Interleaved comparison methods are based on the observation that user clicks are context-dependent, i.e., interpreting them as relative feedback (in relation to surrounding documents) results in more reliable feedback than absolute interpretations [21]. Interleaved comparison methods aggregate clicks to obtain relative comparisons between result rankings, such as those generated by different rankers. Our methods for reusing historical data are based on PI [9, 11]. This interleaved comparison method enables historical data reuse because its probabilistic approach allows ranker comparisons using arbitrary result lists (e.g., result lists previously shown to users that were generated using rankers different from the ones currently compared).

Algorithm 3 Probabilistic Interleave, following [9], to be used as $f(\mathbf{l}_1, \mathbf{l}_2)$ in Algorithm 1

1: **Input**: $o(\mathbf{r}, \mathbf{l}_1, \mathbf{l}_2, \mathbf{c})$, $\mathbf{l}_1$, $\mathbf{l}_2$, τ, κ
2: $\mathbf{r} \leftarrow []$
3: **for** $i(1, 2)$ **do**
4: $\forall d \in \mathbf{l}_i : T_i \leftarrow P_i(d) = \frac{1}{index(\mathbf{l}_i, d)^\tau} Z_{i,d}$
// $Z_{i,d}$ is a normalization factor such that $\sum_{d \in \mathbf{l}_i} P_i(d) = 1$
5: **while** $(len(\mathbf{r}) < \kappa) \wedge ((\exists i : \mathbf{l}_1[i] \notin \mathbf{r}) \vee (\exists i : \mathbf{l}_2[i] \notin \mathbf{r}))$ **do**
6: $l_s \leftarrow 1$ **if** $random\_bit()$ **else** 2
7: $l_o \leftarrow 2$ **if** $l_s - 1$ **else** 1
8: $d_{next} \leftarrow sample\_without\_replacement(T_{l_s})$
9: $remove(T_{l_o}, d_{next})$
10: $append(\mathbf{r}, d_{next})$
// present $\mathbf{r}$ to user and observe clicks $\mathbf{c}$
// then compute the comparison outcome, e.g., using Eqs. 2–5
11: $o \leftarrow o(\mathbf{r}, \mathbf{l}_1, \mathbf{l}_2, \mathbf{c})$
12: **return** $(o, \mathbf{r}, \mathbf{c})$

The baseline version of PI (without historical data) is shown in Algorithm 3. Its first input is a comparison method $o(\cdot)$, that computes a comparison outcome given an interleaved list $\mathbf{r}$, original lists $\mathbf{l}_1$ and $\mathbf{l}_2$, and observed user clicks $\mathbf{c}$ (optionally, historical data $\mathbf{h}$ can be passed in). It also accepts the two lists $\mathbf{l}_1$ and $\mathbf{l}_2$ to be compared, a decay parameter τ, and the maximum desired length of the interleaved result list κ. The first step is to transform $\mathbf{l}_1$ and $\mathbf{l}_2$ into probability distributions over documents T_i (lines 3–4). The shapes of both distributions are identical and are determined by the original result lists and τ, such that the most highly ranked documents of an original result list are the most likely to be sampled. These distributions are used to generate an interleaved result list $\mathbf{r}$, which ensures that all possible permutations of documents $d \in \mathbf{l}_1 \cup \mathbf{l}_2$ can be observed with some probability $P > 0$.

During interleaving, the distribution to be used to contribute a document at a given rank of the interleaved result list $\mathbf{r}$ is randomly selected (lines 6–7). From the selected distribution (T_{l_s}) a document is drawn without replacement (8). The document is removed from the other distribution and appended to $\mathbf{r}$ (9–10). The process is repeated until all documents have been added or $\mathbf{r}$ is filled.

The interleaved result list is then shown to the user in response to the query and user clicks $\mathbf{c}$ are observed, where each entry in $\mathbf{c}$ indicates whether the corresponding document in $\mathbf{r}$ has been clicked. The observed clicks are used by the second step, *comparison*. In this step, the comparison outcome o is computed using $o(\cdot)$. In the baseline version of PI, we use the scoring function from [9]. This approach uses knowledge of the probabilistic interleaving process sketched above to marginalize over possible outcomes as follows. Recall that during interleaving, distributions for contributing documents were selected randomly (lines 6–7). By observing which distribution contributed which document (in an assignment vector $\mathbf{a}$), we could obtain a comparison outcome. However, we can obtain more reliable outcomes by marginalizing over all possible assignments $\mathbf{a}_i \in \mathbf{A}$ that could have led to the observed $\mathbf{r}$, and weighting them by their probability $P(\mathbf{a}|\mathbf{r}, q)$. This marginalized scoring function computes outcomes as follows:

$$o = \sum_{i=1}^{|\mathbf{A}|}(n(\mathbf{a}_i, \mathbf{c}, 1) - n(\mathbf{a}_i, \mathbf{c}, 2))P(\mathbf{a}_i|\mathbf{r}, q). \tag{2}$$

Here, $n(\mathbf{a}, \mathbf{c}, x)$ is a function that returns the number of clicks that, according to $\mathbf{a}$ were contributed by (the distribution based on) the original list $\mathbf{l}_x$. Following [9], we compute $P(\mathbf{a}|\mathbf{r}, q)$ using:

$$P(\mathbf{a}|\mathbf{r}, q) = \frac{P(\mathbf{r}|\mathbf{a}, q)P(\mathbf{a}|q)}{P(\mathbf{r}|q)} \tag{3}$$

$$P(\mathbf{a}|q) = P(\mathbf{a}) = |\mathbf{A}|^{-1} \tag{4}$$

$$P(\mathbf{r}|\mathbf{a}, q) = \prod_{i=1}^{len(\mathbf{r})} P(\mathbf{r}[i]|\mathbf{a}[\mathbf{r}[i]], \mathbf{r}[1, i-1], q), \tag{5}$$

where $P(\mathbf{r}[i])$ denotes the probability of observing document $\mathbf{r}[i]$ at rank i of the interleaved list $\mathbf{r}$ displayed for query q, given that it was contributed by the list specified in assignment $\mathbf{a}[i]$ and documents $\mathbf{r}[1, i-1]$ were already placed on $\mathbf{r}$ (obtained from $T_{1,2}$).

3.4 Reliable Historical Comparison

Based on DBGD and the interleaved comparison method PI, we can now define our first approach for reusing historical data to speed up online learning to rank. To enable this approach, we collect historical data by setting $\lambda > 0$ in Algorithm 1. Then, we use the collected historical data to supplement the interleaved comparisons based on live data as shown in Algorithm 4. We call this approach *reliable historical comparison* (RHC).

Algorithm 4 (RHC) Probabilistic interleaved comparison with reuse of historical data, to be used as $f(\mathbf{l}_1, \mathbf{l}_2)$ in Algorithm 1.

1: **Input**: $o_L(\mathbf{r}, \mathbf{l}_1, \mathbf{l}_2, \mathbf{c})$, $o_H(\mathbf{l}_1, \mathbf{l}_2, \mathbf{r}', \mathbf{l}'_1, \mathbf{l}'_2, \mathbf{c}')$, $\mathbf{r}$, $\mathbf{l}_1$, $\mathbf{l}_2$, $\mathbf{c}$, $\mathbf{h} = n \times (\mathbf{r}'_i, \mathbf{l}'_{i_1}, \mathbf{l}'_{i_2}, \mathbf{c}'_i)$
2: $o_L \leftarrow o_L(\mathbf{r}, \mathbf{l}_1, \mathbf{l}_2, \mathbf{c})$ *// compute live outcome following Eqs. 2–5*
// compute historical outcome, biased (Eqs. 2–5) or unbiased (Eq. 6)
3: $\mathbf{o}_H \leftarrow []$
4: **for** $(\mathbf{r}'_i, \mathbf{l}'_{i_1}, \mathbf{l}'_{i_2}, \mathbf{c}'_i) \in \mathbf{h}$ **do**
5: $\quad append(\mathbf{o}_H, o_H(\mathbf{l}_1, \mathbf{l}_2, \mathbf{r}', \mathbf{l}'_1, \mathbf{l}'_2, \mathbf{c}'))$
6: $\beta_L \leftarrow 1$
7: $\beta_H \leftarrow var(\mathbf{o}_H)$
8: $o_C \leftarrow (\beta_L * mean(\mathbf{o}_H) + \beta_H * mean(o_L))/(\beta_L + \beta_H)$
9: **return** o_C

RHC takes as input two methods for computing outcomes, o_L, which accepts data from one live observation, and o_H, which accepts as input the current target lists as well as one historical observation. Further, RHC takes as input one live observation, i.e., the interleaved list, original lists, and clicks obtained when interleaving the original lists $\mathbf{l}_1$ and $\mathbf{l}_2$ that are currently compared. In addition, it accepts n historical data points that were observed in previous comparisons of two different result lists $\mathbf{l}'_1$ and $\mathbf{l}'_2$. The algorithm first generates the live outcome as before (cf., Algorithm 3), using the live outcome method o_L (line 2). Then, additional outcome estimates are computed using the historical data and $o_H(\cdot)$.

In this paper we instantiate o_H in two ways to explore the effects of bias and variance on this approach. Previous work showed that applying PI directly to historical data results in biased estimates of comparison outcomes [11]. An alternative method, that compensates for bias using importance sampling, is unbiased, but can suffer from high variance when only little data is available. Both methods were previously applied to an evaluation task. Their effectiveness was similar for relatively small amounts of data, while for large amounts of data the unbiased method was more reliable. In contrast, in the online learning to rank task addressed here, we expect the effect of bias and variance to be relatively small, because amounts of historical data are small, and because subsequent ranker pairs are relatively more similar to those used to obtain the historical samples than in the evaluation setting addressed previously.

Our first (biased) instantiation of o_H uses the same scoring method as PI to estimate outcomes for the current target lists given historical data (Eq. 2). It uses the historical $\mathbf{r}'$ and $\mathbf{c}'$ to count clicks given assignments ($n(\mathbf{a}, \mathbf{c}', x)$), but uses distributions $T_{1,2}$ based on the current target lists $\mathbf{l}_1$ and $\mathbf{l}_2$. The resulting comparison method computes outcomes based on historical data but may be biased. Under the current target rankers, document distributions may be different from those under which the historical data was collected. This means that it is not guaranteed that each target ranker has an equal chance of contributing its highly ranked documents to the interleaved list, and to obtain clicks on these documents. As a result, the target list that is more similar to the historical lists has an advantage over the less similar one.

To address the problem of bias when historical data is used for computing interleaved comparison outcomes, we use importance sampling, as proposed in [11]. Importance sampling is a statistical method for compensating for differences between distributions, when data collected under one (original) distribution is used to infer information about a different (target) distribution. This approach is frequently used in e.g., off-policy reinforcement learning [19].

Our second instantiation of o_H (with importance sampling) is:

$$o_{IS} = \sum_{i=1}^{|\mathbf{A}|}(n(\mathbf{a}_i, \mathbf{c}', 1) - n(\mathbf{a}_i, \mathbf{c}', 2))P(\mathbf{a}_i|\mathbf{r}', q')\frac{P(\mathbf{r}'|q')}{P'(\mathbf{r}'|q')}. \tag{6}$$

As in the biased scoring method, $n(\cdot)$ counts the clicks each target list would obtain given an assignment and the original data ($\mathbf{c}'$). The obtained click difference is weighted by the probability of each assignment. In contrast to the biased method, this outcome is then weighted by its probability of occurring under the target distribution ($P(\cdot)$) versus the original (historical) distribution ($P'(\cdot)$). Intuitively, this means that observations that are more likely under the target distribution, and less likely under the original distribution, obtain a high weight and vice versa. It has been shown that outcomes obtained using importance sampling are unbiased (i.e., they converge to the expected outcome under the target distribution in the limit) [23]. While o_{IS} is unbiased, it may suffer from high variance when the target and source distributions are very different from each other, which may lead to unreliable outcome estimates.

After computing the live and historical estimates o_L and $\mathbf{o}_H$, they are combined into a final estimate o_C using the Graybill-Deal estimator [7] (line 6–8). This combined estimator weights the two estimates by the ratio of their variances. It was shown to result in a minimal variance combined estimate when the variances of the individual estimators are known, and to have strictly lower variance than either individual estimate when their variances are estimated on samples of size $n > 10$ [7].

A limitation of combining historical and live estimates according to Algorithm 4 is that for any given comparison we only have one live data point collected under the current target rankers, so that the variance of the live outcome(s) cannot be estimated. Here, we set the weight of the live outcomes to $\beta_L = 1$.[3] Our experiments in §4 below investigate whether this approximation is sufficient for improved performance. We hypothesize that the reliability of comparisons can be improved using RHC, leading to faster learning.

3.5 Candidate Preselection

Our second approach for reusing historical data to speed up online learning to rank for IR uses historical data to improve candidate generation. Instead of randomly generating a candidate ranker to test in each comparison, it generates a pool of candidate rankers, and selects the most promising one using historical data. We hypothesize that historical data can be used to identify promising rankers, and that the increased quality of candidate rankers can speed up learning. We call this second approach *candidate preselection* (CPS).

Algorithm 5 (CPS) Generating candidate rankers with preselection, for use as $g(\delta, \mathbf{w}_t)$ in Algorithm 1.

1: **Input**: $o_H(\mathbf{l}_1, \mathbf{l}_2, \mathbf{r}', \mathbf{l}'_1, \mathbf{l}'_2, \mathbf{c}')$, $\mathbf{w}_t$, δ, ζ, η, $\mathbf{h} = n \times (\mathbf{r}'_i, \mathbf{l}'_{i_1}, \mathbf{l}'_{i_2}, \mathbf{c}'_i)$
2: $\mathbf{e} = []$
// generate candidate pool
3: **for** i in $(i = 1..\eta)$ **do**
4: $\quad append(\mathbf{e}, generate\_candidate(\delta, \mathbf{w}_t))$
// compare and eliminate candidates using historical data
5: **while** $len(\mathbf{e}) > 1$ **do**
6: $\quad \mathbf{p} \leftarrow sample(\mathbf{e}, 2)$
7: $\quad o_H \leftarrow []$
8: $\quad$ **for** $i \; (i = 1..\zeta)$ **do**
9: $\quad\quad (\mathbf{r}'_i, \mathbf{l}'_{i_1}, \mathbf{l}'_{i_2}, \mathbf{c}'_i) \leftarrow sample(\mathbf{h}, 1)$
10: $\quad\quad append(o_H, o_H(l(\mathbf{p}[1].w), l(\mathbf{p}[2].w), \mathbf{r}', \mathbf{l}'_1, \mathbf{l}'_2, \mathbf{c}'))$
11: $\quad$ **if** $mean(o_H) < 0$ **then**
12: $\quad\quad remove(\mathbf{e}, \mathbf{p}[2])$
13: $\quad$ **else if** $mean(o_H) > 0$ **then**
14: $\quad\quad remove(\mathbf{e}, \mathbf{p}[1])$
15: $\quad$ **else**
16: $\quad\quad remove(\mathbf{e}, sample(\mathbf{p}, 1))$
17: **return** $\mathbf{e}[0]$ *// return remaining candidate*

Our implementation of CPS is shown in Algorithm 5, which replaces the method $generate\_candidate(\cdot)$ in our baseline method (cf., Algorithm 1). As input it takes a comparison function $o_H(\cdot)$ that estimates comparison outcomes using historical data, a current weight vector $\mathbf{w}_t$, the step size δ, arguments η and ζ that determine the size of candidate pools and the number of historical comparisons to conduct per ranker pair, and a vector of historical observations $\mathbf{h}$.

The algorithm is called when a new candidate ranker is requested. It first generates a pool of η candidate rankers by calling the original $generate\_candidate(\cdot)$ function (Algorithm 2) (lines 3–4). The most promising ranker is determined in rounds, where in each round a randomly selected pair of rankers (line 6) competes. For each pair, ζ comparisons are performed on historical data points randomly sampled from $\mathbf{h}$ with replacement (8–10). After the individual historical estimates are obtained, their mean is used to determine which ranker to eliminate from the pool. If there is a winner (i.e., $o_H \neq 0$), the losing ranker is removed. Otherwise, one of the rankers is selected to be removed at random. When only one element remains in the candidate pool, it is returned as the most promising candidate.

Our candidate selection approach ensures that a single candidate is selected after a finite $((\eta - 1) \times \zeta)$ number of comparisons. Because only the best candidate needs to be selected, the randomized approach is expected to provide a good balance of effectiveness and efficiency. In cases where the compared candidates perform equally well, only one candidate needs to be retained (chosen randomly).

Like in §3.4 above, we investigate the effect of bias and variance on this approach by implementing the comparison method o_H in two different ways, (1) using the biased (but low variance) method defined by Eqs. 2–5, and (2) using the unbiased (potentially high variance) method that uses importance sampling (Eq. 6).

We hypothesize that CPS can substantially improve the quality of candidate rankers available for online learning, leading to faster learning than using live data only. Regarding the biased and unbiased version of CPS, we expect only small performance differences, as the amount of historical data reused per live comparison is small.

4. EXPERIMENTS

Our experiments are designed to investigate whether online learning to rank for IR can be sped up by using historical data. They are based on an existing simulation framework. This framework combines fully annotated learning to rank data sets with probabilistic user models to simulate user interactions with a search engine that learns online. The use of this framework allows us to investigate characteristics of our proposed learning approaches without the potential risk of hurting a real system's performance. Below, we provide details of the evaluation framework, data sets, and user models, as well as the performance metrics and parameter settings used in our experiments.

The simulation framework works as follows. An incoming user query is modeled as random sampling from a pool of queries provided with a learning to rank data set. The system generates a result list to respond to the query using the features of candidate documents that are provided with the data set (this is similar to ranking candidate documents after an initial matching/filtering step as would be done while interacting with real users). Displaying the generated result list to the user and observing clicks is simulated by applying our user model, which generates clicks probabilistically on the basis of the annotations available with the data set. The clicks are sent back to the retrieval system, where feedback is inferred and learned from. Then, the cycle continues with the next simulated user query.

We conduct all our experiments on the 9 data sets provided as LETOR 3.0 and 4.0 (LEarning TO Rank) [18]. All data sets contain feature vectors that represent the relationships between queries and documents that are typical for various search settings. In addition, the (manually assessed) relevance level of each document-query pair is provided. Finally, all data sets are pre-split by query for 5-fold cross validation.

The following search tasks are implemented: the data set *OHSUMED* models a literature search task, based on a query log of a search engine for the MedLine abstract database. This data set contains 106 queries that implement an informational search task. The remaining 8 data sets are based on TREC Web track tasks run between 2003 and 2008. The datasets *HP2003*, *HP2004*, *NP2003*, and *NP2004* implement navigational tasks, homepage finding and named-page finding respectively. *TD2003* and *TD2004* implement an informational task: topic distillation. All six data sets are based on the .GOV document collection, a crawl of the .gov domain, and contain between 50 and 150 queries and approximately 1000 judged documents per query. A more recent document collection, .GOV2

[3]We also experimented with batches of comparisons where the same original pair was used for several subsequent comparisons. However, the performance loss due to the resulting smaller number of updates outweighed the gain due to improved variance estimates.

formed the basis of *MQ2007* and *MQ2008*. These data sets contain 1700 and 800 queries respectively, but far fewer judged documents per query. The data sets *OHSUMED*, *MQ2007* and *MQ2008* are annotated with graded relevance judgments (3 grades, from 0, not relevant, to 2, highly relevant), while the remaining data sets are labeled using binary assessments.

To generate clicks, we employ a user model based on the Dependent Click Model (DCM) [8],[4] an extension of the Cascade Model [6] that has been shown to be effective in explaining users' click behavior in web search. The model explains position bias (i.e., the observation that higher-ranked results are much more likely to be clicked than lower-ranked ones) by positing that users start examining documents at the top of a result list. For each document they examine, they determine whether the document representation (e.g., consisting of title, snippet and URL) appears promising enough to warrant a click (we model this step of deciding to click with a click probability given some relevance label $P(C|R)$). After each click, users decide whether they are satisfied with the information provided in the clicked document(s) and they want to stop examining further results (with stop probability $P(S|R)$), or if they want to continue examining results.

Table 1: Overview of the click models used.

	click probabilities			*stop probabilities*		
relevance grade	0	1	2	0	1	2
perfect	0.0	0.5	1.0	0.0	0.0	0.0
navigational	0.05	0.5	0.95	0.2	0.5	0.9
informational	0.4	0.7	0.9	0.1	0.3	0.5

The user model instantiations used in our experiments are provided in Table 1. First, the *perfect* click model provides reliable feedback, and is used to obtain an upper bound on performance. The second (*navigational*) and third (*informational*) model reflect the two types of search tasks implemented by our data sets, as well as increasing levels of noise (i.e., smaller differences in click probabilities for different relevance levels). For each instance, the table provides the click and stop probabilities given a relevance grade R. For example, under the navigational model, simulated users would be very likely to encounter a highly relevant document ($P(C|2) = 0.95$), and very likely to stop examining documents once they clicked on such a document ($P(S|2) = 0.9$). Under the informational model, users are less likely to stop, and click probabilities for the different relevance grades are much more similar, resulting in a higher level of noise. For data sets with binary relevance judgments, only the two extremes are used.

Our experiments compare and contrast three baseline runs and four experimental runs:

BI Baseline – learning with live data only, using Balanced Interleave [14, 21] for interleaved comparisons. Balanced Interleave generates interleaved result lists using a mostly deterministic process, where only the starting list is selected at random. Comparisons are made based on the number of clicks each original list would obtain above a cutoff.

TD Baseline – learning with live data only, using Team Draft [20, 21] for interleaved comparisons. Team Draft randomizes interleaving per pair of ranks, and assigns clicks to the original list that contributed a document.

PI Baseline – learning with live data only, using PI (cf., §3.3).

[4]Models that take additional information into account have been shown to more accurately reflect click behavior [27], but these make stronger assumptions rendering experiments unnecessarily complex.

RHC-B Uses historical data to infer more reliable feedback (cf., §3.4), with *biased* comparison outcome estimates (Eq. 2).

RHC-U Uses historical data to infer more reliable feedback (cf., §3.4), with *unbiased* comparison outcome estimates (Eq. 6).

CPS-B Uses historical data for candidate preselection (cf., §3.5) with *biased* comparison outcome estimates (Eq. 2).

CPS-U Uses historical data for candidate preselection (cf., §3.5) with *unbiased* comparison outcome estimates (Eq. 6).

Our main evaluation metric is online performance, measured as the cumulative discounted reward obtained over the course of T interactions between system and user (cf. Eq. 1). This means that we measure the utility of result lists presented to search engine users while learning. Note that, although we run our experiments over a limited number of interactions, discounting ensures that our measured performance is a close approximation of the online performance that could be obtained in an infinite horizon setting.

To approximate the true utility of a search engine result page to a user, we compute Normalized Discounted Cumulative Gain (NDCG) on the top $\kappa = 10$ results shown to the user, a standard evaluation metric in information retrieval [4]:[5]

$$NDCG = \sum_{i=1}^{len(\mathbf{r})} \frac{2^{rel(\mathbf{r}[i])} - 1}{\log_2(i+1)} iNDCG^{-1}. \quad (7)$$

This metric sums over the gain that is based on the relevance label ($rel(\mathbf{r}[i])$) of each document, and divides it by a discount factor (based on the log of the rank i at which the document was presented). This sum is then normalized by the ideal NDCG (iNDCG) that would be obtained on an ideal document ranking.

For each data set, we run experiments over 1000 iterations (i.e., simulated interactions), and repeat each experiment 25 times and average results over all folds and repetitions. Parameters for the DBGD learning algorithm are selected to match those found to work best in previous work ($\mathbf{w}_0$ is initialized to zero, $\alpha = 0.01$, $\delta = 1$, cf., [28]). For the remaining parameters, we report results on one setting (for CPS, $\eta = 6$, $\zeta = 10$, and $\lambda = 10$; for RHC, $\lambda = 10$). The sensitivity to specific parameter settings is analyzed in §6. We test for statistically significant differences using a two-sided student's t-test. To ensure repeatability of our experiments, we make all source code used to obtain our results available online.[6]

5. RESULTS

In this section we present the results of our experiments, described in §4, to answer our main research question: *Can historical interaction data be reused to speed online learning to rank?* In addition to our main question, we also investigate *how* historical data can best be reused (i.e., to improve the reliability of evaluations, as in our RHC approach, or to improve the quality of candidate rankers, as in CPS), and whether and how historical data reuse is affected by bias and variance in outcome estimates based on historical data.

Table 2 shows the online performance obtained on all LETOR 3.0 and 4.0 data sets, for the three click model instantiations specified in Table 1, the three baseline runs BI, TD, PI, and the four experimental runs RHC-B, RHC-U, CPS-B and CPS-U. For reasons discussed below, BI outperforms the other baseline methods. Therefore, we use BI as our baseline for significance testing.

[5]Note that our formulation differs from earlier ones, including the one provided with the LETOR toolkit, where documents at rank 2 are not discounted (cf., [12]). Here, we use the formulation from [4] so that relevance differences at the highest ranks can be detected.

[6]Available from http://ilps.science.uva.nl/resources/online-learning-framework.

		BI	TD	PI	RHC-B	RHC-U	CPS-B	CPS-U
				perfect click model				
1	*HP2003*	107.84	108.94	97.62▼	95.51▼	95.60▼	**118.24▲**	116.72▲
2	*HP2004*	99.82	99.72	89.72▼	87.49▼	88.54▼	**109.12▲**	108.40▲
3	*NP2003*	97.94	98.15	88.67▼	87.03▼	89.05▼	**108.82▲**	108.04▲
4	*NP2004*	102.96	102.72	93.50▼	93.12▼	92.93▼	113.97▲	**114.35▲**
5	*TD2003*	40.38	38.81	36.21▼	34.10▼	33.79▼	**47.26▲**	47.22▲
6	*TD2004*	36.19	35.87	34.55▼	30.82▼	31.60▼	43.96▲	**44.72▲**
7	*OHSUMED*	70.68	70.14	68.29▼	64.23▼	65.29▼	**72.57**	72.36
8	*MQ2007*	59.87	60.18	58.23▼	58.69▽	58.22▼	**64.30▲**	63.60▲
9	*MQ2008*	79.03	77.98	75.57▼	76.08▼	77.09▼	84.35▲	**84.68▲**
				navigational click model				
10	*HP2003*	93.82	93.52	79.15▼	85.29▼	84.22▼	114.93▲	**116.24▲**
11	*HP2004*	83.23	82.54	69.28▼	77.25▼	76.66▼	106.12▲	**107.48▲**
12	*NP2003*	88.00	85.07	74.77▼	78.75▼	80.47▼	106.81▲	**107.58▲**
13	*NP2004*	90.53	88.50	79.43▼	85.81▼	86.84▽	**113.62▲**	112.39▲
14	*TD2003*	34.60	33.20	30.99▼	30.53▼	31.07▼	**44.77▲**	44.56▲
15	*TD2004*	32.71	31.78	30.72▼	27.60▼	27.78▼	**41.11▲**	39.85▲
16	*OHSUMED*	67.54	67.96	65.10▼	62.60▼	62.27▼	68.16	**70.28△**
17	*MQ2007*	58.42	58.92	56.33▼	55.71▼	57.36	61.61▲	**61.63▲**
18	*MQ2008*	76.14	76.32	72.84▼	74.21▽	74.66▽	81.41▲	**81.70▲**
				informational click model				
19	*HP2003*	55.63	55.65	46.87▼	65.54▲	63.92▲	104.46▲	**107.61▲**
20	*HP2004*	42.99	45.02	37.52▽	56.23▲	55.66▲	83.04▲	**89.17▲**
21	*NP2003*	53.38	52.88	45.38▼	65.63▲	64.25▲	103.09▲	**103.34▲**
22	*NP2004*	58.31	57.62	52.32▽	71.48▲	72.81▲	96.20▲	**99.88▲**
23	*TD2003*	22.11	21.99	21.74	25.20▲	26.12▲	38.47▲	**38.86▲**
24	*TD2004*	23.66	22.87	21.60▼	22.35	22.22	29.63▲	**30.27▲**
25	*OHSUMED*	63.39	**64.91**	60.48▼	58.65▼	58.47▼	61.05	64.29
26	*MQ2007*	55.29	54.58	53.99	54.79	54.37	56.35	**57.76▲**
27	*MQ2008*	73.14	71.83	70.42▼	70.89▼	70.42▼	76.63▲	**76.97▲**

Table 2: Online performance (in terms of discounted cumulative reward) when learning with interleaved comparison methods. Best runs per row are highlighted in bold. Statistically significant improvements (losses) from the baseline method *BI* are indicated by △ ($p = 0.05$) and ▲ ($p = 0.01$) (▽ and ▼).

Overall, we see that the highest online performance is achieved by our CPS method for most data sets and click models. The observed improvements over BI are statistically significant with $p < 0.01$, and substantial. For example, for the data set *HP2003*, the highest performance under perfect click feedback is 118.24 (using biased estimates of comparison outcomes), which constitutes an improvement of 8.5% over the best-performing baseline method TD (cf., row 1). The only exception is the data set *OHSUMED*, for which performance under the perfect and informational click models is statistically equivalent for BI and CPS (rows 7 and 25).

To put the obtained absolute online performance scores in perspective, recall that we measure discounted cumulative gain, i.e., high online performance is obtained when a method both learns well (i.e., it achieves high offline performance, in terms of NDCG), and it learns quickly, i.e., after a small number of interactions. In our experimental setup, a method that presented perfect result lists (with NDCG = 1) on all interactions could obtain an online performance of 200.0, while a method that would obtain no reward on the first 500 interactions and perfect results after would achieve an online performance of only 15.0. Scores obtained by our methods fall between these two extremes, indicating that good rankers are learned within a few hundred simulated interactions.

For the baseline methods, which learn from live data only, we find that online performance of BI and TD is very similar, while that of PI is significantly lower for most data sets and click models. To understand why, we compare the offline performance and learning speed of these methods (cf., the offline performance on data set *NP2003* in Figure 1).[7] We see that the final offline performance is very similar (differences are not statistically significant), and that they also learn equally fast. Thus, PI learns as well as BI and TD, but loses online performance due to the increase in randomization during interleaving. Compared to the evaluation setting, where PI was shown to outperform BI and TD when applied to compare rankers over large amounts of data, PI performs worse than expected [9]. PI provides fine-grained information about the magnitude of ranker difference, which leads to more accurate comparisons when outcomes are aggregated over repeated samples. However, in the online learning to rank setting with live data only, ranker comparisons are based on a single data sample, and information about the magnitude of ranker differences is lost. Developing online learning methods that exploit this additional information is a direction for future work.

Our methods that learn from historical data are enabled by PI, meaning that to improve performance over the best-performing baseline, BI, the methods need to learn substantially faster, to overcome the initial performance loss incurred by the randomization inherent to PI. For the CPS method, we see that this is the case. The method achieves much higher online performance than any of the methods

[7]For brevity we present offline performance plots for only one data set. Plots for the remaining data sets are qualitatively similar.

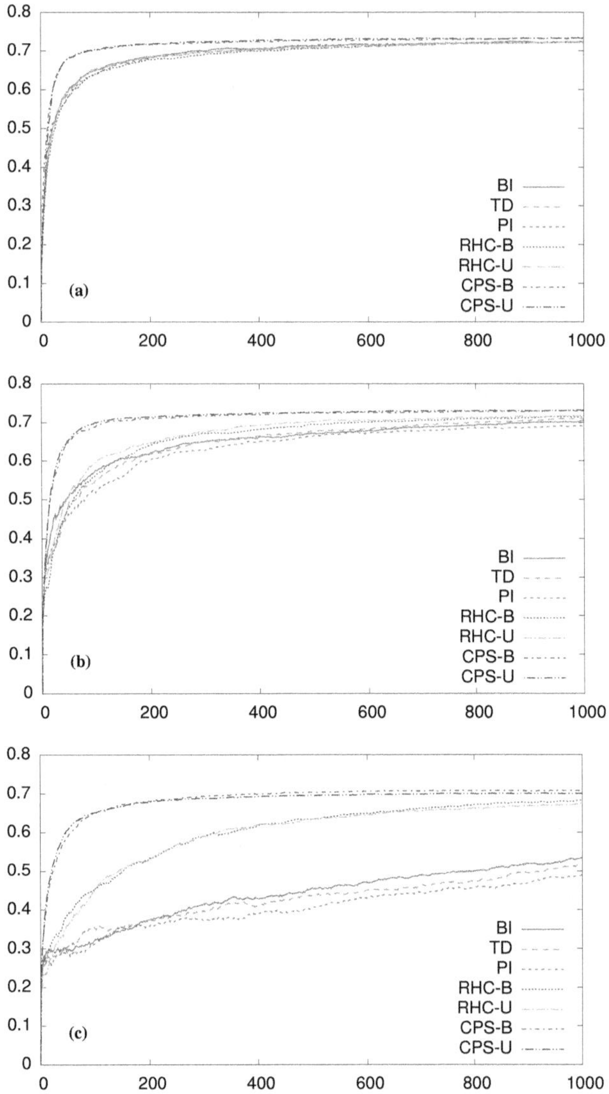

Figure 1: Offline performance (computed on held-out test queries after each learning step) on *NP2003* data set, for the *perfect*, *navigational*, and *informational* click models.

that learn with live data only. Furthermore, the performance gain for reusing historical data is particularly big when click feedback is noisy, with gains up to 107% (row 20). Looking at offline performance (Figure 1), we observe that CPS learns faster than methods that learn from live data only. In particular, the speed-up is biggest for the noisy informational click model, suggesting that the CPS method can effectively limit the effect of noise in click feedback.

Performance for our method RHC is generally lower than that obtained by CPS or the baselines that only take live data into account. However, under noisy feedback (the informational click model) online performance is significantly higher than that obtained by BI on 5 of the 9 data sets (rows 19–23). Comparing again to offline performance, we find that RHC learns as quickly as the baseline methods, but cannot make as effective use of the learned rankers, similar to PI. However, when feedback is noisy, the method does succeed in making comparisons more reliable (cf., part (c) of Figure 1). Thus, we conclude that RHC can effectively leverage historical data to make ranker comparisons more reliable, but this results in performance gains only when click feedback is indeed noisy.

The effect of removing bias is small overall. Of the differences between RHC-B and RHC-U, only that in row 26 (*MQ2007*, informational click model) is statistically significant. This small effect is expected, because for the relatively few samples that are combined in historical outcome estimates (e.g., for $\lambda = 10$), removing bias can only have a small effect on absolute outcomes. However, several patterns do emerge. For RHC, using the unbiased method (RHC-U) improves online performance for 5 of the 9 data sets, and performance decreases in 4 cases. For the navigational click model, differences are smaller, and the trend continues for the informational model. It appears that for RHC, removing bias can slightly improve learning. This can be explained by the direction of the bias. We use the λ most recent historical points. For these, the original and target distributions are expected to be most similar, so bias or variance should be smallest for these samples. Also, the original distribution will typically be biased towards the current best ranker $\mathbf{w}_t$, as it was used before. Therefore, there is a slightly increased chance of observing clicks on documents highly ranked by $\mathbf{w}_t$, giving a disadvantage to the new candidate ranker. This means that, due to this bias, a good candidate may be missed, leading to slower learning. When feedback is noisier, this effect is masked by the noise.

For CPS, the biased version of the method performs slightly better than CPS-U under perfect feedback (none of the differences are statistically significant). However, CPS-U performs better when click feedback is noisier. It appears that, when feedback is very reliable (perfect user model), the increase in noise due to removing bias may slow learning more than can be compensated for by the bias removal. However, increases in click noise can amplify the effect of bias. CPS evaluates several rankers distributed around the current best ranker, $\mathbf{w}_t$. It is itself not evaluated using historical data, but the candidate rankers that generate rankings that are more similar to the current (or previous) best ranker have an advantage. This advantage is stronger when click feedback is noisier, because highly-ranked documents that are not relevant to the query are more likely to be clicked than under more reliable feedback. This bias leads to slower learning and the observed lower online performance for CPS-B under noisy feedback. Overall, we can conclude that the unbiased methods should be preferred over biased methods, especially when click feedback is expected to be noisy.

Our main results show consistently high performance for our CPS method, which can achieve significantly and substantially higher online performance than all other methods tested. We find that reusing historical data using CPS allows faster learning than with current online learning to rank methods that take only live data into account. In the next section, we analyze our results in more detail.

6. ANALYSIS

In this section, we first compare the performance of our methods to supervised learning to rank approaches (§6.1). Then we compare our methods' sensitivity to parameter settings (§6.2 and 6.3).

6.1 Comparison with Previous Work

Most previous work on learning to rank for IR focused on supervised approaches, and measured the offline performance achieved by learners after all training data had been processed. Our approach is fundamentally different, as it learns online, from relative feedback observed on the result lists presented to users. Despite this more limited form of feedback, previous work showed that online learning to rank can achieve competitive offline performance, at least when click feedback is reliable [10].

To allow for some comparison with supervised learning to rank approaches, we show the offline performance achieved by CPS-U in terms or LETOR NDCG at different cutoffs on the perfect and informational click models in Table 3. Despite the degenerate quality of feedback available in the online setting, final performance

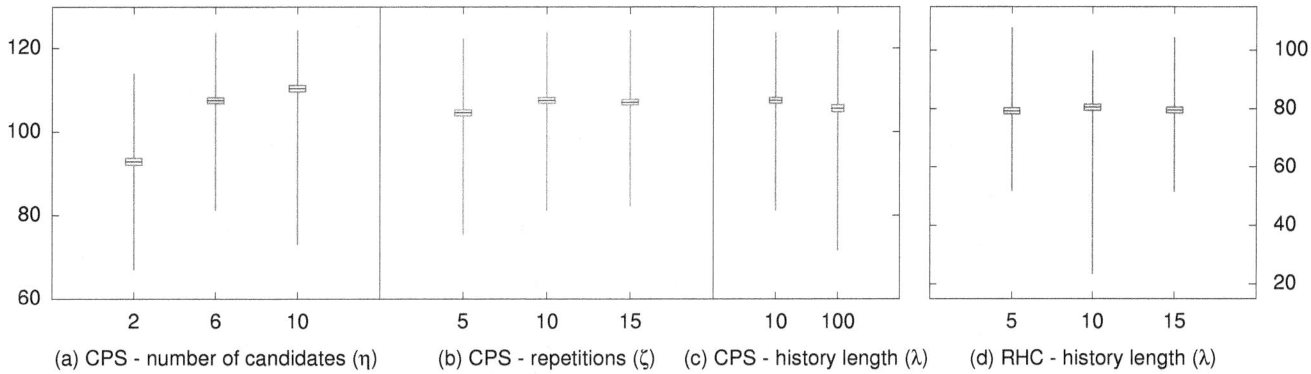

Figure 2: Online performance (min, max, and mean with standard error) after 1000 iterations for different settings of parameters (a) η, (b) ζ, and (c) λ for CPS and (d) λ for RHC on the *NP2003* data set and *navigational* click model.

after 1000 iterations is reasonable, compared to supervised learning to rank methods [18]. For example, final performance of CPS-U under perfect feedback outperforms supervised regression on four out of the seven LETOR 3.0 data sets, and it outperforms other supervised listwise approaches (RankBoost and/or FRank) on three data sets. Even though performance under the much noisier informational feedback is significantly lower, offline performance remains competitive.

	perfect			informational		
	N@1	N@3	N@10	N@1	N@3	N@10
HP2003	0.685	0.745	0.777	0.661	0.715	0.749
HP2004	0.533	0.662	0.719	0.533	0.662	0.719
NP2003	0.524	0.696	0.754	0.508	0.669	0.730
NP2004	0.523	0.684	0.746	0.478	0.632	0.691
TD2003	0.286	0.273	0.273	0.226	0.243	0.249
TD2004	0.307	0.279	0.250	0.188	0.200	0.188
OHSUMED	0.362	0.380	0.367	0.326	0.342	0.335
MQ2007	0.261	0.296	0.331	0.236	0.270	0.306
MQ2008	0.277	0.361	0.461	0.244	0.325	0.431

Table 3: Offline performance after 1000 iterations in terms of LETOR NDCG and cutoffs 1, 3, and 10 for CPS-U under the perfect and informational click models.

6.2 CPS - Sensitivity to Parameter Settings

Above, we reported results for only one set of parameters. Here, we investigate the sensitivity of our CPS method to changes in these parameters. CPS has three parameters: the history length λ (default: 10), the size of the candidate pool η (default: 6), and the number of historical comparisons per candidate pair ζ (default: 10). The algorithm is linear in η and ζ per live update ($O(\eta\zeta)$). An increase in λ does not significantly affect the run time of the algorithm, but only determines the number of historical samples kept in memory, from which the samples for candidate comparisons are selected.

Figure 2 (parts a–c) shows the online performance achieved by CPS-U under the navigational click model on the data set *NP2003* when varying one parameter at a time. For η, the size of the candidate pool, a smaller pool ($\eta = 2$) leads to a decrease in performance of 13.6% percent. Increasing the number of candidates to 10 increases online performance to 110.67, a much smaller change of 2.9%. This suggests that the performance reported above (§5) can be further increased by using larger candidate pools. However, returns are expected to diminish as ever more candidates are used.

For the number of repetitions (ζ), effects are much smaller. Here, increasing ζ to 15 leads to no significant improvement in mean online performance, although comparisons are slightly more reliable (shown by the higher minimum).

Increasing the history length to $\lambda = 100$ significantly decreases the performance of CPS. The reason is that the more recent historical samples used with a smaller λ are collected on ranker pairs that are more similar to the current candidate rankers. When older samples are used instead, the variance of historical outcome estimates increases (under CPS-B, bias would increase), leading to diminished performance.

Overall, we find that performance under CPS can be further improved by increasing the size of the candidate pool. For the remaining parameters, performance is relatively stable and decreases gracefully when less optimal settings are used. Finally, our analysis indicates that additional computational resources are best spent on increasing the size of the candidate pool (η). Although the linear increase in computation is expected to lead to sub-linear performance gains, developers of deployed applications are typically willing to invest in additional computing time when it translates to even small performance gains (while in a scientific setting computational resources limit what experiments are feasible to run).

6.3 RHC - Sensitivity to Parameter Settings

RHC has only one parameter, the history length λ (cf., Algorithms 1 and 4, default: 10). This parameter determines how many historic data points are kept in memory, and are used to compare the current best ranker $\mathbf{w}_t$ to the candidate ranker $\mathbf{w}'_t$. This method is linear in λ per live update.

The sensitivity of RHC-U to changes in λ is shown in Figure 2, part (d). Setting $\lambda = 5$ leads to a statistically significant decrease in online performance of this algorithm. However, this decrease constitutes a performance change of only 1.6%. Increasing the amount of history used to $\lambda = 15$ has no significant effect on online performance. We can conclude that the performance of this algorithm is relatively robust to changes in λ (thus, investing in additional resources to increase λ is not recommended).

7. CONCLUSION

In this paper we investigated whether and how historical data can be reused to speed up online learning to rank for IR. We proposed two approaches for integrating estimates based on historical data with a stochastic gradient descent algorithm for online learning to rank. Our first approach, RHC, uses historical comparison estimates to complement live comparisons and to make them more reliable. Our second approach, CPS, uses historical data for preselecting candidate rankers, thereby improving the quality of the rankers that are evaluated in live interactions with search engine users.

Our experimental evaluation of the proposed methods, based on the 9 LETOR data sets and 3 click models that allowed us to investigate online performance of the methods under varying levels of click noise, yielded several insights. First, we found that the CPS method can substantially and significantly speed up online learning to rank in IR. We observed high gains in online performance over methods that use live data only for all click models. Second, performance gains of CPS were particularly high when click feedback was noisy. This result demonstrates that CPS is effective in compensating for noise in click feedback. Third, RHC was found to make ranker comparisons more reliable. However, positive effects on learning were observed only under noisy feedback and performance gains were lower than those obtained by CPS. Finally, we found that compensating for bias in click feedback had only small effects on online performance but that unbiased variants of our methods generally performed better than biased ones.

This work is the first to show that historical data can be used to significantly and substantially improve online performance in online learning to rank for IR. In addition, our approaches and experiments pointed at interesting directions for future work. While making comparisons themselves more reliable resulted in only minor speed-up in learning, major improvements were obtained when improving the quality of candidate rankers used for learning. This suggests that designing more elaborate candidate selection strategies, possibly taking properties of the solution space into account, is a promising direction for future research.

Acknowledgements

This research was partially supported by the European Union's ICT Policy Support Programme as part of the Competitiveness and Innovation Framework Programme, CIP ICT-PSP under grant agreement nr 250430, the European Community's Seventh Framework Programme (FP7/2007-2013) under grant agreements nr 258191 (PROMISE Network of Excellence) and 288024 (LiMoSINe project), the Netherlands Organisation for Scientific Research (NWO) under project nrs 612.061.814, 612.061.815, 640.004.802, 727.011.-005, 612.001.116, HOR-11-10, the Center for Creation, Content and Technology (CCCT), the Hyperlocal Service Platform project funded by the Service Innovation & ICT program, the WAHSP and BILAND projects funded by the CLARIN-nl program, the Dutch national program COMMIT, by the ESF Research Network Program ELIAS, and the Elite Network Shifts project funded by the Royal Dutch Academy of Sciences.

8. REFERENCES

[1] D. Agarwal, B. Chen, P. Elango, N. Motgi, S. Park, R. Ramakrishnan, S. Roy, and J. Zachariah. Online models for content optimization. In *NIPS'08*, pages 17–24, 2008.

[2] P. Auer, N. Cesa-Bianchi, and P. Fischer. Finite-time analysis of the multiarmed bandit problem. *Machine Learning*, 47(2): 235–256, May 2002.

[3] A. G. Barto, R. S. Sutton, and P. S. Brouwer. Associative search network: A reinforcement learning associative memory. *IEEE Trans. Syst., Man, and Cybern.*, 40:201–211, 1981.

[4] C. Burges, T. Shaked, E. Renshaw, A. Lazier, M. Deeds, N. Hamilton, and G. Hullender. Learning to rank using gradient descent. In *ICML '05*, pages 89–96, 2005.

[5] O. Chapelle, T. Joachims, F. Radlinski, and Y. Yue. Large-scale validation and analysis of interleaved search evaluation. *ACM Trans. Inf. Syst.*, 30(1):6:1–6:41, 2012.

[6] N. Craswell, O. Zoeter, M. Taylor, and B. Ramsey. An experimental comparison of click position-bias models. In *WSDM '08*, pages 87–94, 2008.

[7] F. Graybill and R. Deal. Combining unbiased estimators. *Biometrics*, 15(4):543–550, 1959.

[8] F. Guo, C. Liu, and Y. M. Wang. Efficient multiple-click models in web search. In *WSDM '09*, pages 124–131, 2009.

[9] K. Hofmann, S. Whiteson, and M. de Rijke. A probabilistic method for inferring preferences from clicks. In *CIKM '11*, pages 249–258, 2011.

[10] K. Hofmann, S. Whiteson, and M. de Rijke. Balancing exploration and exploitation in listwise and pairwise online learning to rank for information retrieval. *Information Retrieval*, 2012. doi: 10.1007/s10791-012-9197-9.

[11] K. Hofmann, S. Whiteson, and M. de Rijke. Estimating interleaved comparison outcomes from historical click data. In *CIKM '12*, 2012.

[12] K. Järvelin and J. Kekäläinen. Cumulated gain-based evaluation of IR techniques. *ACM Trans. Inf. Syst.*, 20(4): 422–446, October 2002.

[13] T. Joachims. Optimizing search engines using clickthrough data. In *KDD '02*, pages 133–142, 2002.

[14] T. Joachims. Evaluating retrieval performance using clickthrough data. In J. Franke, G. Nakhaeizadeh, and I. Renz, editors, *Text Mining*, pages 79–96. Physica/Springer, 2003.

[15] J. Langford, A. Strehl, and J. Wortman. Exploration scavenging. In *ICML '08*, pages 528–535, 2008.

[16] L. Li, W. Chu, J. Langford, and R. E. Schapire. A contextual-bandit approach to personalized news article recommendation. In *WWW '10*, pages 661–670, 2010.

[17] L. Li, W. Chu, J. Langford, and X. Wang. Unbiased offline evaluation of contextual-bandit-based news article recommendation algorithms. In *WSDM '11*, pages 297–306, 2011.

[18] T. Y. Liu. Learning to rank for information retrieval. *Found. and Trends in Inf. Retr.*, 3(3):225–331, 2009.

[19] D. Precup, R. Sutton, and S. Singh. Eligibility traces for off-policy policy evaluation. In *ICML'00*, pages 759–766, 2000.

[20] F. Radlinski and N. Craswell. Comparing the sensitivity of information retrieval metrics. In *SIGIR '10*, pages 667–674, 2010.

[21] F. Radlinski, M. Kurup, and T. Joachims. How does clickthrough data reflect retrieval quality? In *CIKM '08*, pages 43–52, 2008.

[22] M. Sanderson. Test collection based evaluation of information retrieval systems. *Found. and Trends in Inf. Retr.*, 4(4): 247–375, 2010.

[23] D. Schuurmans. Greedy importance sampling. In *NIPS '99*, 1999.

[24] A. Strehl, C. Mesterharm, M. Littman, and H. Hirsh. Experience-efficient learning in associative bandit problems. In *ICML '06*, pages 889–896, 2006.

[25] R. S. Sutton and A. G. Barto. *Reinforcement learning: An introduction.* MIT Press, Cambridge, MA, USA, 1998.

[26] M. Szummer and E. Yilmaz. Semi-supervised learning to rank with preference regularization. In *CIKM '11*, pages 269–278, 2011.

[27] D. Xu, Y. Liu, M. Zhang, S. Ma, and L. Ru. Incorporating revisiting behaviors into click models. In *WSDM '12*, pages 303–312, 2012.

[28] Y. Yue and T. Joachims. Interactively optimizing information retrieval systems as a dueling bandits problem. In *ICML'09*, pages 1201–1208, 2009.

[29] Y. Yue, J. Broder, R. Kleinberg, and T. Joachims. The k-armed dueling bandits problem. *Journal of Computer and System Sciences*, 78(5):1538 – 1556, 2012.

Pairwise Ranking Aggregation in a Crowdsourced Setting

Xi Chen*
Carnegie Mellon University
Pittsburgh, PA U.S.A.
xichen@cs.cmu.edu

Paul N. Bennett,
Kevyn Collins-Thompson, Eric Horvitz
Microsoft Research
Redmond, WA U.S.A. 98052
{pauben,kevynct,horvitz}@microsoft.com

ABSTRACT

Inferring rankings over elements of a set of objects, such as documents or images, is a key learning problem for such important applications as Web search and recommender systems. Crowdsourcing services provide an inexpensive and efficient means to acquire preferences over objects via labeling by sets of annotators. We propose a new model to predict a gold-standard ranking that hinges on combining pairwise comparisons via crowdsourcing. In contrast to traditional ranking aggregation methods, the approach learns about and folds into consideration the quality of contributions of each annotator. In addition, we minimize the cost of assessment by introducing a generalization of the traditional active learning scenario to jointly select the annotator and pair to assess while taking into account the annotator quality, the uncertainty over ordering of the pair, and the current model uncertainty. We formalize this as an active learning strategy that incorporates an exploration-exploitation tradeoff and implement it using an efficient online Bayesian updating scheme. Using simulated and real-world data, we demonstrate that the active learning strategy achieves significant reductions in labeling cost while maintaining accuracy.

Categories and Subject Descriptors

I.2.6 [**Artificial Intelligence**]: Learning; H.3.3 [**Information Storage and Retrieval**]: Information Search and Retrieval—*Retrieval models*; H.1.2 [**Information Systems**]: User/Machine Systems—*Human factors*

General Terms

Algorithms, Human Factors

Keywords

Ranking, Crowdsourcing, Pairwise Preference

*This work was performed during an internship at Microsoft Research.

WSDM'13, February 4–8, 2013, Rome, Italy.

1. INTRODUCTION

Obtaining a set of gold-standard labels for a set of objects is a critical step in learning to rank. For example, when determining how to rank the results returned in response to a Web search, the results are often passed through a ranking model that has been learned using a machine learning procedure [13]. In order to learn this model, learning methods typically require a training set of queries and documents where gold-standard labels on relevance with respect to a query have been provided. The learning method optimizes some objective with respect to the labels.

A variety of approaches can be employed to acquire labels. We may obtain binary relevance judgments, graded relevance judgments, or preferences [1]. Among these there may be tradeoffs in the amount of information the label contains and the noise associated with obtaining the label. For example, while a graded relevance judgment on a five-point scale may contain more information than a binary judgment, annotators may also make more errors due to the complexity of assigning finer-grained judgments. One approach to acquiring inputs on rank is to obtain relative preference judgments for pairs of items. This method promises assessments that are easier and faster to obtain, is less prone to assessor error, and enables fine-grained comparisons. Such pairwise assessment may be especially valuable for ranking in tasks with higher numbers of gradations, *e.g.*, assessing reading difficulty into one of the standard 12 American grade levels [3]. Pairwise assessment may also be valuable for inferring global rankings in such settings as developing recommender systems where we desire to order a set of products based on a small number of observed preferences from individual users.

We focus on the task of inferring a gold-standard ranking from a set of preferences over objects given in the form of pairwise comparisons (*i.e.*, i is preferred to j denoted as $i \succ j$). As in any collection of gold-standard data, we seek to obtain the most accurate labeling with minimal labeling cost. To this end, we seek to take advantage of crowdsourcing services, such as Amazon Mechanical Turk, which enables one to programmatically obtain large collections of pairwise comparisons from sets of annotators at low cost. However, the reliability of annotators available via crowdsourcing can vary significantly. In addition, seeking pairwise assessments from the crowd can lead to inconsistent pairs (*e.g.*, $i \succ j$ by one annotator and $j \succ i$ by another annotator; or $i \succ j$, $j \succ k$ and $k \succ i$). Many existing ranking aggregation methods [21, 16, 19, 14, 2, 20] are either incapable of modeling the quality of work by annotators or are inadequate for dealing with inconsistent pairs.

To address the challenge of learning a global ranking in a crowdsourced setting, we introduce the *Crowd-BT* algorithm, which extends the widely used Bradley-Terry model [21] by explicitly incorporating the quality of contributions provided by different annotators. The Crowd-BT algorithm can both appropriately weight annotators' contributions by their annotation quality as well as distinguish between *spammers* and *malicious annotators*: spammers assign random labels,[1] while malicious annotators (or poorly informed annotators) assign the wrong label most of the time.[2] Many existing crowdsourcing algorithms treat assessments provided by spammers or malicious annotators the same as they do assessments of low quality. In contrast, Crowd-BT can exclude pairs labeled by spammers from the modeling while automatically correcting the pairs provided by malicious annotators.

Beyond appropriately handling error, spam, and malicious inputs, we seek to be budget-conscious; we typically prefer to harness fewer labeled samples while achieving reasonably good accuracy. Thus, we seek a formal model of active learning to guide the allocation of effort in crowdsourcing (*e.g.*, see [9]). Most active learning methods [23] assume the availability of an *oracle* that can provide the correct label. In such settings, we only need to decide how to select the next pairwise assessment. We typically do not have access to such expertise in a crowdsourced setting. Thus, we face the challenge of simultaneously selecting the best next pair to be labeled and the best annotator to label the next pair. We shall formulate and study an *exploration-exploitation tradeoff* in crowdsourcing, previously explored in bandit and reinforcement learning. More precisely, *exploration* refers to using pairs with high-confidence labels to test the quality of annotators, while *exploitation* refers to asking for labels for the most uncertain pairs. We need to balance the tradeoff between exploration and exploitation carefully: too much exploration could lead to samples being repeatedly labeled, so that we do not have a sufficient number of unique samples within the assessment budget; however, too much emphasis on exploitation may result in a large number of noisy labels provided by low-quality annotators.

In the remainder of the paper, we first provide background on the Bradley-Terry model and demonstrate how to incorporate annotator quality into the model. We then demonstrate how to address situations that arise in practice via a regularization term before discussing how to optimize the objective function to infer the model parameters. Next, we formalize the active learning problem as an exploration-exploitation tradeoff and derive an approach that enables the efficient updates needed in an active learning setting. Finally, we present a series of experiments with synthetic data to better understand model properties. The experiments with real-world data demonstrate that modeling annotator quality improves inferred ranking quality, and furthermore, that our active learning approach achieves 90% of the best gold-standard accuracy with only 3% of the total labeling cost.

[1] Annotators who either do not actually look at instances, or robots pretending to be human annotators, presumably to quickly receive pay for work.

[2] That is, they label $i \succ j$ whenever $j \succ i$ and vice versa, perhaps because the annotators are malicious or misunderstand the labeling criteria.

2. RELATED WORK

Early work for modeling annotator quality is presented in [5], where the true category of an object is inferred from the crowd. With the availability of programmatic access to human effort via crowdsourcing platforms, a range of studies have applied machine learning to data collected from the crowd. Raykar *et al.* [22] extended Dawid & Skene's work [5] by introducing a logistic classification model to incorporate features of the input data. Wang *et al.* [26] proposed to separate malicious annotators from spammers in a binary classification setting. Our Crowd-BT algorithm extends the latter work to pairwise ranking aggregation problems.

Karger *et al.* [10] proposed an iterative algorithm to infer consensus class labels with asymptotic consistency guarantees. Welinder *et al.* [27] extended Dawid & Skene's work [5] to Bayesian updating procedures. While most of the work in learning from the crowd has focused on classification problems, several studies examine ordinal regression and ranking problems with assessments [22, 25]. For example, the formulation presented by Volkovs & Zemel [25] models annotator quality as the variance term in a logistic formulation and could be used to address our challenge. However, the methodology suffers from the weakness that it cannot distinguish spammers and malicious (or poorly informed) annotators. In addition, Bayesian modeling and active learning with the variance term in their logistic formulation provide more difficult computational challenges.

Cost and efficiency within a budget are important for learning about and harnessing a crowd for problem solving. Costs can be throttled with selective assessments guided by active-learning procedures. Unlike many applications of active learning, in a crowd setting, we cannot assume we have access to an oracle with answers. Yan *et al.* [30] proposed an active learning strategy for binary classification with a crowd. This work mainly focused on selection of an annotator who can provide the most confident label for an actively selected sample. Kamar *et al.* [9] describe methods for guiding the acquisition of votes in a crowdsourcing system for citizen science with a decision-theoretic computation of value of information within a POMDP representation, using a voting rule on a training set to define ground truth.

A great deal of prior work has been devoted to challenges with aggregation of rankings. Methods studied include permutation-based methods (*e.g.*, Mallows [2] and CPS [20] models), matrix factorization methods (*e.g.*, [6]) and score-based probabilistic methods (*e.g.*, Bradley-Terry [21], Plackett-Luce [16, 19] and Thurstone [14] models).

Permutation-based methods are generally computationally expensive while matrix factorization methods lack probabilistic interpretation. Thus, we build our work on score-based methods which are both more suitable for modeling pairwise comparisons and computationally efficient.

In summary, in contrast to previous work in pairwise ranking aggregation, our method can learn annotator quality with a unified model and distinguishes malicious annotators from spammers. More importantly, the active learning strategy proposed in this paper explicitly models the tradeoff between the learning of annotator quality versus the learning of pairwise preference. Our work formalizes this as the important concept of an *exploration-exploitation tradeoff* in active learning with the crowd.

3. CROWD-BT: EXTENDING BRADLEY -TERRY MODEL TO CROWDSOURCING

As mentioned above, we choose to extend the Bradley-Terry model because it has a well-understood probabilistic interpretation, is well-suited to preferences, and can be optimized for computational efficiency. In particular, we extend the Bradley-Terry model [21] to incorporate parameters for individual annotator quality. We first review the basic Bradley-Terry model before demonstrating how annotator quality can be incorporated.

For any two objects X and Y, Bradley-Terry models the probability that X is preferred over Y as $\Pr(X \succ Y) = \frac{\pi_X}{\pi_X+\pi_Y}$, where $\pi_X, \pi_Y > 0$ can be viewed as relevance scores for X and Y respectively (alternative interpretations in other settings are as skill scores or difficulty scores). By defining $\pi_X = \exp\{s_X\}$, we obtain:

$$\Pr(X \succ Y) = \frac{e^{s_X}}{e^{s_Y} + e^{s_Y}} = \frac{e^{(s_X - s_Y)}}{1 + e^{(s_X - s_Y)}}. \quad (1)$$

The Bradley-Terry model can be easily extended to model preferences among a small set of objects:

$$\Pr(X \succ \{Y, Z\}) = \frac{e^{s_X}}{e^{s_X} + e^{s_Y} + e^{s_Z}}. \quad (2)$$

It can also model a chain-complete partial order by decomposing it into pairwise preferences: $\Pr(X \succ Y \succ Z) \doteq \Pr(X \succ Y)\Pr(Y \succ Z)$.

We assume there are N objects $\{o_1, \ldots, o_N\}$ and a pool of K annotators $\{a_1, \ldots, a_K\}$. We denote the set of labeled pairs by the k-th annotator as $S_k = \{(i,j) : o_i \succ_k o_j\}$, where $o_i \succ_k o_j$ represents that the k-th annotator prefers o_i over o_j. Here, we make an implicit assumption that an annotator never simultaneously claims $o_i \succ o_j$ and $o_i \prec o_j$, so that each pair (i, j) in S_k can be ordered by $o_i \succ_k o_j$. Directly applying the Bradley-Terry model without distinguishing each annotator's quality, we have $\Pr(o_i \succ_k o_j) = \frac{e^{s_i}}{e^{s_i}+e^{s_j}}$. Then, pairwise ranking aggregation can be directly formulated into a *log-likelihood maximization problem* as follows:

$$\max_{\mathbf{s}} \sum_{k=1}^{K} \sum_{(i,j)\in S_k} \log\left(\frac{e^{s_i}}{e^{s_i}+e^{s_j}}\right) \quad \text{s.t.} \quad \sum_{i=1}^{N} s_i = 0. \quad (3)$$

Because the objective function on the left of Eq. (3) is *not scale-invariant*: if we increase all s_i by any given constant c, the log-likelihood will remain the same. Therefore, to make the objective identifiable, we use a standard trick (e.g., [8]), which adds one additional constraint, $\sum_{i=1}^{N} s_i = 0$. By maximizing Eq. (3), we can obtain a global ranking over N objects by sorting the obtained $\mathbf{s}$.

When directly applying the Bradley-Terry model in crowdsourcing, as in Eq. (3), each annotator is treated equally and, hence, the model is incapable of capturing the variability in quality of contribution across individual annotators. We now introduce a parameter η_k for the k-th annotator which is defined as the probability that the k-th annotator agrees with the true pairwise preference. In particular, for any pair with the true preference $X \succ Y$:

$$\eta_k \equiv \Pr(X \succ_k Y | X \succ Y). \quad (4)$$

If the k-th annotator is perfect, we have $\eta_k \approx 1$; if he/she is a spammer, we have $\eta_k \approx 0.5$; while if he/she is a malicious or poorly informed annotator, we have $\eta_k \approx 0$. Applying the law of total probability, we have

$$\begin{aligned}\Pr(o_i \succ_k o_j) &= \Pr(o_i \succ_k o_j | o_i \succ o_j)\Pr(o_i \succ o_j) \\ &\quad + \Pr(o_i \succ_k o_j | o_i \prec o_j)\Pr(o_i \prec o_j) \\ &= \eta_k \frac{e^{s_i}}{e^{s_i}+e^{s_j}} + (1-\eta_k)\frac{e^{s_j}}{e^{s_i}+e^{s_j}}. \quad (5)\end{aligned}$$

The log-likelihood $\mathcal{L}(\boldsymbol{\eta}, \mathbf{s})$ thus takes the form

$$\begin{aligned}\mathcal{L}(\boldsymbol{\eta}, \mathbf{s}) &= \sum_{k=1}^{K} \sum_{(i,j)\in S_k} \log \Pr(o_i \succ_k o_j) \quad (6) \\ &= \sum_{k=1}^{K} \sum_{(i,j)\in S_k} \log\left[\eta_k \frac{e^{s_i}}{e^{s_i}+e^{s_j}} + (1-\eta_k)\frac{e^{s_j}}{e^{s_i}+e^{s_j}}\right].\end{aligned}$$

For a perfect annotator with $\eta_k = 1$, $\Pr(o_i \succ_k o_j)$ will reduce to the Bradley-Terry model. For a spammer with $\eta_k = 0.5$, $\Pr(o_i \succ_k o_j) \equiv 0.5$ for any s_i, s_j and hence all the pairs provided by a spammer will not affect our objective in Eq. (7). In other words, once we detect a spammer, we automatically discard all the pairs labeled by him/her. For a malicious annotator with $\eta_k = 0$, we have $\Pr(o_i \succ_k o_j) = \frac{e^{s_j}}{e^{s_i}+e^{s_j}}$, which is equivalent to having $o_j \succ o_i$ provided by a perfect annotator. This means that our model can automatically recover the errors made by a malicious annotator. On the other hand, if $s_i \gg s_j$ (*i.e.*, there is a significant difference between these two objects), we have $\Pr(o_i \succ_k o_j) \approx \eta_k$, which indicates that the probability depends largely on the annotator's quality. If $s_i \approx s_j$, we have $\Pr(o_i \succ_k o_j) \approx 0.5$ which indicates that for two very similar objects, they are indistinguishable regardless of the annotator's quality.

3.1 Thurstone model

A closely related model to the Bradley-Terry model is the Thurstone model [14], which assumes that the score for each object X has a Gaussian distribution $N(S_X, \sigma_X)$. For simplicity, here we only consider the Case V Thurstone model where $\sigma_X = 1$ for all objects. Then, the difference between the score of X and that of Y follows a Gaussian distribution $N(S_X - S_Y, \sqrt{2})$ and thus $\Pr(X \succ Y) = \Phi\left(\frac{S_X - S_Y}{\sqrt{2}}\right)$, where $\Phi(\cdot)$ is the standard Gaussian cumulative distribution function. The likelihood $\mathcal{L}(\boldsymbol{\eta}, \mathbf{s})$ under the Thurstone model thus takes the following form:

$$\mathcal{L}(\boldsymbol{\eta}, \mathbf{s}) = \sum_{k=1}^{K} \sum_{(i,j)\in S_k} \log\left[\eta_k \Phi\left(\frac{s_i - s_j}{\sqrt{2}}\right) + (1-\eta_k)\Phi\left(\frac{s_j - s_i}{\sqrt{2}}\right)\right].$$

To solve this corresponding maximum likelihood problem, we need to evaluate $\Phi(\cdot)$ many times, which involves an integration and hence is computationally more expensive than maximizing Eq. (6). Thus, we adopt the Bradley-Terry model in the paper. However, we note that the performance of Bradley-Terry and Thurstone models have been shown to be very similar [24]; and all the developed methods in this paper can be used in a straightforward way to extend the Thurstone model for use in crowdsourcing.

3.2 Regularization

For better visualization and interpretation, pairwise comparisons are often presented as a comparison graph: if an annotator prefers o_i over o_j, we draw a *directed* edge from o_j to o_i. We first point out that application of the Bradley-Terry

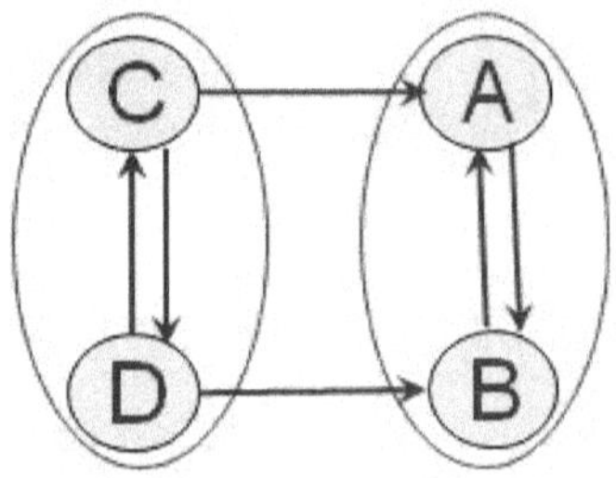

Figure 1: Example of comparison graph.

model in Eq. (3) can face numerical challenges if the underlying comparison graph is not strongly-connected.[3] More specifically, one cannot have a maximizer of the log-likelihood in Eq. (3) when the comparison graph is not strongly-connected. As an example, we consider the comparison graph in Fig. 1 with *two* strongly-connected components in red circles. For *any* given solution s_A, s_B, s_C, s_D, if one adds an arbitrary positive constant c to s_A, s_B and subtracts the constant c from s_C, s_D, then the likelihood terms corresponding to the edges $C \to A$ and $D \to B$ (*i.e.*, $\frac{e^{s_A}}{e^{s_A}+e^{s_C}}$ and $\frac{e^{s_B}}{e^{s_B}+e^{s_D}}$) will always increase, while the likelihood terms corresponding to the edges within each strongly-connected component (*i.e.*, $A \to B$, $B \to A$, $C \to D$ and $D \to C$) will remain the same. Therefore, we could not have a maximizer of the log-likelihood.

This numerical problem can be addressed via the so-called virtual node regularization which has been used in ranking problems under different settings [4, 11]. In particular, we introduce a virtual object (node) o_0 with the score e^{s_0}. We assume that each object o_i is compared to o_0 by a perfect annotator with one virtual win and one virtual loss. Thus, any comparison graph will be made into a strongly-connected one. According to [15], the log-likelihood will then have a unique maximizer. In fact, this amounts to using a regularized form $\mathcal{L}(\boldsymbol{\eta}, \mathbf{s}) + \lambda \mathcal{R}(\mathbf{s})$, where the regularization term $\mathcal{R}(\mathbf{s})$ is defined as:

$$\mathcal{R}(\mathbf{s}) = \sum_{i=1}^{N} \left(\log\left(\frac{e^{s_0}}{e^{s_0}+e^{s_i}}\right) + \log\left(\frac{e^{s_i}}{e^{s_0}+e^{s_i}}\right)\right)$$

and $\lambda > 0$ is the predefined regularization parameter.

3.3 Crowd-BT

The final Crowd-BT formulation for pairwise ranking aggregation in crowdsourcing is essentially a *regularized maximum likelihood problem*:

$$\begin{aligned}
\max_{\boldsymbol{\eta},\mathbf{s}} \quad & \mathcal{L}(\boldsymbol{\eta}, \mathbf{s}) + \lambda \mathcal{R}(\mathbf{s}) \qquad (7)\\
&\doteq \sum_{k=1}^{K} \sum_{(i,j)\in S_k} \log\left[\eta_k \frac{e^{s_i}}{e^{s_i}+e^{s_j}} + (1-\eta_k)\frac{e^{s_j}}{e^{s_i}+e^{s_j}}\right]\\
&\quad + \lambda \sum_{i=1}^{N}\left(\log\left(\frac{e^{s_0}}{e^{s_0}+e^{s_i}}\right) + \log\left(\frac{e^{s_i}}{e^{s_0}+e^{s_i}}\right)\right)\\
\text{s.t.} \quad & 0 \le \eta_k \le 1, \qquad \forall k \in \{1,\ldots,K\}.
\end{aligned}$$

As we can see from Eq. (7), another benefit of this extra regularization is that the constraint $\sum_{i=1}^{N} s_i = 0$ in Eq. (3) is no longer needed if we fix s_0. Recall that this constraint is used to address the scale-invariant problem in the objective function in Eq. (3). Now, in Eq. (7), if we fix s_0, the objective is no longer scale-invariant and hence the constraint $\sum_{i=1}^{N} s_i = 0$ could be dropped.

Let us provide more detailed explanations for the regularization term in Eq. (7). First, as we show in Section 3.2, without the regularization, the corresponding optimization is not well-defined when the graph is not strongly connected, and we will not have a finite solution. Therefore, the regularization is indispensable for comparison graphs that are not strongly connected. Secondly, when the graph is indeed strongly connected, the regularization might change the solution. However, if we set λ to be sufficiently small, the ranking inferred from $\mathbf{s}$ will be the same as that obtained from the un-regularized problem. Interestingly, in many problems, the regularized problem could lead to an even better solution than the un-regularized one as shown in our experiments. In practice, if one only wants to recover the ranking from the un-regularized problem (assuming it is well-defined), one could just use a sufficiently small λ. On the other hand, if gold pairs are available (*i.e.*, samples with the true label provided by experts),[4] one can carefully use them to tune the parameter λ to achieve the best performance on gold samples. Regardless of the optimal choice, we show empirically later that for a broad range of $\lambda \in [0.1, 10]$ our algorithm outperforms the baseline (see Tables 2 and 3).

To maximize the objective $\mathcal{L}(\boldsymbol{\eta}, \mathbf{s}) + \lambda \mathcal{R}(\mathbf{s})$, a natural optimization strategy is the alternating approach [17]: fix $\boldsymbol{\eta}$ and optimize over $\mathbf{s}$; then fix $\mathbf{s}$ and optimize over $\boldsymbol{\eta}$; and iterate over these two steps. In particular, we adopt limited-memory BFGS [17] to optimize $\mathbf{s}$ and the projected Newton method to optimize $\boldsymbol{\eta}$ [12]. We note that as Eq. (7) is a non-concave maximization problem, a good initialization is important to avoid being trapped in local minima. As long as the average quality of the annotators is better than that of spammers, we suggest starting with $\eta_k = 1$ for each annotator and first optimizing over $\mathbf{s}$. In fact, this strategy is better than the traditional multiple random initialization strategy for solving non-convex optimization since we utilize the prior side information of the problem (*i.e.*, most annotators are good). If there are more spammers and malicious annotators (although it may happen rarely in practice), we could initialize η_k by measuring the performance of each annotator on a handful of gold samples. In particular, η_k could be initialized as the ratio of the correct answers on the gold samples.

4. ACTIVE LEARNING

Active learning in crowdsourcing is fundamentally different from traditional active learning in two different aspects: (1) we do not have access to an oracle for labels and (2) beyond selecting pairs to be labeled (exploitation) we also need to probe each annotator's quality (exploration), and carefully balance this exploration-exploitation tradeoff. For pairwise comparison, at each round, we need to choose a triplet *(object i, object j, annotator k)* and ask for the preference between *object i* and *object j* from the annotator *k*.

[3] A directed graph is called strongly-connected if there is a path from each node in the graph to every other node.

[4] In fact, even if there is no expert, one can construct gold pairs from the data. For example, we could treat a pair as a gold sample if more than 10 annotators rank the pair and at least 90% of them agree on the same preference.

Let T be the total budget, i.e., the total number of triplets that we can query. The high-level picture of the active learning in crowdsourcing for our problem is as follows. For each round $t = 1, \ldots, T$ run the following steps:

1. Choose the triplet (o_i, o_j, k) that maximizes the impact on the model uncertainty given the expectation over the annotator k's response.
2. Query the preference between o_i and o_j from the annotator k.
3. Update the model with the elicited preference.

However, there are three major challenges for implementing the above approach. First, the sheer number of possible triplets is $KN(N-1)/2$ so that the maximization in Step 1 is taken over a large space. The second is quantifying the impact on the model uncertainty in a way that also incorporates the notion of an exploration-exploitation tradeoff. The third is how to update the model in a time-efficient manner without re-training the whole model. For the first issue, since the maximization can be solved in a straightforward parallel manner, this challenge can be addressed given enough computational power. For the second issue, we establish a Bayesian framework for our problem and introduce a novel definition of the *expected information gain* by extending the traditional Kullback-Leibler (KL) divergence to incorporate the exploration-exploitation tradeoff. Finally, we introduce an efficient online update of the model parameters using the techniques from [28].

We first extend Crowd-BT into a Bayesian framework to enable the definition of the information gain/model uncertainty and facilitate the development of an online updating method. We assume $\{s_i\}_{i=1}^N$ and $\{\eta_k\}_{k=1}^K$ are independent random variables and introduce a Gaussian prior for each s_i (*i.e.*, $s_i \sim N(\mu_i, \sigma_i)$) and a Beta prior for each η_k (*i.e.*, $\eta_k \sim \text{Beta}(\alpha_k, \beta_k)$). Given a pair labeled by the k-th annotator, $(o_i \succ_k o_j)$, we have the prior

$$p(s_i, s_j, \eta_k) = N(s_i; \mu_i, \sigma_i) N(s_j; \mu_j, \sigma_j) B(\eta_k; \alpha_k, \beta_k)$$

with the likelihood $l(s_i, s_j, \eta_k)$ given in Eq. (5). Then the posterior can be calculated from Bayes' rule. However, since the marginal posterior will be again used as the prior for the coming pairs, it is difficult to directly use the exact inferred posterior. Therefore, we approximate the posterior $p(s_i, s_j, \eta_k | o_i \succ_k o_j)$ using the variational approximation:

$$\begin{aligned} & p(s_i, s_j, \eta_k | o_i \succ_k o_j) = l(s_i, s_j, \eta_k) p(s_i, s_j, \eta_k)/C \qquad (8) \\ & \approx N(s_i; \mu_i^{i\succ_k j}, \sigma_i^{i\succ_k j}) N(s_j; \mu_j^{i\succ_k j}, \sigma_j^{i\succ_k j}) B(\eta_k; \alpha_k^{i\succ_k j}, \beta_k^{i\succ_k j}). \end{aligned}$$

where

$$l(s_i, s_j, \eta_k) = \Pr(o_i \succ_k o_j) = \eta_k \frac{e^{s_i}}{e^{s_i} + e^{s_j}} + (1 - \eta_k) \frac{e^{s_j}}{e^{s_i} + e^{s_j}},$$

is the likelihood function and $C = \Pr(o_i \succ_k o_j)$ is the normalization constant. In particular, we assume s_i, s_j and η_k are (conditionally) independent in posterior, the posterior distributions for s_i and s_j are still Gaussian, and η_k is Beta.

Let us defer the discussion of how to efficiently update the posterior parameters to the next subsection and first present the proposed active learning strategy. For each potential triplet in the pool (o_i, o_j, a_k) (*i.e.*, represents asking the k-th annotator to compare o_i and o_j), we compute the expected information gain:

$$\begin{aligned} \Pr(o_i \succ_k o_j) \quad & \Big(\text{KL}\left(N(\mu_i^{i\succ_k j}, \sigma_i^{i\succ_k j}) || N(\mu_i, \sigma_i)\right) \qquad (9) \\ & + \text{KL}\left(N(\mu_j^{i\succ_k j}, \sigma_j^{i\succ_k j}) || N(\mu_j, \sigma_j)\right) \\ & + \gamma\, \text{KL}\left(\text{Beta}(\alpha_k^{i\succ_k j}, \beta_k^{i\succ_k j}) || \text{Beta}(\alpha_k, \beta_k)\right)\Big) \\ + \Pr(o_i \prec_k o_j) \quad & \Big(\text{KL}\left(N(\mu_i^{i\prec_k j}, \sigma_i^{i\prec_k j}) || N(\mu_i, \sigma_i)\right) \\ & + \text{KL}\left(N(\mu_j^{i\prec_k j}, \sigma_j^{i\prec_k j}) || N(\mu_j, \sigma_j)\right) \\ & + \gamma\, \text{KL}\left(\text{Beta}(\alpha_k^{i\prec_k j}, \beta_k^{i\prec_k j}) || \text{Beta}(\alpha_k, \beta_k)\right)\Big) \end{aligned}$$

where $\text{KL}(\cdot)$ denotes the Kullback-Leibler (KL) divergence. Since we do not know whether $o_i \succ_k o_j$ or not before the pair is labeled, we take the *expected* information gain over the Bernoulli outcome; the computation of $\Pr(o_i \succ_k o_j)$ is shown in the next section (Eq. (15) and Eq. (18)). At each iteration, we choose the triplet (o_i, o_j, a_k) that maximizes Eq. (9). In other words, we use a pure greedy strategy to select the most informative triplet. We also realize that other mixed methods may work better in practice. For example, one can use an ϵ-greedy approach, *i.e.*, with probability $1-\epsilon$ select the triplet that maximizes the expected information gain, else with probability ϵ, select a random triplet.

The expected information gain defined via KL divergence has been a popular utility function in traditional active learning [23] and used for ranking problems [18]. To extend active learning to crowdsourcing, our formulation in Eq. (9) generalizes the traditional expected information gain by introducing an extra parameter γ. In particular, recall that the traditional information gain is simply defined by the KL divergence between the posterior and the prior:

$$\begin{aligned} & \text{KL}\big(p(s_i, s_j, \eta_k | o_i \succ_k o_j) \,||\, p(s_i, s_j, \eta_k)\big) \qquad (10) \\ & = \text{KL}\left(N(\mu_i^{i\succ_k j}, \sigma_i^{i\succ_k j}) \,||\, N(\mu_i, \sigma_i)\right) \\ & + \text{KL}\left(N(\mu_j^{i\succ_k j}, \sigma_j^{i\succ_k j}) \,||\, N(\mu_j, \sigma_j)\right) \\ & + \text{KL}\left(\text{Beta}(\alpha_k^{i\succ_k j}, \beta_k^{i\succ_k j}) \,||\, \text{Beta}(\alpha_k, \beta_k)\right). \end{aligned}$$

As compared to Eq. (10), our formulation in Eq. (9) introduces the parameter γ which represents the tradeoff between exploration and exploitation. A larger γ will give more weight to the KL divergence terms related to annotator quality in the objective in Eq. (9), which means that we are willing to spend more to explore the quality of annotators. On the other hand, a smaller γ will result in relatively more emphasis on exploiting the information in the observed pairwise comparisons. When gold samples are not available, according to our experience, any $\gamma \in [5, 10]$ could lead to much better performance than setting $\gamma = 0$ (*i.e.*, traditional active learning without exploring annotator quality) or $\gamma = 1$ (*i.e.*, traditional information gain defined by KL divergence). Meanwhile, setting γ larger than 10 could lead to too much exploration at the beginning—especially when the budget is limited. Therefore, as a simple rule of thumb, one could set $\gamma = 5$ when the budget is limited while $\gamma = 10$ when the budget is sufficient. Although such a simple rule is by no means an optimal choice of γ, it often leads to superior empirical performance. We can adopt a more sophisticated guideline for the selection of γ. Specifically, we can start from a large γ; and gradually reduce the parameter γ by half for every τ% of the budget (*e.g.*, $\tau = 25$). The reason behind such a dynamic strategy of setting γ is as follows: at the beginning, we may typically have very little knowledge about the quality of annotators, so more exploration should be carried out with a larger γ. As we gradually gather more information about annotator quality, we should do more exploitation instead of exploration using a smaller γ.

4.1 Online Learning

To update the posterior parameters efficiently in Eq. (8), we use a moment-matching strategy. We first approximate the first- and second-order moments for s_i, s_j, η_k under the true posterior distribution and then update the posterior parameters accordingly. To compute $\mathbb{E}(s_i)$, $\mathbb{E}(s_j)$, $\mathrm{Var}(s_i)$, $\mathrm{Var}(s_j)$ under the true posterior, we first integrate out η_k and the marginal posterior for (s_i, s_j) takes the form:

$$f_s(s_i, s_j) N(s_i; \mu_i, \sigma_i) N(s_j; \mu_j, \sigma_j),$$

where

$$f_s(s_i, s_j) = \frac{\alpha_k}{\alpha_k+\beta_k}\frac{e^{s_i}}{e^{s_i}+e^{s_j}} + \frac{\beta_k}{\alpha_k+\beta_k}\frac{e^{s_j}}{e^{s_i}+e^{s_j}}.$$

Let $z_i = \frac{s_i-\mu_i}{\sigma_i} \sim N(0,1)$ and $z_j = \frac{s_j-\mu_j}{\sigma_j} \sim N(0,1)$. We can view $f_s(s_i, s_j)$ as a function of z_i, z_j and rewrite it as:

$$\begin{aligned} f_z(z_i, z_j) = \; & \frac{\alpha_k}{\alpha_k+\beta_k}\frac{e^{\sigma_i z_i+\mu_i}}{e^{\sigma_i z_i+\mu_i}+e^{\sigma_j z_j+\mu_j}} \\ & + \frac{\beta_k}{\alpha_k+\beta_k}\frac{e^{\sigma_j z_j+\mu_j}}{e^{\sigma_i z_i+\mu_i}+e^{\sigma_j z_j+\mu_j}}. \end{aligned}$$

Using the technique from [28], which is essentially the extension of the Stein's Lemma [29], the expectation $\mathbb{E}(z_i)$ can be approximated:

$$\mathbb{E}(z_i) = \mathbb{E}\Big(\frac{\partial f_z(z_i,z_j)/\partial z_i}{f_z(z_i,z_j)}\Big) \approx \frac{\partial \log f_z(z_i,z_j)}{\partial z_i}\Big|_{z_i=z_j=0}.$$

Therefore, we have:

$$\begin{aligned} \mu_i^{i\succ_k j} &= \mathbb{E}(s_i) = \mu_i + \sigma_i \mathbb{E}(z_i) && (11) \\ &\approx \mu_i + \sigma_i^2\left(\frac{\alpha_k e^{\mu_i}}{\alpha_k e^{\mu_i}+\beta_k e^{\mu_j}} - \frac{e^{\mu_i}}{e^{\mu_i}+e^{\mu_j}}\right). \end{aligned}$$

We can interpret this updating rule as follows. For a perfect annotator with $\alpha_k \gg \beta_k$, we have $\frac{\alpha_k e^{\mu_i}}{\alpha_k e^{\mu_i}+\beta_k e^{\mu_j}} \approx 1$ and hence $\mu_i^{i\succ_k j} \approx \mu_i + \sigma_i^2 \frac{e^{\mu_j}}{e^{\mu_i}+e^{\mu_j}}$. This formulation captures the intuition that μ_i should increase when an observation $o_i \succ_k o_j$ is made by a good annotator. Secondly, if $\mu_i \gg \mu_j$, the extra information of observing $o_i \succ_k o_j$ is limited and hence the amount of increase of μ_i, $\sigma_i^2 \frac{e^{\mu_j}}{e^{\mu_i}+e^{\mu_j}}$, is very small. On the other hand, for a random annotator with $\alpha_k \approx \beta_k$, we have $\mu_i^{i\succ_k j} \approx \mu_i$ while for a malicious annotator, $\mu_i^{i\succ_k j} \approx \mu_i - \sigma_i^2 \frac{e^{\mu_i}}{e^{\mu_i}+e^{\mu_j}}$. Similarly, we have:

$$\begin{aligned} \mu_j^{i\succ_k j} &= \mathbb{E}(s_j) = \mu_j + \sigma_j \mathbb{E}(Z_j) && (12) \\ &\approx \mu_j + \sigma_j^2\left(\frac{\beta_k e^{\mu_j}}{\alpha_k e^{\mu_i}+\beta_k e^{\mu_j}} - \frac{e^{\mu_j}}{e^{\mu_i}+e^{\mu_j}}\right) \\ &\approx \mu_j - \sigma_j^2\left(\frac{\alpha_k e^{\mu_i}}{\alpha_k e^{\mu_i}+\beta_k e^{\mu_j}} - \frac{e^{\mu_i}}{e^{\mu_i}+e^{\mu_j}}\right). \end{aligned}$$

We can also derive $\sigma_i^{i\succ_k j}$, $\sigma_j^{i\succ_k j}$ following [28]:

$$\begin{aligned} &\mathrm{Var}(z_i) = \mathbb{E}(z_i^2) - (\mathbb{E}(z_i))^2 \\ &= \left(1+\mathbb{E}\left(\frac{\partial^2 f_z(z_i,z_j)/\partial z_i^2}{f_z(z_i,z_j)}\right)\right) - \mathbb{E}\Big(\frac{\partial f_z(z_i,z_j)/\partial z_i}{f_z(z_i,z_j)}\Big)^2 \\ &= 1+\mathbb{E}\left(\frac{\partial^2 \log f_z(z_i,z_j)}{\partial z_i^2}\right) \approx 1 + \frac{\partial^2 \log f_z(z_i,z_j)}{\partial z_i^2}\Big|_{z_i=z_j=0}. \end{aligned}$$

Then we have:

$$\begin{aligned} &\left(\sigma_i^{i\succ_k j}\right)^2 = \mathrm{Var}(s_i) = \sigma_i^2 \mathrm{Var}(z_i) && (13) \\ &= \sigma_i^2 \max\left(1+\sigma_i^2\left(\frac{\alpha_k e^{\mu_i}\beta_k e^{\mu_j}}{(\alpha_k e^{\mu_i}+\beta_k e^{\mu_j})^2} - \frac{e^{\mu_i}e^{\mu_j}}{(e^{\mu_i}+e^{\mu_j})^2}\right), \kappa\right), \\ &(\sigma_j^{i\succ_k j})^2 = \mathrm{Var}(s_j) = \sigma_j^2 \mathrm{Var}(z_j) && (14) \\ &= \sigma_j^2 \max\left(1+\sigma_j^2\left(\frac{\alpha_k e^{\mu_i}\beta_k e^{\mu_j}}{(\alpha_k e^{\mu_i}+\beta_k e^{\mu_j})^2} - \frac{e^{\mu_i}e^{\mu_j}}{(e^{\mu_i}+e^{\mu_j})^2}\right), \kappa\right). \end{aligned}$$

where the parameter κ is a small constant (*e.g.*, 10^{-4}) to ensure the positivity of variance.

To update α_k and β_k, let $C_1 = \mathbb{E}_N\left(\frac{e^{s_i}}{e^{s_i}+e^{s_j}}\right)$, where $\mathbb{E}_N$ denotes the expectation over the prior Gaussian distribution of (s_i, s_j) and let $C_2 = \mathbb{E}_N\left(\frac{e^{s_j}}{e^{s_i}+e^{s_j}}\right) = 1 - C_1$. The normalization constant $C = \Pr(o_i \succ_k o_j)$ in Eq. (8) can be computed as:

$$\begin{aligned} C &= \int_{[0,1]} (C_1\eta_k + C_2(1-\eta_k))\,\mathrm{Beta}(\eta_k;\alpha_k,\beta_k)\mathrm{d}\eta_k \\ &= \frac{C_1\alpha_k + C_2\beta_k}{\alpha_k+\beta_k}. && (15) \end{aligned}$$

Then we can compute the first and second order moment of η_k as follows:

$$\begin{aligned} \mathbb{E}(\eta_k) &= \frac{1}{C}\int_{[0,1]} \eta_k\,(C_1\eta_k + C_2(1-\eta_k))\,\mathrm{Beta}(\eta_k;\alpha_k,\beta_k)\mathrm{d}\eta_k \\ &= \frac{C_1(\alpha_k+1)\alpha_k + C_2\alpha_k\beta_k}{C(\alpha_k+\beta_k+1)(\alpha_k+\beta_k)}. \\ \mathbb{E}(\eta_k^2) &= \frac{C_1(\alpha_k+2)(\alpha_k+1)\alpha_k + C_2(\alpha_k+1)\alpha_k\beta_k}{C(\alpha_k+\beta_k+2)(\alpha_k+\beta_k+1)(\alpha_k+\beta_k)}. \end{aligned}$$

and update the α_k and β_k as follows:

$$\begin{aligned} \alpha_k^{i\succ_k j} &= \frac{(\mathbb{E}(\eta_k) - \mathbb{E}(\eta_k^2))\mathbb{E}(\eta_k)}{\mathbb{E}(\eta_k^2) - (\mathbb{E}(\eta_k))^2} && (16) \\ \beta_k^{i\succ_k j} &= \frac{(\mathbb{E}(\eta_k) - \mathbb{E}(\eta_k^2))(1-\mathbb{E}(\eta_k))}{\mathbb{E}(\eta_k^2) - (\mathbb{E}(\eta_k))^2} && (17) \end{aligned}$$

Now the challenge is to compute C_1 efficiently. Let $g(s_i, s_j) = \frac{e^{s_i}}{e^{s_i}+e^{s_j}}$ and we take the second-order Taylor expansion of $g(s_i, s_j)$ at (μ_i, μ_j):

$$\begin{aligned} &g(s_i,s_j) \approx g(\mu_i,\mu_j) + (s_i-\mu_i)\nabla_{s_i} g(\mu_i,\mu_j) + \\ &(s_j-\mu_j)\nabla_{s_j} g(\mu_i,\mu_j) + \frac{1}{2}(s_i-\mu_i)^2 \nabla_{s_i,s_i} g(\mu_i,\mu_j) + \\ &(s_i-\mu_i)(s_j-\mu_j)\nabla_{s_i,s_j} g(\mu_i,\mu_j) + \frac{1}{2}(s_j-\mu_j)^2 \nabla_{s_j,s_j} g(\mu_i,\mu_j). \end{aligned}$$

We take the expectation of $g(s_i, s_j)$ under the prior distribution and we obtain C_1. In particular, by the fact that $\mathbb{E}_N(s_i-\mu_i) = \mathbb{E}_N(s_j-\mu_j) = 0$, we have:

$$C_1 \approx \frac{e^{\mu_i}}{e^{\mu_i}+e^{\mu_j}} + \frac{1}{2}(\sigma_i^2+\sigma_j^2)\frac{s^{\mu_i}s^{\mu_j}(s^{\mu_j}-s^{\mu_i})}{(s^{\mu_i}+s^{\mu_j})^3}. \qquad (18)$$

We can use the above closed-form updating rules to infer approximate posterior distributions in constant time. Combining the posterior update rules with our selection criteria based on expected information gain in Eq. (9), the entire active algorithm is presented in Algorithm 1. We note that, after labeling the pairs, we can simply sort $\{\mu_i\}$ to obtain the ranking (which is used in our experiments), or we could rank the objects by using Crowd-BT. In general, solving the optimization of Crowd-BT leads to a slightly better performance than sorting $\{\mu_i\}$ but is also computationally more expensive.

Algorithm 1 Active Ranking Aggregation in Crowd

Input: Prior distribution parameters $\{\mu_i\}$, $\{\sigma_i\}$, $\{\alpha_k\}$, $\{\beta_k\}$, the tradeoff parameter γ and the total budget T.

for $t = 1, \ldots T$ **do**
  Select a pair (o_a, o_b) and an annotator k which maximize the expected information gain in Eq. (9).
  Query the annotator k on the preference between o_a and o_b.
  if $o_a \succ_k o_b$ **then**
    Set $i = a$ and $j = b$
  else
    Set $i = b$ and $j = a$.
  end if
  Update μ_i, μ_j, σ_i, σ_j, α_k and β_k according to Eq. (11), (12), (13), (14), (16) and (17).
end for

Output: Rank objects by sorting the obtained $\{\mu_i\}$.

5. EXPERIMENTS

5.1 Simulated Study

5.1.1 Accuracy for Different Distributions of Annotator Quality

We first conduct experiments with simulated data to test the performance where the average quality of annotators is varied. We assume that there are 100 objects, each with an underlying true score in the range of 1 to 100. We randomly sample 400 pairs of objects and assume that each pair is labeled by 10 different annotators. In this way, we gather 4000 labeled pairs. We assume that the ground truth quality of 100 annotators $\{\eta_k^*\}_{k=1}^{100}$ follow a Beta distribution Beta(α, β). For any pair (o_i, o_j) labeled by the k-th annotator, he/she will claim $o_i \succ_k o_j$ with the probability η_k and vice versa with the probability $1 - \eta_k$. We test our Crowd-BT method Eq. (7) with two different initialization schemes: (1) initialize each η_k by 1, *i.e.*, starting by assuming that all annotators are perfect (Crowd-BT-One) and (2) initialize each η_k by the accuracy on 5 gold pairs with known true relationship (Crowd-Gold); and compare them with the vanilla Bradley-Terry model (BT) in Eq. (3). We evaluate algorithms using the accuracy based on Wilcoxon-Mann-Whitney statistics:

$$\text{ACC} := \frac{\sum_{i,j} \mathbf{I}(y_i > y_j \wedge s_i > s_j)}{\sum_{i,j} \mathbf{I}(y_i > y_j)}, \tag{19}$$

where $\mathbf{y}$ is the true relevance score and $\mathbf{s}$ is the estimated score.

We first vary the distribution of annotator quality and report the accuracy for each distribution in Table 1 with virtual node regularization parameter $\lambda = 0.5$. The sensitivity of λ will be further investigated in another simulated experiment. As we can see from Table 1, when the average quality is above 0.5, the two initialization strategies for Crowd-BT achieve very similar performance and are both better than the Bradley-Terry model. For a difficult scenario with many more malicious annotators, the performance of Crowd-BT with "all ones" initialization is indeed quite bad. However, initialization by a very rough estimate of quality using only five gold pairs will lead to a significant boost in performance. This is because our method has the ability to automatically recover from the errors made by malicious annotators with a reasonable initialization. In summary, when there are more good annotators, which is often the case in practice, we could directly apply Crowd-BT with "all ones" initialization; otherwise, it is necessary to obtain a rough estimate of quality via several gold samples.

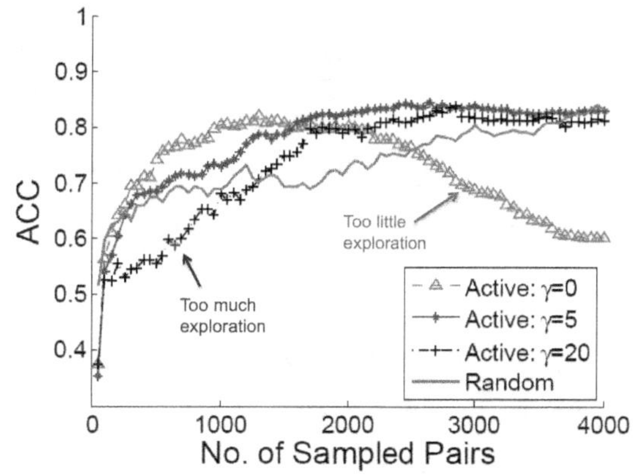

Figure 2: Active Learning with different γ.

5.1.2 Exploration-Exploitation Tradeoff

We now investigate the effect of considering the control of an exploration-exploitation tradeoff in active learning and compare our active learning method with different configurations of the tradeoff to the random selection strategy. In particular, we assume that the true quality for each annotator is drawn from the Beta distribution Beta$(2, 1)$. This is similar to one of the most common settings in practice where we have many good annotators but also some spammers and malicious contributors. We initialize the prior of the quality with Beta$(10, 1)$ to reflect our starting assumption that all annotators are very good. We plot the number of sampled pairs against accuracy by varying the parameter γ. As displayed in Figure 2, the active learning strategy with an appropriate γ (*e.g.*, blue line with $\gamma = 5$) significantly outperforms the random selection strategy. If one uses too small a value for γ (*e.g.*, red line with $\gamma = 0$), the accuracy has a sharp increase at the beginning, but becomes worse as we sample more pairs. This outcome arises because in the absence of enough exploration of annotator quality, we may assign many pairs to bad annotators and thus harm the performance in the long run. On the other hand, if we adopt too large γ (*e.g.*, black line with $\gamma = 30$), the increase in accuracy is slow at the beginning. The main reason for this is that during the first few hundred iterations, we perform too much exploration and hence obtain limited information about pairwise preferences.

We also study the exploration-exploitation tradeoff under different settings of averaged annotator quality. For each distribution of annotator quality and each setting of γ, we calculate the normalized area under the active learning curve. A typical active learning curve is displayed in Figure 2. As presented in Figure 3, in both (a) and (b) with different priors, when the average quality is relatively low (*e.g.*, 0.667), a larger γ (*e.g.*, $\gamma = 5, 10$) performs best, which means that we need more exploration in that scenario. On the other hand, when average quality approaches one, exploration becomes unnecessary and $\gamma = 0$ or $\gamma = 1$ leads to the best performance.

(α, β)	(10, 1)	(5,1)	(2,1)	(2,2)	(1,2)	(1,5)
Average Quality	0.909	0.833	0.667	0.500	0.333	0.166
BT	0.882	0.890	0.800	0.542	0.171	0.144
Crowd-BT-One	**0.899**	**0.918**	**0.869**	0.849	0.109	0.122
Crowd-BT-Gold	**0.899**	0.917	**0.869**	**0.850**	**0.897**	**0.878**

Table 1: Accuracies of different approaches on the simulated datasets. Average Quality is the mean $\alpha/(\alpha+\beta)$ of the Beta distribution. Best performance in each column is in bold.

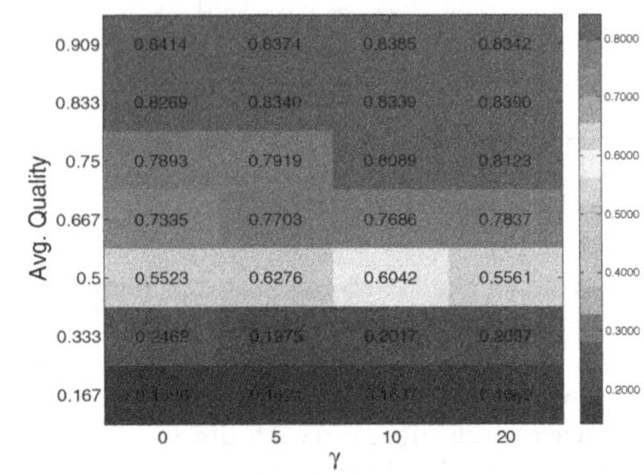

(a) Prior Beta(10, 1)

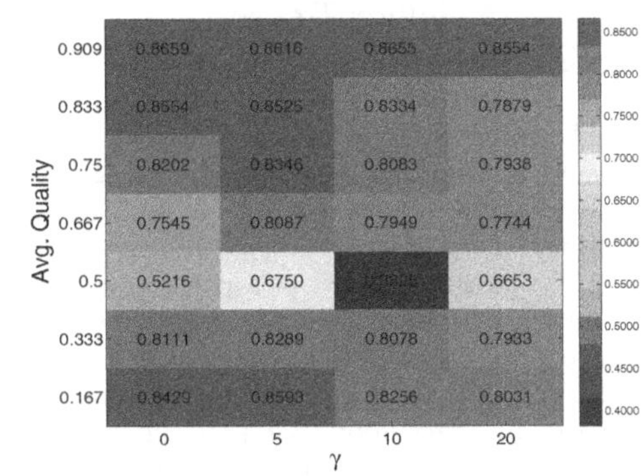

(b) Prior estimated on 5 gold pairs

Figure 3: Normalized area under the active learning curve for different averaged quality and γ.

5.1.3 Virtual Node Regularization

Finally, we conduct a simulated experiment to investigate the effect of the virtual node regularization parameter λ. We generate the synthetic data in a similar manner as in the previous section. Again, we assume that there are 100 objects, each with an underlying true score in the range 1 to 100, and 100 annotators with the ground truth quality $\{\eta_k^*\}_{k=1}^{100}$ following a Beta distribution Beta(2, 1). We randomly sample n pairs of objects and assume that each pair is labeled by $m = (4000/n)$ distinct annotators. We test our Crowd-BT algorithm in Eq. (7) with different virtual node regularization λ under different settings of n and compare the accuracies with that from the Bradley-Terry (BT) model. We report the accuracy and the correlation between the estimated quality $\widehat{\eta}$ and true quality η^* in Table 2. For all settings, Crowd-BT is superior to the baseline Bradley-Terry model. In addition, the correlations between the estimated quality and true quality are very close to one. More interestingly, when n is smaller (*i.e.*, the number of unique pairs is small), we need a larger regularization weight λ to achieve better performance. In fact, when $n = 4000$, it is very likely that the underlying comparison graph is strongly connected and hence we do not need a strong regularization. On the other hand, when $n = 200$, then we have at most 400 directed edges in the graph. In such a sparse graph, strong regularization will help to improve performance.

	ACC
TrueSkill	0.6722 (0.002)
Online-Crowd-BT	0.6822 (0.002)

Table 4: Comparisons of online learning methods on reading level dataset (with all 12,728 pairs).

5.2 Real-World Challenge: Reading Level

We now apply Crowd-BT to the task of ranking documents by their reading difficulty. Our dataset is composed of 491 documents, each assigned a gold-standard reading difficulty level from 1 to 12, as described in [3] in more detail. Using the CrowdFlower crowdsourcing platform,[5] a total of 624 distinct annotators in the United States and Canada were shown representative passages from randomly selected pairs of these documents, and asked to decide which of the two texts was more challenging to read and understand. To help avoid an imbalanced judgment pool that is biased toward a few prolific annotators, each annotator was allowed to contribute a maximum of 40 judgments. We obtained a total of 12,728 pairwise comparisons. The overall quality of annotators on this task is known to be relatively high.

We compare Crowd-BT with $\eta_k = 1$ as the initialization to several competitors: (1) Bradley-Terry (BT) model; (2) for each pair of objects (o_i, o_j), we first use majority vote to obtain the preference between them and apply the BT model (*e.g.*, if 3 annotators claim $o_i \succ o_j$ and 2 claim $o_i \prec o_j$, then we generate a pair $o_i \succ o_j$ as labeled by a perfect annotator); (3) a model proposed in [25] where the difference for annotators is captured by a variance term in the logistic form in Bradley-Terry model. We call this method *Variance-BT*. As the evaluation metric, we again use the accuracy in Eq. (19) as in the simulated experiments which measures the overall accuracy across all pairs in the gold-standard ranking. The results are presented in Table 3. As we can see, Crowd-BT performs the best for any λ, followed by Variance-BT and Majority-Vote-BT, which has the worst performance. We also plot the histogram for the estimated η in Figure 4 and we observe that about half of the annotators are estimated to be perfect annotators on this dataset.

We also compare our Bayesian online Crowd-BT with another well-known online ranking aggregation algorithm: Trueskill [7]. Since the sample ordering in an online algo-

[5] `http://crowdflower.com/`

$n \times m$	4000 × 1			400 × 10			200 × 20		
λ	0.1	0.5	1	0.1	0.5	1	0.1	0.5	1
BT (ACC)	0.849	0.849	0.849	0.803	0.804	0.804	0.745	0.748	0.749
Crowd-BT (ACC)	**0.955**	0.946	0.936	0.893	**0.894**	0.883	0.793	0.803	**0.810**
Crowd-BT Estimate vs. Truth									
Quality Correlation	0.956	0.950	0.945	0.957	0.950	0.947	0.972	0.970	0.967

Table 2: Simulated studies for the virtual node regularization. Best performance in each block is in bold.

	ACC				
	$\lambda = 0.1$	$\lambda = 0.5$	$\lambda = 1$	$\lambda = 10$	$\lambda = 50$
BT	0.6760	0.6796	*0.6815*	0.6802	0.6629
Majority-Vote-BT	0.6686	*0.6700*	0.6688	0.6483	0.6409
Variance-BT	0.6790	0.6835	*0.6862*	0.6828	0.6658
Crowd-BT	**0.6924**	**0.6961**	***0.6978***	**0.6874**	**0.6690**

Table 3: ACC for different methods on reading level dataset (with all 12,728 pairs). Best performance in each column is in bold. Best performance in each row is in italics.

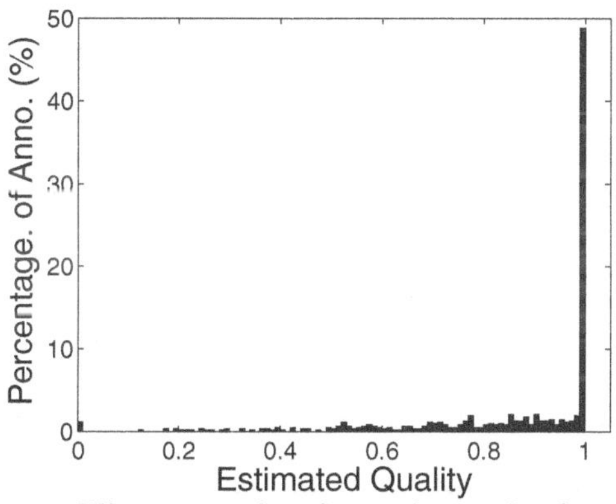

Figure 4: Histogram for the estimated η for different annotators.

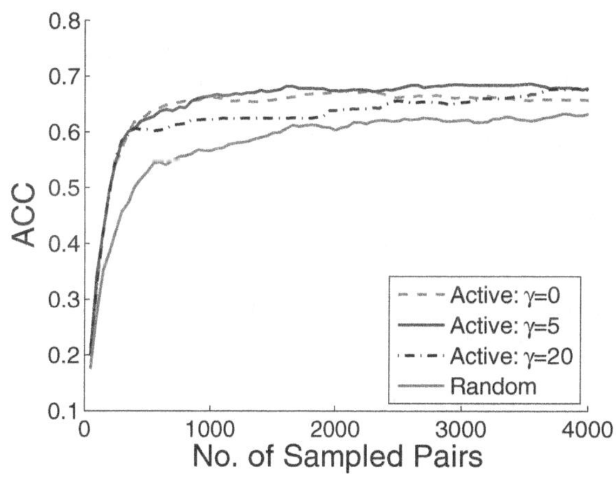

Figure 5: Active learning *vs.* random strategy on reading level dataset.

rithm is random, the results could be slightly different for each run, so we report the mean and standard deviation over 50 runs in Table 4. As we can see, our method improves over the TrueSkill method's accuracy. We note that the performance of the online methods is worse than that of the deterministic methods. The main advantages of online methods are their computational efficiency and the ability to handle streaming data.

Finally, we compare the active-learning strategy with different exploration-exploitation tradeoffs, against the random strategy. For better visualization, we only present the accuracy for the first 4,500 labeled pairs in Figure 5. As captured in the figure, the active learning strategy significantly outperforms the random strategy. The exploration-exploitation tradeoff can also be observed from Figure 5. In particular, the accuracy for $\gamma = 0$ (red line) increases sharply at the beginning; on the other hand, the accuracy for $\gamma = 50$ (black line) increases slowly at the beginning but outperforms the $\gamma = 0$ case after about 3,000 samples. This indicates that different from traditional active learning, the exploration-exploitation tradeoff leveraged by γ is very important for active learning in crowdsourcing. In practice, according to our experience, we suggest choosing $\gamma \in [1, 10]$ to achieve better performance. To further quantify the improvement, we report the number of sampled pairs to first achieve a certain accuracy. In particular, the best accuracy over different methods after sampling all 12,728 pairs is 0.6843. We report the number of sampled pairs to achieve a certain ratio of best accuracy in Table 5. As we can see, the number of pairs needed for the active learning strategy is much smaller than that for the random strategy. With active learning, we can achieve 90% of the best accuracy with only about $400/12,728 \approx 3.14\%$ of the total pairs.

Ratio to best accuracy	$\gamma = 0$	$\gamma = 5$	$\gamma = 20$	Random
98 %	1850	*1400*	3650	7250
95 %	*700*	850	2450	5350
90 %	*400*	450	850	2150

Table 5: Number of pairs required to achieve a specified level of accuracy. Best performance in each row is in italics.

6. CONCLUSIONS AND FUTURE WORK

We have explored the challenge of learning a global ranking from pairwise comparisons via inputs from the crowd. We generalized the widely applied Bradley-Terry model by incorporating annotator quality. We further proposed an active learning strategy that can adaptively sample the next assessment pair and annotator. We introduced and studied an exploration-exploitation tradeoff in active learning with crowdsourcing pairwise comparisons, and demonstrated the importance of the configuration of this tradeoff via empirical studies. Although we developed methods on the foundation provided by the Bradley-Terry model, the proposed methods can be applied to other models for pairwise ranking, such as the Thurstone model [14].

We see several interesting future directions for extending this work. In one direction of research, we see opportunities for reducing the computational cost via narrowing the sampling space for active learning. Heuristics for narrowing the space promise to be valuable. For example, if we are certain about $o_i \succ o_j$ and $o_j \succ o_k$, we may exploit the nearly certain preference between o_i and o_k which can be inferred by the transitivity rule. A second direction of research centers on optimizing in an automated manner both the exploration-exploitation tradeoff parameter γ and virtual node regularization parameter λ. We are also interested in better ways of harnessing limited sets of gold samples in validation sets.

7. ACKNOWLEDGMENTS

We would like to thank T.K. Huang, Denny Zhou and Susan Dumais for helpful discussions and Vaughn Hester for support obtaining information from Crowdflower runs needed for this research.

8. REFERENCES

[1] B. Carterette, P. Bennett, D. Chickering, and S. Dumai. Here or there: Preference judgments for relevance. In *ECIR*, 2008.

[2] C.L.Mallows. Non-null ranking models. *Biometrika*, 44:114–130, 1957.

[3] K. Collins-Thompson and J. Callan. A language modeling approach to predicting reading difficulty. In *HLT*, 2004.

[4] R. Coulom. Computing elo ratings of move patterns in the game of go. Technical report, Université Charles de Gaulle, 2007.

[5] A. P. Dawid and A. M. Skene. Maximum likelihood estimation of observer error-rates using the em algorithm. *Journal of the Royal Statistical Society. Series C (Applied Statistics)*, 28:20–28, 1979.

[6] D. Gleich and L. Lim. Rank aggregation via nuclear norm minimization. In *KDD*, 2011.

[7] R. Herbrich, T. Minka, and T. Graepel. Trueskill(tm): A bayesian skill rating system. In *NIPS*, 2007.

[8] T.-K. Huang, R. C. Weng, and C.-J. Lin. Generalized bradley-terry models and multiclass probability estimates. *Journal of Machine Learning Research*, 7:85–115, 2006.

[9] E. Kamar, S. Hacker, and E. Horvitz. Combing human and machine intelligence in large-scale crowdsourcing. In *AAMAS*, 2012.

[10] D. R. Karger, S. Oh, and D. Shah. Iterative learning for reliable crowdsourcing systems. In *NIPS*, 2011.

[11] K.W.Chang, C. Hsieh., T. Huang, T. Wu, R. Weng, and C.J.Lin. Large-scale ranking by sparse paired comparisons. Unpublished manuscript, 2012.

[12] C. Lin and J. J. More. Newton's method for large bound-constrained optimization problems. *SIAM Journal on Optimization*, 9:1100–1127, 1999.

[13] T. Liu. Learning to rank for information retrieval. *Foundations and Trends in Information Retrieval*, 3:225–331, 2009.

[14] L.L.Thurstone. The method of paired comparisons for social values. *Journal of Abnormal and Social Psychology*, 21:384–400, 1927.

[15] L.R.Ford. Solution of a ranking problem from binary comparisons. *American Math Monthly*, 64:28–33, 1957.

[16] R. Luce. *Individual choice behavior: a theoretical analysis.* Wiley, 1959.

[17] J. Nocedal and S. Wright. *Numerical Optimization.* Springer, 2000.

[18] T. Pfeiffer, X. A. Gao, A. Mao, Y. Chen, and D. G. Rand. Adaptive polling for information aggregation. In *AAAI*, 2012.

[19] R. Plackett. The analysis of permutations. *Applied Statistics*, 24:193–302, 1975.

[20] T. Qin, X. Geng, and T.Y.Liu. A new probabilistic model for rank aggregation. In *NIPS*, 2010.

[21] R.A.Bradley and M. Terry. The rank analysis of incomplete block designs: I. the method of paired comparisons. *Biometrika*, 39:324—345, 1952.

[22] V. Raykar, S. Yu, L. H. Zhao, G. Valadez, C. Florin, L. Bogoni, and L. Moy. Learning from crowds. *Journal of Machine Learning Research*, 11:1297–1322, 2010.

[23] B. Settles. Active learning literature survey. Technical report, University of Wisconsin–Madison, 2009.

[24] K. Tsukida and M. R. Gupta. How to analyze paired comparison data. Technical report, University of Washington, 2011.

[25] M. N. Volkovs and R. S. Zemel. A flexible generative model for preference aggregation. In *WWW*, 2012.

[26] J. Wang, P. G. Ipeirotis, and F. Provost. Managing crowdsourcing workers. In *The 2011 Winter Conference on Business Intelligence*, 2011.

[27] P. Welinder, S. Branson, S. Belongie, and P. Perona. The multidimensional wisdom of crowds. In *NIPS*, 2010.

[28] R. C. Weng and C.-J. Lin. A bayesian approximation method for online ranking. *Journal of Machine Learning Research*, 12:267–300, 2011.

[29] M. Woodroofe. Very weak expansions for sequentially designed experiments: linear models. *The Annals of Statistics*, 17:1087–1102, 1989.

[30] Y. Yan, R. Rosales, G. Fung, and J. G. Dy. Active learning from crowds. In *ICML*, 2011.

Optimizing Parallel Algorithms for All Pairs Similarity Search

Maha Alabduljalil, Xun Tang, Tao Yang
University of California at Santa Barbara, CA 93106, USA
{maha,xtang,tyang}@cs.ucsb.edu

ABSTRACT

All pairs similarity search is used in many web search and data mining applications. Previous work has used comparison filtering, inverted indexing, and parallel accumulation of partial intermediate results to expedite its execution. However, shuffling intermediate results can incur significant communication overhead as data scales up. This paper studies a scalable two-step approach called Partition-based Similarity Search (PSS) which incorporates several optimization techniques. First, PSS uses a static partitioning algorithm that places dissimilar vectors into different groups and balance the comparison workload with a circular assignment. Second, PSS executes comparison tasks in parallel, each using a hybrid data structure that combines the advantages of forward and inverted indexing. Our evaluation results show that the proposed approach leads to an early elimination of unnecessary I/O and data communication while sustaining parallel efficiency. As a result, it improves performance by an order of magnitude when dealing with large datasets.

Categories and Subject Descriptors

H.3.3 [**Information Search and Retrieval**]: Search Process, Clustering; H.3.4 [**Systems and Software**]: Distributed Systems

General Terms

Parallel Algorithms, Performance

Keywords

Similarity search, partitioning, load balancing, filtering

1. INTRODUCTION

All Pairs Similarity Search (APSS) is a core function for many data-intensive applications that identifies a set of objects similar to another under a specified threshold. Examples of such applications include: collaborative filtering for similarity-based recommendations [1], search query suggestions [19], coalition detection for advertisement frauds [17], spam detection [9, 15, 14], web mirrors and plagiarism [21], and near duplicate detection [13, 15].

WSDM'13, February 4–8, 2013, Rome, Italy.

Conducting similarity is a time-consuming process, especially when a massive amount of data is involved. Previous research on expediting the process has used filtering methods and inverted indexing to eliminate unnecessary computations[8, 23, 2]. However, parallelization of such methods is not straightforward given the extensive amount of I/O and communication overhead involved. One popular approach is the use of MapReduce [10] to compute and collect similarity results in parallel using an inverted index [16, 18]. In addition, computation filtering can be applied to avoid unnecessary computation [7]. Unfortunately, the cost of communicating the intermediate partial results is still excessive and such solutions are un-scalable for larger datasets.

Thus we pursue a design that conducts partition-based APSS in parallel without the need for reducer tasks. Furthermore, to avoid unnecessary data loading and comparison, we statically group data vectors into partitions such that the dissimilarity of partitions is revealed in an early stage. In addition, previous works [8, 23, 2, 18, 7] have used characteristics of the partially computed similarity scores to filter out similarity comparisons. These methods can be viewed as dynamic filtering, since they happen at runtime. On the other hand, our approach is a fast static partitioning method that divides the dataset in a way that dissimilar documents are more likely mapped to different machines.

The proposed partitioning performs an early removal of unwanted comparisons which eliminates a significant amount of unnecessary I/O, memory access and computation. We further present a circular partition-based comparison assignment that exploits the computation symmetry and balances the parallel workload. In designing data structure and computation flow of each parallel task, we investigate the trade-offs between different choices for data access. We found that a hybrid combination of forward and inverted indexing can lead to a significantly better performance. The proposed two-step method, called Partition-based Similarity Search (PSS), is more scalable than previously proposed methods and can lead to an order-of-magnitude improvement in performance when dealing with large datasets.

The rest of this paper is organized as follows. Section 2 reviews background and the problem statement. Section 3 gives an overview of PSS. Section 4 describes the partitioning algorithm and the circular load balancing scheme. Section 5 presents the execution of PSS with a hybrid index data structure. Section 6 presents the experimental results and Section 7 concludes this paper.

Task Map(feature t, posting $P(t)$) :
  For each pair of vectors $(d_i, d_j) \in P(t)$ **do**
    Emit $(d_i, d_j, w_{i,t} \times w_{j,t})$.

Task $Reduce(d_i, d_j$, partial scores $s_1, s_2, ...)$:
  Sum partial scores $s_1 + s_2 + ..$ as $Sim(d_i, d_j)$;
  Write $(d_i, d_j, Sim(d_i, d_j))$ if $Sim(d_i, d_j) \geq \tau$.

Figure 1: MapReduce tasks with inverted index for APSS.

2. BACKGROUND

Following the definition in [8], assume a set of n real-valued vectors $D = \{d_1, d_2, \cdots, d_n\}$, and each vector contains at most m non-negative features, $d_i = \{w_{i,1}, w_{i,2}, \cdots, w_{i,m}\}$. For simplicity, each vector is normalized and hence the cosine-based similarity $Sim(d_i, d_j)$ is computed as:

$$Sim(d_i, d_j) = \cos(d_i, d_j) = \sum_{t \in (d_i \cap d_j)} w_{i,t} \times w_{j,t}.$$

Two vectors x, y are considered similar if their similarity score exceeds a threshold τ, namely $Sim(x, y) \geq \tau$.

In many problem domains, for example web text data, input vectors are sparse and a vast majority of feature weights are zero. We denote the 1-norm value of a vector as $\|d_i\|_1$, which is the summation of all its non-zero values. Denote $maxw[d_i]$ to be the maximum feature weight in vector d_i, which is also known as $\|d_i\|_\infty$.

Given n vectors with k features on average per vector, a naïve algorithm computes similarity scores with complexity $O(n^2k)$. While threshold-based computation filtering [20, 6] lowers computation cost, APSS is still expensive for large datasets such as web documents.

Inverted and forward indexing have been studied in [16] to compute top-k similar vectors using MapReduce. Figure 1 shows the pseudo-code of the map and reduce tasks for a simplified APSS algorithm with feature-centric inverted index. Each feature-centric map is assigned a unique set of postings and derives partial similarity scores for all pairs of documents sharing a feature. Reducers then merge these partial scores for each vector pair. Parallel APSS has been studied in [5] for shared memory multi-processor machines where the inverted index is shared among processors to reduce interprocessor communications. There are further techniques to optimize the inverted index code performance: 1) only compute pairs of vectors (d_i, d_j) such that $i < j$ due to the symmetry nature; 2) scale down the size of the map task outputs so that each reduce task handles the partial scores between a document d_i and all other documents [16]; 3) eliminate participation of features that have only one document ID in their postings; and 4) filter additional computations as discussed in the next paragraph. However, even with extensive optimization to filter unnecessary computation, map-reduce communication with the inverted index can increase quadratically as the dataset size scales up and can incur significant synchronization and I/O overhead.

Computation-filtering techniques have also been developed to continuously monitor partially accumulated similarity scores and dynamically detect dissimilar pair of documents. This bases on the given similarity threshold without complete derivation of the similarity value [8, 23]. The key formula used for this filtering is:

$$Sim(d_i, d_j) = \sum_{t \in \chi} w_{i,t} \times w_{j,t} + \sum_{t \in (d_i \cap d_j - \chi)} w_{i,t} \times w_{j,t}. \quad (1)$$

Here, set χ contains the common features that have been scanned and their contributed summation has been computed. The second expression in Formula 1 represents uncomputed summation and can be bounded. For example, an upperbound of the second expression is $maxw[d_i] \times \sum_{t \in (d_i \cap d_j - \chi)} w_{j,t}$. If the sum of the first expression and the bound of the second expression is less than τ, these two vectors are for sure dissimilar and further computations can be omitted.

Similar formulas are discussed in [4, 18, 7] for computation pruning. Also, some of these techniques, [7] for example, can also be applied in a pre-processing step to eliminate lonely documents with no other vectors to be similar to. While we do leverage such dynamic filtering techniques, our focus is to develop an efficient partitioning method for static filtering and parallelism exploitation.

The work in [22] is a parallel algorithm for Jaccard-based similarity computation which filter vectors by assigning them to the same partition if they share a feature. Comparisons are then conducted within each partition exclusively. Such a mapping is more effective for vectors with short lengths. Different long documents that share many features can collide in multiple partitions and this can result in a significant repetition of computation.

Locality Sensitive Hashing (LSH) can be used to derive approximated APSS results [12, 11]. However, LSH's recall is quite low even though precision is fairly high. Besides, a related study [2] shows that exact algorithms can still deliver performance competitive to LSH when inverted indexing and computation filtering methods are applied [8, 23]. Thus we focus on exact APSS in this paper. However, some application-specific preprocessing techniques can be applied to reduce comparison complexity with an approximation. For example, remove stop-words or extremely high frequent features [16]. During our experiments, datasets are pre-processed with such techniques.

3. PARTITION-BASED APSS

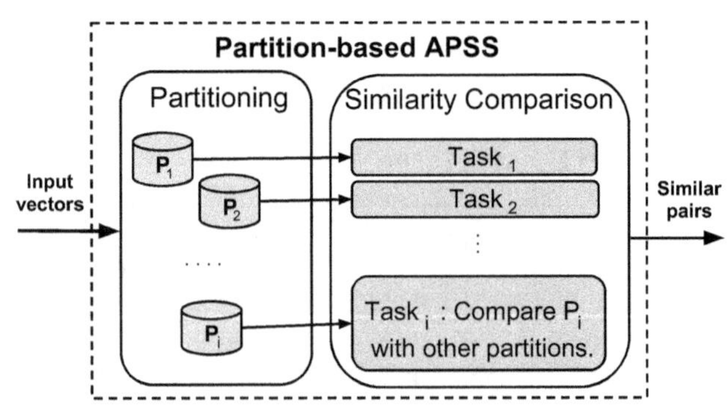

Figure 2: Two-step processing flow of PSS.

In this section, we discuss the overall design of PSS. We assume that PSS runs on a cluster of nodes with multiple CPU cores and can read data from and write data to a distributed file system (DFS) such as Hadoop DFS. The two steps of our algorithm are depicted in Figure 2. We assume that an input dataset is stored in their natural vector-oriented format on the disk storage. For example, each crawled web page is stored as a set of text words (i.e. features) that it contains. Feature-oriented format (statically stored as inverted index) is less preferable since the maintenance is hard as pages get deleted or their contents get updated periodically.

In the design of our algorithm, we use the following strategies to make it scalable.

- First, unlike previous exact APSS approaches with MapReduce, we run a mapper-only scheme with no reducers. In our approach, the dataset is divided into a set of partitions. Each partition is then assigned to a task to be responsible for computing its similarity with another partition if it has a chance to find similar pairs between those two partitions. We adopt this approach because there are enough task-level parallelism and this simple parallelism management avoids I/O and communication overhead among mappers and reducers. This is further described in Section 5.1.
- Second, during the partitioning process, we mark the dissimilarity relationship among those partitions. In this way, communications and comparisons between dissimilar partitions are avoided. The challenge here is to derive an efficient partitioning mechanism that exposes enough parallelism among the partitions. We also exploit the symmetric nature of pairwise comparison and distribute comparisons evenly among tasks whenever possible. We discuss partitioning and circular computation distribution in Section 4.
- Finally, another consideration is the choice of data structures used in each task. In Section 5, we show that hybrid indexing that partially uses forward indexing, can achieve good performance.

Task$_i$:

```
Read the assigned partition of s vectors into area S and
  compute similarity among them;
repeat
  | Read b vectors from another partition into area B;
  | Compare vectors in S with vectors in B;
  | Write comparison results to DFS;
until all input vectors in D are compared.;
```

Figure 3: High level description of a map task in PSS.

The pseudo-code in Figure 3 defines the basic flow of parallel map tasks in a vector-centric approach. The memory used by each task is divided into three areas. Area $\mathcal{S}$ hosts the assigned partition with an average of s vectors, stored in an inverted index format. Area $\mathcal{B}$ stores b vectors fetched from another partition at each comparison step and stored in forward index format. Area $\mathcal{C}$ stores temporary accumulators holding similarity scores.

4. PARTITIONING AND LOAD BALANCING

This section describes an efficient algorithm that derives a mechanism to partition vectors such that dissimilar vectors are assigned to different partitions. This partitioning algorithm allows each task in our framework to completely avoid fetching partitions from DFS which are dissimilar to the partition it owns. We also discuss how to exploit the symmetric nature of comparison to avoid further overheads while assigning partition computations evenly.

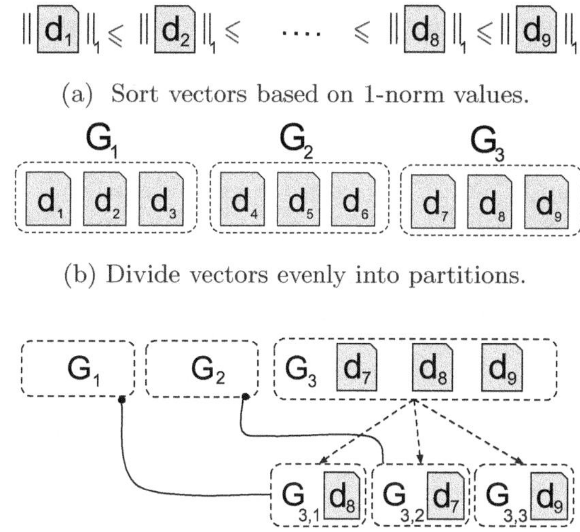

(a) Sort vectors based on 1-norm values.

(b) Divide vectors evenly into partitions.

(c) Partition G_3 further.

Figure 4: Example of static partitioning using 9 vectors.

4.1 Static Partitioning

To determine that two vectors cannot be similar without explicitly computing the product of their features, the following formula based on Formula 1 is used .

$$Sim(d_i, d_j) \leq min(maxw[d_i]\|d_j\|_1, maxw[d_j]\|d_i\|_1) \quad (2)$$

If the upper-bound is less than τ, such document pair cannot be similar and comparison between such pairs can be avoided. This formula shows the relationship between two vectors, the challenge is to find a partitioning of vectors quickly without involving a quadratic complexity.

Our algorithm first sorts all vectors based on their 1-norm value (ie.$\|\cdot\|_1$). Without loss of generality, assume that

$$\|d_1\|_1 \leq \|d_2\|_1 \leq \cdots \leq \|d_n\|_1 .$$

Given a vector d_j, we find another vector d_i in the above sorted list where:

$$\|d_i\|_1 \leq \frac{\tau}{maxw[d_j]}. \quad (3)$$

Vectors d_i and d_j cannot be similar because this implies $Sim(d_i, d_j) \leq maxw[d_j]\|d_i\|_1 \leq \tau$. Moreover, all vectors $d_1, d_2, \cdots d_{i-1}$ cannot be similar to d_j due to the above norm-based sorting. Following this concept, we rapidly find a large number of vectors dissimilar to one vector.

We define τ-$maxw$ ratio of vector d_j as $\frac{\tau}{maxw[d_j]}$. The above analysis shows that a sorted comparison between the 1-norm value and τ-$maxw$ ratio of vectors can facilitate the identification of dissimilar data partitions.

The partitioning procedure is formally described below along with an example illustrated in Figure 4.

- **Step 1**. Sort all vectors by their 1-norm values ($\|\cdot\|_1$) in a non-decreasing order. Divide this ordered list evenly to produces u consecutive groups $G_1, G_2, \cdots, G_u$.

For example, given $d_1, d_2, \cdots, d_9$ in a non-decreasing order of their 1-norm values, shown in Figure 4, the above step produces the following groups:

$$G_1 = \{d_1, d_2, d_3\},\ G_2 = \{d_4, d_5, d_6\},\ G_3 = \{d_7, d_8, d_9\}.$$

- **Step 2**. Partition each group further as follows. For the i-th group G_i, divide its vectors into i disjoint subgroups $G_{i,1}, G_{i,2}, \cdots, G_{i,i}$. With $j < i$, each subgroup $G_{i,j}$ contains all vectors d_x from group G_i satisfying the following inequality:

$$\max_{d_y \in G_j} \|d_y\|_1 \leq \frac{\tau}{maxw[d_x]}.$$

Let $leader(G_j)$ be the maximum vector 1-norm value in group G_j, namely $\max_{d_y \in G_j} \|d_y\|_1$. The above condition can be interpreted as:

* $G_{i,1}$ contains G_i's vectors whose τ-$maxw$ ratio is in the interval $[leader(G_1), leader(G_2))$;
* $G_{i,2}$ contains G_i's vectors whose τ-$maxw$ ratio is in the interval $[leader(G_2), leader(G_3))$;
* $G_{i,i-1}$ contains G_i's vectors whose τ-$maxw$ ratio is greater or equal to $leader(G_{i-1})$.
* $G_{i,i}$ contains vectors from G_i that are not in $G_{i,1}$, $G_{i,2}, \cdots, G_{i,i-1}$.

For the example in Figure 4(c), group G_3 is further divided into:

$$G_{3,1} = \{d_8\}, G_{3,2} = \{d_7\}, G_{3,3} = \{d_9\}.$$

The vectors in G_3 have been compared with the leaders of groups G_1 and G_2 and satisfied:

$$Leader(G_1) = \|d_3\|_1 \quad \leq \frac{\tau}{maxw[d_8]}$$

and

$$Leader(G_2) = \|d_6\|_1 \quad \leq \frac{\tau}{maxw[d_7]}.$$

The *leader* value defines the characteristic of each partition and facilitates the fast partitioning to detect dissimilarity relationship. From the above partitioning algorithm, it is easy to show that the groups derived by the above algorithm satisfy the following property.

PROPOSITION 1. *Given $i > j$, Vectors in $G_{i,j}$ are not similar to ones in any group $G_{k,l}$ where $l \leq k \leq j$.*

This is because as $G_{i,j}$ is not similar to G_j, any leader in groups with index below j has the vector 1-norm value less than $Leader(G_j)$. Thus $G_{i,j}$ is not similar to G_1,G_2, $\cdots, G_{j-1}, G_j$.

Figure 5 illustrates the dissimilarity relationship among the partitioned groups and each edge represents a dissimilar relationship. For example, members of $G_{3,2}$, $G_{4,2}$,$\cdots$, $G_{n,2}$ are not similar to any member in $G_{1,1}$, $G_{2,1}$ or $G_{2,2}$,

The complexity of this partitioning algorithm is $O(n \log n)$. This is because Step 2 of the above algorithm only needs to compare member's τ-$maxw$ ratios with the leaders of each group, $G_1, \cdots G_{i-1}$. Furthermore, it is easy to parallelize this algorithm with a parallel sorting routine that Hadoop provides. The cost of parallel partitioning is relatively small and is less than 3% of the overall execution time of PSS in our experiments.

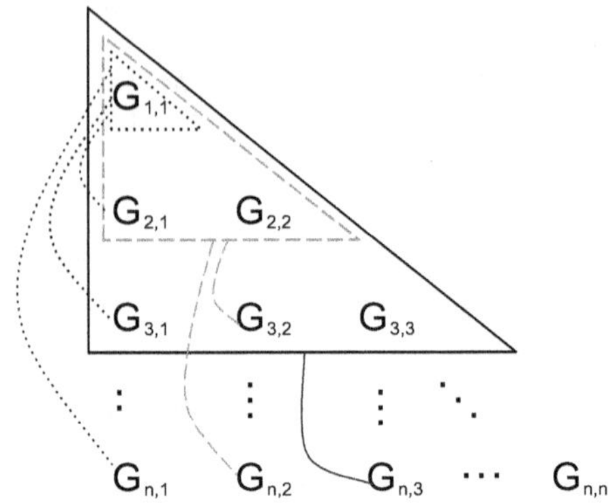

Figure 5: Dissimilarity relationship among partitions.

Step 1 of our static partitioning algorithm uses the 1-norm values to sort vectors. We call it 1-norm guided. Another option is to sort based on the *maxw* value of each vector, then find a point that fulfills the following inequality:

$$maxw[d_j] \leq \frac{\tau}{\|d_i\|_1}. \tag{4}$$

With this sorting, Step 2 is modified to divide group G_i into i disjoint subgroups $G_{i,1}, G_{i,2}, \cdots, G_{i,i}$ using the following criterion. With $j < i$, each subgroup $G_{i,j}$ contains all vectors d_x from group G_i that satisfies the following:

$$\max_{d_y \in G_j} maxw[d_j] \leq \frac{\tau}{\|d_x\|_1}.$$

We call the above alternative partitioning algorithm as ∞-norm guided. The choice of 1-norm or ∞-norm guided partitioning depends on characteristics of the dataset.

To further utilize the above partitioning effectively, we first eliminate the lonely features which only appear in a single vector in the entire dataset. These features do not participate in any similarity computation. We also investigated the elimination of lonely vectors following the definition of $\hat{d}$ from [7], where $\hat{d} = \{\hat{w}_{i,1},\ \hat{w}_{i,2},\ \cdots, \hat{w}_{i,m}\}$. Here $\hat{w}_{i,j} = \max_{d_i \in D}\{w_{i,j}\}$, which is the maximum weight for j-th feature among all vectors. Then, $Sim(d_i, d_j) \leq Sim(d_i, \hat{d})$. If any vector satisfies $Sim(d_i, \hat{d}) \leq \tau$, such vector is a lonely vector and cannot be similar to any vector in the entire dataset. In the datasets we have tested, we have not found enough lonely vectors. However, we find it is useful to exploit partition-level lonely vectors as follows.

Once the static partitions have been derived, we further detect dissimilarity relationships among them using the following procedure.

- For each data partition P_i, compute:

  $$\hat{d}_i = \{\hat{w}_{i,1}, \hat{w}_{i,2}, \cdots, \hat{w}_{i,m}\}$$

  where $\hat{w}_{i,j} = \max_{d_i \in P_i}\{w_{i,j}\}$ and it is the maximum weight for the j-th feature used in set P_i.

- Two partitions P_i and P_k are dissimilar if $Sim(\hat{d}_i, \hat{d}_k) \leq \tau$.

4.2 Partition-oriented Symmetric Comparison and Load Balancing

As the similarity result of two vectors is symmetric, we only need to compare vector d_i from $\mathcal{S}$ with d_j from $\mathcal{B}$ when $i < j$ in Line 4 of Figure 3. There are two approaches available.

- *Statement-level symmetric condition.* Each task reads vectors from all other partitions. The symmetric condition is applied after vectors are fetched into area $\mathcal{B}$, so some effort for data fetching is wasted. The total read I/O traffic for loading data into $\mathcal{B}$ in all tasks is $O(n^2/s)$. Only half of data fetched are actually used for comparisons, thus effective read I/O ratio is only 50%, which represents a significant waste and unnecessary time delay.
- *Partition-level symmetric condition.* A better solution is that the condition of symmetric comparison is applied at the partition level. Namely d_i and d_j are compared only when $PartitionID(d_i) < PartitionID(d_j)$, where $PartitionID()$ is the partition ID where each vector belongs to. With such a condition, Line 3 of Figure 3 only reads other partitions when their partition IDs are bigger than the local partition assigned to the task. Hence read I/O of a task is 100% effective in the sense that all fetched vectors from other partitions are compared.

The disadvantage of the above partition oriented strategy is that fetching vectors from other partitons is highly skewed among the tasks. Let p be the number of partitions. The first task for Partition 0 needs to read all other $(p-1)$ partitions and has the highest I/O and computation load. The second task reads $(p-2)$ partitions for comparison. I/O volume and computation load decrease monotonically as the task identification number increases. Task for partition $(p-2)$ only compares with 1 partition while task for partition $(p-1)$ does not read and compare any other partition. The above skewed distribution affects the load balance.

Given the above considerations, we devise a a *circular* load assignment applied at the partition-level that still exploits the symmetric comparison condition.

- If p is odd, Task i, which handles partition i, compares with the following partition IDs:

  $$(i+1) \bmod p,\ (i+2) \bmod p,\ \cdots,\ (i+\frac{p-1}{2}) \bmod p.$$

- If p is even, Task i $(0 \le i < p/2)$ compares with the following partition IDs:

  $$(i+1) \bmod p,\ (i+2) \bmod p,\ \cdots,\ (i+\frac{p}{2}) \bmod p.$$

  Task i $(p/2 \le i < p)$ compares with the following partition IDs:

  $$(i+1) \bmod p,\ (i+2) \bmod p,\ \cdots,\ (i+\frac{p}{2}-1) \bmod p.$$

In this way, every partition is compared with at most $\frac{p}{2}$ other partitions and the computation load is evenly distributed with a difference of at most one partition. Figure 6 illustrates a case with 5 tasks for 5 partitions.

The circular assignment for a pair of partitions is applied only when these two paritions are not marked as dissimilar by the static partitioning algorithm.

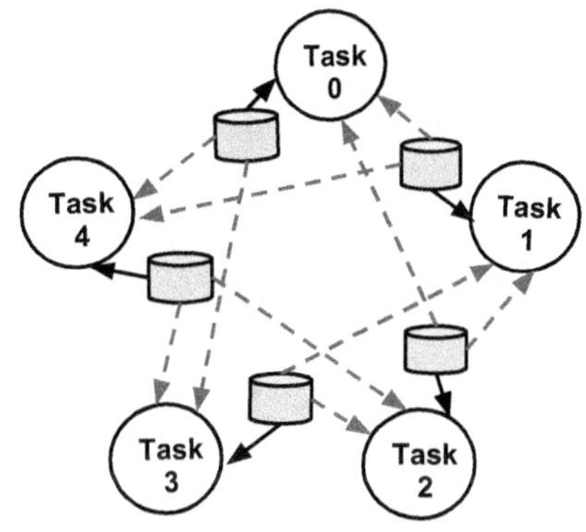

Task i	assigned	compared
0	P_0	P_1, P_2
1	P_1	P_2, P_3
2	P_2	P_3, P_4
3	P_3	P_4, P_0
4	P_4	P_0, P_1

Figure 6: Example of partition-oriented circular comparison assignment. Solid arrows indicate local reads, dotted arrows indicate a likely through network reads. Partition-level comparisons are listed in the right table.

5. RUNTIME DATA STRUCTURE AND TRAVERSAL

In this section we discuss the design of the sparse data structure and traversal method for each task. Feature vectors from a web-scale dataset are often very sparse, and this creates challenges in data structure and access design.

One approach is to maintain the assigned vectors in a forward index format. Namely each vector ID is associated with a list of feature IDs and weights, stored in a compact manner. This forward indexing algorithm proceeds as follows: once each task loads its own s vectors, it starts to fetch a block of b vectors from other partitions into $\mathcal{B}$ and compute similarity one by one between these b vectors and the assigned s vectors. This process repeats until all other potentially similar vectors are fetched and compared. To compute the similarity of *each* vector in area $\mathcal{B}$ to the local vectors, the core of the computation is to traverse through the forward index of *all* these s vectors and accumulate the partial similarity score. If the similarity of a vector pair (d_i, d_j) exceeds the predefined threshold τ, a record of the form $(d_i, d_j, score)$ is appended to the output file.

The drawback of the above forward indexing approach is that it takes time to find the common features between these vectors in $\mathcal{S}$ and a vector in $\mathcal{B}$. Even though this scanning can be shortened by using a skipping technique [25], an inverted index approach is more efficient to exploit the sparse data representation and avoid unnecessary similarity comparison when vectors do not share any features [8, 16, 7]. PSS uses a hybrid approach that combines the use of an inverted index with a forward index at the same time, with the objective of taking advantage from both approaches.

5.1 Hybrid Indexing

Figure 7 describes the function of each PSS task with hybrid indexing, called PSS/HI. Each task loads the assigned vectors in a forward index format and then inverts them locally within area $\mathcal{S}$ (Lines 1,2). It then fetches b vectors from other partitions one at time, which are still in forward index format (Line 4). Compared with a fully inverted index approach (such as the one described in Figure 1), our inverted index data is handled locally by each task at runtime instead of an offline processing to invert the data.

Let d_j be a vector fetched from another partition. For each feature t in d_j (Line 8), the inverted index in area $\mathcal{S}$ is

```
    Task:
1   Read the assigned s vectors into S;
2   Build inverted index of s vectors and find similarity
    within S;
3   repeat
4     Fetch b vectors from another partition into B,
      subject to static partitioning and circular
      assignment constraints;
5     foreach d_j ∈ B do
6       r_j ← ||d_j||_1;
7       InitializeArray(score) of size s;
8       foreach t ∈ d_j and Posting(t) ∈ S do
9         foreach d_i ∈ Posting(t) and
          isCandidate(d_i, d_j) do
10          if score[i]+maxw[d_i]×r_j<τ then
11            (d_i, d_j) is not a candidate;
12          else
13            score[i]=score[i] + w_{i,t}×w_{j,t};
14        r_j ← (r_j − w_{j,t});
15      for i = 1 to s do
16        if score[i] ≥ τ then
17          Write d_i, d_j, score[i];
18  until all required partitions in (D − S) are fetched;
```

Figure 7: Details of each parallel task in PSS/HI.

used to find t's posting localized for the s vectors. Then, the weights of vector d_i in t's posting will contribute a partial score towards $Sim(d_i, d_j)$.

The memory requirement for the temporary partial scores in $\mathcal{C}$ is small, since $\mathcal{C}$ mainly hosts array *score*[ ] and *maxw*[ ] with a size proportional to s.

Lines 6,10 and 14, are the implementation of the dynamic filtering over vector d_j from [8] implied from Formula 1. In Line 9, d_i is a candidate being potentially similar to d_j when it is not marked as dissimilar by the dynamic elimination in Line 11. For the tested benchmark data, dynamic elimination integrated with our scheme does not improve the performance for non-binary feature vectors after static filtering, but actually slows it down due to the additional comparison overhead. Only one binary dataset in our experiments has a relatively small improvement in performance. Thus an alternative would be to disable this dynamic filtering.

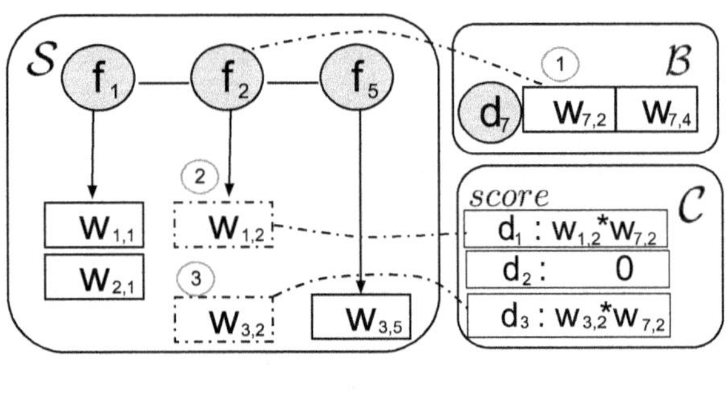

Figure 8: Example of task computation in PSS/HI.

Figure 8 shows one processing example of a task in PSS. When a vector $d_7 = \{w_{7,2}, w_{7,4}\}$ is fetched from another partition and stored in area $\mathcal{B}$, we access the first feature t_2 and traverse its posting in area $\mathcal{S}$. Then each vector weight ($w_{1,2}$ from d_1 and $w_{3,2}$ from d_3 in the example) appearing in t_2's posting is accessed and the partial contribution is accumulated to $score[d_1]$ and $score[d_3]$ in area $\mathcal{C}$.

5.2 Cost Comparison

Here, we analyze briefly the worst-case processing time for a task in PSS using the hybrid indexing and compare it with the forward index approach. By worst-case we mean, none of the computations is dynamically filtered, but every partition needs to be compared with R vectors from other partitions. This simplifies the formula analysis next. As the I/O behavior of both methods is the same, we can safely ignore this part of the comparison and focus on the computational aspect between the two approaches.

In hybrid indexing, there is a small overhead for index inversion of the s vectors assigned to each task. This portion of overhead is negligible because the inverted index is only built once during partition loading and is reused many times during comparison with other partitions. The computation-intensive part is the inner loop, Line 9 in Figure 7. Assume vectors in $\mathcal{S}$ and $\mathcal{B}$ have an average size of k features. Let l be the cost of looking up the posting of a feature in $\mathcal{S}$ where this feature appeared in a vector d_j from $\mathcal{B}$. Term p_s is the average length of postings visited in $\mathcal{S}$, so it estimates the number of iterations for Line 9.

There are 4 memory accesses with a cost of 4δ (Lines 10, 13), namely fetching data items $score[i]$, $w_{i,t}$, $maxw[d_i]$, and writing to $score[i]$. Other items, such as $w_{j,t}$, r_j, and τ, are constants within this loop and can be pre-loaded into registers. These lines also involve 2 pairs of multiplication and addition bringing in a cost of 4ψ, where ψ is the unit execution cost for multiplication or addition. Let T_{HI} be the computation cost of each task in PSS/HI comparing with R vectors from other partitions. Then computation can be estimated as follows.

$$\mathrm{T_{HI}} \approx Rk[l + p_s(4\delta + 4\psi)].$$

For forward indexing along with dynamic computation filtering called PSS/FI, its computation cost can be estimated as follows:

$$\mathrm{T_{FI}} \approx Rk[2s\delta + 4p_s\psi].$$

Considering $s \gg p_s$, $\delta \gg \psi$, and l is insignificant compared to other terms, the cost relative ratio of hybrid and forward indexing can be approximated as:

$$\frac{\mathrm{T_{HI}}}{\mathrm{T_{FI}}} \approx \frac{l + 4p_s\delta + 4p_s\psi}{2s\delta + 4p_s\psi} \approx \frac{2p_s}{s}.$$

We have verified the above ratio in the experiments. For example, the $\frac{p_s}{s}$ ratio of the Twitter dataset is about 9.97×10^{-2}. Thus, ratio $\frac{T_{HI}}{T_{FI}}$ is estimated to be about 20% and the actual ratio is about 9%. This shows that the above analysis helps to reveal the advantage of hybrid indexing over forward indexing.

6. PERFORMANCE EVALUATION

This section describes the performance evaluation of the parallel algorithms for similarity search as discussed earlier in the paper. These algorithms are implemented in Java running with Hadoop MapReduce and tested on a 84-node PC cluster. Each node contains 12 cores (Intel X5650 6-core dual processors) and 24GB of memory. The cluster management provides a batch mode for running jobs submitted through a queue and we were able to use about 20 to 40 machines with a total of 120 to 320 cores. The results reported in this section are an average of three runs.

The evaluation of this section has the following objectives:

- First, we assess the scalability and speedup of PSS/HI using three datasets described next.
- Second, we perform comparative experiments among PSS/HI and the following algorithms:
    - PSS/FI that uses PSS's filtering when applicable but with forward indexing described in Section 5.
    - SII which is an inverted indexing implementation with a dynamic computation filtering as discussed in Section 2.
    - A parallel APSS algorithm from [7], called, SSJ-2R, that uses inverted indexing and dynamic computation filtering.
- Finally, we assess the impact of the proposed static partitioning and circular assignment, and compare 1-norm and ∞-norm guided partitioning.

The datasets used in the experiments are as follows:

- **Twitter dataset**: 19.6 million tweets collected from approximately 2 million unique users. The average number of features per vector is 18.5. The total number of features is 980K and 25% which are lonely features.
- **Clueweb dataset** : 50 million web pages, randomly selected from the Clueweb collection from [3]. The average number of features is 320 per web page with approximately 56% of them are lonely features.
- **Emails dataset**: the raw corpus contained 619,446 messages belonging to 158 users with an average of 757 messages per user. Our preprocessing yielded 516,302 cleaned messages with 107 features on average per message and a total of 448K features.

The datasets are preprocessed to follow a *tf-idf* weighting scheme after filtering stop words and top 0.5% frequent features [16]. We have used threshold τ values 0.9 and 0.7 in the experiments.

6.1 Scalability and Comparative Studies

We first study the parallel time and speedup of PSS/HI when increasing the CPU resource. Figure 9 shows the speedup of PSS/HI in processing Twitter and Clueweb datasets with $\tau = 0.9$. The speedup using q cores is defined as the ratio of parallel time using q cores divided by the serial time when using one core. The performance of PSS/HI scales well as the number of CPU cores increases. With 200 cores, the efficiency for Twitter is about 80% defined as the speedup divided by the number of cores. The efficiency cannot reach 100% because 1) having more cores introduces higher startup cost; 2) having more machines increases the inter-machine communication overhead. The efficiency for the Clueweb dataset is 61%, lower than the 80% efficiency of

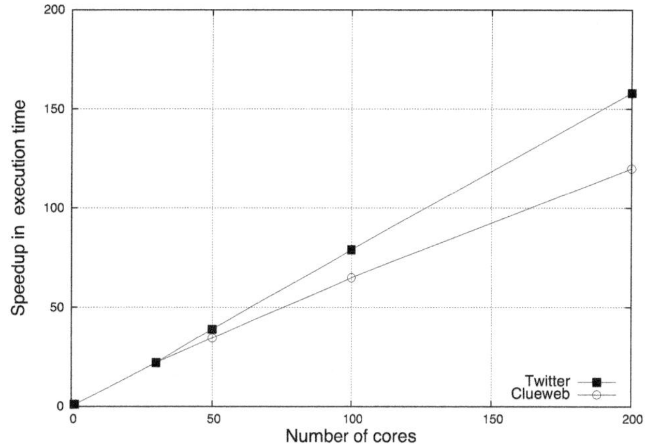

Figure 9: Speedup of PSS/HI while processing 20M Twitter and 50M Clueweb with varied numbers of cores.

Twitter dataset. This is because Clueweb data has higher average number of nonzero features per vector. Also, the tested Clueweb data has much more vectors than Twitter. This results in more map tasks for similarity comparisons, higher startup cost and heavier inter-machine data transfer traffic. Even with such overhead, the overall algorithm performance scales well as the computing resource increases.

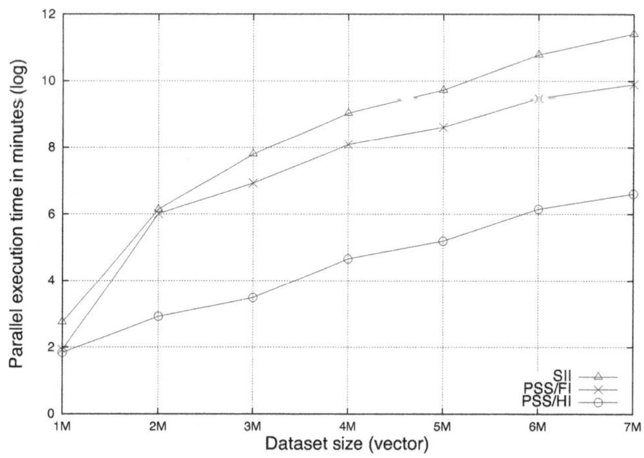

Figure 10: Parallel time on 120 cores of SII, PSS/HI, and PSS/FI over Twitter in *log scale* as data size increases from 1M to 7M with $\tau = 0.9$.

To compare PSS/HI with other algorithms when data size scales up, Figure 10 shows the execution time of PSS/HI, PSS/FI, and SII in log scale when varying the problem size. For a 1 million Twitter dataset, PSS/HI is about 2 times faster than SII while it is similar to PSS/FI's. As data size scales up, we noticed a relatively large gap between PSS/FI and SII. PSS/HI can be up to 25 times faster than SII due to the excessive shuffling between map and reduce tasks. PSS/FI can be up to 10 times slower than STHI because of the slow scanning of common features between vectors in area $\mathcal{S}$ and a vector in area $\mathcal{B}$.

Figure 11(a) shows the parallel time of PSS/HI when dealing with the Clueweb dataset of different sizes using 320 cores. Figure 11(b) shows the relative ratio of the parallel time increase compared to the data size increase, which is defined as:

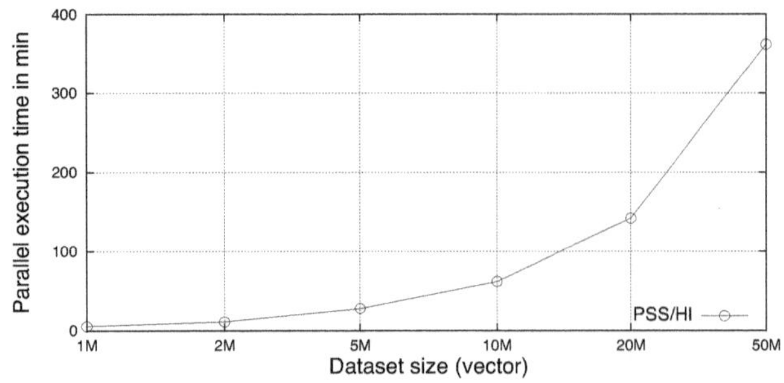

(a)

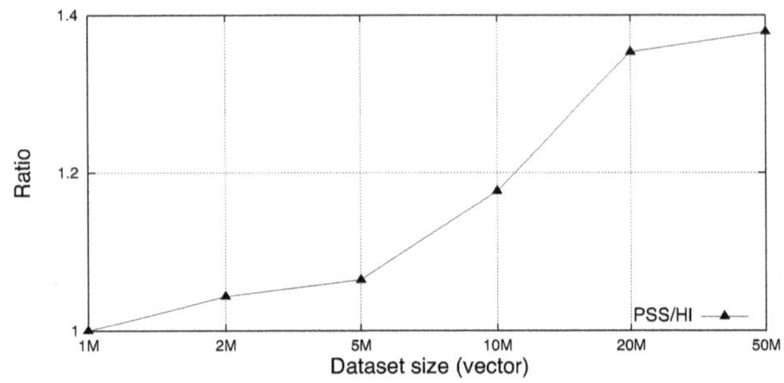

(b)

Figure 11: (a) Parallel time of PSS/HI for Clueweb with 320 cores as the dataset scales from 1M to 50M. (b) The growth ratio of time over data size increases using Formula 5.

$$\frac{PT_n}{PT_{baseline}} / \frac{n}{n_{baseline}} \quad (5)$$

where n is the dataset size and PT_n is the corresponding parallel time. In this case, $n_{baseline}$ is 1M and $PT_{baseline}$ is the parallel time for 1M dataset. The curve shows that PSS/HI exhibits a scalable behavior with a near linear increase of parallel time as the data size increases.

Alg.	Time	3M	5M	7M
PSS/HI	Computation	511.63	1,004.35	1,934.73
	I/O	27.16	49.44	68.59
	Total	538.783	1,053.80	2,003.33
PSS/FI	Computation	6,214.01	12,074.40	21,234.70
	I/O	31.60	56.35	69.44
	Total	5,849.01	11,308.7	19,638.0

Table 1: Average processing time in seconds for computations and I/O of each PSS/FI and PSS/HI map task using Twitter data with varying sizes.

Table 1 explains why PSS/HI outperforms PSS/FI by showing the I/O and computation distribution of each PSS/FI or PSS/HI task in processing the Twitter dataset of different sizes. The I/O time of two algorithms is about the same, while the computation time reduction ratio from PSS/FI to PSS/HI is over 90%. PSS/HI outperforms PSS/FI by exploiting the sparsity of inverted index locally at each machine and arranging memory allocation and data traversal more effectively.

We further compare PSS/HI with another inverted index implementation. Table 2 shows the running time of SSJ-2R when processing a smaller Twitter dataset varying from 60K to 100K. The reducer input column shows the number

Dataset size n	Reducer input	Reducer output	SSJ-2R	PSS/HI
60K	394,123,600	328,778	1,969	158
80K	741,378,156	1,077,014	3,180	216
100K	1,284,741,377	1,428,190	6,180	228

Table 2: Parallel time of SSJ-2R vs. PSS/HI in seconds for processing small Twitter datasets using 10 cores on 5 machines.

of intermediate results as output of map tasks communicated to the reduce tasks. These numbers are reported by Hadoop. The reducer output column is the number of similar vector pairs produced. This table shows large numbers of intermediate results are generated, compared to the size of final output. As the problem size increases, the amount of data shuffled between map tasks and reduce tasks increases significantly. PSS/HI is much faster than SSJ-2R for these tested cases. We are not able to conduct this direct comparison with a larger dataset as the current SSJ-2R code implementation from [7] may have a size limitation.

6.2 Effectiveness of partitioning and circular load balancing

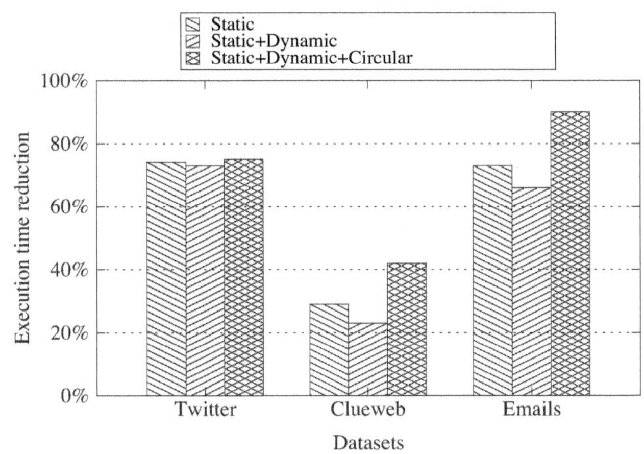

Figure 12: Reduction percentage of execution time when incorporating different optimization techniques. The baseline uses a simple partitioning and statement-level symmetric computation elimination. "Static" implies using static partitioning and filtering over the baseline algorithm. "Static+Dynamic" uses static filtering after partitioning and dynamic filtering over the baseline. "Static+dynamic+Circular" means that all three techniques are applied.

Figure 12 itemizes the percentage of execution time reduction by using the optimization techniques under $\tau = 0.9$. The number of cores allocated is 120 for the Twitter and 10M of Clueweb datasets, and 20 cores for the Email dataset. The baseline is a simpler version of PSS/HI with symmetric comparison filtering. In this baseline version, a comparison of two vectors is skipped if $i < j$, but dynamic computation filtering, static computation filtering with partitioning, or circular assignment is not applied. Each bar represents execution time reduction ratio by using one or more optimization techniques compared to the baseline.

Overall reduction from using all techniques leads to 75%

for Twitter, 42% for Clueweb, and 90% for Emails. Features vectors of these datasets all use non-binary weights.

Static partitioning with dissimilarity detection leads to about 74% reduction for Twitter, about 29% for Clueweb, and about 73% for Emails. Adding the circular assignment contributes an additional 2% for Twitter, 19% for Clueweb, and 14% for Emails.

Dynamic computation filtering after static elimination actually slows down the computation in all these 3 datasets from 1% to 7%. That is because dynamic filtering carries the overhead of extra computation while most dissimilar vectors are already detected by static partitioning. Also even when a vector in $\mathcal{S}$ is detected as dissimilar to another vector from $\mathcal{B}$, the inverted index structure does not change and thus does not reduce the data traversal cost, which is more significant than that of multiplication or addition. Dynamic filtering integrated in our scheme does have some impact for binary vectors.

We have also assessed the impact of the optimization for datasets with binary feature weights. Figure 13 shows the effectiveness of the optimization with a setting similar to Figure 12. Dynamic filtering yields a slight improvement with about 1% reduction for Twitter whose average vector size is relatively short. Static partitioning for dissimilarity detection gains significant reduction while circular assignment is still effective.

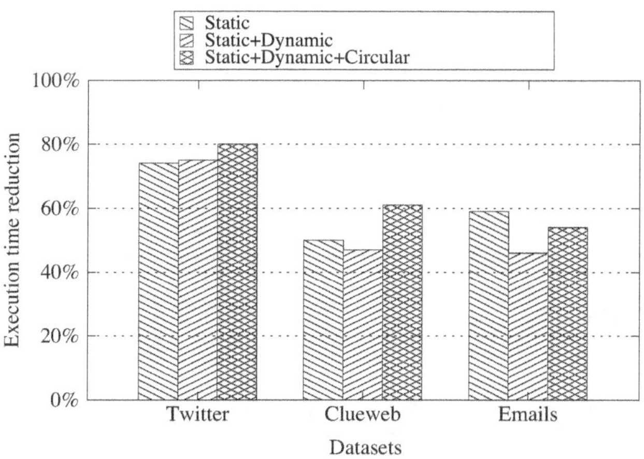

Figure 13: Reduction percentage in execution time under different optimization techniques defined in Figure 12. The data vectors are represented using binary weights.

To materialize the effect of the techniques over the I/O portion of the algorithm, Figure 14 shows the amount of data read I/O reduced by using static partitioning with $\tau = 0.7$ or $\tau = 0.9$ over sampled datasets. This is computed by comparing the total amount of read I/O of PSS/HI algorithm with or without static partitioning. Static partitioning reduces I/O volume by up to 81%.

Figure 15 shows a comparison of total read communication volume reported by Hadoop when using the statement-level and partition-level symmetric comparison discussed in Section 4.2. The results show that the partition-level based one can save up to 50% of the communication volume.

6.3 Partitioning guided by 1-norm and ∞-norm

Table 3 compares the two versions of static partitioning guided by 1-norm or ∞-norm discussed in Section 4.

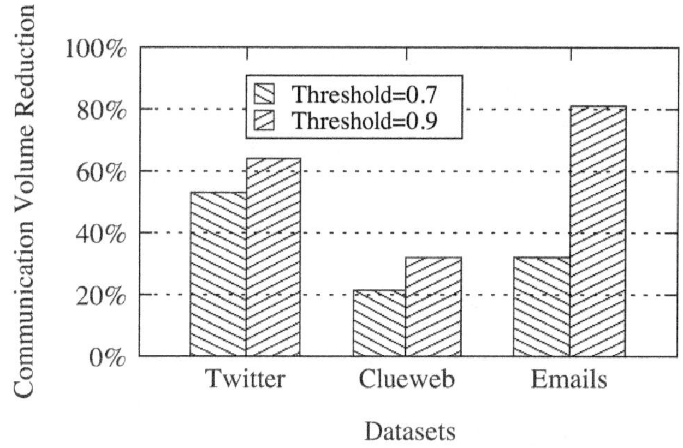

Figure 14: Percentage of the read I/O reduction in bytes, after using the static partitioning under different thresholds.

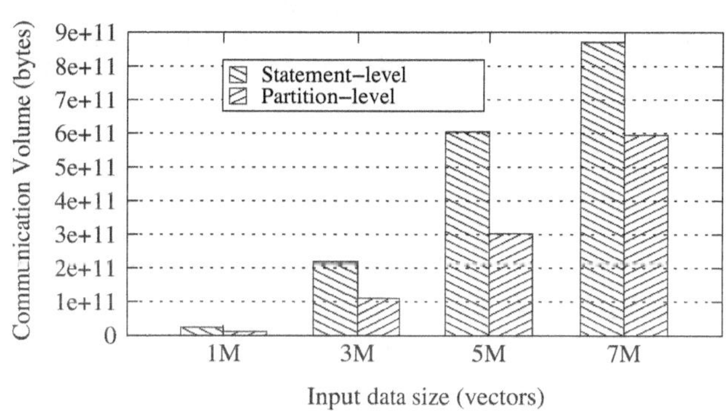

Figure 15: Total communication volume with statement-level symmetric comparison and with partition-level symmetric comparison. The Twitter dataset varies from 1M to 7M vectors.

Datasets	Execution time 1-norm: ∞-norm	Skipped vector pairs 1-norm:∞-norm
Twitter	1.01	1.01
Clueweb	0.88	0.82
Emails	1.09	1.07

Table 3: The second column is relative ratio of execution time between 1-norm ∞-norm guided partitioning. The third column is relative ratio of the number of skipped vector pairs by these two methods.

The table shows the ratio of execution time between these two methods, and also the ratio in terms of the number of skipped vector pairs among the two. The result shows two methods are about the same for Twitter. 1-norm is more effective for Clueweb while the ∞-norm guided method performs better with Emails.

7. CONCLUSIONS

The main contribution of this paper is a two-step partition-based APSS algorithm with 1) an efficient static partitioning and circular assignment for an early removal of unwanted I/O and computations, and 2) a partition-based runtime comparison with a simplified parallelism management and hybrid indexing. Our experiments demonstrate the significant performance gain obtained by PSS. For example, PSS is up to about 25 times faster than a parallel approach that exploits parallelism in partial results accumulation for Twitter dataset and is 10 times faster than a forward indexing scheme. The experiments show that the static partitioning with dissimilarity detection significantly improves performance while circular assignment is also effective. The integration of dynamic computation filtering is not effective as expected and we plan to investigate this issue further. We currently assume the dataset to be static, and our future work is to consider incremental computing algorithms for applications where the dataset is updated continuously [24].

Acknowledgment

We thank Alexandra Potapova and Paul Weakliem for their help in data processing and the anonymous referees for their thorough comments. This work is supported by NSF IIS-1118106 and Kuwait University Scholarship. Equipment access is supported by the Center for Scientific Computing at CNSI/MRL under NSF DMR-1121053 and CNS-0960316. Any opinions, findings, conclusions or recommendations expressed in this material are those of the authors and do not necessarily reflect the views of the National Science Foundation.

8. REFERENCES

[1] G. Adomavicius and A. Tuzhilin. Toward the next generation of recommender systems: a survey of the state-of-the-art and possible extensions. *IEEE Transactions on Knowledge and Data Engineering*, june 2005.

[2] Arvind Arasu, Venkatesh Ganti, and Raghav Kaushik. Efficient exact set-similarity joins. In *Proceedings of the 32nd international conference on Very large data bases*, VLDB '06, 2006.

[3] Language Technologies Institute at Carnegie Mellon University. The clueweb09 dataset, http://boston.lti.cs.cmu.edu/data/clueweb09.

[4] Amit Awekar and Nagiza F. Samatova. Fast matching for all pairs similarity search. In *International Conference on Web Intelligence and Intelligent Agent Technology Workshop*, 2009.

[5] Amit Awekar and Nagiza F. Samatova. Parallel all pairs similarity search. In *International Conference on Information Knowledge Engineering*, 2010.

[6] Ricardo Baeza-Yates and Berthier Ribeiro-Neto. *Modern Information Retrieval.* Addison Wesley, 1999.

[7] Ranieri Baraglia, Gianmarco De Francisci Morales, and Claudio Lucchese. Document similarity self-join with mapreduce. In *ICDM*, 2010.

[8] Roberto J. Bayardo, Yiming Ma, and Ramakrishnan Srikant. Scaling up all pairs similarity search. In *Proceedings of WWW*, 2007.

[9] Abdur Chowdhury, Ophir Frieder, David A. Grossman, and M. Catherine McCabe. Collection statistics for fast duplicate document detection. *ACM Trans. Inf. Syst.*, 20(2):171–191, 2002.

[10] Jeffrey Dean and Sanjay Ghemawat. Mapreduce: simplified data processing on large clusters. In *Proc. of OSDI 2004*.

[11] Jimmy Lin Ferhan Ture1, Tamer Elsayed2. No free lunch: Brute force vs. locality-sensitive hashing for cross-lingual pairwise similarity. 2011.

[12] Aristides Gionis, Piotr Indyk, and Rajeev Motwani. Similarity search in high dimensions via hashing. In *VLDB*, 1999.

[13] Hannaneh Hajishirzi, Wen tau Yih, and Aleksander Kolcz. Adaptive near-duplicate detection via similarity learning. In *Proc. of ACM SIGIR*, pages 419–426, 2010.

[14] Nitin Jindal and Bing Liu. Opinion spam and analysis. In *Proceedings of the international conference on Web search and web data mining*, WSDM '08, pages 219–230, 2008.

[15] Aleksander Kolcz, Abdur Chowdhury, and Joshua Alspector. Improved robustness of signature-based near-replica detection via lexicon randomization. In *Proceedings of KDD*, pages 605–610, 2004.

[16] Jimmy Lin. Brute force and indexed approaches to pairwise document similarity comparisons with mapreduce. In *SIGIR*, 2009.

[17] Ahmed Metwally, Divyakant Agrawal, and Amr El Abbadi. Detectives: detecting coalition hit inflation attacks in advertising networks streams. In *Proceedings of the 16th international conference on World Wide Web*, WWW '07, pages 241–250, 2007.

[18] Gianmarco De Francisci Morales, Claudio Lucchese, and Ranieri Baraglia. Scaling out all pairs similarity search with mapreduce. In *8th Workshop on LargeScale Distributed Systems for Information Retrieval (2010)*, 2010.

[19] Mehran Sahami and Timothy D. Heilman. A web-based kernel function for measuring the similarity of short text snippets. In *Proceedings of the 15th international conference on World Wide Web*, WWW '06, pages 377–386, 2006.

[20] Gerard Salton and Michael J. McGill. *Introduction to Modern Information Retrieval.* McGraw-Hill, Inc., 1986.

[21] Narayanan Shivakumar and Hector Garcia-Molina. Building a scalable and accurate copy detection mechanism. In *Proceedings of the first ACM international conference on Digital libraries*, DL '96, pages 160–168, 1996.

[22] Rares Vernica, Michael J. Carey, and Chen Li. Efficient parallel set-similarity joins using mapreduce. In *Proceedings of the 2010 international conference on Management of data*, SIGMOD '10, 2010.

[23] Chuan Xiao, Wei Wang, Xuemin Lin, and Jeffrey Xu Yu. Efficient similarity joins for near duplicate detection. In *Proceeding of the 17th international conference on World Wide Web*, WWW '08. ACM, 2008.

[24] Shanzhong Zhu, Alexandra Potapova, Maha Alabduljalil, Xin Liu, and Tao Yang. Clustering and load balancing optimization for redundant content removal. In *Proc. of WWW 2012 (21th international conference on World Wide Web), Industry Track*, 2012.

[25] Justin Zobel and Alistair Moffat. Inverted files for text search engines. *ACM Comput. Surv.*, 38(2), July 2006.

Bursty Subgraphs in Social Networks

Milad Eftekhar
Department of Computer Science
University of Toronto
Toronto, ON, Canada
milad@cs.toronto.edu

Nick Koudas
Department of Computer Science
University of Toronto
Toronto, ON, Canada
koudas@cs.toronto.edu

Yashar Ganjali
Department of Computer Science
University of Toronto
Toronto, ON, Canada
yganjali@cs.toronto.edu

ABSTRACT

Data available through social media and content sharing platforms present opportunities for analysis and mining. In the context of social networks, it is interesting to formalize and locate bursts of activities amongst users, related to a particular event and to report sets of socially connected users participating in such bursts. Such collections present new opportunities for understanding social events, and render new ways of online marketing.

In this paper, we model social information using two conceptualized graph models. The first one (the action graph) provides a detailed model of all activities of all users while the second one (the holistic graph) provides an aggregate view on each user in the social media. We also propose two models to define the notion of "burst". The first model (intrinsic burst model) takes the intrinsic characteristics of each user into account to recognize the bursty behaviors; while the second model (social burst model) considers neighbors' influences when identifying bursts. We provide two linear algorithms to detect bursts based on the proposed models. These algorithms have been extensively evaluated on a month of full Twitter dataset certifying the practicality of our approach. A detailed qualitative study of our techniques is also presented.

Categories and Subject Descriptors

H.2.8 [**Database Management**]: Database applications—*Data mining*; J.4 [**Social and Behavioral Sciences**]: Economics

Keywords

Social networks; Information burst; Bursty subgraphs; Twitter

1. INTRODUCTION

Social media have been widely adopted in recent years. Services such as Twitter, Facebook and Google Plus (to name a few) enable millions of individuals to connect with each other, share diverse pieces of information content and interact via a multitude of services (e.g., apps, exchanging messages, etc).

In the vast majority of social media platforms available, there are a few prevailing characteristics of functionality that are common across services. These include a) the formation of an underlying graph structure arising from social connections (e.g., becoming "friends" or following each other's messages) and b) the ability to share and act upon (e.g., like, retweet) diverse pieces of information content. As a result, these two main functions can be conceptualized via a graph in which vertices represent "users" and edges are social connections. Information (in terms of content produced and shared) flows across edges amongst nodes. In addition, content can be acted upon by vertices (users) through (platform dependent) means such as "liking" content or sharing content produced by others ("sharing" or "retweeting"). These and other related actions can be viewed as direct means of content endorsement. With this conceptual view in mind, there are several interesting patterns of activity that can emerge.

Consider for example an external event, such as an outbreak of violence or protest (e.g. recent protests in Tahrir square in Egypt) or a natural disaster (e.g., an earthquake). These events will be reported by several users (vertices in the graph) and such content will rapidly be endorsed (liked, shared, retweeted) by the social connections of these users. These, in turn, will instigate additional rapid content endorsement by additional users causing what is generally referred to as an information cascade in the graph. The rate with which such cascades are formed (i.e., the time delay between content endorsements) commonly points to the importance of the event. It is natural to expect that there are millions of such cascades forming at different time intervals. Being able to quickly identify the most prominent ones (i.e., those that are forming rapidly) will aid in the identification of breaking events or events that are gaining popularity very rapidly in the graph. Such information cascades can be visualized as bursty subgraphs (the set of socially connected users involved in the cascade).

The graph structure along with the information shared by users gives rise to additional interesting activity patterns which in some sense are complementary to the example above. Consider the information shared by all nodes in the graph over the period of some fixed time interval (say one hour). If we have an a priori subject area in mind (e.g., political chatter associated to say Barack Obama) it would be possible to identify subgraphs (sets of socially connected users) that primarily produce and share information related to our target subject area (i.e., Barack Obama) during the time interval of interest. A naïve solution to this problem would be to detect nodes posting more than a specific threshold of related information and report as the solution (subgraphs), the connected components containing these nodes. However, since the distribution of activity is non-uniform among users, this approach would result in numerous spurious transitions in the activity status of users and produce several tiny subgraphs as solutions primarily segmenting larger burst graphs. It is desirable to assign each node with an activity status providing smooth transitions among neighbors and obtain large smooth subgraphs. This is analogous to the goals of the algorithms presented by Kleinberg [9] for the case of document streams.

The bursty subgraphs can be of vast interest for a variety of reasons. Depending on the subject area of interest, they can be important sources of information (e.g., interesting users to follow on twitter given ones interests) or important candidates for word of mouth marketing and (content or display) advertising. Consider for example (further details in the experimental section) one of the trending topics of June 10, 2012 on Twitter, namely "Grand Prix". When we search for bursty subgraphs using the query "grand prix" using the techniques presented herein, we identify several subgraphs consisting of twitter accounts that tweet actively about several facets of grand prix, such as "Canadian formula 1 grand prix", "Thailand open badminton grand prix", "volleyball FIVB world grand prix", "CSI show jumping grand prix, "Kazan FIDE Women Chess grand prix", and "San Marino motorcycle grand prix". These subgraphs, each corresponding to one aspect of our specified topic (namely grand prix), consist of twitter accounts in social proximity that exhibited a lot of activity related to our topic of interest for that day. In addition to providing more context around the topic of interest (that is useful in search; e.g., in query expansion, and diversified search), they provide valuable topical targets for marketing campaigns.

In this paper, we formalize these intuitions and present efficient algorithms to identify such activity patterns in social networks. The notion of information burst has successfully been studied in the content of time series streams and document collections [9,12]. We extend these notions in the context of social networks and formalize problems that concern detecting information bursts in large collections of socially connected users. More formally in this paper, we present and formalize two graph theoretic conceptual models of information sharing. The first (referred to as "action graph") focuses on user actions, timings, and how actions trigger other actions. The second model (referred to as "holistic graph") does not track timestamps and the relationship between individual actions. Instead, it keeps track of all content endorsed (generated or shared) by each user. We also develop two formal approaches to quantify information bursts. The first (called the "intrinsic burst model") treats each user (vertex) as an isolated unit and does not consider the influence of neighboring nodes during burst detection. This is provided to capture the cases in which nodes share a piece of information (in the action graph case) or multiple pieces of information on a particular subject (in the holistic graph model) due to genuine interest without being influenced by their neighbors that actively share or produce related content. The second (called the "social burst model") takes into account neighbor influences during the detection of bursts. This model naturally takes into account the effects of neighbors and their actions or type of information they share.

For each type of graph (action/holistic), we present an *optimal* polynomial solution for the intrinsic burst model. For very large graphs, an optimal linear approach (called $\mathcal{DIBA}$) is presented by simplifying the problem. Furthermore, we present an iterative linear algorithm (called $\mathcal{SODA}$) for the social burst model for each type of graph.

To evaluate our developments, we utilize real data from the Twitter fire hose, namely the set of all tweets flowing through the Twitter service. In Section 4, we evaluate our algorithms at full scale for days worth of twitter data (not samples of it). Both $\mathcal{DIBA}$ and $\mathcal{SODA}$ algorithms can operate on the days worth of full fire hose in seconds on action graphs. On the holistic graph, $\mathcal{DIBA}$ takes about 3 minutes and $\mathcal{SODA}$ takes about 2 hours. In addition we deploy a qualitative study demonstrating the goodness of our findings (Section 4.3).

2. MODELING

Let $U = \{u_1, ..., u_n\}$ be the set of users in a social network. We say that users u_i and u_j are socially connected in the network if there exists a direct social relationship between them (for example they are friends on Facebook or Google Plus or have a follower-folowee relationship on Twitter, etc). We denote by $C = \{c_1, ..., c_m\}$ the set of actions generated by all users. An action in this context is a piece of information (e.g., a document, a status update, a tweet, a retweet, a reply, etc) generated by a user. This section details two graph models (Section 2.1) and two burst models (Section 2.2) formalizing burst definition.

2.1 Graph Models

We present two graph models; the **action graph** (Section 2.1.1) and the **holistic graph** (Section 2.1.2) to represent the users, the content they generate, and their relationships. An action graph represents each action generated by each user (Section 2.1.1), while a holistic graph consolidates all actions generated by each user providing an aggregate view and yielding a simpler model (Section 2.1.2). Action graphs provide an elaborate view over the social network and the actions of each user recording explicitly a timestamp for each action, signifying the time the action occurred. In this graph, time difference between actions plays an essential role in detecting a burst. Holistic graphs on the other hand, simplify this representation by aggregating all actions of a user maintaining only an aggregate view. Burst detection in holistic graphs proceeds by considering the aggregate number of actions related to a particular subject (e.g., "Barack Obama").

2.1.1 Action graph

For each topic, an action graph is a graph $G = (V, E)$ where each node a of the graph represents an action that is related to that topic (**relevant actions**). Given an action (e.g., a post on Facebook or a tweet) and a topic description, there are numerous ways to assess whether the action is relevant to the topic. The specific approach used is totally orthogonal to our discussion. To simplify our presentation, we adopt a simple approach. We describe a topic by a set of keywords S_k (e.g., 'Barack Obama') and declare that the action (i.e., the post) is relevant to the topic if the action contains at least one keyword in S_k. Clearly other more elaborate approaches could be applied and indeed we can incorporate those without affecting our framework.

In this model, each node a of the graph is a relevant action and is associated with a user u, as well as timestamp t. If an action a of user u triggers another action b of user v (for example a retweet, or a reply in Twitter), we add a link from a to b in the graph G. Here, we assume that for each action a, we can identify the set of all actions, $T(a)$, which have triggered a. Notice that in the action graph, it is possible to have an edge between two actions even if the associated users are not directly socially connected (e.g., friends on facebook).

2.1.2 Holistic graph

In the holistic graph $G = (V, E)$, each node v of the graph represents a user. There is an edge between users u and v in E if and only if they are socially connected. Moreover, each node u maintains a weight $w_u = (r_u, d_u)$. The variable r_u is subject/topic specific and represents the fraction of actions of u relevant to a given topic. We use d_u to refer to the total number of actions conducted by u.

2.2 Burst Models

We introduce two models to formalize the notion of a burst: (1) the intrinsic burst model and (2) the social burst model. The former (Section 2.2.1) does not incorporate neighboring effects throughout burst detection. In several cases users act independently (primarily via occurrences of external events, such as during a sports game) and this model is geared towards such cases. The latter (Section 2.2.2) identifies bursts considering the influence of neighbors.

2.2.1 Intrinsic burst model

For a given (action/holistic) graph $G = (V, E)$, a **burst state** $s_v \in \{\mathtt{B}, \mathtt{N}\}$ is associated with each vertex $v \in V$ determining whether v is bursty B or non-bursty N. Note that v represents an action that a user did at a specific time in the action graph model, while it represents a user in the holistic graph model.

Here, we model the process of generating actions by a two state automaton. The two states are "bursty B" and "non-bursty N". This automaton transitions between states with fixed probabilities. The probability to keep the same state is λ; while the probability to change state is $1 - \lambda$. To avoid spurious transitions between bursty and non-bursty states, we require that λ should be greater than 0.5.

At the non-bursty state, the automaton emits actions at a rate γ; while at the bursty state, actions are emitted at a higher rate $\gamma^* > \gamma$ ($\alpha = \frac{\gamma^*}{\gamma} > 1$).

For the case of action graphs, the automaton emits actions with time gaps x according to an exponential probability density function $f_N(x) = \gamma e^{-\gamma x}$ at a rate of $\gamma = \frac{1}{E[x]}$ (the non-bursty state rate) [9]. The exponential density function is a distribution that models the inter-arrival times between events occurring in an independent and continuous manner. The time gap x for each vertex v is defined as the time difference between the timestamp of v and the neighboring vertex with the most recent timestamp prior to v; i.e.,

$$x_v = \min_{u \in N(v): t_u < t_v} t_v - t_u$$

where $N(v)$ is the set of v's neighbors and t_v is v's timestamp.

Holistic graphs do not have timing information. Here, the only parameters available for each node u are d_u, the total number of actions, and r_u, the number of relevant actions (actions that are related to our topic of interest). The automaton emits d_u actions out of which r_u actions are relevant. Assuming a fixed probability of being relevant, the distribution becomes binomial $f_N(r_u, d_u) = \binom{d_u}{r_u}\gamma^{r_u}(1-\gamma)^{d_u - r_u}$ with the rate of $\gamma = R/D$ (the non-bursty state rate) [9, 12]. Here, $R = \sum_{u \in V} r_u$ and $D = \sum_{u \in V} d_u$ are, respectively, the number of relevant actions and the number of all actions generated by all users.

PROBLEM 1. *For graph $G = (V, E)$, identify a burst state assignment $\mathcal{S} = (s_{v_1}, ..., s_{v_{|V|}})$ to maximize*

$$P(\mathcal{S}|G) \sim P(G|\mathcal{S})P(\mathcal{S}) = (\prod_{i=1}^{|V|} f_{s_{v_i}}(v_i)) \times (\prod_{(v_i, v_j) \in E} \lambda_{s_{v_i} s_{v_j}})$$

where $s_{v_i} \in \{\mathtt{B}, \mathtt{N}\}$ is the assigned burst state of v_i, and $f_{s_{v_i}}(v_i)$ determines the probability that the vertex v_i is generated by the bursty or the non-bursty exponential/binomial distribution function. Moreover, $\lambda_{s_{v_i} s_{v_j}}$ equals to λ when $s_{v_i} = s_{v_j}$ and equals to $1 - \lambda$ when $s_{v_i} \neq s_{v_j}$. This problem is equivalent to maximizing

$$\log(P(\mathcal{S}|G)) \sim \sum_{i=1}^{|V|} \log(f_{s_{v_i}}(v_i)) + \sum_{(v_i, v_j) \in E} \log(\lambda_{s_{v_i} s_{v_j}})$$

The bursty subgraphs of G are consisting of nodes with an assigned burst state B.

2.2.2 Social burst model

In accordance with prior observations [2, 8, 11] that the activity of neighbors has an influence on the activity of a node, we present a model that takes the influence of neighbors into account. We aim to assign a **fuzzy burst state** $s_u = s_u^{\mathtt{B}}/s_u^{\mathtt{N}}$ to each vertex $u \in V$ to represent the severity of burst in u. The value $s_u^{\mathtt{B}}$ ($s_u^{\mathtt{N}}$) represents the probability that the vertex u is bursty (non-bursty) and $0 \leq s_u^{\mathtt{N}}, s_u^{\mathtt{B}} \leq 1$. A node u is called bursty in this model, if s_u is bigger than a predetermined threshold $\theta > 1$.

PROBLEM 2. *For a graph $G = (V, E)$, assign a fuzzy burst state $\mathcal{S} = (s_{v_1}, ..., s_{v_{|V|}})$ to members of V to minimize*

$$\mathcal{D} = \sum_{i=1}^{|V|} (s_{v_i} - \frac{P(\mathtt{B}|v_i)}{P(\mathtt{N}|v_i)})^2$$

where for the vertex $v_i \in V$:

$$P(\mathtt{B}|v_i) = f_{\mathtt{B}}(v_i) \prod_{v_j:(v_i, v_j) \in E} (P(\mathtt{B}|v_j)\lambda + P(\mathtt{N}|v_j)(1-\lambda))^{\frac{1}{n_i}}, \quad (1)$$

$$P(\mathtt{N}|v_i) = f_{\mathtt{N}}(v_i) \prod_{v_j:(v_i, v_j) \in E} (P(\mathtt{B}|v_j)(1-\lambda) + P(\mathtt{N}|v_j)\lambda)^{\frac{1}{n_i}}, \quad (2)$$

v_j is a neighbor of v_i, and n_i is the number of v_i's neighbors.

By minimizing $\mathcal{D}$ in Problem 2, we attempt to assign s_i values that are as close (in Euclidean metric) as possible to a set of values satisfying equations 1 and 2.

In these equations, the probability to be bursty B (non-bursty N) depends on two factors: (1) the intrinsic characteristics of nodes to match the probability distribution functions ($f_{\mathtt{B}}(v_i)$, $f_{\mathtt{N}}(v_i)$) and (2) the influence of neighbors ($\prod_{v_j:(v_i,v_j)\in E}(P(\mathtt{B}|v_j)(1-\lambda)+P(\mathtt{N}|v_j)\lambda)^{\frac{1}{n_i}}$). Here, λ $(1-\lambda)$ is the probability to see two neighboring nodes with the same (different) burst state and is defined similar to the intrinsic burst model. Note that the power $1/n_i$ in the second factor provides an equal weight for each of the two mentioned factors in probability calculations. Similarly to Problem 1, the nodes with an assigned burst state B constitute the bursty subgraphs.

2.3 Weighted graphs

We can consider scenarios where the underlying graphs are weighted and social ties (influences) between various pair of individuals have different weights. We note that our models and algorithms still apply on weighted graphs; the generalization is pretty straightforward. In the intrinsic burst model, we need to substitute $\lambda_{s_{v_i}s_{v_j}}$ with $\lambda^{w_{ij}}$ (instead of λ) if $s_{v_i} = s_{v_j}$ and with $(1-\lambda)^{w_{ij}}$ (instead of $1-\lambda$) if $s_{v_i} \neq s_{v_j}$. Here w_{ij} is the weight of the edge between v_i and v_j. Similarly, in the social burst model, we use $\lambda^{w_{ij}}$ instead of λ and $(1-\lambda)^{w_{ij}}$ instead of $1-\lambda$ in Equations 1 and 2.

We utilize the same algorithms (Section 3) for identifying the burst state assignment S on the weighted graphs. Note that the time complexity of the algorithms does not change when we incorporate weights.

3. ALGORITHMS

We address Problem 1 in Section 3.1 and Problem 2 in Section 3.2. We commence with providing a polynomial algorithm to identify the optimal solution of Problem 1 (Section 3.1.1). Although optimal, the complexity can be an issue with large social graphs. Thus, we offer a simplified version of problem 1 in Section 3.1.2 and present a linear algorithm ($\mathcal{DIBA}$) in Section 3.1.3 that optimally solves it. Section 3.2 addresses the social burst detection problem (Problem 2) with suggesting an iterative algorithm ($\mathcal{SODA}$) to solve it (Section 3.2).

3.1 Intrinsic burst detection

3.1.1 The optimal solution

The optimal solution for Problem 1 can be obtained by establishing the equivalence between this problem and the well-known Min Cut problem.

THEOREM 1. *Problem 1 is equivalent to identifying the minimum s-t cut (the Min Cut problem [4]) on weighted graphs.*

For the sake of saving space, we remove the complete proof and content ourselves with the proof sketch.

PROOF SKETCH. Problem 1 can be transformed to associating graph's vertices with a burst state $\mathcal{S}$ such that

$$cost = -\log(P(S|G)) = \sum_{i=1}^{|V|} \log \frac{1}{f_{s_{v_i}}(v_i)} + \sum_{(v_i,v_j)\in E} \log \frac{1}{\lambda_{s_{v_i}s_{v_j}}}$$

is minimized. We provide a bi-directional reduction between Problem 1 and the Min Cut problem.

Assume $G = (V, E)$ is the underlying graph of Problem 1 and $N = (V', E')$ is the graph (flow network) for the Min Cut problem.

Reducing Problem 1 to Min Cut: Problem 1 can be reduced to an instance of the Min Cut problem. The reduction is as follows:

1. For each node $u \in V$, a node u' is added in V'.
2. A source s and a sink t are added to V'.
3. A directed edge is added from the source s to each node $u' \in V'$ with a capacity of $w'_{su'} = \log(\frac{1}{f_{\mathtt{N}}(u)}) > 0$.
4. A directed edge is added from each node $u' \in V'$ to the sink t with a capacity of $w'_{u't} = \log(\frac{1}{f_{\mathtt{B}}(u)}) > 0$.
5. For each pair of neighboring nodes $(u, v) \in E$, two directed edges are added to E' between their corresponding nodes (u', v') with a capacity of $w'_{u'v'} = w_{uv}\log(\frac{\lambda}{1-\lambda}) > 0$.

The cost of the minimum cut identified on N' is equal to the cost of the optimal burst state assignment on G.

Reducing Min Cut to Problem 1: Having the flow network $N = (V', E')$, we create a graph $G = (V, E)$ as follows:

1. For each vertex $u' \in V' - \{s, t\}$ (all nodes except the source s and the sink t), there is a vertex $u \in V$.
2. For each vertex $u \in V$, set $0 < f_{\mathtt{B}}(u) = \frac{1}{\exp(w'_{u't})} < 1$ and $0 < f_{\mathtt{N}}(u) = \frac{1}{\exp(w'_{su'})} < 1$.
3. For each edge $(u', v') \in E'$ (where $u' \neq s$ and $v' \neq t$), add an edge (u, v) in E with the weight $w_{uv} = w'_{u'v'}$.
4. Set $\lambda = \frac{e}{1+e}$.

The cost of the optimum burst state assignment in G is equal to the minimum cut in N'. □

To solve Problem 1, the reduction proposed in the proof of Theorem 1 is utilized to create an instance of Min Cut problem. We can employ the Ford-Fulkerson algorithm [4], Edmonds-Karp algorithm [3], Preflow-Push algorithm or its efficient implementations (Preflow-Push algorithm with FIFO vertex selection rule, Preflow-Push algorithm with dynamic trees) [6] to determine the minimum cut of the created flow network N. Among these algorithms, the most efficient one for sparse graphs (e.g., social networks) is Preflow-Push algorithm with dynamic trees that has a time complexity of $O(|V|\times|E|\times log(|V|^2/|E|))$. After running these algorithms, the network will be divided into two partitions, one containing the source s and the other containing the sink t. We label all nodes in the partition containing the source s as bursty B and all nodes in the other partition as non-bursty N.[1]

[1]We note that a similar approach has been used in image processing domain to solve a problem that attempts to distinguish whether each pixel of a given image belongs to foreground or background [7].

3.1.2 Simplifying the problem

The above algorithm is not practical for very large graphs such as social network graphs. Every day about 30 million unique Twitter users send about 350 million tweets. The corresponding action/holistic graphs are large, making the previously mentioned algorithm impractical. Therefore, we need strictly faster algorithms.

Instead of maximizing the transition probability over all edges, Problem 1 can be simplified by attempting to maximize the transition probability on the edges that are the most likely ones to achieve the smallest transition probabilities (edges that reduce the overall probability of $P(\mathcal{S}|G)$ the most).

PROBLEM 3. *Assign burst states $\mathcal{S} = (s_{v_1}, ..., s_{v_{|V|}})$ to maximize*

$$P(\mathcal{S}|G) = (\prod_{i=1}^{|V|} f_{s_{v_i}}(v_i)) \times (\prod_{i=1}^{|V|} \lambda_{s_{v_i^*} s_{v_i}})$$

where

$$v_i^* = \underset{\substack{v_j: \\ (v_i,v_j)\in E, \\ v_j < v_i}}{\arg\max}\ \psi_{v_i v_j} \tag{3}$$

Here, $\psi_{v_i v_j} = |(f_{\mathtt{B}}(v_i) - f_{\mathtt{N}}(v_i)) - (f_{\mathtt{B}}(v_j) - f_{\mathtt{N}}(v_j))|$ and $v_j < v_i$ means that v_j happens prior to v_i. For nodes v_i with no predecessor, we set $\lambda_{s_{v_i^*} s_{v_i}} = 1$.

The node v_i^*, for each node $v_i \in V$, is a neighboring node such that the probability that it's burst state is different from the burst state of v_i is the maximum among all neighboring nodes of v_i that are prior to v_i. To determine what nodes are prior to others, an ordering between members of V should be defined. In the action graph, the timestamp of nodes can be adopted to make an ordering. In the holistic graph, we can utilize any arbitrary (e.g., random) ordering between vertices.

Problem 3 is equivalent to maximizing

$$\log(P(\mathcal{S}|G)) = \sum_{i=1}^{|V|} \log(f_{s_{v_i}}(v_i)) + \sum_{i=1}^{|V|} \log(\lambda_{s_{v_i^*} s_{v_i}})$$

3.1.3 $\mathcal{DIBA}$: Dynamic programming Intrinsic Burst detection Algorithm

Let $G = (V, E)$ be an action/holistic graph. We aim to distinguish the bursty subgraphs of G according to Problem 3. $\mathcal{DIBA}$ starts by creating a forest $\mathcal{F}$ (a disjoint union of trees) out of G: for each connected component of G, $\mathcal{DIBA}$ identifies a spanning tree. The spanning trees are created by considering v^* (defined in Problem 3) as the parent of each node $v \in V$. The union of these spanning trees create the forest $\mathcal{F}$.

$\mathcal{DIBA}$ examines vertices of $\mathcal{F}$ starting from the leaves, going up to the roots. For any leaf l, $LP(\mathtt{B}|l) = \log(f_{\mathtt{B}}(l))$ and $LP(\mathtt{N}|l) = \log(f_{\mathtt{N}}(l))$ are calculated. Here, for each leaf l, $LP(\mathtt{B}|l)$ is the logarithm of the probability to have the burst state B and $LP(\mathtt{N}|l)$ is the logarithm of the probability to have the burst state N. Moreover, f is the exponential/binomial probability density function. The algorithm, afterwards, traverses the trees of $\mathcal{F}$ bottom-up to reach the roots. For each non-leaf node v, we define and calculate

$$LP(\mathtt{B}|v) = \log(f_{\mathtt{B}}(v)) + \sum_{u\in C(v)} \max(LP(\mathtt{B}|u) + \log(\lambda), LP(\mathtt{N}|u) + \log(1-\lambda)), \tag{4}$$

and

$$LP(\mathtt{N}|v) = \log(f_{\mathtt{N}}(v)) + \sum_{u\in C(v)} \max(LP(\mathtt{B}|u) + \log(1-\lambda), LP(\mathtt{N}|u) + \log(\lambda)), \tag{5}$$

where $C(v)$ is v's children set.

For each tree $\mathcal{T}$ in the forest $\mathcal{F}$, the burst state assignment, $\mathcal{S}_{\mathcal{T}}$, is the chain of burst states for $\mathcal{T}$'s nodes maximizing the value of "$\max(LP(\mathtt{B}|r_{\mathcal{T}}), LP(\mathtt{N}|r_{\mathcal{T}}))$" where $r_{\mathcal{T}}$ is the root of the tree $\mathcal{T}$. The burst state assignment $\mathcal{S}$ is the union of all $\mathcal{S}_{\mathcal{T}}$ for each tree component $\mathcal{T}$ of forest $\mathcal{F}$.

Algorithm 1: $\mathcal{DIBA}$

input : Graph $G = (V, E)$
output: burst state assignment $\mathcal{S} = (s_{v_1}, ..., s_{v_{|V|}})$

// Create a forest $\mathcal{F}$ from G
foreach $v \in V$ **do**
  $parent(v) = v^*$ // Eq. 3
end
// Probability calculations
Traverse $\mathcal{F}$ bottom-up (from leaves to roots):
foreach $v \in V$ **do**
  $\mathtt{B}_v = \log(f_{\mathtt{B}}(v)) + \sum_{u\in C(v)} \max(\mathtt{B}_u + \log(\lambda), \mathtt{N}_u + \log(1-\lambda))$;
  $\mathtt{N}_v = \log(f_{\mathtt{N}}(v)) + \sum_{u\in C(v)} \max(\mathtt{B}_u + \log(1-\lambda), \mathtt{N}_u + \log(\lambda))$;
  $BPointer_v = \arg\max(\mathtt{B}_v + \log(\lambda), \mathtt{N}_v + \log(1-\lambda))$;
  $NPointer_v = \arg\max(\mathtt{B}_v + \log(1-\lambda), \mathtt{N}_v + \log(\lambda))$;
end
foreach *root* $r \in V$ **do**
  $s_r = \arg\max(\mathtt{B}_r, \mathtt{N}_r)$;
end
Traverse $\mathcal{F}$ top-down (from roots to leaves):
foreach $v \in V$ **do**
  $s_v = NPointer_v$;
  if $s_{v^*} =$ "B" **then**
    $s_v = BPointer_v$;
  end
end

The pseudo code of $\mathcal{DIBA}$ is provided in Algorithm 1. Note that in this algorithm, $\mathtt{B}_v$ represents $LP(\mathtt{B}|v)$ (Equation 4) and $\mathtt{N}_v$ represents $LP(\mathtt{N}|v)$ (Equation 5). The variable $BPointer_v$ holds the optimum burst state assignment to node v (an assignment leading to the maximum value of $P(\mathcal{S}|G)$) when the burst state assigned to its parent (v^* in Equation 3) is bursty B. Similarly, $NPointer_v$ is the optimal burst state assigned to v when the parent's assigned burst state is non-bursty N. Moreover, the function "$\arg\max(a, b)$" declares what argument (a or b) has the maximum value. Formally it returns B (bursty) if $a > b$ and returns N (non-bursty) otherwise. At the end of the algorithm, s_v contains the assigned burst state of node $v \in V$.

THEOREM 2. *$\mathcal{DIBA}$ discovers the optimal burst state assignment according to Problem 3 for a graph G.*[2]

THEOREM 3. *The run time of $\mathcal{DIBA}$ on a graph $G = (V, E)$ is $T(G) = \theta(|V| + |E|)$ that is linear in size.*

3.2 Social burst detection

Problem 2 can be represented by a set of $2n$ polynomial equations with $2n$ variables: the variables are $P(\texttt{B}|v_i)$ and $P(\texttt{N}|v_i)$ and the equations are Equations (1), and (2) for each $v_i \in V$. Since discovering the solution for a polynomial equation system is NP-hard [5], we propose an iterative algorithm in Section 3.2.1 to identify the burst state assignment $\mathcal{S}$.

3.2.1 $\mathcal{SODA}$: SOcial burst Detection Algorithm

$\mathcal{SODA}$ is an iterative algorithm to address Problem 2. The goal is to locate the closest values s_{v_i} to $\frac{P(\texttt{B}|v_i)}{P(\texttt{N}|v_i)}$ for each $v_i \in V$ (to minimize the value of $\mathcal{D}$).

By dividing equations 1 and 2 and substituting $\frac{P(\texttt{B}|v_i)}{P(\texttt{N}|v_i)}$ with s_{v_i}, the following equation holds:

$$s_{v_i} = \frac{f_{\texttt{B}}(v_i)}{f_{\texttt{N}}(v_i)} \times \prod_{v_j:(v_i,v_j)\in E} \left(\frac{s_{v_j}\lambda + (1-\lambda)}{s_{v_j}(1-\lambda)+\lambda}\right)^{1/n_i}$$

$\mathcal{SODA}$ initializes the s_{v_i} variables as follows:

$$s^0_{v_i} = f_{\texttt{B}}(v_i)/f_{\texttt{N}}(v_i)$$

In the kth iteration, the algorithm updates the variables' values according to Equation (6).

$$s^k_{v_i} = s^0_{v_i} \times \prod_{v_j:(v_i,v_j)\in E} \left(\frac{s^{k-1}_{v_j}\lambda + (1-\lambda)}{s^{k-1}_{v_j}(1-\lambda)+\lambda}\right)^{1/n_i} \qquad (6)$$

We assume that the convergence is accomplished when $distance = \sum_{i=1}^{|V|}(s^k_{v_i} - s^{k-1}_{v_i})^2 < \epsilon$. In all of our experiments, $\mathcal{SODA}$ converges in a very small number of iterations, usually around 10 for action graphs and 20 for holistic graphs.

The pseudo code of $\mathcal{SODA}$ is presented in Algorithm 2. When this algorithms terminates, the variable s_v holds the assigned burst state of node v.

THEOREM 4. *The run of $\mathcal{SODA}$ on a graph $G = (V, E)$ is $T(G) = \theta(|V|+|E|)\times I$ where I is the number of iterations till convergence achieved.*

4. EXPERIMENTAL RESULTS

To evaluate our algorithms, we use a dataset consisting of 30 days of the Twitter fire hose (May 15, 2012 – June 13, 2012). Each day contains between 300 – 400 million tweets. This dataset is about 25 TB on disk.

Section 4.1 explains how the graph models are created. The results on the run time of all proposed algorithms are presented in Section 4.2 and qualitative results of their output are discussed in Section 4.3.

The algorithms were coded in Java and were evaluated on a computer with 16 cores 2.4GHz (AMD Opteron^{TM} Processor 850) with 100G of memory that is running CentOS 5.5 with kernel version 2.6.18-194.11.1.el5. All algorithms are single-threaded.

[2]Hereafter, we remove all proofs to save space.

Algorithm 2: $\mathcal{SODA}$

```
input : Graph G = (V, E)
output: burst state assignment S = (s_{v_1}, ..., s_{v_|V|})
foreach v ∈ V do
    s^0_v = f_B(v)/f_N(v);
end
K = 0;
distance = Infinity;
while distance ≥ ε do
    k = k + 1;
    s^k_v = s^0_v × ∏_{u:(v,u)∈E} ((s^{k-1}_u λ+(1−λ))/(s^{k-1}_u (1−λ)+λ))^{1/n_v};
    distance = ∑_{v∈V} (s^k_v − s^{k-1}_v)^2;
end
foreach v ∈ V do
    s_v = s^k_v;
end
```

Topic	Queries (ignoring case)
Fire	contains("highparkfire" or "high park fire")
Prix	contains("grandprix" or "grand prix")
Tennis	contains("djokovic" or " nadal " or "#nadal")
Euro 2012	contains("euro2012" or "euro 2012" or "eufa")
Debate 2012	contains("debate2012" or "yosoy132" or "#epn" or "#amlo" or "#quadri" or "#jvm" or "#amlopresidente" or "#marchantiepn")

Table 1: Topics and the associated queries.

4.1 Topics, Modeling, and Parameter Setting

We evaluate our algorithms on 5 popular topics on Jun 10, 2012. These topics are: (1) "Colorado high park fire", (2) "the grand prix race", (3) "French Open 2012 tennis final match between Rafal Nadal and Novak Djokovic", (4) "Euro 2012", and (5) "Mexico Presidential TV debate on June 10". Table 1 presents these topics and the queries used to retrieve the relevant tweets. A tweet is considered as relevant if it matches the corresponding query.

To evaluate the algorithms, we create the action graph and the holistic graph for each of these topics. In the action graph, any relevant tweet is a vertex. The number of relevant tweets varies from about 10 thousand for the "Fire" topic to about 1.1 million for the "Debate 2012" topic. To add edges between the vertices, the sender-recipient information of replies (tweets containing "@" sign) has been utilized. An edge (a, b) is added, in the action graph, between nodes a and b if: a is the value of the "`in_reply_to_status_id`" attribute in the JSON object of b or *(1)* action "b" is in reply to a user" u" (i.e., "@u" exists in the tweet's text of action "b"), and *(2)* "a" corresponds to the last relevant action conducted by user "u" prior to the occurrence of "b".

For the holistic graph, we employ Twitter's social graph created based on one month of tweets. We note that there exist about 27.5 million users in this social graph who tweeted at least once in Jun 10, 2012 (nodes of the holistic graph). Moreover, these users are connected with more than 1.5 billion edges.

In the following experiments, we set the parameters $\lambda = 0.8$ and $\alpha = \gamma^*/\gamma = 2$. Recall that λ is the probability to keep the current burst state in the assumed automaton and α is the increase in the action generation rate for

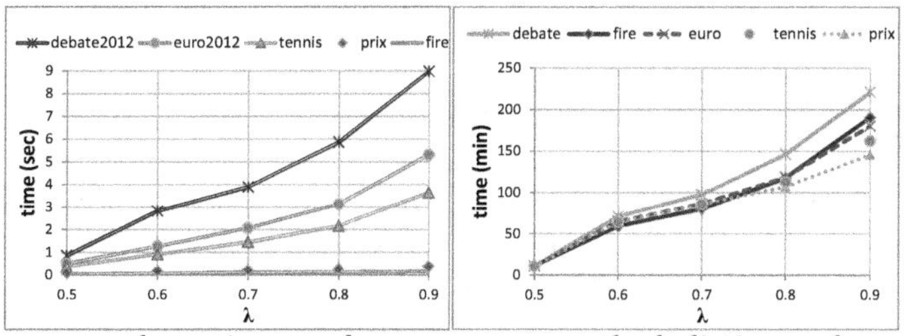

the action graph the holistic graph

Figure 1: The impact of changing λ on the run time of $\mathcal{SODA}$

the bursty state over the non-bursty state. We will analyze how things change when the values of these parameters alter (Sections 4.2 and 4.3.2).

4.2 Time Analysis

There are three parameters that our burst detection algorithms depend on: *(1)* the parameter λ, *(2)* the rate ratio α, and *(3)* the dataset size. This section analyzes how varying these parameters affects the execution time of the algorithms.

Execution time vs λ: Our experiments show that the run time of $\mathcal{DIBA}$ does not depend on the value of λ (as predicted by Theorem 3).

Figure 1 displays how the run time of $\mathcal{SODA}$ increases as λ ascends from 0.5 to 1. When $\lambda = 0.5$, a node is indifferent to the burst state of the neighboring nodes. Thus, the burst state of each node u solely depends on its intrinsic probability ($f_{\mathtt{B}}(u)$ to be bursty, or $f_{\mathtt{N}}(u)$ to be non-bursty). Hence, $\mathcal{SODA}$ converges in the first iteration. When we move farther from 0.5, the dependency to neighbors intensifies. Hence, as the values of burst states continuously change, $\mathcal{SODA}$ needs more iterations to converge and takes more time.

Execution time vs α: Our experiments validate Theorem 3 and show that the run time of $\mathcal{DIBA}$ does not depend on the value of α.

As Figure 2 depicts, initially when α ascends on action graphs, the run time of $\mathcal{SODA}$ grows. Further increase in α , however, reduces the run time. After a certain point, the run time remains unchanged when additional increments take place. As a matter of fact, the run time of $\mathcal{SODA}$ depends on the number of iterations performed and this relates to the number of pairs of neighbors in the graph with different burst states. When $\alpha = 1.1$, many nodes are recognized as non-bursty; hence $d = |(number\ of\ nonbursty\ nodes) - (number\ of\ bursty\ nodes)|$ is large. When α increases, d decreases resulting in a growth in the number of neighboring pairs with non-matching states. Augmenting α further increases d;[3] hence the number of the mentioned pairs reduces; correspondingly the number of iterations required and the associated run time decline.

On the holistic graph, the run time of $\mathcal{SODA}$ remains constant when α raises. In fact, $\mathcal{SODA}$ identifies a big fraction of nodes in holistic graphs as non-bursty (d holds a very big value).[4] Altering α does not have a significant impact

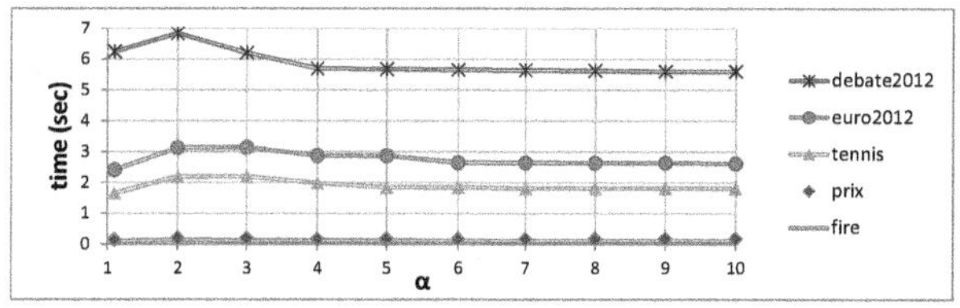

Figure 2: The impact of changing α on the run time of SODA on action graphs.

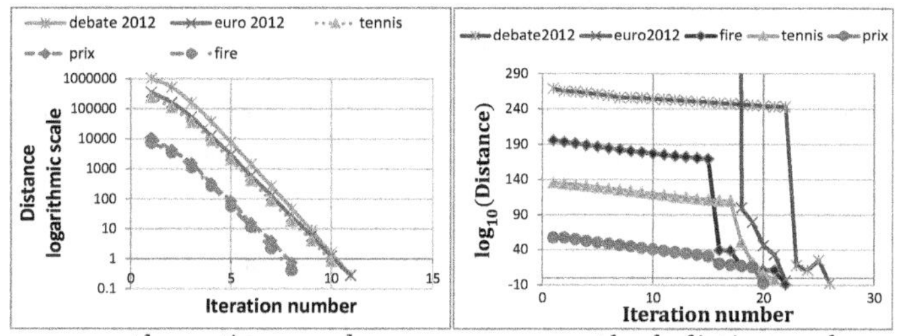

the action graph the holistic graph

Figure 4: The convergence of $\mathcal{SODA}$

on d; hence, the number of iterations (and correspondingly run time) does not change.

Execution time vs graph size: The linear relation between the run time and the graph size is depicted in Figure 3(a)-(b) for $\mathcal{DIBA}$, and (c)-(d) for $\mathcal{SODA}$ on action/holistic graphs. Here, size is sum of the number of nodes and edges in the graph. In the action graph, we measure the size of the graph and the run time of the algorithms for each topic. Note that all topics share the same holistic graph (the only difference is in nodes' weights). Thus, to evaluate the impact of changing holistic graph size on the run time, we run the algorithms on the smaller subsets of this fixed underlying graph and report the average run time (over all topics) for each subset. We note that both algorithms run in seconds on the action graphs; on the holistic graph, $\mathcal{DIBA}$ takes about 3 minutes and $\mathcal{SODA}$ takes about 2 hours in average.

Convergence: In this section, we study how $\mathcal{SODA}$ converges. Note that as $\mathcal{DIBA}$ is not iterative, convergence is not defined there. The $\mathcal{SODA}$ algorithm converges when the distance between the identified solution at the end of the last iteration and the identified solution at the end of its previous iteration is smaller than some threshold. Here, we use a Euclidean distance function. If $S^k = (s_1^k, \ldots, s_n^k)$ is the solution (burst state assignment) at iteration k, we define the distance between iteration k and iteration $k-1$ solutions as $distance = \sum_{i=1}^{n}(s_i^k - s_i^{k-1})^2$. $\mathcal{SODA}$ continues until $distance < 1$. Figure 4 shows that distance declines exponentially as we perform more iterations.

4.3 Qualitative Results

There are two main differences between the subgraphs identified on action graphs and the subgraphs identified on holistic graphs. Firstly, the algorithms on holistic graphs identify bursty users. On action graphs, however, since the algorithms assign burst states to each single action, the output indicates which users with what actions at what

[3]Section 4.3.2 studies the impact of altering α on the number of bursty/non-bursty nodes.

[4]Note that for the discussed topics, more than 26 million users (among 27 million users) have not tweeted about the specified topic ($r_i = 0$) and are non-bursty. The balance between the number of bursty and non-bursty nodes is much better in action graphs, as these graphs are built up on relevant actions.

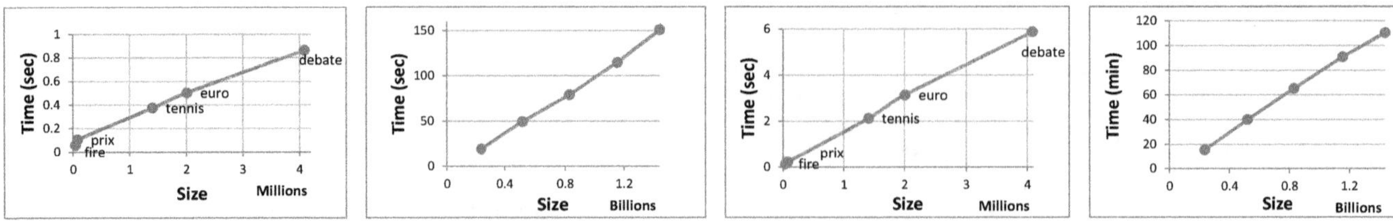

(a) DIBA on action graph (b) DIBA on holistic graph (c) SODA on action graph (d) SODA on holistic graph

Figure 3: The impact of changing size on the run time of DIBA and SODA.

times are bursty. This helps to find out why and based on what actions, a user is considered bursty. Moreover, we can clearly state at what specific times a user was active or inactive. Secondly, the algorithms on the holistic graphs identify subgraphs that are bursty in the whole time interval under analysis. On the action graphs, however, besides these subgraphs, the algorithms can identify subgraphs that are temporarily bursty. We sometimes observe a bunch of continuously arriving actions about some specific topic that disappear as time passes. These actions may have a high rate of generation in a subset time interval but the rate may continuously decreases afterwards. We may see a low rate of generation if we look at these actions cumulatively for the whole time interval hence report them as non-bursty. Analyzing arriving documents with action graphs helps us to detect these temporal bursty subgraphs.

Our observations suggest that the main difference between the top bursty subgraphs identified by DIBA and SODA is that, for a given topic, DIBA locates collections (usually small in size) of highly bursty users who continuously tweet about some topic; while SODA is capable of finding much larger collections of connected users who are bursty as a whole but may contain some nodes that are not bursty if we look at them individually. Since in reality, we similarly see that not all members of an active physical group progressively execute actions (e.g., tweet) on a specified topic, the subgraphs identified by SODA better match with these groups.

In this section, we take a closer look at the top subgraphs identified by the proposed algorithms on the topics discussed in Section 4.1 in order to qualitatively understand the "goodness" of the results. For each case, we retrieve all subgraphs and rank them according to their size (Section 4.3.1). We follow by a demonstration on how the results change when we utilize different parameter values (Section 4.3.2).

4.3.1 Bursty subgraphs

By manually inspecting the subgraphs identified for different topics, we found them meaningful. Here, we choose to report the detected subgraphs for 2 topics ("grand prix" and "high park fire") in detail. Other topics are omitted to save space.

Among the 10 top subgraphs of running SODA for "grand prix" on the action graph, we can find a group of car race fans in different countries talking about the Canadian formula1 grand prix and Pocono 400. Pocono 400 is a "NASCAR Sprint Cup Series stock car race held annually at Pocono Raceway in Long Pond, Pennsylvania".[5] We note that both Canadian formula1 grand prix and Pocono 400 took place on Jun 10, 2012. The other subgraph is created around a joke by the famous spanish driver of the Italian car manufacturer Ferrari "Fernando Alonso" who achieved the 3rd rank in the Canadian grand prix. Fernando said: "If we [Spain] win [in the Spain vs Italy soccer match in euro 2012 happening simultaneously], then maybe I might find there are not too many people on hand to change my tires at the pit stop.!"[6] It is very interesting to note that other subgraphs represent other grand prix matches that happened on the same day on other parts of world. There exist 2 subgraphs of Brazilian volleyball websites and citizens supporting their team in the Brazil vs Poland match for volleyball FIVB world grand prix. Two subgraphs represent Dominican Republic citizens discussing the Dominican Republic vs USA match in Women volleyball grand prix 2012 worldcup. We note that in the larger subgraph (with a size of 813 actions), members mostly live in Santa Domingo the capital of Dominican Republic. Another subgraph contains citizens of Thailand talking about Thailand vs China match on the FIVB grand prix. Two subgraphs contain Indian citizens and Indonesian citizens discussing the victory of "Saina Nehwal", the Indian female winner, and "Sony Dwi Kuncoro", the Indonesian male winner of the Thailand Open Grand Prix Gold badminton tournament. Finally, the last subgraph is composed of Turkish citizens discussing the victory of the Turkish motorcycle racer "Kenan Sofuoglu" in the Supersport world championship's San Marino grand prix event. We note that all of the mentioned races happened on Jun 10, 2012.

When SODA is run on the holistic graph to detect top subgraphs of "grand prix", we notice two differences. First, it does not output any subgraph related to Alonso's joke in Canadian grand prix. The reason is that the mentioned subgraph is bursty in a subset of time not the whole day. Therefore, the action graph shows it as bursty while the holistic graph recognize it as a less bursty event (not in the top ten list). Second, just one subgraph of Brazilian citizens is detected talking about the volleyball grand prix (note that SODA finds two subgraphs in the action graph). In fact, in the action graph, these two subgraphs are separate while in the holistic graph that we incorporate social ties between individuals, these subgraphs are merged. Instead of these two subgraphs, we observe other bursty subgraphs related to the "CSI show jumping grand prix" (qualifying Olympics 2012 games) and "Kazan FIDE Women Chess Grand Prix" both held on June 10.

The top bursty subgraphs detected by running SODA for the "high park fire" topic on action/holistic graphs also rep-

[5] http://en.wikipedia.org/wiki/Pocono_400

[6] http://www.fernandoalonso.com/en/category/fernando-alonso

resent meaningful physical groups. To save space, we report the two top subgraphs. The top subgraph is a collection of Colorado news channels, journalists, nature and animal activists (mostly in Denver, CO). These include "9NEWS Denver", "Denver Channel", "North Forty News" to name a few. The second subgraph is a collection of members of Calvary Chapels churches in some cities of Colorado (e.g., Aurora, CO; Castle Rock, CO) concerned about the impacts of fire.

On the other hand, $\mathcal{DIBA}$ generally locates subgraphs where all users are bursty. For the "high park fire" topic, top subgraphs can be summarized to news networks, active bloggers, and some subgraphs of Colorado residents. For "Grand Prix", top subgraphs are car news networks, and car race lovers. We note that the top subgraphs identified by $\mathcal{DIBA}$ include less than 40 members.

4.3.2 The impact of parameter values on the final results

In this section, we study how modifying α and λ affects the burst state assignments by inspecting the number of identified bursty subgraphs, the size of the largest bursty subgraph, and the final number of bursty nodes for "Euro 2012" topic. We observe similar trends for other topics.

λ on $\mathcal{DIBA}$: Figure 5(a)-(b) displays that the number of bursty nodes and the size of the largest bursty subgraph decrease when $\mathcal{DIBA}$ runs on larger λ values. When λ grows, no change occurs in nodes' f_N and f_B values; however, the role of transition probabilities (providing smoothness in burst state transitions) intensifies in associating burst states. If the burst state of a node v and its parent v^* (Equation 3) is different, the cost of not changing those states increases when λ obtains a higher value. We note that $\mathcal{DIBA}$ identifies a large fraction of nodes in our dataset as non-bursty. Hence, to provide smooth transitions as a result of increasing λ, nodes aim to be non-bursty. Hence, we observe a decreasing trend in the number of bursty nodes and similarly the size of the largest subgraph when λ ascends.

α on $\mathcal{DIBA}$: According to Figure 5(c)-(d), the number of bursty nodes and the maximum size of bursty subgraphs enlarges when α grows to some point and it remains constant afterwards. When we increase α, the role of intrinsic probabilities (f_N and f_B values) intensifies in associating burst states of nodes. When α is small, there are nodes that are individually (according to f values) bursty but are declared as non-bursty and vice versa to provide smooth transitions. When we increase α, we achieve higher $P(S|G)$ values if for these nodes the burst state s_i matches with the individually assigned burst states (solely according to the values of f_N and f_B). As previously mentioned, $\mathcal{DIBA}$ originally has identified a large fraction of nodes in our dataset as non-bursty. Hence, the absolute number of nodes aiming to change state is higher in the (large) non-bursty fraction. Thus, overall, the number of newly announced as bursty nodes increases and accordingly the maximum size of the bursty subgraphs enlarges.

λ on $\mathcal{SODA}$: Figure 6(a) depicts the impact of λ on $\mathcal{SODA}$'s burst state assignment in action graphs. $\mathcal{SODA}$ determines burst states utilizing both intrinsic values and neighbors' influences. When we increase λ, there is more motivation for the neighbors of large (compact) bursty subgraphs to become bursty to match with their large number of bursty neighbors. Thus, the large subgraphs expand. On the other hand, in the small (sparse) bursty subgraphs, some members with many non-bursty neighbors are passionate to change their burst state to non-bursty to match with their neighbors. Therefore, we see some of these subgraphs break into several smaller ones. This results in a higher number of bursty components. Further enlargements of λ causes to make some small bursty subgraphs to totally disappear (all members eventually switch to the non-bursty state) and results in a reduction in the number of bursty components.

As discussed in Section 4.2, on holistic graphs, $\mathcal{SODA}$ identifies a large fraction of nodes as non-bursty. Thus, we see many relatively small (compared to the graph size) bursty subgraphs. When we raise λ, the smoothness in transitions becomes more important. Thus, the members of these small bursty subgraphs (of the holistic graph) start to change state to match with their non-bursty neighbors. Hence, the number of bursty nodes and the size of the largest bursty subgraph will eventually shrink (Figure 6(b)).

α on $\mathcal{SODA}$: To identify the optimal burst state assignment, $\mathcal{SODA}$ initializes s_i to $f_B(i)/f_N(i)$. Hence, in the action graphs, $s_i = \alpha \times e^{(1-\alpha)\gamma x}$. When α grows, two cases happen:

- $x_i \geq 1/\gamma$: the value of s_i decreases.
- $x_i < 1/\gamma$: as we increase α to $\frac{1}{x_i\gamma}$, s_i grows; further increments in α will reduce the value of s_i.

When α increases (to some point β), the large (compact) bursty subgraphs (containing many nodes with $x_i < 1/\gamma$) expand as the s_i value of the members raises and this affect the non-bursty neighbors due to the neighboring influences in $\mathcal{SODA}$. Thus the size of the largest bursty subgraph increases. Farther increments of α has a negative impact on bursty nodes by decreasing s_i values. Hence, we see a degradation happening in the maximum size of the bursty subgraphs. The concave diagram in Figure 6 (c) displays this behavior. Here $\beta = 3$. The same trend is seen for the number of bursty nodes. In the smaller bursty subgraphs with bigger x values, increasing α will result in reducing s_i values, recognizing some members as non-bursty, and breaking the subgraphs. Hence a slightly-increasing trend is seen in the number of bursty subgraphs.

On the holistic graph (Figure 6(d)), since the number of bursty nodes is considerably smaller than the size of the graph, enlarging α will end in lower s_i values for most of the nodes and this reduces the number of bursty nodes and the size of the largest bursty subgraph.

What values are appropriate? One important question here is that "what values should be chosen for parameters α and λ to run $\mathcal{DIBA}$ and $\mathcal{SODA}$?". Two goals are defined in assigning burst states: (1) for each node, the assigned state is in accordance with the time gap (x) or the fraction of relevant actions (r/d) and (2) smooth transitions are provided. The first goal would not be achieved if λ is too high (close to 1) or α is too low (close to 1). The second goal would not be satisfied when λ is too low (close to 0.5) or α is too high (according to Figures 5(c) and 6(c), in average the pick happens when α is close to 4). In fact, a value in the middle would be a good choice for both parameters. For this reason, setting λ to some value around 0.7-0.8 and α to 2-3 seems a reasonable choice.

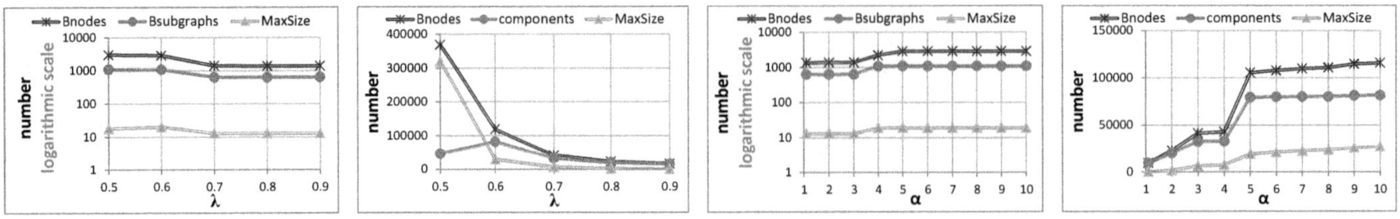

(a) action graph (b) holistic graph (c) action graph (d) holistic graph

Figure 5: The impact of changing parameters on $\mathcal{DIBA}$.

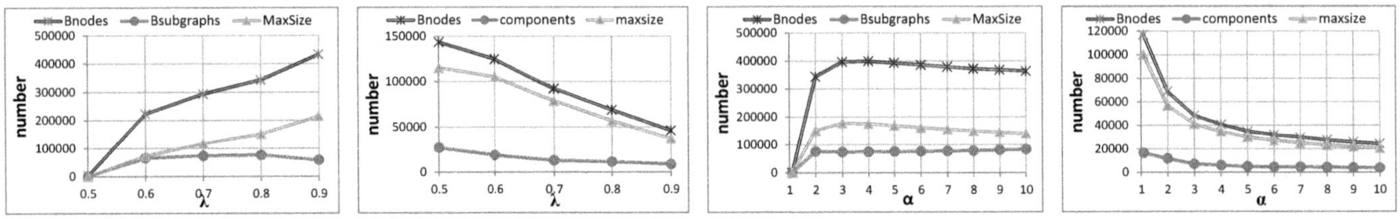

(a) action graph (b) holistic graph (c) action graph (d) holistic graph

Figure 6: The impact of changing parameters on $\mathcal{SODA}$.

5. RELATED WORKS

Identifying bursts of activity has been studied in time-series streams [9] and geographically-focused document collections [12]. Kleinberg [9] utilizes a multi-state automaton to associate time intervals with different levels of burst activity. Our intrinsic burst model is analogous to his approach. Mathioudakis et al. [12] adopt a 2-state automaton to identify spatial bursty regions in a 2D geographical grid. We generalize these works to identifying bursts of activity on social networks without restricting our methods to specific dimensions (e.g., time/geography or combinations thereof).

Burst detection has been also utilized in specific application contexts. Zhu and Shasha [16] proposed algorithms to detect gamma ray bursts in astrophysical data and trading activity bursts in stock exchange data. Kotov et al. [10] detect terms with correlated temporal bursts of mention counts in multiple text streams to recognize major and minor real life events and assist transliteration.

There are numerous recent works utilizing twitter data for research, including [1, 13–15]. Such works address problems orthogonal to ours such as influence identification, correlations between tweets and other data (e.g., stock-market events), personalized news recommendation, etc.

6. CONCLUSION

We proposed several models to characterize and identify information bursts in social networks and presented algorithms to identify bursty subgraphs. We evaluated our algorithms on real twitter data on the entire twitter fire hose. We also presented a quantitative and a qualitative analysis of our results. This work raises several research questions for future work. We are interested to explore applications of our techniques in the web search domain. For instance, we would like to devise a way to utilize the various subgraphs detected (e.g., bursty subgraphs related to various "grand prix" events) to address problems such as diversified search and query expansion. Moreover, we would like to utilize these subgraphs to assign temporal local reputation values to different users and publishers in the social web. Another avenue is to explore the relation between subgraphs' structures and their corresponding topics; i.e., how does the structure of the identified bursty subgraphs (ranging from chains to complete graphs) depend on the topic at hand? We are also interested to the dynamics of bursty subgraphs; i.e., how do these subgraphs evolve over time?

7. REFERENCES

[1] G. De Francisci Morales, A. Gionis, and C. Lucchese. From chatter to headlines: harnessing the real-time web for personalized news recommendation. WSDM, pages 153–162, 2012.

[2] P. Domingos and M. Richardson. Mining the network value of customers. SIGKDD, pages 57–66, 2001.

[3] J. Edmonds and R. M. Karp. Theoretical improvements in algorithmic efficiency for network flow problems. *J. ACM*, 19:248–264, 1972.

[4] J. Ford, L.R. and D. Fulkerson. Maximal flow through a network. *Canadian Journal of Mathematics*, 8:399–404, 1956.

[5] M. R. Garey and D. S. Johnson. *Computers and Intractability; A Guide to the Theory of NP-Completeness*. W. H. Freeman & Co., New York, NY, USA, 1990.

[6] A. V. Goldberg and R. E. Tarjan. A new approach to the maximum-flow problem. *J. ACM*, 35(4):921–940, 1988.

[7] D. M. Greig, B. T. Porteous, and A. H. Seheult. Exact maximum a posteriori estimation for binary images. *Journal of the Royal Statistical Society. Series B*, 51:271–279, 1989.

[8] D. Kempe, J. Kleinberg, and E. Tardos. Maximizing the spread of influence in a social network. SIGKDD, pages 137–146, 2003.

[9] J. Kleinberg. Bursty and hierarchical structure in streams. SIGKDD, pages 91–101, 2002.

[10] A. Kotov, C. Zhai, and R. Sproat. Mining named entities with temporally correlated bursts from multilingual web news streams. WSDM, pages 237–246, 2011.

[11] C. X. Lin, B. Zhao, Q. Mei, and J. Han. Pet: a statistical model for popular events tracking in social communities. SIGKDD, pages 929–938, 2010.

[12] M. Mathioudakis, N. Bansal, and N. Koudas. Identifying, attributing and describing spatial bursts. *VLDB Endowment*, 3(1-2):1091–1102, Sept. 2010.

[13] A. Pal and S. Counts. Identifying topical authorities in microblogs. WSDM, pages 45–54, 2011.

[14] E. J. Ruiz, V. Hristidis, C. Castillo, A. Gionis, and A. Jaimes. Correlating financial time series with micro-blogging activity. WSDM, pages 513–522, 2012.

[15] J. Weng, E.-P. Lim, J. Jiang, and Q. He. Twitterrank: finding topic-sensitive influential twitterers. WSDM, pages 261–270, 2010.

[16] Y. Zhu and D. Shasha. Efficient elastic burst detection in data streams. SIGKDD, pages 336–345, 2003.

Sharding Social Networks

Quang Duong*
Google
qduong@google.com

Sharad Goel*
Microsoft Research
sharadg@microsoft.com

Jake Hofman*
Microsoft Research
jmh@microsoft.com

Sergei Vassilvitskii*
Google
sergeiv@google.com

ABSTRACT

Online social networking platforms regularly support hundreds of millions of users, who in aggregate generate substantially more data than can be stored on any single physical server. As such, user data are distributed, or sharded, across many machines. A key requirement in this setting is rapid retrieval not only of a given user's information, but also of all data associated with his or her social contacts, suggesting that one should consider the topology of the social network in selecting a sharding policy. In this paper we formalize the problem of efficiently sharding large social network databases, and evaluate several sharding strategies, both analytically and empirically. We find that random sharding—the de facto standard—results in provably poor performance even when frequently accessed nodes are replicated to many shards. By contrast, we demonstrate that one can substantially reduce querying costs by identifying and assigning tightly knit communities to shards. In particular, our theoretical analysis motivates a novel, scalable sharding algorithm that outperforms both random and location-based sharding schemes.

Categories and Subject Descriptors

H.2.4 [**Information Systems**]: Database Management—*Systems*; F.2.0 [**Theory of Computation**]: Analysis of Algorithms and Problem Complexity—*General*

Keywords

community detection, sharding, social networks

1. INTRODUCTION

As the popularity of online social networks grows, it becomes increasingly challenging to maintain scalable data infrastructures. In particular, the amount of uploaded user content, including photos, videos, and status messages, far exceeds the storage capacity of any single machine, and thus user data must necessarily be distributed, or sharded, across hundreds or even thousands of servers.

Rapidly retrieving these data poses a particularly challenging problem, as one must support billions of queries each day while balancing latency against memory and bandwidth constraints. The difficulty of the retrieval task is compounded by the fact that users often require access not only to their own data, but also to that of all their social contacts. Such neighborhood queries are the key ingredient in generating popular, personalized user feeds—which present activities from a user's social circle after filtering for recency and relevance—and thus exert considerable strain on existing database systems.

This paper addresses the problem of sharding social networks so as to efficiently execute such neighborhood queries. A simple and oft-used sharding strategy is to randomly assign users to shards. At a high level, however, there are two near-universal features of social networks that suggest one can do substantially better. First, social networks generally contain densely connected communities of users. By ensuring tightly knit clusters of users are assigned to the same shard, one might greatly reduce the number of shards accessed per query. Second, a relatively small number of "locally popular" users (i.e., those that are frequently queried by certain communities) account for a disproportionally large number of shard accesses. Neighborhood queries might thus be further optimized by replicating local celebrities to the appropriate shards, analogous to maintaining a cache of frequently accessed resources. By leveraging these properties, network-aware sharding strategies offer the potential for considerable gains over the alternatives.

Several recent papers have in fact demonstrated the benefits of sharding network data based on correlated access patterns. Karagiannis et al. [8] deploy and evaluate Hermes, an optimization engine for large-scale enterprise email services in which observed communication data are analyzed to co-locate user data based on the implicit social graph. Such co-location reduces storage costs as senders and receivers of an email can access the same physical version of the message, obviating the need for each to keep separate local copies. Agarwal et al. [1] detail and analyze a similar system, Volley, for placing data across geo-distributed servers. Like Hermes, Volley is based on an implicit network extracted from access logs, and the system is shown to considerably reduce storage and bandwidth requirements relative to a baseline strategy of placing resources close to their primary requesters. Similarly, SPAR, a system developed

*Work done while author was at Yahoo! Research

WSDM'13, February 4–8, 2013, Rome, Italy.

by Pujol et al. [13] is designed to facilitate strict co-locality requirements in online social networks—where a user and all its neighbors must reside on the same server—and the objective is to minimize the number of necessary shards.

Past work has approached network-aware sharding from an almost exclusively empirical perspective, focusing on both storage and bandwidth. Here we formalize the problem as minimizing average load across shards, and both derive analytic results and present empirical evaluations. We show that in graph models with strong community structure, random shardings, though the de facto industry standard, are far from optimal and lead to provably worst-case performance. In contrast, by simply mapping communities in these networks to shards, one can greatly reduce the average load exerted by neighborhood queries.

As we show, finding optimal network-aware sharding strategies is an NP-complete problem. Our theoretical analysis, however, motivates a novel, scalable method for community detection, which can in turn be used to lower sharding costs.[1] We validate our approach on two large web-scale datasets, and find that average query load is more than halved relative to random sharding. On the one dataset for which geographic information is available, we further find that network sharding improves on location-aware sharding strategies. The large decrease in average load, however, comes at the expense of creating hotspots (i.e., shards with much higher-than-average loads), particularly in the case of networks with extreme degree skew. We address this problem by replicating, or caching, a relatively small number of local celebrities to shards, a technique that has the additional benefit of reducing average load.

Roadmap. We proceed by formally defining the problem in Section 2, and then proving that random sharding is a poor strategy for minimizing the average load in Section 3. To motivate alternate sharding strategies, we review the stochastic block model for network structure in Section 4 and show that significantly better shardings exist for networks following this model (Theorem 6). After showing that networking sharding is NP-complete in Section 4.3, we develop an algorithm for efficiently sharding large networks in Section 5. We evaluate this method experimentally on two large real-world networks in Section 6, and conclude by discussing open questions in Section 7.

2. PROBLEM STATEMENT

Before formally defining the network sharding problem, we introduce some notation. Let $G = (V, E)$ be a directed graph with $n = |V|$ nodes and $m = |E|$ edges. Let $N(i) = \{j : (i,j) \in E\}$ denote the neighborhood of the i-th node, and $d_i = |N(i)|$ its degree. For convenience we will denote by $N^+(i) = \{i\} \cup N(i)$ the set consisting of the neighborhood of the i-th node and the node itself. For $S, T \subseteq V$, where the subsets are not necessarily disjoint, let $E(S,T) = E \cap (S \times T)$ be the set of edges from S to T. We abbreviate $E(\{i\}, T)$ as $E(i,T)$ and $E(S, \{j\})$ by $E(S,j)$.

Given a graph G, our goal is to cover the n nodes of G with T potentially overlapping sets $S_1, S_2, \ldots, S_T$. We refer to each of these sets as a *shard*, and insist that each shard contain at most M nodes. Semantically, each shard corresponds to the subset of G stored on an individual machine.

[1] Ugander and Backstrom [16] concurrently and independently developed a similar network sharding strategy.

We refer to the collection of shards, $\mathcal{S} = \{S_1, \ldots, S_T\}$, as a *sharding*. We note that if $M \cdot T = n$, the shards are necessarily disjoint; otherwise let $\rho = MT/n > 1$ define the *replication ratio*, which characterizes the level of node duplication in the system.

As described in the introduction, the goal of the system is to support an efficient execution of *neighborhood queries*, queries that retrieve a node i together with all of its neighbors. We refer to the set of all such neighborhood queries as a *query plan* $\mathcal{Q}$, formally defined by a set of indices e_{ij} that indicate where to access node j when executing a neighborhood query for node i:

$$\mathcal{Q} = \{e_{ij}\} \quad 1 \le i \le n, \; j \in N^+(i), \; e_{ij} \in \{1, \ldots, T\}.$$

A query plan is valid for a sharding $\mathcal{S}$ if the nodes are retrieved from shards on which they actually reside (i.e., $j \in S_{e_{ij}}$). For settings without replication ($\rho = 1$), a sharding corresponds to a unique query plan in which nodes access neighbors on their respective shards. When nodes are replicated ($\rho > 1$), however, there are many valid query plans corresponding to a given sharding.

From a query plan it is easy to generate a compatible sharding (i.e., a sharding for which the query plan is valid). Namely, a node is assigned to a given shard if and only if at least one neighborhood query expects to find it there:

$$S_t = \left\{ j \;\middle|\; t \in \bigcup_{i : j \in N^+(i)} \{e_{ij}\} \right\}. \tag{1}$$

We thus consider a query plan to be valid if the induced shards satisfy the capacity constraints $|S_t| \le M$.

In practice, the overall performance of a query plan depends on several factors, including the cost of database accesses, the latency of network connections, and the total network bandwidth consumed. A simple abstraction of these performance metrics is the average query load across shards (i.e., the number of queries processed per unit time per shard). Let λ_i be the rate at which node i queries the system. Denote by $L_{i,t}(\mathcal{Q})$ the load induced by user i on shard t under query plan $\mathcal{Q}$:

$$L_{i,t}(\mathcal{Q}) = \begin{cases} \lambda_i, & \text{if } t \in \bigcup_{j \in N^+(i)} \{e_{ij}\} \\ 0, & \text{otherwise} \end{cases}$$

Then the average load per shard is:

$$\text{load}(\mathcal{Q}) = \frac{1}{T} \sum_{t=1}^{T} \sum_{i=1}^{n} L_{i,t}(\mathcal{Q}). \tag{2}$$

In our analysis, it is helpful to consider the average load generated per user (i.e., the average number of shards accessed per user), which we call the *cost* of a query plan:

$$\text{cost}(\mathcal{Q}) = \frac{1}{n} \sum_{i=1}^{n} \sum_{t=1}^{T} L_{i,t}(\mathcal{Q}). \tag{3}$$

Note that the two measures are scalar multiples of each other as $\text{load}(\mathcal{Q}) = \frac{n}{T}\text{cost}(\mathcal{Q})$. Minimizing cost is thus equivalent to minimizing load, and so we switch between the two formulations as convenient. For simplicity in our presentation we assume that $\lambda_i = \lambda$ for all i (i.e., that all users query the system at the same, constant rate), but note that the results extend to the heterogeneous user setting as well.

We are now ready to formally state the NETWORKSHARDING problem.

PROBLEM 1 (NETWORKSHARDING). *Given a graph G, the total number of shards, T, and a per shard capacity constraint M, find a valid query plan $\mathcal{Q}$ with minimal cost.*

3. RANDOM SHARDING

Under our cost metric the worst one can do is to access a node and each of its neighbors on distinct shards, in which case the cost is approximately the average network degree. As we show below, this is exactly what occurs when one employs the common strategy of randomly assigning nodes to shards regardless of network structure. Theorem 2 formalizes this result, showing that even with substantial replication random sharding leads to near worst-case performance.

THEOREM 2. *Let G be a graph with $n \geq 2$ nodes, and let $T, M \geq 1$ be integers such that $TM \geq n$. Consider a random sharding of G into T shards with capacity M chosen uniformly from all shardings that fill each shard to capacity, and let Q denote an optimal query plan compatible with that sharding. Then if $\rho = TM/n$ is the replication ratio, the expected cost of Q satisfies*

$$\frac{1}{n}\sum_{i=1}^{n} d_i - \frac{\rho M}{n} \cdot \frac{1}{n}\sum_{i=1}^{n} d_i^3 \leq \mathbb{E}\left[cost(\mathcal{Q})\right] \leq 1 + \frac{1}{n}\sum_{i=1}^{n} d_i \quad (4)$$

where d_i is the degree of node i.

Before proving the theorem, we make two observations. First, given a sharding, generating an optimal compatible query plan is in general an NP-complete problem. In particular, it requires solving a set cover problem for each node and its neighbors. Nevertheless, we show that this optimal query plan is necessarily poor when the sharding is chosen uniformly at random. Second, suppose d_i is $O(\log n)$ and the replication ratio is as high as $O(n^{1/2})$. Then even for very high memory capacities—for example, $M = O(n^{1/2-\epsilon})$—we still find that random sharding leads to near worst-case performance.

PROOF. The upper bound follows trivially, since in the worst case each node must access its neighbors and itself in $d_i + 1$ different shards. Likewise, if $M = 1$ then each node must choose different shards for each neighbor, and if $M > n$ then the left-hand side of (4) is negative, so the lower bound holds in these degenerate cases.

To establish the lower bound for $2 \leq M \leq n$, fix a node i, and consider the probability that i has at least two neighbors in the t-th shard, S_t. Applying the union bound over all pairs of i's neighbors, we have

$$\begin{aligned}\mathbb{P}(|N(i) \cap S_t| \geq 2) &\leq \binom{d_i}{2}\binom{n-2}{M-2}\Big/\binom{n}{M} \\ &\leq d_i^2\frac{M(M-1)}{n(n-1)} \leq \left(\frac{d_iM}{n}\right)^2.\end{aligned}$$

Consequently, the probability that i has at most a single neighbor in any of the T shards is at least

$$1 - T\left(\frac{d_iM}{n}\right)^2 = 1 - \frac{\rho M d_i^2}{n}.$$

In this case, i must access at least d_i shards, and the result follows. □

4. A THEORETICAL ANALYSIS OF NETWORK SHARDING

Even when a graph has substantial community structure, Theorem 2 above shows that random shardings, perhaps unsurprisingly, perform poorly at neighborhood queries. In contrast, as we show below, network-aware strategies can perform considerably better when sharding social networks.

4.1 Model Description

Our formal analysis is based on stochastic block model (SBM) networks [7], a simple yet widely used family of networks with community structure. In these models, nodes belong to one of K communities, or blocks, and the probability of an edge between any two nodes depends only on their corresponding block assignments. Specifically, the generative process for a network with n nodes and K blocks is as follows: for each node i, independently roll a K-sided die with bias $\vec{\pi}$ to determine the node's block assignment $z_i \in \{1, \ldots, K\}$; for each ordered pair of nodes (i, j), flip a coin with bias θ_+ (resp. θ_-) for nodes in the same (resp. different) blocks to determine if a directed edge exists from i to j. Formally, for an SBM with parameters $\vec{\pi}$ and $\vec{\theta}$, the marginal distributions for block assignments z_i and edges indicated by A_{ij} are:

$$p(z_i = k|\vec{\pi}) = \pi_k \quad (5)$$

$$p(A_{ij} = 1|z_i, z_j, \vec{\theta}) = \begin{cases} \theta_+ & \text{if } z_i = z_j \\ \theta_- & \text{if } z_i \neq z_j \end{cases}, \quad (6)$$

where $0 < \theta_\pm < 1$, $0 < \pi_k < 1$, and $\sum_{k=1}^{K} \pi_k = 1$.

Networks generated under this model may loosely be characterized as a mixture of Erdos-Renyi networks, with an edge density θ_+ within blocks and θ_- between. In the assortative case ($\theta_+ > \theta_-$), nodes tend to form more edges within than between their blocks, resulting in dense "communities."

4.2 Analysis

Despite their simplicity, stochastic block models capture one of the most salient features of social networks, namely the tendency of individuals to cluster into communities. Moreover, these models immediately illustrate the potential savings from network-aware sharding strategies. By assigning all nodes in a block to the same shard, a node need only access a single shard to retrieve all its in-block neighbors. Thus, in the worst case, nodes only access different shards for each of their out-of-block neighbors, leading to a total cost approximately equal to the average out-of-block degree. In contrast, Theorem 2 shows that the expected cost of a random sharding of this network—in fact, of any network—is approximately the average degree, which is generally substantially larger than the average out-of-block degree.

While the naive sharding strategy of assigning blocks to shards offers considerable gains over a random sharding, one might reasonably wonder if there is further structure embedded in these networks that one can exploit. Theorem 6 below shows that in fact there is not, that the best one can do is to simply leverage the first-order structure of these graphs. While this result is quite believable, rigorously establishing its validity requires a detailed understanding of the structure of Erdos-Renyi graphs.

We proceed by first establishing in Theorem 4 that Erdos-Renyi graphs have no discernible structure one can exploit for sharding. This result follows from an observation by

Bollobás [3] that Erdos-Renyi graphs do not contain large, isolated sets of nodes (Theorem 3). Then, by considering SBMs as a mixture of Erdos-Renyi graphs of different densities, Theorem 6 shows that SBMs are best partitioned by assigning blocks to shards.

THEOREM 3 (BOLLOBÁS [3]). *Suppose $\delta = \delta(n)$ and $D = D(n)$ satisfy $\delta pn \geq 3\log n$, $D \geq 3\log(e/\delta)$ and $D\delta n \to \infty$. Then for every $\epsilon > 0$, $\exists N$ such that for $n \geq N$ and $G \sim G(n,p)$, G satisfies the following property with probability at least $1-\epsilon$: For every $U \subseteq V$ with $|U| = \lceil D/p \rceil$ the set*

$$T_u = \{x \in V \setminus U \mid N(x) \cap U = \emptyset\}$$

has at most δn elements.

Theorem 3 shows that in most Erdos-Renyi graphs, every suitably large set contains a neighbor of most nodes in the network. Importantly, it is not only the case that most large sets are well-connected to the rest of the network, but that in *most graphs, every large set* is well-connected. It is this subtle distinction that constitutes the primary difficulty in establishing the result.

Theorem 4 below recasts the Bollobás result as a statement about sharding, and can be seen as an analog of Theorem 2. Whereas the former result established that completely random *shardings* lead to poor performance, the latter shows that completely random *graphs* can not be efficiently sharded.

THEOREM 4. *Suppose $p = p(n)$ satisfies $p \geq (6\log n)/n$. Then for every $\epsilon > 0$, $\exists N$ such that for $n \geq N$, $G \sim G(n,p)$, and positive integers T, M with $TM = n$, the cost of an optimal query plan $\mathcal{Q}$ satisfies*

$$c_0 \min(T, np) \leq cost_{opt}(\mathcal{Q}) \leq c_1 \min(T, np) \tag{7}$$

with probability $1-\epsilon$, where $c_0 = 1/50$ and $c_1 = 3$.

REMARK 5. *By assuming $TM = n$ in Theorem 4, we exclude the possibility of nodes residing on multiple shards. That is, the result pertains to a traditional sharding in which nodes are partitioned, but not replicated, across machines.*

PROOF. We start with the upper bound. The cost of any query plan is trivially at most $\min(T, \bar{d}+1)$, where $\bar{d}$ is the average degree of G. This value is well concentrated, and a Chernoff bound argument shows that:

$$\mathbb{P}\left(\bar{d} > 2\cdot\mathbb{E}[\bar{d}]\right) \leq \left(\frac{e}{4}\right)^{\mathbb{E}[\bar{d}]} \leq \left(\frac{e}{4}\right)^{(n-1)p} \leq \left(\frac{e}{4}\right)^{5\log n} \leq \frac{1}{n}.$$

Hence, $\mathbb{P}\left(\bar{d} \leq 2np\right) \geq 1-\epsilon/2$ for sufficiently large n, establishing the upper bound.

For the lower bound, suppose $\mathcal{S}$ is a sharding $(S_1, \ldots, S_T)$ of G. Since we assume $TM = n$, $\mathcal{S}$ necessarily partitions the nodes of G, and so there is a unique compatible query plan, which we denote by $\mathcal{Q}$. Since G is undirected, node i accesses the t-th shard if and only if $i \in N(S_t)$ (i.e., if i has a neighbor in S_t). Thus, if $I_A(i)$ indicates whether i is in the set of nodes A, $\text{cost}(\mathcal{Q}) =$

$$\frac{1}{n}\sum_{i=1}^{n}\sum_{t=1}^{T} I_{N(S_t)}(i) = \frac{1}{n}\sum_{t=1}^{T}\sum_{i=1}^{n} I_{N(S_t)}(i) = \frac{1}{n}\sum_{t=1}^{T}|N(S_t)|.$$

In other words, the cost of the query plan can be expressed as the sum of the sizes of each shard's neighborhood.

We next apply Theorem 3 to show that every suitable large node set has a large neighborhood. Specifically, take $\delta = 1/2$ and $D = 6$ in Theorem 3. Then for n sufficiently large and almost all graphs $G \sim G(n,p)$, any vertex set U of size $\lceil 6/p \rceil$ has $|T_U| \leq n/2$. Therefore:

$$|N(U)| \geq n - |U| - \frac{n}{2} \geq \frac{n}{2} - \frac{n}{\log n} \geq \frac{n}{3} \tag{8}$$

where the last inequality follows by taking $n \geq e^6$.

To finish the proof, we consider two cases. First suppose $M \geq \lceil 6/p \rceil$, that the machines have relatively high memory. Then by (8), for almost all graphs G and any sharding S of G, each shard has $|N(S_t)| \geq n/3$. Summing over shards, we have $\text{cost}(\mathcal{Q}) \geq T/3$. So, when memory is high (and thus there are relatively few shards), nodes tend to access a constant fraction of the shards. Alternatively, suppose that the machines have small capacity, that $M < \lceil 6/p \rceil$. In this case, consider the union U of $\lceil \lceil 6/p \rceil / M \rceil$ distinct shards, which, as above, must necessarily have a large neighborhood. Moreover,

$$\sum_{\{t \mid S_t \subseteq U\}} |N(S_t)| \geq |N(U)| \geq \frac{n}{3}. \tag{9}$$

That is, the neighborhood sizes of the constituent shards sum to be relatively large. Finally, the number of such disjoint shard groupings one can form is

$$\left\lfloor \frac{T}{\lceil \lceil 6/p \rceil / M \rceil} \right\rfloor \geq \frac{np}{6+p+Mp} - 1 \geq \frac{np}{14} - 1.$$

Thus, by (9), $\text{cost}(\mathcal{Q}) \geq \frac{np}{42} - 1 \geq \frac{np}{50}$ for n sufficiently large. □

As shown in Theorem 4, Erdos-Renyi graphs do not contain any subtle structure that permits efficient sharding. Using this fact, Theorem 6 demonstrates that SBMs are optimally partitioned by assigning nodes in a block to the same shard. For simplicity we assume the blocks, instead of having binomial size, are of fixed size n/K, and moreover, that the SBM network is undirected.

THEOREM 6. *Suppose $\theta_+(n) \geq \theta_-(n) \geq (6\log n)/n$. Then for every $\epsilon > 0$, $\exists N$ such that for $n \geq N$, $K \geq 2$ an integer, G an undirected SBM graph with blocks of size exactly n/K, and positive integers T, M with $M \geq n/K$ and $TM = n$, the cost of an optimal (G, T, M)-query plan $\mathcal{Q}$ satisfies*

$$c_0 \min(T, n\theta_-) \leq cost_{opt}(\mathcal{Q}) \leq c_1 \min(T, n\theta_-) \tag{10}$$

with probability $1-\epsilon$, where $c_0 = 1/50$ and $c_1 = 3$.

PROOF. Without loss of generality, we assume that nodes are numbered so that ones in the same community are adjacent. For the upper bound, consider the sharding $\mathcal{S}$ in which the first M nodes are placed into the first shard, the second set of M nodes are put into the second shard, and so on. Since communities, which have size n/K, are by assumption smaller than the shards, this sharding results in each community being spread over at most two shards. Consequently, for the unique compatible query plan $\mathcal{Q}$,

$$\text{cost}(\mathcal{Q}) \leq 2 + \frac{1}{n}\sum_{i=1}^{n}|N_-(i)| \tag{11}$$

where $N_-(i)$ is the set of i's neighbors outside of its block. To bound the sum in (11), note that

$$\mathbb{E}\left[\sum_{i=1}^{n} N_-(i)\right] = n^2\frac{K-1}{K}\theta_-,$$

since each of the $n^2(K-1)/2K$ inter-community edges is present with probability θ_- and appears in the sum once from the perspective of each endpoint. Since the probability of each edge being present is independent of the rest, an application of Chernoff bounds allows us to conclude that:

$$\mathbb{P}\left(\frac{1}{n}\sum_{i=1}^{n}|N_-(i)| \leq 2n\theta_-\right) \leq \left(\frac{e}{4}\right)^{n^2\frac{K-1}{K}\theta_-} \leq \left(\frac{e}{4}\right)^{n\log n}$$

Thus, for n sufficiently large, $\text{cost}(\mathcal{Q})$ is bounded by $3n\theta_-$ with probability at least $1-\epsilon/2$. To complete the upper bound, we note that trivially $\text{cost}(\mathcal{Q}) \leq T$.

For the lower bound, starting with G define the (random) graph $\hat{G}$ by independently deleting each intra-community edge with probability $1-\theta_-/\theta_+$. Let $\mathcal{Q}$ and $\hat{\mathcal{Q}}$ denote optimal query plans for G and $\hat{G}$, respectively, Since we only delete edges in constructing $\hat{G}$, $\text{cost}(\mathcal{Q}) \geq \text{cost}(\hat{\mathcal{Q}})$. Moreover, any given intra-community edge is independently present in $\hat{G}$ with probability $\theta_+(\theta_-/\theta_+) = \theta_-$. Since inter-community edges are likewise independently present with probability θ_-, we have $\hat{G} \sim G(n, \theta_-)$. Consequently, by Theorem 4, for n sufficiently large,

$$\begin{aligned}
&\mathbb{P}\left(\text{cost}(\mathcal{Q}) \geq c_0 \min(T, n\theta_-)\right) \\
&\quad \geq \mathbb{P}\left(\text{cost}(\hat{\mathcal{Q}}) \geq c_0 \min(T, n\theta_-)\right) \geq 1 - \frac{\epsilon}{2}
\end{aligned}$$

which completes the proof. □

4.3 Optimal sharding

The preceding analysis suggests that when sharding networks, one should map tightly knit communities to shards. In practice, however, this task is complicated by the fact the we observe only the network, not the community assignments. As we show below, finding an optimal solution to the NETWORKSHARDING problem is in fact NP-complete.

THEOREM 7. *The* NETWORKSHARDING *problem is NP-complete.*

PROOF. The proof is by reduction from the 3-partition problem [5]: Given a set A of $3T$ elements, a bound $B \in \mathbb{Z}^+$, and an integral size w_a for each element $a \in A$ with $B/4 \leq w_a \leq B/2$, find a partition of A into disjoint sets $A_1, \ldots, A_T$ such that for each set i, $\sum_{a \in A_i} w_a = B$. We assume the sum of the weights B is bounded by a polynomial in T—the problem remains hard under this constraint.

From any instance of the 3-partition problem, consider the following instance of the NETWORKSHARDING problem. Associate a clique $G_a = (V_a, E_a)$ on $|V_a| = w_a$ nodes with every element $a \in A$. Then let the network G be the union of the individual cliques, $G = (\cup_a V_a, \cup_a E_a)$; and set the number of shards to T, each with capacity B.

We claim that there is a 3-partition of A iff the cost of the optimal sharding is exactly 1. Suppose first that there is a 3-partition of A into $A_1, \ldots, A_T$ as above. Then a valid sharding is obtained by setting $S_t = \cup_{a \in A_t} V_a$, the capacity constraint is satisfied, and the sharding cost is 1, since all of the neighbors of a node are stored on the same shard.

Conversely, suppose there is a sharding of G with cost 1. It must be the case that each clique G_i is assigned fully to one shard. Thus we can set $A_t = \{a_j : G_j \in S_t\}$. The capacity constraints imply that $\sum_{a \in A_j} w_a = B$ and hence this is a valid 3-partition of A. □

5. A NETWORK SHARDING ALGORITHM

In developing a practical method for network sharding, we are motivated by our key analytic result: stochastic block model networks are optimally sharded by assigning blocks to shards. Accordingly, in the first stage of our algorithm we attempt to infer the block structure of the network, taking a Bayesian approach to the problem. Importantly, even though real-world networks only loosely conform to SBMs, in practice this first step nevertheless partitions social networks into densely connected communities. In the second stage, these inferred blocks are mapped to shards in a way that both respects memory constraints and that takes advantage of any second-order structure in the network. Namely, while the blocks in true SBM networks are simply randomly connected, real-world networks often exhibit between-block structure that can be leveraged to lower sharding costs. In the third and final step, we replicate frequently accessed nodes across shards to further reduce sharding cost and to reduce hotspots among the shards.

5.1 Block inference

Though there is a large literature on community detection, few of the developed methods scale to networks with millions of nodes and billions of edges. In this section we introduce a scalable framework for inferring community structure consistent with our analysis of stochastic block models. Roughly, the algorithm proceeds with nodes iteratively updating their community assignments via a weighted, discounted vote over their neighbors' memberships. Notably, we show that as a special case this technique includes label propagation [14], one of the only existing methods for inferring communities in very large networks. Before discussing this previously unknown connection, we review the work presented in Hofman and Wiggins [6].

The block model presented in Section 4 provides a means of generating random networks with local structure (i.e., blocks). In particular, given parameters for block assignments $\vec{\pi}$ and edge probabilities $\vec{\theta}$, the model specifies the probability $p(\mathbf{A}, \vec{z}|\vec{\theta}, \vec{\pi})$ of observing a network $\mathbf{A}$ with realized block assignments $\vec{z}$. Now, given a network $\mathbf{A}$ one can ask which parameter choices likely generated it. In Bayesian terms, we would like to compute the posterior distribution over parameters

$$p(\vec{z}, \vec{\theta}, \vec{\pi}|\mathbf{A}) = \frac{p(\mathbf{A}, \vec{z}|\vec{\theta}, \vec{\pi})p(\vec{\theta}, \vec{\pi})}{p(\mathbf{A})}, \tag{12}$$

where $p(\vec{\theta}, \vec{\pi})$ quantifies our prior beliefs about parameter values, and $p(\mathbf{A})$ is the marginal likelihood of observing the network under this prior. Unfortunately, however, exact calculation of the normalizing constant $p(\mathbf{A})$ requires summing over all possible block assignments $\vec{z}$, rendering computation of the posterior intractable. Moreover, even if one could compute this posterior, determining the most probable posterior block assignment for a given node again requires iterating through the entire space of possible assignments.

This computational difficulty motivates the variational mean-field approach presented in Hofman and Wiggins [6], a method that performs well in a number of inference tasks [2]. Variational methods facilitate such calculations by rephrasing the inference problem as an optimization over a constrained family of distributions. Although these methods only yield an approximately best assignment of nodes to blocks, they are highly scalable as we explain below.

In applying variational inference, we search for a fully factorized distribution

$$q(\vec{z}, \vec{\pi}, \vec{\theta}) = \left[\prod_{i=1}^{N} q_{z_i}(z_i)\right] q_{\vec{\theta}}(\vec{\theta}) q_{\vec{\pi}}(\vec{\pi}) \tag{13}$$

that is close to the true posterior under the Kullback-Leibler (KL) divergence $D_{KL}[q||p] \equiv \sum_x q(x) \ln \frac{q(x)}{p(x)}$, an (asymmetric) measure on distributions. To find a minimizing function q, we rewrite the divergence as follows:

$$D_{KL}\left[q(\vec{z}, \vec{\pi}, \vec{\theta}) || p(\vec{z}, \vec{\theta}, \vec{\pi} | \mathbf{A})\right] = F_{\mathbf{A}}[q] + \ln p(\mathbf{A}), \tag{14}$$

where

$$F_{\mathbf{A}}[q] = -\mathbb{E}_{q(\vec{z}, \vec{\pi}, \vec{\theta})}\left[\ln \frac{p(\mathbf{A}, \vec{z}, \vec{\pi}, \vec{\theta})}{q(\vec{z}, \vec{\pi}, \vec{\theta})}\right] \tag{15}$$

is termed the variational free energy. Consequently, for a fixed network $\mathbf{A}$, minimization of the free energy $F_{\mathbf{A}}[q]$ is equivalent to minimization of the KL divergence. Furthermore, the expectation in the free energy $F_{\mathbf{A}}[q]$ is by construction taken over a fully factorized distribution, yielding a tractable objective function. In particular, approximate minimization of the free energy can be achieved by iterative coordinate descent over the factors in Equation (13), a procedure guaranteed to find a local optimum of $F_{\mathbf{A}}[q]$. The resulting algorithm—termed variational Bayes—is an extension of expectation-maximization (EM), involving iterative updates of the variational distributions over parameters and block assignments until convergence in the free energy.

Upon convergence, variational Bayes provides an approximate distribution over block assignments for each node. Moreover, as this distribution is fully factorized, we can compute the most probable block assignment for each node. Unfortunately, in the large-scale network setting of interest here, the inference algorithm of Hofman and Wiggins [6] cannot be directly applied. For example, simply storing these distributions in memory is prohibitive: with 10 million nodes and 10,000 blocks, the required storage exceeds that of most commodity machines. To scale variational inference to networks of this size and to complete the connection with traditional label propagation, we dispense with storing the full distributions $q_{z_i}(z_i)$ and instead calculate only the most probable node assignment z_i for each node, known as max-product inference [2].

This modification, while relatively simple, admits an intuitive reinterpretation of approximate Bayesian inference for stochastic block models as a framework for generalized label propagation. The procedure, detailed in Algorithm 1, proceeds as follows: in the "E-step", each node takes a discounted vote over its neighbors' block assignments to determine an updated block assignment; and in the "M-step", the weights J, J' and $\vec{h}$ determining these discounts are updated via expectations over the variational distributions on $\vec{\theta}$ and $\vec{\pi}$. As shown in the Appendix, these expectations are easily calculated as functions of the estimated block sizes and the edge counts within and between blocks. In the limiting case where blocks are assumed to be of uniform size, no discounting is applied and we recover conventional label propagation. The algorithm, termed VBLabelProp, has a low memory footprint—linear in the number of nodes and edges in the network—and its runtime scales linearly with the number of edges.

Algorithm 1 VBLabelProp

Randomly initialize the block assignments $\vec{z}$

repeat

  Estimate the variational distributions $q_{\vec{\theta}}$ and $q_{\vec{\pi}}$ based on the current block sizes and edge counts within and between blocks

  Compute the expected weights J, J', and h:

  $J \leftarrow \mathbb{E}_{q_{\vec{\theta}}}\left[\ln \frac{\theta_+(1-\theta_-)}{\theta_-(1-\theta_+)}\right]$

  $J' \leftarrow \mathbb{E}_{q_{\vec{\theta}}}\left[\ln \frac{1-\theta_-}{1-\theta_+}\right]$

  $\vec{h} \leftarrow \mathbb{E}_{q_{\vec{\pi}}}\left[\ln \frac{1}{\vec{\pi}}\right]$

  Update each node's community assignment by a discounted vote over its neighbors' assignments:

  for $i = 1 \rightarrow N$ **do**

    $z_i \leftarrow \underset{k}{\operatorname{argmax}}\ Jw_k - J'(n_k - \delta_{z_i,k}) - h_k$

    where $w_k = |E(i, B_k)| + |E(B_k, i)|$ is the total number of in and out edges between the i-th node and block $B_k = \{i \mid z_i = k\}$

  end for

until convergence in $F_{\mathbf{A}}[q]$

5.2 Partitioning Blocks

Community detection algorithms such as VBLabelProp provide a means for identifying tightly knit groups of nodes in a network. As discussed in Section 4, by storing these nodes on the same shard we greatly reduce the number of shards accessed when querying a node's neighbors. In practice, however, mapping communities to shards is non-trivial, as the largest communities in a social network can substantially exceed the available capacity of any single machine. Moreover, while Theorem 6 shows that SBMs have no second order structure one can exploit for sharding, in real-world networks we expect there is some gain to be had by intelligently placing well-connected blocks on the same shard. As such, we present BlockShard, a greedy method for assigning blocks to shards that maintains a low sharding cost.

The inputs to BlockShard include the network adjacency matrix $\mathbf{A}$, the inferred communities $\mathcal{B}$ (e.g., as produced by VBLabelProp), and the maximum shard capacity M. The output is a mapping from nodes to shards, with each node appearing only on a single shard, which consequently induces a unique compatible query plan.

The intuition behind BlockShard is to greedily map blocks to shards to minimize the current sharding cost. We start by allocating the largest block to the first shard and, if necessary, overflowing nodes to adjacent shards, filling each to capacity before moving to the next. Subsequent blocks are greedily selected to have highest average in-degree from the current, partially filled shard—or if the current shard is empty, the largest unallocated block is chosen. This condition may be interpreted as selecting the most "popular" block from the perspective of nodes currently allocated to the shard. If the block size exceeds remaining shard capacity, nodes within the selected block are ordered by their in-degree from the current shard and accordingly overflowed to adjacent shards.

Algorithm 2 BlockShard

Input $\mathbf{A}, \mathcal{B}, M, \mathcal{S}$
Sort blocks by decreasing size $|B_k|$
Start with the first shard: $S_t \leftarrow S_1$
while unallocated nodes **do**
  if current shard S_t is empty **then**
    Select the largest unallocated block B_k
  else
    Select the block with the largest average in-degree from shard S_t: $B_k \leftarrow \underset{B}{\operatorname{argmax}} \frac{1}{|B|}|E(S_t, B)|$
  end if
  Sort nodes $i \in B_k$ by decreasing in-degree $|E(S_t, i)|$ from shard S_t
  Place nodes in shards starting with S_t, overflowing to adjacent shards as needed
  Update S_t to the shard containing the last node allocated
end while

Pseudocode for BlockShard is given in Algorithm 2. An efficient implementation is achieved by maintaining an updatable heap over nodes, keyed by their in-degrees from the current shard. Runtime is then linear in the number of edges in the network, as desired for sharding large networks.

5.3 Replicating Nodes

When the total system capacity $M \cdot T$ exceeds the number of nodes n, utilizing excess memory to replicate data offers the potential benefits of decreasing the cost of reads and improving the system's overall fault tolerance. We quantify the amount of excess memory in the system via the replication ratio $\rho = TM/n \geq 1$, and present a simple method to add replication to any valid partitioning of nodes across shards—such as that produced by BlockShard.

One reasonable approach to replication is to simply copy the globally most accessed nodes to a reserved cache on each shard. While providing some improvement in performance, we opt for a variant of this strategy that considers the local structure of each shard, filling the cache with "locally popular" nodes on each shard. In particular, when using BlockShard to partition nodes, we first run the algorithm with an artificially lower shard capacity $M' = \lceil n/T \rceil$ to obtain a partial sharding. Then for each partially filled shard S_t, we rank nodes by their in-degree $|E(S_t, i)|$ from the shard, filling it with the most accessed nodes. Pseudocode for the replication scheme, NodeRep, is given in Algorithm 3.

To construct a valid query plan $\mathcal{Q}$ from the output of NodeRep, we avoid solving the costly set cover problem and instead build an index as follows. Consider the initial partitioning of nodes across shards (i.e., before replication) to define a node's primary shard. When executing a neighborhood query for node i, as many neighbors as possible are retrieved from i's primary shard, with the remaining ones fetched from their respective primary shards. In particular, a node only makes use of the cache on its primary shard. As we show below, this method of replication is particularly effective for heavily skewed degree distributions, achieving substantial reductions in both load and frequency of hotspots among shards.

Algorithm 3 NodeRep

Input $\mathbf{A}, \mathcal{S}, M$
for shard $S_t \in S$ **do**
  while current shard S_t is not full **do**
    Select a node current not in S_t with the largest in-degree $|E(S_t, i)|$ from shard S_t
    Replicate the selected node on shard S_t
  end while
end for

6. EMPIRICAL EVALUATION

We evaluate the performance of the network sharding method developed above on two large social network datasets, showing that this technique reduces average system load over both random sharding and sharding based on geography. We further find that even a small degree of node duplication offers large savings in cost for both random and network-aware shardings. We conclude with a discussion of the variance in load over shards introduced by network sharding.

6.1 Data

We examine two online social networks appropriate for the NetworkSharding problem, as both contain a large number of nodes and edges, and require queries over node neighborhoods. Specifically, we look at the blogging community LiveJournal and the microblog platform Twitter, in which individuals frequently access activity feeds constructed from their local neighborhood of contacts.

Our first dataset comes from a 2004 snapshot of LiveJournal [12], a free online community that allows members to maintain and share journals and blogs. The full network contains over 5.1 million nodes connected by more than 150 million directed edges that specify for each user a set of "friends" whose blogs or journals she "follows". In addition to the network structure, the dataset contains a subset of city, state, and country information for 3.1 million users. We restrict our attention to the network induced by the 1.6 million users for whom all three of these fields are specified. The second network we investigate is a publicly available snapshot of the Twitter social graph [10]. The snapshot, completed in July of 2009, contains more than 41 million user profiles and 1.4 billion directed edges connecting these profiles. Users post short status updates and subscribe to—or "follow"—other users to receive their updates.

6.2 Results

For both the LiveJournal and Twitter datasets, we compare random sharding to BlockShard+VBLabelProp, that is BlockShard with the underlying community structure inferred by VBLabelProp. As noted above, alternative community detection techniques [9, 4, 11, 15] can be substituted for VBLabelProp in the first stage of our network sharding approach. Thus for the moderately-sized LiveJournal network, we also evaluate sharding performance with METIS used in place of VBLabelProp for the community detection phase. Unfortunately, however, while past work has explored community detection on subsets of the Twitter network using such methods [15], memory requirements for METIS are prohibitive in considering the full Twitter network. Finally,

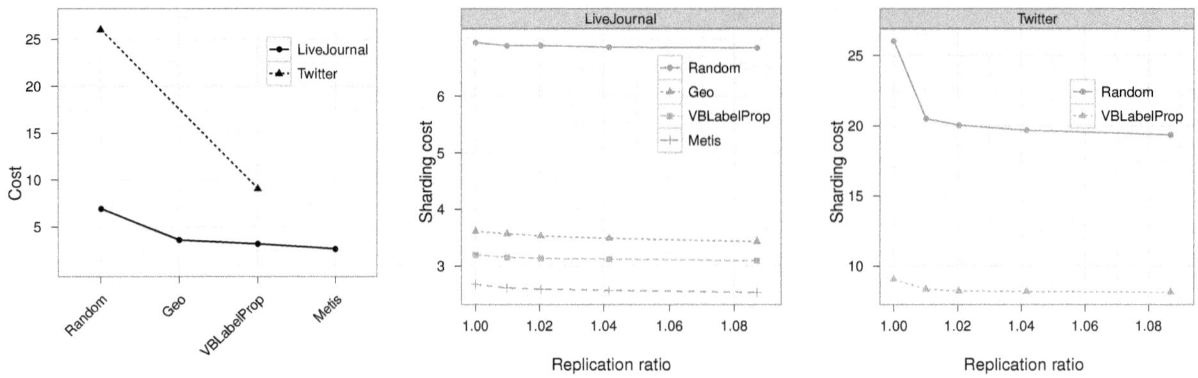

Figure 1: The left panel shows a cost comparison at zero replication. The center and right panels show variation in cost as replication is added to the system.

as geographic information is available for the LiveJournal network, we additionally compare the above methods to location-based sharding on that dataset. In particular, for the Geo baseline, we key each user by a concatenation of their country, state, and city, sort users by this key, and then vertically fill shards in this order.

For both networks we assume that each profile requires roughly 1MB of in-memory space and that shard storage is on the order of 40GB of RAM, leaving a capacity of roughly 40k nodes per shard. As a result, the LiveJournal network requires 50 shards and Twitter requires 1000, at zero replication ($\rho = 1.0$). We set the number of blocks for VBLabelProp to ten times the number of shards. All methods are evaluated in terms of average load and load balance, both with and without replication.

6.2.1 *Average load*

We first examine the average load, or equivalently, the sharding cost in the zero replication setting ($\rho = 1.0$). Figure 1 demonstrates that network-aware sharding offers a substantial reduction in cost over random sharding as well an improvement over geographic sharding. For example, randomly sharding LiveJournal results in an average access of 7 shards per query. While geographic sharding nearly halves this cost, network-aware shardings offer further improvements with VBLabelProp and METIS accessing 3.2 and 2.6 shards on average, respectively. Likewise, randomly sharding Twitter results in the average access of 26 shards per query, while VBLabelProp accesses 9 shards on average. In other words, network-aware shardings result in an approximately 60% reduction in average system load over Random. The observed difference between the two network-aware sharding methods for LiveJournal is likely due to the relatively balanced block sizes obtained by METIS, leading to more efficient allocation of blocks to shards.

Replication. Next we investigate performance when excess storage is used to accommodate popular nodes replicated by NodeRep. We vary the replication ratio ρ from 1.0 (zero replication) to 1.45 (45% replication) for all experiments and examine the relative and absolute changes in cost. Note that we consider "horizontal scaling," wherein an increase in ρ corresponds to an increase in the number of shards $T = T_0\rho$, while holding the capacity per shard M fixed.

Figure 1 shows the change in sharding cost for both LiveJournal (center) and Twitter (right) as we vary the replication ratio, with the points on the far left corresponding to the zero replication ($\rho = 1.0$) results in the left chart of Figure 1. Notably, a small amount of replication in random sharding (1%) for Twitter results in a large reduction in sharding cost (23%), which quickly asymptotes as replication increases further. That is, replicating even a small number of local celebrities to shards results in substantial gains. In contrast, random sharding for LiveJournal admits a relatively modest boost from replication. Intuitively these differences are due to the degree of skew in the two networks—while there is a relatively small population of highly popular celebrity accounts in Twitter, LiveJournal has a less heavy-tailed in-degree distribution.

Geographic and network-aware shardings also benefit from node replication, although to a lesser extent than Random, as these methods have already captured a substantial amount of network structure. Although omitted in the figure, as replication is increased beyond the point of $\rho = 1.09$, performance degrades for both methods: with a fixed shard capacity, increasing ρ effectively reduces the primary storage available on each shard, resulting in fragmentation of local structure and an increase in cost. Thus, while a certain degree of replication improves performance across methods, replication provides diminishing returns from 1% ($\rho = 1.01$) to 9% ($\rho = 1.09$), after which replication tends to slightly degrade system performance.

6.2.2 *Load Balance*

In addition to evaluating system performance in terms of mean load, we now examine load balancing—or expected distribution of load across shards—for the various sharding techniques. Recalling Section 2, we define the load on an individual shard to be the sum of rates over all nodes that access that shard: $L_t = \sum_i L_{i,t}$. Intuitively this captures the expected number of nodes that access shard S_t per unit time. Calculating these rates exactly would require knowledge of user logins and accesses to activity feeds—information which unfortunately is not provided in either dataset. Thus we approximate these rates by assuming a uniform query rate across users.[2]

As we saw above, network-aware sharding more than halves the mean load across shards compared to random sharding. However, as shown in Figure 2, this reduction in mean

[2]Load results are virtually identical under various alternate approximations to query rate.

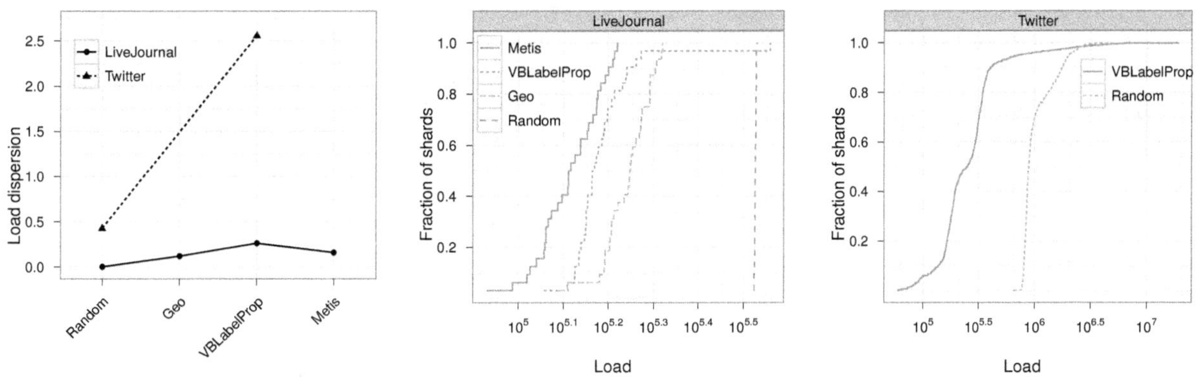

Figure 2: Load across shards for zero replication. The left panel shows standard deviation in load, normalized by mean load. The center and right panels show the cumulative distributions of per-shard load.

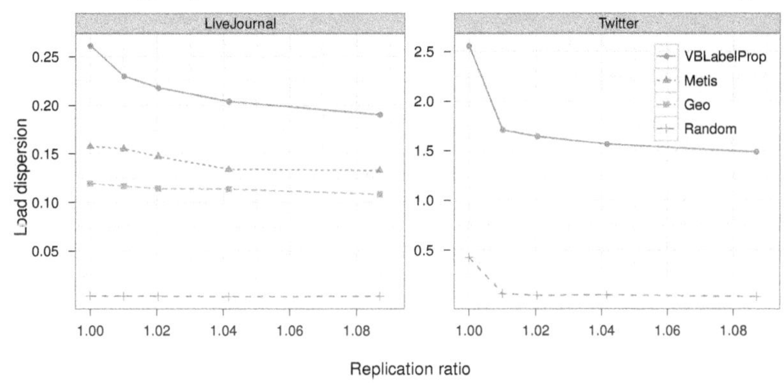

Figure 3: Effect of replication on load balance. The left and right panels show the variation in load dispersion as replication is added to the system for LiveJournal and Twitter, respectively.

load comes at an increase in variance over random sharding. Specifically, we compute the standard deviation over shards normalized by the mean load—termed the "load dispersion"—and plot the results for zero replication in the left panel of Figure 2.

As expected, we see that random sharding has the lowest relative variance across shards followed by geographic sharding. Further details of the cumulative load distribution across shards at zero replication are given for LiveJournal and Twitter in the center and right panels of Figure 2. Increased variance notwithstanding, we see that under network-aware sharding almost all shards (greater than 95%) experience less load compared to random and geographic sharding.

The observed skew under Random is, once again, explained by examining the role of celebrities in the system. Twitter contains an exceedingly small number of profiles (< 100) with hundreds of thousands of followers, after which profile popularity rapidly decreases, with tens of millions of profiles followed by at most a few users. Thus the small fraction ($\approx 10\%$) of shards which host these celebrities receive a disproportionate amount of traffic, accounting for the observed variance.

Replication. Node replication mitigates the load imbalance noted above (Figure 3). As revealed in the difference between the left (LiveJournal) and right (Twitter) panels, a small degree of replication (1%) drastically reduces variance in load for Twitter across both sharding methods, whereas LiveJournal sees more modest improvements. Again, this difference is due to the high degree of skew in popularity on Twitter, where we see that even random sharding experiences a reasonable degree of variance in per-shard load. Similar to the effect of replication on mean load, we see diminishing returns of increasing replication on load balance.

In summary, while the improvement in mean load achieved by network-aware sharding comes at the expense of a slight degradation in load balance, introducing a small degree of replication largely compensates for this effect.

7. DISCUSSION

We have formally defined the NetworkSharding problem and shown that considering network structure significantly improves system performance. Our results hold both in theory, where we show that network-aware sharding results in substantial savings over random sharding for networks with community structure, and in practice, where network-aware sharding via VBLabelProp+BlockShard more than halves the average load for both the LiveJournal and Twitter networks. Moreover, for moderately-sized networks such as LiveJournal, our sharding strategy can incorporate METIS or other state-of-the-art community detection algorithms to realize additional gains. Finally, we find that allowing a small amount of replication further reduces mean load while improving load balance.

Several interesting questions remain. Experiments show that the decrease in average load was accompanied by an increase in variance, and that for a handful of shards load increases under network-aware sharding. We leave open the problem of formulating sharding strategies that improve the load for *all* of the shards. Further possible improvements include online implementations capable of updating sharding assignments as the network evolves.

8. REFERENCES

[1] S. Agarwal, J. Dunagan, N. Jain, S. Saroiu, A. Wolman, and H. Bhogan. Volley: Automated data placement for geo-distributed cloud services. In *Seventh USDI*, pages 2–2, San Jose, CA, 2010.

[2] C. M. Bishop. *Pattern Recognition and Machine Learning.* Springer, New York, 2006.

[3] B. Bollobás. *Random Graphs*, volume 73. Cambridge University Press, 2001.

[4] I. Dhillon, Y. Guan, and B. Kulis. A fast kernel-based multilevel algorithm for graph clustering. In *Eleventh ACM SIGKDD*, Chicago, IL, 2005.

[5] M. Garey and D. Johnson. *Computers and Intractability: A Guide to the Theory of NP-completeness.* WH Freeman & Co. New York, NY, 1979.

[6] J. M. Hofman and C. H. Wiggins. Bayesian approach to network modularity. *Physical Review Letters*, 100:258701, June 2008.

[7] P. Holland. Local structure in social networks. *Sociological Methodology*, 7:1–45, 1976.

[8] T. Karagiannis, C. Gkantsidis, D. Narayanan, and A. Rowstron. Hermes: clustering users in large-scale e-mail services. In *First ACM Symposium on Cloud Computing*, pages 89–100, Indianapolis, IN, 2010.

[9] G. Karypis and V. Kumar. Multilevel algorithms for multi-constraint graph partitioning. In *ACM/IEEE Conference on Supercomputing*, pages 1–13, San Jose, CA, 1998.

[10] H. Kwak, C. Lee, H. Park, and S. Moon. What is twitter, a social network or a news media? In *Nineteenth ACM WWW Conference*, pages 591–600, Raleigh, NC, 2010.

[11] J. Leskovec, K. Lang, A. Dasgupta, and M. Mahoney. Statistical properties of community structure in large social and information networks. In *Seventeenth WWW Conference*, pages 695–704, Beijing, China, 2008.

[12] D. Liben-Nowell, J. Novak, R. Kumar, P. Raghavan, and A. Tomkins. Geographic routing in social networks. *Proceedings of the National Academy of Sciences*, 102(33):11623–11628, Aug. 2005.

[13] J. M. Pujol, V. Erramilli, G. Siganos, X. Yang, N. Laoutaris, P. Chhabra, and P. Rodriguez. The little engine(s) that could: scaling online social networks. In *ACM SIGCOMM Conference*, pages 375–386, New Delhi, India, 2010.

[14] U. N. Raghavan, R. Albert, and S. Kumara. Near linear time algorithm to detect community structures in large-scale networks. *Physical Review E*, 76:036106, Sep 2007.

[15] V. Satuluri, S. Parthasarathy, and Y. Ruan. Local graph sparsification for scalable clustering. In *ACM SIGMOD Conference*, pages 721–732, Athens, Greece, 2011.

[16] J. Ugander and L. Backstrom. Balanced label propagation for partitioning massive graphs. In *Sixth ACM WSDM*, 2013.

APPENDIX

We provide details of the VBLabelProp algorithm omitted from Section 5.1. First, we note that the variational free energy in Equation (15) can be decomposed as the sum of three terms

$$\begin{aligned} F_{\mathbf{A}}[q] = & - \mathbb{E}_q\left[\ln p(\mathbf{A}, \vec{z}|\vec{\theta}, \vec{\pi})\right] - \mathbb{E}_q\left[\ln p(\vec{\theta}, \vec{\pi})\right] \\ & - \mathbb{E}_q\left[\ln q(\vec{\theta}, \vec{\pi})\right], \end{aligned}$$

where all expectations are taken with respect to the variational distribution $q(\vec{z}, \vec{\pi}, \vec{\theta})$. The first term is the expected complete-data likelihood, the second is the cross-entropy between the prior $p(\vec{\theta}, \vec{\pi})$ and $q(\vec{z}, \vec{\pi}, \vec{\theta})$, and the third is the entropy of the variational distribution itself.

The complete-data likelihood can be written as

$$p(\mathbf{A}, \vec{z}|\vec{\theta}, \vec{\pi}) = \theta_+^{m_{++}}(1-\theta_+)^{m_{+-}}\theta_-^{m_{-+}}(1-\theta_-)^{m_{--}}\prod_{k=1}^{K}\pi_k^{n_k},$$

where $m_{++} = \sum_{k=1}^{K}|E(B_k, B_k)|$ is the number of edges contained within blocks, $m_{+-} = \sum_{k=1}^{K} n_k(n_k-1) - m_{++}$ is the number of non-edges contained within blocks, $m_{-+} = m - m_{++}$ is the number of edges between different blocks, $m_{--} = n(n-1) - m - m_{-+}$ is the number of non-edges between different blocks, and $n_k = |B_k|$ is the number of nodes in the k-th block. Taking the logarithm of the likelihood and collecting common terms, we can write this as

$$\begin{aligned} \ln p(\mathbf{A}, \vec{z}|\vec{\theta}, \vec{\pi}) &= Jm_{++} - J'\sum_{k=1}^{K} n_k(n_k-1) - \sum_{k=1}^{K} h_k n_k \\ &+ m\ln\theta_- + [n(n-1)-m]\ln(1-\theta_-) \end{aligned}$$

where we have defined $J = \ln\frac{\theta_+(1-\theta_-)}{\theta_-(1-\theta_+)}$, $J' = \ln\frac{1-\theta_-}{1-\theta_+}$, and $h_k = \ln\frac{1}{\pi_k}$ to be positive for the assortative case ($\theta_+ > \theta_-$). Intuitively we interpret these as follows: J weights the local term involving edges within blocks, while J' and h_k balance this term by global discounts based on the number of possible edges within blocks and block sizes, respectively.

As mentioned in Section 5.1, we assume priors which are conjugate to the specified likelihood terms—namely Beta distributions over θ_+ and θ_- with hyperparameters (α_+, β_+) and (α_-, β_-), respectively, and a Dirichlet distribution over $\vec{\pi}$ with hyperparameters $\vec{\alpha}$. This choice reduces posterior calculations to simple algebraic updates—rather than potentially costly numerical integration—which may be interpreted as adding counts (from observed data) to pseudocounts (specified by hyperparameter values) to determine updated hyperparameter values.

Likewise, expectations under these distributions have relatively simple functional forms. Specifically we have the following values for the expected weights J, J', and $\vec{h}$, as abbreviated in Algorithm 1 for VBLabelProp:

$$\begin{aligned} \mathbb{E}_{q_{\vec{\theta}}}[J] &= \psi(m_{++}+\alpha_+) - \psi(m_{+-}+\beta_+) \\ &- \psi(m_{+-}+\alpha_-) + \psi(m_{--}+\beta_-) \\ \mathbb{E}_{q_{\vec{\theta}}}[J'] &= \psi(m_{--}+\beta_-) - \psi(m_{-+}+\alpha_-+m_{--}+\beta_-) \\ &- \psi(m_{+-}+\beta_+) + \psi(m_{++}+\alpha_++m_{+-}+\beta_+) \\ \mathbb{E}_{q_{\vec{\pi}}}[h_k] &= \psi(n_k+\alpha_k) - \psi(\sum_{k=1}^{K}\alpha_k), \end{aligned}$$

where $\psi(x)$ is the digamma function.

Arrival and Departure Dynamics in Social Networks

Shaomei Wu[*]
Facebook
Menlo Park, CA
shaomei@fb.com

Atish Das Sarma[†]
eBay Research Labs
San Jose, CA
atish.dassarma@gmail.com

Alex Fabrikant
Google Research
Mountain View, CA
fabrikant@google.com

Silvio Lattanzi
Google Research
New York, NY
silviol@google.com

Andrew Tomkins
Google Research
Mountain View, CA
tomkins@google.com

ABSTRACT

In this paper, we consider the natural arrival and departure of users in a social network, and ask whether the dynamics of arrival, which have been studied in some depth, also explain the dynamics of departure, which are not as well studied.

Through study of the DBLP co-authorship network and a large online social network, we show that the dynamics of departure behave differently from the dynamics of formation. In particular, the probability of departure of a user with few friends may be understood most accurately as a function of the raw number of friends who are active. For users with more friends, however, the probability of departure is best predicted by the overall fraction of the user's neighborhood that is active, independent of size. We then study global properties of the subgraphs induced by active and inactive users, and show that active users tend to belong to a core that is densifying and is significantly denser than the inactive users. Further, the inactive set of users exhibit a higher density and lower conductance than the degree distribution alone can explain. These two aspects suggest that nodes at the fringe are more likely to depart and subsequent departures are correlated among neighboring nodes in tightly-knit communities.

Categories and Subject Descriptors

H.1.2 [**Models and Principles**]: :User/Machine Systems; H.2.8 [**Database Management**]: Database Applications—*Data Mining*

General Terms

Theory Measurement

Keywords

social networks, user engagement, social graph analysis

*Part of this research was performed while the author was visiting Google Research, Mountain View.

†Part of this research was performed while the author was working at Google Research, Mountain View.

WSDM'13, February 4–8, 2013, Rome, Italy.

1. INTRODUCTION

There has been significant focus on the dynamics of propagation in social networks, ranging from the actual spread of biological infection [19, 9] to such disparate online phenomena as sharing [4], tagging [18], brand adoption [2, 11], recommendations [15], and joining a community [3]. In many cases, such as the decision to become a member or use a product, the story does not end at adoption. Instead, the user may decide at any point to cease using the product, or to depart the community. It is not clear that a decision of this type, to "reverse" a prior socially-mediated decision to adopt, will follow the same dynamics as the original decision to adopt. In this paper, we study this question in the context of arrivals and departures within social networks.

A natural place to look for models of arrivals and departures is the existing literature on the spread of infectious physical disease. These models often include a recovery component[19, 9], which is akin to a reversal of the decision to become infected. Typically, however, this component assumes that an infected user recovers based on properties of the immune system, without reference to any social process. In our case, we are motivated by the metaphor of a user at a party with friends. The user is more likely to attend upon discovering that some number of friends will also attend. If some or all of the friends then opt to depart, whether for a new party or to just go home, then the original user is much more likely to follow suit. Hence, we anticipate to see the network effect in both arrivals and departures.

We begin to address this question with a basic study of the temporal correlation of arrivals and departures, and show that both processes introduce significant correlation; in fact, we show that time intervals between the departure of friends are more tightly distributed than the equivalent distribution of gaps between arrival of friends.

Assuming social influence has some effect on the temporal correlation, we might consider arrival as the propagation of a "join" virus, and departure as simply the propagation of a new virus, in this case representing the decision to cease usage. However, this formulation is at odds in reality. It is plausible that seeing one friend join a social network, then two, then three, might impel a user to join, as we see in prior work [3]. However, once a user has two hundred friends, will the departure of one, then two, then three friends have a qualitatively different impact on the user's likelihood to depart? Perhaps like the decision to join, the decision to depart depends more on the number of active friends than the number of inactive friends. Or perhaps departure is a fundamentally different decision that depends on an assessment of the pulse of the neighborhood, captured more accurately by the fraction of friends who remain active. At last, departure can be a process that is driven mostly by exogenous factors rather than social forces.

We study this question in the context of the DBLP co-authorship graph and a large social network, and argue that a hybrid of the social influence models could characterize the observed temporal clustering rather accurately. While the number of active friends is known to be a strong predictor of joining a group, for users with twenty or more friends, overall neighborhood activity, measured by the fraction of friends who remain active, is by far the best predictor of likelihood to depart. Surprisingly, this likelihood is linear in the fraction of active friends throughout almost its entire range, and the linear form is identical in both slope and intercept for several different buckets of neighborhood size. Raw counts of inactive friends have low predictive power, and raw counts of active friends, while stronger, remain weak compared to the overall fraction of active friends. On the other hand, for users with fewer than twenty neighbors, the actual count of active friends remains a strong predictor of likelihood to depart. One interpretation of these findings can be that users with few friends rely heavily on the presence of individual friends, while users with more friends stay for the neighborhood atmosphere - they appear one unit closer to departure by each successive fraction of existing friends observed to depart (this phenomena does not apply for the DBLP dataset where many nodes have very small degree).

From this emerging local picture of behavior, we may then ask how arrival and departure dynamics interact with the global structure of the graph. In particular, we seek to understand where departures happen in the graph. It is possible, for example, that departures tend to occur as high-status users in the core of the graph choose to depart in search of the next big thing. Alternately, it is possible that departure happens first at the "fringes" of the graph, and then spreads inwards from there. We study this problem by computing the average induced degree(or density) and conductance of the subgraphs of active and inactive users through time, and comparing these results to thought experiments in which each node decides independently whether to remain active. These experiments allow us to conclude that a core of active nodes remains at much higher internal density than the set of inactive nodes. We also compare the densities observed against the expected density and conductance under a planted degree constraint model. The results suggest that although the inactive set of nodes densifies, its densification is not just a consequence of the degree distribution, but really a consequence of well-connected cluster of nodes from the fringes departing. We reach the picture that departures happen from the fringes and spread to their immediate neighborhoods, while an internal dense core of active nodes survives. We also build a simple model of network evolution based on affiliation networks that incorporates departures and analyze it theoretically to corroborate some of the observed trends.

2. RELATED WORK

There is a large body of work studying the correlation of activity among friends in online communities (see examples in [1, 3, 7, 18, 22]). Most are forms of diffusion research, built on the premise that user engagement is contagious. As such, a user is more likely to adopt new products or behaviors if his friends do so [3, 15]; and large cascades of behavior can be triggered by the actions of a few individuals [11, 21]. With regard to the effect of local structure on the spread of behavior, empirical work has shown a "diminishing returns" on the correlation of activities among network neighbors[3, 22]. Furthermore, the probability of a user adopting a behavior not only correlates with the number of neighbors who have already adopted, but also with the connectivity among his local neighborhood[3, 22].

In addition to research on local influence, a number of theoretical models have been developed to simulate the growth of social networks over time [17, 13, 16]. By modeling the process of nodes arrival and edges creation, these models can generate graphs with observed evolving macro-level structural properties such as degree distribution, edge densification, and diameters shrinking. Although some work in this domain shows that incorporating random deletion of links can induce degree distribution that better matches the observed power-law pattern[10], most existing empirical work focuses on the growth of networks and the increase of activity. Our paper differs by emphasizing the dynamics of user departure from social networks, and the decline of activity. What leads people to depart from social networks? Is inactivity also contagious? Previous studies on user churn in mobile phone networks suggest the existence of social influence at user's disengagement. Dasgupta *et al.* showed in [8] that the probability of a user churning grows with the number of contacts who already churned. Richter *et al.* studied users in groups based on communication intensity[20], finding a strong correlation between individuals' propensity to churn and the group-level characteristics, especially, the (in)activity of the "leader" of the group. Does the same group effect exist when people disengage from a social network? A big difference here is the visibility of the behavior. In the case of a mobile phone network, leaving the service usually involves notifying existing contacts and signaling them about the disengagement; in online social networks, inactivity is less visible and thus may have less influence on others' behavior. However, the extreme case in which all friends depart suggests that there must be some effect. Given such effect, how would a graph evolve structurally after it stops growing, or starts shrinking? There has been some recent theoretical work on modeling the evolution of network structure in the process of "unraveling"[5]. However, built on top of simple game theory principles, these models are not yet examined by empirical data. To our knowledge, this work is the first to address these questions.

3. DATA

In this paper, we study the dynamics of arrival and departure using a snapshot of the DBLP co-authorship graph and a well-known social network. As previous research [3] showed that the co-author network largely reassembles the dynamics of online social networks in forming individual communities, we are interested at testing whether this similarity persists in the forming and degenerating of the entire social graph. The DBLP snapshot that we consider contains 1 million nodes and around 1.8 millions edges, for each author we store his/her co-authors and the year of the last publication. Furthermore for each author to author edge we also store the year of the first publication. In the rest of the paper we will refer to it as DBLP. The social network dataset we study contains millions of users and over a billion edges. For each user, we have the timestamp of signup and last login, and for each edge, we have the timestamp of edge creation. In the rest of the paper we will refer to this network as SN.

To study the pattern of user arrivals and departures, we first describe each user at each timestamp as either active or inactive, based on his most recent activity time. Given a snapshot of the SN network at time t, we consider a user *inactive* if his last login time is earlier than two months prior to t, and consider a user *active* otherwise[1]. Given a snapshot of the DBLP network at time t, we consider a user *inactive* if he/she has not published any paper in the earlier than five year prior to t, and consider a user *active* otherwise. Note that our results do not depend on the time frame that we used. In fact, they hold for two quite different networks and time frames.

4. ARRIVAL AND DEPARTURE CORRELATION AMONG FRIENDS

In this section, we study the basic properties of arrival and departure. We wish to understand whether users typically arrive and/or depart together in social networks. However, we cannot directly compare gaps between arrivals and departures of friends, as networks are not stationary—consider for example the case of a network that grows very rapidly during a brief period, resulting in a flurry of temporally-proximate arrivals, leading to a mistaken conclusion that arrivals tend to be tightly clustered in time. We must therefore normalize in some way against global rates of arrival and departure, which we do by the following technique. Given a snapshot of the network at time t, we consider two samples of user-pairs, one in which the pair of users are friends, and another in which the pair of users is chosen uniformly from all possible pairs[2]. We then consider the distribution of the gap in arrival time between pairs in the two cases. Differences in these distributions will then highlight temporal correlation of arrivals of friends compared to strangers.

To study departures, we adopt the same technique. We consider only inactive users, and generate again a set of pairs of friends, and another set of pairs chosen uniformly at random. For a fixed time t, we define the last login time of inactive users as their departure time. We pick 1M pairs for each of these four sample groups, and compute the Cumulative Distribution Function (CDF) for these distributions.

In Figure 1, we plot the CDF curves, showing the percentage of friends(co-authors)/strangers who joined and left the SN(DBLP) within n days(years) of each other.

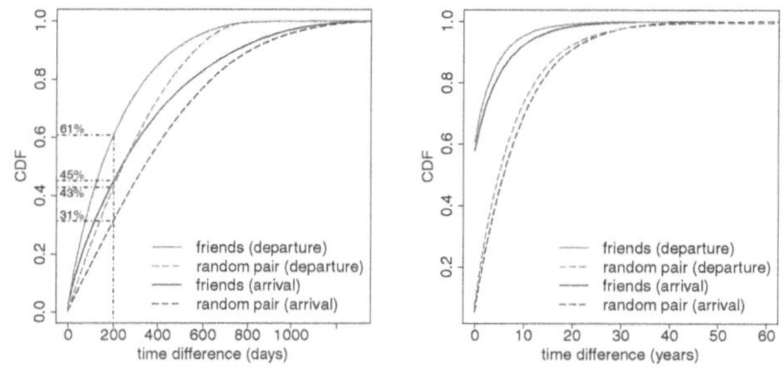

(a) SN (b) DBLP

Figure 1: The CDF curve for the difference in arrival and departure time between friends and random pairs of users.

The CDF for both arrivals and departures of friends lies significantly above the CDF for random pairs, indicating that friends both arrive and depart together, in comparison to the control group of random pairs. As the figure shows, in the case of SN, 43% of random pairs depart within 200 days of one another, while 61% of friends depart within the same period. We find similar pattern in the time interval of arrival - only 31% of random pairs arrive within 200 days, but 45% of friends arrive within the same period. This observation is even more evident in DBLP, where the solid and dashed lines show stronger separation.

To quantify the differences, we plot in Figure 2 the distribution of absolute difference in the CDF values at each time, for arrivals and departures. The correlation of departures in SN is seen to be stronger than the correlation of arrivals, although the two gaps peak around roughly the same value. However, arrivals and departures behave almost identically in DBLP, suggesting the dynamics of arrival and departure are more similar in collaboration networks than in social networks.

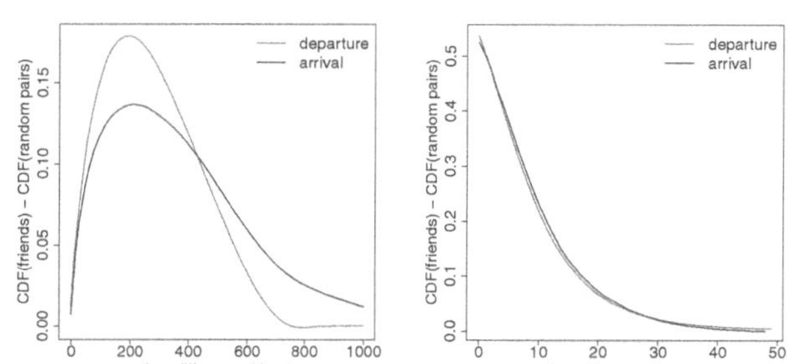

(a) SN (b) DBLP

Figure 2: Gap between CDF curves.

The temporally correlated activities between friends have been observed and modeled before[3, 18, 1], mostly in the form of adopting a new behavior or product within an existing social network. However, given that there is not a single underlying social network that might be accountable for the joining of new users, are those models still applicable in the scenarios of arrival? To answer this question, we will now focus on individual users, and study one's arrival in position of his local neighborhood.

Since we have no information on friendship outside the

[1]As most online social network or social game sites use Monthly-Active-Users(MAU) as a standard way to measure the number of engaged users, we double the cutoff window to 2-month for a more conservative threshold to determine a user has departed.

[2]Technically, it is possible for a random pair to be a pair of friends, however, given the service policy that each user has a rather small upper-bound for the number of friends, the chance of a random pair being friends is negligible.

networks we are studying, we use the eventual set of friends acquired by a user at the snapshot time t to approximate the set of friends he had before arrival, and ask whether those friends join before or after the user. For DBLP, we see the "diminishing returning" curve (Figure 3c) as found in previous research [3]. In SN (Figure 3a), however, the probability of a user signup increases near-linearly as the number of adopted friends increases. The expected fraction of friends joining before the user is 0.5, as the friend network is undirected and each edge contributes one pair in which a joins before b, and one pair with b before a. Thus, for regular graphs (of constant degree), the mean fraction of friends already signed up will be 0.5. The results are shown in Figure 3. True social networks are of course non-regular, and while the distribution of plot (Figure 3b) appears largely symmetrical, there are some outliers. In particular, in SN there are more than 20 times as many users who signed up after all of their eventual friends did, compared to users who signed up before any of their friends. This follows from the many low-degree nodes who join in response to an invitation but do not subsequently engage with the network. In DBLP, the peaks at 0%, 25%, $\frac{1}{3}$, 50%,..., 100% (Figure 3d) can be explained by the substantial number of authors with only one publication, as they have a very small set of co-authors. Although the plot in Figure 3d is largely symmetrical but is slightly skewed to the left. This shows that there are more authors whose collaboration networks grow than ones who stay with their early collaborators. Overall, we posit a weak network effect for new users in both networks, which may not be enough to actively engage users after they sign up.

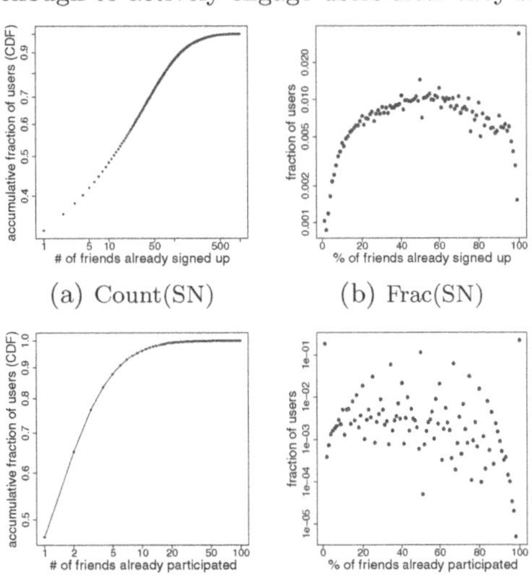

(a) Count(SN) (b) Frac(SN)

(c) Count(DBLP) (d) Frac(DBLP)

Figure 3: Count and fraction of friends signed-up before user.

Our conclusion from these graphs is that friends tend to arrive and depart together, but at least for SN, departures are more tightly clustered than arrivals. We also find interesting nuances in the dynamics of arrivals, that was not noted previously. In the next section, we will look more closely at departures, learning the how neighborhood activities correspond to one's likelihood to depart.

5. LOCAL NEIGHBORHOODS

Figure 1 shows a strong correlation in arrivals and departures for friends; now we will go beyond single-edges and study how such correlation is presented in the entire neighborhood of a node.

5.1 Dependence on local properties

To better understand how a user's departure corresponds to his local community, we look at the probability of a user's departure in relation to the following four properties of the user's neighborhood.

- number of active friends;
- fraction of active friends;
- number of inactive friends;
- number of inactive friends who left in the past 6 months;

We use a similar method as in [3] to calculate the probability of a user becoming inactive, as a function of the number of active friends: we first take two snapshots (t_0, t_1) of the network, three months apart in SN and three years apart in DBLP; we then find all pairs (u, k) such that u is active at the time of first snapshot t_0, and has k friends who are also active at t_0; $p(k)$ is calculated as the fraction of such pairs (u, k) for a given k such that u had left the network at the time of second snapshot t_1. In other words, $p(k)$ is the fraction of active users who left the network in the next three months, given that k friends were active at the first snapshot time. Figure 4a and Figure 4c shows the curves of $p(k)$ at three different t_0. In a similar way, we can fix the fraction of friends f who are active at time t_0, and calculate the probability $p(f)$ of an active user leaving the network as function of f (see Figure 4e). Note that in all figures involving the fraction of active/inactive friends, we exclude all nodes with no friends in SN (around 10% of all active users as of 2011/1/1). Among those users, 35% of them left within three months.

Not surprisingly, Figure 4a, Figure 4c and Figure 4e show that as more and more friends stay active, a user is less and less likely to be inactive. The curve of $p(k)$ (see Figure 4a) also matches very well with what has been seen in other domains [3], exhibiting the "diminishing returns" property. This observation indicates that the marginal gain of having each additional active friend is quite significant for users with a small number of active friends, but rather negligible when a user already has many, say more than 50, active friends. In contrast, in Figure 4e, we do not see such a "diminishing returns" trend, but a steeper, and almost constant rate of decrease in the probability of departure throughout the course when the fraction of active friends increases. This is an interesting observation that has not been previously seen (specifically in various positive influence studies).

To see how the inactivity of the neighborhood determines the departure of a user, we also plot the probability of departure as a function of number of inactive friends, in Figure 4b and Figure 4d. The curves in Figure 4b and Figure 4d show an interesting trend of decreasing slope through time: while the probability of a user departing increases with the growth in the number of inactive friends initially, it becomes more and more insensitive to the value of k in the later curves. This phenomenon is quite intriguing to us: if the departure of friends do have certain predictive power on the departure of the user, as shown in the earlier curves, why is such predictive power diminished so much in the latest years? To answer this question, we note that we are counting the number of inactive friends as prior to the time of each snapshot, but many of them could have been inactive for a long time thus could hardly account for the dynamics of the network

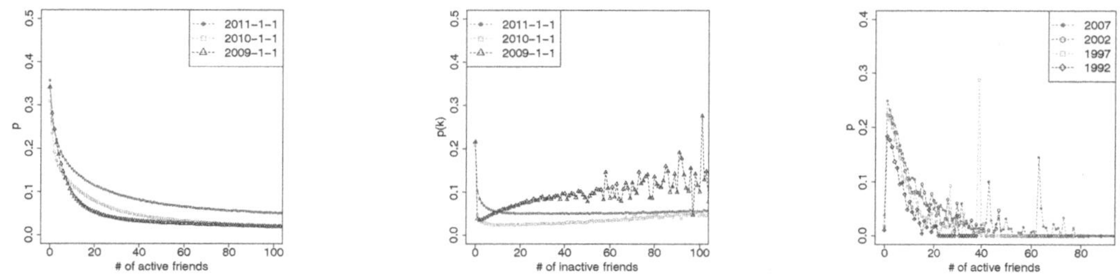

(a) SN, number of active friends (b) SN, number of inactive friends (c) DBLP, number of active friends

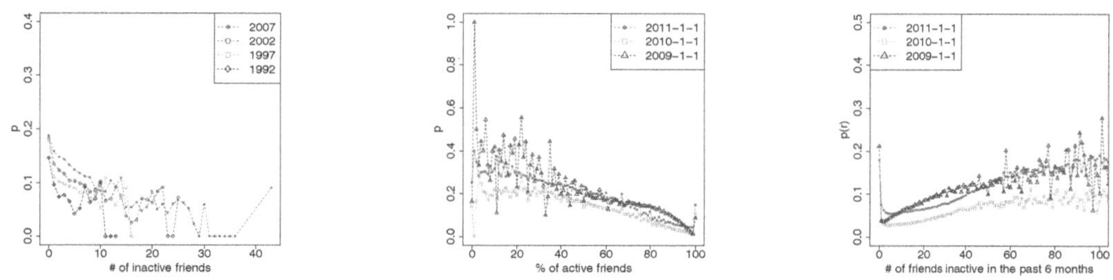

(d) DBLP, number of inactive friends (e) SN, percentage of active friends (f) SN, number of recent inactive friends

Figure 4: Probability of departure as function of different local properties. (a) f(active friend count) in SN; (b) f(inactive friend count) in SN; (c) f(active friend count) in DBLP; (d) f(inactive friend count) in DBLP, (e) f(active friend fraction) in SN; (f) f(inactive friends who left in the past 6 months) in SN.

at the snapshot time. Figure 4f confirms this idea, showing that the curves we see in Figure 4b are somewhat misleading - in general, the probability of user's departure constantly grows with the number of friends r who *recently* became inactive (when r is not too small).

5.2 Interaction between local properties

The results of the previous section provide qualitative evidence that an individual's probability of departure is related to the activeness of his neighborhood. However, does that apply to all users? Do the highly connected users act differently than the more marginally connected ones? Is the probability of departure sensitive to the degeneration of neighborhood, or is it a step function that will only drop once there are less than k active friends, as modeled in [5]? To address these issues, we compute the probability of user's departure in SN in relation to the interaction between local properties. Specifically, in Figure 5a, we divide users into three groups based on their degrees, and plot the probability of departure as a function of the number/fraction of active friends, for each group separately. We note that for users with different levels of connectivity in the network, the curves of $p(f)$ (Figure 5a) are qualitatively identical. This result demonstrates again that the fraction of friends who are active has a stronger effect on the probability of an individual's departure, regardless of the size of the user's neighborhood.

In addition, we aggregate users by the fraction of active/inactive friends, and look at how the probability of departure depends on the number of active/inactive friends for each group (see Figure 5). There are two things we note from Figure 5: First, for users with different fractions of inactive friends, there is a big gap between their probabilities of departure - for example, compared to users with less than 10% friends inactive (blue line in Figure 5c), users who have more than 50% friends inactive (red line in Figure 5c) are 10 times more likely to leave as well. Second, once the user is in an inactive part of the neighborhood, the raw count of inactive friends has little effect in determining the probability of the user's departure (green line in Figure 5b). Note that the blue line in Figure 5b is very noisy because there are very few people in a highly obsolete neighborhood but still with a substantial amount of active friends. We still plot it just to be symmetric with Figure 5c.

5.3 Predict the departure of user

Given a strong correlation between the probability of a user becoming inactive and the inactivity of his friends, the next question is, can we actually predict individuals's departures based on local properties? In this section, we model the departure of users using simple linear regression models and decision tree classifiers. In particular, we will focus exclusively on SN because we have a richer set of features available.

To start, we formalize our problem as a binary classification task in which class 1 is defined as consisting of those users who were active as of Jan 1st, 2011 (t_0) and departed within two months after t_0, and class 0 is defined as consisting of those who stayed active for two months after t_0. We then randomly sample 500K examples for each class, from all the users who were active at t. Note that in our data, there are 90% negative and only 10% positive cases; our sampling scheme provides a more balanced distribution of examples of both classes.

We extract two sets of local features for each user:

- Neighborhood features. The local structural properties of the user's direct neighborhood, including the number of friends who already departed, the number of friends who are active, the number of friends who departed recently (six months prior to t_0), and the fraction of friends who departed recently.
- Activity features. The properties reflecting user's participation to activities in the network, including the number of contents he received, the number of contents he sent, and the number of status updates.

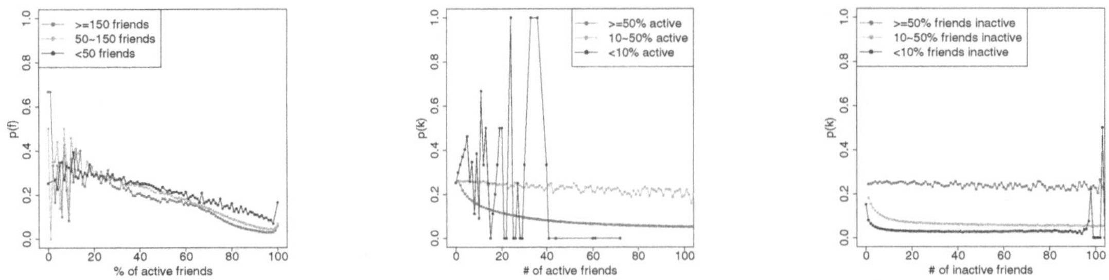

(a) $p \sim$ percentage of active friends (b) $p \sim$ number of active friends (c) $p \sim$ number of inactive friends

Figure 5: Probability of departure as function of local properties, at different levels of active/inactive friend fraction and friend count (snapshot taken at time t =2011/1/1). in SN

Table 1: Predict user departure with decision tree

Feature	*Accuracy*	*F1 pos*	*ROC area*
Neighborhood	0.694	0.694	0.755
Activity	0.730	0.735	0.801
All	0.755	0.761	0.833

To predict the departure of users, we train a simple decision tree (REPTree) classifier on our examples. Table 1 gives the performance of the classifier with different sets of features under 10-fold cross validation.

Table 1 shows that relying on only local features of individuals, the simple decision tree classifier can predict the departure of user with high accuracy (75% with all features, as compared to 50% for always predicting one class). This result demonstrates a strong connection between user's local properties and the propensity of departure. Moreover, comparing across 3 sets of features, we see that although the activity features are most effective, neighborhood features can also provide rather accurate insights on the departure of users.

6. STRUCTURAL TRENDS IN NETWORK TOPOLOGY

In this section, we explore the overall structural changes that occur in the network as a result of the departure of existing users, as well as the steady arrival of new users. Topological changes have been studied in the context of new nodes arriving but here we pay specific attention to how the global structure changes in the process of the departure or decline of user activities.

To get a sense of the how the structure of the network evolves over time, we first study the distribution of edges among active and inactive nodes. Specially, we look at the edges between active nodes (Figure 6a and Figure 6d), edges between inactive nodes (Figure 6b and Figure 6e), and the edges across active and inactive nodes (Figure 6c and Figure 6f), and plot the ratio between the actual number of edges over the expected value over time. The expected number of edges is computed based on the total number of edges, $|E|$, in the network and the number of nodes in each of the active and inactive sets. The expected number of edges of any type is the expected number of edges when the total $|E|$ edges are placed between randomly chosen pairs of nodes.

To understand the overall structure among the sets of active and inactive nodes, we study the density and conductance of these two sub-networks in the rest of this section. Here the active sub-network consists of the active nodes and the edges among them, and the inactive sub-network is similarly defined.

Figure 7 and plots the overall density of the active (7a and 7c) and inactive (7b and 7d) set of nodes, as a function of time. For comparison, we also plot the *expected* densities of the respective sets, as determined by the number of active and inactive nodes and edges and the degree distributions.

We use the definition density of a set of nodes (or average induced degree) used in [6], where the density of a set of nodes is the number of edges between the nodes divided by the number of nodes; i.e. for a set of nodes S, $density(S) = \frac{|E(S,S)|}{|S|}$ (here $E(S,S)$ contains all edges (u,v) such that $u, v \in S$). Therefore, the density of set S is half of the average induced degree of the set of nodes in S. In order to compare the the density we observe for the set of active nodes and the set of inactive nodes, we define an *expected* density for each sub-network. The expected density of the inactive set of nodes could be computed simply as the density of the entire graph times the fraction of inactive nodes.

However, we even use a stronger baseline to see if the trends we observe are a result of a trend more than just that of degrees. Therefore, we compute expected density subject to the overall degree constraints on active and inactive nodes as follows.

Consider each edge as occupying two slots (end points), each slot being in either S_a (the active set of nodes), or S_i (the inactive set of nodes); therefore $S_a \cup S_i = V(G)$. Let the fraction of all these slots that are in S_i be P_i (which is the number of edges going across the active and inactive sub-network plus twice the number of edges in the inactive sub-network); therefore the number of such slots occupied in S_a is $P_a = (1 - P_i)$. Suppose that all the $|E|$ edges were randomly placed in two slots each, with probabilities determined such that in expectation we respect P_i and P_a, then we consider the induced density of this process as the expected density (for respective sub-networks). Notice that this is a more stringent baseline for our comparison. Therefore, an edge is contained in the inactive sub-network with probability P_i^2 and so the expected density of the inactive set is $(|E|P_i^2)/|S_i|$. Similarly the expected density of the active sub-network can be computed.

The plots on these densities in Figure 7 shows that the density of the active set $density(S_a)$ increases rapidly with increase in time. However, as shown in the plot on distribution of edges in Figures 6, as the number of edges in the active sub-network continue growing, the density of the ac-

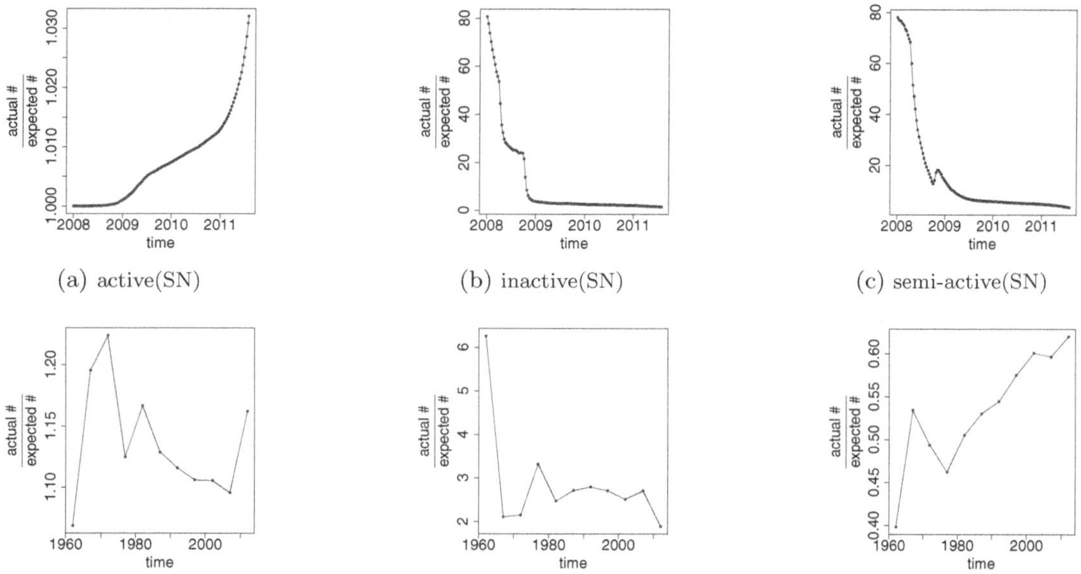

(a) active(SN) (b) inactive(SN) (c) semi-active(SN)

(d) active(DBLP) (e) inactive(DBLP) (f) semi-active(DBLP)

Figure 6: Distribution of edges, indicated by the ratio of actual number of edges over the expected number of edges.

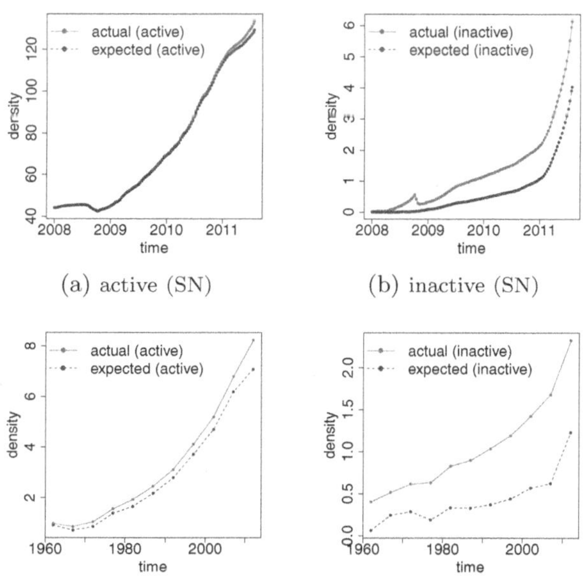

(a) active (SN) (b) inactive (SN)

(c) active (DBLP) (d) inactive (DBLP)

Figure 7: Density of the active and inactive sub-networks

tive sub-network is only marginally higher than its expected density. On contrast, the density of inactive sub-network is significantly higher than the expected density, even conditioned on the degree distribution. This further confirms the fact that departure is correlated across edges, as shown in our local analysis. The nodes that are departing are still probably at the periphery of the network (since the inactive set has much lower density than the active set), but these inactive nodes continue to be internally well-connected because of a higher-than-expected density. This strengthens the evidence from previous sections that a node's likelihood to become inactive is strongly associated with neighboring inactivity.

After studying the connectedness within the active/inactive sub-network separately, we now look at the connection of each sub-network to the rest of social graph, to get a more complete picture about where departures happen and spread in the network. We use conductance to measure the amount of possible connections between different sets of nodes in a network.

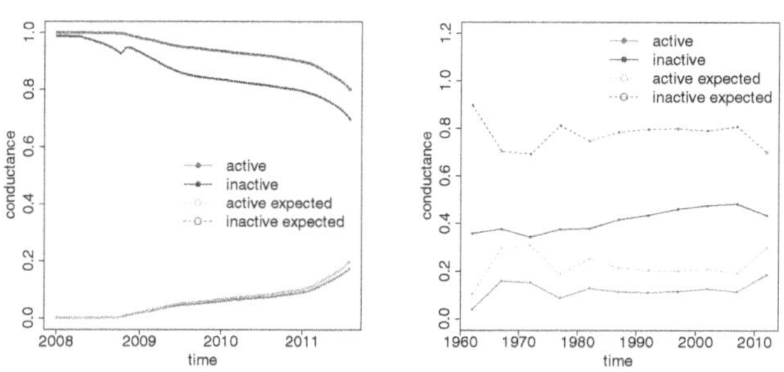

(a) SN (b) DBLP

Figure 8: Conductance of the active and inactive sets

Conductance of a set of nodes S, $\phi(s)$, first defined in [12], is measured as $\phi(S) = \frac{|E(S,V(G)\S)|}{|E(S)|}$. Here $E(S,V(G)\S)$ contains all edges (u,v) such that $u \in S, v \notin S$, and $|E(S)| = 2|E(S,S)|+|E(S,V(G)\S)|$. So notice that conductance is always less than 1, and any set with more than half its edges going across to the complement set has a conductance of more than $\frac{1}{3}$. We again measure the conductance of sets S_a and S_i through time and compare with their expected conductances (see Figure 8). The computation of expected conductance is also performed in a similar manner to as described previously for expected density.

We see a similar trend in conductance (Figure 8) as seen for densities. The conductance of the active set of nodes S_a,

$\phi(S_a)$ remains less than the conductance expected for this set. This suggests that there are fewer edges going across from S_a to the inactive set S_i and far more edges within S_a itself, than would be expected. The conductance plots for the set of inactive nodes however is again more contrasting. $\phi(S_i)$ remains far lower than the expected conductance. Nodes that are becoming inactive continue to have many more edges within, than one would expect. This clearly suggests that the inactive set of nodes are influencing neighbors to inactivity. Yet again, the absolute conductance value still suggests that nodes at the periphery of the network are more susceptible to becoming inactive.

The takeaway from these plots are two fold. Firstly, of course, these trends corroborate our findings from the previous sections suggesting that there is a strong correlation among inactivity in neighboring nodes . However, these plots on global measures such as density and conductance also suggest a picture of the evolving network. With the active sub-network's density being much higher than the inactive, and the inactive set showing higher than expected density and lower than average conductance, we are led to believe that nodes in the *core* of the network are much more likely to survive, while nodes at the periphery are more susceptible to departure, probably by a combination of external forces and the neighborhood inactivity.

7. MODELING THE ARRIVAL AND DEPARTURE DYNAMICS

In this section we introduce a simple evolving model that is able to explain formally the densification of the active part of the network. To the best of our knowledge this is the first model that explains the densification of the edges in a network where nodes and edges join and leave the network. Our model is an extension of the Affiliation Networks model introduced in [14]. [3]

First note that the arrival dynamics are already captured by the Affiliation Networks model, where at each step a node is added with constant probability. In order to model the departure probability we introduce in the Affiliation Network model a departure probability of a node, we define the probability of leaving the network for a node v in a step as

$$P[v_{\ominus}] = f(n) + h(N(v))$$

where $f(n)$ is a function of the size of the network, n, and captures the probability of a node leaving independently of its neighborhood and $h(N(v))$ is the probability of leaving as a function of a node neighborhood, $N(v)$.

In particular we fix $f(n) = \frac{\alpha}{n}$, where α is a constant smaller than 1. Furthermore from figures 4a and 4c we have that $h(N(v)) \propto \left(\frac{1}{|N_{\odot}(v)|}\right)^{\lambda}$, where $N_{\odot}(v)$ is the number of active neighbors of v and α is a constant and $\lambda = g(n)$ where $g(n)$ is function slowly growing with the number of nodes in the network[4]. So we define:

$$P[v_{\ominus}] = \frac{\alpha}{n} + \left(\frac{1}{|N_{\odot}(v)|}\right)^{\lambda}$$

[3]We here study the Affiliation Network model because it gives us a clear way to identify community in the network.
[4]Note that if λ was a constant, all the constant degree nodes would disappear from the networks in a constant number of steps and this is not the case.

Here we only consider the dependency on the number of active friends, since in section 5 we showed empirically that this is the more relevant feature. We now present the affiliation network model and our extension to it, and then apply our extension of the model to explain the densification of the active part of the network.

7.1 Our model

We now recall the Affiliation Network model presented in [14] and explain our extension. In the models there are two graphs that evolve at the same time: a bipartite graph between people and their interests and a social network just on the people. The evolution of the two graphs is described in table 2.

In our extension a node v in P in $B(P, I)$ and $G(P, E)$ can also become inactive. More precisely, with probability $P[v_{\ominus}]$ at each (discrete) timestamp after the first departure time t_d (the time when people start to leave the network), a node becomes inactive with probability $P[v_{\ominus}]$. Hereafter, we assume that t_d is equal to ϵn, where ϵ is a constant and n is the time at which we analyze the network.

7.2 Densification

In this subsection, we prove that, in our network model, the graph induced by the active nodes densifies even when we allow deactivation of the nodes.

THEOREM 1. *There exist small constant value of λ, α and ϵ for which our model densifies in time with high probability.*

Where with high probability we mean probability bigger than $1 - o(1)$. The detailed proof of this theorem is postponed to the appendix but we sketch the main intuitions here.

PROOF. (Sketch) First we notice that from [14] we have that at time t_d there exist several nodes in I of polynomial degree in the bipartite graph $B(P, I)$ and thus a dense community in $G(P, E)$.

Then we prove that even if part of the network is becoming inactive, there is still a significant number of new user joining the dense community. Furthermore the new nodes will tend to add edges(via preferential attachment) to popular existing community. So we have that even if some nodes are becoming inactive, the dense part of the graph is still growing.

The last observation with the analysis of densification presented in [14] implies that the network is still densifying. □

Note that the main proof's idea are in line with our experimental finding; in fact it suggests that most of the nodes that are leaving the network are in the fringes and not in the core part of the graph (that is composed by the dense communities which continue to grow with time).

Finally it is interesting to notice that the preferential attachment, that does not have a strong clustering structure, do not have the densification property. In fact, the density of the preferential attachment model is also always upperbounded by a constant when we allow node deletion. Specifically, the density of the preferential attachment model without node deletion is m, where m is the number of edges added by a new node; and it is $\leq m$ for the model with deletions. To prove this, note that we can attribute inactive nodes to inactivation of the m edges that had been added when the node joined the network.

$B(P, I)$	$G(P, E)$
Fix integers $c_p, c_i > 0$. Fix $\beta \in (0, 1)$. At time 0, the bipartite graph $B_0(P, I)$ is a simple graph with at least $c_p c_i$ edges. At time $t > 0$: **(Evolution of P)** With probability β: A new node v is added to P. A node $v_i \in P$ is chosen as *prototypes* for the new node, with probability proportional to its active degree. c_p edges are "copied" from v_i **(Evolution of I)** With probability $1 - \beta$, a new node v is added to I following a symmetrical process, adding c_i edges to v.	Fix integers c_p, c_i, s. Fix $\beta \in (0, 1)$. At time 0, $G_0(P, E)$ two vertices have an edge between them for every neighbor in I that they have in common in $B_0(P, I)$. At time $t > 0$: **(Evolution of P)** With probability β: A new node v is added to P. An edge between v and another node in P is added with probability p for every neighbor that they have in common in $B(P, I)$. The new node also add s preferential attachment on active edges. **(Edges via evolution of I)** With probability $1 - \beta$: A new edge is added between two nodes active v_1 and v_2 if the new a new common interested has been added

Table 2: Informal description of the evolving model, for a detailed description refer to [14].

8. CONCLUSIONS

We have studied the dynamics of user departure from online social networks and collaboration networks, from the perspectives of local and global network structure. We considered the predictive power of local neighborhoods on the behavior of nodes as well as studied global changes in the network topology. At the local level, we studied individuals and the dynamics in their local neighborhood, measured the probability of user arrival and departure in relation to the activity of their friends. Our findings are threefold: first, there is a strong clustered effect in the timing of departure among friends while this is not as visible in arrivals; second, although both numbers and fractions of neighborhood (in)activity are correlated to the probability of the individual's departure, the fraction of inactive friends has arguably the better predictive power on the departure probability, providing an interesting complement to literature on arrivals which shows number of active friends as the most predictive of these measures; third, once a significant fraction of friends depart, the overall connectivity of individuals in the entire network does not have predictive power as to whether the user will leave the network. At the global level, we looked at the trend of network topological properties over the past few years, showing that as the network evolves, users at the peripheral region of the network are more likely to depart in groups; yet an internal core of the network survives and densifies over time.

We want to emphasize that our results do not prove a causal relationship between the departure of friends and the departure of a user. What we have observed and modeled is only correlated actions among neighbors, and we are aware of the possible factors that can contribute to, or actually lead to, the departure of users. For example, internally, users with similar personal traits may tend to leave the network altogether; externally, the emergence of competing services may draw users away from the original network. Our model provides *one* possible explanation on the emergence of observed pattern, but does not exclude other explanations. Our goal is to offer a space for building better models of how people tune out of social networks, in additional to how they sign up.

9. REFERENCES

[1] A. Anagnostopoulos, R. Kumar, and M. Mahdian. Influence and correlation in social networks. In *KDD'08.*

[2] S. Aral, L. Muchnik, and A. Sundararajan. Distinguishing influence-based contagion from homophily-driven diffusion in dynamic networks. *Proceedings of the National Academy of Sciences*, 2009.

[3] L. Backstrom, D. Huttenlocher, J. Kleinberg, and X. Lan. Group formation in large social networks: membership, growth, and evolution. In *KDD '06.*

[4] E. Bakshy, J. M. Hofman, W. A. Mason, and D. J. Watts. Everyone's an influencer: quantifying influence on twitter. In *WSDM '11.*

[5] K. Bhawalkar, J. Kleinberg, K. Lewi, T. Roughgarden, and A. Sharma. Preventing unraveling in social networks: The anchored k-core problem. In *Automata, Languages, and Programming*, pages 440–451. 2012.

[6] M. Charikar. Greedy approximation algorithms for finding dense components in a graph. In *APPROX '00.*

[7] D. Crandall, D. Cosley, D. Huttenlocher, J. Kleinberg, and S. Suri. Feedback effects between similarity and social influence in online communities. In *KDD '08.*

[8] K. Dasgupta, R. Singh, B. Viswanathan, D. Chakraborty, S. Mukherjea, A. A. Nanavati, and A. Joshi. Social ties and their relevance to churn in mobile telecom networks. In *EDBT'08.*

[9] P. S. Dodds and D. J. Watts. A generalized model of social and biological contagion. *Journal of Theoretical Biology*, 2005.

[10] T. Fenner, M. Levene, and G. Loizou. A stochastic model for the evolution of the web allowing link deletion. *ACM Trans. Internet Technol.*, 2006.

[11] M. Gladwell. *The Tipping Point: How Little Things Can Make a Big Difference.* 2002.

[12] M. Jerrum and A. Sinclair. Conductance and the rapid mixing property for markov chains: the approximation of the permanent resolved. In *STOC '88.*

[13] R. Kumar, J. Novak, and A. Tomkins. Structure and evolution of online social networks. In *KDD '06.*

[14] S. Lattanzi and D. Sivakumar. Affiliation networks. In *STOC'09.*

[15] J. Leskovec, L. A. Adamic, and B. A. Huberman. The dynamics of viral marketing. *ACM Trans. Web*, 2007.

[16] J. Leskovec, L. Backstrom, R. Kumar, and A. Tomkins. Microscopic evolution of social networks. In *KDD '08.*

[17] J. Leskovec, J. Kleinberg, and C. Faloutsos. Graphs

over time: densification laws, shrinking diameters and possible explanations. In *KDD '05*.
[18] C. Marlow, M. Naaman, D. Boyd, and M. Davis. HT06, tagging paper, taxonomy, Flickr, academic article, to read. In *HYPERTEXT '06*.
[19] M. E. J. Newman. Spread of epidemic disease on networks. *Physical Review E*, 2002.
[20] Y. Richter, E. Yom-Tov, and N. Slonim. Predicting customer churn in mobile networks through analysis of social groups. In *SDM*.
[21] E. M. Rogers. *Diffusion of Innovations*. Simon and Schuster, 2003.
[22] D. M. Romero, B. Meeder, and J. Kleinberg. Differences in the mechanics of information diffusion. In *WWW '11*.

10. APPENDIX

THEOREM 2. *There exist small constant values of λ, α and ϵ for which our model densifies in time with high probability.*

PROOF. In order to prove the statement we first analyze the evolution of the high degree interests, in particular we will prove that those interests will continue to grow even after the departure of some nodes from the network. Then we will show that this in turn implies that the network densifies in time.

Let S be the set of nodes in I in $B(P,I)$ such that their degree is bigger or equal to t_d^δ, for a fixed constant $\delta = \frac{1}{10}\left(4+\frac{c_i\beta}{c_p(1-\beta)}\right)^{-1}$. Note that Theorem 1 in [14] implies that $S \neq \emptyset$. Consider a node v in S, note that from construction the $N(v)$ in $B(P,I)$ are a community of size bigger or equal than t_d^δ in $G(P,E)$. Let us call this community $C(v)$.

We will start by showing that the number of active nodes in $C(v)$ for an interest $v \in S$ grows asymptotically as in the model without deletions, finally we will use this property to prove the densification.

Let us call $E^n_{\odot}(v)$ the expected number of active nodes in $C(v)$ at time n, $E^n_{\otimes}(v)$ the number of inactive nodes, e_n the number of edges in $B(P,I)$, and $C_t(v)$ the set of nodes in $N(v)$ as of time t.

We start by bounding $E^n_{\otimes}(v)$. We first upper bound the nodes that become inactive by random choice independently of their neighbors. Let us call them $I_{\otimes}(v)$.

Let W_t be the number of nodes (active or inactive) in $C(v)$ at time t. By Lemma 2 in [14] we have that $W_n \leq k|C_{t_\delta}(v)|$ for some constant $k > 0$.

Now we can bound $E[I_{\otimes}(v)] \leq \sum_{t=t_d}^{n} W_t \frac{\alpha}{n} \leq W_n \frac{\alpha}{n}(n - t_d) = (1-\epsilon)\alpha k|C_{t_\delta}(v)|$. In addition, by applying the Chernoff-Hoeffding's bound we have that $I_{\otimes}(v) \leq (1+\gamma)(1-\epsilon)\alpha k|C_{t_\delta}(v)|$ with probability $1 - o(\frac{1}{n^2})$ for any $\gamma > 0$. So by fixing $\alpha < (1+\gamma)\frac{k(1-\epsilon)}{10}$ we have that $I_{\otimes}(v) \leq \frac{|C_{t_\delta}(v)|}{10}$ with high probability.

We now bound the number of nodes that became inactive at time t because other nodes in their neighborhood have left the network, we call those nodes $D^t_{\otimes}(v)$. To do it we will first prove that for a node in $C(v)$ the probability of becoming inactive because other nodes in their neighborhood is dominated by a simpler random process and use it to upper bound $D^n_{\otimes}(v)$ with $\frac{C_{t_\delta}(v)}{10}$.

First note that until $D^t_{\otimes} \leq \frac{|C_{t_\delta}(v)|}{10}$, $D^t_{\otimes}(v)$ is dominated the random variable X^t that counts the number of heads that are observed when a biased coin, that gives head with probability $\frac{1}{\left(\frac{8C_{t_\delta}(v)}{10}\right)^\lambda} = \frac{1}{\left(\frac{8(\epsilon n)^\delta}{10}\right)^\lambda}$ when the coin is flipped t times.

Note that by fixing $\lambda \geq \frac{1}{\delta}$, we have that X^t in expectation is ≤ 1 for every $t \leq n$ and thus by the Chernoff bound with probability bigger than $1 - o\left(\frac{1}{n^2}\right)$ $X^n \leq \log n$. But $\log n << \frac{C_{t_\delta}(v)}{10}$, thus $X^n << \frac{C_{t_\delta}(v)}{10}$ with probability bigger than $1 - o\left(\frac{1}{n^2}\right)$.

Now $D^{t_\delta}_{\otimes}(v)$ is equal to 0 and it is dominated by X^{t_δ} until $D^t_{\otimes}(v)$ it is smaller than $\frac{C_{t_\delta}(v)}{10}$, but because $X^n << \frac{C_{t_\delta}(v)}{10}$ this implies that $D^t_{\otimes}(v)$ is always dominated by X^{t_δ}a. Thus $D^n_{\otimes}(v) << \frac{C_{t_\delta}(v)}{10}$ with probability bigger than $1 - o\left(\frac{1}{n^2}\right)$.

So we get:

$$E^n_{\otimes}(v) = I_{\otimes}(v) + D_{\otimes}(v) \leq \frac{1|C_{t_\delta}(v)|}{5}$$

with probability at least $1 - o\left(\frac{1}{n^2}\right)$. Hence by union bound and by the fact that $|S|$ is smaller than n we get that with high probability for all the $v \in S$ $E^n_{\otimes}(v) \geq \frac{1|C_{t_\delta}(v)|}{5}$.

Now we want to study how $E^n_{\odot}(v)$ evolves in time. To do it, note that by the bound of $E^n_{\otimes}$ we have that the number of deleted node in $C_t(v)$ is $\leq \frac{1|C(v)|}{5}$ for all $t \geq t_\delta$. Thus the grow of $C(v)$ will dominate the grow of a community that has size $\frac{4|C(v)|}{5}$ at time ϵn in the process without deletion of the nodes. By combining the above property and Lemma 2 in [14] we get that for any $C(v)$ with $v \in S$ the final size of the cluster in the process without deletion and in the process with deletion are just a constant factor away.

Now note that from [14] we know that in the process without deletion the graph densifies because

$$\begin{aligned}
|E_n| &> \sum_{v \in I}(\text{edges generated by a cluster of size I}) \\
&> \sum_{v \in V}(\text{edges generated by a cluster of size I}) \\
&> \sum_{v \in S}(1-\sigma)p(|C(v)|(|C(v)|-1)) \\
&> \sum_{i=n^\delta}^{n}(\#\text{ of nodes of degree } i \text{ in } I)(1-\sigma)pi^2) \\
&> \sum_{i=n^\delta}^{n}\left(\left(\left(\frac{n}{\zeta(-2-\Delta)}\frac{1}{(i)^{2+\Delta}}\right)(1 \pm o(1))\right)(1-\sigma)pi^2\right) \\
&\in \omega(n)
\end{aligned}$$

Where σ is a constant >0, $\zeta()$ is Riemann zeta function and $\Delta = \left(4 + \frac{c_i\beta}{c_p(1-\beta)}\right)^{-1}$.

Thus the densification property in the process without deletion is a consequence of the number of edges in the clusters generated by large interest but we have proved that the size of those interest change by at most a constant factor, so also in the model with deletion the number of the edges is $\omega(n)$ and thus the model densifies in time. □

Three Findings Regarding Privacy Online

Catherine Tucker*
MIT Sloan
100 Main St, E62-533
Cambridge, MA 02142, USA
cetucker@mit.edu

ABSTRACT

The Internet now enables firms to collect detailed and potentially intrusive data about their customers both easily and cheaply. I discuss three empirical results related to customer privacy-protection that is enacted in response to this change.

1. Privacy protection that focuses on obtaining consent appears to lead to less effective advertising. This is based on results from extensive empirical analysis into how effectiveness of online advertising changed in response to the implementation of the E-Privacy Directive in Europe [2].

2. Privacy protection which gives direct control over customers' privacy appears to enhance economic outcomes. This is based on a detailed case study of customer responsiveness to different forms of advertising in the wake of a change in Facebook privacy policies [3].

3. Restricting the length of time that potentially private data is stored appears to have little economic impact. This is based on empirical analysis of aggregate search behavior following a change in the length of time search engines were told they could store search engine query data in Europe [1].

Categories and Subject Descriptors

H.4 [**Information Systems Applications**]: Miscellaneous

Keywords

Economics, Search, Privacy Online

1. REFERENCES

[1] L. Chiou and C. Tucker. Data Storage, Data Privacy and Search Engines. *Mimeo, MIT*, 2012.
[2] A. Goldfarb and C. E. Tucker. Privacy regulation and online advertising. *Management Science*, 57(1):57–71, 2011.
[3] C. Tucker. Social networks, personalized advertising, and privacy controls. *Mimeo, MIT*, 2011.

*All mistakes are mine alone.

WSDM'13, February 4–8, 2013, Rome, Italy.
ACM 978-1-4503-1869-3/13/02.

Optimized Interleaving for Online Retrieval Evaluation

Filip Radlinski
Microsoft
Cambridge, UK
filiprad@microsoft.com

Nick Craswell
Microsoft
Bellevue, WA, USA
nickcr@microsoft.com

ABSTRACT

Interleaving is an online evaluation technique for comparing the relative quality of information retrieval functions by combining their result lists and tracking clicks. A sequence of such algorithms have been proposed [6, 13, 4], each being shown to address problems in earlier algorithms. In this paper, we formalize and generalize this process, while introducing a formal model: We identify a set of desirable properties for interleaving, then show that an interleaving algorithm can be obtained as the solution to an optimization problem within those constraints. Our approach makes explicit the parameters of the algorithm, as well as assumptions about user behavior. Further, we show that our approach leads to an unbiased and more efficient interleaving algorithm than any previous approach, using a novel log-based analysis of user search behavior.

Categories and Subject Descriptors

H.3.3 [**Information Search and Retrieval**]: Information Search and Retrieval.

Keywords: Interleaving, Evaluation, Web Search

1. INTRODUCTION

In most studies retrieval evaluation is performed using manual relevance judgments that assess the relevance of particular documents to particular queries, or by observing user behavior in an actual retrieval system. In both cases, the goals are clear: Sensitivity to small improvements in retrieval quality for a given cost of evaluation, and fidelity to the actual user experience were real users to directly compare particular retrieval systems.

The most common approach involves relevance judgments. Among other benefits, this most easily allows for reproducibility and reusability: A retrieval algorithm can be run on a document collection for a particular query set for which judgments are known. Performance can be measured using any number of metrics such as Mean Average Precision (MAP) [11], Discounted Cumulative Gain (DCG) [11], or Subtopic Recall [16]. Different researchers can apply the same retrieval algorithms to the same collection to reproduce results. Further, the data can be used to evaluate future retrieval methods on the same document collection and query set.

In contrast, online evaluation involves real users searching for actual and current information needs. The users can enter search terms, and documents are retrieved. Based on the user interface (in particular the captions shown by the retrieval system), users select results, reformulate or revise their information need, and continue with other tasks. Their behavior in selecting queries issued and documents clicked can be interpreted as feedback about the documents retrieved. Reproducing an evaluation requires showing new users similar results. If the new users are substantially different, or have substantially different needs or behavior, the outcome may change. Furthermore, a record of behavior given particular documents returned to users does not tell the researcher how the users would have behaved had other documents been shown, so observed behavior is not easily reusable when evaluating new retrieval methods.

However, online evaluation benefits from involving real users, particularly when conducted on real queries in situ. In that case there is no uncertainty in how a judge should interpret the query *sdsu*, nor how to trade off the relevance of new and old documents to the query *wsdm*. All aspects of the users' context and state of knowledge are present, some of which may be difficult to realistically capture in a test collection. Finally, as usage data can be collected essentially for free by any active information retrieval system, its cost can be much lower than that of obtaining sufficient relevance judgments from experts to detect small relevance improvements. For these reasons, we focus on online evaluation.

Among online evaluation approaches in the context of Web search, two methods dominate today: The first involves measuring properties of user responses to retrieval, such as the the time it takes users to click, or the positions of these clicks and other observable behavior [9, 14, 5]. This can be used to compute a score for a given retrieval algorithm that can be compared across systems. The second approach invovles showing users a *combination* of results retrieved by different ranked retrieval algorithms, and observing which results users select from this combination. This is usually termed *interleaved* evaluation. A number of authors have demonstrated the higher sensitivty of the interleaved approach [7, 13, 1], largely due to the within-user comparison that is taking place: The same user with the same information need at the same time is shown the best results proposed by both systems, and directly chooses between them.

Figure 1: Illustrative example of interleaving. Rankings produced by two retrieval functions for the query *napa valley*, are combined into an interleaved combination.

In this paper, we address the question of how to obtain an optimal interleaving algorithm. In particular, a number of interleaving algorithms have been proposed, including Balanced Interleaving [6], Team Draft Interleaving [13] and Probabalistic Interleaving [4]. Further, additional variants of interleaving algorithms, for example involving how credit is assigned for clicks have been proposed [2, 15]. This leads to the question of what the best interleaving algorithm would be, and why. Also, the two most recent interleaving algorithms addressed unexpected flaws in previous algorithms. This suggests that analysis of interleavings algorithm is difficult, and that the properties encoded by each algorithm implicitly make assumptions that are difficult to verify. The designer of an algorithm risks creating new problems, even while fixing existing ones.

We thus invert the problem of deriving an interleaving algorithm: Starting with properties that we wish the algorithm to have, we formulate interleaving as the solution to an optimization problem. We then solve for the algorithm. This is the key contribution of our work. A second contribution is our evaluation method: Following a similar approach to Li et al. [10], we show how different interleaving algorithms can be evaluated on historical log data, without running a new algorithm on new users.

This paper is organized as follows. First, we present interleaved evaluation in detail. We then describe our approach, interleaving as the solution to an optimization problem. After formulating the optimization problem, we show theoretical guarantees and solve for two interleaving algorithms. We conclude with an evaluation comparing our approach with previous interleaving algorithms using a real usage data.

2. INTERLEAVING

An interleaving evaluation compares two retrieval functions R_A and R_B. Rather than showing the results of R_A to some users, and R_B to the rest, both results lists are generated for each query issued and a randomized combination is presented to users, as illustrated in Figure 1.

2.1 Goals of Interleaving

While mixing retrieval results from multiple rankings was first described by Kantor [8], the first interleaving algorithm was detailed and implemented by Joachims [6, 7]. He proposed that the comparison should satisfy:

(a) be blind to the user with respect to the underlying [retrieval functions],

(b) be robust to biases in the user's decision process that do not relate to retrieval quality,

(c) not substantially alter the search experience, and

(d) lead to clicks that reflect the user's preference.

2.2 Previous Algorithms

A number of interleaving algorithms have been proposed that attempt to satisfy these requirements. We focus on three: Balanced, Team Draft and Probabalistic interleaving. In all cases, we suppose that we are wishing to construct an interleaved list of results $A = (a_1, a_2, \ldots)$ and $B = (b_1, b_2, \ldots)$. We denote the interleaved list $I = (i_1, i_2, \ldots)$.

Balanced Interleaving

Balanced interleaving [6] creates a combined list I such that the top-k_I results of I includes the top-k_A of A and the top-k_B of B where for every k_I, values k_A and k_B differ by at most 1. The algorithm runs as follows: First, toss an unbiased coin. The outcome of this coin toss is $t = (A)$ or $t = (B)$. Let there be two pointers p_A and p_B that indicate the rank of the highest ranked document in A and B respectively that is not yet in I. Construct I by greedily appending a_{p_A} whenever $p_A < p_B$, or $p_A = p_B$ and $t = (A)$, and appending b_{p_B} otherwise. Recompute p_A and p_B after each document is added to I.

Team Draft Interleaving

Radlinski et al. proposed Team Draft interleaving [13] based on how sports teams are often assigned in friendly matches: Two captains (each with a preference order over players) toss a coin, then take turns picking players for their team.

In the retrieval setting, the algorithm proceeds similarly: In each iteration, toss an unbiased coin, t. If $t = (A)$, append the next available result from A (i.e. the next highest result in A that is not already in I) to I, followed by the next available result from B. If $t = (B)$, follow the same procedure but with B before A. This process continues, with a coin toss and two results added per iteration. The output is the interleaved list I and a record of which list provided each of the results in I.

Probabilistic Interleaving

Probabilistic interleaving, proposed by Hofmann et al. [4], is similar to Team Draft but allows a richer set of rankings to be constructed. First, rather than taking two results per coin toss, Probabilistic interleaving takes one. In an extreme case, I could be constructed entirely from A (with probability $0.5^{|I|}$), but in expectation A and B contribute the same number of results. Second, when selecting a result to append to I, Team Draft interleaving selects the next available result from a ranking. In Probabilistic Interleaving, results are instead selected with a probability decreasing with the position of the result in the ranking from which it is being selected. Thus, when selecting the first document in I from A, it is most likely that a_1 is selected, less likely that a_2 is selected, even less likely that a_3 is selected, and so forth.

Assigning Credit for Clicks

Having established these three list combination approaches, a way to interpret user clicks in each case is also required. Each interleaving algorithm was presented with a credit assignment rule, while other work has proposed alternate credit assignment approaches (only). It is the combination of list interleaving and credit assignment that comprises an interleaving algorithm, and determines fidelity and sensitivity.

In Balanced interleaving, when clicks are observed, the minimum values of k_A and k_B to generate the list down to the lowest click are computed. Then, $k = max(k_A, k_B)$. The number of clicked documents present in the top k of A is compared to the number of clicked documents in the top k of B. The ranking with the higher count "wins" this ranking instance (also termed *impression*), otherwise it is a tie. If one of the retrieval functions wins more than half of non-tied impressions, Balanced interleaving concludes that this retrieval function is better.

In Team Draft interleaving, each document is assumed to "be on the team" of the ranking from which it was selected: Clicks on this document count as credit for that ranker (each team always has an equal number of documents). The ranker with more credit "wins" each impression. A refinement ignores clicks on results in any identical prefix of both A and B, increasing sensitivity of the algorithm [1].

In Probabalistic interleaving, credit assignment is more sophisticated: Given an interleaved ranking I, all the possible coin toss sequences that could have resulted in I are computed. For each possible sequence of coin tosses, the algorithm computes which retrieval function "wins" using the same logic as with Team Draft. Probabilistic interleaving then assigns a probabalistic outcome to each impression based on how likely each ranker is to have won each impressions across all possible consistent coin toss inputs.

Finally, an assumption implicit in the above is that all clicks on documents are treated equally. Yue et al. [15] showed how to learn a weight for each click to improve sensitivity, for example perhaps treating top-position clicks differently. Hofmann et al. [3] reduce bias by similarly reweighting clicks. Alternatively, Hu et al. [2] proposed to interpret clicks as pairwise preferences over documents.

2.3 Success Criteria and Breaking Cases

Given these alternatives, the question arises of what makes a successful interleaving algorithm. When considering success, we adopt the approach of [12], focusing on fidelity and sensitivity. An interleaving algorithm with good fidelity will tend to agree with other appropriate evaluation methods such as test collections or randomized A/B tests in identifying the better of two retrieval functions. A sensitive algorithm will make efficient use of data, coming to a statistically significant conclusion with fewer interleaved impressions.

Fidelity and sensitivity of interleaving algorithms can be affected by systematic problems in their design, known as breaking cases. Breaking cases are interesting in the current study since they indicate algorithmic problems that we wish to address. More generally, in a practical setting it is useful to know the breaking cases of an algorithm, since a particular comparison (with an 'unlucky' pair of retrieval functions) may systematically have that case more often, which can change or delay the outcome of the comparison.[1]

As shown in [13, 1], $A = (doc_1, doc_2, doc_3)$ and $B = (doc_3, doc_1, doc_2)$ is a breaking case for Balanced interleaving. In particular, a user who clicks at random on one of the documents in the interleaved list will prefer A two out of three times. Team Draft interleaving also draws the wrong conclusions for some pairs of rankings A and B [4, 1]. For instance, if the only relevant and clicked document is doc^*, in expectation Team Draft interleaving prefers neither ranking when $A = (doc_1, doc^*, doc_3)$ and $B = (doc_1, doc_2, doc^*)$, despite one clearly being better for users. Finally, while Probabilistic interleaving avoids these breaking cases, it can show rankings that are very dissimilar from A and B, potentially degrading the user experience.

[1]Note that while these constructed breaking cases are *possible* for the interleaving algorithms, in many real-world evaluations they are not prevalent enough to affect the outcome.

3. OPTIMIZING INTERLEAVING

We now turn to the question of deriving an interleaving algorithm as the solution to an optimization problem. We start by deriving the constraints on this problem.

3.1 Refining Interleaving Goals

Refining the desirable properties presented by Joachims [6], we propose to modify the two last conditions:

(c') The comparison does not substantially alter the search experience, presenting the user with one input ranking, or the other, or a ranking that is "in between" the two.

(d') An interleaved evaluation produces a preference for a ranker if and only if the users prefer the documents returned by that ranker. Specifically:

d'.1 If document d is clicked, the input ranker that ranked d higher is given more credit for the click than the other ranker.

d'.2 In expectation, a randomly clicking user does not create a preference for either input ranker.

These goals will be written formally in Section 3.2. However, we first consider the intuition.

There are two naturally competing goals in an online evaluation: Should rankings be shown to obtain maximally useful relevance information, or should rankings that minimally disrupt the user be shown? Similar to Joachims requirement (c), we argue for the latter as users can quickly abandon an information retrieval system that performs poorly – even if it is doing so for evaluation reasons. In our formulation, (c') aims to guarantee small relevance impact: (1) interleaving two identical lists must yield the same list; (2) if two lists start with the same k documents, the interleaved list must also start with those same k documents; (3) if document d_1 is ranked higher than d_2 in both input rankings, it is also ranked higher in the interleaved ranking; (4) any document shown in the top k by an interleaving algorithm must be in the top k of at least one of the input rankings.

The property (d') limits how credit can be assigned to rankers based on clicks. For example, if a ranking is improved by moving the only relevant document higher (and users click on relevant documents), then the interleaving algorithm must recognize this improvement. Similarly, if clicks are made randomly then there should not be any preference.

Sensitivity

A further goal is for the interleaving algorithm to be as sensitive as possible to changes in ranking quality. This means that it should require the fewest user queries (or impressions) possible to infer a statistically significant preference. While absent from Joachims' original explicit criteria, we will show how to incorporate this as well.

Given these goals, we now show how the interleaving algorithm can be written as the solution to an explcit optimization problem.

3.2 Optimization Framework

Suppose we have two input rankers, R_A and R_B, that we wish to compare. We use lowercase letters to denote documents returned by these rankers, and uppercase letters to denote (ordered) rankings of results. For example, $A(q) = (a_1, \ldots, a_n)$ denotes the results retrieved by R_A for query q. Let $A^k(q)$ denote the (unordered) set of top-k documents $\{a_1, \ldots, a_k\}$. Without loss of generality, for notational simplicity we present the optimization problem for a single fixed query, for example writing A instead of $A(q)$.

Our goal is to obtain an algorithm that, given any two rankings A and B, produces a distribution over interleaved rankings of documents $\mathcal{L}$. The parameter we learn, p_j, is the probability with which each ranking $L_j \in \mathcal{L}$ will be shown to users[2]. For any given $L = (l_1, l_2, \ldots) \in \mathcal{L}$, let $\delta_i(L)$ (subsequently δ_i) be the (real valued) credit assigned to R_A whenever document l_i is clicked. Thus δ_i is positive if ranker R_A receives credit for this document, and negative if ranker R_B receives credit.

We next address randomly clicking users: We would like that for any user who clicks at random there is no preference inferred by the interleaving algorithm for either input retrieval function. However, it is not clear how to formalize this requirement. Instead, we require this to be the case for a specific model random user:[3] Let a randomly clicking user be a user who (1) picks a random threshold k from any distribution, then (2) clicks on $\eta \geq 1$ documents in the top-k of the interleaved list chosen uniformly at random.

We can finally write a formal definition of our constraints, based on the intuition from Section 3.1:

c' The interleaving list L satisfies:

$$\forall k.\ \exists i, j.\ s.t.\ L^k = A^i \bigcup B^j \tag{1}$$

This simply requires that any prefix of L consists of all top i documents from ranking A and all top j documents from ranking B. This means that, for example, the top document of L must be either a_1 or b_1. Similarly, the top two must be $\{a_1, a_2\}$, $\{a_1, b_1\}$ or $\{b_1, b_2\}$.

d'.1 The credit function δ satisfies:

$$rank^*(l_i, A) < rank^*(l_i, B) \Leftrightarrow \delta_i > 0 \tag{2}$$
$$rank^*(l_i, A) > rank^*(l_i, B) \Leftrightarrow \delta_i < 0 \tag{3}$$

where $rank^*(d, R)$ is the rank of document d in R if $d \in R$, and $|R| + 1$ otherwise. Rank positions are numbered from top to bottom, so the highest position has the lowest rank.

d'.2 Given the probability with which each ranking L_j is shown to users,

$$\forall k, \forall \eta,\ E\left[\eta E\left[\delta_i\right]_{i \in 1 \ldots k}\right]_{L_j} = 0 \tag{4}$$

[2]For example, in Balanced interleaving, there would be one or two elements in $\mathcal{L}$, with equal values of p_j. For Team Draft interleaving, there are up to $2^{|L|/2}$.

[3]Other models of random user could be used instead of, or even in addition to, this model.

3.3 Problem Definition

The set of permissible interleaved rankings is:

$$\mathcal{L} = \{L : \forall k, \exists i, j.\ s.t.\ L_k = A_i \bigcup B_j\} \tag{5}$$

The only parameter of the algorithm is the probability p_i with which each ranking $L_i \in \mathcal{L}$ is shown to users. The values of p_i must satisfy

1. Each ranking L_i is shown with a valid probability:
$$p_i \in [0, 1] \tag{6}$$

2. The probabilities add to 1:
$$\sum_{i=1}^{|\mathcal{L}|} p_i = 1 \tag{7}$$

3. The expected credit from a random user is zero:
$$\forall k, \forall \eta,\ \sum_{n=1}^{|\mathcal{L}|} \left(p_n \eta \frac{1}{k} \sum_{i=1}^{k} \delta_i \right) = 0$$
which simplifies to:
$$\forall k,\ \sum_{n=1}^{|\mathcal{L}|} \left(p_n \sum_{i=1}^{k} \delta_i \right) = 0 \tag{8}$$

For any input rankings A and B, and credit function δ_i, the solution values of p_i completely define an interleaving algorithm. The p_i values indicate the probablity with which each ranking is shown to users, and δ_i determines credit assignment.

However, this problem is also usually underconstrained. To produce an interleaved list of length k, there are $k + 1$ constraints but up to 2^k parameters p_i (although in practice usually many fewer, as A and B in Equation 5 are often similar in most real-world comparisons). We can therefore further refine the algorithm by optimizing for sensitivity.

3.3.1 Ensuring Sensitivity

As formulated, this problem allows any ranking that shows any prefix combination of results from A and B to be shown to users. However, as noted earlier, interleaving is more sensitive than comparisons where each ranking is shown to half of users because the same user observes documents from *both* rankers simultaneously and chooses between them. We therefore propose to maximize a sensitivity term subject to the above constraints (Equations 5 through 8).

Intuitively, the solution is to ensure fairness at the impression level: For every ranking shown to users, both rankers should get approximately equal space. While our formulation ensures fairness in expectation, here we wish to maximize it for every impression shown to users. Our goal is also similar to that of Probabilistic interleaving [4], where each impressions is given a real valued score that depends on all possible team assignments that could have generated it, smoothing the preference inferred. However, we instead select impresions that are most sensitive to ranking changes.

We choose a simple model of sensitivity to retain tractability that is a special case of our model in Section 3.2. Suppose that users observe the result at position i with probability

$f(i)$. Assuming a single random click on an interleaved list L, the probability of ranker R_A winning the impression is

$$w_A(L) = \sum_{i:\delta_i > 0} f(i), \quad (9)$$

although we now drop the parameter L from $w_A(L)$ for succinctness. Similarly, the probability of ranker R_B winning the impression, and of the rankers being tied can be written

$$w_B = \sum_{i:\delta_i < 0} f(i) \quad (10)$$

$$w_T = \sum_{i:\delta_i = 0} f(i) \quad (11)$$

Sensitivity can be defined as the uncertainty in the winner of a particular impression. Intuitively, sensitivity should be low if one of the rankers is bound to be preferred, or if the impression is always tied. Conversely, if each ranker would win 50% of impressions with random clicking, sensitivity should be high. We choose the following form of the sensitivity $s(L)$ of a particular ranking L:

$$s(L) = 0 \times w_T + entropy(w_A, w_B) \times (1 - w_T) \quad (12)$$

$$= -\frac{1 - w_T}{w_A + w_B} \log_2 \frac{w_A^{w_A} w_B^{w_B}}{(w_A + w_B)^{w_A + w_B}} \quad (13)$$

Note that if $w_T = 0$, this reduces to the entropy of a binomial outcome. For example, if for a given L, $w_A = w_B = 0.5$, the sensitivity is 1. On the other hand, if $w_T = 1$, $w_A = 1$ or $w_B = 1$, the sensitivity is zero.

The optimized interleaving algorithm thus reduces to maximizing the expected sensitivity (Equation 13) subject to the constraints presented in Equations 5 through 8[4].

An alternative formulation may be to minimize the variance in the expected outcome of the entire interleaving experiment across all impressions, although we leave assessing this to future work. We also note that different sensitivity criteria could be proposed, and be substituted into our approach. This would simply change the optimal probabilities for showing different ranking.

3.3.2 *Secondary Goals*

If we desire, we can also add extra criteria to optimize at the expense of sensitivity. For example, *all else being equal, minimize the frequency with which we show results from ranker R_B*. This might be required, for example, if we are performing high-risk comparisons of a known high quality ranker R_A with an experimental ranker R_B.

3.3.3 *Credit as a Parameter*

One particular difference in this formulation over previous approaches is that the credit function δ is an explicit parameter of the algorithm. This may seem a new parameter, but was in fact implicit in previous algorithms. For instance, Balanced, Team Draft and Probabalistic interleaving approaches each deal with multiple clicks differently. Yet this choice may have a non-trivial impact on the outcome of experiments, and the implicit behavior may not be desired. Rather, an explicit δ means the experimenter can choose the tradeoff, much as judgment based metrics make explicit the tradeoff between documents at different positions. We will consider some examples of credit functions below.

[4]For simplicity, in our evaluation we assume that $f(i)$ in Equations 9 through 11 is proportional to $1/i$

Probabilistic Interleaving encodes a similar idea – credit is assigned based on possible coin toss outcomes, and the closer a document is in R_A and R_B, the smaller its effect when clicked. However, instead of encoding credit in how documents are selected when interleaving, we make it explicit. Yue et al.'s [15] approach is also related, where the weight of each click is learned. Our approach is complimentary: An experimenter can specify a credit function based on where clicks happen, and the importance of e.g. duration of click may be learned using their approach.

3.4 Theoretical Guarantees

In this section we show the theoretical benefits of our approach over previous algorithms.

3.4.1 *Allowed Rankings*

We first consider the class of rankings allowed in $\mathcal{L}$, which are a superset of those produced by Team Draft and Balanced interleaving and a subset of those produced by Probabilistic interleaving.

PROPERTY 1. *The rankings produced by Balanced interleaving are in $\mathcal{L}$.*

PROOF INTUITION. *Balanced interleaving constructs an interleaving by maintaining pointers p_A and p_B to the highest ranked documents in each input ranking but that are not in the interleaved list. It then greedily selects the next document to add to the interleaved list based on the higher pointer, or the coin toss in the event of a tie. The value of i and j in Equation 5 is equal to $p_A - 1$ and $p_B - 1$ when result k is added by the Balanced interleaving algorithm.* □

PROPERTY 2. *The rankings produced by Team Draft interleaving are in $\mathcal{L}$.*

PROOF INTUITION. *Team Draft interleaving involves the two rankers greedily selecting the next available document to add to the interleaved list subject to the coin tosses. The ranks of the last document that is not available for each ranker correspond to the values of i and j in Equation 5.* □

PROPERTY 3. *The rankings produced by Probabilistic interleaving are a superset of $\mathcal{L}$.*

PROOF INTUITION. *Every prefix L^k involves the top i documents from ranking A and top j documents from ranking B. Clearly these could have been selected at random by the Probabilistic interleaving algorithm.* □

We also note that any ranking shown to users by our approach does not misorder more pairs of documents than would be misordered in expectation if half the users were shown the results from ranker A and half the users were shown the results from ranker B:

PROPERTY 4. *For every L^k prefix of length k of any $L \in \mathcal{L}$, the number of misordered pairs of documents between L^k and A^k plus the number of misordered pairs between L^k and B^k is less than or equal to the number of misordered pairs between A^k and B^k.*

PROOF INTUITION. *Let $rank^*(d, R)$ be the rank of document d in R if $d \in R$, and $|R| + 1$ otherwise. For any pair of documents $l_i, l_j \in \mathcal{L}^k$, with $i < j$, there are three cases. One of three cases must hold:*

1. *$rank^*(l_i, A) \leq rank^*(l_j, A), rank^*(l_i, B) \leq rank^*(l_j, B)$ This pair of documents is not misordered with respect to either A or B.*
2. *$rank^*(l_i, A) > rank^*(l_j, A), rank^*(l_i, B) \leq rank^*(l_j, B)$ This pair is misordered between L and A. However, it is also misordered between A and B.*
3. *$rank^*(l_i, A) \leq rank^*(l_j, A), rank^*(l_i, B) > rank^*(l_j, B)$ This pair is misordered between L and B. However, it is also misordered between A and B.*

It is not possible that $rank^*(l_i, A) > rank^*(l_j, A)$ and that $rank^*(l_i, B) > rank^*(l_j, B)$ because l_i could then not be at position i in L: Document l_j would have had to have been selected before l_i could have been selected because it precedes l_i in both A and B. Hence the total number of misordered documents must be bounded as required. □

3.4.2 Comparisons with Previous Algorithms

Balanced interleaving and Team Draft interleaving both have known breaking cases that Optimized interleaving solves:

PROPERTY 5. *The breaking cases with Balanced interleaving do not exist with Optimized interleaving.*

PROOF. *Balanced interleaving is biased when one of the rankings is preferred more often in expectation by a randomly clicking user. The randomly clicking user constraints ensure this does not occur with Optimized interleaving.* □

PROPERTY 6. *The breaking cases where Team Draft interleaving is not sensitive to actual relevance improvements with a single click do not exist with Optimized interleaving.*

PROOF. *The formulation of Optimized interleaving requires that the ranker that places a document higher receives more credit for that document whenever it is clicked. Hence promoting a relevant and clicked document will always be recognized by Optimized interleaving.* □

On the other hand, Probabilistic interleaving can present rankings that degrade the user experience more than Optimized interleaving. Letting $MOP(A, B)$ be the number of pairs of documents misordered between A and B,

PROPERTY 7. *If A and B agree on the order of any pair of documents, there exists a ranking R that can be shown to users by Probabilistic interleaving where $MOP(R, A) + MOP(R, B) > \max_{L \in \mathcal{L}} MOP(L, A) + MOP(L, B)$. In words, Probabilistic interleaving may show rankings that include more disagreements with both input rankers than the ranking with most disagreements shown by Optimized interleaving.*

PROOF OUTLINE. *As shown in Property 4, the number of misordered pairs in any ranking shown by Optimized interleaving is bounded by $MOP(A, B)$. Ranking A is at this bound, and $A \in \mathcal{L}$. Let a_i and a_j with $i < j$ be a pair of documents in the same order in B with smallest i and then smallest j given i. Consider the ranking R that reverses a_i and a_j in A. This ranking can be shown by Probabilistic interleaving. Moreover, $MOP(R, A) \geq 1$. Also, $MOP(R, B) \geq MOP(A, B)$ because only pairs of the form (a_i, a_k) or (a_k, a_j) with $i < k < j$ also change order when a_i and a_j are reversed. Now, it must be that case that $rank(a_k, B) < rank(a_i, B)$ because j has the smallest possible value. After the swap, R and B agree on the order of (a_i, a_k), but disagree on the order of (a_j, a_k) whereas the reverse was true previously. Hence $MOP(R, A) + MOP(R, B) \geq 1 + MOP(A, B) > MOP(A, B)$.* □

3.4.3 Existence of a Solution

It would be useful to know what further requirements on credit functions must be satisfied for there to always exist a solution to the optimization problem for any pair of input rankings A and B. It is clearly essential that for any k, there exist rankings in $L \in \mathcal{L}$ where $\Delta_k(L) = \sum_{i=1}^{k} \delta_i(L)$ are both positive and negative, or that all $\Delta_k(L)$ values are zero: Otherwise Equation 8 has no soluton. Empirically, for the Linear Rank Difference and Inverse Rank credit function examples below there is always a solution for rankings of length up to 10. However, we leave the question of general conditions as future work.

4. EXAMPLES

To obtain an interleaving algorithm, we need to specify a credit function. What form should this function take? We now present three examples that satisfy requirement (d'.1) in Section 3.2, followed by an example of how this impacts the interleaving algorithm obtained.

4.1 Example Credit Functions

Binary Preference

A particularly simple credit function would be to to give all the credit for any clicked document to the ranker that positioned this document higher:

$$\delta_i^{\text{Bin}} = \begin{cases} 1 & \text{if } rank^*(l_i, A) < rank^*(l_i, B) \\ -1 & \text{if } rank^*(l_i, A) > rank^*(l_i, B) \\ 0 & \text{otherwise} \end{cases}$$

Given this credit function, consider Equation 8, with $k = 3$ and input rankings $A = (d_1, d_2, d_3)$ and $B = (d_2, d_3, d_1)$. Under (c') there are three allowed rankings, the two original rankings plus the intermediate ranking (d_2, d_1, d_3). In all three cases a user who clicks randomly to $k = 3$ will assign two thirds of credit to input B. The equation becomes:

$$\sum_{n=1}^{|\mathcal{L}|} (p_n(1 - 1 - 1)) = 0$$

Together with Equation 7, we see that there is no valid solution for p_i. Hence this credit function would be biased and cannot be used. These input rankings are also a breaking case for Balanced interleaving. In fact, this credit function closely resembles that encoded by Balanced interleaving. Note that this credit function also violates the requirement introduced in Section 3.4.3.

Linear Rank Difference

Next consider an approach where the credit assigned to a clicked document is the additional effort that a user would have to spend to find the document in the other ranking:

$$\delta_i^{\text{Lin}} = rank^*(l_i, A) - rank^*(l_i, B), \tag{14}$$

Inverse Rank

A third way we could assign credit for clicks would be to give more weight to changes in rank at the top of a ranking. For example, we could use an inverse-rank credit scoring:

$$\delta_i^{\text{Rank}} = 1/rank^*(l_i, B) - 1/rank^*(l_i, A) \tag{15}$$

Table 1: Interleaved rankings $\mathcal{L}$ for $A = (a, b, c, d)$ and $B = (b, d, c, a)$. For two different credit functions, we show solution display probabilities p with cost constraints $\Delta_1 \ldots \Delta_4$ for each ranking, where $\Delta_j = \sum_{i=1}^{j} \delta_i$. Each allowed ranking has a total of 4 misordered pairs with respect to A and B. For comparison, we show the display probabilities for three other algorithms.

Interleaved	Linear Rank Diff. Cost Constraints					Inverse Rank Cost Constraints					sensi-tivity	Other algorithm ranking probabilities			Misordered Pairs	
Ranking L_i	Δ_1	Δ_2	Δ_3	Δ_4	p_i	Δ_1	Δ_2	Δ_3	Δ_4	p_i	$s(L_i)$	Bal.	TD	Prob.	$L_i \sim A$	$L_i \sim B$
(a, b, c, d)	3	2	2	0	0	3/4	1/4	1/4	0	0	0.83		25%	15.7%	0	4
(a, b, d, c)	3	2	0	0	25%	3/4	1/4	0	0	40%	0.87	50%	25%	18.0%	1	3
(b, a, c, d)	-1	2	2	0	0	-1/2	1/4	1/4	0	0	0.73		25%	11.5%	1	3
(b, a, d, c)	-1	2	0	0	35%	-1/2	1/4	0	0	35%	0.74	50%	25%	13.2%	2	2
(b, d, a, c)	-1	-3	0	0	40%	-1/2	-3/4	0	0	25%	0.60			10.8%	3	1
(b, d, c, a)	-1	-3	-3	0	0	-1/2	-3/4	-3/4	0	0	0.50			6.3%	4	0
other	*disallowed*					*disallowed*								24.3%	*average sum: 5.69*	

4.2 Illustrative Optimization Solutions

Table 1 compares the solutions produced using these credit functions with Balanced (Bal), Team Draft (TD) and Probabilistic (Prob) interleaving for one particular pair of rankings. We now walk through the example in the table.

The left column shows the allowed rankings $\mathcal{L}$ for this pair of input rankings. There are six of them. As shown above, the possible rankings produced by Team Draft and Balanced interleaving are subsets of these six. The *Other algorithm* column shows that each possible ranking for these algorithms is shown equally often. The rankings shown by Probabilistic interleaving are a superset of these six rankings. To illustrate the user impact of interleaving, the rightmost column shows the number of misordered pairs of documents in the interleaved list with respect to the input rankings A and B. While all six allowed rankings are "in between" the input rankings in terms of the total number of misordered pairs, Probabilistic interleaving shows other rankings 24.3% of the time, allowing possibilities such as showing a different document in the top position than was in either input.

Finally, the middle columns describe the optimization problem solved in more detail: The columns Δ_i each represent one constraint of the optimization problem. For instance, the columns Δ_2 show the values of $\delta_1 + \delta_2$ for each L_i. Here, we see that to ensure that in expectation there is no credit from a randomly clicking users given linear credit, the value of p_i in the top four rows must add up to 60% (thus ensuring that in expectation ranker R_A gets credit equal to $2 \times 60\%$ while ranker R_B in expectation gets identical credit in expectation, equal to $3 \times 40\%$). The column labeled $s(L_i)$ shows the sensitivity of each ranking.

5. EMPIRICAL EVALUATION

We finally turn to evaluation based on real user data. To be able to compare all the algorithms in a realistic setting without implementing and running all five at large scale, we devise a log-based approach that allows repeatable comparison of interleaving algorithms. Intuitively, we find queries where a sufficient number of distinct rankings was previously shown that we can imagine that two particular rankings were being interleaved, and take the rankings actually shown to measure the outcome of any interleaving algorithm that would have shown some subset of these rankings.

5.1 Log Collection Details

We would like to simulate the online case offline: Have two rankers providing rankings of documents, and observe these rankings interleaved using different algorithms. Hence we need a log of rankings shown to users and their responses. However, the Web is constantly changing, with new and ephemeral content. Many documents are ranked very few times, particularly lower down in query results. To get a suitable offline collection, we thus take all queries and all sets of top *four* results shown by a commerical search engine over the first six weeks of 2012. As Web search users most often click at top positions, these documents include most clicked documents. We keep all queries with at least four such distinct rankings, each shown at least 10 times, and with at least one user click on one of the top four documents each time[5]. Additionally, we require the distinct rankings not to have been the product of Web search personalization.

As interleaving involves a comparison of two rankings, for each query we must call two rankings A and B. We take the most frequent top-4 ranking as A, and the most dissimilar ranking (i.e. with a difference at the highest position) which was shown at least ten times as B. In the event of a tie in dissimilarity, the most frequent most dissimilar ranking is selected as B. For example, for the query *beef barley soup* we take $A = (d_1, d_2, d_3, d_4)$ and $B = (d1, d_3, d_2, d_4)$, where d_1 is a document on *cooks.com*, d_2 is a document on *southernfood.about.com*, d_3 is a document on *allrecipes.com* and d_4 is on *foodnetwork.com*.

Next, we further filter the logs, restricting ourselves to queries where all possible rankings produced by Team Draft interleaving were shown to users at least ten times, as well as both possible rankings produced by Balanced interleaving.

We end up with 64,251 distinct queries[6]. These can be interpreted as having run Balanced, Team Draft and Optimized interleaving by reweighting actual rankings shown to real users[7]. We can also evaluate Probabalistic interleaving over the subset of possible rankings that were shown.

Table 2 shows an example of the rankings observed for one particular query. On the left, we see which two rankings were selected as A and B. The four rankings produced by Team Draft interleaving, and two produced by Balanced interleaving, are included. For example, the row with (A) (B) in the

[5]These queries had some amount of instability in the top 4 positions due to changes in the Web, different rankers providing users with results, and potentially other reasons.

[6]As can be expected, all queries in this dataset are frequent. Further, we must assume that the intent of the queries does not change during data collection.

[7]For just one query there was no solution for the Inverse Rank credit function optimization since sufficient rankings were not shown to users. We considered this query a tie.

Table 3: Pearson correlation and directional agreement between each pair of interleaving algorithms.

Pearson correlation

	Bal.	TD.	Prob.	Opt:Linear	Opt:Inv
Balanced	-	0.94	0.90	0.93	0.84
Team Draft	0.94	-	0.92	0.93	0.91
Probabilistic	0.90	0.92	-	0.91	0.92
Opt:Delta	0.93	0.93	0.91	-	0.88
Opt:Inverse	0.84	0.91	0.92	0.88	-

Directional agreement

	Bal.	TD.	Prob.	Opt:Linear	Opt:Inv
Balanced	-	94%	87%	94%	92%
Team Draft	94%	-	88%	93%	91%
Probabilistic	87%	88%	-	88%	89%
Opt:Delta	94%	93%	88%	-	95%
Opt:Inverse	92%	91%	89%	95%	-

Team Draft column would be generated by Team Draft if R_A won the first coin toss, and R_B won the second coin toss. These rankings also include those produced by Probabilistic interleaving 63% of the time. We also see the solution produced by our optimization approach for two credit functions presented earlier. Both credit functions result in a different set of four rankings being shown to users than are selected by Team Draft interleaving, and these rankings are not shown equally often. In particular, A and B are not shown to users as they have low sensitivity (see Sec. 3.3.1).

5.2 Scoring Each Query

To compute the interleaving score of each query, we weight each observed ranking with the appropriate probability for each algorithm. We then sample the actually observed click patterns for the ranking, calculating a mean score that would have been observed per query had the query had been shown to many users (assuming the log data is representative).

5.3 Evaluation Results

We compare our optimization approach to previous interleaving algorithms, measuring agreement and sensitivity.

5.3.1 Correlation of Interleaving Algorithms

We first measure the agreement in the scores of the interleaving algorithms across queries. We would expect this to be high, as Team Draft and Balanced interleaving have been shown to both be reliable in previous online evaluations [7, 13, 1, 12]. Table 3 shows the Pearson correlation, as well as directional agreement of each pair of algorithms. As expected, both are very high.

The most interesting cases for further analysis are those where the algorithms disagree. The following four queries have the highest disagreement (most negative product of scores) between Balanced or Team Draft, and an Optimized algorithm. For each, we show the A and B rankings, which was preferred by each algorithm, and a manual assessment.

Balanced vs Optimized: Linear Rank Cost

`query` *shrimp stir fry with vegetables*
`A` (1) cooks.com; (2) chinesefood.about.com; (3) myrecipes.com; (4) allrecipes.com
`B` (4) allrecipes.com; (1) cooks.com; (2) chinesefood.about.com; (3) myrecipes.com;
`Preference` All algorithms prefer ranker A, except Balanced
`Notes` This is a classic case of Balanced bias, as ranking B just promotes the previously fourth result to the top
`Correct` Team Draft, Probabilistic, Opt:Linear and Opt:Inverse

Balanced vs Optimized: Inverse Cost

`query` *siberian rhubarb extract*
`A` (1) drozfans.com; (2) herbalmenopauseremedy.com; (3) ezinearticles.com; (4) bizrate.com
`B` (2) herbalmenopauseremedy.com; (3) ezinearticles.com; (4) bizrate.com; (4) herbalmenopausremedy.com
`Preference` All algorithms prefer ranker A, except Balanced
`Notes` Also a breaking case for Balanced, with ranking B removing the top result from ranking A.
`Correct` Team Draft, Probabilistic, Opt:Linear and Opt:Inverse

Team Draft vs Optimized: Linear Rank Cost

`query` *trutv originals*
`A` (1) trutv.com homepage; (2) hollywoodreporter.com; (3) trutv.com/videos/originals; (4) closinglogos.com
`B` (2) hollywoodreporter.com; (3) trutv.com/videos/originals; (1) trutv.com homepage; (4) closinglogos.com
`Preference` All algorithms except Team Draft prefer A
`Notes` This is the breaking case discussed for Team Draft in Section 2.3: Most clicks are on result (3)
`Correct` Balanced, Probabilistic, Opt:Linear and Opt:Inverse

Team Draft vs Optimized: Inverse Credit

`query` *publix.org oasis*
`A` (1) yoomk.com; (2) publix.org; (3) publix.com; (4) publix.com (sub-page)
`B` (2) publix.org; (3) publix.com; (4) publix.com (sub-page); (5) answers.yahoo.com
`Preference` Balanced and Team Draft prefer ranker A, the others prefer ranker B
`Notes` Most clicks are on publix.org, although a sufficient number are on yoomk.com when shown first to change the outcome for Balanced and Team Draft.
`Correct` Probabilistic, Opt:Linear and Opt:Inverse

Summary

To summarize these four most extreme cases, we see that Balanced was correct once, Team Draft twice, and Probabilistic, Optimized:Inverse and Optimized:Linear in all four.

5.3.2 Agreement with Expert Judgments

Although the previous four cases are informative, we must consider the agreement with expert judgments to have a generalized estimate of the correctness of the interleaving algorithms. We thus take all the queries in our log based set, and intersect them with a large set of previously judged queries. We find 1,664 queries in the intersection.

Table 4 shows the fraction of queries for which each interleaving algorithm agrees directionally with DCG@4, a popular judgment-based relevance metric [11], and the correlation between interleaving and DCG@4 values. Agreement and correlation of the algorithms is similar, but all the agreement values are low, in the mid-50% range. While at first surprising, note that we restrict ourselves to queries with some amount of instability, which is more likely for ambiguous queries. Easy-to-judge queries are often navigational, where the ranking produced by a commercial search engine is likely more stable. One way to bound the agreement is

Table 2: Data for one example query, *hrc*. d_1 is a webpage on http://www.hrc.army.mil/, d_2 is on http://www.hrc.org/, etc.

Label	Generated By: Team Draft	Balanced	Probabilistic	Ranking	Frequency Actually Shown	Optimization Solution: Delta Credit	Inverse Credit
R_A	(A) (A)	(A)	11.8%	d_1, d_2, d_3, d_4	>1000	-	-
	(A) (B)		9.9%	d_1, d_2, d_4, d_3	14	17%	23%
			9.9%	d_1, d_2, d_4, d_5	46	33%	27%
	(B) (A)		11.8%	d_2, d_1, d_3, d_4	19	33%	38%
	(B) (B)	(B)	9.9%	d_2, d_1, d_4, d_3	14	17%	12%
R_B			9.9%	d_2, d_1, d_4, d_5	179	-	-

Table 4: Directionary agreement and Pearson correlation between interleaving algorithms and manual judgments. The differences are not statistically significant. The correlations of Optimized:Linear and Optimized:Inverse are statistically significantly greater than zero (p<0.01).

Algorithm	Directional Agreement	Pearson Correlation
Balanced	52.0%	0.020
Team Draft	52.4%	0.046
Probabilistic	54.2%	0.039
Optimized:Linear	53.1%	0.078
Optimized:Inverse	53.2%	0.065
All algorithms	40.2%	
Any algorithm	63.2%	

to consider the fraction of queries where *any* of the interleaving algorithms agree directionally with DCG@4: This is 63.2% of queries. In fact, the following queries are those with highest average interleaving preference (across all five algorithms) yet disagreeing with judgments:

- `tw` Judgments prefer the Wikipedia page about Taiwan. User prefer to click on the Twitter homepage.
- `tea` Judgments prefer pages about the drink. Users prefer the Texas Education Agency.
- `att webmail` Judgments also give credit to the main AT&T homepage, which is rarely clicked by users.
- `mail` Judgments prefer mail.com, users prefer mail.yahoo.com.
- `torrent` Judges assign some relevance to results about the BitTorrent protocol, while users almost only click on download sites.
- `y` Judgments prefer the Wikipedia page for the letter Y, while users prefer yahoo.com.

We see that in all cases the interleaving evaluation may be correct, suggesting that the judgments used may not always reflect user needs for ambiguous queries.

5.3.3 *Bias Analysis*

We notice that our chosen (most frequent) ranking A is preferred for 53 to 58% of queries, ranking B is preferred for 37% to 41% of queries, with the two rankings tied for 4% to 8% (depending on the algorithm): With all five algorithms, ranking A is preferred on average. This provides a way to evaluate the bias of the different interleaving algorithms.

We summarize the queries by *pattern*, assigning a letter to each Web document such that A is always (a, b, c, d). We can then describe ranking B in terms of these letters[8]. For example, in our dataset, ranker B is (a, c, b, d) for 18,262 queries and (a, b, e, c) for 9,494 queries.

[8]The first document not returned by ranker A but returned by ranker B is assigned e, then f and so forth.

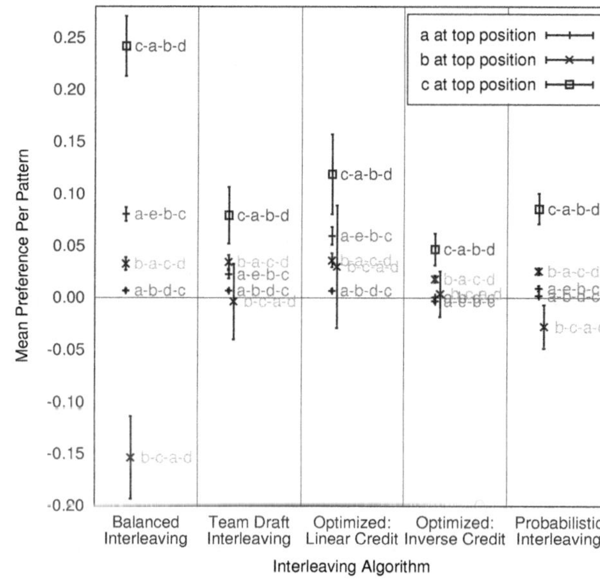

Figure 2: Per-pattern aggregate preference of different interleaving algorithms for selected patterns, showing the relative credit given to different ranking changes.

Figure 2 shows the mean interleaving preference for some example patterns. For instance, across all queries where ranker B mapped to (c, a, b, d) – i.e. the first document returned by ranker B is the same as the third document returned by ranker A, etc – Balanced interleaving generates a mean preference of 0.242. For each ranking pattern, each algorithm generates a preference in favor of ranker A (up) or ranker B (down). Because the most frequent ranking is most often best in our dataset, we expect all points to lie above zero. However, each interleaving algorithm encodes a different relative preference for each pattern, depending on the (previously implicit) credit function. For example, the bias in Balanced interleaving means that (b, c, a, d) is biased against ranker A, and (c, a, b, d) is biased for ranker A. We also see the relative magnitude of different changes. As expected, inserting an originally lower result at higher positions tends to cause a bigger preference.

5.3.4 *Sensitivity Analysis*

Finally, we compare the sensitivity of the different interleaving algorithms. Following [12, 4], we measure the sensitivity of each algorithm by sampling different numbers of

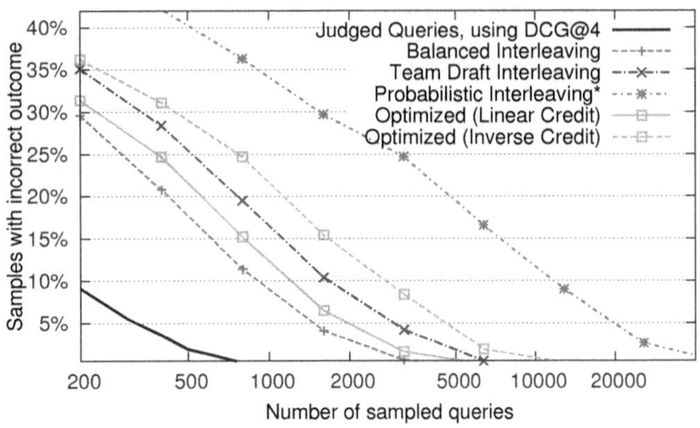

Figure 3: Fraction of bootstrapped simulations that prefer ranker A over ranker B for each interleaving algorithm, as a function of the number of queries sampled.

queries from our log[9] 10,000 times, and observing the fraction of samples for which ranker A is preferred overall. If one of the algorithms reliably prefers A with fewer impressions, it is more sensitive on this collection. Figure 3 shows that the optimized algorithms have comparable sensitivity to previous interleaving algorithms. In particular, we see that the Optimized algorithm with Linear Rank Credit is similarly sensitive to Balanced interleaving, while we showed above that it is less biased. We also note that the apparent poor sensitivity of Probabilistic interleaving may be caused by the nature of our dataset: Only a specific small fraction of the possible rankings that would have been produced by Probabilistic interleaving were present in our dataset, potentially disadvantaging this algorithm. Moreover, in opposition to other algorithms, probabalistic interleaving can make a probabilistic preference from even single-impression queries, where our evaluation technique cannot be applied.

6. CONCLUSION

In this paper we have presented a new approach to online evaluation with interleaving. We show that it is possible to postulate the requirements of interleaving by making explicit the assumptions about the value of user clicks, and solving for the rankings that should be shown to users.

Our key theoretical contribution is to show how to invert the question of obtaining interleaving algorithms: Starting with the desirable properties, we essentially solve for the algorithm. We then show that our interleaving algorithms are an improvement over previous ones. Empirically, we achieve similar correlation with judgments, and sensitivity only second to Balanced interelaving, which is known to be biased in some cases. We also avoid showing users poorer rankings than necessary while making it possible to optimize sensitivity of the algorithm directly.

Our work leaves open a number of questions. First, further theoretical analysis is necessary to show what further restrictions on the credit function optimized must exist to ensure there is always a solution to the optimization problem. Second, futher empirical evaluations by implementing this interleaving algorithm are required to confirm the sensitivity improvements. Finally, by making the credit function a parameter of the optimization framework, we leave its choice as an important parameter. A better understanding of the best credit function to use is clearly necessary.

[9]As the query set is already skewed away from a natural query distribution, queries were sampled uniformly.

Aknowledgments

We thank Martin Szummer, Emine Yilmaz, Michael Taylor and the anonymous reviewers for comments on this work.

7. REFERENCES

[1] O. Chapelle, T. Joachims, F. Radlinski, and Y. Yue. Large scale validation and analysis of interleaved search evaluation. *ACM Transactions on Information Science*, 30(1), 2012.

[2] J. He, C. Zhai, and X. Li. Evaluation of methods for relative comparison of retrieval systems based on clickthroughs. In *Proc. of CIKM*, 2009.

[3] K. Hofmann, F. Behr, and F. Radlinski. On caption bias in interleaving experiments. In *Proc. of CIKM*, 2012.

[4] K. Hofmann, S. Whiteson, and M. de Rijke. A probabilistic method for inferring preferences from clicks. In *Proc. of CIKM*, 2011.

[5] J. Huang, R. W. White, and S. Dumais. No clicks, no problem: Using cursor movements to understand and improve search. In *Proceedings of CHI*, 2011.

[6] T. Joachims. Optimizing Search Engines Using Clickthrough Data. In *Proceedings of KDD*, 2002.

[7] T. Joachims. Evaluating Retrieval Performance using Clickthrough Data. In J. Franke, G. Nakhaeizadeh, and I. Renz, editors, *Text Mining*. Physica/Springer Verlag, 2003.

[8] P. Kantor. National, language-specific evaluation sites for retrieval systems and interfaces. In *International Conference on Computer-Assisted Information Retrieval (RIAO)*, pages 139–147, 1988.

[9] D. Kelly and J. Teevan. Implicit feedback for inferring user preference: A bibliography. *SIGIR Forum*, 37(2), 2003.

[10] L. Li, W. Chu, J. Langford, and X. Wang. Unbiased offline evaluation of contextual-bandit-based news article recommendation algorithms. In *Proc. of WSDM*, 2011.

[11] C. D. Manning, P. Raghavan, and H. Schuetze. *Introduction to Information Retrieval*. Cambridge University Press, 2008.

[12] F. Radlinski and N. Craswell. Comparing the sensitivity of information retrieval metrics. In *Proc. of SIGIR*, 2010.

[13] F. Radlinski, M. Kurup, and T. Joachims. How does clickthrough data reflect retrieval quality. In *Proc. of CIKM*, 2008.

[14] K. Wang, T. Walker, and Z. Zheng. PSkip: Estimating relevance ranking quality from web search clickthrough data. In *Proceedings of KDD*, 2009.

[15] Y. Yue, Y. Gao, O. Chapelle, Y. Zhang, and T. Joachims. Learning more powerful test statistics for click-based retrieval evaluation. In *SIGIR*, 2010.

[16] C. Zhai, W. W. Cohen, and J. Lafferty. Beyond independent relevance: Methods and evaluation metrics for subtopic retrieval. In *Proc. of SIGIR*, 2003.

Mining the Web to Predict Future Events

Kira Radinsky
Technion–Israel Institute of Technology
Haifa, Israel
kirar@cs.technion.ac.il

Eric Horvitz
Microsoft Research
Redmond, WA, USA
horvitz@microsoft.com

ABSTRACT

We describe and evaluate methods for learning to forecast forthcoming events of interest from a corpus containing 22 years of news stories. We consider the examples of identifying significant increases in the likelihood of disease outbreaks, deaths, and riots in advance of the occurrence of these events in the world. We provide details of methods and studies, including the automated extraction and generalization of sequences of events from news corpora and multiple web resources. We evaluate the predictive power of the approach on real-world events withheld from the system.

Categories and Subject Descriptors

I.2.6 [**Artificial Intelligence**]: Learning; I.2.1 [**Artificial Intelligence**]: Applications and Expert Systems

General Terms

Algorithms, experimentation

Keywords

News corpora, predicting future news, learning from Web content

1. INTRODUCTION

Mark Twain famously said that "the past does not repeat itself, but it rhymes." In the spirit of this reflection, we develop and test methods for leveraging large-scale digital histories captured from 22 years of news reports from the New York Times (NYT) archive to make real-time predictions about the likelihoods of future human and natural events of interest. We describe how we can learn to predict the future by generalizing sets of specific transitions in sequences of reported news events, extracted from a news archive spanning the years 1986–2008. In addition to the news corpora, we leverage data from freely available Web resources, including Wikipedia, FreeBase, OpenCyc, and GeoNames, via the LinkedData platform [6]. The goal is to build predictive models that generalize from specific sets of sequences of events to provide likelihoods of future outcomes, based on patterns of evidence observed in near-term newsfeeds. We propose the methods as a means of generating actionable forecasts in advance of the occurrence of target events in the world.

The methods we describe operate on newsfeeds and can provide large numbers of predictions. We demonstrate the predictive power of mining thousands of news stories to create classifiers for a range of prediction problems. We show as examples forecasts on three prediction challenges: proactive alerting on forthcoming disease outbreaks, deaths, and riots. These event classes are interesting in serving as examples of predictions that can serve as heralds for attention for guiding interventions that may be able to change outcomes for the better. We compare the predictive power of the methods to several baselines and demonstrate precisions of forecasts in these domains ranging from 70% to 90% with a recall of 30% to 60%.

The contributions of this work include automated abstraction techniques that move the level of analysis from specific entities to consideration of broader classes of observations and events. The abstractions enlarge the effective sizes of training sets by identifying events as members of more general sets of evidence and outcomes at higher-levels of ontological hierarchies. For example, we can learn from news data about events in specific countries (e.g., Angola and Rwanda) to build classifiers that consider the likelihood of events on a continent (e.g., Africa) or to regions characterized by particular demographic and geological properties. The knowledge that Angola and Rwanda are elements of the broader set of countries comprising Africa is extracted from LinkedData.

As an example, the learning and inference methods can be used to provide alerts about increases in the likelihood of a forthcoming cholera outbreak within a specified horizon. Cholera is a fast-paced infection causing over 100,000 deaths per a year, with a mortality rate exceeding 50% for people with the ailment who do not receive treatment. With prompt rehydration therapy, the mortality rate drops to less than 1%. Alerts about inferred jumps in the likelihoods of future cholera outbreaks based on the monitoring of news stories could assist with the triaging of attention and planning effort. For example, inferred likelihoods of a cholera outbreak over specific periods of time could guide proactive designs for distributing fresh water in areas at raised risk. The methods we describe might one day be used to continue to monitor evolving news stories and to provide automated

WSDM'13, February 4–8, 2013, Rome, Italy.

alerting about the raised likelihood of outcomes of interest. Such predictions could serve as adjuvants to existing monitoring and communication services, such as the World Health Organizations (WHO) Global Alert and Response (GAR) system for coordinating responses to public health emergencies[1]. In tests, we found that automated predictions would have provided an alert a week in advance of several of the outbreaks of cholera (Figure 6).

Experts such as epidemiologists who explore the relationships between the spread of disease and natural disasters make similar inferences. However, such studies are typically few in number, employ heuristic assessments, and are frequently retrospective analyses, rather than aimed at generating predictions for guiding near-term action. In contrast, a computational system has the ability to learn patterns from large amounts of data, can monitor numerous information sources, can learn new probabilistic associations over time, and can continue to do real-time monitoring, prediction, and alerting on increases in the likelihoods of forthcoming concerning events. Beyond knowledge that is easily discovered in studies or available from experts, new relationships and context-sensitive probabilities of outcome can be discovered by a computational system with long tentacles into historical corpora and real-time feeds. As an example, the methods we describe identified a relationship in Angola between droughts and storms that, in turn, catalyze cholera outbreaks. Alerts about a downstream risk of cholera could have been issued nearly a year in advance (Figure 1). Human experts who focus on shorter time horizons may overlook such long-term interactions. Computational systems can consider multiple time granularities and horizons in pursuing the probabilistic influences among events. Beyond alerting about actionable situations based on increased likelihoods of forthcoming outcomes of interest, predictive models can more generally assist by providing guidance when inferences from data run counter to expert expectations. It can be valuable to identify situations where there is a significantly *lower likelihood* of an event than expected by experts based on the large set of observations and feeds being considered in an automated manner. Finally, a system monitoring likelihoods of concerning future events typically will have faster and more comprehensive access to news stories that may seem less important on the surface (e.g., a story about a funeral published in a local newspaper that does not reach the main headlines), but that might provide valuable evidence in the evolution of larger, more important stories (e.g., massive riots).

2. EVENT PREDICTION

We assume that events in the real-world are generated by a probabilistic model that also generates news reports corresponding to these events. We use the text of news stories to build an inferential model of the form $P\big(ev_j(\tau+\Delta)\big|ev_i(\tau)\big)$ for some future event ev_j at time $\tau+\Delta$ and past event ev_i happening at time τ (e.g., today). For example, the model learns that the probability of a news report about a drought (ev_j) happening after a news report about a flood (ev_i) to be 18%. This probability approximates the relationship between the two real-world events.

Given a target future event (such as cholera outbreak), calculating this probability for every possible future time

[1] http://www.who.int/csr/alertresponse/en/

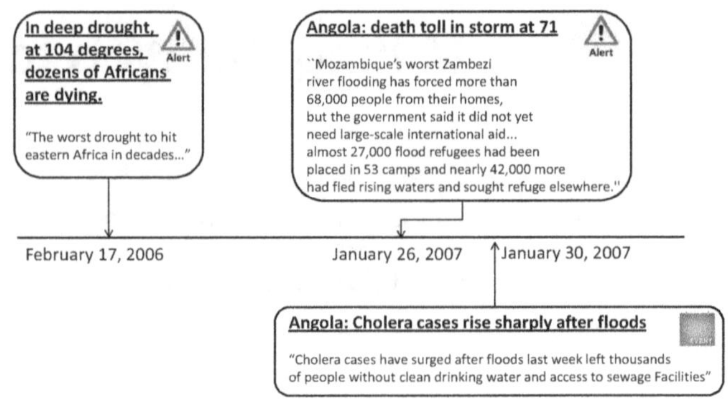

Figure 1: Example of likelihood of cholera rising after a drought followed by storms in Angola. Triangular alert icons represent inferences of significant upswings in likelihood of a cholera outbreak occurring within several days.

$\tau+\Delta$ and every possible ev_i is an intractable problem. We simplify the analysis by focusing on a small subset of event sequence candidates that may be causally linked, and define sets of events ev_i that are linked to target events ev_j in this manner. In particular, we define and extract from the NYT archive news *storylines*—sets of topically cohesive ordered segments of news that include two or more declarative independent clauses about a single story. As an example, the following events form a storyline: {(drought in Africa, 02/17/2006), (storm in Rwanda, 01/26/2007), (flood in Rwanda, 01/27/2007), (cholera outbreak in Rwanda, 01/30/2007)}. We then use such storylines as a heuristic for identifying possible causal relationships among events. The process is performed by clustering news stories with similar text and semantic entities, as detailed in Section 2.1.

We show a componentized view of the method in Figure 2. At the start of the learning phase, the system mines the NYT news corpora and extracts storylines, using techniques adapted from well-known topic tracking and detection algorithms [8, 3, 7], that cluster similar texts together (Section 2.1). We next enrich the storylines with information extracted from Web knowledge sources via the LinkedData project(Section 2.2). We extract a wide variety of facts, including such information as the population density in Rwanda, percentage of land in Rwanda covered by water, and the gross domestic product of the country. We generalize both features and events to increase the number of equivalent samples for constructing predictive models (Section 2.3). For example, we can learn from data about events in specific countries (e.g., Angola and Rwanda) to build classifiers that consider the likelihood of events of interest on a larger scale (e.g., larger continent of Africa) or to regions characterized by particular demographic and geological properties. At the end of the learning phase, the system estimates the probabilities $P\big(ev_j(\tau+\Delta)\big|ev_i(\tau)\big)$ and builds a probabilistic classifier for use in the prediction phase. The classifier can be used to provide real-time probabilities of events of interest, such as an impending "cholera outbreak in Angola" based on the previous knowledge obtained in a storyline about Angola or its generalization, Africa. The classifier we construct provides binary predictions of whether an event will occur following an observed event sequence. In experiments, we also evaluate both the occurrence of the target event and the mean time between the prediction and occurrence. We show results on providing such alerts nearly three weeks prior to the actual predicted event. We leave the prediction of the exact date of events of interest based on specific dynamics to future work.

2.1 Extracting Event Chains

We define and extract news storylines from the NYT archive as a heuristic for identifying potential causal relationships among events. A storyline is a set of topically cohesive ordered segments of news that includes two or more declarative independent clauses about a single story. As an example, a story line about the arrest of Carlos the Jackal includes the stories about verification of his identity, his transport to prison, and so on. Methods for extracting such storylines are referred to as *topic detection and tracking* (TDT) [8]. Topic detection involves identifying a series of linked events in streams of stories. To identify storylines, we modified the Inc.LM method, an approach to topic tracking found to be most successful for this task in several competitions [3]. Consider $Chains \in 2^{2^{|T| \times Time}}$ as the set of all possible storylines, where T is all the news articles and $Time$ is a discrete representation of time. We denote with $t_1 <<_c t_2$ an event represented by the news article t_1 occurring before an event represented by the news article t_2 in a chain $c \in Chains$. We use the notation $t(\tau)$ to represent an event as defined by the appearance of the text t of a news story at time $\tau \in Time$. Under the assumption that causality occurs only within storylines, the prediction challenge is reduced to calculating the probability $P\big(t(\tau_i > \tau)\big|t_j(\tau)\big)$ for $\{t_j | \exists c \in Chains, t_j <<_c t\}$.

Similar to other vector space approaches for topic detection [7], we first cluster documents with similar text. We consider news articles as documents and represent each news article as a vector $(\sigma_1^t \ldots \sigma_n^t)$, such that

$$\sigma_i^t = \mathrm{tf}_{w,t} \cdot \log \frac{|T|}{|\{t' \in T \,|\, w_i \in t'\}|},$$

where $|T|$ is all the news articles, and $\mathrm{tf}_{w,t}$ is the frequency of the word w in article t. We then perform a nearest-neighbor analysis, where we find for each article the k closest (in our experiments $k = 50$) articles to it using a cosine similarity measurement, defined as

$$\mathrm{sim}(t_a, t_b) = \frac{\sum_{i=1}^{N} \sigma_i^{t_a} \sigma_i^{t_b}}{\sqrt{\sum_{i=1}^{N} {\sigma_i^{t_a}}^2} \sqrt{\sum_{i=1}^{N} {\sigma_i^{t_b}}^2}},$$

with a constraint on temporal proximity. Articles are either generated within a threshold time horizon or the date of an article is mentioned in a text of a more recent article in the chain. We performed several experiments using the time threshold on the TDT4 corpus[2], and reached our best performance when limiting the chains to 14 days. This type of analysis has a high recall for identifying articles that cover the same topic, referring to the fraction of relevant instances that are retrieved. However, the procedure has a low precision; a large fraction of the identified instances are false positives. We wish to enhance the precision, while maintaining the high recall. As an approach to reducing the false positives, we overlay a preference that the entropy of the entities $\{e \in Entities\}$ of the story articles C, defined as

$$StoryEntropy(C) = -\sum_{i=1}^{n} P(e_i \in C) \log P(e_i \in C)),$$

grows "slowly" as the story evolves over time. A similar approach has been shown to provide major improvements on a related topic-detection task [2]. We employ conditional random fields (CRF), trained on a heterogeneous corpus [9], to identify entities of the types *location*, *people*, and *organizations*. We define a vector of counts of entities and operations of addition and removal of an article from a chain. We use a greedy algorithm that selects at each step the next best document to add or decides to halt if all remaining documents increase the entropy by more than a threshold amount α, which we evaluate from a validation set. We performed experiments showing that this extension improves precision while maintaining levels of recall (see Section 3.4).

We performed the latter process on an offline corpus. We note that studies have addressed the usage of similar techniques for extraction from online streams of news (e.g., [2]). Such online approaches could be adapted in our approach to forecasting future events.

2.2 Lexical and Factual Features

We seek to infer the probability of a predefined future news event of interest given a vector representing the news events occurring up to a certain time. To perform this task, we create training cases for each target event, where each case is represented using a set of observations or features. We define both *lexical* and *factual* features. We set the label for each case as true only if the text representing the future target event occurs in a document dated at a later time in the chain.

Let $w_1 \ldots w_n$ be the words representing the concepts of the event at time τ and let $a_1 \ldots a_m$ be additional real-world characteristics of the event concepts. We refer to these attributes respectively as *lexical and* factual features. The words w_i are extracted from the text of each news article using the Stanford Tokenizer, and filtered using a list of stop words. The factual characteristics a_i are extracted from the different LinkedData sources, specifically the properties under the type rdf:Property for the event concepts w_i. For example, given the text of the news story title, "Angola: Cholera Cases Rise Sharply After Floods," the feature vector contains both the tokenized and filtered words of the text (Angola, cholera, rise, sharp, flood), and other features describing characteristics of Angola (GDP, water coverage, population, etc.). We map each concept in the event text to a LinkedData concept. If several concepts are matched, we perform disambiguation based on the similarity between the concept text (e.g., its Wikipedia article) and the news article, using a bag-of-words representation.

We denote $f_1(ev) \ldots f_{n+m}(ev)$ to be the features of the event ev (either lexical or factual features). We make a naive simplifying assumption that all features are independent, and describe the probability $P(ev_j(\tau+\Delta)|ev_i(\tau))$ as follows:

$$P(ev_j(\tau + \Delta)|ev_i(\tau)) \propto \prod_{k=1}^{n+m} P\big(ev_j(\tau + \Delta)\big|f_k(ev_i(\tau))\big).$$

[2] http://www.nist.gov/TDT

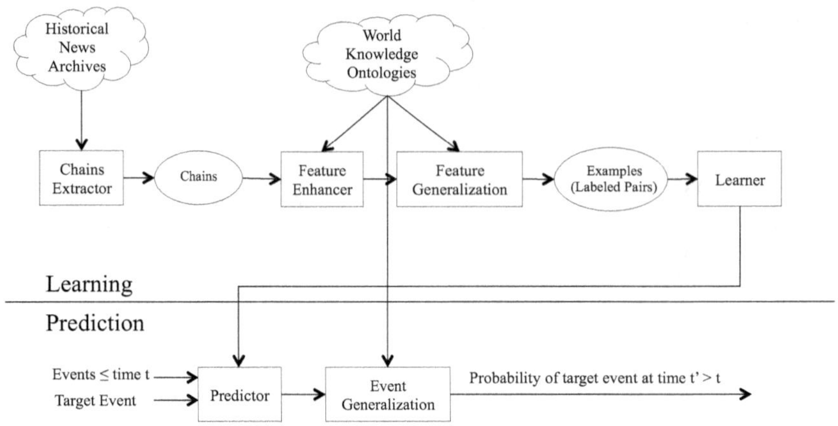

Figure 2: Main components and flow of analysis of event prediction pipeline.

Using Bayes rule, we can derive that

$$P\big(ev_j(\tau+\Delta)\big|f_k(ev_i(\tau))\big) = \frac{P\big(ev_j(\tau+\Delta), f_k(ev_i(\tau))\big)}{P(f_k(ev_i(\tau)))},$$

where $P\big(ev_j(\tau+\Delta), f_k(ev_i(\tau))\big)$ is evaluated from the data by counting how many times the event ev_j happens in the same storyline after an event having the value of feature f_k of the event ev_i at time τ. Similarly, $P(f_k(ev_i(\tau))$ is evaluated from the data by counting the portion of times that an event with this feature value happens in the corpus. We build a predictor based on these learned probabilities. The predictor outputs the probability that each future event represented in the system will occur. Changes in this probability can be noted and thresholds set for alerting.

We may be interested in predicting various characteristics of a future event as *scalar* values. For example, beyond predicting the likelihood that deaths will be associated with a later accident or disruption occurring within a horizon, we may wish to predict the number of people who will perish given the occurrence of a target event that causes or is associated with deaths. To do this, we bin target predictions of numbers of deaths into a set of buckets capturing a mutually exclusive and exhaustive set of ranges of numbers of deaths, e.g., less than ten deaths, greater than 10 but less than 100 deaths, and greater than 100 deaths. We say that ev_j belongs to bin_k, if ev_j holds the bin_k relation. As an example, for the less than 10 deaths bin, we say that $ev_j \in bin_{0-10}$ if the text representing ev_j contained text indicating how many people died and this number was less than 10. We learn predictors that estimate the probability of the event to belong to a certain bin k, $P\big(ev_j(\tau+\Delta), ev_j(\tau+\Delta) \in bin_k \big| ev_i(\tau)\big)$, and output the bin with the highest probability. We present results on a study of the accuracy of inferring the number of deaths caused by an event in Section 3.2.

2.3 Learning to Predict with Abstractions

Event sequences are relatively sparse in the domains we explored. For example, the target event "Rwanda cholera outbreak" appeared only 33 different times in the news archive. Such sparsity may degrade classifier performance due to the poor estimation of both $P\big(ev_j(\tau+\Delta), f_k(ev_i(\tau))\big)$ and $P(f_k(ev_i(\tau)))$. In other cases, the feature values might not appear with high enough frequency in the data for deriving high-confidence inferences about the future. For example, there is not even a single mention of the African country of Comoros in the news corpus. Such sparsity in lexical features can lead to poor estimation of the probability $P\big(ev_j(\tau+\Delta), f_k(ev_i(\tau))\big)$, and therefore to poor predictors. As an example, for the target prediction of the likelihood of a forthcoming large-scale evacuation, a hurricane originating in Comoros might be important information for predicting a storm in nearby countries which might be useful in predicting evacuations in those countries. Similarly, if the system is focused on making predictions about upcoming storms in Comoros, i.e., "storm in Comoros" is the target event, there may not be enough data to evaluate the aforementioned probabilities.

We address the joint challenges of event and feature sparsity via employing procedures for automated abstraction. Instead of considering only "Rwanda cholera outbreak," an event with a small number of historical cases, we consider more general events of the form: "[Country in Africa] cholera outbreak." We turn to world knowledge available on the Web. Some LinkedData resources provide hierarchical ontologies. For example, Fabian et al.[24] created an *isA* ontology from Wikipedia content. This ontology maps Rwanda to the following concepts: Republics, African countries, Landlocked countries, Bantu countries, etc. Similarly, WordNet provides hypernym relations, that map Rwanda to the concept *country*.

We developed a an automated method for guiding abstraction. The method determines when to generalize events and features. As features are evaluated separately, estimations are made about the value of each feature abstraction to enhance the accuracy of predicting the target event. We evaluate for each feature and its abstractions the precision over the training data using cross validation. We note that it is insufficient to measure the precision associated with using an abstracted feature without altering the target event. Consider the abstracted feature [Country in Africa], and the target event "Death in Kigali." The probability of a death in Kigali, the capital of Rwanda, caused by an event in some country in Africa, is small. Therefore, given an event in [Country in Africa], the probability of death being caused by the event in CapitalOf([Country in Africa]) may typically be more appropriate. We now formalize this intuition.

Let the semantic network graph G be an edge-labeled graph, where each edge is a triplet $\langle v_1, v_2, l \rangle$ and l is a predicate (e.g., "CapitalOf"). We look for a path of maximum length k (in our experiments $k = 3$)that connects the concept representing the abstraction and the concepts described in the target event. For example, given a chain where the first event discusses the large attendance at the opera "The Nose," and the second event discusses an award that the opera writer Dmitri Shostakovich receives, we find the following path in the Wikipedia graph, connecting the articles: "The Nose"$\xrightarrow{OperasBy}$Dmitri Shostakovich. Later, we can use a similar observation, observing a large attendance at the opera "The Murder of Comrade Sharik," to predict an award for the opera writer William Bergsma using the path "The Murder of Comrade Sharik"$\xrightarrow{OperasBy}$William Bergsma. Given two events' concepts c_1, c_2, represented by the nodes v_1 and v_2 in G, we call the labels of the k-sized path, connecting v_1 and v_2, an *abstraction path* $abs(c_1, c_2) = l_1, \ldots, l_k$. *Applying an abstraction* on a node v determines the node v' that satisfies the abstraction path, i.e., $ApplyAbs(v, abs(c_1, c_2)) = v'$, s.t $\exists v_i \in V(G)(v, v_1, l_1) \ldots, (v_{k-1}, v', l_k) \in E(G)$.

When inferring probabilities for each entity en in the target event and a feature of the causing event, we iteratively abstract each feature f to a more general concept $gen(f)$, using a semantic hierarchical graph G^H, calculating the abstraction path $abs(f, en)$ (based on the semantic graph G), and instead of $P(ev_j(\tau + \Delta), f_k(ev_i(\tau)))$, we calculate the probability for the more abstract event,

$$P\Bigg(ApplyAbs\Big(ev_j(\tau + \Delta), abs(f_k, en)\Big), gen(f_k)(ev_i(\tau))\Bigg).$$

A similar process is conducted when generalizing the target event. In this case, the probabilities are calculated for the abstracted target event, and the precision is calculated on the concrete target event. For each entity en in the target event and a feature of the causing event, we wish to iteratively abstract each feature f to a more general concept $gen(f)$, using a semantic hierarchical graph G^H (in our experiments we used the IsA and InCategory relations).

Figure 3 shows pseudocode for the abstraction process. Given a target and a possible causative event, the goal of the procedure is to estimate the probability of the causative event or any of its abstractions to cause the target event. The algorithm is given as input several parameters: a target event (e.g., cholera Outbreak in Rwanda), denoted as *target*, and an event occurring at time τ (*cause*), the storylines the system extracted, denoted as *Chains*, the hierarchical graph G^H, the semantic graph (G), and some parameter specifying a maximum degree of abstraction (k). The system evaluates the probability

$$P\Bigg(ApplyAbs\Big(ev_j(\tau + \Delta), abs(f_k, en)\Big), gen(f_k)(ev_i(\tau))\Bigg).$$

At stages 1-2, the system builds a classifier estimating the probability that any of the entities of the lexical features of the causative event precede an appearance of the target event in a text of an event in a storyline. For example, the *bestClassifier* at this stage will have estimations of the probability of "cholera Outbreak in Rwanda" given the entity Kigali (Rwanda's capital). At stage 3, the algorithm iteratively estimates the probability of the target event happening given any of the abstracted features (extracted using the hierarchical graph G^H). For example, one iteration can be the evaluation of the number of times the entity "Capital of Africa" preceded "cholera Outbreak in Rwanda" in our storylines. Stages 3.1-3.2 evaluate the needed transformations to the target event given the abstracted cause entity. For example, instead of looking for cases where an event with an entity belonging to "Capitals in Africa" occurred and an event regarding "cholera Outbreak in Rwanda" followed, we look for examples where an event of the type "cholera Outbreak in Africa" followed. We then train and evaluate new classifier using the transformed training data. If its performance, as measured by cross validation on the training data, is superior to that of the classifier in advance of the abstraction, we update the best classifier found.

3. EXPERIMENTAL EVALUATION

We now describe the experiments that we conducted to test the methodology, and present the results of the studies of inferences performed on a test portion of the news archive held out from the training phase.

3.1 Experimental Setup

In this Section we outline the data we obtained for the experiments, the experimental methodology, and the baselines we compared against.

3.1.1 Data

We crawled and parsed the NYT archive containing news articles for the years 1986–2007. We say that a chain of events belongs to a domain D, if it consists one of the domain relevant words, denoted as $w_i(D)$. For example, for the challenge of predicting future deaths, we consider the words "killed," "dead," "death," and their related terms.[3] For the challenge of predicting future disease outbreak, we consider all mentions of "cholera, " "malaria, " and "dysentery."

During prediction, we hold out from the learning phase a test set of a decade of events for the period of 1998–2007 (the *test period*). We say that a chain is a *test-domain chain* if (1) the dates of all of its events occurred in the test period dates, and (2) the first chronological event in the chain does not contain one of the domain terms, e.g., the first event did not contain a mention of death (otherwise the prediction might be trivial). Formally, let $C = \{e_1 \ldots e_k\}$ be a test chain, thus $\forall i : w_i(D) \notin e_1$.

[3]We consider all the similarity relations in Wordnet: Synonyms, pertainyms, meronyms/holonyms, hypernyms/hyponyms, *similar to*, *attribute of*, and *see also* relations.

Procedure ABSTRACT($target, cause, Chains, G^H, G, k$)

(1) **Foreach** $\{entity \in Entities(cause)\}$

(1.1) $PositiveExamples \leftarrow \{(ev_1, ev_2) | ev_1 <<_{c \in Chains} ev_2, entity \in ev_1, \forall e \in Entities(target) : e \in ev_2\}$

(1.2) $NegativeExamples \leftarrow \{(ev_1, ev_2) | ev_1 <<_{c \in Chains} ev_2, entity \in ev_1, \exists e \in Entities(target) : e \notin ev_2\}$

(2) $bestClassifier \leftarrow Build(PositiveExamples, NegativeExamples)$

(3) **Foreach** $\{entity \in Entities(cause), absEntity \in Abstractions(entity, G^H)\}$

(3.1) $absPaths \leftarrow FindPaths(absEntity, Entities(target), G, k)$

(3.2) $absTargets \leftarrow ApplyAbs(absEntity, absPaths, G)$

(3.2) **Foreach** $absTaret \in absTargets$

(3.2.1) $PositiveExamples \leftarrow \{(ev_1, ev_2) | ev_1 <<_{c \in Chains} ev_2, absEntity \in ev_1, \forall e \in Entities(absTarget) : e \in ev_2\}$

(3.2.2) $NegativeExamples \leftarrow \{(ev_1, ev_2) | ev_1 <<_{c \in Chains} ev_2, absEntity \in ev_1, \exists e \in Entities(absTarget) : e \notin ev_2\}$

(3.2.3) $absClassifier \leftarrow Build(PositiveExamples, NegativeExamples)$

(3.2.4) **If** $CV(bestClassifier, Chains) < CV(absClassifier, Chains)$ $bestClassifier \leftarrow Update(absClassifier)$

(4) **Return** bestClassifier

Figure 3: Procedure for generalizing features via abstraction. *Build* takes as input positive and negative examples and estimates the probability of our target event. *FindPaths* finds all predicate paths of size k between two nodes in the graph given as input. *ApplyAbs* applies the predicate path on a node, returning nodes that are connected to the given node via the predicates of the directed paths. *CV* calculates the precision via cross validation of a classifier on the training data.

3.1.2 Experimental Methodology

For each prediction experiment we first select a target event e_{target} from a test-domain chain. The procedure differs depending on the type of the experiment:

1. Predicting general events in the period 2006–2007. In this type of experiment, a target event is any news headline published during 2006–2007, i.e., we build a classifier for each possible headline.

2. Predicting events in specific three domains: deaths, disease outbreaks, and riots. In this case, any news story containing one of the domain words is selected. Additionally, we validate manually that those events actually contain an event from the domain. If several of the target events exist, we choose the first one appearing chronologically to be the identified target event, i.e., $e_{target} = argmin_j\{e_j | \exists i : w_i(D) \in e_j\}$. As e_{target} is selected from a test-domain chain $j > 1$, i.e., it is not the first event in the chain. That is, we consider only event chains that are not observed by the system during the years 1998–2007, and do not contain words implying the target event within a domain (e.g., the word death) during the first event chain. The first event of the chain is given as input to the system.

In summary, the general events predictions represents prediction of *all* the events in 2006-2007. The system is given an event from 2006–2007 as input, and we measure the success in predicting the event. For the domain-specific predictions (death, disease outbreak, and riots), we manually check to see if the event occurs using the domain representative words or their synonyms as filters. We consider only event chains that are not observed during the years 1998–2008, and do not contain words implying the target event within a domain (e.g., the word death) during the first event chain. The first event of the chain is given as an input.

We train from the data via evaluating the probabilities of e_{target} happening for events occurring up until the date of the first event in the chain. During the test, the algorithm is presented with the first event of the chain e_1 and outputs its prediction about e_{target}. In the experiments, we consider the predictor as indicating that the target event will occur if

$$P(e_{target} | e_1) > P(\neg e_{target} | e_1),$$

i.e., the probability of the event happening given e_1 is bigger than the probability of it not happening. We perform these experiments repeatedly over all the relevant chains, and evaluate for each:

$$\text{precision} = \frac{|\{\text{events reported}\} \cap \{\text{predicted events}\}|}{|\{\text{predicted events}\}|}$$

and

$$\text{recall (sensitivity)} = \frac{|\{\text{events reported}\} \cap \{\text{predicted events}\}|}{|\{\text{events reported}\}|}.$$

3.1.3 Comparative Analysis

We are not aware of any methods in the literature that are aimed at tackling the prediction of probabilities of future news events. Thus, we compare the generated predictions with two baselines:

1. using prior probabilities of the occurrence of an event e given the appearance of its corresponding text in the training set, $P(e)$;

2. using an estimate of how well people do on predicting these types of events.

For the latter, we implement a method [11] that provides approximations of whether people, given two events represented by text of news stories, would agree that the first event implies the truth of the later event. This baseline evaluates the probabilities of co-occurrence in text rather than in time.

		Predicted		
		Few	Tens	Hundreds
Real	Few	40%	6%	1%
	Tens	4%	32%	1%
	Hundreds	1%	6%	9%

Table 2: Confusion matrix showing predicted versus actual number of deaths.

3.2 Prediction Results

We performed experiments evaluating the precision and recall for the general predictions and for each of the different domains. We compare our model (Full model) with the frequency-based model (Frequency), and the co-occurrence-based method (Co-occurrence). The results are presented in Table 1. We observe that in all cases the Full model outperforms the baselines.

We performed additional experiments to evaluate numerical predictions, such as forecasts of numbers of deaths. For this purpose, we searched for specific patterns in the news stories of the form "[number] died" or "[number] killed". The number matching [number] is used as the bin classification. We focus only on chains containing those patterns and evaluate our algorithms on those. In Table 2, we show a confusion matrix for the numbers of deaths. The content of each cell i, j (i is row and j is column) represents the percentage of the data that in reality belongs in bin i and is classified as belonging in bin j. For example, 4% of the events resulting in tens of deaths are predicted erroneously as events associated with only a few (less than ten) deaths. We see high performance in those types of classifications and most mistakes are observed in adjacent bins.

3.3 Algorithm Analysis

We now describe additional experiments performed to measure the performance of the procedures and the contribution of specific components of the analysis.

3.3.1 Gain from Factual Features and Generalization

We first consider the influence of adding different sources of world knowledge on the accuracy of predictions. The results are displayed in Table 3. We consider predictors based solely on lexical features (News alone), on both lexical and factual features (News + factual features), on lexical features and abstractions (News + generalization), and on using all categories of features along with the abstraction procedure (Full model). We find that adding knowledge, either when abstracting or when adding factual features, improves the performance of predictions. We see the biggest performance gain when employing both refinements.

3.3.2 Predicting Times of Forthcoming Events

Table 4 displays the average and median times between the inference-based alerts and the occurrence of reports that embody the target event for the three types of predictions we study. We consider only examples where deaths appear in the news story title and match a handcrafted template (patterns in the text of the form "[number] died" or "[number] killed") to identify certain deaths only on test chains. This procedure results in 951 death predictions. In many cases, we find that the alerts would come more than a week in advance of the target event. We illustrate this phenomenon in Figure 4, where we show predictions of the number of deaths

General Predictions		Death		Disease Outbreak		Riots	
Med.	Avg.	Med.	Avg.	Med.	Avg.	Med.	Avg.
9	21	8	41	12	273	18	30

Table 4: Median and average time between alerts based on inferred probabilities of outcome and target events in the world (days).

that come at a future time within a storyline predicted at different times between the alert and the occurrence of the deaths. A more detailed view of the timing of alerts at two and fifteen days before the event are displayed in Figure 5.

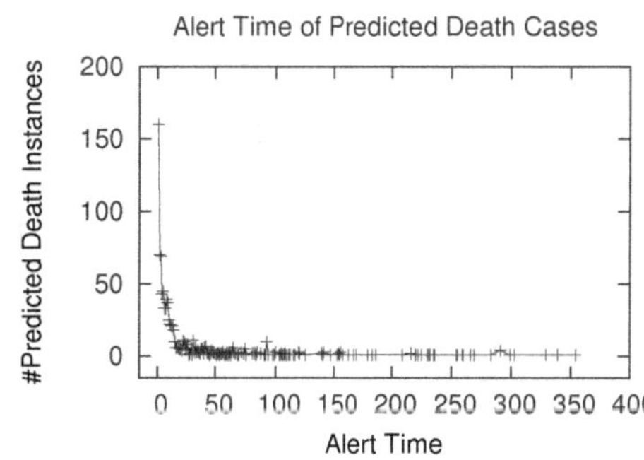

Figure 4: Number of times deaths of any number were predicted as a function of alert time (days before event).

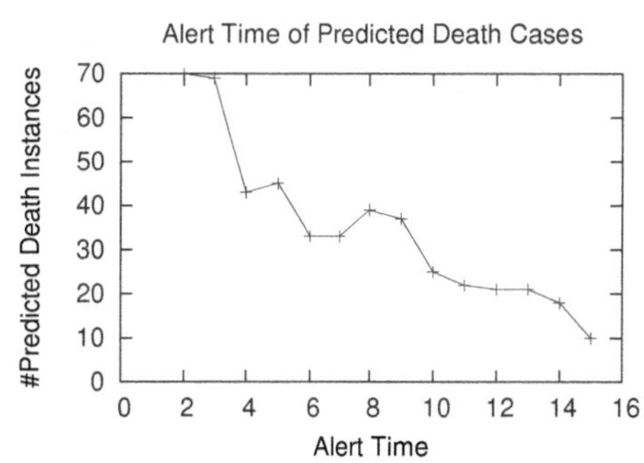

Figure 5: Number of times deaths of any number were predicted as a function of alert time (days before event).

3.4 Event Chain Extraction Evaluation

To evaluate the quality of the extracted event chains, we performed experiments on the TDT4 corpus[4], filtering only NYT articles. This corpus contains about 280,000 documents from the dates 04/01/2003–09/30/2003. Human annotation for labeling storylines was performed by the organizers of the TDT challenge. For each chain, we calculate the average precision—the percentage of articles we extracted as being in a chain that were indeed part of the storyline. We also compute the average recall, the number of articles actually in the chain that the system retrieved. We compared the event chain extractor using the entity entropy measure with

[4] `http://www.nist.gov/TDT`

	General Predictions		Death		Disease Outbreak		Riots	
	Prec.	Recall	Prec.	Recall	Prec.	Recall	Prec.	Recall
Full model	24%	100%	83%	81%	61%	33%	91%	51%
Frequency	<1%	100%	59%	<1%	13%	3%	50%	1%
Co-occurrence	7%	100	46%	61%	40%	<1%	61%	14%

Table 1: Precision and recall of predictions for several domains.

	General Predictions		Death		Disease		Riots	
	Prec.	Rec.	Prec.	Rec.	Prec.	Rec.	Prec.	Rec.
News alone	19%	100%	80%	59%	44%	34%	88%	38%
News + factual features	19%	100%	81%	62%	52%	31%	87%	42%
News + generalization	21%	100%	81%	67%	53%	28%	88%	42%
Full model	24%	100%	83%	81%	61%	33%	91%	51%

Table 3: Precision and recall for different algorithm configurations.

the extractor working without the entropy measure. The results are summarized in Table 5. The results show that, while the recall of text clustering is very high (by 10%), the precision is significantly lower than the methods we have presented (by 30%). We therefore prefer the second method, as it provides more flexibility in training predictive models in a more precise way, with influence on the number of examples used for training the learner.

	Precision	Recall
Text Clustering	34%	**80%**
Text Clustering + Entity Entropy	**70%**	63%

Table 5: Precision and recall for chain extraction procedure.

3.5 Sample Likelihoods and Storylines

The learning and inference methodology we have described can be used to output the probabilities of key transitions of interest from sequences of observations. The system continues to refine its learning with updates of news and related data on the Web. As we mentioned, the system can provide real-time alerting from news stories on sets of specific outcomes that it is monitoring. Examples of statistics of representative learned transition probabilities are displayed in Figure 6. These transition probabilities and mean times to transition highlight the ability of the methods to provide inferences about a variety of levels of abstraction.

We now present details on several additional storylines, along with inferences and timing. Consider the example displayed graphically in Figure 1. On January 26th, 2007, the New York Times published an article about storms and floods in Africa. News of a cholera epidemic were reported four days later. In response to this stream of news, the methodology we describe yields two alerts, one when observing the drought reports in Angola at the beginning of 2006, and another one after news of the reported storms. The system learned from numerous similar incidents in its training set that the likelihood of a cholera outbreak is higher after droughts, specifically as reports on observations of drought are linked to increases in the probability of later reports of water-related disasters, which, in turn, are linked to increases in the likelihood of reports of waterborne diseases. Examples of such transitions and likelihoods include a set of Bangladesh droughts analyzed by the system. 19 significant cases of drought were reported in Bangladesh between 1960–1991 [19]. We observed that in the story lines describing those droughts, a cholera outbreak was reported later in the storyline in 84% of cases. After the 1973 drought, which was responsible for the famine in 1974, the NYT reported on October 13, 1975: "cholera epidemic hits Bangladesh; may prove worse than one that set record in '74...". On March 13 1983, a year after the 1982 drought that "caused a loss of rice production of about 53000 tons while in the same year, flood damaged 36000 tons ...", the NYT published an article entitled, "Bangladesh cholera deaths." Several months later, an article appeared entitled "cholera reportedly kills 500 in 3 outbreaks in Bangladesh". Based on these past story lines the system infers the outbreak of cholera at the end of January in 2007.

The prediction method learns that not all droughts are associated with jumps in the likelihood of such outbreaks of disease. Specific sets of preconditions influence the likelihood of seeing a transition from a report of drought to a report of cholera outbreak. The method was able to recognize that the drought experienced in New York City on March 1989, published in the NYT under the title: "Emergency is declared over drought" would not be associated with a disease outbreak. The only consequence was that New York City declared water curbs, which ended on May 16th of that year. The system estimates that, for droughts to cause cholera with high probability, the drought needs to happen in dense populations (such as the refugee camps in Angola and Bangladesh) located in underdeveloped countries that are proximal to bodies of water.

As an additional example of predictions, we focus on the case of the 1991 cholera epidemic in Bangladesh. This cholera outbreak is estimated to have included 210,000 cases of cholera with more than 8,000 deaths [16]. In our experiments, we found that the running prediction system would have produced an alert four days before the beginning of the cholera outbreak, following observation of the major floods. In Figure 6, we display graphically the storyline detected. The system identifies that reports of major floods with high probability will be followed by reports of significant disease outbreak in Bangladesh. The inferences of the system are supported by a large study of cholera epidemics in Bangladesh [16], based on analyses of government figures, as well as data collected independently in 400 rural areas in Bangladesh between the years 1985Ñ1991. The analysis shows that the number of cholera cases and deaths in 1987 and 1988 is significantly higher than in other years (300,000-1,000,000 cases vs. 50,000 cases in other years). In 1987 and 1988, severe floods occurred in Bangladesh. The study concludes that

Cause	Effect	Probability
Drought	Flood	18%
Flood	cholera	1%
Flood in Rwanda	cholera in Rwanda	67%
Flood in Lima	cholera in Lima	33%
Flood in Country with water coverage > 5%	cholera in Country	14%
Flood in Country with water coverage > 5%, population density > 100	cholera in Country	16%

Table 6: Probability transitions for several examples.

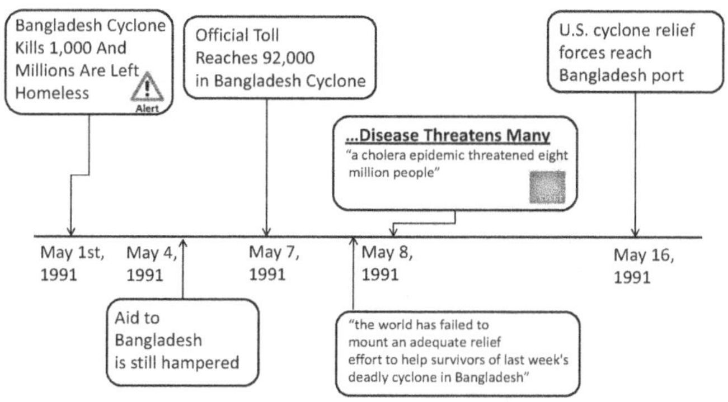

Figure 6: Example of cholera alert following storms in Bangladesh. Triangular alert icons represent inferences of significant upswings in likelihood of forthcoming cholera outbreak.

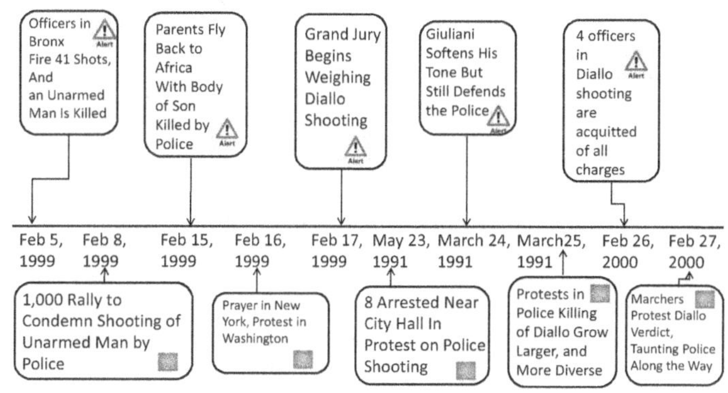

Figure 7: Example of alerts on the likelihood of forthcoming riots after shooting of unarmed minority. Triangular alert icons represent inferences of significant upswings in likelihood of a forthcoming riot.

access to medical care was one of the main reasons for high death rates in many non-rural areas. In areas where appropriate interventions were made at early stages, the death rates were significantly smaller.

We also study examples of prior deaths and riots. In Figure 7, we present a partial storyline and the alerts inferred for the Dialo case of 1999. One of the storylines is presented in detail in Table 7 (Top). The system identified in an automated manner that for locations with large immigrant populations (e.g., Ohio and New York), the shooting of an unarmed person by the police can cause protests. Additional events in the news, such as reports of the funeral of the people who have been killed in similar way, of the beginning of the trial of the policemen who performed the shooting, of support for the policemen, and of the end of the trial are all associated with increases in the likelihood of later reports of protests. A sample storyline at the basis of the inferred probabilities is presented in Table 7 (Bottom).

4. RELATED WORK

Prior related research includes efforts in political science on forecasting forthcoming international political crises from coded event data, including event data extracted from news stories [23]. Research in this realm includes the application of HMMs to identify similarities among attributes that appear to be linked to the development of international crises [22]. Relevant research has also explored predicting riots [13] and the sales of movie tickets [5, 12, 18] from signals derived from social media such as Twitter. Other investigations have leveraged information in text of news and book corpora to qualitatively estimate how multiple aspects of human culture evolve [25, 25, 17]. Other relevant work in search and retrieval has focused correlating logs of queries input to search engines with future events in both traditional media [20] and blogs [1]. Ginsberg et al. [10] used queries for predicting H1N1 influenza outbreaks. Other research has sought to predict how Web content changes. Kleinberg [14, 15] developed general techniques for summarizing the temporal dynamics of textual content and for identifying bursts of terms within content. Similarly, other works [4] build time-series models over publication dates of documents relevant to a query in order to predict future bursts. In other related work, Radinsky et al. [21] extracted generalized templates in the form of "x causes y" from past news. The templates were applied on a present news title, generating a plausible future news title.

In this work, we take a probabilistic approach and perform more general-purpose predictions without relying on templates. We also combine heterogeneous online sources, leveraging world knowledge mined from more than 90 sources on the Web, to enrich and generalize historical events for the purpose of predicting future news.

5. CONCLUSIONS

We presented methods for mining chains of events from 22 years of news archives to provide a methodology that provides real-time predictions about the likelihoods of future world events of interest. The system harnesses multiple Web resources to generalize the events that it learns about and predicts. We discussed how we can learn patterns from large amounts of data, monitor large quantities of information sources, and continue to learn new probabilistic asso-

Date	Title
Jan 16, 1992	Jury in Shooting by Officer Hears Conflicting Accounts
Feb 11, 1992	Closing Arguments Conflict on Killing by Teaneck Officer
Feb 12, 1992	**[Past Event] Officer Acquitted in Teaneck Killing**
Feb 13, 1992	Acquitted Officer Expresses Only Relief, Not Joy
Feb 16, 1992	**[Past Riot] 250 March in Rain to Protest Teaneck Verdict**

Date	Title
Feb 24, 2000	Diallo Jurors Begin Deliberating In Murder Trial of Four Officers
Feb 26, 2000	**[Riot Alert] 4 officers in Diallo shooting are acquitted of all charges**
Feb 26, 2000	Rage Boils Over, and Some Shout 'Murderers' at Police
Feb 26, 2000	Civil Rights Prosecution Is Considered
Feb 27, 2000	**[Riot Event] Marchers Protest Diallo Verdict...**
Feb 27, 2000	2 jurors defend Diallo acquittal

Table 7: Top table: Partial sample of a historical storyline used to infer probabilities. Bottom table: Partial storyline with an alert.

ciations. To demonstrate the approach, we presented the results of several evaluations and representative examples of sequences of events and proactive alerts. We considered as sample inferences predictions about disease outbreaks, riots, and deaths. We believe that the methods highlight directions in building real-time alerting services that predict significant increases in global events of interest. Beyond knowledge that is easily discovered in studies or available from experts, new relationships and context-sensitive probabilities of outcomes can be discovered with such automated analyses. Systems employing the methods would have fast and comprehensive access to news stories, including stories that might seem insignificant but that can provide valuable evidence about the evolution of larger, more important stories. We hope that this work will stimulate additional research on leveraging past experiences and human knowledge to provide valuable predictions about future events and interventions of importance.

6. REFERENCES

[1] E. Adar, D. S. Weld, B. N. Bershad, and S. D. Gribble. Why we search: visualizing and predicting user behavior. In *WWW*, 2007.

[2] A. Ahmed, Q. Ho, J. Eisenstein, E. Xing, A. J. Smola, and C. H. Teo. Unified analysis of streaming news. In *Proc. of WWW*, 2011.

[3] J. Allan, editor. *Topic detection and tracking: event-based information organization.* Kluwer Academic Publishers, Norwell, MA, USA, 2002.

[4] G. Amodeo, R. Blanco, and U. Brefeld. Hybrid models for future event prediction. In *CIKM*, 2011.

[5] S. Asur and B. A. Huberman. Predicting the future with social media, 2010.

[6] C. Bizer, T. Heath, and T. Berners-Lee. Linked data – the story so far. *IJSWIS*, 2009.

[7] J. Carbonell, Y. Yang, J. Lafferty, R. D. Brown, T. Pierce, and X. Liu. Cmu report on tdt-2: segmentation, detection and tracking, 2000.

[8] C. Cieri, D. Graff, M. Libermann, N. Martey, and S. Strassel. Large, multilingual, broadcast news corpora for cooperative research in topic detection and tracking: The tdt-2 and tdt-3 corpus efforts. In *LREC*, 2000.

[9] J. R. Finkel, T. Grenager, and C. Manning. Incorporating non-local information into information extraction systems by gibbs sampling. In *Proceedings of ACL*, 2005.

[10] J. Ginsberg, M. Mohebbi, R. Patel, Brammer, M. L., Smolinski, and L. Brilliant. Detecting influenza epidemics using search engine query data. *Nature*, 457:1012–1014, 2009.

[11] O. Glickman, I. Dagan, and M. Koppel. A probabilistic classification approach for lexical textual entailment. In *Proc. of AAAI*, 2005.

[12] M. Joshi, D. Das, K. Gimpel, and N. A. Smith. Movie reviews and revenues: An experiment in text regression. In *In Proc. of NAACL-HLT*, 2010.

[13] Kalev. Culturomics 2.0: Forecasting large-scale human behavior using global news media tone in time and space. *First Monday*, 15(9), 2011.

[14] J. Kleinberg. Bursty and hierarchical structure in streams. In *KDD*, 2002.

[15] J. Kleinberg. Temporal dynamics of on-line information systems. *Data Stream Management: Processing High-Speed Data Streams. Springer*, 2006.

[16] J. Michel, Y. Shen, A. Aiden, A. Veres, M. Gray, Google Books Team, J. Pickett, D. Hoiberg, D. Clancy, P. Norvig, J. Orwant, S. Pinker, M. Nowak, and E. Aiden. Cholera epidemics in bangladesh: 1985-1991. *Journal of Diarrhoeal Diseases Research (JDDR)*, 10(2):79–86, 1992.

[17] J. Michel, Y. Shen, A. Aiden, A. Veres, M. Gray, Google Books Team, J. Pickett, D. Hoiberg, D. Clancy, P. Norvig, J. Orwant, S. Pinker, M. Nowak, and E. Aiden. Quantitative analysis of culture using millions of digitized books. *Science*, 331:176–182, 2011.

[18] G. Mishne. Predicting movie sales from blogger sentiment. In *In AAAI Spring Symposium*, 2006.

[19] R. Nagarajan. *Drought Assessment.* Springer, 2009.

[20] K. Radinsky, S. Davidovich, and S. Markovitch. Predicting the news of tomorrow using patterns in web search queries. In *WI*, 2008.

[21] K. Radinsky, S. Davidovich, and S. Markovitch. Learning causality for news events prediction. In *Proceedings of WWW*, 2012.

[22] D. Richards, editor. *Political Complexity: Nonlinear Models of Politics.* Ann Arbor: University of Michigan Press, Norwell, MA, USA, 2000.

[23] R. J. Stoll and D. Subramanian. Hubs, authorities, and networks: Predicting conflict using events data, 2006.

[24] F. Suchanek, G. Kasneci, and G. Weikum. Yago: a core of semantic knowledge. In *Proc. of WWW*, 2007.

[25] C. Yeung and A. Jatowt. Studying how the past is remembered: Towards computational history through large scale text mining. In *Proc. of CIKM*, 2011.

Studying Inter-National Mobility through IP Geolocation*

Bogdan State
Stanford University
Stanford, CA, U.S.
bstate@stanford.edu

Ingmar Weber
Qatar Computing Res. Inst.
Doha, Qatar
ingmarweber@acm.org

Emilio Zagheni
Queens College - CUNY
New York, NY, U.S.
emilio.zagheni@qc.cuny.edu

ABSTRACT

The increasing ubiquity of Internet use has opened up new avenues in the study of human mobility. Easily-obtainable geolocation data resulting from repeated logins to the same website offer the possibility of observing long-term patterns of mobility for a large number of individuals. We use data on the geographic locations from where over 100 million anonymized users log into Yahoo! services to generate the first global map of short- and medium-term mobility flows. We develop a protocol to identify anonymized users who, over a one-year period, had spent more than 3 months in a different country from their stated country of residence ("migrants"), and users who spent less than a month in a country different from their country of residence ("tourists"). We compute aggregate estimates of migration probabilities between countries, as inferred from a user's location over the observed period. Geolocation data allow us to characterize also the pendularity of migration flows – i.e., the extent to which migrants travel back and forth between their countries of origin and destination. We use data regarding visa regimes, colonial ties, geographic location and economic development to predict migration and tourism flows. Our analysis shows the persistence of traditional migration patterns as well as the emergence of new routes. Migrations tend to be more pendular between countries that are close to each other. We observe particularly high levels of pendularity within the European Economic Area, even after we control for distance and visa regimes. The dataset, methodology and results presented have important implications for the travel industry, as well as for several disciplines in social sciences, including geography, demography and the sociology of networks.

Categories and Subject Descriptors

H.3.5 [**Information Storage and Retrieval**]: Online Information Services; J.4 [**Social and Behavioral Sciences**]: Sociology

*We are grateful to Yahoo! Research and the Barcelona Media Foundation for their support. State was an intern and Weber an employee of Yahoo Research! during the course of this research. State's work was supported by the Joan Butler Ford Stanford Graduate Fellowship. Additional material is available at: https://sites.google.com/site/studyinginternationalmobility/

WSDM'13, February 4–8, 2013, Rome, Italy.

Keywords

mobility, IP addresses, migrations, tourism

1. INTRODUCTION

International migration is a major source of population growth in several regions of the world, in particular in developed countries, where fertility has fallen under replacement level [23]. Migration processes are complex phenomena that have relevant consequences on societies, economies, culture and the environment. Despite the importance of migration dynamics, our understanding of global human mobility is still quite limited. As a matter of fact, migrations account for a very large source of uncertainty in population projections carried out by the United Nations [9]. One of the reasons for the lack of understanding of migration processes is the limited availability of data on international migration flows. For a substantial number of developing countries, data on migration flows are not collected at all. For developed countries with mature demographic registration systems, data on migration flows are often inconsistent across countries, since different countries collect data for different purposes and thus use different definitions of migration [22].

In this article, we analyze human global mobility using an innovative data source. We track the geographic locations from where anonymized users of a large provider of Internet services (Yahoo!) log in over time. We use geolocation data (from IP addresses) for a period of one year to build a data set on global mobility patterns. The data that we gather provide the most comprehensive and up-to-date picture of human mobility across the world. The data set that we generated is unique for three main reasons. First, migration flows are easily comparable across countries, since we use the same definition of migration consistently. Second, data from digital records show the latest trends, compared to official migration statistics, that are typically published with a considerable lag from the collection period. Third, the nature of our data allows us to analyze mobility on a continuous scale between tourism and longer-term changes of residence.

There is a growing body of literature on the use of geolocated data for the analysis of human mobility. This article complements existing studies in several different ways. For the first time, a data set that covers most countries in the world is used to estimate country-to-country flows of migrants and tourists. Previous work has focused on either tourist itineraries or migration rates from a specific country to the rest of the world. Our work goes beyond a descriptive analysis of human flows across borders: we develop a statistical model to predict flows and to understand the major determinants of migration and tourism patterns.

After a brief review of relevant related work, we provide a thorough explanation of how we built the data set on global mobility. Then we perform a statistical analysis of the new data set. Some of the results confirm classic theories of migrations. Some others open new questions for social sciences and challenge traditional models of migration processes.

2. RELATED WORK

The study of human mobility is inherently an interdisciplinary field. This area of research has been the domain of demographers, geographers, statisticians, sociologists and economists, often working in teams. The recent availability of geographic information (through IP addresses) from where users log into Internet services has made possible unprecedented developments in the study of human mobility. Data mining of geo-located digital records has increasingly become central to the analysis of human movements at a global scale [21], with large implications for social sciences.

There are three main lines of literature in Web data mining that are relevant for our work. A first set of studies has used geolocated records from various sources to evaluate spatial mobility at a city or regional level. For instance, Ferrari et al. [16] analyzed urban patterns, for the city of New York, from Twitter data, whereas Rinzivillo et al. [35] used GPS traces to analyze regional mobility patterns. Routine whereabouts have also been extracted from applications that allow people to share their locations with friends (e.g., from Google Latitude [15] and Foursquare [29]). Mobile phone data have been tracked to understand frequent mobility patterns [6] and regularities in spatio-temporal trajectories of human mobility [19]. The applications of these types of analysis range from identification of urban routines [16] to evaluation of mobility trajectories in case of disasters [24], characterization of traffic jams [17] and inference on social ties from co-occurrence in time and space [10].

A second set of studies has focused on the analysis of tourists, with the goal of improving tourist itineraries or targeting tourists with ad hoc ads. Geo-referenced pictures in Flickr [12, 13], cellphone network data [18] and recommendations posted on the social network service for travelers CouchSurfing [34] have proved useful to reconstruct and improve travel itineraries for tourists.

A third group of studies has looked into longer distance and medium- to long-term movements. For instance, data from a large bill-tracking website, and from trajectories of traceable items, have been used to infer statistical regularities about long distance human mobility [7]. More recently, telecommunications data was used to track changes in individual's social networks as a result of internal migrations in Portugal [31]. Geolocated e-mail data have been used to infer emigration rates for a number of countries [39]. This last paper is the main inspiration for this article. In our work, we complement previous analyses by looking into global mobility (instead of local or regional patterns), by evaluating country-to-country migration flows (instead of overall emigration rates from selected countries), and by providing a statistical model for prediction and analysis of flows of migrants and tourists.

The work that we present in this study is relevant not only to the field of Web data mining, but also to the disciplines of demography, geography and sociology. International mobility is a central research area in social sciences. However, data on flows of migrants, in particular by age and gender, are almost inexistent. When some data exist, they are typically inconsistent across countries because of different definitions of migration and because of different methods of data collection.[1] Data on migration stocks (e.g., number of foreign born residents in a country) often come from censuses and are used to produce summary statistics, like the net migration rate of a country (the difference between immigrants and emigrants, over a period of time, per 1,000 residents). Data on migration flows are more sparse. For European countries, there has been a large effort to harmonize migration data. Thus, for some countries, there are data on flows reported by both the sending and the receiving country. These data have allowed the development of methods intended to generate comparable statistics on flows [2, 11, 22]. More often, data on flows are not available at all. In some cases, time series of migration flows can be roughly estimated indirectly, by evaluating differences over time in migration stocks obtained from census data [3, 36]. The lack of reliable and comparable data on migration flows is one of the main reasons behind the high level of uncertainty in models of global migration.

Web data mining of geo-referenced records has proven useful to provide new and relevant information for migration studies [39]. Statistical analysis of digital records is becoming increasingly influential in disciplines like demography and sociology. Our article complements a descriptive analysis of current global human flows with a statistical model whose results provide a test of classic theories of migration [8] in the contemporary world.

3. DATA SET

Our dataset was extracted from IP address data recorded from the logins of an initial sample of over 100 million anonymized users of Yahoo! Web services, over the period of one year (July 2011 - July 2012). Random numbers were used as user IDs. IP addresses were matched against the latest version of the GeoCityLite database provided by MaxMind[2]. Each user was thus linked with the country from where he/she logged in. Note that though IP-based geolocation has been found to be very noisy at the city level, it is generally considered reliable at the country level [33, 20, 37].

The data underwent a data-cleaning protocol that followed a number of rules. Each user's data were partitioned into "spells"[3] according to the country from where they logged in. A spell was defined as the total amount of time during which a user recorded logins only from within the same country. In addition to imposing the constraint that a user only logged in from the same country for the entire duration of the spell, we kept in our sample only those users whose geographic location, as given by city-level data extracted from the MaxMind database, varied in a plausible manner. Thus, the logins of a user within the same spell were not allowed to move in space at a speed higher than 150 km/h.[4] Our method builds on previous work on inferring location and mobility patterns using series of logins for the same individual over time [32]. Adopting this rule allowed us to remove from the data a great deal of noise that is typically associated with IP geolocation data, oftentimes as a result of users employing proxy servers to connect to the Internet.

Two other rules were implemented when extracting the dataset: we only kept in our dataset those users for whom the cumulative spell duration was of at least 300 days out of 365[5]. As a further

[1]Certain countries consider a migrant a person who moves his or her residence for at least 6 months, other countries use a threshold of 3 months or 1 year. Some countries collect data only on out-migration, some others only on in-migration. Some national statistical offices use data from registration systems, others from sample surveys, etc. [38].

[2]`http://www.maxmind.com/app/geolite`

[3]A spell is understood as the length of time during which a user is assumed to be in one state.

[4]We believe this method is accommodating of most instances of air travel within the same country, given that most individuals are not expected to log in immediately before or after a flight, but at most at a few hours' distance from the moments of take-off and landing.

[5]As a spell is defined as a series of logins from within the same country, the cumulative spell duration is the total number of days during the year for which we can say with relative certitude that the user was in the country, rather than somewhere else. Between

safeguard against noisy geolocations due to proxy servers we eliminated from our sample those individuals who recorded a location spell that lasted less than a day in duration (i.e., those users who went back and forth from the same country during a day, and logged in twice in the same country, but only for a few hours).

A a result of our data-cleaning procedure we obtained a sample of order 10^8 users, each of whom experienced an average of 1.12 spells of contiguous logins from one country. The average length of a spell was 306.00 days, whereas the average cumulative length of all spells was 341.76 days, out of 365 days possible.[6] On average, a user in our sample logged in more than 100 times. Out of all anonymized users, 96.68% spent (tracked) time in only one country, 3.10% spent time in two countries, 0.20% in three countries, and 0.03% spent time in four countries or more.

3.1 Defining Migration Events

Although the concept of migration seems intuitive at first blush, the problem of defining migration is not without its complications. Despite the fact that the United Nations provide recommendations on statistics of international migration [26], there is no universally-accepted definition of what a migrant is. Different countries and statistical agencies often use different definitions of the concept. There have been some efforts to harmonize migration statistics, particularly in Europe (see, for instance [14]). However, most international migration statistics are inconsistent, if existent at all.

The definition of migration used in this paper derives from the observation that a person who migrates during a given year typically spends a considerable amount of time in at least two countries during that year. From this consideration we define a migrant an individual who spends at least 90 days in exactly two countries during the observed timespan of one year. The timespan is not necessarily contiguous: thus we consider a migrant an individual who spends 45 days in country A, followed by 90 days in country B, followed by another 45 days in country A. Our operational definition aims to capture the *process* of migration rather than the *state* of being a migrant. An individual is considered to be potentially participating in migration when he or she moves between countries. The individual may move only once and follow the traditional conceptualization of being an emigrant from the home country or an immigrant to the destination. In this case the individual experiences one migration event. Alternatively, the individual may move between the country of origin and the one of destination multiple times, possibly over the course of a number of years. This type of individual is constantly engaged in the process of migration, and the reality of this increasingly-common pattern is oftentimes inadequately described by classical definitions of migration. Thus we allow individuals to spend their minimum 90 days in each country in multiple spells. A person is thus considered a migrant even if he or she returns to the home country for part of the year, as long as he or she meets the threshold of spending a minimum of 90 days in exactly two countries. This protocol generated a subsample of hundreds of thousands of migrants, about 3% of all individuals who spent more than three months in at least one country.

Our protocol identified individuals moving between countries, but gave us no information about the directionality of a move. To infer the most likely direction of a move we used the individuals' reported country of residence as obtained from the Yahoo! User database from April 2012.[7] The matching protocol further reduced our sample to a size of 223,344 individuals, as we dropped those individuals for whom no home country could be identified (6%), those emigrants whose reported home country was in neither of the two identified countries in which they had spent a considerable amount of time (17%), as well as those individuals whose reported age was lower than 15 or larger than 75 (2%).

3.2 Identifying Short-Term Mobility

Geolocation data allow us to identify not only geographic patterns consistent with international migration, but also movement between countries indicative of short-term mobility ("tourism"). Official definitions of tourism are broad and include "people traveling to and staying in places outside their usual environment for not more than one consecutive year for leisure, business or other purposes" [30]. In this paper, we refer to (international) tourism as short-term trips taken to a particular country, by a person who has a primary residence in a different country. More specifically, we considered tourists those individuals who spent more than three months in exactly one country (considered their primary country of residence), and who spent spells of less than a month in at least one other country (inferred to be the country visited by the individual). As in the case of migration, to be considered a tourist an individual could spend non-contiguous amounts of time in one country, though the cumulative time spent in the visited country could not exceed one month overall. We identified a sample of millions of individuals, about ten times larger than the sample of migrants.

3.3 Normalization Procedure

Our final dataset consists of the conditional probabilities of short- and medium-term mobility out of each country. We defined a mobility flow (migration or tourism) as the total number of individuals from one country (the "origin") who spent at least a certain amount of time in a different country (here referred to as the "destination") during the observed period. We normalized each count against the total numbers of individuals from the country of origin who engaged in short- or medium-term mobility, respectively. Edges (migration flows) corresponding to either 0% or 100% of outgoing flows from a country were dropped (since the log-odds are undefined). The final dataset consists of two weighted directed graphs of migration and tourism flows between countries, where for each node the outgoing edge-weights sum to 1.

4. RESULTS

4.1 Global Inter-Country Mobility

Figure 1 shows inferred worldwide migration patterns according to conditional probabilities of migration. These flows quantify the likelihood that a migrant from one country go to another one. Thus, for each country of origin, the conditional probabilities all sum to one. The lines used to represent migration flows encode three characteristics. Intensity encodes the magnitude of the conditional probability. Line type communicates the number of times individuals travel back-and-forth between two countries during the course of the year. As all individuals undergo migration during the interval of interest, they participate in at least one

two spells the user may be traveling, or simply not logging into his or her account. We imposed this constraint to keep in our sample those users for whom highly consistent location data was available, while leaving some room for inconsistent location data between spells due to international travel.

[6]Our interval included 366 days, but logs for one day were unavailable.

[7]For some individuals in our sample it is possible that this data may have been obtained after the occurrence of the migration event. Given that there is oftentimes considerable latency in users' updating their website profile information, we do not expect this potential delay in data gathering to impact our conclusions in a substantive way.

movement between the two countries. Solid lines on the map indicate those migrant flows where individuals are less than half as likely to return to their home country during the year (where the overall number of travels between the two countries is less than 1.5). Dashed lines indicate migrant flows where individuals have a moderate likelihood of between- country travel (between 1.5 and 2 between-country movements). Dotted lines indicate highly "pendular" migration flows, where it is quite common for individuals to show interspersed spells of time spent in both origin and destination country, with an average of more than 2 movements per individual per year. Color is used to indicate the direction of migrant flows, which are shown as arcs that transition from black to red when moving from the country of origin to the migrants' destination. Thus, a country with a lot of red arcs is mainly a country of immigration while one with mainly black arcs is a country of emigration.

At the global level, data on conditional probabilities of migration show the persistence of migration patterns dominated by geography, language and economics. The United States dominates among global migration destinations, as it is the top destination for 58 (44%) out of the 132 countries with at least 50 migrants represented in the dataset. The United States is followed by Great Britain and France, which represent the top migration destinations for 10 and, respectively, 20 countries in our sample. India and Australia complete the top-five, each figuring as the top migration destination for 7 countries. The findings for short-term stays (broadly classified as tourism) reveal a relatively similar structure as for migration. The United States is the top destination for short-term stays for users coming from 57 (32%) of the 176 countries with more than 50 persons reporting short-term stays in the sample. France is second for short-term stays, being the top destination for 23 countries, followed by India with 13, Spain with 10 and Great Britain with 9.

Comparing Figures 1 and 2 reveals rather similar patterns of both short- and medium-term human mobility, with only a few noticeable differences. The most striking pattern is a web connecting all countries to the United States, followed by a smaller, though still noticeable tendency for many countries to be strongly connected with their former colonial metropolises - France, Spain and England, a trend from which Portugal however seems to be excepted. Another trend is the emergence of regional hubs. India, China, Australia, Brazil and Argentina, as well as South Africa are emerging as both migration and tourist destinations. Given that these countries have been experiencing above-average growth during the past decade, it stands to reason that economic development is a driving factor of choice of both migration and tourist destinations. We provide a more explicit examination of the role of economics in Section 4.3.

4.2 Regional Patterns of Migration

Figures 3 - 8 show migration flows in Europe, Africa, Latin America, the Middle East, South-East Asia and North America, respectively. Within Europe we observe movement from East to West, the main preferred destinations being the U.K., Germany, France, Spain and Italy. Europe likewise shows highly-pendular migration flows, which are represented with dashed and dotted lines, as is evident from the profusion of such lines on the map. Because the map only shows flows originating in countries with at least 50 users that migrate, and given that most African countries do not cross this threshold, there are few visible flows in Africa (portrayed with part of the Middle East in Figure 4). The exceptions are flows from Liberia to Lebanon, as well as from Botswana and Zimbabwe to South Africa. Latin America (Figure 5) shows a broad pattern of regional migration gravitating towards Brazil and Argentina, and, to a lesser extent, towards Mexico and Colombia. There is an interesting observable flow of people from Haiti to the Dominican Republic, as well as from Haiti to Jamaica, possibly as a result of the humanitarian crisis caused by the country's major earthquake in 2010. Another striking migration pattern connects Cuba to Venezuela, otherwise a country of emigration. A local pattern is visible in Central America, with migration flows from Belize, Honduras and El Salvador to Guatemala, as well as from Honduras to Nicaragua and from Nicaragua to Panama. The South East Asian region (Figure 7) is dominated by India, China and Australia, the main poles towards which migrant flows gravitate. India and Saudi Arabia are the centers of migration flows for the Middle East region (Figure 6). The United States attracts most of the migration flows in North America (Figure 8).

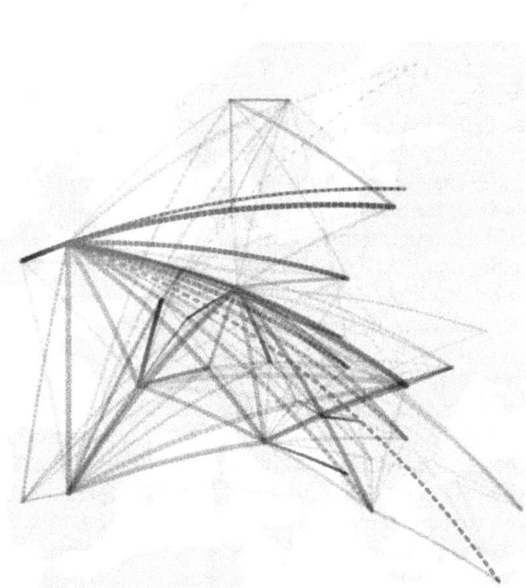

Figure 3: Conditional Probabilities of Migration in Europe Represented flows originate in countries with at least 50 total observed migrants. Line intensity represents conditional propensity of migrating to destination country. Solid lines show flows with less than 1.5 trips between origin and destination; dashed lines indicate between 1.5 and 2 trips per year, and dotted lines show over 2 trips per year. Line thickness indicates observed size of migrant flow.

4.3 Determinants of Mobility

Given the large number of observations obtained from our dataset it is possible to test empirically for the extent to which multiple factors determine mobility choices across the world. To do so we matched our dataset with three other data sources. From [27] we obtained data on colonial ties between countries, travel visa regimes, whether two countries share language and geographic location, Purchasing Power Parity-Adjusted GDP, and the volume of bilateral trade between two countries. From [28] we obtained a measure of distance between countries, weighted by the spatial distribution of their populations. Our analysis also employed current (2011) per-capita GDP figures from the World Bank [1].

Our dataset consists of conditional probabilities of migration and tourism for pairs of origin and destination countries. Because most countries generate repeated observations both as origin and as destination, a typical linear regression (e.g. Ordinary Least Squares)

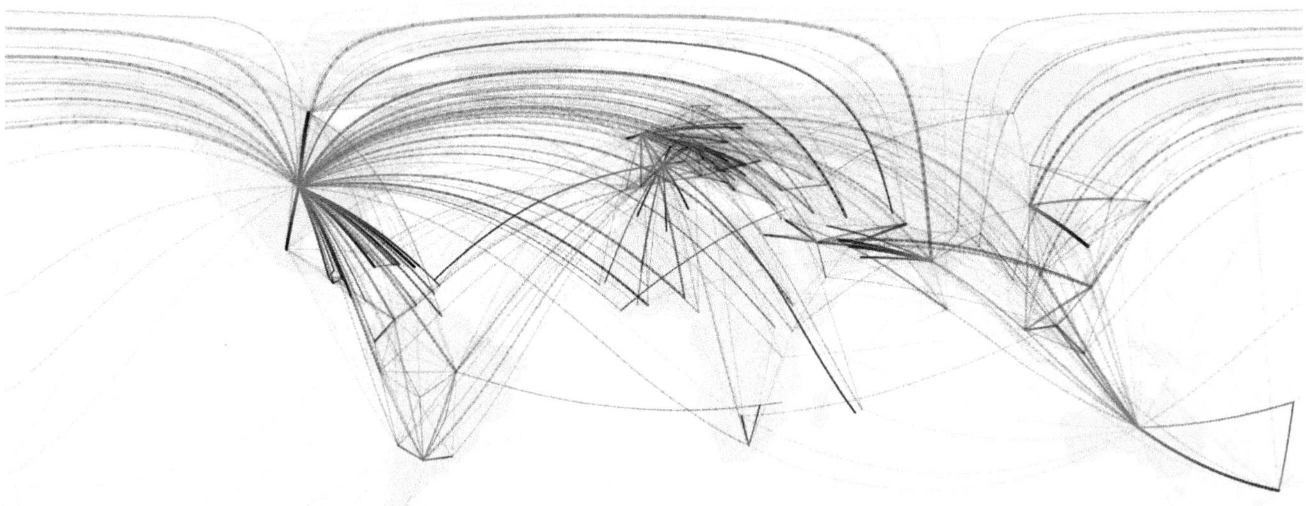

Figure 1: Conditional Probabilities of Migration
Represented flows originate in countries with at least 50 total observed migrants. Line intensity represents conditional propensity of migrating to destination country. Line thickness indicates observed size of migrant flow.

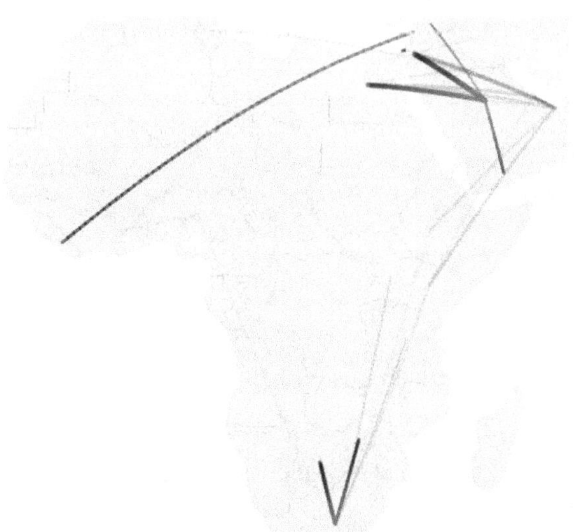

Figure 4: Conditional Probabilities of Migration in Africa

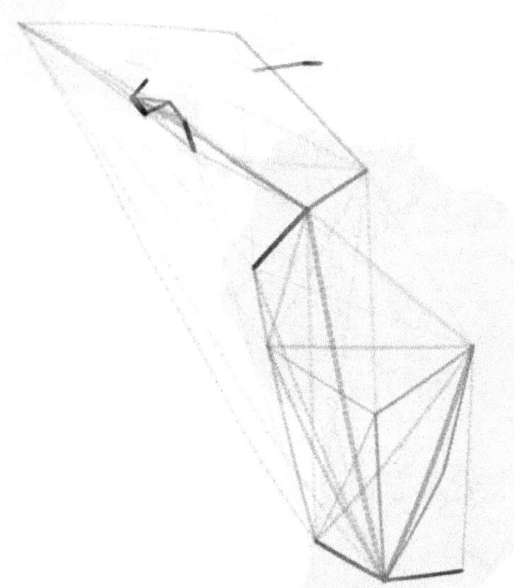

Figure 5: Conditional Probabilities of Migration in Latin America

would lead to biased results due to non-independence of observations. Treating observations about the same country as independent would overweight the amount of information available in them. To correct for this potential source of bias, we use a Linear Mixed Effects model [25], specified as:

$$y = XB + ZU + \epsilon,$$

with y a vector of responses, X the data matrix, B the fixed-effects coefficients, U a vector of "random effects" partitioned according to a classification of the data given by the incidence matrix Z and ϵ, the error component. This specification improves on the typical linear regression since it allows us to partition the error term in each regression into a systematic error component ("random effect"), due to the country of origin, and a random effect, due to the destination, in addition to the fixed effects given by the predictors.

Given that we are trying to predict a conditional probability, the distribution of which is highly skewed towards zero (as most mobility flows are minor ones), we transform the probability into its log-odds ratio, which we use as the Dependent Variable in our analysis.[8] We fit the model using the R package lme4[5]; tests of statistical significance for the estimated coefficients were calculated using MCMC methods provided by the languageR package[4].

Results for the regression analysis are presented in Table 1. The Dependent Variable being log-odds, the coefficients can be interpreted the same way as for a logistic regression. Thus we can see that having a colonial tie to the destination country increases the

[8]The analysis presented here does not include those cases where the observed probability is either 0 or 1, as the log-odds would be undefined.

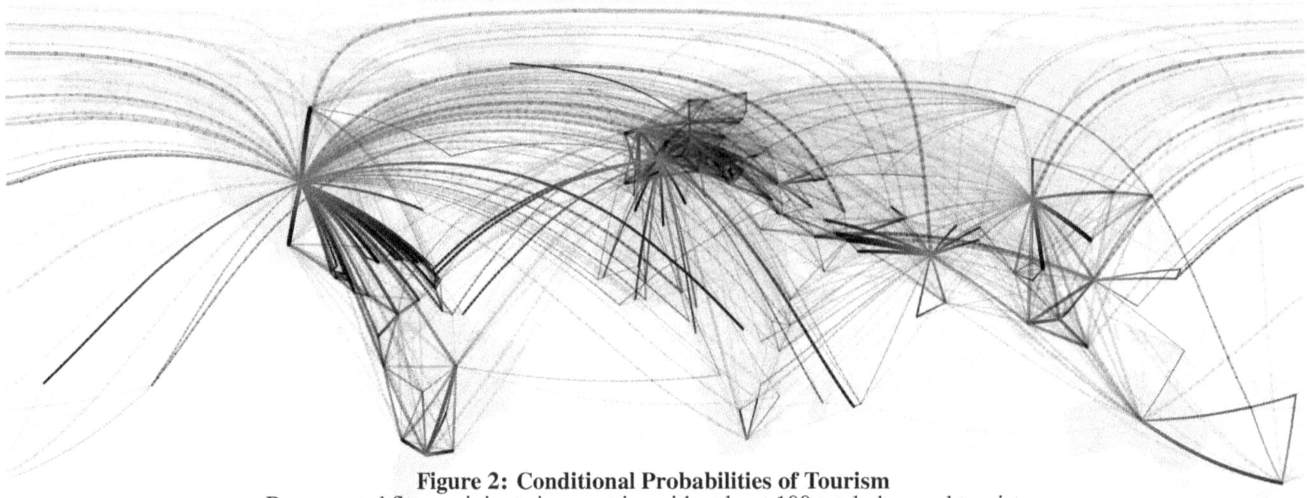

Figure 2: Conditional Probabilities of Tourism
Represented flows originate in countries with at least 100 total observed tourists.

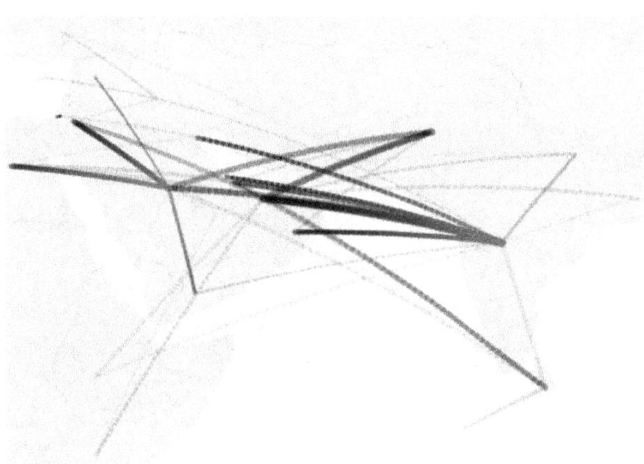

Figure 6: Conditional Probabilities of Migration in the Middle East

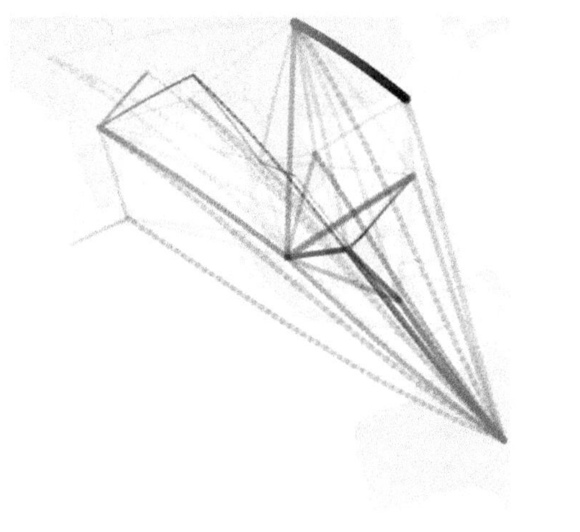

Figure 7: Conditional Probabilities of Migration in South-East Asia and Australia

conditional log-odds of migration by 1.369, which is equivalent to an increase in the odds by a factor of 3.93. Individuals in our sample appear to have close to 4 times higher odds of migrating to a country to which their country of origin has a colonial tie (outside of the British Commonwealth), all else being equal. The respective effect for tourism is $3.23(e^{1.174})$. Commonwealth membership likewise has an effect, a smaller one, on the mobility log-odds, which increase by .345 and .310 in the case of tourism and migration, respectively.

Our analysis reveals that barriers to mobility are more salient in the case of short-term stays than they are in the case of longer-term migrations. A travel visa requirement has an effect comparable (same order of magnitude) to that of a Commonwealth tie, decreasing the log-odds ratio by .236 in the case of migrations, and .410 in the case of tourism. Common language facilitates migration: its presence increases the migration log-odds by .424, but its effect is even more poignant in the case of tourism, the log-odds of which are increased by .846. A one unit increase in the log-weighted distance measure yields a decrease of .686 in the migration log-odds, and of 1.128, roughly twice as much for tourism. Finally, being the same geographic region has a relatively minor effect (with distance accounted for) on the migration log-odds (.117), but an effect three times as large in magnitude (.387) on the log-odds of tourism.

The model presented in Table 1 also explores the influence of the economy in the country of destination – a "pull" factor – on the patterning of mobility. Interestingly, the destination's level of economic development, measured in absolute terms as well as relative to the country of origin's level, seems to have an effect of similar magnitude on short-term as well as long-term mobility. Each additional thousand U.S. dollars in the destination country GDP increases the log-odds ratio of migration by 0.058, and the log-odds of tourism by .095. The ratio between the destination and origin GDP has a smaller, seemingly second-order effect on the mobility log-odds: each unit increase in the ratio adds .007 to the migration log-odds and .004 to the log-odds of short-term mobility. Finally, bilateral trade between origin and destination, measured as

Table 1: Mixed Effects Regression of Conditional Log-Odds of Migration and Tourism

	Migrations			Tourism		
Fixed Effects	Coef	(S.E.)	T-stat.	Coef	(S.E.)	T-stat.
Intercept	-0.355	(0.273)	-1.303	1.934^{***}	(0.267)	7.248
Colonial Tie (non-Commonwealth)	1.369^{***}	(0.117)	11.703	1.174^{***}	(0.103)	11.369
Commonwealth Tie	0.345^{***}	(0.084)	4.114	0.310^{***}	(0.061)	5.082
Visa Required	-0.236^{***}	(0.044)	-5.321	-0.410^{***}	(0.031)	-13.323
Common Language	0.424^{***}	(0.058)	7.270	0.846^{***}	(0.043)	19.465
Log-weighted Distance	-0.686^{***}	(0.027)	-25.609	-1.128^{***}	(0.019)	-58.058
Same Region	0.117^{*}	(0.050)	2.361	0.387^{***}	(0.036)	10.722
Destination GDP / Origin GDP	0.007^{***}	(0.001)	6.300	0.004^{***}	(0.001)	5.570
Destination GDP (PPP-adjusted)	0.058^{***}	(0.010)	5.504	0.095^{***}	(0.016)	5.906
Bilateral Trade	0.035^{***}	(0.003)	10.875	0.032^{***}	(0.003)	11.313
Random Effects	Variance	(S.D.)		Variance	(S.D.)	
Country of Origin	.573	(.757)		.627	(.792)	
Country of Destination	.947	(.973)		1.532	(1.238)	
Residual	.911	(.955)		1.248	(1.117)	
Counts	N	Origins	Destinations	N	Origins	Destinations
	4,641	144	123	9,236	157	125
Log-Likelihood	Model	Baseline	McFadden R^2	Model	Baseline	McFadden R^2
	-6,793	-10,481	.352	-14,671	-23,820	.477
Mean Prediction Error	Model	Baseline	Ratio	Model	Baseline	Ratio
	.290	.370	.784	.265	.457	.580

Source: Mobility Log-Odds extracted from observations of Yahoo! users. Predictors from [27] and [28]. Mean Prediction Error calculated with Training and Test datasets stratified according to country of origin, each containing half of observations in a country of origin. *:, p < .05, **: p < .01, ***: p < .001.

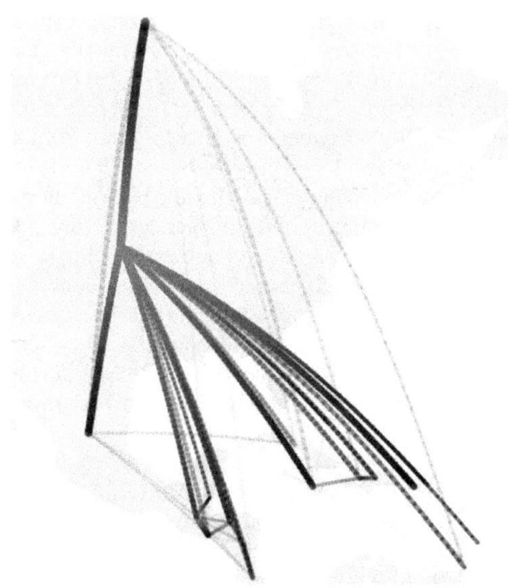

Figure 8: Conditional Probabilities of Migration in North America

a proportion of the origin's internal trade flows, and indicating the overall strength of economic ties between the two countries has an almost identical effect on the log-odds of migration and tourism (.035 and .032, respectively, for every unit increase in the proportion). The importance of economic ties for short-term mobility may seem counter-intuitive, but only if one loses sight of the fact that such mobilities may include business trips, educational travel, as well as short-term employment – all arguably influenced by the destination's economy – in addition to holiday travel.

In addition to fixed effects discussed above, the model includes country-specific random effects, which account for the systematic error components due to every origin and destination country present in the sample. Because the log-odds used as the Dependent Variable in the model are based on conditional probabilities of migration, the random effects for origin and destination countries have different interpretations. Similar to an entropy measure, the origin-specific random effect accounts for the lopsidedness in a country's mobility patterns. While the conditional probabilities of mobility originating in one particular country all sum to one, their logits have a slightly different behavior. The mean log-odds is relatively high for countries with few observed mobility destinations, such as the Republic of Congo or Swaziland, the top two countries of origin in terms of their random effects. At the other end of the spectrum are countries with a large number of observed mobility destinations, as is the case with India and the Philippines for migration.

Destination country random effects offer a more intuitive measure of surprise of a mobility destination, insofar as a country's popularity is not accounted by the fixed effects. The United States is the most "surprising" migration destination, in light of the explanatory variables included in the model. In context, the result is not counter-intuitive: the United States is known to be a popular migration destination for most countries, even though it imposes wide-spread visa restrictions, has few colonial ties, and is separated from most of the world's countries by a considerable distance. The estimated random effect for the United States is 2.56, which translates into an estimated 13-fold increase in the odds ratio of migrating to the United States, compared to the prediction based on the fixed effects. Likewise exceptional is the case of China for tourism, which yields an increase in the log-odds of 4.66. Exponentiated this quantity would predict an 105-fold increase in the odds of visiting China for a short time. This surprising increase should be seen in context however: with a large diaspora spread across the world, China is visited every year by a far larger number of individuals living very far away than distance would predict. The pattern of surprising tourist destinations being those with large and widespread diasporas is likewise supported by the second- and third- highest random effect, associated with India (3.68) and the

Philippines (2.82). Interestingly enough, the effect associated with the United States in the case of tourism (2.72, the fourth-highest) is similar in terms of magnitude to that associated with the country for migration log-odds.

The models show high explanatory power for all of the independent variables. All fixed effect coefficients are significant at the .001 level, with the exception of the coefficient associated with two countries being in the same region (significant at the .05 level), and of the intercept (not significant) in the case of migration. To provide a measure of the model's explanatory power we compute McFadden's R^2 measure, defined as 1 minus the ratio between the log-likelihood of the model and that of a baseline model. Our baseline ("null") model is set up conservatively: it is specified as a Linear Mixed Effects model which includes the same random effects, but only an intercept term for the fixed-effects portion. This baseline provides us with a measure of the extent to which the fixed-effects included in our model explain the variation in the Dependent Variable, the results being .352 for migrations and .477 for tourism.

The analysis was done using the whole data set. To ensure that the improvements in goodness-of-fit we observed were not merely caused by having more degrees of freedom and overfitting, we evaluated the model performance in a prediction setup, separately for migration and tourism, as follows. First, we looked at all source countries which had at least four target countries. Then, for each source country, we split all (source, target) pairs into train and test sets in a balanced, 50-50 manner. For all the train pairs we then fitted a single model to describe the log-odds as described above. To the pairs in the test set the fitted model was applied to obtain log-odds, and these log-odds L were then converted back to probabilities P according to $P = \exp(L)/(1.0 + \exp(L))$. These transition probabilities were then grouped by source country and re-normalized to 1.0. Re-normalization was required as (i) only half the transitions were present in the test set and (ii) a model fitted to log-odds ratios does not guarantee normalization to begin with. The predicted probabilities P_p obtained in this manner were then compared to the observed probabilities P_o and the difference measured according to $\|P_p - P_o\|_1/2$, where the division by 2.0 guaranteed that the error was between 0. 0 for identical probability distributions and 1.0 for orthogonal ones. These errors are shown at the bottom of Table 1.

4.4 Pendular Migration

Europe stands out among world regions due to the extent to which migrations are circular on the continent. Migrants within Europe made an average of 2.52 trips between home and destination country during the year, whereas the next region in terms of mobility - the Americas - registers 0.72 fewer trips per person per year (t = 44.62, dF=39,904, p < .001). The next in terms of mobility is Australia and Oceania, with .26 fewer trips per year than the Americas (t=8.42, dF=1,567, p<.001), followed by Asia, .09 lower than Australia and Oceania (t=2.85, dF=1,479, p=.004). The continent with the least pendularity in intra-continent migrations is Africa, with .09 fewer trips than Asia (t=2.31, dF=569, p=.02).

To discover patterns in the pendularity of world migrations we perform regression analysis of the mean number of trips undertaken between countries (Table 3). We use the same Linear Mixed Effects specification, with random effects on origin and destination countries. In addition to the predictors included in Table 1 we included a dummy variable to account for both origin and destination countries being in the European Economic Area, a region in which our analysis reveals a great deal of pendularity.

The fixed effects estimates reveal no statistically-significant effect for colonial ties, travel visa regimes, having a common language, or the extent of commercial ties. It appears that these factors, while important for the initial decision of migration, lose salience when it comes to influencing migrants' opportunities to return temporarily to their country of origin. Distance has a great deal of influence on pendularity, however: each unit increase in the log-weighted distance measure yields an estimated -.4 reduction in the mean number of trips migrants undertake between two countries. With distance accounted for, having both origin and destination countries in the European Union increases by .322 the mean number of trips, suggesting an important effect of European integration efforts on human mobility.

Table 2: Mean Number of Trips between Origin and Destination Countries, within the same continent

Continent	Mean No. Moves	N
Europe	2.52	25,859
Americas	1.80	35,923
Australia and Oceania	1.54	1,388
Asia	1.45	44,254
Africa	1.36	550

There is likewise a small *negative* effect of both countries being in the same region (-.098). Given that travel between countries in the same geographic region is expected to be easier, this effect appears counter-intuitive. Likewise odd is the effect of the ratio of the destination and origin per-capita GDPs (-.002 for each unit increase). Though small, both effects are significant at the 5% level and demand an explanation. While a thorough explanation is beyond the scope of this paper, we hypothesize that these effects may be due to highly-skilled migrants. We believe that this migrant group is likely to make up a higher proportion of people migrating across regions, as well as between countries of similar GDP levels (especially from one developed country to another). Since these migrants typically command higher salaries and have greater access to flights between their countries of origin and destinations, the potentially greater share of highly-skilled migrants moving across regions and between similar-GDP countries would account for these unexpected effects. A likewise-small, though intuitive effect is presented by the destination country's per-capita GDP: for each additional thousand dollars in the destination's GDP, migrants to that country are likely to undertake .006 more trips between origin and destinations.

Some interesting patterns appear when considering the regression's random effects. Four out of the lowest five origin countries in terms of their random effects (which are, in decreasing order, Egypt, Malta, Tunisia, Yemen, Algeria) are Middle-Eastern countries that experienced turmoil during the recent Arab Spring. Originating in any of these countries was estimated to reduce a migrant's mean number of trips by between 0.36 (for Egypt) and 0.26 (for Algeria). Conversely, four out of the top five random effects (Croatia, Russia, the Czech Republic, Slovenia, and the Netherlands) are from Eastern European countries that are typically a source of economic migrants. Random effects for these countries range between .74 for Croatia and .41 for the Netherlands. There is less of a discernible pattern in terms of destination-specific random effects. Destination countries that consistently reduce pendularity beyond the fixed effects' predictions are Ireland, Slovenia, Latvia, Singapore and Ghana. The (negative) magnitude of their effects ranges between -.20 and -.12. The most pendularity-increasing destinations are, in descending order, Ukraine, Kazakhstan, Hungary, the Czech Republic and Slovakia. Their random effects are between .23 and .32. A potential explanation for the first two countries' high levels of mobility is their proximity to Russia: many highly-mobile, economic migrants move between Russia (and other former Soviet republics) and Ukraine and Kazakhstan. The existence of large cross-border national minorities between the Czech Republic and Slovakia, and Slovakia and Hungary potentially accounts for the high level of pendularity created by these destination countries.

Even when adding a variable for within-EEA migration[9], the predictors have less explanatory power for pendularity than they have for the conditional odds of migration (McFadden's R^2 is .275, and the test Mean Squared Error decreases by only 16% against a baseline model including random effects, when the regression is trained on a stratified dataset containing 50% of all observations and tested on the rest of the observations).

Table 3: Mixed Effects Regression of Mean Number of Trips between Origin and Destination

	Migrations		
Fixed Effects	Coef	(S.E.)	T-stat.
Intercept	4.868***	(0.182)	26.786
Colonial Tie (non-Comm.)	−0.104	(0.094)	−1.104
Commonwealth Tie	−0.035	(0.061)	−0.569
Visa Required	0.005	(0.033)	0.143
Common Language	−0.061	(0.044)	−1.379
Log-weighted Dist.	−0.400***	(0.021)	−19.467
Same Region	−0.098*	(0.039)	−2.509
Both in EEA	0.322***	(0.056)	5.712
Dest. / Origin GDP	−0.002*	(0.001)	−2.246
Dest. GDP (PPP-adjusted)	0.006***	(0.002)	2.899
Bilateral Trade	0.002	(0.003)	−0.608
Random Effects	Variance	(S.D.)	
Country of Origin	.573	(.757)	
Country of Destination	.947	(.973)	
Residual	.911	(.955)	
Counts	N	Origins	Destinations
	4,641	144	123
Log-Likelihood	Model	Baseline	R^2
	-5,668	-7,819	.275
Mean Squared Error	Model	Baseline	Ratio
	.709	.825	.859

Source: Mobility Log-Odds extracted from observations of Yahoo! users. Predictors from [27] and [28]. Mean Prediction Error calculated with Training and Test datasets stratified according to country of origin, each containing half of observations in a country of origin. *: p < .05, **: p < .01, ***: p < .001. McFadden R^2 measure used.

5. CONCLUSIONS

In this article, we presented an innovative method to estimate global flows of migrants and tourists using geo-located logins to Yahoo! Web services. For the first time, we estimated country-to-country flows in a consistent way both for developed and developing countries. Our work shows the unifying power of the Internet. Official migrations statistics are based on inconsistent definitions across countries. The Web brings all countries into a single dimension: once a definition of migration/tourism is chosen, then estimates comparable across countries can be obtained in a straightforward way. The methods that we discussed, and the data set that we generated have the largest potential in developing countries, where no other reliable data sources on migration flows exist.

[9]This was an insignificant predictor when added to models in Table 1, results not reported.

At the global level, we showed the persistence of migration patterns dominated by geography, language, history and economics. The findings for short-term movements (broadly classified as tourism) reveal patterns relatively similar to the ones observed for migration. The United States is the global center in the network of migration flows. We also observed the emergence of regional hubs of migration, like India and China, and a tendency for many countries to connect with their colonies. Individuals in our sample have almost four times higher odds of migrating to a country if they have a colonial tie. A travel visa requirement has an effect on mobility of the same order of magnitude as the one of a Commonwealth tie (but with opposite sign).

The dataset that we produced allows for the analysis of "pendularity" of migration, a phenomenon that is becoming more and more prominent, but that is understudied because of lack of data. We observed a high level of pendular, or circular, movements within the European Union. We also noted that countries that experienced turmoil during the recent Arab Spring tended to have very low levels of pendularity. In other words, people who left those countries had low probabilities of returning, at least for short visits.

Our study opens new and exciting opportunities for interdisciplinary research at the intersection of Web data mining and social sciences. Our study also comes with limitations that open up challenges for future research. Perhaps the most important problem that needs to be addressed is selection bias: individuals observed in our sample may or may not be representative of the entire population for their respective countries. For this study, two facts reassure us about the quality of our dataset and results. First, the regression analyses performed on all the estimated flows give results that are consistent with key findings in the sociological literature. Second, the conditional probabilities of migration that we estimated are consistent with the ones obtained by Guy Abel from census data for the period 1990-2000 [3]. We compared the top five destination countries for each country in our data set with the tables available in the companion website of [3]. Our estimates refer to the period 2011-2012, whereas the published tables are for the period 1990-2000. We observed striking similarities as well as new developments in migratory routes. More than 40% of the top five destinations for each country in Abel's data set are in the top five destinations for the respective countries in our world estimates based on Yahoo! data. The value is even higher (about 50%) if we consider only countries in the developed world. In some cases we observed a persistence of migration routes. For instance, the top destination countries for Italy in [3] are Germany, US, Serbia, France and Spain. All of these countries, except for Serbia, are in the top five destinations for Italy in our data set. Flows between Italy and Serbia at the end of the 1990s might have been related to the beginning and end of a period of political instability in the former Yugoslavia. For the US, we observed a change in traditional routes of migration. In the 1990s, the five top destinations from the US were Mexico, Germany, France, UK and Israel. In our data set, the top five destinations countries from the US are Mexico, China, India, Canada and the Philippines. The new trend is probably related to economic integration and return migration.

Combining geolocation data with social-network data and demographic information opens a series of exciting research questions that we intend to explore in future work. Sociologists of migration have long developed rich theories of migrant identities, immigrant integration, ethnic networks, immigrant entrepreneurship, etc. While these studies have been restricted to small-sample research, the increasing worldwide Internet usage opens promising new avenues to advance our understanding of human mobility.

6. REFERENCES

[1] *World development indicators*. World Bank (data.worldbank.org), 2011.

[2] G. Abel. Estimation of international migration flow tables in europe. *J R Stat Soc Ser A-G*, 173:797–825, 2010.

[3] G. Abel. Estimating global migration flow tables using place of birth data. In *European Population Conference*, 2012.

[4] R. H. Baayen. *languageR: Data sets and functions with "Analyzing Linguistic Data: A practical introduction to statistics"*., 2011. R package version 1.4.

[5] D. Bates and D. Sarkar. Linear mixed-effects models using s4 classes. *See http://cran. r-project. org/web/packages/lme4/index. html*, 2006.

[6] M. Bayir, M. Demirbas, , and N. Eagle. Discovering spatiotemporal mobility profiles of cellphone users. In *WoWMoM*, pages 1–9, 2009.

[7] D. Brockmann and F. Theis. Money circulation, trackable items, and the emergence of universal human mobility patterns. *PERCOM*, 7(4):28–35, 2008.

[8] S. Castles and M. Miller. *The age of migration: International population movements in the modern world*. Palgrave Macmillan, 2003.

[9] N. R. Council. *Beyond Six Billion: Forecasting the World's Population*. National Academies Press, 2000.

[10] D. J. Crandall, L. Backstrom, D. Cosley, S. Suri, D. Huttenlocher, and J. Kleinberg. Inferring social ties from geographic coincidences. *PNAS*, 107(52):22436–22441, 2010.

[11] J. De Beer, R. Raymer, R. Van der Erf, and L. Van Wissen. Overcoming the problems of inconsistent international migration data: A new method applied to flows in europe. *Eur J Popul*, 26(4):459–481, 2010.

[12] M. De Choudhury, M. Feldman, S. Amer-Yahia, N. Golbandi, R. Lempel, and C. Yu. Automatic construction of travel itineraries using social breadcrumbs. In *HT*, pages 35–44, 2010.

[13] M. De Choudhury, M. Feldman, S. Amer-Yahia, N. Golbandi, R. Lempel, and C. Yu. Constructing travel itineraries from tagged geo-temporal breadcrumbs. In *WWW*, pages 1083–1084, 2010.

[14] J. DeWaard and J. Raymer. The temporal dynamics of international migration in Europe: Recent trends. *Demogr Res*, 26(21):543–592, 2012.

[15] L. Ferrari and M. Mamei. Discovering daily routines from google latitude with topic models. In *PERCOM*, pages 432–437, 2011.

[16] L. Ferrari, A. Rosi, M. Mamei, and F. Zambonelli. Extracting urban patterns from location-based social networks. In *GIS-LBSN*, pages 9–16, 2011.

[17] F. Giannotti, M. Nanni, D. Pedreschi, F. Pinelli, C. Renso, S. Rinzivillo, and R. Trasarti. Unveiling the complexity of human mobility by querying and mining massive trajectory data. *VLDB*, 20(5):695–719, Oct. 2011.

[18] F. Girardin, F. Calabrese, F. Fiore, C. Ratti, and J. Blat. Digital footprinting: Uncovering tourists with user-generated content. *PERCOM*, 7(4):36–43, 2008.

[19] M. Gonzalez, C. Hidalgo, and A. Barabasi. Understanding individual human mobility patterns. *Nature*, 453:779–782, 2008.

[20] B. Gueye, S. Uhlig, and S. Fdida. Investigating the imprecision of ip block-based geolocation. In *PAM*, pages 237–240, 2007.

[21] P. Hui, R. Mortier, M. Piorkowski, T. Henderson, and J. Crowcoft. Planet-scale human mobility measurement. In *HotPlanet*, 2010.

[22] D. Kupiszewska and B. Nowok. *International Migration in Europe: Data, Models and Estimates*, chapter Comparability of Statistics on International Flows in the European Union, pages 41–71. John Wiley and Sons Ltd., 2008.

[23] R. Lee. The outlook for population growth. *Science*, 333:569–573, 2011.

[24] X. Lu, L. Bengtsson, and P. Holme. Predictability of population displacement after the 2010 haiti earthquake. *PNAS*, 109(29):11576–11581, 2012.

[25] R. McLean, W. Sanders, and W. Stroup. A unified approach to mixed linear models. *Am Stat*, pages 54–64, 1991.

[26] U. Nations. Recommendations on statistics of international migration. Technical Report Statistical Papers Series M, No. 58, Rev.1, Statistics Division, Department of Economic and Social Affairs, United Nations, New York, 1998.

[27] E. Neumayer. Unequal access to foreign spaces: how states use visa restrictions to regulate mobility in a globalized world. *T I Brit Geogr*, 31(1):72–84, 2006.

[28] E. Neumayer. On the detrimental impact of visa restrictions on bilateral trade and foreign direct investment. *Appl Geogr*, 31(3):901–907, 2011.

[29] A. Noulas, S. S., C. Mascolo, and M. Pontil. An empirical study of geographic user activity patterns in foursquare. In *ICWSM*, pages 570–573, 2011.

[30] W. T. Organization. *Collection of tourism expenditure statistics*, 1995. Technical Manual No. 2.

[31] S. Phithakkitnukoon, F. Calabrese, Z. Smoreda, and C. Ratti. Out of Sight Out of Mind–How Our Mobile Social Network Changes during Migration. In *Third international Social Computing (SocialCom)*, pages 515–520. IEEE, 2011.

[32] A. Pitsillidis, Y. Xie, F. Yu, M. Abadi, G. M. Voelker, and S. Savage. How to tell an airport from a home: techniques and applications. In *Hotnets*, pages 13:1–13:6, 2010.

[33] I. Poese, S. Uhlig, M. A. Kaafar, B. Donnet, and B. Gueye. Ip geolocation databases: unreliable? *CCR*, 41(2):53–56, 2011.

[34] E. Pultar and M. Raubal. A case for space: Physical and virtual location requirements in the couchsurfing social network. In *LBSN*, pages 88–91, 2009.

[35] S. Rinzivillo, S. Mainardi, F. Pezzoni, M. Coscia, D. Pedreschi, and F. Giannotti. Discovering the Geographical Borders of Human Mobility. *Kuenstliche Inteligenz*, 26(3):253–260, 2012.

[36] A. Rogers and J. Raymer. Origin dependence, secondary migration, and the indirect estimation of migration flows from population stocks. *Journal of Population Research*, 22(1):1–19, 2005.

[37] Y. Shavitt and N. Zilberman. A geolocation databases study. *JSAC*, 29(10):2044–2056, 2011.

[38] J. Stillwell, P. Boden, and A. Dennett. *Population Dynamics and Projection Methods*, chapter Monitoring Who Moves Where: Information Systems for Internal and International Migration, pages 115–140. Springer, 2011.

[39] E. Zagheni and I. Weber. You are where you email: Using e-mail data to estimate international migration rates. In *WebSci*, pages 497–506, 2012.

From Machu_Picchu to *"rafting the urubamba river"*: Anticipating information needs via the Entity-Query Graph

Ilaria Bordino[1] Gianmarco De Francisci Morales[2] Ingmar Weber[3]* Francesco Bonchi[4]

[1,2,4]Yahoo! Research Barcelona, Spain [3]Qatar Computing Research Institute, Doha, Qatar

{[1]bordino, [2]gdfm, [4]bonchi}@yahoo-inc.com [3]ingmarweber@acm.org

ABSTRACT

We study the problem of anticipating user search needs, based on their browsing activity. Given the current web page p that a user is visiting we want to recommend a small and diverse set of search queries that are relevant to the content of p, but also non-obvious and serendipitous.

We introduce a novel method that is based on the content of the page visited, rather than on past browsing patterns as in previous literature. Our content-based approach can be used even for previously unseen pages.

We represent the topics of a page by the set of Wikipedia entities extracted from it. To obtain useful query suggestions for these entities, we exploit a novel graph model that we call EQGraph (*Entity-Query Graph*), containing entities, queries, and transitions between entities, between queries, as well as from entities to queries. We perform Personalized PageRank computation on such a graph to expand the set of entities extracted from a page into a richer set of entities, and to associate these entities with relevant query suggestions. We develop an efficient implementation to deal with large graph instances and suggest queries from a large and diverse pool.

We perform a user study that shows that our method produces relevant and interesting recommendations, and outperforms an alternative method based on reverse IR.

Categories and Subject Descriptors

H.3 [**Information Storage and Retrieval**]: H.3.3 **Information Search and Retrieval.**

Keywords

Query Suggestions, Implicit Search, Serendipity, Entity Extraction.

1. INTRODUCTION

Exploring the Web is often a *serendipitous* experience, where users with no pre-existing search objective meander from topic to topic, sometimes discovering unexpected, surprising, and interesting information [16]. Such serendipitous search encounters can be extremely enriching for the users, as they may stimulate their thinking to arrive to particular creative insights [2, 32]. In this scenario, it is interesting to analyze the class of web search queries that are *triggered* by the content of a previously read web page. For example, while reading a news article about the 2012 presidential election results in France, the user might want to read more about the new president and his financial policies, thus issuing a query such as "francois hollande financial policies". Figure 1 shows a real example from our experiments.

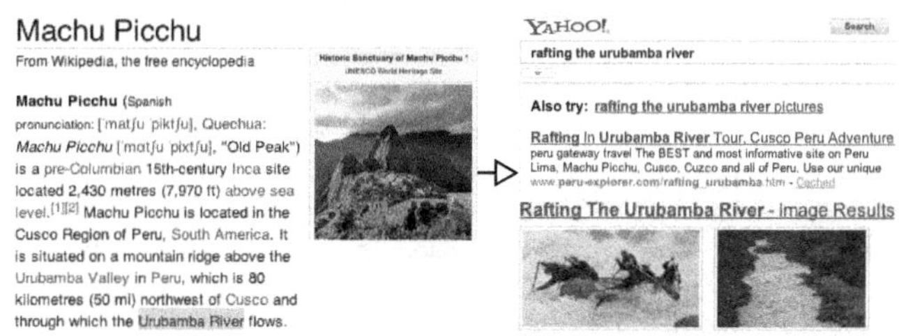

Figure 1: Example of a suggestion produced by our method in our experiments: when reading the Wikipedia page about Machu Picchu, a pre-Columbian Inca site in Peru, we suggest to the user a query about rafting the Urubamba, the river that flows in the valley where Machu Picchu is located.

In this paper we tackle the problem of *anticipating* such newly created information needs. More concretely, given the current web page p that a user is visiting we want to recommend a small and diverse set of search queries that are relevant to the content of p, non-obvious and serendipitous.

Observe that this problem is not just a web search problem *in reverse*, as we are not trying to identify queries that would lead to the page p being ranked highly in the result list. Such queries are mostly obvious given the content of the page, and this is not desirable for our application. Our goal is to identify queries that *stem from* the page, rather than queries that *lead to* the page.

The problem of understanding users' intent and supporting them in the formulation of web search queries has been studied extensively over the last years [3, 4, 6, 13, 30]. However, the standard problem studied is that of recommending new related queries that refine a given search query. In other terms, in the traditional context it is assumed that the user has already explicitly given an indication concerning her intent through a (possibly incomplete) web search query. In this perspective the provided recommendations are *passive*,

*This work was done while the author was at Yahoo! Research Barcelona.

WSDM'13, February 4–8, 2013, Rome, Italy.

in the sense that they only come after a user has submitted one or more queries to a search engine. The reasons behind these queries and what triggered the information need are not taken into account.

Instead, in the scenario we consider in this paper, the user does not need to formulate a query that represents explicitly an information need. The idea is that the user is picked up at an earlier stage during the search process, when she is reading a web page and, potentially, she has not even yet conceived the thought of issuing a web search query at all. The motivation for considering such a scenario is that many information needs of web users are actually triggered by what they browse. This particularly holds for informative pages, such as news and blogs: whenever a user finds something interesting or unclear while reading a page, she might want to go deeper in the matter and, to obtain further information, she might formulate a query.

A recent work by Cheng et al. [10] has proposed to exploit data gathered from search logs and browsing logs to actively predict users' query intent based on the web pages they browse. The model proposed by Cheng et al. is based on the frequent patterns of (page, query) transitions. The basic idea is that of exploiting *"the wisdom of the crowd"*: if after visiting a particular page, many users continue with the same query then the original page is likely to "trigger" the query. One main limitation of this approach is that, being based on frequent patterns, it is more effective for popular pages that have been seen many times by many different users, while it is inherently inapplicable to previously unseen pages. Unfortunately, as discussed above, the kind of pages that are more likely to be an interesting playground for these recommendations are informative pages which are very dynamical in nature and usually have a short life: from few hours to few days. Therefore it is important to develop methods for recommending queries even for new pages.

In this paper we tackle such a goal, by focusing on the content of pages. In particular, given any web page, we build a succinct representation of its subject matter by extracting the main concepts described or discussed in it, in the form of Wikipedia entities. With the aim of obtaining relevant and interesting query recommendations for the entities contained in a page, we devise a novel graph model, which we call EQGraph (*Entity-Query Graph*).

Our model extends the well-known Query-Flow graph [5]. It consists of two distinct sets of nodes, namely Wikipedia entity nodes and query nodes, and three different sets of arcs: entity-entity, query-query, and entity-query. The query-query connections are akin to their counterpart in the Query-Flow graph: the presence of a directed arc between two query nodes indicates a sufficiently high likelihood of submitting the second query after having issued the first one. In the EQGraph each entity is connected to all the queries that contain it. Finally, the entity-entity transitions are equivalent to query-flow transitions at the conceptual level of entities. We draw a directed arc between two entities if a user who issued a query related to the first entity is likely to search for the second entity. We derive these entity-entity transitions from the query-flow transitions by aggregating transitions that are related to the same entities.

We leverage the EQGraph to recommend interesting queries for web pages. We start from the *seed set* of entities contained in the page. To ensure that the seed set contains a sufficiently large number of concepts, we expand the initial set of entities by performing Personalized PageRank computations in the subgraph of the EQGraph induced by all the entity nodes.

In the EQGraph, the entities of interest for a page are connected to the queries that contain them. However, we do not build our final query recommendations for the page by simply looking at these queries. Instead we perform a Personalized PageRank computation for the expanded set of entities in the full EQGraph.

We could use a textual representation of the entities to provide synthetically generated queries. However, we decide to employ real queries to leverage the wisdom of the crowd. Queries that are pointed by multiple entities are more likely to be interesting because they are at the intersection of different topics in a page. The EQGraph naturally captures this intuition: if two entities are related, there will likely be a query that is pointed by both entities.

The EQGraph can be huge. For our experiments, we have built an instance of the graph containing several hundreds of millions nodes and arcs. Running Personalized PageRank computations on such a large graph is potentially a serious performance bottleneck of our query recommendation method. To perform these computations in an efficient and scalable manner, we develop a Giraph[1] implementation of the Personalized PageRank algorithm. Giraph is a Hadoop-based framework for running graph algorithms on large-scale data in parallel by distributing the load on a large number of computers. It is based on the Bulk Synchronous Parallel (BSP) model of computation [34].

We test our method on a large EQGraph extracted from a recent (2012) sample of a Yahoo! query log . We produce query recommendations for a set of 150 pages sampled from Wikipedia, Yahoo! News and Yahoo! Finance. We evaluate the quality of the produced recommendations by performing a user study, and find that our method produces relevant and non-obvious suggestions.

The main contributions of this paper are the following:

- We introduce the EQGraph as a novel object. This object enriches the standard Query-Flow graph [5] with entity nodes. We describe this graph in detail as it has interesting properties in its own right and could be applied to other problems.
- We present a novel method for anticipating information needs that arise from the content of pages that people are browsing. Our method is based on Personalized PageRank computation over the EQGraph.
- We use Wikipedia entities to represent the information items contained in web pages. By leveraging entities, our model is able to generate query recommendations for previously unseen pages.
- We provide an efficient implementation that can deal with very large graphs. We develop a Giraph implementation of the Personalized PageRank algorithm, which could be useful for many other applications.
- We perform a user study that shows that our recommendations are relevant for the content of the page, and that our method based on the EQGraph outperforms an alternative baseline based on reverse IR.

The rest of this paper is organized as follows. Section 2 introduces the basic concepts for the EQGraph, which is then

[1] `http://giraph.apache.org`

presented in Section 3. Section 4 describes how we extract entities from pages and queries, how we expand the initial set of entities extracted from a page, and how we produce the suggestions. In Section 5 we assess the quality of the recommendations produced by our method via a user study. Section 6 reviews related literature and Section 7 concludes.

2. PRELIMINARIES

In the following, we first introduce the basic elements of our model, namely, entities, queries, and the Query-Flow graph. Then we describe the EQGraph in the next section.

Entities. We aim at suggesting relevant and interesting queries to a user browsing a web page. To do so, we need a way to effectively represent the *aboutness* of a page, i.e., the set of topics that the page is related to.

The standard approach to this problem requires to perform two tasks: automatic keyword extraction and word sense disambiguation. The former task identifies the sentences in the input text that capture the relevant concepts discussed in the page. The latter task aims at finding the correct interpretation of any such sentence, thus linking it to the actual concept it represents.

Following the state of the art [14, 17, 24, 25, 26], we perform the sense disambiguation task by linking phrases extracted from web pages to Wikipedia articles. We dub *entity* any concept (person, place, event, etc.) that is defined and described in a Wikipedia page. This choice implicitly limits the set of concepts that we can represent in a web page to the ones that have a Wikipedia page describing them.

We believe that Wikipedia provides a fairly comprehensive list of entities of interest. It is nowadays the largest and most visited knowledge repository on the Web, with millions of pages available in many different languages.

Query log. A query log stores information about the *search actions* of the users of a search engine. The basic record stored in a query log $\mathcal{L}$ is a tuple $\langle q_i, u_i, t_i, V_i, C_i\rangle$ where: q_i is the submitted query, u_i is an anonymized identifier for the user who submitted the query, t_i is a timestamp, V_i is the set of documents returned as results to the query, and C_i is the set of documents clicked by the user. In this paper we ignore information from the results of queries (V_i and C_i).

A *user query session*, or *session*, is defined as a sequence of queries of one particular user issued within a given threshold from each other (typically 30 minutes [5]). A *chain* or *logical session*, or *mission*, is a sequence of queries in the same session that are topically coherent.

Query-Flow graph. The Query-Flow graph [5] is a graph representation of a query log aimed at capturing interesting knowledge about the latent querying behavior of the users, with special focus on the sequentiality of similar queries. The nodes of the Query-Flow graph are all the queries in the query log $\mathcal{L}$, and an arc between two queries indicates that the two queries are likely to be part of the same search mission, in the order given by the direction of the arc.

3. THE EQ GRAPH MODEL

We now present our novel graph model, which we call EQGraph. The EQGraph extends the Query-Flow graph [5] with nodes representing Wikipedia entities, and with arcs between entities, as well as from entities to queries.

Bonchi et al. [8] have recently introduced the *Term-Query graph*, which is a Query-Flow graph augmented with term nodes, and with arcs connecting any term to the queries that contain it. The EQGraph is based on a similar principle, but we use Wikipedia entities rather than terms in virtue of their deeper semantics. Entities capture the concepts of interest for people surfing the Web with less ambiguity. They provide a better representation of the content of a page and a more solid base for our query suggestion task.

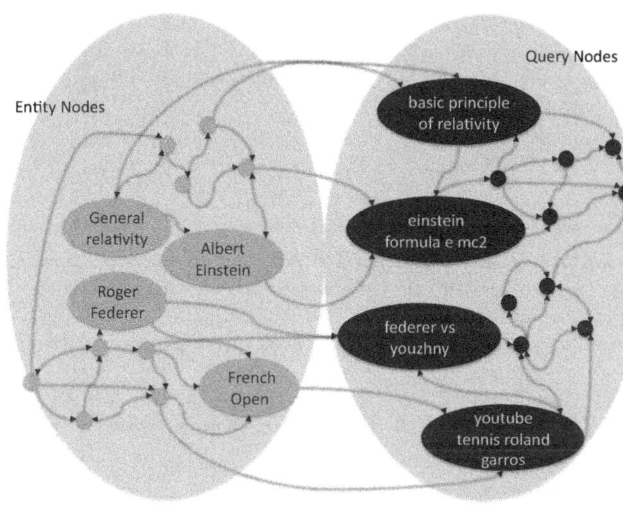

Figure 2: Depiction of the Entity-Query Graph.

More formally, the EQGraph is a directed graph $\mathcal{G} = (\mathcal{N}, \mathcal{A})$ whose nodes and arcs are defined as follows. Let $\mathcal{Q}$ denote all the queries appearing in a query log $\mathcal{L}$, and $\mathcal{E}$ all the entities extracted from the text of such queries. The set of nodes $\mathcal{N}$ contains a node for every entity $e \in \mathcal{E}$, and for every query $q \in \mathcal{Q}$. Specifically, we denote by $\mathcal{N}_\mathcal{E}$ the set of entity nodes, and by $\mathcal{N}_\mathcal{Q}$ the set of query nodes. Thus $\mathcal{N} = \mathcal{N}_\mathcal{E} \cup \mathcal{N}_\mathcal{Q}$. The set of arcs $\mathcal{A}$ is given by the union of three different sets of arcs: $\mathcal{A}_\mathcal{E}$, $\mathcal{A}_\mathcal{Q}$, and $\mathcal{A}_{\mathcal{E}\mathcal{Q}}$.

Query-to-query transitions. Arcs in $\mathcal{A}_\mathcal{Q}$ connect only query nodes, and they have exactly the same semantic as in the original Query-Flow graph model. An arc $q_i \to q_j \in \mathcal{A}_\mathcal{Q}$, with $q_i, q_j \in \mathcal{N}_\mathcal{Q}$, indicates that the two queries q_i and q_j are likely to be part of the same search mission.

Arc $q_i \to q_j$ is assigned a weight $w_Q(q_i \to q_j)$ representing the *chaining probability* that a user issues query q_j consecutively after q_i in a same search mission. The chaining probability of any transition $q_i \to q_j$ is computed by extracting temporal, syntactic and session features that aggregate information from all the sessions where q_i and q_j appear consecutively, and in the given order. We discard arcs whose chaining probability is lower than a minimum threshold, because they represent noisy reformulations that are not likely to be made within a given search mission.

The subgraph ($\mathcal{N}_\mathcal{Q}$, $\mathcal{A}_\mathcal{Q}$) is actually a Query-Flow graph. We follow the settings of the original paper [5] to generate the set of query-to-query arcs $\mathcal{A}_\mathcal{Q}$.

Entity-to-query transitions. To extract entities from queries we use the methodology described in the next section. We denote by $\mathcal{X}_\mathcal{E}(q)$ the set of entities extracted from a query q. We build the set of arcs $\mathcal{A}_{\mathcal{E}\mathcal{Q}}$ by connecting each entity to all the queries that contain it:

$$\mathcal{A}_{\mathcal{E}\mathcal{Q}} = \{e \to q, \text{ s.t. } e \in \mathcal{N}_\mathcal{E}, q \in \mathcal{N}_\mathcal{Q}, e \in \mathcal{X}_\mathcal{E}(q)\}.$$

Any arc $e \rightarrow q \in \mathcal{A}_{\mathcal{EQ}}$ connecting an entity e to a query q is given a weight proportional to the relative frequency of the query q in the log $\mathcal{L}$, with respect to all the queries that contain e. Formally,

$$w_{\mathcal{EQ}}(e \rightarrow q) = \frac{f(q)}{\sum_{q_i | e \in \mathcal{X}_{\mathcal{E}}(q_i)} f(q_i)},$$

where $f(q)$ indicates the frequency of query q in the log $\mathcal{L}$.

Entity-to-entity transitions. Arcs in $\mathcal{A}_{\mathcal{E}}$ connect only entity nodes, and their semantic is intended to be similar to that of arcs in $\mathcal{A}_{\mathcal{Q}}$.

The set of entity nodes $\mathcal{N}_{\mathcal{E}}$ includes all the entities that are contained in the queries in log $\mathcal{L}$. Thus, such entities represent individual concepts of interest, for which people have attempted to gather relevant information by submitting queries to the search engine. In general, an entity can be contained in many different queries, while most of the queries contain just one entity or no entity at all (due to the fact that average query length is very short).

We draw an arc between two entities $e_i \rightarrow e_j \in \mathcal{A}_{\mathcal{E}}$ to indicate that there is high probability that a user who issued one or more queries related to the concept expressed by the first entity e_i, subsequently performs one or more searches related to the concept represented by the second entity e_j.

We build the set $\mathcal{A}_{\mathcal{E}}$ of entity-to-entity arcs starting from the set $\mathcal{A}_{\mathcal{Q}}$ of query-to-query arcs and from the set $\mathcal{A}_{\mathcal{EQ}}$ of the arcs that connect entities to queries.

Given a single transition $q_i \rightarrow q_j \in \mathcal{A}_{\mathcal{Q}}$, let us consider the set of entities $\mathcal{X}_{\mathcal{E}}(q_i)$ extracted from the source query q_i, and the set of entities $\mathcal{X}_{\mathcal{E}}(q_j)$ extracted from the target query q_j. We draw an arc from each entity extracted from the source query, to every entity extracted from the target query. In other words, we derive from $q_i \rightarrow q_j$ a set of transitions $T_{q_i \rightarrow q_j} = \{e_u \rightarrow e_v | e_u \in \mathcal{X}_{\mathcal{E}}(q_i), e_v \in \mathcal{X}_{\mathcal{E}}(q_j)\}$.

Now let $w_{\mathcal{Q}}(q_i \rightarrow q_j)$ be the weight (chaining probability) assigned to arc $q_i \rightarrow q_j$ in our model. With the aim of avoiding to excessively boost the weights assigned to arcs involving popular entities, which may be contained in many queries, we uniformly divide the probability $w_{\mathcal{Q}}(q_i \rightarrow q_j)$ among the $n \cdot m$ entity-entity transitions derived from $q_i \rightarrow q_j$: thus every transition $e_u \rightarrow e_v \in T_{q_i \rightarrow q_j}$ is assigned a probability equal to $p_{q_i \rightarrow q_j}(e_u \rightarrow e_v) = w_{\mathcal{Q}}(q_i \rightarrow q_j)/(n \cdot m)$.

Next, we observe that a given entity-to-entity transition $e_u \rightarrow e_v$ can be derived from multiple query-to-query transitions (all the ones whose source query contains e_u and whose target query contains e_v). Let us assume that there exist r query-to-query transitions $q_{i_s} \rightarrow q_{i_t}$, $i = 1, \ldots, r$ in $\mathcal{A}_{\mathcal{Q}}$ that originate the entity-to-entity transition $e_u \rightarrow e_v$. Let us denote by $p_{q_{i_s} \rightarrow q_{i_t}}(e_u \rightarrow e_v)$, $i = 1, \ldots, r$, the probabilities assigned to transition $e_u \rightarrow e_v$ from each of the r originating $q_{i_s} \rightarrow q_{i_t}$ query-to-query transitions. We aggregate these probabilities to derive the global weight $w_{\mathcal{E}}(e_u \rightarrow e_v)$ that we assign to arc $e_u \rightarrow e_v$ in the EQGraph:

$$w_E(e_u \rightarrow e_v) = 1 - \prod_{i=1,\ldots,r} (1 - p_{q_{i_s} \rightarrow q_{i_t}}(e_u \rightarrow e_v)).$$

Despite the fact that $\mathcal{A}_{\mathcal{Q}}$, which is constructed by following the Query-Flow graph model, does not contain self loops, our procedure for deriving $\mathcal{A}_{\mathcal{E}}$ transitions from $\mathcal{A}_{\mathcal{Q}}$ transitions might lead to the extraction of entity self loops, for example, in the case where the original query-to-query transition is a *specialization*. A specialization [7] is a query reformulation that a user submits when she realizes that her first query was too general given the information need that she had in mind. Thus she formulates a second, more specific query in the attempt of getting a narrower set of results. Typically, the set of words of the specialized query is a superset of the set of words of the first query, thus the entities extracted from the first query are also very likely to be extracted from the second query.

However, we do not include entity self loops in the EQGraph. The scenario for which we introduce our model is that of suggesting relevant queries for web pages, based on the entities they contain. Further in the paper we will show that our recommendation method exploits the entity-entity transitions to perform a preliminary expansion of the initial set of entities extracted from the content of a page. The goal of this entity expansion is to overcome problems that might be encountered when the seed set of entities is particularly poor. We achieve this by performing Personalized PageRank computations on the subgraph of the EQGraph induced by the entity nodes, i.e., the subgraph that contains all the entity nodes, and all the arcs between them. In the computation of Personalized PageRank, self loops could have the effect of boosting the rank of nodes that might not be very close to the preference vector [38].

4. RECOMMENDATION METHOD

We want to suggest to a given user who is browsing a web page p a ranked list Q of k queries such that $q \in Q$ is related to p and *non obvious*.

In this paper we focus on the creation of such a list. We also give a brief overview of the technical aspects of serving these queries, though it is not the main focus of this work.

We decompose the task of finding a set Q of queries that are relevant for a page p into the following subtasks:

1. Extracting a seed set of entities $\mathcal{X}_{\mathcal{E}}(p)$ from p;
2. Expanding $\mathcal{X}_{\mathcal{E}}(p)$ to a larger set of entities $\mathcal{Z}_{\mathcal{E}}(p)$;
3. Obtain queries Q for the expanded set of entities.

Extracting entities from text. To extract entities from a text, which in our framework can be either a web page or a query occurring in a search-engine query log, we first parse the text to identify *surface forms*[2] that are candidate mentions of Wikipedia entities. We add entity candidates to each recognized phrase by retrieving the candidates from an offline Wikipedia database.

To resolve each surface form to the correct Wikipedia entity we apply the machine-learning approach proposed by Zhou et al. [39]. This approach employs a resolution model based on a rich set of both context-sensitive and context-independent features, derived from Wikipedia and various other data sources including web behavioral data.

We then use Paranjpe's *Aboutness* ranking model [26] to rank the obtained Wikipedia entities according to their relevance for the text. This model exploits structural and visual properties of web documents, as well as user feedback derived from search-engine click logs. Paranjpe has shown that his approach, even when trained mainly on head web pages, generalizes and performs well on all kinds of documents, including tail pages.

[2]A surface form is any mention of an entity in the text, e.g., *tomatoes* is a surface form of the entity *Tomato*.

Expanding a list of seed entities. Let p denote a web page for which we want to recommend queries. We perform a Personalized PageRank computation on the graph $\mathcal{G}_{\mathcal{E}} = (\mathcal{N}_{\mathcal{E}}, \mathcal{A}_{\mathcal{E}})$, i.e., the subgraph of the EQGraph that contains all the entities, and all the arcs between them. We use a uniform distribution on the seed set $\mathcal{X}_{\mathcal{E}}(p)$ as preference vector. We build an expanded set of entities denoted $\mathcal{Z}_{\mathcal{E}}(p)$ by taking the top entities with the highest scores in the resulting distribution.

Bonchi et al. [8] use a centerpiece subgraph computation on a Term-Query graph rather than Personalized PageRank to recommend queries related to an input query. In the centerpiece computation, the final distribution is given by the Hadamard product of the single seed-node distributions, rather than by their sum as in Personalized PageRank. The choice of [8] is motivated by the fact that they use a term-centric approach. In order to discover queries that are actually relevant for an input query, they have to identify queries that are related to *most* of the terms in the starting query, rather than just to a few of them. As the number of terms in a query is typically very small, this condition is needed to filter out marginally related queries.

In our scenario the centerpiece approach is not a good choice for two reasons. First, the number of seed-entity distributions that we have to aggregate is much larger. In our experiments, we consider pages that contain at least 5 entities, and we extract a maximum of 100 entities per page. With so many starting points, only extremely connected entities would have a non-zero product. Second, entities have a stronger semantic value compared to terms. Terms are more ambiguous and benefit from the disambiguation power of the centerpiece computation. On the contrary, an entity only needs to be relevant enough for some of the seed entities to be considered relevant for a page, and thus to be included in the expanded set. These two facts motivate our choice of Personalized PageRank.

Obtaining queries for entities. Given the expanded set of entities $\mathcal{Z}_{\mathcal{E}}(p)$ obtained in the previous step, we now want to create a list Q of k related queries to recommend to the user. Our method is similar in spirit to the one considered for the entity expansion step. We still perform a Personalized PageRank computation, but this time on the full EQGraph, by using a uniform distribution over the entities in $\mathcal{Z}_{\mathcal{E}}(p)$ as preference vector. We return the k query nodes $\{q_1, q_2, \ldots, q_k\}$ that achieve the highest scores in the resulting distribution.

As an alternative method, we implement a *Reverse IR* approach that, given a page p, suggests those queries that have the page in the top positions of their search-engine result list. We represent both queries and pages by means of TF/IDF vectors. Given a page p, we compute the cosine similarity between its TF/IDF vector and the vector of any query stored in the query log. We then return the top k queries that achieve the highest similarity.

5. EXPERIMENTS

5.1 System description

We begin the section with a description of how we envision a system that employs our technique. Our objective is to provide online query recommendations while the user is browsing the Web.

The system consists of two parts: back-end and front-end. The back-end is dedicated to the offline computation of the distributions on the EQGraph. The front-end sends requests to the back-end and shows suggested queries to the user. It can be implemented by a browser plugin or a toolbar add-on.

Workflow. The workflow of our system is as follows. First, the front-end extracts the textual content of the current page and cleans it by using a service such as boilerpipe[3] or by using ad-hoc rules for specific domains. The front-end then sends a request with the cleaned content to the back-end.

The back-end receives the text and extracts relevant entities from it. These entities constitute the seed set for the query suggestion. The back-end then uses this set to query the precomputed index of distributions over the EQGraph, then sums the distributions to obtain the top-k queries to suggest. This operation is very similar to answering a query and can be implemented efficiently on the same infrastructure that a web search engine runs on.

Indexing. The EQGraph has 738 627 entity nodes and 121×10^6 query nodes, so the full distribution would have $738\,627 \times 121 \times 10^6 \approx 89 \times 10^{12}$ entries. Even by compressing the lists the space required to store the full distribution is prohibitive. Thus, following Bonchi et al. [8], we propose to use approximate distributions to make our solution viable. Approximation comes in two ways: pruning and bucketing.

Pruning. By storing only the top-p probabilities for each entity, the space requirements are reduced from $|\mathcal{N}_{\mathcal{E}}| \times |\mathcal{N}_{\mathcal{Q}}|$ to $|\mathcal{N}_{\mathcal{E}}| \times p$. The space saving depends on the condition $p \ll |\mathcal{N}_{\mathcal{Q}}|$. The price to pay is introducing some error in the query suggested. However, this error is less critical than the one introduced by Bonchi et al. [8] as we use Personalized PageRank rather then centerpiece computation. In Personalized PageRank the final distribution is the sum of the single entity-specific distributions, rather than their Hadamard product. Thus even if one query is missing from the distribution of one of the entities in the seed, it can still be suggested if it is relevant enough to another entity in such set.

Bucketing. Probabilities can be bucketed together by using buckets with exponentially increasing size, as done by Bonchi et al. [8]. We can then save a single probability for the whole bucket, thus greatly reducing the space occupancy. In our case, error propagation is additive rather than multiplicative, so we have a better approximation. See Bonchi et al. [8] for further details. Entity ids in the same bucket can be easily compressed by using gap coding and Elias gamma coding or similar techniques.

5.2 Building the EQGraph

We build a large EQGraph instance from a recent sample of a Yahoo! (US) query log. We anonymize our dataset by discarding all the queries that contain personally identifiable information, and by aggregating information from all the available user query sessions, without retaining any user identifiers. The sample we consider is very large: it contains 24.3×10^9 queries (1.9×10^9 distinct), and 3.3×10^9 transitions between queries.

Normalization. We preprocess the query log to *clean* queries before presenting them to the users. We employ the following query normalization scheme. Given a query q occurring in the log, we remove stop words and non-alphanumeric characters. We then apply Porter's stemming

[3] `http://boilerpipe-web.appspot.com`

Table 1: The EQ Graph: Basic stats

$\lvert\mathcal{N}\rvert$	$\lvert\mathcal{N}_\mathcal{E}\rvert$	$\lvert\mathcal{N}_\mathcal{Q}\rvert$	$\lvert\mathcal{A}\rvert$	$\lvert\mathcal{A}_\mathcal{E}\rvert$	$\lvert\mathcal{A}_{\mathcal{E}\mathcal{Q}}\rvert$	$\lvert\mathcal{A}_\mathcal{Q}\rvert$
122 421 398	738 627	121 682 771	202 469 003	17 103 835	40 948 844	144 416 324

Table 2: The EQ Graph: Average degree

$\overline{d_\mathcal{N}}$	$\overline{d_{\mathcal{N}_\mathcal{E}}}$	$\overline{d_{\mathcal{N}_\mathcal{Q}}}$	$\overline{in_\mathcal{N}}$	$\overline{in_{\mathcal{N}_\mathcal{E}}}$	$\overline{in_{\mathcal{N}_\mathcal{Q}}}$	$\overline{out_\mathcal{N}}$	$\overline{out_{\mathcal{N}_\mathcal{E}}}$	$\overline{out_{\mathcal{N}_\mathcal{Q}}}$
3.31	101.75	2.71	1.65	23.15	1.52	1.65	78.59	1.19

algorithm [27] and we sort the stemmed terms lexicographically for each query. As a result we obtain a *normalized* query form $\hat{q}$. This normalization scheme maps multiple queries onto the same normalized form $\hat{q}$ and defines an equivalence class for queries. We thus collapse all the queries that are in the same equivalence class onto the same query. We choose the most frequent query inside each class as the *representative* of the class. Finally, we replace every query in the original log with the representative for its class.

Query graph. We then build $\mathcal{N}_\mathcal{Q}$ and $\mathcal{A}_\mathcal{Q}$ by applying the standard Query-Flow graph methodology [5]. Following the original paper, we filter the log by retaining only the queries that have at least 5 occurrences in the log, and the query-to-query transitions that appear at least 2 times.

Entity graph. From the query log we extract the set of entity nodes $\mathcal{N}_\mathcal{E}$ by following the approach described in Section 4. We then proceed to create $\mathcal{A}_{\mathcal{E}\mathcal{Q}}$ and $\mathcal{A}_\mathcal{E}$. $\mathcal{A}_{\mathcal{E}\mathcal{Q}}$ is obtained simply by connecting every entity in $\mathcal{N}_\mathcal{E}$ to all the queries in $\mathcal{N}_\mathcal{Q}$ that contain it. The set of entity-to-entity transitions $\mathcal{A}_\mathcal{E}$ is derived from $\mathcal{A}_\mathcal{Q}$, using the approach described in Section 3. We discard the top 100 entities with highest in-degree in the graph induced by the entity nodes $\mathcal{G}_\mathcal{E} = (\mathcal{N}_\mathcal{E}, \mathcal{A}_\mathcal{E})$. These entities correspond to popular sites such as Yahoo!, Google, Facebook, Twitter, Youtube, etc. They are mostly derived from navigational queries, and they are not interesting for the purposes of our work.

Altogether we obtain an EQGraph that consists of 122.4×10^6 nodes and 202.4×10^6 arcs . Tables 1, 2, and 3 provide basic statistics about the graph. Observe that the subgraph of the entity nodes is much denser than the subgraph of the query nodes. Figure 3 shows the frequency distribution of queries in the query log, which follows a typical power law.

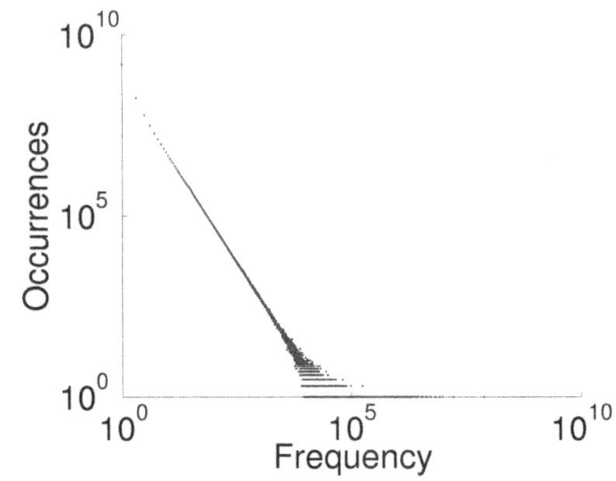

Figure 3: Frequency of queries in the query log

5.3 Personalized PageRank in Giraph

Given a weighted directed graph, Personalized PageRank is a measure of proximity or relevance of a node to a set of query nodes. To compute this measure on the EQGraph we implement Personalized PageRank on Giraph. Giraph is an open-source large-scale graph-processing framework based on Hadoop. It implements the Bulk Synchronous Parallel model of computation on graphs. Its APIs are inspired by the Pregel system [20].

Our implementation takes as input a directed graph, a restart probability α and a preference vector defined on the nodes of the graph, and generates the stationary distribution of a random walker which restarts from a node in the graph according to the preference vector with probability α.

We use the power iteration method to compute the final distribution. As standard practice, we set the restart probability $\alpha = 0.15$ and the number of iterations to 30.

In order to reduce the memory requirements of handling the EQGraph, we develop a compact, array-based node representation which allows fast iteration over the arcs but makes random access very expensive. This choice makes sense in the case of PageRank because at each step we need to iterate over all the arcs of each node.

Our implementation of Personalized PageRank can easily scale to very large graphs with billions of nodes and arcs. The code is open source, available online[4], and will be integrated in a future release of Giraph.

5.4 Testing

Our testset is composed of 150 pages drawn randomly from Wikipedia, Yahoo! News, and Yahoo! Finance.

We filter out pages for which we can detect less than 5 entities. We extract the relevant textual content from each page by using a combination of domain specific ad-hoc rules and automatic tools for detecting templates and stripping HTML. Finally, the textual content of each page is fed to our entity detection module to extract entities. These entities constitute the seed set for each page in our experiments.

We have 5 142 unique entities in our testset. As described before, our system would need to perform 5 142 runs of Personalized PageRank, for the entity expansion set. However, for our offline experiments, we leverage the property that PageRank is additive. By setting the preference vector to a uniform distribution over the (expanded) seed set, we need

[4] `https://issues.apache.org/jira/browse/GIRAPH-191`

Table 3: The EQ Graph: Maximum degree

max $d_{\mathcal{N}}$	max $d_{\mathcal{N}_{\mathcal{E}}}$	max $d_{\mathcal{N}_{\mathcal{Q}}}$	max $in_{\mathcal{N}}$	max $in_{\mathcal{N}_{\mathcal{E}}}$	max $in_{\mathcal{N}_{\mathcal{Q}}}$	max $out_{\mathcal{N}}$	max $out_{\mathcal{N}_{\mathcal{E}}}$	max $out_{\mathcal{N}_{\mathcal{Q}}}$
724 634	186 162	724 634	402 121	8 604	402 121	322 513	186 162	322 513

to run 150 Personalized PageRank computations per step, one for each page.

The first round of Personalized PageRank computations produces the expanded seed set $\mathcal{Z}_{\mathcal{E}}(p)$. We fix $|\mathcal{Z}_{\mathcal{E}}(p)| = 50$ and for each page p we only keep the top entities in the distribution. This pruning would not be necessary given our offline testing methodology as there is no additional overhead in using all of the entities. However, in a more realistic setting, we would like to reduce the number of Personalized PageRank computations that we need to perform and store. Furthermore, pruning lowly related entities helps to remove noise. Note that the entity expansion step adds entities to the seed set only if the seed set size is less than $|\mathcal{Z}_{\mathcal{E}}(p)|$.

The second round of Personalized PageRank computations produces the query recommendations. We return the top 5 query suggestions for each page. For all the pages in our testset, we generate recommendations with our EQGraph algorithm, and with the alternative Reverse IR method introduced in section 4. We obtain 1 392 distinct suggestions.

5.5 Evaluation

We ask 10 assessors[5] to evaluate our query recommendations. Each record given to an assessor consists of a (URL, query) pair. The query links to a search-engine result page. The assessor is asked to browse the starting page in order to understand its topic, then to click on the query and read the snippets of the result page to understand the query. Finally, we ask the assessor to rate the relevance of the suggestion on a 3-point scale: "Related and interesting", "Related but obvious", "Unrelated". The following guidelines are provided:

- *Related and interesting*: the query is relevant to the content of the page and expresses a question that cannot be fully answered by reading the web page. The page and the query are related, and you believe that reading the web page would raise your interest in the topics covered by the query.
- *Related but obvious*: the query is equal to the title of the page or the page is top result in the search result page of the query. Page and query are related, but you believe that reading the page would not raise your interest in the query, e.g. the query does not cover any additional aspect with respect to the page content.
- *Unrelated*: the query and the topics of page are clearly unrelated. You believe it is not possible that browsing that page may raise your interest in the query.

The assessors are also given the option of withholding judgment by selecting the "Undecided" option. This choice is designed for difficult cases or when the page is unreadable (e.g. because the page was not available anymore).

Results. Table 4 summarizes the results of our user study. We report aggregated values for the full testset as well as results broken down by domain. We separate the Wikipedia domain from Yahoo! News and Yahoo! Finance because of their intrinsic differences.

Wikipedia pages are an ideal case for our method: they focus on a single topic but provide many links to continue the exploration, they are very descriptive and easy to understand. They also have a natural affinity with our entity extraction technique that uses Wikipedia pages as entities.

Pages from Yahoo! News and Yahoo! Finance represent a bigger challenge: understanding them is more complex, they present acronyms and jargon that is difficult to decipher, they are also more compact and less descriptive. From technical standpoint, they are less structured and thus harder to clean from HTML tags and templates, so more noise is left in the textual representation of the pages.

EQGraph outperforms Reverse IR in all cases for the "Related and interesting" class. The fraction of interesting suggestions is almost twice as much as the one provided by the baseline for Wikipedia pages (62.7% vs. 33%), and still relevantly higher for the full dataset (58% vs. 36.1%).

As expected, the Reverse IR baseline suggests a large number of obvious queries. This confirms our hypothesis that the problem we are tackling is different from a reverse web search problem. Moreover, we prove that our method addresses exactly the right problem: the number of obvious queries that we suggest to the user is always below 5%.

The price to pay for this *serendipity* is a larger fraction of unrelated queries. Indeed, sometimes the link between a page and a query suggested by the EQGraph is far-fetched and non-obvious. However, this behavior is desired, and in line with research on recommender systems that argues that recommendation is not a prediction task and that accuracy is not the most important metric [21].

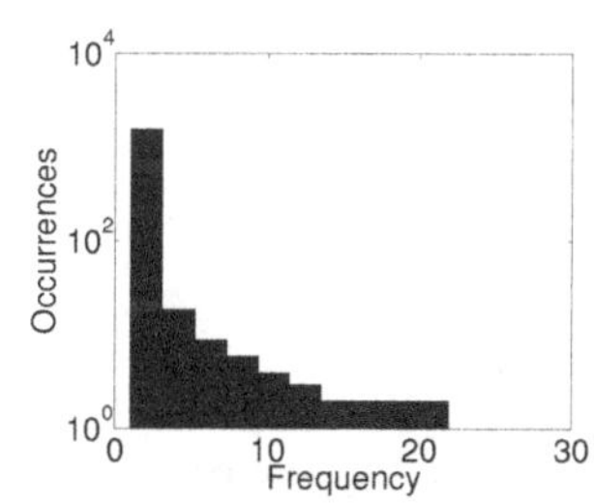

(a) EQGraph

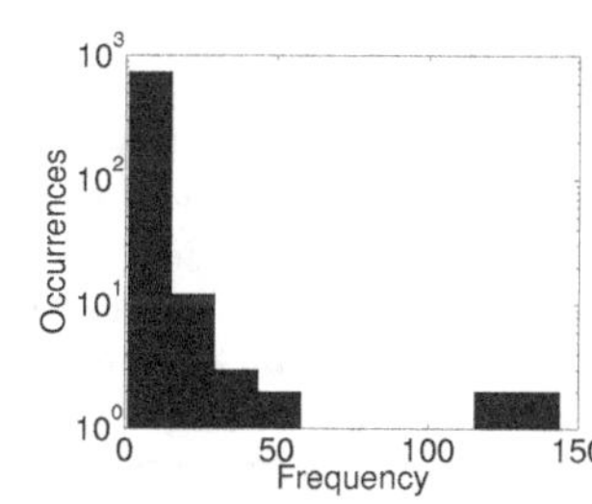

(b) Reverse IR

Figure 4: Frequency of suggested queries

Diversity. We analyze the results of the query suggestions in terms of diversity. Our methodology does not include any explicit result diversification step. However, by leveraging the EQGraph we implicitly take into account the different topics in each page. Figure 4 shows the histogram of the query frequencies for the results provided by our method and the baseline. The results provided by Reverse IR contain many highly-repeated queries, up to 50 times and beyond (on the x axis). There are also a few popular queries with frequency higher than 100. On the contrary, the results obtained via the EQGraph are more diverse and spread out.

[5]The assessors did not include the authors of this paper.

Table 4: **Results obtained with EQGraph, and with Reverse IR baseline**

Testset	Label	EQGraph	Reverse IR
Wikipedia pages	Related and interesting	62.7%	33%
	Related but obvious	3.3%	41.5%
	Unrelated	34%	25.5%
Yahoo! News + Yahoo! Finance	Related and interesting	52%	40%
	Related but obvious	2.3%	34.3%
	Unrelated	45.7%	25.7%
Full testset	Related and interesting	58%	36.1%
	Related but obvious	2.9%	38.4%
	Unrelated	39.1%	25.5%

The highest frequency for a single query in this set is 22, while most of the queries are singleton (note the logarithmic scale on the y axis).

We further explore the diversity of the result sets via lexical analysis. Given the result set returned for a page by a given method, we compute the Levenshtein distance between all of the result pairs in the set. We define the lexical diversity $\mathcal{D}$ of a result set for a page as the sum of all the $\frac{n\times(n-1)}{2}$ distances:

$$\mathcal{D}(p) = \sum_{i,j} \text{Lev}(q_i, q_j) \quad \text{for } i, j \in [1, k] \wedge i < j$$

where q_i, q_j are the queries in the result set of page p and k is the cardinality of the set.

We compute the lexical diversity for each page in our testset and for each method. Then we do a statistical analysis of the distribution of the lexical diversity. We apply a dependent t-test for paired samples to pairs of lexical diversity coming from different methods applied to the same page.

The test shows that the lexical diversity of the queries obtained via the EQGraph is higher than the baseline, and is statistically significant with a confidence level of 0.1%.

Anecdotal evidence. We present example suggestions created by both methods in Table 5. We select examples from Wikipedia as they are easier to understand and exemplify at best the kind of interesting queries we want to suggest.

The queries suggested by Reverse IR almost invariably contain the title of the page in their formulation. For the few queries that are in the form of a question, the page itself contains the answer.

On the contrary, the queries suggested by the EQGraph are mostly about specific aspects related to the main topic of the page. For example the role of osteoblasts and osteoclasts (cells that create and destroy bone tissue) in the process of osteoporosis, a bone disease. Or in the case of Azotemia (a condition of high level of nitrogen compounds like urea and creatinine in the blood), about its possible causes and symptoms such as kidney stones and osmotic diuresis.

6. RELATED WORK

Implicit and Context-Aware Search Predictions. Cheng *et al.* [10] actively predict search intents from user browsing behavior data. The basic idea is that if, after visiting a particular page, many users often continue with the same query then the original page is likely to "trigger" the query. To predict such queries, they learn a model to effectively rank such follow-up queries according to their likelihood of being triggered by the page. They also propose an approximation algorithm to diversify the ranked lists of queries obtained. They test their approach on large-scale user browsing behavior data obtained from a commercial search engine. Though their basic problem, identifying queries likely to be "triggered" by a visited web page, is the same as ours, our work differs significantly. Their approach requires historic browsing information and is not appropriate for previously unseen pages. They focus on identifying relevant (page, query) transitions from an existing candidate set whereas we, with tail pages in mind, focus on the creation of such sets in the first place.

The authors in [19] predict the next query in a session, using both search and click information. Though many of their features used are not applicable for previously unseen URLs, some, such as the DMOZ category of pages visited, are. In their experiments the best features are the previous query and the clicked URL. Their approach is largely orthogonal to ours. We focus on content-based techniques, not on log-based ones. Also, the problem they study has a crucial difference: for predicting the next query, "obvious" queries – often corresponding to repeat queries [31, 33] – are actually good, whereas they are bad for our purposes.

Cao *et al.* [9] propose a hidden markov model for predicting user behavior in a search session. Given a user's session so far, the model can predict the next query, and the urls the user is likely to click. The hidden states in the model describe the user's intent, while observed variables are the queries, and clicks on urls. The probability distributions over queries and urls depend only on the current state, but the state transitions depend on all previous states of the session. Similar to the work in [10] this approach could work in our setting *given enough observed page-to-query transitions.* However, the method fails to suggest queries while browsing *tail* pages, while our approach is not affected by this.

Finally, the problem of query prediction has been studied in the context of *caching* [18]. In caching, the focus is less on the user and more on the system. E.g., the system might benefit from knowing which queries are currently trending to cache their results, but such queries are unlikely to be of use for the problem studied by us.

Query suggestions. There is a large body of work on the problem of query suggestions in the context of web search [22, 5, 15]. Though such work is clearly related, note that our problem is not one of helping users to formulate their *existing* information need. Rather we are interested in possibilities to *create* such needs.

Work on query suggestions that is more closely related to our paper includes [23]. There the authors employ "semantic" information from dbpedia for the suggestions, which at a high level is related to our use of Wikipedia entities. Similarly, the work in [11] is related because the authors also

Table 5: Query suggestions for some Wikipedia pages

Page	EQGraph	Reverse IR
Medulla Oblongata	the pyramidal decussation occurs in the	difference between medulla and medulla oblongata
	location of middle cerebellar peduncles	what does the medulla do
	somatic motor nuclei	medulla
	bilateral middle cerebellar peduncle lesion	medulla oblongata
	cortical tissue running between the medullary pyramids	parts of medulla oblongata
Osteoporosis	function of osteoblasts	bone osteoporosis
	osteoclast and osteoblast	osteoporosis
	vasovagal syncope	medicinenet.com osteoporosis
	symptoms of pulmonary embolism	mayoclinic.com osteoporosis
	partial cauda equina syndrome	osteoporosis fractures
Azotemia	symptoms of kidney stones	creatinine
	coffee and diabetes	why could a creatinine would only go up
	fluid volume deficit related to osmotic diuresis	what is creatinine for
	signs and symptoms of osmotic diuresis	what does creatinine do
	blood urea nitrogen	medicinenet.com creatinine

use *content* of clicked pages in constructing query suggestions, differing from most of the other work in this area. As in our paper, a random walk on a graph model where nodes are queries is applied in [6, 5]. Finally, the work in [30] is related due to its focus on query suggestions for infrequent, long-tail queries. The authors propose the use of *templates* to learn rules such as "[CITY] flight" -> "[CITY] hotel". These rules can then be applied for previously *unseen* queries such as "bertinoro flight -> bertinoro hotel", both as input and output, as long as "bertinoro" is identified as a city. In future work, we will consider a similar approach in our setting: if after reading about a person X the query "X place of birth" is frequently suggested by our system, we could also suggest such a query, even when it is previously unseen for a concrete person Y.

User intent modeling. At a high level, our work is also related to user intent modeling. Note, however, that unlike in search-result ranking our suggestions make an effort to *influence* a user's intent, rather than merely guiding him.

Shen *et al.* [28] focus on the problem of exploiting implicit user feedback to improve the accuracy of a retrieval feedback via context-sensitive language models that combine the current query with the interaction history (previous queries and clicks). Again, our aim is that of *suggesting* the next query, not combining its signal with previous relevance signals.

Agichtein *et al.* [1] show how to incorporate "user behavior" to improve web search. They discuss how to merge two distinct ranked lists, how to re-rank results or how to incorporate the new features in a learning to rank model. Somewhat relevant to our problem is the type of features they use. Apart from traditional CTR information they use information such as "are results below this one ever clicked on the search result page", "is this result typically found via links", or "what's the average dwell time on this web page". In our setting, such features fail for previously unseen pages.

Zhu *et al.* [40] expand the use of browsing information for web search ranking, and other applications. They introduce *ClickRank*, an algorithm to estimate web page importance from browsing information. Finally, [40] discusses novel applications of ClickRank in providing enriched user web search experience.

White *et al.* [36] present a web search interaction feature which, for a given query, provides links to web sites frequently visited by other users with similar information needs. These "popular" destinations complement traditional search results, allowing direct navigation to authoritative resources. Results show that search enhanced-by-destination suggestions outperform other approaches. In a certain sense such "suggestions", rather than search results, are dual to our problem: given a page we want to suggest queries, whereas they suggest pages for a given query.

White and Chandrasekar [35] present a comparative oracle study of techniques to shortcut sub-optimal search trails using labels derived from social bookmarking, anchor text, query logs, and a human-computation game. The authors show that labels can help users reach target pages efficiently, and that shortcuts are most useful when the target is challenging to find. As such shortcuts are derived from *observed* browsing behavior, similar approach would not be applicable for our problem where we are also addressing tail pages.

Xiang *et al.* [37] investigate how to improve web-search results by taking into account "context" information. For example, if a user searches for 'BMW' and then for 'jaguar', it is likely that he is interested in the car rather than the cat. In this work "context" always means the previous query. So a user submits query q_{t-1}, clicks on some results, then submits query q_t. In our setting, one could try modeling the currently browsed page as q_{t-1} and use a similar approach to theirs, but they rely on observing transitions from q_{t-1} to q_t where we want to *suggest* such transitions.

On the general topic of query-intent modeling, [12] and [29] are related as they, respectively, present novel methods for query clustering and query intent classification that leverage user interaction logs.

7. CONCLUSIONS

Suggesting a small and diverse set of search queries that are relevant to the content of the web page currently visited by a user, and that moreover are non-obvious and serendipitous, is an interesting problem which has received (so far) surprisingly little attention. In this paper we tackle such a problem focusing on the content of the page and the entities contained therein. Our proposal is based on a novel graph model which enriches the Query-Flow graph with entity nodes. Our model is content-based and can produce meaningful recommendations even for previously unseen pages.

Our recommendation method is based on a two-step Personalized PageRank computation, whose goal is to expand the set of entities extracted from a page into a richer set of entities, and to associate the entities with relevant query suggestions. We develop an efficient implementation that enables our framework to deal with very large graph instances and suggest queries from a large and diverse pool.

Our experiments show that our recommendations are relevant and serendipitous, outperforming in a user study, a method based on reverse IR. As our method is tailored towards avoiding related-but-obvious recommendation, we sometimes produce some unrelated suggestions. These are easy to identify and can be filtered out by a specialized classifier: we leave this further development for future work, as well as evaluating other expansion strategies and the effect of parameters in the quality of recommendations.

8. ACKNOWLEDGEMENTS

This work was partially supported by the Torres Quevedo Program from the Spanish Ministry of Science and Innovation, co-funded by the European Social Fund.

References

[1] E. Agichtein, E. Brill, and S. Dumais. Improving web search ranking by incorporating user behavior information. In *SIGIR*, pp. 19–26, 2006.

[2] P. André, m. schraefel, J. Teevan, and S. T. Dumais. Discovery is never by chance: designing for (un)serendipity. In *C&C*, pp. 305–314, 2009.

[3] R. Baeza-Yates and A. Tiberi. Extracting semantic relations from query logs. In *KDD*, pp. 76–85, 2007.

[4] R. Baeza-Yates, C. Hurtado, and M. Mendoza. *Query Recommendation Using Query Logs in Search Engines*, volume 3268, pp. 588–596. Springer, 2004.

[5] P. Boldi, F. Bonchi, C. Castillo, D. Donato, A. Gionis, and S. Vigna. The query-flow graph: model and applications. In *CIKM*, pp. 609–618, 2008.

[6] P. Boldi, F. Bonchi, C. Castillo, D. Donato, and S. Vigna. Query suggestions using query-flow graphs. In *WSCD*, pp. 56–63, 2009.

[7] P. Boldi, F. Bonchi, C. Castillo, and S. Vigna. From 'dango' to 'japanese cakes': Query reformulation models and patterns. In *Proc. WI'09*. IEEE CS Press, 2009.

[8] F. Bonchi, R. Perego, F. Silvestri, H. Vahabi, and R. Venturini. Efficient query recommendations in the long tail via center-piece subgraphs. In *SIGIR*, p. to appear, 2012.

[9] H. Cao, D. Jiang, J. Pei, E. Chen, and H. Li. Towards context-aware search by learning a very large variable length hidden markov model from search logs. In *WWW*, pp. 191–200, 2009.

[10] Z. Cheng, B. Gao, and T.-Y. Liu. Actively predicting diverse search intent from user browsing behaviors. In *WWW*, pp. 221–230, 2010.

[11] S. Cucerzan and R. W. White. Query suggestion based on user landing pages. In *SIGIR*, pp. 875–876, 2007.

[12] J. Cui, H. Liu, J. Yan, L. Ji, R. Jin, J. He, Y. Gu, Z. Chen, and X. Du. Multi-view random walk framework for search task discovery from click-through log. In *CIKM*, pp. 135–140, 2011.

[13] B. M. Fonseca, P. Golgher, B. Pôssas, B. Ribeiro-Neto, and N. Ziviani. Concept-based interactive query expansion. In *CIKM*, pp. 696–703, 2005.

[14] J. Hoffart, M. A. Yosef, I. Bordino, H. Fürstenau, M. Pinkal, M. Spaniol, B. Taneva, S. Thater, and G. Weikum. Robust disambiguation of named entities in text. In *EMNLP*, pp. 782–792, 2011.

[15] R. Jones, B. Rey, O. Madani, and W. Greiner. Generating query substitutions. In *WWW*, pp. 387–396, 2006.

[16] R. Kop. The Unexpected Connection: Serendipity and Human Mediation in Networked Learning. *Educational Technology and Society*, pp. 2–11, 2012.

[17] S. Kulkarni, A. Singh, G. Ramakrishnan, and S. Chakrabarti. Collective annotation of Wikipedia entities in web text. In *KDD*, pp. 457–466, 2009.

[18] R. Lempel and S. Moran. Predictive caching and prefetching of query results in search engines. In *WWW*, pp. 19–28, 2003.

[19] K. H.-Y. Lin, C.-J. Wang, and H.-H. Chen. Predicting next search actions with search engine query logs. In *WI*, pp. 227–234, 2011.

[20] G. Malewicz, M. H. Austern, A. J. C. Bik, J. C. Dehnert, I. Horn, N. Leiser, and G. Czajkowski. Pregel: A System for Large-Scale Graph Processing. In *SIGMOD*, pp. 135–145, 2010.

[21] S. M. McNee, J. Riedl, and J. A. Konstan. Being accurate is not enough: how accuracy metrics have hurt recommender systems. In *CHI*, pp. 1097–1101, 2006.

[22] Q. Mei, D. Zhou, and K. Church. Query suggestion using hitting time. In *CIKM*, pp. 469–478, 2008.

[23] E. Meij, M. Bron, L. Hollink, B. Huurnink, and M. de Rijke. Learning semantic query suggestions. In *ISWC*, pp. 424–440, 2009.

[24] R. Mihalcea and A. Csomai. Wikify!: linking documents to encyclopedic knowledge. In *CIKM*, pp. 233–242, 2007.

[25] D. Milne and I. H. Witten. Learning to link with Wikipedia. In *CIKM*, pp. 509–518, 2008.

[26] D. Paranjpe. Learning document aboutness from implicit user feedback and document structure. In *CIKM*, 2009.

[27] M. F. Porter. *An algorithm for suffix stripping*, pp. 313–316. Morgan Kaufmann Publishers Inc., 1997.

[28] X. Shen, B. Tan, and C. Zhai. Context-sensitive information retrieval using implicit feedback. In *SIGIR*, pp. 43–50, 2005.

[29] Y. Shen, J. Yan, S. Yan, L. Ji, N. Liu, and Z. Chen. Sparse hidden-dynamics conditional random fields for user intent understanding. In *WWW*, pp. 7–16, 2011.

[30] I. Szpektor, A. Gionis, and Y. Maarek. Improving recommendation for long-tail queries via templates. In *WWW*, pp. 47–56, 2011.

[31] J. Teevan, E. Adar, R. Jones, and M. A. S. Potts. Information re-retrieval: repeat queries in Yahoo's logs. In *Proc. SIGIR'07*. ACM, 2007.

[32] E. Toms. Information exploration of the third kind: the concept of chance encounters. In *Information Exploration Interfaces @ CHI*, 1998.

[33] S. K. Tyler and J. Teevan. Large scale query log analysis of re-finding. In *WSDM*, pp. 191–200, 2010.

[34] L. G. Valiant. A bridging model for parallel computation. *Communications of the ACM*, 33(8):103–111, 1990.

[35] R. W. White and R. Chandrasekar. Exploring the use of labels to shortcut search trails. In *SIGIR*, pp. 811–812, 2010.

[36] R. W. White, M. Bilenko, and S. Cucerzan. Studying the use of popular destinations to enhance web search interaction. In *SIGIR*, pp. 159–166, 2007.

[37] B. Xiang, D. Jiang, J. Pei, X. Sun, E. Chen, and H. Li. Context-aware ranking in web search. In *SIGIR*, pp. 451–458, 2010.

[38] M. Yazdani and A. Popescu-Belis. Using a Wikipedia-based Semantic Relatedness Measure for Document Clustering. In *TextGgraphs*, pp. 29–36, 2011.

[39] Y. Zhou, L. Nie, O. Rouhani-Kalleh, F. Vasile, and S. Gaffney. Resolving surface forms to Wikipedia topics. In *COLING*, pp. 1335–1343, 2010.

[40] G. Zhu and G. Mishne. Mining rich session context to improve web search. In *KDD*, pp. 1037–1046, 2009.

Personalizing Atypical Web Search Sessions

Carsten Eickhoff
Delft University of Technology
Delft, The Netherlands
c.eickhoff@tudelft.nl

Kevyn Collins-Thompson
Paul N. Bennett
Susan Dumais
Microsoft Research
Redmond, WA, USA
{kevynct,pauben,sdumais}@microsoft.com

ABSTRACT

Most research in Web search personalization models users as static or slowly evolving entities with a given set of preferences defined by their past behavior. However, recent publications as well as empirical evidence suggest that for a significant number of search sessions, users diverge from their regular search profiles in order to satisfy atypical, limited-duration information needs. In this work, we conduct a large-scale inspection of real-life search sessions to further understand this scenario. Subsequently, we design an automatic means of detecting and supporting such atypical sessions. We demonstrate significant improvements over state-of-the-art Web search personalization techniques by accounting for the typicality of search sessions. The proposed method is evaluated based on Web-scale search session data spanning several months of user activity.

Categories and Subject Descriptors

H.1.2 [**Information Systems**]: Models and Principles—*Human Factors*; H.3 [**Information Systems**]: Information Storage and Retrieval

Keywords

Personalized search; user modeling; adaptive interfaces; domain expertise.

1. INTRODUCTION

In recent years, we have seen a strong emerging tendency towards personalizing users' Web search experiences in order to better account for the searcher's individual context [29]. Context, in this case, is often understood as the searcher's previous search history, geo-spatial position, topical interests, and language or literacy background. Most of these are static or slowly-evolving properties of an individual and are typically captured by means of query and interaction log analyses. While personalization functionality has been shown to benefit retrieval performance [29], there are significant situational factors that can influence performance and thus should be taken into account. Domain expertise is one such factor. Depending on the topic searched for, an individual can display significantly different search behavior based on their previous knowledge of the domain at hand [33]. In this work, we investigate instances of users straying from their search profiles to satisfy information needs outside their regular areas of interest. Such atypical information needs can often be triggered by external events (*e.g.*, pending medical treatments, financial deadlines, or upcoming vacations) that explain the unprecedented interest in a previously unseen domain. As an example, a user might in general favor easily-readable documents about sports and be confident in querying, selecting, and understanding this type of information. At the same time, they might display significantly different preferences and skills when pursuing a novel task, such as completing a particularly involved tax form. Due to static modeling of user profiles, atypical information needs are currently poorly represented by Web search engines. Personalizing atypical search sessions in the 'regular' way does not seem appropriate as it assumes topical and behavioral consistency with previous search sessions. Often, this is not the case for atypical searches.

This work advances the state of the art by answering the following three research questions: **(1)** What is the frequency, extent and success rate of users pursuing atypical information needs? Additionally, can we identify common types of information needs for which users diverge from their previous preferences? **(2)** How can we automatically distinguish atypical search sessions from typical ones? **(3)** Can we improve retrieval performance for atypical sessions by re-ranking search results in a typicality-aware fashion? Our investigations are based on manually-annotated log files of the Bing commercial Web search engine.

The remainder of this work is structured as follows: Section 2 gives an overview of previous work on search personalization and expertise modeling. Section 3 introduces the problem domain by investigating the frequency and extent of atypical Web search sessions. Section 4 introduces an automatic method for detecting atypical sessions based on query and interaction logs. Section 5 quantifies the usefulness of applying typicality-aware personalization based on a large-scale query log evaluation, showing significant performance gains at Web scale. In Section 6, we discuss potential extensions of our method and directions for future work. Finally, we conclude by summarizing our findings and their implications on state-of-the-art Web search in Section 7.

WSDM'13, February 4–8, 2012, Rome, Italy.

2. RELATED WORK

Previous related work can be grouped into three categories: **(1)** general search personalization efforts; **(2)** query log analysis with the goal of long-term user modeling; **(3)** investigations of user expertise and content readability.

2.1 Search personalization

A growing number of data sources, such as search history, manually or automatically created preference profiles, and social network information, are being exploited for personalizing the selection of results for users [24, 30]. Approaches to search personalization vary in types of features considered (*e.g.*, language models, topical categories, links or other metadata such as reading level), the time frame chosen (*e.g.*, short-term or long-term profiles), and how the profiles are used (*e.g.*, for ranking or recommendations). Several researchers have shown how profiles that consist of topical representations of users' search interests can be used to personalize search. Gauch and colleagues learned topical user profiles based on browsing history [11] or search history [25], and Ma *et al.* [21] used topical profiles that users specified explicitly. In all cases, user profiles were compared with those of search results and used to re-order search results for individuals. Bennett *et al.* [5] have recently shown how topics from the *Open Directory Project's* (ODP) topology of the Web[1] could be used to personalize search ranking for individuals. Expanding on the PageRank algorithm, Haveliwala [14] proposed a topic-sensitive modification to allow for a direct, more focused scoring of the Web graph given a query's topic or a user's topical preference. Queries and Web content were automatically categorized using the ODP hierarchy in order to facilitate topic-sensitive scoring. Sugiyama *et al.* [26] employed collaborative filtering on users' observed Web search histories for profile building. They compared their approach to exclusively using browsing history and implicit feedback mechanisms, finding significant merit in the use of profile expansion via their proposed method. Teevan *et al.* [29] investigated the potential of re-ranking the top 50 search engine results based on previous user profiles. In particular, the authors explored alternative document representations for search personalization, finding that full-text representations outperformed priority-driven selective keyword models. Li *et al.* [20] developed a dynamic graph-based adaptation scheme modeling a user's general preferences for search personalization, while accounting for changes of interest by incorporating short-term browsing information. In a recent study, Goel *et al.* [12] analyzed the U.S. market's large-scale consumption of movies, music, and Web search results in order to quantify the importance of the 'long tail' of items in those respective categories of popular media. The authors found that the majority of users largely displayed standard tastes in most categories but showed some degree of eccentricity in choices. In this work, we will investigate a related notion, namely, that of atypical search sessions: cases in which users occasionally stray from their personal previous mainstream.

2.2 Long-term user modeling

A special subclass of research on user modeling and search personalization is based on long-term profiles rather than focusing only on the user's immediate history. While being noisier than short-term profiles, this approach has the advantage of being able to detect niche interests or those that surface in long cycles. Matthijs and Radlinski [22] captured users' 3-month Web history across multiple search engines and sites via a browser plug-in. The full resulting log files were used for result re-ranking and showed significant performance improvements over the native ranking of popular search engines. Furthermore, long-term user profiles served as reliable general descriptors of a user's interests. Tan *et al.* [27] presented a language modeling approach that interpolated immediate search history and long-term user profiles in order to improve retrieval performance. They found that short-term profiles contained more useful clues as to the current query's intent, but that adequately-weighted long-term information introduced further performance gains. White *et al.* [32] investigated the usefulness of short-, mid-, and long-term profiles for the task of predicting user interest in Web sites. The authors demonstrated that, depending on the type of information being profiled as well as the type of information need, different profiling durations could be optimal. Finally, Bennett *et al.* [5] showed how long- and short-term profiles could be optimally combined for effective search personalization. They found that long-term models provided the most benefit at the beginning of a session, while short-term models became more important for longer sessions.

2.3 Expertise

Studies of Web search often distinguish between two types of expertise - search expertise (reflecting knowledge of the search process) and domain expertise (reflecting knowledge of the domain or topic of the information need). In one of the early comparisons of Internet information search behavior and success, Hölscher and Strube [15] examined both search and domain expertise. They reported that search experts displayed a richer set of skills, such as selection of tools, query formulation and relevance judgment than novice searchers. Also, experts were found to navigate search interfaces more efficiently. Beyond search skills, Thatcher [31] showed that experts and non-experts followed different strategies to obtain search results, depending on the task. White and Morris [34] conducted a large-scale log analysis of the differences in search behaviors and success of search experts and novices. The authors found that experts generated different types of queries, had shorter and less branchy post-search browse trails, and were generally more successful than novices. More recent work has tried to model strategies of successful searchers. Ageev *et al.* [1] exploited this expertise-dependent difference in search behavior by using a Markov chain approach to predict search success for a range of pre-defined search tasks based on the sequence of actions the searcher had undertaken in the session. One of their main findings was that searchers who are more successful are generally more active (*e.g.*, more queries issued and results clicked) in a given time window. Aula *et al.* [3] analyzed different characteristics of successful and unsuccessful search sessions. Based on a small qualitative lab study and a subsequent large-scale evaluation, they established a range of indicators for user frustration during search sessions that were not yielding the desired results. Most saliently, the authors report longer sessions, question-type queries, the use of advanced query operators and aimless scrolling on the results page for failing searches. We will revisit these findings in Section 4 to employ them for identifying atypical sessions.

[1] http://www.dmoz.org

Beyond the effect of general search expertise on success rates, other recent work has considered the searcher's familiarity with the search topic. Based on a large-scale query log analysis, White *et al.* [33] found significant differences between the search behavior of domain experts and non-experts within the domain of their expertise (but not outside of the domain). The authors found that domain experts generated longer queries with more technical terms, had longer search sessions with more branches, and had greater success in satisfying their information needs than novices. Collins-Thompson *et al.* [6] investigated the use of reading level metadata for search personalization, finding that search ranking could be improved by taking into consideration the user's previous reading level preferences as well as the reading level coherence between a Web page and its result snippet. Kim *et al.* [18] followed up in this direction by jointly modeling reading level and topic preferences to describe users. Their so-called RLT profiles were used to distinguish domain experts from non-experts as well as to identify occurrences of 'stretch' reading behavior, *i.e.*, when users go beyond their usual preferences to satisfy information needs. Their work is central to ours as it observes users temporarily diverging from their profiles to solve particular tasks. In this work, we focus on the in-depth analysis and support of such cases. In a similar effort, Tan *et al.* [28] exploit notions of reading level and text comprehensibility for ranking popular answers on the Web portal *Yahoo! Answers*. According to the searcher's degree of domain expertise, simple *vs.* more technical answers were ranked higher. The research we present in this paper extends previous results by: characterizing the extent to which searchers diverge from their long-term search profiles, and demonstrating how the ability to detect such atypical sessions can be used to improve search personalization.

3. DATA SET

As a starting point for our investigation, we begin with an analysis of real search sessions to get insights into the problem domain. Our data set originates from the proprietary log files of the commercial Web search engine Bing. Our analysis focuses on a 4-month period of query logs from January to April, 2012 submitted by English-speaking U.S. users. We refer to the respective time spans as M1 (January) through M4 (April). Throughout this paper, we will use M3 as our profiling period and M4 to test for atypical sessions. Later, in Section 4, we will also investigate the usefulness of prolonged profiling periods, using M2 and M1 in addition to M3. To gain a first, qualitative insight into the domain, we limit our scope to the 200 most active users. Together, they submitted a total of 679,808 queries in 67,812 sessions. Session boundaries are drawn based on a 30-minute threshold of user inactivity as suggested by several previous studies (*e.g.*, [9, 10]). Since this work is concerned with information seeking behavior, we exclude navigational queries from our inspection in order to get a clearer impression of the difference between normal and atypical *informational* queries. To this end, we employed a list of frequent navigational queries as well as structural heuristics to detect queries encoding domain names or URLs (*e.g.*, those starting with "www." or ending in ".[domain]"). After this pre-processing step, 370,844 queries and 44,059 sessions remained for investigation. On average, users submitted 464 queries in 55 sessions

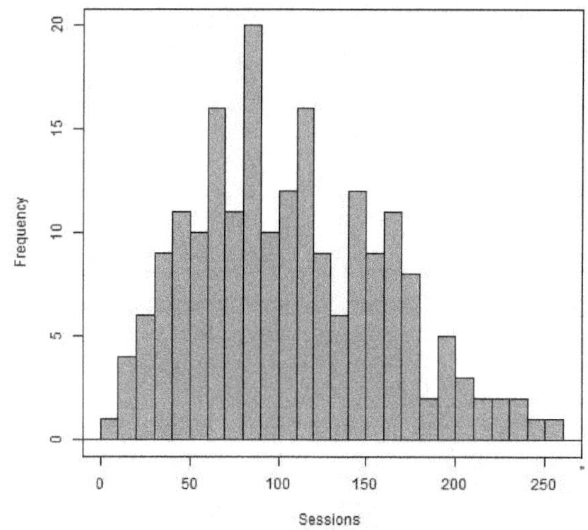

Figure 1: Distribution of session counts across unique users in January 2012.

per month. Figure 1 shows the observed distribution of session counts across users for M1.

3.1 Annotation

In order to get a deeper understanding of the extent and frequency of atypical search sessions, we collected manual labels for all search sessions from M4. Previous work [16, 19] suggests that sessions tend to be topically coherent, often serving a single information need. Based on this observation, we labeled typicality at the session level in order to preserve as much search context as possible. The labeling was facilitated by means of an internal crowdsourcing effort. Prior to this step, all sessions containing *personal identifiable information* (PII), such as names, phone numbers, addresses, social security numbers, *etc.*, as well as identical sessions for the same user, were removed in order to protect the users' privacy and anonymity.

At first, each annotator was shown a condensed profile representing the users' previous search history during the profiling duration (M3). For each clicked result, we automatically determined the topic distribution along the ODP's Web taxonomy. User profiles were summarized using the most common topics per user, *i.e.* those that comprised at least 5% of the overall click volume for that user. To give a more detailed overview of the user's interests, we also provided the three most frequently-issued queries per category. In addition to the topical domain, we incorporated information about the textual complexity of the accessed material. Following previous work [6], we estimated clicked pages' *reading level* (RL) and highlighted easy-to-read material ($RL \leq 4.0$) in green, moderately difficult material ($4.0 < RL < 9.0$) in blue, and advanced resources ($RL \geq 9.0$) in red. This allowed judges to make decisions about typicality using the distribution of topics, and the topic and reading level of individual resources. Figure 2 shows an example of a user profile as presented to the annotators. The judges were then presented with a single search session from M4. All queries, both in the profile as well as

55% Sports/Baseball ("ncaa baseball", "ectb baseball", "pg baseball")
14% Society/Religion_and_Spirituality ("pope benedict bio", "shamanistic travel", "sacred heart newton")
5% Reference/Education ("matlab student version", "umass email", "my math lab")
5% Sports/Hockey ("elmira pioneers", "umass lax", "necbl")

Figure 2: Example of Web search user profile with topical categories and color-encoded reading level.

in the session, were presented as Web search hyperlinks to enable the judges to quickly explore the types of content to which the search led. Analogously to the user profile, session queries were color-encoded by reading level. A short survey probed two main aspects of a session: 1) its typicality for the user, and 2) the degree of importance that the search task shows. The latter is interesting as we assume that atypical search sessions may often relate to important tasks or problems. The survey questions were:

```
1.  How typical is this session for the user whose
profile was shown above?

2.  Now go back to the list of queries in the
session above, and select all queries that support
your decision.

3.  For the queries you selected in #2, do you
think the desired information has high importance
to this user?  (e.g., likely to have lasting
value, or help solve an important problem.)
```

Questions 1) and 3) were rated on a 5-point scale. In addition to the main questions, the judges could give further feedback by means of a free text field. To account for subjectivity and inaccuracies of individual workers, each session was labeled by 5 independent judges. The final label was determined by averaging across the constituent judgments. One of the researchers broke ties that could occur when individual judgments were rejected as the worker had flagged their decision as 'unsure'. The task was offered as a privately sourced task on the crowdsourcing platform Clickworker[2] at a pay level of 5 cents per session, a rate comparable to those suggested in related studies [2]. A grand total of $500 was invested in label acquisition. We followed previous surveys on the design and quality control of crowdsourcing studies [17, 8] by employing a hand-labeled set of gold standard tasks as well as measuring agreement between judges in order to discourage low-quality submissions.

The results showed substantial agreement between workers for the typicality vote. The standard deviation between each individual crowdsourcing judge and the majority vote among all 5 judges was found to be less than one point (0.854). To give an indication of the general task difficulty, we asked 3 expert judges to create redundant annotations for a subset of 100 sessions in a lab-based study using the same interface as the crowdsourcing workers. Among experts, the standard deviation from majority votes was found to be even lower (0.495). Finally, we computed the overlap between majority votes from experts and those from crowdsourcing workers. In the vast majority of cases (82.6%) the two majority votes were identical. Details on this labeling

[2]http://www.clickworker.com

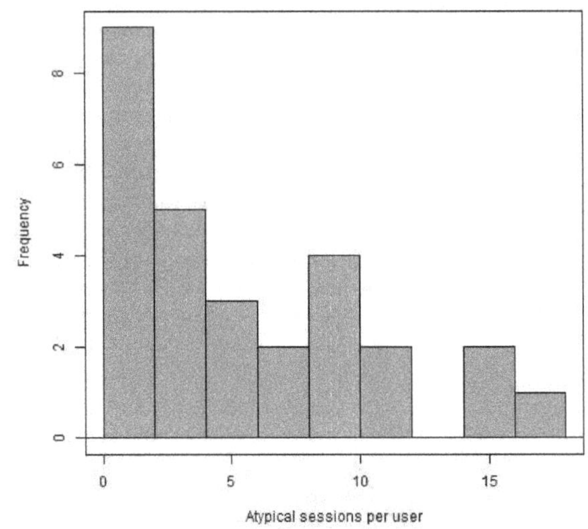

Figure 3: Distribution of atypical search session counts across unique users in April 2012 (M4).

task and construction of the user profile are available in a separate paper [7].

3.2 Data analysis

Out of all 2790 informational search sessions labeled in M4, 166 were found to be atypical given the user's previous profile. Based on M3 profiles, 74% of all users showed at least one atypical search session in M4. On average, each user displayed 5.9 atypical sessions which comprised 7.5% of their overall monthly query volume. Figure 3 shows the distribution of atypical session counts across users. While atypical sessions can be observed for most users, their frequency differed across searchers. The average user was largely coherent in search behavior except for occasional atypical sessions, which is consistent with what Goel *et al.* [12] observed as well. Some, however, regularly explored different topics, making their search history very diverse topically.

As a next step, we compare typical and atypical sessions based on a number of session-level properties. Table 1 shows a juxtaposition across the whole user population. Statistically significant differences between session types are denoted by an asterisk. Significance was tested using a Wilcoxon signed-rank test ($\alpha < 0.05$). Both groups show comparable session lengths with only a slight increase in number of queries submitted in atypical sessions. As we turn to the queries, however, we observe significant differences. Atypical sessions show longer queries (5.23 vs 3.10 terms/query)

Table 1: Properties of typical and atypical sessions.

Type	Frequency	queries/session	terms/query	unique terms/session	SAT. dwell time	SAT. rank	RL	SAT. RL
typical	2624	6.26	3.10	8.93	209 sec	1.5	5.4	3.9
atypical	166	6.69	5.23*	16.07*	180 sec	1.8	5.8	5.3*

Table 2: Divergence from previous session statistics per user.

Type	Frequency	queries/session	terms/query	unique terms/session	SAT. dwell time	SAT. rank	RL	SAT. RL
typical	2624	-0.21	-0.11	-0.80	+15 sec	+0.19	-0.70	-0.40
atypical	166	+0.43	+1.70*	+1.55*	-21 sec	+0.49	-0.09	+1.80*

and also explore the result space more broadly by employing almost twice as many unique terms as regular sessions (16.07 vs 8.93 unique terms/session). Since explicit relevance judgments are not available, previous work frequently accepts clicked results on which the user dwells for at least a threshold amount of time, as relevant given the underlying information need. A commonly-used threshold is a dwell time of at least 30 seconds [9, 10]. We investigated these so-called *satisfied* (SAT) clicks in terms of their dwell time and the rank on which the user clicked. For typical sessions, such clicked pages show significantly longer dwell times (208 vs 180 sec.) and a better user satisfaction in the top ranks (average SAT click rank position of 1.5 vs 1.8) compared to atypical sessions. Finally, turning to textual complexity, we find comparable reading levels of clicked resources for both session types. However, SAT-clicked material in atypical sessions had significantly higher reading difficulty (average level 5.3) than in typical sessions (average level 3.9). In conclusion, we notice a less optimal search experience in atypical sessions along several dimensions - more complex queries, shorter SAT dwell times, lower SAT rank and higher SAT reading level.

In order to rule out the effect of individual users' querying style on these numbers, we now compare typical and atypical sessions per user. To enable this, we collected session statistics for all users in M3 and report the divergence from those observations for M4. Table 2 shows the population-wide averages of this comparison. Generally, typical sessions conform more closely with the user profile than atypical ones. While the differences are less marked than in the global comparison, we can note similar tendencies. For atypical sessions, queries are longer on average (by 1.7 terms) compared to the user's typical sessions, and use a wider selection of unique terms (an average of 1.55 more). Dwell times shrink and rankings are somewhat less optimal. Again, we note a higher textual complexity of documents that satisfy atypical information needs.

These distinct characteristics of typical and atypical search sessions are also reflected in the resulting retrieval performance. An indication of this trend can be found in the number of sessions that are abandoned without a single user click. This occurs 17% more frequently for atypical sessions than for typical ones.

Finally, we are interested in the content and cause of atypical search sessions. We manually grouped the 166 atypical sessions from M4 according to their high-level topic. Table 3 shows an overview of the most prominent resulting categories. Almost half of the atypical search sessions are concerned with health and medical information. Queries in these sessions are often dedicated to getting advice on healthy diets or finding information about causes and cures for certain medical conditions. Technical and computer queries are another major reason for atypical sessions. Typically computer problems such as viruses, or requests for help on diagnostic procedures, can be found in this group. The remaining 30% of atypical queries are distributed across a wide range of topics. Instructions for claiming taxes, preparing foreign recipes, or caring for pets were among the most prominent queries. To set these numbers into perspective, we contrast them with the overall frequencies of the respective categories in the same period. Interestingly enough, we note that many of the dominant topics in atypical sessions occur at significantly different frequencies than in the global collection. For example, medical and technical queries are significantly less common in the set of general queries. On the other hand, generally popular topics such as inquiries about celebrities, sports, or movies are rarely found in the set of atypical sessions.

Table 3: Prominent topics in atypical sessions.

Category	atypical freq.	typical freq.
Medical	49%	3%
Computers	21%	9%
Crafting	7%	3%
Cooking	5%	5%
Pets	4%	2%
Administrative	4%	2%
Travel	3%	7%
Other	7%	69%

With respect to our first research question, we conclude that atypical Web search sessions are events that affect the majority of users. Often, they occur when users seek advice on unfamiliar subjects outside of their topical area of expertise. As the users struggle with finding the appropriate keywords in the unknown domain, many affected queries are natural language questions, a class of queries that is known to often yield inferior result quality [4]. In Section 5, we will demonstrate that state-of-the-art personalization techniques achieve inferior results on atypical sessions.

4. IDENTIFYING ATYPICAL SESSIONS

The previous section summarized the concept and extent of atypical search sessions. In this section, we turn towards automatically identifying atypical search sessions and queries in order to appropriately react to the different nature of the information need. While, ultimately, it would be desirable to classify ongoing sessions to directly benefit retrieval performance, this first investigation of using typicality information for search personalization addresses sessions in a post-hoc fashion. To this end, we propose a two-step approach: First, we model user interests, preferences and querying style in the form of a profile, *e.g.* based on past sessions. Then, for new sessions, we measure the divergence from the existing profile.

4.1 Feature design

Based on the findings summarized in Section 3, as well as previous work, our classification scheme employs 2 distinct types of features: **(1)** Direct observations from the current search session. **(2)** Divergences of the current session from the user profile.

Session-level features

Session length Search sessions within a well-known topical area are typically shorter than those issued by users exploring a novel domain. In the latter case, frequent query reformulations can be expected as the user closes in on the desired information. To measure this effect, we consider the number of queries issued per session. In the previous section, this feature could not be confirmed to indicate session typicality when inspected in isolation. We include it in our classification scheme to test its validity in interplay with other features.

Query length Atypical queries, on average, were found to be longer than typical ones. We use the average number of terms per query as a feature.

Unique terms per session Previously we saw that there are significant differences in how deeply typical and atypical sessions explore a given topic by using a wide or narrow vocabulary. We measure the number of unique terms per session as an indicator of topic exploration *vs.* focused search.

Question query ratio In our qualitative analysis, we observed that many atypical sessions contain natural language questions. To account for this fact, we measure the ratio of queries per session that contain at least one of the following question words: *What, Where, When, Why, Who, How.*

Advanced operator ratio Previous work on the nature of unsuccessful and difficult search sessions [3], found that struggling searchers tend to make more use of otherwise often neglected advanced querying operators. We denote the ratio of queries per session employing at least one of the following advanced operators: *AND*, *OR*, *NOT* and *literal text matches* indicated by quotation marks.

Position of longest query The query editing history has been previously reported to hold information about the success rate of a search session [3]. Successful sessions tend to end in the longest query, as the user has sufficiently narrowed down the scope of the result set. On the other hand, unsuccessful sessions often see several iterations of specifications and generalizations before the search is finally abandoned. In the latter case the longest query can be found in the middle of the search session. We employ this observation by considering the relative position of the longest query as a feature (*i.e.*, the rank of the longest query divided by the overall number of queries in the session).

POS ratios Our analysis of atypical sessions showed a high number of natural language queries. In order to exploit this apparently different syntactic structure of regular and atypical queries, we apply *Part-of-Speech* (POS) tagging and note the relative frequencies of *nouns, verbs, adjectives*, and *miscellaneous constituents* (anything that could not be grouped into one of the previous categories). We assume that natural language queries will display a lower ratio of verbs and nouns but more of the 'syntactic glue', such as prepositions, that fall into the miscellaneous category.

Clicks per query Previous work [1, 33] found domain experts to be more active and to generally explore more results per query than non-experts. We measure the average number of clicks each query receives in order to account for different degrees of user activity and proficiency in the target domain.

SAT clicks per query Similarly to clicks per query, we consider the relative frequency with which SAT clicks (clicks with a dwell time of at least 30 seconds) occur. More frequent SAT clicks can indicate a better ability to formulate successful queries and identify relevant material in the result lists [15].

SAT click ratio In relation to the previous two features, we measure the relative number of satisfied clicks. A high ratio indicates efficient search behavior with targeted clicks on relevant material. Atypical search sessions are expected to display comparably lower ratios.

SAT click dwell time In Section 3, we saw shorter dwell times on the results of atypical sessions. In order to measure the degree to which the current result list satisfies the user, we report the average dwell time of all satisfied clicks in the session.

Median SAT clicked rank Previously, we observed a difference in ranking quality for regular and atypical sessions. For the latter, the user was more often forced to visit lower ranks of the result list. We account for this difference by measuring the median rank per session on which a SAT click was registered.

Reading level When faced with an unfamiliar problem, users are not always able to maintain their usual preferences for (typically lower) textual complexity. Due to the novel domain, they might lack the necessary knowledge for finding adequate, yet easy-to-understand material. Alternatively, the domain might inherently be of a more complex nature. We follow up on this notion by measuring the average reading level (as estimated using the classifier described in [6]) of all clicked search results per session.

SAT-clicked RL Similarly to the previous feature, here we only consider SAT-clicked pages. This distinction has been used in the previous section and was observed to separate regular and atypical search sessions better than considering all clicks.

Topical flags In the previous section, we saw that certain topics are more dominant in the group of atypical queries than others. To reflect this, we include a signal that indicates whether the current session serves, *e.g.* a medical information need. Since the actual distribution of topics underlying the user's information need is unknown, we employ topical classification of clicked results and note the relative frequency at which we observe the following categories: *Medical, Computers, Crafting, Cooking, Pets, Administrative, Travel.*

Unique topics per session Exploratory sessions in a novel topical domain tend to be more diverse than regular ones. Again, we classify all clicked search results into ODP categories and report the number of unique categories per session as a measure of coherence and focus.

Profile-based features

For each session-based feature above, we compute a corresponding divergence feature with respect to the user's profile. More specifically, we compute the difference between the session feature for the current session, and its historical average value across a user's previous sessions. For example, the length of the current session, minus the average session length across the profiling duration, will give the session length divergence feature. Additionally, two new feature types are considered.

Query term divergence For each user, we collect frequency counts of all query terms during the profiling duration. For each new session we do the same. Both profile and session can now be projected into a vector space with one dimension per unique term and frequency counts as components. We measure vocabulary coherence in terms of cosine distance between previous query terms and the current session.

Topic divergence Analogously, we also measure coherence in terms of topics, using cosine distance across topical vectors to account for sudden changes in the general subject domain.

For a high-level understanding of the problem domain, we computed estimates of the informativeness of all previously presented features. Table 4 shows a ranking of the 10 strongest features (out of 34 total) according to *Information Gain* (IG) and a χ^2 test. The feature rankings produced by the respective methods are largely consistent, with a few swaps at lower ranks. The strongest feature overall was the difference in query length from the user's previous profile (query length divergence), followed by the absolute query length. A majority (7 out of 10) of the high-ranking features are directly based on query information. Additional important signals are those based on the reading level of SAT-clicked pages (SAT RL) as well as the estimated difference in page topics (topic divergence). We note a balanced mixture of session- and profile-based features in the top 10.

Table 4: 10 strongest features for identifying atypical search sessions by information gain and χ^2.

Feature	Rank by IG	Rank by χ^2
query length divergence	1	1
query length	2	2
question ratio	3	4
verb ratio divergence	4	3
topic divergence	5	5
longest query position	6	8
SAT RL	7	6
SAT RL divergence	8	7
adjective ratio divergence	9	9
noun ratio	10	10

4.2 Classification

We applied the above features to the binary classification task of predicting whether a session was typical or atypical, relative to a given user's profile. We compared several different classification models, including support vector machines and various regression methods using the Weka toolkit [13]. The data set was split into distinct stratified training (90%) and test (10%) sets, such that no unique user's sessions were present in both sets. The session labels were obtained as described in Sec. 3.1.

Consistently, the best results on the training set were achieved by a logistic regression classifier that reached a final performance of $F_1 = 0.84$ ($P = 0.82$ and $R = 0.86$). When moving from the cross-validation setting on the training set to the previously unseen test set, we observed a final score of $F_1 = 0.74$ ($P = 0.8$ and $R = 0.68$). This number is comparable to a human annotator's accuracy of agreeing with the annotator majority vote label.

We investigated how the amount of previous search history used to compute features affected the classification performance in finding atypical sessions. Figure 4 shows cross-validation performance of the logistic regression classifier as a function of the number of search sessions per user that were used for building profiles. While performance rises quickly across the first sessions per user, scores level out between 18 and 20 sessions. At this point, no significant differences from the previously observed overall performance of $F_1 = 0.84$ can be observed. 95% of our users issued this threshold amount of 20 sessions across 14 days. Using longer search histories beyond this two-week threshold (*e.g.*, from M2 and M1) for profiling did not result in statistically significant performance changes.

With respect to our second research question, we conclude that automatic classification methods based on direct session-level features and divergence-from-profile features can be effective at estimating a search session's degree of typicality. Additionally, we note that a few weeks of query logs (typically between 1 and 2 weeks) were sufficient to make reliable typicality decisions for a given user.

5. RETRIEVAL PERFORMANCE

After examining properties of atypical search sessions (Section 3) and describing an automatic scheme for identifying them (Section 4), we now turn towards improving retrieval performance for atypical search sessions. Previously, we conducted our investigations on a sample of the 200 most active users. Now, we apply those insights to Web-scale retrieval tasks on a much larger dataset, as described next.

5.1 Method

Our study in this section closely follows recent research by Bennett *et al.* [5], and so we summarize that work briefly. In Bennett *et al.*, the authors examined a rich family of mod-

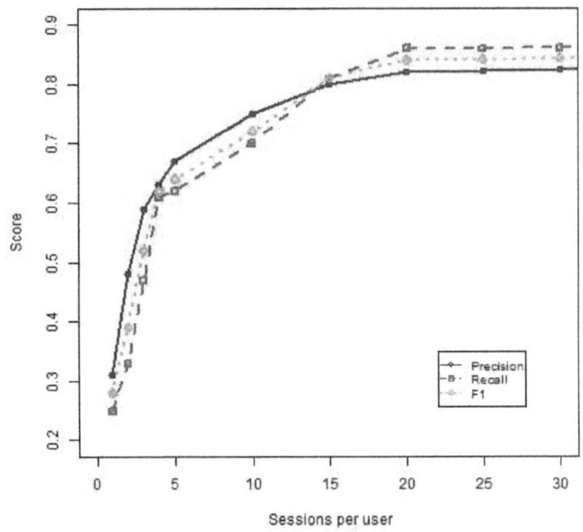

Figure 4: Classification performance as a function of the number of sessions per user in training set.

eling techniques for search personalization, looking at how different scopes of search and interaction history affected search personalization performance. They defined three key scope types: **(1) Session** considers all previous queries and actions from the current session. **(2) Historic** includes all previous actions and queries except for those in the current session. **(3) Aggregate** considers all previous actions before the current query. In addition to temporal extent, they considered several other factors used in earlier personalization research, including related queries and results in the profile. For each related query a score based on the weight of related queries, the similarity of the related results to the current result and the action taken on related results (*e.g.*, click, skip) was computed and used to re-rank the current results. Then, they used a unified re-ranking framework that comprised the following components:

rel(q, u) For each new query q issued by user u, this function returns a set of related past queries q_r from the same user.

view(u) Denotes the temporal view on the user u. Different temporal views can limit the scope of $rel(q, u)$. Possible settings for $view(u)$ are: *session*, *historic* and *aggregate*. Their concrete definitions will be given later in this section.

w(q_r, q, u) Each related query q_r is assigned a relatedness score. We abbreviate it as w_{q_r}.

results(q_r) For each related query q_r, a set of previously returned results d_{q_r} is stored.

sim(d_{q_r}, d) This function determines the similarity between a current result for query q and past results for related query q_r.

action(q_r, d_{q_r}) The action the user took for the previously seen result d_{q_r} for query q_r. Actions, such as SAT clicks, can indicate document relevance [9, 10].

Given the above components, many commonly studied personalization features can be represented as triples of $< q, d, u >$. The feature score $f(q, d, u)$ presented by [5] is:

$$f(q, d, u) = \sum_{q_r \in R} w_{q_r} \sum_{d_{q_r}} sim(d_{q_r}, d) action(q_r, d_{q_r}) \quad (1)$$

where $R = \{q : q \in rel(q, u) \mid q \in view(u)\}$.

A key finding in [5] was that the *aggregate* context scope achieved better overall improvements in MAP of satisfied clicks than either *session* or *historic*. The authors noted that some sessions showed performance losses, which might be attributable to sessions in which users look for very different material than what they are usually interested in. We hypothesize that the atypical sessions studied in this paper are examples of this class of sessions. Thus, as a first step towards personalization of atypical search needs, we investigate the performance of the above personalization framework on typical and atypical search sessions.

5.2 Experiments

To ensure comparability of results, we identically replicated the original experiment setting used in Bennett *et al.*, with the same underlying dataset [5]. Our experiments ranged over an 8-week period based on logs collected in July and August 2011. The selection covers 155,000 unique users and 10.4 million sessions, with an average of 174.4 queries per user and 2.61 queries per session. All reported results are mean values across 5 stratified experiment folds.

The features derived from the above framework were used to train a LambdaMART learning algorithm [35] for re-ranking the top 10 returned results. The goal was to produce an optimized ranking, and following [9], positive judgments were assigned to *satisfied result clicks* (SAT clicks). We estimated session typicality with the logistic regression classifier used in Section 4.

Table 5 compares the MAP re-ranking performance gains using *session*, *historic* and *aggregate* profiles over the original search engine ranking. We are also interested in the proportion of searches that were affected by the re-ranking. Consequently, we report the ratio of sessions whose MAP scores improve to those whose MAP score worsened. MAP scores are computed as the mean of average precision across the top 10 retrieved results. Cases in which the performance on atypical sessions differs significantly from that of typical ones are marked with an asterisk (determined via Wilcoxon signed-rank test at $\alpha < 0.05$-level). We confirmed the previous finding of Bennett *et al.* [5] that aggregate profiles lead to the highest overall performance gains for typical sessions. However, atypical sessions show a very different trend. Session-level information yields the strongest gains, followed by aggregate information. Interestingly, re-ranking using historic (pre-session) profiles is worse than the original ranking for atypical sessions. All performance differences between different information sources for the same class of sessions (*e.g.*, historic vs. aggregate information for typical sessions) are statistically significant.

We now address this difference between personalization performance for typical and atypical search sessions. Rather than uniformly applying one type of search history for personalization, we propose a hybrid approach that uses an initial classification step to predict whether the user is enacting a typical vs atypical session. Then, for all typical

Table 5: Personalization for atypical search sessions.

δ_{MAP}

	session	historic	aggregate
typical	0.0023	0.0047	0.0064
atypical	0.0067*	-0.001*	0.0059*

improved / # worsened

	session	historic	aggregate
typical	1.56	1.26	1.48
atypical	1.79*	0.91*	1.5

sessions, we apply historic personalization, and for atypical sessions, we rely exclusively on session-level information. Table 6 shows the overall performance gains of the proposed hybrid approach compared to both constituent methods in isolation. Significant improvements over **both** constituent methods are marked with an asterisk. Despite the relatively low frequency of atypical sessions, there are substantial gains in overall performance over the original search engine ranking. This tendency is also reflected in the case-based improvement and loss ratios. Atypical sessions see significantly more performance losses than gains when exclusively using historic profiles.

Finally, we conduct the analogous experiment for hybrid session-level and aggregate personalization. Table 7 shows the result of this alternative setup. We can note that the improvements over the original search engine ranking are consistently higher than in the previous case. The gain of the hybrid method over uniform application of aggregate personalization shrinks, yet remains significant. This makes intuitive sense as aggregate histories already inherently contain session-level information. The ratio of improvements and performance losses remains largely stable.

With respect to our third research question, we were able to obtain significant personalization improvements when identifying atypical sessions first and treating them differently from typical ones during re-ranking, by applying short-term session-level personalization rather than the historic or aggregated versions.

6. DISCUSSION AND FUTURE WORK

One important implication of our study is that a user's motivation to succeed at a search, and the corresponding utility they place on finding the information, might be estimated in part *by the effort or risk they are willing to take to get the information*: an application of the classic von Neumann-Morganstern definition of economic utility. By 'risk' we have in mind a compound quantity that captures both a) the uncertainty of relevance for the information sources the user is accessing, as measured by proxy quantities such as how 'unfamiliar' or 'new' a source is for that user, and b) the opportunity cost that the user perceives from accessing these unknown information sources with uncertain payoff compared to accessing a known source with more certain payoff. This is a different dimension of user effort than is captured by existing behavior-oriented measures like user frustration, since it accounts for content-based factors such as the unfamiliarity and difficulty of the material being retrieved, and the quality of alternatives that may be available. We believe these connections to economic utility theory as well as related work on information foraging [23] could be a rich area for further exploration.

Our initial study and modeling of atypical searches could be extended in a number of directions, of which we mention two here. First, over time, certain information needs or topics that were initially atypical may become recurring and thus part of a user's typical profile; the classic example is the search for information on medical conditions that follow initial symptoms, through diagnosis and treatment. More generally, however, it would be important to broaden the class of tasks or needs for which we can model such variability. Second, the findings from our post-hoc analysis of atypical sessions could be applied to online prediction of atypicality, in which we make dynamic predictions of typicality as a user progresses through a session.

7. CONCLUSION

While previous work on search personalization has focused on the problem of matching content to a user profile, we characterize and predict *atypical searches*. For such sessions, matching against the user's existing profile may *not* be accurate or desirable. Atypical searches are particularly interesting because in many cases they correspond to high-motivation needs in which the user exhibits a willingness to stretch their own boundaries for what is familiar or easy. Based on human labeling of 'typical' vs. 'atypical' sessions from several months of commercial search logs, we analyzed topic, reading level, and session-level properties of atypical sessions. We found significant differences between typical and atypical sessions: certain topics such as medical information and technical support were much more likely to arise in atypical sessions, along with query features such as increased term count, more unique terms, and more natural language-type terms. We showed how atypical sessions could be successfully identified using a classification approach that combined session-level and profile-based features. Finally, we showed that the ability to identify atypical sessions results in significant performance gains for search personalization based on short- and long-term user profiles.

8. REFERENCES

[1] M. Ageev, Q. Guo, D. Lagun, and E. Agichtein. Find it if you can: A game for modeling different types of web search success using interaction data. In *SIGIR 2011*. ACM.

[2] O. Alonso and R. Baeza-Yates. Design and implementation of relevance assessments using crowdsourcing. *ECIR 2011*, pages 153–164.

[3] A. Aula, R.M. Khan, and Z. Guan. How does search behavior change as search becomes more difficult? In *CHI 2010*, pages 35–44. ACM.

[4] M. Bendersky and W.B. Croft. Analysis of long queries in a large scale search log. In *Proceedings of the 2009 workshop on Web Search Click Data*, pages 8–14. ACM.

[5] P.N. Bennett, R.W. White, W. Chu, S.T. Dumais, P. Bailey, F. Borisyuk, and X. Cui. Modeling the impact of short-and long-term behavior on search personalization. In *SIGIR 2012*. ACM.

[6] K. Collins-Thompson, P.N. Bennett, R.W. White, S. de la Chica, and D. Sontag. Personalizing web search results by reading level. In *CIKM 2011*, pages 403–412. ACM.

Table 6: Session and historic information for search personalization.

	% improved	% worsened	# improved / # worsened	δ_{MAP}
session	3.32%	2.1%	1.58	0.00247
historic	3.53%	2.83%	1.25	0.00454
session/historic hybrid	4.11%*	2.6%	1.58	0.0055*

Table 7: Session and aggregate information for search personalization.

	% improved	% worsened	# improved / # worsened	δ_{MAP}
session	3.32%	2.1%	1.58	0.00247
aggregate	4.9%	3.31%	1.48	0.00637
session/aggregate	4.83%	3.19%	1.52	0.00639*

[7] C. Eickhoff, K. Collins-Thompson, P.N. Bennett, and S. Dumais. Designing human-readable user profiles for search evaluation. *ECIR 2013*.

[8] C. Eickhoff and A.P. de Vries. Increasing cheat robustness of crowdsourcing tasks. *Information Retrieval*, pages 1–17, 2012.

[9] S. Fox, K. Karnawat, M. Mydland, S. Dumais, and T. White. Evaluating implicit measures to improve web search. *TOIS*, 23(2):147–168, 2005.

[10] J. Gao, W. Yuan, X. Li, K. Deng, and J.Y. Nie. Smoothing clickthrough data for web search ranking. In *SIGIR 2009*, pages 355–362. ACM.

[11] S. Gauch, J. Chaffee, and A. Pretschner. Ontology-based user profiles for search and browsing. *WI-IAT 2003*, pages 219–234.

[12] S. Goel, A. Broder, E. Gabrilovich, and B. Pang. Anatomy of the long tail: ordinary people with extraordinary tastes. In *WSDM 2010*, pages 201–210. ACM.

[13] M. Hall, E. Frank, G. Holmes, B. Pfahringer, P. Reutemann, and I.H. Witten. The Weka data mining software: an update. *SIGKDD Explorations Newsletter*, 11(1):10–18, 2009.

[14] T.H. Haveliwala. Topic-sensitive pagerank: A context-sensitive ranking algorithm for web search. *TKDE 2003*, 15(4):784–796.

[15] C. Hölscher and G. Strube. Web search behavior of internet experts and newbies. *Computer networks*, 33(1):337–346, 2000.

[16] R. Jones and K.L. Klinkner. Beyond the session timeout: automatic hierarchical segmentation of search topics in query logs. In *CIKM 2008*, pages 699–708. ACM.

[17] G. Kazai. In search of quality in crowdsourcing for search engine evaluation. *ECIR 2011*, pages 165–176.

[18] J.Y. Kim, K. Collins-Thompson, P.N. Bennett, and S.T. Dumais. Characterizing web content, user interests, and search behavior by reading level and topic. In *WSDM 2012*, pages 213–222. ACM.

[19] A. Kotov, P.N. Bennett, R.W. White, S.T. Dumais, and J. Teevan. Modeling and analysis of cross-session search tasks. In *SIGIR 2011*, pages 5–14. ACM.

[20] L. Li, Z. Yang, B. Wang, and M. Kitsuregawa. Dynamic adaptation strategies for long-term and short-term user profile to personalize search. *Advances in Data and Web Management*, pages 228–240, 2007.

[21] Z. Ma, G. Pant, and O.R.L. Sheng. Interest-based personalized search. *TOIS*, 25(1):5, 2007.

[22] N. Matthijs and F. Radlinski. Personalizing web search using long-term browsing history. In *WSDM 2011*, pages 25–34. ACM.

[23] Peter Pirolli and Stuart Card. Information foraging in information access environments. In *CHI '95*, pages 51–58.

[24] J. Pitkow, H. Schütze, et al. Personalized search. *Communications of the ACM*, 9(45):50–55, 2002.

[25] M. Speretta and S. Gauch. Personalized search based on user search histories. In *WI-IAT 2005*, pages 622–628. IEEE.

[26] K. Sugiyama, K. Hatano, and M. Yoshikawa. Adaptive web search based on user profile constructed without any effort from users. In *WWW 2004*, pages 675–684. ACM.

[27] B. Tan, X. Shen, and C.X. Zhai. Mining long-term search history to improve search accuracy. In *SIGKDD 2006*, pages 718–723. ACM.

[28] C. Tan, E. Gabrilovich, and B. Pang. To each his own: personalized content selection based on text comprehensibility. In *WSDM 2012*, pages 233–242. ACM.

[29] J. Teevan, S.T. Dumais, and E. Horvitz. Personalizing search via automated analysis of interests and activities. In *SIGIR 2005*, pages 449–456. ACM.

[30] J. Teevan, S.T. Dumais, and E. Horvitz. Potential for personalization. *TOCHI*, 17(1):4, 2010.

[31] A. Thatcher. Web search strategies: The influence of web experience and task type. *Information Processing & Management*, 44(3):1308–1329, 2008.

[32] R.W. White, P. Bailey, and L. Chen. Predicting user interests from contextual information. In *SIGIR 2009*, pages 363–370. ACM.

[33] R.W. White, S.T. Dumais, and J. Teevan. Characterizing the influence of domain expertise on web search behavior. In *WSDM 2009*, pages 132–141. ACM.

[34] R.W. White and D. Morris. Investigating the querying and browsing behavior of advanced search engine users. In *SIGIR 2007*, pages 255–262. ACM.

[35] Q. Wu, C.J.C. Burges, K.M. Svore, and J. Gao. Ranking, boosting, and model adaptation. *Technical Report, MSR-TR-2008-109*, 2008.

Expediting Search Trend Detection via Prediction of Query Counts

Nadav Golbandi
Yahoo! Labs, Haifa, Israel
nadavg@yahoo-inc.com

Liran Katzir*
Microsoft Research,
Advanced Technology Labs,
Herzliya, Israel
lirank@microsoft.com

Yehuda Koren†
Google, Haifa, Israel
yehuda.a.koren
@gmail.com

Ronny Lempel
Yahoo! Labs, Haifa, Israel
rlempel@yahoo-inc.com

ABSTRACT

The massive volume of queries submitted to major Web search engines reflects human interest at a global scale. While the popularity of many search queries is stable over time or fluctuates with periodic regularity, some queries experience a sudden and ephemeral rise in popularity that is unexplained by their past volumes. Typically the popularity surge is precipitated by some real-life event in the news cycle. Such queries form what are known as *search trends*. All major search engines, using query log analysis and other signals, invest in detecting such trends. The goal is to surface trends accurately, with low latency relative to the actual event that sparked the trend.

This work formally defines precision, recall and latency metrics related to top-k search trend detection. Then, observing that many trend detection algorithms rely on query counts, we develop a linear auto-regression model to predict future query counts. Subsequently, we tap the predicted counts to expedite search trend detection by plugging them into an existing trend detection scheme.

Experimenting with query logs from a major Web search engine, we report both the stand-alone accuracy of our query count predictions, as well as the task-oriented effects of the prediction on the emitted trends. We show an average reduction in trend detection latency of roughly twenty minutes, with a negligible impact on the precision and recall metrics.

*Research was conducted while the author was working at Yahoo!

†Research was conducted mainly while the author was working at Yahoo!

WSDM'13, February 4–8, 2013, Rome, Italy.

Categories and Subject Descriptors

H.3.3 [**Information Search and Retrieval**]: Information filtering

Keywords

Search trend detection, query count prediction

1. INTRODUCTION

Major Web search engines continuously receive enormous volumes of queries from all over the world, which together provide a unique perspective into the aggregated interests of the world's population. These interests are reflected in the dynamics of query frequencies, typically visualized as two-dimensional plots of query counts along a time axis. At the two extremes are queries that are perpetually popular and queries that are exceedingly rare; in between are queries that are at times popular. Some queries' popularities exhibit periodic behavior, such as leisure queries whose volume picks up on weekends, seasonal queries, etc. Of particular interest to this work are queries that emerge in popularity in a manner unexplained by their past volumes, typically due to some (non-periodic) news-worthy real-life event that attracted a sudden peak in human attention (see Figure 1). We call these *search trends.*

Algorithmic detection of trending searches is an important and established problem. Indeed, as depicted in Figure 2, today's major search engines all track and report search trends, whether through dedicated experiences (e.g. `trends.google.com`) or as part of associated media sites (e.g. `now.msn.com` and the *"Trending Now"* module on `www.yahoo.com`). Lists of trending searches are of value both to end users, who find them engaging, as well as to editorial staff who can address content creation and curation needs on the trending searches. Consequently, there is business value in algorithms that are able to spot emerging trends as quickly as possible.

Algorithms for detecting search trends should therefore be judged by at least three high-level metrics. The first two are adaptations of the familiar precision and recall metrics, as trend detection algorithms aspire to output as many "true" trends as possible.The third metric concerns the speed of detection, or the latency by which emerging trends are de-

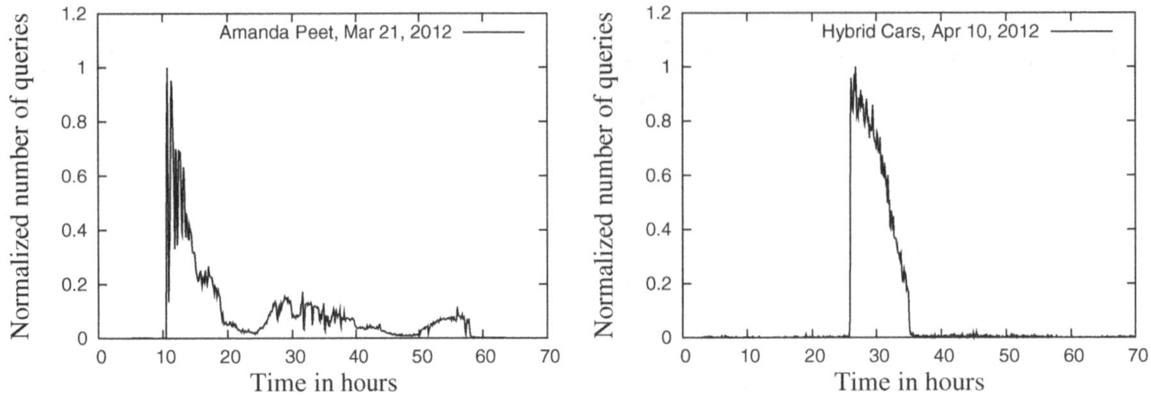

Figure 1: Examples of search trends for the queries "Amanda Peet" (left) and "Hybrid Cars" (right).

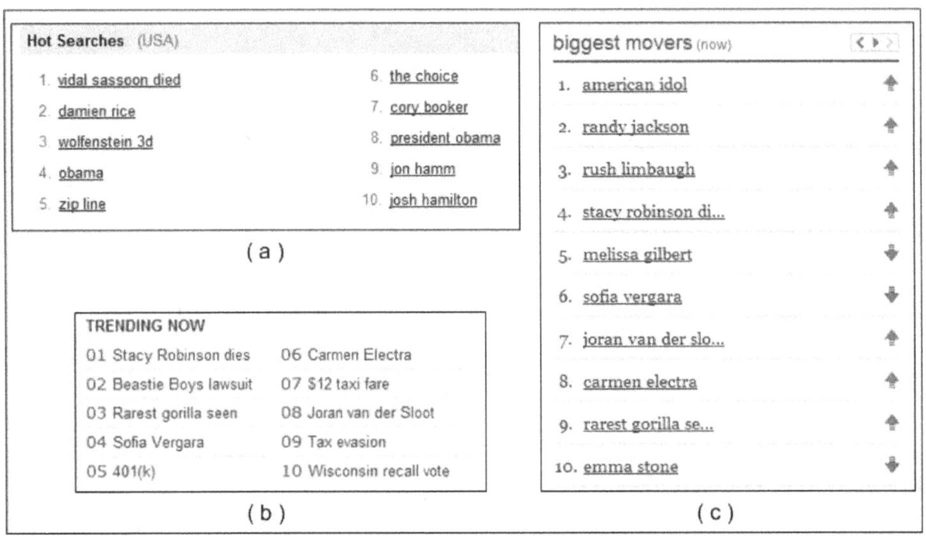

Figure 2: Top 10 "buzzing" trends (a) Google; (b) Yahoo!; and (c) Bing taken on May 10, 2012.

tected. Here latency may be measured in absolute terms, with respect to the occurrence of the news event that sparked the surge in search activity, or in relative terms when comparing two competing algorithms. The first contribution of this work is in defining the three metrics, and in particular the definition of relative latency.

Naturally, a crucial piece of input to search trend detection algorithms is the search log, and in particular query counts over the log. The second and principal contribution of this work is in demonstrating that (near) future query counts can be predicted from recent search activity, and in tapping the predicted counts to expedite trend detection. At a high level, we plug the predicted future query counts into an existing trend detection algorithm that relies on access to query counts. With an ideal (oracle) predictor, this would expedite trend detection by pre-producing future results earlier.

Concretely, we incorporated our predicted query counts into the search trend detection algorithm of Dong et al. [9]. We report both the stand-alone accuracy of our query count predictions, as well as the task-oriented effects on the emitted trends. Our experiments indicate that we were able to detect trends of comparable precision and recall while reducing detection latency by about 20 minutes on average.

The rest of this paper is organized as follows. Section 2 surveys related work. Section 3 details our query count prediction algorithm and its usage for detecting search trends. Section 4 proposes metrics for evaluating trend detection algorithms. Section 5 reports our results, and Section 6 concludes.

2. RELATED WORK

Query counts provide a very strong signal of trending crowd interests. Ginsberg et al. [11] used query counts to predict emerging flu outbreaks. Choi and Varian [6] use public query volumes of Google Trends to predict merchandise sales trends. Along similar lines, Goel et al. [12] showed that consumer behavior is reflected by search volume; specifically, they showed how to predict the billboard score and revenue of a movie. Dong et al. [9] show how to tap query volumes for predicting trending searches. While some works [6, 11] use a week or more of aggregated search data, Dong et al. [9] operate at a much finer resolution (e.g. hourly outputs). Al-Bawab et al. [1] extended [9] to provide a location-aware search trends detection algorithm using geographical properties associated with query log entries.

Chen et al. [5] offers a classification into *stable queries* (perpetually popular queries such as "youtube"), *one time burst* ("octopus paul"), *multiple times burst* ("earthquake"), and *periodic* ("christmas present"). They used this classification in turn to improve ranking results.

Kulkarni et al. [15] offer new insights into changes in query intent given fluctuations of query popularity. For example, a change in a non-periodic query like "earthquake" strongly indicates that an earthquake has occurred. Vlachos et al. [22] use query counts to learn semantic similarity between queries. Their main intuition is that when two queries are semantically similar, the fluctuations of their popularities will be highly correlated.

Zhang et al. [23] present the problem of ranking *recurrent event* queries, e.g. "WSDM 2013", "WSDM 2012", etc. Modern search engines may rank higher "older" pages which have more links and have been clicked on more times. Specifically, when the authors searched for WSDM during May 2012, "WSDM 2012" was the top result, whereas the authors' intent (and probably the main intent for others too) was "WSDM 2013", which was ranked below "WSDM 2011" and "WSDM 2010". During July 2012, the top result was "WSDM 2013". The authors show such queries have distinctly shaped query count graphs. Shokouhi [21] indicates that the seasonal (periodic) nature of queries can be detected using time series analysis. Independently, Chen et al. [4, 5] offered a detection based on the variance, mean, and peak values of the query count.

Efron [10] revisits the term scoring function. The proposed method hypothesizes that a term whose frequency prediction does not fit a linear model should get a higher weight. They learn the auto-regressive linear coefficient and use the difference between the actual count and the predicted count in order to re-weight each term. Note that terms with high weights tend to have low frequencies.

Another line of work used the blogosphere to detect top news stories [16, 17]. They detect in retrospect the "best story of the day". The main tools used are *language models* [18]. Mathioudakis et al [19] provide a framework for online trends detection in Twitter.

While all these prior works offer new signal sources, this work has an orthogonal contribution of predicting the magnitude of the signals, rather than waiting for them to reach a critical mass.

Shimshoni et al. [20] indicate that it is useful to know the query count itself in advance. They observe that over half of the most popular search queries are predictable one year ahead with a relative small error. Predictability is found to be particularly high at certain categories like Health, Food & Drink, and Travel. One use case would be aiding companies in planning advertising campaigns. They used auto-regression, in which the past query count was used to detect periodicity and to produce estimates for future query counts. The emphasis was on long periods of time and high volume queries. The underlining algorithm for predicting the counts is from Cleveland et al. [7]. The prediction task of the current work is different by aiming at a timely identification of emerging trends, which requires the analysis of short-term query frequencies.

Ihler et al. [14] offer a generic way to detect anomalous events in count data using time series analysis. The count data is modeled as a non-homogeneous Poisson process and the transitions to anomalous events are modeled as a Markov chain. They show how to decompose the time series into periodic and non-periodic components. Their algorithm is a classifier into three states, "high", "normal", and "low".

3. TREND PREDICTION ALGORITHM

Given a query log, we describe an algorithm outputting a list of top-k trending searches. First, we formalize the search trend detection problem as follows:

Definition 1 *A search trend at time t is a topic, which around time t suddenly became very popular. It might indicate the topic follows a news item prior to time t.*

Instance: An integer k, and a query log that contains a list of submitted queries along with their submission timestamps.

Objective: Find a list of k topics every regular interval (e.g. every hour) that constitute the top-k search trends.

3.1 Background

3.1.1 Modeling assumptions

A Poisson process is a stochastic process which counts the number of events for a specified time. It is commonly assumed that the count of a specific search query is a Poisson process, as is often the case with count data [3]. However, the Poisson distribution assumes that there are many independent events, each of which has a low probability to occur such that the mean of the total occurrences number is a small constant. This is not the case in our scenario since we are interested in queries where the query count is high and the induced distribution is better approximated with a normal (Gaussian) distribution. Our experiments have shown that although Poisson modeling better predicts low counts, it fails to produce good results when the query count is high. Hence, we assume a normal distribution for query counts, which tends to produce better results for our needs. An additional benefit of the normal distribution assumption is a more convenient modeling scheme that reduces running time.

3.1.2 Data setup

The input for the prediction algorithm is the query log of the Yahoo! search engine. Every search query made by a user is logged with the query string and the respective timestamp. First, every query q is normalized by lower casing, trimming, special character removal, etc. Second, the queries are aggregated in batches of short, regular time intervals of length s (in this work we set $s =$ 1-minute). This results in a time series of counts being associated with each query q. We denote by $c_t(q)$ the number of times q appears in the query log during time-interval $[(t-1)s, ts)$. For each query q the count time-series during $[as, bs)$ is $c_{a+1}(q), c_{a+2}(q), \ldots, c_b(q)$.

For the training phase, we use time-series for a set of *emerging queries*. We define a query as "emerging" whenever there exists (at least) a single hour during which: (1) the number of its submissions is in the hundreds; (2) the first search result for the query is a news item; and (3) the click through rate of the first search result is at least 25%.

q	Query
s	Basic time unit (e.g., 1-minute)
t	Timestamp
$c_t(q)$	q's count during $[(t-1)s, ts)$
l	Length of observed time series per query
m	Length of period for predicting query volume
$x(q,t) \in \mathbb{R}^l$	Training time series for q at timestamp t
$y(q,t) \in \mathbb{R}$	Query count following $x(q,t)$
$\hat{y}(q,t) \in \mathbb{R}$	Predicted query count following $x(q,t)$
n	Number of training examples
p	Number of timeframes per day (e.g., 24)
h	Day time unit (e.g., hour of day)
$h(t)$	Timeframe (hour) corresponding to time t

Table 1: Summary of notations

In case a query satisfies the emerging conditions during several hours, we take its emerging time as the first such hour. For an emerging query q, we extract its time series for the 24-hour period prior to its emerging time and 48-hours since its emerging time. We collected a set of around 1500 such emerging queries, each constituting its own time series. We have $(48+24)60 = 4320$ time-stamped query counts in each time-series. Note that it is possible that many of the counts are zero.

Given an emerging query q and its corresponding time-series, we extract multiple training examples. Each training example corresponds to $l+m$ continuous minutes of the time series. The first l minutes are represented via the vector $x(q,t) \in \mathbb{N}^l$, whose entries are the l-long subsequence of the time series ending at timestamp t. Namely,

$$x(q,t) = (c_{t-l+1}(q), \ldots, c_{t-1}(q), c_t(q)).$$

Additionally, we sum the query counts in the following m minutes, denoted by $y(q,t) = \sum_{j=t+1}^{t+m} c_j(q)$. This work sets $l = 30$ minutes and $m = 60$ minutes (one hour). The training set is composed of all possible $(x(q,t),\ y(q,t))$ pairs. We denote the number of such pairs by n. As we will shortly explain, the goal is to predict the scalar $y(q,t)$ given the vector $x(q,t)$.

Our solution partitions the training examples by their corresponding time of day. We divide the day into p disjoint timeframes. In our implementation $p = 24$, so that we simply split the day into round hours. Accordingly, each training example $(x(q,t),\ y(q,t))$ is assigned to a subset corresponding to the round hour of t. For example "10:13, July 5, 2012" is associated with the 10-th timeframe. Formally, we use the function $h(t)$ to get the timeframe (hour) corresponding to time t. We denote by $\hat{y}(q,t)$ the predicted value of $y(q,t)$. Table 1 summarizes the notations used throughout this paper.

3.1.3 *Trending searches detection*

Since many of the top search queries are quite regular (e.g. navigational and periodical queries), it is not sufficient to output the queries of the highest count volume, but rather a screening process must filter out those queries that are perpetually or periodically popular.

Specifically, we harness a recent search trends detection algorithm [9], which builds a language model [18] from query counts at each time period. The algorithm builds a language model (LM) of queries for the current time, and compares it to several reference language models of past times (typically 1-day, 1-week, and 1-month ago). Trendiness is measured by the difference between the current probability of an n-gram and its highest reference probability. We adopt the notation of [9], and denote by $M_{Q,t}$ the language model of the query log at time t. The algorithm proceeds as follows:

Algorithm 1 (Topic Trend Scoring [9])

1. *Use recent query log history to create the LM*[1].
2. *Estimate trendiness score using*

$$score(q,t,Q) = \log P(q|M_{Q,t}) - \max_i \log P(q|M_{Q,t-r_i})$$
$$= \log \min_i \left(\frac{P(q|M_{Q,t})}{P(q|M_{Q,t-r_i})} \right)$$

3. *Output top-k items.*

Here, the historical reference set $\{t - r_i\}$ is typically {1-day, 1-week, 1-month}-ago. This serves to eliminate most of the natural periodicity of queries.

As reported in [9], Algorithm 1 bases the current LM on the queries of the last hour. In our notation, this means that at time $t = 60$ the LM is built using the actual counts $\sum_{i=1}^{60} c_i(q)$ for each query q. In our work, at the same time $t = 60$, we will typically consider a shorter time period of 30-minutes $(c_{31}(q), c_{32}(q), \ldots, c_{60}(q))$, and based on these past counts we will *predict* the total query volume in the upcoming hour $\sum_{i=61}^{120} c_i(q)$. The LM at $t = 60$ will be computed using the 1-hour predicted counts.

3.1.4 *Auto-regression*

The main tool we use is linear regression [13]. Formally, the input is a set of explanatory vectors $X = (x_1, x_2, \ldots, x_n)$, and a set of response variables $Y = (y_1, y_2, \ldots, y_n)^T$. The model assumption is that $y_i = \beta^T x_i + \epsilon_i$, where ϵ_i is the measurement error and $E(\epsilon_i) = 0$. The goal is to find a vector β such that

$$\hat{\beta} = \arg\min_\beta ||Y - X\beta||_2^2 = \arg\min_\beta \sum_{i=1}^{n} \left(y_i - x_i^T \beta\right)^2$$

When ϵ_i has a normal distribution this model coincides with the maximum likelihood estimator. This is justified when assuming the normal distribution on query counts.

Regularization is often used to prevent overfitting by limiting the complexity of the learned parameters (β). While we have found traditional Ridge [13] and Lasso [13] regularizations beneficial, we achieved better results by using a tailored regularization scheme that accounts for the temporal smoothness expected from the model parameters. The details are given in the next section.

3.2 Predicting query counts

Time-smoothed model.

Given past query counts we build a linear regression model predicting the future query counts. Each training instance consists of the counts for a query over l-minute time interval, followed by the total count in the ensuing m-minute period,

[1]Additional input types were used in [9]. This paper focuses on the main component, namely the query log.

which ought to be predicted. As mentioned earlier, our implementation sets $l = 30$ and $m = 60$. We thus observe a 30-minute history in order to predict the query count over the following 1-hour.

Formally, for every timestamped-query pair (q, t), we define the explanatory vector

$$x(q,t) \in \mathbb{R}^l = (c_{t-l+1}(q), \ldots, c_{t-1}(q), c_t(q))$$

and the response variable

$$y(q,t) = \sum_{j=t+1}^{t+m} c_j(q).$$

Linear regression finds a coefficient vector $\beta \in \mathbb{R}^l$ such that $y(q,t) \sim \beta^T x(q,t)$.

It is important to regularize β in order to avoid overfitting the training examples. To this end, we assume that β's components exhibit temporal smoothness. This is realized by constraining consecutive parameters to change relatively slowly, through penalizing their squared differences. That is, we strive to reduce

$$\sum_{i=1}^{i=l-1} (\beta_i - \beta_{i+1})^2. \quad (1)$$

Such a time-smoothed linear regression model can be solved by a closed formula. We will shortly provide the formula for a more general case to which we now turn.

Time-smoothed, per-hour model.

In practice we have found that the time of day has a substantial effect on autoregressive model of the query counts. Hence, instead of working with a fixed vector β, we let it vary with day time. We split the day into $p = 24$ equal hourly timeframes. Let us denote by $\beta(h) \in \mathbb{R}^l$ the coefficient vector associated with timeframe h (where $0 \leqslant h < p$). We assume that the coefficients change slowly with time and thus employ a cyclical regularization striving to reduce

$$\sum_{h=0}^{h=p-1} ||\beta(h) - \beta(h+1 \mod p)||_2^2. \quad (2)$$

Note that this cyclical regularization is independent of the regularization of Eq. (1), which is still required. Hence, two different smoothing schemes are employed. First we strive to reduce differences between adjacent components (corresponding to adjacent minutes), as per Eq. (1). Second, we strive to reduce differences between components representing the same minute within adjacent timeframes, as per Eq. (2).

We now introduce some notation in order to facilitate a closed formula derivation of the model's parameters. Matrix notation will be used for convenience. We arrange all the $\beta(h)$ vectors, row-wise, in a $p \times l$ matrix B, and denote the l corresponding column vectors as $\beta^{(1)}, \beta^{(2)}, \ldots, \beta^{(l)} \in \mathbb{R}^p$:

$$B = \begin{pmatrix} \beta(1)^T \\ \beta(2)^T \\ \vdots \\ \beta(p)^T \end{pmatrix} = \left(\beta^{(1)}, \beta^{(2)}, \ldots, \beta^{(l)}\right)$$

Note that we regularize B both horizontally and vertically, minimizing differences of adjacent cells in both directions.

Let us first describe the regularization for each $\beta(h)$ and $\beta^{(i)}$ separately, and then combine them all within a single formula. We use $\Gamma(\lambda) \in \mathbb{R}^{l \times l}$ to regulate $\beta(h)$ (temporal line smoothness) and $\Gamma_*(\lambda) \in \mathbb{R}^{p \times p}$ to regulate $\beta^{(i)}$ (temporal cyclic smoothness), where

$$\Gamma(\lambda) = \lambda \left[\begin{pmatrix} I_{l-1 \times l-1} & 0 \\ 0 & 0 \end{pmatrix} - \begin{pmatrix} 0 & I_{l-1 \times l-1} \\ 0 & 0 \end{pmatrix} \right]$$

Thus, $\left|\left|\Gamma(\lambda)\hat{\beta(h)}\right|\right|_2^2 = \lambda^2 \sum_{i=1}^{l-1} (\beta(h)_{i+1} - \beta(h)_i)^2$. Similarly,

$$\Gamma_*(\lambda) = \lambda \left[\begin{pmatrix} I_{p-1 \times p-1} & 0 \\ 0 & 1 \end{pmatrix} - \begin{pmatrix} 0 & I_{p-1 \times p-1} \\ 1 & 0 \end{pmatrix} \right]$$

Note that Γ_* is a circulant matrix in which the first row is $(1, -1, 0, 0, \ldots, 0)$. Thus,

$$\left|\left|\Gamma_*(\lambda)\hat{\beta^{(i)}}\right|\right|_2^2 = \lambda^2 \sum_{h=1}^{p} \left(\beta_h^{(i)} - \beta_{h+1 \mod p}^{(i)}\right)^2.$$

We also introduce a new notation for representing the training data. We will rearrange training examples by their day-time (hour) in order to facilitate applying the matching coefficients $\beta(h)$. Specifically, for each day-time $0 \leqslant h < p$, we row-wise arrange all $x(q,t)$-vectors satisfying $h(t) = h$ within the matrix X_h. The respective $y(q,t)$ values are arranged within the vector Y_h. The whole training set is re-arranged within the matrix $P \in \mathbb{R}^{n \times lp}$ and the vector $Q \in \mathbb{R}^n$, such that $P = \text{diag}(X_1, X_2, \ldots, X_p)$, and $Q = (Y_1^T, Y_2^T, \ldots, Y_p^T)^T$.

Accordingly, we combine all individual regularization matrices together allowing their activation on the whole set of $\beta(h)$ and $\beta^{(i)}$ vectors. We use two $pl \times pl$ matrices defined as

$$\tilde{\Gamma}(\lambda) = \Gamma(\lambda) \otimes I_{p \times p} = \begin{pmatrix} \Gamma(\lambda) & 0 & \ldots & 0 \\ 0 & \Gamma(\lambda) & \ldots & 0 \\ \vdots & \vdots & \ddots & \vdots \\ 0 & 0 & \ldots & \Gamma(\lambda) \end{pmatrix}$$

$$\tilde{\Gamma}_*(\lambda) = \lambda \left[\begin{pmatrix} I & 0 & 0 & \ldots & 0 \\ 0 & I & 0 & \ldots & 0 \\ \vdots & \vdots & \vdots & \ddots & \vdots \\ 0 & 0 & 0 & \ldots & I \end{pmatrix} - \begin{pmatrix} 0 & I & 0 & \ldots & 0 \\ 0 & 0 & I & \ldots & 0 \\ \vdots & \vdots & \vdots & \ddots & \vdots \\ I & 0 & 0 & \ldots & 0 \end{pmatrix} \right]$$

All the blocks in $\tilde{\Gamma}_*(\lambda)$ are of dimension $l \times l$.

Finally, let $\gamma \in \mathbb{R}^{pl}$ be a linearization of $\beta(1), \beta(2), \ldots, \beta(p)$. That is,

$$\gamma = \left(\beta(1)^T, \beta(2)^T, \ldots, \beta(p)^T\right)^T$$

By using the introduced notation, the sought parameters (γ) satisfy

$$\hat{\gamma} = \arg\min_{\gamma} ||Q - P\gamma||_2^2 + \left|\left|\tilde{\Gamma}(\lambda_1)\gamma\right|\right|_2^2 + \left|\left|\tilde{\Gamma}_*(\lambda_2)\gamma\right|\right|_2^2$$

The solution for this optimization problem is given by

$$\hat{\gamma} = \left(P^T P + \tilde{\Gamma}(\lambda_1)^T \tilde{\Gamma}(\lambda_1) + \tilde{\Gamma}_*(\lambda_2)^T \tilde{\Gamma}_*(\lambda_2)\right)^{-1} P^T Q \quad (3)$$

Note that we employ two different regularization coefficients (λ_1, λ_2) in the model, thereby gaining better flexibility. The actual values that we used are $\lambda_1 = 0.15$ and $\lambda_2 = 0.05$, based on holdout set performance. The computational effort involves inverting a $pl \times pl$ matrix, which is feasible for the typical values we use ($p = 24, l = 30$).

The online prediction phase involves computing an inner product with the corresponding model. Formally,

$$\hat{y}(x, y) = \beta(h(t))^T x(q, t) \tag{4}$$

3.3 Tying it all together

We now present Algorithm 2 (see Figure 3) for detecting search trends. To emit trends at time t, Algorithm 2 uses the query log to produce predicted counts for the time-period following t. As mentioned earlier, in our case this means predicting query counts for the following hour. The query prediction procedure is applied to all queries in the query log. The predicted counts are then fed as input into the baseline search trends detection algorithm, Algorithm 1. The baseline algorithm then emits trends based on the predicted future counts rather than on actual past counts.

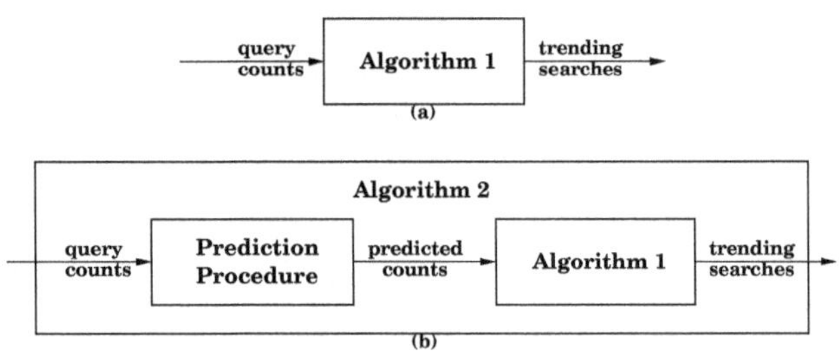

Figure 3: Algorithm 1(3a) and Algorithm 2(3b)

Algorithm 2 (Augmented Topic Trending Scoring)

1. *Use recent query log history to predict future query count.*
2. *Compute search trends by feeding the predicted query count into Algorithm 1.*

To recap, the offline learning algorithm requires (1) a preliminary scan of the query log to find emerging queries (see subsection 3.1.2); (2) a second scan to extract the counts for these emerging queries; and (3) computing Eq (3). Then, the online phase involves predicting - from l recent query counts - the sum of query counts for the next m time slots. Both offline and online phases can be efficiently programmed in the map-reduce framework [8], and were implemented in Hadoop [2].

4. EVALUATION METRICS FOR TREND DETECTION

This section describes the recall, precision and latency metrics by which we judge search trend detection algorithms. We assume that algorithms emit top-k trends every time unit, and that we also have some ground truth GT of true trends (whose number is not necessarily k) per time unit. As we are mostly concerned with the comparison of two competing trend detection algorithms A and B, we will denote by A^t, B^t and GT^t the sets of trends emitted at time t by the two algorithms (k trends per set) and the ground truth, respectively.

When comparing an algorithm's list of trends with the ground truth, one cannot simply compute recall and precision metrics by looking at the lists emitted at time t alone. An algorithm may be late in emitting a true trend, i.e. emit the trend at a later time as compared to the ground truth. In such cases we will still credit the algorithm with discovering a correct trend. Concretely, we define the w-window around time t as $w(t) = [t - w, t + w]$, i.e. span of time starting w time units before t and ending w units after t. Trend comparisons will rely heavily on the notion of time windows.

The *precision at k under window w at time t* of algorithm A is defined as follows:

$$P_k^t(A, w) = \frac{|A^t \bigcap \cup_{j \in w(t)} GT^j|}{k}$$

Since $|A^t| = k$, $P_k^t(A, w) \in [0, 1]$ and equals the fraction of the k trends emitted by A at time t that appear in the ground truth anywhere in the w-window around t. For a time range T (formally, a set of discrete time slots), the *precision at k under window w over T* of algorithm A is defined as the average over the precision values in each time unit $t \in T$, i.e.

$$P_k^T(A, w) = \frac{\sum_{t \in T} P_k^t(A, w)}{|T|}.$$

Often, T, w and k will be implied from context and we will simply use the notation P_k. Note that due to the overlap in time windows and potentially also in trend lists emitted at different times, P_k^T does not measure the fraction of true trends emitted in time range T. Its only interpretation is of the average of precision values over multiple time slots.

In similar fashion, the *recall at k under window w at time t* of algorithm A is defined as follows:

$$R_k^t(A, w) = \frac{|GT^t \bigcap \cup_{j \in w(t)} A^j|}{|GT^t|}$$

This is the fraction of the ground truth trends at time t that appear in A's output anywhere in the w-window around t. For a time range T, the *recall at k under window w over T* of algorithm A is defined as the average of recall values over all time units $t \in T$, i.e.

$$R_k^T(A, w) = \frac{\sum_{t \in T} R_k^t(A, w)}{|T|}.$$

Again, when context allows, we will simply use R_k.

Note that the above definitions allow trends to repeat and be treated independently. In particular, if a trend appears twice in the ground truth, with the appearances separated by $2w + 1$ time slots, an algorithm would need to emit the trend twice to account for both ground truth appearances. This is reasonable, as some real-life entities or topics (e.g. "Lady Gaga") create headlines for different reasons quite frequently, causing what are essentially different search trends.

Moving on to define trend detection latency, here we wish to measure the amount by which one algorithm lags behind or leads another algorithm (or the ground truth) in emitting trends. We will base the measurements only on ground truth trends that were emitted by both A and B, i.e. only on overlapping true trends. The algorithms were already penalized for missing true trends or emitting false ones in the precision and recall metrics.

Formally, let Q be the set of true search trends emitted by both algorithms. For any $q \in Q$, denote by $t^A(q)[t^B(q)]$ the earliest time in which trend q appears in A's [B's] output. The *latency score at k* of A with respect to B is defined as

$$\ell_k(A,B) = |Q|^{-1} \sum_{q \in Q} t^A(q) - t^B(q).$$

This is essentially the average time per overlapping trend by which algorithm A beats (when negative) or lags behind (when positive) algorithm B. Note that $\ell_k(A,B) + \ell_k(B,A) = 0$.

5. EXPERIMENTAL RESULTS

This section reports on two different experiments. In Section 5.1, we measure the success of the query count prediction algorithm. Then, Subsection 5.2 compares the precision, recall, and latency of Algorithm 1 (our baseline) and the prediction-based Algorithm 2. Section 5.3 offers a retrospective look at the prediction scheme.

As described in Section 3, we used the training set to devise a query count prediction model. The test set consists of two parts:

1. Time series of 750 emerging queries, as defined in Subsection 3.1.2. These were used to evaluate the accuracy of query count prediction in Subsection 5.1

2. The entire query log over several weeks. This was used to test the effect of query count prediction for identifying search trends in Subsection 5.2

Datasets statistics are enclosed in Table 2.

From the training set we held out a validation set, consisting of 20% of its queries. The validation set was used to find the optimal values of the regularization coefficients, λ_1 and λ_2 (see Subsection 3.2), where $\lambda_1 = 0.15, \lambda_2 = 0.05$ provided the best results. As mentioned earlier, the sampling rate, s, was set to 1 minute.

5.1 Pure query counts

In Figure 4 we demonstrate the effect of the learning period length, l, on the Root Mean Squared Error(RMSE) of the Time-smoothed model and the Time-smoothed per-hour model. Both models show improvement as l grows, but saturate around 30 minutes. The Time-smoothed per-hour model exhibits a slightly better performance under RMSE.

However, we argue that RMSE is not the most suitable measure of success in this task. In our application of search trend detection, the following claims hold:

- As long as low-count queries are predicted as such, the precise accuracy hardly matters, as low-count queries will not be deemed as trends. Therefore, we should only focus on queries with large real or predicted counts.

- Small prediction errors on high-count queries have little effect on the outcome of the search trend detection system.

- Large underestimation errors (e.g. underestimating by 90% or by 100%) will result in a trend not being identified, regardless of the exact percentage of error.

Therefore, we chose to use another known measure which has a unit penalty for estimating over/under a relative threshold.

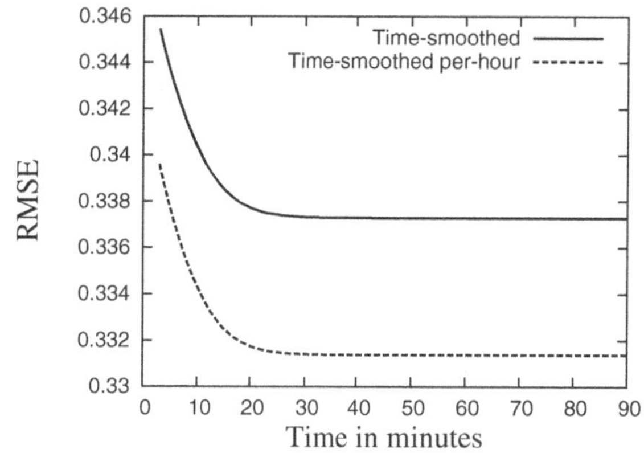

Figure 4: The effect of the learning period length, l, on the RMSE (the lower a curve, the better).

Furthermore, we limit our attention only to queries whose true or predicted count is high enough.

To this end, we used a confidence interval (CI) metric on a subset of queries S of high enough real or predicted counts. The metric measures the fraction of times a prediction falls within reasonable distance from the true value. Formally, we define support set with threshold M, $S(M)$, and the $\text{CI}(\epsilon, M)$ metric as follows:

$$S(M) = \{(y,x,t) \mid \max\{y(x,t), \hat{y}(x,t)\} > M\}$$

$$\text{CI}(\epsilon, M) = \frac{\left|\left\{(1-\epsilon) \le \frac{y(x,t)}{\hat{y}(x,t)} \le (1+\epsilon)\right\} \mid (y,x,t) \in S(M)\right|}{|S(M)|}.$$

Figure 5 shows the effect of the learning period length, l, on the CI(0.25, 600) metric ($S(600) \approx 200{,}000$). The x-axis is the l parameter and the y-axis is the percentage of queries in $S(600)$ whose predicted value over/under-predicts the true value by no more than 25%. The lower curve is for the Time-smoothed model and the upper curve is for Time-smoothed per-hour model. Both prediction algorithms improve as l grows and reach saturation after 30 minutes. Hence, we set $l = 30$. In Figure 6 we show the effect of ϵ on $\text{CI}(\epsilon, 600)$ metric with $l = 30$. It is easy to see that the Time-smoothed per-hour model dominates the Time-smoothed model. Moreover, the gap between the models is about the same for $\epsilon < 0.3$, but the difference diminishes as ϵ grows. In reasonable epsilon range there is a 8.3% (70.93 vs 65.5) improvement between the Time-smoothed model and the Time-smoothed per-hour model. Therefore, we will henceforth use the Time-smoothed per-hour model.

Finally, we show the model of one specific hour (1800–1900 GMT) in the Time-smoothed per-hour mode (see Figure 7). The x-axis is the index in the time series, j, and the y-axis is the value of the matching coefficient in the model, $\beta(h(t))_j$. One can see that the value of $\beta(h(t))_j$ drops when $j - t$ increases and it is virtually zero close to 30.

5.2 Search trend detection

We compare the performance of Algorithm 1 (our baseline) and Algorithm 2. The algorithms were applied at the top of every hour (tt:00). We use editorially-generated ground truth lists, that are constantly updated throughout the day. The editors rely on many input channels, and refresh the list of trending searches by adding and removing

Dates	Type	Experiment	queries type	size
Dec 10, 2011 – Dec 24, 2011 Jan 06, 2012 – Jan 20, 2012	train	query count	only emerging	1500
Mar 03, 2012 – Mar 21, 2012 Jun 12, 2012 – Jul 01, 2012	test	query count search trend	only emerging entire query log	750 undisclosed

Table 2: Train and Test Datasets

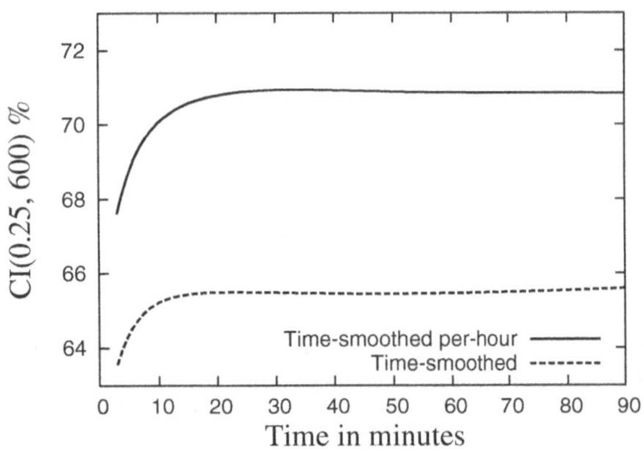

Figure 5: The effect of the learning period length, l, on the CI$(0.25, 600)$ metric (the higher a curve, the better).

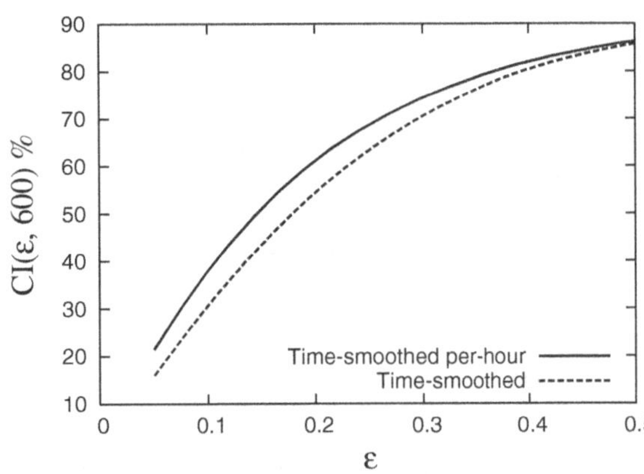

Figure 6: The sensitivity CI$(\epsilon, 600)$ to ϵ.

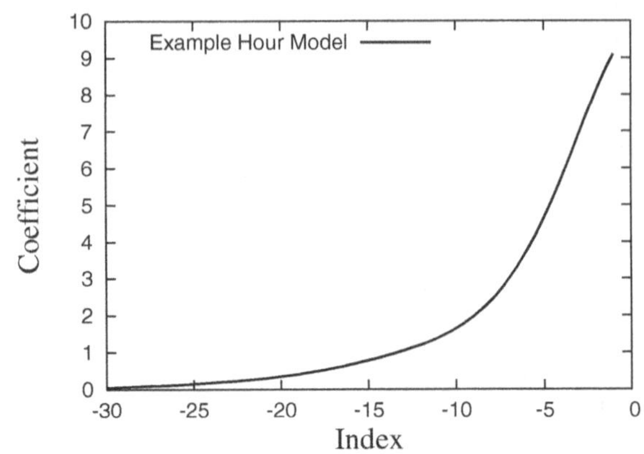

Figure 7: An example of 1800–1900 GMT hour model.

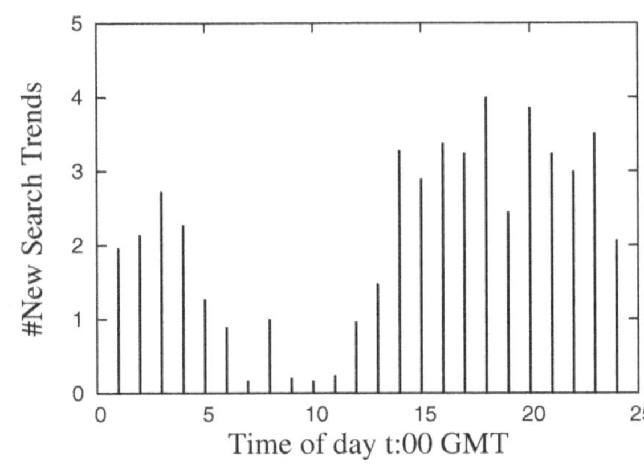

Figure 8: The number of newly introduced search trends in each hour (GMT)

queries. The average number of trends per ground truth list is 72.5. However, The average number of *new* search trends in 24 hours is 50.44. The intersection of two consecutive ground truth lists is thus substantial. Figure 8 shows the distribution of the number of newly introducted search trends per time-of-day. Note that the number of new search trends is low when Eastern Time is 01:00–08:00 (EDT is GMT -4).

Our metrics P_k (Precision), R_k (Recall), and L_k(Latency) are described in Section 4. Figure 9 compares P_k and R_k as a function of k, the number of trends in the output of the algorithms, with a window of $w = 4$ hours. The y-axis is the precision (recall) of Algorithm 2 relative to the precision (recall) of Algorithm 1. Due to business considerations, the actual values of the two algorithms cannot be disclosed. We observe that recall is effectively unchanged, while precision exhibits a negligible decrease. Specifically, the precision relative change ranges in $[0.965, 1]$ and recall relative change ranges in $[0.97, 1.02]$.

Figure 10 compares the latency gain, L_k, as a function of k. The y-axis is L_k in minutes. For a typically interesting value of k, e.g., $k = 10$, the value is 19.37 minutes. This means that on average Algorithm 2 reports a ground truth trend 20 minutes earlier than Algorithm 1. When k further grows, so does the size of the intersection with the ground truth and the latency gain converges to around 15 minutes.

Note that bursty queries (Figure 1) peak soon after they emerge. For the elevated state to strongly affect the 1-hour window of Algorithm 1, it needs to be reached "enough time" before the hourly cutoff. Otherwise, Algorithm 1 will lack signal to declare it as trending, whereas the prediction-fed Algorithm 2 will likely succeed in doing so. Our simulations suggest that the tipping point is at about 20 minutes.

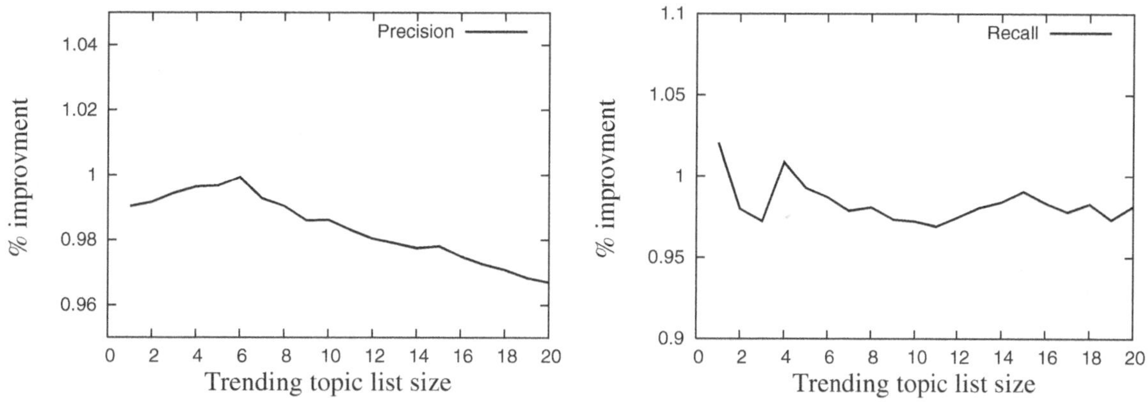

Figure 9: The effect of the trending searches output list size, k, on precision (left) and recall (right).

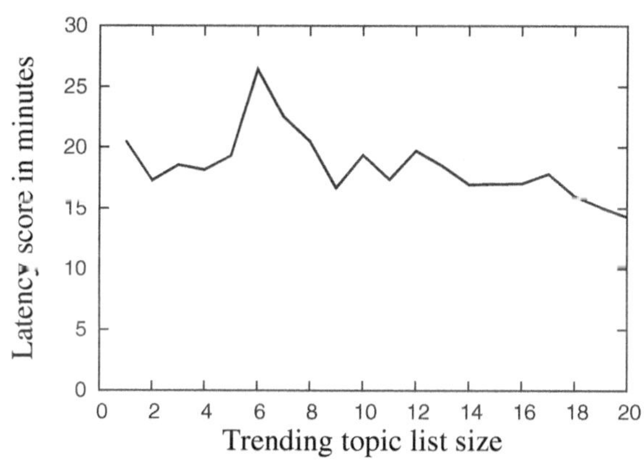

Figure 10: The effect of the trending searches output list size, k, on the latency gain.

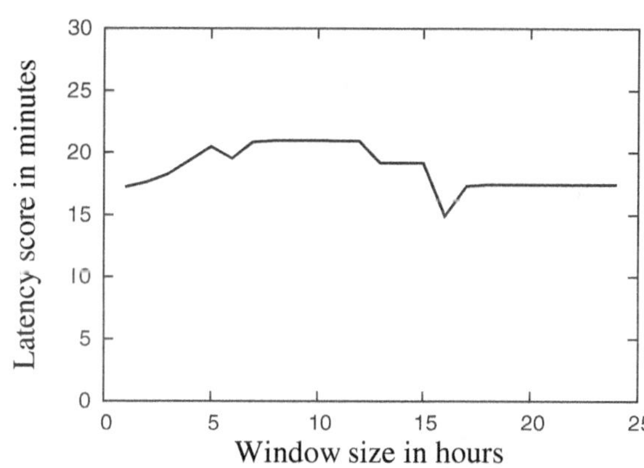

Figure 12: The effect of the window size, w (in hours), on latency, for $k = 10$.

Namely, once a query has been trending for more than 20 minutes, both algorithms are likely to declare it a trend.

Finally, we explore the effect of the window size w (See Section 4) for $k = 10$. Figure 11 demonstrates the relative value of P_{10}/R_{10} over the baseline value of P_{10}/R_{10}. Clearly when w grow so does the effective ground truth, and precision improves. Note that when $w = 4$, precision gets to 99% of its maximal value. The recall curve exhibits a linear increase, indicating that once a trend gets in the ground truth, it remains there for more than a day.

Figure 12 compares latency gains for $k = 10$, L_{10}, as a function of w. Clearly, the effect of w on the latency gain is negligible.

5.3 Discussion

When building query-based language models to detect trends, two seemingly conflicting requirements emerge. First, the language model must be based on "enough" queries so as to estimate query rates with low variance. Second, it must be based as much as possible on "fresh" traffic, in order to adapt to the rapid fluctuations in popularity exhibited by trends (low bias). The approach taken by Algorithm 1 is to consider 60 minutes' worth of query history as both "enough" and "fresh". An alternative perspective of what Algorithm 2 does is that it aggregates recent query submissions with varying weights, based on the time that has passed since their submission. Figure 7 shows the coefficients for a specific hour. The coefficient at $-i$ corresponds to the weight of a query submitted i minutes ago. Observe that the more recent the query is, the higher its weight. The weighting scheme is automatically learned from the data, and by observing the decay in the magnitude of the weights, one learns the length of query submission history that is relevant to near-future query rate prediction (the coefficients approach zero at -30). Next, since the predicted counts give rise to a language model, our scheme can be interpreted as giving recent queries a higher representation in the language model than less recent ones. In essence, we build a time-sensitive language model.

6. CONCLUSIONS

This paper devised a method for predicting query counts in order to detect search trends. We applied the search trend detection algorithm of Dong et al. [9] over predicted near-future query counts rather than over known recent-past count volumes. The main analytical tool in the prediction procedure was linear regression with tailored regularization for inducing two-dimensional temporal smoothness.

The prediction procedure was shown to be effective in approximately predicting high-volume, news-related query

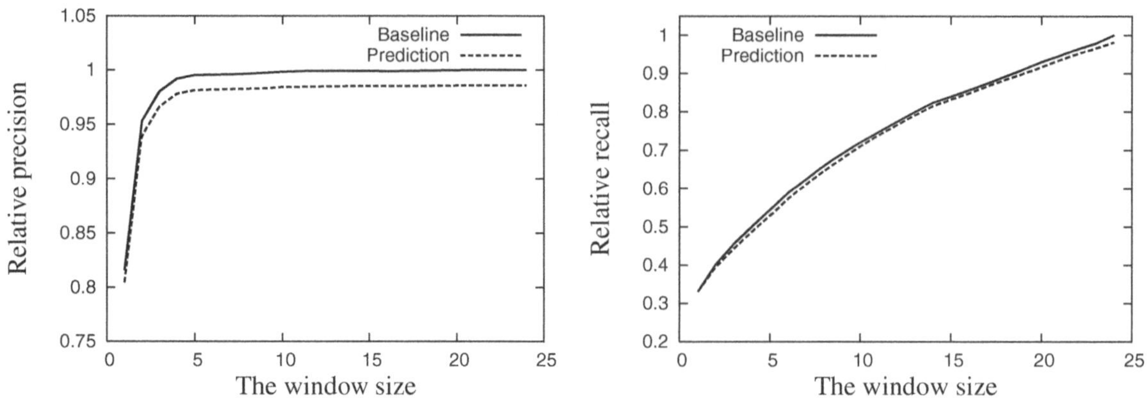

Figure 11: The effect of the window size, w (in hours), on precision (left) and recall (right), for $k = 10$.

counts. Subsequently, the detection algorithm of [9] combined with the prediction procedure was shown to reduce trend detection latency by about 20 minutes on average, while maintaining nearly the same precision and recall levels, as compared to detecting trends based on past counts. A main conclusion from this work is that the short term predictability of non-periodic (trending) query count volume allows reducing the latency of algorithms that rely on this signal.

In addition, an independent contribution of this work is in defining latency, precision and recall metrics for the evaluation of trend detection algorithms.

7. REFERENCES

[1] Z. Al-Bawab, G. H. Mills, and J.-F. Crespo. Finding trending local topics in search queries for personalization of a recommendation system. In *KDD*, 2012.

[2] Apache. *The Apache Hadoop Project.* http://wiki.apache.org/hadoop.

[3] A. C. Cameron and P. K. Trivedi. *Regression Analysis of Count Data.* Cambridge University Press, 1998.

[4] Z. Chen, H. Yang, J. Ma, and J. Lei. A novel ranking approach for periodic queries. *JICS*, 8(16):3973–3980, 2011.

[5] Z. Chen, H. Yang, J. Ma, J. Lei, and H. Gao. Time-based query classification and its application for page rank. *JICS*, 7(9):3149–3156, 2011.

[6] H. Choi and H. Varian. Predicting the Present with Google Trends. Technical report, Google, 2009.

[7] R. B. Cleveland, W. S. Cleveland, J. E. McRae, and I. Terpenning. Stl: A seasonal-trend decomposition procedure based on loess (with discussion). *Journal of Official Statistics*, 6:3–73, 1990.

[8] J. Dean and S. Ghemawat. Mapreduce: simplified data processing on large clusters. *Commun. ACM*, 51(1):107–113, 2008.

[9] A. Dong, Y. Chang, Z. Zheng, G. Mishne, J. Bai, R. Zhang, K. Buchner, C. Liao, and F. Diaz. Towards recency ranking in web search. In *WSDM*, pages 11–20, 2010.

[10] M. Efron. Linear time series models for term weighting in information retrieval. *JASIST*, 61(7):1299–1312, 2010.

[11] J. Ginsberg, M. H. Mohebbi, R. S. Patel, L. Brammer, M. S. Smolinski, and L. Brilliant. Detecting influenza epidemics using search engine query data. *Nature*, 457(7232):1012–1014, Nov. 2008.

[12] S. Goel, J. M. Hofman, S. Lahaie, D. M. Pennock, and D. J. Watts. Predicting consumer behavior with Web search. *Proceedings of the National Academy of Sciences*, 107(41):17486–17490, Oct. 2010.

[13] T. Hastie, R. Tibshirani, and J. Friedman. *The Elements of Statistical Learning: Data Mining, Inference, and Prediction.* Springer, corrected edition, Aug. 2003.

[14] A. T. Ihler, J. Hutchins, and P. Smyth. Learning to detect events with markov-modulated poisson processes. *TKDD*, 1(3), 2007.

[15] A. Kulkarni, J. Teevan, K. M. Svore, and S. T. Dumais. Understanding temporal query dynamics. In *WSDM*, pages 167–176, 2011.

[16] Y. Lee, H.-Y. Jung, W. Song, and J.-H. Lee. Mining the blogosphere for top news stories identification. In *SIGIR*, pages 395–402, 2010.

[17] C. Macdonald, I. Ounis, and I. Soboroff. Overview of the trec 2009 blog track. In *TREC*, 2009.

[18] C. D. Manning and H. Schütze. *Foundations of statistical natural language processing.* MIT Press, Cambridge, MA, USA, 1999.

[19] M. Mathioudakis and N. Koudas. Twittermonitor: trend detection over the twitter stream. In *SIGMOD Conference*, pages 1155–1158, 2010.

[20] Y. Shimshoni, N. Efron, and Y. Matias. *On the Predictability of Search Trends*, 2009.

[21] M. Shokouhi. Detecting seasonal queries by time-series analysis. In *Proceedings of the 34th international ACM SIGIR conference on Research and development in Information Retrieval*, SIGIR '11, pages 1171–1172, New York, NY, USA, 2011. ACM.

[22] M. Vlachos, C. Meek, Z. Vagena, and D. Gunopulos. Identifying similarities, periodicities and bursts for online search queries. In *SIGMOD Conference*, pages 131–142, 2004.

[23] R. Zhang, Y. Konda, A. Dong, P. Kolari, Y. Chang, and Z. Zheng. Learning recurrent event queries for web search. In *EMNLP*, pages 1129–1139, 2010.

News Recommendation via Hypergraph Learning: Encapsulation of User Behavior and News Content

Lei Li
School of Computing and Information Sciences
Florida International University
Miami, FL 33199
lli003@cs.fiu.edu

Tao Li
School of Computing and Information Sciences
Florida International University
Miami, FL 33199
taoli@cs.fiu.edu

ABSTRACT

Personalized news recommender systems have gained increasing attention in recent years. Within a news reading community, the implicit correlations among news readers, news articles, topics and named entities, e.g., what types of named entities in articles are preferred by users, and why users like the articles, could be valuable for building an effective news recommender. In this paper, we propose a novel news personalization framework by mining such correlations. We use hypergraph to model various high-order relations among different objects in news data, and formulate news recommendation as a ranking problem on fine-grained hypergraphs. In addition, by transductive inference, our proposed algorithm is capable of effectively handling the so-called *cold-start* problem. Extensive experiments on a data set collected from various news websites have demonstrated the effectiveness of our proposed algorithm.

Categories and Subject Descriptors: H.3.3[Information Search and Retrieval]: Information filtering

General Terms: Algorithms, Design, Experimentation

Keywords: Personalization, News Recommendation, Hypergraph Learning, Named Entity, Transductive Inference

1. INTRODUCTION

Common research efforts in personalized news recommendation can be divided into two categories: (1)modeling user profiles by analyzing news content in users' consumption history and then retrieving relevant news articles for recommendation (content filtering); and (2)analyzing reading behaviors of users similar to the target user and then recommending items based on the collaborative activities (collaborative filtering). Many hybrid methods, which integrate the above two categories of algorithms, have also been developed. Despite extensive recent advances, several critical issues in news recommendation have not been well explored in previous studies, including *user profiling* (i.e., how to obtain high-quality user profiles from historical consumptions of users?), *news evolving* (i.e., how to recommend news items that are newly published and without enough accessing activities?) and *user cold-start* (i.e., how to provide reasonable recommendation for new users?) [21].

A key step in news recommender systems is to build the readers' preference profiles based on their historical consumption, i.e., the reading history. Traditionally, user profiling is conducted by extracting representative elements (e.g., words or phrases) from the reading history or selecting similar access patterns. However, users' historical consumption may contain a gigantic amount of element correlations, e.g., a group of users like the same topic, which cannot be well captured by the aforementioned profiling paradigms.

Further, online readers tend to prefer some named entities in news articles, e.g., when the event happened, where it happened, who were involved, etc. These types of entities can attract online readers' interest since they contain concise information about the news article itself. Therefore, named entities would be valuable to model users' preferences. However, few research efforts have been reported on utilizing named entities for user profiling. In [12] and [20], named entities extracted from news articles are represented as an entity vector, and then the similarity based on such a vector is calculated for retrieving relevant news items. Such a representation might cause the information loss of news access data, e.g., what type of entities is preferred by a group of users, and therefore render user profiling less effective.

In our work, to address the aforementioned issues, we propose a novel news personalization algorithm by mining the implicit relations among users, news articles, topics and named entities. Motivated by [5], we use a unified hypergraph to model multi-type objects and implicit relations in news reading community. A hypergraph is a generalization of the ordinary graph, in which the edges, called *hyperedges*, are arbitrary non-empty subsets of the vertex set [4]. However, due to the special properties of news articles (e.g., textual content, implicit relation and short shelf life), a straightforward extension of hypergraph modeling on music community cannot be directly applied to news recommendation. Instead, we first partition the hypergraph into multiple fine-grained ones, and further model personalized news recommendation as a ranking problem on fine-grained hypergraphs to recommend news articles.

To the best of our knowledge, our work is the *first journey towards modeling implicit high-order correlations in news reading community via hypergraph*, by considering the special properties of news articles and online readers' behaviors. The contribution of this paper is three-fold:

WSDM'13, February 4–8, 2013, Rome, Italy.

- *A hypergraph representation of news reading community.* We explore implicit correlations among readers, articles, topics and named entities, and represent these relations as a unified hypergraph, by which a user's reading behavior can be well captured (cf. §3.2).
- *A principled framework for news selection.* We partition the hypergraph into fine-grained ones, and then model the recommendation problem as a local selection problem on sub-hypergraphs, instead of global selection on the entire hypergraph (cf. §4.1 and §4.2).
- *A novel strategy for solving "cold-start".* We embrace new users into a specific sub-hypergraph, and then resolve *cold-start* using transductive inference on the hypergraph (cf. §4.3).

Roadmap: §2 presents a brief summary of prior work relevant to personalized news recommendation and hypergraph learning. In §3, we introduce the data model used in our work and formalize the problem. In §4, we discuss how to perform ranking and transductive inference on the hypergraph. Extensive experimental results are reported in §5, and finally §6 concludes the paper.

2. RELATED WORK

2.1 Content-based Methods

Content-based news recommenders construct user profiles based on news content, and recommend for users news articles similar to user profiles in content-wise [10, 12, 22]. The computational representation of news content is the cornerstone of content-based recommenders. In practice, news content is often represented by vector space model or topic models that are widely used in text mining. To calculate the relevance between news items and user profiles, different affinity measurements might be applied, depending on specific strategies of news recommenders. For example, Newsjunkie [12] filters news stories by formal measures of information novelty to custom-tailor newsfeeds based on a user's reading history. [10] tries to obtain users' reading interests from multiple news channels. However, it might be insufficient to simply represent users' profiles by a bag of words for capturing the reading preference of users [20].

2.2 Collaborative filtering

Collaborative filtering based news recommenders model users profiles by analyzing feedbacks of news readers, e.g., click on news articles, and then recommend news based on similar users' behaviors. Therefore, these news recommenders are content-free [9]. Collaborative filtering can be roughly categorized into two groups: memory-based methods [25, 26] (i.e., neighborhood-based recommendation) and model-based approaches [14, 24] (i.e., latent factor based recommendation). Collaborative filtering assumes that the overlap historical consumptions between users exist; however, with the rapid change of both news repository and user repository, it suffers from the well-known *cold-start* problem [27], which renders collaborative filtering less effective.

2.3 Hybrid Approaches

To remedy the inability of both content filtering and collaborative filtering, many researchers investigate the feasibility of combining these two types of methods, and propose hybrid solutions to news recommendation. Representative examples include [6, 7]. Another extensively studied direction in recommendation community is hybrid filtering, which is similar to the problem in our work. Several recently published methods include [2, 3, 17]. However, most hybrid filtering methods either focus on analyzing explicit ratings in the data, or assume that demographic and other auxiliary information of users are available. Although it is possible to incorporate user behaviors into these methods, they still suffer from the difficulty of comprehensively capsuling high-order relations within news reading community.

2.4 Hypergraph Learning

In machine learning problem settings, a typical representation of data is hypergraph, by which the information loss issue resulted from pairwise relationship among objects can be effectively remedied. Hypergraph can help resolve general learning problems, e.g., clustering [13], classification [28, 30] and embedding [34]. Hypergraph learning has been explored in various machine learning areas, such as gene expression classification [16, 29], image retrieval [11, 15, 31], document analysis [18], etc.

Our work is essentially a graph-based hybrid recommendation approach. In [1], social interactions, e.g., comments by news readers, are modeled as a graph and news articles are filtered based on the content and interactions. However, their model failed to consider the implicit relations among news readers, news articles and named entities, which are essential for news recommendation.

What differentiates our work from prior methods is that we model personalized news recommendation as a hypergraph learning paradigm by integrating all implicit correlations among users, news items, topics and named entities into a unified hypergraph, and then recommending news articles via a hypergraph ranking algorithm. The way that we encapsule the data into a hypergraph is similar to [5], in which a music recommendation algorithm is proposed by considering the integration of multiple kinds of social media information and music acoustic-based content. However, the intrinsic characteristics of news recommendation render it different from music recommendation. The differences between these two tasks are summarized as follows:

- Content-wise: News content is composed of words, prone to be associated with topics, whereas music content consists of acoustic features, which are difficult to interpret and understand;
- Evolutionary: News community evolves much faster than music community due to the instantaneity of news articles, i.e., news articles have short shelf life;
- Relation-wise: The relations within news community are mostly implicit, while music community has multiple explicit relations.

Given these differences, the derived hypergraph from a news reading community would be much more complex than the one from a music sharing community. Simply applying the work in [5] to news recommendation might suffer the scalability issue. Therefore, we propose to first partition the hypergraph into more fine-grained ones. Further, our proposed method has the capability of effectively handling the *cold-start* problem in recommendation scenario.

3. DATA MODEL AND PROBLEM STATEMENT

In this section we start by introducing our data model of news reading community and some basic notations, and then we formally state our exploration problem.

3.1 Preliminaries

We follow the definitions in [5, 34] to describe hypergraph preliminaries. We denote $\mathbb{G}(V, E, w)$ as a hypergraph, where V is a finite set of vertices, E is a family of hyperedges on V, and w is a weight function, $w : E \rightarrow \mathbb{R}$. Each hyperedge $e \in E$ contains a list of vertices that belong to V. The degree of a hyperedge e is defined by $\delta(e) = |e|$, i.e., the number of vertices in e. The degree $d(v)$ of a vertex v is defined by $d(v) = \sum_{v \in e} w(e)$, where $w(e)$ is the weight of the hyperedge e. We say that there is a *hyperpath* between vertices v_1 and v_k if there is an alternative sequence of distinct vertices and hyperedges $v_1, e_1, v_2, e_2, \cdots, e_{k-1}, v_k$, such that $\{v_i, v_{i+1}\} \subseteq e_i$ for $1 \le i \le k-1$. We formulate a vertex-hyperedge incidence matrix $\mathbf{H} \in \mathbb{R}^{|V| \times |E|}$ in which each entry $h(v, e)$ is 1 if $v \in e$ and 0 otherwise. Then we have $d(v) = \sum_{e \in E} w(e)h(v, e)$, and $\delta(e) = \sum_{v \in V} h(v, e)$. Let $\mathbf{D}_v$ and $\mathbf{D}_e$ denote the diagonal matrices containing the vertex and hyperedge degrees respectively, and $\mathbf{W}$ the diagonal matrix $|E| \times |E|$ containing the weights of hyperedges.

3.2 Data Model

In news reading community, multiple types of resources are often available for analysis, including users, news articles, representative terms, named entities, etc. Let $\mathbb{U}$ denote the user pool, and $\mathbb{N}$ denote the set of news articles, both of which are the major elements being considered in recommender systems. Further, let $\mathbb{T}^t$ denote the representative terms, or say, topics, and $\mathbb{T}^e$ be the set of named entities involved in the entire news corpus. Notice that in reality, the pools of these four types of resources would be enlarged as there are always news events happening everyday with different topic categories and distinct named entities. In our data model, we name these resources as *Media Objects*. To facilitate the reading, we list some notations in Table 1.

Table 1: Notations in our data model.

$\mathbb{U}$	the user set.	u_i	a particular user.
$\mathbb{N}$	the article set.	n_i	a particular article.
$\mathbb{T}^t$	the topic set.	t_k^t	the k-th topic.
$\mathbb{T}^e$	the entity set.	t_k^e	the k-th entity.

n_i^k	the k nearest neighbors of an article i.
α	the importance factor of content similarities.
E^{UNT^t}	the set of user-article-topic hyperedges.
E^{UNT^e}	the set of user-article-entity hyperedges.
E^{UUN}	the set of user-user-article hyperedges.
E^{UUT^t}	the set of user-user-topic hyperedges.
E^{UUT^e}	the set of user-user-entity hyperedges.
E^{NNT^t}	the set of article-article-topic hyperedges.
E^{NNT^e}	the set of article-article-entity hyperedges.
E^{N^k}	the set of k-nearest-articles hyperedges.

Besides, several relations among objects are implicitly embedded among *media objects*. For example, two users $u_1, u_2 \in \mathbb{U}$ are the fans of NBA star *LeBron James* ($t_i^e \in \mathbb{T}^e$), which is a named entity appearing in news articles of sports event ($t_j^t \in \mathbb{T}^t$). Then there is an implicit relation among these media objects. In our data model, we formalize a hypergraph $\mathbb{G}$ that contains 7 different implicit relations with different objects[1] and 1 implicit relation that considers the similarity graph of news articles:

- E^{UNT^t}: A user reads a news article that describes an event, or a topic. Typically we assign the weight of this hyperedge to be 1. Here we assume that a user would only navigate a news item once.

- E^{UNT^e}: A user reads a news article that embraces a named entity. Similar to E^{UNT^t}, we assign the hyperedge weight as 1.

- E^{UUN}: Two users might read the same news article. We assign the hyperedge weight to be 1.

- E^{UUT^t}: Two users might read news articles with the same topic. The weight $w(e^{u_i u_j t_k^t})$ for this relation is set to be the frequency that both users, u_i and u_j, read articles with the same topic t_k^t, i.e.,

$$w(e^{u_i u_j t_k^t}) = |\{(u_i, u_j, t_k^t)|u_i \in \mathbb{U}, u_j \in \mathbb{U}, t_k^t \in \mathbb{T}^t\}|. \tag{1}$$

We normalize the weight as

$$w(e^{u_i u_j t_k^t}) = \frac{w(e^{u_i u_j t_k^t})}{\sqrt{\sum_{l=1}^{|\mathbb{T}|} w(e^{u_l u_j t_k^t})}\sqrt{\sum_{m=1}^{|\mathbb{U}|} w(e^{u_i u_m t_k^t})}}. \tag{2}$$

The above heuristic normalization aims to penalize the abnormal news readers with dense reading activities. Moreover, in order to treat different types of relations equally, we further normalize the weight as follows:

$$w(e^{u_i u_j t_k^t}) = \frac{w(e^{u_i u_j t_k^t})}{ave(w(e^{u_i u_j \mathbb{T}^t}))}, \tag{3}$$

where $ave(w(e^{u_i u_j \mathbb{T}^t}))$ is the average of normalized weights for users u_i and u_j on different topics.

- E^{UUT^e}: Two users might read news articles containing the same named entity. The weight $w(e^{u_i u_j t_k^e})$ for this relation is set to be the frequency that both users, u_i and u_j, read articles containing the same entity t_k^e. The weight normalization is similar to Eq.(2) and Eq.(3).

- E^{NNT^t}: Two news articles might describe the same or similar topic. We assign the hyperedge weight as 1.

- E^{NNT^e}: Two news articles might contain the same entity. We assign the hyperedge weight to be 1.

- E^{N^k}: In our data model, we also consider the similarity of news articles. We construct a k nearest neighbor (k-NN) news graph based on content-based item similarities. In the hypergraph, a hyperedge of this type is composed of the top k articles similar to the target news item and the target item itself. The weight

[1]It is natural that the edges can be generalized from a pairwise co-occurrence, e.g., an edge incident on a news item and all of its readers. However, the generated incidence matrix would become much denser. For simplicity, we only consider the hyperedges with three vertices. Our algorithm can be extend to hyperedges with arbitrary number of vertices.

$w(e^{n_i^k})$ is the averaged similarity between the target news item and the ones similar to the target, i.e.,

$$w(e^{n_i^k}) = \frac{1}{k}\sum_{j=1}^{k} sim(n_i, n_j), \quad (4)$$

where $sim(n_i, n_j)$ is the similarity between two news articles. In our work, this similarity is calculated using the cosine similarity by considering the content features of news items. We introduce a parameter α to control the relative importance of content-based similarities in the unified hypergraph model. Then, the hyperedge weight is given by

$$w(e^{n_i^k}) = \alpha * w(e^{n_i^k}). \quad (5)$$

Finally, the unified hypergraph of news reading community is composed of 4 types of media objects as vertices and 8 types of object relations as hyperedges. Figure 1 summarizes the aforementioned media objects and relations. By employing the unified hypergraph model, we can effectively capture the high-order relations among various types of media objects without loss of any important information.

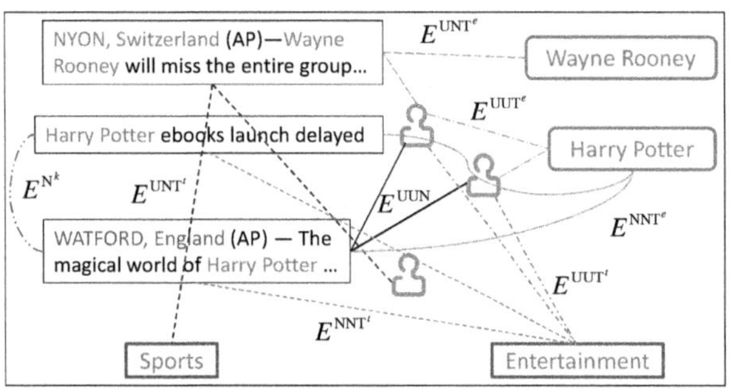

Figure 1: An illustrative example of data model in news reading community.

Based on the data model introduced above, we can derive the vertex-hyperedge incidence matrix **H** (as described in Table 2) and also the weight matrix **W**. The size of both matrices depends on the cardinality of different element sets involved in the matrices, and they are all sparse matrices.

3.3 Problem Statement

In this subsection, we first define the problem of personalized news recommendation, and then analyze the major technical issues for resolving the problem.

PROBLEM (Personalized News Recommendation): *Given a collection of newly-published news articles $\mathcal{N}$ and a target online reader u, recommend a list of news items $\mathcal{S}$ that maximally match u's reading preference.*

It is straightforward to observe that the success of personalized news recommendation depends on two critical subproblems: user profiling and news personalization. The former aims at capturing online users' reading preference, whereas the latter tries to select news items to be optimally consistent to user's preference.

To facilitate user profiling, we define a concept of *news capsule* as follows:

DEFINITION 1. *(News Capsule). A news capsule, $\mathcal{C} = (V^{\mathcal{C}}, E^{\mathcal{C}}, w^{\mathcal{C}})$, is a subset of a given hypergraph $\mathbb{G} = (V, E, w)$, where $V^{\mathcal{C}} = \{U, N, T^t, T^e\} \subset V = \{\mathbb{U}, \mathbb{N}, \mathbb{T}^t, \mathbb{T}^e\}$, i.e., $U \subset \mathbb{U}, N \subset \mathbb{N}, T^t \subset \mathbb{T}^t, T^e \subset \mathbb{T}^e$, and $E^{\mathcal{C}} \subset E$, $w^{\mathcal{C}} \subset w$.*

A capsule $\mathcal{C}$ is said to be *compact* iff $\forall u \in U$, u's reading preference is maximally captured in $\mathcal{C}$. To evaluate how well u's preference is captured, we formalize another definition.

DEFINITION 2. *(Maximality). Given a user u and a news capsule $\mathcal{C}$ that u belongs to, u's reading preference is said to be maximally captured in $\mathcal{C}$ iff most hyperedges that embrace u are within $\mathcal{C}$.*

Then the first technical problem of user profiling in our setting can be defined as follows:

SUBPROBLEM 1 (User Profiling): *Given a hypergraph $\mathbb{G}$ consisting of multiple media objects ($\mathbb{U}, \mathbb{N}, \mathbb{T}^t$ and $\mathbb{T}^e$) associated with a series of object relations (see § 3.2), model users' profiles $\mathbb{P}$ to capture users' reading preferences by news capsules, such that in each news capsule, the maximality is satisfied.*

The well-captured user profiles serve as the basis of personalized news recommendation. We discuss our solution to this subproblem in § 4.1.

Given a collection of newly-published news articles and a target online user's profile, our goal is to recommend to this user a list of news articles that satisfy the user's reading appetite. We expect that by a recommendation list, the user's preference is optimally matched, and also the news list is diverse enough so that the user would not get bored when he/she is navigating news articles.

DEFINITION 3. *(Optimally Matchable). Given a news list l recommended to a user u and u's profile p, l is said to be optimally matchable to u's reading preference only if there is no other list l′ by which the similarity between l′ and p is larger than the one between l and p.*

DEFINITION 4. *(Diversity). Given a news list l recommended to a user u, l is said to be diverse if it matches all of u's different reading interests. A user's reading interest can be categorized by the topics and named entities in the consumption history.*

We now formally define our second problem of selecting a list of news articles from newly-published news collection to maximally match an online user's reading preference.

SUBPROBLEM 2 (News Personalization): *Given a collection of newly-published news articles $\mathcal{S}$ and a user's profile p, select a subset $\mathcal{S}^*$ from $\mathcal{S}$ where $\mathcal{S}^*$ is optimally matchable to p and the diversity of $\mathcal{S}^*$ is maximized, where the diversity denotes distinct topics and named entities in p.*

The essence of personalized news recommendation is well captured in the above problem formation. We discuss our personalization solution in § 4.2.

In reality, with various subjective factors involved in news recommendation, the optimality of both **SUBPROBLEM1** and **SUBPROBLEM2** is difficult to achieve. Many existing news recommenders try to approximately resolve both problems based on certain evaluation criteria. In our work, we employ hypergraph learning to tackle these problems.

4. RECOMMENDATION METHODOLOGY

In this section, we discuss how to approximately address the aforementioned problems via hypergraph learning. The

Table 2: The incidence matrix $\mathbf{H}$ of the unified hypergraph.

	$E^{\mathbb{UNT}^t}$	$E^{\mathbb{UNT}^e}$	$E^{\mathbb{UUN}}$	$E^{\mathbb{UUT}^t}$	$E^{\mathbb{UUT}^e}$	$E^{\mathbb{NNT}^t}$	$E^{\mathbb{NNT}^e}$	$E^{\mathbb{N}^k}$
$\mathbb{U}$	$\mathbb{U}E^{\mathbb{UNT}^t}$	$\mathbb{U}E^{\mathbb{UNT}^e}$	$\mathbb{U}E^{\mathbb{UUN}}$	$\mathbb{U}E^{\mathbb{UUT}^t}$	$\mathbb{U}E^{\mathbb{UUT}^e}$	$\mathbf{0}$	$\mathbf{0}$	$\mathbf{0}$
$\mathbb{N}$	$\mathbb{N}E^{\mathbb{UNT}^t}$	$\mathbb{N}E^{\mathbb{UNT}^e}$	$\mathbb{N}E^{\mathbb{UUN}}$	$\mathbf{0}$	$\mathbf{0}$	$\mathbb{N}E^{\mathbb{NNT}^t}$	$\mathbb{N}E^{\mathbb{NNT}^e}$	$\mathbb{N}E^{\mathbb{N}^k}$
$\mathbb{T}^t$	$\mathbb{T}^tE^{\mathbb{UNT}^t}$	$\mathbf{0}$	$\mathbf{0}$	$\mathbb{T}^tE^{\mathbb{UUT}^t}$	$\mathbf{0}$	$\mathbb{T}^tE^{\mathbb{NNT}^t}$	$\mathbf{0}$	$\mathbf{0}$
$\mathbb{T}^e$	$\mathbf{0}$	$\mathbb{T}^eE^{\mathbb{UNT}^e}$	$\mathbf{0}$	$\mathbf{0}$	$\mathbb{T}^eE^{\mathbb{UUT}^e}$	$\mathbf{0}$	$\mathbb{T}^eE^{\mathbb{NNT}^e}$	$\mathbf{0}$

unified hypergraph defined in § 3.2 is used to model the high-order relations among different types of media objects in news reading community. In order to effectively capture online users' reading preference, we propose to initially partition the entire hypergraph into multiple *news capsules*, by which users' reading behaviors can be stored. Given newly-published news articles, we integrate relevant articles into the capsule that embraces the user, and then perform ranking on this specific news capsule. In this way, we are capable of providing instant news recommendation.

4.1 News Hypergraph Partition

Recall from § 3.3 that a news capsule is a subset of a given hypergraph. We follow the definitions in [34] to describe the hypergraph partition. For a vertex subset $S \subset V$, let S^c denote the complement of S. A hyperedge e is said to be a cut if it is incident with both S and S^c simultaneously. We further denote the *hyperedge boundary* ∂S of S be a hyperedge set consisting of multiple cuts, i.e., $\partial S := \{e \in E | e \cap S \neq \emptyset, e \cap S^c \neq \emptyset\}$, and define the *volume* vol$S$ of S to be the sum of degrees of the vertices in S, i.e., vol$S := \sum_{v \in S} d(v)$. Moreover, we denote the volume of ∂S by

$$vol\, \partial S := \sum_{e \in \partial S} w(e) \frac{|e \cap S||e \cap S^c|}{\delta(e)}. \tag{6}$$

We then formalize the hypergraph partition as

$$\arg\min_{\emptyset \neq S \subset V} \text{Ncut}(S) := vol \partial S (\frac{1}{vol S} + \frac{1}{vol S^c}), \tag{7}$$

which is similar to the normalized cut on ordinary graphs. In this paper, we will not focus on how to resolve the hypergraph partitioning problem. To automatically generate hypergraph partitions (news capsules) with compact representations, we employ the method introduced in [34]. It generalizes a methodology of spectral clustering originally operating on undirected graphs to hypergraphs, which is essentially suitable to the problem setting in our work. We partition the news hypergraph into m disjoint news capsules where m is predefined.

Discussion: The hypergraph built upon a news reading community could be very large. Directly performing graph inference on such a hypergraph would be inefficient. By partitioning the graph into multiple subgraphs, the inference will be performed on a smaller scale, which can improve the efficiency to a great extent. In our work, we employ "cut" to partition the graph, which can be viewed as a hard clustering scheme. Other clustering methods can be applied to our problem setting, e.g., soft clustering that can generate overlapping news capsules. However, this is not our main focus, and therefore we leave it to our future work.

A practical issue suffered by the hypergraph partitioning in our problem setting would be the imbalanced user distribution over different capsules. This issue could be caused by the imbalanced distribution of different types of edges. For example, the edges between news and topics can be much denser than the edges between news and users, and as a result, some capsules might contain very few users, or even no users at all. It is trivial to resolve this issue by considering some constrains (e.g., do not "cut" on user-inside edges) when partitioning the hypergraph.

The partition paradigm is based on not only topical categories, but also the reading behaviors of users, involving the preferences on topics and named entities. In each capsule $\mathcal{C}$, $\forall u \in U$, the *maximality* defined in § 3.3 is suboptimally satisfied based on the partition paradigm. One may argue that a per-user capsule would be more suitable to satisfy the *maximality*; however, such a capsule cannot be used for graph inference.

4.2 News Recommendation via Ranking

Hypergraph partitioning provides us a list of disjoint news capsules, in which the users' reading preferences are encapsulated, including topics, named entities and similar users. In the following, we present our approach in which we model the recommendation as a sub-hypergraph ranking problem.

Formally, given a capsule (or a sub-hypergraph) $\mathcal{C}$, a set of newly-published news articles $\mathcal{S}$ and a target user u within $\mathcal{C}$, we first link articles in $\mathcal{S}$ onto $\mathcal{C}$. To do so, we extract topics and named entities from $\mathcal{S}$ and then compare these objects with the objects in $\mathcal{C}$. In this way, we can not only connect new articles to $\mathcal{C}$, but also add new objects into $\mathcal{C}$. Next, we reconstruct the unified hypergraph based on the enriched $\mathcal{C}$ and get the vertex-hyperedge incidence matrix $\mathbf{H}^{\mathcal{C}}$ and the weight matrix $\mathbf{W}^{\mathcal{C}}$. Since the scale of $\mathcal{C}$ is supposed to be much smaller than the entire hypergraph, the reconstruction would be more efficient. Then the vertex degree matrix $\mathbf{D}_v^{\mathcal{C}}$ and the hyperedge degree matrix $\mathbf{D}_e^{\mathcal{C}}$ are computed based on $\mathbf{H}^{\mathcal{C}}$ and $\mathbf{W}^{\mathcal{C}}$. In the following, we discuss how to perform ranking on a sub-hypergraph by using similar idea of [5].

We define the cost function of $\mathbf{f}$ as follows:

$$Q(\mathbf{f}) = \frac{1}{2} \sum_{i,j=1}^{|V|} \sum_{e \in E} \frac{1}{\delta(e)} \sum_{\{v_i, v_j\} \subseteq e} w(e) \left\| \frac{f_i}{\sqrt{d(v_i)}} - \frac{f_j}{\sqrt{d(v_j)}} \right\|^2 + \mu \sum_{i=1}^{|V|} ||f_i - y_i||^2, \tag{8}$$

where $\mu > 0$ is the regularization factor. To achieve the optimal ranking result, we need to minimize $Q(\mathbf{f})$:

$$\mathbf{f}^* = \arg\min_{\mathbf{f}} Q(\mathbf{f}). \tag{9}$$

For inference, we need to smooth the process as much as possible under the constraint that vertices that are contained by many common hyperedges should have similar ranking scores. As an illustrative example, if two news articles have been accessed by many common users, then both articles will have similar ranking scores. The smoothness can be achieved by minimizing the first term in Eq.(8). We also need to minimize the difference between the obtained ranking scores and the pre-given scores to guarantee that the result will not deviate much from the truth, i.e., to minimize the second term in Eq.(8). After a series of mathematical derivation by [5], we can obtain the optimal $\mathbf{f}^*$ as

$$\mathbf{f}^* = (\mathbf{I} - \gamma \mathbf{A})^{-1}\mathbf{y}, \tag{10}$$

where $\mathbf{A} = (\mathbf{D}_v^{\mathcal{C}})^{-1/2}\mathbf{H}^{\mathcal{C}}\mathbf{W}^{\mathcal{C}}(\mathbf{D}_e^{\mathcal{C}})^{-1}(\mathbf{H}^{\mathcal{C}})^T(\mathbf{D}_v^{\mathcal{C}})^{-1/2}$. Notice that under the constraint of $\mathcal{C}$, the matrix $\mathbf{I} - \gamma\mathbf{A}$ is highly sparse, and therefore the inverse of $\mathbf{I} - \gamma\mathbf{A}$ can be efficiently calculated. $\mathbf{y}$ corresponds a query vector given a user, each entry of which can be either 1 or 0, indicating what topics and entities are preferred by the user. After performing ranking on the sub-hypergraph, we can choose top ranked news articles as the recommendation list.

Discussion: An interesting setup to approximately satisfy the *diversity* requirement defined in § 3.3 is to predefine query scores over different topics $\mathbb{T}^t$ and named entities $\mathbb{T}^e$ within the profile of the target user. Specifically, we can analyze the user's profile and choose the topics and named entities that are ranked high in terms of the accumulated score of the edge weights. For these topics and named entities, the corresponding values in $\mathbf{y}$ can be set to 1 for the query purpose, whereas for other topics and named entities, the values can be set to 0. For example, given a user q with preference over the topic "Basketball" and the named entity "LeBron James", we can specify 1 value for the corresponding two entries in $\mathbf{y}_q$. In addition, we can set 1 value for entries that are related to the user's preference, e.g., "NBA" and "Competitive Sports", which can be obtained using some simple text mining techiniques. In this way, the ranking result can have more diverse content in terms of topics and named entities that are distributed over the target user's profile and related preferences. Therefore the setup of the query vector $\mathbf{y}$ fosters the diversity in the results.

4.3 Transductive Inference on Hypergraph

Our proposed framework is capable of handling the so-called *cold-start* problem, especially for new users. In this subsection, we introduce the strategy of how we can tackle the user cold-start problem. Given a new user q without enough reading history, traditional recommender systems fail to construct a comprehensive user profile due to the data sparsity. Comparatively in our framework, we initially embrace this new user q into a specific capsule (by extracting topics and named entities of the limited consumption history of q and linking them to the capsule). Taking q into the construction of the query vector $\mathbf{y}$, we perform transductive inference on the new capsule to derive the vertices related to q's preference, and finally provide the recommendation list for q.

Specifically, given a news capsule $\mathcal{C} = (V^{\mathcal{C}}, E^{\mathcal{C}}, w^{\mathcal{C}})$, in which the vertices in a subset $S \subset V^{\mathcal{C}}$ have labels in $L = \{1, -1\}$ predefined by the new user q according to q's reading history, our goal is to predict the labels of the remaining unlabeled vertices. Note that for news recommendation, the labels $\{1, -1\}$ indicate whether the user is interested in the corresponding element or not. On the one hand, the inference function should be as *smooth* as possible, i.e., we should assign the same label to all vertices contained in the same hyperedge; moreover, vertices lying on a densely linked sub-hypergraph are likely to have the same label. Thus we define a function

$$\Omega(\mathbf{f}) = \frac{1}{2}\sum_{e\in E}\sum_{\{u,v\}\subseteq e}\frac{w(e)}{\delta(e)}\left\|\frac{f(u)}{\sqrt{d(u)}} - \frac{f(v)}{\sqrt{d(v)}}\right\|^2, \tag{11}$$

which sums the weighted variation of a function on each edge of the capsule. On the other hand, the initial label assignment should be changed as little as possible. Let $\mathbf{y}$ denote the initial label vector, in which the assignments are defined by $y(v) = 1$ or -1 if vertex v has been labeled as positive or negative respectively, and 0 if it is unlabeled. Then we consider the following optimization problem [33]

$$\arg\min_{\mathbf{f}\in\mathbb{R}^{|V|}}\{\Omega(\mathbf{f}) + \mu||\mathbf{f} - \mathbf{y}||^2\}, \tag{12}$$

where $\mu > 0$ is the parameter specifying the tradeoff between the two components. The optimization problem defined in Eq.(12) is similar to the one in Eq.(8). The difference here is that for transudctive inference, our goal is to derive the labels of the unlabeled vertices, whereas for ranking, we try to derive the complete importance order of the vertices. Due to the space limit, we omit the detailed procedure for sovling Eq.(12). In this way, even if a user does not have enough reading history, we can still get enough labeled news items that the user might prefer. Hereby, for new users, we can recommend a list of unordered news articles.

5. EMPIRICAL EVALUATION

In this section, we provide a comprehensive experimental evaluation to show the effectiveness of our proposed hypergraph-based news recommendation algorithm (*Hyper* for short).

5.1 Real-World Data Collection

The data used in our experiment is obtained from multiple news reading portals, ranging from Aug 15th, 2010 to Nov 16th, 2010 [20], which includes news articles and users' access histories. It contains 10 news topic categories, such as sports, movies, politics, etc. We preprocess the data by removing news articles that are rarely accessed (i.e., the accessed frequency is less than 1 per day) and by storing users with frequent online reading behaviors (i.e., users who read news articles everyday and read more than 1 piece of news each day). By preprocessing, some unexpected noise can be removed to ensure the quality of the generated hypergraph. We perform LDA on news articles to extract representative words from each news category, as the topics of the data model[2]. For named entities, we use NLP tools, e.g., GATE [8], to perform information extraction. The media objects and relations contained in this data collection are summarized in Table 3(a) and 3(b), respectively. Note that the number of nearest neighbors, k, in the news similarity graph is not fixed, and therefore the number of hyperedges varies for $E^{\mathbb{N}^k}$.

5.2 Experiments

In this subsection, we first consider the effect of different factors in our unified news hypergraph on the recommendation performance, i.e., by constructing the hypergraph using different combinations of hyperedges; We then investigate

[2]Here each "topic" is represented as a bag of words when constructing the unified hypergraph.

Table 3: Statistics of our news collection.

(a) Objects

Elements	Count
Users	3,280
Articles	58,873
Topics	10
Entities	121,617

(b) Relations

Relations	Count	Relations	Count
E^{UNT^t}	501,239	E^{UUT^e}	402,918
E^{UNT^e}	672,348	E^{NNT^t}	52,136
E^{UUN}	307,652	E^{NNT^e}	176,431
E^{UUT^t}	43,785	E^{N^k}	-

the performance of local selection (selecting articles in specific news capsules) and global selection (selecting articles on the entire hypergraph); Further, we demonstrate the superiority of the transductive inference on news capsules in handling the user *cold-start* problem; We also provide comprehensive comparisons with existing and recently published approaches related to news recommendation.

5.2.1 Evaluation Setup

For evaluation purpose, we divide the entire news data into two disjoint sets, where the first one ranges from Aug 15th, 2010 to Nov 6th, 2010, regarded as the training set, and the remaining falls into the testing set. The training set is used to construct the unified hypergraph, whereas the testing set is regarded as the ground truth for recommendation evaluation. For each user in the testing set, we recommend news items (top@10, top@20 and top@30[3]) to the user at each day of the testing range. For comparison, we compute the averaged F1-score over multiple users and multiple days. We also use Normalized Discount Cumulative Gain (NDCG) to measure the ranking quality of the recommended list based on a user's actual accessing sequence. NDCG at position n is defined as

$$NDCG@n = N(n) \times \sum_{i=1}^{n} \frac{2^{r_i} - 1}{\log_2(i+1)}, \qquad (13)$$

where $N(n)$ is the NDCG at n of the ideal ranking list, and r_i is the relevance rating of item at rank i. In our scenario, $r_i = 1$ if the user has read the recommended news article and 0 otherwise.

5.2.2 Construction of Hypergraph

In our proposed data model, we integrate 8 different hyperedges or object relations into the construction of news hypergraph. Such a hypergraph provides an elegant representation of the news data, encapsulating multiple correlations among different media objects. To evaluate the effect of such a representation in personalized news recommendation, we consider different combinations of hyperedges for hypergraph construction: (1) E^{N^k} (NK): consider news similarities based on users' profiles, which is essentially a content-based method; (2) E^{UUN} (UN): construct the hypergraph using only users' co-visit information, which can be regarded as an example of collaborative filtering; (3) E^{UNT^t}, E^{UUT^t} and E^{NNT^t} (UNT): build hypergraph by considering the topics in news collection and users' access patterns in a hybrid way; and (4) E^{UNT^e}, E^{UUT^e}, E^{NNT^e} (UNE): construct the hypergraph using the entity information, i.e., considering users' preference on specific named entities. We compare the metrics introduced in § 5.2.1, and the results are shown in Figure 2, in which Figure 2(a) demonstrates the performance difference of multiple hypergraph constructions in terms of F1-score, whereas Figure 2(b) shows the ranking performance in terms of NDCG.

[3]The "top@x" means the top ranked x news items being recommended to the user.

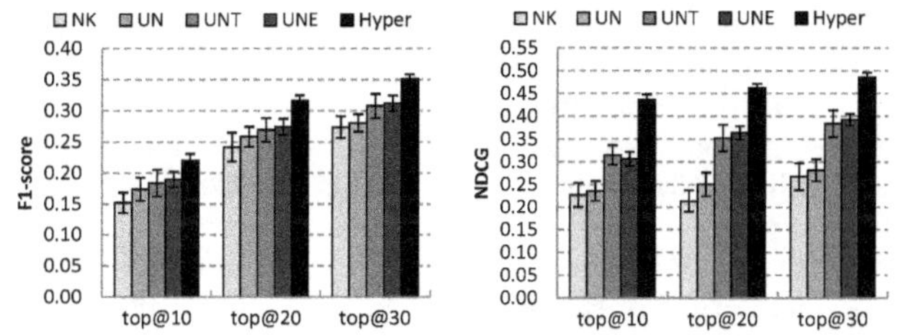

(a) F1-score comparison. (b) NDCG comparison

Figure 2: Performance comparison of different hypergraph constructions.

It is evident that the unified hypergraph model significantly outperforms other constructions of hypergraph from both accuracy and ranking perspective. The reason behind this is straightforward: in our unified model, high-order correlations among different media objects are well-captured, which extensively enrich a user's reading preference and hence make the recommended result more accurate. Besides this, we observe that: (i) The performance of hybrid constructions (i.e., UNT and UNE) is better than uni-edge construction (i.e., NK and UN); and (ii) the result of UNE is comparable with UNT, which means that in real-world news recommender systems, users pay equal or more attention on named entities they prefer, not just the topics that news articles are reporting.

5.2.3 Local Selection V.S. Global Selection

To recommend news articles to a target user, our approach first partitions the entire hypergraph into multiple news capsules, and then locates the capsule that the user belongs to for further recommendation. Such a paradigm can not only expedite the recommendation (since we only consider partial hypergraph), but also improve the accuracy of the recommendation because the information in a news capsule is more specialized than the one in a global perspective. To validate this claim, we choose different values for m (the number of capsules defined in § 4.1) and compare the recommendation results with the one using the entire hypergraph (Global, for short). Figure 3 depicts the comparison.

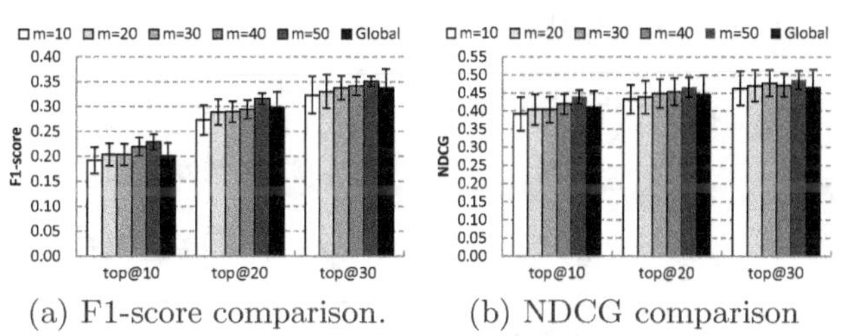

(a) F1-score comparison. (b) NDCG comparison

Figure 3: Performance comparison of local selection with different number of capsules and global selection.

With different m, the performance of our approach varies. *Hyper* achieves the optimal performance when $m = 50$, which is not compatible with the number of topics. By partitioning the entire hypergraph into more capsules, the information within each capsule is more specialized, and therefore a user's reading interest can be modeled in a more fine-grained level. Compared with the global selection, $Hyper_{m=50}$ performs better in terms of both F1-score and NDCG.

We are also interested in the performance details of local selection and global selection. Therefore, for $Hyper_{m=50}$ and global selection, we randomly select 100 users to provide recommendations for them, and then plot the precision and recall pair for each user on top@10, top@20 and top@30 news items recommended to these user. Figure 4 shows the resulted plot. As observed in Figure 4, besides the higher recommendation precision and recall, the performance distribution of *Hyper* is more dense than the one of the global selection, which demonstrates the stability of our proposed local selection strategy.

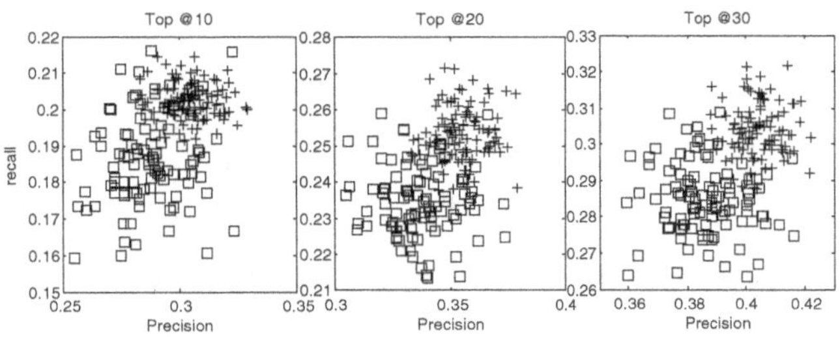

Figure 4: Precision-recall plot for local selection with $m = 50$ and global selection. Remark: "□" denotes users using the global selection strategy; and "+" represents users using the local selection strategy.

5.2.4 Parameter Tuning

In our algorithm, there are several parameters for tuning, i.e., the number of the nearest neighbor k in Eq.(4), the control parameter α in Eq.(5), the regularization factor γ in Eq.(10) and μ in Eq.(12).

Both k and α are related to $E^{\mathbb{N}^k}$ in the data model. To explore the effect of the parameters k and α (the influence of hyperedges relevant to news content similarity), we use F1-score as the evaluation metric. Figure 5 shows the results. We first empirically fix $\alpha = 0.2$ and evaluate the changing of k. Figure 5(a) shows the F1-score measured as a function of k. The optimal value for k is obtained when $k = 70$. We then fix k and evaluate the changing of α. Figure 5(b) shows the F1-score measured as a function of α. The best result is obtained when $\alpha = 0.2$.

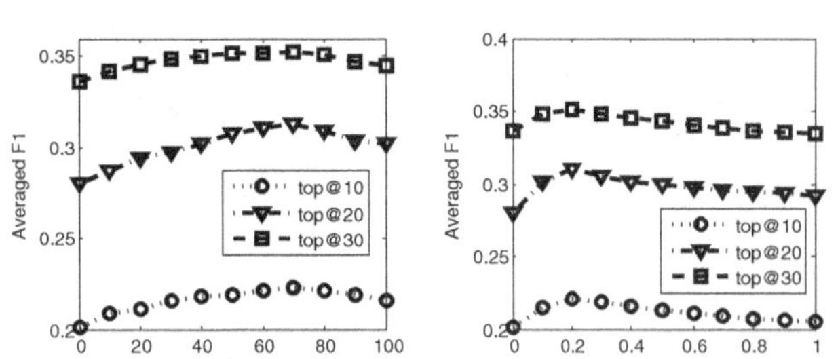

(a) $\alpha = 0.2$ (b) $k = 70$

Figure 5: Parameter Tuning.

The parameters γ and μ are common factors in many hypergraph learning methods. In our experiment, we empirically set γ as 0.9 and μ as 0.1.

5.2.5 Comparison with Other Methods

We also implement several recently published methods: Goo [9], ClickB [23], Bilinear [7], Bandit [19], fLDA [3], and SCENE [20] for comparison. The details of these algorithms are described as follows:

- Goo: The method is essentially a collaborative filtering approach, in which MinHash clustering, PLSI and covisitation counts are taken into account for a unified recommendation paradigm.
- ClickB: In this approach, the profiles of user's news interests are built based on their past click behavior, and then a Bayesian framework for predicting users' current news interests.
- Bilinear: This method maintains profiles of content of interest based on temporal characteristics of the content, e.g., popularity and freshness, and also maintains profiles of users including historical activities. The recommendation is achieved via a feature-based machine learning approach.
- Bandit: The method models recommendation as a contextual bandit problem, in which a learning algorithm sequentially selects articles to serve users based on contextual information about users and articles, while simultaneously adapting its selection strategy based on user-click feedback.
- fLDA: The method regularizes both user and item factors simultaneously through user features and the bag of words associated with each item. It is essentially a hybrid filtering method.
- SCENE: The method assumes the interestingness of news articles with respect to a user could be regressive, and uses the "submodularity" property to model the news selection problem.

Note that the parameters of these baseline methods are optimally tuned in our experiment to ensure the fair comparison. We use F1-score and NDCG to compare these baselines with *Hyper*. The results are shown in Figure 6(a) and 6(b). It is evident that our proposed method significantly outperforms other candidates on both metrics. The results of fLDA and SCENE are comparable to ours. In fLDA, each word in an item is associated with a discrete latent factor often referred to as the topic of the word; item topics are obtained by averaging topics across all words in an item. Therefore, fLDA considers more fine-grained granularity of topics, and consequently obtains reasonable recommendation results. SCENE explicitly takes into account the "submodularity" within users' reading behaviors for recommendation. As we observe, the performance of Goo and ClickB is relatively poor. This is because the recommended lists of both methods are heavily determined by users' co-visiting histories; however, the news data used in the experiments contains a great portion of relatively new users[4], i.e., users

[4]In our dataset, the number of new users is around 400, compared with the total number of users, 3,280.

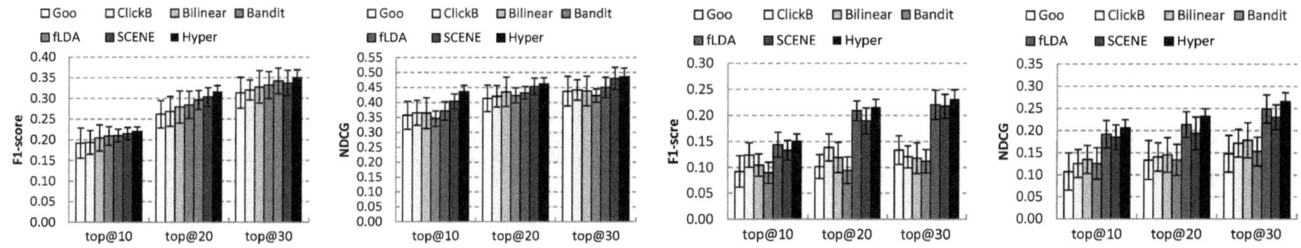

(a) F1-score comparison. (b) NDCG comparison (c) F1-score comparison. (d) NDCG comparison

Figure 6: Performance comparison for regular recommendation and cold-start user recommendation. Remark: (a) and (b) are comparisons of different algorithms on averaged metrics; (c) and (d) are comparisons of different algorithms for the *cold-start* problem of new users.

who read less than 5 news articles per day. Hence, the *cold-start* problem of new users in the dataset causes the poor performance of both methods.

5.2.6 Handling Cold-start

In traditional recommendation methods, the *cold-start* problem cannot be well handled due to the data sparsity. To resolve it, we perform transductive inference on the unified news capsule for new users. The intuition is straightforward: we borrow the concept of inference by utilizing a small set of labeled data to infer the labels of unlabeled data on the hypergraph. Notice that in such a case, we do not focus on the ranking of news articles, but pay more attention on the interestedness of items, i.e., whether the items are preferred by the user or not.

Specifically, we randomly choose 100 users who read news articles less than 5 per day, and then recommend news articles (top@10, top@20 and top@30) for these users. For evaluation purpose, we compare our method with Goo, ClickB, Bilinear, Bandit, fLDA and SCENE. Figure 6(c) and 6(d) shows the comparison results. As shown in Figure 6(c), the *cold-start* problem can be elegantly alleviated by using our proposed method, *Hyper*. The explanation is straightforward: in *Hyper*, we explicitly model the recommendation for new users as transductive inference on a specified news capsule, and meanwhile we consider high-order correlations among different media objects, which significantly complement the data sparsity of new users when performing recommendation. In Figure 6(d) we also observe that although we do not intentionally take the ranking into account, our method surprisingly outperforms the others in terms of NDCG. The reason is that we can provide more news articles in the recommendation list that match a user's reading interest, and thus the quality of ranking is improved consequently. The result of fLDA on cold-start handling is comparable to our performance. For cold-start users, fLDA gives more weight to the prior mean (predicted by user and/or item features) in estimating the factor, and therefore selects news items that are quite relevant to the prior.

5.2.7 Diversity Evaluation

The recommended news list provided by our algorithm shows a great diversity on topic aspects. Such diversity is originated from the sparkle of the query vector **y** designed in § 4.2, by which we can not only specify the target user, but also provide topics and named entities that the user prefers. To evaluate how diverse our recommendation result is, we compare the set diversity [32] among the results of our method and other recommender systems. The set diversity is defined as the *average dissimilarity* of all pairs of news items in the resulted list. Specifically, given a news set $\mathcal{S}$, the *average dissimilarity* of $\mathcal{S}$, $f_d(\mathcal{S})$, is defined as

$$f_d(\mathcal{S}) = \frac{2}{p(p-1)} \sum_{s_i \in \mathcal{S}} \sum_{s_j \in \mathcal{S}, s_j \neq s_i} (1 - sim(s_i, s_j)), \quad (14)$$

where $|\mathcal{S}| = p$, and the dissimilarity of a news pair is $1 - sim(s_i, s_j)$, in which $sim(s_i, s_j)$ denotes the content similarity between the news item s_i and s_j, and it is calculated using the cosine similarity.

For diversity evaluation, we choose the aforementioned methods (Goo, ClickB, Bilinear, Bandit, fLDA and SCENE) as our comparison baselines. We employ the experiment setup similar to the previous section, and then compare the diversities of recommended lists with different cardinalities (top@10, top@20 and top@30). Table 4 shows the averaged diversity for 100 randomly selected users.

Table 4: Diversity evaluation on the result list. (**Bold** indicates the best performance. * indicates the statistical significance at $p < 0.01$ w.r.t. the randomness of selected users.)

Methods	top@10	top@20	top@30
Goo	0.4101	0.3074	0.1105
ClickB	0.4329	0.3128	0.1562
Bilinear	0.4234	0.2517	0.0933
Bandit	0.5056	0.4126	0.2925
fLDA	0.4726	0.3981	0.2705
SCENE	**0.6537***	0.5771	0.4859
Ours	0.6323	**0.5987***	**0.5072***

From the result, we observe that (i) The diversity decreases as the recommended news list enlarges. It is straightforward that when more news articles are selected, the topic distribution of the news list becomes closer to the user's reading interest, and therefore the selected news items are more similar. (ii) The diversity of the recommendation list provided by the baseline methods drops dramatically as the list size increases, since they did not take the diversity into account. (iii) Our proposed method outperforms the others very significantly, except SCENE. SCENE explicitly selects different news items solely from topic-wise for recommendation, and hence the diversity of the result from SCENE is higher more or less. In our work, we consider the interest of news readers by specifying different topics and named entities in the query vector **y**. The diversity decreases very smoothly when we recommend more news items to individual users, compared with other rivals.

6. CONCLUDING REMARKS

In this paper, we propose to use hypergraph learning methods to deal with the issues existed in news recommenders. We first represent news data as a unified hypergraph, in which various correlations among different media objects are integrated into an information capsule. We then decompose the recommendation problem as two subproblems: partitioning and ranking, where the former aims to separate the entire hypergraph into multiple groups, or subcapsules, and the latter is designed to select a list of news articles from a specific capsule and recommend them to a target user (the user is regarded as a query).

In our proposed data model, we simplify the profiling problem by only analyzing a user's reading history (as the profile) without accessing any other auxiliary information. In reality, a news reader might have other information, e.g., demographics, locations, and other social and behavioral patterns. We believe such information can be easily incorporated into our proposed framework, e.g., by encapsuling the user relations within close locations or the same social community into the data model. In our future work, we plan to delve into extending our framework along this direction. In addition, although we intentionally partition the hypergraph into multiple small ones to expedite the procedure, the scalability of our proposed framework is not quite satisfactory. We plan to use distributed environment, e.g. Hadoop, to accelerate the partitioning and recommendation procedure in our future work.

ACKNOWLEDGEMENTS

We thank the reviewers for their valuable comments. The work is supported in part by NSF grants IIS-0546280, DBI-0850203, CCF-0939179, HRD-0833093 and CNS-1126619.

7. REFERENCES

[1] B. Adams, D. Phung, and S. Venkatesh. Social reader: following social networks in the wilds of the blogosphere. In *Proc. of 1st SIGMM workshop on Social media*, pages 73–80. ACM, 2009.

[2] D. Agarwal and B.C. Chen. Regression-based latent factor models. In *Proc. of SIGKDD*, pages 19–28. ACM, 2009.

[3] D. Agarwal and B.C. Chen. flda: matrix factorization through latent dirichlet allocation. In *Proc. of WSDM*, pages 91–100. ACM, 2010.

[4] S. Agarwal, K. Branson, and S. Belongie. Higher order learning with graphs. In *Proc. of ICML*, pages 17–24. ACM, 2006.

[5] J. Bu, S. Tan, C. Chen, C. Wang, H. Wu, L. Zhang, and X. He. Music recommendation by unified hypergraph: Combining social media information and music content. In *Proc. of ACM MM*, pages 391–400. ACM, 2010.

[6] R. Burke. Hybrid systems for personalized recommendations. *Intelligent Techniques for Web Personalization*, pages 133–152, 2005.

[7] W. Chu and S.T. Park. Personalized recommendation on dynamic content using predictive bilinear models. In *Proc. of WWW*, pages 691–700. ACM, 2009.

[8] D.H. Cunningham, D.D. Maynard, D.K. Bontcheva, and M.V. Tablan. GATE: A framework and graphical development environment for robust NLP tools and applications. In *Proc. of ACL*, 2002.

[9] A.S. Das, M. Datar, A. Garg, and S. Rajaram. Google news personalization: scalable online collaborative filtering. In *Proc. of WWW*, pages 271–280. ACM, 2007.

[10] R. Di Massa, M. Montagnuolo, and A. Messina. Implicit news recommendation based on user interest models and multimodal content analysis. In *Proc. of AIEMPro*, pages 33–38. ACM, 2010.

[11] L. Ding and A. Yilmaz. Image segmentation as learning on hypergraphs. In *Proc. of ICMLA*, pages 247–252, 2008.

[12] E. Gabrilovich, S. Dumais, and E. Horvitz. Newsjunkie: providing personalized newsfeeds via analysis of information novelty. In *Proc. of WWW*, pages 482–490. ACM, 2004.

[13] K. George and K. Vipin. Multilevel k-way hypergraph partitioning. *VLSI Design*, 11(3):285–300, 2000.

[14] T. Hofmann. Latent semantic models for collaborative filtering. *ACM Transactions on Information Systems*, 22(1):89–115, 2004.

[15] Y. Huang, Q. Liu, S. Zhang, and D.N. Metaxas. Image retrieval via probabilistic hypergraph ranking. In *Proc. of CVPR*, pages 3376–3383. IEEE.

[16] T.H. Hwang, Z. Tian, R. Kuangy, and J.P. Kocher. Learning on weighted hypergraphs to integrate protein interactions and gene expressions for cancer outcome prediction. In *Proc. of ICDM*, pages 293–302. IEEE, 2008.

[17] A. Karatzoglou, X. Amatriain, L. Baltrunas, and N. Oliver. Multiverse recommendation: n-dimensional tensor factorization for context-aware collaborative filtering. In *Proc. of RecSys*, pages 79–86. ACM, 2010.

[18] D. Li and S. Li. Hypergraph-based inductive learning for generating implicit key phrases. In *Proc. of WWW*, pages 77–78. ACM, 2011.

[19] L. Li, W. Chu, J. Langford, and R.E. Schapire. A contextual-bandit approach to personalized news article recommendation. In *Proc. of WWW*, pages 661–670. ACM, 2010.

[20] L. Li, D. Wang, T. Li, D. Knox, and B. Padmanabhan. Scene: a scalable two-stage personalized news recommendation system. In *Proc. of SIGIR*, pages 125–134. ACM, 2011.

[21] L. Li, D.D. Wang, S.Z. Zhu, and T. Li. Personalized news recommendation: a review and an experimental investigation. *Journal of Computer Science and Technology*, 26(5):754–766, 2011.

[22] L. Li, L. Zheng, and T. Li. Logo: a long-short user interest integration in personalized news recommendation. In *Proc. of RecSys*, pages 317–320. ACM, 2011.

[23] J. Liu, P. Dolan, and E.R. Pedersen. Personalized news recommendation based on click behavior. In *Proc. of IUI*, pages 31–40. ACM, 2010.

[24] D.M. Pennock, E. Horvitz, S. Lawrence, and C.L. Giles. Collaborative filtering by personality diagnosis: A hybrid memory- and model-based approach. In *Proc. of UAI*, pages 473–480, 2000.

[25] P. Resnick, N. Iacovou, M. Suchak, P. Bergstrom, and J. Riedl. GroupLens: an open architecture for collaborative filtering of netnews. In *Proc. of CSCW*, pages 175–186. ACM, 1994.

[26] B. Sarwar, G. Karypis, J. Konstan, and J. Reidl. Item-based collaborative filtering recommendation algorithms. In *Proc. of WWW*, pages 285–295. ACM, 2001.

[27] A.I. Schein, A. Popescul, L.H. Ungar, and D.M. Pennock. Methods and metrics for cold-start recommendations. In *Proc. of SIGIR*, pages 253–260. ACM, 2002.

[28] L. Sun, S. Ji, and J. Ye. Hypergraph spectral learning for multi-label classification. In *Proc. of SIGKDD*, pages 668–676. ACM, 2008.

[29] Z. Tian, T.H. Hwang, and R. Kuang. A hypergraph-based learning algorithm for classifying gene expression and arraycgh data with prior knowledge. *Bioinformatics*, 25(21):2831, 2009.

[30] G. Wachman and R. Khardon. Learning from interpretations: a rooted kernel for ordered hypergraphs. In *Proc. of ICML*, pages 943–950. ACM, 2007.

[31] F. Wu, Y.H. Han, and Y.T. Zhuang. Multiple hypergraph clustering of web images by miningword2image correlations. *Journal of Computer Science and Technology*, 25(4):750–760, 2010.

[32] M. Zhang and N. Hurley. Avoiding monotony: improving the diversity of recommendation lists. In *Proc. of RecSys*, pages 123–130. ACM, 2008.

[33] D. Zhou, J. Huang, and B. Scholkopf. Beyond pairwise classification and clustering using hypergraphs. Technical report, 2005.

[34] D. Zhou, J. Huang, and B. Scholkopf. Learning with hypergraphs: Clustering, classification, and embedding. *Advances in Neural Information Processing Systems*, 19:1601, 2007.

Group Sparse Topical Coding: From Code to Topic

Lu Bai Jiafeng Guo Yanyan Lan Xueqi Cheng
Institute of Computing Technology, Chinese Academy of Sciences, Beijing, China
{bailu, guojiafeng}@software.ict.ac.cn, {lanyanyan, cxq}@ict.ac.cn

ABSTRACT

Learning low dimensional representations of text corpora is critical in many content analysis and data mining applications. It is even more desired and challenging to learn a sparse representation in practice for large scale text modeling. However, traditional probabilistic topic models (PTM) lack a mechanism to directly control the posterior sparsity of the inferred representations; While the emerged non-probabilistic models (NPM) can explicitly control sparsity using sparse constraint like ℓ_1 norm, they convey different limitations in latent representations. To address the existing problems, we propose a novel non-probabilistic topic model for discovering sparse latent representations of large text corpora, referred as *group sparse topical coding* (GSTC). Our model enjoys both the merits of the PTMs and NPMs. On one hand, GSTC can naturally derive document-level admixture proportions in topic simplex like PTMs, which is useful for semantic analysis, classification or retrieval. On the other hand, GSTC can directly control the sparsity of the inferred representations with *group lasso* by relaxing the normalization constraint. Moreover, the relaxed non-probabilistic GSTC can be effectively learned using coordinate descent method. Experimental results on benchmark datasets show that GSTC can discover meaningful compact latent representations of documents, and improve the document classification accuracy and time efficiency.

Categories and Subject Descriptors

H.4.m [**Information Systems Applications**]: Miscellaneous; I.2.7 [**Natural Language Processing**]: Text analysis

General Terms

Algorithms, Experimentation, Performance, Theory

Keywords

Document Representation, Topic Model, Sparse Coding, Group Lasso

WSDM'13, February 4–8, 2013, Rome, Italy.

1. INTRODUCTION

With huge repositories of text data emerged over Web, learning low dimensional representations that captures latent semantics of the data becomes critical for efficiently processing many basic tasks such as classification, clustering, and information retrieval. It is even more desired and challenging to learn a sparse representation in practice for large scale text modeling [27, 31]. For example, it is very often that there are hundreds or thousands of topics within hundreds of millions of documents, while each document or word has only a few salient topical meanings or senses [27, 31]. Such a phenomenon is even more typical in large collections of short text data, like instant messages or tweets. By explicitly learning a sparse representation, we may better discover the salient semantic meanings of a document or word. Moreover, sparse representations have obvious computational benefits, by saving both processing time and storage space [38].

In Recent years, probabilistic topic models (PTM) such as probabilistic latent semantic indexing (PLSI) [16] and latent dirichlet allocation (LDA) [5] have gained remarkable success in text topical modeling. In these models, a document is typically modeled as a finite admixture of latent topics where each topic is a unigram distribution over a given vocabulary. The document-level admixture proportions can be regarded as a low dimensional representation of the document in the topic simplex. However, traditional PTMs lack a mechanism to directly control the posterior sparsity of the inferred representations, since the admixture proportions or topics are normalized distributions. Some attempts have been made to achieve sparsity in PTMs by introducing sparse priors [5] or using posterior regularizations [14, 27]. These methods often cannot yield truly sparse posterior representations due to indirect sparsity bias or the smoothness of the regularizer.

Meanwhile, the emerged non-probabilistic models (NPM) such as matrix factorization [20, 9] and sparse coding [23, 40], provide an elegant way to achieve sparsity by using sparse constraint like ℓ_1 norm [29] or other composite regularizer [33, 30] on the usually unnormalized latent representations. However, while getting the benefits from using the unnormalized latent representations, NPMs lose the clear semantic explanations over the latent representations. That is, the learned document-level latent representations no longer lie on the same topic simplex like PTMs, but could be in quite different scales over different documents. This will lead to difficulty in semantic comparison between documents, and in using the latent representations as robust features for future tasks (e.g., text classification) as shown in our work. Although post-normalization could be conducted over the latent representations of an entire document, the resulted normalized representations no longer represent the admixture proportions.

To address the above problems, we propose a novel non-probabilistic topic model that can discover sparse latent representation (or admixture proportions) of the document, referred as *group sparse topical coding* (GSTC). In our model, each individual word count is consisted of a set of latent word counts, where each latent word count is generated from a Poisson distribution. Thus, we can *reconstruct* the individual word count from a linear combination of topic bases, where the coefficient vectors (i.e. codes) are unnormalized, and the topic bases are unigram distributions over a given vocabulary. We impose group lasso [38] over the unnormalized word codes to achieve the sparsity of the document-level latent representations. The admixture proportion of an entire document can be derived from the learned word codes and topic bases.

Our model enjoys both the merits of the PTMs and NPMs as follows: 1) by using Poisson distribution, GSTC can naturally derive document-level admixture proportions in topic simplex like PTMs; 2) as a non-probabilistic model, GSTC can directly control the sparsity of inferred representations by taking into account the structure of bag of words with group lasso; 3) by relaxing the normalization constraint of admixture proportions, GSTC can be effectively learned using coordinate descent method. All these nice properties make GSTC an appealing alternative formulation of topic models.

We conducted empirical experiments on benchmark datasets and compared GSTC with the state-of-the-art PTMs (i.e. LDA)and NPMs (i.e. NMF and STC). The experimental results show that GSTC can identify sparse and salient topical representations over documents. Moreover, the experiments demonstrate that with the compact representations of documents learned by GSTC, we can largely improve the document classification accuracy and obtain better time efficiency.

2. RELATED WORK

In this section, we will introduce some recent related work on probabilistic topic models, non-probabilistic topic models and sparse techniques.

2.1 Probabilistic Topic Models

Due to the theoretical soundness and explicit interpretation, probabilistic topic models(PTMs) has been widely used for data analysis in various applications such as such as information retrieval [34], network analysis [1], and recommender systems [32]. PTMs provide a clear probabilistic interpretation of the generative process of data. PTMs such as Probabilistic Latent Semantic Analysis (PLSA) and Latent Dirichlet Allocation (LDA) have shown impressive empirical success in practise through the discovery of low-rank hidden structure. Typically, both PLSA and LDA posit that each document is an admixture of latent topics where each topic is a unigram distribution over the terms in a vocabulary. There are quite a lot of work extending these basic probabilistic models by incorporating the auxiliary knowledge as constraints or priors. Cai et al. [7] proposed the Laplacian pLSI(LapPLSI) by incorporating the manifold structure information to smooth the probabilistic density functions. Blei et al. [4] adopted the logistic normal distribution, a more flexible distribution for modeling covariance structure among components, to generate the documents.

However, how to achieve sparsity is a non-trivial problem for PTMs. The major reason lies in the fact that the admixture proportions and topics are normalized distributions in PTMs, leading to the failure of directly applying a sparsity inducing ℓ_1 regularizer as in lasso [29]. Although some alternative methods have been proposed to control sparsity in PTMs , these sparse-biased PTMs are not good in either effects or efficiency. For example, using a weak Dirichlet prior [5] may indirectly introduce some sparse bias over posterior representations. However, the sparsity is mostly resulted from the scarcity of document content and the control of sparsity in this way is very limited. Selecting subset of topics to construct documents is another common strategy [35, 31]. Usually a binomial prior is employed to decide which topics to be selected. Although these models are good in interpretation, the learning might be quite unstable. The major reason lies in the discrete generative process - topic components are either reserved or dropped from models. In this way, small changes in data or parameters can result in very different models. What is more, the optimization for these models is often hard to solve [39, 24]. Some studies tried to directly impose posterior regularizations [14, 27], which often do not obtain truly sparse posterior representations in practice due to the smoothness of the regularizer (e.g., entropic regularizer).

2.2 Non-Probabilistic Topic Models

As an alternative, NPMs such as sparse coding [23] and matrix factorization [20] provide an elegant framework to achieve sparsity. With usually unnormalized code vector or dictionary, NPMs can directly control the sparsity with ℓ_1 norm or other composite regularizer [41, 30]. However, while getting the benefits from the unnormalized codes, NPMs lose the clear semantic explanations over the latent representations of documents. For example, most sparse coding methods [3, 18] only learn flat representations (i.e. the code at word level). One may take post-processing like average or max pooling [36] to achieve representations at document level, but the meaning of the averaged code vector is not clear. Although sparse topical coding (STC) [40] learns a hierarchical topical representations, the document codes (truncated averaging from the word codes) still lacks the semantic interpretation. Besides, matrix factorization methods (e.g. NMF [20] and LSI [9]) learn the latent representations of documents, which are usually unnormalized or even non-positive. (e.g. RLSI [33]). Mapping such learned representations to a topic simplex is not a trivial task. Unlike the existing methods, GSTC is a novel non-probabilistic topic model that can discover sparse admixture proportions of documents.

2.3 Sparse Techniques

The lasso [29] is a widely applied technique to produce sparse model by penalizing the loss function with a ℓ_1 norm. Increasing the ℓ_1 penalty will make more parameters be drawn to zeros instead of reducing all parameters simultaneously as the ℓ_2 norm does. Furthermore, in contrast with the ℓ_0 norm, the ℓ_1 norm is obviously convex. Therefore, the resulting optimization will be convex when the loss function is convex, which can be effectively solved by a variety of optimization algorithms [21, 11]. Actually, lasso can recover the sparse supports of a sparse model from data when the covariates of the model are not too related. Elastic net, a new regularization of the lasso, was further proposed by Zou et al. [41] for an unknown group of variables and for multicollinear predictors. It can be taken as a stabilized version of the lasso, which enjoys a sparse representation and encourages group effects.

However, the lasso lacks a mechanism to contain any prior information about the variables, e.g. some groups of variables should be picked jointly. Some efforts have been made to enforce the estimated models maintain the special sparsity patterns. Especially, group lasso [38] extends the lasso by making the correlated variables selected jointly rather than individual variables. It achieves this by applying a mixed ℓ_1/ℓ_2 norm (the sum (ℓ_1 norm) of the ℓ_2 norms) over different groups of variables. In this way, the predefined sparse pattern is preserved by selecting the group of variables with ℓ_2 norm[37]. Apparently, the group lasso constraint is still convexity, which is a desirable property for developing an efficient algorithm to solve the optimization problem. Other variants of the group lasso are applied in selecting covariates in multi-task learning and enforcing the hierarchical selection of covariates, e.g. covariates are located in a hierarchical structure and one variable is selected if and only if its ancestors are selected as well. Recently, this ℓ_1/ℓ_2 norm for group lasso has been extended to model a more general settings where the groups can be overlapped and nested [17].

3. GROUP SPARSE TOPICAL CODING

GSTC aims to discover document-level sparse latent representation (or admixture proportion) for large scale text corpora, which can be regarded as a sparse representation of the document in the topic simplex. Suppose we are given a collection of documents $\boldsymbol{D}$ with size M, containing words from a vocabulary $\boldsymbol{V}$ with size N. A document is simply represented as a $|I|$-dimension vector $\boldsymbol{d} = \{w_1, ..., w_{|I|}\}$, where $\boldsymbol{I}$ is the index set of words that appear and the n-th entry w_n ($n \in \boldsymbol{I}$) denotes the number of appearances of the specific word in this document. Let $\boldsymbol{\beta} \in \mathbb{R}^{K\times N}$ be a dictionary with K bases, where each base is assumed to be a topic base, i.e. a unigram distribution over $\boldsymbol{V}$. For a given document $\boldsymbol{d}$, GSTC projects $\boldsymbol{d}$ into a semantic space spanned by a set of automatically learned topic bases $\boldsymbol{\beta}$ and directly obtain the unnormalized word code $\boldsymbol{s}_{d,n\cdot} \in \mathbb{R}^K$ for each individual word in document $\boldsymbol{d}$. For simplicity, we use $\boldsymbol{s}_{n\cdot}$ to describe the word code in current document. The admixture proportion of the entire document $\boldsymbol{d}$ can then be derived from the learned word code set $\boldsymbol{s} = \{\boldsymbol{s}_{1\cdot}, ..., \boldsymbol{s}_{|I|\cdot}\}$ and the topic bases $\boldsymbol{\beta}$. To better understand the proposed GSTC model, we start with describing a probabilistic generative procedure.

3.1 Probabilistic Generative Process for GSTC

The basic idea of GSTC is that the appearances of each individual word in a document come from a set of latent topics, where each topic is characterized by a distribution over words. The graphical representation of GSTC is depicted in Figure 1. We first sample a dictionary $\boldsymbol{\beta}$ from a prior distribution (e.g. uniform distribution in this work) on a $(N-1)$-simplex. Then, each document $\boldsymbol{d}$ in a collection $\boldsymbol{D}$ is assumed to be generated by the following process:

1. For each topic $k \in \{1, \dots, K\}$:

   Sample a word code vector $\boldsymbol{s}_{\cdot k} \in \mathbb{R}^N \sim$ M-Laplace(λ).

2. For each observed word $n \in \boldsymbol{I}$:

   For each topic $k \in \{1, \dots, K\}$:

   Sample a latent word count $w_{nk} \sim$ Poisson($s_{nk}\boldsymbol{\beta}_{kn}$).

3. Obtain the word count $w_n = \sum_{k=1}^{K} w_{nk}$.

Several simplifying assumptions are made in our model. We assume that for each document the observed word counts are independent given their latent representations $\boldsymbol{s}$ [40]. We also assume that the latent word counts of a given word over different topics are independent given its latent representation $\boldsymbol{s}$. In the above generative process, the word code vectors under each topic are first generated from a Multi-Laplacian distribution, which is defined as:

$$\text{M-Laplace}(\boldsymbol{s}|0, \lambda^{-1}) \propto \lambda^{N/2} \exp(-\lambda \parallel \boldsymbol{s} \parallel_2). \quad (1)$$

For each individual word appeared in the document, the observed word count w_n is obtained by aggregating the latent word counts over different topics, where each latent word count is generated from a Poisson distribution, that is defined as

$$\text{Poisson}(w_{nk}|s_{nk}\beta_{kn}) \propto (s_{nk}\boldsymbol{\beta}_{kn})^{w_n}(e^{-s_{nk}\beta_{kn}}) \quad (2)$$

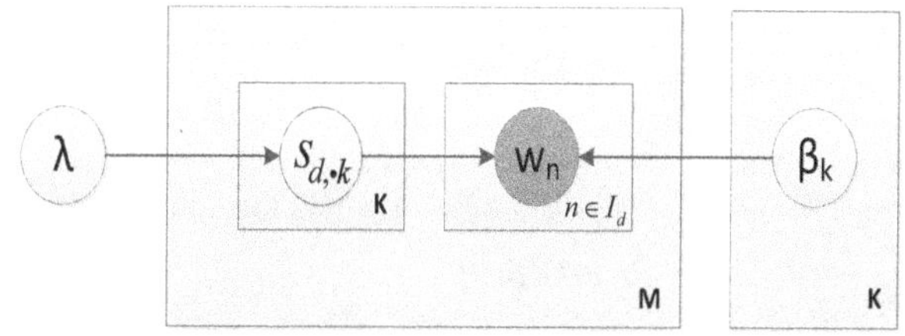

Figure 1: The graphical model of group sparse topical coding.

We choose to use Multi-Laplacian distribution to achieve sparse codes at the document level by taking into account the structure of bag of words. Similar to the relationship between the ℓ_1 norm and Laplace distribution, the multi-Laplacian prior over each group of coefficients turns the classical group-lasso constraints into a MAP-solution in the log-space. The parameter λ in formula 1 has the same role of a fixed Lagrange parameter that deals with the concentration of the probability mass towards zero. Unlike STC which introduces a document code $\boldsymbol{\theta}$, we only model the word code in GSTC and view the document code as a natural by-product, e.g. an simple aggregation of the individual codes of all its words on each topic. To achieve document-level sparse representation, we may expect that there are only a set of topics that convey positive aggregated codes, while others are zero (i.e. all the word codes under that topic are zero). This could be achieved by grouping the word codes under the same topic together and sample the groups of variables from a Multi-laplacian distribution [12, 25]

Moreover, we adopt the Poisson distribution with the *mean* parameter $s_{nk}\boldsymbol{\beta}_{kn}$ to generate the latent word count from the k-th topic w_{nk} due to the following reasons. 1) Since observed word counts as well as latent word counts are non-negative discrete number, it is natural to use Poisson distribution to model such variables. 2) We use the combination as mean parameter to naturally constrain the feasible domains (i.e. non-negative) of word codes for good interpretation. Moreover, imposing non-negativity constraints could potentially result in sparser and more interpretable patterns [20]. 3) Last but not least, Poisson distribution has two nice properties which plays a critical role in GSTC, namely additive property and Moran's property. The additive property says that if $X_1 \sim$ Poisson(τ_1) and $X_2 \sim$ Poisson(τ_2) are independent, then $X_1 + X_2 \sim$ Poisson($\tau_1 + \tau_2$). Based on additive property, we have that the word count w_n follows a Poisson distribution with the mean parameter defined as a linear combination of topic bases $\boldsymbol{s}_{n\cdot}^{\top}\boldsymbol{\beta}_{\cdot n}$, since the latent word counts over different topics are assumed to be independent. Similar methods have been used to define exponential family distributions [22, 6, 40]. The Moran's property further helps us derive the admixture proportions based on the learned word codes and topic bases, which will be discussed later.

3.2 Formulation of GSTC

For a document $\boldsymbol{d}$, the above generative process defines a joint distribution of word codes and word counts shown as below.

$$\begin{aligned} p(\boldsymbol{s}, \boldsymbol{w}|\boldsymbol{\beta}) &= \prod_{k=1}^{K} p(\boldsymbol{s}_{\cdot k}) \left(\prod_{n=1}^{|I_d|} \prod_{k=1}^{K} p(w_{nk}|s_{nk}, \beta_{kn}) \right) \\ &= \prod_{k=1}^{K} p(\boldsymbol{s}_{\cdot k}) \prod_{n=1}^{|I_d|} p(w_n|\boldsymbol{s}_{n\cdot}, \boldsymbol{\beta}), \end{aligned} \quad (3)$$

where $p(\boldsymbol{s}_{\cdot k})$ = M-Laplace($\boldsymbol{s}_{\cdot k}|0, \lambda^{-1}$), $p(w_n|\boldsymbol{s}_{n\cdot}, \boldsymbol{\beta})$ = Poisson($w_n; \boldsymbol{s}_{n\cdot}^{\top}\boldsymbol{\beta}_{\cdot n}$) The hyper-parameter λ is non-negative which can be selected via cross-validation or integrated out by introducing hyper-priors [19,

25]. The second equation is derived according to the additive property of Poisson distribution.

Now, we formally define GSTC as finding the MAP estimate of the above probabilistic model. Given a collection of documents $\boldsymbol{D}$ with size M, GSTC solves the following optimization problem:

$$\begin{aligned}
\min_{\boldsymbol{\Theta},\boldsymbol{\beta}} \mathcal{L}(\Theta,\boldsymbol{\beta}) &= -\ln P(\Theta,\boldsymbol{\beta}|D) \\
&= \min_{\boldsymbol{\Theta},\boldsymbol{\beta}} \sum_{d=1}^{M}\sum_{n=1}^{|\boldsymbol{I}_d|} \ell(\boldsymbol{s}_{d,n\cdot},\boldsymbol{\beta}) + \sum_{d=1}^{M}\sum_{k=1}^{K} \lambda\|s_{d,\cdot k}\|_2 + C \\
&= \min_{\boldsymbol{\Theta},\boldsymbol{\beta}} \sum_{d=1}^{M}\sum_{n=1}^{|\boldsymbol{I}_d|}\left(\sum_{k=1}^{K} s_{d,nk}\beta_{kn} - w_{d,n}\ln(\sum_{k=1}^{K} s_{d,nk}\beta_{kn})\right) \\
&\quad + \sum_{d=1}^{M}\sum_{k=1}^{K}\lambda\|s_{d,\cdot k}\|_2 + C, \\
s.t. &\quad \boldsymbol{s}_{d,n\cdot} \geq 0, \forall d, n \in \boldsymbol{I}_d, \\
&\quad \sum_{n=1}^{N} \beta_{kn} = 1, \forall k,
\end{aligned} \tag{4}$$

where the loss function $\ell(\boldsymbol{s}_{d,n\cdot},\boldsymbol{\beta}) = -\log \text{Poisson}(\boldsymbol{s}_{d,n\cdot}^{\top}\boldsymbol{\beta}_{\cdot n})$, $\Theta = \{\boldsymbol{s}_{d,\cdot\cdot}|\boldsymbol{d} \in \{1,\cdots,M\}\}$, C is a constant. It is shown that minimizing the log-Poisson loss is actually equivalent to minimizing an unnormalized KL-divergence between observed word counts $w_{d,n}$ and their reconstructions $\boldsymbol{s}_{d,n\cdot}^{\top}\boldsymbol{\beta}_{\cdot n}$ [28].

Although the objective function of GSTC is derived from a probabilistic perspective, it can be directly interpreted in a non-probabilistic way. Like the ridge regression, the first part of formula 4 is the reconstruction error for the observed word counts in terms of dictionary $\boldsymbol{\beta}$. The second parts is a Group-lasso, i.e. a mixed ℓ_1/ℓ_2 norm, for the matrix of reconstruction coefficients. This form of regularization promotes solutions that are sparse at the level of *groups* of variables, that is, an entire word code vector under a topic may drop out of the model. This in turn achieves the desired document-level sparse coding.

By optimizing the objective function $\mathcal{L}(\Theta,\boldsymbol{\beta})$, we can learn all the word codes in the document collection as well as the dictionary. As aforementioned, the goal of GSTC is to discover document-level sparse admixture proportions, which can be regarded as a low dimensional representation of the document in the topic simplex. Here we show how to derive the document-level admixture proportion with the learned word codes and dictionary.

As traditional topic models, GSTC assumes that the occurrences of a word in a document may be generated from different topics. Therefore, in GSTC the observed word count w_n is consisted of a set of latent word counts $\{w_{nk}\}_{k=1}^{K}$. If we have known exactly which topic each word occurrence comes from, i.e. the latent word counts $\{w_{nk}\}_{k=1}^{K}, \forall n \in \boldsymbol{I}$ are observed, the document-level admixture proportion would be simply a normalization over the aggregated occurrence counts under different topics. However, since the latent word counts are not observed, we calculate the expected admixture proportion for the document instead.

For this purpose, we first introduce the Moran's property of Poisson distribution.

Lemma 1. ***[Moran's Property of Poisson Distribution]*** *If variables $X_1, X_2, \cdots, X_n$ are independent Poisson random variables with parameters $\tau_1, \tau_2, \cdots, \tau_n$, then*

$$X_i|\sum_{j=1}^{n} X_j \sim Binom\left(\sum_{j=1}^{n} X_j, \frac{\tau_i}{\sum_{j=1}^{n}\tau_j}\right).$$

With the help of Moran's property, the document proportion can be directly derived in GSTC, as shown in the following theorem.

Theorem 1. *Let θ be the topic proportion vector of document d. Assume the document is generated as described in section 3.1, we will have the kth topic proportion $\theta_k = \frac{\sum_{n=1}^{|I|} s_{nk}\beta_{kn}}{\sum_{n=1}^{|I|}\sum_{k=1}^{K} s_{nk}\beta_{kn}}$.*

Proof. Recall that in GSTC, each w_{nk} is independently generated from a Poisson distribution Poisson($\boldsymbol{s}_{nk}\boldsymbol{\beta}_{kn}$) , according to the Moran's property we have:

$$w_{nk}|\sum_{n=1}^{|\boldsymbol{I}|}\sum_{k=1}^{K} w_{nk} \sim \text{Binom}\left(\sum_{n=1}^{|\boldsymbol{I}|}\sum_{k=1}^{K} w_{nk}, \frac{\boldsymbol{s}_{nk}\boldsymbol{\beta}_{kn}}{\sum_{n=1}^{|\boldsymbol{I}|}\sum_{k=1}^{K}\boldsymbol{s}_{nk}\boldsymbol{\beta}_{kn}}\right).$$

Therefore, the expected number of word occurrences from the k-th topic can be expressed as:

$$\begin{aligned}
\mathbb{E}[\textstyle\sum_{n=1}^{|I|} w_{nk}|\sum_{n=1}^{|I|}\sum_{k=1}^{K} w_{nk}] &= \sum_{n=1}^{|I|}\mathbb{E}[w_{nk}|\sum_{n=1}^{|I|}\sum_{k=1}^{K} w_{nk}] \\
&= \sum_{n=1}^{|I|}\left(\left(\sum_{n=1}^{|I|}\sum_{k=1}^{K} w_{nk}\right)\frac{\boldsymbol{s}_{nk}\boldsymbol{\beta}_{kn}}{\sum_{n=1}^{|I|}\sum_{k=1}^{K}\boldsymbol{s}_{nk}\boldsymbol{\beta}_{kn}}\right) \\
&= \left(\sum_{n=1}^{|I|} w_n\right)\left(\frac{\sum_{n=1}^{|I|}\boldsymbol{s}_{nk}\boldsymbol{\beta}_{kn}}{\sum_{n=1}^{|I|}\sum_{k=1}^{K}\boldsymbol{s}_{nk}\boldsymbol{\beta}_{kn}}\right).
\end{aligned} \tag{5}$$

The expected admixture proportion on k-th topic can then be obtained by

$$\begin{aligned}
\theta_k &= \mathbb{E}\left[\frac{\sum_{n=1}^{|I|} w_{nk}}{\sum_{n=1}^{|I|}\sum_{k=1}^{K} w_{nk}}\right] \\
&= \frac{\mathbb{E}[\sum_{n=1}^{|I|} w_{nk}]}{\sum_{n=1}^{|I|} w_n} \\
&= \frac{\left(\sum_{n=1}^{|I|} w_n\right)\left(\frac{\sum_{n=1}^{|I|} s_{nk}\beta_{kn}}{\sum_{n=1}^{|I|}\sum_{k=1}^{K} s_{nk}\beta_{kn}}\right)}{\sum_{n=1}^{|I|} w_n} \\
&= \frac{\sum_{n=1}^{|I|}\boldsymbol{s}_{nk}\boldsymbol{\beta}_{kn}}{\sum_{n=1}^{|I|}\sum_{k=1}^{K}\boldsymbol{s}_{nk}\boldsymbol{\beta}_{kn}}.
\end{aligned} \tag{6}$$

Obviously, the obtained $\{\theta_k\}_{k=1}^{K}$ satisfies $\theta_k \geq 0, \forall k; \sum_{k=1}^{K}\theta_k = 1$. □

3.3 Optimization

The objective function $\mathcal{L}(\Theta,\boldsymbol{\beta})$ is bi-convex, that is, convex over either Θ or $\boldsymbol{\beta}$ when the other is fixed. We omit the proof procedures here which is easy to make. Furthermore, the feasible set is a convex set. Therefore, a typical solution to solve this bi-convex problem is coordinate descent algorithm [21]. The algorithm alternatively performs the optimization over Θ and β as shown in Algorithm 1.

Optimize over Θ: this step aims to find the word codes Θ when dictionary $\boldsymbol{\beta}$ is fixed. Due to the conditional independency, we can perform this step for each document separately by solving the optimization problem:

$$\begin{aligned}
\min_{s} &\sum_{n=1}^{|I|} \ell(\boldsymbol{s}_{n\cdot},\boldsymbol{\beta}) + \sum_{k=1}^{K}\lambda\|\boldsymbol{s}_{\cdot k}\|_2 \\
s.t. &\quad \boldsymbol{s}_{n\cdot} \geq 0 \quad \forall n \in \boldsymbol{I}.
\end{aligned} \tag{7}$$

The above optimization problem cannot directly be solved using traditional gradient methods, since the objective function in formula (7) is not derivable in the domain of $\boldsymbol{s}$. Since the word codes are grouped in terms of topics and each group is separable, here we adopt the block coordinate decent method for this optimization [3,

Algorithm 1 Calculate $\min_{\{s,\beta\}} L(D)$

Require: $T, K \in Z_{+}, \epsilon > 0, D, W$
  for $k = 1 : K$ **do**
    initialize $\beta_{k\cdot} \in \mathbb{R}^{|W|}$ randomly
  end for
  initialize $s \in \mathbb{R}^{|D| \times |W| \times K}$ randomly
  for $t = 1 : T$ **do**
    for $d \in D$ **do**
      Learn Coding of s_d with algorithm 2
    end for
    $l \leftarrow$ calculate loss function value as formula (4)
    if $l - l^{old} < \epsilon$ **then**
      break
    end if
    $l^{old} = l$
    Learn topic β with algorithm 3
  end for
  return s, β

13]. Therefore, we only focus on one group, e.g. the k-th group, and obtain the objective function as:

$$\mathcal{L}(\boldsymbol{s}_{\cdot k}) = \sum_{n=1}^{|\boldsymbol{I}|} (\boldsymbol{s}_{nk}\boldsymbol{\beta}_{kn} - w_n \ln (\boldsymbol{s}_{n\cdot}^{\top}\boldsymbol{\beta}_{\cdot n})) + \lambda \|\boldsymbol{s}_{\cdot k}\|_2. \tag{8}$$

Taking the subderivative on $\boldsymbol{s}_{\cdot k}$, the subgradient equations are

$$\boldsymbol{\beta}_{nk} - \frac{w_n \boldsymbol{\beta}_{nk}}{\boldsymbol{s}_{n\cdot}^{\top}\boldsymbol{\beta}_{\cdot n}} + \lambda \zeta_{nk} = 0; \quad \forall n \in \boldsymbol{I}, \tag{9}$$

where $\zeta_{nk} = \frac{s_{nk}}{\|s_{\cdot k}\|_2}$ when $\boldsymbol{s}_{\cdot k} \neq 0$, and $\boldsymbol{\zeta}_{\cdot k}$ is a k-dimension vector satisfying $\|\boldsymbol{\zeta}_{\cdot k}\|_2 \leq 1$ otherwise. After transforming the formula (9), we get,

$$\|\boldsymbol{\zeta}_{\cdot k}\|_2 = \sqrt{\frac{1}{\lambda} \sum_{n=1}^{|\boldsymbol{I}|} \left(-\boldsymbol{\beta}_{kn} + \frac{w_n \boldsymbol{\beta}_{kn}}{\boldsymbol{s}_{n\cdot}^{\top}\boldsymbol{\beta}_{\cdot n}}\right)^2}. \tag{10}$$

Therefore, we can determine whether the vector of $\boldsymbol{s}_{\cdot k}$ is zero by checking the value of $\|\boldsymbol{\zeta}_{\cdot k}\|_2$. If $\|\boldsymbol{\zeta}_{\cdot k}\|_2 \leq 1$ we set the vector $\boldsymbol{s}_{\cdot k}$ to a zero vector, otherwise we solve the optimization problem in formula (8) using coordinate descent method. Specifically, for each $\boldsymbol{s}_{nk}$, given $\boldsymbol{s}_{jk}, j \neq n$ fixed, the objective function can be written as

$$\mathcal{L}(\boldsymbol{s}_{nk}) \quad = \boldsymbol{s}_{nk}\boldsymbol{\beta}_{kn} - w_n \ln(\boldsymbol{s}_{n\cdot}^{\top}\boldsymbol{\beta}_{\cdot n}) + \lambda \sqrt{\boldsymbol{s}_{nk}^2 + C_{nk}} \tag{11}$$

where $C_{nk} = \sum_{i \in \boldsymbol{I} \wedge i \neq n} \boldsymbol{s}_{ik}^2 \geq 0$ relative to $\boldsymbol{s}_{nk}$ is a constant. $\boldsymbol{s}_{nk}$.
The gradient of formula (11) is

$$\nabla_{\boldsymbol{s}_{nk}} \mathcal{L}(\boldsymbol{s}_{nk}) = (1 - \frac{w_n}{\boldsymbol{s}_{n\cdot}^{\top}\boldsymbol{\beta}_{\cdot n}})\boldsymbol{\beta}_{kn} + \lambda \frac{\boldsymbol{s}_{nk}}{\sqrt{\boldsymbol{s}_{nk}^2 + C_{nk}}}, \tag{12}$$

and the second derivative of $\mathcal{L}(\boldsymbol{s}_{nk})$ is

$$\frac{\partial^2 \mathcal{L}(\boldsymbol{s}_{nk})}{\partial \boldsymbol{s}_{nk}^2} = w_n \beta^2 (\boldsymbol{s}_{n\cdot}^{\top}\boldsymbol{\beta}_{\cdot n})^{-2} + \lambda C_{nk}(\boldsymbol{s}_{nk}^2 + C_{nk})^{-\frac{3}{2}}. \tag{13}$$

Since $\frac{\partial^2 \mathcal{L}(\boldsymbol{s}_{nk})}{\partial \boldsymbol{s}_{nk}^2} > 0$ for $\forall \boldsymbol{s}_{nk}$, the formula (11) is strictly convex with respect to $\boldsymbol{s}_{nk}$. By setting the gradient $\nabla_{\boldsymbol{s}_{nk}} \mathcal{L}(\boldsymbol{s}_{nk}) = 0$ equal to to zero, we have that $\boldsymbol{s}_{nk}$ is the solution of the following quartic

Algorithm 2 Encoding Algorithm in GSTC

Require: s_d, β, D, ϵ
  for $t = 1 : T$ **do**
    for $k = 1 : K$ **do**
      if $\|\boldsymbol{\zeta}_{\cdot k}\|_2 \leq 1$ **then**
        $s_{d,\cdot k} \leftarrow \mathbf{0}$
        continue;
      end if
      for $n = 1 : |I_d|$ **do**
        calculate $s_{d,nk}^{\star}$ by solving Eq. (14)
        $s_{d,nk} \leftarrow \max(s_{d,nk}^{\star}, 0)$
      end for
    end for
    $l \leftarrow$ calculate the loss function value with formula (4)
    if $l - l^{old} < \epsilon$ **then**
      break
    end if
    $l^{old} = l$
  end for
  return s_d

problem:

$$\begin{aligned}
&\left(\boldsymbol{\beta}_{kn}^2(\boldsymbol{\beta}_{kn} + \eta)^2 - \boldsymbol{\beta}_{kn}^2 \lambda^2\right) \boldsymbol{s}_{nk}^4 \\
&- \left(2X_{nk}\boldsymbol{\beta}_{kn}(\boldsymbol{\beta}_{kn} + \eta) + 2\boldsymbol{\beta}_{kn}\lambda^2 B_{nk}\right) \boldsymbol{s}_{nk}^3 \\
&+ \left(X_{nk}^2 + (\boldsymbol{\beta}_{kn} + \eta)^2 \boldsymbol{\beta}_{kn}^2 C_{nk} - B_{nk}^2 \lambda^2\right) \boldsymbol{s}_{nk}^2 \\
&-2X_{nk}(\boldsymbol{\beta}_{kn} + \eta)\boldsymbol{\beta}_{kn} C_{nk} \boldsymbol{s}_{nk} \\
&+X_{nk}^2 C_{nk} = 0 \\
&s.t. \quad \boldsymbol{s}_{nk} \geq 0,
\end{aligned} \tag{14}$$

where $B_{nk} = \sum_{i=1 \wedge i \neq k}^{K} \boldsymbol{s}_{ni}\boldsymbol{\beta}_{in}$ and $X_{nk} = w_n \boldsymbol{\beta}_{kn} - B_{nk}(\boldsymbol{\beta}_{kn} + \eta)$. The feasible solution of $\boldsymbol{s}_{nk}$ is either in the roots of Equation 14) or the boundary point which is zero [40]. Solving this quartic equation is very efficient using modern numerical tools. The detailed encoding algorithm is presented in Algorithm 2.

Optimize over $\boldsymbol{\beta}$: After we have inferred all the latent word codes of the collection, we update the dictionary $\boldsymbol{\beta}$ by minimizing the log-Poisson loss. It is a convex optimization problem which can be efficiently solved with high-performance methods. Here we adopt the limited-memory projected quasi-Newton(L-PQN) algorithm [26] for our problem. The L-PQN algorithm is suitable for large-scale optimization problems where the evaluation of the function is substantially more expensive than the projection onto the constraint set. It fits our problem as the calculation of the loss function is time consuming, while the projecting a vector to a probabilistic simplex can be conducted in linear time [10].

The L-PQN algorithm uses the gradient of loss function for optimization which is defined as Equation (15) for all n, k.

$$\frac{\partial \mathcal{L}(\beta)}{\partial \beta_{kn}} = \sum_{d=1}^{M} \left(s_{d,nk} - \frac{w_{d,n} \cdot s_{d,nk}}{\sum_{k=1}^{K} s_{d,nk}\beta_{kn}} \right). \tag{15}$$

To further speed-up the optimization process, we do not use the coordinate descent algorithm to optimize the $\beta_{k\cdot}$ one by one. Alternatively, we transform the topic matrix β to a large vector $\vec{\beta}$. The $\vec{\beta}$ has $K \times N$ elements, and includes K normalization constraints on every N elements. In this way, we can simultaneously learn the whole topics matrix using L-PQN. The topic learning procedure is described in Algorithm 3, and for the detailed steps of L-PQN one may refer to [26].

Algorithm 3 Topic Learning Algorithm in GSTC

Require: s, β, D

transform matrix β to vector $\vec{\beta}$
$pr \leftarrow$ a function to do simplex projection
$obj \leftarrow$ a function to calculate both the loss value as formula (4)
$grd \leftarrow$ a function to calculate the gradient as formula (15)
$\vec{\beta} \leftarrow$ L-PQN($\beta, s, D, pr, obj, grd$)
transform vector $\vec{\beta}$ back to matrix β
return β

Table 1: Comparison among Different Topic Models

Property	PTMs	NPMs	GSTC
Efficient Sparse Control	No	Yes	Yes
Semantic Interpretation	Yes	No	Yes
Learning Efficiency	Good	Better	Better

3.4 Discussions

GSTC is a non-probabilistic topic model for discovering sparse latent representations of large text corpora. Here we compared GSTC with exiting PTMs and NPMs to show the benefits of GSTC on text modelling. The advantages and weakness of different topic models are summarized in the table 1, and the detailed explanations are presented as follows.

The PTMs (e.g. LDA[5]) construct the document in a probabilistic way, where a document is typically modeled as a finite admixture of latent topics, and each topic is a unigram distribution over a given vocabulary. The document-level admixture proportions can be regarded as a low dimensional representation of the document in topic simplex. When compared with unnormalized document codes (typically obtained by NPMs), such admixture proportions would be beneficial in both understanding and semantic comparison between documents as they clearly convey the relative importance of topics in documents. Besides, when using the latent representations as features for future tasks (e.g. text classification, text clustering and so on), such admixture proportions (within the interval $[0, 1]$) might be more robust and preferred than usually scale-unstrained document codes. GSTC enjoys the merits of latent semantic representations as PTMs. Although GSTC relaxed the normalization constraint in modeling, we can naturally recover the admixture proportions afterwards.

A limitation of PTMs is that it is non-trivial to achieve sparsity since the admixture proportions or topics are normalized distribution. This problem can be well addressed in the non-probabilistic GSTC. Due to the same reason of having to define a normalized likelihood function, another limitation of PTMs is that they usually have to deal with a hard-to-compute *log-sum-exp* function [40]. By relaxing the normalization constraint, the learning problem in GSTC can be effectively solved using coordinate descent method, which has closed-form solutions for updating word codes. Empirical results in Sec 4.4 show that GSTC is much more efficient than LDA in training.

The advantage of NPMs lies in that they provide an elegant framework to achieve sparsity in topic modeling by using sparse constraint like ℓ_1 norm as lasso [21]. As a non-probabilistic model, GSTC enjoys the same merit by directly control the sparsity of inferred representations at document-level with the help of group lasso. Unlike SPC [22] and standard NMF [20, 15] encode all the words in a vocabulary, GSTC only encodes the words with nonzero counts as STC, which makes GSTC more efficient and scalable to large vocabulary. Compared to STC, GSTC has less variables to be estimated since we do not need to model the document codes θ. The additional variables θ make the STC require more data in learning.

One limitation of existing NPMs, as aforementioned, is that they lose the clear semantic explanations over the latent representations. Although some NPMs like STC and NMF can directly learn document-level latent representations, the learned codes no longer lie on the same topic simplex like PTMs, but could be in quite different scales over different documents. Mapping the codes into a semantic simplex is not natural and straightforward. An ad-hoc normalized code vector no longer represents the admixture proportions in topic simplex. While in GSTC, we can derive the expected admixture proportions based on the learned word codes and dictionary.

4. EXPERIMENTS

In this section, we provide both qualitative and quantitative evaluation of GSTC. We first introduce the dataset the baseline methods. Then we conduct extensive experiments to compare the performance of GSTC with some state-of-the-art methods. The empirical results demonstrate the effectiveness and efficiency of the proposed model.

4.1 Dataset and Baseline Methods

We conducted empirical experiments based on the 20-Newsgroup dataset. The 20-Newsgroup is a benchmark text collection widely used in topic modeling, which organizes the postings to Usenet newsgroups into 20 related categories almost evenly. Here we make use of a preprocessed version downloaded from Cai's webpage[1], which includes 18,846 documents and 26,214 distinct words. The vocabulary is generated by stemming each term to its root and removing the stop words.

We evaluation the performance of GSTC by comparing with several state-of-art PTMs and NTMs, including:

- Latent Dirchelet Allocation (LDA). The code of LDA is provided by Blei[2], which employs variational EM in the training process. The Dirichlet parameters are estimated by the Newton-Raphson method [5].
- Sparse Topical Coding (STC). The code of STC is available online[3], which employs the coordinate descent algorithm to learn the model.
- Non-negative Matrix Factorization (NMF). NMF is solved with an alternating constrained least squares algorithm [2].

For comparison fairness, all the baseline methods are initialized randomly similar as GSTC, the training parameters of these models are set according to the original papers' suggestions , and the regularization constants are selected by cross-validation.

4.2 Sparse Latent Representations

To demonstrate the effectiveness in learning meaningful topics by our model, we first show 9 randomly picked learned topics in Table 2. For each topic, we list several top words according to their probabilities under the corresponding topic. Each column is a distinct topic, where the topic labels are produced by human judges for better understanding. Although the top words listed here are in their stemmed form, it is obvious to see that the learned topics are

[1]http://www.zjucadcg.cn/dengcai/Data/TextData.html
[2]http://www.cs.princeton.edu/ blei/lda-c/
[3]http://www.cs.cmu.edu/ junzhu/stc.htm

Table 2: Top words for 4 randomly selected learned topics

COMPUTER	LOVE	DRUG	WEAPON	BICYCLE	TERROR	DIET	MEDICATION	SPACE-FLIGHT
pc	love	drug	weapon	motorcycl	terror	diet	medic	launch
printer	promis	illeg	gun	bike	soldier	vitamin	diseas	orbit
hardware	rose	alcohol	arm	ride	civilian	fat	infect	satellit
software	lie	addict	firearm	guid	iraqi	nutrition	patient	shuttl
system	marriag	heroin	automat	rider	bomber	headach	clinic	solar
lan	marri	cocain	rifl	biker	casualti	dose	diet	mar
inkjet	grave	marijuana	pistol	road	defenseless	intak	syndrom	spacecraft

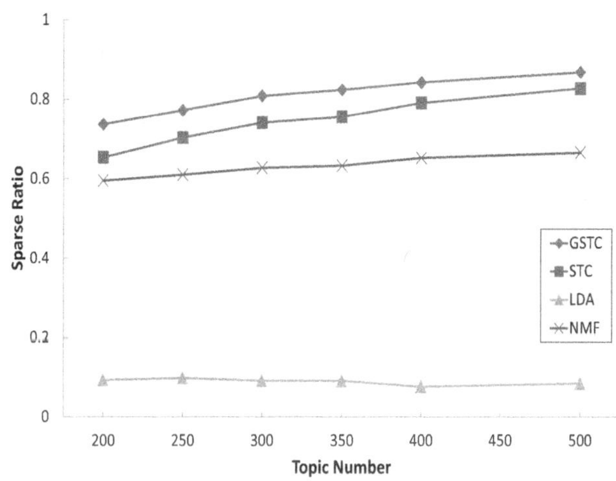

Figure 4: The sparse ratio of document-level latent representations learned by different models.

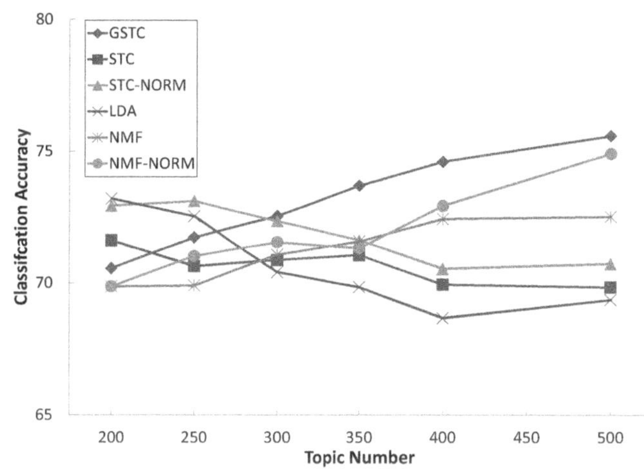

Figure 5: The classification accuracy of different models.

quite clear and semantically concentrated. For example, we can find *pc, hardware*, and *software* in the topic about computer, and *weapon, gun*, and *pistol* in the topic about weapon.

We compare the sparsity of the learned latent representations of documents from different models. We randomly selected two news groups and sampled two documents from each. The inferred latent representations of documents from different models under 500 topics are shown in Fig. 2 and Fig. 3. We can see that LDA tends to learn a broad spectrum of topics for each document, while the other three models can discover more sparse and salient patterns. Take the first document in the autos group as an example, LDA assigned 456 topics to it, while STC, NMF and GSTC discovered 33, 162, and 28 topics respectively. Note that STC seems sparser than GSTC since the document codes learned by STC varies largely and thus some small codes cannot be clearly observed due to the image scale. From Fig. 2 and Fig. 3, we can also find that the document codes learned by STC can be in quite different scales. For example, the most salient document codes in autos group are around 8 while in hardware group are around 11. It is difficult to use such codes to directly explain the importance of topics or conduct semantic comparison between documents.

We further quantitatively evaluate the average sparse ratio on latent representations of documents from different models, as shown in Fig. 4. Not surprisingly, we can see that the representations learned by LDA are very dense. Since there is no direct sparsity control over the posterior representations in LDA, the sparsity in inferred admixture proportions is mainly caused by the data scarcity. Meanwhile, the sparse ratio of NMF is lower than STC and GSTC. It indicates that directly imposing sparse constraints (e.g. lasso or group lasso) can achieve better sparsity than using the non-negative constraints alone. By comparing GSTC and STC, we can see that using group lasso can further improve the sparsity ratio (and classification performance as shown later). The possible reason is that group lasso uses structural information to align variables to sparse and salient factors, and such additional constraints over variables may lead to better sparsity.

4.3 Document Classification

To quantitatively evaluate the quality of learned representations from different models, we report the performance on document classification. Specifically, we use all the 20-newsgroup data to learn the parameters of different models. Then we use the training documents with their inferred representations as features to build multi-class SVM classifiers. Note that in LDA and our GSTC, the inferred latent representations of documents are admixture proportions; while in STC and NMF, the latent representations of documents are unnormalized code vectors. Here we also conducted post-normalization on the document codes and used the normalized codes as input features. We denote the results based on these normalized codes as STC-Norm and NMF-Norm, respectively. We adopted the LIBSVM toolbox[4] as our classifier implementation. The one-against-one approach is employed in multi-class classification by LIBSVM. The train/test split is the same as [8]. We performed cross validation to select the coefficient C of SVM as well as the regularizer parameters in GSTC and STC.

The classification results are depicted in the Fig 5. We can see that GSTC performs better than all the other three models, especial-

[4]http://www.csie.ntu.edu.tw/ cjlin/libsvm/

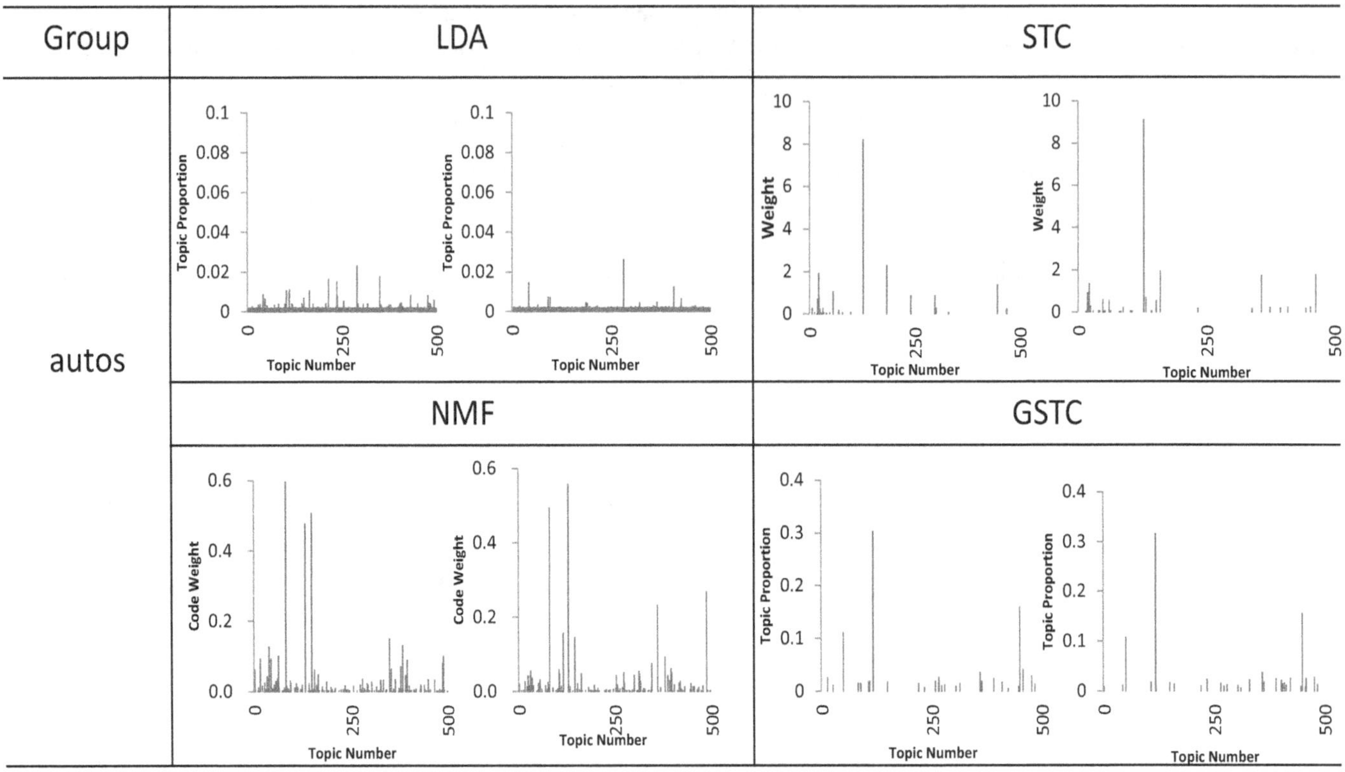

Figure 2: The latent representations of example documents from autos category discovered by different models.

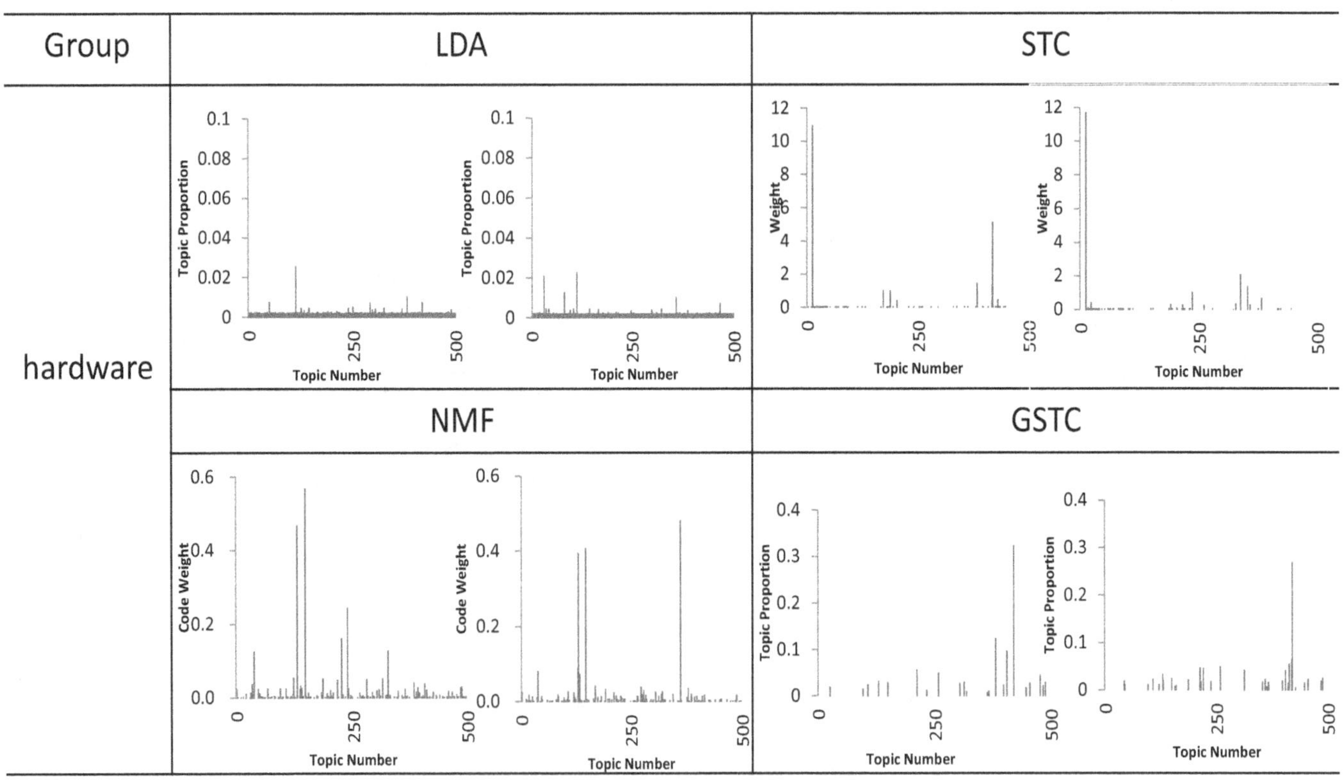

Figure 3: The latent representations of example documents from hardware category discovered by different models.

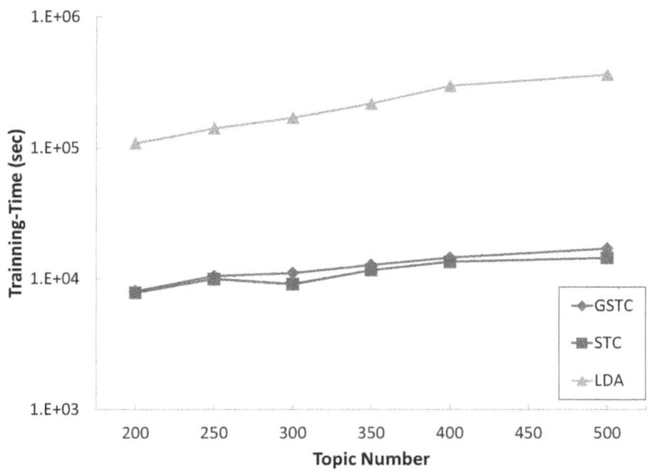

Figure 6: The training time of different models.

ly when the topic number is large. As compared with LDA, we can find that LDA performs well when the topic number is small, but the performance drops when topic number increases. It indicates that by learning compact representations for documents, especially when there are a large number of potential topics in the text corpora, we can achieve better prediction performance. As compared with NMF and STC, one possible reason for the improvement is that GSTC learns the admixture proportions which lay different documents in the topic simplex. Such latent representations may better help compare or classify documents than the unnormalized code vectors which are often in different scales. This can also be verified if we compare STC and NMF with their normalized counterparts respectively, where using normalized features can always performs better. Meanwhile, one may notice that the curve of STC in Fig 5 is downward-sloping. This phenomenon can also be observed in the original paper of STC 5 when topic number is larger than 100. One possible reason is that by setting the same weight over the sparse control and the alignment components (as suggested in [40]), the adaptability of STC may get hurt when topic number become large. Finally, by comparing GSTC with STC-Norm and NFM-Norm, we can see that with the learned admixture proportions, one can obtain better classification accuracy than using the normalized document codes which lack clear semantic explanations.

4.4 Time Efficiency

We further compare the learning efficiency of different models. Since GSTC, LDA and STC are all implemented in C++ while NMF is implemented in Matlab, here we compare the training time of the first three but omit the result of NMF for fair comparison.[5] All the experiments are conducted on the same workstation with a 2.33GHZ intel processor. Each model runs 10 times with random initialization.

Fig 6 shows the average training time of different models. Clearly, both GSTC and STC are much more efficient than LDA. The main reason is that the coordinate descent algorithm employed by both GSTC and STC is much more efficient than the probabilistic inference of LDA. Besides, as the learning process proceeds, the sparse representations obtained by GSTC and STC can further speed-up the learning process, while the LDA almost keeps the same learning speed for every iteration. By comparing GSCT and STC, we can see that both obtain comparable time efficiency in learning. It seems that in GSTC the saving on the cost of explicitly learning the document codes, compensates the cost of solving group lasso rather than lasso in STC.

[5]In fact, it is shown that the time cost of NMF is much worse than STC in the appendix of STC [40]. From our results later, therefore, we may anticipate the running time of NMF will also be longer than GSTC

5. CONCLUSIONS AND FUTURE WORK

In this paper, we present group sparse topical coding (GSTC), a novel non-probabilistic topic model for discovering sparse latent representations (i.e. admixture proportions) of documents over large text corpora. GSTC enjoys both the merits of the PTMs and NPMs. By relaxing the normalization constraint made in PTMs, GSTC can directly control the sparsity of the inferred representations and learn with efficient algorithm. Meanwhile, GSTC can naturally derive document-level admixture proportions as in PTMs with learned word codes and dictionary. Empirical results on benchmark datasets show that GSTC can identify sparse topics, and improve the document classification accuracy and time efficiency.

For the future work, it would be interesting to further consider the sparsity of dictionary, and develop parallel learning algorithm for GSTC for large-scale applications. Besides, we will also try to extend the GSTC by integrating the discriminative features of document, such as document structure, the case of words, label of documents and so on. These discriminative information may help the GSTC learn the codes and topics more accurately and thus further improve the classification performance. Finally, it would also be interesting to apply the GSTC in other fields, such as computer vision and signal processing.

6. ACKNOWLEDGMENTS

This research is funded by the National Natural Science Foundation of China under Grant No. 60933005, No. 61173008, No. 61003166 , No. 61203298, 973 Program of China under Grants No. 2012CB316303, and the National 242 Project of China under Grant No. 2011F65, 2011A001.

7. REFERENCES

[1] E. M. Airoldi, D. M. Blei, S. E. Fienberg, and E. P. Xing. Mixed membership stochastic blockmodels. *J. Mach. Learn. Res.*, 9:1981–2014, June 2008.

[2] R. Albright, J. Cox, D. Duling, A. N. Langville, and C. D. Meyer. Algorithms, initializations, and convergence for the nonnegative matrix factorization. *Matrix*, (919):1–18, 2006.

[3] S. Bengio, F. C. N. Pereira, Y. Singer, D. Strelow, and D. Strelow. Group sparse coding. In *NIPS*, pages 82–89, 2009.

[4] D. M. Blei and J. D. Lafferty. Correlated topic models. In *NIPS*, 2005.

[5] D. M. Blei, A. Y. Ng, M. I. Jordan, and J. Lafferty. Latent dirichlet allocation. *Journal of Machine Learning Research*, 3:2003, 2003.

[6] W. Buntine and A. Jakulin. Discrete component analysis. *Subspace Latent Structure and Feature Selection*, 3940:23–25, 2006.

[7] D. Cai, Q. Mei, J. Han, and C. Zhai. Modeling hidden topics on document manifold. In *Proceedings of the 17th ACM conference on Information and knowledge management*, CIKM '08, pages 911–920, New York, NY, USA, 2008. ACM.

[8] D. Cai, S. Member, X. He, J. Han, and S. Member. Srda: An efficient algorithm for large-scale discriminant analysis. *IEEE Transactions on Knowledge and Data Engineering*, 20(1):1–12, 2008.

[9] S. C. Deerwester, S. T. Dumais, T. K. Landauer, G. W. Furnas, and R. A. Harshman. Indexing by latent semantic analysis. *JASIS*, 41(6):391–407, 1990.

[10] J. Duchi, S. S. Shwartz, Y. Singer, and T. Chandra. Efficient projections onto the L1-ball for learning in high dimensions. In *Proceedings of the 25th international conference on Machine learning*, ICML '08, pages 272–279, New York, NY, USA, 2008. ACM.

[11] B. Efron, T. Hastie, L. Johnstone, and R. Tibshirani. Least angle regression. *Annals of Statistics*, 32:407–499, 2004.

[12] T. Eltoft, T. Kim, and T.-W. Lee. On the multivariate Laplace distribution. *IEEE Signal Processing Letters*, 13(5):300–303, May 2006.

[13] J. Friedman, T. Hastie, and R. Tibshirani. A note on the group lasso and a sparse group lasso. *Arxiv preprint arXiv10010736*, pages 1–8, 2010.

[14] J. Graca, K. Ganchev, B. Taskar, and F. Pereira. Posterior vs Parameter Sparsity in Latent Variable Models. In *Proceedings of NIPS*, 2009.

[15] M. Heiler and C. Schnörr. Learning sparse representations by non-negative matrix factorization and sequential cone programming. *J. Mach. Learn. Res.*, 7:1385–1407, December 2006.

[16] T. Hofmann. Unsupervised learning by probabilistic latent semantic analysis. In *Machine Learning*, page 2001, 2001.

[17] L. Jacob, G. Obozinski, J.-P. Vert, and J.-P. Vert. Group lasso with overlap and graph lasso. In *ICML*, page 55, 2009.

[18] R. Jenatton, J. Mairal, G. Obozinski, and F. Bach. Proximal methods for sparse hierarchical dictionary learning. In *ICML*, pages 487–494, 2010.

[19] M. Kyung, J. Gill, M. Ghosh, and G. Casella. Penalized regression, standard errors, and bayesian lassos. *Bayesian Analysis*, 5(2):369–412, 2010.

[20] D. D. Lee and H. S. Seung. Learning the parts of objects by non-negative matrix factorization. *Nature*, 401(6755):788–791, Oct. 1999.

[21] H. Lee, A. Battle, R. Raina, and A. Y. Ng. Efficient sparse coding algorithms. In *NIPS*, pages 801–808, 2006.

[22] H. Lee, R. Raina, A. Teichman, and A. Y. Ng. Exponential family sparse coding with applications to self-taught learning. In *Proceedings of the 21st international jont conference on Artifical intelligence*, IJCAI'09, pages 1113–1119, San Francisco, CA, USA, 2009. Morgan Kaufmann Publishers Inc.

[23] B. A. Olshausen and D. J. Field. Emergence of simple-cell receptive field properties by learning a sparse code for natural images. *Nature*, 381(6583):607–609, June 1996.

[24] J. Paisley, L. Carin, and D. Blei. Variational inference for stick-breaking beta process priors. In L. Getoor and T. Scheffer, editors, *Proceedings of the 28th International Conference on Machine Learning (ICML-11)*, ICML '11, pages 889–896, New York, NY, USA, June 2011. ACM.

[25] S. Raman, T. J. Fuchs, P. J. Wild, E. Dahl, and V. Roth. The bayesian group-lasso for analyzing contingency tables. In *Proceedings of the 26th Annual International Conference on Machine Learning*, ICML '09, pages 881–888, New York, NY, USA, 2009. ACM.

[26] M. Schmidt, E. V. D. Berg, M. P. Friedl, and K. Murphy. Optimizing costly functions with simple constraints: A limited-memory projected quasi-newton algorithm. In *Proc. of Conf. on Artificial Intelligence and Statistics*, pages 456–463, 2009.

[27] M. Shashanka, B. Raj, and P. Smaragdis. Sparse overcomplete latent variable decomposition of counts data. *Advances in Neural Information Processing Systems 20*, 20(1):1–8, 2008.

[28] S. Sra, D. Kim, S. Sra, D. Kim, and B. Schölkopf. Non-monotonic poisson likelihood maximization. Technical report, 2008.

[29] R. Tibshirani. Regression shrinkage and selection via the lasso. *Journal of the Royal Statistical Society, Series B*, 58:267–288, 1994.

[30] R. Tibshirani, M. Saunders, S. Rosset, J. Zhu, and K. Knight. Sparsity and smoothness via the fused lasso. *Journal Of The Royal Statistical Society Series B*, 67(1):91–108, 2005.

[31] C. Wang and D. Blei. Decoupling Sparsity and Smoothness in the Discrete Hierarchical Dirichlet Process. In Y. Bengio, D. Schuurmans, J. Lafferty, C. K. I. Williams, and A. Culotta, editors, *Advances in Neural Information Processing Systems 22*, pages 1982–1989. 2009.

[32] C. Wang and D. M. Blei. Collaborative topic modeling for recommending scientific articles. In *Proceedings of the 17th ACM SIGKDD international conference on Knowledge discovery and data mining*, KDD '11, pages 448–456, New York, NY, USA, 2011. ACM.

[33] Q. Wang, J. Xu, H. Li, and N. Craswell. Regularized latent semantic indexing. In *SIGIR*, pages 685–694, 2011.

[34] X. Wei and W. B. Croft. Lda-based document models for ad-hoc retrieval. In *Proceedings of the 29th annual international ACM SIGIR conference on Research and development in information retrieval*, SIGIR '06, pages 178–185, New York, NY, USA, 2006. ACM.

[35] S. Williamson, C. Wang, K. A. Heller, and D. M. Blei. The ibp compound dirichlet process and its application to focused topic modeling. In *ICML*, pages 1151–1158, 2010.

[36] J. Yang, K. Yu, Y. Gong, and T. Huang. Linear spatial pyramid matching using sparse coding for image classification. *Computer Vision and Pattern Recognition, IEEE Computer Society Conference on*, 0:1794–1801, 2009.

[37] X. Yang, S. Kim, and E. Xing. Heterogeneous multitask learning with joint sparsity constraints. In Y. Bengio, D. Schuurmans, J. Lafferty, C. K. I. Williams, and A. Culotta, editors, *Advances in Neural Information Processing Systems 22*, pages 2151–2159. 2009.

[38] M. Yuan, M. Yuan, Y. Lin, and Y. Lin. Model selection and estimation in regression with grouped variables. *Journal of the Royal Statistical Society, Series B*, 68:49–67, 2006.

[39] M. Zhou, L. Hannah, D. Dunson, and L. Carin. Beta-negative binomial process and poisson factor analysis. 2011.

[40] J. Zhu and E. P. Xing. Sparse topical coding. In *UAI*, pages 831–838, 2011.

[41] H. Zou and T. Hastie. Regularization and variable selection via the elastic net. *Journal of the Royal Statistical Society, Series B*, 67:301–320, 2005.

TYPiMatch: Type-specific Unsupervised Learning of Keys and Key Values for Heterogeneous Web Data Integration

Yongtao Ma
Institute AIFB
Karlsruhe Institute of Technology
76128 Karlsruhe, Germany
yongtao.ma@kit.edu

Thanh Tran
Institute AIFB
Karlsruhe Institute of Technology
76128 Karlsruhe, Germany
duc.tran@kit.edu

ABSTRACT

Instance matching and blocking, a preprocessing step used for selecting candidate matches, require determining the most representative attributes of instances called keys, based on which similarities between instances are computed. We show that for the problem of learning blocking keys and key values, both generic techniques that do not exploit type information and supervised learning techniques optimized for one single predefined type of instances do not perform well on heterogeneous Web data capturing instances for which the *predefined type is too general*. That is, they actually belong to some subtypes that are not explicitly specified in the data. We propose an unsupervised approach for *learning these subtypes and the subtype-specific blocking keys and key values*. Compared to state-of-the-art supervised and unsupervised learning approaches that are optimized for one single type, our approach improves efficiency as well as result quality. In particular, we show that the proposed strategy of learning subtype-specific blocking keys and key values improves both blocking and instance matching results.

Categories and Subject Descriptors

H.2.8 [**Database Management**]: Database Application—*Data Mining*

Keywords

Information Integration; Heterogeneous Web Data; Unsupervised Learning

1. INTRODUCTION

Especially due to recent trends in Web data publishing, there is a large amount of heterogeneous datasets that are publicly available. Linked Data alone comprises billions of RDF triples that reside in hundreds of datasets [4].

One main problem towards the effective usage of Web data is integration. Besides schema matching, the other main problem in this regard is to resolve differences in the data representation of the same real-world object. It is called *instance matching* (also known as entity resolution, entity co-reference, or record linkage), which is about finding instances (e.g. `Products`) that refer to the same object. One main challenge behind this is to find a few representative attributes (e.g. `title` and `price`), based on which the similarity between instances can be computed. These attributes and their values (so-called *keys* and *key values*) are not only needed for *blocking*, which uses a few simple *blocking keys* to quickly determine candidates and group them together in blocks, but also for the instance matching task in general. Blocking is usually performed as a quick candidate selection step that involves boolean matching, while instance matching employs fuzzy similarity matching with fine-tuned similarity thresholds to further refine the candidates in the blocks.

State-of-the-art approaches for finding blocking keys assume a given schema, which describes the types and attributes associated with instances of these types. Given a particular type, its attributes, and training data for that type, existing approaches derive type-specific keys or more complex similarity matching function predicates that capture the keys as well as the similarity metrics and thresholds [5, 12, 3, 22, 21]. Not relying on training data, an unsupervised approach has been proposed recently to select attributes as keys based on their discriminability and coverage [18]. Basically, the discriminability of an attribute is measured by the diversity of its values such that low-discriminability means that many instances have the same values on that attribute. The coverage of an attribute refers to the number of instances that have that attribute. Intuitively, attributes shall be selected and used as keys when they are covered by many instances and also, discriminate them well. Finding type-specific keys in this supervised or unsupervised fashion is however problematic when the given instances actually belong to *multiple unknown subtypes*, as illustrated by the following example:

EXAMPLE 1. *One example of data that lacks type information is Linked Data as shown in Fig. 1. Based on a 3M sample of instances extracted from several Linked Data sources crawled from the Web, we found that 393,503 of them lack type information, e.g. it is not captured in the data that p_1 is a* `Camera` *(dotted edges indicate the type information that is not captured). Another example is data stored in big tables of enterprise databases. Tab. 1 shows real product data from a data integration project of a product*

WSDM'13, February 4–8, 2013, Rome, Italy.

Table 1: Product table; some words later used as features for illustration purposes, are highlighted.

ID	Title	Price	Brand	Description
p_1	Sony Cyber-Shot DSC-W650	129	Sony	**Sony Cyber-Shot** DSC-W650 **camera** owns14 **megapixel** sensor ... Optical Steady Shot Image stabilization reduces blur, while**photos** Effect modes allow you to get more creative with your photos.
p_2	Sony DSC-W620 Cyber-Shot	112	Sony	Capture true-to-life photos with the **Sony Cyber-shot** DSC-W620 digital **camera**. Boasting a 5x zoom, this 14.1 **megapixel** digital camera captures the most detailed **photos**
p_3	Sony Cyber-Shot DSC-W65	138	Sony	Get high-quality images with the **Sony Cyber-shot** DSC-W650 digital camera. Boasting a 5x optical zoom, this 16.1 **megapixel** digital **camera** produces detailed **photos**.
p_4	Sony Reader PRS-600SC	118	Sony	The **Sony** PRS-600E-Book **Reader** allows readers to store 350 **books** from anywhere. Using **e-link** technology for a paper-like display...
p_5	Sony Reader PRS-600SC	93	Sony	The **Reader** Touch Edition utilizes **E-Ink** screen technology to deliver an amazing, paper-like display...Take your favorite **books** to go with the Reader Touch Edition by **Sony**.
p_6	Sony PRS-T1 6" eBook Reader	129	Sony	The **Sony reader** equipped **E-Ink** Pearl V220 glare-free screen... Books from your local public library or download Google public domain **books**.

management company[1]. *Here, we face the situation where 7M descriptions acquired from different sources are stored in one single product table. The products captured by this data actually belong to many different subtypes. Using four attributes, this table captures instances of type* `Product`, *which actually belong to subtypes such as* `Camera` *and* `eReader`.

This example illustrates the cases where the type is either not specified or too general to be useful. The current supervised solution [21, 22, 3, 12, 5] to that is to treat instances as belonging to one single type and learn blocking keys that are applicable to all of them, e.g. keys for all `Product` instances. Intuitively, when dealing with instances of the type `Camera` (p_1, p_2, and p_3), keys specific to `Camera` might be more useful (e.g. `Model`) than keys learned for `Product` (e.g. `Title`). However, when learned for a single big `Product` table, such camera-specific keys might not be selected because they are not applicable to many table records.

As an alternative to these schema-based type-specific supervised learning solutions, a schema- and type-agnostic approach has been recently proposed to deal with heterogeneous Web data. This approach does not exploit attributes (of specific types) for building keys, but instead, uses unstructured bags of features that can be extracted from the attribute values as key values [14]. They are simply composed of features that do not come with attribute information. Instances are considered similar when their key values overlap, i.e. they have some features in common.

Contributions. In this work, we show that considering the schema and the attributes it captures significantly improves the quality of the results achievable with the schema-agnostic approach [14]. In particular, the quality improves when instead of using the general type [19, 20, 5] , blocking keys are learned for specific subtypes of instances in the data. To this end, we propose an *unsupervised approach* that relies entirely on the data for *learning both the subtypes*, and the *keys and key values specific to these subtypes*. In experiments, we show how this approach can be used for blocking and instance matching. Compared to state-of-the-art instance matching approaches, our solution greatly improves result quality (up to 201.56% improvement in terms of F-measure). Results are also promising when considering the blocking task only. Our approach yields up to 32.62% improvement in terms of reduction ratio over existing solutions for blocking [19]. It is also time efficient when compared against approaches that achieve similar result quality. Compared to the approach that yields second best result quality, our approach is up to several times faster w.r.t. blocking, and achieves similar performance w.r.t. instance matching.

Outline. We provide an overview of the problem and solutions in Sec. 2. The learning of types is presented in Sec. 3. The learning of keys and key values specific to these types is discussed in Sec. 4. We present experiments in Sec. 5, related work in Sec. 6, and conclusions in Sec. 7.

2. OVERVIEW

We consider general Web data, which includes different types such as relational, XML and RDF data. In literatures, this data is often conceived as a graph:

DEFINITION 1. *The* data G *is a tuple* (N, E, L) *where*

- N *is a finite set of nodes. Thereby,* N *is conceived as the disjoint union* $N_I \uplus N_C \uplus N_V$ *with* N_I *representing* instances, N_C *stands for* classes, *and* N_V *stands for* attribute values.
- L *is a finite set of labels, subdivided by* $L = L_N \uplus L_E \uplus type$, *where* L_N *are node labels and* $L_E \uplus type$ *are edge labels.*
- E *is a finite set of edges* $e(n_1, n_2)$ *with* $n_1, n_2 \in N$ *and* $e \in L$. *In particular, we distinguish* attribute edges $E_A \subset E$, *with* $e(n_1, n_2) \in E_A$ *iff* $n_1 \in N_E$ *and* $n_2 \in N_V$ *from* type edges, $type(n_1, n_2) \in E$, $n_1 \in N_I$ *and* $n_2 \in N_C$.

An instance description *of* n_i *refers to the set of attribute-value pairs* $E(n_i) = \{e(n_i, n_j) \in E\}$ *associated with* n_i.

This graph-structured model resembles the RDF model, where classes correspond to RDF classes, instances are RDF resources, and attribute values are RDF literals. A record in a relational database captures an instance and its attribute values. For clarity, we omit relationships, e.g. relations between RDF resources and foreign key relationships between

[1] `http://www.reposito.com/`

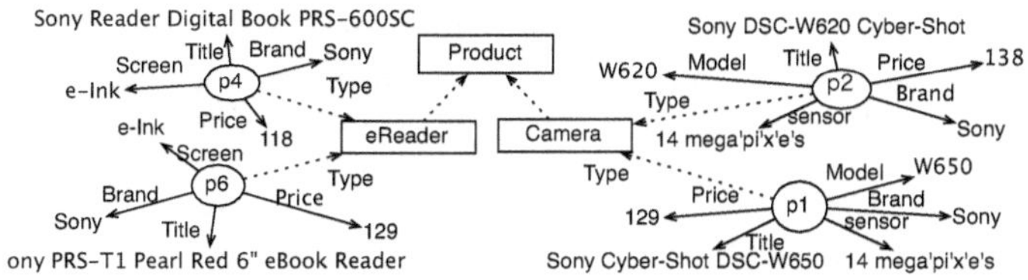

Figure 1: A data graph.

records, because they are not used for instance matching here. The graph for our data example is shown in Fig. 1.

Problem. The overall problem in this work is *instance matching*: given a set of instances and their descriptions, the goal is to detect those that refer to the same real-world object. Existing solutions can be characterized through the tuple $(\sim_I, \sigma)$, where $\sim_I$: $N_I \times N_I \to \mathbb{R}^+$ maps a pair of instances to a similarity value, and they are considered as being the same when that similarity value is higher than the threshold σ. Typically, this instance similarity $\sim_I$ is defined based on the similarity of the attribute values, $\sim_V$: $N_V \times N_V \to \mathbb{R}^+$. Effective *instance matching* involves determining (1) (combinations of) attributes (`Title`, `Price` etc.) and for each of them, (2) the weight indicating its importance, (3) the value representation function, simply referred to as values, (e.g. selecting only the most important words in the values of `Title` and using only the first 3 tokens of each word), (4) the similarity measures (e.g. edit distance and Jaccard similarity) and (5) the similarity thresholds [21, 22, 3, 12, 5].

Often performed as a candidate selection step, *blocking* is typically limited to finding attributes also called *blocking keys* (task 1) and their values (task 3) [12, 2, 24, 14]. They are used without weights and thresholds. The similarity is determined through a predefined boolean function predicate (e.g. exact value matching or value overlap). Previous works [14, 18] use the best ranked attribute [18] as key and all features from its values as key values (schema-based), or the values of attributes combined [14] (omitting attribute information, hence called schema-agnostic). Then, instances are considered as matches and placed into one block when there is an overlap in their value representation (i.e. value overlap is the similarity metric). Resembling the blocking problem, we focus on the tasks 1 and 3 in this instance matching context, i.e. finding attributes and their their value representation:

DEFINITION 2 (FIND BLOCKING KEYS AND KEY VALUES). *Given the data $G(N, E, L)$, we find a conjunction of boolean function predicates (called* blocking scheme*)* $\bigwedge_{e \in L^*} \sim_V^e$ *where* $\sim_V^e$: $N_V^e \times N_V^e \to \{true, false\}$, $N_V^e \subseteq N_V \subset N$ *denotes the values of some* keys $e \in L^*$, *and* $L^* \subset L$ *is the set of* blocking keys. *Blocking maps every instance* $n_i \in N_I$ *to a subset* $N_{B_i} \subseteq N_I \subset N$, *an equivalence class of instances (instances, that according to the blocking scheme, are equivalent to* n_i*) called* block*:* $N_{B_i} = [n_i] = \{n_j \in N_I : n_i, n_j \in N_I, \bigwedge_{e \in L^*} \sim_V^e (n_i, n_j) = true\}$.

EXAMPLE 2. *Tab. 2 shows two blocks obtained using* `Title` *as key and words in* `Title` *as key values. Note instances in the same block overlap on the word* `Sony` *and* `Reader`*. In addition, our approach recognizes that instances belong to the two subtypes* `Camera` *and* `eReader`.

Our Solution. We consider the case where the data might contain instances belonging to multiple unknown subtypes.

Table 2: Example blocks for different subtypes.

Block	ID	Title	Subtype
$block_1$	p_1	**Sony** Cyber-Shot DSC-W650	Camera
	p_2	**Sony** DSC-W620 Cyber-Shot	Camera
	p_3	**Sony** Cyber-Shot DSC-W650	Camera
$block_2$	p_4	Sony **Reader** PRS-600SC	eReader
	p_5	Sony **Reader** PRS-600SC	eReader
	p_6	Sony PRS-T1 6" eBook **Reader**	eReader

Our solution to that is based on the following main ideas: we observe that instances belonging to the same type share the same attributes in the schema, e.g. instances of the type `Product` have `Title` and `Price` as attributes. However, as noted in the example, these attributes we call schema features, are too few to distinguish the different subtypes of instances that exist in our `Product` example. Yet, following this intuition, we can also observe that besides schema features, instances of the same type also have some features in their values in common. For instance, instances of the type `Camera` commonly have `Cyber-Shot` and `camera` in the `Description`. We infer features in values as so-called *pseudo-schema features* when they commonly co-occur in instance descriptions. From these features and the instances in which they co-occur, we then infer different *subtypes*. Intuitively, a subtype is a set of instances that share the same set of pseudo-schema features. Both pseudo-schema features and subtypes learned from the data are then finally exploited for blocking and instance matching: representative attributes are learned for specific subtypes, and as pseudo-schema features characterize a set instead of individual instances, they are excluded from the value representation.

We compare our approach with existing solutions for blocking [19, 14]. Subtype-specific schemes are used in our solution. This represents a major depart from existing blocking and instance matching techniques. Several schemes might be used for blocking (i.e. multiple run blocking [5]). However, they are always applied to all instances. Instance matching is applied separately to candidates within blocks for reason of efficiency. However, we are not aware of any existing instance matching work, which uses different instance matching strategies for instances of different blocks. We use different strategies concerning tasks 1 and 3 for different subtypes to recognize that for improved result quality, their instances have different characteristics, and thus deserve different treatments. Further, we note that while also representing a set of instances, blocks are not the same as subtypes used in this work. Instances in the same blocks refer to the same real-world object, hence share object-specific features. Instances belonging to the same subtype refer to the same class, thus might have different object-specific features but share class-specific features (i.e. pseudo-schema features).

To form a blocking scheme, only the best ranked attribute determined for every subtype is used as key and non-pseudo-schema features are extracted from its value as key values. For finding blocks using such a scheme, there are two strategies: one is to iterate through the instances, as proposed recently [18]; using the features in the key value of a given instance, candidates are retrieved for that instance (*instance-based*); the alternative is to iterate through all features that appear in the instances' key values, and to retrieve all the candidates for a given feature (*feature-based*). For our approach, we use the feature-based strategy and apply value overlap as similarity measure.

Additionally, we show that the subtype-specific attributes and key values are also useful for instance matching. Similar to blocking, different attributes are values are used for different subtypes. Concerning tasks 2, 4 and 5, we assign uniform weights to attributes (i.e. no weighting) and use Jaccard similarity as measure where the threshold is learned using an existing technique [23].

3. LEARNING PSEUDO-SCHEMA FEATURES AND THEIR TYPES

The idea of pseudo-schema features and their use for learning the type semantics of structured data has been presented in our previous work [11]. The focus of that work, called TYPifier, lies in the clustering techniques that can be used for computing a hierarchy of types. In this work, we apply the technique used by TYPifier for identifying pseudo-schema features. However, we note that the hierarchy of types learned by TYPifier is not suitable. Note only does the learning of hierarchy requires more computational effort, it also yields types too fine-grain that have only low coverage of the instances. In this section, we firstly revisit the technique used to identify pseudo-schema features, and then introduce the technique used by TYPimatch to learn a set of types, as opposed to a hierarchy of types.

3.1 Learning Pseudo-schema Features

We observe that many values such as `Cyber-Shot` and `camera` appear in the descriptions of several instances. We aim to find those values, which commonly appear in descriptions of instances that belong to the same type. We call these values pseudo-schema features because just like schema attributes such as `Title` and `Price`, the are specific to one particular type. For identifying these features, we exploit two intuitions: first, candidate pseudo-schema features are those, which *appear in a large number of instance descriptions*; those which *co-occur in a large number of instance descriptions*, form a specific type. We capture co-occurrences through the notion of conditional co-occurrence probability (CCP), and groups of co-occurring features through the feature co-occurrence graph (FCG).

Recall we define the instance description $E(n)$ as a set of attribute-value pairs. From the label of a value node, words can be extracted such that every value can be conceived as a bag of words. $E(n)$ contains a feature f when it has a bag of words (a value) that contains f (we use $f \in E(n)$ to denote this containment). Then, we say a feature f_i co-occurs with another f_j when there is an entity description $E(n)$ that contains both. Through counting co-occurrences of features, we compute the CCP as follows:

DEFINITION 3 (CONDITIONAL CO-OCC. PROBABILITY). *The probability that f_i and f_j co-occur, given f_j, is $p(f_i|f_j) = p(f_i, f_j)/p(f_j) = count(f_i, f_j)/|N_I^{f_j}|$, where $N_I^{f_j} = \{n \in N_I : f_j \in E(n)\}$ denotes all instances having f_j as feature, and $count(f_i, f_j) = |N_I^{f_i} \cap N_I^{f_j}|$, the* co-occurrence count *of f_i and f_j.*

This co-occurrence relation between features is used to construct the FCG:

DEFINITION 4 (FEATURE CO-OCCURRENCE GRAPH). *Given the vocabulary of all features V, the feature* co-occurrence graph *is a labeled directed graph $G' = (N', E', L')$, with nodes $n \in N'$ stand for features in V and edges $w(n_i, n_j) \in E'$ capture the co-occurrence between the two features f_i and f_j, where edge labels L' stand for the conditional co-occurrence probabilities, $w = p(f_i|f_j)$.*

EXAMPLE 3. *The FCG according to the example in Tab. 1 is shown in Fig. 2. For example, because the features* `E-Ink` *and* `Sony` *co-occur, there are the corresponding edges w(*`E-Ink`*,* `Sony`*) and w(*`Sony`*,* `E-Ink`*) in the graph. Note $count$(*`E-Ink`*,* `Sony`*) $= |\{p_4, p_5, p_6\}| = 3$ and there are six instances that have* `Sony` *as feature. Thus, we have 0.5(*`E-Ink`*,* `Sony`*) because p(*`E-Ink`*|*`Sony`*) $=$ $count$(*`E-Ink`*,* `Sony`*)$/N_I^{\texttt{Sony}} = 0.5$. In the same way, we obtain 1.00(*`Sony`*,* `E-Ink`*) (and other edges and weights not shown in the figure).*

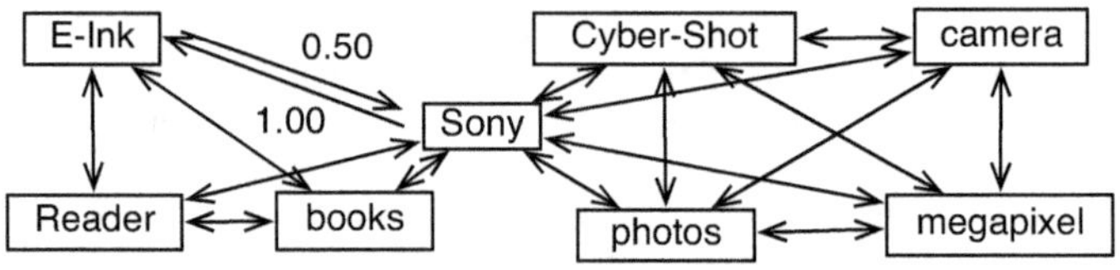

Figure 2: FCG for data in Table 1.

We propose to identify features that are characteristic for sets of instances by searching for maximal cliques in the FCG, i.e. clusters of features that pairwise, highly co-occur as measured in terms of CCP. The computation of pseudo-schema features is performed in two steps, namely computing G' from G (FCG) and extracting maximal cliques from G' ($MaxCliques$) as shown in Alg. 1.

For computing G', Alg. 1 firstly calculates the probabilities $p(f_i|f_j)$, which requires a maximum of $|N_I| \times |N_I|$ steps (simple counting) for computing the co-occurrences of f_i and f_j (because $|N_I|$ is the maximum number of instances that can have f_i or f_j). This has to be performed for all possible feature pairs, a number bounded by $|V| \times |V|$. An undirected edge $\theta(f_i, f_j)$ is created for G' only when both $p(f_i|f_j)$ and $p(f_j|f_i)$ are greater then the given parameter θ. This parameter is used to control the desired amount of pseudo-schema features generated by this procedure. Note that this is not the same as using the joint probability $p(f_i, f_j)$, which is often high when either $p(f_i)$ or $p(f_j)$ is high. This two-ways conditional probability gives a smoother estimate of co-occurrence.

Then, an existing maximal cliques algorithm [13] is applied to this undirected version of the FCG. While MaxCliques is known to be NP-hard, optimized algorithms such as the one we apply can provide fast runtime performance. The amount of edges in the FCG is bounded by $|V|^2$. The size of V is reduced through text processing techniques such as stop words elimination. Further, a large amount of feature pairs is pruned during the construction of the FCG, especially when θ is high.

Finally, only features corresponding to nodes contained in the resulting maximal cliques are kept as pseudo-schema features, the set of nodes $\mathbb{F}_{PS}^*$.

Algorithm 1: Computing maximal feature cliques

```
Input: G(N, E, L), V.
Data: Undirected FCG G'(N', E', L').
Result: F*_PS.
foreach f_i ∈ V do
    foreach f_j ∈ V do
        p(f_i|f_j) := count(f_i, f_j)/|N_I^{f_j}|;
        p(f_j|f_i) := count(f_i, f_j)/|N_I^{f_i}|;
        //Construct undirected edges.;
        if p(f_i|f_j) ≥ θ ∧ p(f_j|f_i) ≥ θ then
            G' := G' ∪ θ(f_i, f_j);
//Extract features from maximal cliques.
F*_PS :=Features (MaxCliques (G'));
return F*_PS;
```

3.2 Learning Types

Every maximal clique represents a cluster of features (i.e. a set of features) that are specific to a particular set of instances. We observe that these clusters are too fine-grained, hence do not directly correspond to the types given in the data. We propose to merge them to form larger clusters capturing types.

Previously, we use *feature co-occurrence* to determine features that are characteristic for sets of instances. To merge clusters, we leverage a similar intuition: we use pairwise *cluster co-occurrence*, i.e. *feature sets co-occurrence*, to determine the distance between clusters. Then, we merge those that frequently co-occur, i.e. are close to each other in terms of this distance metric:

DEFINITION 5 (CLUSTER DISTANCE). *Let $count(f_i, f_j)$ be the co-occurrence count of f_i and f_j and $|N_I^f|$ be the count of instances having f as feature, the distance $d(F_i, F_j)$ between the set of features F_i and F_j is the conditional probability of co-occurrence of features in F_i and F_j,*

$$d(F_i, F_j) = p(F_i|F_j) = \frac{\sum_{f_i \in F_i, f_j \in F_j} count(f_i, f_j)}{\sum_{f \in F_j} |N_I^f|} = \frac{|N_i \cap N_j|}{|N_j|},$$

where N_i (N_j) denotes instances that have at least one element in F_i (F_j) as feature in their description, i.e. for every $n_i \in N_i$ ($n_j \in N_j$) there exists one $f_i \in F_i$ ($f_j \in F_j$), where $f_i \in E(n_i)$ ($f_j \in E(n_j)$).

Two clusters F_i and F_j are merged when they highly co-occur. Equivalently, this co-occurrence means there is a strong overlap between the instances N_i that have some element in F_i and the instances N_j that have some element in F_j as features. Using this distance metric, we merge two clusters F_i and F_j when $d(F_i, F_j) > \epsilon$ and $d(F_j, F_i) > \epsilon$, where ϵ is a parameter used to control the granularity respectively the number of clusters. Clusters resulting from this merging are used as types. In particular, given the resulting cluster F_i, the set of instances that belong to the type captured by F_i is simply N_i, i.e. instances that have some elements in F_i as features.

We note that just like TYPifier [11], the learning of types as proposed above also makes use of pseudo-schema features. However, TYPifier requires complex hierarchical relations between and operators on clusters to perform hierarchical clustering. The method proposed above only uses the distance metric and applies cluster merging as the only operator. When doing hierarchical clustering, not only the features but also the instances representing the clusters have to be processed. For this, features and instances not only have to be merged but also might be added or spitted during the hierarchy construction process. Here, we only need to compute a set of clusters, where the computation stops after merging the clusters represented by the features. Only then, instances have to be considered, i.e. we simply group instances together that are associated with pseudo-schema features representing the same cluster.

We will now learn keys for a specific cluster and use them for blocking instances that belong to that cluster.

4. LEARNING KEYS AND VALUES

The keys are selected based on their ability to discriminate instances, measured in terms of a notion we call instance similarity, while the value representation excludes the pseudo-schema features computed before because they characterize a set instead of individual instances.

4.1 Blocking Key Selection

Intuitively, attributes that are more useful in discriminating instances shall be selected as keys. Because keys capture similarity (thus are called *similarity attributes*), we introduce a notion of instance similarity that distinguishes attributes by their ability to discriminate instances, measured by the number of similarity evidences they provide:

DEFINITION 6 (ATTR.-SPECIFIC INSTANCE SIMILARITY). *Given $G(N, E, L)$ and the similarity relations $\sim_I$ and $\sim_V$ on the instances $N_I \subseteq N$ and attribute values $N_V \subseteq N$, respectively, the* instance similarity *of an attribute e is measured as the number of instances in N_I that are similar, given they all have a similar value for e, i.e. $s(e) = |\{n : n, m \in N_I, m \sim_I n, v(e, m) \sim_V v(e, n)\}|$, where $v(e, x)$ refers to the value of the attribute e of the instance x.*

Note that this notion reflects the intuition behind existing learning-based approaches [21, 22, 3, 12, 5], which aim to learn keys that maximally separate positive examples from negative ones, i.e. keys that lead to a large amount of correct matches (high $s(e)$) when applied against training data. However, obtaining representative examples (for unknown types) is difficult. Thus, we propose to estimate instance similarity based on the *dependencies among attribute values* that can be observed in the data:

DEFINITION 7 (DEPENDENCY). *The strength of* dependency *of an attribute e_i from an attribute e_j, denoted $d(e_i, e_j)$, is inverse to the amount of information carried by values of e_i, given the values of e_j are known. Given $G = (N, E, L)$, $d(e_i, e_j)$ is measured as the entropy of the values of e_i, $N_V^{e_i} = \{n_y | e_i(n_x, n_y) \in E\}$, conditional on val-*

ues of e_j, $N_V^{e_j} = \{n_y | e_j(n_x, n_y) \in E\}$:

$$d(e_i, e_j) = (1 + H(N_V^{e_i} | N_V^{e_j}))^{-1} \quad (1)$$

$$= \left(1 + \sum_{n_j \in N_V^{e_j}} p(n_j) H(N_V^{e_i} | N_V^{e_j} = n_j)\right)^{-1}$$

$$= \left(1 + \sum_{n_i \in N_V^{e_i}, n_j \in N_V^{e_j}} p(n_i, n_j) log \frac{p(n_i)}{p(n_i, n_j)}\right)^{-1} \quad (2)$$

EXAMPLE 4. *For the attributes given in Tab. 1, we obtain* $d(Brand, Title) = 1$ *and* $d(Title, Brand) = 0.43$. *It can be easily observed in the data that given* `Title`, *it is easier to predict the value for* `Brand`, *while given* `Brand` *there are many products with different values for* `Title`.

When an attribute e_j is strongly dependent on an attribute e_i ($d(e_j, e_i)$ is high), it means that if instances have the same value for e_i then the probability they also have the same value for e_j is high. In particular, the conditional entropy used above implies that for any two instances n_i and n_j, $d(e_x, e_i) > d(e_x, e_j)$ means the probability n_i and n_j have the same value for e_x when they have the same value for e_i, is higher than the probability n_i and n_j have the same value for e_x when they have the same value for e_j, i.e. $p(v(n_i, e_x) = v(n_j, e_x) | v(n_i, e_i) = v(n_j, e_i)) > p(v(n_i, e_x) = (n_j, e_x) | v(n_i, e_j) = v(n_j, e_j))$.

We note this notion of dependency correlates with instance similarity: namely, the more other attributes are dependent on e, the higher the amount of evidences e can provide (higher $s(e)$) and hence, the less the amount of additional evidences the other attributes can contribute. We exploit this correlation to estimate $s(e)$ as follows:

PROPOSITION 1. *Let* $Agg : 2^{\mathbb{R}^+} \rightarrow \mathbb{R}^+$ *be a monotonic aggregation function and* L_E^F *be the set of attributes associated with the type* F. *For two attributes* $e_i, e_j \in L_E^F$, *if* $Agg_{e \in L_E^F}(d(e, e_i)) \geq Agg_{e \in L_E^F}(d(e, e_j))$ *then we have* $s(e_i) \geq s(e_j)$.

Alg. 2 computes the instance similarity for every attribute in L_E^F that is associated with a given type F, and stores it in S. Selecting the set of blocking keys L^* is simply done by sorting S and keeping the top ones with highest instance similarity. In this work, we simply use the top-1 attribute as the blocking key, i.e. L^* consists of exactly one attribute.

First, Alg. 2 computes $d(e_i, e_j)$ for every pair of attributes to construct the matrix M. Every combination of values for e_i and e_j has to be considered to derive the probabilities $p(n_i)$ and $p(n_i, n_j)$. At most, these steps of probability computation have to be performed $|N_V^{e_{max}}| \times |N_V^{e_{max}}|$ times (e_{max} denotes the attribute in the data that is associated with the largest number of values). We choose the *sum of dependencies* as an aggregation function for selecting similarity attributes. Then, instance similarities stored in S can be derived from the sums of row values in M. Since probabilities as well as the sums of dependency values in M can be computed in time linear to the size of G, we have this as overall complexity:

THEOREM 1. *Given* $G = (N, E, L)$, S *can be computed in* $\mathcal{O}((|N_V^{e_{max}}| \times |N_V^{e_{max}}|)^{|L_E^F| \times |L_E^F|})$.

Algorithm 2: Computing instance similarities

```
Input: G(N, E, L).
Data: H(N_V^{e_i}, N_V^{e_j}), |L_E^F| × |L_E^F| matrix M.
Result: S.
foreach e_i ∈ L_E^F ⊂ L do
    foreach e_j ∈ L_E^F ⊂ L do
        foreach n_i ∈ N_V^{e_i} = {n_y | e_i(n_x, n_y) ∈ E} do
            foreach n_j ∈ N_V^{e_j} = {n_y | e_j(n_x, n_y) ∈ E}
            do
                H(N_V^{e_i}, N_V^{e_j}) =
                H(N_V^{e_i}, N_V^{e_j}) + p(n_i, n_j) log (p(n_i) / p(n_i, n_j));
        M_ij = (1 + H(i, j))^{-1};
foreach e ∈ L_E^F ⊂ L do
    S_e = s(e) = Σ_{1≤i≤|L_E^F|} M_ei;
return S;
```

Thus, when excluding the effect of maximal clique finding, which operates against the relatively small graph of attributes, both the computation of pseudo-schema features (and the types based on them) and the selection of blocking key can be performed in polynomial time, bounded by the maximum number of instances and values associated with an attribute, and the amount of attributes. In practice, these bounds can be reduced substantially: not all attributes are relevant for blocking. For instance, strategies for ranking and filtering attributes (e.g. attributes too general or too type-specific to be useful for blocking) can be applied. Further, we note that just like other learning algorithms, a smaller amount of representative samples may be chosen instead of using all instances and values. Even without these strategies, the proposed algorithms scale well to large datasets in our experiment.

4.2 Key Value Selection

The idea behind selecting keys also applies for the selection of key values: they should help to discriminate instances. Pseudo-schema features characterize a set of instances well but are less useful in discriminating individual instances. As a result, while they help to identify types, they are less useful in identifying blocks of similar instances, as illustrated by the following example:

EXAMPLE 5. *There are two* `Product` *instances with the* `Title` *"Sony Cyber-Shot DSC-W650" and "Sony DSC-W620 Cyber-Shot". When using all the words in* `Title` *as key values, these two instances exhibit an overlap and thus, would be placed in one block. However, after excluding pseudo-schema features such as* `Sony` *and* `Cyber-Shot`, *features that remain such as* `DSC-W650` *and* `DSC-W620` *are more specific to these two instances (rather than the class they belong to).*

Thus, pseudo-schema features associated with a type are excluded from the value representation of keys that have been selected for that type.

In summary, the output of the two steps discussed before is a blocking scheme for every subtype F, which consists the attribute as key that has highest instance similarity. The key value representation contains all features from its value except those that are in the set of pseudo-schema features.

Table 3: **For each dataset pair: number of instances, attributes, words that appear in attribute values, pseudo-schema features (PS), and mappings indicating two instances are same (ground truth, GT).**

Task	Instances		Words	PS	GT
	Dataset1	Dataset2			
AB	1,081	1,092	7,040	163	1,097
DS	2,616	64,263	89,189	386	5,347

5. EXPERIMENTAL EVALUATION

Our work mainly addresses scenarios where type information is missing. To study the proposed solution, we employ a recent instance matching benchmark [10] that captures data from enterprise databases. We show that recognizing subtypes and learning type-specific attributes and values improve both efficiency and the quality of results. Compared against the best blocking baseline, our approach is up to several times faster and improves result quality measured in terms of reduction ratio (RR) by up to 32.62%, while maintaining similar results for pair completeness (PC). Considering the instance matching task, our solution, when used in combination with standard solutions for other tasks, improves F-measure result by up to 201.56%.

5.1 Datasets and Matching Tasks

We now briefly describe the datasets and matching tasks in the benchmark [10] that are used here. They cover the bibliographic and e-commerce domains. Tab. 3 provides an overview of these datasets.

DBLP-Scholar (DS). These datasets include data from DBLP and Google Scholar. The attributes and values in Google Scholar are automatically extracted from full-text documents, hence contain a number of misspellings and heterogeneous representations of authors and venues. Because one instance in DBLP can be mapped to multiple instances in Google Scholar, the number of GT is larger than the number of instances in DBLP.

Abt-Buy (AB). This matching task is performed between instances of the product dataset from `http://abt.com` and `http://buy.com`. Although all the products are stored in the same tables, they actually represent different subtypes of products, including `computer`, `cell phone`, and `wash machine`. Compared to the other matching tasks featured by this benchmark, the one captured by this pair of datasets is in fact most representative for our scenario of heterogeneous data with multiple unknown types.

5.2 Experimental Setting

In the experiments, we select the four approaches [14, 19, 5, 20] as discussed before as baselines.

Systems. The first two approaches are recent approaches proposed for blocking, while the other twos are state-of-the-art solutions targeting the instance matching task. The first one is the type- and schema-agnostic approach (**Agnostic**), which treats instances as unstructured bags of words extracted from attribute values [14]. The second approach is the unsupervised solution for learning keys based on ranking attributes by discriminability and coverage [19] (**Unsupervised**). It requires setting two parameters: α is used to control the discriminability of a key and β determines if a key should be removed. We swept over parameters and used the optimal configurations with $\alpha = 0.9$ and $\beta = 0.5$. For instance matching, we use a supervised learning approach, which infers the attributes, similarity thresholds etc. from positive and negative examples [5] (**Supervised**). We use 10% of the ground truth mappings as positive examples, and negative examples are generated by combining instances in positive examples [9]. Finally, we use a recent approach, which iteratively cross-fertilizes instance matching results with schema matching results [20] until convergence (**PARIS**). The maxinum number of iterations is set to 5, while PARIS always terminated in less than four iterations in the experiments. PARIS's implementation is available for download. We use that PARIS Java implementation for the experiment, while the other systems were implemented in Java 5.

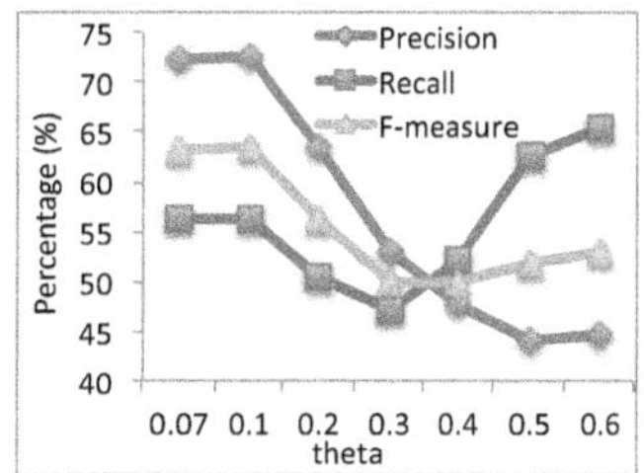

Figure 3: The Effect of θ on Effectiveness.

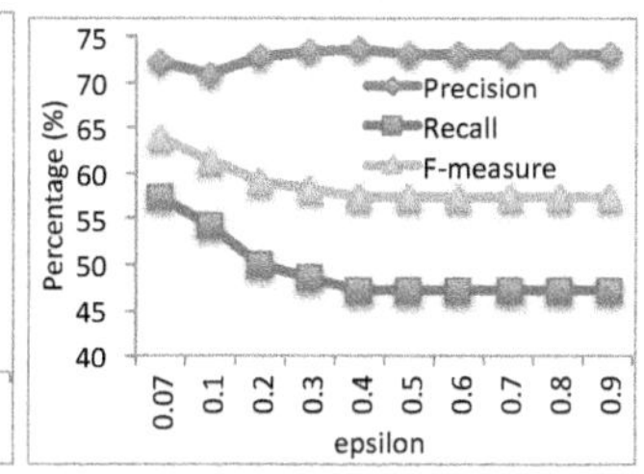

Figure 4: The Effect of ϵ on Effectiveness.

We compare these approaches against our solution, called **TYPiMatch**. As discussed, to solve the task of finding similarity threshold, TYPiMatch applies an existing mechanism that exploits redundancy between thresholds [23]. Also for TYPiMatch, we swept over parameters to find the optimal configuration such that the results presented in these experiments, represent best performances of the studied approaches. As parameters, TYPiMatch uses θ and ϵ to control the amount of pseudo-schema features and clusters, respectively. The effect of these parameters are shown in Figs. 3 and 4. Higher θ results in less pseudo-schema features. We observed that as θ increases, precision decreases and while recall decreases in the beginning (for small values of θ), it also increases with larger values for θ. With less pseudo-schema features available for pruning key values, instance representations contain more features for classes. Using them to find similarity yields more matches (high recall) including incorrect ones (low precision). High ϵ prevents clusters from being merged. Thus, as ϵ increases, the number of clusters increases. To accommodate the increasing number of clusters that are also more fine-grained, TYPiMatch employs a large number of schemes. As a result of this, precision increases while recall decreases. Thus, these two parameters can be used to control the tradeoff between precision and recall. The results presented in the following are for the configuration $\epsilon = 0.07$ and $\theta = 0.1$.

Metrics. We use standard metrics proposed for evaluating blocking and instance matching results. Let S be the result generated by blocking or instance matching approaches, M be the matching pairs, i.e. the ground truth GT, and N the non-matching pairs in the dataset, i.e. all possible pairs of instances but the ones in GT. PC captures the ratio between correct matches as captured in the blocks and all matches in the ground truth, i.e. $PC = \frac{|S \cap M|}{|M|}$. RR measures the relative reduction in the size of the comparison space accomplished by blocking, i.e. $RR = 1 - \frac{|S|}{|M \cup N|}$. Precision ($P$) captures the ratio between correct matches and all generated matches, i.e. $P = \frac{|S \cap M|}{|S|}$. Recall ($R$) is the same as PC, i.e. $R = \frac{|S \cap M|}{|M|}$. F-measure ($F$) considers both P and R, calculated as $F = \frac{2PR}{P+R}$.

All experiments were run on a server with two Intel Xeon 2.8GHz Dual-Core CPUs, using 8GB of main memory, running Linux with kernel version 2.6.18.

5.3 Efficiency of Blocking

Table 4: Performance of learning blocking keys in ms.

	TYPiMatch-Type	TYPiMatch-Key	Unsupervised
Abt	4,572	**1,041**	1,069
Buy		**895**	1,192
DBLP	42,262	**1,679**	1,952
Scholar		10,639	**9,661**

Tab. 4 shows learning times only for TYPiMatch and Supervised because Agnostic simply uses all attributes as keys. Both approaches yield good and fairly comparable performances, requiring only a few seconds to output the keys. We can see that TYPiMatch was slightly faster in learning keys (TYPiMatch-Key), which excludes the times needed to infer the subtypes in the data (TYPiMatch-Type). Unsupervised iterates through the data graph and considers all instances to calculate the discriminability and coverage for each property. Thus, learning time for Unsupervised increases with the size of the dataset. This is also the case with TYPiMatch. It uses dependencies for key selection. Given an attribute, it inspects values associated with instances to calculate dependencies. However, only values owned by more than one instance are relevant. Thus, processing was faster for datasets that contain less duplicate values. Also, we can see that inferring types could be done efficiently. As shown in the TYPiMatch-Type column, this could be done in 4,572 ms for AB, and 42,262 ms for DS.

Table 5: Performance of blocking in ms.

	TYPiMatch	Agnostic	Unsupervised
AB	**9,635**	27,208	18,243
DS	**95,254**	882,626	491,569

Tab. 4 shows blocking times for all three approaches. Note that blocking performance depends on two tasks: (1) retrieving candidates from the index and (2) performing pair-wise similarity computation to filter these candidates. As discussed, an instance-based [18] or a feature-based strategy can be used for candidate retrieval. While Unsupervised uses the former, the other two approaches employ the latter.

TYPiMatch yields best performance while Agnostic is clearly worst. The latter is slow because it employs all words extracted from all attribute values, whereas the other two approaches only use words extracted from the keys. Compared to the baselines, TYPiMatch benefits from decomposing the dataset into n subtypes. Because blocking is performed separately for every subtype, the number of retrieval operations needed equals the number of distinct features associated with every subtype. The total number of features for all subtypes combined is higher than the number of distinct features for the single general type. Accordingly, the total number of retrieval operations is higher for TYPiMatch. However, the total number of candidates retrieved for all subtype features was lower than the total number of candidates retrieved for the general type features. Therefore in total, TYPiMatch spends less time in computing matches. In fact, this can be seen as a "blocking within blocking" strategy, where the data is partitioned into blocks corresponding to subtypes, and subsequently, is further decomposed into more fine-grained blocks. However, we already pointed out in Section 2 that subtypes and blocks resulting from standard blocking are different in many aspects.

Table 6: Effectiveness of blocking in terms of PC and RR, * indicates statistically significant improvements of TYPiMatch over the best baseline, Unsupervised (paired t-test, p<0.05).

	TYPiMatch		Agnostic		Unsupervised		chg% over second best	
	PC	RR	PC	RR	PC	RR	PC	RR
AB	86.14	**94.17**	85.96	26.45	**87.05**	71.01	-1.04*	+32.62*
DS	98.33	**99.64**	98.43	93.16	**99.93**	96.20	-1.60*	+3.58*

5.4 Effectiveness of Blocking

Tab. 6 presents total results for blocking effectiveness for the comparison between our solution and the other two unsupervised approaches. TYPiMatch largely outperforms these two in terms of RR and achieves comparable results for PC. Compared to the second best approach in every setting, TYPiMatch results in -1.32% decrease in PC and and +18.10% increase in RR on average. Intuitively, instances which refer to the same real-world object should belong to the same type. Thus, learning the blocking scheme for every type should be possible without losing PC. However, the scheme obtained for every type is more specific and thus, can improve RR. The results show this is indeed true for the matching tasks in the benchmark, as TYPiMatch yields high quality types that can be used to preserve PC and improve RR. In particular, we note it produces the largest improvement for the AB task. This is because for products captured by these datasets, there exist many different subtypes that exhibit different vocabularies of features. TYPiMatch is able to infer these subtypes and to adopts distinguished words for matching instances with these types. For the DS task, which involves datasets that are well maintained and fairly homogeneous (contain only instances of type `Publication`), TYPiMatch achieves a small improvement.

5.5 Efficiency of Instance Matching

Table 7: Performance of learning instance matching schemes and executing them in ms.

	Learning		Instance Matching		
	TYPiMatch	Supervised	TYPiMatch	Supervised	PARIS
AB	**2,369**	2,784	24,527	66,856	**18,373**
DBLP	6,281	**5,726**	101,070	229,833	**70,479**

For instance matching, this version of TYPiMatch also includes the mechanism for learning threshold [23]. The overall time needed by TYPiMatch for learning keys, key values and thresholds and the time needed by Supervised to learn instance matching scheme, which additionally, also captures the weights, are shown in Tab. 7. These two approaches achieve similar performance. However, Supervised's learning process is non-deterministic. In our experiments, it often did not finish after several hours. This problem has been discussed before [23], which occurs especially when there is a large numbers of attributes that can be used to form the scheme. The results presented for Supervised is an average over five successful runs.

Tab. 7 also shows the performance for instance matching. The process implemented by TYPiMatch for this is similar to the one used for blocking: it consists of feature-based retrieval of candidates and then, for matching them, Jaccard similarity as well as the learned thresholds are employed. As discussed, due to the use of types, this processing resembles a "blocking within instance matching" strategy. TYPiMatch retrieves candidates for subtype features and match these subtype candidates. We can see this strategy yields better performance when analyzing the differences between TYPiMatch and Supervised. While the learning techniques they employ are different, the resulting scheme employed by both these approaches for matching are of the same type, i.e. keys, values and thresholds (and weights). Just like TYPiMatch, Supervised applies feature-based candidate retrieval and uses such a scheme for matching. However, TYPiMatch needs only half of the time taken by Supervised. This is because TYPiMatch retrieves and matches instances belonging to subtypes (using different schemes), Supervised applies its scheme to all candidates. Even though TYPiMatch requires a higher number of retrieval operations, it yields better overall performance because it reduces the number of pairwise similarity computation. However, we note this strategy employed by TYPiMatch is different to the standard pipeline of computing candidates via blocking and refining candidates using an instance matcher. TYPiMatch does not physically partition the data into different blocks. Using features from a subtype-specific scheme, candidates retrieved might belong to that corresponding subtype as well as some other subtypes. Hence, blocks are actually formed online during feature-based retrieval and also, they might be overlapping. Moreover, they are more coarse-grained, corresponding to classes of entities instead of individual real-world objects.

PARIS is the fastest. We observed that this is mainly because PARIS is very aggressive in pruning candidates. Often, candidates are only kept when they have identical attribute values. While this largely increases performance, it leads to low recall when the data contains more noises, as discussed in the following.

5.6 Effectiveness of Instance Matching

Tab. 8 presents results for instance matching effectiveness. TYPiMatch largely outperforms the other two approaches in terms of F-measure. We can see from the results that the product matching task AB is more difficult, where F-measures values obtained by all approaches are lower than for the other task. This is because the product descriptions contain a large amount of noisy text, while the bibliographic data employed in that benchmark is more structured.

Because Supervised randomly picks positive examples, the schemes it learns vary in different runs. We calculate the average for five runs. We observed that Supervised's strategy of learning the threshold from the skyline of negative examples tends to produce low values. As the result, Supervised covers most positive matches and thus, leads to high recall. However, this comes at the cost of very low precision.

The poor performance on the AB matching task suggests that PARIS is not successful with dealing with noises in textual descriptions. PARIS can propagate evidences when the same values at the data or schema level can be found. However, this task involves many products, which refer to the same object, but due to noises in the data, these matching instances greatly vary in their values for `name` and `price`. PARIS's performance was better for the DS task. As a general observation, PARIS tends to be more aggressive in pruning results compared to the other approaches. This leads to high precision but low recall.

6. RELATED WORK

Throughout the paper, we have discussed our previous work on TYPifier [11] and the most related approaches applicable to the problem of learning blocking keys and key values [14, 18] as well as more complex instance matching schemes that also include similarity metrics and thresholds [23, 5, 3, 12]. We pointed out that as opposed to existing solutions, we learn keys and key values that are specific for subtypes derived from the data. Here, we provide a broader overview of solutions for the instance matching problem.

Efficient Instance Matching. For efficiency, there exist several *similarity join algorithms* for efficient similarity comparison [6, 1, 16]. They can be used to compute candidate matches based on the blocking scheme learned by our approach, where the conjunction of similarity function predicates acts as the join predicate. By filtering candidates, *blocking approaches* aim to reduce the number of similarity comparisons [12, 2, 24, 14]. The attributes learned by our approach can be used for instance matching in general and as blocking keys that can be quickly processed to produce candidates, in particular.

Attribute-based Matching. For improving the quality of matching results, there are approaches that specifically focus on the matching at the level of fields (attributes). To this category belong the various proposals for measuring similarities, from character-based metrics (e.g. edit distance) to token-based metrics that consider the rearrangements of words [7]. A recent approach measures the degrees of matching based on probability estimates [20] (and cross-fertilizes them by incorporating and propagating evidences at the data and schema level). In this work, we simply assume a given similarity metric that can be used for blocking.

Supervised Learning. For matching at the level of instances (records), there are supervised learning techniques, which use decision trees to learn combinations of similarity functions, both for effective instance matching [21, 22] and for quick blocking [12]. This class of algorithms performs worst than SVM models [3]. The quality of instance matching results achieved through SVM models could be further improved by a recent approach that reduces the learning of similarity function predicates to the maximum rectangle problem [5]. We compare our approach to this learning-based approach [5] in the experiment.

Semi-Supervised Learning. There are also semi-supervised techniques based on probabilistic graphical models. In fact, it has been shown that many existing instance matching approaches including the blocking solution here can be specified in terms of Markov Logic formulas and reformulated as a Markov Logic learning problem [17]. However, this involves learning both the structure (formulas) and their weights. The current solution [17] still requires the logic for matching to be manually specified as Markov Logic formulas.

Unsupervised Learning. Probabilistic graphical mod-

Table 8: Effectiveness of instance matching in terms R, P and F; * indicates statistically significant improvements of TYPiMatch over the best baseline, Supervised for AB, and PARIS for DS (paired t-test, p<0.05).

	TYPiMatch			Supervised			PARIS			chg% over second best		
	R	P	F	R	P	F	R	P	F	R	P	F
AB	**56.70**	**72.49**	**63.63**	55.79	13.01	21.10	2.55	12.44	4.24	+1.63*	+457.19*	+201.56*
DS	75.28	76.49	**75.88**	**79.66**	5.76	10.74	41.18	**89.08**	56.32	+82.81*	-14.13*	+34.73*

els were also used for unsupervised instance matching. Common to all these approaches is the observation that instance matching can be formulated as a standard classification task, where instances are classified as matching or non-matching [8]. For instance, latent binary variables in a hierarchical graphical model were used to model whether attributes match or not [15]. While in principle, the problem of learning blocking keys tackled here could be formulated as a classification problem, different learning techniques may be needed due to the large amount of classes.

7. CONCLUSION

For the problem of matching instances, we provide a solution to solve the subtasks of selecting discriminative attributes and representing their values. This solution is derived for every subtype learned from the data to recognize that in some datasets, instances cannot be assumed to be of one particular type but may actually belong to multiple unknown subtypes. We showed in experiments that our approach of using subtype-specific keys and values improved both blocking and instance matching. In experiments, we show how this approach can be used for blocking and instance matching. Compared to state-of-the-art instance matching approaches, our solution greatly improves result quality (up to 201.56% improvement in terms of F-measure). Considering the blocking task, our approach yields 32.62% improvement in terms of reduction ratio. It is also time efficient when compared against approaches that achieve similar result quality. Currently, we focus on selecting keys and their values. One direction for future work is to apply this subtype-specific strategy to other tasks in instance matching such as learning similarity metrics and thresholds.

8. REFERENCES

[1] A. Arasu, V. Ganti, and R. Kaushik. Efficient exact set-similarity joins. In *VLDB*, pages 918–929, 2006.

[2] M. Bilenko, B. Kamath, and R. J. Mooney. Adaptive blocking: Learning to scale up record linkage. In *ICDM*, pages 87–96, 2006.

[3] M. Bilenko and R. J. Mooney. Adaptive duplicate detection using learnable string similarity measures. In *KDD*, pages 39–48, 2003.

[4] C. Bizer, T. Heath, and T. Berners-Lee. Linked data - the story so far. *International Journal of Semantic Web and Information System*, 5(3):1–22, 2009.

[5] S. Chaudhuri, B.-C. Chen, V. Ganti, and R. Kaushik. Example-driven design of efficient record matching queries. In *VLDB*, pages 327–338, 2007.

[6] S. Chaudhuri, V. Ganti, and R. Kaushik. A primitive operator for similarity joins in data cleaning. In *ICDE*, page 5, 2006.

[7] W. W. Cohen. Integration of heterogeneous databases without common domains using queries based on textual similarity. In *SIGMOD Conference*, pages 201–212, 1998.

[8] I. Fellegi and A. Sunter. A Theory for Record Linkage. *Journal of the American Statistical Association*, 64(328):1183–1210, 1969.

[9] R. Isele and C. Bizer. Learning linkage rules using genetic programming. In *OM*, 2011.

[10] H. Köpcke, A. Thor, and E. Rahm. Evaluation of entity resolution approaches on real-world match problems. *PVLDB*, 3(1):484–493, 2010.

[11] Y. Ma, T. Tran, and V. Bicer. Typifier: Inferring the type semantics of structured data. In *ICDE, to appear*, 2013.

[12] M. Michelson and C. A. Knoblock. Learning blocking schemes for record linkage. In *AAAI*, 2006.

[13] P. R. J. Östergård. A fast algorithm for the maximum clique problem. *Discrete Applied Mathematics*, 120(1-3):197–207, 2002.

[14] G. Papadakis, E. Ioannou, C. Niederée, and P. Fankhauser. Efficient entity resolution for large heterogeneous information spaces. In *WSDM*, pages 535–544, 2011.

[15] P. D. Ravikumar and W. W. Cohen. A hierarchical graphical model for record linkage. In *UAI*, pages 454–461, 2004.

[16] S. Sarawagi and A. Kirpal. Efficient set joins on similarity predicates. In *SIGMOD Conference*, pages 743–754, 2004.

[17] P. Singla and P. Domingos. Entity resolution with markov logic. In *ICDM*, pages 572–582, 2006.

[18] D. Song and J. Heflin. Automatically generating data linkages using a domain-independent candidate selection approach. In *International Semantic Web Conference (1)*, pages 649–664, 2011.

[19] D. Song, J. Heflin, and J. Heflin. Automatically generating data linkages using a domain-independent candidate selection approach. In *International Semantic Web Conference (1)*, pages 649–664, 2011.

[20] F. M. Suchanek, S. Abiteboul, and P. Senellart. Paris: Probabilistic alignment of relations, instances, and schema. *PVLDB*, 5(3):157–168, 2011.

[21] S. Tejada, C. A. Knoblock, and S. Minton. Learning object identification rules for information integration. *Information System*, 26(8):607–633, 2001.

[22] S. Tejada, C. A. Knoblock, and S. Minton. Learning domain-independent string transformation weights for high accuracy object identification. In *KDD*, pages 350–359, 2002.

[23] J. Wang, G. Li, J. X. Yu, and J. Feng. Entity matching: How similar is similar. *PVLDB*, 4(10):622–633, 2011.

[24] S. E. Whang, D. Menestrina, G. Koutrika, M. Theobald, and H. Garcia-Molina. Entity resolution with iterative blocking. In *SIGMOD Conference*, pages 219–232, 2009.

Robust Query Rewriting using Anchor Data

Nick Craswell
Bing, Microsoft
Bellevue, USA
nickcr@microsoft.com

Bodo Billerbeck
Bing, Microsoft
Melbourne, Aus
bodob@microsoft.com

Dennis Fetterly
Microsoft Research
Mountain View, USA
fetterly@microsoft.com

Marc Najork
Microsoft Research
Mountain View, USA
najork@microsoft.com

ABSTRACT

Query rewriting algorithms can be used as a form of query expansion, by combining the user's original query with automatically generated rewrites. Rewriting algorithms bring linguistic datasets to bear without the need for iterative relevance feedback, but most studies of rewriting have used proprietary datasets such as large-scale search logs. By contrast this paper uses readily available data, particularly ClueWeb09 link text with over 1.2 billion anchor phrases, to generate rewrites. To avoid overfitting, our initial analysis is performed using Million Query Track queries, leading us to identify three algorithms which perform well. We then test the algorithms on Web and newswire data. Results show good properties in terms of robustness and early precision.

Categories and Subject Descriptors

H.3.3 [**Information Retrieval**]: Retrieval Models

General Terms

Algorithms, Experimentation

Keywords

Query rewriting, anchor text

1. INTRODUCTION

Web search is typified by fast light-weight interaction. In a 2006 Web search log, the median query length was two words, the median click count was one and the median rank of clicked results was one [34]. These median values could hardly be more extreme, compared to other IR applications where significant time is spent on query reformulation and viewing multiple relevant results, for example [2]. Given the characteristics of Web search, it is natural that Web search evaluation focuses on achieving good early precision given short user queries, while also focusing on scaling to large collections [18].

Another characteristic of Web search that has attracted less attention from the research community is the importance of query response time. Web search results are typically returned in under one second, and experiments that introduce a delay of 100 to 400 milliseconds have demonstrated a significant impact on user engagement [24, 8], with users performing fewer queries and becoming less likely to click. This creates a balancing act. Improving early precision is positive for users, but if this increases response time by hundreds of milliseconds, the overall effect on users may be negative.

Some algorithms have been developed and published which translate, expand or adjust the query based on large-scale linguistic resources such as search logs and document sets, for example [12, 21, 16, 20]. Many of these rewriting methods can be run quickly, without requiring any extra search against a document corpus, so they are suitable for applications where response time is critical. They may also rewrite the query conservatively. An approach which adds fewer terms to the query can be executed more efficiently.

This paper follows that approach, of using linguistic resources to rewrite queries, with the goal of improving retrieval effectiveness. We follow the approach of Dang and Croft [13], using a large anchor graph as a linguistic resource for query rewriting. Despite its contribution in defining the anchor graph, that paper took a semi-manual approach, assuming the user can choose the most effective formulation from a set of automatically generated candidates. Here our contribution is to introduce new algorithms that achieve statistically significant improvements in retrieval effectiveness in a fully automatic setting. The new algorithms, which adopt the random walk approach of [11], show good effectiveness in early precision and robustness.

2. RELATED WORK

Query-document mismatch is a fundamental problem in information retrieval, with one solution being pseudo-relevance feedback (PRF), employing two rounds of retrieval. The first uses the original query, then the top-k results are mined for additional vocabulary terms. The second round uses the expanded query, which typically is a mixture of the original query terms and expansion query terms.

PRF can improve both precision and recall of web search [32]. However, given the constraints on response time men-

WSDM'13, February 4–8, 2013, Rome, Italy.

tioned in the introduction, we note that PRF introduces a significant extra delay to query processing. Query execution may be massively parallel, accessing many index servers and many document summarization servers [3]. However, certain parts of the process are sequential, with three major sequential phases being query expansion (if any), retrieval and summarization. These must be sequential, since retrieval can not commence until the query is finalized, and summarization can not commence until the top-k results have been identified.

To take expansion terms from the top-k documents, for example building a relevance model [23], their content, or some representation of their language model, must be processed. Computationally this may have comparable cost to the document summarization phase at the end of retrieval. Therefore, to apply PRF an extra round of retrieval and summarization is required during the initial query-expansion phase, and this must be complete before retrieval of the user's results can begin. This is even true for expansion against a reduced corpus such as Wikipedia [33, 15, 29]. For example, the Wikipedia-based expansion method of Elsas *et al.* [15] retrieves the top 1000 documents for the user's query from Wikipedia.

Instead of PRF, or in addition to it, query rewriting may be based on linguistic resources such as anchor text or query logs. These resources can potentially be accessed with $O(1)$ lookups or with efficient data structures such as a trie [7]. The rewritten query can be a spelling correction, a suggestion for the user, or a query that can be mixed with the user's query to improve retrieval effectiveness.

Jones *et al.* [21] take the user's query and rewrite it to form a modified query. Their application is an advertising scenario where recall is important and documents have few words. Papers on spelling correction [7, 16] assume that the user's query is ill-formed and attempt to correct it. Such models operate at the character level, whereas algorithms which introduce synonyms operate at the word level. Despite this difference, in other ways the algorithms are related, for example using a dataset of translation probabilities. In general they use linguistic datasets, for example a large-scale set of query reformulations from web searching users [21], the text from a set of 50 million web pages [16] or Wikipedia [30].

Cui *et al.* [12] carry out query expansion using a bipartite click graph, connecting a query node to a URL node if a click has been observed. They then extended the graph to encompass words in queries and words in documents. Craswell and Szummer [11] also use the click graph, performing a random walk to find a probability distribution over nodes from any given starting node.

Dang and Croft [13] induce a bipartite graph with similar properties to the click graph, based on anchor text from document hyperlinks. One advantage of this approach is that web crawls and anchor data are more freely available for academic and commercial purposes. For example, when building an enterprise search engine it is unlikely that there will ever be sufficient usage logs on that service to build good language and translation models for query rewriting. However, there is some chance that anchor text from the corpus or from external corpora can be used to build a query rewriting system.

While improved precision can be a good indication of the usefulness of a system, another – related – aspect is reliability: even if precision on average is greatly increased, the results of an expansion method may be perceived to be worse than that of a baseline system if for some queries precision is markedly reduced. Smeaton and Van Rijsbergen [27] found as early as 1982 that not all queries benefit from the same expansion method. More recently this problem has gained greater popularity amongst information retrievalists. For instance, Harman and Buckley [17] confirm Smeaton's and Van Rijsbergen's insight and a number of papers followed their workshop, such as this by Collins-Thompson [10], who defines query expansion as a risk/reward problem in a machine learning framework and achieves good robustness. Robust retrieval has also become a major focus of TREC [28] and remains a widely studied problem.

Kraft and Zien [22] find in a user study that sourcing expansion terms from anchor text using rank aggregation over the anchor frequency and lengths in word and characters is superior than sourcing those terms from the document collection. In this work, they find anchors for expansion that contain the full query as an exact match.

Amitay et al. [1] use queries instead of anchors to aid with retrieval. While acknowledging the practice to *stuff* a document with keywords gained from in-links, they instead pre-expand a document with queries that were used earlier in a user session that eventually ended with a user visiting the target page. They record modest improvements in precision measures, but decreased the number of query reformulations needed by users to find pages markedly. In a sense, this work inverts our approach by adding text to the target documents and thus avoiding query expansion all together. Similarly, [14] use session queries as implicit annotations, but also add explicit annotations as well as anchor text to target documents. They find that while difficult to obtain explicit annotations are very useful, implicit annotation can lead to an increase in early precision.

3. REWRITING ALGORITHMS ON THE ANCHOR GRAPH

An anchor graph $\mathcal{G} = (\mathcal{A}, \mathcal{U}, \mathcal{E})$ represents the anchor text descriptions in a hypertext corpus. It is a bipartite graph, connecting anchors $\mathcal{A}$ and URLs $\mathcal{U}$. An edge (a, u) exists in $\mathcal{E}$ if there are one or more links to URL u with anchor text a. This form of graph was introduced by Dang and Croft [13] and is analogous to the bipartite click graph, so we will begin with adapting click graph random walk algorithms [11].

Each edge in $\mathcal{E}$ has a weight, and we use those weights to calculate transition probabilities of the random walk. In the click graph work, the edge weight was a click count [12]. Here we weight (a, u) according to how often a was used to describe u. A problem is that a single author can easily create a large number of links, for example by putting the same link at the bottom of every page on a large site. Hence we count the number of unique linking hostnames that use a to describe u.

We generate our anchor graph $\mathcal{G}$ from the ClueWeb09 corpus, which has edges such as (*facebook*, `http://facebook.com`) and (*click here*, `http://trec.nist.gov`). In the cases where a ClueWeb09 page links to a document outside the corpus, we still use that u and (a, u) data, since we do not need any information about u other than its links from ClueWeb09 documents. Overall our graph has $|\mathcal{A}| = 1.26$ billion unique anchors and $|\mathcal{U}| = 4.82$ billion unique URLs.

```
Output of Q2Q algorithm:
q = new york department of labor

1.  P(new york state department of labor|q) = 0.115 [6,
0.08]
2.  P(nys department of labor|q) = 0.039 [6,0.19]
3.  P(department of labor|q) = 0.039 [5,0.01]
4.  P(new york|q) = 0.037 [8,0.00]
5.  P(new york labor department publications|q) = 0.018
[1,0.048]
...
208.  P(job source|q) = 4.98E-04 [1,0.02]
209.  P(employer information|q) = 4.98E-04 [1,0.01]
210.  P(http://w|q) = 4.98E-04 [1,0.00]
211.  P(employment resources|q) = 4.98E-04 [1,0.00]
212.  P(employment|q) = 4.98E-04 [1,0.00]
```

Figure 1: Example output of the Q2Q algorithm, for the query *new york department of labor*. The random walk probability is indicated, as well as [I,J] being URL set intersection size and Jaccard similarity.

We identify 27.4 billion links, which collapse to $|\mathcal{E}| = 5.96$ billion edges once we identify the distinct (a, u) pairs.

In the remainder of this section we introduce three anchor-driven query rewriting algorithms which we call query-to-query, phrase-to-phrase, and hybrid.

3.1 Query-to-Query Translation

Our query-to-query (Q2Q) algorithm first identifies the user's query in the anchor data $\mathcal{A}$, via an exact string match, after case folding and removing punctuation. If there is no match, then Q2Q produces no output. From the anchor node, the algorithm identifies all anchors that can be reached in two steps as candidate rewrite queries. For example, the query *new york department of labor* appears as an anchor in $\mathcal{A}$, and has 21 edges in $\mathcal{E}$. From the 21 URL nodes in $\mathcal{U}$ we reach 212 anchor nodes in $\mathcal{A}$.

Having identified all two-step candidates, we then calculate features that indicate a good rewrite. Our primary feature is the random walk probability [11] from a two-step forward random walk with no self-transition probability. As in that paper, the transition probability is calculated based on edge weights, with the probability of following an edge being the edge's weight divided by the total incident edge weights of the node. Exploring other edge weighting and random walk parameters is left for future work.

We calculate two additional Q2Q features based on the URLs adjacent to q and q'. Let U_q and $U_{q'}$ be the set of URL nodes adjacent to q and q' respectively. One feature is the number of URLs co-cited by q and q', which is the cardinality of the intersection $|U_q \cap U_{q'}|$. The other feature is the Jaccard similarity of the URL sets, which is $|U_q \cap U_{q'}|/|U_q \cup U_{q'}|$. The Jaccard similarity is related to the random walk probability, but is also affected by the degree of q'. If we were to increase $|U_{q'}|$ purely by connecting q' to URLs outside U_q, the random walk probability $P(q'|q)$ would be unaffected, but Jaccard similarity would decrease.

Figure 1 shows some examples of Q2Q feature values. The highest-scoring rewrites under random walk probability and Jaccard similarity are at positions 1 and 2 respectively, and seem strongly related to the original query. The highest-scoring rewrite on intersection size is *new york*, which misses the Department of Labor aspect of the original query. There are also a large number of rewrites with intersection size of 1 which tend to be of low quality. For the remainder of the paper we post-filter the Q2Q results to remove candidates with intersection size of only one or two, which greatly reduces the set of rewrites we need to consider.

Using the Million Query Track queries, we noticed two problematic patterns in the Q2Q rewrites. First, some rewrites simply shorten the query, for example *new york dmv* rewritten as *new york*. Second, some rewrites contain Web noise words, for example adding the word *site* or replacing the query with *click here*. Since only a small number of noise words showed up in top rewrites, we found we could build the list by hand with a small amount of manual effort: *free*, *wikipedia*, *www*, *click*, *here*, *com*, *org*, *site*, *website*, *more* and *link*. Under the assumption that removing words via query shortening or adding noise words are unlikely to be helpful, we removed all such rewrites from consideration. A more comprehensive analysis of noise words is left as future work.

To implement the Q2Q rewriting algorithm, the Q2Q rewrites can be calculated offline for each node in $\mathcal{A}$. Then online a single lookup in a hash table can be used to access rewrites of the user's query (if any). If we know ahead of time the number of rewrites that will be used, we need store only those in the table.

3.2 Phrase-to-Phrase Translation

The Q2Q algorithm relies on having a query which already appears in $\mathcal{A}$. We can consider a broader range of rewrites by translating parts of queries, as in [21]. Rather than adapting the machine learning approach of this paper to our setting, we attempt to identify algorithms with no parameters that perform well. Such algorithms are easier to implement and reproduce since no training data and parameter tuning are required. In a setting with sufficient training data, our algorithms can be used as features in a larger model.

Our algorithms P2P and HYB are somewhat related to noisy channel models [26, 7] and statistical machine translation. A noisy channel model over search queries assumes that the user has a well-formed query in mind, but accidentally typed a noisy version of that query. Given the noisy query *sigir acomodation* one part of the model tells us about likely translations, that *acomodation* is a likely mistake for a user who meant *accommodation*. The other part tells us the likelihood of the target query *sigir accommodation*. In the context of machine translation this is called the target language model.

Our application differs from spelling correction models [7, 16], in that we operate over correctly spelled TREC queries. Rather than suggesting a replacement of the user's query, we combine the original query with one or more rewrites, with the goal of improving retrieval effectiveness. Unlike spelling correction, where the suggested query is typically much more likely than the query the user typed, we find effectiveness can increase even if the rewrite is less likely than the original.

For example, given the query *rental cars*, our translation features suggest candidate translations for *rental* such as *hire* and *vacation*. The target model tells us that *rental cars* is the most likely formulation of the three, *hire cars* is an order of magnitude less likely, and *vacation cars* is extremely rare. We may then find that performing retrieval with a weighted combination of *rental cars* and *hire cars* can improve retrieval effectiveness. Allowing rewrites that are less likely than the original query is appropriate because we have not assumed that the original query was noisy.

For translation data we have two algorithms, called P2P and HYB. The P2P (phrase-to-phrase) model is a substitution model as in [21], taking the translations from the pairs used in the Q2Q data. For example, if the anchor *tool rental company* is within two steps of the anchor *tool hire company* (co-citing one or more URLs) this provides some phrase-to-phrase evidence that $p = rental$ and $p' = hire$ are related. We use an alignment that drops shared words from one or both ends of the queries (in this case *tool* and *company*), then if something was removed and the remainder is non-empty we have an alignment. The translation data is built over all Q2Q pairs, such that $P(hire|rental) = l/L$, where l counts how many times alignment produced (p, p') and L counts how many times p was aligned with anything $(p, *)$.

```
P2P translation data:
p = rental

1.  P(rentals|p) = 0.215
2.  P(hire|p) = 0.123
3.  P(rent|p) = 0.044
4.  P(for rent|p) = 0.012
5.  P(vacation|p) = 0.010
...
550.  P(bracelet|p) = 3.12E-04
551.  P(hub|p) = 3.12E-04
552.  P(talent|p) = 3.12E-04
553.  P(project|p) = 3.12E-04
554.  P(web site|p) = 3.12E-04
```

Figure 2: Example translation data from the Q2Q algorithm, for the phrase *rental*. The translation probabilities for the 554 translated phrases sum to 1, and are proportional to how many Q2Q pairs produced each translation.

The HYB (hybrid) algorithm is a hybrid between the other two. Q2Q translates the entire query using whole-anchor data (Figure 1). P2P translates part of the query using data from anchor substitutions (Figure 2). HYB translates part of the query using whole-anchor data (Figure 1). Its translation probability is simply the random walk probability from the Q2Q dataset. Using our ClueWeb09 anchor graph, the difference between P2P and HYB translations can be quite pronounced, as shown in the example data in Figure 2 and Figure 3.

To use the P2P and HYB algorithms we also need to consider target probability. This helps us choose whether *rental* should translate to *hire* or *vacation*, depending on the context *rental* appears in. For example *hire cars* is more likely than *vacation cars*, yet *florida vacation properties* is more likely than *florida hire properties*. We use two target models. One is an anchor frequency histogram, in fact we use the total incident edge weight for that node in $\mathcal{A}$. Matching the candidate rewrite against this histogram is sufficient to make the target likelihood decisions described above, see Figure 4 for example data. The other target model we use is a language model over a large set of Web data, made available via API by Microsoft Research[1], as described by Huang *et al.* [19]. Other target models could also be considered, such as one derived from the ClueWeb09 body text itself.

```
HYB translation data:
p = rental

1.  rentals - 0.022 [99]
2.  car rentals - 0.017 [70]
3.  calendar - 0.003 [7]
4.  luxury automobile rental - 0.002 [1]
5.  netflix - 0.001 [6]
...
4475.  company name - 9.43E-07 [1]
4476.  passages of lorem ipsum - 9.43E-07 [1]
4477.  pizhichilphoto gallery - 9.43E-07 [1]
4478.  media - 9.43E-07 [1]
4479.  booking - 9.43E-07 [1]
4480.  if you want to advertise...  - 9.43E-07 [1]
```

Figure 3: Example translation data from the HYB algorithm, for the one-word phrase *rental*. The random walk probability is indicated, as well as [I] the URL set intersection size.

```
Anchor histogram data:
anchors ending in the word cars

1.  used cars - 11426
2.  new cars - 5396
3.  find local rental cars - 2743
4.  hybrid cars - 1832
5.  rental cars - 1649
...
245461.  zymol products for my cars - 1
245462.  zz top bob seger cars - 1
245463.  zz tops cars - 1
245464.  zz+ used cars - 1
245465.  zzz cars - 1
```

Figure 4: Example anchor histogram data, for all anchors ending in the word *cars*. The frequency is the total incident edge weight of that node in $\mathcal{G}$.

To implement P2P or HYB, we precompute translations for each phrase in the anchor graph. Then given a k-word query we do a hash table lookup for each phrase to find its translations, and a further lookup of the target probability of each translated query. We note that each of our candidates is produced by applying exactly one translation. Adding more translations can be achieved by incorporating multiple single-translation rewrites into the expanded search.

Using the Million Query Track queries, we noticed some translations to stopwords, so manually built a small list of cases to avoid: *about, an, and, are, as, at, be, but, by, com, for, from, how, if, in, is, it, of, on, or, that, the, this, to, was, what, when, where, which, who, will, with, would, www, a, i* and *org*. Building such a list requires a small amount of manual effort, a more comprehensive study of translation stopwords is left for future work.

4. ANALYSIS

The previous section introduced the rewriting algorithms of Q2Q, P2P and HYB, but each algorithm has multiple possible variants. This section explores various alternatives, and finalizes the choice of algorithms before our experimental evaluation.

Dataset

To avoid overfitting, our analysis uses a queryset that is disjoint from our test sets. We choose the 2009 Million Query (MQ) Track queries [9], minus the 50 shared with the Web Track. Each of the 637 queries has very few judged documents, so we do not believe the results here are as reliable as those of our main experiments. Our goal instead is to

[1]Microsoft Web N-gram Services - `http://web-ngram.research.microsoft.com/`

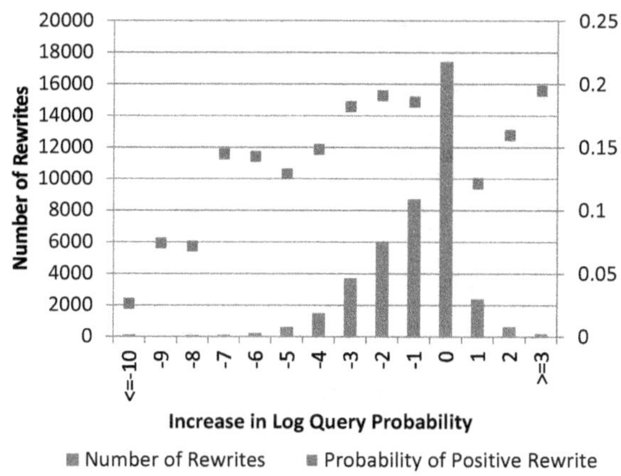

Figure 5: Differences in query log probability between rewrite and original, using Web language model data. Rewrites of higher frequency than the original are relatively rare, and do not seem to be significantly more likely to be positive according to our MQ judgments.

generate a very large number of rewrites for each query, and get a general view of which rewriting methods look promising. Performing this preliminary analysis allows us to make some decisions, and thus make fewer decisions on the test set(s).

The unfiltered output of the three algorithms for 637 queries is more than 1.3 million different query-rewrite pairs, the vast majority of which score low on all our features. To identify a more promising set of rewrites we apply the filters described in the previous section, and also remove all HYB and P2P rewrites with zero frequency in the anchor target model. These filters allow us to identify 41,639 rewrites, for which we gather target language model data via API. For each rewrite we also retrieve results from ClueWeb09 category A, ranking according to BM25F using title, body, anchor and URL fields.

Target Language Model

In introducing our algorithms we discussed the noisy channel model, which would tend to rewrite from a less frequent to a more frequent query. The rewrite should be more likely because the original query is noisy, and noise would tend to move from a likely query to a less likely one. We also considered an alternative hypothesis that the user's initial query is well formed, so it can be beneficial to rewrite to a less likely query, as in the *rental/hire cars* example.

To test this we identified a language model likelihood for each of our queries and rewrites. Then in Figure 5, the difference in likelihood between the rewrite and original query are the horizontal axis with one bin for each order of magnitude. We see that many rewrite candidates are as likely or less likely than the original query, which is not surprising. Using the MQ judgments, we then flag rewrites that had at least one relevant document in the top-1000 as *positive*, and plot the probability of drawing a positive rewrite from each bin. Results show that there are many cases where a less-frequent rewrite is positive. Generating the same graph using the ClueWeb09 anchor text histogram instead of language modeling probability showed a very similar pattern. We therefore will consider rewriting algorithms that have weak or no preference for more likely rewrites.

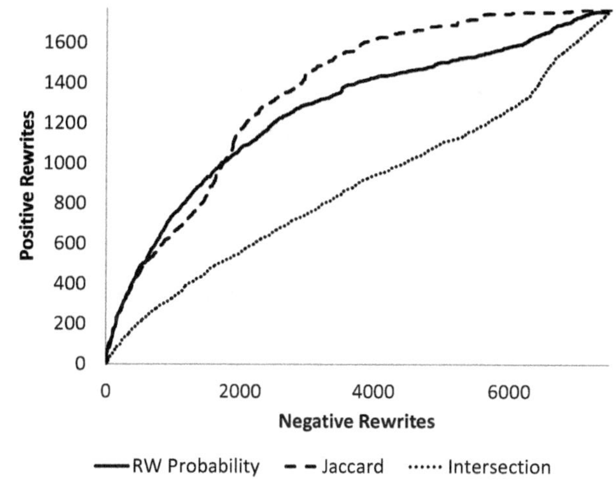

Figure 6: ROC curves analyzing all Q2Q rewrites, as indicated by the three different Q2Q features.

Q2Q Variants

The rewrites generated by Q2Q can be ordered by random walk probability, intersection size or Jaccard coefficient. To analyze these alternatives, we flag each Q2Q rewrite as positive if a document relevant to the original query occurs in the top-1000, and negative otherwise. Under this relatively weak definition of a positive rewrite, Q2Q produces 1,773 positive and 7,480 negative rewrites.

Figure 6 presents the results if we rank all Q2Q rewrites by each of the three potential features. The intersection signal is close to the diagonal, indicating there is little useful signal left after having used the feature as a threshold to cut down from our initial 1.3 million rewrites. The random walk probability and Jaccard similarity both seem like stronger signals, with random walk performing slightly better early on. The performance of the Jaccard similarity later in the ranking suggests that a combination of the two features could be a good alternative, but for simplicity we choose to use random walk scoring for Q2Q data in the remainder of this study.

P2P and HYB Variants

The previous analysis used all 41,639 query-rewrite pairs. We now consider several forms of our translation algorithms intended to choose the best rewrite for each query. We will also evaluate Q2Q as a reference point, using mean reciprocal rank (MRR) as our metric. Due to judgment sparsity many rewrites return results lists that are largely unjudged, so we chose MRR to give us an indication of where relevant documents are returned instead of focusing on top-20 precision or on recall.

Given the target language model analysis in Figure 5, we focus on comparing different target model variants. In one variant HYB0 there is no target language model. Given a query with w words, HYB0 finds all possible translations of n-grams in the query of length up to $w-1$, and applies the most likely one according only to the HYB (random walk) probability. HYB1 is the same, but rewrites which

Algo	microsoft home	my own background check
P2P0	ms home	my own criminal records
P2P1	ms home	personal background check
P2P2	windows home	my own business
P2P3	microsoft website	personal background check
HYB0	www.microsoft.com home	my h. david kotz named new inspector general at sec check
HYB1	microsoft corporation home	my own visit
HYB2	here home	my own background
HYB3	microsoft website	my own website
Q2Q	microsoft frontpage	–

Table 1: Rewrites for TREC Million Query Track queries 20591 and 20110. Most algorithms find good rewrites for *microsoft home*, while for query *my own background check* many rewrites do not seem useful.

have zero frequency in the anchor histogram are eliminated. HYB2 is like HYB1 but multiplies the HYB probability by the language model likelihood of the rewrite query. HYB3 is like HYB1, and comparable to HYB2, but instead multiplies the HYB probability by the anchor histogram probability of the rewrite query. If Figure 5 were incorrect, and we should prefer higher-frequency queries all other things being equal, then we would expect HYB2 or HYB3 to perform best.

The variants of P2P are the same as for HYB, with variants being: no filtering, filtering on existence in anchor, incorporating a language model probability and incorporating anchor histogram probability.

Example query rewrites are given in Table 1, showing the strongest rewrite for each algorithm. The examples show some typical patterns, such as the relatively sparse Q2Q having no output in one case, and HYB0 producing a nonsensical rewrite. Table 2 presents the MRR results. In this paper we present metrics multiplied by 100 for readability, so MRR of 1.1 is actually 0.011. The MRR results are low for this corpus due to the very small number of judgments per topic and the relatively large corpus. Unlike Figures 6 and 5 which considered thousands of rewrites, this table considers only the best rewrite for each query according to each ranking, so is potentially the most susceptible to noise. However, the results are consistent with Figure 5. The variants of types 2 and 3 perform not as well as the type 1 variants, for both HYB and P2P. The type 0 variants perform worst, indicating that some target model is necessary, but its most useful function is to filter out nonsense rewrites such as *vacation cars*.

The table also presents the coverage of each approach, since in some cases there are no possible rewrites. The 0 variants with no filter rewrite the most queries, although the filtered variants still have better coverage than Q2Q. Q2Q rewrites around a third of queries compared to the translation approaches, but the MRR on the – relatively few – rewritten queries is good.

5. RETRIEVAL EXPERIMENTS

Having finalized our rewriting algorithms, we test them on the TREC robust04 test collection (250 topics), the TREC GOV2 test collection (150 topics) and the ClueWeb09 adhoc test collection (150 topics). To set parameters in each case we use three-fold cross validation, choosing parameters on two folds and testing on the third, then present overall results for the three test folds.

Our unexpanded baseline is the default Indri language model (LM) ranking, and our expansion baseline is the Indri

	MRR	Queries	Affects	Data
P2P0	1.1	602	Phrase	P2P
P2P1	2.0	545	Phrase	P2P-AnchorFilter
P2P2	1.6	545	Phrase	P2P-LMProb
P2P3	1.9	545	Phrase	P2P-AnchorProb
HYB0	1.4	570	Phrase	Q2Q
HYB1	4.0	508	Phrase	Q2Q-AnchorFilter
HYB2	2.8	508	Phrase	Q2Q-LMProb
HYB3	2.6	508	Phrase	Q2Q-AnchorProb
Q2Q	1.1	179	Query	Q2Q

Table 2: MRR results on Million Query Track data. P2P1 and HYB1 perform best. Filtering for existence in anchor data (AnchorFilter) performs better than also multiplying by a target likelihood (LMProb or AnchorProb). Q2Q has lower MRR, though achieves this by rewriting only 179 queries.

		P@5	P@10	P@20	MAP	GMAP
LM	nostem	46.1	40.2	33.5	22.4	12.2
RM	nostem	*45.9*	40.6	34.5	26.5*†	12.3
QR	nostem	46.8	41.7*	34.4*	23.3*	13.0*
LM	stemmed	47.2	42.0	35.2	24.5	13.8
RM	stemmed	47.4	42.7	36.4*	28.1*†	*13.6*
QR	stemmed	47.4	42.8*	35.5	24.9*	14.1

Table 3: Overall results for robust04, with cross validation optimizing for MAP. Annotations: (*) Significantly better than LM with $p < 0.05$, (*italics*) numerically worse than LM and (†) significant difference between RM and QR with $p < 0.05$.

implementation of Relevance Model (RM) relevance feedback [23]. The latter model has multiple parameters, in our cross-validation we set three parameters: original query weight, number of PRF documents and number of terms. In all our Indri experiments we use Dirichlet smoothing ($\mu = 2500$).

For comparison with RM we incorporate our three best rewriting algorithms (P2P1, HYB1, Q2Q) into algorithm QR, which has two parameters. One parameter r is the maximum number of rewrites to take from each algorithm. The other parameter w is the total weight assigned to rewrite queries. Our query formulation in Indri is a `#weight` combination of queries, each in its own `#combine`. The original query has weight 1.0, and each of k rewrites has weight w/k. Since there are three rewriting algorithms that each produce zero or more rewrites for a given input query, $k \leq 3r$.

In our cross validation setting, it would have been possible to tune both parameters separately for each of the three rewriting algorithms, and possibly use each algorithm's probability as a confidence score to further weight each rewrite. This would likely give a significant increase in effectiveness, but restricting ourselves to two parameters makes our approach more comparable with RM.

Overall results for robust04 are presented in Table 3, for an index with no stemming and also an index with Porter stemming. The cross validation optimization is towards mean average precision (MAP), and RM achieves significantly better MAP than QR and the language modeling (LM) baselines. However, it is numerically worse than the unexpanded baseline LM on some early precision measures and on geometric mean average precision (GMAP) [25]. The latter metric is intended to penalize a system for reducing

		P@5	P@10	P@20	MAP	GMAP
LM	nostem	46.1	40.2	33.5	22.4	12.2
RM	nostem	47.0	42.9*	35.5*	25.5*†	14.2*†
QR	nostem	47.1	42.2*	34.5*	23.5*	13.2*
LM	stemmed	47.2	42.0	35.2	24.5	13.8
RM	stemmed	47.7	43.7*	36.7*†	26.9*†	14.8*†
QR	stemmed	48.0	42.9*	35.4	24.9*	14.0

Table 4: Overall results for robust04 with cross validation optimizing for GMAP.

		P@5	P@10	P@20	MAP	GMAP
LM	nostem	56.8	55.5	52.6	27.0	19.0
RM	nostem	*54.9*	*54.5*	*51.3*	28.2*	*18.4*
QR	nostem	60.5*†	57.0†	55.0*†	28.7*	20.4*†
LM	stemmed	57.8	54.5	51.0	29.4	21.0
RM	stemmed	*55.8*	55.3	52.0	31.0*†	*20.5*
QR	stemmed	58.5†	56.1*	52.7*	29.9*	21.5

Table 5: Overall results for GOV2 with cross validation optimizing for MAP.

average precision (AP) towards zero, for example a small drop from AP=80 is penalized much less than a small drop from AP=1.

Given that RM had a numerical reduction in GMAP when optimizing for MAP, we conducted the same cross validation targeting GMAP itself. With that target, RM no longer has a loss in GMAP (Table 4) at the cost of losing about one point of MAP in absolute terms.

Overall results for GOV2 are presented in Table 5 for cross-validation optimizing for MAP and Table 6 for cross-validation optimizing for GMAP. The results in both cases are for an index with no stemming and also an index with Porter stemming. Cross validation with target MAP yields significant improvements over the baseline when stemming is not applied. However, RM again has a numerical (not significant) loss in GMAP, and QR is significantly better than RM on that metric. Note that the t-test for GMAP is conducted on log(AP) values.

When cross validation targets GMAP, QR reaches a very similar solution in terms of our target metrics, possibly because it is restricted to a single parameter (rewrite weight). The RM approach improves on GMAP but becomes worse on all other metrics than it was in MAP optimization. The next section analyzes this effect in more depth.

In Web collections, indexes typically allow unstemmed queries, for example so that a search for *david hawking* is not met with documents about a hawk or some hawks, or even Tennessee politician David Hawk. Thus for ClueWeb09 experiments we do not apply Porter stemming, and thus rely on RM and QR to introduce stem variants where appropriate. We also fix the number of rewrites for QR to 1, exploring a one-dimensional parameter space, instead of two-dimensional.

In our ClueWeb09 experiments, we did not build an Indri index, due to the size of category A English subset. Instead we ran the system from [6] and tested for significant gains due to rewriting over a baseline with unexpanded queries. Overall results are presented in Table 7, with cross validation optimized for NDCG@20. We found that optimizing for NDCG@20 yielded marginally better results in terms of statistical significance, but having done so ERR@20 was more likely to be the significant metric. Here we show just those

		P@5	P@10	P@20	MAP	GMAP
LM	nostem	56.8	55.5	52.6	27.0	19.0
RM	nostem	*55.7*	55.8	*52.6*	28.2*	19.2
QR	nostem	60.5*†	57.0	54.6*†	28.5*	20.2*
LM	stemmed	57.8	54.5	51.0	29.4	21.0
RM	stemmed	*56.5*	55.8*	52.2*	30.5*	21.2
QR	stemmed	58.1	55.6	52.5*	30.0*	21.5

Table 6: Overall results for GOV2 with cross validation optimizing for GMAP.

Rewrite	Variant	ERR@20	NDCG@20
	NONE	14.3	24.1
QR	HYB1	14.3	24.0
QR	P2P1	14.7*	24.4*
QR	Q2Q	14.7	24.3
QR	ALL (1 param)	14.9*	24.4
QR	ALL (3 param)	15.2*	24.5

Table 7: Overall results for ClueWeb09, with cross validation optimizing for NDCG@20. Significant improvements are for P2P1, for all three algorithms with a shared weight and for all three algorithms with three separate weights.

	Target	P@5	P@10	P@20	MAP	GMAP
RM	P@5	46.3	42.2	35.9	27.3	14.0
RM	P@10	45.9	43.1	36.4	26.6	14.7
RM	P@20	46.4	42.9	36.5	27.1	14.6
RM	MAP	47.4	42.7	36.4	28.1	13.6
RM	GMAP	47.7	43.7	36.7	26.9	14.8
Range:		1.8	1.5	0.8	1.5	1.2
QR	P@5	48.0	42.9	35.5	25.0	14.1
QR	P@10	47.9	43.3	35.6	25.1	14.1
QR	P@20	48.6	42.8	35.9	25.1	14.2
QR	MAP	47.4	42.8	35.5	24.9	14.1
QR	GMAP	48.0	42.9	35.4	24.9	14.0
Range:		1.2	0.5	0.5	0.2	0.2

Table 8: Optimizing for different target metrics on robust04, with stemming. RM has a broader range of possible outcomes.

results, targeting NDCG@20. Best results are obtained with rewrites from three algorithms, and a marginal numerical improvement from using one weight per algorithm rather than a shared weight as in our robust04 and GOV2 experiments.

5.1 Robustness and Parameter Settings

Our overall evaluation results indicated mixed results for RM, that were very positive on MAP but sometimes negative on early precision and GMAP. The cause of this, and a comparison to QR, can be seen in Figure 7. The impact of QR on AP is small, yet it achieves consistent gains across our metrics, many of which are statistically significant. The GOV2 results also indicated that RM parameters optimized for one metric may be sub-optimal on another. This section studies these properties of RM, and compares to QR, with some further analysis of parameter settings.

In our first analysis, we repeat the cross validation for each of our five effectiveness measures. The goal is not to observe a significant improvement, but to analyze the variability of

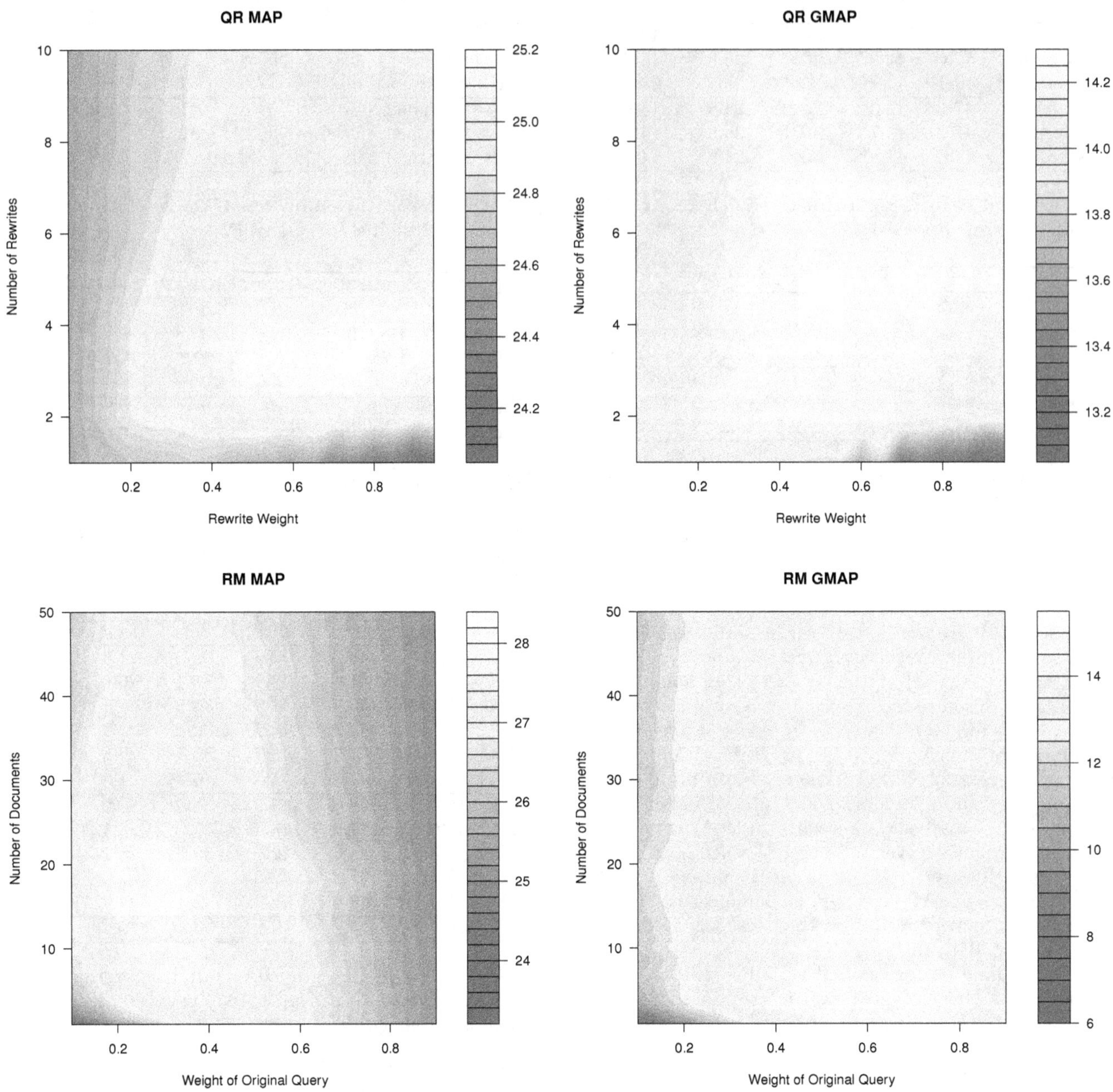

Figure 8: Parameter sensitivity for RM and QR on robust04, with stemming. Note that the plots for RM and QR can not be compared with each other, as they consider different parameters. Comparing the two QR plots, the optimum for MAP has good GMAP, and vice versa. For the RM plots the optima differ more, so there is a tradeoff between MAP and GMAP.

test performance under the different training targets. The experiment is related to experiments on varying training targets in Learning to Rank [31].

The variability of RM performance under different parameter settings is somewhat greater than the variability of QR (Table 8). This could be seen as a good property of RM, that it is powerful enough to be optimized for different metrics. To increase the power of QR approaches, perhaps more linguistic data could be incorporated, with exposure of more weighting parameters and a more sophisticated construction of the overall Indri query. RM's variability could also be seen as a disadvantage, since it has no parameter setting that is optimal for all metrics. For example, training on MAP gives the lowest GMAP, vice versa.

Comparing these results to the Learning to Rank results in [31], we see the same pattern, that our best results for a test metric are not always achieved when using the same metric for training. However, unlike that study QR can achieve good results when training on early precision.

Figure 8 presents an analysis of the difference between MAP and GMAP for the two algorithms. The figure indicates a parameter sweep rather than cross validation, though

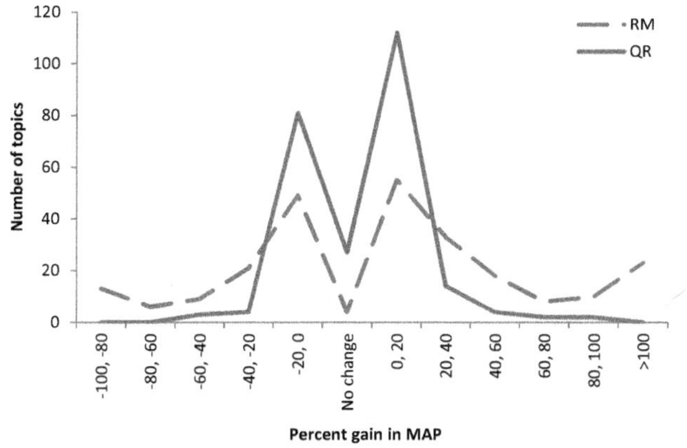

Figure 7: Robustness histogram for robust04 MAP, corresponding to Table 3 and with stemming. Our other experiments showed a similar pattern. RM has more topics at the extremes, including more with $>100\%$ gain in MAP.

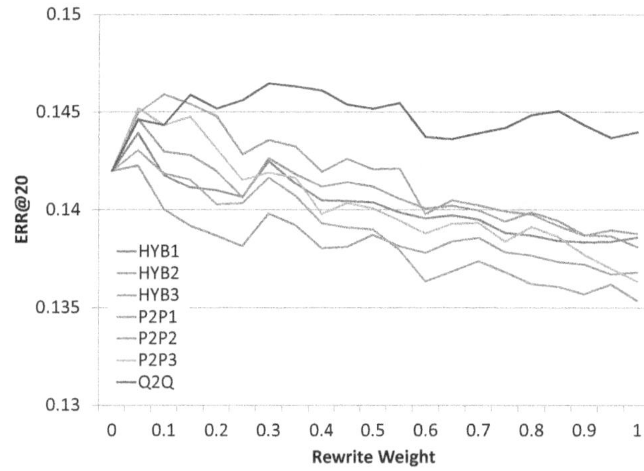

Figure 9: Parameter sensitivity for the best rewrite from each algorithm on ClueWeb09. Best ERR@20 is achieved at low weights for algorithms P2P1, HYB1, and Q2Q.

it uses the same full parameter grids as in our cross validation experiments. Note that due to the design of the algorithms the horizontal axes are reversed: QR has more effect as the rewrite weight increases (moving right), while RM has more effect when the original query weight decreases (moving left). Note also that the scales of the plots are different, and shown to the right in each case. Since RM has three parameters, for the purposes of this plot we hold the number of terms constant at its best value (20).

The stability of results for QR may be explained by the top two plots in Figure 8. The parameter settings for which MAP is optimal are similar to the parameter settings where GMAP is optimal. This is the likely explanation for the robustness of the algorithm. By contrast, the bottom two plots show the parameter settings for RM. If the goal is to optimize MAP, then the best parameter settings are with just under 20 documents and 0.4 weight on the original query, which means 0.6 weight on the relevance model. The parameter settings for optimal GMAP put much more weight on the original query, and may use fewer pseudo-relevant documents. This may explain the relatively poor GMAP performance of RM, since any choice of parameter settings is a tradeoff between MAP and GMAP.

Finally, we consider the parameter sensitivity of single rewriting algorithms on ClueWeb09, including rewriting algorithms that were evaluated in Table 2 on Million Query Track data. The results on adhoc Web Track data in Figure 9 indicate that HYB1, P2P1 and Q2Q were indeed the best algorithms, and are best applied at low weight.

6. CONCLUSIONS

We introduce several robust algorithms for query rewriting. Our general approach is to take a large linguistic dataset, in this case the ClueWeb09 anchor data, and use these to build translation and target models. We then apply these to generate rewrites of robust04, GOV2 and ClueWeb09 Web Track queries, and perform retrieval based on a mixture of original and rewrite queries.

Having introduced the general form of three algorithms, we chose specific variants Q2Q, P2P1 and HYB1 based on analysis of tens of thousands of rewrites. The analysis indicated that a useful rewrite need not be more likely than the user's original query, consistent with the hypothesis that query rewriting can be useful even if the user's query was not "noisy".

Compared to a traditional PRF baseline, our QR algorithms do not have higher average precision, but have better early precision and are more robust. They yield significant improvements over an unexpanded baseline, and avoid losses in metrics that may be important to users such as early precision and geometric mean average precision. Under cross validation training, the QR approach yields consistent gains even if the target metric is changed, whereas the PRF baseline is much less stable, forcing a choice between higher MAP or higher GMAP.

Overall our results indicate our new QR approaches are competitive with traditional PRF without the need for two rounds of retrieval, making it a practical alternative for real-world systems where users care about early precision, response time and robustness. This can be achieved across collections, applying algorithms based on ClueWeb09 data to unrelated test collections robust04 and GOV2.

We note that approaches based on external linguistic resources can potentially be improved simply by adding more linguistic data. This suggests some promising follow-up work would be to identify more such resources, in particular resources that can provide within-language translations, in this case English-to-English. A further promising avenue would be to integrate such rewriting algorithms with query weighting approaches such as [4, 5]. With large-scale linguistic data for query rewriting, plus an integrated retrieval model, significant further improvements in retrieval effectiveness may be achievable.

7. ACKNOWLEDGMENTS

Thanks to Milad Shokouhi for his advice on good practices with Indri and RM parameter tuning and Dan Liebling for his help with obtaining the ClueWeb09 collection.

8. REFERENCES

[1] E. Amitay, A. Darlow, D. Konopnicki, and U. Weiss. Queries as anchors: selection by association. In *Proc. of the sixteenth ACM conference on Hypertext and hypermedia*, HYPERTEXT '05, pages 193–201, New York, NY, USA, 2005. ACM.

[2] J. R. Baron, D. D. Lewis, and D. W. Oard. TREC-2006 legal track overview. In *Proc. of TREC 2006*, 2006.

[3] L. Barroso, J. Dean, and U. Holzle. Web search for a planet: The Google cluster architecture. *Micro, IEEE*, 23(2):22 – 28, March-April 2003.

[4] M. Bendersky, D. Metzler, and W. B. Croft. Parameterized concept weighting in verbose queries. In *Proc. of the 34th International ACM SIGIR Conference on Research and Development in Information Retrieval*, SIGIR '11, pages 605–614, 2011.

[5] M. Bendersky, D. Metzler, and W. B. Croft. Effective query formulation with multiple information sources. In *Proc. of the 5th ACM International Conference on Web Search and Data Mining*, WSDM '12, pages 443–452, 2012.

[6] B. Billerbeck, N. Craswell, D. Fetterly, and M. Najork. Microsoft research at TREC 2011 web track. In *20th Text Retrieval Conference*, 2011.

[7] E. Brill and R. C. Moore. An improved error model for noisy channel spelling correction. In *Proc. of the 38th Annual Meeting on Association for Computational Linguistics*, ACL '00, pages 286–293, 2000.

[8] J. Brutlag. Speed matters for Google web search. Technical report, Google, 2009.

[9] B. Carterette, V. Pavlu, H. Fang, and E. Kanoulas. Million query track 2009 overview. In *Proc. of TREC 2009*, 2009.

[10] K. Collins-Thompson. Reducing the risk of query expansion via robust constrained optimization. In *Proc. of the 18th ACM Conference on Information and Knowledge Management*, CIKM '09, pages 837–846, 2009.

[11] N. Craswell and M. Szummer. Random walks on the click graph. In *Proc. of the 30th Annual International ACM SIGIR Conference on Research and Development in Information Retrieval*, SIGIR '07, pages 239–246, 2007.

[12] H. Cui, J.-R. Wen, J.-Y. Nie, and W.-Y. Ma. Probabilistic query expansion using query logs. In *Proc. of the 11th International Conference on World Wide Web*, WWW '02, pages 325–332, 2002.

[13] V. Dang and B. W. Croft. Query reformulation using anchor text. In *Proc. of the 3rd ACM International Conference on Web Search and Data Mining*, WSDM '10, pages 41–50, 2010.

[14] P. A. Dmitriev, N. Eiron, M. Fontoura, and E. Shekita. Using annotations in enterprise search. In *Proc. of the 15th international conference on World Wide Web*, WWW '06, pages 811–817, New York, NY, USA, 2006. ACM.

[15] J. L. Elsas, J. Arguello, J. Callan, and J. G. Carbonell. Retrieval and feedback models for blog feed search. In *Proc. of the 31st Annual International ACM SIGIR Conference on Research and Development in Information Retrieval*, SIGIR '08, pages 347–354, 2008.

[16] J. Guo, G. Xu, H. Li, and X. Cheng. A unified and discriminative model for query refinement. In *Proc. of the 31st Annual International ACM SIGIR Conference on Research and Development in Information Retrieval*, SIGIR '08, pages 379–386, 2008.

[17] D. Harman and C. Buckley. The NRRC Reliable Information Access (RIA) workshop. In *Proc. of the 27th Annual International ACM SIGIR Conference on Research and Development in Information Retrieval*, SIGIR '04, pages 528–529, 2004.

[18] D. Hawking and N. Craswell. The very large collection and web tracks. In E. Voorhees and D. Harman, editors, *TREC: Experiment and Evaluation in Information Retrieval*. MIT Press, 2005.

[19] J. Huang, J. Gao, J. Miao, X. Li, K. Wang, F. Behr, and C. L. Giles. Exploring web scale language models for search query processing. In *Proc. of the 19th International Conference on World Wide Web*, WWW '10, pages 451–460, 2010.

[20] A. Jain, U. Ozertem, and E. Velipasaoglu. Synthesizing high utility suggestions for rare web search queries. In *Proc. of the 34th International ACM SIGIR Conference on Research and Development in Information Retrieval*, SIGIR '11, pages 805–814, 2011.

[21] R. Jones, B. Rey, O. Madani, and W. Greiner. Generating query substitutions. In *Proc. of the 15th International Conference on World Wide Web*, WWW '06, pages 387–396, 2006.

[22] R. Kraft and J. Zien. Mining anchor text for query refinement. In *Proc. of the 13th international conference on World Wide Web*, WWW '04, pages 666–674, New York, NY, USA, 2004. ACM.

[23] V. Lavrenko and W. B. Croft. Relevance based language models. In *Proc. of the 24th Annual International ACM SIGIR Conference on Research and Development in Information Retrieval*, SIGIR '01, pages 120–127, 2001.

[24] S. Levy. *In the Plex: How Google Thinks, Works, and Shapes Our Lives*. Simon & Schuster, 2011.

[25] S. Robertson. On GMAP – and other transformations. In *Proc. of the 15th ACM International Conference on Information and Knowledge Management*, CIKM '06, pages 78–83, 2006.

[26] C. Shannon, N. Petigara, and S. Seshasai. A mathematical theory of communication. *Bell System Technical Journal*, 27:379–423, 1948.

[27] A. F. Smeaton and C. J. Van Rijsbergen. The retrieval effects of query expansion on a feedback document retrieval system. *The Computer Journal*, 26(3):10–18, 1983.

[28] E. M. Voorhees. The TREC robust retrieval track. *SIGIR Forum*, 39:11–20, June 2005.

[29] Y. Xu, G. J. Jones, and B. Wang. Query dependent pseudo-relevance feedback based on Wikipedia. In *Proc. of the 32nd International ACM SIGIR Conference on Research and Development in Information Retrieval*, SIGIR '09, pages 59–66, 2009.

[30] X. Xue, W. B. Croft, and D. A. Smith. Modeling reformulation using passage analysis. In *Proceedings of the 19th ACM international conference on Information and knowledge management*, CIKM '10, pages 1497–1500, New York, NY, USA, 2010. ACM.

[31] E. Yilmaz and S. Robertson. On the choice of effectiveness measures for learning to rank. *Inf. Retr.*, 13:271–290, June 2010.

[32] S. Yu, D. Cai, J.-R. Wen, and W.-Y. Ma. Improving pseudo-relevance feedback in web information retrieval using web page segmentation. In *Proc. of the 12th International Conference on World Wide Web*, WWW '03, pages 11–18, 2003.

[33] W. Zhang and C. Yu. UIC at TREC 2006 blog track: a notebook paper. In *Proc. of TREC 2006*, 2006.

[34] Y. Zhang and A. Moffat. Some observations on user search behavior. In *Proc. of the 11th Australasian Document Computing Symposium*, pages 1–8, 2006.

Wiki3C: Exploiting Wikipedia for Context-aware Concept Categorization

Peng Jiang[†], Huiman Hou[‡], Lijiang Chen[†], Shimin Chen[†], Conglei Yao[§], Chengkai Li[¶], Min Wang[†]

[†]HP Labs China, Beijing, China

[‡]Baidu Inc., Beijing, China

[§]Tencent Inc., Beijing, China

[¶]University of Texas at Arlington, Arlington, TX, USA

[†]{pengj, lijiang.chen, shimin.chen, min.wang6}@hp.com

[‡]humanhou@hotmail.com, [§]ycl.pku@gmail.com, [¶]cli@cse.uta.edu

ABSTRACT

Wikipedia is an important human generated knowledge base containing over 21 million articles organized by millions of categories. In this paper, we exploit Wikipedia for a new task of text mining: Context-aware Concept Categorization. In the task, we focus on categorizing concepts according to their context. We exploit article link feature and category structure in Wikipedia, followed by introducing Wiki3C, an unsupervised and domain independent concept categorization approach based on context. In the approach, we investigate two strategies to select and filter Wikipedia articles for the category representation. Besides, a probabilistic model is employed to compute the semantic relatedness between two concepts in Wikipedia. Experimental evaluation using manually labeled ground truth shows that our proposed Wiki3C can achieve a noticeable improvement over the baselines without considering contextual information.

Categories and Subject Descriptors

I.2.7 [**Artificial Intelligence**]: Natural Language Processing – *Text analysis.*

General Terms

Algorithms, Experimentation.

Keywords

Context-aware concept categorization, Wikipedia, text mining.

1. INTRODUCTION

Wikipedia is a rich human-generated knowledge base containing over 21 million articles organized into millions of categories. A number of prior studies utilize category information in Wikipedia to enrich the representation of text in various text mining tasks, including text classification [1, 2], text clustering [3, 4], word sense disambiguation [5, 6], information retrieval [7, 8], similarity computing [9, 10], taxonomy building [11], and so on. The main methodology of text enrichment in these works is to map text tokens to Wikipedia concepts and further to Wikipedia categories. However, a concept in Wikipedia usually has many categories. Some categories are irrelevant to the text from which a concept is extracted. Most previous works treat all Wikipedia categories equally without considering their relative importance in different specific contexts.

In this paper, we introduce and study a new task to solve the above problem: context-aware concept categorization by Wikipedia. In this task, we are interested in ranking categories for a concept to determine which categories describe it better with respect to a particular textual context. It leads us to a more fine-grained understanding of concepts in their contexts. The understanding can help enrich unstructured text by its relevant semantic information.

Figure 1 illustrates an example of the task of context-aware concept categorization. There are two paragraphs of text, from which concepts are extracted by an existing tool [12] and are underlined. For instance, both paragraphs in Figure 1 contain the concept "*Iron Man*". Each extracted concept corresponds to a Wikipedia article. The top portion of Figure 1 shows that the Wikipedia article for "*Iron Man*" belongs to 22 Wikipedia categories. [1] These categories bear different importance in different contexts. For instance, consider two particular categories "*Film characters*" and "*Characters created by Stan Lee*" of "*Iron Man*", which are in boldface in Figure 1. Between these two categories, "*Film characters*" is the more relevant one in the context of Paragraph 1, whereas "*Characters created by Stan Lee*" is more relevant with regard to Paragraph 2. Our task is to rank all categories of "*Iron Man*" according to their relevance to the contextual information where the concept is extracted.

Context-aware concept categorization provides a fine-grained understanding of extracted concepts. As shown in the above example, the same concept is captured by quite different categories in different contexts. In addition, context-aware categorization is a form of in-depth understanding of important aspects of concepts in particular textual contexts. Through this task, one can derive context-aware important categories that are at higher level of abstraction than individual concepts.

WSDM'13, Feb 4–8, 2013. Rome, Italy.

[1] Articles in Wikipedia are assigned to multiple categories, which represent major topics of the articles. Each category may contain a number of child articles.

"Iron Man" belongs to 22 categories in Wikipedia:

1968 comic debuts | 1996 comic debuts | 1998 comic debuts | 2005 comic debuts | 2008 comic debuts | 2011 comic debuts | Comics characters introduced in 1963 | Characters created by Don Heck | Characters created by Jack Kirby | **Characters created by Stan Lee** | Comics adapted into films | Fictional business executives | Fictional characters from New York | Fictional cyborgs | Fictional engineers | Fictional inventors | Fictional scientists | Fictional socialites | **Film characters** | Iron Man | Marvel Cinematic Universe characters | Marvel Comics titles

Paragraph 1 that contains "Iron Man":

In The Avengers, Nick Fury, director of the peacekeeping organization S.H.I.E.L.D., recruits **Iron Man**, Captain America, the Hulk and Thor to form a team that must stop Thor's adoptive brother Loki from enslaving the human race.

Category: Film characters, ……

Paragraph 2 that contains "Iron Man":

He co-created Spider-Man, the Hulk, the X-Men, the Fantastic Four, **Iron Man**, Thor, and many other fictional characters, introducing complex, naturalistic characters and a thoroughly shared universe into superhero comic books.

Category: Characters created by Stan Lee, ……

Figure 1. An example of context-aware concept categorization. Different categories should be chosen for the same concept "Iron Man" in different paragraphs.

Previous studies have attained considerable success in exploiting Wikipedia for many text analysis tasks by identifying concepts in text and linking them to Wikipedia articles [12, 13]. The task of context-aware concept categorization proposed in this paper moves one step further. It is worth mentioning that, while Wikipedia provides a gold standard of ground truth for the task of concept extraction (i.e., the hyperlinks in Wikipedia articles to other Wikipedia articles representing such ground truth), it does not provide ground truth for context-aware concept categorization. Therefore, although supervised or semi-supervised techniques can be effectively applied in concept extraction [12, 14, 15], we design an unsupervised and domain-independent approach for concept categorization.

Context-aware concept categorization is related to but different from text categorization (a.k.a. document classification). While the latter converts text into vector, and aims to label it with one or more predefined categories, concept categorization requires a finer-grained analysis to rank categories in the granularity of concept. Moreover, context-aware concept categorization is different from word sense disambiguation task. As shown in Figure 1, "*Iron Man*" in the two paragraphs refers to a same concept without ambiguity. In this work, we focus on compute the different relevance of categories for a given concept according to context. Being lack of description in Wikipedia Category, we represent category for ranking by two kinds of article sets: child article and split article. The set of child article includes Wikipedia articles under a given category, while the set of split article includes articles that are the sub-components of the given category' name. By leveraging the relatedness between each article in the two article sets and concepts in context, we combine the contextual relevance to rank categories for a concept. The relatedness measuring is based on the comparison of link structures[2] in Wikipedia articles. In order to address the bias problem caused by the incompleteness in Wikipedia, we propose a probabilistic model. In the model, any unseen link in a concept can have a probability of occurrence which is proportional to that of the link given by the concept's category.

The main contributions of this paper are two folds. First, to the best of our knowledge, we are the first to introduce and study the problem of context-aware concept categorization. Second, we present an unsupervised and domain-independent approach for this task. Experimental evaluation using manually labeled ground truth shows the effectiveness of our approach.

The remainder of the paper is organized as follows: Section 2 describes our approach to the task of context-aware concept categorization. Evaluation of both accuracy and efficiency of our solution is presented in Section 3. In Section 4, we make a brief discussion of related work. Finally, Section 5 concludes the paper and discusses future work.

Table 1. Symbols used in this paper.

Symbols	Description
a	An article in Wikipedia
$In(a)$	Link set in a
T	Set of concepts extracted from a piece of text
t	A concept in Wikipedia
$r(t_i, t_j)$	Semantic relatedness of concept t_i and t_j
C_i	Set of categories of concept t_i in Wikipedia
c_{ij}	A category of concept t_i
$ch(c)$	Set of child articles in category c
$ch'(c)$	Set of filtered child articles in category c
$sp(c)$	Set of split articles for category c
$R(t, c)$	Relevance of category c to concept t
$T_{context_i}$	Set of contextual concepts of t_i
D	Window size for contextual concepts
μ	Dirichlet smoothing parameter
α	Weight parameter of two category representations
β	Weight Parameter to control the influence of context
K	Pseudo size of $ch'(c)$

[2] Link structure is an important feature of Wikipedia. Underlinked words in a Wikipedia article are typically linked to another relevant Wikipedia page.

2. WIKI3C: CONTEXT-AWARE CONCEPT CATEGORIZATION

In the task of context-aware concept categorization, we are given 1) a set of concepts extracted from an input text, and 2) a list of categories defined in Wikipedia for each concept. We aim at ranking the categories for each concept according to their relevance to the particular textual context surrounding the concept.

In this section, we first present the basic idea of our solution, and then describe each component of our solution in detail. Table 1 summarizes some symbols that are frequently used in this paper.

2.1 Overview of Our Approach

Given a target concept with the surrounding textual context, and the concept's corresponding categories, the task is to rank these categories by exploring the surrounding textual context. For example, in paragraph 1 of Figure 1, the context of the target concept "*Iron Man*" contains several concepts surrounding it, such as "*The Avengers*", "*Nick Fury*", "*S.H.I.E.L.D*", "*Captain America*", etc. Similarly, in Paragraph 2, the context of "*Iron Man*" includes "*fictional characters*", "*naturalistic*", "*shared universe*", etc. The number of contextual concepts is determined by the window size parameter D, provided that the contextual concepts must be in the same paragraph as the target concept.

Figure 2 illustrates the basic idea of our approach. The rectangular box T represents the set of concepts extracted from the input text. $t_i \in T$ is a target concept, represented by "*Iron Man*" in Figure 2. $T_{context_i} \subset T$ is the set of contextual concepts for t_i. In this case, the window size D is set to 2. We denote C_i as the set of categories of t_i. $c_{ij} \in C_i$ is one category of t_i, such as "*Film characters*". In Wikipedia, each category has little description. In order to rank the categories according to their relevance to the context, we investigate two types of Wikipedia article sets to represent a category. The first set is $ch(c_{ij})$ that contains all the child articles of category c_{ij} in Wikipedia. The second set is denoted as $sp(c_{ij})$ with all articles generated directly from the name of category c_{ij}. We will describe the two types of article sets and their usage in the following two subsections.

2.2 Child Article Selection

To represent category c_{ij}, we can select all the child articles $ch(c_{ij})$ in c_{ij}. $ch(c_{ij})$ can be obtained from the category page in Wikipedia. In this way, the relevance between c_{ij} and a contextual concept in $T_{context_i}$ can be measured by the average relatedness between each article in $ch(c_{ij})$ and the concept in $T_{context_i}$.

However, there are biases in Wikipedia. For example, given a concept "*Physics*" in $T_{context_i}$, we consider two categories "*Swiss physicists*" and "*American physicists*". Intuitively the two categories should have a similar relevance to "*Physics*". However category "*Swiss physicists*" is more relevant to "*Physics*" than category "*American physicists*". What happens is that "*Swiss physicists*" has 44 child articles, while "*American physicists*" has 1206 child articles in Wikipedia. Most of the 44 child articles of "*Swiss physicists*" contain long descriptions and have a large number of links with the article corresponding to "*Physics*". Therefore they can achieve higher relatedness with "*Physics*". On the other hand, most of the 1206 child articles of "*American physicists*" describe less famous American physicists, and are very short with few links shared with "*Physics*". Therefore, they are considered as irrelevant to "*Physics*". As such, the average relevance between all articles in category "*American physicists*" and "*Physics*" is significantly biased. It shows that categories that contain few but long articles tend to have higher relevance to a given concept. This seems unfair.

To resolve the above problem, we use K articles with the highest relatedness with other articles in the category to represent the category regardless of the actual number of articles. K is the pseudo size of category. This will remove "unpopular" or "uncompleted" child articles to maintain the size of $ch(c)$ to K. Another benefit of category filtering is that it can shorten the time of relatedness computation. Algorithm 1 selects child articles in $ch(c)$ by the following steps:

1) If the count of links of an article in $ch(c)$ is less than *Threshold*, delete the article.
2) If the size of $ch(c)$ is greater than K, calculate the total relatedness between each article and all the other articles in $ch(c)$. Then delete the article with the smallest total relatedness.
3) Repeat step 2) until the size of $ch(c)$ is equal to K.

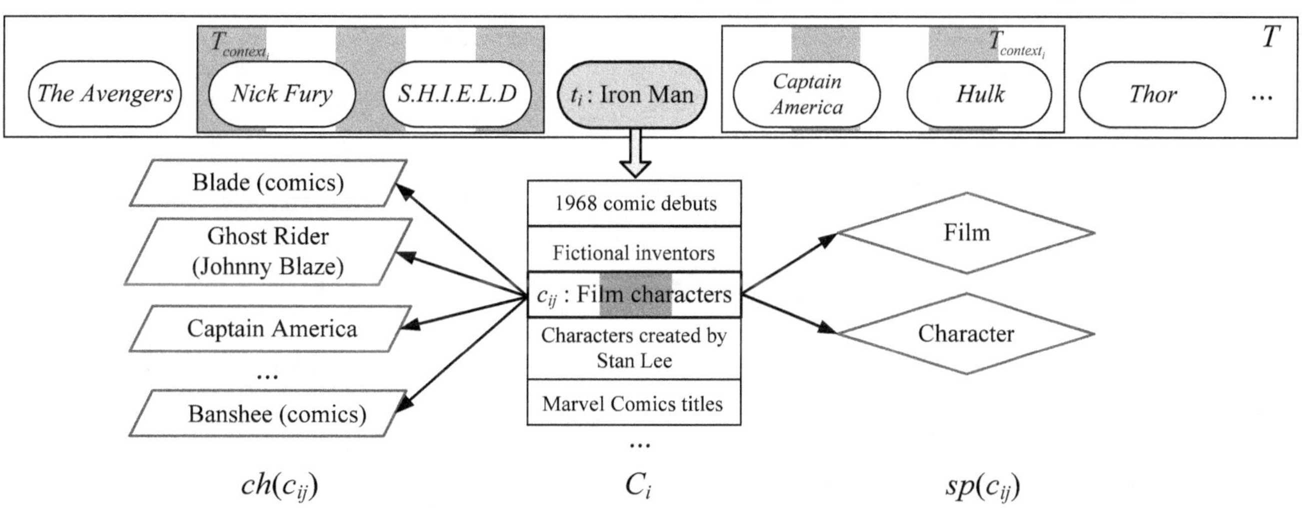

Figure 2. An illustration of the computation of relevance for a category using two article sets.

Algorithm 1: Child articles filtering

```
Input: ch(c)
Output: filtered ch(c)
Const Threshold, K;
foreach a ∈ ch(c) do
    if |In(a)| < Threshold then
        ch(c).delete(a);
    end
end
while |ch(c)| > K do
    min ← |ch(c)| × 1.0;
    foreach a_i ∈ ch(c) do
        total ← 0;
        foreach a_j ∈ ch(c) and i ≠ j do
            total ← total + r(a_i, a_j);
        end
        if total < min then
            min ← total;
            a_min ← a_i;
        end
    end
    ch(c).delete(a_min);
end
return ch(c)
```

Algorithm 1 first deletes noise in a category. The threshold parameter is set to 3 in our experiment. Then Algorithm 1 finds and deletes the article that is most irrelevant to others in a category until the size of *ch*(*c*) is equal to *K*. The relatedness computation will be discussed in Section 2.4. The filtering algorithm does not require any contextual information. Therefore, we perform it offline. We denote the filtered *ch*(*c*) as *ch'*(*c*) in the rest of the paper.

If a category has less than *K* articles before filtering, we can use the article with minimum relatedness as supplements. This will be discussed in detail in Section 2.4.3. Figure 2 shows several child articles for category "*Film characters*", including "*Blade (comics)*", "*Ghost Rider (Johnny Blaze)*", "*Captain America*", "*Banshee (comics)*", etc.

2.3 Split Article Selection

Another way to represent a category is to use variants of the category's name. For the example of category "*Swiss physicists*" and "*American physicists*", it is natural to expect the two categories to have similar relevance to the concept "*Physics*" since their names contain a common concept "*physicists*". Another example is "*American physicists*" and "*American chemists*" with the common concept "*American*" in their names. Therefore it is natural to expect them to have similar relevance when their context contains concept such as "*America*". To support this intuition, we split the name of a category into many sub-components if they are valid Wikipedia articles. Compared to articles in $ch(c_{ij})$, the concepts corresponding to split articles are more general. We denote the set of split articles for category c_{ij} as $sp(c_{ij})$ and expect it to serve as a complement for $ch(c_{ij})$.

To measure the relevance between concept *t* and category c_{ij}, we compute the relatedness between each article in $sp(c_{ij})$ and *t*. Unlike relatedness computation using child articles in Section 2.4.3, we select the maximum relatedness rather than average relatedness. That means we select the split article with the maximum relatedness with contextual concept to represent c_{ij}. It is because the relevance of each member in $sp(c_{ij})$ may vary greatly. Therefore, it is not appropriate to use all split articles to represent *c* and compute the average relatedness as the relevance of c_{ij}. For example, "*America*" is a contextual concept and "*American physicists*" is a category for a target concept. The relatedness between the concept "*America*" and a split article "*American*" of category "*American physicists*" is 1, while the relatedness between "*America*" and the other split article "*Physicist*" will be much smaller. Intuitively, it is better to use "*America*" to represent category "*American physicists*" in this context. Computing maximum relatedness matches this intuition. Figure 2 shows two split articles "*Films*" and "*Character*" for category "*Film Characters*".

Now we have two approaches to representing a category in Wikipedia. In the next section, we present our approach to ranking categories using these two representations.

2.4 Category Ranking

Before presenting the category ranking function, we first introduce the computation of semantic relatedness between concepts. We use link structure to represent concepts in our approach. There are two kinds of links in Wikipedia: inlink (incoming link) is the article with links toward the target article while outlink (outgoing link) is the article referred by the target article. Inlink and outlinks behave similar and both are good indicators of relevance [16].

2.4.1 Basic Model

In this model, we represent concept *t* by an link set *In*(*a*), where *a* is the corresponding article of *t* in Wikipedia. According to the representation, we can compute the semantic relatedness between two concepts t_i and t_j by the following formula:

$$r(t_i,t_j)=\frac{|In(a_i)\cap In(a_j)|}{|In(a_i)\cup In(a_j)|} \tag{1}$$

where a_i and a_j are the corresponding Wikipedia articles for concept t_i and t_j respectively. The above formula employs the link structure in Wikipedia to measure the relatedness between two articles. It assumes that the more links shared by the two concepts, the more related they are. In addition, the number of link shared is normalized by the size of $In(a_i) \cup In(a_j)$. This model is simple and intuitive, but has the following weakness. In some cases, two articles in the same category have no shared links. The relatedness between them would be zero, even though they belong to the same category. This is because Wikipedia is human generated knowledge base and some articles corresponding to "unpopular" concepts may be quite short and incomplete. In order to solve this problem, we introduce the following probabilistic model.

2.4.2 Probabilistic Model

In the probabilistic model, we represent a concept *t* as a probability distribution over links. Different from the basic model, we assume an unseen link (outlink) in *t* to have a probability of occurrence. The probability is proportional to that of the link given by all categories that *t* belongs to. The probabilistic model θ_t for *t* can be estimated as follows:

$$p(link\mid\theta_t)=\frac{n(link;t)+\mu p(link\mid C)}{|t|+\mu} \tag{2}$$

where $n(link;t)$ is the number of times *link* appears in the article corresponding to t. $|t|$ is the number of links in t. μ is a Dirichlet parameter and will be determined in experiment. C is the set categories that t belongs to. $p(link|C)$ can be estimated as follows:

$$p(link \mid C) = \frac{\sum_{c \in C} \sum_{a \in c} |n(link; a)|}{\sum_{c \in C} \sum_{a \in c} |a|} \tag{3}$$

where c is a category of t in C. a is an article belongs to c. $|a|$ is the number of links in a. According to Formula 2, each concept in c shares all links of c with the probabilistic related to the frequency of the link occurring in c. The semantic relatedness between two concepts t_i and t_j can be measured as follows:

$$r(t_i, t_j) = -D(\theta_i \| \theta_j) - D(\theta_j \| \theta_i) \tag{4}$$

where $D(\theta_i \| \theta_j)$ is the KL-divergence of θ_i and θ_j:

$$D(\theta_i \| \theta_j) = \sum_{link} p(link \mid \theta_i) \log \frac{p(link \mid \theta_i)}{p(link \mid \theta_j)} \tag{5}$$

The more t_i relates to t_j, the smaller $D(\theta_i \| \theta_j)$ is. If t_i and t_j are the same concept, $D(\theta_i \| \theta_j)$ equals 0. Therefore, we use the negative KL-divergence to measure the relatedness.

2.4.3 Category Ranking Approach

Based on the models introduced in the above section, the relevance between a category c and a concept t can be computed as follows:

$$\begin{aligned} R(t,c) &= \alpha R(t, ch'(c)) + (1-\alpha) R(t, sp(c)) \\ &= \alpha \frac{1}{K} \sum_{t_i \in ch'(c)} r(t, t_i) + (1-\alpha) \max_{t_i \in sp(c)} r(t, t_i) \end{aligned} \tag{6}$$

where $R(t, ch'(c))$ is the relatedness between t and filtered child articles $ch'(c)$. $R(t, sp(c))$ is the relatedness between t and split articles $sp(c)$. The reason to use the maximum relatedness instead of average relatedness can be found in Section 2.3. α in Formula (6) is a parameter used to control the influence weight of two category representations. K is the pseudo size of each category. If the size of $ch'(c)$ is less than K, we can use the concept with minimum relatedness with t as supplement:

$$t_{\min} = \arg\min_{t_i} r(t, t_i) \tag{7}$$

Thus $R(t, ch'(c))$ in Formula (6) can be rewritten as:

$$R(t, ch'(c)) = \frac{1}{K} \left(\sum_{i=1}^{n'} r(t, t_i) + (K - n') r(t, t_{\min}) \right) \tag{8}$$

where n' is actual size of $ch'(c)$. We use the article in $ch'(c)$ with the minimum relatedness as supplement and keep the size of each category to K, so that each child article has the same contribution to the relevance of different-sized categories. For example, if in category A, the relatedness of two articles is 0.8 and 0.2 respectively; whereas the relatedness of three articles in category B is 0.8, 0.3 and 0.3 respectively. Obviously, B should be more relevant than A. But if we use the actual size to average the impact of each article, category A would rank higher than category B.

Given n concepts $T = \{t_1, t_2, \dots, t_n\}$ extracted from a paragraph, we use $T_{Context_i} = \{t_{i-D}, \dots, t_{i-1}, t_{i+1}, \dots, t_{i+D}\}$ to represent all contextual concepts for a target concept t_i. D is the contextual window size which determines how many concepts surrounding t_i will be considered as contextual concepts. Suppose there are m predefined categories $C_i = \{c_{i1}, c_{i2}, \dots, c_{ij}, \dots, c_{im}\}$ that t_i belongs to. The scoring function for category is defined as follows:

$$score(t_i, c_{ij}) \overset{\text{rank}}{=} \frac{\beta}{|T_{context_i}|} \sum_{t' \in T_{context_i}} R(t', c_{ij}) + (1-\beta) R(t_i, c_{ij}) \tag{9}$$

where $R(t', c_{ij})$ is the relevance between a contextual concept t' and a category c_{ij} of the target concept t_i. On the other hand, $R(t_i, c_{ij})$ is the relevance between the target concept t_i and its category c_{ij} without considering the context. We observe that the relevance values of a target concept to its own categories may vary. For example, for the concept "*Iron Man*", its category "*Marvel Comics title*" is more relevant than its category "*Fictional socialites*" without considering the context. Formula (9) takes into account the impact of the relevance without the context in category ranking. $R(t_i, c_{ij})$ and $R(t', c_{ij})$ can be computed by Formula (6). β is a parameter used to control the influence weight of context. If $\beta = 0$, the approach will be simplified to use only the information of the target concept without using the context of the target concept. Finally, we compute the ranking score for every category c_{ij} in C_i, and then rank the categories in descending order of the score.

3. EXPERIMENTS

This paper aims at exploiting Wikipedia for context-aware concept categorization. In line with this, we select two baselines in our experiments for comparative studies: (1) Ranking randomly for categories (Random). (2) Approach only using target concept but not the context surrounding it (Without context). Note that baseline 1 only utilize the basic knowledge structures in Wikipedia, and are just used to prove the intention of concept categorization. Baseline 2 is used to evaluate the contextual impact on the task of concept categorization.

We perform experiments for the two strategies of article selection discussed in Section 2.2 and 2.3, and compare our basic model and probabilistic model mentioned in Section 2.4.

3.1 Data Set and Evaluation

Currently, there is no available dataset in the community for the evaluation of concept categorization task. Therefore, we manually label a test set as the ground truth. We randomly select 100 English articles from Wikipedia for fine-grained labeling. The concepts in the articles have already been labeled by Wikipedia, and are used as given knowledge in our labeling process of the experiment. Our objective is to select relevant categories among all categories for each target concept according to the context.

We develop a category labeling tool. In our tool, each evaluation user can browse each article in Wikipedia with concepts marked in a different color from the main text. The reason to select Wikipedia article is that all concepts are linked unambiguously by editors. He/she can click on each concept and get all candidate categories of the clicked concept. Evaluation users can select the relevant categories according to textual context. We merge their labeled result together to obtain a final ground truth: only if it is checked by more than one user, a category is selected for the ground truth. In this way, the ground truth enables us to know whether or not a category is relevant to the concept given its context. Finally, we labeled 3072 concepts that belong to 29044 categories (7780 relevant categories). We notice that each concept has an average of 9.5 categories, of which only 2.5 are relevant according to the ground truth.

In our experiments, Wiki3C ranks all the categories for a concept according to its context and compares the rank results with the ground truth. We use MAP (Mean average precision), R-precision (R-prec) and bpref as evaluation metrics [17] to measure the quality of category ranking.

3.2 Overview of Experimental Results

Table 2 shows the performance comparison among all the approaches. Overall, all context-aware approaches outperform the three baselines. It proves that category selection is related to context, which is the basic assumption for the task of context-aware concept categorization in this paper. Moreover, baseline 1 only uses basic category structure information without any computation of relatedness. Their performance is much worse than that of baseline 2 uses the relatedness between the target concept and its categories. This proves the Wikipedia categories are not equal for a given concept.

In the context-aware approaches, we compare the performances of basic model and probabilistic model with different article selection strategies. Overall, the probabilistic model outperforms basic model. In addition, using filtering algorithm to select top K child articles can improve the performance significantly. We will discuss about it in Section 3.3.3. As shown in Figure 4, we can see that the curve of probabilistic model using filtered child articles is the closest to the upper right-hand corner of the graph, and achieves the best performance (MAP = 0.7542) with an improvement of 15.2% over baseline 2. This indicates that probabilistic model using filtered child articles is superior to the others. Moreover, child article selection strategy outperforms split article selection in both models. Furthermore, using the filtering algorithm in child article selection demonstrates a further improvement (4.3% for basic model and 2.0% for probabilistic model). The performance of the combination between the two selection strategies will be discussed in Section 3.3.2.

Table 2. Performance comparison.

Approach	MAP	R-prec	bpref
Random (baseline 1)	0.5245	0.4304	0.4213
Without context (baseline 2)	0.6546	0.5504	0.5389
Basic model (child)	0.6979	0.5942	0.5868
Basic model (child + filter)	0.7279	0.6142	0.6088
Basic model (split)	0.6679	0.5613	0.5414
Probabilistic model (child)	0.7392	0.6382	0.6321
Probabilistic model (child + filter)	**0.7542**	**0.6512**	**0.6411**
Probabilistic model (split)	0.6942	0.5932	0.5845

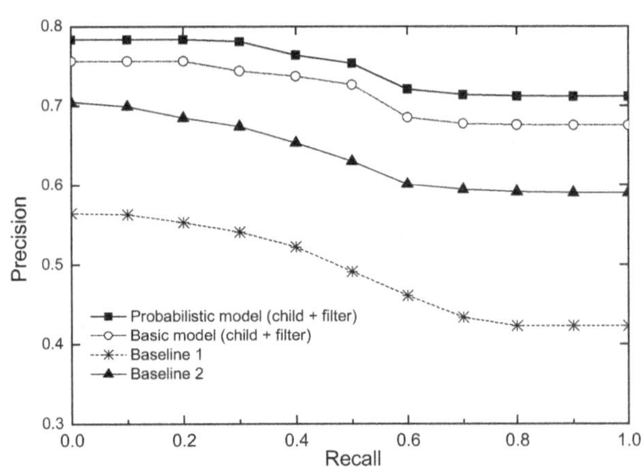

Figure 3. Comparison of recall-precision curves among different approaches.

3.3 Analysis of Parameters

3.3.1 *Parameter D*

In our approach, we use the concepts surrounding a target concept as the context. The concepts in the same paragraph with the target concept are considered as contexts and their number is determined by the window size parameter D. We experiment with D varying from 1 to 10 to see its impact on the quality of category ranking. In Figure 4, we notice that the performances of all approaches improve gradually as D increases (MAP of the approach without using context is constant at 0.6546). But when D is approaching 10, the performance deteriorates slightly. An explanation is that concepts separated by a significant distance are also less relevant than concepts located closer to each other. If D is set too large, some unrelated and noise contextual concepts will be included.

In particular, for the approaches that only use split articles, their performance does not change much when D varies, since the number of split articles for a category is often small (less than 5), and some of them are context-independent. However, compared to the baseline approach, using contextual information improves MAP from 0.6546 to 0.6942 (6.0% increase for probabilistic model) and 0.6669 (1.9% increase for basic model) respectively. For the approaches that using child articles, the performance increases significantly as D increases. It reaches the best performance when D = 8, after which the performance stays roughly the same. Therefore, D is fixed to 8 in other experiments.

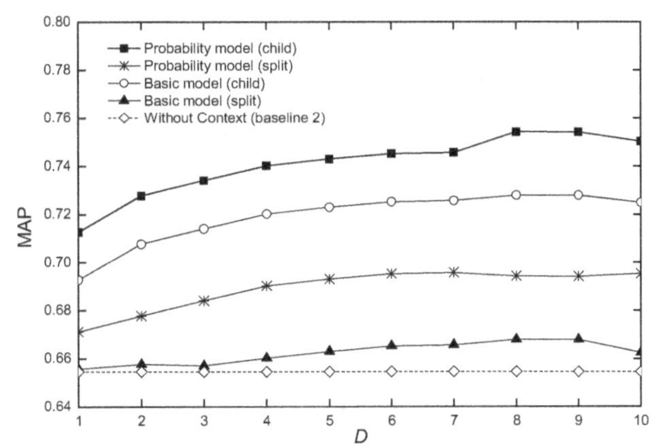

Figure 4. Performance sensitivity to window size *D*.

3.3.2 *Parameter α and β*

In our approach, there are two main parameters that should be determined in our experiments: α and β. The parameter β in Formula (9) controls influence of context for category ranking. Specifically, β is used to adjust the ratio of target concept's relevance and contextual relevance in the ranking model. Figure 5(a) shows the effect of varying β from 0 to 1, with a step up size of 0.1. In this experiment, we set α = 1, thus, we actually only use the child articles to represent a category. Clearly, the introduction of contextual concepts can significantly improve the performance. But when β is approaching 1, the performance deteriorates sharply, though it is still better than without using contextual concepts. For the basic approach, the performance keeps improving until β = 0.6, while the best performance occurs when β = 0.7 for the probabilistic model.

As mentioned in Section 2.2 and 2.3, both the split articles and child articles can represent a category. We combine them together to calculate the ranking score for a category. In Formula (6), α is a weight parameter to control the proportion of child articles in the linear combination. Figure 5(b) shows how MAP varies accordingly with α when β is fixed at 0.7. The best performances of probabilistic model and basic model are reached at $\alpha = 1.0$. Clearly, the combination does not achieve better performance than using child articles alone. In the solution of split article selection, we expect to find a generalized concept that can best represent the category. This leads to categories with similar name having a similar relevance and some feature will be lost in these categories. For example, 7 categories of the concept "*Iron Man*" contain a common split article "*Character (film)*". Therefore, they may have a similar relevance to the context in Paragraph 1 of Figure 1. But in fact, the correct category "*Film characters*" should be more relevant than others such as "*Comics characters introduced in 1963*", "*Characters created by Stan Lee*", etc. In conclusion, child articles are more effective than split articles to represent categories in the task of context-aware concept categorization.

3.3.3 Parameter K and μ

Another two key parameters that should be determined in our approach are K and μ. K is used for the child article selection in Section 2.2. It can be considered as a pseudo category size to filter noise and irrelevant articles in a category. Figure 6(a) shows that the performance increases significantly as K increases. However, when K exceeds 10, the performance deteriorates gradually. When K is large enough, we actually select all child articles to represent a category without filtering. In the other experiments, we set $K = 8$, which is optimal for all models in this experiment.

According to Formula (2), μ is the Dirichlet prior for smoothing. Because some articles corresponding to "unpopular" concepts in Wikipedia may be very short and incomplete, their relevance always tends to be zero even though they belong to the same category. The introduction of μ makes unseen link of an article have a probability of occurrence. The probability is proportional to that of the link given by all categories that the concept belongs to. Thus, each concept shares some links that belong to the common categories. Figure 6(b) demonstrates the changing performance by changing μ from 0 to 4000. When μ increases, the performances of the two strategies of article selection improve until $\mu = 1000$. After that, the performances deteriorate slightly and start to stabilize. It is worth to mention that when μ is too large, each concept tends to have a similar distribution as that of the categories to which it belongs. Therefore, each concept loses its own features. Specifically, the performance of selecting child articles to represent categories can be improved significantly by the introduction of μ; whereas the impact of μ is relatively small for the approach using split article selection. This is because we actually use only one article to represent a category. The selected article has the maximum relatedness among all split articles for the category, and is relatively long and complete. Besides, split articles usually correspond to general concepts. So the bias mentioned above is small.

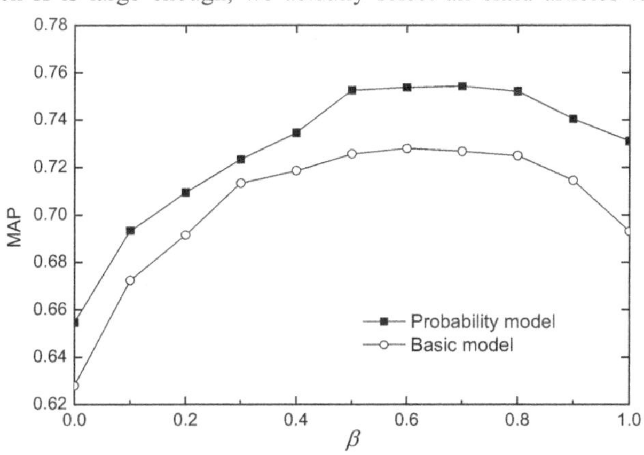

(a) MAP sensitivity to β

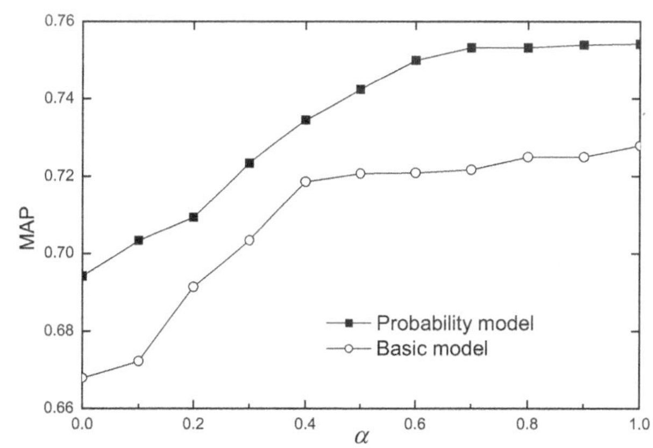

(b) MAP sensitivity to α

Figure 5. Performance sensitivity to α and β.

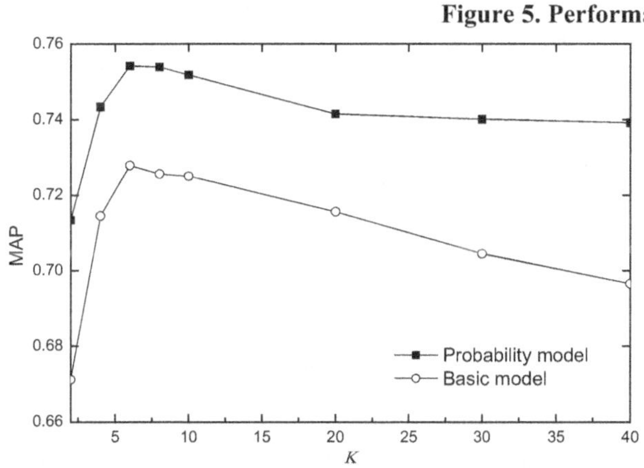

(a) MAP sensitivity to K

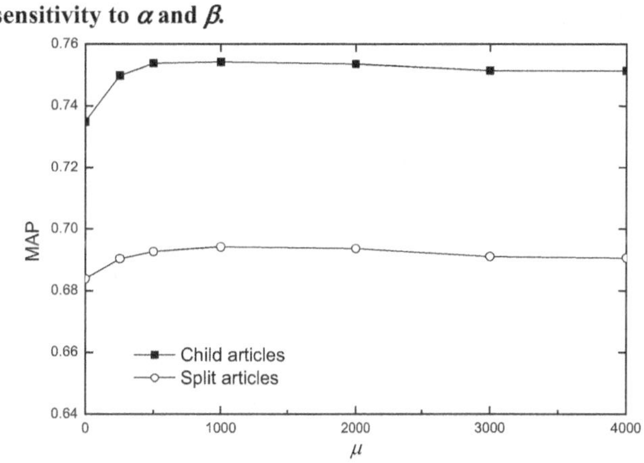

(b) MAP sensitivity to μ

Figure 6. Performance sensitivity to μ and K.

4. RELATED WORK

The work described in this paper mainly uses the knowledge in Wikipedia. Previous work using Wikipedia mainly focuses on semantic relatedness computing, word sense disambiguation, text classification and clustering. Völkel et al. [18] provide an extension to be integrated in Wikipedia that allows the typing of links between articles and the specification of typed data inside the articles to be easy-to-use. Strube and Ponzetto [19] are the first to propose a Wikipedia based approach to computing measures of semantic relatedness. Gabrilovich and Markovitch [2] enrich document representation through Wikipedia to improve the performance of text categorization. Empirical results prove that this knowledge-intensive representation brings text categorization to a qualitatively new level of performance across a diverse collection of datasets. They [10] also propose explicit semantic analysis to measure semantic relatedness. With their approach, they employ text classification techniques to explicitly represent the meaning of any text in terms of Wikipedia-based concepts. In addition, due to the use of Wikipedia concepts, their model is easy to be explained to human users. Cucerzan [20] uses Wikipedia structured knowledge for named entity disambiguation task. Through a process of maximizing the agreement between the contextual information extracted from Wikipedia and the context of a document, as well as the agreement among the category tags associated with the candidate entities, the implemented system shows high disambiguation accuracy on both news stories and Wikipedia articles. Banerjee et al.[21] propose a method of improving the accuracy of clustering short texts by enriching their representation with additional features from Wikipedia. Compared to traditional bag of words representation, the Wikipedia based enriched representation can improve the clustering accuracy significantly.

Within the community of information retrieval (IR) and information extraction (IE), there are various studies related to Wikipedia [14, 15, 22-25]. In 2007, INEX [26, 27] introduces an entity ranking track that aims to evaluate the entity retrieval in Wikipedia. In TREC entity track [28] which aims at finding related entities on the Web, many approaches use Wikipedia as an external resource for query expansion, named entity recognition or entity type detection. Wu and Weld [14] propose an open IE system which performs a self-supervised learning to distill relations from natural-language text. Their system constructs training data by heuristically matching Wikipedia infobox attribute values with corresponding sentences.

The following work is particularly relevant to this paper. Milne and Witten [29] use Wikipedia Link-based Measure (WLM) to compute the semantic relatedness between two articles. Unlike other techniques based on Wikipedia, WLM is able to provide accurate measures efficiently, using only the links between articles rather than their textual content. They [12] also use link to cross-refer documents with Wikipedia. Mihalcea and Csomai [13] propose Wikify, the first system to extract concepts from text documents and link them to Wikipedia articles. Their system extracts keyword automatically and disambiguates word sense by linking concepts extracted from document to the corresponding Wikipedia pages. Our work extends the above studies by ranking the Wikipedia categories of the extracted concepts according to their context, and it can be used in text classification, text cluster, IR and IE.

5. CONCLUSION

Wikipedia produces rich category information that can be used in many text mining tasks, such as text classification, text clustering, word sense disambiguation, etc. However, Wikipedia category representation for each concept is simplistic: a concept contains a number of categories, without considering their relevance to the context where the concept appears. In this paper, we introduce and study the task of ranking categories based on context. We aim at categorizing extracted concepts based on contextual information. It provides an in-depth understanding of concepts in a specific context and generates context-aware categories that are of higher level than concepts. It goes one step further than classical text mining task in Wikipedia, such as semantic relatedness computing, word sense disambiguation, concept extraction, etc.

This paper proposes an unsupervised learning solution to the task of context-aware concept categorization, named Wiki3C. In the solution, we treat the extracted concepts surrounding a target concept as context, followed by ranking the categories of target concept according to the relevance to the context. Two strategies of article selection are chosen to represent category. In addition, we use a probabilistic model to compute the semantic relatedness between concepts. Experimental results prove the effectiveness of Wiki3C. It is worth mentioning that there is still huge potential for further research to improve the performance for context-aware concept categorization. Another interesting future research issue is to apply the results of context-aware concept categorization to other related task, such as text classification, text clustering, topic modeling, contextual online advertising, etc.

6. ACKNOWLEDGMENTS

We would like to express our gratitude to the anonymous reviewers for their insightful feedbacks. The author Chengkai Li is partially supported by HP Labs Innovation Research Program award.

7. REFERENCES

[1] X.-H. Phan, et al. Learning to classify short and sparse text & web with hidden topics from large-scale data collections. In *Proceedings of the 17th international conference on World Wide Web*, Beijing, China, pages 91-100, 2008.

[2] E. Gabrilovich and S. Markovitch. Overcoming the brittleness bottleneck using wikipedia: enhancing text categorization with encyclopedic knowledge. In *proceedings of the 21st national conference on Artificial intelligence - Volume 2*, Boston, Massachusetts, pages 1301-1306, 2006.

[3] X. Hu, et al. Exploiting Wikipedia as external knowledge for document clustering. In *Proceedings of the 15th ACM SIGKDD international conference on Knowledge discovery and data mining*, Paris, France, pages 389-396, 2009.

[4] D. Carmel, et al. Enhancing cluster labeling using wikipedia. In *Proceedings of the 32nd international ACM SIGIR conference on Research and development in information retrieval*, Boston, MA, USA, pages 139-146, 2009.

[5] S. Cucerzan. Large-Scale Named Entity Disambiguation Based on Wikipedia Data. In *Proceedings of the 2007 Joint Conference on Empirical Methods in Natural Language Processing and Computational Natural Language Learning*, Prague, pages 708-716, 2007.

[6] R. Bunescu and M. Pasc. Using Encyclopedic Knowledge for Named Entity Disambiguation. In *Proceedings of the 11th Conference of the European Chapter of the Association for*

Computational Linguistics (EACL), Trento, Italy, pages 2006.

[7] J. Pehcevski, et al. Entity ranking in Wikipedia: utilising categories, links and topic difficulty prediction. *Inf. Retr.*, 13(5):568-600, 2010.

[8] Y. Li, et al. Improving weak ad-hoc queries using wikipedia as external corpus. In *Proceedings of the 30th annual international ACM SIGIR conference on Research and development in information retrieval*, Amsterdam, The Netherlands, pages 797-798, 2007.

[9] G. Katz, et al. Using Wikipedia to boost collaborative filtering techniques. In *Proceedings of the fifth ACM conference on Recommender systems*, Chicago, Illinois, USA, pages 285-288, 2011.

[10] E. Gabrilovich and S. Markovitch. Computing semantic relatedness using Wikipedia-based explicit semantic analysis. In *Proceedings of the 20th international joint conference on Artifical intelligence*, Hyderabad, India, pages 1606-1611, 2007.

[11] S. P. Ponzetto and M. Strube. Deriving a large scale taxonomy from Wikipedia. In *Proceedings of the 22nd national conference on Artificial intelligence - Volume 2*, Vancouver, British Columbia, Canada, pages 1440-1445, 2007.

[12] D. Milne and I. H. Witten. Learning to link with wikipedia. In *Proceedings of the 17th ACM conference on Information and knowledge management*, Napa Valley, California, USA, pages 509-518, 2008.

[13] R. Mihalcea and A. Csomai. Wikify!: linking documents to encyclopedic knowledge. In *Proceedings of the 16th ACM conference on Conference on information and knowledge management,* Lisbon, Portugal, pages 233-242, 2007.

[14] F. Wu and D. S. Weld. Open Information Extraction using Wikipedia. In *Proceedings of the 48th Annual Meeting of the Association for Computational Linguistics*, pages 118-127, 2010.

[15] E. Hovy, et al. Toward completeness in concept extraction and classification. In *Proceedings of the 2009 Conference on Empirical Methods in Natural Language Processing: Volume 2 - Volume 2*, Singapore, pages 948-957, 2009.

[16] J. Kamps and M. Koolen. Is Wikipedia link structure different? In *Proceedings of the Second ACM International Conference on Web Search and Data Mining*, Barcelona, Spain, pages 232-241, 2009.

[17] B. Chris and M. V. Ellen. Retrieval evaluation with incomplete information. In *Proceedings of the 27th annual international ACM SIGIR conference on Research and development in information retrieval*, Sheffield, United Kingdom, pages 25-32, 2004.

[18] M. Völkel, et al. Semantic Wikipedia. In *Proceedings of the 15th international conference on World Wide Web*, Edinburgh, Scotland, pages 585-594, 2006.

[19] M. Strube and S. P. Ponzetto. WikiRelate! computing semantic relatedness using wikipedia. In *proceedings of the 21st national conference on Artificial intelligence - Volume 2*, Boston, Massachusetts, pages 1419-1424, 2006.

[20] S. Cucerzan. Large Scale Named Entity Disambiguation Based on Wikipedia Data. In *The EMNLP-CoNLL Joint Conference*, Prague, 2007.

[21] S. Banerjee, et al. Clustering short texts using wikipedia. In *Proceedings of the 30th annual international ACM SIGIR conference on Research and development in information retrieval*, Amsterdam, The Netherlands, pages 787-788, 2007.

[22] D. N. Milne, et al. A knowledge-based search engine powered by wikipedia. In *Proceedings of the sixteenth ACM conference on Conference on information and knowledge management*, Lisbon, Portugal, pages 445-454, 2007.

[23] D. P. T. Nguyen, et al. Relation extraction from wikipedia using subtree mining. In *Proceedings of the 22nd national conference on Artificial intelligence - Volume 2*, Vancouver, British Columbia, Canada, pages 1414-1420, 2007.

[24] K. Balog, et al. Entity search: building bridges between two worlds. In *Proceedings of the 3rd International Semantic Search Workshop*, Raleigh, North Carolina, pages 1-5, 2010.

[25] Y. Yan, et al. Unsupervised relation extraction by mining Wikipedia texts using information from the web. In *Proceedings of the Joint Conference of the 47th Annual Meeting of the ACL and the 4th International Joint Conference on Natural Language Processing of the AFNLP: Volume 2 - Volume 2*, Suntec, Singapore, pages 1021-1029, 2009.

[26] G. Demartini, et al. Overview of the INEX 2009 entity ranking track. In *INEX 2009*, pages 256–264, 2009.

[27] P. V. Arjen, et al. Overview of the INEX 2007 Entity Ranking Track. In *Focused Access to XML Documents: 6th International Workshop of the Initiative for the Evaluation of XML Retrieval*, pages 245-251, 2008.

[28] B. Krisztian, et al. Overview of the TREC 2009 Entity Track. In *Proceedings of TREC-2009*, Gaithersburg, USA, 2009.

[29] D. Milne and I. H. Witten. An Effective, Low-Cost Measure of Semantic Relatedness Obtained from Wikipedia Links. In *Proceeding of AAAI Workshop on Wikipedia and Artificial Intelligence: an Evolving Synergy*, pages 25-30, 2008.

Crawling Deep Web Entity Pages

Yeye He[*]
Univ. of Wisconsin-Madison
Madison, WI 53706
heyeye@cs.wisc.edu

Dong Xin
Google Inc.
Mountain View, CA, 94043
dongxin@google.com

Venkatesh Ganti
Google Inc.
Mountain View, CA, 94043
vganti@google.com

Sriram Rajaraman
Google Inc.
Mountain View, CA, 94043
sriramr@google.com

Nirav Shah
Google Inc.
Mountain View, CA, 94043
nshah@google.com

ABSTRACT

Deep-web crawl is concerned with the problem of surfacing hidden content behind search interfaces on the Web. While many deep-web sites maintain document-oriented textual content (e.g., Wikipedia, PubMed, Twitter, etc.), which has traditionally been the focus of the deep-web literature, we observe that a significant portion of deep-web sites, including almost all online shopping sites, curate structured entities as opposed to text documents. Although crawling such entity-oriented content is clearly useful for a variety of purposes, existing crawling techniques optimized for document oriented content are not best suited for entity-oriented sites. In this work, we describe a prototype system we have built that specializes in crawling entity oriented deep-web sites. We propose techniques tailored to tackle important subproblems including query generation, empty page filtering and URL deduplication in the specific context of entity oriented deep-web sites. These techniques are experimentally evaluated and shown to be effective.

Categories and Subject Descriptors: H.2.8 Database Application: Data Mining

Keywords: Deep-web crawl, web data, entities.

1. INTRODUCTION

Deep-web crawl refers to the problem of surfacing rich information behind the web search interface of diverse sites across the Web. It was estimated by various accounts that the deep-web has as much as an order of magnitude more content than that of the surface web [10, 14]. While crawling the deep-web can be immensely useful for a variety of tasks including web indexing [15] and data integration [14], crawling the deep-web content is known to be hard. The difficulty in surfacing the deep-web has inspired a long and fruitful line of research [3, 4, 5, 10, 14, 15, 17, 22, 23].

In this paper we focus on entity-oriented deep-web sites. These sites curate structured entities and expose them through search interfaces. Examples include almost all online shopping sites (e.g., ebay.com, amazon.com, etc.), where each entity is typically a product that is associated with rich structured information like item name, brand name, price, and so forth. Additional examples of entity-oriented deep-web sites include movie sites, job listings, etc. Note that this is to contrast with traditional document-oriented deep-web sites that mostly maintain unstructured text documents (e.g., Wikipedia, PubMed, etc.).

Entity-oriented sites are very common and represent a significant portion of the deep-web sites. The variety of tasks that entity-oriented content enables makes the general problem of crawling entities an important problem.

The practical use of our system is to crawl product entities from a large number of online retailers for advertisement landing page purposes. While the exact use of such entities content in advertisement is beyond the scope of this paper, the system requirement is simple to state: We are provided as input a list of retailers' websites, and the objective is to crawl high-quality product entity pages efficiently and effectively.

There are two key properties that set our problem apart from traditional deep-web crawling literature. First, we specifically focus on the entity-oriented model, because of our interest in product entities from online retailers, which are entity-oriented deep-web sites in most cases. While existing general crawling techniques are still applicable to some extent, the specific focus on entity-oriented sites brings unique opportunities. Second, a large number of entity sites (online retailers) are provided as input to our system, from which entity pages are to be crawled. Note that with thousands of sites as input, the realistic objective is to only obtain a *representative* content coverage of each site, instead of an *exhaustive* one. Ebay.com, for example, has hundreds of thousands of listings returned for the query "iphone"; the purpose of the system is not to obtain all iphone listings, but only a representative few of these listings for ads landing pages. This goal of obtaining representative coverage contrasts with traditional deep-web crawl literature, which tends to deal with individual site and focus on obtaining exhaustive content coverage. Our objective is more in line with the pioneering work [15], which also operates at the Web scale but focuses on general web content.

We have developed a prototype system that is designed specifically to crawl representative entity content. The crawling process is optimized by exploiting features unique to entity-oriented sites. In this paper, we will focus on describing important components of our system, including query generation, empty page filtering and URL deduplication.

Our first contribution is to show how query logs and knowledge bases (e.g., Freebase) can be leveraged to generate entity queries for crawling. We demonstrate that classical techniques for infor-

[*]Work done while author at Google, now at Microsoft Research.

WSDM'13, February 4–8, 2013, Rome, Italy.

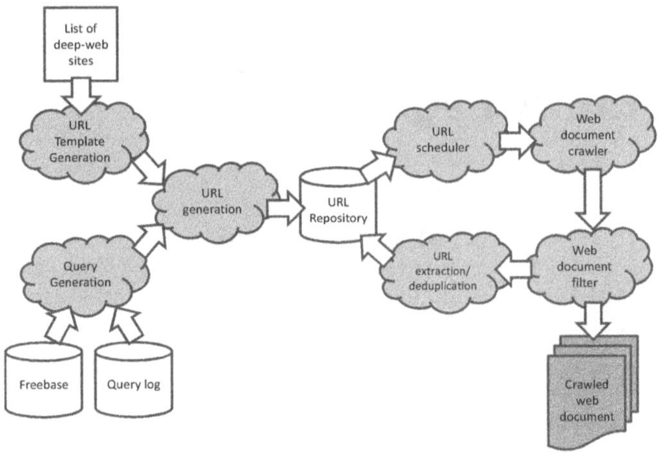

Figure 1: Overview of the entity-oriented crawl system

mation retrieval and entity extraction can be used to robustly derive relevant entities for each site, so that crawling bandwidth can be utilized efficiently and effectively (Section 5).

The second contribution of this work is a new empty page filtering algorithm that removes crawled pages that fail to retrieve any entities. This seemingly simple problem is nontrivial due to the diverse nature of pages from different sites. We propose an intuitive filtering approach, based on the observation that empty pages from the same site tend to be highly similar (e.g., with the same page layout and the same error message). In particular, we first submit to each target site a small set of queries that are intentionally "bad", to retrieve a "reference set" of pages that are highly likely to be empty. At crawl time, each newly crawled page is compared with the reference set, and pages that are highly similar to the reference set are predicted as empty and filtered out from further processing. This weakly-supervised approach is shown to be robust across sites on the Web (Section 6).

Additionally, we observe that the search result pages typically expose additional deep-web content that deserves a second round of crawling, which is an interesting topic that has been overlooked in the literature. In order to obtain such content, we identify promising URLs on the result pages, from which further crawling can be bootstrapped. Furthermore, we propose a URL deduplication algorithm that prevents URLs with near-identical results from being crawled. Specifically, whereas existing techniques use content analysis for deduplication which works only after pages are crawled, our approach identifies the semantic relevance of URL query segments by analyzing URL patterns, so that URLs with similar content that differ in non-essential ways (e.g., how retrieved entities are rendered and sorted) can be deduplicated. This approach is shown to be effective in preserving distinct content while reducing the bandwidth consumption (Section 7).

2. SYSTEM OVERVIEW

Deep-web sites	URL templates
ebay.com	*www.ebay.com/sch/i.html?**_nkw={query}**&_sacat=All-Categories*
chegg.com	*www.chegg.com/search/?**search_by={query}***
beso.com	*www.beso.com/classify?search_box=1**&keyword={query}***
...	...

Table 1: Example URL templates

In this section we explain each component of our system in turn at a very high level. The overall architecture of our system is illustrated in Figure 1.

URL template generation. At the top left corner the system takes a list of domain names of deep-web sites as input, and an example of which is illustrated in the first column of Table 1. The URL template generation component then crawls the home-pages of these sites, extracts and parses the web forms found on the home-pages, and produces URL templates. Example URL templates are illustrated in the second column of Table 1. Here the boldfaced "**{query}**" represents a wild-card that can be substituted by any keyword query (e.g., "iphone"); the resulting URL can be used to crawl deep-web content as if the web forms are submitted.

Query generation and URL generation. The query generation component at the lower left corner takes the Freebase [6] and query logs as input, outputs queries consistent with the semantics of each deep-web site (for example, query "iphone" may be generated for sites like amazon.com or ebay.com but not for tripadvisor.com).

Such queries can then be plugged into URL templates to substitute the "{query}" wild-card to produce final URLs, which will be stored in a central URL repository. URLs can then be retrieved from the URL repository and scheduled for crawling at runtime.

Empty page filter. It is inevitable that some URLs corresponding to previously generated queries will retrieve empty or error pages that contain no entity. Once pages are crawled, we move to the next stage, where pages are inspected to filter out empty ones. The process of filtering empty pages is critical (to avoid polluting downstream operations), but also non-trivial, for different sites indicate empty pages in disparate ways. The key insight here is that empty pages from the same site tend to be highly similar. So we intentionally retrieve a set of pages that are highly likely to be empty, and filter out any crawled pages from the same site that are similar to the reference set. Remaining pages with rich entity information can then be used for a variety of purposes.

URL extraction/deduplication. Additionally, we observe that a significant fraction of URLs on search result pages (henceforth referred to as "second-level URLs", to distinguish from the URLs generated using URL template, which are "first-level URLs") typically link to additional deep-web content. However, crawling all second-level URLs indiscriminately is wasteful due to the large number of second level URLs available. Accordingly, in this component, we filter out second-level URLs that are less likely to lead to deep-web content, and dynamically deduplicate remaining URLs to obtain a much smaller set of "representative" URLs that can be crawled efficiently. These URLs then iterate through the same crawling process to obtain additional deep-web content.

3. RELATED WORK

The aforementioned problems studied in this work have been explored in the literature to various extents. In this section, we will describe related work and discuss key differences between our approach in this work and existing techniques.

URL template generation. The problem of generating URL templates has been studied in the literature in different contexts. For example, authors in [4, 5] looked at the problem of identifying searchable forms that are deep-web entry points, from which templates can then be generated. The problem of parsing HTML forms for URL templates has been addressed in [15]. In addition, authors in [15, 20] studied the problem of assigning combinations of values to multiple input fields in the search form so that content can be retrieved from the deep-web effectively.

In our URL template generation component, search forms are parsed using techniques similar to what was outlined in [15]. However, our analysis shows that generating URL templates by enumerating values combination in multiple input fields can lead to an inefficiently large number of templates and may not scale to the number of websites that we are interested in crawling. As will be discussed in Section 4, our main insight is to leverage the fact that for entity-oriented sites, search forms predominantly employ one text field for keyword queries, and additional input fields with good "default value" behavior. Our URL template generation based on this observation provides a tractable solution for a large number of potentially complex search forms without significantly sacrificing content coverage.

Query generation and URL generation. Prior art in query generation for deep web crawl focused on bootstrapping using text extracted from retrieved pages [15, 17, 22, 23]. That is, a set of seed queries are first used to crawl pages. The retrieved pages are analyzed for promising keywords, which are then used as queries to crawl more pages recursively.

There are several key reasons why existing approaches are not very well suited for our purpose. First of all, most previous work [17, 22, 23] aims to optimize coverage of *individual* sites, that is, to retrieve as much deep-web content as possible from one or a few sites, where success is measured by percentage of content retrieved. Authors in [3] go as far as suggesting to crawl using common stop words "a, the" etc. to improve site coverage when these words are indexed. We are in line with [15] in aiming to improve content coverage for a large number of sites on the Web. Because of the sheer number of deep-web sites crawled we trade off complete coverage of individual site for incomplete but "representative" coverage of a large number of sites.

The second important difference is that since we are crawling entity-oriented pages, the queries we come up with should be entity names instead of arbitrary phrases segments. As such, we leverage two important data sources, namely query logs and knowledge bases. We will show that classical information retrieval and entity extraction techniques can be used effectively for entity query generation. To our knowledge neither of these data sources has been very well studied for deep-web crawl purposes.

Empty page filtering. Authors in [15] developed an interesting notion of *informativeness* to filter search forms, which is computed by clustering *signatures* that summarize content of crawled pages. If crawled pages only have a few signature clusters, then the search form is *uninformative* and will be pruned accordingly. This approach addresses the problem of empty pages to an extent by filtering uninformative forms. However, this approach operates at the level of search form / URL template, it may still miss empty pages crawled using an informative URL template.

Since our system generates only one high-quality URL template for each site, filtering at the granularity of URL templates is likely to be ill-suited. Instead, our approach considers in this work filters at page level — it can automatically distinguishes empty pages from useful entity pages by utilizing intentionally generated bad queries. To our knowledge this simple yet effective approach has not been explored in the literature.

A novel page-level empty page filtering technique was described in [20], which labels a result page as empty, if either certain predefined error messages are detected from the "significant portion" of result pages (e.g., the portion of the page formatted using frames, or visually laid out at the center of the page), or a large fraction of result pages are hashed to the same value. In comparison, our approach obviates the need to recognize the significant portion of result pages, and we use content signature instead of hashing that is more robust against minor page differences.

URL deduplication. The problem of URL deduplication has received considerable attention in the context of web crawling and indexing [2, 8, 13]. Current techniques consider two URLs as duplicates if their content are highly similar. These approaches, referred to as *content-based URL deduplication*, proposes to first summarize page contents using content sketches [7] so that pages with similar content are grouped into clusters. URLs in the same cluster are then analyzed to learn URL transformation rules (for example, it can learn that `www.cnn.com/story?id=num` is equivalent to `www.cnn.com/story_num`).

Figure 2: A typical search interface (ebay.com)

In this paper, instead of looking at the traditional notion of page similarity at the content level, we view page similarity at the semantic level. That is, we view pages with entities from the same result set (but perhaps containing different portions of the result, or presenting with different sorting orders) as semantically similar, which can then be deduplicated. This significantly reduces the number of crawls needed, and is in line with our goal of obtaining representative content coverage given the sheer number of websites crawled.

Using semantic similarity, our approach can analyze URL patterns and deduplicate *before* pages are crawled. In comparison, existing content-based deduplication not only requires pages to be crawled first for content analysis, it would not be able to recognize the semantic similarity between URLs and would require billions of more URLs crawled.

Authors in [15] pioneered the notion of presentation criteria, and pointed out that crawling pages with content that differ only in presentation criteria are undesirable. Their approach, however, deduplicates at the level of search forms and cannot be used to deduplicate URLs directly.

4. URL TEMPLATE GENERATION

As input to our system, we are given a list of entity-oriented deep-web sites that need to be crawled. Our first problem is to generate URL templates for each site that are equivalent to submitting search forms, so that entities can be crawled directly using URL templates.

As a concrete example, the search form from ebay.com is shown in Figure 2, which represents a typical entity-oriented deep-web search interface. Searching this form using query "ipad 2" without changing the default value "All Categories" of the drop-down box is equivalent to using the URL template for ebay.com in Table 1, with wild-card "{query}" replaced by "ipad+2".

The exact technique that parses search forms is developed based on techniques proposed in [15], which we will not discuss in details in the interest of space. However, our experience with URL template generation leads to two interesting observations worth mentioning.

Our first observation is that for entity-oriented sites, the main search form is almost always on home pages instead of somewhere deep in the site. The search form is such an effective information retrieval paradigm that websites are only too eager to expose them. A manual survey suggests that only 1 out of 100 randomly sampled sites does not have the search form on the home page (www.arke.nl). This obviates the need to use sophisticated techniques to locate search forms deep in websites (e.g., [4, 5]).

The second observation is that in entity-oriented sites, search forms predominantly use one main text input fields to accept keyword queries (a full 93% of sites surveyed have exactly one text field to accept keyword queries). At the same time, other non-text input fields exhibit good "default value" behavior (94% of sites out of the 100 sampled are judged to be able to retrieve entities using default values without sacrificing coverage).

Since enumerating values combination in multiple input fields

Deep-web sites	sample queries from query logs
ebay.com	cheap iPhone 4, lenovo x61, ...
bestbuy.com	hp touchpad review, price of sony vaio, ...
booking.com	where to stay in new york, hyatt seattle review, ...
hotels.com	hotels in london, san francisco hostels, ...
barnesandnobel.com	star trek books, stephen king insomnia, ...
chegg.com	harry potter book 1-7, dark knight returns, ...

Table 2: Example queries from query logs

(e.g., [15, 20]) can lead to an inefficiently large number of templates and may not scale to the number of websites that we are interested in crawling, we leverage aforementioned observation to simplify URL template generation by producing one template for each search form. Specifically, only the text field is allowed to vary (represented by a placeholder "{query}") while others fields will take on default values, as shown in Table 1. In our experience this provides a more tractable way to generate templates than the previous multi-value enumeration approach that works well in practice. We will not discuss details of template generation any further in the interest of space.

5. QUERY GENERATION

After obtaining URL templates for each site, the next step is to fill relevant keyword query into the "{query}" wild-card to produce final URLs. The challenge here is to come up with queries that match the semantics of the sites. A dictionary-based brute force approach that sends every known entity to every site is clearly inefficient – crawling queries like "ipad" on tripadvisor.com does not make sense, and will most likely result in an empty/error page.

We utilize two data sources for query generation: query logs and knowledge-bases. Our main observation here is that classical techniques in information retrieval and entity extraction are already effective in generating entity queries.

5.1 Entity extraction from query logs

Query logs refer to keyword queries searched and URLs clicked on search engines (e.g., Google). Conceptually query logs make a good candidate for query generation in deep-web crawls — queries with high number of clicks to a certain site is an indication of the relevance between the query and the site, submitting such queries through the site's search interface for deep-web crawl thus makes intuitive sense.

We used Google's query logs with the following normalized form $< keyword\_query, url\_clicked, num\_times\_clicked >$. To filter out undesirable queries (e.g., navigational queries), we only consider queries that are clicked for at least 2 pages in the same site, for at least 3 times.

Although query logs contain rich information, it is also too noisy to be used directly for crawling. Specifically, queries in the query logs tend to contain extraneous tokens in addition to the central entity of interest. However, it is not uncommon for the search interface on deep-web sites to expect only entity names as queries. Figure 3 serves as an illustration of this problem. When feeding a search engine query "HP touchpad reviews" into the search interface on deep-web sites, (in this example, ebay.com), no results are returned (Figure 3a), while searching using only the entity name "HP touchpad" retrieves 6617 such products (Figure 3b).

This issue above is not isolated. On the one hand, search engine queries typically contain tokens in addition to entity mentions, which either specify certain aspects of entities of interest (e.g., "HP touchpad review", "price of chrome book spec"), or are simply natural language fragments (e.g., "where to buy iPad 2", "where to stay in new york"). On the other hand, many search interfaces only expect clean entity queries. This is because a significant portion of

(a) search with "hp touchpad reviews"

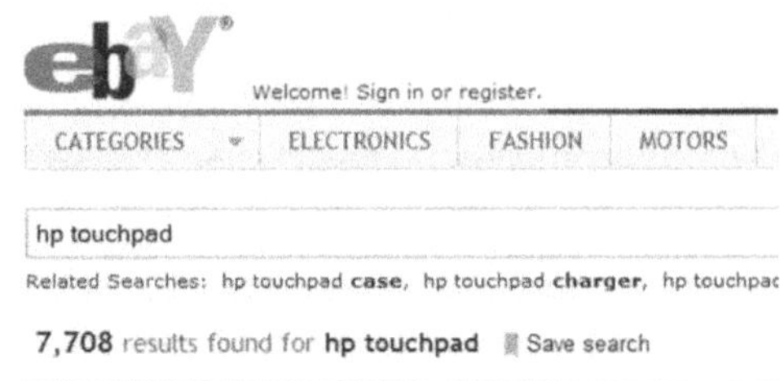

(b) search with "hp touchpad"

Figure 3: An example of Keyword-And based search interface

entity sites employ the simple Keyword-And mechanism, where *all* tokens in the query have to be matched in a tuple before the tuple can be returned (thus the no match problem in Figure 3b). Even if the other conceptual alternative, Keyword-Or is used, the presence of extraneous tokens can promote spurious matches and lead to less desirable crawls.

We reduce the aforementioned problem to entity extraction from query logs. Or to view it the other way, we clean the search engine queries by removing tokens that are not entity related (e.g., removing "reviews" from "HP touchpad reviews", or "where to stay in" from "where to stay in new york", etc.).

In the absence of a comprehensive entity dictionary, it is hard to tell if a token belongs to (ever-growing) entity names and their name variations, abbreviations or even typos. At the same time, the diverse nature of the query logs makes it all the more valuable, for it captures a wide variety of entities and their name variations.

Inspired by an influential work on entity extraction from query logs [18], we first identify common patterns in query logs that are clearly not entity related (e.g., "reviews", "specs", "where to stay in" etc.) by leveraging known entities. Query logs can then be "cleaned" to extract entities by removing such patterns.

Specifically, we first obtained a dump of the Freebase data [6] — a manually curated repository with about 22M entities. We then find the maximum-length subsequence in each search engine query that matches Freebase entities as an entity mention. The remaining tokens are treated as entity-irrelevant prefix/suffix. We aggregate distinct prefix/suffix across the query logs to obtain common patterns ordered by their frequency of occurrences. The most frequent patterns are likely to be irrelevant to entities and need to be cleaned.

EXAMPLE 1. *Table 2 illustrates the sample queries with mentions of Freebase entity names underlined. Observe that this entity recognition this way is not perfect. For example, the query "where to stay in new york" for booking.com has two matches with Freebase entities, the match of "where to" to a musical release with that name, and the match of "new york" as city name. Since both matches are of length two, we obtain the false suffix "stay in new york" (with an empty prefix) and the correct prefix "where to stay in" (with an empty suffix), respectively. However, when all the prefix/suffix in the query logs are aggregated, the correct prefix "where*

Deep-web sites	sample queries from query logs
ebay.com	iPhone 4, lenovo, ...
bestbuy.com	hp touchpad, sony vaio, ...
booking.com	where to, new york, hyatt, seattle, review, ...
hotels.com	hotels, london, san francisco, ...
barnesandnobel.com	star trek, stephen king, ...
chegg.com	harry potter, dark knight, ...

Table 3: Example entities extracted for each deep-web site

to stay in" occurs much more frequently and should clearly stand out as a entity irrelevant pattern.

Another potential problem is that Freebase may not contain all possible entities. For example in the query "hyatt seattle review" for booking.com, the first two tokens "hyatt seattle" refer to the Hyatt hotel in Seattle, which however is absent in Freebase. Using Freebase entities "hyatt" (a hotel company), and "seattle" (a location) will be recognized separately. However, with prefixes/suffixes aggregation, the suffix "review" is so frequent across the query logs such that it will be recognized as an entity-irrelevant pattern. This can be used to clean the query to produce entity "hyatt seattle".

Our experiments using Google's query log (to be discussed in Section 8) will show that this simple approach of entity extraction by pattern aggregation is effective in producing entity queries.

5.2 Entity expansion using knowledge-bases

While query logs provide a good set of initial seed entities, its coverage for each site depends on the site's popularity as well as the item's popularity (recall that the number of clicks is used to predict the relevance between the query and the site). Even for highly popular sites, there is a long tail of less popular items which may not be captured by query logs.

On the other hand, we observe that there exists manually curated entity repositories (e.g., Freebase), that maintain entities in certain domains with very high coverage. For example. Freebase contains comprehensive lists of city names, books, car models, movies, etc. Such categories, if matched appropriately with relevant deep-web sites, can be used to greatly improve crawl coverage. For example, names of all locations/cities can be used to crawl travel sites (e.g., tripadvisor.com, booking.com), housing sites (e.g., apartmenthomeliving.com, zillow.com); names of all known books can be useful on book retailers (amazon.com, barnesandnoble.com), book rental sites (chegg.com, bookrenter.com), so on and so forth. In this section, we consider the problem of expanding the initial set of entities using Freebase.

Recall that we can already extract Freebase entities from the query logs for each site. Table 3, for example, contains lists of entities extracted from the sample queries in Table 2. Thus, for each site, we need to bootstrap from these seed entities to expand to Freebase entity "types" that are relevant to each site's semantics.

We borrow classical techniques from information retrieval: if we view the multi-set of Freebase entity mentions for each site as a document, and the list of entities in each Freebase type as a query, then the classical *term-frequency, inverse document frequency* (TF-IDF) ranking can be applied.

For each Freebase type, we use TF-IDF to produce a ranked list of deep-web sites by their similarity scores. We then "threshold" the sorted list using a relative score. That is, we include all sites with scores above a fixed percentage, τ, of the highest similarity score in the same Freebase type as matches. Empirically results in Section 8 show that setting $\tau = 0.5$ achieves good results and is used in our system. This approach is significantly more effective than other alternatives like Cosine or Jaccard Similarity [21], with precision reaching 0.9 for $\tau = 0.5$.

6. EMPTY PAGE FILTERING

Once the final URLs are generated, pages can be crawled in a fairly standard manner. The next important issue that arises is to filter empty pages with no entity in them, in order to avoid polluting downstream pipelines. However, different sites can display disparate error messages, from textual messages (e.g., "sorry, no items is found", "0 item matches your search", etc.), to image-based error messages. While such messages are easily comprehensible for humans, it is difficult to detect automatically across all different sites. The presence of dynamically generated ads content further complicates the problem of detecting empty pages.

We develop a page-level filtering approach that filters out crawled pages that fail to retrieve any entities. Our main observation is that empty pages from the same site are typically extremely similar to each other, while empty pages from different sites are normally very different. Ideally we should obtain "sample" empty pages for each deep-web site, with which newly crawled pages can be compared. To do so, we generate a set of "background queries", that are long strings of arbitrary characters that lack any semantic meanings (e.g., "zzzzzzzzzzzzz", or "xyzxyzxyzxyz"). Such queries, when searched on deep-web sites, will almost certainly generate empty pages. In practice, we generate N (10 in our experiments) such background queries in order to be robust against the rare case where a bad "background query" accidentally matches some records and produces a non-empty page. We then crawl and store the corresponding "background pages" as the reference set of empty pages. At crawl time, each newly crawled page is compared with background pages to determine if the new page is actually empty.

Our content comparison mechanism uses a signature based page summarization techniques also used in [15]. The signature is essentially a set of tokens that are descriptive of the page content, but also robust against minor differences in page content (e.g., dynamically generated advertisements). [1] We then calculate the Jaccard Similarity between the signature of the newly crawled page and the "background pages", as defined below.

DEFINITION 1. *[21] Let S_{p_1} and S_{p_2} be the sets of tokens representing the signature of the crawled page p_1 and p_2. The **Jaccard Similarity** between S_{p_1} and S_{p_2}, denoted Sim_{Jac} (S_{p_1}, S_{p_2}), is defined as Sim_{Jac} $(S_{p_1}, S_{p_2})= \frac{S_{p_1} \cap S_{p_2}}{S_{p_1} \cup S_{p_2}}$*

The similarity scores are averaged over the set of N "background pages", and if the average score is above certain threshold θ, we label the newly crawled page as empty. As we will show in experiments, this approach is very effective in detecting empty pages across different websites (with an overall precision of 0.89 and a recall of 0.9).

7. SECOND-LEVEL CRAWL

7.1 The motivation for second level crawl

We observe that the first set of pages crawled using URL templates often contain URLs that link to additional deep-web contents. In this work, we refer to the first set of pages obtained through URL templates as "first-level pages" (because they are one click away from the homepage), and those pages that are linked from first-level pages as "second-level pages" (and the corresponding URLs "second-level URLs"). There are at least a few common cases in which crawling second-level pages can be useful.

[1] Our signatures are generated using a proprietary method also used in [15], the details of which is beyond the scope of this paper. In principle well-known content summarization techniques like [7, 16] can be used in place.

(a) "Related queries" on first-level pages

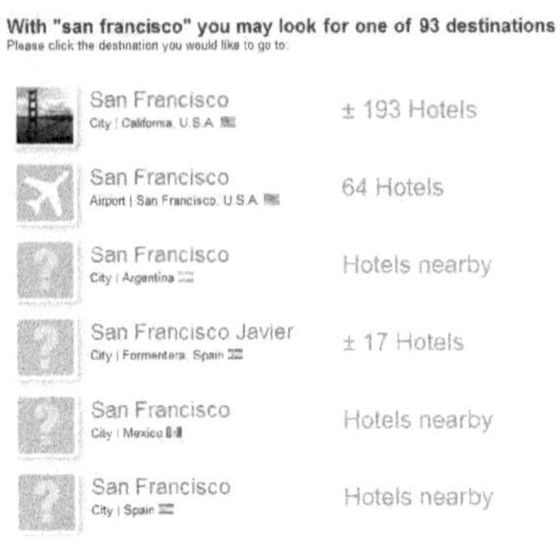

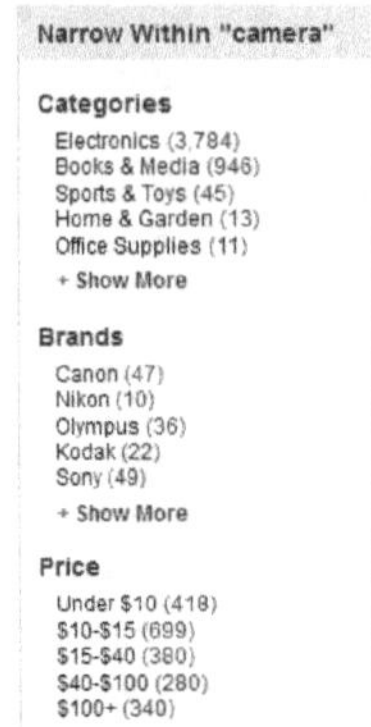

(b) Disambiguation pages (c) Faceted search

Figure 4: Examples for which second-level crawl is desirable

In the first category, when a query is searched, an additional set queries relevant to the original query are displayed. This is known as query expansion [19], which aims to help users to reformulate their queries. Figure 4a is a screen-shot of such an example. When the original query "iphone 4" is searched, the returned page displays queries related to the original query, like "iphone 3gs", "iphone 4 case", etc. Since these queries are maintained and suggested by individual sites, they can in most cases lead to valid deep-web content, thus improving content coverage.

Figure 4b shows another scenario for second-level crawl. In this example, when the query "san francisco" is searched, a disambiguation page is returned containing multiple cities with that name. Following second-level URLs on the disambiguation page is needed in order to expose rich deep-web content (lists of hotels in this case).

Second-level crawls are also desirable for sites that employ the "faceted search/browsing" paradigm [11]. In faceted search, returned entities are presented in a multi-dimensional, faceted manner. In the example shown in Figure 4c when "camera" is searched, a "multi-faceted" entity classification is returned along with a large set of results, to allow users to drill-down using additional criteria (e.g., category, brand, price etc.). Conceptually, this is equivalent to adding an additional predicate to the original entity retrieval query, which amounts to a new query. Accordingly, such URLs are also desirable for further crawling.

We also note that crawling second-level URLs using our simplified URL template with default values can achieve similar effects as exhaustively template generation by enumerating all possible values combinations (Section 4). In this example website in Figure 4c where query "camera" is searched with default category "All-categories", the second-level URL for category "Electronics" actually corresponds to searching "camera" with sub-category "Electronics" selected.

Furthermore, while the previous multi-field enumeration approach would search for a query with all value combination e.g., searching for "camera" with the (inconsistent) sub-categories "pets" or "furnitures" that would lead to empty pages, our approach is data driven — typically faceted search links are exposed only when there exists deep-web content matching the searching criteria (category "pets" will not display when "camera" is searched). As a result, our approach is more likely to retrieve content successfully.

www.buy.com/sr/searchresults.aspx?qu=gps&sort=4&from=7&mfgid=-652&page=1 *www.buy.com/sr/searchresults.aspx?qu=gps&sort=5&from=7&mfgid=-652&page=1* ... *www.buy.com/sr/searchresults.aspx?qu=gps&sort=4&from=8&mfgid=-652&page=1* *www.buy.com/sr/searchresults.aspx?qu=gps&sort=4&from=9&mfgid=-652&page=1* ... *www.buy.com/sr/searchresults.aspx?qu=gps&sort=4&from=7&mfgid=-652&page=2* *www.buy.com/sr/searchresults.aspx?qu=gps&sort=4&from=7&mfgid=-652&page=3* ...
www.buy.com/sr/searchresults.aspx?qu=gps&sort=4&from=7&mfgid=-1755&page=1 *www.buy.com/sr/searchresults.aspx?qu=gps&sort=5&from=7&mfgid=-1755&page=1* ...
www.buy.com/sr/searchresults.aspx?qu=tv&sort=4&from=7&mfgid=-1001&page=1 *www.buy.com/sr/searchresults.aspx?qu=tv&sort=5&from=7&mfgid=-1001&page=1* ...

Table 4: Duplicate cluster of second-level URLs

7.2 URL extraction and filtering

While *some* second-level URLs are desirable, not all second-level URLs should be crawled for efficiency as well as quality reasons. First, there are on average a few dozens second-level URLs for each first-level page crawled. Crawling all these second-level URLs becomes very costly at large scale. Furthermore, a significant portion of these second-level URLs are in fact entirely irrelevant with no deep-web content (many URLs are static and navigational, for example browsing URLs, login URLs, etc.), which need to be filtered out.

We filter URLs by using *keyword-query arguments*. Keyword-query argument is the URL argument immediately prior to the "{query}" wild-card in URL templates. For example, in Table 1, "_nkw=" is the keyword-query argument for ebay.com. Similarly we have "search_by=" for chegg.com, and "keyword=" for beso.com. The presence of the keyword-query argument in a given domain is in general indicative that the page is dynamically generated with keyword predicates and is thus likely to be deep-web related. We observe that filtering URLs by keyword-query arguments significantly reduces the number of URLs — typically by a factor of 3-5 — while still preserves desirable second-level URLs that lead to deep-web content.

7.3 URL deduplication

We observe that after URL filtering, there are groups of URLs that are different in their text string but really lead to similar or nearly identical deep-web content. In this section we propose to deduplicate second-level URLs to further reduce the number of URLs that need to be crawled.

To take a closer look at second-level URLs, we use URLs extracted from buy.com in Table 4 as an example to illustrate. Dynamical URLs generated by deep-web form submission generally follow the W3C URI recommendations [1], where the part of URL string after "?" is the so-called *query string*, and each component separated by "&" (or ";") is a *query segment* that consists of a pair of *argument* and *value* connected by an "=".

The observation here is that each query segment typically corresponds to a query predicate. Take the first URL in Table 4 as an example, the query segment "qu=gps" indicates that returned entities should contain the keyword "gps". "Sort=4" specifies that the list of entities should be sorted by price from low to high (where 4 is an internal encoding for that sorting criterion); "from=7" is an internal tracking parameter to record which URL was clicked that leads to this page; "mfgid=-652" is a predicate that selects manufacturer Garmin (where -652 is again an internal encoding), and finally "page=1" retrieves the first page of matching entities (typically each page only presents a limited number of entities, thus not all results can be displayed on one page). While the exact URL encodings of query strings vary wildly from site to site, such map-

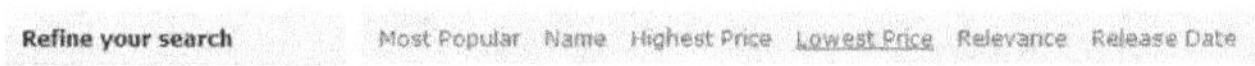

Figure 5: Second-level URLs from different sorting criteria

pings from query segments to logical query predicates generally exist across different sites.

In this particular example, if this URL query string is to be written in SQL, it would correspond to the query below:

```
SELECT * FROM db
WHERE description LIKE '%gps%'
AND manufacturer = 'Garmin'
ORDER BY price DESC
LIMIT 20; -- number of entities per page
```

The second URL in Table 4 differs from the first one in the segment "sort=5", which sorts entities by release date. They actually correspond to different sorting tabs in the result page, as illustrated in Figure 5, and there exist many additional sorting criteria, each of which corresponds to a second-level URL.

Recall that we aim to recover a representative content coverage of each site — obtaining exhaustive coverage for a large number of site is unrealistic and also unnecessary. With that in mind, we only need to crawl one of these two example URLs (and other similar URLs with different sorting criteria) discussed above by "deduplicating" them — after all, crawling entities with similar properties but different sorting criteria only produce marginal benefit.

Similarly, the third and fourth URL in Table 4 differ from the first URL in the segment "from=". This is only for internal tracking purposes so that source of the click can be identified. While the URL strings are different in the "from=" part, the content they lead to are identical and thus also need to be deduplicated.

Lastly, the fifth and sixth URL in the Table differ from the first URL in the "page=" segment. This is to retrieve different portion of the result set as the number of entities presented on each page tends to be limited. Again with the goal of recovering representative content coverage, we would want to avoid iterating over the complete result set by crawling all results that span different pages with the use of URL deduplication.

Given this requirement, existing content-based URL deduplication (e.g., [2, 8, 13]) is clearly insufficient. To see why this is the case, consider the first and second URL in Table 4 that retrieves the same result set but use different sorting criteria. Since the result set can span multiple pages, a different sorting order can produce a totally different result page. Existing techniques that analyze content similarity will not be able to recognize the semantic similarity between these two pages. Similarly content based deduplication will treat the fifth and sixth URL as distinct pages instead of semantic duplicates, thus wasting significant crawling bandwidth. In this paper we propose an approach that analyzes URL argument patterns and deduplicates URLs even before any pages are crawled.

7.3.1 Pre-crawl URL deduplication

In this work we propose to analyze the patterns of second-level URLs before they are crawled, and use a new definition to capture both content similarity as well as the similarity in the semantics of queries that are used to retrieve deep-web content.

First, we categorize query segments into three groups, (1) *selection segments* are query segments that correspond to selection predicates and can affect the set of result entities (e.g., "qu=gps" and "mfgid=-652" in the example URLs discussed above, which are essentially predicates in the `where` clause of the SQL query); (2) *presentation segments* are query segments that do not change the result set, but only affect how the set of entities are presented (e.g., "sort=4" or "page=1" in the example URL); and lastly, (3) *content irrelevant segments* are query segments that have no immediate impact on the result entities (e.g., the tracking segment "from=7").

We then define two URLs as **semantic duplicates** if the corresponding selection queries have the same set of selection segments. More specifically, if queries corresponding to two URL strings return the same set of entities, then irrespective of how the entities are sorted or what portion of result set are presented, the two URLs are considered to be duplicates to each other. We can alternatively state that two URLs are considered as semantic duplicates if they differ only in content irrelevant segments or presentation segments.

While the reason of disregarding "content irrelevant segments" are straightforward, the rationale behind ignoring *presentation segments* goes back to our goal of obtaining "representative coverage" for each site. Exhaustively crawling the complete result set in different sorting orders provides marginal benefits; crawling one page for each distinct set of selection predicates is deemed sufficient.

EXAMPLE 2. *We use example URLs in Table 4 to illustrate our definition of semantic duplicates. The first group of URLs all correspond to the same selection predicates (i.e., "qu=gps" and "mfgid=-652") but differ only in content irrelevant segments ("from="), or presentation segments ("sort=", "page="). Crawling any one URL from this group will provide representative coverage.*

On the other hand, URLs from the first group and second group differ in selection segment "mfgid=?", where "mfgid=-652" represents "Garmin" while "mfgid=-1755" is for "Tomtom". The selection queries would retrieve two different sets of entities, thus should not be considered as semantic duplicates.

It can be seen that our *semantics-based URL deduplication* is a more general notion that goes beyond simply content-based similarity. Our approach is not based on any content analysis. Rather, it hinges on the correct identification of the categories of query segments by URL pattern analysis.

On the high level, our approach is based on two key observations. First, search result pages in the same site are likely to be generated from the same template and are thus highly *homogeneous*. That is, for the same site, the structure, layout and content of result pages share much similarity (which include deep-web URLs embedded in result pages that we are interested in).

Second, given page homogeneity, we observe that almost *all* result pages in the same site share certain presentation logics or other content-irrelevant functionalities. In the example of URLs extracted from buy.com we discussed above, almost all result pages can sort entities by price, or advance to the second page of entities in the result set. Each page also implements the site-specific click-tracking functionality. These presentation logics translates to the same presentation segments ("sort=4" and "page=2"), and content-irrelevant segments ("from=7"), respectively, which can be found in almost every result page.

With these observations, we propose to take all URLs embedded in a result page as a unit of analysis. We then aggregate the frequency of query segments and identify segments that commonly occur across many different pages in the same site. The fact that these query segments in almost all pages indicates that they are not specific to the input keyword query, and are thus likely to be either presentational (sorting, page number, etc.), or content irrelevant (internal tracking, etc.).

On the other hand, selection segments, like manufacturer name ("mfgid=-652" for "Garmin") in the previous example, are much more sensitive to the input queries. Only when queries related to GPS are searched, will the segment representing manufacturer "Garmin" ("mfgid=-652") appear. Pages crawled for other entities (e.g., laptops or cameras or furnitures) are likely to contain a different set of query segments for manufacturers. A specific query segment (argument/value pair) is likely to exist on *some*, but not *all* crawled pages.

To capture this intuition we define a notion of prevalence at the query segment (argument/value pair) level and also at the argument level.

DEFINITION 2. *Let $\mathcal{P}_s$ be the set of search result pages from the same site s, and $p \in \mathcal{P}_s$ be one such page. Further denote $D(p)$ as the set of query segments (argument-value pairs) in second-level URLs extracted from p, and $D(\mathcal{P}_s) = \cup_{p \in \mathcal{P}_s} D(p)$ as the union of all possible segments.*

*The **prevalence** of an argument-value pair (a, v), denoted as $r(a, v)$, is $r(a, v) = \frac{|\{p | p \in \mathcal{P}_s, (a,v) \in D(p)\}|}{|\mathcal{P}_s|}$.*

*The **prevalence** of an argument a, denoted as $r(a)$, is the average prevalence value of argument-value pairs with the same argument a, or $r(a) = \frac{\sum_{(a,v) \in D(\mathcal{P}_s)} r(a,v)}{|\{(a,v)|(a,v) \in D(\mathcal{P}_s)\}|}$.*

Intuitively, the prevalence of an argument-value pair specifies the ratio of pages from site s that contain the argument-value pair in the second-level URLs. For example if the URL with the argument-value pair "sort=4" that sorts items by price exist in 90 out of 100 result pages from buy.com, its prevalence is 0.9. The prevalence of an argument is just the average over all possible values of this argument (the prevalence of argument "sort=", for example, is averaged from "sort=1", "sort=2", etc.). The average prevalence score at argument level is a more robust indicator of the prevalence of an argument.

Since query segments with arguments that have a high prevalence score tend to be either content irrelevant, or presentational, we set a threshold score θ, such that any argument with prevalence higher than θ are considered to be *semantically-irrelevant* (for example if "sort=" has a high enough prevalence score, all URLs that differ only in query segments "sort=?" can be deduplicated, because crawling the same set of entities with all possible sorting orders are deemed as unnecessary). On the other hand, if an query segment's argument has prevalence lower than θ it is assumed to be a selection segment, which is relevant to the result set of entities.

After identifying semantically-irrelevant arguments, second-level URLs from the same site can then be partitioned by disregarding these irrelevant arguments into different buckets, as in Table 4. URLs in the same bucket are treated as semantic duplicates, and only one URL in the same partition needs to be crawled[2].

To sum up, our deduplication algorithm takes second-level URLs on the same result page as a unit of analysis instead of analyzing URLs individually. This has the advantage of providing more context for analysis and producing robust prediction through aggregation. Note that our analysis is possible because result pages returned from the search interface tend to be homogeneous. Web pages in general are much more heterogeneous and this page-oriented URL deduplication may not work well in a general web crawl setting.

8. EXPERIMENTS

In this section, we will discuss key experimental results for the query generation, empty page filtering, and URL deduplication, respectively.

Query extraction from query logs. Recall that in Section 5.1, we first identify frequent patterns that are likely to be entity irrelevant using pattern aggregation, which are then used to extract entities from query logs.

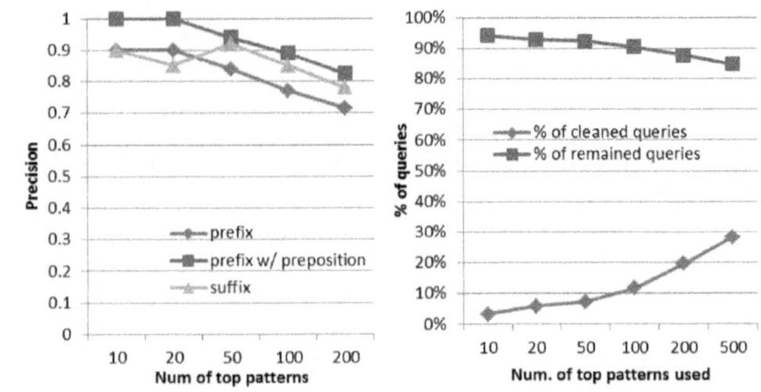

(a) Impact of removing top patterns (b) Top pattern precision

Figure 6: Removing top patterns

In this experiment, we used 6 month's worth Google's query logs, and entities in Freebase as seed entities. In order to evaluate whether patterns produced by our approach is truly entity-irrelevant or not, we asked a domain expert to manually label top 200 patterns, as correct predictions (irrelevant to entities) or incorrect predictions (relevant to entities), by looking at 5 sample queries with and without each pattern. We do not observe much ambiguities since only top patterns were labeled.

Table 5 lists the top 10 most frequent prefix and suffix patterns we produced. The presence of preposition in the prefix is also good indication that the prefix is not relevant to any entity so such patterns is also aggregated in the second column. In this table, patterns that are relevant to entities (and are thus mislabeled) are underlined. It is clear from the table that most patterns found this way are indeed not related to entity mentions. Removing such patterns allows us to obtain a cleaner set of entity names ranging from song/album names ("lyrics", "lyrics to", etc.), location/attraction names ("pictures of", "map of", "where to stay in" etc.), to various product names ("review", "price of", etc.).

Top prefix	Top prefix with prep.	Top suffix
how	lyrics to	lyrics
watch	pictures of	download
samsung	list of	wiki
download	map of	torrent
is	history of	online
which	lyrics for	video
free	pics of	review
the	lyrics of	mediafire
best	facts about	pictures

Table 5: Top 10 common patterns

In Figure 6a we summarize the precision for top 10, 20, 50, 100 and 200 patterns. Not surprisingly, the precision decreases as more number of patterns are included.

Figure 6b shows the percentage of queries in the query logs that contain top patterns, thus illustrating the impact of query cleaning using top patterns. At top 200 about 19% of the queries will be cleaned using our approach. The total number of distinct queries also reduces by 12%, for after cleaning some queries become duplicate with existing ones. This reduces the number of unnecessary crawls, and also improves the quality of the resulting pages (when extraneous information like "review", "price of" is included spurious matches are promoted and the search results are less clean accordingly).

Entity expansion using Freebase. In Section 5.2, we discussed entity expansion using Freebase using extracted seed entities. At

[2]Note that we pick one random URL to crawl rather than removing irrelevant query segments, because there are cases in which removing query segments breaks the URL and lead to error pages.

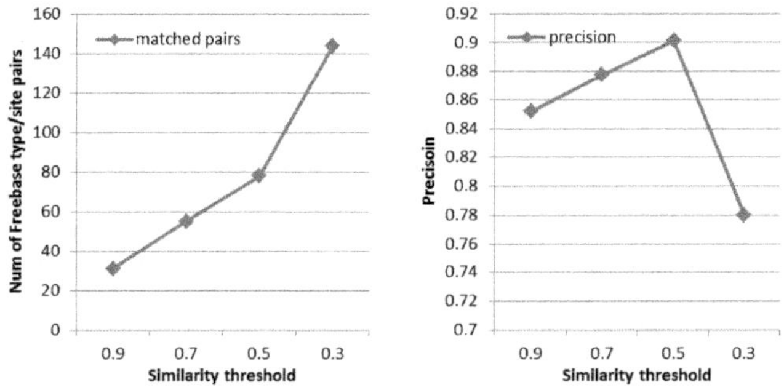

(a) Num. of matched pairs (b) Precision of matched pairs

Figure 7: Effects of different score threshold

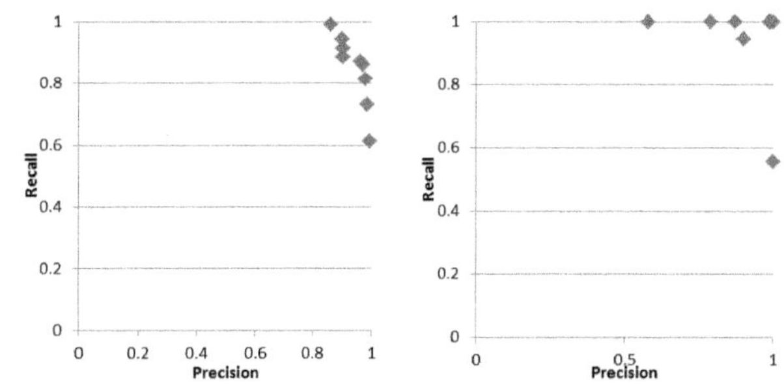

(a) Vary score threshold (b) Using different sites

Figure 8: Precision/recall of empty page filtering. (8a): Each dot in the graph represents precision/recall of a different score threshold; (8b): Each dot represents results from a different website.

the highest level Freebase data are grouped into "domains", or categories of relevant topics, like automotive, book, computers, etc., in the first column in Table 6. Within each domain, there is a list of "types," each of which consists of manually curated entities with names and relationships. For example, the domain film contains types including film (list of film names), actor (list of actor names) and performance (which actor performed in which film relation).

Domain name	Top types	# of types	# of instances
Automotive	trim_level, model_year	30	78,684
Book	book_edition, book, isbn	20	10,776,904
Computer	software, software_comparability	31	27,166
Digicam	digital_camera, camera_iso	18	6,049
Film	film, performance, actor	51	1,703,255
Food	nutrition_fact, food, beer	40	66,194
Location	location, geocode, mailing_address	167	4,150,084
Music	track, release, artist, album	63	10,863,265
TV	tv_series_episode, tv_program	41	1,728,083
Wine	wine, grape_variety_composition	11	16,125

Table 6: Freebase domains used for query expansion

Domain:type name	matched deep-web sites
Automotive:model_year	stratmosphere.com, ebay.com
Book:book_edition	christianbook.com, netflix.com, barnesandnoble.com
Computer:software	booksprice.com
Digicam:digital_camera	rozetka.com.ua, price.ua
Food:food	fibergourmet.com, tablespoon.com
Location:location	tripadvisor.com, hotels.com, apartmenthomeliving.com
Music:track	netflix.com, play.com, musicload.de
TV:tv_series_episode	netflix.com, cafepress.com
Wine:wine	wineenthusiast.com

Table 7: Sample Freebase matches (incorrect ones are underlined)

Since not all Freebase domains are equally applicable for deep-web crawl purposes (e.g., chemistry ontology), for human evaluation purposes we only focus on the 5 largest Freebase types in 10 widely applicable domains listed in Table 6. We also restrict our attention in 100 high-traffic online retailers that we are most interested in. We asked a domain expert to manually label, for each pair of <website, Freebase type> result, whether the matching is correct. That is, whether entities in the Freebase type can be used to retrieve valid product entities from the matching website. In order not to overestimate the matching precision, we intentionally ignore matches for general-purpose sites that span multiple product categories (ebay.com, nextag.com, etc.), by considering such matches as neither correct nor incorrect.

Figure 7a shows the total number of matched Freebase-type / site pairs and Figure 7b illustrates the matching precision. As we can see, while the number of matched pairs increases as the threshold decreases, there is a significant drop in matching precision when threshold decreases from 0.5 to 0.3. Empirically a threshold of 0.5 is used in our system.

Table 7 illustrates example matches between Freebase types and deep-web sites. Top 3 matches of the largest type in each Freebase domain are listed (in some cases only 1 or 2 matches are above the relative threshold). Overall this produces good quality matches to Freebase types, which in turn greatly improves crawling coverage.

Empty page filtering. To evaluate the effectiveness of our empty page filtering approach (Section 6), we randomly selected 10 deep-web sites from a list of high-traffic sites (namely, booking.com, cdiscount.com, ebay.com, ebay.com.uk, marksandspencer.com, nordstrom.com, overstock.com, screwfix.com, sephora.com, tripadvisor.com), and manually identified their respective error messages (e.g., "Your search returned 0 items" is the error message used by ebay.com). This manual approach, while accurate, does not scale to a large number of websites. It does, however, enables us to build the ground truth — any page crawled from the site with that particular message is regarded as an empty page (negative instances), and pages without such message are treated as non-empty pages (positive instances). We can then evaluate the precision and recall of our algorithm, where precision and recall are defined as

$$precision = \frac{|\{\text{pages predicted as non-empty}\}|\cap|\{\text{pages that are non-empty}\}|}{|\{\text{pages predicted as non-empty}\}|}$$

$$recall = \frac{|\{\text{pages predicted as non-empty}\}|\cap|\{\text{pages that are non-empty}\}|}{\{|\text{pages that are non-empty}|\}}$$

Figure 8a shows the precision/recall graph of empty page filtering when varying the threshold score θ from 0.4 to 0.95. We observe that setting threshold to a low value, say 0.4, achieves high precision (predicted non-empty pages are indeed non-empty) at the cost of significantly reducing recall to around only 0.6 (many non-empty pages are mistakenly labeled as empty because of the low threshold). At threshold 0.85 the precision and recall are 0.89 and 0.9, respectively, which is a good empirical setting that we used in our system.

Figure 8b plots the precision/recall of individual deep-web site for empty page filtering. Other than a cluster of points at the upper-right corner, representing sites with almost perfect precision/recall, there is only one site with relative low precision and another one with relative low recall.

URL deduplication. To understand the effectiveness of our semantic URL deduplication technique (Section 7.3), we used the same set of 10 entity sites used in empty page filtering, and manually label all URL arguments above the threshold 0.01 as either semantically relevant or irrelevant for deduplication purposes. Note that we cannot afford to inspect all possible arguments, because websites can typically use a very large number of arguments in URLs. For example, we found 1471 different arguments from overstock.com, 1243 from ebay.co.uk, etc. Furthermore, ascertaining semantic relevance of arguments that appear very infrequently can

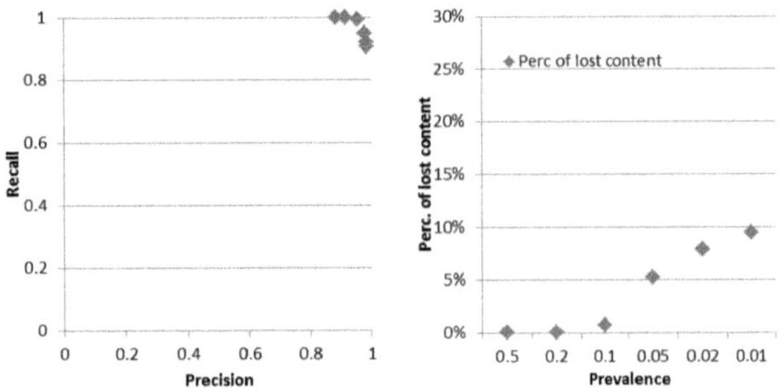

(a) Argument level results (b) URL level recall

Figure 9: Precision/recall of URL deduplication. (9a): Each dot represents argument precision/recall at different prevalence value; (9b): Each dot represents lost URL at different prevalence value.

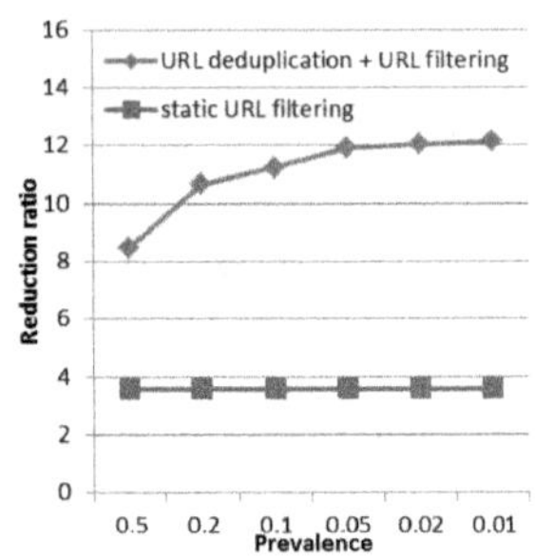

Figure 10: Reduction ratio of URL deduplication

be increasingly hard. As a result we only evaluate arguments with prevalence score of at least 0.01, and identified a total of 152 arguments that are semantically relevant.

Figure 9a shows the precision/recall of URL deduplication at the argument level. Each data point corresponds to a threshold at a different value that ranges from 0.01 to 0.5. Recall that our prevalence based algorithm predicts an argument as irrelevant if its prevalence score is over the threshold. This predication is deemed correct if the argument is manually labeled as irrelevant (because it is presentational or content-irrelevant). At threshold 0.1, our approach has a precision of 98% and recall of 94%, respectively, which is a good empirical value we use for our crawl system.

The second experiment in Figure 9b shows the recall at URL level. An argument mistakenly predicted as irrelevant by our algorithm will cause URLs with that argument to be incorrectly deduplicated. In this experiment, in addition to using all arguments manually labeled as relevant in the ground truth, we treat unlabeled arguments with prevalence lower than 0.1 as relevant (which we cannot manually verify however due to the sheer size of such infrequent arguments). We then evaluate the percentage of URLs mistakenly deduplicated (percentage of the loss in content that should have been crawled) due to the mis-prediction. The graph shows that at 0.1 level, only 0.7% of URLs are incorrectly deduplicated.

Finally, Figure 10 compares the reduction ratio of second-level URLs between our approach and the simpler approach of using URL filtering only (which filters out static URLs and URLs without the keyword-query segment, e.g., _nkw= for ebay.com). As can be seen, URL filtering alone accounts for a reduction ratio of 3.6. Our approach of using semantic URL deduplication on top of URL filtering achieves a roughly 10 fold reduction in the number of URLs, which is 2.3 to 3.4 times more reduction than using URL filtering alone, depending on the prevalence threshold. This amounts to significant saving given that the number of second-level URLs extracted from results pages are on the order of billions.

9. CONCLUSION

In this work we develop a prototype system that focuses on crawling entity-oriented deep-web sites. We leverage characteristics of these entity sites, and propose optimized techniques that improve the efficiency and effectiveness of the crawl system.

While these techniques are shown to be useful, our experience points to a few areas that warrant future studies. For example, in the template generation, our parsing approach only handles HTML "GET" forms but not "POST" forms or javascript forms, which reduces site coverage. In query generation, although Freebase-based entity expansion is useful, certain sites with low traffic or diverse traffic do not get matched with Freebase types effectively using query logs alone. Utilizing additional signals (e.g., entities bootstrapped from crawled pages) for entity expansion is an interesting area. Efficiently enumerate entity query for search forms with multiple input fields is another interesting challenge.

Given the ubiquity of entity-oriented deep-web sites and the variety of uses that entity-oriented content can enable, we believe entity-oriented crawl is a useful research effort, and we hope our initial efforts in this area can serve as a springboard for future research.

10. REFERENCES

[1] HTML 4.01 Specification, W3C recommendations. http://www.w3.org/addressing/url/4_uri_recommentations.html.

[2] Z. Bar-yossef, I. Keidar, and U. Schonfeld. Do not crawl in the dust: different urls with similar text. In *Proceedings of WWW*, 2006.

[3] L. Barbosa and J. Freire. Siphoning hidden-web data through keyword-based interfaces. In *Proceedings of SBBD*, 2004.

[4] L. Barbosa and J. Freire. Searching for hidden web databases. In *Proceedings of WebDB*, 2005.

[5] L. Barbosa and J. Freire. An adaptive crawler for locating hidden-web entry points. In *Proceedings of WWW*, 2007.

[6] K. D. Bollacker, C. Evans, P. Paritosh, T. Sturge, and J. Taylor. Freebase: a collaboratively created graph database for structuring human knowledge. In *Proceedings of SIGMOD*, 2008.

[7] A. Z. Broder, S. C. Glassman, M. S. Manasse, and G. Zweig. Syntactic clustering of the web. In *Proceedings of WWW*, 1997.

[8] A. Dasgupta, R. Kumar, and A. Sasturkar. De-duping urls via rewrite rules. In *Proceeding of the 14th ACM SIGKDD international conference on Knowledge discovery and data mining*, Proceedings of KDD, 2008.

[9] J. Guo, G. Xu, X. Cheng, and H. Li. Named entity recognition in query. In *Proceedings of SIGIR*, Proceedings of SIGIR, 2009.

[10] B. He, M. Patel, Z. Zhang, and K. C.-C. Chang. Accessing the deep web. *Commun. ACM*, 50, 2007.

[11] M. A. Hearst. UIs for faceted navigation recent advances and remaining open problems. In *Proceedings of HCIR*, 2008.

[12] A. Jain and M. Pennacchiotti. Open entity extraction from web search query logs. In *Proceedings of ICCL*, 2010.

[13] H. S. Koppula, K. P. Leela, A. Agarwal, K. P. Chitrapura, S. Garg, and A. Sasturkar. Learning url patterns for webpage de-duplication. In *Proceedings of WSDM*, 2010.

[14] J. Madhavan, S. R. Jeffery, S. Cohen, X. luna Dong, D. Ko, C. Yu, and A. Halevy. Web-scale data integration: You can only afford to pay as you go. In *Proceedings of CIDR*, 2007.

[15] J. Madhavan, D. Ko, L. Kot, V. Ganapathy, A. Rasmussen, and A. Halevy. Google's deep web crawl. In *Proceedings of VLDB*, 2008.

[16] G. S. Manku, A. Jain, and A. D. Sarma. Detecting near-duplicates for web crawling. In *Proceedings of WWW*, 2007.

[17] A. Ntoulas. Downloading textual hidden web content through keyword queries. In *JCDL*, 2005.

[18] M. Paşca. Weakly-supervised discovery of named entities using web search queries. In *Proceedings of CIKM*, 2007.

[19] Y. Qiu and H.-P. Frei. Concept based query expansion. In *Proceedings of SIGIR*, 1993.

[20] S. Raghavan and H. Garcia-Molina. Crawling the hidden web. Technical report, Stanford, 2000.

[21] P.-N. Tan and V. Kumar. *Introduction to Data Mining*.

[22] Y. Wang, J. Lu, and J. Chen. Crawling deep web using a new set covering algorithm. In *Proceedings of ADMA*, 2009.

[23] P. Wu, J.-R. Wen, H. Liu, and W.-Y. Ma. Query selection techniques for efficient crawling of structured web sources. In *Proceedings of ICDE*, 2006.

Using Early View Patterns to Predict the Popularity of YouTube Videos

Henrique Pinto, Jussara M. Almeida, Marcos A. Gonçalves
Computer Science Department
Universidade Federal de Minas Gerais, Brazil
{hpinto, jussara, mgoncalv}@dcc.ufmg.br

ABSTRACT

Predicting Web content popularity is an important task for supporting the design and evaluation of a wide range of systems, from targeted advertising to effective search and recommendation services. We here present two simple models for predicting the future popularity of Web content based on historical information given by early popularity measures. Our approach is validated on datasets consisting of videos from the widely used YouTube video-sharing portal. Our experimental results show that, compared to a state-of-the-art baseline model, our proposed models lead to significant decreases in relative squared errors, reaching up to 20% reduction on average, and larger reductions (of up to 71%) for videos that experience a high peak in popularity in their early days followed by a sharp decrease in popularity.

Categories and Subject Descriptors

C.4 [**Computer Systems Organization**]: Performance of Systems - *Measurement techniques*; H.3.5 [**Information Storage and Retrieval**]: Online Information Services - *Web-based services*

General Terms

Experimentation, Measurement

Keywords

popularity prediction; YouTube; regression models

1. INTRODUCTION

The increasing popularity of Web 2.0 applications brings along an enormous and ever growing amount of user generated content. Take for instance the YouTube video sharing system, which often figures among the top 3 most popular applications on the Web [1]. It has been reported that YouTube users upload 72 hours of video per *minute*[1], and that the total amount of content uploaded to YouTube in 60 days is equivalent to all content that would have been broadcasted for 60 years, without interruption, by NBC, CBS and ABC altogether [9]. Given such staggering content upload rate, it is unsurprising that the distribution of popularity across different contents on YouTube, as well as on other Web applications, is very uneven: most content garners very little attention whereas a small amount of it attracts millions of views [4, 16].

In this context, predicting content popularity is of great importance to support and drive the design and management of various services. For example, in online marketing, the information about the expected future popularity of a certain type of content can be useful for planning advertising campaigns and estimating costs. Accurately predicting content popularity is also key to support effective information services (e.g., recommendation and searching services) [3]. Popularity prediction can help identifying possible bottlenecks due to poor recommendation and search engines and improving the quality of such services by extending current result ranking strategies to take the estimated future popularity into account [8].

There have been recent efforts towards building models to predict the popularity of online content using various techniques such as reservoir computing [17], stochastic models of user behavior [12] and biology-inspired survival analysis techniques [11]. Towards that goal, Szabo and Huberman first observed that the log-transformed long-term popularity of a given content is strongly correlated with its early popularity [15]. Based on this observation, they proposed a simple model that predicts the total number of views (i.e., the popularity) of a piece of content at a target date t_t, based on a linear function of its *total number of views* at an earlier *reference date* t_r ($t_r < t_t$). That is, their model states that the future popularity is related to the early one by a constant factor α, which depends only on the target and reference dates and not on any specific information of the content itself, and can be fitted by linear regression.

While the reported results produced by the Szabo and Huberman (S-H) model are reasonably accurate, especially given its simplicity, the model does have shortcomings. In particular, two different pieces of content may have very similar popularity at the same reference date and yet exhibit distinct popularity behaviors thereafter. Take, for instance, the two real YouTube videos whose popularity curves, in terms of the daily number of views for the first 30 days, are shown in Figure 1. After 7 days since upload, both videos have very similar total number of views: 10,665 for video A,

[1] `http://www.youtube.com/t/press_statistics`

WSDM'13, February 4–8, 2013, Rome, Italy.

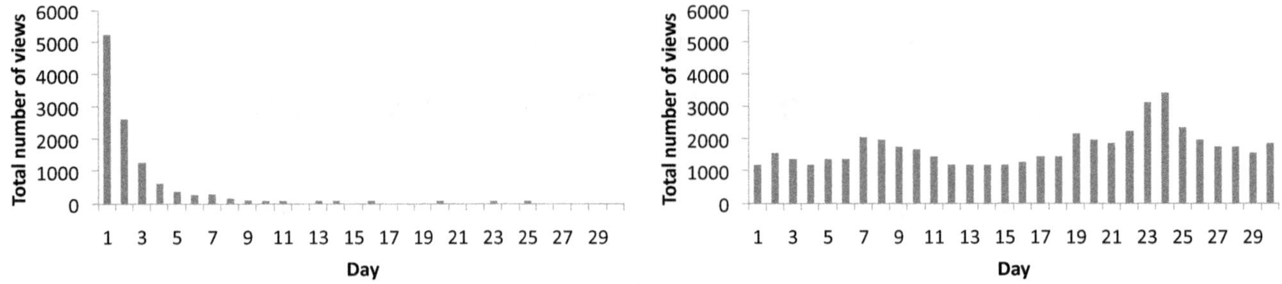

(a) Video A: 10,665 at t_r=7; 12,060 views at t_t=30

(b) Video B: 10,070 views at t_r=7; 51,851 views at t_t=30

Figure 1: Number of views per day during the first 30 days of life of two YouTube videos

and 10,070 for video B. Thus, the S-H model would predict, using data from these days (t_r=7), that both videos would have similar total number of views on the 30th day since upload (t_t=30). Yet, they end up with very different total popularities: whereas Figure 1-a) shows a final aggregate popularity that barely exceeds 12,000 views, the video in Figure 1-b) ends up attracting more than 50,000 views during the same period. This example illustrates that different YouTube videos (and online content in general) may experience very different *popularity evolution patterns*. Indeed, Crane and Sornette have distinguished four different popularity evolution patterns among YouTube videos [5], which are explained in terms of a combination of endogenous (i.e., user interactions within the system) and exogenous factors (i.e., external events), as further discussed in Section 2.

Thus, we here investigate whether the *view patterns* of a video during its early days in the system up to a reference date t_r lead to more accurate predictions of its total number of views at a target date t_t, in comparison to simply using the total view count up to t_r (as done by the S-H model).

We propose two new popularity prediction models. The first is a multivariate linear regression model, the ML model, that, building on the S-H model, incorporates information about historical patterns. It is motivated by the observation that if one is monitoring the number of views of a video for t_r days, these days are not all equally important to predict its future popularity. Thus, like the S-H model, our model relies only on the number of views up to a reference date t_r, but it assigns different weights to each monitored day, thus allowing us to distinguish between videos with roughly the same number of views at t_r but very different popularity curves (as in Figure 1).

Our second prediction model, referred to as MRBF, is an extension of the ML model that aims to exploit the different popularity patterns a video can follow in a more explicit way. By measuring the similarity of a video and known examples from the training set, and changing the prediction based on this information, it is able to adapt to the different patterns in a more direct way, leading to further improvements in prediction accuracy.

We evaluate our models, comparing them against the S-H model, on two datasets of YouTube videos. One consists of popular videos that appear on the world-wide top lists kept by YouTube, and the other contains videos sampled according to a random procedure [6]. For each such dataset, we also measure how well each model performs, in terms of prediction error, for various values of t_r and t_t as well as for videos that exhibit different popularity evolution patterns (as defined in [5]). We find that our models significantly improve prediction accuracy over the S-H model. For instance, when predicting the popularity of a video at the end of a month (t_t=30) using only data from the first week (t_r=7), the ML model leads to reductions in prediction error of 13% and 15%, on average, for videos on the top and random datasets, respectively. The MRBF model further reduces the prediction errors by 6% on each dataset, leading to total reductions in error over the S-H baseline of 19% and 21% for the top and random datasets, respectively.

Our models exploit the same data used by the S-H model, with little extra cost in practice (see discussion in Section 3.3). We find that such accuracy improvements can provide real benefits to services that exploit future popularity estimates. Moreover, we find that for specific patterns of views, our models perform especially well. For example, for videos in the random dataset that exhibit very high peaks followed by sharp decreases in popularity (as in Figure 1-a), the MRBF model leads to an accuracy gain of 71% over the S-H model.

Motivated by a question left open by Szabo and Huberman [15], we also evaluated whether building specialized models for each YouTube video category leads to more accurate popularity predictions. However, we found that this type of model specialization has little impact on prediction error (except in a single case), because the videos in most categories follow the same general popularity evolution patterns,. Thus a global model, trained on videos of all categories, can adequately predict the popularity of videos in any category.

The rest of this paper is organized as follows. Section 2 discusses related work, whereas Section 3 formally presents both the S-H and our new popularity prediction model. Our evaluation methodology and main results are discussed in Sections 4 and 5, respectively. Section 6 concludes the paper.

2. RELATED WORK

There have been several efforts towards analyzing the popularity of online content. For example, Cha *et al.* studied the popularity cycle of YouTube videos [4], finding that they have, on average, long life times, and that around 80% of the videos watched on a day are older than one month, although the most popular video tends to be one that has been recently uploaded. Figueiredo *et al.* characterized the popularity evolution patterns of YouTube videos and studied the impact of different types of referrers on such patterns [6], whereas Rodrigues *et al.* analyzed the characteristics of groups of duplicates of the same YouTube video, finding that they often have different popularities [13].

Crane and Sornette analyzed the popularity evolution patterns of YouTube videos, identifying four main classes, which they explained in terms of endogenous and exogenous effects [5]. According to them, the majority of the videos experience no marked peak in popularity: they either attract little attention or experience some popularity fluctuation that can be explained through a simple stochastic process. They referred to these videos as *Memoryless*. In contrast, the other videos experience bursts in popularity, being further categorized into *Viral*, *Quality* or *Junk* videos. *Viral* videos experience a popularity peak that emerges through a word-of-mouth epidemic-like internal propagation process. Their popularity increases slowly, up to a peak, decreasing also slowly afterwards. *Quality* videos experience a very sudden peak in popularity, possibly due to some external event (such as being featured on the first page of YouTube), and a slow decay afterwards as users propagate the videos among themselves. *Junk* videos also experience a burst of popularity, but, in contrast, they do not spread through the social network and thus their popularity drops quickly afterwards. The videos in Figures 1-(a) and 1-(b) are, respectively, in the *Junk* and *Memoryless* classes. The authors also offered an alternative classification procedure of videos into *Viral*, *Quality* and *Junk* based on the fraction of views on the peak day. In Section 5.1, we analyze the accuracy of the popularity prediction models for videos in each of these classes.

Popularity prediction has also been the goal of a few recent studies. Lerman and Hogg predicted the popularity of Digg[2] stories by modeling user behavior explicitly as a stochastic process [12]. They considered aspects of the user interface of the system, as well as the social dynamics of voting due to the *friends* feature. They model the user interaction with the system in terms of actions, such as visiting the home page, clicking on the "next" link to go to the second page, visiting the friends page, voting on a news item and others, and considered how these actions influence popularity. They found that there are two main components for explaining popularity evolution: a story's inherent *quality* and *social influence*. While their model produced good results for Digg content, its effectiveness on a system like YouTube is questionable. This is because YouTube has many more internal features and mechanisms, allowing a richer variety of user interactions, which can ultimately impact popularity. Thus, modeling YouTube user behavior and its impact on content popularity becomes much more complex. In particular, in order for a user behavior model such as the one proposed on [12] to perform well on a system like YouTube, external factors (e.g., search and links in other web sites), which significantly influence popularity [6], should also be taken into account and explicitly modeled.

Wu *et al.* [17] proposed a model based on *reservoir computing*, a special type of neural network, to predict the near future popularity of videos based on popularity data from the previous days. However, their strategy can be affected by randomization effects, as the hidden layer weights are set to randomly chosen *fixed* values, and it takes a number of iterations until the outputs reflect the data instead of the random weights. Moreover, the proposed model does not outperform simpler strategies, such as the Szabo-Huberman model, in large datasets, as reported by the authors.

Lee *et al.* [11] proposed a model to predict the likelihood that a thread in discussion forums will still be popular in the future. They used biology-inspired *survival analysis* techniques that take certain "risk factors" as input. Examples of such factors are: the total number of comments and the time between the thread's creation and the first comment. Their model is built on the assumption that measures of the actual popularity are not available, which may be too restrictive for popularity prediction on such systems. On YouTube, in particular, this is unrealistic, as the system makes such data publicly available. Moreover, we found that the risk factors used by their model are highly correlated with the number of views of the videos in our datasets, bringing no improvements to our models.

Yin *et al.* [18] proposed a model that predicts the expected popularity ranking of items. In many systems, users can express positive or negative opinions about items (such as "like/dislike" on YouTube). Through an empirical study, they noticed that users display two personalities: they are either "Conformers", voting according to the opinion of the majority, or "Mavericks", who vote in disagreement with the majority. They argued that an individual user exhibits both of these personalities to different degrees, and that when a user votes on a specific item, one of these personalities prevails. Based on this, they created a model for user behavior and used the early votes to develop a function to rank items based on their potential popularity. They evaluated their proposed ranking function on a dataset collected from JokeBox[3], a popular iPhone application that allows users to post and vote on jokes. The proposed method outperformed many other strategies when tasked with predicting the top-k most popular jokes. One disadvantage of their method, though, is that it requires full information about users' votes in order to build user profiles. This information is not publicly available in many systems, including YouTube, either due to scale issues, or privacy issues, or both.

In contrast to these efforts, Szabo and Huberman analyzed the popularity of YouTube videos and Digg stories, noting that the long term popularity of online content is strongly correlated with its early popularity in a logarithmic scale [15]. Based on that observation, they proposed a very simple linear popularity prediction model. Given its simplicity and promising results for different applications, we here choose the Szabo and Huberman model, which is further described in Section 3.2, as baseline for evaluating our new strategies.

3. POPULARITY PREDICTION MODELS

We start our discussion of the popularity prediction models by presenting the criterion adopted for evaluating their performance (Section 3.1). We then present the baseline S-H model (Section 3.2) as well as our ML (Section 3.3) and MRBF (Section 3.4) models, discussing how each model tries to optimize the adopted performance criterion. The goal of all the prediction models is to predict the future popularity,

[2]Digg (`http://digg.com`) is a news aggregator website where users can post links to stories, votes and comments.

[3]`http://itunes.apple.com/us/app/all-in-1-joke-box-no-adsunlimited/id363494433?mt=8`

in terms of *total number of views*, of a video at t_t, given data from the first t_r days ($t_r < t_t$).

3.1 Performance Criterion

As in [15], we use the Relative Squared Error (RSE) to evaluate the performance of the prediction models. Let $N(v,t)$ be the total number of views video v receives up to day t ($N(v,0) = 0$), and $\hat{N}(v,t_r,t_t)$ be the total number of views *predicted* for v at target date t_t based on data from the first t_r days. The RSE for this prediction is given by:

$$RSE = \left(\frac{\hat{N}(v,t_r,t_t)}{N(v,t_t)} - 1\right)^2 \tag{1}$$

For a collection C of videos, the mean Relative Squared Error (mRSE) is defined as the arithmetic mean of the RSE values for all videos in C[4], that is:

$$mRSE = \frac{1}{|C|} \cdot \sum_{v \in C} \left(\frac{\hat{N}(v,t_r,t_t)}{N(v,t_t)} - 1\right)^2 \tag{2}$$

We here adopt the RSE, instead of the absolute quadratic error because, for various services for which popularity prediction is useful (e.g., search engine and content recommendation), relative errors tend to be more relevant and meaningful than absolute ones, particularly given the great variability in popularity across different contents [4].

3.2 Szabo-Huberman (S-H) Model

Szabo and Huberman [15] observed a high linear correlation between the log-transformed early and future popularities of online content up to a normally distributed noise. Based on this observation, they expressed the future popularity of a piece of content v as:

$$\hat{N}(v,t_r,t_t) = \alpha_{t_r,t_t} \cdot N(v,t_r) \tag{3}$$

where parameter α_{t_r,t_t} is independent of the video v. This means that, for fixed t_r and t_t, the future popularity of v is related to its early one by a constant factor.

For any given pair (t_r, t_t), we can compute the optimal value for α_{t_r,t_t} in a given training set C of videos, by plugging the expression for $\hat{N}(v,t_r,t_t)$ in Equation 2, taking its derivative and equating it to zero. This procedure leads to:

$$\alpha_{t_r,t_t} = \frac{\sum_{v \in C} \frac{N(v,t_r)}{N(v,t_t)}}{\sum_{v \in C} \left(\frac{N(v,t_r)}{N(v,t_t)}\right)^2} \tag{4}$$

Computing this optimal value for the model parameter can be done in $O(n)$ on a training set with n examples.

3.3 Multivariate Linear (ML) Model

The S-H model uses as input the total number of views of a video up to day t_r. We here consider that, instead of having only one number, we sample the total number of views at regular intervals up to the same t_r date, thus computing the number of views received *per sampling interval*, which can be seen as popularity *deltas* up to t_r. Unless otherwise stated, we here assume daily samplings for simplicity, although the model itself makes no assumption on the sampling rate.

Our proposed multivariate linear (ML) model predicts the popularity of a video at t_t as a linear function of these popularity deltas. The linear assumption is reasonable given the strong linear correlation between early and future popularities observed in [15]. Yet, the model is more powerful than the S-H model as it allows the assignment of different "weights" to each sampling interval.

More formally, let $x_i(v)$ be the number of views received by video v on the i-th day since its upload ($x_i(v) = N(v,i) - N(v,i-1)$). The *feature vector* $X_{t_r}(v)$ is defined as:

$$X_{t_r}(v) = (x_1(v),\, x_2(v),\, \ldots, x_{t_r}(v))^T$$

and we estimate the popularity of the video v at t_t as:

$$\hat{N}(v,t_r,t_t) = \Theta_{(t_r,t_t)} \cdot X_{t_r}(v) \tag{5}$$

where $\Theta_{(t_r,t_t)} = (\theta_1,\, \theta_2,\, \ldots,\, \theta_{t_r})$ is the vector of *model parameters* and depends only on t_r and t_t.

Given a training set C, t_r and t_t, we can compute the optimal values for the elements of $\Theta_{(t_r,t_t)}$ as the ones that minimize the mRSE on C, i.e.:

$$\underset{\Theta_{(t_r,t_t)}}{\arg\min} \frac{1}{|C|} \sum_{v \in C} \left(\frac{\Theta_{(t_r,t_t)} \cdot X_{t_r}(v)}{N(v,t_t)} - 1\right)^2 \tag{6}$$

The hypothesis is that $\hat{N}(v,t_r,t_t)$ is a linear function, and $N(v,t_t)$ a scalar. Thus, it follows that:

$$\frac{\Theta_{(t_r,t_t)} \cdot X_{t_r}(v)}{N(v,t_t)} = \Theta_{(t_r,t_t)} \cdot \left(\frac{X_{t_r}(v)}{N(v,t_t)}\right)$$

Let $X_v^* = \frac{X_{t_r}(v)}{N(v,t_t)}$. We express the optimization problem as:

$$\underset{\Theta_{(t_r,t_t)}}{\arg\min} \frac{1}{|C|} \sum_{v \in C} \left(\Theta_{(t_r,t_t)} \cdot X_v^* - 1\right)^2, \tag{7}$$

which is an ordinary least squares (OLS) problem that can be solved via a singular value decomposition [2], with complexity $O(np^2)$, where n is the number of training examples and p the number of model parameters. We assume that $n \geq p$.

The S-H model is a special case of this multivariate linear model, with the added restriction that $\theta_1 = \theta_2 = \cdots = \theta_{t_r}$. As such, the aggregate results, in terms of mRSE, provided by our model should be always either equal or better than those generated by the S-H model, although this is not guaranteed for individual videos. One possible drawback of our ML model, though, is that the number of parameters is not fixed, but increases linearly with t_r. We believe, however, that this would not be an issue in practice because: (1) one would usually not observe the popularity for very long before the prediction; and (2) if the total number of samples, and thus the number of parameters, is too large, we can reduce it by using a larger sampling interval (for example, weekly instead of daily).

3.4 MRBF Model

By assigning different weights to different days in the observed history of the video, the ML model is able to capture some information about the popularity evolution patterns of videos. However, it is still limited by using a single set of parameters for all videos. The different popularity patterns display very different behaviors, and thus it is likely

[4]We note that the RSE is not defined for videos that have zero views at the target date. However, we find that only a very small fraction (below 1.5%) of the videos in our datasets have zero views at all target dates we considered. Thus, we disregard those videos when computing mRSE values.

that exploring particular aspects of each pattern can lead to improved prediction accuracy.

One possible approach for solving that problem is to create different, specialized models for each pattern. Applying those models, though, is problematic, because it requires choosing the most appropriate model for the video for which we want to predict the future popularity, which ultimately implies that we have to be able to predict, a priori, based solely on the early view measures, the overall popularity pattern the video will follow. This is a hard, still open problem.

We opt here for a different approach. Instead of building a classifier for predicting the popularity pattern of videos, we build a new model that takes into account the similarity (in terms of early views, up to t_r) between the video and known examples from the training set, and uses this similarity to adapt the popularity prediction. This new model extends the ML model using additional features that measure the similarity between the video for which one wishes to predict the future popularity and some specific examples from the training set. Using these extra features, we can tweak the popularity prediction to better capture some particular aspect of certain types of videos. In essence, we still keep a single-parameter-set ML model, but alter that prediction based on the similarity to certain videos. Assuming that the videos from the training set used for this computation encompass the various popularity patterns, we are (indirectly) incorporating information about the pattern of the video for which we are predicting the future popularity, and adapting the prediction model to it.

For measuring the similarity between videos, we use Radial Basis Functions (RBFs). A radial basis function is a real-valued function whose value depends only on the distance between its inputs and a given point, the *center* [7]. Given a training set video v_c, we create a Gaussian RBF with it as the center to capture its similarity with a target video v as follows:

$$RBF_{v_c}(v) = e^{\left(-\frac{||X(v)-X(v_c)||^2}{2\cdot\sigma^2}\right)}, \quad (8)$$

where σ is a parameter and $X(v)$ is the ML model feature vector for the video v.

We select an uniform random sample of examples from the training set and use these as centers for RBF features. For each video v, we then compute $RBF_{v_c}(v)$ and use it as one of the features in the prediction model. We call this model the MRBF model, and formally define it as:

$$\hat{N}(v,t_r,t_t) = \underbrace{\Theta_{(t_r,t_t)} \cdot X(v)}_{\text{ML Model}} + \underbrace{\sum_{v_c \in C} \omega_{v_c} \cdot RBF_{v_c}(v)}_{\text{RBF Features}} \quad (9)$$

where C is the set of training set examples chosen as centers and ω_{v_c} is the model weight associated with the RBF feature for v_c used for prediction purposes.

In order to use the MRBF model, we must first set appropriate values for α, σ and the number of training set examples chosen as centers. There is no a priori best value for any of these parameters. We experimented with many values for each of them and chose to use the values that provided the lowest prediction error in a cross-validation set.

Once these parameters are set, training the MRBF model consists of finding optimal values for the Θ and ω_{v_c} model parameters. In order to do so, we could perform regular linear regression, as we did for the ML model. Notice that the MRBF model as defined in Equation 9 is mathematically equivalent to:

$$\hat{N}(v,t_r,t_t) = \Theta^*_{(t_r,t_t)} \cdot X^*_{t_r}(v) \quad (10)$$

where Θ^* is the Θ vector with the w_{v_c} parameters appended to it and $X^*(v)$ is the $X(v)$ vector with the values of the corresponding RBF functions appended to it – i.e., the RBF features can be simply treated as additional features in the original feature and parameter vectors. Equation 10 is in exactly the same format as Equation 5 that describes the ML model. Thus, it can be solved using the same OLS technique. However, due to the extra features, we are at increased risk of overfitting our training set. To reduce this problem, we opted to use Ridge regression [7] instead.

Ridge regression is a regression method that works in a very similar manner to the ordinary least squares (OLS) method, but additionally imposes a penalty on the sizes of the coefficients. In our ML model, which is based on OLS regression, we expressed the optimization problem as defined in Equation 7. This equation implies that we want to find the value for the parameter vector $\Theta^*_{(t_r,t_t)}$ that minimizes the prediction error. For Ridge regression, we add an extra term to the optimization problem that penalizes solutions where the norm of $\Theta^*_{(t_r,t_t)}$ is large:

$$\arg\min_{\Theta^*_{(t_r,t_t)}} \frac{1}{|C|}\left(\sum_{v\in C}\left(\Theta^*_{(t_r,t_t)} \cdot X^*_v - 1\right)^2\right) + \alpha \cdot ||\Theta^*_{(t_r,t_t)}||^2$$

where α is a parameter that controls how large the penalty for larger coefficients can be. The effect of penalizing solutions with large norms is that we avoid overfit, as usually solutions with smaller coefficients tend to have higher generalization power [7]. We tested this by comparing the errors of the MRBF model in training and test sets. If overfit occurred, we would expect the error in the training set to be much lower than the error in the test set. We found, however, that for reasonable values of α, the error in the test set is very close to the error on the training set.

4. DATASETS

We evaluate our ML and MRBF models, comparing them against the S-H model, on two datasets of YouTube videos. For both datasets, we choose to focus on videos with at least 30 days in the system, varying t_t from 30 to 100. Our datasets are:

- *Top*: YouTube maintains various per-country and world-wide top lists (e.g., most viewed, most commented, most responded videos), allowing users to browse them in different time scales (top of the day, week, month and top of all time). Each such top list contains one hundred videos. This dataset contains videos from all world-wide top lists provided by YouTube. 27,212 videos were collected through this procedure.

- *Random*: we also would like to evaluate the prediction models on a random sample of YouTube videos. As the system does not provide a means to collect a truly random sample of all its videos, alternative sampling procedures must be adopted. We here use a dataset consisting of videos collected in a procedure that is based on random topics. First, 30,000 entities (i.e., words and proper names) were randomly selected from the Yago lexical ontology [14]. Each such entity was then fed as query to the YouTube search engine, and the first result was collected. Overall, this resulted in 24,484 unique videos.

For both datasets, the view count data for each video was extracted from the video statistics frame provided by YouTube, where it is shown in graph form, plotted using the Google Charts API[5]. The API call to plot the graph was intercepted and the plotted points were collected. Each graph contains at most 100 points. This means that, for videos with at most 100 days of life, the system maintains complete information about the daily view counts, whereas for older videos some daily view counts are missing. For example, if a video is in the system for 300 days, then the graph will be plotted with 100 points, each point corresponding to a 3-day interval. For such videos, we used linear interpolation to infer the missing points. We note that the interpolation may impact the prediction results. However, we repeated our experiments considering only videos with complete information, finding that the qualitative results are not affected, and that the mRSE values for models trained on the interpolated data are actually slightly higher than those obtained with models trained only on videos that do not require interpolation, for the S-H, the ML and the MRBF models. Nevertheless, we choose to present, in the next section, results that include videos for which interpolation was used, due to the small number of videos with complete information in our datasets.

We noticed that many videos in YouTube do not have statistics available. Since these statistics represent key input data for our prediction experiments, we removed from the datasets these videos with missing information. We also removed videos that were in the system for less than 30 days. After applying these filters, our Top and Random datasets were left with 5,834 and 16,123 videos, respectively.

5. EXPERIMENTAL RESULTS

In this section, we discuss the main experimental results of the S-H model and our new ML and MRBF model. These results were produced using 10-fold cross validation. That is, each dataset was randomly divided into 10 equal-sized folds. 9 folds were used as training set from which model parameters are learned, and the other fold was used as test set. We repeated the same process 10 times, using a different fold as test set each time. We report average results across all 10 test sets along with corresponding 95% confidence intervals (except in the charts, where the intervals are omitted to improve readability).

We divide our experimental analysis in three parts. First, in Section 5.1, we analyze in details the performance of the S-H model and of our ML model, explain how and why the latter outperforms the baseline. Then, in Section 5.2, we compare the ML model to the MRBF model, discussing what is the impact in popularity prediction of adding the RBF features to the ML model. Finally, in Section 5.3 we discuss our experiment in creating specialized models for each YouTube category.

[5]`http://code.google.com/apis/chart/`

5.1 ML and S-H Model Results

Figure 2-a) shows mRSE values for both S-H and our new ML models when predicting the popularity for a target date t_t equal to 30 days and various values of reference date t_r, for videos in the random dataset. Note that if t_r is too small, there is very little extra information that our ML model can benefit from, and thus both models perform very similarly. On the other hand, if almost the total popularity history is used (i.e., t_r is close to t_t), the errors are so small that there is little space for improvements. In any case, predicting popularity in this latter scenario is of little practical use. More importantly, Figure 2-a) shows that, outside these two extreme scenarios, the ML model leads to significant mRSE reductions over the S-H model, with gains in precision of over 20%. For example, if we use $t_r = 12$ days, the mRSE produced by the ML and by the S-H models are 0.081 ± 0.009 and 0.104 ± 0.008, respectively, leading to an error reduction of 22%, on average. For smaller values of t_r, the gains are reduced but still significant (e.g., 15% for t_r equal to 7 days).

Figure 2-b) and 2-c) show similar patterns for results produced for the top dataset and $t_t = 30$, as well as for the random dataset and $t_t = 100$. In the latter case, the reductions in mRSE values are even larger. For instance, if we use $t_r = 40$ to predict for $t_t = 100$, the mRSE produced by the ML and S-H models are 0.1112 ± 0.0024 and 0.1679 ± 0.0025, respectively, yielding a 33% error reduction on average.

To further understand the performance of the ML model, we separately analyze the mRSE values produced by both models for videos with different popularity evolution patterns. Towards that goal, we group the videos in our datasets into the four classes identified by Crane and Sornette [5], namely *Memoryless*, *Viral*, *Junk* and *Quality*, following the approach adopted in [5, 6]. To identify Memoryless videos, a Chi-Square test was applied to determine whether the time series describing the popularity evolution of each video follows a Poisson process. Videos for which the test failed were further classified into Viral, Junk and Quality based on the fraction f of views on the most popular day: videos with $f \leq 35\%$ were classified as Viral, videos with $f > 65\%$ as Junk, and the others were classified as Quality.

Table 1 shows the mRSE results produced by all three models, for both random and top dataset, considering t_r=7 and t_t=30. Results for other values of t_r and t_t are qualitatively similar, being thus omitted. Aggregate as well as per-class results are shown[6]. In each case, results for the most accurate model are shown in bold (including statistical ties at 95% confidence level). The table also shows the model equations for the S-H and ML models, indicating the optimal parameters found during training (parameters for the MRBF models were omitted for space). We will first analyze the results for the ML and S-H models, and defer the analysis of the MRBF results until Section 5.2.

The overall mRSE reductions achieved with our ML model over the baseline, across all classes, are 15% and 13% for the random and top datasets, respectively. It produces significant error reductions for videos in most classes while reaching statistical ties in a few others. The gains are especially large for *Junk* videos in the random dataset (69% on average) (see discussion below). Such a large reduction in pre-

[6]These results are produced by one global S-H model, one global ML model, and one global MRBF model, built from the complete training set.

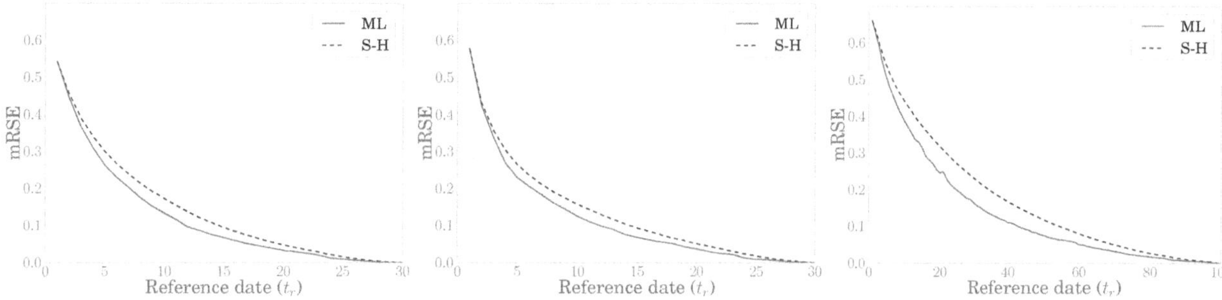

(a) t_t = 30 days, random dataset (b) t_t = 30 days, top dataset (c) t_t = 100 days, random dataset

Figure 2: Model Prediction Errors (mRSE) as Function of Reference Date t_r for Various Target Dates t_t

Table 1: Prediction Errors for S-M, ML, and MRBF Models for Videos with Various Popularity Evolution Patterns (mRSE and 95% confidence intervals, t_r=7, t_t=30).

Videos in the Random Dataset				
Popularity Class	**Number of Videos**	**S-H Model**	**ML Model**	**MRBF Model**
Overall	16123	0.2382 ± 0.0038	0.2022 ± 0.0043	$\mathbf{0.1892 \pm 0.0032}$
Memoryless	3449	0.3351 ± 0.0099	0.2929 ± 0.0120	$\mathbf{0.2641 \pm 0.0111}$
Viral	11504	0.2086 ± 0.0040	0.1788 ± 0.0041	$\mathbf{0.1713 \pm 0.0040}$
Junk	222	0.4588 ± 0.0283	$\mathbf{0.1402 \pm 0.0274}$	$\mathbf{0.1268 \pm 0.0319}$
Quality	948	0.1921 ± 0.0124	$\mathbf{0.1707 \pm 0.0283}$	$\mathbf{0.1490 \pm 0.0199}$
Videos in the Top Dataset				
Popularity Class	**Number of Videos**	**S-H Model**	**ML Model**	**MRBF Model**
Overall	5813	0.2121 ± 0.0074	0.1837 ± 0.0081	$\mathbf{0.1723 \pm 0.0071}$
Memoryless	5130	0.2104 ± 0.0081	$\mathbf{0.1820 \pm 0.0088}$	$\mathbf{0.1740 \pm 0.0084}$
Viral	401	0.3096 ± 0.0234	0.2612 ± 0.0228	$\mathbf{0.1845 \pm 0.0242}$
Junk	78	$\mathbf{0.0560 \pm 0.0226}$	$\mathbf{0.0360 \pm 0.0236}$	0.0929 ± 0.0358
Quality	204	$\mathbf{0.1236 \pm 0.0314}$	$\mathbf{0.1315 \pm 0.0330}$	$\mathbf{0.1373 \pm 0.0479}$

Model Equations for Random Dataset:

S-H model : $\hat{N}(v, 7, 30) = 1.92 \cdot N(v, 7)$

ML model: $\hat{N}(v, 7, 30) = 1.22 \cdot x_1(v) + 1.24 \cdot x_2(v) + 1.36 \cdot x_3(v) + 1.52 \cdot x_4(v) + 2.23 \cdot x_5(v) + 2.33 \cdot x_6(v) + 6.15 \cdot x_7(v)$

Model Equations for Top Dataset:

S-H model : $\hat{N}(v, 7, 30) = 1.41 \cdot N(v, 7)$

ML model: $\hat{N}(v, 7, 30) = 1.19 \cdot x_1(v) + 1.02 \cdot x_2(v) + 1.16 \cdot x_3(v) + 1.36 \cdot x_4(v) + 1.35 \cdot x_5(v) + 1.47 \cdot x_6(v) + 4.82 \cdot x_7(v)$

diction error, even if for a small fraction of the videos, may have significant impact on infrastructure management and sizing decisions as well as on the effectiveness of popularity-based information retrieval services [8], particularly given that the predictions made by the original S-H model are great overestimations, as we verified experimentally.

Junk videos are characterized by a sudden, high peak in the daily number of views followed by a steep decrease. Through some external mechanism (e.g., being featured in national news, or trending on a service like Twitter), these videos attract a burst of popularity at some point in time, but they are not *interesting* enough to continue being popular in the long run. By analyzing Junk videos in our two datasets, we found that around 90% of the videos classified as Junk in both datasets have their popularity peak at most 3 days after upload. By assigning lower weights to the first days in the range used as input (see model equations at the bottom of Table 1), the ML model produces much better predictions for such videos, compared to the S-H model. In other words, the ML model recognizes that a video that is still receiving a significant number of views after 7 days in the system is much more likely to continue receiving even more views after 30 days than a video that received a large number of views in the first two or three days with very few daily views afterwards. For *Junk* videos in the top dataset, the mRSE produced by the S-H model is already very small, leaving little room for improvements. Thus, for that dataset, both models produce results that are statistically tied.

Figures 2(a-c) allow us to determine the minimum number of daily samples (i.e., minimum t_r) so as to keep model errors below a given threshold, for the given target date t_t. For example, for t_t=30, we need to set t_r equal to at least 8 to keep the mRSE of our ML model below 0.2, for videos in the random dataset. We now extend this analysis, considering various values of t_t, and plotting, in Figure 3, mRSE results as function of the fraction of the total period up to the target date that must be monitored and sampled (i.e., $\frac{t_r}{t_t}$).

Figure 3-a) shows that our ML model is very insensitive to variations in the target date, that is, it is able to maintain the same average prediction error while still predicting longer into the future, provided that the same fraction of popularity history is sampled. The same is true, to some

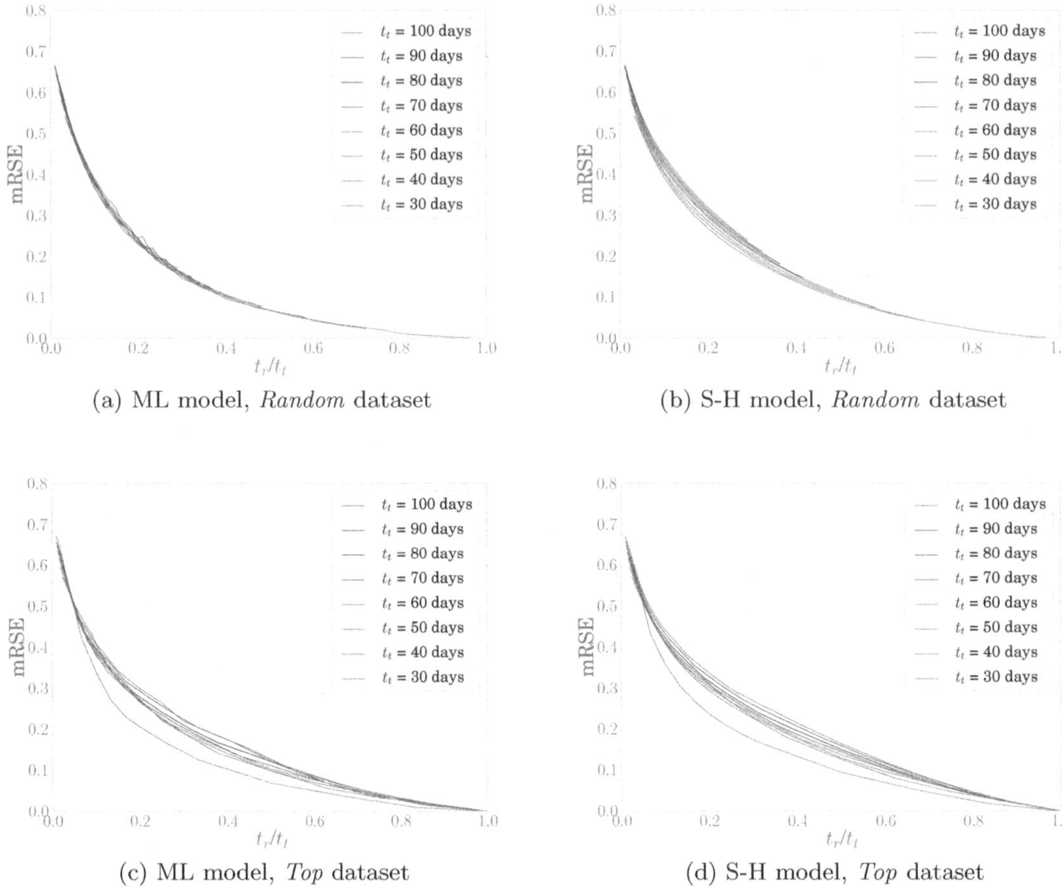

(a) ML model, *Random* dataset

(b) S-H model, *Random* dataset

(c) ML model, *Top* dataset

(d) S-H model, *Top* dataset

Figure 3: Model Prediction Errors (mRSE) as Function of Fraction of History Monitored and Sampled.

extent, for the S-H model, although, having fixed the desired average prediction error, Figure 3-b) shows a slight trend towards an increase in the required fraction of history sampled as we increase the target date. This trend is more clear, for both models, in the Top dataset, as shown in Figures 3(c,d). We conjecture that the reasons for this different behavior are related to the distribution of popularity evolution patterns among the videos in both datasets, shown in Table 1 (column "Number of Videos"). Note that the vast majority of the videos in the Top dataset (88%) are in the *Memoryless* class. The popularity curves of these videos have no marked peak but rather some random fluctuations. The absence of some clear trend makes it harder to make accurate predictions. Thus, having fixed the fraction of history to be sampled, the further into the future the target date is, the harder the prediction becomes. In contrast, almost 70% of the videos in the Random dataset are classified as *Viral*, corresponding to videos with a clear trend in the popularity curve, which makes both models, and particularly our ML model, less sensitive to variations in the target date, for a fixed fraction of history sampled.

5.2 MRBF Model Results

Finally, we evaluate our extension of the ML model to include RBF features, the MRBF model. As described in Section 3.4, there are three main parameters we need to set in order to instantiate this model. The first, and simplest, is the number of RBF features to include. The two remaining parameters are σ, which controls the sphere of influence for each RBF feature, and α, which controls the tradeoff between minimizing the prediction error and minimizing the norm of the model parameter vector.

We used grid search to choose the best values for these parameters for our datasets. For each fold, the training set was split into a training subset and a cross-validation set. For each parameter, we selected a range of possible values. We then tested every combination of values for the parameters by training the model on the training subset and evaluating it on the cross-validation set. Afterwards, we selected the optimal values for the parameters as the ones that minimized the average error on the cross-validation set across all folds. Finally, we applied the model trained with these values to our test set.

For the number of RBF features, we considered using 100, 200, 500 and 1000 centers. The centers for each of these features were videos chosen uniformly at random from the training set. Suprisingly, we found very little variation in prediction error between these numbers, with all values being statistically equivalent. We report the numbers for the scenario where 100 RBF features are used, as using fewer centers leads to fewer model parameters and thus lower computational cost.

For α, we considered the values 10^0, 10^{-1}, 10^{-3}, 10^{-4}, 10^{-5}, 10^{-6}, and 10^{-9}. For σ, we first considered all non-negative integer multiples of 100 up to 1000, in an initial pass $(0, 100, 200, 300, \ldots, 1000)$. After observing the most promising value of σ among those, we performed a finer-grained search near it.

Table 1 shows the mRSE for MRBF model on both datasets, compared to the ML and the S-H models. Once again, we choose to present only the results for $t_t = 30$ days and $t_r = 7$ days, as the results for other target and reference dates are qualitatively similar. Table 2 shows the optimal parameter values for the model found through grid search for this scenario.

Table 2: Optimal values for the model parameters found by the grid search ($t_t = 30$, $t_r = 7$)

Parameter	Random Data Set	Top Data Set
# centers	100	100
σ	10.0	390.0
α	10^{-5}	10^{-9}

In both datasets, the MRBF model outperforms the ML model by a statistically significant amount (as measured by a paired t-test[10]). The reduction in mRSE compared to ML is of about 6% on both datasets. Compared to the S-H model, the reduction in mRSE reaches 21% and 19% on the Random and Top datasets, respectively.

One important question is where these gains in prediction accuracy come from. In order to shed some light on this issue, we measured how well the ML and MRBF models behave with respect to the popularity evolution patterns proposed by Crane & Sornette[5]. These results are also shown in Table 1.

In both datasets, we noticed a significant reduction in prediction error for the second largest class (Memoryless in the Random dataset and Viral in the Top dataset). We believe this behavior can be explained by the global model being biased towards the largest class, and the second largest class still being large enough that a reasonable number of videos of that class were chosen as centers of RBF features, thus allowing the MRBF model to better handle those videos. In both datasets, the reduction in prediction error for videos of the largest class was below the overall average.

For Quality videos, we noticed no reduction in prediction error in the Top dataset and a somewhat large but not statistically significant reduction in prediction error in the Random dataset. For Junk videos, we noticed an insignificant reduction in prediction error in the Random dataset and a very large *increase* in prediction error in the Top dataset. Junk and Quality videos are the two smallest classes in our datasets and, as such, we expect that very few videos of these classes were chosen as centers, thus limiting the ability of the model to deal with these videos effectively. However, these classes still have lower average relative squared errors than Memoryless and Viral videos.

5.3 Model Specialization

Last, we investigated whether building specialized models for specific categories of videos helps boosting model performance, reducing prediction errors. This was motivated by a conjecture, raised by Szabo and Huberman [15], that videos in different YouTube categories (e.g., "Comedy", "Education", "Music", "News and Politics", etc) might have different popularity profiles, and thus might benefit from specialized models. The authors raised this question but left it open.

To test this conjecture, we built specialized MRBF models for each video category. The parameters for each such specialized model were learned based on training examples from that category only. We compared the performance of the specialized models against that of a global model, built using training examples from all categories. We found, however, that the mRSE results of the specialized models were statistically tied with those produced by the global model for all categories in both datasets, with only one exception. That exception was the "Music" category in the Top dataset: videos in that category have an mRSE of 0.2756 ± 0.0326 in the global model, but only 0.2295 ± 0.0409 when predicted using the specialized model.

The reason for these results is related to the distributions of video popularity evolution patterns across different video categories. For the Random dataset, we found that the distribution of video popularity evolution patterns is about the same for all categories: the large majority of the videos are *Viral*, followed by a sizable but noticeably smaller number of *Memoryless* videos, and fewer *Quality* and *Junk* videos. Since most categories have videos with the same overall patterns, building specialized models does not lead to significant improvements. The same conclusion holds for the Top dataset: almost all videos there are *Memoryless*, regardless of the category, with smaller numbers of *Viral*, *Junk* and *Quality* videos. The Music category is an exception in that it has an even higher fraction of *Memoryless* videos than other categories: 97% of its videos, compared to 89% on the entire dataset. We believe that this difference in the distribution of popularity patterns explains why we observed a reduction in mRSE for this category.

6. CONCLUSIONS AND FUTURE WORK

The rate at which new content is uploaded to YouTube, and to other Web applications in general, has reached unprecedented marks. Whereas some pieces of content become instant hits, others experience a growing increase of attention, and the vast majority are of limited interest. In face of such a very uneven popularity distribution and heterogeneous popularity evolution patterns, system administrators may greatly benefit from accurate predictions of content future popularity to guide their infrastructure sizing and management decisions and online marketing strategies as well as improve the effectiveness of information retrieval services.

We here proposed two new models for predicting the future popularity of a given content using, as input, daily samples of the content's popularity measures up to a given reference date. We have tested our models on two datasets of YouTube videos, comparing their accuracy against that of a state-of-the-art baseline approach that predicts future popularity based only on the aggregate popularity up to the same reference date. We found that, by assigning different weights to different popularity samples within the monitoring period, our model is able to better distinguish between videos with different popularity evolution patterns, which leads to significant reductions in average prediction errors. We also found that by exploring the similarity between the video and known examples from the training set through RBF functions, we are able to reduce prediction errors even further, by adapting the prediction to better handle some specific kinds of videos.

Other avenues we intend to pursue include investigating the impact on prediction accuracy of introducing other variables to our models. For example, other sources of information about the video itself could be exploited for that purpose. Indeed, we experimented with variables such as daily samples of number of comments, number of ratings and number of users who "favorited" the video, as these pieces of information are also available in the video statistics panel. However, since these measures tend to be highly correlated with the number of views, introducing them to a linear regression model does not help. Alternatively, information related to the *user* who posted the video, such as number of subscribers, number of friends, might be more useful. In fact, Rodrigues *et al.* [13] noticed that user information is a major factor in explaining why duplicate copies of the same video end up having different popularities. Thus, we intend to investigate whether introducing user-related variables to our model improves its accuracy.

Our MRBF model was a first step at considering the popularity evolution pattern of the video at prediction time. There are other possible approaches for this task, though. A different approach is to explore the problem of directly predicting the popularity evolution pattern that a video will follow based only on observations up to the reference date. With this information, it would be possible to use different popularity prediction models for each pattern. We believe this can lead to reduced prediction errors due to exploring the differences between patterns in a more explicit form than what the MRBF model does. Thus, we believe that is the main line for future work, and the one we intend to pursue.

ACKNOWLEDGEMENTS

This research is partially funded by the Brazilian National Institute of Science and Technology for Web Research (MCT/CNPq/INCT Web Grant Number 573871/2008-6), and by the authors' individual grants from CNPq, CAPES and Fapemig.

7. REFERENCES

[1] Alexa.com. Alexa top 500 global sites. `http://www.alexa.com/topsites`, 2011. [Online; acessed 2-November-2011].

[2] S. Boyd and L. Vandenberghe. *Convex optimization*. Cambridge University Press, 2004.

[3] M. Cha, H. Kwak, P. Rodriguez, Y. Ahn, and S. Moon. Analyzing the video popularity characteristics of large-scale user generated content systems. *ACM Trans. on Networking*, 17(5), 2009.

[4] M. Cha, H. Kwak, P. Rodriguez, Y.-Y. Ahn, and S. Moon. I tube, you tube, everybody tubes: analyzing the world's largest user generated content video system. In *Proc. ACM Internet Measurement Conference*, 2007.

[5] R. Crane and D. Sornette. Robust dynamic classes revealed by measuring the response function of a social system. *Proc. National Academy of Sciences*, 105(41), 2008.

[6] F. Figueiredo, F. Benevenuto, and J. Almeida. The tube over time: Characterizing popularity growth of youtube videos. In *Proc. Conference of Web Search and Data Mining* , 2011.

[7] J. Friedman, T. Hastie, and R. Tibshirani. *The elements of statistical learning*, volume 1. Springer Series in Statistics, 2001.

[8] M. Gonçalves, J. Almeida, L. Santos, A. Laender, and V. Almeida. On popularity in the blogosphere. *Internet Computing*, 14(3), 2010.

[9] V. Heffernan. Uploading the avant-garde. `http://www.nytimes.com/2009/09/06/magazine/06FOB-medium-t.html`, 2009. [Online; acessed 2-November-2011].

[10] R. Jain. *The art of computer systems performance analysis*. John Wiley & Sons, 2008.

[11] J. Lee, S. Moon, and K. Salamatian. An approach to model and predict the popularity of online contents with explanatory factors. In *Int'l. Conf. on Web Intelligence and Intelligent Agent Technology*, 2010.

[12] K. Lerman and T. Hogg. Using a model of social dynamics to predict popularity of news. In *Proc. World Wide Web Conference*. ACM, 2010.

[13] T. Rodrigues, F. Benevenuto, V. Almeida, J. Almeida, and M. Gonçalves. Equal but different: A contextual analysis of duplicated videos on youtube. *Springer Journal of the Brazilian Computer Society*, 16(3), 2010.

[14] F. Suchanek, G. Kasneci, and G. Weikum. Yago: a core of semantic knowledge. In *Proc. World Wide Web Conference*, 2007.

[15] G. Szabo and B. Huberman. Predicting the popularity of online content. *Communic. of ACM*, 53(8), 2010.

[16] F. Wu and B. Huberman. Novelty and collective attention. *Proc. National Academy of Sciences*, 104(45), 2007.

[17] T. Wu, M. Timmers, D. De Vleeschauwer, and W. Van Leekwijck. On the use of reservoir computing in popularity prediction. In *Proc. Conference on Evolving Internet*, 2010.

[18] P. Yin, P. Luo, M. Wang, and W.-C. Lee. A straw shows which way the wind blows: Ranking potentially popular items from early votes. In *Proc. WSDM 2012*, 2012.

Geo Topic Model: Joint Modeling of User's Activity Area and Interests for Location Recommendation

Takeshi Kurashima*, Tomoharu Iwata+, Takahide Hoshide*, Noriko Takaya* and Ko Fujimura*
*NTT Service Evolution Labs., NTT Corporation
+NTT Communication Science Labs., NTT Corporation
*1-1 Hikari-no-oka, Yokosuka-Shi, Kanagawa, 239-0847 Japan
+2-4 Hikaridai, Seika-Cho, Soraku-gun, Kyoto, 619-0237 Japan
{kurashima.takeshi,iwata.tomoharu,hoshide.takahide,takaya.noriko,fujimura.ko}@lab.ntt.co.jp

ABSTRACT

This paper proposes a method that analyzes the location log data of multiple users to recommend locations to be visited. The method uses our new topic model, called *Geo Topic Model*, that can jointly estimate both the user's interests and activity area hosting the user's home, office and other personal places. By explicitly modeling geographical features of locations and users, the user's interests in other features of locations, which we call latent topics, can be inferred effectively. The topic interests estimated by our model 1) lead to high accuracy in predicting visit behavior as driven by personal interests, 2) make possible the generation of recommendations when the user is in an unfamiliar area (e.g. sightseeing), and 3) enable the recommender system to suggest an interpretable representation of the user profile that can be customized by the user. Experiments are conducted using real location logs of landmark and restaurant visits to evaluate the recommendation performance of the proposed method in terms of the accuracy of predicting visit selections. We also show that our model can estimate latent features of locations such as art, nature and atmosphere as latent topics, and describe each user's preference based on them.

Categories and Subject Descriptors

H.2.8 [**Database Management**]: Database Applications—*Data Mining*

General Terms

Algorithms

Keywords

Topic model, Location recommendation

1. INTRODUCTION

In recent years, social media has become ubiquitous and important for social networking and user-generated content sharing. In the tourism and food domains, more and more people are sharing their experiences on photo sharing sites (e.g. Flickr [10] and Google Picasa [14]), social networking services (e.g. foursquare [11] and Facebook [9]), travel communities (e.g. TripAdvisor [27]), and restaurant review sites (e.g. Tabelog [26], yelp [29] and ZAGAT.com [31]). Mining and modeling the visit behavior contained in this tremendous volume of location log data is an important task, because it will provide people with efficient ways to develop the most satisfying plan of action.

In this paper, we propose a method for recommending new locations that are potentially interesting to users based on a new topic model, called *Geo Topic Model*. We define a location as a uniquely identified specific site, including landmark and restaurant. Our concept is based on understanding the processes that underlie a user's decision about where and what to visit in the future; the location that the user will visit depends on 1) user's daily-life range and 2) user's topic interest.

We have two criteria for designing a method to recommend locations. First, recommending locations that match the user's interests is important. For example, if the user is interested in the arts, we would expect the recommender system to emphasize locations associated with art such as art museums and picture galleries. Our approach is motivated by the success of using topic models to analyze human behavior log data [7, 19, 18]. A topic model is a hierarchical Bayesian model, in which a user (document) is modeled as a mixture of topics, and a topic is modeled as a probability distribution over locations (words). However, when we use existing topic models to analyze visit behavior based on location log data, we are unable to discover the users' interests in the features (latent topics) of locations such as "art" and "nature". In the tourism and food domains, the user's choice of items is largely influenced by her/his geographical coordinates, and locations in the user's immediate neighborhood are likely to be chosen. The estimated topic, therefore, groups nearby locations, and most of the topics are used to describe the user's spatial area of activity. Thus existing topic models tend to recommend easily accessible but uninteresting locations to the user.

Second, augmenting location recommendations with feedback is important. When a user is not satisfied with the first suggestions, she/he would like to review the estimated user profile in order to understand why and how the recommendations were made, and customize it to receive better recommendations. Providing an interpretable representation of the user profile is very useful for understanding the original user information and reformulating the profile, resulting in improved recommendation performance. Existing collaborative filtering methods can make use of the travel histories of a group of similar users (i.e., user-based collaborative filtering) or a set of similar locations (i.e., location-based collaborative filtering) to generate location recommendations. The main

WSDM'13, February 4–8, 2013, Rome, Italy.

disadvantage of the method is that the learnt latent space is not easy to interpret. The user of a recommender system based on existing collaborative filtering methods can not easily understand why and how the recommendations were made.

With these criteria in mind, we develop a machine learning algorithm for recommending geographical locations. Our key idea is to model the user's interests separately from location accessibility. By modeling user's spatial area of activity based on geographical features of visited locations (i.e. latitude and longitude coordinates), the user's interests in other latent features (latent topics) of locations can be inferred effectively. Furthermore, we use annotation data of each location to construct a meaningful representation of latent features (latent topics). Thus our proposed model can generate an interpretable representation of each user profile; it can be presented alongside location recommendations and customized by the user if necessary.

Our proposed model can yield impressive results when recommending interesting locations in two scenarios: 1) recommending locations in the vicinity of the user's daily life areas and 2) recommending locations when the user is in less familiar areas. Recommendations for the user's daily life generated by our model are easy to access from the user's home, office, and other personal places, and suit the user's interests. The latent topics estimated from our model lead to high accuracy in predicting the visit behavior as driven by personal interests. We also introduce a recommendation method customized for a user in the mobile environment who wants to find locations to suit her immediate surroundings; the recommended locations are easy to access from the user's current position, and match the user's interests. Even when the user visits a new place (e.g. sightseeing and business trips), this method can generate recommendations from the user's topic interests learned from the characteristics found in the user's location log.

We demonstrate the effectiveness of the proposed model using real-life location logs of landmark and restaurant visits. We show the utility of our model by generating recommendations in two areas: daily life and those yet to be visited. We also analyze the content of estimated latent topics using annotation data of locations and find that our model can lucidly describe each user's interests in terms of latent features of locations such as art, nature, construction, popularity and atmosphere.

In summary, the major contributions of this paper include:

- Geo Topic Model: learns the user's activity area and personal interests in the latent features of locations simultaneously;
- A recommendation method that presents easy-to-access and interesting locations for 1) a user in daily life and 2) a traveler in an unfamiliar territory;
- A method of discovering latent features (latent topics) of landmarks/restaurants from the actual logs of visited landmarks/restaurants and an interpretable description of the user's interest based on latent features (latent topics).

This paper is organized as follows: The next section describes related works. Section 3 defines our research problem and presents our proposed model and recommendation methods. Section 4 uses actual location logs to confirm the effectiveness of the proposed model, and Section 5 concludes this paper.

2. RELATED WORK

2.1 Behavior Modeling for Recommendation

Collaborative filtering, the traditional approach to recommendation, makes use of the location logs of a group of similar users (i.e., user-based collaborative filtering) or a set of similar locations (i.e., location-based collaborative filtering) to generate location recommendations. Most successful collaborative filtering methods are based on latent factor models; one technique, matrix factorization, offers good performance [25]. Matrix factorization allows us to represent users and items in a shared low-dimensional space, and predict whether the user will like an item from the inner product of their latent representations. Among latent factor models, matrix factorization performs well for behavior prediction, but its main disadvantage is that the learnt latent low-dimensional space is not easy to interpret.

Analyzing human behaviors using probabilistic topic models yields a more interpretable representation of users and locations than latent factor models. Topic modeling algorithms are used to discover a set of latent features of locations (topics) from the location histories of multiple users (a collection of documents), where a latent feature (topic) is a probabilistic distribution over locations (words). Topic models also provide an interpretable low-dimensional representation of the user's interests, where interests are modeled as a mixture of location features (topics). We can discover the latent feature of locations based on what types of locations are contained, and understand the user's preference profile based on the latent feature of the locations that he or she likes. We adopt a topic modeling approach to realize our goal of obtaining knowledge that offers a deeper understanding of the decision-making process (i.e. answer the question, "how do we decide where to visit next?").

Probabilistic Latent Semantic Analysis (PLSA) [16, 17] and Latent Dirichlet Allocation (LDA) [4] are two representative topic models; they have been successfully used in a wide variety of applications such as information retrieval, language modeling, and modeling the interests underlying human behavior. For example, Das et al. use a linear model to combine recommendations from different algorithms including PLSA for generating personalized recommendations from Google News [7]. We proposed the Topic Tracking Model for analyzing purchase behavior; it captures interests and temporal changes in item trends [18]. The discovery of patterns in the navigational behavior of Web users based on PLSA was tackled by [19].

In the tourism domain, we adopted the topic model for estimating user's interests based on geo-tag based histories on Flickr [20]. The method proposed in [20] has, unfortunately, difficulty in recommending locations that suit the user's preference because most of the latent topics describe the user's immediate area of activity (i.e. the estimated topic of existing topic models groups nearby locations). The topic-based model proposed in [30] also infers an area (a set of nearby locations) that could have similar functions (e.g. residential, commercial and entertainment area in a city). This is one of the major problems when analyzing location histories, and the challenge tackled by this study is to estimate the user's interests by considering the extent of the user's geographical range.

2.2 GPS Trajectory Mining

Data mining from GPS trajectories gathered by mobile devices is somewhat related to our work because its main goal is to predict where a person may be going. GPS point data is assumed to contain only the information of location (latitude and longitude) and timestamp; a GPS trajectory is a time series of points. Ashbrook et al. apply a Markov model to GPS data in an attempt to model traveler behavior [2]. Their assumption is that the location that the tourist will move to next depends on the current and recently visited locations. Zheng et al. applied a graph mining method to a GPS dataset generated by 107 users in order to extract major sightseeing spots and classical travel routes between them [34, 32]. Several papers have mined travel routes and itineraries linking popular landmarks from the GPS trajectories of multiple users [20, 1, 5]. Sequential pattern mining from GPS trajectories was also performed by Monreale et al. [23]. Zheng et al. proposed hierarchical-graph-based measurement for estimating the similarity between multiple users' movements [33]. Leung et al. proposed CLM graph extraction from GPS trajectory data with a User-Activity-Location tripartite data structure [21]. Their model assumes that the temporal sequence of visited locations represents the user's activity. This is because most users visit several locations in order to perform a specific activity (e.g. go to office and its nearest station for work). The methods that depend on the sequential patterns found in GPS trajectories are designed for capturing the current temporal-spatial properties in user activities. Different from these methods, we want to predict the next location assuming that the user's actions are being driven by her/his personal interests (e.g. vacation spot, place to eat on the weekend).

2.3 Location-Based Recommender System

There are some related studies on mobile city guide applications that can personalize the user's recommendations. COMPASS is a tourist guide system that makes recommendations after considering user profile, schedule, shopping list, time since last visit and context such as weather and traffic conditions [28]. MobyRec is a context-aware mobile recommender system that allows preferences to be specified for restaurants etc. [24]. However, these systems require the user's stated query or initially specified interests. Ours generates recommendations using only location log data; the user does not have to explicitly enter her/his profile, interests or queries.

Based on extensive field work in Tokyo, Bellotti et al. designed and developed a location recommender system that infers user activity (e.g. "eating" and "shopping") and preference [3]. Their work is similar to our work in that they attempt to generate recommendations based on the user's implicit (inferred) interests. Their system, however, combines the results from a variety of existing recommendation models in an ad hoc fashion depending on the user's context or pre-defined rules. No new recommendation model is proposed in [3]. Again, this paper proposes a new probabilistic model specialized for recommending locations.

3. PROPOSED MODEL

In this section, we first describe the proposed Geo Topic Model, and the recommendation method based on the model for predicting visit behavior in daily life. We then describe how the recommendation method supports a mobile user who visits a new place.

3.1 Geo Topic Model

Suppose that we have a set of N users $\boldsymbol{U} = \{u\}_{u=1}^{N}$ and a set of I locations $\boldsymbol{I} = \{i\}_{i=1}^{I}$. Each location is associated with geotag r_i, which represents the latitude and longitude coordinates of the location in a shared bi-axial space. Each user has a visited-location log denoted by $\boldsymbol{x}_u = \{x_{u1}, ..., x_{uM_u}\}$, where x_{um} represents the mth visited location of user u, and $x_{um} \in \boldsymbol{I}$. Our research problem is simple, and is described as follows; given a user's location log $\boldsymbol{x}_u$, the task is to recommend a set of locations that the user will want to visit next. The notations used are summarized in Table 1.

We make the following two assumptions about visit behavior in daily life:

1. The location that the user visits next largely depends on the user's activity areas, i.e. areas that encompass her home, office, and other personal places. For example, a user whose office is located in Manhattan is much more likely to visit Grand Central Station than Newark Pennsylvania Station because Grand Central Station is much closer.
2. The choice of what to do next is also determined by the user's interests. For example, a user who is interested in art is likely to visit the Metropolitan Museum of Art while a user who is interested in sports is likely to visit Yankee Stadium.

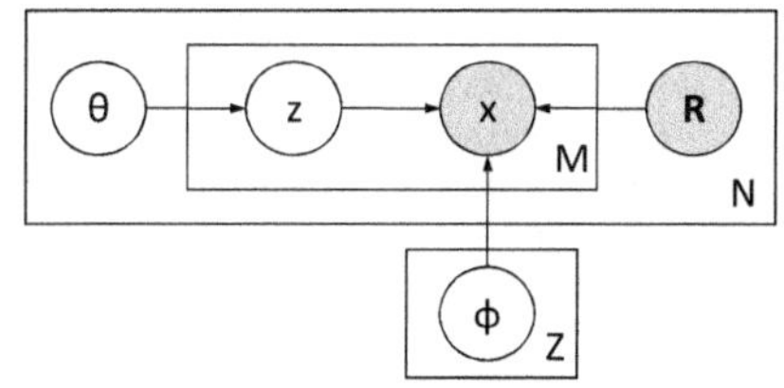

Figure 1: Graphic model representation of Geo Topic Model. Shaded and hollow nodes indicate observed and latent variables, respectively.

Table 1: Notation

Symbol	Description
$\boldsymbol{U}$	set of users
u	user, $u \in \boldsymbol{U}$
$\boldsymbol{I}$	set of locations
i	location, $i \in \boldsymbol{I}$
z	latent topic
M_u	number of locations in the history of user u
x_{um}	the mth visited location of user u, $x_{um} \in \boldsymbol{I}$
$\boldsymbol{x}_u$	location log of user u denoted by $\boldsymbol{x}_u = \{x_{u1}, ..., x_{uM_u}\}$
r_i	geotag of location i represented by latitude and longitude coordinates in bi-axial space
$\boldsymbol{R}_u$	the set of geotags of locations of user u denoted by $\boldsymbol{R}_u = \{r_{x_{um}}\}_{m=1}^{M_u}$
θ_{uz}	probability that topic z is chosen by user u
$\boldsymbol{\theta}_u$	topic proportions of user u denoted by $\boldsymbol{\theta}_u = \{\theta_{uz}\}_{z=1}^{Z}$
ϕ_{zi}	probability that location i is chosen for topic z
$\boldsymbol{\phi}_z$	location proportions of topic z denoted by $\boldsymbol{\phi}_z = \{\phi_{zi}\}_{i=1}^{I}$
N	number of users
I	number of locations
Z	number of latent topics
β	bandwidth parameter for the width of the activity area

Our model incorporates these assumptions by assuming the following generative process of visit locations. Each user has user-dependent topic proportions $\boldsymbol{\theta}_u = \{\theta_{uz}\}_{z=1}^{Z}$ that represent the interests of the user, where $\sum_z \theta_{uz} = 1$, $\theta_{uz} \geq 0$, and Z is the number of latent topics. For each visit, topic z is chosen according to $\boldsymbol{\theta}_u$, and then location x is generated depending on both topic-specific parameters $\boldsymbol{\phi}_z = \{\phi_{zi}\}_{i=1}^{I}$ and the set of geotags of previously visited locations: $\boldsymbol{R}_u = \{r_{x_{um}}\}_{m=1}^{M_u}$. Here, ϕ_{zi} represents how likely location i is to be visited given topic z. The proposed model is illustrated in Figure 1, where shaded and hollow nodes indicate observed and latent variables, respectively.

In our model, the probability that user u with geotag history $\boldsymbol{R}_u$ visits location i is calculated by the following equation:

$$P(i|u, \boldsymbol{R}_u, \boldsymbol{\Theta}, \boldsymbol{\Phi}) = \sum_{z=1}^{Z} P(z|u, \boldsymbol{\Theta}) P(i|z, \boldsymbol{R}_u, \boldsymbol{\Phi}), \quad (1)$$

where $\Theta = \{\theta_u\}_{u=1}^{N}$, $\Phi = \{\phi_z\}_{z=1}^{Z}$, and $P(z|u,\Theta) = \theta_{uz}$. $P(i|z, R_u, \Phi)$ represents the probability that location i is chosen from topic z after consideration of the user's geotags R_u. We assume that a location that is close to the locations visited by the user is more likely to be visited. Probability $P(i|z, R_u, \Phi)$ can be written as follows:

$$P(i|z, R_u, \Phi) = \frac{1}{C} \exp(\phi_{zi}) \sum_{r \in R_u} \exp(-\frac{\beta}{2}\|r_i - r\|^2), \quad (2)$$

where $\|\cdot\|$ represents the Euclidean norm in the geographical space, $C = \sum_{i' \in I} \exp(\phi_{zi'}) \sum_{r \in R_u} \exp(-\frac{\beta}{2}\|r_{i'} - r\|^2)$ is the normalization constant, and β is a parameter describing the width of each activity area. As bandwidth parameter β is decreased, the width of the activity area increases. The first factor, $\exp(\phi_{zi})$, implies the contribution of interest in choosing a location. Parameter ϕ_{zi} represents the probability that location i is chosen for topic z; existing topic models such as PLSA also have this parameter. If latent topic z represents "art", location i associated with art, such as a museum or a theater, is likely to be chosen as the topic. The second factor $\sum_{r \in R_u} \exp(-\frac{\beta}{2}\|r_i - r\|^2)$ implies the contribution of the user's movement potential. Location i that is near the visit locations in the user's visit log x_u is likely to be chosen. If the user often visits restaurants on the city's main street, other restaurants on the street are likely to be chosen. By using the geographical features of visited locations to explicitly model the user's spatial area of activity, we can effectively estimate other latent features (latent topics) of locations and the user's interest in them (i.e. user-dependent topic proportions).

The number of parameters of the proposed model is $N(Z-1)+ZI$, where there are many fewer latent topics than users and locations ($Z \ll N$ and $Z \ll I$). The proposed method has the same order of computational cost as PLSA because the number of parameters in PLSA is $N(Z-1) + Z(I-1)$. Topic models, including ours, can establish a low-dimensional representation of the location of a user (expressed as user $*$ location matrix), so we can represent $N * I$ probabilities with fewer parameters.

3.2 Parameter Estimation

We use maximum likelihood to estimate the parameters in the proposed model. The unknown parameters are a set of topic probabilities Θ and a set of location parameters Φ. All unknown parameters are represented by $\Psi = \{\Theta, \Phi\}$.

Parameter log likelihood is, given a set of user location logs $X = \{x_u\}_{u=1}^{N}$, derived as follows:

$$L(\Psi|X) = \sum_{u=1}^{N} \sum_{m=1}^{M_u} \log \sum_{z=1}^{Z} \theta_{uz} P(x_{um}|z, R_u, \Phi). \quad (3)$$

The log likelihood can be maximized with the EM algorithm [8]. The conditional expectation of the complete-data log likelihood is represented as follows:

$$Q(\Psi|\hat{\Psi}) = \sum_{u=1}^{N} \sum_{m=1}^{M_u} \sum_{z=1}^{Z} P(z|u,m;\hat{\Psi}) \log \theta_{uz} P(x_{um}|z, R_u, \Phi), \quad (4)$$

where $\hat{\Psi}$ represents the current estimate, and $P(z|u,m;\hat{\Psi})$ represents the topic posterior probability of the mth location of user u given the current estimate. In E-step, we use Bayes rule to compute the topic posterior probability:

$$P(z|u,m;\hat{\Psi}) = \frac{P(z|u,\Theta)P(x_{um}|z, R_u, \Phi)}{\sum_{z'=1}^{Z} P(z'|u,\Theta)P(x_{um}|z', R_u, \Phi)}, \quad (5)$$

where $P(x_{nm}|z, R_u, \Phi)$ is calculated by (2). In M-step, the next estimate of topic proportion θ_{uz} is given by:

$$\hat{\theta}_{uz} = \frac{\sum_{m=1}^{M_u} P(z|u,m;\hat{\Psi})}{\sum_{z'=1}^{Z}\sum_{m=1}^{M_u} P(z'|u,m;\hat{\Psi})}. \quad (6)$$

The next estimates of ϕ_z can not be solved in closed form. Therefore, we estimate them by maximizing $Q(\Psi|\hat{\Psi})$ through the use of a gradient-based numerical optimization method such as the quasi-Newton method [22]. The gradient of ϕ_z w.r.t. ϕ_z is as follows:

$$\frac{\partial Q}{\partial \phi_z} = \sum_{u=1}^{N}\sum_{m=1}^{M_u} P(z|u,m;\hat{\Psi}) - \sum_{u=1}^{N}\sum_{m=1}^{M_u} P(z|u,m;\hat{\Psi}) P(x_{um}|z, R_u, \Phi). \quad (7)$$

By iterating the E-step and the M-step until convergence, we obtain a local optimum solution for Ψ. The number of topics Z and width parameter β can be estimated by using cross validation.

3.3 Recommendation to Suit Current Position

In the previous sections, we described Geo Topic Model, a probabilistic model that predicts locations to visit. The recommendations generated from our model have two features; 1) easy to access from the user's home, office, and other familiar locations 2) and match user's interests. This type of information need occurs often in daily life. In this section, we show another recommendation method customized for a user in the mobile environment. The prevalence of location-aware devices enables the user to search for local information using his current position (i.e. GPS point) as an implicit search query. A mobile user wants to search for locations that suit her/his current position when she/he is in an unfamiliar territory. This type of information need occurs in several situations such as sightseeing, traveling, and business trips. The required properties of these recommendations are 1) offer immediate access from the user's current position 2) and match user's interests. The first property is addressed by using the current position as a substitute for the area of activity. The second property is addressed by using parameters Φ and Θ in the same way as used for generating daily life recommendations.

Suppose that the user's current position is c, as identified by latitude and longitude coordinates. Given the user's visit log x_u and c, the task is to recommend a set of personalized locations that the user will want to visit next. The probability that user u at position c visits location i is given by the following equation:

$$P(i|u, c, \Theta, \Phi) = \sum_{z=1}^{Z} P(z|u,\Theta)P(i|z, c, \Phi), \quad (8)$$

where the probability that location i is visited given topic z and current position c is as follows:

$$P(i|z, c, \Phi) = \frac{\exp(\phi_{zi})\exp(-\frac{\beta}{2}\|r_i - c\|^2)}{\sum_{i' \in I}\exp(\phi_{zi'})\exp(-\frac{\beta}{2}\|r_{i'} - c\|^2)}, \quad (9)$$

where we assume that the probability depends on the Euclidean distance from the current position (latitude and longitude coordinates in bi-axial space).

An important characteristic of our model, described in the previous section, is that it can extract the latent features (topics) of locations beyond just their geographical positions. Once user-dependent topic proportions θ_u (and a set of location parameters Φ) are estimated from the location log formed in her/his own hometown, recommendations based on the user's topic interests can be generated anywhere since spatially-disbursed locations are grouped in each latent topic of our model. Furthermore, our method satisfies a key requirement of mobile recommender systems; it must generate real-time recommendations according to the current position. This is because the probability $P(i|u, c, \mathbf{\Theta}, \mathbf{\Phi})$ can be calculated with low computational cost by using (8) and (9) without parameter estimation. User-dependent topic proportions $\boldsymbol{\theta}_u$ do not strongly vary with her/his position.

4. EXPERIMENTS

This section evaluates the performance of the proposed method by conducting quantitative experiments on a location log of visits to restaurants and landmarks. Two quantitative experiments were conducted based on two scenarios; one is recommending locations to a user who wants to know interesting locations in his daily-life range (Section 4.1), the other is recommending locations to a user who wants to know interesting locations while traveling (Section 4.2). Finally, we analyze the content of estimated latent topics (position and types of locations grouped in each topic of our model) using the annotations attached to each location, and compare them to the output of an existing topic model (Section 4.3).

4.1 Experiment 1: Behavior Prediction Accuracy in Daily Life

4.1.1 Dataset

Our experiment used restaurant reviews from Tabelog and a Flickr-sourced geotag collection. Tabelog, which provides restaurant information, has successfully collected a large number of customer reviews. According to our research, at least 2,500,000 customer reviews of about 680,000 restaurants in Japan, uploaded by over 260,000 users, are available on Tabelog. A set of reviews of each user can be taken as the location log of restaurants the user visited. We generated four types of location log datasets from Tabelog data; location logs for Tokyo, Osaka, eastern Japan (including Tokyo, Kanagawa and Saitama prefectures) and western Japan (including Osaka, Kyoto and Hyogo prefectures). For each region, we first crawled the restaurant data including geotags (latitude and longitude), and reviews of crawled restaurants were then downloaded. A set of reviews of each user was then translated into a location log. We eliminated users traveling through or to these destinations using the static location information annotated by each user in order to evaluate prediction accuracy for local inhabitants.

We also collected large-scale-sets of geotagged photographs on Flickr using the site's public API. The geotagged photographs of each user can be assumed to be the user's personal location log. We generated three types of location log datasets from Flickr data; location logs for New York City, San Francisco and Los Angeles. For each city, geotagged photos taken within 50km from the city center were crawled. Given a collection of photos with geolocations, we automatically extracted often-photographed landmarks in the city because we want to recommend popular locations. We define a landmark as a uniquely identified specific location within the city; such as a sightseeing spot, a store, a building, a bridge, an outlet, and so on. We used *mean-shift* clustering to extract often-photographed landmarks from a set of geotags on Flickr since the previous work by Crandall et al. showed that the mean-shift procedure was effective for landmark extraction from spatial data [6]. Based on the results of landmark detection, each location in a location log was converted into one of the landmarks found by the mean-shift procedure. This yielded a set of location logs of visit landmarks from the Flickr-sourced geotag collection. Details of

Table 2: Location log data. Users who visited fewer than five locations were omitted from each. Restaurants reviewed by fewer than one hundred, forty, one hundred and fifty users were omitted from the data for Tokyo, Osaka, eastern Japan and western Japan, respectively. Each dataset had about the same number of recommended restaurants. Landmarks visited by fewer than ten users were also omitted from Flickr-sourced data.

Region	Logs	Locations	Ave. log length
Tokyo	6,257	910	14.872
Osaka	2,304	763	15.995
Eastern Japan	7,326	1,067	14.871
Western Japan	3,531	956	15.245
New York City	3,363	967	9.778
San Francisco	4,433	1,030	12.231
Los Angeles	2,848	943	11.686

the number of users (location logs) and the number of locations (landmarks) to be recommended are shown in Table 2.

4.1.2 Model Comparison

We evaluate the validity of our model in terms of its accuracy in predicting behavior in daily life. This is because, according to a previous survey, prediction accuracy is by far the most commonly used measure for evaluating the performance of recommender systems [15]. We compared the Geo Topic Model against the following four probabilistic models:

Multinomial model: recommends locations based on popularity. Popularity can be calculated by using the multinomial probability distribution over locations $P(i)$.

Kernel model: recommends locations based on user's activity area. New locations close to visited locations are likely to be recommended.

$$P_K(i|u) = \frac{\sum_{r \in \boldsymbol{R}_u} \exp(-\frac{\beta}{2}\|r_i - r\|^2)}{\sum_{i' \in \boldsymbol{I}} \sum_{r \in \boldsymbol{R}_u} \exp(-\frac{\beta}{2}\|r_{i'} - r\|^2)}. \quad (10)$$

Topic model: recommends locations based on user interest as estimated by the PLSA model.

$$P_T(i|u) = \sum_{z \in \boldsymbol{Z}} P(z|u)P(i|z). \quad (11)$$

Kernel-Topic model: recommends locations based on user's activity area and interests. This model is the linear combination of the Kernel model and the topic model (PLSA) as follows:

$$P_{KT}(i|u) = \alpha P_K(i|u) + (1-\alpha)P_T(i|u), \quad (12)$$

where α is a parameter that balances the influence of Kernel and Topic models.

We used data excluding the last visited locations of all users as training data to infer the model, and predicted the last visited locations of all users as test data. Thus, the number of training sets equals the number of location logs (users) in Table 2, the number of test sets also equals the number of location logs (users) in Table 2. Since the model predicts the next location likely to be visited by the user, we employed the 5-best (accuracy) prediction of visited locations as the evaluation metric. In other words, we calculated the percentage of visited locations contained in the set of 5-highest items over all test examples. The results of 5-best (accuracy) prediction of visited location are shown in Figure 2. In

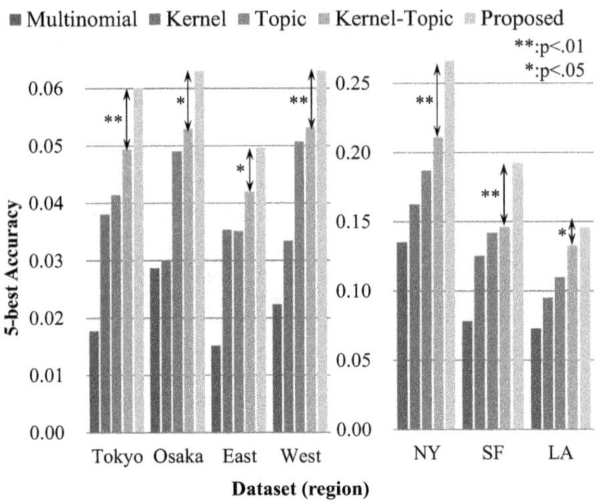

Figure 2: Comparisons of 5-best (accuracy) predictions of daily-life behavior. X-axis plots the datasets.

Table 3: Best parameter values as identified in the first experiment. β was chosen from 10, 10^2, 10^3, 10^4, 10^5, 10^6, 10^7 and 10^8. Z was set in the range of 3 to 50.

Model	Region	β	Z	α
Kernel-Topic	Tokyo	10^5	22	0.2
	Osaka	10^6	13	0.1
	Eastern Japan	10^5	15	0.3
	Western Japan	10^6	19	0.1
	New York City	10^2	5	0.9
	San Francisco	10^3	20	0.5
	Los Angeles	10^2	16	0.7
Proposed	Tokyo	10^4	8	-
	Osaka	10^4	7	-
	Eastern Japan	10^3	9	-
	Western Japan	10^3	10	-
	New York City	10^3	9	-
	San Francisco	10^2	7	-
	Los Angeles	10^3	6	-

this figure, the X-axis plots datasets and the Y-axis plots the 5-best (accuracy) prediction. We used the sign test to determine the statistical significance between the proposed model and the baselines. To sum up, for both data sets, the proposed model yields better 5-best (accuracy) prediction than Multinomial, Kernel, Topic model or Kernel-Topic model, and the differences are significant (two-sided sign test: $p < 0.05$). This shows that the proposed method can appropriately predict the user's visit behavior in regular/daily life because it recommends locations by considering both the user's activity area and interests. Furthermore, unlike the Kernel-topic model, our model does not need not to estimate the value of α because it can automatically learn the influence of location and interest in parameter estimation (i.e. automatically decide which to emphasize).

Note that best parameter values of all models, except Multinomial model, were determined using 5-fold cross validation; they are summarized in Table 3. Parameters that influence the performance of our method are the number of topics Z and bandwidth parameter β. In our model, as bandwidth parameter β is decreased, the width of the activity area increases. For example, restaurants in eastern Japan (western Japan) are distributed more widely than those in Tokyo (Osaka), so the estimated β of eastern Japan (western Japan) is smaller than that of Tokyo (Osaka). Furthermore, best parameters of Z of eastern Japan (western Japan) are larger than those of Tokyo (Osaka) since eastern Japan (western Japan) has more and a wider variety of restaurants than Tokyo (Osaka).

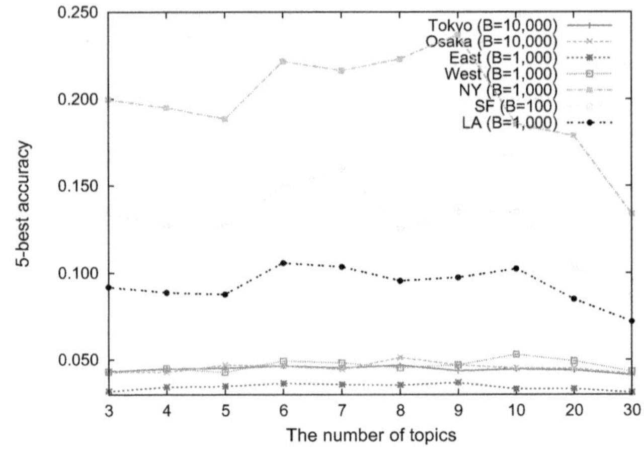

Figure 3: 5-best (accuracy) predictions of daily-life behavior of the proposed model with different numbers of topics. The X-axis plots Z. The Y-axis plots the averaged 5-best (accuracy) prediction across 5 runs.

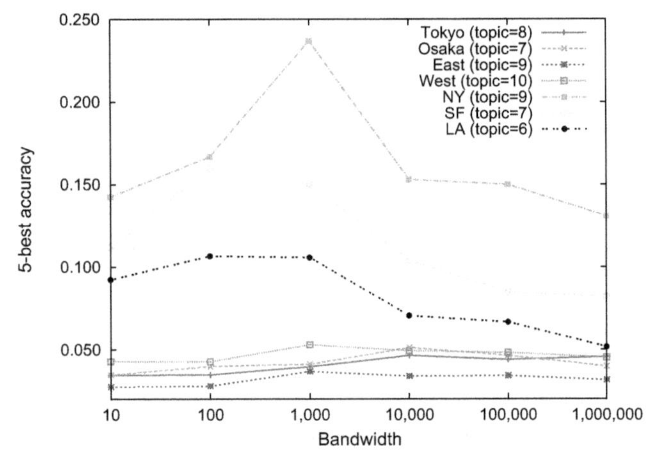

Figure 4: 5-best (accuracy) predictions of daily-life behavior of the proposed model with different bandwidth parameters. The X-axis plots β. The Y-axis plots the averaged 5-best (accuracy) prediction across 5 runs.

Figure 3 shows the results of 5-fold cross validation of the 5-best (accuracy) predictions of the proposed model with different numbers of topics (for each dataset, bandwidth parameter β is set to the best parameter value). When the number of topics is small, the 5-best prediction accuracy is low. The scores of both datasets are maximized at about 10, and after that, it gradually decreases with further increases in the number of topics. The results of 5-fold cross validation of 5-best (accuracy) predictions of the proposed model at different values of β are shown in Figure 4 (for each dataset, the number of topics, Z, is set to the best parameter value). These results show that setting the appropriate number of topics and best bandwidth parameter β can yield better recommendation performance.

Table 4: Location log data used in the second experiment. Users who visited fewer than five restaurants and Restaurants reviewed by fewer than one hundred users were omitted from each dataset.

Home - Destination	Restaurants (home/destination)	Logs	Ave. length
East - West	1424 (1103/321)	1,558	24.335
West - East	1424 (321/1103)	820	19.162

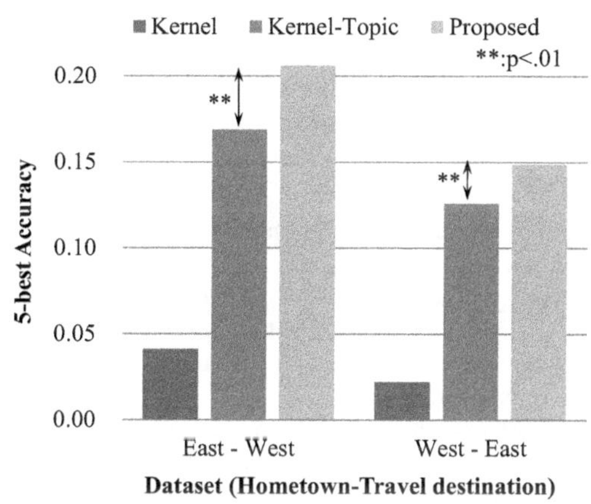

Figure 5: Comparisons of 5-best (accuracy) predictions of travel behavior. The X-axis plots datasets and the Y-axis plots the 5-best prediction accuracy averaged across all runs.

4.2 Experiment 2: Travel Behavior Prediction Accuracy

Our method was tested by recommending locations to suit the user's position while traveling (see part 3.3). In this section, we show that our method can predict visit locations while traveling with higher accuracy than is possible with the baselines. The dataset used in our experiments was generated from crawled Tabelog data. Details of the data collection and generation procedure are as follows. We first crawled users living in eastern Japan (Tokyo, Kanagawa, and Saitama prefecture). For each user, the location logs of her/his hometown and travel destination were then downloaded. Travel destinations were western Japan (including Osaka, Kyoto and Hyogo prefecture). Only users who visited restaurants in both western and eastern Japan were chosen from the users living in eastern Japan (i.e. each location log had to contain restaurants in both eastern Japan and western Japan). The dataset holds travel behavior log data because there is a great distance (about 500 kilometers) between these regions. In the evaluation, we predicted the visited restaurants in western Japan while traveling based on the location log of her/his hometown (eastern Japan). The converse dataset consists of location logs of users living in western Japan, and was used to predict travel destinations in eastern Japan from location logs for western Japan. Tokyo station and Osaka station were set as the user's current position while traveling east and west, respectively, since they are the start points of most travelers. Details of the number of users (location logs) and the number of restaurants to be recommended are shown in Table 4.

We compared three probabilistic models that can incorporate the user's current position information: Kernel model, Kernel-topic model and the proposed model. Kernel model recommends locations in the order of distance from the current position. Kernel-topic model recommends locations based on user's current position and interests estimated by existing topic model (PLSA). As is the case in the first experiment, we employed the 5-best (accuracy) predictions of restaurant visit as the evaluation metric. We tested prediction accuracy by leave-one-out cross validation. That is to say, one data was used for testing, and the others were used for training. This was repeated using each of the location log entries as a test set. So the number of tests equals the number of location log entries as shown in Table 4. Figure 5 shows the 5-best (accuracy) predictions averaged across all runs. We also used the sign test to determine the statistical significance of the differences between the average 5-best (accuracy) predictions of the proposed and the baselines. For each dataset, the result of the sign test was $p < 0.01$ (two-sided sign test). The results show that the proposed model is significantly better than the baselines in terms of the prediction accuracy of travel behavior because it generates recommendations by using user interests that do not specifically depend on user's activity area.

Table 5: Best parameter values in the second experiment. β was chosen from 10, 10^2, 10^3, 10^4, 10^5, 10^6, 10^7 and 10^8. Z was set from 5 to 50 with interval of 5. α was chosen from 0.1 to 0.9 with interval of 0.1

Model	Hometown - Travel destination	β	Z	α
Kernel-Topic	East - West	10^2	5	0.9
Kernel-Topic	West - East	10^2	10	0.7
Proposed	East - West	10^3	10	-
Proposed	West - East	10^3	10	-

All comparative models were run using the best parameters estimated using 5-fold cross validation, see Table 5. As to the proposed model, we used the best combination of Z and β from among all possible combinations. As to the Kernel-topic model, we used the best combination of Z, β and α from among all possible combinations. The two datasets used in this experiments were generated by combining two types of location logs; the location logs of eastern and western Japan used in the first experiment. Thus the best parameters, Z and β, of the combined dataset in the second experiment are almost the same as those of the location logs of eastern and western Japan in the first experiment.

4.3 Experiment 3: Topic Extraction

An important characteristic of probabilistic latent topic models is that they provide an interpretable low-dimensional representation of the users or locations. In this section, we qualitatively discuss the differences between the data-driven topics identified by Geo Topic Model and PLSA model.

Maps in Figure 6 shows the high-probability locations given the topics extracted by the proposed model and PLSA from the Flickr-sourced location log data used in the first experiment (New York City and San Francisco). The top 30 landmarks for each topic and each region are mapped on the map interface based on their geotags; the color of the mapped icon represents the topic. As shown, compared with our model, the PLSA model tends to group nearby locations together due to their positions. On the other hand, in the proposed model, each topic contains landmarks without any undue weighting from their positions. This means that the topics of the proposed model represent location-independent features of landmarks.

So what types of locations are grouped in each latent topic of our model? In order to answer this question, we further analyzed the estimated topics using the annotations (tags) associated with each landmark on the Flickr site. These annotations indicate the location names, the photographic subjects and the content of activity and are attached by the Flickr users. We extracted representative tags of each topic.

Details of the representative tag extraction procedure are as follows. Suppose that we have tag g and a set of tags G. For each topic z, we calculated the $lift$ value of tag g in order to extract representative tags specific to each topic. Given topic z, the $lift$ value of tag g is calculated as follows:

$$Lift_z(g) = \frac{P(g|z)}{\sum_{z' \in \mathbf{Z}} P(g|z')P(z')}. \quad (13)$$

$Lift$, one of the measures for discovering interesting rules or patterns, is the ratio of $P(g|z)$ over the average for the population as a whole [12]. $Lift$ takes a low value for noisy tags that appear in all topics such as "nyc" and "sf" since it considers the global occurrence probability of g. $P(g|z)$ is the probability that tag g is chosen from topic z, and calculated as follows:

$$P(g|z) = \frac{1}{C} \sum_{i \in \mathbf{I}} \exp(\phi_{zi}) P(g|i), \quad (14)$$

where $C = \sum_{i' \in \mathbf{I}} \exp(\phi_{zi'})$ is the normalization constant, and $P(g|i)$ is the probability that tag g is chosen from landmark i, and calculated as follows:

$$P(g|i) = \frac{H(g,i)}{H(i)}. \quad (15)$$

$H(i)$ is the number of users who visited landmark i, and $H(g,i)$ is the number of users who annotated landmark i with tag g.

High-value tags of the topics of the proposed model and PLSA are shown in the lower part of each map in Figure 6. Topics from 1 to 10 are ranked in descending order of $P(z) = \sum_{u \in \mathbf{U}} P(z|u)P(u)$ as estimated by each model. For both cities, the most probable topics (topic 1) as estimated by our model group famous sightseeing spots including Central Park, Guggenheim Museum, Golden Gate Bridge and Palace of Fine Arts Theatre. These location, contained in the most probable topic (i.e. topic 1), are interesting to sightseers. Other topics from 2 to 10 in our model tend to group a set of landmarks in terms of their features (e.g. nature, sea, construction, art, entertainment, sports, great views, and driving). On the other hand, each topic in PLSA is likely to contain location names, and does not contain tags that clearly identify location features.

As shown in Figure 6, one of the important characteristics of the recommender system based on our model is that it provides interpretable representations of latent topics. Each latent topic is transformed into an easy-to-understand representation such as popularity, art and nature. Furthermore, for each user u, estimated topics are ranked by user interest $\boldsymbol{\theta}_u$ as estimated and provided together with location recommendations. This offers user interaction for increasing recommendation satisfaction. For example, if a user is not satisfied with the initial location recommendations, the user first looks at the list of topics and understands the implicit estimation of profile information. Next, the user explicitly indicates which topics are interesting; At which point, our system reformulates the location recommendations based on $\boldsymbol{\phi}_z$, the location proportions of specified topic z.

Topic extraction is also performed using the location logs of restaurant visits. High-value tags of the topics of the proposed model and PLSA are shown in Table 6 and Table 7, respectively. We used Tabelog-based location log data from Tokyo, and the number of topics of the proposed model and PLSA were set to 10. As shown in Table 7, the high-probability tags of each topic are, in the PLSA model, pretty much the same. For example, topics 2, 4, 7 and 8 have almost all the same tags. On the other hand, in our model, restaurants appear to be grouped according to their features such as taste of food, atmosphere, and cooking style. For example, restaurants grouped in topic 3 are preferred by users who like sweet-tasting foods, while restaurants in topics 1 and 9 are preferred by users who like spicy or salty foods. The restaurants with a nice atmosphere in topics 4, 5 and 7 tend to be chosen by users on social dates (e.g. French restaurants and wine bars). Topics 2 and 6 tends to contain Japanese restaurants that serve tempura, sushi, soba and yakitori, while topics 8 and 10 tend to contain the restaurants that serve a wider variety of international cuisines such as American, Vietnamese and Spanish foods. The results show that ours can learn and extract latent features of locations from other type of location log data (i.e. location log data of restaurant visits).

5. CONCLUSION

This paper proposed Geo Topic Model to estimate both the user's interest and the user's spatial area of activity, simultaneously. By using the geographical features of visited locations to explicitly model the user's spatial area of activity, we can effectively estimate the user's interests in the latent features of locations beyond just their geographical positions.

The recommendation method based on Geo Topic Model meets the two criteria of a truly effective recommender system; one is recommending locations that match user's interests, and the other is augmenting location recommendations with the estimated user profile that can be customized as desired. We conducted quantitative experiments using Tabelog-based and Flickr-based real location log data to compare Geo Topic Model against other probabilistic models in terms of prediction accuracy of behavior. The results show that the latent topics estimated by our model lead to high accuracy in predicting the next location to be visited as driven by personal interest. We also showed a method for expressing latent topics in everyday language; we analyzed the content of estimated latent topics using annotation data of each location, and found that our model discovered latent topics related to art, nature, construction, great views, atmosphere and so on from actual logs of visited locations. This enables the recommender system to explain the estimated user profile in an easy-to-understand way since the user's interest can be represented as a probability distribution over the topics.

As the first and most important step, we showed the effectiveness of our proposed model in terms of the restaurant and landmark recommendation tasks which are the most popular services. A future direction is to incorporate more information such as user features to improve the performance and meet more practical information needs. Our future work also includes an evaluation in the field. The offline evaluations using behavior log data conducted in our experiments are an important starting point for exploring the validity and effectiveness of our model, but are only one approach to evaluating models and recommendation methods. We will let real users in realistic mobile settings evaluate the real strengths of our approach.

6. REFERENCES

[1] Y. Arase, X. Xie, T. Hara, and S. Nishio. Mining people's trips from large scale geo-tagged photos. In *MM '10*, pages 133–142, 2010.

[2] D. Ashbrook and T. Starner. Using GPS to learn significant locations and predict movement across multiple users. *Personal and Ubiquitous Computing*, 7(5):275–286, 2003.

[3] V. Bellotti, B. Begole, E. H. Chi, N. Ducheneaut, J. Fang, E. Isaacs, T. King, M. W. Newman, K. Partridge, B. Price,

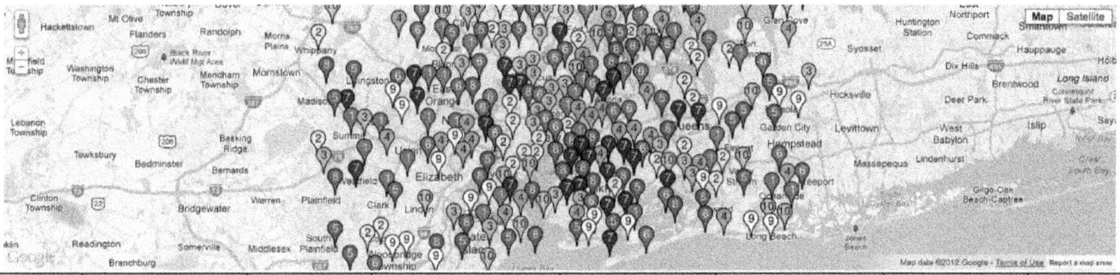

topic 1	topic 2	topic 3	topic 4	topic 5	topic 6	topic 7	topic 8	topic 9	topic 10
centralpark	ferry	construction	art	yankeestadium	cityscape	garden	livemusic	beach	spring
guggenheim	bird	architecture	bar	coneyisland	liberty	flowers	graffiti	zoo	bike
met	sunset	chelsea	streetart	baseball	batterypark	prospectpark	music	vacation	bicycle
fifthavenue	lake	show	soho	summer	panorama	green	party	animals	color
rockefeller	boat	urban	dumbo	mets	skyline	nature	waterfront	garden	library

Geo Topic Model - New York City

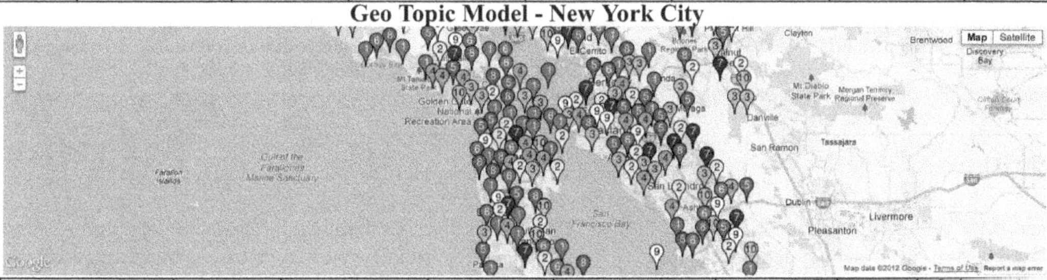

topic 1	topic 2	topic 3	topic 4	topic 5	topic 6	topic 7	topic 8	topic 9	topic 10
goldengate	woods	ship	store	landscape	graffiti	concert	sausalito	bike	coast
palaceoffinearts	goldengatepark	alcatraz	hotel	marin	art	live	urban	bicycle	sailing
downtown	trees	sunrise	house	sunrise	color	fireworks	cafe	bus	summer
presidio	muirwoods	sea	dinner	sea	mural	show	bar	ship	bakerbeach
chinatown	park	bridge	marketstreet	coast	haightashbury	livemusic	restaurant	birds	bike

Geo Topic Model - San Francisco

topic 1	topic 2	topic 3	topic 4	topic 5	topic 6	topic 7	topic 8	topic 9	topic 10
met	parkslope	greenwichvillage	newark	coneyisland	yankees	jerseycity	libertyisland	harlem	jerseycity
guggenheim	prospectpark	soho	ice	neon	mets	airport	ellisisland	upperwestside	bridge
columbuscircle	astoria	eastvillage	jersey	beach	bronx	statenisland	statueofliberty	library	statenisland
centralpark	williamsburg	jfk	nature	island	queens	ferry	statenisland	broadway	astoria
fifthavenue	eastvillage	lowereastside	tree	parade	eastriver	newark	batterypark	centralpark	trees

PLSA - New York City

topic 1	topic 2	topic 3	topic 4	topic 5	topic 6	topic 7	topic 8	topic 9	topic 10
prison	palaceoffinearts	alameda	giants	goldengatepark	airport	muirwoods	oceanbeach	marinheadlands	mission
alcatraz	presidio	oakland	embarcadero	castro	sfo	sausalito	pacificocean	coast	mural
island	marina	eastbay	soma	museum	berkley	marincounty	museum	marin	hill
pier39	fishermanswharf	berkeley	baseball	oceanbeach	baybridge	marin	soma	marincounty	house
presidio	pier39	train	baybridge	garden	baseball	marinheadlands	alameda	pacificocean	bart

PLSA - San Francisco

Figure 6: The top five representative tags for topics estimated by our model and PLSA. We use the location logs in New York City and San Francisco. Bandwidth parameter β of our model is set to the best parameter as estimated in the first experiment. The number of topics is 10. For each topic, z, tags are ordered according to $Lift_z(g)$. An interface is implemented using Google Maps API [13].

Table 6: The top five representative tags for topics estimated by our model. We use the location logs of Tokyo. The number of topics is 10, and bandwidth parameter β of proposed model is set to the best parameter as estimated in the first experiment.

topic 1	topic 2	topic 3	topic 4	topic 5	topic 6	topic 7	topic 8	topic 9	topic 10
ramen	soba	cafe	Italian food	French dish	broiled meat	bar	hamburger	Indian curry	seafood
cold noodle	broiled eel	cake	French dish	broiled eel	beef giblets	shouchu	sandwich	Indian food	Spanish cuisine
dumpling	wheat noodle	chocolate	wine	tempura	yakitori	sake	steak	curry	Vietnamese food
dan dan noodle	beef giblets	bread	pasta	sushi	chicken	pub	pizza	Thai dish	western dish
Chinese noodle	tempura	bagel	pizza	soba	kebab	wine	western dish	Thai curry	Thai dish

Table 7: The top five representative tags for topics estimated by PLSA. We use the location logs of Tokyo. The number of topics is 10.

topic 1	topic 2	topic 3	topic 4	topic 5	topic 6	topic 7	topic 8	topic 9	topic 10
cafe	ramen	French dish	ramen	broiled meat	cafe	ramen	ramen	soba	French dish
cake	cold noodle	Italian food	western dish	Italian food	cake	Italian food	cold noodle	wheat noodle	western dish
bread	Indian curry	sushi	cold noodle	French dish	Italian food	French dish	wheat noodle	curry	cafe
chocolate	Indian food	wine	curry	Chinese food	hamburger	cold noodle	dumpling	western dish	chicken
bagel	curry	Chinese food	dumpling	cafe	French dish	pizza	Indian curry	cafe	hamburger

P. Rasmussen, M. Roberts, D. J. Schiano, and A. Walendowski. Activity-based serendipitous recommendations with the magitti mobile leisure guide. In *CHI '08*, pages 1157–1166, 2008.

[4] D. M. Blei, A. Y. Ng, and M. I. Jordan. Latent dirichlet allocation. *Journal of Machine Learning Research*, 3:993–1022, 2003.

[5] M. D. Choudhury, M. Feldman, S. Amer-Yahia, N. Golbandi, R. Lempel, and C. Yu. Automatic construction of travel itineraries using social breadcrumbs. In *HT '10*, pages 35–44, 2010.

[6] D. Crandall, L. Backstrom, D. Huttenlocher, and J. Kleinberg. Mapping the world's photos. In *WWW '09*, pages 761–770, 2009.

[7] A. S. Das, M. Datar, A. Garg, and S. Rajaram. Google news personalization: scalable online collaborative filtering. In *WWW '07*, pages 271–280, 2007.

[8] A. P. Dempster, N. M. Laird, and D. B. Rubin. Maximum likelihood from incomplete data via the EM algorithm. *Journal of the Royal Statistical*, 39(1):1–38, 1977.

[9] Facebook. http://www.facebook.com/.

[10] Flickr. http://www.Flickr.com/.

[11] foursquare. http://foursquare.com/.

[12] L. Geng and H. J. Hamilton. Interestingness measures for data mining: a survey. *ACM Computing Surveys*, 38(3), 2006.

[13] Google Maps. http://maps.google.com/.

[14] Google Picasa. http://picasa.google.com/.

[15] J. L. Herlocker, J. A. Konstan, L. G. Terveen, and J. T. Riedl. Evaluating collaborative filtering recommender systems. *ACM Transaction on Information systems*, 22(1):5–53, 2004.

[16] T. Hofmann. Probabilistic latent semantic analysis. In *UAI '99*, pages 289–296, 1999.

[17] T. Hofmann. Collaborative filtering via gaussian probabilistic latent semantic analysis. In *SIGIR '03*, pages 259–266, 2003.

[18] T. Iwata, S. Watanabe, T. Yamada, and N. Ueda. Topic tracking model for analyzing consumer purchase behavior. In *IJCAI '09*, pages 1427–1432, 2009.

[19] X. Jin, Y. Zhou, and B. Mobasher. Web usage mining based on probabilistic latent semantic analysis. In *KDD '04*, pages 197–205, 2004.

[20] T. Kurashima, T. Iwata, G. Irie, and K. Fujimura. Travel route recommendation using geotags in photo sharing sites. In *CIKM '10*, pages 579–588, 2010.

[21] K. W. T. Leung, D. L. Lee, and W. C. Lee. CLR: a collaborative location recommendation framework based on co-clustering. In *SIGIR '11*, pages 305–314, 2011.

[22] D. C. Liu and J. Nocedal. On the limited memory BFGS method for large scale optimization. *Mathematical Programming*, 45(3):503–528, 1989.

[23] A. Monreale, F. Pinelli, R. Trasarti, and F. Giannotti. WhereNext: a location predictor on trajectory pattern mining. In *KDD '09*, pages 637–646, 2009.

[24] F. Ricci and Q. N. Nguyen. Acquiring and revising preferences in a critique-based mobile recommender system. *IEEE Intelligent Systems*, 22(3):22–29, 2007.

[25] R. Salakhutdinov and A. Mnih. Probabilistic matrix factorization. In *NIPS '08*, pages 1257–1264, 2008.

[26] Tabelog. http://tabelog.com/.

[27] TripAdvisor. http://www.tripadvisor.com/.

[28] M. van Setten, S. Pokraev, and J. Koolwaaij. Context-aware recommendations in the mobile tourist application COMPASS. In *AH '04*, pages 235–244, 2004.

[29] yelp. http://www.yelp.com/.

[30] J. Yuan, Y. Zheng, and X. Xie. Discovering regions of different functions in a city using human mobility and POIs. In *KDD '12*, pages 186–194, 2012.

[31] ZAGAT.com. http://www.zagat.com/.

[32] V. W. Zheng, Y. Zheng, X. Xie, and Q. Yang. Collaborative location and activity recommendations with GPS history data. In *WWW '10*, pages 1029–1038, 2010.

[33] Y. Zheng, L. Zhang, Z. Ma, X. Xie, and W. Y. Ma. Recommending friends and locations based on individual location history. *ACM Transactions on the Web*, 5(1), 2011.

[34] Y. Zheng, L. Zhang, X. Xie, and W. Y. Ma. Mining interesting locations and travel sequences from GPS trajectories. In *WWW '09*, pages 791–800, 2009.

Latent Factor Models with Additive and Hierarchically-smoothed User Preferences

Amr Ahmed *
Google Inc.
amra@google.com

Bhargav Kanagal*
Google Inc.
bhargav@google.com

Sandeep Pandey*
Twitter
spandey@twitter.com

Vanja Josifovski*
Google Inc.
vanjaj@google.com

Lluis Garcia Pueyo*
Google Inc.
lgpueyo@google.com

Jeff Yuan
Yahoo! Research
yuanjef@yahoo-inc.com

ABSTRACT

Items in recommender systems are usually associated with annotated attributes such as brand and price for products; agency for news articles, etc. These attributes are highly informative and must be exploited for accurate recommendation. While learning a user preference model over these attributes can result in an interpretable recommender system and can hands the cold start problem, it suffers from two major drawbacks: data sparsity and the inability to model *random effects*. On the other hand, latent-factor collaborative filtering models have shown great promise in recommender systems; however, its performance on rare items is poor. In this paper we propose a novel model LFUM, which provides the advantages of both of the above models. We learn user preferences (over the attributes) using a personalized *Bayesian* hierarchical model that uses a combination (*additive model*) of a globally learned preference model along with user-specific preferences. To combat data-sparsity, we smooth these preferences over the item-taxonomy using an efficient forward-filtering and backward-smoothing inference algorithm. Our inference algorithms can handle both discrete attributes (e.g., item brands) and continuous attributes (e.g., item prices). We combine the user preferences with the latent-factor models and train the resulting collaborative filtering system end-to-end using the successful BPR ranking algorithm. In our extensive experimental analysis, we show that our proposed model outperforms several commonly used baselines and we carry out an ablation study showing the benefits of each component of our model.

Categories and Subject Descriptors

G.3 [**Probability And Statistics**]: Statistical Computing; I.2.6 [**Computing Methodologies**]: Artificial Intelligence-Learning

General Terms

Algorithms, Experimentation, Performance

*The work was performed at Yahoo! Research.

WSDM'13, February 4–8, 2013, Rome, Italy.

Keywords

Recommendation, Latent Variable Models, Collaborative Filtering, Inference, Factor Models

1. INTRODUCTION

Personalized recommender systems are ubiquitous with applications to computational advertising, content suggestions, e-commerce and search engines. These systems use the past behavior of users to recommend items to them that are likely to be of interest. Significant advancements have been made in recent years to improve the accuracy of such personalized recommendation systems and to scale the algorithms to large amount of data.

One of the most extensively used techniques in these recommendation systems is the latent factor model and its variants [2, 13, 14, 16] (see Koren et al. [15] for an excellent survey). The key idea behind latent factor models is to project the users and items into a smaller dimensional space (such lower dimensional projections are called *factors*), thereby clustering similar users and items. Subsequently, the interest (similarity) of a user to an unrated item is measured and the most similar item(s) is recommended to the user. While factor models have been very successful with the Netflix contest top performers [5, 13] and tag recommendation [19] being some of the success stories, these models have certain shortcomings. Much of these techniques do not take into account, the auxiliary information that is typically associated with items. In most domains, the items being recommended have a rich set of attributes which are highly indicative of users' preferences, i.e., they determine the users' intent to purchase the item. For instance, in the movie recommendation application, there is information about the director, lead actor, duration of the movie, time of release, all of which play a significant role in the user selecting the movie. Movies that have reputed directors are usually chosen despite lack of user interest as modeled by a latent factor model. In the retail product recommendation, we have attributes such as the brand and price that determines user's interest in the product. The other disadvantage with this approach is that of sparsity, commonly referred to as the *cold-start* problem.

In order to leverage such auxiliary information, there has been a number of efforts to build content-based recommender systems [6]. While content-based approaches work well in the presence of cold-start, they are outperformed by the latent factor models in warm-start scenarios, i.e., when we have enough training data. Hybrid recommendation models [9, 8, 6] that combine collaborative and content information have been proposed to overcome this issue. However, as we will show in our experiments, these hybrid methods are expensive to to train and does not perform well when the

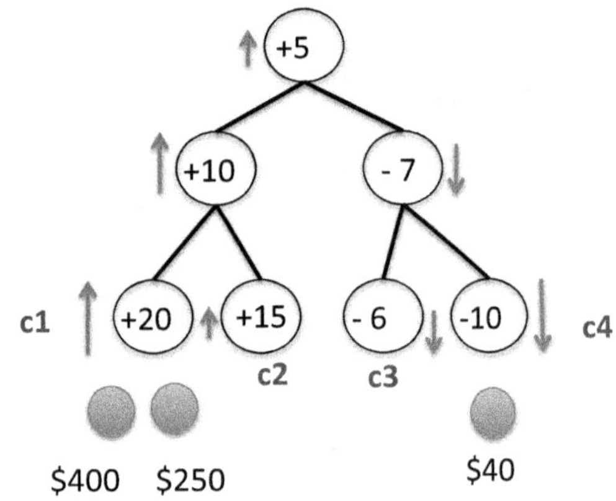

Figure 1: Illustrating the role of hierarchy and additive model in learning user preferences. Each internal node gives the user preferred mean price as an addition over the global mean price at the same node. The user bought items shaded at the leaves of the tree and our model inferred the number inside each internal node of the user's tree. See Section 3.1 for more details.

attributes of the items live in a very high-dimensional space. Furthermore, it is not easy to augment these hybrid models with additional background information, such as a taxonomy over items.

In this paper we propose the LFUM (Latent Factor augmented with User preferences Model) which combines latent factor models along with a user preference models for improving personalization in recommendation. A key to our model is that we capture the user preferences over each of the item attributes, using an addition of a global preference model and a per-user personalized preference model. We smooth these user preferences over a *taxonomy* of the items, to alleviate the aforementioned sparsity problem. Taxonomies are commonly available for many domains [1, 12]. For example, consider the price attribute: Suppose that Alice bought an expensive laptop. In this case, our model can learn that Alice buys `electronics` items at a price $200 more than the global average. The preferences in our model are learned using a *hierarchical additive* model. We develop an efficient forward filtering, backward-smoothing algorithm over the taxonomy. Continuing with the above example, if Alice buys expensive electronics, then that increases the likelihood that she would purchase an expensive phone (even though she has not purchased any phone). We support both discrete-valued (e.g., brand) and continuous-valued (e.g., price) attributes. For continuous variables, we extend the well known Kalman filtering/smoothing [11] algorithm to multiple interacting hierarchies using an additive model. Furthermore, we combine these user preferences with a latent factor model and optimize an efficient lower bound on the joint objective function using the Bayesian personalized ranking algorithm of Rendle et al. [18]. We apply LFUM to the real world problem of *smart ad* selection for Display advertising and demonstrate significant improvements in the recommendation accuracy using our approaches.

Outline: The rest of this paper is organized as follows. First in Section 2 we establish notations, formalize the problem and review relevant background. Then in Section 3 we describe detail our model. In Section 4 we give an efficient inference algorithm and in Section 5-6 we show a comprehensive evaluation of our model against several baseline. Section 7 covers related work and we conclude in Section 8.

2. PRELIMINARIES

In this Section we provide background for the various concepts in the paper. We begin with the notations used in the paper and explain commonly used recommender systems in the literature, namely latent factor models and hybrid recommender systems.

2.1 Notations

Let $\mathcal{I}$ be a set of items and $\mathcal{U}$ be a set of users. For each $u \in \mathcal{U}$, we let $\mathcal{I}_u$ denote the set of items the user interacted with (ex. purchased before). Each item $I \in \mathcal{I}$ is described by a set of continuous (such as price) and discrete (such as brand) attributes. We let $I.x$ denote a continuous attribute of I and $x \in \mathcal{X}$, where $\mathcal{X}$ is the set of continuous attributes. Similarly, we let $I.y$ denote a discrete attribute of I for $y \in \mathcal{Y}$, where $\mathcal{Y}$ is the set of discrete attributes. In addition, each item is associated with a category. We use $\pi(I)$ to denote the category of item I. The categories themselves are arranged in a tree-like taxonomy (or a hierarchy). For a given node in the tree, say n, we abuse notation a a bit, and we let $\pi(n)$ denote the parent of node n in the tree, and $\mathcal{I}_n$ denotes the children of node n. If n is a leaf category, then $\mathcal{I}_n$ is a set of items, and if n is an internal node, then $\mathcal{I}_n$ is a set of subcategories. We let L denote the depth of the tree, where the root is at level 0 and the leaf categories are at level $L-1$. We also use $T(n)$ to denote the subtree rooted at node n. Our goal is to learn user preferences over attributes for each category in the tree and subsequently, use these preferences to augment a factor model, thereby improving recommendation of items to users.

2.2 Latent Factor Models

The input to a recommender system is a sparse (partially populated) user-item matrix where the entries correspond to an interaction between a user and an item – either in terms of a rating or a purchase. The goal of the recommender system is to predict, for each user u, a ranked list of items. We assume that each user u and item i can be represented by latent factors $\mathbf{v_u}$ and $\mathbf{v_i}$ respectively, which are vectors of size $1 \times K$. User u's affinity/interest in item i (denoted by z_{ui}) is assumed to follow this model:

$$z_{ui} = \langle \mathbf{v_u}, \mathbf{v_i} \rangle$$

The learning problem here is to determine the best values for $\mathbf{v_u}$ and $\mathbf{v_i}$ (for all users u and all items i) based on the given rating matrix; we denote these parameters by Γ. While traditional approaches to matrix factorization try to regress over the known entries of the matrix, a more successful approach is the recently proposed Bayesian personalized ranking (BPR) [18]. Here, the trick is to do regression directly over the *ranks* of the items, rather than the actual ratings since the goal is to construct ranked lists. Also, we only have *implicit feedback* from the users (i.e., we will have a rating between 1 to 5, but only know that the user made a purchase). In this case, regression over the actual numbers of purchases is not meaningful. The main objective in BPR is to discriminate between items bought by the user from those that were not bought. In other words, we need to learn a ranking function R_u for each user u that ranks u's interesting items higher than the non-interesting items. In other words, if item i appears in user u's purchase list B_u and item j does not appear in B_u, then we must have $R_u(i) > R_u(j)$. For this, we need to have: $z_{ui} > z_{uj}$. Based on the above arguments, our likelihood function $p(R_u|\Gamma)$ is:

$$p(R_u|\Gamma) = \prod_{u \in U} \prod_{i \in B_u} \prod_{j \notin B_u} \sigma(z_{ui} - z_{uj})$$

Following Rendle et al. [18], we approximate the non-smooth, non-differentiable expression $z_{ui} > z_{uj}$ using the logistic sigmoid function $\sigma(z_{ui} - z_{uj})$, where $\sigma(z) = \frac{1}{1+e^{-z}}$. We use a Gaussian prior $N(0, \sigma)$

over all the factors in Γ and compute the MAP (maximum a posteriori) estimate of Γ. The posterior over Γ (which needs to be maximized) is given by:

$$\begin{aligned} p(\Gamma|R_u) &= p(\Gamma)p(R_u|\Gamma) \\ &= p(\Gamma)\prod_{u\in U}\prod_{i\in B^u}\prod_{j\notin B_u}\sigma(z_{ui}-z_{uj}) \end{aligned}$$

2.3 Hybrid Recommender Systems

As described in Section 1, hybrid recommender systems [6] combine latent factor models along with the content-based approaches based on user and item features. Much of the approaches work by first fitting a regression function over the item features against the target feedback and subsequently modeling the residual with a latent factor model. We can represent hybrid recommender systems in our context using the following affinity expression.

$$z_{ij} = \langle v_u, v_i\rangle + \sum_{x\in\mathcal{X}} W_x i.x + \sum_{y\in\mathcal{Y}} W_y i.y$$

The first term in the expression corresponds to the traditional latent factor model. In the second term, W_x denotes the weights for each of the discrete attribute set $\mathcal{X}$ (Note that we abuse notation slightly: $i.x$ corresponds to the value of attribute x of item i). Similarly, the third term corresponds to the weights learned over the continuous attributes. In practice, we can extend hybrid recommender systems to learn both the weights and the user/item factors simultaneously. However, such an approach is problematic in two aspects: First, the weights are learned over all the users, thus we cannot model user personalization. Further more, we cannot learn per user weights owing to the sparsity of the data. In addition, it is unclear how to learn weights for the continuous attributes without discretizing them and as such introducing additional noise. In the next section we will introduce our LFUM which addresses these problems in a principled way.

3. AUGMENTED LATENT FACTOR MODELS: LFUM

This section describes our proposed approach, a Latent Factor augmented with a User preference Model (LFUM). We will begin by first describing the intuition behind the model and then give a formal description. Our model is a hybrid model that combines the observed item attributes with a latent factor model. However, our model is novel since it doesn't learn a regression function over item attributes but rather learn a user-specific probability distribution over item attributes. Let us define $q_x(i.x|u)$ to be the probability that user u likes item i based on item's i value of attribute x. We abuse notation slightly and write $q_x^u(i.x)$ to denote $q_x(i.x|u)$. One could imagine that we can combine these probabilities for each attributed and learn a linear function that predicts the user affinity to each item. However, the observed attributes might not be enough to explain why the user would buy item i instead of item j. For example, the user might prefer item i over item j based on an attribute that is not observed (for instance, the shape or the color of the item). Therefore, we define $P(R_u|\Gamma, q)$ to denote the *ranking* probabilities for user i. As we made explicit in this probability, the raking depends on q and is parameterized by a set of parameters Γ to be defined later. Our goal thus is to solve the following optimization problem:

$$\begin{aligned} &\max_{\Gamma}\prod_u P(R_u|\Gamma) \\ =\ &\max_{\Gamma}\int_q P(q)\prod_u P(R_u|\Gamma, q)dq \qquad (1) \end{aligned}$$

where $q = \{q_x(.)\}_{x\in\mathcal{X}} \cup \{q_y(.)\}_{y\in\mathcal{Y}}$, is the product probability of all item attributes. In essence, Eq (1) treats q as a *hidden variable* and integrates over it to define the marginal observed rankings for all users. There are several advantages to treating q as a hidden variable: 1) it makes it easier to combine continuous and discrete attributes (with varying cardinalities) as we map each attribute's contribution into a number between [0,1]; 2) treating q as a probability distribution opens the door for using several hierarchical smoothing that combats data sparsity and allows us to introduce regularization in a principled way. To fully define our model we need to answer the following three questions:

1. How to define q for both discrete and continuous attributes?
2. How to define $P(R_u|\Gamma, q)$?
3. How to optimize the seemingly intractable objective function in Eq (1)?

In the following two subsections, we will answer the first two questions and then in Section 4, we will tackle the third question.

3.1 User Preference Models

3.1.1 *The Intuition: Background Subtraction*

Before delving into the technical details of the generative process, we begin by giving an overview of our model. Let us assume that items represent products, and that we have only one continuous attribute (price of the item), and one discrete attribute (brand of the item). Moreover, let the nodes in the taxonomy represent product categories. Let us first consider preferences over item prices. Given the items purchased in the dataset, one could postulate that there is a global (across-users) average price for each category, this is not the average price of items under the category, but rather the average price of the *actual purchases* of items under the category. For example, under the category `smart phones`, the average price of phones purchased by the users is say \$200 even though the average price of the distinct phones might be much higher (or lower). However, this modeling assumption is rather inadequate as it ignores user personalized preferences over the category. To remedy that, we could hypothesize that users' personal preferences can be modeled as an addition over the global preference. For example, a user might be more inclined to buy expensive smart phones and as such her mean price over this category is above the category's global mean price. Similarly, another user might have a mean price that is much smaller than the global mean price, i.e. she prefers to buy the cheapest smart phones. Therefore, we can look at the global price of a given category as the average across all users, and we can model each user's preferences as an addition over it (either positive or negative).

However there is a problem with this approach as it ignores the taxonomy. It is quite natural to assume that both the global and personalized preferences are smooth over the taxonomy. This has the advantage of combating data sparsity. To see this point, we refer the reader to Figure 1. This figure depicts the preferences of a given user over the prices of different categories. In this figure, we observed two purchases of this user under category $c1$ and we deduced from them, that under category $c1$, the user's average price is above the global average price. Moreover, we observed a single purchase from this user under category $c4$ and we concluded that the user prefers inexpensive items under this category (i.e the user average price is below the global average price). However, what can we say about the user's preferences over categories $c2$ and $c3$? Intuitively we expect $c2$ to follow the same pattern as $c1$ and $c3$ to follow the same pattern as $c4$. However, the exact deviations from the global mean prices depend on two factors: First, how confident

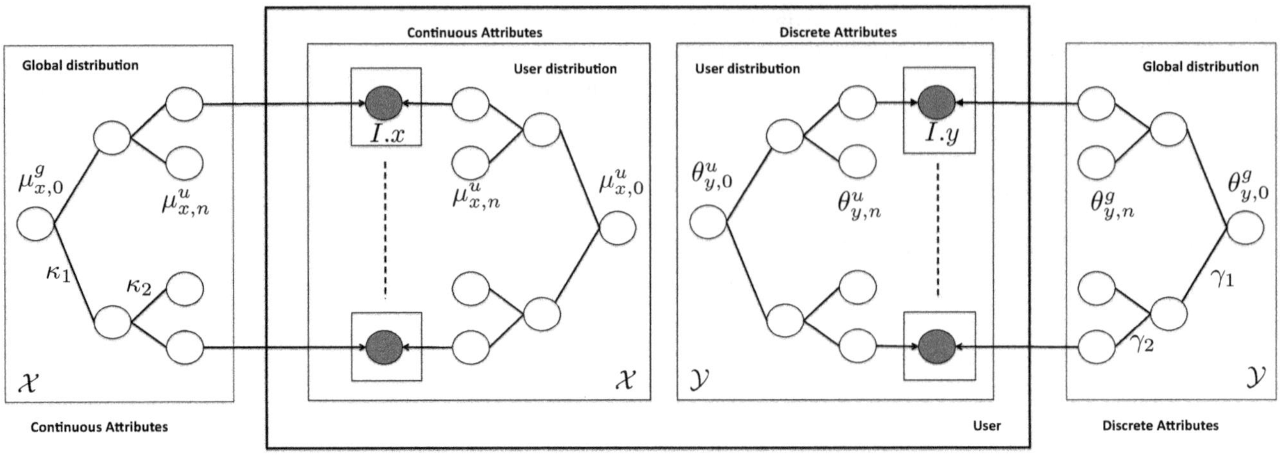

Figure 2: The graphical model, see text for more details, Section 2 for notations and Algorithm 1 for the full generative process

we are about our estimate for $c1$ and $c4$ and second, the variance of prices over the tree (we will formalize these notions in the generative process shortly). However, the main message of this figure is that given a few observations about each user, we could still have a hypothesis about each user's preferences over *all* the categories in the tree. Informally, this is possible, since we can pool data across users to create hypotheses about the global preferences and then use these hypotheses to draw conclusions about each user (a process called smoothness – Section 4).

The same intuition applies also to discrete attributes such as the brand of the item. Given all purchases, one could form a global brand preference over each category and then use it as a prior over the preferences of each user. This process is known in the literature as smoothness with a background model. However, this process alone does not achieve smoothness over close-by nodes in the taxonomy. For example, let us assume that a user bought an iPhone, i.e a smart phone with "Apple" as the brand. Since smart phone is a subcategory of "electronic gadget", we could infer that this user prefers to also buy other "Apple" products under other subcategories of "electronic gadgets", such as "laptops" for instance. However, if we don't observe any purchase from the user under the "electronic gadgets" category, we might *shrink* our estimate of the user's preferences over "electronic gadgets" to the global distribution. We will see that our model achieves this property using an additive model as we detail below.

3.1.2 The Generative Model

Armed with the above intuitions, we are now ready to detail the generative process with reference to Figure 2 and Algorithm 1. For a continuous attribute x, we let $\mu^g_{x,n}$ denotes the global mean value of this attribute at node n in the taxonomy. We connect those means over the tree using a Gaussian-cascade process, where each node's value acts as the mean of a normal distribution that is used to generate the children of node n. Put it another way, the mean of node n is generated from a normal distribution centered at the mean value of its parent in the tree. The variance of this normal distribution depends on the level of the node n, and we denote it as $\kappa_{Level(n)}$. We expect the variance to be high for levels close to the root and small for levels close to the leaf categories. Similarly, for each user, we let $\mu^u_{x,n}$ denotes user u's deviation at node n from the global mean at the same node. Again we connect those user-specific deviations over the tree using a Gaussian-Cascade process with the same variances used in the global process. We use the same variances since estimating a user-specific variance is prone to over-fitting. Moreover, those variances act as priors and during inference we compute a posterior value for each user based on his observations (see Section 4.1). Finally, for each user, we observe a set of purchased items under each leaf category (depicted as shaded nodes in Figure 2 and as I^u_n in the generative process, i.e. item purchased by

Algorithm 1 Description of the generative model

Require: set of users U , set of items I
Generate global preferences:
for all $x \in \mathcal{X}$ // *Continuous Attributes* **do**
  for all categories n starting from the root downward: **do**
    Draw $\mu^g_{x,n} \sim N(\mu^g_{s,\pi(n)}, \kappa_{\text{Level}(n)})$
  end for
end for
for all $y \in \mathcal{Y}$ // *Discrete Attributes:* **do**
  for all categories n starting from the root downward: **do**
    Draw $\theta^g_{y,n} \sim \text{Dir}(\gamma_{\text{Level}(n)}\theta^g_{y,\pi(n)})$
  end for
end for
Generate User Preferences
for all $u \in \mathcal{U}$ **do**
  for all $x \in \mathcal{X}$ // *Continuous Attributes* **do**
    for all categories n starting from the root downward: **do**
      Draw $\mu^u_{x,n} \sim N(\mu^u_{x,\pi(n)}, \sigma_{\text{Level}(n)})$
    end for
  end for
  for all $y \in \mathcal{Y}$ // *Discrete Attributes:* **do**
    for all categories n starting from the root downward: **do**
      Draw $\theta^u_{y,n} \sim \text{Dir}(\gamma_{\text{Level}(n)}\theta^u_{y,\pi(n)})$
    end for
  end for
  Generate Attributes of Items the user interacted with
  for all $i \in \mathcal{I}_u$ **do**
    for all $x \in \mathcal{X}$ **do**
      $i.x \sim N(\mu^g_{x,\pi(i)} + \mu^u_{x,\pi(i)}, \kappa_L)$
    end for
    for all $y \in \mathcal{Y}$ **do**
      $i.y \sim \text{Multinomial}(\theta^u_{y,\pi(i)} + \gamma_L\theta^g_{y,\pi(i)})$
    end for
  end for
end for

the user under leaf category n). The final step in the generative process is to generate the attributes of those items from a normal distribution centered at the sum of the global mean and the user-specific deviation under each category (step 27). The variance of this distribution is κ_L where L is the depth of the tree (recall that the leaf categories, which are the parents of the items, appear at level $L-1$ in the tree) . We should note here that the item attributes are not user specific, however, we still generate them for each user but rather from a different user-specific distribution. This is the key step that allows the model to connect global means with each user local mean as we will see during posterior inference. Put in another way, the item attributes acts as constraints that forces the model during inference to factor the observed prices into a global and user-specific components.

We model the discrete attributes of the items in a similar fashion but with a Dirichlet-Multinomial cascade instead (step 7-11 for the global distributions and 19-23 for the user specific distributions). Recall that the Dirichlet is the conjugate prior for the Multinomial distribution. Usually a Dirichlet distribution is specified as $Dir(\rho)$ for a given parameter vector ρ, thus the mean and variance of the sampled multinomials depend on ρ. A more expressive way of specifying a Dirichlet distribution is as $Dir(\gamma\theta)$, here γ acts as the variance and θ acts as the mean. The higher the value of γ the less the variance of the distribution. We use this representation to connect nodes over the taxonomy as the case of the Gaussian distribution with θ playing the role of μ and γ playing the role of κ (see steps 9 and 21). We expect γ to be small for nodes close to the root (to give high variances) and high for nodes close to the leaf (to give small variances). Finally to generate the discrete attributes of items purchased by a user, we use an additive model that combines the global and local distributions of the item's category (step 30). In this case, we weight the global preference by a scalar value γ_L which specifies how much the user preference can deviate from the global distribution (this plays the same role as κ_L in step 27).

3.2 Item Ranking: $P(R_u|\Gamma, q)$

How can we use the learned user preferences to perform recommendation? In other words, how can we define the item preference ranking probabilities, $P(q)\prod_u P(R_u|\Gamma, q)$? Using the principle of BPR, we first let z_{ui} denotes user u's affinity towards item i and we define it as follows:

$$z_{ui} = \sum_{x\in\mathcal{X}} \alpha_x q_x^u(i.x) + \sum_{y\in\mathcal{Y}} \beta_y q_y^u(i.y) + \epsilon_{ui} \tag{2}$$

where α and β are attribute-specific weights that determine the importance of this attribute in computing the affinity. The preference probability is computed as follows:

$$q_x^u(i.x) = N(\mu_{x,\pi(i)}^g + \mu_{x,\pi(i)}^u, \kappa_L) \tag{3}$$

$$q_y^u(i.y) = \text{Multinomial}(\theta_{y,\pi(i)}^g + \gamma_L \theta_{y,\pi(i)}^u)) \tag{4}$$

The final component in computing z_{ui} is thus ϵ_{ui} which is a random noise that accounts for interactions not explained by the observed attributes (which is termed as a random effect model in the statistics literature [10]). We model ϵ_{ui} using a latent factor model as follows:

$$\epsilon_{ui} =< v_u, v_i > \tag{5}$$

where $<.,.>$ denotes dot product and $v_u \in \mathcal{R}^K$ is the user factor and $v_i \in \mathcal{R}^K$ is the item factor. The parameters of this system are:

$\Gamma = \{\alpha_x\}_{x\in\mathcal{X}}, \{\beta_y\}_{y\in\mathcal{Y}}, \{v_u\}_{u\in\mathcal{U}}$ and $\{v_i\}_{i\in\mathcal{I}}$.

4. PARAMETER LEARNING

We seek to optimize the following objective function:

$$\max_\Gamma \int_q P(q) \prod_u P(R_u|\Gamma, q)dq$$

However, this objective integrates over the space of all probability distributions, which makes the optimization intractable. To remedy this, we instead optimize the following variational lower bound:

$$\max_\Gamma \int_q P(q) \prod_u P(R_u|\Gamma, q)dq \tag{6}$$

$$\geq \max_\Gamma \prod_u P(R_u|\Gamma, \hat{q}) \tag{7}$$

where $\hat{q}$ is the map estimate of q, i.e., the best distribution q that explains the user preferences over the item attributes. The above lower bound gives rise to the following simple algorithm. First learn the map estimate of q using the observed attributes of the items bought by each user, and then use $\hat{q}$ to learn the value of Γ that best explains the item rankings by each user, R_u. We will tackle each of these problems in the following sections.

4.1 Posterior Inference of Preferences

Given a set of user-item interactions, the goal is to learn a posterior distribution over q, $\hat{q}$. This is equivalent to learning the posterior values of the global parameters μ^g, θ^g and the posterior values of the user specific parameters μ^u, θ^u. We address the continuous case in Section 4.1.1 and the discrete case in Section 4.1.2.

4.1.1 The Continuous Case

Let $\mathcal{I}_u$ be the set of items purchased by a given user, and let $\mathcal{I}_g$ the set of all purchased items by all users. Our goal is to compute $P(\mu_x^g|\mathcal{I}_g)$ and $P(\mu_x^u|\mathcal{I}_g, \mathcal{I}_u)$ for all users u and for all attributes x, where $\mu_x^g = (\mu_0^g, \mu_1^g, \cdots, \mu_N^g)$, and $\mu_x^u = (\mu_0^u, \mu_1^u, \cdots, \mu_N^u)$, where N is the total number of nodes in the taxonomy. We give below the inference algorithm for a given attribute x, thus the following algorithm is repeated for each attribute separately.

The problem of this posterior computation is the dependencies between μ_x^g and μ_x^u for all $u \in \mathcal{U}$ because of the additive form of the observation model (Step 27 in Algorithm 1). Therefore we resort to an **alternating algorithm** similar to loopy belief propagation, that computes each of these quantities conditioned on the other. Lets first assume that we know μ_g^x. Thus conditioning on μ_x^g, the inference problem over user's means **decouples** into a set of $|\mathcal{U}|$ independent problems. For user u, we just need to compute $P(\mu_x^u|\mathcal{I}_u, \mu_x^g)$. Once we compute this quantity for all users, we alternate and compute $P(\mu_x^g|\mathcal{I}_g, \{\mu_x^u\}_{u\in\mathcal{U}})$. We **repeat this alternating procedure** until convergence, where convergence is assessed by measuring changes in the value of μ_x^g. The algorithm is summarized below:

1. Repeat
   (a) $\forall u \in \mathcal{U}$:
      i. Compute $P(\mu_x^u|\mathcal{I}_u, \mu_x^g)$.
   (b) Compute $P(\mu_x^g|\mathcal{I}_g, \{\mu_x^u\}_{u\in\mathcal{U}})$
2. Until convergence.

We focus here first on $P(\mu_x^u|\mathcal{I}_u, \mu_x^g)$. This inference problem is known in the literature as multi-scale Kalman filter [11], albeit with a **shifted observations** here. Recall that the value of the x attribute of all items I in $\mathcal{I}_u$ are generated from a normal distribution with mean $= \mu^g_{x,\pi(I)} + \mu^u_{x,\pi(I)}$. Since we hold μ^g_x fixed, this is equivalent to generating the values $I.x - \mu^g_{x,\pi(I)}$ for all $I \in \mathcal{I}_u$ form the leaf categories of the user tree $\mu^u_{x,\pi(I)}$, which is exactly the posterior inference problem addressed by the multi-scale KF algorithm [11].

The multi-scale KF algorithm [11] proceeds in two stages: upward phase (from the leafs to the root) and downward phase (from the root to leaf). The upward phase is known as the filtering phase. In this phase we compute the posterior probability of each node conditioned on its immediate children. Once we reach the root of the tree, the root has now received information from all nodes in the tree, and we move to the second downward phase known as the smoothing phase. In this phase, we propagate information down the tree to get the posterior mean of each node conditioned on the whole tree (not only its children). The recursive equations for both phases are given below in the following two subsections and interested readers can refer to [11] for more details. We first define the following quantities used by both the forward and backward phase:

$$\Psi_n = \sum_{i=1}^{\text{Level}(n)} \kappa_i \tag{8}$$

$$F_n = \Psi_{\text{Level}(n)-1}\left[\Psi_{\text{Level}(n)}\right]^{-1}$$

where Ψ_n is the prior variance of node n and F is the prior covariance between the mean of node n and its parent.

Filtering: upward phase

We begin at node n at level $L-1$ on the tree. The children of this node are the shifted attributes of the items purchased by the user under category n, $\mathcal{I}_{u,n}$. We compute the probability of this node based on those children, $P(\mu^u_{x,n}|\mu^g_{x,n}, \mathcal{I}_{u,n}) = N(\phi^u_{x,n}, \sigma^u_{x,n})$, where ϕ, σ are given as follows:

$$\sigma^u_{x,n} = \frac{\Psi_n \kappa_L}{\kappa_L + |\mathcal{I}_{u,n}|\Psi_n} \tag{9}$$

$$\phi^u_{x,n} = \frac{\sigma^u_{x,n}}{\kappa_L} \sum_{I \in \mathcal{I}_{u,n}} I.x - \hat{\mu}^g_{x,n} \tag{10}$$

We repeat the above computations for all nodes n at Level $L-1$. We then move one level at a time upward computing $P(\mu^u_{x,n}|\mu^g_{x,n}, \mathcal{I}_{u,T(n)}) = N(\phi^u_{x,n}, \sigma^u_{x,n})$ for each node n at levels $L-2, L-3, \cdots, 0$ as follows, where $T(n)$ is the tree rooted at node n as defined in Section 2:

- For all nodes $m \in \mathcal{I}_n$. i.e. the children of node n under consideration, compute the following:

$$\phi^u_{x,n|m} = F_m \phi^u_{x,m} \tag{11}$$

$$\sigma^u_{x,n|m} = F^2_m \sigma^u_{x,m} + F_m \kappa_{\text{level}(m)} \tag{12}$$

  where the above computes the filtering probability of node n conditioned on child m only (denoted by $n|m$ above).
- Now combine those estimates to find the filtering probability of node n based on all of its children as follows:

$$\sigma^u_{x,n} = \left[\Psi_n^{-1} + \sum_{m \in \mathcal{I}_n} [\sigma^u_{x,n|m}]^{-1} - \Psi_n{}^{-1}\right]^{-1} \tag{13}$$

$$\phi^u_{x,n} = \sigma^u_{x,n} \sum_{m \in \mathcal{I}_n} \phi^u_{x,n|m} [\sigma^u_{x,n|m}]^{-1} \tag{14}$$

Smoothing: downward phase

The recurrence in the upward phase ends at the root of the tree. and we now have the posterior probability of root itself from the filtering phase, that is $\hat{\mu}^u_{x,0} = \phi^u_{x,0}$ and $\hat{\sigma}^u_{x,0} = \sigma^u_{x,0}$, where we note that the posterior probability of each node n in the tree is distributed as $N(\hat{\mu}^u_{x,n}, \hat{\sigma}^u_{x,n})$. Now we propagate this information down the tree computing the posterior probability of each node n by combining the filtering probabilities from its children, with the smoothed probability from its parent as follows:

$$\hat{\mu}^u_{x,n} = \phi^u_{x,n} + \sigma^u_{x,n} F_n \left[\hat{\mu}^u_{x,\pi(n)} - \mu^u_{x,\pi(n)|n}\right]\left[\sigma^u_{x,\pi(n)|n}\right]^{-1} \tag{15}$$

$$\hat{\sigma}^u_{x,n} = \sigma^u_{x,n} + \sigma^u_{x,n}{}^2 F_n{}^2 \left[\hat{\sigma}^u_{x,\pi(n)} - \sigma^u_{x,\pi(n)|n}\right]\left[\sigma^u_{x,\pi(n)|n}\right]^{-2} \tag{16}$$

where the quantities $\pi(n)|n$ are those computed in the upward phase (Eq 11,12).

The above concludes the multi-scale Kalman Filtering Algorithm. It scales linearly with the number of nodes in the tree and as such it is efficient. Once we compute the smoothed posterior values for each user, we now repeat the same algorithm but over the global tree. The equation remains exactly the same, except that Eq 9 and 10 become:

$$\sigma^g_{x,n} = \frac{\Psi_n \kappa_L}{\kappa_L + |\mathcal{I}_{g,n}|\Psi_n} \tag{17}$$

$$\phi^g_{x,n} = \frac{\sigma^g_{x,n}}{\kappa_L} \sum_{u \in \mathcal{U}} \sum_{I \in \mathcal{I}_{u,n}} I.x - \hat{\mu}^u_{x,n} \tag{18}$$

which means that the observation to the global tree are shifted by each user's smoothed posterior mean. The rest of the steps of the upward and downward recurrences remains the same.

4.1.2 The Discrete Case

In this subsection we address the similar posterior problem addressed in the previous subsection but over discrete attributes. Our goal is to compute $P(\theta^g_{y,n}|\mathcal{I}_g)$ and $P(\theta^u_{y,n}|\mathcal{I}_g)$. We could use a similar alternating algorithm similar to the one described for the continuous case. At each step of this algorithm we run a Dirichlet-Multinomial algorithm called *Forward filtering, backward sampling* [20] and iterate it until convergence. However, this approach is expensive as it is slow to converge. Hence, we resort to an approximation algorithm due to [7] known as the maximum-path algorithm over trees. This algorithm proceeds in two phases as well: upward phases and downward phases. In the upward phase, we generate *pseudo* observations for internal nodes in the tree given the observations at their children. In the downward phase, we smooth each node's distribution with its parent. We give the algorithm below for the user specific distribution and then for the global distribution. Let $C^u_{y,n}$ be the counts of observed values of attribute y at node n. C is a vector whose components gives the observed counts for each possible value of y. For example, if y is the brand, then each component of C would contains the number of items purchases from this brand at node n. If n is a leaf category, then C is already observed.

- Upward phase: in which, we compute $C^u_{y,n}$ for all nodes n above the leaf category levels (at the leaf C is observed).

$$C^u_{y,n} = \sum_{m \in \mathcal{I}_n} C^u_{y,m} \tag{19}$$

  Which has the intuitive interpretation that $C^u_{y,n}$ is just the sum of the observed counts at the subtree rooted at node n.
- Downward phase: Once we reach the root in the upward phase, we compute the smoothed distribution of the root node as follows:

$$\hat{\theta}^u_{y,0} = \text{Normalize}(C^u_{y,0} + \gamma_0) \tag{20}$$

where Normalize just makes the input vector sums to one. We then proceed downward computing the smoothed distribution at all *internal* nodes as follows:

$$\hat{\theta}^u_{y,n} = \text{Normalize}(C^u_{y,n} + \gamma_{\text{Level}(n)}\hat{\theta}^u_{y,\pi(n)}) \quad (21)$$

The above algorithm computed the posterior over θ^u_y for each user and then we ran it again to compute the global distribution θ^g_y. The same equation above holds except that at the leaf categories $C^g_{y,n}$: for a leaf category n θ^g_y is computed using $\mathcal{I}_{g,n}$ which is the set of observed purchases from all users under category n. Finally, the posterior distribution used to predict how user u is likely to purchase an item under a leaf category n is computed using: $\text{Normalize}(C^u_{y,n} + \gamma_{\text{Level}(n)}\hat{\theta}^u_{y,\pi(n)} + \gamma_{\text{Level}(n)}\hat{\theta}^g_{y,n})$.

4.1.3 *Summary*

To summarize, given a set of continuous item attributes $\mathcal{X}$ and discrete item attributes $\mathcal{Y}$, our goal is to learn a user preference over each of them. This preference is learned as a distribution over those attributes. To combat sparsity, we parametric these distribution as an additive model of two parts: a global component which is shared across all the users, and a user-specific components that *shifts* the global component to personalize the distribution. We learn those two parts for each continuous and discrete attribute using upward-downward algorithms. In the case of continuous attributes, we use an iterative multi-scale Kalman algorithm until convergence. And in the discrete case we use a non-iterative two pass approximate algorithm. Each of these algorithms scales linearly with the number nodes of the tree. We noticed in practice that the iterative Kalman filtering algorithm converges in 5 to 10 iterations. While the output of these algorithm are useful by itself as we demonstrated in Figure 1, we use it as input to augment a latent-factor model to perform the end-end recommendations as we detail in the next subsection Finally, we treat the variances over the edges of the trees κ_i and γ_i as parameters and we estimate them using cross validation with regard to their effect of the end-end recommendation. To reduce the number of parameters we use the following parameterization :

$$\kappa_i = \frac{\kappa}{i} \qquad \gamma_i = \gamma * i \quad (22)$$

This parameterization implements our intuition that the variances of the parameters dimension as we go down the tree.

4.2 Learning Item Ranking Parameters: Γ

In this subsection, we describe how to find the Γ that maximizes $P(R|\Gamma, q)$. We decided to exploit recent advances in learning factorization models and rely on the so-called discriminative Bayesian personalized ranking (BPR) which has been shown to significantly outperform generative training [18].Based on Section 2, we seek to optimize the following log-likelihood function:

$$\begin{aligned} p(\Gamma|R_u, q) &= p(\Gamma)p(R_u|\Gamma, q) \quad (23) \\ &= p(\Gamma)\prod_{u\in U}\prod_{i\in\mathcal{I}_u}\prod_{j\notin\mathcal{I}_u} p(z_{ui} > z_{uj}|\Gamma, q) \end{aligned}$$

where, we approximate the non-smooth, non-differentiable expression $x_{ui} > x_{uj}$ using the logistic sigmoid function $\sigma(x_{ui} - x_{uj})$, where $\sigma(z) = \frac{1}{1+e^{-z}}$, which results in maximizing:

$$\sum_u \sum_{i\in\mathcal{I}_u} \sum_{j\notin\mathcal{I}_u} \ln\sigma(z_{ui} - z_{uj}) - \lambda||\Gamma||^2 \quad (24)$$

where, λ is the regularization constant which arise from a Gaussian prior over the parameters. and $||\Theta||^2$ is given by the following expression:

$$||\Gamma||^2 = \sum_u ||v_u||^2 + \sum_i ||v_u||^2 + \sum_{x\in\mathcal{X}} \alpha_x^2 + \sum_{y\in\mathcal{Y}} \beta_y^2$$

We use stochastic gradient descent to optimize the above function. At each iteration, we pick a triplet (u, i, j) where the user u bought item i and did not buy item j and define its associated loss $L(u, i, j)$ as follows:

$$\begin{aligned} L(u,i,j) &= \ln\sigma(z_{ui} - z_{uj}) - \lambda||\Gamma||^2 \\ &= \ln\sigma\Big[\langle v_u, v_i - v_j\rangle + \sum_{x\in\mathcal{X}} \alpha_x\big(q^u_x(i.x) - q^u_x(j.x)\big) \\ &+ \sum_{y\in\mathcal{Y}} \beta_y\big(q^u_y(i.y) - q^u_y(j.y)\big)\Big] - \lambda||\Gamma||^2 \end{aligned}$$

Now, we need to compute the gradients of $L(u, i, j)$ with respect to the parameters $\Gamma = \{v_u, v_i, v_j, \alpha_x, \beta_y\}$ and perform a gradient step over those parameters. It is quite straightforward to show that this would give rise to the following update rules:

$$\begin{aligned} v_u &= v_u + \rho\Big(c_{uij}(v_i - v_j) - \lambda v_u\Big) \\ v_i &= v_i + \rho\Big(c_{uij}v_u - \lambda v_i\Big) \\ v_j &= v_j + \rho\Big(-c_{uij}v_u - \lambda v_j\Big) \\ \alpha_x &= \alpha_x + \rho\Big(c_{uij}(q^u_x(i.x) - q^u_x(j.x)) - \lambda\alpha_x\Big) \\ \beta_x &= \beta_x + \rho\Big(c_{uij}(q^u_y(i.y) - q^u_y(j.y)) - \lambda\beta_y\Big) \end{aligned} \quad (25)$$

Where ρ is the learning rate and $c_{uij} = 1 - \sigma(z_{ui} - z_{uj})$. We iterate sampling a tuple and updating the parameters until convergence (we used 100 epochs, where each epoch is a pass over the training data).

4.2.1 *Hierarchical Extension: hLFUM*

Since we have access to a taxonomy over items, we can also constraint the item factors to be smooth over the taxonomy using an additive model as follows. Recall that items appear at level L in the taxonomy. We define v_i as follows:

$$v_i = \sum_{l=0}^{L} w_{\pi^l(i)} \quad (26)$$

where $\pi^l(i)$ is the lth parent of item i in the taxonomy. And w_n is a latent factor assigned to each internal node in the taxonomy. Thus for two sibling items i, i', they will share all the nodes starting from their parent up until the root, and as such only differ on $w_i, w_{i'}$ in the above summation and such $v_i, v_{i'}$ would become close to each other in the latent space. A similar additive model have been proposed before in [17]. The update rules in (25) for v_u, α_x, β_y remains the same using v_i defined in (26). A new update rule for w should be added and can be derived using the chain rule as follows:

$$\begin{aligned} w_{\pi^l(i)} &= w_{\pi^l(i)} + \rho\Big(c_{uij}v_u - \lambda w_{\pi^l(i)}\Big), l = 0, 1, \cdots L \\ w_{\pi^l(j)} &= w_{\pi^l(j)} + \rho\Big(-c_{uij}v_u - \lambda w_{\pi^l(j)}\Big), l = 0, 1, \cdots L \end{aligned}$$

which means that we update each weight on the path form the root to the item using the same gradient we used to update v_i in (25) before (this is easy to see from the chain rule over (26)).

5. EXPERIMENTAL SETUP

5.1 Dataset

To evaluate our proposed models, we used a log of user online transactions obtained from a major search engine, email provider and online shopping site and join it with a dataset of user conversion on display advertising where the ads correspond to products. The dataset contains information about the historical purchases of users over a period of 3 months and their response to display advertising Ads shown to them. We fully anonymize the users by dropping the original user identifier and assigning a new, sequential numbering of the records. For anonymity reasons, we report results over a sample of the above data. In the sample, we have about 40,000 users with average 2.3 purchases/ad response. We have 500,000 distinct individual products that are purchased/clicked upon in the dataset, which is mapped to a publicly available shopping taxonomy [1] which gives the price and the brand for each item as well. We use price as an example of a continuous attribute and brand as an example of a discrete attribute. The (resulting) taxonomy we use has about 1.5 million individual products in the leaf level organized into a taxonomy 3 levels deep, with around 1500 nodes at lowest level, 270 at the middle level and 23 top level categories. For each user, we select a transaction and mark all subsequent transactions/ad responses into the test dataset. All previous transactions/ ad responses are used for training. The last transaction/ad response in the training dataset is used for cross-validation and first transaction/ad response in the test dataset is used for prediction and reporting the error estimates.

5.2 Metrics

We use the AUC metric described below to compare our model with the baseline systems. AUC is a commonly used metric for testing the quality of rank orderings. Suppose the list of items to rank is X and our test transaction is B. Also suppose $r(x)$ is the numerical rank of the item x according to our model (from $1 \dots n$). Then, the formula to compute AUC is given by:

$$\frac{1}{|B||X \setminus B|} \sum_{x \in B, y \in X \setminus B} \delta(r(x) < r(y))$$

While we could have used an alternate metric such as precision/recall at a given rank in the list, it requires selecting a suitable rank value. In contrast, AUC combines the prediction performance over all ranks into a single number and is therefore convenient to use.

6. EVALUATION

In this subsection, we study the performance of our proposed model LFUM and compare it with several baselines. We user the following system for comparison:

- LFUM is the model proposed in this paper with NO taxonomy over the item factors.
- hLFUM is the model proposed in this paper with a taxonomy over the item factors.
- LF is a latent factor model. i..e uses no item attributes
- hLF is latent factor model with a taxonomy over the item factors.
- UM: is a user preference model only. That is no latent factors are used. We just train the smoothed user preferences. (i.e. we set ϵ_{ui} to zero)
- HybridLF: this is the hybrid LF model described in Section 2.3.

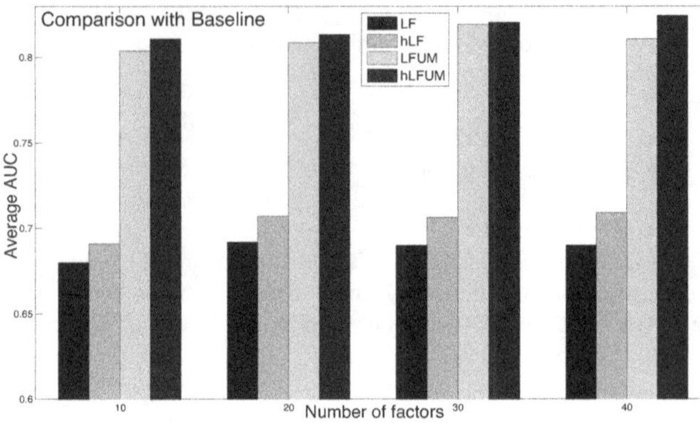

Figure 3: Comparing LFUM and hLFUM against several baselines along different number of factors

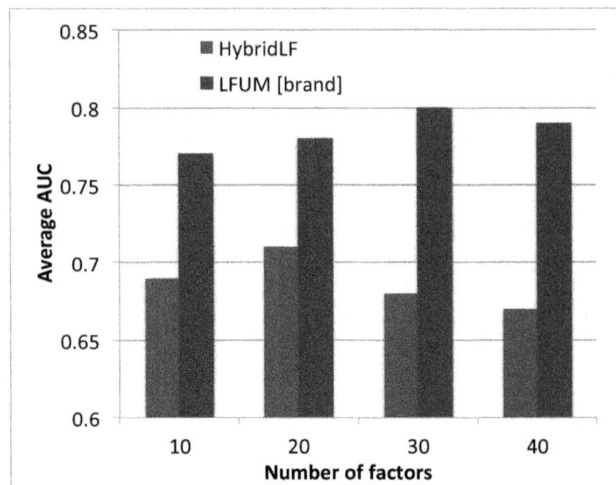

Figure 4: Comparing our approach LFUM with a fancier version of the standard hybridLF described in Section 2.3. The figure shows that our approach is more efficient in utilizing the extra information (brand in this case).

All models are trained using the BPR algorithm and all regularization parameters are tuned on a validation set.

6.1 Comparison to Baselines

in Figure 3 we compare LF, hLF, LFUM and hLFUM over different number of factors. As evident form the figure hLFUM and LFUM significantly outperformed models that ignore user preferences. Notice that LF does not use taxonomy in any way but hLF used taxonomy to constraint the item factors and combat sparsity. Nevertheless, hLF is till lagging even behind LFUM which does not impose a taxonomy constraint over the latent factors. It should be noted that both LFUM and hLFUM used taxonomy to smooth the user preferences, but only hLFUM used the taxonomy to smooth the item factors as well.

Second, we compare with the standard HybridLF model from Section 2.3. To make the comparison fair we only use the brand attribute to avoid introducing any bias in the result due to improper thresholding of the price attribute (note that our model does not need any such thresholding but we still use only the brand attribute in this experiment). The range of the brand attribute is 17K, thus we have $\mathcal{Y} = 17K$, since we need to add a binary variable for each brand. Furthermore, to make the HybridLF stronger, we stipulate that $W_y = W_y^u + W_y^0 + W_y^c$, i.e., we use an additive model to define W_y that combines user-specific weights with background

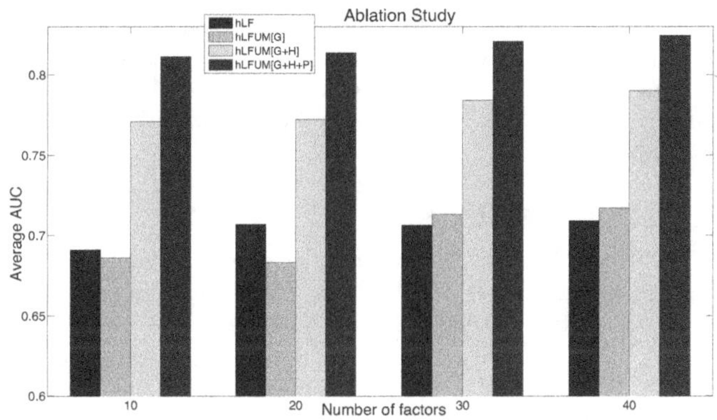

Figure 5: Studying the effect of the method used to learn user preferences on the final performance of our model. The figure shows that each part of our construction adds to the final result

weights W_y^0 and the item's category weights. We found that this form performed the best as opposed to using a global only weight vector, W_y^0, or a user-specific only weight vector, W_y^u. The results are shown in Figure 4. As evident, our model outperforms that baseline which confirms that our approach does not suffer from attributes with high cardinalities and that our model makes better use of the item attributes.

6.2 Ablation Study

In this subsection we study the contribution of each part of our model to understand the source of our improvement over the baselines. In Figure 5, we first study the smoothness effect over the user preference models. We parameterize LFUM and hLFUM with the the technique used to compute the user preferences over items as follows:

- G: means that we ignore the user specific distribution and the hierarchy and only compute the global preferences over each leaf category individually and use it for all users.
- G+H: same as G but we in addition we use the tree to smooth the computation of the global preferences over item attributes. However , no user personalization is used.
- G+H+P: is the full model described in Section 3 where the preferences are computed using an additive process smoothed over the taxonomy.

We compare these configurations against a hLF model by varying the number of factors. As obvious from this figure using only the global preference with no smoothing results in minimal improvement and sometime even degrade performance for small number of factors. As the number of factors increases, the model learned to user the extra factor to counter that detrimental effect. However, smoothing those global preference over the tree improves the performance. At first this might be puzzling, but this effect can be attribute to the wisdom of the crow effect. In other words, if the majority of the users prefer a given brand, then there is a chance that recommending this brand under a category that interest the user already (which can be inferred from the LF part of the model) would help the recommendation process. Finally adding user personalization significantly improved the result.

In Figure 6 we performed another ablation study to study if the improvement brought by LFUM are only due to the item preferences. In this case we compare the UM model against LFUM using 40 factors and by varying the technique used to smooth the preferences. As shown in this figure, while UM is still a strong baseline, LFUM outperforms it which shows the importance of using a latent factor model to account for the unobserved sources that draws the user to a given item.

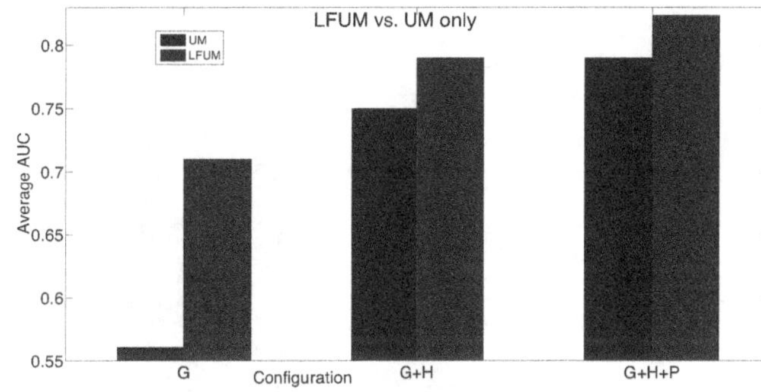

Figure 6: Comparing the performance of the full model against a model that only uses items' attributes

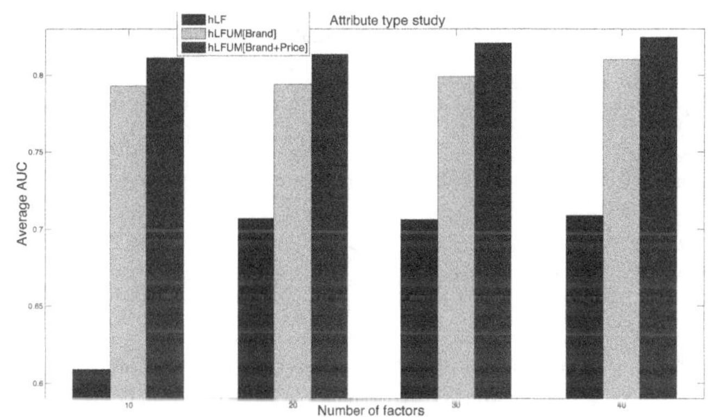

Figure 7: Studying the effect of different attribute types on the final result

6.3 Study of Attribute Type

In this subsection we study the effect of attribute type on the final result. We compare three models: hLF, hLFUM trained with brand preferences only and hLFUM model trained with both brand and price preferences. Both LFUM and hLFUM uses the default preference learning mechanisms (G+H+P). As can be seen from the result both attributes bring improvements, although we notices in general that brand preferences brings more improvements due to brand-loyalty: a user who like "Apple" product for instance, would still buy "Apple" product even if "Apple" increase the price of its products. Nevertheless, price by itself still provides a strong signal.

6.4 Effect of Item Frequency

We compare the performance of our approach hLFUM and with the baseline hLF as the frequency of items changes. As shown in Figure 8, our approach significantly outperforms the baseline especially when the item frequency is small (i.e. cold-start items). We omit the result of hybrid LF as it was worse than hLF as we showed in Figure 4

7. RELATED WORK

There is a wealth of literature about latent factor models for recommendation (see [15] for a survey). Conventional recommendation algorithms do not use user/item attributes, which can limit their performance when the feedback data is sparse. In recent work, several authors propose to augment the latent factor model with item

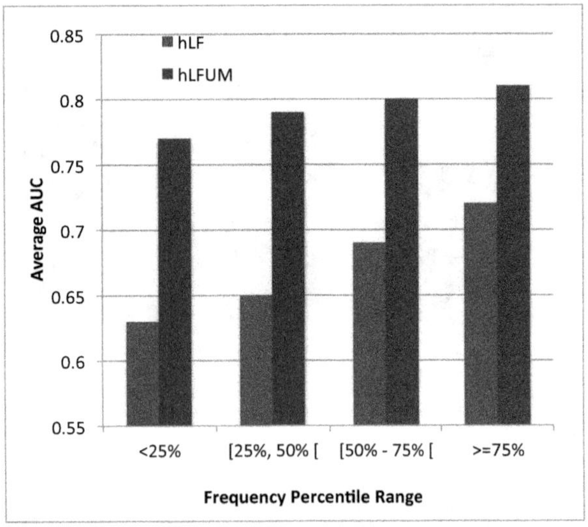

Figure 8: Illustrating the difference in performance between hLF and hLFUM as a function of item's popularity. Each cell in the x-axis represent items in a given frequency percentile range. Note that our approach consistently gives good results across different frequency ranges. Number of factors = 30.

and user attributes. This work was pioneered by Agarwal et al. [2]. However, the authors used very high-dimensional item and user attributes and use them to constraint the projection of users and items into the latent space. In contrast, in our work we only use few attributes (two in our study, brand and price) and therefore this approach is not applicable in our settings. Moreover our approach is unique as it first uses an additive model to preprocess the attributes before combining them with the latent factor model. This has the advantage of turning a discrete attribute with a large cardinality into a single informative feature. For instance, an alternative approach is to add a binary feature for each distinct brand, however that will produce a lot of noise and significantly slow down learning.

Our work is also related to hybrid recommender systems which combine two or more techniques, such as content and collaborative-filtering, to make recommendations [6]. We make several novel contributions in this work. We derive user preferences (e.g., brand, price) in terms of the global preference model and a per-user personalized model. The former captures the global trend and is very useful for sparse users, while the latter allows us to capture the individual characteristics for the dense users. In other words, for new users we leverage the global model, and as we get more and more data about a user, his/her preference model gets increasingly personalized. Moreover, we exploit the taxonomy while learning these preference models (in contrast to Yu et al. [21]). This allows us to deal with sparsity, e.g., preferences over different phones can be propagated to understand preferences over siblings in the hierarchy such as computers, printers, as well as parents such as electronics.

8. CONCLUSIONS

In this paper we presented a novel approach to integer content-based and latent factor based models. We learn a user preference model over item attributes that factors out common parts shared across users via an additive model, thus allowing user preferences to be represented in a discriminative fashion. Moreover, we showed how to integrate these learned preferences with a latent factor model and train the resulting system end-end to optimize a Bayesian discriminative ranking loss function. Our approach can handle continuous and discrete attributes and the complexity of learning and inference is weakly dependent no the cardinalities of the item attributes. We demonstrated the efficacy of our approach in a smart ad retrieval task with very promising results over several baselines. In the future we plan to incorporate the dynamics of user interests [4] and scale our inference to hundred of millions of users using techniques from [3]

9. REFERENCES

[1] Pricegrabber. http://www.pricegrabber.com/.

[2] D. Agarwal and B.-C. Chen. Regression-based latent factor models. In *KDD*, pages 19–28, 2009.

[3] A. Ahmed, M. Aly, J. Gonzalez, S. Narayanamurthy, and A. J. Smola. Scalable inference in latent variable models. In *WSDM*, pages 123–132, 2012.

[4] A. Ahmed, Y. Low, M. Aly, V. Josifovski, and A. J. Smola. Scalable distributed inference of dynamic user interests for behavioral targeting. In *KDD*, pages 114–122, 2011.

[5] J. Bennett, S. Lanning, and N. Netflix. The netflix prize. In *In KDD Cup and Workshop in conjunction with KDD*, 2007.

[6] R. D. Burke. Hybrid recommender systems: Survey and experiments. *User Model. User-Adapt. Interact.*, 12(4):331–370, 2002.

[7] P. Cowans. Probabilistic document modelling. 2006.

[8] A. Gunawardana and C. Meek. Tied boltzmann machines for cold start recommendations. In *RecSys*, pages 19–26, 2008.

[9] A. Gunawardana and C. Meek. A unified approach to building hybrid recommender systems. In *RecSys*, pages 117–124, 2009.

[10] P. D. Hoeff. Bilinear mixed effects models for dyadic data. *Journal of the American Statistical Assosciation*, 2005.

[11] A. W. K. Chou and A. Benveniste. Multiscale recursive estimation, data fusion, and regularization. *IEEE Transactions on Automatic Control*, 39(3), 1994.

[12] N. Koenigstein, G. Dror, and Y. Koren. Yahoo! music recommendations: modeling music ratings with temporal dynamics and item taxonomy. In *RecSys*, 2011.

[13] Y. Koren. Factorization meets the neighborhood: a multifaceted collaborative filtering model. In *KDD*, pages 426–434, 2008.

[14] Y. Koren. Collaborative filtering with temporal dynamics. In *KDD*, pages 447–456, 2009.

[15] Y. Koren and R. M. Bell. Advances in collaborative filtering. In *Recommender Systems Handbook*, pages 145–186. 2011.

[16] Y. Koren, R. M. Bell, and C. Volinsky. Matrix factorization techniques for recommender systems. *IEEE Computer*, 42(8):30–37, 2009.

[17] A. Mnih. Taxonomy-informed latent factor models for implicit feedback. In *KDD Cup, KDD 2011*, 2011.

[18] S. Rendle, C. Freudenthaler, Z. Gantner, and L. Schmidt-thieme. L.s.: Bpr: Bayesian personalized ranking from implicit feedback. In *UAI*, 2009.

[19] S. Rendle and L. Schmidt-Thieme. Pairwise interaction tensor factorization for personalized tag recommendation. In *WSDM*, 2010.

[20] Y. W. Teh, M. I. Jordan, M. J. Beal, and D. M. Blei. Hierarchical dirichlet processes. Dec. 2006.

[21] K. Yu, J. D. Lafferty, S. Zhu, and Y. Gong. Large-scale collaborative prediction using a nonparametric random effects model. In *ICML*, page 149, 2009.

App Recommendation: A Contest between Satisfaction and Temptation

Peifeng Yin[†] Ping Luo[§] Wang-Chien Lee[‡] Min Wang[♯]

[†,‡]Department of Computer Science & Engineering, Pennsylvania State University
[§,♯]Hewlett Packard Labs China, Beijing, China
{[†]pzy102, [‡]wlee} @cse.psu.edu, {[§]ping.luo, [♯]min.wang6}@hp.com

ABSTRACT

Due to the huge and still rapidly growing number of mobile applications (apps), it becomes necessary to provide users an app recommendation service. Different from conventional item recommendation where the user interest is the primary factor, app recommendation also needs to consider factors that invoke a user to replace an old app (if she already has one) with a new app. In this work we propose an Actual-Tempting model that captures such factors in the decision process of mobile app adoption. The model assumes that each owned app has an *actual* satisfactory value and a new app under consideration has a *tempting* value. The former stands for the real satisfactory value the owned app brings to the user while the latter represents the estimated value the new app may seemingly have. We argue that the process of app adoption therefore is a contest between the owned apps' *actual values* and the candidate app's *tempting value*. Via the extensive experiments we show that the AT model performs significantly better than the conventional recommendation techniques such as collaborative filtering and content based recommendation. Furthermore, the best recommendation performance is achieved when the AT model is combined with them.

Categories and Subject Descriptors

H.3.3 [**Information Storage and Retrieval**]: Information Search and Retrieval

General Terms

Algorithms, Performance

Keywords

Smartphone Apps, App recommendation, Contest

1. INTRODUCTION

The popularity of smart phones accelerates the growth of mobile applications, or *apps* for short. As Apple reported, there have been over 500,000 apps available in iPhone's app store[1]. Moreover, there have been 25 million app downloads by March, 2012 [12]. With so many apps providing different functions (e.g., games, utility, books, etc.), it is difficult for users to find right apps they are looking for via keywords search [36]. Therefore, there is an urgent need to provide an effective app recommendation service.

Recommendation services have been deployed for many types of items such as books [18], music [7], movies [15] and even point-of-interests [38, 39]. Compared with those items, mobile apps have a unique characteristics, i.e., a downloaded app may affect the adoption of alternative apps. Most conventional items (e.g., books, movies, locations) are for *one-shot consumption*. For these products, users are typically ready or even glad to receive more new and similar items when they finish "consuming" old ones (e.g., reading books, watching movies, vising locations). Mobile apps are different. Once an app is downloaded, it serves the user continuously, thus referred to as *continuous consumption*, which may affect the user's decision of downloading some alternative apps[2]. For example, if a user has owned a weather forecast app, she is less likely to download another one that provides exactly the same function. Therefore, an app recommendation service may want to avoid such a recommendation.

While avoiding recommendation of similar items for continuous assumption may sound intuitive, via an analysis of user downloading log, we observed that some users did download multiple similar apps (weather forecast, for example)[3]. Before detailing this we first consider a common process of app downloading. Usually a user enters an app store, which would provide her a list of apps, as shown in Figure 1a. Among those candidate apps, the user may pick one and tap the screen to view its detailed information, e.g., description, screenshots, reviews, etc., as shown in Figure 1b. If the user decides to download the app, she may click "install". If not, she may simply return to the app list. We summarize the process as *pick-and-take*, where "pick" represents the user's behavior of viewing the details of an app and "take" means the user downloads the app.

We argue that picking some app from a pool to view is affected by the users' interests since users can see the app titles while browsing the app list. On the other hand the decision

WSDM'13, February 4–8, 2013, Rome, Italy.

[1]http://www.apple.com/iphone/apps-for-iphone/

[2]We are aware that some apps are equal to electronic books and belong to one-shot consumption. However, most of them are to provide some utility which can continuously serve the user.

[3]Please refer to Section 5 for detailed description of the data.

to download the app is influenced by the contest between the already-owned apps and the candidate one. Specifically, people download apps to satisfy their needs. Thus, the apps' "satisfactory value", or marginal utility [33] is an important factor. However, such value remains unknown until the app is installed and used by the user. What prompting the user to download an app is its seeming attractiveness. Therefore, in this work we introduce the notions of *actual value* and *tempting value* to denote the assessment of satisfactory and attractiveness in mobile apps. The former refers to the real satisfactory value of the app after it is used and the latter stands for the estimated satisfactory value that the app seems to bring. Whether to download some app or not is thus a result of the contest between the owned apps' actual values and the candidate's tempting value.

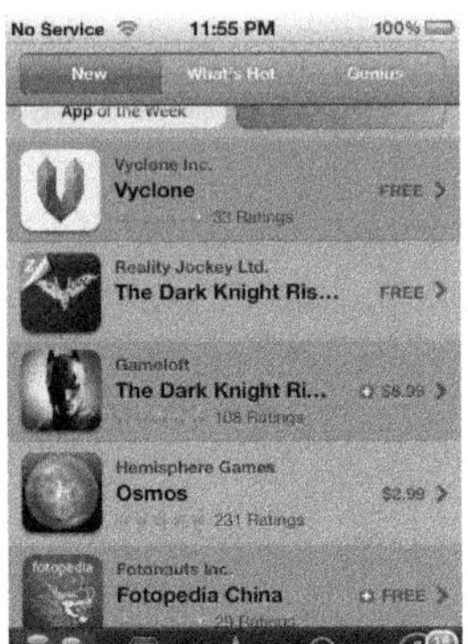

(a) App list.

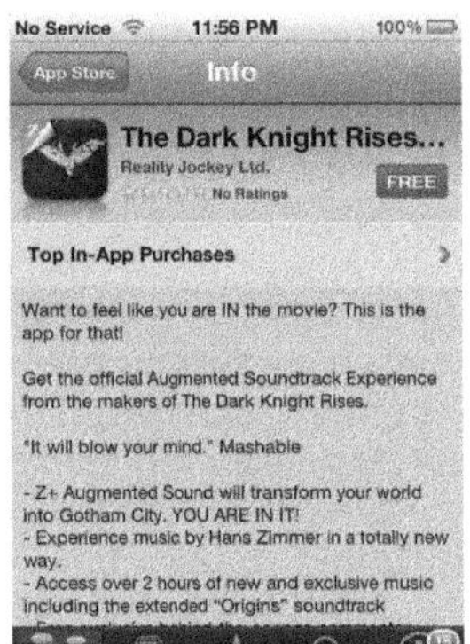

(b) App's detailed information page.

Figure 1: Screenshots of app store

Specifically, consider two apps, one owned by the user while the other is the candidate. There are basically two possible contest results between them. Firstly, if the candidate's tempting value is larger than the other's actual value, the user is more likely to download the new app. On the other hand, if the tempting value is smaller than the actual value, the user would probably not install the new app. For example, suppose the user has installed an app for weather forecast and now there is a new one available in the app store. If the app looks better than the owned one (e.g., more fancy screenshots), the user may probably download it. If the app does not seem to provide some attractive new features or powerful functions (i.e., the tempting value is no larger than the actual value), the user may not consider to install it.

In summary the process of an app download, as mentioned above, consists of two stages, namely pick to view and then download it. User interests and the contest between satisfaction and temptation are in play respectively in these two stages. Conventional recommendation techniques, which do not consider the latter one, may fail to provide successful recommendation when directly applied. We use examples in Figure 2 to illustrate scenarios where user-based collaborative filtering (UCF), item-based collaborative filtering (ICF) and content-based recommendation (CBR) fail to make good recommendation, respectively. UCF finds a set of users similar to the target user and recommends items accessed by those similar users to the target user. In Figure 2a, two users have shared a few apps, represented as *App Group*. UCF will thus treat them as similar users and recommend App_1 to u_2 and App_2 to u_1. However, if App_1's actual value is larger than App_2's tempting value, u_1 will reject the recommended App_2. Also, recommendation to u_2 will fail if the App_2 has an actual value larger than App_1's tempting value. Similarly for ICF and CBR, failing to incorporate the app contest results in ineffective recommendation.

As shown above, the phenomenon of app contest is an important factor in app adoption and thus should be incorporated in app recommendation. In this work, we aim to model such phenomenon by mining the actual value (AV) and tempting value (TV) of each app. Generally they can be learned via the users' view/download sequences. With no loss of generality, consider two apps app_i and app_j, of which app_i is owned by the user and app_j is being viewed. There are two possible results, i.e., i) the user downloads app_j, and ii) the user does not download app_j. Let n_{ij} denote the number of people falling in case i) while m_{ij} denote the number of people in case ii). Intuitively, large n_{ij} and small m_{ij} indicate app_i's AV is larger than app_j's TV. Similarly, small n_{ij} and large m_{ij} suggest that the app_i's AV is smaller than app_j's TV. The details regarding learning model parameters are discussed in Section 3.2.

Usually, a user has owned several apps when she is viewing a candidate app. Intuitively not all of them may affect the user's decision. For example, a game app is unlikely to be selected for comparison when the user is considering whether to download a weather forecast app. Here we introduce a new metric *function overlap*, ranging from 0 to 1 to measure the similarity between two apps. The function overlap is 1 when two apps offer exactly the same function, e.g., weather forecast. On the other hand, function overlap is 0 if two apps are totally different, e.g., a game app and a weather forecast app. Generally, a larger function overlap between two apps suggests a higher probability of contest between them. In this work, while our focus is not on quantifying function overlap, we provide a reasonable measure based on each app's description. The details are provided in Section 2.2.

In summary, our contributions are four-folds:

- We reveal two item access patterns, i.e., one-shot consumption and continuous consumption. Also we point out a decision in app download is affected by two factors, i.e., user interest and app contest.
- We analyze why the state-of-the-art recommendation techniques, i.e., UCF, ICF and CBR, may fail in recommending apps due to app contest.
- We propose an Actual-Tempting model to capture the contest between apps and integrate it into app recommendation.
- We conduct extensive experiments to evaluate our AT model as well as collaborative filtering and content-based recommendation. The result shows that performance of conventional recommendation techniques is improved by incorporating the AT model.

The rest of the paper is organized as follows. Section 2 formulates the app recommendation problem and introduces the solution framework. It also briefly describes the quantification of function overlap. Section 3 provides details of our AT model. Section 4 gives a discussion on the AV and TV of each app. Section 5 evaluates the model as well as the baseline. Section 6 gives a literature review of related work. Finally Section 7 concludes the whole paper and briefly discusses our future work.

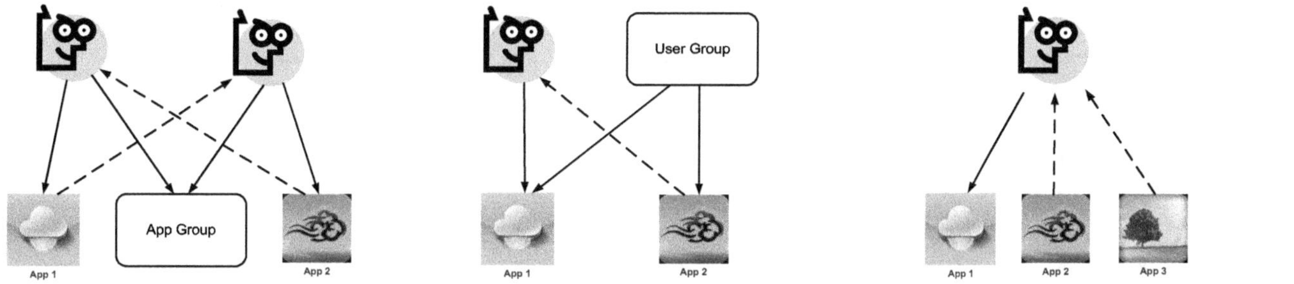

(a) User-based Collaborative Filtering (b) Item-based Collaborative Filtering (c) Content-based Recommendation

Figure 2: Three scenarios of failed recommendation. The solid arrow means the user downloads the app while the dashed arrow indicates the particular app is recommended to the user.

2. PRELIMINARIES

In this section we first formulate the app recommendation as a ranking problem. Then, we provide a simple method to measure the function overlap between two apps. Finally, we propose a ranking framework, which consists of two parts, i) user-interest ranking, and ii) app-contest ranking.

2.1 Problem Formulation

Generally, to recommend apps to a target user, the system selects a number, say k, apps from a pool of candidate apps and sort them based on the probability that the target user may download them. Formally let u_t denote the target user to whom the recommendation would be delivered, and $S = \{app_1, \cdots, app_n\}$ denote the list of candidates among which app_j is the jth app in the list. The top-k app recommendation is to select k apps that are most likely to be downloaded by the target user u_t. The formal definition is shown in Definition 1.

DEFINITION 1 (TOP-k APP RECOMMENDATION). *Given a list of candidate apps S, the top-k recommendation is to form a subset S' s.t. $\forall app_{j_1} \in S', app_{j_2} \in S \wedge app_{j_2} \notin S'$, the user u_t is more likely to download app_{j_1} than app_{j_2}.*

2.2 Computation of Function Overlap

As mentioned in Section 1, the precondition that the user would make comparison of two apps is that these two apps should provide similar functions, or exactly, how much one app's function overlaps with the other's. While our focus is on the app contest, we only provide a feasible method to compute the function overlap. Formally, let $w_{ij} \in [0, 1]$ denote the function overlap between app_i and app_j, where small values indicate tiny function overlap and vice versa.

Supposedly an app's function is reflected in its description. Thus we use such information to indirectly quantify the function overlap. Specifically, we treat it as a document and use LDA [4] to learn the latent topic distribution for it. As such, each app is represented as a vector showing its distribution over the discovered latent topics. Then the function overlap of two apps is computed as the cosine similarity of their vectors. Let $\boldsymbol{f}$ denote the topic distribution of the app, the computation of function overlap between app_i and app_j is shown in Equation (1).

$$w_{ij} = \frac{\boldsymbol{f}_i \cdot \boldsymbol{f}_j}{||\boldsymbol{f}_i|| \times ||\boldsymbol{f}_j||} \quad (1)$$

where $(\cdot)$ represents the vector dot multiplication.

2.3 Ranking Framework

As described earlier the user behaviors in the mobile app market can be summarized as a *pick-and-take* process. First, when a user browses the app list she can see the titles and logos of the apps and thus know their basic functions. Thus, which apps are selected to view is mainly decided by the user's interests. Then, after she view the details of an app the contest between satisfaction and temptation plays a major role to decide to download it or not.

Therefore, in the scenario of app recommendation, there are two aspects to consider, user's interest and the app contest. The former suggests what kind of apps may attract the user while the latter considers the contest between the new app and old ones the user has already installed. Therefore, the ranking consists of two parts, user-interest ranking and app-contest ranking, which are linearly combined. Formally, the ranking score of an app app_i for the target user u_t is defined in Equation (2).

$$\texttt{Rank}(u_t, app_i) = \alpha\texttt{UIR}(u_t, app_i) + (1-\alpha)\texttt{ACR}(u_t, app_i) \quad (2)$$

where $\alpha \in [0, 1]$ is a balancing parameter.

The first part $\texttt{UIR}(\cdot)$ measures how interesting the candidate app is, which can be implemented by any conventional recommendation technique. The second part $\texttt{ACR}(\cdot)$ consider the app contest and thus is the focus of this study.

3. ACTUAL-TEMPTING MODEL

In this section we describe the details of our AT model. We first introduce the general idea of the actual value and tempting value of each app as well as how they affect the user's app-downloading behaviors. Then we discuss how to learn such latent values for each app via users' action sequence. Finally we give the ranking function of AT model.

3.1 Model of Actual and Tempting Value

We assume that each app has two user-independent latent parameters, referred to as *actual value (AV)* and *tempting value (TV)*. The first one stands for the real satisfaction the app brings to the user while the second one is the estimated satisfaction the app may provide. The AV only exists after the user downloads and uses the app while the TV is obtained when the user views the app and evaluates whether it is worth downloading. Generally speaking, a large TV suggests that the app looks quite attractive and is therefore likely to motivate the user to download it.

Different apps may have functional overlap with each other,

Table 1: List of Symbols

u	The index over users
i, j	The index over apps
app_i	The ith mobile app
a_i	The actual value of app_i
t_i	The tempting value of app_i
v_{ij}	The contest result of app_i and app_j
r_{uj}	The user u's action (download or not) to app_j
$A_{u,j}$	The collection of apps owned by u when viewing app_j
n_{ij}	The number of users who owned app_i and later download app_j
m_{ij}	The number of users who owned app_i and later does not download app_j

which becomes a factor the user may consider when deciding whether to download an app or not. For example, if the user already owns an app for weather forecast, then it is not very likely for her to download another one of the same function. However, a close check on the real data reveals that some users did download multiple apps of the same function, which can be naturally explained using the notion of AV-TV. Suppose there are two apps app_i and app_j serving the same function (e.g., weather forecast), the user already downloads app_i and is viewing the information of app_j. We argue that the process of decision-making involves the contest between the value of these two apps, or exactly, the AV of app_i and the TV of app_j. Specifically, if the app_i's AV is larger than the app_j's TV, the user may not download the app_i. On the other hand, if the app_i's AV is smaller than the app_j's TV, the user may be tempted to download the app_j since it is likely to bring her better user experience.

Formally, let a and t respectively denote the AV and TV of an app, p_{ij} stands for the probability that the user u owns app_i but downloads app_j later. We assume that the p_{ij} satisfies a Beta distribution whose parameters are app_i's a_i and AV and app_j's TV t_j, as shown in Equation (3).

$$P(p_{ij}|a_i, t_j) = \mathsf{Be}(p_{ij}; t_j, a_i) = \frac{\Gamma(a_i + t_j)}{\Gamma(a_i)\Gamma(t_j)}(p_{ij})^{t_j - 1}(1-p_{ij})^{a_i - 1} \quad (3)$$

where $\Gamma(x) = (x-1)!$ is a Gamma function.

Figure 3 shows the probability density function of p_{ij} for different combinations of (a_i, t_j). As is easily seen, for small a_i and large t_j, the generated probability p_{ij} is close to 1, indicating a high probability for the user to download app_j. On the other hand, if the a_i is large and t_j is small, the generated p_{ij} tends to be small, leading to a low probability of downloading app_j.

To model the app contest, we take two steps. Firstly, we give the probability of contest between two apps. Then we extend it to a general case, where contest occurs between one and a group of apps.

Contest between two apps.

Let $v_{ij} \in \{-1, 1\}$ denote the contest result between app_i and app_j, where -1 means the user does not download app_j (which loses the contest) and 1 means app_j is downloaded (wins the contest). Given two apps app_i and app_j, the v_{ij} satisfies a Bernoulli process whose parameter p is generated by a Beta distribution. Specifically the probability of v_{ij} is

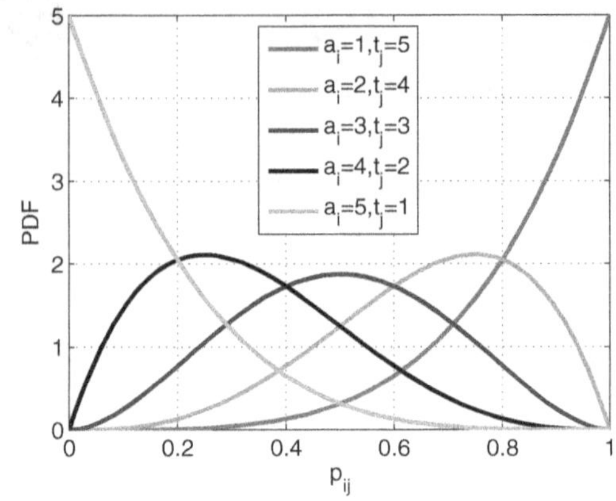

Figure 3: Probability density function of p_{ij} for different combination of (a_i, t_j).

shown in Equation (4).

$$\begin{aligned} P(v_{ij}|a_i, t_j) &= \int_0^1 \left(v_{ij}p_{ij} + \frac{1 - v_{ij}}{2}\right) \mathsf{Be}(p_{ij}; t_j, a_i) dp_{ij} \\ &= v_{ij} \int_0^1 p_{ij}\mathsf{Be}(p_{ij}; t_j, a_i) dp_{ij} + \frac{1 - v_{ij}}{2} \\ &= \frac{t_j}{t_j + a_i} \cdot v_{ij} + \frac{1 - v_{ij}}{2} = -\frac{a_i}{t_j + a_i} \cdot v_{ij} + \frac{1 + v_{ij}}{2} \end{aligned} \quad (4)$$

Contest between one and a group of apps.

Now we extend Equation (4) to a more general case. We assume that there exists a quantification method to compute the function overlap between any two apps. For two apps app_i and app_j, let $w_{ij} \in [0, 1]$ represent their function overlap. Suppose the user u now is viewing app_j and is considering whether to download it. At this time point, let $A_{u,j}$ denote the collection of apps u has already owned. Intuitively, the user would choose similar apps as reference to decide whether to download a new app. It is highly possible that she has installed multiple similar apps but we have no way to know which one affects her final decision. Thus we assume that for app contest, every owned app is likely to affect the final decision and the probability of choosing app_i for comparison is positively proportional to its function overlap with app_j.The probability of $r_{uj} \in \{1, -1\}$ can thus be written as in Equation (5).

$$P(r_{uj}|A_{u,j}, t_j) = \prod_{app_i \in A_{u,j}} P(v_{ij} = r_{uj}|a_i, t_j)^{\tau_{u,i,j}} \quad (5)$$

where $\tau_{u,i,j} \in \{1, 0\}$ is a binary value indicating whether the app_i is selected by the user u for comparison when she is viewing app_j and $P(\tau_{u,i,j} = 1) \propto w_{ij}$.

3.2 Model Learning

Here we describe the details of learning parameters for each app's AV and TV. The observed data is a series of logs sorted by the time stamp. Each log has such format as $(u, app_j, A_{u,j}, r_{uj})$, where u is the unique user id, app_j is the app the user is viewing, $A_{u,j}$ is the collection of apps already owned by the user and r_{uj} is the final action the user takes. When $r_{uj} = -1$, the user does not download

app_j and $r_{u,j} = 1$ means the user downloads the app. Let $\boldsymbol{A}$ and $\boldsymbol{T}$ denote the AV and TV for apps appearing in the data $\mathcal{D}$. The learning process is to find proper values for $\boldsymbol{A}$ and $\boldsymbol{T}$ such that the log-likelihood of observing $\mathcal{D}$ is maximized as shown in Equation (6).

$$\begin{aligned}\log P(\mathcal{D}|\boldsymbol{A},\boldsymbol{T}) &= \sum_u \sum_j \boldsymbol{I}_{uj} \log P(r_{uj}|A_{u,j}, t_j) \\ &= \sum_u \sum_j \boldsymbol{I}_{uj} \sum_{app_i \in A_j^u} \tau_{u,i,j} \log P(v_{ij}|a_i, t_j)\end{aligned} \tag{6}$$

where $\boldsymbol{I}_{uj}$ is binary indicator where 1 means the user u has viewed (and even downloaded) app_j.

Since we do not really know which apps are selected for comparison when she views app_j, $\tau_{u,i,j}$ is unknown. Here we adopt the idea of Expectation-Maximization where the expected value of $\tau_{u,i,j}$ is computed and then the log-likelihood is maximized.

$$E_\tau(\log P(\mathcal{D}|\boldsymbol{A},\boldsymbol{T})) = \sum_{u,j} \boldsymbol{I}_{uj} \sum_{app_i \in A_j^u} E(\tau_{u,i,j}) \log P(v_{ij}|a_i, t_j)$$

$$\propto \sum_u \sum_j \boldsymbol{I}_{uj} \sum_{app_i \in A_j^u} w_{ij} \log P(v_{ij}|a_i, t_j) =_{DEF} \mathfrak{L}(\boldsymbol{A},\boldsymbol{T}) \tag{7}$$

We further transform Equation (7) by introducing two new values, n_{ij} and m_{ij}. The former one counts the number of people who own app_i and later download app_j while the latter one is the number of people who own app_i but do not download app_j after viewing it. Mathematically, these two values are defined in Equation (8).

$$\begin{aligned} n_{ij} &= \sum_u \boldsymbol{I}_{uj} \cdot \frac{1 + r_{uj}}{2} \cdot \mathbf{1}_{app_i \in A_{u,j}} \\ m_{ij} &= \sum_u \boldsymbol{I}_{uj} \cdot \frac{1 - r_{uj}}{2} \cdot \mathbf{1}_{app_i \in A_{u,j}} \end{aligned} \tag{8}$$

These two values can help remove the u from the objective function. Semantically, each log can be interpreted as one or multiple logs describing the contest between two apps. For example, given a log (u, app_j, A_j^u, v_j^u), we can unfold it to such set of data $S = \{(app_i, app_j, w_{ij} \cdot v_{ij} | app_i \in A_j^u)\}$. The learning is to find proper values for $\boldsymbol{A}$ and $\boldsymbol{T}$ such that the probability of these unfolded data is maximized. Now the objective function $\mathfrak{L}(\boldsymbol{A},\boldsymbol{T})$ can be written as Equation (9).

$$\begin{aligned}\mathfrak{L}(\boldsymbol{A},\boldsymbol{T}) &= \sum_j \sum_u \boldsymbol{I}_{uj} \sum_{app_i \in A_j^u} w_{ij} \log P(v_{ij}|a_i, t_j) \\ &= \sum_i \sum_{j \neq i} w_{ij} (n_{ij} \log P(1|t_j, a_i) + m_{ij} \log P(-1|t_j, a_i)) \\ &= \sum_i \sum_{j \neq i} w_{ij} \left(n_{ij} \log \frac{t_j}{t_j + a_i} + m_{ij} \log \frac{a_i}{a_i + t_j} \right)\end{aligned} \tag{9}$$

The parameters can be learned via gradient descent with the partial differentiation to each a_i and t_j, shown as in Equation (10).

$$\begin{aligned} \frac{\partial \mathfrak{L}}{\partial a_i} &= \sum_{j \neq i} w_{ij} \left(\frac{m_{ij}}{a_i} - \frac{n_{ij} + m_{ij}}{a_i + t_j} \right) \\ \frac{\partial \mathfrak{L}}{\partial t_j} &= \sum_{i \neq j} w_{ij} \left(\frac{n_{ij}}{t_j} - \frac{m_{ij} + n_{ij}}{t_j + a_i} \right) \end{aligned} \tag{10}$$

3.3 AT Ranking

With the learned actual value and tempting value for each app, recommendation can be made considering the possible contest result between new app and those owned by the user. As mentioned above, when the user is viewing an app, each of her owned apps is likely to affect the decision and the probability of influence is proportional to the function overlap between these two apps. The ranking score given by the AT model is the expected value of action r_{uj} where 1 for download and -1 for not.

Given two apps app_i and app_j, of which app_i is owned by the user and app_j is the one under review. With Equation (4) giving the probability, the expected value of v_{ij} can be computed in Equation (11).

$$E(v_{ij}|a_i, t_j) = 1 \cdot \frac{t_j}{a_i + t_j} + (-1) \cdot \frac{a_i}{a_i + t_j} = \frac{t_j - a_i}{a_i + t_j} \tag{11}$$

Given a set of apps $A_{u,j}$ owned by the target user u_t, the ranking score for app_j is the expected value for r_{uj}.

$$\begin{aligned}\mathtt{AT}(u_t, app_j) &= E(r_{uj}|A_{u_t,j}, t_j) \\ &\propto \sum_{app_i \in A_{u_t,j}} w_{ij} E(v_{ij}|a_i, t_j) = \sum_{app_i \in A_{u_t,j}} w_{ij} \cdot \frac{t_j - a_i}{a_i + t_j}\end{aligned} \tag{12}$$

4. ANALYSIS AND DISCUSSION

We use a data set containing 5,661 apps and 3,308 users' view-download record to learn our AT model. Details of the data set are described later in Section 5. Then we analyze the learned actual and tempting value for these apps. Generally, we aim to explore the following two apsects, i) the indication of actual and tempting values, ii) the hint of the difference between actual and tempting values.

4.1 The Indication of Actual and Tempting Values

The core idea of the AT model is that each app has two latent values, actual value and tempting value. The former is the real value the app may bring to the user once she downloads and uses it. The latter is the value estimated by the user when viewing it. In other words, the actual value reflects the real satisfaction of an app while the tempting value suggests the expectation of the app to the user. To demonstrate such claims, we crawled these apps' ratings from the app store and compare them with the apps' actual values. Also, we scanned the original records and computed for each app its number of downloads with regarding to the total number of viewing. Results are shown in Figure 4.

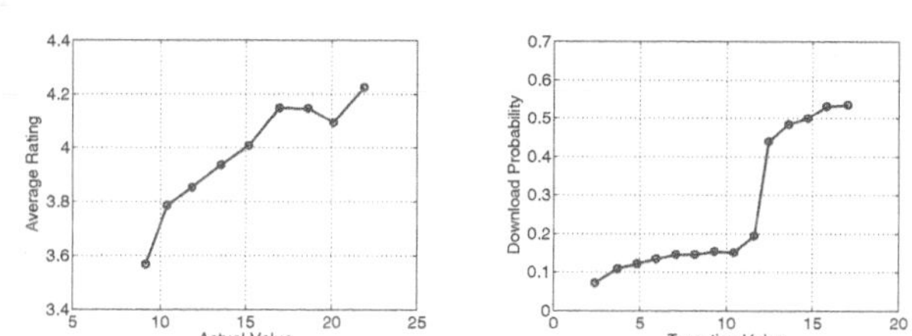

(a) Meaning of app's actual value (b) Meaning of app's tempting value

Figure 4: Meaning of app's actual and tempting value

Figure 4a displays the relationship between actual value and app rating in the app store. Among all apps, we firstly find a minimum as well as maximum actual value. Next we equally divide this range into 9 groups and assign each app a group according to its learned actual value. Then for each group, we calculate the average ratings of apps. It can be seen that the two have a positive correlation where larger actual value suggests a higher rating. Since the app's rating in app store reflects the app's quality in some way, we show that the actual value of our AT model captures the app's quality to some degree.

Figure 4b displays the relationship between tempting value and app's download probability. Similar to the above steps, we group the apps into 14 bins based on their learned tempting values. Then for each group, we calculate the average proportion of download numbers over view numbers, referred to as *download probability*. It can be easily seen that with the growth of tempting value, the download probability is also increasing. Given that the user has no idea of the app's real quality before downloading it, the tempting value thus suggests the degree of attraction the app looks.

4.2 The Hint of Actual-Tempting Difference

After a careful check on the learned model, we note that there exists apps whose actual value and tempting value are not equal, and the difference may vary from app to app. Thus we are curious about the hint behind such difference. In Apple's app store, each app is assigned a category. Accordingly, we group apps and for each category calculate the average difference between its actual value and tempting value. The results are shown in Figure 5.

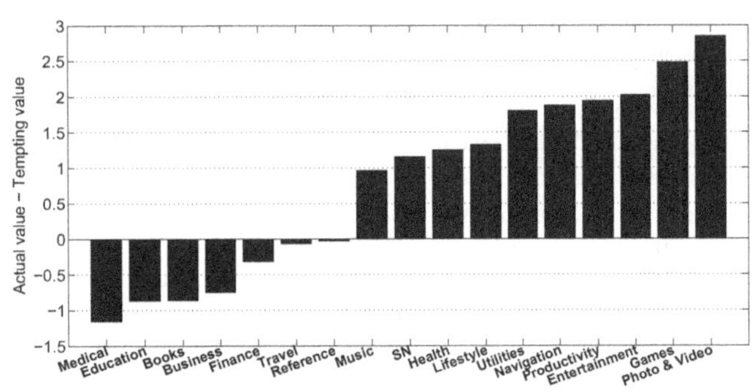

Figure 5: Actual-tempting difference with regarding to app category. Note that negative value means the app's actual value is smaller than its tempting value and vice versa.

Note that for apps in the same category, negative actual-tempting difference may lead to a continuous downloading of similar apps. The most straightforward example is the category Books. In app store, apps of this category are usually some electric books or comics, e.g., G. A. Henty Books[4], Pocket God Comics[5] etc. These apps are similar to conventional items (e.g., real books) where the consumption is one-shot, i.e., users are ready to receive new items once finishing old ones.

Another interesting app category is those whose actual value and tempting value are quite close. Similar actual and tempting value means the app's real value is easy to estimate and one knows what to expect before downloading. The representative example is the category Reference. Apps in this category usually provide guidance or instructions, e.g., MW3 Facts and Guide[6], Encyclopedia of Guns[7]. Users clearly know these apps' function before downloading. Therefore the difference between actual and tempting values is nearly zero.

Finally some apps have higher actual values than tempting values. Apps falling in this type are more likely to block users from downloading other similar apps since on average their actual values are larger than tempting values. In reality, these apps usually have strong function overlap and downloading similar ones is unnecessary. For example, one is less likely to download two radio players in Music category. Also, in Social Networking (SN), once a user is using one (e.g., Facebook), she is unwilling to switch to another (e.g., Google+).

5. EVALUATION

In this section we conduct extensive experiments to demonstrate the effectiveness of our AT model as well as other recommendation techniques. We also evaluate the performance of hybrid recommendation that integrates AT model into collaborative filtering and the content-based recommendation techniques, respectively.

5.1 Data Preprocess

We used the data logged from an iPhone app, namely, *Limited-time Free*[8], which collects information of iPhone apps that become available for free for a limited time in the Apple App Store. When a user runs the app, she is given a list of apps that are free for a limited time, as shown in Figure 6a. When the user clicks an app from the list, the detailed description as well as its running screenshots are displayed (Figure 6b). When the user decides to download the app, she clicks the "Get" button, which leads her to the app store. Also, if she does not want to download the app, the user can return to the app list by clicking the "Back" button. Compared with the official Apple App Store as shown in Figure 1, the user interface of this software is very much similar and thus we can safely claim that users follow the same *pick-and-take* pattern when downloading apps via this one. The system records these two types of actions for each user, i.e., the user's picking some particular app to view detailed information and her downloading some app. By analyzing each log entry, we know which apps the user has downloaded and which apps the user viewed only (but has not downloaded). We use the afore-described data for evaluation.

We further process the log as follows. We remove users who have conducted less than 100 actions and then remove apps that have less than 10 visitors. The resulted data set consists of 3,308 users and 5,661 apps. Among these users, we randomly select 25% as target users to receive recommendation. For each target user, we mask their most recent 25% log entries by default. Recommendation is evaluated by observing how many masked logs are recovered in the recommendation list.

5.2 Evaluation Metrics

In the experiment, we use "relative" *precision* and *recall* to measure the recommendation performance of the recommen-

[4]http://itunes.apple.com/app/id397900901

[5]http://itunes.apple.com/app/id380752345

[6]http://itunes.apple.com/app/id479406467

[7]http://itunes.apple.com/app/id368360223

[8]http://itunes.apple.com/app/id440230030

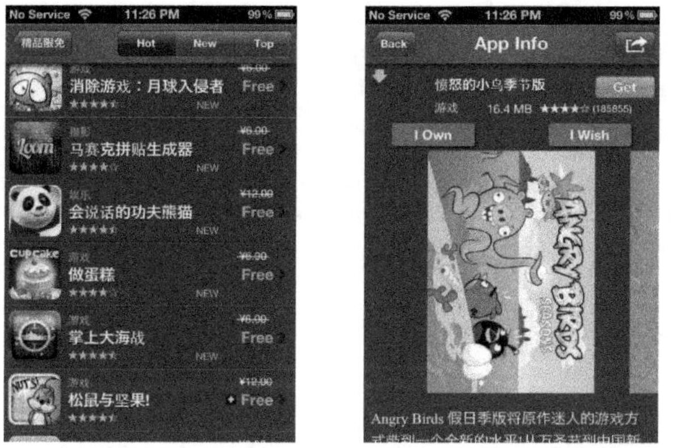

(a) Screenshot of app list. (b) Screenshot of app's detailed information page.

Figure 6: Screenshots of Limited-free app

dation technique under examination improves over a random recommender. Given a recommendation list l sorted in descending order of the ranking score, we refer to those that are previously masked from the log as "hit". Let $hit(k)$ denote the number of hit in a top-k list, and H is the total number of masked items. The absolute precision and recall are defined in Equation (13) as follows.

$$precision@k = \frac{hit(k)}{k} \qquad recall@k = \frac{hit(k)}{H} \tag{13}$$

Let S denote the total number of candidate items, the precision and recall in a top-k list of a random recommender system is $\frac{H}{S}$ and $\frac{k}{S}$ [41]. Therefore, the relative precision and recall is defined in Equation (14).

$$\begin{aligned} \text{r-}precision@k &= \frac{precision@k}{H/S} = \frac{hit(k)\cdot S}{kH} \\ \text{r-}recall@k &= \frac{recall@k}{k/S} = \frac{hit(k)\cdot S}{kH} \end{aligned} \tag{14}$$

As shown, the relative precision and recall are the same and thus we only show one of them in the experiment result. Furthermore, the groundtruth data contains two types of items (apps), i) those viewed and downloaded by the user, and ii) those viewed only by the user. Naturally an ideal recommendation would rank items in first group as high as possible and rank those in second group as low as possible. Accordingly we evaluate these two types of items separately. In the experiment we first sort the recommended apps in a descent order based on the ranking score and count how many of top-k ranked apps are really downloaded by the target user in the masked ground truth data. This performance is denoted as P_{pos}. Then we resort the list in an ascending order and count how many of top-k ranked apps are only viewed but not downloaded by the target user, denoted as P_{neg}. For both metrics, higher value indicates a better recommendation performance.

5.3 Baseline

In the evaluation, we mainly consider two conventional recommendation techniques, i.e., collaborative filtering (CF) and content-based recommendation (CBR). Specifically we use probabilistic matrix factorization (PMF) [22] to realize CF and support vector machine (SVM), implemented by LIBSVM [5] to realize CBR. PMF has been widely used in previous works [23, 1, 17, 2] as an implementation of collaborative filtering. It is highly flexible and easy to extend. SVM displays good performance in classification and its probabilistic extension [20, 40] can be used for ranking.

As mentioned above, apps viewed by the user are either downloaded or not. In the user-item matrix, we assign 1 to the element if the corresponding app is downloaded by the user and set the value as -1 if the app is only viewed but not downloaded by the user. For SVM, we use the description of the app as the feature vector. Also, apps are labeled as positive example if they are downloaded and those that are only viewed are labeled as negative example.

Besides pure PMF and SVM, we also displays performance of hybrid methods that linearly combine any of two solutions, including PMF & SVM, PMF & AT and SVM & AT.

5.4 General Performance

We firstly evaluate the general performance of all recommendation techniques. For hybrid ones, we try different weighting parameters and display the result of the optimal one. The results are shown in Figure 7.

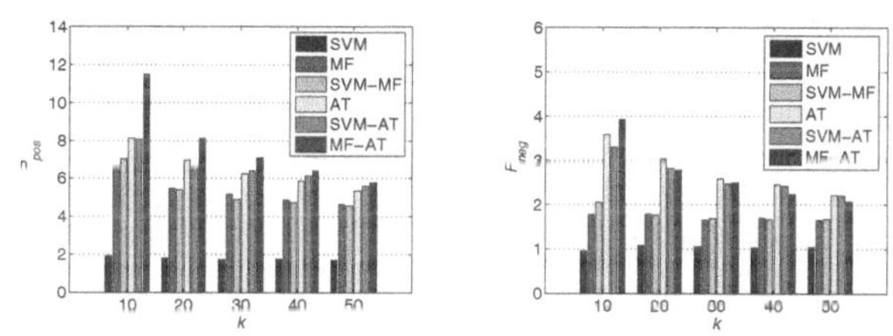

(a) P_{pos} (b) P_{neg}

Figure 7: General performance of examined techniques.

It can be easily seen that the AT model as well as solutions that have incorporated the AT model outperform others. Note that the AT model takes into consideration the effect of contest between apps when making recommendation. Its better performance confirms our argument that in mobile app recommendation, the app contest is an important factor to be considered. Also, those hybrid methods that incorporates the AT model, i.e., SVM-AT and MF-AT, achieve better performance than the pure AT model. This is because AT, emphasizing on unique relationships between apps, are complementary to other techniques that capture users' interests. Therefore optimal performance is obtained when these techniques are integrated together. Finally, SVM performs worse than MF in terms of P_{pos}, but outperforms MF in terms of P_{neg}.

The former observation indicates that the impact of app contest is more significant to content-based recommendation than to collaborative filtering. This can be explained as follows. Recall that in Figure 2c we show how content-based recommendation may fail in app recommendation. Its idea of recommending items similar to those appeared in a user's historical log is susceptible to the app contest. The latter one is caused by imbalanced classification problem [6, 34]. In the records, the proportion of download log is relatively small compared to view log, because users would usually view multiple apps before downloading one. This situation leads to an imbalanced training data set for SVM which is biased towards a strong class (i.e., apps that are viewed only by the user) when conducting classification.

5.5 Experiment on Mask Ratio

In this set of experiment we evaluate the performance of our AT model with regarding to different size of test data, i.e., mask ratio. After randomly selecting a group of target users, we mask a proportion of their most recent app view/download log and check how many of them are recovered by the AT model. The number of masked log is mask ratio. The default value is 25%. In this experiment adjust this ratio to different values, i.e., 10%, 50%, 75% and 90%, where large value indicates small training data. Results are shown in Figure 8.

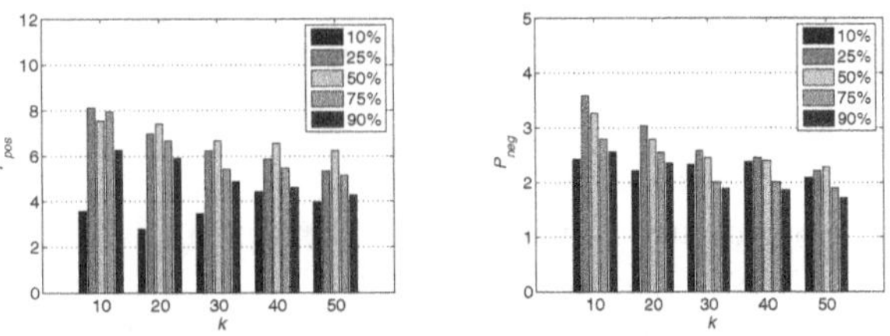

(a) P_{pos} (b) P_{neg}

Figure 8: Experiment on mask ratio

From the figures we can see that when the mask ratio increases from 25% to 90%, the performance degrades. This is reasonable as the training data is decreasing, resulting in an inaccurate learned model. Therefore the recommendation precision suffers. On the other hand, when ratio increases from 10% to 25%, the performance is improving due to the increase of test data. When the mask ratio is 10%, the proportion of masked apps in the recommendation pool is very tiny which makes the recommendation quite difficult to hit the masked ones. Therefore the performance is poor. When the test data is properly increased, the performance improvement is be expected.

5.6 Experiment on Balancing Parameters

In this experiment we demonstrate how much improvement the AT model brings to collaborative filtering and content-based recommendation with different balancing parameters. Recall in Equation (2) the ranking score is the linear combination of two. In the experiment, we combine the AT model respectively with MF and SVM, where the balancing parameters are denoted as α_{mf} and α_{svm}.

The balancing parameter α_{mf} controls the weight of collaborative filtering in the final ranking score. When α_{mf} is set to 0, the recommendation is reduced to pure AT while $\alpha_{mf} = 1$ transforms the model to the pure CF. Figure 9 shows the impact of α_{mf} to the recommendation performance, where optimal one is achieved when $\alpha_{mf} = 0.2$.

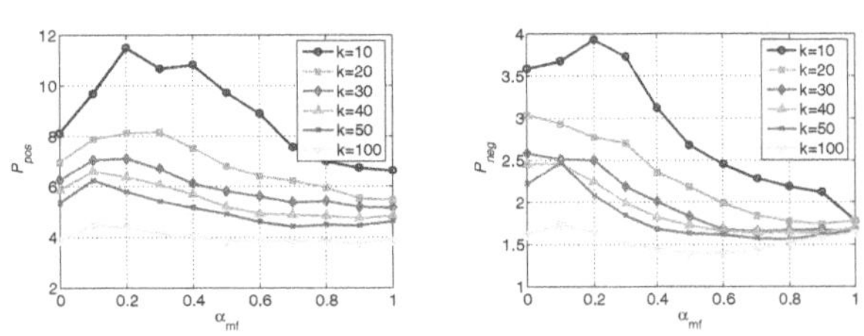

(a) P_{pos} (b) P_{neg}

Figure 9: Experiment on α_{mf}

Next we test the hybrid of content-based recommendation and AT model with regarding to different values for α_{svm}. Note that when $\alpha_{svm} = 0$, the hybrid one is reduced to AT model. And when $\alpha_{svm} = 1$, the solution is equal to content-based recommendation. As shown in Figure 10, the performance is improved when two methods are combined and the optimal performance is achieved when $\alpha_{svm} = 0.1$. Also, recall that when CF is combined with AT, the optimal balance weight is 0.2. The smaller weight for CBR indicates that the contest effect has a larger impact on its performance.

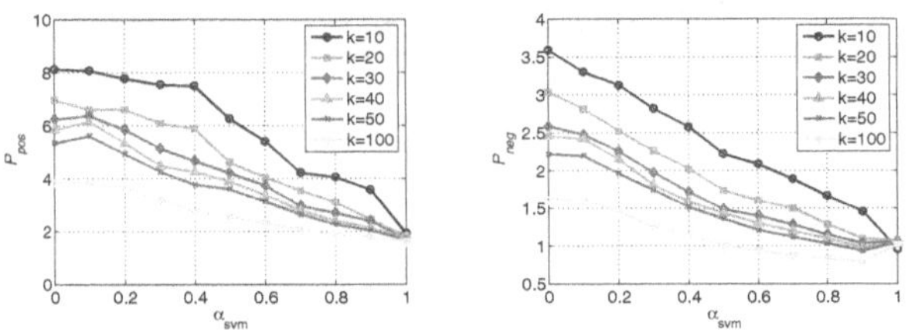

(a) P_{pos} (b) P_{neg}

Figure 10: Experiment on α_{svm}

5.7 Experiment on No. of Iterations

In the final set of experiments, we evaluate the performance of the AT model with regarding to different number of iterations. In gradient descent, we set the learning speed as 0.001. The results are shown in Figure 11.

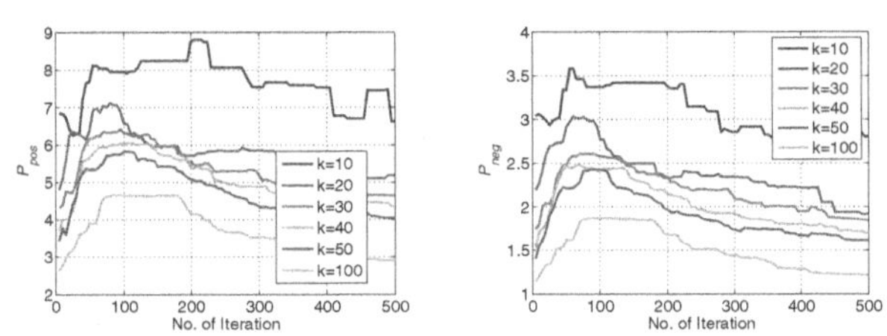

(a) P_{pos} (b) P_{neg}

Figure 11: Experiment on different No. of iterations

As can be seen in Figure 11a and Figure 11b, the performance of the AT model is optimal near the 60th iteration in terms of both P_{pos} and P_{neg}. When the iteration number exceeds 60, the performance is degrades, indicating the model is over-fit.

6. RELATED WORK

Due to the popularity of smart phones and growing number of mobile app made available, a number of research works on the mobile app recommendation have appeared in the literature [35, 36, 9, 11]. However, most of them focus on how to collect extra information via the phones in order to help improve recommendation. In [35] several app usage patterns have been identified. In [36, 9], app's usage data is collected to quantify user's rating on downloaded apps. In [11], GPS sensor information is exploited to provide context-aware app recommendation. Those works are complementary to ours in terms of app recommendation. In this work, we mainly focus on a unique phenomenon in mobile app adoption, i.e., *app contest*, which makes mobile app recommendation different from conventional item recommendation where current recommendation techniques, e.g., CF and CBR, are directly applicable.

Conventional recommendation techniques are generally classified into three categories, collaborative filtering, content-based recommendation and hybrid of the two. In the following we give a brief review of the first two as well as their implementation techniques. Finally we review recent works that consider item relationship in recommendation.

6.1 Collaborative Filtering and Probabilistic Matrix Factorization

Collaborative filtering (CF) is a well known recommendation approach that has been widely studied and adopted. The core idea is that users of similar interests may display similar ratings on similar items. Specifically, if a recommendation is made based on similar users (those who have accessed the same items as the target user has), it is referred to as *user-based CF* [13]. On the other hand, if a recommendation is made based on similar items (those that have been accessed by the same set of people), it is referred to as *item-based CF* [25].

As mentioned in [10], CF algorithms can be roughly classified into neighborhood models and latent factor models. Matrix factorization (MF) is one of the most successful realizations of latent factor models and is superior to classic nearest-neighbor techniques [14]. The general idea of MF is that users and items are associated with several latent factors and the observed user item rating matrix is the multiplication of the two. These latent factors are learned by minimizing a loss function, which is defined as the sum-squared distance between observed and simulated entries [28]. Then Rennie et. al. [29, 21] modified such a loss function by constraining the norms of user and item feature vectors.

In [22], Salakhutdinov and Mnih proposed probability distribution on the latent feature vectors and developed *probabilistic matrix factorization (PMF)*. In their work, they derived the loss function in terms of probability theory and correlated those heuristically-defined loss function with standard Gaussian distribution. Based on the idea of PMF, many variants and extensions have been proposed so far, e.g., [23, 1, 17, 2]. Readers can resort to [26, 27] for a general picture.

In this work we adopt the basic PMF proposed in [22] as the implementation of CF. Our goal is to demonstrate the importance of app contest in app recommendation and performance would be improved when combined with our AT model.

6.2 Content-based Recommendation and Support Vector Machine

The content-based recommendation (CBR) is an outgrowth and continuation of information filtering research [3]. It recommends items similar to the target user's profile. A typical CBR consists of three steps, i.e., content analyzer (or item representation), user profile learning and content filtering [16]. The first one is about how to model items' feature. The second and third one are usually bound together.

For textual items, the feature modeling has been widely studied for information retrieval where items are usually represented as bag-of-word with TF/IDF [24] or latent topic distribution [30]. The latter one is proved to be more precise and thus in this work we use the popular Latent Dirichlet Analysis (LDA) [4] to model the apps' features.

Major methods of user-profile learning, as mentioned in [19, 16], are k-nearest neighbor, Naive Bayes classifier and linear/nonlinear classifier. The first one is inefficient at classification time [16]. The second one suffers unsatisfactory performance for diversified length of items' textual content and unbalanced training sample [16]. Therefore in this work we choose Support Vector Machine (SVM) [32] as it is shown to be a good classifier in text categorization [31] and has been adopted by previous works (e.g., [40, 8]) as basis of CBR. Furthermore, the probabilistic extension [20, 40] makes it capable of ranking tasks as in our work.

6.3 Item Relationship in Recommendation

Few works considered the impact of item relationship in recommendation except for two recent works [37, 33], where the relationship is modeled by introducing the concept of "utility".

In [37], Yang et. al. proposed *Collaborative Competitive Filtering (CCF)* to model the user choice process. They argued that when the user is given a few items, they are competing to win the user's favor. Our work is different. Firstly, in [37] they model the item competition among candidate items, but in this work we aim to model the contest between old items (apps) and new one. Also, the scenario is different. In [37], user first searched for similar items and selected only one of them. In our case, the recommended apps are not necessarily similar. Even if they are, the user can select (download) all of them since the cost is not high[9].

In [33], Wang et. al. modeled the user purchase behavior in E-commerce by maximizing the marginal net utility. Specifically they proposed a utility function where each item has decreasing benefit as the purchasing quantity increases, based on the Law of Diminishing Marginal Utility. The app recommendation in our work differs from conventional shopping behavior in two ways. Firstly, there is no concept of "quantity" in app downloading. The user does not need to repetitively download one app as she might do when purchasing some conventional items, e.g., food, tickets. For app, there is only binary value, i.e., download or not. Secondly, in [33], the increase of some item can always bring some utility, although the value is decreasing as the quantity increases, which is not true in our case. For example, if the user already has a weather forecast app and suppose it works perfectly well, downloading any similar app brings nothing but occupance of smart phone's storage space. Thus, the assumption in [33] is not applicable to app recommendation.

7. CONCLUSION AND FUTURE WORK

In this work we proposed the AT model to exploit the app contest phenomenon for app recommendation. Generally we assume each app has two latent values, i.e., *actual value* and *tempting value*. The former stands for the real value the app brings to the user while the latter represents the satisfactory value it looks to have. The app recommendation needs to consider both user's interest and the app contest. App download involves a comparison between the actual satisfactory values of owned apps and the tempting value of a new app. By conducting extensive experiments, we demonstrate that our AT model outperforms conventional recommendation techniques (i.e., CF and CBR) that only captures user's

[9]All apps we studied in this work are free when the user views them

interests. Moreover, optimal recommendation is achieved when both parts are integrated.

In the proposed model, the actual and tempting values are treated as latent attributes of apps and learned via users' action sequence. While this technique is quite popular in latent factor model, it is rather interesting to understand what really determines the actual and tempting values for an app. In future works we plan to conduct a comprehensive study on this point.

8. REFERENCES

[1] D. Agarwal and B.-C. Chen. flda: matrix factorization through latent dirichlet allocation. In *WSDM*, pages 91–100, 2010.

[2] N. Barbieri and G. Manco. An analysis of probabilistic methods for top-n recommendation in collaborative filtering. In *ECML/PKDD (1)*, pages 172–187, 2011.

[3] N. J. Belkin and W. B. Croft. Information filtering and information retrieval: two sides of the same coin? *Commun. ACM*, 35(12):29–38, 1992.

[4] D. M. Blei, A. Y. Ng, and M. I. Jordan. Latent dirichlet allocation. *J. Mach. Learn. Res.*, 3:993–1022, 2003.

[5] C.-C. Chang and C.-J. Lin. LIBSVM: A library for support vector machines. *ACM Transactions on Intelligent Systems and Technology*, 2:27:1–27:27, 2011.

[6] N. V. Chawla, N. Japkowicz, and A. Kotcz. Editorial: special issue on learning from imbalanced data sets. *SIGKDD Explor. Newsl.*, 6(1):1–6, 2004.

[7] H.-C. Chen and A. L. P. Chen. A music recommendation system based on music data grouping and user interests. In *CIKM*, pages 231–238, 2001.

[8] K.-W. Cheung, J. T. Kwok, M. H. Law, and K.-C. Tsui. Mining customer product ratings for personalized marketing. *Decis. Support Syst.*, 35(2):231–243, 2003.

[9] E. Costa-Montenegro, A. B. Barragáns-Martínez, and M. Rey-López. Which app? a recommender system of applications in markets: Implementation of the service for monitoring users' interaction. *Expert Syst. Appl.*, 39(10):9367–9375, 2012.

[10] P. Cremonesi, Y. Koren, and R. Turrin. Performance of recommender algorithms on top-n recommendation tasks. In *RecSys*, pages 39–46, 2010.

[11] C. Davidsson and S. Moritz. Utilizing implicit feedback and context to recommend mobile applications from first use. In *CaRR*, pages 19–22, 2011.

[12] D. Graziano. Apple's app store reaches 25 billion downloads. *http://www.bgr.com/2012/03/05/apples-app-store-reaches-25-billion-downloads/*, 2012.

[13] J. L. Herlocker, J. A. Konstan, A. Borchers, and J. Riedl. An algorithmic framework for performing collaborative filtering. In *SIGIR*, pages 230–237, 1999.

[14] Y. Koren, R. M. Bell, and C. Volinsky. Matrix factorization techniques for recommender systems. *IEEE Computer*, 42(8):30–37, 2009.

[15] G. Lekakos and P. Caravelas. A hybrid approach for movie recommendation. *Multimedia Tools Appl.*, 36(1-2):55–70, 2008.

[16] P. Lops, M. de Gemmis, and G. Semeraro. Content-based recommender systems: State of the art and trends. In *Recommender Systems Handbook*, pages 73–105. 2011.

[17] H. Ma, D. Zhou, C. Liu, M. R. Lyu, and I. King. Recommender systems with social regularization. In *WSDM*, pages 287–296, 2011.

[18] R. J. Mooney and L. Roy. Content-based book recommending using learning for text categorization. In *DL*, pages 195–204, 2000.

[19] M. J. Pazzani and D. Billsus. Content-based recommendation systems. In *The Adaptive Web: Methos and Strategies of Web Personalization*, pages 325–341. Springer-Verlag, 2007.

[20] J. C. Platt. *Probabilities for SV Machines*, pages 61–74. MIT Press, 2000.

[21] J. D. M. Rennie and N. Srebro. Fast maximum margin matrix factorization for collaborative prediction. In *ICML*, pages 713–719, 2005.

[22] R. Salakhutdinov and A. Mnih. Probabilistic matrix factorization. In *NIPS*, 2007.

[23] R. Salakhutdinov and A. Mnih. Bayesian probabilistic matrix factorization using markov chain monte carlo. In *ICML*, pages 880–887, 2008.

[24] G. Salton. *Automatic Text Processing: The Transformation, Analysis, and Retrieval of Information by Computer.* Addison-Wesley, 1989.

[25] B. Sarwar, G. Karypis, J. Konstan, and J. Riedl. Item-based collaborative filtering recommendation algorithms. In *WWW*, pages 285–295, 2001.

[26] H. Shan and A. Banerjee. Generalized probabilistic matrix factorizations for collaborative filtering. Technical report, University of Minnesota, Twin Cities, 2010.

[27] H. Shan and A. Banerjee. Generalized probabilistic matrix factorizations for collaborative filtering. In *ICDM*, pages 1025–1030, 2010.

[28] N. Srebro and T. Jaakkola. Weighted low-rank approximations. In *ICML*, pages 720–727, 2003.

[29] N. Srebro, J. D. M. Rennie, and T. Jaakkola. Maximum-margin matrix factorization. In *NIPS*, 2004.

[30] M. Steyvers and T. Griffiths. *Handbook of Latent Semantic Analysis*, chapter Probabilistic Topic Models.

[31] J. T. Text categorization with support vector machines : Learning with many relevant features. *ECML*, pages 137–142, 1998.

[32] V. N. Vapnik. *The nature of statistical learning theory.* Springer-Verlag New York, Inc., 1995.

[33] J. Wang and Y. Zhang. Utilizing marginal net utility for recommendation in e-commerce. In *SIGIR*, pages 1003–1012, 2011.

[34] G. M. Weiss. Mining with rarity: a unifying framework. *SIGKDD Explor. Newsl.*, 6(1):7–19, 2004.

[35] Q. Xu, J. Erman, A. Gerber, Z. Mao, J. Pang, and S. Venkataraman. Identifying diverse usage behaviors of smartphone apps. In *IMC*, pages 329–344, 2011.

[36] B. Yan and G. Chen. Appjoy: personalized mobile application discovery. In *MobiSys*, pages 113–126, 2011.

[37] S.-H. Yang, B. Long, A. J. Smola, H. Zha, and Z. Zheng. Collaborative competitive filtering: learning recommender using context of user choice. In *SIGIR*, pages 295–304, 2011.

[38] M. Ye, P. Yin, and W.-C. Lee. Location recommendation for location-based social networks. In *GIS*, pages 458–461, 2010.

[39] M. Ye, P. Yin, W.-C. Lee, and D. L. Lee. Exploiting geographical influence for collaborative point-of-interest recommendation. In *SIGIR*, pages 325–334, 2011.

[40] K. Yu, A. Schwaighofer, and V. Tresp. Collaborative ensemble learning: combining collaborative and content-based information filtering via hierarchical bayes. In *UAI*, pages 616–623, 2003.

[41] T. Zhou, Z. Kuscsik, J.-G. Liu, M. Medo, J. R. Wakeling, and Y.-C. Zhang. Solving the apparent diversity-accuracy dilemma of recommender systems. *Proceedings of the National Academy of Sciences*, 107:4511–4515, 2010.

Threading Machine Generated Email

Nir Ailon
Technion & Yahoo! Research
Techion, Haifa 32000, Israel
nailon@yahoo-inc.com

Zohar S. Karnin
Yahoo! Research
MATAM, Haifa, 31905, Israel
zkarnin@ymail.com

Edo Liberty
Yahoo! Research
MATAM, Haifa, 31905, Israel
edo@yahoo-inc.com

Yoelle Maarek
Yahoo! Research
MATAM, Haifa, 31905, Israel
yoelle@ymail.com

ABSTRACT

Viewing email messages as parts of a sequence or a thread is a convenient way to quickly understand their context. Current threading techniques rely on purely syntactic methods, matching sender information, subject line, and reply/forward prefixes. As such, they are mostly limited to personal conversations. In contrast, machine-generated email, which amount, as per our experiments, to more than 60% of the overall email traffic, requires a different kind of threading that should reflect how a sequence of emails is caused by a few related user actions. For example, purchasing goods from an online store will result in a receipt or a confirmation message, which may be followed, possibly after a few days, by a shipment notification message from an express shipping service. In today's mail systems, they will not be a part of the same thread, while we believe they should. In this paper, we focus on this type of threading that we coin "causal threading". We demonstrate that, by analyzing recurring patterns over hundreds of millions of mail users, we can infer a causality relation between these two individual messages. In addition, by observing multiple causal relations over common messages, we can generate "causal threads" over a sequence of messages. The four key stages of our approach consist of: (1) identifying messages that are instances of the same email type or "template" (generated by the same machine process on the sender side) (2) building a causal graph, in which nodes correspond to email templates and edges indicate potential causal relations (3) learning a causal relation prediction function, and (4) automatically "threading" the incoming email stream. We present detailed experimental results obtained by analyzing the inboxes of 12.5 million Yahoo! Mail users, who voluntarily opted-in for such research. Supervised editorial judgments show that we can identify more than 70% (recall rate) of all "causal threads" at a precision level of 90%. In addition, for a search scenario we show that we achieve a precision close to 80% at 90% recall. We believe that supporting causal threads in email clients opens new grounds for improving both email search and browsing experiences.

WSDM'13, February 4–8, 2013, Rome, Italy.

Categories and Subject Descriptors

H.4.3 [**Information Systems Applications**]: Communications Applications—*Electronic Email*

Keywords

Email Threading, User Experience, Algorithms, Models, Frequent sets and patterns

1. INTRODUCTION

Web mail has become one of the largest sources of user generated content today, significantly bigger than the Web. The volume of email going through Web mail services such as Windows Live Hotmail (recently re-branded as Outlook.com), Yahoo! Mail and Gmail, today's largest email providers [3], keep growing. Some analysts even predict that the number of email accounts will increase from 3.1 billion in 2011 to nearly 4.1 billion by 2015, [7].

Even if personal communications seem to increasingly move away from mail toward social media such as Facebook or instant messaging applications, especially with the younger generations [4, 15], email retains its value as an asynchronous method of communication with commercial entities or organizations. One key characteristics of these entities is that they regularly and automatically generate messages and send them to individual users.

Machine-generated messages dominate email traffic, as we have verified on Yahoo! mail, and detail later. It is also clear that the volume of machine-generated email will keep growing. Among these machine-generated messages, while some are of critical importance like an e-ticket, a car rental reservation, a bill to pay, or a new password, others are almost spammy, like hotel newsletters, or obsolete mailing list subscriptions. Most users do not take the time to clean up their inboxes, never define a single folder [10], and have to turn to the usual search and browse mechanisms when tracking important messages. One convenient mechanism to navigate one's inbox is "threads" or "conversations" that visually link related messages.

The task of *email threading* consists of identifying sequences (threads) of messages related to a single logical conversation, event or action. The most common type of email thread is a group of email messages that have been exchanged by a common list of senders and recipients via the mail reply/forward mechanisms. They can be extracted by purely syntactic methods, through the analysis of the senders and recipients in the mail headers and more importantly by observing the shared subject lines. Indeed, in these "syntactic threads" the subject lines are similar modulo the addition of the prefixes '`Re:`' for reply and '`Fw:`' for forward, possibly multiple times. Other threading header field based mechanisms were defined in RFCs 822 [5] and 2822 [13]. These suggest email clients should endow forwarded or replied messages with a special "**`In-Reply-To`**" field header and include the original message identifier. Clearly when such fields exist threading becomes straightforward.

This, however, happens almost solely for personal (individual or multi-party) conversations. Automated messages that are caused by a same action will not be identified as a thread. This is because separate email messages in these threads have different subject lines and content. In many cases, they do not even the share the same sender.

We argue here that it is critical to offer some kind of threading mechanism dedicated to machine-generated email simply because already today it represents the majority of the volume of email traffic. Indeed, we have analyzed the inbound (non-spam) traffic of Yahoo! mail over a period of one month, simply counting the number of messages originating from a same sender. We verified that more than 60% of the overall traffic originated from mass senders in multiple domains (manually classified via editors) such as social (facebook, linked in, etc.), commerce (ebay, amazon, etc.), finance, shopping, travel, etc. as illustrated in Figure 1. We also sampled[1] the bodies and subject lines of the mass senders' messages and verified they were clearly automatically generated, as expected. Indeed each of us can easily recognize in their inboxes these messages derived from a same boilerplate, where only user specific information such as name, address, date, purchase good, confirmation number, etc. differ. In the same Figure 1, the categories labeled "Personal", "Other", "Miscellaneous", and "Unknown" contain mostly personal conversations.

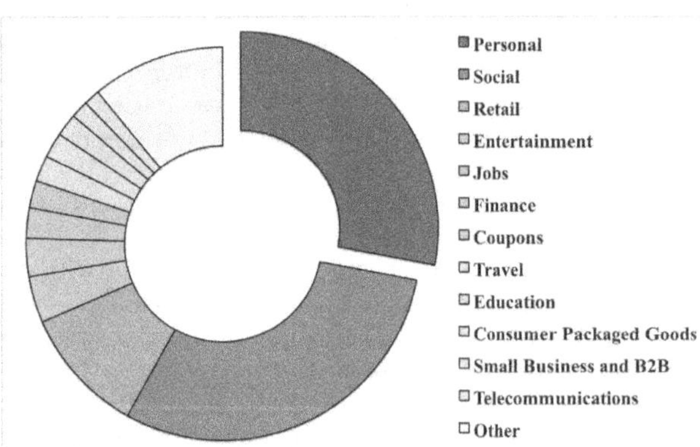

Figure 1: Distribution of email traffic per domain over a month of Yahoo! mail traffic.

[1]All email studies reported here that involved looking at subject lines or bodies were conducted exclusively on the inboxes of users who had voluntarily opted in for such research.

Given the mass volume of these machine-generate email messages and the fact that we can only expect it to grow in the future, we argue here that it is critical to help users naivgate it in a more convenient way. One first step in this direction is to define and offer a new type of threading that takes advantage of this mass volume in order to provide a new type of threading abstraction. We introduce in this paper the notion of "causal threading", which is a specific type of thread dedicated to machine-generated email messages.

We define a causal thread as a sequence of messages that originate from a same cause and are thus logically linked. Consider the following example of a user who clicked on a "**`I forgot my password`**" button on a site she is registered to. She might first get an email message entitled "**`change your password`**" with a link taking her to a dedicated "**`change your password`**" page on the site, and then a second message entitled "**`your password has been changed`**" containing the new password and informing her that her password has been successfully changed. Clearly these messages are strongly related, as they pertain to one action that spans several stages, yet today's threading mechanisms will not group them together as they are not seen as part of a same conversation. Moreover, most such machine-generated messages are one directional, they are inbound messaged often without a return channel[2]. Yet, we argue that these messages are part of a same logical thread as the second message is an automatic result of the action taken on the first message. In other words, as the second message can be traced back to the first message as its "cause", we want to link them into the same causal thread. Consider now this more complex example, in which a user purchased an electronic device from an online mass retailer. He will first get from the retailer a message that the order was placed, then possibly a message from the delivery service with the tracking number, and another one confirming delivery. Finally he might even get another message from the retailer thanking him and including instructions for returning the device if not satisfied. All these messages would not belong to the same syntactic thread. Indeed, not only do they not share the same subject lines (as in the previous example) but also involve different senders that were not part of a same conversation at any time. We propose here to group them in the same causal thread that will link them in a logical order to the source or cause of the thread.

Our approach is based on the intuition that since these messages are machine generated and sent over and over, modulo minor user-specific variations, to large volume of users we should be able to observe causality patterns between them.

We propose to first identify, over very large amounts of email data, these similar messages that share a common sender and variations of subject lines. We refer to these as *email templates*, and will define them more formally later on. Note that for performance we do not, at this stage, consider the body of messages.

Given these email templates that represent an abstraction of machine-generated mail, we propose to learn causality relations offline over a very large corpus of email data. Our process consists of three offline stages and one online stage:

1. We first learn email templates over a very large repre-

[2]In fact, many of such automated messages explicitly ask the recipient *not* to respond.

sentative sample of email data and devise an efficient procedure that associates any new incoming message with its template, as well as return the list of variables instantiated by the message. This stage is detailed in Section 2.

2. We then learn, offline, a "causal graph" over email templates, as explained in Section 3. Given the causal graph, one can estimate the likelihood that one message follows another.

3. In addition, we learn a "causality prediction function" that takes as input a pair of email messages, produces a list of features that rely on the causal graph, and outputs a confidence score to whether the first message caused the second. This function is critical to deciding whether the second message should follow the first one in the same thread. This step relies on a supervised data set. The features produced in the step are detailed in Section 4.

4. Given the causality prediction function, we thread the incoming emails, in an online manner, by appending a newly received email to its most likely predecessor (i.e., assigning the new email to the same thread as its chosen predecessor) or decide that it is the beginning of a new thread when all candidate predecessors are given an insufficient score. We describe this process in Section 5.

The unsupervised offline process needs to be conducted on a regular basis to account for the arrival of new mass senders on the market, or template updates as service providers keep changing their infrastructures. The supervised phase of learning the confidence function need not be updated so often as it is a function of features that are independent of the exact templates. Once the templates, causal graph and confidence function are learned, actual threading can be conducted online. The causal threading process serves the inbound message stream. It associates each incoming message, at arrival time, with a thread identifier, while maximizing a utility function parametrized by the confidence score, as detailed in Section 5.

The contributions of our work are three-fold: We introduce the notion of "email template" for machine-generated email and define a new mechanism for identifying them efficiently. We propose a method for efficiently learning relations between these templates, over millions of users' inboxes, so as to infer causality. We introduce the notion of "causal threading" and propose an efficient mechanism for dynamically assembling causal threads as messages are delivered to the email system.

2. EMAIL TEMPLATES

By analyzing inbound traffic it is possible to identify these near similar messages from a same sender, and separate the boilerplate from the variables parts. The idea is to find frequent subsequences of words in email subject lines shared by many messages originating from a same sender. For example, an email sent by "`usps.com`" whose subject line is "`Your package number 2049862-56 is on its way`" will be rare if not unique. But, the regular expression "`Your package number * is on its way`" , where the wild-card character "`*`" can match any number of words or characters, will match a great number of subject lines in messages sent by "`usps.com`".

Following the above intuition, each machine-generated message can be mapped into a tuple formed by a static template and a list of variables. For example, consider the message e sent by "`usps.com`" whose subject line is "`Your package number 2049862-56 is on its way`". The template identifier $\tau(e)$ would be formed by concatenating the sender name and the regular expression matching best a great number of subject lines, namely "`usps.com: Your package number * is on its way`" and vars(e) would be a list containing a single element: "`2049862-56`''.

Given a stream of messages, it is an interesting computational task to identify the templates and extract the variables. We refer to this process as templating. Note that the proposed threading introduced in this paper is independent from the templating process, and should work in a similar manner with any other templating technique. The templating technique we apply here is rather simple yet effective. Templates are extracted for the most frequent senders by analyzing the subject lines of the messages originating from that sender. The probability that the subject line of a message from "`usps.com`" matches the regular expression "`Your package number * is on its way`" is higher than some small constant. Obtaining these regular expressions from raw data is standard practice in data mining. See [9, 2, 1] for examples of efficient techniques for association rule mining.

In our system, we found that removing long numbers, unique identifiers, proper names, and all other non frequent words (those whose probability is below some small constant) almost always results in the exact template. There is some subtlety in identifying either overspecified or underspecified templates but this goes beyond the scope of this paper.

In what follows, we assume that given any machine generated mail e, one can efficiently compute both a template identifier $\tau(e)$, and a list of variable values[3] vars(e).

3. LEARNING THE CAUSALITY GRAPH

The input to the system is a set of N anonymized users $\{1,\ldots,N\}$. For each user, i, we are given a set of n_i inbound messages $\{e^i_1,\ldots,e^i_{n_i}\}$, collected between time t_{begin} and t_{end}. For clarity, e^i_j denotes the j'th email in user i's inbox. The inbound email streams are chronologically sorted, namely, $t(e^i_{j_1}) < t(e^i_{j_2})$ for all i and $j_1 < j_2$. We denote by $\tau(e^i_j)$, vars(e^i_j) and $t(e^i_j)$ the template, variables, and arrival time of email j to user i, respectively. We use $\mathcal{T}$ to denote the space of templates occuring in our data (see Section 2 for details on discovering the templates). Many messages do not fit into any template, for example, personal email. These can be ignored since they are irrelevant in the context of automated mail threading. From this point on, our notation assumes that all messages in the system match a valid template.

Let $\Delta = t_{\text{end}} - t_{\text{begin}}$ denote the length of the time window in which data is collected. For each[4] $\tau \in \mathcal{T}$, define $\lambda(\tau)$ to

[3]We note that in practice, given a set $\mathcal{T}$ of templates, one can construct in linear time, a *trie*-like database that would support these types of queries in constant time.

[4]We abuse notations and refer to τ both as a function and a template.

be the average number of times template τ was observed in a single time unit:

$$\lambda(\tau) = \frac{|\{(i,j) : i \in [N],\ j \in [n_i],\ \tau(e^i_j) = \tau\}|}{N\Delta}.$$

We posit that the number of appearances of a template τ per time unit in a stream is distributed Poisson with parameter $\lambda(\tau)$. This means that the probability of observing template τ at least k times within an interval of δ units is estimated by $\text{Poiss}(\lambda(\tau)\delta, k) = e^{-\lambda(\tau)\delta}(\lambda(\tau)\delta)^k/k!$.

In order to identify statistical relations between the appearance of two distinct templates $\tau, \tau_{\text{caus}} \in \mathcal{T}$, we define a window size parameter δ. We then count the conditional frequency of τ_{caus} given τ as follows:

$$C(\tau, \tau_{\text{caus}}) = \Big|\{(i, j_1, j_2) \ : \ i \in [N],\ j_1 < j_2,\ t(e^i_{j_2}) < t(e^i_{j_1}) + \delta \le t_{\text{end}},\ \tau(e^i_{j_1}) = \tau_{\text{caus}},\ \tau(e^i_{j_2}) = \tau\}\Big|.$$

In words, $C(\tau, \tau_{\text{caus}})$ counts the number of times templates τ and τ_{caus} appeared within δ time units in one user's stream, where τ_{caus} appears before τ. In order to infer a potential causal connection $\tau \to \tau_{\text{caus}}$ (read: τ was caused by τ_{caus}), we compare the prior probability of observing τ in an arbitrary window of length δ to the probability of observing τ in a window of length at most δ following an appearance of τ_{caus}.

Our directed, weighted causal graph $G_{\mathcal{T}} = (V_{\mathcal{T}}, E_{\mathcal{T}}, W_{\mathcal{T}} : E_{\mathcal{T}} \mapsto \mathcal{R}^+)$ is constructed as follows. Its nodes correspond to templates $V_{\mathcal{T}} = \mathcal{T}$. The weight function is in fact defined for any pair of vertices:

$$W_{\mathcal{T}}(\tau, \tau_{\text{caus}}) = \frac{\Pr[\tau \text{ appears in the } \delta\text{-window after } \tau_{\text{caus}}]}{\Pr[\tau \text{ appears in a } \delta\text{-window}]} = \frac{C(\tau, \tau_{\text{caus}})/C(\tau_{\text{caus}})}{1 - e^{-\lambda(\tau)\delta}},$$

where

$$C(\tau) = \Big|\Big\{(i, j_1) \ : \ i \in [N],\ t(e^i_{j_1}) + \delta \le t_{\text{end}},\ \tau(e^i_{j_1}) = \tau\Big\}\Big|.$$

In words, $W_{\mathcal{T}}(\tau, \tau_{\text{caus}})$ is the ratio between the number of times the pair of templates τ and τ_{caus} co-appeared in a window of length δ and the expected number of times τ would appear after τ_{caus} assuming an independence between the appearance of τ and of τ_{caus} (the *null* hypothesis). We kept only arcs $\tau \to \tau_{\text{caus}}$ for which the weight $W_{\mathcal{T}}(\tau, \tau_{\text{caus}}) \ge 1$. For scalability reasons, we also restricted the out degree of each vertex to be at most 20.

3.1 Causality Graph: Construction and Interpretation

We implemented the algorithm described above using email streams from 12.5 million users, over a time span of $\Delta = 2$ months. We took the window interval parameter δ to be 17 days. The set of templates, $\mathcal{T}$, was limited to a set of 11646 templates.

To remove noise factors for infrequent templates, we used a smoothing factor for the weight ratio calculation. Specifically, in the calculation of $W_{\mathcal{T}}(\tau, \tau_{\text{caus}})$, we have artificially added a constant number of appearances of τ_{caus} followed by a time window of length δ in which τ appeared exactly $\mathbb{E}$[number of appearnaces of τ in a δ−window] many times. Formally, we set

$$W_{\mathcal{T}}(\tau, \tau_{\text{caus}}) = \frac{C(\tau, \tau_{\text{caus}}) + \beta\lambda(\tau)}{(C(\tau_{\text{caus}}) + \beta)(1 - e^{-\lambda(\tau)\delta})}$$

where β is a smoothing parameter. See Figure 2 for an excerpt from the resulting causal graph.

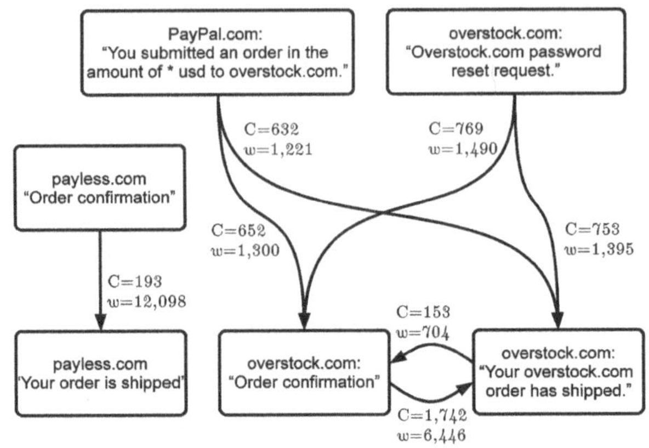

Figure 2: A snippet of the learned causal graph. Note that, for example, shipping notices tend to follow order confirmations. An interesting insight is that users who intend to purchase online often forget their password and thus a password reset precedes the purchase. This is a common structure across many vendors.

Although the causal graph is not the only ingredient in the final threading algorithm (see Section 4 below), some interesting facts can already be observed from it. If we consider the semantic meaning of templates we can identify template types which repeat across many senders. These include all password change confirmations, payment due notices, shipping alerts, service begin/end confirmation, etc. By aggregating statistical behavior on the type level we gain a lot of insights into the global flow of machine generated messages. See Figure 3 for examples for such insights.

In what follows, we assume the learned graph is fixed, and denote it by $G_{\mathcal{T}} = (V_{\mathcal{T}}, E_{\mathcal{T}}, W_{\mathcal{T}})$, where $V_{\mathcal{T}} \subseteq \mathcal{T}$, $W_{\mathcal{T}} : E_{\mathcal{T}} \mapsto \mathcal{R}^+$ denotes the arc weights, as described above.

4. PREDICTING CAUSALITY

While the end goal is to thread a sequence of email messages, a crucial building block is the ability to evaluate the likelihood that one email is caused by another. The causality relation of a pair of messages cannot be derived solely from the causality relation between their templates. Clearly, a purchase confirmation and a shipment notice a year apart are not related. We assert that the likelihood that a message e_i is caused by the message e_j is a function F of a list of features of the (ordered) tuple (e_j, e_i). In what follows we describe these features along with some insights. The function F is learned in a supervised manner; the exact learning process is explained in Section 6.

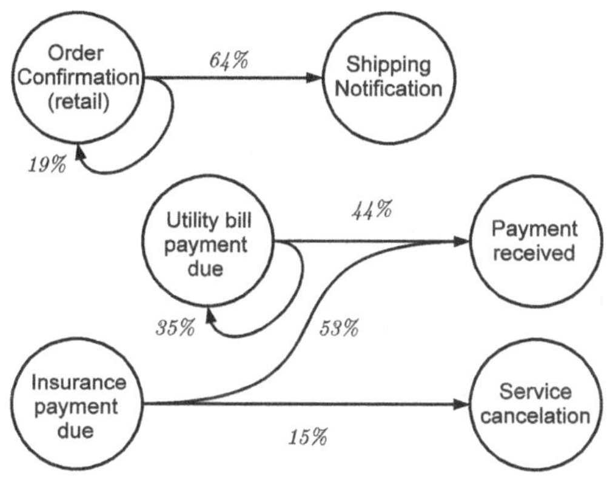

Figure 3: We present here the transition probability graph between types. The figure shows a very small portion of this graph in a classic automaton-like layout. Taking utility bill payments as an example, we see that 44% of the times they are followed by a confirmation of the payment being received. Yet, in 35% of the cases, a second payment notification is followed.

We note that for every feature described below, two features are actually created; one for an ordered pair (e_i, e_j) and another for the same pair reversed (e_j, e_i). The motivation is that a causal connection between a pair of email types is anti-symmetric while a spurious relation is in many cases symmetric.

4.1 Time Difference Features

Every arc a in the causality graph corresponds to an ordered pair of templates that tend to appear in temporal proximity. We endow each arc with the empirical mean $\mu_{\text{timediff}}(a)$ and standard deviation $\sigma_{\text{timediff}}(a)$ of the time difference between the appearance of the first and the second in the pair. When considering threading e_i and e_j with the corresponding arc $a = (\tau(e_i), \tau(e_j))$, we include the feature

$$\frac{|t(e_i) - t(e_j) - \mu_{\text{timediff}}(a)|}{\sigma_{\text{timediff}}(a)}$$

This measures the deviation of the arrival time difference between e_i and e_j from its expected value.

To further sharpen this feature, we created another cleaner version thereof in which the calculation of $\mu_{\text{timediff}}(a)$ and $\sigma_{\text{timediff}}(a)$ excluded the top and bottom 10 percentiles of the observed time differences. This cleanup was designed to reduce the effect of the following scenario occurring in the causality graph creation step. Consider a user who changed her password twice within two weeks. Changing a password usually includes a thread of two messages with templates in the spirit of 'how to change your password' and 'your password has been changed'. These two messages tend to arrive at very close time intervals. Forgetful users who change their password, say, twice in two weeks, are considered outliers for the purpose of computing the time difference. Our cleanup method is likely to avoid such noise.

In addition to the time difference information, we also computed edge weights as described in Section 3, using 4 different values of the time interval parameter δ. The different values were 4 minutes, 1 hour, 1 day and 17 days. The rationale for computing the different weight variants was that causality relations between templates happens at varying time resolutions. Note that we do not create a new graph for the different values of δ. The set of arcs is still determined by $\delta = 17$ days (as explained in Sections 3 and 3.1). We simply endow the arcs with multiple weights.

4.2 Variable Match Features

A variable match may be very significant when determining the causality relation between two emails. For example, in template pairs of the type: '`order #number# confirmation`' and '`shipment for order #number#`', a match in the variable '`#number#`' is very significant. On the other hand, there are cases where a variable match is not as significant. Consider the two templates: '`the itinerary of your flight from #location1# to #location2#`' and '`changes in your flight from #location1# to #location2#`'. A match in only one of the location variables does not mean that the two emails are connected. It is not unlikely for the two emails to discuss different flights while '`#location1#`' is simply the user's city of residence.

We introduce variable match features into threading decision making as follows. Consider an arc $a = (\tau_1, \tau_2)$ in the causality graph, and assume that templates τ_1 and τ_2 are endowed with non-empty variable lists.

In the causality graph learning step, given an instance of τ_1 and τ_2 appearing within time interval δ, the corresponding *variable match pattern* is a bipartite graph with the variables of τ_1 on the left, the variables of τ_2 on the right, and an edge between two variables if their value is identical in the two corresponding emails. For each possible variable match pattern M, we compute a weight that is defined as $W_{\mathcal{T}}(a)$, except that only occurrences of τ_1, τ_2 with variable match pattern M are counted.

The feature we output for messages e_1, e_2 with templates τ_1, τ_2 is the weight of the corresponding variable match pattern. Additionally, we provide a binary feature indicating whether the variable match pattern contains at least one variable match.

4.2.1 Matching Variables to Sender Domain Names

An additional type of match can occur between the variables of the template corresponding to one email and the domain of the sender of the other. Here, an example where this connection is meaningful for our purpose. One message from '`racingbuy.com`' with subject '`Your order confirmation`', the other email from '`paypal.com`' with subject '`Your purchase from racing buy`'. The corresponding feature we introduced in the system is a textual measure of similarity between the sender domain name of one email and a variable of the other. In case more than one variable exists, the maximal similarity measure is chosen as the feature.

4.3 Periodicity Features

We say that a template is periodic if its instances appear periodically in users' inbound mailboxes. Common examples include: daily quotes, weekly newsletter or monthly bills. In such cases, a false causality arc might be created due to *spurious relationships*. In statistics, two events have a *spurious relationship* when neither causes the other, but both are caused by a third event. In our case, the third event is e.g.

the beginning of a month. We elaborate on spurious relationships and the problem they present in Section A. We add features indicating periodicity as follows. For each template τ we compute both the average and the standard deviation of the *time difference* between its consecutive appearances in users' email streams. Denote these statistics by period_av(τ) and period_std(τ). For each causality graph arc (τ_1, τ_2), we add log(period_av(τ_i)) and log(period_std(τ_i)) for $i = 1, 2$ as features, totaling 4 numerical features. Note that we use logarithms because the important information is the ratio between the standard deviation and the mean, which is captured by difference of logarithms, which in turn, can be captured by a linear classifier.

5. SERVING AN INBOUND MAIL STREAM: THREADING

After a template graph is created offline and the causality prediction function is learned, the system is ready to provide online threading service to the email stream. The task is to process each of the user's incoming emails one at a time and decide whether it continues an existing thread or starts a new one. Fix a user, and let $\{e_1, e_2, \dots\}$ denote the stream of messages arriving into her inbox[5].

We now think of the stream $\{e_1, e_2, \dots\}$ of inbound messages as a vertex set $V_\mathcal{E}$ of a sequentially revealed graph. There is also a special vertex $e_0 \in V_\mathcal{E}$ which corresponds to no email. In this notation, the goal is to endow $V_\mathcal{E}$ with a set of arcs $E_\mathcal{E}$. When node e_i is revealed the algorithm must output a single arc (e_i, e_j) for some $0 \leq j < i$. We think of e_j as being the parent of e_i and denote it by $e_j = \text{par}(e_i)$. The choice must meet the following conditions. Either $j = 0$ in which case we say that e_i starts a new thread. If $j > 0$ then it must be the case where $(\tau(e_i), \tau(e_j)) \in E_\mathcal{T}$ and $0 < t(e_i) - t(e_j) \leq \delta$ where δ is the same window size parameter used in Section 3. In this case we say that e_i continues a thread by being appended to $e_j = \text{par}(e_i)$.

We refer to the process of selecting the arc $(e_i, \text{par}(e_i))$ upon arrival of e_i as *threading*. Note that there may be cases where $\text{par}(e_{i_1}) = \text{par}(e_{i_2}) > 0$ for some $i_1 \neq i_2$. This means that we are allowing threads to *split*. There is a good reason for allowing splitting, an example being that of *piecemeal shopping cart delivery*: A user purchases a cartload of goods from an aggregate vendor. The vendor sends a confirmation and receipt message for the entire purchase. Then the products are processed and shipped by separate sub-vendors. Each of those will result in a separate thread of email notifications. Naturally, those threads continue (or are caused by) the original online purchase.

5.1 Optimal Log-Likelihood Threading

Let (e_i, e_j) be a pair of email messages. We abuse notations and denote by $F(e_i, e_j)$ the score given by the function F (as defined in Section 4) when given as input the features extracted from (e_i, e_j). We consider $F(e_i, e_j)$ as an estimated probability for e_j being the parent of e_i. Define the score of a threading output at step n, i.e. after handling n emails, as

$$\sum_{i \in [n] : \text{par}(e_i) \neq e_0} - \log \left(F \left(e_i, \text{par}(e_i) \right) \right) .$$

[5]Since in this stage we deal with only one user we omit the email superscript indicating the user index.

By our construction, maximizing the score is equivalent to maximizing the log-likelihood of the chosen threading given a pairwise independence statistical model on email messages. Moreover, the following greedy threading algorithm always ensures a maximal score. Upon arrival of e_i, choose $\text{par}(e_i)$ to be

$$\text{par}(e_i) = \text{argmax}_{0 \leq j < i} F(e_i, e_j) \tag{5.1}$$

We define $F(e_i, e_0)$ as the probability of e_i being the first member in its thread, which is equal to

$$\prod_{0 < j < i} (1 - F(e_i, e_j))$$

assuming pairwise independence. Note that had we not allowed threads to split, this greedy online step would not have ensured optimality. Another important note is that eventually our threading process does not completely follow the maximum log-likelihood model, but rather appends the newly arrived message to an existing thread only when the probability corresponding to the best candidate predecessor exceeds some threshold (a parameter of the model). The main reason for using a threshold-based threading rather than the maximum log-likelihood is that the regime of the problem dictates a need for very large precision rates; a requirement that is not necessarily provided by the log-likelihood model yet is provided by the latter model.

6. EXPERIMENTS AND RESULTS

6.1 Labeled Data

We obtained editorially annotated thread information for a dataset consisting of 10,606 examples. An example is an inbound email e along with a set of email messages $e_1, \dots, e_m$ received prior to e in the same mailbox which consists of candidate *causes* of e. We refer to e as the *target* email message, and to $e_1, \dots, e_m$ as *candidate email messages*.

The editorial examples were randomly collected from the Yahoo! inbound mail stream only from users who voluntarily opted-in specifically to allow such research to be performed. From each such user, only a handful of machine-generated messages that matched our templates were picked. More specifically, for a randomly chosen message e, the set of candidate messages taken from that user are those suspected of causing e, namely, those for which $(\tau(e), \tau(e_i)) \in E_\mathcal{T}$. For each message (either target or candidate), only the following information was made available to Yahoo! employed editors: sender, obfuscated subject line, and delivery time. Subject line obfuscation garbled identifiable information such as: names, numbers, dates, places, etc. (appearing as template variables). For each target message, the editors were asked to indicate which (if any) of the candidate messages was the cause of the target message as previously defined. The instructions that were given to editors are listed below.

We collected a total of 10,606 such examples, with a total of 13,701 candidate email messages. In other words, each target email message had an average number of roughly 1.3 candidates. Since "No preceding email" was also an option, each instance gave rise to an average of roughly 2.3 options to choose from. The small number of candidates is critical for modern email services to be able to make this choice at delivery time, for each and every inbound message. Out of the 10,606 instances 4,504 labels indicated a thread contin-

Instructions given to editors to label data:
You are given a target (input) email message and a handful of other email messages that arrived shortly before it. Please mark *at most one message* that is causally related to the target (input) email message or naturally precedes it and was caused by a common action.

1. If more than one preceding email exists mark the most recent one.
2. If no causally related preceding email exists mark 'No preceding email'.
3. If there is no way to make a valid judgment, e.g., foreign language, missing information, etc. mark 'No Judgment' (NJ).

target		
From	**Subject line**	**Time Stamp**
chegg.com	your returned chegg book has been processed	6pm 5/24
candidates		
From	**Subject line**	**Time Difference**
chegg.com	returning your chegg textbook	8 hours prior
	No preceding email	
	NJ	

Table 1: A simple editorial example. The editors were asked to indicate whether the target email should or should not be appended to the candidate email to create (or continue) a thread.

target		
From	**Subject line**	**Time Stamp**
ebay.com	your invoice for ebay purchases apple iphone 3gs 8gb black smartphone 170730882108	7pm 4/9
candidates		
From	**Subject line**	**Time Difference**
ebay.com	updates for your purchase from thegeex apr 07 12	1 hour prior
ebay.com	your ebay item sold apple iphone 3gs 8gb black smartphone 170730882108	1 day prior
ebay.com	ebay invoice notification for saturday march 31 2012	4 days prior
members .ebay.com	re details about item jgdsne02 sent a message about comcast arris tg262 docsis 3 modem wireless 210038603616	5 days prior
	No preceding email	
	NJ	

Table 2: An editorial example where there are a number of possible candidate emails. Here, the target email should continue the thread ending with the second candidate email. This example also shows that simply threading emails by sender and time difference cannot succeed.

uation, 4800 were indicated to be the first in their thread and 1302 were not identified (the option "NJ" was chosen).

6.2 Editorial Data Creation

The straightforward way to create the editorial data is to sample a set of email messages and for each sampled message e, output the following instance: The email message e is the target email message and the candidates $c_1, \ldots, c_n$ are all of the email messages in the same inbox, received in the appropriate time window, for which the arc $(\tau(e), \tau(c_i))$ appears in the causality graph.

This sample is problematic due to the following reason. The number of candidates per email averages at 6.05 meaning that even if all of the instances were positive, the number of positive pairs is only a sixth of the data. We sampled 200 instances without the mentioned filtering and found that 39 (19.5%) were positive meaning that the estimated percentage of positive examples is slightly more than 3%. Due to this skewness, it is not practical to obtain sufficiently many editorially labeled positive examples and we must use some unsupervised initial filtering. An added bonus of the quick filtering process is that the drop in the average number of instances (from 6.05 to 1.3) translates into a more efficient classifier, which is very important in a large scale system such as an email service.

Our unsupervised filtering is done as follows: A possible candidate c for an email message e is removed if either the weight of the corresponding arc $(\tau(e), \tau(c))$ is smaller than 12 or the ratio between its weight and that of the inverse arc $(\tau(c), \tau(e))$ is smaller than 3. To assess the cost of this processing to the recall, we sampled 200 instances without the mentioned filtering and found (via manual labeling of editors) that in 24 of these instances, the correct answer was removed in the unsupervised filtering stage. It follows that our preprocessing stage yields an approximate multiplicative penalty of 0.88 to the recall rate. Notice that the precision can also be affected by this filtering. This may occur when the true candidate was filtered yet the classifier predicted a different parent. Though theoretically possible, none of the 200 labeled examples emitted such an error, meaning that the penalty for the precision is negligible.

6.3 The Learning Model

We divided our labeled data into training, validation and test portions. Their respective sizes were set to 60, 20 and 20 percent (of instances). The trained model is a real function mapping between pairs of email messages (a target e and a candidate e') and a confidence score. The higher the confidence is, the stronger our belief that e' is the actual parent of e in the same causal thread. Specifically, given a new email message e and a candidate parent e', we compute the vector valued feature extraction function described in Section 4 $\bar{f}(e, e') = (f_1, f_2, \ldots)$, and compose the result with a classifier given by a learning system (described below).

Notice that the editors did not provide labels per a pair

of target e and candidate e', but rather a choice of one or no candidate from a list. To use this information for learning, each instance of target e and candidates $e_1, \ldots, e_m$ was converted into m pairs $(e, e_1), \ldots, (e, e_m)$. If an editor chose e_i as the actual parent of e, then (e, e_i) was taken as a positive instance, and $(e, e_1), \ldots, (e, e_{i-1}), (e, e_{i+1}), \ldots, (e, e_m)$ were taken as negative ones. If the editor marked no parent (e.g. that e begins a new thread) then all m pairs were taken as negative instances. We trained an AD tree classifier [6]. We also considered other classifiers such as logistic regression; while their results are comparable, AD trees performed slightly better.

Since our conversion method produced a skewed data set of significantly more negative examples than positive ones, we introduced a parameter $\alpha_1 > 0$ and gave each positive instance a weight of $\alpha_1 \cdot m$ where m is the number of candidate for that instance. The intuition for the m factor is two-fold. First, it results in a (roughly) balanced weight of positive and negative examples. Second, a candidate that tends to have a lot of competition (i.e. many other candidates) would intuitively require a higher score to be chosen by the classifier than a candidate that tends to have zero or little competition. We also distinguished between two types of negative instances. The first type results from an instance in which the new email began a new thread (none of the candidates was chosen as the actual parent). The second type is a pair (e, e') of target e and a candidate e' distinct from the actual candidate e'' the editor marked. The latter example should intuitively have a smaller weight as it could be the case that a candidate e' is a moderately fine choice for a parent of e but a better candidate was found. Negative examples of the latter type received a weight of α_2, where $\alpha_2 > 0$ is another tuning parameter, while the first type was given a unit weight.

The testing and validation were performed as follows. Denote the learned function mapping a feature vector to a confidence by h. Given a target e and candidates $e_1, \ldots, e_m$ we computed $h(\bar{f}(e, e_1)), \ldots, h(\bar{f}(e, e_m))$ and identified $e^* = \operatorname{argmax}_{e' \in \{e_1, \ldots, e_m\}} h(\bar{f}(e, e'))$. We also introduced another threshold parameter $\beta > 0$. If the confidence $h(\bar{f}(e, e^*))$ was greater than β, we predicted a causal relation, i.e. that e^* was the actual parent of e. Otherwise we predicted that e began a new thread. A correct prediction for an instance is one where we predict the same parent option as the editor. We measured the performance by computing the precision-recall plot for the actual positive examples, i.e. the examples in which the editorials marked that e did not begin a new thread.

The parameters $\alpha_1, \alpha_2, \beta$ where chosen to optimize the $F_{0.5}$ measure w.r.t. the stated precision-recall over the validation set. We used $F_{0.5}$ rather than the F_1 score since in our setting, low recall is more acceptable than low precision. Once we determined the parameters, we ran the test on the test portion of the data with various values of β to obtain the precision-recall plots in figure 4.

6.4 Baseline: Causal Graph Independent Features

To measure the amount of information hiding in the causal graph, we compared our results to the following baseline. For each pair of messages, we omit all features that depended on the causal graph in any way. Specifically, we left only two features; the domain similarity and time difference. We

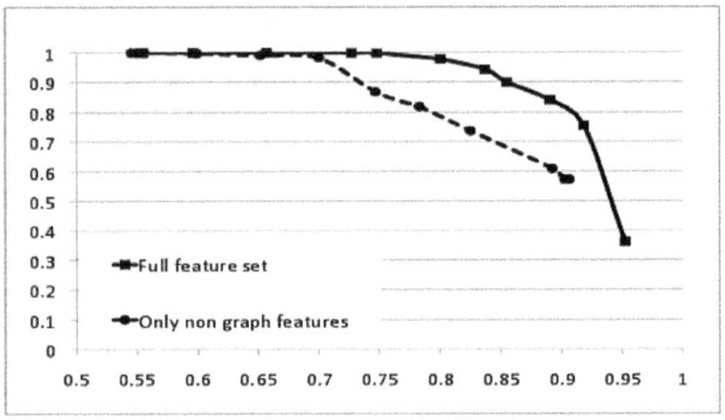

Figure 4: Precision (on the x-axis) versus recall (y-axis) curves for the threading process and baseline. As can be seen from the plot, features extracted from the template causality graph are extremely helpful. From a practical standpoint, such results can already be presented to users with $\sim$ 90% precision at $\sim$ 80% recall. Notice that due to the preliminary filtering of candidates, the true recall is a product of 0.88.

mention that this baseline still somewhat depends on the graph because the graph edge set was used in the first place for selecting editorial instances. Nevertheless, the algorithm using the complete set of features is significantly superior to the baseline as seen in figure 4. Specifically, by using the additional graph related features we increase (absolutely, not relatively) the recall rate by 15%-20%. Moreover, this is achieved in the range of the precision values, which is large enough to be presented to users.

7. RELATED WORK

Our work intersects several lines of research. The first typically known as *association rule mining* (see for example [1, 8]) refers to the problem of identifying statistical dependence between sets of items appearing in logical shopping carts. Such rules allow the vendor to apply sophisticated pricing and discounting strategies. Our work differs from this line of work in that no logical shopping cart exists here. The stream of inbound emails for a user, for our purpose, is an infinite object revealed over time. The association rules we mine have a temporal nature in that we search for repetitive patterns over relatively small time windows. Additionally, the rules are not symmetric in the sense that the relation 'caused by' is anti-symmetric as opposed to 'correlated with', which is the relation of interest in the case of logical shopping carts.

Another relevant line of research is that of identifying semantic threads based on statistical text similarity [16, 11, 12, 17]. This problem has been studied both in the context of email and newsgroups, where threading can be offered to the end user as a valuable feature for navigating through a large corpus.

Yeh et. al [17], in addition to using semantic tools to identify threads, report their study on identifying threads using payloads planted in a protocol used by a propietary mail client. Such information allows very precise thread identification, but the approach is limited to identification of threads in which all parties use this proprietary protocol.

Our work is different in multiple ways. First, our threads define logical connections between inbound messages *only*, whereas semantic threading uses bidirectional information towards identifying so called conversations between two (or more) parties. Outbound messages are not used in our scenario, and often do not exist. Additionally, we seek to predict association rules to within almost the same precision as the trivial tag based thread prediction, while maintaining a reasonable recall rate.

To the best of our knowledge, this is the first work, dealing with causal threading of automated email messages. The only previous work we can compare ourselves to is that on threading of personal email messages, in other words, of conversations. The comparison is difficult because the problems are almost completely different. We still make the following note of comparison. In both [11] and [12], a single message e was given to a threading algorithm as "query", and the algorithm outputted a ranked list of messages suspected as belonging to the same thread as e. Both [11] and [12] evaluate their system over a set of query messages known a priori to belong to a thread of size *more than one*. Hence it was known (by experiment design) that e was associated to another message, the question was only *which*. Assuming the first message on the retrieved list was taken as the suggested related message, the algorithm in [12] succeeded in around 35% of the times. The algorithm in [11] claimed precision of 71% using a similar evaluation method (note that the datasets were different). It is difficult to compare these result with ours, because our algorithm was measured also against messages that were not associated with any other message by way of threading. Quoted from [11]: *"Of course, these figures are for messages that are known to have a parent message. An operational system would need not only to distinguish among potential parents, but also to detect whether or not the message had a parent at all"*. Such detection is performed by neither [11] nor [12]. Nevertheless, our proposed system clearly outperforms these benchmarks.

8. CONCLUSION

In this paper, we introduced a method for building a new type of thread, coined "causal thread", specially adapted to machine-generated email. Our approach leverages the fact that machine-generate messages are typically sent by mass senders to a very large number of users. By automatically learning causality patterns, offline, across millions of users, we could develop mechanisms that allow to identify causal threads at delivery time.

It is important to stress that our solution is fully scalable and can be adopted by large scale email service providers. First, our threading procedure is very efficient and can be integrated into the email delivery pipeline without causing delays or bottlenecks. Second, the entire process is language independent. This is crucial for large email providers since they typically support numerous different languages. The only seemingly language-dependent portion of our process is the editorial judgment. Bear in mind, however, that the features used to predict causality are language independent. Moreover, the exact same kind of training data is naturally generated by users when they, for example, indicate a threading mistake.

Furthermore, our process identifies non trivial threads spanning different senders, possibly over long periods of time. This, while still correctly dealing with *interleaving* threads, which occur, for example, when a user makes multiple independent purchases almost at the same time, possibly from the same vendor.

Finally, we achieve high threading precision, while delivering a reasonable recall rate. This is crucial for a positive user experience while browsing email. For the email search scenario, our system allows extremely high recall rate (almost 90%) while maintaining a precision of close to 80%.

9. REFERENCES

[1] Rakesh Agrawal, Tomasz Imielinski, and Arun N. Swami. Mining association rules between sets of items in large databases. In *SIGMOD Conference*, pages 207–216, 1993.

[2] Rakesh Agrawal and Ramakrishnan Srikant. Fast algorithms for mining association rules in large databases. In *Proceedings of the 20th International Conference on Very Large Data Bases*, VLDB '94, pages 487–499, San Francisco, CA, USA, 1994. Morgan Kaufmann Publishers Inc.

[3] Mark Brownlow. Email and web mail statistics. *Email Marketing Reports*, October 2011. http://www.email-marketing-reports.com/metrics/email-statistics.htm.

[4] comScore Inc. The 2010 US digital year in review. comScore Whitepaper, February 2011. http://www.comscore.com/Press_Events/Presentations_Whitepapers/2011/2010_US_Digital_Year_in_Review.

[5] D. Crocker. Standard for the format off arpa internet text messages, August 1982.

[6] Yoav Freund and Llew Mason. The alternating decision tree learning algorithm. In *ICML*, pages 124–133, 1999.

[7] The Radicati Group. Email statistics report, 2011-2015, May 2011. http://www.radicati.com/?p=7269.

[8] Jochen Hipp, Ulrich Güntzer, and Gholamreza Nakhaeizadeh. Algorithms for association rule mining - a general survey and comparison. *SIGKDD Explorations*, 2(1):58–64, 2000.

[9] Ruoming Jin and Gagan Agrawal. An algorithm for in-core frequent itemset mining on streaming data. In *Proceedings of the Fifth IEEE International Conference on Data Mining*, ICDM '05, pages 210–217, Washington, DC, USA, 2005. IEEE Computer Society.

[10] Yehuda Koren, Edo Liberty, Yoelle Maarek, and Roman Sandler. Automatically tagging email by leveraging other users' folders. In *KDD*, pages 913–921, 2011.

[11] David D. Lewis and Kimberly A. Knowles. Threading electronic mail: a preliminary study. *Inf. Process. Manage.*, 33:209–217, March 1997.

[12] Einat Minkov, William W. Cohen, and Andrew Y. Ng. Contextual search and name disambiguation in email using graphs. In *Proceedings of the 29th annual international ACM SIGIR conference*, SIGIR '06, pages 27–34. ACM, 2006.

[13] Ed. P. Resnick. Internet message format, 2001.

[14] George Rebane and Judea Pearl. The recovery of causal poly-trees from statistical data. *Int. J. Approx. Reasoning*, pages 1–1, 1988.

[15] Alexia Tsotsis. Comscore says you don't got mail: Web email usage declines, 59% among teens. *TechCrunch*, Feb 2011.

[16] Yi-Chia Wang, Mahesh Joshi, William Cohen, and Carolyn Rosé. Recovering implicit thread structure in newsgroup style conversations. In *Proceedings of the 2nd International Conference on Weblogs and Social Media (ICWSM II)*, 2008.

[17] Jen-Yuan Yeh and Aaron Harnly. Email thread reassembly using similarity matching. In *Proceedings of Collaboration, Electronic messaging, Anti-Abuse and Spam Conference (CEAS)*, 2006.

APPENDIX

A. SPURIOUS RELATIONSHIPS

The goal we set out to achieve in this reseasrch was to identify *strong causality* between emails. By this we mean that we are interested in identifying threads of inbound automatically generated messages, emanating from a single event driven by the user. The method used for identifying these causal relations are purely statistical. A well known problem with this approach [14] is the following. Consider three events X, Y and Z and the following two cases: (i), event X causes Z (ii), event Y causes both X and Z. In the second case X and Z are not related by a *causal relationship* but rather by a *spurious relationship.* If Y is not observed, then both cases are indistinguishable, because the pair (X, Z) appears to be statistically dependent. Thus, a false causality relation might be inferred.

The main source of false causality in our data are *monthly recurring emails.* Credit card companies usually send a report to the cardholder on the same day monthly (e.g. every first of the month). Many users hold cards from more than one credit card company, and many hold cards from the same two major credit card companies. Hence, it may appear that one credit card statement causes the other. In reality these emails are both caused by an unobserved event, namely, the beginning of the month. It is easy to eliminate these false effects by identifying monthly recurring emails, and forcing them *not* to continue threads. (Starting threads is still allowed and useful: Often a "*thank you for your payment*" template appears shortly after the bill arrives and continues the thread.)

A slightly different type of statistical phenomenon one should be aware of is known as frequent item sets. This problem is well known among data miners who analyze purchase data at supermarkets (either traditional or online). The idea there is to identify pairs (or tuples) of items that are bought together in the same cart with some noticeable statistical significance. This allows the store to apply sophisticated pricing and discounting strategies. We refer the reader to the survey [1, 8]. For the purpose of this work, we do not view pairs of frequent actions as threads. Consider the following example: Users who order streaming movies from online providers are more likely to place an online order for pizza (from a different vendor) shortly thereafter. Everyone would agree that the relationship between the action of ordering the movie and ordering the pizza should not be considered causal for the purpose of threading the corresponding emails. We have noticed that the weight assigned to such connections in our data, albeit high with strong statistical significance, is well below that of arcs corresponding to actual thread connections. Careful thresholding of arc weights in $G_{\mathcal{T}}$ typically eliminates this problem.

Predicting Content Change on the Web

Kira Radinsky*
Technion–Israel Institute of Technology
Haifa, Israel
kirar@cs.technion.ac.il

Paul N. Bennett
Microsoft Research
Redmond, WA, USA
paul.n.bennett@microsoft.com

ABSTRACT

Accurate prediction of changing web page content improves a variety of retrieval and web related components. For example, given such a prediction algorithm one can both design a better crawling strategy that only recrawls pages when necessary as well as a proactive mechanism for personalization that pushes content associated with user revisitation directly to the user. While many techniques for modeling change have focused simply on past change frequency, our work goes beyond that by additionally studying the usefulness in page change prediction of: the page's content; the degree and relationship among the prediction page's observed changes; the relatedness to other pages and the similarity in the types of changes they undergo. We present an expert prediction framework that incorporates the information from these other signals more effectively than standard ensemble or basic relational learning techniques. In an empirical analysis, we find that using page content as well as related pages significantly improves prediction accuracy and compare it to common approaches. We present numerous similarity metrics to identify related pages and focus specifically on measures of temporal content similarity. We observe that the different metrics yield related pages that are qualitatively different in nature and have different effects on the prediction performance.

Categories and Subject Descriptors

H.3.7 [**Information Storage and Retrieval**]: Digital Libraries; I.5.4 [**Pattern Recognition**]: Applications

Keywords

Web Change Prediction, Web Dynamics, Web Crawling

1. INTRODUCTION

In many retrieval frameworks, web pages are often treated as static documents. However, in reality, pages are dynamic channels whose contents change with time. Some pages, like news entry points, change on a daily basis with regularity. While others, like faculty home pages, may be updated with far less frequency and regularity. These changes may involve significant changes in content, the addition or deletion of hyperlinks, or the addition of hyperlinks to previously unknown web pages. Furthermore, these changes in content drive changes in the query distribution that lead to a page, and impact the relevance of a page to the query.

The ability to predict key types of changes can be used in a variety of settings. For example, accurate prediction of a significant change in page content enables an improved incremental crawling strategy that only recrawls pages when necessary [18]. Similarly, accurate prediction of a new hyperlink to a previously unknown (i.e., non-indexed) web page, enables one to efficiently discover pages that should be indexed. In a personalized retrieval setting, accurate prediction of re-visitation to a page with new content enables one to push new content to a user.

When modeling any variable of interest as a function of time, it is natural to consider the past observed values as a basic means of prediction [8]. For example, in this setting, when predicting whether a page will change, we can simply predict based on the change frequency for the page observed over some past historical window. However, there are other signals that provide information beyond change frequency.

In particular, the content of a page enables better prediction of its change [4, 24, 23]. It provides a finer distinction of the degree of change that a page is undergoing, and the relationship among these changes. For example, in a series of ten days, a page may experience small changes on every day or large changes. These changes in content might be similar to each other or vastly dissimilar. For a page that experiences vastly dissimilar changes on a regular basis, the changes may be considered more significant (since the content change implies a need for reindexing). On the other hand, similar changes with the same regularity may be considered less significant. To distinguish these cases, the appropriate features need to be encoded.

Pages that are related to the prediction page may also change in a similar, although not necessarily, synchronous fashion [24, 23, 9, 12, 13]. These pages would then provide a useful signal for determining whether the prediction page will change. The *strength* and the *type* of the relationship between those pages is likely to be indicative of how well one can predict the change of the other. In the web setting, natural choices of relationship types include: distance in the web graph, similarity in content, and similarity in temporal change pattern. We explore all of these relationship types and evaluate their relative contributions over the page's content alone. In particular, our exploration of similarity in content *over time* through the use of cross-correlation and the dynamic time warping (DTW) algorithm is especially

*This research was performed while the author was at Microsoft Research.

WSDM'13, February 4–8, 2012, Rome, Italy.

novel. Both of these provide more robust computation of similar temporal change patterns by dealing with the case where content between two pages may be correlated in time but slightly out of phase.

Additionally, even after identifying other related information sources, there is a question as to how to best incorporate this information into a machine learning algorithm. We develop an expert combination approach where the experts are selected according to their degree of "relatedness" and demonstrate the superiority of this modeling choice to other combination and relational learning techniques.

This paper is organized as follows: In Section 2 we describe the related work. In Section 3, we present the formal problem description and outline the challenges and research questions. We then present a general characterization of the types of information sources available when predicting page change using past history (Section 4.1). Using this characterization, we develop specific feature sets that capture aspects of each of these information sources in a useful way for modeling change (Section 4.2). In particular, in addition to the past history of a page's change, we also incorporate features based on the page content of the page as well as the content of *related* pages. For each information source we provide several algorithms to combine the information in a learning setting. In particular, we present a novel algorithm to combine the information in an expert prediction framework (Section 5). We examine techniques for identifying related pages, including pages that are close in the web graph, pages with similar content, and pages with correlated content across time – where the last two prove to be especially effective (Section 6). Finally, in an empirical study, we not only demonstrate the effectiveness of our methods, but also explore alternative modeling choices, analyze the qualitative differences in the expert selection methods, and present the superiority of our prediction methods in a crawling application, which strives to maximize the *freshness* of its index (how many pages in the index remain up-to-date as compared with the online web copies).

2. RELATED WORK

Attempting to predict the probability of a web page changing is not a new problem and has been studied by a variety of researchers [9, 8, 4, 24, 23]. This has primarily been motivated by the incremental web crawling setting [18]. In this setting, recrawling a web page is linked to the probability of its change, and the goal is to maximize some tradeoff between freshness and coverage of a web index. A crawl policy that optimizes this tradeoff usually focuses only on the probability of change for pages that do not change too often or very rarely. The reason for this is that, under certain assumptions, recrawling pages that change very frequently dominates crawl resources and actually hurts the overall utility of a crawl by ensuring only these very frequently changing pages are kept fresh [10, 7, 22]. In line with these studies, we restrict our study to pages above a minimum threshold of change and below a maximum threshold.

However, while freshness may be one metric for measuring the utility of recrawling a web page, it may not reflect impact on the user of a search engine. As a result, Wolf *et al.* [25] look at minimizing embarrassment – the probability a search engine user clicks on a result URL whose live page doesn't match the query. This introduces a notion of the negative utility a user may experience but not what gains may be experienced from crawling. Therefore, Pandey & Olston [19] consider a user-centric utility. This

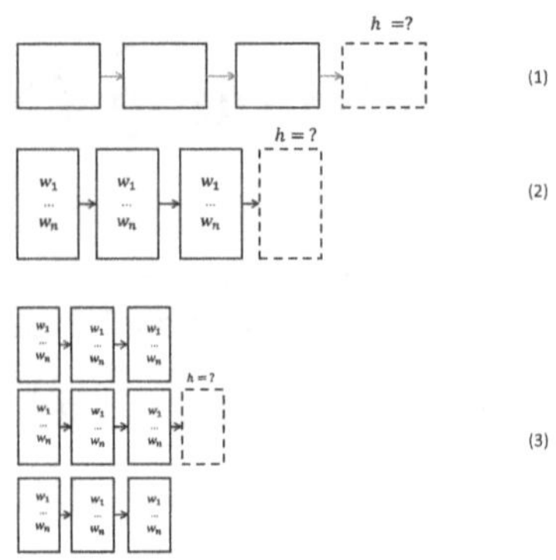

Figure 1: Fully observed setting. Each square represents a page, where w_i are the page contents. (1) 1D setting (2) 2D setting [3, 6] (3) 3D setting

utility weights each page by: (1) an observed query load on a search engine, and (2) the impact that downloading a new copy of the page has on the search ranking (as estimated via previous change). Similarly, Ali & Williams [3] measure the impact under a specific query load of several simple prediction schemes. They found that simply recrawling pages whose previous two observed snapshots changed by more than (approximately) 20 words significantly reduced crawling compared to recrawling all recently changed pages. This policy also maintained effective ranking as measured under the query load. In line with these, we restrict ourselves to predicting significant changes to a search page. In our case, we define this as cases where the page's change relative to the last observed snapshot is above a significance threshold (as defined in Equation 1).

In terms of methods of predicting change, several works [6, 11, 7] use past change-frequency and change-recency of a page, typically together with an assumption of a Poisson process, in order to predict whether the page will change. This is essentially equivalent to our baseline model described in Section 5.1. Both Barbosa *et al.* [4] and Tan & Mitra [23] demonstrate that using content-based features can improve prediction over just change-frequency alone [6]. The first of these works primarily uses static features (content features, such as file size available from a single snapshot) in addition to change history, while the second also considers dynamic features (features that change between two snapshots, such as the cosine similarity between the page contents). In our work, we focus on dynamic content features since we are concerned with predicting *significant* content change, and as argued by Ali & Williams [3], many of those static features are usually predictive of any type of change (e.g., new advertisements, images, etc.), that are usually uninteresting or do not impact indexing. Nevertheless, our methods are general and could easily incorporate such additional features.

Fetterly *et al.* [13] note that not only is the previous degree of content change a good predictor of future change, but that change is also correlated at the top-level domains of web pages. Cho & Ntoulas [9] exploited this type of correlation structure at the website level by using a sample of webpages from a website to estimate the change probability of any page from the website. Tan *et al.* [24, 23] extend this idea to the more general case by clustering pages based on static and dynamic content features into clusters that are more homogeneous in terms of change patterns before conducting the sampling based approach. Both of these can be viewed as methods of identifying related pages. We also identify related pages, but use them to directly predict the probability of change without having sampled from the current time slice. Additionally, we investigate directly estimating relatedness via temporal content similarity – which could easily be used to cluster in a sampling based approach.

In contrast to previous work: (1) we focus on the task of predicting *significant* changes rather than any change to a web page; (2) we develop a wide array of dynamic content-based features that may be useful for the more general temporal mining case beyond crawling; (3) we explore a wide variety of methods to identify related pages including content, web graph distance, and temporal content similarity – where the last is both especially novel and effective; (4) we derive a novel expert prediction framework that effectively leverages information from related pages without the need for sampling from the current time slice.

3. PROBLEM FORMULATION

We consider the general setting where we want to estimate a function h for each page. This h can indicate several types of page change (Section 3.1). This function can be estimated using different information types (Section 3.2), which have different observability when estimating h (Section 3.3).

3.1 Types of Web Page Change

Let O be a finite set of pages, and let $h : O \times \mathfrak{T} \rightarrow \mathbb{R}$ be a temporal goal function, that provides information about the state of a page $o \in O$ at time $t \in \mathfrak{T}$, where $\mathfrak{T}$ is a discrete representation of time. Depending on the targeted application, a function h can be defined in numerous ways. For example, the change may be:

1. Whether the page $o \in O$ changed significantly. This can be used to identify when a page is stale enough to be recrawled.
2. Whether the change in page $o \in O$ corresponds to a change from non-relevant previous content to relevant current content for some specified query load. The function not only indicates whether the page is stale, but also that the change will result in the page being surfaced for a query.
3. Whether there is a new out link from page $o \in O$. This helps indicate when recrawling a page will lead to discover a new portion of the web graph, discover new anchor text, or impact link analysis metrics.

We focus on page changes of type 1, although our approach is readily applicable to the other change types. We consider a *significant page change* to be a change in content between the content vector at time t and the content vector at time $t+1$ whose word distribution is different in a statistically significantly sense (as measured by a chi-squared test) from that of the previous day. That is, the p-value produced by performing the test satisfies:

$$p^{\chi^2}(\text{ContentDist}(t), \text{ContentDist}(t+1)) < 0.05 \qquad (1)$$

3.2 Information Sources

As we discussed before, when estimating h for each page, we can consider several types of information. In many previous studies [6, 11, 7, 3], only information about the changing object was used, e.g., the change rate of the specific page. We propose a general-unifying framework (formally discussed in Section 4.1) of the possible information types, ranging from only information about the changing object to information about all the other related objects. We divide the information types into the following information settings:

1. 1D setting: In this setting, only information about h of the page itself in previous time-stamps is used to estimate h. For example, only information involving the rate of the page change itself is used to estimate future page change. This setting was explored in the past [11, 7], and we consider it as one of the baselines.
2. 2D setting: In this setting, a wider range of information about the page h itself is used to estimate h. We consider the page as an entity with features which can be used to understand its future h, e.g., future change rate. This setting was explored by several works [3, 6], and we consider it as one of the baselines as well.
3. 3D setting: In this setting, not only is the information about the specific page used, but also the relations to the other pages are considered in determining the probability of a future h value of a page, e.g., the future change of a page.

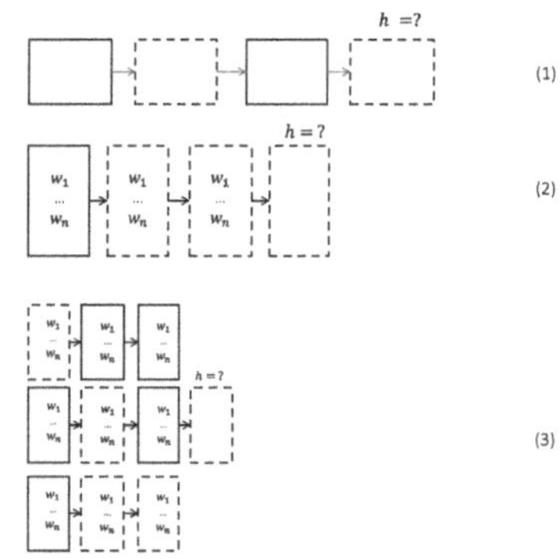

Figure 2: Partially observed setting.

3.3 Information Observability

In a *fully-observed scenario*, at each time stamp t, all the above information from the previous n time stamps is available. This is a scenario, where, given a set of k periodically observed pages over a period of n, the goal is to induce a function h that can be used to estimate page changes within this group in the following time-stamp. Figure 1 illustrates the three information settings in the fully-observed scenario.

The more general scenario, is a *partially-observed scenario*, where only partial information about the objects in previous times is given. That is, at each time stamp t, only the information about some subgroup is available to the learner. This is an online scenario, where, for example a crawling system doesn't observe the information about non-crawled pages. It only crawls pages it believes to have changed, and therefore only information about those crawled pages is given to the learner to induce an approximation of h. The three information settings in the partially-observed scenario are illustrated in Figure 2.

In this work we focus on the fully-observed setting and provide algorithms based on the 1D, 2D and 3D settings. We wish to derive insights and understanding of this setting before generalizing to the partially-observable scenario. Additionally, in Section 8.3 we empirically show a simple application of our algorithms for the partially-observed setting, where the objects are iteratively sampled to gain more information. Section 4.1 formalizes the problem from a machine learning perspective, and Section 5 outlines our algorithmic solution to the problem.

4. SOLUTION FRAMEWORK

In this section, we formalize the learning problem and provide an algorithmic framework for predicting change. Unlike standard learning algorithms that assume a static feature set and a single object type, we present a formalism that handles temporal features, derived from both single and multiple objects over time. We then discuss the specific features for page change prediction that we build using this framework.

4.1 Formal Framework

Let O be a set of objects. Let $C \subseteq O$ be a goal concept. In our problem, O is the set of pages and C is the set of changing pages. In the traditional (binary) supervised learning setup, we define the goal function $h : O \rightarrow \{0,1\}$, where $h(o) = 1 \leftrightarrow o \in C$. Let $E = \{\langle o_1, h(o_1)\rangle, ..., \langle o_K, h(o_K)\rangle\}$, where $o_i \in O$ and $h(o_i) \in \{0,1\}$, be a set of training examples. To extend the basic setup to include classes and features that dynamically change over time, we assume $\mathfrak{T} = \{0, 1, ..., \infty\}$ to be a discrete representation of time. We define $h : O \times \mathfrak{T} \rightarrow \{0,1\}$ to be a *temporal goal function*, and $E = \{\langle\langle o_1, t_1\rangle, h(o_1, t_1)\rangle, ..., \langle\langle o_K, t_n\rangle, h(o_K, t_n)\rangle\}$ to be a set of *temporal training examples*, where $o_i \in O$, $t_j \in \mathfrak{T}$ and $h(o_i, t_j) \in \{0,1\}$.

The basic algorithm for predicting page change, as currently used in many applications [6, 11, 7], is prediction based on the $h(o_i, t_j)$ of past training examples of o_i. Using the previous notation, we call this information setting the *1D setting*, as it only utilizes the class (in our case, page change) behavior.

Let $F = \{f_1, ..., f_{|F|}\}$ be a set of feature functions, where $f_i : O \rightarrow Im(f_i)$. A traditional learning algorithm takes E and F as input and produces a hypothesis $\hat{h}$ which is a good approximation of h. We define $F = \{f_1, ..., f_{|F|}\}$ to be a set of *temporal feature functions*, where $f_i : O \times \mathfrak{T} \rightarrow Im(f_i)$. That is, $f_i(o,t)$ is the value of the feature i of object o at time t. A *temporal learning algorithm* receives as input E and F and produces a temporal hypothesis $\hat{h}$.

Traditionally in machine learning, the building blocks of a classifier $\hat{h}(o)$ are the features of the object $f_1(o), \ldots, f_{|F|}(o)$, e.g., changes in a page might depend only on its features, e.g., its terms. In our extended framework, $\hat{h}(o,t)$ can use, in addition to $f_i(o,t)$, also $f_i(o,t')$ for $t' < t$. For example, the page change might depend on the change direction values over the last several days. Using the previous notation, we call this information setting a *2D setting*, as it only utilizes the features of the page itself.

Alternatively, in our framework, $\hat{h}(o,t)$ can use features of other objects, $f_i(o', t')$ for $o' \neq o, t' < t$. For example, changes in other pages from previous observable times. We also assume a relation function $R_i : O \times O \leftarrow R$ between the objects. These functions can also be considered as a weighted graph structure over the objects. Thus, $\hat{h}(o,t)$ can use features of only related objects using metrics over the structure of relations R_i. In the most general setup, $\hat{h}(o,t)$ can combine the above two approaches and use $f_i(o', t')$ for $t' < t$ and $o' \neq o$. For example, to determine whether a certain page will change tomorrow, the classifier can use various parameters of other pages over the last week. A more extended view of the features f_i, are those that take into account several objects in an aggregated feature, i.e., $f_i : O^K \rightarrow Im(f_i)$. For example, a feature that determines the content similarity of the predicted page o with the other objects that are fed as input to produce $\hat{h}(o,t)$. In the previous notation, we call this setting a *3D setting*, as it utilizes the features of the page itself and other pages as well.

4.2 Framework Implementation

The previous section discussed the formal framework of the information sources. We now discuss the specific features that we implement for content change prediction.

4.2.1 2D Features

Given the time of classification t, the goal is to predict whether page A will change at time $t + \sigma$, where σ is the prediction interval. We denote the representation of a page to be classified at time t as $A(t)$. Let l be the regression parameter, i.e., the window size from which features are generated. For example, for $l = 2$ we create page features using its behavior over the last 2 time stamps (not to be confused with the number of examples n, which is the number of objects usually fed into a classifier). We define the following features for learning page change:

1. Frequency of change in page A during the window l. This feature is equivalent to the information captured by the baseline in Section 5.1.

2. Term unigram probability distribution of the words in page $A(t)$: $\{\frac{c_{i,A(t)}}{\sum_j c_{j,A(t)}}\}$ where $c_{i,A(t)}$ is the number of occurrences of the considered term (w_i) in page $A(t)$, and the denominator is the sum of number of occurrences of all terms in page $A(t)$, that is, the size of the document $A(t)$. These features are meant to capture the intuition that particular words on a page might be predictive of page change. For example, on a local organization's page the words "upcoming meeting" might be predictive of a change that notes of the meeting will soon be posted.

3. Features representing the magnitude of the change vector between the content at every time point in the window and the content of the page at time t. Formally, a set of l features representing how big of a change A experienced compared to each previous day in the window: $\{||A(t) - A(t-i)|| | i \in [1 \ldots l]\}$. Intuitively, the magnitude of change in content between the last observed content (t) and the content on any given day in the window may be predictive of change. For example, a stable set without change may increase the chance of no change. While a series of small changes may presage an upcoming update. This will be dependent on the particular page and these features provide the expressiveness to learn such behaviors.

4. For each pair of prediction-interval separated timesteps in the window, we define features measuring the magnitude of the change vector in page content in a single timestep. Formally, a set of l features representing how big of a change A was experiencing compared to previous days in the window: $\{||A(t-i) - A(t-i-\sigma)|| | i \in [1 \ldots l]\}$. Intuitively, this captures the magnitude of change typically seen given the prediction interval size.

5. Features representing whether the page changed on every time in the window. We define change of page at time t as:

$$\text{change}(A(t)) = \begin{cases} 1 & \text{if } A(t) \text{ changed} \\ 0 & \text{if } A(t) \text{ did not change} \end{cases}$$

We consider the following features: change($A(t-1)$), ..., change($A(t-l)$) representing whether the page changed significantly on the days before the prediction. Intuitively, these features are useful when an upcoming change might be predicted by any change (or lack thereof) a fixed number of days in the past or a regularity of change/stability might indicate a continuation of the pattern.

4.2.2 3D Features

Additionally, we can incorporate features of other pages B on the web. Their change and features might also reflect on the change in page A. The first five types of features we define are exactly analogous to those defined in Section 4.2.1, and they are meant to capture similar motivations but with the shift that if the feature types from the same page are useful, then the same ones from a related page may prove useful. We also add two new feature types targeted at representing the relationship between the two pages. We define the following set of features for each page B:

1. Frequency of change in page B during the window l.
2. Term unigram probability distribution of the words in page $B(t)$: $\{\frac{c_{i,B(t)}}{\sum_j c_{j,B(t)}}\}$.
3. A set of l features representing how big of a change B experienced compared to previous days in the window: $\{||B(t)-B(t-i)|||i \in [1\ldots l]\}$.
4. A set of l features representing how big of a change B was experiencing compared to previous days in the window: $\{||B(t-i)-B(t-i-\sigma)|||i \in [1\ldots l]\}$.
5. Feature change$_{t-\sigma-1}(B), \ldots,$ change$_{t-l}(B)$ representing whether the page changed significantly on the days before the prediction.
6. A set of l features representing the similarity of page B to the prediction page A: $\cos(A(t), B(t))$. Intuitively, the degree of content similarity of the pages at time $t \in [t \ldots t-l]$ may indicate the strength of predictivity between the pages.
7. A set of l features representing the similarity in change of page B to the content of page A. Formally, let $\delta(B)_i = B(t) - B(t-i)$, and $i \in [1\ldots l]$, thus this feature is defined as: $\cos(\delta(B), A)$. Intuitively, not only may the degree of content similarity be indicative of the relationship strength, but also the similarity between the content of B that changed and A's full content. We also consider a set of l features representing the similarity of the changes of page B to the changes of the prediction page A: $\cos(\delta(B(t-i)), \delta(A(t-i))$ for $i \in [1\ldots l]$.

5. LEARNING ALGORITHMS

In this section we outline the specific algorithms based on the solution framework we described in the previous section.

5.1 Baseline Algorithm

The basic algorithm for predicting page change, as currently used in many applications [6, 11, 7], is prediction based on the probability of the page to change significantly based on the past training examples. That is, $h(o_i, t_j) = 1$ with probability:

$$p(h(o_i,t_j) = 1 \mid h(o_i,t_k) \in E \text{ where } t_k < t_j \text{ and } (t_j - t_k) \leq l).$$

The parameter l is typically referred to as a window size and is a user-specified parameter.

5.2 Single Expert Algorithm

The single expert is an algorithm that represents the pages with a set of features. Given M time stamps, we create training examples with the features described in Section 4.2.1. For example, if we want to predict for 5 days in the future ($\sigma = 5$) and we have a total of 300 days for training, we can prepare training objects for a learner. Each object is made of features of l days, where l is the regression parameter. For example, for $l = 3$ a total of $300 - \sigma - l + 1 = 293$ examples are created to train a learner with. Given prediction interval σ, each example is labeled with the h value of the page in σ time stamps, i.e., $h(o, t+\sigma)$. Those E examples are used to train a classifier C. In our experiments we use SVM classifiers for this purpose.

During prediction, the set of the above features is extracted for the test instance and given as input to C. In our example, we are given another set of consecutive 21 days (separate from training period), from which $21-\sigma-l+1 = 14$ testing objects are created, on which the learner will be tested. In this work we consider the case where $\sigma = 1$ and $l = 1$, i.e., we observe the page as it is today and predict how it will be tomorrow. We then output the prediction of the classifier.

5.3 Algorithms Using Related Objects

In this section we discuss algorithms that consider both the page's features and features of other pages. We first present a novel algorithm that models the related pages as experts, and follows a voting scheme (Section 5.3.1) In order to investigate whether this framework is in fact advantageous we also investigate several alternative mechanisms for incorporating information from related pages: an algorithm that collects the information of the other sources into a single expert (Section 5.3.2), and algorithms that use multiple models to boost performance (Section 5.3.3).

5.3.1 Multiple-Experts Algorithm

In this section we propose a novel algorithm, that performs a temporal relational choice of experts. By temporal experts we mean related pages that predict change. The novel algorithm we present here takes into consideration the structure of the object-relations network, and builds relational experts. Each page will be considered an expert, and will include the features described in Section 4.2.1 and Section 4.2.2 (features are calculated in respect to page $A(t)$ – the object of classification). Each expert is trained with the target function, h, of the *relevant page*. Intuitively, each expert can predict based on the changes it experienced, its content and similarity to page A at time t and previous times, whether page A will experience a change in the future. For example, if we wish to predict a change in an Information Retrieval professor's page, we might train a classifier based on the features of the WSDM page, where the label would be whether the professor's page changed or not.

While the combination of the pages decision can be done using any ensemble combination method we use weighted majority voting (see weighting techniques in Section 6). Formally, given prediction interval σ, for each object $o \in O$ train a classifier using examples (with the features described in Section 4.2.2) and labeled with the h value of the page A in σ time stamps, i.e., $h(o, t+\sigma)$. Those examples are used to train a classifier C (in our experiments we use SVM classifiers for this purpose). Eventually O classifiers are trained.

During prediction, for each classifier C_i (corresponding to an object o_i), the set of the above features is extracted for the test instance and given as input to C_i. We then output the combined prediction of the classifier by selecting the majority weighted vote. See full algorithm in Figure 3.

Procedure MULTIPLE EXPERTS($WeakLearner, O, o_{target}$)
  Train:
  Foreach $o_j \in O$
    $E(o_j) = \{ \langle f_1^t(o_j, t_i), \ldots, f_n^t(o_j, t_i) \rangle, h(o_{target}, t_i + \sigma) | \}$
    Call *WeakLearner* with $E(o_j)$,
      and receive the hypothesis classifier h_j
    Add h_j to the ensemble, ξ
  Test: Given an unlabeled instance o_{target} at time t
    Evaluate the ensemble $\xi = \{h_1, \ldots, h_{|O|}\}$ on $o_{target}(t)$
    Let $V_{t,j} = \begin{cases} R_i(o_{target}, o_j) & \text{if } h_t \text{ picks class } c_j \\ 0 & \text{otherwise} \end{cases}$
    be the vote given to class c_j by classifier h_t
    Obtain total vote received by each class
      $V_j = \sum_{t=1}^{T} v_{t,j}$ for $j \in \{0, 1\}$
    Return the class that receives the highest total vote.

Figure 3: Temporal experts algorithm. The inputs are a weak learner, the pages O and the page to be classified o_{target}. R_i is a weighting of the relation between two objects. The prediction interval is σ.

5.3.2 Relational-Union Algorithm

In many relational learning scenarios relational features are created by collecting features over related objects, which are then fed into a classifier. This type of prediction has been used widely on the web [15]. One such example is the ad-click prediction problem [21]. Here the nodes are the ads, bids and queries, and the edges are the relations between the three. The goal is to predict a certain click on an ad. Similarly here, the nodes are the pages and the edges are the hyperlinks. The goal is to predict a certain page change.

Given M time stamps, we create training examples with the features described in Section 4.2.2. Given prediction interval σ, each example is labeled with the h value of the page of prediction in σ time stamps, i.e., $h(o, t+\sigma)$. Those E examples are used to train a classifier C. In our experiments we use SVM classifiers for this purpose. During prediction, the set of the above features is extracted for the test instance and given as input to C, which provides the prediction.

5.3.3 Relational-Stacking Algorithms

Stacking methods use multiple models to improve prediction over just a single model. Stacking algorithms, similar to the previous models, combine many features from related objects, and then train several "base" models either by bagging or reweighting the example distribution (boosting) before combining these models in the final model output.

Bagging [5] is one such method, where randomly sampled examples from the training set are used to train different base models. The base models predictions are then combined, where every model has an equal weight. Let k be the number of base models and let E be the set of examples as in Section 5.3.2. Given a training set of size $|E|$, this method generates k new training sets, each of size $|E|$, by sampling examples from the original training set uniformly and with replacement. A model is trained for each of the k training sets, and combined by majority voting. This method was shown to be useful in improving many linear models [5].

An extension of this idea, is **Boosting**. Intuitively, instead of randomly choosing instances, the ensemble model is built incrementally, where every new base model is trained

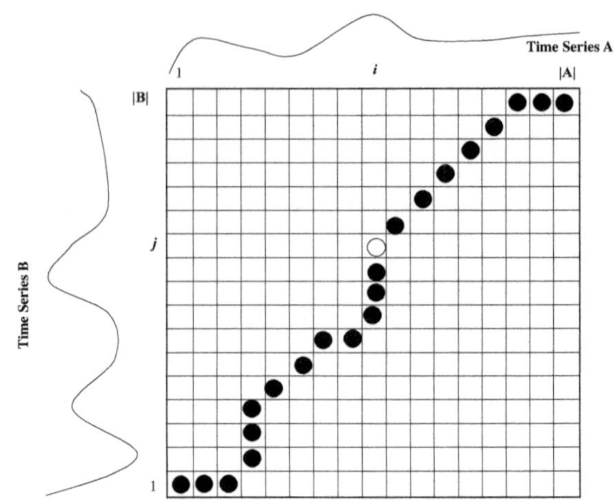

Figure 4: DTW finds the best alignment between time series A and B by maintaining the illustrated cost matrix $C(i, j)$.

with the training instances that previous models did not perform well on. Let E be the examples (as mentioned in Section 5.3.2), k number of base models, and let C be a classifier. AdaBoost [14] defines a vector of weights W for each example in E. It is first initialized as: $W_0(j) = \frac{1}{|E|}$. The algorithm performs k iterations, at each iteration reweighing the examples and retraining a classifier C_i with the weighted examples. The examples are reweighed in the following way:

$$W_{i+1}(j) = \frac{W_i(j) \exp(-\alpha_t y_j C_i(x_j))}{Z_i}$$

where Z_i is a normalization factor, $C_i(x)$ is the prediction of the classifier at iteration i for example x, and $\alpha_i = \frac{1}{2}\ln\frac{1-\epsilon_i}{\epsilon_i}$ is the weighted error rate at iteration i, where $\epsilon_i = \sum_{j=1}^{|E|} W_i(j)[y_j \neq h_t(x_j)]$ is the error rate at iteration i. The output of the ensemble model is a combination of the k base models created at the end of each iteration weighted by the error α_i they experienced.

6. EXPERT SELECTION

The number of pages on the web, and therefore the number of temporal experts (or number of 3D features as used by the relational algorithm), is extremely large. Due to this computational considerations, only a subset of the pages in O can be considered and monitored for every page. Based on our formalism from Section 4.1, we assumed a relation function $R_i : O \times O$ between the objects. We explore several such functions that choose the experts to monitor for every page – what we refer to as the *Expert Selection* problem.

Let p be the page whose h value is being predicted, and let e be a candidate expert. Given a predefined constant k of pages the system is capable of monitoring, the goal of an expert selection algorithm is to find the k experts such that the prediction accuracy of page h values is the highest. Notice that simple cross validation is a hard task due to its computation complexity (selecting all possible set of experts). We next present several heuristic algorithms for estimation of these experts.

6.1 Graph Distance KNN

We hypothesize that pages that are linked to one another in the web graph have higher probability of experiencing similar changes. In this case, we identify the experts for a page by using in-links and out-links and finding the closest neighbor using a single step using an undirected representation of the links. In other words, the experts are selected using a K-nearest-neighbors procedure in the web graph, and we weight each page equally ($R_i(o, neighbor(o) = 1)$. We used a web graph based on a sample of 22 million web pages (reached from good reputation sites seed) and 345 million edges, extracted from a web crawl performed in 2006 (for more information see [17]), at the same time the content crawling was performed.

6.2 Content Similarity KNN

We hypothesize that content similarity is a potential catalyst of mutual page changes. As the expert and the page discuss similar topics, a change in one might lead to a change in the other. Each page can be represented in some vector space with a predefined distance metric, and then a k nearest algorithm can be applied to find the most similar experts in content. In this work, we represent each page as a bag of words and the distance metric chosen is the cosine similarity (i.e., $R_i(o, neighbor(o) = cos(text(o), text(neighbor(o)))$.

6.3 Temporal Content Similarity KNN

The above mentioned approaches can be considered as finding k nearest neighbors in some static snapshot (either the web graph or web content). In this section, we also leverage the content change dynamics of the pages. The change patterns of the expert and the page over time are essential information to understand their mutual temporal behavior. Intuitively, a good predictive expert of change will have some correlation in content not just at a static time, but also will tend to trend in change together with the predicted page across a range of time – although one may lag/lead the other. Furthermore, the change correlation will be in similar topics. That is, the temporal correlation of the content-similarity of the change behavior of the two pages is high. We explore the monitoring of content similarity using cross-correlation and dynamic time warping (DTW). Similar temporal semantic modeling techniques have been used successfully in the past to improve semantic relatedness tasks [20]. Cross-correlation is a measure of similarity of two time series as a function of some time-lag applied to them, and defined as

$$\frac{\sum_i [(ts_1[i] - E(ts_1)) \cdot (ts_2[i-d] - E(ts_2))]}{N \cdot \sigma_{ts_1} \sigma_{ts_2}},$$

where $d = 1 \ldots N$ is a possible delay, N is the minimal time series length, σ is the time series variance, and E is the means of the corresponding series. The delay with the best correlation is chosen as the similarity. DTW (see Figure 5), on the other hand is a measure of similarity of two time series as a function of both time-lag and speed. For example, DTW will give high score to the similarity of page A and page B, even if A changes more than B, but they still have a similar change pattern, i.e., B is influenced by some of the changes in A. DTW is a dynamic programming algorithm, that tries to find an optimal match of the time series by stretching and compressing section of those time series. It holds a cost matrix C, where $C(i, j)$ is the minimum distance between two points of the time series i and j (see illustration in Figure 4). Cross-correlation can be thought of a simple case of DTW, where only diagonal steps are allowed in the matrix.

We define *temporal content similarity* over time as the weighted combination of the correlation over the words in

```
Procedure DTW(ts1, ts2, C)
  n ← Min(|ts1|, |ts2|)
  dtw(ts1, ts2) ← new [|ts1| × |ts2|]
  For i = {1...n}
    dtw(i, 1) ← dtw(i − 1, 1) + C(i, 1)
    dtw(1, i) ← dtw(1, i − 1) + C(1, i)
  For i = {1...n}
    For j = {1...n}
      dtw(i, j) = |ts1(i) − ts2(j)|+
            Min(dtw(i − 1, j), dtw(i, j − 1), dtw(i − 1, j − 1))
  Return dtw(n, n)
```

Figure 5: Dynamic time warping algorithm (DTW)

the two documents. Let a document d be represented by a sequence of words $w_1, \ldots, w_m$. Let $t_1, \ldots, t_T$ be a sequence of consecutive discrete time points (e.g., days). We define the *dynamics* of a word w in a document d to be the time series of its frequency of appearance in d:

$$\mathrm{Dyn}(w, d) = \langle \mathrm{tfidf}(w, d(t_0)), \ldots, \mathrm{tfidf}(w, d(t_T)) \rangle$$

where $d(t_i)$ us the snapshot of document d at time t_i.

Let Q be a correlation function between time series (such as DTW or cross-correlation). We define a distance metric between p and e as follows:

$$\mathrm{Distance}(p, e) = \sum_{i=1}^{k} \omega(w_i)[Q(\mathrm{Dyn}(w_i, p), \mathrm{Dyn}(w_i, e))]$$

where $\omega(w_i)$ is a weighting function for every word, which can represent how dominant the word was in past changes, how many times it changed, etc. In our work we consider a simple version where the function represents the significance of the word for the document in the last snapshot of page: $\omega(w_i) = \mathrm{tfidf}(w_i, p(T))$. As before, the closest k experts can now be selected using the distance metric Distance, and the weights are the values of their correlation.

7. EXPERIMENTAL SETUP

We implemented the 1D, 2D and 3D algorithms and conducted a variety of experiments to test their performance, compared to the state of the art in the prediction literature.

7.1 Dataset

We evaluate our method on a real-world data collection. The data consists of 54,816 pages crawled on an hourly basis for a 6 months period (2007-06-30 till 2007-12-31). We collected URLs from the logs of logged-in users of the Microsoft Live Search toolbar. The pages to crawl were not random, but rather driven by user visitation patterns. We are interested in pages whose change is going to affect the satisfaction of many users, and therefore we sampled pages from those visited by 612,000 people for a five week period. For more information see the work by Adar et al. [2]. In order to prevent trivial predictions, we filtered out pages that exhibit a constant behavior, e.g., pages that either change all the time or don't at all. Additionally, for pages below a change frequency threshold (whose change patterns appear to be random), one can recrawl them on an infrequent schedule paying an amortized cost for having a stale copy. Let change$(o, t) = 1$ if the page o changes at time t, and change$(o, t) = 0$ otherwise. We require $|\{t|\,\mathrm{change}(o, t) \neq \mathrm{change}(o, t+1)\}| \geq \alpha$, where in our experimentation $\alpha = 0.3$, i.e., that page changes behavior at least in 30% of the data.

1D features [11, 7] (Baseline)	2D features [3, 6] (Single Expert)	3D features (Multiple Experts)
54.84%	62.93%	**72.72%**

Table 1: Prediction accuracy average on a sliding window. Results statistically significant using a t-test ($p < 0.05$) when compared to Multiple Experts.

Relational Union	Relational Stacking		Multiple Experts
	Boosting	Bagging	
62.91%	63.44%	63.58%	**72.72%**

Table 2: Prediction accuracy using different relational algorithms. Results statistically significant using a t-test ($p < 0.05$) when compared to Multiple Experts.

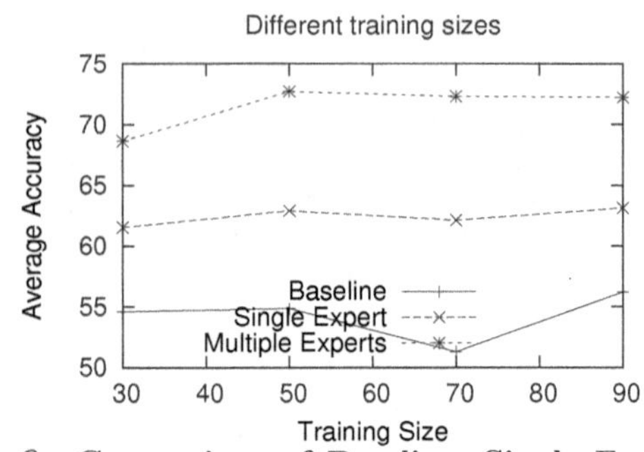

Figure 6: Comparison of Baseline, Single Expert and Multiple Experts over different training sizes. Each point in the graph represents the prediction accuracy (y label) of every of the method using the specified size of training examples (x label).

7.2 Empirical Methodology

In order to perform correct statistical evaluations of the algorithms over sufficient data, the empirical evaluation over each dataset is performed as follows:

- In each prediction, for each algorithm, we use the previous n days as training examples (we experimented on several n values). We construct each example where the task is to predict what happens on the following day ($\sigma = 1$). In order to construct each example the two days previous are used for the dynamic change features ($l = 1$).

- We repeated the predictions $|O|$ (number of pages) times. Each time, a different page was used as the target of prediction.

For each training set of size n and the consecutive test day, all algorithms train on all but last time point in the training set, and classify o_i with the resulting classifier. The classifier always takes as input the last ($l = 1$) time points. We use the same SVM polynomial classifier (degree=3) to implement all of the learning approaches to control for variance. All parameters of the learning algorithm were calibrated on the training data. The accuracy of a prediction algorithm for a page is averaged over all sliding windows (i.e., over $t_n - (t_1 + \sigma)$ predictions).

8. RESULTS

In this section we discuss the different experiments we have conducted. We first start with the main result showing that the use of information found in other pages provides higher precision for page change prediction. We then proceed with different analysis experiments of our algorithm.

8.1 Main Result

The accuracy results of all algorithms are presented in Table 1, with $k = 20$ experts selected using the cross-correlation method, trained with training size of $n = 50$. These particular values, as well as the number of experts and selection of cross-correlation as the primary temporal selection method, were chosen over a small sample of data. We investigate sensitivity of performance of these methods to varying choices of the amount of history used (n) as well as the number of experts selected (k) in Sections 8.2. Each value in the table represents an average performance over all objects. The results provide evidence that the temporal experts outperform the single experts and baseline, and that the single experts outperform the baseline (both results are statistically significant, as measured by a paired t-test).

We further experiment with different training sizes (Figure 6). There was a statistical significant difference in all periods of times in favor of the multiple expert approach, and the single expert approach outperformed the baseline over all training sizes. The behavior of the algorithm exhibits almost constant behavior over the different training sizes, indicating that a crawler only monitoring the last 30 days of every page can perform with high accuracy. All learning algorithms performed poorly with less than 30 training examples, and therefore are not shown in the graph.

8.2 Parameter Selection Analysis

In this section we analyze the different multiple experts algorithms, the different expert selection method and how the number of experts affects performance.

8.2.1 *Different Expert Algorithms*

The accuracy results of all algorithms are presented in Table 2, with 20 experts selected using the cross-correlation method, trained with a training size of 50. We observe that the multiple experts algorithm we have suggested in this paper reaches the highest performance (significant as measured by a paired t-test), providing evidence that this type of mechanism is appropriate for combining information from multiple sources. We conclude that, although all algorithms were trained using the same set of features, just combining the features without the taking into account the structure, whether one trains a simple classifier, bags, or boosts, is not enough.

8.2.2 *Expert Selection Methods*

In this section we present the results for the different expert selection methods (see Table 3). We performed a paired t-test on the results, and found statistical significance difference between the cross-correlation approach and the non-temporal approaches with p-value $p < 0.05$. However, we found no statistical significance between the different temporal content approaches. All expert selection algorithms show statistically significantly higher performance than the performance of methods using 2D and 1D features.

The results provide an interesting viewpoint on the change behavior and its indicators. Although graph distance may seem an intuitive measure for the web, it provides little impact for change prediction. Correlation over time in the same topics is the more beneficial approach in those cases.

Graph Distance	Content Similarity	Temporal Content Similarity	
		Cross-Correlation	DTW
64.40%	67.27%	**72.72%**	70.33%

Table 3: Prediction accuracy average of multiple experts using the different selection algorithms. Results statistically significant using a t-test ($p < 0.05$) when compared to DTW.

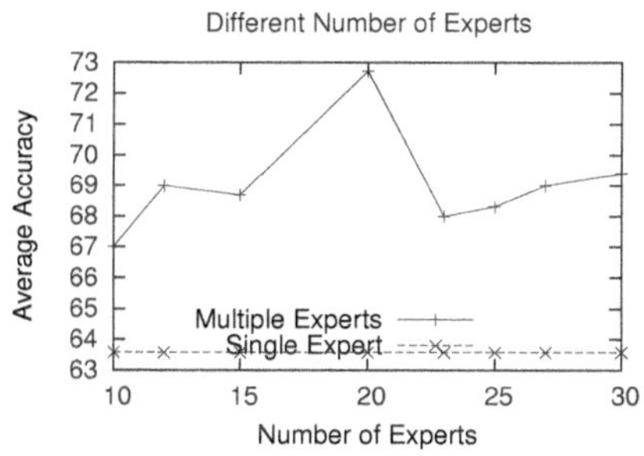

Figure 7: Number of experts as a function of accuracy. Each point in the graph represents the prediction accuracy (y label) of the multiple experts algorithm using the specified size of experts (x label).

8.2.3 *Number of Selected Experts*

In this section we investigate the performance of the multiple expert algorithm as a function of the number of selected experts. We show the results in Figure 7. While there is some sensitivity in performance to the number of experts selected, the gains over the single expert using the 2D features is robust across a range of values for number of experts. Up to 20 experts it seems the system gains more precision by the addition of more experts. However, after reaching this performance peak the addition of other features seems to be adding unnecessary noise to the system. Additionally, we see that even a small number of experts has enough predictive power for predicting page content change.

8.3 Application to Crawling: Maximizing Freshness

We show an application of our work to a crawling task in which the goal is to maximize the freshness of the indexed pages. It is standard practice to assume that the set of crawled pages is fixed and to assume a maximum crawl rate r [18]. We set a crawling limit of 10% of the total number of pages to simulate a setting where the number of pages to be crawled far exceeds the crawling resources, and adopt a scheduling policy that targets to re-visit pages as closely as possible to their change frequency by flipping a biased coin based on the estimated change probability. This probability is estimated by fitting logistic regression models (Platt recalibration [1]) to the outputs of the SVM classifier for the multiple and single experts, and for the baseline it is estimated based on the page frequency. We follow a batch crawling scenario, therefore the classifiers are not re-trained during the crawling period. Once a page is selected to be crawled it is used to update the training of all the methods. We compare the overall freshness of the index using different methods of estimating this probability as a function of the number of days the crawl was performed. Figure 8 shows the performance according to average freshness as a function of the number of observed crawling days (*i.e.*, the amount of data available to train the classifier). Both the 2D and 3D methods improve over the baseline with significant

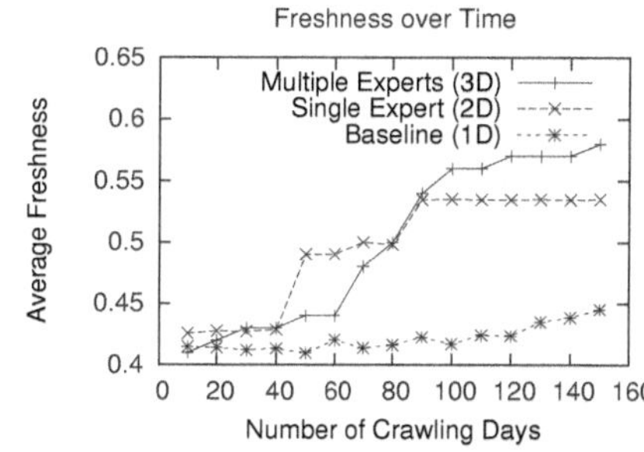

Figure 8: Freshness as a function of crawling days

gains in freshness occurring after observing 50 days of crawl data. The 3D method shows performance on par with the 2D method after 80 days with superior and significant performance after 100 days of crawl data. Overall, the results show the superiority of the 3D algorithm over the baseline after a small number of days were sampled and over the 2D approach after a moderate number of days, showing that the approach is also applicable for when some of the features are missing (as presented in the partially-observed setting).

9. DISCUSSION

In this section we give some qualitative examples to provide insight into the multiple experts and expert selection algorithms. We then also discuss how our methods can be efficiently calculated and scaled.

9.1 Qualitative Examples

In this section we provide some qualitative examples of the prediction results.

An example where related page expert selection outperforms the 1D and 2D approaches is for the URL `http://www.thekirkreport.com/archives.html`. This is a URL irregularly giving updates on stock trading. The content similarity KNN method (Section 6.2) chose the page of the American first credit union `http://www.amerfirst.org/`, that provides updates on rates, credits and loans. And indeed, in many of the times that the kirkreport had changes, it followed a significant update of all the rates on the amerfirst site. However, using simple content similarity pages as experts might also yield unsatisfactory result for change prediction. For example, the experts selected for the Southern Methodist university (`http://smu.edu/`, were other university sites such as the university of Windsor `http://www.uwindsor.ca`, and the university of Vermont `http://www.uvm.edu/`. Although all the above university pages change frequently, their change is usually due to updating university news, such as awards and local news. Therefore using those experts as indicators for the change in smu was unhelpful. As we use the page itself as an expert of its own change, in this case the ensemble algorithm weighted the smu page very high, yielding similar results to the 2D approach.

Those type of errors were easily fixed by the temporal content similarity method using cross-correlation (Section 6.3), that not only takes content into account, but also the actual correlation across time. For example, the best correlating pages for `http://www.boxofficeindia.com` were `http://www.musicnmovies.com` and `http://www.bollywoodworld.com`, as the pages experience change in the same topics when a new movie comes out to the theater.

The graph distance similarity (Section 6.1) usually selects pages with no clear connection to the temporal dynamics; therefore the experts extracted using this method are not satisfactory. For example, for the URL `http://www.mtv.com/music/video` the experts selected were relevant pages such as a radio site `http://www.ksidradio.com`, but also irrelevant pages, such as a wrestling site `http://prwrestling.com`. For comparison, the cross-correlation experts for this same URL were `http://www.mtv.com/ontv/dyn`, `http://www.imdb.com/Sections/Quotes` and `http://www.newsoftheworld.co.uk/story_pages`. The first URL is an aggregate of new content in MTV, the second indicates a new popular movie that indicates new YouTube films about it, the last one is a correlation indicating that after specific news events there will be a new YouTube movie.

9.2 Efficient Calculation

In this work we showed that information from related pages strongly contributes to better page change detection. We investigated numerous ways of identifying such related pages – either by graph distance, content similarity or temporal content similarity. We have showed empirically that the temporal content similarity methods outperform the first two. However, identifying those related pages can be computationally expensive. Fortunately, several methods have been proposed in the literature, that can be used to speed up identifying such pages in an efficient way. For example, Keogh and Pazzani [16] discuss several ways of efficiently identifying similar time series in a large database. The method reduces the size of every time series by providing a method to divide it into frames, on which a time-series similarity algorithm can later be performed. The algorithm was applied using DTW algorithm, but the extension to the application of cross-correlation is similar.

Additional concern in such large scale prediction tasks is that storing snapshots from multiple iterations is prohibitively expensive. However, the cross-correlation method for finding temporal experts, that had the best performance in our empirical study, can be computed online without the need to actually store the previous snapshots. As more information arrives the correlation can be updated with only the correlation of the new snapshot. We saw in the empirical study that gains in performance asymptote after 30 days of historical data. Some classifiers can be trained online as well, preventing the need to keep the last snapshots. Additionally, in our experiments the object used for prediction is composed of only the past two snapshots ($l = 1$), and we did not see a significant higher gain when using bigger l values. This result is akin to the result by Ali & Williams [3], that showed that simply using only the previous two snapshots of a page to determine when to recrawl significantly reduces crawling compared to recrawling all recently changed pages.

10. CONCLUSIONS

In this paper we tackled the problem of predicting significant content change on the web. Our results shed light on how and why content changes on the web, and how it can be predicted. We explored several information sources that can be used to predict such change – the commonly used frequency of change, the page content and related pages content. We have seen that the addition of the page content improves prediction when compared to simple frequency-based prediction. Additionally, the addition of information of related pages content improves over the usage of page's content alone. We experimented with several methods for selecting related pages, and have shown that related pages that correlate over time in their content change contain valuable information for page content change prediction. We have investigated several ways of combining information from related pages, and proposed a novel algorithm that outperformed the common learning mechanisms.

11. REFERENCES

[1] B. S. A. J. Smola, P. Bartlett and D. Schuurmans. *Advances in Large Margin Classifiers*. MIT Press, 1999.

[2] E. Adar, J. Teevan, S. Dumais, and J. Elsas. The web changes everything: Understanding the dynamics of web content. In *Proc. of WSDM*, 2009.

[3] H. Ali and H. E. Williams. What's changed? measuring document change in web crawling for search engines. In *SPIRE*, pages 28–42, 2003.

[4] L. Barbosa, A. Salgado, F. de Carvalho, J. Robin, and J. Freire. Looking at both the present and the past to efficiently update replicas of web content. In *Proc. of WIDM Workshop*, 2005.

[5] L. Breiman. Bagging predictors. *ML*, 24(2):123–140, 1996.

[6] J. Cho and H. García-Molina. The evolution of the web and implications for an incremental crawler. In *Proc. of VLDB*, 2000.

[7] J. Cho and H. García-Molina. Effective page refresh policies for web crawlers. *TODS*, 28(4):390–426, 2003.

[8] J. Cho and H. García-Molina. Estimating frequency of change. *TOIT*, 3(3):256–290, 2003.

[9] J. Cho and A. Ntoulas. Effective change detection using sampling. In *Proc. of VLDB*, 2002.

[10] E. Coffman, Z. Liu, and R. Weber. Optimal robot scheduling for web search engines. *Journal of Scheduling*, 1(1), 1998.

[11] J. Edwards, K. McCurley, and J. Tomlin. An adaptive model for optimizing performance of an incremental web crawler. In *Proc. of WWW*, 2001.

[12] D. Fetterly, M. Manasse, M. Najork, and J. L. Wiener. A large-scale study of the evolution of web pages. In *Proc. of WWW*, 2003.

[13] D. Fetterly, M. Manasse, M. Najork, and J. L. Wiener. A large-scale study of the evolution of web pages. *Software Practice and Experience*, 1(1), 2003.

[14] Y. Freund, R. Iyer, R. E. Schapire, and Y. Singer. An efficient boosting algorithm for combining preferences. *JMLR*, 4:933–969, 2003.

[15] L. Getoor and L. Mihalkova. Exploiting statistical and relational information on the web and in social media. In *Proc. of WSDM*, 2011.

[16] E. Keogh and M. Pazzani. Scaling up dynamic time warping for datamining applications. In *Proc. of KDD*, 2000.

[17] J. Leskovec, S. Dumais, and E. Horvitz. Web projections: learning from contextual subgraphs of the web. In *Proc. WWW*, 2007.

[18] C. Olston and M. Najork. Web crawling. *Foundations and Trends in Information Retrieval*, 4(3):175–246, 2010.

[19] S. Pandey and C. Olston. User-centric web crawling. In *Proc. of WWW*, pages 401–411, 2005.

[20] K. Radinsky, E. Agichtein, E. Gabrilovich, and S. Markovitch. A word at a time: Computing word relatedness using temporal semantic analysis. In *Proc. of WWW*, 2011.

[21] M. Richardson, E. Dominowska, and R. Ragno. Predicting clicks: estimating the click-through rate for new ads. In *Proc. of WWW*, 2007.

[22] D. Shahaf, Y. Azar, E. Lubetzky, and E. Horvitz. Optimal web crawling. Technical Report, April 2011.

[23] Q. Tan and P. Mitra. Clustering-based incremental web crawling. *TOIS*, 28(4), 2010. Article 17.

[24] Q. Tan, Z. Zhuang, P. Mitra, and C. Giles. A clustering-based sampling approach for refreshing search engine's database. In *Proc. of WebDB Workshop*, 2007.

[25] J. Wolf, M. Squillante, P. Yu, J.Sethuraman, and L.Ozsen. Optimal crawling strategies for web search engines. In *Proc. of WWW*, 2002.

Triplex Transfer Learning: Exploiting both Shared and Distinct Concepts for Text Classification

Fuzhen Zhuang
Key Laboratory of Intelligent Information Processing, Institute of Computing Technology, Chinese Academy of Sciences
zhuangfz@ics.ict.ac.cn

Ping Luo
Hewlett-Packard Labs, China
ping.luo@hp.com

Changying Du*
Key Laboratory of Intelligent Information Processing, Institute of Computing Technology, Chinese Academy of Sciences
ducy@ics.ict.ac.cn

Qing He
Key Laboratory of Intelligent Information Processing, Institute of Computing Technology, Chinese Academy of Sciences
heq@ics.ict.ac.cn

Zhongzhi Shi
Key Laboratory of Intelligent Information Processing, Institute of Computing Technology, Chinese Academy of Sciences
shizz@ics.ict.ac.cn

ABSTRACT

Transfer learning focuses on the learning scenarios when the test data from target domains and the training data from source domains are drawn from similar but different data distribution with respect to the raw features. Some recent studies argued that the high-level concepts (e.g. word clusters) can help model the data distribution difference, and thus are more appropriate for classification. Specifically, these methods assume that all the data domains have the same set of shared concepts, which are used as the bridge for knowledge transfer. However, besides these shared concepts each domain may have its own distinct concepts. To address this point, we propose a general transfer learning framework based on non-negative matrix tri-factorization which allows to explore both shared and distinct concepts among all the domains simultaneously. Since this model provides more flexibility in fitting the data it may lead to better classification accuracy. To solve the proposed optimization problem we develop an iterative algorithm and also theoretically analyze its convergence. Finally, extensive experiments show the significant superiority of our model over the baseline methods. In particular, we show that our method works much better in the more challenging tasks when distinct concepts may exist.

*Changying Du is also with the Graduate University of Chinese Academy of Sciences.

WSDM'13, February 4–8, 2013, Rome, Italy.

Categories and Subject Descriptors

I.2.6 [**Artificial Intelligence**]: Learning–Machine Learning

Keywords

Triplex Transfer Learning; Distribution Mismatch; Non-negative Matrix Tri-factorization; Common Concept; Distinct Concept

1. INTRODUCTION

Traditional classification algorithms often fail to obtain satisfying performance, since in many emerging real-world applications, new test data usually come from different data sources with different but semantically-related distributions. For example, to build a news portal for any of the Fortune 500 companies we want to classify the everyday news about this company into some classes, such as "product-related", "financial report, business and industry analysis", "stock review", "merger and acquisition related" and so on. The traditional classification model learned from the news of a company may not perform well on the news of another company since these two companies may have different business areas and thus the distributions on the raw words in the two news corpora may be different. To reduce the manual efforts in labeling the training data in the new domain leads to a vast amount of studies in transfer learning (also referred to as domain adaptation, cross-domain learning) [1, 2, 3, 4, 5, 6, 7, 8, 9, 10, 11, 12]. It aims at adapting the classification models trained from the source domains to the target domains with different data distributions.

Although the source and target domains have different data distributions in raw word features, many recent studies exploit the commonality between different domains for knowledge transfer [5, 9, 11, 12]. In these studies the high-level *concepts* (i.e. *word clusters* and *topics*) are utilized with the observation that *different domains may use different key words to express the same concept while the association between the concepts and the document classes may be stable across domains* [11]. In this paper we refer to the set of key words in expressing a concept as the ***extension*** of this concept, in other words, the extension of a concept can be described as the distribution over words. In the other hand, we refer to the association between the concept and the document classes as the concept ***intension***, which can also be expressed as the indication to a document class. With these terminologies the widely used observation actually says that the extension of a concept may be different in different domains while its intension is stable across all the domains. This basic observation motivated these recent studies to use the stable concept intension as the bridge for knowledge transfer.

It is clear that most of the previous works assume that all the data domains share the same set of concepts with their respective stable intensions. However, it is not always true since some *distinct concepts* may exist in the data domains. For example, there may be some concepts in a text corpus, which are totally irrelevant to the content of another corpus. Thus, these distinct concepts in Definition 1 have both different extensions and different intensions.

DEFINITION 1 (DISTINCT CONCEPTS). *A concept is distinct when it has both different extension and different intension with any other concepts.*

Additionally, all the shared concepts can be further divided into two groups, namely *alike concepts* and *identical concepts*, defined as follows. The *alike concepts* have the same intension but different extension with others'. They are actually widely used in previous works. Meanwhile, there may be some concepts with both the same intension and the same extension with others' as shown in [12]. They are the *identical concepts.*

DEFINITION 2 (ALIKE CONCEPTS). *A concept is alike to some other ones when it has the same intension but different extension with others'.*

DEFINITION 3 (IDENTICAL CONCEPTS). *A concept is identical with some other ones when it has both the same intension and the same extension with others'.*

Table 1: The Three Kinds of Concepts

		Extension	Intension
Shared	Identical Concepts	*same*	*same*
	Alike Concepts	*different*	*same*
Non-shared	Distinct Concepts	*different*	*different*

These three kinds of concepts are summarized in Table 1. They may all exist in the multiple corpora. However, all the previous works never consider these three kinds of concepts together for classification, and only address them separately or partially. For example, CoCC [5] models the identical concepts only. MTrick [9] explores the associations between word cluster and document class for cross-domain classification, thus actually considers the alike concepts only. DKT [11] adopts the similar idea with MTrick for cross-language web page classification. Recently, DTL (Dual Transfer Learning) [12] is proposed to model alike and identical concepts together. Therefore, an ideal model should handle the alike, identical, and distinct concepts simultaneously. Motivated by this observation, we propose a general framework based on non-negative matrix tri-factorization (NMTF) techniques, which considers all these concepts jointly. We believe that the more flexibility in modeling the data may improve the classification accuracy. Since our model considers the three kinds of concepts, we call it TRIplex Transfer Learning (i.e. TriTL for short). For the sake of clarity, the differences of the four previous methods and our model are summarized in Table 2.

Table 2: The Comparison of Models

	Alike	Identical	Distinct
CoCC [5]		√	
MTrick [9]	√		
DKT [11]	√		
DTL [12]	√	√	
TriTL	√	√	√

To highlight the contributions of this work, we summarize them as follows.

1. We deeply analyze the commonalities and distinctions between the source and target domains, and find that there are also some distinct concepts in each of data domain.
2. We introduce distinct concepts into transfer learning. Together with alike and identical concepts we propose a triplex transfer learning model to model them simultaneously based on non-negative matrix tri-factorization. An iterative algorithm is developed to solve the proposed matrix factorization problem, and its theoretical analysis on algorithm convergence is also provided.
3. We conduct the systematic experiments to show the superiority of TriTL over the compared methods. In particular, we show that our method works much better in the more challenging tasks when distinct concepts may exist.

The rest of this paper is organized as follows, Section 2 briefly introduces the preliminary knowledge and notations, followed by the detailed formalization and solution of the proposed model TriTL in Section 3. Section 4 gives the experimental results. We summarize the related works in Section 5, and Section 6 concludes. Finally, the theoretical analysis of the iterative algorithm is given in Appendix.

2. PRELIMINARY KNOWLEDGE

In this section, we first give the notations used throughout this paper, and then briefly introduce the non-negative matrix tri-factorization (NMTF) technique and its notions.

2.1 Notations

We use calligraphic letters to represent sets, such as $\mathcal{D}$ is used to denote data set. The data matrices are written in upper case, such as X and Y, and $X_{[i,j]}$ indicates the i-th row and j-th column element of matrix X. Also, we use $\mathbb{R}$ and $\mathbb{R}_+$ to denote the set of real numbers and nonnegative real numbers respectively. Finally, $\mathbf{1}_m$ is used to represent a column vector with size m, and its elements are all equal to 1. For clarity, the frequently-used notations and denotations are summarized in Table 3.

2.2 Non-negative Matrix Factorization

Non-negative matrix factorization (NMF) technique has been widely used for text and image classification in the last

Table 3: The Notation and Denotation

$\mathcal{D}$	The data set
X	The word-document co-occurrence matrix from a domain
m	The number of words
n	The number of documents
c	The number of document classes
r	The index of domain
s	The number of source domains
t	The number of target domains
k_1	The number of identical concepts
k_2	The number of alike concepts
k_3	The number of distinct concepts
F	The matrix for the word clusterings
S	The matrix for the association between word clusters and document classes
G	The matrix for the document labeling
$\top$	Denotes the transposition of matrix

decade [13, 14, 15, 16]. Our model is based on the non-negative matrix tri-factorization, and the basic formula is

$$X_{m\times n} = F_{m\times k}S_{k\times c}G^{\top}_{n\times c}, \tag{1}$$

where X is the word-document matrix, and m, n, k, c are the numbers of words, documents, word clusters, and document classes respectively, $G^{\top}$ is the transposition of G. Conceptually, the matrix of F contains the information on word clusterings. G denotes the document labeling information, and S denotes the association between word clusterings and document classes [9]. In this paper, each column of F refers to a concept and each row of G refers to a document. The details on these matrices will be addressed later.

Here we also introduce some concepts about NMF, which are used in Section 3 and Appendix.

Definition 4 (Trace of Matrix). *Given a data matrix $X \in \mathbb{R}^{n\times n}$, the trace of X is computed as*

$$tr(X) = \sum_{i=1}^{n} X_{(ii)}. \tag{2}$$

Actually, the trace of matrix can also be computed when the matrix is not a phalanx. Without losing any generality, let $m < n$ and $X \in \mathbb{R}^{m\times n}$, then $tr(X) = \sum_{i=1}^{m} X_{(ii)}$.

Definition 5 (Frobenius Norm of Matrix). *Given a data matrix $X \in \mathbb{R}^{m\times n}$, the frobenius norm of X is computed as*

$$||X|| = \sqrt{\sum_{i=1}^{m}\sum_{j=1}^{n} X^2_{[i,j]}}. \tag{3}$$

The properties of the trace and frobenius norm are as follows,

Property 1. *Given a matrix $X \in \mathbb{R}^{m\times n}$, then*

$$tr(X^TX) = tr(XX^T). \tag{4}$$

Property 2. *Given matrices $X, Y \in \mathbb{R}^{m\times n}$, then*

$$tr(a\cdot X + b\cdot Y) = a\cdot tr(X) + b\cdot tr(Y). \tag{5}$$

Property 3. *Given a matrix $X \in \mathbb{R}^{m\times n}$, then*

$$||X||^2 = tr(X^TX) = tr(XX^T). \tag{6}$$

3. TRIPLEX TRANSFER LEARNING

Motivated by the observation on the three kinds of concepts, we divide F and S into three parts respectively. Namely, $F = [F^1_{m\times k_1}, F^2_{m\times k_2}, F^3_{m\times k_3}]$ $(k_1 + k_2 + k_3 = k)$, where F^1 refers to the word clusterings for the identical concepts, F^2 refers to the word clusterings for the alike concepts, and F^3 refers to the word clusterings for the distinct concepts. Correspondingly, the association S can be denoted as $S = \begin{bmatrix} S^1_{k_1\times c} \\ S^2_{k_2\times c} \\ S^3_{k_3\times c} \end{bmatrix}$, where S^1 refers to the association between the identical concepts and document classes, S^2 refers to the association between the alike concepts and document classes, and S^3 refers to the association between the distinct concepts and document classes. Thus Eq.(1) can be rewritten as,

$$\begin{aligned} X_{m\times n} &= F_{m\times k}S_{k\times c}G^T_{n\times c} \\ &= [F^1_{m\times k_1}, F^2_{m\times k_2}, F^3_{m\times k_3}] \begin{bmatrix} S^1_{k_1\times c} \\ S^2_{k_2\times c} \\ S^3_{k_3\times c} \end{bmatrix} G^{\top}_{n\times c}. \end{aligned} \tag{7}$$

Based on Eq.(7), we will formulate the transfer learning framework in the following.

3.1 Problem Formalization

Supposed we have $s + t$ data domains, denoted as $\mathcal{D} = (\mathcal{D}_1, \cdots, \mathcal{D}_s, \mathcal{D}_{s+1}, \cdots, \mathcal{D}_{s+t})$. Without loss of generality, we assume the first s domains are source domains with the document labels, i.e., $\mathcal{D}_r = \{x^{(r)}_i, y^{(r)}_i\}|^{n_r}_{i=1}$ $(1 \le r \le s)$, and the left t domains are target domains without any label information, i.e., $\mathcal{D}_r = \{x^{(r)}_i\}|^{n_r}_{i=1}$ $(s+1 \le r \le s+t)$. n_r is the number of documents in data domain $\mathcal{D}_r$. Let $X = (X_1, \cdots, X_s, X_{s+1}, \cdots, X_{s+t})$ be the word-document co-occurrence matrices of $s + t$ domains, then the objective function is formulated as follows,

$$\mathcal{L} = \sum_{r=1}^{s+t} ||X_r - F_rS_rG_r^{\top}||^2 \tag{8}$$

where $X_r \in \mathbb{R}^{m\times n_r}_+$, $F_r \in \mathbb{R}^{m\times k}_+$, $S_r \in \mathbb{R}^{k\times c}_+$ and $G_r \in \mathbb{R}^{n_r\times c}_+$.

As described earlier, we divide the word clustering matrix F_r into three parts $F_r = [F^1, {F^2}_r, {F^3}_r]$ $(F^1 \in \mathbb{R}^{m\times k_1}_+$, ${F^2}_r \in \mathbb{R}^{m\times k_2}_+$, ${F^3}_r \in \mathbb{R}^{m\times k_3}_+$, $k_1 + k_2 + k_3 = k)$. Here, since F^1 refers to the word clusterings on the identical concepts it is shared in all the domains (note that F^1 does not have the sub-index of r). While ${F^2}_r$ and ${F^3}_r$ refers to the word clusterings on the alike and distinct concepts they are different in different domains (note that ${F^2}_r$ and ${F^3}_r$ do have the sub-index of r).

Similarly, S_r can be expressed as $S_r = \begin{bmatrix} S^1 \\ S^2 \\ {S^3}_r \end{bmatrix}$ $(S^1 \in \mathbb{R}^{k_1\times c}_+$, $S^2 \in \mathbb{R}^{k_2\times c}_+$, ${S^3}_r \in \mathbb{R}^{k_3\times c}_+)$. Here, S^1 (S^2) are the associations between the identical (alike) concepts and document classes. Thus, they are shared in all the domains (note that S^1 and S^2 do not have the sub-index of r). However, ${S^3}_r$ represents the association between distinct concepts and document classes. Thus, it is domain dependent (note that ${S^3}_r$ does have the sub-index of r).

Therefore, the objective function in Eq.(8) can be rewritten as follows,

$$\mathcal{L} = \sum_{r=1}^{s+t} ||X_r - F_r S_r G_r^\top||^2 = \sum_{r=1}^{s+t} ||X_r - [F^1, F^2{}_r, F^3{}_r] \begin{bmatrix} S^1 \\ S^2 \\ S^3{}_r \end{bmatrix} G_r^\top||^2. \quad (9)$$

Considering the constraints to F_r and G_r, we come to the optimization problem as

$$\min_{F_r, S_r, G_r} \mathcal{L}$$
$$s.t. \sum_{i=1}^{m} F^1{}_{[i,j]} = 1, \sum_{i=1}^{m} F^2{}_{r[i,j]} = 1, \sum_{i=1}^{m} F^3{}_{r[i,j]} = 1, \sum_{j=1}^{c} G_{r[i,j]} = 1. \quad (10)$$

Here, the constraints inform that the sum of the entries in each column of F equals to 1 and the sum of the entries in each row of G equals to 1. In other words, each column of F refers to the word distribution of a concept while each row of G refers to the probabilities that a document belongs to the different document classes.

3.2 The Solution to TriTL

To solve the optimization problem in Eq.(10), we derive an iterative algorithm. According to the properties of the trace and frobenius norm, the minimization of Eq.(10) is equal to minimize the following objective function,

$$\begin{aligned}
\mathcal{L} =& \sum_{r=1}^{s+t} ||X_r - [F^1, F^2{}_r, F^3{}_r] \begin{bmatrix} S^1 \\ S^2 \\ S^3{}_r \end{bmatrix} G_r^\top||^2 \\
=& \sum_{r=1}^{s+t} tr(X_r^\top X_r - 2 \cdot X_r^\top [F^1, F^2{}_r, F^3{}_r] \begin{bmatrix} S^1 \\ S^2 \\ S^3{}_r \end{bmatrix} G_r^\top \\
&+ G_r \begin{bmatrix} S^1 \\ S^2 \\ S^3{}_r \end{bmatrix}^\top [F^1, F^2{}_r, F^3{}_r]^\top [F^1, F^2{}_r, F^3{}_r] \begin{bmatrix} S^1 \\ S^2 \\ S^3{}_r \end{bmatrix} G_r^\top) \\
=& \sum_{r=1}^{s+t} tr(X_r^\top X_r - 2 \cdot X_r^\top A_r - 2 \cdot X_r^\top B_r - 2 \cdot X_r^\top C_r \\
&+ G_r {S^1}^\top {F^1}^\top A_r + G_r {S^2}^\top {F^2_r}^\top B_r + G_r {S^3_r}^\top {F^3_r}^\top C_r \\
&+ 2 \cdot G_r {S^1}^\top {F^1}^\top B_r + 2 \cdot G_r {S^1}^\top {F^1}^\top C_r + 2 \cdot G_r {S^2}^\top {F^2_r}^\top C_r) \\
& s.t. \sum_{i=1}^{m} F^1{}_{[i,j]} = 1, \sum_{i=1}^{m} F^2{}_{r[i,j]} = 1, \\
& \sum_{i=1}^{m} F^3{}_{r[i,j]} = 1, \sum_{j=1}^{c} G_{r[i,j]} = 1,
\end{aligned} \quad (11)$$

where $A_r = F^1 S^1 G_r^\top$, $B_r = F^2{}_r S^2 G_r^\top$, $C_r = F^3{}_r S^3{}_r G_r^\top$.

The partial differentials of $\mathcal{L}$ are as follows,

$$\frac{\partial \mathcal{L}}{\partial F^1} = \sum_{r=1}^{s+t} (-2 \cdot X_r G_r {S^1}^\top + 2 \cdot A_r G_r {S^1}^\top + 2 \cdot B_r G_r {S^1}^\top + 2 \cdot C_r G_r {S^1}^\top), \quad (12)$$

$$\frac{\partial \mathcal{L}}{\partial F^2{}_r} = -2 \cdot X_r G_r {S^2}^\top + 2 \cdot B_r G_r {S^2}^\top + 2 \cdot A_r G_r {S^2}^\top + 2 \cdot C_r G_r {S^2}^\top, \quad (13)$$

$$\frac{\partial \mathcal{L}}{\partial F^3{}_r} = -2 \cdot X_r G_r {S^3_r}^\top + 2 \cdot C_r G_r {S^3_r}^\top + 2 \cdot A_r G_r {S^3_r}^\top + 2 \cdot B_r G_r {S^3_r}^\top, \quad (14)$$

$$\frac{\partial \mathcal{L}}{\partial S^1} = \sum_{r=1}^{s+t} (-2 \cdot {F^1}^\top X_r G_r + 2 \cdot {F^1}^\top A_r G_r + 2 \cdot {F^1}^\top B_r G_r + 2 \cdot {F^1}^\top C_r G_r), \quad (15)$$

$$\frac{\partial \mathcal{L}}{\partial S^2} = \sum_{r=1}^{s+t} (-2 \cdot {F^2_r}^\top X_r G_r + 2 \cdot {F^2_r}^\top B_r G_r + 2 \cdot {F^2_r}^\top A_r G_r + 2 \cdot {F^2_r}^\top C_r G_r), \quad (16)$$

$$\frac{\partial \mathcal{L}}{\partial S^3{}_r} = -2 \cdot {F^3_r}^\top X_r G_r + 2 \cdot {F^3_r}^\top C_r G_r + 2 \cdot {F^3_r}^\top A_r G_r + 2 \cdot {F^3_r}^\top B_r G_r, \quad (17)$$

$$\frac{\partial \mathcal{L}}{\partial G_r} = -2 \cdot X_r^\top F_r S_r + 2 \cdot G_r S_r^\top F_r^\top F_r S_r. \quad (18)$$

Note that when $r = \{1, \cdots, s\}$, G_r is the true label information, so we just need to solve G_r when $r = \{s+1, \cdots, s+t\}$. Since $\mathcal{L}$ is not concave, it is hard to obtain the global solution by applying the latest non-linear optimization techniques. In this work we develop an alternately iterative algorithm, which can converge to a local optimal solution.

In each round of iteration these matrices are updated as

$$F^1{}_{[i,j]} \leftarrow F^1{}_{[i,j]} \cdot \sqrt{\frac{[\sum_{r=1}^{s+t} X_r G_r {S^1}^\top]_{[i,j]}}{[\sum_{r=1}^{s+t} (A_r G_r {S^1}^\top + B_r G_r {S^1}^\top + C_r G_r {S^1}^\top)]_{[i,j]}}}, \quad (19)$$

$$F^2{}_{r[i,j]} \leftarrow F^2{}_{r[i,j]} \cdot \sqrt{\frac{[X_r G_r {S^2}^\top]_{[i,j]}}{[B_r G_r {S^2}^\top + A_r G_r {S^2}^\top + C_r G_r {S^2}^\top]_{[i,j]}}}, \quad (20)$$

$$F^3{}_{r[i,j]} \leftarrow F^3{}_{r[i,j]} \cdot \sqrt{\frac{[X_r G_r {S^3_r}^\top]_{[i,j]}}{[C_r G_r {S^3_r}^\top + A_r G_r {S^3_r}^\top + B_r G_r {S^3_r}^\top]_{[i,j]}}}, \quad (21)$$

$$S^1{}_{[i,j]} \leftarrow S^1{}_{[i,j]} \cdot \sqrt{\frac{[\sum_{r=1}^{s+t} {F^1}^\top X_r G_r]_{[i,j]}}{[\sum_{r=1}^{s+t} ({F^1}^\top A_r G_r + {F^1}^\top B_r G_r + {F^1}^\top C_r G_r)]_{[i,j]}}}, \quad (22)$$

$$S^2{}_{[i,j]} \leftarrow S^2{}_{[i,j]} \cdot \sqrt{\frac{[\sum_{r=1}^{s+t} {F^2_r}^\top X_r G_r]_{[i,j]}}{[\sum_{r=1}^{s+t} ({F^2_r}^\top B_r G_r + {F^2_r}^\top A_r G_r + {F^2_r}^\top C_r G_r))]_{[i,j]}}}, \quad (23)$$

$$S^3{}_{r[i,j]} = S^3{}_{r[i,j]} \cdot \sqrt{\frac{[{F^3_r}^\top X_r G_r]_{[i,j]}}{[{F^3_r}^\top C_r G_r + {F^3_r}^\top A_r G_r + {F^3_r}^\top B_r G_r]_{[i,j]}}}, \quad (24)$$

$$G_{r[i,j]} \leftarrow G_{r[i,j]} \cdot \sqrt{\frac{[X_r^\top F_r S_r]_{[i,j]}}{[G_r S_r^\top F_r^\top F_r S_r]_{[i,j]}}}. \quad (25)$$

After the calculation of each round of iteration, F^1, ${F^2}_r$, ${F^3}_r$, G_r are normalized using Eq.(26) to satisfy the equality constraints,

$$\begin{aligned} {F^1}_{[i,j]} &\leftarrow \frac{{F^1}_{[i,j]}}{\sum_{i=1}^m {F^1}_{[i,j]}}, {F^2}_{r[i,j]} \leftarrow \frac{{F^2}_{r[i,j]}}{\sum_{i=1}^m {F^2}_{r[i,j]}}, \\ {F^3}_{r[i,j]} &\leftarrow \frac{{F^3}_{r[i,j]}}{\sum_{i=1}^m {F^3}_{r[i,j]}}, G_{r[i,j]} \leftarrow \frac{G_{r[i,j]}}{\sum_{j=1}^c G_{r[i,j]}}. \end{aligned} \quad (26)$$

The detailed procedure of this iterative algorithm is described in Algorithm 1. In this algorithm, the data matrices are normalized such that $X_{r[i,j]} = \frac{X_{r[i,j]}}{\sum_{i=1}^m X_{r[i,j]}}$, G_r $(1 \le r \le s)$ are assigned as the true label information. Specifically, $G_{r[i,u]} = 1$ if the i-th document belongs to the u-th class, else $G_{r[i,v]} = 0$ $(v \ne u)$. F^1 and ${F^2}_r$ are initialized as the word clustering results by PLSA [17]. Specifically, We combine all the data from source and target domains, and conduct the PLSA implemented by Matlab[1]. We set the number of topics as $(k_1 + k_2)$, and obtain the word clustering information $W \in \mathbb{R}_+^{m\times(k_1+k_2)}$. W is divided into two parts $W = [W^1, W^2]$ $(W^1 \in \mathbb{R}_+^{m\times k_1}$, $W^2 \in \mathbb{R}_+^{m\times k_2})$, then F^1 is initialized as W^1 and ${F^2}_r$ is assigned as W^2. Finally, ${F^3}_r$ is randomly initialized, and ${F^3}_{r[i,j]} = \frac{{F^3}_{r[i,j]}}{\sum_{i=1}^m {F^3}_{r[i,j]}}$. After the computation of Algorithm 1, we can conduct the classification of target domain data according to G_r $(s+1 \le r \le s+t)$. The convergence analysis of Algorithm 1 can be referred in Appendix.

Algorithm 1 Triplex Transfer Learning (TriTL) Algorithm

Input: The source domains $\mathcal{D}_r = \{x_i^{(r)}, y_i^{(r)}\}|_{i=1}^{n_r}$ $(1 \le r \le s)$, target domains $\mathcal{D}_r = \{x_i^{(r)}\}|_{i=1}^{n_r}$ $(s+1 \le r \le s+t)$, and the corresponding data matrices $X_1, \cdots, X_s, X_{s+1}, \cdots, X_{s+t}$. The data matrices are normalized such that $X_{r[i,j]} = \frac{X_{r[i,j]}}{\sum_{i=1}^m X_{r[i,j]}}$, G_r $(1 \le r \le s)$ are assigned as the true label information. The parameters k_1, k_2, k_3, and the number of iterations T.

Output: F^1, ${F^2}_r$, ${F^3}_r$, S^1, S^2, ${S^3}_r$ $(1 \le r \le s+t)$, and G_r $(s+1 \le r \le s+t)$.

1. **Initialization:** The initializations of ${F^1}^{(0)}$, ${{F^2}_r}^{(0)}$, ${{F^3}_r}^{(0)}$ are detailed in Section 3.2; ${S^1}^{(0)}$, ${S^2}^{(0)}$, ${{S^3}_r}^{(0)}$ are randomly assigned, and ${G_r}^{(0)}$ $(s+1 \le r \le s+t)$ are initialized as the probabilistic output by supervised learning models, such as Logistic Regression (LR) [18] in the experiments.
2. $k := 1$.
3. Update ${F^1}^{(k)}$ according to Eq.(19);
4. **For** $r := 1 \rightarrow s+t$
   Update ${{F^2}_r}^{(k)}$ according to Eq.(20) and ${{F^3}_r}^{(k)}$ according to Eq.(21);
5. **end**
6. Update ${S^1}^{(k)}$ according to Eq.(22) and ${S^2}^{(k)}$ according to Eq.(23);
7. **For** $r := 1 \rightarrow s+t$
   Update ${{S^3}_r}^{(k)}$ according to Eq.(24);
8. **end**
9. **For** $r := s+1 \rightarrow s+t$
   Update ${G_r}^{(k)}$ according to Eq.(25);
10. **end**
11. Normalize ${F^1}^{(k)}$, ${{F^2}_r}^{(k)}$, ${{F^3}_r}^{(k)}$, ${G_r}^{(k)}$ according to Eq.(26);
12. $k := k+1$. If $k < T$, then turn to Step 3.
13. Output ${F^1}^{(k)}$, ${{F^2}_r}^{(k)}$, ${{F^3}_r}^{(k)}$, ${S^1}^{(k)}$, ${S^2}^{(k)}$, ${{S^3}_r}^{(k)}$ and ${G_r}^{(k)}$.

4. EXPERIMENTAL EVALUATION

In this section, we systemically demonstrate the effectiveness of the proposed transfer learning framework TriTL. In the experiments, we only focus on binary text classification and there are only one source domain and one target domain, i.e., $s = 1$ and $t = 1$. Note that TriTL is a general model, which can handle multi-class classification problems and multiple source and target domains, i.e., $s > 1$ and $t > 1$.

4.1 Data Preparation

20Newsgroups[2] is one of the benchmark data sets for evaluate transfer learning algorithms, which is widely used in previous works [1, 3, 19, 20]. This corpus has approximately 20,000 newsgroup documents, which are evenly divided into 20 subcategories. Some similar subcategories are grouped into a top category, e.g., the four subcategories *sci.crypt*, *sci.electronics*, *sci.med* and *sci.space* belong to the top category *sci*. The four top categories and their subcategories are depicted in Table 4.

Firstly, We construct the transfer learning tasks using the approach in [9]. For example, for the data set *rec vs. sci*, we randomly select a subcategory from *rec* as positive class and a subcategory from *sci* as negative class to produce the source domain. The target domain is similarly constructed, thus in totally 144 $(P_4^2 \cdot P_4^2)$ classification tasks are generated for data set *rec vs. sci*. However, in this traditional setting the source and target domains are both drawn from the same top categories, thus they may tend to share all the concepts.

Secondly, to validate our model TriTL can effectively exploit the distinct concepts, we further construct another type of classification tasks. For example, for the classification task generated from *rec vs. sci* from the above approach, we replace one subcategory from the target domain as another subcategory from the top category *comp* or *talk*. In this new type of classification tasks the source and target domains are not drawn from the same top categories, thus they would have their own distinct concepts.

This way, we can construct additional 384 $(144 \div 3 \times 8)$ classification tasks. Among all these 384 tasks we first run the supervised learning model Logistic Regression (LR) [18] on each of them. Then, we select the ones whose accuracies from LR are from 50% to 55% (this is only slightly better than the random classification, thus they might be much difficult). In summary, we have 65 such tasks for the experiments.

4.2 Experimental Setting

Compared algorithms: We compare our model TriTL with some state-of-the-art baselines, including

[1] http://www.kyb.tuebingen.mpg.de/bs/people/pgehler/code/index.html.

[2] http://people.csail.mit.edu/jrennie/20Newsgroups/.

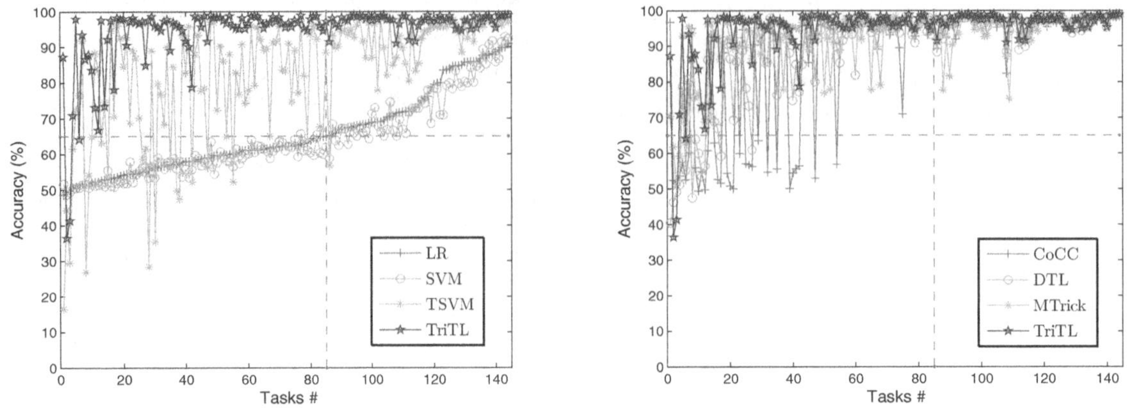

(a) TriTL vs. LR, SVM, TSVM (b) TriTL vs. CoCC, DTL, MTrick

Figure 1: The Performance Comparison among LR, SVM, TSVM, CoCC, DTL, MTrick and TriTL on data set *rec vs. sci*

Table 4: The top categories and their subcategories

Top Categories	Subcategories
comp	*comp.{graphics, sys.mac.hardware}* *comp.sys.ibm.pc.hardware* *comp.os.ms-windows.misc*
rec	*rec.{autos, motorcycles}* *rec.sport.{baseball, hockey}*
sci	*sci.{crypt, med, electronics, space}*
talk	*talk.politics.{guns, mideast, misc}* *talk.religion.misc*

- The supervised algorithms: Logistic Regression (LR) [18], Support Vector Machine (SVM) [21];
- The semi-supervised algorithm: Transductive Support Vector Machine (TSVM) [22];
- The cross-domain methods: Co-clustering based Classification (CoCC) [5], MTrick [9] and Dual Transfer Learning [12].

Parameter setting: In TriTL, we set $k_1 = 20$, $k_2 = 20$, $k_3 = 10$ and $T = 100$. The baseline methods LR is implemented by Matlab[3], SVM and TSVM are given by SVM^{light}[4]. The parameters of CoCC, MTrick and DTL are set as the default ones in their original papers, except that for DTL, we normalize the data matrix the same as this paper, i.e., $X_{[i,j]} = \frac{X_{[i,j]}}{\sum_{i=1}^{m} X_{[i,j]}}$, rather than $X_{[i,j]} = \frac{X_{[i,j]}}{\sum_{i=1}^{m}\sum_{j=1}^{n} X_{[i,j]}}$ in their paper. Experimental results in Section 4.3 show that, this slight change of normalization results in significant improvement of DTL.

We use the classification accuracy as the evaluation metric,

$$auc = \frac{|\{d | d \in \mathcal{D} \wedge f(d) = y\}|}{n}, \quad (27)$$

where y is the true label of document d, n is number of documents and the function $f(d)$ gives d a prediction label.

4.3 Experimental Results

4.3.1 Comparison on the Traditional Transfer Learning Tasks

We compare TriTL with LR, SVM, TSVM, CoCC, DTL and MTrick on the data set *rec vs. sci*, and all the results of the 144 classification tasks are recorded in Figure 1 and Table 5. In figure 1, the 144 tasks are sorted by the increase order of the performance of LR. The lower accuracy of LR indicates that it is harder to transfer the knowledge from source domain to target domain. Also, these classification tasks are separated into two parts, the left side of red dotted line in figure 1 represents the problems with accuracy of LR lower than 65%, while the right higher than 65%. Table 5 lists the corresponding average performance.

From these results, we have the following findings.

- TriTL is significantly better than the supervised learning algorithms LR and SVM, and the semi-supervised method TSVM.
- TriTL significantly outperforms all the compared transfer learning algorithms CoCC, MTrick and DTL with the statistical test. In Talble 5, TriTL achieves the best results in term of the average performances, no matter the classification tasks with accuracy of LR lower or higher than 65%. This improvement might be due to the synthesized effectiveness in modeling all the three concepts. When the accuracy of LR is lower than 65%, the degree of distribution difference between source and target domains might be large. Thus, modeling the distinct concepts in TriTL may improve the performance. On the other hand, when the accuracy of LR higher than 65% the data distributions of the source and target domains might be similar. Thus, modeling the identical concepts may work. Therefore, our model TriTL is much flexible under different situations.
- When the accuracy of LR is lower than 65%, MTrick is better than DTL, and DTL is better than CoCC, which coincide with our expectation. In these difficult tasks, the degree of distribution difference between source and target domains might be large. There might not be any identical concepts shared in the source and target domains. Thus, modeling the identical concepts in DTL and CoCC might deteriorate the performance.

[3]http://research.microsoft.com/∼minka/papers/logreg/.
[4]http://svmlight.joachims.org/.

Table 5: Average Performances (%) on 144 Tasks of Data Set *rec vs. sci*

Data Set		LR	SVM	TSVM	CoCC	DTL	MTrick	TriTL
	Lower	57.41	56.78	75.73	79.69	84.29	90.44	**92.23**
rec vs. sci	*Higher*	75.77	73.48	91.66	96.18	96.56	95.53	**97.19**
	Total	65.57	64.20	82.81	87.02	89.75	92.70	**94.43**

- When the accuracy of LR higher than 65%, the compared transfer learning algorithms perform similarly. However, we still can find that DTL is slightly better than CoCC, and CoCC slightly outperforms MTrick. The reason might be that modeling the identical concepts in DTL and CoCC improves the performance when the data distributions of the source and target domains are similar.

4.3.2 Comparison on the New Type of Transfer Learning Tasks

To further validate the effectiveness of TriTL, we construct the other 65 transfer learning tasks which are detailed in Section 4.1. The average accuracy values of these 65 tasks using all the methods are given in Table 6. From this table, it can be found that TriTL once more obtains the best results. In Table 6, MTrick is better than DTL, and DTL outperforms CoCC. These results are consistent to the analysis in Section 4.3.1 when the accuracy of LR is lower than 65%.

Table 6: Average Performances (%) on 65 Much Harder Transfer Learning Tasks

LR	SVM	TSVM	CoCC	DTL	MTrick	TriTL
52.45	51.81	74.32	69.66	75.34	78.45	**80.93**

4.4 Parameter Sensitivity

Here we investigate the parameter sensitivity of our model TriTL. There are three parameters in TriTL, including the number of identical concepts k_1, the number of alike concepts k_2, and the number of distinct concepts k_3. To verify that TriTL is not sensitive to the parameter setting, we relax the sampling ranges of these three parameters. Specifically, after some preliminary test we bound the parameters $k_1 \in [15, 25]$, $k_2 \in [15, 25]$ and $k_3 \in [5, 15]$, and evaluate them on 10 randomly selected tasks from the 144 classification problems of *rec vs. sci*. We randomly sample 10 combinations of parameters, and all the results are shown in Table 7. The 12th and 13th row respectively represents the average accuracy and variance of each tasks under the 10 combinations of parameters. The last row is the result using the default parameters adopted in this paper.

It is obvious that in Table 7, the mean performance of the 10 combinations of parameters for each task is almost the same as the one using the default parameters, and the variance is very small. These results show that TriTL is not sensitive to the parameter setting when they are sampled from some predefined bounds.

4.5 Algorithm Convergence

In this section, we also empirically check the convergence of the iterative algorithm to TriTL. We randomly choose 6 tasks from the data set *rec vs. sci*, and the results are shown in Figure 2. In these figures, the x-axis denotes the number of iterations, and the left and right y-axis denotes the prediction accuracy and the objective value in Eq.(10), respectively. Both prediction accuracy and objective value can converge within 100 iterations, and the value of objective function in Eq.(10) decreases along with the iterating process, which coincides with the theoretic analysis.

5. RELATED WORKS

This section we summarize the related works of transfer learning, which has aroused large amounts of interest and research in recent years. Here we group the previous works of transfer learning into three categories, i.e., feature based, instant weighing based and model combination based transfer learning.

Feature based methods can further be divided into two categories, i.e., feature selection and feature mapping. Feature selection based methods are to identify the common features (at the level of raw words) between source and target domains, which are useful for transfer learning [23, 5, 24]. Jiang et al. [23] argued that the features highly related to class labels should be assigned to large weights in the learnt model, thus they developed a two-step feature selection framework for domain adaptation. They first selected the general features to build a general classifier, and then considered the unlabeled target domain to select specific features for training target classifier. Uguroglu et al. [24] presented a novel method to identify variant and invariant features between two data sets for transfer learning. Feature space mapping based methods are to map the original high-dimensional features into a low-dimensional feature space, under which the source and target domains comply with the same data distribution [25, 26, 27]. Pan et al. [25] proposed a dimensionality reduction approach to find out this latent feature space, in which supervised learning algorithms can be applied to train classification models. Gu et al. [26] learnt the shared subspace among multiple domains for clustering and transductive transfer classification. In their problem formulation, all the domains have the same cluster centroid in the shared subspace. The label information can also be injected for classification tasks in this method. Gupta et al. [28] proposed a nonnegative shared subspace learning for social media retrieval. However, their algorithm does not consider the alike concepts and can not be directly used for transfer classification.

Instance weighting based approaches re-weight the instances in source domains according to the similarity measure on how they are close to the data in the target domain. Specifically, the weight of an instance is increased if it is close to the data in the target domain, otherwise the weight is decreased [20, 29, 30]. Dai et al. [20] extended boosting-style learning algorithm to cross-domain learning, in which the training instances with different distribution from the target domain are less weighted for data sampling, while the training instances with the similar distribution to the target domain are more weighted. Jiang et al. [29] proposed a general instance weighting framework, which has been validated to work well on NLP tasks. Wan et al. [30] first aligned the feature spaces in both domains utilizing some

Table 7: **The Parameter Effect for Performance (%) of Algorithm TriTL**

Sampling ID	k_1	k_2	k_3	Problem ID 1	2	3	4	5	6	7	8	9	10
1	20	22	15	97.11	97.37	98.01	98.72	98.86	96.81	97.76	98.91	91.54	94.91
2	16	22	15	97.24	97.37	97.96	98.65	98.86	97.01	97.64	98.93	91.59	95.03
3	19	24	10	97.23	97.22	97.91	98.79	98.86	96.89	97.59	98.91	91.76	94.84
4	19	21	8	97.06	97.14	97.98	98.77	98.88	97.01	97.71	98.89	90.94	95.11
5	18	17	10	97.35	97.22	97.71	98.69	98.86	96.99	97.66	98.89	91.93	94.94
6	15	22	9	96.94	97.39	97.59	98.74	98.91	97.03	97.66	98.89	91.88	94.93
7	18	25	14	97.24	97.53	97.60	98.62	98.91	96.79	97.66	98.93	91.71	94.73
8	24	24	10	96.96	97.41	97.82	98.64	98.86	97.08	97.71	98.94	90.92	94.98
9	19	17	9	97.13	97.12	97.84	98.71	98.86	96.99	97.64	98.89	92.10	94.86
10	24	20	9	97.06	96.99	97.87	98.76	98.86	96.96	97.69	98.89	91.41	95.06
Mean				97.13	97.28	97.83	98.71	98.87	96.96	97.67	98.91	91.58	94.94
Variance				0.017	0.027	0.023	0.003	0.000	0.009	0.002	0.000	0.158	0.013
This paper	20	20	10	97.21	97.43	97.82	98.71	98.88	97.02	97.67	98.91	91.49	94.90

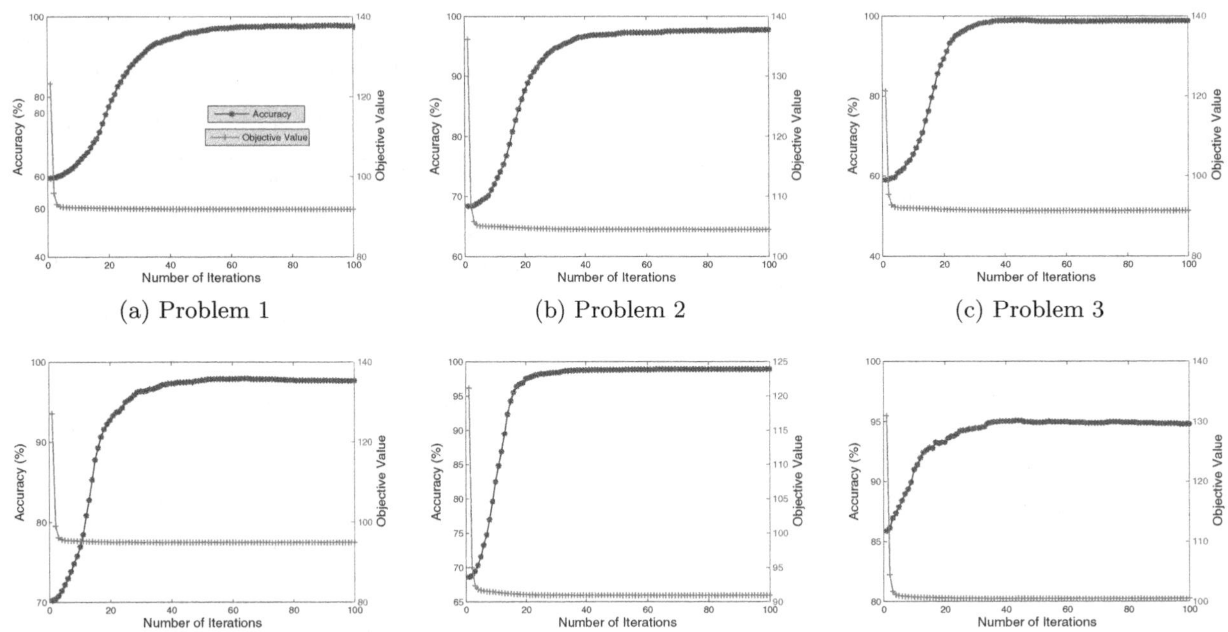

(a) Problem 1 (b) Problem 2 (c) Problem 3

(d) Problem 4 (e) Problem 5 (f) Problem 6

Figure 2: Number of Iterations vs. the Performance of TriTL and Objective Value.

on-line translation service, and then proposed an iterative feature and instance weighting (Bi-Weighting) method for cross-language text classification.

Model combination based methods aim at giving different weights to the classification models in an ensemble [3, 31]. Gao et al. [3] proposed a dynamic model weighting method for each test example according to the similarity between the model and the local structure of the test example in the target domain. Dredze [31] developed a new multi-domain online learning framework based on parameter combination from multiple classifiers for a new target domain.

However, there has not yet transfer learning algorithm systemically analyzes the commonalities and speciality between source and target domains, and model them together. This work belongs to the feature based methods, and simultaneously model the three commonalities and specific characteristic between source and target domains. Moreover, we design a new type of experiments to validate the effectiveness of our model.

6. CONCLUSIONS

In this paper, we systemically analyze the three kinds of concepts, namely identical, alike and distinct concepts, among the source and target domains. By considering them altogether we propose a general model model TriTL based on nonnegative matrix tri-factorization. Then, an alternately iterative algorithm is developed to solve the proposed optimization problem. Finally, we construct two types of transfer learning tasks, on which we conduct the systematic experiments. It shows that TriTL always significantly outperforms the compared methods under different situations of the source and target domain.

It is worth mentioning that TriTL is a general model, which can tackle multiple source domains, multiple target domains and multi-class classification problems. Furthermore, we can easily incorporate unlabeled source domain data and labeled target domain data into this model.

7. ACKNOWLEDGEMENTS

The work is supported by the National Natural Science Foundation of China (No. 61175052, 60975039, 61203297, 60933004, 61035003), National High-tech R&D Program of China (863 Program) (No.2012AA011003).

8. REFERENCES

[1] S. J. Pan and Q. Yang. A survey on transfer learning. *IEEE Transactions on Knowledge and Data Engineering*, 22(10):1345–1359, 2010.

[2] W. Y. Dai, Y. Q. Chen, G. R. Xue, Q. Yang, and Y. Yu. Translated learning: Transfer learning across different feature spaces. In *Proceedings of the 22nd NIPS*, 2008.

[3] J. Gao, W. Fan, J. Jiang, and J. W. Han. Knowledge transfer via multiple model local structure mapping. In *Proceedings of the 14th ACM SIGKDD*, pages 283–291, 2008.

[4] J. Gao, W. Fan, Y. Z. Sun, and J. W. Han. Heterogeneous source consensus learning via decision propagation and negotiation. In *Proceedings of the 15th ACM SIGKDD*, pages 339–348, 2009.

[5] W. Y. Dai, G. R. Xue, Q. Yang, and Y. Yu. Co-clustering based classification for out-of-domain documents. In *Proceedings of the 13th ACM SIGKDD*, pages 210–219, 2007.

[6] P. Luo, F. Z. Zhuang, H. Xiong, Y. H. Xiong, and Q. He. Transfer learning from multiple source domains via consensus regularization. In *Proceedings of the 17th ACM CIKM*, pages 103–112, 2008.

[7] G. R. Xue, W. Y. Dai, Q. Yang, and Y. Yu. Topic-bridged plsa for cross-domain text classification. In *Proceedings of the 31st ACM SIGIR*, pages 627–634, 2008.

[8] W. Y. Dai, O. Jin, G. R. Xue, Q. Yang, and Y. Yu. Eigen transfer: a unified framework for transfer learning. In *Proceedings of the 26th ICML*, pages 193–200, 2009.

[9] F. Z. Zhuang, P. Luo, H. Xiong, Q. He, Y. H. Xiong, and Z. Z. Shi. Exploiting associations between word clusters and document classes for cross-domain text categorization. In *Proceedings of the 10th SIAM SDM*, pages 13–24, 2010.

[10] F. Zhuang, P. Luo, Z. Shen, Q. He, Y. Xiong, Z. Shi, and H. Xiong. Collaborative dual-plsa: mining distinction and commonality across multiple domains for text classification. In *Proceedings of the 19th ACM CIKM*, pages 359–368. ACM, 2010.

[11] H. Wang, H. Huang, F. Nie, and C. Ding. Cross-language web page classification via dual knowledge transfer using nonnegative matrix tri-factorization. In *Proceedings of the 34th ACM SIGIR*, pages 933–942. ACM, 2011.

[12] M. Long, J. Wang, G. Ding, W. Cheng, X. Zhang, and W. Wang. Dual transfer learning. In *Proceedings of the 12th SIAM SDM*, 2012.

[13] C. Ding, T. Li, W. Peng, and H. Park. Orthogonal nonnegative matrix t-factorizations for clustering. In *Proceedings of the 12th ACM SIGKDD*, pages 126–135. ACM, 2006.

[14] T. Li, V. Sindhwani, C. Ding, and Y. Zhang. Knowledge transformation for cross-domain sentiment classification. In *Proceedings of the 32nd ACM SIGIR*, pages 716–717. ACM, 2009.

[15] F. Wang, T. Li, and C. Zhang. Semi-supervised clustering via matrix factorization. In *Proceedings of The 8th SIAM SDM*, pages 1041–1048, 2008.

[16] T. Li, C. Ding, Y. Zhang, and B. Shao. Knowledge transformation from word space to document space. In *Proceedings of the 31st ACM SIGIR*, pages 187–194. ACM, 2008.

[17] T. Hofmann. Unsupervised learning by probabilistic latent semantic analysis. *Journal of Machine Learning*, pages 177–196, 2001.

[18] David Hosmer and Stanley Lemeshow. *Applied Logistic Regression.* Wiley, New York, 2000.

[19] D. Zhang, J. He, Y. Liu, L. Si, and R.D. Lawrence. Multi-view transfer learning with a large margin approach. In *Proceedings of the 17th ACM SIGKDD*, pages 1208–1216. ACM, 2011.

[20] W. Y. Dai, Q. Yang, G. R. Xue, and Y. Yu. Boosting for transfer learning. In *Proceedings of the 24th ICML*, pages 193–200, 2007.

[21] B. E. Boser, I. Guyou, and V. Vapnik. A training algorithm for optimal margin classifiers. In *Proceedings of the 5th AWCLT*, 1992.

[22] T. Joachims. Transductive inference for text classification using support vector machines. In *Proceedings of the 16th ICML*, 1999.

[23] J. Jiang and C. X. Zhai. A two-stage approach to domain adaptation for statistical classifiers. In *Proceedings of the 16th ACM CIKM*, pages 401–410, 2007.

[24] S. Uguroglu and J. Carbonell. Feature selection for transfer learning. *Machine Learning and Knowledge Discovery in Databases*, pages 430–442, 2011.

[25] S. J. Pan, J. T. Kwok, and Q. Yang. Transfer learning via dimensionality reduction. In *Proceedings of the 23rd AAAI*, pages 677–682, 2008.

[26] Q. Q. Gu and J. Zhou. Learning the shared subspace for multi-task clustering and transductive transfer classification. In *Proceedings of 9th ICDM*, pages 159–168. IEEE, 2009.

[27] S.J. Pan, I.W. Tsang, J.T. Kwok, and Q. Yang. Domain adaptation via transfer component analysis. *IEEE TRANSACTIONS ON NEURAL NETWORKS*, 22(2):199–210, 2011.

[28] S.K. Gupta, D. Phung, B. Adams, T. Tran, and S. Venkatesh. Nonnegative shared subspace learning and its application to social media retrieval. In *Proceedings of the 16th ACM SIGKDD*, pages 1169–1178. ACM, 2010.

[29] J. Jiang and C. X. Zhai. Instance weighting for domain adaptation in nlp. In *Proceedings of the 45th ACL*, pages 264–271, 2007.

[30] C. Wan, R. Pan, and J. Li. Bi-weighting domain adaptation for cross-language text classification. In *Proceedings of 22nd IJCAI*, pages 1535–1540, 2011.

[31] M. Dredze, A. Kulesza, and K. Crammer. Multi-domain learning by confidence-weighted parameter combination. *Machine Learning*, 79(1):123–149, 2010.

[32] L. Lee and D. Seung. Algorithms for non-negative matrix factorization. volume 13, pages 556–562, 2001.

[33] C. Ding, T. Li, W. Peng, and H. Park. Orthogonal nonnegative matrix tri-factorizations for clustering. In *Proceedings of the 12th ACM SIGKDD*, pages 126–135, 2006.

[34] D.D. Lee and H.S. Seung. Learning the parts of

objects by non-negative matrix factorization. *Nature*, 401(6755):788–791, 1999.

APPENDIX

To study the convergence of update rules in Eqs. (19) through (26), we first check the convergence of F^1 when the rest parameters are fixed. According to Eq. (10), we formulate the optimization problem with constraints as the following Lagrangian function,

$$\begin{aligned}\mathcal{G}(F^1) =& \sum_{r=1}^{s+t} ||X_r - F_r S_r G_r^\top||^2 \\ &+ tr[\boldsymbol{\lambda}({F^1}^\top \mathbf{1}_m - \mathbf{1}_{k_1})({F^1}^\top \mathbf{1}_m - \mathbf{1}_{k_1})^\top],\end{aligned} \tag{28}$$

where $\boldsymbol{\lambda} \in \mathbb{R}^{k_1 \times k_1}$ is a diagonal matrix. Omitting the items, which are independent of F^1, Eq. (28) becomes

$$\begin{aligned}\mathcal{G}(F^1) =& \sum_{r=1}^{s+t} tr(-2 \cdot X_r^\top F^1 S^1 G_r^\top + G_r {S^1}^\top {F^1}^\top A_r \\ &+ 2 \cdot G_r {S^1}^\top {F^1}^\top B_r + 2 \cdot G_r {S^1}^\top {F^1}^\top C_r) \\ &+ tr[\boldsymbol{\lambda}({F^1}^\top \mathbf{1}_m \mathbf{1}_m^\top F^1 - 2 \cdot \mathbf{1}_{k_1} \mathbf{1}_m^\top F^1)],\end{aligned} \tag{29}$$

Then the differential is

$$\begin{aligned}\frac{\partial \mathcal{G}}{\partial F^1} =& \sum_{r=1}^{s+t}(-2 \cdot X_r G_r {S^1}^\top + 2 \cdot A_r G_r {S^1}^\top + 2 \cdot B_r G_r {S^1}^\top \\ &+ 2 \cdot C_r G_r {S^1}^\top) + 2 \cdot \mathbf{1}_m(\mathbf{1}_m{}^\top F^1 - \mathbf{1}_{k_1}{}^\top)\boldsymbol{\lambda},\end{aligned} \tag{30}$$

LEMMA 1. *Using the update rule (31), Equation (29) will monotonously decrease.*

$$F^1{}_{[i,j]} \leftarrow F^1{}_{[i,j]} \cdot \sqrt{\frac{[\sum_{r=1}^{s+t} X_r G_r {S^1}^\top + \mathbf{1}_m \mathbf{1}_{k_1}{}^\top \boldsymbol{\lambda}]_{[i,j]}}{[\sum_{r=1}^{s+t} D_r + \mathbf{1}_m \mathbf{1}_m{}^\top F^1 \boldsymbol{\lambda}]_{[i,j]}}}, \tag{31}$$

where $D_r = A_r G_r {S^1}^\top + B_r G_r {S^1}^\top + C_r G_r {S^1}^\top$.

PROOF. To prove Lemma 1 we describe the definition of auxiliary function [32] as follows.

DEFINITION 6 (AUXILIARY FUNCTION). *A function* $\mathcal{Q}(Y, \widetilde{Y})$ *is called an auxiliary function of* $\mathcal{T}(Y)$ *if it satisfies*

$$\mathcal{Q}(Y, \widetilde{Y}) \geq \mathcal{T}(Y), \mathcal{Q}(Y, Y) = \mathcal{T}(Y), \tag{32}$$

for any $Y, \widetilde{Y}$.

Then, define

$$Y^{(t+1)} = arg\min_Y \mathcal{Q}(Y, Y^{(t)}). \tag{33}$$

Through this definition,

$$\mathcal{T}(Y^{(t)}) = \mathcal{Q}(Y^{(t)}, Y^{(t)}) \geq \mathcal{Q}(Y^{(t+1)}, Y^{(t)}) \geq \mathcal{T}(Y^{(t+1)}).$$

It means that the minimizing of the auxiliary function of $\mathcal{Q}(Y, Y^{(t)})$ ($Y^{(t)}$ is fixed) has the effect to decrease the function of $\mathcal{T}$.

Now we can construct the auxiliary function of $\mathcal{G}$ as,

$$\begin{aligned}\mathcal{Q}(F^1, F^{1'}) =& \\ &\sum_{i=1}^{m}\sum_{j=1}^{k_1}\{-2 \cdot (\sum_{r=1}^{s+t} X_r G_r {S^1}^\top)_{[i,j]} F^{1'}{}_{[i,j]}(1 + \log \frac{F^1{}_{[i,j]}}{F^{1'}{}_{[i,j]}}) \\ &- 2 \cdot (\mathbf{1}_m \mathbf{1}_{k_1}{}^\top \boldsymbol{\lambda})_{[i,j]} F^{1'}{}_{[i,j]}(1 + \log \frac{F^1{}_{[i,j]}}{F^{1'}{}_{[i,j]}}) \\ &+ (\sum_{r=1}^{s+t} A_r{}' G_r {S^1}^\top + \mathbf{1}_m \mathbf{1}_m{}^\top F^{1'} \boldsymbol{\lambda})_{[i,j]} \frac{F^1{}_{[i,j]} F^1{}_{[i,j]}}{F^{1'}{}_{[i,j]}} \\ &+ [\sum_{r=1}^{s+t}(B_r G_r {S^1}^\top + C_r G_r {S^1}^\top)]_{[i,j]}(F^{1'}{}_{[i,j]} + \frac{F^1{}_{[i,j]} F^1{}_{[i,j]}}{F^{1'}{}_{[i,j]}})\},\end{aligned}$$

where $A_r{}' = F^{1'} S^1 G_r^\top$. Obviously, when $F^1 = F^{1'}$ the equality $\mathcal{Q}(F^1, F^{1'}) = \mathcal{G}(F^1)$ holds. Also we can prove the inequality $\mathcal{Q}(F^1, F^{1'}) \geq \mathcal{G}(F^1)$ holds using the similar proof approach in [33]. Then, while fixing $F^{1'}$, we minimize $\mathcal{Q}(F^1, F^{1'})$. The differential of $\mathcal{Q}(F^1, F^{1'})$ is

$$\begin{aligned}&\frac{\partial \mathcal{Q}(F^1, F^{1'})}{\partial F^1{}_{[i,j]}} = \\ &- 2 \cdot (\sum_{r=1}^{s+t} X_r G_r {S^1}^\top)_{[i,j]} \frac{F^{1'}{}_{[i,j]}}{F^1{}_{[i,j]}} - 2 \cdot (\mathbf{1}_m \mathbf{1}_{k_1}{}^\top \boldsymbol{\lambda})_{[i,j]} \frac{F^{1'}{}_{[i,j]}}{F^1{}_{[i,j]}} \\ &+ 2 \cdot (\sum_{r=1}^{s+t} A_r{}' G_r {S^1}^\top + \mathbf{1}_m \mathbf{1}_m{}^\top F^{1'} \boldsymbol{\lambda})_{[i,j]} \frac{F^1{}_{[i,j]}}{F^{1'}{}_{[i,j]}} \\ &+ 2 \cdot [\sum_{r=1}^{s+t}(B_r G_r {S^1}^\top + C_r G_r {S^1}^\top)]_{[i,j]} \frac{F^1{}_{[i,j]}}{F^{1'}{}_{[i,j]}}.\end{aligned}$$

Let $\frac{\partial \mathcal{Q}(F^1, F^{1'})}{\partial F^1{}_{[i,j]}} = 0$, we can obtain Eq.(31). Thus, the update rule (31) decreases the values of $\mathcal{G}(F^1)$. Then, Lemma 1 holds. □

The only obstacle left is the calculation of the Lagrangian multipliers $\boldsymbol{\lambda}$. Actually, $\boldsymbol{\lambda}$ in this problem is to drive the solution to satisfy the constrained condition that the sum of the values in each column of F^1 is 1. Here we adopt the normalization technology in [34, 9] to satisfy the constrains regardless of $\boldsymbol{\lambda}$. Specifically, in each iteration we use Eq.(26) to normalize F^1. After normalization, $\mathbf{1}_m \mathbf{1}_{k_1}{}^\top \boldsymbol{\lambda}$ is equal to $\mathbf{1}_m \mathbf{1}_m{}^\top F^1 \boldsymbol{\lambda}$ which are both constants, therefore, the effect of Eq.(26) and Eq.(19) can be approximately equivalent to Equation (31) when only considering the convergence. In our solution, we adopt the approximate update rule of Eq.(19) by omitting the items which depends on $\boldsymbol{\lambda}$ in Eq.(31). We can use the similar method to analyze the convergence of the update rules for $F^2{}_r$, $F^3{}_r$, S^1, S^2, $S^3{}_r$ $(1 \leq r \leq s+t)$, G_r $(s+1 \leq r \leq s+t)$ in Eqs. (20), (21), (22), (23), (24), (25), (26) respectively.

THEOREM 1 (CONVERGENCE). *After each round of iteration in Algorithm 1 the objective function in Eq.(10) will not increase.*

According to the lemmas for the convergence analysis on the update rules for F^1, $F^2{}_r$, $F^3{}_r$, S^1, S^2, $S^3{}_r$ $(1 \leq r \leq s+t)$, G_r $(s+1 \leq r \leq s+t)$, and the Multiplicative Update Rules [32], each update step in Algorithm 1 will not increase Eq. (10) and the objective has a lower bounded by zero, which guarantee the convergence. Thus, the above theorem holds.

Have You Done Anything Like That? Predicting Performance Using Inter-category Reputation

Marios Kokkodis
mkokkodi@stern.nyu.edu

Panagiotis G. Ipeirotis
panos@stern.nyu.edu

Leonard N. Stern School of Business, New York University
New York, New York 10012, USA
and
oDesk Research
Redwood City, California 94063, USA

ABSTRACT

Online labor markets such as oDesk and Amazon Mechanical Turk have been growing in importance over the last few years. In these markets, employers post tasks on which remote contractors work and deliver the product of their work. As in most online marketplaces, reputation mechanisms play a very important role in facilitating transactions, since they instill trust and are often predictive of the future satisfaction of the employer. However, labor markets are usually highly heterogeneous in terms of available task categories; in such scenarios, past performance may not be a representative signal of future performance. To account for this heterogeneity, in our work, we build models that predict the performance of a worker based on prior, category-specific feedback. Our models assume that each worker has a category-specific quality, which is latent and not directly observable; what is observable, though, is the set of feedback ratings of the worker and of other contractors with similar work histories. Based on this information, we build a multi-level, hierarchical scheme that deals effectively with the data sparseness, which is inherent in many cases of interest (i.e., contractors with relatively brief work histories). We evaluate our models on a large corpus of real transactional data from oDesk, an online labor market with hundreds of millions of dollars in transaction volume. Our results show an improved accuracy of up to 47% compared to the existing baseline.

Categories and Subject Descriptors

H.4 [**Information Systems Applications**]: Miscellaneous

Keywords

Online labor markets; Reputation; Task performance prediction; Bayesian modeling

WSDM'13, February 4–8, 2013, Rome, Italy.

1. INTRODUCTION

Online labor markets are growing in importance: Statistics from oDesk show an exponential growth in total hours worked per week since 2004, and the company is currently reporting transactions of more than 500, 000 hours of work-time billed per week.[1] Mechanical Turk,[2] a micro-work site, receives hundreds of thousands of dollars worth of new jobs every day.[3] In these markets, employers post tasks on which contractors work and deliver the product of their work online.

Work is mainly an "*experience good,*" meaning it is difficult to observe the quality of the deliverable in advance [19]. A key solution to resolve this uncertainty is the use of online reputation systems, which provide signals about the past performance of workers [6]. Reputation signals are predictive of the quality of users' future performance, in a wide variety of online communities e.g., online reviews, question and answering communities and others [5, 17, 18]. Consequently, it is rational to assume that employers, who have limited knowledge of the skills and abilities of a remote contractor, often consult the history of past transactions to understand better whether a contractor is qualified and suitable for the task at hand.

The implicit assumption of most existing reputation systems is that the past history, for which a participant has been rated for, is similar to the future tasks in which the participant will engage in. However, what happens when, say, a worker switches to a new type of task? For example, what happens when a contractor with a background in web development decides to work on a graphic design task? What can we say regarding the possible outcome of a programming task, for a worker with history in technical writing? In general, are reputations transferable across categories and predictive of future performance? How can we estimate task affinity and use the information to best estimate expectations of future performance?

As a novel contribution of this paper, we propose a set of predictive models that use Bayesian inference to estimate the future performance of a user based on category-specific past performance. Specifically, we assume that the category-specific qualities (or skills) of a user are *latent and not directly observable.* However, these skills are reflected into a set of other *measurable* characteristics, such as employer ratings for past projects. Based on these past ratings, we build models that are capable of connecting past performance *across categories*

[1] `http://www.odesk.com`
[2] `http://www.mturk.com`
[3] `http://mturk-tracker.com/arrivals/`

to predict performance in a new category for which we have either no, or very few, past data points. Since for many category pairs we lack sufficient data to build robust predictors (e.g., from English-Russian translation to web development), we also present a hierarchical model that compensates for the inherent sparseness by using training data from higher-level, more general categories, to compute the cross-category predictive power of past ratings.

For our experimental evaluation, we first present some synthetic experiments that illustrate the effect of various parameters in the performance of our model, showing that our model outperforms existing baselines. Next, we present experiments with *real* data, consisting of hundreds of thousands of real transactions across tens of different categories from the oDesk marketplace, which capture histories of hundreds of thousands of different contractors. We demonstrate how different categories are correlated with each other, and whether past performance in a given category contains predictive information about performance in another. Our results show that our techniques that explicitly take into account category-specific reputation demonstrate significant improvement (of up to 47%) in estimating the feedback score of a worker's next task compared to the existing baseline.

Our bottom line result is clear and simple: Reputation schemes stand to benefit significantly if they adjust the feedback scores of the participating users to take into account the type of task that a user is expected to complete (or has already completed), as well as the user's past category-specific performance history. For example, the "stars" in the profile of a user bidding for a translation work may be more influenced by past writing tasks compared to past programming tasks. Or even when presenting statistics for the author of a review, the history statistics of the user (e.g., "written 100 reviews, with 98% usefulness") can be adjusted to take into consideration the type of the past reviews (e.g., for a camera review to put more weight on past ratings on digital cameras, and not so much weight on reviews about shoes).

2. BACKGROUND

Reputation systems: There are many studies of online reputation mechanisms and how such mechanisms resolve various information asymmetries [6, 7]. Common reputation systems use the average of past performance across all transactions, often adding a time-discounting mechanism, or weighting feedback ratings by the size of the transaction. In our work, we explore how past, *task-specific* reputation can be used to predict future performance on *different types* of tasks. We are not aware of other studies that compartmentalize the past reputation of an agent in a market in order to understand better the ability of a worker to carry out a specific type of task.

Two other major streams of research that relate to our work (and to reputation systems, in a more general sense) are research on helpfulness of online reviews and research on community question answering (*CQA*).

Estimating helpfulness of online reviews: Various approaches have been proposed to predict review helpfulness that exploit different sets of features: Soo-Min Kim et al. [14] use review length, uni-grams and product rating; O'Mahony and Smyth use readability tests [20]; Otterbacher and Arbor [21] use the topical relevancy, the believability and the objectivity of the review; and Danescu-Niculescu-Mizil et al. [5] use the difference of a product evaluation with other evaluations of the same product. Furthermore, Liu et al. [17] take into account the reviewer's expertise, the writing style of the review, as well as the timeliness of the review. Lu et al. [18] include in their predictive feature sets information about the author's identities and their social networks. Lappas and Gunopoulos [15] propose a framework for capturing the overall consensus of the reviewers, on a given subset of item attributes. Tsaparas et al. [24] propose algorithms for selecting a comprehensive set of a few, high-quality reviews that cover many different aspects of the reviewed item.

Our work is orthogonal and complementary to these efforts: in many settings (e.g., online labor markets), we cannot extract features of the past submitted work, and in settings where we can, these extra features are orthogonal to the idea of creating category-specific features.

Closely related to our work, Ghose and Ipeirotis examine how the overall history of the reviewer (along with other textual features of a review such as its subjectivity and readability levels) affects the helpfulness of a review [9]. Our proposed approach, instead of just using the average past reputation of a user, exploits also the correlation among given topic categories and provides more accurate quality estimates.

Selecting quality answers in community question answering: A lot of research has been conducted in the past that aims to predict the quality of online answers in "Community Question Answering" platforms. In that direction, Jeon et al. [13] propose a framework that uses non-textual features such as click counts. Liu et al. [16] present a prediction model of customers' satisfaction in the "Yahoo! Answers" platform. Similarly, Agichtein et al. [2] address the task of identifying high quality content in *CQA* platforms by exploiting community feedbacks (such as links between items, and explicit ratings). Furthermore, Bian et al. [3] develop a semi-supervised coupled mutual reinforcement framework for extracting high quality content answers, that requires only relatively few labeled examples. Suryanto et al. [23] propose a different framework to design methods that select high-quality answers from a *CQA* site by considering both the answer's quality and relevance. Shah and Pemrantz [22] use Amazon Mechanical Turk workers to label the quality of the answers, and then they use these labels to train classifiers that select the highest quality answers.

Closely related to our work, Adamic et al. [1] cluster forum categories according to content characteristics and study patterns of interactions among users. In particular Adamic et al. relate categories based on user participation and estimate the user's interests' entropy values. Using these values, they observe that lower entropy is correlated with receiving higher answer ratings, but only for categories where factual expertise is required. Their work deviates from ours in that it does not use prior, category-specific quality to predict the current user quality, as well as in the fact that the authors correlate categories based on user replies and not on how user participation is associated with the quality of completed tasks.

3. PROBLEM FORMULATION

In this section, we present a set of increasingly sophisticated methods for estimating future ratings for a worker, given the past rating history. We start with a simple binomial Bayesian model that learns the (latent) quality from a user's past ratings in the same category using a binary measurement: whether the feedback will be positive or negative; next, we show how to handle multi-degree ratings using a multinomial model. Then we move and discuss our latent-variable model that assumes that each worker has multiple, latent, and interdependent qualities across categories, which we try to estimate by observing the

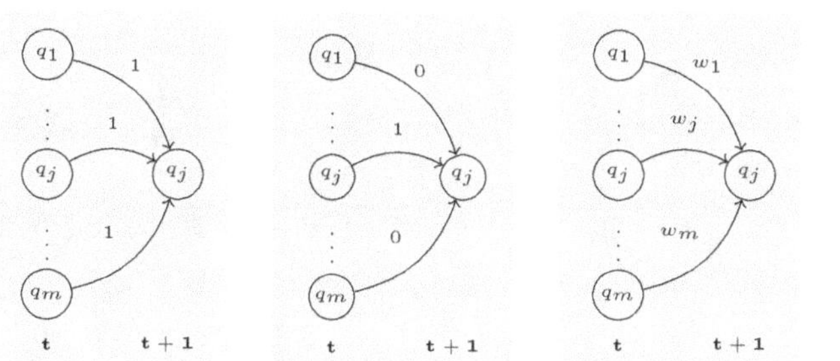

(a) Feedback from all past tasks treated equal. (b) Only feedback from tasks in the same category counts. (c) Adjusting feedback score by affinity.

Figure 1: Different ways of estimating the quality of a new task in category j. worker , (b) aggregating only history in the specific weights to

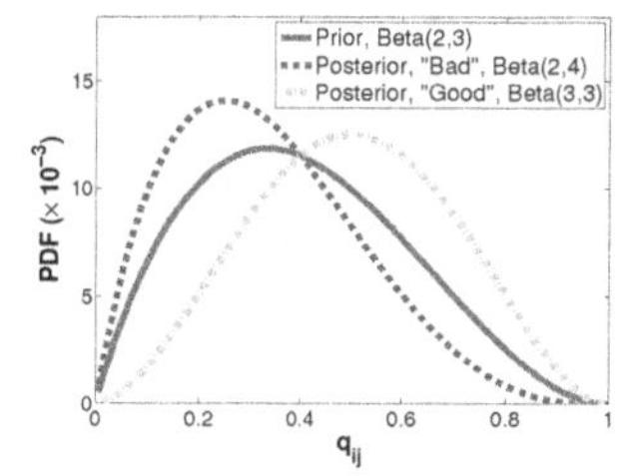

Figure 2: Prior and posterior distributions comparison for both "Bad" and "Good" outcomes.

ratings received by a variety of users across categories. Finally, we propose the creation of hierarchical models that are able to successfully deal with heterogeneous environments and the resulting data sparseness.

In all our models, we assume that we have m categories of tasks (e.g., Software Development, Multimedia & Design, Sales & Marketing). We further assume that each user is endowed with a set of m category-specific, latent qualities. We denote with $q_{ij} \in [0, 1]$ the quality of a user i in category j ($j \in \{1, \ldots, m\}$). The category-specific quality q_{ij} is the probability that, given a task in category j, user i will receive a specific rating for the task. Our goal is to estimate q_{ij} by observing the user's past performance; needless to say, we are mainly interested in improving the vanilla averaging mainly in cases where past feedback in a given category is sparse.

In Figure 1 we show a schematic description of the existing baselines and of our approach. In particular, Figure 1(a) shows the existing baseline, which provides an estimation of the next task's quality by uniformly aggregating *all feedback ratings from past tasks*, irrespectively of the affinity of past tasks to the current one. Figure 1(b) focuses on estimating the quality of a new task in a specific category by only using past information from completed tasks in the exact same category, ignoring feedback from other categories. Finally, our model in Figure 1(c) assigns different weights to each category's feedback, and uses these weights to predict the expected rating for the new task. We discuss this approach in Section 3.2.

3.1 Learning from past ratings, within category

In this case we assume that a user has completed enough tasks in category j and has enough feedback ratings, so that we can use the user's prior performance in this specific category to predict the performance for a new task in this category.

3.1.1 Binomial Approach

We start with a very simple setting; we examine the case where a user is performing tasks only within a category j, and the performance rating on these tasks is strictly binary, either "good" or "bad". Given a past history of n tasks within the given category, and assuming that we know the current quality q_{ij} of the worker i in category j, we expect the number x of completed tasks rated as "good" to follow a binomial distribution:

$$\Pr(x|q_{ij}; n) = \binom{n}{x} q_{ij}^{x} (1 - q_{ij})^{n-x}$$

Now, by using basic concepts of Bayesian statistics [8], we can try to infer q_{ij} based on the number of "good" and "bad" completed tasks. Specifically, if we assume some prior distribution $q_{ij} \sim Beta(\alpha, \beta)$, by applying Bayes' theorem we get that:

$$\Pr(q_{ij}|x; n) = \frac{p(x|q_{ij}; n) p(q_{ij})}{\int_0^1 p(x|q_{ij}, n) p(q_{ij}) dq_{ij}}$$

which is known to follow $Beta(\alpha + x, n - x + \beta)$.

Figure 2 shows an example. Assuming a prior distribution $Beta(2, 3)$, we show the resulting probability distribution functions for the two possible outcomes, "Bad" ($Beta(2, 4)$) and "Good" ($Beta(3, 3)$). We can observe the shift to the right (i.e., improved quality) when we have a successful outcome, and to the left (i.e., downgraded quality) otherwise.

3.1.2 Multinomial Approach

In reality, binary feedback is typically used for small tasks (e.g., on Amazon Mechanical Turk). For more complex tasks, we often see reputation systems that have multiple grades for feedback (e.g., 5-star ratings are common). To extend the previous model to account for a range of discrete outcomes, we use a multinomial distribution of K possible outcomes (instead of just two):

$$\Pr(\mathbf{x}|\mathbf{q}_{ij}; n) = \binom{n}{x_1, \ldots, x_K} \prod_{k=1}^{K} q_{ijk}^{x_k} ,$$

where the vector $\mathbf{x} = (x_1, \ldots, x_K)$ encodes the past feedback with x_k being the number of times that outcome k occurred in the past. The value q_{ink} captures the probability that the work of worker i in category j will be of quality k. The conjugate prior for $\mathbf{q}_{ij}$ is be the Dirichlet distribution (see [8] for more details), with a vector hyperparameter $\boldsymbol{\alpha}$: $\Pr(\mathbf{q}_{ij}|\boldsymbol{\alpha}) \sim \mathcal{D}(\boldsymbol{\alpha})$. Using a Dirichlet prior and after observing the past feedback $\mathbf{x}$, the posterior distribution becomes:

$$\Pr(q_{ijk}|\mathbf{x}, \boldsymbol{\alpha}) \sim \mathcal{D}(x_k + \alpha_k)$$

Instead of the approaches presented here, we could adapt approaches from item response theory (IRT) [11], for the task at hand. However, most techniques in IRT do not work well with relatively sparse data. IRT models work well for standardized tests, trying to estimate the skills of students that complete tens and hundreds of questions, and identical questions are repeated across thousands of students. Furthermore, there is little focus on inter-task correlations of performance, which is the focus of our work. We present our approach next.

3.2 Learning across categories

In practice, we often have insufficient history within a category and the distribution of $p(q_{ij}|x,n)$ does not provide much information. This results in a q_{ij} distribution with high variance, as well as in very uncertain estimates. A naive approach to estimate q_{ij} would be to simply treat every single past feedback as equal, or, potentially taking a moving average to give higher weight to recent tasks. However, we often have the intuition that even though someone may have no experience in a given category (e.g., in developing Android applications), the past experience in some other, related categories (e.g., iPhone development) can be predictive of future performance in a new category. Conversely, some categories may give no useful information; for example past experience as an administrative assistant does not give much information about the ability to carry out a translation task from Chinese to English.

In our model, we assume that the quality of worker i for a category j (q_{ij}) can be estimated based on our knowledge of the history and values q_{ik}, for other categories, as well as the overall average quality of the user, q_i, as reflected in the past ratings.[4] Since q_{ij} are probability values, we use the method presented by Clemen and Winkler [4] to *combine probability estimates from multiple, correlated sources*:

$$\text{logit}(q_{ij}) = \sum_{k=1}^{m} \alpha_{jk}\text{logit}(q_{ik}) + \beta_j \text{logit}(q_i) + \varepsilon_{ij}$$

where α_{jk}, β_j are data-specific coefficients, ε_{ij} is a random disturbance, and logit is defined as follows:

$$\text{logit}(x) = \log(\frac{x}{1-x}) \Leftrightarrow \text{logit}^{-1}x = \frac{\exp(x)}{1+\exp x}$$

Since we can observe the full feedback history of the worker, we use *panel data* [10] and estimate the quality $q_{ij}(t+1)$ at time $t+1$, given the feedback ratings until time t. The resulting equation that we use is the following:

$$\text{logit}(q_{ij}(t+1)) = \sum_{k=1}^{m} \alpha_{jk}\text{logit}(q_{ik}(t)) + \beta_j \text{logit}(q_i(t)) + \varepsilon_{ij} \quad (1)$$

or in matrix notation, for all the available categories that we examine:

$$\begin{bmatrix} \text{logit}(q_{i1}(t+1)) \\ \dots \\ \text{logit}(q_{im}(t+1)) \end{bmatrix} = \begin{bmatrix} \alpha_{11} & \dots & \alpha_{1m} & \beta_1 \\ \dots & \dots & \dots & \dots \\ \alpha_{m1} & \dots & \alpha_{mm} & \beta_m \end{bmatrix} \begin{bmatrix} \text{logit}(q_{i1}(t)) \\ \dots \\ \text{logit}(q_{im}(t)) \\ \text{logit}(q_i(t)) \end{bmatrix} + \begin{bmatrix} \varepsilon_{i1} \\ \dots \\ \varepsilon_{im} \end{bmatrix}$$

The parameters of Equation 1 can be easily computed using regression.

3.3 Estimating quality distributions

We showed before that in the binomial (multinomial) case, $\Pr(q_{ij}|.)$ follows some *Beta* (*Dirichlet*) distribution. However, to use the regression in Equation 1 we need numeric values for q_{ij} and not distributions. As a result, in order to use the acquired knowledge of the distribution of values of q_{ij} within a framework that allows only scalar values, we use the following two techniques:

[4] The q_i factor can be considered as a global smoothing factor in the model, which we know to be correlated with the q_{ik} values.

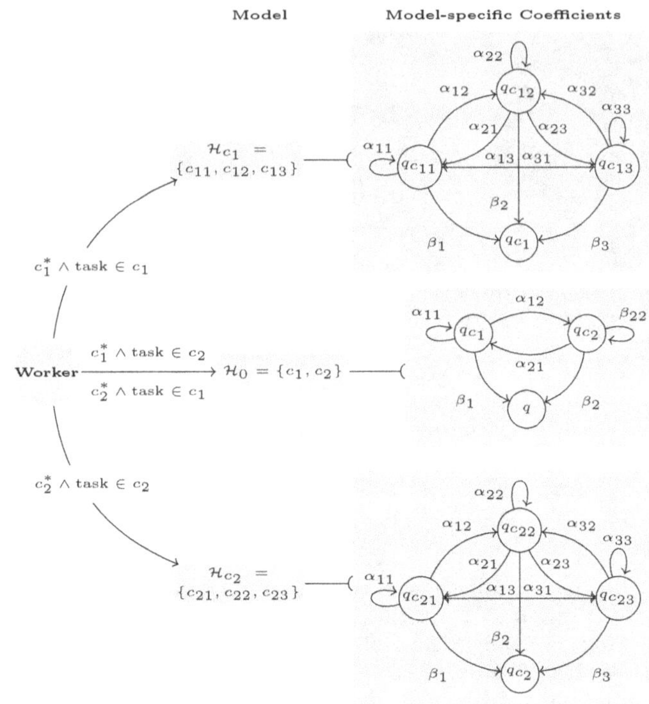

Figure 3: Model selection for a user with the majority of past tasks in category c_l^* and current task in category c_l, where $l = \{1, 2\}$. In the presented example, $L = 2, L_1 = L_2 = 3$.

- **Point Estimate (PE)**: We set q_{ij} to be a mean of the user's resulting distribution. In particular, for the binomial case, for a prior $Beta(\alpha, \beta)$, the value of q_{ij} is:

$$q_{ij} = \frac{x+\alpha}{n+\alpha+\beta}$$

For the multinomial model, with a prior $\mathcal{D}(\boldsymbol{\alpha})$, where $\boldsymbol{\alpha} = (\alpha_1, \dots, \alpha_k, \dots, \alpha_K)$, the mean value of q_{ij} is:

$$q_{ij} = \frac{1}{K}\sum_{k=1}^{K} k \cdot \frac{x_k + \alpha_k}{n + \sum_{k=1}^{K} \alpha_k}$$

- **Random Sampling (RS)**: With this approach, we instantiate the values q_{ij} by sampling multiple random values from the associated distribution.[5] For the multinomial model, in order to sample from the resulting Dirichlet distribution, we follow the procedure described by Gelman et al. [8]: we draw values $d_1, \dots, d_K$ from K independent Gamma distributions, $Gamma(x_k+\alpha_k, x_k+\alpha_k)$, and we then estimate q_{ijk} as follows:

$$q_{ijk} = \frac{d_k}{\sum_{k=1}^{K} d_k}$$

3.4 Dealing with sparseness

So far we have discussed how we can predict the quality for a new task, given the history of a worker across all available categories. However, when the number of categories grows, we

[5] In our work, we sample 30 values from the underlying distribution.

often face problems of data sparseness: there are not enough points to adequately estimate, in a robust manner, the coefficients of Equation 1 (i.e., we end up overfitting the training data and get poor results when dealing with unseen data).

To deal with sparsity, we propose to pair our technique with a hierarchical clustering algorithm. In particular, we cluster categories into L number of abstract groups, for which we have enough "*transitional data points*" to estimate the necessary coefficients. By transitional data points we mean that there is a sufficient number of users that worked in both categories, allowing us to estimate the predictive power of feedback in one category to predict future performance in another.

These categories represent the top level model, $\mathcal{H}_0 = \{c_1, \ldots, c_l, \ldots, c_L\}$. Then, by decomposing each abstract category c_l in the top level, we can create a number of second level models, each one with L_l number of categories. For example, if we decompose category c_1, we will get $\mathcal{H}_{c_1} = \{c_{11}, c_{12}, \ldots, c_{1L_1}\}$; if we decompose category c_2 we will get $\mathcal{H}_{c_2} = \{c_{21}, c_{22}, \ldots, c_{2L_2}\}$, etc. By repeatedly applying this procedure we can reach a desired category-specific detail level, where all categories in a specific set will have enough data points for the necessary coefficients' estimation.

Now that we have different models at different levels, we need to choose which one suits best for each user. To do that, we follow the procedure shown in Figure 3: we first find the abstract category in the highest level model $\mathcal{H}_0$ that contain the majority of the worker's past tasks. Say this category is c_l^*. If the current task that we examine and want to predict its quality is also of the same category c_l^*, we use the coefficients of the model in the lower level that decomposes c_l^*, $\mathcal{H}_{c_l^*}$. Otherwise, we use the coefficients of $\mathcal{H}_0$. We move to lower levels in a similar fashion. The example illustrated in Figure 3 assumes a specific case where $L = 2$, and $L_1 = L_2 = 3$. Note that in this approach, all three models have different coefficients (rightmost column of diagrams in Figure 3).

4. EXPERIMENTAL SETUP

In this section, we discuss the experimental setup we use to evaluate our approaches. We start by discussing the different tuning parameters for our model, and then present the evaluation metrics and the baselines that we use.

4.1 Threshold Parameters

We use three parameters to evaluate our models. For the Binomial Model, we use parameter $\theta \in (0, 1)$ which is a threshold that separates "good" outcomes from the "bad" (i.e., $q > \theta$ is a "good" outcome while $q \leq \theta$ is a "bad" outcome). For the multinomial approach, we use a parameter for the number of discrete classes (K). Finally, for both of our approaches, we use a History Threshold, (η), that represents the minimum number of completed tasks that a worker needs to complete *across all categories* before our model provides a prediction; of course, for workers with very limited history (i.e., one or two tasks) the predictions are going to be worse than with workers with longer histories. By varying the η value, we want to examine what is the lower bound for getting good performance, even for workers with limited number of ratings.

4.2 Evaluation Metrics

Our goal here is twofold: first, we want to have good predictive performance when predicting the quality of a new task; second, we are interested in understanding whether there are significant correlations among different task categories. To estimate the accuracies of our approach, we use the mean absolute error (MAE) across all tasks in our test set, which we define as follows:

$$MAE = \frac{1}{N}\sum_{t=1}^{N}|\hat{q}_t - \bar{q}_t|$$

where N is the total number of tasks in our test set, $\hat{q}_t$ is the predicted quality of task t and $\bar{q}_t$ the actual feedback score of task t. We compare our results with the baselines by computing the MAE percentage *improvement*, which we define as follows:

$$Improvement\% = \frac{MAE_{Baseline} - MAE_{model}}{MAE_{Baseline}}$$

4.3 Baseline Methods

The baselines we use to compare our results predict the quality of a new task by uniformly considering the past history of a worker in all categories. For our binomial approach, the predicted baseline quality $\hat{q}_{ij}^{(Bin)}$ of a new task by worker i in category j at time $T+1$ will be:

$$\hat{q}_{ij}^{(Bin)}(T+1) = \frac{1}{N_i(T)}\sum_{t=1}^{N_i(T)} \mathbf{1}_{\{\bar{q}_{ij}(t)>\theta\}}$$

where $\mathbf{1}_{\{\bar{q}_{ij}(t)>\theta\}}$ is the indicator function for "good" outcomes, and $N_i(T)$ is the total number of completed tasks by worker i at time T. Similarly, for the multinomial approach, the baseline predictions $\hat{q}_{ij}^{(Mult)}$ is:

$$\hat{q}_{ij}^{(Mult)}(T+1) = \frac{1}{N_i(T) \times K}\sum_{k=1}^{K}\sum_{t=1}^{N_i(T)} k\mathbf{1}_{\{\bar{q}_{ij}(t)\in(\frac{k-1}{K},\frac{k}{K}]\}}$$

5. SYNTHETIC DATA EXPERIMENTS

In this section, we describe the synthetic experiments we ran to study the effect of various parameters (see Section 4.1) on our algorithms. We conducted the experiments with synthetic data, in addition to the experiments with real data described in Section 6, in order to understand better the performance of our algorithms under different settings, something that is not directly possible with real data.

5.1 Data Generation

Dense data, simple model: We first generated data that is "dense" enough and for which we can build our models as described in Section 3.2. Specifically, we generated m different categories, where $m \in \{3, 5, 7\}$, and we randomly assigned prior probabilities across these categories. Next, we randomly created an $m \times m$ transition matrix, where the element in the i-th row and j-th column represents the probability that given a completion of a task in category i at time t the next task (at time $t+1$) will be in category j.

Next, for each user i in our synthetic dataset, we created a quality vector $\mathbf{q_i} = [q_{i1}, \ldots, q_{im}]$ for all available categories. This vector $\mathbf{q_i}$ describes the probability that the user will successfully complete a task in category j. Then, each user is assumed to randomly complete between 10 and 50 tasks. We pick the category distribution as follows: Based on the global category distribution we estimated before, we pick an initial category for each user; then, based on the transition matrix, we draw the next task category for the user and we continue the random walk until exhausting the tasks. Knowing the category of the task, we pick a performance for the task using

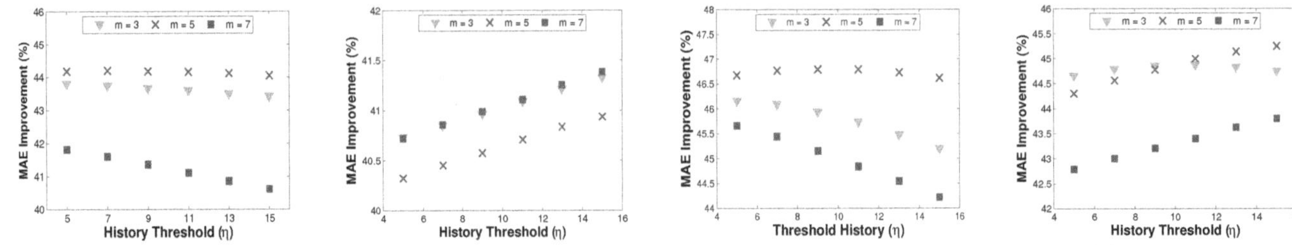

(a) $\theta = 0.5$, PE (b) $\theta = 0.5$, RS (c) $\theta = 0.6$, PE (d) $\theta = 0.6$, RS

Figure 4: Synthetic Experiment: the *improvement* of our models compared to the existing baselines, as measured by "mean absolute error" (MAE) for the (a) Binomial model point estimate (PE) and random sampling (RS), for different number of categories ($m = 3, 5, 7$), and different θ-thresholds ($\theta \in \{0.5, 0.6\}$).

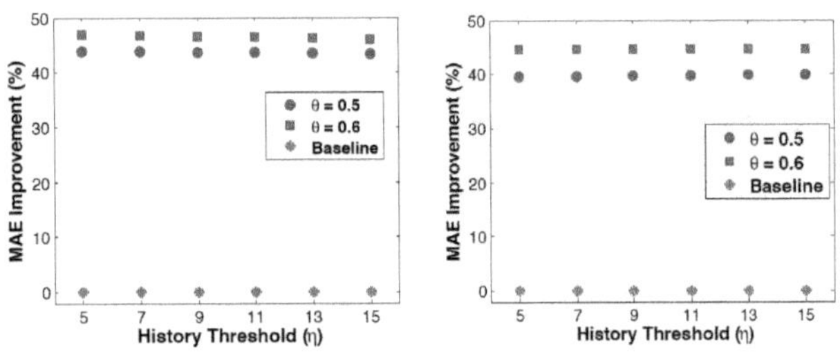

(a) PE (b) RS

Figure 5: Synthetic Experiment - Hierarchical Model: the *improvement* of our hierarchical model compared to the baselines, as measured by "mean absolute error" (MAE) for point estimate (PE) and random sampling (RS), for different θ-thresholds.

the latent quality values q_{ij}. For the binomial case, and for a task in category j we conduct a Bernoulli trial with probability of having "good" performance being q_{ij}. Analogously, for the multinomial case.

Sparse data, hierarchical model: To evaluate the robustness of our hierarchical approach, we created three higher-level categories (clusters), which in turn consist of three lower-level categories. In contrast with the dense case, the transition matrix has low probability values when transitioning across clusters (less than 0.05), and high probability to transition in the same category or in other categories within the same cluster. In this way, we simulate a scenario where users have expertise in one category and in a few other similar ones, and they continue to show a preference for tasks from these categories.

5.2 Results for Synthetic Data

After generating our data, we split it into training and test sets, based on users; the same user could not be both in the training and test data sets. Then, we use the training sets to build our models and the test sets to evaluate them.

In the "dense data" case, we build simple models (no hierarchies). Figures 4(a) to 4(d) show the results. We can see that in all different settings we tried (different θ values, different number of categories, different history thresholds η) our approach outperforms the baselines. Note that we report the *improvement* over the baseline, so any value above 0 indicates better performance than the baseline. We further notice that the improvement does not significantly vary with the number of categories (m) or the history threshold (η), which is a good sign: This indicates that our approach scales nicely with an increasing number of categories, and can also work with limited work histories, respectively.

Next, in Figures 5(a) and 5(b) we present the results of our hierarchical model implementation with sparse data. Similarly with before, we observe that our hierarchical approach provides a significant improvement compared to existing baselines. Further, we notice again that this improvement is sustained across the different values of θ-threshold and history threshold η, indicating again that our approach works with limited work histories, even with sparse data.

6. REAL DATA EXPERIMENTS: ODESK

In this section we apply our approaches to real transactional data from the online labor site oDesk.com.[6] We examine whether we can improve the prediction of feedback ratings for contractors that perform a task through oDesk. In addition, we also conducted experiments using data from Amazon.com product reviews; we examined the performance of *reviewers*, measured as the usefulness of the submitted product reviews, but due to space restrictions and due to the qualitatively similar results, we do not include Amazon results in this paper. We focus instead solely on the oDesk dataset, which we believe is inherently more interesting: For product reviews there is already a significant amount of literature (e.g., [14, 17, 20, 21]) that can predict the quality of a review using purely textual analysis; we do not have such an ability for online work contracts so we believe that the usefulness of our models is higher in the oDesk setting.

6.1 Data

oDesk is a global job marketplace with a plethora of tools targeted to businesses that intend to hire and manage remote workers. The company reports more than 500,000 hours of work billed per week as well as an exponentially growing transaction volume of more than $300 million USD per year.

For all our experiments, we build and test our models on real oDesk transactional data. In particular, we analyze a total of 666,229 completed tasks by 115,436 individual workers, along with their feedback scores. We vertically (i.e., by user) split this data into training and test sets. More specifically, we randomly choose 90% of the total workers and their related tasks as our training set, and we consider the remaining 10% of the data to be our test set. In all of our experiments, we

[6]The data set is available, on request, through oDesk.

Level	Coeff.	Correlates Categories
Gen. ($\mathcal{H}_0$)	α_{11}	Technical - Technical
	α_{12}	Technical - Non Technical
	β_1	Technical - Overall
	α_{21}	Non Technical - Technical
	α_{22}	Non Technical - Non Technical
	β_2	Non Technical - Overall
Technical ($\mathcal{H}_{c_1}$)	α_{11}	Software developer - Software developer
	α_{12}	Software developer - Web developer
	α_{13}	Software developer - Design & Multimedia
	β_1	Software developer - Overall
	α_{21}	Web developer - Software developer
	α_{22}	Web developer - Web developer
	α_{23}	Web developer - Design & Multimedia
	β_2	Web developer - Overall
	α_{31}	Design & Multimedia - Software developer
	α_{32}	Design & Multimedia - Web developer
	α_{33}	Design & Multimedia - Design & Multimedia
	β_3	Design & Multimedia - Overall
Non Technical ($\mathcal{H}_{c_2}$)	α_{11}	Writing - Writing.
	α_{12}	Writing - Administration
	α_{13}	Writing - Sales & Marketing
	β_1	Writing - Overall
	α_{21}	Administration - Writing
	α_{22}	Administration - Administration
	α_{23}	Administration - Sales & Marketing
	β_2	Administration - Overall
	α_{31}	Sales & Marketing - Writing
	α_{32}	Sales & Marketing - Administration
	α_{33}	Sales & Marketing - Sales & Marketing
	β_3	Sales & Marketing - Overall

Table 1: Interpretation of different coefficients in all three levels.

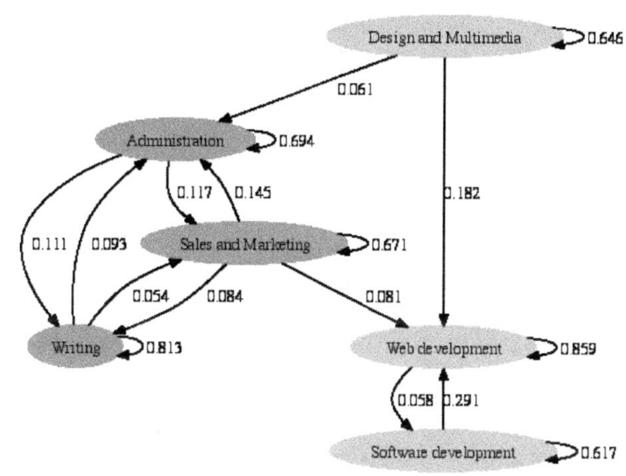

Figure 7: Transition probabilities across different categories in our training dataset. The graph shows only transitions with probability greater than 0.05.

build models on the training set, and evaluate them on the test set. In this way, we ensure that the resulting performance evaluation metrics are not due to overfitting the data.

An instance in our datasets consists of the worker id, the category of the completed task, and the average feedback score that the specific worker received for that task.

In the oDesk platform specifically, after a user completes a task, the employer supplies feedback scores (in integers of 0 to 5) in the following six fields: "Availability" ($f1$), "Communication" ($f2$), "Cooperation" ($f3$), "Deadlines" ($f4$), "Quality" ($f5$), "Skills" ($f6$). The average of these scores divided by 5 represents the observed quality of the specific task ($\bar{q}$):

$$\bar{q} = \frac{1}{5}(\frac{\sum_{i=1}^{6} f_i}{6}), \;\; \bar{q} \in [0, 1] \cdot \tag{2}$$

The feedback score distribution in the training set is skewed towards high scores, with a mean value of 0.89, i.e., approximately 4.5/5 in a five-star scale. Intuitively, this can be explained by the user survival patterns in online communities: users that receive low feedback scores are unable to get hired again, so they leave the marketplace (or rejoin with different credentials). On the other hand, users that receive high feedback scores, tend to continue to use the marketplace. Thus, the majority of the marketplace users end up having high feedback scores. Notice that such skewed distributions of ratings are very common across many different marketplaces [12].

6.2 oDesk hierarchical models

In our experiments, we examine a set of the following six categories: "Software Developer", "Web Developer", "Design & Multimedia", "Writing", "Administration" and "Sales & Marketing". Figure 7 shows the transition probabilities with values above 0.05, across our categories. The graph shows the probability that, given that a user has just completed a task in category j will next complete a task in category k. We can observe that users, with relatively high probability, choose to complete tasks in the same category (e.g., they choose to remain in web development with probability 0.859). This is intuitively expected, since it shows a reasonable preference of the workers to keep choosing to work on tasks that are familiar with and build on their expertise. A natural, but incorrect, conjecture would be that inter-category performance would not matter much in such a setting, where users stay often within the same category. We will demonstrate, however, that properly leveraging past performance data from other categories can improve significantly the prediction of their future performance.

An important characteristic of the graph is the natural clustering of the nodes in the transition matrix: on the right, we have the "technical" categories, while on the left part of the graph we have a cluster of the "non-technical" categories, that can be characterized as the "Knowledge Process Outsourcing (KPO)" categories. This indicates that our categories are heterogeneous, and as a result, our transitional data points across categories are very sparse. To deal with the sparseness, we use the methodology described in Section 3.4. In particular, we choose $L = 2$, meaning that our top-level model deals with only two abstract categories: $\mathcal{H}_0 = \{$"Technical", "Non-Technical"$\}$. We name this model "**Generic**". Then we decompose each one of the two abstract categories into the following, more fine grained category sets:

- "**Technical**", $\mathcal{H}_{c_1} = \{$"Software developer", "Web developer", "Design & Multimedia"$\}$, and
- "**Non-technical**", $\mathcal{H}_{c_2} = \{$ "Writing", "Administration", "Sales & Marketing" $\}$.

To estimate the quality for worker i, we proceed as follows: We first estimate the necessary coefficients α_{jk} and β_j for three different models: the higher-level model, with $m = 2$, and the categories in $\mathcal{H}_0$, the lower-level technical model, with $m = 3$ and the categories in $\mathcal{H}_{c_1}$, and the lower level non-technical model, with $m = 3$ and the categories in $\mathcal{H}_{c_2}$. Then, we characterize the type of worker i as "Technical" or "Non-technical"

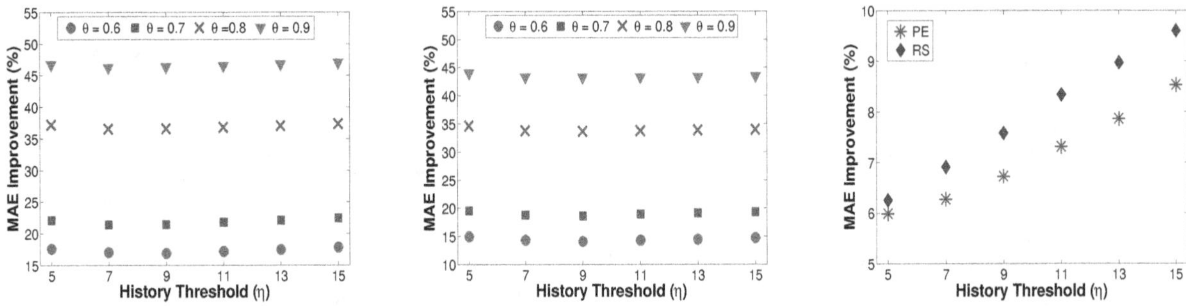

(a) Binomial Model,(PE) (b) Binomial Model,(RS) (c) Multinomial Model

Figure 6: The *improvement* of our models compared to the existing baselines, as measured by "mean absolute error" (MAE) for the (a) Binomial model point estimate (PE), (b) random sampling (RS), and (c) for the Multinomial model approaches.

based on the majority of her past tasks (i.e., $c_l^* \in$ {"Technical", "Non-technical"}). Given the task's category at time $t+1$ and the type of worker, we predict the quality of the task using the most appropriate model as determined by the process in Figure 3. Table 1 shows the coefficients for each model along with the categories that they correlate.

6.3 Experimental Procedure

We conducted our experiments as follows: for each of our models, we first use the training data, to compute the $logit(q_{ij})$ values for each reviewer i in the set and for each category j, following the point estimate (PE) and random sampling (RS) approaches, described in Section 3.3. We then use regression with panel data [10] to estimate the coefficients a_{jk} and β_j for the model. We repeat the process for all possible combinations of thresholds θ and η.

Tuning Parameters: By considering the skewness of our training data distribution in our experiments (see also Section 6.1), we use various discrete threshold values for θ. In particular we assume that $\theta \in \{0.6, 0.7, 0.8, 0.9\}$. For each of these thresholds, the prior class probabilities ("bad" - "good") are respectively (11.5% vs. 88.5%), (13.6% vs. 86.4%), (19% vs. 81%), and (24.3% vs. 76.7%). Intuitively, low threshold values, result in higher skews. For the multinomial approach, we choose $K = 5$ and uniformly split the $[0, 1]$ interval into 5 buckets. Tasks with $\bar{q} \leq 0.2$ fall in bucket 1, tasks with $0.2 < \bar{q} \leq 0.4$ fall in bucket 2, and so on. Intuitively, K can also be seen as the discrete star rating, 1 to 5. Finally, we evaluate each one of our models for discrete values of $\eta \in \{5, 7, 9, 11, 13, 15\}$.

Prior Distributions: Our models suggest that we have to pick some reasonable prior distributions. Specifically, for our binomial approach, we assume that $q_{ij} \sim Beta(9, 1)$ (i.e., $\alpha = 9, \beta = 1$). The selection is not random, since it represents a belief that is close to the real prior expectation in the marketplace (which is captured by the feedback scores in our training set). Note here that we further experimented with many other priors, including the uniform prior $Beta(1, 1)$. The results were not significantly different across our evaluations, so we kept the $Beta(9, 1)$ as prior, which reflects our prior knowledge about the marketplace. Similarly, for our multinomial approach, we choose a parameter vector $\boldsymbol{\alpha} = (2, 1, 1, 4, 8)$. Again this selection aims to capture the marketplace's biases, first toward high scores and second toward scores at the extremes of the distribution.

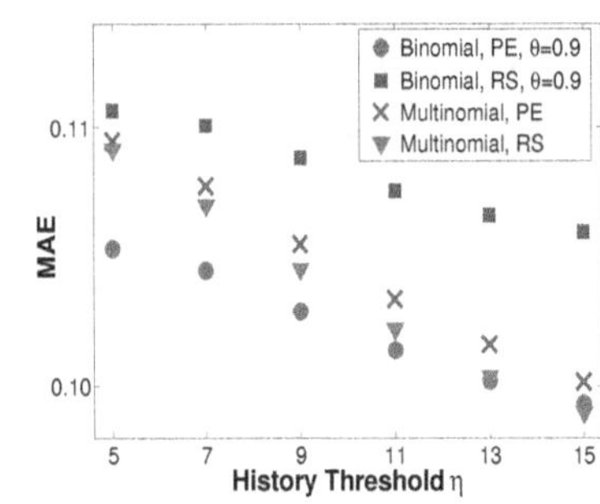

Figure 8: MAE values for each model and each proposed approach, for different values of η.

6.4 Experimental Results

6.4.1 *Performance Analysis*

In Figure 6(a) we show the percentage improvement for our binomial model, using the point estimate (PE) approach, for different threshold θ values. As one might expect, higher θ thresholds lead to better results for our model, as the data set becomes more balanced and training becomes more effective with more data in the minority class ("bad"). Specifically, for $\theta = 0.9$, the case with the more evenly balanced classes and therefore the highest underlying uncertainty, we achieve up to 47% improved performance. In the case with very skewed data (i.e., most cases are "good"), our model results in a MAE improvement of 16%. The history threshold η appears to have a very small effect in the MAE improvement, indicating that our algorithm works well even with very small worker histories.

In Figure 6(b), we show the percentage improvement for the Random Sampling (RS) approach, for the binomial model and for different values of θ. The results are very similar to those of the point estimate approach. Our maximum improvement, compared to the previous approach, is now a bit lower, 43.5%. we achieve this maximum with higher θ threshold. Similar to the point estimate approach, the worst case scenario of our model provides an MAE improvement of 13%. Once again,

Model	Level	Approach	α_{11}	α_{12}	α_{13}	β_1	α_{21}	α_{22}	α_{23}	β_2	α_{31}	α_{32}	α_{33}	β_3
Binomial	Generic ($\mathcal{H}_0$)	PE	-0.902 (0.200)	1.437 (0.188)	-	1.110 (0.101)	-1.165 (0.342)	1.088 (0.152)	-	1.691 (0.292)	-	-	-	-
		RS	0.433 (0.019)	0.512 (0.064)	-	0.467 (0.065)	0.441 (0.009)	0.468 (0.098)	-	0.492 (0.039)	-	-	-	-
	Technical ($\mathcal{H}_{c_1}$)	PE	-0.661 (0.215)	1.149 (0.187)	0.782 (0.076)	0.358 (0.051)	-0.362 (0.113)	0.877 (0.098)	0.725 (0.048)	0.433 (0.115)	-0.265 (0.165)	0.650 (0.155)	0.669 (0.027)	0.609 (0.112)
		RS	0.341 (0.028)	0.412 (0.029)	0.343 (0.048)	0.316 (0.046)	0.353 (0.031)	0.378 (0.029)	0.354 (0.028)	0.323 (0.065)	0.362 (0.022)	0.373 (0.045)	0.327 (0.020)	0.335 (0.043)
	Non-Technical ($\mathcal{H}_{c_2}$)	PE	-0.439 (0.193)	0.947 (0.090)	0.556 (0.130)	0.537 (0.092)	-0.446 (0.171)	0.642 (0.048)	0.835 (0.124)	0.610 (0.109)	-0.398 (0.165)	0.545 (0.102)	0.588 (0.074)	0.853 (0.098)
		RS	0.349 (0.035)	0.412 (0.037)	0.329 (0.068)	0.306 (0.062)	0.340 (0.022)	0.351 (0.048)	0.396 (0.048)	0.348 (0.059)	0.320 (0.030)	0.337 (0.066)	0.338 (0.052)	0.409 (0.042)
Multinomial	Generic ($\mathcal{H}_0$)	PE	-0.477	1.372	-	1.330	-0.111	1.058	-	0.933	-	-	-	-
		RS	0.433	0.325	-	0.286	0.373	0.278	-	0.371	-	-	-	-
	Technical ($\mathcal{H}_{c_1}$)	PE	0.844	-0.021	0.976	0.312	0.297	0.541	0.575	0.829	0.137	0.308	0.938	0.941
		RS	0.525	0.185	0.168	0.144	0.543	0.094	0.265	0.174	0.475	-0.004	0.334	0.307
	Non-Technical ($\mathcal{H}_{c_2}$)	PE	0.339	0.725	0.314	0.692	0.364	0.781	0.567	0.433	0.574	0.497	0.416	0.521
		RS	0.423	0.299	0.115	0.184	0.385	0.232	0.280	0.169	0.402	0.172	0.192	0.256

Table 2: The regression coefficients (resulting from the train set), broken down by model/level/approach. Numbers in parenthesis represent the standard deviations of the means across all θ values.

the history threshold η does not appear to significantly affect the MAE improvement.

Next, in Figure 6(c), we present the results for our multinomial model. Compared to the binomial model, the improvement is lower, but this might be related to the fact that the baseline for this model is more fine-grained than that used in the binomial case. The maximum achieved improvement is 9.6% for the random sampling approach (RS) and for $\eta = 15$, while the minimum MAE improvement is 6%, for $\eta = 5$ and for the point estimate approach (PE). We make two important observations here: first, compared to before, the *RS* approach provides slightly better results than the *PE* approach, and second, η threshold seems to have an increased effect on the achieved accuracies. Intuitively, the latter means that the multinomial model learns better from the outcome of each task than the binomial, and hence, it improves its predictions as history increases.

Finally, in order to give a presentation of integrated results, in Figure 8 we compare the actual MAE values for each of our models, for both approaches PE and RS. Note that for the binomial approach, we choose threshold $\theta = 0.9$ since that is the value with which our models achieve their highest accuracy. The first thing to observe here is that there is a significant difference between the PE and RS approaches of our binomial Model. On the other hand, for the multinomial model, the two approaches give very similar accuracies. Next, we can see that our multinomial approach benefits more from longer worker histories compared to the binomial as performance increases more as the threshold η increases.

6.4.2 *Coefficient Analysis*

To evaluate our coefficient estimates, we use both a quantitative and a qualitative approach. In particular, for the binomial model, we estimate the standard deviation of the means across all possible θ values for both the point estimate and random sampling approaches. Second, we interpret the meaning of these coefficients with respect to the oDesk environment.

In Table 2 we present all of the coefficients, broken down by model, level, and approach. For all the coefficients of the Binary model we show the mean and its standard deviation (in parentheses) across all the possible values of θ; we notice that the variances are very small among the coefficients of our binomial model. These low variances across different regressions also imply that these coefficients accurately capture correlations across different task categories, meaning they can be used to better interpret inter-category relations in the marketplace.

Finally, we notice that the β coefficients tend to be higher on non-technical task categories. This has an interesting explanation, and also serves as a reason for including the global quality as a factor in the regression The key reason for this is the relative easiness with which a worker can move across non-technical categories: As a rule of thumb, there is no specific training or difficult-to-acquire skill to perform many of the tasks in these categories.[7] For example, a worker who performs an "Administrative" task is likely to have an easier time switching to a "Sales & Management" task than a worker switching from "Software Development" to "Sales & Marketing". As a result, we can argue that the overall quality across the non-technical categories is more informative (higher coefficient) compared to the overall quality across all technical categories.

7. DISCUSSION AND FUTURE WORK

In this work we built different Bayesian hierarchical models that predict the quality of a new task performed by an on-line worker, by assigning different weights to the worker's observed category-specific qualities. We evaluated our methods by using hundreds of thousands of transactions from oDesk, an on-line labor market, and we demonstrated that our methods provide more accurate results than existing baselines. Based on our resulting coefficients, we were further able to note specific relations across different categories of the oDesk marketplace. In the future, we plan to expand the process to even more fine-grained categories, or even to deal with transitions across skills (e.g., "jquery" and "node.js"). In such a setting, with potentially thousands of micro-categories, we intend to study the building of hierarchical models in more detail. For example, we could create hierarchies by clustering categories based on their respective skillsets (e.g., the skillset {java,sql} could be one category, the skillset {php,javascript,ruby} could be a different category etc.).

In our current work we did not account for the effect of time. In our problem definition, we assign the same weight to a prior task, as long as it comes from the same category, independent of the time that has passed since then. This might not be quite accurate, since, in the majority of the tasks, a worker

[7] Translation is a notable exception in this rule of thumb.

acquires more expertise and improves his skills by completing more and more additional tasks. In the future, we intend to extend our models by including timestamps as a component of each completed task.

A key thing to mention is that our current model is predictive and not necessarily causal. A basic characteristic of predictive models such as the one we propose here is that they capture the behavior of the existing system, as-is. For example, we may predict that a worker who has worked as virtual assistant in the past, with good ratings, is also going to be a good transcriptionist. However, this is a result of a training set in which the workers applied to the jobs they wanted to get. So, such a tool should *not* be used to recommend jobs to workers as this will modify the self-selection process, and by extension the underlying data generation process, potentially rendering our model invalid. Our algorithm can best be applied to modify the rating scores shown to the employers when they pick workers, as this "interference" is not expected to change much the self-selection process of applying for jobs.

A desirable feature of our proposed algorithms is their broadness: they can be easily adapted for various kinds of marketplaces, which are interested in estimating the quality of their users. For example, as mentioned in Section 6, we have already experimented with predicting the usefulness of product reviews on Amazon.com, by analyzing the usefulness of prior reviews posted by a user, and examining their category distribution. Our results, not included in the current paper for space reasons, are similar in nature with the oDesk results and illustrate the benefits of this approach. We believe that most reputation systems can benefit from using approaches similar to ours, instead of relying on simple average values.

8. REFERENCES

[1] L. Adamic, J. Zhang, E. Bakshy, and M. Ackerman. Knowledge sharing and yahoo answers: everyone knows something. In *Proceedings of the 17th international conference on World Wide Web*. ACM, 2008.

[2] E. Agichtein, C. Castillo, D. Donato, A. Gionis, and G. Mishne. Finding high-quality content in social media. In *Proceedings of the international conference on Web search and web data mining*. ACM, 2008.

[3] J. Bian, Y. Liu, D. Zhou, E. Agichtein, and H. Zha. Learning to recognize reliable users and content in social media with coupled mutual reinforcement. In *Proceedings of the 18th international conference on World Wide Web*. ACM, 2009.

[4] R. Clemen and R. Winkler. Unanimity and compromise among probability forecasters. *Management Science*, 36(7), 1990.

[5] C. Danescu-Niculescu-Mizil, G. Kossinets, J. Kleinberg, and L. Lee. How opinions are received by online communities: a case study on amazon. com helpfulness votes. In *Proceedings of the 18th international conference on World Wide Web*. ACM, 2009.

[6] C. Dellarocas. The digitization of word of mouth: Promise and challenges of online feedback mechanisms. *Management science*, 49(10), 2003.

[7] C. Dellarocas. Reputation mechanisms. *Handbook on Economics and Information Systems*, 2006.

[8] A. Gelman, J. Carlin, H. Stern, and D. Rubin. *Bayesian Data Analysis*. Chapman & Hall/CRC, 2004.

[9] A. Ghose and P. G. Ipeirotis. Estimating the helpfulness and economic impact of product reviews: Mining text and reviewer characteristics. *TKDE*, 23(10), 2011.

[10] W. Greene. *Econometric analysis*. Prentice Hall, 2007.

[11] R. Hambleton. *Fundamentals of item response theory*, volume 2. Sage Publications, Incorporated, 1991.

[12] N. Hu, J. Zhang, and P. A. Pavlou. Overcoming the j-shaped distribution of product reviews. *Commun. ACM*, 52(10), 2009.

[13] J. Jeon, W. Croft, J. Lee, and S. Park. A framework to predict the quality of answers with non-textual features. In *Proceedings of the 29th annual international conference on Research and development in information retrieval*. ACM, 2006.

[14] S. Kim, P. Pantel, T. Chklovski, and M. Pennacchiotti. Automatically assessing review helpfulness. In *Proceedings of the 2006 Conference on Empirical Methods in Natural Language Processing*, 2006.

[15] T. Lappas and D. Gunopulos. Efficient confident search in large review corpora. *Machine Learning and Knowledge Discovery in Databases*, 2010.

[16] Y. Liu, J. Bian, and E. Agichtein. Predicting information seeker satisfaction in community question answering. In *Proceedings of the 31st annual international conference on Research and development in information retrieval*. ACM, 2008.

[17] Y. Liu, X. Huang, A. An, and X. Yu. Modeling and predicting the helpfulness of online reviews. In *Eighth IEEE International Conference on Data Mining, 2008. ICDM'08*. IEEE, 2008.

[18] Y. Lu, P. Tsaparas, A. Ntoulas, and L. Polanyi. Exploiting social context for review quality prediction. In *Proceedings of the 19th international conference on World Wide Web*. ACM, 2010.

[19] P. Nelson. Information and consumer behavior. *The Journal of Political Economy*, 78(2), 1970.

[20] M. O'Mahony and B. Smyth. Using readability tests to predict helpful product reviews. In *Adaptivity, Personalization and Fusion of Heterogeneous Information*, 2010.

[21] J. Otterbacher. 'helpfulness' in online communities: a measure of message quality. In *Proceedings of the 27th international conference on Human factors in computing systems*. ACM, 2009.

[22] C. Shah and J. Pomerantz. Evaluating and predicting answer quality in community qa. In *Proceeding of the 33rd international conference on Research and development in information retrieval*. Citeseer, 2010.

[23] M. Suryanto, E. Lim, A. Sun, and R. Chiang. Quality-aware collaborative question answering: methods and evaluation. In *Proceedings of the Second ACM International Conference on Web Search and Data Mining*. ACM, 2009.

[24] P. Tsaparas, A. Ntoulas, and E. Terzi. Selecting a comprehensive set of reviews. In *Proceedings of the 17th ACM SIGKDD international conference on Knowledge discovery and data mining*. ACM, 2011.

Learning Multiple-Question Decision Trees for Cold-Start Recommendation

Mingxuan Sun
College of Computing
Georgia Tech.
msun3@gatech.edu

Fuxin Li
College of Computing
Georgia Tech.
fli@cc.gatech.edu

Joonseok Lee
College of Computing
Georgia Tech.
jlee716@gatech.edu

Ke Zhou
College of Computing
Georgia Tech.
kzhou@gatech.edu

Guy Lebanon
College of Computing
Georgia Tech.
lebanon@cc.gatech.edu

Hongyuan Zha
College of Computing
Georgia Tech.
zha@cc.gatech.edu

ABSTRACT

For cold-start recommendation, it is important to rapidly profile new users and generate a good initial set of recommendations through an interview process — users should be queried adaptively in a sequential fashion, and multiple items should be offered for opinion solicitation at each trial. In this work, we propose a novel algorithm that learns to conduct the interview process guided by a decision tree with multiple questions at each split. The splits, represented as sparse weight vectors, are learned through an L_1-constrained optimization framework. The users are directed to child nodes according to the inner product of their responses and the corresponding weight vector. More importantly, to account for the variety of responses coming to a node, a linear regressor is learned within each node using all the previously obtained answers as input to predict item ratings. A user study, preliminary but first in its kind in cold-start recommendation, is conducted to explore the efficient number and format of questions being asked in a recommendation survey to minimize user cognitive efforts. Quantitative experimental validations also show that the proposed algorithm outperforms state-of-the-art approaches in terms of both the prediction accuracy and user cognitive efforts.

Categories and Subject Descriptors

H.3.3 [**Information Search and Retrieval**]: Information filtering; I.2.6 [**Artificial Intelligence**]: Learning

General Terms

Algorithms, Performance, Experimentation

Keywords

Recommender systems, Cold-start problem, Collaborative filtering, Decision tree

1. INTRODUCTION

Recommender systems have been established as a critical tool for many business applications with significant economic impact. Successful systems span a variety of platforms, including Amazon's book recommendations, Netflix's movie recommendations, and Pandora's music recommendations. A popular and effective approach to recommendations is collaborative filtering, which focuses on detecting users with similar preferences and recommending items favored by the like-minded [3, 13, 11, 15]. However, the system would fail to provide recommendations when no preference information is gathered from a new user, which is known as the cold-start problem [6, 17, 22].

Rapid profiling of new users is a key challenge in cold-start recommender systems. One direct way to solicit the preferences of new users is going through an initial interview process [17]. In the interview, the recommender system asks users to provide opinions on selected items and constructs rough user profiles. Asking too few questions may lead to inaccurate estimation of user profiles and the system is unable to provide satisfactory recommendations, while asking too many questions may cause users to abandon the interview. A good interview is targeted at discovering user interests with minimum interactions. Specifically, the process should focus on (1) increasing the recommendation accuracy and (2) minimizing user interaction efforts.

An adaptive interview process is known to improve the accuracy, compared with previous approaches such as methods based on meta-features or a static set of interview questions. Many state-of-the-art work [17, 27, 6] have championed decision trees [4] as a natural fit for adaptive interviews of new users. In a primitive form of the decision tree, each node asks for user opinions on one item and users are directed to subtrees based on whether their answer is *like*, *dislike* or *unknown*. Finally, the average preference of training users within each leaf node is used to generate the recommendation list.

However, most users do not have the luxury to go through the entire item set, thus the system needs to serve a majority of users who have seen only tiny percentage of the items. In this case the constructed decision trees are often extremely unbalanced with the *unknown* branch capturing more than 80% of the users at each split (Figure 1, upper). Many users have to repeatedly select *unknown* multiple times before locating any item they know about. In this case, not only did the system gain little valuable information on users' interests, but the users also easily get bored and may opt out of the system prematurely.

For a better cold-start recommender system, we advocate designs focusing on asking multiple questions at each trial. Displaying multiple questions on one screen increases the chance that a user knows at least one of them and thus allowing for solicitation of more valuable information. This was also suggested by some experimental studies that show users prefer providing opinions on multiple items at a trial [17]. However, within the collaborative filtering context, there has not been much existing work that focuses on building a single decision tree with each node asking multiple questions.

The major contribution of this paper is to develop a tree learning algorithm for cold-start collaborative filtering with each node asking multiple questions. There are two key technical challenges to overcome in learning such a tree structure. First, with multiple questions at each node, it becomes substantially more expensive to search over all possible splits. Instead, we rely on a framework of minimizing expected prediction loss with L_1 regularization to find each split. Second, when asking multiple questions, users with different opinions would be grouped into the same node, and making predictions by averaging training user responses within each node is no longer sufficient. We propose to learn a regressor within each node making use of all the answers from the root to the present node. In our experiments, the algorithm is shown to be able to improve the performance of the cold-start recommendation system. One example of the tree with multiple questions is shown in Figure 1 (lower).

In addition to the prediction accuracy, another essential component for profiling new users is minimizing user efforts in the interaction. Critical features influencing user cognitive efforts include the number of items to ask at each trial, as well as the type of answers collected from the users. User response in common recommender systems can be binary or 5-star rating scale. The 5-star rating response is expected to be more informative than a binary response but it may take more user time. However, few existing work provides a quantitative analysis on the efforts that users would spend on different interfaces.

This issue is addressed in our second contribution which analyzes different strategies in terms of both the prediction accuracy and user efforts. A user study, preliminary but first in its kind, is performed to measure user efforts by the interaction time. Tree-models that ask different number of questions and different type of questions (binary/5-scale) are shown randomly to different users through a web interview interface. The average time spent on each scenario is measured and we are thus able to measure the accuracy against average user interaction time, which reveals the configurations that work best in real-life scenarios. The current quantitative user study that compares $1-4$ questions in both binary and 5-star formats is new, to the best of our knowledge.

2. RELATED WORK

There have been a substantial body of literature on collaborative filtering (CF) recommendations, which can largely be classified into memory and model based methods. Memory-based CF methods predict the ratings of items based on the similarity between the test user and training users [20, 3,

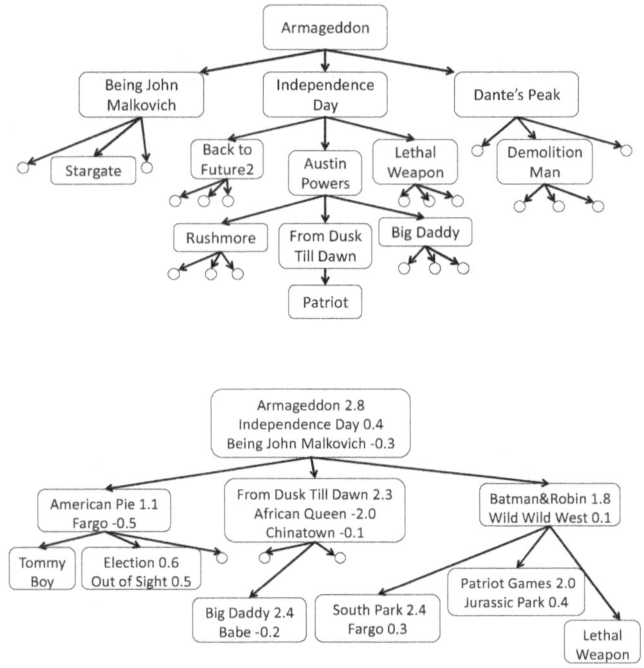

Figure 1: The interview trees learned from the movielens1M dataset. A circle denotes a leaf node with recommendation results. Top: each node asks a single question. The first 5 levels are shown from the 10-level learned tree. Users are branched to left, middle and right subtrees according to the answers *like*, *unknown* and *dislike* respectively. It can be seen that the middle branch of the tree is much longer than the other branches. Bottom: each node asks multiple questions. The first 3 levels out of a total 5 are shown. Users are branched to left, middle and right subtrees according to equation (3) given the answers and corresponding weights.

10]. Similarity measures include Pearson correlation [20] and Vector cosine similarity [3, 10]. Other memory-based CF methods include item-based CF [21] and a non-parametric probabilistic method based on ranking preference similarities [24]. Model-based CF includes user and item clustering, Bayesian networks [3], and probabilistic latent variable models [15, 26, 11]. The state-of-the-art methods, including the Netflix competition winner, are mostly based on matrix factorization. The factorized matrix can be used to fill out the unobserved entries of the user-rating matrix in a way similar to latent factor analysis [19, 13].

One difficulty in recommender system is that the performance is affected by factors such as number of users, number of items, and observed total ratings. Unified models have been proposed in [1, 7, 22] by combining both CF methods and content features such as the genre, actor and director of a movie. These methods generally achieve better prediction accuracy on the items that few or no users have ever rated.

Several studies focus on eliciting preference for new users to solve the cold-start problem. It has been demonstrated in [16] that a good elicitation strategy should increase the prediction accuracy with minimum user interaction. Several approaches construct a short interview in which users are asked to provide information on selected items. Earlier attempts [17, 18] construct a static seed set based on the item popularity and informativeness. A later work [5] proposes a greedy algorithm to select the seed set that minimizes the prediction error. The performance of seed-based methods is unsatisfactory because items selected in batch are not adaptive to user responses in the interview process. Active learning methods for collaborative filtering [2, 8, 12, 9] select questions according to criteria such as minimizing the expected distance to the true user model, although these methods are not efficient enough for online user interview.

The IGCN algorithm proposed in [18] uses pre-defined user clusters to adaptively select questions in the interview. An alternative approach using decision trees is also mentioned in [18], where each node is a question and users are directed to subtrees based on their responses. The idea was later developed in [6] as a more disciplined approach that fits the decision tree to user ratings. To improve the prediction accuracy with missing data, the work [27] further integrates the decision tree with matrix factorization to fit the user ratings with a latent factor analysis. The limitation is that only one item is selected to ask at each node of the decision tree. It is highly likely that the user does not know any items in the first several interactions and the estimation would be inaccurate. One alternative suggested in [6] is selecting multiple items to ask at each interaction by bootstrapping multiple trees. The method first generates random trees and then select the best few whose linear combinations fit the training data best. However, this tends to ask more questions compared to building a single tree with multiple questions at each split, because each of the shallow trees would more likely be full and in that case, the number of questions increases linearly with the number of trees.

In this paper, we propose a tree learning algorithm for collaborative filtering with each node asking multiple questions. In contrast to the work [6], our algorithm enables optimization-based estimation procedures for not only the prediction of user profiling but also the selection of questions. Our algorithm achieves significant improvements in terms of the prediction accuracy and user interaction time. Furthermore, it is able to handle heterogeneous preference information including binary and 5-star rating responses.

Existing user study in [17, 18] is measuring the user efforts by the number of pages they views before they rate a minimum number of items for the initial interview. Our user study seeks to discover both the efficient number of questions on each screen, and whether binary or 5-star is more effective in discovering user preferences.

3. DECISION TREE FOR COLD-START

In cold-start recommendations, we assume nothing about new users and an interview process is performed to ask the user a set of questions. For example, in the movie recommendation system, we ask a user questions in the form "Do you like the movie *50 first dates*?" and the user answers *like*, *dislike* and *unknown*, or provides 5-scale ratings, etc. Based on the answers, the system would adaptively ask another set of questions, gradually refine user preference and recommend a set of movies in the end.

In the adaptive interview, we would like to learn a function that maps user responses to user preference profiles from training data. Formally, let r_{ij} denote the observed rating of training user i for item j, where $i = 1, 2, \ldots, m$ and $j = 1, 2, \ldots, n$. The pairs (i, j) are stored in the set $O = \{(i, j) \mid r_{ij} \text{ is observed}\}$. Denote $O_i = \{j \mid r_{ij} \text{ is observed}\}$ the set of items user i rated, $O^j = \{i \mid r_{ij} \text{ is observed}\}$ the set of users that rate item j. Assume there are possible n questions to ask, let x denote the user answer, which is a n-dimensional vector and each entry takes value in the set $\{-1, 0, 1\}$ corresponding to *dislike*, *unknown* and *like*. Given each training user i with the answer x_i, our goal is to learn a user profile $T(x_i)$ that predicts the rating of this user on all the items.

In the simplest form, the user profile $T(x_i)$ is an n dimensional vector with each dimension representing the predicted rating of item j. However, such a representation is computationally challenging and hard to learn in large corpora with thousands or millions of items. A common technique in recommender systems is to obtain lower dimensional models for both users and items by minimizing a prediction loss function between the predicted ratings and true ratings of users. That is,

$$\min_{T,V} \sum_i \sum_{j \in O_i} (r_{ij} - T(x_i)^\top v_j)^2, \tag{1}$$

where $T(x_i)$ is a k-dimensional vector, $V = [v_1, v_2, \ldots, v_n]$ is a $k \times n$ matrix, and v_j is a k-dimensional vector representing the profile for item j. Usually, T and V are optimized using matrix factorization methods, such as PCA, NMF or nuclear-norm based matrix completion.

A decision tree structure is a natural fit for adaptive interviews where each node corresponds to one or multiple questions to ask. According to the evaluation of a user's answers, the user will be directed to subtrees. Once the user reaches the leaf node, the recommendation list is provided using the user preference learned from training data. Thus, the mapping function $T(x)$ should be viewed as a function induced from the decision tree, which is constructed from training user ratings in a top-down approach. For each node N in the tree, we learn a distinct function $T_N(x)$ for that node. During test time, a user is first assigned to a node based on his/her answers to the interview, then the function in that node is used to obtain his/her user profile.

We adopt the framework in (1) for V and will discuss the details for obtaining V in Section 3.4. However, our main contribution lies in determining the decision tree split with multiple questions, as well as learning the user profile function in each node. Therefore we discuss these first in Section 3.1 - 3.3.

3.1 Multiple Question Decision Tree Construction

In this subsection, we propose our approach of learning to ask multiple questions at each decision tree split. For this goal, there are two challenges to overcome. First, the number of possible questions can be quite large (e.g., we may have $n \sim 10^5$ in movie recommendation system) and searching over all possible splits becomes a combinatorial problem with a prohibitive $\binom{n}{l}$ possibilities to evaluate where l is the number of questions at each node. We solve this problem by relaxing it as an L_1 regularized optimization. Second, since we are keeping the structure of the tree with 3 branches, it is possible that users with different opinions would enter the same node. Therefore different from other decision tree approaches (e.g. [27]), a non-constant function T needs to be learned separately for each node. We solve this second problem by training a linear regressor within each node using all the previously obtained answers as input.

For splitting with multiple items, the idea is to optimize for a sparse weight vector on each item that has only a few non-zeros. Formally, let w denote the weight of items, which is a n-dimensional vector. Let l denote the maximum number of questions at each split. Training users at the current node are split into 3 child nodes L, D and U according to the linear combination of the answers $x_i^\top w$.

We use a modified logistic probability model to determine the split. Let p_i, q_i denote the probability that user i belongs to the L, and D branch respectively:

$$p_i = \frac{1}{1 + c\exp(-x_i^\top w)},$$
$$q_i = \frac{1}{1 + c\exp(x_i^\top w)}. \quad (2)$$

The three subgroups are defined as:

$$\begin{aligned} L(w) &= \{i | p_i > q_i,\ p_i > 1 - p_i - q_i\}, \\ D(w) &= \{i | q_i > p_i,\ q_i > 1 - p_i - q_i\}, \\ U(w) &= \{i | 1 - p_i - q_i \geq \max(p_i, q_i)\}, \end{aligned} \quad (3)$$

where c is a parameter controlling the likelihood of falling into different groups. In practice, we find that $c = 2$ works best. In such a case, a user belongs to the L group when $x_i^\top w$ is positive, the D group when $x_i^\top w$ is negative, and the middle group U only when the user answers none of the questions, as shown in Figure 2.

Ideally, we need to optimize such an objective function

$$\begin{aligned} \min_{w, T_L, T_D, T_U} & \sum_{i \in L(w)} \sum_{j \in O_i} (r_{ij} - T_L(x_i)^\top v_j)^2 \\ & + \sum_{i \in D(w)} \sum_{j \in O_i} (r_{ij} - T_D(x_i)^\top v_j)^2 \\ & + \sum_{i \in U(w)} \sum_{j \in O_i} (r_{ij} - T_U(x_i)^\top v_j)^2 \\ \text{s.t.} \ & \|w\|_0 \leq l, \end{aligned} \quad (4)$$

where T_L, T_D and T_U are the profile functions for the nodes L, D, U, and $\|w\|_0$ denotes the number of non-zeros in w. The objective function first divides the training users into three child nodes, and then computes the squared error within each child node. The goal is to minimize the sum of errors in all the three child nodes. In addition, the constraint $\|w\|_0 \leq l$ determined that w cannot have more than l non-zeros.

We would adopt an alternating minimization strategy that optimizes w and T_L, T_D, T_U iteratively. However, the optimization of w is a complicated non-convex combinatorial problem, therefore we make relaxations to solve it with continuous optimization. In the next two subsections we discuss separately the optimization of w and the computation of T_L, T_D, and T_U.

3.2 Optimization Relaxations

In order to update the weight vector w in (4) with continuous optimization, we adopt two relaxations. The first is to relax the hard partitioning L, D, and U into a soft partitioning, with the probability of x belonging to the subgroups L, D and U to be p_i, q_i, and $1 - p_i - q_i$, respectively. This makes the main objective function smooth in w.

The second relaxation is to append a penalty term on $\|w\|_1$ to the objective function, instead of a hard constraint on the number of nonzeros $\|w\|_0$. This L_1 relaxation approach has been popular in machine learning and signal processing in recent years. The L_1 term is convex and there exist efficient methods to optimize a smooth objective function with such a penalty term [23].

Let $\bar{m}$ denote the number of users reaching the current node, our relaxation problem computes w which minimizes the weighted prediction loss:

$$\begin{aligned} \min_w & \sum_{i=1}^{\bar{m}} p_i \sum_{j \in O_i} (r_{ij} - T_L(x_i)^\top v_j)^2 \\ & + \sum_{i=1}^{\bar{m}} q_i \sum_{j \in O_i} (r_{ij} - T_D(x_i)^\top v_j)^2 \\ & + \sum_{i=1}^{\bar{m}} (1 - p_i - q_i) \sum_{j \in O_i} (r_{ij} - T_U(x_i)^\top v_j)^2 + \lambda \|w\|_1. \end{aligned} \quad (5)$$

To solve (5), we adopt a projected scaled sub-gradient optimization [23]. This algorithm computes the Hessian only for the nonzero part of the current w, and adopts linear-time Barzilai-Borwein subgradient steps for the rest. It is suitable for our task because of its fast convergence rate thanks to the incorporated second-order information, and each iteration is a linear-time operation. The only cubic-time computation is to compute the Hessian inverse on the nonzeros. Since we have usually less than 5 nonzeros, this step would normally take constant time.

By changing the parameter λ, we can find solutions with different numbers of nonzeros in w. In practice, we first binary search between 0 and λ_{max} to find λ_0 such that the number of nonzero entries of w is between 1 and l. Then we search around λ_0 with a finer step size, locating l different solutions with $1, 2, \ldots, l$ nonzeros respectively. From this solution set, we select the one that minimize (5) without the penalty term.

The optimization for w is still non-convex, therefore a good choice of starting point is important. We choose the starting point as the best 1-item question found by the approach in [27] and set $w_s = 1$ and $w_j = 0$ $(j = 1, 2, \ldots, n, j \neq s)$ as our initial value. We find this scheme to work well in practice.

3.3 Computing User Profile Functions

We adopt a linear regression model in each node in order to map different user answers to preferences. The input to the linear model would be all the previous answers that the user has submitted and the output is the user profile. The nodes deeper down the tree would have more information since more answers have been submitted by the user to arrive at the node.

Formally, let t $(t < n)$ denote the number of asked items from the root till the current node, $\bar{x}_i$ denote the answer of user i, which is a $t + 1$ dimensional vector including a constant dimension $\bar{x}_{i0} = 1$. Our linear model is $T_L(x_i) = Z_L \bar{x}_i$, $T_D(x_i) = Z_D \bar{x}_i$ and $T_U(x_i) = Z_U \bar{x}_i$, where Z_L, Z_D and Z_U are $(t + 1) \times k$ matrices for each individual node in the next level.

We try to best approximate all the observed scores r_{ij} within the node, using all the obtained answers $\bar{x}_i$ and the current item profiles v_j. This gives the following optimization problem:

$$Z_L = \arg\min_Z \sum_{i \in L(w)} \sum_{j \in O_i} (r_{ij} - (Z^\top \bar{x}_i)^\top v_j)^2,$$
$$Z_D = \arg\min_Z \sum_{i \in D(w)} \sum_{j \in O_i} (r_{ij} - (Z^\top \bar{x}_i)^\top v_j)^2,$$
$$Z_U = \arg\min_Z \sum_{i \in U(w)} \sum_{j \in O_i} (r_{ij} - (Z^\top \bar{x}_i)^\top v_j)^2. \quad (6)$$

It turns out that each has a closed form solution:

$$z_L = \left(\sum_{i \in L(w)} \sum_{j \in O_i} (\bar{x}_i \bar{x}_i^\top) \otimes (v_j v_j^\top) \right)^{-1} \left(\sum_{i \in L(w)} \sum_{j \in O_i} r_{ij} (\bar{x}_i \otimes v_j) \right),$$
$$z_D = \left(\sum_{i \in D(w)} \sum_{j \in O_i} (\bar{x}_i \bar{x}_i^\top) \otimes (v_j v_j^\top) \right)^{-1} \left(\sum_{i \in D(w)} \sum_{j \in O_i} r_{ij} (\bar{x}_i \otimes v_j) \right),$$
$$z_U = \left(\sum_{i \in U(w)} \sum_{j \in O_i} (\bar{x}_i \bar{x}_i^\top) \otimes (v_j v_j^\top) \right)^{-1} \left(\sum_{i \in U(w)} \sum_{j \in O_i} r_{ij} (\bar{x}_i \otimes v_j) \right), \quad (7)$$

where z_L, z_D and z_U are large column vectors formed by concatenating the column vectors of the matrices Z_L, Z_D, and Z_U respectively, and $\otimes$ denotes the matrix Kronecker product. The regression inside each node allows different answers to be mapped to different ratings, thus solving the problem of contradicting opinions for different users within a node. At each node, we alternatively optimize (5) and (6) until convergence.

When the amount of training data becomes small along the path reaching the leaf node, the estimation of user profiles may overfit. Following previous papers [27], we apply hierarchical regularization at the current node so that the coefficients of profile Z_L, Z_D and Z_U are shrinking towards the ones at its parent node. For example, the solution with regularization for Z_L is:

$$Z_L = \arg\min_Z \sum_{i \in L(w)} \sum_{j \in O_i} (r_{ij} - (Z^\top \bar{x}_i)^\top v_j)^2 + \lambda_z ||Z - Z_0||^2, \quad (8)$$

where Z_0 is the estimation at the parent node padded with zeros to reach the size of Z at the child node.

3.4 Item Profile Construction

The item profile is initialized using a nonlinear matrix factorization method based on Gaussian process latent variable models [14]. Given an initialized profiles v_j, we can construct a tree T using the algorithm in section 3.1. Given the decision tree T, the user profile estimated at leaf nodes of the tree is $T(x_i) = (Z_k^\top x_i)$, where x_i is the user responses along the path. We then update item profiles v_j $(j = 1, 2, \ldots, n)$ with regularized least square regression:

$$v_j = \arg\min_{v_j} \sum_{i \in O^j} (r_{ij} - v_j^\top T(x_i))^2 + \lambda_v ||v_j||^2. \quad (9)$$

A closed form solution for v_j exists as shown in [27].

3.5 Computational Complexity

The full algorithm is summarized in Algorithms 1 and 2. The computational complexity for updating item profiles v_j for all $j = 1, 2, \ldots, n$ is $O(n|O^j|_{max} k^2 + nk^3)$, where n is the number of items, $|O^j|$ is the number of users who rated item j, and k is the dimension of latent space. For the tree construction, at each node, the complexity for running the split algorithm in [27] is $O(\sum_{i \in users} |O_i|^2 + nk^3)$, the complexity for optimizing w and Z by (5) is $O(\alpha \sum_{i \in users} |O_i| n + \alpha t^3 k^3)$, where $|O_i|$ is the number of observed ratings of user i at the node, α is the iterations, and t is the maximum number of questions asked in the path. The complexity for building the whole tree is thus $O(d \sum_{i=1}^m |O_i| n + \beta n k^3 + \beta t^3 k^3)$, where d is the depth of the tree and β is the number of nodes in the tree. In practice, the tree depth d is no more than 6, the maximum number of questions t is no more than 20, and k is usually selected from 10 to 20.

Algorithm 1 Optimization for Tree Model and Item Profiles

```
Require: The training data R = r_ij|(i,j) ∈ O.
Ensure: Estimated decision tree T and item profile v_j (j = 1,2,...,n).
Initialize v_j (j = 1,2,...,n) using [14].
while not converge do
    Fit a decision tree T using Algorithm 2.
    Update v_j using Equation (9).
end while
return T and v_j (j = 1,2,...,n).
```

Algorithm 2 Optimization for Tree Model

```
function FitTree(UsersAtNode)
Find the best single item s using [27].
Initialize w with all zeros but w_s = 1.
while not converge do
    Compute Z_L, Z_D, and Z_U using Equation (7).
    Update w using Equation (5).
end while
Split users into three groups L(w), D(w) and U(w).
if square error reduces after split and depth < maxDepth then
    call FitTree(L(w)), FitTree(D(w)) and FitTree(U(w)) to construct subtrees.
end if
return T with T(x) = (Z_k^T x)^T V, if x falls in the k-th node in the decision tree.
end function
```

4. EXPERIMENTS

We examine the estimation framework on three movie recommendation datasets: Movielens1M, EachMovie and Netflix. The details of each dataset are shown in Table 1. The Netflix data we used is a random sample containing about half of the original movies and a quarter of the original users. The prediction performance is evaluated on the test set S with the root mean square error (RMSE), which is defined as:

$$RMSE = \sqrt{\frac{1}{|S|} \sum_{(i,j) \in S} (\hat{r}_{i,j} - r_{i,j})^2}, \quad (10)$$

where $\hat{r}_{i,j}$ and $r_{i,j}$ are the predicted and ground truth ratings for user i and item j, respectively.

We seek to answer three questions in the following:

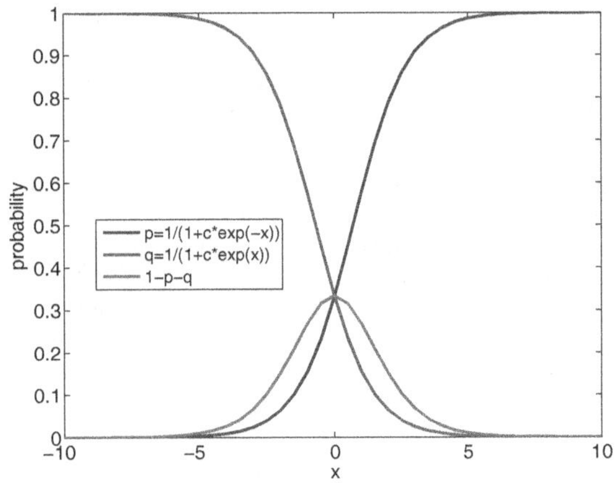

Figure 2: Probabilities of being in the three groups with $c = 2$.

1. For new users, how does the proposed algorithm perform in terms of the prediction accuracy comparing to baselines? How does the performance improve with respect to the number of screens and questions?
2. How many questions do we ask on each screen in order to minimize user interaction time?
3. What types of user responses are more informative and less time-consuming?

In the end, we summarize and analyze insights on how many items to query on each screen, what types of answers users can employ, and how prediction accuracy changes with different settings.

Table 1: Dataset Description

Dataset	Users	Items	Ratings	Scale
MovieLens1M	6040	3952	1,000,209	$1-5$
EachMovie	72,916	1628	2,811,983	$1-6$
Netflix	120,000	8000	11,670,175	$1-5$

4.1 Cold-Start Prediction Accuracy

In this experiment, we randomly split the data into a training and a test set, each containing 75% and 25% users, respectively. The parameters λ_z and λ_v in the algorithm are selected by 4-fold cross validation on the training set. The dimensionality for the profile, k is fixed to be 15. All the ratings in the training set are used to construct the decision tree. The test set is further split into two disjoint sets: answer and evaluation sets, which contain 75% and 25% rated items for each test user. The answer set is used to simulate the responses of test users in the interview process. The evaluation set is used to evaluate the prediction accuracy after the interview process. The question is in the form "Do you like item j?". For example in the movie recommendation, the question is "Do you like movie *50 first date*?" For binary answer type, where a user is expected to answer *like*, *dislike* and *unknown*, we follow the standard settings [18, 6, 27] and simulate test user responses as the following:

$$x_{ij} = \begin{cases} 1 & (i,j) \in O \text{ and } r_{ij} > 3 \\ -1 & (i,j) \in O \text{ and } r_{ij} <= 3 \\ 0 & (i,j) \notin O. \end{cases} \quad (11)$$

For the EachMovie dataset where the rating scale is $1-6$, we use $r_{ij} > 4$ instead.

Figure 3 compares the performance of our model with several standard baselines. One is the single-question decision tree with matrix factorization, denoted as $w1_{Base}$ [27]. This model has been shown in [27] as the strongest tree model with single-question splits. The other is bootstrapping tree model $w4_{Base}$ [6] which generates random decision trees, and select k-best ones to form a linear combination. In our experiments, the tree generation method in [6] always performs worse than the one in [27]. Therefore in $w4_{Base}$ we adopted the bootstrapping methodology in [6] with the tree generation method from [27], in order for a fairer comparison. We used the best parameters as reported in [27] and [6].

It has been shown that $1 \leq k \leq 5$ is practical for online interview. We set $k = 4$. Our models $w2$, $w3$, and $w4$ are the trees with maximum number of questions at each node being 2, 3, and 4 respectively.

For all methods, the prediction error measured in RMSE decreases as more questions have been asked (Figure 3). In the first row of Figure 3, our models $w2, w3$ and $w4$ have a big advantage over $w1_{Base}$ when the error is measured per screen, since in each screen we have definitely solicited more information than $w1_{Base}$. The model $w4_{Base}$ also performs better than $w1_{Base}$ in this sense. But more notably, our models $w3$ and $w4$ outperform $w4_{Base}$, which shows the advantage of our multiple-question tree model versus a linear combination of multiple bootstrapped trees.

In the second row in Figure 3 where we compare performance versus number of questions, we see no major difference between $w1_{Base}$ and $w2, w3, w4$ when relatively few questions have been asked. However, our multiple-question tree model is able to ask more questions and further reduce the prediction error, whereas in $w1_{Base}$, the performance cannot improve with trees more than $6-7$ layers, because at this time the number of training users in each leaf node is already very small, essentially making further splits very susceptible to overfitting. The model $w4_{Base}$ in this row showed its inefficiency in needing to ask more questions to obtain the same performance, which comes from the redundancy and inefficient use of information from the multiple trees.

In the third row, we compare performance versus the expected time that users spend in the interview process measured from our user study, described in the next subsection. In this case, $w1_{Base}$ is comparable with our models when relatively few questions have been asked. However, our improvement is more significant if the user is going to spend more than 20 seconds in the recommender system. In that case the performance of single-question decision trees starts to saturate, but our models continue to provide more and more accurate recommendations to the user.

Table 2 shows an example of a user's responses and the recommendation list.

4.2 User Study

In this user study, we measure the expected time that users spend on the interview process through an online interview. Once a user logs in, the interview script loads the precomputed tree model and displays questions of the node on one screen. It proceeds to another screen after the user submits answers. The interview process ends when the user

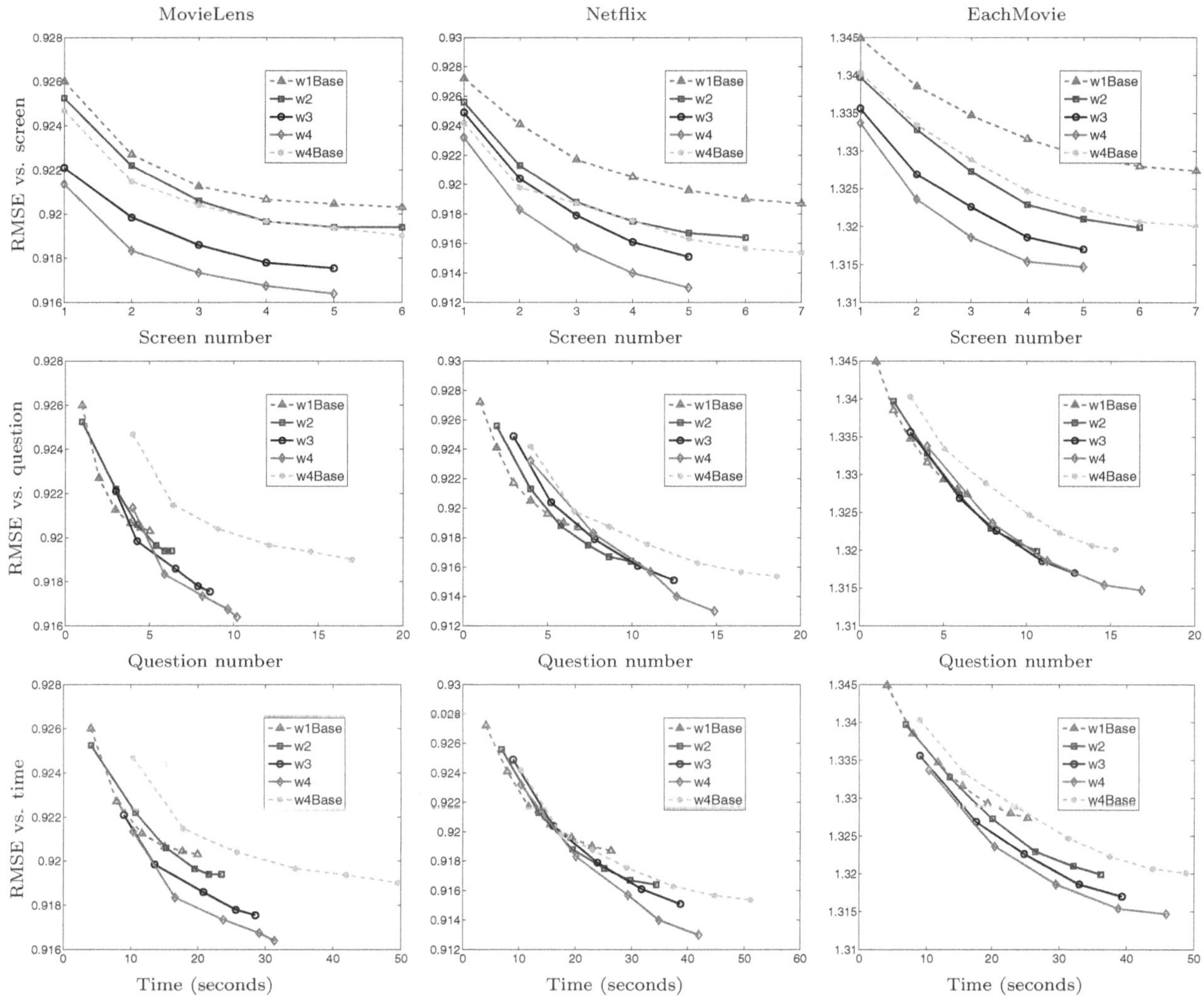

Figure 3: The prediction RMSE with respect to screen number, question number and user time on three datasets. We compare our methods asking 2, 3 and 4 questions with baseline $w1_{Base}$ asking single question and baseline $w4_{Base}$ asking 4 questions. For all methods, the prediction error measured in RMSE decreases as the screen number, question number increases. The first and second row shows that methods asking $2, 3, 4$ questions on each screen performs better than asking one question $w1_{Base}$. The time in the third row is the expected time users spend in the interview process measured from our user study.

reaches a leaf node of the tree model. The trees are always downloaded fully into the local computer in order to save network communication time. There are 8 precomputed tree models in total. For tree models labeled as $w1_{Binary}$, $w2_{Binary}$, $w3_{Binary}$ and $w4_{Binary}$, users are asked 1, 2, 3, and 4 questions maximum at each node respectively and provides binary answers *dislike*, *like*, or *unknown*. For another 4 tree models $w1_{Rate}$, $w2_{Rate}$, $w3_{Rate}$, and $w4_{Rate}$, user responses are in $1-5$ rating scale. A random tree type will be selected when a user logs in. The users are instructed to answer the questions at their first sight, in order to avoid the situation that users linger on a particular page too long, or even search the internet to find particular answers.

In total we are able to collect responses from 76 users. Figure 4 shows our interview web interface. Table 3 compares the expected time to answer k questions on one screen. It reveals that the time increment for users to answer more questions per screen is usually sublinear, with answering 2 questions around 1.5 times slower than asking 1 question, and answering 4 questions around 2.5 times slower. Answering rating scale questions usually adds $2.5-3.5$ seconds to all the 4 settings ($1-4$ questions). The time difference between a rating scale answer and a binary answer seems not to have strong dependency with the number of questions. We suspect this phenomenon still comes from the sparsity of the data: with 4 questions per page, usually the user would not have seen all movies on a page therefore he/she only has to provide ratings for $1-2$ of them.

Figure 5 compares the time of the interview process by asking different number of questions per screen. It can be seen that $w1_{Rate}$ does not seem to be a much better option than $w1_{Binary}$ because the time increases significantly without too many questions being asked. However, the fraction of time increased from $w4_{Binary}$ to $w4_{Rate}$ seems not too big. Although $w4_{Rate}$ costs the longest time (over 50 seconds for 4 screens), it is able to obtain about 14 rated

Table 2: **A user's responses to the first two screens of the interview process each with 4 questions, followed by the recommendation list.**

(a) Interview Questions

Screen	Questions	Responses
1	The Royal Tenenbaums	Unknown
	Lost in Translation	Like
	Independence Day	Unknown
	Being John Malkovich	Unknown
2	How to Lose a Guy in 10 Days	Like
	Miss Congeniality	Like
	Pulp Fiction	DisLike
	Taxi Driver	Unknown

(b) Top-5 Recommendations

Rank	Movie Title
1	Indiana Jones and the Last Crusade
2	The Sixth Sense
3	The Green Mile
4	Life Is Beautiful
5	Toy Story

Table 3: A comparison of average time to answer n questions on one screen. When the number of questions per screen increases, the increase in the response time is sublinear.

Binary User Response

Ask l questions	$l = 1$	$l = 2$	$l = 3$	$l = 4$
Time (seconds)	4.4097	6.7267	7.8841	10.4232

Rating Scale User Response

Ask l questions	$l = 1$	$l = 2$	$l = 3$	$l = 4$
Time (seconds)	6.9339	9.5906	10.1404	13.8569

responses, comparing to less than 5 rated responses from $w1_{Rate}$ in 35 seconds.

We plot in Figure 6 the prediction performance for these different settings. The performance differs with data, in MovieLens, the setting $w4_{Binary}$ with asking 4 questions for binary answers performs the best. In the Netflix data, the main advantage of a rated response is that it can achieve superior recommendation performance, with longer surveys. However, time-wise it has only a very small advantage if the total time spent on the survey is less than 30 seconds. In the EachMovie data however, a rated response is always significantly better than a binary one in all accounts. This study can provide material to support decisions in deploying cold-start recommender systems: if the goal is a short survey, then using either binary or rated responses should have no major difference, while rated responses could have a slight advantage. However if the goal is a longer survey for more accurate user responses, it is more likely that seeking rated responses from the user would perform better.

5. CONCLUSIONS

In this paper we propose a new algorithm to learn decision trees with multiple dimensions selected for each split, for applications in cold-start recommender systems. Based on L_1 regularization, a relaxation formulation is proposed to optimize for each split. The new tree has users with heterogeneous answers in the same node. Therefore regressors are learned within each node based on previously given answers. Experiments show that the algorithm outperforms state-of-the-art approaches in terms of both the prediction accuracy and user cognitive efforts. A user study is conducted to understand the efficient number and format of questions being asked in a movie recommendation survey. The conclusion is that the multiple movies per screen approach is more favorable to single movie per screen approach, and asking for a rated response is more beneficial than a binary response, especially in longer surveys.

The current framework focuses on collaborative filtering recommendation and it does not take into account the content features such as user information and item attributes. In the future, we may learn to ask questions based on hybrid information of varying degree of granularity (e.g., genre, subgenre, director, actor, user age). Moreover, there are other types of strategies to explore in terms of minimizing user efforts. One example suggested in [25] supplies a list of items and asks the users to choose some from them. Another similar cold-start problem is to learn the profile for new items by asking a few experienced users to rate them. In this case, asking multiple users at each trial would also be preferable because some users may not respond to a particular question. We suspect that there are some duality between this cold-start item problem and the current one, and the current framework can be extended to handle this new task.

Figure 4: Interview web interface with 2 types of user input. Upper: binary. Bottom: rating scale.

6. ACKNOWLEDGMENTS

Part of the work was supported by NSF IIS-1116886 and a Yahoo! Faculty Research and Engagement award.

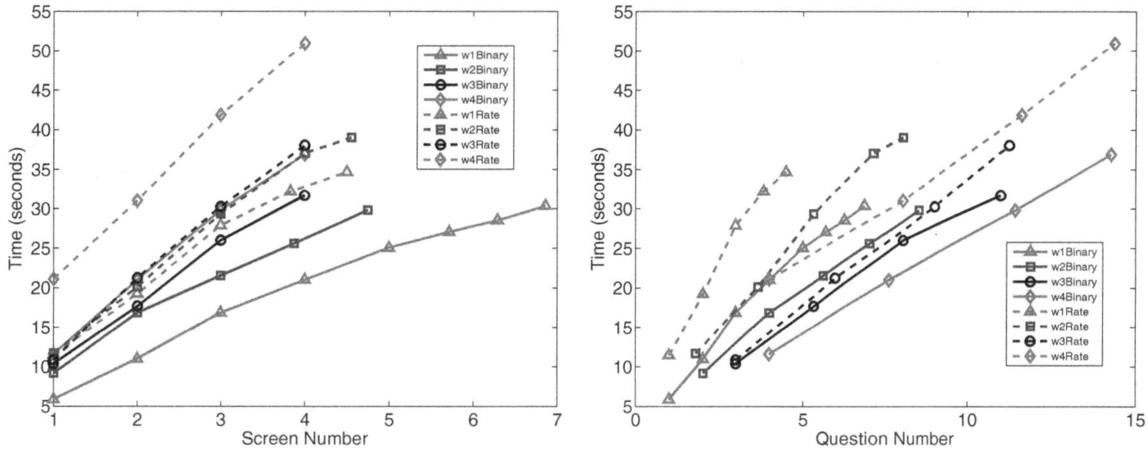

Figure 5: Time of the interview process with different question number per screen. The horizontal axis of left figure is the number of screen and the horizontal axis of right figure is the averaged number of accumulated questions.

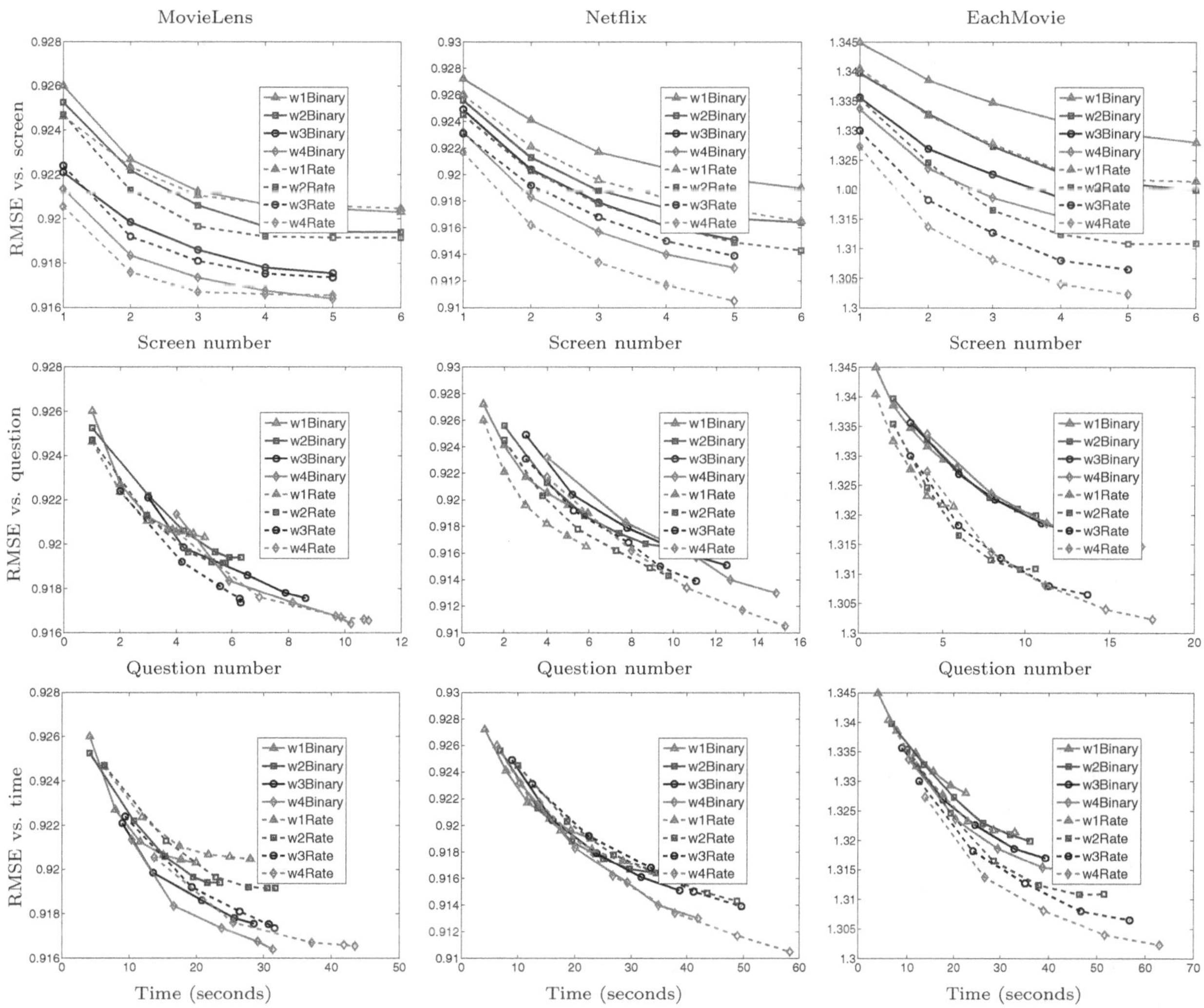

Figure 6: The prediction RMSE with respect to screen number, question number and user time on three datasets given different types of user answers. The *Binary* type expects users to answer *like* and *dislike*. $w2_{Binary}$, $w3_{Binary}$ and $w4_{Binary}$ are the tree models with 2, 3 and 4 questions on each screen respectively. In the *Rate* type, user chooses from a 5-star rating scale. $w2_{Rate}$, $w3_{Rate}$ and $w4_{Rate}$ are the tree models with 2, 3 and 4 questions on each screen respectively. Generally, rating scale provides richer information than binary answers, which leads to better prediction accuracy. On the other hand, rating scale may take more user time than binary answers.

7. REFERENCES

[1] D. Agarwal and B. Chen. Regression-based latent factor models. In *Proc. of the ACM SIGKDD*, pages 19–28. ACM, 2009.

[2] C. Boutilier, R. Zemel, and B. Marlin. Active collaborative filtering. In *Proceedings of the Nineteenth Conference on Uncertainty in Artificial Intelligence*, pages 98–106, 2003.

[3] J. Breese, D. Heckerman, and C. Kadie. Empirical analysis of predictive algorithms for collaborative filtering. In *Proc. of Uncertainty in Artificial Intelligence*, 1998.

[4] L. Breiman, J. Friedman, R. Olshen, and C. Stone. *Classification and Regression Trees.* Wadsworth and Brooks, Monterey, CA, 1984.

[5] N. Golbandi, Y. Koren, and R. Lempel. On bootstrapping recommender systems. In *Proceedings of the 19th ACM international conference on Information and knowledge management*, pages 1805–1808. ACM, 2010.

[6] N. Golbandi, Y. Koren, and R. Lempel. Adaptive bootstrapping of recommender systems using decision trees. In *Proceedings of the fourth ACM international conference on Web search and data mining*, pages 595–604. ACM, 2011.

[7] A. Gunawardana and C. Meek. Tied boltzmann machines for cold start recommendations. In *Proceedings of the 2008 ACM conference on Recommender systems*, pages 19–26. ACM, 2008.

[8] A. Harpale and Y. Yang. Personalized active learning for collaborative filtering. In *Proc. of ACM SIGIR Conference*, pages 91–98. ACM, 2008.

[9] L. He, N. Liu, and Q. Yang. Active dual collaborative filtering with both item and attribute feedback. In *AAAI*, 2011.

[10] J. L. Herlocker, J. A. Konstan, A. Borchers, and J. Riedl. An algorithmic framework for performing collaborative filtering. In *Proc. of ACM SIGIR Conference*, 1999.

[11] T. Hofmann. Latent semantic models for collaborative filtering. *ACM Transactions on Information Systems*, 22(1):115, 2004.

[12] R. Jin and L. Si. A bayesian approach toward active learning for collaborative filtering. In *Proceedings of the 20th conference on Uncertainty in artificial intelligence*, pages 278–285, 2004.

[13] Y. Koren. Factor in the neighbors: Scalable and accurate collaborative filtering. *ACM Transactions on Knowledge Discovery from Data*, 4(1):1–24, 2010.

[14] N. D. Lawrence and R. Urtasun. Non-linear matrix factorization with gaussian processes. In *Proc. of the ICML*, 2009.

[15] D. M. Pennock, E. Horvitz, S. Lawrence, and C. L. Giles. Collaborative filtering by personality diagnosis: A hybrid memory- and model-based approach. In *Proc. of the Conference on UAI*, 2000.

[16] P. Pu and L. Chen. User-involved preference elicitation for product search and recommender systems. *AI Magazine*, 29(4):93, 2009.

[17] A. Rashid, I. Albert, D. Cosley, S. Lam, S. McNee, J. Konstan, and J. Riedl. Getting to know you: learning new user preferences in recommender systems. In *Proceedings of the 7th international conference on Intelligent user interfaces*, pages 127–134. ACM, 2002.

[18] A. Rashid, G. Karypis, and J. Riedl. Learning preferences of new users in recommender systems: an information theoretic approach. ACM, 2008.

[19] J. Rennie and N. Srebro. Fast maximum margin matrix factorization for collaborative prediction. In *Proc. of the International Conference on Machine Learning*, 2005.

[20] P. Resnick, N. Iacovou, M. Suchak, P. Bergstrom, and J. Riedl. Grouplens: an open architecture for collaborative filtering of netnews. In *Proc. of the Conference on CSCW*, 1994.

[21] B. Sarwar, G. Karypis, J. Konstan, and J. Reidl. Item-based collaborative filtering recommendation algorithms. In *Proc. of the International Conference on World Wide Web*, 2001.

[22] A. I. Schein, A. Popescul, L. H. Ungar, and D. M. Pennock. Methods and metrics for cold-start recommendations. In *Proc. of ACM SIGIR Conference*, pages 253–260. ACM, 2002.

[23] M. Schmidt. *Graphical Model Structure Learning with L1-Regularization.* PhD thesis, The University of British Columbia, 2010.

[24] M. Sun, G. Lebanon, and P. Kidwell. Estimating probabilities in recommendation systems. In *Proc. of the International Conference on Artificial Intelligence and Statistics*, 2011.

[25] S. Yang, B. Long, A. Smola, and H. Zha. Collaborative-competitive ltering: Learning recommender using context of user choice. In *Proc. of ACM SIGIR Conference*, 2011.

[26] K. Yu, S. Zhu, J. Lafferty, and Y. Gong. Fast nonparametric matrix factorization for large-scale collaborative filtering. In *Proc. of ACM SIGIR Conference*, 2009.

[27] K. Zhou, S. Yang, and H. Zha. Functional matrix factorizations for cold-start recommendation. In *Proc. of the ACM-SIGIR conference*, pages 315–324, 2011.

Online Multi-modal Distance Learning for Scalable Multimedia Retrieval

Hao Xia, Pengcheng Wu, Steven C.H. Hoi
School of Computer Engineering
Nanyang Technological University
Singapore 639798
{xiah0002,wupe0003,chhoi}@ntu.edu.sg

ABSTRACT

In many real-word scenarios, e.g., multimedia applications, data often originates from multiple heterogeneous sources or are represented by diverse types of representation, which is often referred to as "multi-modal data". The definition of distance between any two objects/items on multi-modal data is a key challenge encountered by many real-world applications, including multimedia retrieval. In this paper, we present a novel online learning framework for learning distance functions on multi-modal data through the combination of multiple kernels. In order to attack large-scale multimedia applications, we propose Online Multi-modal Distance Learning (OMDL) algorithms, which are significantly more efficient and scalable than the state-of-the-art techniques. We conducted an extensive set of experiments on multi-modal image retrieval applications, in which encouraging results validate the efficacy of the proposed technique.

Categories and Subject Descriptors

H.3.3 [**Information Storage and Retrieval**]: Retrieval models; H.2.8 [**Database Applications**]: Image databases

General Terms

Algorithms, Experimentation

Keywords

Online Learning; Graph Laplacian; Multi-modal Distance; Multimedia Retrieval

1. INTRODUCTION

Similarity search plays a fundamental role in a variety of multimedia retrieval tasks [29, 25, 11, 19, 7, 52], which has been extensively studied in multimedia and computer vision fields, especially for Content-Based Image Retrieval (CBIR) [38, 18, 34]. The crux of similarity search is to find some proximity function that can effectively measure distance/similarity between images [1, 30, 33]. In a conventional CBIR system, given images represented in a vector space, the typical choices of such proximity functions are Euclidean distance and its variants, which are often not flexible enough to measure the proximity of images due to the nature of the fixed rigid functions.

In recent years, researchers have noticed the limitations of conventional rigid proximity functions for visual similarity search. To address this issue, one group of active research is the Distance Metric Learning (DML) studies [13, 18, 36, 28, 46, 17, 47], which usually learn to optimize the Mahalanobis distance metric on some vector space to improve visual similarity search for various multimedia retrieval applications. Despite their successes for improving visual similarity search, most existing DML studies are limited in that they usually do not effectively handle the distance measure of multi-modal data that may originate from multiple resources and not necessarily be represented in a vector space.

Recently, the Multiple Kernel Partial Order Embedding (MKPOE) [32] has attempted to address this limitation by adopting multiple kernel learning techniques for integrating multiple sources of heterogeneous data into a single, unified distance space. Despite their pioneering study, MKPOE is limited in two key aspects: (i) it cannot preserve the intrinsic geometric structure of the underlying data, which has been shown to be able to improve the performance of many related applications; (ii) it has poor efficiency and scalability, which cannot be applied to large-scale applications.

To overcome the limitations of MKPOE, this paper proposes a novel Online Multi-modal Distance Learning (OMDL) scheme, which exploits the local dependency of underlying data distributions to enhance the learning efficacy of MKPOE, and further improves the efficiency and scalability by exploring online learning techniques.

The OMDL task is however very challenging because it must on one hand learn an optimal distance function for each kernel in each modality, and on the other hand determine an optimal combination of multiple kernels in building the final distance function with all modalities. To attack the challenges, we propose an online learning algorithm for OMDL, which learns both the optimal distance function with each individual kernel and the optimal combination of multiple kernels in an effective and scalable online learning framework. In particular, we apply the online passive aggressive learning technique [8] to learn the distance function for each individual kernel, and the Hedging learning technique to learn the optimal combination weights of multiple kernels, from a sequence of triplet training data.

WSDM'13, February 4–8, 2012, Rome, Italy.

As a summary, our main contributions include:

- We propose a novel OMDL framework, which exploits local dependency of underly data distribution for learning distance on multi-modal data using multiple kernels via an online learning scheme.
- We present effective OMDL algorithms, which learn both the optimal proximity function with an individual kernel and the optimal combination of multiple kernels in an efficient and scalable online learning approach.
- We conduct an extensive set of experiments to evaluate the performance of the proposed technique for multi-modal image retrieval on several image data sets, in which the encouraging results show clear advantages of OMDL over the state-of-the-art techniques.

The rest of this paper is organized as follows. Section 2 reviews related work. Section 3 gives some preliminaries of related techniques in literature. Section 4 introduces the problem definition and presents the proposed online learning algorithm for OMDL. Section 5 discusses the experimental results, and section 6 sets out the conclusion of this work.

2. RELATED WORK

This section reviews related work which can be generally grouped into two major categories as follows.

2.1 Distance Metric Learning

Distance Metric Learning (DML) from side information has been actively studied in CBIR for years. In general, most DML works aim to learn an optimal distance metric in the family of Mahalanobis distances, which can be viewed as an equivalent problem of learning an optimal linear embedding of original data, where Euclidean distance can be adopted to measure proximity between the embedded objects.

In literature, various DML techniques have been proposed in both machine learning [4, 48, 43] and multimedia communities [18, 36, 10, 28, 45, 50, 45, 47]. Some well-known techniques include Relevant Component Analysis (RCA) [4], Discriminative Component Analysis (DCA) [18], Large Margin Nearest Neighbor (LMNN) [43], Information-Theoretic Metric Learning (ITML) [22], Regularized Metric Learning [36], and Laplacian Regularized Metric Learning (LRML) [17], and so on.

We also note that several kernel-based distance metric learning algorithms [6, 51, 52, 22] were proposed for learning distance functions in CBIR. Despite their successes, most existing DML studies are limited in that they usually do not effectively handle the distance measure of multi-modal data that may originate from multiple resources and not necessarily be represented in vector space.

2.2 Multiple Kernel Learning

Our work is also closely related to Multiple Kernel Learning (MKL) studies [27, 39], which aim to find the optimal combination of multiple kernels for learning classifiers towards a given classification task. Exemplar algorithms include the convex optimization [27], the Semi-Infinite Linear Program (SILP) approach [39], and the level method [49]. In addition, several recent studies [54, 23] address multiple kernel learning for multi-class and multi-labeled data, and some other works aim at improving its efficiency and generality [41, 42, 21].

Despite sharing the common goal of finding the optimal combination of multiple kernels, our technique differs significantly from the existing MKL studies in two key aspects. First, we aim to learn kernel-based distance functions for multimedia search tasks while conventional MKL studies often address classification tasks. Second, the training data used by conventional MKL studies are in the regular form of single data instances with class label, while the training data in our problem are in the form of triplet instances.

Recently, the Multiple Kernel Partial Order Embedding (MKPOE) [32] adopts multiple kernel learning techniques for integrating multiple sources of heterogeneous data into a single, unified distance space. Our work is partially inspired to overcome the limitations of MKPOE by adopting graph Laplacian to capture the underlying data structure so as to improve the effectiveness of MKPOE, and tackling the efficiency and scalability issue by solving the learning problem via online learning.

We should note that this work was also inspired by our previous work on Online Multiple Kernel Learning [24, 16]. The OMKL technique was proposed to learn classifiers by finding an optimal combination of multiple kernels for classification tasks, while the goal of this work is to learn the distance function from triplets for multimedia retrieval [16]. Unlike the regular classification task, special care is needed in the design of algorithms to handle the triple constraints for multimedia retrieval.

3. PRELIMINARIES

To better motivate our work, in this section, we introduce an important previous work, i.e., Multiple Kernel Partial Order Embedding (MKPOE) [32], for learning distance with multiple kernels. For problem setting, assume we are given a set of n objects $\mathcal{X} = \{\mathbf{x}_i | i = 1, 2, \ldots, n\}$, and a collection of triplet constraints $\mathcal{C} = \{(i_t, j_t, k_t), t = 1, 2, \ldots, T\}$, where each triplet (i_t, j_t, k_t) indicates that object $\mathbf{x}_{i_t}$ is similar to object $\mathbf{x}_{j_t}$, but dissimilar to object $\mathbf{x}_{k_t}$. For simplicity, we will simply denote $\mathbf{x}_{i_t}$ as $\mathbf{x}_i$ for the rest of discussion.

We first consider the case of learning distance with a single kernel. In particular, it first maps the data into a Reproducing Kernel Hilbert Space (RKHS) [2] $\mathcal{H}$ via a feature map ϕ with corresponding kernel function $\kappa(\mathbf{x}, \mathbf{y}) = \langle \phi(\mathbf{x}), \phi(\mathbf{y}) \rangle_{\mathcal{H}}$; then the data is mapped to $\mathbb{R}^d$ by a linear projection $\mathbf{M} : \mathcal{H} \to \mathbb{R}^d$. The embedding function $g : \mathcal{X} \to \mathbb{R}^d$ is therefore the composition of the projection $\mathbf{M}$ with ϕ:

$$g(\mathbf{x}) = \mathbf{M}(\phi(\mathbf{x})) \tag{1}$$

It is further extended to the multiple kernel case by defining the embedding function as the concatenation:

$$g(\mathbf{x}) = (\mathbf{M}^p(\phi^p(\mathbf{x})))_{p=1}^m \tag{2}$$

where the index of kernel $p \in \{1, 2, \ldots, m\}$ and $(\cdot)_{p=1}^m$ denotes concatenation. By invoking the representer theorem [35] for each $\mathbf{M}^p$:

$$\mathbf{M}^p = \mathbf{N}^p(\mathbf{\Phi}^p)^\top \tag{3}$$

where $\mathbf{N}^p \in \mathbb{R}^{d \times n}$ is a real-valued matrix, $\mathbf{\Phi}^p$ is a matrix representation of $\mathcal{X}$ in $\mathcal{H}$ (i.e., $\mathbf{\Phi}_i^p = \phi^p(\mathbf{x}_i)$ for $\mathbf{x}_i \in \mathcal{X}$).

So the embedding function can now be written as:

$$g(\mathbf{x}) = (\mathbf{M}^p(\phi^p(\mathbf{x})))_{p=1}^m = (\mathbf{N}^p \mathbf{K}_\mathbf{x}^p)_{p=1}^m \tag{4}$$

where $\mathbf{K}_\mathbf{x}^p$ is the column vector formed by evaluating the kernel function κ^p at $\mathbf{x}$ against $\mathcal{X}$.

Further we use a Positive Semi-Definite (PSD) matrix $\mathbf{W}^p = (\mathbf{N}^p)^\top(\mathbf{N}^p)$. The optimization problem of MKPOE can be formally written as follows:

$$\min_{\mathbf{W}^p,\xi} \quad \sum_{p=1}^{m} tr(\mathbf{W}^p\mathbf{K}^p) + \frac{\beta}{|\mathcal{C}|}\sum_{\forall(i,j,k)\in\mathcal{C}} \xi_{ijk} \tag{5}$$

$$s.t. \quad d(\mathbf{x}_i,\mathbf{x}_j) \doteq \sum_{p=1}^{m}(\mathbf{K}_i^p - \mathbf{K}_j^p)^\top \mathbf{W}^p(\mathbf{K}_i^p - \mathbf{K}_j^p)$$

$$d(\mathbf{x}_i,\mathbf{x}_j) + 1 \le d(\mathbf{x}_i,\mathbf{x}_k) + \xi_{ijk},\ \xi_{ijk} \ge 0, \forall(i,j,k)\in\mathcal{C}$$

$$\mathbf{W}^p \succeq \mathbf{0} \quad p = 1,2,\ldots,m$$

where $\mathbf{K}^p$ is the kernel matrix corresponding to κ^p, $\mathbf{K}_i^p$ is the i-th column of it, and β is a trade-off parameter.

4. ONLINE MULTI-MODAL DISTANCE LEARNING (OMDL)

4.1 Overview

In this section, we present a framework of Online Multi-modal Distance Learning (OMDL) using multiple kernels. We first give our formulation of multi-modal distance learning and then propose the online algorithms.

4.2 Multi-modal Distance Learning

Let us denote by $f(\mathbf{x}_i,\mathbf{x}_j)$ a similarity function that measures the similarity between any two data points $\mathbf{x}_i$ and $\mathbf{x}_j$, and $\mathbf{S} \in \mathbb{R}^{n\times n}$ is a similarity matrix where each element $S_{ij} = f(\mathbf{x}_i,\mathbf{x}_j) \ge 0$. Note that $f(\cdot,\cdot)$ does not have to be a kernel function that satisfies the Mercer's condition. Given n data instances, a kernel matrix $\mathbf{K}$ can be expressed as $\mathbf{K} = \mathbf{V}'\mathbf{V} \succeq \mathbf{0}$, where $\mathbf{V} = [\mathbf{v}_1,\ldots,\mathbf{v}_n]$ is the matrix of the embedding of the n data instances. The regularizer of the kernel matrix $\mathbf{K}$, which captures the local dependency [15, 14, 53] between the embeddings of $\mathbf{v}_i$ and $\mathbf{v}_j$ (i.e., the low dimensional embedding [37] of similar instances should be similar w.r.t. the similarity S_{ij}) can be defined as:

$$\begin{aligned}\Omega(\mathbf{V},\mathbf{S}) &= \frac{1}{2}\sum_{i,j=1}^{n} S_{ij}\|\frac{\mathbf{v}_i}{\sqrt{D_i}} - \frac{\mathbf{v}_j}{\sqrt{D_j}}\|_2^2 \\ &= tr(\mathbf{VLV}') = tr(\mathbf{LK})\end{aligned} \tag{6}$$

where $\mathbf{L}$ is the graph Laplacian matrix defined as:

$$\mathbf{L} = \mathbf{I} - \mathbf{D}^{-1/2}\mathbf{S}\mathbf{D}^{1/2} \tag{7}$$

where $\mathbf{D} = diag(D_1, D_2,\ldots,D_n)$ is a diagonal matrix with the diagonal elements defined as $D_i = \sum_{j=1}^{n} S_{ij}$. By incorporating graph Laplacian regularizer, we can formulate the optimization problem of the proposed multi-modal distance learning:

$$\min_{\mathbf{W}^p,\xi} \quad \sum_{p=1}^{m} tr(\mathbf{K}^p\mathbf{W}^p\mathbf{K}^p\mathbf{L}^p) + \frac{\beta}{|\mathcal{C}|}\sum_{\forall(i,j,k)\in\mathcal{C}} \xi_{ijk} \tag{8}$$

$$s.t. \quad d(\mathbf{x}_i,\mathbf{x}_j) \doteq \sum_{p=1}^{m}(\mathbf{K}_i^p - \mathbf{K}_j^p)^\top \mathbf{W}^p(\mathbf{K}_i^p - \mathbf{K}_j^p)$$

$$d(\mathbf{x}_i,\mathbf{x}_j) + 1 \le d(\mathbf{x}_i,\mathbf{x}_k) + \xi_{ijk},\ \xi_{ijk} \ge 0, \forall(i,j,k)\in\mathcal{C}$$

$$\mathbf{W}^p \succeq \mathbf{0} \quad p = 1,2,\ldots,m$$

In the above, the first regularizer term of the objective function enforces the smoothness of the distance on the manifold, which is the key difference as compared to the previous MKPOE approach. The above optimization can be solved by applying projected gradient descent by following a solution similar to MKPOE [32]. However, such an approach can be computationally intensive, which is hardly scalable for large-scale application. In the following, we will present an online learning algorithm to tackle this challenge.

4.3 Algorithms for OMDL

In this section, we present an online learning scheme which aims to sequentially updates the multi-modal distance function from a sequence of triplet constraints. In particular, given any received triplet constraint (i,j,k), it can be used to update two sets of target variables: (i) the parameters of the distance function defined on each individual kernel, i.e., $\mathbf{W}^p, p = 1,2,\ldots,m$ and (ii) the combination weights assigned to different kernels, denoted as $\mu_p, p = 1,2,\ldots,m$. Figure 1 shows the system flow of the proposed OMDL algorithm which learns distance functions from a sequence of triplet constraints.

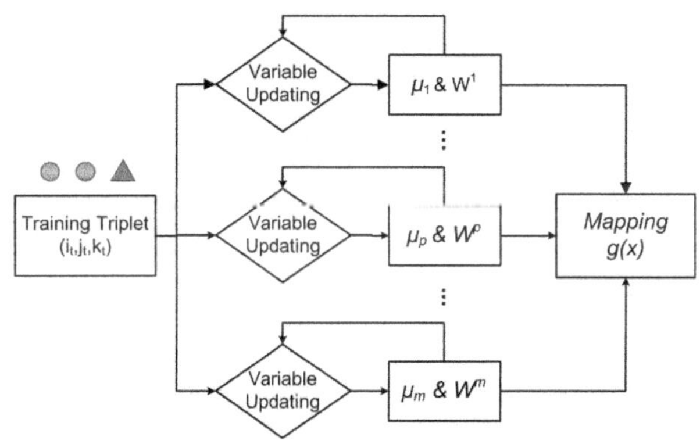

Figure 1: The system flow of the proposed OMDL algorithm from a sequence of training triplets.

Given these variables, the class of the combined kernel can be expressed as:

$$\mathbf{K}_\mu = \sum_{p=1}^{m}\mu_p\mathbf{K}^p\mathbf{W}^p\mathbf{K}^p \tag{9}$$

Correspondingly, the embedding function is:

$$g(\mathbf{x}) = (\sqrt{\mu_p}\mathbf{N}^p\mathbf{K}_\mathbf{x}^p)_{p=1}^m \tag{10}$$

The inner products between embedded points take the form:

$$\begin{aligned}\mathbf{A}_{ij} &= \langle g(\mathbf{x}_i), g(\mathbf{x}_j)\rangle \\ &= \sum_{p=1}^{m}(\sqrt{\mu_p}\mathbf{N}^p\mathbf{K}_i^p)^\top(\sqrt{\mu_p}\mathbf{N}^p\mathbf{K}_j^p) \\ &= \sum_{p=1}^{m}\mu_p(\mathbf{K}_i^p)^\top(\mathbf{N}^p)^\top(\mathbf{N}^p)(\mathbf{K}_j^p)\end{aligned} \tag{11}$$

Thus, the squared Euclidean distance can be expressed as:

$$\begin{aligned}d(\mathbf{x}_i,\mathbf{x}_j) &= \|g(\mathbf{x}_i) - g(\mathbf{x}_j)\|^2 \\ &= \sum_{p=1}^{m}\mu_p(\mathbf{K}_i^p - \mathbf{K}_j^p)^\top(\mathbf{N}^p)^\top(\mathbf{N}^p)(\mathbf{K}_i^p - \mathbf{K}_j^p) \\ &= \sum_{p=1}^{m}\mu_p d_p(\mathbf{x}_i,\mathbf{x}_j)\end{aligned} \tag{12}$$

Therefore, the key challenges of online multi-modal distance learning are to find effective and efficient solutions for solving both W^p and μ_p at each online learning round.

4.3.1 Algorithm on a Single Kernel

We first start by presenting the solution for online distance learning on a single kernel.

By following the principle of online passive aggressive learning [8], we can rewrite the formulation of the Online Distance Learning (ODL) as the following optimization for a single triplet (i, j, k) at some round t:

$$\begin{aligned} \min_{\mathbf{W},\xi} \quad & \frac{1}{2}\|\mathbf{W}-\mathbf{W}_{t-1}\|_F^2 + C_1 tr(\mathbf{KWKL}) + C_2\xi \quad (13) \\ s.t. \quad & d(\mathbf{x}_i,\mathbf{x}_j) \doteq (\mathbf{K}_i-\mathbf{K}_j)^\top \mathbf{W}(\mathbf{K}_i-\mathbf{K}_j) \\ & d(\mathbf{x}_i,\mathbf{x}_j)+1 \le d(\mathbf{x}_i,\mathbf{x}_k)+\xi,\ \xi \ge 0 \\ & \mathbf{W} \succeq \mathbf{0} \end{aligned}$$

where $\|\cdot\|_F$ denotes the Frobenius norm.

In the following, we derive the solution to the ODL problem. At first, we solve the optimization problem without considering the PSD constraint, i.e., $\mathbf{W} \succeq \mathbf{0}$. Then the PSD constraint is applied by projecting onto the feasible set. The following proposition shows the analytic solution to the optimization without the PSD constraint.

PROPOSITION 1. *The closed-form solution to the optimization task in (13) can be expressed as follows:*

$$\mathbf{W} = \mathbf{W}_{t-1} - C_1\mathbf{KLK} - \tau\mathbf{K}(\mathbf{E}_{ij}-\mathbf{E}_{ik})\mathbf{K} \quad (14)$$

where τ *is calculated by*

$$\tau = \min\{C_2, \frac{h(l_{t-1})}{\|\mathbf{K}(\mathbf{E}_{ij}-\mathbf{E}_{ik})\mathbf{K}\|_F^2}\} \quad (15)$$

$h(x) = \max\{0,x\}$ *is the hinge loss function,* $\mathbf{E}_{ij} = (\mathbf{e}_i - \mathbf{e}_j)(\mathbf{e}_i-\mathbf{e}_j)^\top$ *and*

$$\begin{aligned} l_{t-1} &= -C_1 tr(\mathbf{KLKK}(\mathbf{E}_{ij}-\mathbf{E}_{ik})\mathbf{K}) \\ &\quad + tr(\mathbf{W}_{t-1}\mathbf{K}(\mathbf{E}_{ij}-\mathbf{E}_{ik})\mathbf{K}) + 1 \end{aligned}$$

PROOF. We define the Lagrangian as:

$$\begin{aligned} f(\mathbf{W},\xi,\lambda,\tau) &= \frac{1}{2}\|\mathbf{W}-\mathbf{W}_{t-1}\|_F^2 + C_1 tr(\mathbf{KWKL}) + C_2\xi \\ &\quad -\lambda\xi + \tau(1-\xi+\langle \mathbf{W}, \mathbf{K}(\mathbf{E}_{ij}-\mathbf{E}_{ik})\mathbf{K}\rangle_F) \end{aligned}$$

where $\lambda \ge 0$ and $\tau \ge 0$ are Lagrangian multipliers. By setting $\frac{\partial f(\mathbf{W},\xi,\lambda,\tau)}{\partial \mathbf{W}} = 0$, we have the following:

$$\mathbf{W} - \mathbf{W}_{t-1} + C_1\mathbf{KLK} + \tau\mathbf{K}(\mathbf{E}_{ij}-\mathbf{E}_{ik})\mathbf{K} = 0 \quad (16)$$

and therefore

$$\mathbf{W} = \mathbf{W}_{t-1} - C_1\mathbf{KLK} - \tau\mathbf{K}(\mathbf{E}_{ij}-\mathbf{E}_{ik})\mathbf{K} \quad (17)$$

Next by setting $\frac{\partial f(\mathbf{W},\xi,\lambda,\tau)}{\partial \xi} = 0$, we have:

$$C_2 - \lambda - \tau = 0 \quad (18)$$

Since $\lambda \ge 0$, we have $\tau \le C_2$. Thus, we have the following:

$$\begin{aligned} & f(\tau) \\ = \ & \frac{1}{2}\|\mathbf{W}-\mathbf{W}_{t-1}\|_F^2 + C_1 tr(\mathbf{KWKL}) + \tau \\ & + \tau\langle \mathbf{W}, \mathbf{K}(\mathbf{E}_{ij}-\mathbf{E}_{ik})\mathbf{K}\rangle_F \\ = \ & \frac{1}{2}\|\mathbf{W}-\mathbf{W}_{t-1}\|_F^2 - tr(\mathbf{W}(\mathbf{W}-\mathbf{W}_{t-1})) + \tau \\ = \ & -\frac{1}{2}\|\mathbf{W}-\mathbf{W}_{t-1}\|_F^2 - tr(\mathbf{W}_{t-1}(\mathbf{W}-\mathbf{W}_{t-1})) + \tau \\ = \ & -\frac{1}{2}\|C_1\mathbf{KLK} + \tau\mathbf{K}(\mathbf{E}_{ij}-\mathbf{E}_{ik})\mathbf{K}\|_F^2 \\ & + C_1 tr(\mathbf{W}_{t-1}\mathbf{KLK}) + \tau tr(\mathbf{W}_{t-1}\mathbf{K}(\mathbf{E}_{ij}-\mathbf{E}_{ik})\mathbf{K}) + \tau \end{aligned}$$

Further, by setting $\frac{\partial f(\tau)}{\partial \tau} = 0$, we have

$$\begin{aligned} & \frac{\partial f(\tau)}{\partial \tau} \\ = \ & -C_1 tr(\mathbf{KLKK}(\mathbf{E}_{ij}-\mathbf{E}_{ik})\mathbf{K}) - \tau\|\mathbf{K}(\mathbf{E}_{ij}-\mathbf{E}_{ik})\mathbf{K}\|_F^2 \\ & + tr(\mathbf{W}_{t-1}\mathbf{K}(\mathbf{E}_{ij}-\mathbf{E}_{ik})\mathbf{K}) + 1 \\ = \ & 0 \end{aligned}$$

Thus, we have

$$\tau = \frac{l_{t-1}}{\|\mathbf{K}(\mathbf{E}_{ij}-\mathbf{E}_{ik})\mathbf{K}\|_F^2} \quad (19)$$

where

$$\begin{aligned} l_{t-1} &= -C_1 tr(\mathbf{KLKK}(\mathbf{E}_{ij}-\mathbf{E}_{ik})\mathbf{K}) \\ &\quad + tr(\mathbf{W}_{t-1}\mathbf{K}(\mathbf{E}_{ij}-\mathbf{E}_{ik})\mathbf{K}) + 1 \end{aligned}$$

Combining the fact that $\tau \le C_2$, we have

$$\tau = \min\{C_2, \frac{l_{t-1}}{\|\mathbf{K}(\mathbf{E}_{ij}-\mathbf{E}_{ik})\mathbf{K}\|_F^2}\} \quad (20)$$

Further by considering $\tau \ge 0$, we have:

$$\tau = \min\{C_2, \frac{h(l_{t-1})}{\|\mathbf{K}(\mathbf{E}_{ij}-\mathbf{E}_{ik})\mathbf{K}\|_F^2}\} \quad (21)$$

where $h(x) = \max\{0,x\}$ is the hinge loss function. □

4.3.2 Algorithm on Multiple Kernels

We now extend the above online distance learning on a single kernel to the setting of online multi-modal distance learning with multiple kernels. In particular, we tackle the challenges of the online multi-modal distance learning task by two steps: (i) we apply the previous online distance learning algorithm for learning distance function for each individual kernel; and (ii) we attempt to find the optimal combination of multiple kernels using the Hedging online learning algorithm by following the similar idea in [24]. Specifically, we denote by $\mu_p(t)$ the combination weight of the p-th kernel at t-th learning round. We iteratively update the following combination weight according to the online learning performance:

$$\mu_p(t) = \mu_p(t-1)\eta^{z_p(t)} \quad (22)$$

where $\eta \in (0,1)$ is a discounting parameter, and $z_p(t)$ is an indicator which outputs 1 when $d_p(\mathbf{x}_i,\mathbf{x}_j) > d_p(\mathbf{x}_i,\mathbf{x}_k)$, and 0 otherwise. The details of the proposed OMDL algorithm are shown in Algorithm 1.

Algorithm 1 Online Multi-modal Distance Learning (OMDL)

INPUT:

- n objects $\mathcal{X} = \{\mathbf{x}_i | i = 1, 2, \ldots, n\}$
- m kernel matrices $\mathbf{K}^p, p = 1, 2, \ldots, m$
- m graph Laplacian matrices $\mathbf{L}^p, p = 1, 2, \ldots, m$
- tradeoff parameter $C_1 > 0, C_2 > 0$
- discount weight $\eta \in (0, 1)$

```
Initialize: W_0^p = I, μ_p(0) = 1, p = 1, 2, ..., m
for t = 1, 2, ..., T do
  receive a triplet (i, j, k)
  for p = 1, 2, ..., m do
    compute τ_t^p in (15).
    compute W_t^p in (14).
    PSD projection: λ_i ↦ max(0, λ_i), i = 1, 2, ..., n
    if d_p(x_i, x_j) > d_p(x_i, x_k) then
      z_p(t) = 1
    else
      z_p(t) = 0
    end if
    update μ_p(t) = μ_p(t − 1) η^{z_p(t)}
  end for
end for
```

OUTPUT: mapping $g : \mathcal{X} \to \mathbb{R}^{m \times n}$

4.4 Fast OMDL Algorithm

In this section, we propose a fast OMDL algorithm by low rank approximation (OMDL-LR). Specifically, instead of learning a high dimensional matrix $\mathbf{W}$ of $d \times d$, we attempt to learn a matrix $\mathbf{W}_{LR}$ of dimensionality $d_{LR} \times d_{LR}$ ($d_{LR} \ll d$). Following [5], we generate a $d \times d_{LR}$ random projection matrix $\mathbf{P}$ based on Gaussian distribution, and use $\mathbf{P}\mathbf{W}_{LR}\mathbf{P}^\top$ to approximate $\mathbf{W}$. Once the random projection matrix is chosen, it is straightforward for improving the rest of the algorithm by projecting the columns of kernel values accordingly, i.e., $\mathbf{K}_i \leftarrow \mathbf{P}^\top \mathbf{K}_i$. One may also consider other low-rank approximation methods, such as Nyström [44].

5. EXPERIMENTS

To evaluate our proposed scheme, we first test it on small-scale data sets. Then we apply it in image retrieval applications on some standard benchmark data sets. At last we report the results on a large-scale image retrieval data set.

5.1 Experimental Testbed

We form our experimental testbed[1] by adopting three publicly available image data sets. These three data sets have been widely used for the benchmark of image retrieval, classification and recognition tasks.

The first testbed is the "Caltech256" database[2], which has been widely adopted for object recognition and image retrieval tasks [12, 26, 9, 7]. This database contains 256 object categories (excluding the background category) and a total of 30607 images. Following the similar experiments as the previous work [7], we pick 10, 20 or 50 out of the 256 classes to form three subsets (the same sets as used in [7]), which are named as "Caltech10", "Caltech20", and "Caltech50", respectively.

[1]`http://www.cais.ntu.edu.sg/~chhoi/OMDL/`

[2]`http://www.vision.caltech.edu/Image_Datasets/Caltech256/`

The second testbed is the "Corel5000" database [18]. The image testbed consists of real-world photos from COREL image CDs. It has 50 categories, with each category contains exactly 100 images that are randomly selected from relevant examples in the COREL image CDs.

The third testbed is the "ImageCLEF" database[3], which is a medical image data set for image retrieval benchmark evaluation. To examine the scalability, we also combine "ImageCLEF" with a collection of 1,000,000 social images crawled from Flickr, which is named "ImageCLEF+". For the Flickr images, we treat all of them as the background noise, which are mainly used to test the scalability of our algorithms.

5.2 Experimental Setup

For each data set, we randomly select a subset from each class to make sure that all classes have the same number of images as the one has least images in the original data set. This can avoid the performance being dominated by some single class of large number of images. Based on the data set, we then randomly select 50% examples from each class to form a training set, 10% examples to form a validation set, 10% examples to form a query set, and the rest 30% examples to form the test set for retrieval evaluation. The validation set is mainly used to determine the best parameters and the best cases of the compared algorithms.

We need to generate side information in the forms of triplet and pairwise training instances. In our approach, we generate side information by sampling triplet constraints from the feedback of images in the training set. The feedback information is simply derived from class labels in this study, which can be collected from the relevance feedback mechanism in a practical CBIR system [20]. Specifically, we select 40% from the training set to form the training queries and the rest as the database pool. For each training query, we generate 5 triplets. A triplet (q, p^+, p^-) is generated by first randomly choosing an image p^+ from the database pool which belongs to the same class as the training query q, then choosing another image p^- from the database pool which belongs to another class. As a result, two pairwise constraints, $(q, p^+, +1)$ and $(q, p^-, -1)$, can be derived from (q, p^+, p^-). For the small-scale experiment, the triplets for validation (test) are generated in the similar manner as that of the training set, but restrict q from validation (query) set, p^+ and p^- from the test set. The final results are averaged over 5 random sets of training data. We measure both mean and standard deviation of the results, and highlight the best case by performing student t-tests with the significance level $\alpha = 0.05$.

The performance of the small-scale experiment is evaluated by the prediction accuracy on triplets from the test set. For the image retrieval experiments, we evaluated the performance by standard performance metrics for multimedia retrieval. Specifically, for each query image, all the images in the database are ranked according to their similarities to the query. We can measure the precision at top n ranked images by computing the number of top-n images of the same class label as the query image. We also adopt the standard mean Average Precision (mAP) [31] to evaluate the retrieval result. In particular, the Average Precision (AP) value is the area under precision-recall curve for a query. The mAP value is calculated based on the average AP value of all the queries. The precision value is the ratio of relevant

[3]http://imageclef.org/

Table 1: Experimental results on three small-scale data sets

Dataset	Metric	Kernel-Best	Kernel-U	Kernel-W	MKPOE	OMDL	OMDL-LR
Caltech(S)	accuracy std	0.4700 ±0.0000	0.6200 ±0.0000	0.5900 ±0.0000	0.6967 ±0.0681	**0.7933** **±0.0058**	**0.7900** **±0.0100**
	time(s) std	-	-	-	150.5669 ±1.1985	5.6428 ±0.0793	**0.4364** **±0.0088**
Corel(S)	accuracy std	0.6900 ±0.0000	0.6200 ±0.0000	0.6700 ±0.0000	0.7167 ±0.0153	**0.8067** **±0.0351**	**0.7967** **±0.0306**
	time(s) std	-	-	-	149.4588 ±1.3813	5.6499 ±0.3046	**0.4446** **±0.0262**
ImageCLEF(S)	accuracy std	0.7700 ±0.0000	0.7400 ±0.0000	0.7500 ±0.0000	0.8600 ±0.0300	**0.9333** **±0.0058**	**0.9333** **±0.0289**
	time(s) std	-	-	-	152.1280 ±0.5545	5.6533 ±0.0050	**0.4364** **±0.0071**

examples over the total retrieved examples, while recall is the ratio of the relevant examples retrieved over the total relevant examples in the database.

Two parameters for the proposed OMDL algorithm are set as follows: (i) k — the number of nearest neighbors for graph Laplacian $\mathbf{L}$ is set to 5 for the small-scale experiment in Table 1 and 50 for the image retrieval applications in Table 2; (ii) d_{LR} — the dimensionality of the low-rank matrix $\mathbf{W}_{LR}$ for OMDL-LR is set to 20 for the small-scale experiment and 100 for the image retrieval application. Finally, all the experiments were running in MATLAB on a Linux machine with 3GHz Intel CPU and 16GB RAM.

5.3 Feature Descriptors and Kernel Functions

Here we describe feature descriptors for image representation and the set of kernel functions used.

5.3.1 *Feature Descriptors for Image Representation*

We adopt both global and local feature descriptors to extract features for representing images.

For global features, we extract five kinds of features from images, including (1) color histogram and color moments (81 dimensions), (2) edge direction histogram (37 dimensions), (3) Gabor wavelets transform (120 dimensions), (4) Local Binary Pattern (59 dimensions), and (5) GIST features (512 dimensions). These global features have been widely adopted in previous CBIR studies.

For local features, we extract the bag-of-words features using two types of descriptors: (i) the SIFT descriptor, in which we adopt the Hessian-Affine interest region detector with threshold 500; and (ii) the SURF descriptor, in which we use the SURF detector with threshold 500. For the clustering step, we adopt a forest of 16 kd-trees and search 2048 neighbors to speed up the clustering task. Finally, we adopt the TF-IDF weighing scheme to generate the final bag-of-words for the local features. By choosing different descriptors (SIFT/SURF) and vocabulary sizes (200/1000), we totally extracted four kinds of local features: SIFT200, SIFT1000, SURF200 and SURF1000.

We apply PCA to all kinds of features and keep the first 50 dimensions (if the original dimension is less than 50, we keep all dimensions) to improve the efficiency of the experiment.

5.3.2 *Kernel Functions*

In the above, we represent each image in our database by a total of 9 types of different features. Based on these features, we can build a series of kernel functions on these features. Specifically, we adopt RBF kernel functions to build kernels on each kind of feature, which thus results in a total of 9 different kernels. RBF kernel is computed as $\kappa(\mathbf{x}, \mathbf{x}') = \exp(-\frac{d(\mathbf{x},\mathbf{x}')}{\gamma})$, where $d(\cdot, \cdot)$ is the Euclidean distance, the kernel parameter γ is selected as the mean of the pairwise distance.

5.4 Experiment I: Learning Distance on Small-Scale Data Sets

In this section, we follow the same setting as [32]. We build 3 small-scale data sets from the above benchmark data sets by first choosing 10 object categories, and then randomly sampling 20 examples from each category. We name them "Caltech(S)", "Corel(S)" and "ImageCLEF(S)" respectively. We adopt 5 kernels built from global features described in section 5.3 augmented by a set of kernels with five "noise" kernels, each of which was generated by sampling random points from the unit sphere in $\mathbb{R}^3$ and applying the RBF kernel.

5.4.1 *Comparison Algorithms*

In this experiment, we implemented the following algorithms for comparison:

- Kernel-Best: we test the performance of all the kernels on the validation set by adopting kernel value as similarity, and then select the best kernel with the highest performance;
- Kernel-U: we build a new kernel as the uniform combination of all kinds of kernels;
- Kernel-W: we test the performance of all kinds of kernels on the validation set by adopting kernel value as similarity, and then build a kernel as the weighted combination of all kinds of kernels where the weight is computed as e^{mAP_p}, $p = 1, 2, \ldots, m$;
- MKPOE: the existing MKPOE algorithm in [32];
- OMDL: the proposed algorithm in Algorithm 1;
- OMDL-LR: the proposed fast OMDL algorithm in Section 4.4 which learns a low rank matrix by random projection to speed up OMDL.

5.4.2 Experimental Results

Table 1 summarizes the experimental results of the compared algorithms on three small-scale data sets. Some observations can be drawn from the results as follows.

First, we can see that both Kernel-U and Kernel-W beat Kernel-Best on "Caltech(S)", but fail on the other two data sets. This implies that kernel combination is possible to improve the performance, but if the combination weight is not assigned appropriately, it could even decrease the performance.

Second, we found that MKPOE significantly outperforms Kernel-Best, Kernel-U, and Kernel-W, which shows the importance of learning the multi-modal distance.

Third, we found that OMDL not only significantly improves the accuracy performance of MKPOE, but also spends much less time. On average, OMDL is about 30 times faster than MKPOE.

Finally, OMDL-LR can further improve the efficiency while maintain comparable performance with OMDL. On overage, OMDL-LR is about 450 times faster than MKPOE.

5.5 Experiment II: Learning Distance for Medium-scale Image Retrieval Applications

In this section, we examine the proposed algorithm on some medium-scale image retrieval data sets, which have been widely used for benchmarking.

5.5.1 Comparison Algorithms

To examine the efficacy of the proposed algorithms extensively, we have compared our technique with a variety of state-of-the-art algorithms as follows:

- Kernel-Best: we test the performance of all the kernels on the validation set by adopting kernel value as similarity, and then select the best kernel with the highest performance;
- RCA-Best: we train RCA [3] model on the training set for all the features and test each model on the validation set, and then select the best feature with the highest mAP for RCA;
- KRCA-Best: we train KRCA [40] model on the training set for all the kernels and test each model on the validation set, and then select the best kernel of the highest mAP for KRCA;
- LMNN-Best: we train LMNN [43] model on the training set for all the features and test each model on the validation set, and then select the best feature of the highest mAP for LMNN;
- OASIS-Best: we train OASIS [7] model on the training set for all the features and test each model on the validation set, and then select the best feature of the highest mAP for OASIS;
- Kernel-Con: we build a kernel on the concatenation of all kinds of features together;
- RCA-Con: we concatenate all kinds of features together first, and then run RCA;
- KRCA-Con: we concatenate all kinds of features together first, and the run KRCA;
- LMNN-Con: we concatenate all kinds of features together first, and then run LMNN;
- OASIS-Con: we concatenate all kinds of features together first, and then run OASIS;
- Kernel-U: we build a new kernel as the uniform combination of all kinds of kernels;
- Kernel-W: we test the performance of all kinds of kernels on the validation set by adopting kernel value as similarity, and then build a kernel as the weighted combination of all kinds of kernels where the weight is computed as e^{mAP_p}, $p = 1, 2, \ldots, m$;
- OMDL-LR: the proposed fast OMDL algorithm in Section 4.4 which learns a low rank matrix by random projection to speed up OMDL.

Remark. We note that we will only apply OMDL-LR to the rest experiments and exclude MKPOE and OMDL because of two key reasons: (i) MKPOE is not practical for large data sets due to its extremely low efficiency, which can be seen from the previous experiment; (ii) OMDL-LR is able to improve the efficiency of OMDL while maintaining comparable learning efficacy.

5.5.2 Experimental Results

Table 2 summarizes the experimental results of mAP performance of the compared algorithms on some standard benchmark data sets, and Figure 2 illustrates the details of the top-n precision results on one of the data sets. We can draw some observations from the results as follows.

First, by comparing Kernel-Best with Kernel-U and Kernel-W, it is obvious that kernel combination can lead to better performance, and the weighted combination outperforms uniform combination.

Second, we found that those methods based on concatenated feature outperform those based on best feature in some cases, such as "Corel5000" and "ImageCLEF" , but fail on the other data sets. This implies that feature concatenation is not optimal to combine different kinds of features.

Finally, by examining the results of OMDL-LR, we found that it outperforms the other algorithms on all the data sets. This promising result shows that the proposed OMDL algorithm is able to learn an effective distance function on multi-modal data.

5.6 Experiment III: Learning Distance for Large-scale Image Retrieval Applications

In this section, we apply the proposed algorithm on a large-scale image retrieval application to test its scalability. The data set we use is "ImageCLEF+", which is a combination of "ImageCLEF" and 1 million social photos crawled from Flickr. The compared algorithms are the same as those in the previous section. Experimental results of mAP performance are shown in the last column of Table 2. Figure 3 also illustrate the details of the top-n precision results.

Similar observations can be drawn from these results. Kernel combination (Kernel-U and Kernel-W) can lead to better performance than Kernel-Best, and the weighted combination outperforms uniform combination. Those methods based on concatenated feature outperform those based on best feature on this data set. And it is obvious that OMDL-LR outperforms all the other algorithms. The promising results show that the proposed algorithm can learn an effective distance function with multi-modal data for large-scale image retrieval applications.

Table 2: Experimental results of distance learning for image retrieval applications.

Algorithm	Metric	Caltech10	Caltech20	Caltech50	Corel5000	ImageCLEF	ImageCLEF+
Kernel-Best	mAP	0.2315	0.1657	0.1010	0.1789	0.4090	0.0959
	std	±0.0000	±0.0000	±0.0000	±0.0000	±0.0000	±0.0000
RCA-Best	mAP	0.2343	0.1714	0.1012	0.1801	0.4709	0.1098
	std	±0.0003	±0.0001	±0.0001	±0.0001	±0.0004	±0.0002
KRCA-Best	mAP	0.2489	0.1867	0.1087	0.2113	0.5497	0.1078
	std	±0.0004	±0.0003	±0.0001	±0.0002	±0.0012	±0.0008
LMNN-Best	mAP	0.2365	0.1696	0.1049	0.1909	0.4939	0.1069
	std	±0.0013	±0.0014	±0.0002	±0.0002	±0.0013	±0.0019
OASIS-Best	mAP	0.2472	0.1852	0.1010	0.1797	0.4325	0.1062
	std	±0.0036	±0.0052	±0.0000	±0.0054	±0.0087	±0.0115
Kernel-Con	mAP	0.2115	0.1609	0.0998	0.2518	0.3959	0.1598
	std	±0.0000	±0.0000	±0.0000	±0.0000	±0.0000	±0.0000
RCA-Con	mAP	0.2173	0.1699	0.1040	0.2591	0.5044	0.2176
	std	±0.0001	±0.0002	±0.0000	±0.0002	±0.0006	±0.0009
KRCA-Con	mAP	0.2404	0.1955	0.1114	0.3240	0.5797	0.1936
	std	±0.0008	±0.0001	±0.0001	±0.0002	±0.0012	±0.0005
LMNN-Con	mAP	0.2419	0.1781	0.1097	0.2768	0.5373	0.2272
	std	±0.0009	±0.0013	±0.0002	±0.0005	±0.0021	±0.0030
OASIS-Con	mAP	0.2350	0.1633	0.1001	0.2518	0.4518	0.1560
	std	±0.0044	±0.0043	±0.0004	±0.0077	±0.0119	±0.0047
Kernel-U	mAP	0.2536	0.2133	0.1247	0.3310	0.4415	0.2554
	std	±0.0000	±0.0000	±0.0000	±0.0000	±0.0000	±0.0000
Kernel-W	mAP	0.2557	0.2148	0.1253	0.3321	0.4602	0.2682
	std	±0.0000	±0.0000	±0.0000	±0.0000	±0.0000	±0.0000
OMDL-LR	mAP	**0.3377**	**0.2498**	**0.1356**	**0.3639**	**0.6136**	**0.3147**
	std	**±0.0047**	**±0.0025**	**±0.0004**	**±0.0068**	**±0.0098**	**±0.0220**

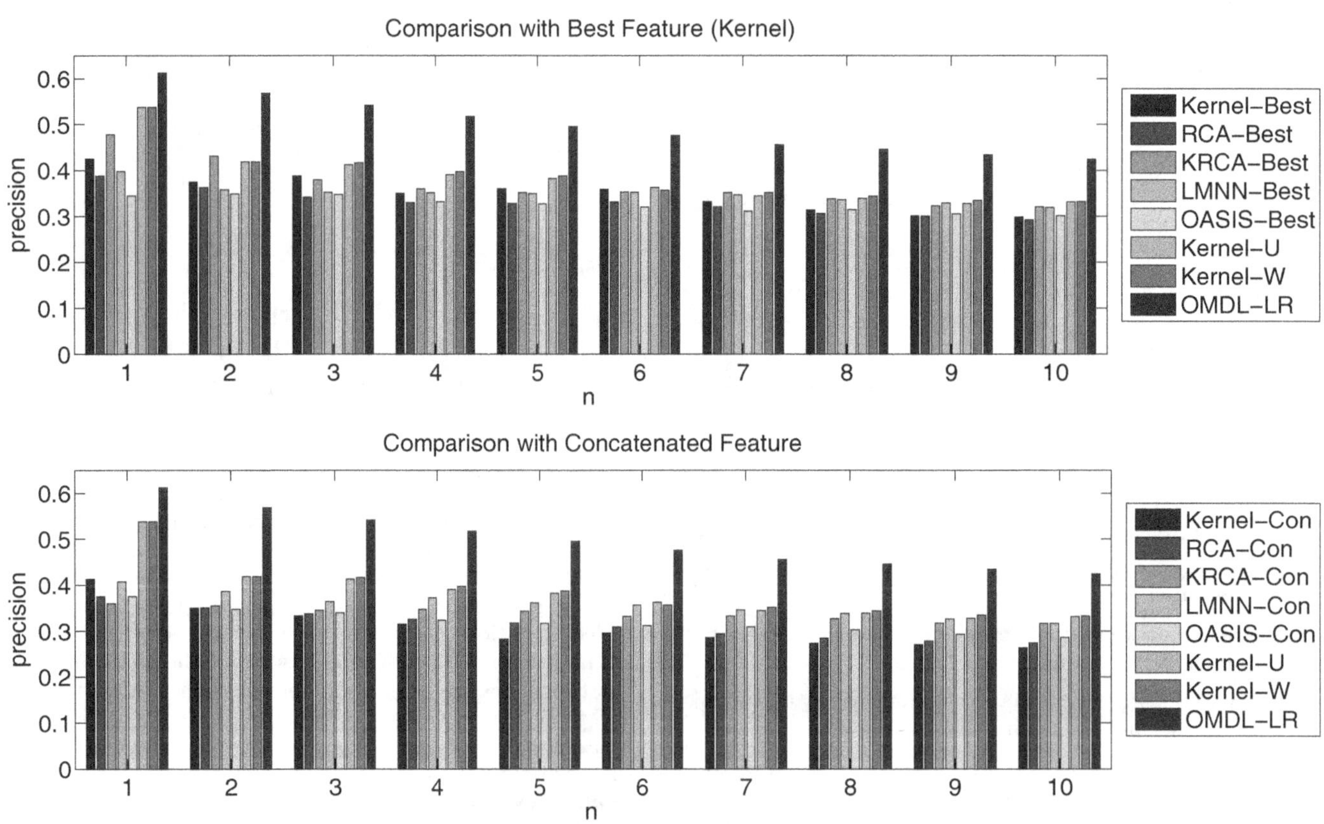

Figure 2: Top-n precision of retrieval results on "Caltech10" data set.

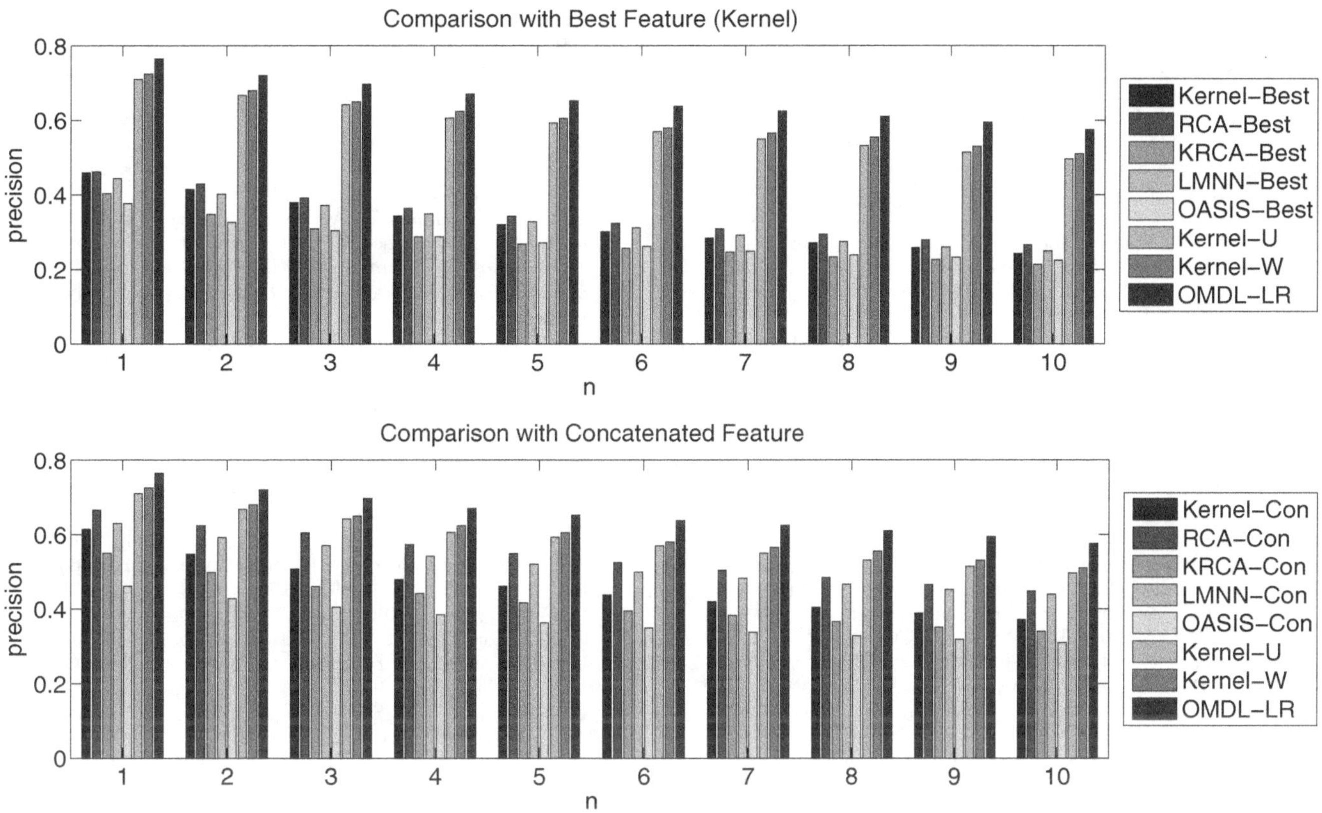

Figure 3: Top-n precision of retrieval results on "ImageCLEF+" data set.

6. CONCLUSIONS

This paper addressed an important challenge of learning proximity functions on multi-modal data for multimedia retrieval. Unlike the previous Multiple Kernel Partial Order Embedding (MKPOE) which suffers from poor efficiency and scalability, this paper proposed a novel framework of Online Multi-modal Distance Learning (OMDL), which on one hand enhances the learning efficacy of MKPOE by exploiting underlying data distribution via the graph Laplacian, and on the other hand significantly improves the efficiency and scalability via an online learning scheme. In this paper, we developed efficient online learning algorithms and extensively evaluated the proposed OMDL algorithms on several public image data sets. The empirical results showed that the proposed OMDL algorithms are not only more effective than the MKPOE technique, but also significantly more efficient and scalable for large-scale applications. Future work will explore theoretical analysis of our technique.

Acknowledgments

This work was in part supported by Singapore MOE Academic tier-1 grant (RG33/11) and Microsoft Research grant.

7. REFERENCES

[1] S. Aksoy and R. M. Haralick. Probabilistic vs. geometric similarity measures for image retrieval. In *Proceedings of IEEE Conference on Computer Vision and Pattern Recognition*, pages 2357–2362, 2000.

[2] N. Aronszajn. Theory of reproducing kernels. *Transactions of the American Mathematical Society*, 68(3):337–404, 1950.

[3] A. Bar-Hillel, T. Hertz, N. Shental, and D. Weinshall. Learning distance functions using equivalence relations. In *International Conference on Machine Learning*, pages 11–18, 2003.

[4] A. Bar-Hillel, T. Hertz, N. Shental, and D. Weinshall. Learning a mahalanobis metric from equivalence constraints. *Journal of Machine Learning Research*, 6:937–965, 2005.

[5] E. Bingham and H. Mannila. Random projection in dimensionality reduction: applications to image and text data. In *KDD*, pages 245–250, 2001.

[6] H. Chang and D.-Y. Yeung. Kernel-based distance metric learning for content-based image retrieval. *Image Vision Comput.*, 25(5):695–703, 2007.

[7] G. Chechik, V. Sharma, U. Shalit, and S. Bengio. Large scale online learning of image similarity through ranking. *Journal of Machine Learning Research*, 11:1109–1135, 2010.

[8] K. Crammer, O. Dekel, J. Keshet, S. Shalev-Shwartz, and Y. Singer. Online passive-aggressive algorithms. *Journal of Machine Learning Research*, 7:551–585, 2006.

[9] P. V. Gehler and S. Nowozin. On feature combination for multiclass object classification. In *ICCV*, pages 221–228, 2009.

[10] A. Globerson and S. Roweis. Metric learning by collapsing classes. In *Advances in Neural Information Processing Systems*, 2005.

[11] D. Grangier and S. Bengio. A discriminative kernel-based approach to rank images from text queries. *IEEE Trans. Pattern Anal. Mach. Intell.*, 30(8):1371–1384, 2008.

[12] G. Griffin, A. Holub, and P. Perona. Caltech-256 object category dataset. Technical Report 7694, California Institute of Technology, 2007.

[13] G. Guo, A. K. Jain, W.-Y. Ma, and H.-J. Zhang. Learning similarity measure for natural image retrieval with relevance feedback. *IEEE Transactions on Neural Networks*, 13(4):811–820, 2002.

[14] S. C. H. Hoi and R. Jin. Active kernel learning. In *Proceedings of International Conference on Machine Learning*, pages 400–407, 2008.

[15] S. C. H. Hoi, R. Jin, and M. R. Lyu. Learning nonparametric kernel matrices from pairwise constraints. In *Proceedings of International Conference on Machine Learning*, pages 361–368, 2007.

[16] S. C. H. Hoi, R. Jin, P. Zhao, and T. Yang. Online multiple kernel classification. *Machine Learning*, 2012. to appear.

[17] S. C. H. Hoi, W. Liu, and S.-F. Chang. Semi-supervised distance metric learning for collaborative image retrieval and clustering. *ACM Trans. Multimedia Comput. Commun. Appl.*, 6(3):18:1–18:26, Aug. 2010.

[18] S. C. H. Hoi, W. Liu, M. R. Lyu, and W.-Y. Ma. Learning distance metrics with contextual constraints for image retrieval. In *IEEE Conference on Computer Vision and Pattern Recognition*, New York, US, June 17–22 2006.

[19] S. C. H. Hoi and M. R. Lyu. A multimodal and multilevel ranking scheme for large-scale video retrieval. *IEEE Transactions on Multimedia*, 10(4):607–619, June 2008.

[20] S. C. H. Hoi, M. R. Lyu, and R. Jin. A unified log-based relevance feedback scheme for image retrieval. *IEEE Trans. KDE*, 18(4):509–204, 2006.

[21] A. Jain, S. V. N. Vishwanathan, and M. Varma. Spg-gmkl: Generalized multiple kernel learning with a million kernels. In *Proceedings of the ACM SIGKDD Conference on Knowledge Discovery and Data Mining*, August 2012.

[22] P. Jain, B. Kulis, J. V. Davis, and I. S. Dhillon. Metric and kernel learning using a linear transformation. *Journal of Machine Learning Research*, 13:519–547, 2012.

[23] S. Ji, L. Sun, R. Jin, and J. Ye. Multi-label multiple kernel learning. In *Advances in Neural Information Processing Systems*, 2008.

[24] R. Jin, S. C. H. Hoi, and T. Yang. Online multiple kernel learning: Algorithms and mistake bounds. In *ALT*, pages 390–404, 2010.

[25] Y. Jing and S. Baluja. Visualrank: Applying pagerank to large-scale image search. *IEEE Trans. Pattern Anal. Mach. Intell.*, 30(11):1877–1890, 2008.

[26] A. Kumar and C. Sminchisescu. Support kernel machines for object recognition. In *ICCV*, pages 1–8, 2007.

[27] G. R. G. Lanckriet, N. Cristianini, P. Bartlett, L. E. Ghaoui, and M. I. Jordan. Learning the kernel matrix with semidefinite programming. *Journal of Machine Learning Research*, 5:27–72, 2004.

[28] J.-E. Lee, R. Jin, and A. K. Jain. Rank-based distance metric learning: An application to image retrieval. In *Proceedings of IEEE Conference on Computer Vision and Pattern Recognition*, Anchorage, AK, 2008.

[29] M. S. Lew, N. Sebe, C. Djeraba, and R. Jain. Content-based multimedia information retrieval: State of the art and challenges. *ACM Trans. Multimedia Comput. Commun. Appl.*, 2(1):1–19, 2006.

[30] B. Li, E. Y. Chang, and Y.-L. Wu. Discovery of a perceptual distance function for measuring image similarity. *Multimedia Syst.*, 8(6):512–522, 2003.

[31] C. D. Manning, P. Raghavan, and H. Schütze. *Introduction to information retrieval.* Cambridge University Press, 2008.

[32] B. McFee and G. R. G. Lanckriet. Learning multi-modal similarity. *Journal of Machine Learning Research*, 12:491–523, 2011.

[33] A. Qamra, Y. Meng, and E. Y. Chang. Enhanced perceptual distance functions and indexing for image replica recognition. *IEEE Trans. Pattern Anal. Mach. Intell.*, 27(3):379–391, 2005.

[34] R. Rahmani, S. A. Goldman, H. Zhang, S. R. Cholleti, and J. E. Fritts. Localized content-based image retrieval. *IEEE Trans. Pattern Anal. Mach. Intell.*, 30(11):1902–1912, 2008.

[35] B. Schölkopf, R. Herbrich, and A. J. Smola. A generalized representer theorem. In *COLT/EuroCOLT*, pages 416–426, 2001.

[36] L. Si, R. Jin, S. C. H. Hoi, and M. R. Lyu. Collaborative image retrieval via regularized metric learning. *ACM Multimedia Systems Journal*, 12(1):34–44, 2006.

[37] V. Sindhwani, P. Niyogi, and M. Belkin. Beyond the point cloud: from transductive to semi-supervised learning. In *ICML*, pages 824–831, 2005.

[38] A. W. M. Smeulders, M. Worring, S. Santini, A. Gupta, and R. Jain. Content-based image retrieval at the end of the early years. *IEEE Trans. PAMI*, 22(12):1349–1380, 2000.

[39] S. Sonnenburg, G. Rätsch, C. Schäfer, and B. Schölkopf. Large scale multiple kernel learning. *Journal of Machine Learning Research*, 7:1531–1565, 2006.

[40] I. W. Tsang, P. ming Cheung, and J. T. Kwok. Kernel relevant component analysis for distance metric learning. In *IEEE International Joint Conference on Neural Networks (IJCNN)*, pages 954–959, 2005.

[41] M. Varma and B. R. Babu. More generality in efficient multiple kernel learning. In *Proceedings of International Conference on Machine Learning*, pages 1065–1072, 2009.

[42] S. V. N. Vishwanathan, Z. sun, N. Ampornpunt, and M. Varma. Multiple kernel learning and the smo algorithm. In *NIPS*, pages 2361–2369, 2010.

[43] K. Weinberger, J. Blitzer, and L. Saul. Distance metric learning for large margin nearest neighbor classification. In *Advances in Neural Information Processing Systems*, pages 1473–1480, 2006.

[44] C. Williams and M. Seeger. Using the nyström method to speed up kernel machines. In *Advances in Neural Information Processing Systems 13*, pages 682–688. MIT Press, 2001.

[45] L. Wu, S. C. H. Hoi, R. Jin, J. Zhu, and N. Yu. Distance metric learning from uncertain side information with application to automated photo tagging. In *ACM Multimedia*, pages 135–144, 2009.

[46] L. Wu, S. C. H. Hoi, and N. Yu. Semantics-preserving bag-of-words models and applications. *Trans. Img. Proc.*, 19(7):1908–1920, July 2010.

[47] P. Wu, S. C. H. Hoi, P. Zhao, and Y. He. Mining social images with distance metric learning for automated image tagging. In *Proceedings of the fourth ACM international conference on Web search and data mining*, WSDM '11, pages 197–206, Hong Kong, China, 2011. ACM.

[48] E. P. Xing, A. Y. Ng, M. I. Jordan, and S. Russell. Distance metric learning with application to clustering with side-information. In *Advances in Neural Information Processing Systems*, 2002.

[49] Z. Xu, R. Jin, I. King, and M. R. Lyu. An extended level method for efficient multiple kernel learning. In *Advances in Neural Information Processing Systems*, 2008.

[50] L. Yang, R. Jin, L. B. Mummert, R. Sukthankar, A. Goode, B. Zheng, S. C. H. Hoi, and M. Satyanarayanan. A boosting framework for visuality-preserving distance metric learning and its application to medical image retrieval. *IEEE Trans. Pattern Anal. Mach. Intell.*, 32(1):30–44, 2010.

[51] D.-Y. Yeung and H. Chang. A kernel approach for semisupervised metric learning. *IEEE Transactions on Neural Networks*, 18(1):141–149, 2007.

[52] J. Zhuang and S. C. H. Hoi. A two-view learning approach for image tag ranking. In *Proceedings of the fourth ACM international conference on Web search and data mining*, WSDM'11, pages 625–634, Hong Kong, China, 2011.

[53] J. Zhuang, I. W. Tsang, and S. C. H. Hoi. A family of simple non-parametric kernel learning algorithms. *Journal of Machine Learning Research*, 12:1313–1347, 2011.

[54] A. Zien and C. S. Ong. Multiclass multiple kernel learning. In *Proceedings of International Conference on Machine Learning*, pages 1191–1198, Corvalis, Oregon, 2007.

Unsupervised Graph-based Topic Labelling using DBpedia

Ioana Hulpuş, Conor Hayes, Marcel Karnstedt
Digital Enterprise Research Institute (DERI)
National University of Ireland
Galway, Ireland
{*first.last*}@deri.org

Derek Greene
School of Computer Science and Informatics
University College Dublin
Dublin, Ireland
Derek.Greene@ucd.ie

ABSTRACT

Automated topic labelling brings benefits for users aiming at analysing and understanding document collections, as well as for search engines targetting at the linkage between groups of words and their inherent topics. Current approaches to achieve this suffer in quality, but we argue their performances might be improved by setting the focus on the structure in the data. Building upon research for concept disambiguation and linking to DBpedia, we are taking a novel approach to topic labelling by making use of structured data exposed by DBpedia. We start from the hypothesis that words co-occuring in text likely refer to concepts that belong closely together in the DBpedia graph. Using graph centrality measures, we show that we are able to identify the concepts that best represent the topics. We comparatively evaluate our graph-based approach and the standard text-based approach, on topics extracted from three corpora, based on results gathered in a crowd-sourcing experiment. Our research shows that graph-based analysis of DBpedia can achieve better results for topic labelling in terms of both precision and topic coverage.

Categories and Subject Descriptors

E.1 [**Data Structures**]: Graphs and networks; H.3.1 [**Information Storage and Retrieval**]: Content Analysis and Indexing—*Linguistic processing*; H.3.5 [**Information Storage and Retrieval**]: Information Search and Retrieval—*Selection process*

Keywords

Topic labelling; Graph centrality measures; DBpedia; Latent Dirichlet Allocation (LDA);

1. INTRODUCTION

One of the most popular approaches for identifying the subject matter of a collection of documents is to determine its inherently addressed topics. Several methods have been proposed for probabilistic topic modelling, such as Latent Dirichlet Allocation (LDA) [2], Pachinko Allocation [11] or Probabilistic Latent Semantic Analysis (pLSA) [7]. They model the documents as a mixture of topics, where each topic is treated as a probability distribution over words. As such, topics consist of groups of co-occurring words, ranked by their relevance. Such models are largely used in the domain of text analysis for summarising big document corpora.

Typically users have then to interpret these sets of words in order to label the underlying concepts for further processing and classification. Labelling in this context refers to finding one or a few single phrases, or better concepts, that sufficiently describe the topic in question. This can become a cumbersome task when a corpus is summarised by some hundreds of topics. In this light, automatic topic labelling becomes an important problem to solve in order to support users in their task to efficiently and conveniently analyse, understand and explore document collections. Besides that, it further promises benefits for web search engines, as it allows clustering groups of words under the same umbrella term.

Furthermore, there is an increased interest in research on linking text documents to external knowledge bases that are often created collaboratively by communities and validated by multiple experts. Many benefits are expected to result from this integration, in areas like information retrieval, classification and knowledge discovery and visualisation. One of best known multidomain knowledge bases is DBpedia[1], which extracts structured information from Wikipedia in the form of an openly accessible, consensus driven semantic graph of concepts and relations. This paper describes an approach to automatically extract topic labels by linking the inherent topics of a text to concepts found in DBpedia and mining the resulting semantic topic graphs. Our aim is not only to find a good label itself, but also to integrate the topic into a knowledge base to support subsequent exploitation and navigation of related concepts. An important aspect of our work is therefore to relate a topic label with a URI identifying a concept, which opens the way for facilitating knowledge exploration in DBpedia – and far beyond, based on its rich linkage within Linked Open Data project.

We argue that current approaches for topic labelling based on content analysis capture the essence of a topic only to a limited extent. Mainly, because they do not focus on the structure behind the concepts, nor on the navigation and exploration of these topics. We hypothesise that concepts co-occurring in the text are also closely related in the DB-

[1]`http://dbpedia.org`

WSDM'13, February 4–8, 2013, Rome, Italy.

pedia graph. Using graph centrality measures, we are able to identify the concepts that are most likely to represent the topics and are therefore suited to label them. Our contribution can be summarised as follows:

1. We propose a novel approach for topic labelling that relies only on structured data – and provides means to fully exploit its potential. The method does not require any pre-processing and can thus be run directly on-line against queryable knowledge bases like DBpedia.
2. The approach is suited for finding a good label *and* for integrating the topic into a knowledge base to support subsequent exploitation and navigation of related concepts.
3. We show that graph-based algorithms can be used with success to label topics and that they provide richer knowledge than purely text-based methods.
4. We present a thorough comparative evaluation, based on human judgements about the quality of labels, collected through a crowd-sourcing experiment.

Section 2 discusses related work, and in Section 3 we briefly overview the overall framework that comprises the topic modelling proposed in this work. Based on a motivating example, we formalise the problem statement and introduce the general principle of our solution. We present our approach for graph-based topic labelling in Section 4. We examine particular important aspects of our approach and compare it to the standard text-based approach in terms of precision and topic coverage in Section 5. This evaluation is based on the results from a crowd-sourcing experiment involving texts from three different document corpora. Finally, we conclude in Section 6.

2. RELATED WORK

Several works [15, 12, 10] consider topic labelling in the same scenario as we do, where topics represented by a set of words have to be labelled. A second relevant area considers labelling of document clusters [24, 3, 17, 21]. Similar to the first scenario, document clusters are often summarised as a collection of the most prominent words they contain. The third related direction deals with annotations for indexing [4, 23, 14], also called automatic topic identification [4]. In contrast to identifying exactly one or a couple of labels, this aims for identifying as many as possible concepts that are strongly related to the document in question. Despite these different application domains, the various approaches are better distinguished by the techniques they use.

A significant part of the approaches *extracts* the most likely label from the text, such as [17, 24, 15]. An important drawback is that they rely on the assumptions that (i) the correct label can be found in the documents, and that (ii) the corpus is rich enough to identify a label with confidence. However, this is not always the case. For example, a cluster of documents might be about *artificial intelligence* without mentioning the phrase. On the other hand, it might contain many more specialised phrases that cannot be related just based on the text (e.g., *probabilistic reasoning* and *first-order logic*). This problem can be overcome by the use of external data sources. Besides the work in hand, this idea motivates a wide range of recent research [21, 3, 12, 10, 4, 23, 14].

The probably most popular external knowledge base for this purpose is Wikipedia. Usually, a Wikipedia dump is pre-processed into a local data structure that is subsequently analysed in order to extract suitable labels. [21] manipulates the Wikipedia dump by deconstructing it into a collection of minipages corresponding to subsections of Wikipedia article. The label for the document cluster is selected out of the sections' headings. Besides using Wikipedia, the authors of [10] also query the Google web search engine to obtain label candidates. [4] uses the entire English Wikipedia to build a so-called *encyclopedic graph*. In this graph, the nodes represent Wikipedia articles and their categories. Afterwards, a biased PageRank algorithm is used to weight the nodes of the graph with respect to the queried key-phrases. Unfortunately, the work does not provide enough details to be able to reconstruct the graph. The approach proposed by [23] uses a simplified spreading activation algorithm on the graph consisting of Wikipedia articles and their categories. It relies on the cosine similarity between article texts and the texts of the target documents. While also being graph-based, the work presents only very small scale "informal evaluation". All the aforementioned approaches using Wikipedia strongly differ from our approach, as they analyse the content of Wikipedia articles in order to decide on the proper label. This makes the algorithms hard to adapt to data sources that are less rich in content and do not contain encyclopedic text about concepts Our approach is fully structured and independent of the content of Wikipedia articles.

Another topic-labelling approach using an external data source is [12]. This approach differs from our work and the aforementioned ones by relying on a tree-structured external data source, the Open Directory Project[2]. The authors model each node of the hierarchy as a list of words and compare the topics to label with the nodes in the hierarchy based on various similarity measures. Using a novel algorithm, they select and reuse the label of the most similar node. However, this approach is particularly suited for use-cases providing a given hierarchy that has to match the clusters of the corpus. For less constrained scenarios, as we illustrate in Section 3.2, we see strict usage of tree-shaped knowledge bases as problematic.

Our approach differs from all the above works from three perspectives: First, it uses only structured data in order to identify the labels, which strictly correspond to concepts found in DBpedia. Second, the analysed graphs are not pre-processed off-line. Thus, it can be used entirely on-line by querying knowledge bases, such as the DBpedia SPARQL endpoint[3]. Third, for identifying suitable labels, we adapt and experiment with popular graph-based centrality measures that have not been used before for this task.

3. OVERVIEW

The topic labelling approach proposed in this work is part of a larger framework supporting automated topic analysis, called *Canopy*. Figure 1 illustrates its overall architecture. In this section, we present an overview of the system and formally define the problem that this work focuses on. We also introduce the main notation and terms used throughout the paper.

[2] http://www.dmoz.org

[3] dbpedia.sparql.endpoint

3.1 The Canopy Framework

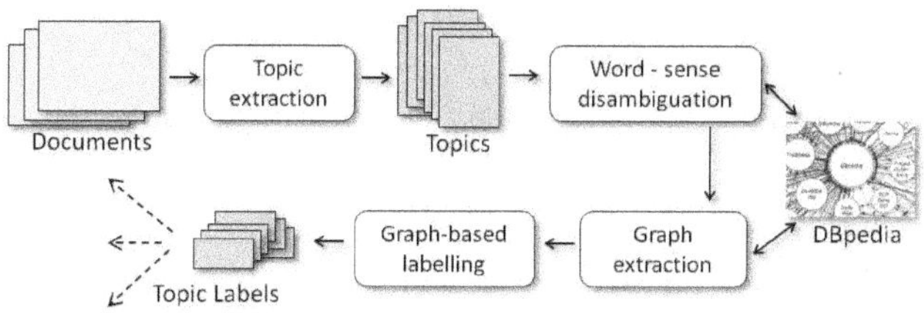

Figure 1: *Canopy* framework for automated topic analysis

At the time of writing this paper, Canopy consists of four main components: the topic extraction, the word-sense disambiguation (WSD), the graph extraction and the graph-based labelling. These are the basic building blocks on top of which we envision a range of possible application scenarios: corpus summarisation, visualisation, browsing and extraction of new knowledge by uncovering latent dependencies and relations between topics or domains, etc.

The topic extraction applies the LDA probabilistic topic model [2] to extract *topics* from a corpus of documents. For the sake of generality, we consider each topic θ as a set of *words* (rather than a probability distribution over words). In previous work [9], we have demonstrated a novel graph-based approach to WSD that addresses the linking problem. The WSD determines a set $\mathbf{C}^\theta$ of DBpedia *concepts*, where each $C \in \mathbf{C}^\theta$ represents the identified *sense* of one of the top-k words of a topic θ. Usually, it is neither feasible nor required to relate all top-k words to a concept.

In this paper, we propose a solution for the third and fourth stage of the Canopy process, which together provide the actual topic labelling. In the following, we provide a motivating example and then formalise the underlying problem.

3.2 Example

An intuitive approach for labelling topics represented by a set of concepts $\mathbf{C}^\theta$ is to determine a minimum spanning tree encompassing all $C \in \mathbf{C}^\theta$ from an according hierarchical knowledge base. The least common subsumer in such a tree could then be chosen as a label. However, this would most often produce very generic terms, very close to the root of the overall hierarchy of concepts. This is mainly due to the nature of probabilistic topic models, which do not necessarily group concepts of the same type. Consider a topic θ described by [**`patient, drug, hospital, health, professional`** ...]. All top five words come from very different branches of a standard knowledge base like WordNet. In this case, the least common subsumer is the very root of the WordNet hierarchy: *Entity*. Similarly, in DBpedia's structure of categories, the least common subsumer is *Life*. However, a considerably good label would be *Health* itself, *Healthcare* or even *Medicine*. *Healthcare* is the least common subsumer of **`patient, drug`** and **`hospital`**, and a child of *Health*. *Medicine*, however, is only subsuming **`drug`**.

In order to identify good labels we can thus not rely on the simple least common subsumer. This motivates us to to exploit graph specific methods on graph-based knowledge repositories, in our case DBpedia. The example also illustrates the main challenges of this approach, which we formalise next.

3.3 Problem Statement and General Approach

In this paper, we consider the task of topic labelling independent of the way the topics have been linked and disambiguated to DBpedia concepts. We formulate the problem as follows: Let $\mathbf{C}^\theta$ be a set of n DBpedia concepts C_i, $i = 1,..,n$, that correspond to a subset of the top-k words representing one topic θ. The problem is to identify the concept $\mathcal{C}^*$ from all available concepts in DBpedia, such that the relation $r(\mathbf{C}^\theta, \mathcal{C}^*)$ is optimised. Thus, the main challenges are:

1. to extract an appropriate set of concepts from DBpedia as candidates for $\mathcal{C}^*$, and

2. to define r, which quantifies the strength of the relation between the concepts $C_i \in \mathbf{C}^\theta$ and $\mathcal{C}^*$, in a way resulting in topic labels that are meaningful for humans.

We propose to extract a good candidate set by extracting a *topic graph* $\mathbf{G}$ from DBpedia consisting of the close neighbours of concepts C_i and the links between them (*graph extraction*). Then, we investigate how to define the relation r by analysing the conceptual graph of DBpedia underlying $\mathbf{G}$. We adopt principles from social network analysis to identify in $\mathbf{G}$ the most prominent concepts for labelling a topic θ (*graph-based labelling*).

4. GRAPH-BASED TOPIC LABELLING

The intuition behind our approach is that as the concepts of a topic are related, they should lie close in the DBpedia graph. This implies that by expanding from each such concept for a few hops, all the topic concepts will ideally form one connected graph. The graph extraction phase uses this inutition to address the problem of finding label candidates. The sense graph of each concept is defined as follows:

Definition 1. The *sense graph* of a concept C_i is an undirected graph $G_i = (V_i, E_i, C_i)$, where V_i is the set of nodes and E_i is the set of edges connecting the nodes. $C_i \in V_i$ is a DBpedia concept called the *seed concept* or *seed node* of graph G_i.

The topic graph $\mathbf{G}$ is a union of the sense graphs of one topic. It is passed as the result of the graph extraction phase to the actual graph-based labelling step.

Definition 2. Let $\mathbf{C}^\theta = \{C_1, .., C_n\}$ be the set of DBpedia concepts corresponding to the disambiguated senses of the words in the latent topic θ, and let $G_i = (V_i, E_i, C_i)$ be the sense graph corresponding to C_i, $\forall i \in 1,..,n$. Then, if $\mathbf{V} = \bigcup V_i$, and $\mathbf{E} = \bigcup E_i$, then $\mathbf{G} = (\mathbf{V}, \mathbf{E}, \mathbf{C}^\theta)$ is called the *topic graph* of θ, and the concepts $C_i \in \mathbf{C}^\theta$ are the *seed concepts* or *seed nodes* of $\mathbf{G}$.

The second problem, to define a measure for assessing the goodness of all candidate topics, is solved by applying adapted graph centrality measures on the topic graph. This is based on the assumption that a good topic label should be a central node in the topic graph, with respect to the seed nodes. We discuss the benefits of different centrality measures, the reasons for adapting and the resulting formulae for computing them in Section 4.3.

4.1 DBpedia Graph Extraction

The objective of the graph extraction is to identify candidate *concepts* from DBpedia suited to label the topic and to provide an entry point for further knowledge exploration. Starting from the seed node, we want to follow edges of certain type (i.e., "properties") to reach other nodes representing candidate concepts (i.e., "entities" identified by URIs). Because the topic labelling can be seen as assigning classes to topics, we focus mainly on the DBpedia class structure. DBpedia provides three different classification schemata for things, which we describe below. While there is overlap between them, each is derived from a different part of Wikipedia using different processes. As such, our approach will combine the data from these schemata to build topic graphs rather than strict concept hierarchies.

Wikipedia Categories The Wikipedia categorisation system provides a valuable source for categorising the concepts found in DBpedia. It contains 740,000 categories whose structure and relationships are represented by the Simple Knowledge Organization System Vocabulary (prefixed by `skos:`) [25]. The linkage between DBpedia concepts and Wikipedia categories is defined using the `subject` property of the DCIM terms vocabulary (prefixed by `dcterms:`) [8]. We can then extract a category's parent and child categories by querying for the properties `skos:broader` and `skos:broaderOf`. This structure is not a proper hierarchy as it contains cycles [1].

YAGO The YAGO vocabulary represents an ontology automatically extracted from Wikipedia and WordNet [6]. It is linked to DBpedia and contains 365,372 classes. Classes are organised hierarchically and can be navigated using the `rdfs:type` property and `rdfs:subClassOf` property. For example, the DBpedia entity *dbres:Elvis_Presley* has property `rdfs:type` *yago:wikicategory_American_rock_singers*, which in turn has a `rdfs:subClassOf` property of *yago:wordnet_singer_110599806*.

DBpedia Ontology The DBpedia ontology is a shallow, cross-domain ontology that has been manually created based on the most commonly used infoboxes in Wikipedia [1]. It contains 320 classes organised into a subsumption hierarchy. In a similar way to the YAGO approach, DBpedia concepts can be navigated following the `rdfs:subClassOf` and `rdfs:type` properties.

Given a topic θ, for each concept $C_i \in \mathbf{C}^\theta$, we extract a sense graph G_i by querying for all nodes lying at most two hops away from C_i, recursively taking into account all existing edges of type `skos:broader`, `skos:broaderOf`, `rdfs:subClassOf`, `rdfs:type` and `dcterms:subject`. We then merge the sense graphs together, obtaining the topic graph $\mathbf{G}$. The decision to use a distance of two-hops was made after several experiments with node expansions. Expanding the nodes of coherent topics to three hops tended to produce very large graphs and introduce a lot of noise.

Figure 2 exemplifies the graph extraction phase. At the top, it shows four sense graphs for a topic consisting of four DBpedia concepts or 'resources' (prefixed as `dbres:`): `dbres:Energy`, `dbres:Atom`, `dbres:Electron` and `dbres:Quantum`. The dark nodes represent the seed nodes corresponding to these concepts. At the bottom, the figure shows the topic graph obtained by merging them.

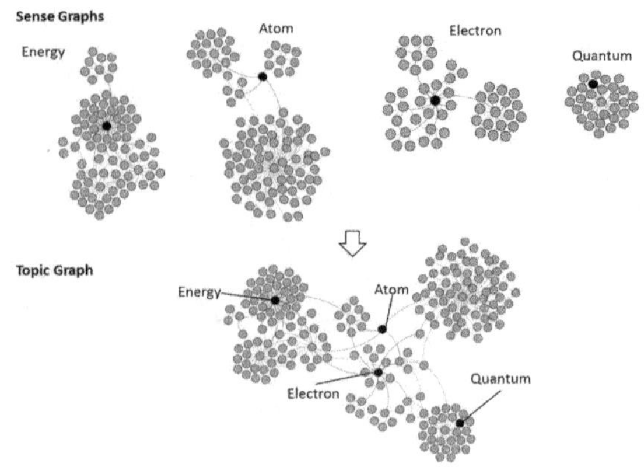

Figure 2: Four sense graphs merged into one topic graph.

One problem we face in the DBpedia graph is that concepts are often linked with Wikipedia administrative categories (e.g., `Category:Pages_containing_deleted_templates`), nodes referring to ethimology (e.g., `Category:Latin_loanwords`) and with very generic LOD concepts (e.g., `owl:Thing`, `owl:Class`, `skos:core#Concept`, etc.). These nodes create a range of shortcuts between concepts that do not reflect relationships we are interested in. For example, if all concepts are considered an instance of `skos:core#Concept`, then there will be a path of length two between *any* two concepts.

To overcome this, we automatically created a list of *stop URIs* that tries to cover this type of nodes. We created that list by navigating the higher levels of the category hierarchy rooted at the node `Category:Contents`. We made the list of 865 identified stop URIs publicly available[4], as it was generated in May 2012.

4.2 Graph Connectivity

An important hypothesis in our work is that the sense graphs of one topic are more likely to become connected than random concepts in DBpedia. In order to validate this, we ran some experiments on the ground truth data we collected in a previous user study on concept linking and disambiguation [9]. This data consists of 111 topics that had all the top-7 words manually linked and disambiguated by human users against DBpedia concepts or WordNet synsets. We used only the DBpedia concepts and computed for each topic a measure of pairwise concept seed connectivity after two hops.

$$PairConnectivity^{\mathbf{C}^\theta} = \frac{\sum\limits_{C_i \in \mathbf{C}^\theta; C_j \in \mathbf{C}^\theta} \mathbf{1}\{V_i \cap V_j \neq \emptyset\}}{|\mathbf{C}^\theta|(|\mathbf{C}^\theta| - 1)}$$

where $\mathbf{1}\{.\}$ represents the indicator function, V_i/V_j represent the set of nodes of the sense graphs seeded by C_i/C_j.

We compared the obtained average Pair Connectivity over all 111 topics to the same measure applied to identical 111 groups of DBpedia concepts formed by randomising the initial topics, and inserting random noise. For the case of ground truth concepts we obtained an average of 0.46 with standard deviation 0.09, while the random groups had an average pair connectivity of 0.07 and standard deviation 0.02. These values indicate that the connectivity of seed concepts obtained from correctly linking and disambiguating topics

[4]`http://uimr.deri.ie/sites/StopUris`

to DBpedia is not accidental. Throughout the remaining of this paper, we consider seed concepts that are not connected to the main component as noise, and ignore them from our computation. At the same time, we introduce the term *core concept* to refer to the seed concepts that belong to the main connected component, which similarly is called *core component*.

Figure 3 gives an example on the evolution of the topic words towards the topic labels. In the illustrated example, the topic consists of fifteen words. Out of these words, only eleven *seed concepts* were obtained after linking and disambiguating to DBpedia. Further on, after the graph extraction that we just described, only the nine underlined concepts became connected in the graph, so they became *core concepts*. The other two seed concepts remained disconnected. This exemplifies how noise concepts (i.e. resulting from wrong disambiguation) are implicitly isolated.

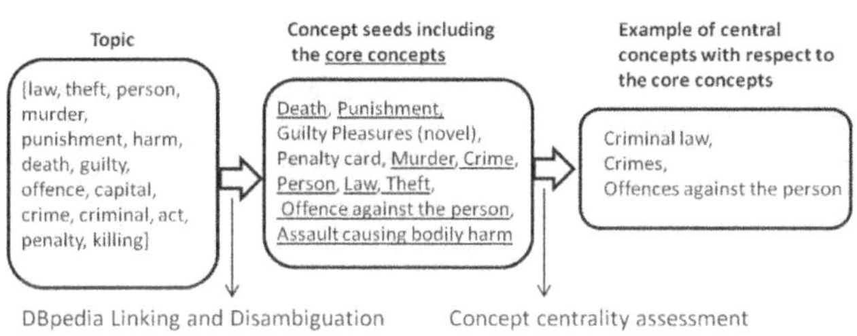

Figure 3: Evolution from topic words to candidate labels.

Intuitively, nodes central to the core component offer themselves as good labels for the topic. In the following section, we focus on defining this "centrality" and detailing our suggested approach for identifying the most central concepts with respect to the core concepts.

4.3 Centrality Measures and Labelling

As previously discussed, relying upon subsumption relationships tends to produce very generic topic labels. Instead our approach is to build a topic graph from which we can analyse the contributions that each node makes to the structure of the graph. As our graph is a semantic graph, we hypothesise that nodes that play important structural role in the graph also have an important semantic relationship to the seed concepts. We select our candidate labels from these nodes. In this section, we discuss how several centrality measures proposed in literature are suited for this task and introduce adaptations required in our case. We use the example in Table 1 throughout this section to illustrate our argumentation. It shows the top-3 concepts that the methods discussed below produce for one example topic.

Centrality measures are a well-known concept in (social) network science. They are used to identify nodes (or actors) that are most important (and thus, central) for the network, an objective in line with our own requirements. Different criteria for importance, suitable for different purposes and scenarios, led to a range of centrality measures proposed in the literature [20]. Two of the most popular ones are:

Closeness centrality: a node is important if it lies close to all of the other nodes in the network. In the context of topics, nodes with high closeness centrality indicate concepts that are closely related to all other concepts of the topic graph.

Betweenness centrality: a node is important if it facilitates the flow of information between other nodes in the graph. In a semantic network, nodes with high betweenness centrality are the nodes that establish short connections between the other nodes in the graph.

These properties intuitively recommend themselves for identifying labels. However, particularly the betweennness centrality is strongly biased towards nodes with high degree, or nodes that are central in large local groups of nodes. This holds even stronger for another centrality measure, the degree centrality, which directly reflects the node degrees. Table 1 shows that "Chemistry" is ranked high by both measures. This concept, part of `Atom`'s sense graph, lies at the center of the large node group in the top right of the topic graph in Figure 2.

In general, centrality measures compute the importance of a node with respect to all other nodes. This means, all network nodes contribute with the same weight to its score. However, in the case of topic labelling, we are particularly interested in the seed concepts, as it is their combination that defines the topic.

We therefore propose to adapt the centrality measures so that they focus on the seed nodes, rather than to all the nodes of the graph. We call these adapted measures *focused centralities*. This focus on seed nodes reduces the impact that broad concept nodes have due to their high degree and that of dense local clusters due to their sheer size – as explained above for Figure 2. Table 1 illustrates that the focused variants indeed determine, in comparison to their non-focused counterparts, concepts that are more related to the seed concepts.

Although popular, closeness and betweenness centrality rely on shortest paths only. The assumption that the spread of information is best modelled by the use of shortest paths has been questioned [19, 22]. Some alternatives have been suggested, which consider all paths in a network rather than just the shortest paths. Two such measures are:

Information centrality [22]: Related to the closeness centrality, the information of a path is inverse proportional to its length. This measure aggregates the information of all paths connecting a node with other nodes.

Random walk betweenness centrality [19]: As its name suggests, this measure is a variation of the betweenness centrality. It roughly measures how often a node is traversed by a random walker going from any node in the network to another.

Again, Table 1 illustrates the impact these measures can have. Information centrality and random walk betweenness centrality rank *Particle Physics* highest. This is a more discriminative and therefore better candidate for labelling the example topic than the rather broad *Fundamental Physics Concepts*, ranked highest by the variants based on only shortest paths.

In the following, we explain how to compute the finally chosen set of centrality measures. For simplicity, we assume that the topic graph **G** consists of the core component only.

Focused Closeness Centrality: fCC. The average shortest distance l_i from a node i to all other nodes in a graph $G = (V, E)$ is computed as

$$l_i = \frac{1}{|V|} \sum_{v_j \in V} d_{ij} \quad ,$$

where d_{ij} is the length of the shortest path between nodes v_i and v_j. The closeness centrality CC is calculated as the

Rank	Degree	Closeness Centrality on all graph (CC)	Focused Closeness Centrality (fCC)	Focused Information Centrality (fIC)	Betweenness Centrality on all graph (BC)	Focused Betweenness Centrality (fBC)	Focused Random Walk Betweenness (fRWB)
1	Chemistry	Thermodynamic Properties	Fundamental Physics Concepts	Particle Physics	Chemistry	Fundamental Physics Concepts	Particle Physics
2	Energy	Thermodynamic Free Energy	Physics	Fundamental Physics Concepts	Fundamental Physics Concepts	Particle Physics	Quantum Mechanics
3	Quantum Mechanics	Orbits	Classical Mechanics	Quantum Mechanics	Energy	Quantum Mechanics	Fundamental Physics Concepts

Table 1: Example top-3 labels for topic: [`atom, energy, electron, quantum, classic, orbit, particle`]

inverse of this average:

$$CC_i = \frac{1}{l_i} = \frac{|V|}{\sum\limits_{v_j \in V} d_{ij}} .$$

In our case, the adapted *focused closeness centrality* fCC is computed as:

$$fCC'_i = \begin{cases} \frac{n}{\sum\limits_{c_j \in \mathbf{C}^\theta} d_{ij}} & v_i \notin \mathbf{C}^\theta; \\ \frac{n-1}{\sum\limits_{c_j \in \mathbf{C}^\theta} d_{ij}} & v_i \in \mathbf{C}^\theta; \end{cases} ,$$

where n is the number of seed nodes in $\mathbf{G}$. Note that if $v_i \in \mathbf{C}^\theta$, there are only $n-1$ other seed nodes in $\mathbf{C}^\theta$ and thus we use $n-1$ as denominator.

Focused Information Centrality: fIC. The information centrality in a graph $G = (V, E)$ is computed as follows:

1. Define a $|V| \times |V|$ matrix B containing the elements:
$$b_{ij} = \begin{cases} 0 & \text{if } v_i \text{ and } v_j \text{ are incident} \\ 1 & \text{otherwise} \end{cases}$$
$$b_{ii} = 1 + degree(v_i) .$$
2. The information contained in the combined path between v_i and v_j is given by:
$$I_{ij} = (c_{ii} + c_{jj} - 2c_{ij})^{-1} ,$$
where c_{ij} are the elements of the matrix $C = B^{-1}$.
3. For a node v_i the information centrality IC is then computed as:
$$IC_i = \frac{|V|}{\sum\limits_{v_j \in V} 1/I_{ij}} .$$
In our case, the *focused information centrality* fIC is computed as:
$$fIC_i = \begin{cases} \frac{n}{\sum\limits_{c_j \in \mathbf{C}^\theta} 1/I_{ij}} & v_i \notin \mathbf{C}^\theta; \\ \frac{n-1}{\sum\limits_{c_j \in \mathbf{C}^\theta} 1/I_{ij}} & v_i \in \mathbf{C}^\theta; \end{cases} .$$

Focused Betweenness Centrality: fBC. For the betweenness centrality, we have to be aware that for every pair of nodes there might exist several shortest paths that pass through the node of interest. The betweenness centrality BC of a node v_i in a graph $G = (V, E)$ is computed as:

$$BC_i = \frac{\sum\limits_{v_s, v_t \in V \wedge s<t} \frac{x^i_{st}}{g_{st}}}{|V|(|V|-1)/2} ,$$

where x^i_{st} is the number of shortest paths between v_s and v_t that pass through node v_i. g_{st} is the total number of shortest paths between v_s and v_t. $(|V|-1)(|V|-2)/2$ is the total number of pairs of nodes that exist in G, excluding v_i. The *focused betweenness centrality* fBC is computed as:

$$fBC_i = \begin{cases} \frac{\sum\limits_{v_s, v_t \in \mathbf{C}^\theta \wedge s<t} \frac{x^i_{st}}{g_{st}}}{n(n-1)/2} & v_i \notin \mathbf{C}^\theta \\ \frac{\sum\limits_{v_s, v_t \in \mathbf{C}^\theta \wedge s<t} \frac{x^i_{st}}{g_{st}}}{(n-1)(n-2)/2} & v_i \in \mathbf{C}^\theta \end{cases} .$$

Focused Random Walk Betweenness Centrality: $fRWB$. Finally, the random walk betweenness RWB in a graph $G = (V, E)$ is computed by the following steps:

1. $L = D - A$, where D is a diagonal matrix containing the degrees of the nodes and A is the adjacency matrix of G. The matrix L is called the Laplacian matrix.
2. $T_r = L_r^{-1}$, where L_r is called the reduced Laplacian. It is obtained from L by removing any single row r and the corresponding column. T_r is the reduced Laplacian's inverse.
3. The matrix T is obtained from T_r by adding a row of zeros and a column of zeros on position r.
4. RWB_i for v_i is then computed as:
$$RWB_i = \frac{\sum\limits_{v_s, v_t \in V \wedge s<t} I_i^{(st)}}{(1/2)|V|(|V|-1)} ,$$
where $I_i^{(st)}$ is the so-called intensity, from this measure's association to the current flowing through an electrical circuit [19].
$$I_i^{(st)} = 1/2 \sum_{v_j \in V} A_{ij} |T_{ij} - T_{it} - T_{js} + T_{jt}| .$$
The averaging factor $(1/2)|V|(|V|-1)$ again is the number of all pairs of nodes in the graph.

For the *focused random walk betweenness* $fRWB$, we limit the computation to all paths between all pairs of seed nodes:

$$fRWB_i = \begin{cases} \frac{\sum\limits_{v_s, v_t \in \mathbf{C}^\theta \wedge s<t} I_i^{(st)}}{(1/2)n(n-1)} & v_i \notin \mathbf{C}^\theta; \\ \frac{\sum\limits_{v_s, v_t \in \mathbf{C}^\theta \wedge s<t} I_i^{(st)}}{(1/2)(n-1)(n-2)} & v_i \in \mathbf{C}^\theta; \end{cases} .$$

The above measures fCC, fIC, fBC and $fRWB$ are the ones that we experimented with for defining the target function r, which quantifies the strength of the relation between each candidate concept and all other concepts in the topic graph $\mathbf{G}$. The graph-based labelling ranks all nodes of $\mathbf{G}$ by the chosen centrality measure and presents the top ones to the user as topic-label candidates. In the following section, we present an evaluation of the overall approach and the different centrality measures.

5. EXPERIMENTS AND EVALUATION

In this section, we describe our experiments and the results we gained on the basis of a crowd-sourcing experiment. One objective is to show the suitability of the centrality measures we propose in Section 4.1 and the differences we can observe in applying them. We discuss the chosen measures and the standard text-based method we compare to in Section 5.1. The data we used in the experiments is described in Section 5.2, including a brief analysis of the impact of removing stop URIs. Section 5.3 presents an overview of the user study, a crucial requirement for obtaining the comparative results discussed in Section 5.4. Finally, we inspect the stability of our approach in terms of the number of seed nodes in Section 5.5.

5.1 Evaluated Methods

Pearson Correlations	fCC	fBC	fIC	$fRWB$
Degree	0.3365	0.4889	0.5072	0.6620
fCC	1	0.4432	**0.7967**	0.5118
fBC		1	0.4967	**0.8923**
fIC			1	0.6436
$fRWB$				1

Table 2: Correlation of the focused centrality measures

To keep the requirements of the user study in meaningful limits, we decided to ask the users to only evaluate fIC and $fRWB$. First, each is strongly correlated with one of the measures not evaluated and they are weakly correlated with each other. Second, by considering all paths of the topic graphs they take more information about the network topology into account than their shortest path relatives. We show the corresponding Pearson correlation coefficients in Table 2.

An important aspect is to compare our methods based on only structured data from DBpedia, to approaches that use only the documents to extract labels. We thus compare to the state-of-the-art text-based approach (TB) as described in [15]. Out of the two algorithms the authors suggest, we implemented the one for which they reported better results, the so-called "first-order relevance". The main idea is to represent candidate labels l as multinomial distribution of words $p(w|l)$. This probability represents the percentage of documents containing the word w out of the documents containing the label l. Then, a good topic label shows a distribution that is similar to the latent topic's distribution, measured using the Kullback-Leibler (KL) divergence (zero if a label perfectly matches the distribution of a topic). This value is computed as the expectation E of point-wise mutual information (PMI) between the label l and the topic words given the context D (i.e. the document corpus). The score s of a label is thus computed as:

$$s(l,\theta) = E_\theta[PMI(w,l|D)] = \sum_w (p(w|\theta)PMI(w,l|D)) \quad .$$

As in [15], for labelling we select the 1,000 most frequent noun phrases extracted from the corpus with the NLP Noun-Chunker [5] and rank them by s.

[5]http://opennlp.sourceforge.net/

5.2 Data

For evaluating our approach and the different centrality measures, we require topics extracted and linked to DBpedia. To generate this, we ran LDA [13] on three corpora, and linked and disambiguated them using the method presented in [9]. The three corpora used are:

- The British Academic Written English Corpus (BAWE) [18] consists of 2,761 documents of proficient assessed student writing, ranging in length from about 500-5,000 words. The documents are fairly evenly distributed across four broad disciplinary areas (Arts and Humanities, Social Sciences, Life Sciences and Physical Sciences) covering 35 concrete disciplines.

- The BBC [5] corpus consists of 2,225 documents from the BBC news website corresponding to stories in five topical areas from 2004-2005: business, entertainment, politics, sport, and technology.

- The StackExchange [6] dataset consists of all discussion threads from nine forums of the StackExchange website. We chose forums that matched the general knowledge of the users participating in the user study: wordpress, webmasters, web applications, photography, gaming, game development, android, cooking and bicycles. We merged all posts of a single thread in one document and the final dataset consists of 3,709 documents, roughly 400 documents per domain on average.

We chose these three corpora because of the different text style they exhibit. We expect that the graph-based methods will be less sensitive to the text style than the text-based labelling method.

With respect to the user study, we aimed for evaluating 200 topics. Apart from the size, a user study also provides constraints by the actual user base and their background knowledge. First, topics should be understandable and coherent. To measure a topic's coherence, we used the measure published in [16] and computed as:

$$coherence(\theta; \mathbf{w}^{(\theta)}) = \sum_{m=2}^{M} \sum_{l=1}^{m-1} \log \frac{D(w_m^{(\theta)}, w_l^{(\theta)})+1}{D(w_l^{(\theta)})},$$

where $\mathbf{w}^{(\theta)} = \{w_1^{(\theta)}, .., w_M^{(\theta)}\}$ represents the set of top-M most probable words of the topic θ, $D(w)$ represents the number of documents containing the word w at least once, and $D(w, w')$ represents the number of documents containing words w and w', at least once each.

We extracted 150 topics from BAWE, 50 topics from BBC and 50 topics from StackExchange ranging from medium to high coherence. Afterwards, we manually removed 30 BAWE topics that were very specific and required domain knowledge clearly outside the expertise of our users, for example from chemistry and biology. Similar, we removed 18 BBC topics (mainly from sport and politics, which contained many names of persons that would require explicit familiarity) and 2 too technical StackExchange topics. The final 200 topics contained 120 from BAWE, 32 from BBC and 48 from StackExchange.

In order to assess the impact of stop-URIs (Section 4.1), we compared topic graphs that were created before and after excluding them. We observed that when they are included in the graph, 90% of the extracted topic graphs consisted of

[6]http://stackexchange.com/

only one connected component. This number goes down to 16% when excluding them. However, the remaining 84% of graphs contain one core component that connects on average 69% of the seed concepts. Sense graphs that did not connect to this core remained isolated.

We argue that the removal of stop-URIs results in much cleaner data. As the disambiguation algorithms have an accuracy of 70-80%[9], we have to assume 20-30% of noise among all concept seeds. When including stop-URIs, the achieved graph connectivity can be considered a 'fake' connectivity, as they bring together most of the concepts that would otherwise be isolated. For all the following experiments we therefore made sure not to extract the graph beyond the stop-URIs, and analysed only the core connected component of each topic graph.

5.3 User Study

In order to comparatively evaluate the three methods, we created a web interface to gather input from human annotators. For each randomly selected topic, annotators were given the top 5 labels produced by the three evaluated methods: TB, $fRWB$ and fIC. The labels were listed in a randomised order. The first letter of each label was capitalised so that this could not influence the users perception on the label. For each label, the annotators had to choose between: "Good Fit", "Too Broad", "Related but not a good label" and "Unrelated". There was no restriction on how many "Good Fit" labels a topic could have, so users could choose none or several. In the final data set for evaluation, each label has been annotated by exactly three different annotators. There were 54 annotators in total.

We computed the Fleiss Kappa for the inter-annotator agreement in two cases: (i) on all four classes, and (ii) on two classes obtained by collapsing "Good Fit" and "Too Broad" as well as combining "Related but not a good label" and "Unrelated". For the first case we obtained a value of 0.27, and 0.38 for the second case. These values are very much in line with the agreement obtained by [14] for the task of topic indexing. As these values correspond to the level of fair to moderate agreement, this shows that, although topic labelling is a subjective task, a certain trend in users' preferences can be observed.

5.4 Comparative Evaluation

We evaluated two types of tests. The first one, which we call *Good Fit*, counts a Hit for a method if the recommended label was annotated as "Good Fit" by at least 2 annotators. The second type of test, called *Good-Fit-or-Broader*, counts a Hit for a method if the recommended label was annotated as "Good Fit" or as "Too Broad" by at least two annotators. This second type is aiming at a scenario of (hierarchical) classification. We expect the relation between specialised terms and general vocabulary hard to be captured using only text, but easier using structured data.

We compare the three chosen methods based on *Precision* and *Coverage*, taking the top-1 to top-5 suggested labels into account. Precision for a topic at top-k is computed as:

$$\text{Precision@}k = \frac{\#\text{Hits with rank} <= \text{k}}{k} \quad .$$

Then, we compute the average precision over all topics. As we cannot compute recall, due to the lack of ground truth, we define Coverage as the proportion of topics for which a method has found at least one Hit:

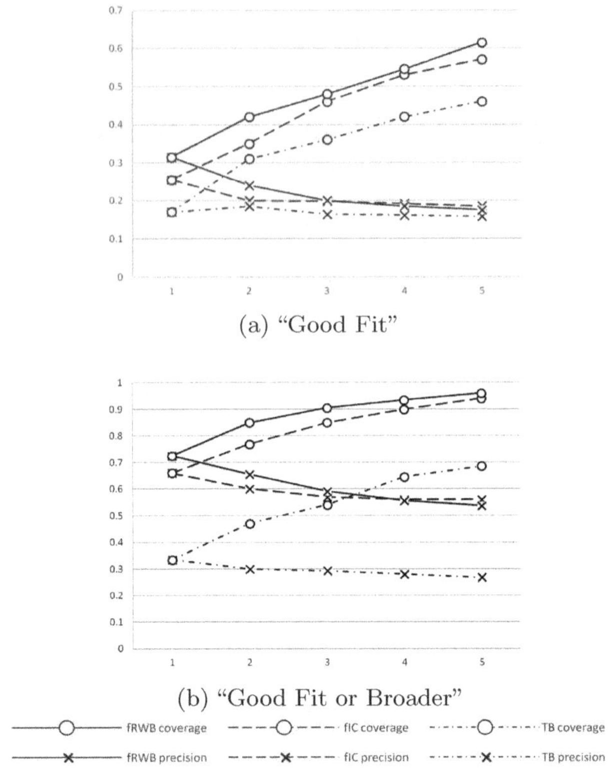

(a) "Good Fit"

(b) "Good Fit or Broader"

Figure 4: Precision and Coverage (y axis) @top-k (x axis) for combined corpora.

$$\text{Coverage@}k = \frac{\#\text{topics with at least one Hit at rank<=k}}{\#\textit{topics}} \quad .$$

Figures 4a 4b show the results for all topics combined. Figure 5 shows the results for each individual corpus.

The results indicate two advantages of our graph-based methods over the text-based one: a better coverage over all topics and a much higher ability to identify broader concepts. For the case of Good Fit, the precision values for all methods are comparable. An important difference can be seen for the precision@1 which is 31% for $fRWB$ while the text-based method achieves 17%. Regarding coverage, $fRWB$ has a Good Fit label among the top-5 in 61% of the cases, fIC in 57% and the TB in 46%.

The graph-based methods achieve significantly better results than the text-based one, in the Good-Fit-or-Broader test. In 72% of the cases the top-1 label retrieved by $fRWB$ was either a Good Fit or a Too Broad label. fIC scores 0.66 and TB 0.335. This shows that our approach is better suited for a classification scenario. This also confirms the intuition that the text-based labelling methods encounter problems identifying broader terms. As for coverage on all corpora, $fRWB$ achieves 96% in top-5, while fIC covers 94% and TB 68%.

The analysis of the different corpora provides interesting insights also. Particularly the StackExchange fora corpus highlights differences. All three methods have their worst precision on the Good Fit test on this corpus, being almost constantly under 20%. As expected, this corpus poses problems especially for the text-based method, whose coverage@5 in the Good Fit test is 0.35, with $fRWB$ scoring 0.6.

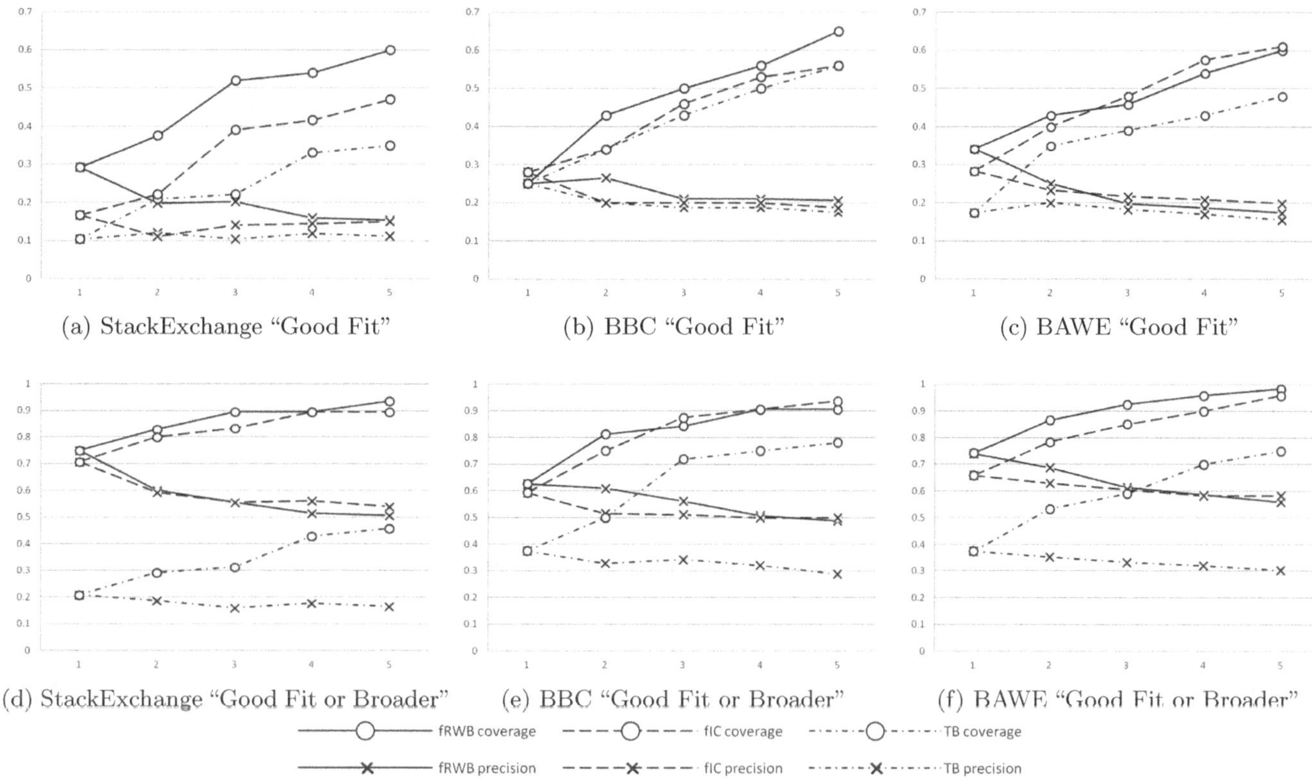

(a) StackExchange "Good Fit" (b) BBC "Good Fit" (c) BAWE "Good Fit"

(d) StackExchange "Good Fit or Broader" (e) BBC "Good Fit or Broader" (f) BAWE "Good Fit or Broader"

Figure 5: Precision and Coverage (y axis) @top-k (x axis) for the three corpora.

On the same corpus, in the Good-Fit-or-Broader test, TB has a coverage@5 of 45% whereas the $fRWB$ scores 93% and fIC 90%. Regarding the Good-Fit-or-Broader test on each corpus, the coverage@5 of $fRWB$ and fIC reaches more than 90%. More variation is seen in the converage@5 of the TB method, which is 78% on the BBC corpus, slightly lower on the BAWE corpus, while on StackExchange it results in its worst coverage@5 of less than 50%.

These results show that the graph-based methods on DBpedia can achieve better results than the standard text-based methods. The text-based method is also more sensitive to the type of text. The graph-based methods are able to retrieve better labels without a high drop in quality for forum text. The biggest difference is observed in their bias towards broader labels as compared to the text-based method. More experiments are needed with other knowledge bases than only DBpedia in order to conclude if the bias towards broader labels is due to the nature of graph-based measures or due to the nature of concepts in DBpedia. However, the results indicate that the graph-based labelling is more suited for recommendation scenarios where a good coverage is more important than a good precision.

5.5 Stability of Graph Measures

Topic labelling using external knowledge strongly depends on the quality of the linking of topic words. In our experiments, the disambiguation algorithm received the top 15 words of each topic. Usually, there are topic terms that cannot be linked, because they do not have a corresponding DBpedia concept. Moreover, we also want to support cases when the input topics are not necessarily probabilistic latent topics, for instance if they are extracted from a phrase, and contain very few words. Therefore, we analyse the impact of the number of disambiguated concepts. We achieve this by inspecting the number of concepts in core connected component of the topic graph.

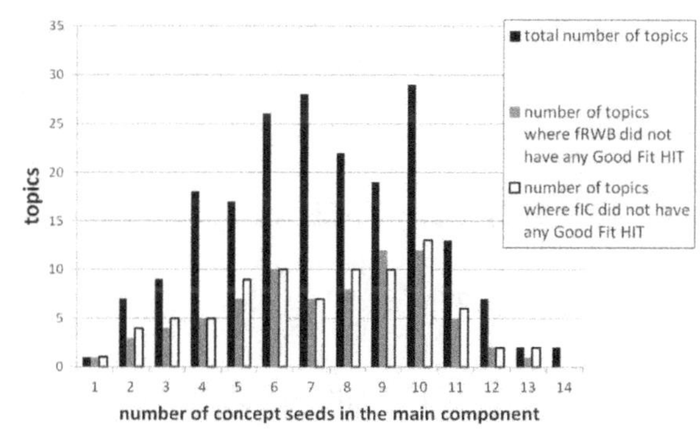

Figure 6: Influence of number of seed nodes

We selected the topics for which the graph-based methods did not find any label annotated with Good Fit by at least two annotators. Then, we statistically checked if the number of core concepts in these cases is biased in comparison to all topics. Figure 6 shows the distributions. For each method, we computed the Chi Square Goodness of Fit statistic with respect to the distribution of all topics. In both cases, there was no significant difference between the mistaken topics distribution and the distribution of all topics. For $fRWB$ we obtained $\chi^2(13, n = 77) = 7.10, p > 0.10$, and for fIC we obtained $\chi^2(13, n = 85) = 7.44, p > 0.10$.

This result has an important practical significance, as it shows that even with less than 5 core concepts the labelling can be as successful as with more than 5 or even more than 10 core concepts. We also analysed with how many seed concepts the different centrality measures converge to the final set of top-5 labels. We noticed that for all measures, the first 5 concept seeds already established at least 2 labels of the final top-5 set. We also observed that fCC is not very sensitive to new concepts once it identified concepts very close to its seed concepts, while fBC and $fRWB$ are most sensitive to each individual seed concept.

6. CONCLUSION AND FUTURE WORK

In this work, we investigated approaches for graph-based topic labelling using DBpedia. We extract the DBpedia subgraph of topic concepts and adapt network centrality measures to identify concepts that promise to be good labels for a topic. On the basis of a crowd-sourcing experiment, we showed that the graph-based approaches perform constantly better than a state-of-the-art text-based method. The most important improvements are (i) better corpus coverage, and (ii) much higher ability to identify broader labels. We envisage applications that support users in the tasks of topic-labelling and navigation – either by recommending a set of top labels or by recommending exploration directions.

However, none of these approaches is yet ready for fully automated labelling. In this perspective, we continue our research by investigating graph patterns (e.g., density of the topic graph) that could identify particular centrality measures suited in particular situations.

Linking topics from a corpus to external knowledge bases like DBpedia has more benefits than just topic labelling. For example, relations and similarities between different topics can be identified based on the graph overlap between topics. The extent to which topics overlap or are similar to one another can help the user assess the suitability of the chosen number of topics. Finally, a network of topics is obtained for a corpus that can serve as basis for corpus navigation. There are many interesting research directions in the area of graph mining to topic / document analysis, and the work presented here is barely scratching the surface.

7. ACKNOWLEDGEMENTS

This work was jointly supported by Science Foundation Ireland (SFI) partly under Grant No. 08/CE/I1380 (Lion-2) and partly under Grant No. 08/SRC/I1407 (Clique: Graph and Network Analysis Cluster), and by the European Union (EU) under grant no. 257859 (ROBUST integrating project).

8. REFERENCES

[1] C. Bizer, J. Lehmann, G. Kobilarov, S. Auer, C. Becker, R. Cyganiak, and S. Hellmann. Dbpedia-a crystallization point for the web of data. *JWS*, 7(3):154–165, 2009.

[2] D. Blei, A. Ng, and M. Jordan. Latent dirichlet allocation. *J. Mach. Learn. Res.*, 3:993–1022, 2003.

[3] D. Carmel, H. Roitman, and N. Zwerdling. Enhancing cluster labeling using wikipedia. In *SIGIR '09*, pages 139–146, 2009.

[4] K. Coursey, R. Mihalcea, and W. Moen. Using encyclopedic knowledge for automatic topic identification. In *CoNLL '09*, pages 210–218, 2009.

[5] D. Greene and P. Cunningham. Practical solutions to the problem of diagonal dominance in kernel document clustering. In *ICML'06*, pages 377–384, 2006.

[6] J. Hoffart, F. M, S. K. Berberich, G. Weikum, and I. Saclay. Yago2: A spatially and temporally enhanced knowledge base from wikipedia. *Commun. ACM*, 2009.

[7] T. Hofmann. Probabilistic latent semantic analysis. In *Uncertainty in Artificial Intelligence (UAI '99)*, pages 289–296, 1999.

[8] http://dublincore.org/. DCMI: The Dublin Core Metadata Initiative, 2012. [accessed 07-August-2012].

[9] I. Hulpuş, C. Hayes, M. Karnstedt, and D. Greene. An eigenvalue based measure for word-sense disambiguation. In *FLAIRS 2012*, 2012.

[10] J. H. Lau, K. Grieser, D. Newman, and T. Baldwin. Automatic labelling of topic models. In *ACL: Human Language Technologies*, pages 1536–1545, 2011.

[11] W. Li and A. McCallum. Pachinko allocation: Dag-structured mixture models of topic correlations. In *ICML '06*, pages 577–584, 2006.

[12] D. Magatti, S. Calegari, D. Ciucci, and F. Stella. Automatic labeling of topics. In *Intelligent Systems Design and Applications*, pages 1227–1232, 2009.

[13] A. K. McCallum. Mallet: A machine learning for language toolkit. http://mallet.cs.umass.edu, 2002.

[14] O. Medelyan, I. H. Witten, and D. Milne. Topic indexing with wikipedia. In *Workshop on Wikipedia and Artificial Intelligence (WIKIAI '08)*, 2010.

[15] Q. Mei, X. Shen, and C. Zhai. Automatic labeling of multinomial topic models. In *SIGKDD '07*, pages 490–499, 2007.

[16] D. M. Mimno, H. M. Wallach, E. M. Talley, M. Leenders, and A. McCallum. Optimizing semantic coherence in topic models. In *EMNLP '11*, pages 262–272, 2011.

[17] M. Muhr, R. Kern, and M. Granitzer. Analysis of structural relationships for hierarchical cluster labeling. In *SIGIR '10*, pages 178–185, 2010.

[18] H. Nesi, S. Gardner, P. Thompson, and P. Wickens. British academic written english (bawe) corpus. *Universities of Warwick, Reading and Oxford Brookes, under funding from ESRC (RES-000-23-0800)*, 2007.

[19] M. Newman. A measure of betweenness centrality based on random walks. *Social networks*, 27:39–54, 2005.

[20] M. Newman. *Networks. An Introduction.* Oxford University Press, 2010.

[21] T. Nomoto. Wikilabel: an encyclopedic approach to labeling documents en masse. In *CIKM '11*, pages 2341–2344, 2011.

[22] K. Stephenson and M. Zelen. Rethinking centrality: Methods and examples. *Social Networks*, 11:1 – 37, 1989.

[23] Z. Syed, T. Finin, and A. Joshi. Wikipedia as an ontology for describing documents. In *ICWSM '08*, 2008.

[24] P. Treeratpituk and J. Callan. Automatically labeling hierarchical clusters. In *Conference on Digital Government Research*, pages 167–176, 2006.

[25] W3C. SKOS: Simple Knowledge Organization System. `http://www.w3.org/2004/02/skos/`, 2009.

Estimating Content Concreteness for Finding Comprehensible Documents

Shinya Tanaka[1], Adam Jatowt[1,2], Makoto P. Kato[1] and Katsumi Tanaka[1]

[1]Graduate School of Informatics,
Kyoto University, Yoshida-honmachi, Sakyo-ku
606-8501 Kyoto, Japan
{s.tanaka,adam,kato,tanaka}@dl.kuis.kyoto-u.ac.jp

[2]Japan Science and Technology Agency
4-1-8 Honcho, Kawaguchi-shi, Saitama
332-0012 Tokyo, Japan

ABSTRACT

Document comprehensibility is one of key factors determining document quality and, in result, user's satisfaction. Relevant web pages are of little utility if they are incomprehensible or impose too much cognitive burden on readers. Traditional measures of text difficulty focus often on syntactic factors of text such as sentence length, word length, syllable count, or they utilize fixed list of common terms. However, document comprehensibility depends on many factors, of which concreteness and the ease of concept visualization are crucial ones. In this paper, we first propose a method for predicting the concreteness of terms using SVM regression. We then extend it to calculating document concreteness level. The experimental results indicate satisfactory accuracy in estimating both term and document concreteness as well as demonstrate positive correlation between the document concreteness and comprehensibility. Our ultimate goal is to enable comprehension-driven search, which will return both relevant and comprehensible results.

Categories and Subject Descriptors

H.3.3 [Information Storage and Retrieval]: Information Search and Retrieval

General Terms

Algorithms, Measurements

Keywords

concreteness, abstractness, comprehensibility, readability, information retrieval

1. INTRODUCTION

Comprehensibility, defined as "the ease of understanding", is one of the significant factors of the utility of documents. The gap between a text and a reader measured, for example, in school grade levels, determines whether the text is readable or not. Texts about complex topics (e.g., on scientific, philosophical or legal issues) can be easily comprehensible for educated and skilled readers; however, for a significant fraction of readers, they constitute considerable cognitive burden. According to the National Adult Literacy Survey (NALS) [21] about 21% of the adult population in USA (around 40 million) have low literacy skills, which are defined as reading at the 6 grade level or below. Another 27% (around 50 million) have limited literacy ability, defined as lacking reading and numeric proficiency to function adequately in society. This situation effectively limits information accessibility causing documents in collections like Britannica or Wikipedia, and many others, to be poorly comprehensible for relatively large population of users, especially, when it comes to difficult topics.

While comprehensibility depends on different factors such as syntactic difficulty measured by surface text features (e.g. sentence or word length) or document coherence, we focus on concreteness which is regarded as a key aspect of content comprehensibility [23, 26]. Consider the following two passages about symptoms of Parkinson's disease.

1. Parkinson's disease affects movement, producing motor symptoms. Non-motor symptoms, which include autonomic dysfunction, neuropsychiatric problems (mood, cognition, behavior or thought alterations), and sensory and sleep difficulties, are also common.[1]

2. Patient will begin to notice early signs of Parkinson's. These may include mild shaking or tremors in one limb. Patients may experience occasional loss of balance. Patient may begin to experience symptoms on both sides of their body. Shaking may regularly occur in all limbs. Uncontrollable shaking affects patient's ability to walk, stand, and maintain balance. Patient may encounter difficulty handling otherwise simple tasks.[2]

Passage 2 contains more concrete words and seems easier to read than the passage 1. It should help non-expert users understand and also imagine the symptoms of Parkinson's

[1]http://en.wikipedia.org/wiki/Parkinson's_disease [27th November, 2012]

[2]http://www.googobits.com/articles/1527-guide-to-parkinsons-disease.html [27th November, 2012]

WSDM'13, February 4–8, 2013, Rome, Italy.

disease to greater extent than the passage 1, which has been actually taken from Wikipedia. It would be beneficial for many users to receive documents with contents characterized by similar comprehensibility degree to the one of passage 2 for difficult queries such as "Parkinson's disease".

Concreteness does not only affect understanding but it also has direct impact on user interest and attitude to text. Readers may find a text with too many generalizations and abstractions boring, confusing or vague. Specific content seems to have greater impact on readers than abstract, general one, because it involves their memories of sensory experiences; often, virtually making them feel, see, hear, touch, smell, and taste through reading. The good style of writing is thus to capture reader's attention by arousing his or her senses with many concrete words [23, 26].

In addition, interest and attitude to information seem to have direct relation to its remembering as human memory is known to be driven by emotions [2]. Consider the case when one tries to teach a child to be careful. Simply saying "It is dangerous to go out at night" will have lesser effect than providing the child with information on concrete, specific experiences. While it is well-known that humans learn by abstracting concrete cases through generalization, which allows them to apply the obtained knowledge to similar situations, when provided only with abstract explanations they often have problems with comprehension and remembering.

In principle, concrete words (e.g. "car", "table") refer to physical entities that can be observed by at least one of the senses [22]. On the other hand, abstract words indicate abstract objects, such as ideas or concepts (e.g. "democracy" or "love") which are hard to be materially perceived by humans. According to previous studies [22, 26] concrete terms can be represented by two psycholinguistic attributes: *perceivability* and *imageability*. Perceivability is defined as the ability to sense the object, while imageability is the ability to imagine the object easily and quickly. In this paper we propose estimating the concreteness degree of words through SVM regression [29] equipped with a range of diverse features that are related to the concepts of perceivability and imageability. As a training set we use manual labels stored in Medical Research Council Psycholinguistic Database (MRCDB)[3] which is an established source in psycholinguistic research field. Next, we extrapolate the term-level concreteness to the document-level one to enable estimation of document comprehensibility. Although the effect of concreteness on comprehensibility has been already studied in psycholinguistic field, to the best of our knowledge, this is the first attempt for estimating term- and document-level concreteness in an automatic fashion.

We make the following contributions in this paper: (a) we propose a new research problem of evaluating concreteness of documents in order to improve reading comprehension, (b) we describe method for estimating term-level concreteness and then extend it into evaluating concreteness of documents, (c) we show the results of the experimental evaluation of both the methods and, lastly, (d) we perform additional experimentation for investigating the co-occurrence of concrete/abstract terms on Wikipedia and for estimating query concreteness.

The reminder of this paper is organized as follows. Section 2 surveys the related work. In Section 3 we describe our methodology for estimating concreteness of terms and documents. In Sections 4 and 5 we report experimental results for the term- and document-level concreteness estimation, respectively, while in Section 6 we provide general discussion. Finally, Section 7 concludes the paper and outlines our future work.

2. RELATED WORK

2.1 Psychological Studies of Concreteness

Concrete and abstract concepts are commonly defined by the reference to perceivability [8, 17]. Concrete entities are considered to be physical entities with characteristic shapes, parts, materials, and so on, whereas abstract entities lack physical attributes [8, 17]. Concreteness is also defined by imageability [26, 22], which measures how quickly and easily people can imagine a given referent. Some terms arouse a sensory experience such as a mental picture or sound very quickly and easily, whereas others may arouse a sensory experience slowly or with difficulty. For example, think of the terms "banana" or "fact". "Banana" would probably arouse an image relatively easily, whereas "fact" would most likely do so with difficulty.

Most of the previous works focused on defining the concreteness of terms and measuring it on the basis of manual evaluation. For instance, Paivio *et al.* [22] asked subjects to rate concreteness and imageability of words on 7-point scale. The main finding was that abstract words are harder to understand than concrete words. Three theories have been proposed to explain this phenomenon: the *dual-coding theory*, *age of acquisition hypothesis* and *context availability model*. The *dual-coding theory* [22, 24] is the oldest one and assumes the existence of two parallel systems: the logogen denoting the verbal system and the imagen - the human's image system. The difference between the concrete and abstract terms is that the former activate both the systems while being more strongly associated with the imagen system, whereas abstract words tend to activate only the logogen system. On the other hand, the *age of acquisition hypothesis* [24] binds the difficulty of abstract terms with their later acquisition during the language development process. Due to the time gap subjects have simply less exposure to them and hence experience greater difficulty in comprehending and remembering abstract concepts. The last theory, the *context availability model* [24], models word comprehension by means of a complex information retrieval system operating on human's knowledge base. The slower retrieval of abstract terms is due to their weaker associations with contextual knowledge in comparison to more concrete words.

2.2 Readability Measures

Several readability measures have been proposed due to the practical needs for estimating text reading ease (e.g., textbooks, legal contracts or technical manuals). The widely accepted definition of readability can be found in [9]: "The sum total (including all the interactions) of all those elements within a given piece of printed material that affect the success a group of readers have with it. The success is the extent to which they understand it, read it at an optimal speed, and find it interesting". This definition is quite general and emphasizes the impact of diverse factors on the ease of understanding.

[3]http://www.psy.uwa.edu.au/mrcdatabase/uwa_mrc.htm [27th November, 2012]

Despite the composite, multi-construct character of comprehensibility, most traditional readability indexes such as Flesch Reading Ease [12] or Coleman Liau Index [5] are calculated by the category of simple, syntactic measures such as the count of syllables, words and the length of sentences. Flesch Reading Ease, one of the earliest standard measures, defines readability as a function of word length and sentence length. This approach is simple to implement but sensitive to outliers. Another category of metrics focuses on difficulty levels of words themselves to achieve a more robust measure. A typical approach here is to use a predefined list of common or easy words (e.g., New Dale-Chall Formula [4]). However, due to a dynamic character of language, the static list requires continuing updates.

Other studies cast the problem to classifying texts according to reading levels. For example, Collins-Thompson and Callan [6] use statistical language modeling and multinomial Naïve Bayes classification for readability measure of English and French. This line of research exploits various features ranging from surface text ones (e.g., word length) to discourse-level features (e.g., the number of entities involved in a text) and from a manually compiled list of vocabulary to statistical language modelling. Contextual approach to readability estimation was proposed by Akamatsu *et al.* [1]. The authors employed biased random walk for finding easy or difficult pages on the Web based on the hypothesis that pages with similar comprehensibility levels are relatively more likely to be linked with each other than those with very different levels.

Other studies have investigated automatic and adaptive models [7] for personalizing web search results by their readability levels. However, none of the above works focused explicitly on estimating abstractness and concreteness qualities of terms or documents.

2.3 Information Retrieval and Concreteness

To the best of our knowledge, concreteness has not been explicitly incorporated into document retrieval, although some works proposed including readability measures into web search or returning content depending on user age and thus related to his or her mental capabilities.

Eickoff *et al.* [10] classified web pages into those suitable for children and those not following the topical and non-topical approach. They employed a range of diverse features such as common readability measures, presentation styles, numbers of multimedia on pages, link ratios, etc. Nakatani *et al.* [20] measured word detailedness and topicality based on analysis of links in Wikipedia in order to employ them in web search. The main hypothesis was that a Wikipedia article about a detailed word has most of their inlinks originating from articles in the same category as the one of the target article. Coh-Metrix [14] is a tool that comprehensively analyzes texts based on various measures of cohesion, language and readability. Abstractness and text vagueness are discussed in the context of this work. Although average imageability and concreteness scores of texts are provided by the system, these are based on the fixed list of judged words obtained from MRCDB database; hence, the scores are not algorithmically determined.

Considering image retrieval, current image search engines return results which are of good quality when the query contains concrete terms. On the other hand, search results for abstract query such as "summer" or "happiness" are often not satisfactory. To improve image search results for an abstract term query, Kato *et al.* [16] proposed to retrieve more concrete terms which are associated with the input abstract concept and then to substitute them for this concept. Sun and Bhowmick [25] proposed *image tag visual clarity* to evaluate the effectiveness of a tag in describing the visual content of its annotated images. The objective was to improve the effectiveness of image search engines. Larson *et al.* [19] predicted sizes of visually-depicted objects in images based on mining linguistic patterns within web search results such as "the <tag> in his hand", "the <tag> in her pocket", "the <tag> on the horizon", etc. where <tag> is a given object.

3. MEASUREMENT OF CONCRETENESS

In this section, we describe features used to estimate the concreteness of terms with SVM regression model and then propose the measure for document concreteness. Note that in the current implementation we have focused only on nouns which are key information bearing elements of text.

3.1 Estimating Concreteness of Terms

Automatically judging how much terms are concrete and abstract is not trivial. An intuitive approach would be a topic-based one by assuming that common terms in documents, for example, on psychology or philosophy tend to be abstract. However, this solution would not be practical as it would require large datasets of annotated documents on high number of diverse topics. In addition, not all documents and terms in abstract domains are actually abstract. We decided to follow a non-topical approach and determine term concreteness/abstractness based on their non-topical, and hence, more general features. We selected 21 features grouped in 8 categories: (1) visual representativeness and popularity, (2) diversity of annotations, (3) co-occurrence with sense verbs, (4) number of senses, (5) depth in ontology tree, (6) number of hyponyms, (7) sentiment level, and (8) term length. We describe each group in turn.

Visual Representativeness and Popularity

Imageability of terms indicates how easily and quickly people can imagine the referent of terms. To estimate word's imageability we propose to analyze the degree of *visual representativeness* of a term, which we define as the extent to which the term is used for describing photos or, in general, images. The reasoning behind this hypothesis is that words used frequently to describe photos or images have high probability to be concrete, since the photos and images usually show concrete objects as perceived by a sense of vision. We necessarily make an assumption here that in most of the cases photos or images are annotated with terms that represent the displayed objects. We measure the popularity of using a given word to annotate photos, $\text{Popularity}_{\text{photo}}(t)$ and images, $\text{Popularity}_{\text{image}}(t)$. In addition, we also capture the word's popularity on the web, $\text{Popularity}_{\text{web}}(t)$, according to the hypothesis that common words could represent concrete objects which people see in everyday life.

In particular, we measure the frequency of a term t in the search index of the Bing web search[4], $\text{Freq}_{\text{web}}(t)$, the frequency of a term t in the Bing image search, $\text{Freq}_{\text{image}}(t)$, and the frequency of a term t in Flickr[5], $\text{Freq}_{\text{photo}}(t)$. As these frequencies range vastly we represent the features using

[4]http://www.bing.com [27th November, 2012]

[5]http://www.flickr.com [27th November, 2012]

logarithms.

$$\begin{array}{lll} \textbf{f1} & \text{Popularity}_{\text{web}}(t) & = \log_{10}(\text{Freq}_{\text{web}}(t)+1) \\ \textbf{f2} & \text{Popularity}_{\text{image}}(t) & = \log_{10}\left(\text{Freq}_{\text{image}}(t)+1\right) \\ \textbf{f3} & \text{Popularity}_{\text{photo}}(t) & = \log_{10}\left(\text{Freq}_{\text{photo}}(t)+1\right) \end{array}$$

Since some words, especially, the popular ones, could be used for annotating images just by chance, we also normalized $\text{Freq}_{\text{image}}(t)$ and $\text{Freq}_{\text{photo}}(t)$ by the popularity of words in text domain approximated by their popularity on the web, $\text{Popularity}_{\text{web}}(t)$. Then, additional features **f4** and **f5** are calculated as below.

$$\begin{array}{lll} \textbf{f4} & \frac{\text{Popularity}_{\text{image}}(t)}{\text{Popularity}_{\text{web}}(t)} & = \frac{\log_{10}\left(\text{Freq}_{\text{image}}(t)+1\right)}{\log_{10}(\text{Freq}_{\text{web}}(t)+1)} \\ \textbf{f5} & \frac{\text{Popularity}_{\text{photo}}(t)}{\text{Popularity}_{\text{web}}(t)} & = \frac{\log_{10}\left(\text{Freq}_{\text{photo}}(t)+1\right)}{\log_{10}(\text{Freq}_{\text{web}}(t)+1)} \end{array}$$

The last two features can be interpreted as the degrees of word's visual representativeness, or, the rate of word's popularity in the visual vs. textual domain.

Diversity of Annotations

In shared image databases users usually add annotations for stored contents. We hypothesize that when many diverse annotations are added for photos related to a given term t, the term might be abstract. This is because an abstract concept can have many interpretations and instantiations, and, often, there are several ways to represent its meaning. For example, a tag "happiness" could be used for annotating an image of a smiling child playing with a dog, a couple walking together, a person driving elegant car, a luxurious house and so on. We describe the number of annotations which are added for contents related to a term t as $\#\text{Annotations}(t)$ and the corresponding number of unique annotations as $\#\text{Annotations}_{\text{uniq}}(t)$.

For capturing these measures, we used social tagging data derived from Flickr. Since in Flickr users sometimes submit multiple photos with exactly same tags due to their similar theme or just for convenience, we applied a simple filtering scheme. A given photo is skipped if there is another photo submitted by the same user that has identical tag set.

After applying the filtering we took up to 500 top ranked photos from the search results for a query t, denoted as $\text{Photos}(t) = \{photo_1, photo_2, \cdots, photo_n\}$ where $0 \leq n \leq 500$. The number of tags of photos in $\text{Photos}(t)$ is $\#\text{Tags}(t)$ and the number of unique tags is $\#\text{Tags}_{\text{uniq}}(t)$. Note that tags containing stop words and the search query t itself were eliminated. The features **f6** and **f7** were calculated as follows.

$$\begin{array}{lll} \textbf{f6} & \#\text{Annotations}(t) & = \frac{\#\text{Tags}(t)}{n} \\ \textbf{f7} & \#\text{Annotations}_{\text{uniq}}(t) & = \frac{\#\text{Tags}_{\text{uniq}}(t)}{n} \end{array}$$

Co-occurrence with Sense Verbs

As mentioned before, concreteness is often defined in terms of perceivability. Concrete terms should commonly occur with verbs which denote senses such as *see*, *hear*, or *taste*. We use verbs representing sensory experience, called sense verbs, to represent 5 basic senses: sight, hearing, taste, smell, and touch. The average co-occurrence rate of a term t with the sense verbs is defined as $\text{SenseVerbs}_{\text{avg}}(t)$ and is measured using the window size of a single sentence.

For instance, let a set of verbs related to sight be $\text{Verbs}_{\text{sight}} = \{\text{see, sees, saw, seen}\}$. The co-occurrence between a term t and verbs related to sight is calculated as:

$$\text{Cooc}_{\text{sight}}(t) = \sum_{v \in Verbs_{\text{sight}}} \frac{\text{Freq}_{\text{web}}(\text{"}v * t\text{"})}{\text{Freq}_{\text{web}}(v \vee t)}$$

In the implementation, we use phrase search. An asterisk * matches more than 0 terms or does not match any terms in the same sentence. $\text{Cooc}_{\text{hearing}}$, $\text{Cooc}_{\text{taste}}$, $\text{Cooc}_{\text{smell}}$, and $\text{Cooc}_{\text{touch}}$ are calculated in a similar way.

Note however that some terms co-occur with only one sense. For example, a noun "photo" often co-occurs with a verb *see*, while rarely co-occurring with the other sense verbs. We thus use not only the average but also the maximum co-occurrence rating of a term t with sense verbs denoted as $\text{SenseVerbs}_{\text{max}}(t)$. The features **f8** and **f9** are calculated as follows.

$$\begin{array}{lll} \textbf{f8} & \#\text{SenseVerbs}_{\text{max}}(t) & = \max(\text{Cooc}_{\text{sight}}(t), \text{Cooc}_{\text{hearing}}(t), \\ & & \quad \text{Cooc}_{\text{taste}}(t), \text{Cooc}_{\text{smell}}(t), \\ & & \quad \text{Cooc}_{\text{touch}}(t)) \\ \textbf{f9} & \#\text{SenseVerbs}_{\text{avg}}(t) & = \frac{1}{5}(\text{Cooc}_{\text{sight}}(t) + \text{Cooc}_{\text{hearing}}(t) \\ & & \quad +\text{Cooc}_{\text{taste}}(t) + \text{Cooc}_{\text{smell}}(t) \\ & & \quad +\text{Cooc}_{\text{touch}}(t)) \end{array}$$

Number of Senses

A term often has more than one meaning. For example, according to WordNet [6], the nouns "reason" and life have 6 and 14 senses, respectively, while "tree" and "plant" have 3 and 4 senses, respectively.

We hypothesize that when the number of senses of a term t is high, t might be abstract. Hence we propose the number of senses obtained from WordNet, $\#\text{Senses}(t)$, that a term t has as another feature (**f10**).

Depth in Ontology Tree

The relation of concreteness of terms with their depth in an ontology tree has been pointed out in [11]. Similar idea was investigated in [18] for the purpose of subjectivity classification. We consider ontology to be a hierarchical structure constructed of relations such as is-a and part-of relations. Note that the depth of a term t in the ontology is usually different for its different senses. For example, the 4 senses of a noun "plant" in the WordNet ontology tree have depths of 7, 5, 9, and 11. We denote the depth of the most frequently used sense of a term, t as $\text{Depth}_{\text{freq}}(t)$ (**f11**) and the average depth of the senses of a term t as $\text{Depth}_{\text{avg}}(t)$ (**f12**). Both mean the distance in the ontology tree from the root to a target sense.

Number of Hyponyms

The number of hyponyms a term has appears to be related to the level of its generality. We hypothesize that when the number of hyponyms which a term t has is large, t might be abstract. Same as for the features based on the depth in the ontology tree, the number of hyponyms also depends on different senses of a term. We thus use two features, the number of hyponyms of the most frequently used sense, $\#\text{Hyponyms}_{\text{freq}}(t)$ (**f13**) and the average number of hyponyms of all the senses of t, $\#\text{Hyponyms}_{\text{avg}}(t)$ (**f14**).

Sentiment Level

Intuitively, abstract terms tend to arouse positive or negative sentiments. For example, according to SentiWordNet[7], which is a lexical resource providing sentiment values to

[6]http://wordnet.princeton.edu/ [27th November, 2012]

[7]http://sentiwordnet.isti.cnr.it/ [27th November, 2012]

Wordnet synsets, "opportunity" arouses positive sentiment, whereas "regret" arouses negative sentiment. On the other hand, concrete terms (e.g., "tree", "road") might be more objective and to lesser extent associated with sentiment than abstract ones. We select positivity, negativity and objectivity values of terms as other features for SVM regression. Same as for some of the previously introduced features, the values can differ for different term senses. We thus define the positivity, negativity and objectivity values of the most frequently used sense of a term t as $\text{Positivity}_{\text{freq}}(t)$ (**f15**), $\text{Negativity}_{\text{freq}}(t)$ (**f16**), and $\text{Objectivity}_{\text{freq}}(t)$ (**f17**), respectively. The average positivity, average negativity, and average objectivity values of the senses of a term t are represented by $\text{Positivity}_{\text{avg}}(t)$ (**f18**), $\text{Negativity}_{\text{avg}}(t)$ (**f19**), and $\text{Objectivity}_{\text{avg}}(t)$ (**f20**), respectively.

Term Length

According to the rule of the least-effort in human communication as proposed by Zipf [30], the most frequent words tend to be short. These are often words describing common objects surrounding humans. In English, many abstract nouns are formed by adding noun-forming suffixes (-ness, -ity, -tion, -ism) to adjectives, verbs or other nouns (e.g. "happiness", "circulation", "serenity" and "communism"). We thus set a hypothesis that the longer the number of characters in a term, the more abstract the term might be. The number of characters of a term t, $\#\text{Characters}(t)$, is selected as feature **f21**.

3.2 Estimating Concreteness of Documents

In this section we estimate the concreteness of documents by using the calculated concreteness levels of terms. We propose two methods: (1) *average concreteness* and (2) *maximum concreteness*. The first one is based on the hypothesis that concrete documents contain many concrete terms. Let, $Conc(t)$ be the concreteness score of term t, D be a document and $|D|$ be the number of terms in D:

$$\text{Conc}_{\text{doc}}^{\text{avg}}(D) = \frac{1}{|D|}\sum_{t\in D}\text{Conc}(\text{t}) \quad (1)$$

The second method, *maximum concreteness*, is based on the assumption that documents consist of abstract paragraphs and concrete paragraphs. The intuition behind this method is that often a short, yet concrete paragraph, such as the one with concrete examples or instances of abstract concepts makes a difference between document understanding and confusion.

The estimation of document concreteness consists then of 2 steps: (1) calculating the concreteness of paragraphs in a document, and (2) using the calculated paragraph scores to derive the concreteness of the document.

Let a document D be considered as a set of paragraphs: $D = \{P_1, P_2, \cdots, P_L\}$ where P_i is a paragraph in D. We then represent P_i as a sequence of terms $P_i = (t_1, t_2, \cdots, t_M)$. For each paragraph P in D we calculate the concreteness of P as follows.

$$\text{Conc}_{\text{par}}(P) = \frac{1}{|P|}\sum_{t\in P}\text{Conc}(\text{t}) \quad (2)$$

Finally, the concreteness of a document D is estimated as follows.

$$\text{Conc}_{\text{doc}}^{\text{max}}(D) = \max\left(\text{Conc}_{\text{par}}(P_1), \cdots, \text{Conc}_{\text{par}}(P_N)\right)$$

4. EVALUATION OF TERM-LEVEL CONCRETENESS

4.1 Dataset and Evaluation Metrics

We use the Medical Research Council Psycholinguistic Database (MRCDB) version 2.0 as a dataset and WordNet 3.0, Flickr, and SentiWordNet 3.0 as external knowledge bases. MRCDB contains 150,837 terms and provides information on 26 different linguistic properties, although, information about every property is not available for each term. In MRCDB 8,288 terms have perceivability ratings[8], and 9,240 terms have imageability ratings. The ratings were derived from merging 3 sets of norms: Paivio [22], Toglia and Batting [27], and Gilhooly and Logie [13]. The 3 sets of norms correlated highly and were merged by adjusting both the means and standard deviations. The scores were obtained from two groups of evaluators and are expressed as integer values ranging in the interval [100, 700]. 28 evaluators (12 males) estimated perceivability, and 30 evaluators (15 males) estimated imageability. Perceivability was rated in 7-point numerical scale from 1 (one cannot experience the referent of a target term by his or her sense) to 7 (one can easily experience the referent of a target term, such as objects, materials, and people). Similarly, the imageability of terms was rated in 7-point numerical scale from 1 (one cannot imagine the referent of a target term quickly and easily) to 7 (one can easily and quickly imagine the referent of a target term). In the experiments, we used nouns which have perceivability rating and imageability rating in MRCDB, and which, at the same time, are contained in WordNet as nouns. In total, there were 3,455 nouns satisfying these conditions. We then used both the perceivability ratings and the imageability ratings of these terms as the target values for SVM regression. As the ratings range in the interval [100, 700] we have normalized them to fit into the interval [0, 1] by min-max normalization.

As mentioned before, the earlier studies defined concreteness by two psycholinguistic attributes, perceivability and imageability. Therefore we define the concreteness as follows:

$$\text{Conc}_{\text{MRC}}(t) = \frac{1}{2}\left\{\text{Perc}_{\text{MRC}}(t) + \text{Imag}_{\text{MRC}}(t)\right\}$$

$\text{Perc}_{\text{MRC}}(t)$ is the perceivability rating of a term t in MRCDB, and $\text{Imag}_{\text{MRC}}(t)$ is the imageability rating of t in MRCDB. Table 1 shows the minimum rating, the maximum rating, the average rating, and the standard deviation of perceivability, imageability rating and the combined rating of 3,455 nouns in MRCDB. The Pearson's correlation coefficient between the perceivability and imageability ratings of 3,455 nouns in MRCDB is 0.826. This represents a strong positive correlation between the both measures.

Table 1: The statistics of 3,455 nouns in MRCDB used for the experiment.

Measure	min	max	Avg.	S.D.
Perceivability	0.097	0.950	0.578	0.195
Imaginability	0.048	0.945	0.620	0.175
Concreteness	0.152	0.923	0.609	0.177

[8]In fact, perceivability scores are termed "concreteness" in MRCDB although their sense is closer to the notion of perceivaility as indicated in the description of user study.

In order to evaluate the correlation between two lists of values, we used three measurements: Pearson's correlation coefficient, Kendall's τ, and Root Mean Square Error (RMSE). The values for Pearson's correlation coefficient and Kendall's τ range in the interval [-1, 1]. Large or small values imply that there is positive or negative correlation between two input lists, while a value of 0 implies the lack of such correlation. Values for RMSE are more than or equal to 0. Small RMSE values imply small differences between the input value pairs.

4.2 Results

We used SVM[light] [15] implementation with standard parameterization for SVM regression. SVM was trained first on imageability scores and then on perceivability scores.

We denote the perceivability and imageability scores of term t estimated by using SVM regression as $\mathrm{Perc}_{\mathrm{SVM}}(t)$ and $\mathrm{Imag}_{\mathrm{SVM}}(t)$, respectively. We then estimate the concreteness of a term t, $\mathrm{Conc}_{\mathrm{SVM}}(t)$ using perceivability ratings and imageability ratings estimated by SVM regression.

$$\mathrm{Conc}_{\mathrm{SVM}}(t) = \frac{1}{2}\left(\mathrm{Perc}_{\mathrm{SVM}}(t) + \mathrm{Imag}_{\mathrm{SVM}}(t)\right) \quad (3)$$

Table 2 shows the results. The correlations between $\mathrm{Perc}_{\mathrm{MRC}}(t)$ and $\mathrm{Perc}_{\mathrm{SVM}}(t)$ measured by Pearson's correlation coefficient, Kendall's τ, and the Root Mean Square Error are 0.671, 0.492, and 0.145, respectively. The correlations between $\mathrm{Imag}_{\mathrm{MRC}}(t)$ and $\mathrm{Imag}_{\mathrm{SVM}}(t)$ are 0.675, 0.502, and 0.129, respectively. These results indicate reasonably strong positive correlation. It also appears that imageability can be estimated slightly more accurately. However, we managed to achieve better results on the concreteness measure. The correlations between the concreteness of terms using MRCDB, $\mathrm{Conc}_{\mathrm{MRC}}(t)$, and the proposed concreteness, $\mathrm{Conc}_{\mathrm{SVM}}(t)$, are 0.688, 0.508, and 0.128, respectively. These results indicate that our method can successfully estimate word concreteness scores as compared to the labelled data in MRCDB. For better understanding of the results, in Table 4 we show 10 terms which have the largest or smallest perceivability, imageability and the concreteness rating estimated by using SVM regression.

Table 2: Results of term-level concreteness estimation

Measure	Pearson's r	Kendall's τ	RMSE
Perceivability	0.671	0.492	0.145
Imageability	0.675	0.502	0.129
Concreteness	0.688	0.508	0.128

Next, we looked at the statistics of the scores generated by our approach. Table 3 shows the statistics of $\mathrm{Perc}_{\mathrm{SVM}}(t)$, $\mathrm{Imag}_{\mathrm{SVM}}(t)$ and the concreteness score, $\mathrm{Conc}_{\mathrm{SVM}}(t)$. We notice that the perceivability ratings estimated by SVM regression have smaller standard deviation than the target ratings in MRCDB (see Table 1). Similar smoothing effect is observed for imageability.

Table 3: The statistics of SVM regressions results

Measure	min	max	Avg.	S.D.
Perceivability	-0.016	1.010	0.601	0.132
Imaginability	0.105	1.017	0.623	0.116
Concreteness	0.085	1.001	0.612	0.122

Table 4: Top 10 terms having largest or smallest ratings estimated by SVM regression

Terms with the largest perceivability scores, $\mathrm{Perc}_{\mathrm{SVM}}(t)$
cattle, portrait, deer, cow, shrub, tree, robin, boat, moose, feline
Terms with the smallest perceivability scores, $\mathrm{Perc}_{\mathrm{SVM}}(t)$
competence, exactitude, ingratitude, comradeship, insufficiency, importance, integrity, infallibility, virtue, misconception
Terms with the largest imageability scores, $\mathrm{Imag}_{\mathrm{SVM}}(t)$
portrait, cattle, boat, sunlight, cow, grass, dusk, deer, sunset, mare
Terms with the smallest imageability scores, $\mathrm{Imag}_{\mathrm{SVM}}(t)$
besieger, exactitude, disparagement, ingratitude, increment, impotency, competence, profiteer, interposition, loquacity
Terms with the largest concreteness scores, $\mathrm{Conc}_{\mathrm{SVM}}(t)$
portrait, cattle, cow, boat, deer, robin, tree, grass, dusk, sunlight
Terms with the smallest concreteness scores, $\mathrm{Conc}_{\mathrm{SVM}}(t)$
exactitude, competence, ingratitude, insufficiency, besieger, infallibility, impotency, condescension, loquacity, comradeship

4.2.1 *Feature Selection*

We evaluate the importance of each feature with 5-fold cross-validation and 3 measurements: Pearson's correlation coefficient, Kendall's τ, and RMSE. The mechanism of feature selection is based on finding the least effective feature **f** in the set of all features *Features*, and then removing **f** from *Features* step by step.

Table 5 lists the transition of the three evaluation metrics during the feature selection. The values in step 0 are the values which are estimated by SVM regression using all the 21 features. Each column in Table 5 shows the pairs of removed feature and the measured value of our evaluation metrics.

Feature **f20** (the average objectivity of the senses of a term) is the most important feature used in SVM regression for perceivability, and feature **f3** (the rating how much a term is related to photos) is the most important feature for imageability. Features **f3** and **f11** (the depth of the most common sense) are important for both perceivability and imageability. On the other hand, features based on capturing average values over different senses of a term such as **f9**, **f14** are not very helpful. The performance should thus improve if the actual sense of a word is considered. Surprisingly, **f5** (the ratio of popularity of a term in Flickr vs. popularity on the web) performs poorly, while a very similar feature **f4** (the ratio of popularity of a term in image search engine vs. popularity on the web) is quite significant. This is probably due to the fact that shared photo databases such as Flickr do not contain large variety of images when compared to the data captured by image search engines. For example, images of tourist places tend to be more common in Flickr than the images of less interesting objects such as hammer or sponge.

4.3 Term Co-occurrence and Concreteness

We complete the analysis of term-level concreteness by investigating another possible approach to its evaluation.

We expected a tendency that abstract nouns co-occur with other abstract nouns more frequently than with concrete nouns. Similarly, we also suspected that concrete nouns co-occur with concrete nouns more frequently than with abstract nouns. If these assumptions would be true, then the near context of a term could serve as an additional signal for concreteness estimation. To investigate the hypothesis regarding the correlation between the concreteness of terms and their co-occurrence we used the article content of En-

Table 5: The change in average Pearson's correlation coefficient, Kendall's τ, and RMSE

step	$\text{Perc}_{\text{SVM}}(t)$						$\text{Imag}_{\text{SVM}}(t)$					
	Pearson		Kendall		RMSE		Pearson		Kendall		RMSE	
0	–	0.668	–	0.489	–	0.145	–	0.671	–	0.499	–	0.130
1	**f5**	0.669	**f14**	0.490	**f5**	0.145	**f5**	0.673	**f6**	0.499	**f5**	0.129
2	**f14**	0.669	**f17**	0.490	**f14**	0.145	**f1**	0.673	**f20**	0.499	**f1**	0.129
3	**f16**	0.669	**f8**	0.490	**f16**	0.145	**f9**	0.673	**f8**	0.499	**f19**	0.129
4	**f19**	0.669	**f9**	0.490	**f19**	0.145	**f14**	0.673	**f1**	0.500	**f17**	0.129
5	**f8**	0.669	**f2**	0.490	**f8**	0.145	**f13**	0.673	**f5**	0.500	**f8**	0.129
6	**f9**	0.670	**f18**	0.490	**f9**	0.145	**f20**	0.673	**f9**	0.500	**f13**	0.129
7	**f2**	0.670	**f15**	0.490	**f2**	0.145	**f18**	0.674	**f17**	0.500	**f14**	0.129
8	**f6**	0.669	**f5**	0.490	**f18**	0.145	**f8**	0.674	**f13**	0.500	**f6**	0.129
9	**f18**	0.669	**f6**	0.489	**f17**	0.145	**f19**	0.674	**f15**	0.500	**f16**	0.129
10	**f17**	0.669	**f19**	0.488	**f6**	0.145	**f6**	0.674	**f14**	0.500	**f9**	0.129
11	**f13**	0.667	**f13**	0.487	**f13**	0.146	**f15**	0.674	**f19**	0.500	**f15**	0.129
12	**f10**	0.665	**f10**	0.485	**f10**	0.146	**f21**	0.673	**f12**	0.498	**f21**	0.129
13	**f15**	0.663	**f16**	0.483	**f15**	0.146	**f17**	0.671	**f18**	0.496	**f18**	0.130
14	**f12**	0.660	**f12**	0.479	**f12**	0.147	**f12**	0.669	**f4**	0.492	**f12**	0.130
15	**f7**	0.652	**f7**	0.470	**f7**	0.148	**f10**	0.666	**f21**	0.489	**f4**	0.130
16	**f21**	0.635	**f21**	0.459	**f21**	0.151	**f4**	0.664	**f10**	0.486	**f10**	0.131
17	**f4**	0.619	**f4**	0.443	**f4**	0.153	**f16**	0.653	**f16**	0.474	**f20**	0.132
18	**f1**	0.592	**f1**	0.422	**f1**	0.157	**f7**	0.631	**f7**	0.458	**f7**	0.136
19	**f11**	0.532	**f11**	0.359	**f11**	0.166	**f2**	0.608	**f11**	0.431	**f2**	0.139
20	**f3**	0.415	**f3**	0.287	**f3**	0.196	**f11**	0.344	**f2**	0.230	**f11**	0.448
21	**f20**	–	**f20**	–	**f20**	–	**f3**	–	**f3**	–	**f3**	–

glish Wikipedia [9]. In particular, we examined the relation between the co-occurrence of terms in the same sentences and their concreteness ratings as provided in MRCDB.

Let #Sentences (t) be the number of sentences which contain a term t. The Jaccard Coefficient between any two terms, t and u, is calculated by the following equation.

$$\text{Jaccard}(t,\ u) = \frac{\#\text{Sentences}\,(t \wedge u)}{\#\text{Sentences}\,(t \vee u)}$$

To proceed we make two sets that include adjustable portions of terms according to their perceivability or imageability scores (terms are ranked by their scores):

$$Terms_{\text{high}} = \{\text{terms in highest } x\%\},$$
$$Terms_{\text{low}} = \{\text{terms in lowest } x\%\}.$$

The co-occurrence rate between the two sets of terms, $Terms_i$ and $Terms_j$, is then calculated as the average Jaccard coefficient between terms from these two sets.

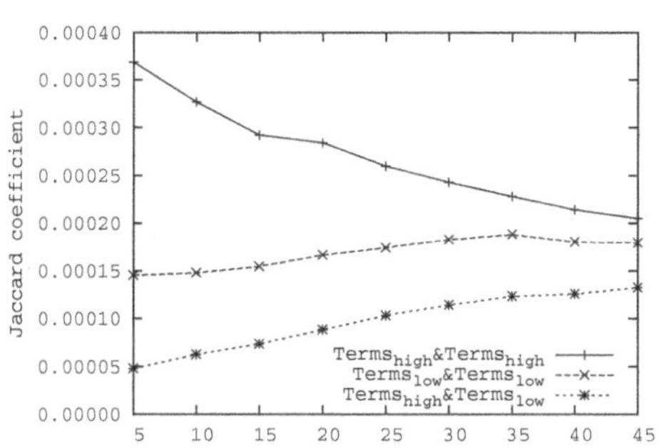

Figure 1: Average Jaccard Coefficient results of two sets of terms for perceivability

Figures 1 and 2 show the results according to the used rate of top-scored terms in the two term sets (i.e., x%). We can observe significant differences between term co-occurrence levels at different sizes of term sets. For example, at $x = 5$ the average co-occurrence between the little perceivable terms or between the highly perceivable terms is 3 and 7 times higher, respectively, than the average co-occurrence between terms in which one has high and the other has low perceivability scores. These results suggest that concrete terms may tend to co-occur with other concrete terms more than with abstract ones. The co-occurrence score of a term with manually labelled examples of concrete terms could be then another feature for SVM.

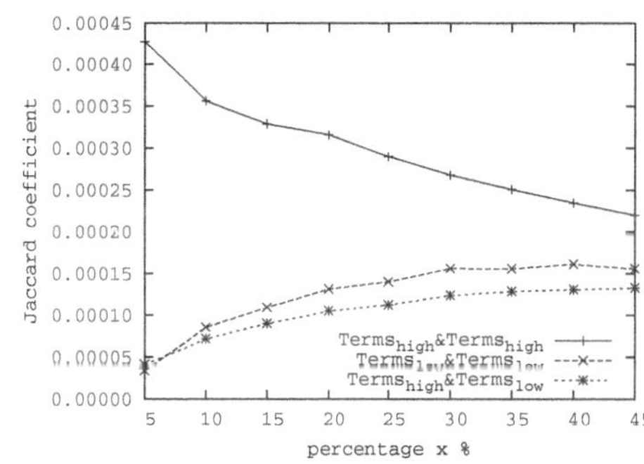

Figure 2: Average Jaccard Coefficient results of two sets of terms for imageability

5. EVALUATION OF DOCUMENT-LEVEL CONCRETENESS

Although we obtained satisfactory results the estimation of term-level concreteness, we wanted to investigate whether it is feasible to estimate the concreteness of the whole documents based on the concreteness scores of their contained terms. In this section we report the results of the second experiment to measure the accuracy of document-level concreteness estimation.

5.1 Settings

To create dataset for the second experiment we have collected web pages from the Yahoo! web search engine[10]. We have used 50 queries, among which, 33 queries were manually selected from TREC Million Query Track 2007, 2008 and 2009 [3], and 17 were selected from the titles of

[9]Wikipedia dump of July 2011.

[10]http://www.yahoo.com [27th November, 2012]

Wikipedia articles. We have tried to collect both abstract (e.g., "rationalism", "good moral character") and concrete queries (e.g., "copper penny", "apple laptops") in order to have documents with different concreteness degrees. In total, we had 35 abstract and 15 concrete queries. The top 10 returned search results were collected for each query. Next, we removed HTML tags, Javascript and any multimedia files, and captured the core content of each document. Finally, we extracted two top paragraphs filtering out the ones with less than 400 characters.

Such processed documents were then shown to 5 evaluators who rated them in terms of concreteness and comprehensibility using the 5-point Likert scale ("very low", "low", "neutral", "high", and "very high"). The evaluators were in their 20's and 30's, had higher education degrees and were not experts in any of the topics of test queries. Besides the concreteness and comprehensibility judgements, the evaluators were also asked to rate the relevance of each document to its associated query. By this we wanted to eliminated spam or completely irrelevant documents. The relevance choices were as follows: "irrelevant (spam)", "neutral" and "relevant". After the documents have been evaluated, we removed those that were judged as irrelevant or neutral. The criteria for removal were as follows, (a) a document received at least one "irrelevant (spam)" vote from any of five judges or (b) at least three judges labelled the document as "neutral". After this step we had in total 305 labelled documents. Note that we have decided to choose a relatively high number of judges rather than extending the size of document collection according to the intuition that both concreteness and comprehensibility are subjective and may depend on user's knowledge. The inter-evaluator agreement of the scores assigned by the five judges was measured by average Kendall's τ coefficient. The result was 0.568 for concreteness and 0.624 for comprehensibility indicating reasonably high agreement among judges. To assign a single concreteness and comprehensibility score to each document we took the median of five scores provided by the evaluators.

5.2 Results

5.2.1 Correlation between Concreteness and Comprehensibility

We first investigate our initial assumption that concrete texts help users better understand documents. We show the results of the correlation between the ground truth scores (i.e., the median of the scores by five judges) of concreteness and comprehensibility. The Kendall's τ correlation coefficient between the concreteness and comprehensibility is 0.385 ($p < 0.0001$). This is moderate positive correlation indicating that concreteness and comprehensibility of documents are somehow correlated, although the correlation is not very high. Moreover, we have found that concrete documents are much more likely to be comprehensible than abstract ones as evidenced by the conditional probabilities, $P(\text{High Comp}|\text{High Conc}) = 0.971$, and $P(\text{High Comp}|\text{Low Conc}) = 0.491$. Similarly, incomprehensible documents are less likely to be concrete than comprehensible ones, $P(\text{High Conc}|\text{Low Comp}) = 0.067$, and $P(\text{High Conc}|\text{High Comp}) = 0.723$. High Conc and High Comp indicate here the scores, "high", and "very high", while Low Conc and Low Comp indicate the scores, "low", and "very low" for the concreteness and comprehensibility, respectively. These results indicate the usefulness of concrete texts when it comes to content understanding.

In addition, we investigated correlation between readability metrics and comprehensibility. By this we wanted to check whether using readability measures only would be enough to determine document comprehensibility. We have used here the following measures, Flesch Reading Ease (FRE) [12], New Dale Chall (NDC) [4] and Lexical Density (LD) [28]. As mentioned before, FRE calculates document readability based on the combined measure of sentence and word length, while NDC estimates the expected school grade level of a text based on the average sentence length and the number of "difficult" words. To distinguish "easy" words from difficult ones NDC uses the list of 3,000 common words in English. Lastly, LD estimates the rate of content words (e.g., nouns, adjectives, verbs, etc.) to the total number of words in a document including grammatical words. Intuitively, documents with high lexical density should contain much information (e.g., academic papers) and may thus be poorly understandable by readers. To calculate LD we have used POS tagger available in the Natural Language Toolkit[11] (NLTK).

Table 6 shows the correlation between documents' comprehensibility and their readability. We can see that the assumption that readability formulas only such as FRE and NDC can successfully estimate how easy documents are is generally not correct. When compared to the above-reported correlation between the document concreteness and comprehensibility, these results suggest that concreteness is an important factor of document comprehensibility that cannot be simply captured by the surface document characteristics such as sentence length, word length, or POS tag distribution.

Table 6: Kendall's τ coefficient between the readability and the comprehensibility. A parenthetical value indicates the p value.

$Conc^{gt}_{doc}$	Readability Measures		
	FRE	NDC	LD
0.385 (0.000)	0.215 (0.000)	0.335 (0.000)	-0.111 (0.003)

5.2.2 Evaluation of Document Concreteness Measure

For evaluation we use two baselines, *name entity score* and *generality score*. The first one calculates the rate of named entities in text using NLTK toolkit according to the intuitive assumption that named entities usually indicate concrete entities. The second baseline calculates average term commonness in a document using a large English corpus. It is expressed as follows:

$$\text{Generality}\,(D) = \frac{1}{|D|}\sum_{t \in D} \ln \text{cf}\,(t) \quad (4)$$

where cf (t) is the term frequency of t in the Corpus of Contemporary American English[12] (COCA). COCA is a balanced, up-to-date corpus containing about 450 million words from documents of diverse genres. The intuition behind this choice is the assumption that documents containing popular words should be on average more concrete than the ones

[11]http://nltk.org [27th November, 2012]

[12]http://corpus.byu.edu/coca [27th November, 2012]

with less popular words. For example, a blog describing someone's daily life or dining experience should contain on average more common words than scientific paper on astrophysics or a discourse about philosophy. We are aware that this hypothesis may not be always true and there are still many documents that describe abstract topics using relatively popular words (e.g., "love", "sadness"). We note that as our work is the first attempt for automatic estimation of document concreteness we could not use any standard evaluation benchmark or other similar systems.

First, we calculate the correlation of the concreteness scores given by judges and the scores assigned by $Conc^{avg}_{doc}$ and $Conc^{max}_{doc}$, as described in Section 3.2. The results are shown in Table 7 and indicate that the proposed methods produce significantly better results than the baselines. Interestingly, the *name entity scoring* is characterized by the negative correlation with the concreteness scores. Thus it is not necessarily true that documents with many named entities are concrete. The results of the Mean Average Precision and nDCG measures (see Table 8) confirm also the higher effectiveness of our approach when compared to the baselines. However, we notice from these results that it is difficult to conclude which method, $Conc^{avg}_{doc}$ or $Conc^{max}_{doc}$, performs better.

For a more complete analysis we show the 11-points interpolated precision-recall graph in Figure 3. To plot the grap, first, we ranked all the documents based on the calculated concreteness score. Then we considered documents having "high" or "very high" median score as *true documents*. Looking at the Figure 3 we can notice that the precision at 10% recall drops significantly, although it is still relatively high (over 60%). We can explain it as an increased difficulty to predict correct concreteness for the documents that did not achieve top ranks. In other words, it is relatively easy to determine the correct concreteness levels of documents with plenty of concrete terms but more difficult to do it for documents with moderate number of terms. The precision values until the middle recall range remain relatively stable (e.g., Precision = 60% at Recall = 50%).

We note here that the relatively simple extension from the term-level to document-level concreteness produces already good results. One improvement of this approach would involve estimating concreteness levels of phrases and sentences. Consider, for example, the expression "lipstick on a pig". While both the nouns in this expression are concrete, their combination refers to rather abstract concept.

Table 7: Kendall's τ coefficient between the ground truth and concreteness predicted by each method. A parenthetical value indicates the p value.

Baseline methods		Proposed methods	
Named entity score	Generality score	$Conc^{avg}_{doc}$	$Conc^{max}_{doc}$
-0.0255 (0.507)	0.101 (0.009)	0.362 (0.000)	**0.364** (0.000)

5.3 Estimating Query Concreteness

We are also interested whether there is any correspondence between query concreteness and search results' concreteness. In other words, we wish to know whether abstract queries return on average abstract documents and, correspondingly, whether concrete queries result in on average concrete search results. To test these assumptions we have measured conditional probabilities of the average

Table 8: Average MAP and nDCG over all the queries.

	Baseline methods		Proposed methods	
	Named entity score	Generality score	$Conc^{avg}_{doc}$	$Conc^{max}_{doc}$
MAP	0.666	0.664	**0.796**	0.793
nDCG@1	0.693	0.750	0.830	**0.835**
nDCG@3	0.756	0.810	**0.847**	0.845
nDCG@5	0.826	0.855	0.886	**0.890**

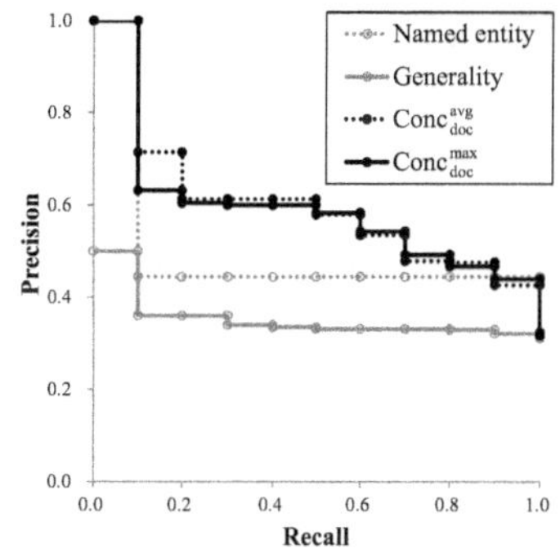

Figure 3: A 11-points interpolated precision curve.

document concreteness/abstractness (using ground truth scores) depending on the query characteristics (as calculated by our method). The results indicate that documents returned in response to a concrete query are likely to be concrete ($P(ConcD|ConcQ) = 0.779$), while ones returned in response to an abstract query are likely to be abstract ($P(AbstD|AbstQ) = 0.685$). We think that the concreteness value of query itself could be a good predictor of the average concreteness level of the returned search results. This could be used by search engines to dynamically adapt their ranking mechanisms depending on the expected query "difficulty" represented by its concreteness/abstractness score in a similar way as approaches to query performance prediction (relevance viewpoint). This forms our future work.

6. DISCUSSION

6.1 Search Considering Document Concreteness

Conventional search engines do not seem to directly consider concreteness of web pages when ranking search results. Currently, users have to manually find web pages which contain concrete contents. Typically, they do it either by skimming through search results or by reformulating their initial queries to achieve more concrete results. Considering the latter, in the previous example of Parkinson's disease, users could append keywords, such as "experience" and "symptoms" to the initial query "Parkinson's disease". However, the ability to find such keywords depends on users' experience and expertise, hence, novice or inexperienced users may have difficulty with conceptualizing appropriate terms. Imagine a legal document about a newly established law written in a fairy abstract and complicated way. A novice, non-expert user may require texts about concrete, real-life cases to study the law in practice in order to better understand its meaning and application scope. Yet, it may be difficult for the user to come up with keywords leading to pages describing the specific cases of this law. While state-of-the-art web search engines offer query suggestions given the input query string, the returned candidates do not necessarily lead to retrieving more concrete documents. In general, there is no systematic way to retrieve concrete documents neither to support users in finding such documents, for example, by suggesting query extensions that would return more concrete results. We think that incorporating concreteness/abstractness judgements into IR systems could become a valuable enhancement. In the future we plan to propose concreteness/abstractness query expansion model in order to support users in the search for more comprehensible, concrete contents.

6.2 Abstract Documents

We focused in this work on finding concrete web pages. However, concrete documents may be sometimes too long and users might have difficulty to read and memorize them. Certain readers, such as more proficient or knowledgeable ones, may actually prefer to read abstract texts. Although, in general, concrete documents help readers understand the topic of documents, concrete documents lack information which abstract documents contain. For example, think of the documents about the effects of Parkinson's disease. In abstract documents, one of the effects of Parkinson's disease is *motor symptoms*. In concrete documents, the effects of Parkinson's disease are *loss of balance*, *shaking in limbs*, and *slow walk*. In many cases, it is difficult for users to induce abstract rules, theories, or concepts from concrete cases and examples. In the above example, *motor symptoms* covers *loss of balance*, *shaking in limbs* and *slow walk*, yet, many users could have difficulties to abstract into *motor symptoms* from these concrete descriptions. We believe that finding abstract web pages could be also useful sometimes and we do not exclude this case.

7. CONCLUSION AND FUTURE WORK

Concrete contents help to understand abstract, complex concepts, are more easily remembered and are often more attractive to users. However, despite these well-known phenomena, no reasonable solution has been proposed until now for supporting users in finding concrete and thus more comprehensible documents. In this paper, we describe method for evaluating the concreteness of words using machine learning and then extrapolate it to the estimation of concreteness on the document-level. A wide number of signals are explored and the evaluation is conducted on term-level as well as on the document-level. In addition, we discuss the problems and applications of the concreteness estimation in IR and provide additional experimentation for directing further studies. In the future we would like to focus on the previously mentioned directions as well as on the interplay between the concreteness and relevance of documents.

8. ACKNOWLEDGEMENTS

This work has been supported in part by the project: Grants-in-Aid for Scientific Research (No. 24240013) from MEXT of Japan.

9. REFERENCES

[1] K. Akamatsu, N. Pattanasri, A. Jatowt, and K. Tanaka. Comprehensibility of web pages based on link analysis. In *WI'11*, pages 40–46. IEEE, 2011.

[2] L. Cahill and J. L. McGaugh. A novel demonstration of enhanced memory associated with emotional arousal. *Consciousness and Cognition*, 4(4):410–421, 1995.

[3] B. Carterette, V. Pavlu, H. Fang, and E. Kanoulas. Million query track 2009 overview. In *TREC '09*, 2009.

[4] J. Chall. *Readability Revisited: The New Dale-Chall Readability Formula*. Brookline Books/Lumen Editions, 1995.

[5] M. Coleman and T. L. Liau. A computer readability formula designed for machine scoring. *Journal of Applied Psychology*, 60:283–284, 1975.

[6] K. Collins-Thompson and J. Callan. A language modeling approach to predicting reading difficulty. In *HLT-NAACL*, pages 193–200, 2004.

[7] K. Collins-Thompson, S. de la Chica, and D. Sontag. Personalizing web search results by reading level. In *CIKM'11*, pages 403–412. ACM, 2011.

[8] D. Crystal. *The Cambridge encyclopedia of the English language*. Cambridge University Press, 1995.

[9] E. Dale and J. Chall. The concept of readability. *Elementary English*, 26(23), 1949.

[10] C. Eickhoff, P. Serdyukov, and A. P. de Vries. A combined topical/non-topical approach to identifying web sites for children. In *WSDM '11*, pages 505–514.

[11] T. Faaß, L. Kaczmirek, and A. Lenzner. Psycholinguistic determinants of question difficulty: A web experiment. In *7th International Conference on Social Science Methodology*, 2008.

[12] R. Flesch. A new readability yardstick. *Journal of Applied Psychology*, 32(3):221–233, 1948.

[13] K. J. Gilhooly and R. H. Logie. Age-of-acquisition, imagery, concreteness, familiarity, and ambiguity measures for 1,944 words. *Behavior Research Methods*, 12(4):395–427, 1980.

[14] A. C. Graesser, D. S. McNamara, M. M. Louwerse, and Z. Cai. Coh-metrix: analysis of text on cohesion and language. *Behavior Research Methods, Instruments, and Computers*, 36(2):193–202, 2004.

[15] T. Joachims. *Making large-scale support vector machine learning practical*, pages 169–184. MIT Press, Cambridge, MA, USA, 1999.

[16] M. Kato, H. Ohshima, S. Oyama, and K. Tanaka. Can social tagging improve web image search? In *WISE'08*, pages 235–249. Springer, 2008.

[17] J. Krug and X. Xu. Imagery, context availability, contextual constraint, and abstractness. In *Proceedings of the 23rd Annual Conference of the Cognitive Science Society*, pages 1134–1139. Erlbaum, 2001.

[18] D. Lambov, G. Dias, and J. Graca. Multi-view learning for text subjectivity classification. In *1st Workshop on Computational Approaches to Subjectivity and Sentiment Analysis*, 2010.

[19] M. Larson, C. Kofler, and A. Hanjalic. Reading between the tags to predict real-world size-class for visually depicted objects in images. In *MM'11*, pages 273–282. ACM, 2011.

[20] M. Nakatani, A. Jatowt, and K. Tanaka. Easiest-first search: towards comprehension-based web search. In *CIKM'09*, pages 2057–2060. ACM, 2009.

[21] U. D. of Education Office of Educational Research and Improvement. Adult literacy in america, 2002. `http://nces.ed.gov/pubs93/93275.pdf` [27th November, 2012].

[22] A. Paivio, J. C. Yuille, and S. A. Madigan. Concreteness, imagery, and meaningfulness values for 925 nouns. *Journal of Experimental Psychology*, 76(1, Part 2):1–25, 1968.

[23] R. Rumbo. English composition 1: Using specific and concrete diction. `http://www2.ivcc.edu/rambo/eng1001/eng1001_diction.htm` [27th November, 2012].

[24] P. Schwanenflugel. *Why are Abstract Concepts Hard to Understand?*, pages 223–250. 1991.

[25] A. Sun and S. Bhowmick. Quantifying visual-representativeness of social image tags using image tag clarity. In *Social Media Modeling and Computing*, pages 3–23. Springer, 2011.

[26] J. T. and E. Richardson. *Imagery, concreteness, and lexical complexity*, volume 27 of *2*, pages 211–223. Psychology Press, 1975.

[27] M. P. Toglia and W. F. Battig. Handbook of semantic word norms. *John Wiley & Sons, Inc., One Wiley Drive, Somerset, New Jersey 18873*, page 152, 1978.

[28] J. Ure. *Lexical density and register differentiation*, pages 443–452. London: Cambridge Univ. Press, 1971.

[29] V. N. Vapnik. *The nature of statistical learning theory*. Springer-Verlag New York, Inc., 1995.

[30] G. K. Zipf. *Human behavior and the principle of least effort*. Addison-Wesley, Cambridge, (Mass.), 1949.

Translating Related Words to Videos and Back through Latent Topics

Pradipto Das
CSE Dept., SUNY Buffalo
Buffalo, NY 14260
pdas3@buffalo.edu

Rohini K. Srihari
CSE Dept., SUNY Buffalo
Buffalo, NY 14260
rohini@cedar.buffalo.edu

Jason J. Corso
CSE Dept., SUNY Buffalo
Buffalo, NY 14260
jcorso@buffalo.edu

ABSTRACT

Documents containing video and text are becoming more and more widespread and yet content analysis of those documents depends primarily on the text. Although automated discovery of semantically related words from text improves free text query understanding, translating videos into text summaries facilitates better video search particularly in the absence of accompanying text. In this paper, we propose a multimedia topic modeling framework suitable for providing a basis for automatically discovering and translating semantically related words obtained from textual metadata of multimedia documents to semantically related videos or frames from videos. The framework jointly models video and text and is flexible enough to handle different types of document features in their constituent domains such as discrete and real valued features from videos representing actions, objects, colors and scenes as well as discrete features from text. Our proposed models show much better fit to the multimedia data in terms of held-out data log likelihoods. For a given query video, our models translate low level vision features into bag of keyword summaries which can be further translated using simple natural language generation techniques into human readable paragraphs. We quantitatively compare the results of video to bag of words translation against a state-of-the-art baseline object recognition model from computer vision. We show that text translations from multimodal topic models vastly outperform the baseline on a multimedia dataset downloaded from the Internet.

Categories and Subject Descriptors

I.2.7 [**Computing Methodologies**]: Artificial Intelligence—*Natural Language Processing*

General Terms

Algorithms, Experimentation

Keywords

multimedia topic models; video to text summarization

1. INTRODUCTION

In recent years there has been an abundance of multimedia data in the form of video contents from television networks, video uploads to websites and so on. However, organizing such data by integrating the semantic content of the videos is a very difficult problem. On the other hand, summarizing videos directly into text summaries can lead to significant improvements in many end-user applications—multimedia search experience, content based advertisements [33], helping the visually impaired and so on. In this paper we concern ourselves with two language agnostic tasks: **i)** Building a topic modeling framework to model multimedia documents consisting of videos and textual metadata and **ii)** using the topic modeling framework to predict bag-of-word summaries for a new video belonging to a previously known category. The first task helps us discover semantically related concepts in the text through latent topics and translating them to topically related videos or frames. The second task takes a test video and generates intermediate text keywords ideal for natural language generation.

Figure 1: An example of the task of video summarization

As a further addition we also experiment with efficient natural language sentence generation from the predicted bag of words (henceforth BoW) using language models and confidence of syntactic parse tree generation following a simple template. The first two tasks, though, are the focus of this paper. Fig. 1 shows some keyframes of two sample videos from our training dataset and the short summaries written by human annotators. This dataset is discussed in Section 1.1. *In our paper, translation from video to text is synonymous to summarizing a video with a set of textual keywords.*

It seems intuitive that a topic model which incorporates low level vision features representing objects, actions, color and scenes and correspond those to the text summaries should have a better chance of describing the multimedia data. We thus seek representations of visual data that mimic the subject-verb-object-scene quadruplet structure of English sentences in terms of subject, object and scene nouns as well as verbs. Additionally illumination gives rise to color which differentiates one object from another and is often expressed as adjectives. Objects, actions and color can be visualized using specific word concepts and can be counted over time thus lending themselves to quantization but scene represents global energy distributions which pervade the arrangement of objects and is thus better represented as real values.

In the context of this paper, our training data consists of videos and associated summaries. The training data is also available with event category labels for e.g. "boarding event" and topic modeling video documents in each event can allow us to discover "sub-topics" e.g. "skateboarding", "snowboarding" and "surfing". Of course, our topic models do not include any event label bias and can be applied on the overall dataset as well. However we will see shortly that doing so can be very unappealing to end users when summaries need to be generated.

Apart from the topical analysis of video documents, the problem of generating summaries directly from videos also has significant end user appeal. We emphasize that the video summarization/translation task in this paper is to describe an entire video firstly as a bag of salient keywords i.e. BoW, and then, as a further addition, use simple Natural Language Generation (henceforth NLG) techniques to summarize the bag of words into a human readable paragraph of text wherever possible. Translating and generating summaries from a video can always be looked upon as finding the right information need which is paramount to any search problem.

Video summarization in our context is different from image annotation mentioned in early literature [27] and in more modern ones [18]. If we perfectly annotate all objects and actions in each frame correctly, we can probably use a standard topic modeling technique [5] to figure out the themes in the multimedia documents. However, detecting objects [15] and scenes [22] in images and actions [11] and keyframes [14] in videos in a reliable manner are open problems in the computer vision community [18]. Most of these detection techniques fall in the domain of supervised learning and require large amounts of annotated data. Video annotation task is a particularly laborious process even though tools like VATIC [29] have been written to ease the effort (for an interactive demo of the tool, see VATIC's website[1]). Also firing thousands of detectors to accurately label even a single keyframe of an unknown video leads to many false positives. This is particularly true of the videos *in-the-wild* i.e. videos downloaded from the Internet where there are plenty of resolution problems, severe motion blurs, camera shakes etc. These are the videos that we experiment with in this paper.

We view the video to text translation/summarization problem in the light of multidocument summarization of plain text documents which has been popularized by the Text Analysis Conference[2] (TAC). In the multidocument summarization track of TAC, participants are given document sets (docsets) of newswire articles typically belonging to 5 major event types like "Health and Safety," "Accidents and Natural Disasters" etc. and are asked to generate a fixed length fluent summary of the documents in each docset. A docset in the TAC setting is unique in that it contains a set of documents that are relevant for a particular information need like "Cyclone Katrina." The system summaries are scored in several ways including the most reliable manual way using PYRAMID [21] evaluation but systems usually are tuned w.r.t. the automatic ROUGE [16] scoring. By analogy, we assume that each docset here corresponds to a video and contains a sequence of frames and a set of keyframes. At test time we are given unknown event specific videos without any text summary. For measuring system performance, we generate summaries of videos and evaluate them using the recall oriented ROUGE-1 score to measure the percent overlap of the words in the short ground truth summaries.

Figure 2: An example of vocabulary intrusion in the task of video summarization. Best viewed with magnification

A key concern in generating a BoW summary of a video is the vocabulary intrusion problem. Fig. 2 shows an example of vocabulary intrusion in the task of video summarization that arises out of topic modeling on the entire vocabulary of the corpus. If we consider a vocabulary of V words—the probability of getting the top L words correctly in the summary is $(1/V)(1/(V-1))...(1/(V-L+1))$. If V is large (such as 2000) then the probability is very low. Further, if the entire vocabulary is used, then intrusive words describing other but related event categories like "birthday, flash mob, dance, parade, fish" can appear with high probability (see a possible predicted BoW summary in Fig. 2 from a topic model(Fig. 3b) trained over all events with number of topics set to 200). This problem is mitigated by first classifying the test video into its corresponding event category (Section 4.4) and then using a topic model to predict the BoW summary. In the absence of the event labels, this direction improves readability and is much faster.

The novelty in our new approach to topic modeling video documents with textual metadata is the use of the right features for the videos and augmenting basic topic models for joint modeling with those features along with text. We represent each video in terms of objects, actions, color (represented with discrete distributions) and scenes (represented with Normal distributions with unknown means and variances) and try to find a translation space that translates the pattern of these features to a permutation in language vocabulary. Such a representation of a video is both intuitive and logical. We observe that the interplay of the full spectrum of representations (Section 4) indeed yield the highest likelihoods to held out test data than those using partial representations (Section 4.1).

1.1 Dataset Description

The dataset that we use for the video summarization task is released as part of NIST's 2011 TRECVID Multimedia Event Detection (MED) evaluation set[3]. The dataset consists of a collection of Internet multimedia content posted to the various Internet video hosting sites. The training set is organized into 15 event categories, some of which are: *1) Attempting a board trick 2)Feeding an animal 3)Landing a fish 4)Wedding ceremony 5) Working on a woodworking project* etc.

We use the videos and their textual metadata in all the 15 events as training data. There are 2062 clips with summaries in the training set with almost equal distribution amongst the events. The test set which we use is called the Transparent Development (Dev-T) collection. The Dev-T collection includes positive instances of the first 5 training events and near positive instances for the last 10 events—a total of 630

[1]http://mit.edu/vondrick/vatic/

[2]http://www.nist.gov/tac/2011/Summarization/

[3]http://www.nist.gov/itl/iad/mig/med11.cfm

videos labeled with event category information (and associated human synopses which are to be compared against for summarization performance). Each summary is a short and very high level description of the entire video and ranges from 2 to 40 words but on average **10** words (with stopwords). We remove standard English stopwords and retain only the word morphologies (not required) from the synopses as our training vocabularies. The proportion of videos belonging to events 6 through 15 in the Dev-T set is much low compared to the proportion for the other events since those clips are considered to be "related" instances which cover only part of the event category specifications. The performances of our topic models are evaluated on those kinds of clips as well. The numbers of videos in events 6 through 15 in the Dev-T set are {4,9,5,7,8,3,3,3,10,8} while there are around 120 videos per event for the first 5 events. All other videos in the Dev-T set neither have any event category label nor are identified as positive, negative or related videos and we do not consider these videos in our experiments.

1.2 Evaluation Measures

We measure the predictive performance of the topic models using the Evidence Lower BOunds (ELBO) on held-out test set—the Dev-T collection *with* summaries, as well as the predictive ELBO for BoW summary generation on the held-out Dev-T collection *without* summaries (Section 4.1). ELBO is just log likelihood and is directly related to measuring average perplexity of the model per observed textual word [5, 4]. We also evaluate our BoW summaries using the ROUGE scorer. ROUGE measures the n-gram overlap for system generated summaries to the ones written by annotators and the scores are interpreted in terms of recall. Usually 4 gold standard summaries are needed for evaluation but here we use the base case of using only one short summary as a reference summary per video on this dataset. While summarizing, since our primary task is to evaluate only the BoW summaries generated from a video, we use the ROUGE-1 unigram measure. We evaluate 5 and 10 keywords long BoW summaries respecting the average length of the short human summaries. Since we are considering videos in the Dev-T set with event category information, we can use the ROUGE evaluation setup of multidocument summarization as used in TAC. If the categories are not known, we can multiply the ROUGE scores with the event classification accuracies to obtain lower bounds (see Section 4.4 for lower bounds on classification accuracies). Evaluations with higher order n-grams are not needed for unigram translations. We do not use manual evaluations since the data cannot be released for public verifications.

The task of discovering topically related words is mostly evaluated w.r.t ELBO. We use the topic models from [4] as baselines. We modify the GM-LDA model in [4] following [26] to use discrete visual data and name the model MMLDA—"MM" stands for the multinomials for text as well as the multinomials for the visual words. We implement a deterministic optimization framework for MMLDA instead of the non-deterministic sampling as in [26]. The Corr-LDA model in [4] is also extended by using Normal-Wishart priors and named Corr-MGLDA (M for Multinomials and G for Gaussians). For evaluating video to text summarization based on ROUGE-1 scores, we use a non-topic model based automatic image annotation tool as the baseline for video labeling by using labels aggregated from keyframes. Our topic model based video summarization methods outperform the state-of-the-art image to text translation model [15] applied on video keyframes in terms of ROUGE-1 scores of the predicted keyword summaries.

2. RELATED WORK

Makadia et al. [18] uses nearest neighbor and label transfer techniques to annotate images suitable for the image retrieval task. However, we can not directly apply their methods as the individual frames/keyframes of the videos in our dataset are not annotated. Based on the size and genre of our dataset, such annotations prove very expensive and we do not follow that direction. Further, we are interested in the task of direct natural language summarization of the entire video and not specific annotation of a vast majority of possible objects, actions and scenes in every frame/keyframe of the video. The closest work to our task is by Yang et al. [34] where low level object and scene classifiers are used to obtain object and scene labels in an *image*. These are then combined using background language models and Hidden Markov Models to predict a natural language sentence that automatically includes the best possible verb i.e. action. *We will observe in Section 4.4 that* ***actions****, which are intrinsic to videos, are important event discriminators.* Further, none of above mentioned methods can discover related concepts as latent topics and translate them into related frames.

In the domain of topic modeling of images with captions, the Corr-LDA model has recently been extended to handle a multinomial feature space in [25] with different number of topics for visual word type and textual word type. The model learns an association from the topic proportions over image domain to those over text domain through a regression formulation. However, during prediction, this dependency needs to be marginalized out anyways. Also, if we quantize every type of real valued vision feature using some clustering algorithm such as K-means into C clusters, then each C represents a parameter of the final model and performance analysis become that much more difficult. Ahmed et al. [1] uses Gaussian feature vectors and mention Normal-Wishart priors but do not use them—they use uniform priors in a non-deterministic sampling framework instead.

On the other hand the Continuous Relevance Model (CRM) [13] and Multiple Bernoulli Relevance Model (MBRM) [8] assume different, nonparametric density representations of the joint word-image space. CRM gets rid of the latent factor representation and achieves non-parameterization. The dataset used in [8] for MBRM has hierarchical word annotations which are handled using multiple Bernoulli models rather than multinomial distributions. In our dataset, multinomial distributions are sufficient since the summaries read like very short documents with repeated word morphologies.

Detecting objects can often be seen as an important step towards identifying the main topic of a video and generating a BoW summary. To that end, Torresani et al. [28] transform an image feature vector into a another lower dimensional feature vector whose values are the outputs of several category classifiers (which are named "classemes" in their paper). We take a similar approach to convert Object Bank [15] (OB) feature vectors to high level sparse histogram of object detectors to be used in our discrete video data representation and as *baseline* for video to text translation. To extract OB features, keyframes are identified to reduce computational time. Keyframe detection is a research topic in its own right, where some recent ones include more involved techniques [14] using Transfer Learning from accompanying text transcripts. However, the keyframes extracted using the change in color histogram [35] satisfy our purposes.

In the domain of topic modeling of videos, the Hidden Topic Markov Model in [32] does not incorporate both text and visual words in a single framework and also does not use a fuller representation of videos as we do. A Markovian assumption is also imposed in [10] for modeling actions and identifying behaviors (with no automatic labeling), however, we can safely ignore frame dependence because our action features are derived using temporal windows and activity tracking is not an objective in this paper. The reformulations of LDA and CTM using class labels and without any temporal dynamics in [30] also target activity classification. To the best of our knowledge this is the first work to use mixed membership topic models for video to text summarization which *can* eliminate frame-wise object annotations.

The proposed models are discussed in the following section in as much depth as possible. The use of asymmetric Dirichlet priors over the topic proportions helps us achieve better sparsity in topics. However, this also leads to singularities in precision matrices conditioned on topics when Normal-Wishart priors for real valued data are not used.

3. THE PROPOSED MODELS

In this section we describe our proposed topic models for multimedia documents. We call the model in Fig. 3d MMGLDA, short for Multinomial-Multinomial-Gaussian LDA, and the model in Fig. 3e to Corr-MMGLDA, short for correspondence MMGLDA. In our context, the correspondence LDA model [4] places a probabilistic constraint on the correspondence of summary words to Gaussian observations—a word is likely to be generated by the topic which is agreed upon by most of the Gaussian instances in the video document. Since the real valued GIST features (see Section 4) "summarize" a scene in an image, we want a stronger influence of the topic of the scene on the summary text. This assumption is relaxed in MMGLDA. Of course the correspondence could have been established between the discrete observations only or both discrete and real valued ones but conditioned on the current dataset, we want more flexibility in topics for sampling discrete observations. We avoid overly complicated topic models and instead go for better data representations and supporting models with just the right amount of complexity.

In MMGLDA, for a multimedia document d, it is possible to have different topics competing for each occurrence of w_m. In Corr-MMGLDA, the number of such modes is constrained to be much fewer. The asymmetric $\boldsymbol{\alpha}$ can yield few additional modes which group co-occurring data dominant in densities or masses in separate latent topics. This phenomenon is observed for a larger number of latent topics.

Table 1 explains the symbols used in the two proposed topic models. Everywhere in this paper, we assume that K is the number of topics. The generative processes for the proposed models are illustrated below:

For each video document $d \in 1, ..., D$
  Choose a topic proportion $\boldsymbol{\theta}|\boldsymbol{\alpha} \sim Dir(\boldsymbol{\alpha})$
  For each position h in d
    Choose topic indicator $z_h|\theta \sim Mult(\boldsymbol{\theta})$
    Choose a discrete video "word" $w_h|z_h = k, \boldsymbol{\rho} \sim Mult(\boldsymbol{\rho}_{z_h})$
  For each real valued observation o in d
    Choose topic indicator $z_o|\theta \sim \mathcal{N}(\boldsymbol{\mu}, \boldsymbol{\Lambda}^{-1})$
    Choose a real valued $\mathbf{w}_o|z_o = k, \boldsymbol{\mu}, \boldsymbol{\Lambda}^{-1} \sim \mathcal{N}(\boldsymbol{\mu}_{z_o}, \boldsymbol{\Lambda}_{z_o}^{-1})$

Symbol	Meaning (*r.v. = random variable*)
D	total number of multimedia "documents"
M	total number of discrete text features per multimedia document $d \in \{1, ..., D\}$
H	total number of discrete visual features in a multimedia document $d \in \{1, ..., D\}$
O	total number of real valued visual features per multimedia document $d \in \{1, ..., D\}$
$\boldsymbol{\alpha} = \{\alpha_1, ..., \alpha_K\}$	r.v. for asymmetric Dirichlet prior for the document level topic proportions
$\boldsymbol{\theta}_d$	r.v. for document level latent topic proportions
$\boldsymbol{\rho}$	corpus level topic multinomials over discrete video features
$\boldsymbol{\beta}$	corpus level topic multinomials for textual words
$\boldsymbol{\mu}$	means of topic Gaussians for the real valued features from videos
$\boldsymbol{\Lambda} = (\boldsymbol{\Sigma}^{-1})$	precision (inverse covariance) matrices of topic Gaussians for the real valued features from videos
y_m in Figs. 3b, and 3d	indicator variable for a sample from $\boldsymbol{\theta}_d$ for discrete text features
y_m in Figs. 3c and 3e	indicator variable for *document level* real valued datum correspondences
z_h	indicator variable for a sample from $\boldsymbol{\theta}_d$ for discrete visual features
z_o	indicator variable for a sample from $\boldsymbol{\theta}_d$ for real valued visual features
w_m	r.v. for textual word at position m in document d; vocabulary size of V
w_h	r.v. for vision oriented discrete feature at position h in document d; vocabulary size $corrV_H$
$\mathbf{w}_o$	r.v. for the oth Gaussian feature vector with a dimensionality of P in document d

Table 1: Meanings of the variables used in the models

For each position m in video d
  Choose $y_m \sim Uniform(1, ..., O)$ (for Fig. 3e)
  or Choose $y_m|\theta \sim Mult(\boldsymbol{\theta})$ (for Fig. 3d)
  Choose a word $w_m \sim p(w_m|z_{y_m}, \boldsymbol{\beta})$ (for Fig. 3e)
  or Choose a word $w_m \sim p(w_m|y_m, \boldsymbol{\beta})$ (for Fig. 3d)

In all further notations, $\mathbf{w}_M$ is the ensemble of observed random variables that represent summary words in the dth multimedia document. Similar notations hold for $\mathbf{w}_O$, $\mathbf{w}_H$ and the indicators $\mathbf{y}$ and $\mathbf{z}$. In this paper, the text vocabularies are event specific and of size 312 words on average.

Fig. 3a shows the Object Bank [15] (OB) baseline that we initially used to translate videos to text. The boxes labeled OB_1, ..., OB_N are the individual object detectors in Object Bank. The positive responses of the detectors lead towards identifying the label of the objects in the keyframes and hence translating the entire video. We choose this baseline to verify the difficult nature of our dataset—there is a 10% overlap between OB's vocabulary and the test set vocabulary, and we should expect to see at least 2-5% recall in ROUGE-1 recall scores for most events based on a 40-50% ROUGE-1 recall achieved by the best 100-word multidocument text summarization systems in TAC competitions.

3.1 Inference on Latent Variables

We use the Variational Bayesian Expectation Maximization (VB-EM) [2, 31] algorithmic framework as the optimization framework. An advantage of VB-EM is that it is deterministic.

The derivations for the MMG class of topic models become sufficiently complicated due to the need for using priors over the parameters governing the real valued observations. Since the nature of the modes for topic proportions is not

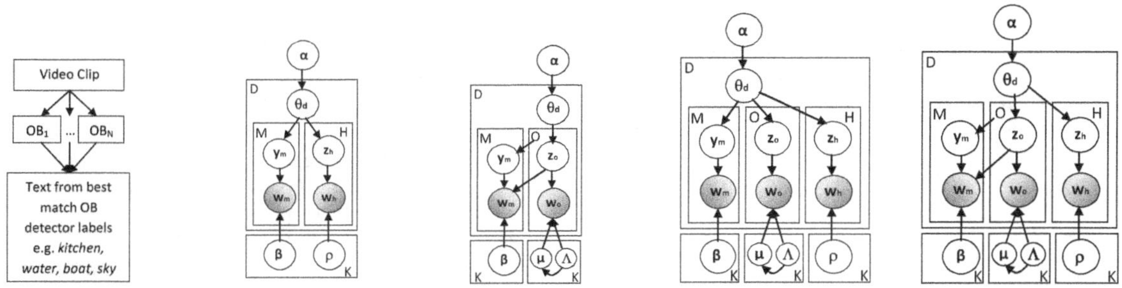

(a) Object Bank object detection model [15] (b) MMLDA [4, 26] (c) Corr-MGLDA [4] (extended) (d) MMGLDA (proposed) (e) Corr-MMGLDA (proposed)

Figure 3: Graphical model representations of existing topic models and proposed extensions— Figs. 3d and 3e. In this paper, we extend the model in Fig. 3c i.e. the Corr-LDA model in [4] with Normal-Wishart priors over parameters for real valued observations as well.

known in advance, singularities arising out ill-conditioned topic covariance matrices must be handled. This problem is mitigated in a principled way by introducing independent Normal-Wishart priors governing the mean vectors and precision matrices of the Gaussians conditioned on the topics. Since both $\boldsymbol{\mu}$ and $\boldsymbol{\Lambda}$ are unknown we cannot factorize $p(\boldsymbol{\mu}, \boldsymbol{\Lambda})$ directly because the variance of the distribution over μ is a function of $\boldsymbol{\Lambda}$. Instead we use combinations of Normal-Wishart priors on each Gaussian component as:

$$p(\boldsymbol{\mu}, \boldsymbol{\Lambda}) = \prod_{k=1}^{K} \mathcal{N}(\boldsymbol{\mu}_k | \mathbf{m}_0, (\kappa_0 \boldsymbol{\Lambda}_k)^{-1}) \mathcal{W}(\boldsymbol{\Lambda}_k | \mathbf{W}_0, \nu_0) \quad (1)$$

where $\boldsymbol{\Sigma}_k^{-1} = \boldsymbol{\Lambda}_k$ is the precision matrix for the kth factor or topic. This is similar to the mixture model used in [19]. To preserve the dependence between the means and covariances, a *partially* factorized tractable q distribution with "free" variational parameters $\boldsymbol{\gamma}$, $\boldsymbol{\phi}$, $\boldsymbol{\phi}^{(O)}, \boldsymbol{\phi}^{(H)}$ (for every multimedia document $d \in D$) is imposed by

$$q(\boldsymbol{\theta}, \mathbf{y}, \mathbf{z}_O, \mathbf{z}_H | \boldsymbol{\gamma}, \boldsymbol{\phi}, \boldsymbol{\phi}^{(O)} \boldsymbol{\phi}^{(H)}) = \left[\prod_{d=1}^{D} q(\boldsymbol{\theta}_d | \boldsymbol{\gamma}_d) \left[\prod_{m=1}^{M_d} q(y_{d,m} | \boldsymbol{\phi}_{d,m}) \prod_{o=1}^{O_d} q(z_{d,o} | \boldsymbol{\phi}_{d,o}^{(O)}) \prod_{h=1}^{H_d} q(z_{d,h} | \boldsymbol{\phi}_{d,h}^{(H)}) \right] \right] \prod_{i=1}^{K} q(\boldsymbol{\mu}_i, \boldsymbol{\Lambda}_i) \quad (2)$$

with $\boldsymbol{\theta_d} \sim Dirichlet(\boldsymbol{\gamma_d})$, $z_{d,o} \sim Mult(\boldsymbol{\phi}_{d,o}^{(O)})$ and $z_{d,h} \sim Mult(\boldsymbol{\phi}_{d,h}^{(H)})$. The maximum likelihood (ML) estimates of free parameters are found by optimizing the lower bound on $\log p(\mathbf{w}_M, \mathbf{w}_H, \mathbf{w}_O | \boldsymbol{\alpha}, \boldsymbol{\beta}, \boldsymbol{\rho}, \boldsymbol{\mu}, \boldsymbol{\Lambda})$.

The hyperparameters for α in the asymmetric Dirichlet case (the concentration parameter and the base measure) and κ_0, ν_0, $\mathbf{m}_0$ and $\mathbf{W}_0$ are not shown in Figs. 3c, 3d and 3e and in equ. 2 above. Also $\boldsymbol{\phi}$ are the free parameters of the variational summary_word multinomials over Gaussian_observations in the correspondence multimodal models or summary_word multinomials over topics in the plain multimodal models; $\boldsymbol{\phi}^{(O)}$ are the free parameters of the variational Gaussian_observation multinomials over topics and similarly for $\boldsymbol{\phi}^{(H)}$ for discrete visual features.

The variational posterior distribution $q(\boldsymbol{\mu}_k, \boldsymbol{\Lambda}_k)$ does not factorize into the product of the marginals, but we can always write it as $q(\boldsymbol{\mu}_k, \boldsymbol{\Lambda}_k) = q(\boldsymbol{\mu}_k | \boldsymbol{\Lambda}_k) q(\boldsymbol{\Lambda}_k)$. Then we use the result from mean field theory[24, 31] that says that the log of the optimal solution for factor q_j is obtained by considering the log of the joint distribution over all hidden and observed variables and then taking the expectation with respect to all of the other factors $\{q_i\}$ for $i \neq j$ i.e. for visible and hidden variable ensembles V and H, $\log q_j^*(H_j) = E_{i \neq j}[\log p(V, H)] + const.$ This results in a Normal-Wishart distribution and is given by:

$$q(\boldsymbol{\mu}_k, \boldsymbol{\Lambda}_k) = \mathcal{N}(\boldsymbol{\mu}_k | \mathbf{m}_k, (\kappa_k \boldsymbol{\Lambda}_k)^{-1}) \mathcal{W}(\boldsymbol{\Lambda}_k | \mathbf{W}_k, \nu_k) \quad (3)$$

where $\boldsymbol{\Sigma}_k^{-1} = \boldsymbol{\Lambda}_k$ is the precision matrix for the kth factor or topic. The expression in Equ. 3 is obtained by first writing out the expression for $\log q^*(.)$ and selecting those terms that involve $\boldsymbol{\mu}_k$ and $\boldsymbol{\Lambda}_k$. This yields:

$$\log q^*(\boldsymbol{\mu}, \boldsymbol{\Lambda}) = \sum_{i=1}^{K} \log p(\boldsymbol{\mu}_i, \boldsymbol{\Lambda}_i) + \sum_{d=1}^{D} \sum_{o=1}^{O_d} \sum_{i=1}^{K} \phi_{d,o,i}^{(O)} \log \mathcal{N}(\mathbf{w}_{d,o} | \boldsymbol{\mu}_i, \boldsymbol{\Lambda}_i^{-1}) + const \quad (4)$$

Note that the variance of the distribution over $\boldsymbol{\mu}_k$ is a function of $\boldsymbol{\Lambda}_k$. The random variables $\mathbf{m}_k$ and $\mathbf{W}_k$ can be thought of as surrogates to $\mathbf{m}_0$ and $\mathbf{W}_0$ and that κ_k and ν_k surrogates to κ_0 and ν_0 but conditioned on latent topic k. The expressions for these variables, which are also used in the M-Step updates, can be found in Equs. 23, 24, 22 and 25. These expressions are obtained by matching the moments of $\boldsymbol{\mu}_k$ and $\boldsymbol{\Lambda}_k$ to the Normal and Wishart distribution expressions. The optimal solution for $q^*(\boldsymbol{\mu}_k, \boldsymbol{\Lambda}_k)$ depends on the moments evaluated with respect to the distributions of other variables, and so the variational update equations are coupled and must be solved iteratively. Following [5, 4], let us now write down the objective functional, $\mathcal{L}_{(.)}$, to be maximized which acts as the lower bound to the true data log likelihood. We have **for the MMGLDA model**,

$$\begin{aligned} \mathcal{L}_{MMG} &= E_q[\log p(\boldsymbol{\theta}|\boldsymbol{\alpha})] + E_q[\log p(\mathbf{y}_M|\boldsymbol{\theta})] \\ &+ E_q[\log p(\mathbf{w}_M|\mathbf{y}_M, \beta)] + E_q[\log p(\mathbf{z}_O|\boldsymbol{\theta})] \\ &+ E_q[\log p(\mathbf{w}_O|\mathbf{z}_O, \boldsymbol{\mu}, \boldsymbol{\Lambda})] + E_q[\log p(\boldsymbol{\mu}, \boldsymbol{\Lambda}|\mathbf{m}_0, \mathbf{W}_0, \kappa_0, \nu_0)] \\ &+ E_q[\log p(\mathbf{z}_H|\boldsymbol{\theta})] + E_q[\log p(\mathbf{w}_H|\mathbf{z}_H, \boldsymbol{\rho})] - E_q[\log q(\boldsymbol{\theta}, \mathbf{y}_M, \\ &\mathbf{z}_O, \mathbf{z}_H, \boldsymbol{\mu}, \boldsymbol{\Lambda}|\boldsymbol{\gamma}, \boldsymbol{\phi}, \boldsymbol{\phi}^{(O)}, \boldsymbol{\phi}^{(H)}, \mathbf{m}, \mathbf{W}, \boldsymbol{\kappa}, \boldsymbol{\nu})] \end{aligned} \quad (5)$$

We only highlight the derivations for the expressions: $E_{q_{[\boldsymbol{\mu}_i, \boldsymbol{\Lambda}_i]}}\left[\frac{\ln|\boldsymbol{\Lambda}_i|}{2} - \frac{(\mathbf{w}_o - \boldsymbol{\mu}_i)' \boldsymbol{\Lambda}_i (\mathbf{w}_o - \boldsymbol{\mu}_i)}{2}\right]$, $E_{q_{[\boldsymbol{\mu}_i, \boldsymbol{\Lambda}_i]}}[\log p(\boldsymbol{\mu}_i, \boldsymbol{\Lambda}_i)]$ and $E_{q_{[\boldsymbol{\mu}_i, \boldsymbol{\Lambda}_i]}}[\log q(\boldsymbol{\mu}_i, \boldsymbol{\Lambda}_i)]$. In the variational Bayesian setting, the expression:

$$E_{q_{[\boldsymbol{\mu}_i, \boldsymbol{\Lambda}_i]}}\left[(\ln|\boldsymbol{\Lambda}_i|)/2 - ((\mathbf{w}_o - \boldsymbol{\mu}_i)^\top \boldsymbol{\Lambda}_i (\mathbf{w}_o - \boldsymbol{\mu}_i))/2\right]$$

needs to be evaluated in the log likelihood calculation for every video document d to update the free distributions given the current parameter values. The term $\left[\frac{\ln|\boldsymbol{\Lambda}_i|}{2}\right]$ is the normalization factor of the Gaussians and its expectations can cause the log likelihood to be positive. We therefore only evaluate $E_{q_{[\boldsymbol{\mu}_i, \boldsymbol{\Lambda}_i]}}\left[-((\mathbf{w}_o - \boldsymbol{\mu}_i)^\top \boldsymbol{\Lambda}_i (\mathbf{w}_o - \boldsymbol{\mu}_i))/2\right]$

for the per document updates and subtract the log of the exponentials of the aggregations as an approximation. We independently derive and mention only the final expressions for the following variables due to space constraints and self containment of this paper:

$$E_{q_{[\mu_i,\Lambda_i]}}[\ln|\Lambda_i|] = \sum_{p=1}^{P}\psi\left(\frac{\nu_i+1-p}{2}\right)+P\ln 2+\ln|\mathbf{W}_i| \quad (6)$$

$$E_{q_{[\mu_i,\Lambda_i]}}\left[(\mathbf{w}_o-\mu_i)'\Lambda_i(\mathbf{w}_o-\mu_i)\right] = P\kappa_i^{-1}+\nu_i\left((\mathbf{w}_o-\mathbf{m}_i)'\mathbf{W}_i(\mathbf{w}_o-\mathbf{m}_i)\right) \quad (7)$$

$$E_{q_{[\mu,\Lambda]}}[\log q(\mu,\Lambda)] = \sum_{i=1}^{K}\left\{\frac{1}{2}\ln\hat{\Lambda}_i+\frac{P}{2}\ln\frac{\kappa_i}{2\pi}-\frac{P}{2}-H[q(\Lambda_i)]\right\} \quad (8)$$

$$H[q(\Lambda_i)] = -\ln Z(\mathbf{W}_i,\nu_i)-\frac{(\nu_i-P-1)}{2}\ln\hat{\Lambda}_i+\frac{\nu_i P}{2}, \text{ where} \quad (9)$$

- $Z(\mathbf{W}_i,\nu_i) = |\mathbf{W}_i|^{-\nu_i/2}\left(2^{\nu_i P/2}\pi^{P(P-1)/4}\prod_{p=1}^{P}\Gamma\left(\frac{\nu_i+1-p}{2}\right)\right)^{-1}$
- $\ln\hat{\Lambda}_i = E_q[\ln|\Lambda_i|] = \sum_{p=1}^{P}\psi\left(\frac{\nu_i+1-p}{2}\right)+P\ln 2+\ln|\mathbf{W}_i|$

Note that Ψ is the digamma function. For the expression $\sum_{i=1}^{K}E_{q_{[\mu_i,\Lambda_i]}}[\log p(\mu_i,\Lambda_i)]$, we have:

$$\sum_{i=1}^{K}E_{q_{[\mu_i,\Lambda_i]}}[\log p(\mu_i,\Lambda_i)] = \frac{1}{2}\sum_{i=1}^{K}\left\{P\ln(\frac{\kappa_0}{2\pi})+\ln\hat{\Lambda}_i-\frac{\kappa_0 P}{\kappa_i}-\kappa_0\nu_i(\mathbf{m}_i-\mathbf{m}_0)'\mathbf{W}_i(\mathbf{m}_i-\mathbf{m}_0)\right\}+K\ln Z(\mathbf{W}_0,\nu_0)+\frac{\nu_0-P-1}{2}\sum_{i=1}^{K}\ln\hat{\Lambda}_i-\frac{1}{2}\sum_{i=1}^{K}\nu_i Tr(\mathbf{W}_0^{-1}\mathbf{W}_i) \quad (10)$$

Using the lower bound $\mathcal{L}_{MMG}$, the ML estimations of the hidden variables in video document d can be obtained using Lagrange Multipliers on $\phi^{(H)}$, $\phi^{(O)}$ and ϕ as follows:

$$\phi^{(H)}_{d,h,i}\propto\exp\left\{\psi(\gamma_{d,i})-\psi(\sum_{j=1}^{K}\gamma_{d,j})+\log\rho_{i,w_{d,h}}\right\} \quad (11)$$

$$\phi^{(O)}_{d,o,i}\propto\exp\left\{\psi(\gamma_{d,i})-\psi(\sum_{j=1}^{K}\gamma_{d,j})+E_{q_{[\mu_i,\Lambda_i]}}\left[(\ln|\Lambda_i|)/2-((\mathbf{w}_o-\mu_i)'\Lambda_i(\mathbf{w}_o-\mu_i))/2\right]\right\} \quad (12)$$

$$\phi_{d,m,i}\propto\exp\left\{\psi(\gamma_{d,i})-\psi(\sum_{j=1}^{K}\gamma_{d,j})+\log\beta_{i,w_{d,m}}\right\} \quad (13)$$

$$\gamma_{d,i}=\alpha_i+\sum_{m=1}^{M_d}\phi_{d,m,i}+\sum_{o=1}^{O_d}\phi^{(O)}_{d,o,i}+\sum_{h=1}^{H_d}\phi^{(H)}_{d,h,i} \quad (14)$$

For the Corr-MMGLDA model, $E_q[\log p(\mathbf{w}_M|\mathbf{z}_{\mathbf{y}_M},\beta)]$ expands out to be:

$$\sum_{m=1}^{M}\sum_{i=1}^{K}\left(\sum_{o=1}^{O}\phi_{m,o}\phi^{(O)}_{o,i}\right)\log\beta_{i,w_m} \quad (15)$$

Also,

$$E_q[\log q(\mathbf{y}_M|\phi_{\mathbf{y}_M})] = \sum_{m=1}^{M}\sum_{o=1}^{O}\phi_{m,o}\log\phi_{m,o} \quad (16)$$

and $E_q[\log p(\mathbf{y}_M|O)]$ is constant for all m in d. Equation (15) is a computational bottleneck because finding the confidence of the word w_m on topic i necessitates the elimination of uncertainties of w_m's dependence on $\mathbf{w}_o$ and $\mathbf{w}_o$'s dependence on topic i. This is also a strong point since the marginalization suggests a stronger influence of a topic on a summary word if that influence is justified by most $\mathbf{w}_o$s.

Using a similar lower bound $\mathcal{L}_{Corr-MMG}$ for Corr-MMGLDA, the ML estimations of the hidden variables in video d can be obtained as follows:

$$\phi^{(H)}_{d,h,i}\propto\exp\left\{\psi(\gamma_{d,i})-\psi(\sum_{j=1}^{K}\gamma_{d,j})+\log\rho_{i,w_{d,h}}\right\} \quad (17)$$

$$\phi^{(O)}_{d,o,i}\propto\exp\left\{\psi(\gamma_{d,i})-\psi(\sum_{j=1}^{K}\gamma_{d,j})+E_{q_{[\mu_i,\Lambda_i]}}\left[\frac{\log|\Lambda_i|}{2}-\frac{(\mathbf{w}_o-\mu_i)'\Lambda_i(\mathbf{w}_o-\mu_i)}{2}\right]+\sum_{m=1}^{M_d}\phi_{d,m,o}\log\beta_{z_{y_m},w_{d,m}}\right\} \quad (18)$$

$$\phi_{d,m,o}\propto\exp\left\{\sum_{i=1}^{K}\phi^{(O)}_{d,o,i}\log\beta_{i,w_{d,m}}\right\} \quad (19)$$

$$\gamma_{d,i}=\alpha_i+\sum_{o=1}^{O_d}\phi^{(O)}_{d,o,i}+\sum_{h=1}^{H_d}\phi^{(H)}_{d,h,i} \quad (20)$$

3.2 Model Parameter Estimations

Before deriving the expressions for the maximum a posteriori and maximum likelihood estimates of the parameters of the proposed models using moment matching (Section 3.1) and derivatives w.r.t the parameters of the functional $\mathcal{L}_{(.)}$ let us define the following quantities for each topic i:

$$N_i=\sum_{d=1}^{D}\sum_{o=1}^{O_d}\phi^{(O)}_{d,o,i}; \qquad \bar{\mathbf{x}}_i=\frac{1}{N_i}\sum_{d=1}^{D}\sum_{o=1}^{O_d}\phi^{(O)}_{d,o,i}\mathbf{w}_{d,o}$$

$$\mathbf{S}_i=\frac{\sum_{d=1}^{D}\sum_{o=1}^{O_d}\phi^{(O)}_{d,o,i}(\mathbf{w}_{d,o}-\bar{\mathbf{x}}_i)(\mathbf{w}_{d,o}-\bar{\mathbf{x}}_i)'}{N_i} \quad (21)$$

By using moment matching techniques on Equ. 3, we obtain the following MAP expressions in general for each topic i:

$$\kappa_i=\kappa_0+N_i \quad (22)$$

$$\mathbf{m}_i=\frac{1}{\kappa_i}(\kappa_0\mathbf{m}_0+N_i\bar{\mathbf{x}}_i) \quad (23)$$

$$\mathbf{W}_i^{-1}=\mathbf{W}_0^{-1}+N_i\mathbf{S}_i+\frac{\kappa_0 N_i}{\kappa_0+N_i}(\bar{\mathbf{x}}_i-\mathbf{m}_0)(\bar{\mathbf{x}}_i-\mathbf{m}_0)' \quad (24)$$

$$\nu_i=\nu_0+N_i \quad (25)$$

Further, using some algebraic manipulations and utilizing Lagrange Multipliers for β and ρ for each topic i, we obtain:

For the MMGLDA model:

$$\rho_{i,j}\propto\sum_{d=1}^{D}\sum_{h=1}^{H_d}\sum_{j=1}^{corrV_H}\phi^{(H)}_{d,h,i}\delta(w_{d,h},j) \quad (26)$$

$$\beta_{i,j}\propto\sum_{d=1}^{D}\sum_{m=1}^{M_d}\sum_{j=1}^{V}\phi_{d,m,i}\delta(w_{d,m},j) \quad (27)$$

For the Corr-MMGLDA model:

$$\beta_{i,j}\propto\sum_{d=1}^{D}\sum_{m=1}^{M_d}\sum_{j=1}^{V}\left(\sum_{o=1}^{O}\phi_{d,m,o}\phi^{(O)}_{d,o,i}\right)\delta(w_{d,m},j) \quad (28)$$

The update for parameters $\rho_{i,j}$ remain the same. To optimize the $\boldsymbol{\alpha}$ parameters, we follow the corresponding expressions in [5] and optimize using Newton's iterative gradient based method using backtracking line search.

For predicting a bag of words summary from an ensemble of low level features of video document d and the learnt $p(w_v|z_v = k, \boldsymbol{\beta})$, we permute the vocabulary V for the new test video as:

$$p(w_v|\mathbf{w}_O, \mathbf{w}_H) \approx \sum_{o=1}^{O}\sum_{i=1}^{K} \phi_{d,o,i}^{(O)} p(w_v|\boldsymbol{\beta}_i) + \sum_{h=1}^{H}\sum_{i=1}^{K} \phi_{d,h,i}^{(H)} p(w_v|\boldsymbol{\beta}_i) \tag{29}$$

4. EXPERIMENTAL SETUP AND RESULTS

Here we briefly mention the descriptors that we use to represent the videos. To represent actions, we use features known as Histogram of Oriented Gradients in 3D (HOG3D) [11]. The gradient directions are binned by mapping them to 10 polar meridian and 6 polar parallel planes and then treating half spaces to be equivalent. We resized the video frames such that the largest dimension (height or width) was 160 pixels, and extracted HOG3D features from a dense sampling of frames. Our HOG3D parameters resulted in a 300-dimensional feature vector using support volumes of dimension $2 \times 2 \times 5$ and 5×3 polar co-ordinate bins. We then use K-means clustering to create a 1000-word codebook following [3] from a random sampling of the training data.

Color histogram features are also used as part of the discrete visual data. We use 512 RGB color bins and histograms are computed on densely sampled frames. Due to large deviations in the extremities of the color spectrum, we use the histogram between the 15th and 85th percentiles averaged across a video and counts normalized to lie in [1,100].

Finally we use Object Banks [15] for a histogram pattern of positive object detections. OB transforms an image into a 44604 dimensional concatenated feature vector for each of the 177 *off-the-shelf* object detectors that are currently used. Each entry within a 252 dimensional detection feature vector represents the distance from the decision hyperplane midway within the margins for different scale-space transformations of the image. The object labels in OB cover only about 10% of the summary words (246 out of 2687 for the training set and 166 out of 1219 for the Dev-T set). Keyframes used for these features are extracted using the change in color histogram method [35] and the positive OB responses are quantized following classemes in [28]. Thus $\mathbf{w}_H$ in Figs. 3b, 3d and 3e consists of codebook histograms from HOG3D, color and OB. Needless to say, the contributions of these *off-the-shelf* object detectors are not significant at all.

The real valued features we use in our video representation are those representing scenes as mentioned in [22]. The scene property by itself induces image summarization in a way that is consistent with human perception of vision [23]. A set of perceptual dimensions is proposed along the boundary viewpoint (e.g. depth, openness, expansion, perspective) and along the content viewpoint (e.g. naturalness, roughness, ruggedness, etc.) which represent the dominant *spatial structure* of a scene. These features are named GIST features as is common parlance in computer vision literature. To compute these features, we have used the setup in [7] leading to a 960-dimensional descriptor for each frame. We calculate GIST features for every 10th frame.

To save computational time, the GIST features are projected into lower dimensions using Principle Component Analysis (PCA). PCA is done on the training data across all event categories to remove the dependence of the visual descriptors on specific events. We first visualize the lower (15, 30 and 60) dimensional GIST features in two dimensions using t-statistic based stochastic neighbor embedding (t-SNE) [17], however, the separations look more or less the same and do not yield conclusive evidence of choosing the right number of dimensions. By inspecting the plots from t-SNE, we choose 15 dimensions and validate the choice by both manually inspecting the eigenvalues and experimentally cross-validating with the baseline Corr-MGLDA topic model (Fig. 3c). 30 or 60 dimensional features decreased the ELBO of the model. We do not select further lower dimensions based on significance of the eigenvalues. Each $\mathbf{w}_o$ in Figs. 3c, 3d and 3e represents a frame in 15 dimensions corresponding to a GIST feature vector.

4.1 Model Log Likelihoods and Topics

In this section, we evaluate the topic models in terms of ELBO on the held-out Dev-T set acting as a test set (with the human summaries) for posterior inference and as a prediction set (without human summaries) for BoW summary generation. Multinomial parameters are seeded and Gaussian parameters are randomly initialized. The base measures

Model	Topic 1	Topic 2	Topic 3	
Corr-MMGLDA	wed couple ceremony church ring footage exchange bride groom helicopter	wed ceremony bride groom church flower vow exchange ring walk kiss outdoors	wed Hawai US beach guest place footage scene ring minister lei Kailua	Wedding ceremony
Corr MGLDA-PDS	wed ceremony couple bride groom church flower exchange vow	wed ceremony bride groom couple flower church man outdoors vow	wed ceremony bride groom couple flower church man outdoors vow	

Table 2: 3 latent topics for an event from proposed 5-topic Corr-MMGLDA and Corr-MGLDA-PDS models. The topics from Corr-MGLDA-PDS are similar as a result of high values of α_k obtained after running Corr-MGLDA-PDS on scaled i.e. normalized data. The topics from Corr-MMGLDA are qualitatively far superior and indicates sub-events of the "Wedding ceremony" event.

of $\boldsymbol{\alpha}$ are initialized to 0.1 and normalized while its concentration parameter is set to 10. An issue with the real valued features is the influence of data normalization on the ELBOs from the topic models. We have observed that when the data is not normalized to lie within $[0,1]^P$, the sequence of ELBOs from Corr-MGLDA during EM often indicate suboptimality even during training. The "PDS" suffix (in the table and all other figures) means "Positive Data Scaling" i.e. each real valued vector is sum-normalized to $[0,1]^P$ independently.

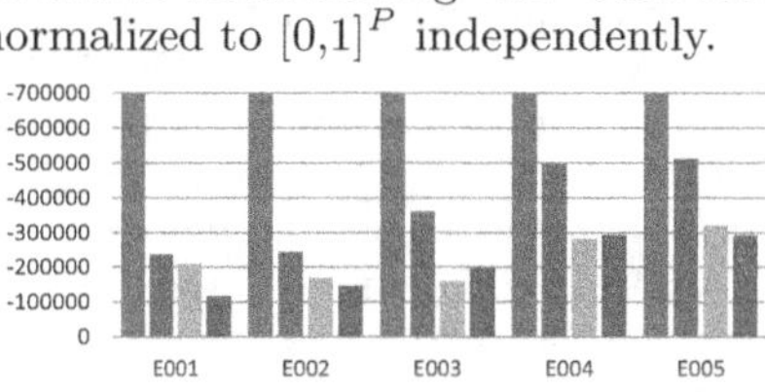

Figure 4: Test ELBOs on events E001-E005 in the Dev-T set. Lower is better.

The PDS normalization fixes this problem and raises ELBOs for Corr-MGLDA significantly but convergence is slower. However in the latter setting, the values of α_k become large which destroys sparsity in topics. This is possibly due to strong overlap of modes within the $[0,1]^P$ hypercube where one dimension is severely correlated with the others. Examples of such topics on the "Wedding Ceremony" event is given in Table 2 where all topics are almost alike and lose subjective interpretability.

The new topic models with both Multinomial and Gaussian distributions on the video features do not suffer from the data scaling problem. It is possible that the mean parameter space for the tractable distributions over both discrete and real valued observations prevents co-ordinate ascent steps to dwell in suboptimal regions that could arise out of extreme values in the real valued data alone.

Although the Normal-Wishart priors act as regularizers, automatically tuning $\mathbf{W}_0$ using another level of priors or from the data itself is not used here. In general optimization with tractable distributions and parameter constraints (e.g. non-negativity, boundedness and positive definiteness) can be non-convex [31].

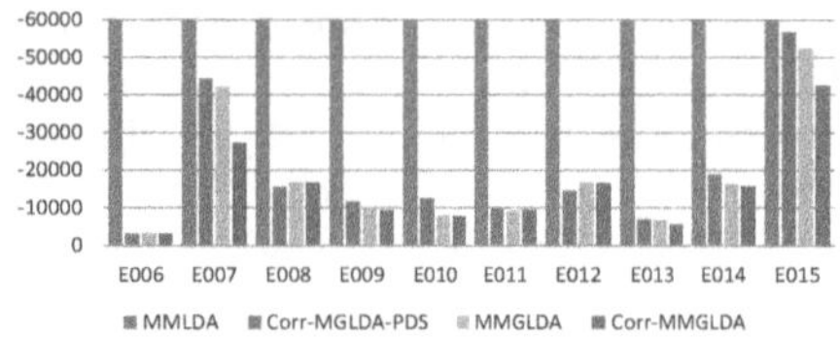

Figure 5: Test ELBOs on events E006-E015 from Dev-T set. Lower is better

Figures 4 and 5 show the test ELBOs of MMGLDA and Corr-MMGLDA versus the MMLDA model and the Corr-MGLDA model with PDS. The ELBOs for MMLDA are off the charts (at least three to four times the cut-off shown in the graphs). For the first 5 events, the videos contain positive instances of the events in Dev-T set. For this subset of events, the MMGLDA family of models outperform the best version of Corr-MGLDA in terms of ELBOs (i.e. with PDS). Figures 4 and 5 are obtained using K=20 topics—K being set through 5-fold cross-validation. For the last 10 events (Fig. 5), the videos contain only related instances of the events in Dev-T set—dissimilar to the training configuration i.e. the annotators are unsure about the relevance of the videos to the event category. In this case, Corr-MGLDA-PDS do not perform worse in general since the GIST features are *global* features [22].

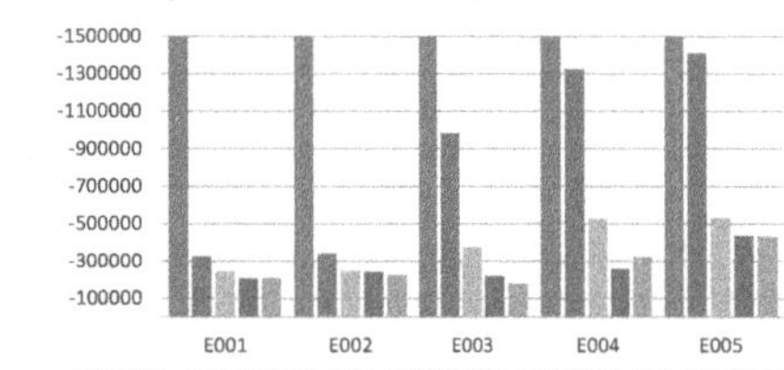

Figure 6: Prediction ELBOs on first 5 event for Dev-T set. Lower is better.

The prediction performance on the first 5 events is shown in terms of ELBO in Fig. 6 for the same value of K. Fig. 6 shows that MMLDA does not perform well in terms of word prediction ELBO measure. We can also see the effects of sub-optimality when PDS is suppressed for Corr-MGLDA (Corr-MGLDA in Fig. 6). MMGLDA and Corr-MMGLDA again perform comparably and outperforms Corr-MGLDA-PDS on the first 5 events except E002—"feeding an animal"—a very complex event for computer vision.

For events 6 through 15, the prediction ELBO graphs also look very similar to that in Fig. 5 (not shown here due to space constraints). PDS on our proposed MMGLDA family shows even better ELBOs, but topic sparsity problems mitigate only a little and we do not report those here. All these experiments are run using $\mathbf{m}_0$ set to $\mathbf{0}$, $\mathbf{W}_0$ set to a broader prior $\mathbf{I}$, the identity matrix, ν_0 set to P and κ_0 set to 1. Normalizing the data to lie in $[0,1]^P$ with $\mathbf{I}$ as priors for $\mathbf{\Lambda}_k$s leads to sharing of topic responsibilities of the real valued data by only a few Gaussians thereby contributing much less to the overall log-likelihood.

It is also observed that the means of the ELBOs of our proposed models are significantly less negative (i.e. better) at 95% confidence level (using paired t-test) than the existing topic models during cross-validation on the training set. For most events, ELBOs for proposed models with K=10 are not statistically worse either and show slightly higher ROUGE-1 scores for some events. Figure 7 shows the macro average of test ELBOs across all the 15 events in the Dev-T set. We omit the line graph for MMLDA as it is out of axis limits. The graphs confirm the superior fit of our proposed models to a natural representation of multimedia (test) data.

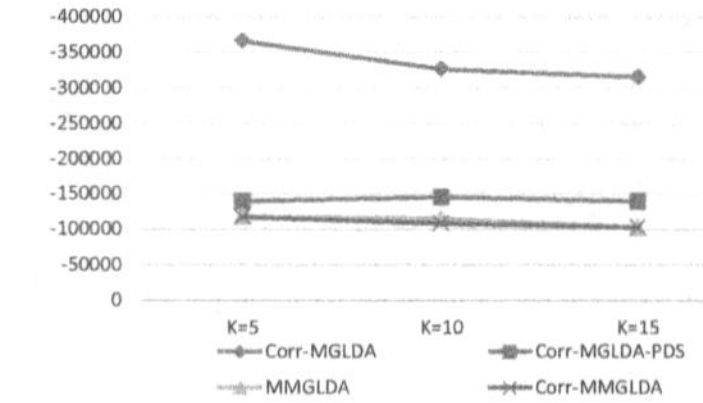

Figure 7: Average test ELBOs on all events in the Dev-T set for different topics. Lower is better.

4.2 Translating Related Words to Videos

Table 3 shows how latent topics can first be used to discover most probable related words from unstructured text which can then be translated to most probable frames from one or more videos (and hence the videos themselves). The frames correspond to $\mathbf{w}_o$s in Fig. 3 and Table 1.

We observe from Table 3 how topics 6 and 10 decompose the "Flash mob gathering" event into its constituent sub-themes. While topic 6 describes flash mob dances in outdoors and near plazas, topic 10 focuses on a flash mob in Hollywood posing in Star Wars costumes and light sabers along with the famous miniature robot R2D2. Due to space constraints we cannot show more samples of numerous such examples.

Topic 6: mob flash dance people mall outdoors large gather woman public plaza

Topic 10: Hollywood dog star wars robot light saber R2D2 eye lens blvd fight street

Table 3: 2 latent topics for "Flash mob" event from a 10-topic Corr-MMGLDA

Table 4 shows the inter-translation of modalities for topic 10 from MMGLDA corresponding to that in Table 3 from Corr-MMGLDA. Note how the topic loses specificity (e.g. misses "R2D2", "light," "saber" within the top few words) and focuses on generality (e.g. flash mob). Topic 6 for MMGLDA is exactly the same as that for Corr-MMGLDA. Table 5 shows log of the ratio: $\frac{\alpha_k}{|\mathbf{\Lambda}_k|}$ for the two proposed

Topic 10: place fight fake public event gather flash mob music star outdoors war

Table 4: Topic 10 for the "Flash mob" event from a 10-topic MMGLDA

models and gives us a hint on how "broad" a topic k may be vs. how much variance in the visual summary is it able to capture. A relatively higher value of the ratio means that a topic captures more variance and hence the volume captured by the determinant of the inverse covariance matrix $\mathbf{\Lambda}_k$, i.e. $|\mathbf{\Lambda}_k|$, through its spanning eigenvectors is proportionally less. For MMGLDA, this ratio is always relatively lower in our setting and this means that the model captures more generic patterns first giving rise to a lower $|\mathbf{\Lambda}_k|^{-1}$.

The last column in Table 5 is the average of the ratios for the other topics from the two models for event eight. The ratios can be large for a more general topic (e.g. topic 6 in Table 3) owing to a higher $\boldsymbol{\alpha}_k$ too. Although, all values are close due to the use of the broader prior, $\mathbf{I}$, it is observed that Corr-MMGLDA discovers related words which are qualitatively superior. However, the corresponding most probable frames are almost similar for both models in most cases. Translating related words to frames is best judged manually, but, the ratio we use here can be a viable alternative.

Model	k=6	k=10	$\text{avg}_{k\neq\{6,10\}}$
Corr-MMGLDA	104.628	8.164	40.2398
MMGLDA	104.623	8.102	40.0702

Table 5: $\log \frac{\alpha_k}{|\mathbf{\Lambda}_k|}$ values for topics in event 8

4.3 Translating/Summarizing Videos To Text

Table 6 reports the ROUGE-1 (henceforth R-1) scores of the predicted 5 to 10 keyword summaries from the different models when compared with the corresponding short human synopses. Sometimes full sentences cannot be generated from the predicted words due to a deficient language model. This and the short nature of human synopses are the primary reasons why we perform only R-1 evaluation. Some examples of the sentences/phrases are shown in Fig. 8.

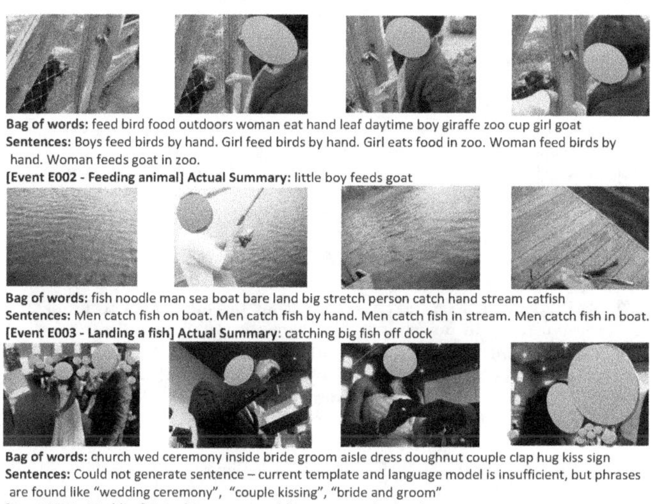

Figure 8: Bag of keywords and sentence translations from our proposed MMGLDA (K = 20) for some clips from events 2, 3 and 4 from the Dev-T set. Best viewed in color and magnification.

In Table 6, OB is the Object Bank baseline (see just ahead of Section 3.1)—it confirms the difficulty of detecting objects on this dataset. The quantized OB responses perform poorly since a-priori it is hard to know which object detectors will be needed and existing but irrelevant object detectors can produce an unpredictable pattern of false positives. Creating object models for every genre of data requires expensive annotation efforts. Even if there is a 100% overlap between our training vocabulary and object models, the R-1 scores for OB *may* only increase by 10-folds which is still low.

Purely multinomial topic models showing lower ELBOs can perform quite well in BoW summarization. MMLDA assigns likelihoods based on success and failure of *independent* events and failures contribute highly negative terms to the log likelihoods but this does not indicate the model's summarization performance where low probability terms are pruned out. Gaussian components can partially remove the *independence* through covariance modeling and fit the data better at the cost of higher time and space complexity. The R-1 scores from MM(G)LDAs are comparable for 5 and 10 keywords with no statistical difference, however, a possible reason for lower R-1 scores for Corr-MMGLDA model is that due to better correspondence to the topic of the GIST energy in the scene, when a topically relevant but non-summary word is chosen upfront, more related but non-summary words are also drawn in. As future research, we also like to do a principled initialization of Gaussian parameter priors as in [19].

	Model	n=5	n=10	OB
E001	MMLDA	0.182	0.248	0.0*
	Corr-MGLDA-PDS	0.187	0.257	
	MMGLDA	0.179	0.245	
	Corr-MMGLDA	0.139*	0.192*	
E002	MMLDA	0.186	0.249	0.0*
	Corr-MGLDA-PDS	0.182	0.242	
	MMGLDA	0.186	0.237	
	Corr-MMGLDA	0.143*	0.176*	
E003	MMLDA	0.221	0.265	0.012* =1%
	Corr-MGLDA-PDS	0.233	0.263	
	MMGLDA	0.228	0.267	
	Corr-MMGLDA	0.171*	0.230	
E004	MMLDA	0.265	0.302	0.0*
	Corr-MGLDA-PDS	0.263	0.292	
	MMGLDA	0.264	0.321	
	Corr-MMGLDA	0.221	0.247*	
E005	MMLDA	0.167	0.213	0.005* =0.5%
	Corr-MGLDA-PDS	0.180	0.208	
	MMGLDA	0.165	0.205	
	Corr-MMGLDA	0.129*	0.142*	
6-15 Avg.	MMLDA	0.216	0.252	0.001* =0.1%
	Corr-MGLDA-PDS	0.211	0.258	
	MMGLDA	0.210	0.243	
	Corr-MMGLDA	0.179*	0.221	

Table 6: Individual and average ROUGE-1 scores on the events—best results from 10/20 latent topics are shown. The value of n represents the top-n most probable keywords. A (*) means significantly **worse** performance at 95% confidence to {MM,MMG}LDAs. These results are only reported for the same hyperparameter settings.

However, the high scores with Corr-MGLDA-PDS is entirely co-incidental—the topics are more or less uniform and each one covers parts of the sub-events equally. Further, each $\mathbf{w}_o$'s density over those topics is uniform enough to not achieve a reasonable permutation. The same thing happens when PDS is used for our MMGLDA family of models and the summaries completely lose subjective appeal although R-1 scores improve considerably. This is similar to the *qualitatively degenerate approach*—taking the top n frequent words from the event vocabulary and using those as summaries for **every** test video. The scores for MMLDA and MMGLDA are also comparable to this setting. Quantification of the permutation quality has not been done.

Scores in Table 6 need to be multiplied by the event classification accuracies to obtain lower bounds for clips having no event labels. The scores become competitive for larger n and much larger K if we topic model on the entire corpus.

4.3.1 Natural Language Generation

To translate a video into multiple sentences from predicted keywords, we use an ordered-sequence template as <subject, verb, object, preposition, scene-noun>. Language models from the data at hand is used to prune impossible sequences. The subjects, objects, verbs and nouns extracted from the training synopses using dependency grammars and POS models appear in each generated sentence only once.

We use the parser in [12] to score the sequence of words following the template. The sentences are ordered according to bigram and parse tree scores. When complete sentences cannot be generated due to a deficient language model, we output possible bigrams and trigrams (see E004 in Fig. 8). Similar corpus based sentence generation techniques can be found in [34, 9] but NLG is a research topic in its own right.

4.4 Event Classification

Fig. 9 shows 5-fold cross-validation on the 15-event training set and also the test accuracies on Dev-T set for event classification. A c-SVM classifier from the libSVM [6] package is used with default settings for multiclass classification. Although around 50% classification accuracy can be easily achieved using the discrete visual features that we use, higher accuracies can be obtained using better kernels, fusion of classifiers and optimizing Detection-Error-Tradeoff curves while cross validating [20]. However, these discussions are outside the scope of this paper.

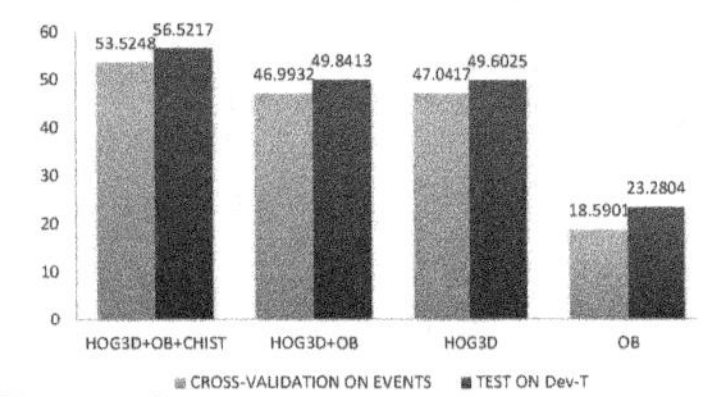

Figure 9: Event detection accuracies for cross-validation (light gray bars) and test (dark gray bars) with different features

5. CONCLUSION

Our new topic models show better fits to multimedia data representation consisting of discrete and real valued features from videos as well as accompanying short textual synopses. In general Corr-MMGLDA improves on text to video translation while the non-correspondence versions perform better in video to text summarization. Video summarization through topic models significantly out-perform that through state-of-the-art object detectors and thus can be used as new baselines. Our NLG component has suffered from severe data sparsity and impoverished language models and we wish to overcome these using external knowledge bases.

ACKNOWLEDGEMENTS This work was supported by the Intelligence Advanced Research Projects Activity (IARPA) via Department of Interior National Business Center contract number D11PC20069. The U.S. Government is authorized to reproduce and distribute reprints for Governmental purposes notwithstanding any copyright annotation thereon. Disclaimer: The views and conclusions contained herein are those of the authors and should not be interpreted as necessarily representing the official policies or endorsements, either expressed or implied, of IARPA, DOI/NBC, or the U.S. Government. We thank Honeywell ACS Labs, Simon Fraser Univ. & Kitware Inc. for support in feature extraction and the anonymous reviewers for their comments.

6. REFERENCES

[1] A Ahmed, E. P. Xing, W. W. Cohen, and R. F. Murphy. Structured correspondence topic models for mining captioned figures in biological literature. In *SIGKDD*, 2009.

[2] M. J. Beal. *Variational Algorithms for Approximate Bayesian Inference*. PhD thesis, UCL, 2003.

[3] P. Bilinski and F. Bremond. Evaluation of local descriptors for action recognition in videos. In *ICCV*, 2011.

[4] D. Blei and M. Jordan. Modeling annotated data. In *SIGIR*, 2003.

[5] D. M. Blei, A. Ng, and M. I. Jordan. Latent dirichlet allocation. *JMLR*, 3:993–1022, 2003.

[6] C. Chang and C. Lin. LIBSVM: A library for support vector machines. *ACM TIST*, 2:27:1–27:27, 2011.

[7] M. Douze, H. Jégou, H. Sandhawalia, L. Amsaleg, and C. Schmid. Evaluation of gist descriptors for web-scale image search. In *CIVR*, pages 19:1–19:8, 2009.

[8] S. L. Feng, R. Manmatha, and V. Lavrenko. Multiple bernoulli relevance models for image and video annotation. In *CVPR*, 2004.

[9] A. Gupta, Y. Verma, and C. V. Jawahar. Choosing linguistics over vision to describe images. In *AAAI*, 2012.

[10] T. M. Hospedales, S. Gong, and T. Xiang. A markov clustering topic model for mining behaviour in video. In *ICCV*, 2009.

[11] A. Klaser, M. Marszalek, and C. Schmid. A spatio-temporal descriptor based on 3d-gradients. In *BMVC*, 2008.

[12] D. Klein and C. D. Manning. Accurate unlexicalized parsing. In *ACL*, 2003.

[13] V. Lavrenko, R. Manmatha, and J. Jeon. A model for learning the semantics of pictures. In *NIPS*. 2004.

[14] L. Li, K. Zhou, G. Xue, H. Zha, and Y. Yu. Video summarization via transferrable structured learning. In *WWW*, 2011.

[15] L-J. Li, H. Su, E. P. Xing, and L. Fei-fei. Object bank: A high-level image representation for scene classification and semantic feature sparsification. In *NIPS*, 2010.

[16] C-Y. Lin and E. Hovy. Automatic evaluation of summaries using n-gram co-occurrence statistics. In *NAACL HLT*, 2003.

[17] L. V. D. Maaten and G. Hinton. Visualizing high-dimensional data using t-sne. *JMLR*, 9(Nov):2579–2605, 2008.

[18] A. Makadia, V. Pavlovic, and S. Kumar. A new baseline for image annotation. In *ECCV*, pages 316–329, 2008.

[19] N. Nasios and A.G. Bors. Variational learning for gaussian mixture models. *IEEE Transactions on Systems, Man, and Cybernetics, Part B: Cybernetics*, 36(4):849 –862, 2006.

[20] P. Natarajan et al. BBN VISER. In *TRECVID MED*, 2011.

[21] A. Nenkova and R. Passonneau. Evaluating content selection in summarization: The pyramid method. In *HLT-NAACL*, 2004.

[22] A. Oliva and A. Torralba. Modeling the shape of the scene: A holistic representation of the spatial envelope. *Int. J. Comput. Vision*, 42(3):145–175, 2001.

[23] A. Oliva and A. Torralba. Building the gist of a scene: the role of global image features in recognition. *Progress in Brain Research*, 155(1):23–36, 2006.

[24] G. Parisi. *Statistical Field Theory*. Addison-Wesley, 1988.

[25] D. Putthividhya, H. T. Attias, and S. S. Nagarajan. Topic regression multi-modal latent dirichlet allocation for image annotation. In *CVPR*, 2010.

[26] D. Ramage, P. Heymann, C. D. Manning, and H. Garcia-Molina. Clustering the tagged web. In *WSDM*, 2009.

[27] R. K. Srihari. Piction: A system that uses captions to label human faces in newspaper photographs. In *AAAI*, 1991.

[28] L. Torresani, M. Szummer, and A. Fitzgibbon. Efficient object category recognition using classemes. In *ECCV*, 2010.

[29] C. Vondrick, D. Patterson, and D. Ramanan. Efficiently Scaling Up Video Annotation with Crowdsourced Marketplaces. In *ECCV*, 2010.

[30] Yang W. and Greg M. Human action recognition by semi-latent topic models. *IEEE PAMI*, 31(10):1762–1774, 2009.

[31] M. J. Wainwright and M. I. Jordan. *Graphical Models, Exponential Families, and Variational Inference*. Now Publishers Inc., Hanover, MA, USA, 2008.

[32] J. Wanke, A. Ulges, C. Lampert, and T. Breuel. Topic models for semantics-preserving video compression. In *MIR*, 2010.

[33] M. J. Welch, J. Cho, and W. Chang. Generating advertising keywords from video content. In *CIKM*, 2010.

[34] Y. Yang, C. L. Teo, H. Daumé III, and Y. Aloimonos. Corpus-guided sentence generation of natural images. In *EMNLP*, 2011.

[35] H. J. Zhang, C. Low, S. Smoliar, and J. Wu. Video parsing, retrieval and browsing: an integrated and content-based solution. In *ACM MM*, 1995.

What's in a Name? An Unsupervised Approach to Link Users across Communities*

Jing Liu
Harbin Institute of Technology
Harbin 150001, P.R. China
jliu@ir.hit.edu.cn

Fan Zhang
Nankai University
Tianjin 300071, P.R.China
zhangfan555@gmail.com

Xinying Song
Microsoft Research
Redmond, WA 98052, USA
xinson@microsoft.com

Young-In Song
NHN Corporation
Seoul, Korea
youngin.song@gmail.com

Chin-Yew Lin
Microsoft Research Asia
Beijing 100080, P.R. China
cyl@microsoft.com

Hsiao-Wuen Hon
Microsoft Research Asia
Beijing 100080, P.R. China
hon@microsoft.com

ABSTRACT

In this paper, we consider the problem of linking users across multiple online communities. Specifically, we focus on the *alias-disambiguation* step of this user linking task, which is meant to differentiate users with the same usernames. We start quantitatively analyzing the importance of the *alias-disambiguation* step by conducting a survey on 153 volunteers and an experimental analysis on a large dataset of About.me (75,472 users). The analysis shows that the *alias-disambiguation* solution can address a major part of the user linking problem in terms of the coverage of true pairwise decisions (46.8%). To the best of our knowledge, this is the first study on human behaviors with regards to the usages of online usernames. We then cast the *alias-disambiguation* step as a pairwise classification problem and propose a novel unsupervised approach. The key idea of our approach is to automatically label training instances based on two observations: (a) rare usernames are likely owned by a single natural person, e.g. **pennystar88**[1] as a positive instance; (b) common usernames are likely owned by different natural persons, e.g. **tank** as a negative instance. We propose using the n-gram probabilities of usernames to estimate the rareness or commonness of usernames. Moreover, these two observations are verified by using the dataset of Yahoo! Answers. The empirical evaluations on 53 forums verify: (a) the effectiveness of the classifiers with the automatically generated training data and (b) that the rareness and commonness of usernames can help user linking. We also analyze the cases where the classifiers fail.

Categories and Subject Descriptors

H.4 [**Information Systems Applications**]: Miscellaneous

*This work was done when Jing Liu and Fan Zhang were visiting students at Microsoft Research Asia, and Young-In Song worked as a researcher at Microsoft Research Asia.

[1]We use pseudo usernames in this paper to protect people's privacy.

WSDM'13, February 4–8, 2013, Rome, Italy.

General Terms

Algorithms, Experimentation

Keywords

Social network, User linking, Pairwise classification

1. INTRODUCTION

In recent years, the unprecedented amount of data from online communities such as online forums, community-based question answering (cQA), and micro blogs is becoming available for fundamental research on social networks such as user influence estimation [32], user expertise estimation [17], community structure analysis [23], etc. However, most work has concentrated on single communities (i.e. without crossing websites) due to the lack of explicit links between users across communities. Building such links is not a trivial matter as we will show later.

Zafarani et al. [33] first formalized the task of user linking as linking users across multiple communities who belong to a single natural person in the real world. Linking users across sites can enable many applications. For example, it can be used for understanding user migration patterns in social media [14] and allows community owners to learn how to retain or increase site traffic; it can be used for aggregating the public profile data of users (belonging to one natural person) from different communities to solve the cold-start problem in recommendation or personalization [1, 19]; it can protect users from privacy risks arising from large amounts of publicly available user information [18, 19]; it can enable users to keep up-to-date with their online friends from different communities in an integrated environment [29]; it can be used to create cross-community expert recommendation systems and mine influential people on a global social graph.

The task of user linking aims to solve the problem of linking users across multiple online communities. These users are identifiable by their usernames. This task can be divided into two steps. In the first step, we determine the set of the same usernames appearing in multiple communities and develop algorithms to decide if a username in this set is owned by a single natural person. We call this step the *alias-disambiguation* step, i.e. differentiating users under the same usernames. In the second step, we deal with a natural person using different usernames across sites. We call this step the *alias-conflation* step, i.e. finding a natural person using different usernames. In this paper, we focus on the first step, i.e. the *alias-disambiguation* step and leave the *alias-conflation* step for future work. Our survey of 153 volunteers and an analysis of a data set crawled from About.me[2] (75,472 users) show that the solution of *alias-disambiguation* can address a major part of the user linking problem in terms of the coverage of true pairwise decisions (46.8%, see Section 3.3). Specifically, 89.17% of participants in our survey reported that they prefer to use one main username across multiple communities. This implies that most of their online activities can be linked through their main usernames. A similar finding was also reported by [33] that 59% of their sampled users identified themselves with the same usernames across social networks. In addition, this problem cannot be trivially solved, since the baseline of treating two identical usernames always belonging to a single natural person only achieves an accuracy of 56.44% on a data set of 122 usernames.

We cast the *alias-disambiguation* step of user linking task as a pairwise classification problem. Given any two users from two different communities under the same username, a classifier is learned to decide whether these two users belong to a single natural person. Supervised methods are very effective but require manually annotated training corpora. To learn such a classifier without manually labeled data, we propose a novel unsupervised approach to automatically generate training data and then apply a standard machine learning method to learn classifiers. Our evaluation results show the classifiers trained with the automatically generated training data are effective. This method achieves an accuracy of 92.08% over a set of forum data consisting of 53 travel forums, 7.2 million threads, and 1.94 million users. Simply assuming the same usernames are always owned by a single natural person has an accuracy of 56.44%.

The key idea of our approach for automatic acquisition of training data is based on the following two observations:

- Rare usernames are likely owned by a single natural person, e.g. **pennystar88** (positive case).
- Common usernames are likely owned by different natural persons, e.g. **tank** (negative case).

Using n-gram probability of a username that estimates rareness or commonness of a username, training instances can be automatically assigned positive (low n-gram probability) or negative (high n-gram probability) labels. These two observations are supported by the data collected from Yahoo! Answers[3] in which a single username can be used by multiple natural persons. Please see Section 4 for more details.

The main contributions of this paper are:

- We demonstrate the importance of the *alias-disambiguation* step by conducting a survey and an experimental analysis on a dataset of About.me (see Section 3). To the best of our knowledge, it is the first study on human behavior on the usage of online usernames.
- We show that the rareness of a username measured by its n-gram probability is a good indicator of how likely it belongs to a single natural person (see Figure 4).
- We demonstrate how to automatically create a labeled training data set with the knowledge of the n-gram probability of a username (see Section 4).
- We verify the effectiveness of the classifiers trained with the automatically generated training data. We also examine the cases where our classifiers would fail. (see Section 6).

The remaining of this paper is organized as follows. Section 2 summarizes related work. In Section 3, we formally define the user linking problem and show the importance of *alias-disambiguation* step. Section 4 analyzes the relationship between n-gram probability of a username and its ownership, and shows how to utilize the n-gram probability of a username to automatically create a labeled training data set. Section 5 describes the features and models we propose. Section 6 describes evaluation setups, reports the experimental results and gives detail analysis. We conclude this paper in Section 7 and discuss future work.

2. RELATED WORK

2.1 User Linking across Communities

To the best of our knowledge, there has not been much research conducted on the problem of user linking. Zafarani et al. [33] firstly formalized the problem and proposed a web search based approach to address it. This approach is mainly based on two assumptions: (a) the URL of a user profile page contains the corresponding username; (b) a user profile page usually contains another username that is used by the same natural person on another community. However, our experiments suggest that these two assumptions do not hold for 75.47% of the cases in the data we collected. (see Section 6).

Iofciu et al. [12] focused on linking users in tagging systems and proposed a method to linearly combine the edit distances of usernames and the similarities between the tags provided by users. The proposed techniques are dependent on specific types of social networks (e.g. tagging services).

[29, 25, 19] collected user profiles from multiple social networks and proposed representing user profiles in vectors, of which each dimension corresponds to a profile field (e.g. username, description, profile image, location, etc.). Once the profile vectors are generated, both unsupervised and supervised approaches can be applied to link users. Vosecky et al. [29] used (unsupervised) comparison algorithms to compute the similarity scores between the user vectors, and those with scores larger than a pre-defined threshold are deemed to be the same person. [25, 19] used similarity vectors derived from annotated users as training instances, and upon which supervised classifiers are trained. The supervised approaches achieve high accuracy with regards to the user linking task. However, the types of identifiable personal information [22] are very different from site to site. Since it is impossible to manually label training instances for each online community, the above mentioned supervised approaches are not easily scaled. To address this challenge, we propose a novel unsupervised approach to automatically generate training instances, which can be adapted to any type of online communities trivially.

Another major limitation of the existing techniques is their dependencies on user profile pages to be publicly available [29, 25, 19], which is actually not the case for many online communities. Detailed analysis can be found in our experiments in Section 6. In our approach, we only collect personal identifiable information from the public user gen-

[2]`https://about.me`

[3]`http://answers.yahoo.com`

erated content (UGC) pages, which are accessible in most online communities.

2.2 De-anonymization on Social Networks

Researchers from data security and privacy area considered that linking the records from different anonymized databases may expose sensitive privacy information of the users [3, 22]. The main findings can be summarized into two categories: (a) It is pointed out that rare attribute values in high-dimensional sparse data sets can help de-anonymization [20, 10]. (b) [21, 15] found that an anonymized network can be successfully re-identified by only utilizing the structures of the social networks, because the online friends (neighbors) of a natural person are usually a similar group of people on different social graphs. In this paper, we have similar hypothesis on structure features for user linking (see Section 5).

2.3 Authorship Classification

Authorship classification is a task that identifies the authors of articles according to their writing styles by analyzing the corresponding article content. The findings in authorship classification can also help user linking. Novak et al. [24] proposed a language model based approach for authorship classification in online forums. In this paper, we use language model for feature extraction in the user linking task. Rao et al. [27] found that the usages of function words are indicative of authorship identification in mailing lists. We also make use of function words for user linking.

2.4 Entity Resolution

User linking is similar to several problems that have been studied for decades across multiple research communities. Examples include *coreference resolution* in natural language processing [6, 4, 28], where different mentions of the same underlying entity in free texts should be linked; *record linkage* in databases [5, 9], where two records from databases referring to the same real-world object should be identified; *people name disambiguation* in information retrieval [26, 13], which aims to assign documents to their authors with the same name, given thousands of documents belonging to different persons with the same name. Such problems fall under the umbrella-term *entity resolution* [5].

The state-of-the-art systems for addressing these problems mainly adopt two types of supervised approaches: (a) pairwise classification [4, 28] and (b) supervised and semi-supervised clustering [6, 5, 26, 13]. Given a username shared by multiple users, a graph of the corresponding users (nodes) can be constructed. However, the graphs of many usernames only contain two or three nodes (Figure 5). The clustering approaches cannot work well in such cases. Hence, in this paper, we cast the *alias-disambiguation* step as a pairwise classification problem. The supervised approaches usually outperforms unsupervised approaches in *entity resolution* tasks [9, 26]. However, it is expensive to manually annotate data sets for training. To address this challenge, we propose a method for automatic acquisition of training data.

To summarize the relationship to previous methods, our approach (1) automatically generates training instances by utilizing two characteristics of usernames; (2) models the *alias-disambiguation* step as a pairwise classification problem; (3) and explores the problem by using public UGC pages instead of the user profile pages, which are private in many online communities.

3. PROBLEM STATEMENTS

In this section, we first formally define the two steps of user linking: (a) the *alias-disambiguation* step and (b) the *alias-conflation* step (Section 3.1). In this paper, we focus on the first step, the *alias-disambiguation* step, and leave the *alias-conflation* step for future work. We demonstrate the importance of the *alias-disambiguation* step for the user linking problem by conducting a survey (Section 3.2) and an analysis on About.me (Section 3.3). The survey was completed by 153 volunteers including college students and full-time employees, who were invited by email or instant message (IM). The survey results provided us insight into human behavior with regards to the usage of online usernames. Specifically, 89.17% of the participants in our survey reported that they prefer using one main username across multiple communities. This implies that most of their online activities can be linked through their main usernames. Inspired by this observation, we further conducted an analysis on a large data set (75,472 users) crawled from About.me. The analysis results show that the *alias-disambiguation* step can address a major part of the user linking problem. Hence, the *alias-disambiguation* step is a valid starting point to solve the user linking problem.

3.1 Problem Definition

Let C denote a set of all communities, and $c \subseteq C$ denote a community. For each community c, there is a set U_c of all users who have registered in c. For a user $u \subseteq U_c$, let $id(u)$ denote the natural person to whom the user u belongs, and let $I(u)$ present all the publicly available information about the user u, including the username (denoted as $I(u).username$), the avatar (denoted as $I(u).avatar$), the location (denoted as $I(u).location$), all the posts written by him or her (denoted as $I(u).posts$), etc. The task of linking users across multiple communities can be divided into two steps: (a) the *alias-disambiguation* step and (b) the *alias-conflation* step. The formal definitions of these two steps are given as follows:

Alias-disambiguation step of user linking. The aim is to differentiate users under the same usernames. Formally, given two users $u \subseteq U_c$ and $u' \subseteq U_{c'}$ from two different communities c and c', and all the publicly available information about them $I(u)$ and $I(u')$, with the constraint that two users sharing the same username, the objective is to learn a function f to decide whether these two users belong to the same natural person. That is,

$$f(u,u') = \begin{cases} 1 & \text{if } id(u) = id(u') \\ 0 & \text{otherwise} \end{cases} \quad (1)$$
$$\text{subject to } I(u).username = I(u').username$$

Alias-conflation step of user linking. The goal is to find a natural person using different usernames. Formally, given two users $u \subseteq U_c$ and $u' \subseteq U'_c$ from two different communities c and c', and all the publicly available information about them $I(u)$ and $I(u')$, with the constraint that two users having different usernames, the objective is to learn a function g to decide whether these two users belong to the same natural person. That is,

$$g(u,u') = \begin{cases} 1 & \text{if } id(u) = id(u') \\ 0 & \text{otherwise} \end{cases} \quad (2)$$
$$\text{subject to } I(u).username \neq I(u').username$$

Table 1: **The distribution of #usernames used by participants**

#usernames	1	2	3	4	>4
%participants	13.04%	28.99%	27.54%	12.32%	18.12%

In this paper, for any user u, we obtain his or her publicly available information $I(u)$ from public UGC pages, rather than user profile pages that have been used in other work [29, 25, 19] since user profile pages are private in many communities. We will show this in Section 6.

3.2 Survey

We conducted a survey to explore the way in which people manage their usernames across online communities. To the best of our knowledge, it is the first study on human behavior with regards to the usage of online usernames.

Survey Content In addition to collecting the basic demographic information about participants, the survey asked a series of questions, starting with whether participants have ever participated in at least one online community. If they have done so, they were asked several follow-up questions about their frequency of using online communities and the number of usernames they use across all online communities in which they participate. Additionally, we asked participants who reported using more than one username whether they used one as a main username, and the reason they prefer to use one main username. We also asked the reason they use more than one username.

Participants This survey was completed by 153 people. All of the participants were invited via email or IM. 56.86% of the participants were male and 43.14% were female. 54.9% of the participants were aged 18 $\sim$ 26, 42.48% aged 27 $\sim$ 35 and only 1.96% aged 36 and over. 43.14% were university students and 56.86% were full-time employees. Most of the participants are heavy users of the internet, e.g. 67.97% spent approximately more than 20 hours on the internet per week on average, and 25.49% spent 5 $\sim$ 20 hours per week on average.

138 participants (90.20%) reported that they had participated in online communities before. 60.87% reported that they participate in online communities everyday. 15.94% participate weekly (e.g. 1 $\sim$ 2 times one week). 15.94% participate monthly (e.g. 1 $\sim$ 2 times one month). 9.42% participate rarely (e.g. 1 $\sim$ 2 times one year). We also collected the types of online communities in which they have participated. 69.93% have participated in social networks (e.g. microblog); 65.36% have participated in online forums; 54.25% have participated in blog community; 46.41% have participated in question and answering community.

Analysis Table 1 shows the distribution of the number of usernames used by the participants in online communities. We can observe that most participants (81.88%) used a small number of usernames (1−4) across online communities. Specifically, 89.17% of the participants who used more than one username reported that they used one as their main username across multiple communities. This implies that the *alias-disambiguation* step can link most of their activities in online communities. Additionally, they prefer to use

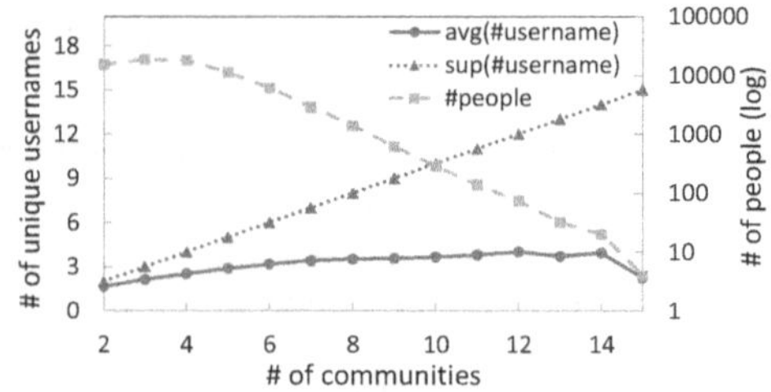

Figure 1: # of unique usernames w.r.t # of communities

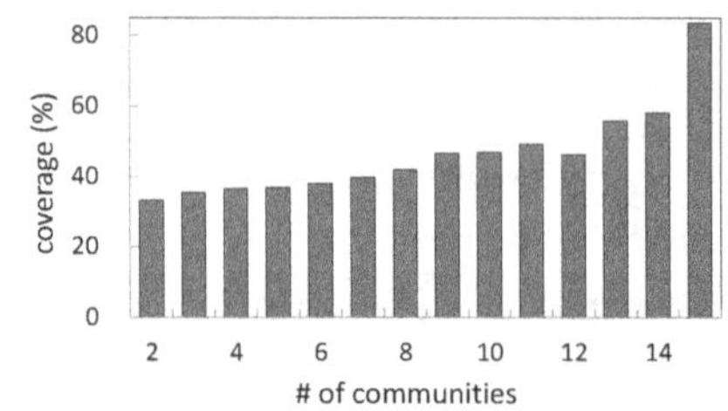

Figure 2: Coverage of true pairwise decisions in *alias-disambiguation* step

one main username across multiple communities due to two main reasons: (a) 79.53% reported that they wanted to minimize their efforts in remembering usernames across multiple communities. (b) 15.75% reported that a unique username would help them build their online reputation and make them more easily identified by other people. This observation tells us that people try to reduce the number of usernames they use. However, 86.96% of participants use more than one username (see Table 1). Two main reasons behind this phenomenon includes: (a) 58.26% reported that their preferred (main) usernames already had been used by other people at some communities, so they have to choose other usernames; (b) 21.74% reported that they would like to keep their online privacy by using different usernames in different communities to avoid de-anonymization.

3.3 Analysis on About.me

About.me is an online name card service, where people manually aggregate the links to their profile pages in other communities into one single personal page, which points to everything they do around the web. We crawled 75,472 public personal pages from About.me that show at least two involved communities and extracted all the usernames they used in those communities. There were 15 different communities in our data set (e.g. Twitter, LinkedIn and Flickr). On average, each person participated in 3.92 communities and had 2.44 usernames.

In Figure 1, people are categorized into 14 buckets according to the number of communities they participated in. The dash line (green) gives the number of people in each bucket. The dotted line (red) gives the upper bound of the number of unique usernames people can use in each bucket (i.e. the number of communities one participates in). The solid line (blue) indicates the average number of unique usernames people use in each bucket (i.e. the number of communities they participated in). From Figure 1, it can be seen that the average number of unique usernames used by one person only slightly increases as the number of the involved communities increases (the solid line). This implies people

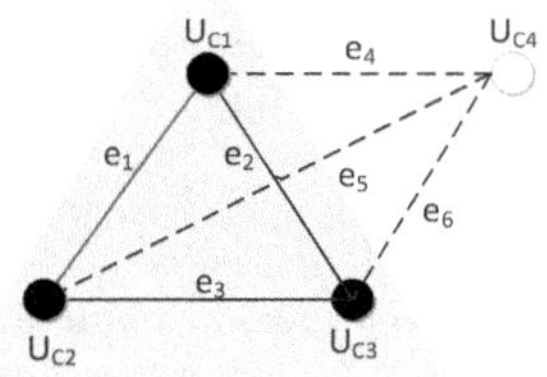

Figure 3: Example

tend to keep only a few usernames, i.e. 2 - 4, even if they participate in multiple online communities.

To quantitatively analyze how important solving the *alias-disambiguation* step is to approach the user linking problem, we conducted a further analysis of About.me. Linking all users belonging to one natural person is viewed as a number of separate pairwise decisions, where a true pairwise decision (tp) correctly links two users belonging to one natural person. Let $\sup(tp_1)$ and $\sup(tp_2)$ be the upper bound of the number of true pairwise decisions in the *alias-disambiguation* step and in the whole user linking problem, respectively. The ratio of $\sup(tp_1)$ and $\sup(tp_2)$ (called *coverage*) is the proportion of the true pairwise decisions in the user linking problem that can be covered by perfectly solving the *alias-disambiguation* step. This *coverage* is the best contribution the *alias-disambiguation* step can make to the user linking problem. It can be computed as follows:

$$coverage = \sup(tp_1)/\sup(tp_2) \tag{3}$$

Taking Figure 3 as an example, one natural person participates in four communities, c_1 (as user u_{c_1}), c_2 (as user u_{c_2}), c_3 (as user u_{c_3}) and c_4 (as user u_{c_4}). She uses one username across c_1, c_2 and c_3 (i.e. the usernames of u_{c_1}, u_{c_2} and u_{c_3} are the same), and uses another one in c_4. The user linking problem is to link the four nodes (u_{c_1}, u_{c_2}, u_{c_3} and u_{c_4}) together. Each of the 6 edges (e_1, e_2, ..., e_6) in Figure 3 indicates one true pairwise decision. In Figure 3, $\sup(tp_1)$ is 3 (i.e. 3 edges, e_1, e_2 and e_3), and $\sup(tp_2)$ is 6 (i.e. 6 edges, e_1, e_2, ..., e_6). Hence, the *coverage* of the *alias-disambiguation* step in Figure 3 is 50% (i.e. 3/6).

In Figure 2, people are categorized into 14 buckets according to the number of communities they participated in, and the bucket sizes illustrate the *coverage* value discussed above. The average *coverage* is 46.8%. Hence, it is important to solve the *alias-disambiguation* step. If the data about activity levels of users can be used, we believe that the *coverage* weighted by activity levels will be higher since 89.17% of our survey participants using more than one username reported that they use one main username in most online communities.

From Figure 2, we can observe that the *coverage* becomes higher with the increment of the number of communities people participated in. This implies that if one person participates in more communities, she prefers to spend less effort in managing her online usernames by using fewer usernames.

4. AUTOMATIC ACQUISITION OF TRAINING DATA

As we described in Section 1 and 2, we cast the *alias-disambiguation* step of user linking task as a pairwise classification problem. Supervised methods are very effective but require manually annotated training corpora. Moreover, the types of personal information are very different from site to site. It is impossible to manually label training instances for every online community. To address these challenges, we propose a novel unsupervised approach to automatically label training data for the user linking task.

The key idea of our approach is based on the following observations:

- Rare usernames are likely owned by a single natural person, e.g. **pennystar88** and **travelbag62**.
- Common usernames are likely owned by different natural persons, e.g. **tank** and **blues**.

In Section 3, we already observed that some people tend to use one main username across different communities to make it easier to remember usernames or to build their online reputation. To achieve these goals, they have to make their author names unique, for example, **pennystar88**. Hence, it is likely that two users sharing a rare username belong to a single natural person, so that the most rare usernames can be utilized for automatically labeling positive training instances. In contrast, it is unlikely that two users sharing a common username belong to a single natural person. Since there is a high probability that multiple natural persons prefer the common username. Hence, the most common usernames can be utilized for automatically labeling negative training instances. We propose using the n-gram probability of a username to estimate the rareness or commonness of a username (Section 4.1). Based on these two observations, we propose an algorithm to automatically label positive (low n-gram probability) or negative (high n-gram probability) training instances (Section 4.2).

4.1 N-gram Probabilities of Usernames

In this section, we use the n-gram probability of a username to estimate the rareness or commonness of the username, which is similar to [16]. Usually, when people select their usernames, they would like to use combinations of word sequences (one or more words) as their usernames. The word sequences may present people's real names, their birthdays, their hobbies, etc. For example, **pennystar88** might be composed of **penny**, **star** and **88** or **pen**, **ny**, **star** and **88**. The n-gram probability of a username is the n-gram probability of the word sequence of which the username consists. If the n-gram probability of a username is very low, the username is likely a rare username. If the n-gram probability of a username is very high, the user name is likely a common username.

Since it is not allowed to have spaces in usernames at many sites, we should first segment usernames and then estimate their n-gram probabilities. For example, **travelbag62** is segmented into **travel**, **bag** and **62**. We then treat the username segmentation task as a standard word breaking problem. Following the method proposed by [30], the task of username segmentation is

$$\hat{s} = \arg\max_{s \subseteq \Omega} P(s|a) = \arg\max_{s \subseteq \Omega} P(a|s)P(s) \tag{4}$$

Here, $s = (w_1, w_2, w_3, \ldots, w_{|s|})$ is a segmentation of a username a (without spaces) and the $\hat{s}$ is the objective segmentation with the maximum a posteriori, where $|s|$ denotes the number of words in the segmentation s. Let $|a|$ present the number of characters in a, and the size of the set of all possible segmentations Ω is $2^{|a|-1}$. In addition, $P(a|s)$

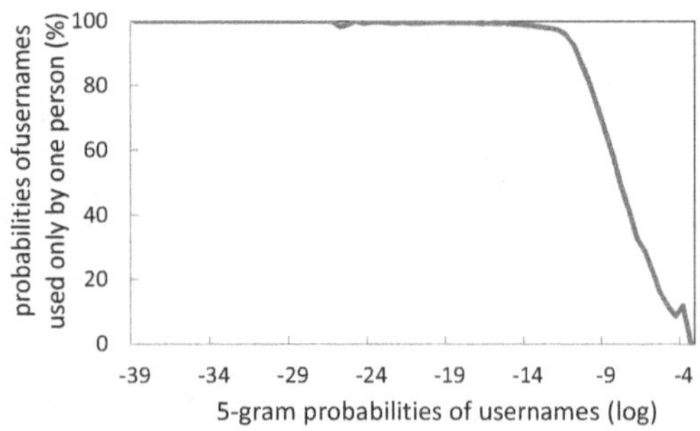

Figure 4: The distribution of username n-gram probability

and $P(s)$ are called the transformation and the segmentation prior model, respectively. In this paper, we use the word synchronous beam search approach proposed by [30] to estimate $P(a|s)$ and $P(s)$ and use the web n-gram service provided by [31] to estimate the n-gram probability. In this paper, we use the 5-gram based on the title corpus provided by the web n-gram service.

4.2 Automatic Acquisition of Training Data

Based on the two observations described above, we propose two intuitive assumptions for automatic acquisition of training data:

- **Assumption 1**: if the n-gram probability of a username is very low, it is likely that only one natural person uses it as his or her username.
- **Assumption 2**: if the n-gram probability of a username is very high, it is likely that more than one natural person uses it as a username.

We verify these two assumptions by using the data crawled from Yahoo! Answers, where different users are allowed to use the same username. Multiple users sharing the same username in Yahoo! Answers can be differentiated by their unique profile page URLs. There are 69 million question answering threads and 14 million unique users in our data set. We first counted the frequency of each unique username (i.e. the number of users using a given username) in the whole data set, and then sampled 299,716 unique usernames used by 673,037 unique users to verify our assumptions. In Figure 4, all the sampled usernames are categorized into buckets according to the n-gram probabilities of usernames after word breaking (estimated by the method in Section 4.1). The solid line shows the probabilities of usernames (with certain n-gram probabilities) used by only one person in Yahoo! Answers. From the solid line in Figure 4, we can observe that, (a) when the n-gram probability of a username is very low, it is likely that the username would be used by only one person; (b) when the n-gram probability of a username is very high, it is unlikely that the username would be used by one person. The experimental results verify our assumptions. Additionally, it can be observed that the solid curve in Figure 4 can be fitted by a logistic function of the n-gram probability of a username. Then, the fitted logistic function can be used for new usernames. We will show the details in Section 5.2.

Based on these two assumptions, we propose an approach to automatically label training data for user linking. Alg. 1 shows the details of our approach. The key idea of our approach is to utilize the n-gram probabilities of usernames for automatic acquisition of training instances, where each instance is a pair of users sharing the same username. We first estimate the n-gram probability of each username by using Alg. 1 (Line 2 $\sim$ 4). A given instance (i.e. one pair of users) with a username that has very low n-gram probability is assigned a true positive label, since it is likely that the username is used by only one person (Line 6 $\sim$ 8). In contrast, an instance with very a high n-gram probability username should be assigned a negative label, since it is very likely that the corresponding username is used by more than one person as their username (Line 9 $\sim$ 11).

Algorithm 1 Automatically Labeling Training Data

Input: A set S of n pairs of users sharing the same usernames from m communities
Output: A set Ω of labeled training instances

```
1: Ω ← {}
2: for each d = (u_c, u_c') in S do        ▷ d is a pair of users sharing the same username
3:     d.username ← I(u_c).username
4:     d.p ← EstimateNgramProb(d.username) ▷ segment the username and then estimate its n-gram probability
5: L ← SortByUsernameNgramProb(S)          ▷ L is a list of paired users and is in ascending order
6: for each d = (u_c, u_c') in SelectTopOnePercent(L) do
7:     d.label ← positive                  ▷ assign positive label
8:     Ω ← Ω ∪ {d}
9: for each d = (u_c, u_c') in SelectLastOnePercent(L) do
10:    d.label ← negative                  ▷ assign negative label
11:    Ω ← Ω ∪ {d}
12: return Ω
```

5. OUR APPROACH TO LINKING USERS

We view the *alias-disambiguation* step of the user linking task as a pairwise classification problem. Given any two users (from two different communities) sharing the same username, the objective is to learn a classifier which decides whether these two users belong to one person. As a test case, we focus on linking users from different online forums. Our approach for user linking includes two main phases: automatic acquisition of training data (Section 4.2) and a standard classification procedure. In Section 5.1, we describe the features used for user linking. We introduce the classification models in Section 5.2.

5.1 Features

In this paper, we do not consider the user profile pages for feature extraction, since many communities keep user profile pages private (See details in Section 6.5). As we described in Section 3.1, we only extract features from public UGC pages (e.g. forum thread pages). Taking an online forum as a test case, there are three categories of features extracted from forum thread pages: (a) user meta data based features; (b) social relationship based features; (c) post content based features.

5.1.1 User Meta Data based Features

Usually, there is some user meta data (e.g. avatar, location) displayed on the content pages (e.g. forum thread pages).

Avatar We observed that some people would like to put the same avatars on different communities they participated in. One possible motivation is that it can help people build their online reputation and enable others to recognize them through the unique avatars. We use a standard downsampling method of digital image processing to check whether two avatars (images) are the same [11].

Location If the locations provided by two users are the same or part-of relationship, it is likely that these two users belong to one person. We use Google Map API[4] to check whether two locations are the same or part-of relationship.

Signature We observe that some users prefer to use the same or similar signature on different sites. We employ Jensen-Shannon divergence [8], which is a symmetric measure of distance between two probability distributions, to measure the difference between two signatures.

5.1.2 Social Relationship based Features

Co-Author In online communities, users have social relationships with each other via interactions. In an online forum, we define two users (from one forum) as co-authors, if they participated in one forum thread. We observed that two persons may co-author with each other in two different forums. Hence, given two users (sharing the same username) from two different forums, we extract a real value co-author feature, which counts the number of their common co-authors with the same usernames.

5.1.3 Post Content based Features

Function words Rao et al. [27] found that the usage of function words is an effective feature for authorship classification. Since function words are specific English words that are usually independent of the topic of the content, and the usage of function words correlates with the writing style of an author. We employ Jensen-Shannon divergence to measure the difference between two frequency distributions of function words.

The first n and the last n words One of our interesting observations is that some users would like to use certain words at the beginning or the ending of posts. For example, a user with a username **bob** usually used "cheers, bob ☺" as the last words in a post. Some users would like to use "hi all," when asking questions. We use Jensen-Shannon divergence to measure the difference between the frequency distributions of the first n and the last n words by two users ($n = 3$).

5.2 Classification Models

In this section, we propose two models for the pairwise classification phase. In **Model 1**, a support vector machine (SVM) model with RBF kernel [7] is trained upon the automatically labeled training data (Section 4.2), with the features introduced in the previous section. Given a set of training instances $T = \{(\mathbf{x}_i, y_i)\}$, where $\mathbf{x}_i \in \mathbb{R}^n$ is a feature vector with a label $y_i \in \{1, 0\}$. The learned model makes decisions based on the output of the function $f(\mathbf{x})$,

$$f(\mathbf{x}) = sign(\mathbf{w} \cdot \mathbf{x} + b) \tag{5}$$

where $\mathbf{x}$ is a given testing instance, and the parameters $\mathbf{w}$ and b are optimized on the training set. It is noteworthy that the username n-gram probability is not included in the feature set of **Model 1**. Since the training instances are labeled according to the n-gram probabilities, this feature can easily dominate when appearing in the feature set.

[4] `http://code.google.com/apis/maps`

Table 2: Statistics of top forums

Forum	#Threads	#Users
Disboards	$1,937K$	$169K$
Tripadvisor	$1,026K$	$522K$
Cruisecritic	$923K$	$233K$
Lonelyplanet	$699K$	$265K$
Bikeforums	$565K$	$114K$
Advrider	$312K$	$74K$

However, the n-gram probability of a username should be an effective indicator for the user linking task. We propose incorporating it in our proposed **Model 2**. Recall the prior knowledge of the username n-gram probability learned from Yahoo! Answers (Figure 4 in Section 4.2): (a) If the n-gram probability of a username is very low, it is highly likely that the username is used by only one natural person; (b) With the increment of the n-gram probability, the likelihood of the corresponding username being used by only one natural person becomes lower. As we mentioned in Section 4.2, the solid curve in Figure 4 can be fitted by a logistic function. Given the n-gram probability θ of a username, a probability $P(y = 1|\theta)$ can be estimated, which indicates how likely the username is used by only one natural person. The logistic function adopted is defined as:

$$P(y = 1|\theta) = \frac{1}{1 + e^{-\alpha(\theta - \beta)}} \tag{6}$$

where θ is the n-gram probability of the given username. Parameters α and β are learned from Yahoo! Answers ($\alpha = 0.6270$ and $\beta = -7.4212$). To utilize both the priori knowledge of the n-gram probability and the learned SVM model which makes use of other features, we design a new objective function $f'(\mathbf{x}; \theta)$ in **Model 2**:

$$f'(\mathbf{x}; \theta) = \begin{cases} 1 & \text{if } P(y = 1|\mathbf{x}; \theta) > \mu \\ 0 & \text{otherwise} \end{cases} \tag{7}$$

where

$$P(y = 1|\mathbf{x}; \theta) = \lambda P(y = 1|\theta) + (1 - \lambda) P(y = 1|\mathbf{x})$$

Unlike in Equation (5), $P(y = 1|\mathbf{x})$ is the probabilistic output of the SVM model (i.e. **Model 1**), which can be derived from LIBSVM [7]; λ controls the contributions of the n-gram probability priori and the SVM predictions, and it is set to $P(y = 1|\theta)$ in this paper. When a username n-gram probability is low, **Model 2** relies more on the username related information $P(y = 1|\theta)$ due to the high $P(y = 1|\theta)$ value; when the n-gram probability becomes higher, **Model 2** is more dependent on the predictions of the SVM model $P(y = 1|\mathbf{x})$, which takes other features into consideration.

6. EXPERIMENTS

6.1 Data Set

We collected 53 travel related forums and crawled the public forum thread pages from these forums (until June 2011). We manually developed one template for each forum to extract the structured data (e.g. username, avatar, location, signature and post content) from the forum thread pages.

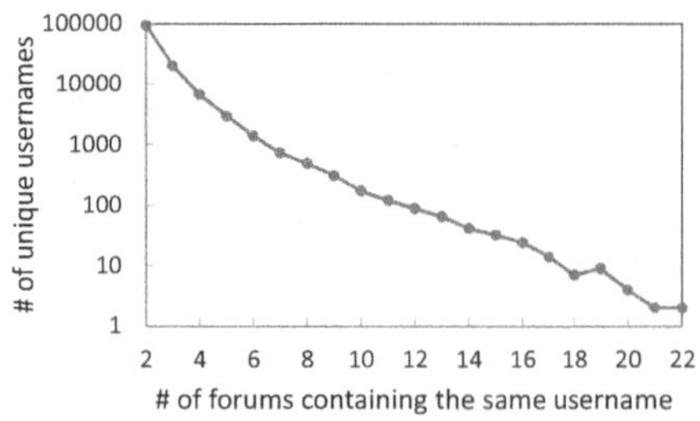

Figure 5: The frequency distribution of usernames

The data set includes 7.2 million forum threads and 1.94 million users. Table 2 shows the number of threads and the number of users in the biggest 6 sites. It should be noted that one username only can be allowed for one person to use in each of the 53 forums. There are totally 325,139 pairs of users sharing the same usernames extracted from the data set and 127,088 corresponding unique usernames. Our approach (Alg. 1) generated 1462 training instances (i.e. pairs of users), including 961 positive instances and 601 negative instances.

Figure 5 illustrates the frequency distribution of the same username being used in multiple forums. Each point in the plot specifies the number of unique usernames (corresponding to the y axis) which are observed in x forums (corresponding to the x axis). From the distribution it can be seen that most of the usernames that are used across forums only occur in a few forums (2 or 3), therefore resulting in sparse connections between users sharing the same usernames. Since clustering techniques are more useful for tasks involving richer and denser relationships, the clustering techniques widely used in *entity resolution* tasks [6, 5, 26, 13] are not suitable in these cases. Hence, we view this task as a pairwise classification problem.

6.2 Ground Truth

To evaluate our approaches, we hired one assessor to annotate the ground truth. The annotation of ground truth for this task is expensive. We developed a tool that helps the assessor quickly explore (a) user profile pages that have more detailed information about users and (b) users' post contents to make judgements. The information that the assessor can use to annotate data includes but is not limited to:

- The personal information about users on profile pages, e.g. avatar, personal interests, occupation, location;
- The information describing users themselves or their families in post contents or signatures, e.g. "... my family of five. Two adults, and three children ...", "... I'm planning a wedding October ...", etc;
- Similar questions posted on different forums with close dates;
- The places where (or the time when) they traveled according to their post contents or signatures;
- The URLs of blogs or homepages linked from their profile pages or signatures;
- Two people know each other, so they (frequently) interact with each other in different forums.

We randomly sampled and annotated 122 user pairs. There are 57 pairs labeled as positive instances, 44 pairs labeled as negative instances and 21 instances we cannot determine.

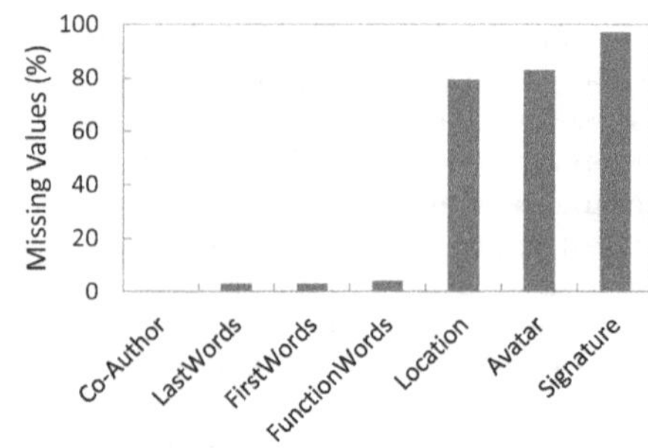

Figure 6: The percentage of missing values for each feature

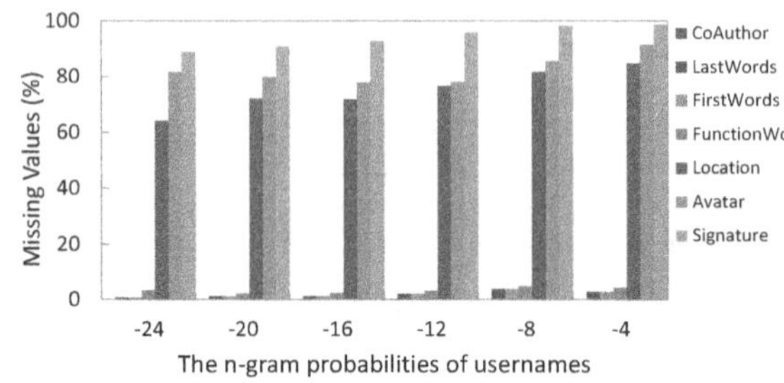

Figure 7: The percentage of missing values for each feature w.r.t n-gram probabilities of usernames

6.3 Evaluation Metrics

We employ the standard evaluation metrics in information retrieval to evaluate: accuracy (denoted as Acc), precision (denoted as P), recall (denoted as R) and F_1-measure (denoted as F_1), which are defined as follows:

$$Acc = \frac{tp + tn}{tp + tn + fp + fn}$$

$$P = \frac{tp}{tp + fp}, R = \frac{tp}{tp + fn}, F_1 = \frac{2PR}{P + R}$$

where tp indicates the number of true positives, tn indicates the number of true negatives, fn indicates the number of false negatives and fp indicates the number of false positives.

6.4 Missing Values of Features

We examine the problem of missing values of features in the dataset. Figure 6 shows the percentage of missing values for each feature in our dataset. It can be observed that some of the features (e.g. location, avatar and signature) have large proportion of missing values. Actually, a similar problem has been reported in [19]. However, Malhotra et al. [19] avoid this problem by selecting the communities where there is no large proportion of missing values.

The presence of missing values in a dataset can affect the performance of a classifier trained on the dataset containing missing values [2]. Several methods have been proposed to treat missing data. Acuna et al. [2] carried out experiments and found that case deletion (CD) is the most effective method for a dataset where there is a large proportion of missing values. This method discards all instances (cases) with missing values for at least n features (we use $n = 2$).

Table 3: Overall results

Method	Prec.	Rec.	F_1	Acc.
Baseline	0.5644	1.0000	0.7215	0.5644
Model 1	0.8571	0.6316	0.7273	0.7327
Model 2 ($\mu = 0.8$)	0.9455	0.9123	0.9286	0.9208
Model 2 ($\mu = 0.7$)	0.9000	0.9474	0.9231	0.9109
Model 2 ($\mu = 0.6$)	0.8636	1.0000	0.9268	0.9109
Model 2 ($\mu = 0.5$)	0.8382	1.0000	0.9120	0.8911

Table 4: Experimental results on two subsets

Method	Accuracy on Set1 (size=59)	Accuracy on Set2 (size=42)
Baseline	0.6441	0.1220
Model 1	0.8571	0.6441
Model 2 ($\mu = 0.8$)	0.9322	0.9048

We further examine the missing values problem over different n-gram probabilities of usernames. Figure 7 shows the percentage of missing values for each feature according to different n-gram probabilities of usernames. We can observe that the proportion of missing values for each feature becomes higher with the increment of the n-gram probability of a username. Recall the results of our survey (Section 3.2), 15.75% participants reported that a unique username would help them build their online reputation and make them easily identified by other people. Similarly, one possible reason behind the above phenomenon (Figure 7) is that the person a using unique username (low n-gram probability) prefers to maintain their online reputation via a unique avatar, signature etc. This would result in the different performances of our classifier on the instances with different n-gram probabilities. We will provide detailed results in Section 6.5.

6.5 Experimental Results

We first examine the possibility of applying the previous approaches to this task. Most previous methods [29, 25, 19] are heavily dependent on the accessability of user profile pages. However, user profile pages are private at many online communities. Among the 53 forums in our data set, 45.28% of forums have user profile pages that are private. Zafarani et al. [33] proposed a web search based approach, which is dependent on: (a) the URL of a user profile contains the corresponding username; (b) the user profile pages of usernames should be publicly available. However, only 24.53% of forums in our data set meet these two conditions.

We then empirically evaluated three methods. The simplest baseline is to treat all pairs of users sharing the same usernames as positive instances. We also examined our proposed **Model 1** and **Model 2**.

Table 3 shows the experimental results on the whole set of ground truth. The baseline of treating two identical usernames always belonging to a single natural person only achieves an accuracy of 56.44%. This tells us that the *alias-disambiguation* step is not a trivial task. Both **Model 1** and **Model 2** outperform the baseline. **Model 1** gives an accuracy of 73.27%. It shows that our classifier on the automatically training data is reasonably effective. **Model 2**, which additionally utilizes the priori knowledge of usernames learned from Yahoo! Answers, gives the best performance. It shows that the rareness or commonness of usernames can help user linking.

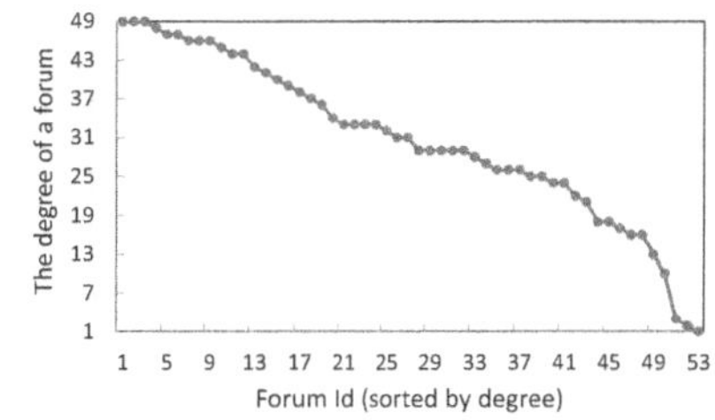

Figure 8: Degree distribution of the forum graph

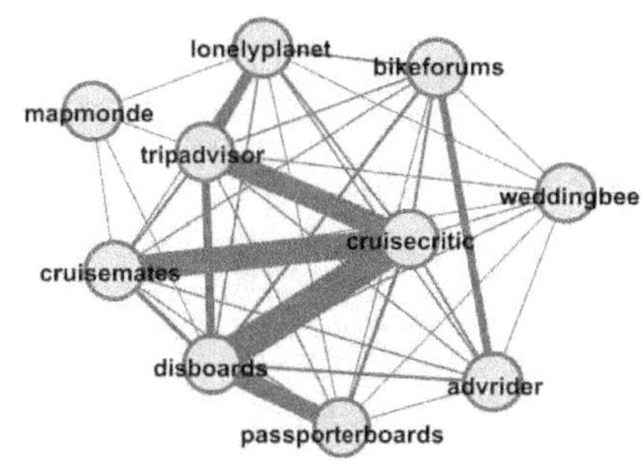

Figure 9: The graph of top 10 forums

Additionally, we found that **Model 2** gives higher recall and lower precision with the increment of the threshold μ.

We further investigated the cases where **Model 1** performs poorly. We separated the ground truth into two subsets: (a) the set of instances with n-gram probabilities lower than a threshold θ (named Set 1); (b) the set of instances with the n-gram probabilities higher than the threshold θ (named Set 2). In this paper, we set the threshold θ to be -7.42, since we learned from Yahoo! Answers (Figure 4) that when the n-gram probability of a username is higher than -7.42, the probability of the username used by only one person is lower than 50.0%. Table 4 shows the performances of the three methods on the two subsets. From Table 4, we can see that **Model 1** performs much better on Set 1 than on Set 2. As we described in Section 6.4, this is due to the fact that there is a larger proportion of missing values for each feature in Set 2 than in Set 1.

6.6 Analysis on the Graph of Forums

In this section, we examine the effectiveness of our proposed method (**Model 2**) by analyzing the graph of forums. A graph of forums can be constructed by using the linked user pairs: if there is one pair of users from two forums linked together, there is an undirected edge between these two forums (nodes). The weight of each edge is the number of linked user pairs between the corresponding two forums.

We first apply our proposed method (**Model 2**) on the 53 travel related forums. There are 68,349 user pairs (21.02%) linked according to the classification results of our method. Then, the graph of forums can be constructed. Figure 8 shows the degree distribution of the constructed forum graph. From Figure 8, we can observe that all 53 forums are connected to at least one other forum. Figure 9 shows the subgraph of the 10 biggest forums. The width of the edge is proportional to the weight of the edge. It is expected that two forums with similar topics share common users. Hence, the width of the edge between two forums with similar topics should be wide. We have several interesting observations from Figure 9:

- There is a strong connection between Cruisecritic and Cruisemates, since the main discussion topics on both forums are cruise;
- There is a strong connection between Bikeforums and Advrider, since the topic of these two forums is cycling;
- There is a strong connection between Disboards and Passporterboards, since both of them focus on Disney World;
- The strong connection between Tripadvisor and Lonelyplanet is due to their similar board hierarchies for discussing world travel.

7. CONCLUSIONS

In this paper, we focus on the *alias-disambiguation* step of the user linking task. We quantitatively analyze the importance of this step by conducting a survey and an experiment. The analysis shows that the *alias-disambiguation* solution can address a major part of the user linking problem in terms of the coverage of true pairwise decisions (46.8%). Morever, 89.17% of participants in our survey reported that they prefer to use one main username across multiple communities. To the best of our knowledge, it is the first study on the human behavior of the usage of online usernames. We then propose an unsupervised approach for user linking, which utilizes the rareness and commonness of usernames measured by their n-gram probabilities to automatically label training instances. The empirical evaluation verifies the effectiveness of the classifiers with the automatically generated training data. It also shows that the rareness and commonness of usernames can help user linking. We further analyze the cases where our classifiers would fail.

Future work may follow two paths: (a) investigate *alias-conflation* step by using the SVM model (**Model 1**) that is learned from the *alias-disambiguation* step and does not rely on usernames; (b) employ blocking techniques with pairwise classification models to efficiently explore this problem on a larger scale data set.

8. ACKNOWLEDGEMENT

The authors thank Jie Cai for her helpful discussions and supports on this work.

9. REFERENCES

[1] F. Abel, N. Henze, E. Herder, and D. Krause. Interweaving public user profiles on the web. In *Proceedings of UMAP*, 2010.

[2] E. Acuna and C. Rodriguez. The treatment of missing values and its effect on classifier accuracy. *Classification, Clustering, and Data Mining Applications*, 2004.

[3] L. Backstrom, C. Dwork, and J. Kleinberg. Wherefore art thou r3579x?: anonymized social networks, hidden patterns, and structural steganography. In *Proceedings of WWW*, 2007.

[4] E. Bengtson and D. Roth. Understanding the value of features for coreference resolution. In *Proceedings of EMNLP*, 2008.

[5] I. Bhattacharya and L. Getoor. Collective entity resolution in relational data. *ACM Transactions on Knowledge Discovery from Data (TKDD)*, 1(1), 2007.

[6] J. Cai and M. Strube. End-to-end coreference resolution via hypergraph partitioning. In *Proceedings of COLING*, 2010.

[7] C. Chang and C. Lin. Libsvm: a library for support vector machines. *ACM Transactions on Intelligent Systems and Technology (TIST)*, 2(3), 2011.

[8] T. Cover, J. Thomas, J. Wiley, et al. *Elements of information theory*, volume 6. 1991.

[9] A. Elmagarmid, P. Ipeirotis, and V. Verykios. Duplicate record detection: A survey. *IEEE Transactions on Knowledge and Data Engineering (TKDE)*, 19(1), 2007.

[10] D. Frankowski, D. Cosley, S. Sen, L. Terveen, and J. Riedl. You are what you say: privacy risks of public mentions. In *Proceedings of SIGIR*, 2006.

[11] R. Gonzalez and R. Woods. *Digital image processing*. 2002.

[12] T. Iofciu, P. Fankhauser, F. Abel, and K. Bischoff. Identifying users across social tagging systems. In *Proceedings of ICWSM*, 2011.

[13] D. Kalashnikov, Z. Chen, S. Mehrotra, and R. Nuray-Turan. Web people search via connection analysis. *IEEE Transactions on Knowledge and Data Engineering (TKDE)*, 20(11), 2008.

[14] S. Kumar, R. Zafarani, and H. Liu. Understanding user migration patterns in social media. In *Proceedings of AAAI*, 2011.

[15] S. Labitzke, I. Taranu, and H. Hartenstein. What your friends tell others about you: Low cost linkability of social network profiles. In *Proceedings of SNAKDD*, 2011.

[16] J. Liu, X. Song, J. Jiang, and C. Lin. An unsupervised method for author extraction from web pages containing user-generated content. In *Proceedings of CIKM*, 2012.

[17] J. Liu, Y. Song, and C. Lin. Competition-based user expertise score estimation. In *Proceedings of SIGIR*, 2011.

[18] K. Liu and E. Terzi. A framework for computing the privacy scores of users in online social networks. In *Proceedings of ICDM*, 2009.

[19] A. Malhotra, L. Totti, W. Meira, P. Kumaraguru, and V. Almeida. Studying user footprints in different online social networks. In *Proceedings of CSOSN*, 2012.

[20] A. Narayanan and V. Shmatikov. Robust de-anonymization of large sparse datasets. In *Proceedings of S&P*, 2008.

[21] A. Narayanan and V. Shmatikov. De-anonymizing social networks. In *Proceedings of S&P*, 2009.

[22] A. Narayanan and V. Shmatikov. Myths and fallacies of personally identifiable information. *Communications of the ACM*, 53(6), 2010.

[23] M. Newman. Communities, modules and large-scale structure in networks. *Nature Physics*, 8(1), 2011.

[24] J. Novak, P. Raghavan, and A. Tomkins. Anti-aliasing on the web. In *Proceedings of WWW*, 2004.

[25] A. Nunes, P. Calado, and B. Martins. Resolving user identities over social networks through supervised learning and rich similarity features. In *Proceedings of SAC*, 2012.

[26] Y. Qian, Y. Hu, J. Cui, Q. Zheng, and Z. Nie. Combining machine learning and human judgment in author disambiguation. In *Proceedings of CIKM*, 2011.

[27] J. Rao and P. Rohatgi. Can pseudonymity really guarantee privacy. In *Proceedings of USENIX*, 2000.

[28] W. Soon, H. Ng, and D. Lim. A machine learning approach to coreference resolution of noun phrases. *Computational Linguistics*, 27(4), 2001.

[29] J. Vosecky, D. Hong, and V. Shen. User identification across multiple social networks. In *Proceedings of NDT*, 2009.

[30] K. Wang, C. Thrasher, and B. Hsu. Web scale nlp: A case study on url word breaking. In *Proceedings of WWW*, 2011.

[31] K. Wang, C. Thrasher, E. Viegas, X. Li, and B. Hsu. An overview of microsoft web n-gram corpus and applications. In *Proceedings of NAACL*, 2010.

[32] J. Weng, E.-P. Lim, J. Jiang, and Q. He. Twitterrank: finding topic-sensitive influential twitterers. In *Proceedings of WSDM*, 2010.

[33] R. Zafarani and H. Liu. Connecting corresponding identities across communities. In *Proceedings of ICWSM*, 2009.

Big Data, Lifelong Machine Learning and Transfer

Qiang Yang
Huawei Noah's Ark Lab
5F, Core Building 2, Hong Kong
Science Park
Shatin, Hong Kong
http://www.cse.ust.hk/~qyang

ABSTRACT

A major challenge in today's world is the Big Data problem, which manifests itself in Web and Mobile domains as rapidly changing and heterogeneous data streams. A data-mining system must be able to cope with the influx of changing data in a continual manner. This calls for Lifelong Machine Learning, which in contrast to the traditional one-shot learning, should be able to identify the learning tasks at hand and adapt to the learning problems in a sustainable manner. A foundation for lifelong machine learning is transfer learning, whereby knowledge gained in a related but different domain may be transferred to benefit learning for a current task. To make effective transfer learning, it is important to maintain a continual and sustainable channel in the life time of a user in which the data are annotated. In this talk, I outline the lifelong machine learning situations, give several examples of transfer learning and applications for lifelong machine learning, and discuss cases of successful extraction of data annotations to meet the Big Data challenge.

Categories and Subject Descriptors

D.3.3 [**Algorithms**] Machine Learning

General Terms

Algorithms,

Keywords

Big Data, Lifelong Machine Learning, Transfer Learning, Mobile Intelligence

WSDM'13, February 4–8, 2013, Rome, Italy.
ACM 978-1-4503-1869-3/13/02.

Balanced Label Propagation for Partitioning Massive Graphs

Johan Ugander
Center for Applied Mathematics
Cornell University
Ithaca, NY
jhu5@cornell.edu

Lars Backstrom
Facebook
Menlo Park, CA
lars@fb.com

ABSTRACT

Partitioning graphs at scale is a key challenge for any application that involves distributing a graph across disks, machines, or data centers. Graph partitioning is a very well studied problem with a rich literature, but existing algorithms typically can not scale to billions of edges, or can not provide guarantees about partition sizes.

In this work we introduce an efficient algorithm, *balanced label propagation*, for precisely partitioning massive graphs while greedily maximizing edge locality, the number of edges that are assigned to the same shard of a partition. By combining the computational efficiency of label propagation — where nodes are iteratively relabeled to the same 'label' as the plurality of their graph neighbors — with the guarantees of constrained optimization — guiding the propagation by a linear program constraining the partition sizes — our algorithm makes it practically possible to partition graphs with billions of edges.

Our algorithm is motivated by the challenge of performing graph predictions in a distributed system. Because this requires assigning each node in a graph to a physical machine with memory limitations, it is critically necessary to ensure the resulting partition shards do not overload any single machine.

We evaluate our algorithm for its partitioning performance on the Facebook social graph, and also study its performance when partitioning Facebook's 'People You May Know' service (PYMK), the distributed system responsible for the feature extraction and ranking of the friends-of-friends of all active Facebook users. In a live deployment, we observed average query times and average network traffic levels that were 50.5% and 37.1% (respectively) when compared to the previous naive random sharding.

Categories and Subject Descriptors

G.2.2 [**Mathematics of Computing**]: Discrete Mathematics—*Graph Theory, Graph Algorithms*

General Terms

Algorithms, Measurement

Keywords

graph clustering, graph partitioning, label propagation, social networks

1. INTRODUCTION

In Plato's *Phaedrus*, Socrates tells us that a key principle of rhetoric is the ability to divide ideas "where the natural joints are, and not trying to break any part, after the manner of a bad carver" [15]. This, too, is the goal of graph partitioning: breaking a graph at its natural joints.

In this work, we present an algorithm for finding 'joints' in graphs of particularly massive proportions, with an emphasis on the Facebook social graph consisting of over 800 million nodes and over 68 billion edges [19]. The algorithm we present uses label propagation to relocate inefficiently assigned nodes while respecting strict shard balancing constraints. We show how this *balanced label propagation algorithm* can be formulated as a convex optimization problem that reduces to a manageable linear programming problem. The algorithm is fundamentally iterative, where each iteration entails solving a linear program.

While we find that our algorithm performs well under random initialization, by initializing the algorithm with a greedy geographic assignment, we find that it is possible to effectively achieve convergence within a single step of the update algorithm, while random initialization requires many iterations to slowly converges to a less performative solution.

Our algorithm has the ability to follow arbitrary partition size specifications, a generalization of the more common goal of symmetric partitioning [10]. This functionality makes it possible to use the greedy efficiency of label propagation when considering partitions that are not symmetric by creation, but might still benefit from label propagation. Specifically, the geographic initialization we consider is not symmetric, yet balanced label propagation can still be used to considerably improve the partitioning.

Label propagation unfortunately offers no formal performance guarantees with respect to the graph partitioning objective, and neither does our modification. It is worth remarking that the basic problem of constrained graph partitioning, bisecting a graph into two equal parts with as few crossing edges as possible, is the well known NP-hard *minimum bisection problem* [8], with the best known approximation algorithm being a $O(\sqrt{n}\log n)$-factor approximation [6]. Knowing this, our goal has been to develop a highly scalable algorithm that can deliver precise partition size guarantees while performing well at maximizing edge locality in practice.

People You May Know. After presenting our algorithm and analyzing its performance on both the Facebook social graph and a LiveJournal graph, we then present the results of a full deployment of the partitioning scheme for the Facebook friend recommendation system, 'People You May Know' (PYMK). This system computes, for a given user u, and each friend-of-friend (FoF) w of u a feature vector $x_{u,w}$ of graph metrics based on the local structure between u and w. The system then uses machine learning to rank all the suggestions w for u, based on the feature vector $x_{u,w}$, as well as demographic features of u and w.

Due to the size of the graph and high query volume, Facebook has built a customized system for performing this task. Each user u is assigned to a specific machine m_u (this assignment is what we are optimizing). When a FoF query is issued for a user u, it must be sent to machine m_u. Then, for each $v \in N(u)$, a query must be issued to the machine m_v, to retrieve the nodes two hops from u. The results of these queries are then aggregated to compute the features that are input to the machine learning phase, which outputs the final ranked list of FoFs.

Our goal is to perform our graph sharding such that, as often as possible, $m_v = m_u$ for $v \in N(u)$. By doing this well, we can reduce the number of other machines that we need to query, and also reduce the total amount of data that needs to be transferred over the network, increasing overall system throughput and latency. We are constrained by the fact that machines have a limited amount of memory, which puts a hard cap on the size of each shard.

At the outset, it is important to note that it is not actually clear that a sophisticated sharding will be a performance win in this application. When naively sharding a graph, one typical approach is to assign nodes to machines by simply taking the modulus of the user ID; see Figure 1. The advantage of this approach is that the machine location of a node is directly encoded in the user ID. Using a non-trivial sharding requires extensive additional lookups in a *shard map*, as well as an additional network operation at the start of the query where the initial request is forwarded to the appropriate machine hosting the subject of the query. The shard map for all 800 million nodes must also be mirrored in memory across all machines.

As we will see in our ultimate demonstration, the cost of this additional complexity is greatly overshadowed by the improvements in locality that can be had. The novel graph sharding algorithm we introduce, combined with the intelligent initialization based on geographic metadata, is able to produce a sharding across 78 machines where 75.2% of edges are local to individual machines. In the conclusion to this work, we deploy the resulting sharding on Facebook's 'People You May Know' realtime service, and observe dramatic performance gains in a realtime environment.

The main distinction when designing an algorithm applicable at Facebook's scale is that the full graph can not be easily stored in memory. Realistically, this means that the only admissible algorithms are those that examine the graph in streaming iterations. One iteration of our balanced label propagation algorithm takes a single aggregating pass over the edge list, executable in MapReduce, and then solves a linear program with complexity dependent on the number

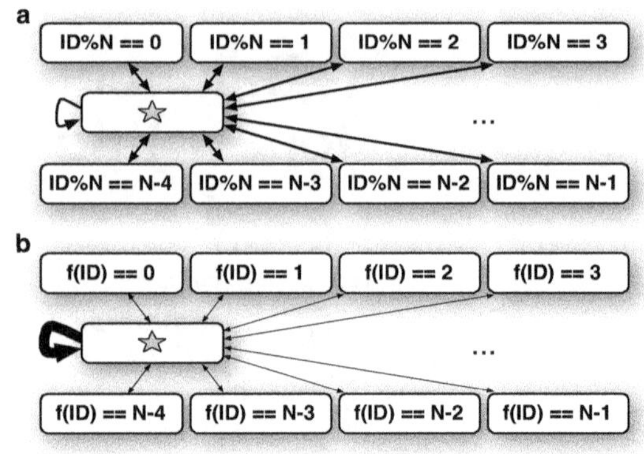

Figure 1: Sharding the neighbors of a node across N machines. (a) Aggregating properties of the neighbors when the edge list is sharded according to node ID mod N. (b) Aggregating when the edge list is sharded according to a shardmap f. The goal of an efficient shard map is to greatly increase the likelihood that a node is located on the same shard as its neighbors.

of machines, not the size of the graph. A final assignment step takes a single streaming pass over the nodes, again in MapReduce, to redefine their assignments. Recent work on streaming graph partitioning [17] produced notable performance using a single greedy iteration, but the results were obtained within a framework that did not naturally lend itself to additional iteration.

Organization of the paper. Section 2 presents the details of the balanced label propagation algorithm. Section 3 discusses a geographic initialization that, when possible, greatly improves performance. In Section 4, we evaluate the algorithm and its ability to shard the Facebook social graph and a publicly availably LiveJournal graph dataset. In Section 5, we study a deployment of the sharding to load-balance Facebook's PYMK service. We conclude with Section 6 by discussing future directions for work on this problem.

2. BALANCED LABEL PROPAGATION

Label propagation was first proposed as an efficient method for learning missing labels for graph data in a semi-supervised setting [20]. In such a setting, unlabeled nodes iteratively adopt the label of the plurality of their neighbors until convergence, making it possible to infer a broad range of traits that are fundamentally assortative along the edges of a graph.

In a context very similar to graph partitioning, label propagation has been found to be a very efficient technique for network community detection [16], the challenge of finding naturally dense network clusters in an unlabeled graph [7]. In this context, each node of a graph is initialized with an individual label, and label propagation is iterated where nodes again update their labels to the plurality of their neighbor's labels.

Network community detection and graph partitioning are very similar challenges, with two key differences. First, community detection algorithms need not and should not require *a priori* specification of the number or size of graph communities to find. Second, community detection algorithms ought to support overlapping communities, while graph partitions seek explicitly disjoint structure. While some partitioning applications may benefit from assigning nodes to multiple partitions, the Facebook social graph we aim to partition has a modest maximum degree of 5,000, and so we restrict our investigation to creating true partitions.

Label propagation fails to detect overlapping communities [7], though an adaptation does exist [9]. But this failure of the ordinary label propagation algorithm in fact makes it a strong candidate for graph partitioning. The remaining difficulty is therefore that label propagation provides no way of constraining the sizes of any of the resulting community partitions. Our contribution address precisely this difficulty.

A previous attempt to 'constrain' label propagation utilizes an optimization framework with a cost penalty to encourage balanced partitions [3], but this approach does not offer constraints in a formal sense. The constraint-based algorithm we introduce in this work offers the possibility of precisely constraining the size of all the resulting shards – it is in fact not limited to constraints that produce balanced partitions. It is also worth noting that the previous cost penalty approach lacks the computational efficiency of label propagation, and the largest graph that framework was originally tested on contained just 120,000 edges.

2.1 Partition constraints

The goal of our balanced label propagation algorithm is to take a graph $G = (V, E)$ and produce a partition $\{V_1, \ldots, V_n\}$ of V, subject to explicitly defined size constraints. The algorithm is capable of enforcing arbitrary size constraints in the form of lower bounds S_i and upper bounds T_i, such that $S_i \leq |V_i| \leq T_i$, $\forall i$. These constraints can easily take the form of balanced constraints, targeting exact balance $S_i = \lfloor |V|/n \rfloor$ and $T_i = \lceil |V|/n \rceil$, $\forall i$, or operating with leniency, $S_i = \lfloor (1-f)|V|/n \rfloor$ and $T_i = \lceil (1+f)|V|/n \rceil$, for some fraction $f > 0$.

To initialize the algorithm, we begin by randomly assigning nodes to shards, in proportions that are feasible with respect to these sizing constraints.

2.2 The constrained relocation problem

Given an initial feasible sharding, we wish to maintain the specified balance of nodes across shards between iterations. The key challenge is however that some shards will be more popular than others. In fact, under ordinary label propagation without any balance constraints, labelling all nodes with the same single label is a trivial equilibrium. Because we won't be able to move all nodes, our greedy approach is to sychronously move those nodes that stand to increase their colocation count (the number of graph neighbors they are co-located with) the most.

Given a constraint specification, we now formalize our greedy relocation strategy as a maximization problem subject to the above constraints. Consider therefore the nodes that are assigned to shard i but would prefer to be on shard j. Order these nodes according to the number of additional neighbors they would be co-located with if they moved, from greatest increase to least increase, labeling them $k = 1, \ldots, K$. Let $u_{ij}(k)$ be the change in utility (co-location count) from moving the kth node from shard i to j.

Let $f_{ij}(x) = \sum_{k=1}^{x} u_{ij}(k)$ be the *relocation utility function* between shard i and j, the total utility gained from moving the leading x nodes from i to j. Observe that because $u_{ij}(k) \geq 0$ and $u_{ij}(k) \geq u_{ij}(k+1)$ for all k (since they are ordered), all $f_{ij}(x)$ are increasing and concave.

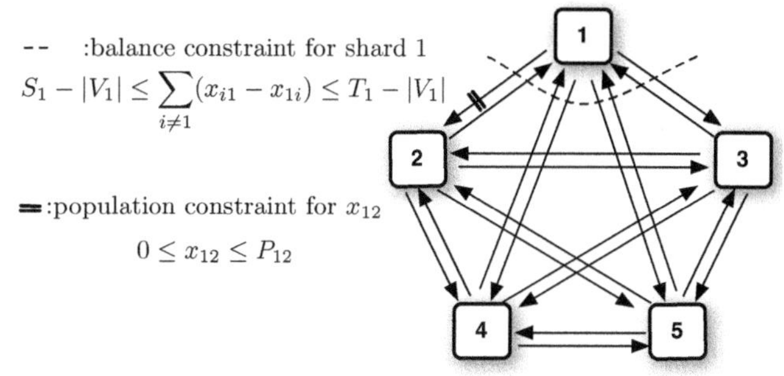

Figure 2: Illustration of the constraints for balanced label propagation applied to five shards. Each shard has a two-sided balance constraint, while each pair of shards has a population constraint.

Our goal can then be formulated as a concave utility maximization problem with linear constraints.

PROBLEM 1 (CONSTRAINED RELOCATION). *Given a graph $G = (V, E)$ with the node set partitioned into n shards $V_1, \ldots, V_n$, and size constraints $S_i \leq |V_i| \leq T_i$, $\forall i$, the constrained relocation problem is to maximize:*

$$\max_X \textstyle\sum_{i,j} f_{ij}(x_{ij}) \quad s.t. \tag{1}$$

$$\begin{array}{rcccl} S_i - |V_i| & \leq & \sum_{j \neq i}(x_{ij} - x_{ji}) & \leq & T_i - |V_i|, \ \forall i \\ 0 & \leq & x_{ij} & \leq & P_{ij}, \ \forall i, j. \end{array} \tag{2}$$

Here P_{ij} is the number of nodes that desire to move from shard i to j, and $f_{ij}(x)$ is the relocation utility function between shard i and j, both derivable from the graph and the partition.

For an illustration of the constraints, see Figure 2.

When the above problem is considered under continuous values of x_{ij}, we will now show that it reduces to a fully tractable optimization problem. Note that relaxing these integrality constraints on all x_{ij} is a fully reasonable approximation as long as the number of nodes seeking to be moved between each pair of shards is large.

We aim to rewrite the above optimization problem as a linear program. Notice that all f_{ij} are piecewise-linear concave functions. To see this, notice that the slope of f_{ij} is constant across all intervals where the ordered users have the same derived utility. As a consequence of this, we obtain the following straight-forward lemma.

LEMMA 1. *Assuming a bounded degree graph G, the objective function in Problem 1, $f(x) = \sum_{i,j} f_{ij}(x_{ij})$, is a piecewise-linear concave function, seperable in x_{ij}.*

PROOF. The separability is clear from the fact that the f_{ij} depend on different variables. Since users are atomic and the graph is of bounded degree, there are a finite number of utilities, and the sum is therefore also piecewise linear. Since the nodes are sorted in order of decreasing utility, the function is concave. □

Recall that any piecewise linear concave function $f(x)$: $\mathbb{R}^n \to \mathbb{R}$ can be written as $f(x) = \min_{k=1,\ldots,\ell}(a_k^T x + b_k)$, for some choices of a_k's and b_k's. For our problem, all the a_k's and b_k's are scalar. Now, also recall the following [5].

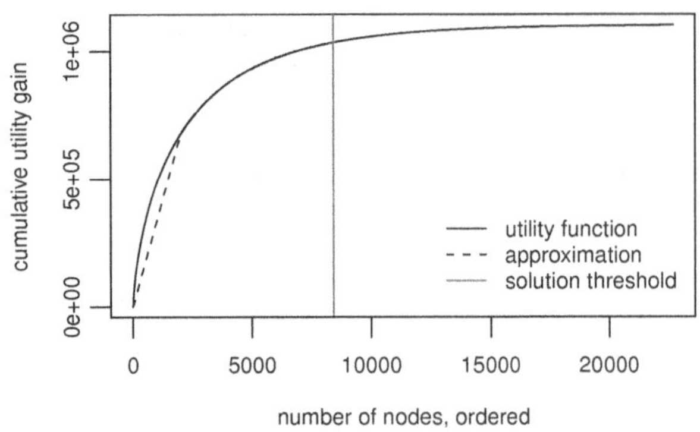

Figure 3: The piecewise-linear utility function for moving nodes from one shard to another, from an example problem iteration. The discontinuous derivates are imperceivable. The utilty approximation shown allows for a significant reduction in the number of constraints in the LP. The red line indicates the threshold found in the optimal solution for balanced propagation: here 8,424 of the 22,728 nodes that wanted to move were moved.

LEMMA 2. *Let* $x \in \mathbb{R}^n$ *and* $f(x) = \min_{k=1,\ldots,\ell}(a_k^T x + b_k)$ *be a piecewise linear concave function. Maximizing* $f(x)$ *subject to* $Ax \leq b$ *is then equivalent to:*

$$\max z \quad s.t. \tag{3}$$

$$\left\{ \begin{array}{rcl} Ax & \leq & b \\ a_k^T x + b_k & \geq & z, \quad \forall k. \end{array} \right. \tag{4}$$

Utilizing these two lemmas, we can thus solve the concave maximization problem in Problem 1 using a linear program.

THEOREM 2. *Consider a bounded degree graph* $G = (V, E)$. *Under continuous* x_{ij}, *the constrained relocation problem can be written as*

$$\max_{X,Z} \sum_{i,j} z_{ij} \quad s.t. \tag{5}$$

$$\begin{array}{rcccl} S_i - |V_i| & \leq & \sum_{j \neq i}(x_{ij} - x_{ji}) & \leq & T_i - |V_i|, \ \forall i \\ 0 & \leq & x_{ij} & \leq & P_{ij}, \ \forall i,j \\ & & -a_{ijk}x_{ij} + z_{ij} & \leq & b_{ijk}, \ \forall i,j,k, \end{array} \tag{6}$$

where all a_{ijk} *and* b_{ijk} *derive directly from the relocation utility functions* f_{ij}. *Assuming* n *shards and at most* K *unique utility gains achieved by nodes that would like to move, this constitutes a linear program with* $2n(n-1)$ *variables and at most* $2n^2 + Kn(n-1)$ *sparse constraints.*

Since the most utility a node can gain is its degree, and furthermore only a small set of nodes in real world graphs have high degree, it becomes unlikely that all pairs of shards will observe nodes seeking large utility gains. Thus, in practice the number of constraints is typically small. For $m = 78$ and $K = 100$, this would imply a linear program with 12,012 variables and 612,768 constraints, which is fully manageable by a basic LP solver owing to the extensive sparsity of the matrix of constraints.

2.3 Iteration

Procedurally, an iteration of this algorithm differs very little from an iteration of ordinary label propagation. First, determine where every node would prefer to move, and how much each node would gain from its preferred relocation. Second, sort the node gains for each shard pair and construct the Constrained Relocation linear program. Third, solve the linear program, which determines how many nodes should be moved, in order, between each shard pair. Fourth, move these nodes. This constitutes one iteration.

When compared to ordinary label propagation, the only difference is that rather than moving every node that asks to move, our algorithm pauses, solves a linear program, and then proceeds to move as many nodes as possible without breaking the balance. As with ordinary label propagation, the bulk of the work lies in determining where every node would prefer to move (which requires examining every edge in the graph). The entire balancing procedure has a complexity that depends principally on the number of shards and is nearly independent of the graph size (the number of constraints per shard pair, K, can depend weakly on the graph size in practice).

2.4 Approximating utility gain

If the number of constraints becomes limiting, we note that it is possible to greatly reduce the number of constraints by a very slight approximation of the objective function. We emphasize that constraint satisfaction is still guaranteed under this approximation, it is merely the utility gain of the iteration that is approximated.

Observe that for each shard pair, the handful of nodes that stand to gain the most are likely to be contribute relatively unique utility levels, and so contribute many of the constraints in the problem. This is rather unnecessary, since those nodes are highly likely to move. Thus, by disregarding the unique utility levels of the first C nodes, all very likely to move, and approximating them by the mean gain of this population, we can greatly reduce the number of constraints. To exemplify this approximation, in Figure 3 we show one of the piecewise linear concave utility functions from a problem instance, corresponding to movement between two shards, and the threshold on the number of users that were allowed to be moved in the optimal solution.

3. GEOGRAPHIC INITIALIZATION

When applying greedy algorithms to intricate objective functions, initialization can dramatically impact performance. For the balanced label propagation algorithm presented in the previous section, random initialization — in proportions that are feasible with respect to the sizing constraints — might be considered an adequate initialization. However, by using node data to initialize our assignment, we find that we can improve on both the number of iterations and the final sharding quality. How well one can do in this initial assignment depends on what auxiliary node information is available. For example, on the web one might use domain, or in a computer network one might use IP-address. In the case of the Facebook social network, we find that geographical information gives us good initial conditions. Thus, in this section we will examine an initial graph partitioning based on a geographic partitioning in the absence of any graph structure.

Facebook's geolocation services assign all 800 million users to one of approximately 750,000 cities wordwide. The idea behind our geographic partitioning is to harness the intuitive and well-studied properties of geography as a strong basis for graph assortativity in social networks: individuals have an elevated tendency to be friends with people geographically close to them [2].

A key challenge, however, when partitioning a realtime service based on geographic information, is the heterogeneity of traffic between geographies. When balanced propagation is run under random initialization, it is our experience that the local improvements made by the algorithm tend to not discover any large-scale geographic structure. Yet some parts of the world are much more active on Facebook than others, and as a result, they have more friends and their friend-of-friend calculations are much more expensive. As a result, it is desirable to configure the geographic initialization so that shards with higher than average degree contain fewer nodes, and shards with a lower than average degree contain more.

To achieve this, instead of cutting up the geographic space to form shards of exactly equal population, we consider a more general cost model, based on the number of users in each city and also on the average degree of users in that city. Note that in this particular sharding challenge we are most concerned with sharding node attributes, and the distribution of the graph (as an edge list) is not as central a concern, but instead we are considering average degree as a means of distributing computational load. For each city c with population n_c and average degree d_c, the cost of the city is given by $\text{Cost}(c) = n_c(1 + \lambda d_c)$, where λ is a weight parameter determined by the proportion of node attribute data to edge attribute data to be sharded. For our applications we used $\lambda = 1/d_{avg}$, the reciprocal of the average degree across the graph.

3.1 Balloon partitioning algorithm

The partitioning algorithm we will present here constructs shards centered at the most populated cities in the data set, beginning with the most populated city not yet assigned to a shard, and grows circular 'balloons' around these cities.

This balloon algorithm, illustrated in Figure 4, consists of a single iterated loop. For each of the $i = 1, \ldots, n$ shards, the goal is to obtain shards each with $(\sum_c \text{Cost}(c))/n$ in cost assigned to them. The algorithm first finds the city C with the largest unassigned cost. The city C is selected as the center-point of a new shard, and all cities with a non-zero remaining cost are sorted according to their geodesic distance from C. Since edges in the social network are overwhelmingly internal to countries, a negative distance reward is introduced to all cities in the same country as C. This ensures that the algorithm finishes assigning each country completely before moving on to another country. Beginning with C, the algorithm progresses down the sorted list of cities, and while there is capacity, it assigns each city to the shard currently being constructed. When the algorithm does change countries, a new negative distance reward is given to cities in that country. Eventually, when there is not enough capacity in the current shard to accommodate an entire city, a fractional assignment is noted, and the cost is subtracted from the remaining cost of that city.

The result is n shards, centered over population centers, each containing all nodes within a certain radius of the central city, adaptively configured such that each shard is of equal burden under the cost model. A handful of cities are assigned to multiple shards according to a fractional division. The map of cities to shards is used to assign nodes to shards, and for those cities with distributed fractional assignments (at most n of the 750,000 cities), simple randomization is used, distributing nodes in such cities proportional to the fraction of the cost mapped to each shard. A map of the Facebook social graph partitioned into 234 partitions is shown in Figure 6.

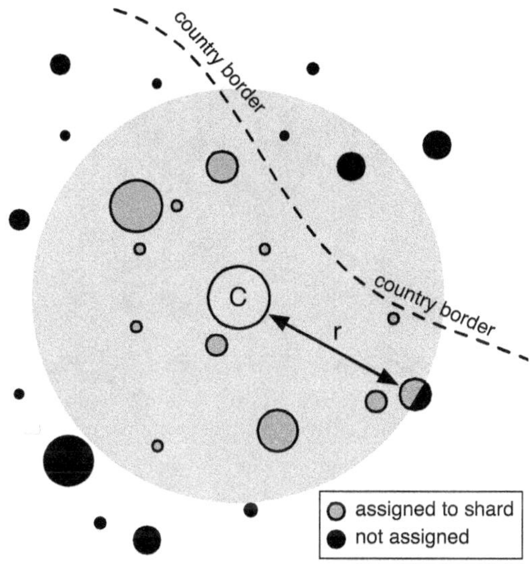

Figure 4: Geometric illustration of the greedy geographic initialization of a shard, with cities as circles with radii indicating cost. The algorithm centers itself at the most costly remaining city, C, and then fills a shard with the cities closest to that city, with a penalty for crossing national borders. When the shard is full, fractional assignments are made.

After performing an initial aggregation of the social graph, this assignment algorithm operates only on the set of cities and not on the social graph itself, making it possible to quickly run this complete assignment on a single machine in a single processor thread in seconds, with no actual graph analysis being necessary.

It should be noted that the geographic sharding performed here is ultimately static, and as new users register to join the site, these users can be assigned in accordance with the map from cities to shards. We note that as the geographic distribution of Facebook users slowly changes over time, resharding may be useful.

3.2 Oversharding

Selecting shards for a real-time graph computation service from a geographic initialization has another serious practical challenge that we have not yet discussed. For the purposes of load-balancing a service that handles real-time requests, it is important to mitigate potentially problematic peak loads that result from assigning geographically concentrated regions to the same shard. A three day window of user traffic is shown in Figure 5, where we see that local geographic regions experience much more volatile peak loads than the full site on average. Our solution to this problem was to create 3 times more shards than there are machines, and then sort shards by the longitude of their most populated city. The shards are then distributed cyclically across the n machines so that, e.g., shard 1, $(n + 1)$, and $(2n + 1)$ in longitudinal order are assigned to the same machine.

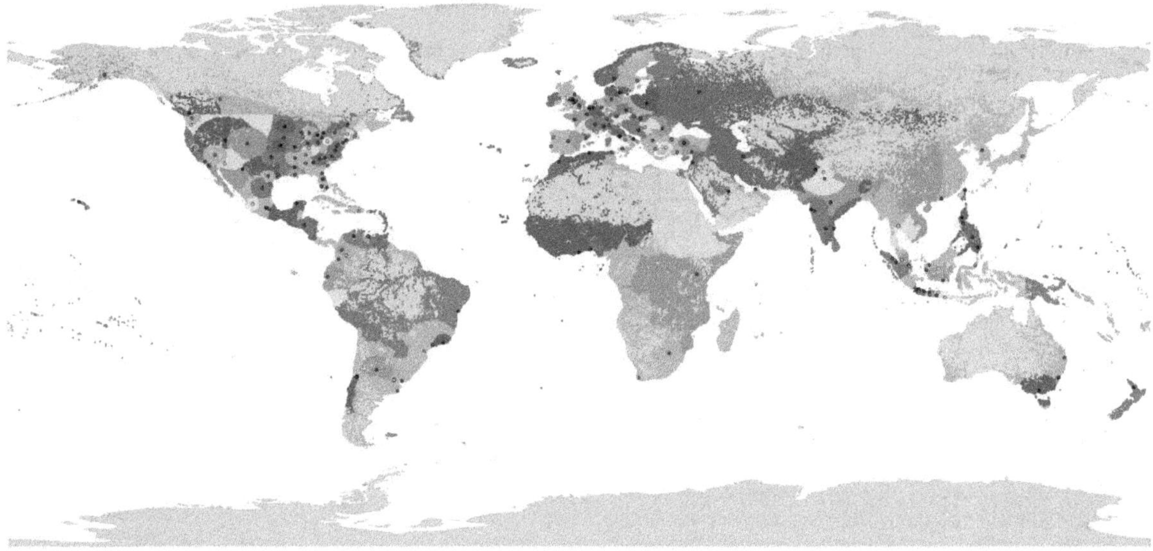

Figure 6: Output of the greedy geographic initialization algorithm for the $\sim 750,000$ known cities, obtaining 234 shards of equal cost, with each shard's most costly city marked. As described in the text, the algorithm is aware of national borders.

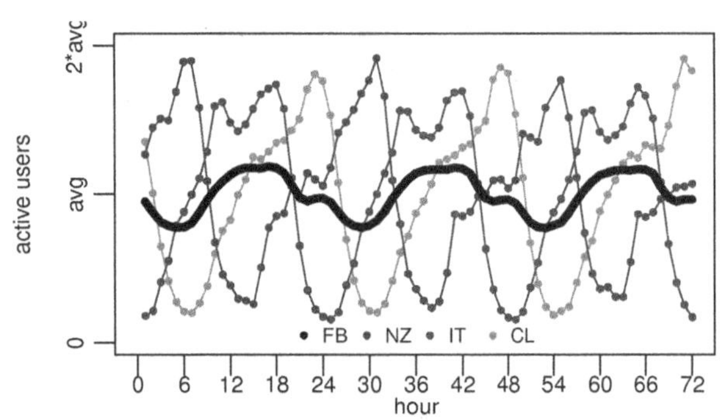

Figure 5: User traffic differences between countries. Comparing traffic for New Zealand, Italy, and Chile to that of Facebook as a whole, the intraday variability in users accessing the site from a single country far exceeds the variability of the site as whole.

4. EVALUATING PERFORMANCE

In this section we discuss the performance of our balanced label propagation algorithm as a graph cutting procedure applied to the Facebook social graph, under both random and geographic initialization. In Section 5 we evaluate shardings of this graph when deployed for a realtime graph computation service. To align the discussion between the two sections, we evaluate the algorithm by sharding the graph into 78 shards, where the service we evaluate later will consist of 78 machines, evenly split across two server racks. We also provide a comparison to performance on a publicly available social graph collected from LiveJournal [1].

4.1 Sharding the Facebook social graph

For the random initialization, all shards of the partition were constrained to symmetrically balanced node counts. Meanwhile, for the geographic initialization, partition size constraints were inherited from the output of the geographic balloon algorithm initialization, where partition node counts were tuned to mitigate the differences in average degree between different parts of the globe, as discussed in the previous section. All iterations were allowed a five percent leniency, $f = 0.05$, and utility approximation was used within the constrained relocation problem for the leading $5,000$ nodes between each shard pair.

The matrix of shard-shard edge counts resulting from both geographic and random initialization are shown in Figure 7, while the convergence properties observed when iterating the algorithm are shown in Figure 8. We observe that initializing the algorithm with a greedy geographic assignment greatly accelerates the convergence of the algorithm. Using geographic initialization, before even beginning the propagation we see that 52.7% of edges are locally confined. After a single propagation, fully 71.5% of edges are local, and after four iterations this rises to 75.2%.

For the geographic initialization instance, we overshard by a factor of 3, meaning that 234 virtual shards were distributed to 78 actual shards. When oversharding for distributed computation, it is useful to distribute closely related shards across machines located on the same physical rack. While this does not effect the fraction of edges that are local to individual machines, the order in which the shards are assigned does effect the cross-rack traffic. Machines within the same rack have relatively fast high-bandwidth connections compared with machine in different racks, where all traffic must pass through a switch. Since the service we study later is split across two racks, we distribute our 234 geographic shards across the 78 machine shards by splitting them into two block groups. The first block was set to contain all shards centered in countries in North America, Africa and Oceania, and the second block contains all shards centered in South America, Europe and Asia, with shards centered in the Middle East balancing between the two sets. The two-block structure is clearly visible in Figure 7, but we reiterate that it does not effect the local edge fraction.

For comparison, we investigate the performance of the algorithm when initialized with a random distribution, also

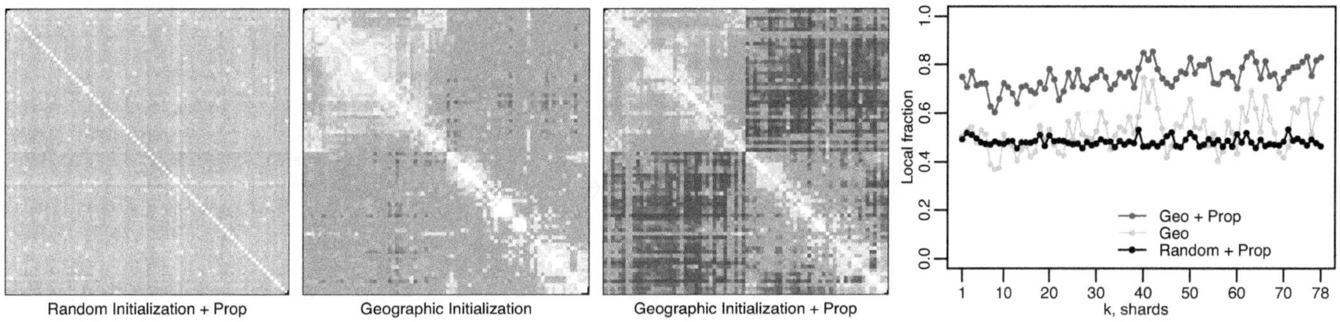

Figure 7: Matrices of edges between 78 shards under three different shardings: Balanced label propagation with random initialization, the sharding produced by the geographic initialization, and balanced label propagation after geographic initialization. All matrices share the same logarithmic color scale, saturated to make the structure of the random initialization visible. The fraction of local edges for each shard is also shown.

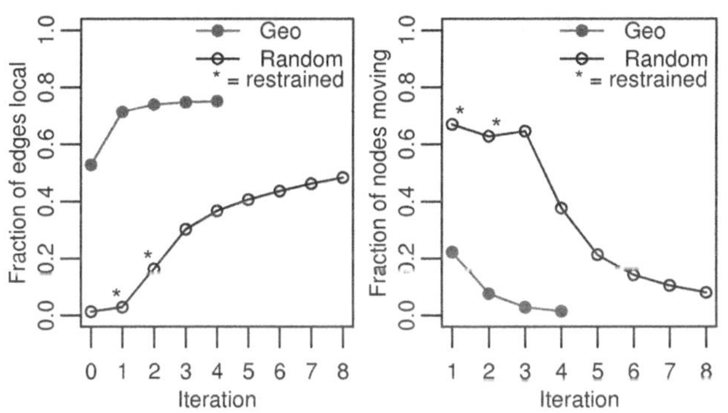

Figure 8: Iterating the balanced label propagation algorithm with 78 shards, from a geographic and random initialization. Left: the fraction of edges that are local as the balanced propagation is iterated. Right: the fraction of nodes that are moved in each iteration.

shown in Figure 8. After 8 iterations, this random initialization achieved a local fraction of 44.8%.

When nodes are initially distributed at random, it implies that a node's neighbors are initially distributed uniformly across all shards. For graphs where nodes possess many neighbors, as in the Facebook social graph, this implies that it can take many iterations until the initial symmetry of the random initialization is broken. In an important demonstration of how label propagation functions, we observed that applying our balanced label propagation algorithm from a random initial condition meant that 96.7% of nodes were relocated during the first iteration, a chaotic shuffling that slows the algorithm's ability to converge. To address this, in the random initialization shown here, the linear program constraints were modified to only move nodes that claimed to gain 2 or more additional neighbors post-propagation. This 'restrained' modification meant that only 67.0% of nodes were relocated during the first iteration. This 'restraint' was used during the first two steps of the random initialization algorithm, as denoted in the Figure 8, after which it was removed and ordinary balanced label propagation was performed.

Why should one bother to move nodes that only stand to gain one additional neighbor co-location? As another instructive highlight of how balanced label propagation operates, nodes that are mostly indifferent to moving offer very useful 'slack' for the linear program: by moving them, it is possible to balance the constraints while still moving many nodes who stand to make larger gains.

The Facebook social graph is enormous, and these computations do not come cheaply. The graph aggregations required for a single iteration utilizes approximately 100 CPU days (2395 CPU hours) on Facebook's Hadoop cluster. For comparison, a simple two-sided join aggregation of the graph edge list (such as computing a shard-shard matrix in Figure 7) uses 72 CPU days. Once the aggregations have been performed, the linear program is solved in a matter of minutes on a single machine using lpsolve [4].

While the randomly initialized algorithm only achieves 44.8% locality compared to 75.2% locality for the geographic initialization, the random initialization produces an impressively homogenous sharding free of 'hot' shard-shard connections. It would be interesting to iterate the random initial algorithm further, but running the random initialization for 8 iteration utilized approximately 800 CPU days. Examining the properties of balanced label propagation more throughly on modest graphs would be important future work.

4.2 LiveJournal comparison

Because the Facebook social graph is not publicly available, we also report the performance of our algorithm when attempting to partition a large publicly available social network dataset, LiveJournal [1]. The LiveJournal graph, collected in 2006, is a directed graph consisting of of 4.8 million nodes and 69.0 million arcs. Because we are principally interested in partitioning undirected graphs, we consider the undirected graph consisting of 4.8 million nodes and the 42.9 million unique edges that remain and disregarding directionality.

The resulting graph is more than 20 times smaller than the Facebook graph by node count and more than 1000 times smaller by edge count. The average degree is only 8.8, making partitioning much less challenging. Because the public LiveJournal graph lacks complete geographic information, we consider only random initialization. We consider the performance of cutting the graph into 20, 40, 60, 80, and 100 symmetric shards, with five percent leniency ($f = 0.05$) and no approximation of the utility gain. Splitting into 20 shards took less than 3 minutes using a single threaded C++ im-

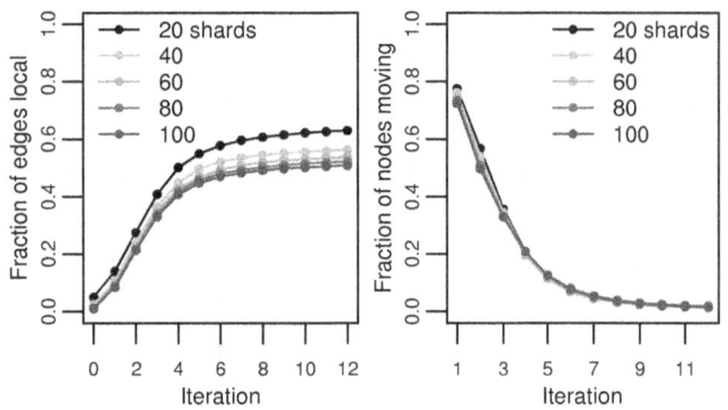

Figure 9: Balanced label propagation applied the LiveJournal social graph, partitioning the graph into 20, 40, 60, 80, and 100 shards. Left: the fraction of edges that are local as the balanced propagation is iterated. Right: the fraction of nodes that are moved in each iteration.

plementation, while splitting into 40 shards took 8 minutes, and splitting into 100 shards took 88 minutes.

The results from partitioning the LiveJournal graph are shown in Figure 9, where we see that when partitioning the LiveJournal graph into 20 parts, 63% of edges are local to a single partition. Impressively, when the algorithm is scaled up to 100 shards, fully 51% of edges are local to a single partition. Overall, we observe that the fraction of edges that are local is nearly unchanged when increasing the number of shards from 40 to 100. We interpret this performance to be a consequence of the greedy nature of the algorithm, as the algorithm principally exploits local graph relocations that are significantly below the scale of any of the shard sizes, while global improvements are less possible. A further investigation of this scaling behavior in relation to studies of natural social network cluster sizes [11] would make for interesting future work.

5. REALTIME DEPLOYMENT

In this section, we present the results of a large-scale experiment where the sharding algorithm we develop is evaluated in a realtime distributed graph computation service: Facebook's 'People You May Know' (PYMK) service for suggesting friend recommendations.

Many pages on Facebook occasionally feature a small module presenting users with 'People You May Know'. The PYMK service has contributed significantly to the growth of Facebook, accounting for around 40% of all friending on Facebook. The friend suggestions that populate this module are mostly (but not exclusively) generated by the system described in this work.

5.1 People You May Know

The PYMK system computes, for a given user u, and each friend-of-friend (FoF) of u, w, a feature vector $x_{u,w}$ of graph metrics based on the local structure between u and w. The system then uses machine learning to rank all the suggestions w for u, based on the graph-based feature vector $x_{u,w}$, as well as demographic features of u and w. The system described here returns the top 100 suggestions for each user (out of a potential of many thousands of FoFs). Regeneration of suggestions is performed when a user logs in to Facebook and no recent suggestions for the user are found in the cache.

The PYMK service consists of 78 machines split across two racks (there are 40 machines to a rack, but one machine per rack is reserved as a backup). All 78 machines feature 72 GB of memory, which is used to store two in-memory indexes. First, a mirrored data structure containing basic demographic data of all 800 million users (19 GB). Second, a sharded index containing the friendlist data of those users assigned to the individual machine (~40 GB). All in-memory indexes are stored as open-addressed hash tables. To handle the full query volume, a number of identical copies of this 78 machine system run in parallel.

Prior to the optimizations presented in this paper, users were assigned to machines based on their user ID mod 78, see Figure 1. This naive sharding has a direct advantage over any sophisticated sharding in that the shard ID is encoded directly in the user ID. Introducing the more sophisticated shardings used in this paper requires adding an additional data structure serving as a *shard map*, mirrored on all machines, to map the 800 million user IDs to shard IDs.

The evaluation we perform examined three separate instances of the PYMK service operating in parallel, receiving identical and evenly balanced shares of the service load, differing only with regard to their sharding configuration. The three systems were:

- **Baseline sharding**: assigning users by the modulus sharding, 'user ID % 78'.
- **Geographic sharding**: assigning users using 234 geographic shards, with no label propagation.
- **Propagated sharding**: one step of balanced label propagation after geographic initialization.

Because of resource constraints we were only able to test three parallel systems, and did not deploy a propagated sharding featuring random initialization, which required much more iteration and achieved worse edge localization than the unpropogated geographic initialization.

First, we characterize the impact of our sharding by evaluating our algorithm's ability to concentrate requests to few machines, reporting on the number of machines queried across requests. Next, because intelligent sharding disadvantages the PYMK service by requiring an additional round of requests (as described in the introduction), we evaluate the algorithm's ability to reduce to total query time of FoF requests, with particular attention to the slowest machine, as well as the ability to reduce the total cross-machine network traffic within the full system.

The evaluation was performed during the three day period September 20-22, 2011. Because the evaluation required the dedication of considerable hardware resources (6 racks of machines, in total 240 machines), testing on exactly identical hardware configurations was not possible (it was important to test the three systems in parallel so that no external events could impact the results). All machines featured 72GB of memory, while the machines in the baseline system and the geographic system featured 12 CPUs and the machines in the propagated system featured 24 CPUs, all 2.67 GHz Intel Xeon processors. This difference of CPU resources is one of the main reasons we focus our analysis on hardware invariant performance evaluations such as request concentration and network traffic measurements.

5.2 Request concentration

Here we consider the concentration of requests in a real-time setting, recording the number of machines accessed per query. Because the PYMK system has to wait for the slowest query response before performing ranking, the number of machines queried is an important performance characteristic. By waiting for fewer machines, the expected time needed to wait until the slowest machine has returned data can be significantly decreased.

Baseline performance. In the baseline system, users are sharded by their Facebook user ID modulus 78. Prior to the sharding optimizations in this paper, the distribution of requests on each machine was not instrumented, and because there were significant architectural changes to the service when the sharding optimization was introduced, the baseline system was not upgraded to include instrumentation.

Fortunately, the trailing digits of a user's ID are uncorrelated from the trailing digits of the user IDs of their friends, and thus the question of how many machines are queried during an average aggregation can be computed directly given only the degree distribution of the graph.

Consider a graph sharded across m machines. Let X_i, $i = 1, \dots, m$ be the Bernoulli random variables indicating whether a given user has a friend on machine i. Let $Y = \sum_{i=1}^{m} X_i$ be the total number of machines that are queried when this user's friends data is aggregated. By the law of total probability,

$$Pr(Y = k) = \sum_d Pr(Y = k | \deg(u) = d) \cdot Pr(\deg(u) = d),$$

where $\deg(u)$ is the degree of the user, and $Pr(\deg(u) = d)$ is the empirical Facebook degree distribution. Focusing on the term $Pr(Y = k | \deg(u) = d)$,

$$Pr(Y = k | \deg(u) = d) = Pr\left(\sum_{i=1}^{m} X_i = k | \deg(u) = d\right),$$

where X_i are Bernoulli distributed random variables. To derive the distribution of X_i, notice that, $\forall i$,

$$\begin{aligned} Pr(X_i = 1 | \deg(u) = d) &= \\ &= 1 - Pr(X_i = 0 | \deg(u) = d) \\ &= 1 - (1 - 1/m)^d. \end{aligned}$$

Thus, we see that $X_i \sim \text{Bernoulli}(1-(1-1/m)^d)$, $\forall i$. While these m variables are identically distributed, they are unfortunately not independent.

Since the variables X_i are not independent, we resort to a simple Monte Carlo simulation of the distribution $Pr(Y = k | \deg(u) = d)$ for a uniformly sharded system. Combing this distribution with the empirical degree distribution from PYMK queries, $Pr(\deg(u) = d)$, gives us the theoretical request concentration distribution for the baseline system.

Results. In Figure 10, we compare the distribution of requests as measured for the two algorithms and computed for the baseline system. Note that our measurement of request concentration is not affected by differences in hardware or traffic volumes between the three systems.

The median number of non-local machines queried for the baseline, geographic, and once-propagated shardings were 59, 12, and 9 machines, respectively. Notice that under the old naive system, the most common occurrence was that friend lists had to be aggregated from all 77 non-local machines, while the modes for the new shardings are 6 non-local machines for the geographic sharding and 3 non-local machines for the once-propagated sharding.

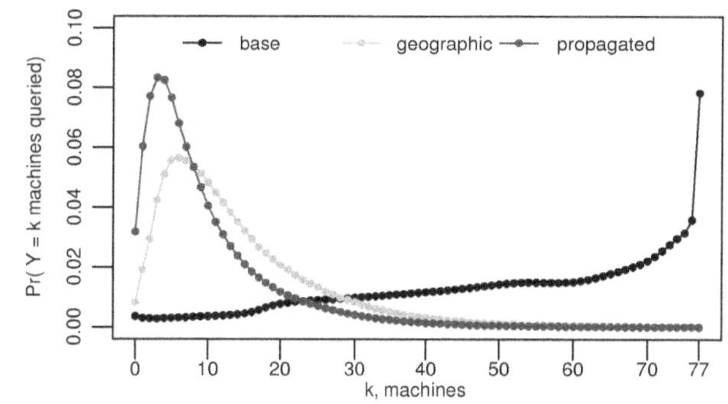

Figure 10: Number of non-local machines queried per request during friend-of-friend calculations in PYMK. The median number of machines queried for the baseline, geographic, and once-propagated shardings were 59, 12, and 9 machines, respectively.

5.3 Query time and network traffic

Here we report on the relative performance of the three systems with regard to query time and network traffic. While the hardware specifications of the three PYMK services were not identical, with the propagated sharding operating with twice as many CPUs per machine, we still report the query times, noting that each query was run in a single thread, and that for the most part, the number of cores per machine did not come into play. The baseline and geographic systems were run on identical hardware, and in any event the bandwidth comparisons are independent of the machine specifications and can thus be taken at face value.

The time-averages of the average machine query times for the baseline, geographic, and once-propagated shardings were 109ms, 68ms, and 55ms, respectively. The time-averages of the maximum machine query times were 122ms, 106ms, and 100ms, respectively (not plotted). Notice that the geographic system, which operated on hardware identical to the baseline system, featured an average query time only 62.3% of the baseline system. The total improvement when comparing to the propagated system was an average query time only 50.5% of the baseline system.

Recall that the two optimized systems being tested are disadvantaged compared to the baseline system because they must perform an additional query redirection, since the web tier does not possess a copy of the shard map and doesn't know which of the 78 machines the user lives on.

Meanwhile, when we turn to network traffic, the time-averages of the average machine traffic for the baseline, geographic, and once-propagated shardings were 35.3 MB/s, 21.8 MB/s, and 13.1 MB/s, respectively. The time-averages of the maximum machine traffic (not plotted) were 103.6 MB/s, 68.0 MB/s, and 51.0 MB/s, respectively. The systems were configured to be equally load-balanced, each handling equal thirds of the total traffic. Thus, the machines in the propagated system saw network traffic levels only 37.1% of the baseline system machines.

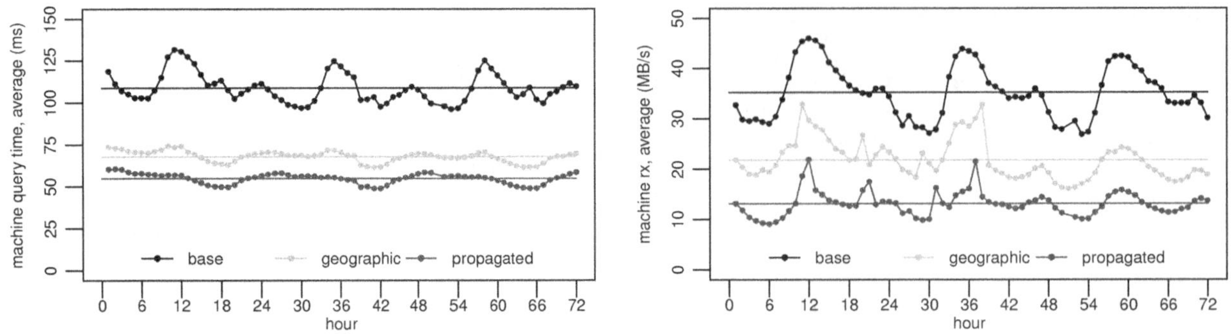

Figure 11: Query time and network traffic for the three different shardings applied to the PYMK service. Because network traffic is instrumented on a machine level, the data also captures daily traffic bursts which correspond to loading data into the service. For this reason, momentary outliers should be considered benign.

6. DISCUSSION

The problem of clustering a graph for community detection is a widely studied active area of research within computer science and physics [13, 14]. In this work, we approach the rather different challenge of graph partitioning. We develop and evaluate a novel algorithm, balanced label propagation, for partitioning a graph while managing these challenges.

We show that by using intelligent partitioning in the context of load-balancing a realtime graph computation service, we are able to dramatically outperform a baseline configuration. While a random initialization of our balanced label propagation algorithm produces an impressive sharding, we show that by using user metadata we can derive a sharding that is greatly superior to a random initialization while still maintaining uniformity in shard sizes. These techniques were applied to a single system in this work, but we believe that they are broadly applicable to any graph computation system that distributes graphs across many machines.

7. ACKNOWLEDGMENTS

We thank Jon Kleinberg for helpful discussions. This work was supported in part by NSF grants IIS-0910664 and IIS-1016099.

8. REFERENCES

[1] L. Backstrom, D. Huttenlocher, J. Kleinberg, X. Lan. Group formation in large social networks: membership, growth, and evolution. In *KDD*, 44–54, 2006.

[2] L. Backstrom, E. Sun, C. Marlow. Find me if you can: improving geographical prediction with social and spatial proximity. In *WWW*, 61–70, 2010.

[3] M.J. Barber, J.W. Clark. Detecting network communities by propagating labels under constraints. *Physical Review E*, 80:026129, 2009.

[4] M. Berkelaar. The lpsolve package. *http://lpsolve.sourceforge.net*, 2011.

[5] S.P. Boyd, L. Vandenberghe. *Convex optimization.* Cambridge University Press, 2004.

[6] U. Feige, R. Krauthgamer. A polylogarithmic approximation of the minimum bisection. In *FOCS*, 105–115, 2000.

[7] S. Fortunato. Community detection in graphs. *Physics Reports*, 486:75–174, 2010.

[8] M.R. Garey, D.S. Johnson, L. Stockmeyer. Some simplified NP-complete graph problems. *Theoretical computer science*, 1(3):237–267, 1976.

[9] S. Gregory. Finding overlapping communities in networks by label propagation *New Journal of Physics*, 12:103018, 2010.

[10] G. Karypis, V. Kumar. Multilevel k-way partitioning scheme for irregular graphs. *J. Parallel Distrib. Computing* 48(1):96–129, 1998.

[11] J. Leskovec, K. Lang, A. Dasgupta, M. Mahoney. Community structure in large networks: natural cluster sizes and the absence of large well-defined clusters. *Internet Mathematics* 6(1):29–123, 2009.

[12] D. Liben-Nowell, J. Novak, R. Kumar, P. Raghavan, A. Tomkins. Geographic routing in social networks. *PNAS*, 102:11623, 2005.

[13] P.J. Mucha, T. Richardson, K. Macon, M.A. Porter, and J.P. Onnela. Community structure in time-dependent, multiscale, and multiplex networks. *Science*, 328:876, 2010.

[14] M.E.J. Newman, M. Girvan. Finding and evaluating community structure in networks. *Physical Review E*, 69:026113, 2004.

[15] H.N. Fowler. *Plato: Phaedrus*, Loeb Classical Library, 1971.

[16] U.N. Raghavan, R. Albert, S. Kumara. Near linear time algorithm to detect community structures in large-scale networks. *Physical Review E*, 76:036106, 2007.

[17] I. Stanton, G. Kilot. Streaming graph partitioning for large distributed graphs. *KDD*, 1222–1230, 2012.

[18] A. Thusoo, JS Sarma, N Jain, Z Shao, P Chakka, N Zhang, S Antony, H Liu, R Murthy. Hive – a petabyte scale data warehouse using hadoop. In *ICDE*, 996–1005, 2010.

[19] J. Ugander, B. Karrer, L. Backstorm, C. Marlow. The anatomy of the Facebook social graph. Arxiv preprint arXiv:1111.4503, 2011.

[20] X. Zhu, Z. Ghahramani. Learning from labeled and unlabeled data with label propagation. CMU CALD Tech Report CMU-CALD-02-107, 2002.

GOP Primary Season on Twitter: "Popular" Political Sentiment in Social Media

Yelena Mejova
Yahoo! Research
Barcelona, Spain
ymejova@yahoo-inc.com

Padmini Srinivasan, Bob Boynton
University of Iowa, IA, USA
padmini-srinivasan@uiowa.edu
bob-boynton@uiowa.edu

ABSTRACT

As mainstream news media and political campaigns start to pay attention to the political discourse online, a systematic analysis of political speech in social media becomes more critical. What exactly do people say on these sites, and how useful is this data in estimating political popularity? In this study we examine Twitter discussions surrounding seven US Republican politicians who were running for the US Presidential nomination in 2011. We show this largely negative rhetoric to be laced with sarcasm and humor and dominated by a small portion of users. Furthermore, we show that using out-of-the-box classification tools results in a poor performance, and instead develop a highly optimized multi-stage approach designed for general-purpose political sentiment classification. Finally, we compare the change in sentiment detected in our dataset before and after 19 Republican debates, concluding that, at least in this case, the Twitter political chatter is not indicative of national political polls.

Categories and Subject Descriptors

H.3.3 [**Information Search and Retrieval**]: General

General Terms

Social media; Political discourse; Sentiment analysis

Keywords

Human factors, experimentation, performance

1. INTRODUCTION

Originally dealing largely with product reviews [15], social media-driven sentiment analysis (SA) has recently expanded its target to encompass political discourse. Using NLP and data mining tools, the goal is to determine the author's political *stance* (i.e. attitude adopted with respect to an issue) [18, 9], diverging from the standard practice of focussing on sentiment defined as *positive* or *negative*.

WSDM'13, February 4–8, 2013, Rome, Italy.

Analysis of such data is important, considering the attention social media has been getting in the news. Following Barack Obama's 2008 Presidential campaign, the world saw the "crowning of the Internet as the king of all political media" [20]. Online activity indicators such as number of fans on Facebook, followers on Twitter, and likes on YouTube have been seen as indicators of a galvanized base, which ultimately contributed to Obama's victory [13]. Since then, not only has traditional media started paying more attention to political discussions on social media, but several research papers have been published claiming a connection between social media and public polls and even election outcomes. For example, Tumasjan et al. [19] examine Twitter messages about the 2009 German federal election and find that the mere number of messages reflects the election result and even comes close to traditional election polls, concluding that Twitter can be considered a valid indicator of political opinion.

However, some studies show little correlation between the sentiment found on Twitter to that of general public as measured using standard polling techniques. For example, O'Connor et al [14] find no correlation between the 2008 election polls and the support seen in Twitter messages for Obama. They further find that sentiment for McCain (Obama's rival) and Obama slightly correlate (instead of being inversely related). They do find the discussion volume for Obama to have a correlation to the polls, postulating that simple attention may be related with popularity, at least for Obama. Some researchers have came out cautioning against treating social media as a "black box" and letting wishful thinking cloud the analysis of sentiment in political sphere [5]. Metaxes et al. [12], for example, find that electoral predictions using various previously published methods on Twitter data is no better than chance. Among these techniques are discussion volume, lexicon-driven sentiment classification, and user-specific political leaning estimation. Still, some researchers continue to use lexicon-driven classifiers without evaluating their performance [1, 7, 19]. In leu of recent news media and political campaign attention to political discourse online, it is imperative, then, to better understand the nature and limitations of this data.

Thus, we attempt to closely examine the nature of political speech on social media, and evaluate its predictive power of real-world phenomena. In this paper, we examine the discussion surrounding the 2012 GOP Presidential candidate selection process. Throughout 2011 and 2012, the US Republican party chooses a nominee for the 2012 Presidential election. This process is highly public, and includes many television appearances and debates. By developing a large annotated corpus, we examine the sentiments expressed about these politicians, and the users expressing them.

Furthermore, instead of using a lexicon-driven system, we implement and test a data-driven political sentiment classifier. Recently, similar systems employing data mining techniques have been used to identify stances in ideological debates [18] and predictive opinions [8]. Instead, we provide an evaluation of a highly optimized multi-stage approach designed for general-purpose political sentiment classification.

In short, this project contributes the following to the political analysis of social media:

1. We build and optimize a multi-stage data-driven sentiment classifier.
2. We analyze sentiment expression in a large sample of Twitter messages, and show the differences between groups of users varying in posting frequency.
3. We perform sentiment tracking experiments in which we compare the sentiment found before and after 19 debates to public opinion polls.
4. We contribute an annotated dataset spanning the second half of 2011 and seven popular Republican Presidential nominee candidates, totaling 6,400 documents annotated for relevance, sentiment about the politician, sentiment intensity, and various stylistic measures.

2. RELATED WORK

The recent role of social media in political actions in US, Middle East, and elsewhere around the world has produced a gamut of studies on mining of political speech online. A report on Social Media in the Arab World recognizes "the pivotal role of the microblogging [Twitter] site [...]" and "the role that social media will continue to play in Tunisia, Egypt, and the rest of the Arab world" [6]. Thus, from tracking discussions of political debates [3] to predicting election outcomes [19], social media has become a gold mine for political sentiment research. For example, [10] use social media to determine whether news sources are biased in favor of covering one political party more than another. Focusing on representation of political figures in Twitter, [16] have developed a way to detect *astroturf* (politically-motivated speech which creates appearance of widespread support for a candidate or opinion). Elections have been studied through the lens of social media: [11] examine the usage patterns of social media by US political parties in the 2010 Midterm Election, whereas [4] look at the conversations surrounding German political parties during the 2009 Federal Elections and Saez-Trumper et al. [17] further improve on their approach by considering only the unique authors in the analysis.

However, recent papers such as those by Gayo-Avello, Meta-xas, and Mustafaraj [5, 12] question the power of social media to predict political phenomena. Partially, their skepticism stems from the questionable quality of sentiment analysis tools which are applied to the problem. In particular, sentiment lexicons used to detect the polarity of individual words and phrases suffer from vocabulary mismatch and a lack of context sensitivity. Instead, they propose to go "one step further" and use the machine learning approach. They further acknowledge the complex nature of political discourse, and the need for a deeper understanding of political conversation. In this paper we address both of these concerns by annotating thousands of political tweets for political agreement, sentiment strength, and style, and evaluate experimentally this data's predictive power.

3. DATA COLLECTION

We begin by describing the political speech dataset we have created for the purpose of political sentiment analysis. This data is available upon request.

Using Twitter Search API we collected tweets mentioning various politicians, the names of which have been manually composed into queries in order to increase precision. The collected tweets span a year, over the period of January 1, 2011 to January 11, 2012 and include tweets about the politicians listed in Table 1. These are some of the Republican politicians who joined the race for Republican nomination for the US Presidential Election of 2012. Some of these joined later in the year, and thus tweets about them do not span the full year. Figure 1 shows the discussion volume (in number of tweets mentioning the politician in a week). Notice that the discussion becomes more lively towards the end of the year. Guided by these trends, we select a time span in which to sample the data for each politician – choosing months in which sufficient posting activity is seen. The rightmost two columns of Table 1 show the time spans and the number of tweets sampled from that time span. The sampling was done in a random uniform fashion within each month, and duplicates and retweets were removed.

The subset, totaling in 6,400 tweets was annotated by a group of political science students as a part of class project. Each annotator was given the name of the target politician and a set of tweets. For each tweet, she decided whether the tweet was about the politician by making a *Relevance* judgment. If the tweet was relevant, she would decide on whether the tweet was *For* or *Against* the politician, had *Mixed* opinion, or was *Neutral*. We also allowed for a *Can't Tell* option. Furthermore, if the tweet was *For* or *Against* the politician, the annotator needed to select the *Intensity* of the opinion. Finally, several stylistic features of the text were collected: whether tweet contained *Sarcasm*, *Humor*, *Swearing*, or a *Quote*. Some of the tweets were annotated by several (maximum of three) annotators, and majority vote or third annotation broke ties in the cases of disagreement.

Table 2 shows annotator agreement as percentage overlap of the labels. The most difficult tasks proved to be *Sentiment* and *Intensity*. Because these are not binary tasks (for sentiment, for example, there are five classes), these numbers are reasonable. Thus, we look at the sentiment data in steps: first we determine agreement in *subjectivity* (distinction between {*For*, *Against*, *Mixed*} and {*Neutral*}), then in *polarity* (*For* versus *Against*). Subjectivity proves to be a harder task than polarity. That is, once it is known that the tweet is subjective, it becomes easier to gauge polarity. The labeling interface also allowed annotators to resolve some of their disagreements. Out of these, 19.0% were about *Relevance*, 73.1% about *Subjectivity* and only 7.9% about *Polarity*. As a measure of the human classification performance, these figures put an upper bound to the performance we would expect from our automated classification algorithms.

Table 1: Republican Presidential nomination race dataset statistics

	Full Dataset		Annotated Subset	
Politician	**Time Span**	**# Tweets**	**Time Span**	**# Tweets**
Michele Bachmann	1/13/11 - 1/11/12	2,006,034	6/1/11 - 1/1/12 (excluding Oct.)	1,400
Newt Gingrich	1/1/11 - 1/11/12	1,725,271	11/1/11 - 1/1/12	600
Herman Cain	5/26/11 - 1/11/12	1,514,739	9/1/11 - 1/1/12	1,000
Rick Perry	5/27/11 - 1/11/12	1,641,646	7/1/11 - 1/1/12	1,400
Mitt Romney	1/4/11 - 1/11/12	3,170,260	10/1/11 - 1/1/12	800
Ron Paul	1/5/11 - 1/11/12	2,342,392	10/1/11 - 1/1/12	800
Rick Santorum	1/2/11 - 1/11/12	1,125,602	12/1/11 - 1/1/12	400

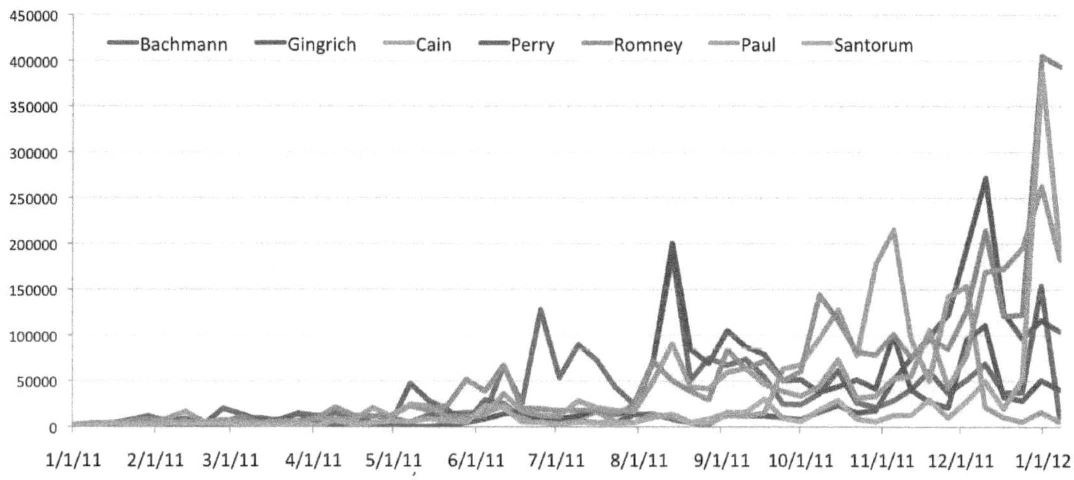

Figure 1: Tweet volume for individual politicians in full dataset

4. SENTIMENT ANALYSIS

Table 3 shows the relevance and sentiment statistics for each politician and their aggregates based on manually annotated data. One of the most striking features is high percentage of relevant documents – 94.8% on average. The accuracy of our retrieval method – querying Twitter Search API using politician's names – supports the widespread use of this technique in the literature [3, 2, 19]. Looking at sentiment annotations, nearly 10% of the tweets were labeled as *Can't Tell*, with Gingrich having the highest %, and another 25% as Neutral, leaving 65% of the documents with subjective labels. We also observe the dominant sentiment class to be Against, with a notable exception of Ron Paul, whose For tweets outnumber Against nearly 2 to 1.

Following [3], we summarize sentiment expressed in these documents by subtracting the number of Against tweets from For, resulting in a summary score of expressed sentiment. In general, the number of For and Against documents reflects the overall posting rate, but with Against at a greater rate. An example is shown for Cain in Figure 2, the rest omitted for brevity. The sentiment score is positive at the beginning of Mr. Cain's campaign. But as for most other politicians, it quickly becomes negative. Again, the exception is Ron Paul whose sentiment score is positive throughout.

We also examine the intensity associated with each of the sentiments in Table 4. Tweets with Neutral sentiment show the least number of excited and passionate tweets, whereas those with For sentiment show the greatest. Note that a politically neutral tweet can still be excited, such as in ambiguous questioning: *"Did Michele Bachmann Jump the Shark by Suggesting HPV Vaccine Can Cause "Mental Retardation"? http://t.co/48zMcaN"*. However, we find that on average 78% of the tweets are not particularly more intense than "normal".

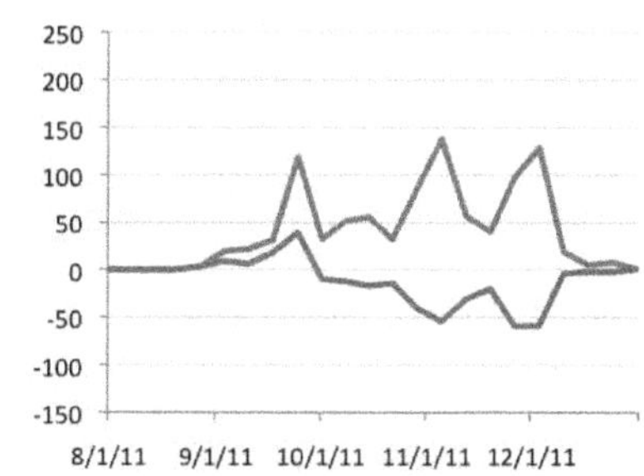

Figure 2: Volume (blue) and sentiment score (red) for Herman Cain

Table 5 shows the distribution of various stylistic features across tweets about each politician and in For and Against

Table 2: Annotator agreement as percentage label overlap

	Relev.	Sent.	Subj.*	Pol.*	Int.	Sarc.	Humor	Swear.	Quote
Bachmann	0.871	0.493	0.802	0.924	0.460	0.854	0.751	0.975	0.865
Gingrich	0.572	0.271	0.379	0.569	0.212	0.587	0.533	0.598	0.526
Cain	0.816	0.436	0.700	0.807	0.452	0.762	0.677	0.845	0.758
Perry	0.792	0.436	0.652	0.784	0.420	0.782	0.654	0.819	0.733
Romney	0.826	0.446	0.642	0.817	0.404	0.861	0.828	0.872	0.850
Paul	0.794	0.374	0.651	0.616	0.478	0.791	0.737	0.828	0.733
Santorum	0.726	0.407	0.560	0.710	0.369	0.728	0.678	0.742	0.723
Average	0.793	0.425	0.660	0.776	0.416	0.784	0.701	0.839	0.760

Table 3: Subset relevance and sentiment statistics

				Sentiment (counts)					Sentiment (%)				
	total	relevant	rel %	for	aga	mix	neu	ctt	for	aga	mix	neu	ctt
Bachmann	1400	1295	92.5	115	728	31	317	105	8.9	56.2	2.4	24.5	8.1
Gingrich	600	575	95.8	69	218	20	160	108	12.0	37.9	3.5	27.8	18.8
Cain	1000	947	94.7	202	450	23	203	71	21.3	47.5	2.4	21.4	7.5
Perry	1400	1340	95.7	126	743	39	297	135	9.4	55.4	2.9	22.2	10.1
Romney	800	760	95.0	104	310	32	254	60	13.7	40.8	4.2	33.4	7.9
Paul	800	758	94.8	303	161	31	166	97	40.0	21.2	4.1	21.9	12.8
Santorum	400	389	97.3	76	150	19	128	16	19.5	38.6	4.9	32.9	4.1
Total/Avg	6400	6064	94.8	995	2760	195	1525	592	16.4	45.5	3.2	25.1	9.8

Table 4: Intensity associated with different sentiments (percent of total)

	For	Against	Mixed	Neutral	All
Passionate	8.3	6.6	3.5	0.9	6.6
Excited	19.5	15.2	18.8	2.2	15.4
Normal	72.2	78.2	77.6	97.0	78.0

tweets separately. We find 21.6% of all tweets in the dataset to be humorous and 7.4% sarcastic. These are not evenly distributed between the politicians. For example, discussion about Bachmann and Cain are especially laden with sarcasm and humor. Strikingly, 40% of Against tweets are humorous, compared to only 5.7% of those For the politician. They are also more likely to contain swear words. Discussion about Mitt Romney, the politician to ultimately become the official republican Presidential nominee, shows much less of such rhetoric. We also note that a humorous tweet is 76.7% likely to also be sarcastic (but sarcastic tweets is only 26.2% likely to be humorous). This connection between sarcasm and humor would be an interesting future study.

5. USER STRATIFICATION

We further examine data by stratifying the users, as in Mustafaraj et al. [13], who discover that political discussion is dominated by power users (a *vocal minority*), leaving the opinions of the rest (the *silent majority*) underrepresented in a corpus which has been randomly sampled. We expand their analysis by characterizing these two groups in terms of sentiment they tend to express. As predicted, user posting behavior in our dataset follows power law – with few users posting thousands of messages and a vast majority posting very few. We separate all users in our dataset into five quintiles according to their posting behavior (see Table 6). To do this, we separate the users into groups where each group is responsible for roughly a fifth of all content. The first group consists of 78.5% of all users in the dataset, in which users post an average of 1.7 tweets (that's over the span of a year). The most active group, however, consists of just 0.2% of all users, but it generated 15.9% of the tweets with an average of 4,164.5 tweets/year per user.

Figures 3 show sentiment and stylistic features of the tweets from each of the user group. Additional Twitter-specific features (bottom four) were extracted using regular expressions. The results are shown for Ron Paul and other politicians separately, because of the unusually positive overall sentiment of Mr. Paul's subset. We see many tendencies: the vocal group tends to be more for and less against the politician, and post more neutral tweets. It is also less sarcastic or humorous, but is more likely to use hashtags and links, and to retweet. They are unlikely to post a tweet without any hashtags, links or retweet ("Only text"). Ron Paul tweets show the same trends, except for the prominence of For sentiment.

Upon examining a selection of users from most and least vocal (around 70 users from each group), we note that whereas all users from the least vocal group were accounts owned by individuals (many of which had very few tweets), only 65% were individual accounts in the vocal group. These accounts have thousands of followers, and many have their own blogs or websites: 31% of the vocal group were campaigning for some political cause, and the last 4% were news sites.

The significance of these peculiarities is that the vast difference in posting frequency of these users skews the overall sentiment of the data. When polls measure favorability, each polled person is counted equally. This is not the case when each tweet is counted as a "vote". Thus, counting users instead of individual tweets may be a better approach when comparing sentiment expressed on Twitter to traditional polls.

In summary, our annotated dataset reveals a discussion

Table 5: Stylistic features (percent of total)

	All Relevant				For				Against			
	sarc	humor	swear	quote	sarc	humor	swear	quote	sarc	humor	swear	quote
Bachmann	13.8	28.8	4.8	17.9	1.7	7.0	0.0	13.9	23.4	44.1	8.0	22.7
Gingrich	3.3	13.7	2.3	11.0	0.0	4.3	0.0	14.5	8.7	30.7	6.0	16.5
Cain	10.8	29.0	6.5	20.4	3.5	6.9	2.0	22.8	19.8	52.9	12.4	25.3
Perry	6.5	29.6	3.3	10.2	2.4	4.8	4.0	7.1	11.0	47.8	4.8	12.5
Romney	2.4	7.6	0.4	4.1	1.9	3.8	0.0	3.8	4.2	11.9	1.0	6.1
Paul	3.6	9.0	1.6	19.7	2.0	6.6	1.7	22.4	13.0	24.2	3.7	25.5
Santorum	3.9	15.9	1.8	4.9	1.3	2.6	0.0	5.3	8.7	37.3	4.7	5.3
All	7.4	21.6	3.3	13.6	2.1	5.7	1.4	15.8	14.7	40.3	6.5	17.2

Table 6: Users grouped by posting behavior (in original dataset)

Group #	# of users	% of all users	tweets generated	% of all tweets	tweets/user
1	2,461,806	78.5	3,133,990	23.2	1.7
2	505,786	16.1	2,805,942	20.7	7.6
3	130,398	4.2	2,728,078	20.2	29.1
4	34,559	1.1	2,710,589	20.0	124.3
5	5,278	0.2	2,147,345	15.9	4164.5

65% of which is opinionated speech, which is laden with humor and sarcasm. It showed the power-users to be more for the politician they are tweeting about, and to be less sarcastic, humorous, and use fewer swear words. The sample set also contains links (in 55.2% of sampled tweets), hashtags (31%), and retweets (36.4%). Compare these to a general subset we collected to estimate general Twitter use consisting of 5 million tweets, 13.0% of which had links, 16.5% had hashtags and 13.1% retweets. The opinionated speech is mostly biased against the politicians (except for the case of Ron Paul), and in which users with different posting behaviors exhibit different biases.

The skewed negative bias, the prevalence of humor and sarcasm, and the dominance of power users in the political discourse data all may negatively impact classification performance. Next, we apply a machine learning approach to political sentiment classification.

6. CLASSIFICATION

In this section, we develop a political sentiment classifier and evaluate it using our labeled dataset. We build the classification models using SVMlight[1], which gives us some flexibility for tuning of the class selection. Using Lingpipe[2] tokenizer, we extract 1-, 2-, and 3-grams as a feature vector. Punctuation and special characters were not removed at this step and no stemming was performed on the words in order to capture twitter-specific features such as hashtags, mentions, and emoticons. Preliminary studies showed it to be beneficial to compute the models for the dataset as a whole instead of building one for each politician, and we take this approach.

Overall design of our model is shown in Figure 4. The classification is done in two stages. First, three binary classifiers (one for detecting For, Against, and Neutral sentiments) each produce a score indicating the extent to which the document belongs to that class. These are then used to determine the label of the document by the final classifier.

[1]http://svmlight.joachims.org/

[2]http://alias-i.com/lingpipe/

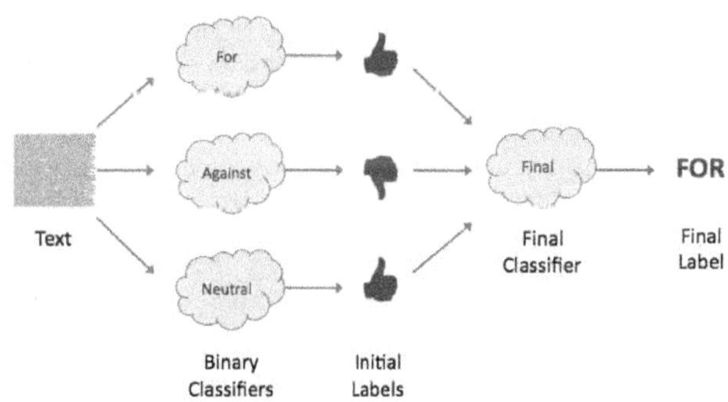

Figure 4: Multi-step classification design

The accuracy, and the average precision, recall, and f-score measures for the un-tuned classifier are shown in the Table 7 under Default SVMLight. Notice that in overall performance the Accuracy is computed for the final classifier instead of taking an average of individual class accuracies, showing the overall accuracy instead of by-class accuracy. Due to the low recall for minority classes – For and Neutral – the overall accuracy is rather low. We attempt to improve this performance by tuning the two steps of the algorithm. To determine the class of a document SVMlight looks at the polarity of a score, which ranges roughly between -1 and 1. The magnitude of this score can be considered as the confidence of the classifier. Thus we introduce a notion of "cutoff", such that if the score is greater than the cutoff, the class decision is accepted. Furthermore, we may also want to change the value 0 as being the class cross-over point. We can "bias" the classifier by shifting this point closer toward -1 or 1. That is, if we change the cross-over point to -0.2, all documents in the range of [-0.2, 0.0] are now considered in the positive class instead of negative. We use a tuning set to determine the best values of the cutoff and bias by examining performance metrics at various values of these two parameters. We choose the best bias and cutoff

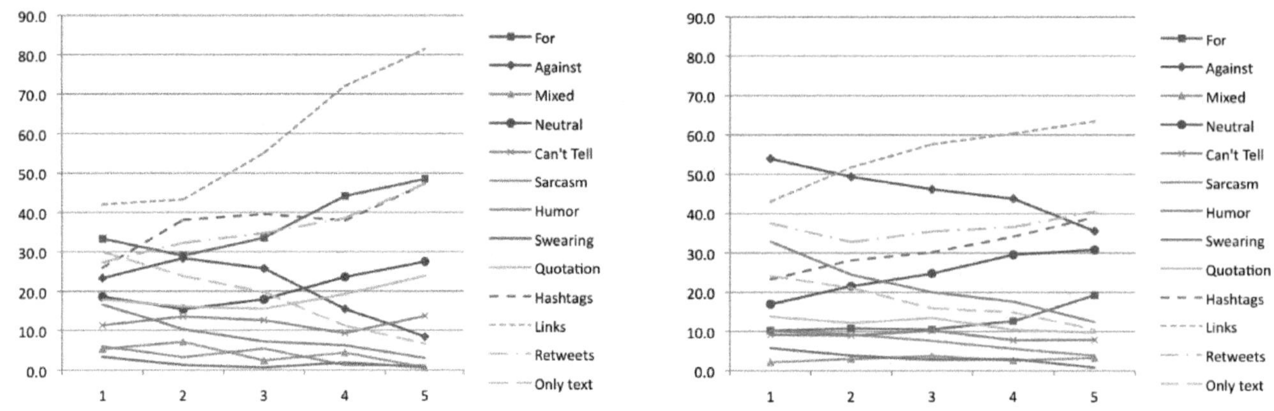

Figure 3: Sentiment and stylistic features within stratified user groups from least vocal (1) to most vocal (5), left: excluding Ron Paul, right: Ron Paul only

values at which at least half of all documents are being classified. These are 0.2 cutoff and 0.8 bias for For and Neutral classifiers and 0.5 cutoff and 0.5 bias for Against classifier.

In order to improve the performance of the final classifier, instead of using heuristics for determining the final class label, we train a logistic regression classifier (using Weka) using the outputs of the three classifiers as features. The final classification performance is shown in Table 7 under Tuned SVMLight + Regression.

To further optimize our classifier we also tried anonymizing the data set by replacing the names of the target politicians with a bogus feature, but such approach did not yield a superior performance. It may be the case that politician's names have distinguishing qualities which aid the classifier in its task (Ron Paul, for example, is likely to be highly associated with the For class).

7. TRACKING SENTIMENT

Using classifier developed in previous section we now track change in sentiment. We focus on the time spans around Republican debates taking place during the 2011. A list of these debates was collected from 2012 Presidential Election News website[3]. We also collect the poll numbers for each of our politicians from Real Clear Politics[4], a website which collects information from national polls including Gallup, Rasmussen, Reuters, and others. Figure 5 shows the poll numbers for the seven politicians with vertical lines at the debates (19 in total).

For each debate, we collect a sample of 10,000 documents 5 days before and 5 days after the debate. The five-day window was chosen to accommodate the fact that the polls are not updated on a daily basis. We then apply Tuned SVMlight + Regression classifier to assign labels to the sampled documents. Our goal is to predict the change of sentiment that often happens around debates. We compare the change in predicted class to that of the polls. Not all seven politicians participated at all of the polls, and our data did not cover some of the debates. The final experiment consisted of 104 predictions of sentiment change for a politician before and after debate. We take several approaches to estimating sentiment change:

- For: number of For documents after the debate minus before
- Against: number of Against documents before the debate minus after (reversed in order to show change in favorability)
- For-Against: number of For documents minus Against documents after the debate minus the same before
- For-Against Mod: same as For-Against, with For numbers boosted according to the average For to Against ratio (estimated using training set)
- * (U): same as above, but normalizing contribution of each tweet by the number of tweets the author has in the sample: $\frac{tweet\_polarity:\{-1,+1\}}{\#tweets\_by\_user}$
- Volume: number of all documents after the debate minus before

The performance of these approaches for each candidate is shown in Table 8. We also show the performance of a baseline based on the historical sentiment change in the polls: we predict sentiment change for a politician after a given debate according to the majority of sentiment changes in the previous debates for a that politician. For example, by the fourth debate in which Ron Paul participated, we have witnessed two debates after which the sentiment about him becomes more positive and one in which it becomes more negative, so we guess a positive change. Looking at prediction accuracy, we see different predictors performing differently for each politician. Ron Paul's sentiment change can be predicted quite well just by looking at the volume of conversation about him (which tends to be positive, unlike for the other candidates). Change in For and in Against documents showed different results. For example, the change in For documents predicts Romney sentiment change much better than the Against, but this is reversed for Herman Cain. Furthermore, normalizing the contribution of tweet

[3]http://www.2012presidentialelectionnews.com/2012-debate-schedule/2011-2012-primary-debate-schedule/

[4]http://www.realclearpolitics.com/epolls/2012/president/us/republican_presidential_nomination-1452.html

Table 7: SVMlight combined classifiers

Default SVMlight

	Accuracy	Avg Prec	Avg Rec	Avg F-measure
Overall performance	0.269	0.595	0.357	0.295
	Accuracy	Precision	Recall	F-measure
For	0.849	0.740	0.037	0.071
Against	0.578	0.680	0.556	0.612
Neutral	0.432	0.750	0.095	0.168
Other	0.475	0.211	0.738	0.328

Tuned SVMlight

	Accuracy	Avg Prec	Avg Rec	Avg F-measure
Overall performance	0.476	0.511	0.445	0.440
	Accuracy	Precision	Recall	F-measure
For	0.855	0.590	0.225	0.326
Against	0.594	0.681	0.553	0.610
Neutral	0.521	0.522	0.440	0.478
Other	0.632	0.251	0.561	0.347

Tuned SVMlight + Regression

	Accuracy	Avg Prec	Avg Rec	Avg F-measure
Overall performance	0.544	0.529	0.432	0.434
	Accuracy	Precision	Recall	F-measure
For	0.852	0.551	0.249	0.344
Against	0.592	0.565	0.836	0.674
Neutral	0.634	0.496	0.503	0.500
Other	0.826	0.503	0.139	0.218

sentiment by number of tweets posted by its user (U) increases the match for For and Against approaches. However, not any one of the approaches correlates well with the official poll results, and none are statistically better than the baseline. After computing Pearson correlation between these measures and the poll numbers, we also see very low numbers, with highest at 0.08.

We examine further the latest of the examined debates, one which took place on Jan 7, 2012. According to the polls, Gingrich did very poorly around the same time, seeing his numbers go from 27.4 (on Jan 2) to 16.6 (on Jan 11). The reverse is true for Santorum, whose numbers went from 4 (on Jan 2) to 15.8 (on Jan 11). The majority of these popular tweets are anti-Gingrich jokes, with only one pro-Gingrich tweet. Also note that the popular jokes do not seem to be propagating because of an organized effort (such as in tweet supporting Gingrich – "RT our new video"), and they do not link to outside sources, but they are propagated just because the users thought they were worthy of sharing with others. For Santorum, the popular tweets also look quite bleak, with all of them jokes, and very few have Twitter-specific features which would make the tweet more searchable and retweetable (like hashtags, links, or pleas for users to retweet). We conclude that, although an expression of sentiment, much of tweeting may not be considered "serious" political discussion.

8. DISCUSSION & FUTURE WORK

The overall tendency towards the Against class in our dataset, as well as the fact that sentiment we find around the debates does not correspond well to that found in national polls suggests that political discourse on Twitter is not indicative of that of the nation as a whole. Because the politicians we examine in this project are Republicans (with possible exception of Ron Paul who has claimed to be Libertarian), it may be the case that an overall leaning of Twitter is more liberal. This may also be supported by Twitter's young user base (mostly under 30)[5]. A future analysis of the conversation about both Republicans and Democrats, as well as the users most active in this conversation, would shed more light on this issue.

Ron Paul, a libertarian politician who has been known for his young user base[6], proves to be an exception to the rule on many occasions. Although ultimately his campaign was unsuccessful, the overwhelming support he receives on social media is unusual. It would be interesting to compare his campaign to that of Barack Obama (a democrat) during the 2008 Presidential Election, who also has successfully used internet to rally a young base.

One could argue that comparing immediate reactions on Twitter to real-world events does not account for a lag in news and opinion propagation through the social network. Instead, one can check whether Twitter sentiment is predictive of or responsive to the national polls by "shifting" the times at which the sentiments are compared, for instance, by comparing earlier Twitter sentiment to later national polls. We may find a delayed response in Twitter to debates or other newsworthy events, but it would be even more interesting to find a sentiment which is first expressed in Twitter, and then in national polls. Second, we may examine polls which focus on a particular demographic, perhaps a younger

[5]http://www.sysomos.com/insidetwitter/

[6]http://www.huffingtonpost.com/2012/01/12/ron-paul-young-voters_n_1202616.html

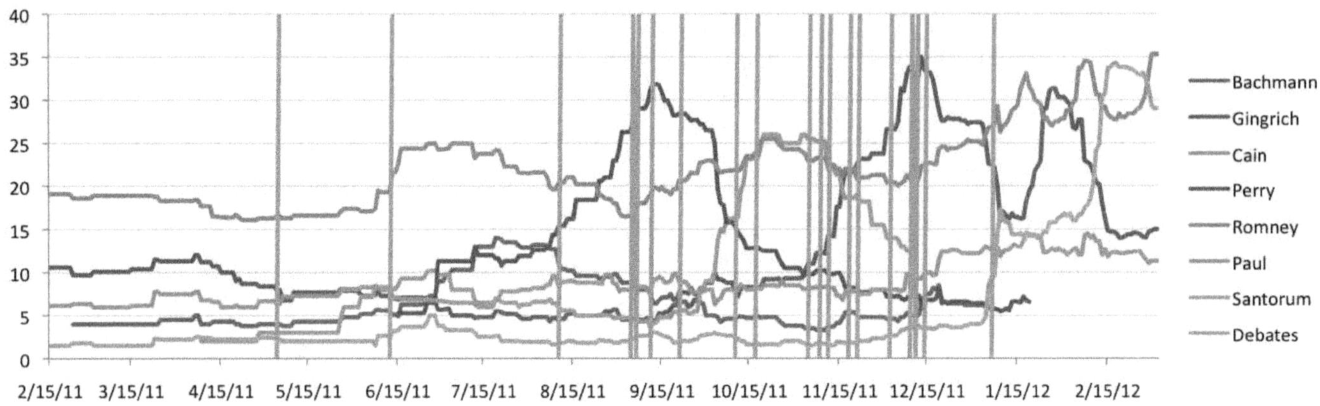

Figure 5: Polls (approval %) for seven select politicians with debate days marked by vertical lines

Table 8: Predicting change in sentiment before and after debates: accuracy

	Bachmann	Gingrich	Cain	Perry	Romney	Paul	Santorum	Avg
For (T)	66.7	50.0	38.5	46.2	78.6	53.3	56.3	55.77
For (U)	60.0	55.6	30.8	53.8	78.6	60.0	68.8	58.65
Against (T)	53.3	44.4	69.2	61.5	28.6	40.0	50.0	49.04
Against (U)	66.7	38.9	61.5	61.5	42.9	40.0	50.0	50.96
For-Against (T)	60.0	50.0	69.2	61.5	28.6	46.7	50.0	51.92
For-Against (U)	60.0	55.6	69.2	53.8	28.6	40.0	56.3	51.92
For-Against Mod (T)	66.7	50.0	69.2	46.2	35.7	46.7	43.8	50.96
For-Against Mod (U)	60.0	50.0	69.2	53.8	35.7	40.0	50.0	50.96
Volume	53.3	66.7	46.2	46.2	57.1	73.3	50.0	56.73
Majority baseline	56.7	63.9	46.1	69.2	67.9	46.7	56.2	58.10

population, or that which is more likely to express political opinion online. Similarly, there may be network characteristics which relate to sentiment, with "authorities" having more influence on Twitter sentiment.

Finally, as Mustafaraj et al. [13] point out, uniform sampling of data may be detrimental to political predictions. More research into the effect of influential bloggers and Twitter users, as opposed to the rest of the users, on the predictive power of statistical algorithms could be useful in limiting the amount and improving the quality of social media data that is useful.

9. CONCLUSION

The most striking feature of our political data was an overwhelming negative bias toward all politicians with an average ratio of 3.76 Against to 1 For tweets, except for Ron Paul who shows 0.53 to 1 ratio. The negative sentiment is sometimes matched by the positive at the beginning of the politician's campaign, but as a rule quickly returns to an overall negative sentiment. These negative documents are often humorous (40.3%) and/or sarcastic (14.7%), and sometimes contain swear words (6.5%). This, and the amount of polarity skew, makes polarity classification of political discourse difficult.

By stratifying the users by the frequency of their postings, we find distinctly differing behaviors between the "silent majority" and "vocal minority" (terms coined by Mustafaraj et al. [13]). The vocal group tends to be more For and less Against the politician, it is less sarcastic and humorous, and is more likely to use hashtags, links, and retweet. Thus, if one counts users instead of tweets (as in traditional polls), the negative sentiment would be even more pronounced. Indeed, it may be useful to use stratified sampling paying special attention to the opinions of individual users.

Using this dataset, we build and test a classifier to detect For, Neutral, and Against sentiments. We find that using out-of-the-box tools works nearly the same as the majority baseline, and only after some thorough tuning we improve overall accuracy from 0.269 to 0.544. We conclude that it is indeed a difficult task, and that researchers tracking political sentiment on Twitter should be wary of using untuned out-of-the-box tools without evaluation.

Using this classifier, we track sentiment expressed about each of the politicians change before and after 19 republican debates. We compare this sentiment to national polls, and find that overall the sentiment we find in the tweets does not well correspond to that in the polls. Examining the most popular tweets further, we find them mostly to be joking banter about the politicians, all negative – even for the politicians whose national poll numbers were improving. More future work must be done in order to determine whether this truly points to an overall anti-republican or liberal-leaning bias in the Twittersphere.

10. REFERENCES

[1] J. Bollen, A. Pepe, and H. Mao. Modeling public mood and emotion: Twitter sentiment and socio-economic phenomena. *World Wide Web Conference (WWW)*, 2010.

[2] M. D. Conover, J. Ratkiewicz, M. Francisco, B. Goncalves, F. Menczer, and A. Flammini. Political polarization on twitter. *International Conference on Weblogs and Social Media (ICWSM)*, 2011.

[3] N. A. Diakopoulos and D. A. Shamma. Characterizing debate performance via aggregated twitter sentiment. *Conference on Human Factors in Computing Systems (CHI)*, 2010.

[4] A. Feller, M. Kuhnert, T. O. Sprenger, and I. M. Welpe. Divided they tweet: The network structure of political microbloggers and discussion topics. *International Conference on Weblogs and Social Media (ICWSM)*, 2011.

[5] D. Gayo-Avello, P. T. Metaxas, and E. Mustafaraj. Limits of electoral predictions using twitter. *International Conference on Weblogs and Social Media (ICWSM)*, 2011.

[6] J. Ghannam. Social media in the arab world: Leading up to the uprisings of 2011. *A Report to the Center for International Media Assistance*, Febuary 2011.

[7] S. Gonzalez-Bailon, R. E. Banchs, and A. Kaltenbrunner. Emotional reactions and the pulse of public opinion: Measuring the impact of political events on the sentiment of online discussions. *http://arxiv.org*, 2010.

[8] S.-M. Kim and E. Hovy. Crystal: Analyzing prediction opinions on the web. *Proceedings of the Joint Conference on Empirical Methods in Natural Language Processing and Computational Natural Language Learning (EMNLP-CoNLL)*, 2007.

[9] W.-H. Lin, T. Wilson, J. Wiebe, and A. Hauptmann. Which side are you on? identifying perspectives at the document and sentence level. *Conference on Natural Language Learning (CoNLL)*, 2006.

[10] Y.-R. Lin, J. P. Bagrow, and D. Lazer. More voices than ever? quantifying media bias in networks. *International Conference on Weblogs and Social Media (ICWSM)*, 2011.

[11] A. Livne, M. Simmons, E. Adar, and L. Adamic. The party is over here: Structure and content in the 2010 election. *International Conference on Weblogs and Social Media (ICWSM)*, 2011.

[12] P. Metaxas, E. Mustafaraj, and D. Gayo-Avello. How (not) to predict elections. *International Conference on Social Computing*, 2011.

[13] E. Mustafaraj, S. Finn, C. Whitlock, and P. T. Metaxas. Vocal minority versus silent majority: Discovering the opinions of the long tail. *International Conference on Social Computing*, 2011.

[14] B. O'Connor, R. Balasubramanyan, B. R. Routledge, and N. A. Smith. From tweets to polls: Linking text sentiment to public opinion time series. *International AAAI Conference on Weblogs and Social Media (ICWSM)*, 2010.

[15] B. Pang and L. Lee. Thumbs up?: sentiment classification using machine learning techniques. *Conference on Empirical Methods in Natural Language Processing (EMNLP)*, 10:79–86, 2002.

[16] J. Ratkiewicz, M. D. Conover, M. Meiss, B. Goncalves, A. Flammini, and F. M. Menczer. Detecting and tracking political abuse in social media. *International Conference on Weblogs and Social Media (ICWSM)*, 2011.

[17] D. Saez-Trumper, W. Meira, and V. Almeida. From total hits to unique visitors model for election's forecasting. *International Conference on Web Science*, 2011.

[18] S. Somasundaran and J. Wiebe. Recognizing stances in ideological on-line debates. *NAACL HLT Workshop on Computational Approaches to Analysis and Generation of Emotion in Text*, 2010.

[19] A. Tumasjan, T. O. Sprenger, P. G. Sandner, and I. M. Welpe. Predicting elections with twitter: What 140 characters reveal about political sentiment. *Association for the Advancement of Artificial Intelligence Conference (AAAI)*, 2010.

[20] M. Wagner. Obama election ushering in first internet presidency. http://www.informationweek.com/news/government/ 212000815, 2008.

Towards Twitter Context Summarization with User Influence Models

Yi Chang[†], Xuanhui Wang[¶], Qiaozhu Mei[§], Yan Liu[‡]
[†]Yahoo! Labs, Sunnyvale, CA 94089
[¶]Facebook, Menlo Park, CA 94025
[§]University of Michigan, Ann Arbor, MI 48109
[‡]University of Southern California, Los Angeles, CA 90089
yichang@yahoo-inc.com, xuanhui@fb.com, qmei@umich.edu, yanliu.cs@usc.edu

ABSTRACT

Twitter has become one of the most popular platforms for users to share information in real time. However, as an individual tweet is short and lacks sufficient contextual information, users cannot effectively understand or consume information on Twitter, which can either make users less engaged or even detached from using Twitter. In order to provide informative context to a Twitter user, we propose the task of Twitter context summarization, which generates a succinct summary from a large but noisy Twitter context tree. Traditional summarization techniques only consider text information, which is insufficient for Twitter context summarization task, since text information on Twitter is very sparse. Given that there are rich user interactions in Twitter, we thus study how to improve summarization methods by leveraging such signals. In particular, we study how user influence models, which project user interaction information onto a Twitter context tree, can help Twitter context summarization within a supervised learning framework. To evaluate our methods, we construct a data set by asking human editors to manually select the most informative tweets as a summary. Our experimental results based on this editorial data set show that Twitter context summarization is a promising research topic and pairwise user influence signals can significantly improve the task performance.

Categories and Subject Descriptors

H.3.1 [**Information Storage and Retrieval**]: Content Analysis and Indexing - abstracting methods

General Terms

Algorithms, Experimentation

Keywords

Twitter Context Tree, Summarization, User Influence Model

1. INTRODUCTION

Twitter, the most popular micro-blogging site, has become a phenomenon in recent years. On Twitter, users post messages with the limit of 140 characters, which are called *tweets*. Unlike most of other online social network sites such as Facebook, Twitter users can follow each other and such a relationship is not reciprocal: a Twitter user does not need to follow back if the user is followed by another. Being a *Twitter follower* means that the user will receive all tweets from other users that he/she follows. A Twitter follower could re-broadcast a tweet to its own followers by *retweeting* or *replying* to the tweet.

As each individual tweet is short, users cannot effectively understand or consume information on Twitter due to lack of context. If an ordinary Twitter user follows a celebrity Twitter user, the follower will receive all original tweets from the celebrity. Unfortunately, most replies to the original tweets by other Twitter users are not available to this follower, although these replies may potentially contain useful information. For example, a tweet by Justin Bieber just contains a single hashtag "#prayforjapan" and an URL during the period of Japan earthquake in 2011. More than 1100 replies to this tweet to express their suggestions, compassion, or appreciation (Table 2 shows an example), but all these replies are not available to any individual follower of Justin Bieber. Even if a Justin Bieber's follower also follows several users who replied to Justin's original tweet, those replies may not be connected appropriately to the original tweet. It could be even worse whenever a follower just receives a replied tweet but not the original tweet: without proper context, it might be difficult to understand what the reply is really about. All these obstacles prevent users from effectively understanding or consuming information on Twitter, which can either make users less engaged or even detached from using Twitter.

In this paper, we propose the task of Twitter context summarization, which generates a succinct summary from a large but noisy Twitter context tree, to help users effectively understand the contextual information. A *Twitter context tree* is defined as a tree structure of tweets which are connected with reply relationship, and the root of a context tree is its original tweet. We do not consider retweet relationship in constructing Twitter context tree, since retweets usually do not provide any extra textual information, which is necessary for contextual information. Yet retweet signals are not totally ignored in this paper, since retweet information can be leveraged to indicate the quality of a tweet. Imaging a Twitter user receives either a root tweet or a replied tweet from its followees, we can identify the context tree that it belongs to, and automatically generate a summary out of it. The generated summary would be presented in a succinct form along with the tweet, which helps the user to quickly understand the whole contextual information. In the real application, we always keep the root tweet as part of the summary since it provides critical information in terms of context, however, we exclude the root tweet in evaluating the summarization accuracy.

An intuitive approach for the task of Twitter context summarization is to apply traditional text-based methods which are either abstraction or extraction [22, 15]. In the extraction based methods, we can treat each tweet as a sentence, a Twitter context tree as a document. However, the major challenges of extraction based Twitter context summarization include: 1) Tweet texts are short and informal, thus a Twitter context tree could contain too much noisy data; 2) There are rich interactions among Twitter users, which can be potentially useful to generate high quality summary. Unfortunately, text-based summarization methods are not designed to leverage such type of information.

To improve Twitter context summarization, our main idea is to leverage user influence models, which project user interaction information onto a Twitter context tree. There are mainly two types of user influence models, called pairwise user influence model and global user influence model: the former considers pairwise influence between two entities, while the latter investigates the influence among all entities. For the task of Twitter context summarization, we explore the pairwise user influence between the Twitter user generating the root tweet and any Twitter user sending replies, using Granger Causality influence model [12]. If a user is strongly influenced by the user generating the root tweet, chances are his replies are strongly coherent with the root tweet, and such a reply is more likely to be an appropriate summary candidate than other replies. A global user influence model investigates the relative importance of each user via user interactions among them. Intuitively, the more important user would less likely to generate a low quality tweet. In this paper, we will use PageRank algorithm [4] to generate the propagated global user influence signals.

Both text-based signals and user influence signals are represented as features, and we further propose to combine them in a supervised learning framework. To evaluate our methods, we construct a data set by asking editors to manually select the most informative tweets as a summary. Our experimental results based on this editorial data set show that Twitter context summarization is a promising research topic, and pairwise user influence signals can significantly improve the task performance. In real application, we could still rely on the supervised learning method with a relatively small training data, since non-text features are very limited.

The rest of the paper is organized as follows. We first review the related work in Section 2, and then analyze characteristics of Twitter context trees in Section 3. We introduce user influence models in Section 4, and describe our methods of summarization with different type of features in Section 5. The editorial data is described in Section 6 and our experimental results are presented in Section 7. Finally, we conclude our paper in Section 8.

2. RELATED WORK

Text summarization [15] has been a well established research area in the last decades. Recent research has been focused on summarization beyond textual information, such as using clickthrough data for web-page summarization [27], using temporal information for summarization [31], leveraging reviews or comments for opinion summarization [19], learning to rank for summarization [26], etc.

Most of the prior work on Twitter data summarization are about topic level summarization. Clustering algorithms are introduced [14] to explore the topic of multi-post extractive Twitter summarization, with frequency based, graph based, and cluster based methods, to select multiple posts that conveyed information about a given topic without being redundant. However, without leveraging user interaction information in Twitter, the simple frequency based summarizer produced the best results both in F-measure scores. Chakrabarti and Punera [7] formalized the problem of summarizing event-tweets and give a solution based on learning the underlying hidden state representation of the event via Hidden Markov Models, which is proposed to complement Twitter stream event detection problem [21]. Brendan O'Connor et. al. [20] presented a demo system to summarize sentiment based on syntactic filtering and near-duplicate detection. Sharifi et al. [25] summarized Twitter hot topics through finding the most commonly used phrase that encompasses the topic phrase. Unfortunately, rich user interaction signals are ignored in these papers.

Existing studies on Twitter influence are based on Twitter users, tweets or Twittersphere. Bakshy et al. [2] investigated the attributes and relative influence based on Twitter follower graph, and concluded that word-of-mouth diffusion can only be harnessed reliably by targeting large numbers of potential influencers, thereby capturing average effects. Hopcroft et al. [13] studied the Twitter user influence based on two-way reciprocal relationship prediction. Weng et al. [29] extended PageRank algorithm to measure the influence of Twitter users, and took both the topical similarity between users and link structure into account. Kwak et al. [16] study the topological and geographical properties on the entire Twittersphere and they observe some notable properties of Twitter, such as a non-power-law follower distribution, a short effective diameter, and low reciprocity, marking a deviation from known characteristics of human social networks.

3. TWITTER CONTEXT TREE ANALYSIS

In our task, a Twitter context tree is constructed by tweets connected with reply relationship, and the root of the context tree is its original tweet. Twitter context trees are also called Twitter conversations in [23], and the authors revealed the size of the majority of trees is very small and the distribution of the tree sizes roughly follows a power law. In this section, we conduct further analysis on the Twitter context trees with respect to temporal growth and depth distributions.

For the task of Twitter context summarization, we are more interested in those large Twitter context trees to which summarization is more desired. In our analysis, we collect 40,583 large Twitter context trees from March 7th to March 20th in 2011. Each context tree contains more than 100 tweets, and overall there are 9.4 millions tweets. Among

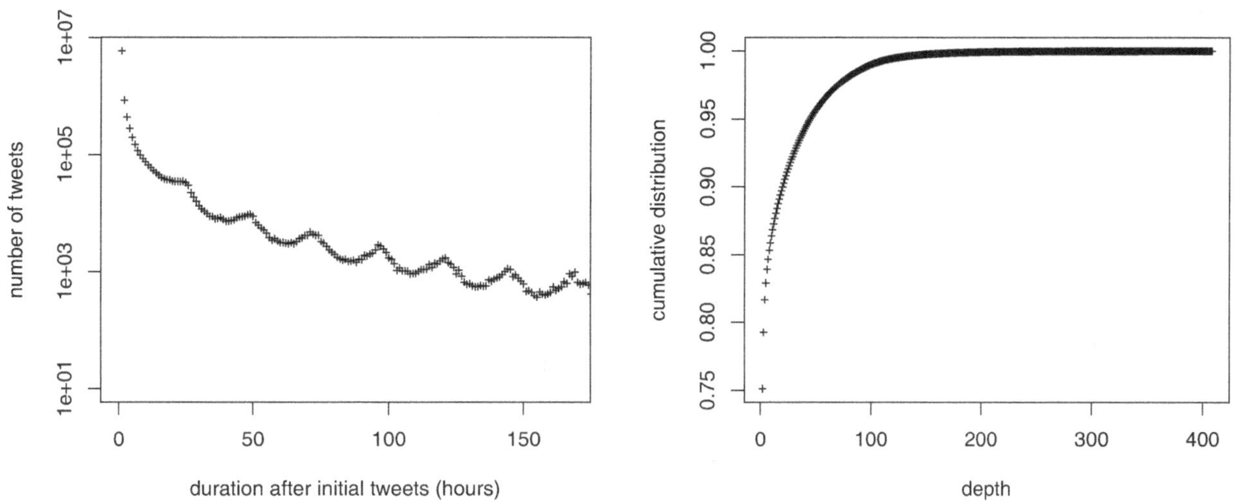

(a) Number of Tweets over Time

(b) Cumulative Distribution over Tree Depth

Figure 1: Statistics of Large Twitter Context Trees

them, 833 out of 40,583 Twitter context trees contain more than 1000 tweets, and the largest context tree contains 17,084 tweets. Based on these 40,583 context trees, we have some interesting observations as follows.

Given that Twitter is a real-time service, we first analyze the temporal growth of the Twitter context tree in Figure 1(a) where y-axis is the the number of tweets and x-axis is the *relative* temporal distance from the original tweets, measured by hours. Overall, about 63.18% of replies are generated within the first hour, which shows that Twitter can propagate information quite fast and a meaningful context tree can be formed very quickly. Interestingly, the number of replied tweets forms a declining wave curve over time. A close look at the two adjacent peaks shows that the gap is about 24 hours, which corresponds to the daily patterns of Twitter usage: there are more users during the days but less users during the late nights.

The next question is whether the tree structure can help the summarization task. Figure 1(b) shows the cumulative distribution of the number of tweets over depth in context trees, assuming the root of each tree has the depth of 0. Surprisingly, the structures of these Twitter context trees are highly skewed, and more than 75% of tweets are at depth 1. This means that most tweets reply to their corresponding root tweets directly, and the interactive dialogs are not popular on Twitter. In the other word, there is very few real dialog-based conversations on Twitter, therefore we prefer to call those trees as Twitter context trees, instead of Twitter conversations.

One presumable reason of the shallow tree structure is the loose organization of Twitter information, as Twitter fails to offer interesting replies for users to interact with, or provides little context of a reply for users to understand, as we discussed in Section 1. Although the deepest paths can reach 407 levels, those deep paths only account for a tiny fraction. Figure 1(b) suggests that that most context trees are wide and shallow. For the task of Twitter context summarization, it is difficult to leverage context tree structure information to extract a dialog snippet as the summary of the context tree. Therefore, in this paper, we ignore dialog information, and organize all tweets within a Twitter context tree as a stream of tweet candidates.

In addition, as the dialog information cannot be effectively used, the information extracted from each Twitter context tree is very limited. Therefore, it is necessary for us to leverage information beyond each individual context tree.

4. USER INFLUENCE MODELS

Twitter, as one of the most important micro-blogging platforms, contains rich user interaction information, which can be leveraged to improve Twitter context summarization. As the user interactions extracted from each Twitter context tree is limited, in this paper we mainly explore those user influence signals which can be derived from the data beyond each Twitter context tree. There are mainly two types of social influence models, called pairwise user influence model and global user influence model: the former considers pairwise influence between two Twitter users, while the latter investigates the influence among all Twitter users.

4.1 Granger Causality Influence Model

Granger Causality Influence Model is a time series based pairwise influence model for mining causality. The motivation of using this influence model for summarization is: if we could mine the causality relationship between two Twitter users based on time series data, we can know that a user u has strong influence on a user v; in this case, when u issues a tweet and causes a big Twitter context tree, those tweets in the context tree published by v are more likely to be a summary candidate than other tweets.

Granger Causality is originally proposed in the area of econometrics [12], and its basic idea is that a cause should be helpful in predicting its future effects, beyond what can be predicted solely based on its past values. That is to say, a time series data x is to *Granger cause* another time series data y, if and only if regressing for y in terms of both past values of y and x is statistically significantly more accurate than regressing for y in terms of past values of y only. Let $\{x_t\}_{t=1}^T$ to be lagged variables of x and $\{y_t\}_{t=1}^T$ for y, and let $\vec{x}_t$ denote, in general, $\langle x_i \rangle_{i=1}^t$. T is the predefined window size.

$$y_t \approx A \cdot \vec{y}_{t-1} + B \cdot \vec{x}_{t-1} \tag{1}$$

$$y_t \approx A \cdot \vec{y}_{t-1} \tag{2}$$

After performing these 2 regressions, and then applying a significance test, if the regression model from equation (1) is statistically significantly better than the regression model from equation (2), then x is called a Granger cause of y.

In particular, we implement Lasso-Granger method [1], which applies regression to the neighborhood selection problem, given the fact that the best regression result for that variable with the least squared error will have non-zero coefficients only for those variables in the neighborhood. The Lasso algorithm use an L1-penalty term, and its output $\vec{w}$ minimizes the sum of average squared error of regression, plus the L1-norm of the coefficients,

$$\vec{w} = \text{argmin} \frac{1}{n} \sum_{(\vec{x},y) \in S} |\vec{w} \cdot \vec{x} - y|^2 + \lambda ||\vec{w}||_1 \tag{3}$$

where S is the input data, n is the number of data points in S, and λ is a weight parameter to be tuned. Algorithm 1 summarizes the Lasso Granger method in details. We use $Lag(X, T)$ to denote the lagged version of data X; $FullyConnectedFeatureGraph(X)$ denotes the fully connected graph defined over the features; $Lasso(y, X^{lag})$ denotes the set of temporal variables receiving a non-zero coefficient by the Lasso algorithm.

Algorithm 1 Lasso Granger Method

Procedure: Lasso-Granger (X, T)

- $X^{lag} \leftarrow Lag(X, T)$
- $G = \langle V, E \rangle \leftarrow FullyConnectedFeatureGraph(X)$
- $w^y = Lasso(y, X^{lag})$, y is the root of Tree D
- **for** $(x, y) \in E$ **do**
  - orient (x, y) as $x \rightarrow y$, if $x_t \in w^y$ for some t but $y_t \notin w^x$ for all t
  - orient (x, y) as $y \rightarrow x$ if $y_t \in w^x$ for some t but $x_t \notin w^y$ for all t
  - place an un-oriented edge (x, y) $x \leftrightarrow y$, if $x_t \in w^y$ for some t and $y_t \in w^x$ for some t
  - place no edge between (x, y), otherwise
- **end for**
- **return** $G_{feature}^{causal}$

In this paper, we run Lasso Granger method for each Twitter context tree to explore the Granger cause between the Twitter user of root tweet and any replied Twitter user. We collect all tweets, from March 7th to March 20th 2011, posted by every Twitter user who appears in the 10 context trees, which is described on Section 6 in details. Overall, there are 6.5 million extra tweets collected, which is far beyond the local information within the context trees. We treat all tweets posted by a user within a day as one document, and run LDA [3] to generate a topic probability vector for each day, which is a data point in our time series data for the user. Empirically, we choose the LDA topic number to be 5, and set window size T to be 3, and then generate a feature vector, called Granger Causality influence feature for all the users.

4.2 Pagerank Influence Model

Pagerank Influence Model is a user influence model based on the relationship among Twitter users. It measures how influential a user is with respect to general Twitter users. There are mainly 3 different relationship among Twitter users, follower relationship, reply relationship, and retweet relationship. Follower relation attracts most existing researches [2, 16, 29]. Unfortunately, such a relationship is not readily available. What's more, [28] showed that reply or retweet graphs can carry more topical relevance than follower graph. Therefore, we focus on reply and retweet relationship in this paper. We construct the reply or retweet relations between users within the same context tree based on user-user activity, and all these relations are directed. For each user u, it has a directed edge to each user v if u has a reply or a retweet to v's tweet in our twitter data and thus we can have a global user graph G.

Intuitively, if a user has been replied or retweeted by many users, a natural assumption is that a tweet published by this user will likely influence all those users and thus its influence is higher. In the task of Twitter context summarization, those tweets whose authors have high influence would be preferred to be selected in the summary. To capture this, we build the following projected graph for twitter tree D: $G_D = (V_D, E_D)$, where V_D is the set of authors of tweets in D and E_D is the projected graph from G on V_D:

$$E_D = \{(u, v) | u \in V_D, v \in V_D, (u, v) \in G\}.$$

Thus, for each Twitter context tree, we can construct an adjacent matrix M to represent G_D. To capture the user influence, we apply the PageRank algorithm [4]: Assume $\hat{M}$ is row normalized matrix and we can compute the following equation as

$$\vec{\pi} = \vec{\pi} \cdot [(1 - \gamma)\hat{M} + \frac{\gamma}{|V_D|} \vec{e} \cdot \vec{e}^T],$$

while $\vec{\pi}$ is the vector of PageRank score, $\vec{e}^T$ is the transpose of $\vec{e}$, and $\vec{e}$ is a column vector with each entry as 1 and γ is a parameter (usually 0.15) to make the solution stable. Each entry in $\vec{\pi}$ corresponds to the estimation of the author's influence within the Twitter context tree.

5. SUMMARIZATION METHOD

Besides user influence signals introduced on Section 4, we also include text-based signals, popularity signals and temporal signals to provide a solid experimental baseline. In addition, we introduce how to utilize different types of signals in a supervised learning framework for summarization in details.

5.1 Text-based Signals

Traditional summarization tasks are purely text-based approaches and there are quite a few mature methods [15, 9, 17]. Among them, the centroid based method, although simple, is one of the most effective and robust ones for text-based summarization [22]. We will also compare it with many other text-based methods in the our task. In this paper, we assign scores to a candidate tweet based on the following two centroid-based methods. For each tweet d in a tree D, we represent it as a TFIDF vector $\vec{d}$ in the vector space model [24], and then compute similarity to the root vector $\vec{r}$, and similarity to the centroid vector $\vec{c}$, which is defined as

$$\vec{c} = \frac{\sum_{d \in D} \vec{d}}{|D|}.$$

We use the commonly used cosine similarity in our paper to assign two features for each d.

$$\cos(\vec{d}, \vec{r}) = \frac{\vec{d} \cdot \vec{r}}{||\vec{d}|| \cdot ||\vec{r}||} \text{ and } \cos(\vec{d}, \vec{c}) = \frac{\vec{d} \cdot \vec{c}}{||\vec{d}|| \cdot ||\vec{c}||}.$$

We thus name these features as *SimToRoot* and *Centroid* respectively, to leverage the text information: the similarity to the root tweet is to measure how much a tweet would be related to the initiator's content; the similarity to the centroid is to measure how representative a tweet is with respect to the whole tree.

5.2 Popularity Signals

Popularity is an important factor to Twitter context summarization. On the one hand, those popular tweets, if selected as part of the context summary, would benefit more users to find direct context; on the other hand, for those tweets with higher popularity, chances are that their quality is better. Although popularity does not immediately mean high quality but they can be positively correlated. In this paper, we consider 3 types of signals representing tweet popularity: number of replies, number of retweets, and number of followers for a given tweet's author. All these signals can be directly extracted from the Twitter context trees as features. Yet these popularity features are highly skewed, e.g., the followers of a popular elite Twitter user could reach tens of millions, while most of the long tail Twitter users barely have more than 100 followers. In this paper, we normalize these popularity signals with corresponding z-score,

$$z_i = \frac{x_i - \mu}{\sigma}$$

where μ is the mean of the vector $\vec{x} = [x_1, x_2, ...]$, and σ denotes its standard deviation.

5.3 Temporal Signals

Temporal signals can also provide valuable information for Twitter context summarization due the real-time characteristics of Twitter. According to Figure 1(a), 63.18% of replies are generated within the first hour, and the number of replies declines quickly over time. Therefore, for a context tree summary, its temporal distribution should be similar to the overall temporal distribution of the Twitter context tree. In this paper, we first fit the age of tweets in a context tree into an exponential distribution. Then for each tweet, we compute its temporal signal as the likelihood of sampling its age from the fitted exponential distribution. Intuitively, this will give a high score for those replies which appear earlier in the context tree.

Note that geographical information can be also considered as informative signals. We do not explore it in this paper mainly because the information is not available in our data set. The geographical information is usually associated with Twitter users (not individual tweet) and some past work [8] showed that only 26% of the users have their locations at the city level. Predicting the geographical information is possible but can be highly involved and we leave this exploration as future work.

5.4 Supervised Learning Framework

Given the above signals, we could convert them as features, then cast the Twitter context summarization task into a supervised learning problem. After training a model, we could predict a few tweets as its summary for all tweets in a new context tree. As the positive examples and negative examples in the training data are highly skewed, non linear SVM [5] performs poorly. In this paper, we choose Gradient Boosted Decision Tree (GBDT) algorithm [10] to learn a non-linear model.

GBDT is an additive regression algorithm consisting of an ensemble of trees, fitted to current residuals, gradients of the loss function, in a forward step-wise manner. It iteratively fits an additive model as:

$$f_r(x) = H_r(x; \Theta) + \lambda \sum_{r=1}^{H} \beta_r H_r(x; \Theta_r)$$

such that certain loss function $L(y_i, f_H(x+i))$ is minimized, where $H_r(x; \Theta_r)$ is a tree H at iteration r, weighted by parameter β_r, with a finite number of parameters, Θ_r and λ is the learning rate. At iteration r, tree $H_r(x; \beta)$ is induced to fit the negative gradient by least squares. That is

$$\hat{\Theta} := \operatorname{argmin}_{\beta} \sum_{i}^{N} (-G_{ir} - \beta_r H_r(x_i); \Theta)^2$$

where G_{ir} is the gradient over current prediction function

$$G_{ir} = \left. \frac{\partial L(y_i, f(x_i))}{\partial f(x_i)} \right|_{f=f_{r-1}}$$

The optimal weights of trees β_t are determined by

$$\beta_r = \operatorname{argmin}_{\beta} \sum_{i}^{N} L(y_i, f_{r-1}(x_i) + \beta H(x_i, \theta))$$

6. EDITORIAL DATA SET

To the best of our knowledge, there is no data set available to evaluate Twitter context summarization. Thus, we conduct a pilot study to construct such an editorial data set in our work.

As celebrities are highly influential in Twitter [30], celebrities initiated tweets would lead to large context trees. We manually select 10 Twitter context trees from March 7th to March 20th, 2011. Among these 10 context trees, 4 are initiated by Lady Gaga, who is the most popular elite user on Twitter, and 6 are initiated by Justin Bieber, who is extremely popular among teenagers. From another perspective, 4 out of 10 context trees are about Japan Tohoku earthquake and tsunami, another 4 context trees are related to music shows, while the remaining 2 are just gossip context trees. The largest context tree contains 11,394 tweets, and the smallest context tree includes 1,106 tweets. On average, there are 4,265 tweets among these 10 context trees, yet they are very wide and shallow: assuming the root of each tree has the depth of 0, 91.43% of these tweets are at depth 1, although the deepest branch has a depth of 54, the average depth is only 1.33.

-	Editor 1	Editor 2	Editor 3	Editor 4	Editor 5
Editor 1	-	0.295	0.239	0.307	0.239
Editor 2	0.433	-	0.317	0.433	0.283
Editor 3	0.292	0.264	-	0.361	0.236
Editor 4	0.458	0.441	0.441	-	0.305
Editor 5	0.276	0.224	0.224	0.237	-
Consensus	**0.618**	**0.552**	**0.539**	**0.618**	**0.447**

Table 1: Consistency among the editors and with the Consensus.

Time	Tweet Content
00:00	#prayforjapan http://youtu.be/o9tJW9MDs2M
02:03	@justinbieber i can't listen to #pray without crying; i hope people are thinking about #japan with your song in mind.
03:09	@justinbieber I love that you care for japan and they are in everyones prayers lets get others to notice the devastation it has caused #PRAY
04:43	@justinbieber An assembly at school was about you and your charity work...it changed so many peoples opinions <3 #prayforjapan x
06:26	@justinbieber PRAY is by far one of the most genuine songs I've heard in a while. Well played sir. #prayforjapan
07:00	@justinbieber Don't be afraid of how big the TSUNAMI is. Show to the Tsunami how BIG your GOD is. Lets #PRAYFORJAPAN. Have faith. trust GOD
16:34	@justinbieber Hi! I live in Tokyo, Japan. We are still scared. We need your help!! #NeverSayNever

Table 2: An Example of Twitter context tree Summary

One goal of this pilot study is to assess the difficulty of generating a summary by human. Thus, we only focus on the 10 trees but ask 5 human editors for judgements for every tree to study the inter-editor agreement. In our guideline, we ask each human editor to first read the root tweet and open any URL inside to have a sense of what the root tweet is about. Then, the editor scans through all candidate tweets to get a sense of the overall set of data. Finally, the editor selects 5 to 10 tweets ordered sequentially as the summary, which respond or extend the original tweets by providing extra information about it. Thus, for each tree, we will have 5 independent judgements. Comparing with many other data sets in NLP and IR community, this data set is relatively small. However, it is very difficult and time-consuming to generate such a manual labeled data set, as each editor need to look through all tweets in a context tree to get a sense of topic at the beginning, and then go through each tweet carefully according to previously selected tweets to avoid duplication in the summary.

We study the inter-editor agreement by computing the asymmetric consistency measure as follows. Given two editors and their selected summary sets S_1 and S_2, the two consistency measures are

$$\frac{|S_1 \bigcap S_2|}{|S_1|} \text{ and } \frac{|S_1 \bigcap S_2|}{|S_2|}.$$

Table 1 indicates the overall consistencies among these 5 editors. For example, for the pair of <Editor 1, Editor 2>, 0.295 means 29.5% sentences in the summary of Editor 1 are also included in the summary of Editor 2. Comparing with document summarization such as [27], Table 1 shows that Twitter context summarization is more difficult to human editors. Compared with a document which usually is written by a couple of authors in a more coherent way, a Twitter context tree is informal and less coherent given that many users participate in the context tree without knowing what others have talked about.

In order to combat the relatively low consistency among different editors, we construct a consensus judgement set by only including those tweets which are selected by at least 2 editors. We end up with 6 to 9 tweets for each context tree. In the last row of Table 1, we show the consistency between the consensus and all the 5 editors. We can see that the consistency is improved a lot. In our experiments, we use the consensus data set as our ground truth to evaluate different methods.

Table 2 shows an example of Twitter context summary. Given a very short tweet by Justin Bieber, which only contains a hashtag and a URL, without clicking the URL, most of the users do not know what Justin is talking about. These 6 replied tweets selected by human editors extend the original tweets from diverse perspectives, which provide users enough context information to understand the original tweet. In addition, 5 out of 6 summary tweets are generated within the first 10 minutes, which convinces the importance of the temporal signal.

7. EXPERIMENTS

We conduct our experiments using the editorial data set described in Section 6. Our main goal is to evaluate the usefulness of the user influence signals proposed for the Twitter context summarization task. As the root tweet provide critical information for a context tree, we should always keep the root tweet as part of the summary. In our experiment, we exclude the root tweet from both the editorial data sets and automatic generated summaries for summarization evaluation.

7.1 Evaluation Metrics

We use the ROUGE [18] package[1] to evaluate the generated summaries. ROUGE measures the overlapping units between the human labeled ground truth summaries and the algorithmic generated ones. The units can be n-grams or word sequences. Formally, given a summary S which consists of a few sentences and a human selected summary S_{human}, ROUGE-n metrics are defined as:

$$\text{Rec(ROUGE-n)} = \frac{\sum_{s\in S_{\text{human}}}\sum_{n\text{-gram}\in s}\text{count}_{\text{match}}(n\text{-gram})}{\sum_{s\in S_{\text{human}}}\sum_{n\text{-gram}\in s}\text{count}(n\text{-gram})}$$

$$\text{Prec(ROUGE-n)} = \frac{\sum_{s\in S_{\text{human}}}\sum_{n\text{-gram}\in s}\text{count}_{\text{match}}(n\text{-gram})}{\sum_{s\in S}\sum_{n\text{-gram}\in s}\text{count}(n\text{-gram})}$$

$$\text{F(ROUGE-n)} = \frac{2\times\text{Prec(ROUGE-n)}\times\text{Rec(ROUGE-n)}}{\text{Prec(ROUGE-n)}+\text{Rec(ROUGE-n)}}$$

where $\text{count}_{\text{match}}(n\text{-gram})$ is the maximum number of n-gram co-occurring in both S and S_{human}; $\text{count}(n\text{-gram})$ is the number of n-grams in S.

In this paper, we use ROUGE-1 and ROUGE-2 as two instantiations of ROUGE-n metrics. In addition, we also use the ROUGE-L which use the longest common subsequence as the units in ROUGE metrics.

7.2 Methods for Comparison

Many different methods have been proposed for document summarization and a few packages are available for text-based summarization tasks. In this paper, we compare with the following text-based summarization method:

- Centroid: We use the single centroid feature which are described in Section 5.1. Tweets are ranked based on this feature.
- SimToRoot: Similarly, we can use the single SimToRoot feature described in Section 5.1 and rank all the tweets accordingly.
- Linear: We linearly combine Centroid and SimToRoot together with a parameter α. In our experiment we set $\alpha = 0.8$ which is the optimal value based on cross-validation.
- Mead: Mead[2] is a publicly available summarization package designed for single document or multi-document summarization [22]. It considers multiple information for each sentence, including text representativeness, sentence position, sentence length, etc. To use Mead, we treat each twitter tree as a document: Each tweet is a sentence and all the tweets are ordered by their publishing time. We apply the Mead package with their default setting to generate summaries.
- LexRank: LexRank[3] builds a sentence to sentence graph and use the centrality to select sentences [9]. This method has been included in the Mead package and we use the implementation in the package.
- SVD: Another method is based on the singular value decomposition [11]. To adapt this method, we construct a tweet by term matrix using the TF-IDF vectors of all tweets in a context tree. SVD is applied on this matrix, and the candidate tweets are selected as follows: each entry in a left eigenvector corresponds to a tweet. Starting from the most significant one, select the tweet which has the highest entry value and then iterate to the next left eigenvector. In this way, a ranked list of tweets will be output.

[1]http://berouge.com

[2]http://www.summarization.com/mead/

[3]http://clair.si.umich.edu/clair/lexrank/

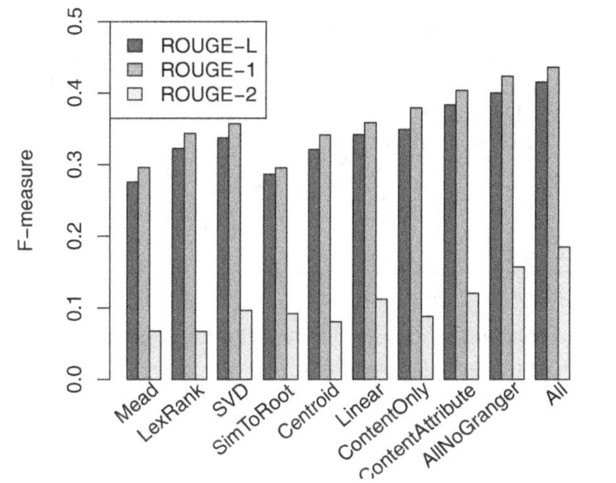

Figure 2: Overall comparison of different methods.

To incorporate user influence information as features on top of text related features, we use GBDT to train and test with 10-fold cross-validation. We also tried SVM with different non-linear kernels, their performance is much worse than GBDT. To demonstrate the usefulness of different type of user interaction features, we try different feature combinations as follows:

- ContentOnly: We only use text-related features defined in Section 5.1.
- ContentAttribute: We combine text-based features, popularity features and temporal features, which are described in Section 5.
- AllNoGranger: This variant use all the features except the Granger causality influence feature.
- All: We use all features, including text-based, popularity, temporal, and user influence features together in our learning setting.

7.3 Experimental Results

We report our experimental results in this subsection. For each summarization method, we have a rank list of sentences. Thus, the ROUGE F-measure can be defined over any top m sentences. In the following, unless stated explicitly, we use F-measure@10 as the primary metric for comparison.

7.3.1 Overall Comparison

In Figure 2, we compare all the methods using the F-measure of all three ROUGE metrics. The first 7 methods are text-based baselines and the last 3 methods incorporate user interaction information. From this figure, we have the following observations: (1) All the text-based approaches perform relatively worse than learning based methods. Among all the text-based ones, the Linear is the best

Table 3: **Improvement over the Linear method. Notation * and ** means the improvement over the Linear method are significant at level 0.1 and 0.05; † means the improvement over the ContentAttribute method are significant at level 0.1**

	ContentAttribute	AllNoGranger	All
ROUGE-L	12.1%*	17.0%*	21.4%**†
ROUGE-1	12.5%*	17.9%*	21.4%**†
ROUGE-2	7.0%	39.7%	64.4%*

one and the next to it is the SVD method. Comparing Linear with SimToRoot and Centroid, the performance is improved. This shows that both information are useful in our summarization. (2) The last 3 methods are much better than all the text-based methods. For example, using ROUGE-L as the metric, we can improve over the Linear method 12% by ContentAttribute, 17% by AllNoGranger, and 21% by All. In Table 3, we compute the relative improvement over the Linear method for the last 3 methods. Most of the improvement are significant at level 0.1. (3) We also compare among the last three methods. It can be seen that the global user influence information can help. The t-test shows that the improvement of All over ContentAttribute is significant at level 0.1, which AllNoGranger is not significant. This results indicate the usefulness of our causality based influence model.

As we observed in Table 3, ROUGE-2 is not significant even if the improvement is about 40%. To understand this, we plot the performance of the four methods compared in Table 3 for each query in Figure 3. By comparing the figures horizontally, we can see that ROUGE-2 has extremely large variance over 10 different Twitter context trees. This observation may be due to the informally formatted tweets. For example, some tweets usually have repeated words like "love love love" to express their emotions, some Internet words like "lol", etc. All these could make the text-based ROUGE-2 less stable.

7.3.2 The Impact of Summary Length

The F-measure is a harmonic mean of precision and recall. Different length of summary will yield different results. In Figure 4, we plot the F-measure@N using the ROUGE-L as the metric where we vary N from 1 to 20. As we can see in this figure, the F-measure increases along with the the summary length. It peaks at around N=10 and becomes saturated or drops slightly when N is larger than 10. Intuitively, when the length is small, we will have a high precision but lower recall. A long summary can improve the recall but decrease the precision. Compared with the Linear method, all our method is more robust along with N. In our editorial data set, we have about 6 to 9 tweets selected by the editors. This means that many tweets are not informative. In our automatic summarization tasks, the results suggests that setting N = 10 is a good choice to balance precision and recall.

7.4 Discussions

A good summary should have good quality but with less redundancy. In all of our methods, we do not consider the diversity. Then the question is whether diversification techniques such as Maximum Margin Relevance (MMR) [6] can benefit a method. In this section, we take the top 50 tweets

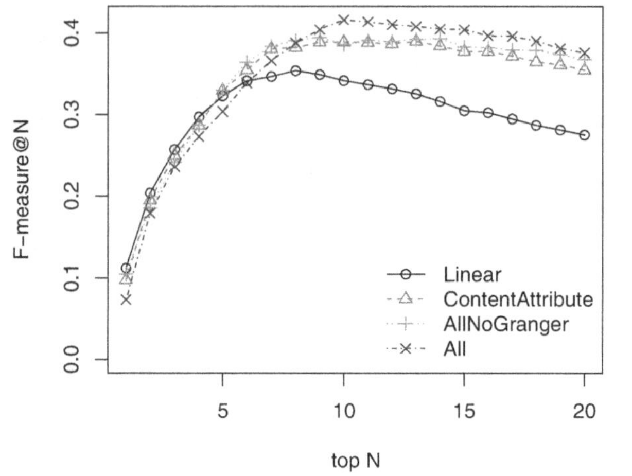

Figure 4: F-measure along with the top N results.

Table 4: The average pairwise similarity between tweets in a summary.

	Linear	AllNoGranger	All
Mean	0.4722	0.0811	0.0864
Stdev	0.2080	0.0392	0.0474

from the ranked list of a method and take this as an input for MMR. We use the following implementation to diversify the results:

$$(1-\lambda)\text{score}(t) - \lambda \max_{\tau \in S}\{\cos(\vec{t}, \vec{\tau})\}$$

where score(t) is the output score of t from a method, S is the set of tweets already selected, λ is the parameter to control the degree of diversity. In MMR, we use the cosine similarity over the tweet text features to measure the redundancy. MMR is a greedy algorithm and we set S as empty in the beginning. Iteratively, we select a tweet which has the maximum marginal value in the above formula, until we obtain 10 tweets.

We compare the impact of MMR on different methods in Figure 5 using the ROUGE-L as the metric. From this figure, we can see that only the Linear method can benefit from the diversity component, while the other two can not. In order to understand this, we compute the average pairwise similarity among the top 10 results of a summary and compare the three methods based on it. The results are shown in Table 4. Clearly, the Linear method is much more redundant compared with our methods. Even though our learning-based methods does not explicitly model the diversity, our training examples are diversified and the user influence features we proposed can contribute to model diversity.

In this paper, we use the GBDT algorithm for learning. We also tried to use SVM based methods[5], but due to the small amount of positive examples and the high non-linear property of our learning task, SVM yielded pretty poor results and take a long time to converge. GBDT is a boosting approach, we show the impact of decision tree numbers in Figure 6. We can see that the performance increases along with the number of trees and drops afterwards. This means that GBDT can gradually pick-up the signals from our fea-

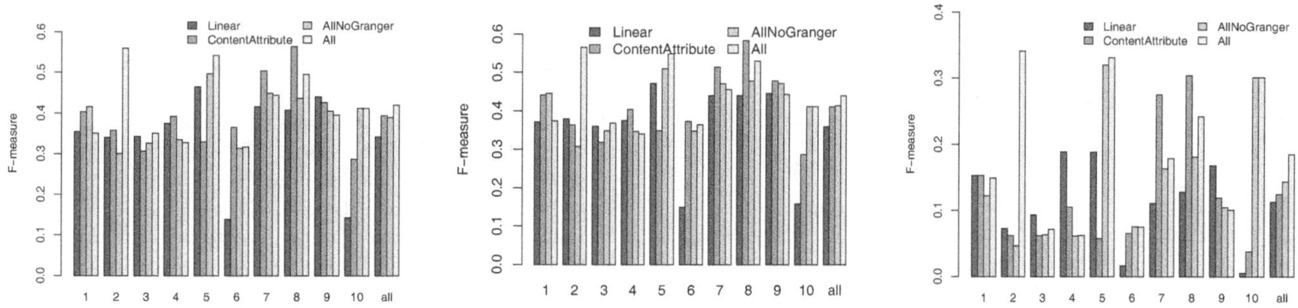

(a) ROUGE-L (b) ROUGE-1 (c) ROUGE-2

Figure 3: Results on each individual twitter context tree.

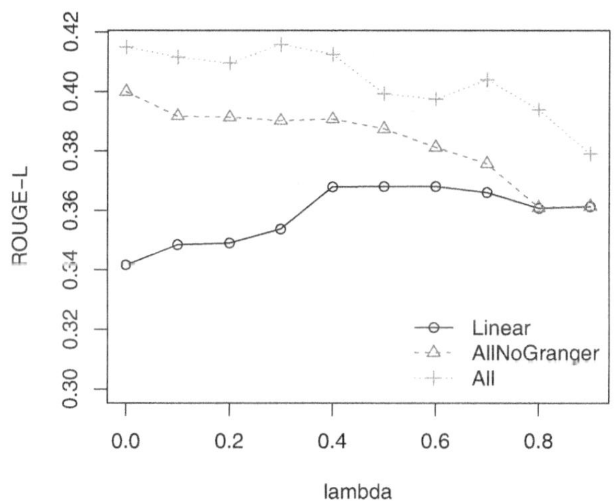

Figure 5: The impact of MMR on ROUGE-L.

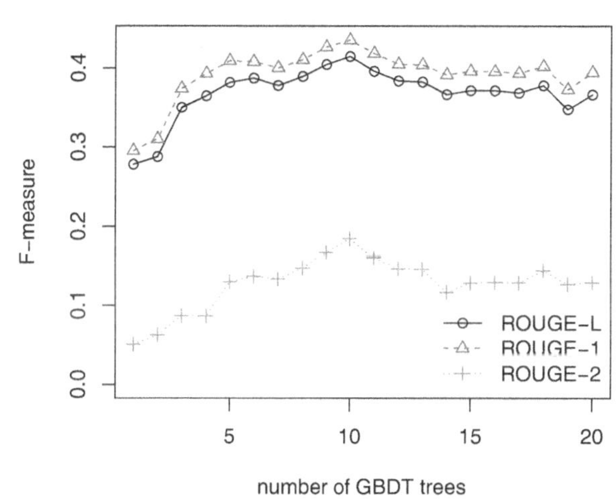

Figure 6: Performance change along with the number of decision trees in GBDT.

tures for the summarization task. Combined with the MMR results, this result shows that GBDT is an effective to learn to generate a summary with diversity incorporated.

8. CONCLUSION AND FUTURE WORK

In this paper, we propose the problem of the Twitter context summarization, which is to help users get more context information when using Twitter. Traditional summarization methods only consider text information, and we leverage pairwise and global user influence models to improve text-based summarization. All signals are converted into features, and we cast Twitter context summarization into a supervised learning problem. To evaluate our methods, we collect an editorial data set in which 5 human editors are employed to generate a summary for each context tree. Analysis shows that twitter summarization is more difficult than general document summarization. Based on the editorial data set, our experimental results show that user influence information is very helpful to generate a high quality summary for each Twitter context tree. In particular, Granger Causality influence model provides the most effective user influence feature among all.

Our work can be extended as follows. As a supervised learning method requires more editorial data set, how to provide a semi-supervised method, which is learned from user engagement instead of editorial labels, is a natural direction in the next step. In addition, it is valid to consider how to leverage geographical information for more complicated twitter context summarization. In the future, it will be interesting to study whether the same methodology can be used for other user-generated contents such as comments on news articles or comments on Facebook pages. Furthermore, how to incorporate other information such as the readability of tweets and the contents of contained URLs into summarization is also an interesting and challenging research direction.

9. ACKNOWLEDGMENTS

This research was supported by the NSF research grants IIS-1134990 and the U.S. Defense Advanced Research Projects Agency (DARPA) award No. W911NF-12-1-0034. The views and conclusions contained herein are those of the authors and should not be interpreted as representing the official policies or endorsements, either expressed or implied, of any of the above organizations or any person connected with them.

10. REFERENCES

[1] A. Arnold, Y. Liu, and N. Abe. Temporal causal modeling with graphical granger methods. In *Proceedings of the ACM Conference on Knowledge Discovery and Data Mining (KDD)*, pages 66–75, 2007.

[2] E. Bakshy, J. M. Hofman, W. A. Mason, and D. J. Watts. Everyone's an influencer: quantifying influence on twitter. In *Proceedings of International conference on Web Search and Data Mining (WSDM)*, 2011.

[3] D. M. Blei, A. Y. Ng, and M. I. Jordan:. Latent dirichlet allocation. *Journal of Machine Learning Research*, 3:993–1022, 2003.

[4] S. Brin and L. Page. The anatomy of a large-scale hypertextual web search engine. *Proceedings of International Conference on World Wide Web (WWW)*, 1998.

[5] C. J. C. Burges. A tutorial on support vector machines for pattern recognition. *Data Mining and Knowledge Discovery*, 2(2):121–167, 1998.

[6] J. G. Carbonell and J. Goldstein. The use of mmr, diversity-based reranking for reordering documents and producing summaries. In *Proceedings of the Annual ACM SIGIR Conference*, pages 335–336, 1998.

[7] D. Chakrabarti and K. Punera. Event summarization using tweets. In *Proceedings of ICWSM*, 2011.

[8] Z. Cheng, J. Caverlee, and K. Lee. You are where you tweet: a content-based approach to geo-locating twitter users. In *Proceedings of the 19th ACM international conference on Information and knowledge management*, CIKM '10, pages 759–768, 2010.

[9] G. Erkan and D. R. Radev. Lexrank: Graph-based lexical centrality as salience in text summarization. *Journal of Artificial Intelligence Research (JAIR)*, 22:457–479, 2004.

[10] J. H. Friedman. Greedy function approximation: A gradient boosting machine. *Annals of Statistics*, 29(5):1189–1232, 2001.

[11] Y. Gong and X. Liu. Video summarization and retrieval using singular value decomposition. In *Multimedia Systems, Vol 9*, pages 157–168, 2003.

[12] C. W. J. Granger. Investigating causal relations by econometric models and cross-spectral methods. In *Econometrica*, pages 37: 424–438l, 1969.

[13] J. E. Hopcroft, T. Lou, and J. Tang. Who will follow you back?: reciprocal relationship prediction. In *Proceedings of ACM International Conference on Information and Knowledge Management (CIKM)*, pages 1137–1146, 2011.

[14] D. Inouye and J. K. Kalita. Comparing twitter summarization algorithms for multiple post summaries. In *Proceedings of SocialCom/PASSAT*, pages 298–306, 2011.

[15] K. S. Jones. Automatic summarising: The state of the art. In *Information Processing and Management*, pages 1449–1481, 2007.

[16] H. Kwak, C. Lee, H. Park, and S. B. Moon. What is twitter, a social network or a news media. In *Proceedings of 19th International World Wide Web Conference (WWW)*, 2010.

[17] C.-Y. Lin. From single to multi-document summarization. In *Proceedings of the Annual Meeting of the Association for Computational Linguistics (ACL)*, 2002.

[18] C.-Y. Lin. Rouge: a package for automatic evaluation of summaries. In *Proceedings of the Workshop on Text Summarization Branches Out (WAS)*, 2004.

[19] J. Liu, Y. Cao, C.-Y. Lin, Y. Huang, and M. Zhou. Low-quality product review detection in opinion summarization. In *Proceedings of the Conference on Empirical Methods on Natural Language Processing (EMNLP)*, pages 334–342, 2007.

[20] B. O'Connor, M. Krieger, and D. Ahn. Tweetmotif: Exploratory search and topic summarization for twitter. In *Proceedings of ICWSM*, 2010.

[21] S. Petrovic, M. Osborne, and V. Lavrenko. Streaming first story detection with application to twitter. In *Proceedings of HLT-NAACL*, pages 181–189, 2010.

[22] D. R. Radev, H. Jing, M. Sty, and D. Tam. Centroid-based summarization of multiple documents. *Information Processing and Management*, 40(6):919–938, 2004.

[23] A. Ritter, C. Cherry, and B. Dolan. Unsupervised modeling of twitter conversations. In *Proceedings of HLT-NAACL*, pages 172–180, 2010.

[24] G. Salton, A. Wong, and C. S. Yang. A vector space model for automatic indexing. *Communications of the ACM*, 18(11):613–620, 1975.

[25] B. Sharifi, M.-A. Hutton, and J. K. Kalita. Summarizing microblogs automatically. In *Proceedings of HLT-NAACL*, pages 685–688, 2010.

[26] C. Shen and T. Li. Learning to rank for query-focused multi-document summarization. In *Proceedings of ICDM*, 2011.

[27] J.-T. Sun, D. Shen, H.-J. Zeng, Q. Yang, Y. Lu, and Z. Chen. Web-page summarization using clickthrough data. In *Proceedings of the Annual ACM SIGIR Conference*, pages 194–201, 2005.

[28] M. J. Welch, U. Schonfeld, D. He, and J. Cho. Topical semantics of twitter links. In *Proceedings of the fourth ACM international conference on Web search and data mining*, WSDM '11, pages 327–336, 2011.

[29] J. Weng, E.-P. Lim, J. Jiang, and Q. He. Twitterrank: finding topic-sensitive influential twitterers. In *Proceedings of International conference on Web Search and Data Mining (WSDM)*, pages 1137–1146, 2010.

[30] S. Wu, J. M. Hofman, W. A. Mason, and D. J. Watts. Who says what to whom on twitter. In *Proceedings of International World Wide Web Conference (WWW)*, 2011.

[31] R. Yan, L. Kong, C. Huang, X. Wan, X. Li, and Y. Zhang. Timeline generation through evolutionary trans-temporal summarization. In *Proceedings of the Conference on Empirical Methods on Natural Language Processing (EMNLP)*, pages 433–443, 2011.

Exploiting Social Relations for Sentiment Analysis in Microblogging

Xia Hu†, Lei Tang‡, Jiliang Tang†, Huan Liu†
†Arizona State University, Tempe, AZ 85287, USA
‡@WalmartLabs, San Bruno, CA 94066, USA
{xiahu, jiliang.tang, huan.liu}@asu.edu, leitang@acm.org

ABSTRACT

Microblogging, like Twitter[1], has become a popular platform of human expressions, through which users can easily produce content on breaking news, public events, or products. The massive amount of microblogging data is a useful and timely source that carries mass sentiment and opinions on various topics. Existing sentiment analysis approaches often assume that texts are independent and identically distributed (i.i.d.), usually focusing on building a sophisticated feature space to handle noisy and short messages, without taking advantage of the fact that the microblogs are networked data. Inspired by the social sciences findings that sentiment consistency and emotional contagion are observed in social networks, we investigate whether social relations can help sentiment analysis by proposing a Sociological Approach to handling Noisy and short Texts (*SANT*) for sentiment classification. In particular, we present a mathematical optimization formulation that incorporates the sentiment consistency and emotional contagion theories into the supervised learning process; and utilize sparse learning to tackle noisy texts in microblogging. An empirical study of two real-world Twitter datasets shows the superior performance of our framework in handling noisy and short tweets.

Categories and Subject Descriptors

H.3.3 [**Information Storage and Retrieval**]: Information Search and Retrieval—*Classification*; I.2.7 [**Artificial Intelligence**]: Natural Language Processing

General Terms

Algorithm, Performance, Experimentation

Keywords

Sentiment Classification, Microblogging, Twitter, Noisy and Short Texts, Social Context, Social Correlation

[1]`https://twitter.com/`

WSDM '13, February 4–8, 2013, Rome, Italy.

1. INTRODUCTION

Microblogging services are extensively used to share information or opinions in various domains. With the growing availability of such an opinion-rich resource, it attracts much attention from those who seek to understand the opinions of individuals, or to gauge aggregated sentiment of mass populations. For example, advertisers may want to target users who are enthusiastic about a brand or a product in order to launch a successful social media campaign. Aid agencies from around the world would like to monitor sentiment evolutions before, during, and after crisis to assist recovery and provide disaster relief. The sheer volumes of microblogging data present opportunities and challenges for sentiment analysis of these noisy and short texts.

Sentiment analysis has been extensively studied for product and movie reviews [32], which differ substantially from microblogging data. Unlike standard texts with many words that help gather sufficient statistics, the texts in microblogging only consist of a few phrases or 1-2 sentences. Also, when composing a microblogging message, users may use or coin new abbreviations or acronyms that seldom appear in conventional text documents. For example, messages like "It is cooooooool", "OMG :-(", are intuitive and popular in microblogging, but some are not formal words. It is difficult for machines to accurately identify the semantic meanings of these messages, though they provide convenience in quick and instant communications for human beings. Existing methods [2, 8] rely on pre-defined sentiment vocabularies [39], which are highly domain-specific.

Meanwhile, microblogging platforms often provide additional information other than text. For example, in Figure 1, we depict two kinds of data available in microblogging. Figure 1(a) shows the content of messages, in the form of a message-feature matrix. Traditional methods measure the similarity between text documents (messages) purely based on content information. A distinct feature of microblogging messages is that they are potentially networked through user connections, which may contain useful semantic clues that are not available in purely text-based methods. Besides content information, relations between messages can be represented via a user-message matrix and a user-user interaction matrix, as shown in Figure 1(b). Traditional methods, if applied directly to the microblogging data, do not utilize the social relation information.

In social sciences, it is well-established that emotions and sentiments play a distinct role in our social life and correlate with our social connections. When experiencing emotions, people do not generally keep the emotions to themselves,

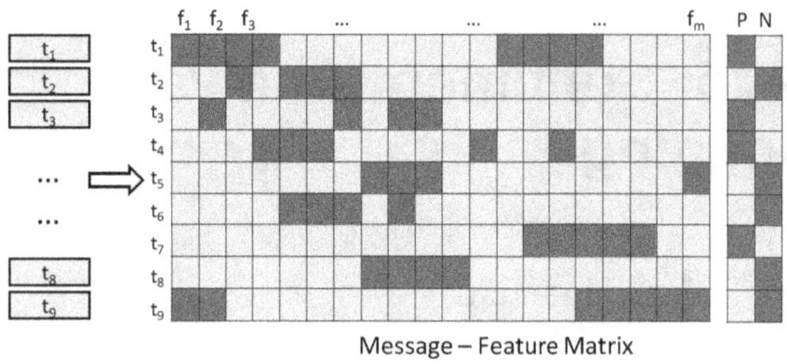

(a) Data Representation of Message Content

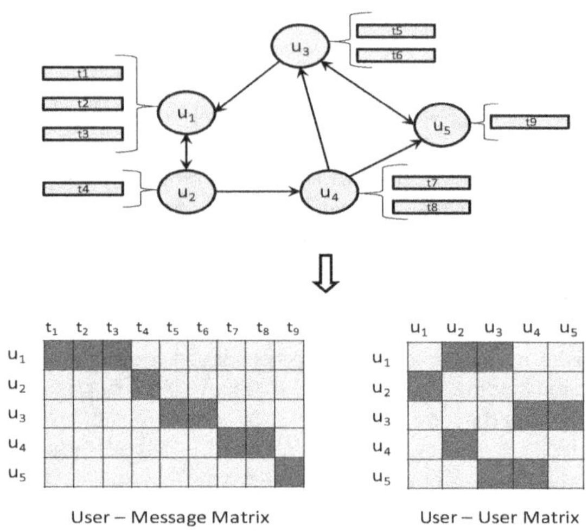

(b) Data Representation of Social Relations

Figure 1: Data Representation of Text and Social Relation Information in Microblogging

but rather, they tend to *show* them [19]. Also, people tend to "catch" others' emotions as a consequence of facial, vocal, and postural feedback, which has been recognized as *emotional contagion* [10] in social sciences. Emotional contagion may be important in personal relationships because "it fosters behavioral synchrony and the tracking of the feelings of others moment-to-moment even when individuals are not explicitly attending to this information" [10]. As a consequence of emotional contagion, Fowler and Christakis [6] reported the spread of happiness in a social network. Two social processes, selection and influence, are proposed to explain the phenomenon [22]: people befriend others who are similar to them (*Homophily* [26]), or they become more similar to their friends over time (*Social Influence* [25]). Both explanations suggest that connected individuals are more likely to have similar behaviors or hold similar opinions. Inspired by this sociological observation, we explore the utilization of social relation information to facilitate sentiment analysis in the context of microblogging.

In this paper, we aim to provide a supervised approach to sentiment analysis in microblogging by taking advantage of social relation information in tackling the noisy nature of the messages. In particular, we first investigate whether the social theories exist in microblogging data. Then we discuss how the social relations could be modeled and utilized for supervised sentiment analysis. Finally, we conduct extensive experiments to verify the proposed model. The main contributions of this paper are as follows:

- We formally define the problem of sentiment analysis in microblogging to enable the utilization of social relations for sentiment analysis;
- By verifying the existence of two social theories in microblogging, we build sentiment relations between messages via social relations;
- We present a novel supervised method to tackle the noisy and short texts by integrating sentiment relations between the texts; and
- We empirically evaluate the proposed *SANT* framework on real-world Twitter datasets and elaborate the effects of social relationships on sentiment analysis.

The remainder of this paper is organized as follows. In Section 2, we review related work. In Section 3, we formally define the problem we study. In Section 4, we conduct a study to verify the social theories. In Section 5, we propose a novel framework *SANT* for supervised sentiment analysis. In Section 7, we report empirical results. We conclude and present the future work in Section 8.

2. RELATED WORK

Recently, sentiment analysis on microblogging, which is considered to be an opinion-rich resource, has gained huge popularity and attracted researchers from many disciplines [3, 18, 20, 30]. Bollen et al. [3] proposed to measure the sentiments on Twitter over time, and compared the correlation between sentiments and major events, including the stock market, crude oil prices, elections and Thanksgiving. Also, Kim et al. [20] examined a tweet dataset about Michael Jackson's death to gain insight into how emotion is expressed on Twitter. O'Connor et al. [30] used sentiment analysis to automatically label the sentiments of tweets about politicians, and found strong correlation between the aggregated sentiment and the manually collected poll ratings.

Sentiment classification has been studied for years on various text corpus, like newspaper articles [33], movie reviews [31], and product reviews [5, 11, 23]. The basic idea of the methods is to build a sophisticated feature space, which can effectively represent the sentiment status of the texts. Existing methods, which are designed for traditional i.i.d. text data, cannot effectively make use of the abundant social relation information contained in microblogging. Following the methods for traditional texts, there are some existing efforts in the community on the microblogging data. Alec et al. [8] presented the results of machine learning algorithms for classifying the sentiments of Twitter messages using distant supervision. Barbosa and Feng [2] explored the linguistic characteristics of how tweets are written and the meta-information of words for sentiment classification. The ideas of the methods are consistent with traditional ones, ignoring the social relation information.

Some efforts have been made to explore the effect of external information sources [37, 41], especially social network information [35, 36], on sentiment analysis. Speriosu et al. [35] proposed to incorporate labels from a maximum entropy classifier, in combination with the Twitter follower graph. They simply used a user's followers as separate features and combined them with the content matrix. Tan et al. [36] proposed to improve user-level sentiment analysis of different topics [16] by incorporating social network information. However, our task is document-level sentiment classification, which has finer granularity than their work. In addition, our method simultaneously utilizes social relation information and handles noisy, short texts in microblogging.

3. PROBLEM STATEMENT

The problem we study in this paper is different from traditional sentiment classification since the latter normally only considers the content information. In this section, we first present the notations and then formally define the problem of sentiment classification on microblogging messages.

We use boldface uppercase letters (e.g., $\mathbf{A}$) to denote matrices, boldface lowercase letters (e.g., $\mathbf{a}$) to denote vectors, and lowercase letters (e.g., a) to denote scalars. The entry at the ith row and j^{th} column of a matrix $\mathbf{A}$ is denoted as $\mathbf{A}_{ij}$. $\mathbf{A}_{i*}$ and $\mathbf{A}_{*j}$ denote the ith row and j^{th} column of a matrix $\mathbf{A}$, respectively. $\|\mathbf{A}\|_1$ is the ℓ_1-norm and $\|\mathbf{A}\|_F$ is the Frobenius norm of matrix $\mathbf{A}$. Specifically, $\|\mathbf{A}\|_1 = \sum_{i=1}^{m}\sum_{j=1}^{n}|\mathbf{A}_{ij}|$ and $\|\mathbf{A}\|_F = \sqrt{\sum_{i=1}^{m}\sum_{j=1}^{n}|\mathbf{A}_{ij}|^2}$.

Given a corpus $\mathbf{T} = [\mathbf{X}, \mathbf{Y}] \in \mathbb{R}^{n\times(m+c)}$, where $\mathbf{X} \in \mathbb{R}^{n\times m}$ is the content matrix, $\mathbf{Y} \in \mathbb{R}^{n\times c}$ is the sentiment label matrix, n is the number of messages, m is the number of features and c is number of sentiments, as shown in Figure 1(a). For each message in the corpus $\mathbf{T} = \{\mathbf{t}_1, \mathbf{t}_2, \dots, \mathbf{t}_n\}$, $\mathbf{t}_i = (\mathbf{x}_i, \mathbf{y}_i) \in \mathbb{R}^{m+c}$ consists of microblogging message content and sentiment label, where $\mathbf{x}_i \in \mathbb{R}^m$ is the message feature vector and $\mathbf{y}_i \in \mathbb{R}^c$ is the sentiment label vector. Following previous work [8, 35], in this paper, we focus on polarity sentiment classification, i.e., $c = 2$. It is practical to extend this setting to a multi-class sentiment classification task. $\mathbf{u} = \{u_1, u_2, \dots, u_d\}$ is the user set, where d is the number of distinct users in the corpus. $\mathbf{U} \in \mathbb{R}^{d\times n}$ is a user-message matrix, as shown as the left matrix in Figure 1(b). In the user-message matrix, $\mathbf{U}_{ij} = 1$ (red frame in the figure) denotes that message $\mathbf{t}_j$ is posted by user u_i. $\mathbf{F} \in \mathbb{R}^{d\times d}$ is the user-user matrix, as shown in Figure 1(b). In the matrix, $\mathbf{F}_{ij} = 1$ (red frame in the figure) indicates that user u_i is connected by user u_j. The graph is a directed graph, thus $\mathbf{F}$ is asymmetric.

With the notations above, we formally define sentiment classification of microblogging messages as:

Given a corpus of microblogging messages $\mathbf{T}$ *with their content* $\mathbf{X}$ *and corresponding sentiment labels* $\mathbf{Y}$*, social relations for this corpus including the user-message relation* $\mathbf{U}$*, and user-user following relation* $\mathbf{F}$*, we aim to learn a classifier* $\mathbf{W}$ *to automatically assign sentiment labels for unseen messages (i.e., test data).*

4. DATA AND OBSERVATIONS

Before we proceed to our solution, in this section, we first introduce real-world data used in this work and present some explorations whether social theories have any impacts on sentiment analysis.

4.1 Data

Subsets of two publicly available Twitter datasets are employed: Stanford Twitter Sentiment (STS) and Obama-McCain Debate (OMD). Both datasets consist of raw tweets with their corresponding sentiment labels.

Table 1: Statistics of the Datasets

	STS	*OMD*
# of Tweets	22,262	1,827
# of Users	8,467	735
Max Degree of the Users	897	138
Min Degree of the Users	1	1
Ave. Tweets per User	2.63	2.49

The first dataset is the Stanford Twitter Sentiment (STS)[2]. Go et al. [8] created a collection of 40216 tweets with polarity sentiment labels to train a sentiment classifier. However, it lacks social network information among users in this dataset. We further refined the Twitter dataset according to authors' social relation information, which is the complete follower graph[3] crawled by Kwak et al. [21] during July 2009. According to the social network, we filter tweets whose authors have no friends or have published fewer than two tweets. Finally, it leaves a corpus of 22,262 tweets that consists of 11959 positive tweets and 10303 negative ones.

The second dataset is the Obama-McCain Debate (OMD)[4]. This dataset consists of 3,269 tweets posted during the presidential debate on September 26, 2008 between Barack Obama and John McCain [34]. The sentiment label of each tweet was annotated through Amazon Mechanical Turk[5]. Each tweet was manually labeled by at least three Turkers. In our experiment of polarity sentiment classification, we use tweets with sentiment labels. The majority of votes for a tweet is taken as a gold standard. In order to obtain the social relation information, we use the same social network as in refining the STS dataset. All the tweets whose authors have no friends or have published fewer than two tweets are filtered. This results in a corpus of 1,827 tweets, in which 747 have positive labels and 1080 have negative labels.

The statistics of the datasets are summarized in Table 1.

4.2 Social Theories in Microblogging

In social sciences, Fowler and Christakis [6] found that the spread of happiness appears to reach up to three degrees of separation in a social network. Recently, researchers reported the phenomenon of sentiment diffusion [27] in online social networks based on the theory of emotional contagion [10] between friends. The analysis indicates that, in terms of sentiment, social theories such as *Sentiment Consistency* [1] and *Emotional Contagion* [10] could be helpful for sentiment analysis. Sentiment Consistency suggests that the sentiments of two messages posted by the same user are more likely to be consistent than those of two randomly selected messages. Emotional Contagion reveals that the sentiments of two messages posted by friends are more likely to be similar than those of two randomly selected messages.

The two theories are derived from offline surveys and conversations. We would like to validate whether the two social theories hold true in microblogging data. For each of the theories, we form a null hypothesis: in terms of sentiment, there is no difference between relational data and random data. We test the hypotheses on each of the two datasets.

[2] http://www.stanford.edu/~alecmgo/cs224n/

[3] http://an.kaist.ac.kr/traces/WWW2010.html/

[4] https://bitbucket.org/speriosu/updown/src/5de483437466/data/

[5] https://www.mturk.com/

The sentiment difference score between two messages is defined as $\mathbf{T}_{ij} = ||\mathbf{y}_i - \mathbf{y}_j||_2$, where $\mathbf{y}_i$ is the sentiment label of message $\mathbf{x}_i$. To verify the existence of Sentiment Consistency, we construct two vectors $\mathbf{sc}_t$ and $\mathbf{sc}_r$ with equal number of elements. Each element of the first vector $\mathbf{sc}_t$ is obtained by calculating the sentiment difference score between $\mathbf{x}_i$ and $\mathbf{x}_j$, which are posted by the same user. Each element in the vector corresponds to a pair of related messages. The element of the second vector represents the sentiment difference score between $\mathbf{x}_i$ and another random message $\mathbf{x}_r$ in the corpus. We perform a two-sample t-test on the two vectors $\mathbf{sc}_t$ and $\mathbf{sc}_r$. The null hypothesis is that there is no difference between the two vectors, $H_0 : \mathbf{sc}_t = \mathbf{sc}_r$; the alternative hypothesis is that the sentiment difference between messages with Sentiment Consistency relation is less than those without, $H_1 : \mathbf{sc}_t < \mathbf{sc}_r$. Similarly, we construct another two vectors $\mathbf{ec}_t$ and $\mathbf{ec}_r$, and perform a two-sample t-test on the two vectors for verifying Emotional Contagion. The null hypothesis is $H_0 : \mathbf{ec}_t = \mathbf{ec}_r$ and the alternative hypothesis is $H_1 : \mathbf{ec}_t < \mathbf{ec}_r$. The t-test results, p-values, show that there is strong evidence (with the significance level $\alpha = 0.01$) to reject the null hypothesis in both tests on the two datasets. In other words, we observe the existence of what Sentiment Consistency and Emotional Contagion suggest in microblogging data. This preliminary study paves the way for our next study: how to explicitly model and utilize these social theories for sentiment classification task.

5. A SOCIOLOGICAL APPROACH - SANT

In this section, we first introduce data representation and modeling for message content, and then discuss how we model relations between messages based on the social theories. Finally, we present how to employ sparse learning to handle noisy and high-dimensional data.

5.1 Modeling Message Content

To find a better text representation for sentiment analysis, Pang and Lee [33] conducted experiments to investigate the effectiveness of different features on sentiment classification. Their two major findings are (1) although different feature construction methods, like N-grams, Part of Speech, adjectives, sentiment vocabulary, have comparable performance, the unigram model with term presence (but not frequency) as feature weight achieves the best results; and (2) no stemming or stop-word lists are used because some of them may carry sentiment information. Thus, we employ the unigram model to construct our feature space, use term presence as the feature weight, and do not perform stemming or remove stop-words. It is noted that our framework is not confined to the unigram model. We can also use other text representation methods for specific sentiment classification tasks.

The widely used method Least Squares is employed to fit the learned model to message content. In terms of multiclass classification problems, the Least Squares aims to learn c classifiers by solving the following optimization problem:

$$\min_{\mathbf{W}} \quad \frac{1}{2}||\mathbf{X}^T\mathbf{W} - \mathbf{Y}||_F^2, \tag{1}$$

where $\mathbf{W}$ represents the learned classifiers. This formulation is a traditional supervised classification method, where the messages are assumed to be independent and identically distributed. This method has been well studied, and it has a closed-form solution.

5.2 Modeling Message-Message Relations

In this subsection, we introduce our formulation to utilize social relations for sentiment analysis, and answer the question: "How can social relations be explicitly integrated into the sentiment classification framework?".

In order to transform user-centric social relations into sentiment relations between messages, we employ the social theories discussed in Section 4.2. Given the user-message matrix $\mathbf{U}$ and user-user matrix $\mathbf{F}$, the message-message sentiment relation matrix for *Sentiment Consistency* ($\mathbf{A}sc$) is defined as $\mathbf{A}sc = \mathbf{U}^T \times \mathbf{U}$, where $\mathbf{A}sc_{ij} = 1$ indicates that $\mathbf{t}_i$ and $\mathbf{t}_j$ are posted by the same user, and sentiments of the two messages are similar. The message-message sentiment relation matrix for *Emotional Contagion* ($\mathbf{A}ec$) is defined as $\mathbf{A}ec = \mathbf{U}^T \times \mathbf{F} \times \mathbf{U}$, where $\mathbf{A}ec_{ij} = 1$ indicates that the author of $\mathbf{t}_i$ is a friend of the author who wrote $\mathbf{t}_j$, and sentiments of the two messages are similar. Note that the $\mathbf{A}sc$ is a symmetric matrix and $\mathbf{A}ec$ is not. The following derivations in this paper are based on the message-message sentiment relation matrix $\mathbf{A}$, which can be obtained as either the sentiment relation $\mathbf{A}sc$, $\mathbf{A}ec$, or the combination $\mathbf{A} = \mathbf{A}sc + \theta\mathbf{A}ec$, where θ controls the weight of two different sentiment relations in the model. In this paper, we focus on studying the effects of different sentiment relations on the sentiment classification performance, but not ways to combine them. We can simply combine these two relations with equal weight $\theta = 1$ to construct a relation matrix.

Based on the discussion above, to integrate sentiment relations between messages in sentiment classification, the basic idea is to build a latent connection to make two messages as close as possible if they are posted by the same user (*Sentiment Consistency*) or two users are follower/friend with each other (*Emotional Contagion*). Under this scenario, it can be mathematically formulated as solving the following objective function.

$$\begin{aligned} &\frac{1}{2}\sum_{i=1}^{n}\sum_{j=1}^{n}\mathbf{A}_{ij}||\hat{\mathbf{Y}}_{i*} - \hat{\mathbf{Y}}_{j*}||^2 \\ &= \sum_{k=1}^{c}\hat{\mathbf{Y}}_{*k}^T(\mathbf{D} - \mathbf{A})\hat{\mathbf{Y}}_{*k} \\ &= tr(\mathbf{X}^T\mathbf{W}\mathcal{L}\mathbf{X}^T\mathbf{W}), \end{aligned} \tag{2}$$

where $tr(\cdot)$ is the trace of a matrix. $\hat{\mathbf{Y}} = \mathbf{X}^T\mathbf{W}$ is the fitted value of the sentiment label $\mathbf{Y}$. $\mathcal{L} = \mathbf{D} - \mathbf{A}$ is the Laplacian matrix [4], where $\mathbf{A} \in \mathbb{R}^{n \times n}$ is a message-message sentiment relation matrix to represent a direct graph. $\mathbf{A}_{ij} = 1$ indicates that message t_i has relation with message t_j, and $\mathbf{A}_{ij} = 0$ otherwise. $\mathbf{D} \in \mathbb{R}^{n \times n}$ is a diagonal matrix with $\mathbf{D}_{ii} = \sum_{j=1}^{n}\mathbf{A}_{ij}$ indicating its diagonal element is the degree of a message in relation matrix $\mathbf{A}$.

As Laplacian matrix $\mathcal{L}$ is positive semi-definite, Eq. (2) can be rewritten as:

$$\begin{aligned} &tr(\mathbf{W}^T\mathbf{X}\mathcal{L}\mathbf{X}^T\mathbf{W}) \\ &= ||\mathbf{W}^T\mathbf{X}\mathcal{L}^{\frac{1}{2}}||_F^2, \end{aligned} \tag{3}$$

For different message-message relations, we use different sentiment relation matrices $\mathbf{A}$ to obtain the Laplacian matrices $\mathcal{L}$. The optimization formulation, which integrates sentiment relations into the learning process, is defined as:

$$\min_{\mathbf{W}} \quad \frac{1}{2}||\mathbf{X}^T\mathbf{W} - \mathbf{Y}||_F^2 + \frac{\alpha}{2}||\mathbf{W}^T\mathbf{X}\mathcal{L}^{\frac{1}{2}}||_F^2, \tag{4}$$

where α is the regularization parameter to control the contribution of sentiment relation information.

5.3 Handling the Noisy & Short Texts – A Sparse Formulation

Compared with texts in traditional media, another distinct feature of texts in microblogging is that they are noisy and short [12, 14, 38], which leads to two problems. First, text representation models, like "bag of words" or n-gram, often lead to a high-dimension feature space because of the large-scale size of the dataset and vocabulary. Second, the short and noisy texts make the data representation very sparse. This high-dimension sparse representation poses significant challenges to building an interpretable model with high prediction accuracy.

To retain original information in the texts, we do not filter the terms according to any domain-specific sentiment vocabularies. When people speed-read through a text, they may not fully parse the sentence but instead seek a sparse representation for the incoming text using a few phrases or words [13]. Thus, we propose to provide a sparse reconstruction for the classification feature space. Recently, sparse regularization has been widely used in many data mining applications to obtain more stable and interpretable models. A natural approach for our problem is the lasso [7], the penalization of the ℓ_1-norm of the estimator. The ℓ_1-norm based linear reconstruction error minimization can lead to a sparse representation for the texts, which is robust to the noise in features. The multi-class classifier can be learned by solving the following optimization problem.

$$\min_{\mathbf{W}} \quad \frac{1}{2}||\mathbf{X}^T\mathbf{W} - \mathbf{Y}||_F^2 + \beta||\mathbf{W}||_1, \tag{5}$$

where β is the sparse regularization parameter. In the objective function, the first term is least squares loss. The second term is ℓ_1-norm regularization on weight matrix $\mathbf{W}$, which causes some of the coefficients to be exactly zero. Thus the lasso does a kind of continuous subset selection and also controls the complexity of the model. Further, we introduce the Laplacian regularization discussed in Section 5.2 to Eq. (5). The sentiment classification of microblogging data can be formulated as the following optimization problem.

$$\min_{\mathbf{W}} \quad \frac{1}{2}||\mathbf{X}^T\mathbf{W} - \mathbf{Y}||_F^2 + \frac{\alpha}{2}||\mathbf{W}^T\mathbf{X}\mathcal{L}^{\frac{1}{2}}||_F^2 + \beta||\mathbf{W}||_1, \tag{6}$$

where α and β are postive regularization parameters. By solving Eq. (6), the sentiment label of each message can be predicted by

$$\arg\max_{i\in\{p,n\}} \quad \mathbf{x}^T\mathbf{w}_i. \tag{7}$$

Next, we introduce an efficient algorithm to solve the optimization problem in Eq. (6).

6. ALGORITHMIC DETAILS

Since $||\mathbf{W}||_1$ is non-differentiable, the proposed objective function in Eq. (6) is non-smooth. In this section, we introduce an efficient algorithm to solve the optimization problem, and discuss its convergence rate and time complexity.

6.1 Optimization Algorithm for *SANT*

Motivated by [24, 29, 9], we propose to solve the non-smooth optimization problem in Eq. (6) by optimizing its equivalent smooth convex reformulations.

THEOREM 1. *Eq. (6) can be reformulated as a constrained smooth convex optimization problem:*

$$\min_{W\in\mathcal{Z}} \; f(\mathbf{W}) = \frac{1}{2}||\mathbf{X}^T\mathbf{W} - \mathbf{Y}||_F^2 + \frac{\alpha}{2}||\mathbf{W}^T\mathbf{X}\mathcal{L}^{\frac{1}{2}}||_F^2, \tag{8}$$

where,

$$\mathcal{Z} = \{\mathbf{W}| \; ||\mathbf{W}||_1 \leq z\}, \tag{9}$$

$z \geq 0$ is the radius of the ℓ_1-ball, and there is a one-to-one correspondence between β and z.

REMARK 1. *The relationship between β and z is not critical because the optimal values of both are unknown. The two parameters are usually tuned using cross-validation. A sufficiently small z will cause some of the coefficients to be exactly zero, thus it also does a kind of continuous subset selection.*

Proof. The Hessian matrix of the objective function in Eq. (8) is positive semi-definite, thus the objective function $f(\mathbf{W})$ is convex and differentiable. It is easy to verify that $||\mathbf{W}||_1$ is a valid norm because it satisfies the three norm conditions, including the triangle inequality $||\mathbf{A}||_1 + ||\mathbf{B}||_1 \leq ||\mathbf{A}+\mathbf{B}||_1$. Since any norm defines a convex set, $\mathcal{Z}$ is a closed and convex set.

As we can see, our problem defines a convex and differentiable function $f(\mathbf{W})$ in a closed and convex set $\mathcal{Z}$. Thus this problem is a constrained smooth convex optimization problem, which completes the proof. □

We first consider the optimization problem in Eq. (8) without the constraint part $W \in \mathcal{Z}$, and it is defined as:

$$\min_{\mathbf{W}} f(\mathbf{W}). \tag{10}$$

It is known that, in gradient descent method, $\mathbf{W}_{t+1}$ is updated in each step as:

$$\mathbf{W}_{t+1} = \mathbf{W}_t - \frac{1}{\lambda_t}\nabla f(\mathbf{W}_t) \tag{11}$$

where λ_t is the step size, which is determined by the line search according to the Armijo-Goldstein rule. The smooth part of the optimization problem can be reformulated equivalently as a proximal regularization [17] of the linearized function $f(\mathbf{W})$ at $\mathbf{W}_t$, which is formally defined as:

$$\mathbf{W}_{t+1} = \arg\min_{\mathbf{W}} G_{\lambda_t,\mathbf{W}_t}(\mathbf{W}), \tag{12}$$

where,

$$G_{\lambda_t,\mathbf{W}_t}(\mathbf{W}) = f(\mathbf{W}_t) + \langle\nabla f(\mathbf{W}_t), \mathbf{W} - \mathbf{W}_t\rangle + \frac{\lambda_t}{2}||\mathbf{W} - \mathbf{W}_t||_F^2. \tag{13}$$

Considering the equivalence relationship and the constraints $\mathcal{Z}$, we propose to solve Eq. (8) through the following iterative step,

$$\mathbf{W}_{t+1} = \arg\min_{\mathbf{W}\in\mathcal{Z}} G_{\lambda_t,\mathbf{W}_t}(\mathbf{W}), \tag{14}$$

By ignoring terms that are independent of $\mathbf{W}$ in Eq. (13), the objective function in Eq. (14) boils down to:

$$\mathbf{W}_{t+1} = \arg\min_{\mathbf{W}\in\mathcal{Z}} \|\mathbf{W} - \mathbf{U}_t\|_F^2, \tag{15}$$

where $\mathbf{U}_t = \mathbf{W}_t - \frac{1}{\lambda_t}\nabla f(\mathbf{W}_t)$ and actually the solution of $\mathbf{W}$ is the Euclidean projection of $\mathbf{U}_t$ on $\mathcal{Z}$. $\nabla f(\mathbf{W}_t)$ is the gradient of $f(\mathbf{W}_t)$, and in our paper $\nabla f(\mathbf{W}_t)$ is defined as:

$$\nabla f(\mathbf{W}_t) = \mathbf{X}\mathbf{X}^T\mathbf{W}_t - \mathbf{X}\mathbf{Y}^T + \alpha\mathbf{X}\mathcal{L}\mathbf{X}^T\mathbf{W}_t. \tag{16}$$

Eq. (14) can be decomposed into n subproblems as:

$$\mathbf{w}_{t+1}^j = \arg\min_{\mathbf{w}^j\in\mathcal{Z}^j} \|\mathbf{w}^j - \mathbf{u}_t^j\|_2^2, \tag{17}$$

where $\mathbf{u}_t^j$, $\mathbf{w}^j$ and $\mathbf{w}_t^j$ are the j-th rows of $\mathbf{U}_t$, $\mathbf{W}$ and $\mathbf{W}_t$, respectively. $\mathcal{Z}^j$ is defined on $\|\mathbf{w}^j\|_1$. Given β, the Euclidean projection has a closed form solution as follows,

$$\mathbf{w}_{t+1}^j = \begin{cases} (1 - \frac{\beta}{\lambda_t\|\mathbf{u}_t^j\|})\mathbf{u}_t^j & \text{if } \|\mathbf{u}_t^j\| \geq \frac{\beta}{\lambda_t} \\ 0 & \text{otherwise} \end{cases} \tag{18}$$

The above method has the convergence ratio of $\frac{1}{\epsilon}$. As discussed in [24], our constrained smooth convex optimization problem can be further accelerated to achieve the optimal convergence $\frac{1}{\sqrt{\epsilon}}$. In particular, this accelerated algorithm is based on two sequences $\mathbf{W}_t$ and $\mathbf{V}_t$ in which $\mathbf{W}_t$ is the sequence of approximate solutions, and $\mathbf{V}_t$ is the sequence of search points, which is an affine combination of $\mathbf{W}_t$ and $\mathbf{W}_{t-1}$ as:

$$\mathbf{V}_t = \mathbf{W}_t + \gamma_t(\mathbf{W}_t - \mathbf{W}_{t-1}), \tag{19}$$

where γ_t is the combination coefficient. The approximate solution $\mathbf{W}_{t+1}$ is computed as a "gradient" step of $\mathbf{V}_t$ through $G_{\lambda_t,\mathbf{V}_t}$. Then the detailed algorithm about *SANT* with this accelerated optimization solution is shown in Algorithm 1.

In the algorithm, we use Nesterov's method [29] to solve the optimization problem in Eq. (6) from line 5 to 22. It is the line search algorithm for λ_t according to the Armijo-Goldstein rule from line 8 to 15. In line 20, η_t is set according to [24]. Based on the algorithm, we can have the solution to the convex optimization problem, and obtain the sentiment class label by Eq. (7).

Algorithm 1: *SANT*: Sentiment Analysis for Noisy Texts with Social Relations

Input: $\{\mathbf{X}, \mathbf{Y}, \mathbf{U}, \mathbf{F}, \mathbf{W}_0, \lambda_1, \alpha, \beta\}$
Output: $\mathbf{W}$

1: Initialize $\eta_0 = 0$, $\eta_1 = 1$, $\mathbf{W}_1 = \mathbf{W}_0$, $t = 1$
2: $\mathbf{A}sc = \mathbf{U}^T \times \mathbf{U}$, $\mathbf{A}ec = \mathbf{U}^T \times \mathbf{F} \times \mathbf{U}$
3: $\mathbf{A} = \mathbf{A}_{sc} + \mathbf{A}_{ec}$
4: Construct Laplacian matrix $\mathcal{L}$ from $\mathbf{A}$
5: **while** Not convergent **do**
6: Set $\mathbf{V}_t = \mathbf{W}_t + \frac{\eta_{t-1}-1}{\eta_t}(\mathbf{W}_t - \mathbf{W}_{t-1})$
7: Set $\nabla f(\mathbf{W}_t) = \mathbf{X}\mathbf{X}^T\mathbf{W}_t - \mathbf{X}\mathbf{Y}^T + \alpha\mathbf{X}\mathcal{L}\mathbf{X}^T\mathbf{W}_t$
8: **loop**
9: Set $\mathbf{U}_t = \mathbf{V}_t - \frac{1}{\lambda_t}\nabla f(\mathbf{W}_t)$
10: Compute $\mathbf{W}_{t+1}$ according to Eq. (18)
11: **if** $f(\mathbf{W}_{t+1}) \leq G_{\lambda_t,\mathbf{V}_t}(\mathbf{W}_{t+1})$ **then**
12: $\lambda_{t+1} = \lambda_t$, break
13: **end if**
14: $\lambda_t = 2 \times \lambda_t$
15: **end loop**
16: $\mathbf{W} = \mathbf{W_{t+1}}$
17: **if** stopping criteria satisfied **then**
18: break
19: **end if**
20: Set $\eta_{t+1} = \frac{1+\sqrt{1+4\eta_t}}{2}$
21: Set $t = t + 1$
22: **end while**
23: $\mathbf{W} = \mathbf{W_{t+1}}$

6.2 Convergence and Complexity Analysis

In this subsection, we discuss the convergence rate and time complexity of the proposed Algorithm 1.

The convergence rate of Algorithm 1 is elaborated in the following theorem.

THEOREM 2. *[17] Assume that $\{\mathbf{W}_t\}$ is the sequence obtained by Algorithm 1, then for any t we have,*

$$f(\mathbf{W}_{t+1}) - f(\mathbf{W}^\star) \leq \frac{2\hat{L}_f\|\mathbf{W}^\star - \mathbf{W}_1\|_F^2}{(t+1)^2}, \tag{20}$$

where $\hat{L}_f = \max(2L_f, L_0)$, L_0 is an initial guess of the lipschitz continuous gradient L_f of $f(\mathbf{W})$ and $\mathbf{W}^\star$ is the solution of $f(\mathbf{W})$.

Proof. The detailed proof of the above theorem can be found in [17]. This theorem shows that the convergence rate of Algorithm 1 is $O(\frac{1}{\sqrt{\epsilon}})$ where ϵ is the desired accuracy. □

Based on the theorem, the algorithm will converge in $\frac{1}{\sqrt{\epsilon}}$ iterations, now we discuss time complexity of the proposed method *SANT* at each iteration. Given a collection of n messages with the feature space m, the objective function Eq. (6) consists of three components. First, for the least squares loss function, it costs $O(mn)$ floating point operations for calculating the function value and gradient of the objective function. Second, for the ℓ_1-norm regularization part, the time complexity is $O(2n)$ based on the Euclidean projection algorithm [24]. Third, the Laplacian regularization part, the time complexity is also $O(mn)$. Therefore, we can solve the objective function in Eq. (6) with a time complexity of $O(\frac{1}{\sqrt{\epsilon}}(mn + 2n + mn)) = O(\frac{1}{\sqrt{\epsilon}}(mn))$.

7. EXPERIMENTS

In this section, we present empirical evaluation results to assess the effectiveness of our proposed framework, and answer the question: "Can social relations improve sentiment classification of microblogging messages?". In particular, we evaluate the proposed method on the two datasets introduced in Section 4. Impacts brought by size of training set, different relations and other factors that appear to affect the experiment are further discussed.

7.1 Performance Evaluation

Below we first present the finding of comparing *SANT* with the classical text-based sentiment classification methods, and then with the models that incorporate social relations in sentiment classification.

7.1.1 Comparison with Text-based Methods

In the first set of experiments, we use classification accuracy as the performance metric, and compare the proposed framework *SANT* with following text-based methods:

Table 2: Sentiment Classification Accuracy on STS Dataset

	$D_{10\%}$ (gain)	$D_{25\%}$ (gain)	$D_{50\%}$ (gain)	$D_{100\%}$ (gain)
LS	0.670 (N.A.)	0.704 (N.A.)	0.720 (N.A.)	0.713 (N.A.)
Lasso	0.699 (+4.22%)	0.722 (+2.56%)	0.746 (+3.50%)	0.759 (+6.38%)
MinCuts	0.677 (+0.93%)	0.705 (+0.27%)	0.727 (+0.89%)	0.757 (+6.10%)
LexRatio	0.699 (+4.25%)	0.746 (+5.97%)	0.753 (+4.55%)	0.763 (+6.94%)
SANT	**0.764 (+13.90%)**	**0.778 (+10.56%)**	**0.793 (+10.02%)**	**0.796 (+11.52%)**

Table 3: Sentiment Classification Accuracy on OMD Dataset

	$D_{10\%}$ (gain)	$D_{25\%}$ (gain)	$D_{50\%}$ (gain)	$D_{100\%}$ (gain)
LS	0.615 (N.A.)	0.634 (N.A.)	0.654 (N.A.)	0.660 (N.A.)
Lasso	0.626 (+1.81%)	0.663 (+4.62%)	0.698 (+6.76%)	0.709 (+7.49%)
MinCuts	0.659 (+7.16%)	0.664 (+4.80%)	0.674 (+3.06%)	0.697 (+5.64%)
LexRatio	0.613 (-0.18%)	0.633 (-0.22%)	0.655 (+0.18%)	0.659 (-0.06%)
SANT	**0.685 (+11.51%)**	**0.717 (+13.04%)**	**0.748 (+14.47%)**	**0.763 (+15.72%)**

- *LS*: Least squares [7] is a widely used supervised classification method for i.i.d. data.
- *Lasso*: Lasso [7] on tweet content only. This is one of the most popular sparse learning methods.
- *MinCuts*: Pang and Lee [31] utilized contextual information via the minimum-cut framework to improve polarity-classification accuracy. In the experiment, we use MinCuts package provided by the freely available software LingPipe[6].
- *LexRatio*: The methods [30, 40] count the ratio of sentiment words, from OpinionFinder subjectivity lexicon[7], in a tweet to determine its sentiment orientation. Due to its unsupervised setting, *LS* is used for the tweets do not contain any sentiment words.

There are three important parameters in our experiments, including α, β in Eq. (6) and θ in Section 5.2. All three parameters are positive. α is the parameter to control the contribution of sentiment relation information, β is the sparse regularization parameter, and θ is the parameter to combine the two sentiment relations. As a common practice, α and β are tuned via cross-validation. In the experiments, we set $\alpha = 0.05$ and $\beta = 0.1$ for general experiment purposes. We set $\theta = 1$ which means the two sentiment relation matrices are simply combined with equal weight.

Experimental results of the methods on the two datasets, STS and OMD, are respectively reported in Table 2 and 3. In the experiment, we used five-fold cross validation. To test the sensitivity of *SANT* to different sizes of training data, in the tables, $D_{percentage}$ denotes the amount of data used for training as a percentage of whole training dataset. For example, in each round of the experiment, 80% of the whole dataset is used for training. $D_{50\%}$ means we chose 50% of 80% thus using 40% of the whole dataset as training data. The test dataset is always 20% of the whole dataset. In the tables, "gain" represents the percentage improvement of the methods as compared to the traditional *LS* method. In the round of the experiment, the result denotes the average score of 10 test runs. By comparing the results of different methods, we draw the following observations:

(1) Compared with the text-based methods, *SANT* achieves consistently better performance on both datasets with different sizes of training data. The highest improvement with respect to *LS* is obtained on the OMD dataset when the training dataset is D_{100}. We apply t-test to compare *SANT* with the best methods *MinCuts* and *LexRatio*. The experiment results demonstrate that, by exploiting social relations, our proposed model is able to achieve significant improvement (with the significance level $\alpha = 0.01$) as compared to the state-of-the-art methods.

(2) The sparse learning based method *Lasso* achieves better performance than least squares based method *LS*. This shows that a sparse solution of the feature space is an effective way to tackle with noisy microblogging data. The introduction of sparse regularization has positive impacts on the proposed sentiment classification method.

(3) It is noted that the proposed *SANT* also achieves significant improvement with respect to the baseline methods when using a small training dataset. It outperforms the *LS* baseline of 13.90% and 11.51% in the two datasets using only 10% as the training dataset, which demonstrates that our proposed method is robust to a training dataset with small number of training samples. In addition, *SANT* achieves better performance with only 10% training data comparing with *LS* with all training data. It indicates that, by integrating social relation information, our proposed model can significantly save labeling cost. We will discuss the sensitivity of our proposed method to various sizes of training datasets in Section 7.2.

In summary, the proposed model consistently achieves better performance than the state-of-the-art methods based on text alone. It suggests that the social relation information positively help improve sentiment classification. In the next subsection, we compare *SANT* with the models that make use of social relations.

7.1.2 Incorporating Social Relations

To further evaluate *SANT*, in the second set of experiments, we use the following methods in this set of experiments; in other words, all methods utilize social relation information in classification.

[6]`http://alias-i.com/lingpipe/`

[7]`http://www.cs.pitt.edu/mpqa/opinionfinder_1.html`

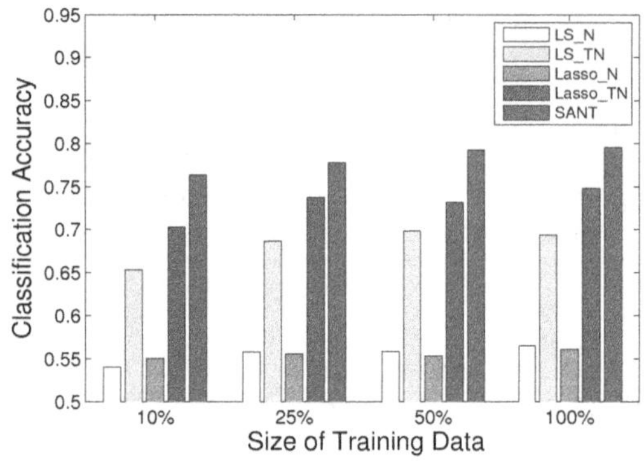

Figure 2: Sentiment Classification on STS Dataset

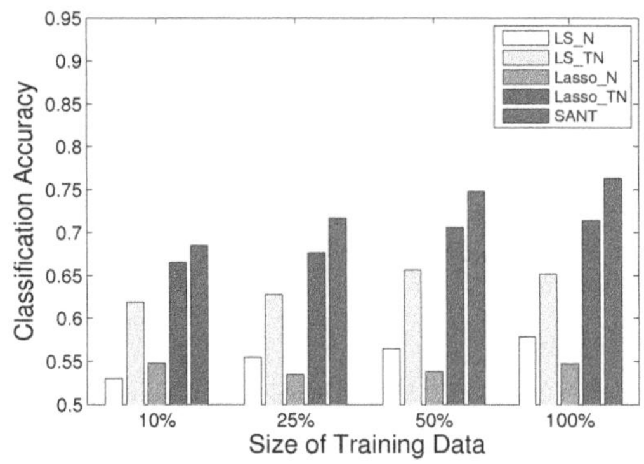

Figure 3: Sentiment Classification on OMD Dataset

- *LS_N* : Least squares is applied on sentiment relation information only. Following previous work [35], tweet-tweet relation information is used as feature expansion for each tweet. If a tweet t_i is related to another tweet t_j, we add the tweet id t_j as a feature into t_i's feature vector. The following *LS_TN*, *Lasso_N* and *Lasso_TN* methods use the same technique to integrate sentiment relation information between tweets.

- *LS_TN*: Least squares on tweet content and sentiment relation information together. A sentiment relation matrix is utilized as a feature augmentation of the content feature space. The final feature space is constructed with the equally weighted combination of content matrix and tweet-tweet sentiment relation matrix.

- *Lasso_N*: Lasso on sentiment relation information only. This is the sparse version of the method LS_N.

- *Lasso_TN*: Lasso on tweet content and sentiment relation information together. This is the sparse version of the method *LS_TN*. The relation information between tweets is employed as a simple feature expansion, which differs from our proposed method.

Following parameter and experiment settings discussed in the first experiment, we conduct the baseline methods on the two Twitter datasets with different percentages of training data. The classification performance of the methods are

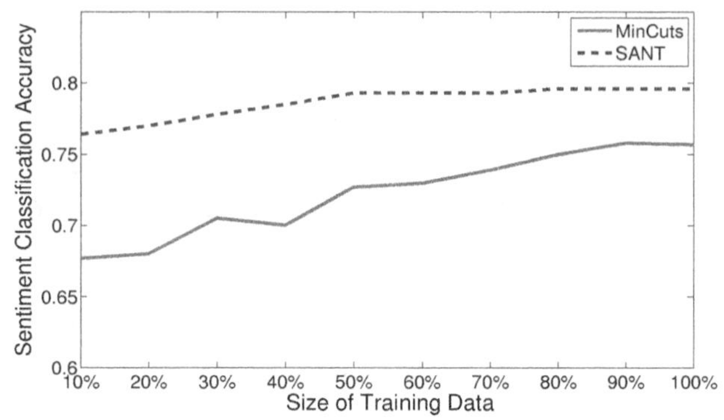

Figure 4: Sensitivity of *SANT* to Training Data Sizes on STS

plotted in Figures 2 and 3, from which we can draw the following observations:

(1) Among the five methods, *SANT* achieves the best performance on both datasets with different sizes of training data. It indicates that, comparing with other methods of incorporating social relations, our proposed model successfully utilize the social relations for sentiment analysis.

(2) *LS_TN* and *Lasso_TN* achieve better performance than *LS_N* and *Lasso_N*. In addition, the social relation information based methods *LS_N* and *Lasso_N* are slightly better than randomly ($accuracy = 0.5$) assigning a sentiment label to the messages. The results demonstrate that it is inaccurate to rely on sentiment relation information only to determine the sentiment of a microblogging message.

In summary, the existing methods perform differently in sentiment classification. In some cases, the use of social relation information does not help performance improvement. It suggests that the way of using social relations is also important. The superior performance of the proposed method *SANT* validates its excellent use of social relation information in sentiment analysis.

7.2 Sensitivity to Training Data Sizes

One difficulty in sentiment analysis is the lack of manually labeled training data. The publicly available datasets are always insufficient for training purposes in supervised learning methods. We showed that our proposed method is robust to small size of training data in Tables 2 and 3. In order to further investigate the sensitivity of the proposed *SANT* framework to the size of training data, in Figure 4, we plot the sentiment classification accuracy with training data from 10% to 100% on the STS dataset.

In the figures, we compare the performance of *SANT* and *MinCuts*. *SANT* consistently outperforms *MinCuts* with different sizes of training data. Compared with the results from using the whole training dataset, *SANT* achieves greater improvement with respect to *MinCuts* when the size of training data is small. *SANT* does not show significant changes when the size of the training data changes, which demonstrates that our proposed method is not sensitive to training data sizes. This property has its significance due to the widely existed "lack of manually labeled training data" problem in sentiment classification tasks.

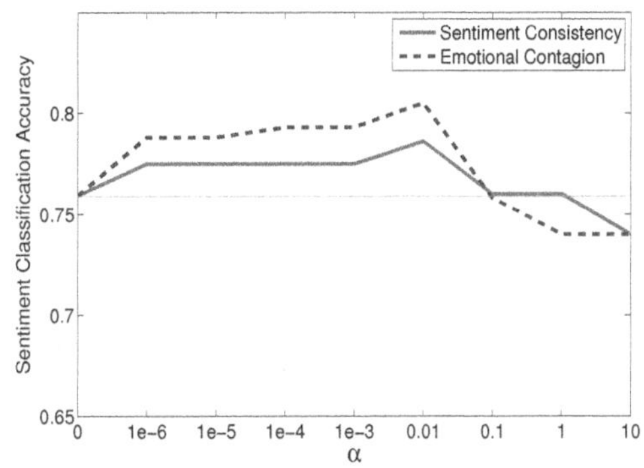

(a) STS Dataset

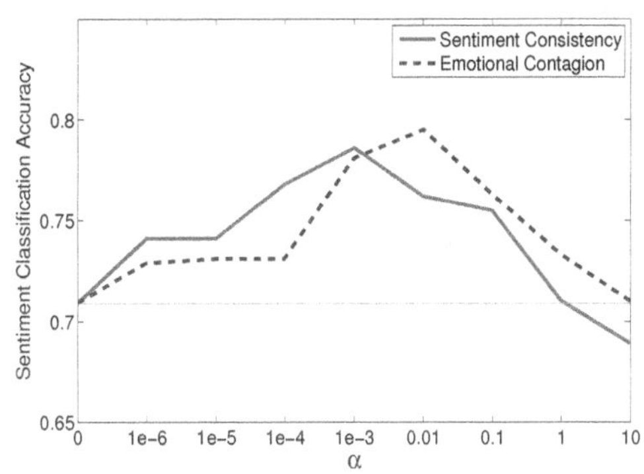

(b) OMD Dataset

Figure 5: Performance Variation of *SANT*

7.3 Effect of Sentiment Relations

In the experiments, we combined the two sentiment relations with equal weight. To further understand the effect of each relation on the performance of sentiment classification, experiments are conducted with separate sentiment relation on the two datasets. The parameter α controls the contribution of sentiment relation to the model. We varied the value of α from 0 to 10. The results are presented in Figures 5(a) and 5(b). The red curve shows the performance of "Sentiment Consistency" (SC), the blue dotted curve depicts the performance of "Emotional Contagion" (EC), and the green line is baseline without sentiment relation information.

In Figures 5(a) and 5(b), the curves of SC reach the peak at $\alpha = 0.01$ and $\alpha = 0.001$ respectively. For most parameter settings, the classification accuracy with SC is higher than the baseline. This demonstrates that, with only one sentiment relation, $SANT$ can improve the sentiment classification performance as well. When the value of parameter α is not too extreme, SC is not sensitive to the parameter setting. This is an appealing property of the proposed method because it is not necessary to make much effort to tune the parameter. The method can consistently achieve good performance with a large range of parameter settings. The trend of curve EC is similar to SC in the figures.

With different parameter settings, the two relations achieve comparable results. Intuitively, the first sentiment relation SC should have a stronger impact to the model than EC relation. A potential reason is that the constructed matrix of SC is much more sparse than the latter one.

7.4 Multi-Class Sentiment Classification

As discussed in Section 3, following [8, 35], we focused on the polarity sentiment classification task in this paper. It is observed that many tweets do not show clear emotions in real-world applications. Users may post objective expressions about entities and events. For example, in the OMD dataset used in our experiment, besides tweets with positive and negative sentiments, we still have tweets in other categories. In this case, our proposed model can be easily applied to this application, which classifies the tweets as positive, negative and neutral. We next present some preliminary results.

We added the tweets with neutral and other as sentiment labels in the OMD data to construct a three class dataset. The dataset consists 3,269 tweets with the class label as positive, negative and neutral. We compared the performance of our proposed model $SANT$ with the baseline methods LS and *LexRatio*. Among the three methods, our proposed method has the best performance at 58.3% and it achieves 11.66% improvement as compared to LS. Although the focus of this paper is polarity sentiment classification, our method is quite general to be applied to real-world multi-class (> 2) sentiment analysis applications.

8. CONCLUSIONS AND FUTURE WORK

Different from texts in traditional media, microblogging texts are noisy, short, and embedded with social relations, which presents challenges to sentiment analysis. In this paper, we propose a novel sociological approach ($SANT$) to handle networked texts in microblogging. In particular, we extract sentiment relations between tweets based on social theories, and model the relations using graph Laplacian, which is employed as a regularization to a sparse formulation. Thus the proposed method can utilize sentiment relations between messages to facilitate sentiment classification and effectively handle noisy Twitter data. We further develop an optimization algorithm for $SANT$. Experimental results show that the user-centric social relations are helpful for sentiment classification of microblogging messages. Empirical evaluations demonstrate that our framework significantly outperforms the representative sentiment classification methods on two real-world datasets, and $SANT$ achieves consistent performance for different sizes of training data, a useful feature for sentiment classification.

This work suggests some interesting directions for future work. For example, it would be interesting to investigate the contributions of different sentiment relations to sentiment classification. Other information, like spatial-temporal patterns, could be potentially useful to measure the sentiment consistency of people as well [28]. For example, people in Miami might be happier about the temperature than people in Chicago during winter time. We can further explore how sentiments diffuse in the social network and how people's sentiments correlate with internal (their friends) and external (public events [15]) factors. With the analysis, it is possible for us to understand the differences of sentiment between the online world and physical world.

Acknowledgments

We thank the anonymous reviewers for their comments. This work is, in part, supported by ONR (N000141110527) and (N000141010091).

9. REFERENCES

[1] R. Abelson. Whatever became of consistency theory? *Personality and Social Psychology Bulletin*, 1983.

[2] L. Barbosa and J. Feng. Robust sentiment detection on twitter from biased and noisy data. In *Proceedings of ACL*, 2010.

[3] J. Bollen, A. Pepe, and H. Mao. Modeling public mood and emotion: Twitter sentiment and socio-economic phenomena. *CoRR, abs/0911.1583*, 2009.

[4] F. Chung. *Spectral graph theory*. Number 92. Amer Mathematical Society, 1997.

[5] X. Ding and B. Liu. The utility of linguistic rules in opinion mining. In *Proceedings of SIGIR*, 2007.

[6] J. Fowler and N. Christakis. The dynamic spread of happiness in a large social network. *BMJ: British medical journal*, 2008.

[7] J. Friedman, T. Hastie, and R. Tibshirani. The elements of statistical learning, 2008.

[8] A. Go, R. Bhayani, and L. Huang. Twitter sentiment classification using distant supervision. *Technical Report, Stanford*, 2009.

[9] Q. Gu and J. Han. Towards feature selection in network. In *Proceedings of CIKM*, 2011.

[10] E. Hatfield, J. Cacioppo, and R. Rapson. Emotional contagion. *Current Directions in Psychological Science*, 1993.

[11] M. Hu and B. Liu. Mining and summarizing customer reviews. In *Proceedings of SIGKDD*, 2004.

[12] X. Hu and H. Liu. Text analytics in social media. *Mining Text Data*, pages 385–414, 2012.

[13] X. Hu, N. Sun, C. Zhang, and T.-S. Chua. Exploiting internal and external semantics for the clustering of short texts using world knowledge. In *Proceedings of CIKM*, pages 919–928, 2009.

[14] X. Hu, L. Tang, and H. Liu. Enhancing accessibility of microblogging messages using semantic knowledge. In *Proceedings of the 20th CIKM*, 2011.

[15] Y. Hu, A. John, D. Seligmann, and F. Wang. What were the tweets about? topical associations between public events and twitter feeds. *ICWSM*, 2012.

[16] Y. Hu, A. John, F. Wang, and S. Kambhampati. Et-lda: Joint topic modeling for aligning events and their twitter feedback. In *AAAI*, 2012.

[17] S. Ji and J. Ye. An accelerated gradient method for trace norm minimization. In *ICML*, 2009.

[18] S. Kamvar and J. Harris. We feel fine and searching the emotional web. In *Proceedings of WSDM*, pages 117–126, 2011.

[19] D. Keltner and G. Bonanno. A study of laughter and dissociation: Distinct correlates of laughter and smiling during bereavement. *Journal of Personality and Social Psychology*, page 687, 1997.

[20] E. Kim, S. Gilbert, M. Edwards, and E. Graeff. Detecting sadness in 140 characters: Sentiment analysis of mourning michael jackson on twitter. 2009.

[21] H. Kwak, C. Lee, H. Park, and S. Moon. What is twitter, a social network or a news media? In *Proceedings of WWW*, 2010.

[22] K. Lewis, M. Gonzalez, and J. Kaufman. Social selection and peer influence in an online social network. *PNAS*, pages 68–72, 2012.

[23] B. Liu. Sentiment analysis and opinion mining. *Synthesis Lectures on Human Language Technologies*, pages 1–167, 2012.

[24] J. Liu, S. Ji, and J. Ye. Multi-task feature learning via efficient l 2, 1-norm minimization. In *Proceedings of UAI*, 2009.

[25] P. Marsden and N. Friedkin. Network studies of social influence. *Sociological Methods & Research*, 1993.

[26] M. McPherson, L. Smith-Lovin, and J. Cook. Birds of a feather: Homophily in social networks. *Annual review of sociology*, pages 415–444, 2001.

[27] M. Miller, C. Sathi, D. Wiesenthal, J. Leskovec, and C. Potts. Sentiment flow through hyperlink networks. In *Proceedings of ICWSM*, 2011.

[28] A. Mislove, S. Lehmann, Y. Ahn, J. Onnela, and J. Rosenquist. Pulse of the nation: Us mood throughout the day inferred from twitter. 2010.

[29] Y. Nesterov and I. Nesterov. *Introductory lectures on convex optimization: A basic course*. 2004.

[30] B. O Connor, R. Balasubramanyan, B. Routledge, and N. Smith. From tweets to polls: Linking text sentiment to public opinion time series. In *Proceedings of ICWSM*, 2010.

[31] B. Pang and L. Lee. A sentimental education: Sentiment analysis using subjectivity summarization based on minimum cuts. In *Proceedings of ACL*, 2004.

[32] B. Pang and L. Lee. Opinion mining and sentiment analysis. *Foundations and Trends in Information Retrieval*, pages 1–135, 2008.

[33] B. Pang, L. Lee, and S. Vaithyanathan. Thumbs up?: sentiment classification using machine learning techniques. In *Proceedings of EMNLP*, 2002.

[34] D. Shamma, L. Kennedy, and E. Churchill. Tweet the debates: understanding community annotation of uncollected sources. In *Proceedings of the first SIGMM workshop on Social media*, pages 3–10. ACM, 2009.

[35] M. Speriosu, N. Sudan, S. Upadhyay, and J. Baldridge. Twitter polarity classification with label propagation over lexical links and the follower graph. In *Proceedings of the First Workshop on Unsupervised Learning in NLP*, 2011.

[36] C. Tan, L. Lee, J. Tang, L. Jiang, M. Zhou, and P. Li. User-level sentiment analysis incorporating social networks. In *Proceedings of SIGKDD*, 2011.

[37] J. Tang and H. Liu. Feature selection with linked data in social media. In *SDM*, 2012.

[38] J. Tang, X. Wang, H. Gao, X. Hu, and H. Liu. Enriching short texts representation in microblog for clustering. *Frontiers of Computer Science*.

[39] J. Wiebe, T. Wilson, and C. Cardie. Annotating expressions of opinions and emotions in language. *Language Resources and Evaluation*, 39:165–210, 2005.

[40] T. Wilson, J. Wiebe, and P. Hoffmann. Recognizing contextual polarity in phrase-level sentiment analysis. In *Proceedings of HLT and EMNLP*, 2005.

[41] X. Zhao, G. Li, M. Wang, J. Yuan, Z.-J. Zha, Z. Li, and T.-S. Chua. Integrating rich information for video recommendation with multi-task rank aggregation. In *Proceedings of ACM MM*, 2011.

Connecting Comments and Tags: Improved Modeling of Social Tagging Systems

Dawei Yin† Shengbo Guo^S Boris Chidlovskii^S
Brian D. Davison† Cedric Archambeau^S Guillaume Bouchard^S
†Dept. of Computer Science and Engineering, Lehigh University, Bethlehem, PA, USA
^{S}Xerox Research Center Europe, Grenoble, France

ABSTRACT

Collaborative tagging systems are now deployed extensively to help users share and organize resources. Tag prediction and recommendation can simplify and streamline the user experience, and by modeling user preferences, predictive accuracy can be significantly improved. However, previous methods typically model user behavior based only on a log of prior tags, neglecting other behaviors and information in social tagging systems, e.g., commenting on items and connecting with other users. On the other hand, little is known about the connection and correlations among these behaviors and contexts in social tagging systems.

In this paper, we investigate improved modeling for predictive social tagging systems. Our explanatory analyses demonstrate three significant challenges: coupled high order interaction, data sparsity and cold start on items. We tackle these problems by using a generalized latent factor model and fully Bayesian treatment. To evaluate performance, we test on two real-world data sets from Flickr and Bibsonomy. Our experiments on these data sets show that to achieve best predictive performance, it is necessary to employ a fully Bayesian treatment in modeling high order relations in a social tagging system. Our methods noticeably outperform state-of-the-art approaches.

Categories and Subject Descriptors

H.3.3 [**Information Storage and Retrieval**]: Information Search and Retrieval; H.2.8 [**Database Management**]: Database applications—*Data Mining*; H.3.1 [**Information Storage and Retrieval**]: Content Analysis and Indexing; H.1.2 [**Models and Principles**]: User/Machine Systems—*Human Information Processing*

Keywords

social tagging; tag recommendation; personalized tag prediction; personalized comment recommendation; co-factorization

WSDM'13, February 4–8, 2013, Rome, Italy.

1. INTRODUCTION

Collaborative tagging systems have become widely used for sharing and organizing resources in recent years. In social bookmarking, as one type of collaborative tagging system, users can add metadata in the form of descriptive terms, called tags, to describe web resources. Social bookmarking systems have been utilized successfully in many areas, such as web search [5], personalized search [36], web resource classification [39] and clustering [26]. However, the major bottleneck for large scale applications of social tagging systems is that only a small number of web resources have manually assigned tags, compared to the size of the Web. Therefore, systems that can automatically tag web resources are needed. On the other hand, from the user's perspective, a system that can provide suggestions and recommendations when users are about to assign tags to new resources can improve human-computer interactions and organization of the knowledge base as well.

Motivated by the needs described above, researchers have considered how to build systems to recommend or predict tag usage. Early work in this area, such as Hotho et al. [14] and Lipczak et al. [18], has demonstrated two basic approaches—content-based and graph-based methods—to tackle the problem. Recent work, including Rendle et al. [27] and Yin et al. [38, 37], show how personalized tag recommenders that take the user's previous tagging behaviors into account usually have better performance. However, most previous methods for social tagging system only model user behavior based on the log of prior tags [27] and item content [18, 38], neglecting the other behaviors and information found in real-world social tagging systems. In such social tagging systems, there exist many other artifacts of user activities, such as comments on items [4] and social connections with other users. Unlike tags which are usually personalized descriptions of the item, users' comments on the items are user-generated opinionated texts. Although they share some similar patterns of behaviors (both are user-generated texts for specific items), they have different properties and aims. Personalized tag prediction has been studied for several years, but comment prediction, which is quite different from traditional opinion mining, is rarely investigated. Recently, Agarwal et al. [4] develop personalized comment recommendation via factor models but they do not predict the content (e.g., term frequency) of personalized comments which could potentially help in the interpretation of comments and be applied to improve sentiment analysis of comments. In addition, the effects of mutual reinforcement across contexts such as user-tag-item and user-comment-item are still unknown.

In addition to user-generated tags and comments, users are often also able to denote friendship (via links) with other users. All of these activities provide potential hints for tag prediction, comment prediction and prediction of other user behaviors. By analyzing all of these activities, we can better capture users' preferences and make more accurate recommendations, but many of these activities are coupled and their effects on each other are not easily modeled.

In this paper, we systematically investigate the coupled activities of users and their mutual effects in a social tagging system. Our explanatory analyses show that the main challenges in modeling tagging systems are from three points: coupled high order interaction, data sparsity, and cold start on items. We tackle these problems by proposing a generalized Bayesian probabilistic latent factor model which can be tailored to fit the tagging system. We conduct empirical evaluations on two public data sets—Flickr and Bibsonomy. The experiments show that in social tagging systems, a user's commenting and tagging behaviors are highly correlated and can be mutually inferred, which has not been explored previously. The contributions of this paper are summarized as follows:

1. To better model social tagging systems, we propose a novel generalized latent factor model which is based on a Bayesian approach.
2. We find that connecting comments and tags within the same model permits mutual reinforcement and improves overall performance.
3. Experiments on real-world data show that our Bayesian methods can achieve much better performance than the probabilistic version of our model, due to the sparsity of the high-order relational data in social media. Our model significantly outperforms state-of-the-art methods.

The paper is organized as follows: Section 2 discusses related work. We present preliminary experiments in Section 3. Section 4 presents the proposed model, followed by describing an efficient and scalable approach developed for estimating the model parameters in Section 5. Section 6 presents the empirical evaluations of the proposed approach on both data sets. Section 7 concludes the paper.

2. RELATED WORK

Personalized tag recommendation, as a special case of collaborative filtering, is a recent topic in recommender systems. Two main directions for these systems are content-based approaches and graph-based approaches.

Content-based methods, which usually encode users' preferences from textual information within items (e.g., web pages, academic papers, tags), can predict tags for new users and new items. State-of-the-art content-based tag recommendation systems [18, 37] utilize several tag sources including item content and the user's previous history to build profiles for both users and tags. New tags are checked against user profiles, which are a rich, but imprecise source of information about user interests. The result is a set of tags related both to the resource and user.

Graph-based approaches, which usually have stronger assumptions than content-based ones (e.g., every user, every item and every tag has to occur in at least p posts), can often provide better performance. An example of early work is FolkRank, introduced by Hotho et al. [14], which is an adaptation of PageRank that can generate high quality recommendations and is shown to be empirically better than previously proposed collaborative filtering models [16]. Guan et al. [10] propose a framework based on the graph Laplacian to model interrelated multi-type objects involved in a tagging system. More recently, factorization models (also considered as graph-based approaches) have shown success on personalized tag recommendation problems. Symeonidis et al. [33] propose a method based on Higher-Order-Singular-Value-Decomposition (HOSVD), which corresponds to a Tucker Decomposition (TD) model optimized for square-loss where all not observed values are learned as 0s. Rendle et al. [27, 28] present a better learning approach for TD models, which is to optimize the model parameters for the AUC (area under the ROC-curve) ranking statistic. The main problem of the graph-based methods is that they can only predict tags for certain groups of existing users and web resources. Thus, a better tag recommender should be able to recommend tags for new users or new web resources, and still have reasonably good performance.

Non-personalized tag recommenders—i.e., for a given item they recommend to all users the same tags—have also attracted attention (e.g., [12, 32]). However, Rendel et al. [27] shows that personalized tag recommendation systems empirically outperform the theoretical upper bound for any non-personalized tag recommender.

Existing opinion mining or sentiment analysis studies [8, 15, 19] focus on summarizing and classifying comments, and discard higher-order relations for user-comment-item. In contrast, we focus on predicting users' opinions (i.e., the terms used) for an item instead of simply classifying the comment contents. Recently, Agarwal et al. [4] develop personalized comment recommendation via factor models but they do not predict the content (e.g., term frequency) of personalized comments.

There exist a number of latent factor methods. One related method is collective matrix factorization from Singh and Gordon [31] which provides a general framework to model multi-relational data, extending many previous approaches for matrix factorization in the presence of additional features. These extensions of matrix factorization/factor analysis tend to be limited to two or three relations to take into account contextual information (such as user-specific and movie-specific features) in a recommender system [42, 1, 2, 20]. For instance, Zhu et al. [42] propose to make use of links and content for web page classification. More recently, Agarwal and Chen [3] incorporate explicit features of users and items into latent factor models, and Ma et al. [20] propose to improve recommendation quality based on social regularization. However, these methods only model two factor data and cannot be directly used in a social tagging system which is naturally a higher-order system.

More generally, co-factorization models [11, 40, 41] make recommendations across multiple contexts or domains. While the framework proposed by Singh and Gordon [31] is fairly general, the key weakness is that it does not enable the handling of high-order relations, such as that needed in a social tagging system and it does not use Bayesian estimation to tackle the problem of data sparsity. Modeling higher or-

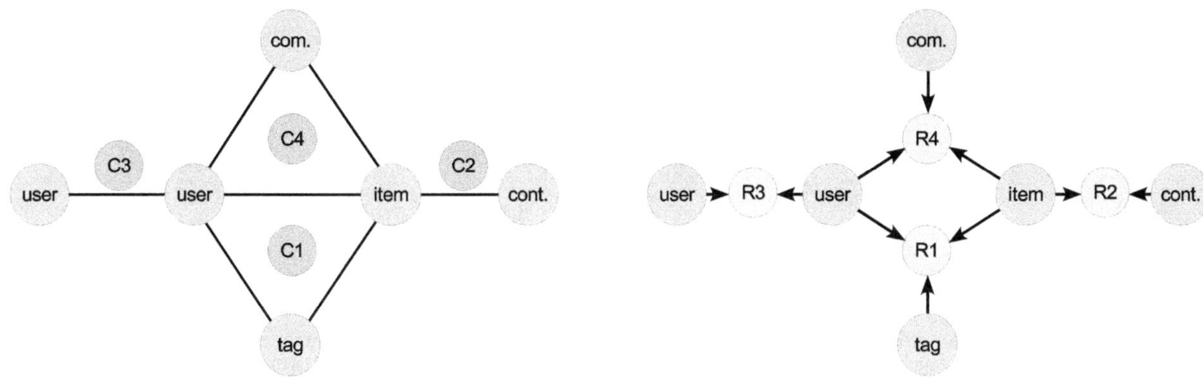

(a) Clique relations among the entity types serve as contexts

(b) Bipartite graph between relations and entity types

Figure 1: An example of four relations on five entity types in a social tagging system. R_1 is the tag post context (user-tag-item), R_2 is the item-content context (item-content feature), R_3 is the social network context (user-user) and R_4 is the comment context (user-comment-item).

der data in social media is often neglected in existing factor models.

3. PRELIMINARY EXPERIMENTS

In this section, we review characteristics of social tagging systems and describe the challenges and problems in modeling user behaviors such as tagging and commenting.

Unlike traditional collaborative filtering and recommendation tasks, in social tagging systems, a user's tagging and commenting activities generate relations involving more than two types of entities. In contrast, most traditional work focuses on second order relations that involve just two types of entities (e.g., user-item). In social tagging systems, the posts (that is, each tag produced by a user for an item) are by nature third order data [28, 27, 38, 37] that we consider as a triple (user-tag-item). Figure 1(a) shows that in a tagging system, users, tags and items pairwise interact and compose a clique. Similarly, users, tags and comments also interact pairwise. For the tag and comment prediction tasks, we cannot drop any one of user, tag/comments, or item. By involving the temporal factor, it even becomes fourth order data [37]. However, these types of higher order relations have rarely been studied due to the complexity and difficulty in modeling and inference.

On the other hand, the relational data from different contexts are coupled together. In Figure 1(a), we can see the social tagging entity relations: there exist four cliques in this social tagging system (user-tag-item, user-comment-item, user-user, item-content). Within these cliques, all involved entities interact with all others. Activities within these cliques are also strongly correlated with each other: for instance, activities where users comment on items or where users rate items share two of the same types of entity—user and item. With Figure 1(a), after recognizing the cliques, we can define them as contexts. Each context can be considered a type of observation individually and generated by the associated entities. In Figure 1(b), we see the directed bipartite graph, which describes which entities contribute to the process of generating each context. These contexts are frequently coupled together by sharing the same entities, increasing the difficulty of modeling.

3.1 Data sets

In this section, we conduct some simple analysis on two data sets: Flickr and Bibsonomy. The main data set is from Flickr. We crawl the data from **Flickr** by using the social-network connectors (Flickr API).[1] This data set includes 2,866 users, 60,339 tags, 32,752 comment terms and 46,733 items (e.g., images), leading to the four relations shown in Figure 1(b). The remaining dataset is a public dataset. The **Bibsonomy** dataset is from the ECML PKDD 09 Discovery Challenge Workshop[2] which includes two relations: user-tag-item and item-content.

In order to observe the variety of user interests in both datasets, for each user, we calculate and plot the total number of tags, and the total number of posts. In Figure 2(a), we can see that the two datasets have different properties and users form two clusters. In Bibsonomy, users typically apply a larger variety of tags across fewer posts, suggesting that their interests are more varied. In contrast, the users in Flickr use fewer tags and their interests are more focused, reusing their tags many times. This suggests that it may be easier to track user interests in Flickr.

3.2 Coupled higher-order system

We now conduct some simple analyses for different relations. At first, we check the distribution of tags and terms in the comments. Figure 2(b) shows a linear relationship between the of number of tags/terms and the frequency of tags/terms in log scale. We can see that the distributions over both tags and comment terms are very similar and show two straight lines with the same slope in the log-log plot. In the (user, comment, item) relation, among the 21,881 records where a user comments on an item, 8,307 records show that the user also tags the same item, meaning if a user comments on an item there will be around 1/3 chance that the user will also contribute a tag on that item. This

[1]http://www.flickr.com/services/api/

[2]http://www.kde.cs.uni-kassel.de/ws/dc09/

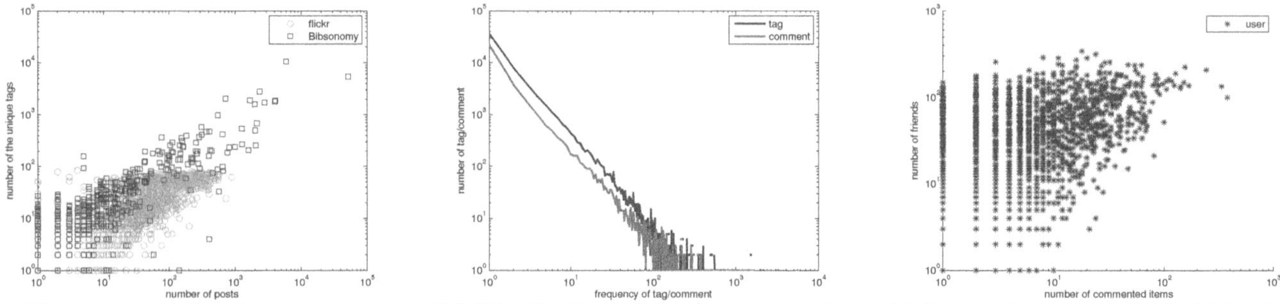

(a) The number of unique tags as a function of the number of posts for each user across datasets

(b) Distribution of tag/comments frequency in Flickr

(c) For each user, number of friends as a function of the number of commented items in Flickr

Figure 2: Representative analyses for different activities.

Table 1: Fractions of new users, items, or tags in samples from each data set.

	Bibsonomy	Flickr
New/Total Users	41/668	23/1000
New/Total Items	602/668	1000/1000
New/Total Tags	321/2207	175/4123

evidence shows the strong connection between the relation (user, comment, item) and the relation (user, tag, item).

Figure 2(c) shows the coupling between user-user interaction and commenting activity. From the figure, we can see that most users are located on the upper left portion of the Figure. Some users with many friends may NOT comment at all (or very little) but users who frequently comment items usually have many friends. We also note that the inverse does not hold.

3.3 Cold start

As in our earlier work in tag prediction [38, 37], we employ online evaluation[3] in which only training posts which have earlier timestamps than those of the test posts are used. Note that this implies that the available training data is different for each test post and, for items tagged earlier in the timeline, fewer training data are available. While the online evaluation approach naturally fits the real-world case in which every post is used for testing a model trained on all prior posts, its feasibility depends highly on the efficiency of the training method as a new model may be necessary for each post. Instead, we can estimate the performance of the complete system by performing evaluation on only a sample of test posts, and largely avoid model-building efficiency concerns for the purpose of evaluation of effectiveness.

We utilize the online evaluation model and conduct time-sensitive sampling experiments on two data sets. For the Bibsonomy dataset, we use the same sampling dataset as in Yin et al. [38] which includes 668 test posts. For Flickr, we randomly choose 1000 posts. In all cases we effectively simulate a system running—the tagging system operates in an incremental mode. The data set statistics (shown in Table 1) demonstrate that in Bibsonomy data, we face a new user (a user which is not in any prior data) in 6.1% of the cases, and in 90.1% of the time users are trying to bookmark a "new item" not previously seen by the system. In addition, there is 13.9% chance that users would use new tags (which do not appear in the system before).

This shows that most of the time (i.e., 86.1% of posts) it is feasible to predict tags based only on past tags. The other dataset also shows similar distributions. Thus, in the real world, the principal difficulty is to handle cases in which existing users try to tag new items and therefore strictly graph-based recommenders (e.g., [27, 28]) will not be able to make recommendations most of the time. This also suggests that incorporating external information, such as item or comment content into the model might help process these cold start cases.

3.4 Data sparsity

Another notorious problem in most social media systems is data sparsity. Here, we define the number of observations over the total number of entries in the relations as the density of the data. For comparison, in one MovieLens data set[4], there are 1,000,000 ratings for 6,000 users and 4,000 movies, so the data density is just 4.17%, rendering it 95.83The sparsity of data is even more serious when the relation is higher-order and coupled in a social tagging system: in our Flickr data, there are 373,125 records of the user-tag-item relation, so the density of the context user-tag-item is 4.6170×10^{-8} $(373125/(2866 \times 60339 \times 46733))$, and for the context user-comments-item, there are 218161 records, so its density is 3.8518×10^{-8} $(218161/(2866 \times 60339 \times 32752))$. Similarly in our Bibsonomy data, the data density is 3.52×10^{-8}. Thus, data sparsity is dauntingly higher in social tag data than the traditional two-dimensional recommendation problem. The serious problem of sparsity in higher order relations strongly suggests Bayesian treatment. Previous work has already shown the significant advantage of the Bayesian approach in processing sparse data, such as in the comparison of LDA [6] to PLSA [13] and BPMF [29] to PMF [30].

4. MULTI-RELATIONAL DATA MODEL

To address the problems described above in Section 3, here we propose a novel latent factor model to handle coupled

[3]In this paper, online mode means an incremental mode of a real tagging system rather than real-time tag prediction.

[4]http://www.grouplens.org/node/73

K	Number of entity types.
N_k	Number of entities of type k.
D	Latent feature dimension.
V	Number of relations.
Θ_k	Latent features for entities of type k.
R_v	Set of relation v observations.
M_v	Total number of observations of relation v.
S_v	List of indices identifying the types of relation v.
α_v^{-1}	Variance of the observations of relation v.

Table 2: Summary of the notation used.

higher-order data in social tagging systems. We describe a Bayesian treatment to learn the parameters in the model.

An activity performed by a user in a specific social tag context induces a relation; for instance, the activity consisting of the triple (user-comment-item) is a 3-order relation with three types of entities. Let us consider a coupled higher order relational dataset with K types of entities. There are V possible relations among the entities and, for each entity type $k \in \{1, \dots, K\}$, there are N_k possible entities. Each relation $v \in \{1, \dots, V\}$ is associated with the list S_v of the entity types involved in relation v, that is $S_v = (S_{v1}, \dots, S_{v|S_v|})$ with $S_{vj} \in \{1, \dots, K\}$. Relations are then encoded by multi dimensional arrays, where dimension j is indexed by entity type S_{vj}. The data associated with relation v are the observed triplets $\mathcal{D} = (v_m, \mathbf{i}_m, r_m)_{m=1}^{M}$ where for the mth observation, $v_m \in \{1, \dots, V\}$ is the index of the relation and $\mathbf{i}_m = (i_{m1}, \dots, i_{m|S_{v_m}|})$ is a list of entity indices identifying the observation with value $r_m \in \mathbb{R}$.

Our probabilistic multi-relational data model assumes that each entity can be represented by a latent (i.e., unobserved) continuous feature vector in $\mathbb{R}^D$, where D is typically small (e.g., of the order of 10 or 100). The low-dimensional latent features are denoted by $\boldsymbol{\Theta} = (\Theta_1, \dots, \Theta_K)$, where $\Theta_k = (\boldsymbol{\theta}_{k1}, \dots, \boldsymbol{\theta}_{kN_k})^T \in \mathbb{R}^{N_k \times D}$ contains the feature vectors associated to entity type k.

A summary of notation is shown in Table 2. To facilitate understanding of the notation, we consider the example described in Figure 3 where there are four relations and five entity types: u for users, i for items, f for item features, t for tags and c for comment terms. The four relations are coupled together by linking the same types of entities. Two of these four relations linking different entity types forms a 3-dimensional array, while the other two relations are encoded as two 2-dimensional arrays. To this end, we can define S as $\{S_1, S_2, S_3, S_4\}$, where $S_1 = \{u, i, t\}$, $S_2 = \{i, f\}$, $S_3 = \{u, u\}$ and $S_4 = \{u, c, i\}$.

Figure 4 shows the graphical model for multi-relational data factorization. The model assumes multilinear links in order to predict the mean of the observations given the latent features of the corresponding entities. Formally, this means that for an observation of relation v with indices $\mathbf{i} = (i_1, \dots, i_{|S_v|})$, the mean of the observation r is a multi-dimensional dot-product $\langle ., \cdots, . \rangle$ defined as

$$\langle \boldsymbol{\Theta}_{\mathbf{i}} \rangle = \langle \theta_{i_1}, \cdots, \theta_{i|S_v|} \rangle = \sum_{d=1}^{D} \prod_{k \in S_v} \theta_{k i_k d} \ .$$

Note that for binary relations, this is equivalent to a standard vectorial dot-product. In this paper, the distribution of the observations is assumed to be Gaussian with relation-dependent variances α_v^{-1}. This assumption can be relaxed easily to model other types of generalized linear models such as Poisson or Bernoulli distributions. Assuming independent observations, the likelihood of total observations $\mathcal{D}$ is given by

$$\begin{aligned} p(\mathcal{D}|\boldsymbol{\Theta}) &= \prod_{(v,\mathbf{i},r)\in\mathcal{D}} p(r|\theta_{S_{v1}i_1}, \dots, \theta_{S_{v|S_v|}i_{|S_v|}}, \alpha_v) \\ &= \prod_{(v,\mathbf{i},r)\in\mathcal{D}} \mathcal{N}(r|\sum_{d=1}^{D} \prod_{k\in S_v} \theta_{k i_k d}, \alpha_v^{-1}) \\ &= \prod_{(v,\mathbf{i},r)\in\mathcal{D}} e^{-\ell(\sum_{d=1}^{D} \prod_{k\in S_v} \theta_{k i_k d}, r; \alpha_v)}, \end{aligned}$$

where $\ell(\bar{r}, r; \alpha) = \frac{\alpha}{2}(r - \bar{r})^2 - \frac{1}{2}\log\frac{\alpha}{2\pi}$ is the quadratic loss.

We also assume that the prior distributions over $\Theta_1, \dots, \Theta_K$ are independent isotropic Gaussian distributions with type-dependent variances $\sigma_1^2, \dots, \sigma_K^2$:

$$p(\Theta_k|\sigma_k^2) = \prod_{j=1}^{N_k} \mathcal{N}(\theta_{kj}|0, \sigma_k^2 \mathbf{I}).$$

Now that we have presented the model, the remaining problem is to infer the latent variables $\boldsymbol{\Theta}$ given the observations. We consider the *Maximum a Posteriori* (MAP) estimator of $\boldsymbol{\Theta}$. The problem is therefore a simple minimization problem of a smooth and differentiable objective function equal to the negative log-likelihood:

$$\min_{\boldsymbol{\Theta}} \mathcal{O}, \quad \text{where} \quad \mathcal{O} := -\log p(\mathcal{D}|\boldsymbol{\Theta}, \boldsymbol{\alpha}) - \log p(\boldsymbol{\Theta}|\boldsymbol{\sigma}) \qquad (1)$$

and $\boldsymbol{\alpha} = (\alpha_1, \dots, \alpha_V)$ and $\boldsymbol{\sigma} = (\sigma_1, \dots, \sigma_K)$.

Two approaches to solve the optimization problem are *stochastic gradient descent* (SGD) and *alternating least squares* (ALS). ALS is a block-coordinate descent algorithm which minimizes Equation (1) with respect to one of the types, say Θ_k by fixing all others and repeats the same procedure for each Θ_k sequentially, ensuring that each step decreases the objective function. The procedure is repeated until convergence. The inner optimization problems are ordinary least squares which can be solved optimally. However, there is evidence from the tensor factorization literature that this procedure is not always effective because there are often strong dependencies between the feature values of the different types [25]. In addition, our method targets very large data sets for which even one pass through the data can be slow. This setting favors SGD-type algorithms since every gradient estimation is much cheaper than their batch counterpart (i.e., using standard unconstrained optimization tools such as L-BFGS [23]). This type of first-order optimization technique can be formally justified by a bias-variance argument, remarking that the ultimate goal of the

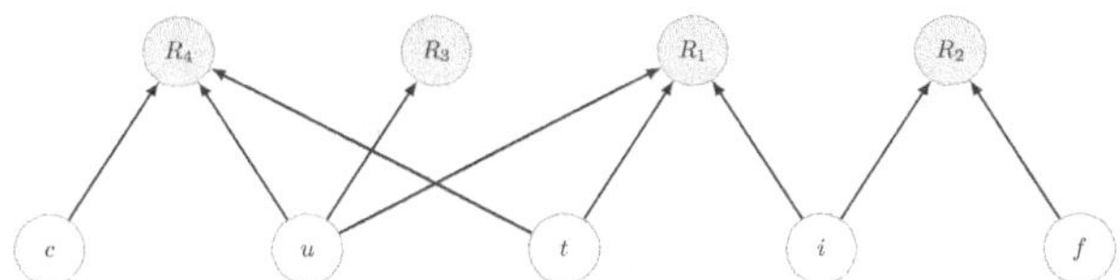

Figure 3: A bipartite graph representation of tagging system shown in Fig 1(b)

estimation procedure is not the minimization of the objective (1), but the minimization of its expectation $\mathbb{E}[\mathcal{O}]$ under the sample distribution [7].

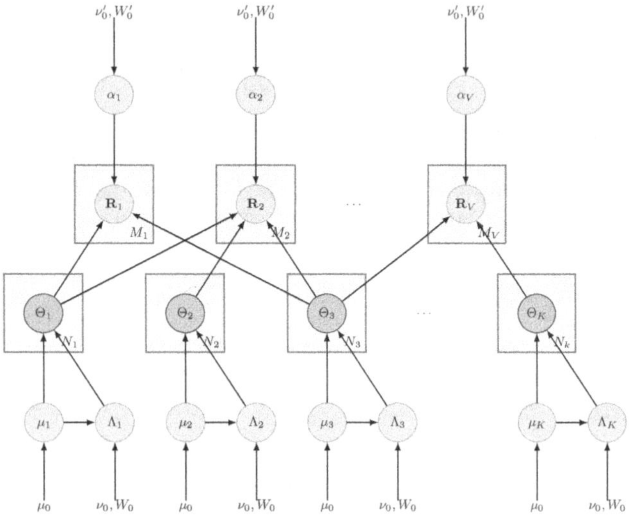

Figure 4: Sample Bayesian probabilistic multi-relational data factorization graphical model. $R_1, \ldots, R_V$ are the observed relations. $\Theta_1, \ldots, \Theta_K$ are the latent features associated to the K entity types. $\alpha_1, \ldots, \alpha_V$ are the unobserved precisions (inverse variances) associated with the observed relations, and similarly $\mu_1, \mu_2, \ldots, \mu_k$ and $\Lambda_1, \Lambda_2, \ldots, \Lambda_k$ are the unobserved mean and variances associated with latent features.

4.1 Bayesian Treatment

The performance of the probabilistic model is tied to the careful tuning of the hyper-parameter when model parameters Θ are estimated by maximum a posteriori probability (MAP) [29]. When the hyper-parameters are not properly tuned, such a point estimation—MAP—is often vulnerable to overfitting, especially when the data is large and sparse.

Instead of using MAP, an alternative estimation scheme that may avoid these problems is a fully Bayesian treatment, which integrates out all model parameters and hyper-parameters, arriving at a predictive distribution of future observations given observed data. Because this predictive distribution is obtained by averaging all models in the model space specified by the priors, it is less likely to over-fit a given set of observations.

A graphical overview of our entire model is in Figure 4, and each component is described below.

In this paper, we assume the observations follow a Gaussian distribution. As in the probabilistic model, this assumption can also be relaxed easily to model other types of generalized linear models such as Poisson or Bernoulli distributions. For each observation $(v, \mathbf{i}, r) \in \mathcal{D}$, we have

$$r|\Theta_{\mathbf{i}} \sim \mathcal{N}(\langle \mathbf{\Theta}_{\mathbf{i}} \rangle, \alpha_v), \text{ where } (v, \mathbf{i}, r) \in \mathcal{D}$$

The prior distribution for hidden feature Θ is assumed to be Gaussian too, but the mean and the precision matrix (inverse of the covariance matrix) may take arbitrary value:

$$\theta_{kj} \sim \mathcal{N}(\mu_k, \Lambda_k^{-1}), \quad j = 1 \ldots N_k$$

The key ingredient of our fully Bayesian treatment is to view the hyper-parameter $\Phi_k \equiv \{\mu_k, \Lambda_k\}$ also as a random variable, leading to a predictive distribution for an unobserved rating $(v, \mathbf{i}, \hat{r})$

$$p(\hat{r}|\mathcal{D}) = \int\int p(\hat{r}|\Theta_{\mathbf{i}}, \alpha_v) p(\Theta_{\mathbf{i}}, \alpha, \Phi_{\mathbf{i}}|\mathcal{D}) d\{\Theta_{\mathbf{i}}, \alpha_v\}, d\{\Phi_{\mathbf{i}}\}$$

For convenience, we also define $\Phi_{\mathbf{i}} = \{\Phi_{i_1}, \ldots \Phi_{i_{|S_v|}}\}$. We then need to choose a prior distribution for the hyper-parameters. For the Gaussian parameter, we choose the conjugate distribution as priors that facilitate subsequent computation:

$$p(\alpha_v) = \mathcal{W}(\alpha_v|W_0', v_0')$$
$$p(\Phi_k) = p(\mu_k|\Lambda_k)p(\Lambda_k) = \mathcal{N}(\mu_0, (\beta_0\Lambda_k)^{-1})\mathcal{W}(\Lambda_k|W_0, v_0)$$

Here $\mathcal{W}$ is the Wishart distribution of a $D \times D$ random matrix Λ with v_0 degrees of freedom and a $D \times D$ scale W_0:

$$\mathcal{W}(\Lambda|W_0, v_0) = \frac{|\Lambda|^{(v_0 - D - 1)/2}}{C} \exp(-\frac{\mathrm{Tr}(W_0^{-1}\Lambda)}{2})$$

where C is a normalizing constant. There are several parameters in the hyper-priors: $\mu_0, \rho_0, \beta_0, W_0, v_0, W_0', v_0'$, which reflect our prior knowledge about the specific problem and can be treated as constants during training. In fact, Bayesian learning is able to adjust them according to the training data, and varying their values (within in a reasonably large range) has little impact on the final prediction, as is often observed in Bayesian estimation procedures [35].

5. INFERENCE

One can represent the predictive distribution of the relation value r given observation $(v, \mathbf{i}, r) \in \mathcal{D}$ by marginalizing over model parameters:

$$p(\hat{r}|\mathcal{D}) = \int\int p(\hat{r}|\Theta_{\mathbf{i}}, \alpha_v) p(\Theta_{\mathbf{i}}, \alpha, \Phi_{\mathbf{i}}|\mathcal{D}) d\{\Theta_{\mathbf{i}}, \alpha_v\}, d\{\Phi_{\mathbf{i}}\}$$

Often the exact predictive disribution is intractable; thus one relies on approximate inference such as sampling based on Markov chain Monte Carlo (MCMC) [21, 22]. For instance, MCMC can be used to approximate the predictive distribution of Eq. 2:

$$p(\hat{r}|\mathcal{D}) = \frac{1}{L}\sum_{l=1}^{L} p(\hat{r}|\Theta_{\mathbf{i}}^{(l)})$$

where the sample $\Theta_{\mathbf{i}}^{(l)}$ is generated by running a Markov chain whose stationary distribution is the posterior distribution over the model parameters and hyper-parameter Θ, Φ.

One of the simplest MCMC algorithms is Gibbs sampling [9], which cycles through the latent variables, sampling each one from the conditional distribution given the current values of all other variables. Gibbs sampling is typically used when these conditional distributions can be sampled from easily. In this section we give detailed derivation for the conditional distributions of model parameters and hyper-parameters which are required for implementing Gibbs sampling. Note that with our model assumptions, the joint posterior distribution can be factorized as

$$p(\Theta, \alpha, \Phi|\mathcal{D}) \propto \prod_{(v,\mathbf{i},r)\in\mathcal{D}} p(r|\theta_{S_{v1}i_1}, \ldots, \theta_{S_{v|S_v|}i_{|S_v|}}, \alpha_v)$$
$$\prod_k [p(\Theta_k|\Phi_k)p(\Phi_k)] \prod_v p(\alpha_v) \quad (2)$$

5.1 Hyper-parameters

We start with the derivation of the conditional distributions of the model hyper-parameters. For each v, α_v follows the Wishart distribution. By using the conjugate prior to α_v, we have the conditional distribution of α_v given R_v, Θ following the Wishart distribution:

$$p(\alpha_v|\mathcal{D}_v, \Theta) = \mathcal{W}(\alpha_v|W_0^*, v_0^*) \quad (3)$$

where

$$\begin{aligned} v_0^* &= v_0' + |\mathcal{D}_v|, \\ (W_0^*)^{-1} &= W_0'^{-1} + \sum_{(v,\mathbf{i},r)\in\mathcal{D}_v} (r - \langle\mathbf{\Theta}_\mathbf{i}\rangle)^2. \end{aligned}$$

Next, we derive the conditional probability for Φ_k. Our graphical model (Fig. 4) assumption suggests that it is conditionally independent of all the other parameters given Θ_k. We thus integrate out all the random variables in Eq. 2 except Θ_k, and obtain the Gaussian-Wishart distribution:

$$p(\Phi_k|\Theta_k) = N(\mu_k|\mu_0^*, (\beta_0^*\Lambda_k)^{-1})\mathcal{W}(\Lambda_k|W_0^*, v_0^*), \quad (4)$$

where

$$\mu_0^* = \frac{\beta_0\mu_0 + N_k\bar{\theta}_k}{\beta_0 + N_k}, \ \beta_0^* = \beta_0 + N_k, \ v_0^* = v_0 + N_k;$$

$$(W_0^*)^{-1} = W_0^{-1} + N_k\bar{S} + \frac{\beta_0 N_k}{\beta_0 + N_k}(\mu_0 - \bar{\theta}_k)(\mu_0 - \bar{\theta}_k)^T,$$

$$\bar{\theta}_k = \frac{1}{N_k}\sum_{j=1}^{N_k}\theta_{ki}, \ \bar{S} = \frac{1}{N_k}\sum_{j=1}^{N_k}(\theta_{kj} - \bar{\theta}_k)(\theta_{kj} - \bar{\theta}_k)^T.$$

5.2 Model-parameters

The remaining conditional distributions are for model parameters Θ_k, and we describe the derivation of these distributions in this section. According to the graphical model (Fig. 4), its conditional distribution factorizes with respect to the individual entities:

$$p(\Theta_k|\mathcal{D}, \Theta_{-k}, \alpha, \Phi_k) = \prod_{j=1}^{N_k} p(\theta_{kj}|\mathcal{D}, \Theta_{-k}, \alpha, \Phi_k)$$

$$p(\theta_{kj}|\mathcal{D}, \Theta_{-k}, \alpha, \Phi_k) = \mathcal{N}(\theta_{kj}|\mu_{kj}^*, (\Lambda_{kj}^*)^{-1}) \quad (5)$$

where

$$\begin{aligned} \mu_{kj}^* &= (\Lambda_{kj}^*)^{-1}(\Lambda_k\mu_k + \sum_{v\in\{v'|k\in S_{v'}\}} \alpha_v \sum_{(v,\mathbf{i},r)\in\mathcal{D}_v, kj\in\mathbf{i}} rQ_{(v,\mathbf{i},r)}) \\ \Lambda_{kj}^* &= \Lambda_k + \sum_{v\in\{v'|k\in S_{v'}\}} \alpha_v \sum_{(v,\mathbf{i},r)\in\mathcal{D}_v, kj\in\mathbf{i}} Q_{(v,\mathbf{i},r)}Q_{(v,\mathbf{i},r)}^T \\ Q_{(v,\mathbf{i},r)} &= \frac{\prod_{n=1}^{|S_v|}\theta_{S_{v,n},i_n}}{\theta_{kj}} \end{aligned}$$

6. EXPERIMENTS

We conduct systematic experiments to evaluate the two versions of our proposed model, named PRA (Probabilistic Relational-data Analysis) and BPRA (Bayesian Probabilistic Relational-data Analysis) on two data sets: Flickr and Bibsonomy.[5]

[5]To facilitate replication of experiments, sourcecode and datasets are available upon request.

Algorithm 1 Gibbs sampler for Relational Data Analysis

INPUT: hyper-prior parameters $\{\mu_0, \rho_0, \beta_0, W_0, v_0, W_0', v_0'\}$
OUTPUT: model parameters $\{\Theta\}$

Initialize model parameters $\{\Theta^{(1)}\}$
for $l = 1, ..., L$, **do**
  Sample the hyper-parameters according to Eq. {3, 4 }, respectively:

$$\begin{aligned} \alpha_v^{(l)} &\sim p(\alpha_v|\mathcal{D}, \Theta^{(1)}) \text{ where } v = 1, \ldots, V \\ \Phi_k^{(l)} &\sim p(\Phi_k|\mathcal{D}, \Theta_k^{(1)}) \text{ where } k = 1, \ldots, K \end{aligned}$$

  Sample the model parameters in parallel according to Eq. {5}:
  for $k = 1, \ldots, K$ **do**
    for each latent factor

$$\theta_{kj}^{(l+1)} \sim p(\theta_{kj}|\mathcal{D}, \Theta_{1:k-1}^{(l+1)}, \Theta_{k+1:K}^{(l)}, \alpha^{(l)}, \Phi^{(l)}) \text{ where } j = 1, \ldots, N_k \text{and } k \neq t$$

  end for
end for

6.1 Evaluation and Comparison Methods

As there are different kinds of responses (such as binary, term frequency and real value) in our recommendation tasks across multi-contexts, we employ Root Mean Square Error (RMSE) as our primary measurement for all contexts. In our Bayesian probabilistic relational-data model, we simply set $\mu_0, \rho_0, \beta_0, W_0, v_0, W_0', v_0'$ all equal to one or identity vector and $D = 20$ for the dimension of latent factors, on all three data sets. Our experiments also show that the performance is fairly robust to changes to the hyper-prior.

In the following experiments, we compare our methods with four state-of-the-art latent factor methods:

- Salakhutdinov's Probabilistic Matrix Factorization (PMF) [30]: collaborative filtering using probabilistic matrix factorization which treats activities as independent.
- Bayesian Probabilistic Matrix Factorization (BPMF) proposed by Salakhutdinov et al. [29]: the Bayesian version of PMF.
- Rendle's Tensor Factorization (TF) [27, 28] which handles high-order relational data for tag prediction and showed prior success in the graph-based tag recommendation task.
- Bayesian Probabilistic Tensor Factorization (BPTF) proposed by Xiong et al. [35] which models temporal collaborative filtering, and whose extension is straightforward to model higher order relational data such as user-tag-comments.

6.2 Flickr Experiments

6.2.1 *Data set*

The Flickr data has been briefly described in Section 3. This data set includes 2,866 users, 60,339 tags, 32,752 comment terms and 46,733 items (e.g., images), leading to four relations. The relation $S_1 = (u, t, i)$ indicates that user u tags item i with tag t. The relation $S_2 = (i, f)$ characterizes item i with a 1024-dimension feature vector f extracted according to [24], which are of real numbers. The relation $S_3 = (u_1, u_2)$ encodes a partially observed adjacency matrix representing the explicitly expressed friendship relations among users. For instance, if user u_1 and u_2 are friends, then the value at (u_1, u_2) and (u_2, u_1) are both equal to 1, 0 otherwise. The relation $S_4 = (u, c, i)$ indicates that user u comments on item i using word c, and this relation can be described by term frequency (positive integers).

In the first relation, the problem of interest is tag prediction, that is, to predict tags that users will assign to items. We need to model relation S_1, for which the Flickr data set has a total of 373,125 records with time stamps. The data is partitioned into training and test sets based on the time stamp of April 1st 2010. In total, there are 2,613,388 observations for training and 205,880 observations for testing. Note that there are only positive samples of tags available for the Flickr data set, so we sample 50 tags at random as negative examples for training. For the relation user-comment-item, where users could make some comments on a specific item, we try to predict the term frequency in the comments and the data also are split into training and test data set similarly, resulting in 1,366,068 training observations and 341,043 testing observations.

As mentioned above, we also have two more contexts: for image content, we characterize image i by a feature vector f of 1024-dimensional visual features according to Perronnin and Dance [24]; the social context is also comprised of binary typed observations, which contain 1,377,548 training observations and 342,576 test observations.

6.2.2 Analysis of relations and their co-effects

Some explanatory analysis has been presented in Section 3. A social tagging system is a coupled higher-order data system and multiple contexts are coupled together. Here, we will show that by using our methods together with Bayesian treatment, predictive accuracy can be mutually improved.

We first conduct two versions of our model: PRA for MAP version and BPRA for Bayesian version. In Table 3, it can be seen that the Bayesian method clearly outperforms the MAP version (in all scenarios), due to the high data sparsity. In Figure 5(a), we show the convergence of our Bayesian model BPRA which starts sampling with parameters based on the results of PRA. We can see that after around 50 epochs, the performance on two relations converge. In the following sections, we will use Bayesian version for analysis and comparison.

Another interesting question is: do coupled relations lead to mutually improved prediction performance? We conduct experiments on modeling different relations with several combinations to study this question. The tasks are described in Section 6.2.1 for different relations and the results are shown in Table 3. The first four rows of the table indicate that best performances are achieved for all four relations when modeling them together. The following three rows (rows 5-7) of the table indicate the performance of modeling three relations (C1, C2, C4). Similarly, the results of modeling (C1, C3, C4) and (C1, C4) are shown in the remaining rows. Taking the prediction of Context 1 (C1: user-tag-item) relation as an example: the best performance is 0.3073 in modeling all four relations, 0.3177 in modeling the three relations (C1, C3, C4), and degrades to 0.3465 when only modeling the relation (C1, C4) together. Comparable results for comment prediction are also shown in Figure 5(c).

6.2.3 Comparison with existing methods

We report the evaluation of our models together with comparisons to state-of-the-art approaches introduced earlier. Bayesian Probabilistic Matrix Factorization and its Bayesian treatment are popular methods and have shown success in traditional collaborative filtering. In our experiments with binary contexts, we compare our methods with PMF and BPMF. Since TF and BPTF can model the tag prediction and comment prediction tasks, we compare our methods with them in such higher-order contexts.

We summarize the results in Table 3. While Section 3 showed that over 90% of real-world cases are cold start problems and the graph-based methods (such as Hotho's Folkrank and Rendle's tensor factorization) will not work on such cases, we still compare to the state of the art method—tensor factorization. The results show that Rendle's TF performs the worst in tag prediction, because it only models a single relation without encoding external information of items. Intuitively the external information of items (e.g., comments, features) is more critical to the tag prediction task. This result agrees with [38]. For the cold start problem, the external information of items is essential for tag prediction because most items do not exist in the training data.

In the comment prediction context, we see similar results; tensor factorization performs the worst because of the lack of external information and data sparsity. Xiong's method—Bayesian Tensor Factorization—is much better, but our methods still achieve the best performance. In both tag and comment prediction, the experiments show that in such a real-world case, tensor factorization is insufficient and Bayesian treatment on tensor factorization can improve performance significantly because of the data sparsity. We also note that with more information in the model, the performance of our approach improves, e.g., with social relation information (C3), we can see that both tag and comment prediction improves.

Overall, we can see that for all methods, the Bayesian

Table 3: RMSE of 4 relations for Flickr data set. Context 1 for users tagging items (user-tag-item), Context 2 for item content (item-feature), Context 3 for social interaction (user-user) and Context 4 for users' comments on item (user-item-comments)

	BPRA	PRA	PMF	BPMF	TF	BPTF
C1	**0.3073**	0.3599	N/A	N/A	0.8226	0.3520
C2	0.9215	0.9627	0.9913	**0.9004**	N/A	N/A
C3	**0.1828**	0.2053	0.1841	0.1878	N/A	N/A
C4	**0.3478**	0.3676	N/A	N/A	0.4185	0.3593
C1	0.3449	0.4450	N/A	N/A	0.8226	0.3520
C2	0.9198	0.9630	0.9913	0.9004	N/A	N/A
C4	0.3516	0.3681	N/A	N/A	0.4185	0.3593
C1	0.3177	0.3984	N/A	N/A	0.8226	0.3520
C3	0.1858	0.2298	0.1841	0.1878	N/A	N/A
C4	0.3482	0.4241	N/A	N/A	0.4185	0.3593
C1	0.3465	0.7843	N/A	N/A	0.8226	0.3520
C4	0.3530	0.3656	N/A	N/A	0.4185	0.3593

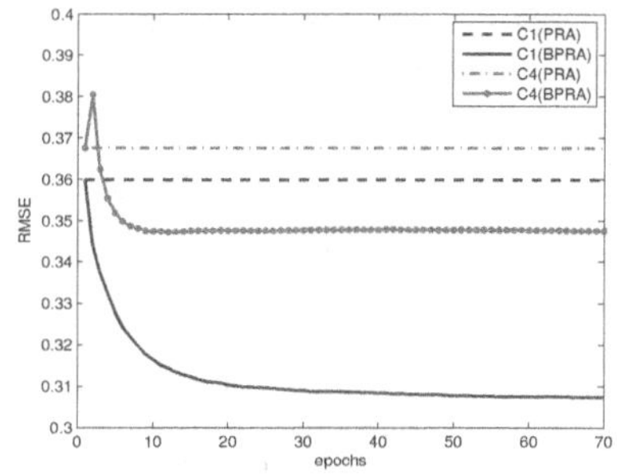

(a) BPRA vs. PRA on Flickr

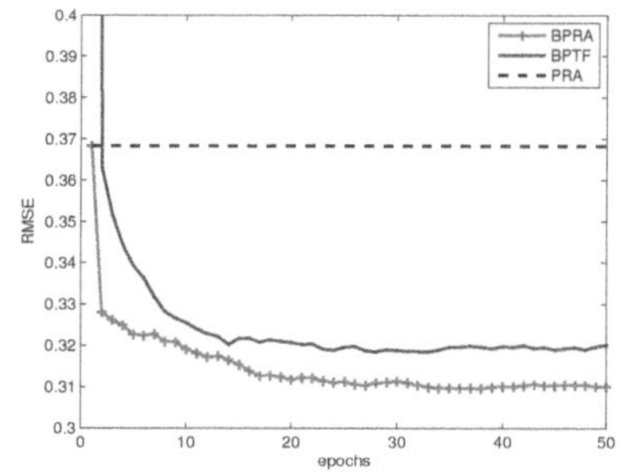

(b) Experiments on Bibsonomy

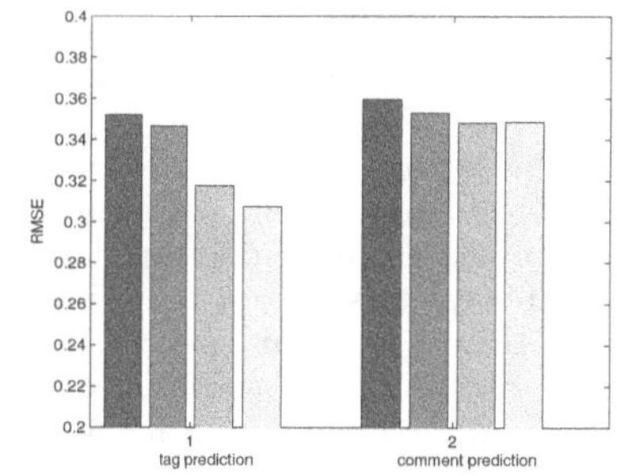

(c) RMSE decreasing with more contexts on Flickr

Figure 5: Experimental results for different activities exhibited in the two data sets.

versions always outperform the MAP version respectively, due to the sparsity of the data. Our model outperforms all four recent nontrivial methods—PMF, TF, BPMF, BPTF in the comments context, social network context and tag context. We also notice that in the item feature relation, our model is slightly worse than BPMF. That is because our model tries to maximize the total likelihood for all relations.

6.3 Bibsonomy Experiments

The second data set used to evaluate our model is Bibsonomy—the bookmark data set of the ECML-PKDD'09 Discovery Challenge. This data set involves 2,679 users, 263,004 items, 56,424 tags, 262,336 posts and 1,401,104 records. Clearly, this is also a very sparse data set, whose density is only 3.52×10^{-8}. Each post is associated with a time stamp, and each item contains textual content. In this experiment, we show that the single graph-based model cannot work in the real world (where the data set is split by time stamp). By incorporating content into the model, prediction accuracy can be significantly improved. To generate a descriptor for the items, we first use the bag-of-words language model and then use Latent Dirichlet Allocation [6] to produce a latent factor for each item. There are only two relations for this data set: $S_1 = (u, t, i)$, where user u tag item i with tag t, and $S_2 = (i, f)$, where each item i is described by a 100-dimensional feature f. To model S_1, we use a time stamp of August 1st 2008 to distinguish training and testing sets with 7,214,426 and 1,585,179 observations respectively.

We show the results for Bibsonomy in Table 4. At first, we compare the two versions of our model: BPRA is still clearly much better than PRA, benefiting from handling sparse data well. Similarly, in Figure 5(b), we show the convergence of our Bayesian model BPRA which starts sampling with parameters based on the results of PRA. We can see that after around 50 epochs, performance converges. The convergence in Bibsonomy experiments is consistent with our Flickr experiments. We also compare our methods with the baselines. Similarly, BPMF and BPTF outperform PMF and TF respectively. The experiments on this data set also verify the necessity of employing Bayesian treatment in social relational data.

TF almost fails to solve the task specified by (user-tag-item) relation without item external information, because as we have shown in Section 3, most items in a tagging log are

Table 4: RMSE on the Bibsonomy data set. Context 1 for users tagging items (user-tag-item) and Context 2 for item content (item-feature)

	BPRA	PRA	PMF	BPMF	TF	BPTF
C1	**.3097**	0.3484	N/A	N/A	1.0409	0.3455
C2	**1.0088**	1.0118	1.7387	1.1025	N/A	N/A

new items. The results of our model are consistent with the Flickr data: our model noticeably decreases the RMSE for the tag prediction task. The performance for both relations can lead to significant improvements: 0.3097 in the (user-tag-item) relation and 1.0088 in the (item-feature) relation respectively. This also confirms that the two contexts can mutually reinforce the performance of the model. Overall, like in Flickr experiments, our Bayesian model noticeably outperforms all other methods in the Bibsonomy data set.

7. CONCLUSION AND FUTURE WORK

In this paper, we examined how to model predictive social tagging systems. We found that user activity modeling in social tagging systems suffers from coupled high order interaction, data sparsity, and the cold start problem. We tackled these problems with a novel generalized latent factor model and Bayesian treatment. We found that in social tagging systems, the user-comment-item and user-tag-item relations can be mutually inferred based on common latent factors and thus improve prediction performance, which has not been explored previously.

Our novel latent factor model can handle multiple activities, such as commenting within tagging systems and can do so simultaneously and demonstrate predictive superiority over state-of-the-art methods. Our experiments on two real-world data sets also show the advantage of employing a fully Bayesian treatment to boost the performance of point estimation when modeling high order relations.

There are many possible extensions to the current approach, either in terms of scalability or in terms of modeling. A first direction is to investigate how to incorporate temporal factors into the model. Temporal factors have been shown to be important by a number of previous efforts[37, 17, 35]. A significant improvement is expected through incorporating temporal factors.

Secondly, in our experiments, we found that different contexts, e.g., tag context and comments context may have different convergence speeds. One possible solution is that one could add a *core tensor* in each of the factored matrices and tensors, as is done in Tucker decomposition for tensors [34]. It enables a more flexible parameterization of the problem thanks to the use of relation-specific core tensors.[6] It will also enable entity specific latent dimensions $D_1, \cdots, D_k$ instead of the constant dimension D used for all the entities.

While the proposed algorithm can scale to hundreds of thousands of observations, it requires several hours to converge. A possible solution is to utilize deterministic approximate inference techniques such as variational Bayes to further improve the convergence speed and enable the possibility of using gradient descent algorithms instead of Gibbs sampling.

Another potentially interesting follow-up of this work is the study of very large data sets, for which distributed algorithms can be designed thanks to the decomposable formulation of the loss. The on-the-fly computation of predictions might be also of interest in order to obtain near real-time responses.

8. REFERENCES

[1] E. Acar, T. G. Kolda, and D. M. Dunlavy. All-at-once optimization for coupled matrix and tensor factorizations. In *MLG*, 2011.

[2] R. Adams, G. Dahl, and I. Murray. Incorporating side information in probabilistic matrix factorization with gaussian processes. In *UAI*, pages 1–9, 2010.

[3] D. Agarwal and B.-C. Chen. Regression-based latent factor models. In *SIGKDD*, pages 19–28, 2009.

[4] D. Agarwal, B.-C. Chen, and B. Pang. Personalized recommendation of user comments via factor models. In *EMNLP*, pages 571–582, 2011.

[5] S. Bao, G. Xue, X. Wu, Y. Yu, B. Fei, and Z. Su. Optimizing web search using social annotations. In *WWW*, 2007.

[6] D. M. Blei, A. Y. Ng, and M. I. Jordan. Latent Dirichlet allocation. *JMLR*, 3:993–1022, 2003.

[7] L. Bottou and O. Bousquet. The trade-offs of large scale learning. In *NIPS*, volume 20, pages 1161–168, 2008.

[8] X. Ding, B. Liu, and P. S. Yu. A holistic lexicon-based approach to opinion mining. In *WSDM*, pages 231–240, 2008.

[9] S. Geman and D. Geman. Stochastic relaxation, Gibbs distributions, and the Bayesian restoration of images. *IEEE TPAMI*, 6(6):721–741, November 1984.

[10] Z. Guan, J. Bu, Q. Mei, C. Chen, and C. Wang. Personalized tag recommendation using graph-based ranking on multi-type interrelated objects. In *SIGIR*, pages 540–547, 2009.

[11] S. K. Gupta, D. Phung, B. Adams, T. Tran, and S. Venkatesh. Nonnegative shared subspace learning and its application to social media retrieval. In *SIGKDD*, 2010.

[12] P. Heymann, D. Ramage, and H. Garcia-Molina. Social tag prediction. In *SIGIR*, pages 531–538, 2008.

[13] T. Hofmann. Probabilistic latent semantic analysis. In *UAI*, pages 289–296, 1999.

[14] A. Hotho, R. Jäschke, C. Schmitz, and G. Stumme. Information retrieval in folksonomies: Search and ranking. In *The Semantic Web: Research and Applications*, Lecture Notes in Computer Science, chapter 31, pages 411–426. 2006.

[15] M. Hu and B. Liu. Mining and summarizing customer reviews. In *SIGKDD*, pages 168–177, 2004.

[6]Tucker decomposition is a strict generalization of the Parafac decomposition

[16] R. Jäschke, L. Marinho, A. Hotho, L. Schmidt-Thieme, and G. Stumme. Tag recommendations in folksonomies. In *PKDD*, pages 506–514, Berlin, Heidelberg, 2007.

[17] Y. Koren. Collaborative filtering with temporal dynamics. In *KDD*, pages 447–456, 2009.

[18] M. Lipczak, Y. Hu, Y. Kollet, and E. Milios. Tag sources for recommendation in collaborative tagging systems. In *ECML/PKDD Discovery Challenge Workshop (DC09)*, 2009.

[19] B. Liu, M. Hu, and J. Cheng. Opinion observer: analyzing and comparing opinions on the web. In *WWW*, 2005.

[20] H. Ma, D. Zhou, C. Liu, M. R. Lyu, and I. King. Recommender systems with social regularization. In *WSDM*, 2011.

[21] N. Metropolis and S. Ulam. The Monte Carlo methods. *JASA*, 44(247):335–341, 1949.

[22] R. M. Neal. Probabilistic inference using Markov Chain Monte Carlo methods, 1993.

[23] J. Nocedal. Updating quasi-newton matrices with limited storage. *Mathematics of Computation*, 35, 1980.

[24] F. Perronnin and C. R. Dance. Fisher kernels on visual vocabularies for image categorization. In *CVPR*, 2007.

[25] M. Rajih, P. Comon, and R. A. Harshman. Enhanced line search: A novel method to accelerate PARAFAC. *SIAM J. Matrix Anal. Appl.*, 30:1128–1147, 2008.

[26] D. Ramage, P. Heymann, C. D. Manning, and H. Garcia-Molina. Clustering the tagged web. In *WSDM*, 2009.

[27] S. Rendle, L. Balby Marinho, A. Nanopoulos, and L. Schmidt-Thieme. Learning optimal ranking with tensor factorization for tag recommendation. In *SIGKDD*, 2009.

[28] S. Rendle and L. Schmidt-Thieme. Pairwise interaction tensor factorization for personalized tag recommendation. In *WSDM*, pages 81–90, 2010.

[29] R. Salakhutdinov and A. Mnih. Bayesian probabilistic matrix factorization using Markov chain Monte Carlo. In *ICML*, pages 880–887, 2008.

[30] R. Salakhutdinov and A. Mnih. Probabilistic matrix factorization. In *NIPS*, pages 1257–1264, 2008.

[31] A. P. Singh and G. J. Gordon. Relational learning via collective matrix factorization. In *SIGKDD*, pages 650–658, 2008.

[32] Y. Song, L. Zhang, and C. L. Giles. A sparse gaussian processes classification framework for fast tag suggestions. In *CIKM*, pages 93–102. ACM Press, 2008.

[33] P. Symeonidis, A. Nanopoulos, and Y. Manolopoulos. Tag recommendations based on tensor dimensionality reduction. In *RecSys*, pages 43–50. ACM Press, 2008.

[34] L. Tucker. Some mathematical notes on three-mode factor analysis. *Psychometrika*, 31:279–311, 1966.

[35] L. Xiong, X. Chen, T.-K. Huang, J. Schneider, and J. G. Carbonell. Temporal collaborative filtering with bayesian probabilistic tensor factorization. In *SDM*, 2010.

[36] S. Xu, S. Bao, B. Fei, Z. Su, and Y. Yu. Exploring folksonomy for personalized search. In *SIGIR*, pages 155–162, 2008.

[37] D. Yin, L. Hong, Z. Xue, and B. D. Davison. Temporal dynamics of user interests in tagging systems. In *AAAI*, pages 1279–1285, 2011.

[38] D. Yin, Z. Xue, L. Hong, and B. D. Davison. A probabilistic model for personalized tag prediction. In *KDD 2010*.

[39] Z. Yin, R. Li, Q. Mei, and J. Han. Exploring social tagging graph for web object classification. In *SIGKDD*, 2009.

[40] J. Yoo and S. Choi. Bayesian matrix co-factorization: Variational algorithm and cramer-rao bound. In *ECML/PKDD*, 2011.

[41] Y. Zhang, B. Cao, and D.-Y. Yeung. Multi-domain collaborative filtering. In *UAI*, 2010.

[42] S. Zhu, K. Yu, Y. Chi, and Y. Gong. Combining content and link for classification using matrix factorization. In *SIGIR*, pages 487–494, 2007.

Co-Factorization Machines: Modeling User Interests and Predicting Individual Decisions in Twitter

Liangjie Hong Aziz S. Doumith Brian D. Davison
Dept. of Computer Science and Engineering, Lehigh University, Bethlehem, PA, USA
{lih307, asd309, davison}@cse.lehigh.edu

ABSTRACT

Users of popular services like Twitter and Facebook are often simultaneously overwhelmed with the amount of information delivered via their social connections and miss out on much content that they might have liked to see, even though it was distributed outside of their social circle. Both issues serve as difficulties to the users and drawbacks to the services.

Social media service providers can benefit from understanding user interests and how they interact with the service, potentially predicting their behaviors in the future. In this paper, we address the problem of simultaneously predicting user decisions and modeling users' interests in social media by analyzing rich information gathered from Twitter. The task differs from conventional recommender systems as the cold-start problem is ubiquitous, and rich features, including textual content, need to be considered. We build predictive models for user decisions in Twitter by proposing Co-Factorization Machines (CoFM), an extension of a state-of-the-art recommendation model, to handle multiple aspects of the dataset at the same time. Additionally, we discuss and compare ranking-based loss functions in the context of recommender systems, providing the first view of how they vary from each other and perform in real tasks. We explore an extensive set of features and conduct experiments on a real-world dataset, concluding that CoFM with ranking-based loss functions is superior to state-of-the-art methods and yields interpretable latent factors.

Categories and Subject Descriptors: H.3.3 [**Information Storage and Retrieval**]: Information Search and Retrieval; H.4 [**Information Systems Applications**]: Miscellaneous

Keywords: Latent Factor Models; Recommender Systems; Collaborative Filtering; Twitter

1. INTRODUCTION

In the current online social media ecosystem, users are able to connect and communicate with each other utilizing rich multimedia content, including text, images, video, and audio. These communication streams allow users to be informed instantly of the latest updates from their social connections. As a result, the aggregated social content has become a powerful tool for monitoring critical information in various situations, such as natural disasters and political upheavals.

Although services like Twitter and Facebook provide platforms for users to obtain fresh information, two issues prevent them from being sufficiently relevant, causing deterioration of user experience and engagement. First of all, when facing a large amount of content from their social connections, users simply cannot consume it in an effective and efficient way, leading to the problem of *information overload*. On the other hand, information for a user is usually limited in scope to the user's social connections. Thus, it is difficult for a user to obtain information distributed outside of their circle, even though it might match their interests, leading to the problem of *information shortage*. Users may spend a significant amount of time filtering and searching for relevant information in social media. From the perspective of service providers, it is also very important to understand how users interact with the systems through a variety of actions such as re-posting (retweets), replying and commenting. It is also indispensable to track what in which users are interested, induced from the content requested and generated by them. Therefore, social media services can filter and recommend content to users based on their the history of previous interactions and interests.

The task of understanding users' behaviors and their interests has a number of challenges. First, although the number of items (updates, tweets, etc.) generated by users in such services may be huge, few of them impact a particular user, making the interaction data sparse. Second, new users and new content items flow into the system continuously. Thus, the "cold start" problem tends to be severe in these social platforms, compared to traditional information systems. In addition, a tremendous amount of content is rich yet noisy. Simple information retrieval or topical modeling techniques may not be sufficient to capture users' interests.

The problem tackled in this paper has strong links to research in recommender systems and collaborative filtering. From the perspective of recommender systems, the task can be cast as building a list of relevant content items to users based their social connections and interests. Thus, many collaborative filtering techniques are applicable to the task. However, on the other hand, as we mentioned, social content systems are much more dynamic than traditional recommender systems: many new items are pushed into the system every second. Therefore, recommender systems need to be adapted to this novel situation.

State-of-the-art collaborative filtering models are based on latent factor models (LFM), partially due to their superior performance in the Netflix competition [17]. However, the basic assumption for standard LFM is to exploit a user-item interaction matrix and cannot handle arbitrary features easily. Although some of newly

WSDM'13, February 4–8, 2013, Rome, Italy.
Copyright 2013 ACM 978-1-4503-1869-3/13/02 ...$15.00.

proposed frameworks such as [1, 7], based on LFM, can consider features, fundamental modeling assumptions prevent them from handling high-order interaction data (e.g., tensors). In addition, current extensions to LFM [2, 25, 28] which incorporate rich text information are usually cumbersome, requiring complicated inference algorithms which cannot scale to large datasets. Moreover, researchers in collaborative filtering are realizing that pointwise-based measurement may no longer be appropriate and so a handful of ranking-based metrics are proposed. However, no work to date has compared them systematically on real world datasets.

In this work, we study the problem of modeling users' behaviors by focusing on one particular decisions, retweets, in Twitter and try to understand users' interests. Our method can be easily extended to model multiple types of users' decisions as well. We use a state-of-the-art recommendation model, Factorization Machines FM [22], to model user decisions and user-generated content simultaneously. Our contributions can be summarized as follows:

- We propose Co-Factorization Machines (CoFM), which deal with two (multiple) aspects of the dataset where each aspect is a separate FM. This type of model can easily predict user decisions while modeling user interests through content at the same time.
- We apply Factorization Machines to text data with constraints. Thus, the resulting method can mimic state-of-the-art topic models and yet benefit from the efficiency of a simpler form of modeling.
- For user decision modeling, we compare a number of ranking-based loss functions. We introduce the newly proposed WARP loss [26], which has been successfully applied in text and image retrieval tasks (e.g., [31, 32]), into the context of recommendation.
- We apply our proposed methods to the problem of modeling personal decision making in Twitter and explore a wide range of features, revealing which types of features contribute to the predictive modeling and how content features help with the prediction.

We next review several directions of related work. In Section 3, we review FM: its basic settings and learning procedure. In Section 4, we formalize CoFM with different strategies of shared latent features. In Section 5, we compare and discuss a variety of loss functions. In Section 6, we describe features used in our model. In Section 7, we report the experiments with the discussions of datasets and baselines used. We conclude the paper in Section 8.

2. RELATED WORK

In this section, we review three lines of relevant research work: 1) collaborative filtering and ranking, 2) collaborative filtering with content integration, and 3) Twitter user and content modeling. We link them with our tasks and discuss the novelty of our work as well.

Recommender systems which utilize LFM have gained significant attention because they were used by the winning team of the Netflix Prize. However, simple LFM cannot easily be coupled with additional information (features) in other recommendation scenarios. Recently, researchers have explored how traditional LFM can be enhanced by exploiting rich features generated by users. Three main paradigms are proposed for this purpose. The first paradigm is "Regression Based Factor Models" (RBFM) and its extensions, proposed by Agarwal, Chen and colleagues [1, 2, 3, 36], which have been successfully used in a variety of recommendation scenarios, such as social networks [33, 34], professional networks and content recommendation. The basic idea behind RBFM is to replace zero-mean Gaussian distributions usually used in a simple LFM with regression-based means. Thus, RBFM adds another layer of regression on top of LFM, which can incorporate different types of features effectively. However, RBFM can only handle 2-order data interactions and thus high-order data structures (e.g., tensors) cannot be modeled. In addition, the proposed method, training with Monte Carlo EM, is inefficient and cannot scale to large scale datasets easily. The second paradigm is called "Factorization Machines" (FM), proposed by Rendle et al. [22]. FM can handle, in theory, arbitrary orders of interactions between variables and naturally deal with features. However, the existing formalism of FM has not been explored with topical modeling of content and pairwise preferences learning has not been discussed in the context of FM. The last paradigm is called "Feature-based matrix factorization" (FBMF), proposed by Chen et al. [7], which is to combine LFM with linear regression. As noted by Rendle [22], similar to RBFM, FBMF cannot handle high-order interactions either. Additionally, FBMF can be viewed as a special case of FM.

Traditional collaborative filtering methods are trained and evaluated on pointwise-based measures, such as Root-Mean-Square-Error (RMSE) and Mean-Square-Error (MSE), essentially measuring how accurate each single prediction is, regardless of how items are presented to users. Although the use of RMSE gained popularity through the Netflix prize competition, ranking-based measures might be more appropriate than pointwise-based measures since users are presented a ranked list of items calculated by recommendation systems. Thus, it would be more natural to optimize the ranked list directly. Some recent advances in recommender systems lie in this direction. For instance, Weimer et al. [29] extended the maximum margin matrix factorization method (MMMF) by optimizing a surrogate loss function approximating the NDCG ranking measure, a ranking-based metric commonly used in the Information Retrieval (IR) community. However, the method proposed in the paper is complicated and arguably hard to scale to large datasets. A margin ranking criterion, an ordinal loss, is introduced from the field of IR to collaborative filtering by Weimer et al. [30] in the context of MMMF, which is a direct extension of the hinge loss for Support Vector Machines. This max-margin loss essentially minimizes AUC, which is the area under the ROC curve [4, 31]. A smooth version of hinge loss which is also to minimize AUC, called Bayesian personalized ranking, is proposed by Rendle et al. [23] and has yielded superior performance in tag recommendation. Recently, Balakrishnan and Chopra [5] proposed a two-stage procedure for collaborative ranking. Their proposal is to first train a matrix factorization model for users and items and treat latent factors as features to feed into a standard learning-to-rank framework. Koren and Sill [18] proposed a method to embed ordinal regression into matrix factorization by predicting a full distribution over all ranks. An interesting point is that this method is indeed a pointwise method. With a slightly different approach, Yang et al. [34] studied user behaviors when browsing a list of items. The proposed framework includes two loss functions that are comparable to multinomial logic model and a margin ranking criterion but have more intuitive explanations. Though different ranking-based loss are proposed, they are never compared.

Some recent developments in collaborative filtering have demonstrated the power to integrate rich content from articles and scientific papers with user decisions to provide better recommendation results. For instance, Agarwal and Chen [2] extended RBFM with a latent Dirichlet allocation prior for latent factor models. A similar approach was investigated by Shan and Banerjee [25] as well. Wang and Blei [28] proposed a method to combine matrix factorization with probabilistic topic modeling for recommending scientific papers. The method cannot easily leverage additional features. One significant advantage of these joint modeling methods is that latent factors obtained through content modeling can reveal interpretable meanings to latent spaces and thus provide a unique way to uncover some hidden structures of the data. However, all these methods require complicated inference algorithms which are not easily to scale to large datasets.

Recommender systems have been built specifically for Twitter. For instance, Kim and Shim [16] argued that Twitter does not offer to find the most interesting tweet messages for users. The authors proposed a probabilistic model derived from Probabilistic Latent Semantic Analysis (PLSA) for collaborative filtering to recommend potential followers to users in Twitter. The method does not consider any explicit features at all. Due to the fact that Twitter users form a information network, researchers have tried to use undirected graphical models to model such networks. For example, Yang et al. [35] used a factor graph to model the spread of tweets. Lin et al. [20] proposed a generic joint inference framework for topic diffusion and evolution in social network communities based on Gaussian Random Fields, which also cannot integrate with rich features. Similarly, Peng et al. [21] proposed a method based on Conditional Random Fields (CRF) to predict how likely a tweet will be retweeted by a user. The proposed method suffered from the difficulty to efficiently perform inference on graph-like CRFs. Duan et al. [9] studied how learning to rank approaches can be used in ranking tweets. They explored a number of features and used 20 query terms as input to train a RankSVM as the model. In the present work, we do not have explicit queries while modeling user decisions and user-generated content. Hong et al. [14] and Uysal and Croft [27] trained classifiers to predict whether a tweet will be retweeted. However, the classifiers they trained are universal for all users and hence cannot provide personalized results. Recently, Chen et al. [6] utilized FBMF with a wide range of features to recommend tweets for users on Twitter. However, the proposed method cannot provide much insight on how content contributes to users' decisions and only one type of ranking loss function is used without comparisons. In all, these methods either do not handle arbitrary features or do not obtain summarized content (topics) from Twitter messages, preventing us from further understanding how users' decisions are made. In this work, we will perform these two tasks simultaneously.

3. MODELING TWITTER BY FM

In this section, we first review the basic settings of FM with a discussion of how it can be used for different types of responses. Then, we detail how FM can fit into the task of modeling Twitter data, which is a predictive modeling for user responses and a topic coding model for content.

3.1 Factorization Machines

Here we briefly review FM, a state-of-the-art framework for latent factor models with rich features. For a detailed description, please refer to Rendle [22]. We start from a design matrix $\mathbf{X} \in \mathbb{R}^{D \times P}$, where the ith row $\mathbf{x}_i \in \mathbb{R}^P$ denotes one data instance with P real-valued variables and where y_i is a response for the data instance. We use s_i to represent our estimation of y_i based on $\mathbf{x}_i$. In many tasks, the goal is to make the discrepancy between s_i and y_i as small as possible. The factorization machine (FM) model of order $d = 2$ for $f(y_i \mid \mathbf{x}_i, \mathbf{\Theta}) = s_i$ can be defined as:

$$s_i = \beta_0 + \sum_{j=1}^{P} \boldsymbol{\beta}_j \mathbf{x}_j + \sum_{j=1}^{P} \sum_{j'=j+1}^{P} \mathbf{x}_{i,j} \mathbf{x}_{i,j'} \sum_{k=1}^{K} \boldsymbol{\theta}_{j,k} \boldsymbol{\theta}_{j',k} \quad (1)$$

where k is the dimensionality of the factorization and the model parameters $\mathbf{\Theta} = \{\beta_0, \boldsymbol{\beta}, \boldsymbol{\theta}\}$ are: $\beta_0 \in \mathbb{R}$, $\boldsymbol{\beta} \in \mathbb{R}^P$ and $\boldsymbol{\theta} \in \mathbb{R}^{P \times K}$. The form of FM (Equation 1) is very general and can be used in many applications. In order to cope with different tasks, we can define an exponential family distribution over $P(y_i \mid s_i)$ similar to that utilized in [19], as $P(y_i \mid s_i) = h(y_i, \mathbf{\Phi}) \exp\left[\eta(\lambda; s_i)^T T(y_i) - A\left(\eta(\lambda; s_i)\right)\right]$ where λ is the **natural** parameter of the family. For instance:

- **Gaussian response**: For normal rating prediction problems, y_i can be treated as a real-valued response drawn from a Gaussian distribution. Thus, we scale s_i with a known variance. $\eta = s_i/\sigma^2$, $A = s_i^2/2\sigma^2 = \sigma^2\eta^2/2$ and $h = \frac{1}{\sqrt{2\pi\sigma}} \exp(-\frac{1}{2\sigma^2} y_i^2)$ where σ^2 is the variance. Thus, the expectation $\mathbb{E}[T(y)] = s$.
- **Poisson response**: For word counts, y_i can be treated as the indicator of word index, drawn from a Poisson distribution. Thus, $\eta = s_i$, $A = \exp(s_i)$ and $h = \frac{1}{y_i!}$. The expectation $\mathbb{E}[T(y)] = \exp(s) = \lambda$.
- **Binary (Bernoulli) response**: For binary decisions, y_i is usually treated as 0 or 1. Thus, $\eta = s_i$, $A = \log(1 + \exp(s_i))$. The expectation $\mathbb{E}[T(y)] = \frac{\exp(s)}{1+\exp(s)}$.

One important aspect of FM is that the model can mimic the structure of many state-of-the-art models like matrix factorization, pairwise interaction tensor factorization, SVD++ and neighborhood models in one unified framework, as demonstrated by Rendle [22].

FM can be learned in several ways, including maximum a posteriori (MAP) estimation and Bayesian inference. In this paper, we stick to MAP learning, which is to maximize the log likelihood through stochastic gradient descent (SGD) or alternating least squares. An equivalent view is to minimize a loss between the reconstructed response $f(y_i \mid \mathbf{x}_i, \mathbf{\Theta})$ and the true response y_i as $\arg\min_{\mathbf{\Theta}} \sum_i l(f(y_i \mid \mathbf{x}_i, \mathbf{\Theta}), y_i) + \mathcal{R}(\mathbf{\Theta})$ where l is a certain loss function and $\mathcal{R}$ is a regularization term for $\mathbf{\Theta}$.

3.2 Modeling User Decisions and Content

In this paper, we focus on extending FM to model Twitter data. We have two goals to achieve for understanding and modeling user behaviors in Twitter. First, we wish to uncover what kind of items with which users interact through various actions (e.g., retweets, replies and favorites) and what features contribute to the mechanism that causes certain pieces of information to be shared across social connections. Second, content is of great importance in Twitter and thus it is vital to discover topics in which users are interested and how these topics influence users' decisions. As mentioned earlier, we wish to predict users' decisions as accurately as possible while discerning topics from the huge amount of user-generated content at the same time.

For the first task, we focus on a binary response y_d for each tweet d: whether the tweet will be retweeted by a target user $u^{(t)}$. We use $u^{(a)}$ denote the author of the current tweet d. For each tweet, we use $\mathbf{x}_d$ to represent a list of explicit features for tweet d, which might include features about $u^{(t)}$ and $u^{(a)}$, and $\boldsymbol{\theta}_d$ to represent a list of latent features (factors) discovered through modeling. For the purpose of discussion, we compose a simple feature vector consisting of one categorical feature to indicate its author and one categorical feature to indicate the index of the tweet. Following the definition of FM (Equation 1), we can have an estimation of y_d based on $\mathbf{x}_d$ and $\boldsymbol{\theta}_d$ as $f(s_d \,|\, \mathbf{x}_d, \boldsymbol{\theta}_d)$:

$$s_d = \beta_0 + \boldsymbol{\beta}_u + \boldsymbol{\beta}_d + < \boldsymbol{\theta}_u, \boldsymbol{\theta}_d > \quad (2)$$

This is the exact form of traditional matrix factorization for collaborative filtering where the $\boldsymbol{\theta}$ are treated as latent factors for users and items (tweets). Since y_d is a binary response, we can also have a binary version as $y_d \sim \text{Bernoulli}\big(\delta(s_d)\big)$ where δ is the sigmoid function. For user decisions $\mathbf{y}$, one natural criteria for a reasonable model is to predict them as accurately as possible by specifying some error based loss functions (e.g., squared error loss). Alternatively, we can provide a ranked list of items for each user and measure how well these ranked lists approximate user actions. The latter view goes beyond pointwise evaluation and learning process for recommendation systems and has been studied extensively recently (e.g., [17, 34]). Later, we will further explore this idea.

For the second task, we will model terms in each tweet d. We denote s_{dv} to represent our estimation of the raw word count of term v in tweet d, w_{dv}, which is the response in this task. The vector $\mathbf{x}_{di}$ is used to represent features of term i in tweet d. In order to explain things more clearly, we change $\boldsymbol{\beta}$ for s_{dv} to $\boldsymbol{\alpha}$ and latent factors to $\boldsymbol{\phi}$. We use two simple indicator features here. More specifically, for each s_{dv}, we associate one categorical feature to indicate the term index and another one to indicate the tweet index. Following a similar argument, s_{dv} is a function of all features $f(s_{dv} \,|\, \mathbf{x}_{dv}, \boldsymbol{\phi}_{dv})$:

$$s_{dv} = \alpha_0 + \boldsymbol{\alpha}_d + \boldsymbol{\alpha}_v + < \boldsymbol{\phi}_v, \boldsymbol{\phi}_d > \quad (3)$$

The inner product between $\boldsymbol{\phi}_v$ and $\boldsymbol{\phi}_d$ is of interest. For $\boldsymbol{\phi}_d$, it is a K-dimensional vector and it can be treated as code for tweet d, playing a similar role as $P(z \,|\, \theta)$ in traditional topic models like probabilistic latent semantic analysis (PLSA) or latent Dirichlet allocation (LDA). The only difference is that $\boldsymbol{\phi}_d$ is not constrained to rest on the simplex. For $\boldsymbol{\phi}_v$, it is a K-dimensional vector for term v and it can be treated as a $P(z \,|\, v)$. Using $\boldsymbol{\phi}_v$ for all terms, we construct the following matrix:

$$\mathbf{M} \in \mathbb{R}^{K \times V} \quad \text{where } \mathbf{M}_{\cdot,v} = \boldsymbol{\phi}_v$$

where each column of $\mathbf{M}$ is set to $\boldsymbol{\phi}_v$. Therefore, each row of $\mathbf{M}$ can be treated as $P(v \,|\, z)$ **without** normalization. In order to recover a similar modeling power from topic models, we add the following constraints to the parameters:

$$\sum_v \boldsymbol{\phi}_{kv} = 1 \text{ for all } k, \boldsymbol{\phi}_{kv} \geq 0 \text{ ; and, } \boldsymbol{\phi}_{dk} \geq 0 \text{ ;}$$

Thus, we have a normalized matrix $\mathbf{M}$, resembling a conventional topic matrix. We can further restrict all $\boldsymbol{\alpha}$ to be non-negative, resulting in a non-negative decomposition of the term matrix. In such a setting, the content modeling behaves like a simpler topic model than its more complicated counterparts. If we view the terms in a tweet as count data, we can use the Poisson distribution and thus have $w_{di} \sim \text{Poisson}\big(\exp(s_{di})\big)$. On the other hand, since terms are sparse in tweets where one term will most likely appear only once in a single tweet, an alternative parametrization is to use the Bernoulli distribution $w_{di} \sim \text{Bernoulli}\big(\delta(s_{di})\big)$. Note that other explicit features, which are not discussed here, can be incorporated into the model easily.

Thus, we can have use FM to model two tasks separately. However, it might be better if we can jointly model these two aspects of the data together. In this paper, we propose several methods to simultaneously perform these two tasks.

4. CO-FACTORIZATION MACHINES

In many application scenarios, we may have multiple views. For instance, each tweet is associated with two types of important aspects to be modeled: 1) user action responses and 2) terms. In this subsection, we introduce Co-Factorization Machines (CoFM) to address the problem of modeling multiple aspects of data. Following the setting described in Equation 2 and Equation 3, we have two separate FMs to model two aspects of the **same** tweet where the two aspects are not linked together. Notice that we have learned two different latent representations of the same tweet: $\boldsymbol{\theta}_d$ and $\boldsymbol{\phi}_d$. Linking two factorization machines might be possible if these two latent representations of the tweet can be coupled in certain ways. Indeed, there exist several design choices to combine these two modeling processes. We present three paradigms below.

4.1 CoFM through shared features

One natural approach to link two latent representations of the **same** tweet is to treat one type of latent representation as a set of features and feed it into another modeling process. More specifically, we plug $\boldsymbol{\phi}_d$ into Equation 2 and have:

$$s_d = \beta_0 + \boldsymbol{\beta}_u + \boldsymbol{\beta}_d + < \boldsymbol{\beta}_{\boldsymbol{\phi}_d}, \boldsymbol{\phi}_d > + < \boldsymbol{\theta}_u, \boldsymbol{\theta}_d >$$
$$+ \sum_{k=1}^{K} \boldsymbol{\phi}_{d,k} < \boldsymbol{\theta}_u, \boldsymbol{\theta}_{\boldsymbol{\phi}_{d,k}} > + \sum_{k=1}^{K} \boldsymbol{\phi}_{d,k} < \boldsymbol{\theta}_d, \boldsymbol{\theta}_{\boldsymbol{\phi}_{d,k}} > \quad (4)$$

Here, the third term $< \boldsymbol{\beta}_{\boldsymbol{\phi}_d}, \boldsymbol{\phi}_d >$ is a simple regression part by using latent factors obtained from content. The last two terms are of interest. Each latent factor in $\boldsymbol{\phi}_d$ is **re-weighted** by the interaction between its projection to the latent space of $\boldsymbol{\theta}$ and corresponding user/tweet latent factors. In other words, the last two terms can be re-written as:

$$\sum_{k=1}^{K} \boldsymbol{\phi}_{d,k} < \boldsymbol{\theta}_u, \boldsymbol{\theta}_{\boldsymbol{\phi}_{d,k}} > + \sum_{k=1}^{K} \boldsymbol{\phi}_{d,k} < \boldsymbol{\theta}_d, \boldsymbol{\theta}_{\boldsymbol{\phi}_{d,k}} > =$$
$$< \boldsymbol{\phi}_d, \boldsymbol{\omega}_{u,\boldsymbol{\phi}} > + < \boldsymbol{\phi}_{di}, \boldsymbol{\omega}_{d,\boldsymbol{\phi}} >$$

where $\boldsymbol{\omega}$ are weights that each element is obtained from the interaction between the latent factors $\boldsymbol{\theta}$ and linear mapping vector $\boldsymbol{\theta}_{\boldsymbol{\phi}}$. This kind of mapping is similar in spirit that used by Gantner et al. [11]. The same process can be used for $w_{i,v}$ as well. If the shared feature mechanism is indeed a feature re-weighting scheme, another re-weighting approach might also be possible. Instead of using $\boldsymbol{\theta}_{\boldsymbol{\phi}}$ to map each dimension in $\boldsymbol{\phi}$ to $\boldsymbol{\theta}$, we treat $\boldsymbol{\phi}$ as the latent representation of a **missing** feature $\omega_{\boldsymbol{\phi}}$. The corresponding equation is:

$$s_d = \beta_0 + \boldsymbol{\beta}_u + \boldsymbol{\beta}_d + \boldsymbol{\beta}_{\omega_{\boldsymbol{\phi}}} \omega_{\boldsymbol{\phi},d} + < \boldsymbol{\theta}_u, \boldsymbol{\theta}_d >$$
$$+ \omega_{\boldsymbol{\phi}} < \boldsymbol{\theta}_u, \boldsymbol{\phi}_d > + \omega_{\boldsymbol{\phi}} < \boldsymbol{\theta}_d, \boldsymbol{\phi}_d > \quad (5)$$

Under this formalism, $\omega_{\boldsymbol{\phi}}$ is a missing feature and can be treated as weights for interactions between $\boldsymbol{\theta}$ and $\boldsymbol{\phi}$. Comparing Equation 5 and Equation 4, we can see that the second formalism has fewer parameters to be estimated and more intuitive motivations. In this paper, we use the second formalism.

4.2 CoFM through shared latent space

The methods introduced in the previous section assume that the latent representations obtained by different aspects of the model are different. A simpler approach is to assume that the latent factor of $\boldsymbol{\theta}_d$ is exactly the same as $\boldsymbol{\phi}_d$. Therefore, some parts of the latent factors of the same tweet are shared across different aspects. If we use $\boldsymbol{\eta}$ to indicate the shared latent factors, the two aspects under this formalism are as follows:

$$s_d = \beta_0 + \boldsymbol{\beta}_u + \boldsymbol{\beta}_d + < \boldsymbol{\theta}_u, \boldsymbol{\eta}_d >$$
$$s_{d,v} = \alpha_0 + \boldsymbol{\alpha}_d + \boldsymbol{\alpha}_v + < \boldsymbol{\phi}_v, \boldsymbol{\eta}_d > \quad (6)$$

This formalism shares the idea of matrix co-factorization used in relational learning scenarios.

This approach would be convenient when multiple factors will be shared. For instance, for each term, we can add one more categorical feature to indicate the author of the tweet and therefore obtain a latent representation of its author through content modeling:

$$s_d = \beta_0 + \boldsymbol{\beta}_u + \boldsymbol{\beta}_d + < \boldsymbol{\eta}_u, \boldsymbol{\eta}_d >$$
$$s_{d,v} = \alpha_0 + \boldsymbol{\alpha}_d + \boldsymbol{\alpha}_v + \boldsymbol{\alpha}_u + < \boldsymbol{\phi}_v, \boldsymbol{\eta}_d > + < \boldsymbol{\phi}_v, \boldsymbol{\eta}_u >$$
$$+ < \boldsymbol{\eta}_u, \boldsymbol{\eta}_d >$$

where the factors for user u and tweet d are shared in two aspects.

4.3 CoFM via latent space regularization

The discussions in Sections 4.1 and 4.2 represent two variations of how to work with two latent representations of the tweet. One can regularize two such representations such that they do not reside too far away from each other. A simple approach is to impose the following regularization on the model:

$$\lambda_{\phi,\theta} ||\boldsymbol{\phi}_d - \boldsymbol{\theta}_d||_F^2$$

where $\lambda_{\phi,\theta}$ is a regularization parameter. Under this assumption, we can also view that one latent factor is drawn from the multivariate normal distribution with the mean as another latent factor:

$$\boldsymbol{\phi}_d \sim \text{MVN}(\boldsymbol{\theta}_d, \lambda_{\phi,\theta}^{-1}\mathbf{I})$$

This will recover the formalism from Wang and Blei [28]. An additional possibility is suggested in Agarwal and Chen [3] where a "global" representation is assumed. The "local" representation is drawn from the "global" representation by a multivariate normal distribution. Thus, a third latent representation will be introduced if this approach is used.

5. LEARNING WITH COFM

In this section we formalize the FM learning problem in an optimization framework. The discrepancy between the estimation s_i by FM/CoFM and the true value y_i can be measured by loss functions. Different choices of loss functions may lead to significant changes in performance as we will see in the experiments. Traditionally, pointwise error-based loss functions are widely used in latent factor models, which are widely used in recommender systems. Here, we discuss how different loss functions fit into the FM/CoFM framework and how the overall learning algorithm proceeds.

5.1 Optimization with content

For the task of modeling content in Twitter, two possible loss functions come from two assumptions (Poisson or Bernoulli distributions). We have the following optimization task:

$$\text{Opt(C)} = \arg\min_{\boldsymbol{\Phi},\boldsymbol{\alpha}} \sum_{d=1}^{D}\sum_{v=1}^{V} l_C(w_{dv}, f(s_{dv} \mid \mathbf{x}_{dv}, \boldsymbol{\alpha}, \boldsymbol{\Phi}))$$
$$+ \sum_{j=1}^{P_1} \lambda_{\alpha,j}\boldsymbol{\alpha}_j^2 + \sum_{j=1}^{P_1} \lambda_{\phi,j} ||\boldsymbol{\phi}_j||_F^2$$
$$\text{s.t.:} \boldsymbol{\alpha} \geq 0,\ \boldsymbol{\phi}_{kv} \geq 0, \forall k, v;\ \boldsymbol{\phi}_k \in \mathcal{P}, \forall k \in K;\ \boldsymbol{\phi}_{dk} \geq 0, \forall d, k \quad (7)$$

where P_1 is the number of features used for each term v in each tweet d and $\mathcal{P}$ is a $(K-1)$-simplex. We consider the following loss functions for this task:

- Log Poisson loss: $l^{LP}(w_{dv}, s_{dv}) = -w_{dv}\log s_{dv} + s_{dv}$. Minimizing this loss is actually equivalent to minimizing an unnormalized KL-divergence between observed counts w_{dv} and their reconstructions s_{dv}.
- Logistic loss: $l^{LG}(w_{dv}, s_{dv}) = \log[1 + \exp(-w_{dv}s_{dv})]$. Minimizing this loss is essentially performing logistic regression. Here, we only consider on/off of a term v in tweet d, dismissing its possible multiple occurrences.

The optimization problem in Equation 7 can be efficiently solved according to two facts: 1) Due to the property of *multilinearilty* [22], the model is linear with respect to each model parameter when others are fixed and, 2) Proposition 1 in [37] states that the optimal value of a single parameter when other are fixed is the maximum between zero and the value obtained by a non-constrained version of the same problem. Also, efficient methods (e.g., [10]) exist to project real-valued vectors onto the simplex. Therefore, this optimization problem is solvable.

5.2 Optimization with user decisions

For modeling user decisions, we also formalize the problem as an optimization problem as follows:

$$\text{Opt(U)} = \arg\min_{\boldsymbol{\Theta},\boldsymbol{\beta}} \sum_{d=1}^{D} l_U(y_d, f(s_d \mid \mathbf{x}_d, \boldsymbol{\beta}, \boldsymbol{\Theta}))$$
$$+ \sum_{j=1}^{P_2} \lambda_{\beta,j}\boldsymbol{\beta}_j^2 + \sum_{j=1}^{P_2} \lambda_{\theta,j} ||\boldsymbol{\theta}_j||_F^2 \quad (8)$$

where P_2 is the number of features used for each tweet d. Unlike content modeling, no constraints are put onto the parameter space. For pointwise loss functions, we consider:

- Squared error loss: $l^S(y_d, s_d) = (y_d - s_d)^2$, which is for regression problems with Gaussian responses.
- Logistic loss: l^{LG}, the same as the loss used in modeling content.
- Huber loss:

$$l^H(y_d, s_d) = \begin{cases} \frac{1}{2}\max(0, 1 - y_d s_d)^2 \text{if } y_d s_d > 0 \\ \frac{1}{2} - y_d s_d & \text{otherwise} \end{cases}$$

  This is the one-sided variant of Huber's robust loss function. It is convex and continuously differentiable. The loss is mentioned in Yang et al. [33].

It has been demonstrated that pointwise loss functions may not be appropriate for recommender tasks when users choose items from a list of items prepared by the system [8]. In such cases, we wish to adopt more advanced loss functions which consider pairwise preferences. For each target user u, we can construct a set of tweets which are originated by other users and retweeted by u, denoted as $\mathcal{C}_u^+$. Note that these tweets could be originated by u's friends or any other users who are not connected to u. On the contrary, we denote all other tweets from u's friends which are not retweeted by u as $\mathcal{C}_u^-$. Therefore, for each user u, there exists a huge set of tweets which are outside of u's network and are treated as unknown and not considered in the following loss functions. In this work, we focus on pairwise loss functions:

Margin ranking criterion (MRC):

$$l^M(x_1, x_2) = \sum_{x_1 \in \mathcal{C}_u^+} \sum_{x_2 \in \mathcal{C}_u^-} \max[0, 1 - f(x_1) + f(x_2)]$$

which considers all pairs of positive and negative labels, and assigns each a cost if the negative label is larger or within a "margin" of 1 from the positive label. Optimizing this loss is similar to optimizing the area under the curve of the receiver operating characteristic curve. That is, all pairwise violations are considered equally if they have the same margin violation, independent of their position in the list. For this reason the margin ranking loss might not optimize precision at k very accurately. This loss function is proposed in Herbrich et al. [12] and used in many IR tasks (e.g., [15, 4]).

Bayesian personalized ranking (BPR):

$$l^B(x_1, x_2) = \sum_{x_1 \in C_u^+} \sum_{x_2 \in C_u^-} -\log[\delta(f(x_1) - f(x_2))]$$

where δ is a sigmoid function. This loss is proposed in Rendle et al. [23] and has been used in tag recommendation (e.g., [24]) and yielded superior performance. This can be viewed as a smooth version of MRC.

Weighted Approximately Ranked Pairwise loss (WARP): This loss, proposed in Usunier et al. [26], has been successfully applied in image retrieval tasks [31] and IR tasks [32]. Here, we discuss its application in recommender systems. The idea of WARP is to focus more on the top of the ranked list where the top k positions are those we care about, comparing to MRC and BPR where no notion of ranked list is introduced. By using the precision at k measure, one can weigh the pairwise violations depending on their position in the ranked list. WARP is defined as an error function as follows:

$$\text{err}_{\text{WARP}} = \sum_{\mathbf{x}_i \in C_u^+} L[rank(f(\mathbf{x}_i))] \tag{9}$$

where $rank(f(\mathbf{x}_i))$ is the rank of a positive labeled instance $\mathbf{x}_i \in C_u^+$ given by $rank(f(\mathbf{x}_i)) = \sum_{\mathbf{x}' \in C_u^-} \mathbb{I}[f(\mathbf{x}') \geq f(\mathbf{x}_i)]$ where $\mathbb{I}(x)$ is the indicator function, and $L(\cdot)$ transforms this rank into a loss: $L(r) = \sum_{j=1}^{r} \tau_j$, with $\tau_1 \geq \tau_2 \geq \cdots \geq 0$. The idea of the $rank$ function is to compute the violations where negative instances are ranked higher than the positive ones and the L function is to transform violations into a loss. Different choices of τ define different importance of the relative position of the positive examples in the ranked list. In particular:

- For $\tau_i = 1$ for all i we have the same AUC optimization as margin ranking criterion.
- For $\tau_1 = 1$ and $\tau_{i>1} = 0$ the precision at 1 is optimized.
- For $\tau_{i \leq k} = 1$ and $\tau_{i>k} = 0$ the precision at k is optimized.
- For $\tau_i = 1/i$ a smooth weighting over positions is given, where most weight is given to the top position, with rapidly decaying weight for lower positions. This is useful when one wants to optimize precision at k for a variety of different values of k at once.

In this work, we use $\tau_i = 1/i$. It is difficult to directly optimize WARP due to the discrete nature of indicator functions. In addition, since the number of negative instances is significantly larger than positive instances, the $rank$ function is inefficient to be calculated. Before we tackle these issues, the form of Equation 9 can be readily re-written as (see [31] for details):

$$\text{err}_{\text{WARP}} = \sum_{\mathbf{x}_i \in C_u^+} \frac{L[rank(f(\mathbf{x}_i))] \sum_{\mathbf{x}' \in C_u^-} \mathbb{I}[f(\mathbf{x}') \geq f(\mathbf{x}_i)]}{rank(f(\mathbf{x}_i))}$$

with the convention $0/0 = 0$ when the correct label y is top-ranked. We replace the indicator function by using the margin function $\max(0, 1 - f(\mathbf{x}_i) + f(\mathbf{x}'))$. In order to approximate the $rank$ function, for a given positive instance, one draws negative instances until the one which violates the indicator function. Thus, we approximate $rank(f(\mathbf{x}_i))$ by using $\left\lfloor \frac{D^- - 1}{N} \right\rfloor$ where $\lfloor\cdot\rfloor$ is the floor function, D^- is the number of items in C_u^- and N is the number of trials of sampling until a violating pair is found. The approximation only requires local knowledge of negative instances, making it easily to be calculated per user for our case.

Competitive softmax loss (SOFTMAX):

$$P(y_i = 1 \mid C_u) = \frac{\exp(f(s_i \mid \mathbf{x}_i))}{\sum_{\mathbf{x}_i} \exp(f(s_i \mid \mathbf{x}_i))} \text{ for all } \mathbf{x}_i \in C_u \tag{10}$$

This loss is introduced by Yang et al. [34] and is motivated by the idea that users are presented a list of items and they choose items based on the "utility" they will receive if the item is chosen. Here, we assume that the utility for item i consists of two components $s_i + e_i$ where s_i encodes the intrinsic interest of the item to the target user and e_i is a stochastic error term reflecting the uncertainty and complexity of the choice process. We choose s_i to be the outcome from the predictive model (e.g., FM, CoFM). If the error term e_i is independently and identically distributed as a Weibull distribution, the probability item i is chosen is exactly as Equation 10, which is essentially a multinomial logic model.

Competitive hinge loss (HINGE): Following a similar assumption that a user chooses items based on their utilities, we can formalize the problem of distinguishing positive instances from negative ones as a problem of classification. Therefore, the key idea of HINGE loss is that the utility difference between a positive item and negative items would be greater than **random errors**, namely:

$$\mathbb{I}(y_i == 1) f(s_i \mid \mathbf{x}_i) > \frac{1}{|C_u^-|} \sum_{\mathbf{x}_i \in C_u^-} \mathbb{I}(y_i == 0) f(s_i \mid \mathbf{x}_i)$$

With this spirit, a pairwise preference learning problem can be formalized as follows:

$$l^H = \min \sum_{t=1}^{|C_u^+|} \xi_t$$

$$\text{s.t.: } f(s_t \mid \mathbf{x}_t) - \frac{1}{|C_u^-|} \sum_{\mathbf{x}_i \in C_u^-} f(s_i \mid \mathbf{x}_i) \geq 1 - \xi_t \text{ and } \xi_t \geq 0,$$

$$\forall \mathbf{x}_t \in C_u^+$$

where ξ are introduced parameters to be optimized. This loss reflects the insight that user decisions are usually made by comparing alternatives and considering the differences in potential utilities. In other words, the marginal utility between user choice and the average of non-choices is maximized. This loss is also introduced in Yang et al. [34].

All of these ranking-based loss functions were proposed in different contexts and never compared in recommender systems. From the discussion above, it is clear that WARP is the only loss function considering the relative positions between positive instances. Meanwhile, both SOFTMAX and HINGE consider the set of positive and negative instances as a whole, rather than MRC and BPR only deal with pairwise preferences. In addition to what has been discussed here, other ranking based loss measures are also proposed. For instance, Koren and Sill proposed the OrdRec approach [18], which is based on a pointwise ordinal model. The idea of OrdRec is to predict a full probability distribution of the expected item ratings, rather than only a single score for an item. However, this is not desirable in our setting in that we only care about relevant items ranked at the top. Thus, it is not necessary (and even impossible in practice) to predict a full distribution over

Algorithm 1: The sketch of the algorithm to optimize Equation 11. This is one iteration over the whole dataset.

for $u = 1$ **to** $|U|$ **do**
  Optimize Opt(U) for $\boldsymbol{\theta}_d$, $\boldsymbol{\theta}_u$ **and** $\boldsymbol{\beta}$:
    Perform stochastic gradient descent for pointwise loss functions or rank-based loss functions.
  Optimize Opt(C) for $\boldsymbol{\phi}_d$ **and** $\boldsymbol{\alpha}$:
    Perform stochastic gradient descent for log-Poisson loss or logistic loss
Optimize Opt(C) for $\mathbf{M}$
  Perform gradient descent to obtain the current optimal value for the topic matrix

all positions. Other researchers have tried to optimize NDCG directly. However, this is either done by approximation [29] or by a two-stage approach [5], which might be sub-optimal.

5.3 Summary

Putting things together, a CoFM framework for learning a model for user decisions and content understanding can be formalized as:

$$\text{Opt(CoFM)} : \ \text{Opt(U)} + \pi\text{Opt(C)} \tag{11}$$

where π is a parameter to balance two objective functions. By choosing different coupling strategies introduced in Section 4 and different loss functions, Opt(CoFM) can effectively perform predictive modeling and maximum likelihood estimation of content at the same time. We adopt a hybrid of SGD and coordinate descent to optimize Equation 11, which is sketched in Algorithm 1. We iterate the whole dataset by performing SGD for predictive modeling and content modeling while fixing the topic matrix. After one iteration, we optimize the topic matrix by gradient descent. Since we restrict $\mathbf{M} \in \mathcal{P}$, an efficient method [10] can achieve this task.

6. FEATURES

Here we discuss the features used in our models. These features utilize the content of tweets that users have generated. All of these features try to capture users' interests. Features are divided into five groups: 1) categorical features, 2) content profiles, 3) relevance scores, 4) latent topic model features, and 5) content meta features, where each group has multiple features.

Categorical Features: The key idea of FM/CoFM is to use both indicator features and explicit features together to obtain competitive performance in predictive tasks. For modeling user decisions, we use three categorical features: 1) target user id, 2) neighbor user id and 3) the tweet id. For content modeling, we use the term id and the tweet id as features.

Content Features: For "content profiles" we utilize features to characterize what users have posted and what their friends have posted. For each tweet i, let $\boldsymbol{w}_i$ be the term vector for this tweet. Let $u(i)$ be the author of the tweet i. For user u, we construct three user profiles as follows:

- **Content Profile**: Let $\text{CP}(u) = \sum_{i=1}^{D} \mathbb{I}[u(i) == u]\mathbf{w}_i$. This is essentially the concatenation of all term vectors generated by user u.
- **Neighborhood Profile**: Let $\text{NP}(u) = \sum_{u' \in N(u)} C(u')$ where $N(u)$ is a set of friend users of user u.
- **Retweet Profile**: Let $\text{RP}(u) = \sum_{i=1}^{D} \mathbb{I}[u(i) == u \wedge r(i) == 1]\mathbf{w}_i$ where $r(i)$ is a binary indicator for whether tweet i is a retweet or not.

These profile features will capture the interests of users at a fine-grained level. One drawback of these features is that they capture the long-term interests of users. For new tweets, they remain the same and would be less discriminative. Thus, we introduce the second group of features, characterizing how relevant a new tweet is against user profiles. Let $\mathcal{R}(\mathbf{w}_1, \mathbf{w}_2)$ be a relevance measurement between term vector $\mathbf{w}_1$ and $\mathbf{w}_2$. Thus, we have the following relevance scores:

- **Content Relevance**: $\mathcal{R}(\mathbf{w}_i, \text{CP}(u))$, measuring the similarity of the incoming tweet to the user's content profile.
- **Neighborhood Relevance**: $\mathcal{R}(\mathbf{w}_i, \text{NP}(u))$, measuring the similarity of the incoming tweet to the user's neighborhood profile.
- **Retweet Relevance**: $\mathcal{R}(\mathbf{w}_i, \text{RP}(u))$, measuring the similarity of the incoming tweet to the user's retweet profile.

We use dot product as the relevance measure although many other IR relevance scores could also apply. Both "content profiles" and "relevance scores" utilize term level information to determine the features. In addition to these features directly related to the content generated by the users, other meta information also might be useful:

- **Length of Tweet**: Number of characters used in tweet i.
- **Hash Tag Count**: Number of hash tags used in tweet i.
- **Hash Tag History**: How many times the hash tag appears in $u(i)$'s retweets.
- **URL Count**: The number of URLs used in tweet i.
- **URL Domain History**: How many times the URL domain appears in $u(i)$'s retweets.
- **Retweet Count**: The number of times tweet i has been retweeted so far.

Local Graph & User Features: These features potentially characterize how popular and how well connected a user is. Intuitively, a popular user who has many friends and followers can be actively passing information by retweeting messages.

- **Mention Count**: The number of times user u is mentioned in other tweets.
- **Friend Count**: The number of friends user u follows.
- **Follower Count**: The number of followers user u has.
- **Status Count**: The number of tweets user u has published.
- **Account Age**: Number of years user u appeared on Twitter.

User Relationship Features: Relation features refer to those features which represent the relationship between a target user u_i and his/her friend u_j.

- **Co-Friends Score**: This feature estimates the similarity of friend sets of the target user u_i and his/her friend u_j.
- **Co-Follow Score**: This feature estimates the similarity of follower sets of the target user u_i and his/her friend u_j.
- **Mention Score**: The number of times u_i mentions u_j.
- **Retweet Score**: The number of times u_i retweets u_j.
- **Mutual Friend**: Whether u_i and u_j are mutual friends.

The similarity measure used is the Jaccard coefficient.

Temporal Features: We estimate user u's activity level at time t as $h_u(t)$, which is calculated by the average number of tweets he/she published in a periodical time slot, e.g., every Monday. With the estimated response time Δt, the number of accumulated tweets can be written as: $r_u(\Delta t) = \sum_{j \in F(u)} \int_{t^w}^{t^w+\Delta t} h_j(t)\, dt$, as proposed by Peng et al. [21]. We calculate both activities using period of a day and a week.

In our case, all features are pre-calculated through a Hadoop cluster and can be processed efficiently.

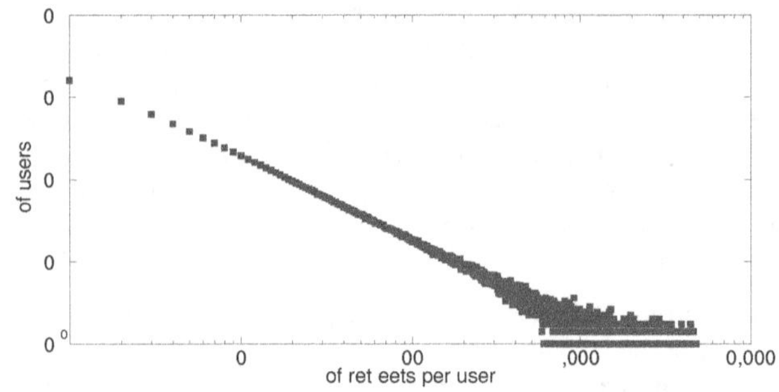

Figure 1: The sparsity of retweets per user.

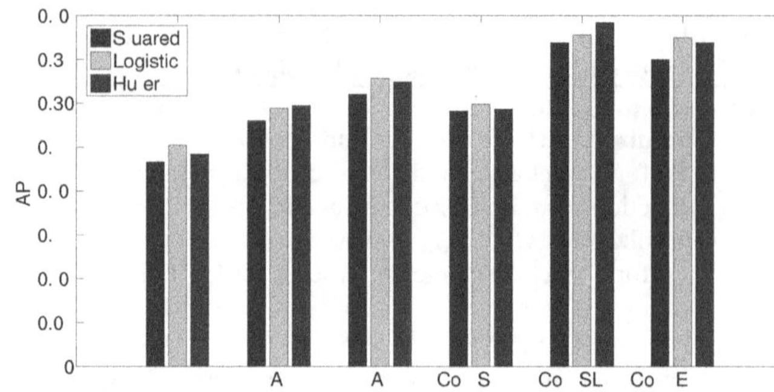

Figure 2: The comparison of pointwise loss functions.

7. EXPERIMENTS

To prepare our dataset, we first monitored the Twitter public stream for one month in June 2012 and extracted users who post at least ten tweets including at least one retweet during this time period, resulting in 765,386 target users with approximately 11M tweets. For all these target users, we 1) crawled all their historical posts and 2) traced who they retweeted from and crawled all their posts as well. In this fashion, we obtained 4,327,816 neighbor users with 27M tweets, resulting in a dataset that is significantly larger than any previous work for similar tasks. For each target user u, we treat all tweets from his/her neighbor users as incoming tweets. If a tweet d from incoming tweets are retweeted by user u, d is treated as a positive instance, and negative otherwise. We plot the unnormalized distribution of number of retweets per user in Figure 1, demonstrating that a great number of users only retweet a limited number of times while some users retweet thousands of times.

We adopt rank-based metrics to evaluate the effectiveness of different models. We borrow Mean Average Precision (MAP) from the IR community. We define "precision" at position k (Precision@k) of all incoming items for a particular user as $(\#\text{ of retweets in top positions})/k$. Then an average measure across all top m positions (Average Precision) for user u is defined as $(\sum_{k=1}^{m} \text{Precision@k} \times l_k)/(\#\text{ of retweets for ranked list of user } u)$ where l_k is a binary indicator whether the position k has been retweeted or not and m is the total number of positions evaluated. Note that Average Precision is evaluated per user. We can average it across all users, resulting in the MAP measure, as used similarly in [6, 13].

In order to mimic a realistic evaluation environment, we adopt a time-based evaluation process, significantly differing from Chen et al. [6] where a **fixed** ratio of training vs. testing dataset is used. (It is not clear whether the ratio is kept according to the time order.) In addition, we do not use cross validation as it violates the time order of data, yielding unfair advantages to certain models. Here, for each user, we split all incoming tweets into n consecutive time periods with **equal** number of tweets in each time period. We train models on one time period and test them on the next. This is a balance between cross validation and online training and testing. In our experiments, we set $n = 5$.

We compare several aspects of proposed methods and other state-of-the-art baselines (some details omitted for space):

- **Matrix factorization** (MF): Categorical features, the target user id and the tweet id are used to feed into FM, yielding a MF model with biases, which is a solid baseline in many collaborative filtering tasks.
- **Matrix factorization with attributes** (MFA): In addition to the categorical features used in MF, we add explicit features into the model, which essentially mimic the state-of-the-art latent factor models with features [1, 33, 7] as mentioned by Rendle [22].
- **Collaborative personalized tweet recommendation** (CPTR): This is the model proposed in [6], which is a variation of MFA where the item factors for a tweet are decomposed into term factors and neighboring user factors. This is a state-of-the-art method for the task. We re-implement their approach under the framework of FM.
- **Factorization machines with attributes** (FMA): In contrast to two categorical features, we add one more categorical feature, the neighbor user id, into the model, resulting in a pairwise tensor factorization model with "target user-item-neighbor user" interactions.
- CoFM **with shared features** (CoFM-SF): This is the model introduced in Section 4.1 with the same indicator features as FMA for user decisions. We use term id and tweet id as two categorical features for content modeling. The latent factors for the tweet are shared through the tweet id. Thus, we have a pairwise tensor interaction model for user decisions and a topic coding model for content.
- CoFM **with shared latent spaces** (CoFM-SL): This is the model introduced in Section 4.2. The feature setting is the same as CoFM-SF.
- CoFM **with latent space regularizations** (CoFM-REG): This is the model introduced in Section 4.3. The feature setting is the same as CoFM-SF.

For the sake of simplicity, we fix all regularization parameters to 1 and tune π, the balance parameter of predictive modeling and content modeling in Equation 11. We report the performance of $\pi = 0.3$, which is the best in our experiments. We also tune K, the dimensionality of latent factors in FM/CoFM, from 10 to 250. We report the performance of $K = 150$, which is the best in the experiments. For CPTR, we fix $K = 200$, which is used in [6]. For content modeling, we do not observe significant differences between using log-Poisson loss and logistic loss. Thus, for generality, we report the results based on log-Poisson loss.

Predictive Results: We compare the predictive power of different models. First, we demonstrate how loss functions affect performance, starting from pointwise loss functions. For MF, MFA and FMA, we compare using three pointwise loss functions: squared error loss, logistic loss and Huber loss. For CoFM-SF, CoFM-SL and CoFM-REG, we use the same three loss functions for predictive modeling while fixing log-Poisson loss for content modeling. Since CPTR is fixed to pairwise learning, we exclude it from the experiment. The result is shown in Figure 2. The first observation is that the performance of MF which only uses user-item interactions

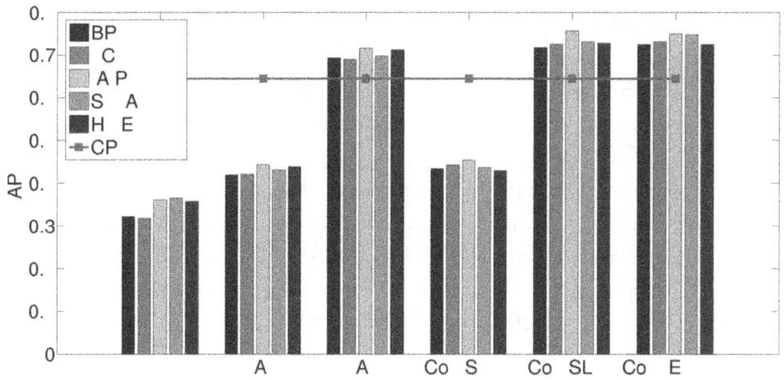

Figure 3: The comparison of ranking-based loss functions.

Table 1: Examples of topics are shown. The terms are top ranked terms in each topic. The topic names shown in bold are given by the authors.

Entertainment
album music lady artist video listen itunes apple produced movies #bieber bieber new songs
Finance
percent billion bank financial debt banks euro crisis rates greece bailout spain economy
Politics
party election budget tax president million obama money pay bill federal increase cuts

is significantly worse than the ones utilizing explicit features. The second observation is that logistic loss and Huber loss is consistently better than squared error loss. This might be due to the reason that we only have binary responses (retweets), similar to what is reported in Yang et al. [33]. The third observation is that CoFM-SL and CoFM-REG are noticeably better than all other methods. This validates our discussion in Section 4 that these two paradigms can be viewed as variants of many successful co-factorization models where the predictive aspect can benefit from the content modeling aspect. On the other hand, CoFM-SF performs poorly and even cannot match the performance of FMA. We conjecture that this is because the data is too sparse such that additional parameters induced by CoFM-SF cannot be effectively learned. We also observe that FMA performs better than MFA, indicating that ternary interactions "target user-item-neighbor user" can indeed capture the dynamics between users on Twitter, compared to "target user-item" binary interactions.

In addition to pointwise loss functions, we also compare performance of different models with ranking-based loss functions, as shown in Figure 3. The green line in the bar chart is the performance of CPTR since it is trained with BPR. Comparing the results to pointwise loss functions, the overall performance is significant higher, indicating that ranking-based loss functions are indeed better for the task. Also, the discrepancy between different models becomes larger, compared to pointwise loss functions. For instance, FMA, CoFM-SL and CoFM-REG are much better than the others, where all three are above CPTR significantly. In addition, CoFM-SL and CoFM-REG are consistently $3\% - 4\%$ better (depending on the specific ranking-based loss function) than FMA in absolute MAP scores across 5 split of data. Overall, WARP achieves competitive performance consistently for all models.

Content Modeling: We explore how topics are learned through the modeling. From the formalism in Section 5.1, the matrix $\mathbf{M}$

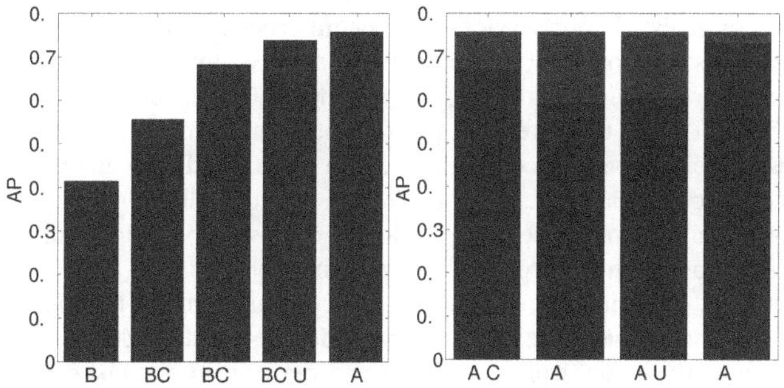

Figure 4: The impact of different groups of features. The effect of "add on" is shown on the left and the effect of "take out" is on the right. For both figures, "A", "B", "C", "G", "U" and "T" stand for "All", "Base model", "Content feature", "Graph feature", "User feature" and "Temporal feature" respectively.

can be interpreted as a topic matrix as in standard PLSA/LDA. Thus, we can describe topics as in other topic models by ranking terms in probabilities. This is superior to CPTR [6] where term factors are not in the simplex. We show some example topics in Table 1. We can see that these topics are easily recognized and have the benefit of normal topic models while we do not have cumbersome Bayesian style formalism and expensive inference algorithms in the model. Note, however, that content modeling is not only for explanatory analysis—it is indeed helpful for prediction tasks. From Figures 2 and 3, we can see that CoFM which utilizes content modeling has better performance in general, and especially for CoFM-SL and CoFM-REG which can outperform state-of-the-art methods significantly.

Feature Analysis: We study how different types of features contribute to the predictive power of the model. Instead of using methods like χ^2 to calculate the correlation between feature values with respect to classification labels, we adopt the following two straightforward methods. First, we start from a base model CoFM-SL using WARP without any explicit features, which is the best model from previous experiments, and then add one group of features consecutively. This method, denoted as "add on", shows the contribution of each group of features as it is added into the model. The second method, denoted as "take out", starts with a complete model and removes one group of features to see how performance drops accordingly. The results for "add on" and "take out" are shown in Figure 4. For "add on", it is clear that each group of features contributes to the final performance of the model and "Temporal" features have the least marginal gain. The most gains come from "Content" features and "Local Graph" features. This observation is consistent with [14]. For "take out", the red square in each bar in the figure represents the performance deduction for the corresponding feature group. Again, "Temporal" features have the least impact on performance while removal of "Local Graph" features hurts performance much more than that of "Content" features. From both "add on" and "take out", it seems that "Local Graph" plays an important role in the performance, followed by "Content" features. This suggests that social connections are important in determining retweets as well as content factors.

8. CONCLUSION

Users of social media services are often simultaneously overwhelmed with the amount of information delivered via their social connections and miss out on content that they might have liked to see. Both issues serve as difficulties to the users and drawbacks to the services. These services can benefit from understanding user interests and how they interact with the service, potentially predicting their behaviors in the future. We propose Co-Factorization Machines (CoFM) to address the problem of simultaneously predicting user decisions and modeling content in social media by analyzing rich information gathered from Twitter. The task differs from conventional recommender systems as the cold-start problem is ubiquitous, and rich features, including textual content, need to be considered. Additionally, we discuss and compare ranking-based loss functions in the context of recommender systems, shedding light on how they vary from each other and perform in real tasks, providing the first work in this direction. We explore a large number of features and conduct experiments on a real-world dataset, concluding that CoFM with ranking-based loss functions is superior to state-of-the-art methods and yields interpretable latent factors.

Acknowledgements

This material is based upon work supported in part by the National Science Foundation under Grant Number IIS-0803605.

9. REFERENCES

[1] D. Agarwal and B.-C. Chen. Regression-based latent factor models. In *KDD*, pages 19–28, 2009.

[2] D. Agarwal and B.-C. Chen. fLDA: matrix factorization through latent dirichlet allocation. In *WSDM*, pages 91–100, 2010.

[3] D. Agarwal, B.-C. Chen, and B. Long. Localized factor models for multi-context recommendation. In *KDD*, pages 609–617, 2011.

[4] B. Bai, J. Weston, D. Grangier, R. Collobert, K. Sadamasa, Y. Qi, C. Cortes, and M. Mohri. Polynomial semantic indexing. In *NIPS*, pages 64–72, 2009.

[5] S. Balakrishnan and S. Chopra. Collaborative ranking. In *WSDM*, pages 143–152, 2012.

[6] K. Chen, T. Chen, G. Zheng, O. Jin, E. Yao, and Y. Yu. Collaborative persoanlized tweet recommendation. In *SIGIR*, 2012.

[7] T. Chen, Z. Zheng, Q. Lu, W. Zhang, and Y. Yu. Feature-based matrix factorization. Technical report, Apex Data & Knowledge Management Lab, Shanghai Jiao Tong University, 2011.

[8] P. Cremonesi, Y. Koren, and R. Turrin. Performance of recommender algorithms on top-n recommendation tasks. In *RecSys*, pages 39–46, 2010.

[9] Y. Duan, L. Jiang, T. Qin, M. Zhou, and H.-Y. Shum. An empirical study on learning to rank of tweets. In *COLING*, pages 295–303, 2010.

[10] J. Duchi, S. Shalev-Shwartz, Y. Singer, and T. Chandra. Efficient projections onto the l1-ball for learning in high dimensions. In *ICML*, pages 272–279, 2008.

[11] Z. Gantner, L. Drumond, C. Freudenthaler, S. Rendle, and L. Schmidt-Thieme. Learning attribute-to-feature mappings for cold-start recommendations. In *ICDM*, pages 176–185, 2010.

[12] R. Herbrich, T. Graepel, and K. Obermayer. Large margin rank boundaries for ordinal regression. In *Advances in Large Margin Classifiers*, pages 115–132. MIT Press, 2000.

[13] L. Hong, R. Bekkerman, J. Adler, and B. D. Davison. Learning to rank social update streams. In *SIGIR*, pages 651–660, 2012.

[14] L. Hong, O. Dan, and B. D. Davison. Predicting popular messages in twitter. In *WWW Companion*, pages 57–58, 2011.

[15] T. Joachims. Optimizing search engines using clickthrough data. In *KDD*, pages 133–142, 2002.

[16] Y. Kim and K. Shim. Twitobi: A recommendation system for twitter using probabilistic modeling. In *ICDM*, pages 340 –349, 2011.

[17] Y. Koren. Factor in the neighbors: Scalable and accurate collaborative filtering. *ACM Transactions on Knowledge Discovery from Data (TKDD)*, 4(1):1:1–1:24, Jan. 2010.

[18] Y. Koren and J. Sill. OrdRec: an ordinal model for predicting personalized item rating distributions. In *RecSys*, pages 117–124, 2011.

[19] H. Lee, R. Raina, A. Teichman, and A. Y. Ng. Exponential family sparse coding with applications to self-taught learning. In *IJCAI*, pages 1113–1119, 2009.

[20] C. Lin, Q. Mei, J. Han, Y. Jiang, and M. Danilevsky. The joint inference of topic diffusion and evolution in social communities. In *ICDM*, pages 378 –387, dec. 2011.

[21] H.-K. Peng, J. Zhu, D. Piao, R. Yan, and Y. Zhang. Retweet modeling using conditional random fields. In *ICDM Workshops*, pages 336–343, 2011.

[22] S. Rendle. Factorization machines with libFM. *ACM TIST*, 3(3):57:1–57:22, May 2012.

[23] S. Rendle, C. Freudenthaler, Z. Gantner, and S.-T. Lars. BPR: Bayesian personalized ranking from implicit feedback. In *UAI*, pages 452–461, 2009.

[24] S. Rendle and L. Schmidt-Thieme. Pairwise interaction tensor factorization for personalized tag recommendation. In *WSDM*, pages 81–90, 2010.

[25] H. Shan and A. Banerjee. Generalized probabilistic matrix factorizations for collaborative filtering. In *ICDM*, pages 1025–1030, 2010.

[26] N. Usunier, D. Buffoni, and P. Gallinari. Ranking with ordered weighted pairwise classification. In *ICML*, pages 1057–1064, 2009.

[27] I. Uysal and W. B. Croft. User oriented tweet ranking: a filtering approach to microblogs. In *CIKM*, pages 2261–2264, 2011.

[28] C. Wang and D. M. Blei. Collaborative topic modeling for recommending scientific articles. In *KDD*, pages 448–456, 2011.

[29] M. Weimer, A. Karatzoglou, Q. V. Le, and A. Smola. CofiRank - maximum margin matrix factorization for collaborative ranking. In *NIPS*, pages 1593–1600, 2007.

[30] M. Weimer, A. Karatzoglou, and A. Smola. Adaptive collaborative filtering. In *RecSys*, pages 275–282, 2008.

[31] J. Weston, S. Bengio, and N. Usunier. Large scale image annotation: learning to rank with joint word-image embeddings. *Machine Learning*, 81(1):21–35, Oct. 2010.

[32] J. Weston, C. Wang, R. Weiss, and A. Berenzweig. Latent collaborative retrieval. In *ICML*, 2012.

[33] S.-H. Yang, B. Long, A. Smola, N. Sadagopan, Z. Zheng, and H. Zha. Like like alike: joint friendship and interest propagation in social networks. In *WWW*, pages 537–546, 2011.

[34] S.-H. Yang, B. Long, A. J. Smola, H. Zha, and Z. Zheng. Collaborative competitive filtering: learning recommender using context of user choice. In *SIGIR*, pages 295–304, 2011.

[35] Z. Yang, J. Guo, K. Cai, J. Tang, J. Li, L. Zhang, and Z. Su. Understanding retweeting behaviors in social networks. In *CIKM*, pages 1633–1636, 2010.

[36] L. Zhang, D. Agarwal, and B.-C. Chen. Generalizing matrix factorization through flexible regression priors. In *RecSys*, pages 13–20, 2011.

[37] J. Zhu and E. P. Xing. Sparse topical coding. In *UAI*, pages 831–838, 2011.

Wikipedia Entity Expansion and Attribute Extraction from the Web Using Semi-supervised Learning *

Lidong Bing Wai Lam
Department of Systems Engineering and Engineering Management
The Chinese University of Hong Kong
{ldbing, wlam}@se.cuhk.edu.hk

Tak-Lam Wong
Department of Mathematics and Information Technology
The Hong Kong Institute of Education
tlwong@ied.edu.hk

ABSTRACT

We develop a new framework to achieve the goal of Wikipedia entity expansion and attribute extraction from the Web. Our framework takes a few existing entities that are automatically collected from a particular Wikipedia category as seed input and explores their attribute infoboxes to obtain clues for the discovery of more entities for this category and the attribute content of the newly discovered entities. One characteristic of our framework is to conduct discovery and extraction from desirable semi-structured data record sets which are automatically collected from the Web. A semi-supervised learning model with Conditional Random Fields is developed to deal with the issues of extraction learning and limited number of labeled examples derived from the seed entities. We make use of a proximate record graph to guide the semi-supervised learning process. The graph captures alignment similarity among data records. Then the semi-supervised learning process can leverage the unlabeled data in the record set by controlling the label regularization under the guidance of the proximate record graph. Extensive experiments on different domains have been conducted to demonstrate its superiority for discovering new entities and extracting attribute content.

Categories and Subject Descriptors

H.4.m [**Information Systems Applications**]: Miscellaneous

Keywords

Information Extraction, Entity Expansion, Proximate Record Graph, Semi-supervised Learning

* The work described in this paper is substantially supported by grants from the Research Grant Council of the Hong Kong Special Administrative Region, China (Project Code: CUHK413510) and the Direct Grant of the Faculty of Engineering, CUHK (Project Codes: 2050476 and 2050522). This work is also affiliated with the CUHK MoE-Microsoft Key Laboratory of Human-centric Computing and Interface Technologies.

WSDM'13, February 4–8, 2013, Rome, Italy.

1. INTRODUCTION

As a remarkable and rich online encyclopedia, Wikipedia provides a wealth of general knowledge about various aspects. Some Wikipedia articles have a structured information block known as infobox, as exemplified in Figure 1, typically on the upper right of the Wikipedia page. An infobox is composed of a set of attribute name and value pairs that summarize the key information of the entity. Infobox was extensively explored in some existing projects such as DBpedia [1], Freebase [4], and YAGO [29].

Although Wikipedia already covers a large number of popular entities, many entities have not been included. Figure 2 presents a fragment of a Web page containing a semi-structured list that describes some cartoon films. After manual checking, we find that quite a number of cartoons in this list have not been covered by Wikipedia. For example, no existing Wikipedia entities describe the cartoons numbered 2, 3, 100 and 101. On the other hand, the ones numbered 319 to 321 in the same list are well contained by Wikipedia and each of them has a description article and an infobox. Therefore, with these records that are already described by some Wikipedia entities as clues, we may infer that the remaining records in the same list shown in Figure 2 are talking about the same type of entities. For example, one can infer that, from the record 100, there exists a cartoon with title "`What's Buzzin' Buzzard`" which does not exist in Wikipedia. Furthermore, considering the infobox of cartoon entity "`One Droopy Knight`" as shown in Figure 1 and its corresponding data record, i.e. record 320 in Figure 2, one can infer that the text fragment "`Directed by Michael Lah`" in the record 320 is related to the director attribute and its value. As a result, one can further infer that the director attribute of the newly discovered entity "`What's Buzzin' Buzzard`" is associated with the value "`Tex Avery`". Some other attributes of the new entity can be obtained similarly.

Inspired by the above observation, we develop a new framework to achieve the goal of new entity discovery and attribute extraction for Wikipedia categories by mining the rich and valuable semi-structured data records on the Web as exemplified in Figure 2. Our framework makes use of a few existing seed Wikipedia entities and their infoboxes automatically extracted from a particular category as clues to discover more entities of this category. It can leverage the existing infoboxes of the seed entities to automatically harvest attribute content of the newly discovered entities. Entity attribute extraction is essential for the usability of the entities in downstream applications such as knowledge base construction.

One Droopy Knight	
	Droopy series
Directed by	Michael Lah
Produced by	William Hanna Joseph Barbera
Story by	Homer Brightman
Narrated by	Bill Thompson
Voices by	Bill Thompson Daws Butler

Figure 1: The infobox of a cartoon entity.

As noticed by previous works [6, 9, 36, 40], semi-structured data records have inherent advantages in the presentation of similar entities sharing common attributes, and these entity records are usually arranged in a layout format that has some regularities, but not following a strictly fixed template. As estimated by Elmeleegy et al., 1.4% of Web pages contain lists (formatted with <dl>, <ol>, or <ul>) that can be extracted into relational tables [9]. Another estimation shows that 1.1% of the tables (formatted with <table>) on the Web contain high-quality relational-style data [6]. Since the <table> tag is commonly used for formatting and navigation, the absolute number of relational tables is very large. Note that some semi-structured data record sets are arranged in a much more complicated format than simply with <ol>, <ul> or <table> tags. Therefore, semi-structured data exists in large amount on the Web. Such kind of data records are collected as the source from which we discover new entities and their attributes.

With respect to the goal of discovering entities from the Web given some seed entities, some existing works on entity set expansion can tackle this task to some extent. Entity set expansion takes a few user given seed entities of a particular class as input, and aims at collecting more entities of the same class. SEAL [33] explores the "list" style of data records, which can be considered as a simplified kind of semi-structured data records mentioned above, to discover more entities to expand a given entity set. Specifically, it extracts named entities with wrappers [34], each of which is a pair of character-level prefix and suffix. The work [13] by Gupta and Sarawagi also processes the "list" style of data records to extract entity names and their attributes. It takes several user input data records, including entity names and attribute values, as seeds to discover more entities as well as similar specified attributes by a trained semi-Markov Conditional Random Field (semi-Markov CRF) [27] based extractor. This method requires considerable manual effort when applying it on large number of domains. Some other works focus on a more general problem setting for the task of entity set expansion [22, 23, 25]. They first obtain a set of candidate entities by some linguistics techniques such as pattern-based method. Then the similarity of a candidate with the seeds is calculated using their context distributions on the Web or Web queries. Because of the general setting, the targeted classes have coarser granularity such as city, country, etc. Moreover, these methods are not able to conduct attribute extraction of the new entities.

With respect to the goal of entity attribute extraction, some existing works [14, 30, 37, 38] train extractors on the free text of Wikipedia articles that are automatically annotated with the corresponding articles' infoboxes. Different from their direction, we explore the semi-structured data records which exist in large quantity on the Web. For example, we can extract the entity attributes of release date, director, etc. from the semi-structured list of the page shown in Figure 2. Since each data record describes one entity, the extracted attribute information can be connected to the correct subjects (i.e. entities) automatically. Consequently, our entity discovery and attribute extraction framework eliminates some error-prone operations such as coreference resolution and disambiguation.

2: CLEANING HOUSE
Rel 2/19/38
Supervised by Robert Allen

3: BLUE MONDAY
Rel 4/2/38
Supervised by William Hanna
... ...
... ...
100: WHAT'S BUZZIN' BUZZARD?
Rel 11/27/43
Directed by Tex Avery; Animation: Ed Love, Ray Abrams, Preston Bla

101: THE STORK'S HOLIDAY
Rel 10/23/43
Directed by George Gordon; Animation: Michael Lah, Rudy Zamora, C
Al Grandmain; Story: Otto Englander, Webb Smith
... ...

319: SCAT CATS
Rel 7/26/57
Directed by Joseph Barbera and William Hanna;
Animation: Kenneth Muse, Carlo Vinci, Lewis
Marshall; Story: Homer Brightman; Layout: Dick
Bickenbach; Backgrounds: Robert Gentle

320: ONE DROOPY KNIGHT
Rel 12/6/57
Directed by Michael Lah; Animation: Bill Schipek, Ken Southworth, Ir
Story: Homer Brightman; Layout: Ed Benedict; Backgrounds: F. Monte

321: FEEDIN' THE KIDDIE
Rel 6/7/57
Directed by Joseph Barbera and William Hanna; Animation: Irvin Spen
Ray Patterson; Layout: Dick Bickenbach; Backgrounds: Don Driscoll; I
ORPHAN.

Figure 2: A Web page fragment of cartoon list.

Although semi-structured data is abundant on the Web and its inherent advantages are appealing for the task of entity discovery and attribute extraction, one big challenge of this task is that the number of available seed entities is typically very limited. As shown by the work [13], when the seed number is small, the trained semi-Markov CRF based extractor cannot perform well. However, it is time consuming and labor force intensive to prepare more seed entities' as well as their attributes. Semi-supervised approaches are proposed to ease the difficulty of lacking enough training data by taking the unlabeled data into account [12, 28]. In this paper, we propose a semi-supervised learning framework to extract the entities and their attribute content from the semi-structured data record sets. Our framework first derives training examples from a few data records by using the seed Wikipedia entities and their infoboxes as automatic labeling knowledge. We employ semi-Markov CRF as the basic sequence classification learning model. Due to the limited number of seed entities, the derived training examples are usually not sufficient to train a reliable model for extracting the entities and their attributes. A semi-supervised learning model with CRF is developed to solve this problem by exploiting the unlabeled data in the semi-structured data record set. To connect the derived training examples and the unlabeled records in the semi-supervised learning, a proximate record graph with each node representing one data record is constructed. Armed with the pairwise sequence alignment based similarity measure between the record nodes in the graph, the labels of derived training examples can regularize the labels of directly or indirectly aligned segments in the unlabeled records effectively.

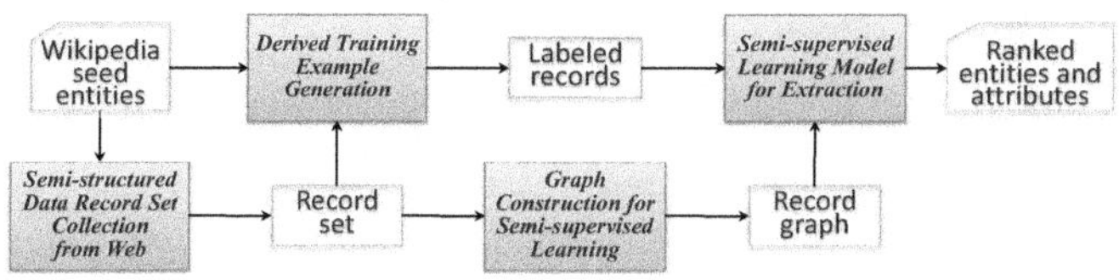

Figure 3: Architecture of our framework.

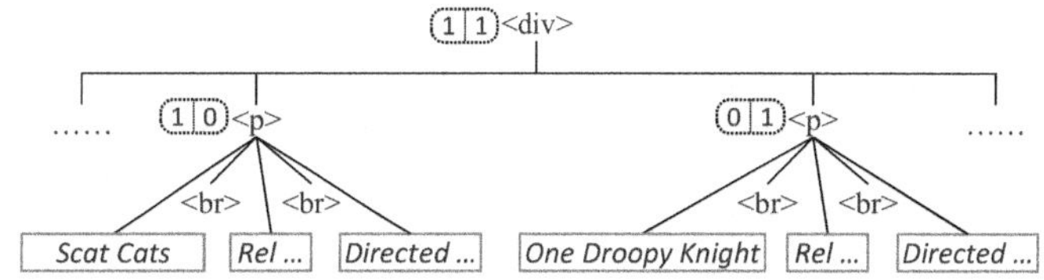

Figure 4: The DOM of the record set in Figure 2.

2. FRAMEWORK OVERVIEW

A Wikipedia category contains a set of existing entities. Taking the "`MGM animated short films`" category as an example, its existing entities include "`Scat Cats`", "`One Droopy Knight`", etc. Each single entity may have an infobox, as exemplified in Figure 1, which contains a set of attributes. Each attribute is a name-value pair (n, V), where n is the attribute name and V is the set of values. In Figure 1, an example of attribute is ("`Produced by`", {"`William Hanna`", "`Joseph Barbera`"}). Given a Wikipedia category C with several existing entities and infoboxes automatically extracted from C as clues, our framework aims at discovering more entities for the category C as well as extracting the attributes for the newly discovered entities. For discovering new entities, one example is the entity "`What's Buzzin' Buzzard`" found in the semi-structured list shown in Figure 2 and the director attribute of this new entity is "`Tex Avery`".

The architecture of our framework is depicted in Figure 3. First, the component of semi-structured data record set collection aims at automatically obtaining from the Web a collection of semi-structured data record sets which provide the sources for new entity discovery and attribute extraction. Given a Wikipedia category C, it takes several seed entities $\mathcal{S}$ automatically extracted from C as clues for constructing a synthetic query to retrieve Web pages. Then semi-structured data record sets that likely contain new entities and attributes are automatically detected from the retrieved pages. One example of such record set is given in Figure 2. Let $\mathcal{D}$ denote a record set discovered from a Web page. Some records in $\mathcal{D}$, corresponding to the seed entities in $\mathcal{S}$, are called *seed records*. The remaining records likely describe some new entities as well as their attribute values. In each record, the key information of the entity described is presented with text segments, such as cartoon name (i.e. entity name of this cartoon), release date, director, etc. The component of semi-supervised learning model for extraction in our framework aims at detecting these desirable text segments. Considering the characteristics of the task, we formulate it as a sequence classification problem. Our classification problem is different from the standard learning paradigm since we do not have manually labeled training examples. Instead, our framework automatically derives the training examples from the seed records. Such labels are known as *derived labels* and the labeled records are known as *derived training examples*. For instance, consider the record 320 in Figure 2 corresponding to the seed entity "`One Droopy Knight`" in Figure 1, our framework automatically derives labels for the text fragments corresponding to the entity name and attribute values in this record to generate a derived training example.

Let $\mathcal{D}_L$ denote the set of derived training examples in $\mathcal{D}$. Our goal is to predict the labels of text fragments for each remaining record in $\mathcal{D}$. We employ semi-Markov Conditional Random Field (semi-Markov CRF) [27] as the basic sequence classification learning model. Typically, the amount of $\mathcal{D}_L$ is quite limited, so the trained classifier by pure supervised learning would not perform well. A semi-supervised learning model is developed to solve this problem by exploiting the data records in $\mathcal{D} - \mathcal{D}_L$, which is called unlabeled data and denoted as $\mathcal{D}_U$. A proximate record graph, with each node of the graph representing one data record in $\mathcal{D}$, is proposed based on the proximate relation of records. This graph is employed to guide the regularization of the posterior label distribution of the records in $\mathcal{D}_U$ during the semi-supervised learning process. Then the labels of the records in $\mathcal{D}_U$ are inferred based on the regularized posterior. The data records in $\mathcal{D}_U$ with inferred labels are taken into account in the subsequent iteration of the training process. Finally, the new entities and their attributes extracted from different data record sets are integrated together. Then a ranking criterion is applied to return a ranked list of the entities together with their attributes.

3. SEMI-STRUCTURED DATA RECORD SET COLLECTION

As mentioned in the overview, given a Wikipedia category C, a seed entity set $\mathcal{S}$ is automatically selected from C. These seed entities are used for constructing a synthetic query to retrieve Web pages which are expected to contain semi-structured data record sets as exemplified in Figure 2. The synthetic query is composed of the seed entity names and the nouns in the category title. In addition, the query term "list" is added because this term is often used in the page titles and article titles of the desirable Web pages. One sample synthetic query for "`MGM animated short films`" category is ⟨scat cats, one droopy knight, [mgm, film, list]⟩, where the square brackets denote optional query terms. The synthetic query is then submitted to Google API to retrieve relevant documents, and the pages from Wikipedia are excluded.

In each Web page obtained above, we need to detect the semi-structured data record set describing a group of targeted entities. To do so, we design a method with two steps, namely, candidate record region identification, and record segmentation. To identify the possible record region, we make use of the seed entities as clues. We first build the DOM tree of the page and assign a flag array to each inner node of it. The number of flags in the array is equal to the number of the seed entities in $\mathcal{S}$. Each flag indicates whether the corresponding entity appears in the sub-tree rooted at the current node. After that, the flag array of each node is set following the post-order traversal. Finally, we identify the DOM node which has all 1's in its flag array, and none of its descendants meets this condition. For example, the DOM tree of the list in Figure 2 with the flag array added is shown in Figure 4, and <div> is the DOM node that satisfies the condition.

The sub-tree identified above is the candidate region in the page that may contain the desirable record set. Next, we need to conduct data record segmentation to segment the sub-trees of the identified DOM node (e.g. <div>) into separate data records. Several methods may be adopted to handle this task such as MDR [18], DEPTA [39], and our previous work RST [3]. Different from MDR and DEPTA which assume a fixed length of generalized nodes, RST provides a unified search based solution for record region detection and segmentation. In this framework, we employ and modify the RST method so that it only detects the records within the identified DOM tree (e.g. the tree in Figure 4). Meanwhile, the top down traversal search is not needed here since we already know that the record region's root should be the root of this sub-tree (e.g. <div> in Figure 4). Note that this method is able to eliminate regions that cannot be segmented into records since these regions are probably not record regions.

4. SEMI-SUPERVISED LEARNING MODEL FOR EXTRACTION

In our framework, the extraction of new entities and their attributes from a particular data record set is formulated as a sequence classification problem. Recall that $\mathcal{D}$ is a semi-structured data record set identified from a Web page. Each data record $\mathbf{x}_i$ in $\mathcal{D}$ is composed of a sequence of text tokens and HTML tags. Hence, it can be represented by a token sequence $\mathbf{x}_i = x_i^1 \cdots x_i^{|\mathbf{x}_i|}$. Since some records in $\mathcal{D}$ correspond to the seed entities known as seed records, we attempt to automatically identify the text fragments corresponding to entity names and attribute values based on the infobox information. For example, consider the sample data record 320, i.e., the cartoon "`One Droopy Knight`" in Figure 2. By using the infobox of the seed Wikipedia entity as given in Figure 1, the text fragment "`ONE DROOPY KNIGHT`" is identified as the entity name and labeled with "ENTITY_NAME" label. The text fragment "`Michael Lah`" is identified as the director attribute value of the cartoon and labeled with "DIRECTED_BY" label. Unlike traditional labels that are provided by human, the above labels are automatically derived from the infobox and called derived labels. The label "OTHER" is used to label the tokens that do not belong to the entity names and attribute values.

After the seed records are automatically labeled with the derived labels, we obtain a set of derived training examples denoted as $\mathcal{D}_L = \{(\mathbf{x}_i, \mathbf{s}_i)\}$, where $\mathbf{s}_i = s_i^1 \cdots s_i^{|\mathbf{s}_i|}$ and $s_i^q = \langle t_i^q, u_i^q, y_i^q \rangle$ is a token segment with the beginning index t_i^q, the ending index u_i^q, and the derived label y_i^q. Our goal is to predict the labels of the text fragments for each record in the remaining part of $\mathcal{D}$, namely $\mathcal{D}_U = \mathcal{D} - \mathcal{D}_L$, so as to extract new entity names and their attribute values described by the record. The details of the component for generating the derived training examples will be presented in Section 5.

We adopt the semi-Markov CRF [27] as the basic sequence classification learning model. As mentioned, the amount of $\mathcal{D}_L$ is quite limited since only a few seed entities are given. As a result, the performance of the trained classifier with the ordinary supervised learning is limited. To tackle this problem, we develop a semi-supervised learning model which exploits the data records in $\mathcal{D}_U$. To better utilize $\mathcal{D}_U$, a graph-based component is designed to guide the semi-supervised learning process. Specifically, we propose

1: **input**: record set $\mathcal{D}$ $(\mathcal{D}_L \cup \mathcal{D}_U)$
2: $\mathcal{D}_U^{(0)} \leftarrow \mathcal{D}_U$, $n \leftarrow 0$
3: $\Lambda^{(0)} \leftarrow$ train semi-Markov CRF on $\mathcal{D}_L$
4: $\mathcal{G} \leftarrow$ construct proximate record graph on $\mathcal{D}$
5: $\hat{\mathbf{P}} \leftarrow$ calculate empirical distribution on $\mathcal{D}_L$
6: **while** *true* **do**
7: $\quad \mathbf{P} \leftarrow$ estimate label distribution for each record $\mathbf{x}_i$ in $\mathcal{D}$ with $\Lambda^{(n)}$
8: $\quad \mathbf{P}^* \leftarrow$ regularize $\mathbf{P}$ with $\hat{\mathbf{P}}$ according to graph $\mathcal{G}$
9: $\quad \tilde{\mathbf{P}} \leftarrow$ interpolate distributions of $\mathbf{P}^*$ and $\mathbf{P}$
10: $\quad \mathcal{D}_U^{(n+1)} \leftarrow$ inference label of $\mathcal{D}_U$ with $\tilde{\mathbf{P}}$
11: $\quad$ **if** $\mathcal{D}_U^{(n+1)}$ same as $\mathcal{D}_U^{(n)}$ **or** $n = maxIter$ **then**
12: $\quad\quad$ **goto** Line 17
13: $\quad$ **end if**
14: $\quad \Lambda^{(n+1)} \leftarrow$ train semi-Markov CRF on $\mathcal{D}_L \cup \mathcal{D}_U^{(n+1)}$
15: $\quad n \leftarrow n + 1$
16: **end while**
17: **return** $\mathcal{D}_U^{(n+1)}$

Figure 5: The algorithm of our Semi-supervised Learning Model.

a graph called proximate record graph where each node of the graph represents a record in $\mathcal{D}$. Each edge represents the connected data records with high degree of similarity in both of text content and HTML format. The high-level pseudo-code of our semi-supervised learning algorithm is given in Figure 5. At the beginning, we train the initial parameters of the semi-Markov CRF on $\mathcal{D}_L$ in Line 3. Before performing the semi-supervised learning, the construction of the proximate record graph $\mathcal{G}$ is conducted using the records in $\mathcal{D}$ in Line 4. The details of the construction will be discussed in Section 4.1. In Lines 7 and 8, the proximate record graph $\mathcal{G}$ guides the regularization of the posterior label distribution $\mathbf{P}$ of the records. The details are presented in Section 4.3. In Lines 9 and 10, the regularized distribution $\mathbf{P}^*$ is interpolated with the original posterior distribution $\mathbf{P}$ to produce an updated label distribution $\tilde{\mathbf{P}}$ which is used in the inference to get the predicted labels for the records in $\mathcal{D}_U$. The details are presented in Section 4.4. Then, if the stopping conditions in Line 11 are not met, the algorithm proceeds to the next iteration, and the records in $\mathcal{D}_U$ with the inferred labels in the current iteration are involved in the semi-Markov CRF training in Line 14 as discussed in Section 4.5. Finally the labeling results of $\mathcal{D}_U$ in the last iteration are returned as the output.

After all record sets corresponding to category C are processed, the extracted entities and attribute values are integrated together. The details are described in Section 4.6.

4.1 Proximate Record Graph Construction

A proximate record graph $\mathcal{G} = (\mathcal{D}, \mathcal{E})$ is an undirected weighted graph with each record in $\mathcal{D}$ as a vertex and $\mathcal{E}$ is the edge set. Recall that each record $\mathbf{x}_i$ in $\mathcal{D}$ is represented by a token sequence $\mathbf{x}_i = x_i^1 \cdots x_i^{|\mathbf{x}_i|}$. Each edge $e_{ij} = (\mathbf{x}_i, \mathbf{x}_j)$ connecting the vertices $\mathbf{x}_i$ and $\mathbf{x}_j$ is associated with a weight w_{ij} calculated as:

$$w_{ij} = \begin{cases} \mathbb{A}(\mathbf{x}_i, \mathbf{x}_j) & if\ \mathbf{x}_i \in \mathbb{K}(\mathbf{x}_j)\ or\ \mathbf{x}_j \in \mathbb{K}(\mathbf{x}_i) \\ 0 & otherwise \end{cases}, \quad (1)$$

where $\mathbb{A}$ is a pairwise sequence alignment function returning a score in $[0, 1]$ which indicates the proximate relation between the two record sequences of $\mathbf{x}_i$ and $\mathbf{x}_j$. $\mathbb{K}(\cdot)$ is a function that can output the top k nearest neighbors. In the proximate record graph, only the vertices (i.e., records) sharing similar format and content will be connected by the edges. Taking the record set given in Figure 2 as an example, $\mathbf{x}_i$ denotes the token sequence obtained from the data record number i. There are edges such as $(\mathbf{x}_{319}, \mathbf{x}_{320})$ and $(\mathbf{x}_{319}, \mathbf{x}_{321})$. However, it is unlikely that there is an edge between $\mathbf{x}_2$ and $\mathbf{x}_{319}$.

To design the alignment function $\mathbb{A}$, we employ a modified Needleman-Wunsch algorithm [21] which performs a global alignment on two sequences using the dynamic programming technique. In particular, we use unit penalty per gap, zero penalty per matching, and infinite penalty per mismatching. The overall alignment penalty of two sequences is converted and normalized into a similarity score in $[0, 1]$. Considering data records $\mathbf{x}_2$ and $\mathbf{x}_3$ in Figure 2, their token sequences are "<p> *DIGIT : cleaning house*
 rel DATE $\cdots$", and "<p> *DIGIT : blue monday*
 rel DATE $\cdots$" respectively. The alignment result is illustrated as below:

$$\begin{array}{llllll} <p> & DIGIT: & cleaning\ house & - & - &
\ rel \cdots \\ | & | & & & & |\quad | \\ <p> & DIGIT: & - & - & blue\ monday &
\ rel \cdots \end{array}$$

where "-" represents a gap token. After sequence alignment, we obtain a set of aligned token pairs $\mathcal{A}^t_{ij} = \{(x^m_i, x^n_j)\}$, where (x^m_i, x^n_j) indicates that x^m_i from $\mathbf{x}_i$ and x^n_j from $\mathbf{x}_j$ are aligned. Furthermore, we can also define the set of aligned segment pairs of $\mathbf{x}_i$ and $\mathbf{x}_j$:

$$\begin{aligned} \mathcal{A}^s_{ij} &= \{(s^q_i, s^r_j)\} \\ s.t.\ & (a).\neg\exists(x^m_i, x^n_j) \in \mathcal{A}^t_{ij} \wedge x^m_i \in s^q_i \wedge x^n_j \in s^r_j, and \\ & (b).(x_i^{t^q_i-1}, x_j^{t^r_j-1}) \in \mathcal{A}^t_{ij} \wedge (x_i^{u^q_i+1}, x_j^{u^r_j+1}) \in \mathcal{A}^t_{ij}, and \\ & (c).u^q_i - t^q_i \leq maxL \wedge u^r_j - t^r_j \leq maxL. \end{aligned}$$

The first condition constrains that an aligned segment pair does not contain any aligned token pairs. The second condition constrains that the left (right) neighboring tokens of the segment pair are aligned. The last condition constrains that the length of both segments should be less than or equal to the maximum length $maxL$. In the above example, one aligned segment pair is ("*cleaning house*", "*blue monday*"). Note that the alignment relation between segments is transitive. Therefore, although $\mathbf{x}_2$ and $\mathbf{x}_{319}$ are not directly connected by an edge, the segments "*cleaning house*" and "*scat cats*" can still be aligned indirectly with the paths from $\mathbf{x}_2$ to $\mathbf{x}_{319}$ in $\mathcal{G}$.

As shown by the above example, it is beneficial to make the labels of aligned segments favor towards each other. The reason is that the text fragments having the same label in different records often share the same or similar context tokens. Meanwhile, they are often presented in the similar relative locations in their own token sequences. The aligned segments generated from our pairwise sequence alignment algorithm can capture the above two characteristics at the same time. The context tokens of some "OTHER" segments may also be similar to that of the desirable segments. The "OTHER" segments in the unlabeled records are often directly or indirectly aligned to the "OTHER" segments in the labeled records. The label regularization in the semi-supervised learning can help predict the correct labels for such situations.

4.2 Semi-Markov CRF and Features

As mentioned in the overview of our framework in Section 2, our semi-supervised extraction model employs semi-Markov CRFs [27] as the basic classification learning model. In particular, a linear-chain CRF model is used. Let $\mathbf{s}_i = s^1_i \cdots s^{|\mathbf{s}_i|}_i$ denote a possible segmentation of $\mathbf{x}_i$, where $s^q_i = \langle t^q_i, u^q_i, y^m_i\rangle$ as defined above. Then the likelihood of $\mathbf{s}_i$ can be expressed as:

$$P(\mathbf{s}_i|\mathbf{x}_i;\Lambda) = \frac{1}{Z(\mathbf{x}_i)} \exp\{\Lambda^T \cdot \sum_q \mathbf{f}(y^{q-1}_i, s^q_i, \mathbf{x}_i)\}, \quad (2)$$

where $\mathbf{f}$ is a feature vector of the segment s^q_i and the state of the previous segment. Λ is the weight vector that establishes the relative importance of all the features. $Z(\mathbf{x}_i)$ is a normalizing factor.

To avoid the risk of overfitting with only a few derived training examples in our problem setting, the only feature template used in our framework is the separator feature:

$$f_{j,j',t,t',d}(y^{q-1}_i, s^q_i, \mathbf{x}_i) = \mathbf{1}_{\{y^q_i=d\}} \mathbf{1}_{\{x_i^{t^q_i-j}=t\}} \mathbf{1}_{\{x_i^{u^q_i+j'}=t'\}}, \quad (3)$$

where $j, j' \in \{1, 2, 3\}$. t and t' vary over the separators such as delimiters and tag tokens in the sequence $\mathbf{x}_i$. d varies over the derived labels of the record set from where $\mathbf{x}_i$ originates. This class of features are unrelated to the previous state, so the feature vector $\mathbf{f}$ can be simplified to $\mathbf{f}(s^q_i, \mathbf{x}_i)$ in our framework.

4.3 Posterior Regularization

In Lines 7 and 8 of the semi-supervised learning model shown in Figure 5, the posterior label distribution is regularized with the guidance of the proximate graph $\mathcal{G}$. Once the parameters of the CRF model are trained, the posterior probability of a particular segment s^q_i in the sequence $\mathbf{x}_i$, denoted by $P(s^q_i|\mathbf{x}_i;\Lambda)$, can be calculated as:

$$P(s^q_i|\mathbf{x}_i;\Lambda) = \frac{1}{Z'} \exp\{\Lambda^T \cdot \mathbf{f}(s^q_i, \mathbf{x}_i)\}, \quad (4)$$

where $Z' = \Sigma_y \exp\{\Lambda^T \cdot \mathbf{f}(\langle t^q_i, u^q_i, y\rangle, \mathbf{x}_i)\}$. Let the vector $\mathbf{P}_{s^q_i} = (P(\langle t^q_i, u^q_i, y\rangle|\mathbf{x}_i;\Lambda))^T$ denote the posterior label distribution of s^q_i. To regularize this distribution with the proximate graph $\mathcal{G}$, we minimize the following function:

$$O(\mathbf{P}) = O_1(\mathbf{P}) + \mu O_2(\mathbf{P}), \quad (5)$$

where μ is a parameter controlling the relative weights of the two terms. $O_1(\mathbf{P})$ and $O_2(\mathbf{P})$ are calculated as in Equations 6 and 7:

$$O_1(\mathbf{P}) = \sum_{\mathbf{x}_i \in \mathcal{D}_L} \sum_{b=1}^{|\mathbf{x}_i|} \sum_{s:\langle b, b+l-1, y\rangle}^{\substack{s.t. 1 \leq l \leq maxL, \\ b+l-1 \leq |\mathbf{x}_i|}} \|\hat{\mathbf{P}}_s - \mathbf{P}_s\|, \quad (6)$$

$$\begin{aligned} O_2(\mathbf{P}) &= \sum_{(\mathbf{x}_i, \mathbf{x}_j) \in \mathcal{E}} w_{ij} \Big(\sum_{(x^m_i, x^n_j) \in \mathcal{A}^t_{ij}} \|\mathbf{P}_{x^m_i} - \mathbf{P}_{x^n_j}\| \\ &+ \sum_{(s^q_i, s^r_j) \in \mathcal{A}^s_{ij}} \|\mathbf{P}_{s^q_i} - \mathbf{P}_{s^r_j}\| \Big), \end{aligned} \quad (7)$$

where $\|\cdot\|$ is the Euclidean norm. $\hat{\mathbf{P}}_s$ is the empirical label distribution of the segment s in $\mathbf{x}_i$. When $l > 1$, $\hat{P}(\langle b, b+$

$l-1, y\rangle|\mathbf{x}_i)$ is calculated as:

$$\hat{P}(\langle b, b+l-1, y\rangle|\mathbf{x}_i) = \sum_{b \le m \le b+l-1} \hat{P}(\langle m, m, y\rangle|\mathbf{x}_i)/l, \quad (8)$$

and $\hat{P}(\langle m, m, y\rangle|\mathbf{x}_i)$ is obtained from the derived label sequence of $\mathbf{x}_i$. In Equation 5, the term $O_1(\mathbf{P})$ regularizes the estimated posterior distribution of the derived training examples in $\mathcal{D}_L$ with the original empirical labeling. The term $O_2(\mathbf{P})$ regularizes the estimated posterior distribution of the aligned token and segment pairs.

To achieve efficient computation, we employ the iterative updating method to obtain the suboptimal solution $\mathbf{P}^*$ of Equation 5. The updating formulae are:

$$\mathbf{P}'_{s_i^q} = \hat{\mathbf{P}}_{s_i^q} \mathbf{1}_{\{\mathbf{x}_i \in \mathcal{D}_L\}} + \mu \sum_{(\mathbf{x}_i, \mathbf{x}_j) \in \mathcal{E}} w_{ij} \sum_{(s_i^q, s_j^r) \in \mathcal{A}_{ij}^s} \mathbf{P}_{s_j^r}, \quad (9)$$

and

$$\mathbf{P}'_{x_i^m} = \hat{\mathbf{P}}_{x_i^m} \mathbf{1}_{\{\mathbf{x}_i \in \mathcal{D}_L\}} + \mu \sum_{(\mathbf{x}_i, \mathbf{x}_j) \in \mathcal{E}} w_{ij} \sum_{(x_i^m, x_j^n) \in \mathcal{A}_{ij}^t} \mathbf{P}_{x_j^n}, \quad (10)$$

where $\mathbf{P}$ is the old estimation from the last iteration. Note that after each iteration, $\mathbf{P}'$ should be normalized so as to meet the condition $\|\mathbf{P}'\|_1 = 1$, where $\|\cdot\|_1$ is the ℓ_1 norm. Then $\mathbf{P}'$ will be regarded as the old estimation for the next iteration.

4.4 Inference with Regularized Posterior

In Lines 9 and 10 of the algorithm shown in Figure 5, the obtained $P^*(s_i^q|\mathbf{x}_i)$ in the regularization is employed to adjust the original $P(s_i^q|\mathbf{x}_i; \Lambda)$ which is calculated with the parameters obtained from the training in the last iteration. The interpolation function is given in Equation 11:

$$\tilde{P}(s_i^q|\mathbf{x}_i; \Lambda) = (1-v)P^*(s_i^q|\mathbf{x}_i) + vP(s_i^q|\mathbf{x}_i; \Lambda), \quad (11)$$

where v is a parameter controlling the relative weights of P^* and P. Then we calculate the new feature value related to s_i^q on $\mathbf{x}_i$ as $\tilde{P}(s_i^q|\mathbf{x}_i; \Lambda) * Z'$. This value is utilized in the Viterbi decoding algorithm to infer new label sequences for the records in $\mathcal{D}_U$.

Recall that the proximate graph $\mathcal{G}$ captures the alignment relation between similar segments and this relation is transitive. Therefore, the decoded labels with the interpolated posterior distribution favor towards the labels of their aligned neighboring segments.

4.5 Semi-supervised Training

As shown in Line 11 of the algorithm in Figure 5, if the inferred labels of the records in $\mathcal{D}_U$ from the previous step are the same as the ones obtained in the last iteration, the semi-supervised learning process terminates. Otherwise, if n is still smaller than the maximum iteration number, the records in $\mathcal{D}_U$ with new labels will be taken into consideration in the next iteration of the training process. In this training, we maximize the penalized log likelihood function as shown below:

$$\begin{aligned} \ell(\Lambda^{(n)}) &= \eta \sum_{(\mathbf{x}_i, \mathbf{s}_i) \in \mathcal{D}_L} \log P(\mathbf{s}_i|\mathbf{x}_i; \Lambda^{(n)}) \quad (12) \\ &+ (1-\eta) \sum_{(\mathbf{x}_i, \mathbf{s}_i^*) \in \mathcal{D}_U^{(n)}} \log P(\mathbf{s}_i^*|\mathbf{x}_i; \Lambda^{(n)}) + \gamma\|\Lambda^{(n)}\|, \end{aligned}$$

where η is a parameter controlling the relative weights of the contribution from the records in $\mathcal{D}_L$ and $\mathcal{D}_U$. The term $\gamma\|\Lambda^{(n)}\|$ is the Euclidean norm penalty factor weighted by γ. $\mathbf{s}_i^*$ is the segmentation of $\mathbf{x}_i$ inferred from the previous step. Obviously, the above objective function is still concave and it can thus be optimized with the efficient gradient descent methods such as L-BFGS [19].

4.6 Result Ranking

In our semi-supervised leaning model for extraction as shown in Figure 5, each data record set is processed separately. Thus, the same entity may be extracted from different record sets where it appears with its different variant names. Before ranking the result entities, we first conduct entity deduplication. The number of occurrence of the same entity is counted during the deduplication process. Then the entities are ranked according to their number of occurrence. After entity deduplication, the attributes of the same entity collected from different record sets are integrated together, and they are also deduplicated and ranked similarly. The details of variant collecting and approximate string matching utilized in the deduplication will be presented in Section 5 since they are also used in the generation of derived training examples.

5. DERIVED TRAINING EXAMPLE GENERATION

As mentioned before, in a semi-structured data record set $\mathcal{D}$, the seed records refer to the data records that correspond to the seed entities in $\mathcal{S}$. The goal of derived training example generation is to automatically identify seed records in $\mathcal{D}$ and determine the sequence classification labels for these records using the information of the seed infoboxes. Since such labels are not directly provided by human as in the standard machine learning paradigm, we call them derived labels. Moreover, the records, after determining the derived labels, are called derived training examples. The generation task can be decomposed into two steps, namely, seed record finding and attribute labeling.

To find the seed record in $\mathcal{D}$ for a seed entity E, we first find the records that contain E's name or its variants as a sub-sequence. The name variants are obtained from synonym in WordNet and the redirection relation in Wikipedia. If the entity name is a person name detected by YagoTool[1], we also collect its variants by following the name conventions, such as middle name removal, given name acronym, etc. In addition, we allow an approximate string matching as supplement in case that the collected variants are not sufficient. The found records are regarded as candidate seed records of E, and the matching sub-sequences are regarded as the candidate record name segments. If multiple record name segments are found in one candidate seed record, the one that has the smallest index in the record is retained and the others are discarded. We adopt this strategy because the subject of a record, i.e. the record name segment, is usually given in the very beginning of the record [8]. When multiple candidate seed records are found for E, the one whose record name segment has the smallest index in its own token sequence is returned as the seed record. This treatment can handle the case that the entity name of E appears as an attribute value or plain text in other non-seed records.

[1] http://www.mpi-inf.mpg.de/yago-naga/javatools/

The found record name segment of the seed record is labeled with the derived label "ENTITY_NAME".

The seed records found above compose the derived training set $\mathcal{D}_L$. The procedure of labeling the attribute values in these seed records is similar to the labeling of the entity name. The attribute values for labeling are collected from the seed entities' infoboxes and their variants are obtained in a similar manner as above. In addition, we use YagoTool to normalize the different formats of date and number types. The variant set of each attribute value goes through the same procedure above for entity name except that we only search the value variant in its own seed record. The derived labels of attribute values are obtained from the seed entity's infobox, such as "DIRECTED_BY", "STORY_BY", etc. After the labeling of attribute values, the remaining unlabeled parts in the seed records are labeled with "OTHER".

6. EXPERIMENTS

6.1 Experiment Setting

We collect 16 Wikipedia categories as depicted in Table 1 to evaluate the performance of our framework. These categories are well-known so that the annotators can collect the full set of the ground truth without ambiguity. Therefore, the experimental results are free from the annotation bias. Moreover, some of these categories are also used in the experimental evaluation of existing works, such as SEAL [33] which will also be compared in our experiments.

To obtain the ground truth of entity elements, the annotators first check the official Web site of a particular category if available. Normally, the full entity list can be found from the Web site. For example, the teams of NBA can be collected from a combox in the home page. For the categories that do not have their own official Web sites such as African country, our annotators try to obtain the entity elements from other related organization Web sites, e.g. the Web site of The World Bank. In addition, the entity lists of some categories are also available in Wikipedia.

Wikipedia already contains articles for some entities in the above categories, and quite many of these articles have well maintained infoboxes. This is helpful for us to collect the ground truth attribute values with high quality for conducting the evaluation of the attribute extraction results. For each entity, the annotators collect the ground truth attribute values for each attribute that also appeared in the seed entities' infoboxes of the same category. Since these infoboxes are used to generate the derived training examples, the extracted attribute values have the same label set as the derived label set from these infoboxes. Hence, the collected ground truth attribute values can be used to evaluate the results. During the collection of attribute values, if the entity exists in Wikipedia and has a good quality infobox, our annotators use the infobox first. After that, they search the Web to collect the values for the remaining attributes.

For each category, the semi-structured data collection component randomly selects two seed entities from the existing ones in Wikipedia to generate a synthetic query. This query is issued to Google API to download the top 200 hit Web pages. The discovery of entities and the extraction of their attributes are carried out with the semi-structured record sets detected from the downloaded pages. This procedure is executed 3 times per category so as to avoid the possible bias introduced by the seed entity selection. The average of these 3 runs is reported as the performance on this category. It is worthwhile to notice that when three or more seeds are available, we can enhance the performance by generating several synthetic queries with different combinations of the seeds and aggregate the results of these synthetic queries. For example, three synthetic queries each of which involves two seeds can be generated from three seed entities.

Table 1: The details of the Wikipedia categories collected for the experiments.

Category ID	Category Name	# of entities
1	African countries	55
2	Best Actor Academy Award winners	78
3	Best Actress Academy Award winners	72
4	Best Picture Academy Award winners	83
5	Counties of Scotland	33
6	Fields Medalists	52
7	First Ladies of the United States	44
8	Leone d'Oro winners	57
9	Member states of the European Union	27
10	National Basketball Association teams	30
11	Nobel laureates in Chemistry	160
12	Nobel laureates in Physics	192
13	Presidents of the United States	44
14	Prime Ministers of Japan	66
15	States of the United States	50
16	Wimbledon champions	179

In our framework, the parameter setting is chosen based on a separate small development data set. The tuned parameters are $\mu = 0.1$, $\upsilon = 0.2$, and $\eta = 0.01$. In the proximate record graph construction, each vertex is connected to its 3 nearest neighbors. The iteration numbers are 20 and 10 for regularization updating and semi-supervised learning respectively. Following the setting in [27], $maxL$ and γ are set to be 6 and 0.01.

6.2 Entity Expansion

For entity expansion, we conduct comparison with two methods. The first one is a baseline that employs supervised semi-Markov CRF as the extraction method (called CRF-based baseline). It also makes use of the collected semi-structured record sets by our framework as the information resource and takes the derived training examples in our framework as the training data to perform supervised learning. The second comparison method is an existing work, namely SEAL [33]. SEAL also utilizes the semi-structured data on the Web to perform entity set expansion. It generates a character-level wrapper for each Web page with the seed entities as clues. We collect 200 results from the system[2] Web site of SEAL per seed set per category.

Both precision and recall are used to evaluate the ranking results of entity discovery. We first report the result of precision at K (P@K) where K is the number of entities considered from the top of the ranked output list by a method. For each method, the value of K varies over 5, 20, 50, 100, and 200. The results of entity discovery of different methods are given in Table 2. It can be observed that all three methods achieve encouraging performance. Their average P@5 values are 0.94, 0.90 and 0.90 respectively. This demon-

[2]http://www.boowa.com/

Table 2: The precision performance of entity discovery of different methods.

	Our framework					CRF-based baseline					SEAL				
#	@5	@20	@50	@100	@200	@5	@20	@50	@100	@200	@5	@20	@50	@100	@200
1	1.00	1.00	0.94	0.48	0.25	1.00	0.90	0.80	0.47	0.25	1.00	1.00	0.92	0.47	0.25
2	1.00	1.00	0.94	0.76	0.38	1.00	0.90	0.84	0.68	0.38	1.00	1.00	0.92	0.71	0.38
3	1.00	0.95	0.92	0.67	0.35	1.00	0.90	0.82	0.58	0.31	1.00	0.85	0.74	0.48	0.29
4	1.00	1.00	0.98	0.81	0.41	1.00	0.93	0.90	0.77	0.41	1.00	1.00	0.98	0.79	0.40
5	0.53	0.43	0.28	0.16	0.11	0.40	0.35	0.28	0.16	0.11	0.40	0.40	0.22	0.12	0.07
6	1.00	1.00	0.94	0.50	0.25	1.00	0.95	0.84	0.43	0.25	1.00	1.00	0.86	0.46	0.24
7	1.00	0.93	0.72	0.42	0.21	0.93	0.85	0.60	0.41	0.21	1.00	0.80	0.62	0.40	0.21
8	0.87	0.85	0.74	0.44	0.24	0.73	0.68	0.48	0.34	0.24	0.80	0.72	0.51	0.26	0.14
9	0.80	0.72	0.46	0.23	0.12	0.60	0.55	0.44	0.23	0.12	0.80	0.55	0.42	0.22	0.12
10	1.00	1.00	0.54	0.28	0.14	1.00	0.93	0.48	0.25	0.14	1.00	1.00	0.52	0.27	0.14
11	1.00	0.95	0.90	0.88	0.66	1.00	0.87	0.84	0.68	0.52	1.00	0.95	0.86	0.71	0.48
12	1.00	0.97	0.86	0.84	0.73	1.00	0.83	0.78	0.62	0.58	1.00	0.95	0.92	0.57	0.52
13	1.00	1.00	0.80	0.41	0.21	1.00	0.93	0.72	0.37	0.19	1.00	0.98	0.76	0.39	0.20
14	1.00	1.00	0.84	0.52	0.32	1.00	0.95	0.76	0.44	0.30	1.00	0.98	0.82	0.42	0.30
15	1.00	1.00	0.95	0.48	0.24	1.00	0.93	0.88	0.48	0.24	1.00	1.00	0.96	0.48	0.24
16	0.80	0.68	0.52	0.33	0.19	0.67	0.62	0.48	0.33	0.18	0.47	0.35	0.34	0.25	0.14
avg.	0.94	0.91	0.77	0.52	0.31	0.90	0.82	0.68	0.46	0.28	0.90	0.85	0.71	0.44	0.26
P-value in pairwise t-test						0.014	9.90E-08	1.25E-05	0.002	0.025	0.074	0.011	0.004	0.001	0.010

strates that semi-structured data on the Web is very useful in this task. Therefore, making use of the semi-structured Web data to enrich some categories of Wikipedia is a feasible and practical direction. On average, the performance of our framework with semi-supervised learning extraction is better than SEAL. One reason for the superior performance is that our framework detects the semi-structured data record region before the extraction. This can eliminate the noise blocks in the Web pages. The character-level wrapper of SEAL may be affected by these noise blocks. In addition, with only a few seeds, the character-level wrapper of SEAL cannot overcome the difficulty caused by the cases that the seed entity names have inconsistent contexts. For example, one seed name is embedded in a tag <font> while the other seed name is not. The wrapper induction procedure will be misled by this inconsistency. Moreover, when the text segments of the names have similar format contexts as that of other segments of the records, the obtained wrapper will also extract more false positives. The CRF-based baseline also suffers from the above context related difficulties. Our semi-supervised learning method can cope with this problem by taking the unlabeled data records into account. Specifically, the sequence alignment based proximate record graph regularizes the labels according to the alignment relation so as to overcome the difficulties brought in by the ambiguous context. We conduct pairwise t-test using a significance level of 0.05 and find that the improvements of our framework are significant in most cases. The P-values in the significance tests are given in the last row of Table 2.

We manually check some categories with low performance. One major type of error for Category 9 is due to the non-EU European countries, such as "Ukraine" and "Switzerland". When we retrieve the semi-structured data records from the Web, the seeds of EU member countries also serve as the seeds for non-EU European countries in a counterproductive manner. For the category of Scotland county, many noisy place names are extracted. The main reason is that the entity names in this category are also widely used to name other places all over the nations of British Commonwealth. Consequently, the collected large amount of noisy semi-structured data records affect the performance.

We also report the recall of different methods in Table 3. Since the number of the ground truth entities in different categories varies from dozens to near 200, the recall values are calculated at different K values of the result list, namely 50, 100, and 200. If the ground truth number is no more than a particular K value, the recall for this K value is calculated. On average, our framework outperforms SEAL by about 7%. One reason is that the noise output of SEAL affects the ranking of the true positives, and some of them are ranked lower. Another possible reason is that the search engine cannot return sufficient number of semi-structured record sets. This also affects the performance of our framework.

6.3 Attribute Extraction

Another major goal of our framework is to extract attribute values for the detected entities. SEAL does not perform entity attribute extraction, therefore, we only report the performance of our framework and the CRF-based baseline. For each domain, we only examine the extracted attributes of the correct entities in its answer entity list and report the average precision at different K values from 1 to 10 in all domains. Note that about one fifth correctly extracted entities do not have detected attributes and they are excluded from this evaluation.

The result of attribute extraction performance is given in Figure 6. It can been seen that our framework can perform significantly better than the CRF-based baseline with a difference about 11% on average at different K levels. It is worth emphasizing that our framework can achieve 16% improvement on average when K is no more than 5. It indicates that our framework is rather robust. We manually check the extracted attributes of CRF-based baseline and find that besides noise segments, it sometimes wrongly identifies the name of an entity as an attribute value. The reason is that the CRF-based baseline only depends on the separator fea-

Table 3: The precision performance of entity discovery of different methods.

# \ K	Our framework 50	Our framework 100	Our framework 200	CRF baseline 50	CRF baseline 100	CRF baseline 200	SEAL 50	SEAL 100	SEAL 200
1	–	0.91	0.94	–	0.89	0.94	–	0.89	0.94
2	–	0.79	0.87	–	0.78	0.84	–	0.79	0.82
3	–	0.74	0.83	–	0.68	0.83	–	0.62	0.79
4	–	1.00	1.00	–	0.95	1.00	–	0.97	0.99
5	0.45	0.52	0.71	0.44	0.52	0.71	0.35	0.39	0.45
6	–	1.00	1.00	–	0.92	1.00	–	0.92	1.00
7	0.81	1.00	1.00	0.72	0.97	1.00	0.74	0.90	0.95
8	–	0.71	0.84	–	0.62	0.80	–	0.41	0.51
9	0.84	0.92	0.96	0.81	0.92	0.96	0.81	0.88	0.96
10	0.96	1.00	1.00	0.86	0.89	1.00	0.93	0.96	1.00
11	–	–	0.81	–	–	0.66	–	–	0.61
12	–	–	0.74	–	–	0.59	–	–	0.52
13	0.93	0.97	1.00	0.86	0.88	0.90	0.89	0.90	0.93
14	–	0.83	1.00	–	0.75	1.00	–	0.76	1.00
15	0.98	1.00	1.00	0.92	1.00	1.00	1.00	1.00	1.00
16	–	–	0.19	–	–	0.18	–	–	0.16
avg.	0.83	0.88	0.87	0.77	0.85	0.84	0.79	0.80	0.79

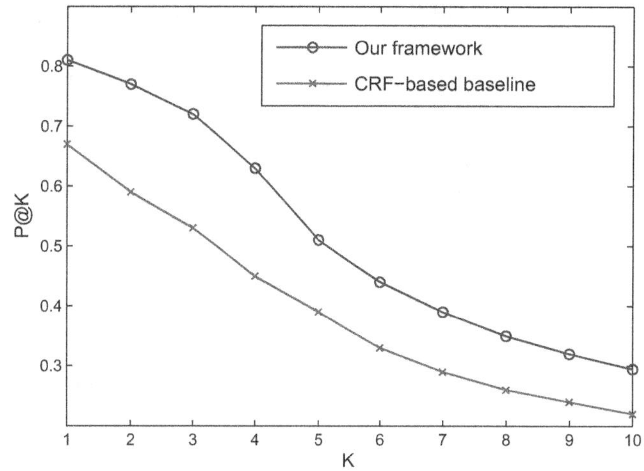

Figure 6: The attribute extraction performance of our framework and the CRF-based baseline.

tures to identity segments. Thus they cannot distinguish those segments with similar context tokens. Our framework can handle these cases by regularizing the label distribution with the proximate record graph as guidance. As a result, noise segments can be regularized to favor towards the segments labeled as "OTHER" in the derived training examples. Similarly, the segments of the entity name and the attribute value with similar context tokens can also be properly identified. In addition, it can be seen that the attributes of higher rank have better precision. Specifically, our framework can output 2 true positive attribute values among the top 3 extracted attribute results. It is because the important attributes of an entity are repeatedly mentioned in different data record sets, such as the capital and GDP of an African country, the party and spouse of a US president, etc. Therefore, they are ranked higher according to the counted occurrence time. We also find that some correct attributes are not ranked very high. One possible reason is due to the simple design of the final ranking method which only counts the number of occurrence of the extracted attributes.

7. RELATED WORK

SEAL [33] exploits "list" style of data, which can be considered as a simplified kind of semi-structured data records in this paper, to discover more entities for expanding a given entity set. They extract named entities with wrappers, each of which is composed of a pair of character-level prefix and suffix [34]. However, they do not perform record region detection, consequently the wrappers may extract noise from the non-record regions of the page. Context distribution similarity based methods [23, 25] utilize the context of the seed entities in the documents or Web search queries to generate a feature/signature vector of the targeted class. Then the candidate entities are ranked according to the similarity of their feature vectors with the class's vector. Different from the above methods that explore positive seed instances only, Li et al [16] proposed a learning method that takes both positive and unlabeled learning data as input and generates a set of reliable negative examples from the candidate entity set. Then the remaining candidates are evaluated with the seeds as well as the negative examples. Ensemble semantics methods [7, 26] assemble the existing set expansion techniques as well as their information resources to boost the performance of a single approach on a single resource. The output of named entity recognition [20] can serve as one source to perform set expansion [23, 25, 26]. All the above methods cannot extract attributes of the discovered entities.

Entity set acquisition systems [5, 10] do not need input seeds. They leverage domain independent patterns, such as "is a" and "such as", to harvest the instances of a given class. Open information extraction [2, 11] and table semantifying [17, 31, 32] focus more on extracting or annotating large amount of facts and relations. The methods of weakly-supervised attribute acquisition [22, 24] can also be applied in identifying important attributes for the categories. Thus, the existing infoboxes can be polished, and the non-infobox categories can obtain proper attributes to establish their own infobox schemata.

Among the semi-supervised CRF approaches, one class of methods consider data sequence granularity [12, 15, 35]. Precisely, these methods incorporate one more term in the objective function of CRF. This term captures the conditional entropy of the CRF model or the minimum mutual information on the unlabeled data. The extra term can be interpreted by information theory such as rate distortion theory. However, the objective function does not possess the convexity property any more. Subramanya et al. also constructed a graph to guide the semi-supervised CRF learning in part-of-speech tagging problem [28]. This method regularizes the posterior probability distribution on each single token in a 3-gram graph. Its n-gram based graph construction is not applicable to the problem tackled here. The reason is that the length of our desirable text segments cannot be fixed in advance. In contrast, our proximate record graph can capture both record level and segment level similarities at the same time. Furthermore, the proximate record graph is also able to capture the position information of a text segment in the alignment so that the aligned segments with higher chance describing the same functionality components of different records.

8. CONCLUSIONS AND FUTURE WORK

In this paper, a framework of Wikipedia entity expansion and attribute extraction is presented. This framework takes a few seed entities automatically collected from a particular category as well as their infoboxes as clues to harvest more entities as well as attribute content by exploiting the semi-structured data records on the Web. To tackle the problem of lacking sufficient training examples, a semi-supervised learning model is proposed. A proximate record graph is designed, based on pairwise sequence alignment, to guide the semi-supervised learning. Extensive experimental results can demonstrate that our framework can outperform a state-of-the-art existing system. The semi-supervised learning model achieves significant improvement compared with pure supervised learning.

Several directions are worth exploring in the future. One direction is to investigate how to perform derived training example generation with the article of the seed entity when its infobox does not exist. Another direction is to detect new attributes in the semi-structured data record sets that are not mentioned in the infoboxes. Such new attributes are valuable to populate the relations in knowledge bases.

9. REFERENCES

[1] S. Auer, C. Bizer, G. Kobilarov, J. Lehmann, R. Cyganiak, and Z. Ives. Dbpedia: a nucleus for a web of open data. In *ISWC/ASWC*, pages 722–735, 2007.

[2] M. Banko, M. J. Cafarella, S. Soderl, M. Broadhead, and O. Etzioni. Open information extraction from the web. In *IJCAI*, pages 2670–2676, 2007.

[3] L. Bing, W. Lam, and Y. Gu. Towards a unified solution: data record region detection and segmentation. In *CIKM*, pages 1265–1274, 2011.

[4] K. Bollacker, C. Evans, P. Paritosh, T. Sturge, and J. Taylor. Freebase: a collaboratively created graph database for structuring human knowledge. In *SIGMOD*, pages 1247–1250, 2008.

[5] M. J. Cafarella, D. Downey, S. Soderland, and O. Etzioni. Knowitnow: fast, scalable information extraction from the web. In *HLT*, pages 563–570, 2005.

[6] M. J. Cafarella, A. Halevy, D. Z. Wang, E. Wu, and Y. Zhang. Uncovering the relational web. In *WebDB*, 2008.

[7] A. Carlson, J. Betteridge, R. C. Wang, E. R. Hruschka, and T. M. Mitchell. Coupled semi-supervised learning for information extraction. In *WSDM*, pages 101–110, 2010.

[8] E. Crestan and P. Pantel. Web-scale table census and classification. In *WSDM*, pages 545–554, 2011.

[9] H. Elmeleegy, J. Madhavan, and A. Halevy. Harvesting relational tables from lists on the web. *Proc. VLDB Endow.*, 2:1078–1089, 2009.

[10] O. Etzioni, M. Cafarella, D. Downey, S. Kok, A.-M. Popescu, T. Shaked, S. Soderland, D. S. Weld, and A. Yates. Web-scale information extraction in knowitall (preliminary results). In *WWW*, pages 100–110, 2004.

[11] O. Etzioni, A. Fader, J. Christensen, S. Soderland, and Mausam. Open information extraction: The second generation. In *IJCAI*, pages 3–10, 2011.

[12] Y. Grandvalet and Y. Bengio. Semi-supervised learning by entropy minimization. In *NIPS*, pages 529–536. 2004.

[13] R. Gupta and S. Sarawagi. Answering table augmentation queries from unstructured lists on the web. *Proc. VLDB Endow.*, 2:289–300, 2009.

[14] R. Hoffmann, C. Zhang, and D. S. Weld. Learning 5000 relational extractors. In *ACL*, pages 286–295, 2010.

[15] F. Jiao, S. Wang, C.-H. Lee, R. Greiner, and D. Schuurmans. Semi-supervised conditional random fields for improved sequence segmentation and labeling. In *ACL*, pages 209–216, 2006.

[16] X.-L. Li, L. Zhang, B. Liu, and S.-K. Ng. Distributional similarity vs. pu learning for entity set expansion. In *ACLShort*, pages 359–364, 2010.

[17] G. Limaye, S. Sarawagi, and S. Chakrabarti. Annotating and searching web tables using entities, types and relationships. *Proc. VLDB Endow.*, 3:1338–1347, 2010.

[18] B. Liu, R. Grossman, and Y. Zhai. Mining data records in web pages. In *KDD*, pages 601–606, 2003.

[19] D. C. Liu and J. Nocedal. On the limited memory bfgs method for large scale optimization. *Mathematical Programming*, 45:503–528, 1989.

[20] D. Nadeau and S. Sekine. A survey of named entity recognition and classification. *Lingvisticae Investigationes*, 30:3–26, 2007.

[21] S. Needleman and C. Wunsch. A general method applicable to the search for similarities in the amino acid sequence of two proteins. *Journal of Molecular Biology*, 48:443–453, 1970.

[22] M. Paşca. Organizing and searching the world wide web of facts – step two: harnessing the wisdom of the crowds. In *WWW*, pages 101–110, 2007.

[23] M. Paşca. Weakly-supervised discovery of named entities using web search queries. In *CIKM*, pages 683–690, 2007.

[24] M. Paşca and B. V. Durme. Weakly-supervised acquisition of open-domain classes and class attributes from web documents and query logs. In *ACL*, pages 19–27, 2008.

[25] P. Pantel, E. Crestan, A. Borkovsky, A.-M. Popescu, and V. Vyas. Web-scale distributional similarity and entity set expansion. In *EMNLP*, pages 938–947, 2009.

[26] M. Pennacchiotti and P. Pantel. Entity extraction via ensemble semantics. In *EMNLP*, pages 238–247, 2009.

[27] S. Sarawagi and W. W. Cohen. Semi-markov conditional random fields for information extraction. In *NIPS*, pages 1185–1192, 2004.

[28] A. Subramanya, S. Petrov, and F. Pereira. Efficient graph-based semi-supervised learning of structured tagging models. In *EMNLP*, pages 167–176, 2010.

[29] F. M. Suchanek, G. Kasneci, and G. Weikum. Yago: A large ontology from wikipedia and wordnet. *Web Semant.*, 6:203–217, 2008.

[30] F. M. Suchanek, M. Sozio, and G. Weikum. Sofie: a self-organizing framework for information extraction. In *WWW*, pages 631–640, 2009.

[31] P. Venetis, A. Halevy, J. Madhavan, M. Paşca, W. Shen, F. Wu, G. Miao, and C. Wu. Recovering semantics of tables on the web. *Proc. VLDB Endow.*, 4:528–538, 2011.

[32] J. Wang, B. Shao, H. Wang, and K. Q. Zhu. Understanding tables on the web. Technical report, 2010.

[33] R. C. Wang and W. W. Cohen. Language-independent set expansion of named entities using the web. In *ICDM*, pages 342–350, 2007.

[34] R. C. Wang and W. W. Cohen. Character-level analysis of semi-structured documents for set expansion. In *EMNLP*, pages 1503–1512, 2009.

[35] Y. Wang, G. Haffari, S. Wang, and G. Mori. A rate distortion approach for semi-supervised conditional random fields. In *NIPS*, pages 2008–2016. 2009.

[36] T.-L. Wong and W. Lam. Learning to adapt web information extraction knowledge and discovering new attributes via a bayesian approach. *IEEE Trans. on Knowl. and Data Eng.*, 22:523–536, 2010.

[37] F. Wu and D. S. Weld. Autonomously semantifying wikipedia. In *CIKM*, pages 41–50, 2007.

[38] F. Wu and D. S. Weld. Open information extraction using wikipedia. In *ACL*, pages 118–127, 2010.

[39] Y. Zhai and B. Liu. Web data extraction based on partial tree alignment. In *WWW*, pages 76–85, 2005.

[40] J. Zhu, Z. Nie, J.-R. Wen, B. Zhang, and W.-Y. Ma. Simultaneous record detection and attribute labeling in web data extraction. In *KDD*, pages 494–503, 2006.

Retweet or not? Personalized Tweet Re-ranking

Wei Feng Jianyong Wang
Tsinghua National Laboratory for Information Science and Technology
Department of Computer Science and Technology, Tsinghua University, Beijing 100084, China
feng-w10@mails.tsinghua.edu.cn, jianyong@tsinghua.edu.cn

ABSTRACT

With Twitter being widely used around the world, users are facing enormous new tweets every day. Tweets are ranked in chronological order regardless of their potential interestedness. Users have to scan through pages of tweets to find useful information. Thus more personalized ranking scheme is needed to filter the overwhelmed information. Since retweet history reveals users' personal preference for tweets, we study how to learn a predictive model to rank the tweets according to their probability of being retweeted. In this way, users can find interesting tweets in a short time. To model the retweet behavior, we build a graph made up of three types of nodes: users, publishers and tweets. To incorporate all sources of information like users' profile, tweet quality, interaction history, etc, nodes and edges are represented by feature vectors. All these feature vectors are mapped to node weights and edge weights. Based on the graph, we propose a feature-aware factorization model to re-rank the tweets, which unifies the linear discriminative model and the low-rank factorization model seamlessly. Finally, we conducted extensive experiments on a real dataset crawled from Twitter. Experimental results show the effectiveness of our model.

Categories and Subject Descriptors

H.3.3 [**Information Storage and Retrieval**]: Information Search and Retrieval—*Information Filtering, Retrieval Models, Selection Process*

Keywords

Social Media; Recommender System

1. INTRODUCTION

With 500 million active users and 340 million tweets generated every day[1], Twitter is one of the leading social networking and microblogging service providers in the world. A tweet is a text message of up to 140 characters generated by users. Users can follow their friends, idols and any other kind of information sources to keep up with their latest tweets. Tweets can be shared along the followee-follower links so that more users are informed. The sharing action is referred as retweet. Retweet behavior is the key part behind the information spreading in Twitter.

[1]http://en.wikipedia.org/wiki/Twitter

When a user logs in to Twitter, tweets are ranked in chronological order regardless of their potential interestedness. Users have to scan through pages of tweets to find important information. Thus a more personalized ranking scheme is needed to deal with the overwhelmed updates. Since retweet history can be considered as explicit feedbacks of one's preference for tweets, we can learn a predictive model to find what tweets are likely to attract one's attention. Tweets can be re-ranked according to their probability of being retweeted. This re-ranking scheme will help users find the important tweets that are missed since last login in a short time. Personalized re-ranking can serve as a complementary information filtering tool to the current system.

While some work [2, 3, 7, 12] has been done in studying the retweet behavior, they mainly focused on the global factors, i.e., predicting popular tweets in the whole social network or in the perspective of information spreading[11, 14]. Different from previous work, our work is focused on local factors at the individual level, i.e., building a predictive model that serve for each user.

Our contributions are summarized as follows:

- We propose a novel problem called personalized tweet re-ranking to help users deal with overwhelmed tweets. To the best of our knowledge, we are among the first to study retweet behavior at the individual level.
- We propose a general graph model to analyze retweet behavior. All sources of information can be converted to the feature vectors of nodes and edges. The graph model is fully extensible to new features.
- Based on the graph, we propose a feature-aware factorization model which unifies the linear discriminative and the low-rank factorization models seamlessly.
- We have conducted extensive experiments on a real dataset crawled from Twitter. Our model is proved to be more effective than the existing models.

The rest of the paper is organized as follows: In Section 2, we give a formal definition of our problem and discuss the drawbacks of the existing methods. In Section 3, we introduce our basic framework and all kinds of features. Our feature-aware matrix factorization model is introduced in

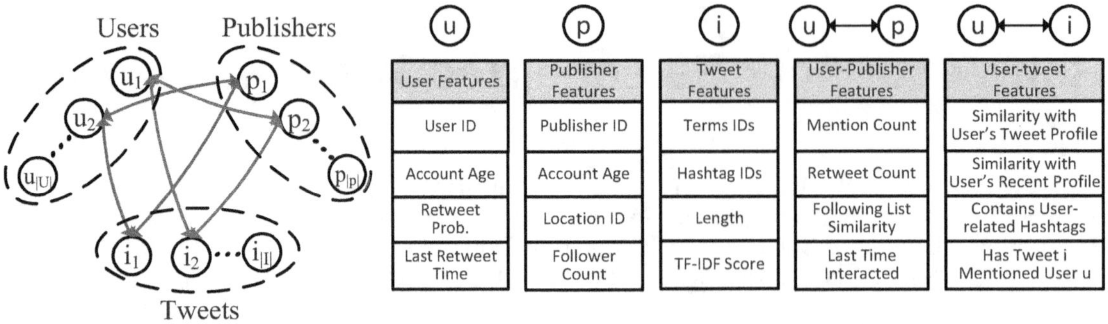

Figure 1: Retweet behavior modeled by a graph. Nodes and edges are represented by features. Some typical features are listed here.

Section 4. Section 5 describes our experimental study on a dataset crawled from Twitter, where we show that our model is more effective than the existing models. In Section 6, we introduce the related work. Finally, we conclude the paper in Section 7.

2. PRELIMINARIES

2.1 Problem Statement

Every time a user signs in to Twitter, she/he will get the latest 20 tweets[2] on the home page. As the user rolls down to the bottom, the client will pull another 20 tweets until the user stops scanning. The whole process is called a session in our paper. Usually only a small number of tweets will be retweeted in a session. The goal of Personalized Tweet Re-Ranking (PTR) is to rank the tweets that are more likely to be retweeted at the front of the list for each session.

Let U, P, I denote the user set, publisher set and tweet set[3], respectively. Since a tweet can be received by multiple users, we define a tweet as a tuple $<u, p, i, t, r_{upi}>$ where

- $u \in U$ is the receiver of the tweet, $p \in P$ is the publisher of the tweet, $i \in I$ is tweet itself.
- t is the timestamp of the session indicating when user u saw tweet i.
- r_{upi} is a binary constant indicating whether this tweet is retweeted by user u. r_{upi} can be viewed as the class label or u's binary rating for tweet i.

Formally, the goal of PTR is to predict r_{upi} for each new tweet. Let $\widehat{r}_{upi}$ denote the predicted rating, there are two ways to judge whether $\widehat{r}_{upi}$ is a good approximation of r_{upi}:

- **Point-wise Approach**. This approach tries to find the best boundary to separate the positive tweets from the negative tweets. When r_{upi} is 1, $\widehat{r}_{upi}$ should also be close to 1.
- **Pair-wise Approach**. This approach tries to find the best $\widehat{r}_{upi}$ so that $\widehat{r}_{upi}$ and r_{upi} can generate the same ranking order. $\widehat{r}_{upi}$ is not limited to have a similar value with r_{upi}.

More details will be discussed in Section 4.3.

[2]The exact number may be different in different clients.

[3]Tweet set can be viewed as item set in traditional recommender systems

2.2 Drawbacks of Matrix Factorization

In this section, we will discuss the reason why existing matrix factorization techniques cannot be directly applied to PTR and what are the differences between PTR and traditional recommendation task.

In the setting of matrix factorization, low-dimension vectors $\mathbf{p}_u$ and $\mathbf{p}_i$ are learned for each user u and item i respectively to approximate the original user-item rating matrix. Let r_{ui} denote user u's rating to item i, r_{ui} is predicted according to the following equation [4]

$$\widehat{r}_{ui} = \mu + b_u + b_i + \mathbf{p}_u^T \mathbf{p}_i \tag{1}$$

where μ is the global bias, b_u and b_i are the biases for user u and item i, respectively. There are two challenges that cannot be solved by the traditional matrix factorization models:

- Tweets have much stronger temporal effects than traditional items like movies and songs. On the one hand, users usually prefer new tweets. On the other hand, most new tweets have barely no feedbacks from users, since other users may have not seen them yet. Moreover, with the low cost of composing tweets, tweets are generated with a much higher frequency than traditional items. In this case, most tweets in the test set may not exist in the training set at all. Experimental results in Section 5.4 empirically prove this.
- The auxiliary information is much richer than the traditional user-item rating data. For example, a tweet can contains URLs, medias and hashtags. All of them can be viewed as indicators to the content quality. The times and frequency that users interact with each other will indicate whether they will keep interacting in the future. The number of followers and the fraction of tweets being retweeted can indicate a user's authority. Traditional matrix factorization lacks support for the auxiliary information.

3. FRAMEWORK

In this section, we first introduce the graph model. Then we introduce our basic framework.

Recall a tweet is defined as a tuple $<u, p, i, t, r_{upi}>$ in Section 2.1. There are three entities involved during the retweet action: user u, publisher p and tweet i itself. It is intuitive to construct a graph to illustrate the involved factors in retweet behavior. The graph is shown in Figure 1. Now we give a formal definition of the graph.

Definition 1. (**Retweet Graph**) Retweet behavior can be represented as a graph G = (V, E) where

- V = $U \cup P \cup I$. Three types of nodes are involved: users, publishers, and tweets.

- E = <u, p>∪<u, i>∪<p, i>. <u, p> represents u's trust to p. <u, i> represents the content interestedness of tweet i to u. <p, i> represents the fact that p is the publisher of tweet i.

As shown in Figure 1, nodes and edges in the retweet graph have rich auxiliary information. To incorporate all sources of information, each node is represented by a feature vector $\mathbf{x}_m$ ($m \in \{u,p,i\}$) and each edge is also represented by a feature vector $\mathbf{x}_{um}$ ($m \in \{p,i\}$)[4]. These features will finally be mapped to node weights and edge weights.

We assume that a retweet action is mainly influenced by two types of factors:

- **Node Weights**. Node weights can be interpreted as whether user u is willing to retweet, whether publisher p is likely to be retweeted, whether tweet i has a high quality, etc. Based on the specific node features, node weights can incorporate multiple meanings.

- **Edge Weights**. Edge weights can describe relations like whether user u and publisher p are close friends, and whether tweet i is interesting to user u. Again, all the information can be contained in the edge feature.

According to the above assumption, we designed the prediction function:

$$\widehat{r}_{upi} = \sum_{m\in\{u,p,i\}} f_m + \sum_{m\in\{p,i\}} f_{um} + \sum_{m\in\{p,i\}} \mathbf{g}_u^T \mathbf{g}_m \quad (2)$$

where f_m is a function that maps a node feature vector to node weight, f_{um} is a function that maps the edge feature vector to edge weights. $\mathbf{g}_u^T \mathbf{g}_m$[5] is a term representing the factorization part. In this paper, four relations are factorized: user-publisher, user-location, user-term, and user-hashtag. Unlike the user-tweet relation, the above relations are all much denser. But our framework is not limited to the above four relations. It is fully extensible to new relations. The details will be discussed in Section 4.

In the next two subsections, we will introduce the node features and edge features used in f_m ($m \in \{u,p,i\}$) and f_{um} ($m \in \{p,i\}$). Some of the features are designed to be calculated in realtime (incrementally) to catch the temporal effects. All the node features marked by '*' are further used in the factorization term $\mathbf{g}_u^T \mathbf{g}_m$.

3.1 Node Features

3.1.1 Tweet Features

Term IDs/Hashtag IDs*. Although it is not common to use IDs as features, they have special meaning in our model. According to Equation 2, f_i will map term IDs to their latent biases. These latent biases can be viewed as the automatically learned term weights, which can serve as complements to the hand-crafted TF-IDF scores. $\mathbf{g}_i$ will map term IDs to low-dimension latent vectors. Each dimension can be regarded as a latent topic. Each latent vector is a distribution over these topics. $\mathbf{g}_u^T \mathbf{g}_i$ will calculate the interestedness of the terms for user u. More details will be discussed in Section 4.

Has geography/hashtag/multimedia/URL/mention. This set of boolean features is used to indicate the content quality. For example, a tweet with multimedia like an video or an image will be more likely to be noticed. If a tweet mentions the user, the user will be more likely see it.

Length and average TF-IDF score. Both the features describe the content quality.

Retweet count and time span since last time being retweeted. Both the features are calculated in realtime and can be updated incrementally. They are used to capture tweets with a high spreading speed.

Time span since created. This feature measures the freshness of the tweet. Since fresh tweets carry new information, they tend to be more valuable than older tweets.

3.1.2 Publisher Features

Publisher ID*. Like term IDs and hashtag IDs, publisher IDs in f_p will be mapped to latent biases, which represent the prior probabilities of publishers' tweets being retweeted. This reflects the idea that tweets from authorities are more likely to be retweeted than tweets from common publishers. Besides the latent biases, $\mathbf{g}_p$ will map publisher IDs to low-dimension latent vectors, which have the same space with low-dimension vectors of terms or hashtags. Each dimension represents a topic and the value at the dimension represents the publisher's authority on this topic. Finally, user u's trust to publisher p is calculated by $\mathbf{g}_u^T \mathbf{g}_p$. More details will be introduced in Section 4.

Location ID*. Location IDs represents the cities or countries extracted from publishers' profiles. This feature is used to capture the spatial effects like local events and language preferences. Followers that have a strong preference toward a location will also likely to be interested in publishers in this location. f_p maps location IDs to their latent biases, which represent activeness of locations. $\mathbf{g}_p$ maps location IDs to latent vectors. Each vector represents a distribution over the k latent topics. Finally, the topic distribution of a publisher is partially influenced by her/his location.

Prior probability of being retweeted and time span since last time being retweeted. Both the features are used to measure the probability of the publisher's tweets getting retweeted. They can filter publishers that seldom get attentions and capture popular publishers.

Authority score. The authority score is defined as the ratio between the follower count and the followee count. This feature states the social status of the publisher. High authorities are likely to have much more followers than followees.

Is verified. Verified publishers tend to earn more trust.

Mention count. If a publisher is frequently mentioned, she/he is more likely to be popular and has more interactions than other publishers.

Account Age. From this feature we can know how long a user has participated in Twitter. Older accounts tend to be more influential in the social network.

[4]Since <p, i> has little connection with whether user u will retweet tweet i, we will mainly focus on the other edges in this paper, i.e., <u, p> and <u, i>.

[5]The function value of $\mathbf{g}_u$ is a vector. For convenience, we also use $\mathbf{g}_u$ to represent a vector.

3.1.3 User Features

User ID*. Like publisher IDs, f_u will map user IDs to latent biases, which state their willingness to retweet. $\mathbf{g}_u$ will map user IDs to low-dimension latent vectors, which states the user's preferences for each latent topic. User u's trust to publisher p is defined as $\mathbf{g}_u^T\mathbf{g}_p$. Tweet i's interestedness to u will be calculated according to $\mathbf{g}_u^T\mathbf{g}_i$.

Prior probability of retweet and time span since last retweet. As a complement to users' biases, this feature also describes users' willingness to retweet. However, this feature is hand crafted. It is computed by n_{ret}/n_{recv}, where n_{ret} and n_{recv} are the number of tweets retweeted and received respectively before timestamp t. The time span since last retweet will indicate how long a user has not retweeted. These features can filter users that seldom retweet and catch active users that often retweet.

Account Age. This feature is the same with the account age of publishers.

3.2 Edge Features

3.2.1 User-Publisher Features

Similarity of tweet profiles. Users and publishers are represented by terms in their tweets. All the tweets (originally posted and retweeted) are integrated into a single document. The tweet profile is a term vector with TF-IDF weighting scheme of all the tweets. The similarity between a user and a publisher is defined as the similarity of their tweet profiles in the term vector space. This feature is used to measure the user-publisher similarity in the long term.

Similarity of recent tweet profiles. Each user and publisher are represented by their latest ten tweets. This feature can describe whether the user and the publisher focus on the the same topic recently. We want to catch the short term interests. Users' recent tweet profiles are updated incrementally in realtime.

Similarity of self-descriptions. Users can write self-descriptions to introduce themselves. The similarity is defined as the cosine distance of their description in the vector space model.

Similarity of the following lists. This feature is defined as the Jaccard similarity of the following lists of the user and the publisher. We assume that similar users tend to follow similar publishers.

Are friends/Is same location/same time zone. 'Are friends' refers to whether users and publishers follow each other, while 'Is same location' and 'Is same time zone' are used to find whether they are close in physical world.

Ratio of their authority score/Are both verified. Recall that 'Authority score' is defined as the ratio of follower count and followee count. According to whether a user and a publisher are verified, we have four different combinations, i.e., user is verified but publisher is not verified, etc. We want to know whether users and publishers have comparable influence.

Mention count/Retweet count/Reply count/Time span since last interaction. This set of feature describes the closeness between the user and the publisher. We assume users with many interactions in the past tend to keep interacting in the future. These feature are calculated in realtime and can be updated incrementally.

3.2.2 User-Tweet Features

Similarity of the tweet and the user's tweet profile. Recall that a user's tweet profile is a TF-IDF vector of all his tweets. This feature describes the content similarity between the tweet and the user's tweet profile.

Similarity of the tweet and the user's recent tweet profile. Recall that a user's recent tweet profile is a TF-IDF vector of his lastest ten tweets. This feature describes whether this tweet is related to user's short term interests.

Has mentioned the user/Has hashtags related to the user. If the tweet has mentioned the user, he will be informed to see this tweet. Hashtags related to user u are defined as the hashtags used or retweeted by user u.

3.3 Nodes and Edges as Feature Vectors

In this section, we introduce some details about how these features are used in our algorithm.

There are two types of features involved in this paper:

- **Numeric features**. Numeric features are normalized to have mean equals to zero and standard deviation equals to one.
- **Categorical features**(including boolean features). A categorical feature with k categories is converted to a sparse vector of length k. The i-th entry corresponds to the i-th category. Take user ID as an example. Suppose user ID ranges from 1 to 5. u_2 will be represented by $(0, 1, 0, 0, 0)^T$. For features like term IDs and hashtag IDs, the feature vector is normalized to sum to 1. Take term IDs for example. Suppose the content of tweet i is 'WSDM is coming' and the dictionary is {1:WSDM, 2:is, 3:coming, 4:data, 5:mining}. Tweet i can be represented by $\mathbf{x}_i = (1, 1, 1, 0, 0)^T$. Normalizing $\mathbf{x}_i$ by the number of nonzero entries, i.e., three, we have $\mathbf{x}_i = (\frac{1}{3}, \frac{1}{3}, \frac{1}{3}, 0, 0)^T$. Without normalization, term IDs of long tweets will dominate other features.

Missing feature values are specially handled in our task.

- **Numeric features**. If a numeric feature is missing, it will be marked as 'NA' and a new boolean feature is added and set to true. A suitable weight can be found in the training process to replace the missing value. For example, if a user's tweets have never been retweeted, the feature 'last time being retweeted' is missing. So we add new boolean feature $x_{new} = 1$ with weight θ_{new}. During the training process, $\theta_{new}x_{new}$ is used to represent the missing value. With enough training examples, a proper θ_{new} will be learned. For non-missing values, the added boolean feature is false.
- **Categorical features**. If a categorical feature has missing values, a new category is added to represent all the missing values. Take hashtag IDs as an example. For tweets that do not have hashtags, we add a new hashtag 'NULL' to represent the missing hashtag.

4. FEATURE-AWARE FACTORIZATION MODEL

In this section, we will discuss how to incorporate all the features in our model. We will introduce the meaning of Equation 2 in two steps: Section 4.1 introduces the definitions of f_m and f_{um} $(m \in \{p, i\})$. Section 4.2 introduces the definition of $\mathbf{g}_u^T\mathbf{g}_m$ $(m \in \{p, i\})$.

4.1 Feature-based Approach

When only considering f_m and f_{um}, Equation 2 is equivalent to

$$\widehat{r}_{upi} = \sum_{m\in\{u,p,i\}} f_m + \sum_{m\in\{p,i\}} f_{um} \quad (3)$$

where f_m maps a node feature vector $\mathbf{x}_m$ to the node weight and f_{um} maps an edge feature vector $\mathbf{x}_{um}$ to the edge weight. In the simplest case, f_m is defined to be a linear combination of all the node features:

$$f_m = \boldsymbol{\theta}_m^T \mathbf{x}_m \quad (4)$$

where $\boldsymbol{\theta}_m$ is the feature weight vector that stores the importance of each dimension. f_{um} is also defined to be the linear form:

$$f_{um} = \boldsymbol{\theta}_{um}^T \mathbf{x}_{um} \quad (5)$$

where $\boldsymbol{\theta}_{um}$ is the feature weight vector corresponding to edge feature vector $\mathbf{x}_{um}$.

With the definition of f_m and f_{um}, we discuss the meaning of user ID and publisher ID in feature vectors. Suppose user ID and publisher ID both range from 1 to 5. When other features are ignored, u_1 can be represented by $\mathbf{x}_{u_1} = (1,0,0,0,0)^T$ and p_2 can be represented by $\mathbf{x}_{p_2} = (0,1,0,0,0)^T$. According to Equations 4 and 5, we have

$$\widehat{r}_{u_1p_2i} = \boldsymbol{\theta}_{u,1} + \boldsymbol{\theta}_{p,2} \quad (6)$$

where $\boldsymbol{\theta}_{m,k}$ represents the k-th entry of vector $\boldsymbol{\theta}_m$. $\boldsymbol{\theta}_{u,1}$ and $\boldsymbol{\theta}_{p,2}$ represent the general biases of u_1 and p_2. $\boldsymbol{\theta}_{u,1}$ states u_1's willingness to retweet while $\boldsymbol{\theta}_{p,2}$ states the probability of the tweets of p_2 being retweeted. With enough training instances and an effective loss function, appropriate $\boldsymbol{\theta}_{u,1}$ and $\boldsymbol{\theta}_{p,2}$ will be found. These learned biases can be treated as complementary to hand-crafted features like 'prior probability of retweet' and 'prior probability of being retweeted' introduced in Section 3.1.

With the understanding of user ID and publisher ID, it is easy to understand the meaning of term IDs. Suppose the content of tweet i is 'WSDM is coming' and the dictionary is {1:WSDM, 2:is, 3:coming, 4:data, 5:mining}. When only term IDs are considered, tweet feature vector $\mathbf{x}_i$ is $(1,1,1,0,0)^T$. To avoid long tweet dominating the ranking score, we normalize each entry by the text length, which makes $\mathbf{x}_i$ equal to $(\frac{1}{3},\frac{1}{3},\frac{1}{3},0,0)^T$. According to Equations 4 and 5, we have

$$\widehat{r}_{upi} = (\boldsymbol{\theta}_{i,1} + \boldsymbol{\theta}_{i,2} + \boldsymbol{\theta}_{i,3})/3 \quad (7)$$

where $\boldsymbol{\theta}_{i,1}$, $\boldsymbol{\theta}_{i,2}$ and $\boldsymbol{\theta}_{i,3}$ are automatically learned term importance. $(\boldsymbol{\theta}_{i,1} + \boldsymbol{\theta}_{i,2} + \boldsymbol{\theta}_{i,3})/3$ describes the content quality of tweet i. $\boldsymbol{\theta}_{i,k}$ can be considered as a complement to TF-IDF score of term k.

Now we discuss why tweet ID is not a good option for tweet features. Recall that in Section 2.2 we argue that tweets have stronger temporal effects. Since only a small number of recent tweets can attract users' attention, most tweet biases will have no training data at all. Unlike tweets, most users, publishers and terms are likely to exist in both training data and test data.

Finally we discuss the meaning of f_{up} and f_{ui} in Equation 3. f_{up} and f_{ui} are edge weights of <u, p> and <u, i>, respectively. <u, p> represents how much u trusts p. <u, t> can be considered as the interestedness of t to u. While node weights provide a prior knowledge of each object, edge weights contain more personalized information. Unlike node weight, edge weights are different for each different instances. Thus they are considered to be more effective, which is also empirically proved in Section 5.5.

So far, all the edge features (i.e., similarities between nodes) are hand-crafted. In the next section, we will discuss how factorization techniques can be used to serve as complements to the hand-crafted features.

4.2 Feature-aware Factorization Model

The basic idea of $\mathbf{g}_m$ ($m \in \{u,p,i\}$) is to learn a k-dimension latent vector for each dimension of the node feature, where k is usually a number from 50 to 200. Each latent vector can be viewed as a distribution of preferences over the k latent topics. $\mathbf{g}_u^T\mathbf{g}_p$ represents the similarity of user u and publisher p over k latent topics. $\mathbf{g}_u^T\mathbf{g}_p$ and $\mathbf{g}_u^T\mathbf{g}_i$ can serve as complements to f_{up} and f_{ui}, where similarities are calculated from hand-crafted features.

Like f_m, $\mathbf{g}_m$ is defined to be a linear form:

$$\mathbf{g}_m = \boldsymbol{\Phi}_m \mathbf{x}_m \quad (8)$$

where $\boldsymbol{\Phi}_m$ is a $k \times |\mathbf{x}_m|$ matrix.

$\mathbf{g}_m$ in the special form. We use $\mathbf{g}_i$ as an example to explain the meaning of $\mathbf{g}_m$. According to the node features introduced in Section 3.1, tweet i can be represented by its terms and hashtags, i.e., $\mathbf{x}_i = (\mathbf{x}_i^{term}, \mathbf{x}_i^{tag})^T$. Corresponding to $\mathbf{x}_i^{term}$ and $\mathbf{x}_i^{tag}$, $\boldsymbol{\Phi}_i$ can also be rewritten to two blocks, i.e., $\boldsymbol{\Phi}_i = [\boldsymbol{\Phi}_i^{term}, \boldsymbol{\Phi}_i^{tag}]$. $\mathbf{g}_i$ is computed by

$$\begin{aligned}\mathbf{g}_i &= [\boldsymbol{\Phi}_i^{term}, \boldsymbol{\Phi}_i^{tag}] \begin{bmatrix} \mathbf{x}_i^{term} \\ \mathbf{x}_i^{tag} \end{bmatrix} \\ &= \boldsymbol{\Phi}_i^{term}\mathbf{x}_i^{term} + \boldsymbol{\Phi}_i^{tag}\mathbf{x}_i^{tag}\end{aligned} \quad (9)$$

We can see that $\mathbf{g}_i$ is made up of two components, i.e., $\boldsymbol{\Phi}_i^{term}\mathbf{x}_i^{term}$ and $\boldsymbol{\Phi}_i^{tag}\mathbf{x}_i^{tag}$. $\boldsymbol{\Phi}_i^{term}\mathbf{x}_i^{term}$ represents the latent vectors inferred from terms while $\boldsymbol{\Phi}_i^{tag}\mathbf{x}_i^{tag}$ represents the latent vectors inferred from hashtags. Suppose the content of tweet i is '#WSDM# #Data Mining# WSDM is coming'. The term dictionary is {1:WSDM, 2:is, 3:coming, 4:data, 5:mining} and the hashtag dictionary is {1:WSDM, 2:Data Mining, 3:Machine Learning}. Accoring to the dictionaries, we have $\mathbf{x}_i^{term} = (\frac{1}{3},\frac{1}{3},\frac{1}{3},0,0)^T$ and $\mathbf{x}_i^{tag} = (\frac{1}{2},\frac{1}{2},0)^T$. Plug $\mathbf{x}_i^{term}$ and $\mathbf{x}_i^{tag}$ into Equation 9, we have

$$\begin{aligned}\mathbf{g}_i &= \boldsymbol{\Phi}_i^{term}\mathbf{x}_i^{term} + \boldsymbol{\Phi}_i^{tag}\mathbf{x}_i^{tag} \\ &= \frac{\boldsymbol{\Phi}_{i,1}^{term} + \boldsymbol{\Phi}_{i,2}^{term} + \boldsymbol{\Phi}_{i,3}^{term}}{3} + \frac{\boldsymbol{\Phi}_{i,1}^{tag} + \boldsymbol{\Phi}_{i,2}^{tag}}{2}\end{aligned} \quad (10)$$

where $\boldsymbol{\Phi}_{i,k}$ represents the k-th column of $\boldsymbol{\Phi}_i$. When $\mathbf{x}_i^{term} = (\frac{1}{3},\frac{1}{3},\frac{1}{3},0,0)^T$, only the first three columns of $\boldsymbol{\Phi}_i^{term}$ are retained. '$(\boldsymbol{\Phi}_{i,1}^{term} + \boldsymbol{\Phi}_{i,2}^{term} + \boldsymbol{\Phi}_{i,3}^{term})/3$' in the above equation represents the averaged latent vector for term IDs. '$(\boldsymbol{\Phi}_{i,1}^{tag} + \boldsymbol{\Phi}_{i,2}^{tag})/3$' represents the averaged latent vector for hashtag IDs. $\mathbf{g}_i$ is a combination of these two latent vectors.

$\mathbf{g}_m^T\mathbf{g}_n$ in the special form. Now we explain the meaning of $\mathbf{g}_u^T\mathbf{g}_i$ in Equation 2. According to Equation 8, we have $\mathbf{g}_u = \boldsymbol{\Phi}_u\mathbf{x}_u$. $\mathbf{g}_u^T\mathbf{g}_i$ is computed as the following

$$\begin{aligned}\mathbf{g}_u^T\mathbf{g}_i &= (\boldsymbol{\Phi}_u\mathbf{x}_u)^T(\boldsymbol{\Phi}_i\mathbf{x}_i) \\ &= (\boldsymbol{\Phi}_u\mathbf{x}_u)^T(\boldsymbol{\Phi}_i^{term}\mathbf{x}_i^{term} + \boldsymbol{\Phi}_i^{tag}\mathbf{x}_i^{tag}) \\ &= (\boldsymbol{\Phi}_u\mathbf{x}_u)^T(\boldsymbol{\Phi}_i^{term}\mathbf{x}_i^{term}) + (\boldsymbol{\Phi}_u\mathbf{x}_u)^T(\boldsymbol{\Phi}_i^{tag}\mathbf{x}_i^{tag})\end{aligned} \quad (11)$$

where $(\mathbf{\Phi}_u\mathbf{x}_u)^T(\mathbf{\Phi}_i^{term}\mathbf{x}_i^{term})$ represents user u's preference to tweet i's terms, and $(\mathbf{\Phi}_u\mathbf{x}_u)^T(\mathbf{\Phi}_i^{tag}\mathbf{x}_i^{tag})$ represents user u's preference to tweet i's hashtags.

Now we discuss the meaning of $\mathbf{g}_u^T\mathbf{g}_p$. According to publisher features introduced in Section 3.1, a publisher can be represented by $\mathbf{x}_p = (\mathbf{x}_p^{ID}, \mathbf{x}_p^{loc})$, where $\mathbf{x}_p^{ID}$ is a feature vector of publisher IDs and $\mathbf{x}_p^{loc}$ is a feature vector of location IDs. Similar to $\mathbf{g}_u^T\mathbf{g}_i$, $\mathbf{g}_p^T\mathbf{g}_p$ is calculated by

$$\begin{aligned}\mathbf{g}_u^T\mathbf{g}_p &= (\mathbf{\Phi}_u\mathbf{x}_u)^T(\mathbf{\Phi}_p\mathbf{x}_p) \\ &= (\mathbf{\Phi}_u\mathbf{x}_u)^T(\mathbf{\Phi}_p^{ID}\mathbf{x}_p^{ID} + \mathbf{\Phi}_p^{loc}\mathbf{x}_p^{loc}) \\ &= (\mathbf{\Phi}_u\mathbf{x}_u)^T(\mathbf{\Phi}_p^{ID}\mathbf{x}_p^{ID}) + (\mathbf{\Phi}_u\mathbf{x}_u)^T(\mathbf{\Phi}_p^{loc}\mathbf{x}_p^{loc})\end{aligned} \tag{12}$$

where $(\mathbf{\Phi}_u\mathbf{x}_u)^T(\mathbf{\Phi}_p^{ID}\mathbf{x}_p^{ID})$ represents user u's preference to publisher p, and $(\mathbf{\Phi}_u\mathbf{x}_u)^T(\mathbf{\Phi}_p^{loc}\mathbf{x}_i^{loc})$ represents user u's preference to publisher p's location.

Combining Equation 11 with Equation 12, we can find that four matrices (relations) are factorized in our problem: user-term matrix, user-hashtag matrix, user-publisher matrix, and user-location matrix.

$\mathbf{g}_m$ in the general form. Now we discuss $\mathbf{g}_m$ $(m \in \{u, p, i\})$ in a more generalized setting. Suppose node m has k_m features, then we have $\mathbf{x}_m = (\mathbf{x}_m^1, \mathbf{x}_m^2, ..., \mathbf{x}_m^{k_m})^T$ and $\mathbf{\Phi}_m = (\mathbf{\Phi}_m^1, \mathbf{\Phi}_m^2, ..., \mathbf{\Phi}_m^{k_m})$. According to Equation 8, $\mathbf{g}_m$ is calculated according to the following equation

$$\begin{aligned}\mathbf{g}_m &= \left[\mathbf{\Phi}_m^1, \mathbf{\Phi}_m^2, ..., \mathbf{\Phi}_m^{k_m}\right]\left[\mathbf{x}_m^1, \mathbf{x}_m^2, ..., \mathbf{x}_m^{k_m}\right]^T \\ &= \sum_{q=1}^{k_m} \mathbf{\Phi}_m^q\mathbf{x}_m^q\end{aligned} \tag{13}$$

where $\mathbf{\Phi}_m^q\mathbf{x}_m^q$ is a latent vector for node feature vector $\mathbf{x}_m^q$. $\mathbf{g}_m$ is a combination of these latent vectors.

$\mathbf{g}_m^T\mathbf{g}_n$ in the general form. According to Equation 13, we $\mathbf{g}_m^T\mathbf{g}_n$ is calculated by

$$\begin{aligned}\mathbf{g}_m^T\mathbf{g}_n &= (\sum_{q=1}^{k_m} \mathbf{\Phi}_m^q\mathbf{x}_m^q)^T(\sum_{p=1}^{k_n} \mathbf{\Phi}_n^p\mathbf{x}_n^p) \\ &= \sum_{q=1}^{k_m}\sum_{p=1}^{k_n} (\mathbf{\Phi}_m^q\mathbf{x}_m^q)^T(\mathbf{\Phi}_n^p\mathbf{x}_n^p)\end{aligned} \tag{14}$$

The above equation states that similarity between node m and node n is the summation of pair-wise dots of node m's latent vectors and node n's latent vectors.

Connections with traditional matrix factorization models. Our feature-aware factorization model can be considered as an extension of the traditional matrix factorization model. In the simplest case, our model can be degraded to the matrix factorization model defined by Equation 1.

We can illustrate the connections with an example. Suppose user ID and publisher ID all range from 1 to 5. When only user ID and publisher ID are considered, node feature of u_1 is $\mathbf{x}_{u_1} = (1, 0, 0, 0, 0)^T$ and node feature of p_2 is $\mathbf{x}_{p_2} = (0, 1, 0, 0, 0)^T$. According to Equation 2, the similarity term $\mathbf{g}_u^T\mathbf{g}_p$ is calculated by

$$\begin{aligned}\mathbf{g}_u^T\mathbf{g}_p =& (\mathbf{\Phi}_u\mathbf{x}_{u_1})^T(\mathbf{\Phi}_p x_{p_2}) \\ =& \mathbf{\Phi}_{u,1}^T\mathbf{\Phi}_{p,2}\end{aligned} \tag{15}$$

where $\mathbf{\Phi}_{i,j}$ represents the j-th column of matrix $\mathbf{\Phi}_i$. Plug $\mathbf{g}_u^T\mathbf{g}_p$ and $f_u^Tf_p$ into Equation 2 and ignore other features, where $f_u^Tf_p$ for u_1 and p_2 has been explained in Equation 6, we have

$$\widehat{r}_{u_1p_2i} = \boldsymbol{\theta}_{u,1} + \boldsymbol{\theta}_{p,2} + \mathbf{\Phi}_{u,1}^T\mathbf{\Phi}_{p,2} \tag{16}$$

The above equation has the same form as Equation 1. This means feature-aware matrix factorization can be degraded to matrix factorization if only user ID and item ID are used as features.

To summarize, our feature-aware factorization model learns latent biases and vectors for each node feature. In this paper, we only consider five types of node features: user ID, publisher ID, location ID, term IDs, and hashtag IDs. Our model is fully extensible to new features, as long as the model has not over-fitted the problem.

4.3 Loss Function

In the previous section we have defined parameters $\boldsymbol{\theta}_m$, $\boldsymbol{\theta}_{um}$ and $\mathbf{\Phi}_m$ in Equations 4, 5, and 8. The ranking score $\widehat{r}_{upi}$ is dependant on these parameters. To find the best parameter, we need a good loss function to measure whether $\widehat{r}_{upi}$ is a good approximation of r_{upi}. Two types of loss functions are considered in this paper:

Point-wise Loss. Point-wise approach is similar to a binary classification task. Whenever the real label r_{upi} is 1, the predicted score $\widehat{r}_{upi}$ should be close to 1. First we choose the logistic function to transform $\widehat{r}_{upi}$ to (0, 1) interval:

$$\widehat{r}'_{upi} = \sigma(-\widehat{r}_{upi}) \tag{17}$$

where $\sigma(x) = 1 \;/\; (1 + e^{-x})$. The loss function is defined as

$$\begin{aligned}l(\boldsymbol{\theta}_m, \boldsymbol{\theta}_{um}, \mathbf{\Phi}_m) = -r_{upi}\log\widehat{r}'_{upi} + (r_{upi} - 1)\log(1 - \widehat{r}'_{upi}) \\ + regularzation\end{aligned} \tag{18}$$

The *regularzation* term will be introduced at the end of the section. Now we explain the meaning of the loss function. Suppose $r_{upi} = 1$, the above loss function will be $\log(\widehat{r}'_{upi})$. If $\widehat{r}'_{upi}$ is close to 1, the loss is zero. If $\widehat{r}'_{upi}$ is close to 0, the loss will be close to positive infinite. Our goal is to minimize the loss function so that $\widehat{r}'_{upi}$ is always close to r_{upi}.

Pair-wise Loss. Pair-wise loss focuses on the relative ranking order instead of the difference between $\widehat{r}_{upi}$ and r_{upi}. When a negative example is ranked higher than a positive example, a loss is generated. AUC is such a metric that measures the probability of ranking a positive example higher than a negative example. Let T^+ and T^- denote the indices of positive tweets and negative tweets, respectively. AUC is defined as

$$AUC = \frac{\sum_{p=1}^{|T^+|}\sum_{q=1}^{|T^-|}\mathbb{I}(\widehat{r}_{u_pp_pi_p} - \widehat{r}_{u_qp_qi_q})}{|T^+||T^-|} \tag{19}$$

where $\mathbb{I}(x)$ is 1 when $x > 0$, otherwise $\mathbb{I}(x)$ is 0. Since sigmoid function can be considered as a smoothed version of $\mathbb{I}(x)$ and is differentiable, we replace $\mathbb{I}(x)$ with sigmoid function. The final pair-wise loss function is defined as

$$\begin{aligned}l(\boldsymbol{\theta}_m, \boldsymbol{\theta}_{um}, \mathbf{\Phi}_m) =& \frac{\sum_{p=1}^{|T^-|}\sum_{q=1}^{|T^+|}\sigma(\widehat{r}_{u_pp_pi_p} - \widehat{r}_{u_qp_qi_q})}{|T^+||T^-|} \\ &+ regularzation\end{aligned} \tag{20}$$

Note that we have changed the order of positive examples and negative examples in the above equation, since we want to minimize the loss function. Now it represents the probability of ranking a negative example higher than a positive example, which can be viewed as the loss.

Regularization. Regularization is used to punish big parameters so that the model is not over-fitted. We use L2-norm regularization. Suppose node m have k_m feature components, the regularization term is defined as

$$regularization = \sum_{m\in\{u,p,i\}} \lambda_m ||\boldsymbol{\theta}_m||^2 + \sum_{m\in\{p,i\}} \mu_m ||\boldsymbol{\theta}_{um}||^2 + \sum_{m\in\{u,p,i\}} \sum_{q=1}^{k_m} \lambda_{m,q} ||\boldsymbol{\Phi}_m^q||^2 \quad (21)$$

where λ_m, $\lambda_{m,q}$ and μ_m are regularization parameters that control the the sensitiveness to big parameters, which are often set empirically. [10] has proposed an efficient method to find the optimal regularization parameters.

4.4 Parameter Learning

The parameters are learned by minimizing the loss function with stochastic gradient descent. The basic idea of stochastic gradient descent is to calculate the gradient with respect to each training instance and move a tiny step along the descent direction according to the gradient. The step size is controlled by a parameter called *learning rate*. As long as the *learning rate* is not too large, parameters are guaranteed to converge to a global or local optima. Now we briefly list the gradient of Equation 18 and Equation 20.

Let $\boldsymbol{\omega}$ denote the parameter set, i.e., $\boldsymbol{\omega} = \{\boldsymbol{\theta}_m, \boldsymbol{\theta}_{um}, \boldsymbol{\Phi}_m\}$. The gradient of Equation 18 is

$$\frac{\partial l}{\partial \boldsymbol{\omega}} = (r_{upi} - \widehat{r}'_{upi}) \frac{\partial \widehat{r}_{upi}}{\partial \boldsymbol{\omega}} \quad (22)$$

The gradient of Equation 20 is

$$\frac{\partial l}{\partial \boldsymbol{\omega}} = \frac{\sum_{p=1}^{|T^-|} \sum_{q=1}^{|T^+|} \frac{\partial \sigma(err_{pq})}{\partial \boldsymbol{\omega}}}{|T^+||T^-|} \left(\frac{\partial \widehat{r}_{u_p p_p i_p}}{\partial \boldsymbol{\omega}} - \frac{\partial \widehat{r}_{u_q p_q i_q}}{\partial \boldsymbol{\omega}} \right) \quad (23)$$

where $err_{pq} = \widehat{r}_{u_p p_p i_p} - \widehat{r}_{u_q p_q i_q}$ and $\frac{\partial \sigma(err_{pq})}{\partial \boldsymbol{\omega}} = \sigma(err_{pq})[1 - \sigma(err_{pq})]$. Both the above equations need to compute $\frac{\partial \widehat{r}_{upi}}{\partial \boldsymbol{\omega}}$. According to Equation 2, $\frac{\partial \widehat{r}_{upi}}{\partial \boldsymbol{\omega}}$ is computed as follows

$$\frac{\partial \widehat{r}_{upi}}{\partial \boldsymbol{\theta}_m} = \mathbf{x}_m + 2\lambda_m \boldsymbol{\theta}_m \quad (24)$$

$$\frac{\partial \widehat{r}_{upi}}{\partial \boldsymbol{\theta}_{um}} = \mathbf{x}_{um} + 2\mu_m \boldsymbol{\theta}_{um} \quad (25)$$

$$\frac{\partial \widehat{r}_{upi}}{\partial \boldsymbol{\Phi}_u^k} = \boldsymbol{\Phi}_p \mathbf{x}_p + \boldsymbol{\Phi}_i \mathbf{x}_i + 2\lambda_{u,k} \boldsymbol{\Phi}_u^k \quad (26)$$

Since $\frac{\partial \widehat{r}_{upi}}{\partial \boldsymbol{\Phi}_p^k}$ and $\frac{\partial \widehat{r}_{upi}}{\partial \boldsymbol{\Phi}_i^k}$ have similar form with $\frac{\partial \widehat{r}_{upi}}{\partial \boldsymbol{\Phi}_u^k}$, we do not list them. With gradients with respect to each parameter in $\boldsymbol{\omega}$, $\boldsymbol{\omega}$ is updated according to the following iterative equation

$$\boldsymbol{\omega}^{(t+1)} = \boldsymbol{\omega}^{(t)} - lr * \frac{\partial l(\boldsymbol{\omega}^{(t)})}{\partial \boldsymbol{\omega}^{(t)}} \quad (27)$$

where lr is the *learning rate* that controls how far to move along the descent direction and is set empirically.

4.5 Complexity Analysis

Suppose the dimension of node features and edge features are respectively n_{node} and n_{edge}. The dimension of $\boldsymbol{\Phi}_m$ $(m \in \{u,p,i\})$ is set to $k \times n_{node}$. Since node contains features like user ID and publisher ID, n_{node} can represent the data size. According to edge features introduced in Section 3.2, n_{edge} does not grow with the data size. Thus n_{edge} can be considered as a constant and $n_{edge} \ll n_{node}$.

Space Complexity. All the parameters stay in main memory during the training process. The time complexity of $\boldsymbol{\theta}_m$ $(m \in \{u,p,i\})$ and $\boldsymbol{\theta}_{um}$ $(m, \in \{p,i\})$ is $O(c_1 n_{node} + c_2 n_{edge})$, where c_1 and c_2 represent the number of types of nodes and edges. The space complexity of $\boldsymbol{\Phi}_m$ $(m \in \{u,p,i\})$ is $O(c_1 k n_{node})$. Since training data is read line by line and each line can be dropped immediately after the gradients are calculated, they are not accounted. So the total space complexity is $O(k n_{node} + n_{edge})$. The space grows linearly with the data size.

Time Complexity. First we discuss the time complexity of the training process. Suppose we have n training instances. For each instance, the parameters corresponding to non-zero features are updated. For example, for a user node with user ID=1, only the first column of $\boldsymbol{\Phi}_u$ will be updated. Let F denote the average number of non-zero node features $(F \ll n_{node})$, the time complexity of updating $\boldsymbol{\theta}_m$, $\boldsymbol{\theta}_{um}$ and $\boldsymbol{\Phi}_m$ parameters is $O(c_1 F + c_2 n_{edge} + c_1 k F)$. Since kF dominates $c_2 n_{edge}$, the cost for updating parameters is O(kF). Suppose we need R rounds to converge. The total time complexity is O(nkFR). Since k and F are small constants, the final complexity of training is O(nR). The time complexity of prediction is the same with the complexity of updating parameters, i.e., $O(kF)$. Since both k and F are small constants, the time complexity of prediction is O(1).

5. EXPERIMENTAL STUDY

5.1 Dataset

We crawled Twitter with a breadth-first strategy on the user graph using Twitter's REST API[6]. The dataset in this paper was crawled from April to June, 2012. Each user's latest 3200 tweets[7], profile and following list were crawled. Once a user's following list is crawled, every user on the following list are further crawled. Finally we are able to simulate users' browsing history (i.e., what tweets were received and what tweets were retweeted). All the terms are lowercased and stemmed.

Since users do not have time to see all the tweets, we split the browsing history into sessions to filter the missed tweets. Suppose tweet i has been retweeted by user u. Since there are 20 tweets per page, a session is defined to be a tweet set made up of three parts: (1) tweet i itself (2) fifteen tweets before i (3) five tweets after i. Sessions that have overlaps will be merged into one. Finally, the statistics of our dataset is shown in Table 1.

We split the dataset into training set and test set at time point of May 14th, 2012. The ratio of training set and the test set is about 3:1. The statistics of overlaps between Test Set and Training Set are shown in Table 2. From the table we can see that only 2% tweets in the test set occurs

[6]https://dev.twitter.com/docs

[7]This number is limited by Twitter.

Table 1: Dataset Statistics

Users	Tweets	Sessions	Terms	Tags	Locations
28,420	2,132,533	119,206	554,820	148,476	8,255

Table 2: Overlap between Test Set and Train Set

Users	Tweets	Terms	Hashtags	Locations
93.6%	2%	67%	43%	93.8%

in the training set. This indicates that performing matrix factorization on user-tweet matrix cannot work. The rest of the columns are more suitable for matrix factorization since they are much more denser.

5.2 Evaluation Metric

We use Mean Average Precision (MAP) to measure the performance. Suppose we have a session that contains n tweets. The Average Precision (AP) of this session is calculated by

$$AP = \frac{\sum_{k=1}^{n}(P@k \times isRetweeted(k))}{number\ of\ retweeted\ tweets} \tag{28}$$

where k represents the position from 1 to n, $isRetweeted(k)$ is 1 when the $k-th$ tweet is retweeted, otherwise $isRetweeted(k)$ is 0. MAP is the mean of the APs for all sessions.

5.3 Models for Evaluation

Recommendation with Social Regularization (SocRS). This method is proposed in [5] to incorporate social networks into traditional matrix factorization. When adapted to our problem, we minimize the following loss function:

$$\min_{U,V} L_2(R,U,V) = \frac{1}{2}\sum_{i=i}^{m}\sum_{j=1}^{n} I_{ij}(R_{ij} - U_i^T V_j)^2$$
$$+ \frac{\beta}{2}\sum_{i=i}^{m}\sum_{f\in F^+(i)}^{n} Sim(i,f)||U_i - U_f||^2 + \lambda_1||U||^2 + \lambda_2||V||^2 \tag{29}$$

where β is weight of social factors, U is the set of latent vectors for users and publishers, $F^+(u)$ is the set of friends of u, $Sim(i,f)$ is the similarity between u_i and u_f. u_i and u_f are represented as a vector of their retweeted tweets, respectively. $Sim(i,f)$ is defined to be the Jaccard similarity between u_i and u_f. The final rating $\widehat{r}_{upi}$ is $U_i^T U_p$. The method assumes that friends tend to have similarity interests, thus their latent vector U_i and U_f should be similar. This baseline is used to prove that matrix factorization on user-tweet matrix will not work even when social networks are incorporated to address the sparsity of user information.

Non-personalized Retweet Prediction (RP). [3] and [7] explored tweet features and publisher features to predict whether a tweet will get retweeted regardless of which user retweets it. This baseline can be viewed as a special form of our model where only tweet features and publisher features are considered. This baseline is used to prove the need for personalization.

Feature-based Model (Feat). This method only considers hand-crafted node and edge features and thus is a simplified version of our method. $\mathbf{g}_u^T\mathbf{g}_p$ and $\mathbf{g}_u^T\mathbf{g}_i$ are ignored in Equation 1. This method is used to measure the contributions from hand-crafted features.

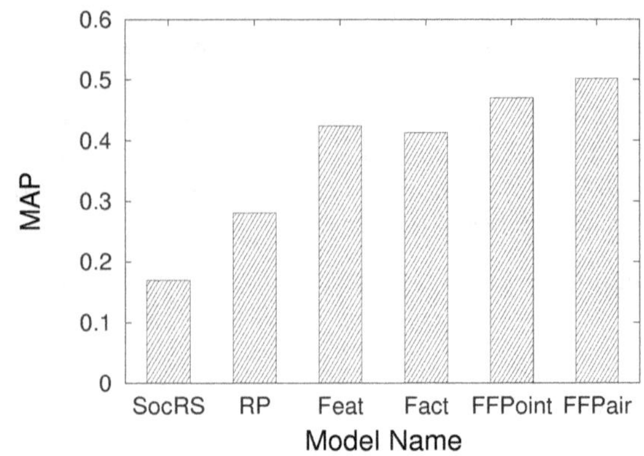

Figure 2: Comparision of all models

Table 3: Comparison of all models

Model	SocRec	RP	Feat	Fact	FFPoint	FFPair
MAP	0.176	0.281	0.424	0.413	0.47	0.502

Factorization-based Model (Fact). This method only considers automatically learned latent biases and vectors. Thus this is another simplified version of our method. All the hand-crafted feature are ignored. Only features corresponding to latent biases and latent vectors are retained in Equation 2. This method is used to measure the contributions from the factorization part.

Feature-aware Factorization Model with Point-wise Loss (FFPoint). This is our proposed model with point loss function. Compared with *Feat* and *Fact*, this model can prove the advantages of combining feature-based model and factorization-based model.

Feature-aware Factorization Model with Pair-wise Loss (FFPair). This method is used to prove the advantages of using pair-wise loss function. Compared with point-wise loss function, pair-wise loss function further employs the session context information.

All the experiments were conducted on a server with Intel Xeon E5405 2.00GHz CPU and 10G memory. The algorithms are implemented in Java with the support of matrix library jblas[8] for fast matrix/vector manipulation.

5.4 Overall Results

The overall results are shown in Figure 2 and Table 3. First we analyze why *SocRS* and *RP* cannot solve the problem. Recall that according to Table 2, only 2% tweets in the test set also exist in the training set. So it is not surprised *SocRS* has the the worst performance. By using publisher features and tweets features, *RP* is able to outperform *SocRS*. However, its performance is much worse than the personalized model. This indicates that the interestedness of a tweet varies from user to user. Only considering publisher's authority and tweet's quality is not enough. Personalization plays an important role in the retweet behavior.

Now we discuss some indications by comparing *Feat* with *Fact*. With hand-crafted user-publisher features and user-tweet features, *Feat* has a big improvement over *RP*. A major difference between PTR and traditional matrix factorization models can be found here: PTR has rich features

[8]http://jblas.org/

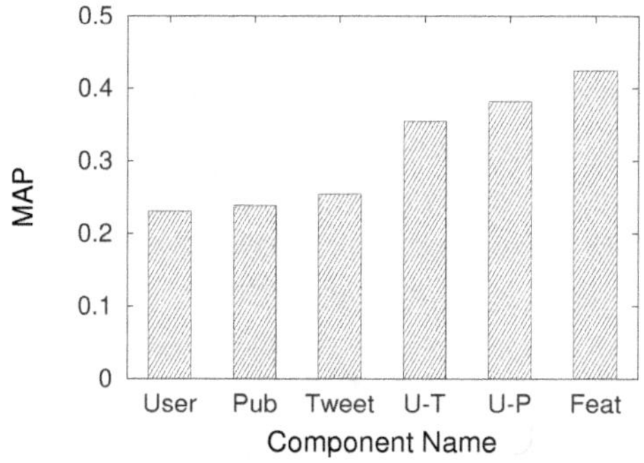

Figure 3: Contribution of each component in Feat

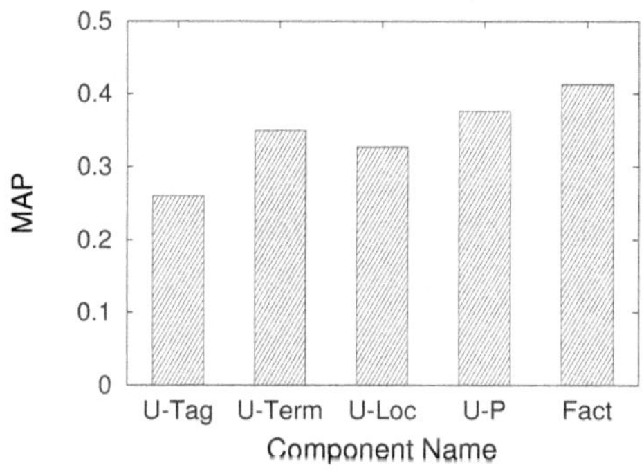

Figure 4: Contribution of each component in Fact

to indicate the similarity between a user and an item[9] while traditional matrix factorization only has a user-item rating matrix. In fact, the MAP of *Feat* is even slightly higher than *Fact*. However, this does not indicate *Feat* is better than *Fact*. The main advantage of *Fact* is that it does not need any feature engineering work. All the latent biases and vectors are automatically learned from the data. The similarity between a user and a publisher is directly calculated by $\mathbf{g}_u^T\mathbf{g}_p$. So is for user-tweet similarity. Moreover, the improvement of *Feat* over *Fact* is quite marginal.

Finally, we analyze the results of *FFPoint* and *FFPair*. By combining features with factorization models, the MAP of *FFPoint* is further improved. This indicates that feature-based model and factorization-based model can be complementary to each other. Comparing *FFPair* with *FFPoint*, we can find that the MAP is improved again by replacing point-wise loss function with pair-wise loss function. Since the loss is minimized according to each session instead of each single tweet, the pair-wise loss function is able to catch the context of user's choice. Thus using pair-wise loss function can lead to a better performance.

5.5 Contribution of Each Component

To measure the contribution of each component, we compare models trained for each component of *Feat* and *Fact*.

Components of Feat. According to Equation 3, *Feat* is made up of node features and edge features. The performance of models corresponding to each component is shown in Figure 3, where 'U-T' and 'U-P' represent user-tweet edge features and user-publisher edge features, respectively. Since node features does not consider personalized information and are mapped to basic biases, each of them has relative poor performance when used alone. On the contrast, user-tweet features and user-publisher features play an important role in this model. User-publisher features are more effective than user-tweet features. Since a tweet has only up to 140 characters, it is difficult to find explicit features to measure the interestedness of the tweet to the user. By resorting to user-publisher features, the user's preference toward the tweet is more predictable. Finally, when all features are combined, we get the *Feat* model analyzed in Section 5.4.

[9]Items are tweets and publishers in our setting.

Table 4: Training Time per Tweet (ms)

Loss Func	Feat	U-P	U-Term	FeatFact
Point-wise	0.34	0.46	11.40	13.12
Pair-wise	1.02	0.67	13.43	16.08

Table 5: Predicting Time per Tweet (ms)

Feat	U-P	U-Term	FeatFact
0.18	0.16	2.58	3.22

Components of Fact. According to $\mathbf{g}_u^T\mathbf{g}_i$ defined in Equation 11 and $\mathbf{g}_u^T\mathbf{g}_p$ defined in Equation 12, four relations are factorized in *Fact*: user-hashtag, user-term, user-publisher, and user-location relation. When trained alone, the performance is shown in Figure 4, where 'U-Tag', 'U-Term', 'U-Loc' and 'U-P' represent user-tag, user-term, user-location, and user-publisher relation, respectively. According to Table 2, the overlap of hashtags in training set and test set is the smallest. Thus about half of the latent biases and latent vectors of the hashtags cannot get trained. Thus the contribution of user-tag relation is the smallest. user-term and user-location relation are proved to be more effective. This indicates users tend to prefer tweets of some certain topics and areas. Finally, like the 'U-P' component in *Feat*, user-publisher relation in *Fact* is also proved to be the most effective component. Although overlaps of users and locations in the training set and test set are both very high, user-publisher relation is considered as a finer-grained interaction than user-location relation. Thus user-publisher relation is more effective than user-location relation.

5.6 Efficiency Issue

In this section, we first analyze the training time and predicting time of each component in Equation 2. Then we compare the time cost of point-wise loss function and pair-wise loss function. The training time and prediction time of each component are shown in Table 4 and Table 5, respectively. 'Feat' represents the feature-based component made up of f_m and f_{um} in Equation 2. 'FeatFact' is the complete model defined by Equation 2. Since 'U-Loc' and 'U-Tag' have similar training time and predicting time with 'U-P', we do not list them in the tables.

Efficiency of Each Component Comparing training time of different components in the 'point-wise' row, we find that feature-based component and 'U-P' are much more efficient than 'U-Term'. Since a tweet can contain up to 140 different terms but only one publisher, the training time and predicting time of 'U-Term' is 1-140 times faster than 'U-P'. Although 'U-Term' has dominated most of the time and seems to be costly, the final predicting time of 'FeatFact' is 3.22 ms per tweet. This is considered to be fast enough for online response. Note that all the original terms are considered in our model. Since a tweet may contain many meaningless terms, keyword extraction or simple TF-IDF based filtering can be performed to find out potentially important terms to represent the tweets. Once the tweet is shortened, the efficiency will be further improved.

Point-wise Loss vs. Pair-wise Loss. The predicting time of point-wise approach and pair-wise approach are the same since they both use Equation 2 for prediction. So we only compare the training time. Comparing the 'Point-wise Loss' row with 'Pair-wise Loss' row in Table 4, we can find that pair-wise approach is slower than point-wise but the difference is quite small. Suppose a session contains two positive tweets and eight negative tweets. For point-wise approach, the loss is calculated on ten tweets. However, for pair-wise approach, the loss is calculated on each pair of positive tweets and negative tweets, i.e. $2\times 8 = 16$ tweets. In our dataset, most sessions only contain one or two positive tweets. Thus pair-wise approach is just slightly slower than the point-wise approach.

6. RELATED WORK

Many work have been done in studying retweet behavior in the macro perspective [2, 3, 7, 8, 12]. Boyd[2] studied some basic issues about retweet behavior: how people retweet, why people retweet and what people retweet. He found that retweet provides a way to let users make conversations with each other. Hong[3] studied how to predict the popularity of messages measured by the number of future retweets. In their work, content features, temporal information and metadata of tweets and publishers are explored. Suh[12] and Petrovic[7] explored tweet features like URLs and hashtags, and publisher features like followers/followees count and account age. Compared with our model, these work tried to find useful node features to predict whether a tweet will be retweeted regardless of who will retweet the tweet. To the best of our knowledge, personalized tweet re-ranking has very limited work. [6] and [13] are considered to be most relevant to our problem. Macskassy[6] claimed that the majority of users do not retweet that tweets similar to their own tweets. When content similarity is considered, the predicting performance can be improved. Uysal[13] further explored user-publisher and user-tweet features. Both of them belongs to pure feature-based approach and mainly focus on finding hand-crafted node features and edge features. Compared with our model, the automatically learned latent biases and vectors are dropped. Thus they are very similar to our baseline 'feature-based model'.

In terms of feature-aware factorization models, [1] and [9] are considered to be most relevant. Agarwal[1] proposed a regression-based prior for the latent vectors, which has similar form with our definition of g_m. The regression-based prior in [1] is mainly based on numeric features. In our work, the latent vectors are learned for each categorical features so that more relations can be incorporated in the factorization model. The practical meaning is quite different. Rendle[9] proposed a general factorization machine, which performs all pair-wise interactions between node features. However, the general form does not exist in our problem. Publisher-tweet interaction is empirically found to have little connection with whether user u will retweet tweet i.

7. CONCLUSIONS

In this paper, we proposed a novel problem called personalized tweet re-ranking. We modeled retweet behavior as a graph made up of users, publishers and tweets. To incorporate all sources of information, nodes and edges are represented by feature vectors. According to the graph model, we designed feature-aware factorization model that can fully explore all the information in the graph for prediction. We aim to propose a general prediction framework. Like SVM for classification task, users only need to specify the node features and edge features. Our feature-aware factorization model will build a predicting model based on the features.

8. ACKNOWLEDGMENTS

This work was supported in part by National Natural Science Foundation of China under Grant No. 61272088 and 60833003, National Basic Research Program of China (973 Program) under Grant No. 2011CB302206. This work is partially done when the authors visited SA Center for Big Data Research hosted in Renmin University of China. This Center is partially funded by a Chinese National "111" Project "Attracting International Talents in Data Engineering and Knowledge Engineering Research".

9. REFERENCES

[1] D. Agarwal and B.-C. Chen. Regression-based latent factor models. In *KDD*, pages 19–28, 2009.

[2] D. Boyd, S. Golder, and G. Lotan. Tweet, tweet, retweet: Conversational aspects of retweeting on twitter. In *HICSS*, pages 1–10, 2010.

[3] L. Hong, O. Dan, and B. D. Davison. Predicting popular messages in twitter. In *WWW (Companion Volume)*, pages 57–58, 2011.

[4] Y. Koren. Factorization meets the neighborhood: a multifaceted collaborative filtering model. In *KDD*, pages 426–434, 2008.

[5] H. Ma, D. Zhou, C. Liu, M. R. Lyu, and I. King. Recommender systems with social regularization. In *WSDM*, pages 287–296, 2011.

[6] S. A. Macskassy and M. Michelson. Why do people retweet? anti-homophily wins the day! In *ICWSM*, 2011.

[7] S. Petrovic, M. Osborne, and V. Lavrenko. Rt to win! predicting message propagation in twitter. In *ICWSM*, 2011.

[8] D. Ramage, S. T. Dumais, and D. J. Liebling. Characterizing microblogs with topic models. In *ICWSM*, 2010.

[9] S. Rendle. Factorization machines with libfm. *ACM TIST*, 3(3):57, 2012.

[10] S. Rendle. Learning recommender systems with adaptive regularization. In *WSDM*, 2012.

[11] D. M. Romero, W. Galuba, S. Asur, and B. A. Huberman. Influence and passivity in social media. In *ECML/PKDD (3)*, pages 18–33, 2011.

[12] B. Suh, L. Hong, P. Pirolli, and E. H. Chi. Want to be retweeted? large scale analytics on factors impacting retweet in twitter network. In *SocialCom/PASSAT*, pages 177–184, 2010.

[13] I. Uysal and W. B. Croft. User oriented tweet ranking: a filtering approach to microblogs. In *CIKM*, 2011.

[14] J. Yang and S. Counts. Predicting the speed, scale, and range of information diffusion in twitter. In *ICWSM*, 2010.

Overlapping Community Detection at Scale: A Nonnegative Matrix Factorization Approach

Jaewon Yang
Stanford University
crucis@stanford.edu

Jure Leskovec
Stanford University
jure@cs.stanford.edu

ABSTRACT

Network communities represent basic structures for understanding the organization of real-world networks. A community (also referred to as a module or a cluster) is typically thought of as a group of nodes with more connections amongst its members than between its members and the remainder of the network. Communities in networks also overlap as nodes belong to multiple clusters at once. Due to the difficulties in evaluating the detected communities and the lack of scalable algorithms, the task of overlapping community detection in large networks largely remains an open problem.

In this paper we present BIGCLAM (Cluster Affiliation Model for Big Networks), an overlapping community detection method that scales to large networks of millions of nodes and edges. We build on a novel observation that overlaps between communities are densely connected. This is in sharp contrast with present community detection methods which implicitly assume that overlaps between communities are sparsely connected and thus cannot properly extract overlapping communities in networks. In this paper, we develop a model-based community detection algorithm that can detect densely overlapping, hierarchically nested as well as non-overlapping communities in massive networks. We evaluate our algorithm on 6 large social, collaboration and information networks with *ground-truth* community information. Experiments show state of the art performance both in terms of the quality of detected communities as well as in speed and scalability of our algorithm.

Categories and Subject Descriptors: H.2.8 **[Database Management]**: Database Applications – *Data mining*
General Terms: Algorithms, theory, experimentation.
Keywords: Network communities, Overlapping community detection, Matrix factorization.

1. INTRODUCTION

A large body of work in computer science, statistics, applied mathematics, and statistical physics has been devoted to identifying community structure in complex networks (see [8, 28, 32] for surveys of this area). A community (also referred to as a module or a cluster) is intuitively thought of as a group of nodes with more interactions amongst its members than between its members and the remainder of the network [10]. Such groups of nodes (*i.e.*, communities) are often interpreted as organizational units in social networks [7, 29], functional units in biochemical networks [17], ecological niches in food web networks [10], or scientific disciplines in citation and collaboration networks [3].

WSDM'13, February 4–8, 2013, Rome, Italy.

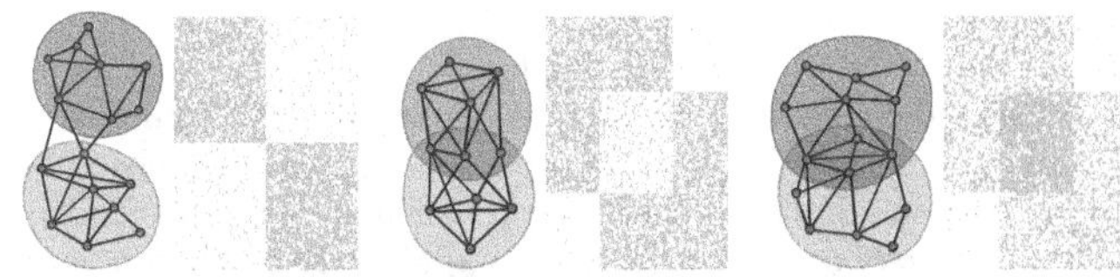

(a) No overlaps (b) Sparse overlaps (c) Dense overlaps

Figure 1: Three views on the structure of network communities. Present view of (a) two non-overlapping and (b) two overlapping communities. Present methods assume that the nodes in the overlap are less-well connected (b). We find densely connected community overlaps (c). Left: Network; Right: Corresponding adjacency matrix.

Even though methods for identifying overlapping as well as hierarchically-nested communities in networks have been considered in the past [1, 2, 25, 32], identifying meaningful communities in large networks has proven to be a challenging task [9, 20, 34]. Most methods have trouble scaling to large networks, and the lack of reliable "ground truth" makes evaluation of detected communities surprisingly difficult. Thus, while networks have been extensively-studied, and the existence and properties of communities in small networks is by now well-understood [1, 2, 10, 25], it is still not clear how to identify realistic overlapping communities in very large networks that are increasingly common.

Present work: Empirical observations. Our work starts with a novel, and in retrospective very intuitive, observation that overlaps of communities tend to be more densely connected than the non-overlapping parts [33, 35]. In particular, we empirically observe that the more communities a pair of nodes shares the more likely they are connected in the network. For example, people sharing multiple hobbies (*i.e.*, interest based communities) have a higher chance of becoming friends [23], researchers with many common interests (*i.e.*, many common scientific communities) are more likely to work and publish together [26].

Even though intuitive our observation is very subtle and represents a radical new view of networks communities and has important consequences for network community detection [33, 35]. To put our observation in the context, we first give a quick overview of recent developments in the network community detection. Traditionally, the emergence of communities in networks has been understood through the strength-of-weak-ties theory [12]. This theory led researchers to conceptualize networks as consisting of dense clusters that are linked by a small number of weak ties (Figure 1(a)). Graph partitioning [28, 30], modularity optimization [24] as well as betweenness centrality [10] based community detection methods all assume such view of network communities and thus aim to identify edges that can be cut in order to separate the network into a set of non-overlapping clusters.

In social as well as other types of networks nodes can belong to multiple communities simultaneously, which leads to overlapping community structure [25]. However, we noticed that practically all present overlapping community detection methods (for example [1, 2, 25]) make a hidden (and so far undocumented) assumption that community overlaps are *less densely* connected than the non-overlapping parts of communities (Figure 1(b)) [33, 35]. This leads to an unnatural modeling assumption that the *more* communities a pair of nodes shares, the *less* likely it is they are connected. Figure 1(b) illustrates the unnatural structure of community overlaps emerging under such assumption.

In contrast, we find an increasing relationship between the number of shared communities and the probability of nodes being connected by an edge [33, 35]. A direct consequence of this observation is that parts of the network where communities overlap tend to be *more densely* connected (Figure 1(c)) [35]. Even though very natural, the observation stands in sharp contrast to present definitions of network communities. More importantly, today's community detection methods (for example, [1, 2, 25]) cannot correctly identify such dense community overlaps. Present methods either mistakenly identify the overlap as a separate community or merge two overlapping communities into a single one [35].

Present work: Large-scale community detection via matrix factorization. Building on the above observation the goal of this work is to detect communities in a given large unlabeled undirected network. This means that, for every node in a given large undirected network, we aim to discover the communities it belongs to. To achieve this we develop a novel community detection method that allows for discovering any combination of densely overlapping, non-overlapping, as well as hierarchically nested communities.

We build on models of affiliation networks [5, 18] and develop the BIGCLAM (Cluster Affiliation Model for Big Networks). In BIGCLAM communities arise due to shared community affiliations of nodes. We explicitly model the affiliation strength of each node to each community. We assign each node-community pair a non-negative latent factor which represents the degree of membership of a node to the community. We then model the probability of an edge between a pair of nodes in the network as a function of the shared community affiliations.

We identify network communities by fitting the BIGCLAM model to a given large undirected network. Our goal is to estimate non-negative latent factors that model the membership strength of each node to each community. By combining the state-of-the-art non-negative matrix factorization methods [19] with block stochastic gradient descent [21] we achieve gains both in the quality of detected communities as well as in scalability of the method. We improve by a factor of 10 the size of the largest networks that overlapping community detection methods could process in the past.

An additional contribution of our work is improved evaluation. So far community detection methods have mostly been evaluated anecdotally on small networks. In contrast, we identify social, collaboration, information and biological networks with explicitly labeled ground-truth communities [34]. This allows for quantitative evaluating by assessing how well detected communities correspond to the ground-truth communities [34]. Experiments reveal that BIGCLAM discovers overlapping as well as non-overlapping community structure more accurately than present state-of-the-art methods [1, 2, 25, 27]. Moreover, BIGCLAM scales well beyond the current overlapping community detection methods. Experiments show that BIGCLAM achieves near linear running time while other methods exhibit quadratic or exponential running time. We process networks of more than 35 million edges which improves by a factor of 10 the size of the largest networks that overlapping community detection methods could process in the past. BIGCLAM improves over the current state of the art in both the scalability as well as the quality of detected communities. Code as well as all the data are available at `http://snap.stanford.edu`.

2. RELATED WORK

Our BIGCLAM is an example of a bipartite affiliation network model [5, 18, 36]. Affiliation networks have been extensively studied in sociology [5] as a metaphor of classical social theory concerning the intersection of persons with groups, where it has been recognized that communities arise due to shared group affiliations [5, 29]. In affiliation network models, nodes of the social network are affiliated with communities they belong to and the links of the underlying social network are then derived based on the node community affiliations. Whereas classical models assume binary node-community affiliations, in our model we also consider the strength of an affiliation which provides additional modeling flexibility.

BIGCLAM formulates community detection as a variant of non-negative matrix factorization (NMF) [15, 19, 21]. Similar to NMF, we aim to learn factors that can recover the adjacency matrix of a given network. However, BIGCLAM has two important improvements. First, most of NMF research pays relatively little attention to interpreting the latent factors. The primary goal there is to estimate the missing entries of the matrix (*e.g.*, as in the Netflix competition). On the other hand, BIGCLAM aims to learn latent factors which represent community affiliations of nodes. Second, instead of using a Gaussian distribution [15, 19] or logistic link function [14], we optimize the model likelihood of explaining the links of the observed network. Our formulation of likelihood allows us to compute a gradient of the factor matrix in near-constant time, which is significant improvement over existing NMF methods where the complexity of computing such gradient is *linear* in the number of rows of the matrix (*i.e.*, nodes of the network). In practice, computing the gradient in near-constant time makes our algorithm about 1,000 times faster.

In terms of scalability most overlapping community detection methods scale to networks with at most thousands of nodes [2, 22, 25]. The largest network processed with overlapping community detection methods is a mobile phone network of 800,000 nodes and 2.8 million edges [1]. Non-overlapping community detection algorithms, which solve a simpler problem, have been applied to networks with millions of nodes [6, 16]. Our methods presented here can process networks with tens of millions of edges while also obtaining state of the art quality of detected communities.

3. EMPIRICAL OBSERVATION

We motivate the development of our model by empirically studying the structure of communities and community overlaps in networks. We fist describe the network datasets with explicit ground-truth communities and then present our empirical findings.

Networks with ground-truth communities. To study the connectivity structure of community overlaps, we now describe networks with explicitly labeled ground-truth communities. To define such ground-truth, we collected 6 large social, information and collaboration networks where nodes explicitly state their community memberships [34]. Defining ground-truth communities will also help us later in evaluating the performance various methods (Section 6).

Dataset	N	E	C	S	A
LiveJournal	4.0 M	34.9 M	310 k	40.06	3.09
Friendster	120 M	2,600 M	1.5 M	26.72	0.33
Orkut	3.1 M	120 M	8.5 M	34.86	95.93
Youtube	1.1 M	3.0 M	30 k	9.75	0.26
DBLP	0.43 M	1.3 M	2.5 k	429.79	2.57
Amazon	0.34 M	0.93 M	49 k	99.86	14.83

Table 1: Dataset statistics. N: number of nodes, E: number of edges, C: number of communities, S: average community size, A: community memberships per node. M denotes a million and k denotes one thousand. On average 95% of all communities overlap with at least one other community.

First, we briefly describe the 6 networks [34][1]. The first 4 networks are online social networks: the LiveJournal blogging community, the Friendster online network, the Orkut social network, and the Youtube social network. Users in these networks create groups which other users then join. Such groups are formed over specific interests, hobbies, affiliations, and geographical regions. For instance, LiveJournal categorizes communities into the following types: culture, entertainment, expression, fandom, life/style, life/ support, gaming, sports, student life and technology. There are over 100 communities with 'Stanford' in their name, and they range from communities based around different classes, student ethnic communities, departments, activity and interest based groups, varsity teams, etc. We use such user-defined groups as ground-truth communities. A user can belong to zero, one or more ground-truth communities and thus ground-truth communities can overlap. The largest network among these online social networks is Friendster, which has 120 million nodes, 2.6 billion edges and 1.5 million ground-truth communities.

We also consider the Amazon product co-purchasing network where the nodes represent products and edges connect commonly co-purchased products. Each product (*i.e.*, node) belongs to one or more hierarchically nested product categories. We use each product category to define a ground-truth community. Members of the same community share a common function or a role. Ground-truth communities in the Amazon network can be overlapping or hierarchically nested. Last we also use the collaboration network of DBLP where nodes represent authors/actors and edges connect nodes that have co-authored a paper. Since research communities stem around conferences or journals, we use publication venues as ground-truth communities in DBLP.

The networks we consider show a nice range of scale in all measures (Table 1): The size of networks ranges from hundreds of thousands to hundreds of millions of nodes and edges and the number of ground-truth communities varies from hundreds to millions. Last, the networks represent a wide range of edge densities, numbers of explicit communities, as well as amounts of community overlap.

In our previous work [33, 34, 35] we found the above definitions of ground-truth to be reliable and robust. In particular, while the networks we consider here come from a variety of domains, span a wide range of network sizes and edge densities, we find our observations and results to be consistent and robust across all of them. The consistency and robustness of results make us confident in our methodology and empirical observations.

In order to express all networks in a consistent way we represent each network as an unweighted undirected static graph. Because members of the same group may be disconnected in the network, we treat each connected component of the group as a separate ground-truth community. We allow ground-truth communities to overlap because a node can belong to multiple groups at once.

[1]Networks are available at `http://snap.stanford.edu`.

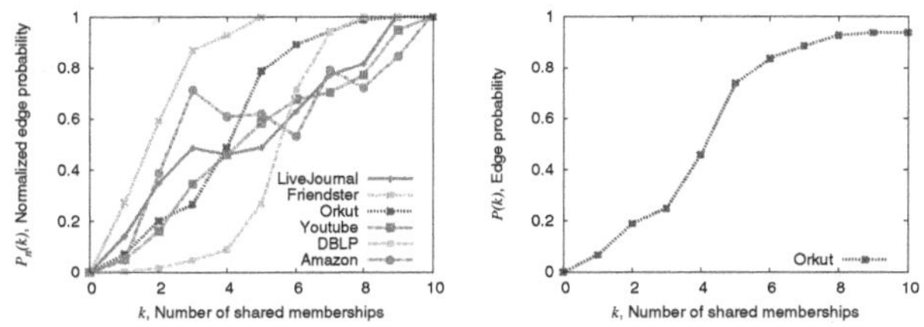

(a) Edge probability (b) Orkut

Figure 2: (a) Normalized edge probability as a function of common memberships k. Probabilities are scaled so that maximum value over k is one. (b) Edge probability in the Orkut network, plotted as an absolute value. We conclude overlaps are more densely connected than single communities.

Observation: Community overlaps are dense. Having defined ground-truth communities, we now empirically study the structure of ground-truth communities. We find that ground-truth communities heavily overlap. On average 95% of all communities overlap with at least one other community and only 15% of community's members belong to only that community. We thus examine the structure of community overlaps by measuring the probability of a pair of nodes being connected given that they belong to k common communities, *i.e.*, the nodes reside in the overlap of same k communities. Figure 2(a) plots this probability for all six datasets. For visualization we scale each probability curve so that the maximum value of each curve over k is 1. Under the current assumption that overlaps are less dense than non-overlaps, the probability curves would decrease as k increases. In contrast, we notice an increasing relationship for all datasets, *i.e.*, the *more* communities a pair of nodes has in common, the *higher* the probability of an edge. This means that nodes residing in overlaps are more densely connected each other than the nodes in a single community [35].

To demonstrate how the edge probability changes as k increases, we plot the edge probability (without scaling) measured in the Orkut network as a function of the number of common communities k in Figure 2(b). Similar to all large networks, Orkut is extremely sparsely connected — the background probability of a random pair of nodes being connected is $\approx 10^{-5}$ — the increase in edge probability is highly significant. For example, if a pair of nodes has 2 communities in common, the probability of an edge is nearly 0.20. The edge probability increases by 10^4 times (from 10^{-5} to 10^{-1}) as soon as the pair share two communities.

Overall, in all the datasets we consistently observe similar and robust behavior: The probability of a pair of nodes being connected approaches 1 as the number of common communities increases [35]. While in online social networks the edge probability exhibits a diminishing-returns-like growth, in DBLP, it appears to follow a threshold-like behavior.

Discussion. In retrospective, the above observation is very intuitive and thus so much more surprising. For pairs of nodes that belong to multiple common communities, edges often exist due to one dominant reason. Thus, nodes in the overlaps will have higher chance of being connected because they belong to multiple communities. Many examples to support this. For example, people sharing multiple hobbies or belonging to several common institutions have a higher chance of becoming friends [23], researchers with many common interests are more likely to work together [26], and proteins involved in multiple common functional modules are more likely to interact [17].

The observation that the probability of an edge *increases* as a function of the number of shared communities means that nodes in the overlap of two (or more) communities are more likely to be

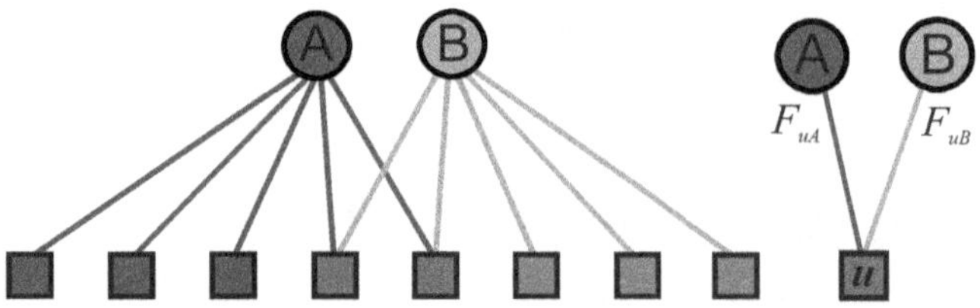

(a) Community Affiliation Network (b) Weight for affiliation

Figure 3: (a) Bipartite community affiliation graph. Circles: Communities, Squares: Nodes of the underlying network. Edges indicate node community memberships. Edges with zero weight are not shown. (b) Each affiliation edge from node u to community c has strength $F_{uc} \geq 0$.

connected. Thus, our finding suggests communities overlap as illustrated in Figure 1(c) where the overlap of the two communities is more densely connected than each single community. However, we note that our finding is in sharp contrast to the currently predominant view of network communities which is based on two fundamental social network theories: triadic closure [31] and strength-of-weak-ties [12]. This leads to the picture of network communities as illustrated in Figure 1(a) which suggests that homophily in networks operates in small pockets where nodes gather in dense non-overlapping clusters. Extending these two theories to the overlapping communities leads to the unnatural structure of community overlaps as illustrated in Figure 1(b): Community overlaps are *less densely* connected than the groups themselves. Our results show the contrary. As a consequence this means that present overlapping community detection methods [1, 2, 25] which rely on the assumption of sparse overlaps fail to correctly identify dense community overlaps. They would either merge two overlapping communities into a single cluster or identify the overlap as a separate cluster [35].

Last, we also note that the observation that community overlaps are denser than communities themselves nicely extends the notion of homophily in networks [23]. The 'strength of weak ties' [12] suggests that homophily in networks operates in small pockets where inside the pocket nodes link strongly among themselves, and weakly to other pockets. Our work extends the understanding of homophily. We are discovering *pluralistic homophily* where the similarity of one node to another is the number of shared affiliations, not just their similarity along a single dimension. This view of tie formation is consistent with the works of Simmel [29] on the web of affiliations, and Feld [7] on focused organization of social ties. In both of these views networks consist of overlapping "tiles" or "social circles" that serve as organizing principles of nodes in networks.

4. CLUSTER AFFILIATION MODEL

Next we present the *Cluster Affiliation Model for Big Networks* (BIGCLAM), a probabilistic generative model for graphs that reliably captures the organization of networks based on community affiliations. Our model has three main ingredients:

The first ingredient is based on Breiger's work [5] which recognized that communities arise due to shared group affiliations [5, 7, 29]. We represent node community memberships with a bipartite affiliation network that links nodes of the social network to communities that they belong to (Figure 3(a)).

The second ingredient stems from the fact that people tend to be involved in communities to various degrees. Therefore, we assume that each affiliation edge in the bipartite affiliation network has a nonnegative weight. The higher the node's weight of the affiliation to the community the more likely is the node to be connected to other members in the community.

The last ingredient of our model is based on the fact that, when people share multiple community affiliations (*e.g.*, co-workers who attended the same university), the links between them stem for one dominant reason (*i.e.*, shared community). This means that for each community a pair of nodes shares we get an independent chance of connecting the nodes. Thus, naturally, the more communities a pair of nodes shares, the higher the probability of being connected.

Figure 3 illustrates our model. We start with a bipartite graph where the nodes at the bottom represent the nodes of the social network G, the nodes on the top represent communities C, and the edges M indicate node community affiliations. We denote the bipartite affiliation network as $B(V, C, M)$.

The flexibility of the affiliation network allows us to model a wide range of network community structures. Figure 4 illustrates the structure of the network as well as the corresponding node-community affiliation network. Figure 4(a) shows an affiliation graph of a network with two non-overlapping communities. The affiliation graph in Figure 4(c) represents hierarchical community structure where communities A and C are nested inside community B. Finally, Figure 4(b) shows an example of overlapping communities. These three very different examples demonstrate that the flexibility of the affiliation network structure allows BIGCLAM to simultaneously model any combination of non-overlapping, hierarchically nested as well as overlapping communities in networks.

From node-community affiliations to the edges of the network. To generate a network $G(V, E)$ given a bipartite community affiliation $B(V, C, M)$ we need to specify the process that generates the edges E of G given the affiliation network B. We consider a simple parameterization where we assign a nonnegative weight F_{uc} between node $u \in V$ and community $c \in C$. ($F_{uc} = 0$ means no affiliation.) Given F, we assume that each community c connects its member nodes depending on the value of F. In particular, each community c connects its member nodes u, v with probability $1 - \exp(-F_{uc} \cdot F_{vc})$. Each community c creates edges independently. However, if a pair of nodes gets connected multiple times, the duplicate edges are not included in the graph $G(V, E)$. Since each community c connects u, v independently with probability $1 - \exp(-F_{uc} \cdot F_{vc})$, the edge probability between u and v is $1 - \exp(-\sum_c F_{uc} \cdot F_{vc})$ and thus increasing in the number of shared communities.

DEFINITION 1. *Let F be a nonnegative matrix where F_{uc} is a weight between node $u \in V$ and community $c \in C$. Given F, the* BIGCLAM *generates a graph $G(V, E)$ by creating edge (u, v) between a pair of nodes $u, v \in V$ with probability $p(u, v)$:*

$$p(u, v) = 1 - \exp(-F_u \cdot F_v^T), \tag{1}$$

where F_u is a weight vector for node u ($F_u = F_{u\cdot}$).

The process in Eq. 1 suggests the following probabilistic interpretation. Assume an undirected weighted network where pairs of nodes have a latent interaction of non-negative strength X_{uv}. However, we only observe an undirected unweighted version of network $G(V, E)$ where a pair of nodes u, v is connected if the corresponding $X_{uv} > 0$. Now consider that nodes u, v generate an interaction of strength $X_{uv}^{(c)}$ within each community c using a Poisson distribution with mean $F_{uc} \cdot F_{vc}$. Then the total amount of interaction X_{uv} between nodes u and v is the sum of $X_{uv}^{(c)}$:

$$X_{uv} = \sum_c X_{uv}^{(c)}, \quad X_{uv}^{(c)} \sim Pois(F_{uc} \cdot F_{vc}).$$

Then, due to the additivity of the Poisson random variable, $X_{uv} \sim Pois(\sum_c F_{uc} \cdot F_{vc})$, and the edge probability ($\text{P}(X_{uv} > 0)$) is the same as $p(u, v)$ in Eq. 1.

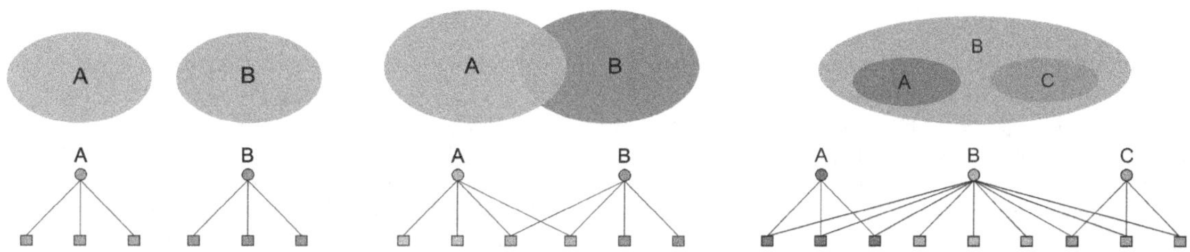

(a) Non-overlapping (b) Overlapping (c) Nested

Figure 4: BIGCLAM allows for rich modeling of network communities: (a) non-overlapping, (b) overlapping, (c) nested. In (a) we assume that nodes in two communities connect with small prob. ε (refer to the discussion in the main text).

$$P(X_{uv} > 0) = 1 - P(X_{uv} = 0) = 1 - \exp(-\sum_c F_{uc} \cdot F_{vc})$$

Note that node u with higher F_{uc} is more likely to be connected to other members of c as $X_{uv}^{(c)}$ will have a higher mean.

Note that this process naturally generates an increasing relationship between edge probability and the number of shared communities. This is due to the fact that nodes that share multiple community memberships receive multiple chances to create a link. For example, pairs of purple nodes in the overlap of communities A and B in Figure 3(a) get two chances to create an edge. First they create an edge with probability $1 - e^{-F_{uA} \cdot F_{vA}}$ (due to the membership to community A) and then also an edge with probability $1 - e^{-F_{uB} \cdot F_{vB}}$ (due to membership to community B). The edge probability between these nodes is $1 - e^{-(F_{uA} \cdot F_{vA} + F_{uB} \cdot F_{vB})}$. If they were to reside in the non-overlapping region of A, they would be linked with probability $1 - e^{-F_{uA} \cdot F_{vA}}$, which is smaller than $1 - e^{-(F_{uA} \cdot F_{vA} + F_{uB} \cdot F_{vB})}$.

ε-Community. In the formulation of Equation 1, BIGCLAM does not allow for the edges between the nodes u and v that do not share any common communities since for such nodes $F_{uc} \cdot F_{vc} = 0$ for all c. To allow for edges between nodes that do not share any community affiliations, we assume an additional community, called the ε-community, which connects *any* pair of nodes with a very small probability ε. We find that setting ε to be the background edge probability between a random pair of nodes ($\varepsilon = 2|E|/|V|(|V|-1)$) works well in practice. For all our experiments we set $\varepsilon \approx 10^{-8}$.

5. COMMUNITY DETECTION

Now that we defined the BIGCLAM model, we explain how to detect network communities using the model. Given an unlabeled undirected network $G(V, E)$, we aim to detect K communities by *fitting* the BIGCLAM (*i.e.*, finding the most likely affiliation factor matrix $\hat{F} \in \mathbb{R}^{N \times K}$) to the underlying network G by maximizing the likelihood $l(F) = \log P(G|F)$ of the underlying G:

$$\hat{F} = \underset{F \geq 0}{\operatorname{argmax}}\, l(F), \tag{2}$$

where

$$l(F) = \sum_{(u,v) \in E} \log(1 - \exp(-F_u F_v^T)) - \sum_{(u,v) \notin E} F_u F_v^T.$$

For now, we assume the number of communities K is given. We will describe later how to automatically estimate K.

The optimization problem of Eq. 2 can be viewed as a variant of nonnegative matrix factorization (NMF) [19] where we learn $F \in \mathbb{R}^{N \times K}$ that best approximates the adjacency matrix A of a given network G. By representing a negative log-likelihood $-l(F)$ as a loss function D and $1 - exp(\cdot)$ as a link function, we can represent the problem as follows:

$$\hat{F} = \underset{F \geq 0}{\operatorname{argmin}}\, D(A, f(FF^T))$$

The benefit of using matrix factorization approach is increased scalability. Overlapping community detection methods have been developed to analyze small networks [1, 2], and most methods rely on combinatorial optimization which is hard to scale. On the other hand, for nonnegative matrix factorization many efficient techniques exist [15, 21].

BIGCLAM modifies the existing NMF methods [15, 19, 21] and adapts them to large networks. While NMF methods use l_2 norm as an objective function, l_2 norm is not suitable for modeling binary adjacency matrices [14]. Instead, BIGCLAM employs log-likelihood as a loss function. Additional benefit is that for sparsely connected networks (which real networks are) our formulation allows for near-constant time gradient computation (l_2 takes linear time) which in practice speeds up our algorithm for a factor of 100.

Solving the optimization problem. To solve the problem in Eq. 2, we adopt a block coordinate gradient ascent algorithm [15, 21]. In particular, we update F_u for each u with the other F_v fixed, *i.e.*, we update the memberships of one node with fixing the membership of all other nodes. The main reason is that if we fix all F_v, then the problem of updating F_u becomes a convex optimization problem. We solve the following subproblem for each u:

$$\underset{F_{uc} \geq 0}{\operatorname{argmax}}\, l(F_u), \tag{3}$$

where

$$l(F_u) = \sum_{v \in \mathcal{N}(u)} \log(1 - \exp(-F_u F_v^T)) - \sum_{v \notin \mathcal{N}(u)} F_u F_v^T,$$

where $\mathcal{N}(u)$ is a set of neighbors of u. To solve this convex problem, we use projected gradient ascent. The gradient can be computed straightforwardly.

$$\nabla l(F_u) = \sum_{v \in \mathcal{N}(u)} F_v \frac{\exp(-F_u F_v^T)}{1 - \exp(-F_u F_v^T)} - \sum_{v \notin \mathcal{N}(u)} F_v$$

We compute a step size using backtracking line search [4]. After update, we project F_u into a space of nonnegative vectors by setting $F_{uc} = \max(F_{uc}, 0)$.

For a large network with more than a million nodes, this coordinate ascent is not very scalable as making a single step of coordinate ascent (*i.e.*, computing $l(F_u)$ and $\nabla l(F_u)$) takes linear time $O(N)$. However, we reduce the complexity to $O(|\mathcal{N}(u)|)$ by computing $\sum_{v \notin \mathcal{N}(u)} F_v$ efficiently. In particular, we notice:

$$\sum_{v \notin \mathcal{N}(u)} F_v = (\sum_v F_v - F_u - \sum_{v \in \mathcal{N}(u)} F_v) \tag{4}$$

By storing $\sum_v F_v$, we can compute $\sum_{v \notin \mathcal{N}(u)} F_u F_v^T$ in time $O(|\mathcal{N}(u)|)$. Given that real-world networks are extremely sparse ($|\mathcal{N}(u)| \ll N$), we can update F_u for a single node u in near-constant time. We iteratively update F_u for each u and stop the iteration if the likelihood does not increase (increase less than 0.001%) after we update F_u for all u. In practice this speeds up our algorithm for two orders of magnitude and makes it practical to run it on networks with millions of nodes and edges.

Determining community affiliations. After we learn $\hat{F}$, we still have to determine whether u belongs to community c or not from the value of F_{uc}. To achieve this, we ignore the membership of node u to community c if F_{uc} is below some threshold δ. Otherwise ($F_{uc} \geq \delta$), we regard u as belonging to c. We set δ so that if two nodes belong to community c, then their edge probability is higher than the background edge probability ε (see Section 4).

$$\varepsilon \leq 1 - \exp(-\delta^2)$$

Solving this inequality, we set the value of $\delta = \sqrt{-\log(1-\varepsilon)}$. Note we also experimented with other values of δ and found that our choice for δ gives overall good performance.

Initialization. To initialize F, we use locally minimal neighborhoods [11]. Neighborhoods $N(u)$ of node u is a community of u and its neighbors, and $N(u)$ is locally minimal if $N(u)$ has lower conductance than all the $N(v)$ for nodes v who are connected to u. Recently, Gleich et al. [11] empirically showed that the locally minimal neighborhoods are good seed sets for community detection algorithms. For a node u' who belongs to a locally minimal neighborhood k, we initialize $F_{u'k} = 1$, otherwise $F_{u'k} = 0$.

Choosing the number of communities. To find the number of communities K, we adopt the approach used in [2]. We reserve 20% of node pairs as a hold out set. Varying K, we fit the BIGCLAM model with K communities on the 80% of node pairs and then evaluate the likelihood of BIGCLAM on the hold out set. The K with the maximum hold out likelihood will be chosen as the number of communities. When the network is too small (*e.g.*, has less than 50 edges), we use K that achieves the smallest value of the Bayes Information Criterion:

$$BIC(K) = -2l(\hat{F}) + NK \log|E|$$

Implementational details. Since the objective function of our optimization problem is not the l_2 norm, the methods for least squares NMF such as multiplicative update [19] or alternating least squares [15] are not applicable. We experimented with the cyclic coordinate descent method (CCD) [15] which optimizes F_{uc} for each u and each c by the Newton's method, but the method converged slower than our block coordinate ascent method. The main reason for this is that the number of subproblems that we have to solve in CCD grows linearly with K, the number of communities. In matrix factorization, usually K (the rank of F) is assumed to be a very small constant [15, 21]; however, in our problem K increases as the size of the underlying network grows.

Connection to other affiliation network models. Last we also briefly describe the connection between BIGCLAM and other affiliation network models. In particular, we consider the AGM [35, 33] which can also model densely overlapping network community structure. Similarly to BIGCLAM, AGM generates $G(V,E)$ given a bipartite community affiliation $B(V,C,M)$. In contrast to BIGCLAM, AGM assigns a single parameter p_c to every community c. Given $B(V,C,M)$ and $\{p_c\}$, AGM models the edge probability $p(u,v)$ as follows:

$$p(u,v) = 1 - \prod_{c \in C_{uv}} (1 - p_c).$$

where C_{uv} is a set of communities that u and v have in common.

One can also detect community structure by fitting AGM to a given network $G(V,E)$ (*i.e.*, finding affiliation graph B and parameters $\{p_c\}$) by maximizing the log-likelihood [33]:

$$\underset{P,\{p_c\}}{\operatorname{argmax}} \sum_{(u,v)\in E} \log p(u,v) + \sum_{(u,v)\notin E} \log(1 - p(u,v)) \quad (5)$$

This results in a combinatorial optimization problem that is very hard to solve. Solving the problem requires a combinatorial search over all possible affiliation graphs B. However, there is an exponential number ($2^{N \cdot K}$) of possible affiliation graphs B.

We now show that fitting BIGCLAM (Eq. 2) can also be derived by relaxing the fitting problem of AGM (Eq. 5) into a continuous optimization problem. We begin by stating Eq. 1 in a new form:

$$p(u,v) = 1 - \prod_{c \in C_{uv}} (1 - p_c) = 1 - \prod_c (1 - p_c)^{M_{uc} M_{vc}},$$

where M_{uc} is an indicator variable whether node u belongs to community c. By replacing $1 - p_c = \exp(-\alpha_c)$ with $\alpha_c \geq 0$, we can express the equation as a linear form of M and α_c:

$$p(u,v) = 1 - \exp(-\sum_c M_{uc} \alpha_c M_{vc}).$$

We then further simplify the equation by letting $\tilde{M}_{uc} = \sqrt{\alpha_c} M_{uc}$.

$$p(u,v) = 1 - \exp(-\tilde{M}_u \tilde{M}_v^T).$$

Note that we did not use any approximation so far. So the maximum likelihood estimation of the model is still a combinatorial optimization problem ($\tilde{M}_{uc} \in \{\sqrt{\alpha_c}, 0\}$). $\tilde{M}_{uc} \in \{\sqrt{\alpha_c}, 0\}$ means that if node u belongs to c, it would be connected to other member nodes in c with the factor $\sqrt{\alpha_c}$. Therefore, we can interpret $\tilde{M}_{uc}$ as the level of participation of u in community c, which then determines edge probability of u to other nodes in c. Basically, we can replace $\tilde{M}_{uc}$ with a *continuous* membership F_{uc} which can be any nonnegative number. This way we actually model a level of participation of each node in a particular community as members with the higher value of F_{uc} will be more likely to connect to other members of c.

$$p(u,v) = 1 - \exp(-F_u F_v^T).$$

Now, we transform the problem of Eq. 5 into a continuous optimization problem:

$$\hat{F} = \underset{F \geq 0}{\operatorname{argmax}} \sum_{(u,v)\in E} \log(1 - \exp(-F_u F_v^T)) - \sum_{(u,v)\notin E} F_u F_v^T.$$

In other words, we can view the optimization problem of BIGCLAM as a continuous relaxation of the combinatorial optimization problem of fitting AGM. BIGCLAM can be considered as a relaxed version of AGM in the sense that it models community affiliation as continuous variables. With BIGCLAM, finding the most probable community affiliation is equivalent to factorizing the adjacency matrix of the underlying network with nonnegative factors.

6. EXPERIMENTS

We proceed by evaluating the performance of BIGCLAM and comparing it to the state-of-the-art community detection methods on a range of networks from a number of different domains and research areas.

6.1 Experiments on synthetic networks

Using synthetic networks we investigate the scalability and convergence of the BIGCLAM optimization problem.

Convergence of BIGCLAM. Non-negative matrix factorization is non-convex which means that gradient based approaches do not guarantee to find an optimal solution. To verify that our fitting algorithm does not suffer too much from local optima, we conduct the following experiment on synthetic networks. We generated 100 synthetic networks using the AGM model [35]. For each of these networks, we then fit BIGCLAM using 10 different random starting points and attempt to recover the true community affiliations.

In 98% of cases our fitting algorithm finds true communities with reliable accuracy (F1-score of node community memberships higher than 0.85), and in 27% of cases our algorithm discovers the communities almost perfectly (F1-Score > 0.95). This result suggests that the optimization space has several local optima which almost equivalent to the global optimum.

Scalability of BIGCLAM. We also evaluate the scalability of BIGCLAM by measuring the running time on the networks of increasing sizes.For comparison, we compare the runtime of the following overlapping community detection methods:

- NMF: Least squares non-negative matrix factorization. We solve the following problem: $\text{argmax}_{F_{uk}\geq 0} ||A - F \cdot F^T||_F$ where A is an adjacency matrix of a given network. We used a projected gradient descent as we do with BIGCLAM.
- BIGCLAM(Naive): BIGCLAM without the optimization in Eq. 4.
- LC: Link Clustering method [1].
- CPM: Clique Percolation method [25].
- MMSB: Mixed-Membership Stochastic Blockmodel [2].

Link Clustering, Clique Percolation Method and Mixed Membership Stochastic Blockmodels are considered the state-of-the-art overlapping community detection methods. We used the implementation of LC and CPM in the Stanford Network Analysis Platform[2]. For MMSB we used publicly-available 'LDA' R package. For CPM, we use the clique size $k = 5$ for CPM. For MMSB, we set the number of communities to detect to $K = 10$. We also consider NMF and BIGCLAM (Naive) so that we can compare the performance gain due to the optimization described in Eq. 4.

Figure 5 shows the results. NMF, BIGCLAM(Naive) and MMSB scale to networks of around 1,000. LC and CPM scale to networks of about 10,000 and then their runtime becomes prohibitively large. On the other hand BIGCLAM can process networks with hundreds of thousands of nodes within 20 minutes. This means that BIGCLAM can easily process networks 10 to 100 times larger than other approaches (and while also more accurately detecting communities). Last, note that the optimization of BIGCLAM defined in Eq. 4 speeds up the algorithm for around 100 times and is thus essential for making BIGCLAM scale to large networks.

6.2 Experiments using real ground-truth

We also examine the performance of BIGCLAM using the 6 networks with ground-truth communities that we described in Section 3. In these networks nodes explicitly state their ground-truth community memberships which allows us to quantify the 'accuracy' of community detection methods by evaluating the level of correspondence between detected and ground-truth communities.

Experimental setup. We are given an unlabeled undirected network G (with known ground-truth communities C^*) we aim to discover communities $\hat{C}$ such that discovered communities $\hat{C}$ closely match the ground-truth communities C^*.

[2]SNAP: http://snap.stanford.edu/snap

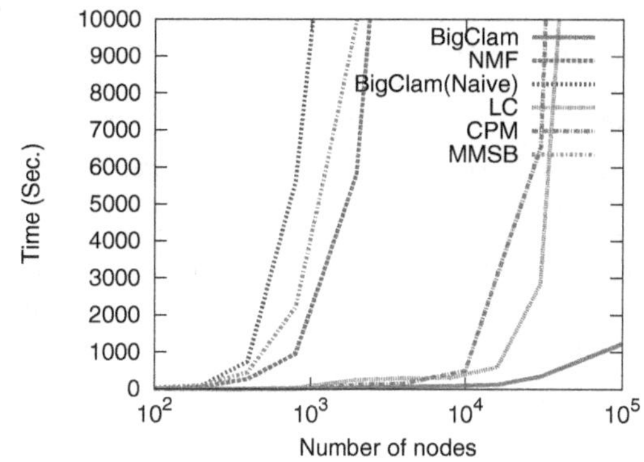

Figure 5: Algorithm runtime comparison. BIGCLAM runs 10 to 100 faster than competing approaches.

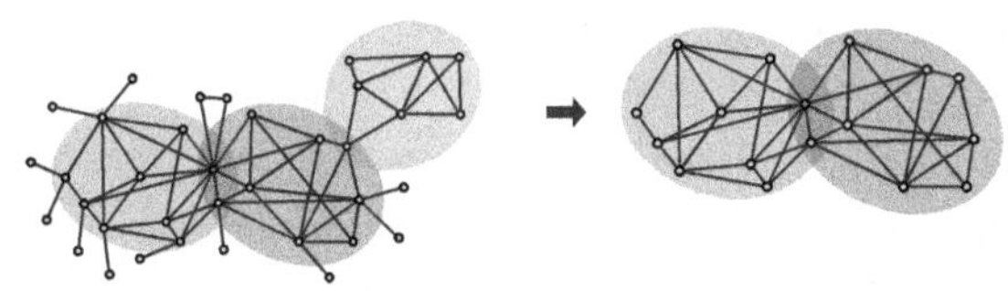

Figure 6: Sampling subnetworks of G.

Even though our algorithm can process the networks described in Table 1, *all* the baseline methods do not scale to networks of such size. To allow for comparison between our and the baseline methods we use the following evaluation scenario where the goal is to obtain a large set of relatively small subnetworks with overlapping community structure. To obtain one such subnetwork we pick a random node u in the given graph G that belongs to at least two communities. We then take the subnetwork to be the induced subgraph of G consisting of all the nodes that share at least one ground-truth community membership with u. Figure 6 illustrates how a subnetwork (right) is created from $G(V, E)$ (left) based on the red node u. Note that on average 95% of all ground-truth communities overlap which means that this procedure does not bias towards overlapping communities. In our experiments we created 500 different subnetworks for each of the six datasets.

Baselines for comparison. For baselines we choose three most prominent overlapping community detection methods: Link clustering (LC) [1], Clique Percolation Method (CPM) [25], and the Mixed-Membership Stochastic Block Model (MMSB) [2].

These methods have a number of parameters that need to be set. For CPM, we set the clique size $k = 5$ since the number of communities discovered by CPM with $k = 5$ best approximates the true number of communities. For MMSB, we have to set the number of communities K as an input parameter. We use the Bayes Information Criterion to choose K. While we require "hard" community memberships, MMSB returns stochastic node memberships to each of the K communities. Thus, we assign a node to a community if the corresponding stochastic membership is non-zero. We also considered Infomap [27], which is the-state-of-the-art non-overlapping community detection method. We omit the results as the performance of the method was not competitive.

Evaluation metrics. The availability of ground-truth communities allows us to *quantitatively* evalute the performance of community detection algorithm. Without ground-truth such evaluation is simply not possible. For evaluation we use metrics that quantify the level of correspondence between the detected and the ground-truth communities. Given a network $G(V, E)$, we consider a set of ground truth communities C^* and a set of detected communities $\hat{C}$ where each ground-truth community $C_i \in C^*$ and each detected community $\hat{C}_i \in \hat{C}$ is defined by a set of its member nodes. To quantify the level of correspondence of $\hat{C}$ to C^* we consider:

- **Average F1 score.** To compute the F1 score, we need to determine which $C_i \in C^*$ corresponds to which $\hat{C}_i \in \hat{C}$. We define F1 score to be the average of the F1-score of the best-matching ground-truth community to each detected community, and the F1-score of the best-matching detected community to each ground-truth community:

$$\frac{1}{2}(\frac{1}{|C^*|}\sum_{C_i \in C^*} F1(C_i, \hat{C_{g(i)}}) + \frac{1}{|\hat{C}|}\sum_{\hat{C}_i \in \hat{C}} F1(C_{g'(i)}, \hat{C}_i))$$

  where the best matching g and g' is defined as follows:

$$g(i) = \operatorname*{argmax}_j F1(C_i, \hat{C}_j), \quad g'(i) = \operatorname*{argmax}_j F1(C_j, \hat{C}_i)$$

  and $F1(C_i, \hat{C}_j)$ is the harmonic mean of Precision and Recall.

- **Omega Index [13]** is the accuracy on estimating the number of communities that each pair of nodes shares:

$$\frac{1}{|V|^2}\sum_{u,v \in V} \mathbf{1}\{|C_{uv}| = |\hat{C_{uv}}|\}$$

  where C_{uv} is the set of ground-truth communities that u and v share and $\hat{C_{uv}}$ is the set of detected communities that they share.

- **Normalized Mutual Information** adopts the criterion used in information theory to compare the detected communities and the ground-truth communities. Normalized Mutual Information has been proposed as a performance metric for community detection. Refer to [8] for details.

- **Accuracy in the number of communities** is the relative accuracy between the detected and the true number of communities, $1 - \frac{||C^*| - |\hat{C}||}{2|C^*|}$.

For all metrics higher values mean more "accurately" detected communities, *i.e.*detected node community memberships better correspond to ground-truth node community memberships. Maximum value of 1 is obtained when the detected communities perfectly correspond to the ground-truth communities.

Results on ground-truth communities. For each community detection method and each dataset we measure the average value of the 4 evaluation metrics over the 500 subnetworks sampled using the procedure described above. Then, for each evaluation metric separately we scale the scores of the methods so that the best performing community detection method achieves the score of 1. Finally, we compute the composite performance by summing up the 4 normalized scores. If a method outperforms all the other method in all the scores, then its composite performance is 4.

Figure 7 displays the composite performance of the methods over all six networks. On average, the composite performance of BIGCLAM is 3.60, which is 79% higher than that of Link clustering (2.01), 45% higher than that of CPM (2.47), and 15% higher than that of MMSB (3.14). The absolute average value of Omega Index of BIGCLAM over the 6 networks is 0.47, which is 24% higher than Link clustering (0.38), 26% higher than CPM (0.37), and 30% higher than MMSB (0.36). In terms of absolute values of scores, BIGCLAM archives the average F1 score of 0.60, average Omega index of 0.47, Mutual Information of 0.22 and accuracy of the number of communities of 0.43.

Overall, BIGCLAM gives superior overall performance. This means that, while BIGCLAM is two orders of magnitude more scalable than competing approaches, it also achieves superior performance in the quality of detected communities. On 4 out of 6 networks BIGCLAM performs best by a big margin. However, we note that on DBLP and Amazon MMSB is the winning method mostly due to BIGCLAM scoring very badly on a single individual metric (Number of communities on DBLP, Ω-index on Amazon). This occurs due to the fact that BIGCLAM uses a single parameter ε to model the edge probability between all pairs of different communities (ε-Community in Section 4), while MMSB uses one parameter for each pair of communities. With more parameters, MMSB can fit these networks better. Note that BIGCLAM could be easily extended to include a distinct parameter for the edge probability between each pair of communities.

6.3 Experiments on networks in Ahn et al. [1]

We further evaluate BIGCLAM using performance benchmarks from Ahn et al. [1]. For this experiment we adopt exactly the same data, evaluation metrics and experimental setup as in [1]. Note that these networks do not contain information about ground-truth communities. However, nodes in these communities contain attributes and [1] used "purity" metrics as surrogates for the quality of detected communities. The idea behind evaluation metrics here is that good communities have low diversity of member nodes' features.

Experimental setup. We use the same seven different networks as in [1]: 5 biological networks, a network of Wikipedia pages and a word association network For further details about these datasets, refer to [1]. We also adopt the same data-driven measures defined in [1]: Community Coverage, Overlap Coverage, Community Quality, Overlap Quality. All networks are small, so we apply the community detection methods to full networks. Moreover, the metrics are heavily biased towards methods that find a large number of communities, so we fit BIGCLAM using the same number of communities as detected by LC (*i.e.*, the algorithm developed in [1]).

Results. Following [1] we compute the composite performance by normalizing the scores the same way as we did in the experiments with ground-truth communities. Figure 8 shows the composite performance of the four methods. The BIGCLAM achieves best composite performance in 4 networks, and the second best in three networks. In all these cases MMSB slightly outperforms BIGCLAM due to BIGCLAM's bad performance on the Overlap Coverage metric.Overlap Coverage is defined as the average number of communities that a node belongs to [1]. This metric is extremely ill posed since assigning nodes to more communities always improves the score. Since any non-zero stochastic membership found by MMSB is regarded as a valid community membership, the MMSB achieves extremely high score on the Overlap Coverage metric. Nevertheless, on average, the BIGCLAM achieves a composite performance score of 3.06, outperforming Link clustering (2.67) by 14%, Clique percolation (1.50) by 102%, and MMSB (2.84) by 8%.

6.4 Experiments on large networks

In addition to better accuracy, another strength of BIGCLAM is its scalability. To test this, we apply BIGCLAM to large real-world networks. We were able to run BIGCLAM on 4 (full) networks from Table 1: LiveJournal, Youtube, Amazon, and DBLP.

To reduce the memory requirements of our method, we aim to find sparse latent factors. We achieve this by adding l_1 regularization term to Eq. 2 and optimize:

$$\operatorname*{argmax}_{F_{uc} \geq 0} l(F) - \lambda \sum_{u,c} |F_{uc}|$$

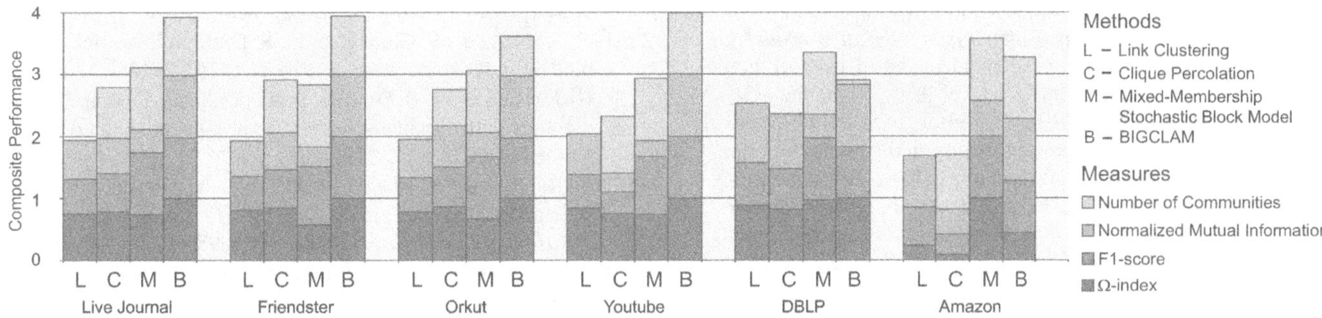

Figure 7: Performance of detecting ground-truth communities. While being 10 to 100 times faster than competing approaches BIGCLAM also achieves overall best performance in the "accuracy" of detected communities.

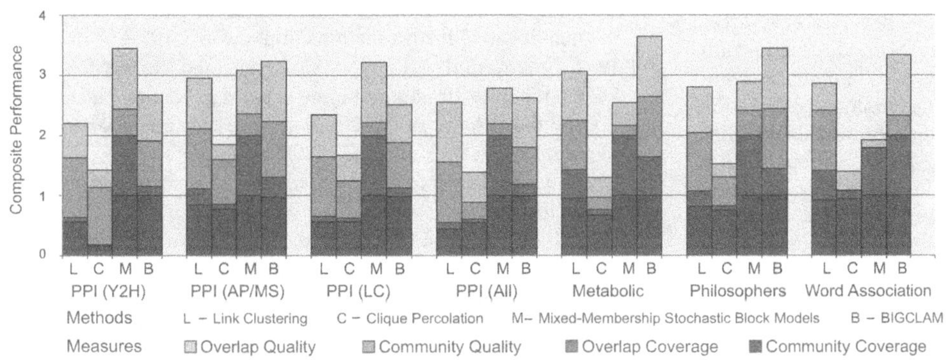

Network	N	E
PPI (Y2H)	1,647	2,518
PPI (AP/MS)	1,004	8,319
PPI (LC)	1,213	2,556
PPI (All)	1,647	12,784
Metabolic	1,042	8,756
Philosophers	1,218	5,972
Word Association	5,018	55,232

Figure 8: Experiments on the data and evaluation metrics used in Ahn et al. [1]. N: Number of the nodes, E: Number of the edges.

Since l_1 regularization introduces sparsity to matrix F, we only need to keep track of latent factors with non-zero value, which decreases the memory requirements of our method. We use $\lambda = 10$ for Amazon, Youtube, and DBLP and $\lambda = 5000$ for LiveJournal. We update F_u (Solving Eq. 3) for multiple nodes in parallel. With 20 threads, it takes about one day to fit BIGCLAM to the LiveJournal network (4M nodes, 35M edges).

As our baselines from the previous experiments do not scale to these networks, we consider two well-known graph partitioning methods as baselines: Metis [16] and Graclus [6]. For Graclus and Metis, we set the number of communities to detect K to be the number of ground-truth communities and use the same K for BIGCLAM as well.

Similarly to experiments in Figure 7, we measure the accuracy of detected communities using F-1 score and Omega index (NMI is omitted as all the methods perform the same). Moreover, notice that grund-truth communities in our data are partially annotated as some nodes might not indicate their memberships.This means it is important to quantify the Recall of a given method. We define Recall as the average Recall of best-matching detected communities:

$$Recall(C^*, \hat{C}) = \frac{1}{|C^*|} \sum_{C_i \in C^*} Rc(C_i, \hat{C_{g(i)}})$$

where $\text{Rc}(C_i, \hat{C}_j)$ is the recall of $\hat{C}_j$ under the best matching g.

Since the two baselines (Graculus and Metis) perform very similarly in all metrics, we take just the best value among the two in each case rather than showing the result of baselines separately. For each network and each score, we pick the best score x among the two baselines and compute the relative improvement of BIGCLAM over the x, *i.e.*, $\frac{Score(\text{BIGCLAM})-x}{x}$. Table 2 shows the relative improvement of BIGCLAM over the baselines. For example, 0.21 for F-1 in LiveJournal means that BIGCLAM achieves 21% higher F-1 score than the best baseline (Metis in this case).

Dataset	Ω-Index	F-1	Recall
LiveJournal	2.70	0.21	0.43
Youtube	1.60	0.39	0.82
Amazon	0.00	0.00	0.23
DBLP	0.10	0.03	0.29
Average	1.10	0.16	0.44

Table 2: Relative improvement of BIGCLAM over Metis and Graclus in detecting communities in large scale networks. Positive value indicates that BIGCLAM outperforms the baselines.

Overall, BIGCLAM outperforms the baselines in nearly all cases. On average, BIGCLAM achieves 110% higher Omega index, 16% higher F-1 score, and 44% higher average Recall, which means that BIGCLAM achieves 57% relative improvement on average among the three scores. Furthermore, BIGCLAM outperforms the baselines in every measure and every network. The absolute value of the scores of BIGCLAM is 0.11 (Omega index), 0.13 (F-1 score), and 0.32 (Recall). Overall, the results emphasize the need for a scalable and accurate overlapping community detection method as graph partitioning methods fail to detect overlapping communities. Results demonstrate that BIGCLAM could be the needed solution.

7. CONCLUSION

In this paper we developed a novel large scale community detection method that accurately discovers the overlapping community structure of real-world networks. We identified a set of networks where nodes explicitly state their ground-truth community membership and studied the connectivity of ground-truth communities and their overlaps. We observed that the overlaps of communities are more densely connected than the non-overlapping parts of communities, which is in sharp contrast to assumptions made by present community detection models and methods. Based on this observation, we then developed the *Cluster Affiliation Model for Big Networks* (BIGCLAM), a conceptual model of network community structure, which naturally produces dense community overlaps. We then presented an efficient algorithm to fit BIGCLAM to a given network. Our fitting algorithm builds on the research of nonnegative matrix factorization and scalable to networks with million nodes. Experiments show that the BIGCLAM outperforms the state-of-the-art community detection methods in accurately discovering network communities as well as the overlaps between communities. Furthermore, BIGCLAM can detect community structure in the LiveJournal network which is more than 10 times bigger than the previously largest network considered for overlapping community detection.

Our work has several implications: First, our analysis sheds light on the organization of complex networks and provides new directions for research on community detection. Second, ground-truth communities offer a reliable way for evaluating community detection methods. Third, large scale overlapping community detection by BIGCLAM can broaden our understanding of organizing principles of large scale networks. And last, BIGCLAM opens up a new possibility to combine the advances in community detection and nonnegative matrix factorization. More generally, a shift in perspective from sparse to dense community overlaps represents a new way of studying networks and provides a unifying framework for network community detection.

Acknowledgements. This research has been supported in part by NSF IIS-1016909, CNS-1010921, IIS-1149837, IIS-1159679, DARPA XDATA, DARPA GRAPHS, Albert Yu & Mary Bechmann Foundation, Allyes, Boeing, Docomo, Intel, Samsung, Alfred P. Sloan Fellowship and the Microsoft Faculty Fellowship.

8. REFERENCES

[1] Y.-Y. Ahn, J. P. Bagrow, and S. Lehmann. Link communities reveal multi-scale complexity in networks. *Nature*, 466:761–764, 2010.

[2] E. M. Airoldi, D. M. Blei, S. E. Fienberg, and E. P. Xing. Mixed membership stochastic blockmodels. *JMLR*, 2007.

[3] L. Backstrom, D. Huttenlocher, J. Kleinberg, and X. Lan. Group formation in large social networks: membership, growth, and evolution. In *KDD '06*, 2006.

[4] S. Boyd and L. Vandenberghe. *Convex Optimization*. Cambridge University Press, 2004.

[5] R. L. Breiger. The duality of persons and groups. *Social Forces*, 53(2):181–190, 1974.

[6] I. Dhillon, Y. Guan, and B. Kulis. Weighted graph cuts without eigenvectors: A multilevel approach. *IEEE PAMI*, 29(11):1944–1957, 2007.

[7] S. L. Feld. The focused organization of social ties. *American J. of Sociology*, 86(5):1015–1035, 1981.

[8] S. Fortunato. Community detection in graphs. *Physics Reports*, 486(3-5):75 - 174, 2010.

[9] S. Fortunato and M. Barthélemy. Resolution limit in community detection. *PNAS*, 104(1):36–41, 2007.

[10] M. Girvan and M. Newman. Community structure in social and biological networks. *PNAS*, 99(12):7821–7826, 2002.

[11] D. F. Gleich and C. Seshadhri. Neighborhoods are good communities. In *KDD '12*, 2012.

[12] M. S. Granovetter. The strength of weak ties. *American J. of Sociology*, 78:1360–1380, 1973.

[13] S. Gregory. Fuzzy overlapping communities in networks. *J. of Stat. Mech.: Theory and Experiment*, 2011.

[14] C.-J. Hsieh, K.-Y. Chiang, and I. S. Dhillon. Low-rank modeling of signed networks. In *KDD '12*, 2012.

[15] C.-J. Hsieh and I. S. Dhillon. Fast coordinate descent methods with variable selection for non-negative matrix factorization. In *KDD '11*, 2011.

[16] G. Karypis and V. Kumar. Multilevel k-way partitioning scheme for irregular graphs. *Journal of Parallel and Distributed Computing*, 48:96–129, 1998.

[17] N. Krogan et al. Global landscape of protein complexes in the yeast Saccharomyces cerevisiae. *Nature*, 440(7084):637–643, 2006.

[18] S. Lattanzi and D. Sivakumar. Affiliation networks. In *STOC '09*, 2009.

[19] D. D. Lee and H. S. Seung. Learning the parts of objects by non-negative matrix factorization. *Nature*, 1999.

[20] J. Leskovec, K. J. Lang, A. Dasgupta, and M. W. Mahoney. Community structure in large networks: Natural cluster sizes and the absence of large well-defined clusters. *Internet Mathematics*, 6(1):29–123, 2009.

[21] C.-J. Lin. Projected gradient methods for nonnegative matrix factorization. *Neural Computation*, 2007.

[22] J. J. McAuley and J. Leskovec. Learning to discover social circles in ego networks. In *NIPS*, 2012.

[23] M. McPherson, L. Smith-Lovin, and J. M. Cook. Birds of a feather: Homophily in social networks. *Annual Review of Sociology*, 27:415–444, 2001.

[24] M. Newman. Modularity and community structure in networks. *PNAS*, 103(23):8577–8582, 2006.

[25] G. Palla, I. Derényi, I. Farkas, and T. Vicsek. Uncovering the overlapping community structure of complex networks in nature and society. *Nature*, 435(7043):814–818, 2005.

[26] W. W. Powell, D. R. White, K. W. Koput, and J. Owen-Smith. Network dynamics and field evolution: The growth of interorganizational collaboration in the life sciences. *American J. of Sociology*, 110(4):1132–1205, 2005.

[27] M. Rosvall and C. T. Bergstrom. Maps of random walks on complex networks reveal community structure. *PNAS*, 105:1118–1123, 2008.

[28] S. Schaeffer. Graph clustering. *Computer Science Review*, 1(1):27–64, 2007.

[29] G. Simmel. *Conflict and the web of group affiliations*. Simon and Schuster, 1964.

[30] U. von Luxburg. A tutorial on spectral clustering. Technical Report 149, MPI for Biological Cybernetics, August 2006.

[31] D. J. Watts and S. H. Strogatz. Collective dynamics of small-world networks *Nature*, 393:440–442, 1998.

[32] J. Xie, S. Kelley, and B. K. Szymanski. Overlapping community detection in networks: the state of the art and comparative study *ACM Computing Surveys*, 45:4, 2013.

[33] J. Yang and J. Leskovec. Community-affiliation graph model for overlapping network community detection. In *ICDM '12*, 2012.

[34] J. Yang and J. Leskovec. Defining and evaluating network communities based on ground-truth. In *ICDM '12*, 2012.

[35] J. Yang and J. Leskovec. Structure and overlaps of communities in networks. In *SNAKDD '12*, 2012.

[36] E. Zheleva, H. Sharara, and L. Getoor. Co-evolution of social and affiliation networks. In *KDD '09*, 2009.

LaFT-Tree: Perceiving the Expansion Trace of One's Circle of Friends in Online Social Networks

Jun Zhang[1,2,3,4] Chaokun Wang[2,3,4] Jianmin Wang[2,3,4] Philip S. Yu[5]
[1] Department of Computer Science and Technology, Tsinghua University
[2] School of Software, Tsinghua University
[3] Tsinghua National Laboratory for Information Science and Technology
[4] Key Laboratory for Information System Security, Ministry of Education
[5] Department of Computer Science, University of Illinois at Chicago
zhang-jun10@mails.tsinghua.edu.cn, {chaokun, jimwang}@tsinghua.edu.cn, psyu@uic.edu

ABSTRACT

Many patterns have been discovered to explain and analyze how people make friends. Among them is the triadic closure, supported by the principle of the transitivity of friendship, which means for an individual the friends of her friend are more likely to become her new friends. However, people's motivations under this principle haven't been well studied, and it's still unknown that how this principle works in diverse situations.

In this paper, we try to study this principle deeply based on the behavior modeling. We study how one expands her egocentric network via her friends, also called intermediaries, based on the transitivity of friendship. We propose LaFT-Tree, a tree-based representation of friendship formation inspired from triadic closure. LaFT-Tree provides a hierarchical view of the flat structure of one's egocentric network by visualizing the expansion trace of one's egocentric network. We model people's friend-making behaviors using LaFT-LDA, a generative model for LaFT-Tree learning.

The proposed model is evaluated on both synthetic and real-world social networks and experimental results demonstrate the effectiveness of LaFT-LDA for LaFT-Tree inference. We also present some interesting applications of the LaFT-Tree, showing that our model can be generalized and benefit other social network analysis tasks.

Categories and Subject Descriptors

H.2.8 [**DATABASE MANAGEMENT**]: Database Applications—*Data mining*; J.4 [**SOCIAL AND BEHAVIORAL SCIENCES**]: Sociology

General Terms

Algorithms, Human Factors, Experimentation, Design

Keywords

Triadic Closure; Transitivity of Friendship; LaFT-Tree; Intermediary Inference; Link Formation; Link Prediction; Social Networks

1. INTRODUCTION

Understanding the evolution of social networks is always an appealing and challenging subject for its intricacy. Although most existing research has focused on the structural properties of either a certain snapshot of networks or multiple snapshots of evolving networks, the microscopic growth dynamics have also been studied recently. A number of patterns have been discovered to explain and analyze how people make friends, including *preferential attachment* [19], *triadic closure* [14][23], *reciprocity* [20][9] and *homophily* [18][5]. Among them, *triadic closure* has been shown as one of the most frequent processes of link formation [14]. The sociological principle for triadic closure is the *transitivity of friendship* [22], which says that there is an increased chance that a friendship will form between two people if they already have a friend in common [22][8]. Though the transitivity of friendship has been proved effective in modeling the network evolution [14] and predicting future link formations [23][7], the deep factors which make this principle work haven't been well studied yet. A simple question is, is it equally likely for one to close all possible open triadic structures involved of her?

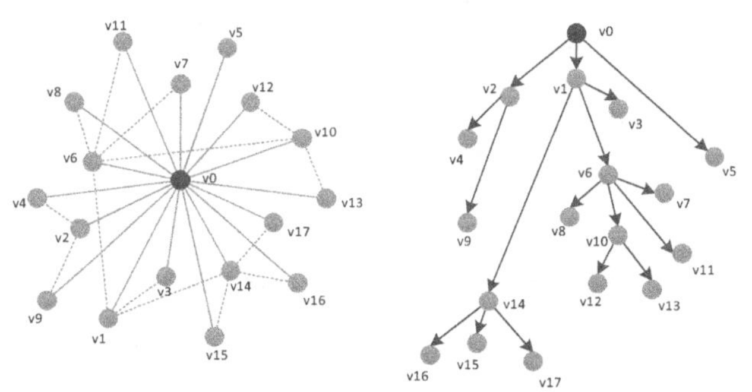

(a) The egocentric network

(b) The LaFT-Tree

Figure 1: An egocentric network with v_0 as the ego and the corresponding LaFT-Tree of v_0. In the LaFT-Tree, the nodes are labeled and arranged vertically according to the time when they became friends of v_0.

In this paper, we investigate the friendship transitivity by modeling the friend-making behaviors in online social networks. We study triadic closure events from the perspective of an active individual. As mentioned above, people are more likely to create friendships with the friends of their current friends. In this sense, one's current friends can be regarded as her potential *intermediaries* who will introduce new friends to her. However, not all the current friends have equal influence on one's social behaviors. Specifically, for two individuals who have many common friends and become friends later, we would like to distinguish the contributions of each common friend and identify the most important intermediary. The question we're interested in is, *who knows whom via whom?*

To formulate this problem, we propose the **Latent Friendship Transitivity Tree (*LaFT-Tree*)**. LaFT-Tree is a tree-based representation for the growth process of one's egocentric social network. It consists of the person we are interested in (referred to as the *ego*), and the ego's friends. Figure 1(a) shows an egocentric network with v_0 as the ego. The solid lines show the friendships between v_0 and each of her friends, while the dashed lines show the friendships among v_0's friends. Figure 1(b) shows the inferred LaFT-Tree for v_0 using our algorithm introduced later in this paper. In the LaFT-Tree, the nodes are labeled and arranged vertically according to the time when they became friends of v_0. The root refers to the ego v_0, while other nodes represent v_0's friends. The path from the root to each node indicates all the intermediaries who have most likely promoted the friendship between the ego and each node in chronological order.

By visualizing the transitivity of friendship, LaFT-Tree provides new perspectives for understanding the evolving social networks. First of all, the LaFT-Tree presents a hierarchical view of the flat structure of one's egocentric network, by showing the formation process of the network driven by the transitivity of friendship. This enables us to gain insight into the evolving structure of social networks. Furthermore, each node in the LaFT-Tree is a possible expansion point of one's ego-centric networks, via whom one can expand her friend circles by making new friends. From the LaFT-Tree we can see not only one's preference for friends, but also her preference for friend-recommenders. In addition, as each branch of the LaFT-Tree shows various potential to grow at different times, LaFT-Tree can reveal the time dynamics about the expansion trend of one's friend circles, and thus can be utilized to predict the future shape of the network.

Taking Figure 1(b) as example, we can see that v_0 knows v_1, v_2 and v_5 directly, and then by v_1 she connects to v_6, via whom she knows more friends including v_7, v_8 and v_{10} later. It can be inferred that v_0 prefers to make friends with the friends of v_6. In other words, v_6 seems an important expansion point of v_0's friend circles. Based on this observation, we can guess that more friends of v_6 will become friends of v_0 in the future than that of others. However, as the time progresses, we see recently v_0 makes more new friends via v_{14}. Thus, the network may tend to expand along with the direction of v_{14} in the future.

Nevertheless, the intermediaries are usually not observable in most online social networks. Thus the challenge is how to infer the LaFT-Trees, in other words, the intermediaries for each friendships, based on the expansion history of the social network. In this paper, we propose to solve this problem by behavior modeling. We design the *LaFT-LDA*, a generative model to capture the effects of hidden choices of friends through which other friendships are formed. LaFT-LDA models the friend-making behaviors in a generative manner, in which firstly an ego selects an intermediary, and one of the current friends of the intermediary is then selected as the ego's new friend. LaFT-LDA can be inferred from data with timestamped links and be utilized for learning the structure of LaFT-Trees effectively.

To the best of our knowledge, this is the first time the transitivity of friendship is deeply investigated and expressed using LaFT-Trees. The contributions of this paper are concluded as follows:

- We propose the LaFT-Tree, a latent structure to formulate the transitivity of friendship and capture the evolution process of one's egocentric network using a hierarchical representation.
- We develop LaFT-LDA, a probabilistic generative model for learning the LaFT-Trees from social networks, given the timestamped relationship creation and interaction histories.
- We conduct experiments on both synthetic and real-world datasets for evaluation and demonstrate the effectiveness of our model for the LaFT-Trees learning.
- We apply LaFT-LDA and LaFT-Tree in real applications, showing the capability of the LaFT-Tree for modeling the network growth and analyzing the network properties.

The rest of this paper is organized as follows. We introduce the concepts of LaFT-Tree and formulate our problem in Section 2. Methods of learning the LaFT-Trees are developed in Section 3. In Section 4 we conduct experimental study on both synthetic and real-world datasets to evaluate our model. Then we present some interesting applications of our model in Section 5. We discuss related work in Section 6 and conclude this study in Section 7.

2. PROBLEM FORMULATION

In this section, we introduce the concepts related to LaFT-Tree and formulate the LaFT-Tree inference problem.

Let $\mathbb{G} = [G_{t_1}, G_{t_2}, \cdots, G_{t_n}]$ denote an evolving social network where $G_{t_i} = (V_{t_i}, E_{t_i})$ is a directed graph denoting the snapshot of the network at time t_i. Each node in V_{t_i} represents an individual in the network, and the edges in E_{t_i} indicate the friendships among them. The nodes $\mathbb{V}$ and edges $\mathbb{E}$ of $\mathbb{G}$ are defined as the union of the counterparts of all the snapshots respectively.

We use T_i to denote the period $(t_{i-1}, t_i]$ and ΔG_{T_i} to denote the new nodes and edges appearing during period T_i; thus we have $G_{t_i} = G_{t_i - 1} \cup \Delta G_{T_i}$. We define the function $\tau : E \rightarrow \mathbb{R}$ which maps each friendship to its building time. Furthermore, for each snapshot G_{t_i} we have a corresponding interaction set $X_{T_i} \subset V_{t_i} \times V_{t_i}$ which denotes the interactions among individuals in T_i. The interactions include co-authoring a paper in scholar collaboration network, leaving a message on Facebook, etc.

It should be noted that although the network $\mathbb{G}$ is defined to be directed, the problem discussed in this paper is also applicable to undirected networks as the latter can be transformed to directed networks easily.

In this paper, we study how $\mathbb{E}$ evolves in social networks, i.e. the formation of people's friendships. Based on the transitivity of friendship, when two individuals become friends, we assume their common friends act as the role of "*intermediaries*". To distinguish the various influence of each common friend on the formation of the new friendship, we define the *friendship propagation probability* $p(z|\langle u, v\rangle)$ which denotes the probability that u gets to know v via z. We use $\mathcal{F}_t(u)$ to denote the set of friends of u at t, and $\mathcal{F}_t(u, v)$ to denote the set of common friends of u and v at t.

Definition 1. (**LaFT-Tuple**) For three nodes u, z and v in $\mathbb{V}$, (u, z, v) is named as a *LaFT-Tuple* if the following constraints hold:

1. $\exists\langle u, z\rangle, \langle z, v\rangle, \langle u, v\rangle \in \mathbb{E}$, and $\tau(u, z) < \tau(u, v)$ and $\tau(z, v) < \tau(u, v)$;
2. $\forall z' \in \mathcal{F}_{\tau(u,v)}(u, v), p(z|\langle u, v\rangle) > p(z'|\langle u, v\rangle)$.

The LaFT-Tuple (u, z, v) can also be denoted as $u \rightarrowtail z \twoheadrightarrow v$, which implies the most possible friendship propagation among

Table 1: The notations for LaFT-LDA

U	# of individuals
N_u, V_u	# of new friends and interactions of u
$F(i)$	The current friend set of individual i
$Y(i)$	The new friend set of individual i
$X(i)$	The interaction collection of individual i
θ_u	The intermediary preference distribution of u
ϕ_u	The friendship strength distribution of u
$z_{u,y}$	The intermediary assignment of the friendship $u \rightarrow y$
α, β	The prior parameters for θ, ϕ respectively
$\Omega_{u,z}$	# that u has selected z as an intermediary
$\Lambda_{u,v}$	# that u has interacted with v
$\Psi_{z,y}$	# that z has recommended y for others

them, i.e. z acts the intermediary via whom u knows v. Furthermore, occasionally one may make new friends without intermediaries. In this situation we take the ego u as the *pseudo-intermediary* and denote the LaFT-Tuple as (u, u, v).

Concatenating the LaFT-Tuples we can get the LaFT-Trace.

Definition 2. **(LaFT-Trace)** A *LaFT-Trace* $\mathcal{R}(u \rightsquigarrow z_n) = (u \rightarrowtail z_1 \twoheadrightarrow z_2 \twoheadrightarrow \cdots \twoheadrightarrow z_n)$ is a directed path with u as the starting node and z_n as the destination. In this path, for any adjacent nodes z_i and z_{i+1}, except the starting node u, (u, z_i, z_{i+1}) is a LaFT-Tuple.

The LaFT-Trace $\mathcal{R}(u \rightsquigarrow z_n) = (u \rightarrowtail z_1 \twoheadrightarrow z_2 \twoheadrightarrow \cdots \twoheadrightarrow z_n)$ represents the process through which u gets to know z_n: she knows z_1 first, and then knows z_2 via z_1. She makes new friends along this path continuously, and finally connects to z_n introduced by z_{n-1}. In other words, the LaFT-Trace $\mathcal{R}(u \rightsquigarrow z_n)$ shows how the transitivity has promoted the friendship between u and z_n.

It should be noted that the recurrence property holds for LaFT-Trace. For any intermediary node z_i in the LaFT-Trace $\mathcal{R}(u \rightsquigarrow z_n)$, $\mathcal{R}(u \rightsquigarrow z_i) = (u \rightarrowtail z_1 \twoheadrightarrow z_2 \twoheadrightarrow \cdots \twoheadrightarrow z_{i-1} \twoheadrightarrow z_i)$ is also a legal LaFT-Trace indicating how u gets to know z_i.

Based on the LaFT-Trace, we can define the **Latent Friendship Transitivity Tree** (*LaFT-Tree*).

Definition 3. **(LaFT-Tree)** For any node u in $\mathbb{G}$, a *LaFT-Tree* $\mathcal{T}(u)$ is a tree structure defined for node u which satisfies the following constraints:

1. The set of nodes contained in $\mathcal{T}(u)$ is equal to $\{u\} \bigcup \mathcal{F}(u)$, and u is the root of $\mathcal{T}(u)$;
2. For any node v in $\mathcal{T}(u)$ except u, the only path from u to v in $\mathcal{T}(u)$ is the *LaFT-Trace* $\mathcal{R}(u \rightsquigarrow v)$.

Now we can formulate our problem as follows:

LaFT-Tree Inference Problem. Given an evolving social network $\mathbb{G} = [G_{t_1}, G_{t_2}, \cdots, G_{t_n}]$ and the associated interaction sets $\mathbb{X} = [X_{t_1}, X_{t_2}, \cdots, X_{t_n}]$, the LaFT-Tree inference problem is to infer the LaFT-Trees for every individual in $\mathbb{G}$.

3. LEARNING THE LAFT-TREE

In this section, we first propose a generative model, *LaFT-LDA*, which adopts the idea of LDA (Latent Dirichlet Allocation) [3] to model the friend-making behaviors naturally. And then we present the inference framework of LaFT-LDA and the learning algorithm for LaFT-Tree by applying LaFT-LDA in cascade.

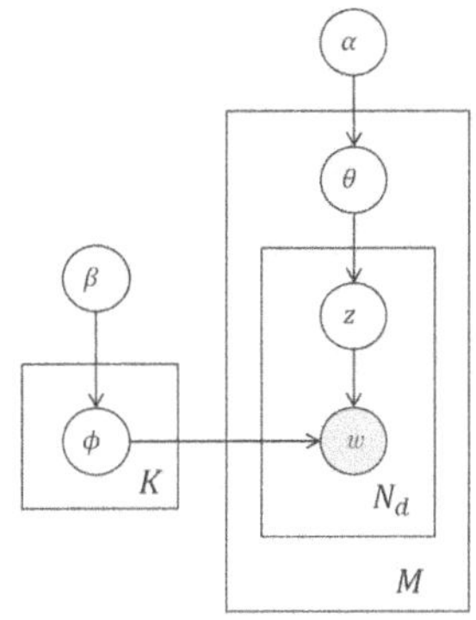

(a) LDA

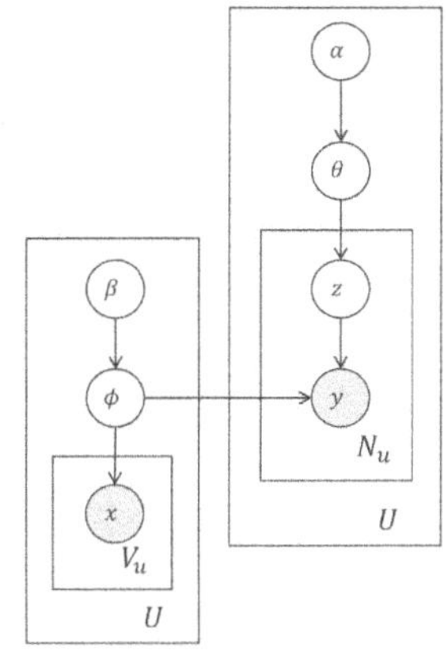

(b) LaFT-LDA

Figure 2: The LDA and LaFT-LDA Model

3.1 The LaFT-LDA Model

The LaFT-Tree is proposed based on the principle of transitivity of friendships, which says that one is likely to create new friendships with the friends of her current friends. This principle inspires us to model one's friend-making behavior using such process: Each time the ego selects one of her current friends as the intermediary first, and then chooses one of the intermediary's friends as her new friend. In this process, the ego's preference for intermediaries and the "recommendation" of the selected intermediary for new friends are critical for the formation of the new relationship. This is similar with the generative process of documents in LDA [3] (as shown in Fig. 2(a)), an unsupervised machine learning technique to identify latent topic structure from large document collection.

The basic elements for LaFT-Tree are the LaFT-Tuples. For each LaFT-Tuple (u, z, v) we regard it as the result of a 2-step process: u selects z as an intermediary and via z she makes friends with v. Formally, we propose the **LaFT-LDA** to infer the LaFT-Tuples. LaFT-LDA is a probabilistic generative model for the social behaviors in social networks. We note that the social behaviors discussed here include the friend-making behaviors and social interaction behaviors. LaFT-LDA applies to a period T_i and tries to capture the intermediation effect in the expansion of one's egocentric network in this period. The basic assumption for LaFT-LDA is that in the given period all the behaviors are independent with each other but follow some specific hidden distributions. In the following we omit the subscript T_i for brevity unless specifically stated.

We model individuals' social behaviors using the *intermediary preference distribution* θ and the *friendship strength distribution* ϕ. The former describes one's preference for intermediaries when making new friends, while the latter models the closeness between one and each of her friends. The closeness can be captured in two ways: the frequency of their interactions and one's willingness to recommend her friends to others.

Now we describe the generative process for the friendships and interactions in a social network in a specific period as follows. For the details of the notations please refer to Table 1.

1. Sample the number of individuals $U \sim$ Poisson (ϵ).
2. For each individual u, sample $V_u \sim$ Poisson(ξ).
   (a) Sample $\phi_u \sim$ Dir(β_u).
   (b) For each of the V_u interaction partners, x:

i. Sample an existing friend of u, $x \sim \phi_u$, as another anticipant of the interaction

3. For each individual u, sample $N_u \sim$ Poisson(ζ).

   (a) Sample $\theta_u \sim$ Dir(α_u).

   (b) For each of the N_u new friends, y:

      i. Sample an intermediary $z \sim \theta_u$

      ii. Sample a new friend $y \sim \phi_z$

The graphical representation of LaFT-LDA is shown in Fig. 2(b). We model each intermediary as the distribution over her friends, i.e. the individuals that may make recommendations to her, and the set of new friendships of an ego as the distribution over her intermediaries. Unlike traditional LDA [3] which defines the distributions over the whole space, we use heuristic pruning to improve the inference efficiency. We assume only the current friends of an ego may act as her intermediaries, and an intermediary can only recommend her current friends. Thus we add the constraint that for each individual her intermediary preference distribution and friendship strength distribution are only defined over her current friends. Each individual maintains a unique sampling space for herself. Correspondingly, the prior distributions for θ and ϕ are also restricted to be defined on the pruned space. That's why the prior parameters α and β need to be defined for each individual u and are placed within the big box labelled U in the graphical model shown in Fig. 2(b).

3.2 Model Inference

We apply Gibbs sampling technique to infer the LaFT-LDA and further obtain the LaFT-Tuples. Gibbs sampling is a special case of Markov-Chain Monte Carlo (MCMC) methods, which can emulate high-dimensional probability distributions by the stationary behavior of a Markov chain.

We express the joint probability of all observed and unobserved data with the hidden distributions integrated out, as follows:

$$P(Z, X, Y; \alpha, \beta) = \prod_{u=1}^{U} \frac{B(\Omega_u + \alpha_u)}{B(\alpha_u)} \cdot \prod_{u=1}^{U} \frac{B(\Lambda_u + \Psi_u + \beta_u)}{B(\beta_u)} \tag{1}$$

where $B(\cdot)$ is the multinomial Beta function.

The key of Gibbs sampling is to update the estimation for hidden variables iteratively. In LaFT-LDA, the only hidden variable is z. In each iteration of Gibbs sampling, we sample z for each new friendship i according to the conditional probability $p(z_i|Z_{-i}, X, Y; \alpha, \beta)$. Y and X are the new friendship and the interaction data respectively, and Z is estimation for the intermediary for each friendship. Z_{-i} is the current estimation except z_i.

The sampling probabilities can be estimated by

$$\begin{aligned} p(z_i|Z_{-i}, X, Y; \alpha, \beta) &= \frac{p(Z, X, Y; \alpha, \beta)}{p(Z_{-i}, X, Y; \alpha, \beta)} \\ &= \frac{\Omega_{u_i,z_i} + \alpha_{u_i,z_i} - 1}{\sum_{z \in F(u_i)} (\Omega_{u_i,z} + \alpha_{u_i,z}) - 1} \\ &\cdot \frac{\Lambda_{z_i,y_i} + \Psi_{z_i,y_i} + \beta_{z_i,y_i} - 1}{\sum_{v \in F(z_i)} (\Lambda_{z_i,v} + \Psi_{z_i,v} + \beta_{z_i,v}) - 1} \end{aligned} \tag{2}$$

Given the estimations for all unobserved data, we can estimate the hidden distributions:

Algorithm 1 LaFT-LDA Inference using Gibbs Sampling

Require:
The snapshot network $G_{t_{i-1}}$ at time t_{i-1}
The increment of the network in period T_i, ΔG_{T_i}
The interaction set in period T_i, X_{T_i}
Ensure:
The hidden distributions θ, ϕ
The intermediary estimations Z
Initialize F, Y using $G_{t_{i-1}}, \Delta G_{T_i}$ respectively
Assign intermediaries for each new friendship randomly
while not finished **do**
  for each individual u who has new friends **do**
    for each new friend $y \in Y(u)$ **do**
      Sample intermediary using Eq. 2
    end for
  end for
end while
Update distributions θ, ϕ using Eq. 3 - 4
for each new friendship $\langle u, y \rangle$ **do**
  Set $z_{u,y}$ using the most frequent intermediary assignments for this friendship
end for
return θ, ϕ, Z

$$\theta_{u,z} = \frac{\Omega_{u,z} + \alpha_{u,z}}{\sum_{z' \in F_u} (\Omega_{u,z'} + \alpha_{u,z'})} \tag{3}$$

$$\phi_{z,v} = \frac{\Lambda_{z,v} + \Psi_{z,v} + \beta_{z,v}}{\sum_{v' \in F_z} (\Lambda_{z,v'} + \Psi_{z,v'} + \beta_{z,v'})} \tag{4}$$

Now we present the inference framework in Algorithm 1. At the beginning, it initializes the friends set F before period T_i, and the new friendships Y that emerge in T_i. Then it randomly picks intermediary for each new friendship. For each friendship each common friend is a candidate intermediary. In each iteration the intermediary assignments are updated using Eq. 2. The iteration is repeated until convergence or the count of iterations reaches a given threshold, and then the hidden distributions are estimated using Eq. 3-4. This algorithm cannot give the exact intermediaries due to its sampling nature; however, we can get the approximate intermediaries by selecting the most frequent one from the repetitive samples.

For each period we apply the LaFT-LDA to infer all the intermediaries z for each friendship and thus get the LaFT-Tuples; further we concatenate the LaFT-Tuples to get the LaFT-Traces, which can be united to build the final LaFT-Trees.

3.3 Learning LaFT-Tree with Cascade LaFT-LDA

By splitting the evolving social network $\mathbb{G}$ into discrete snapshots $G_{t_1}, G_{t_2}, \cdots, G_{t_n}$ and inferring the LaFT-LDA model on each snapshot independently, we can get the LaFT-Tuples, the elements of the LaFT-Trees for each period respectively. However, it's inaccurate for modeling the network evolution because in each period LaFT-LDA only considers the new behaviors but ignores the knowledge of the previous behavior history.

For learning the complete evolving LaFT-Trees, we apply the LaFT-LDA in cascade, during which the subsequent models can inherit the knowledge learned from the earlier models.

As the prior parameters of the LaFT-LDA bring important priori knowledge to the model, we infer the cascade LaFT-LDA by allowing the knowledge in the previous periods be transferred into the next period by the prior parameters. We define the prior parameters of the LaFT-LDA for period T_i using the linear combination of the accumulated knowledge from previous models encoded by their prior parameters and the new knowledge encoded by the statistics in the last period T_{i-1}. Specifically, we define:

$$\alpha_{u,z}^{(T_i)} = \lambda \cdot \alpha_{u,z}^{(T_{i-1})} + \Omega_{u,z}^{(T_{i-1})} \quad (5)$$

$$\beta_{u,v}^{(T_i)} = \lambda \cdot \beta_{u,v}^{T_{i-1}} + \Lambda_{u,v}^{(T_{i-1})} + \Omega_{u,v}^{(T_{i-1})} \quad (6)$$

where λ is the cascade damping factor. A higher λ allows the subsequent models to inherit more priori information from the earlier models.

For the new friends, which are also the new candidate intermediaries, of each ego, the prior parameters can be initialized with the default values α_0 and β_0. However, we can incorporate the priori knowledge from the learned LaFT-Trees in previous models to distinguish the intermediaries with various importance. The LaFT-Tree shows the multiple growth traces of one's circle of friends, and the importance of the paths in the tree are different. A new node locating at an important path is assumed to have a higher value for the prior parameter. Thus we let the new intermediary partially inherent the prior parameters of its parent on the LaFT-Tree of the ego; that means, the prior parameters of the new intermediary is proportional to that of its parent intermediary.

In summary, the cascade LaFT-LDA allows knowledge accumulation via prior parameters of the models and the learned LaFT-Trees in the model inference on the sequential snapshots. By applying the LaFT-LDA in cascade, we can get the up-to-date evolving LaFT-Trees for the evolving social network.

4. EXPERIMENTAL EVALUATION

In this section, we evaluate the effectiveness of the proposed LaFT-LDA for LaFT-Tree inference. As the LaFT-Tuples are the basic components of LaFT-Trees, we focus on the inferred LaFT-Tuples instead of the complete LaFT-Trees. For each friendship $\langle u, v \rangle$, we try to infer the most possible intermediary z which forms the LaFT-Tuple (u, z, v).

4.1 The Synthetic Data

It's difficult to evaluate the soundness of our proposed inference algorithms for the LaFT-Tree on real data because the intermediaries are completely unobservable in online social networks. Thus we conduct experiments on synthetic data which simulate the evolution of social networks, during which the effect of the intermediaries is considered. Our goal here is to generate synthetic networks and the corresponding LaFT-Trees, and then try to recover the original LaFT-Trees based on the evolution history of the network and the interaction history among the nodes.

Our synthetic model assumes that the evolution of the network is driven by the LaFT-LDA model, in other words, based on the friendship transitivity principle. We generate the synthetic network $\mathbb{G}$ in each periods as follows. The set of nodes V_{T_0} is initialized to contain U_0 nodes firstly. In each of the following periods T_i, ΔU new individuals, and a number of new friendship edges and interaction edges are added to G_{T_i} respectively. For each user, the count of new friendships and interactions follow the Gaussian distribution with mean as N and V respectively. The new friendships and interactions are sampled according to the similar generative process described in Section 3.1. Each time when one makes new friends, the algorithm produces a probability deciding whether she makes new friend directly or via an existing friend as the intermediary. For the former situation, a new friend is sampled randomly; for the latter, she will first choose an intermediary according to the intermediary preference distribution and then choose one of the friends of the intermediary according to the friendship strength distribution. Similarly, the interactions are generated according to the friendship strength distributions.

Table 2: The count of pseudo ground-truth LaFT-Tuples collected from each dataset in each year.

Year	**dblp**	**astro-ph**	**cond-mat**	**hep-ex**	**hep-th**	**nucl-ex**
1992	1292	-	-	-	-	-
1993	2052	-	-	-	28	-
1994	2340	32	-	-	74	-
1995	2880	164	40	-	120	-
1996	3166	394	112	-	102	142
1997	4252	690	302	-	202	66
1998	5214	2818	462	-	226	78
1999	6731	4926	792	214	254	574
2000	8470	7352	1310	132	254	736
2001	9566	11206	1820	344	296	1628
2002	12131	12196	2428	590	386	1222
2003	17110	17010	3370	250	412	1782
2004	22010	24150	4672	372	440	2908
2005	29660	28938	4800	686	456	2256
2006	35040	42892	6098	764	480	5390
2007	43984	50594	6474	878	626	5728
2008	49971	57460	9000	2624	794	9164
2009	57978	78472	9818	4726	684	11028
2010	67278	110338	11850	8876	842	14590
2011	73220	124048	12798	17464	842	20142

4.2 The Real-world Data

We construct 6 real-world datasets from DBLP[1] and Arxiv[2]. DBLP is a computer science bibliography and Arxiv is an archive for electronic preprints of scientific papers in the fields of mathematics, physics, etc. We construct the dataset **dblp** from DBLP and 5 datasets from Arxiv including **astro-ph** (Astrophysics), **cond-mat** (Condensed Matter), **hep-ex** (High Energy Physics - Experiment), **hep-th** (High Energy Physics - Theory) and **nucl-ex** (Nuclear Experiment).

It's usually intractable to observe the real intermediaries in real-world social networks. Luckily, scholar collaborative network is a kind of common social networks and reveals some features which may benefit our evaluation. Many scientific papers are written by more than two authors; thus, via this paper we can say one of the authors created friendships with all of others. Taking a paper written by A, B and C as instance, if A and B have never collaborated with each other but both of them have co-authored with C before, we can assume C acted as the intermediary via whom A and B knew each other. Thus we can say (A, C, B) and (B, C, A) are two *pseudo ground-truth LaFT-Tuples*. Based on this assumption, we collect these pseudo ground-truth LaFT-Tuples in real-world scholar collaborative networks as ground truth to evaluate the intermediary inference performance of our model. In some sense, this can also be regarded as the co-author prediction task. The statistics of the pseudo ground-truth LaFT-Tuples we collect from each dataset are shown in Table 2.

4.3 Baselines

We consider the two variants of our LaFT-LDA model: *Standalone LaFT-LDA* and *Cascade LaFT-LDA*. The former infers the LaFT-LDA model in each period independently while the latter allows knowledge accumulation by inferring LaFT-LDA in cascade. We compare them with two baseline methods:

[1]DBLP: http://dblp.uni-trier.de/

[2]Arxiv: http://arxiv.org/

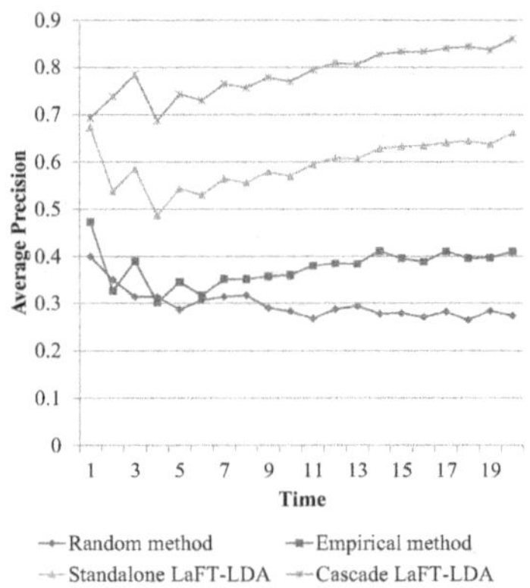

(a) $N = 5$

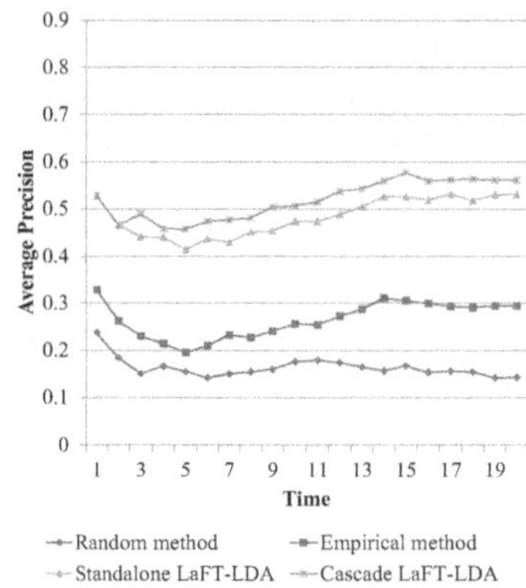

(b) $N = 10$

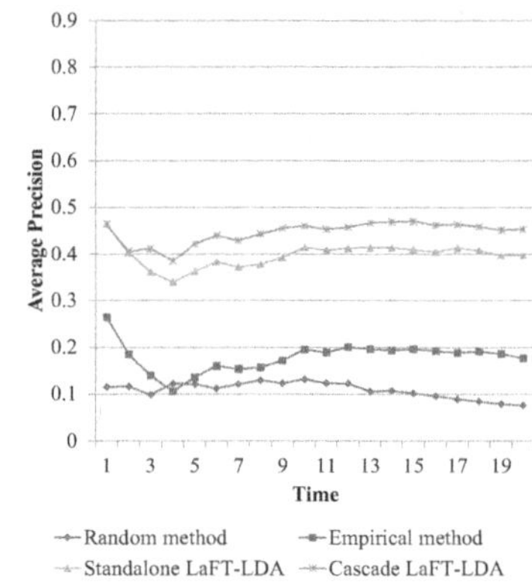

(c) $N = 15$

Figure 3: The evaluation results for intermediary inference on synthetic networks generated by the method described in Section 4.1. Here, we set $U_0 = 50, \Delta U = 50, n = 20$, and observe how the performance varies with N. For *Cascade LaFT-LDA* we set the cascade damping factor $\lambda = 0.5$.

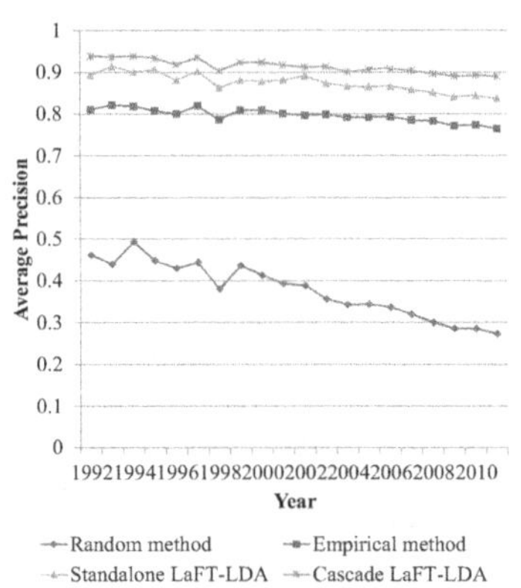

(a) dblp

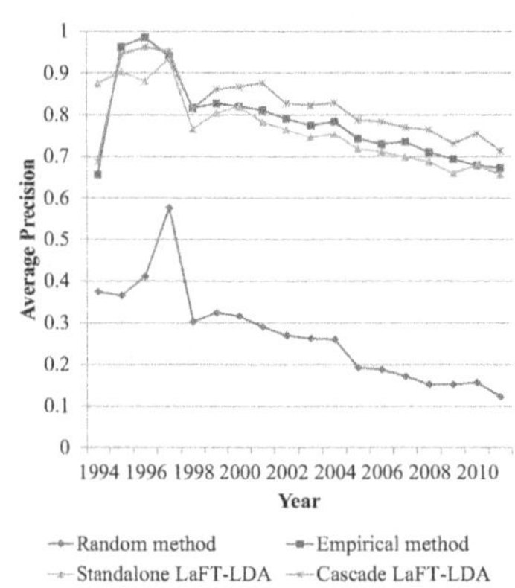

(b) astro-ph

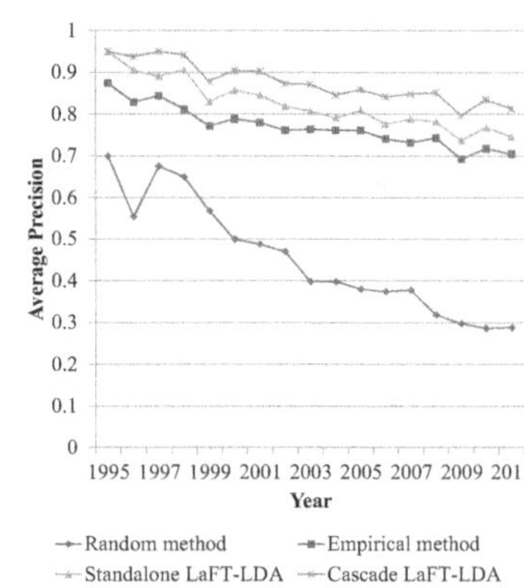

(c) cond-mat

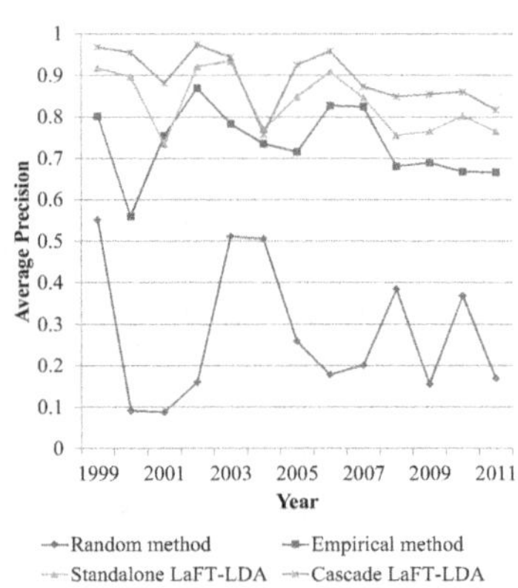

(d) hep-ex

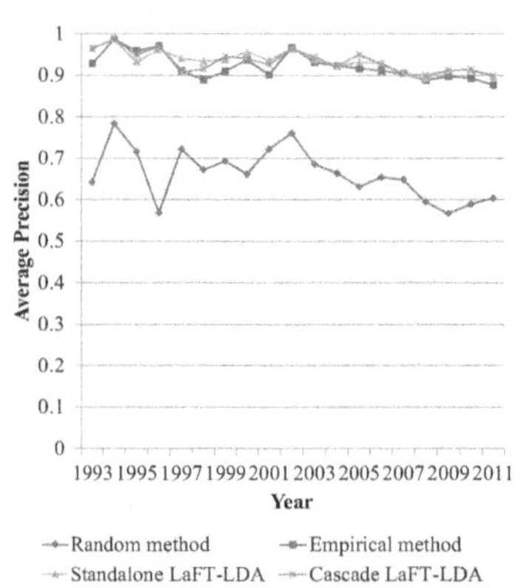

(e) hep-th

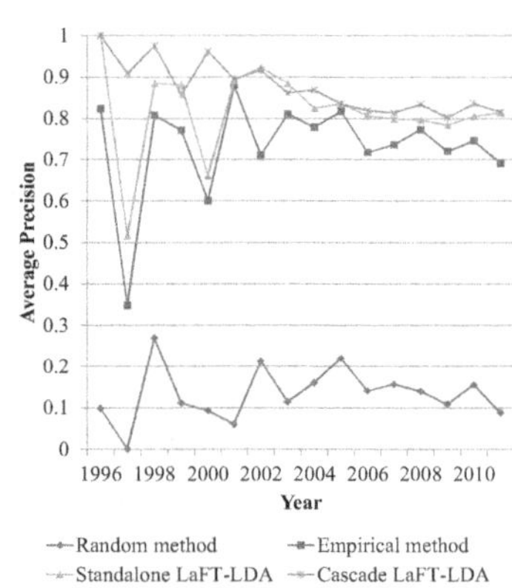

(f) nucl-ex

Figure 4: The intermediary inference results on the real-world datasets.

- *Random method*: For each friendship $\langle u, v \rangle$, select one of their common friends randomly as the intermediary.

- *Empirical method*: For each friendship $\langle u, v \rangle$, each common friend is a candidate and the one with most common friends with u is selected as the inferred intermediary.

4.4 Results on Synthetic Data

We conduct this experiment on the synthetic data generated by the method described in Section 4.1. In order to evaluate how the performance varies with the sparsity of the network, we make the network grow with different speed. Due to the assumption that only one intermediary is considered for each friendship, our models

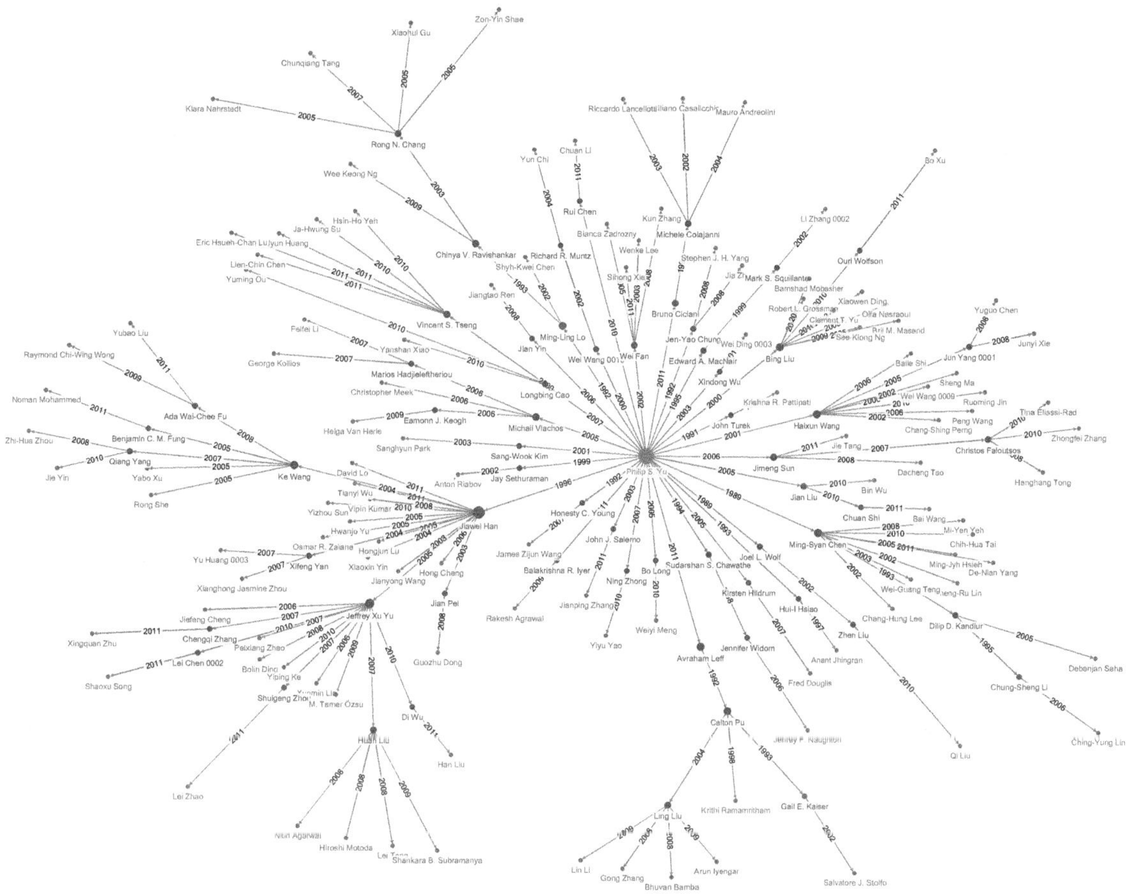

Figure 5: The Inferred LaFT-Tree of *Philip S. Yu*

also just infer the top-1 most likely intermediary. Thus, we only report the average precision of the models because the recall gives no other information. The results are shown in Figure 3.

We can see that both *Standalone LaFT-LDA* and *Cascade LaFT-LDA* outperform other methods on all of the datasets. This benefits from the capability of LaFT-LDA for capturing the latent friendship propagation traces. Furthermore, we observe that in the early periods, the *Standalone LaFT-LDA* and *Cascade LaFT-LDA* show similar performance, however, the latter outperforms the former quickly in the following periods. This results demonstrate the effect of knowledge accumulation by prior knowledge.

Besides, all of the models show worse performance when the grow speed becomes faster, i.e. when in each period more new friendships are established in the network. If one makes many new friends in an interval, it'll become difficult to distinguish the features of these friends from each other, which leads to the confused distributions. However, our *LaFT-LDA* models show more powerful capability of capturing the hidden distributions no matter how the network grows.

4.5 Results on Real-world Data

Figure 4 shows the average precision of intermediary inference on the real-world datasets. We can see that the *LaFT-LDA* Models outperform the baselines in most occasions. This confirms that in real world the transitivity of friendship really plays important role in the formation of friendships and the intermediaries really exist as co-authors connecting two disconnected people. It's also proved that *LaFT-LDA* is effective for inferring the intermediary and predicting the co-authors. The *Cascade LaFT-LDA* always performs better than the *Standalone LaFT-LDA*, demonstrating the effect of knowledge accumulation in cascades. Furthermore, we can see the *empirical method* achieves higher precision than the *random method*. The *empirical method* considers the one who has the most common friends with the ego as the intermediary based on the empirical assumption that one is more likely to make new friends via the friend with whom she has more common friends. However, it ignores the sequential relationship among the social behaviors and cannot model the actual contribution of each intermediary on the link formations. On the contrary, by modeling the generative process of each friendship based on the principle of transitivity of friendship, our *LaFT-LDA* models achieve promising performance.

4.6 A Case Study on DBLP

In this section, we take *Philip S. Yu* as an example to show the effectiveness and informativeness of our proposed LaFT-Tree. The LaFT-Tree of *Philip S. Yu* inferred from the **dblp** dataset is shown in Figure 5. The root of the tree is *Philip S. Yu*, marked with red, and each of other nodes is a researcher who has ever co-published at least one paper with *Philip S. Yu*. The blue nodes represent the intermediaries of *Philip S. Yu* and the green nodes are co-authors via whom *Philip S. Yu* hasn't made new friendships yet. Other non-intermediary co-authors are omitted for brevity.

We can see that *Jiawei Han* leads the largest subtree, implying that *Philip S. Yu* is likely to build friendships with the co-authors of

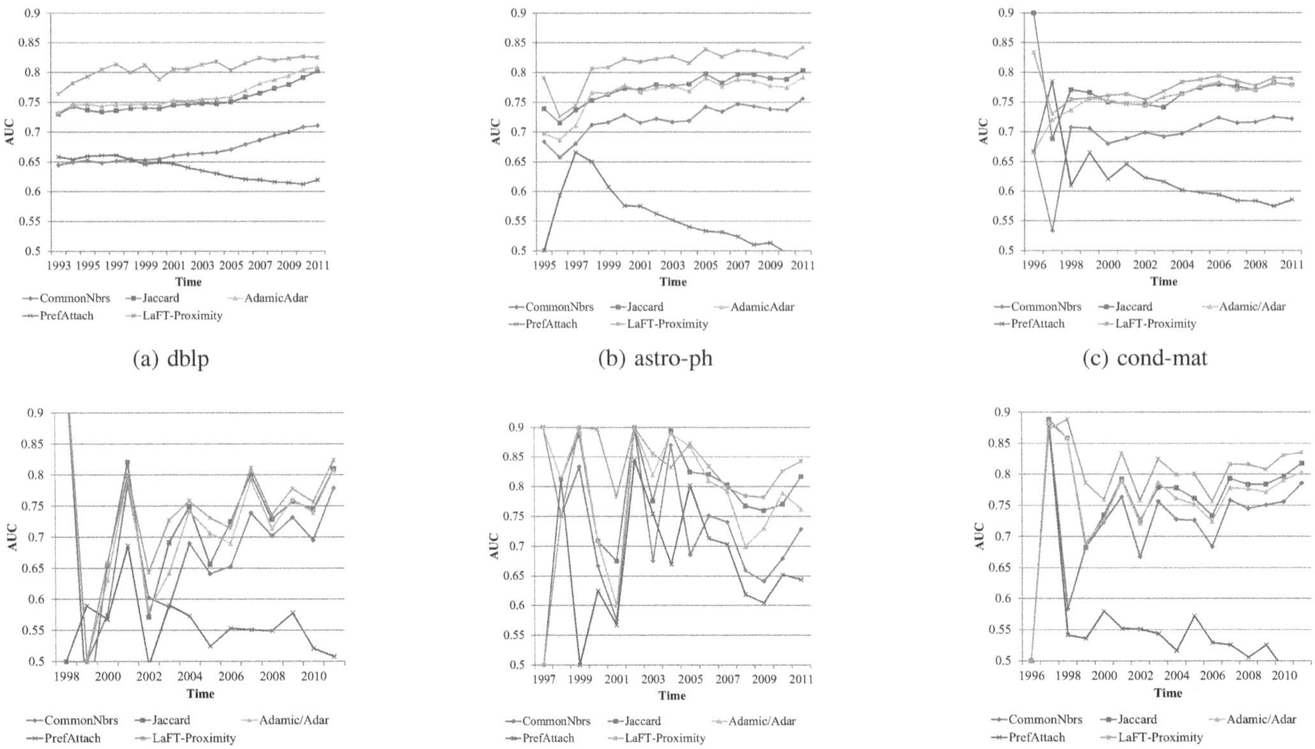

(a) dblp (b) astro-ph (c) cond-mat

(d) hep-ex (e) hep-th (f) nucl-ex

Figure 6: The link prediction performance on 6 real-world datasets.

Jiawei Han. Furthermore, two subbranches growing from *Ke Wang* and *Jeffrey Xu Yu* of the *Jiawei Han*'s branch are also luxuriant, showing the closeness of *Philip S. Yu* with this community.

The variance of *Philip S. Yu*'s preference for friends and intermediaries is also revealed by this tree. Since *Philip S. Yu* knew *Haixun Wang* at 2001, he co-authored with many friends of the latter in the following years. However, *Vincent S. Tseng*, *Bing Liu*, *Ling Liu* and *Huan Liu* become important intermediaries of *Philip S. Yu* in recent years. *Ming-Syan Chen* should be a close intermediary of *Philip S. Yu* for that the former keeps recommending new friends to the latter since their friendship was created at 1989.

5. APPLICATIONS

In this section, we apply the LaFT-Tree and LaFT-LDA in other interesting tasks and illustrate the generality of our model. Specifically, based on our model, we propose LaFT-Proximity for link prediction, LaFT-Patterns for analyzing the expansion traces of social networks and a family of LaFT-Centrality measures for evaluating the importance of nodes in social networks.

5.1 LaFT-Proximity for Link Prediction

Among the applications is link prediction, a classical task which aims to predict the new links given the current social network. One of the most common approaches is based on the topological proximity, assuming that the similar nodes are likely to become friends in the future [17] . As LaFT-LDA models people's social behaviors, we can get a new topological proximity measure, **LaFT-Proximity** for link prediction, with the effect of the intermediaries taken into consideration:

$$\text{LaFT-Proximity}(u, v) = \sum_{z \in \mathcal{F}(u,v)} \theta_{u,z} \cdot \phi_{z,v}. \quad (7)$$

5.1.1 Experimental Study

We evaluate LaFT-Proximity in the link prediction tasks on the real-world datasets introduced in Section 4.2. Given a snapshot of the evolving network $\mathbb{G}$ at time t_i, we predict the new links in t_{i+1}. In this problem, we only predict the new born edges without considering the new born vertices, and for each ego we only consider the 2-hop neighbors as candidate friends since 2-hop connections are dominant in link formations [14].

We compare LaFT-Proximity with some other popular topological proximity measures, including *Common Neighbors*, *Jaccard Coefficient*, *Adamic / Adar* and *Preferential Attachment.* For the details of these measures one can refer to [17]. Due to the goal of this task is to demonstrate the potential of LaFT model for link prediction, we just use the basic popular measures and don't devote to highly complicated, maybe more powerful, algorithms. We use popular AUC (Area Under the ROC Curve) to evaluate the performance of the aforementioned measures.

Figure 6 displays the AUC value of the link prediction results on each dataset and in each year. We can see that *LaFT-Proximity* achieves the best performance on almost all of the datasets. *Preferential Attachment* is always the worst and *Common Neighbours* comes next. Both *Jaccard Coefficient* and *Adamic/Adar* measure the proximity of two nodes by distinguishing the importance of their common friends based on the structural features. Unlike them, *LaFT-Proximity* is based on the transitivity of friendship, a fundamental sociological principle for explaining link formation, and regard the common friends as potential intermediaries with various influence on the expansion of one's friend circles. By modeling the friend-making behaviors with one's preference for intermediaries and new friends taken into consideration, *LaFT-Proximity* performs better than other measures.

Table 3: The top 10 researchers in *data mining* in 2011 ranked by various centrality measures.

PageRank	LaFT-Intermediation	LaFT-Recommendation	LaFT-Hub	LaFT-Authority
Jiawei Han	Jiawei Han	Hector Garcia-Molina	Philip S. Yu	Jiawei Han
Philip S. Yu	Christos Faloutsos	Christos Faloutsos	Huan Liu	Huan Liu
Christos Faloutsos	Gerhard Weikum	Jiawei Han	Wei Wang	Yiyu Yao
Gerhard Weikum	Hector Garcia-Molina	Philip S. Yu	Jiawei Han	Jeffrey Xu Yu
Hector Garcia-Molina	Philip S. Yu	Gerhard Weikum	Jeffrey Xu Yu	Philip S. Yu
Bing Liu	Hans-Peter Kriegel	C. Lee Giles	Jian Pei	Charu C. Aggarwal
Ke Wang	Daniel A. Keim	Huan Liu	Gerhard Weikum	Jian Pei
Jian Pei	Beng Chin Ooi	Hans-Peter Kriegel	Jon M. Kleinberg	Jaideep Srivastava
C. Lee Giles	Bing Liu	Daniel A. Keim	Haixun Wang	Bing Liu
Daniel A. Keim	C. Lee Giles	Beng Chin Ooi	Beng Chin Ooi	Xifeng Yan

5.2 LaFT-Patterns

The LaFT-Traces show one's friend-making sequences and such behavior sequences may contain valuable information about how people usually expand their friend circles. We're interested in whether there exist some sequence patterns for one to make new friends. We define the frequent subsequences of the LaFT-Traces as *LaFT-Patterns*, denoted by $(s_1, s_2, \cdots, s_n)$. The pattern means that someone who is a friend of s_1 will likely be a friend of s_2 later, and then a friend of s_n in the future.

We apply PrefixSpan algorithm [21] on our LaFT-Traces collection learned from the **dblp** dataset. In the area of *data mining*, the length-5 patterns with highest support include (*Alon Y. Levy, Jayant Madhavan, Philip A. Bernstein, Raghu Ramakrishnan, Jeffrey F. Naughton*), (*Beng Chin Ooi, Hongjun Lu, Aoying Zhou, Wen Jin, Jian Pei*) and (*Daniel P. Lopresti, Richard J. Lipton, Avrim Blum, Prabhakar Raghavan, Jon M. Kleinberg*). Among the length-4 patterns are (*Shih-Fu Chang, John R. Smith, Chung-Sheng Li, Philip S. Yu*), (*Daniel P. Lopresti, Richard J. Lipton, Avrim Blum, Prabhakar Raghavan*), (*Baile Shi, Zengping Tian, Hongjun Lu, Beng Chin Ooi*), (*Beng Chin Ooi, Jiawei Han, Philip S. Yu, Jian Pei*). *Jian Pei*, *Jon M. Kleinberg*, *Philip S. Yu* and *Jiawei Han* appear in most of the identified patterns, implying that they are among the most active researchers.

LaFT-Patterns show important axes of the whole structure of the network and indicate how people expand their networks in every circle. Given the LaFT-Pattern (*Beng Chin Ooi, Jiawei Han, Philip S. Yu, Jian Pei*), we can infer that someone who is a friend of *Beng Chin Ooi* is likely to become a friend of *Jiawei Han* and then connects to *Philip S. Yu* and *Jian Pei* later. This pattern also reveals that many people associate with *Philip S. Yu* via some paths including *Jiawei Han* and make friends with *Jian Pei* benefiting from the recommendations of *Jiawei Han* and *Philip S. Yu*.

5.3 LaFT-Centrality Family

People's intermediary preference and friendship strength provide new perspectives for calculating the importance of nodes w.r.t. their influence on the network evolution. We incorporate the two distributions, θ and ϕ, into the popular PageRank and HITS algorithms as the personalized weights, yielding a family of centrality measures. Specifically, *LaFT-Intermediation Centrality* uses the intermediary preference as personalized weights in PageRank and thus produces the most important intermediaries, while *LaFT-Recommendation Centrality* takes the friendship strength in PageRank and ranks the individuals based on the extent to which others would like to recommend them to their friends. Adapting with HITS, *LaFT-Hub Centrality* ranks the individuals high if via them others may get to know new friends of high quality, and *LaFT-Authority Centrality* ranks them high if many important individuals will recommend them to their friends. All the four measures analyze the importance of the individuals in the network from the role of them in promoting the network evolution.

The top 10 researchers in the domain of *data mining* ranked by various measures are shown in Table 3. We can conclude that *Jiawei Han* and *Christos Faloutsos* are the most important intermediaries, and *Hector Garcia-Molina* and *Christos Faloutsos* are most likely to be introduced to others. From another perspective, via *Philip S. Yu* and *Huan Liu* people can know most authoritative researchers, while most influential researchers will recommend *Jiawei Han* and *Huan Liu*, etc.

6. RELATED WORK

The evolution of social networks has attracted considerable attention recently from both the macroscopic and microscopic perspectives. In macroscopic view, researchers focused on the varying global properties of the networks [12][15]. Many evolution models have been proposed to model the evolving social networks, including Preferential Attachment [1], Copying Model [13] and Forest Fire Model [15], etc. In microscopic view, researchers studied the formation and variation of the links in the network. It has been formulated as the link prediction task since the seminal work of Liben-Nowell and Kleinberg [17]. Furthermore, people are also interested in the patterns which describe how the network evolves [14] and how people make friends [10]. They've found many interesting patterns, such as *preferential attachment* [19], *triadic closure* [14][23], *reciprocity* [20][9] and *homophily* [18][5]. Besides, researchers also studied the general evolution patterns with arbitrary structures [16][2].

Triadic closure has been noticed by sociologists long ago. Simmel provided several theoretical rationales for proffering the triad as the basic social unit and theorized that people with common friends are more likely to create friendships [24]. This theory then was applied by Krackhardt and Handcock to explain the evolution of triangle closures [11]. Triadic closure has also been explained using the transitivity of friendship [22]. Recently, the role of triadic closure was further investigated and it was found that most of the links are likely to close triangles, i.e., connect people with common friends [14]. Golder and Yardi found that transitivity and reciprocity ties can increase the likelihood of forming relationships in Twitter [7]. Romero and Kleinberg developed a formalization and methodology for studying the directed triadic closure process, and provided evidence for its important role in the formation of links on Twitter [23]. Triadic closure has also been utilized for friend recommendation [4] and network evolution prediction [6]. However, it hasn't been studied that how the triadic closure works in various situations. In this paper, we conduct in-depth research on triadic closure based on behavior modeling.

Simmel analyzed the roles of the participants in the triadic structure and pointed out the possible role of the third person in interactions as mediation and brokerage, referred to as *intermediaries* in this paper. Nevertheless, it's still unknown how the third person will affect or promote the new link. Yin et al. studied the link prediction problem taking the intermediary into consideration and regarded the link formation as the result of the pseudo recommendation of the intermediate node [25]. They decomposed the adjacency matrix of the current social network into two matrixes, one of which presents the intermediary preference probability and the other presents the recommendation acceptance probability. Unlike their work which analyzes the pseudo intermediary effect in a static snapshot of the network, we try to find the real intermediaries and study how the intermediaries contribute to the link formations.

7. CONCLUSION

Can we go further in explaining the link formation in social networks? Inspired by the famous sociological principle, i.e. the transitivity of friendship, and several classical work which proved the importance of intermediaries in creating new friendships, we study the link formation using behavior modeling. Specifically, we study the triadic closure, one of the most frequent patterns in the network evolution. In this paper, while most new links form triangles, we further argue that some nodes are particularly favored when this happens.

In such a world, we propose the LaFT-Tree, a tree-based representation of friendship formation which captures the growing process of one's egocentric network driven by the triadic closure. Furthermore, we propose a generative model, LaFT-LDA, to model the social behaviors in social networks. LaFT-LDA can be inferred from data with timestamped links and utilized to solve the question of "who are the most likely intermediaries that connect the ego and others", and further build the LaFT-Trees. The model is evaluated on synthetic data and DBLP/Arxiv collaboration networks. In addition, we also present interesting applications of the LaFT-Tree and LaFT-LDA for social network analysis, illustrating the generality of our model on other problems and the capability for understanding the evolving structure of social networks.

8. ACKNOWLEDGMENTS

We would like to thank the anonymous reviewers for their valuable comments and suggestions to improve this paper. This work is supported in part by the National Natural Science Foundation of China (No. 61170064, No. 61073005, No. 61133002), the National Basic Research Program of China (No. 2012AA011002) and the National HeGaoJi Key Project (No. 2010ZX01042-002-002-01), and Philip S. Yu is partially supported by US NSF through grants IIS-0905215, CNS-1115234, IIS-0914934, DBI-0960443, and OISE-1129076, US Department of Army through grant W911NF-12-1-0066, Google Mobile 2014 Program and KAU grant.

9. REFERENCES

[1] A.-L. Barabĺési and R. Albert. Emergence of scaling in random networks. *Science*, 286(5439):509–512, 1999.

[2] M. Berlingerio, F. Bonchi, B. O. R. Bringmann, and A. Gionis. Mining graph evolution rules. In *ECML PKDD '09*, pages 115–130, 2009.

[3] D. M. Blei, A. Y. Ng, and M. I. Jordan. Latent dirichlet allocation. *J. Mach. Learn. Res.*, 3:993–1022, Mar. 2003.

[4] M. J. Brzozowski and D. M. Romero. Who should i follow? recommending people in directed social networks. In *ICWSM'11*, 2011.

[5] M. De Choudhury. Tie formation on twitter: Homophily and structure of egocentric networks. In *SocialCom/PASSAT '11*, pages 465–470, 2011.

[6] M. Doroud, P. Bhattacharyya, S. F. Wu, and D. Felmlee. The evolution of ego-centric triads: A microscopic approach toward predicting macroscopic network properties. In *SocialCom/PASSAT '11*, pages 172–179, 2011.

[7] S. A. Golder and S. Yardi. Structural predictors of tie formation in twitter: Transitivity and mutuality. In *SocialCom/PASSAT '10*, pages 88–95, 2010.

[8] M. S. Granovetter. The Strength of Weak Ties. *The American Journal of Sociology*, 78(6):1360–1380, 1973.

[9] J. Hopcroft, T. Lou, and J. Tang. Who will follow you back?: reciprocal relationship prediction. In *CIKM '11*, pages 1137–1146, 2011.

[10] H. Hu and X. Wang. How people make friends in social networking sites - a microscopic perspective. *Physica A: Statistical Mechanics and its Applications*, 391(4):1877–1886, 2012.

[11] D. Krackhardt and M. S. Handcock. Heider vs simmel: emergent features in dynamic structures. In *Proceedings of the 2006 conference on Statistical network analysis*, ICML'06, pages 14–27, 2007.

[12] R. Kumar, J. Novak, and A. Tomkins. Structure and evolution of online social networks. In *KDD '06*, pages 611–617, 2006.

[13] R. Kumar, P. Raghavan, S. Rajagopalan, D. Sivakumar, A. Tomkins, and E. Upfal. Stochastic models for the web graph. In *FOCS '00*, pages 57 –65, 2000.

[14] J. Leskovec, L. Backstrom, R. Kumar, and A. Tomkins. Microscopic evolution of social networks. In *KDD '08*, pages 462–470, 2008.

[15] J. Leskovec, J. Kleinberg, and C. Faloutsos. Graph evolution: Densification and shrinking diameters. *ACM Trans. Knowl. Discov. Data*, 1(1), 2007.

[16] C. W.-k. Leung, E.-P. Lim, D. Lo, and J. Weng. Mining interesting link formation rules in social networks. In *CIKM '10*, pages 209–218, 2010.

[17] D. Liben-Nowell and J. Kleinberg. The link prediction problem for social networks. In *CIKM '03*, pages 556–559, 2003.

[18] M. McPherson, L. Smith-Lovin, and J. M. Cook. Birds of a feather: Homophily in social networks. *ANNUAL REVIEW OF SOCIOLOGY*, 27:415–444, 2001.

[19] M. E. J. Newman. Clustering and preferential attachment in growing networks. *PHYS.REV.E*, 64:025102, 2001.

[20] V.-A. Nguyen, E.-P. Lim, H.-H. Tan, J. Jiang, and A. Sun. Do you trust to get trust? a study of trust reciprocity behaviors and reciprocal trust prediction. In *SDM '10*, pages 72–83, 2010.

[21] J. Pei, J. Han, B. Mortazavi-Asl, H. Pinto, Q. Chen, U. Dayal, and M. Hsu. Prefixspan: Mining sequential patterns by prefix-projected growth. In *ICDE '01*, pages 215–224, 2001.

[22] A. Rapoport. Spread of information through a population with socio-structural bias: I. assumption of transitivity. *Bulletin of Mathematical Biology*, 15:523–533, 1953.

[23] D. M. Romero and J. Kleinberg. The directed closure process in hybrid social-information networks, with an analysis of link formation on twitter. In *ICWSM '10*, 2010.

[24] G. Simmel and K. H. Wolff. *The Sociology of Georg Simmel*. Free Press, 1964.

[25] D. Yin, L. Hong, and B. D. Davison. Structural link analysis and prediction in microblogs. In *CIKM '11*, pages 1163–1168, 2011.

A Peek into the Future: Predicting the Evolution of Popularity in User Generated Content

Mohamed Ahmed
NEC Laboratories Europe
Heidelberg, Germany
ahmed@neclab.eu

Stella Spagna
Dept. of Inf. Engineering
Univ. of Pisa, Italy
stella.spagna@iet.unipi.it

Felipe Huici
NEC Laboratories Europe
Heidelberg, Germany
huici@neclab.eu

Saverio Niccolini
NEC Laboratories Europe
Heidelberg, Germany
niccolini@neclab.eu

ABSTRACT

Content popularity prediction finds application in many areas, including media advertising, content caching, movie revenue estimation, traffic management and macro-economic trends forecasting, to name a few. However, predicting this popularity is difficult due to, among others, the effects of external phenomena, the influence of context such as locality and relevance to users, and the difficulty of forecasting information cascades.

In this paper we identify patterns of temporal evolution that are generalisable to distinct types of data, and show that we can (1) accurately classify content based on the evolution of its popularity over time and (2) predict the value of the content's future popularity. We verify the generality of our method by testing it on YouTube, Digg and Vimeo data sets and find our results to outperform the K-Means baseline when classifying the behaviour of content and the linear regression baseline when predicting its popularity.

Categories and Subject Descriptors

H.3.3 [**Information Search and Retrieval**]: Clustering

General Terms

Algorithm, Measurement

Keywords

Social Media, Time Series Clustering

1. INTRODUCTION

The large and growing body of user-generated content available on the Internet (e.g., blogs, videos, news postings, etc.) presents important opportunities for both understanding how users utilise the Internet and enhancing their experiences. Amongst the challenges here is the accurate forecasting of the popularity of contents to users.

Numerous proposals have been made for applications to make use of popularity information. These include media advertising [14, 22, 30], trend forecasting [2, 20, 22, 28], movie revenue estimation [5], traffic management [4, 9, 13], understanding the collective behaviour of users [11, 21, 36], election prediction [6, 32, 34] and macro economic trend forecasting [3, 35, 37].

However, predicting the popularity of content is difficult for many reasons. Among these, the effects of external phenomena (e.g., media, natural, geo-political) are difficult to incorporate into models [11, 24]. While cascades of information are difficult to forecast [10]. Finally, the underlying context of content such as locality, relevance to users, and resonance/impact, are often difficult to decipher [7].

In this work, we show that content popularity can be predicted without making too many assumptions regarding the underlying phenomena. To do so, we take a two-step approach. First, we categorise the behaviour of content overtime to reveal distinct patterns of popularity growth (over time) that generalise the variety of different behaviours displayed by large numbers of content. Second, based on this result we show that it is possible to predict the future popularity of content (with high accuracy) by tracing the types of popularity growth behaviour that contents display over time.

In this work, we define a simple and easily generalised feature space (Section 3), and show that it can be used to accurately categorise the behaviour of content (Section ??) and predict the evolution of its popularity (Section 5). We validate our methods using three very different data sets (Section 4). Finally, we compare our results against a baseline of K-Means for the clustering and linear regression for the prediction and show that we are able to significantly outperform both at categorising and predicting the popularity growth behaviour of content.

2. RELATED WORK

Given the breadth of this topic, it is unsurprising that there have been many approaches to address the problem of content popularity prediction. This section covers other works in the field and contrasts them with ours.

Feature space: Numerous works [2, 16, 18, 26, 27, 30] study how features that describe the underlying social net-

WSDM'13, February 4–8, 2013, Rome, Italy.

work of the users that generate and use content can be leveraged to predict its popularity. The authors in [20, 24, 25, 31] study how features that take into account comments related to the content (e.g., comments found in blogs) can be used to predict popularity. Our approach differs from these in that we use a more general feature space (simply the number of hits associated with content and their timings) so as not to over-specialise for a particular application context.

Clustering: A number of works have studied the shape of the attention paid to content over time. The works in [11, 21] show that the popularity evolution of YOUTUBE videos and TWITTER messages can be categorised based on whether the stimuli that triggers them comes from within or outside the system and whether or not the users can spread news about the event. Adar et al. [1] use dynamic time warping [19] to reveal the correlation between search queries from different content sources and show that some of this information can be used to predict whether the queries at one source (e.g., blogs) trigger queries at another (e.g., web search). Laniado and Mika [23] show that the Twitter Hashtags that represent "valuable" identifiers have distinct temporal behaviours. Finally, Yang and Leskovec [36] show that the attention paid to content over time can be characterised to reveal generalisable patterns of temporal popularity evolution.

In this work we categorise the behaviour of content over time to reveal distinct patterns of popularity growth. We show that relatively a few classes of behaviour can be used to capture population growth patterns exhibited by large numbers of different contents. Unlike previous work, we build a transition model based on the classes of behaviour identified and use this information to predict the future popularity of content.

Prediction: Amongst others [9, 10, 29] show that there is a correlation in the views that content receives over time. There are however relatively few works that forecast a value for the actual popularity of content. Lee et al. [24, 25] use survival analysis to evaluate the probability that a given content will receive more than some x number of hits. Hong et al. [17] develop a coarse multi-class classifier based approach to determine whether a given TWITTER Hashtag will be retweeted $x < (0, 100, 10000, \infty)$ times. Similarly, Lakkaraju and Ajmera [22] use Support Vector Machines to predict whether a given content will fall in a group that attracts $x < (10\%, 25\%, 50\%, 75\%, 100\%)$ of the "attention" in a system, while Jamali and Rangwala [18] predict the popularity of content using an entropy measure based on the "user-interest peak" and the "co-participatory network". Finally Szabo and Huberman [29] present a linear regression model based on the number of views; this method is applied by [7, 16, 26, 31] to build predictive popularity based on applying regression to different feature spaces.

In this work we show that a predictor based on modelling the transitions that content makes between being a member of different classes of behaviour (over time) outperforms the linear regression method commonly used in other papers (Section 5.1).

3. MODELLING THE TIME-EVOLUTION OF POPULARITY

The goal of content popularity prediction is to accurately estimate the number of hits associated with a given content object at some time in the future, based on the observation of its past behaviour.

In this section we formally define the content popularity problem, starting from the time series of the cumulative number of hits a given content attracts. We give the feature space based on the time series, and the similarity measure used to relate content. We then show how similar content may be clustered using the Affinity Propagation algorithm [15] and based on the results of the clustering, how the behaviour of individual content over time can be predicted.

The difficulty with defining a feature space for evaluating content behaviour is finding an acceptable trade-off between accuracy and over-specialisation to the application. Incorporating complex features such as social network variables, content context and other approaches reduces the generality of the feature space.

In this work we use general and publicly observable variables to predict content popularity. Specifically, we look only at the number of hits associated with content, and the timings of those hits. Based on this, we define (i) a two-variable feature space that captures the magnitude and timings of the attention content attracts from users; and (ii) a correlation-based similarity metric to group individual content based on how much alike they are in either the number of hits they attract or the timings of those hits.

To predict the popularity of content, we take a two-step approach. In the first step we cluster the data to produce a set of discretised temporal classifiers that capture the patterns of popularity evolution that contents display. In the second step, we model the probabilistic transitions that contents make between these clusters over time, and use this information to predict the future popularity of content (see Figure 1).

Our results (see Section ?? and Section 5) show that the feature space we define is generalisable to different data sets (tested on 3 distinct ones) and suitable for accurately predicting the popularity of content.

3.1 Problem Definition

Given the observations made of some N contents over a period of time T, we define $x_i(t), i \in N, t \in T$ to represent the number of hits received by content i at time t. $x_i(t)$ may be sampled to produce W windows each of length $l = \lceil \frac{T}{W} \rceil$, such that the generic element of the series is $x_i[n], n \in W$.

Given the resulting time windows, our goals are: i) to extract features that capture the particular behaviour of the content, that is, its growth in popularity relative to other observed content; ii) to use these features to derive a set of $|M| < |N|$ behaviour-sets that group together contents sharing similar properties, e.g., all contents whose popularity saturates quickly[1]; and iii) given the resulting M behaviour-sets over the W windows, to predict the future popularity of content by deriving the transition table for moving between behaviours-sets over W.

3.2 Feature Space

Because the popularity of content can be differentiated by how many hits each content attracts and when those hits arrive, we define a two-dimensional feature vector to capture this. The first feature vector is termed SA and captures the *Share of (user) Attention* a content object attracts with respect to all other observed contents at some time interval.

[1]Throughout the paper we use saturation to mean the time it takes for content to receive 90% of all their hits.

The second feature vector, termed $nROC$, captures the *normalised Rate of Change* in the attention attracted, again at some time interval.

In greater detail, the SA feature vector is a function of the number of hits some content receives, relative to the hits received by other monitored content. This is expressed as:

$$SA_i[n] = f\left(x_i[n], x_j[n], i, j \in N\right) \quad (1)$$

In the simplest case, $f(.)$ defines the ratio of $x_i[n]$ to the total number of hits ($\sum_{j \in N} x_j[n]$) in the measured interval n. However, the definition $f(.)$ is clearly subject to the application. For example, if content displays a high variance in the number of hits received, then taking a simple ratio may overestimate the impact of some contents over others. In our case, we take the ratio of the number of hits a content receives in the interval to the maximum number of hits received by contents in the interval, defined as:

$$SA_i[n] = \frac{x_i[n]}{\max\limits_{j \in N}(x_j[n])} \quad (2)$$

This measures the relative magnitude in the popularity of content i with respect to the most popular content in the set of observed contents during the interval n. Using a relative measure means that the feature is unaffected by exogenous behaviours such as diurnal patterns [8] in content use.

The $nROC$ feature, on the other hand, captures when attention is paid to content by tracking the relative change in the number of hits a content receives over time. The generic value of the $nROC$ vector is defined as:

$$nROC_i[n] = \frac{ROC_i[n]}{\max(1, \max\limits_{j \in (0, n-1)}(ROC_i[j]))} \quad (3)$$

where $ROC_i[n] = (x_i[n] - x_i[n-1])$ is the rate of change in the number of hits during the interval, and the denominator takes a range between 1 and the maximum rate of change experienced by the content thus far.

The normalisation in Equation 3 relates the number of hits a content attracts during the interval ($x_i[n]$), to the maximum it has attracted in past intervals ($\max\limits_{j \in (0, n-1)}(ROC_i[j])$), and has the following properties:

$$nROC_i[n] = \begin{cases} 0 & \text{//no hits attracted} \\ ROC_i[n] & \text{//at the first change in the \# of hits} \\ < 0 & \text{//\# hits per interval is decreasing} \\ \geq 1 & \text{//\# hits per interval is increasing} \end{cases} \quad (4)$$

3.3 Measure of similarity

The similarity between two contents at a given time interval captures to what degree they are amplitude and/or phase synchronised. In other words, it measures to what extent two contents attract similar numbers of hits (SA) or experience growth at the same time ($nROC$). For this work we define a negative similarity measure[2] such that $s_{i,j} = -1$ indicates the least similarity between the contents and $s_{i,j} = 0$ the highest.

[2]The Affinity Propagation algorithm defined in Section 3.4 requires a negative similarity measure.

With respect to the SA feature, the similarity between contents i, j is a measure of the distance between the magnitudes of their popularity based on their cross-correlation. Because the time series of two contents ($x_i[n], x_j[n]$, $\forall n$) form two piecewise constant waveforms, we may use their cross-correlation to measure their similarity as a function of a time-lag applied to one of them. Taking the maximum of the cross-correlation gives us a measure of maximum overlapping area between the waveforms. The result is normalised to a value between 0 and 1 by dividing by the auto-correlation. The SA similarity between contents i, j is therefore defined as:

$$sS_{i,j}(SA) = -(1 - \frac{g(SA_i, SA_j)}{max(h(SA_i), h(SA_j))}) \quad (5)$$

where the function $g(.)$ is the maximum value of the discrete convolution of i and j, and $h(.)$ is the maximum value of the auto-correlation, given by:

$$\begin{aligned} g(SA_i, SA_j) &= \max\{\textstyle\sum_k SA_i[n-k] \cdot SA_j[k]\} \quad (6) \\ h(SA_i) &= max\{\textstyle\sum_k SA_i[n-k] \cdot SA_i[k]\} \quad (7) \end{aligned}$$

With respect to the $nROC$ feature, the similarity between two contents i, j ($sR_{i,j}$) over an interval conveys the overlap in the periods where the contents experience a change in the number of hits they receive. This is defined as a negative cosine similarity, given by:

$$sR_{i,j}(n) = -(1 - \frac{\sum_{k \in n} nROC_i^*(k) \cdot nROC_j^*(k)}{\|nROC_i^*\| \cdot \|nROC_j^*\|}) \quad (8)$$

where $nROC_i^* \in (0, 1)$ is the normalisation of the feature vector to $\max(nROC_i[n])$, $\forall n$ and $\|nROC^*\|$ is its norm.

Given the time series of two contents, the definition in Equation 8 takes on values proportional to the time between jumps in the number of hits attracted by the content. The similarity is maximum (0) when two time series are in phase (they jump at the same time instant) and -1 when their jump phases do not overlap.

For each time window in W, we can now construct two square ($|N| \times |N|$) similarity matrices representing the SA ($SA = [sS_{i,j}]_{|N| \times |N|}$) and SR ($SR = [sR_{i,j}]_{|N| \times |N|}$) similarities defined. We use these as input to the clustering algorithm defined in the next section.

3.4 Clustering

For clustering we use the Affinity Propagation (AP) algorithm [15] because it is able to handle non-linear dependencies between data and does not require us to predefine the number of clusters to seek, which helps to reduce the complexity of the training phase.

In brief, AP is a message passing algorithm which initially considers all data points, referred to as nodes, as potential centroids. Nodes exchange messages that are used to calculate their eligibility as centroids, and as the algorithm converges, nodes with low eligibility are discarded. The two main drawbacks of AP are (i) its computational cost and (ii) when using the Euclidean distance to measure similarity (as suggested in [15]) it has a tendency to produce a large number of clusters.

To address the first problem we use a sparse matrix representation, and reduce the number of messages exchanged by not considering nodes whose similarity falls below a given threshold. Fixing the similarity between data points in this way also enables us to tune the classification accuracy of the algorithm; for example, we can increase the intra-cluster similarity by demanding higher correlation between similar data points. The second problem is addressed by our definition of the similarity measure, which is able to reduce the number of clusters without sacrificing the classification accuracy.

Applying this modified clustering algorithm results in a set M where each element consists of a set of clusters for a particular time window. More formally, $M = \{M_1 \dots M_W\}$, where W is the set windows, and each cluster set in $M_{i \in W} = \{m_1 \dots m_m\}$ is composed of the set of clusters identified in the ith time window.

3.5 Prediction

In order to predict the popularity of content, we model the transition probabilities between the members of the cluster set M defined in the previous section. As depicted in Figure 1, because the classification process associates each content in N with exactly one centroid in each time window, tracking the centroids that a given object is associated with over time gives the evolution of that object's popularity.

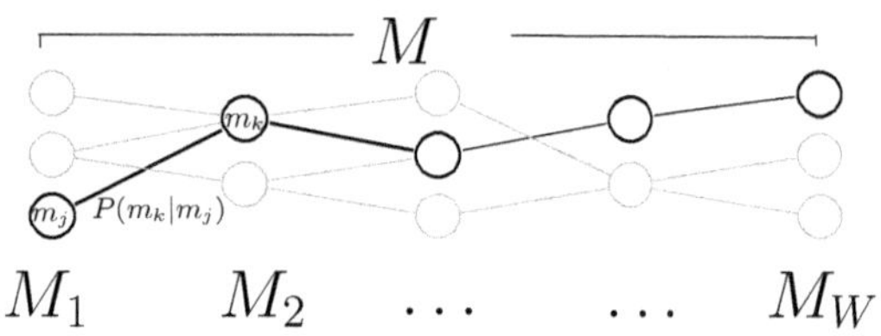

Figure 1: Simple path transition graph depicting the movement of a given content object between clusters over different time windows.

Given the generic time window w, the basic observation here is that the cluster set M forms a directed acyclic graph ($G = (V, E)$), with the vertices being the centroids ($V = M_w$) and the edges the transition probabilities between them. Because each centroid is associated with a given time window, the probability of the k'th centroid in time window w (m_k^w) is given by the ratio of the number of contents associated with the centroid ($mem(m_k^w)$) to the number of classified contents in the time window ($mem(M_w)$). This is expressed as:

$$P(m_k^w) = \frac{mem(m_k^w)}{mem(M_w)} \tag{9}$$

Therefore, the probability of any given content ending up in the centroid m_k^w is the joint probability of all paths leading to m_k^w.

More importantly, given a particular path that a content takes between time windows $1 \dots w$, ($p = \{m_j^1, \dots, m_j^w\}, j \in M_w$), we can evaluate popularity of the content at time $w + r$ by identifying the centroid at the end of the maximum likelihood path between the path (p) and all the centroids in M_{w+r} (m^*), given as:

$$m^* = \underset{j \in M_{w+r}}{\arg\max} \left(\frac{P(m_j)P(p|m_j)}{\sum_{h=1}^{w} P(m_j)|P(M_h|m_j)} \right) \tag{10}$$

where the numerator is the conditional probability of all paths going through p and ending in m_j, and the denominator the probability of all paths ending in m_j.

Evaluating Equation 10 can easily become computationally intractable. If the number of nodes involved is moderate it is possible to use exact inference to marginalise the probability of all paths between m_k^w and m_k^{w+r}, or to directly apply the Viterbi algorithm [33] to do a greedy search for the maximum likelihood path. When this is not possible, we can take advantage of Monte-Carlo methods to approximate the probabilities of the possible paths contents may take as given in Algorithm 1.

The algorithm takes as input the set of distinct paths in the graph and a path length (l). These are then used to sample the graph G and approximate the likelihood of given paths. The final output is a set of transition tables (for different path lengths) which approximate the transition probabilities of contents over time.

```
input : graph_paths, path_length
output: path_distribution
begin
    path_dist = zeros(path_length)
    repeat
        for i=1 to path_length do
            trial_path = path_dist[i] + random_permutation
            if trial_path ∉ graph_paths then
                continue
            end
            m_j = trial_path[path_length])
            p = trial_path[0 : path_length − 1])
            all_paths = Σ P(m_j)|P(graph_paths|m_j)
            ratio = P(m_j)P(p|m_j) / all_paths
            a = random(0, 1)
            if ratio > a then
                path_dist[i]+ = 1 /* trial_path accepted */
            else
                continue /* keep the old sate */
            end
            /* Viterbi path approximation given by:
            likely_path = argmax(path_dist) */
    until n times;
end
```

Algorithm 1: Monte Carlo sampling for the ML path.

4. DATA SETS

This section describes the data sets used in this work, listing their key differences and then discusses the pre-processing applied to generate the feature space used later in the clustering process. Table 1 gives the three data sets used in our experiments. The YouTube and Vimeo data sets consist of the number of views contents receive, while the Digg data set consists of the number of user votes contents receive. All the data sets were collected by directly crawling the relevant websites.

As well as differing in their content, size and sampling granularity, the data sets come from applications that display different popularity evolution characteristics. For example, Digg contents show an average popularity saturation time of around $68hrs$ and Vimeo an average of almost 16.1 months, while YouTube shows a multi-modal pattern, with two peaks at 18 and 27.6 months. The data sets also differ in how content becomes popular. For example, the Vimeo data set displays both the smallest average number of hits per-content and smallest average rate of change (making long periods of samples redundant). At the other extreme, popular Digg contents shows the greatest average rate of change in the number of hits per time interval, with

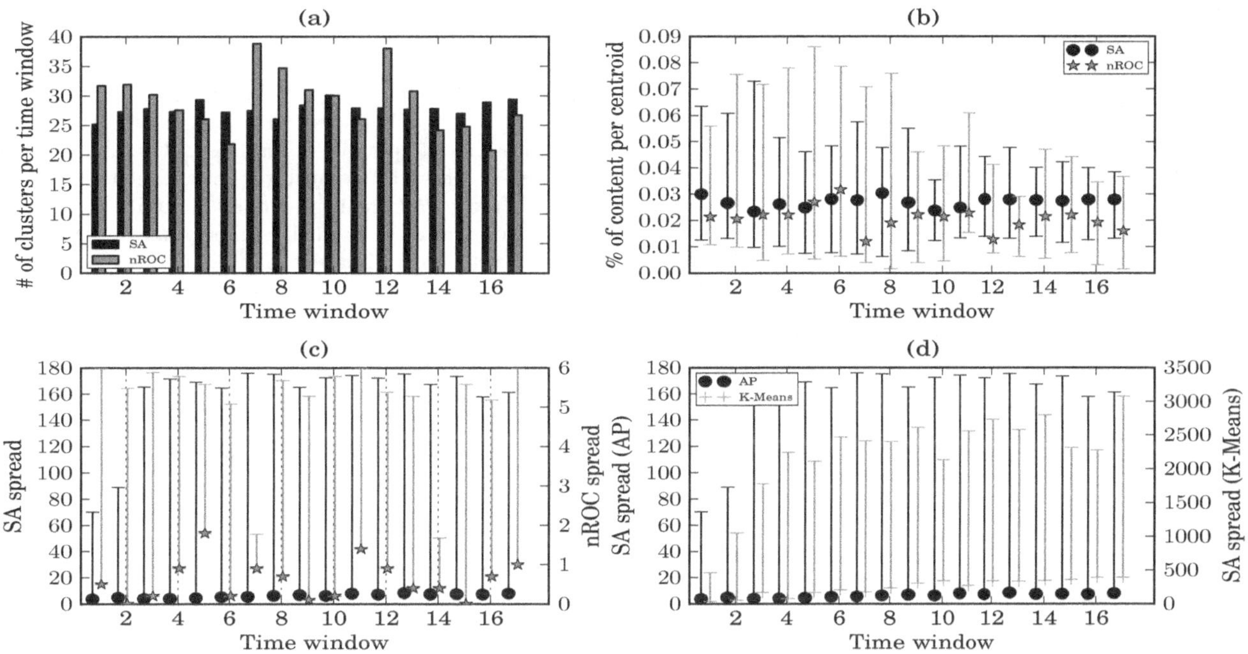

Figure 2: Digg data cluster properties. (a) The median number of clusters identified when using each feature vector. (b) The median, min and max percentage of number of contents associated with each cluster. (c) The median and max cluster spread given in terms of the number of hits (SA) and time shift ($nROC$). It is worth noting that 97.5% of content associated with clusters has a radius under half the max distance from the median of the cluster. Finally, (d) the K-Means cluster spread where K is equal to the number of clusters identified by the Affinity Propagation algorithm at the time window.

Name	# of contents	Dates	Granularity
DIGG	$87x10^3$	11/'07 - 12/'07	1 / 10 mins
VIMEO	$12x10^3$	12/'05 - 04/'10	1 / 30 mins
YOUTUBE	$1.44x10^6$	05/'06 - 11/'11	1 / 468 hrs (max)

Table 1: The experimental data sets. The data sets were chosen because they difference in their size, temporal span/granularity, and the contents' popularity growth behaviour. The sample granularity for YouTube ranges between 1/24hrs to 1/486hrs.

some contents experiencing a significant growth burst within 7hrs of submission and then saturating within 25hrs. This is in contrast to YOUTUBE contents which display very long growth periods lasting weeks to months.

The YOUTUBE data set is interesting because of the length of time it covers, its low temporal granularity and the content popularity growth longevity displayed by some contents.

For each content in the YOUTUBE data set we have only 100 sample points that are uniformly distributed between the contents' upload and crawl dates. This means that depending on the age of the content each sample point summarises the number of hits received in 1 to 19 days.

4.1 Data set processing

To process the data, we first create the slotted time windows described in Section 3.1. The window sizes are chosen experimentally to either smooth the time series (DIGG) or reveal interesting movements (VIMEO).[3]

Digg: For the DIGG data set, we temporally aligned the data such that all sampled objects start at time zero. Although this has the effect of inflating the number of hits per given interval (since we are now considering all objects per time interval), because the sampling interval is constant, the normalisation to calculate the SA feature is not biased. To construct the SA and $nROC$ feature vectors, we use 4hr windows composed of 30 minute slots. Therefore, given the original data (with 10min sample intervals), each window is composed of eight 30 minute slots.

YouTube: Because of its large temporal span and coarse granularity, the YOUTUBE data set allows us to explore the effectiveness of identifying similar content based on the shape of its popularity growth. This means that we can look at identifying similar contents of different ages based on whether their popularity curves evolve in the same way - by comparing them at the same relative portions in their life time, e.g. the number of hits attracted when objects are at 50% of their observed lifetime. For this reason, we do not temporally align YOUTUBE contents to compare only objects of the same age. Again based on experimentation, the YOUTUBE feature vectors are composed of 10 sample windows.

Vimeo: Although the VIMEO data set has a high temporal granularity, the average variance of the number of views per content over time is the lowest - popularity growth is on average very slow, making it difficult to see interesting

[3]We experimented with using volatility measures [12] to determine the window size, but the results were not very convincing in helping to analytically determine the length of windows.

behaviour. For this reason, each VIMEO window contains 3428 samples, equal to two months of observations.

Finally, all experiments in the next sections are conducted by performing repeated random sub-sampling.
presenting the results of the classification process, we first look at the properties of clusters identified by the AP algorithm. This enables us to better understand the clustering results we obtain and to compare them against the performance of our baseline implementation of K-Means.

Figure 2 illustrates the properties of the clusters identified for the DIGG data set. First, we see that the number of clusters per time window ($|M|$) is four orders of magnitude less than the number of content objects (Figure 2a and Table 1). This in effect vindicates the hypothesis that a small number of behaviour patterns underlie the range of temporal popularity evolution we observe in the data. Second, the median number of objects per cluster is not skewed with respect to either feature (Figure 2b). We find that at the extreme, the most populous cluster at a given time window contains at most 30% more objects than the median in the time window (Figure 2b).

The median cluster spread reveals (Figure 2c) that the clusters identified are very tightly packed, the $nROC$ spread - which represents the phase shift between a given content and its associated centroid - reflecting the difference in time between when a given content and its associated centroid experience their biggest jumps in popularity in a given time window, is on the median $1-2$ slots ($30-60$mins) and in the worst case 6 slots (3hrs) for a few outliers ($< 97.5\%$ of centroid members). Comparing the results obtained with the $K-$Means baseline reveals the compactness of the clusters produced. Figure 2d highlights this by comparing the SA spread when using Affinity Propagation and K-Means (for the same features).

For the VIMEO data set, we find that the number of clusters identified tends to be roughly between $1-6\%$ of the data set size ($100-600$ centroids). For YOUTUBE the number of clusters ranges between $0.1-0.4\%$ of the contents per time-interval. The large number of clusters here (in absolute terms) results from the low granularity of the data set, and the lack of temporal realignment to compare objects at absolute points in their lifetime.

Similar to the DIGG result, applying $K-$Means to the VIMEO and YOUTUBE data sets, gives an even larger cluster spread - reflecting the long-tail distribution of the number of hits attracted by contents. Both the median and maximum cluster spread from Affinity Propagation (AP) are always at least an order of magnitude less than the baseline when using the same data and feature space. The impact of this as we will see in the next section is that using $K-$Means results in a poorer classifier for the data set. Further, the compactness of the clusters generated by AP means that we can have a relatively small upper-bound on the prediction error when using the results to predict the popularity of content.

4.2 Accuracy of Clustering

Figure 3 gives the classification error for the clusters identified. The error here is defined as the normalised mean squared error (MSE) in terms of the distance between a classified object and its associated centroid. With regard to the SA feature, distance is the difference in the number of hits attained, while for the $nROC$ feature, the distance is the number of time window slots between when the object experiences its biggest jump and when the centroid does.

From Figure 3, we see that the median classification error for the SA feature on DIGG is between $4-15\%$ of the number of hits associated with a centroid, while for the $nROC$ feature this is between $1.3-16\%$. In practise, an average SA error of 10% in the first time window means a 35 hit difference between a content and its associated centroid. With regard to the sample maximum this is 350 hits, while in the last time window 10% translates on average to 110 hits. Regarding the $nROC$ feature, the maximum error is bounded by the number of slots in the window, and an error of 16% translates to approximately 1.5hrs difference between when content and its centroid experience their biggest jumps.

It is worth pointing out that the upward trend in the $nROC$ error for DIGG data in Figure 3 is somewhat misleading. In absolute numbers (not reported here), during early time windows, the $nROC$ values are large ($>> 1$) as contents attract the vast majority of their hits, while in the last time windows, contents attract very few hits (typically single digits over the 4hr time window). As a result, the $nROC$ values are very small ($0-0.1$) but have a high dispersion, which accounts for the high normalised error.

Regarding the YOUTUBE data set, the $nROC$ feature shows a worst case error of approximately 70%. This is equal to 7 samples, while the median values are $20-30\%$. The poor performance here is due to the lack of temporal alignment of the data. However, given that the 100 sample points associated with a given YOUTUBE content may represent anything from 100 days to over 5 years, a worst case of 70% still shows considerable accuracy in identifying the shape of the jumps in popularity that content experiences. In comparison, with temporally-aligned and higher granularity VIMEO data, we get a $nROC$ error that is bounded under 25% of the centroid's jump time for 95% of the data.

On the SA feature, for YOUTUBE we obtain an error of less than 14% in the worst case, while for the VIMEO the worst case is less than 6%. To contextualise these numbers, the cluster spread for YOUTUBE in the first time interval is $1,000$ hits for the highest outlier, $3,000$ for the second time interval and $3,500$ for the last time interval. Therefore, a worst-case error of 10% in the first time interval equates to 100 hits; a maximum error of 13% in the second time interval represents 390 hits and a maximum error of 2% in the last time interval is 70 hits. For the VIMEO data set, the cluster spread is 50 hits for the first time interval and 25 for the last, giving a maximum worst case error of 30 hits in the first time window.

In comparison with the baseline implementation of K-means, on the DIGG data set (again using the same SA feature space) we obtain a worst case median classification error of 50% and max of 200% compared with AP (16% median, 26% max). This error is even worse for the VIMEO and YOUTUBE data sets (reflecting the power law distribution in the video views). For YOUTUBE and VIMEO, we obtain a worst case median and max classification error of $\approx 150\%, 900\%$ and $\approx 250\%, 700\%$, respectively.

In contrast to related works [17, 22] which classify content to be a member of broad classes of behaviour (i.e. *not popular*, *popular*, *very popular*), these results show that we are accurate at classifying content based on the number of hits they accumulate. For example, when classifying the number of hits for a DIGG contents 8hrs after submission we obtain

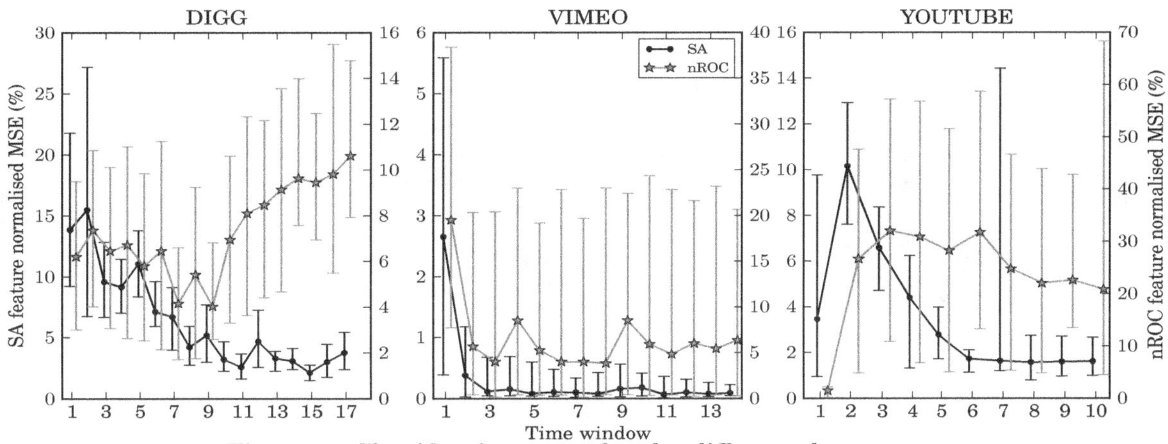

Figure 3: Classification error for the different data sets.

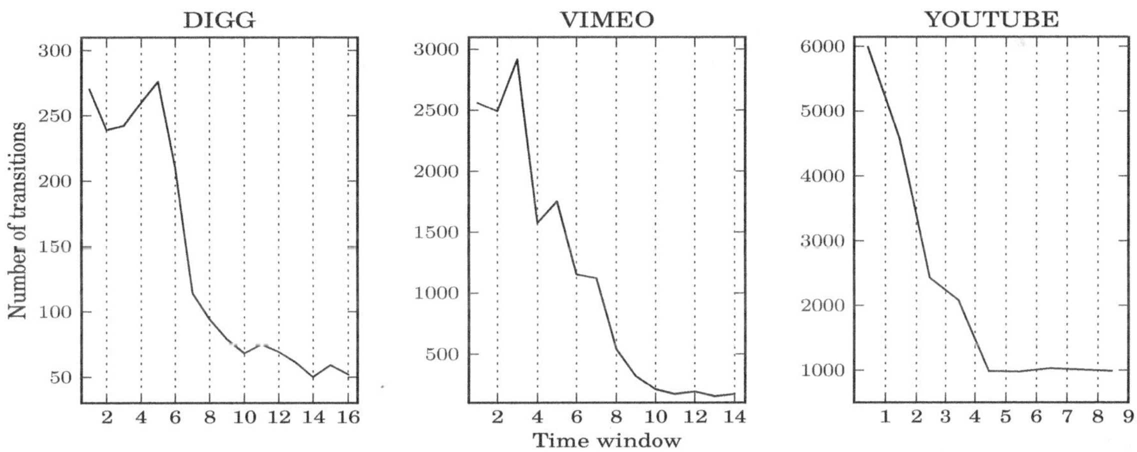

Figure 4: Number of distinct transitions per time window.

an error of 16% median and 26% max.[4] After 24hrs, this value falls to 7% median, 9% max; in contrast, the work in [16] reports an error of 40% after 24hrs.

5. POPULARITY PREDICTION

This section presents our popularity prediction results. We start by discussing the properties of the transitions that contents make when associated with different clusters over their lifetime. We then look at the prediction accuracy of applying the maximum likelihood path prediction to identify the popularity of content. Finally we compare our results against a baseline of linear regression.

As discussed in Section 3.5, the final output of the clustering process is the set of cluster sets identified for each time window ($M = \{M_1, \ldots, M_W\}$). Now, given some object x_i that at time t is classified to be a member of cluster m_j^t, our goal is to predict the most likely cluster that x_i will belong to at time $t+k$, termed m_j^{t+k}. This translates to identifying the centroid at the end of the maximum likelihood path between m_j^t and all the centroids in M_{t+k}.

Before presenting the results of the prediction process, we first look at the transition properties between clusters, that is the paths that the different contents trace as they transition from cluster to cluster over time. Figure 4 illustrates the number of distinct cluster transitions content makes over the time windows. The early stages of content popularity growth show the highest number of transitions, reflecting the high dispersion in the number of hits initially accumulated by content. As the popularity of contents saturates, the number of transitions stabilises, converging to the number of clusters identified per time window.

Figure 5 illustrates the results when using the SA feature vector, giving the error when predicting the future popularity of content based on its cluster membership. Here, the *prediction horizon* refers to how far in the future we project, and the error refers to the normalised mean squared prediction error (MSPE), which normalises the difference between the classified object's number of hits and the number of hits of the centroid it is associated with, to the number of hits at the centroid.

For instance, looking at the one-step (t_{i+1} given t_i) predictions errors in Figure 5, for DIGG we obtain an error between $18.1 - 1.02\%$ (compared to $48 - 23\%$ for linear regression, see Section 5.1), where the first number refers to the first window when there is minimal information about a content's behaviour and the last number refers to the last time window.[5] Similarly, we obtain low prediction errors for the other data sets; $27 - 2.9\%$ for VIMEO, and $19.7 - 1.6\%$ for YOUTUBE.

With regard to the $nROC$ feature, using the one-step pre-

[4]Where max represents less than 5% of all content.

[5]The prediction error in the last time window is very low because it captures a point when content objects have saturated in their popularity; this is reflected in the number of cluster transitions converging as shown in Figure 4.

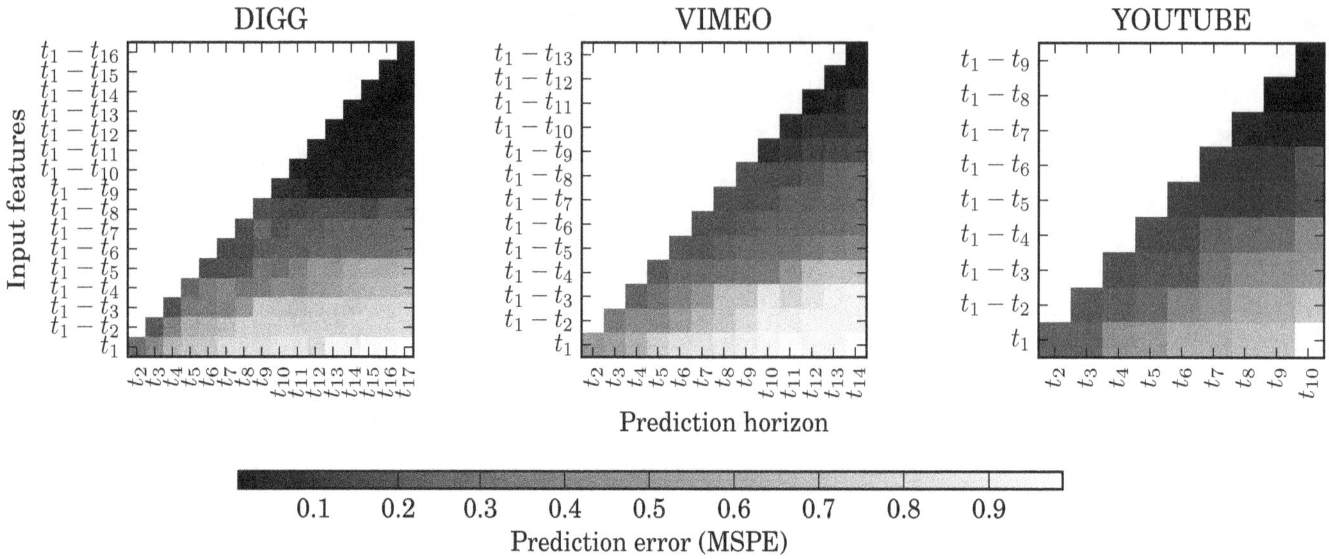

Figure 5: The *SA* feature prediction error. Given as input the cluster(s) that a given content is associated with from time t_i to t_j (the y-axis), the graph gives the MSPE (the x-axis) for time t_k where k is the prediction horizon.

diction, we find the same general trend in the convergence of the prediction error over time. We obtain a 20.3 − 3.2% error for DIGG, 35 − 6.9% for VIMEO, and finally 52.6 − 8.1% for YOUTUBE.

In our analysis so far we have used the entire span of sample points in our data sets. But are there certain sample points or time windows that have more impact in achieving small prediction errors? To answer this question, we began by dividing a content's popularity evolution into three phases: *initialisation*, during which content achieves 0 − 10% of its hits; *growth*, where content gains 10 − 90% of its hits; and *saturation*, where it receives 90%+ of hits.

In brief, having observed that fewer transitions (convergence) results in lower prediction errors, we would like to examine the relationship between the number of transitions and the phases just defined. To highlight this relationship, Figure 6 plots the distribution of the time it takes for content to achieve 10% of its lifetime views (i.e., enter the growth phase)[6] alongside the number of distinct transitions between centroids that contents experience over time.

From Figure 6, we see that the end of the distribution (at 24hrs) coincides with the highest rate of change in the number of cluster transitions as the majority of contents enter the growth phase, meaning that after this point the number of transitions starts to converge and the prediction error decreases. In effect the greatest improvement in the prediction accuracy is observed at point where contents start to attract hits - reflecting the entry into growth phase.

This result leads us to understand that in order to accurately predict the future popularity of content, it is not necessary to use all the points in the feature space - i.e., provide a long history of observations to the prediction process, but rather to choose the most informative subset of points. Specifically, feature points that correspond to when content enters its popularity growth phase have the biggest impact in reducing the prediction error.

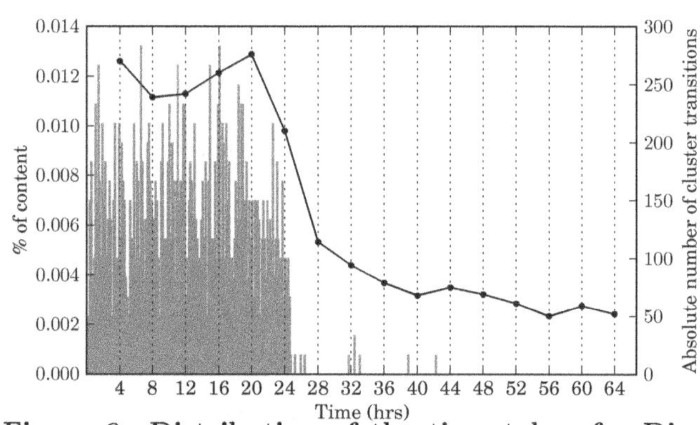

Figure 6: Distribution of the time taken for Digg content to achieve 10% of its lifetime hits (enter the growth phase) alongside the number of centroid transitions.

To better understand this, Figure 7 shows how the prediction error drops as content starts to enter the growth phase (the y-axis gives the MSPE from a given time window t all the way to the last window in each data set). From the figure, we see that the biggest change in the prediction error comes during the initial part of the growth phase (the shaded area).

The practical side effect is, contents that attract a high volume of hits in a short time are identified quickly. Further, this result has the potential to affect how the inputs used to predict popularity are selected, since the points in the feature space corresponding to the beginning of the growth phase contribute most to reducing the prediction error. It is also worth pointing out that identifying the beginning of this growth phase is relatively easy since it corresponds to the point where the rate of change in the number of hits starts to increase the fastest.

[6]Not including all contents with less than 10 hits in their life time.

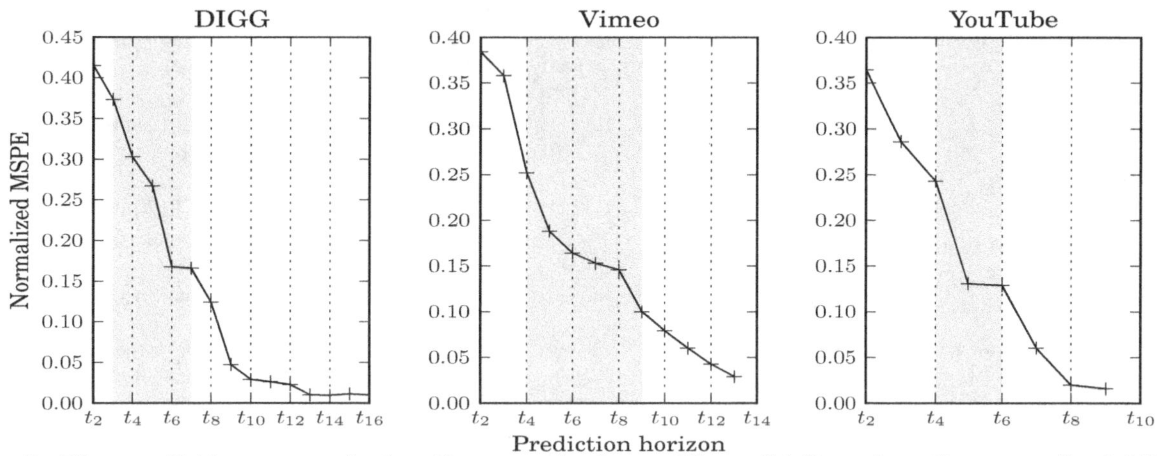

Figure 7: The prediction errors during the growth phase. The solid line gives the normalised MSPE from window t_i to the last window, while the shaded area gives the length of the growth phase (the time taken to accumulate 10% of hits) for 85% of contents.

5.1 Linear Regression Comparison

In this section we compare our results against the baseline implementation of linear regression, the most popular regression technique applied to content popularity prediction (see [7, 16, 26, 29, 31] amongst others).

Figure 8 gives the prediction error obtained when applying linear regression to the DIGG data as suggested by [29], alongside our results (labelled maximum likelihood). Following the author's suggestion, given the number of hits at time t, the linear regression predicts the number of hits that the content expects to achieve $t + k$ steps ahead.

We find that after 4hrs of observations, linear regression obtains a median error of 49% (70% max), after 8hrs the error falls to 29%, and continues to fall, converging slowly to a median error of 23% after 24hrs. Our results, on the other hand start at 18% median error at 4hrs (25% max), after 8hrs (representing two time windows) we have an error of 13%, and after 24hrs this falls to 10%. At the end (after 68hrs) the regression error converges to a minimum of 17%, while our error at this point (the 16th time window) is at 1.0%.

These results are not particular to the DIGG data set: when applied to the VIMEO and YOUTUBE data sets, the median prediction error converges to 24.2% and 29.7% respectively. In comparison, for both data sets our method converges to a median error of under 3.5%. Looking more closely at the result, we believe that the relative poor performance of linear regression is best explained by looking at the coefficient of variation of the data ($\frac{\sigma}{\mu}$) as depicted in Figure 8. This shows that linear regression simply follows the dispersion of the data samples, while in contrast our method takes advantage of the correlations identified by the clustering process.

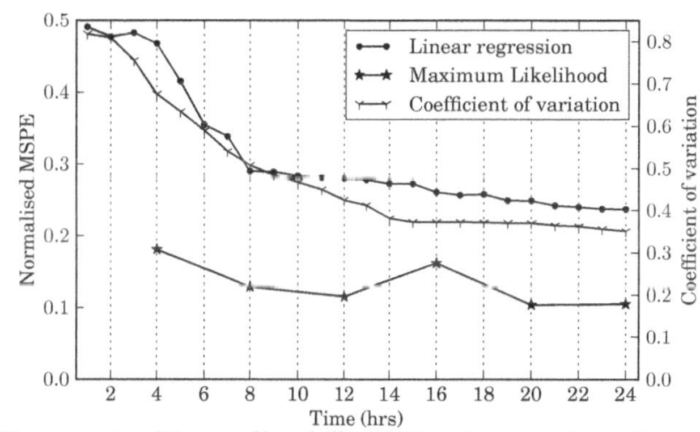

Figure 8: Normalised MSPE when using linear regression (dotted line), along side our method (starred line) for 1-step ahead prediction. From the figure we see that the linear regression tracks the coefficient of variation of the data (crossed line).

6. CONCLUSION AND FURTHER WORK

In this work we presented a novel method to characterise and predict the time evolution of popularity in user generated content. We defined an application agnostic feature space to capture the patterns of behaviour that contents display overtime. Our results show that: (i) we can accurately and in a fine-grained manner classify the behaviour of content based only on the number of hits it receives and (ii) based on our classification results we can construct accurate and again fine-grained predictive models. We have applied our method to three distinct data sets and shown that it is capable of performing better than the baselines of K-Means and linear regression as well as comparable work in the area.

Accurate classification and early prediction have direct relevance to a large number of application areas, including content caching [13], where network caching strategies could be improved by making them proactive; and advertising [22], where advertising strategies can be devised to react to the expected popularity of content (e.g., place a cheap ad on the page of a video that will become popular later).

As future work we are looking into how to extend our method to handle variable-length time windows and heterogeneous data mixtures. We are looking to move away from the offline training method presented in this paper to an online method that can dynamically build classifiers as new data comes in. More specifically, we are looking to replace the Affinity Propagation algorithm with mixture models in order to be able to represent centroids as PDFs and support online updating.

7. ACKNOWLEDGEMENTS

This publication is based on work performed in the framework of the Project COAST-ICT-248036, which is partially funded by the European Community. We would like to thank Christian Wallenta and Nishanth Sastry for sharing data sets with us and the reviewers for their helpful suggestions.

References

[1] E. Adar, D. S. Weld, B. N. Bershad, and S. S. Gribble. Why we search: visualizing and predicting user behavior. In *WWW'07*, 2007.

[2] N. Agarwal, H. Liu, L. Tang, and P. S. Yu. Identifying the influential bloggers in a community. In *WSDM '08*, 2008.

[3] W. Antweiler and M. Z. Frank. Is all that talk just noise? the information content of internet stock message boards. *The Journal of Finance*, 59(3):1259–1294, Jun 2004.

[4] D. Applegate, A. Archer, V. Gopalakrishnan, S. Lee, and K. K. Ramakrishnan. Optimal content placement for a large-scale vod system. In *Co-NEXT '10*, 2010.

[5] S. Asur and B. A. Huberman. Predicting the future with social media. In *WI-IAT '10*, 2010.

[6] R. Balasubramanyan, B. R. Routledge, and N. A. Smith. From Tweets to Polls: Linking Text Sentiment to Public Opinion Time Series. In *ICWSM'10*, 2010.

[7] R. Bandari, S. Asur, and B. A. Huberman. The pulse of news in social media: Forecasting popularity. *CoRR*, abs/1202.0332, 2012.

[8] Y. Borghol, S. Mitra, S. Ardon, N. Carlsson, D. Eager, and A. Mahanti. Characterizing and modeling popularity evolution of user-generated videos. In *IFIP Performace*, 2011.

[9] M. Cha, H. Kwak, P. Rodriguez, Y.-Y. Ahn, and S. Moon. I tube, you tube, everybody tubes: analyzing the world's largest user generated content video system. In *IMC'07*, 2007.

[10] M. Cha, A. Mislove, and K. P. Gummadi. A measurement-driven analysis of information propagation in the flickr social network. In *WWW '09*, 2009.

[11] R. Crane and D. Sornette. Robust dynamic classes revealed by measuring the response function of a social system. *PNAS*, 105(15469), 2008.

[12] R. Cumby, S. Figlewski, and J. Hasbrouck. Forecasting Volatility and Correlations with EGARCH models. *Journal of Derivatives*, 1:51–63, 1993.

[13] J. Famaey, T. Wauters, and F. De Turck. On the merits of popularity prediction in multimedia content caching. In *Integrated Network Management*, 2011.

[14] F. Figueiredo, F. Benevenuto, and J. Almeida. The tube over time: Characterizing popularity growth of youtube videos. In *WSDM'11*, February 2011.

[15] B. J. Frey and D. Dueck. Clustering by passing messages between data points. *Science*, 315:972–976, 2007.

[16] T. Hogg and K. Lerman. Social dynamics of digg. *CoRR*, abs/1202.0031, 2012.

[17] L. Hong, O. Dan, and B. D. Davison. Predicting popular messages in twitter. In *WWW (Companion Volume)*, 2011.

[18] S. Jamali and H. Rangwala. Digging digg: Comment mining, popularity prediction, and social network analysis. In *WISM '09*, 2009.

[19] E. J. Keogh and C. A. Ratanamahatana. Exact indexing of dynamic time warping. *KAIS*, 7(3):358–386, 2005.

[20] S.-D. Kim, S.-H. Kim, and H.-G. Cho. Predicting the virtual temperature of web-blog articles as a measurement tool for online popularity. In *CIT '11*, 2011.

[21] H. Kwak, C. Lee, H. Park, and S. Moon. What is Twitter, a social network or a news media? In *WWW '10*, 2010.

[22] H. Lakkaraju and J. Ajmera. Attention prediction on social media brand pages. In *CIKM '11*, 2011.

[23] D. Laniado and P. Mika. Making sense of twitter. In *ISWC'10*, 2010.

[24] J. G. Lee, S. Moon, and K. Salamatian. An approach to model and predict the popularity of online contents with explanatory factors. In *WI-IAT*, 2010.

[25] J. G. Lee, S. Moon, and K. Salamatian. Modeling and predicting the popularity of online contents with cox proportional hazard regression model. *Neurocomputing*, 76(1):134–145, 2012.

[26] K. Lerman and T. Hogg. Using a model of social dynamics to predict popularity of news. *CoRR*, abs/1004.5354, 2010.

[27] J. Leskovec, A. Krause, C. Guestrin, C. Faloutsos, J. VanBriesen, and N. Glance. Cost-effective outbreak detection in networks. In *SIGKDD'07*, 2007.

[28] D. A. Shamma, J. Yew, L. Kennedy, and E. F. Churchill. Viral actions: Predicting video view counts using synchronous sharing behaviors. In *ICWSM*, 2011.

[29] G. Szabo and B. A. Huberman. Predicting the popularity of online content. *Commun. ACM*, 53:80–88, August 2010.

[30] A. Tatar, J. Leguay, P. Antoniadis, A. Limbourg, M. D. de Amorim, and S. Fdida. Predicting the popularity of online articles based on user comments. In *WIMS '11*, 2011.

[31] M. Tsagkias, W. Weerkamp, and M. de Rijke. News comments: exploring, modeling, and online prediction. In *ECIR'2010*, 2010.

[32] T. O. S. Tumasjan, P. G. Sandner, and I. M. Welpe. Predicting elections with Twitter: What 140 characters reveal about political sentiment. In *ICWSM'10*, 2010.

[33] Wikipedia. Viterbi algorithm, August 2012. [Online; accessed 30-Nov-2012].

[34] C. Williams and G. Gulati. What is a social network worth? Facebook and vote share in the 2008 presidential primaries. *Annual Meeting of the American Political Science Association*, 2008.

[35] H. F. X. Zhang and P. A. Gloor. Predicting asset value through twitter buzz. In *Advances in Collective Intelligence*, 2011.

[36] J. Yang and J. Leskovec. Patterns of temporal variation in online media. In *WSDM '11*, 2011.

[37] X. Zhang, H. Fuehres, and P. Gloor. Predicting Stock Market Indicators Through Twitter: "I hope it is not as bad as I fear". *Procedia - Social and Behavioral Sciences*, 26, Oct 2011.

Online Community Detection in Social Sensing

Guo-Jun Qi
Department of Electrical and Computer Engineering
University of Illinois at Urbana-Champaign
Urbana, IL
qi4@illinois.edu

Charu C. Aggarwal
IBM T.J. Watson Research Center
Yorktown Heights, NY
charu@us.ibm.com

Thomas S. Huang
Department of Electrical and Computer Engineering
University of Illinois at Urbana-Champaign
Urbana, IL
huang@ifp.uiuc.edu

ABSTRACT

The proliferation of location and GPS data streams which are collected in a wide variety of participatory sensing applications has created numerous possibilities for analysis of the underlying patterns of activity. Typically, the spatio-temporal patterns arising from such activity can be analyzed in order to determine the latent community structure in the underlying data. In this paper, we will examine the problem of online community detection from the location data collected from such social sensing applications in real time. Such data brings numerous challenges associated with it, in that they can be of a relatively large scale, and can be extremely noisy from the perspective of both data representation and analysis. Furthermore, the community structure in the underlying data cannot be directly inferred from the shape of the underlying trajectories, since a considerable amount of variation may exist in terms of trajectories of individuals belonging to the same community. In this paper, we will design *online* algorithms for community detection in social sensing applications. Our algorithm uses a robust and efficiently updateable model with the use of Gibbs sampling, and we will show its effectiveness and efficiency for social sensing applications.

Categories and Subject Descriptors

H.2.8 [**Databases Management**]: Database Applications

Keywords

Social Sensing

1. INTRODUCTION

The proliferation of mobile phones and a wide variety of other hardware with embedded and wearable sensors have resulted in a tremendous amount of GPS and trajectory data in a wide variety of applications. Such data can often be mined in order to determine the useful communities from the underlying data. A number of recent hardware advancements have lead to the increased importance of social sensing applications:

- The increasing accessibility of wearable sensors with GPS-enabled devices has made it much easier to track and collect individual locations in mobile sensing applications.
- The rapid popularization of smartphone technology with GPS abilities has increased our ability to collect spatio-temporal data in the context of a wide variety of applications.

Such spatiotemporal data can often be very useful for determining communities with the use of spatial and temporal co-location information between different entities. Nevertheless, the process of determining such communities can be extremely noisy and challenging because of a wide variety of reasons:

- At any given time, a pair of entities could be present at the same location purely by chance. It is only on the basis of repeated interactions between the pair of entities *over different times* that the entities may be said to belong to the same community.
- In many cases, the repeated co-location of communities may not occur over continuous periods in time. This is quite different from many trajectory clustering models, which tend to determine clustering behavior of trajectories on the basis of their shape, and the behavior over contiguous time stamps.
- GPS data is usually highly incomplete, as a result of which the locations of only a subset of the entities may be available at a given moment in time. Therefore, the community maintenance process must be highly cognizant of the errors and noise in the underlying data.
- Locations which have *higher selectivity* in terms of enabling the interaction of a small number of participants *at a given time* are often more indicative of community behavior. In locations containing an extremely large number of participants, the spatial proximity of a pair of participants may often not be quite as indicative of community behavior unless the two participants are extremely close to one another over a long period of time. In this context, the inherent errors of data collection may play a role, because an error of a few meters in location tracking in a spatial region of very high density may be significant, whereas it may not be quite

WSDM'13, February 4–8, 2013, Rome, Italy.

as significant in a spatial region of low density. Thus, the significance of the co-location of a pair of entities should be evaluated in the context of the density of the point of co-location.

- The underlying communities may often evolve over time, as new interactions are observed between different participants. Therefore, one can incorporate temporal information in the community detection process in order to perform the detection in real time. While recent interactions may be very relevant, the history of previous interactions should also play an important role in the community detection process.

The main challenge in the modeling process is to use all the different statistical indicators of community formation in a balanced way in order to continuously determine and track the underlying communities in real time. For example, while a considerable amount of work has been done recently in the area of trajectory clustering [4, 11, 13, 14, 17, 18], most of these methods are not designed for online community detection. Furthermore, most of these methods impose the constraint of either similar trajectory shape, or the occurrence of two objects at the same location over *consecutive* snapshots.

In this context, the problem of determining swarms in spatio-temporal data was proposed in [18], which determines groups of objects which occur together at possibly non-consecutive snapshots. However, this work requires significant global pre-processing of the trajectories, and has several constraints in the context of *real-time* community-detection:

- The work in [18] decouples the spatial and temporal aspects of the problem by performing a static (spatial) pre-clustering of the objects at *each time stamp* with the use of an off-the-shelf algorithm for further temporal analysis. In a sense, the spatial component of the problem is largely abstracted out by this work. This may not be practical in real applications, and the quality and speed of the approach is highly dependent on the quality of the (off-the-shelf) algorithm used for spatial pre-clustering. Thus, if hundreds of thousands of time-stamps are collected, such a spatial pre-clustering would need to be performed at *each time-stamp* to begin with. Such an approach cannot be used for real-time applications, especially in cases, where a large number of objects and time-stamps are involved. The de-coupling of the spatial and temporal aspects of an inherently spatio-temporal problem (and the subsequent de-emphasis on the spatial component by using an off-the-shelf spatial clustering algorithm) is also not qualitatively the most effective design. This can lead to a tremendous loss of information in the spatial pre-clustering phase.

- The purpose of clustering and community detection is to report a small number of groups of related entities, which further allows for easy assimilation and a concise representation. However, the work in [18] may determine hundreds of thousands of swarms by using a temporal frequent-pattern mining like approach on the pre-clustered data. The reported swarms may be highly overlapping, and in many cases, the total number of swarms reported may be greater than the number of objects being tracked. This does not serve the purposes of a problem such a community detection very well.

In this paper, we design a *real time* and *online* approach for determining the set of continuously evolving communities from the locations of a set of users. Different from traditional methods, the approach is real-time and continuous, and is not based on trajectory shape. It is also different from link prediction, which is typically based on very long term analysis, and typically cannot be performed in real time. Our approach uses relatively limited location information for the analysis process, and is also different from most of the (offline) pattern-based co-location clustering methods.

This paper is organized as follows. The remainder of this section discusses related work. In Section 2, we formulate and motivate the problem and introduce notations. In Section 3, we propose an *Infinite Community Dynamic Random Field (IC-DRF) model* to capture the community structure in the context of object locations and their dynamics. In Section 4, a Gibbs Sampling algorithm is presented for efficient incremental inference of community configurations of objects at each time stamp. In Section 5, we experimentally compare our approach with other state-of-the-art algorithms. Section 6 contains the conclusions and summary.

1.1 Related work

The problem of community detection is generally defined in the form of a clustering of the underling network [8, 19, 10, 16, 15]. A survey of a number of important algorithms for community detection is provided in [6]. Discussion of important statistical properties of web communities is discussed in [16]. Evolutionary characteristics of dynamic communities are studied in [2, 7, 8]. The problem of community detection has also been studied in the context of combining node and edge content in order to improve its effectiveness [21, 25, 27].

Social sensing [1] has recently found increasing interest because of the increasing importance of mobile phones and participatory sensing technology. Recent work has extensively studied common properties [9, 20, 22] of common spatio-temporal social networks, which reveal the link patterns between people in these networks. The work in [24] is more closely related to the problem of link prediction, though is not designed for real-time analysis. In this context, a considerable amount of work has been performed for trajectory clustering [4, 11, 13, 14, 17, 18]. Most of this work is either designed for discovering trajectories with *similar shapes* or in determining objects which occur together at consecutive time stamps. In practice, objects in the same community very rarely show similar trajectories, and the communities may be determined only on the basis of proximity to one another over significant periods of time. Furthermore, most of the existing work is applicable only for *offline* community detection, where most of the data is already available. For example, the swarms proposed in [18], determine *temporally co-occurring patterns of entities* from *spatially pre-clustered data*, though such an approach has limited applicability for real time community detection, because of the reasons discussed in the introduction section.

2. PROBLEM DEFINITION

We denote the set of actors tracked by the social sensing application by $\mathcal{O} = \{o_1, \cdots, o_n, \cdots\}$. Their geographical locations at each time stamp are denoted by $\mathcal{L}^{(t)} = \{l_1^{(t)}, \cdots, l_n^{(t)}, \cdots\}$. Since we propose a probabilistic model in this paper, we will readily handle the missing location data, which may occur as a result of failure of the device. Thus $\mathcal{L}^{(t)}$ does not need to contain the complete set of locations for all objects at each time. Our goal is to dynamically maintain a community partition of these moving objects into a set of the communities based on the trajectory information of their locations up to the current time stamp.

PROBLEM 1. *Given a set of actors $\mathcal{O}$, along with a set of streaming locations $\mathcal{L}$, continuously maintain the set of communities from the actors $\mathcal{O}$ in real time.*

We denote the community assignment variable of each of the actors in the social sensing application by $\mathcal{Z}^{(t)} = \{z_1^{(t)}, \cdots, z_n^{(t)}, \cdots\}$, where $z_i^{(t)} \in \{1, 2, \cdots, \}$ is the community index for o_i at time t. In order to determine the community membership of these different participants, we use their location information, such that the objects, which are frequently close to one another are more likely to be in the same community. Intuitively, a good community structure will have low intra-community distance, and high inter-community distance across different communities. This can be quite challenging because of the temporal non-transitivity of distances; two objects which are consistently far away from one another, may frequently each be close to a third object, but never at the same time. This leads to challenges about how the community structure may be consistently defined in online fashion. In the next section, we will define a Dynamic Random Field (DRF) which uses this criterion to yield a probabilistic measurement over the possible configurations of community membership of all the participants.

Moreover, as a dynamic model, DRF should capture the evolution of objects from one community to another over time. We know that an object does not evolve between different communities with equal probability. For example, as long as the object location does not change too much, an object is more likely to stay in the current community unless its locations relative to the other objects in the same community changes dramatically. If the community membership of an object changes, we can expect that it is more likely to join in join in a closer community than the other distant ones. The DRF model will be able to seamlessly use the spatial and temporal components in online fashion in order to capture the dynamic changes of moving objects between communities. This increases the robustness and effectiveness of the community detection model.

The community structure of the moving participants evolves dynamically as their locations change over time. For example, some communities may merge with each other as their member objects encounter each other more frequently; on the other hand, a new community might appear as some objects depart from an existing community in order to show an independent pattern of behavior. Therefore, the number of communities can change dynamically as the geographical layout of objects change over time. This suggests that we cannot pre-decide the number of communities, especially when the natural granularity of the underlying communities is inherently dynamic. Therefore, the number of communities needs to be dynamically determined, on the basis of their spatial patterns and the corresponding evolution dynamics.

In the next section, we will present an Infinite Community - Dynamic Random Field (*IC-DRF*) which derives the evolving community structure from both the spatial trajectory patterns and the community evolution dynamics. The number of communities is automatically determined both from the current spatial dynamics and the temporal history of previous community structures.

3. INFINITE COMMUNITY - DYNAMIC RANDOM FIELDS

In this section, we will define an Infinite Community - Dynamic Random field (*IC-DRF*) model to determine the dynamic community structure in the social sensing problem. Specifically, the *IC-DRF* defines a sequence of probabilistic measures on the community configuration of objects over time based on their locations. The model derives the most probable configuration of community assignment to the moving objects by effectively comparing the intra-community distances between objects with inter-community distances over time.

This model has the following advantages:

1. As compared with many spatial community models, *IC-DRF* does not need to assume any specific prior knowledge about the spatial distribution of the members of each community. Actually, the spatial distribution of members can vary significantly in different communities. For example, people who travel together in dense regions (such as a mall) are usually expected to be much closer to one another as compared with those that travel in a mountain area. The *IC-DRF* model is flexible to varying community scales without the need for specializing to the spatial scale of a particular community.

2. The nonparametric Bayesian construction of this paper obviates the need to pre-decide the number of communities in the *IC-DRF* model. Instead, we assume a possibly infinite number of communities, so that the number of communities are dynamically determined in online fashion based on the spatio-temporal patterns of objects. In real-life applications, the number of communities are rarely constant, since they can evolve, merge and split because of variations in the underlying social interactions. A model which assumes countably infinite communities can simultaneously capture the dynamic changes in the number and structure of communities in a principled manner;

3. The *IC-DRF* model can maintain the community configuration of objects in an online manner. This is critical for social sensing applications, in which real-time analysis is usually an important goal.

To the best of our knowledge, *IC-DRF* is the first model to develop an online and dynamic approach for integrated spatio-temporal evolution and dynamic community analysis. Furthermore, this approach requires no prior knowledge. Straightforward applications of existing nonparametric Bayesian models assume prior knowledge about the spatial distribution of the objects. This is usually not flexible enough to capture the dynamic changes of object locations over time. The *IC-DRF* model defines a prior-independent energy function for minimization, which yields the most probable configuration of community membership of the underlying objects.

3.1 Complete Probabilistic Model

Next, we will introduce the *IC-DRF* model for community detection. Let the community assignment from time instants 1 through T be denoted by $\mathcal{Z}^{(1:T)} = \{\mathcal{Z}^{(1)}, \mathcal{Z}^{(2)}, \cdots, \mathcal{Z}^{(T)}\}$. We define the following probability distribution $P(\cdot)$ for community assignment model from time instants 1 to T with the use of the notations introduced in the previous section:

$$P(\mathcal{Z}^{(1:T)}|\mathcal{L}^{(1:T)}, \gamma, \pi) \propto \prod_{t=1}^{T} \exp(-E(\mathcal{Z}^{(t)}|\mathcal{L}^{(t)})) \prod_{t=2}^{T} P(\mathcal{Z}^{(t)}|\mathcal{Z}^{(t-1)}, \pi) P(\mathcal{Z}^{(1)}|\gamma) \quad (1)$$

The intuitive explanation for the different components of this model are as follows:

- The expression $E(\mathcal{Z}^{(t)}|\mathcal{L}^{(t)})$ (which is described in more detail in the next subsection) defines an energy function which measures the consistency of object locations for the community structure at each time t. In practice, we will use the exponentiated potential function $\exp(-E(\mathcal{Z}^{(1)}|\mathcal{L}^{(1)}))$ of the energy function for analysis.
- The notations $P(\mathcal{Z}^{(1)}|\gamma)$ and $P(\mathcal{Z}^{(t)}|\mathcal{Z}^{(t-1)}, \gamma, \mu, \alpha)$ (for $t > 1$) represent the probability measures for the initial community assignment $\mathcal{Z}^{(1)}$ and the dynamic community assignment $\mathcal{Z}^{(t)}$ at time $t > 1$, conditional on the assignment $\mathcal{Z}^{(t-1)}$ at time $t-1$, respectively. We use the naive Bayes assumption to factorize these probability functions over the different objects.

  $$P(\mathcal{Z}^{(1)}|\gamma) = \prod_{o_i \in \mathcal{O}} P(z_i^{(1)}|\gamma) \quad (2)$$

  Also, for each $t > 1$, we have:

  $$P(\mathcal{Z}^{(t)}|\mathcal{Z}^{(t-1)}, \pi) = \prod_{o_i \in \mathcal{O}} P(z_i^{(t)}|z_i^{(t-1)}, \pi) \quad (3)$$

  Here γ is the model parameter for the initial community assignment with $P(Z_i^{(1)} = k|\gamma) = \gamma_k$, and $\pi = \{\pi_1, \pi_2, \cdots\}$ are the parameters for the community evolution probability, where $\pi_k = [\pi_{k1}, \pi_{k2}, \cdots,]$ gives the probability that a member of community k evolves to another community l in the next time stamp, i.e., $P(z_i^{(t)} = l|z_i^{(t-1)} = k, \pi) = \pi_{kl}$.

In the following, we will impose the Hierarchical Dirichlet Process (HDP) prior on the model parameters γ and π, and give a joint probability of community configurations by marginalizing out γ and π over the HDP prior:

$$P(\mathcal{Z}^{(1:T)}|\mathcal{L}^{(1:T)}) \propto \int_{\gamma,\pi} \prod_{t=1}^{T} \exp(-E(\mathcal{Z}^{(t)}|\mathcal{L}^{(t)})) \times \prod_{t=2}^{T} P(\mathcal{Z}^{(t)}|\mathcal{Z}^{(t-1)}, \pi) P(\mathcal{Z}^{(1)}|\gamma) P(\gamma, \pi) d\gamma d\pi \quad (4)$$

We can see that marginalization of the model parameters couples all the community configurations $\mathcal{Z}^{(1:T)}$ together, where the community configuration at each time stamp no longer depends only on its directly preceding community configuration as in Eq. (1). Therefore, the *IC-DRF* model captures the community evolution dynamics in the history in order to determine the most probable community assignments at each time by maximizing the above probability. This will become clear after we define the priors for $\boldsymbol{\lambda}$ and π.

3.2 Location-Sensitive Energy Function

In this subsection, we will formally define the afore-mentioned location-sensitive community energy function to model the spatial structure of communities. Given the current community configuration $\mathcal{Z}^{(t)}$ of objects, we define the energy function as follows:

$$E(\mathcal{Z}^{(t)}|\mathcal{L}^{(t)}) = E_{\text{intra}}(\mathcal{Z}^{(t)}|\mathcal{L}^{(t)}) - E_{\text{inter}}(\mathcal{Z}^{(t)}|\mathcal{L}^{(t)}) \quad (5)$$

where

$$E_{\text{intra}}(\mathcal{Z}^{(t)}|\mathcal{L}^{(t)}) = \frac{\sum_{i \neq j} d_{ij}^{(t)} \delta \left[\left[z_i^{(t)} = z_j^{(t)}\right]\right]}{\sum_{i \neq j} \delta \left[\left[z_i^{(t)} = z_j^{(t)}\right]\right]} \quad (6)$$

and

$$E_{\text{inter}}(\mathcal{Z}^{(t)}|\mathcal{L}^{(t)}) = \frac{\sum_{i \neq j} d_{ij}^{(t)} \delta \left[\left[z_i^{(t)} \neq z_j^{(t)}\right]\right]}{\sum_{i \neq j} \delta \left[\left[z_i^{(t)} \neq z_j^{(t)}\right]\right]} \quad (7)$$

The last two equations represent the average of inter- and intra-community distances, and where $d_{ij}^{(t)}$ is the distance between object o_i and o_j computed from their locations l_i and l_j at time stamp t, $\delta [\![\cdot]\!]$ is the indicator function which outputs 1 if its condition holds, and outputs 0 otherwise. The first term on the right hand side of the equation computes the average distance between objects in the same community, and the second term computes the average distance between objects in the different community. Minimizing the above energy function will lead to a community configuration for objects that minimizes the average intra-community distance relative to the average inter-community distance over time.

It is worth noting that the number of communities do not need to be pre-decided a-priori. The afore-mentioned energy function handles different numbers of communities in a graceful and uniform way. As we will see in the next subsection, the number of communities can be automatically determined from the dynamic model for community evolution, as it relates to the spatial layout of the objects over time. The energy function also does not make any assumptions about the spatial scales of the underlying communities. In other words, no assumptions are made about how close two objects need to be to one another over time in order to belong to the same community. Thus the proposed model is adaptive and flexible in its ability to discover communities over a wide range of spatial scales.

Finally, we also notice that in some cases, some additional content (or meta-information) about moving community members is available, which can be valuable for the community detection process. For example, in a mobile application, the transportation modes of mobile devices may be available. It is clear that when two objects often have the same transportation mode, in addition to spatial locality, this is more likely to be indicative of similar community membership. Such hints can be seamlessly incorporated into our model by incorporating the following additional term into the energy function:

$$E_{\text{status}}(\mathcal{Z}^{(t)}|\mathcal{S}^{(t)}) = \sum_{i \neq j} \delta \left[\left[z_i^{(t)} = z_j^{(t)}\right]\right] \delta \left[\left[s_i^{(t)} \neq s_j^{(t)}\right]\right] \quad (8)$$

Here, $s_i^{(t)}$ is the indicator from a set of L statuses $\{1, 2, \cdots, L\}$, and $\mathcal{S}^{(t)} = \{s_i^{(t)}|i = 1, 2, \cdots\}$ is the set of the statuses of all objects at time t. This energy function supports the membership of objects into the same community, when they frequently have similar status.

3.3 Infinite Community Evolution Model

To model the possibly infinite number of communities in *IC-DRF*, we adopt a Hierarchical Dirichlet Process (HDP) distribution to impose the prior on the model parameters $\boldsymbol{\gamma}$ and $\boldsymbol{\pi}$ in Eq. (1). We also use the *stick-breaking construction* [23] in order to perform the modeling. While a detailed introduction of this construction is beyond the scope of this paper, we briefly describe how it is applied in the context of this paper. The stick breaking construction imposes a prior on the probability $\boldsymbol{\gamma}$ of community assignment for each object. Suppose we have a stick with unit length. At each time, the stick-breaking construction draws γ_i by breaking a portion, which is determined by the Beta distribution Beta$(1, \alpha)$, from the remaining stick. The larger the concentration parameter α, the more the number of communities that are constructed. The HDP process introduces a two-level prior to capture the community evolution. In the first level, $\boldsymbol{\gamma}$ is drawn from the stick-breaking construction [23] with a concentration parameter α, i.e.,

$$\boldsymbol{\gamma} \sim \mathrm{GEM}(\alpha) \tag{9}$$

Here, GEM denotes the initials of the authors[1] of the stick breaking convention [23].

Each probability $\boldsymbol{\pi}_k$ from $\boldsymbol{\pi}$, denotes the transition probability from community k. This probability is assumed to be drawn from the Dirichlet Process DP$(\beta, \boldsymbol{\gamma})$ with concentration parameter θ.

$$\boldsymbol{\pi}_k \sim \mathrm{DP}(\theta, \boldsymbol{\gamma}), k = 1, 2, \cdots$$

Thus, all transition probabilities $\{\boldsymbol{\pi}_k\}_{k=1}^{+\infty}$ are drawn from Dirichlet Processes with the same base distribution $\boldsymbol{\gamma}$.

As in Eq. (4), we can obtain the joint probability of the community configurations by marginalizing out $\boldsymbol{\gamma}$ and $\boldsymbol{\pi}$ over the afore-mentioned HDP prior. This results in a two-level probabilistic model that can be explained by the Chinese Restaurant process [3]. Suppose there exists an object in community k at the current moment. Then, the HDP prior assumes that at the top level, the probability that an object in community k evolves to community l is proportional to the number of the times that the same transition occurs before; and with probability proportional to θ, an oracle sampling process is invoked for modeling at the bottom level. At the bottom level, the oracle process determines the probability that an object evolves to community l is proportional to the number of the times that community l has been sampled by this oracle process; and with probability proportional to α, the object becomes the solitary member of a newly created community. We refer interested readers to [3] for more details on the HDP prior.

4. GIBBS SAMPLING FOR IC-DRF

The Gibbs sampling process is critical in efficient online maintenance of the social sensing model, while retaining a high level of accuracy. Based on the probabilistic model of Eq. 4, our goal is to incrementally maintain the most probable community configurations. In other words, we aim to maximize the following conditional probability given the previous community configurations and the current member locations:

$$\begin{aligned} \mathcal{Z}^{(T)\star} &= \arg\max_{\mathcal{Z}^{(T)}} P(\mathcal{Z}^{(T)}|\mathcal{Z}^{(1:T-1)}, \mathcal{L}^{(T)}) \\ &= \arg\max_{\mathcal{Z}^{(T)}} P(\mathcal{Z}^{(T)}, \mathcal{Z}^{(1:T-1)}|\mathcal{L}^{(T)}) \end{aligned} \tag{10}$$

The above optimization problem is computationally intractable, because it has an exponentially large solution space in terms of the number of objects. Therefore, we use Gibbs sampling to perform a faster approximation. In Gibbs sampling, we need to compute the conditional probability of the community assignment for one object given the community assignments of the other objects in each step. Then, a new community assignment of each object is sequentially drawn from this conditional probability to replace the old one.

In our *IC-DRF* approach, consider the community configuration $\mathcal{Z}^{(1:T-1)}$ at time $T-1$. At this point, we need to sample the community assignment $z_j^{(T)}$ for each object o_j at time T in sequence conditioned on the community assignments $\mathcal{Z}_{-j}^{(T)}$ of the other objects. Here, $\mathcal{Z}_{-j}^{(T)}$ denotes the community assignments of the objects at time T leaving out $z_j^{(T)}$. According to the Chinese Restaurant process, the conditional probability $P(z_j^{(T)} = l|\mathcal{Z}^{(1:T-1)}, \mathcal{Z}_{-j}^{(T)})$ can be computed by a two-level process depending on whether the oracle process is invoked. We use $u_j^{(T)} = 1$ to indicate that the oracle is invoked or $u_j^{(T)} = 0$ otherwise.

At the top level, when the oracle is not invoked ($u_j^{(T)} = 0$), the probability of assigning object o_j to community l is as follows:

$$\begin{aligned} &P(z_j^{(T)} = l, u_j^{(T)} = 0|\mathcal{Z}^{(1:T-1)}, \mathcal{Z}_{-j}^{(T)}, z_j^{(T-1)} = k) \\ &\propto n_{k\to l,-j}^{(1:T)} \exp(-E(z_j^{(T)}, \mathcal{Z}_{-j}^{(T)}|\mathcal{L}^{(t)})) \end{aligned} \tag{11}$$

Here, we emphasize that object o_j has been assigned to community k at time $T-1$ in the condition, i.e., $z_j^{(T-1)} = k$; and $n_{k\to l,-j}^{(1:T)}$ is the number of the times of community evolutions from community k to l, leaving out the evolution of object o_j at time $T-1$, i.e.,

$$\begin{aligned} n_{k\to l,-j}^{(1:T)} &= \sum_{o_i\in O}\sum_{t=2}^{T-1} \delta\left[\left[z_i^{(t-1)} = k, z_i^{(t)} = l\right]\right] \\ &+ \sum_{o_i\in O, i\neq j} \delta\left[\left[z_i^{(T-1)} = k, z_i^{(T)} = l\right]\right] \end{aligned} \tag{12}$$

Otherwise, the probability of invoking the oracle process is as follows:

$$\begin{aligned} &P(u_j^{(T)} = 1|\mathcal{Z}^{(1:T-1)}, \mathcal{Z}_{-j}^{(T)}, z_j^{(T-1)} = k) \\ &\propto \alpha f_{\text{oracle}}(z_j^{(T)}, \mathcal{Z}_{-j}^{(T)}|\mathcal{L}^{(t)}) \end{aligned} \tag{13}$$

Here, $f_{\text{oracle}}(z_j^{(T)}, \mathcal{Z}_{-j}^{(T)}|\mathcal{L}^{(t)})$ denotes the expected value of the potential function when the oracle process is invoked:

$$\begin{aligned} &f_{\text{oracle}}(z_j^{(T)}, \mathcal{Z}_{-j}^{(T)}|\mathcal{L}^{(t)}) \\ &= \sum_{l=1}^{L_{\max}} \frac{m_{l,-j}^{(1:T)}}{m_{\cdot,-j}^{(1:T)} + \theta} \exp\left(-E(z_j^{(T)} = l, \mathcal{Z}_{-j}^{(T)}|\mathcal{L}^{(t)})\right) \\ &+ \frac{\theta}{m_{\cdot,-j}^{(1:T)} + \theta} \exp\left(-E(z_j^{(T)} = \text{new}, \mathcal{Z}_{-j}^{(T)}|\mathcal{L}^{(t)})\right) \end{aligned} \tag{14}$$

where $L_{\max}$ is the number of the existing communities so far, and $m_{l,-j}^{(1:T)}$ is the number of the times that community

[1]Griffiths, Engen and McCloskey

l has been chosen by the oracle for the objects excluding object j at time T, i.e.,

$$m_{l,-j}^{(1:T)} = \sum_{o_i \in O} \sum_{t=1}^{T-1} \delta \left[\left[z_i^{(t)} = l, u_i^{(t)} = 1 \right]\right] + \sum_{o_i \in O, i \neq j} \delta \left[\left[z_i^{(T)} = l, u_i^{(T)} = 1 \right]\right] \tag{15}$$

and

$$m_{\cdot,-j}^{(1:T)} = \sum_{l=1}^{L_{\max}} m_{l,-j}^{(1:T)} \tag{16}$$

Combining Eq. (11) and Eq. (13), we have the following sampling probability to decide which community is sampled to be assigned to object o_j at the top level, or instead the oracle is invoked as follows:

$$P(z_j^{(T)} = l, u_j^{(T)} = 0 | \mathcal{Z}^{(1:T-1)}, \mathcal{Z}_{-j}^{(T)}, z_j^{(T-1)} = k) = \frac{n_{k \to l,-j}^{(1:T)} \exp(-E(z_j^{(T)}, \mathcal{Z}_{-j}^{(T)} | \mathcal{L}^{(t)}))}{\alpha f_{oracle}(z_j^{(T)}, \mathcal{Z}_{-j}^{(T)} | \mathcal{L}^{(t)}) + \sum_{s=1}^{L_{\max}} n_{k \to s,-j}^{(1:T)} \exp(-E(z_j^{(T)} = s, \mathcal{Z}_{-j}^{(T)} | \mathcal{L}^{(t)}))} \tag{17}$$

and

$$P(u_j^{(T)} = 1 | \mathcal{Z}^{(1:T-1)}, \mathcal{Z}_{-j}^{(T)}, z_j^{(T-1)} = k) = \frac{\alpha f_{\text{oracle}}(z_j^{(T)}, \mathcal{Z}_{-j}^{(T)} | \mathcal{L}^{(t)})}{\alpha f_{\text{oracle}}(z_j^{(T)}, \mathcal{Z}_{-j}^{(T)} | \mathcal{L}^{(t)}) + \sum_{s=1}^{L_{\max}} n_{k \to s,-j}^{(1:T)} \exp(-E(z_j^{(T)} = s, \mathcal{Z}_{-j}^{(T)} | \mathcal{L}^{(t)}))} \tag{18}$$

If $u_i^{(T)} = 1$ is sampled at the top level, the oracle is invoked, and we have the following conditional probability of sampling an existing community for $z_j^{(T)}$:

$$P(z_j^{(T)} = l | \mathcal{Z}_{-j}^{(T)}, u_j^{(T)} = 1) \propto m_{l,-j}^{(1:T)} \exp(-E(z_j^{(T)}, \mathcal{Z}_{-j}^{(T)} | \mathcal{L}^{(t)})) \tag{19}$$

Otherwise, we have a new community sampled for o_j:

$$P(z_j^{(T)} = \text{new} | \mathcal{Z}_{-j}^{(T)}, u_j^{(T)} = 1) \propto \theta \exp(-E(z_j^{(T)} = \text{new}, \mathcal{Z}_{-j}^{(T)} | \mathcal{L}^{(t)})) \tag{20}$$

Algorithm 1 summarizes the Gibbs sampling procedure for community configuration $\mathcal{Z}^{(T)}$ at each time T. We can see that the only role of the previously determined configurations $\mathcal{Z}^{(1:T-1)}$ in this sampling procedure is to count the statistics n and m for each object. Hence, we only need to store and keep these counts updated at each time. Actually, we only need these counts and the community assignments for objects at the previous time $\mathcal{Z}^{(T-1)}$ in order to perform the sampling procedure. The other information in $\mathcal{Z}^{(1:T-1)}$ can be disregarded. This will save space for storing the past community information and make the online inference process of the *IC-DRF* model more efficient.

In each sampling step, only the community assignment for one object changes, and the assignments for the other objects remain the same. Therefore, when we compute the location-sensitive energy, we do not need recompute it. Instead, we can store the total values of intra-community and inter-community distances in two auxiliary variables and update them with the changed community assignment in each sampling step. Moreover, since we will use DBSCAN to cluster all the GPS locations to a much smaller number of semantic locations in real systems, the distances between these semantic locations can be precomputed and stored in a lookup matrix. This will save a lot of computing time in sampling procedure. Thus, the computational complexity in each time stamp is $O(|\mathcal{O}|L_{\max}^2 D)$, which is linear to the number of objects $|\mathcal{O}|$. This shows that our algorithm can well scale to large number of objects.

The model of this paper also ensures that the community membership of an object is determined by its presence in a community over a significant period of time rather than at one occasional moment, which we refer to as *temporal consistency*. To reflect such temporal consistency, we add a positive value n_0 to the community evolution count $n_{k \to k,-j}^{(1:T)}$ for each community k. The larger n_0 is, the longer one community tends to last over time with a stronger temporal consistency effect. This is because it is not sufficient to determine the community assignment of an object only based on its location at a particular moment. Community members may be co-located at a location by chance. Moreover, the reported object locations can be erroneous and noisy, because of the inherent limitations of such location tracking technology. The temporal consistency of our community assignment approach can reduce the negative impact of the limitations of data collection, and make our approach more robust in real scenarios.

5. EXPERIMENTAL RESULTS

In this section, we evaluate the proposed *IC-DRF* model compared with the other state-of-the-art algorithms. We will evaluate the approach for effectiveness, efficiency, and the effectiveness of incorporating content information.

5.1 Data Sets

We evaluate the proposed algorithm on the *GeoLife* data set [28], which recorded the trajectories of 164 users with GPS devices from April 2007 to October 2009 in the city of Beijing, China. It contains more than 12,000 different GPS trajectories over 139,310 kilometers in geographical scale.

Most of these trajectories were recorded at a sampling of 1-5 seconds or every 5-10 meters per point. This is not necessarily desirable, since locations do not change very significantly in small time frames. In the experiments, we apply the DBSCAN to cluster all recorded geo-locations to a set of "semantic" places. Our idea is the frequently visited locations correspond to some places with specific activity semantic meaning. For example, they can be a meeting room in a business building, a fitness facility, or a restaurant. Such geo-location clustering algorithms have been applied in literature [28] to automate the discovery of semantic places, and good performances have been observed on GeoLife dataset. Thus, we believe people who visit these semantic places simultaneously can be considered to be involved in the same activity. We construct the trajectory for each user by connecting their visited semantic places, and sample the trajectories every 10 minutes to form the dynamic networks at a set of discrete time stamps for community detection. The data set also contains the transportation modes, such as walk, bike, bus and car & taxi, associated with some users. We can use them as meta-information for user status in the energy function as Subsection 3.2. However, the transportation modes are incomplete in the data set, and we will simply skip them in the energy function when they are missing.

Since our metrics will require a ground-truth for evaluation purposes, we used the social similarity between users [29]. The degree of social closeness ranged from +1 (close) to −1 (not close). Figure 1 illustrates the social relations be-

Algorithm 1: Online inference for community configuration

Input: The community configurations $\mathcal{Z}^{(1:T-1)}$ from time 1 to $T-1$, α, θ and the number of sampling loops D
Output: The sampled community assignments.
Randomly initialize $\mathcal{Z}^{(T)}$ and compute the number of existing community $L_{\max}$ according;
for $d = 1$ **to** D **do**
  foreach object o_j **do**
    Count $n^{(1:T)}_{k\to l,-j}$ and $m^{(1:T)}_{l,-j}$ based on $\mathcal{Z}^{(1:T-1)}$ and the currently sampled $\mathcal{Z}^{(T)}$;
    Compute the conditional probabilities in Eq. (17) and (18):

$$P(z_j^{(T)} = l, u_j^{(T)} = 0|\mathcal{Z}^{(1:T-1)}, \mathcal{Z}^{(T)}_{-j}, z_j^{(T-1)} = k) = \frac{n^{(1:T)}_{k\to l,-j}\exp(-E(z_j^{(T)}, \mathcal{Z}^{(T)}_{-j}|\mathcal{L}^{(t)}))}{\alpha f_{\text{oracle}}(z_j^{(T)}, \mathcal{Z}^{(T)}_{-j}|\mathcal{L}^{(t)}) + \sum_{s=1}^{L_{\max}} n^{(1:T)}_{k\to s,-j}\exp(-E(z_j^{(T)}=s, \mathcal{Z}^{(T)}_{-j}|\mathcal{L}^{(t)}))}$$

    and

$$P(u_j^{(T)} = 1|\mathcal{Z}^{(1:T-1)}, \mathcal{Z}^{(T)}_{-j}, z_j^{(T-1)} = k) = \frac{\alpha f_{\text{oracle}}(z_j^{(T)}, \mathcal{Z}^{(T)}_{-j}|\mathcal{L}^{(t)})}{\alpha f_{\text{oracle}}(z_j^{(T)}, \mathcal{Z}^{(T)}_{-j}|\mathcal{L}^{(t)}) + \sum_{s=1}^{L_{\max}} n^{(1:T)}_{k\to s,-j}\exp(-E(z_j^{(T)}=s, \mathcal{Z}^{(T)}_{-j}|\mathcal{L}^{(t)}))};$$

    Sample $z_j^{(T)}$ and $u_j^{(T)}$ based on the above probabilities;
    if $u_j^{(T)} = 1$ **is sampled then**
      Compute the conditional probabilities according to Eq. (19) and (20):

$$P(z_j^{(T)}|\mathcal{Z}^{(T)}_{-j}, u_j^{(T)} = 1) = \begin{cases} \frac{m^{(1:T)}_{l,-j}\exp(-E(z_j^{(T)}=l, \mathcal{Z}^{(T)}_{-j}|\mathcal{L}^{(t)}))}{\sum_{s=1}^{L_{\max}} m^{(1:T)}_{s,-j}\exp(-E(z_j^{(T)}=s, \mathcal{Z}^{(T)}_{-j}|\mathcal{L}^{(t)})) + \theta\exp(-E(z_j^{(T)}=\text{new}, \mathcal{Z}^{(T)}_{-j}|\mathcal{L}^{(t)}))}, & \text{an existing community } l \text{ is sampled for } z_j^{(T)} \\ \frac{\theta\exp(-E(z_j^{(T)}=new, \mathcal{Z}^{(T)}_{-j}|\mathcal{L}^{(t)}))}{\sum_{s=1}^{L_{\max}} m^{(1:T)}_{s,-j}\exp(-E(z_j^{(T)}=s, \mathcal{Z}^{(T)}_{-j}|\mathcal{L}^{(t)})) + \theta\exp(-E(z_j^{(T)}=\text{new}, \mathcal{Z}^{(T)}_{-j}|\mathcal{L}^{(t)}))}, & \text{a new community is sampled for } z_j^{(T)} \end{cases};$$

      Sample $z_j^{(T)}$ based on the above probabilities;
      if $z_j^{(T)} = new$ **is sampled then**
        $L_{\max} \leftarrow L_{\max} + 1$;
        $z_j^{(T)} = L_{\max}$;
      end
    end
  end
end

tween these 164 users. The colors near the red end denote stronger social relations between users, whereas the colors near the blue end illustrate the weaker social relations.

5.2 Evaluation Metrics

We used the following three metrics at different time stamps to evaluate the community detection results, and reported the average values of the metrics over the intervals of three years (i.e., 2007, 2008 and 2009) for reporting purposes. This compares the performance changes of different algorithms over years.

- **Pearson:** The first measure was the Pearson's coefficient between the ground truth social relations and the detection results. For each pair of users, we denote their *detected* social relation as +1 if they belong to the same community (as found by the algorithm), and −1 otherwise. Then, we computed the Pearson's coefficient between the *ground truth* social relations and the *detected* social relations. Higher values of the Pearson's coefficients are indicative of good community structure in terms of correspondence with the ground truth.
- **INTRA:** This is the average of intra-community (ground-truth) social closeness. This metric is computed by averaging the social closeness over all pairs of intra-community users. A large value of INTRA suggests that the users assigned to the same community are more likely to be familiar with one another. In an indirect sense, this metric measures the true positives in the community detection results.
- **INTER:** This is the average of inter-community social closeness. This metric is computed by averaging the (ground-truth) social closeness over all pairs of inter-community users. A small value of INTER indicates that the users assigned to the different communities are not likely to be socially close to each other. In this sense, the negated INTER measures the true negatives in the community detection result.

5.3 Baselines

We compared the proposed *IC-DRF* model with three other community detection algorithms: (1) *ObjectGrowth* [18] which finds the swarms of moving objects in the same community;(2) *Dynamic stochastic block model (DSBM)* [26] which extends the stochastic block model to dynamic social

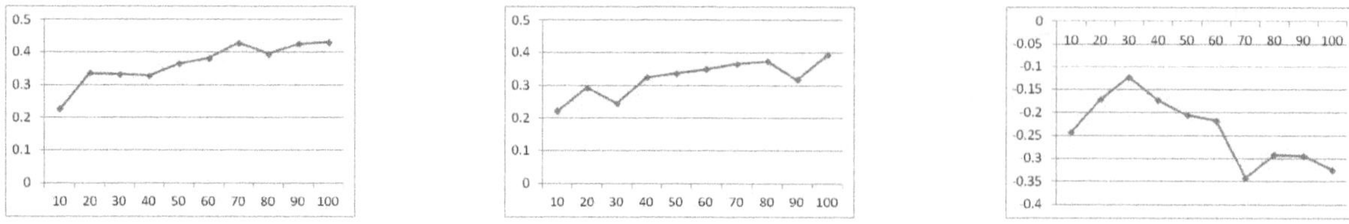

(a) Pearson v.s. α (b) INTRA v.s. α (c) INTER v.s. α

Figure 2: Parameter sensitivity of quality with respect to α, which influences new community formation.

Table 1: Comparison of different community detection algorithms on the *GeoLife* data set between 2007-2009. The best performance is highlighted in bold.

Algorithms	2007			2008			2009		
	Pearson	*INTRA*	*INTER*	*Pearson*	*INTRA*	*INTER*	*Pearson*	*INTRA*	*INTER*
ObjectGrowth	0.2537	0.3043	-0.1124	0.2654	0.2374	-0.153	0.2759	0.2941	-0.1361
DSBM	0.2453	0.1829	-0.1657	0.2631	0.2971	-0.1232	0.2748	0.2637	-0.1489
dIRM	0.2542	0.2818	-0.1208	0.2742	0.2816	-0.1398	0.297	0.2941	-0.1569
IC-DRF	**0.3430**	**0.3302**	**-0.1864**	**0.3606**	**0.3256**	**-0.2081**	**0.3956**	**0.3168**	**-0.2557**

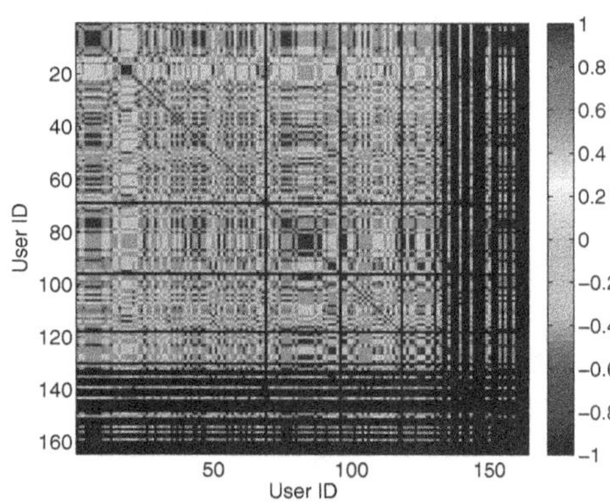

Figure 1: Illustration of social closeness between users. The social closeness between the user ranges from from a value of 1 (the closest) to -1 (the least close). Several users with IDs after 130 have very weak social connections with others. These users tend to form isolated communities with smaller size.

networks. This model also considers the dynamic evolution between communities in a transition probabilistic model;(3) *Dynamic Infinite Relational Model (dIRM)* [12] which also extends the *DSBM* to consider the dynamic and time-sensitive changes in the structure of the relational data.

5.4 Results

In Table 1, we report the results of the four compared algorithms on three time segments of the *GeoLife* data set. In order to show the experimental results over different periods, we evaluated the community detection results on three segments, corresponding to the 2007, 2008, and 2009 years. We reported the average value of Pearson, INTRA and INTER over these periods.

It is evident that the proposed *IC-DRF* model achieves the best performance over all the temporal segments among the compared algorithms in terms of all metrics. Furthermore, the performance improves over the different years, because a larger number of GPS data points progressively improves the incrementally updated probabilistic model over time. In general, the community evolution counts became more stable and robust as the repeated patterns in the community evolution dynamics were learned by the probabilistic model of *IC-DRF*. Thus the model estimation improved over time, and is manifested in the more accurate results for later periods in the community detection process. This is particularly useful in the context of applications in which the community detection process is likely to be executed over long periods of time.

The results reported above are obtained with $\alpha = 80$, $\theta = 80$ and $n_0 = 20$. While the number of communities is determined in a data-driven manner, the value of α still continues to have some indirect influence on it, since it affects the rate of new community formation. Therefore, it is useful to test the impact of α on the quality of the underlying communities. In Figure 2, we illustrate the parameter sensitivity of the *IC-DRF* model in terms of three metrics when α changes from 10 to 100. We can see that as long as α is not too small, the performance does not change too much. This shows the robustness of the approach. Moreover, Figure 2(a) illustrates the variation in the number of communities with respect to different values of α. As we expect, the number of communities tend to increase with larger values of α.

5.5 Computational Efficiency Results

We also studied the computational efficiency of the *IC-DRF* model for updating the community configurations in each time stamp. Since our approach uses an online incremental inference paradigm, it is critical for the model to be efficient enough to make simultaneous decisions about the evolution dynamics of community membership of different users in an incremental way. Recall that our use of

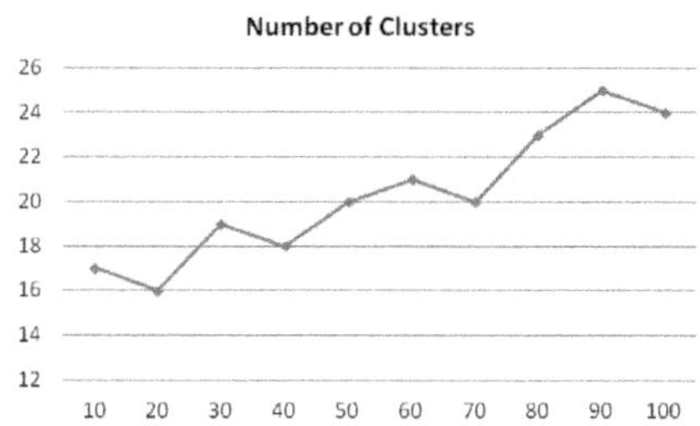

(a) Number of clusters v.s. α

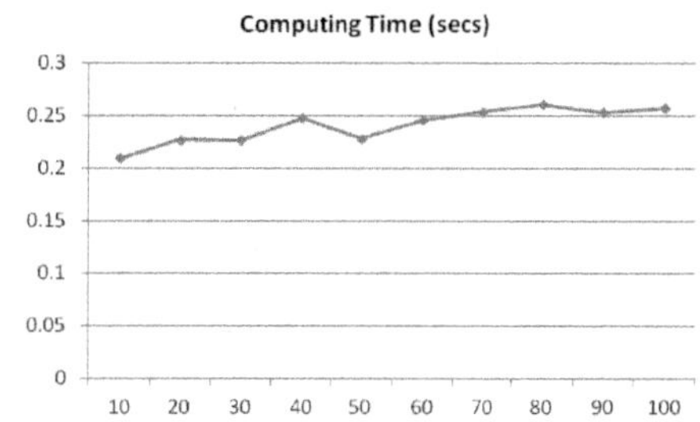

(b) Computational time v.s. α

Figure 3: The variation in (a) the number of communities and (b) computational time (seconds) of *IC-DRF* with α.

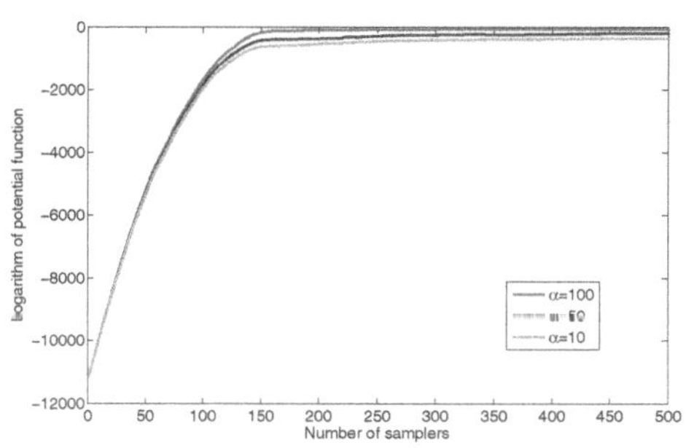

Figure 4: The potential function with increasing number of samples. From about the 160th samplers, the sampling algorithm begins to converge. After about 300 samplers, the potential function closely converges to the maximum value. This indicates that the most probable community configuration can be robustly obtained at that point.

the Gibbs sampling process is motivated by its efficiency in maintaining the incremental model. Our approach is influenced by some parameters in Gibbs sampling process, such as α, since it indirectly influences the number of communities. Figure 3(b) illustrates the computational time versus α. The value of α is illustrated on the X-axis, whereas the computational time is illustrated on the Y-axis. It is evident that while the computational time changes with α, the sensitivity is relatively small. Therefore, the computational efficiency also tends to be quite robust with α.

We also illustrated the efficiency of the Gibbs sampling process in terms of its convergence behavior over a small number of samples. Specifically, we plot the logarithm of the potential function with increasing number of Gibbs samplers in Figure 4. Recall that the potential function is the sum of the energy function and the logarithm of HDP likelihood. The number of Gibbs samples are illustrated on the X-axis, whereas the potential function is illustrated on the Y-axis. We can see that after about 160 samples, the potential function converges to the maximum value (as averaged over all users). We further note that the potential function values were recorded at the early second loop of the Gibbs sampling. Therefore, after the second loop of Gibbs sampling, we can stop and obtain the most probable community configuration with these parameters. This demonstrates the Gibbs sampling process can efficiently infer the most probable community assignment.

5.6 Incorporating Content Information: Transportation Modes

Finally, we show the impact of incorporating additional content-based meta-information into the community detection process, as discussed at the end of subsection 3.2. We will investigate that the additional labeling information can improve the community detection accuracy. Specifically, we use the transportation modes in the data set as the meta-information. These are incorporated in the energy function, as discussed in subsection 3.2. Table 2 presents the results by comparing the models with and without transportation modes in the *IC-DRF* model. We can see that the model with transportation modes performs better than its counterpart, which did not use the transportation modes. We can also see that the value of INTER metric is improved more than the value of INTRA metric. It is reasonable and expected, because users that belong to different communities can sometimes be recognized by very wide variation in their transportation modes. On the the other hand, the improvement of INTER is not obvious since two users in the same transportation mode do not necessarily belong to the same community. It is important to recognize that this additional meta-information is simply additional knowledge to *improve* the community detection process, for which the primary model is the probabilistic spatio-temporal analysis. The transportation modes simply provide additional information for more effective community discovery. Nevertheless, this is a useful feature to incorporate in the detection process, since additional meta-information is often available in many sensing scenarios.

6. CONCLUSION

In this paper, we investigated the dynamic and evolving community formation from the social structure implied by the distance behavior of mobile sensors. The proposed *IC-DRF* algorithm defines dynamic random fields over time that can determine and adjust the community structures on the basis of the evolving spatio-temporal locality. At the same time, the number of communities is determined dynamically and automatically at any given time, so that the model is

Table 2: Comparison of *IC-DRF* model with and without content information (transportation modes). The best performance is highlighted in bold.

	without using transportation modes			with using transportation modes		
Dataset	Pearson	INTRA	INTER	Pearson	INTRA	INTER
2007	0.3430	**0.3302**	-0.1864	**0.3458**	0.2924	**-0.2116**
2008	0.3606	0.3256	-0.2081	**0.3811**	**0.3494**	**-0.2172**
2009	0.3956	0.3168	**-0.2557**	**0.3999**	**0.3309**	-0.2508

able to effectively adapt to global changes in the granularity of the natural community structure. An efficient Gibbs sampling algorithm is used in order to speed up the approach, so that it can be used in an online incremental manner. This makes the *IC-DRF* sufficiently scalable in order to handle large amounts of incoming GPS data in real time. The experimental results on the real dataset show the effectiveness of the proposed model as compared to other state-of-the-art algorithms.

Acknowledgments

Research was sponsored by the Army Research Laboratory under Cooperative Agreement Number W911NF-09-2-0053 and National Science Foundation (NSF) under Grant IIS-1144111. Mr. Guo-Jun Qi was also supported in part by an IBM fellowship.

7. REFERENCES

[1] C. Aggarwal, T. Abdelzaher. *Social Sensing.* Managing and Mining Sensor Data, Springer, 2013.

[2] L. Backstrom, D. P. Huttenlocher, J. M. Kleinberg, X. Lan. Group formation in large social networks: membership, growth, and evolution, *KDD*, 2006.

[3] M.J. Beal, Z. Ghahramani, C. Rasmussen. The infinite hidden Markov Model, *NIPS Conference*, 2001.

[4] M. Benkert, J. Gudmundsson, F. Hubner, T. Wolle. Reporting flock patterns, *COMGEO*, 2008.

[5] C. Aggarwal, H. Wang. *Managing and Mining Graph Data*, Springer, 2010.

[6] C. Aggarwal. *Social Network Data Analytics*, Springer, 2011.

[7] D. Chakrabarti, R. Kumar, A. Tomkins. Evolutionary clustering, *KDD*, 2006.

[8] Y. Chi, X. Song, D. Zhou, K. Hino, B. L. Tseng. Evolutionary spectral clustering by incorporating temporal smoothness, *KDD*, 2007.

[9] E. Cho, S. Myers, J. Leskovec. Friendship and Mobility: User Movement In Location-Based Social Networks. *KDD*, 2011.

[10] A. Clauset, M. E. J. Newman, C. Moore. Finding community structure in very large networks, *Phys. Rev. E 70, 066111*, 2004.

[11] J. Gudmundsson, M. van Kreveld. Computing longest duration flocks in trajectory data. *GIS*, 2006.

[12] K. Ishiguro, T. Iwata, N. Ueda, J. Tenenbaum. Dynamic Infinite Relational Model for Time-varying Relational Data Analysis, *NIPS*, 2010.

[13] H. Jeung, M. L. Yiu, X. Zhou, C. Jensen, H. Shen. Discovery of Convoys in Trajectory Databases. *VLDB*, 2008.

[14] P. Kalnis, N. Mamoulis, S. Bakiras. On discovering moving clusters in spatio-temporal data. *SSTD*, 2005.

[15] R. Kumar, P. Raghavan, S. Rajagopalan, A. Tomkins. Trawling the web for emerging cyber-communities, *Computer Networks*, 31(11-16), pp. 1481–1493, 1999.

[16] J. Leskovec, K. J. Lang, A. Dasgupta, M. W. Mahoney. Statistical properties of community structure in large social and information networks, *WWW*, 2008.

[17] J.-G. Lee, J. Han, K.-Y. Whang. Trajectory Clustering: A Partition and Group Framework, *SIGMOD*, 2007.

[18] Z. Li, B. Ding, J. Han, R. Kays. Swarm: Mining Relaxed Temporal Moving Object Clusters, *VLDB Conference*, 2010.

[19] Y.-R. Lin, J. Sun, P. Castro, R. Konuru, H. Sundaram, A. Kelliher. Extracting community structure through relational hypergraphs, *WWW*, 2009.

[20] A. Noulas, S. Scellato, C. Mascolo, M. Pontil. An empirical study of geographic user activity patterns in foursquare, *ICWSM*, 2011.

[21] G. Qi, C. Aggarwal, T. Huang. Community Detection with Edge Content in Social Media Networks, *ICDE Conference*, 2012.

[22] S. Scellato, A. Noulas, R. Lambiotte, and C. Mascolo. Socio-spatial properties of online location-based social networks, *ICWSM*, 2011.

[23] J. Sethuraman. A constructive definition of dirichlet priors, *Statistica Sinica*, 4:639–650, 1994.

[24] D. Wang, D. Pedreschi, C. Song, F. Giannotti, A. Barabasi. Human mobility, social ties, and link prediction, *KDD*, 2011.

[25] T. Yang, R. Jin, Y. Chi, S. Zhu. Combining link and content for community detection: a discriminative approach, *KDD*, 2009.

[26] T. Yang, Y. Chi, S. Zhu, Y. Gong, R. Jin. Detecting communities and their evolutions in dynamic social networks: a Bayesian approach, *Maching Learning*, 82: pp. 157–189, 2011.

[27] Y. Zhou, H. Cheng, J. X. Yu. Graph clustering based on structural/attribute similarities, *PVLDB*, 2(1), pp. 718–729, 2009.

[28] Y. Zheng, L. Zhang, X. Xie, W.-Y. Ma. Mining interesting locations and travel sequences from GPS trajectories, *WWW*, 2009.

[29] V. Zheng, B. Cao, Y. Zheng, X. Xie, Q. Yang. Collaborative Filtering Meets Mobile Recommendation: A User centered Approach, *AAAI*, 2010.

Distinguishing Topical and Social Groups Based on Common Identity and Bond Theory

Przemyslaw A. Grabowicz[§] [*] Luca Maria Aiello[†] Víctor M. Eguíluz[§] Alejandro Jaimes[†]

[§]{pms,victor}@ifisc.uib-csic.es
IFISC (CSIC-UIB)
Palma de Mallorca, Spain

[†]{alucca, ajaimes}@yahoo-inc.com
Yahoo! Research
Barcelona, Spain

ABSTRACT

Social groups play a crucial role in social media platforms because they form the basis for user participation and engagement. Groups are created explicitly by members of the community, but also form organically as members interact. Due to their importance, they have been studied widely (e.g., community detection, evolution, activity, etc.). One of the key questions for understanding how such groups evolve is whether there are different types of groups and how they differ. In Sociology, theories have been proposed to help explain how such groups form. In particular, the common identity and common bond theory states that people join groups based on identity (i.e., interest in the topics discussed) or bond attachment (i.e., social relationships). The theory has been applied qualitatively to small groups to classify them as either topical or social. We use the identity and bond theory to define a set of features to classify groups into those two categories. Using a dataset from Flickr, we extract user-defined groups and automatically-detected groups, obtained from a community detection algorithm. We discuss the process of manual labeling of groups into social or topical and present results of predicting the group label based on the defined features. We directly validate the predictions of the theory showing that the metrics are able to forecast the group type with high accuracy. In addition, we present a comparison between declared and detected groups along topicality and sociality dimensions.

Categories and Subject Descriptors

H.3.5 [**Online Information Services**]: Web-based services; H.1.2 [**User/Machine Systems**]: Human information processing;

*P.A.G. has performed the research while visiting Yahoo! Research Barcelona.

WSDM'13, February 4–8, 2013, Rome, Italy.

General Terms

Algorithms, Experimentation, Measurement

Keywords

Social Media, Groups, Bond theory, Identity theory, Flickr

1. INTRODUCTION

A longstanding theory about the creation of social communities affirms that people join groups driven by either strong personal ties with other members or by the interest in the group as a whole. As a result, depending on the prevalent motivation of members, spontaneously generated groups can be categorized as either *social* or *topical*. This theory is known as "common identity and common bond" [22] and assumes that the two types of groups have distinct and well recognizable traits that characterize them.

In recent years, the theory has been widely commented and elaborated by social scientists from a theoretical perspective and through small-scale experiments [26, 29, 24], but a validation over large-scale datasets together with the development of rigorous, automated methodologies to distinguish the group types is missing. Indeed, the availability of big data from social media platforms provides the opportunity to study the dynamics of the online communities from a data-mining perspective [19, 21, 14]. None of those experiments, however, have been directly aimed at verifying the common identity and common bond theory.

The design of a technique to detect the group type based on the common identity and common bond principles would first contribute to a strong validation of the theory itself and, on the other hand, would provide a general framework for automatic classification of user groups in online social media. Such a classification would have direct impact on the ability of describing the structure of online social networks along the axes of sociality and topicality and, consequently, on the possibility of better user characterization.

We contribute to fill this gap by proposing a set of general metrics based on the theory. We show that the metrics' values computed on a large corpus of groups extracted from Flickr confirm the cardinal points of the theory and are indeed good predictors of the group type. In addition, we repeat the same analysis on groups identified by a graph-based community detection algorithm. This allows us to compare the user-generated communities to the automatically detected ones not only from a structural perspective but also along the dimensions of sociality and topicality. Since community detection techniques have been largely employed in recent years to describe the structure of complex social systems [8], the need for a clearer assessment of the meaning of the detected clusters has been often expressed from different angles [15, 31], but never completely satisfied. With our study we also contribute to shed light on this matter.

To the best of our knowledge, this is the first attempt of formalization of the common identity and common bond theory, and of its validation over a large and diverse set of user communities. The obtained results can open a new perspective on the semantic interpretation of implicit and explicit user groups in social media.

Our main contributions can be summarized as follows:

- Translation of the common identity and common bond theory into general metrics applicable to social graphs. An insightful characterization of a large group dataset from Flickr is performed using the proposed metrics.
- Comparison between user-defined groups and groups discovered by a community detection algorithm, both in terms of their overlap and their properties of sociality and topicality.
- Design of a method to predict whether a group is social or topical, based on the defined metrics. Prediction on the user-generated groups from the Flickr data yields surprisingly good results.

The rest of the paper is structured as follows. In Section 2 we overview related work. In Section 3 we describe the main principles of the common identity and common bond theory and propose their practical translation into general metrics, and in Section 4 we introduce the Flickr dataset we use to test these metrics. In Section 5 we describe the process of gathering a ground truth about group topicality or sociality through an editorial process. In Section 6 we provide a comparison between user-created Flickr groups and groups identified by a community detection algorithm in terms of their overlap, then we study the properties of the defined metrics computed over declared and detected groups and in particular over the subsets of groups labeled as social or topical in the ground truth that we produced. Finally, in Section 7 we show that we can accurately predict the group type by combining the defined metrics.

2. RELATED WORK

The spontaneous aggregation of people in communities has been widely studied in social science as one of the fundamental processes driving the global dynamics of social ecosystems [18] and as a factor driving the formation of the social identity of individuals [27].

Since the emergence of online social media, the global structure, evolution and dynamics of social groups have been investigated over large-scale and heterogeneous datasets [12]. Evolution of groups has been characterized as a very broad phenomenon [19, 5] that is dependent on the nature of the group [6], its intrinsic fitness [11] and on the density of social ties connecting its members [2]. Dependency of activity and connectivity on group size has been studied in several platforms [13, 14, 10], showing relations to Dunbar's theory on the upper bound of around 150 stable social relationships for an average human [7]. Besides activity, similarity between users is an important dimension in modeling individual users in groups [28], particularly given that, to a large extent, social media users tend to aggregate following the homophily principle [1]. Nevertheless, similarity is not necessarily the best indicator for group activity and longevity, as diversity of content shared between group members is a relevant factor to keep alive the interest of members [17].

At a finer scale, social communities can be described in terms of user engagement. From a quantitative perspective, the amount of participation of members in activities related to the group is varied and dependent on group size [3]. Intra-group activity has been characterized in terms of propensity of people to reply to questions of other members [30], coherence of discussion topics [9], or item sharing practices [21]. Modeling inner activity of groups has helped in finding effective strategies to predict future group growth or activity [14], recommend group affiliation, or enhance the search experience on social platforms [20].

Social and thematic components of communities have been widely studied in social science, most of all within the common identity and common bond theory on which the present work is based [22, 26, 24]. Nevertheless, the principles behind the theory have never been translated into practical methods to categorize groups, nor tested on large datasets. On the other hand, data-driven studies have investigated social and thematic components separately when characterizing groups [5]. Preliminary insights on the interweavement between such dimensions have been given in exploratory work on Flickr, where signals of correlation between social density and tag dispersion in groups is shown [23]. In this paper, we go far beyond that point, defining metrics that can be used to predict if a group is social or topical and testing their effectiveness against a reliable ground truth.

Besides the analysis of user-created groups, the study of automatically detected groups through community detection algorithms has attracted much interest lately [8]. Detected communities are supposed to represent meaningful aggregations of people where dense or intense social exchanges take place among members [13]. Nevertheless, even if synthetic methods to verify the quality of clusters have been proposed [15], the question of whether such artificial groups capture some notion of community perceived by the users remains open. If on the one hand the computation of cluster-goodness metrics over user-created groups can give useful hints about their structural cohesion [31], on the other hand a direct comparison between user-created groups and detected communities is still missing, particularly in terms of the amount of sociality or topical coherence they embed.

3. TOPICAL AND SOCIAL GROUPS

Notions of *community* and social *group* have been widely studied in the behavioral sciences [25, 27]. It has been shown that the internal dynamics of social groups emerge from the combination of complex cognitive processes such as sense of membership, influence between people, fulfillment of individual and collective needs inside the group, and shared emotional connections [18]. Based on such widely accepted theoretical foundations, sociological theories have been formulated to disentangle all of these complex aspects.

In the following subsections, we provide a high-level description of one of the most known theories on group formation and propose a translation of its main cornerstones into general metrics that can be applied on social graphs.

3.1 Identity and Bond Theory

The *common identity and common bond theory* describes social groups along the dimensions of topicality and sociality [22, 24]. According to the theory, the attachment to a group, as well as the permanence and involvement in it, can be explained in terms of common *identity* or common *bond*. Identity-based attachment holds when people join a group based on their interest in the community as a whole or in a well-defined common theme shared by all of the members. People whose participation is due to identity-based attachment may not directly engage with anyone and might even participate anonymously. Conversely, bond-based attachment is driven by personal social relations with other specific members, and thus the main theme of the group may be disregarded. The two processes result in two different group types, that for simplicity we name "*topical*" for identity-based attachment and "*social*" for bond-based attachment.

In practice, groups can be formed from a mix of identity and bond-based attachment, but very often they tend to lean more towards either sociality or topicality. According to the theory, the group type is related with the *reciprocity* and the *topics* of discussion. Members of social groups tend to have reciprocal interactions with other members, whereas interactions in topical groups are generally not directly reciprocated. In addition, topics of discussion tend to vary drastically and cover multiple subjects in social groups, while in topical groups discussions tend to be related to the group theme and cover specific areas. According to the theory, social groups are founded on individual relationships between their members, therefore it is harder for newcomers to join and integrate with members that already have strong relationships between each other. One implication of this is that social groups are vulnerable to turnover, since the departure of a person's friends may influence his own departure. Topical groups, on the other hand, are more open to newcomers and more robust to departures.

3.2 From theory to metrics

Based on the theoretical principles described above, it is possible to construct metrics to differentiate between the two types of groups. In particular, it is possible to quantify the reciprocity of interactions, and the topicality of the information exchanged between group members. We adopt a very general *multidigraph* model that fits most of the current social media platforms. Members are represented as nodes, and each distinct *interaction* between any two members is represented by a directed arc. Nodes can belong to multiple *groups* and we associate, with each group, a bag of user-generated *terms* (e.g., tags, group posts).

Next, we describe: i) *reciprocity* metrics, used to quantifying group sociality, ii) *entropy* of terms, to determine how much the topics of discussion vary within a group, and iii) *activity* metrics, to measure the liveliness of the group.

3.2.1 Reciprocity

Reciprocity occurs whenever a user interacts with another user and that user responds her at any time later with the same type of interaction. We define *intra-reciprocity* of a group g as:

$$r_g^{\text{int}} = \frac{E_g^{\text{int,rec}}/2}{E_g^{\text{int,rec}}/2 + E_g^{\text{int,nrec}}}, \tag{1}$$

where $E_g^{\text{int,rec}}$ and $E_g^{\text{int,nrec}}$ are, respectively, the number of reciprocated and non-reciprocated links internal to the group g. Correspondingly, the *inter-reciprocity* at the border of the group is defined by r_g^{ext}, accounting for the reciprocity between members and non-members.

We normalize the intra-reciprocity score using the average reciprocity value $\langle r_g^{\text{int}} \rangle$ over all groups:

$$t_g = \frac{r_g^{\text{int}}}{\langle r_g^{\text{int}} \rangle}. \tag{2}$$

The larger the intra-reciprocity, the higher the probability that the group is social. Alternatively, to compensate for the effect of the correlation between reciprocity and the number of internal interactions, and to account for local effects, the intra-reciprocity can be normalized by the inter-reciprocity:

$$u_g = \frac{r_g^{\text{int}} + 1}{r_g^{\text{ext}} + 1}. \tag{3}$$

We add 1 to both numerator and denominator to reduce the fluctuations of u_g at low values of r_g^{ext}. This relative reciprocity compares the reciprocity between the members with their reciprocity toward people not belonging to the group. It reflects how sociality of group members distinguishes itself from the environment.

3.2.2 Topicality

The set of terms $T(g)$ associated with a group indicates the topical diversity of the group. Thus we measure the entropy of the group as

$$H(g) = -\sum_{t \in T(g)} p(t) \cdot \log_2 p(t), \tag{4}$$

where $p(t)$ is the probability of occurrence of the term t in the set $T(g)$. The higher the entropy, the greater is the variety of terms and, according to the theory, the more social the group is. Conversely, the lower the entropy, the more topical the group is. In addition, since not all groups have the same number of terms and the entropy value grows with the total number of terms, we introduce the *normalized entropy* h_g, which is normalized by the average value of entropy for the groups with the same number of terms:

$$h_g = \frac{H(g)}{\langle H(f) \rangle_{|T(g)|=|T(f)|}}. \tag{5}$$

3.2.3 Activity

Even if, for the considered theory, activity is not a discriminative factor between social and topical groups, it is useful to characterize the liveliness of a community. Activity is quantified in terms of the number of internal interactions normalized by the expected number of internal interactions for a set of nodes with the same degree sequence:

$$a_g = \frac{E_g^{\text{int}}}{(D_g^{\text{in}} D_g^{\text{out}})/E}. \tag{6}$$

D_g^{in} and D_g^{out} are total numbers of interactions originated by members of the group g or being targeted to members of

comments	favorites	contacts	decl. g.	det. g.
238M	112M	71M	504K	646K

Table 1: Total number of interactions and declared/detected groups.

this group, where E is the total number of interactions in the network. If this property has a value higher than 1 then the number of interactions internal to the group is higher than the number of interactions expected in a random scenario with the same group activity volume.

Another way of measuring activity of a group is by comparing density of its internal interactions with the density of its external interactions:

$$b_g = \frac{E_g^{\text{int}}/(s_g(s_g-1))}{E_g^{\text{ext}}/(2(N-s_g)s_g)}, \quad (7)$$

where s_g is the cardinality of group g and N is total number of nodes in the network. Values of b_g greater than 1 indicate a density of internal interactions higher than interactions between the group and the rest of the network. This metric effectively compares intensity of interactions between members of the groups with the intensity of their interactions with the entire network.

4. DATASET AND PREPROCESSING

The wide variety of user groups and the richness of interaction types make Flickr an ideal platform for our study. We use only public, anonymous data retrievable via the Flickr public API, until the end of 2008. Table 1 summarizes the data described below.

4.1 User interactions

We collected three types of pairwise, directed interactions:

Comments. User u comments on a photo of user v. This interaction is *mediated* through the photo. We filter out the comments of users on their own photos, obtaining a total of 238M comments.

Favorites. User u marks one of user v's photos as a *favorite.* The interaction is mediated through the favorited photo. We extract 112M favorite interactions.

Contacts. User u adds user v among his contacts. Social contacts in Flickr are directed and may be reciprocated. One person can choose another person as his contact only once and the relation remains in the same state until the contact is removed. There are 71M contacts in our dataset.

4.2 Groups

Users of Flickr can create, moderate and administer their own groups. Most groups are open, so users can join without an invitation. Others are only by invitation and joining requires the administrator's permission. There are over 500K groups in our Flickr dataset.

In addition to user-created groups (we refer to them as *declared*), we analyze the sociality and topicality properties of groups that are not defined by users but are instead found by community detection algorithms (we name these *detected* groups). We applied the OSLOM community detection algorithm [16] over the entire network of social contacts in our dataset. We choose OSLOM because it detects overlapping communities, which is a natural feature of real groups. Moreover, OSLOM has performed well in recent community detection benchmarks [15] and it outperformed other algorithms we tested. OSLOM detected 646K groups.

4.3 Tags

We use *tags* of the photos as terms for our model. The primary set of photos from which we extract tags is the *photo pool* of the group (i.e., the photos uploaded to the group by its members). Photo pools are available for declared groups only. In addition, in both declared and detected groups, the interactions between members of the group that are mediated through photos (i.e., comments, favorites) result in two additional photo sets from which tags are extracted. We process the three tag sets separately (pool, comments, favorites), and for each of them we compute the normalized entropy (h_g^{pool}, h_g^{com}, h_g^{fav}).

5. GROUP LABELING

To determine whether the defined metrics correctly capture the sociality and topicality of groups, we compare them against a reliable ground truth. We asked human editors to label groups based on well-defined guidelines extracted directly from the common identity and common bond theory [24]. For the labeling we randomly selected groups meeting the following requirements: i) more than 5 members, ii) more than 100 internal comments, iii) relative activities a_g^{com} and b_g^{com} higher than 10^2. The third requirement ensured us that the selected groups were active well above the expected values in a random case. After this selection we obtained over 34K declared groups and over 33K detected groups. We describe the labeling process of such groups in detail in the following subsections.

5.1 Information provided to editors

The labeling is based on the human capability of processing the semantics and sentiment behind text and photos. The labeling was performed to generate a ground truth of "social" and "topical" groups. The editors were asked to make judgments in this respect and were presented with the following information for each group:

Group profile. The Flickr group profile consists of the group name, description by the creator of the group, discussion board, photo pool, and map of places where photos uploaded to the group pool were taken. This information is available only for declared groups.

Comments. We provide text of all comments that happen between the members. Comments are shown in chronological order and are grouped by thread, if they appear under the same photo. Additionally we also include a link to the photo.

Tags. Editors are shown the list of the 5 most frequent tags attached to the photos that mediate the internal comments to the group. The list is sorted alphabetically.

5.2 Labeling guidelines

Human labelers were shown the information described above and asked to categorize groups as either *social, topical* or *unknown.* The last case is reserved for groups for which text is written in a language unknown to the labeler, making the task impossible to accomplish. Intentionally, no *unsure* category was allowed to keep the categorization strictly binary, as the theory does. Some groups can be both topical and social, and therefore difficult to categorize, but for the sake of clarity and conformity with the theory we kept the categorization as a binary task. Editors were provided with specific instructions on how to recognize social and topical groups, and on how to perform the categorization. The guidelines are summarized as follows:

I. Comments and photos. By examining comments and photos, find traces of people who know each other or who have a personal relationship. Knowing each other's real names, spending time together, co-appearing in photos, sharing common past experiences, referencing mutually known places, and disclosing personal information are all signals of the presence of a social relationship [4]. The predominance of friendly and colloquial comments (e.g., jokes, laughter) is another element distinguishing social groups from topical groups. In topical groups, the atmosphere is more formal and comments tend to be more impersonal [26]. Examples of impersonal comments include expressing appreciation for photos, praising the photographers, thanking them for their work, or commenting on any particular topic in a neutral way. As a rule of thumb, if many personal comments are detected, then the sociality of the group should be considered high. If such comments are not many (e.g., just between small subsets of members), but the overall atmosphere of the interaction is rather personal and friendly, then we consider the sociality of this group as fairly present. If, on the other hand, comments are mainly impersonal and neutral, sociality has to be considered low, in favor of higher topicality.

II. Tags and description. Read the tags and the profile description of the group. If the tags are semantically consistent then the topicality of the group should be considered high, and even higher if the name and description of the group corresponds to the content of the tags. In some cases, tags or group descriptions can contain words indicating personal relations or events (e.g., "wedding", "grandpa", names, etc.), indicating a higher sociality of the group. Tags can also contain names of specific locations. Geo-characterized tags can be reasserted by looking at the map of places where photos were taken. Such tags are a good indication that the sociality of the group is present, but that has to be confirmed through the inspection of comments.

The editors labeled the groups after judging the two aspects above. If both tags and comments are highly social or topical, then the choice of label is straightforward. If the tags are highly topical and the comments are not social then the group is labeled as topical, and vice versa. If the tags are a bit topical and comments highly social then the group is labeled as social. The labelers were asked to read as many comments as needed to arrive to a fairly clear decision.

5.3 Group examples

To provide a sense of how the defined guidelines were applied in practice, we describe two examples. The first one is a group titled "Airlines Austrian", tagged with labels "aircraft", "airport" and "spotting." Photos are from different countries in Europe and the vast majority of them depict airplanes. Members are very active in commenting and writing comments related on the aircraft theme (e.g., "I just love this airplane, the TU-154M is just a plane Boeing or Airbus could never design"). In this case, all of the features are aligned with the concept of topical group defined in the guidelines. The second group is named "Camp Baby 2008" and it is described in the main page as a collection of photos of a two-day event for young mothers taking place at a specific location. Photos depict people attending the event and interacting with each other with a friendly attitude. Tags and comments often contain names of individuals and references to past common experiences (e.g., "I love Mindy and can not wait to see her again!!"). Although the group has a specific topic, its social component is very strong.

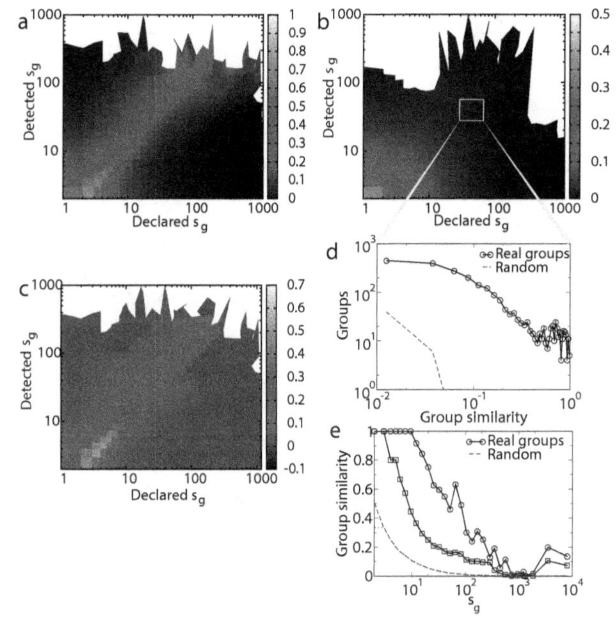

Figure 1: Jaccard similarity between declared and detected groups as a function of their sizes. Diagonal shows an interesting pattern (a) which is not reproduced by randomized groups (b). We subtract (b) from (a) and plot the result in (c), and a histogram of similarity values for a sample of groups lying at the diagonal in (d). For groups of various sizes, we plot 91th and 99th percentiles of similarity between declared and detected groups (e).

In practice, more ambiguous cases can occur and, ultimately, the decision of the labeler has an arbitrary component, as in every complex annotation process. Nevertheless, the defined guidelines gave the labelers precise instructions and, as described next, we recurred to multiple independent editors to assess the quality of the extracted ground truth.

5.4 Labeling outcome

A total of 101 declared groups and 69 detected groups were labeled by 3 people: two of the authors and an independent labeler who was not aware of the type of study nor of the purpose of the labeling. The inter-labeler agreement, measured as Fleiss' Kappa, is 0.60 for the declared groups, meaning that there exists good agreement between labelers.

In order to assess the quality of the labels, we also counted the number of messages exchanged between group members. The counting was done anonymously in aggregate and the content of the messages was not accessed. Groups labeled as social contain around twice as many messages between their members compared to topical groups of similar size. Even if this does not constitute a proof of higher sociality, intuitively people who get in touch via one-on-one communication are more likely to have a more intimate social relationship.

The Kappa value for detected groups is around 0.44, revealing lower agreement. A factor that partially determined

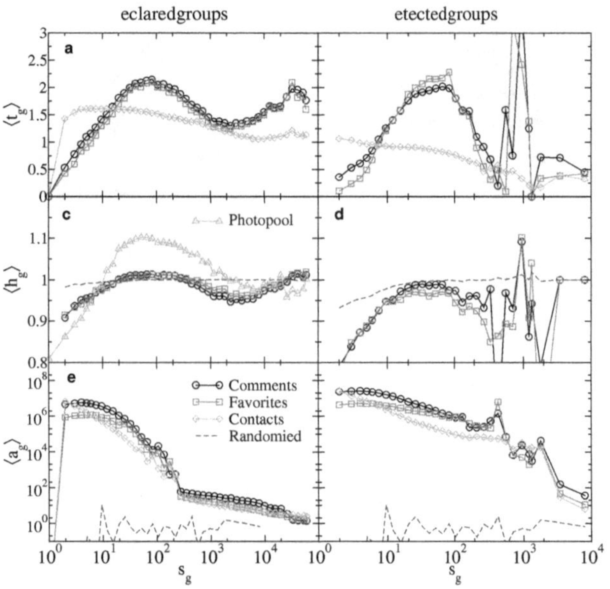

Figure 2: Dependency of normalized reciprocity (a-b), normalized entropy (c-d) and relative activity (e-f) on size of groups for comments, favorites, contacts and photo pools, for declared and detected groups. Blue dashed line is for randomized photos (c-d) and groups (e-f).

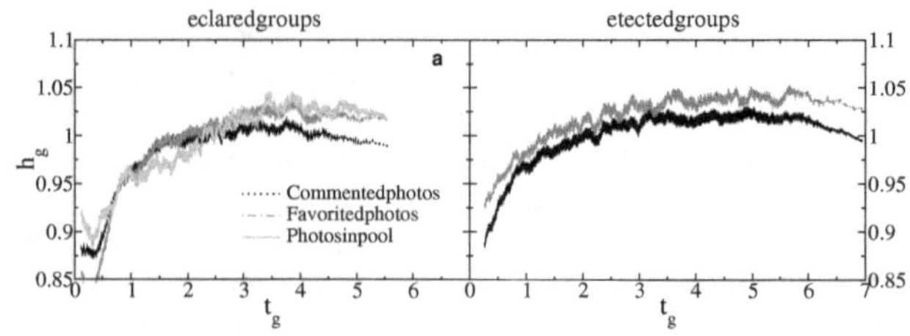

Figure 3: Correlation between reciprocity of comments inside a group and entropy of photos commented or favorited between its members, or belonging to the photo pool of this group, for declared and detected groups.

such result is the lack of information about the group's profile, since it is not available for detected groups. Another cause of the disagreement is a higher variability in the comments. This may be because we use a network of contacts for the purpose of finding clusters and defining detected groups, which may not be the best proxy of personal relations.

In total we label 565 distinct declared groups and 126 distinct detected groups. We characterize them in the following section.

6. CHARACTERIZATION OF GROUPS

We begin the analysis with a direct comparison of the overlap between the declared and detected groups. Then we characterize the two sets of groups in terms of the metrics we introduced in Section 3.2. Finally, we study the relation between the labels of the declared groups annotated by the editors and the values of the metrics. Additionally, we report ratios of groups labeled as social and topical among both declared, and detected groups.

6.1 Membership overlap of declared and detected groups

The groups from the two sets share typical properties of groups found in on-line social networks. The distribution of sizes of groups in both cases is heavy-tailed and close to power-laws (not shown due to space limits). Declared groups tend to be much bigger, having on average 61 members versus 7 members in detected groups.

To test if the groups from the two sets overlap, and to what extent, we measure the Jaccard similarity between their sets of members. Similarity is computed for all declared-detected group pairs and for each detected group we select the declared one with the highest similarity value as the best match. We plot the average similarity of the best matches as a function of the size of groups in Fig. 1a. Zero values of similarity are not taken into account for these averages. For the purpose of comparison with a null model, in Fig. 1b we draw the same plot after randomly reshuffling the members of detected groups, while preserving their sizes. We observe that the two plots differ in values significantly along the diagonal, and that the difference between them is substantial, as shown in Fig. 1c, meaning that indeed detected groups are, to some extent, similar to the declared ones. Further insights are shown in Fig. 1d, where we depict the distribution of similarities of pairs of groups extracted from a small sector of the diagonal, having between 32 and 64 members. The figure shows that there exist multiple detected groups which overlap significantly with declared groups, and that randomized groups do not show this pattern. This holds for groups of all sizes, as shown in Fig. 1e, in which we plot the 91th and 99th percentiles of the best match similarity for detected groups of various sizes (e.g., 1% of detected groups of size 20 have similarity with declared groups higher than 0.75, while for the randomized case 1% of the groups have similarity higher than just 0.05). Therefore, in some cases the community detection algorithm finds groups which are also defined by users (i.e., declared groups). We present evidences that this does not occur by chance through the comparison with the randomized case. Nevertheless, a substantial overlap is found for just a small percentage of groups. Most of the group pairs have similarity close to 0. Consequently, the similarity of detected groups to the best-matching declared groups is 0.082, while for the randomized detected groups it is not much lower, yielding 0.058.

6.2 Statistical properties of metrics

Besides directly comparing membership overlap, we study the variation of the metrics defined in Section 3.2 with the group size. Reciprocity and normalized entropy have a wide local maximum for groups of sizes between 50 and 100 members, both for declared and detected groups, as shown in Figs. 2a-d. This holds for all interactions and all sets of tags, with the exception of contacts, for which the curves are relatively flat. A similar local maximum has been found in a recent study [13] for pairwise interactions in Twitter by various community detection algorithms. We perform a randomization of photos between groups, keeping the number of photos per group fixed. The normalized entropy calculated for the shuffled photos stays close to 1, as expected, and the maximum disappears. A possible interpretation of the existence of the maximum is that these sizes tend to correspond to social groups, while bigger groups are more frequently

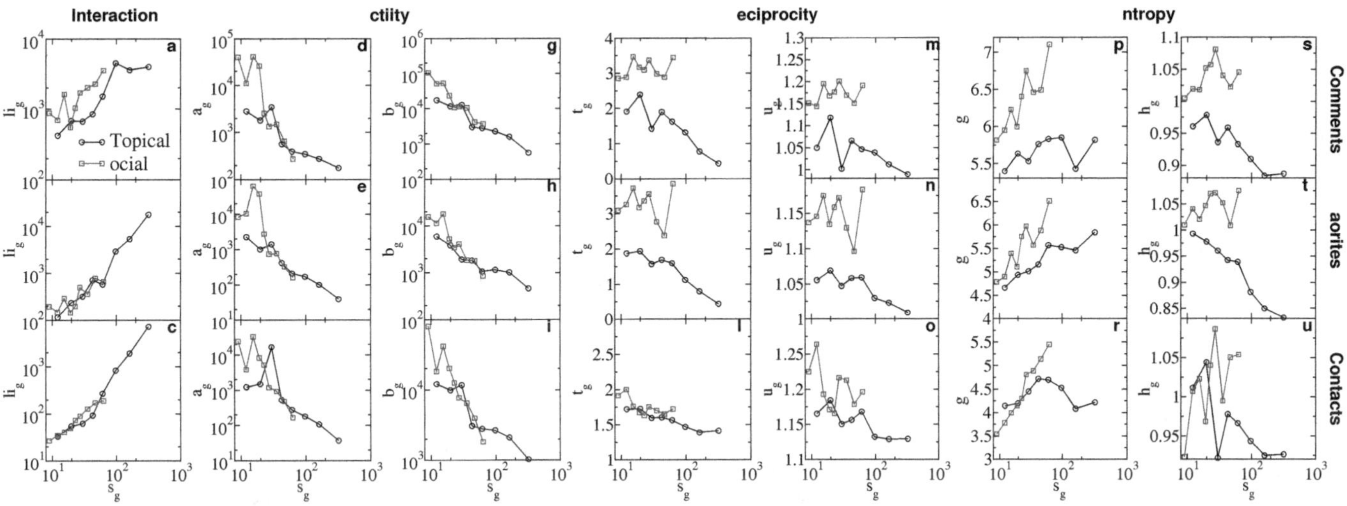

Figure 4: Averages of various topical (black circles) and social (blue squares) groups as a function of their size. Each point corresponds to 30 groups.

topical. Further findings to support this interpretation are presented in the next subsection.

Strong correspondence of the maxima for normalized entropy and reciprocity suggests that these properties are correlated, as shown in Fig. 3. While it may be natural to explain the correlation between reciprocity of comments and normalized entropy based on commented photos, it is not clear why we also find a positive correlation with normalized entropy based on other sets of photos. A possible interpretation is that high intra-reciprocity leads to wider variety of topics covered inside of that group, and vice versa.

The values of relative activity both in declared and detected groups are very high, as presented in Figs. 2e,f. As expected, activity of randomized groups exhibits values around 1 for all group sizes. For real groups instead, the value of relative activity decreases with the size of groups and gets close to 1 for very large ones. This may be caused by the fact that larger groups cannot be as integrated as smaller groups and the social commitment of their members towards other members of the group drops due to limited human capabilities. Additionally, we observe that the activity decay for declared groups occurs sharply between groups of size 100 and 200, in agreement with Dunbar's theory on the upper bound of the number of stable relationships manageable by a human. The activity drop for detected groups is continuous and much more moderate (Fig. 2f), since community detection algorithms tend by design to output node clusters with high numbers of connections between them.

6.3 Relation between metrics and group label

Here we analyze properties and values of the metrics for groups labeled through the editorial process. First, the ratio of groups labeled as social differs between declared and detected groups. In declared groups we find around 48% social groups, whereas among detected groups almost 69% are labeled as social. Additionally, we picked 50 detected groups among the ones that are the most similar to declared groups. Specifically, we selected them randomly from the 99th percentile shown in Fig. 1. These groups have significant overlap with declared groups and should share similar properties. Indeed, the ratio of groups labeled as social among them is closer to that of declared groups and equal to 53%. We conclude that detected groups are more likely to be social than declared ones. It is a somewhat expected result, since clustering algorithms detect dense parts of a network, and so they are inclined to detect areas with more reciprocal connections. Note that the theory envisions more reciprocal relations in social groups. Thus, community detection algorithms are more likely to find social groups, however, determining to what extent it happens is not trivial.

One of the expectations is that bond-based groups should not be very large, as the human capacity for stable relationships is limited. As pointed in Section 6.2, the Dunbar number can be considered as a possible cap for the size of such groups, while topical groups do no yield such a restriction. In line with this expectation, we find that declared groups labeled as social have on average 35 members, whereas groups labeled as topical have on average around 172 members.

We find insightful differences and similarities in various properties, which we explore in detail in Fig. 4. We plot them as a function of the size of groups as they vary drastically with it, and one needs to compare groups of similar sizes in order to draw unbiased conclusions.

First, there are almost no differences in the number of photos (not shown), favorites, and contacts (as in Figs. 4b,c) inside social and topical groups. The number of comments is, however, around 2 times higher in social groups than in topical groups of similar size (Fig. 4a). More differences can be found when looking at relative activity (Figs. 4d-i), which compares the interaction internal to the group with the overall activity level of users belonging to groups. In all three types of interaction the relative activity metrics for social groups yield values from 2 to over 10 times higher than for topical groups. These metrics compare activity internal to the group with activity external to it. Therefore this result may reflect a stronger focus or even a possible isolation of members belonging to social groups from the rest of people they interact with.

More importantly, we observe large differences in values of reciprocity and relative reciprocity of comments and favorites. Social groups exhibit significantly higher reciprocity than topical groups (Figs. 4j-o), in line with common iden-

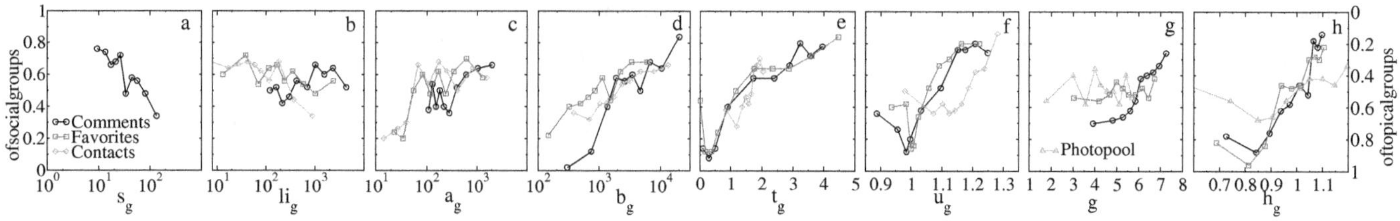

Figure 5: Dependence of fraction f of groups labeled as social on various metrics: based on comments, favorites, contacts and photo pools. The remaining $(1-f)$ groups are topical. Each point corresponds to 50 groups.

tity and common bond theory. There is no difference in reciprocity of contacts, and a plausible interpretation is that contacts do not reflect personal relations between connected users. Possibly, since contacts do not need to be reciprocal, users often add people they do not know and do not interact with as contacts. Finally, we observe much higher values of entropy and normalized entropy in social groups than in topical ones (Figs. 4p,q,s,t). This holds for the tags extracted from photos commented, and favorited between members. Assuming that tags of photos represent topics of interaction, the result is consistent with bond attachment. It is expected for members of bond-based groups to cover many different topics and areas in their interactions, whereas members of identity-based groups focus their interactions on specific topics. However, this does not hold for the tags extracted from photo pool of the group (Figs. 4r,u). Apparently, the content of the photo pool does not always reflect well the interactions and relations between members of the group.

Additionally, we plot the fraction of groups labeled as social with respect to group size, activity, reciprocity, and entropy (Fig. 5). The size of the groups correlates negatively as expected (Fig. 5a). The correlations with the number of interactions and relative activity a_g are rather weak (Figs. 5b,c), whereas surprisingly there is a strong dependency on relative activity b_g (Fig. 5d). For the lowest values of b_g^{com}, 95% of the groups are topical, while for the highest, 80% of the groups are social. High values of b_g can mean stronger group-focus, or even an isolation of the group members from the rest of people they interact with. It may relate to the fact that it is hard to enter bond-based groups due to strong relations existing between their members and because high investment is required to create such relations with them [24]. Direct reciprocity of interactions, with the exception of contacts, correlates strongly with social groups (Figs. 5e,f). We strongly expected this result based on bond attachment. Furthermore, we found that the entropy of tags correlates with social groups, but entropy based on other sources does not (Fig. 5g). However, we find that our normalized entropy performs much better than this, and a strong correlation is found both for tags extracted from comments and from favorites (Fig. 5h). This shows that the normalized entropy of tags may be the most proper way of measuring topical diversity of communications of a set of people.

7. GROUP TYPE DETECTION

The properties of labeled social and topical groups tend to confirm the validity of the principles identified by the common identity and common bond theory. A stronger confirmation would directly come from the ability of the defined metrics to predict the tendency of a group towards sociality or topicality. To this end, we propose and compare two methods to predict the group type and we test their accuracy over the corpus of the labeled groups.

7.1 Prediction methodology

The first approach we use is a linear combination of the metrics. To this end, we select the features that are the most related to the sociological theory and for which we built specific metrics, i.e., t_g, u_g and h_g. Each of them is applied to the 3 different interaction types and bags of tags, which produces a total of 9 values. We transform the values of the metrics into their t-statistics by subtracting the average value and dividing them by the standard deviation of the distribution. Then we weight the normalized scores evenly by dividing them by the total number of metrics considered and we finally sum them up to obtain a single *score* S_g. All of the components are supposed to score high for social groups. Therefore, the higher the value of the score, the higher the chance that the group is social rather than topical. To convert the score into a binary label, a fixed threshold above which groups are predicted to be social must be selected. Using this approach, we aim at testing if those metrics, based on the theory, can be successful in predicting the type of group (social or topical).

The second approach relies on machine-learning methods that use the metrics' values as features. Features are combined in a classifier that is first trained on a sample of labeled data to learn a prediction model. The trained classifier then outputs a binary prediction for any new group instance defined in the same feature space. Due to the limited size of our corpus of labeled groups, we estimate the classifier performance using 10-fold cross validation. We report results on a Rotation Forest classifier, which performed best in comparison to several algorithms implemented in WEKA. For the classifier we used a wider set of features than for the linear combination approach, namely: group size s_g and E_g^{int}, a_g, b_g, t_g, u_g, $H(g)$, h_g, each applied to the 3 different interaction types and bags of tags. This results in a total of 22 features. We selected such a wide set of features to test if indeed the metrics proposed to distinguish between the social and topical groups are the best ones for the task. The relative predictive power of the features is measured through a feature selection algorithm.

7.2 Prediction results

The ratio of groups labeled as social increases quickly with the score S_g, as shown in Fig. 6a. This summarizes the findings of previous sections, suggesting that the features embedded in the score are able to capture well the nature of the groups. The higher the score, the higher the probability

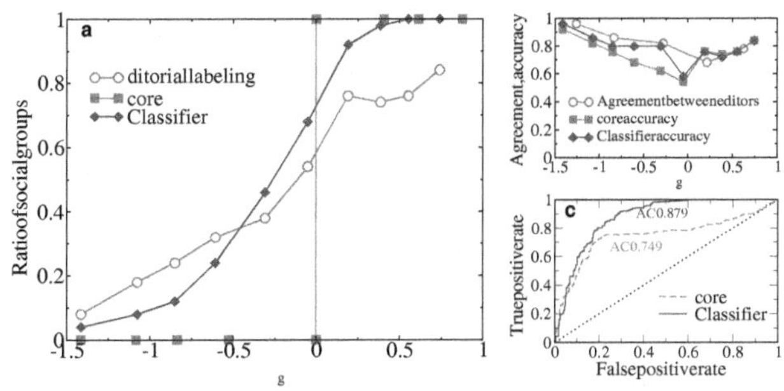

Figure 6: Comparison between prediction methods. a) Ratio of groups labeled as social versus the score. The same ratio is plotted for the score-based (threshold at 0) and trained classifier predictions. b) The accuracy of prediction of the two techniques and agreement between two of the labelers against the S_g values. c) ROC curves for the prediction with the two different techniques.

that the group is social; the lower, the more topical. When the score is around zero, groups can be either social or topical, or both, meaning that a decision on the nature of the group may be more difficult. If we fix the threshold for the S_g value in order to perform a binary group classification, it is clear that several misclassifications will occur, especially around the threshold value. An example for threshold at 0 is shown in Fig. 6a. Conversely, the classifier performs much better and achieves the ratio that adheres much more to the actual ratio of social and topical groups.

Both methods, however, fail more frequently for groups with mixed social and topical features. The prediction accuracies of the classifier and of the score-based predictions have an evident drop of performance around 0 (Fig. 6b). The accuracy at the extreme values of the score is close to 0.95, while it falls below 0.6 for groups with a score close to 0. On the other hand, this drop appears also in the agreement between two of the human labelers, measured as a ratio of groups that have been given the same label. Apparently, this is a shortcoming of the binary classification itself, as opposed to multi-label classification.

The overall performance of the two approaches can be compared fairly through ROC curves (Fig. 6c), which astray from the selection of a fixed threshold. The curve for the classifier (computed for the 10-fold cross validation) always performs better, and this is reflected in the considerably higher AUC value and accuracy, as shown in Tab. 2.

In addition, to determine the most predictive features, we rank the features using Chi-square feature selection. The top 5 features are, in decreasing order of importance: h_g^{com}, t_g^{com}, u_g^{com}, h_g^{fav}, and b_g^{com}. The selected set is the optimal for the prediction performance: retraining the classifier on such restricted set of features results in stable performance, as shown in Tab. 2. The top 4 most predictive features correspond directly to the expectations of the theory and results of the analysis from Section 6. Reciprocity-based metrics and normalized entropy are significantly more predictive than other features. The high position of relative activity b_g^{com} is rather unexpected. However, we have already remarked on its importance and commented on its interpretation in Section 6.

Method	Accuracy	AUC
Score	0.763	0.749
Classifier	0.801	0.879
Classifierχ^2_{top5}	0.803	0.872

Table 2: Group type prediction performance using i) the score with threshold at 0, ii) 10-fold cross validation on a Rotation Forest classifier trained on all the features, or iii) the same classifier trained on the set of top-5 predictive features, according to the Chi Squared feature selection.

8. CONCLUSIONS

Common identity and common bond theory indicates a high-level characterization of topical and social groups. We propose metrics capturing reciprocity of interactions and entropy of user-generated terms, to realize the concepts discussed in the theory and to measure sociality and topicality of groups. We label a number of groups from Flickr as either topical or social and we leverage this ground truth to show that the metrics, combined with a machine-learning approach, predict the group type with high accuracy. Moreover, we note that the degree of isolation of the group activity from the rest of the social network, measured in terms of more personal interactions, is a good predictor of the group type, in addition to the elements identified in the theory. Besides the main prediction results, the supporting analysis of the group properties in terms of the identified dimensions confirms the theory from different angles and highlights other interesting findings. In particular, dependencies of the metrics with the group size confirm previous observations about the effective size of social communities, peaking around rather small sizes and being limited by a cap of 100-200 members.

The study is complemented with a comparison of the structure and sociality and topicality traits between declared groups and groups from community detection algorithms. Detected groups do not overlap much with declared groups on average, but they match sensibly more than the random case for groups of comparable sizes. Furthermore, detected groups are more often social than the declared ones.

Findings from the present work open new opportunities for characterization of social communities and of their members. Extensions to the study include a more exhaustive extraction of detected groups using a different network than the network of contacts e.g., we find mutual comments to carry more social traits than the contacts do. Another interesting extension could be multi-label classification of groups, in order to better categorize groups with mixed social and topical components.

Acknowledgments

The authors would like to thank Gideon Zenz for his helpful suggestions and contributions. This research is partially supported by EU's FP7/2007-2013 under the ARCOMEM and SOCIALSENSOR projects, by the CDTI (Spain) under the CENIT program, project CEN-20101037 "Social Media", and by MICINN (Spain) through Grant TIN2009-14560-C03-01, and by MINECO (Spain) and FEDER (EU) through projects MODASS (FIS2011-247852) and FISICOS (FIS2007-60327). P.A.G. acknowledges support from the JAE Predoc program of CSIC (Spain).

9. REFERENCES

[1] L. M. Aiello, A. Barrat, R. Schifanella, C. Cattuto, B. Markines, and F. Menczer. Friendship prediction and homophily in social media. *ACM Trans. Web*, 6(2):9:1–9:33, 2012.

[2] L. Backstrom, D. Huttenlocher, J. Kleinberg, and X. Lan. Group formation in large social networks: membership, growth, and evolution. In *12th ACM SIGKDD international conference on Knowledge discovery and data mining - KDD'06*, page 44, New York, New York, USA, 2006.

[3] L. Backstrom, R. Kumar, C. Marlow, J. Novak, and A. Tomkins. Preferential behavior in online groups. In *International conference on Web search and web data mining - WSDM'08*, pages 117–128, New York, NY, USA, 2008.

[4] N. L. Collins and L. C. Miller. Self-disclosure and liking: A meta-analytic review. *Psychological Bulletin*, 166(3):457–475, 1994.

[5] A. Cox, P. Clough, and S. Siersdorfer. Developing metrics to characterize Flickr groups. *Journal of the American Society for Information Science and Technology*, 62(1):493–506, 2011.

[6] J. N. Cummings, B. Butler, and R. Kraut. The quality of online social relationships. *Comm. of the ACM*, 45(7):103–108, 2002.

[7] R. I. M. Dunbar. The social brain hypothesis. *Evolutionary Anthropology*, 6:178–190, 1998.

[8] S. Fortunato. Community detection in graphs. *Physics Reports*, 486(3-5):75–174, 2010.

[9] P. A. Gloor and Y. Zhao. Analyzing Actors and Their Discussion Topics by Semantic Social Network Analysis. In *Conference on Information Visualization*, IV '06, pages 130–135, Washington, DC, USA, 2006.

[10] B. Goncalves, N. Perra, and A. Vespignani. Modeling Users' Activity on Twitter Networks: Validation of Dunbar's Number. *PLoS ONE*, 6(8):e22656, 2011.

[11] P. A. Grabowicz and V. M. Eguíluz. Heterogeneity shapes groups growth in social online communities. *Europhys. Lett.*, 97(2):28002, 2012.

[12] P. A. Grabowicz, J. J. Ramasco, and V. M. Eguiluz. Dynamics in online social networks. *arXiv*:1210.0808, 2012.

[13] P. A. Grabowicz, J. J. Ramasco, E. Moro, J. M. Pujol, and V. M. Eguiluz. Social Features of Online Networks: The Strength of Intermediary Ties in Online Social Media. *PLoS ONE*, 7(1):e29358, 2012.

[14] S. R. Kairam, D. J. Wang, and J. Leskovec. The life and death of online groups: predicting group growth and longevity. In *5th ACM international conference on Web search and data mining*, WSDM'12, pages 673–682, New York, NY, USA, 2012.

[15] A. Lancichinetti, S. Fortunato, and F. Radicchi. Benchmark graphs for testing community detection algorithms. *Physical Review E*, 78:046110, 2008.

[16] A. Lancichinetti, F. Radicchi, J. J. Ramasco, and S. Fortunato. Finding Statistically Significant Communities in Networks. *PLoS ONE*, 6(4):e18961, 2011.

[17] P. J. Ludford, D. Cosley, D. Frankowski, and L. Terveen. Think different: increasing online community participation using uniqueness and group dissimilarity. In *Proceedings of the SIGCHI Conference on Human Factors in Computing Systems*, CHI '04, pages 631–638, New York, NY, USA, 2004.

[18] D. W. McMillan and D. M. Chavis. Sense of community: A definition and theory. *Journal of Community Psychology*, 14(1):6–23, 1986.

[19] A. Mislove, M. Marcon, K. P. Gummadi, P. Druschel, and B. Bhattacharjee. Measurement and analysis of online social networks. In *7th ACM SIGCOMM conference on Internet measurement - IMC '07*, pages 29–42, San Diego, California, USA, 2007.

[20] R.-A. Negoescu, B. Adams, D. Phung, S. Venkatesh, and D. Gatica-Perez. Flickr hypergroups. In *17th ACM international conference on Multimedia*, MM'09, pages 813–816, New York, NY, USA, 2009.

[21] R. A. Negoescu and D. Gatica-Perez. Analyzing flickr groups. In *International conference on Content-based image and video retrieval*, CIVR'08, pages 417–426, New York, NY, USA, 2008.

[22] D. A. Prentice, D. T. Miller, and J. R. Lightdale. Asymmetries in attachments to groups and to their members: Distinguishing between common-identity and common-bond groups. *Personality and Social Psychology Bulletin*, 20(5):484–493, 1994.

[23] C. Prieur, N. Pissard, J. Beuscart, and D. Cardon. Thematic and social indicators for Flickr groups. In *Proceedings of International Conference on Weblogs and Social Media - ICWSM'08*, 2008.

[24] Y. Ren, R. Kraut, and S. Kiesler. Applying Common Identity and Bond Theory to Design of Online Communities. *Organization Studies*, 28(3):377–408, 2007.

[25] S. Riger and P. J. Lavrakas. Community ties: Patterns of attachment and social interaction in urban neighborhoods. *American Journal of Community Psychology*, 9:55–66, 1981.

[26] K. Sassenberg. Common bond and common identity groups on the Internet: Attachment and normative behavior in on-topic and off-topic chats. *Group Dynamics Theory Research And Practice*, 6(1):27–37, 2002.

[27] H. Tajfel. *Social identity and intergroup relations.* Cambridge University Press, 1982.

[28] L. Tang, X. Wang, and H. Liu. Group profiling for understanding social structures. *ACM Trans. Intell. Syst. Technol.*, 3(1):15:1–15:25, 2011.

[29] S. Utz and K. Sassenberg. Distributive justice in common-bond and common-identity groups. *Group Processes and Intergroup Relations*, 5(2):151–162, 2002.

[30] H. T. Welser, E. Gleave, D. Fisher, and M. Smith. Visualizing the Signatures of Social Roles in Online Discussion Groups. *The Journal of Social Structure*, 8(2), 2007.

[31] J. Yang and J. Leskovec. Defining and evaluating network communities based on ground-truth. In *Proceedings of the ACM SIGKDD Workshop on Mining Data Semantics*, MDS'12, pages 3:1–3:8, New York, NY, USA, 2012.

Modeling the Impact of Lifestyle on Health at Scale

Adam Sadilek
Dept. of Computer Science
University of Rochester
Rochester, NY, USA
sadilek@cs.rochester.edu

Henry Kautz
Dept. of Computer Science
University of Rochester
Rochester, NY, USA
kautz@cs.rochester.edu

ABSTRACT

Research in computational epidemiology to date has concentrated on estimating summary statistics of populations and simulated scenarios of disease outbreaks. Detailed studies have been limited to small domains, as scaling the methods involved poses considerable challenges. By contrast, we model the associations of a large collection of social and environmental factors with the health of particular individuals. Instead of relying on surveys, we apply scalable machine learning techniques to noisy data mined from online social media and infer the health state of any given person in an automated way. We show that the learned patterns can be subsequently leveraged in descriptive as well as predictive fine-grained models of human health. Using a unified statistical model, we quantify the impact of social status, exposure to pollution, interpersonal interactions, and other important lifestyle factors on one's health. Our model explains more than 54% of the variance in people's health (as estimated from their online communication), and predicts the future health status of individuals with 91% accuracy. Our methods complement traditional studies in life sciences, as they enable us to perform large-scale and timely measurement, inference, and prediction of previously elusive factors that affect our everyday lives.

Categories and Subject Descriptors

H.1.m [**Information Systems**]: Miscellaneous

General Terms

Algorithms, Experimentation, Human Factors

Keywords

Online social networks, machine learning, computational epidemiology, ubiquitous computing, geo-temporal modeling

WSDM'13, February 4–8, 2013, Rome, Italy.

Figure 1: Visualization of the health and location of a sample of Twitter users in New York City. Sick people are colored red, whereas healthy individuals are green. Major pollution sources are highlighted in purple, and ZIP code boundaries are shown with white outlines. This paper explores to what extent online social media can be used to quantify and predict the impact of a large collection of environmental and lifestyle factors on our health. Our web application is available at http://fount.in.

1. INTRODUCTION

How does a new factory affect the health of residents in the city? How does your social status impact your health? Do visits to gyms decrease your susceptibility to communicable diseases? How about visits to bars, or riding the subway? Such questions are traditionally difficult and costly to answer at a population scale. Existing methods resort to surveys of individuals and medical providers, which require extensive amount of human effort to complete, cost large amounts of money, and sample only a small fraction of people in a population. By contrast, we apply machine learning techniques to Twitter data and automatically estimate the health state of any individual on the basis of his or her online communication. Throughout the text, we refer to the frequency of self-reports of sickness in a user's Twitter updates as user's *health estimate* or simply user's *health* for brevity.

By leveraging the text of geo-tagged tweets, along with the social network structure, we quantify the interplay between a number of important factors and human health. We consider environmental and socioeconomic factors (such as pollution, education, and poverty), as well as social aspects of life (such as encounters and friendships with sick people). Furthermore, we do this at no cost, and without any active user participation. This enables us to operate with a significantly larger number of subjects than previous work in life sciences.

For instance, every thirtieth resident of New York City appears in our dataset.[1] Since Twitter users do not, in general, constitute a representative sample of a population, it is unknown to what extent our results generalize to people who do not participate in online social media. Nonetheless, as we will see, the patterns we find are in agreement with previous epidemiological work. Even if it turns out that the mechanisms we explore here operate in a fundamentally different way within the population at large, our methods still capture a considerable fraction of people. Globally, the prevalence of social media usage is significant, and is increasing: 13% of online adults use Twitter, most of them daily and often via a phone [39].

As a result, this large online population creates a vast "organic" sensor network composed of individuals reporting on their activities, social interactions, and events around them. All of this activity streams in real-time and is often annotated with context including GPS location and images. In this work, we leverage this sensor network to model public health. We capture this important domain in a unified statistical model that measures the impact of various aspects of people's behavior on their health, and allows us to control for a number of confounding factors. Specifically, we show the following:

- Features mined from social media account for up to 54% variance in health of individual Twitter users.
- Physical proximity to pollution sources negatively impacts public health in a measurable way.
- One's online social status has a definite positive association with one's health.
- Encounters and social ties with ill individuals have a large negative impact on one's health.
- The quality of one's neighborhood is associated with one's health.
- One's health state revealed on Twitter can be predicted across individuals with 91% accuracy on the basis of geospatial and relationship data inferred from the Twitter stream.

2. SIGNIFICANCE OF RESULTS

Consider the amount of resources and human effort required to determine how complex social and environmental factors affect the health of millions of people in a large metropolitan area. This paper demonstrates that the expenditure can be, in fact, negligible when we concentrate on users of online social media. We show that fine-grained

Figure 2: This figure shows the health status of people within a social network of the user u at the center. Each edge represents one of u's friendships, and the color denotes the health of the corresponding friend. Note the patterns in geographical as well as social distribution of sickness. For instance, friends on the east side of the Hudson River tend to be sicker than friends from Manhattan. Is this due to an outbreak of flu in the New Jersey school district? Or is it because the sick individuals lead more stressful lives? In this work, we begin to tease these intimately tied factors apart.

signals mined from online social media complement traditional coarse-grained offline data, such as census statistics. We view the methods described in this paper as the first step towards real-time public health analysis that enables individuals as well as public officials to make more informed decisions.

3. MOTIVATION

A large body of research in life sciences studied the effect of a variety of factors on animal and human health. For instance, researchers have established that, among monkeys, immune function can be directly influenced by social status. Experimentally controlled manipulations in social rank were found to lead to widespread changes in gene expression related to immune function. Social rank and immune function were found to be directly correlated, *i.e.*, better social status yields a stronger immune system, as measured by counting anti-bodies in blood samples [42].

Proximity to "green" places, such as urban parks, has been linked to improved resistance to allergies [21] and reduction in stress [40]. Another study showed that even the short-term improvement of pollution levels during Beijing Olympics has a measurable impact on people's health [33].

However, most experiments in this space involved relatively small numbers of individuals—typically less than a

[1] More than 19 million people live in the NYC metropolitan area: http://www.census.gov/popest/metro/

hundred, rarely thousands such as the NHLBI-MESA Study involving 6,500 subjects [5]. Furthermore, because of the amount of human effort required in these controlled studies (physical setup, drawing blood samples, analysis requiring expensive equipment *etc.*), the results and insights come with a significant cost and delay. Additionally, ethical constraints preclude arbitrary controlled experiments with human subjects.

As a result, many important mechanisms remain poorly understood. For example, the link between social status and increased risk of contracting an infectious disease in humans still presents an open question [37]. Parts of the puzzle have been solved. Stress has been found to increase the incidence of common cold, mononucleosis [10], and to activate latent viruses [1]. However, the overall picture remains unclear and incomplete. In this paper, we propose a complementary approach to the traditional small-scale biological and sociological studies. By applying machine learning techniques to large-scale data mined from online social networks, we can quantify the impact of a large collection of social and environmental factors on human health. Since our models are fully unsupervised, they can be updated in real-time as new data and evidence come in.

Let us give a concrete example of how we model the association between social status and health. In this work, we measure a person's social status by network properties, such as PageRank, reciprocity of their relationships, and various centrality measures, as well as by features derived from user interactions, *e.g.*, how many times a person's messages get forwarded or "liked", how many times people mention the person's name. As a proxy for the strength of an immune system of any given person, we use the number of days the person indicates an illness in their online communication. In agreement with [42], we find a strong negative correlation ($R = -0.27$, $p \ll 0.0001$) between people's social status and the frequency with which they get sick (Fig. 4).

Social status is just one of more than sixty factors affecting human health we consider in this paper. These include diverse features ranging from intensity of contact with ill individuals to pollution exposure.

The United States has the world's largest health inequality across society, where the gap of life expectancy of the most and the least advantaged segments of the population is over 20 years [41]. It has been reported that this difference is partly due to differences in social status, but many aspects of the phenomenon remain unexplained [37]. The level of detail and timeliness of the signals we mine from people's online social activities enable us to capture a number of confounding factors that were previously invisible.

For instance, we can explore complex geographical, environmental, and social patterns with fine-granularity and at a large scale as shown in Fig. 2. By fusing this information with public data on pollution sources within a single view, we can begin to quantify the emergent patterns (Fig. 1). This is specific example of our vision of the future of public and personal health management enabled by an automated unification of public and personal data sets. As a result, our work allows governments as well as individuals to model and understand the interplay between health, location, environment, and social factors more effectively.

Before we dive into the details of our approach, we will discuss the limitations that apply to any indirect method of modeling public health.

4. LIMITATIONS

This paper describes our approach to public health modeling that we view as a complement to existing work in epidemiology. Any given dataset carries with it a set of biases and our Twitter dataset is no exception. For example, younger people and minorities are disproportionately present on Twitter as compared to the overall makeup of the population [39]. The results of this study apply directly to the health of Twitter users inferred from their online communication. The health state of each user is captured within a gradient from "sick" to "healthy" with respect to influenza-like illness, but does not further distinguish between specific kinds of ailments. Some users may never self-report (stoics) and others may report being sick when they are not (hypochondriacs). We remove some of this bias by counting the sick *days* for each user, but ground truth is required to control for this effect more explicitly.

Our models are exposed to much noisier data than one finds in a typical survey in life sciences. One component of the noise comes from the text classification process, but evaluation on a held-out set shows that it's small. Additional noise is in the location data and its interpretation. For example, a person tweeting on a sidewalk in front of a bar may be recorded as "visiting" the bar. In most instances, it is next to impossible to determine whether he actually did visit the venue from Twitter data alone. To some extent, we mitigate the rate of false positives by capturing each factor in a number of complementary ways. For example, we also record the distance to the nearest bar and the mean distance to all bars.

While people do not tweet from every location they visit and do not declare every friend online, much of the missing data can be "filled in" by data mining their past behavior [4, 8, 34]. We note that currently used methods suffer from similar confounding effects. For example, infected people who do not visit a doctor, or do not respond to surveys are virtually invisible to the traditional methods. Similarly, efforts such as Google Flu Trends can only observe individuals who search the web for certain types of content when sick. A fully comprehensive coverage of a population will require a combination of diverse methods, and application of AI techniques—like the ones presented in this work—capable of *inferring* the missing information. An important part of our future work, as described at the end of this paper, is to study how estimates based on Twitter users can be adjusted to reflect properties of the general population.

5. DATA

Our experiments are based on data obtained from Twitter, a popular micro-blogging service where people post message updates at most 140 characters long. The forced brevity encourages frequent mobile updates, as we show below. Relationships between users on Twitter are not necessarily symmetric. One can follow (subscribe to receive messages from) a user without being followed back. When users do reciprocate following, we say they are *friends* on Twitter. There is anecdotal evidence that Twitter friendships have a substantial overlap with offline friendships [20]. Twitter launched in 2006 and has been experiencing an explosive growth since then. As of April 2012, over 500 million accounts are registered on Twitter.

Figure 3: A snapshot of Twitter activity overlaid on top New York City public transit map. By merging geo-tagged tweets with the known locations of transit routes, we can model the impact of public transit usage on the health of specific individuals.

Using the Twitter Search API[2], we collected a sample of public tweets that originated from the New York City (NYC) metropolitan area. The collection period was one month long and started on May 19 2010, shortly after U.S. Census 2010 data has been recorded. We periodically queried Twitter for all recent tweets within 100 kilometers of the NYC city center in a distributed fashion. Altogether, we have logged nearly 16 million tweets authored by more than 630 thousand unique users. To put these statistics in context, the entire NYC metropolitan area has an estimated population of 19 million people. Since this work studies the effects environment, location, and co-location have on human health, we concentrate on users that posted more than 100 GPS-tagged tweets during the one-month data collection period. We refer to them as *geo-active users*, and our dataset contains 6,237 such individuals.

5.1 User Privacy

Our research demonstrates that much can be inferred and predicted about specific individuals. This allows users with open profiles to consider the implications of such setting and enables them to make an informed decision about their online behavior. Our methods are useful at an anonymized level as well, as they can extract aggregate information from individuals for the benefit of others. For example, we show that one's social status is significantly tied with one's health. Government officials as well as public advocacy groups can use such insights to make a stronger case for a policy change. Personalized results can be reported directly to the authenticated user.

We recognize that there are substantial privacy questions ahead. We believe the issues ultimately reduce to a cost-benefit analysis. Specifically, by quantifying the trade-offs between the *value* our automated systems create versus loss of user privacy. In the future, we envision each person will be able to set—either explicitly or implicitly via an auction scheme—a dollar valuation on his or her privacy, and online services will take that preference into account when collecting, analyzing, and using customer data. In one extreme, one may decide to risk sharing all data, make money on it, and get more personalized services. On the other hand, one may set tight privacy filters and pay for online services. This may lead to a new open marketplace with public data [3].

[2]http://search.twitter.com/api/

6. BACKGROUND

Support vector machine (SVM) is an established model of data in machine learning [12]. We learn an SVM for linear binary classification to accurately distinguish between tweets indicating the author is afflicted by an ailment and all other tweets.

Linear binary SVMs are trained by finding a hyperplane defined by a normal vector w with the maximal margin separating it from the positive and negative datapoints. Finding such a hyperplane is inherently a quadratic optimization problem given by the following objective function

$$\min_{w} \frac{\lambda}{2}||w||^2 + \mathcal{L}(w, D), \tag{1}$$

where λ is a regularization parameter controlling model complexity, and $\mathcal{L}(w, D)$ is the hinge-loss over all training data D given by

$$\mathcal{L}(w, D) = \sum_{i} \max\left(0, 1 - y_i w^T x_i\right). \tag{2}$$

The optimization problem in Equation 1 can be solved efficiently and in a parallel fashion using stochastic gradient descend methods [38].

Class imbalance, where the number of examples in one class is dramatically larger than in the other class, complicates virtually all machine learning. For SVMs, prior work has shown that transforming the optimization problem from the space of individual datapoints $\langle x_i, y_i\rangle$ in matrix D to one over *pairs* of examples $\langle x_i^+ - x_j^-, 1\rangle$ yields significantly more robust results [23]. (x_i^+ denotes feature vectors from the positive class ($y_i = +1$), whereas x_j^- denotes negatively labeled data points ($y_j = -1$).) This method is often referred to as ROC Area SVM because it directly maximizes the area under the ROC curve of the model.

Measures of centrality mathematically capture the "importance" of a node in a (social) network. Some measures, such as degree centrality, are local and depend only on the immediate neighborhood of a node. Other methods, including PageRank and betweenness centrality, capture the global properties of the network as well. For an excellent general overview of computational analysis of social networks at large see [15].

Regression analysis is a statistical technique of quantifying the relationship between one or more independent variables and a dependent response variable. In this work, we apply regularized least-squares regression model with elastic net algorithm [45]. This formalism encourages grouping of strongly correlated independent variables, and enables variable selection in a principled way.

Decision trees are models of data encoded as rules induced from examples [6]. Intuitively, in our domain, a decision tree represents a series of questions that need to be asked and answered in order to estimate the health quality of a person, based on his or her attributes and contextual features. During decision tree learning, features are evaluated in terms of information gain with respect to the labels and the best candidates are subsequently selected for each inner node of the tree. Our implementation uses *regression* decision trees, where each leaf contains a continuous label.

As described below, we also employ decision trees for feature selection, since they intrinsically rank features by their information content.

7. METHODS

This section presents the methods we use to quantify and predict people's health from their location and activities recorded online. In short, we begin by inferring the health state of any given Twitter user on the basis of the content of his or her online communication. We then data mine a large collection of features for each individual. The features jointly describe the context of people's lives in terms of location, their environment, and social activities. We subsequently capture the associations between the contextual features and people's health via statistical analysis. Finally, we explore the *predictability* of health from the induced factors. The following subsections describe each of these steps in detail.

7.1 Health State Inference

We build upon previous work on classification of short text messages [13, 31, 35] and learn a support vector machine classifier C that accurately identifies tweets that indicate their author is ill. C is trained by directly optimizing the area under the ROC curve, as is therefore robust even in the presence of strong class imbalance, where for every health-related message there are more than 1,000 irrelevant ones. We use C to distinguish between tweets indicating the author is afflicted by an ailment (we call such tweets "sick"), and all other tweets (called "other" or "normal").

As SVM features, we use all unigram, bigram, and trigram word tokens that appear in the training data. For example, a tweet *"I feel sick."* is represented by the following feature vector:

$$\left(i, feel, sick, i\ feel, feel\ sick, i\ feel\ sick\right).$$

Overall, our SVM operates in more than 1.7 million dimensions, where each dimension represents a word or a phrase extracted from training data. Before tokenization, we convert all text to lower case, strip punctuation and special characters, and remove mentions of user names (the "@" tag) and re-tweets (analogous to email forwarding). However, we do keep hashtags (such as "#sick"), as those are often relevant to the author's health state, and are particularly useful for disambiguation of short or ill-formed messages. Table 1 lists examples of significant features found in the process of learning C.

We use the SVM cascade learning procedure described in [35]. Evaluation of C on a held-out set shows 0.98 precision and 0.97 recall with respect to labels agreed upon by human annotators. Ground truth for each tweet was obtained by asking five Amazon Mechanical Turk workers to label the tweet as either "sick" or "other" and subsequently extracting the majority vote.

7.2 Modeling Associations: Environment, Lifestyle, and Health

From the online activities of each geo-active user, we mine a number of features that describe the context of his or her life in terms of location, environment, and social interaction. We describe the **health** of individuals using two random variables: the expected number of sick days, and the normalized cumulative probability mass of sickness given by

$$P_S = \frac{1}{|M|} \sum_{t \in M} \Pr\left[t \text{ is sick}\right],$$

where M is the set of tweets of a given user. A sick day is defined as a calendar day during which the user wrote at least one "sick" tweet. Throughout the paper, we will use the term *health quality* to denote $-P_S$.

Positive Features		Negative Features	
Feature	**Weight**	**Feature**	**Weight**
sick	0.9579	sick of	−0.4005
headache	0.5249	you	−0.3662
flu	0.5051	lol	−0.3017
fever	0.3879	love	−0.1753
feel	0.3451	i feel your	−0.1416
coughing	0.2917	so sick of	−0.0887
being sick	0.1919	bieber fever	−0.1026
better	0.1988	smoking	−0.0980
being	0.1943	i'm sick of	−0.0894
stomach	0.1703	pressure	−0.0837
and my	0.1687	massage	−0.0726
infection	0.1686	i love	−0.0719
morning	0.1647	pregnant	−0.0639

Table 1: Examples of positively and negatively weighted significant features of our SVM model C.

We quantify one's **social status** with PageRank, reciprocity of following, the number of times other people mention the user, and a collection of centrality measures (degree, communicability, eigenvector, betweenness, load, flow, and closeness). The *reciprocity* of friendships between high school students has been shown to be a strong predictor of social status of individuals [30]. Namely, low-rank individuals frequently (and wishfully) list highly ranked students as their friends, but the relationship is not reciprocated. Most stable and mutual friendships occur between people of the same rank. We find that all measures of social rank are highly cross-correlated ($R > 0.73, p \ll 0.0001$) and have almost identical predictive power, explaining over 24% of the variance in health.

Leveraging the estimated health state of all individuals in our dataset along with their GPS location, we extract the number of **physical encounters** with sick people. The noise in GPS signal in areas with tall buildings throughout New York City can be up to hundred meters. Therefore, we consider two individuals co-located if they appear within hundred meters of each other within a time window (slack) of length T. While this method is likely to overestimate the number of actual encounters with other Twitter users, we find that it serves as a good proxy for the actual level of exposure to infected individuals. In this work, we consider time windows of lengths 1, 4, and 24 hours. Based on declared Twitter friendships (*i.e.*, mutual following of geo-active users), we count the number of **sick friends** each user has.

Using Google Places API,[3] we download GPS coordinates of all bars, night clubs, transit stations, public parks, and gyms in the greater New York City area. Transit stations include major bus stops, subway stations, and train, ferry

[3]https://developers.google.com/places/documentation/

and airport terminals. We consider a total of 25 thousand venues in these categories (see Fig. 3). Using the geo-tags of individual tweets, we calculate the mean shortest distance to each venue type and the number of *visits* to each venue. A visit is measured as tweeting within 100 meters of a venue. These metrics capture aspects of the **behavior** and **lifestyle** of each person. For instance: How often do they frequent bars versus gyms? How much time they spend in crowded public transportation?

Another type of "venue" we consider are major **pollution** sources obtained from the U.S. Environmental Protection Agency.[4] These include factories, power plants, transportation hubs, and other sites emitting significant amounts of volatile chemical compounds, particulate matter, CO, NO_x, SO_2, and other harmful chemicals. We model over 1,700 pollution sites within NYC (see Fig. 1).

We would like to tie in datasets that do not have GPS annotations. For instance the U.S. census contains rich **socioeconomic characteristics** of the entire nation. We tie our geo-tagged tweets with census data by inferring each person's home ZIP code, which then serves as a key into the census dataset. The GPS coordinates of person x home is estimated by fitting a two-dimensional Gaussian to all x's locations between 1am and 6am. The mean of this Gaussian is taken as the most likely home location. We then look up the corresponding ZIP code in the GeoNames.org database.

The average New York City ZIP code zone has an area of 3.6 km^2 and can be walked across in less than 20 minutes. The ZIP code areas are shown in Fig. 1. We can now associate each person with the context derived from the 2010 census—the most recent census available.[5] We focus on three broad characteristics of a person's neighborhood: poverty, education, and race. Poverty is measured in terms of fraction families and individuals below poverty line, the number of abandoned housing units, and the prevalence of social security dependence. Education captures proportion of people over 25 with various levels of education (from elementary school to a doctorate). The race factor includes proportion of different races and ethnic groups.

For each person, we induce 62 features based on the factors described in this section. In Section 8, we will see how these features correlate and associate with people's health, but let us first describe how we use them for health *prediction*.

7.3 Health Prediction

We are interested in how do the features we discuss above generalize across individuals. We explore this by learning a regression decision tree on a training set of subjects and evaluate on the remaining test set. The decision tree additionally reveals the relative importance of the individual features—with the most informative feature at the root and increasingly insignificant features towards the leaves. We prevent overfitting by pruning the tree on the basis of 10-fold cross-validation.

8. EXPERIMENTS AND RESULTS

This section reports the experimental results we obtained and closely follows the structure of the Methods section above. Unless otherwise noted, all results reported are statistically significant at the 0.001 level ($p < 0.001$).

[4] http://www.epa.gov/air/emissions/

[5] http://www.census.gov/main/www/access.html

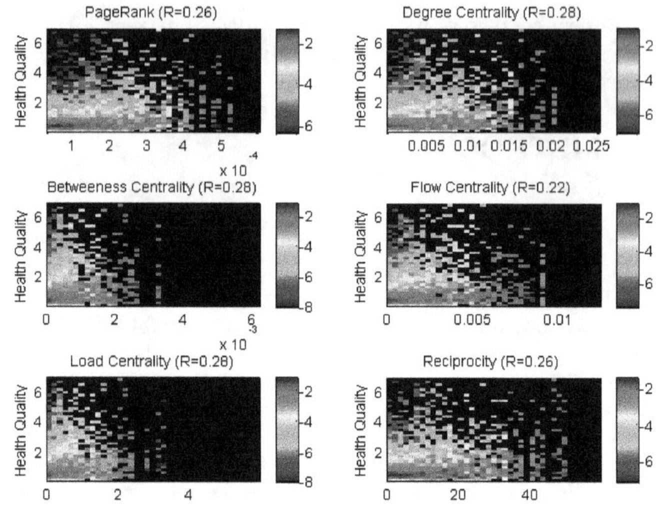

Figure 4: This figure shows the interplay between people's social status and their health. Each pane shows a different measure of social status (plotted on the horizontal axes). The vertical axes show the expected amount of time a person is healthy. A column x in each figure shows the log-probability distribution $\log(\mathbf{Pr}[\mathbf{health}|\mathbf{centrality} = x])$. We see that the people who often get sick (bottom rows in each pane) are more likely of low social status, whereas people with high social rank enjoy better health. The correlation coefficient R for each measure of social status is shown on top. The positive association between rank and health is consistent across all measures of centrality considered.

Fig. 4 shows the interplay between six different measures of social rank and people's health. We see a common pattern independent of the particular centrality measure: the higher the social status, the better the health. While low-rank individuals are concentrated on the "frequently sick" side of the spectrum (on the bottom of each pane), highly ranked subjects (on the right side of each pane) are more uniformly distributed and often attain high health scores.

Applying regression analysis, we quantify the associations between our factors and health (Fig. 5). All measures of social rank are mutually strongly correlated and positively associated with health quality. Proximity to pollution sources is the single most correlated feature with P_s (closer proximity $\Leftrightarrow$ worse health). Visit to polluted sites are also strongly associated with health (more visits $\Leftrightarrow$ worse health).

In agreement with prior work [21], we found a small but significant positive correlation between visits of public parks and health quality.

Fig. 6 shows the fraction of variance in cumulative probability of sickness (P_S) explained by various subsets of our factors (across all subjects).

We see that census data exhibits small correlation scores and explains little variance in health. While the individual contributions of poverty, education, and race are small, they jointly account for 8.7% of variance that is unexplained by other factors. The actual effect of these factors is likely to be even higher, however. In New York City, the ZIP code areas are relatively large compared to the diversity and den-

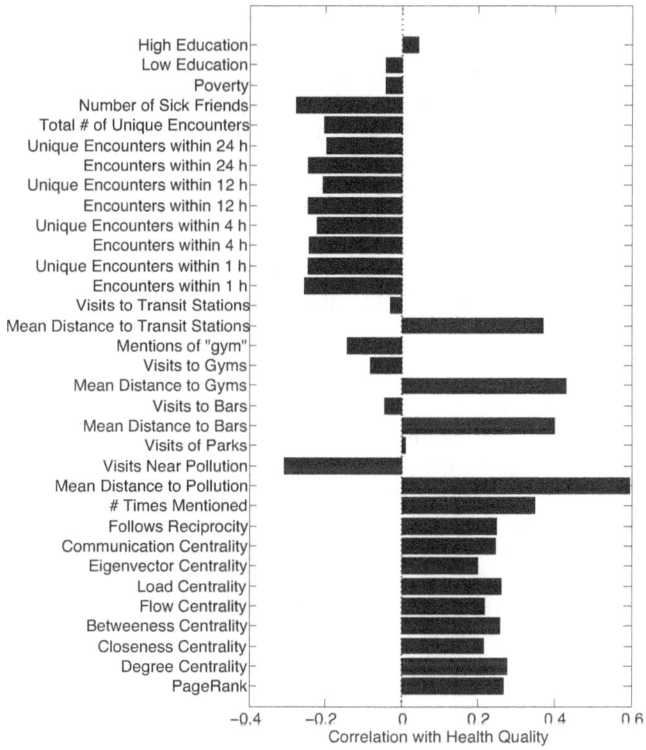

Figure 5: Results of regularized regression analysis with the negative cumulative probability of sickness ($-P_S$) as the dependent variable. Proximity to polluted sites and encounters with sick individuals are negatively correlated with people's health quality, whereas high centrality corresponds with good health. Note the positive association between social rank and health quality, irrespective of the measure of social status. Features derived from census data (education and poverty) have small but significant effect.

sity of the city population. As a result, a single ZIP code often contains people on both extremes of any given factor considered in this study. This suggests that the fine-grained data available in online social media does open novel opportunities for increasingly comprehensive models of public health.

From Figures 5 and 6, we see that subjects' activities regarding bars, gyms, and public transit all appear to have a common association with health: avoiding those venues is connected to better health. For gyms, the effect is mildly stronger (in a statistically significant way) as compared to bars and public transit. Interestingly, mentioning the word "gym" in online communication is also associated with worse health. Future work will explore possible confounders and shed more light on the interplay between these important lifestyle factors.

For health prediction, we use 80% randomly selected subjects to induce a regression decision tree D_1 that predicts the expected number of sick days (Fig. 7), and D_2 that predicts the cumulative probability of sickness P_S. Evaluation on the remaining 20% of the subjects shows that D_1 achieves 91% accuracy, and D_2 is within 8% of the actual P_S value more than 95% of the time. We see that the decision tree induced

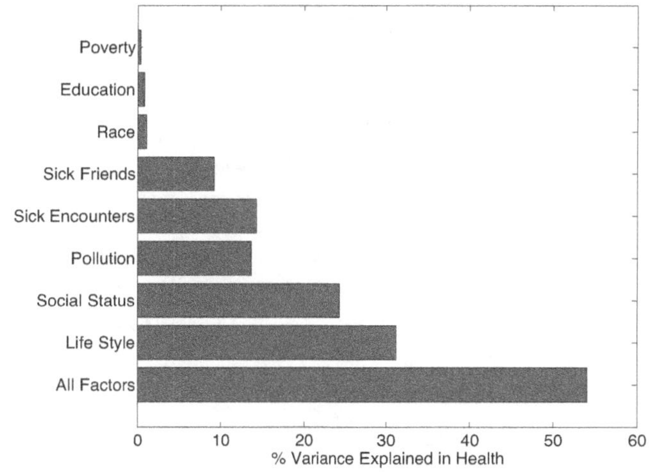

Figure 6: Fraction of variance in health ($-P_S$) explained by various subsets of our factors. All features jointly account for more than 54% of the total variance. The first three factors (Poverty, Education, and Race) are derived from census data for user's home ZIP code. See Section 7.2 for explanation of the composition of the factors.

meaningful sequences of features, and it will be interesting to see if such insights can guide the design of a *controlled* epidemiological study that explores the effects further.

We consider two baselines: random and most-frequent. The former draws the predicted number of sick days from a Gaussian distribution learned from training data, whereas the most-frequent baseline always outputs the mode of the labels in training data. They achieve 15% and 64% accuracy, respectively, when predicting the number of individuals' sick days.

9. RELATED WORK

Since the famous cholera study by John Snow (1855), much work has been done in capturing the mechanisms of epidemics. There is ample previous work in computational epidemiology on building relatively coarse-grained models of disease spread via differential equations and graph theory [2, 29], by harnessing simulated populations [16], and by analysis of official statistics [19]. Such models are typically developed for the purposes of assessing the impact a particular combination of an outbreak and a containment strategy would have on humanity or ecology [7]. However, the above works focus on simulated populations and hypothetical scenarios. By contrast, we address the problem of predicting the health of *real-world* populations composed of individuals embedded in a fine social structure. As a result, our work makes a step towards understanding the impact of complex intertwined factors affecting our health.

Traditionally, public health is monitored via surveys and by aggregating statistics obtained from healthcare providers. Such methods are costly, slow, and may be biased. Recently, digital media has been successfully used to significantly reduce the latency and improve the overall effectiveness of public health monitoring. Perhaps most notably, Google Flu Trends models the prevalence of flu via analysis of geolocated search queries[18].

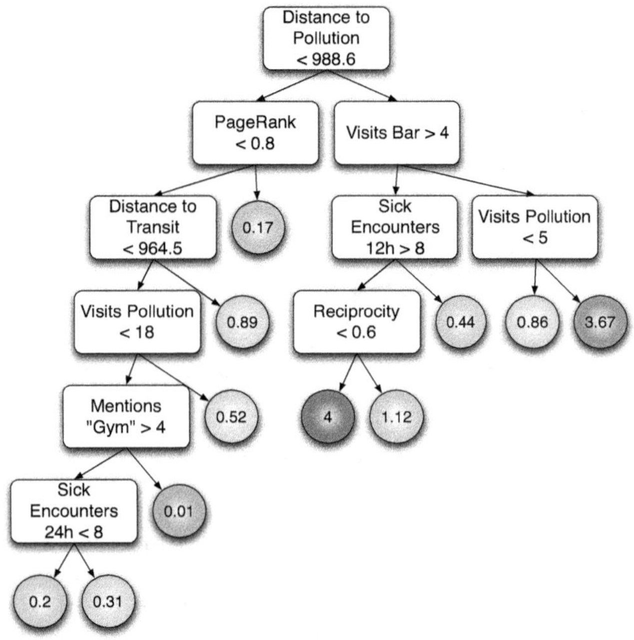

Figure 7: Decision tree predicting the expected number of sick days. The tree has been pruned to an optimal level using 10-fold cross-validation. To estimate the number of sick days for a new individual, we start at the root of the tree and evaluate the inequality in the root. If it evaluates to true, we traverse the left subtree, otherwise we recurse on the right subtree. We see, for example, that highly ranked subjects who avoid pollution sources tend to be healthier than people who frequent bars, encounter too many sick individuals, and have unreciprocated relationships.

Eubank *et al.* began to leverage more fine-grained information, including people's activities [16]. They developed a simulation tool (EpiSims) that leverages synthetic—but statistically realistic—human mobility to study the spread of infectious diseases over a metropolitan area. We see an important continuity from such simulations to real-time tracking of human behavior. For example, as we have seen, our NYC dataset contains 1/30 of the residents. We can simulate the remainder of the population, while "seeding" the system with realistic parameters *learned* from live data. For example, people's home locations or social encounters are no longer drawn from coarse distributions, but rather inferred from online activities.

In the context of social media, [25] explore augmenting the traditional notification channels about a disease outbreak with data extracted from Twitter. By manually examining a large number of tweets, they show that self-reported symptoms are the most reliable signal in detecting if a tweet is relevant to an outbreak or not. This is because people often do not know what their true problem is until diagnosed by an expert, but they can readily write about how they feel. Researchers have also concentrated on capturing the overall *trend* of a particular disease outbreak, typically influenza, by monitoring social media [13, 26, 9]. [17] use information actively submitted by cell phone users to model aggregate public health. However, scaling such systems poses considerable challenges.

Other researchers focus on a more detailed modeling of the *language* of the tweets and its relevance to public health in general [31], and to influenza surveillance in particular [11]. Paul *et al.* develop a variant of topic models that captures the symptoms and possible treatments for ailments, such traumatic injuries and allergies, that people discuss on Twitter. In a follow-up work [32] begin to consider the geographical patterns in the prevalence of such ailments, and show a good agreement of their models with official statistics and Google Flu Trends.

Our previous work has shown that people's interactions recorded in online social networks can be used to learn very specific and fine-grained models of the spread of contagious disease [35, 36]. However, prior work considered only rudimentary features based on immediate user co-location and social ties. In this paper, we include more than forty additional factors based not only on interpersonal interactions, but also on the environment, quality of one's neighborhood, socioeconomic status, and lifestyle. Furthermore, we show that the factors we induce generalize across individuals and have a strong predictive power within our population of Twitter users.

In life sciences, the positive correlation between social rank and strength of an immune system has been found in rhesus monkeys by performing controlled experiments on a small number of subjects [42]. In human studies, social status has been estimated indirectly. Socioeconomic status (SES) has been widely used as a proxy for people's social rank [44]. A strong correlation between SES and health has been documented in a large number of contexts, in countries with egalitarian and socialized medical care, and even for diseases whose outcomes are largely unaffected by the quality of health care. Interestingly, even when controlling for risk factors often associated with low SES, such as smoking and unhealthy diet, SES is still the dominant factor. Subsequent studies have shown that *subjective* SES is a better predictor of a person's health than a global measure SES.

For example, in the US, the higher the income inequality in a given region, the worse the health of the population there [24] (and also the higher the prevalence of firearm ownership [22]). Position in a civil servant hierarchy is another potential proxy for social status. A pioneering study of [28] has found that the risk of heart disease grows as one's occupational rank decreases. In this paper, we use the declared social network of Twitter users and their online interactions to determine the social rank of any given individual.

While we do not yet have a comprehensive understanding of the biological and psychological mechanisms that link social status to disease susceptibility, partial explanations have been proposed. Low social rank often leads to less control over one's life, imbalance between work effort and reward, lack of autonomy, less respect from the general society, fewer means and options available to resolve difficult situations, *etc.* [27]. This renders low-rank individuals more vulnerable to stress, in the developed world mostly *psychological* stress. The negative impact of stress on health is well documented. Stress induces metabolic and endocrine changes that in turn lead to increased risk of disease [37].

However no studies to date have resolved the impact of people's social status on the prevalence of diseases, or the spread of infectious diseases, throughout a large-scale population over extended periods of time. In this paper, we demonstrate that large-scale data mining enables us to fill some of these gaps without any active user participation. As a result, we can improve our understanding of human behavior and begin to quantify—in a scalable fashion—important phenomena affecting our everyday lives. At the same time, our approach complements, but does not replace, controlled longitudinal studies (*e.g.*, [28, 14, 37]) that uncover the detailed biological mechanism behind diseases and capture signal that is, at present, too weak to be detectable online.

10. CONCLUSIONS AND FUTURE WORK

This paper focuses on data mining diverse, noisy, and incomplete sensory data over large numbers of individuals. We show that the induced patterns can be subsequently leveraged in descriptive as well as predictive models of the health of a population of Twitter users at scale. We find that the raw sensory data linked with the content of users' online communication, explicit as well as implicit online social interactions, and relationships are extremely rich information sources. The fine granularity and pervasiveness of the data allows us to model phenomena that have been previously out of reach. We consider environmental factors (such as pollution and poverty) as well as social aspects of life (such as encounters and friendships with sick and healthy people). Furthermore, we do this at no cost, and without any active user participation.

Our methods enable us to shed additional light on important questions in public health that have been either too expensive or outright impossible to answer. In the process, we have drawn parallels to work done in other scientific fields, including epidemiology, immunology, and sociology, and shown how our methods complement previous results and bring new insights.

Our current work concentrates on two areas: effective ways of validating disease models with ground truth about people's health, and expanding the set of environmental factors our models capture. The first area builds on research in traditional epidemiology and active learning, and will enable us to learn more *specific* health models that capture the "offline" part of the population as well.

Consider the following pyramid model of public health. On the base of the pyramid, we have the entire population. In the middle of the pyramid are users of online social media who we can access. At the top of the pyramid is a small—but strategically selected—sample of individuals from the general population (which includes some of the social media users) for whom we have detailed records about their health. These include subjects who respond to online medical surveys, take at-home rapid tests, or even get tested at a nearby medical lab and share the results.

Traditionally, epidemiological studies are based on data collected from the top of the pyramid. This paper addresses the middle of the pyramid. We believe a *hybrid* approach will enable knowledge gained at any level in the pyramid to "trickle down". For example, by applying automated machine learning techniques described in this paper to the large mass of people in online social media, we can bootstrap the top of the pyramid to make well-founded predictions about the general population at the bottom of the pyramid. This will infuse epidemiological models with additional structure and parameters learned from detailed timely data, so that fewer factors need to be modeled via simulation. However, information could also "trickle up", where the latent behavior of the hidden population influences predictions even for individuals on top.

The second area focuses on modeling the interplay between a wider range of personal, social, environmental and health factors. For example: What exact impact eating habits have on one's health, and the health of related people? Animal studies have shown that *personality* plays a significant role in the perception of one's social rank, which in turn modulates the impact of the social status on one's health [43]. Similar processes are likely to occur in human societies as well. For instance, a phlegmatic person may be less affected by his or her low rank. However, these mechanisms prove difficult to capture using current techniques. By contrast, our work builds a foundation that makes such studies possible. For example, the language model used here to infer the health state of an individual can be augmented to estimate the personality type of a person. Finally, our models enable mobile applications that inform the user about health risks around him in real-time, opening opportunities for complex social studies of human behavior at scale.

11. ACKNOWLEDGMENTS

Figures 1-3 in this paper are taken from our web application developed with Sean Brennan, Martin Janda, Andrew Abumoussa, and Hao Chen (http://fount.in). This research was partly funded by ARO grant W911NF-08-1-0242, ONR grant N00014-11-10417, OSD grant W81XWH-08-C07-40, and a gift from the Kodak Company.

12. REFERENCES

[1] R. Ader and N. Cohen. Conditioning and immunity. *Psychoneuroimmunology*, 2:3–34, 2001.

[2] R. Anderson and R. May. Population biology of infectious diseases: Part I. *Nature*, 280(5721):361, 1979.

[3] C. Aperjis and B. Huberman. A market for unbiased private data: Paying individuals according to their privacy attitudes. *Arxiv.org*, 2012.

[4] L. Backstrom and J. Leskovec. Supervised random walks: predicting and recommending links in social networks. In *WSDM 2011*, pages 635–644. ACM, 2011.

[5] D. Bild, D. Bluemke, G. Burke, R. Detrano, A. Diez Roux, A. Folsom, P. Greenland, R. Kronmal, K. Liu, J. Nelson, et al. Multi-ethnic study of atherosclerosis: objectives and design. *American Journal of Epidemiology*, 156(9):871–881, 2002.

[6] L. Breiman et al. *Classification and Regression Trees.* Chapman & Hall, New York, 1984.

[7] P. Chen, M. David, and D. Kempe. Better vaccination strategies for better people. In *Proceedings of the 11th ACM conference on Electronic commerce*, pages 179–188. ACM, 2010.

[8] E. Cho, S. A. Myers, and J. Leskovec. Friendship and mobility: User movement in location-based social networks. *ACM SIGKDD International Conference on Knowledge Discovery and Data Mining (KDD)*, 2011.

[9] R. Chunara, J. Andrews, and J. Brownstein. Social and news media enable estimation of epidemiological patterns early in the 2010 Haitian cholera outbreak. *The American Journal of Tropical Medicine and Hygiene*, 86(1):39–45, 2012.

[10] S. Cohen, D. Tyrrell, and A. Smith. Psychological stress and susceptibility to the common cold. *New England journal of medicine*, 325(9):606–612, 1991.

[11] N. Collier, N. Son, and N. Nguyen. OMG U got flu? Analysis of shared health messages for bio-surveillance. *Journal of Biomedical Semantics*, 2011.

[12] C. Cortes and V. Vapnik. Support-vector networks. *Machine learning*, 20(3):273–297, 1995.

[13] A. Culotta. Towards detecting influenza epidemics by analyzing Twitter messages. In *Proceedings of the First Workshop on Social Media Analytics*, pages 115–122. ACM, 2010.

[14] F. Destefano, E. Eaker, S. Broste, D. Nordstrom, P. Peissig, R. Vierkant, K. Konitzer, R. Gruber, and P. Layde. Epidemiologic research in an integrated regional medical care system: the marshfield epidemiologic study area. *Journal of clinical epidemiology*, 49(6):643–652, 1996.

[15] D. Easley and J. Kleinberg. *Networks, Crowds, and Markets: Reasoning About a Highly Connected World.* Cambridge University Press, 2010.

[16] S. Eubank, H. Guclu, V. Anil Kumar, M. Marathe, A. Srinivasan, Z. Toroczkai, and N. Wang. Modelling disease outbreaks in realistic urban social networks. *Nature*, 429(6988):180–184, 2004.

[17] C. Freifeld, R. Chunara, S. Mekaru, E. Chan, T. Kass-Hout, A. Iacucci, and J. Brownstein. Participatory epidemiology: use of mobile phones for community-based health reporting. *PLoS medicine*, 7(12):e1000376, 2010.

[18] J. Ginsberg, M. Mohebbi, R. Patel, L. Brammer, M. Smolinski, and L. Brilliant. Detecting influenza epidemics using search engine query data. *Nature*, 457(7232):1012–1014, 2008.

[19] B. Grenfell, O. Bjornstad, and J. Kappey. Travelling waves and spatial hierarchies in measles epidemics. *Nature*, 414(6865):716–723, 2001.

[20] A. Gruzd, B. Wellman, and Y. Takhteyev. Imagining Twitter as an imagined community. In *American Behavioral Scientist, Special issue on Imagined Communities*, 2011.

[21] I. Hanski, L. von Hertzen, N. Fyhrquist, K. Koskinen, K. Torppa, T. Laatikainen, P. Karisola, P. Auvinen, L. Paulin, M. Mäkelä, et al. Environmental biodiversity, human microbiota, and allergy are interrelated. *Proceedings of the National Academy of Sciences*, 2012.

[22] D. Hemenway, B. Kennedy, I. Kawachi, and R. Putnam. Firearm prevalence and social capital. *Annals of Epidemiology*, 11(7):484–490, 2001.

[23] T. Joachims. A support vector method for multivariate performance measures. In *ICML 2005*, pages 377–384. ACM, 2005.

[24] I. Kawachi. The health of nations: Why inequality is harmful to your health author: Ichiro kawachi, bruce p. kennedy, publisher: New p. 2006.

[25] M. Krieck, J. Dreesman, L. Otrusina, and K. Denecke. A new age of public health: Identifying disease outbreaks by analyzing tweets. *Proceedings of Health WebScience Workshop, ACM Web Science Conference*, 2011.

[26] V. Lampos, T. De Bie, and N. Cristianini. Flu detector-tracking epidemics on Twitter. *Machine Learning and Knowledge Discovery in Databases*, pages 599–602, 2010.

[27] M. Marmot. Status syndrome. *JAMA: the journal of the American Medical Association*, 295(11):1304–1307, 2006.

[28] M. Marmot, G. Rose, M. Shipley, and P. Hamilton. Employment grade and coronary heart disease in british civil servants. *Journal of Epidemiology and Community Health*, 32(4):244–249, 1978.

[29] M. Newman. Spread of epidemic disease on networks. *Physical Review E*, 66(1):016128, 2002.

[30] M. Newman. A measure of betweenness centrality based on random walks. *Social networks*, 27(1):39–54, 2005.

[31] M. Paul and M. Dredze. A model for mining public health topics from Twitter. *Technical Report. Johns Hopkins University. 2011.*, 2011.

[32] M. Paul and M. Dredze. You are what you tweet: Analyzing Twitter for public health. In *Fifth International AAAI Conference on Weblogs and Social Media*, 2011.

[33] D. Q. Rich, H. M. Kipen, W. Huang, G. Wang, Y. Wang, P. Zhu, P. Ohman-Strickland, M. Hu, C. Philipp, S. R. Diehl, S.-E. Lu, J. Tong, J. Gong, D. Thomas, T. Zhu, and J. J. Zhang. Association between changes in air pollution levels during the beijing olympics and biomarkers of inflammation and thrombosis in healthy young adultsair pollution, inflammation, and thrombosis. *The Journal of the American Medical Association*, 307(19):2068–2078, 2012.

[34] A. Sadilek, H. Kautz, and J. P. Bigham. Finding your friends and following them to where you are. In *Fifth ACM International Conference on Web Search and Data Mining*, 2012. (Best Paper Award).

[35] A. Sadilek, H. Kautz, and V. Silenzio. Modeling spread of disease from social interactions. In *Sixth AAAI International Conference on Weblogs and Social Media (ICWSM)*, 2012.

[36] A. Sadilek, H. Kautz, and V. Silenzio. Predicting disease transmission from geo-tagged micro-blog data. In *Twenty-Sixth AAAI Conference on Artificial Intelligence*, 2012.

[37] R. Sapolsky. Social status and health in humans and other animals. *Annual Review of Anthropology*, pages 393–418, 2004.

[38] S. Shalev-Shwartz, Y. Singer, and N. Srebro. Pegasos: Primal estimated sub-gradient solver for svm. In *Proceedings of the 24th international conference on Machine learning*, pages 807–814. ACM, 2007.

[39] A. Smith. Pew internet & american life project. *http://pewresearch.org/pubs/2007/twitter-users-cell-phone-2011-demographics*, 2011.

[40] C. W. Thompson, J. Roe, P. Aspinall, R. Mitchell, A. Clow, and D. Miller. More green space is linked to less stress in deprived communities: Evidence from salivary cortisol patterns. *Landscape and Urban Planning*, 105(3):221 – 229, 2012.

[41] B. I. Truman et al. CDC health disparities and inequalities report. *Morbidity and Mortality Weekly Report*, 2011.

[42] J. Tung, L. Barreiro, Z. Johnson, K. Hansen, V. Michopoulos, D. Toufexis, K. Michelini, M. Wilson, and Y. Gilad. Social environment is associated with gene regulatory variation in the rhesus macaque immune system. *Proceedings of the National Academy of Sciences*, 2012.

[43] C. Virgin Jr and R. Sapolsky. Styles of male social behavior and their endocrine correlates among low-ranking baboons. *American Journal of Primatology*, 42(1):25–39, 1997.

[44] R. Wilkinson. *Mind the gap*. Weidenfeld & Nicolson, 2000.

[45] H. Zou and T. Hastie. Regularization and variable selection via the elastic net. *Journal of the Royal Statistical Society: Series B (Statistical Methodology)*, 67(2):301–320, 2005.

Collective Inference for Network Data with Copula Latent Markov Networks

Rongjing Xiang
Departments of Computer Science
Purdue University
rxiang@cs.purdue.edu

Jennifer Neville
Departments of Computer Science and Statistics
Purdue University
neville@cs.purdue.edu

ABSTRACT

The popularity of online social networks and social media has increased the amount of *linked* data available in Web domains. Relational and Gaussian Markov networks have both been applied successfully for classification in these relational settings. However, since Gaussian Markov networks model joint distributions over *continuous* label space, it is difficult to use them to reason about uncertainty in discrete labels. On the other hand, relational Markov networks model probability distributions over *discrete* label space, but since they condition on the graph structure, the marginal probability for an instance will vary based on the structure of the subnetwork observed around the instance. This implies that the marginals will not be *identical* across instances and can sometimes result in poor prediction performance. In this work, we propose a novel latent relational model based on *copulas* which allows use to make predictions in a discrete label space while ensuring identical marginals and at the same time incorporating some desirable properties of modeling relational dependencies in a continuous space. While copulas have recently been used for descriptive modeling, they have not been used for collective classification in large scale network data and the associated conditional inference problem has not been considered before. We develop an approximate inference algorithm, and demonstrate empirically that our proposed Copula Latent Markov Network models based on approximate inference outperform a number of competing relational classification models over a range of real-world relational classification tasks.

Categories and Subject Descriptors

I.2.m [**Computing Methodologies**]: Artificial Intelligence—*Miscellaneous*

General Terms

Algorithms

Keywords

Collective Inference, Relational Learning

1. INTRODUCTION

With the emergence of online social networks and social media, there are many web domains which consist of not only a set of data instances, but also the observed relationships (e.g., hyperlinks) that naturally encode statistical dependencies among the data instances. Collective classification methods (see e.g. [26]) aim to exploit such dependencies among the instances in order to improve predictive performance compared to conventional learning methods that assume independent and identically distributed (IID) instances. For example, in online social networks, it may be of interest to predict a user's missing profile information, such as their political view or gender. Collective classification models predict the missing profile labels in the network *jointly* based on the observed labels on other related nodes in the network, as well as other observed attributes.

Existing collective classification approaches can be grouped into two main categories. The first category of methods attempt to summarize the network information as "relational" features and then combine them with each instance's local features while learning a conventional classifier, e.g. [12, 28]. While this feature-construction type of approach can be used with any arbitrary IID learning algorithm, recent research has shown that it is often more accurate to learn, and reason with, the dependencies among the class labels of linked examples. This has motivated research in a second category of methods, which use Markov networks, or other probabilistic graphical models, to represent the *joint* distribution of attributes in relational data, e.g. [29, 25, 22]. These joint models have been shown to perform well when applied for *relational* inference, and thus have been popular in the statistical relational learning community.

As a general class of models, *relational Markov networks*[1] provide a principled framework to represent a joint distribution over the class labels $\mathbf{Y}$ in a network, conditioned on the graph structure G and the observed attributes $\mathbf{X}$: $p(\mathbf{Y}|\mathbf{X}, G)$. Although several methods have been developed to learn relational Markov networks from relational data, and empirical performance when the models are applied for prediction is often good, the models have several limitations. First, since the model is conditioned on the rela-

[1]Relational Markov networks are discriminative probabilistic models that can be viewed as conditional random fields applied to heterogeneous graphs.

tional structure, the prediction for an instance i will vary based on the observed structure of G. Although, the relational structure is indeed the very thing that relational models are trying to exploit, the marginal probability for i: $p(y_i|\mathbf{x}_i) = \sum_{\mathbf{y}_{\setminus y_i}} p(\mathbf{y}|\mathbf{x}_i)$, will vary when it is inferred with the same probabilistic model p but using different observed subgraphs G from the underlying domain (which often comprises a single, infinite network). This can lead to poor behavior in the model, and is a reason why in some cases relational models perform worse than IID classifiers that just model $p(y_i|\mathbf{x}_i)$. Moreover, since it models the full joint distribution, the relational Markov network representation does not allow us to explicitly specify the form of the marginal probability distribution (e.g., $p(y_i|\mathbf{x}_i) = f(y_i, \mathbf{x}_i, \boldsymbol{\theta})$), which makes it difficult to impose any constraint of equality on the marginals.

Second, [34] showed that the relative performance of relational Markov networks with parameters estimated by different methods, i.e., maximum likelihood (MLE) and maximum pseudolikelihood (MPLE), is not consistent as the amount of labeled instances varies in the test network. This is because when the model family is misspecified (which is typically the case for real network data), discrete Markov network models estimated with MLE-type approaches are often afflicted by *under propagation* error when the test network is abundantly labeled, while those estimated with MPLE-type approaches are often afflicted by *over propagation* error when the test network is sparsely labeled.

In contrast to relational Markov networks which model probability distributions over the discrete label space $\mathbf{y}$, *Gaussian Markov networks* model joint distributions over the *continuous* label space [37, 16]. Due to their harmonic property, Gaussian Markov networks usually exhibit better performance when the model is largely misspecified and in practice algorithms based on Gaussian Markov networks have been shown to perform well in relational domains. Many simple *collective classification* algorithms can be interpreted as instantiations of a Gaussian Markov network that is combined with a particular inference procedure for prediction—for example, iterative weighted voting [13] and personalized page rank [36, 30, 10]. Although these Gaussian Markov network models often provide a solid baseline that is hard to outperform, the models also have several limitations. First, since they model continuous attributes, they do not provide probability distributions over the discrete label space. Although thresholding approaches are typically used to transform the continuous predictions into discrete labels, the continuous representation makes it hard to (1) argue about uncertainty in the discrete labels or justify the thresholding of predictions, and (2) to formally analyze the dependence structure of the network data from the model. Moreover, the relational attributes are not typically incorporated into the model, i.e., $p(\mathbf{y}|G)$ is used instead of $p(\mathbf{y}|\mathbf{X}, G)$. While there is some work that attempts to move beyond this to learn kernel functions between linked instances [38], to date, there is not a systematic framework for learning Gaussian Markov networks with attributes in relational settings.

To address these issues and combine the strengths of Gaussian Markov networks' continuous representation with the strengths of relational Markov network methods for learning the dependencies among relational attributes, in this work we propose a novel latent relational model based on copulas [21]. The copula approach allows us to make the intuitively reasonable assumption of identical marginals an explicit constraint in the model. This provides a mechanism to remove the "independent" but not the "identical" from the conventional IID assumption when we model dependencies in relational datasets. While such a model is conceptually desirable for network data, to the best of our knowledge, copulas have not been applied to predictive tasks in real world network datasets.

Copulas were first explored in statistics and have attracted attentions from the machine learning community recently [6, 11, 32, 24] due to their flexibility in modeling the dependence among random variables. However, to date, the primary focus on copulas has been for descriptive modeling such as density estimation, clustering and feature selection, instead of directly applying the copula ideas into discriminative or predictive modeling. On the other hand, the fact that copulas enable the separation of dependence from marginals facilitates new approaches to jointly model networked instances while at the same time incorporating the general advantage of IID models that can use the attributes on instances. Due to the distributional transformations involved in copulas, conditional inference—which is the central task in our setting of collective classification in network data—is not straightforward and has not previously been studied. The contributions of our work is thus two-fold:

- First, we develop a copula latent Markov network model for network data. The model differs from existing copula based models in that it reasons about the dependence among the *latent* label tendency, instead of directly among the labels. Moreover, the proposed model elegantly extends a general class of IID classifiers based on the reformulation of IID probabilistic models from a latent variable perspective.

- Second, we design a message passing based scheme to solve the conditional inference problem in the copula model. This approximate inference approach is scalable for collective classification tasks in networks of tens of thousands of nodes, and is furthermore amenable to parallel implementations for even larger scale applications.

The rest of the paper is organized as follows. In Section 2, we begin with a description of a latent variable model reformulation of a general class of IID classifiers to motivate our proposed approach. Building on this formulation, in Section 3 we derive a copula latent Markov network (CLMN) model which unifies the homogeneous marginal classifiers and the dependence among the latent effects into a joint probabilistic model over the network data. In section 4, we design a message passing inference procedure for the collective classification task using CLMNs. In section 5 the CLMN model is compared with several alternative collective classification methods, and we show empirically that our copula-based approach outperforms several state-of-art relational classifiers over a range of real-world relational classification scenarios. Section 6 reviews related work and Section 7 concludes the paper.

2. LATENT VARIABLE VIEW OF PROBABILISTIC CLASSIFIERS

Our proposed model aims to extend an *IID* probabilistic classifier into a *collective* relational classifier, while still retaining all but the *independence* property of the original classifier. We first outline a latent variable view of probabilistic classifiers, to motivate and describe the approach. While a latent variable interpretation is well known for the probit regression model, analogous interpretations apply to a more general class of probabilistic classifiers.

Consider a binary classification task: $\mathbf{x} \mapsto y$, where $\mathbf{x} \in \mathcal{R}^d, y \in \{-1, 1\}$. Most probabilistic classifiers exploit the use of continuous, monotonically increasing functions $F(\eta) : \mathcal{R} \mapsto [0, 1]$ to map the observed attributes $\mathbf{x}$ to a class label y. Typically η is further modeled as a function of the input attributes $\mathbf{x}$ and a parameter vector $\mathbf{w}$: $\eta := \eta(\mathbf{x}; \mathbf{w})$, resulting in a binary classification model: $p(y=1) = F(\eta(\mathbf{x}; \mathbf{w}))$. Any generalized linear model with binary response fits into this class of models. For example, when $\eta(\mathbf{x}; \mathbf{w}) = \mathbf{w}^T\mathbf{x}$, $F(\cdot) = \frac{1}{1+e^{-\cdot}}$, we obtain the logistic regression model.

When the function F satisfies a further condition:

$$\lim_{a \leftarrow -\infty} F(a) = 0, \lim_{a \rightarrow +\infty} F(a) = 1$$

there always exists a continuous random variable $z \in \mathcal{R}$ for which F is the CDF. Let $f := F'$, i.e., the corresponding PDF of the distribution F. If we assume that the distribution is symmetric around zero (i.e., the CDF satisfies $F(a) = 1 - F(-a)$), we can then relate the class label y to the *sign* of a latent variable z sampled from f with a location shift $\eta(\mathbf{x}; \mathbf{w})$. More specifically, the probabilistic classification model $p(y_i|\mathbf{x}_i)$ can be thought of as modeling the following generative process:

$$\begin{aligned} z_i &\sim p(z_i = z|\mathbf{x}_i = \mathbf{x}) = f(z - \eta(\mathbf{x}_i; \mathbf{w})), \\ y_i &= sign(z_i) \end{aligned} \tag{1}$$

The equivalence is clear to see when the latent variable z is integrated out: $p(y = 1) = \int_0^{+\infty} f(z - \eta(\mathbf{x}; \mathbf{w})) = 1 - F(-\eta(\mathbf{x}; \mathbf{w})) = F(\eta(\mathbf{x}, \mathbf{w}))$.

The corresponding graphical model for this interpretation of probabilistic classifiers is shown in Figure 1(a). As a concrete example, consider the case of logistic regression where $F(\cdot) = \frac{1}{1+e^{-(\cdot)}}$, $p(z) = f(z - \eta(\mathbf{x}, \mathbf{w})) = \frac{e^{-(z-\eta(\mathbf{x},\mathbf{w}))}}{(1+e^{-(z-\eta(\mathbf{x},\mathbf{w}))})^2}$. In this case, $p(z)$ is the PDF of a logistic distribution with mean $\eta(\mathbf{x}, \mathbf{w})$ and scale 1. As another example, in the case of the probit classifier, z is a normal random variable with mean $\eta(\mathbf{x}, \mathbf{w})$ and variance 1. With some abuse of notation, hereinafter, we will use f_i to denote $f(z_i - \eta(\mathbf{x}_i; \mathbf{w}))$, the PDF of z_i, and F_i to denote its CDF.

Here the latent variable z_i for each data instance i can be interpreted as the latent tendency for instance i to have a positive label y_i. Besides capturing discriminative information from the input attributes $\mathbf{x}_i$, z_i can also capture other effects that are not present in $\mathbf{x}_i$, but which also contribute to determining y_i. When no information other than the attributes $\mathbf{x}$ is available, these additional effects can only be modeled as *random* effects (as in the model above). However, in relational domains when links among data instances are observed, the correlation among the class labels of linked instances is an example of such an additional effect, and can thus be interpreted as dependencies among the latent variables $\mathbf{z}$. In short, this latent variable view provides a way to decouple the random effects from the deterministic effects of $\mathbf{x}$ on $\mathbf{y}$, so that we can focus on modeling the correlations among the random effects.

We will use this view to combine the two aspects of relational data—the across-instance *relational* dependence structure and the *instance* level dependence of y_i on $\mathbf{x}_i$—into a coherent probabilistic model, while respecting and making use of the typical assumption of homogeneous (i.e., identically distributed) data instances. Copulas provide an ideal solution for this, since they separate marginal distributions from the joint distribution. Using a copula approach, we can learn a single (identical) marginal model $p(z|\mathbf{x})$ tied across all data instances, while also incorporating the relational dependence in the joint distribution over $\mathbf{z}$. Furthermore, the latent variable representation allows us to incorporate the strengths of Gaussian Markov networks through the relational dependence among the continuous $\mathbf{z}$, while at the same time modeling the uncertainty in the discrete label space $\mathbf{y}$. Our modeling idea differs from previous copula based models [29, 25, 22] in that it is a discriminative model and can be applied directly to classification tasks. As a result, the associated conditional inference task has not been considered before and we develop approximate inference algorithms to make it tractable for large networks. We discuss our proposed model in detail next.

3. COPULA LATENT MARKOV NETWORKS

Assuming that we would like to use some joint probability model Φ of our choice to model the dependence structure among $z_1, z_2, \ldots, z_n$ in a network of n nodes, but each marginal z_i has to be from a specified distribution $F_i(z_i)$. Then based on Sklar's theorem, we can use Φ to model the dependencies among a set of auxiliary variables $t_1, t_2, \ldots, t_n$ and use a copula function to facilitate the transformation from Φ to a joint distribution $F(z_1, z_2, \ldots, z_n)$ with the desired marginals.

An n-copula is an n-dimensional distribution function with n univariate margins distributed as $U(0, 1)$. The following theorem is fundamental in copula modeling:

THEOREM 1 (SKLAR'S THEOREM.). *Let Φ be an n-dimensional distribution function with marginal distribution functions Φ_1, Φ_2, ..., Φ_n. Then there exists an n-copula C such that for all $(t_1, t_2, \ldots, t_n)$:*

$$\Phi(t_1, t_2, \ldots, t_n) = C(\Phi_1(t_1), \Phi_2(t_2), \ldots, \Phi_n(t_n)).$$

If $\Phi_1, \Phi_2, \ldots, \Phi_n$ are all continuous then C is unique.

Define $\Phi_i^{(-1)}(u) = \inf\{x : \Phi(x) \geq u\}$ as the quasi-inverse of Φ_i. Then as a result of Theorem 1, for all $(u_1, \ldots, u_n) \in [0, 1]^n$:

$$C(u_1, \ldots, u_n) = \Phi(\Phi_1^{(-1)}(u_1), \ldots, \Phi_n^{(-1)}(u_n))$$

While the copula formulation provides ways to study the joint CDF Φ (and later F), we will primarily work with the PDF ϕ (and f) for the benefit of applying well established dependence models and inference algorithms in machine learning. In the following corollary, we make precise what we mean by "a joint probability density over $z_1, z_2, \ldots, z_n$ with the required marginals f_i and the desired dependence structure ϕ."

COROLLARY 1. *Let $f_1, f_2, \ldots, f_n$ denote the marginal PDFs of continuous variables $z_1, z_2, \ldots, z_n \in \mathcal{R}$, and let $F_1, F_2, \ldots, F_n$ denote the corresponding marginal CDFs. Let $\phi(t_1, t_2, \ldots, t_n)$ be an arbitrary, continuous joint density function over n random variables $t_1, \ldots, t_n \in \mathcal{R}$, with the respective joint CDF denoted by Φ. Then:*

1. *There exist a unique copula function C over Uniform(0,1) variables and a unique joint distribution function F such that the marginal distributions of F are exactly F_i, and the joint distribution satisfies:* $F(z_1,\ldots,z_n) = C(u_1,\ldots,u_n) = \Phi(\Phi_1^{(-1)}(u_1),\ldots,\Phi_n^{(-1)}(u_n))$, *where* $u_i = F_i(z_i)$.

2. *Let* $c := \frac{\partial^n C}{\partial u_1 \ldots \partial u_n}$, *i.e., the* copula density. *Then the joint density function f of F is given as follows:*

$$f(z_1,z_2,\ldots,z_n) = c(u_1,\ldots,u_n)\prod_{i=1}^{n} f_i(z_i) \tag{2}$$

$$= \frac{\phi(t_1,t_2,\ldots,t_n)}{\prod_{i=1}^{n}\phi_i(t_i)}\prod_{i=1}^{n} f_i(z_i)$$

where $u_i = F_i(z_i)$ *and* $t_i = \Phi_i^{(-1)}(u_i)$.

PROOF. By Sklar's theorem, since Φ is continuous, there exists a unique C such that, for any instantiation $(t_1,t_2,\ldots,t_n)$, $\Phi(t_1,t_2,\ldots,t_n) = C(\Phi_1(t_1),\Phi_2(t_2),\ldots,\Phi_n(t_n))$. On the other hand, since z_i are continuous variables, the inverse CDF function $F_i^{(-1)}$ is uniquely defined. Therefore, we define a joint distribution function F over $\mathbf{z}$ point wise. For any $\mathbf{z} \in \mathcal{R}^n$, let $u_i = F_i(z_i)$, and let $F(z_1,\ldots,z_n) = C(u_1,\ldots,u_n)$. Then $F(z_1,\ldots,z_n) = C(u_1,\ldots,u_n) = \Phi(\Phi^{(-1)}(u_1),\ldots,\Phi^{(-1)}(u_n))$, i.e., C is the unique copula distribution function and F is the unique CDF that satisfy the required condition and we have shown part 1.

Now consider the PDF $f(z_1,z_2,\ldots,z_n) = \frac{\partial^n F}{\partial z_1 \partial z_2,\ldots,\partial z_n}$. By the chain rule,

$$f = \frac{\partial^n F}{\partial z_1 \partial z_2,\ldots,\partial z_n} = \frac{\partial^n C}{\partial u_1 \ldots \partial u_n}\prod_{i=1}^{n}\frac{\partial F_i}{\partial z_i} = c\prod_{i=1}^{n} f_i$$

Moreover,

$$\frac{\partial^n C}{\partial u_1 \ldots \partial u_n}\prod_{i=1}^{n} f_i = \frac{\partial^n \Phi}{\partial t_1 \ldots \partial t_n}\prod_{i=1}^{n}\frac{\partial \Phi_i^{-1}}{\partial u_i}\prod_{i=1}^{n} f_i$$

$$= \frac{\partial^n \Phi}{\partial t_1 \ldots \partial t_n}\prod_{i=1}^{n}\frac{1}{\phi_i(t_i)}\prod_{i=1}^{n} f_i = \frac{\phi(t_1,\ldots,t_n)}{\prod_{i=1}^{n}\phi_i(t_i)}\prod_{i=1}^{n} f_i$$

Therefore, $f(z_1,z_2,\ldots,z_n) = c(u_1,\ldots,u_n)\prod_{i=1}^{n} f_i(z_i) = \frac{\phi(t_1,t_2,\ldots,t_n)}{\prod_{i=1}^{n}\phi_i(t_i)}\prod_{i=1}^{n} f_i(z_i)$. Thus we obtain Equation (2). □

Now, we will use Equation (2), and combine it with Equation (1), to model the joint probability over the labels in a relational network. We can interpret the model with the following generative process. First, a joint set of auxiliary variables $t_1,t_2,\ldots,t_n$ is sampled from ϕ. Then the marginal CDFs Φ_i are used to transform each t_i to a uniform $[0,1]$ variable u_i, and each quasi-inverse $F_i^{(-1)}$ is used to obtain z_i from u_i, i.e., $z_i = F_i^{(-1)}(u_i) = F_i^{(-1)}(\Phi_i(t_i))$. Finally the $y_1,y_2,\ldots,y_n$ can be computed directly from $z_1,z_2,\ldots,z_n$. This generative process is summarized as follows.

- Generate $(t_1,t_2,\ldots,t_n) \sim \phi$.
- Apply the transformation: $u_i = \Phi_i(t_i)$ so that $\mathbf{u}$ follows the copula distribution C corresponding to Φ.
- Apply the transformation: $z_i = F_i^{(-1)}(u_i)$.
- Label: $y_i = sign(z_i)$.

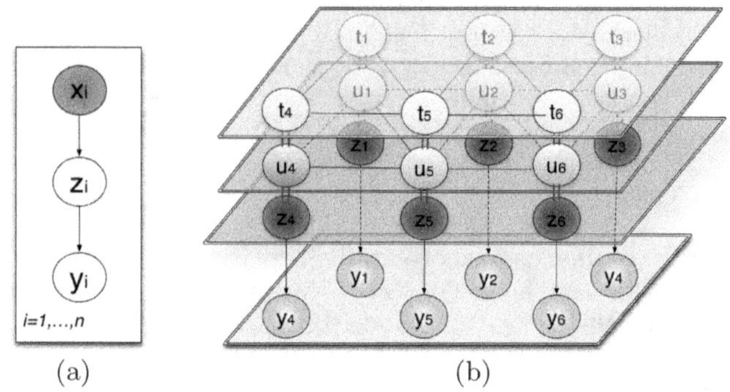

Figure 1: The two facets of a CLMN. (a) The graphical model representation of independent probabilistic classification, which is also the marginal facet of a CLMN. (b) The dependence facet of a CLMN.

Combining Equation (2) with (1), we obtain the joint likelihood over $y_1,y_2,\ldots,y_n$ and $z_1,z_2,\ldots,z_n$:

$$p(y_1,\ldots,y_n,z_1,\ldots,z_n) \tag{3}$$

$$= \frac{\phi(t_1,t_2,\ldots,t_n)}{\prod_{i=1}^{n}\phi_i(t_i)}\prod_{i=1}^{n}\left(f_i(z_i)I_{y_i=sign(z_i)}\right)$$

where $t_i = \Phi^{(-1)}(u_i)$, $u_i = F_i(z_i)$, and I is the indicator function. i.e., $\delta = 1$ if $y_i = sign(z_i)$, otherwise $\delta = 0$. The modeling task is then divided into two subproblems: the dependence modeling ϕ over the auxiliary variables $t_1,t_2,\ldots,t_n$, where t_i is simply the distributionally transformed version of z_i, and the marginal modeling $f_i(z_i)$. In addition, we see from Corollary 1 that switching from the discrete label domain to the continuous latent variable has resulted in the additional advantage of the uniqueness property of the copula construction. We will choose F_i and f_i to be a model from the family described in Section 2, i.e., they represent the discriminative probabilistic model of the binary label and the latent continuous variable respectively, conditioned on the attributes $\mathbf{x}_i$ and parameterized by $\mathbf{w}$. In our experiments, we use a logistic model. Thus, the marginal of z_i follows a logistic distribution—which resembles the normal distribution but with a heavier tail.

Next we consider the problem of modeling the dependence over the auxiliary variables $t_1,t_2,\ldots,t_n$. The dependence structure over continuous variables can be conveniently modeled using a Gaussian Markov network (GMN) with node potentials and edge potentials as follows:

$$\phi(\mathbf{t}) = \frac{1}{Z}\exp\left(-\frac{1}{2}\left(\sum_{i,j:(i,j)\in E}(t_i-t_j)^2\right)-\frac{\epsilon}{2}\sum_{i=1}^{n}t_i^2\right)$$

$$= \frac{1}{Z}\exp\left(-\frac{1}{2}\mathbf{t}^T(\epsilon\mathbf{I}+\Delta)\mathbf{t}\right) \tag{4}$$

where the normalization factor $Z = (2\pi)^{n/2}(|\epsilon\mathbf{I}+\Delta|)^{-1/2}$ and Δ is the graph Laplacian:

$$\Delta = \text{diag}(\text{Degree}_1,\text{Degree}_2,\ldots,\text{Degree}_n) - \mathbf{A}$$

where $\mathbf{A}$ is the adjacency matrix of the undirected data network or, in the case when the data network is a directed graph with adjacency matrix $\tilde{\mathbf{A}}$, let $\mathbf{A} = \frac{1}{2}(\tilde{\mathbf{A}}+\tilde{\mathbf{A}}^T)$, so that $\mathbf{A}$ is symmetric. Thus, ϕ defines a multivariable Gaussian distribution over $t_1, t_2, \ldots, t_n$ with precision matrix $\epsilon\mathbf{I} + \Delta$. The term $\epsilon\mathbf{I}$ is commonly adopted in practical implementation of GMNs for numerical stability. $\epsilon > 0$ ensures that the precision matrix is of full rank, so the Gaussian distribution is not intrinsic.

Summary: While the generic CLMN model is represented by Equation 2 and is described by the sampling process above Equation 3, the model specification in our implementation can be summarized as follows:

- *Dependence structure*—Joint PDF ϕ over latent variables $\mathbf{t}$:

$$\phi(\mathbf{t}) = \frac{1}{Z}\exp\left(-\frac{1}{2}\left(\sum_{i,j:(i,j)\in E}(t_i - t_j)^2\right) - \frac{\epsilon}{2}\sum_{i=1}^{n} t_i^2\right)$$

- *Marginal structure*—each PDF f is an independent classifier of latent variable z:

$$f_i(z_i|\mathbf{w}, \mathbf{x}_i) = \frac{e^{-(z_i - \mathbf{w}^T\mathbf{x}_i)}}{(1 + e^{-(z_i - \mathbf{w}^T\mathbf{x}_i)})^2}$$

- *Glue between joint dependence and marginal models*—marginal CDF transform:

$$\Phi_i(t_i) = u_i = F_i(z_i)$$

- *Classification*—discrete label is determined from latent variable sign:

$$y_i = sign(z_i)$$

Discussion of GMN dependence model.

Our choice of GMNs as the dependence model is inspired by its empirical success on relational collective classification tasks. The GMN provides a probabilistic modeling view of two popular collective classification models: iterative weighted voting with relaxed labels (WV) [13] and personalized page rank (PPR) [36, 10]. Based on the Neuman series expansion of the graph Laplacian (see e.g., the walk-sum analysis of GMNs by [16]), it can be shown that these approaches are related to GMNs and latent GMNs respectively. First, given a set of labeled instances L and their true labels $\mathbf{y}_L^*$, the MAP solution $p(y_i|\mathbf{y}_L^*)$ of the GMN model in Equation 4 results in label scores (for each unlabeled node i) that equal to those of the WV algorithm at convergence. Second, the PPR algorithm converges to the MAP of $p(y_i|\mathbf{y}_L^*)$ for a latent Gaussian Markov network (LGMN) that uses the normalized Laplacian $\tilde{\Delta}$ (instead of the Laplacian Δ in Equation 4). Each observation y_i is a noisy version of a latent variable, just like in CLMNs, but with a Gaussian noise. While the GMN reformulation of the WV method is well known to the relational learning community, it appears that the probabilistic modeling extension of PPR has not been explored before. Although the above LGMN reformulation of PPR considers noise in the observations, it does not make full use of such latent variable modeling because the actual observations y_i^* should binary instead of real-valued. Therefore, to improve it, one can simply modify the observation part $f(y_i|z_i)$ using a logistic or a probit function—indeed, this is the common approach taken when a Gaussian model is applied in classification tasks (e.g., in Gaussian process classifiers), and in our experiments we include a LGMN for comparison. Unlike PPRs, this LGMN model is no longer analytically solvable, and inference techniques similar to those for the CLMN model would need to be employed. On the other hand, they do not share the CLMN advantages that allow for easy incorporation of node attributes and learning the model using general independent classifiers.

4. USING CLMNS FOR COLLECTIVE CLASSIFICATION

We explore the utility of CLMNs in collective classification tasks, where a network of linked data instances $(\mathbf{x}_1, y_1), (\mathbf{x}_2, y_2), \ldots, (\mathbf{x}_n, y_n)$ is observed. A subset of the data instances, $j \in L$, are labeled and the goal is to infer labels for the remainder of the instances, $i \in U$.

4.1 Parameter learning

Before applying CLMNs for collective classification, we need to learn the parameters $\mathbf{w}$ in the marginal model f. Thanks to the marginal preserving property of copulas, parameter estimation for CLMNs can be simple and efficient.

A commonly explored learning approach for copula-based models consists of two stages (see e.g. [6, 4]). First, the marginal distribution is estimated as if we were learning from IID data instances. Second, fixing the estimated marginals, the dependence model is estimated. In the proposed CLMN model, since there is no parameter in the dependence model, only the first stage is involved, i.e., we only need to train the marginal classifier $p(y|\mathbf{x})$ using the observed class labels $y_i \in \{+1, -1\}$ and the attributes $\mathbf{x}_i$ of labeled instances (while ignoring the unlabeled instances) using the typical learning algorithm for the chosen classifier. In this work, we use an $\ell 2$ regularized logistic regression model with parameters $\mathbf{w}$, which we train by gradient-based optimization methods.

We note that this learning approach is also supported by statistical learning theory for dependent data (see e.g. [35]): Under reasonable mixing conditions—i.e., instances that are remote in the network are weakly dependent of each other—the learned marginal classifiers would converge to the optimal one within the model family as the number of labeled instances in the network increases. On the other hand, consider an alternative learning approach that maximizes the joint log-likelihood (conditioned on labeled instances) over the whole observed network. In application domains of our interest, typically only a single network (e.g., a subnetwork of the whole domain) is used for training and inference. There has been little theoretical analysis as to whether, or under which conditions, a joint approach to learning will converge in this setting—as the size of the single training/test network grows. Moreover, empirical results have suggested that such a joint approach is not robust when the model family is misspecified [5].

4.2 Approximate Inference

While learning is relatively well studied for copula based models in the literature, little attention has been paid to the problem of conditional inference, especially for large scale network data. Collective classification with the CLMN model corresponds exactly to the conditional inference problem, which is the central problem we attempt to address in developing CLMN algorithms. During collective classification, we need to apply the model with the estimated parameters $\hat{\mathbf{w}}$ to predict the label probabilities of the unlabeled data instances $i \in U$. Exact inference of the posterior is intractable.

For approximate inference in graphical models with continuous variables, there have been two commonly explored strategies: Nonparametric Belief Propagation (NBP) [27] Expectation Propagation (EP) [18]. While the former uses a nonparametric representation for local messages, the latter explores parametric forms to approximate the messages. For our CLMN model, we need to compute the CDFs and inverse CDFs of the approximate marginals of t_i, and the parametric approximation employed by EP makes this computation straightforward. In addition, EP has already been successfully applied to other large scale probabilistic inference problems such as Gaussian process classification (e.g. [8]). Therefore, we propose an approximation inference algorithm based on EP in this work. Since the developed algorithm uses a distributed message passing scheme, it is amenable to parallel implementation and is thus feasible for applications to large scale networks.

The inference task is to estimate $p(\mathbf{y}_i|\mathbf{y}_L, \mathbf{x}, \mathbf{w})$ for $i \in U$ given the observed labels $\mathbf{y}_L$, the attributes of all nodes $\mathbf{x}_1, \mathbf{x}_2, \ldots, \mathbf{x}_n$, and the parameters $\mathbf{w}$.

$$p(y_i|\mathbf{y}_L, \mathbf{x}, \mathbf{w}) = \int_{z_i \in \mathcal{R}} p(y_i|z_i)p(z_i|\mathbf{y}_L, \mathbf{x}, \mathbf{w})\mathrm{d}z_i$$
$$= \int_{\mathbf{t} \in \mathcal{R}^n} p\Big(y_i|z_i = F^{(-1)}(\Phi_i(t_i))\Big)\, p(\mathbf{t}|\mathbf{y}_L, \mathbf{x}, \mathbf{w})\mathrm{d}\mathbf{t}$$

where the last step follows from the copula transformation. Using Equation (3), the posterior is:

$$p(\mathbf{t}|\mathbf{y}_L, \mathbf{x}, \mathbf{w}) \propto \phi(t_1, t_2, \ldots, t_n) \prod \frac{g_i(z_i)}{\phi_i(t_i)} \quad (5)$$

where $z_i = F_i^{-1}(\Phi_i(t_i))$ and

$$g_i(z_i) = \begin{cases} f_i(z_i; \mathbf{w}, \mathbf{x}) & \text{if } i \in U \\ f_i(z_i; \mathbf{w}, \mathbf{x}) I_{y_i^* = sign(z_i)} & \text{if } i \in L \end{cases}$$

Exact inference of the posterior is intractable, so we develop an approximation inference algorithm based on Expectation Propagation (*EP*) [18].

Since $p(\mathbf{t}|\mathbf{y}_L)$ is intractable, we first proceed by finding an approximate distribution $q(\mathbf{t})$ for it. Specifically, we make a fully factored approximation $q = \prod_i q_i(t_i)$. Each approximation factor q_i is in the Gaussian form: $q_i(t_i; \lambda_i, h_i) = e^{-\frac{1}{2}\lambda_i t_i^2 + h_i t_i^2}$. The approximation factors are updated based on a message passing scheme. We denote the messages sent from node i to node j by $m_{i \to j}(t_j)$. The messages are also in Gaussian forms: $m_{i\to j}(t_j) = e^{-\frac{1}{2}\tilde{\lambda}_{i\to j} t_j^2 + \tilde{h}_{i \to j} t_j}$. Under the EP scheme, when updating each factor q_i, the KL divergence $KL(p||q)$ is minimized locally—which leads to the matching of first and second order moments in the cases where the approximation factors are Gaussian. We give the detailed message passing scheme in Algorithm 1. While the communications of messages between neighboring nodes (i.e., Steps 2a and 2c of Algorithm 1) are akin to those of loopy belief propagation in a Gaussian Markov network [31], the moment matching during incorporating the factor $\frac{g_i(z_i)}{\phi_i(t_i)}$ (i.e., Step 2b of the algorithm) cannot be done analytically, and numerical integration is needed. The required integral

Algorithm 1 Approximate inference of $p(\mathbf{t}|\mathbf{y}_L)$ using message-passing EP

Input: Network structure, observed labels $\mathbf{y}_L^*$, the marginals f_i and ϕ_i for $i = 1, \ldots, n$.
Step 1: Initialize the messages $m_{i\to j}$ by $\tilde{h}_{i \to j} = 0, \tilde{\lambda}_{i \to j} = 0$.
for each iteration **do**
  for each instance $i = 1, 2, \ldots, n$ **do**
    Step 2a: Collecting messages from neighboring nodes (where ∂i denotes i's Markov blanket):

$$\hat{\lambda}_i = \sum_{j \in \partial i} \tilde{\lambda}_{j \to i}, \quad \hat{h}_i = \sum_{j \in \partial i} \tilde{h}_{j \to i}$$

    Step 2b: Compute $\lambda_i^{\text{new}}, h_i^{\text{new}}$ by matching the moments of $q_i(t_i; \lambda_i^{\text{new}}, h_i^{\text{new}})$ with those of $\frac{g_i(z_i)}{\phi_i(t_i)} q_i(t_i; \hat{\lambda}_i, \hat{h}_i)$
    Step 2c: Compute the messages to the neighboring nodes:

$$\tilde{\lambda}_{i\to j} = -\Delta_{ij}^2 / \lambda_{i\setminus j}^{\text{new}}, \quad \tilde{h}_{i \to j} = -\Delta_{ij} h_{i \setminus j}^{\text{new}} / \lambda_{i\setminus j}^{\text{new}}$$

    where $\lambda_{i\setminus j}^{\text{new}} = \lambda_i^{\text{new}} - \tilde{\lambda}_{j\to i}$, and $h_{i\setminus j}^{\text{new}} = h_i^{\text{new}} - \tilde{h}_{j \to i}$.

    Step 2d: Update q_i: $\lambda_i := \lambda_i^{\text{new}}, h_i := h_i^{\text{new}}$.
  end for
end for
Step 3: Return the mean μ_i and variance v_i of the pseudo-marginals q_i: $\mu_i = h_i/\lambda_i, v_i = 1/\lambda_i$.

is of the form $\Gamma = \int \gamma(t) \frac{g_i(F_i^{-1}(\Phi_i(t_i)))}{\phi_i(t_i)} \mathcal{N}(t_i|\hat{\mu}_i, \hat{v}_i)$ where $\hat{\mu}_i = \hat{h}_i/\hat{\lambda}_i, \hat{v}_i = 1/\hat{\lambda}_i$, and $\gamma(t)$ is either t or t^2. This integral has a complicated shape, so care must be taken to obtain an accurate estimate. For labeled instances $i \in L$, we apply importance sampling to compute Γ: sample z_i from the truncated distribution F_i, where the left interval $(-\infty, \mathbf{w}^T\mathbf{x}_i)$ is truncated if $y_i^* = +1$, and otherwise the right interval $(\mathbf{w}^T\mathbf{x}_i, +\infty)$ is truncated. In practice we sample the respective truncated uniform variables u, transform it using inverse CDF to obtain samples of t_i, and then weight the samples using $\mathcal{N}(\hat{\mu}_i, \hat{v}_i)/\phi_i(t_i)$, which is of a Gaussian form. For unlabeled instances $i \in U$, we apply a Metropolis Hasting method due to [20]. In each step, we sample s from $\mathcal{N}(\hat{\mu}, \hat{v})$, and then move from the old sample t^{old} with a step size δ: $t^{\text{new}} = \delta s + \sqrt{1-\delta^2} t^{\text{old}}$, t^{new} is then accepted with probability $\min\left(1, \frac{f_i(F_i^{-1}(\Phi_i(t^{\text{new}})))\phi_i(t^{\text{old}})}{f_i(F_i^{-1}(\Phi_i(t^{\text{old}})))\phi_i(t^{\text{new}})}\right)$.

After obtaining the posterior pseudo marginals q_i from Algorithm 1, we can use the variables z_i transformed from t_i for prediction. The full collective classification procedure using CLMNs is shown in Algorithm 2. In practice, we observe that Algorithm 1 converges to a good solution within a constant number of iterations. Since the complexity of each EP iteration is $O(|E|)$, the complexity of Algorithm 1 is $O(|E|)$. To find the marginals of the latent Markov network in Step 1 of Algorithm 2, we can compute the full covariance matrix, i.e., the inverse of the Laplacian (with ϵ added to the diagonal elements). Since the networks in our applications are usually sparse, Step 1 typically scales as $O(n^2)$, although it may be accelerated to $O(n)$ by using further approximations. For example, since only the marginal variance of each node in the latent Gaussian Markov network needs to be computed, the wavelet based approximation developed by [15] may be applied for this purpose.

Algorithm 2 Collective classification for unlabeled data instances $i \in U$.

Input: Network structure, attributes $\mathbf{x}_1, \dots, \mathbf{x}_n$, observed labels $\mathbf{y}_L^*$, and the marginal model f_i.
Step 1: Compute graph Laplacian Δ and the marginals ϕ_i in the dependence model.
Step 2: Apply Algorithm 1 to find the pseudo marginals $q_i(t_i)$ for $i = 1, \dots, n$.
for each unlabeled instance $i \in U$ **do**
  Numerically evaluate the posterior mean $\hat{y}_i$ by sampling t_i from q_i and computing z_i by marginal CDF transform.
end for

5. EXPERIMENTS

In this section, we evaluate our proposed CLMN model on several real world network datasets from different domains, and demonstrate its effectiveness by comparing it with state-of-art relational classifiers.

5.1 Comparison methods

We consider representative approaches from the following major related methods:

Marginal only classifiers (LR). The baseline logistic regression classifier with $\ell 2$ regularization, which is the same as the marginal model for CLMNs in our experiments, is included to show the effectiveness of using attribute information alone.

Simple iterative collective classifiers (GMN). We include the widely-used, simple collective classifier—iterative weighted voting [13] where we apply the equivalent Gaussian Markov network [37] formulation to directly compute the MAP $\hat{\mathbf{y}}_U = \text{argmax}_{\mathbf{y}_U} p(\mathbf{y}_U|\mathbf{y}_L^*)$, which gives the relaxed label predictions of iterative weighted voting.

Personalized Page Rank collective classifiers (PPR). As mentioned in Section 3, another class of random-walk based classifiers, Personalized Page Rank, have also been widely applied to network data [36, 30, 10].

Latent Gaussian models (LGMN). In contrast to the relaxed labeling approach taken in GMNs, here we use a natural probabilistic model over the binary label space, while using the GMN to model the dependence structure over latent variables z_i. Here z_i determines the labels y_i through a noisy link function. This LGMN model falls into the general category of latent Gaussian models. In our experiments, we use the probit link function and apply EP for approximate inference. We note that we also experimented with the logistic link function for the LGMN model but observed that it performed worse than the probit link function in this setting, possibly due to the fact that the logistic-Gaussian factor cannot be analytically integrated and approximation degrades performance.

Relational feature based classifiers (SocDim). Instead of modeling the joint dependency of the labels, methods in this category extracts network-based features and combine them with other features to be applied in a conventional classifier. We include the recently proposed latent social dimension [28] approach from this category for comparison. The SocDim method uses top eigenvectors of the modularity matrix [23] of the graph as relational features. In our experiments, the top 200 eigenvectors are extracted, and we apply these features with a logistic regression classifier.

Relational Markov Networks (RMN). These methods attempt to model the statistical dependency among the labels, just like the CLMN model does. We include the widely applied relational Markov network [29] for comparison. We learn RMN parameters using a recently developed component likelihood based approach [33], which has been shown to enjoy desirable theoretical properties. We apply the model for collective classification using Gibbs sampling of 100,000 iterations.

Proposed CLMN model. In the implementation of the CLMN model, we specify ϵ in the dependence model to be 1, and the step size δ in the Metropolis Hasting algorithm to be 0.7. We run EP for 40 iterations during inference. Furthermore, to ensure proper convergence of the EP algorithm, we employ the common strategy of partial updates on the messages based on a dampening factor. More specifically, at each iteration k, we apply a step size $\alpha = e^{-0.125k}$, and the messages are updated as $q_i = (q_i^{\text{new}})^{\alpha}(q_i^{\text{old}})^{1-\alpha}$. Correspondingly, the practical updates applied in Step 2d of Algorithm 1 are: $\lambda_i := \alpha\lambda_i^{\text{new}} + (1-\alpha)\lambda_i$, $h_i := \alpha h_i^{\text{new}} + (1-\alpha)h_i$.

In all experiments, we sample part of data network to be the labeled set (i.e., $L \subset V_G$), and then learn the parameters of the LR, SocDim, RMN and CLMN models based on the labeled instances in L (no parameter estimation is involved in the other models). We then test all the models for prediction on the unlabeled instances (i.e., $U = V_G - L$). All results are averaged over 5 trials with different labelings.

5.2 Datasets

We apply the methods to four real-world network datasets drawn from E-Commerce, social network, social media, relational, and biological domains.

Facebook.

This dataset includes user profile attributes as well as friendship links among users. Our sample network consists of 6,694 users, which comprise a set of students from a university's Facebook network. The relational graph is constructed using the friendship links. We consider the classification tasks based on political views ("Conservative" or not). We use the users' gender, relationship status and religious view from their public profile as attributes.

IMDB.

This dataset is drawn from the Internet Movie Database (www.imdb.com). We used a sample of 1,068 movies released in the U.S. between 1996 and 2001. The binary classification task is to predict movie opening weekend returns (> $2 million or not). We construct the relational graph by linking two movies together if they share the same producer. Two movie genre attributes (comedy, action) are used.

Amazon.

We use the subset of the Amazon co-purchasing network [9] which comprise of DVDs. After filtering DVDs with very few ratings, we obtain a network of 13,522 nodes. The links are extracted based on the "Customers Who Bought This Item Also Bought" field in the raw data. We include the average rating and 24 top level genres as the attributes on each node, and predict whether the DVD is a best seller (sales rank threshold: 20,000).

Gene.
This dataset is collected from KDD Cup 2001 (www.cs.wisc.edu/dpage/kddcup2001/). It is a relational dataset containing information about the yeast genome at the the protein level and consists of 1,243 nodes. We predict protein localization ("nucleus" or not) from the interaction structure and 41 binary attributes associated with genes/proteins. These attributes belong to four different types: Essential (4), Phenotype (11), Chromosome (16) and Function (13). We use this dataset mainly to demonstrate the superior ability of the CLMN model to combine attributes and network structures. While most proprietary data from social or web domains naturally contain rich attribute information about the nodes and they are usually incorporated when developing any real application for such domains, the publicly-available datasets that contain both heterogeneous network topologies and informative attributes are sparse. Therefore, we include the gene dataset to demonstrate the broader applicability of the CLMN model.

5.3 Experimental results

In the first set of experiments, we test the performance of these methods on each of the above datasets, while varying the percentage of labeled instances in the network, and sampling the labeled nodes randomly. The experimental results are shown in Figures 2(a)-2(d). Our proposed CLMN model consistently outperforms the other models across all tasks, in some cases by a large margin, demonstrating its superior ability for relational classification. The SocDim approach is a close runner-up in many cases, demonstrating the usefulness of sophisticated relational feature construction methods that effectively flattens network structural information. The GMN model, albeit simple, achieves reasonable accuracy when there is enough correlation in the data, confirming the findings by previous work [14]. The performance of RMNs is rather unstable across different settings, especially when the labeled proportion is small, possibly due to the large learning variance associated with RMNs. Unlike the other models that use both network and attribute information (CLMNs and GMNs), RMNs sometimes perform even worse than the baseline independent classifier LR.

The effect of clustered labeled nodes.
In some applications, labeling is performed by exploring local clusters of the underlying single network. This is not consistent with our previous experiment where instances are labeled randomly throughout the network. To understand the effects of clustered labeling on model performance, we consider the following labeling procedure: given a *dispersion parameter* p, at each step, with probability p we pick an unlabeled node at random to generate a new cluster; with probability $1-p$ the current cluster is expanded greedily by adding an unlabeled node which maximizes the linkage to nodes that are already in the current cluster. Clearly, when $p = 1$, this procedure is equivalent to random sampling as in the previous experiment; when $p = 0$, if the underlying network consists of only one connected component, this procedure would result in one highly connected cluster. The experimental results on the Facebook data with labeled proportion of 0.4 is plotted in Figure 2(e). Other labeled proportions exhibit similar trends. Except for SocDim, all relational classifiers tend to perform relatively poorly when the labeled nodes are highly clustered ($p \leq 0.2$). While the performance of CLMN, LGMN and GMN consistently improves as the labeled nodes are further spread out (p increases), the RMN model demonstrates a different trend—it performs rather poorly when the labeled nodes are highly isolated (e.g., $p = 1$). This is because the sampled graph needs to match the structure of the underlying network in order for RMNs to learn the collective classification model well. In particular, marginal distributions in RMNs estimated from the labeled subnetwork differ more significantly from that of the underlying whole network when p is large.

The effect of attributes.
As stated before, the primary goal of our CLMN model is to better combine individual and relational information in the data. Thus, we evaluate the ability of CLMNs to utilize attribute information more carefully in comparison with SocDim and RMNs, by varying the number of attributes used in the model. The results are plotted in Figure 2(f). We include the LR method for comparison as well since it directly shows the usefulness of the different groups of attributes. The GMN model, for which the performance remains unchanged, is also included to show the proportion of the gains due to the relational information. We found that when no attributes or only a few informative attributes are used, the performance of CLMNs and RMNs is essentially the same, while the SocDim approach cannot exploit the relational information adequately. As the amount of informative features increases, the performance of SocDim catches up, while the RMN approach tends to suffer. Overall, this demonstrates the superior ability of CLMNs to utilize attributes in relational settings through the assumption of identical marginal classifiers.

6. RELATED WORK

A large body of research work has focused on latent variable models for relational data [3, 1, 17]. However, unlike CLMNs, which are conditioned on network structures, these are generative models and attempt to model network structures. They are typically applied to link prediction or collaborative filtering tasks. The latent variables in these approaches typically represent the latent block structure of the network data, instead of the latent tendency of activating a certain label as in the case of CLMNs.

Latent Gaussian models such as latent GMNs [38] and relational Gaussian processes [2] have been applied to graph-based node classification. However, they are usually applied in IID scenarios for semi-supervised prediction, where the attributes are used to construct the graph. In our relational tasks, there are natural links among the data instances (e.g., articulated freindships). While it is possible to further incorporate attributes in latent GMNs, the associated hyper-parameter learning is usually difficult. Our copula approach provides a solution to the problem of integrating network and attribute information in latent Gaussian models.

An alternative, widely applied approach to combining network structures and attributes in a unified probabilistic model is based on discrete Markov networks. Variants of this approach include relational Markov networks [29], Markov logic

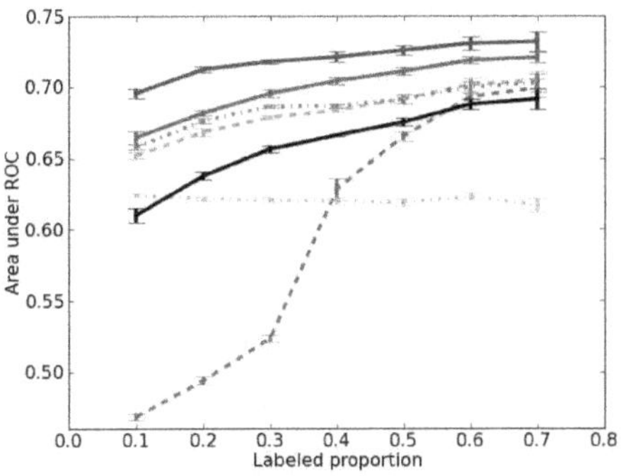

(a) Facebook.

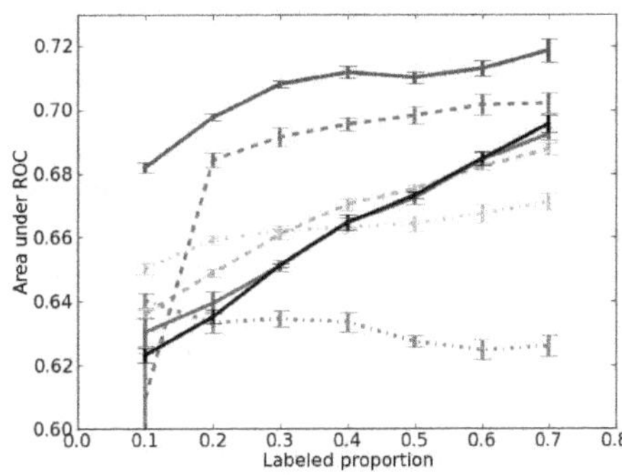

(b) Amazon.

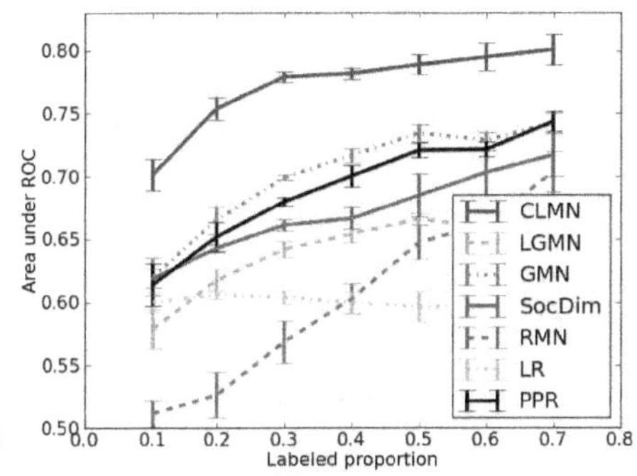

(c) IMDB.

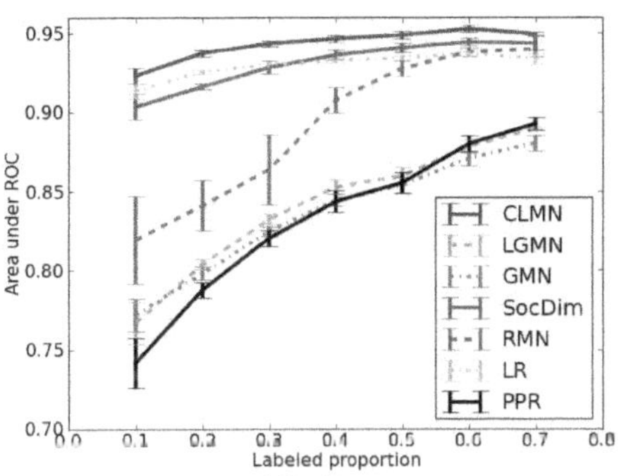

(d) Gene.

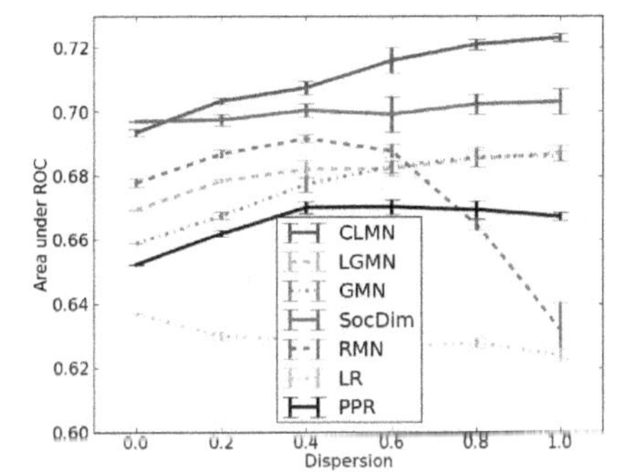

(e) Dispersion of labels.

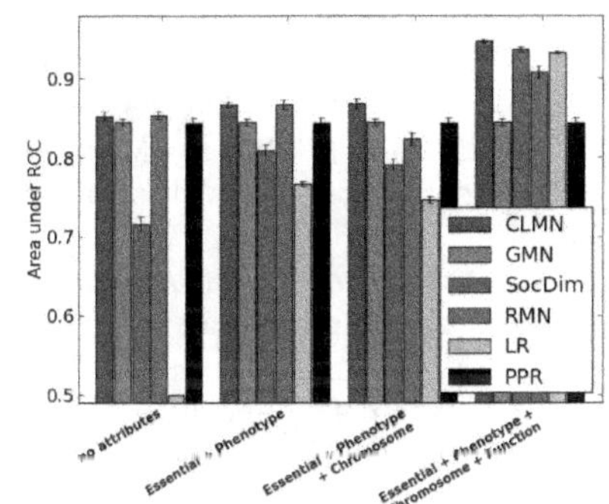

(f) Number of individual attributes.

Figure 2: Classification performance on real networks. (a) to (d): AUCs as the proportion of labeled data is varied. (e): Classification results on Facebook data with 40% of the nodes labeled. The dispersion of the labeled nodes is varied from 0 (contiguous subgraph) to 1 (nodes selected at random throughout the network). (f): Classification results on gene data when sets of individual node attributes, of varying size, are used.

networks [25] and relational dependency networks [22]. These models are based on clique templating, i.e, the same form of clique potentials (e.g., edge potentials) and parameters are tied across the whole network. In contrast to CLMN's "homogeneous marginal" assumption, the probabilistic meaning of the "homogeneous potential" assumption is unclear.

Copulas were developed in statistics and have been widely applied to finance and economics [4, 21]. In machine learning, copula approaches have received much attention lately [6, 11, 32, 24], but they have been used in rather different ways than our proposed model—i.e., the applications revolve around density estimation, clustering and other descriptive modeling tasks rather than prediction. As such, to our knowledge, conditional inference methods have not previously been developed for copula models.

7. CONCLUSIONS AND FUTURE WORK

In this paper, we have developed a new discriminative probabilistic model for relational classification in network data. The proposed model is based on: (1) the intuitive assumption that instances in a network are interdependent but nevertheless should be "identically distributed", and (2) a reasoning about the correlations among latent effects that cannot be explicitly explored using independent probabilistic classifiers. We are thus able to extend a generic conventional probabilistic classifiers into a relational classifier. Based on the copula construction, our proposed CLMN model is able to combine the benefits of modeling relational dependencies, with the ability to incorporate attributes, in a general probabilistic classification model. To apply the model for collective classification in large networks, we develop an approximate inference algorithm based on message passing, which has been demonstrated to achieve high classification accuracy on a variety of real network datasets. Note that since both matrix inversion (Step 1 of Algorithm 2) and message passing (Step 2 of Algorithm 2) are immediately parallelizable, a parallel implementation of our collective classification algorithm is straightforward. Therefore, due to its scalability and its robust performance across different settings, the proposed CLMN approach provides an ideal solution for collective classification in online systems such as social network and social media.

There are several future directions that we would like to explore with this work. First, we plan to investigate hyperparameter learning for the dependence model so that we can learn the graph Laplacian instead of fixing it when there are link attributes available. While an obvious starting point in this direction is an EM-EP algorithm, more sophisticated methods (e.g. [19]) may be explored to improve the learning quality. Moreover, *active label acquisition* for the CLMN model is worth studying in the scenarios when labeling costs are high. We may investigate this issue by using the covariance structure of the Gaussian Markov network [7].

Acknowledgement

This research is supported by NSF under grant numbers CCF-0939370 and IIS-1149789. The U.S. Government is authorized to reproduce and distribute reprints for governmental purposes notwithstanding any copyright notation hereon. The views and conclusions contained herein are those of the authors and should not be interpreted as necessarily representing the official policies or endorsements either expressed or implied, of the NSF or the U.S. Government.

8. REFERENCES

[1] E. M. Airoldi, D. M. Blei, S. E. Fienberg, and E. P. Xing. Mixed membership stochastic blockmodels. *J. Mach. Learn. Res.*, 9:1981–2014, June 2008.

[2] W. Chu, V. Sindhwani, Z. Ghahramani, and S. S. Keerthi. Relational learning with gaussian processes. In *NIPS*, pages 289–296, 2006.

[3] P. D. Hoff, A. E. Raftery, M. S. Handcock, and M. S. H. Latent space approaches to social network analysis. *J. Amer. Stat. Assoc.*, 97:1090–1098, 2001.

[4] H. Joe. *Multivariate Models and Dependence Concepts.* Chapman and Hall, London, 1997.

[5] G. Kim, M. Silvapulle, and P. Silvapulle. Comparison of semiparametric and parametric methods for estimating copulas. *Computational Statistics and Data Analysis*, 51:2836■2850, 2007.

[6] S. Kirshner. Learning with tree-averaged densities and distributions. In *NIPS*, Vancouver, Canada, 2007.

[7] A. Krause and C. Guestrin. Nonmyopic active learning of gaussian processes: An exploration-exploitation approach. In *ICML*, pages 449–456, 2007.

[8] M. Kuss, C. E. Rasmussen, and R. Herbrich. Assessing approximate inference for binary gaussian process classification. *JMLR*, 6:1679–1704, 2005.

[9] J. Leskovec, L. A. Adamic, and B. A. Huberman. The dynamics of viral marketing. *ACM Trans. Web*, 1(1), May 2007.

[10] F. Lin and W. W. Cohen. Semi-supervised classification of network data using very few labels. In *ASONAM '10*, 2010.

[11] H. Liu, J. Lafferty, and L. Wasserman. The nonparanormal: Semiparametric estimation of high dimensional undirected graphs. *J. Mach. Learn. Res.*, 10:2295–2328, Oct. 2009.

[12] Q. Lu and L. Getoor. Link-based classification. In *ICML*, 2003.

[13] S. Macskassy and F. Provost. A simple relational classifier. In *Proceedings of the 2nd Workshop on Multi-Relational Data Mining, KDD2003*, 2003.

[14] S. Macskassy and F. Provost. Classification in networked data: A toolkit and a univariate case study. *JMLR*, 8(May):935–983, 2007.

[15] D. Malioutov, J. Johnson, M. J. Choi, and A. Willsky. Low-rank variance approximation in gmrf models: Single and multiscale approaches. *Signal Processing, IEEE Transactions on*, 56(10):4621 –4634, oct. 2008.

[16] D. M. Malioutov, J. K. Johnson, and A. S. Willsky. Walk-sums and belief propagation in gaussian graphical models. *J. Mach. Learn. Res.*, 7:2031–2064, December 2006.

[17] K. T. Miller, T. L. Griffiths, and M. I. Jordan. Nonparametric latent feature models for link prediction. In *NIPS*, 2009.

[18] T. P. Minka. Expectation propagation for approximate bayesian inference. In *Proceedings of the 17th Conference in Uncertainty in Artificial Intelligence*, UAI '01, pages 362–369, 2001.

[19] I. Murray and R. P. Adams. Slice sampling covariance hyperparameters of latent Gaussian models. In *NIPS*, pages 1723–1731, 2010.

[20] R. M. Neal. Regression and classification using gaussian process priors. *Statistics*, 6:475–501, 1998.

[21] R. B. Nelsen. *An Introduction to Copulas.* Springer, 2006.

[22] J. Neville and D. Jensen. Relational dependency networks. *J. Mach. Learn. Res.*, 8:653–692, 2007.

[23] M. E. J. Newman. Finding community structure in networks using the eigenvectors of matrices. *Physical Review E*, 74(3), July 2006.

[24] B. Poczos, Z. Ghahramani, and J. Schneider. Copula-based kernel dependency measures. In *ICML*, 2012.

[25] M. Richardson and P. Domingos. Markov logic networks. *Mach. Learn.*, 62(1-2):107–136, 2006.

[26] P. Sen, G. Namata, M. Bilgic, L. Getoor, B. Galligher, and T. Eliassi-Rad. Collective classification in network data. *Ai Magazine*, 29(3), 2008.

[27] E. B. Sudderth, A. T. Ihler, W. T. Freeman, and A. S. Willsky. Nonparametric belief propagation. In *Proceedings of IEEE Computer Society Conference on Computer Vision and Pattern Recognition*, 2003.

[28] L. Tang and H. Liu. Relational learning via latent social dimensions. In *KDD*, pages 817–826, 2009.

[29] B. Taskar, P. Abbeel, and D. Koller. Discriminative probabilistic models for relational data. In *UAI*, 2002.

[30] H. Tong, C. Faloutsos, and J.-Y. Pan. Fast random walk with restart and its applications. In *ICDM*, pages 613–622, 2006.

[31] Y. Weiss and W. T. Freeman. Correctness of belief propagation in gaussian graphical models of arbitrary topology. *Neural Computation*, 13:2173–2200, 2001.

[32] A. G. Wilson and Z. Ghahramani. Copula Processes. In *NIPS*, page 11, 2010.

[33] R. Xiang and J. Neville. Relational learning with one network: An asymptotic analysis. In *AISTATS*, 2011.

[34] R. Xiang and J. Neville. Understanding propagation error and its effect on collective classification. In *ICDM*, 2011.

[35] B. Yu. Rates of convergence for empirical processes of stationary mixing sequences. *Ann. Probab.*, 22(1), 1994.

[36] D. Zhou, O. Bousquet, T. N. Lal, J. Weston, and B. SchŽlkopf. Learning with local and global consistency. In *NIPS*, pages 321–328, 2004.

[37] X. Zhu, Z. Ghahramani, and J. Lafferty. Semi-supervised learning using gaussian fields and harmonic functions. In *ICML '03*, 2003.

[38] X. Zhu, J. Lafferty, and Z. Ghahramani. Semi-supervised learning: From gaussian fields to gaussian processes. Technical report, School of CS, CMU, 2003.

Influence Diffusion Dynamics and Influence Maximization in Social Networks with Friend and Foe Relationships*

Yanhua Li†, Wei Chen§, Yajun Wang§ and Zhi-Li Zhang†
†Dept. of Computer Science & Engineering, Univ. of Minnesota, Twin Cities, Minneapolis, MN, US
§ Microsoft Research Asia, Beijing, China
{yanhua,zhzhang}@cs.umn.edu,{weic,yajunw}@microsoft.com

ABSTRACT

Influence diffusion and influence maximization in large-scale online social networks (OSNs) have been extensively studied because of their impacts on enabling effective online viral marketing. Existing studies focus on social networks with only friendship relations, whereas the foe or enemy relations that commonly exist in many OSNs, e.g., Epinions and Slashdot, are completely ignored. In this paper, we make the first attempt to investigate the influence diffusion and influence maximization in OSNs with both friend and foe relations, which are modeled using positive and negative edges on signed networks. In particular, we extend the classic voter model to signed networks and analyze the dynamics of influence diffusion of two opposite opinions. We first provide systematic characterization of both short-term and long-term dynamics of influence diffusion in this model, and illustrate that the steady state behaviors of the dynamics depend on three types of graph structures, which we refer to as balanced graphs, anti-balanced graphs, and strictly unbalanced graphs. We then apply our results to solve the influence maximization problem and develop efficient algorithms to select initial seeds of one opinion that maximize either its short-term influence coverage or long-term steady state influence coverage. Extensive simulation results on both synthetic and real-world networks, such as Epinions and Slashdot, confirm our theoretical analysis on influence diffusion dynamics, and demonstrate that our influence maximization algorithms perform consistently better than other heuristic algorithms.

Categories and Subject Descriptors

E.1 [**Data**]: Data Structures; H.3.3 [**Information Systems**]: Information Storage and Retrieval—*Information Search and Retrieval*

General Terms

Theory, Algorithms, Design

Keywords

Signed social networks, voter model, influence maximization

*This study was done partly when Yanhua Li was a summer intern at Microsoft Research Asia.

WSDM'13, February 4–8, 2013, Rome, Italy.

1. INTRODUCTION

As the popularity of online social networks (OSNs) such as Facebook and Twitter continuously increases, OSNs have become an important platform for the dissemination of news, ideas, opinions, etc. The openness of the OSN platforms and the richness of contents and user interaction information enable intelligent online recommendation systems and viral marketing techniques. For example, if a company wants to promote a new product, it may identify a set of influential users in the online social network and provide them with free sample products. They hope that these influential users could influence their friends, and friends of friends in the network and so on, generating a large influence cascade so that many users adopt their product as a result of such word-of-mouth effect. The question is how to select the initial users given a limited budget on free samples, so as to influence the largest number of people to purchase the product through this "word-of-mouth" process. Similar situations could apply to the promotion of ideas and opinions, such as political candidates trying to find early supporters for their political proposals and agendas, government authorities or companies trying to win public support by finding and convincing an initial set of early adopters to their ideas.

The above problem is referred to as the *influence maximization* problem in the literature, which has been extensively studied in recent years [8–10, 15, 16, 19, 23, 34, 36]. In these studies, several influence diffusion models are proposed to formulate the underlying influence propagation processes, including linear threshold (LT) model, independent cascade (IC) model, voter model, etc. A number of approximation algorithms and scalable heuristics are designed under these models to solve the influence maximization problem.

However, all existing studies only look at networks with positive (i.e., friend, altruism, or trust) relationships, where in reality, relationships also include negative ones, such as foe, spite or distrust relationships. In Ebay, users develop trust and distrust in agents in the network; In online review and news forums, such as Epinions and Slashdot, readers approve or denounce reviews and articles of each other. Some recent studies [11, 21, 22] already look into the network structures with both positive and negative relationships. As a common sense exploited in many existing social influence studies [8–10, 15, 19], positive relationships carry the influence in a positive manner, i.e., you would *more likely* trust and adopt your friends' opinions. In contrast, we consider that negative relationships often carry influence in a reverse direction — if your foe chooses one opinion or votes for one candidate, you would *more likely* be influenced to do the opposite. This echoes the principles that "the friend of my enemy is my enemy" and "the enemy of my enemy is my friend". Structural balance theory has been developed based on these assumptions in social science (see Chapter 5 of [13] and the references therein). We acknowledge that in real social networks, people's reactions to the influence from their friends or foes could be complicated, i.e., one could take the opposite opinion of what her foe suggests for one situation or topic, but may adopt the suggestion from the same person for a different topic, because she trusts her foe's expertise in that particular topic. In this study, we consider the influence diffusion for a single topic, where one always takes the opposite opinion of what her foe suggests. This is our first attempt to model influence diffusion in signed networks, and such topic-dependent simplification is commonly employed in prior influence diffusion studies on unsigned networks [8–10, 15, 16, 19]. Our work aims at providing a mathematical analysis on the influence diffusion dynamic incorporated with negative relationship and applying our analysis to the algorithmic problem of influence maximization.

1.1 Our contributions

In this paper, we extend the classic voter model [12, 18] to incorporate negative relationships for modeling the diffusion of opinions in a social network. Given an unsigned directed graph (digraph), the basic voter model works as follows. At each step, every node in the graph randomly picks one of its *outgoing* neighbors and adopts the opinion of this neighbor. Thus, the voter model is suitable to interpret and model opinion diffusions where people's opinions may switch back and forth based on their interactions with other people in the network. To incorporate negative relationships, we consider signed digraphs in which every directed edge is either positive or negative, and we consider the diffusion of two opposite opinions, e.g., black and white colors. We extend the voter model to signed digraphs, such that at each step, every node randomly picks one of its outgoing neighbors, and if the edge to this neighbor is positive, the node adopts the neighbor's opinion, but if the edge is negative, the node adopts the opposite of the neighbor's opinion (Section 2).

We provide detailed mathematical analysis on the voter model dynamics for signed networks (Section 3). For short-term dynamics, we derive the exact formula for opinion distribution at each step. For long-term dynamics, we provide closed-form formulas for the steady state distribution of opinions. We show that the steady state distribution depends on the graph structure: we divide signed digraphs into three classes of graph structures — balanced graphs, anti-balanced graphs, and strictly unbalanced graphs, each of which leads to a different type of steady state distributions of opinions. While balanced and unbalanced graphs have been extensively studied by structural balance theory in social science [13], the anti-balanced graphs form a new class that has not been covered before, to the best of our knowledge. Moreover, our long-term dynamics not only cover strongly connected and aperiodic digraphs that most of such studies focus on, but also weakly connected and disconnected digraphs, making our study more comprehensive.

We then study the influence maximization problem under the voter model for signed digraphs (Section 4). The problem here is to select at most k initial white nodes while all others are black, so that either in short term or long term the expected number of white nodes is maximized. This corresponds to the scenario where one opinion is dominating the public and an alternative opinion (e.g. a competing political agenda, or a new innovation) tries to win over supporters as much as possible by selecting some initial seeds to influence on. We provide efficient algorithms that find optimal solutions for both short-term and long-term cases. In particular, for long-term influence maximization, our algorithm provides a comprehensive solution covering weakly connected and disconnected signed digraphs, with nontrivial computations on influence coverage of seed nodes.

Finally, we conduct extensive simulations on both real-world and synthetic networks to verify our analysis and to show the effectiveness of our influence maximization algorithm (Section 5). The simulation results demonstrate that our influence maximization algorithms perform consistently better than all other heuristic algorithms. To the best of our knowledge, we are the first to study influence diffusion and influence maximization in signed networks, and the first to apply the voter model to this case and provide efficient algorithms for influence maximization under voter model for signed networks.

Due to space constraints, some of the proofs and additional materials are omitted and delegated to our technical report [24].

1.2 Related work

In this subsection, we discuss the topics that are closely related to our problem, such as: (1) influence maximization and voter model, (2) signed networks, and (3) competitive influence diffusion.

Influence maximization and voter model. Influence maximization has been extensively studied in the literature. The initial work [19] proposes several influence diffusion models and provides the greedy approximation algorithm for influence maximization. More recent works [8–10, 15, 16, 23, 34] study efficient optimizations and scalable heuristics for the influence maximization problem. In particular, the voter model is proposed in [12, 18], and is suitable for modeling opinion diffusions in which people may switch opinions back and forth from time to time due to the interactions with other people in the network. Even-Dar and Shapira [15] study the influence maximization problem in the voter model on simple unsigned and undirected graphs, and they show that the best seeds for long-term influence maximization are simply the highest degree nodes. As a contrast, we show in this paper that seed selection for signed digraphs are more sophisticated, especially for weakly connected or disconnected signed digraphs. More voter model related research is conducted in physics domain, where the voter model, the zero-temperature Glauber dynamics for the Ising model, invasion process, and other related models of population dynamics belong to the class of models with two absorbing states and epidemic spreading dynamics [1, 30, 38]. However, none of these works study the influence diffusion and influence maximization of voter model under signed networks.

Signed networks. The signed networks with both positive and negative links have gained attentions recently [3, 20–22]. In [21, 22], the authors empirically study the structure of real-world social networks with negative relationships based on two social science theories, i.e., balance theory and status theory. Kunegis et al. [20] study the spectral properties of the signed undirected graphs, with applications in link predictions, spectral clustering, etc. Borgs et al. [3] proposes a generalized PageRank algorithm [35] for signed networks with application to online recommendations, where the distrust relations are considered as adversarial or arbitrary user behaviors, thus the outgoing relations of distrusted users are ignored while ranking nodes. Our algorithm can also be viewed as a node ranking algorithm that generalizes the PageRank algorithm, by treating distrust links as generating negative influence rather than ignoring distrusted users' opinions, and thus our ranking method is different from [3]. Overall, none of the above work studies influence diffusion and influence maximization in signed networks.

Competitive influence diffusion. A number of recent studies focus on competitive influence diffusion and maximization [2, 4, 6, 7, 17, 29], in which two or more competitive opinions or innovations are diffusing in the network. Although they consider two or more competitive or opposing influence diffusions, they are all on unsigned networks, different from our study here on diffusion with both positive and negative relationships.

2. VOTER MODEL ON SIGNED NETWORKS

We consider a weighted directed graph (digraph) $G = (V, E, A)$, where V is the set of vertices, E is the set of directed edges, and A is the weighted adjacency matrix with $A_{ij} \neq 0$ if and only if $(i, j) \in E$, with A_{ij} as the weight of edge (i, j). The voter model was first introduced for unsigned graphs, with nonnegative adjacency matrices A's. In this model, each node holds one of two opposite opinions, represented by black and white colors. Initially each node has either black or white color. At each step $t \geq 1$, every node i randomly picks one outgoing neighbor j with the probability proportional to the weight of (i, j), namely $A_{ij}/\sum_\ell A_{i\ell}$, and changes its color to j's color. The voter model also has a random walk interpretation. If a random walk starts from i and stops at node j at step t, then i's color at step t is j's color at step 0.

In this paper, we extend the voter model to signed digraphs, in which the adjacency matrix A may contain negative entries. A positive entry A_{ij} represents that i considers j as a friend or i trusts j, and a negative A_{ij} means that i considers j as a foe or i distrusts j. The absolute value $|A_{ij}|$ represents the strength of this trust or distrust relationship. The voter model is thus extended naturally such that one always takes the same opinion from his/her friend, and the opposite opinion of his/her foe. Technically, at each step $t \geq 1$, i randomly picks one outgoing neighbor j with probability $|A_{ij}|/\sum_\ell |A_{i\ell}|$, and if $A_{ij} > 0$ (edge (i, j) is positive) then i changes its color to j's color, but if $A_{ij} < 0$ (edge (i, j) is negative) then i changes its color to the opposite of j's color. The random walk interpretation can also be extended for signed networks: if the t-step random walk from i to j passes an even number of negative edges, then i's color at step t is the same as j's color at step 0; while if it passes an odd number of negative edges, then i's color at step t is the opposite of j's color at step 0.

Table 1: Notations and terminologies

$G = (V, E, A)$, $\bar{G} = (V, E, \bar{A})$	G is a signed digraph, with signed adjacency matrix A and $\bar{G}$ is the unsigned version of G, with adjacency matrix $\bar{A}$
A^+, A^-	A^+ (resp. A^-) is the non-negative adjacency matrix representing positive (resp. negative) edges of G, with $A = A^+ - A^-$ and $\bar{A} = A^+ + A^-$.
$\mathbf{1}$, π, x_0, x_t, x, x_e, x_o	Vector forms. All vectors are $\|V\|$-dimensional column vectors by default; $\mathbf{1}$ is all one vector, π is the stationary distribution of an ergodic digraph $\bar{G}$; x_0 (resp. x_t) is the white color distribution at the beginning (resp. at step t); x is the steady state white color distribution; x_e (resp. x_o) is the steady state white color distribution for even (resp. odd) steps.
d, d^+, d^-, D	d, d^+, and d^- are weighted out-degree vectors of G, where $d = \bar{A}\mathbf{1}$, $d^+ = A^+\mathbf{1}$, and $d^- = A^-\mathbf{1}$; $D = diag[d]$ is the diagonal degree matrix filled with entries of d.
$P, \bar{P}$	$P = D^{-1}A$ is the signed transition matrix of G and $\bar{P} = D^{-1}\bar{A}$ is the transition probability matrix of $\bar{G}$.
$v_Z, \hat{v}_S, \hat{v}_{Z,S_Z}$	Given a vector v, a node set $Z \subseteq V$, v_Z is the projection of v on Z. Given a partition $S, \bar{S}$ of V, $\hat{v}_S$ is signed such that $\hat{v}_S(i) = v(i)$ if $i \in S$, and $\hat{v}_S(i) = -v(i)$ if $i \notin S$. Given a partition $S_Z, \bar{S}_Z$ of Z, $\hat{v}_{Z,S_Z}$ is taking the projection of v on Z first, then negating the signs for entries in $\bar{S}_Z$.
$I, \hat{I}_S, B_Z$	I is the identity matrix. $\hat{I}_S = diag[\hat{\mathbf{1}}_S]$ is the signed identity matrix. B_Z is the projection of a matrix B to $Z \subseteq V$.

Given a signed digraph $G = (V, E, A)$, let $G^+ = (V, E^+, A^+)$ and $G^- = (V, E^-, A^-)$ denote the unsigned subgraphs consisting of all positive edges E^+ and all negative edges E^-, respectively, where A^+ and A^- are the corresponding non-negative adjacency matrices. Thus we have $A = A^+ - A^-$. Similar to unsigned digraphs, G is *aperiodic* if the greatest common divisor of the lengths of all cycles in G is 1, and G is *ergodic* if it is strongly connected and aperiodic. A *sink component* of a signed digraph is a strongly connected component that has no outgoing edges to any nodes outside the component. When studying the long-term dynamics of the voter model, we assume that all signed strongly connected components are ergodic. We first study the case of ergodic graphs, and then extend it to the more general case of weakly connected or disconnected graphs with ergodic sink components. Table 1 provides notations and terminologies used in the paper.

3. ANALYSIS OF VOTER MODEL DYNAMICS ON SIGNED DIGRAPHS

In this section, we study the short-term and long-term dynamics of the voter model on signed digraphs. In particular, we answer the following two questions.

(i) Short-term dynamics: Given an initial distribution of black and white nodes, what is the distribution of black and white nodes at step $t > 0$?

(ii) Convergence of voter model: Given an initial distribution of black and white nodes, would the distribution converge? If so, what is the steady state distribution of black and white nodes?

3.1 Short-term dynamics

To study voter model dynamics on signed digraphs, we first define the *signed transition matrix* as follows.

Definition 1 (Signed transition matrix). *Given a signed digraph $G = (V, E, A)$, we define the* signed transition matrix *of G as $P = D^{-1}A$, where $D = diag[d_i]$ is the diagonal matrix and $d_i = \sum_{j\in V} |A_{ij}|$ is the weighted out-degree of node i.*

Next proposition characterizes the dynamics of the voter model at each step using the *signed transition matrix*.

Proposition 1. *Let $G = (V, E, A)$ be a signed digraph and denote the initial white color distribution vector as x_0, i.e., $x_0(i)$ represents the probability that node i is white initially. Then, the white color distribution at step t, denoted by x_t can be computed as*

$$x_t = P^t x_0 + (\sum_{i=0}^{t-1} P^i)g^-, \qquad (1)$$

where $g^- = D^{-1}A^-\mathbf{1}$, i.e. $g^-(i)$ is the weighted fraction of outgoing negative edges of node i.

PROOF. (Sketch) Based on the signed digraph voter model defined in Section 2, x_t can be iteratively computed as

$$x_t(i) = \sum_{j\in V} \frac{A^+_{ij}}{d_i} x_{t-1}(j) + \sum_{j\in V} \frac{A^-_{ij}}{d_i}(1 - x_{t-1}(j)). \qquad (2)$$

The matrix form of eq.(2) yields Eq.(1). □

3.2 Convergence of signed transition matrix

Eq.(1) infers that the long-term dynamic, i.e., the vector x_t when t goes to infinity, depends critically on the limit of P^t and $\sum_{i=0}^{t-1} P^i$. We show below that the limiting behaviors of the two matrix sequences are fundamentally determined by the structural balance of signed digraph G, which connects to the social balance theory well studied in the social science literature (cf. [13]). We now define three types of signed digraphs based on their balance structures.

Definition 2 (Structural balance of signed digraphs). *Let $G = (V, E, A)$ be a signed digraph.*

1. **Balanced digraph**. *G is* balanced *if there exists a partition $S, \bar{S}$ of nodes in V, such that all edges within S and $\bar{S}$ are positive and all edges across S and $\bar{S}$ are negative.*
2. **Anti-balanced digraph**. *G is* anti-balanced *if there exists a partition $S, \bar{S}$ of nodes in V, such that all edges within S and $\bar{S}$ are negative and all edges across S and $\bar{S}$ are positive.*
3. **Strictly unbalanced digraph**. *G is* strictly unbalanced *if G is neither balanced nor anti-balanced.*

The balanced digraphs defined above correspond to the balanced graphs originally defined in social balance theory. It is known that a balanced graph can be equivalently defined by the condition that all circles in G without considering edge directions contain an even number of negative edges [13]. On the other hand, the concept of anti-balanced digraphs seems not appearing in the social balance theory. Note that balanced digraphs and anti-balanced digraphs are not mutually exclusive. For example, a four node circle with one pair of non-adjacent edges being positive and the other pair being negative is both balanced and anti-balanced. However, for studying long-term dynamics, we only need the above categorization for aperiodic digraphs, for which we show below that balanced digraphs and anti-balanced digraphs are mutually exclusive.

Proposition 2. *An aperiodic digraph G cannot be both balanced and anti-balanced.*

With the above proposition, we know that balanced graphs, anti-balanced graphs, and strictly unbalanced graphs indeed form a classification of aperiodic digraphs, where anti-balanced graphs and strictly unbalanced graphs together correspond to unbalanced graphs in the social balance theory. We identify anti-balanced graphs as a special category because it has a unique long-term dynamic behavior different from other graphs. An example of anti-balanced graphs is a graph with only negative edges. In general, anti-balanced graphs could be viewed as an extreme in which many hostility exist among individuals, e.g., networks formed by bidders in auctions [5, 33].

The next lemma characterizes the limiting behavior of P^t of ergodic signed digraphs with all three balance structures. Given a signed digraph $G = (V, E, A)$, let $\bar{G} = (V, E, \bar{A})$ corresponds to its unsigned version ($\bar{A}_{ij} = |A_{ij}|$ for all $i, j \in V$). When $\bar{G}$ is ergodic, a random walk on $\bar{G}$ has a unique stationary distribution, denoted as π. That is, $\pi^T = \pi^T \bar{P}$, where $\bar{P} = D^{-1}\bar{A}$ is the transition probability matrix for $\bar{G}$. Henceforth, we always use $S, \bar{S}$ to denote the corresponding partition for either balanced graphs or anti-balanced graphs.

Lemma 1. *Given an ergodic signed digraph $G = (V, E, A)$, let $\bar{G} = (V, E, \bar{A})$ be the* unsigned *digraph. When G is balanced or strictly unbalanced, P^t converges, and when G is anti-balanced, the odd and even subsequences of P^t converge to two opposite matrices, i.e.,*

$$\begin{aligned}
&\textit{Balanced } G\textit{:} && \lim_{t\to\infty} P^t = \hat{\mathbf{1}}_S \hat{\pi}_S^T\\
&\textit{Strictly unbalanced } G\textit{:} && \lim_{t\to\infty} P^t = \mathbf{0}\\
&\textit{Anti-balanced } G\textit{:} && \lim_{t\to\infty} P^{2t} = \hat{\mathbf{1}}_S \hat{\pi}_S^T\\
& && \lim_{t\to\infty} P^{2t+1} = -\hat{\mathbf{1}}_S \hat{\pi}_S^T,
\end{aligned}$$

The above lemma clearly shows different convergence behaviors of P^t for three types of graphs. In particular, P^t of anti-balanced graphs exhibits a bounded oscillating behavior in long term.

Now, we consider a weakly connected signed digraph $G = (V, E, A)$ with one ergodic sink component G_Z with node set Z, which only has incoming edges from the rest of the signed digraph G_X with node set $X = V \setminus Z$. Then, the signed transition matrix P has the following block form.

$$P = \begin{bmatrix} P_X & P_Y \\ \mathbf{0} & P_Z \end{bmatrix}, \tag{3}$$

where P_X and P_Z are the block matrices for components G_X and G_Z, and P_Y represents the one-way connections from G_X to G_Z. Then, the t-step transition matrix P^t can be expressed as

$$P^t = \begin{bmatrix} P_X^{(t)} & P_Y^{(t)} \\ \mathbf{0} & P_Z^{(t)} \end{bmatrix}, \tag{4}$$

where $P_X^{(t)} = P_X^t$, $P_Z^{(t)} = P_Z^t$ and $P_Y^{(t)} = \sum_{i=0}^{t-1} P_X^i P_Y P_Z^{t-1-i}$. When G_Z is balanced or anti-balanced, we use $S_Z, \bar{S}_Z$ to denote the partition of Z defining its balance or anti-balance structure. Then, we denote column vectors

$$u_b = (I_X - P_X)^{-1} P_Y \hat{\mathbf{1}}_{Z,S_Z}, \tag{5}$$

$$\text{and } u_u = (I_X + P_X)^{-1} P_Y \hat{\mathbf{1}}_{Z,S_Z}. \tag{6}$$

The reason that $I_X - P_X$ is invertible is because $\lim_{t\to\infty} P_X^t = \mathbf{0}$, which is in turn because there is a path from any node i in G_X to nodes in Z (since Z is the single sink), and thus informally a random walk from i eventually reaches and then stays in G_Z. The same reason applies to $I_X + P_X$.

Let π_Z denote the stationary distribution of nodes in G_Z, and $\hat{\pi}_{Z,S_Z}$ is signed, with $\hat{\pi}_{Z,S_Z}(i) = \pi_Z(i)$ for $i \in S_Z$, and $\hat{\pi}_{Z,S_Z}(i) = -\pi_Z(i)$, otherwise. Lemma 2 discloses the convergence of P^t given various balance structures of G_Z.

Lemma 2. *Given the formulation in Eq.(4), we have*

$$\begin{aligned}
&\textit{Balanced } G_Z\textit{:} && \lim_{t\to\infty} P^t = \begin{bmatrix} \mathbf{0} & u_b \hat{\pi}_{Z,S_Z}^T \\ \mathbf{0} & \hat{\mathbf{1}}_{Z,S_Z} \hat{\pi}_{Z,S_Z}^T \end{bmatrix}\\
&\textit{Strictly unbalanced } G_Z\textit{:} && \lim_{t\to\infty} P^t = \mathbf{0}\\
&\textit{Anti-balanced } G_Z\textit{:} && \lim_{t\to\infty} P^{2t} = \begin{bmatrix} \mathbf{0} & -u_u \hat{\pi}_{Z,S_Z}^T \\ \mathbf{0} & \hat{\mathbf{1}}_{Z,S_Z} \hat{\pi}_{Z,S_Z}^T \end{bmatrix}\\
& && \lim_{t\to\infty} P^{2t+1} = \begin{bmatrix} \mathbf{0} & u_u \hat{\pi}_{Z,S_Z}^T \\ \mathbf{0} & -\hat{\mathbf{1}}_{Z,S_Z} \hat{\pi}_{Z,S_Z}^T \end{bmatrix}
\end{aligned}$$

Weakly connected digraphs with multiple ergodic sinks or disconnected digraphs can be similarly analyzed.

3.3 Long-term dynamics

Based on the structural balance classification and the convergence of signed transition matrix discussed above, we are now ready to analyze the long-term dynamics of the voter model on signed digraphs. Formally, we are interested in characterizing x_t with $t \to \infty$, i.e.,

$$x = \lim_{t\to\infty} x_t = \lim_{t\to\infty} (P^t x_0 + (\sum_{i=0}^{t-1} P^i) g^-). \tag{7}$$

If the even and odd subsequences of x_t converge separately, we denote $x_e = \lim_{t\to\infty} x_{2t}$, $x_o = \lim_{t\to\infty} x_{2t+1}$.

In the following theorem, we first discuss the long-term dynamics of voter model on ergodic signed digraphs.

Theorem 1. *Let $G = (V, E, A)$ be an ergodic signed digraph, we have*

$$\text{Balanced } G: \quad x = \hat{\mathbf{1}}_S \hat{\pi}_S^T (x_0 - \tfrac{1}{2}\mathbf{1}) + \tfrac{1}{2}\mathbf{1} \quad (8)$$

$$\text{Strictly unbalanced } G: \quad x = \tfrac{1}{2}\mathbf{1} \quad (9)$$

$$\text{Anti-balanced } G: \quad x_e = \hat{\mathbf{1}}_S \hat{\pi}_S^T (x_0 - \tfrac{1}{2}\mathbf{1}) + \tfrac{1}{2}\mathbf{1} \quad (10)$$

$$x_o = -\hat{\mathbf{1}}_S \hat{\pi}_S^T (x_0 - \tfrac{1}{2}\mathbf{1}) + \tfrac{1}{2}\mathbf{1} \quad (11)$$

Theorem 1 has several implications. First of all, for strictly unbalanced digraphs, each node has equal steady state probability of being black or white, and it is not determined by the initial distribution x_0. Secondly, anti-balanced digraphs has the same steady state distribution as the corresponding balanced graph for even steps, and for odd steps, the distribution oscillates to the opposite ($x_o = \mathbf{1} - x_e$).

For a balanced ergodic digraph G with partition $S, \bar{S}$, it is easy to check that it has the following two equilibrium states: in one state all nodes in S are white while all nodes in $\bar{S}$ are black; and in the other state all nodes in S are black while all nodes in $\bar{S}$ are white. We call these two states the *polarized states*. Using random walk interpretation, we show in the following theorem that with probability 1, the voter model dynamic converges to one of the above two equilibrium states.

Theorem 2. *Given an ergodic signed digraph $G = (V, E, A)$, if G is balanced with partition $S, \bar{S}$, the voter model dynamic converges to one of the polarized states with probability 1, and the probability of nodes in S being white is $\hat{\pi}_S^T(x_0 - \frac{1}{2}\mathbf{1}) + \frac{1}{2}$. Similarly, if G is anti-balanced, with probability 1 the voter model dynamic oscillates between the two polarized states eventually, and the probability of nodes in S being white at even steps is $\hat{\pi}_S^T(x_0 - \frac{1}{2}\mathbf{1}) + \frac{1}{2}$.*

Theorem 3 introduces the long-term dynamics of the weakly connected signed digraphs. We consider weakly connected G with a single sink ergodic component G_Z, and use the same notations as in Section 3.2.

Theorem 3. *Let $G = (V, E, A)$ be a weakly connected signed digraph with a single sink component G_Z and a non-sink component G_X. The long term white color distribution vector x is expressed in two parts:*

$$x^T = \lim_{t\to\infty} x_t^T = [x_{XY}^T, x_Z^T].$$

where x_Z is the limit of x_{tZ} on G_Z with initial distribution x_{0Z} and is given as in Theorem 1, and vector x_{XY} is given below with respect to the balance structure of G_Z:

$$\text{Balanced } G_Z: \quad x_{XY} = \tfrac{1}{2}\mathbf{1}_X + u_b \hat{\pi}_{Z,S_Z}^T (x_{0Z} - \tfrac{1}{2}\mathbf{1}_Z)$$

$$\text{Strictly unbalanced } G_Z: \quad x_{XY} = \tfrac{1}{2}\mathbf{1}_X$$

$$\text{Anti-balanced } G_Z, \text{ even } t: \quad x_{XY,e} = \tfrac{1}{2}\mathbf{1}_X - u_u \hat{\pi}_{Z,S_Z}^T (x_{0Z} - \tfrac{1}{2}\mathbf{1}_Z)$$

$$\text{Anti-balanced } G_Z, \text{ odd } t: \quad x_{XY,o} = \tfrac{1}{2}\mathbf{1}_X + u_u \hat{\pi}_{Z,S_Z}^T (x_{0Z} - \tfrac{1}{2}\mathbf{1}_Z),$$

where u_b and u_u are defined in Eq.(5) and Eq.(6).

Theorem 3 characterizes the long-term dynamics when the underlying graph is a weakly connected signed digraph with one ergodic sink component. We can see that the results for balanced and anti-balanced sink components are more complicated than the ergodic digraph case, since how non-sink components are connected to the sink subtly affects the final outcome of the steady state behavior. In steady state, while the sink component is still in one of the two polarized states as stated in Theorem 2, the non-sink components exhibit more complicated color distribution, for which we provide probability characterizations in Theorem 3. Our results can be readily extended to the case with more than one ergodic sink components and disconnected digraphs. When the network only contains positive directed edges, the voter model dynamics can be interpreted using digraph random walk theory [25–28].

4. INFLUENCE MAXIMIZATION

With the detailed analysis on voter model dynamics for signed digraphs, we are now ready to solve the influence maximization problem. Intuitively, we want to address the following question: *If only at most k nodes could be selected initially and be turned white while all other nodes are black, how should we choose seed nodes so as to maximize the expected number of white nodes in short term and in long term, respectively?*

4.1 Influence maximization problem

We consider two types of short-term influence objectives, one is the *instant influence*, which counts the total number of influenced nodes at a step $t > 0$; the other is the *average influence*, which takes the average number of influenced nodes within the first t steps. These two objectives have different implications and applications. For example, political campaigns try to convince voters who may change their minds back and forth, but only the voters' opinions on the voting day are counted, which matches the *instant influence*. On the other hand, a credit card company would like to have customers keep using its credit card service as much as possible, which is better interpreted by the *average influence*. When t is sufficiently large, it becomes the long-term objective, and long-term average influence coincides with long-term instant influence when the dynamic converges.

Formally, we define the *short-term instant influence* $f_t(x_0)$ and the *short-term average influence* $\bar{f}_t(x_0)$ as follows:

$$f_t(x_0) := \mathbf{1}^T x_t(x_0) \text{ and } \bar{f}_t(x_0) := \frac{\sum_{i=0}^t f_i(x_0)}{t+1}. \quad (12)$$

Moreover, we define *l*ong term influence as

$$f(x_0) := \lim_{t\to\infty} \frac{\sum_{i=0}^t f_i(x_0)}{t+1}. \quad (13)$$

Note that when the dynamic converges (e.g. ergodic balanced or ergodic strictly unbalanced graphs), $f(x_0) = \lim_{t\to\infty} f_t(x_0)$. For ergodic anti-balanced graphs (or sink components), it is essentially the average of even- and odd-step limit influence.

Given a set $W \subseteq V$, Let e_W be the vector in which $e_W(j) = 1$ if $j \in W$ and $e_W(j) = 0$ if $j \notin W$, which represents the initial seed distribution with only nodes in W as white seeds. Let e_i be the shorthand of $e_{\{i\}}$. Unlike unsigned graphs, if initially no white seeds are selected on a signed digraph G, i.e., $x_0 = \mathbf{0}$, the instant influence $f_t(\mathbf{0})$ at step t is in general non-zero, which is referred to as the *ground influence* of the graph G at t. The influence contribution of a seed set W does not count such ground influence, as shown in definition 3.

Definition 3 (Influence contribution). *The* instant influence contribution *of a seed set W to the t-th step instant influence objective, denoted by $c_t(W)$, is the difference between the instant influence at step t with only nodes in W selected as seeds and the ground influence at step t: $c_t(W) = f_t(e_W) - f_t(\mathbf{0})$. The* average influence contribution $\bar{c}_t(W)$ *and* long-term influence contribution $c(W)$ *are defined in the same way: $\bar{c}_t(W) = \bar{f}_t(e_W) - \bar{f}_t(\mathbf{0})$ and $c(W) = f(e_W) - f(\mathbf{0})$.*

We are now ready to formally define the influence maximization problem.

Definition 4 (Influence maximization). *The* influence maximization *problem for short-term instant influence is finding a seed set* W *of at most* k *seeds that maximizes* W*'s instance influence contribution at step* t*, i.e., finding* $W_t^* = \arg\max_{|W|\le k} c_t(W)$*. Similarly, the problem for average influence and long-term influence is finding* $\bar{W}_t^* = \arg\max_{|W|\le k} \bar{c}_t(W)$ *and* $W^* = \arg\max_{|W|\le k} c(W)$*, respectively.*

We now provide some properties of influence contribution, which lead to the optimal seed selection rule. By Eq.(1), we have

$$c_t(W) = f_t(e_W) - f_t(\mathbf{0}) = \mathbf{1}^T x_t(e_W) - \mathbf{1}^T x_t(\mathbf{0}) = \mathbf{1}^T P^t e_W. \tag{14}$$

Let $c_t(i)$ be the shorthand of $c_t(\{i\})$, and let $c_t = [c_t(i)]$ denote the vector of influence contribution of individual nodes. Then $c_t^T = [c_t(i)]^T = \mathbf{1}^T P^t$. When $t \to \infty$, the long term influence contributions of individual nodes are obtained as a vector c:

$$c^T = \lim_{t\to\infty} \frac{\sum_{i=0}^t c_i^T}{t+1} = \lim_{t\to\infty} \frac{\mathbf{1}^T \sum_{i=0}^t P^i}{t+1}. \tag{15}$$

When P^t converges, we simply have $c^T = \mathbf{1}^T \lim_{t\to\infty} P^t$. (16)

Lemma 3 below discloses the important property that the influence contribution is a linear set function.

Lemma 3. *Given a white seed set* W*,* $c_t(W) = \sum_{i\in W} c_t(i)$*,* $\bar{c}_t(W) = \sum_{i\in W} \bar{c}_t(i)$*, and* $c(W) = \sum_{i\in W} c(i)$*.*

Given a vector v, let $n^+(v)$ denote the number of positive entries in v. By applying Lemma 3, we have the optimal seed selection rule for instant influence maximization as follows.

Optimal seed selection rule for instant influence maximization. *Given a signed digraph and a limited budget* k*, selecting top* $\min\{k, n^+(c_t)\}$ *seeds with the highest* $c_t(i)$*'s,* $i \in V$*, leads to the maximized instant influence at step* $t > 0$.

Note that the influence contributions of some nodes may be negative and these nodes should not be selected as white seeds, and thus the optimal solution may have less than k seeds. The rules for average influence maximization and long-term influence maximization are patterned in the same way. Therefore, the central task now becomes the computation of the influence contributions of individual nodes. Below, we will introduce our SVIM algorithm, for Signed Voter model Influence Maximization.

4.2 Short-term influence maximization

By applying Definition 3 and Lemma 3, we develop SVIM-S algorithm to solve the short-term instant and average influence maximization problem, as shown in Algorithm 1.

Algorithm 1 Short-term influence maximization SVIM-S

- **INPUT:** Signed transition matrix P, short-term period t, budget k;
- **OUTPUT:** White seed set W.
- $c_t = \mathbf{1}$; $\bar{c}_t = \mathbf{1}$;
- **for** $i = 1 : t$ **do**
  - $c_t^T = c_t^T P$;(for instant influence maximization.)
  - $\bar{c}_t = \bar{c}_t + c_t$; (for average influence maximization.)
- $W =$ top $\min\{k, n^+(c_t)\}$ (resp. $\min\{k, n^+(\bar{c}_t)\}$) nodes with the highest $c_t(i)$ (resp. $\bar{c}_t(i)$) values, for instant (resp. average) influence maximization.

SVIM-S algorithm requires t vector-matrix multiplications, each of which takes $|E|$ times entry-wise multiplication operations. Hence the total time complexity of SVIM-S is $O(t \cdot |E|)$.

4.3 Long-term influence maximization

We now study the long-term influence contribution c and introduce the corresponding influence maximization algorithm SVIM-L. We will see that the computation of influence contribution c and seed selection schemes depends on the structural balance and connectedness of the graph. While seed selection for balanced ergodic digraphs still has intuitive explanations, the computation for weakly connected and disconnected digraphs is more involved and less intuitive.

4.3.1 *Case of ergodic signed digraphs*

When the signed digraph $G = (V, E, A)$ is ergodic, Lemma 4 below characterizes the long-term influence contributions of nodes, with respect to various balance structures.

Lemma 4. *Consider an ergodic signed digraph* $G = (V, E, A)$*. If* G *is* balanced*, with bipartition* S *and* $\bar{S}$*, the influence contribution vector* $c = (|S| - |\bar{S}|)\hat{\pi}_S$*. If* G *is* anti-balanced *or* strictly unbalanced*,* $c = \mathbf{0}$*.*

Based on Lemma 4, Algorithm 2 summarizes how to compute the long-term influence contribution c on ergodic signed digraphs.

Algorithm 2 $c = ergodic(G)$

- **INPUT:** Signed transition matrix P.
- **OUTPUT:** Long term influence contribution vector c
- Detect the structure of ergodic signed digraph G;
- **if** G is balanced, with bipartition S and $\bar{S}$ **then**
  - Compute stationary distribution π of $\bar{P}$;
  - $c = (|S| - |\bar{S}|)\hat{\pi}_S$;
- **else**
  - $c = \mathbf{0}$;

Lemma 4 suggests that for ergodic balanced digraphs, we should pick the larger component, e.g., S, if $|S| > |\bar{S}|$, and select the top $\min\{k, |S|\}$ nodes from S with the largest stationary distributions as white seeds. Selecting these nodes will make the probability of the larger component being white the largest.

4.3.2 *Case of weakly connected signed digraphs*

We first consider a weakly connected signed G which has a single ergodic sink component G_Z with only incoming edges from the remaining nodes $X = V \setminus Z$.

Lemma 5. *Consider a weakly connected digraph* $G = (V, E, A)$ *with a single ergodic sink component* G_Z*. If* G_Z *is* balanced*, with partition* S_Z *and* $\bar{S}_Z$*, the long term influence contribution vector* $c^T = [c_X^T, c_Z^T]$*, where* $c_X = \mathbf{0}_X$ *and* $c_Z = (\mathbf{1}_X^T u_b + |S_Z| - |\bar{S}_Z|)\hat{\pi}_{Z,S_Z}$*. If* G *is* anti-balanced *or* strictly unbalanced*,* $c = \mathbf{0}$*.*

Lemma 5 indicates that influence contribution of the balanced ergodic sink component is more complicated than that of the balanced ergodic digraph. This is because the sink component affects the colors of the non-sink component in a complicated way depending on how non-sink and sink components are connected. Therefore, the optimal seed selection depends on the calculation of the influence contributions of each sink node, and is not as intuitive as that for the ergodic digraph case.

More sink components. When there exist $m > 1$ ergodic sink components, i.e., $G_{Z1}, G_{Z2}, \cdots, G_{Zm}$, the rest of the graph G is considered as a single component G_X. Then the signed transition matrix P and P^t can be written as

$$P = \begin{bmatrix} P_X & P_{Y1} & \cdots & P_{Ym} \\ \mathbf{0} & P_{Z1} & \mathbf{0} & \mathbf{0} \\ \mathbf{0} & \mathbf{0} & \ddots & \mathbf{0} \\ \mathbf{0} & \mathbf{0} & \mathbf{0} & P_{Zm} \end{bmatrix}, P^t = \begin{bmatrix} P_X^t & P_{Y1}^{(t)} & \cdots & P_{Ym}^{(t)} \\ \mathbf{0} & P_{Z1}^t & \mathbf{0} & \mathbf{0} \\ \mathbf{0} & \mathbf{0} & \ddots & \mathbf{0} \\ \mathbf{0} & \mathbf{0} & \mathbf{0} & P_{Zm}^t \end{bmatrix}$$

where $P^{(t)}_{Yi} = \sum_{j=0}^{t-1} P_X^j P_{Yi} P_{Zi}^{t-1-j}$. Hence, each sink ergodic component P_{Zi} along with P_X independently follows Lemma 5. Algorithm 3 below summarizes how to compute the node influence contributions of weakly connected signed digraphs. Note that by our assumption, we consider all sink components to be ergodic.

Algorithm 3 $c = weakly(G)$

INPUT: Signed transition matrix P.

OUTPUT: Influence contribution vector c.

Detect the structure of the weakly connected signed digraph G, and find its $m \geq 1$ signed ergodic sink components $G_{Z1}, \cdots, G_{Zm}$;

for $i = 1 : m$ **do**

  if G_{Zi} is balanced with partition $S_{Zi}, \bar{S}_{Zi}$ **then**

    Compute stationary distribution π_{Zi} of $\bar{P}_{Zi}$;

    $u_{bi} = (I_X - P_X)^{-1} P_{Yi} \hat{\mathbf{1}}_{Zi,S_{Zi}}$;

    $c_{Zi} = (\mathbf{1}_X^T u_{bi} + |S_{Zi}| - |\bar{S}_{Zi}|)\hat{\pi}^T_{Zi,S_{Zi}}$;

$c = [\mathbf{0}_X; c_{Z1}; \cdots ; c_{Zm}]$

4.3.3 General case and SVIM-L algorithm

Given the above systematic analysis, we are now in a position to summarize and introduce our SVIM-L algorithm which solves the long-term voter model influence maximization problem for general aperiodic signed digraphs.

In general, a signed digraph consists $m \geq 1$ disconnected components, within each of which the node influence contribution follows Lemma 5. The long-term signed voter model influence maximization (SVIM-L) algorithm is constructed in Algorithm 4.

Algorithm 4 Long-term influence maximization SVIM-L

INPUT: Signed transition matrix P, budget k.

OUTPUT: White seed set W.

Detect the structure of a general aperiodic signed digraph G, and find the $m \geq 1$ disconnected components $G_1, \cdots, G_m$;

for $i = 1 : m$ **do**

  $c_{G_i} = weakly(G_i)$;

$c = [c_{G_1}; \cdots ; c_{G_m}]$;

$W =$ top $\min\{k, n^+(c)\}$ nodes with the highest $c(i)$ values.

Complexity analysis. We consider $G = (V, E, A)$ to be weakly connected, since disconnected graph case can be treated independently for each connected component for the time complexity. SVIM-L algorithm consists of two parts. The first part extracts the connectivity and balance structure of the graph, which can be done using depth-first search with complexity $O(|E|)$. The second part uses Algorithm 3 to compute influence contributions of balanced ergodic sink components. The dominant computations are on the stationary distribution π_{Zi}'s and $(I_X - P_X)^{-1}$, which can be done by solving a linear equation system and matrix inverse in $O(|Z_i|^3)$ and $O(n_X^3)$, respectively, where $n_X = |X|$. Let b be the number of balanced sink components in G, n_Z be the number of nodes in the largest balanced sink component. Thus SVIM-L can be done in $O(bn_Z^3 + n_X^3)$ time. Alternatively, we can use iterative method for computing both π_{Zi}'s and $\mathbf{1}_X^T(I_X - P_X)^{-1}$, if the largest convergence time t_C of P_{Zi}^t's and P_X^t is small[1]. In this case, each iteration step involves vector-matrix multiplication and can be done in $O(m_B)$ time, where m_B is the number of edges of the induced subgraph G_B consisting of all nodes in the balanced sink components and X. Note that m_B and t_C are only related to subgraph G_B, which could be significantly smaller than G, and thus $O(t_C m_B)$ could be much smaller than the time of naive iterations on the entire graph. Overall SVIM-L can be done in $O(|E| + \min(bn_Z^3 + n_X^3, t_C m_B))$ time.

[1]Note that the convergence time of digraphs could be large [31,32], and even exponentially large at the worst case.

5. EVALUATION

In this section, we first use both synthetic datasets and real social network datasets to demonstrate the efficacy of our short-term and long-term seed selection schemes by comparing the performances with four baseline heuristics. Then, we evaluate how much the short-term and long-term influence can be improved by taking the edge signs into consideration.

5.1 Performance comparison with baseline heuristics

For different scenarios, we compare our SVIM-L and SVIM-S algorithms with four heuristics, i.e., (1) selecting seed nodes with the highest weighted outgoing degrees (denoted by $d^+ + d^-$ in the figures), (2) highest weighted outgoing positive degrees (denoted by d^+), (3) highest differences between weighted outgoing positive and negative degrees (denoted by $d^+ - d^-$), and (4) randomly selecting seed nodes (denoted by "Rand"), where in our evaluations, we run random seed selection 1000 times, and compare the average number of white nodes between our algorithm and other heuristics. Our evaluation results demonstrate that our seed selection scheme can increase up to 72% long-term influence, and 145% short-term influence over other heuristics.

5.1.1 Synthetic datasets

In this part, we generate synthetic datasets with different structures to validate our theoretical results.

Dataset generation model. We generate six types of signed digraphs, including balanced ergodic digraphs, anti-balanced ergodic digraphs, strictly unbalanced ergodic digraphs, weakly connected signed digraphs, disconnected signed digraphs with ergodic components, and disconnected signed digraph with weakly connected components (WCCs). All edges have unit weights. The following are graph configuration details.

We first create an unsigned ergodic digraph $\bar{G}$ with 9500 nodes, which has two ergodic components $\bar{G}_A$ and $\bar{G}_B$, with [3000, 6500] nodes and $[3000, 6500] \times 8$ random directed edges, respectively. Moreover, there are 3000×8 random directed edges across $\bar{G}_A$ and $\bar{G}_B$. Ergodicity is checked through a simple connectivity and aperiodicity check. Given $\bar{G}$, a *balanced digraph* is obtained by assigning all edges within $\bar{G}_A$ and $\bar{G}_B$ with positive signs, and those across them with negative signs. Then, an *anti-balanced digraph* is generated by negating all edge signs of the balanced ergodic digraph. To generate a *strictly unbalanced digraph*, we randomly assign edge signs to all edges in $\bar{G}$ and make sure that there does not exist a balanced or anti-balanced bipartition.

Moreover, we generated a *disconnected signed digraph* and a weakly connected signed digraph for our study. We first generate 5 ergodic unsigned digraphs, $\bar{G}_1, \cdots, \bar{G}_5$ with [500, 200, 800, 300, 2700] nodes and $[500, 200, 800, 300, 2700] \times 8$ edges, respectively. Then, we group $G_{23} = (G_2, G_3)$ and $G_{45} = (G_4, G_5)$ to form two ergodic balanced digraphs, and generate a strictly unbalanced ergodic digraph G_1 by randomly assigning signs to edges in $\bar{G}_1$. Three disconnected components G_1, G_{23}, G_{45} together form a disconnected signed digraph. To form a *weakly connected signed digraph*, we place in total 3000 random direct edges from G_1 to the balanced ergodic components G_{23} and G_{45}, where the nodes in subgraph G_1 only have outgoing edges to G_{23} and G_{45}. Moreover, we combine the above generated balanced ergodic digraph and the weakly connected signed digraph together forming a larger *disconnected signed digraph, with the weakly connected signed digraph as a component*.

Fig. 1-Fig. 6 present the evaluation results for one set of digraphs, where we observe that all digraphs we randomly generated exhibit consistent results. Our tests are conducted using Matlab on a standard PC server.

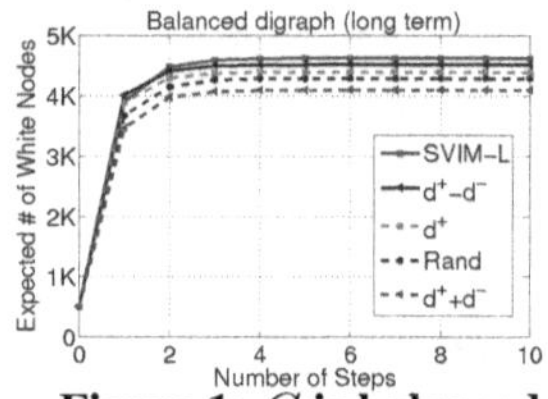

Figure 1: G is balanced

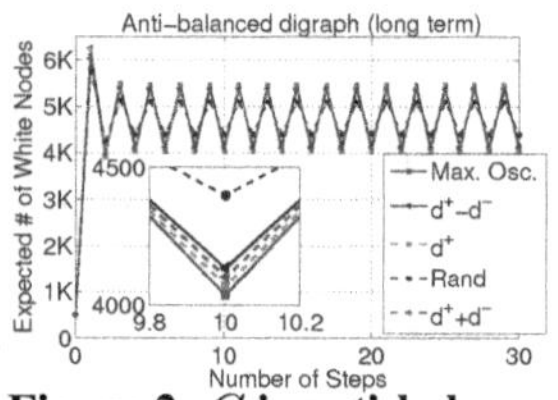

Figure 2: G is anti-balanced

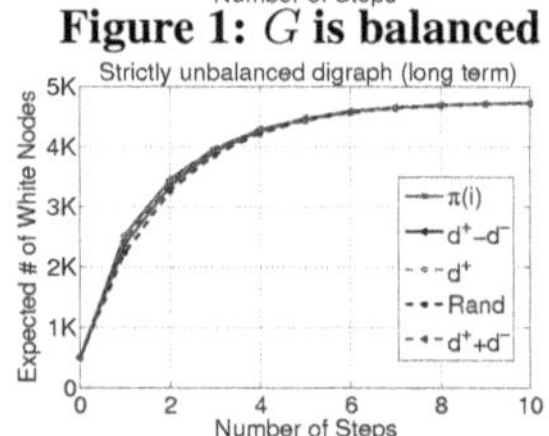

Figure 3: G is strictly unbalanced

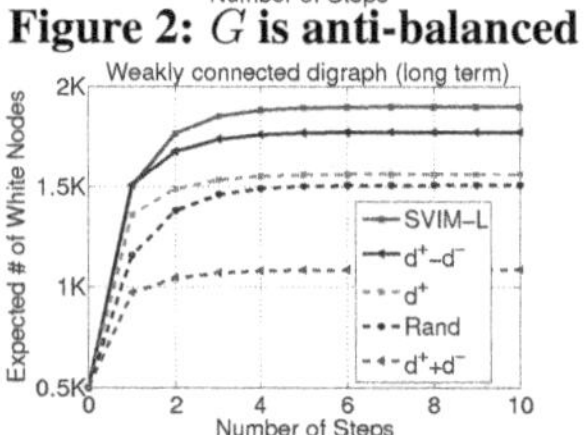

Figure 4: G is weakly connected

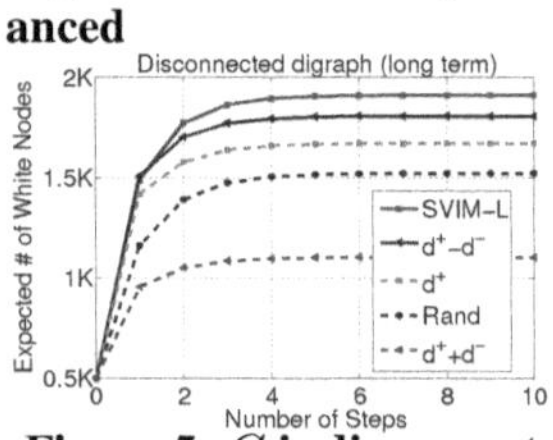

Figure 5: G is disconnected

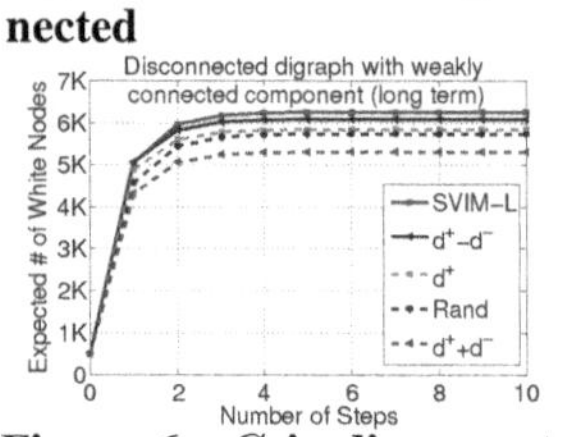

Figure 6: G is disconnected with WCC

Long-term influence maximization. In the evaluations, we set the influence budget as $k = 500$, and compare the average numbers of white nodes over steps between our algorithm and other heuristics. Fig. 1 shows that in the balanced ergodic digraph, SVIM-L algorithm achieves the highest long-term influence over other heuristics. When applying a heuristic seed selection scheme, denoted by $\mathtt{H}$, $f_t^{\mathtt{H}}$ represents the number of white nodes at step $t(\geq 1)$. Similarly, denote $f_t^{\mathtt{SVIM}}$ as the number of white nodes at step $t(\geq 1)$ for SVIM algorithm. We consider $\Delta f_t(\mathtt{SVIM}, \mathtt{H}) = (f_t^{\mathtt{SVIM}} - f_t^{\mathtt{H}})/f_t^{\mathtt{H}}$ as the influence increase of SVIM over the heuristic algorithm $\mathtt{H}$ at step t. The maximum influence increase is the maximum $\Delta f_t(\mathtt{SVIM}, \cdot)$ among all steps $(t \geq 1)$ and all heuristics. Hence, in Fig. 1, we see that our SVIM-L algorithm outperforms all other heuristics. Especially, a maximum of 14% influence increase is observed for $t \geq 4$ with $4.68k$ and $4.1k$ white nodes for SVIM-L and random selection scheme, respectively. In the rest of this section, we will use the maximum influence increase as a metric to illustrate the efficacy of our SVIM algorithm. Fig. 2 shows the clear oscillating behavior on the anti-balanced ergodic digraph, and the average influence is the same for all algorithms. In fact, we also designed an algorithm to maximize the oscillation in this case, but due to space constraint we omit it in this paper. The inset shows that our algorithm (denoted as "Max. Osc.") indeed provides the largest oscillation. Fig. 3 shows the results in strictly unbalanced graph case, where the long-term influences of all algorithms converge to $4750 = |V|/2$, which matches Theorem 1. Fig. 4 and Fig. 5 show that SVIM-L algorithm performs the best, and it generates $5.6\% - 72\%$ long-term influence increases after the sixth step over other heuristics in the weakly connected signed digraph and the disconnected signed digraph. Fig. 6 shows that in a more general signed digraph, which consists of a weakly connected signed component and a balanced ergodic component, SVIM-L algorithm outperforms all other heuristics with up to 17% more long term influence, which occurs for $t \geq 4$. In general, we see that for weakly connected and disconnected digraphs, SVIM-L has larger winning margins over all other heuristics than the case of balanced ergodic digraphs (Fig. 4–6 vs. Fig.1). We attribute this to our accurate computation of influence contribution in the more involved weakly connected and disconnected digraph cases. Moreover, in all cases, the dynamics converge very fast, i.e., in only a few steps, which indicates that the convergence time of voter model on these random graphs are very small.

Table 2: Statistics of Epinions datasets

# of nodes	131580
# of edges	840799
# of positive edges	717129
# of negative edges	123670
# of nodes in largest SCC	41441
# of edges in largest SCC	693507
# of positive edges in largest SCC	614314
# of negative edges in largest SCC	79193
# of strongly connected components	88361

5.1.2 Real datasets

We conduct extensive simulations using real datasets, such as Epinions and Slashdot datasets, to validate our theoretical results and evaluate the performance of our SVIM algorithm.

Epinions Dataset. Epinions.com [14] is a consumer review online social site, where users can write reviews to various items and vote for or against other users. The signed digraph is formed with positive or negative directed edge (u, v) meaning that u trusts or distrusts v. The statistics are shown in Table 2. We compare our short-term SVIM-S algorithm with four heuristics, i.e., $d^+ + d^-$, d^+, $d^+ - d^-$ and random seed selection, on the entire Epinions digraph as well as the largest strongly connected component (SCC).

Our tests are conducted on both Epinions dataset and its largest strongly connected component (SCC), where the largest SCC is ergodic and strictly unbalanced. We first look at the comparison of instant influence maximization (*at* step t) among various seed selection schemes. Fig. 7-10 shows the expected maximum instant influence at each step by different methods. Note that since the initial seeds selected by SVIM-S algorithm hinge on t, the values on the curve of our selection scheme are associated with different optimal initial seed sets. On the other hand, the seed selections of other heuristics are independent to t, thus the corresponding curves represent the same initial seed sets. We choose the budget as 500 and 6000 in our evaluations, i.e., selecting at maximum 500 or 6000 initial white seeds. From Fig. 7-10, SVIM-S algorithm consistently performs better, and in some cases, e.g., Fig. 9, it generates $16\% - 145\%$ more influence than other heuristics at step 1.

Next we compare the seed selection schemes for maximizing the average influence *within* the first t steps. Fig. 11-14 show the expected maximum average influence within the first t steps by different methods. Again, the values on the curve of SVIM-S algorithm are associated with different initial seed sets. Fig. 11-14 show that with different budgets, i.e., 500 and 6000 seeds, SVIM-S algorithm performs better than all other heuristics, where in Fig. 13 a maximum of 64% more influence is achieved at $t = 8$. Moreover, in all these figures, we observe that our seed selection scheme results in the highest long-term influence over other heuristics.

Moreover, from Fig. 7-14, we observe that as t increases, the influences (i.e., the expected number of white nodes), for SVIM-S and all heuristics except for random seed selection schedule, increase for small t's, and then decrease and converge to the stationary state. In contrast, from Fig. 1-6, the influence increases monotonically with t. This happens because Epinions dataset (as

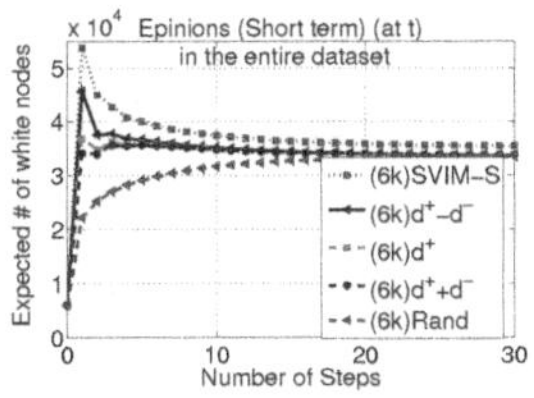

Figure 7: Instant influence in Epinions data with $k = 6k$

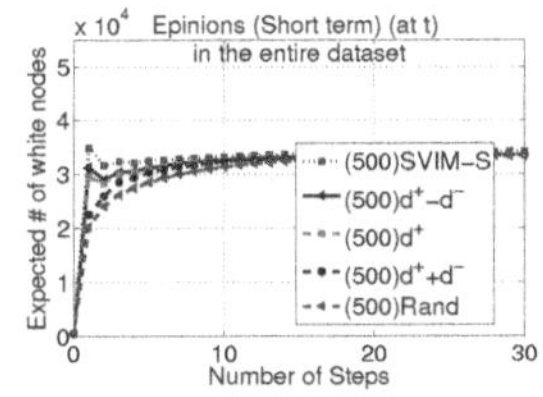

Figure 8: Instant influence in Epinions data with $k = 500$

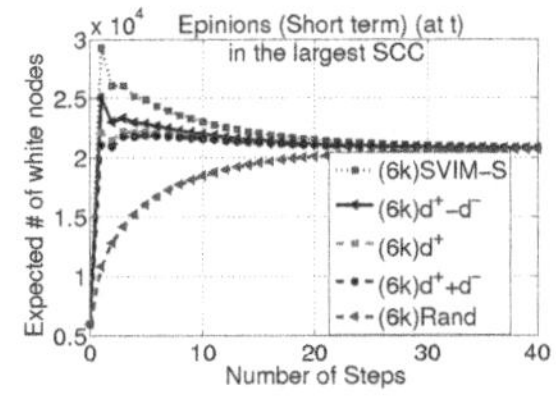

Figure 9: Instant influence in SCC with $k = 6k$

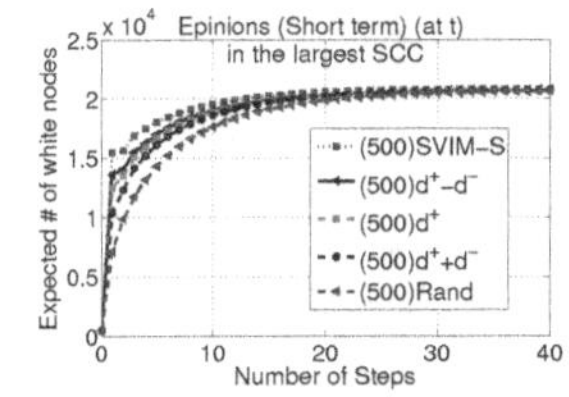

Figure 10: Instant influence in SCC with $k = 500$

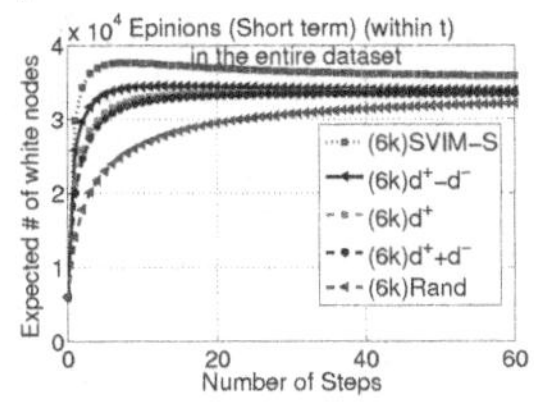

Figure 11: Average influence in Epinions data with $k = 6k$

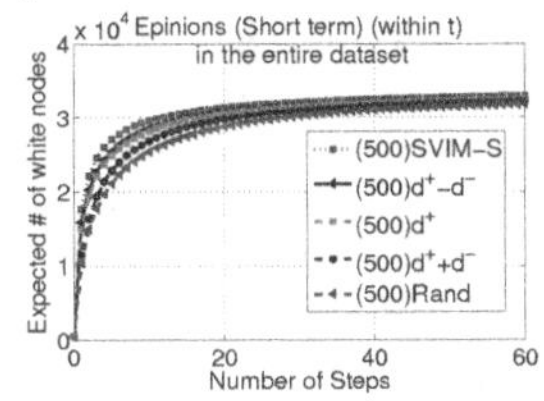

Figure 12: Average influence in Epinions data with $k = 500$

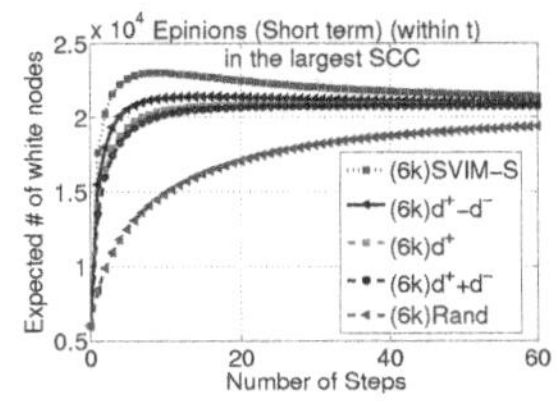

Figure 13: Average influence in SCC with $k = 6k$

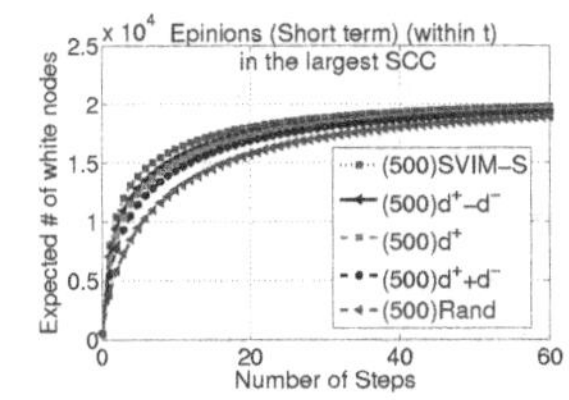

Figure 14: Average influence in SCC with $k = 500$

well as many real network datasets) has large portion (around 80%) of nodes in the non-sink components, where to maximize the long-term influence, only nodes in sink components should be selected, which governs the long-term influence dynamics of the whole graph, namely, sink nodes have higher long-term influence contributions. However, for short-term influence maximization, nodes with higher chances to influence more nodes in a few steps generally have large number of incoming links, which are able to influence a large number of nodes in either sink or non-sink components in a short period of time. Hence, in signed digraphs with large non-sink component, given a sufficiently large budget, the short-term influence can definitely outnumber the long-term influence. Our evaluations confirm this explanation. This interesting observation also leads to a problem that given a budget k, how to find the optimal time step t that generates the largest influence among all possible t's. We leaves this problem as our future work.

We also evaluate our SVIM-S algorithm on the entire slashdot dataset [22, 37] and its largest strongly connected component, where the results are delegated to our technical report [24] due to the limited space. In the simulations, similar results are obtained as that with Epinions dataset, where our SVIM-S algorithm performs the best among all methods tested, especially in the early steps.

Moreover, the convergence times for both real-world datasets are fast, in a few tens of steps, indicating good connectivity and fast mixing property of real-world networks. In summary, our evaluation results on both synthetic and real-world networks validate our theoretical results and demonstrate that our SVIM algorithms for both short term and long term are indeed the best, and often have significant winning margins.

5.2 The impacts of signed information

Unlike Epinions and Slashdot, many online social networks such as Twitter are simply represented by unsigned directed graphs, where friends and foe relationships are not explicitly represented on edges. Without edge signs, two types of information may be mis-represented or under-represented: (1) one may follow his foes for tracking purpose, but this link may be mis-interpreted as friend or trust relationship; and (2) one may not follow his foes publicly to avoid being noticed, but his foes may still generate negative influence to him. In this section, we investigate how much influence gain can be obtained by taking the edge signs into consideration, thus illustrate the significance of utilizing both friend and foe relationships in influence maximization.

Taking the synthetic networks and Epinions dataset (used in Sec 5.1) as examples, we apply our SVIM algorithm to compute the optimal initial seed sets in the original signed digraphs, and two types of "sign-missing" scenarios, i.e., the unsigned digraphs with only original positive edges (denoted by "Positive" graphs) and with all edges labeled by the same signs (denoted by "Sign ignored" graphs). Then, we examine the performances of those three initial seed sets in original signed digraphs.

Fig. 15-18 show the evaluation results, where the seed sets obtained by considering edge signs perform consistently better than those using unsigned graphs. In synthetic networks, we observed $5\% - 16\%$ more influence in balanced digraph for $t \geq 6$ (See Fig. 15), and $11.7\% - 58\%$ more influence in weakly connected digraph for $t \geq 6$ (See Fig. 16). Moreover, in Epinions dataset from Fig. 17-18, there is no impact on the long-term influence, since the underlying graphs are strictly unbalanced. However, in short term, the results demonstrate that taking edge signs into consideration always performs better, which generates at maximum of 38% and 21% more influence for the entire dataset (See Fig. 17) and the largest SCC (See Fig. 18), respectively. Both maximums occur at step 1. These results clearly demonstrate the necessity of utilizing sign information in influence maximization.

6. CONCLUSION

In this paper, we propose and study voter model dynamics on signed digraphs, and apply it to solve the influence maximization problem. We provide a rigorous mathematical analysis to completely characterize the short-term and long-term dynamics, and provide efficient algorithms to solve both short-term and long-term influence maximization problems. Simulation results on both synthetic and real-world graphs demonstrate that our influence maximization (SVIM) algorithms consistently outperform other heuristic algorithms.

There exist several open problems and future directions. One open problem is the convergence time of voter model dynamics on signed digraphs. For balanced and anti-balanced ergodic digraphs, our results show that their convergence times are the same as the corresponding unsigned digraphs. For strictly unbalanced ergodic digraphs and more general weakly connected signed digraphs, the problem is quite open. A future direction is to study influence diffusion in signed networks under other models, such as the voter model with a background color, the independent cascade model, and the linear threshold model.

7. ACKNOWLEDGEMENT

We would like to thank Christian Borgs and Jennifer T. Chayes for pointing out the relations between the signed digraph voter

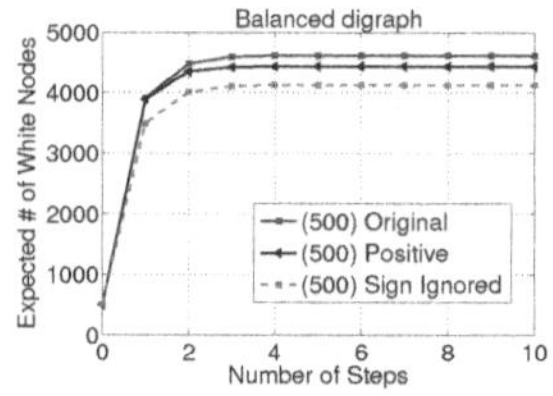

Figure 15: Synthetic balanced digraph

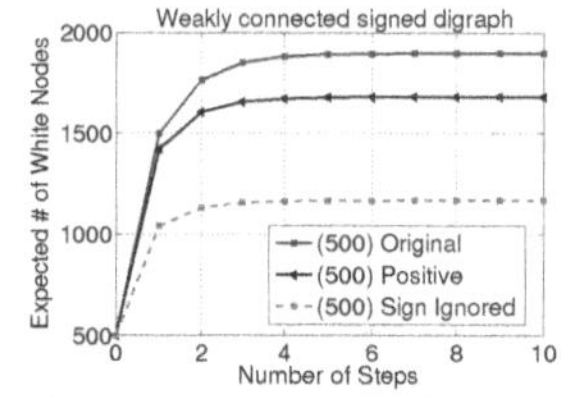

Figure 16: Synthetic weakly connected digraph

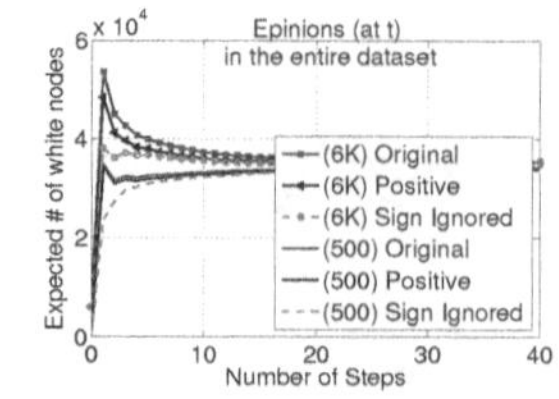

Figure 17: Epinions (the entire dataset)

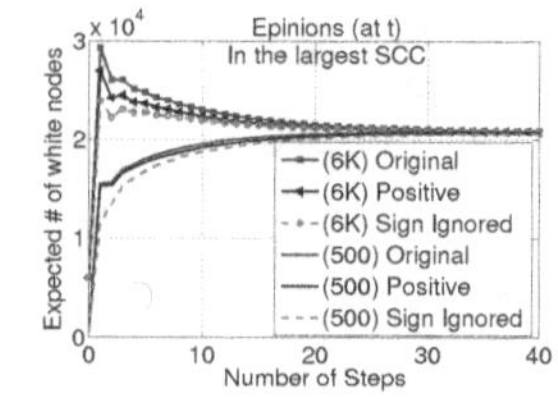

Figure 18: Epinions (the largest SCC)

model and concepts in physics, such as Ising model and Gauge transformations. We also thank Zhenming Liu for many useful discussions on this work.

8. REFERENCES

[1] M. Ángeles Serrano, K. Klemm, F. Vazquez, V. Eguíluz, and M. San Miguel. Conservation laws for voter-like models on random directed networks. *Journal of Statistical Mechanics: Theory and Experiment*, 2009:P10024, 2009.

[2] S. Bharathi, D. Kempe, and M. Salek. Competitive influence maximization in social networks. In *WINE*, 2007.

[3] C. Borgs, J. Chayes, A. Kalai, A. Malekian, and M. Tennenholtz. A novel approach to propagating distrust. *Internet and Network Economics*, 2010.

[4] A. Borodin, Y. Filmus, and J. Oren. Threshold models for competitive influence in social networks. In *WINE*, 2010.

[5] F. Brandt, T. Sandholm, and Y. Shoham. Spiteful bidding in sealed-bid auctions. In *IJCAI*, 2007.

[6] C. Budak, D. Agrawal, and A. E. Abbadi. Limiting the spread of misinformation in social networks. In *WWW*, 2011.

[7] W. Chen, A. Collins, R. Cummings, T. Ke, Z. Liu, D. Rincón, X. Sun, Y. Wang, W. Wei, and Y. Yuan. Influence maximization in social networks when negative opinions may emerge and propagate. In *SDM*, 2011.

[8] W. Chen, C. Wang, and Y. Wang. Scalable influence maximization for prevalent viral marketing in large-scale social networks. In *KDD*, 2010.

[9] W. Chen, Y. Wang, and S. Yang. Efficient influence maximization in social networks. In *KDD*, 2009.

[10] W. Chen, Y. Yuan, and L. Zhang. Scalable influence maximization in social networks under the linear threshold model. In *ICDM*, 2010.

[11] K. Chiang, N. Natarajan, A. Tewari, and I. Dhillon. Exploiting longer cycles for link prediction in signed networks. 2011.

[12] P. Clifford and A. Sudbury. A model for spatial conflict. *Biometrika*, 60(3):581, 1973.

[13] D. Easley and J. Kleinberg. *Networks, crowds, and markets: reasoning about a highly connected world.* Cambridge, 2010.

[14] Epinions. Dataset. *http://www.epinions.com/.*

[15] E. Even-Dar and A. Shapira. A note on maximizing the spread of influence in social networks. In *WINE*, 2007.

[16] A. Goyal, W. Lu, and L. V. S. Lakshmanan. Simpath: An efficient algorithm for influence maximization under the linear threshold model. In *ICDM*, 2011.

[17] X. He, G. Song, W. Chen, and Q. Jiang. Influence blocking maximization in social networks under the competitive linear threshold model. In *SDM*, 2012.

[18] R. Holley and T. Liggett. Ergodic theorems for weakly interacting infinite systems and the voter model. *The annals of probability*, 1975.

[19] D. Kempe, J. Kleinberg, and E. Tardos. Maximizing the spread of influence through a social network. In *KDD*, 2003.

[20] J. Kunegis, S. Schmidt, A. Lommatzsch, J. Lerner, E. W. D. Luca, and S. Albayrak. Spectral analysis of signed graphs for clustering, prediction and visualization. In *SDM*, 2010.

[21] J. Leskovec, D. Huttenlocher, and J. Kleinberg. Predicting positive and negative links in online social networks. In *WWW*, 2010.

[22] J. Leskovec, D. Huttenlocher, and J. Kleinberg. Signed networks in social media. In *CHI*. ACM, 2010.

[23] J. Leskovec, A. Krause, C. Guestrin, C. Faloutsos, J. M. VanBriesen, and N. S. Glance. Cost-effective outbreak detection in networks. In *KDD*, 2007.

[24] Y. Li, W. Chen, Y. Wang, and Z.-L. Zhang. Influence diffusion dynamics and influence maximization in social networks with friend and foe relationships. *arXiv:1111.4729 [cs.SI]*, Nov 2011.

[25] Y. Li and Z.-L. Zhang. Random walks on digraphs: A theoretical framework for estimating transmission costs in wireless routing. In *INFOCOM*, 2010.

[26] Y. Li and Z.-L. Zhang. Random walks on digraphs, the generalized digraph laplacian and the degree of asymmetry. *WAW*, 2010.

[27] Y. Li and Z.-L. Zhang. Digraph laplacian and the degree of asymmetry. *Internet Mathematics*, 8(4), 2012.

[28] Y. Li and Z.-L. Zhang. Random walks and green's function on digraphs: A framework for estimating wireless transmission costs. *IEEE/ACM Transactions on Networking*, PP(99):1–14, 2012.

[29] H. Ma, H. Yang, M. R. Lyu, and I. King. Mining social networks using heat diffusion processes for marketing candidates selection. In *CIKM*, 2008.

[30] N. Masuda and H. Ohtsuki. Evolutionary dynamics and fixation probabilities in directed networks. *New Journal of Physics*, 11:033012, 2009.

[31] A. Mohaisen, H. Tran, N. Hopper, and Y. Kim. On the mixing time of directed social graphs and security implications. In *ASIACCS*, 2012.

[32] A. Mohaisen, A. Yun, and Y. Kim. Measuring the mixing time of social graphs. In *IMC*, 2010.

[33] J. Morgan, K. Steiglitz, and G. Reis. The spite motive and equilibrium behavior in auctions. *The BE Journal of Economic Analysis & Policy*, 2(1):1102–1127, 2003.

[34] R. Narayanam and Y. Narahari. Determining the top-k nodes in social networks using the shapley value. In *AAMAS*, 2008.

[35] L. Page, S. Brin, R. Motwani, and T. Winograd. The pagerank citation ranking: Bringing order to the web. *Technical report, Stanford University*, 1998.

[36] N. Pathak, A. Banerjee, and J. Srivastava. A generalized linear threshold model for multiple cascades. In *ICDM*, 2010.

[37] Slashdot. Dataset. *http://slashdot.org/.*

[38] V. Sood, T. Antal, and S. Redner. Voter models on heterogeneous networks. *Physical Review E*, 77(4):041121, 2008.

Modeling Dynamic Behavior in Large Evolving Graphs

Ryan A. Rossi
Jennifer Neville
Purdue University
{rrossi, neville}@purdue.edu

Brian Gallagher
Keith Henderson
Lawrence Livermore National Laboratory
{bgallagher, keith}@llnl.gov

ABSTRACT

Given a large time-evolving graph, how can we model and characterize the temporal behaviors of individual nodes (and network states)? How can we model the behavioral transition patterns of nodes? We propose a temporal behavior model that captures the "roles" of nodes in the graph and how they evolve over time. The proposed *dynamic behavioral mixed-membership model* (DBMM) is scalable, fully automatic (no user-defined parameters), non-parametric/data-driven (no specific functional form or parameterization), interpretable (identifies explainable patterns), and flexible (applicable to dynamic and streaming networks). Moreover, the interpretable behavioral roles are generalizable and computationally efficient. We applied our model for (a) identifying patterns and trends of nodes and network states based on the temporal behavior, (b) predicting future structural changes, and (c) detecting unusual temporal behavior transitions. The experiments demonstrate the scalability, flexibility, and effectiveness of our model for identifying interesting patterns, detecting unusual structural transitions, and predicting the future structural changes of the network and individual nodes.

Categories and Subject Descriptors

H.2.8 [**Database Applications**]: Data Mining

General Terms

Algorithms, Experimentation

Keywords

Graph mining, dynamic network models, dynamic roles

1. INTRODUCTION

In recent years, we have witnessed a tremendous growth in both the variety and scope of network datasets. In particular, network datasets often record the interactions and/or transactions among a set of entities—for example, personal communication (e.g., email, phone), online social network interactions (e.g., Twitter, Facebook), web traffic between servers and hosts, and router traffic among autonomous systems. A notable characteristic of these *activity* networks, is that the structure of the networks change over time (e.g., as people communicate with different friends). These temporal dynamics are key to understanding system *behavior*, thus it is critical to model and predict the network changes over time. An improved understanding of temporal patterns will facilitate for example, the development of software systems to optimally manage data flow, to detect fraud and intrusions, and to allocate resources for growth over time.

Although some recent research has focused on the analysis of dynamic networks [17, 3, 5, 12, 4, 21], there has been less work on developing *models* of temporal behavior in large scale network datasets. There has been some work on modeling temporal events in large scale networks [2, 31] and other work that uses temporal link and attribute patterns to improve predictive models [26]. In addition, there is work on identifying clusters in dynamic data [5, 27] but these methods focus on discovering underlying communities over time—sets of nodes that are densely connected together. In contrast, we are interested in uncovering the *behavioral* patterns of nodes in the graph and modeling how those patterns change over time. In the simple example below, the red node is a "star-center" and the blue represents peripheral nodes. At some later time, the top nodes transition to a "near-clique" while the two bottom nodes become inactive.

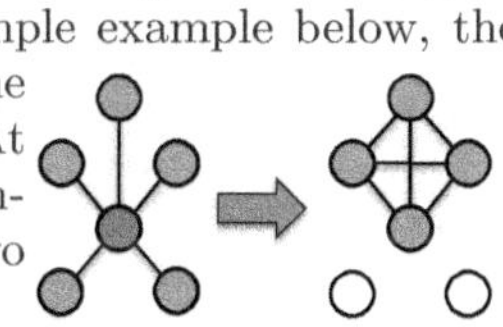

The recent work on dynamic mixed-membership stochastic block models (dMMSB: [9, 30]), is to our knowledge, one of the only methods suitable for modeling node-centric properties over time. The dMMSB model identifies groups of nodes with similar patterns of linkage and characterizes how group memberships change over time. However, dMMSB assumes a specific parametric form where the groups are defined through linkage to specific nodes (i.e., in particular types of groups) rather than more general forms of node behavior over dynamic node sets. More importantly the dMMSB estimation algorithm is not scalable, which makes the method unsuitable for analysis of large graphs.

In this work, we aim to develop a descriptive model to answer the following questions for dynamic network datasets:

1. **Identify dynamic patterns in node behavior.** What types of high level temporal patterns and trends do the

WSDM'13, February 4–8, 2013, Rome, Italy.

data exhibit? Are behaviors cyclical or predictable? Do nodes have different behavioral patterns?

2. **Predict future structural changes.** Can we predict when a node's role will change (e.g., a node with high in-degree transitions to a node with high betweenness)? Is the overall structure of the graph becoming more or less predictable over time?
3. **Detect unusual transitions in behavior.** Are there nodes and/or points in time with significantly different behavioral patterns?

To facilitate the investigation of these questions, we propose to model node "roles" and how they change over time. Informally, *roles* can be viewed as sets of nodes that are more structurally similar to nodes inside the set than outside whereas communities are sets of nodes with more connections inside the set than outside. Specifically, to focus on *node behavior* (rather than the complimentary concept of community finding) we use non-parametric feature-based roles.

Using these non-parametric roles, which can generalize to new unseen nodes, we propose a novel *dynamic behavioral mixed-membership model* (DBMM) suitable for large, unbounded, time-evolving networks. The DBMM discovers features (i.e., using the graph and intrinsic attributes), extracts these features for all timesteps, and automatically learns behavioral "roles" for nodes at each timestep. The number of behavioral roles are selected automatically using MDL or AIC. Afterwards, we learn behavior transition matrices for each node (i.e., given a node role r_i, what is the probability of transitioning to r_j at the next point in time).

Our proposed DBMM technique allows us to investigate the properties of temporal networks and understand both global and local behaviors, detect anomalies, as well as predict future structural changes. The main strengths of the approach include:

- ⋆ **Automatic.** The algorithm doesn't require user-defined parameters.
- ⋆ **Scalable.** The learning algorithm is linear in the number of edges in the time-interval under consideration. It is also easily parallelizable as features, roles, transition models can be learned independently at each time.
- ⋆ **Non-parametric and data-driven.** The model structure (i.e., number of parameters) and more generally the parameterization depends on the properties of the time-evolving network.
- ⋆ **Interpretable and intuitive.** The DBMM is based on an intuitive behavioral representation (structural properties) of the network and individual nodes. It identifies explainable patterns, trends, and aids in understanding the underlying dynamic process.
- ⋆ **Flexible.** The definition of behavior in our model can be tuned for specific applications. The algorithm is applicable for all types of time-evolving networks.

We demonstrate the application our our model on several real world datasets, showing that it both accurately predicts future structural changes as well as identifying interesting temporal patterns and anomalies. We discuss the scalability of the approach and notably we apply the DBMM to networks with up to 300,000 nodes and 4 million edges—datasets that are orders of magnitude larger than could be modeled with dMMSBs.

2. DYNAMIC BEHAVIORAL MODEL

Our goal is to model the behavioral roles of nodes and their evolution over time. Given a sequence of network snapshots (graphs and attributes), the Dynamic Behavioral Mixed Membership Model (DBMM) consists of (1) automatically learning a set of representative features, (2) extracting features from each graph, (3) discovering behavioral roles (4) iteratively extracting these roles from the sequence of network snapshots over time and (5) learning a predictive model of how these behaviors change over time. As an aside, let us note that DBMM is a *scalable general framework* for analyzing temporal behavior as the model components can be replaced by others and each component can be appropriately tuned for any application (e.g., for the feature set, any feature construction system from [25] can conceivably be used).

2.1 Data Model for Temporal Networks

Given a dynamic network $\mathcal{D} = (\mathcal{N}, \mathcal{E})$, where $\mathcal{N}$ is the set of nodes and $\mathcal{E}$ is the set of edges in $\mathcal{D}$, a network snapshot $\mathcal{S}_t = (\mathcal{N}_t, \mathcal{E}_t)$ is a subgraph of $\mathcal{D}$ where $\mathcal{E}_t$ are the edges in $\mathcal{E}$ active at time t and $\mathcal{N}_t$ are the endpoints of the edges $\mathcal{E}_t$.

2.2 Representing Network Behavior

The idea is to discover a set of underlying roles, which together describe the behaviors observed in the network, and then assign a probability distribution over these roles to each node in the network, which explain that node's observed behavior. Roles are extracted via a two-step process.

Feature Discovery. The first step is to represent each active node in a given snapshot graph $\mathcal{S}_t$ using a set of representative features. For this task, we leverage [14]. The method constructs degree and egonet measures (in / out, weighted, ...), then aggregates these measures using sum (or mean) creating recursive features. After each aggregation step, correlated features are pruned using logarithmic binning. The aggregation proceeds recursively, until there are no new features. Formally, we discover a set of features at time t denoted $\boldsymbol{V}_t$ such that $\boldsymbol{V}_t$ is an $n_t \times f$ matrix where n_t is the number of active nodes and f is the number of features learned from the snapshot graph $\mathcal{S}_t$. The features are extracted for each network snapshot resulting in a sequence of node-feature matrices, denoted $\boldsymbol{V} = \{\boldsymbol{V}_t : t = 1, ..., t_{max}\}$.

Role Discovery. The next step is to automatically discover groups of nodes (representing common patterns of behavior) based on their features. For this purpose, we use Non-negative Matrix Factorization (NMF) to extract roles [15] and extend it for a sequence of graphs. Given a sequence of node-feature matrices, we generate a rank-r approximation $\boldsymbol{G}_t\boldsymbol{F} \approx \boldsymbol{V}_t$ where each row of $\boldsymbol{G}_t \in \mathbb{R}^{n \times r}$ represents a node's membership in each role and each column of $\boldsymbol{F} \in \mathbb{R}^{r \times f}$ represents how membership of a specific role contributes to estimated feature values. For constructing the "closest" rank-r approximation we use NMF (multiplicative update method) because of interpretability and efficiency, though any other method for constructing such an approximation may be used instead (SVD, spectral decomposition). More formally, given a non-negative matrix $\mathbf{V}_t \in \mathbb{R}^{n_t \times f}$ and a positive integer $r < \min(n_t, f)$, find non-negative matrices $\mathbf{G}_t \in \mathbb{R}^{n_t \times r}$ and $\mathbf{F} \in \mathbb{R}^{r \times f}$ that minimizes the functional,

$$f(\mathbf{G}_t, \mathbf{F}) = \frac{1}{2}||\mathbf{V}_t - \mathbf{G}_t\mathbf{F}||_F^2$$

Table 1: Dataset characteristics. The number of learned features and roles provide intuition about the underlying generative process and also indicates the amount of complexity present in the network.

Dataset	Features	Roles	Nodes	Edges	|T|	length
TWITTER RELATIONSHIPS	1325	12	310,809	4,095,627	41	1 day
TWITTER (COPENHAGEN)	150	5	8,581	27,889	112	3 hours
FACEBOOK	161	9	46,952	183,831	18	1 day
EMAIL-UNIV	652	10	116,893	1,270,285	50	60 min
NETWORK-TRACE	268	11	183,389	1,631,824	49	15 min
INTERNET AS	30	2	37,632	505,772	28	3 months
ENRON	173	6	151	50,572	82	2 weeks
IMDB	45	3	21,257	296,188	28	1 year
REALITY	99	5	97	31,694	46	1 month

We iteratively estimate the node-role memberships for each network snapshot $\boldsymbol{G} = \{\boldsymbol{G}_t : t = 1, ..., t_{max}\}$ given $\boldsymbol{F}$ and $\boldsymbol{V} = \{\boldsymbol{V}_t : t = 1, ..., t_{max}\}$ using NMF. Afterwards, we have a sequence of matrices $\boldsymbol{G}_1, \boldsymbol{G}_2, ..., \boldsymbol{G}_t, ..., \boldsymbol{G}_{t_{max}}$ where each active node at time t is represented with their current role memberships.

The number of structural roles r is automatically selected using Minimum Description Length (MDL) criterion. However, AIC or any model selection may be used instead. Intuitively, learning more roles, increases model complexity, but decreases the amount of errors. Conversely, learning less roles, decreases model complexity, but increases the amount of errors. In this way, MDL selects the number of behavioral roles r such that the model complexity (number of bits) and model errors are balanced. Naturally, the best model minimizes, *number of bits* + *errors*. See [15] for more details.

2.3 Behavioral Transition Model

Given a sequence of dynamic behaviors $\boldsymbol{G} = \{\boldsymbol{G}_t : t = 1, ..., t_{max}\}$, we can learn a model of how behavior in our network changes over time. More formally, given two behavioral snapshots, $\boldsymbol{G}_{t-1}$ and $\boldsymbol{G}_t$, we learn a transition matrix $\boldsymbol{T} \in \mathbb{R}^{r \times r}$ that approximates the change in behavior from time $t-1$ to t. The transition matrix $\boldsymbol{T}$ represents how likely a node is to transition from role r_i to role r_j for that particular time interval:

$$\boldsymbol{T} = \begin{bmatrix} z^{(r_1 \to r_1)} & z^{(r_1 \to r_2)} & \dots & z^{(r_1 \to r_m)} \\ z^{(r_2 \to r_1)} & z^{(r_2 \to r_2)} & \dots & z^{(r_2 \to r_m)} \\ \vdots & \dots & \ddots & \dots \\ z^{(r_m \to r_1)} & z^{(r_m \to r_2)} & \dots & z^{(r_m \to r_m)} \end{bmatrix}$$

where $\boldsymbol{T}$ is estimated using NMF such that $\boldsymbol{G}_{t-1}\boldsymbol{T} \approx \boldsymbol{G}_t$.

In the simple form of the model presented above, we learn $\boldsymbol{T}$ using only a single transition (i.e., $t-1$ to t). However, we also propose variations that leverage more available data by considering multiple transitions (*stacked model*) or that smooth over a sequence of transitions using kernel functions (*summary model*). We discuss these in detail next.

2.3.1 Stacked Transition Model

The stacked model uses the training examples from the k previous timesteps. More formally, the stacked model is defined as,

$$\begin{bmatrix} \boldsymbol{G}_{t-1} \\ \boldsymbol{G}_{t-2} \\ \vdots \\ \boldsymbol{G}_{k-1} \end{bmatrix} \boldsymbol{T} \approx \begin{bmatrix} \boldsymbol{G}_{t} \\ \boldsymbol{G}_{t-1} \\ \vdots \\ \boldsymbol{G}_{k} \end{bmatrix}$$

where $k = t - w$ and w is the window size; typically $w = 10$. Let us denote the stacked behavioral snapshots as $\boldsymbol{G}_{k:t}$ where $k : t$ represents all the training examples from timestep k to timestep t.

2.3.2 Summary Transition Model

This class of models uses k previous timesteps to weight the training examples at time t using some kernel function. The exponential decay and linear kernels are used in this work. The temporal weights can be viewed as probabilities that a node behavior is still active at the current time step t, given that it was observed at time $(t-k)$. We define the summary behavioral snapshot $\boldsymbol{G}_{S(t)}$ as a weighted sum of the temporal role-memberships up to time t as follows, $\boldsymbol{G}_{S(t)} = \alpha_1 \boldsymbol{G}_k + ... + \alpha_{w-1}\boldsymbol{G}_{t-1} + \alpha_w \boldsymbol{G}_t = \sum_{i=k}^{t} K(\boldsymbol{G}_i; t, \theta)$ where α determines the contribution of each snapshot in the summary model.

In addition to exponential and linear kernels, we experimented with the inverse linear and also tried various θ values. Overall, we found the linear kernel (and exponential) to be the most accurate with $\theta = 0.7$. Nevertheless, the optimal θ will depend on the type of dynamic network and the volatility.

2.4 Remarks

For each type of transition model (e.g., stacked or summary), we may learn a *global transition model* that describes how the behavior of the network as a whole changes over time or we may learn a *local transition model* for each individual node. The local transition model describes more precisely how the behavioral roles of that individual node change over time. We can estimate the local transition model for a node i as $\boldsymbol{G}_{t-1}^{(i)}\boldsymbol{T}^{(i)} \approx \boldsymbol{G}_t^{(i)}$ using NMF. The global transition model for the network is estimated in exactly the same way as described above in §2.3.

We have found the summary model to be the best performer for prediction tasks because of its ability to smooth over multiple timesteps. However, for precisely this reason, the summary model is more difficult to interpret. Therefore, we use the summary model for prediction tasks and the stacked representation for data analysis tasks, due to its interpretability. Let us note that to achieve better accuracy in predictions, one may also estimate local transition models for each node and use these for predicting a node's future role memberships. All of these options make our model flexible for use in a variety of applications.

We also experimented with other variants of the DBMM transition model, including a stacked-summary hybrid and multi-state models, which make an explicit distinction between transitions from activate states and transitions from

Features	S-Center	S-Edge	Bridge	Clique
S-Center	**0.08**	0.25	0.34	0.33
S-Edge	0.27	**0.11**	0.25	0.37
Bridge	0.29	0.20	**0.17**	0.34
Clique	0.24	0.24	0.29	**0.23**

Roles	S-Center	S-Edge	Bridge	Clique
S-Center	**0.07**	0.25	0.33	0.35
S-Edge	0.28	**0.10**	0.22	0.40
Bridge	0.29	0.18	**0.16**	0.37
Clique	0.24	0.25	0.29	**0.22**

Table 2: Validating DBMM's ability to distinguish patterns. Note C is row-normalized.

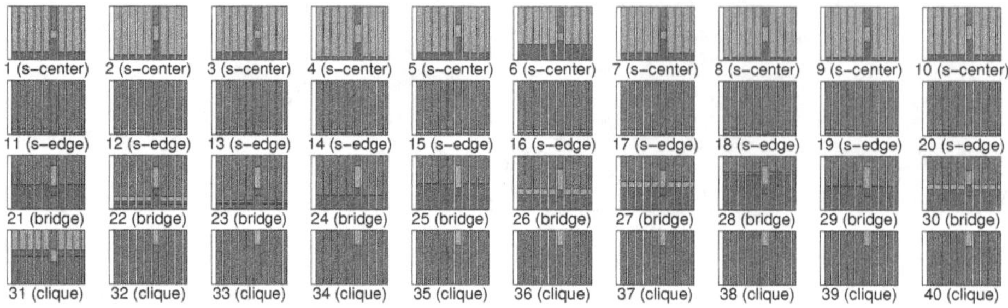

Figure 1: The pattern of each node is listed below the mixed-membership plot whereas the colors represent roles learned from our model. For simplicity, the node's pattern-type is kept stable over time. Strikingly, the DBMM clearly reveals the underlying patterns of the nodes as each pattern has a distinct signature in terms of the role distribution. For instance, the blue role of a bridge node indicates the local similarity with that of a star-edge node (low degree,...) while the red role captures the bridges more global and intrinsic property of acting as a backbone for the other nodes. The other patterns are even more straightforward to interpret. We also inject a type of global anomaly at $t = 6$ (bridges connecting to each other) which is clearly revealed as such in the plots.

inactive states. However, we opted in favor of the simpler stacked and summary models because none of these other models provided an obvious advantage.

While our model currently assumes the role definitions are somewhat stationary, we have found that these roles generalize and can even be applied across different networks. Nevertheless, to remove this assumption, we could simply track the loss over time and recompute the roles when it surpasses some threshold.

3. EXPLORATORY ANALYSIS

This section explores the effectiveness of DBMM for dynamic network analysis tasks.

3.1 Datasets & Structural Analysis

We apply the DBMM model using a variety of dynamic networks from different domains [23]. See Table 1 for details. Interestingly, we find a relationship between the complexity of DBMM and the complexity present in the graph. This is clearly clearly shown in Table 1 by analyzing simple measures generated from the DBMM behavioral representation such as the number of learned features and the number of roles. For instance, the Internet AS topology has some hierarchical structure or recurring patterns of connectivity among ISPs and therefore our model discovers only 30 features. This is in contrast to networks with more complex patterns of connectivity such as twitter and other transaction networks like the email network. In these cases, the links are instantaneous and might only last for some duration of time, thus making more complex structures more likely.

3.2 Experiments on Synthetic Data

In this section, we demonstrate the ability of DBMM to distinguish between common graph patterns (and consequently recover the synthetic roles). For this task, we design a simple graph generator that constructs graphs probabilistically with four main patterns: 'center of a star', 'edge of a star', bridge nodes (connecting stars/cliques), and clique nodes. After constructing the graph, we validate that the DBMM model captured these patterns by measuring if the extracted features and roles represent the known probabilistic patterns. We do this by computing the pairwise euclidean distance matrix $\boldsymbol{D}$ using the initial feature matrix $\boldsymbol{V}$ (and role-membership matrix $\boldsymbol{G}$). Let r_i denote the actual pattern of node i, and $\mathcal{P} = \{(i,j)|r_i = p,\ r_j = q\}$ then $C_{p,q} = \sum_{(i,j)\in\mathcal{P}} D_{i,j}$.

Clearly, the roles and features from nodes of the same pattern are shown to be more similar than the others (smaller values along the diagonal). See Table 2.3. Additionally, the patterns that are structurally similar to one another are represented as such by our model (star-center and clique). In Fig. 1, we visualize the mixed-memberships of 10 randomly chosen nodes from each pattern-type. Each pattern has a distinct and consistent signature in terms of the role distribution.

3.3 Interpretation & Analysis

We start with an illustrative example of applying DBMM to a large IP trace network, shown in Figure 2. We first plot the time-evolving mixed-memberships from four nodes shown in Figure 2(b) and then visualize their corresponding transition models in Figure 2(a). In the time-evolving mixed-memberships, inactivity is represented by white bars whereas in the transition models inactivity corresponds to the last row/column. The transition models are learned using the stacked representation which aids in the understandability and interpretation of the roles and their modeled transitions.

The time-evolving mixed-memberships for each of the four example nodes in Figure 2(b) show distinct patterns from one another which are easy to identify. The four patterns represented by these nodes can be classified as having the following patterns of structural behavior,

1. **Structural Stability.** This node's structural behavior (and communication pattern) doesn't is relatively stable over the time.

2. **Homogeneous.** The node for the most part takes on a single behavioral role.
3. **Abrupt transition.** Their structural behavior changes abruptly. In the IP-network, it could be that the IP was released and someone was assigned it or perhaps that the machine was compromised and began acting maliciously.
4. **Periodic activity.** The node has periodic activity, but maintains similar structural behavior. In the case of the IP-communication network, this machine could be infected and every 30 minutes sends out a communication to the master indicating it's connected and "listening".

For the four example nodes, we show their transition models in Figure 2(a). The transition models represent the probability of transitioning or taking on the structural behavior of role j given that your current role (or main role) is role i. For instance, node 2 homogeneously takes on the red role over time as discussed previously. From Figure 2(c), we see that the red role is "role 9", and looking back at the node's learned transition model, we find that column 9 contains most of the mass, which represents that their is a high probability of transitioning from any other role to the red role. As shown in the mixed-memberships over time, this is exactly what is expected. As another example, we find that node 4 usually transitions from a mix of active roles to the inactive role (i.e., the inactive role is represented by column/row eleven). Therefore, we would expect our learned transition model to capture this by placing most of the mass on the last column, representing the probability of going inactive after having a mix of active roles in the previous timestep, which is exactly what we see in the fourth transition model.

Instead of providing subjective or anecdotal evidence for what the roles represent, we interpret the roles of the DBMM with respect to well-known node measurements (e.g., degree, clustering coefficient, betweenness,...). We extend the analytical tools from [15] for use in interpreting the role dynamics. The first technique interprets the roles using the dynamic node-role memberships $\boldsymbol{G}_t$ and a node measure matrix $\boldsymbol{M}_t \in \mathbb{R}^{n\times m}$ to compute a non-negative matrix $\boldsymbol{E}_t$ such that $\boldsymbol{G}_t\boldsymbol{E}_t \approx \boldsymbol{M}_t$. The node measurements used are betweenness, biconnected components, PageRank, clustering coefficient, and degree. The matrix $\boldsymbol{E}_t$ represents the contributions of the node measures to the roles at time t. We report average contributions over time.

Figure 2(c) shows this quantitative interpretation of roles for the IP network. Intuitively, the first role represents nodes with high PageRank, while role five represents nodes with high betweenness, whereas role nine represents nodes with large clustering coefficient. The other roles represent more specialized structural motifs that were not captured by the set of traditional measures used for interpretation.

The DBMM can be used to understand the temporal behavior across a variety of time-evolving networks. Figure 3 shows another example for an email communication network. Just as before, we can identify significant trends and patterns and interpret these using the role interpretations from Figure 3(b). One notable behavioral pattern in the email communications is that most users have a set of roles for the daytime and a different set for night. Intuitively, one set of roles is work related and the other is more personal/family related (see nodes 1 & 2, among others). We also find nodes that have inconsistent or unstable behavior over the time, such as 17, 18, 19, among others. Additionally, some nodes have relatively stable structural behavior

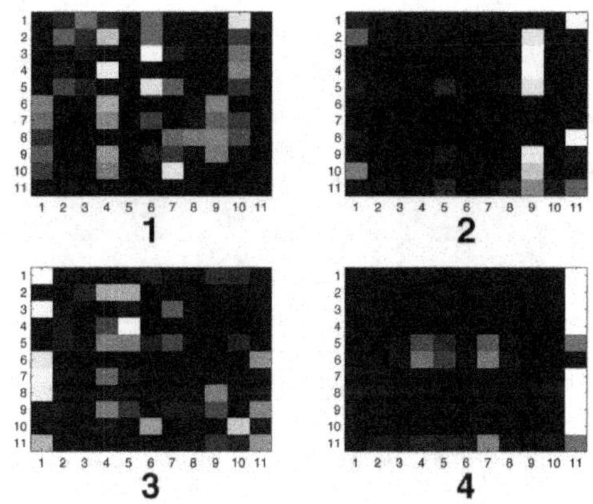

(a) Transition Models

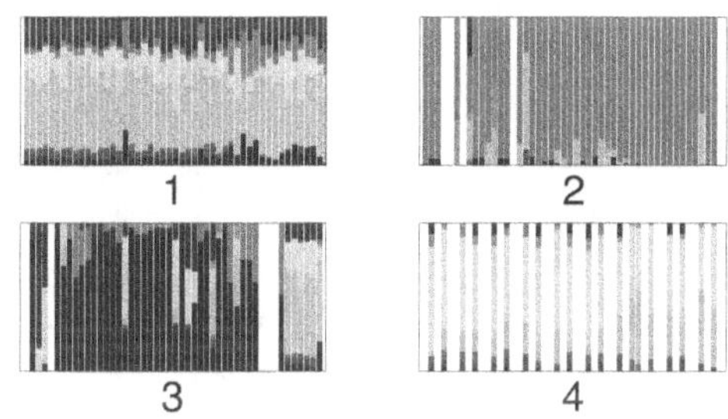

(b) Time-evolving Mixed-Memberships

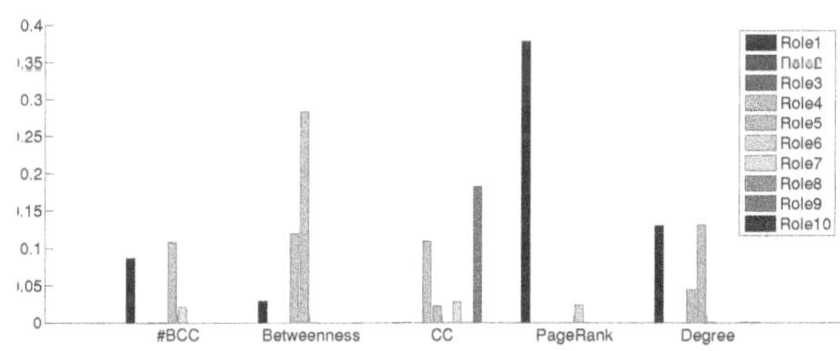

(c) Role Interpretation

Figure 2: The DBMM transition model effectively captures the diverse temporal behavior of hosts in a computer network. (a) Transition matrices for 4 hosts. The y-axis represents the role the node transitions from, the x-axis is the role we transition to. Inactivity is represented by the last row/column. (b) Corresponding role-memberships over time. The x-axis represents time while the y-axis represents the role distribution at each point in time. Each distinct color represents a learned role. (c) Characteristics of individual roles.

over the two days, such as node 4. This is also unusual, since one might expect a user's behavior to change from the work hours to the evening/night. However, users that are consistently dominated by multiple active roles are of importance (may serve in managerial or leadership roles), since they connect to groups of nodes with different types of structural patterns (see nodes 5-7).

3.4 Clustering Temporal Behaviors

Lastly to show the patterns of the learned transition matrices, we cluster nodes based on their temporal behaviors. We find that this clustering reveals the underlying structural patterns of the evolving mixed-memberships. Formally, let

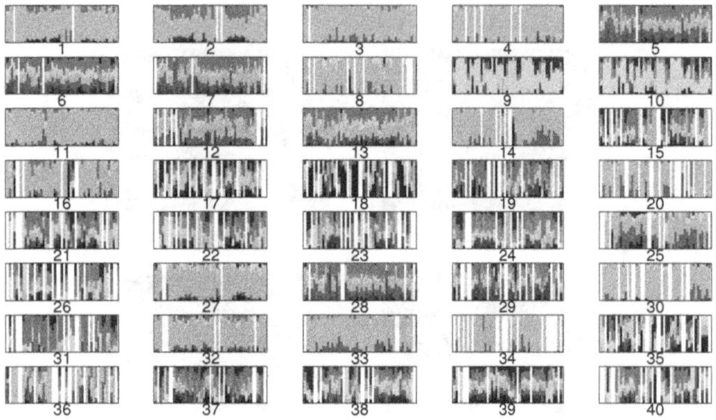

(a) Time-evolving Mixed-Memberships (Email)

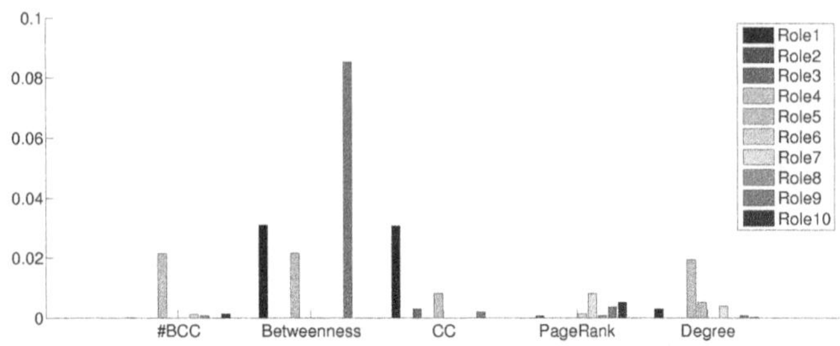

(b) Email Role Interpretation

Figure 3: The DBMM model allows us to uncover patterns of behavior in an email network. (a) evolving memberships for a group of nodes and (b) the characteristics associated with the roles.

$\boldsymbol{T}^{(i)}$ and $\boldsymbol{T}^{(j)}$ be the transition matrices of two nodes i and j. Then we create an $r \times r$ vector from each of the node transition models and define a similarity function between these vectors.

First we estimate a single transition model $\boldsymbol{T}$ for each node using the stacked model. We then compute an $n \times n$ similarity matrix using Frobenious loss between the transition matrices from the nodes. Next, we apply the classical k-means clustering algorithm to cluster the nodes by their transition matrices. Afterwards, we compute the closest rank-k approximation (k = 2 or 3) of the similarity matrix. The nodes are plotted using the low-rank approximation and labeled using the previous clustering algorithm. To reveal the structural transition pattern, we then compute the average dynamic mixed-membership for each cluster using only the nodes from that cluster.

This clustering method reveals common structural trends and patterns between nodes. For instance, this technique may group nodes together that share similar transitional patterns such as nodes with stable roles vs. nodes with more dynamic roles or nodes with high activity vs. nodes with low activity. An example is provided in Figure 4. For clarity in the visualization, we randomly selected a small subset of nodes from the 183,389 candidates and identified common transition patterns among them. The first visualization in Figure 4(a) identifies four distinct well-separated clusters of nodes with similar transition models. Figure 4(b) shows the average dynamic behavioral mixed-membership for each cluster. This visualization shows that each cluster represents a unique structural transition pattern between the nodes. The structural patterns can be interpreted using the previous role interpretation from Figure 2(c). This technique can be used for general exploratory analysis such

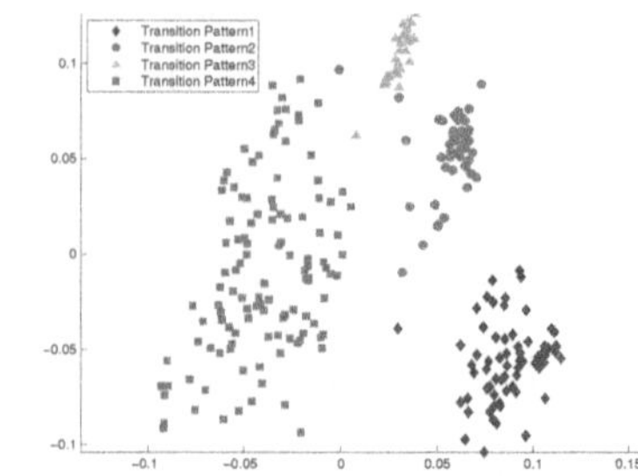

(a) Transition Clustering

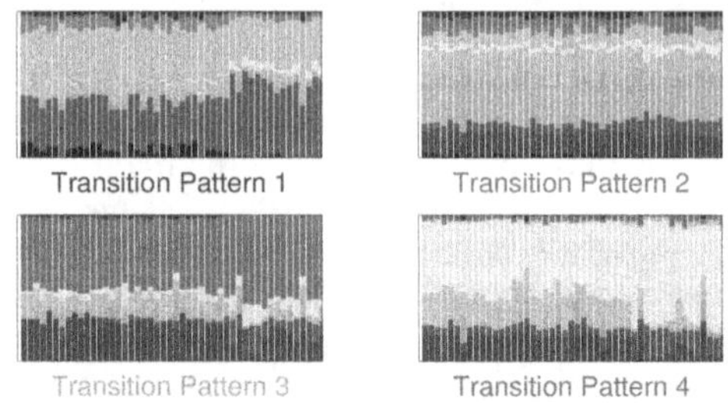

(b) Dynamic Mixed-Membership Patterns

Figure 4: The DBMM model provides an intuitive means of clustering nodes that exhibit similar patterns of behavior over time. (a) identifies four distinct clusters of nodes with similar transition patterns. (b) provides a sense of the behavior of each cluster in terms of the average role-membership over time. Again, we see that DBMM captures differences in both overall static behavior (i.e., the specific roles that dominate) and in patterns of how behaviors (i.e., roles) change over time.

as characterizing the patterns and trends of nodes or eventually used as a means to detect anomalies or nodes that do not fit any transition pattern.

4. PREDICTING FUTURE BEHAVIOR

In this section, we further validate the utility of the DBMM model by demonstrating its ability to predict the future behavior of nodes. This could be useful for optimizing caches on the Web, or for improving dynamic social recommendation systems, among many others.

Models. The goal is to accurately predict $\boldsymbol{G}_{t+1}$ given $\boldsymbol{G}_{s(t)}$, the summary behavioral snapshot described in Section 2.3.2. Our primary means of predicting $\boldsymbol{G}_{t+1}$ is using our DBMM summary transition model $\boldsymbol{T}$ as follows: $\hat{\boldsymbol{G}}_{t+1} = \boldsymbol{G}_t \ \boldsymbol{T}$. We compare this summary model to two sensible baselines: *PrevRole* and *AvgRole*. PrevRole simply assigns each node the role distribution from the previous time t. That is, $\hat{\boldsymbol{G}}_{t+1} = \boldsymbol{G}_t$. AvgRole assigns each node the average role distribution over all nodes at time t. The AvgRole model can be expressed as $\hat{\boldsymbol{G}}_{t+1} = \boldsymbol{G}_t \ \boldsymbol{T}_A$ where $\boldsymbol{T}_A$ is estimated from $\boldsymbol{G}_t = [1] \ \boldsymbol{T}$. Essentially, PrevRole assumes node behavior does not change from each point in time to the next and AvgRole assumes that all nodes exhibit the average behavior of the network.

Evaluation. We consider two strategies for evaluating our predictive models: (a) compare the predicted $\hat{\boldsymbol{G}}_{t+1}$ to the true $\boldsymbol{G}_{t+1}$ using a loss function (we use the Frobenious norm) and (b) Use $\hat{\boldsymbol{G}}_{t+1}$ to predict the modal role of each node at time $t+1$ and evaluate these predictions using a multi-class

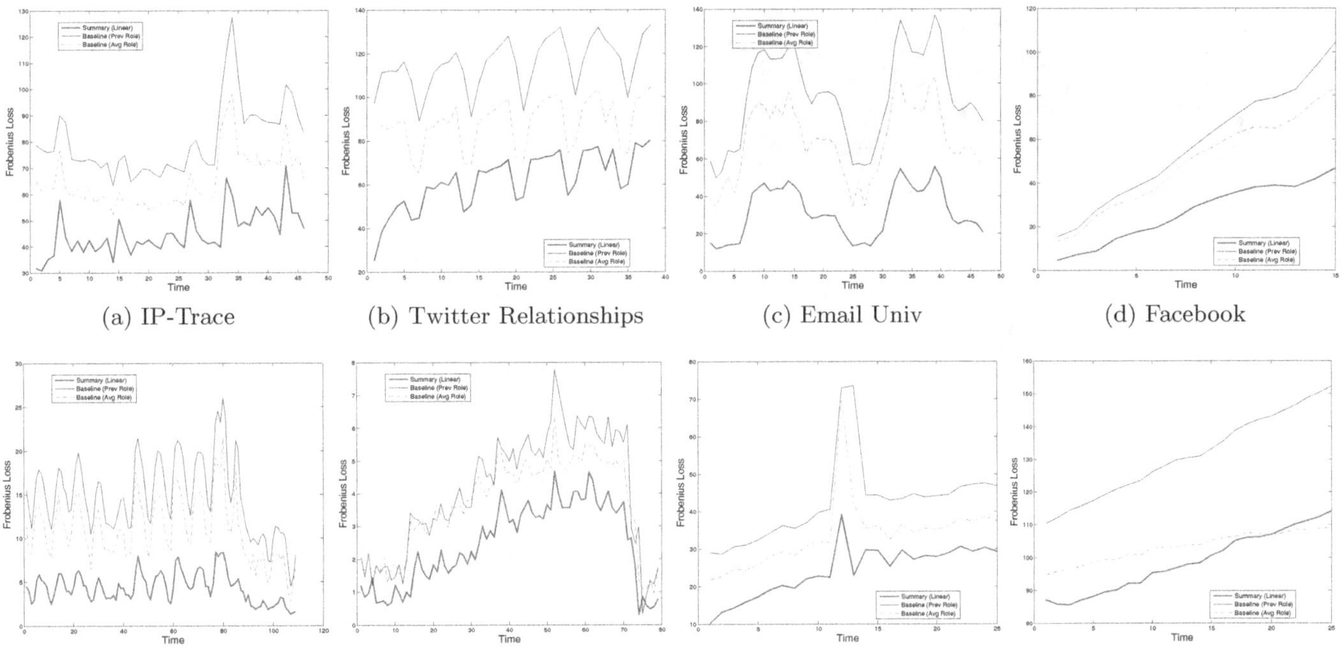

(a) IP-Trace (b) Twitter Relationships (c) Email Univ (d) Facebook

(e) Twitter Copenhagen (f) Enron (g) IMDB (h) Internet AS

Figure 5: The DBMM transition model accurately predicts future behavior of individual nodes (i.e., mixed role membership) compared to sensible baseline models.

AUC (Area Under the ROC curve) measure. We describe each of these strategies more formally below.

Frobenious Loss on $\boldsymbol{G}$. The goal here is to estimate $\boldsymbol{G}_{t+1}$ as accurately as possible. The approximation error between the estimated node memberships $\hat{\boldsymbol{G}}_{t+1} = \boldsymbol{G}_t \boldsymbol{T}_{t+1}$ and the true node memberships $\boldsymbol{G}_{t+1}$ is defined as $||\boldsymbol{G}_{t+1} - \hat{\boldsymbol{G}}_{t+1}||_F$

Structural Prediction with Multi-class AUC. This is a multi-class classification task where the true class label for node i is the modal role from the ith row of $\boldsymbol{G}_{t+1}$ (i.e., the role with maximum membership for this node). The predicted class label for node i is the modal role from the ith row of $\hat{\boldsymbol{G}}_{t+1}$.

We evaluate the predictions using a generalization of AUC extended for multi-class problems. In particular, we compute the AUC of all combinations of labels and take the mean (also known as Total AUC) [13]. The difficulty of the prediction task varies based on the number of roles discovered, complexity of the network evolution, and the type of time-evolving network (e.g., transactional vs. stable).

Results. Figure 5 demonstrate that the DBMM summary transition model is an effective predictor across the range of experiments. With few exceptions, DBMM outperforms both baselines for all data sets and timesteps. This is even true for the more complex time-evolving networks such as Twitter, email, and the IP-traces, which are more transactional with rapidly evolving network structure. For brevity, some findings were omitted, for others see [23].

In addition to validating the DBMM model, both figures offer some interesting insights into the characteristics of time-evolving networks. For example, an increase in loss over time may indicate a "concept drift" where behavior in the network has evolved to the point where the current roles can no longer adequately explain node behavior. This effect is seen most prominently in Figures 5(b), 5(d), 5(g) and 5(h). Interestingly, the drift we see in Figure 5(h) agrees with the current understanding that the underlying evolutionary process of the Internet AS is not constant, as was previously believed [19, 29]. Most notably, there is recent evidence of the Internet topology transitioning from hierarchical to a flat topological structure [7, 6].

Furthermore, the figures provide insights into behavioral anomalies, such as the spike we see in Figure 5(g). The spike in loss indicates the significant deviation of the node roles at a specific time.

Finally, in the large Twitter Relationships network, we see seasonality among the role transitions. In particular, we find that the users generally behave significantly different over the weekends, seen by the increase in loss on these days. Intuitively, we would expect users to be tweeting about different topics and using the system in different manner than they do during the work days. The Twitter Copenhagen network captures the more locally-temporal seasonality; that is users behave differently during the daytime and the night-time hours.

5. ANOMALOUS DYNAMIC PATTERNS

We further demonstrate the use of DBMMs for detecting anomalies in time-evolving networks. In particular, we formulate this problem with respect to identifying nodes that have *unusual structural transition patterns*. For instance, a node might transition from being a hub (i.e., a node with many people linking to it) to a node with low degree.

5.1 Node Transition Anomalies

While there are many ways to define an anomaly detection technique with respect to the DBMM model, we propose an intuitive algorithm shown in Alg. 1 that uses a node's transition model for predicting the network memberships at $t+1$. The anomaly score is the difference between the predicted network mixed-memberships and the ground-truth mixed-memberships. Therefore, the score represents the divergence of that nodes transitions from the entire network. One sim-

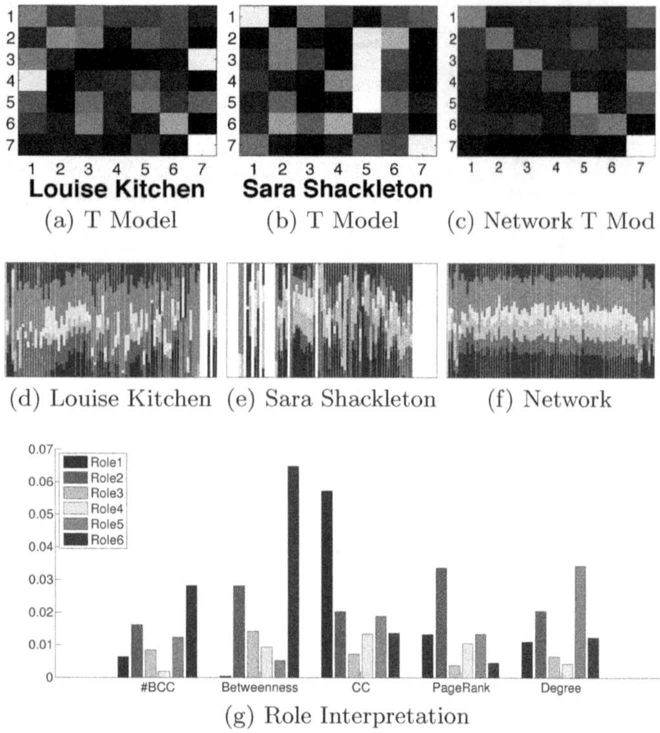

(a) T Model (b) T Model (c) Network T Mod

(d) Louise Kitchen (e) Sara Shackleton (f) Network

(g) Role Interpretation

Figure 6: The DBMM transition model provides an effective means of automatically discovering and visualizing nodes with anomalous temporal behavior. (a)-(b) are the transition models for two of the most anomalous nodes in the Enron email network compared to (c) the normal network transition model. (d)-(f) show the corresponding role memberships over time. (g) shows the characteristics of roles.

ple example is shown in Figure 6(a) where we find Louise Kitchen as having unusual behavioral transitions.

5.2 Time-varying Node Anomalies

For detecting the specific time interval in which a node has unusual behavior we use the previous method with a few subtle distinctions. The global and node models are estimated at each *timestep* (in a sort of streaming fashion) using the stacked representation with a shorter window (for leveraging past training examples). The final result is a ranked list of potential node anomalies for each timestep, shown in Figure 8. The justification for such an approach is that nodes may become anomalous or have unusual behavior only for a specified time interval. In the case of IP-communications, it is unlikely for the behavior of an IP-address to remain unusual as IP-addresses are released/expires and users are assigned entirely new IP-addresses. These types of dynamic anomalies are shown in Figure 8.

5.3 Anomalous Structural Transitions

We first interpret the roles and their temporal variation quantitatively as shown in Figure 6(g) and then provide some simple examples of nodes that have unusual behavior transitions. Intuitively, the first role represents nodes with high clustering coefficient, the second role represents mainly nodes with high pagerank, while the third and fourth roles represent some type of combination of these properties indicating a more complex structural motif that is not

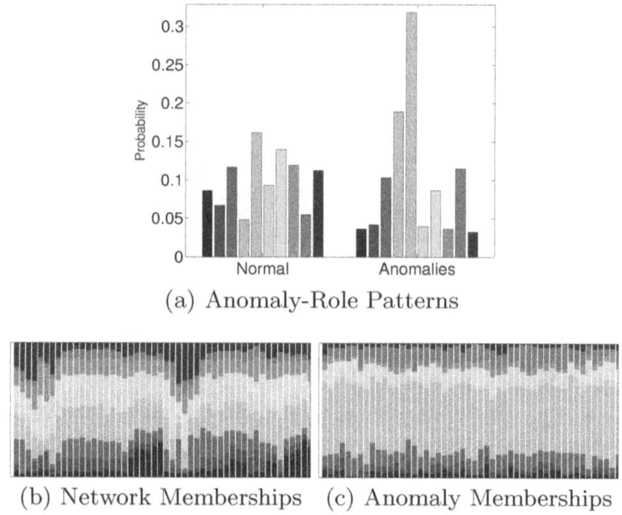

(a) Anomaly-Role Patterns

(b) Network Memberships (c) Anomaly Memberships

Figure 7: The DBMM anomaly detector effectively captures differences in both static and dynamic behavior in an email network. (a) shows that normal and anomalous nodes (top-100) differ in their role distribution (i.e., overall static behavior). (b)-(c) show that normal and anomalous nodes also differ in how their behavior changes over time, with anomalies exhibiting more stable behavior over time than normal.

sufficiently represented by the selected node metrics. However, the fifth role represents nodes with high degree and the sixth role represents nodes that are articulation points or that have high betweenness. Additionally, by analyzing the neighbors roles dynamically, we find that nodes with high clustering coefficient primarily are neighbors to nodes with high betweenness or high degree (this plot has been removed for brevity).

In Figure 6(e), we find Louise Kitchen, one of the Enron executives who was involved in the Fraud, as having unusual behavioral transitions. Further examination of the network transition model and the average evolution of the behavioral mixed-memberships provide further insights into his abnormal activities. In particular, there are two main role transitions ($r_3 \rightarrow r_7$ and $r_4 \rightarrow r_1$) in Louise Kitchen's transition model that are in contradiction with the network transition model shown in Figure 6(c). Furthermore, analyzing the individual changes to the mixed-memberships over time compared with the average behavioral mixed-memberships provides additional insight. For instance, the first two mixed-memberships vectors of Louise Kitchen are mainly red and then begin to deviate significantly with seemingly no un-

Algorithm 1: Anomalous Structural Transitions

Input: $\mathbf{G} = \{\boldsymbol{G}_t : t = 1, ..., t_{max}\}$ (evolving mixed-memberships)

Output: $\mathbf{x}$ (vector of anomalous scores)

for $i \leftarrow 1$ **to** n **do**

  $\boldsymbol{T}^{(i)} \in \mathbb{R}^{r \times r} \leftarrow NMF(\boldsymbol{G}^{(i)}_{1:t-1}, \boldsymbol{G}^{(i)}_{2:t})$

  $\hat{\boldsymbol{G}}_{t+1} = \boldsymbol{T}^{(i)} \cdot \boldsymbol{G}_t$

  $\mathbf{x}^{(i)} = \left\| \hat{\boldsymbol{G}}_{t+1} - \boldsymbol{G}_{t+1} \right\|_F$

end

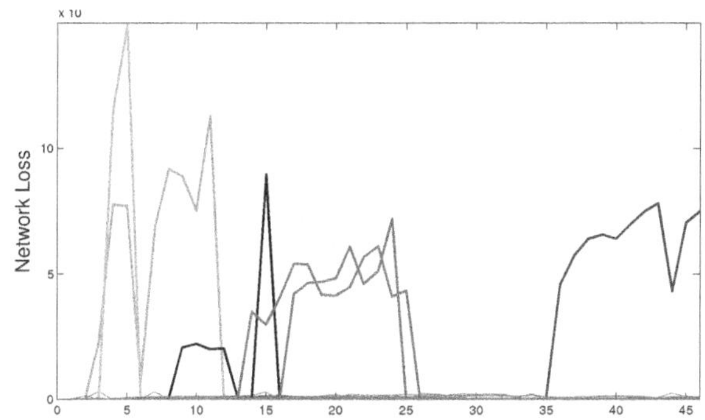

(a) Time-varying Anomalies

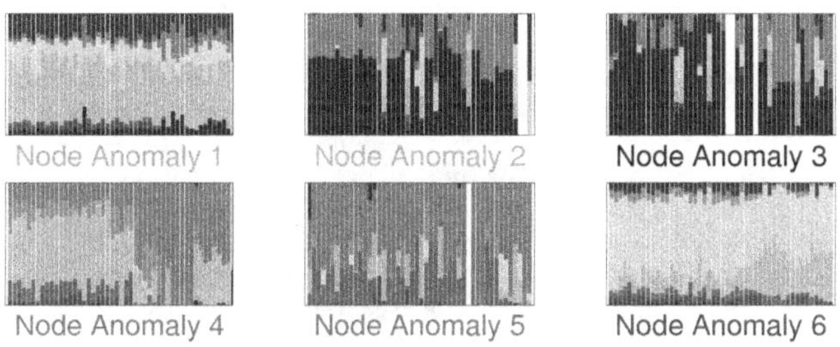

(b) Evolving memberships of the time-varying anomalies

Figure 8: The DBMM model allows us to find nodes that are anomalous for only short periods of time and normal otherwise. Such temporally local anomalies are often impossible to find using static graph analysis because brief abnormal periods are drowned out by mostly normal behavior. (a) shows examples of short lived anomalies in a computer network. (b) shows the corresponding behavior over time for each node in detail.

derlying correlation or pattern between the role transitions. Moreover, there is not any significant correlation between Louise's mixed-memberships and the average memberships at each point in time.

In addition, we also identify interesting patterns of the nodes with unusual behavioral transitions in Figure 7. In particular, the DBMM anomaly detector effectively captures differences in both static and dynamic behavior in an email network. Interestingly, in 7(b), normal users exhibit a clear cyclical pattern which indicates that normal nodes have a set of roles during the day and another set at night (which agrees with intuition). In contrast, the anomalies 7(c) have stable roles over the time that barely fluctuate.

Figure 8 also indicates that the DBMM model allows us to find nodes that are anomalous for only short periods of time and normal otherwise. Such temporally local anomalies are often impossible to find using static graph analysis because brief abnormal periods are drowned out by mostly normal behavior. 8(a) shows examples of short lived anomalies in a computer network. 8(b) shows the corresponding behavior over time for each node in detail.

Synthetic Data. In a separate set of experiments, we further validate our "unusual structural transition" anomaly detector by injecting anomalies into synthetic data (see § 3.2). Initially, the dynamics of nodes are predefined to have normal transitions between patterns (e.g., star-center to clique). Then we inject some nodes with anomalous transition behavior by randomly transitioning to an abnormal pattern which we define as star-edge to clique. For 200 repeated simulations, we achieve high accuracy (88.5%) in detecting the anomalous behavior.

Table 3: Performance Analysis of the Dynamic Behavioral Mixed-Membership Model. The dMMSB takes a day to handle 1,000 nodes [30], while our model takes only 8.44 minutes for 8,000 nodes.

Dataset	Nodes	Edges	Performance
ENRON	151	50,572	117.51 sec
TWITTER (COPEN)	8,581	27,889	506.61 sec
FACEBOOK	46,952	183,831	1,468.65 sec
INTERNET AS	37,632	505,772	1,922.85 sec
NETWORK-TRACE	183,389	1,631,824	16,138.71 sec

6. SCALABILITY AND COMPLEXITY

Most importantly, our dynamic role model is linear in the number of edges. Let n be the number of nodes, f be the number of features, r be the number of roles and t be the number of timesteps. The feature discovery is $O(t(mf + nf^2))$ [14]. For the NMF step, we use the multiplicative update method which has worst case $O(tnfr)$. The transition models is $O(tnr^2)$ using the multiplicative update method. Thus, the running time of DBMM is linear in the number of edges, specifically, $O(t(mf + nfr + nr^2))$. The time-scale t is usually small compared to the edges (even when the time-scale corresponds to minutes or seconds in the IP-trace data). A more accurate bound can be stated in terms of the maximum number of edges at any given timestep.

Our model is capable of handling realistic networks such as social and technological networks consisting of millions of nodes and edges. This is in contrast to a similar dynamic mixed-membership models that have been recently proposed such as the dMMSB [30, 9]. These models are quadratic in the number of nodes and therefore unable to scale to the realistic networks with the number of edges in the millions. Furthermore, these models have been typically used for visualizing trivial sized networks of 18 nodes up to 1,000 nodes. This is in contrast to our work where we apply DBMM not only for visualizations, but for a variety of analysis tasks using large dynamic networks.

Moreover, the dMMSB can handle 1,000 nodes in a day [30] (See page 30), while our model handles ≈8,000 nodes in 506.61 seconds (or 8 minutes and 26 seconds) shown in Table 3. We provide performance results for other larger datasets of up to 183,389 nodes and 1,631,824 edges. In all cases, even for these large networks with over a million edges, our model takes less than a day to compute and the performance results show the linearity of our model in the number of edges. For the scalability experiments, we recorded the performance results using a commodity machine Intel Core i7 @2.7Ghz with 8Gb of memory.

In addition, the proposed DBMM model is also trivially parallelizable (e.g., using Hadoop/MapReduce on Amazon EC2/Cloud) as features, roles, and transition models can be learned at each timestep independent of one another.

7. RELATED WORK

There has been an abundance of work in analyzing dynamic networks. However, the majority of this work focuses on dynamic patterns [10, 17, 16, 22, 27], temporal link prediction [8], anomaly detection [1], dynamic communities [18, 28, 11], dynamic ranking [20, 24], and many others [31, 12].

In contrast, we propose a scalable temporal behavioral model that captures the node behaviors over time and consequently learns a predictive model for how these behaviors evolve over time. Perhaps the most related work is that of [9] where they develop the dMMSB model to identify roles in the graph and how these memberships change over time. However, this type of mixed-membership model assumes a specific parametric form, which is not scalable (1,000 nodes takes a day to model), and where the groups are defined through linkage to specific nodes (in particular types of groups) rather than more general node behavior or structural properties [30]. This is in contrast to our proposed model, which is based on our intuitive behavioral representation and can be interpreted quantitatively. In addition, our model is not tied to any single notion of behavior and thus is flexible in the roles discovered and generalizable. Moreover, not only do we evaluate our model on detecting unusual behavior, identifying explainable patterns and trends, and for clustering nodes with respect to their transition patterns, but we apply our model on large real-world networks to demonstrate its scalability. To the best of our knowledge, our proposed model is the first scalable dynamic mixed-membership model capable of identifying explainable patterns and trends on large networks.

8. CONCLUSIONS

We proposed a dynamic behavioral mixed-membership model for large networks and used it for identifying interesting and explainable patterns and trends. Moreover, we demonstrated its scalability on a variety of real-world temporal networks and provided striking performance results. The experiments have shown the scalability, flexibility, and effectiveness of our model for identifying interesting patterns, detecting unusual structural transitions, and predicting the future structural changes of the network and individual nodes.

Acknowledgments

This work was performed under the auspices of the U.S. Department of Energy by Lawrence Livermore National Laboratory under Contract DE-AC52-07NA27344. This research was also supported by ARO and NSF under contract numbers W911NF-08-1-0238, IIS-1017898, IIS-0916686. The views and conclusions contained herein are those of the authors and should not be interpreted as necessarily representing the official policies or endorsements either expressed or implied, of ARO, NSF or the U.S. Government.

9. REFERENCES

[1] J. Abello, T. Eliassi-Rad, and N. Devanur. Detecting novel discrepancies in communication networks. In *ICDM*, 2010.

[2] S. Asur, S. Parthasarathy, and D. Ucar. An event-based framework for characterizing the evolutionary behavior of interaction graphs. In *SIGKDD*, 2007.

[3] L. Backstrom, D. Huttenlocher, J. Kleinberg, and X. Lan. Group formation in large social networks: membership, growth, and evolution. In *KDD*, 2006.

[4] M. Cha, A. Mislove, and K. P. Gummadi. A Measurement-driven Analysis of Information Propagation in the Flickr Social Network. In *WWW*, 2009.

[5] D. Chakrabarti, R. Kumar, and A. Tomkins. Evolutionary clustering. In *KDD*, 2006.

[6] A. Dhamdhere and C. Dovrolis. Ten years in the evolution of the internet ecosystem. In *SIGCOMM*, 2008.

[7] A. Dhamdhere and C. Dovrolis. The internet is flat: modeling the transition from a transit hierarchy to a peering mesh. In *In CoNEXT*, page 21, 2010.

[8] D. Dunlavy, T. Kolda, and E. Acar. Temporal link prediction using matrix and tensor factorizations. *TKDD*, 5(2):10, 2011.

[9] W. Fu, L. Song, and E. Xing. Dynamic mixed membership blockmodel for evolving networks. In *ICML*, pages 329–336. ACM, 2009.

[10] M. Gotz, J. Leskovec, M. McGlohon, and C. Faloutsos. Modeling blog dynamics. In *ICWSM*, 2009.

[11] D. Greene, D. Doyle, and P. Cunningham. Tracking the evolution of communities in dynamic social networks. In *ASONAM*, 2010.

[12] H. Habiba, Y. Yu, T. Berger-Wolf, and J. Saia. Finding spread blockers in dynamic networks. In *ASONAM*, 2008.

[13] D. Hand and R. Till. A simple generalisation of the area under the roc curve for multiple class classification problems. *Machine Learning*, 45(2):171–186, 2001.

[14] K. Henderson, B. Gallagher, L. Li, L. Akoglu, T. Eliassi-Rad, H. Tong, and C. Faloutsos. It's Who You Know: Graph Mining Using Recursive Structural Features. In *SIGKDD*, pages 1–10, 2011.

[15] K. Henderson, B. Gallagher, L. Li, L. Akoglu, T. Eliassi-Rad, H. Tong, and C. Faloutsos. RolX: Role Extraction and Mining in Large Networks. In *KDD*, 2012.

[16] J. Leskovec, L. Adamic, and B. Huberman. The dynamics of viral marketing. *TWEB*, 1(1):1–39, 2007.

[17] J. Leskovec, J. Kleinberg, and C. Faloutsos. Graphs over time: densification laws, shrinking diameters and possible explanations. In *KDD*, 2005.

[18] Y. Lin, Y. Chi, S. Zhu, H. Sundaram, and B. Tseng. Analyzing communities and their evolutions in dynamic social networks. *TKDD*, 3(2):8, 2009.

[19] P. Mahadevan, D. Krioukov, M. Fomenkov, X. Dimitropoulos, et al. The Internet AS-level topology: three data sources and one definitive metric. *ACM SIGCOMM CCR*, 36(1):17–26, 2006.

[20] J. O'Madadhain, J. Hutchins, and P. Smyth. Prediction and ranking algorithms for event-based network data. *SIGKDD Explorations*, 7(2):30, 2005.

[21] R. Pan and J. Saramaki. Path lengths, correlations, and centrality in temporal networks. *arXiv:1101.5913*, 2011.

[22] S. Papadimitriou, J. Sun, and C. Faloutsos. Streaming pattern discovery in multiple time-series. In *VLDB*, 2005.

[23] R. Rossi, B. Gallagher, J. Neville, and K. Henderson. Modeling temporal behavior in large networks: A dynamic mixed-membership model. In *LLNL-TR-514271*, 2011.

[24] R. Rossi and D. Gleich. Dynamic pagerank using evolving teleportation. In *WAW*, pages 126–137. LNCS 7323, 2012.

[25] R. Rossi, L. McDowell, D. Aha, and J. Neville. Transforming graph data for statistical relational learning. *Journal of Artificial Intelligence (JAIR)*, 2012.

[26] R. Rossi and J. Neville. Time-evolving relational classification and ensemble methods. In *PAKDD*, 2012.

[27] J. Sun, C. Faloutsos, S. Papadimitriou, and P. Yu. Graphscope: parameter-free mining of large time-evolving graphs. In *KDD*, 2007.

[28] L. Tang, H. Liu, J. Zhang, and Z. Nazeri. Community evolution in dynamic multi-mode networks. In *SIGKDD*, pages 677–685. ACM, 2008.

[29] X. Wang, X. Liu, and D. Loguinov. Modeling the Evolution of Degree Correlation in Scale-Free Topology Generators. In *INFOCOM*, 2007.

[30] E. Xing, W. Fu, and L. Song. A state-space mixed membership blockmodel for dynamic network tomography. *Ann. Appl. Stat.*, 4(2):535–566, 2010.

[31] J. Yang and J. Leskovec. Patterns of temporal variation in online media. In *WSDM*, 2011.

On the Streaming Complexity of Computing Local Clustering Coefficients*

Konstantin Kutzkov
IT University of Copenhagen
Copenhagen, Denmark
konk@itu.dk

Rasmus Pagh
IT University of Copenhagen
Copenhagen, Denmark
pagh@itu.dk

ABSTRACT

Due to a large number of applications, the problem of estimating the number of triangles in graphs revealed as a stream of edges, and the closely related problem of estimating the graph's clustering coefficient, have received considerable attention in the last decade. Both efficient algorithms and impossibility results have shed light on the computational complexity of the problem. Motivated by applications in Web mining, Becchetti et al. presented new algorithms for the estimation of the *local* number of triangles, i.e., the number of triangles incident to *individual* vertices. The algorithms are shown, both theoretically and experimentally, to efficiently handle the problem. However, at least two passes over the data are needed and thus the algorithms are not suitable for real streaming scenarios.

In the present work, we consider the problem of estimating the clustering coefficient of individual vertices in a graph over n vertices revealed as a stream of m edges. As a first result we show that any one pass randomized streaming algorithm that can distinguish a graph with no triangles from a graph having a vertex of degree d with clustering coefficient $> 1/2$ must use $\Omega(m/d)$ bits of space in expectation.

Our second result is a new randomized one pass algorithm estimating the local clustering coefficient of each vertex with degree at least d. The space requirement of our algorithm is within a logarithmic factor of the lower bound, thus our approach is close to optimal. We also extend the algorithm to local triangle counting and report experimental results on its performance on real-life graphs.

Categories and Subject Descriptors

F.2.2 [**Analysis of Algorithms and Problem Complexity**]: Nonnumerical Algorithms and Problems

*Work supported by the Danish National Research Council under the Sapere Aude program.

Keywords

Graph algorithms, Streaming, Local clustering coefficient, Triangle counting

1. INTRODUCTION

The last decades have witnessed a rapid growth of available data. Many of the best known algorithms assume random access to the input, and this turns out to be an infeasible requirement for many real-life problems. This motivates the *(semi-) streaming* model of computation where only one or a small number of sequential scans of the input are allowed. The model has become a ubiquitous computational paradigm and considerable progress has been made towards a better understanding of the complexity of many basic algorithmic problems.

Graphs are a ubiquitous representation of relationships between objects in real-life problems. Many applications require knowledge of certain structural properties of a given graph which will allow a better analysis of the original problem. The clustering coefficient of a graph, introduced in [32], gives the probability that two of the neighbors of a vertex chosen at random are connected by an edge. It provides important information about the structure of the graph and the existence of local communities. The computation of the clustering coefficient of a graph, and the closely related problem of computing the total number of triangles in a graph revealed as a stream of edges, have received considerable attention. Becchetti et al. [6] showed that for certain applications in Web mining the computation of the clustering coefficient of individual vertices is required, and presented a semi-streaming algorithm for the problem. In this paper we study whether the problem admits an efficient solution in a real streaming scenario when only one pass over the input graph is allowed.

2. PRELIMINARIES

Notation.

Let $G = (V, E)$ be a simple undirected graph without loops. We denote the number of vertices V by n and the number of edges E by m. An edge between the vertices u and v is written as (u, v). We assume a total order on vertices in V and since our graph is undirected and loopless we will consider only edges (u, v) with $u < v$. $N_G(v) = \{u \in V : (u, v) \in E\}$ is the *neighborhood* of v. The *degree* of a vertex v is $d_v = |N_G(v)|$, i.e., the number of edges adjacent to v. An r-*clique* K_r in G is a subgraph of G on r vertices such that for any vertex pair u, v in K_r there exists an edge $(u, v) \in E$. A *triangle* is a 3-clique. $T_v = \frac{1}{2}|\{(u, w) \in E : (u, v) \in E, (v, w) \in E\}|$ is the number of triangles containing v. A *2-path centered at* v is a triple of vertices (u, v, w) such that there exist edges $(u, v), (v, w)$ and u and w are called the *endpoints* of the 2-path (u, v, w). A triangle on the vertices u, v, w is denoted by $\langle u, v, w\rangle$. The *clustering coefficient* of a vertex v of degree at least two, denoted as C_v, is defined as the ratio of triangles containing v to the number of 2-paths centered at v. More formally, we define

$$C_v = \frac{2T_v}{d_v(d_v - 1)}$$

The *global* clustering coefficient of G is

$$G_G = \frac{1}{n} \sum_{v \in V : d(v) \geq 2} C_v.$$

Note that we define the local clustering coefficient only for vertices of degree at least two. In the literature the clustering coefficient of vertices of degree less than two traditionally has been set to either 0 or 1, or declared to be meaningless. As discussed in several works, see e.g. [18, 26], the different definitions have resulted in different results. Therefore, in order to avoid confusions, we consider only graphs with vertices of degree at least two. This is also justified by the real-life graphs we consider in our experiments, since they do not contain vertices of degree less than two.

Probability theory.

We assume that the reader is familiar with basic definitions from probability theory. In the analysis of our algorithms we will use these inequalities:

- *Markov's inequality* Let X be a random variable. Then for every $\lambda > 1$:

$$\Pr[X \geq \lambda E[X]] \leq \frac{1}{\lambda} \tag{1}$$

- *Chebyshev's inequality.* Let X be a random variable and $s > 0$. Then

$$\Pr[|X - E[X]| \geq s] \leq \frac{V[X]}{s^2} \tag{2}$$

- *Chernoff's inequality.* We will use the following form of the inequality:

  Let $X_1, \ldots, X_\ell$ be ℓ independent identically distributed Bernoulli random variables and $E[X_i] = \mu$. Then for any $\varepsilon > 0$ we have

$$\Pr[|\frac{1}{\ell}\sum_{i=1}^{\ell} X_i - \mu| > \varepsilon\mu] \leq 2e^{-\varepsilon^2\mu\ell/2} \tag{3}$$

A family $\mathcal{F}$ of functions from V to a finite set S is *k-wise independent* if for a function $f : V \to S$ chosen uniformly at random from $\mathcal{F}$ it holds

$$\Pr[f(v_1) = c_1 \wedge f(v_2) = c_2 \wedge \cdots \wedge f(v_k) = c_k] = \frac{1}{s^k}$$

for $s = |S|$, distinct $v_i \in V$ and any $c_i \in S$ and $k \in \mathbb{N}$.

A family $\mathcal{H}$ of functions from V to a finite totally ordered set S is called *(ε, k)-min-wise independent* if for any $X \subseteq V$ and $Y \subseteq X$, $|Y| = k$, for a function h chosen uniformly at random from $\mathcal{H}$ it holds

$$\Pr[\max_{y \in Y} h(y) < \min_{z \in X \setminus Y} h(z)] = (1 \pm \varepsilon)\frac{1}{\binom{|X|}{k}}$$

We will refer to a function chosen uniformly at random from a k-wise independent family as a k-wise independent function.

We will say that an algorithm returns an *(ε, δ)-approximation* of some quantity q, if it returns a value $\tilde{q}$, such that $(1 - \varepsilon)q \leq \tilde{q} \leq (1 + \varepsilon)q$, with probability at least $1 - \delta$ for any $0 < \varepsilon, \delta < 1$.

The streaming model.

We assume that the input graph is read as a stream of edges. In the literature, two models have been considered. In the *incidence list* stream model for each vertex $u \in V$ the edges $(u, v_1), \ldots, (u, v_{d_u})$, i.e., all edges adjacent to u, are revealed in succession. In an *adjacency stream* model edges arrive in arbitrary order. Clearly, the incidence list model provides more information and algorithms analyzed in this model are usually better than algorithms assuming the adjacency stream model. Our results apply to the adjacency stream model.

3. PREVIOUS WORK

Counting the number of triangles in a graph and computing its clustering coefficient are widely studied problems, with applications ranging from computational biology to mining social networks. It is known that unlike random Erdös-Rényi graphs [14], real-life graphs are characterized by high clustering coefficients, see for instance [2], and the clustering coefficient is an important metric for mining knowledge about the original data. For example, Coleman [11] and Portes [25] use the clustering coefficient when analyzing human behaviour in social networks, and Becchetti et al. [6] used it for the detection of spamming activity in large-scale Web graphs. The best known exact algorithm [3] uses as a subroutine matrix multiplication and runs in time $O(n^\omega)$, where $\omega = 2.3727$ is the best known exponent for rectangular matrix multiplication [30]. The algorithm also counts exactly the number of triangles per vertex. Note however that this algorithm is mainly of theoretical importance since it requires random access to the graph, and thus the graph has to fit in memory. Also, currently known asymptotically fast matrix multiplication algorithms do not admit an efficient implementation for realistic input sizes.

Several authors presented sampling based algorithms for the estimation of the *global* number of triangles in a (semi)-streaming setting [5, 9, 12, 16, 21, 24, 28, 29]. Building upon results from linear algebra, researchers proposed techniques for approximate triangle counting not relying on sampling [4, 27]. The closely related problem of estimating the global clustering coefficient was considered in [10, 26]. The algorithm by Schank and Wagner [26] is based on sampling and requires two passes over the input graph. The algorithm was improved to work in a single pass by Buriol et al. [10] at the price of a slightly increased time and space complexity. Motivated by the problem of detection of emerging web communities by analyzing the Web graph [22], Buriol et al. [10] studied the problem of counting bipartite cliques of small size. The more general problem of estimating the number of graph minors of fixed size was studied by Bordino et al [7].

Despite of the fact that researchers have considered applications involving counting the number of triangles per vertex [13, 23], only recently the problem of estimating the *local* number of triangles was rigorously studied by Becchetti et al. [6]. The authors propose two algorithms working in a *semi-streaming* fashion such that the input graph is stored on an external device and a few sequential scans over it are allowed. The algorithms are based on min-wise permutation hashing [8]. Both algorithms use $O(n)$ main memory. However, the first algorithm also requires sequential writing to a persistent storage device and uses $O(m)$ external memory. The second algorithm works only in main memory but one cannot theoretically prove that the algorithm achieves an arbitrarily good approximation of the number of triangles at individual vertices. It is easy to adjust the algorithms to work in two passes but there is no straightforward extension of the approach running in a single pass over the input, thus it is not suitable for real streaming applications.

Our contribution.

Algorithms working in only one pass over the input are important since they can be used in real streaming scenarios and thus have a wider range of applications. We study the complexity of estimating the local clustering coefficient by randomized algorithms in one pass over the input from two perspectives:

1. *Lower bound.* We show that any one pass randomized algorithm detecting with error probability at most $1/3$ if there exists a vertex of degree at least $2d$ with clustering coefficient at least $1/2$ needs $\Omega(m/d)$ bits. This holds even if we guarantee that if there exists any triangle, there exists a vertex with clustering coefficient at least $1/2$.

2. *Upper bound.* We design a randomized one pass algorithm deciding with constant error probability whether a given vertex of degree d or more has a clustering coefficient above a given constant threshold α using $O(\frac{m}{d})$ words. More precisely, we achieve an (ε, δ)-approximation of the clustering coefficient α of all vertices of degree at least d in time $O(\frac{m}{\alpha\varepsilon^2}\log\frac{1}{\varepsilon}\log\frac{n}{\delta})$ and space $O((\frac{m}{d}+\log\frac{1}{\varepsilon})\frac{1}{\alpha\varepsilon^2}\log\frac{n}{\delta})$ for any $\delta, \varepsilon, \alpha > 0$. We extend our algorithm to also estimate the number of triangles per high-degree vertex. At the end we provide an experimental evaluation of the algorithm.

In case d is no larger than the average degree, the space usage is $\Omega(n)$ bits so we are in the semi-streaming domain in terms of space usage. Our algorithm has space usage $o(n)$ whenever the fraction of vertices with degree d or more is sufficiently small. This is the case for many real-life graphs.

Note that the lower bound is given in bits while the upper bound is terms of the number of sampled edges, i.e. machine words of $O(\log n)$ bits each. Thus, for a fixed vertex the lower and upper bound match up to a logarithmic factor.

4. LOWER BOUND

We begin with a negative result that will show the limitations of any randomized one pass algorithm detecting vertices with high clustering coefficient. Lower bounds on the complexity of global triangle counting have been shown in several works [5, 16, 33].

THEOREM 1. *Let $G = (V, E)$ be a simple undirected graph without loops over m edges. Any randomized streaming algorithm, performing only one pass over the edges of G and being able to distinguish between a graph where all vertices of degree $2d = o(\sqrt{m})$ have a clustering coefficient 0, and a graph where there is a vertex of degree $2d$ with clustering coefficient at least $1/2$, with error probability $1/3$, must use $\Omega(m/d)$ bits in expectation.*

PROOF. Let DETECTCLUSTEREDVERTICES be a randomized streaming algorithm detecting vertices with high clustering coefficient in G. Assume without loss of generality that $m/(2d)$ is integer. We show that if DETECTCLUSTEREDVERTICES uses s bits of memory, this would imply a protocol for the SET DISJOINTNESS problem on strings $x, y \in \{0,1\}^{m/(2d)}$ using s bits of communication. This problems has answer 1 if there exists an index i such that $x_i = y_i = 1$, and answer 0 otherwise. By existing lower bounds on the randomized communication complexity of SET DISJOINTNESS [19] this implies that $s = \Omega(m/d)$ bits are needed for any constant error probability smaller than 1.

Denote by x_i the ith bit in the string x. We will reduce the SET DISJOINTNESS problem to detecting vertices with clustering coefficient more than $1/2$ in a graph revealed as a stream of edges in the adjacency stream model. Let $W^x = \{w_1^x, \ldots, w_d^x\}$, $W^y = \{w_1^y, \ldots, w_d^y\}$, $U^x = \{u_1^x, \ldots, u_d^x\}$, $U^y = \{u_1^y, \ldots, u_d^y\}$ be four sets of d vertices each. The reader is referred to Figure 1 for a graphical description of our construction. We read $x \in \{0,1\}^{m/(2d)}$ bit by bit and create a vertex v_i for the ith index in x. If $x_i = 0$, then we feed DETECTCLUSTEREDVERTICES with the d edges (v_i, u_j^x), $1 \le j \le d$. If $x_i = 1$, then we feed DETECTCLUSTEREDVERTICES with the d edges (v_i, w_j^x), $1 \le j \le d$. We proceed with the bits in y in the same way but we create edges (v_i, u_j^y) and (v_i, w_j^y).

After processing x and y we add d^2 edges (w_i^x, w_j^y), $1 \le i, j \le d$, for $w_i^x \in W^x, w_j^y \in W^y$. Now it is easy to see that the graph contains a triangle if and only if there exists an i such that $x_i = y_i = 1$, and in this case the clustering coefficient of v_i is $d^2/\binom{2d}{2} > 1/2$, otherwise all vertices have clustering coefficient 0. Also, each vertex v_i has degree exactly $2d$, the total number of vertices is $m/(2d) + 4d$ and for $d = o(\sqrt{m})$ the number of edges is $m + d^2 = O(m)$. Thus, we have reduced the SET DISJOINTNESS problem for input strings $x, y \in \{0,1\}^{m/(2d)}$ to the problem of distinguishing between vertices of degree d with clustering coefficient 0 or more than $1/2$ in streamed graphs over $O(m)$ edges. We conclude that DETECTCLUSTEREDVERTICES needs $\Omega(m/d)$ bits for graphs over m edges. □

One can extend the above proof such that the vertices v_i can also have odd degree in a trivial way. For a better readability we choose not to present this extension here.

The above lower bound supports the intuition that the space requirements of any randomized one pass algorithm for estimating the clustering coefficient of individual vertices, should not depend only on the value of the coefficient but also on the vertex degree. In order to estimate the clustering coefficient of a given vertex v we need some kind of sampling of 2-paths centered at v for which we can check whether they are a part of a triangle. But to obtain a good estimate of low degree vertices, without any prior knowledge about the degree distributions in the graph, we need a low sampling probability, which in turn results in many sampled edges.

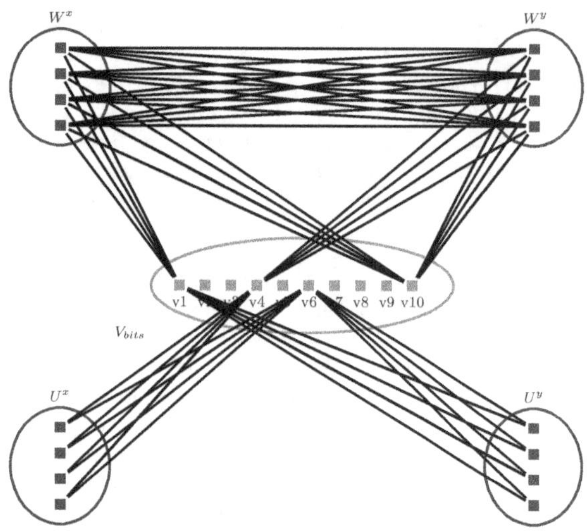

Figure 1: An example of a hard instance for our lower bound construction. The edges going out from v_1 denote that $x_1 = 1$ and $y_1 = 0$. Similarly, we see that $x_4 = 0$ and $y_4 = 1$, while $x_6 = y_6 = 0$ and $x_{10} = y_{10} = 1$. Only v_{10} among the considered vertices is part of a triangle and has a clustering coefficient larger than 1/2.

5. ONE PASS ALGORITHM

In this section we present a randomized one pass algorithm estimating the clustering coefficient of vertices of degree above some threshold d. In Section 5.1 we first give some intuition what are the difficulties for the estimation of the clustering coefficient in only one pass and then describe the main idea behind the new algorithm. A thorough description and theoretical analysis of our algorithm is given is Section 5.2. In Section 5.3 we show how to extend the algorithm to local triangle counting for high-degree vertices. In Section 5.4 we conclude with an experimental evaluation of the performance of the algorithm on real-life graphs.

5.1 Intuition

A straightforward idea for the estimation of the clustering coefficient in only one pass of high degree vertices is to sample independently each incoming edge with a certain probability p. Then in the sparsified graph we compute the clustering coefficient for all vertices. This sparsification approach is essentially the Doulion algorithm [28, 29], which was shown to accurately estimate the number of triangles in a graph given as a stream of edges. Let us consider a vertex v contained in a triangle $\langle u, v, w\rangle$. The probability that we will sample the 2-path (u, v, w) is p^2 while the probability to sample the triangle $\langle u, v, w\rangle$ is p^3. Thus, we have to multiply by $1/p$ the clustering coefficient we have computed for each vertex in the sparsified graph in order to obtain in expectation the true clustering coefficient. But this means that the estimates obtained from the sparsified graph need to be very accurate in order to obtain a concentration around the expected value with high probability, which in turn implies a large value for the sampling probability p resulting in large space consumption.

A simple algorithm can work as follows: for each vertex v we sample independently a number of 2-paths (u, v, w) and for each of them check whether the edge (u, w) exists in the graph. The approach can be implemented in three passes over the edges. In the first pass we find a set of candidate vertices of degree at least d. This can be done by a frequent items mining algorithms, e.g. [20], in space $O(m/d)$ such that each vertex of degree d or more is guaranteed to be among the candidates. In a second pass we determine the set of vertices of degree d or more and the exact degree of each of them. Then for each vertex v of degree d or more we sample a number of 2-paths (u, v, w) and check whether the edge (u, w) appears in the stream, this can be done for example using reservoir sampling [31] as shown in [9]. It is easy to show that the sketched algorithm will compute an (ε, δ)-approximation of a vertex of degree at least d and clustering coefficient α in space $O(\frac{m}{d\varepsilon^2\alpha}\log\frac{1}{\delta})$

In the next section we show how to combine the above two approaches to work for high degree vertices in only one pass over the input graph achieving essentially the same space complexity. We will use the idea of *monochromatic sampling* [24]. Basically, we randomly color the vertices and then take an edge in the sample iff its endpoints have the same color. Clearly, if two of the edges of a triangle are sampled, the third edge must also be sampled. Thus, for a sampled 2-path (u, v, w), after processing the stream of edges we can check whether there exists a triangle $\langle u, v, w\rangle$. The sampling probability for a triangle $\langle u, v, w\rangle$ is the same as for the 2-path (u, v, w), namely p^2.

5.2 The algorithm

A high-level pseudocode description of our algorithm is given in Figure 2. The main method is EstimateClusteringCoefficients. It reads the input graph as a stream of edges in arbitrary order. First we run K independent copies of SparsifyGraph in parallel. Assume we have defined a k-wise independent function $f : V \to [0, 1]$[1], for a k that will be specified later. Let C be a natural number denoting the number of colors. Then we sample each incoming edge (u, v) iff $\lfloor Cf(u)\rfloor = \lfloor Cf(v)\rfloor$, where $\lfloor r\rfloor$ denotes that the real number r is mapped to the biggest integer smaller than (or equal to) r, i.e., we map to one of C colors. At the end we obtain a sparsified graph where all edge endpoints have the same color. Obviously, if $C = d$, we expect sparsified graphs with m/d edges. In order to control the space usage of the algorithm, we check after each edge has been sampled whether not more than t edges are sampled, for a user-defined t. If this is the case, then the algorithm breaks its execution and returns an empty graph.

Clearly, if we have sampled a 2-path (u, v, w), then, if existent, we must have also sampled the edge (u, w). In CheckTwoPaths for each vertex with at least two sampled neighbors we choose the two of these neighbors for which f gives the smallest value and check whether the considered 2-path is part of a triangle. We will show that the expected value is an almost unbiased estimator of the clustering coefficient of vertex v such that the bias depends on how independent is the coloring function. Assume we return $R \le K$ nonempty graphs. At the end, for each vertex v with at least $R/2$ sampled 2-paths (u, v, w) we output as an estimate of the clustering coefficient α_v the ratio of triangles to 2-paths centered at v obtained from the samples.

[1]In fact, f maps V to a discrete set uniformly distributed on the unit interval.

THEOREM 2. *Let $G = (V, E)$ be a graph over n variables revealed as a stream of m edges. Let further $K = \frac{4}{\alpha\varepsilon^2}\log\frac{n}{\delta}$, $C = d/4$ colors, $f_i : V \to [0,1]$, $1 \le i \le K$, be k-wise independent, such that $k = O(\log\frac{1}{\varepsilon})$, and $t = 9m/d$. Then* ESTIMATECLUSTERINGCOEFFICIENTS *returns an (ε, δ)-approximation of the clustering coefficient for all vertices of degree at least d and clustering coefficient at least α for any $\varepsilon, \alpha, \delta > 0$. The expected running time of the algorithm is $O(\frac{m}{\alpha\varepsilon^2}\log\frac{1}{\varepsilon}\log\frac{n}{\delta})$ and the worst case space complexity is $O((\frac{m}{d} + \log\frac{1}{\varepsilon})\frac{1}{\alpha\varepsilon^2}\log\frac{n}{\delta})$.*

PROOF. Let us assume that we run K parallel instances of SPARSIFYGRAPH. In the following we will obtain a bound on K that will guarantee the claimed bounds. We will estimate the probability for each of three "bad" events that lead to an incorrect estimate.

Assume first that for a given vertex v we have sampled $\ell \le K$ 2-paths (u_i, v, w_i), each in one of the copies of the algorithm run in parallel. For a given non-empty sparsified graph G_S^i, $1 \le i \le \ell$, introduce an indicator random variable $X_i, 1 \le i \le \ell$, such that $X_i = 1$ iff $(u_i, w_i) \in G_S^i$, i.e., if u, v, w form a triangle. We first show that for a random enough coloring function f_i, $E[X_i]$ is an almost unbiased estimator of α. Let v's clustering coefficient be α_v and let us define a function $h : N(v) \to [0,1]$ as $h(u) = (f(u) - f(v)) \bmod 1$ for $u \in N(v)$. It is easy to see that the two vertices u, w yielding the smallest values $h(u)$ and $h(w)$ are those yielding the smallest values $f(u)$ and $f(w)$ larger than $f(v)$. Thus, under the assumption that $|N_v(G_S)| \ge 2$, choosing the two neighbors of v in G_S with the smallest values given by f corresponds to choosing the two vertices in $N_v(G)$ with the smallest values given by h. If f is k-wise independent under the assumptions that $f(v)$ evaluates to a certain value, we have that h is $(k-1)$-wise independent. For $k = O(\log\frac{1}{\varepsilon})$, h is then $(\varepsilon, 2)$-min-wise independent, see [15] for the state-of-the-art result. Thus, the chosen pair of vertices is sampled almost uniformly at random among all pairs of v's neighbors and we have $(1-\varepsilon)\alpha_v \le E[X_i] \le (1+\varepsilon)\alpha_v$.

We return $\tilde{\alpha}_v = \frac{1}{\ell}\sum_{i=1}^{\ell} X_i$ as an estimation of α_v. The functions f_i are independent and thus the colorings are also independent. Consequently the indicator random variables X_i are independent, thus by applying Chernoff's inequality and using $\varepsilon < 1$ we bound the probability that $\tilde{\alpha}_v$ is not an $(1 \pm 3\varepsilon)$-approximation is upper bounded by $2^{-\varepsilon^2\alpha_v\ell/2}$. Since $\alpha \le \alpha_v$, we need

$$\ell = \frac{\log 3}{\varepsilon^2\alpha}\log\frac{n}{\delta}$$

such that the error probability for a single vertex is bounded by $\frac{\delta}{3n}$. Thus, the error probability of the estimate for *any* vertex is $\delta/3$.

Second, let us assume that the K parallel instances return R non-empty graphs, i.e., in R cases we have not sampled more than the allowed t edges. We estimate how many independent colorings, each for $C = d/4$ colors, are needed such that we obtain at least $\ell = \frac{\log 3}{\varepsilon^2\alpha}\log\frac{n}{\delta}$ samples for a vertex of degree at least d. Consider a given vertex v with $d_v \ge d$. We have $\frac{d}{4}$ colors and thus a sampling probability of $\frac{4}{d}$. We introduce an indicator random variable $X_1, \ldots, X_{d_v}$ for each neighbor u_i of v, denoting whether $f(v) = f(u_i)$. Let $X = \sum_{i=1}^{d_v} X_i$. We want to bound $\Pr[X \le 1]$. Clearly, we have $E[X] = \frac{4d_v}{d} \ge 4$. The X_i are $\{0, 1\}$-valued, and w.l.o.g. we can assume that f is 3-wise independent, therefore it is easy to see that $V[X] \le E[X]$. Thus, we can set $s = E[X] - 1$ in Chebyshev's inequality and obtain

$$\Pr[|X - E[X]| \ge E[X] - 1] \le \frac{V[X]}{(E[X]-1)^2}$$

$$\le \frac{E[X]}{(E[X]-1)^2} \le \frac{4}{9}$$

for $d_v \ge d$. Now, we introduce an indicator random variable Y_i^v for vertex v of degree at least d, denoting whether enough edges have been sampled in the ith sparsified graph, $1 \le i \le S$. Clearly, $E[Y_i^v] \ge 5/9$. Since the colorings are independent, we can apply again Chernoff's inequality and bound the probability for not enough sampled edges. Therefore, if we have

$$R = 2\frac{\log 3}{\varepsilon^2\alpha}\log\frac{n}{\delta}$$

the probability that in $\ell = \frac{\log 3}{\varepsilon^2\alpha}\log\frac{n}{\delta}$ graphs for any vertex of degree at least d we have less than two sampled neighbors, is upper bounded by $\delta/3$.

Finally, we have to consider the possibility that too many edges have been sampled and the algorithm returns an empty graph. By simply applying Markov's inequality for a sampling probability $\frac{4}{d}$ we get that with probability $4/9$ more than $\frac{9m}{d}$ edges are sampled. We apply again Chernoff's inequality. Running

$$K = 4\frac{\log 3}{\varepsilon^2\alpha}\log\frac{n}{\delta}$$

copies in parallel, we bound the probability that too many edges are sampled in more than $R = 2\frac{\log 3}{\varepsilon^2\alpha}\log\frac{n}{\delta}$ of the copies, to $\delta/3$.

Summing up, the probability that either too many edges are sampled, or not enough neighbors for a vertex of degree d are sampled, or the algorithm does not return an $(1 \pm \varepsilon)$-approximation of the clustering coefficient for vertices of degree at least d, is $3(\delta/3) = \delta$ for $0 < \delta < 1$.

A $O(\log\frac{1}{\varepsilon})$-wise independent function can be defined in $O(\log\frac{1}{\varepsilon})$ machine words and evaluated in time $O(\log\frac{1}{\varepsilon})$. Note that for a approximation parameter ε that can be described in constant number of machine words, $\log\frac{1}{\varepsilon}$ is constant. Storing the adjacency lists of the vertices in the sparsified graphs in hashtables, we can achieve expected constant update time per incoming edge. The sampling of 2-paths and checking whether they are contained in a triangle can thus be done in expected linear time in the size of the sparsified graph. The size of the hash table H is clearly bounded by the number of sampled edges in the R non-empty graphs and the expected time for update and look-up is constant. The time and space complexity of the algorithm follow then immediately from the above discussion. □

The size of the input graph.

In the above analysis we assume that the number of edges and vertices are known in advance. If this is not the case, one can start with a conservative choice for the number of colors and, if too many edges have been sampled, scale the sampling probability, i.e., increase the number of colors. When presenting the implementation of our algorithm we discuss more details about this, but we omit the rigorous description of this extension.

SameColor

Input: a k-wise independent function $f : V \to [0,1]$, number of colors C, vertices u and v

```
if ⌊Cf(u)⌋ = ⌊Cf(v)⌋ then
    return true
else
    return false
```

SparsifyGraph

Input: stream of edges E, number of colors C, k-wise independent function $f : V \to [0,1]$, threshold t

```
G_S = ∅
for each edge (u, v) ∈ E do
    if SameColor(f, C, u, v) then
        G_S = G_S ∪ (u, v).
        if |G_S| > t then
            return the empty graph.
Return G_S.
```

CheckTwoPaths

Input: a sparsified graph G_S

```
for each vertex v ∈ G_S such that |N_{G_S}(v)| ≥ 2 do
    choose the two neighbors u, w, u < w, from N_{G_S}(v)
    with the smallest f(u) and f(w)
    sampled(v) = true
    if (u, w) ∈ G_S then
        X_△(v) = 1 //there is a triangle
    else
        X_△(v) = 0 //no triangle
Return a set of pairs (v, X_△(v)) such that v ∈ V and
sampled(v)
```

EstimateClusteringCoefficients

Input: a stream of edges E, a family of K k-wise functions $f_i : V \to [0,1]$, number of colors C, Hashtable $H\langle V, \langle \text{Int}, \text{Int}\rangle\rangle$, int K, threshold t

```
Run in parallel K copies of SparsifyGraph(E, C, f_i, t)
for each of R returned non-empty sparsified graph G_S^i
do
    V_P = CheckTwoPaths(G_S^i)
    for each (v, X_△(v)) ∈ V_P do
        if v ∉ H then
            p_v = t_v = 0
        else
            get (v, (p_v, t_v)) from H
        p_v++
        if X_△(v) == 1 then
            t_v++
        put (v, (p_v, t_v)) in H
for each (v, (p_v, t_v)) ∈ H with p_v ≥ R/2 do
    Return (v, t_v/p_v).
```

Figure 2: A high-level pseudocode description of the algorithm.

5.3 Local triangle counting

It is easy to extend the algorithm to count the local number of triangles for vertices of sufficiently high degree. All we need is to also estimate the number of 2-paths per high-degree vertex. Indeed, we already have the necessary components for the analysis. In the following theorem we show how to estimate the degree of a vertex for which we have sampled at least $R/2$ times at least two neighbors and that for high degree vertices we can obtain a high quality estimate of the degree. We will use the same notation as in the proof of Theorem 2.

Theorem 3. *Let $G = (V, E)$ be a graph over n variables revealed as a stream of m edges. There exists a randomized one pass algorithm achieving an (ε, δ)-approximation of the number of triangles centered at each vertex of degree at least d and a clustering coefficient at least α in expected time $O(\frac{m}{\alpha\varepsilon^2}\log\frac{1}{\varepsilon}\log\frac{n}{\delta})$ and worst case space complexity $O((\frac{m}{d}+\log\frac{1}{\varepsilon})\frac{1}{\alpha\varepsilon^2}\log\frac{n}{\delta})$ for any $\varepsilon, \alpha, \delta > 0$.*

Proof. Consider a vertex v of degree $d_v \geq d$. We first show how to obtain an approximation of d_v. Assume we extend EstimateClusteringCoefficients in the following way. For each vertex with at least one sampled neighbor we record the number of sampled neighbors in each sparsified graph.

Assume we return $S = \frac{3}{\varepsilon'^2}\log\frac{n}{\delta}$ non-empty sparsified graphs for some $\varepsilon' > 0$ that will be specified later. Let us logically divide them into $\log\frac{n}{\delta}$ groups of $\frac{3}{\varepsilon'^2}$ graphs. In each group for each sparsified graph we introduce an indicator random variable X_i, $1 \leq i \leq d_v$, for each of the d_v neighbors of v. Let $X = \sum_{i=1}^{\frac{3d_v}{\varepsilon'^2}} X_i$, i.e., X is the sum of the X_i in all groups. Clearly, $E[X] = \frac{3d_v}{d\varepsilon'^2}$. Also, we can assume that the coloring function is 3-wise independent and the $\frac{3}{\varepsilon'^2}$ colorings are independent, thus we have $V[X] \leq E[X]$. We apply Chebyshev's inequality with $s = \varepsilon' E[X]$:

$$\Pr[|X - E[X]| \geq \varepsilon' E[X]] \leq \frac{V[X]}{\varepsilon'^2 E[X]^2} \leq \frac{1}{\varepsilon'^2 E[X]} = \frac{d}{3d_v} \leq \frac{1}{3}$$

In each of the $\log\frac{n}{\delta}$ groups we then estimate d_v as $\frac{d\varepsilon'^2 X}{3}$, which is with probability at least $2/3$ $(1\pm\varepsilon')$-approximation of d_v. Now we return the median of the estimates, $\tilde{d}_v$, in the $\log\frac{n}{\delta}$ groups. The colorings in the groups are independent and a standard application of Chernoff's inequality yields that the median will not be an $(1\pm\varepsilon')$-approximation of d_v with error probability δ/n. Summing up, the error probability for any vertex is bounded by δ.

An estimate of the number of triangles at v is now $\binom{\tilde{d}_v}{2}\tilde{\alpha}_v$, where $\tilde{\alpha}_v$ is an $(1\pm\varepsilon')$-approximation of the clustering coefficient α_v. With some algebra one can obtain that this yields an $(1\pm 7\varepsilon')$-approximation of the number of triangles at v.

The bounds on the running time and the space complexity of the algorithm easily follow from Theorem 2 and the above discussion. □

For the case of directed graphs the algorithm can be extended to distinguish between the four possible kinds of triangles [6] a high-degree vertex can be involved in. The only difference is that we will count only the kind of triangles we are interested in. We defer the description of the extension to the full version of the paper.

5.4 Experiments

We implemented our algorithm in Java and ran experiments on a Windows machine with an Intel Core i5 with 2.66 GHz clocked processor with 3 MB Cache. The available RAM memory was 4 GB. Due to the relatively small amount of memory, we ran the copies of SPARSIFYGRAPH sequentially, thus we will not report results on the running time. It is clear that this modification does not affect in any way the estimates obtained by our algorithm. For our coloring function we created random numbers $r(v)$, $v \in V$, in the interval $[0, 1)$ by reading for each vertex 64 random bits from the Marsaglia Random Number CDROM[2]. Then for a given number of colors C two vertices u, v have the same color iff $\lfloor C \cdot r(u) \rfloor = \lfloor C \cdot r(v) \rfloor$. When the graph size is not known in advance, one can dynamically adjust the sampling probability as follows. Once we have that too many edges have been sampled, we double the number of colors, $C = 2C$, and throw away edges that are not any more monochromatic.

We performed experiments on several graphs and chose to present results for two representative graphs, which we think illustrate best the advantages and limitations of the algorithm. Also, we present only experiments on the estimation of the local clustering coefficient, since the estimates on the local number of triangles yield identical observations.

The first graph, Web-BerkStan, is taken from the SNAP library [3]. It is a directed Web graph in which an edge (u, v) shows that there is a link from a page u in the domain berkeley.edu to a page v in the domain stanford.edu. We made the graph undirected such that there is an edge (u, v) for pages u and v connected by a link in either direction and removed loops. The resulting graph consists of 680,485 vertices and 15,190,579 edges.

Following [10] we created a graph MovieActors1000 from the Internet Movie Database[4]. From a set of 1,000 movies, with at least 10 actors starring, we created an undirected graph such that an edge (u, v) records that the actors u in v star together in at least one movie. The resulting graph has 19,037 vertices and 6,501,181 edges.

Clearly, the first graph Web-BerkStan is very sparse, average degree of 22.323, while MovieAvtors1000 is a relatively dense graph with an average degree of 341.502. Also, the degree distribution in Web-BerkStan is quite skewed, the largest degree being 84,290 while the largest degree in MovieActors1000 is only 2,542.

The number of edges in the two graphs is of the same order, thus we compared the results for a fixed sparsification rate of 0.001 and a varying number of parallel copies of SPARSIFYGRAPH. For the two graphs we computed exactly the clustering coefficient for vertices of degree at least 1,000. Note that we chose a smaller sampling probability than the one given by Theorem 2 such that estimates for vertices of degree at least 1,000 will be reported with high probability. The reason is that allows a clearer overview of (dis)advantages of the algorithm for the two considered graphs. In Web-BerkStan there are 568 vertices of degree at least 1,000, while in MovieActors1000 there are 1,161 such vertices. The average clustering coefficient for the considered high-degree vertices for Web-BerkStan is 0.030141, while for MovieActors1000 it is 0.466.

[2]http://www.stat.fsu.edu/pub/diehard/cdrom/

[3]http://snap.stanford.edu/data/

[4]http://www.imdb.com/

Let H be the set of vertices of degree at least 1,000 for which estimates were reported and let $h = |H|$. Let further C_v be the exact clustering coefficients for vertices $v \in H$ and $\tilde{C}_v$ be the corresponding approximation we obtain. Following [6] we evaluated our algorithm with respect to the following measures:

1. Average relative error.

$$\sum_{v \in H} \frac{|C_v - \tilde{C}_v|}{C_v}$$

2. Pearson correlation coefficient.

$$r = \frac{h \sum_{v \in H} C_v \tilde{C}_v - \sum_{v \in H} C_v \sum_{v \in H} \tilde{C}_v}{\sqrt{(h \sum_{v \in H} C_v^2 - (\sum_{v \in H} C_v)^2)(h \sum_{v \in H} \tilde{C}_v^2 - (\sum_{v \in H} \tilde{C}_v)^2)}}$$

3. Spearman's rank correlation.

   Let *Exact* and *Approx* be two sets containing the exact and approximated clustering coefficients. Sorting *Exact* and *Approx* in decreasing order, for each vertex $v \in H$ we define $\text{dist}(v) = r_{Exact}(C_v) - r_{Approx}(\tilde{C}_v)$, where $r_S(x)$ is the rank of the element $x \in S$ in the sorted sequence S. Then the Spearman's rank correlation is defined as $\rho = 1 - \frac{6 \sum_{v \in H} \text{dist}(v)^2}{h(h^2-1)}$

For a number of parallel copies of the algorithm, varying between 50 and 400, we evaluated the quality of the achieved estimates. Note that this means that the sparsification factor is between 5% and 40%. We report estimates on the clustering coefficient of vertices $v \in V$ for which in at least half of the copies a 2-path centered at v was recorded.

Our first observation is that the larger skew in degree distributions in Web-BerkStan results in a higher recall in reported results for vertices of degree 1,000 or more. For Web-BerkStan for all number of parallel copies estimates for more than 80% of the high degree vertices were reported while for MovieActors1000 the recall never exceeded 50%.

Not surprisingly, the larger the number of samples the better approximation is achieved. Figures 3 and 4 show the achieved approximation of clustering coefficient of reported high-degree vertices for the two graphs for a sparsification ratio of 20%. The approximation is tighter for the MovieActors1000 graph while for Web-BerkStan it is more dispersed but this is due to the larger clustering coefficients in the former graph. This is also confirmed by the plot in Figure 5 where we see that the average relative error is much smaller for MovieActors1000. However, the correlation of the estimates of the clustering coefficient for high degree vertices and its true value is comparable for the two graphs as can be seen in Figures 6 and 7.

The above evaluation, as well as other experiments we performed but not report here, lead to the following observations:

- For graphs with a very skewed degree distribution we can report good estimates only for a fraction of the vertices if we want to achieve notable space savings. This is in accordance with the result in Theorem 1 and we believe that this is the best one can hope for. On the other hand the high degree vertices are correctly identified.

- For graphs with a lighter skew in the degree distribution however, our algorithm is able to yield good results for a reasonably big proportion of the vertices. A drawback is that it becomes more difficult to detect all high degree vertices.
- Even in cases when the estimates do not approximate very good the exact values, as in Web-BerkStan, there is a clear correlation between estimates and exact values.

It is worth noting that we did not perform experiments on the large Web-scale graphs considered in [6]. For the full version of the paper we are planning to present a more thorough experimental evaluation on datasets from different domains.

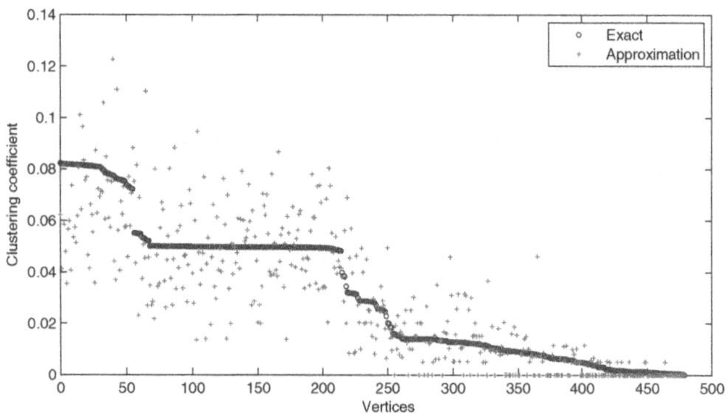

Figure 3: Exact and approximated clustering coefficients of high degree vertices for Web-BerkStan.

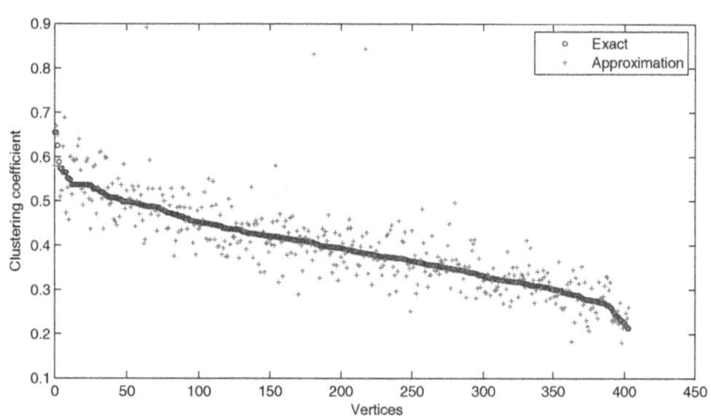

Figure 4: Exact and approximated clustering coefficients of high degree vertices for MovieActors1000.

6. FUTURE DIRECTIONS

We have presented results on the streaming complexity of randomized algorithms estimating the local clustering coefficient. The upper and lower bound on the space usage almost match. We believe that our algorithm is almost optimal in terms of space requirements and an open question is to obtain a tight bound on the space complexity of the problem. Also, it would be interesting whether a similar lower bound is possible for the incidence list stream model.

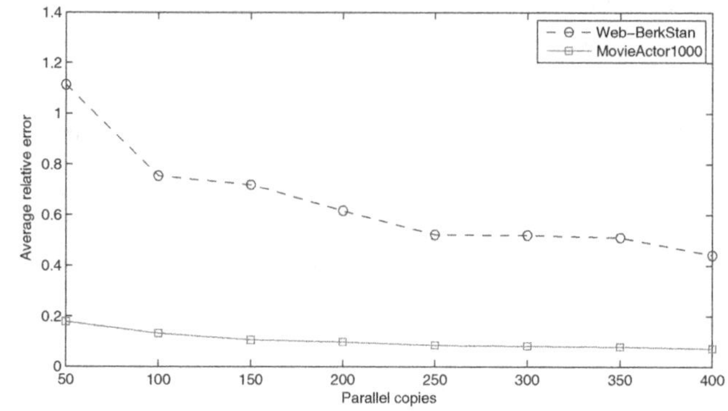

Figure 5: Average relative error for a varying number of parallel copies for the two graphs.

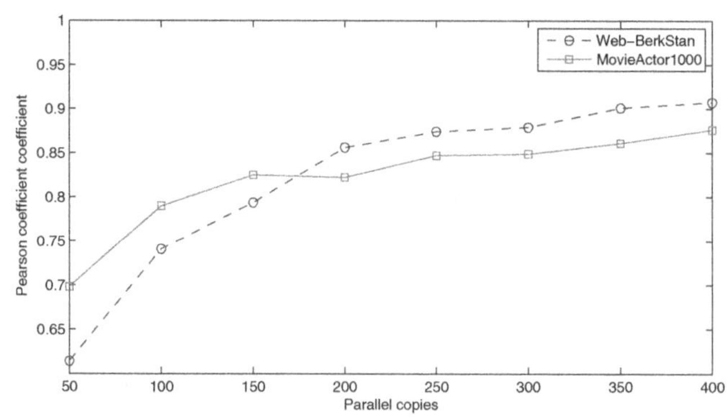

Figure 6: Pearson correlation coefficient for a varying number of parallel copies for the two graphs.

We expect that certain heuristics can improve the running time performance of our algorithm. For example, for many vertices we sample more than two neighbors and we can check for more 2-paths whether they are involved in a triangle. However, one should not consider 2-paths sharing an edge since this will increase the variance of the estimates and the bounds in Theorem 2 will not hold any more.

Also, the advantages of monochromatic sampling compared to naïve sampling of edges become more pronounced if one wants to count the number of k-cliques or more generally dense subgraphs of fixed size, both locally and globally, for $k > 3$. For example, inspired by concrete applications in Web mining, Bordino et al. [7] present an extension of the approach by Buriol et al. [9] to counting graph minors of fixed size. Many of the graph minors are dense, thus it is interesting to study whether using monochromatic sampling one can design better algorithms.

An interesting direction is to study whether one can combine our approach with ideas from L_p sampling in order to obtain an algorithm for the more general problem of processing dynamic graph streams, where edge deletions are also allowed, see e.g. [1, 17].

Acknowledgements.

We thank Paolo Boldi for useful discussions in the early stage of this work.

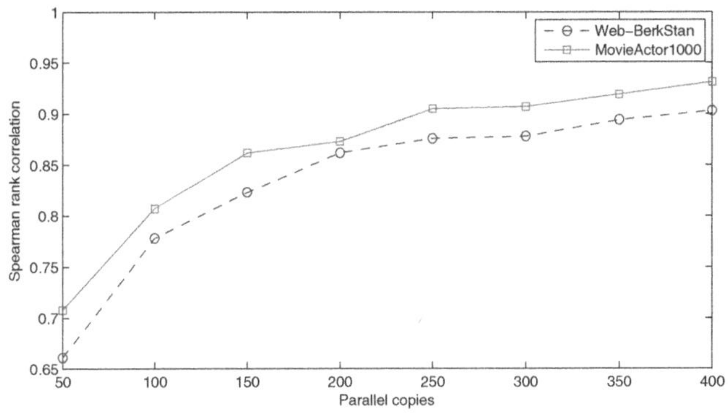

Figure 7: Spearman rank correlation for a varying number of parallel copies for the two graphs.

7. REFERENCES

[1] K. J. Ahn, S. Guha, A. McGregor. Graph sketches: sparsification, spanners, and subgraphs. *PODS 2012*: 5–14

[2] R. Albert, A.-L. Barabási. Statistical mechanics of complex networks. *Rev. Mod. Phys. 74*, 47–97 (2002)

[3] N. Alon, R. Yuster, U. Zwick. Finding and Counting Given Length Cycles. *Algorithmica* 17(3): 209–223 (1997)

[4] H. Avron. Counting triangles in large graphs using randomized matrix trace estimation. *Large-Scale Data Mining: Theory and Applications (KDD Workshop)*, 2010.

[5] Z. Bar-Yossef, R. Kumar, D. Sivakumar. Reductions in streaming algorithms, with an application to counting triangles in graphs. *SODA 2002*: 623–632

[6] L. Becchetti, P. Boldi, C. Castillo, A. Gionis. Efficient algorithms for large-scale local triangle counting. *TKDD 4(3)*: (2010)

[7] I. Bordino, D. Donato, A. Gionis, S. Leonardi. Mining Large Networks with Subgraph Counting. *ICDM 2008*: 737–742

[8] A. Z. Broder, M. Charikar, A. M. Frieze, M. Mitzenmacher. Min-Wise Independent Permutations. *STOC 1998*: 327–336

[9] L. S. Buriol, G. Frahling, S. Leonardi, A. Marchetti-Spaccamela, C. Sohler. Counting triangles in data streams. *PODS 2006*: 253–262

[10] L. S. Buriol, G. Frahling, S. Leonardi, C. Sohler. Estimating Clustering Indexes in Data Streams. *ESA 2007*: 618–632

[11] J. S. Coleman. Social capital in the creation of human capital. *American Journal of Sociology, 94*: 95–120, 1988

[12] D. Coppersmith, R. Kumar. An improved data stream algorithm for frequency moments. *SODA 2004*: 151–156

[13] J.-P. Eckmann and E. Moses. Curvature of co-links uncovers hidden thematic layers in the world wide web. *PNAS, 99(9)*:5825–5829, 2002.

[14] P. Erdös, and A. Rényi. On the evolution of random graphs. *Publ. Math. Inst. Hungar. Acad. Sci. 5* 17–61, 1960

[15] G. Feigenblat, E. Porat, A. Shiftan. Exponential time improvement for min-wise based algorithms. *Inf. Comput. 209(4)*: 737–747 (2011)

[16] H. Jowhari, M. Ghodsi. New Streaming Algorithms for Counting Triangles in Graphs. *COCOON 2005*: 710–716

[17] H. Jowhari, M. Saglam, G. Tardos. Tight bounds for L_p samplers, finding duplicates in streams, and related problems. *PODS 2011*: 49–58

[18] M. Kaiser. Mean clustering coefficients: the role of isolated nodes and leafs on clustering measures for small-world networks. *New J. Phys. 10*, 2008.

[19] B. Kalyanasundaram, G. Schnitger. The Probabilistic Communication Complexity of Set Intersection. *SIAM J. Discrete Math. 5(4)*: 545–557 (1992)

[20] R. M. Karp, S. Shenker, C. H. Papadimitriou. A simple algorithm for finding frequent elements in streams and bags. *ACM Trans. Database Syst. 28*: 51–55 (2003)

[21] M. N. Kolountzakis, G. L. Miller, R. Peng, C. E. Tsourakakis. Efficient Triangle Counting in Large Graphs via Degree-based Vertex Partitioning. *Internet Mathematics*, to appear

[22] R. Kumar, P. Raghavan, S. Rajagopalan, A. Tomkins. Trawling the Web for Emerging Cyber-Communities. *Computer Networks* 31(11-16): 1481–1493 (1999)

[23] M. E. J. Newman. The structure and function of complex networks. *SIAM Review*, 45(2):167–256, 2003

[24] R. Pagh, C. E. Tsourakakis. Colorful triangle counting and a MapReduce implementation. *Inf. Process. Lett. 112(7)*: 277–281 (2012)

[25] A. Portes. Social capital: Its origins and applications in modern sociology. *Annual Review of Sociology, 24(1)*:1–24, 1998.

[26] T. Schank, D. Wagner. Approximating Clustering Coefficient and Transitivity. *J. Graph Algorithms Appl. 9(2)*: 265–275 (2005)

[27] C. E. Tsourakakis. Fast Counting of Triangles in Large Real Networks without Counting: Algorithms and Laws. *ICDM 2008*: 608–617

[28] C. E. Tsourakakis, U. Kang, G. L. Miller, C. Faloutsos. DOULION: counting triangles in massive graphs with a coin. *KDD 2009*: 837–846

[29] C. E. Tsourakakis, M. N. Kolountzakis, G. L. Miller. Triangle Sparsifiers. *J. of Graph Algorithms and Appl. 15(6)*: 703–726 (2011)

[30] V. Vassilevska Williams. Multiplying matrices faster than Coppersmith-Winograd. *STOC 2012*, 887–898

[31] J. S. Vitter. Random Sampling with a Reservoir. *ACM Trans. Math. Softw.* 11(1): 37–57 (1985)

[32] D. J. Watts, S. H. Strogatz. Collective dynamics of "small world" networks. *Nature, 393:* 440–442, 1998.

[33] S. Zhang. Streaming Algorithms Measured in Terms of the Computed Quantity. *COCOON 2007*: 338–348

Learning Query and Document Similarities from Click-through Bipartite Graph with Metadata

Wei Wu
Microsoft Research Asia
Beijing, China, 100080
wuwei@microsoft.com

Hang Li*
Microsoft Research Asia
Beijing, China, 100080
hangli.hl@huawei.com

Jun Xu†
Microsoft Research Asia
Beijing, China, 100080
xu.jun@huawei.com

ABSTRACT

We consider learning query and document similarities from a click-through bipartite graph with metadata on the nodes. The metadata contains multiple types of features of queries and documents. We aim to leverage both the click-through bipartite graph and the features to learn query-document, document-document, and query-query similarities. The challenges include how to model and learn the similarity functions based on the graph data.

We propose solving the problems in a principled way. Specifically, we use two different linear mappings to project the queries and documents in two different feature spaces into the same latent space, and take the dot product in the latent space as their similarity. Query-query and document-document similarities can also be naturally defined as dot products in the latent space. We formalize the learning of similarity functions as learning of the mappings that maximize the similarities of the observed query-document pairs on the enriched click-through bipartite graph. When queries and documents have multiple types of features, the similarity function is defined as a linear combination of multiple similarity functions, each based on one type of features. We further solve the learning problem by using a new technique called Multi-view Partial Least Squares (M-PLS). The advantages include the global optimum which can be obtained through Singular Value Decomposition (SVD) and the capability of finding high quality similar queries. We conducted large scale experiments on enterprise search data and web search data. The experimental results on relevance ranking and similar query finding demonstrate that the proposed method works significantly better than the baseline methods.

Categories and Subject Descriptors

H.3.3 [**Information Storage and Retrieval**]: Information Search and Retrieval—*Retrieval models*

*The author's current affiliation is Noah's Ark Lab of Huawei Technologies

†The author's current affiliation is Noah's Ark Lab of Huawei Technologies

Keywords

similarity learning, click-through, multi-view partial least squares

1. INTRODUCTION

Many tasks in Information Retrieval (IR) rely on similarities between pairs of objects. In relevance ranking, given a query, one retrieves the most relevant documents and ranks them based on their degrees of relevance to the query. The relevance between a query and a document can be viewed as a kind of similarity. In query reformulation or rewriting, queries that convey similar search intents but in different forms are created to reformulate the original query, so that the documents better meeting the users' information need can be properly retrieved and ranked. The original query and reformulated queries are in fact similar queries. In query suggestion, queries with related intents are recommended to the user, to help the user to search other useful information. Those queries are also similar queries. In all these tasks, we need to measure similarities between two objects, either query-document or query-query.

Similarity functions are usually defined based on the features of queries and documents. The relevance models in IR, including Vector Space Model (VSM) [24], BM25 [20], and Language Models for Information Retrieval (LMIR) [19, 37] can all be viewed as similarity functions between query and document feature vectors [35, 33]. Similarity between a query and a document is calculated as similarity between term frequency vectors or n-gram vectors. Similarly, queries are represented as vectors in a term space or n-gram space, and the dot product or cosine is taken as a similarity function between them [38, 36]. All the methods utilize features to calculate similarity functions and we call them feature based methods.

Recently, mining query and document similarities from a click-through bipartite graph has been proposed (cf., [7, 18]). The click-through bipartite graph, which represents users' implicit judgments on query-query, document-document, and query-document relevance relations, has been proved to be a valuable source for measuring the similarities. For example, queries which share many co-clicked documents may represent similar search intents, and they can be viewed as similar queries [4, 31][1]. These methods only rely on the structure of a bipartite graph. We call them graph based methods.

In this paper, we consider leveraging information from both a click-through bipartite graph and features to measure query and document similarities. In other words, this is about how to combine the feature based methods and graph based methods. As far as we know, this problem was not well studied previously. We formalize the issue as that of learning query and document similarities from a click-through bipartite graph with metadata on the

[1]In this paper query similarity and document similarity are defined from the viewpoint search intents.

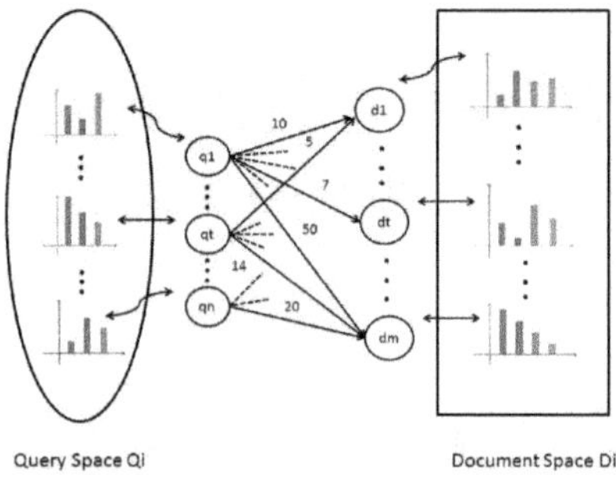

Figure 1: Click-through bipartite graph with metadata on nodes, representing queries and documents in feature spaces and their associations.

nodes representing multiple types of features. The features may come from multiple sources. For example, for queries, the content, the semantic classes, and the user information can be defined as features; for documents, features can be extracted from the URLs, titles, bodies, and anchor texts. Formally, we assume that there is a query-document bipartite graph. The bipartite graph consists of triplets (q,d,t), where q denotes a query, d denotes a document, and t denotes the number of clicks between q and d. Besides, we assume that the queries and documents on the graph have multiple types of features. For each type i ($i \geqslant 1$), queries and documents are represented as vectors in the query space $\mathcal{Q}_i$ and the document space $\mathcal{D}_i$. $\mathcal{Q}_i$ and $\mathcal{D}_i$ are subspaces of the Euclidian spaces $\mathbb{R}^{s_{qi}}$ and $\mathbb{R}^{s_{di}}$, where s_{qi} and s_{di} represent the dimensionalities of the Euclidean spaces. $\mathcal{Q}_i$ and $\mathcal{D}_i$ may or may not be the same space, which means that queries and documents may be either homogeneous or heterogeneous data. Figure 1 illustrates the relationships.

Our goal is to accurately and efficiently learn the similarity functions from the enriched click-through bipartite graph. There are several challenges: 1) how to model the similarity functions based on the complicated graph data, particularly when there are multiple types of features; 2) how to accurately learn the similarity functions; 3) how to efficiently perform the learning task. We propose a method that solves all the problems in a theoretically sound way.

1) Specifically, for each type of features, we use two linear mappings to project the query vectors in the query space and the document vectors in the document space into the same latent space. We take the dot product of the images in the latent space as the similarity function between the query and document vectors. Figure 2 illustrates the method. The dot product in the latent space is also taken as the similarity function between query and query and the similarity function between document and document. The two mappings are supposed to be different, because of the difference between the query space and document space. The final similarity functions are defined as linear combinations of similarity functions from different feature types.

2) We learn the mappings and combination weights using the enriched click-through bipartite graph data. The number of clicks between queries and documents indicates similarities between queries and documents. We formalize the learning method as an optimization problem, in which the objective is to maximize the similarities of the observed query-document pairs on the click-through bipartite graph. We regularize the combination weights with ℓ_2 norm and we make orthogonal assumptions on the mappings. We propose a new machine learning technique called Multi-view Partial Least Squares (M-PLS) to learn the linear mappings. M-PLS extends the Partial Least Squares (PLS) technique to a multi-view learning method (multiple feature types). When there is only one type of features (one view), M-PLS degenerates to the conventional PLS. Moreover, if there is no metadata used, then M-PLS becomes equivalent to Latent Semantic Indexing (LSI) and thus our method can also be regarded as an extension of LSI. We prove that although the optimization problem is not convex, the globally optimal solution of M-PLS can be easily obtained. We also conduct theoretical analysis on the method, and point out that it has two properties that enable the method to capture query-query similarity well (this is also true for document-document similarity), although the learning of it is not explicitly incorporated into the formulation.

3) The learning task can be efficiently performed through Singular Value Decomposition (SVD). First, we employ the power method to build an SVD solver. After that, we solve a simple quadratic program to learn the optimal combination weights. We show that the quadratic program has a closed-form solution.

The learned similarity functions can be applied to relevance ranking and similar query finding. In relevance ranking, the query-document similarity function can be directly used as a model for retrieval and ranking. In addition, it can also be used as a feature of a learning to rank model. In similar query finding, the similar queries found with the query-query similarity function can be utilized in tasks such as query suggestion and query reformulation.

We conducted experiments on large scale enterprise search data and web search data. The results on relevance ranking and similar query finding show that our method significantly outperforms the baseline methods. Specifically, in relevance ranking, we compare our method with the state of the art feature based methods such as BM25, graph based methods such as random walk and their linear combinations. Our method not only significantly outperforms the feature based methods and graph based methods, but also significantly performs better than their linear combinations. In similar query finding, we use examples to demonstrate the capability of our method on finding high quality similar queries. When compared with the baseline methods such as random walk and cosine similarity, our method significantly outperforms the feature based methods and graph based methods, and is comparable with the best linear combination. Particularly, we find our method performs better than the baselines on tail queries, and the results also strongly support the conclusion of our theoretical analysis.

Our contributions in this paper include: 1) proposal of learning query and document similarities from an enriched click-through bipartite graph; 2) proposal of a new learning method called M-PLS to perform the learning task; 3) theoretical proof of the properties of the proposed method and empirical demonstration of the effectiveness of the method.

The rest of the paper is organized as follows: in Section 2, we conduct a survey on related work. Then, we define the similarity learning problem in Section 3. After that, we explain our method based on M-PLS in Section 4. Experimental results are reported in Section 5, and Section 6 concludes the paper and provides some future research directions.

2. RELATED WORK

Partial Least Squares (PLS) [21] refers to a class of algorithms in statistics that aims to model the relations between two or more sets of data by projecting them into a latent space. The underlying idea of PLS algorithms is to model collinearity between different data sets. Since the first work by Wold [32], many variants of PLS have been developed and applied into many tasks such as regression [27], classification [3] and dimension reduction [26]. In practice, PLS has been successfully applied in chemometrics [21], biometrics [6], computer vision [26] and graph mining [23]. In this paper, we extend PLS to M-PLS and employ M-PLS in web search. If

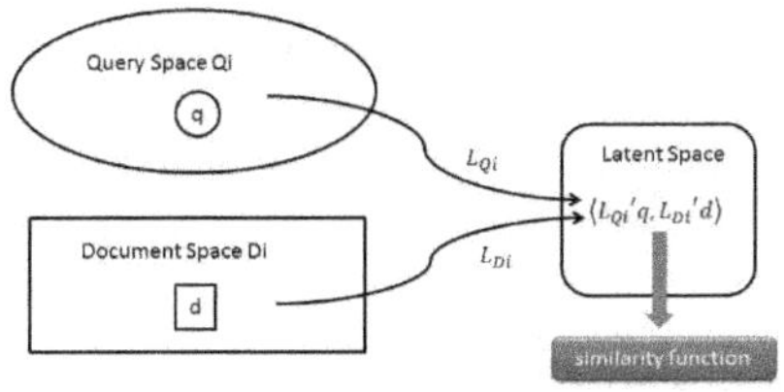

Figure 2: Projecting queries and documents from the query space and document space into a latent space using two linear mappings L_{Q_i} and $L_{\mathcal{D}_i}$. The dot product in the latent space is taken as the similarity function.

there is only one type of features in the query space as well as in the document space, our similarity learning problem degenerates to a problem which can be directly solved by PLS.

Canonical Correlation Analysis (CCA) [13] or its kernelized version KCCA [11, 12] is an alternative method to PLS . Both attempt to learn linear mapping functions to project objects in two spaces into the same latent space. The difference between CCA and PLS is that CCA learns cosine as a similarity function and PLS learns dot product as a similarity function. In our work, we choose PLS instead of CCA, because it is easier to enhance the efficiency of the former. In CCA it is necessary to compute the inverse of large matrices [2], which is computationally expensive.

Measuring query and document similarities is always an important research topic in IR. Existing work on query and document similarities can be divided into two groups: feature based methods and graph based methods. In the former group, Vector Space Model (VSM) [24], BM25 [20], and Language Models for Information Retrieval (LMIR) [19, 37] make use of features, particularly, n-gram features to measure query-document similarities. As pointed out by Xu et al. [35] and others that these models can be viewed as models using the dot product between a query vector and a document vector as the query-document similarity function. Similarly, queries can also be represented as n-grams, and the cosine or dot product can be utilized as the similarity function between them [38, 36]. In [36], queries are represented as n-gram vectors, and a cosine similarity function is learned by using distance metric learning. In [5], the authors propose calculating query similarity with term and n-gram features enriched with a taxonomy of semantic classes. In [2], queries are represented as vectors in a high dimensional space with each dimension corresponding to a document. The click frequency on a document is used as the value of the corresponding dimension. In the latter group, graph based methods exploit the structure of a click-through bipartite graph to learn the query-query, document-document, and query-document similarities. For example, Latent Semantic Indexing (LSI) [9] can be employed, which uses SVD to project queries, documents and terms into a latent space, and calculates query-document, query-query, and document-document similarities through the dot product of their images in the latent space. In [15, 1], the authors propose determining the similarity of a pair of objects based on the similarity of other pairs of objects, and the final similarity measure is iteratively calculated on a bipartite graph. A click-through bipartite graph can also be used in clustering of similar queries [4, 31]. Craswell and Szummer [7] extend the idea and propose adopting a backward random walk process on a click-through bipartite graph to propagate similarity. Our method aims to leverage both features and a click-through bipartite graph to more accurately learn the similarities.

[2] `http://en.wikipedia.org/wiki/Canonical_correlation`

Learning to rank refers to supervised learning techniques for constructing ranking models using training data [16, 17]. The problem of learning to rank is different from that of similarity learning in this paper. We leverage a click-through bipartite graph with metadata to learn similarities between queries and documents, while in learning to rank one constructs a ranking model to predict a ranking list of documents with respect to a query. The similarity learned with our method can be employed as a feature of a learning to rank model, and the similarity learning in this paper can be viewed as feature learning for learning to rank.

Methods for learning similarities between objects by utilizing bipartite graphs built from multiple sources have also been studied. In [8], term relations and document relations are integrated into a document-term bipartite graph. In [29], the authors extend LSI when information from different types of bipartite graphs is available. In [34], the authors use a unified relationship matrix to represent different types of objects and their relations. In [18], matrix factorization is simultaneously conducted on two bipartite graphs, a user-query bipartite graph and a query-document bipartite graph. In [10], similarity scores are first calculated by the LMIR model and then the scores are propagated on a click-through bipartite graph to find similar queries. The method proposed in this paper is different from these existing methods. In our method, we make use of both a click-through bipartite graph and multiple types of features on the nodes. In that sense, we combine feature based methods and graph based methods. In contrast, the existing methods are all graph-based methods and they use either more than one bipartite graph or a graph with more than one type of relations.

The method proposed in this paper is also related to multi-view learning [22] in machine learning. In multi-view learning, instances are assumed to have multiple types of features and the goal is to exploit the different types of features to learn a model. In our work, we assume that queries and documents on a click-through bipartite graph have multiple types of features, which is similar to the assumption in multi-view learning. Our work is unique in that we perform multi-view similarity learning on an enriched click-through bipartite graph. Our method of Multi-view PLS can be regarded as an extension of PLS to multi-view learning.

The similarity learning problem studied in this paper is not limited to search, and it can be potentially extended to other applications such as recommendation system and online advertisement. Recently, Wang et al. [28] propose a method for advertisement in a setting similar to ours. We learn query and document similarities from a bipartite graph with metadata, while they predict possible clicks between users and advertisements on a network with metadata. Note that there is significant difference between our method and their method. First, they only measure similarity between users and advertisements (corresponding to queries and documents), while we also measure query-query and document-document similarities. Second, their method assumes that the latent space is predefined and is independent from the similarity function, while in our method the latent space as well as its similarity function are learned from data.

3. PROBLEM FORMULATION

Let $\mathcal{G} = (\mathcal{V}, \mathcal{E})$ denote a click-through bipartite graph. $\mathcal{V} = Q \bigcup D$ is the set of vertices, which consists of a set of query vertices $Q = \{q_i\}_{i=1}^m$ and a set of document vertices $D = \{d_i\}_{i=1}^n$. $\mathcal{E}$ is the set of edges between query vertices and document vertices. The edge $e_{ij} \in \mathcal{E}$ between query vertex q_i and document vertex d_j is weighted by the click number t_{ij}. We assume that $\mathcal{G}$ is an undirected graph. Besides, we assume that there exists rich metadata on the vertices of the graph. The metadata consists of l types of features ($l \geqslant 1$). The features may stand for the content of queries and documents and the clicks of queries and documents on the bipartite graph [2], as will be seen in Section 5. For each type i ($1 \leqslant i \leqslant l$), query $q \in Q$ and document $d \in D$ are represented as vectors in space Q_i and space $\mathcal{D}_i$, respectively, where Q_i and $\mathcal{D}_i$ are subspaces of the Euclidean spaces $\mathbb{R}^{s_{qi}}$ and $\mathbb{R}^{s_{di}}$. Figure 1 illustrates the relationships.

Our goal is to leverage both the click-through bipartite graph and the features to learn query and document similarities. The similarities may include query-document similarity, query-query similarity, and document-document similarity. In this paper we only study query-document similarity and query-query similarity. The same method can be applied to learning of document-document similarity. Formally, we learn two similarity functions $f(q,d)$ and $g(q,q')$ given $\mathcal{G}$ and $\{(Q_i,\mathcal{D}_i)\}_{i=1}^l$. Similarity function $f(q,d)$ measures the similarity between query $q \in Q$ and document $d \in D$, and similarity function $g(q,q')$ measures the similarity between queries $q, q' \in Q$.

The question is then how to model the similarity functions $f(q,d)$ and $g(q,q')$, and how to accurately and efficiently learn the similarity functions. We propose learning the similarity functions by linearly projecting the queries and documents in the query spaces and document spaces into latent spaces. For each type of feature space $(Q_i,\mathcal{D}_i)$, we learn two linear mappings L_{Q_i} and $L_{\mathcal{D}_i}$. L_{Q_i} is an $s_{qi}\times k_i$ dimensional matrix which can map a query q from Q_i to the k_i dimensional latent space $\mathcal{K}_i$, and $L_{\mathcal{D}_i}$ is an $s_{di}\times k_i$ dimensional matrix which can map a document d from $\mathcal{D}_i$ to the k_i dimensional latent space $\mathcal{K}_i$. We assume that $\forall i,\ k_i \leqslant \min(s_{qi}, s_{di})$. L_{Q_i} and $L_{\mathcal{D}_i}$ are different mapping functions due to the difference between Q_i and $\mathcal{D}_i$. Given $q \in Q$ and $d \in D$, the images in the latent space $\mathcal{K}_i$ are $L_{Q_i}^\top q$ and $L_{\mathcal{D}_i}^\top d$, respectively. We define similarity functions $f_i(q,d)$ and $g_i(q,q')$ as $f_i(q,d) = q^\top L_{Q_i} L_{\mathcal{D}_i}^\top d$, $g_i(q,q') = q^\top L_{Q_i} L_{Q_i}^\top q'$. In other words, we take the dot products of images of queries and documents in the latent spaces as similarity functions. The final similarity functions $f(q,d)$ and $g(q,q')$ are defined as linear combinations of $\{f_i(q,d)\}_{i=1}^l$ and $\{g_i(q,q')\}_{i=1}^l$: $f(q,d) = \sum_{i=1}^l \alpha_i f_i(q,d)$, $g(q,q') = \sum_{i=1}^l \alpha_i g_i(q,q')$, where $\alpha_i \geqslant 0$ is a combination weight.

We learn the mappings $\{(L_{Q_i}, L_{\mathcal{D}_i})\}_{i=1}^l$ and combination weights $\{\alpha_i\}_{i=1}^l$ from the click-through bipartite graph $\mathcal{G}$ and the features $\{(Q_i,\mathcal{D}_i)\}_{i=1}^l$. Specifically, we view the click number of a query-document pair as an indicator of their similarity. We learn $\{(L_{Q_i}, L_{\mathcal{D}_i})\}_{i=1}^l$ and $\{\alpha_i\}_{i=1}^l$ by maximizing the similarities of the observed query-document pairs on the click-through bipartite graph. The underlying assumption is that the higher the click number is, the more similar the query and the document are in the latent spaces.

Finally, we consider the following learning problem:

$$\underset{\{(L_{Q_i},L_{\mathcal{D}_i})\}_{i=1}^l,\{\alpha_i\}_{i=1}^l}{\arg\max} \sum_{e_{uv}\in\mathcal{E}} \sum_{i=1}^l \alpha_i \cdot \left(t_{uv} \cdot q_u^{i\top} L_{Q_i} L_{\mathcal{D}_i}^\top d_v^i\right), \tag{1}$$

where q_u^i and d_v^i represent the feature vectors of query q_u and document d_v in Q_i and $\mathcal{D}_i$, respectively. t_{uv} represents the click number between q_u and d_v on the click-through bipartite graph $\mathcal{G}$.

Note that an alternative method for learning query and document similarities from $\mathcal{G}$ and $\{(Q_i,\mathcal{D}_i)\}_{i=1}^l$ is to concatenate different types of feature vectors of queries as well as different types of feature vectors of documents and learn two mappings for queries and documents with the two concatenated vectors. The method is a special case of the learning method (1). We compare the performances of our proposed method (1) and this alternative method in Section 5.

Objective function (1) may go to infinity, since there are no constraints on the mappings $\{(L_{Q_i}, L_{\mathcal{D}_i})\}_{i=1}^l$ and the weights $\{\alpha_i\}_{i=1}^l$. The features $\{(q_u^i, d_v^i) \mid e_{uv} \in \mathcal{E}, 1 \leqslant i \leqslant l\}$ are also not bounded. We consider adding proper constraints to the mapping functions $\{(L_{Q_i}, L_{\mathcal{D}_i})\}_{i=1}^l$ and the weights $\{\alpha_i\}_{i=1}^l$, as shown in the next section.

4. MULTI-VIEW PARTIAL LEAST SQUARES

We further formalize the learning problem in (1) as a constrained optimization problem. We propose a new learning technique called Multi-view Partial Least Squares (M-PLS) to solve the problem, which is a multi-view learning version of PLS. We prove that the problem has a globally optimal solution. The optimal mappings can be obtained by Singular Value Decomposition (SVD) and the optimal weights can be obtained by quadratic programming. We present the algorithm and its time complexity. We also conduct theoretical analysis to demonstrate that our method has the capability to find high quality similar queries, although query-query similarity is not directly represented in the formulation.

4.1 Constrained Optimization Problem

First, we normalize the feature vectors such that $\forall u,v,i$, $\|q_u^i\| = 1$ and $\|d_v^i\| = 1$. Second, we add orthogonal constraints on the mapping matrices $\{(L_{Q_i}, L_{\mathcal{D}_i})\}_{i=1}^l$. Finally, we introduce ℓ_2 regularization on the weights $\{\alpha_i\}_{i=1}^l$.

The similarity learning method is re-formalized as

$$\underset{\{(L_{Q_i},L_{\mathcal{D}_i})\}_{i=1}^l,\{\alpha_i\}_{i=1}^l}{\arg\max} \sum_{e_{uv}\in\mathcal{E}} \sum_{i=1}^l \alpha_i \cdot \left(t_{uv} \cdot q_u^{i\top} L_{Q_i} L_{\mathcal{D}_i}^\top d_v^i\right) \tag{2}$$

$$\text{subject to} \quad L_{Q_i}^\top L_{Q_i} = I_{k_i\times k_i},\ L_{\mathcal{D}_i}^\top L_{\mathcal{D}_i} = I_{k_i\times k_i},\ \alpha_i \geqslant 0,\ \sum_{i=1}^l \alpha_i^2 \leqslant 1,$$

where $k_i \leqslant \min(s_{qi}, s_{di})$ is a parameter and $I_{k_i\times k_i}$ is an identity matrix. A larger k_i means preserving more information in the projection for the type of feature. Although problem (2) is not convex, we can prove that the globally optimal mappings $\{(L_{Q_i}, L_{\mathcal{D}_i})\}_{i=1}^l$ can be obtained by Singular Value Decomposition (SVD), and the globally optimal weights $\{\alpha_i\}_{i=1}^l$ can be obtained by quadratic programming with a closed-form solution.

4.2 Globally Optimal Solution

Basically, there are two steps in finding the global optimum. First, for each type of features, we find the optimal mappings through solving SVD. Second, we determine the optimal combination weights.

Specifically, the objective function (2) can be re-written as

$$\begin{aligned}
&\sum_{e_{uv}\in\mathcal{E}} \sum_{i=1}^l \alpha_i \cdot \left(t_{uv} \cdot q_u^{i\top} L_{Q_i} L_{\mathcal{D}_i}^\top d_v^i\right) \\
&= \sum_{i=1}^l \alpha_i \cdot \mathrm{trace}\left(\sum_{e_{uv}\in\mathcal{E}} t_{uv} \cdot q_u^{i\top} L_{Q_i} L_{\mathcal{D}_i}^\top d_v^i\right) \\
&= \sum_{i=1}^l \alpha_i \cdot \mathrm{trace}\left(L_{\mathcal{D}_i}^\top \Big(\sum_{e_{uv}\in\mathcal{E}} t_{uv} d_v^i q_u^{i\top}\Big) L_{Q_i}\right) \\
&= \sum_{i=1}^l \alpha_i \cdot \mathrm{trace}\left(L_{\mathcal{D}_i}^\top M_i L_{Q_i}\right),
\end{aligned}$$

where M_i is defined as $\sum_{e_{uv}\in\mathcal{E}} t_{uv} d_v^i q_u^{i\top}$.

Suppose that $\forall i,\ k_i \leqslant \min(s_{qi}, s_{di})$, the following theorem indicates that the global optimum of the optimization problem

$$\underset{L_{Q_i},L_{\mathcal{D}_i}}{\arg\max}\ \mathrm{trace}\left(L_{\mathcal{D}_i}^\top M_i L_{Q_i}\right) \tag{3}$$

$$\text{subject to} \quad L_{Q_i}^\top L_{Q_i} = I_{k_i\times k_i},\ L_{\mathcal{D}_i}^\top L_{\mathcal{D}_i} = I_{k_i\times k_i}$$

can be reached through SVD of M_i:

THEOREM 4.1. *$\forall k_i \leqslant \min(s_{qi}, s_{di})$, the globally optimal solution of problem (3) exists. Furthermore, suppose that $M_i = U_i\Sigma_i V_i^\top$,* *where Σ_i is an $s_{di} \times s_{qi}$ diagonal matrix with singular values $\lambda_1^i \geqslant \lambda_2^i \geqslant \ldots \lambda_{p_i}^i \geqslant 0$, $p_i = \min(s_{qi}, s_{di})$, $U_i = (u_1^i, u_2^i, \ldots, u_{s_{di}}^i)$ where $\{u_j^i\}$ are left singular vectors, and $V_i = (v_1^i, v_2^i, \ldots, v_{s_{qi}}^i)$ where $\{v_j^i\}$ are right singular vectors. The global maximum is given by $\sum_{j=1}^{k_i} \lambda_j^i$ and the global optimum $\hat{L}_{Q_i}$ and $\hat{L}_{\mathcal{D}_i}$ are given by $\hat{L}_{Q_i} = (v_1^i, v_2^i, \ldots, v_{k_i}^i)$ and $\hat{L}_{\mathcal{D}_i} = (u_1^i, u_2^i, \ldots, u_{k_i}^i)$, respectively.*

The proof is given in Appendix. With Theorem 4.1, if we define $\Lambda_i = \sum_{j=1}^{k_i} \lambda_j^i$, then we can re-write problem (2) as

$$\max_{\substack{\{(L_{Q_i}, L_{\mathcal{D}_i})\}_{i=1}^l, \{\alpha_i\}_{i=1}^l \\ L_{Q_i}^\top L_{Q_i} = L_{\mathcal{D}_i}^\top L_{\mathcal{D}_i} = I_{k_i \times k_i}, \alpha_i \geqslant 0, \sum_{i=1}^l \alpha_i^2 \leqslant 1}} \sum_{e_{uv} \in \mathcal{E}} \sum_{i=1}^l \alpha_i \cdot \left(t_{uv} \cdot q_u^{i\top} L_{Q_i} L_{\mathcal{D}_i}^\top d_v^i\right)$$

$$= \max_{\substack{\{\alpha_i\}_{i=1}^l \\ \alpha_i \geqslant 0, \sum_{i=1}^l \alpha_i^2 \leqslant 1}} \sum_{i=1}^l \alpha_i \max_{\substack{\{(L_{Q_i}, L_{\mathcal{D}_i})\}_{i=1}^l \\ L_{Q_i}^\top L_{Q_i} = L_{\mathcal{D}_i}^\top L_{\mathcal{D}_i} = I_{k_i \times k_i}}} \sum_{e_{uv} \in \mathcal{E}} \left(t_{uv} \cdot q_u^{i\top} L_{Q_i} L_{\mathcal{D}_i}^\top d_v^i\right)$$

$$= \max_{\substack{\{\alpha_i\}_{i=1}^l \\ \alpha_i \geqslant 0, \sum_{i=1}^l \alpha_i^2 \leqslant 1}} \sum_{i=1}^l \alpha_i \Lambda_i. \tag{4}$$

It can be proved that problem (4) has a closed-form global optimum. The optimal weights are given by

$$\hat{\alpha}_i = \frac{\Lambda_i}{\sqrt{\sum_{i=1}^l \Lambda_i^2}}, \quad 1 \leqslant i \leqslant l. \tag{5}$$

It is easy to verify that when $l = 1$, problem (2) becomes a problem solvable by Partial Least Squares (PLS) [21, 25]. The orthogonal assumptions on the mapping matrices make it feasible to employ PLS to solve the problem. Therefore, our method of Multi-view PLS is an extension of PLS.

If we assume that only the click-through bipartite graph is used, i.e., no feature is used, then problem (2) becomes equivalent to Latent Semantic Indexing (LSI) on the click-through bipartite graph [9][3]. In other words, LSI is a special case of our method.

In problem (2), we consider using ℓ_2 norm to regularize the weights $\{\alpha_i\}_{i=1}^l$. An alternative method would be to use $\sum_{i=1}^l \alpha_i \leqslant 1$ (i.e., ℓ_1 norm) to regularize them. However, such a regularization will make the final solution become $\alpha_i = 1$, if $\Lambda_i = \max_{1 \leqslant j \leqslant l} \Lambda_j$, and $\alpha_i = 0$, otherwise. This is a degenerative solution and is not desirable. The ℓ_2 regularization in our method does not suffer from the problem.

4.3 Learning Algorithm

The learning algorithm is described in Algorithm 1. The algorithm contains two steps. First, for each type of feature, it calculates M_i, and solves SVD of M_i to learn the linear mappings. Then, it calculates the combination weights using (5).

At Step 2.*a*, it is necessary to calculate M_i. Suppose that there are n_q queries on the click-through bipartite graph $\mathcal{G}$. Each query has on average κ_q clicked documents. Then for each type of feature, the worst case time complexity of calculating M_i is of order $O(n_q \cdot \kappa_q \cdot s_{qi} \cdot s_{di})$, where s_{qi} and s_{di} denote the dimensionalities of query space Q_i and document space $\mathcal{D}_i$, respectively. Although s_{qi} and s_{di} can be very large, the query vectors and document vectors are usually very sparse. This can make the average time complexity much smaller than the worst case time complexity. Suppose that each dimension of query vectors has on average c_{qi} non-zero values, and each document vector has on average c_{di} non-zero values. The average time complexity of calculating M_i becomes of order $O(s_{qi} \cdot \kappa_q \cdot c_{di})$. Since c_{qi} and c_{di} are much smaller than n_q and s_{di}, M_i can be calculated very efficiently.

Algorithm 1

1: Input: click-through bipartite graph $\mathcal{G} = (\mathcal{V}, \mathcal{E})$, feature spaces $\{(Q_i, \mathcal{D}_i)\}_{i=1}^l$, parameters $\{k_i\}_{i=1}^l$.
2: For each type of feature space $(Q_i, \mathcal{D}_i)$
   a. Calculate M_i using $\sum_{e_{uv} \in \mathcal{E}} t_{uv} d_v^i q_u^{i\top}$.
   b. Calculate SVD of M_i.
   c. Take the first k_i left singular vectors $(u_1^i, u_2^i, \ldots, u_{k_i}^i)$ as $\hat{L}_{\mathcal{D}_i}$, and first k_i right singular vectors $(v_1^i, v_2^i, \ldots, v_{k_i}^i)$ as $\hat{L}_{Q_i}$.
   d. Calculate Λ_i using $\sum_{j=1}^{k_i} \lambda_j^i$.
3: Calculate combination weight $\hat{\alpha}_i$ using equation (5).
4: Output: similarity functions:
   a. $\forall q, d,\ f(q, d) = \sum_{i=1}^l \hat{\alpha}_i \cdot q^{i\top} \hat{L}_{Q_i} \hat{L}_{\mathcal{D}_i}^\top d^i$.
   b. $\forall q, q',\ g(q, q') = \sum_{i=1}^l \hat{\alpha}_i \cdot q^{i\top} \hat{L}_{Q_i} \hat{L}_{Q_i}^\top q'^i$.

We empirically find in our experiments that sparse query and document feature vectors also make the matrix M_i sparse. In our experiments, the ratio of non-zero elements in the matrix M_i is not larger than 0.5%. Therefore, we can employ the power method (cf., [30]) to build an SVD solver. It is an iterative algorithm, and after i iterations, the ith largest singular values can be obtained. Suppose that there are C non-zero elements in matrix M_i. The time complexity for calculating each singular value is $O(C + k_i \cdot \max(s_{qi}, s_{di}))$, and the total time complexity is $O(k_i \cdot C + k_i^2 \cdot \max(s_{qi}, s_{di}))$. Since M_i is sparse and C is much smaller than $s_{qi} \cdot s_{di}$, when k_i is small, SVD of M_i can be solved efficiently.

4.4 Query Similarity

Problem (2) is formalized as learning of query-document similarity. Actually the optimization can also help learning of query-query similarity (equivalently document-document similarity). Here, we show that our method is able to find high quality similar queries as well. Under the orthogonal assumptions, the results of problem (2) have two properties which can guarantee that the performance of the method on similar query finding is high as well.

For a specific feature type i, if the similarity between $q, q' \in Q_i$ is high, then the similarity between images of q and q' in the latent space is also high, provided that k_i is sufficiently large. Formally, we assume that there is a small number $\varepsilon/2 > 0$ such that $q^\top q' \geqslant 1 - \varepsilon/2$ (i.e., they have high similarity because $q^\top q' \leqslant 1$). Since $\|q\| = \|q'\| = 1$, we have $\|q - q'\|^2 = \|q\|^2 + \|q'\|^2 - 2q^\top q' \leqslant \varepsilon$. Suppose that $L_{Q_i} = (l_1^{Q_i}, \ldots l_{k_i}^{Q_i})$. We have

$$\|L_{Q_i}^\top q - L_{Q_i}^\top q'\|^2 = (q - q')^\top \sum_{j=1}^{k_i} l_j^{Q_i} l_j^{Q_i \top} (q - q') = \sum_{j=1}^{k_i} |\langle l_j^{Q_i}, q - q' \rangle|^2.$$

Since $L_{Q_i}^\top L_{Q_i} = I_{k_i \times k_i}$, we have

$$\|L_{Q_i}^\top q - L_{Q_i}^\top q'\|^2 = \sum_{j=1}^{k_i} |\langle l_j^{Q_i}, q - q' \rangle|^2 \leqslant \|q - q'\|^2 \leqslant \varepsilon.$$

Thus, we have $q^\top L_{Q_i} L_{Q_i}^\top q' \geqslant (\|L_{Q_i}^\top q\|^2 + \|L_{Q_i}^\top q'\|^2 - \varepsilon)/2$. This inequality indicates that for a specific feature type i, if the similarity between two queries q and q' is high in the feature space Q_i, then the similarity between their images in the latent space is determined

[3]LSI is usually used for learning the similarity between term and document from a term-document bipartite graph.

by their norms in the space. The square of the norm of query q in the latent space can be calculated as

$$||L_{Q_i}^{\top}q||^2 = q^{\top}L_{Q_i}L_{Q_i}^{\top}q = q^{\top}\sum_{j=1}^{k_i} l_j^{Q_i} l_j^{Q_i\top} q = \sum_{j=1}^{k_i} |\langle l_j^{Q_i}, q\rangle|^2. \quad (6)$$

Since usually $k_i \leqslant s_{qi}$, we have $||L_{Q_i}^{\top}q||^2 \leqslant ||q||^2 = 1$. With a sufficiently large k_i, we can assume that $||L_{Q_i}^{\top}q||^2 \geqslant 1 - \delta$, and $||L_{Q_i}^{\top}q'||^2 \geqslant 1 - \delta$, where $\delta \geqslant 0$ is a small number. Thus, we obtain $q^{\top}L_{Q_i}L_{Q_i}^{\top}q' \geqslant 1 - \delta - \frac{\varepsilon}{2}$. Note that δ monotonically decreases when k_i increases. In an extreme case, when $k_i = s_{qi}$, $\delta = 0$ holds. We call this property *inheritance*. This property ensures that when sufficient information is preserved in the latent space (i.e., k_i is sufficiently large), similar queries in the original feature space will also be similar in the latent space.

Second, suppose that $q_1, q_2 \in Q_i$, $d_1, d_2 \in \mathcal{D}_i$, and $q_1' = L_{Q_i}^{\top}q_1$, $q_2' = L_{Q_i}^{\top}q_2$, $d_1' = L_{\mathcal{D}_i}^{\top}d_1$, and $d_2' = L_{\mathcal{D}_i}^{\top}d_2$. If we assume that q_1' and d_1', q_2' and d_2', and d_1' and d_2' are similar pairs with high similarity, then when k_i is sufficiently large, we can obtain high similarity between q_1' and q_2'. Formally, we assume that there is a small number $\varepsilon > 0$ such that $q_1'^{\top}d_1' \geqslant 1 - \varepsilon/18$, $q_2'^{\top}d_2' \geqslant 1 - \varepsilon/18$, and $d_1'^{\top}d_2' \geqslant 1 - \varepsilon/18$. We have $||q_1' - q_2'|| \leqslant ||q_1' - d_1'|| + ||d_1' - d_2'|| + ||q_2' - d_2'||$. Since $q_1' = L_{Q_i}^{\top}q_1$ and $d_1' = L_{\mathcal{D}_i}^{\top}d_1$, similar to the analysis of equation (6), we have $||q_1'|| \leqslant ||q_1|| = 1$ and $||d_1'|| \leqslant ||d_1|| = 1$. We know that $||q_1' - d_1'||^2 = ||q_1'||^2 + ||d_1'||^2 - 2q_1'^{\top}d_1' \leqslant \varepsilon/9$. Similarly, we can get $||q_2' - d_2'||^2 \leqslant \varepsilon/9$ and $||d_1' - d_2'||^2 \leqslant \varepsilon/9$. Thus, we obtain $||q_1' - q_2'||^2 \leqslant \varepsilon$. Similarly to the analysis above, we can say that with a sufficiently large k_i, we can have the similarity between q_1' and q_2' large enough. We call this property *transitivity*. The property ensures that when sufficient information is preserved in the latent space, we can derive similar query pairs from similar query-document pairs. The property needs high similarity between documents in the latent space. The condition can be easily met, because document similarity can be preserved with the "inheritance" property.

In our experiments, we find that the inheritance property and the transitivity property can really help us on finding high quality similar queries. We also give an example to support our theoretical analysis.

5. EXPERIMENTS

We conducted experiments to test the performance of the proposed method on relevance ranking and similar query finding. We used two data sets: enterprise search data and web search data.

5.1 Data Sets

We collected one year click-through data from an enterprise search engine of an IT company and one week click-through data from a commercial web search engine. We built two click-through bipartite graphs with the data. If there are more than 3 clicks between a query and a document, we added a link between them. In other words we discarded the links between queries and documents whose click frequency is lower than or equal to 3. Finally, there are 51,699 queries and 81,186 documents on the bipartite graph of enterprise search data, and there are 94,022 queries and 111,631 documents on the bipartite graph of web search data. Each query has on average 2.44 clicked documents in the enterprise bipartite graph and each query has on average 1.74 clicked documents in the web bipartite graph.

We extracted features from the two click-through data sets as metadata on the bipartite graphs. In this paper, we only considered two types of metadata because our focus in this paper is verification of the effectiveness of the proposed method. First, we took the words in queries and the words in URLs and titles of documents as features, referred to as "word features". Words were stemmed and stop words were removed. With word features, each query is represented by a tf-idf vector in the query space, and each document is also represented by a tf-idf vector in the document space. Each dimension of the query space corresponds to a unique term and so does each dimension of the document space. Note that the two spaces are of high dimension and very sparse. For the enterprise search data, there are 9,958 unique terms. For the web search data, the dimensionality of term space is 101,904. Next, we followed [2] and took the numbers of clicks of documents as features of queries and the numbers of clicks of queries as features of documents. We call the features "graph features", because they are derived from the bipartite graphs. Each query is represented by a vector of click numbers in the query space and each document is represented by a vector of click numbers in the document space. Each dimension of the query space corresponds to a document on the click-through bipartite graph, and similarly each dimension of the document space corresponds to a query on the click-through bipartite graph. The dimensionalities of the two spaces are also very high, while the densities of the two spaces are very low.

In addition, we obtained relevance data consisting of judged query-document pairs from the search engine in a different time period. We also collected relevance data in the enterprise in a different time period. There are five level judgments, including "Perfect", "Excellent", "Good", "Fair", and "Bad". To make comparisons with baseline methods, we removed the queries that are not on the click-through bipartite graphs. There are 1,701 queries and associated documents having judgments in the enterprise search data. Each query has on average 16 judged documents. The number of judged queries is 4,445 in the web search data, and each query has on average 11.34 judged documents. We randomly split each data set and used half of them for tuning model parameters and the other half for model evaluation.

In summary, for both the web data and the enterprise data, we learned models on a click-through bipartite graph with metadata, tuned model parameters on some relevance data, and evaluated model performances on other relevance data.

5.2 Experiment Setup

We consider four alternatives to learn a similarity function using our method: 1) Only word features are used. We denote the model as M-PLS$_{\text{Word}}$; 2) Only graph features are used. We refer to the model as M-PLS$_{\text{Bipar}}$; 3) The vectors from the word feature space and the vectors from the graph feature space are concatenated to create long vectors. The corresponding space is the Cartesian product of the word feature space and the graph feature space. We call the model M-PLS$_{\text{Conca}}$; 4) We apply our method to learn a similarity function assuming that queries and documents have two types of features and we learn a linearly combined similarity function. We call the model M-PLS$_{\text{Com}}$.

As baselines, we consider feature based methods, graph based methods, and their linear combinations. In relevance ranking, we take BM25 as an example of feature based methods. We choose LSI on click-through bipartite graph and random walk (RW for short) [7] as examples of graph based methods. We also linearly combine LSI and RW with BM25. In similar query finding, besides LSI and RW, we adopt as baseline methods cosine similarity of two query vectors represented with graph features and cosine similarity of two query vectors represented with word features. We denote them as Cos$_{\text{B}}$ and Cos$_{\text{W}}$, respectively. We also linearly combine Cos$_{\text{B}}$, LSI, and RW with Cos$_{\text{W}}$.

Table 1: Weights in combination methods on two data sets

Model	Components	Combination weights	
		Enterprise	Web
Relevance ranking			
LSI+BM25	(LSI,BM25)	(0.9, 0.1)	(0.8, 0.2)
RW+BM25	(RW,BM25)	(0.9, 0.1)	(0.8, 0.2)
Similar query finding			
Cos_B+Cos_W	(Cos_B,Cos_W)	(0.5, 0.5)	(0.5, 0.5)
LSI+Cos_W	(LSI,Cos_W)	(0.5, 0.5)	(0.5, 0.5)
RW+Cos_W	(RW,Cos_W)	(0.5, 0.5)	(0.5, 0.5)

To evaluate the performances of different methods in relevance ranking, we employ NDCG [14] at positions of 1, 3, and 5 as evaluation measures. For similar query finding, we evaluated the quality of similar queries found by each method. First, 500 queries were randomly sampled from the data for model evaluation and their top 3 most similar queries by each method were collected. We manually judged the quality of the similar queries. The final results are presented in pos-com-neg graphs, where "pos" represents the ratio of queries for which our method provides higher quality similar queries, "com" represents the ratio of queries on which the performances of our method and the baseline methods are comparable, and "neg" represents the ratio of queries on which the baseline methods do a better job.

5.3 Parameter Setting

We set the parameters of the methods in the following way. In BM25, the default setting is used. There are two parameters in random walk (RW for short): the self-transition probability and the number of transition steps. Following the conclusion in [7], we fixed the self-transition probability as 0.9 and chose the number of transition steps from $\{1, \ldots, 10\}$. We found that RW reaches a "stable" state with a few steps. In the experiments on both the web and enterprise data sets, after 5 steps we saw no improvement on the data for parameter tuning in terms of the evaluation measures. Therefore, we set 5 as the number of transition steps of RW on both data sets.

In LSI, M-PLS_{Word}, M-PLS_{Bipar}, M-PLS_{Conca}, and M-PLS_{Com}, the parameter is the dimensionality of the latent space. We set the dimensionalities in the range of $\{100, 200, \ldots, 1000\}$ for both the enterprise search data and the web search data. We found that when we increase the dimensionality of the latent space, the performances of LSI, M-PLS_{Word}, M-PLS_{Bipar}, M-PLS_{Conca}, and M-PLS_{Com} are all improved on the data for parameter tuning. The larger the dimensionality is, the better the performance is. On the other hand, a large dimensionality means that we need to calculate more singular values and use more computation power. Therefore, we finally chose 1000 as the dimensionalities of the latent spaces for LSI, M-PLS_{Word}, M-PLS_{Bipar}, M-PLS_{Conca}, and M-PLS_{Com} on both data sets.

In the combination models, the weights are also parameters. In LSI+BM25 and RW+BM25 for relevance ranking, LSI+Cos_W, R-W+ Cos_W, and Cos_B+ Cos_W for similar query finding, we chose the combination weights within $\{0.1, 0.2, \ldots, 0.9\}$. For relevance ranking the weights were determined based on the results on the data for parameter tunning. For similar query finding we found that the results of LSI+Cos_W, RW+ Cos_W, and Cos_B+ Cos_W are not sensitive to the combination weights. Therefore, we only report their results under uniform weights. Table 1 shows the weights in each combination model. Note that in M-PLS_{Com}, the combination weights are chosen automatically using equation (5).

Table 2 shows the properties of matrices for computing SVD in each method. We can see that although the matrices have high dimensionalities, they are really sparse, and thus it is possible to conduct SVD on them efficiently.

Table 2: Properties of SVD matrices in each method

	Dimension	Density
Enterprise search data		
M-PLS_{Com}	9958×9958, 81186×51699	0.4%, 0.08%
M-PLS_{Word}	9958×9958	0.4%
M-PLS_{Bipar}	81186×51699	0.08%
M-PLS_{Conca}	91144×61657	0.5%
LSI	81186×51699	0.003%
Web search data		
M-PLS_{Com}	101904×101904, 111631×94022	0.008%, 0.01%
M-PLS_{Word}	101904×101904	0.008%
M-PLS_{Bipar}	111631×94022	0.01%
M-PLS_{Conca}	213535×195926	0.01%
LSI	111631×94022	0.002%

Table 3: Relevance ranking result on enterprise search data

	NDCG@1	NDCG@3	NDCG@5
M-PLS_{Com}	**0.715**	**0.733**	**0.747**
M-PLS_{Conca}	0.700	0.728	0.742
M-PLS_{Word}	0.688	0.718	0.739
M-PLS_{Bipar}	0.659	0.684	0.705
BM25	0.653	0.657	0.663
RW	0.654	0.683	0.700
RW+BM25	0.664	0.688	0.705
LSI	0.656	0.676	0.695
LSI+BM25	0.692	0.701	0.712

5.4 Experimental Results

5.4.1 Relevance Ranking Results

Table 3 and Table 4 give the evaluation results on relevance ranking for the two data sets. We can see that on both data sets, our method M-PLS_{Com} not only outperforms the state of the art feature based methods such as BM25 and graph based methods such as RW, but also performs better than their linear combinations. We conducted sign test on the improvements of M-PLS_{Com} over the baseline methods. The results show that all the improvements are statistically significant ($p < 0.01$).

M-PLS_{Conca} also performs well on both data sets. The higher complexity of it makes it less attractive than M-PLS_{Com} (Note that the matrix of M-PLS_{Conca} for SVD has a high dimensionality and is dense). Therefore it is better to conduct multi-view PLS instead of single view PLS. M-PLS_{Bipar} performs worst among the alternatives of our method. This may be because 1) the features of M-PLS_{Bipar} are more sparse (cf., Table 2); 2) both the features and the similarities (i.e., click numbers) in learning of M-PLS_{Bipar} are from the click-through bipartite graph and there is overlap between them.

More interestingly, we find that when we linearly combine our method M-PLS_{Com} with BM25, the performances of our method can be further improved, indicating that our method M-PLS_{Com} is complementary to BM25. Table 5 shows the results. Note that the learned linear combination model can be viewed as a simplified learning to rank model.

5.4.2 Similar Query Finding Results

We show the performance of the proposed method on similar query finding. We compared M-PLS_{Com} with other baseline methods on the two data sets. In each data set, we evaluated the quality

Table 4: Relevance ranking result on web search data

	NDCG@1	NDCG@3	NDCG@5
M-PLS$_{\text{Com}}$	**0.681**	**0.731**	**0.739**
M-PLS$_{\text{Conca}}$	0.676	0.728	0.736
M-PLS$_{\text{Word}}$	0.674	0.726	0.732
M-PLS$_{\text{Bipar}}$	0.612	0.680	0.693
BM25	0.637	0.690	0.690
RW	0.655	0.704	0.704
RW+BM25	0.671	0.718	0.716
LSI	0.588	0.665	0.676
LSI+BM25	0.649	0.705	0.706

Table 5: Performances of combination of M-PLS$_{\text{Com}}$ and BM25 on relevance ranking

	NDCG@1	NDCG@3	NDCG@5
Enterprise search data	0.727	0.737	0.749
Web search data	0.697	0.740	0.745

of similar queries of 500 random queries found by each method. Finally, we presented the comparisons through pos-com-neg graphs.

Figure 3 and Figure 4 show the results. We can see that M-PLS$_{\text{Com}}$ significantly outperforms the feature based methods and graph based methods, including Cos$_\text{B}$, Cos$_\text{W}$, LSI and RW. Our method performs better on more than 15% queries from the enterprise data and on more than 25% queries from the web data. Only on less than 7% queries from the enterprise data and less than 3% queries from the web data, our method performs worse. We conducted sign test, and the results show that all the improvements are statistically significant ($p < 0.01$). Among the combined models, Cos$_\text{B}$ + Cos$_\text{W}$ and RW + Cos$_\text{W}$ perform comparably well, and our method still outperforms them. However, the improvement of our method over those methods is not so significant.

We investigated the reasons that the methods can or cannot achieve high performance in similar query finding. First, we found that Cos$_\text{B}$, LSI and RW are good at handling head queries, since they all rely on co-clicks on the click-through bipartite graph to calculate query similarity. Among them, RW performs a little better than Cos$_\text{B}$. This may be because similarity on the bipartite graph can be propagated by RW. In contrast, for tail queries, we cannot expect these methods to have good performances. In an extreme case, if a query only has one clicked document and the document is only clicked by the query, then no similar queries can be found for the query. We call this kind of query "isolated island". Second, no matter whether two queries have co-clicked documents, if they share some words, they are likely to be judged as similar queries by Cos$_\text{W}$. Therefore, Cos$_\text{W}$ is good at handling queries sharing terms. This is especially true for tail queries, since tail queries tend to be longer. However, if two similar queries do not share any term, their similarity cannot be captured by Cos$_\text{W}$. The problem is called "term mismatch", and becomes serious when the queries have spelling errors, abbreviations, and concatenations. The two types of methods (either use click graph or use terms) are complementary, and thus when combined together, it is possible to find similar queries with higher probability.

We found that on most queries our method M-PLS$_{\text{Com}}$ performs equally well with the combination baseline Cos$_\text{B}$ + Cos$_\text{W}$. Sometimes, the two methods even give the same top 3 most similar queries. It indicates that click-through bipartite graph and features are really useful for similar query finding. On the other hand, we also found that our method can work very well for some really difficult queries on which graph based methods and word based methods fail. The result demonstrates that our method really has the capability to leverage the enriched click-through bipartite graph to learn query similarities.

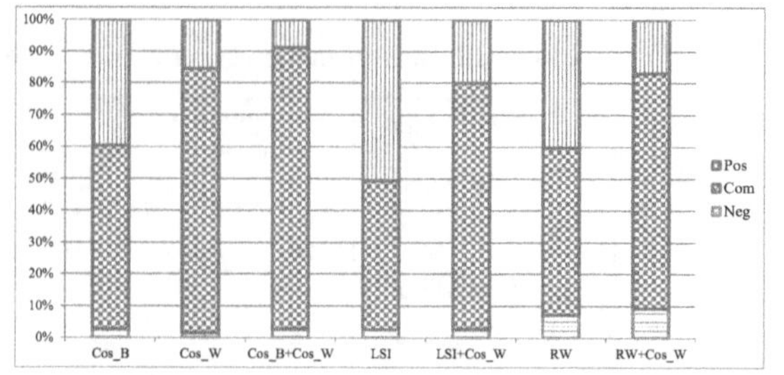

Figure 3: Similar query evaluation on enterprise search data.

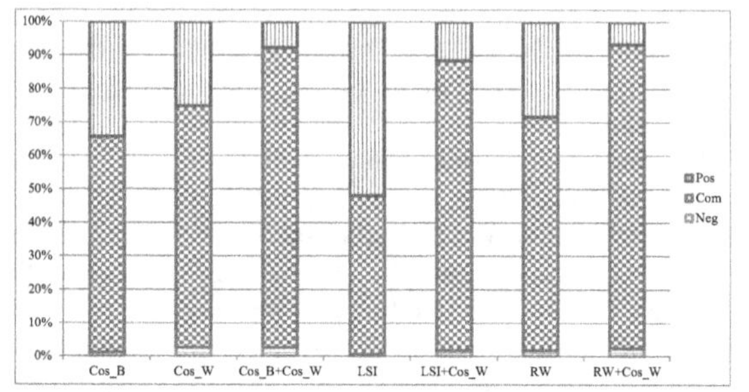

Figure 4: Similar query evaluation on web search data.

Table 6 shows some examples on the similar queries found by M-PLS$_{\text{Com}}$. We can see that M-PLS$_{\text{Com}}$ is able to find high quality similar queries, even for some "difficult" queries, which contain typos, abbreviations, concatenations and rare words. For the tail queries consisting of rare words, usually it is very hard for the baseline methods to find their similar queries, because they only have a few clicks. Nonetheless, M-PLS$_{\text{Com}}$ is still able to find similar queries for them, which is really surprising.

Finally, we particularly investigated the performance of our method on tail queries on the web data, since the web data set is larger and more sparse than the enterprise data set. We treat queries with total click numbers less than 10 on the click-through bipartite graph as tail queries. There are totally 212 tail queries in the 500 samples from the web data. Figure 5 gives the "pos-com-neg" comparison results. We can see that on tail queries, our method M-PLS$_{\text{Com}}$ performs even better than itself on the whole sample set. We further investigated the reasons that our method is capable of finding high quality similar queries in the tail. Table 7 shows an example. The query 'walmartmoneycard' is a concatenation, and is also an isolated island. As a result, for Cos$_\text{B}$, LSI and RW, no similar queries can be found. Cos$_\text{W}$ suffers from term mismatch, and thus only those queries that can exactly match 'walmartmoneycard' are returned. The combination methods can only use Cos$_\text{W}$, and thus return the same results with Cos$_\text{W}$. These baseline methods cannot find similar queries for 'walmartmoneycard'. In contrast, M-PLS$_{\text{Com}}$ can work better than the baseline methods. We found that the key reason is that our method can effectively use the click-through bipartite graph, specifically similar documents on the graph. The query 'walmartmoneycard' has a clicked document `https://www.walmartmoneycard.com/`, and its similar query 'wal-mart prepaid visa activation' also has a clicked document `https://www.walmartmoneycard.com/walmart/homepage.aspx`. Through the optimization, both the similarity between 'wal-

Table 6: Examples of similar queries found by M-PLS$_{Com}$

Original Query	Similar Queries
Spelling Errors	
dictonary	web dictionary
	onlinedictionary
	dictionery
wickapedia	www.wikipedia.org
	wikepedia
	www.wikipedia.com
gooole.com	wwww.google.com
	www.gooogle
	www.goolgle.com
Abbreviations	
fl.lottery	lottery florida
	florida lottery numbers
	florida lottery results
ym	yahoo messanger
	yahoomessenger
	yahoo im messenger
bofa online banking	bank america online banking
	bank of america online
	www.bank of america online banking
Concatenations	
dickssportinggoods	dicks sporting goods
	dicks sporting good store
	dicks sporting goods coupons
googlenews	google news
	goggle news
	news.google.com
peoplesearch	search people
	people search
	yahoo people search
Tail Queries	
star wars anniversary edition lego darth vader fighter	www.star wars legos.com
	star wars legos
	star wars lego
american express online account summary	american express account online
	american express account
	american express online
read full books online free	read books online free
	free online books to read
	read books online

Table 7: Result on a difficult query

Query: walmartmoneycard	
M-PLS$_{Com}$	www.walmartmoneycard.com
	walmartmoneycard.com
	wal-mart prepaid visa activation
Cos$_B$, LSI, RW	N / A
	N / A
	N / A
Cos$_W$	www.walmartmoneycard.com
	walmartmoneycard.com
	N / A
Cos$_B$ + Cos$_W$, LSI + Cos$_W$, RW+ Cos$_W$	www.walmartmoneycard.com
	walmartmoneycard.com
	N / A

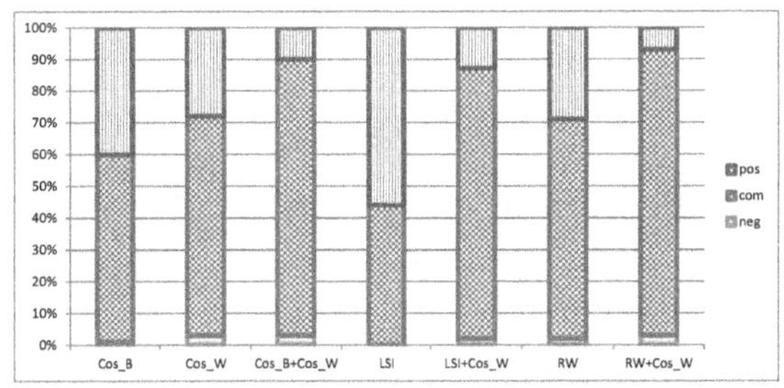

Figure 5: Similar query evaluation on the tail queries from web search data.

martmoneycard' and `https://www.walmartmoneycard.com/` and the similarity between 'wal-mart prepaid visa activation' and `https://www.walmartmoneycard.com/walmart/homepage.aspx` are maximized in the latent space (they are 0.71 and 0.53, respectively). Moreover, since the two documents share a common term 'walmartmoneycard' in the term space, their similarity is also captured in the latent space through the learning process of our method (with similarity 0.47). Therefore, with the two similar documents as a bridge, our method can connect the two queries and treat them as similar queries.

6. CONCLUSION AND FUTURE WORK

In this paper, we have studied the issue of learning query and document similarities from a click-through bipartite with metadata. The click-through bipartite represents the click relations between queries and documents, while the metadata represents multiple types of features of queries and documents. We aim to leverage both the click-through bipartite and features to perform the learning task. We have proposed a method that can solve the problem in a principled way. Specifically, for each type of features, we use two different linear mappings to project queries and documents into a latent space. Then we take the dot product in the latent space as the similarity function between query-document pairs. Similarities between query-query and document-document pairs are simultaneously defined. The final similarity function is defined as a linear combination of similarity functions from different types of features. We learn the mappings and combination weights by maximizing the similarities of the observed query-document pairs on the click-through bipartite graph, and make orthogonal assumptions on the mappings and regularize the weights using ℓ_2 norm. We have proved that the learning problem has a global optimum. The mappings can be obtained efficiently through Singular Value Decomposition (SVD) and the weights can be obtained from a closed-form solution of a quadratic program. It turns out to be a new learning method as an extension of Partial Least Squares, referred to as Multi-view PLS. We have theoretically analyzed the proposed method, and demonstrated its capability on finding high quality similar queries (also similar documents). We have conducted experiments on large scale enterprise search and web search data to test the performance of our method. The results not only indicate that our method can significantly outperform the state of the art methods on relevance ranking and similar query finding, but also verify the correctness of our theoretical analysis.

As future work, we want to further enhance the efficiency of our method and test its performance on larger data sets. To achieve the goal, we may need to parallelize the learning algorithm. We want to incorporate the similarity learned by our method into a large learning to rank system and investigate whether the similarity can improve the performance of the learning to rank system. We also want to study the kernelization of our method, so that our method is still applicable when kernel matrices instead of features are available.

7. REFERENCES

[1] I. Antonellis, H.G. Molina, and C.C. Chang. Simrank++: Query rewriting through link analysis of the click graph. *VLDB*, 1(1):408–421, 2008.

[2] R. Baeza-Yates and A. Tiberi. Extracting semantic relations from query logs. In *SIGKDD*, pages 76–85, 2007.

[3] M. Barker and W. Rayens. Partial least squares for discrimination. *Journal of chemometrics*, 17(3):166–173, 2003.

[4] D. Beeferman and A. L. Berger. Agglomerative clustering of a search engine query log. In *KDD*, pages 407–416, 2000.

[5] A. Broder, P. Ciccolo, E. Gabrilovich, V. Josifovski, D. Metzler, L. Riedel, and J. Yuan. Online expansion of rare queries for sponsored search. In *WWW'09*, pages 511–520, 2009.

[6] H. Chun and S. Kelecs. Sparse partial least squares regression for simultaneous dimension reduction and variable selection. *Journal of the Royal Statistical Society: Series B (Statistical Methodology)*, 72(1):3–25, 2010.

[7] N. Craswell and M. Szummer. Random walks on the click graph. In *SIGIR*, pages 239–246, 2007.

[8] B.D. Davison. Toward a unification of text and link analysis. In *SIGIR'03*, 2003.

[9] S. Deerwester, S. Dumais, G. Furnas, T. Landauer, and R. Harshman. Indexing by latent semantic analysis. *JASIS*, 41:391–407, 1990.

[10] H. Deng, M.R. Lyu, and I. King. A generalized co-hits algorithm and its application to bipartite graphs. In *KDD'09*, 2009.

[11] D.R. Hardoon and J. Shawe-Taylor. Kcca for different level precision in content-based image retrieval. In *Proceedings of Third International Workshop on Content-Based Multimedia Indexing, IRISA, Rennes, France*, 2003.

[12] D.R. Hardoon and J. Shawe-Taylor. Sparse canonical correlation analysis. *stat*, 1050:19, 2009.

[13] D.R. Hardoon, S. Szedmak, and J. Shawe-Taylor. Canonical correlation analysis: An overview with application to learning methods. *Neural Computation*, 16(12):2639–2664, 2004.

[14] K. Jarvelin and J. Kekalainen. Ir evaluation methods for retrieving highly relevant documents. In *SIGIR' 00*, pages 41–48, 2000.

[15] G. Jeh and J. Widom. Simrank: a measure of structural-context similarity. In *SIGKDD*, pages 538–543, 2002.

[16] H. Li. Learning to rank for information retrieval and natural language processing. *Synthesis Lectures on Human Language Technologies*, 4(1):1–113, 2011.

[17] T.Y. Liu. Learning to rank for information retrieval. *Foundations and Trends in Information Retrieval*, 3(3):225–331, 2009.

[18] H. Ma, H.X. Yang, I. King, and M. R. Lyu. Learning latent semantic relations from clickthrough data for query suggestion. In *CIKM*, pages 709–718, 2008.

[19] J.M. Ponte and W.B. Croft. A language modeling approach to information retrieval. In *SIGIR' 98*, pages 275–281, 1998.

[20] S. E. Robertson, S. Walker, S. Jones, M. Hancock-Beaulieu, and M. Gatford. Okapi at trec-3. In *TREC*, 1994.

[21] R. Rosipal and N. Krämer. Overview and recent advances in partial least squares. *Subspace, Latent Structure and Feature Selection*, pages 34–51, 2006.

[22] S. Rüping and T. Scheffer. Learning with multiple views. In *Proc. ICML Workshop on Learning with Multiple Views*, 2005.

[23] H. Saigo, N. Krämer, and K. Tsuda. Partial least squares regression for graph mining. In *SIGKDD*, pages 578–586, 2008.

[24] G. Salton and M. McGill. *Introduction to Modern Information Retrieval*. McGraw-Hill, Inc., New York, NY, USA, 1986.

[25] P.J. Schreier. A unifying discussion of correlation analysis for complex random vectors. *Signal Processing, IEEE Transactions on*, 56(4):1327–1336, 2008.

[26] W.R. Schwartz, A. Kembhavi, D. Harwood, and L.S. Davis. Human detection using partial least squares analysis. In *ICCV*, pages 24–31, 2009.

[27] R.D. Tobias. An introduction to partial least squares regression. In *Proceedings of the Twentieth Annual SAS Users Group International Conference*, pages 1250–1257, 1995.

[28] C. Wang, R. Raina, D. Fong, D. Zhou, J. Han, and G. Badros. Learning relevance from heterogeneous social network and its application in online targeting. In *SIGIR'11*, 2011.

[29] X. Wang, J.T. Sun, Z. Chen, and C.X. Zhai. Latent semantic analysis for multiple-type interrelated data objects. In *SIGIR*, pages 236–243, 2006.

[30] J.A. Wegelin. A survey of partial least squares (pls) methods, with emphasis on the two-block case. *Technical Report, No.371, Seattle: Department of Statistics, University of Washington*, 2000.

[31] J.R. Wen, J.Y. Nie, and H.J. Zhang. Query clustering using user logs. *ACM Trans. Inf. Syst.*, 20(1):59–81, 2002.

[32] H. Wold. Path models with latent variables: the nipals approach. *Quantitative sociology: International perspectives on mathematical and statistical modeling*, pages 307–357, 1975.

[33] W. Wu, J. Xu, H. Li, and O. Satoshi. Learning a robust relevance model for search using kernel methods. *JMLR*, 12:1429–1458, 2011.

[34] W. Xi, E.A. Fox, W. Fan, B. Zhang, Z. Chen, J. Yan, and D. Zhuang. Simfusion: measuring similarity using unified relationship matrix. In *SIGIR*, pages 130–137. ACM, 2005.

[35] J. Xu, H. Li, and Z.L. Zhong. Relevance ranking using kernels. In *AIRS '10*, 2010.

[36] J.F. Xu and G. Xu. Learning similarity function for rare queries. In *WSDM*, pages 615–624, 2011.

[37] C.X. Zhai and J. Lafferty. A study of smoothing methods for language models applied to information retrieval. *ACM Trans. Inf. Syst.*, 22(2):179–214, 2004.

[38] Z. Zhang and O. Nasraoui. Mining search engine query logs for query recommendation. In *WWW*, pages 1039–1040, 2006.

APPENDIX

We give the proof of Theorem 4.1 here.

PROOF. Suppose that $L_{\mathcal{Q}_i} = \left(l_1^{\mathcal{Q}_i}, \ldots, l_{k_i}^{\mathcal{Q}_i}\right)$, and $L_{\mathcal{D}_i} = \left(l_1^{\mathcal{D}_i}, \ldots, l_{k_i}^{\mathcal{D}_i}\right)$. Objective function (3) can be re-written as $\sum_{j=1}^{k_i} l_j^{\mathcal{D}_i \top} M_i l_j^{\mathcal{Q}_i} = \sum_{j=1}^{k_i} \langle l_j^{\mathcal{D}_i}, M_i l_j^{\mathcal{Q}_i} \rangle$. Since $M_i = \sum_{w=1}^{p_i} \lambda_w^i u_w^i v_w^{i\top}$, we have

$$\langle l_j^{\mathcal{D}_i}, M_i l_j^{\mathcal{Q}_i} \rangle = \langle l_j^{\mathcal{D}_i}, \sum_{w=1}^{p_i} \lambda_w^i u_w^i v_w^{i\top} l_j^{\mathcal{Q}_i} \rangle = \sum_{w=1}^{p_i} \lambda_w^i \langle u_w^{i\top} l_j^{\mathcal{D}_i}, v_w^{i\top} l_j^{\mathcal{Q}_i} \rangle$$

$$\leqslant \sum_{w=1}^{p_i} \lambda_w^i |\langle u_w^i, l_j^{\mathcal{D}_i} \rangle| |\langle v_w^i, l_j^{\mathcal{Q}_i} \rangle|$$

$$= \lambda_{k_i}^i \sum_{w=1}^{p_i} |\langle u_w^i, l_j^{\mathcal{D}_i} \rangle| |\langle v_w^i, l_j^{\mathcal{Q}_i} \rangle| + \sum_{w=1}^{k_i} (\lambda_w^i - \lambda_{k_i}^i) |\langle u_w^i, l_j^{\mathcal{D}_i} \rangle| |\langle v_w^i, l_j^{\mathcal{Q}_i} \rangle|$$

$$+ \sum_{w=k_i+1}^{p_i} (\lambda_w^i - \lambda_{k_i}^i) |\langle u_w^i, l_j^{\mathcal{D}_i} \rangle| |\langle v_w^i, l_j^{\mathcal{Q}_i} \rangle|$$

$$\leqslant \lambda_{k_i}^i \sum_{w=1}^{p_i} |\langle u_w^i, l_j^{\mathcal{Q}_i} \rangle| |\langle v_w^i, l_j^{\mathcal{Q}_i} \rangle| + \sum_{w=1}^{k_i} (\lambda_w^i - \lambda_{k_i}^i) |\langle u_w^i, l_j^{\mathcal{D}_i} \rangle| |\langle v_w^i, l_j^{\mathcal{Q}_i} \rangle|$$

Since $\|l_j^{\mathcal{Q}_i}\| = \|l_j^{\mathcal{D}_i}\| = 1$ and $\{u_w^i\}_{w=1}^{p_i}$ and $\{v_w^i\}_{w=1}^{p_i}$ are orthonormal, we have $\sum_{w=1}^{p_i} |\langle u_w^i, l_j^{\mathcal{D}_i} \rangle| |\langle v_w^i, l_j^{\mathcal{Q}_i} \rangle| \leqslant \left[(\sum_{w=1}^{p_i} \langle u_w^i, l_j^{\mathcal{D}_i} \rangle^2)(\sum_{w=1}^{p_i} \langle v_w^i, l_j^{\mathcal{Q}_i} \rangle^2)\right]^{\frac{1}{2}} \leqslant \|l_j^{\mathcal{Q}_i}\| \cdot \|l_j^{\mathcal{D}_i}\| = 1$. Thus, we know $\langle l_j^{\mathcal{D}_i}, M_i l_j^{\mathcal{Q}_i} \rangle \leqslant \lambda_{k_i}^i + \sum_{w=1}^{k_i} (\lambda_w^i - \lambda_{k_i}^i) |\langle u_w^i, l_j^{\mathcal{D}_i} \rangle| |\langle v_w^i, l_j^{\mathcal{Q}_i} \rangle|$. By taking summation on both sides, we obtain $\sum_{j=1}^{k_i} \langle l_j^{\mathcal{D}_i}, M_i l_j^{\mathcal{Q}_i} \rangle \leqslant k_i \lambda_{k_i}^i + \sum_{w=1}^{k_i} (\lambda_w^i - \lambda_{k_i}^i)(\sum_{j=1}^{k_i} |\langle u_w^i, l_j^{\mathcal{D}_i} \rangle| |\langle v_w^i, l_j^{\mathcal{Q}_i} \rangle|)$. From this inequality, we obtain

$$\sum_{w=1}^{k_i} \lambda_w^i - \sum_{j=1}^{k_i} \langle l_j^{\mathcal{D}_i}, M_i l_j^{\mathcal{Q}_i} \rangle \geqslant \sum_{w=1}^{k_i} (\lambda_w^i - \lambda_{k_i}^i)(1 - \sum_{j=1}^{k_i} |\langle u_w^i, l_j^{\mathcal{D}_i} \rangle| |\langle v_w^i, l_j^{\mathcal{Q}_i} \rangle|).$$

Since $L_{\mathcal{Q}_i}^{\top} L_{\mathcal{Q}_i} = I_{k_i \times k_i}$ and $L_{\mathcal{D}_i}^{\top} L_{\mathcal{D}_i} = I_{k_i \times k_i}$, we have

$$\sum_{j=1}^{k_i} |\langle u_w^i, l_j^{\mathcal{D}_i} \rangle| |\langle v_w^i, l_j^{\mathcal{Q}_i} \rangle| \leqslant \left[(\sum_{j=1}^{k_i} \langle u_w^i, l_j^{\mathcal{D}_i} \rangle^2)(\sum_{j=1}^{k_i} \langle v_w^i, l_j^{\mathcal{Q}_i} \rangle^2)\right]^{\frac{1}{2}} \leqslant \|u_w^i\| \cdot \|v_w^i\| = 1.$$

Thus, $\sum_{j=1}^{k_i} \langle l_j^{\mathcal{D}_i}, M_i l_j^{\mathcal{Q}_i} \rangle \leqslant \sum_{w=1}^{k_i} \lambda_w^i$.

Particularly, letting $l_j^{\mathcal{D}_i} = u_j^i$ and $l_j^{\mathcal{Q}_i} = v_j^i$, we can obtain the global maximum. □

Optimizing Budget Constrained Spend in Search Advertising

Chinmay Karande*
chinmayk@fb.com

Aranyak Mehta
aranyak@google.com

Ramakrishnan Srikant
srikant@google.com

Google Research
Mountain View, CA, USA

ABSTRACT

Search engine ad auctions typically have a significant fraction of advertisers who are budget constrained, i.e., if allowed to participate in every auction that they bid on, they would spend more than their budget. This yields an important problem: selecting the ad auctions in which these advertisers participate, in order to optimize different system objectives such as the return on investment for advertisers, and the quality of ads shown to users. We present a system and algorithms for optimizing such budget constrained spend. The system is designed be deployed in a large search engine, with hundreds of thousands of advertisers, millions of searches per hour, and with the query stream being only partially predictable. We have validated the system design by implementing it in the Google ads serving system and running experiments on live traffic. We have also compared our algorithm to previous work that casts this problem as a large linear programming problem limited to popular queries, and show that our algorithms yield substantially better results.

Categories and Subject Descriptors

G.1.6 [**Optimization**]: Linear Programming; K.6.0 [**General**]: Economics

Keywords

Budget Optimization, Online Advertising

1. INTRODUCTION

Search ad auctions have emerged as the primary model for monetizing the value provided by search engines. Advertisers use phrases (keywords) to specify the set of queries they are interested in, and bid the cost they are prepared to pay per click on their ad. For each search query, the set of ads to show, the order in which they are shown, and the cost per click for each shown ad are determined via an auction.

*The author is currently at Facebook, Inc., Menlo Park, CA, USA. The work described in this paper was done while the author was at Google.

WSDM'13, February 4–8, 2013, Rome, Italy.

Each advertiser also specifies a daily budget, which is an upper bound on the amount of money they are prepared to spend each day. While many advertisers use bids as the primary knob to control their spend and never hit their budget, there exists a significant fraction of advertisers who would spend more than their budget if they participated in every auction that their keywords match. Search engines often provide an option to automatically scale the advertiser's bids [1, 2], but a substantial fraction of budget constrained advertisers do not opt into these programs. For these advertisers, the search engine has to determine the subset of auctions the budget constrained advertiser should participate in. This creates a dependence between auctions on different queries, and leads to essentially a matching or an assignment problem of advertisers to auctions.

In this paper, we consider the problem of *optimized budget allocation*: allocating advertisers to queries such that budget constraints are satisfied, while simultaneously optimizing a specified objective. Prior work in this area has often chosen revenue as the objective to optimize. However, the long term revenue of a search engine depends on providing good value to users and to advertisers. If users see low quality ads, then this can result in ad-blindness and a drop in revenue. If advertisers see low return on investment (ROI), then they will reduce their bids and budgets, again resulting in a drop in revenue. Thus, we explore two other objectives in this paper: improving quality, and advertiser ROI.

Paper Outline We describe the problem of optimized budget allocation in Section 2, followed by related work in Section 3. We present our algorithms and system design in Section 4, and discuss certain key properties of the algorithm in Section 5. In Section 6, we show that our algorithms yield substantially better results than prior work and also describe the results of experiments on live traffic. We conclude with some closing thoughts in Section 7.

2. PROBLEM DEFINITION

Let A be the set of advertisers, and Q the set of queries. Each advertiser $a \in A$ comes with a daily budget B_a. Let $G(A, Q, E)$ be a bipartite graph such that for $a \in A$ and $q \in Q$, edge $(a, q) \in E$ means that an ad of a is eligible for the auction for query q (a's keywords match q). Let $\texttt{ctr}_{(a,q)}$ be the probability of a click on a's ad for q, and $\texttt{bid}_{(a,q)}$ be the amount a is willing to pay per click. (Note that $\texttt{ctr}_{(a,q)}$ is the position-independent CTR, i.e., the probability of a click at some chosen fixed position. In other words, $\texttt{ctr}_{(a,q)}$ does not depend on the position of the ad.)

When a query q arrives, the eligible ads a for q are ranked by $\texttt{bid}_{(a,q)}\texttt{ctr}_{(a,q)}$ and shown in that order. Denoting the jth ad in the order as a_j, the cost per click of a_j is set as

$$\texttt{cpc}(a_j) = \texttt{bid}_{(a_{j+1},q)}\texttt{ctr}_{(a_{j+1},q)}/\texttt{ctr}_{(a_j,q)}$$

This is known as the generalized second price (GSP) auction (see, e.g., [25, 14, 6]).

Let T_a denote the spend of the advertiser a if a participates in all the auctions for which a is eligible via the keyword match (ignoring a's budget). If $T_a > B_a$, the advertiser is budget constrained, and the search engine has to limit (or throttle) the set of auctions in which the advertiser participates.

Objectives. For budget constrained advertisers, the search engine can select to optimize different objectives such as:

- the quality of the ads shown, e.g., maximize the position-independent predicted click-through rate,
- reduce advertiser cost-per-click (maximize the number of clicks), or
- increase advertiser ROI.

We do not have full knowledge of the graph G, but only information from past data, i.e., the graphs from previous days. We also require practical algorithms which work online, i.e., given the next query, decide, in sub-second response time, which ad impressions to show. We can now define the problem as follows.

The Optimized Budget Allocation Problem: Given information about the past as $G'(A, Q', E')$ including the bids and CTR for each advertiser-query pair, the budget B_a, for each advertiser a, and a specified objective function to optimize: For each query arriving in an online stream of queries Q, decide which advertisers should participate in the auction.

3. RELATED WORK

There have been two broad approaches to optimizing budget constrained spend: allocation and bid modification. Allocation treats bids as fixed, and allows only decisions about whether the advertiser should participate in the auction. This is our setting, where we are constrained to not change bids, but only optimize allocations.

The second approach, bid modification, is in a setting where bids can be changed. This body of work typically considers the problem from the advertiser's perspective, and assumes full knowledge of the information that advertisers typically have (such as the value of clicks or conversions). However, this work can also be adapted to be applicable from a search engine's perspective, for advertisers who have opted in and allow the search engine to change their bids.

We next describe the related work in the allocation and bid modification approaches.

Allocation The paper by Abrams et al. [5] is the closest to our work. They solve the offline problem (with complete knowledge of future query frequency) for *head* queries (the most popular search queries) in the GSP auction setting using a linear program (LP), to optimize search engine revenue or advertiser clicks per dollar. Thus their approach yields an optimal solution to the click maximization problem in the general GSP setting. However, there are two reasons why this work is not the final word on the allocation approach. First, the LP can only run over head queries due to resource constraints, which brings up an interesting question: Can a non-optimal algorithm that runs over the entire query stream beat an optimal algorithm that is restricted to the head? Second, the LP formulation can yield solutions that are clearly unfair, in that the allocation for some advertisers is very different from what the advertiser would choose for themselves for that objective (see Section 5). Hence it is unclear whether LP solutions can be deployed by search engines.

A second stream of work focused on optimizing search engine revenue in a first price auction. Mehta et al. [22] and Buchbinder et al. [9] both provide an online approximation algorithm for optimizing revenue, with a best possible approximation guarantee of $1 - 1/e \simeq 63\%$, for the scenario in which we do not know anything about the future distribution of queries. In contrast, we assume that we can predict future distributions of queries, albeit noisily. Mahdian et al. [21] extended the algorithm from [22] to provide guarantees in the setting when we have unreliable estimates. [19, 13] analyzed revenue maximization in an average case setting where queries arrive in a random order, or are picked i.i.d from a distribution. All the above papers focus solely on search engine revenue, assume a first price auction, and do not consider multiple slots or positions. We focus on optimizing very different objectives, such as user experience and advertiser ROI, in the second price GSP auction, with multiple slots and positions.

There has been considerable related work in budget allocation for display ads, e.g., [11, 12, 15, 16, 26]. This work also does not consider second price auctions, or the objectives we study.

There has also been work on designing new incentive compatible auctions in the presence of bidders with budget constraints, initiated by [4, 8]. Our goal is to optimize budgets in the context of the GSP auction used by search engines, and hence we do not consider alternate auction designs.

Bid Modification The second approach [7, 10, 17, 20, 24] studies the advertiser's problem of bidding optimally in order to maximize ROI (or some notion of utility). Changing bids in such a manner is an alternate solution to dealing with budget constrained advertisers: if the advertiser permits, the search engine can scale bids down until the advertiser is no longer budget constrained. However, despite the availability of a free option to automatically scale bids [1], a substantial fraction of budget constrained advertisers have not opted in to use this product. For these advertisers, the search engine (as a policy decision) has to use the allocation approach, not bid modification. Hence the work on bid modification, while clearly an appealing alternative, is not applicable in our setting.

Despite the lack of applicability, it would be interesting to understand how optimized budget allocation fares against bid scaling. We compare our algorithms to bid scaling in Section 6.

4. ALGORITHMS

Given the problem of optimizing budget constrained spend, the first step is to neither over- nor under-spend.[1] The naive way to do this is to let advertisers participate in auctions until they hit their budget, and then make them ineligible for the rest of the day. Clearly, this will yield very biased traffic to the advertiser, and also skew auction competition towards the earlier part of the day. The next simplest approach, which does not have these drawbacks, is *Vanilla Probabilistic Throttling* (VPT).

For each advertiser a, define:

- B_a: the remaining budget for the day (or time period).
- T_a: the remaining maximum spend for the rest of the day, i.e., the total spend if the advertiser had unlimited budget.

We now define the **Vanilla Probabilistic Throttling** algorithm:

```
For each arriving query q:
    For each budget constrained advertiser a:
        Flip a coin with P[Heads] = B_a/T_a.
        If heads, a participates in the auction.
```

Figure 1: Vanilla Probabilistic Throttling (VPT)

If our estimate of T_a is accurate, then each advertiser spends very close to her budget in expectation (and with high probability, by Chernoff bounds). Advertisers also receive a representative sample of the traffic they are eligible for.

4.1 Optimized Throttling

We now present algorithms for optimizing one or more of the following objectives:

- average quality of ads shown, represented by CTR.
- clicks per dollar,
- conversions per dollar,
- the advertiser's profit, using the difference between the bid and the cost per click as the estimate of profit.

For the chosen objective, given a candidate ad impression i (i.e., for a specific query and advertiser), we compute a metric $\theta(i)$ which tracks the desired objective. Given a choice between two impressions (for the same advertiser), we would prefer to show the impression with the higher value of the metric. For example, if the objective is quality, the metric could be the position-independent predicted click-through rate of the advertiser for this query, reflecting our desire to show higher-quality impressions. Conceptually, we would like to rank all the impressions for an advertiser by the desired metric, and choose the impressions with the highest metric score until the budget is filled.

[1]While most advertisers are clearly budget constrained or unconstrained, advertisers at the margin may switch back-and-forth between the two states, based on traffic. It is straightforward to handle these marginal cases. For ease of exposition, we ignore this issue in the paper; however our implementation does handle these cases gracefully.

To achieve this goal, our algorithm uses a third input, the rank $R_{\theta,a}$ of an impression for a given advertiser a and metric θ. Define

- $F_{\theta,a}(\mu)$: Estimated fraction of maximum spend T_a for which $\theta(i) \leq \mu$. In other words, F is the estimated cumulative distribution function of θ.
- $R_{\theta,a}(\mu) = 1 - F_{\theta,a}(\mu)$.

The lower the value of the rank R, the better the impression scores on our metric.

We now define the **Optimized Throttling** algorithm:

```
For each arriving query q:
    For each budget constrained advertiser a:
        If R_θ,a(θ(i)) ≤ B_a/T_a, then a
        participates in the auction.
```

Figure 2: Algorithm OT

While the algorithm appears to be a straightforward greedy algorithm, there are several subtleties:

- The algorithm yields a solution that is "fair" to each advertiser (formally defined, and proved in Section 5).
- The algorithm yields an optimal fair solution under certain constraints. While we can find many examples where the constraints don't hold, the constraints hold often enough that the algorithm is not too far from optimal in practice.
- We have transformed the domain from the space of queries to the distribution of some property of queries. Predicting the frequency of queries in the tail is intractable. Predicting the distribution of specific properties of the queries in the tail is very tractable (for properties we use in our algorithms).
- The choice of metric lets us optimize a wide range of objectives, or combinations of objectives (discussed next).

We now define five instantiations of OT, corresponding to the four objectives we listed earlier, and a fifth objective that combines quality and clicks:

	Objective	θ(i)
OT-CTR	Ad quality	$\mathtt{ctr}_i$
OT-CLICKS	Clicks	$1/\mathtt{cpc}_i$
OT-PROFIT	Profit	$(\mathtt{bid}_i - \mathtt{cpc}_i)/\mathtt{cpc}_i$
OT-CONVERSIONS	Conversions	$\mathtt{cvr}_i\mathtt{val}_i/\mathtt{cpc}_i$
OT-CTR-PROFIT	Blend	$\frac{\mathtt{ctr}_i(\mathtt{bid}_i - \mathtt{cpc}_i)}{\mathtt{cpc}_i}$

Figure 3: Instantiations of OT

The first metric, $\mathtt{ctr}_i$ is straightforward: we are using position-independent predicted CTR as a proxy for quality. (Of course, one could use any arbitrary quality metric instead of CTR.)

To understand the next three metrics, it is helpful to multiply the numerator and denominator by the position-dependent predicted CTR. For example, in OT-CLICKS, the numerator now becomes the expected number of clicks, and the denominator the expected cost, and the ratio is the clicks per dollar. Since the total spend is fixed for budget constrained advertisers, optimizing clicks is equivalent to optimizing clicks per dollar. [2]

For OT-PROFIT, assuming that $\texttt{bid}_i$ is the value to the advertiser, $\texttt{bid}_i - \texttt{cpc}_i$ is the expected profit to the advertiser if there is a click on this impression. So the metric for OT-PROFIT is the expected profit per dollar of spend.

For OT-CONVERSIONS the metric is the expected conversion value per dollar, given the value of a conversion on this impression $\texttt{val}_i$, and a model that predicts the conversion rate $\texttt{cvr}_i$. Building machine learning models for estimating $\texttt{cvr}_i$ is beyond the scope of the paper. However, we will note the existence of commercial systems that estimate $\texttt{cvr}_i$ given advertiser-specific conversion data, e.g., [2]. Advertisers do not necessarily need to provide conversion data in order to benefit from the techniques in the paper. One can build models for estimating conversion rate that are not advertiser-specific, e.g., we found that $\texttt{ctr}_i$ is correlated with $\texttt{cvr}_i$.

The final metric simply multiplies the metric for CTR and profit. The intuition is that for advertisers with a lot of variance on CTR but not much on profit, the algorithm will focus on CTR. Similarly for advertisers with more variance on profit than CTR, the algorithm will focus on profit. Thus if the search engine cares about both CTR and advertiser profit, the blended metric will likely yield better results than simply averaging the results of the individual metrics.

4.2 System design and implementation

We next describe our implementation of the algorithm in the production Google ads serving system. Our system has three primary components:

- estimating B_a/T_a,
- estimating and compressing $R_{\theta,a}$, and
- using the estimates at serving time.

We will use OT-CTR to illustrate the techniques used, and discuss any differences between OT-CTR and the other instantiations as they come up.

Estimating B_a/T_a: This component estimates the *impression probability* $\texttt{ip}$, where $\texttt{ip}$ is defined as B_a/T_a. In other words, $\texttt{ip}$ is the probability with which we should allow an impression of the advertiser to participate in an auction, in order to show her impressions uniformly through the remainder of the day, and exhaust her budget at the end of the day. We estimate $\texttt{ip}$ using traffic information from the past, and using the available budget. Given the inherent noise in traffic, a feedback loop is used at frequent intervals to adjust the probability. Clearly, the more accurate the estimate of $\texttt{ip}$, the more the gains from optimization.

Estimating and compressing $R_{\theta,a}$: We use historical data to compute the cumulative distribution function $F_{\theta,a}$. $R_{\theta,a}$ is a trivial transformation of $F_{\theta,a}$. In the rest of this section, we will drop the subscripts and refer to $R_{\theta,a}$ as R (purely for ease of exposition). Since a search engine has a large number of advertisers, we would like to compress the information in R at serving time. We compress R into a histogram H.

Recall that R is only used to answer the question of whether $R(\theta(i))$ is less than $\texttt{ip}$ ($= B_a/T_a$). So if the estimate of $\texttt{ip}$ was very stable, we need just two buckets in the histogram H, with the boundary at the value c^* such that $R(c^*) = \texttt{ip}$. With two buckets, we would need just 8 bytes of data per budget constrained advertiser: the value c^* and the value of $R(c^*)$.

We may choose to create additional buckets around the threshold c^*, based on the tradeoff between increased gains from choosing the highest scoring impressions (see below) versus memory constraints. For each bucket m in H excluding the last bucket, we store the bucket boundary and the value of R at the bucket boundary. We refer to these histograms as *throttling parameters.*

Using the estimates at serving: When a query arrives, we need to determine, for each budget constrained advertiser a, whether a participates in the auction. The input consists of the histogram H, the current value of $\texttt{ip}$, and the value of $\theta(i)$ for the current impression i. Let $\theta(i)$ be in bucket m. Let $H_b(m)$ denote the upper boundary of bucket m, and let $H_r(m) = R(H_b(m))$. Then the advertiser participates in the auction with the following probability:

$$\begin{cases} 1, & \text{if } H_r(m) \le \texttt{ip} \\ 0, & \text{if } H_r(m-1) \ge \texttt{ip} \\ \frac{\texttt{ip} - H_r(m-1)}{H_r(m) - H_r(m-1)}, & \text{otherwise} \end{cases}$$

The first two cases are straightforward, and follow directly from the goal that we (do not) show the impression if it is (not) in the top $\texttt{ip}$ fraction of spend. In the third case, the probability that the impression is in the top $\texttt{ip}$ fraction of spend is given by $(\texttt{ip} - H_r(m-1))/(H_r(m) - H_r(m-1))$, and hence we show the impression with that probability.

Implementation: We have built our data collection pipeline on top of Google's *sawzall* [23] infrastructure, which allows us to process historical query data in parallel. The throttling parameters generated by the data collection pipeline is written to the *Google File System (GFS)* [18]. The data is stored in the *protocol buffer* format [3], which reduces the storage requirement as well as make the transfer and processing of the data more efficient. From GFS, the throttling parameters data is picked up by the *ads data push* system, which writes it to one of its data channels. The ads serving system gets the updated throttling parameters through this channel.

Interactions between budget constrained advertisers: Out of the metrics in Figure 3, $\texttt{ctr}_i$, $\texttt{bid}_i$, $\texttt{cvr}_i$ and $\texttt{val}_i$ are all functions purely of the impression, and do not change based on the other ads in the auction. However, $\texttt{cpc}_i$ is a function of the runner-up, since we use a second-price auction. We analyzed the logs, and found that budget constrained ads are more likely to be next to budget unconstrained ads than budget unconstrained ads. However, we will have instances with consecutive budget constrained ads. We use an iterative technique for improving the performance of the online algorithms in these cases.

The intuition behind the iterative technique is to run sev-

[2]Some metrics like $\texttt{ctr}_i$ are purely a function of the impression. However, metrics like $\texttt{cpc}$ may change based on the other ads in the auction. We discuss this issue in Section 4.2.

eral (simulated) iterations of the auction. In each iteration, we compute the metric θ for each budget constrained advertiser (including those that do not participate in the auction in the current iteration), and based on the value of the metric, decide whether that advertiser participates in the next iteration. Note that an impression may be removed in one iteration and re-enter in a subsequent iteration. While we cannot prove convergence, in practice this often converges in a few rounds, or at least leads to an improved solution over simply using the value of θ from the first iteration.

5. KEY PROPERTIES OF ALGORITHM

The overall effectiveness of the algorithm depends on two factors: the accuracy of the prediction of future traffic (total traffic and the distribution of the metric), and the intrinsic effectiveness of the algorithm. To understand the latter, we analyze the algorithm on the offline version of the problem, in which the advertiser-query graph is known. We will focus on the instantiations with a linear objective: OT-CLICKS, OT-PROFIT and OT-CONVERSIONS. For non-linear objectives such as CTR, optimality with even a single budget constrained advertiser may require allocation in a manner that is clearly against the advertiser's interest. So algorithms like OT-CTR which are designed to both be good for advertisers and improve quality cannot be optimal.

We first consider the special case of a single budget constrained advertiser, and show that our algorithm is optimal for linear objectives. We then discuss the issue of fairness when there are multiple budget constrained advertisers, and show by example that linear programming can yield solutions that are optimal but not fair. When we restrict the space of solutions to fair solutions, we show that our algorithm yields an optimal solution even with multiple budget constrained advertisers, as long as there are no adjacent budget constrained advertisers in a given auction. Obviously, we do get adjacent budget constrained advertisers in the real world – but the optimality result with that constraint suggests that the algorithm will perform well in practice.

For ease of exposition, we will choose the simplest instantiation, OT-CLICKS as the representative algorithm in the proofs. It is straightforward to sketch out similar proofs for OT-PROFIT and OT-CONVERSIONS.

5.1 Optimal For A Single Budget Constrained Advertiser

We start by proving that given $G(A, Q, E)$ and a single budget constrained advertiser $a \in A$, OT-CLICKS maximizes clicks per dollar for a. While the proof is obvious, it is useful as a building block to more interesting results.

Given an advertiser a, we define:

- E_a to be the set of impressions in queries where a is eligible to participate in the auction, and
- $I_a \subseteq E_a$ to be the set of impressions where a participates in the auction.

The total expected clicks is $\sum_{i \in I_a} \alpha_i \mathtt{ctr}_i$, where α_i is the position normalizer. For fixed budget, maximizing clicks per dollar is the same as maximizing total clicks, which is captured by the following linear program: Given a, find

$$\underset{I_a \subseteq E_a}{\mathtt{Max}} \sum_{i \in I_a} \alpha_i \mathtt{ctr}_i \ , \quad s.t. \quad \sum_{i \in I_a} \mathtt{spend}_i \leq B_a \qquad (1)$$

- Rank the impressions $i \in E_a$ in order of decreasing $1/\mathtt{cpc}_i$.
- Pick the top impressions in E_a according to this ranking until the budget runs out, i.e. the largest prefix I_a, s.t. $\sum_{i \in I_a} \mathtt{spend}_i \leq B_a$, and at most one additional fractional impression to finish the budget.

Figure 4: Offline-OT-CLICKS-Single-Advertiser

Without fractional impressions, this is the integral knapsack problem. Since one click is a tiny fraction of advertiser spend, we allow the choice of one fractional impression, thereby converting the problem to a fractional knapsack problem. Observing that $\mathtt{spend}_i = \alpha_i \mathtt{ctr}_i \mathtt{cpc}_i$ and therefore $\alpha_i \mathtt{ctr}_i / \mathtt{spend}_i = 1/\mathtt{cpc}_i$, we get the algorithm in Figure 4, which is a simple greedy algorithm, using the ratio of the expected value from the click to the cost of the click. Theorem 1 follows from the well known optimality of the greedy strategy for the fractional knapsack problem, and its proof is omitted here.

THEOREM 1. *Offline-OT-CLICKS-Single-Advertiser computes an optimal solution to the ROI maximization problem for a single budget constrained advertiser.*

5.2 Fair Allocations

We begin with the following definition of an optimal allocation:

Definition 1. We call an allocation **optimal** if it maximizes

$$\frac{\sum_{a \in A} w_a \sum_{i \in I_a} \alpha_i \mathtt{ctr}_i}{\sum_{a \in A} w_a}$$

over all possible allocations (given the $w_a \geq 0$, which are arbitrary advertiser specific weights).

However, this definition has the problem that in trying to maximize the weighted average of advertiser ROI, we may end up sacrificing the interests of some advertisers, as the following example illustrates.

EXAMPLE 1. There are two budget constrained bidders, a and b, each with a budget of \$100. There are two different queries q_1 and q_2, each with 100 instances. q_1 has a minimum reserve cpc of \$1, and q_2 has a reserve of \$2 (one may replace the reserves by an unconstrained bidder, keeping the example unchanged). The bidders bid the following values for the queries (a does not bid on q_2):

	q_1	q_2
a	20	–
b	10	10
min	1	2

For ease of exposition, we assume that the CTR is equal for all advertisers and query pairs, in both positions. To maximize total clicks, or equivalently, clicks per dollar, the optimal solution is to let a participate in q_1, and b in q_2. Then a gets 100 clicks and b gets 50, giving a total of 150 clicks at a cost-per-click of \$1.33. But this solution is not fair to b, who would rather show for q_1 and get a cpc of \$1 and hence 100 clicks instead of 50. In this scenario a would get only 10 clicks at a cpc of \$10, giving a total of 110 clicks at an average cpc of \$1.81. □

Example 1 motivates the following definition:

Definition 2. We define an allocation $I \subseteq E$ to be a **fair allocation** for the clicks objective, if $\forall\ a \in A$:

a. The expected spend of a is equal to B_a (a exhausts its budget), or $I_a = E_a$ (we show every impression of a it is eligible for).

b. Given the allocation of other advertisers (i.e. $I \backslash I_a$), I_a maximizes the total expected clicks that a can obtain within its budget.

We call an allocation I an **optimal fair allocation** if it is a fair allocation, and it maximizes

$$\frac{\sum_{a \in A} w_a \sum_{i \in I_a} \alpha_i \mathtt{ctr}_i}{\sum_{a \in A} w_a}$$

among all fair allocation (where the $w_a \geq 0$ are arbitrary advertiser specific weights).

We can similarly define fair allocations and optimal fair allocations for the profit objective and the conversions objective.

In Example 1, the allocation which maximizes the sum (giving 150 clicks) is not a fair allocation, while allocating both a and b to q_1 is (even though this reduces the total clicks to 110). We note that our definition of fair allocation is analogous to that of a *Nash equilibrium* in games.

5.3 Optimal Fair Allocation When No Adjacent Budget Constrained Advertisers

When there are multiple budget constrained advertisers, a natural local algorithm is to cycle over the different advertisers until convergence, running Algorithm Offline-OT-Clicks-Single-Advertiser for each advertiser a. In the remainder of this section we analyze this algorithm, which is defined in Figure 5.

In a GSP auction, there are two ways in which the introduction or removal of an impression i of one budget constrained advertiser can effect an impression i' of another:

- i can change the cpc of i'
- i can change the position of i', and hence the expected spend from i'.

Due to this interaction, it is unclear whether Algorithm Offline-OT-Clicks always yields an optimal fair allocation. However we will show that it does converge to a optimal fair allocation when there are no adjacent budget constrained bidders, i.e., in the auction ranking of all eligible bidders, there are no consecutive budget constrained bidders. The key property is that in such a scenario, the cpc of a budget constrained impression is independent of other budget constrained impressions (even though the position may change

1. Begin with an allocation with only budget unconstrained advertisers.
2. For each budget constrained advertiser $a \in A$ (in turn):
   –Run Offline-OT-Clicks-Single-Advertiser for a.
   –Update I.
3. If the allocation has not converged, go to step 2.

Figure 5: Algorithm Offline-OT-Clicks.

due to the insertion or removal of other budget constrained impressions). As an aside, this key property also holds for first price auctions, and the following results also hold for first price auctions.

Given this property, for each advertiser a, the 1 / cpc ordering of the impressions in E_a is fixed throughout the algorithm, independent of the allocations of the other advertisers. From the definition, it is easy to see that every fair allocation has the property that for each $a \in A$, I_a is a prefix of this fixed ordering of E_a, since a non-prefix would violate Property (b) in Definition 2. By definition of the algorithm, this is true also for the allocations produced during every step of the algorithm. We call allocations with this property *prefix-allocations*.

Lemma 2. *Algorithm Offline-OT-Clicks converges to a fair allocation if there are no adjacent constrained bidders in any query.*

Proof. Fix an advertiser a, and consider the allocation to a in each round. We claim that the prefix chosen for a only increases in length in subsequent rounds. Since for each advertiser the prefix cannot increase indefinitely, this means that the algorithm converges to some allocation, say I^*. Property (a) in Definition 2 holds for I^* because of the termination condition of Offline-OT-Clicks. Property (b) holds by definition of Offline-OT-Clicks-Single-Advertiser, which is run in every round of Offline-OT-Clicks.

It remains to prove the claim that the prefix for a can only increase in each round. Suppose this is true up to the time we process advertiser a in round k. In between the times we process a in rounds k and $k+1$, the algorithm may have introduced impressions of other advertisers in the auctions for which we show a's impressions in round k. The only effect this can have on a's impression is to possibly lower its position, and therefore of its expected spend. Thus, in round $k+1$, the algorithm may need to pick a longer prefix to finish a's budget. □

For two prefix-allocations I, J, we say $I \prec J$ if for every advertiser $a \in A$, the prefix length in I is at most the prefix length in J, and therefore $I_a \subseteq J_a$.

Lemma 3. *Let I^* be the fair allocation that Algorithm Offline-OT-Clicks converges to (when there are no adjacent constrained bidders). Then*

$$I^* \prec I, \textit{ for all fair allocations } I$$

Proof. If this is not true for some fair allocation I, then consider the *first time* during the run of the algorithm that some advertiser a's prefix becomes longer than its prefix in I. Comparing to I, the algorithm's current allocation has all advertisers $a' \neq a$ with smaller or equal prefixes. Thus the position normalizers of a's impressions are larger or equal during this step of the algorithm than in the allocation I. This implies that the prefix of a in the current allocation should be shorter or equal than that in I, since the expected spend in each auction is at least that in I, a contradiction. □

Note that Lemma 3 implies that there is a unique $\prec$-minimal fair allocation, and that the algorithm converges to it.

THEOREM 4. *Algorithm Offline-*OT-CLICKS *converges to an optimal fair allocation if there are no adjacent constrained bidders in any query.*

PROOF. From Lemma 2 we know that the algorithm converges to a fair allocation I^*. From Lemma 3 we get that for every advertiser a, and every fair allocation I, a's prefix in I^* is no longer than its prefix in I. Thus a spends the same amount of money (in expectation) in I^* as in I, but spends it on a subset $(I^*)_a \subseteq I_a$ such that impressions in $I_a \backslash (I^*)_a$ have lower (or equal) ratios of value of click to cost of click, as impressions in $(I^*)_a$. This implies that a gets at least as much total expected value in I^* as in I, in turn implying that I^* maximizes any weighted average (over advertisers) of the total expected value obtained, among all fair allocations. □

As mentioned earlier, it is easy to prove similar statements about other linear objectives such as optimizing profit and optimizing conversions.

6. EMPIRICAL EVALUATION

We report two types of experiments below, offline simulations to compare different optimized allocation solutions, and live experiments on Google traffic. We start with a description of prior approaches: LP and BidScaling.

6.1 LP and BidScaling

6.1.1 Linear Programming

Assuming complete knowledge of the data, a theoretical benchmark for any budget allocation algorithm can be obtained via linear programming [5]. For any query q, let s denote the set of bidders chosen to participate in the auction by an allocation mechanism. Let $\mathcal{C}(q)$ be the collection of all such sets, generated by *any* conceivable algorithm. Clearly, we can completely specify an allocation policy by specifying for each query q, the set $s \in \mathcal{C}(q)$ of bidders permitted by the algorithm to participate in the auction for q.

We can then attempt to discover the best allocation policy (for a given linear objective, say click maximization) using linear programming. Let N_q be the number of times query q appears in the data and x_{qs} be the number of times the set s of bidders is selected for query q. For a bidder $i \in s$, let cpc_{qsi} and ctr_{qsi} be the cost-per-click and click-through rate for i in the auction for q. Let α_{si} be the position normalizer for impression i. Let B_i be the budget of bidder i. Then, we can discover the best allocation policy that maximizes total clicks provided to budget constrained advertisers as the solution of the following linear program:

$$\max \sum_{q,s,i} \alpha_{si}\text{ctr}_{qsi}x_{qs}$$

$$\text{Allocation constraint:} \quad \sum_{s} x_{qs} \leq N_q \quad \forall q$$

$$\text{Budget constraint:} \quad \sum_{q,s} \text{cpc}_{qsi}\alpha_{si}\text{ctr}_{qsi}x_{qs} \leq B_i \quad \forall i$$

One can optimize for other linear metrics, such as revenue by suitably changing the objective function. It is not possible to directly optimize for non-linear metrics such as CTR.

The advantage of LP (compared to our approach) is that the LP fully incorporates interactions between different budget constrained advertisers. However, even the most efficient LP solvers cannot solve linear programs on the volume of data a search engine sees in a day. Thus we have to limit LP to the head portion of query traffic, and use an approach such as Vanilla Probabilistic Throttling on the long tail.

6.1.2 Bid Scaling

Both the OT algorithms and the LP formulation work under the constraint that the bidder's inputs (bids) can not be changed by the search engine, but they can only be throttled. Bid Scaling algorithms go outside this design space by lowering the bids of the constrained bidders appropriately. As we discussed in Section 1, bid scaling is not an option for our problem. Nevertheless, it is interesting to compare our approach against bid scaling.

Our bid scaling algorithm finds one bid multiplier per bidder and applies it to all the advertiser's bids, similar to the Budget Optimizer product in Google Adwords [1]. The multiplier is calculated so as to spend exactly the bidder's budget.

6.2 Simulation Methodology

We conducted simulations using a 20% sample of all US queries made over a week to the Google search engine. We sorted queries by the total impressions for that query (summed over all query instances), and picked the queries with the most impressions as the "head" queries for the LP. The number of queries in the head was chosen so that the LP could run in memory. (Note that as we move from the head to the tail, each query has relatively few instances. So even doubling the memory will not substantially increase the fraction of revenue or clicks covered by the "head" queries.) For each set (head and tail), we computed an appropriate budget for that set by scaling down the total budgets. For each query we also have the candidate ads together with the relevant metrics, namely, the bid and the predicted CTR. Our simulation is offline, i.e., the set of queries and candidates is fixed. Since all the algorithms we simulate are time independent (as opposed to some of the bid scaling algorithms studied earlier, e.g., [22, 9, 13, 16, 15]), we do not need to worry about the time-arrival order of the queries.

We simulated the following throttling algorithms for our first set of comparisons:

1. VPT: Vanilla Probabilistic Throttling.
2. OT-CLICKS: Optimized Throttling, objective is clicks (or inverse of cpc).

3. OT-CTR: Optimized Throttling, objective is CTR.
4. BidScaling, as described in Section 6.1.2
5. LP-Clicks: Click maximizing Linear Program on head queries.

6.3 Results

We show the changes in various objectives relative to the baseline of Vanilla Probabilistic Throttling (VPT). It is important to note that while we expect the overall conclusions to carry over to an online setting where the query distribution changes over time, the exact numbers will change. In general, the gains from optimized budget allocation or bid scaling will be significantly lower in live experiments due to changes in query traffic. For this reason, as well as data confidentiality, we omit the scale from our graphs below.

6.3.1 Comparison with LP

Figure 6 shows the change in clicks per dollar for budget constrained advertisers for each of the algorithms. The first set of numbers, "head", show the results when we artificially restrict all the algorithms to operate over the same set of head queries as LP-Clicks, with VPT on the tail. Since LP-Clicks is not just optimal, but can also generate solutions that are not fair (unlike the other algorithms), it is not surprising that LP-Clicks outperforms the alternatives.

However, when we allow the algorithms to optimize over the entire dataset – the "all" numbers – the algorithms that can use the full data dramatically outperform LP-Clicks. In fact, even OT-CTR, which is optimizing CTR and not CPC, yields a higher drop in CPC (or equivalently, more clicks per dollar) than LP-Clicks. The reason for the poor performance of LP-Clicks is that the LP can be run only on the head, and even though the head queries account for a substantial portion of revenue, they are relatively homogeneous – the potential gains from optimization are more in the tail than the head. We found that this held for the other metrics as well, i.e., the substantial majority of the gains from optimization came from the tail queries.[3]

6.3.2 Comparison with BidScaling

The other interesting comparison in Figure 6 is between OT-Clicks and BidScaling. BidScaling performs slightly better than OT-Clicks when restricted to head queries, as many advertisers may appear for a relatively small number of queries in the head. Thus OT-Clicks, which doesn't have the flexibility to scale bids, has a bit less room to maneuver. Over all queries, OT-Clicks has much more scope to differentiate between queries, and hence does slightly better than BidScaling.

However, OT-Clicks may be getting the gains by dropping high bid, high cpc clicks which might still yield more profit for the advertiser than low bid, low cpc clicks. Figure 7 shows how the algorithms do on estimated profit-per-dollar: the sum of the bids minus the total cost, divided by the total cost, over all budget constrained campaigns. (From this

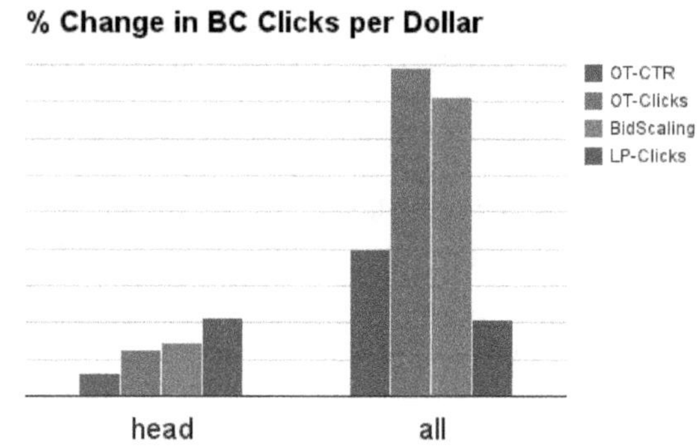

Figure 6: Impact on clicks-per-dollar, over budget constrained campaigns. The baseline is VPT.

point, all figures represent performance using all queries, not just the head.) Here OT-Clicks does much worse than BidScaling, though it is still positive. In fact, even OT-CTR beats OT-Clicks. OT-Profit, which attempts to optimize profit, yields similar results to BidScaling.

As discussed in the introduction, user experience (quality of ads) is as important as advertiser ROI for long-term success. At first glance, one might expect that optimizing clicks per dollar would yield similar results to optimizing CTR: doesn't a higher click-through rate mean more clicks? However, what matters for optimizing clicks per dollar (with a fixed budget) is the cost per click, not the click-through rate.

Figure 8 shows the change in CTR for each of the algorithms. OT-CTR dramatically outperforms all other algorithms, not surprising since it is the only algorithm explicitly trying to optimize quality. Interestingly, while both OT-Profit and BidScaling gave similar gains in profit-per-dollar, their effect on quality is quite different: OT-Profit improves CTR, while BidScaling reduces CTR.

6.3.3 Multiple Objectives

We now present results with metrics that blend the CTR and profit objectives. In Section 4 we had conjectured that blended metrics might yield better results than individual metrics, since different advertisers may have better scope for optimization along different dimensions. Figures 9 and 10 show the impact of two blended metrics: $\mathtt{ctr}(\mathtt{bid}_i - \mathtt{cpc}_i)/\mathtt{cpc}$, and $\mathtt{ctr}^2(\mathtt{bid}_i - \mathtt{cpc}_i)/\mathtt{cpc}$. Notice that OT-CTR-Profit, which uses the former as the metric, almost matches OT-Profit on profit-per-dollar, while yielding significantly higher gains in CTR than OT-Profit. OT-CTR2-Profit further increases CTR gains, for a bit more drop in profit-per-dollar. In addition to validating our conjecture that blended metrics may yield better results, such blended metrics let the search engine pick any arbitrary point in a curve that trades gains in user quality for gains in advertiser value.

6.3.4 Summary

For optimizing clicks-per-dollar, OT-Clicks dramatically outperformed LP-Clicks by using all the data. For optimizing profit-per-dollar, OT-Profit matched BidScal-

[3]An implementation of LP that used more resources could narrow the gap by increasing the fraction of queries covered by the "head". However, as the number of distinct queries increases rapidly for each fraction of additional coverage, every doubling of resources will only yield incremental gains.

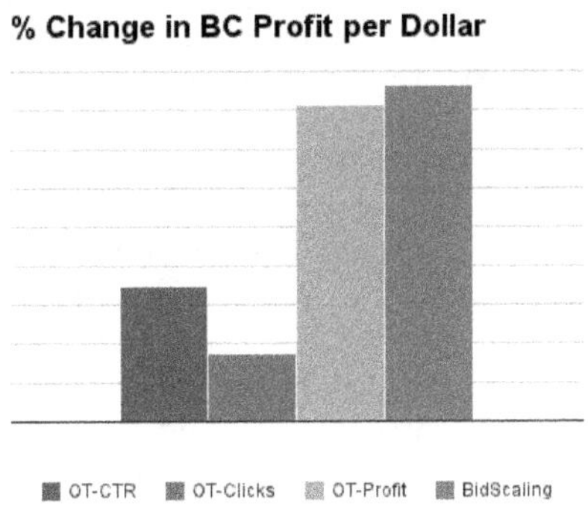

Figure 7: Impact on profit-per-dollar, over budget constrained campaigns. The baseline is VPT.

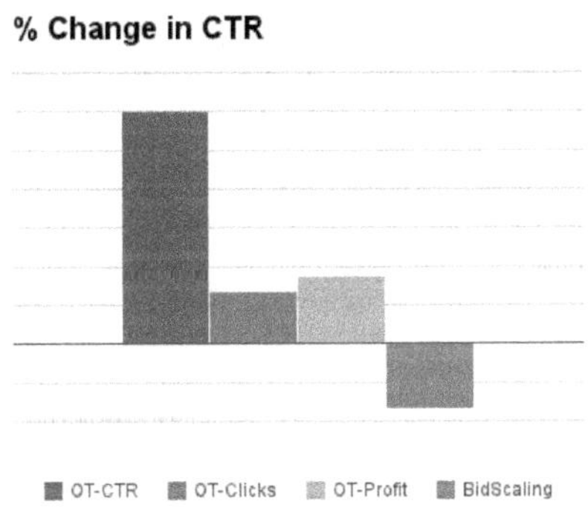

Figure 8: Impact on CTR (including all campaigns). The baseline is VPT.

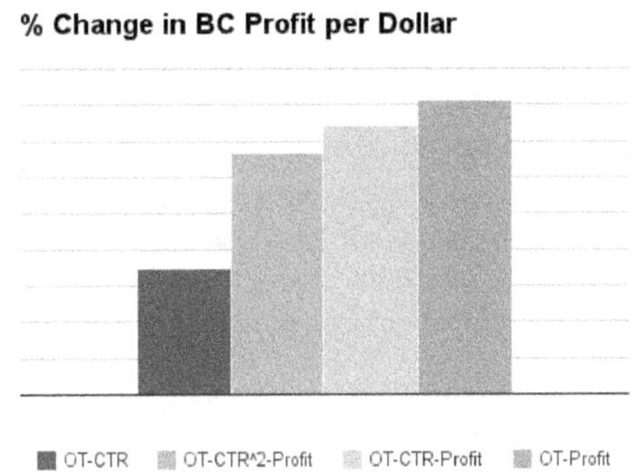

Figure 9: Multiple objectives: impact on Profit-per-dollar. The baseline is VPT.

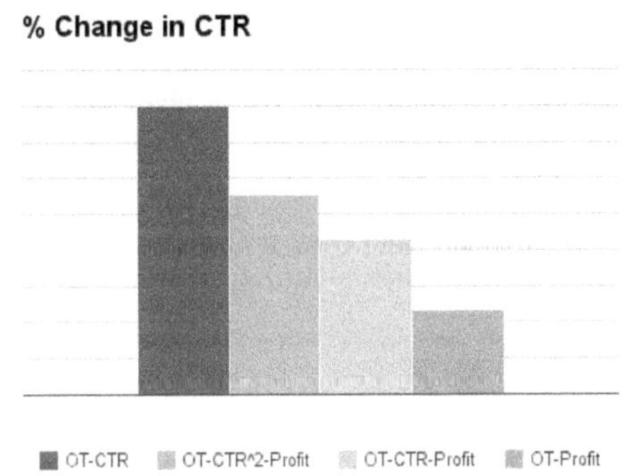

Figure 10: Multiple objectives: impact on CTR. The baseline is VPT.

ING on profit-per-dollar, while yielding better CTR (quality for users). If the primary goal was quality, OT-CTR blew away the other algorithms, while still improving advertiser profit-per-dollar and clicks-per-dollar. Finally, blending multiple metrics can yield better results than a single metric, since different advertisers have more scope for optimization along different metrics.

One might wonder whether implementation of such techniques would incentivize budget unconstrained advertisers to lower their budgets and become budget constrained. The answer is negative: BIDSCALING did slightly better than OT-PROFIT from an advertiser's perspective (ignoring quality for users), and BIDSCALING only used the information available to the search engine, not the additional information available to the advertiser. With additional information about conversion rates for each keyword, or the true value of each click (rather than using the bid as the proxy for value), the advertiser easily get better ROI by optimizing their campaign (versus becoming budget constrained).

6.4 Live Traffic Experiments

We implemented our algorithms in Google's production ad serving system, and ran experiments on live traffic, with both OT-CTR and BIDSCALING. The results were consistent with our simulations, though the magnitude of the gains was significantly less than in the simulations, since we have complete knowledge of future queries in the simulations, unlike the partial predictability of live traffic.

For OT-CTR, the experiments showed statistically significant improvements in quality for users, clicks, and conversions, while revenue was neutral – a Pareto improvement to all objectives. Gains in conversions per dollar were significantly higher than the gains in clicks per dollar, since CTR is correlated with conversion rate. Thus by shifting spend to ads with higher CTR, we also increased the number of conversions.

7. CONCLUSION

We studied the problem of allocating budget constrained spend in order to maximize objectives such as quality for users, or ROI for advertisers. We introduced the concept of fair allocations (analogous to Nash equilibriums), and constrained the space of algorithms to those that yielded fair allocations. We were also constrained (in our setting) to not modify bids. We proposed a family of *Optimized Throttling* algorithms that work within these constraints, and can be used to optimize different objectives. In fact, they can be tuned to pick an arbitrary point in the tradeoff curve between multiple objectives.

Prior approaches such linear programming and bid scaling

are not applicable in our setting: linear programming yields unfair allocations, and bid scaling changes bids. It was nevertheless interesting to study how much of a penalty (if any) our algorithms pay for working within these constraints (fair allocations, fixed bids). We found that, surprisingly, our algorithms dramatically outperform linear programming – by being fast enough to use all the data rather than being limited to head queries. Our algorithms are also competitive with bid scaling on advertiser metrics, while yielding better ad quality for users.

The Optimized Throttling algorithms are designed for implementation in a high throughput production system. The computation overhead at serving time is negligible: just a few comparisons. The algorithms also have a minimal memory footprint, as little as 8 bytes (plus hash table overhead) per advertiser. Finally, they are robust with respect to errors in estimating future traffic, since they only need the total volume of traffic and the distribution of the chosen metric, not the number of occurrences of each query. We validated our system design by implementing our algorithms in the Google ads serving system, and running experiments on live traffic. The experiments showed significant improvements in both advertiser ROI (conversions per dollar) and user experience.

Acknowledgments: We thank Anshul Kothari for his contributions to the algorithms and system design.

8. REFERENCES

[1] Google automatic bidding product. `http://adwords.google.com/support/aw/bin/answer.py?hl=en&answer=113234`.

[2] Google conversion optimizer product. `http://www.google.com/adwords/conversionoptimizer/`.

[3] Protocol buffers. Website, 2008. `http://code.google.com/p/protobuf`.

[4] Z. Abrams. Revenue maximization when bidders have budgets. In *SODA*, 2006.

[5] Z. Abrams, S. Keerthi, O. Mendelevitch, and J. Tomlin. Ad delivery with budgeted advertisers: a comprehensive lp approach. *J. Electronic Commerce Research*, 9(1), 2008.

[6] G. Aggarwal, A. Goel, and R. Motwani. Truthful auctions for pricing search keywords. In *EC*, 2006.

[7] C. Borgs, J. Chayes, N. Immorlica, K. Jain, O. Etesami, and M. Mahdian. Dynamics of bid optimization in online advertisement auctions. In *Proc. of the 16th international conference on World Wide Web*, pages 531–540. ACM, 2007.

[8] C. Borgs, J. Chayes, N. Immorlica, M. Mahdian, and A. Saberi. Multi-unit auctions with budget-constrained bidders. In *EC*, pages 44–51, 2005.

[9] N. Buchbinder, K. Jain, and J. Naor. Online Primal-Dual Algorithms for Maximizing Ad-Auctions Revenue. In *ESA*, 2007.

[10] M. Cary, A. Das, B. Edelman, I. Giotis, K. Heimerl, A. Karlin, C. Mathieu, and M. Schwarz. Greedy bidding strategies for keyword auctions. In *Proc. of the 8th ACM conference on Electronic commerce*, pages 262–271. ACM New York, NY, USA, 2007.

[11] D. X. Charles, M. Chickering, N. R. Devanur, K. Jain, and M. Sanghi. Fast algorithms for finding matchings in lopsided bipartite graphs with applications to display ads. In *ACM Conference on Electronic Commerce*, pages 121–128, 2010.

[12] Y. Chen, P. Berkhin, B. Anderson, and N. Devanur. Real-time bidding algorithms for performance-based display ad allocation. In *KDD*, pages 1307–1315. ACM, 2011.

[13] N. R. Devanur and T. P. Hayes. The adwords problem: online keyword matching with budgeted bidders under random permutations. In *ACM Conference on Electronic Commerce*, pages 71–78, 2009.

[14] B. Edelman, M. Ostrovsky, and M. Schwarz. Internet Advertising and the Generalized Second-Price Auction. *American Economic Review*, 97(1):242–259, 2007.

[15] J. Feldman, M. Henzinger, N. Korula, V. S. Mirrokni, and C. Stein. Online stochastic packing applied to display ad allocation. In *ESA (1)*, pages 182–194, 2010.

[16] J. Feldman, N. Korula, V. S. Mirrokni, S. Muthukrishnan, and M. Pál. Online ad assignment with free disposal. In *WINE*, pages 374–385, 2009.

[17] J. Feldman, S. Muthukrishnan, M. Pal, and C. Stein. Budget optimization in search-based advertising auctions. In *EC*, 2007.

[18] S. Ghemawat, H. Gobioff, and S.-T. Leung. The Google File System. In *19th ACM Symposium on Operating Systems Principles*, 2003.

[19] G. Goel and A. Mehta. Online budgeted matching in random input models with applications to Adwords. In *SODA*, 2008.

[20] K. Hosanagar and V. Cherepanov. Optimal bidding in stochastic budget constrained slot auctions. In *EC*, 2008.

[21] M. Mahdian, H. Nazerzadeh, and A. Saberi. Allocating online advertisement space with unreliable estimates. In *EC*, 2007.

[22] A. Mehta, A. Saberi, U. V. Vazirani, and V. V. Vazirani. Adwords and generalized online matching. *J. ACM*, 54(5), 2007.

[23] R. Pike, S. Dorward, R. Griesemer, and S. Quinlan. Interpreting the data: Parallel analysis with sawzall. *Scientific Programming Journal*, 13:277–298, 2005.

[24] P. Rusmevichientong and D. Williamson. An adaptive algorithm for selecting profitable keywords for search-based advertising services. In *EC*, 2006.

[25] H. Varian. Position auctions. *International Journal of Industrial Organization*, 25(6):1163–1178, 2007.

[26] E. Vee, S. Vassilvitskii, and J. Shanmugasundaram. Optimal online assignment with forecasts. In *ACM Conference on Electronic Commerce*, pages 109–118, 2010.

Characterizing and Supporting Cross-Device Search Tasks

Yu Wang
Emory University
Atlanta, GA 30322 USA
yu.wang@emory.edu

Xiao Huang
Microsoft
Bellevue, WA 98004 USA
xiaohua@microsoft.com

Ryen W. White
Microsoft Research
Redmond, WA 98052 USA
ryenw@microsoft.com

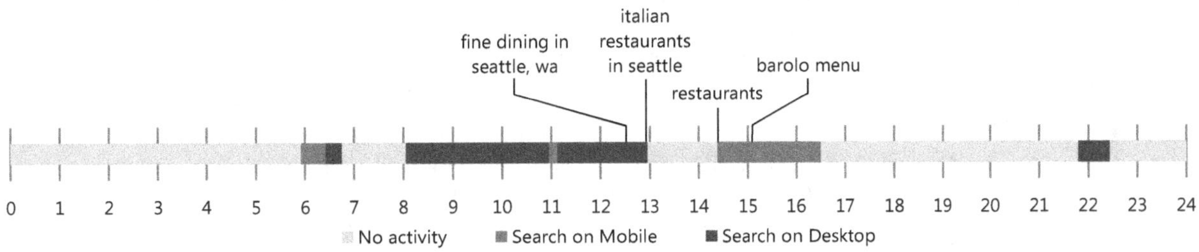

Figure 1. Search activities on mobile and desktop of a fictitious user over the course of a single day. Numbers denote hours from midnight. Queries of interest (relevant to the body of the paper) are included above the figure for reference.

ABSTRACT
Web searchers frequently transition from desktop computers and laptops to mobile devices, and vice versa. Little is known about the nature of cross-device search tasks, yet they represent an important opportunity for search engines to help their users, especially those on the target (post-switch) device. For example, the search engine could save the current session and re-instate it post switch, or it could capitalize on down-time between devices to proactively retrieve content on behalf of the searcher. In this paper, we present a log-based study to define and characterize cross-device search behavior and predict the resumption of cross-device tasks. Using data from a large commercial search engine, we show that there are discernible and noteworthy patterns of search behavior associated with device transitions. We also develop learned models for predicting task resumption on the target device using behavioral, topical, geospatial, and temporal features. Our findings show that our models can attain strong prediction accuracy and have direct implications for the development of tools to help people search more effectively in a multi-device world.

Categories and Subject Descriptors
H.3.3 [**Information Storage and Retrieval**]: Information Search and Retrieval – *search process; selection process*

Keywords
Cross-device search; Slow search; Search tasks; Personalization.

1. INTRODUCTION
Search tasks can involve multiple queries across multiple sessions, and require significant effort to complete, especially if the task is complex [31]. Modern search engines have started shifting their goal from simply achieving better result ranking for individual queries to assisting users in completing such tasks [10][28]. The recent proliferation of mobile devices such as smartphones and tablets allows Web searchers to tackle these search tasks almost anytime, anywhere. Figure 1 presents an example of cross-device behavior for a fictitious (but representative) user searching for information on Italian restaurants on his desktop before continuing the task on his mobile device. Better support for task continuation could help the user resume his restaurant search when mobile. Such *contiguous* cross-device tasks—those resumed soon on the post-switch device—are our focus in this paper. According to our analysis of device switching (shown in Section 5.3.2), around 15% of switches involve contiguous tasks.

WSDM'13, February 4–8, 2013, Rome, Italy.

Switching between devices may be expensive for contiguous tasks. The user has to remember what he was searching for and what has already been searched, which can be difficult when multiple search tasks are active simultaneously. One solution is sharing all search history across all devices. However, this is insufficient since the user might not necessarily resume a search task with a previously searched query and managing one's search history can be challenging from a smartphone. To provide a smooth transition among search devices and aid users in completing tasks on multiple devices, more sophisticated support is needed.

Cross-device behavior has been studied in the human factors community, but not with an emphasis on search [8]. Cross-session search tasks have been studied, but not across devices [20]. Mobile and desktop search have been studied separately [15], but the transitions between them have not been examined. A detailed study of cross-device searching and the development of tools to support this activity are therefore timely and necessary. This paper makes a significant contribution as the first study in this important area.

The specific research contributions of our work are fourfold:

- Define cross-device search tasks as a key research challenge and an opportunity for search engines to help people better perform search tasks that span devices. We demonstrate via empirical study the prevalence of cross-device searches.
- Characterize cross-device task transitions, including identifying patterns in device transitions and exploring the temporal, geospatial, and topical aspects of cross-device searching.
- Develop predictive models to estimate which search tasks will be resumed following device switching. Prediction occurs at different time points, including before a full device switch is observed (when they abandon the pre-switch device) and after device switching (given that they visit the homepage of the search engine on their post-switch device). The model integrates a rich set of features of cross-device searching behavior.

- Perform experiments using the search log from a large commercial search engine and show that our model significantly outperforms a task-continuation baseline, based on prior work that lacks access to information on cross-device behavior.

The remainder of the paper is structured as follows. Section 2 describes related work on desktop and mobile search, multi-device usage, and cross-session search tasks. We characterize cross-device searching in Section 3 and present the details of our prediction models in Section 4. The findings of the prediction experiments are presented in Section 5. We discuss the findings and their implications in Section 6 and conclude in Section 7.

2. RELATED WORK

In this paper our focus is on tasks spanning multiple sessions and multiple devices. Related work falls in the following areas: (1) characterizing search behavior on desktop and mobile, (2) multi-device behavior, and (3) cross-session search tasks.

Search behavior has been studied intensively in recent years. Log data from search engines have proven to be extremely valuable in studying how people search in naturalistic settings across a wide variety of different search intents in desktop or mobile search environments. Recent research on search behavior on the desktop has primarily involved automated analysis and prediction of aspects of search behavior for individual queries [29] and single search sessions [1][4][34], using search logs. Other more qualitative studies have focused on a deeper understanding of the nature and motivations behind the pursuit of searchers' information goals [19][21].

Studies of search in a mobile setting have examined the characteristics of search queries submitted from mobile devices, analyzing behavior along different dimensions such as geographic location and search interface used [33]. Others have performed detailed studies to understand mobile search intent and the influence of contextual factors on them. Church and Smith [7] carried out a four-week diary study of mobile information needs, focusing on the intent behind them, the topics users are interested in and the impact of mobile contexts such as location and time. Teevan et al. [32] showed that local searches tend to be highly contextual, influenced by geographic features, temporal aspects, and the searcher's social context. They showed that mobile searchers are often in transit, and tend to seek out information related to their destination rather than their current location.

Research on comparing and contrasting search behavior on multiple devices is also relevant [14][15][21]. Kamvar and Baluja [14] presented a large scale study of search patterns on Google's mobile search interface. They compared search patterns between phones, personal digital assistants (PDAs), and conventional computers and examine the search queries and their categories as well as other aspects of their interaction such as query input speeds and click-through. Kamvar et al. [15] presented a similar log-based comparison of search patterns on different devices, with the explicit goal of understanding how mobile search tasks differ on computers versus mobile devices. Their results suggest that search usage is typically more focused for the average mobile user than for the average desktop computer user, but search behavior on high-end phones resembles desktop search behavior more so than it does mobile. Li et al. [21] studied good abandonment of search results between desktop and mobile (where users do not click but are still satisfied with the results). They show that good abandonment is significantly higher in mobile search than in desktop-based search.

All of these analyses consider search behavior within a single query or search task on different devices independently. They do not consider two key things: (1) transitions between devices, and (2) search tasks that extend over time. We highlight related work in each of these two areas in the remainder of this section.

Multi-device usage patterns have been actively studied. Studies have shown that user activities tend to span multiple devices [4] and frustrating experiences on mobile devices will drive users to complete their tasks on desktops [17]. Karlson et al. [18] analyzed the usage log of desktop and mobile phone from a user study, and they showed smartphones had become a primary tool to access the internet. They also pointed out that tasks cannot be easily carried over between devices due to the lack of support. We are try to address in this work, especially in support of Web searching across devices. Kane et al. [16] conducted a study focused on Web browsing usage patterns across devices. Their results indicated sharing browsing information between devices could help improve Web browsing on mobile devices. However, to our knowledge, there has been no work specifically focused on cross-device search tasks.

There is growing interest in using long-term search log data to build models of users' interests. Previous work has tried to automatically identify queries on the same task. Mei et al. [26] proposed a framework to study sequences of search activities and focused on simple prediction and classification tasks, ranging from predicting whether the next click will be on an algorithmic result to segmenting the query stream into goals and missions. Teevan et al. [29] showed, via query log analysis, that nearly 40% of queries were attempts to re-find previously encountered results. Aula et al. [4] studied the search and information re-access strategies of experienced Web users using a survey. They found that people often have difficulty remembering the queries they used originally to discover information of interest. MacKay and Watters [25] explored a variety of Web-based information seeking tasks and found that almost 60% of complex information gathering tasks continued across sessions. Liu and Belkin [23] examined the structure (parallel or dependent) of tasks that extend across different search sessions. Jones and Klinkner [13] proposed methods to partition a query stream into research missions and goals, where each mission corresponds to a set of related information needs and may include multiple search goals.

Some explicit support has also been proposed to help people manage long-running tasks. *SearchBar* [27] is a system that proactively and persistently stores query histories, browsing histories, and users' notes and ratings. SearchBar supports multi-session investigations by assisting with task context resumption and information re-finding. *SearchPad* [10] is a system that automatically identifies research missions and presents a search workspace comprising previous queries and results related to the mission. SearchPad uses measures of topic coherence between pairs of consecutive queries and user engagement to identify such research missions. This work was further extended to group queries into mission-coherent clusters based on search behavior [3]. Kotov et al. [20] modeled cross-session information needs and addressed the challenge of identifying all previous queries in a user's search history on the same task as the current query, and predicting whether a user will return to the task in future sessions. They developed classifiers for these two tasks and through evaluation using labeled data from search logs showed that their classifiers can perform both tasks effectively. We use classifiers trained on similar features a baseline for some of the analysis presented later in the paper. Agichtein et al. [2] perform log analysis to understand, characterize, and automatically detect search tasks that will be continued in the near future. They identify intents, topics, and search behavior patterns associated with long-running sessions that are likely to be continued. They also developed an effective task-continuation prediction algorithm that significantly outperforms state-of-the-art classifiers and humans.

The research described in this paper extends previous work in a number of ways. First, we focus on search tasks spanning multiple devices, an area that is gaining importance but has not been explored in detail. Previous studies on mobile and desktop search have focused on the device types independently. Second, we provide the first characterization of cross-device task transitions, including key statistics on the nature of the switches, such as the role of topic, time, and location in cross-device tasks. Third, we develop models to accurately predict task continuation across devices before the switch and once it has been observed. Importantly, we focus on predicting whether the user will resume the search task immediately on another device. This is a different and more challenging task than predicting resumption at some point in the near future; a problem that others have tackled [2][20].

3. CHARACTERIZING CROSS-DEVICE SEARCH BEHAVIOR

We begin by formally defining cross-device search and providing overview statistics about the data that we used in this study. We then examine several characteristics of search across devices, focusing on temporal, geospatial, and topical dimensions.

3.1 Definition

The search activities of a user are usually represented as a stream of temporally-ordered queries. Query streams provide rich information about users' search interests and search tasks. To better capture the search intent of users, the concept of a search session is employed to segment the query stream into fragmented units for analysis. Here we define a typical search session using a 30-minute timeout as its boundaries in the stream. This definition has been used to identify sessions in previous work [34].

A *device switch* is defined as the act of moving between a pair of devices (e.g., personal computer→smartphone). A search session consists of one or more queries, but in our analysis, we do not permit a search session to span multiple devices. In other words, the queries within the same session always occur on a single device. As a result, switching between devices must involve at least two sessions, the *pre-switch* session and the *post-switch* session.

More precisely, let $Q = \{q_1, q_2, \dots, q_i, \dots, q_n\}$ be the query stream of a user, where q_i is the i-th query in the stream. For each q_i ($1 \le i \le n$), there is a 3-tuple (t_i, s_i, d_i) associated with it, where t_i is the timestamp of the query q_i, s_i represents the session of q_i, and d_i defines the device where q_i has been issued. $\mathcal{S}$ is the personal search history comprising user search activity from Q in the time period before s_i. We therefore define cross-device search as:

DEFINITION: *A cross-device search is represented as a 7-tuple,*

$$(\mathcal{S}, q_i, q_{i+1}, s_i, s_{i+1}, d_i, d_{i+1}).$$

And the following conditions need to be satisfied: (1) q_i is the last query in session s_i; (2) q_{i+1} is the first query in session s_{i+1}; (3) d_i and d_{i+1} are two different devices.

The device-switching behavior starts at time t_i and ends at time t_{i+1}. We define q_i as the pre-switch query, s_i as pre-switch session, and s_{i+1} as post-switch session. One of the tasks in this study is to predict whether the search task of q_i will be resumed in the immediate following post-switch session s_{i+1}, referred to as a contiguous cross-device task. All the queries in s_{i+1} are defined as post-switch queries, and q_{i+1} is the first query in the post-switch session. Later in this paper (Section 5.3.2), we will show that q_{i+1} is most likely to be related to continuing the task of q_i among all queries in the post-switch session. Device-switching reveals rich information about the user, including device preferences for searching and the timespan and changing geolocation during the switch.

Table 1. Dataset used in this study.

Number of Days		31
Number of Users		39,081
Number of Sessions	Desktop	709,610
	Mobile	301,028
	Total	1,010,638
Number of Queries	Desktop	3,023,582
	Mobile	667,091
	Total	3,690,673
Number of Switches		158,324

Table 2. Count of switches in two dimensions: direction of the switches across textual relation between switch-related queries.

	Desktop-to-Mobile	Mobile-to-Desktop
Same-query switch	10,480 (6.6%)	5,282 (3.3%)
Different-query switch	69,441 (43.9%)	73,121 (46.2%)

3.2 Dataset Description

In this study, we focus on the switching between two devices: the personal computer (PC) also referred to as "desktop" in this paper[1], and the smartphone. Queries issued on both devices are collected from 39,081 users over one month. Queries are mined from the logs of both modalities respectively and then joined using a persistent user identifier. For each query, we also recorded its timestamp and geolocation (only at the city level), allowing for temporal and geospatial characteristics to be studied. Table 1 shows a basic description of our dataset. Note that all the users in the collection must have used both devices in the period from April 15 to May 15, 2012.

Directionality of device switching: Intuitively, desktop-to-mobile switching may occur when the search is interrupted and the user needs to change his location before resuming (e.g., to catch public transit). Mobile-to-desktop switching may indicate that the user is returning from other events. Since two switching directions imply different search scenarios and suggest different applications, we treat the two directions separately.

Same-query switch vs. different-query switch: When the user issues the same query before and after the switch, it is then reasonable to claim that the search task is resumed after the switch. More formally, if $q_i = q_{i+1}$, the task of q_i is resumed in the post-switch session s_{i+1}. The textual relationship between q_i and q_{i+1} may be a strong indicator of contiguous cross-device tasks.

Table 2 shows the count of cross-device search in two dimensions, directionality and the textual relation within the switch. The substantial volume of same-query switches indicates that contiguous cross-device search tasks may often exist in users' searching activities. One interesting fact is that when users switch from desktop to their mobile phones, they are more likely to resume search tasks with the same query: 6.6% of queries for Desktop-to-Mobile versus 3.3% of queries for Mobile-to-Desktop. Note that distribution of *users* among the four quadrants is similar to that shown in Table 2.

In practice, switching from desktop to mobile may be more challenging for users because typing and resuming search tasks on mobile is likely to be more difficult due to the restricted typing area and high mobility of smartphones. To provide smooth transitions

[1] Note that that our definition of desktops may also include laptops, since we were unable to distinguish them in our log data.

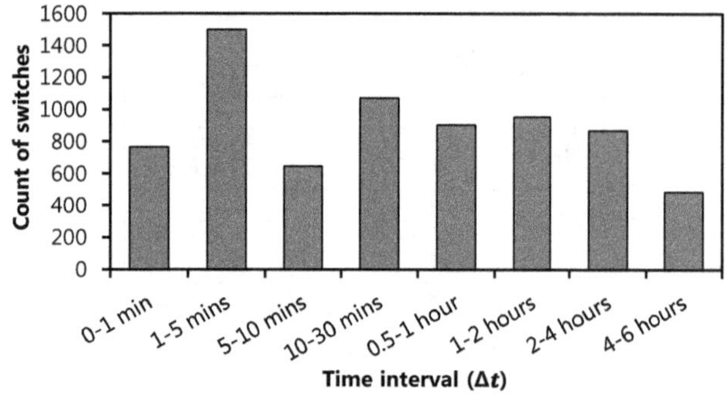

Figure 2. Time interval distribution of same-query switches.

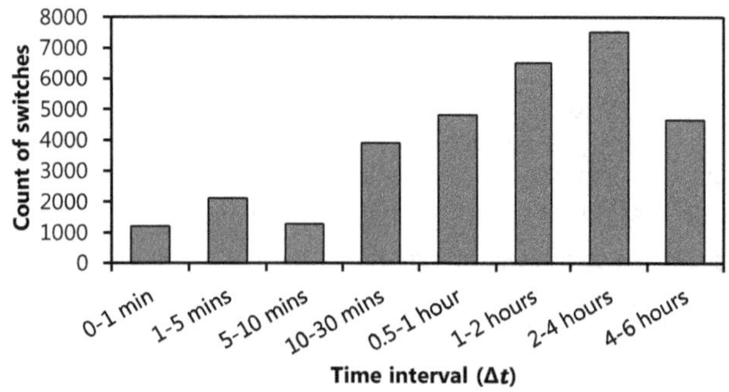

Figure 3. Time interval distribution of different-query switches.

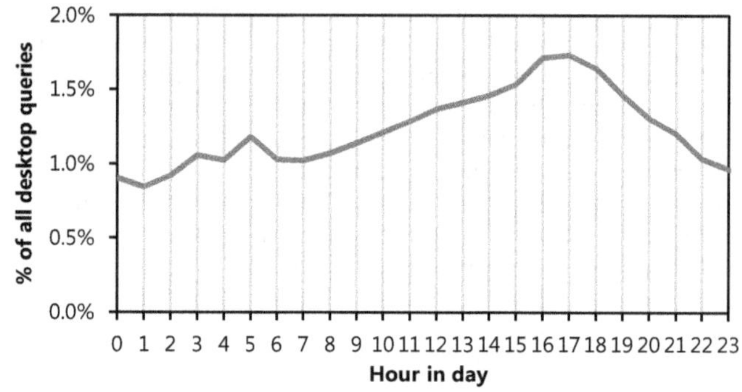

Figure 4. Percentage of pre-switch queries on desktop over time.

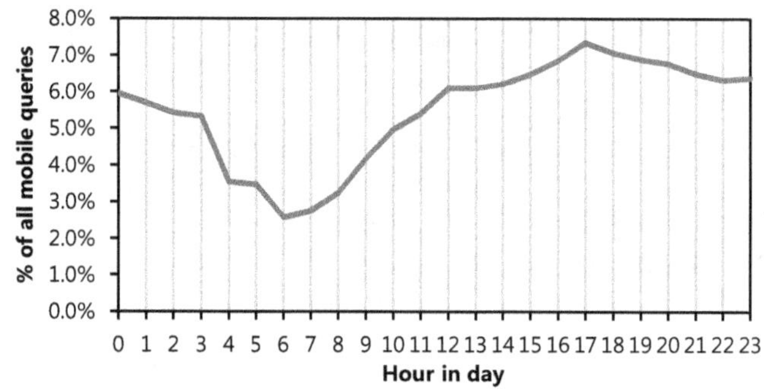

Figure 5. Percentage of post-switch queries on mobile over time.

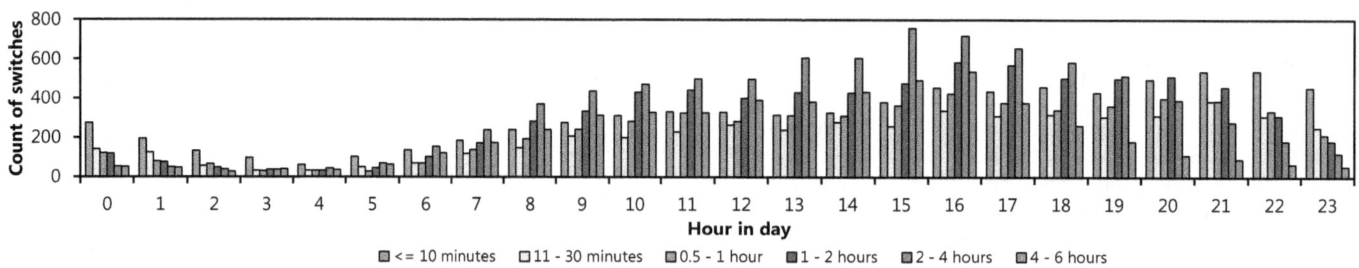

Figure 6. Distribution of switching time interval (Δt) as a function of hour in the day. Order of legend entries corresponds to the order of the bars.

from desktop to mobile as proposed in Section 6, our work tries to predict whether the search task will be resumed post switch. Particularly, we are interested in providing a better mobile search experience by knowing which tasks will be continued when the user leaves the desktop and lands on his phone. For the rest of the paper, we target ***Desktop-to-Mobile*** switches.

3.3 Temporal Characteristics

Cross-device search behavior starts with the pre-switch query and ends with the start of the post-switch session. One intuitive question is the duration of the switch. To answer this question we compute the distribution of the interval Δt, defined as $(t_{i+1} - t_i)$.

Six-hour limit: The time interval exhibits a long-tail distribution, and the longest switch spans several weeks. However, the long-term device-switching is not the focus here, especially since such distal resumptions are more likely to be connected to persistent interests rather than an active search task that the system can directly assist with at the time that the switch occurs. Again, the point of this study is to investigate *contiguous* cross-device search tasks. Therefore we set a six-hour threshold, which covers 50% of the switches, to filter out long-term cross-device searches. Following this filtering, the distribution of switch direction and textual relationship is still similar to Table 2. For the rest of Section 3, all statistics are computed from switches spanning at most six hours.

Figure 2 and Figure 3 show the distributions of Δt for same-query switches and different-query switches. For same-query switches users tend to resume searching on mobile within a short period of time; over 40% of same-query device switches occur within ten minutes of t_i. However, for different-query switches, the transition will take longer perhaps because the user is not actively engaged in a search task. These two figures imply that time interval is another indicator of task-resuming switches.

Another interesting question about the temporal aspect of cross-device search is when users are most likely to leave the desktop (t_i) and what time they will start searching on mobile (t_{i+1}). Intuitively, the searching on desktop might be interrupted around the time when people get off work, and would probably use the smartphone to keep searching (e.g., on transit during the commute). Note that the rates of leaving desktop and starting to use mobile are also affected by the total number of queries issued on both devices. To show the real distribution of t_i and t_{i+1}, the rates are normalized by the search volume on each of the devices over time.

Figures 4 and 5 show the distribution of pre-switch queries and post-switch queries occur over the day. It is evident that users are more likely to begin switching (leaving the desktop) around 4-5PM. Meanwhile, most post-switch queries (starting to use mobile) appear around 5PM. Also, users tend to stop searching on desktop late at night (the rate of leaving desktop is increasing), and the probability of starting search on mobile is very low at late night. These trends align well with people's work-life rhythms.

We have explored time interval distributions of cross-device search and the likelihood of starting the switch over time in a day. The combination of these two temporal aspects could give us more insight of device-switching behavior. Particularly, we are trying to learn if Δt is sensitive to t_i, the start time of the switch.

Figure 6 shows the distribution of $(t_{i+1} - t_i)$ over the hour in the day of t_i. We can see there are noteworthy patterns of the duration of the device-switches over time. For example, if the user leaves the desktop around 3-4PM, he will be more likely to resume the search in 2-4 hours. However, the situation would be very different if the user leaves desktop around midnight (hour 0 in the figure), where he is more likely to resume the search within 10 minutes. Being able to estimate the return time based on time of day is potentially useful for search engines to prepare for searches on mobile. The distribution in Figure 6 may offer a way to predict when the user will start searching on mobile given only knowledge of desktop behavior. We leverage time-of-day and other temporal features in the prediction models described later.

3.4 Geospatial Characteristics

One of the most common reasons for users to search on mobile is the limited mobility of desktop. We suspected that cross-device search may involve a change in location. In our dataset, geospatial information is available at town or city level (e.g., Seattle, WA) based on the same information from the internet providers on desktop and on the mobile device. A comparison of the location before and after the switch shows that one third of the switches (33%) involved a shift in location to a different town or city than before the switch. This is less surprising if you consider the large number of conurbations (i.e., extensive urban areas comprising multiple towns or cities) in the United States. Later in this paper (Section 5.5), we will show that geospatial properties of the switching event (such as average speed during the switch) can help predict contiguous cross-device search tasks.

Since we focus on desktop-to-mobile switches in this analysis, we also observe the change of user's location within the post-switch session. To measure the extent of the change in geolocation within the post-switch session, at least two queries and corresponding geo-coordinates are required. Table 3 provides the percentage of post-switch sessions where the user is moving.

Table 3. Mobility of post-switch session (mobile).

Single query session	Multiple query session	
	Moving session	Stationary session
60.6%	5.3%	34.2%

Among all the multi-query sessions, around 13.3% sessions have non-zero moving speed. Such a scenario suggests that the user is resuming their task while travelling, where interaction with the phone may be more difficult than usual and they may want information about their destination not their current location [32].

3.5 Topical Characteristics

Topic level information has been extensively employed to capture users' search intent and construct models of their search tasks [2][35]. We wanted to understand how the post-switch queries are affected by the topic of the pre-switch query. To do so, we study the *sustainability* of query topics during device switching.

Let z_i be the topic of pre-switch query q_i, and z_{i+1} be the topic of post-switch query q_{i+1}. If the topic of post-switch query is affected by the pre-switch query, the conditioned probability $p(z_{i+1}|z_i)$ will be very different from the global probability $p(z_{i+1})$. Otherwise, these two probabilities will be similar. Particularly, we study the difference between $p(z_{i+1} = z|z_i = z)$ and $p(z_{i+1} = z)$ for several popular topic z. We call $p(z_{i+1} = z|z_i = z)$ as the "sustainability" of topic z because it measures the degree to which topic z will be resumed after the device-switching. To operationalize this topic modeling for our experiments, we ran a proprietary classifier on switch-related queries, which could assign multiple topics to a query, resulting in the sum of the probabilities of all topics exceeding one. Figure 7 shows the distribution of the probabilities described above for each of the topics in our dataset.

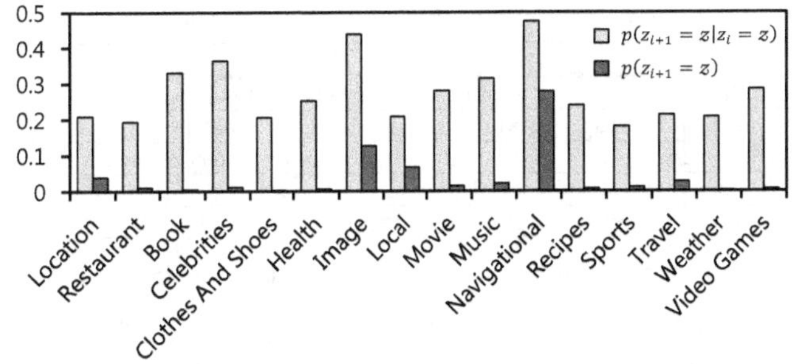

Figure 7. Sustainability and global popularity of query topics.

Figure 7 compares the overall popularity $(p(z_{i+1} = z))$ and sustainability $(p(z_{i+1} = z|z_i = z))$ of the query topics. It shows that the topic distributions of post-switch queries are strongly dependent on the topics of pre-switch queries. We can also tell that users prefer certain topics. For example, *Book*, *Celebrities* and *Music* are more sustainable than other topics. *Image* and *Navigational* are most likely to be resumed in part because of their high overall popularity.

It is clear that there are a number of important temporal, geolocation, and topical attributes in cross-device search. In the next section, we leverage these insights to explore the prediction of contiguous cross-device search tasks.

4. PREDICTING CROSS-DEVICE SEARCH

Before proceeding, we formally define contiguous cross-device search tasks based on the definition of cross-device search in Section 3.1. After that, the features used to capture the contiguous cross-device search tasks will be introduced.

4.1 Definition

A stated earlier, a cross-device search is defined by a 7-tuple, including the personal search history $\mathcal{S}$, the pre-switch and post-switch queries q_i and q_{i+1}, the pre-switch and post-switch sessions s_i and s_{i+1}, and the devices used before and after the switch. Since we only focus on the desktop-to-mobile switches, the definition could be simplified by excluding the device components.

Given a cross-device search, we are trying to predict whether the task of query q_i is continued by any of the queries in the post-switch session s_{i+1}. The following Boolean function f is introduced to judge if two queries belong to the same search task:

$$f(q_m, q_n) = \begin{cases} True & \text{if } q_m \text{ and } q_n \text{ belong to the same task,} \\ False & \text{else.} \end{cases}$$

Then the ground truth for the prediction will be:

$$\vee_{q_j \in s_{i+1}} f(q_i, q_j) \quad (1)$$

Again, q_i is the pre-switch query and s_{i+1} is the post-switch session. By comparing q_i with every query q_j in the post-switch session and take the inclusive OR operation with the results, the final

Table 4. Features for query pair relevance function f.

Name	Description
EditDistance	Editing distance between two queries
NumTermOverlap	Number of overlapping terms in two queries
QueryTermJaccard	Jaccard coefficient of two query term sets
IsSameQuery	Boolean, true if two queries are identical
IsSubsetQuery	Boolean, true if one query contains the other

Table 5. Performance of the query-pair relevance function f.

Accuracy	Positive Precision	Positive Recall	Negative Precision	Negative Recall
0.92	1.00	0.67	0.91	1.00

ground truth for the cross-device search $(\mathcal{S}, q_i, q_{i+1}, s_i, s_{i+1})$ is obtained. Our prediction task is therefore to predict the result of function (1) using features extracted from $(\mathcal{S}, q_i, q_{i+1}, s_i, s_{i+1})$.

In a real setting, the prediction has to be made before post-switch queries are issued, otherwise, the prediction becomes trivial for many applications. In Section 5, we will study the performance of our predictive model when features from different components of the definition are added incrementally.

4.2 The Choice of Function f

Function f measures the relevance between two queries in terms of searching tasks. One option is to ask human labelers to determine the relevance for every query pair. However, this approach is not feasible on a large scale.

In order to obtain the ground truth for all cross-device searches in our dataset, we need a lightweight function f. The three authors of this paper labeled 200 randomly chosen pre- and post-switch query pairs. Fleiss' Kappa (κ) was 0.90, signifying almost perfect agreement for this task. We then train a Support Vector Machine (SVM) classifier using the manual labels and features listed in Table 4 chosen based on [20]. We use the trained SVM classifier as function f. The results based on five-fold cross-validation on function f against the human judgments (Table 5) show that f is accurate on the positive class and can capture two thirds of related-query pairs.

4.3 Features

We temporally segment the device-switching process into five stages and design features accordingly. These five stages include: (1) User's searching history $\mathcal{S}$; (2) Pre-switch session s_i; (3) Pre-switch query q_i; (4) The transition, time period from t_i to t_{i+1}; (5) Post-switch session s_{i+1}. Table 7 lists the features for each stage. As we discuss later, features from (4) could be used to predict task resumption once the user is at the search engine homepage on their mobile device. Feature set (5) is included for completeness.

Using function f to group queries into search tasks: since function f is designed to judge the relevance of query pairs, we therefore apply f to every pair of queries in user's search history, and then cluster queries into groups. Each group of queries represents a certain search task. By observing how the group of queries distributes on desktop and mobile, we compute entropy-based features and cross-device features.

Suppose G_i is the i-th group in the user's search history, and it consists of k queries, $G_i = \{q_{i_1}, q_{i_2}, \dots, q_{i_k}\}$. Among these k queries, l of them are issued on desktop and $(k-l)$ queries are on mobile. Then the device entropy of G_i is:

$$\frac{l}{k}\log\frac{k}{l} + \frac{k-l}{k}\log\frac{k}{k-l}$$

Not only entropy-based features are computed from query groups, some cross-device-related features also group queries into search tasks. The purpose is to capture the individual device preferences for different tasks. For example, the history feature *NumOfRelevantCrossDevice* counts the number of tasks spanning both devices; the pre-switch query feature *NumRelatedQuerySwitch* counts the number of contiguous cross-device searches on the tasks of q_i.

Table 6. Features used to predict contiguous cross-device search tasks. "B" indicates the features used in baseline method.

Name	Description
Features from Search History $\mathcal{S}$	
NumOfDesktopQuery[B]	Number of queries issued on desktop
NumOfMobileQuery	Number of queries issued on mobile
PercentageDesktopQuery[B]	Percentage of queries issued on desktop
PercentageMobileQuery	Percentage of queries issued on mobile
PercentageDesktopTime[B]	Percentage of searching time on desktop
PercentageMobileTime	Percentage of searching time on mobile
NumOfSession[B]	Number of search sessions
NumOfContiguousSwitch	Number of contiguous cross-device tasks
NumOfRelevantCrossDevice	Number of search tasks on both devices
EntropyAvg	Average device entropy of same-task queries
EntropySum	Total device entropy of same-task queries
EntropyWeighted	Weighted device entropy of same-task queries
Features from Pre-switch Session s_i	
NumOfQuery[B]	Number of queries within session s_i
TimeSpanPreSess[B]	Temporal length of session s_i (in minutes)
NumOfLocationQuery[B]	Number of location queries in session s_i
AvgDistancePreSess[B]	Average distance from current location to locations mentioned in session s_i
Features from Pre-switch Query q_i	
GlobalFrequency	Historical frequency of q_i in the entire dataset
PersonalFrequency	Frequency of q_i in personal search history $\mathcal{S}$
NumExactQueryDesktop[B]	Number of same queries as q_i on desktop in $\mathcal{S}$
NumExactQueryMobile	Number of same queries as q_i on mobile
NumRelatedQueryDesktop[B]	Number of related queries as q_i on desktop
NumRelatedQueryMobile	Number of related queries as q_i on mobile
NumExactQuerySwitch	Number of switches that pre-switch query and post-switch query are the same as q_i
NumRelatedQuerySwitch	Number of switches that pre-switch query and post-switch query are both relevant to q_i
PreQueryContiguousSwitch	Number of contiguous cross-device tasks of q_i
NumOfRelatedQueryInSess[B]	Number of queries relevant to q_i in session s_i
NumOfTerm[B]	Number of terms in query q_i
PreQueryCategory[B]	The search topic of query q_i
PreQueryHour[B]	The hour component of t_i
PreQueryDayofWeek[B]	The day of week of t_i
IsWeekday[B]	True if t_i is weekday
HasLocation[B]	True if q_i contains location
PreQueryDistance[B]	Distance from current location to q_i location
HasLocalService[B]	Boolean, true if q_i contains local service
Features from the Transition (t_i~t_{i+1})	
TimeIntervalSwitch	The timespan between t_i and t_{i+1}
GeoDistanceSwitch	Distance between where q_i and q_{i+1} are issued
IsSameLocationSwitch	True if q_i and q_{i+1} occur at the same place
AvgSpeedSwitch	Average travelling speed during the switch
Features from Post-switch Session s_{i+1}	
TimeSpanPostSess	The temporal length of session s_{i+1}
PostQueryCategory	The search topic of query q_{i+1}
PostQueryHour	The hour component of t_{i+1}
GeoDistancePostSess	The distance travelled within session s_{i+1}
AvgSpeedPostSess	Average travelling speed within session s_{i+1}

4.4 Baseline Features

Previous work focuses on predicting the resumption of cross-session search tasks on desktop computers [2][20]. In contrast, our work predicts task-resuming in post-switch sessions by considering the search behaviors on *both* desktop and mobile. We use desktop search features (marked as "B" in Table 6) as a baseline, which contains search history-based features, pre-switch session features, and pre-switch query features, making them good comparators for other features in these stages. Additionally, features from transition and post-switch session are evaluated in Section 5.

4.5 Evaluation Metrics

One of the potential applications of our work is to help users resume their search tasks after device-switching in a way that reminds users

Table 7. Statistics of the dataset used in the experiments.

Item	Value
Number of users (switching frequency ≥ 15)	2,125
Number of potential cross-device search tasks (Pre-switch query with personal frequency ≤ 5 and global frequency ≤ 10)	17,235
Number of all cross-device searches (Without pre-switch query frequency limits)	29,839

Table 8. Statistics of human labeling data.

	Labeling Task #1	Labeling Task #2
Number of labels	800	800
Number of positive labels	238	119
Agreement (Fleiss' κ)	0.037	0.509

Table 9. Percentage of the task-resuming queries (first query on task) in post-switch session over positions.

Position in post-switch session	1	2	Other
Percentage	89.2%	8.9%	1.9%

of the search task that they might continue. This requires high precision for positive cases to avoid providing users with irrelevant recommendations. Therefore, we evaluate the performance of our approach against baseline method using accuracy, positive precision, positive recall, and area under the receiver-operator-characteristic curve (AUC) as the metrics of interest.

5. EXPERIMENTS

The dataset and labels used in the experiments are introduced in Sections 5.1–5.3. We then report the performance of baseline method and our approach in Section 5.4. As an additional experiment, the human performance on predicting contiguous cross-device search tasks is also provided (Section 5.4). Finally, we analyze the feature weights in the learned model by measuring their χ^2 value and information gain against labels (Section 5.5).

5.1 Dataset

The dataset used in the evaluation is a subset of the one introduced in Section 3.2, which only involves the device-switching from desktop to mobile. In addition, we also apply several constraints.

Search tasks vs. Long-term search interests: Popular queries, such as [facebook] and [youtube], have better chance to be resumed and are therefore easier to predict. However, they do not necessarily represent search tasks but rather are long-term search interests. Accordingly, we try to distinguish the search tasks from long-term search interests among all cross-device searches by limiting the frequency of pre-switch queries. Particularly, pre-switch queries (q_i) with personal frequencies (for the current user, within one month) of 5 or less, and global frequency (over all users, within one month) of 10 or less will be selected as potential search tasks. Note that we also run an experiment to test the performance of our predictive models if we retain these popular queries.

Device-switching frequency: We notice that the personal device-switching frequency follows a long-tail distribution, which means many users only switch several times within one month. Users with low switching frequency may not provide much information about daily cross-device search behavior. As a result, we only keep the users with at least 15 switches (within one month).

Table 7 shows the summary of the dataset used in evaluation.

5.2 Experimental Setup

In the experiments, we investigate the problem of predicting contiguous cross-device search tasks in two aspects: (1) the performance of our approach versus the baseline model; (2) the performance of the predictive model by adding features of different stages

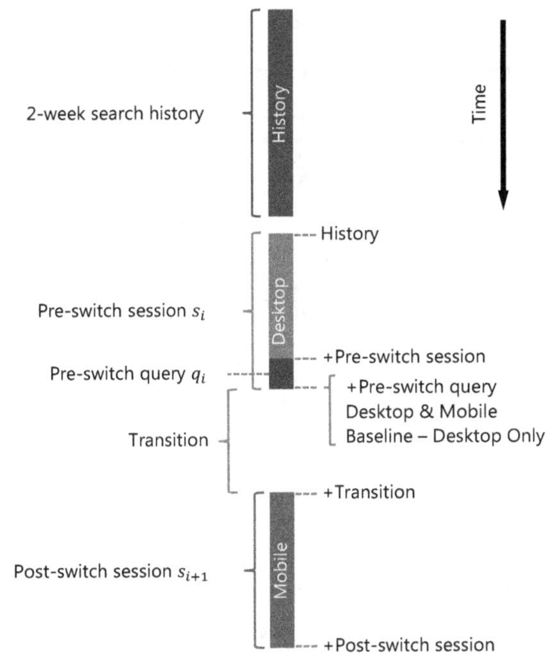

Figure 9. Timeline visualization of the various feature classes that are compared (on the right) and the point where these features are generated in *Q* in the experiments we perform.

(introduced in Section 4.3) incrementally. We leave two-weeks of search history data (around half of the dataset) for training the history-based features (shown in Table 6), which are designed to capture individual preferences of devices for search tasks. Then five-fold cross-validation is applied on the other half of the data to measure the performance of different classifiers.

Figure 9 shows points in the timeline where each model makes the prediction. Each model builds on the features that are available beforehand. For example, the system *+Pre-switch query* uses features from *History + Pre-switch session + Pre-switch query*. In the experiments, the model *Desktop & Mobile* and *+Pre-switch query* are identical. The purpose of having *Desktop & Mobile* is to highlight the comparison between our approach and the baseline method. We use Multiple Additive Regression Trees (MART) for classification [11]. The advantages of MART include model interpretability (e.g., a ranked list of features is generated), facility for rapid training and testing, and robustness against noisy labels and missing values.

5.3 Labeling

In Section 3, switches were defined to occur within six hours of the terminal search on the original device. However, if we imposed this temporal threshold on the labeled data, it would reveal something about the future (i.e., that the next query is on a different device and is within six hours) and could bias the labels. Therefore, for labeling, we do not impose the six-hour switch threshold. Instead, we simply label pairs of consecutive queries issued on different devices, irrespective of their inter-query time. Labels are obtained in two ways: automatic labeling and annotation from human labelers. Meanwhile, as a separate prediction task, we also investigate how well the judges can predict contiguous cross-device search tasks.

5.3.1 Automatic Labeling

To obtain labels for all the cross-device searches in our dataset, automatic task labeling is applied. We use function *f* (introduced in Section 4.2) to annotate the data. According to the performance reported in Table 5, the automatic labeler has a reliable precision. In total, 9.3% of the tasks were labeled as resumed post-switch.

Table 10. Performance of predicting contiguous cross-device search tasks with automatic labels. (indicates statistical significance at $p \leq 0.01$ using paired t-tests compared to the Baseline)**

	Accuracy	Positive Precision	Positive Recall	AUC
Baseline -- Desktop Only	0.903	0.337	0.037	0.646
Desktop & Mobile	**0.907****	**0.504****	**0.145****	**0.757****
History	0.880	0.250	0.142	0.661
+ Pre-switch Session	0.899	0.381	0.130	0.679
+ Pre-switch Query	0.907	0.504	0.145	0.734
+ Transition	**0.910**	0.544	**0.184**	0.781
+ Post-switch Session	**0.910**	**0.568**	0.169	**0.806**

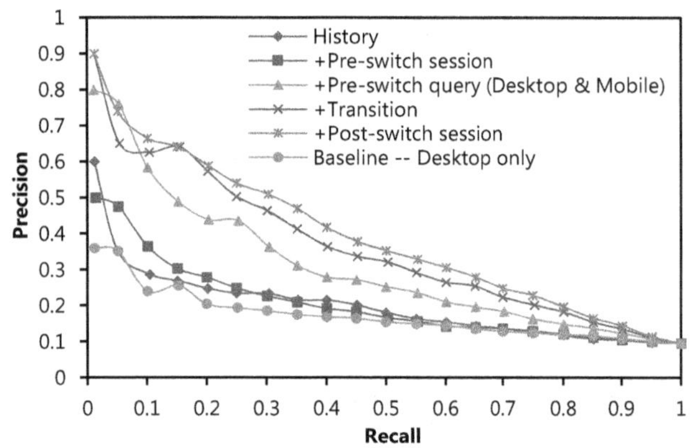

Figure 10. Precision-recall curve of predicting contiguous cross-device search tasks with automatic labels.

5.3.2 Human Labeling

Human annotators are assigned to two labeling tasks as following:

Labeling Task #1: Given the most recent search history (up to 5 queries) and the pre-switch query, annotators are asked to predict if the search task of pre-switch query will be resumed on mobile.

Labeling Task #2: Given the most recent search history (up to 5 queries), the pre-switch query, and the post-switch session, annotators are asked to label every query in the post-switch session if it belongs to the same search task as the pre-switch query.

Note that Task #1 differs from Task #2 in that it requires the judge to predict whether the task will be resumed using only pre-switch behavior. In Task #2, pre- and post-switch behavior is used.

Each of our five judges sees 200 switching instances. Inter-judge agreement is computed from the 50 overlapping labeling instances among the annotators. The remaining 150 instances were unique to each judge. This results in 800 distinct switch labels. Note that to increase the size of our training data, we included the overlapping instances and used the consensus label from all judges to label those instances. All 50 labels could be assigned this way (i.e., no ties).

The ground truth for our predictions is obtained from labeling task #2, and the human performance on predicting contiguous cross-device search tasks is measured from labeling task #1. We hired five annotators for each labeling task and provided them with the same detailed instructions about the judgment task, including example labels. The results are reported in Table 8. Labeling task #1 has poor agreement ($\kappa = 0.037$), suggesting that predicting task continuation is challenging even for human annotators. However, labeling task #2 has moderate agreement ($\kappa = 0.509$), implying that it is less difficult to judge also given the post-switch queries. Note that this task also shows that 14.9% of device switches comprise a contiguous search task, which is higher than the 9.3% reported by automatic labeling, likely because our judges are able to make inferences about task continuations that extend beyond the query overlap features used by the automated approach.

Table 11. Performance of predicting contiguous cross-device search tasks with human labels. (indicates statistical significance at $p \leq 0.01$ using paired t-tests compared to the Baseline).**

	Accuracy	Positive Precision	Positive Recall	AUC
Human	0.676	0.203	0.407	–
Baseline -- Desktop Only	0.827	0.162	0.025	0.548
Desktop & Mobile	**0.829**	**0.347****	**0.100****	**0.587****
History	0.823	0.271	0.084	0.560
+ Pre-switch Session	0.835	0.281	0.083	0.601
+ Pre-switch Query	0.829	0.347	**0.100**	0.587
+ Transition	0.837	0.324	0.083	**0.600**
+ Post-switch Session	**0.841**	**0.420**	0.099	0.592

Table 12. Performance of predicting contiguous cross-device search tasks (and long-term search interests) with automatic labels. (and * indicates statistical significance at $p \leq 0.01$ and $p \leq 0.05$ paired t-tests compared to the Baseline)**

	Accuracy	Positive Precision	Positive Recall	AUC
Baseline -- Desktop Only	0.911	0.770	0.472	0.924
Desktop & Mobile	**0.918****	**0.785***	**0.530****	**0.931****
History	0.878	0.558	0.390	0.911
+ Pre-switch Session	0.887	0.622	0.385	0.911
+ Pre-switch Query	0.918	0.785	0.530	0.931
+ Transition	0.919	0.779	0.542	0.933
+ Post-switch Session	**0.924**	**0.812**	**0.558**	**0.935**

As part of the human labeling, judges also indicate *which* queries in the post-switch session represent a continuation of the pre-switch search task. Table 9 shows that 89% of the task-resuming queries appear as the first query in post-switch session. This suggests that task-resumption support could be useful to searchers if we can accurately predict whether they are likely to resume. For example, if resumption is predicted when they are on the search engine homepage, we could populate the search box with their pre-switch query. Doing this for all queries (without prediction) could annoy users.

5.4 Results

We now present the results of the prediction experiments. Three groups of results are reported in this section. We begin by comparing the different feature classes on how well they predict the cross-device search tasks (with constrained pre-switch query frequency) identified using the automatically-generated labels.

Table 10 shows that *Desktop & Mobile* outperforms the baseline system. The big gap on both positive precision and recall between our system and the baseline system indicates the usefulness of the proposed features. The precision-recall curve in Figure 10 provides strong evidence that using cross-device search behavior can more accurately predict the task-resuming on mobile than the features of desktop search only. Also, the performance of the predictive model grows steadily as the feature classes are added.

The results in Table 11 are from human labels rather than the automatic labels described in Section 5.3.2. Similarly, the proposed model outperforms the baseline. However, we see a decrease in the performance of most systems by using the human labels. One of the reasons is that there are not enough positive cases in human labeled data for the classifier to learn a good decision boundary. The results of the human prediction task are also included in Table 11 (alongside *Human*). Unlike the mechanism of a classifier, human annotated labels are binary and there is no threshold to sweep, therefore AUC for human performance is not computed. Interestingly, our system attains higher positive precision than the human labelers, but lower positive recall. This implies the use of different prediction strategies by the annotators than encoded in the classifiers. Further analysis is needed to understand the nature of these differences.

Table 12 reports the performance on predicting all cross-device searches, which does not constrain the frequency of pre-switch queries (i.e., not excluding popular queries such as [facebook] and [youtube]). As expected, the prediction becomes less challenging because it is easier to capture users' long-term search interests and the frequent queries have better chance to be searched again, or resumed, in the future. But we can still see that the proposed system outperforms the baseline, especially on positive recall.

5.5 Feature Analysis

We now turn our attention to the features which contribute most to the prediction task. In order to show the effectiveness of the proposed features, we compute the χ^2 values and information gain of all the features against the automatic labels.

Table 13 ranks the top 10 features according to their χ^2 value. It clearly shows that users' search behavior on mobile (e.g., *NumRelatedQueryMobile*) and the cross-device search behavior features (e.g., *PreQueryContiguousSwitch*) are very effective in prediction. In addition, the temporal and geospatial features *during* the switch also show substantial weights for prediction. For comparison, we also analyze features against the automatic labels on all cross-device searches (including popular queries). Table 14 lists the top 10 features from that analysis. Not surprisingly, several baseline features appear on the list (e.g., *PersonalFrequency*). However, some cross-device behavior features (e.g., *NumOfContiguousSwitch*) and some transition-related features (e.g., *AvgSpeedSwitch*) still exhibited high evidential weights.

Table 13. The χ^2 value and info gain of features, ranked by χ^2 value.

Features	χ^2	Info Gain
NumRelatedQueryMobile	491.23172	0.031685
TimeIntervalSwitch	378.00423	0.024016
PreQueryContiguousSwitch	342.97317	0.020403
NumRelatedQuerySwitch	315.34983	0.020822
AvgSpeedSwitch	295.76765	0.022745
GeoDistanceSwitch	270.39483	0.020108
NumOfContiguousSwitch	235.27217	0.020083
EntropyAvg	221.82945	0.015446
NumRelatedQueryDesktop	172.73978	0.015161
IsSameLocationSwitch	95.81413	0.009118

Table 14. The χ^2 value and info gain of features on all cross-device searches (including frequent pre-switch queries), ranked by χ^2 value.

Features	χ^2	Info Gain
PreQueryContiguousSwitch	4225.69191	0.149665
NumRelatedQueryMobile	3969.11066	0.147362
NumExactQueryMobile	3408.70987	0.116981
NumOfContiguousSwitch	2755.01591	0.107953
PersonalFrequency	2711.70148	0.106203
NumExactQuerySwitch	2125.13168	0.074743
EntropyAvg	1716.86159	0.063697
PercentageMobileTime	1706.9318	0.059069
PercentageDesktopTime	1706.9318	0.059069
AvgSpeedSwitch	1545.90011	0.067262

6. DISCUSSION AND IMPLICATIONS

We have defined and presented a characterization of cross-device search and developed predictive models that can estimate whether a user will immediately resume on a mobile device the last search task they were attempting on their desktop computer. Our characterization shows interesting variations in switching over time, some topics are more likely to be associated with a switch, and that switching locations is often part of device switching. We also show that we can accurately predict contiguous cross-device task resumption, including more accurately than humans.

Although this is the first study, to our knowledge, to investigate cross-device search tasks specifically, the current trend toward multi-device use [8], suggests a need for further research in this area. For example, the findings that we present in this paper are focused on transitions from desktop to mobile search. However, switches in the opposite direction are also popular and need further exploration. Our early analysis of the Mobile-to-Desktop switches shows that they happen in much less time than Desktop-to-Mobile switches. One explanation for this is that switches in that direction are more related to searcher dissatisfaction with the mobile search results or general search experience on mobile (an assertion supported by non-search studies [17]). Additionally, since we do not interact with the users directly, we cannot be sure that users are actually continuing the same task. We need to work with users to fully understand task resumption, as well as directly measure other factors such as search satisfaction and device-switch motivations.

Beyond further research to better understand and characterize cross-device search tasks, we can also develop support to help searchers perform cross-device searching at different points in the switch, including support for so-called "slow search" (where an instant search-engine response may not be required). The predictive models described in this paper can have direct utility here. We can offer help at two particular points: (1) immediately following the session on the pre-switch device, and (2) on visiting the search engine homepage on the post-switch device.

Immediately following pre-switch session: Accurately predicting future task resumption at this point means that the search engine can perform actions on the users' behalf to maximize the downtime between task termination and resumption. Examples of what the search engine could do during this time include:

- Proactively save recent session state into server memory or disk cache for rapid access when the task is resumed.
- Try different ranking algorithms that may be less efficient but more effective, or issue multiple related queries and blend or summarize the results. The engine could also re-run recent abandoned queries, favoring quality over speed.
- Start a reconnaissance agent [23] to proactively retrieve content from the Web that pertains to the user's current task.
- Pose the query to a question answering site such as Yahoo! Answers (answers.yahoo.com), if the query is sufficiently descriptive to be posed as a question.

Our classifiers are important here because many of these actions are resource intensive and we do not want to perform them for all queries. One alternative to the prediction is to provide users with a way to tell the system that they will resume soon. This requires an additional action from users, which they may forget or be unwilling to perform, and it may not always be clear to the user at termination time that resumption is likely. A combination of such a capability plus prediction may work best, but testing is needed.

On visit to homepage: Once the user visits the homepage of the search engine on the pre-switch device we have access to features about the transition between devices that we show are useful in the task continuation prediction. Examples of support include:

- Provide the user with the option to explicitly resume their task. This would restore their state to that before the switch.
- Prefer pre-switch queries in auto-completion drop-downs or automatically populate the search box on homepage. Given

the difficulty that users can experience with typing on mobile devices [12], such support may speed up query entry.

We could also provide support on the basis of the queries on the post-switch device, which our results suggested could lead to even more accurate task-continuation prediction. Previous studies have shown that leveraging signals from recent session behavior can yield significant performance gains [5][35]. Extending a mobile search session back to the immediately-preceding desktop session may help address the "cold start" problem of insufficient context to personalize early queries on mobile devices [5].

7. CONCLUSIONS AND FUTURE WORK

As people's use of search technology transitions from a single device to multiple devices, understanding and supporting search tasks across those devices is becoming increasingly important. In this paper we have presented the first study of cross-device search tasks, focusing on users' continuing tasks immediately between devices. We analyzed a large set of device switches from logs of a search engine to understand the characteristics of switching. We showed that there were interesting patterns in the temporal, geospatial, and topical aspects of cross-device searching. We also developed classifiers capable of predicting whether users were going to resume a recently-terminated search task on their mobile device at different points in time, including immediately after they terminate the task and once they visit the search engine homepage on the device they are switching to. This affords a range of different types of search support that could be employed to help users tackle tasks that span different devices. Future work will focus on improving the accuracy of our classifiers, and designing and deploying task-continuation support to help users as they search across multiple devices.

REFERENCES

[1] E. Agichtein, E. Brill, and S. Dumais. Improving web search ranking by incorporating user behavior information. *SIGIR '06*, 19–26, 2006.

[2] E. Agichtein et al. Search, interrupted: understanding and predicting search task continuation. *SIGIR '12*, 315–324, 2012.

[3] L.M. Aiello et al. Behavior-driven clustering of queries into topics. *CIKM '11*, 1373–1382, 2011.

[4] A. Aula, N. Jhaveri, and M. Käki. Information search and re-access strategies of experienced Web users. *WWW '05*, 583–592, 2005.

[5] P.N. Bennett et al. Modeling and measuring the impact of short and long-term behavior on search personalization. *SIGIR '12*, 185–194, 2012.

[6] H. Cao et al. Context-aware query suggestion by mining click-through and session data. *SIGKDD '08*, 875–883, 2008.

[7] K. Church and B. Smyth. Understanding the intent behind mobile information needs. *IUI '09*, 245–256, 2009.

[8] ComScore. Digital omnivores: how tablets, smartphones and connected devices are changing U.S. digital media consumption habits. ipmark.com/pdf/Omnivoros.pdf (July 4, 2012).

[9] D. Dearman and J.S. Pierce. "It's on my other computer!": computing with multiple devices. *CHI '08*, 767–776, 2008.

[10] D. Donato et al. Do you want to take notes? identifying research missions in Yahoo! Search Pad. *WWW '10*, 321–330, 2010.

[11] J.H. Friedman, T. Hastie, and R. Tibshirani. *Additive logistic regression: A statistical view of boosting.* Technical Report, Department of Statistics, Stanford University, 1998.

[12] N. Henze, E. Rukzio, and S. Boll. Observational and experimental investigation of typing behavior using virtual keyboards on mobile devices. *SIGCHI '12*, 2659–2668, 2012.

[13] R. Jones and K. Klinkner. Beyond the session timeout: automatic hierarchical segmentation of search topics in query logs. *CIKM '08*, 699–708, 2008.

[14] M. Kamvar and S. Baluja. A large scale study of wireless search behavior: google mobile search. *SIGCHI '06*, 701–709, 2006.

[15] M. Kamvar et al. Computers and iphones and mobile phones, oh my!: a logs-based comparison of search users on different devices. *WWW '09*, 801–810, 2009.

[16] S.K. Kane et al. Exploring cross-device web use on PCs and mobile devices. *INTERACT*, 722–735, 2009.

[17] A.K. Karlson et al. Mobile taskflow in context: a screenshot study of smartphone usage. *SIGCHI '10*, 2009–2018, 2010.

[18] A.K. Karlson et al. Working overtime: patterns of smartphone and PC usage in the day of an information worker. *Pervasive '09*, 398–405, 2009.

[19] M. Kellar, C. Watters, and M. Shepherd. A field study characterizing Web-based information-seeking tasks. *JASIST*, 58(7): 999–1018, 2007.

[20] A. Kotov et al. Modeling and analysis of cross-session search tasks. *SIGIR '11,* 5–14, 2011.

[21] J. Li, S. Huffman, and A. Tokuda. Good abandonment in mobile and PC internet search. *SIGIR '09*, 43–50, 2009.

[22] Y. Li and N.J. Belkin. A faceted approach to conceptualizing tasks in information seeking. *IP&M*, 44(6): 1822–1837, 2008.

[23] H. Lieberman, C. Fry, and L. Weitzman. Exploring the web with reconnaissance agents. *CACM*, 44(8): 69–75, 2002.

[24] J. Liu and N.J. Belkin. Personalizing information retrieval for multi-session tasks: The roles of task stage and task type. *SIGIR '10*, 26–33, 2010.

[25] B. MacKay and C. Watters. Exploring multi-session web tasks. *CHI '08*, 1187–1196, 2008.

[26] Q. Mei et al. An analysis framework for search sequences. *CIKM '09*, 1991–1994, 2009.

[27] D. Morris, M.R. Morris, and G. Venolia. SearchBar: a search-centric Web history for task resumption and information re-finding. *SIGCHI '08*, 1207–1216, 2008.

[28] A. Singla, R.W. White, and J. Huang. Studying trailfinding algorithms for enhanced web search. *SIGIR '10*, 443–450, 2010.

[29] A. Spink et al. From e-sex to e-commerce: Web search changes. *IEEE Computer*, 35(3): 107–109, 2002.

[30] J. Teevan et al. Information re-retrieval: repeat queries in Yahoo's logs. *SIGIR '07*, 151–158, 2007.

[31] J. Teevan et al. The perfect search engine is not enough: a study of orienteering behavior in directed search. *SIGCHI '04*, 415–422, 2004.

[32] J. Teevan et al. Understanding the importance of location, time, and people in mobile local search behavior, *MobileHCI '11*, 77–80, 2011.

[33] J. Yi, F. Maghoul, and J. Pedersen. Deciphering mobile search patterns: a study of Yahoo! mobile search queries. *WWW '08*, 257–266, 2008.

[34] R.W. White and S.M. Drucker. Investigating behavioral variability in Web search. *WWW '07*, 21–30, 2007.

[35] R.W. White, P.N. Bennett, and S.T. Dumais. Predicting short-term interests using activity-based search context. *CIKM '10*, 1009–1018, 2010.

Learning to Rank for Spatiotemporal Search

Blake Shaw, Jon Shea, Siddhartha Sinha, Andrew Hogue
Foursquare
568 Broadway
New York, NY
{blake, jonshea, ssinha, ahogue}@foursquare.com

ABSTRACT

In this article we consider the problem of mapping a noisy estimate of a user's current location to a semantically meaningful point of interest, such as a home, restaurant, or store. Despite the poor accuracy of GPS on current mobile devices and the relatively high density of places in urban areas, it is possible to predict a user's location with considerable precision by explicitly modeling both places and users and by combining a variety of signals about a user's current context. Places are often simply modeled as a single latitude and longitude when in fact they are complex entities existing in both space and time and shaped by the millions of people that interact with them. Similarly, models of users reveal complex but predictable patterns of mobility that can be exploited for this task. We propose a novel spatial search algorithm that infers a user's location by combining aggregate signals mined from billions of foursquare check-ins with real-time contextual information. We evaluate a variety of techniques and demonstrate that machine learning algorithms for ranking and spatiotemporal models of places and users offer significant improvement over common methods for location search based on distance and popularity.

Categories and Subject Descriptors

H.2.8 [**Database Applications**]: Spatial databases; H.2.8 [**Database Applications**]: Data Mining; I.5.1 [**Pattern Recognition**]: Statistical

Keywords

spatial search, machine learning, learn to rank, spatiotemporal models, location data, data mining, geocoding, information retrieval, foursquare, human mobility, mobile devices

1. INTRODUCTION

Today's location-aware mobile devices have dramatically increased the availability and usefulness of location information. Many applications take advantage of the ability of these devices to report a user's location in terms of latitude and longitude, providing useful services to the user such as maps, driving directions, tourist guides, photo sharing, and more. Other services allow users to store content that has been "geotagged" with a location and share it with friends.

Several applications go one step further than raw coordinates, attaching a *semantically meaningful* name to a location. The coarsest form of this labeling involves using a reverse geocoding service [2] to find a city or neighborhood name for a given location. Examples include Twitter, which allows users to attach a location to a tweet, displaying it as a city or neighborhood, and Facebook, which tags most posts by default with a user's current city.

These coarse location names provide some context, but in many cases it is desirable to be significantly more granular when choosing a name for a location. For example, Instagram allows users to choose a specific location when sharing a photo, such as "Washington Square Park" or "The Blind Tiger." Similarly, foursquare, Path, and other mobile applications allow users to "check in" at a specific location such as a restaurant or museum. Tying users and their data to specific, semantically meaningful locations enables these services to provide richer experiences, such as showing the user relevant and timely information like a menu from a restaurant or a tip from a friend about what to order [31]. Moreover, identifying precise locations facilitates the sharing and aggregation of local information. For example, a user of foursquare can see not only recent places their friends have checked into, but also which of their friends have endorsed nearby venues.

Unfortunately, mapping a user's location to a database of known points of interest is complicated by several factors. While location services such as GPS, WiFi, and cell-tower triangulation can provide accuracies under 10 meters under ideal conditions [35], results in real-world environments are substantially worse, with median accuracies of 70 meters (see Figure 1). Additionally, many areas of the world are extremely dense in terms of semantically meaningful locations; in many urban environments, interesting locations may even be located directly above or below each other. Finally, while a user's history may be useful in determining their location [7, 18], the system must still provide accurate results even for users with little or no history.

Despite these difficulties, there are many benefits to an accurate system for finding specific, semantically meaningful names for a given set of coordinates. Tuning such a system for high recall in the top few results allows users to choose their location from a list of results and more easily share and

WSDM'13, February 4–8, 2012, Rome, Italy.

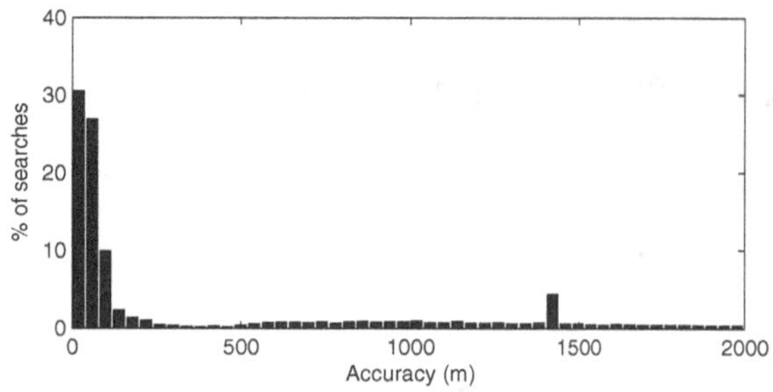

Figure 1: Distribution of reported location accuracy from 26,532 randomly sampled worldwide searches on foursquare. The median is 70 meters, and the mean is 551 meters.

retrieve local information. Alternatively, a system with high precision in the first position could be used to automatically label a user's location or content with a specific location name, or to tie together multiple pieces of content into a coherent grouping about a particular place. Furthermore, such a system could be used to trigger highly contextual notifications, such as transit information when a user enters a train station, or targeted deals when a user enters a store.

In this article, we describe the development, training, and evaluation of the spatial search engine that powers the foursquare application and API. We first introduce our approach to modeling people and places using check-in data, and then describe how these models can be used for retrieval and ranking. We focus on using machine learning techniques to create an optimal ranking function, which learns from large amounts of implicit feedback. Finally, we demonstrate the fully working system and evaluate its performance in a variety of real-world situations, showing significant improvement over common methods for location search and previously reported results.

1.1 Related Work

The growing ubiquity of GPS-enabled consumer mobile devices has only recently enabled the study of user location at the scale described in the current work. Lian and Xie [18] describe a similar system for mapping a user to a point of interest (POI) trained on data from 545 users in a single city using a database of approximately 16,000 points of interest. The system uses several features, such as distance, time, POI popularity, and user history, to train a model that predicts a user's location with 64.5% recall in the top 5 results. Our work improves these results by introducing several new features, more robust models, and significantly more training data (in terms of both size and diversity) to search a much larger database of locations.

Similar techniques regarding context and personalization have been applied in the area of local business search and web search. Lane et al. [17] report relevance improvements of up to ten times in local search relevance by including simple context and behavioral similarity features in a ranking model. Church and Smyth [10] demonstrate the efficacy of including user-, location-, and time-dependent features in mobile web search. Many techniques incorporate signals mined from query logs to improve search results [34, 32].

Outside of the realm of search, significant work has been done with respect to analyzing and describing GPS data

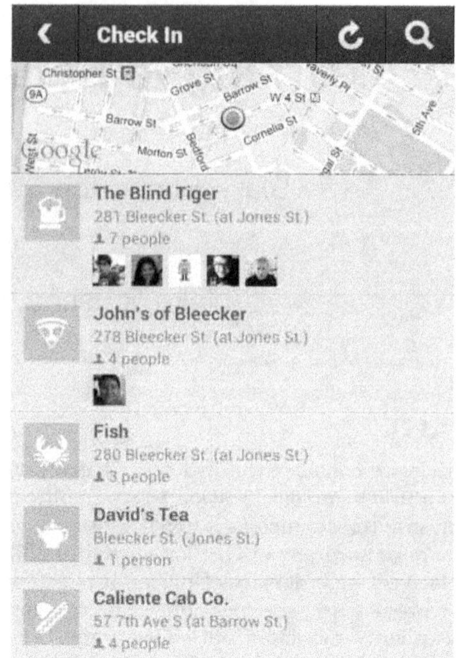

Figure 2: The check-in screen of the foursquare application where a user searches for nearby venues and selects a venue to check in to.

collected over time from users. Ashbrook and Starner [6, 7] cluster GPS locations to model significant locations and predict user movements using a Markov model. Gonzalez et al. [13] develop similar models to predict where a user will be based on their history. Liao et al. [19] predict significant locations for a given user using hierarchical conditional random fields, while Marmasse and Schmand [21] describe a similar system to collect GPS trails and prompt the user to label the significant locations. Furthermore, many techniques combine social and location-based signals to significantly boost the accuracy of models for predicting user location as well as determining attributes of social relationships [30, 8, 28, 20].

Geolocating other types of data has also received substantial attention. Systems for mapping text to a location have been described for tweets [9], blogs [11], and web pages [5] using a variety of lexicographic and user features. Similarly, Serdyukov et al. [29] describe techniques for mapping photos to geographic coordinates using language models and user annotations.

1.2 Venue Search in Foursquare

Foursquare is a location-based service which handles more than 5 million check-ins each day, mapping each to one of more than 40 million locations worldwide. Foursquare has accumulated over 2.5 billion historical check-ins.[1] These actions are enabled by a search engine that maps user locations into a database of points of interest with high accuracy. This service is also provided as an API for external developers to add location mapping to their applications [1].

Figure 2 shows the check-in screen from the foursquare

[1]As of August 2012.

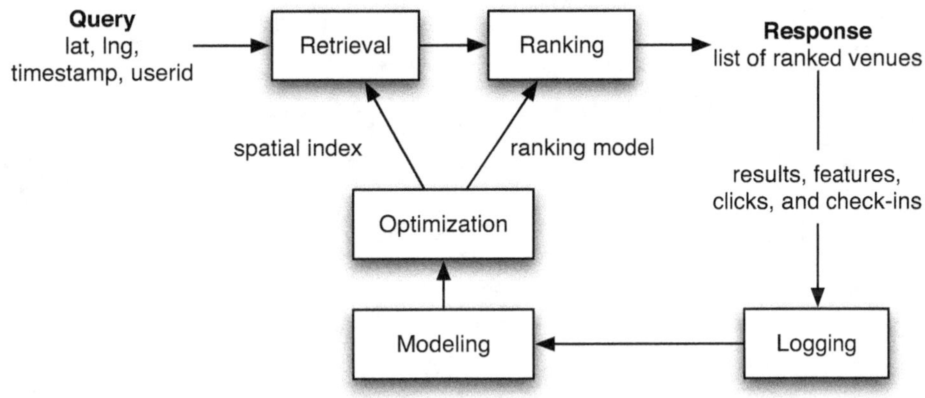

Figure 3: Overview of our system architecture. There are two main stages to responding to a query to produce a response: retrieval, where a spatial index is used to generate a set of candidate venues, and ranking where a machine-learned ranker is used to sort the response venues. Data is then logged from the search process and used offline for modeling and optimization.

application. Upon pressing the "Check in" button, the application sends the user's ID and current location to the server. The user ID is a unique identifier that is used to retrieve the user's history, friends, interests, and other personalized information used for ranking. The user's location is reported by the mobile device, and includes latitude, longitude, and a horizontal accuracy reading. A timestamp is generated at query time on the server in UTC, and is used to identify historical patterns in venue popularity for ranking.

The interface presents the user with a list of nearby locations, along with a map for context. The locations shown are chosen based on a variety of factors outlined below, including their popularity, distance from the user, and compatibility with the user's history. In particular, the current number of other users checked into each venue is displayed, which can help give the user an indication of the current popularity of the venues. For similar reasons, avatars for any of the user's own friends that are currently checked in are also shown. An icon indicating the location's primary category (e.g. Pub or Pizza Place) is also displayed to provide context for the user.

In certain situations, if the location in which the user is interested is not returned, they may perform an explicit textual query to find the correct venue. We term these searches *query* searches, to differentiate them from the *nearby* searches described above. We do not describe the system for query searches in this paper, but it is an extension of the techniques described here using standard text retrieval methods.

If the user still cannot find the desired location after a query search, they are offered the option of creating a new venue in the database. This venue is immediately included in the search engine and made available to the user (and others) to check in to. In this way, the system can adapt to new and missing locations and other recall failures.

Relative to other search systems, foursquare's check-in search has the benefit that the user provides direct feedback about the correct answer to their query by checking into that location after their search. Even in cases where the system fails to provide an accurate answer using nearby search, the user will often use query search to find the correct venue and check into it (26% of foursquare's searches include a text query). We use these sequences of user queries (also called *sessions*) as important training data when determining which features are the best predictors of the correct result.

2. ARCHITECTURE

The goal of a spatial search engine is to accurately retrieve and rank candidate venues which best match a query. Each query consists of a user, timestamp, and location $q_i = (u, t, l)$, where the location consists of a latitude, longitude, and an estimate of horizontal accuracy. Figure 3 gives an overview of our system architecture for mapping a query to a ranked list of venues. For each query we first generate a candidate set of venues $S_i = \{v_1, v_2, ...v_{m_i}\}$ using a coarse spatial index. We then compute features for each query-venue pair $F(q_i, v_j) = \mathbf{x}_{i,j} \in \mathbb{R}^d$, where the d features capture various relationships between each query and the candidate venue, such as distance, prior personal history of the user, etc. The response set R_i consists of the venues in the candidate set S_i rank ordered by some function of the features $G(\mathbf{x}_{i,j})$. For example, a simple linear model, represented as a vector of weights $\mathbf{w} \in \mathbb{R}^d$, would yield $G(\mathbf{x}_{i,j}) = \mathbf{w}^\top \mathbf{x}_{i,j}$. For each query-venue pair we then observe a value $y_{i,j} \in \{0, 1\}$ which indicates whether the user actually checked into venue v_j after performing query q_i.

In this section, we will focus on three main aspects of our system architecture. In Section 2.1 we discuss various ways for modeling places and people that are useful for both retrieval and feature generation. Then in Section 2.2 we describe how we generate the candidate set S_i for a given query. We then discuss in Section 2.3 how we construct features $F(q_i, v_j)$ and how we learn different ranking functions $G(\mathbf{x}_{i,j})$ by optimizing learn-to-rank algorithms using implicit feedback.

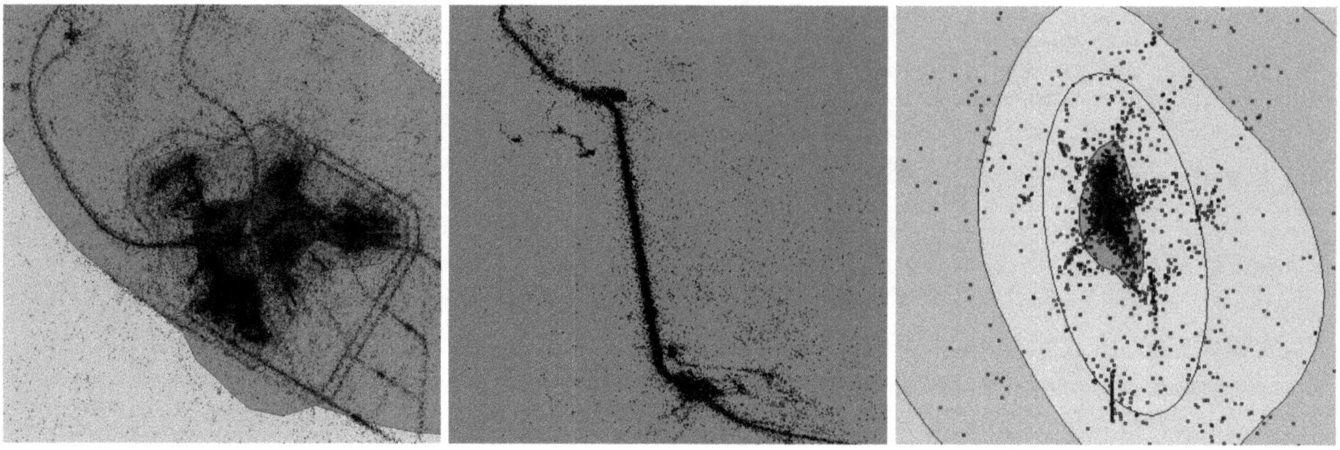

(a) JFK Airport (b) Golden Gate Bridge (close up) (c) The Blind Tiger

Figure 4: The spatial distribution of check-ins at different venues reveals complex patterns. The coordinates of check-ins for each venue are plotted in black. The colors represent a probability distribution modeled as a mixture of bivariate Gaussians, ranging from red (high probability) to blue (low probability). Although individual GPS estimates are noisy, in aggregate these estimates produce accurate reproductions of a venue's shape. Note the fine detail in the runways and terminals of JFK (left), and the clear outline of the Golden Gate Bridge (middle). Even for small venues such as the bar, The Blind Tiger (right), we see a non-uniform shape, that captures the nearby geography of streets and patterns in the noise associated with check-ins at that venue.

2.1 Modeling People and Places

Every check-in helps define exactly where a place is on the surface on the earth. Consider creating a spatial model for John F. Kennedy Airport in New York City from the 442 thousand historical check-ins that have occurred there. In Figure 4(a), we see that despite each individual GPS estimate being prone to noise, the aggregate of these estimates provides an accurate picture of the venue – one can easily make out the runways and terminals when the coordinates of all users' check-ins at the venue are plotted. A spatial model allows us to evaluate the probability that a set of location coordinates l belongs to a specific venue v: $P(l \mid v)$. Figure 4 shows the spatial models for a variety of different venues.

The simplest spatial model we compute from check-ins is based on the latitude and longitude of the center of the venue's check-ins, $l_{c(v)}$. We compute $l_{c(v)}$ by taking all check-ins to a venue, $c(v)$, removing outliers, and taking the mean of both the latitudes and longitudes. Then given a query location l, we approximate a distance-based spatial score as:

$$P(l \mid v) \approx \left(\frac{d}{\text{dist}(l, l_{c(v)}) + d}\right)^e$$

where we set $d = 50$ meters, $e = 4$, and $\text{dist}(l, l_{c(v)})$ is calculated by the Haversine formula. As we will show in Section 3.1, using a distance-based score by itself is a relatively poor predictor of the correct venue for a given set of location coordinates, particularly in dense urban areas. To address this problem, we also consider building probabilistic models of the shape of a venue and the distribution of the observed GPS noise as a mixture of bivariate Gaussians:

$$P(l \mid v) = \sum_k c_k g(l|\mu_k, \Sigma_k),$$

where $g(l, \mu_k, \Sigma_k)$ represents a bivariate Gaussian with mean μ_k and covariance Σ_k evaluated at location l, and c_k represents the mixing proportions. The parameters for this model can be learned via expectation maximization [23].

Each check-in also reveals information about the times at which places are popular. For example, Figure 5 shows the check-in rate over the course of a week for 3 different venues. We define this temporal signal as the probability that a check-in at a venue happens at a specific hour of the week, and estimate this probability using maximum likelihood:

$$P(t \mid v) = \frac{\text{\# of check-ins at wh}(t)}{\text{total \# of check-ins}},$$

where $\text{wh}(t)$ is the hour of the week corresponding to time t. This signal is vital for distinguishing between venues which are close in distance but popular at different times, for example a bar that is next to a bakery. We also calculate a variety of real-time signals about venues as well. We use an exponential moving average of check-ins/day to measure the current popularity of venues. We also maintain a count of the number of people who are currently checked into the venue, defined as those users who have been at the venue less than 3 hours and have not yet checked into another place.

People have been shown to be very predictable in terms of their mobility patterns [13], and Lian and Xie have shown that people's past check-in behavior is a strong predictor of future check-ins [18]. Furthermore, De Domenico et al. show that the locations of a user's friends is highly predictive of a user's location [20]. We observe that 73.1% of foursquare check-ins occur at venues to which the user has been before, and 62% of a user's check-ins are at places to which their friends have been before. Thus we also use personalized signals mined from a user's check-ins and other actions as well as their social connections to improve venue search for these users.

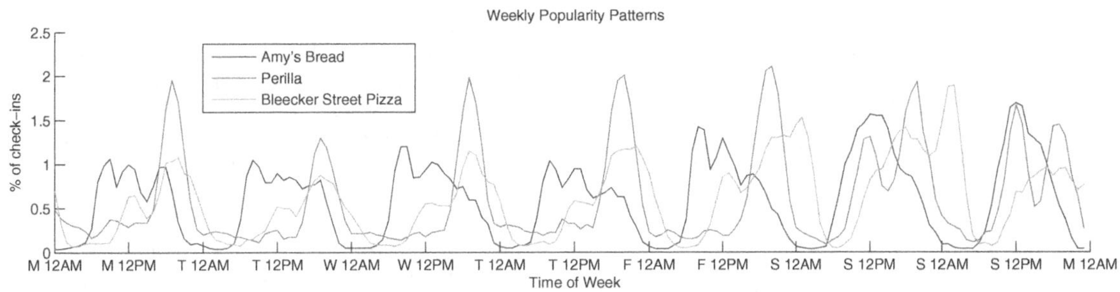

Figure 5: Places have distinct temporal signatures based on when they are popular during the week. Here we see normalized weekly check-ins for 3 venues within a 1 block radius in the West Village of New York City: Amy's Bread, a cafe which serves breakfast and lunch; Perilla, a nice restaurant that serves dinner and brunch on the weekends, and Bleecker Street Pizza, popular for both dinner and late night food on weekends.

2.2 Retrieval

The first step in our spatial search process is to retrieve a set of candidate venues for a given query. The primary source of these candidates is a geospatial index which we query for the m most popular venues closest to the user's query position. The current system uses $m = 150$ as a tradeoff between recall and performance considerations.

Unfortunately, due to poor accuracy in the position reported at query time, this initial query can fail to retrieve the desired venue under a variety of different circumstances. The geospatial query is particularly problematic in dense urban areas. For example, in some areas of Manhattan retrieving the 150 venues closest to a given position will result in an effective search radius of less than 75 meters (approximately the median of reported location accuracy as reported in Figure 1). Additionally, because venues are indexed by their the center point (computed as described in Section 2.1), the geospatial query can fail when the desired venue itself is particularly large. In these cases, the query position might physically exist within the venue's boundary, but nonetheless still be a considerable distance from the venue's indexed center point. For example, a user who searches for an airport while sitting on the airport's runway might be 1000 meters or more from the position at which the airport is indexed, which is usually near the center of the airport terminal.

To mitigate these shortcomings, we retrieve supplemental candidates from three other sources. We query the last 6 months of the user's check-in history for any venues within 1000 meters of the user's current location. We include these venues in the candidate set even if they were not retrieved by the geospatial query. Similarly, we include any venue within 1200 meters at which the user has a friend who is currently checked in. Finally, we keep a list of several hundred of the most frequently checked into large venues in the world (such as airports), and include these in the candidate set if they are within a few kilometers of the query position.

Our geospatial index is built on top of the S2 Geometry Library, open sourced by Google.[2] S2 models spherical geometries by mapping the sphere to a cube, and then recursively dividing each face of the cube into four child squares, which it refers to as "cells". There are 31 levels of cells, starting with the faces of the cube itself, which are level 0. Each cell has a 64-bit identifier called its "cell ID". For a sphere the size of the Earth, a typical level 30 S2 cell has an area of less than 1 cm^2.

The S2 representation has several benefits. Mapping a latitude and longitude to any of the 31 S2 cell IDs which contain it is very efficient. Similarly, given two S2 cell IDs, determining containment is a single bitwise operation. Additionally, given a geometric region on a sphere, the S2 library can efficiently compute a set of S2 cells which cover that region. The number of cells in this "cover" can be tuned by choosing larger or smaller cells at a given point, at the expense of a less accurate representation of the given region.

Using the S2 library, it is easy to build a performant geospatial search system on top of any standard database or key-value store.[3] For each venue in our index, we add an indexed field to the key-value store which contains a list of the 31 S2 cell IDs which contain the venue, one for each S2 level. At query time, we compute the set of S2 cell IDs which cover the query region. We restrict the query to that region by adding those S2 cell IDs to the query as a boolean OR (Figure 6).

In order to find our target of approximately 150 candidate venues, we need to scale the size of the retrieval region based on the expected density of venues in that region. That is, we need to retrieve from a smaller region in areas where venues are dense (for example, metropolitan areas) than we do in areas where venues are sparse. To solve this problem we compute "venue density", which is defined as the number of venues per unit area in a given region. In practice, we choose the region to be a reasonably-sized S2 level (level 15, roughly 250 meters on a side), and calculate the venue density for every S2 cell at that level using an offline process. We use this density to automatically scale the query radius to retrieve approximately the desired number of venues given the density of the query location.

The complete venue retrieval process is thus:

1. Calculate the S2 cell at the chosen venue density S2 level for the user's reported location.
2. Look up the venue density for that cell, and calculate the estimated radius, r, that will retrieve approximately 150 venues for that density.
3. Calculate an S2 covering of the spherical cap within r of the query position.

[2] S2 Geometry Library, http://code.google.com/p/s2-geometry-library

[3] We have built our geospatial index on top of the Apache Solr project, http://lucene.apache.org/solr/.

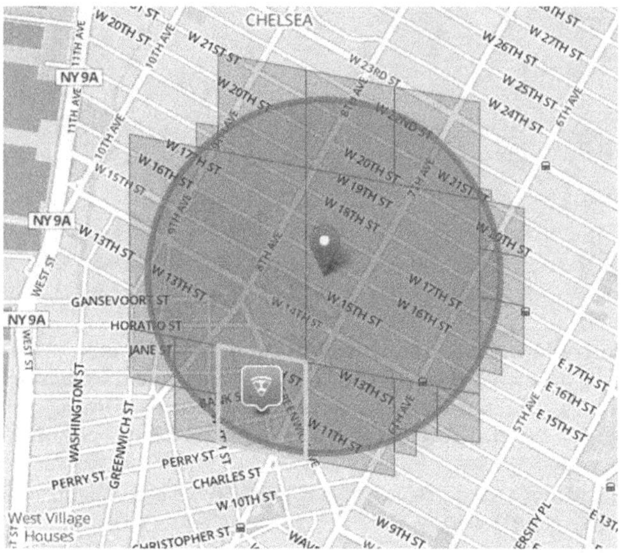

Figure 6: An example of an S2 cell-based retrieval. The query area is shown by the red circle around the query location. The set of S2 cells used for retrieval (known as a "cover") is shown as red polygons (note that an S2 cover is an approximation of the given region). The desired venue is shown as a pin on the map, with its enclosing S2 cell highlighted in yellow.

4. Query the index to retrieve all of the venues which are indexed with any of the cell IDs in the covering to get a list of nearby candidate venues.

5. Concatenate the nearby candidate venues with the supplementary retrieval sources (venues that the user has visited previously, venues that the user's friends are checked in at, and large venues that are nearby).

At the end of the retrieval process, we have between 150 and 250 candidate venues, along with supplementary information about the venues' history, shape, popularity over time, and other factors. In parallel, we have also retrieved the user's own history and preferences, as well as information about their friends and their friends' histories. All of this information is fed into the ranking system.

2.3 Ranking

Many state-of-the-art search systems rely on machine learning to create models for ranking [12, 27]. Traditionally, the data for training such models is generated by people explicitly annotating previously logged search results. There are a few drawbacks to this approach. First, it is time-consuming and expensive to collect explicit feedback at a large scale. Second, it is difficult for annotators to make judgements about personalized results, thus making this approach less desirable for use in a highly personalized search product such as foursquare's. Consider the case where two users perform a search from approximately the same location in a shopping mall. The desired result depends heavily on their personal preferences making it difficult for an annotator to label the correct result given only the list of nearby shops.

An alternative approach that has recently gained popularity is based on interpreting the implicit behavior of users as they are interacting with search results. Such implicit feedback is often available at a large scale and is easy to collect. Unfortunately, implicit feedback is ambiguous. Clicks, the most common form of implicit feedback in search, do not necessarily indicate that users have found the right result. Clicks are biased towards the top results and are often accidental. Users reformulate queries or abandon the search if the clicked results are not satisfactory. Joachims et al. have made great progress in interpreting clicks by extracting pairwise preferences [16] using query chains [15] and randomly modifying the presentation of search results [26].

In this work, we use a different form of implicit feedback: check-ins. A check-in at one of the venues in the search results is an unambiguous endorsement of that result by the user. Using this labeling technique, we can construct a training set consisting of features and labels for each candidate venue $\mathbf{x}_{i,j}$ and $y_{i,j}$ for $j = 1 \ldots m_i$ of each query q_i, where $y_{i,j}$ denotes the binary label for the jth result in the candidate set for the ith query. The label is 1 if the user checked into the venue and is 0 otherwise.

2.3.1 Data Collection

From the perspective of collecting data, a search query and a check-in are distinct and independent actions. Depending upon the version of the foursquare product, a check-in can immediately follow a query or it may have a few intermediate steps (e.g. viewing additional information about a venue prior to checking in). Each of these user actions is associated with independent calls to foursquare services running over a large pool of machines. Each call to a foursquare service results in an event log being written by the service to a distributed log collection mechanism.[4]

The candidate results R_i and the derived ranking features $F(q_i, v_j) = \mathbf{x}_{i,j}$ for $j = 1 \ldots m_i$ used to train our search algorithm are recorded in the server event logs whenever a user performs a search query q_i. Since many of our models and indices are updated continuously, regenerating the exact feature values that were used to rank the results for a query in the past is difficult. Instead, the candidate venues and their corresponding features are pushed to logs at the time of the query, removing the need for regenerating features altogether.

To derive training data from event logs, we use automated MapReduce jobs written in Scala [24] and Pig [25]. The first step in the process joins the independent logs into user "sessions" which contain all actions taken by a user during a given time frame (e.g. opening the application, performing a nearby check-in search, performing a query search for "The Blind Tiger", then checking in to a specific venue). Each session involving either a nearby or query search is then categorized as successful or not if it also includes a corresponding check-in.

Next, we sample a specified number of successful search sessions and split them into training, validation, and test sets. This process extracts from the logs all candidate venues, their features, and their original rank as presented to the user. It then joins these with other datasets containing exploratory features, allowing us to evaluate the efficacy of these features without implementing them at production scale. The training and test sets are then exported as files

[4] Apache Flume, https://cwiki.apache.org/flume/

Feature	Description
Spatial score	$P(l \mid v)$
Timeliness	$P(t \mid v)$
Popularity	Smoothed estimate of expected check-ins/day at the venue
Here now	# of users currently checked in to the venue at query time
Personal History	# of previous visits from the user at the venue
Creator	1 if the user created the venue, 0 otherwise
Mayor	1 is the user is the mayor of the venue, 0 otherwise[5]
Friends Here Now	# of the user's friends currently checked in at query time
Personal History w/ Time of Day	# of previous visits from the user at the venue at the same time of the day

Table 1: Overview of the features used for ranking. General signals (top) capture information about the user's proximity to a venue as well as information about when the venue is popular and to what degree. Personalized signals (bottom) capture past interactions between the user (and his friends) with the venue.

that can be used with various machine learning packages for model training and exploration.

2.3.2 *Features*

The primary features for ranking are derived from models of venues and users as described in Section 2.1. In addition to the scores derived from these models we construct features using contextual information about the users and venues at the time of the query. These contextual signals are updated in real time throughout our system. We also derive features using the social relationships between users. Each of these features is generated and logged at query time. In Table 1, we see an overview of the features used by our search ranking algorithm.

2.3.3 *Metrics*

We use 3 different metrics to evaluate the performance of a ranking R_i given query q_i and labels $y_{i,j}$: precision at position 1 (P@1):

$$\text{P@1} = y_{i,1},$$

recall at 5 (R@5):

$$\text{R@5} = \sum_{j=1}^{5} y_{i,j},$$

and normalized discounted cumulative gain (NDCG) [14]:

$$\text{NDCG@5} = \frac{1}{Z_i} \sum_{j=1}^{5} \frac{2^{y_{i,j}} - 1}{\log(1+j)},$$

where $y_{i,j}$ indicates that the result shown at position j for query i was the location the user checked into, and Z_i is the normalizing constant chosen such that a perfect ranking would result in an NDCG of 1 for each query. Each of these metrics can then be averaged over all n queries in our evaluation set to measure the performance of different ranking functions.

2.3.4 *Optimization*

We consider 3 training procedures for learning the function $G(\mathbf{x}_{i,j})$ which combines features into a rankable score: linear regression, coordinate ascent, and LambdaMART. For the linear regression model, we simply learn a set of weights $\mathbf{w}$ where $G(\mathbf{x}_{i,j}) = \mathbf{w}^\top \mathbf{x}_{i,j}$. The weights are learned such that the L2 loss is minimized:

$$\mathbf{w} = argmin_{\mathbf{w}} \sum_{i,j} ||\mathbf{w}^\top \mathbf{x}_{i,j} - y_{i,j}||_2.$$

The coordinate ascent training procedure similarly learns a set of linear weights but can be used to optimize metrics other than L2 loss and has thus proved to be very useful for search ranking [22]. LambdaMART has been shown to provide significant lift in search ranking tasks [33] by constructing an ensemble of decision trees which non-linearly combine features. We use MATLAB for our linear regression implementation and use RankLib for implementations of coordinate ascent and LambdaMART [3].

[5]On foursquare, the "mayor" of a venue is the person who has been there more days than any other foursquare user in the last 60 days.

3. EXPERIMENTS

We present a variety of experiments which evaluate different aspects of our search algorithm. We start by evaluating the impact of modeling places using spatiotemporal probability distributions, as compared to the most common baseline technique of simply using distance. We then demonstrate the performance of variants of our search algorithm which use different sets of features and optimization procedures. We compare these to baseline methods based on distance, popularity, and user history.

3.1 Spatiotemporal Models

To better understand how spatiotemporal models of venues improve unpersonalized venue search in dense urban areas, we present an experiment that compares different spatiotemporal models for predicting check-ins in a small 10-block radius of downtown Manhattan. Figure 7 shows a sample of the 143 thousand check-ins that have occurred at 127 popular venues near Bleecker and Jones St. color-coded by venue. We have removed any venues from this set with less than 100 check-ins (which represents less than 5% of the total number of check-ins). The dataset is then divided 90%/10% into training and testing sets.

Given only the latitude, longitude, and timestamp of each check-in, the goal is to predict which venue a user checks into (precision @1). We consider three models for this task. The baseline model simply selects the nearest venue based on distance. The spatial Gaussian mixture model uses a probabilistic model, as described in Section 2.1. The num-

Figure 7: A scatterplot showing a sample of the 143 thousand check-ins that have occurred in the few blocks near the corner of Bleecker and Jones St. in Manhattan. Each check-in is color-coded by the venue to which it belongs. We see that although some popular venues can easily be distinguished from others nearby, there is a substantial overlap of check-ins in some areas which makes discrimination difficult.

Model	P@1
Baseline (nearest by distance)	0.130
Spatial Gaussian mixture model	0.193
Spatiotemporal models	0.277

Table 2: Comparison of different models of venues. We see that using more complex spatial models and incorporating temporal signals greatly improves the accuracy of the search algorithm.

Model	P@1
Random	0.009
Spatial only	0.201
User history only	0.358
Popularity only	0.143
Linear regression: spatial + temporal	0.230
Linear regression: spatial + temporal + popularity	0.251
Linear regression: all features	0.434
Coordinate ascent: all features w/ nonlinear pairs	0.493
LambdaMART: all features	0.531

Table 3: The precision of various models and sets of features in ranking venue search results.

ber of Gaussians was limited between 1 and 5 and selected via cross-validation. A venue is then predicted by finding the venue which maximizes the probability under this spatial distribution. The full spatiotemporal model uses the mixture of Gaussians, the timeliness feature, as well as popularity combined as a linear sum of log-likelihoods.

Table 2 shows the test accuracy of the 3 different models. We see that modelling venue shape offers 46% lift over a simple distance-based algorithm, and incorporating timeliness and relative popularity yields a 112% lift in performance.

3.2 Learning to Rank

In this section, we describe our experiments to determine the optimal features and training procedure for our search algorithm. Using the methodology discussed in Section 2.3.1, we collected 38 thousand examples of successful worldwide venue searches, randomly sampled from the week of 6/24/12, where a user selected the correct venue from a rank-ordered list presented to them. Our goal is to create a better ranking algorithm which ranks the correct venues at a higher position. The 38 thousand venue searches are comprised of over 4 million candidate venues and are split 70%/15%/15% into training, validation, and test sets respectively. The models for these venues were built using 282 million check-ins, collected over the 2 years prior to the query date.

We explore a variety of different combinations of features and models, including linear regression, coordinate ascent, and LambdaMART [33]. For the coordinate ascent model, we use domain knowledge to construct explicit cross-products that capture important non-linearities (such as spatial score $\times$ popularity). The LambdaMART algorithm automatically captures non-linearites by forming an ensemble of 2000 decision trees. Table 3 summarizes the performance of these different techniques in terms of precision at 1 on the held-out test set. The NDCG@5 for our best model is 0.686, and recall @5 is 0.822. Figure 9 shows our recall as rank increases. We see that using our best model, we find the correct result in one of the top 5 positions in 82% of searches and in the top 10 positions in 91% of searches.

The results in Table 3 indicate that distance and personal history are informative features; however their individual performance is poor when compared to a full model trained using a combination of many features. We also find that linear models can perform poorly for ranking when many features are combined. Carefully constructing non-linear pairs of features or using a robust non-linear model such as LambdaMART is crucial for combining many disparate signals into an accurate model.

3.3 Analysis

To better understand when venue search is difficult we more closely examine how the performance of our search algorithm degrades based on varying degrees of personal history, venue density, and reported horizontal accuracy from the GPS of the mobile device. In Figure 8(a), we see the performance of the linear model as a function of the number of nearby venues a user has been to when they perform a search. Because users are more likely to check into venues they have visited before, the model performs best when there are a small number of venues nearby that a user has previously visited. As the number of nearby venues in the user's history increases, this history has less predictive value, and the accuracy of the model decreases. In Figure 8(b), we see performance as a function of the number of venues within a 1km radius of the user's query. As expected, we observe

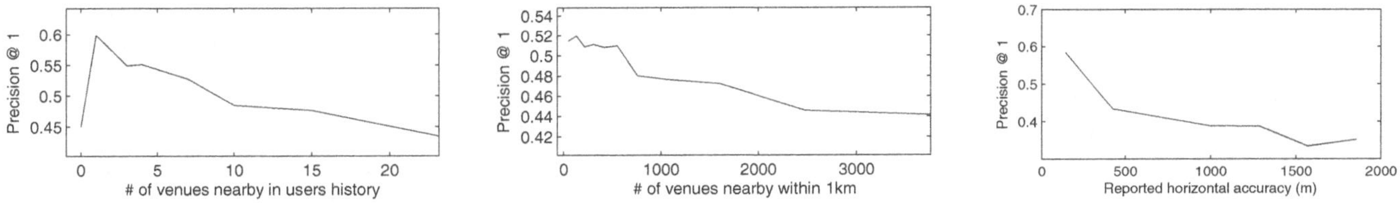

(a) User History vs. Precision (b) Venue Density vs. Precision (c) Reported Accuracy vs. Precision

Figure 8: Many factors influence the precision of venue search: the familiarity of users with nearby venues (left), the density of nearby venues (middle), and the reported horizontal accuracy from the mobile device (right).

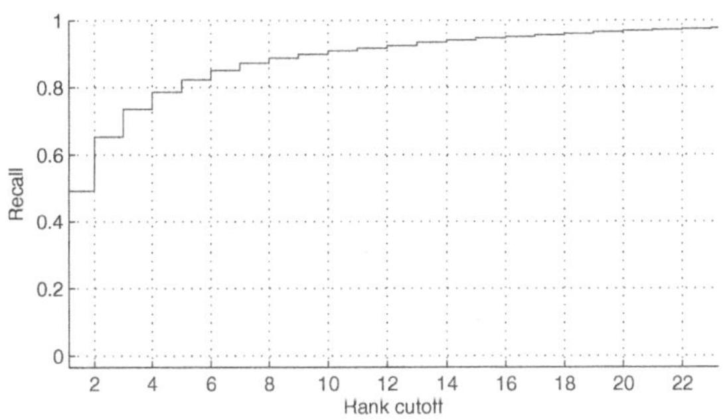

Figure 9: Recall as a function of the rank cut-off.

that performance is higher in areas with fewer venues, and degrades in dense urban areas. Similarly, Figure 8(c) shows that as the horizontal accuracy reported by the device increases, performance also degrades.

4. DISCUSSION

There are now over 5 billion consumer mobile devices in the world that are constantly reporting a signal of latitudes, longitudes, and timestamps [4]. As location data become more pervasive, the need to map these signals to semantically meaningful locations becomes increasingly important. In this article, we have demonstrated a spatial search engine for mapping noisy location estimates from mobile devices to points of interest. Furthermore, we show that simple baseline techniques for this task, such as those based on distance and popularity, are insufficient for accurately predicting a user's location. By leveraging machine learning algorithms for ranking and rich spatiotemporal models of places and users, our spatial search engine achieves significant lift in performance over these common baselines as well as previously reported results.

4.1 Future Work

We aim to incorporate more sophisticated models of user behavior by exploiting additional metadata such as categories of venues and demographics of users (e.g. age, gender, etc.). These additional signals would allow us to better distinguish between nearby venues that are frequented by different types of people (e.g. a nail salon next to barber shop). Furthermore, a better model of user dynamics could improve accuracy as well, by leveraging information about common transitions between locations (both for the user as well as in aggregate).

We plan to improve the modeling of venues in the retrieval stage of our search algorithm to better incorporate venue shapes (building on the Gaussian mixture models described in Section 2.1) instead of points, eliminating the need for supplementary retrieval of large venues. We also plan to incorporate weather information, modeling the popularity changes of venues under different situations (e.g. parks are more popular when it is sunny and art galleries are more popular when the weather is inclement).

We are striving towards a venue search system that can support not only millions of explicit nearby searches every day but millions of implicit searches as well, generated by users' mobile devices as users explore their cities. A passive venue search system would react to changes in a user's location and present relevant local information, such as details of nearby events, tips from friends, or suggestions about where to go next. Every location update can act as a search into local real-time information, surfacing highly contextual results that can help people better understand and navigate the real world.

5. REFERENCES

[1] foursquare API. http://developer.foursquare.com.

[2] Geonames.org reverse geocoding services. http://www.geonames.org/export/reverse-geocoding.html.

[3] Ranklib. http://people.cs.umass.edu/ vdang/ranklib.html.

[4] The World in 2011 – ICT Facts and Figures. http://www.itu.int/ITU-D/ict/facts/2011/material/ICTFactsFigures2011.pdf.

[5] E. Amitay, N. Har'El, R. Sivan, and A. Soffer. Web-a-where: geotagging web content. In *Proceedings of the 27th Annual International ACM SIGIR Conference on Research and Development in Information Retrieval*, pages 273–280. ACM, 2004.

[6] D. Ashbrook and T. Starner. Learning significant locations and predicting user movement with gps. In *Proceedings of the Sixth International Symposium on Wearable Computers. (ISWC 2002).*, pages 101–108. IEEE, 2002.

[7] D. Ashbrook and T. Starner. Using gps to learn significant locations and predict movement across multiple users. *Personal and Ubiquitous Computing*, 7(5):275–286, 2003.

[8] Lars Backstrom, Eric Sun, and Cameron Marlow. Find me if you can: improving geographical prediction with

social and spatial proximity. In *Proceedings of the 19th international conference on World wide web*, WWW '10, pages 61–70, New York, NY, USA, 2010. ACM.

[9] Z. Cheng, J. Caverlee, and K. Lee. You are where you tweet: a content-based approach to geo-locating twitter users. In *Proceedings of the 19th ACM International Conference on Information and Knowledge Management*, pages 759–768. ACM, 2010.

[10] K. Church and B. Smyth. Who, what, where & when: a new approach to mobile search. In *Proceedings of the 13th International Conference on Intelligent User Interfaces*, pages 309–312. ACM, 2008.

[11] C. Fink, C. Piatko, J. Mayfield, T. Finin, and J. Martineau. Geolocating blogs from their textual content. In *Working Notes of the AAAI Spring Symposium on Social Semantic Web: Where Web 2.0 Meets Web 3.0.* AAAI Press, 2009.

[12] J. Fürnkranz and E. Hüllermeier. Pairwise preference learning and ranking. *Machine Learning: ECML 2003*, pages 145–156, 2003.

[13] M.C. Gonzalez, C.A. Hidalgo, and A.L. Barabási. Understanding individual human mobility patterns. *Nature*, 453(7196):779–782, 2008.

[14] K. Järvelin and J. Kekäläinen. IR evaluation methods for retrieving highly relevant documents. In *Proceedings of the 23rd Annual International ACM SIGIR Conference on Research and Development in Information Retrieval*, SIGIR '00, pages 41–48. ACM, 2000.

[15] T. Joachims, L. Granka, Bing Pan, H. Hembrooke, F. Radlinski, and G. Gay. Evaluating the accuracy of implicit feedback from clicks and query reformulations in web search. *ACM Transactions on Information Systems (TOIS)*, 25(2), April 2007.

[16] T. Joachims, L. Granka, B. Pang, H. Hembrooke, and G. Gay. Accurately interpreting clickthrough data as implicit feedback. In *Proceedings of the 28th International ACM SIGIR Conference on Research and Development in Information*, pages 154–161, 2005.

[17] N.D. Lane, D. Lymberopoulos, F. Zhao, and A.T. Campbell. Hapori: context-based local search for mobile phones using community behavioral modeling and similarity. In *Proceedings of the 12th ACM International Conference on Ubiquitous Computing*, pages 109–118. ACM, 2010.

[18] D. Lian and X. Xie. Learning location naming from user check-in histories. In *Proceedings of the 19th ACM SIGSPATIAL International Conference on Advances in Geographic Information Systems*, pages 112–121. ACM, 2011.

[19] L. Liao, D. Fox, and H. Kautz. Extracting places and activities from gps traces using hierarchical conditional random fields. *The International Journal of Robotics Research*, 26(1):119–134, 2007.

[20] A. Lima M. De Domenico and M/ Musolesi. Interdependence and predictability of human mobility and social interactions. *Proceedings of the Nokia Mobile Data Challenge Workshop*, June 2012.

[21] N. Marmasse and C. Schmandt. Location-aware information delivery with commotion. In *Handheld and Ubiquitous Computing*, pages 361–370. Springer, 2000.

[22] Donald Metzler and W. Bruce Croft. Linear feature-based models for information retrieval. *Information Retrieval*, 10(3):257–274, June 2007.

[23] T.K. Moon. The expectation-maximization algorithm. *Signal Processing Magazine, IEEE*, 13(6):47–60, 1996.

[24] M. Odersky, P. Altherr, V. Cremet, B. Emir, S. Maneth, S. Micheloud, N. Mihaylov, M. Schinz, E. Stenman, and M. Zenger. An overview of the scala programming language. Technical report, Technical Report IC/2004/64, EPFL Lausanne, Switzerland, 2004.

[25] C. Olston, B. Reed, U. Srivastava, R. Kumar, and A. Tomkins. Pig latin: a not-so-foreign language for data processing. In *Proceedings of the 2008 ACM SIGMOD International Conference on Management of Data*, SIGMOD '08. ACM, 2008.

[26] F. Radlinski and T. Joachims. Minimally invasive randomization for collecting unbiased preferences from clickthrough logs. In *Proceedings of the 21st National Conference on Artificial Intelligence (AAAI)*, pages 1406–1412, 2006.

[27] M. Richardson, A. Prakash, and E. Brill. Beyond pagerank: machine learning for static ranking. In *Proceedings of the 15th International World Wide Web Conference (WWW)*, pages 707–715. ACM, 2006.

[28] Adam Sadilek, Henry Kautz, and Jeffrey P. Bigham. Finding your friends and following them to where you are. In *Proceedings of the fifth ACM international conference on Web search and data mining*, WSDM '12, pages 723–732, New York, NY, USA, 2012. ACM.

[29] P. Serdyukov, V. Murdock, and R. Van Zwol. Placing flickr photos on a map. In *Proceedings of the 32nd International ACM SIGIR Conference on Research and Development in Information Retrieval*, pages 484–491. ACM, 2009.

[30] M. Terry, E.D. Mynatt, K. Ryall, and D. Leigh. Social net: using patterns of physical proximity over time to infer shared interests. In *CHI'02 Extended Abstracts on Human Factors in Computing Systems*, pages 816–817. ACM, 2002.

[31] M. A. Vasconcelos, S. Ricci, J. Almeida, F. Benevenuto, and V. Almeida. Tips, dones and todos: uncovering user profiles in foursquare. In *Proceedings of the Fifth ACM International Conference on Web Search and Data Mining*, WSDM '12, pages 653–662, New York, NY, USA, 2012. ACM.

[32] Petros Venetis, Hector Gonzalez, Christian S. Jensen, and Alon Halevy. Hyper-local, directions-based ranking of places. *Proc. VLDB Endow.*, 4(5):290–301, February 2011.

[33] Q. Wu, C. J. Burges, K. M. Svore, and J. Gao. Adapting boosting for information retrieval measures. *Information Retrieval*, 13(3):254–270, June 2010.

[34] J. Yi, F. Maghoul, and J. Pedersen. Deciphering mobile search patterns: a study of yahoo! mobile search queries. In *Proceeding of the 17th International World Wide Web Conference (WWW)*, pages 257–266. ACM, 2008.

[35] P.A. Zandbergen. Accuracy of iPhone locations: A comparison of assisted GPS, WiFi and cellular positioning. *Transactions in GIS*, 13:5–25, 2009.

Maguro, A System for Indexing and Searching over Very Large Text Collections

Knut Magne Risvik, Trishul Chilimbi, Henry Tan, Chris Anderson, Karthik Kalyanaraman
Microsoft Corporation
{knutmr, trishulc, htan, chand, karthk}@microsoft.com

ABSTRACT

Maguro is a system for efficiently searching very large collections of text content of up to 1 trillion documents at low cost. Search engines span across content that is very dynamic and highly augmented with metadata to the tail content of the web. A long tail distribution of content calls for different trade-offs in the design space for good efficiency across the entire index range. Maguro is designed for the long tail of content with less dynamics and less metadata, but very good cost efficiency. Maguro is part of the serving stack in Bing and allows us to scale the index significantly better.

Categories and Subject Descriptors

H.3.4 [**Information Storage and Retrieval**]: Systems and Software – *Distributed systems;* H.3.3 [**Information Storage and Retrieval**]: Information Search and Retrieval – *Search process.*

Keywords

Index serving; Scalability

1. INTRODUCTION

Designing an efficient index serving system to comprehensively index the entire World Wide Web is extremely challenging. Given the versatility of the content on the web, it makes sense for Bing to use a portfolio of technologies for efficient and cost effective index serving for different subsets of the web. The head of the web has extreme dynamics in both content and references, and the amount of information external to the page itself (links, anchors, tweets, likes, shares, etc.) are in many cases vastly larger than the content itself. The number of external signals to determine the actual search engine ranking of a head object is large, and the requirements to handle these dynamics drives the index serving system design. Moving into the web's extremely long tail of content, very few signals outside the content itself exists, and the scale of the web tail drives the requirements for us to build a very efficient index serving system for this content.

The storage hierarchy economics implies that we need to utilize hard drives to handle the web tail in an efficient manner. Maguro is designed to index any atom from a web page (word, n-gram, tuple, and feature) and to distribute the index of each atom across hard disks and machines to optimize the retrieval cost, hence enabling a flexible model for trading off efficiency for retrieval features at fine granularity. Maguro's use of hard drives enables it to index more documents per machines as well as a large selection of compound atoms, such as n-grams and tuples. In addition, Maguro's atom partitioned serving architecture reduces the number of machines that need to participate in every query as compared to a document partitioned serving architecture that involves all machines[13][16][14]. Finally, Maguro takes advantage of its phrase-based indexing with n-gram and tuple based query formulation to additionally reduce both the number of machines that must participate in each query as well as the computation needed to answer the query.

Maguro achieves 12x cost efficiency improvement over Bing's baseline search engine that serves head content on the same hardware, and over 40x improvement, when run on hardware with a faster network interconnect. By reducing the number of machines that participate in computing the query results, Maguro is able to demonstrate better latency scaling characteristics and enables providing fast and consistent query response even when indexing and serving a large collection of tail documents.

The rest of the paper is organized as follows. Section 2 talks about overall search engine architecture, introduces the funnel architecture for how we design search engines and helps motivate the Maguro system design based on hardware and scale trends. Section 3 presents the overall Maguro system architecture along with descriptions of the key building blocks. Section 4 provides experimental evaluation of the Maguro system. Finally, Section 5 covers related work, and Section 6 concludes the paper. Protecting Bing's business interests requires us to reduce some level of detail and omit additional information that may have been appropriate. Examples of this include the details of the hash function used, query formulation algorithm, posting list compression, and the omission of absolute numbers from the graphs in Section 4.

2. BACKGROUND

A search engine [13][4][3] is a very complex system operating with multiple large components. Overall, one model of a search engine can be broken down into:

1) Selection and crawling. Using a map of the webgraph to select what documents to schedule

WSDM'13, February 4–8, 2013, Rome, Italy.

for fetching, and a crawler to efficiently download and discover these.

2) Index building by inverting the content of documents into efficient inverted indexes for searching.
3) Matching and ranking documents upon user queries.
4) A search engine user interface to handle the dialog with the user.

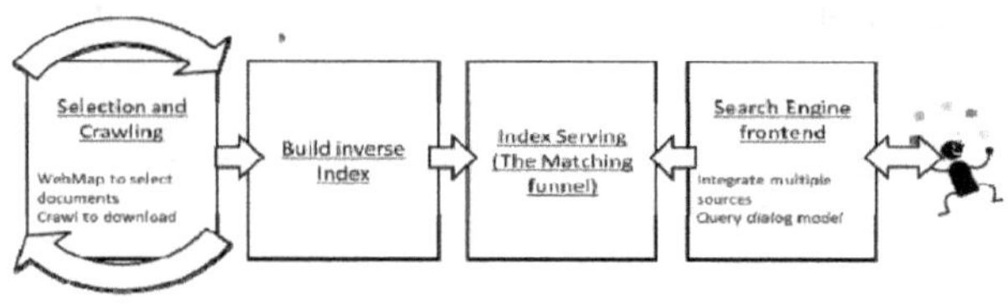

Figure 1: Anatomy of a search engine

2.1 The Matching Funnel

We break matching and ranking down into multiple phases that are sequenced in a funnel. A rational breakdown can be:

1) L0 – Matching. Given a query, find all candidate matches for the query.
2) L1 – Preliminary ranking and pruning. The number of matches from stage 1 can be very large, so stage 2 is using efficient and preliminary ranking to prune away matches that are unlikely to be part of the final answer.
3) L2 – Final ranking and sorting. Based on the pruned results from stage 2, use a full featured ranking system to derive final scores and sort the matches.

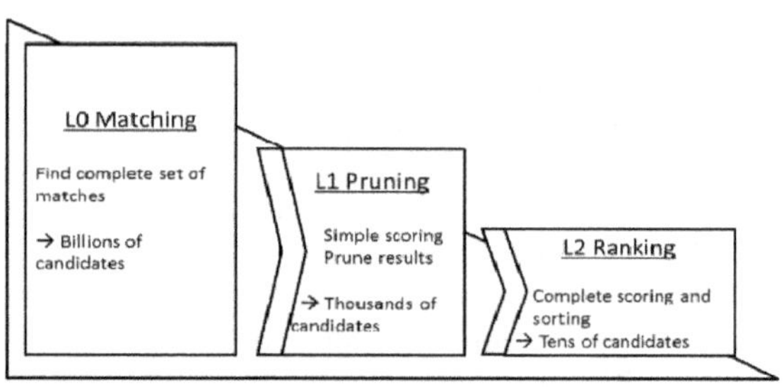

Figure 2: Search matching funnel

This is illustrated above, and Maguro covers both L0 and L1 in this model, and uses pre-computed scores to prune the lists in L1.

2.2 Hardware Trends

Running a search engine at extreme scale implies a relentless focus on cost efficiency. To the extent possible, datacenters are made up of commodity components. When considering the index serving problem at large scale, recent hardware trends open up and suggest specific architectural directions. In particular we take into account trends in 3 major areas:

1) *HDD cost trends*: HDD storage cost is significantly lower than other storage systems, and currently trending at around \$0.05/Gbyte. The technology is expecting to be able to increase the density of storage at least 50x, so there seems to be no immediate physical barrier to be hit here. The challenge is to scale throughput and latency, which is more stagnant.
2) *The evolution of SSD*: Flash-based storage has rapidly entered the stage as a viable storage layer. Since 2007 the cost per GB of SSD has dropped from 120x the cost of HDD to around 25x the cost of HDD, and it has huge advantages in latency of access. Though, there are challenges in lifetime management and write cycles handling.
3) *10Gbit commodity networks*: With the introduction of 10Gbit networking, the bandwidth between machines enables remote storage to be as fast as local storage. Architecturally, this opens up the ability to do more global computation across machines, and this is a key element in the scalability of the Maguro serving platform.

3. MAGURO SYSTEM OVERVIEW

Maguro breaks the searchable index into disjoint segments that are queried in parallel. These segments can be selected based on different criteria such as language, region, topic or static rank. Inside a segment, the index is again distributed onto leaf nodes of computing. At the top, a *CorpusRoot* orchestrates querying across segments, while inside a segment, the *SegmentRoot* handles query execution and result computation. Each leaf node contains an *L01Matcher* component and an *L2Ranker* component that implements the search funnel. Overall the architecture can be illustrated as below.

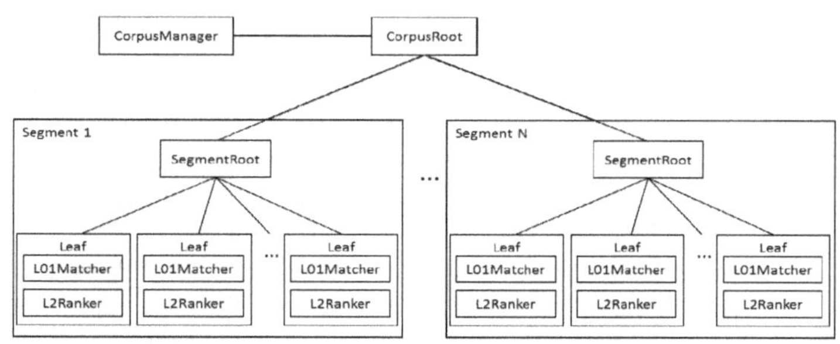

Figure 3: Maguro architecture overview

3.1 Basic Data Model and atom-based indexing

The fundamental data model for Maguro is a mapping from an atom to a list of documents containing the atom called a posting list, e.g:

(atom → {(docid, attributes)}

Documents to be indexed are represented as stream of tokens, e.g (w_1, w_2, w_3, …), and Maguro generates atoms from the following logic:

1) All unigrams/words in the stream are atoms.
2) All n-grams (up to a given n) are considered as atoms.

3) A selection of all n-grams (beyond length n) are considered as atoms.

4) A selection of known n-grams of arbitrarily length are considered as atoms.

5) A selection of all tuples (w_i, w_j) are considered as atoms.

The selection process is based on several a-priori distributions from the document corpus and query logs. From the candidate set above, Maguro generates a set of atoms (a_1, a_N) for each document, as a mix of unigrams along with n-grams and tuples that we collectively refer to as phrases. The primary location for the posting lists is on hard-drive, and hence Maguro is more sensitive to the length of each posting list, rather than the total space used for all postings. This makes it feasible to generate posting lists for a large number of atoms and potentially reduce the number of IOPS and the length of each transfer due to richer atoms. For example, the posting list length of n-gram "*ab*" is typically 1/1000 times smaller than the length of the posting lists for its constituent unigrams, *a* and *b*.

The posting lists are generated as the join of documents for a given atom:

$$P = (atom \rightarrow \{(docid,\ score)\})$$

Here, the score is a pre computed ranking score, *Rank_L1(query, doc)* with atom itself as the query. We refer to this score as the *L1 Score*. The total index is then the union of all posting lists for all atoms.

3.2 Partitioning the index by atoms

Maguro distributes the index across machines inside a segment by the hash value of each atom. This is similar to global indexing schemes described extensively in the literature [13][16][14]. Hence for a given doc, the postings will be scattered over potentially all the machines inside a segment, implying the need for query execution to coordinate fetching results from the machines.

Partitioning the index by atom instead of document is driven by the desire to utilize hard-disk efficiently. For a given query, the number of IO requests with this scheme is linear to the number of atoms in the query, as compared to a document partitioning model that will issue IO requests for each atom on each machine. Hence if we have a query of 10 words, which is quite feasible after query augmentation and analysis, each segment in an atom partitioned configuration will do O(10) IO operations. If the data was partitioned by documents, and assuming that N machines are needed to index the entire document corpus, we are looking at significantly more IO operations O(10*N). The amortized amount of IO operations in document partitioned models is prohibitive, and hence most search engines will use DRAM or SSD to store such an index, where the IOPS capacity is way higher. Typically, this implies that each node has many fewer documents (say 20M), and a significantly wider fan-out. While the throughput of such a DRAM/SSD based index is expected to be higher, the impact of wide fanout is higher latency variations, and typically this is compensated with large capacity buffers to have less latency flux. Latency is an extremely important element of large-scale online services, and as we will show later in this paper, the lower fanout enables us to run with smaller capacity buffers, making the disk based index very attractive.

3.3 Efficient atom lookup

The search index on each machine comprised of inverted posting lists is organized as a multi-level hash-based index. We use a custom hash function that is fast to compute and has almost zero collisions even when indexing trillions of atoms, while still using a small number of bits for space efficiency. The hash-structure is organized in three levels across DRAM, SSD, and HDD with the most popular atoms in DRAM and the least popular ones on HDD. Atom popularity is determined by occurrence frequency in query logs and the document corpus. When N machines participate in a Maguro segment, the amount of atoms accessible without going to HDD is proportional to N x (DRAM size reserved + SSD size reserved), which is sufficient to ensure that the vast majority of query atoms can be efficiently looked up without accessing HDD. This lookup only provides summary statistics about the atom and requires an additional HDD lookup to retrieve the posting list.

Maguro uses such a hash-based structure because efficient atom lookup is crucial to our phrase-based query formulation where a large candidate set of atoms are examined prior to selecting the subset of atoms whose posting lists need to be examined and intersected. Since not all phrases (n-grams, tuples) are present in our index we need to quickly determine if the atom exists in the index along with other information such as occurrence frequency and score distribution that is important for effective query formulation.

3.4 Handling long posting lists

Maguro's efficiency primarily arises from using HDD to index a much larger number of documents per machine. In addition, since it uses a global indexing scheme [13][16][14] each machine's inverted posting list comprises all documents indexed by the segment. Consequently, posting lists, especially for popular atoms, can grow extremely large and require special consideration for efficient processing. This issue is partially addressed by aggressively indexing and using phrases (n-grams, tuples) in query formulation, which have significantly smaller posting lists as compared to unigrams. In addition, Maguro tiers posting lists based on a posting's pre-computed L1 score. High scoring postings are placed in tier 0, the next set of postings are placed in tier 1, and finally, tier 2 is a catch-all tier that contains all remaining postings. Query planning takes this tiering of posting lists into account while formulating the query. Tier 0 postings are always examined by all queries and the size of tier 0 is tuned to strike a balance between HDD IOPS, transfer latency, and L1 score cutoff for query relevance. Tier 2 postings are too long to store on a single machine and are distributed across all machines in the segment. They are also too long to transfer in a timely manner over the network and are locally intersected against rarer query atoms with shorter posting lists. The results of this intersection are communicated over the network and aggregated. Cascading query execution that we describe later can choose to use tier 1 and occasionally tier 2 postings when there are insufficient high scoring results from examining only tier 0 postings.

3.5 Query planning

The sharding of the index data across machines calls for more logic in coordinating the query execution. Maguro builds a query plan upon receiving an augmented and parsed query. A query plan is a hierarchical set of instructions that each leaf node is capable of executing. The results of the execution will be sent to a different machine or kept on the local machine for further processing. The instructions use the notion of a sequence as the result of the instruction, which is an addressable array structure. Maguro has an instruction set with the following basic operations:

Operation	Semantics
ATOMSEQ(a)	Generate a result sequence for the atomic unit a. Results returned sorted by document with approximate ranking (L1 doc ranks).
NEARSEQ(a_1, a_2)	Generate a result sequence for the tuple of atoms a_1 and a_2 that are near each other (predefined to be k). Results returned sorted by document with approximate ranking.
ADJSEQ(a_1,a_2, ...a_N)	Generate a result sequence for the exact phrase composed of the atoms a_1..a_N.
AND(s_1, s_2, ..., s_N, ∂)	Perform a ranking intersection of all sequences in the argument list, computing the rank as $\partial(R(s_1), R(s_2), \ldots, R(s_N))$ where ∂ would default to the sum.
SOFTAND(s_1, s_2, ..., s_N, ∂)	Perform a ranking soft intersection of all sequences in the argument list, computing the rank as $\partial(R(s_1), R(s_2), \ldots, R(s_N))$ where ∂ would default to the sum. The intersection softly converts into a union operator when stream hits natural boundaries due to tiering posting lists.
OR(s_1, s_2, ..., s_N, ∂)	Perform a ranking union of all sequences in the argument list, computing the rank as $\partial(R(s_1), R(s_2), \ldots, R(s_N))$ where ∂ would default to the max over the set.
ANDNOT(s_0, s_2, ..., s_N)	Perform a disjunction of the first sequence and the N-1 following atomic sequences, not impacting ranking already found in s0.
RELAXEDAND(s_1, s_2, ..., s_N, m, ∂)	Perform a relaxed AND where m of N atoms need to be present for the intersection to be considered "successful".
FILTER(s_1, s_2, ..., s_N, ∂)	Filter a set of sequences based on document attributes ∂, like language, spam or porn.
WAND(s_1, w_1, s_2, w_2,..., s_N, w_N, ∂)	Perform a ranking intersection with weights on each atom and a threshold ∂, to trigger a "successful" match.

In addition, each instruction also carries metadata about what machine to execute the instruction on, and expected external consumers of the resulting sequence.

Since the query from an end user has no strict Boolean language or constructs in the common case, we need to reformulate the query into a stricter model. Operators like *RelaxedAnd* are helpful to enable a bit more "fuzziness" in the evaluation of the query, and this has positive impact in overall relevance especially for a tail index aiming at good recall [5].

3.6 Query execution

The query execution performance of Ma guro is strongly correlated to the ability to use n-gram and tuple atoms in the query. The actual formulation of the query for execution on a Maguro segment is currently based on different aspects:

1) **Signals from query analysis and augmentation.** Bing uses multiple techniques to detect entities, indicate phrase and tuple connections in the query, as well as tag it with classification metadata. This is a rich set of rules, and Maguro uses these signals to formulate parts of the query terms into n-gram and tuple atoms.
2) **Atom statistics itself**. Upon dictionary data extraction in Maguro, we have available statistics about the frequency and score of each atom. This data is stored in the index along with the atom and used to make late-binding decisions about where n-gram and tuple formulations make sense.
3) **Network topology and load state on nodes**. Since queries can be hierarchically evaluated and shipped across the network between machines, we also take the load and topology into account when planning execution. This enables us to dynamically make trade-offs between minimal

execution time and avoiding resource congestion. The load and resource state data is continuously updated, and available to any node doing the query planning.

4) **Cascading operations.** Maguro has the capability of cascading query operations through early short-circuit of Boolean expressions. For instance can a query "foo bar" be executed as "ngram(foo,bar) OR (term(foo) AND term(bar))", where we only evaluate the OR after knowing the statistics of the ngram(foo,bar)."

The leaf machine nodes in a Maguro segment have 3 roles, namely *SegmentRoot*, *L01Matcher* and *L2Ranker*. For L01Matcher, each node has an atom-based partition of the entire reverse index. For the L2Ranker, we partition the ranking data needed across the segment of machines with a uniform distribution and place this data on SSD. Hence, each machine has a range of documents, $D_i..D_j$, for which it has ranking information. Figure 4 illustrates this along with our query execution workflow.

Query execution takes place as follows:

1) Any machine can be a *SegmentRoot*, and for each query a random machine is selected. The query is routed down to one of the *SegmentRoot* machines, and the machine computes the query plan as described above.
2) During query execution, the root machine that is the *SegmentRoot* selected in step 1 for the query calls out to the *L01Matchers* holding posting lists for each atom in consideration in the query plan, or it even sends partial query plans out to other nodes for execution. A map of all machines in the segments (with partition and load information) is locally available in any machine to guide routing.
3) Eventually, the root machine assembles the final result set.
4) The top N results are selected for second-level ranking, and again the map is consulted to find the required *L2Rankers* to do the final ranking of the top N results.
5) The re-ranked results are aggregated and returned to the calling service.

This process is done in parallel on each segment, and is illustrated in steps below:

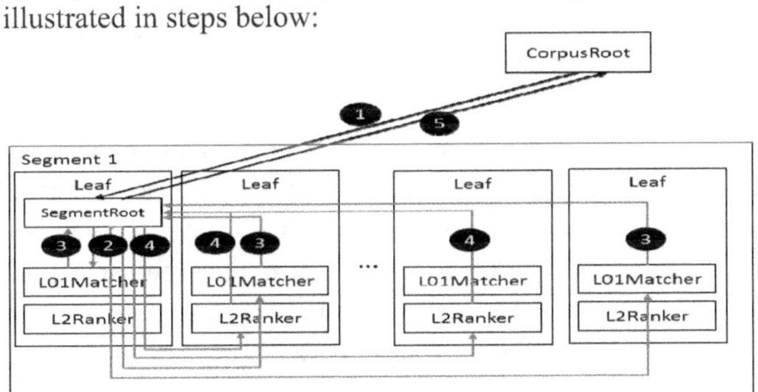

Figure 4 - Life of a query in Maguro

3.7 Fault-tolerant serving operations

Fault-tolerant operations are crucial to running an online search engine. It is also important to have stable performance and fast failovers. The failure scenarios to handle within a Maguro segment are as follows:

1) **Machine failure.** A machine(s) is failing due to software or hardware problems.
2) **Network partition.** A machine is only reachable from a subset of the expected network, hence the network has an error.
3) **Load hotspot occurring on machine.** Machines fail queries or are very slow in answering queries due to high load.
4) **Slow or partially failing machine.** Disk errors, or general outlier characteristics occur on a machine.
5) **Planned maintenance.** Updating a service requires it to gracefully finish its current tasks and shut down. Also merging, updating and OS upgrades have this same code path.

All machines in a Maguro segment have a map of what it perceives as the state of each machine in the segment. This map is used both for marking failed nodes and partitions as well as for dynamic query planning and load balancing. The map holds the following information for all nodes in the segment:

Field	Description
Node	Network address of the node
State	Overall state of machine (UP, DOWN, PROBATION)
L01Load	Load information for the L01 processes on the node
L2Load	Load information for the L2 processes on the node
L01Partitions	List of partitions for L01Matching on this node
L2Partitions	List of partitions for L2 ranking on this node
CPU state	Total load state for CPU
Disk state	Total load state for disks on this machine
Network	Total load state for network on this machine
Connection Status	Immediate status of the remote connection

Failures are detected by multiple mechanisms:

1) **Peer-based watchdogs.** Each machine in a segment is responsible for watching a set of other machines by monitoring heartbeat requests from other machines. Lack of response will have a machine moved into PROBATION state. If it is a

temporal failure and does not recur, it will be moved back into UP state. Otherwise it will be marked as DOWN by the watchdog and eventually that state is shared.

2) **Absolute watchdogs.** Maguro operates in the Microsoft-based cluster management system [10] that also holds dedicated watchdogs; these will ping and send sanity RPC requests to machines and trigger DOWN state settings if no response occurs.
3) **Failure detection in calling remote machines.** Every call to a remote machine for query execution can fail, and repeated failures causes a machine to be first placed in a probation state.
4) **Self-detection**. Machines can also mark themselves as bad from internal failures and errors detected in serving software or through periodic integrity checks being run.

When a machine is marked as DOWN, it can return to an UP state by self-fixing and transitioning through PROBATION mode. When a machine registers that there is consensus in the map that it is DOWN, it can run a set of verifications about its ability to serve. If these pass, it can register itself into PROBATION mode. When the probation state is registered across the segment, other machines will probe connectivity and serving availability and gradually form a consensus that the machine is ok, and can get back into the UP state. A machine with permanent failure due to hardware failure(s) will be fixed by replacing with a spare machine. Once the repair process is completed the new machine will be tagged as UP.

The map that carries the machine states is updated across the segment by means of two mechanisms. In regular update mode, a simple gossip protocol is used where each node shares its current map with others. Each receiving node will update its own map based on the receiving maps by accumulating load and serving state information across the segment machines. This protocol will never reach consensus on load information, but it will give a balanced view of load across the segment machines, so that a query plan will never generate amplifications around hotspots. In addition, a subset of machines in a segment form a Paxos protected quorum [11] to make consistent decision about state changes (DOWN to PROBATION, PROBATION to UP).

3.8 Continuous Index Updates

Maguro generates a relatively large index through exploding the number of atoms indexed per document. Maguro Index Build employs a true delta update mechanism. There is a continuous stream of new and updated documents coming in from the crawl and document processing systems. The documents classified as tail documents are accumulated and processed in a batch for processing efficiency. The computational nature of building index updates maps very well to the computing paradigm championed in Cosmos/Scope [7] and the Dryad engine [9].

3.8.1 Building the index

The continuous stream of tail documents flowing from the crawl and document processing subsystem are assigned and accumulated into the appropriate Maguro segment streams (Queues) in Cosmos. When the count of unprocessed documents for a segment exceeds a threshold, an index build job (SCOPE job) is spawned to process the accumulated documents to build index updates for the segment.

An index build job processes a batch of documents and produces the following index update artifacts which constitutes a mutation to the index served by the segment.

1) Inverted Index updates: These constitute updates to the inverted index that is used to match user queries against documents served by the segment. Every document is processed to produce a set of hit records {Atom Bucket, Atom Id, Document Id, Ranking payload} for the document. Since Maguro employs an atom partitioned inverted index within each segment, the hit records are grouped first by the atom bucket, then grouped by the atom Id, ordered by the Document Id and output into a set of inverted index update files (1 per atom bucket).

2) Forward index updates : These constitute updates to the per document index used for final ranking (L2 ranking) for the set of candidate documents that matched the user query. Every document is processed to produce a set of per document index records {Document Bucket, Document Id, per document index blob}. Since this index is partitioned by document within each segment, the document records are grouped by document bucket, ordered by document id and output into a set of forward index update files (1 per doc bucket).

3) URL to Document Id Mapping: Since Maguro is a large scale index (dealing with potentially a trillion documents), it is expensive for the index build sub system to assign a globally unique document id to every document. The Document Id employed by an Index Build Job is typically only guaranteed to be temporally unique (perhaps within the context of a single job/mutation). Each serving segment in Maguro employs its own scheme of document id assignment to identify a document uniquely in its index. The index build

job also outputs the URL→Document Id map employed in the mutation which is used by the segment nodes to remap the index build document ids to the actual serving document ids for the documents that got processed in the mutation.

3.8.2 Updating serving index

Each Index node in the Maguro segment monitors a special location in cosmos to check if there are any new updates produced for its segment. When new updates are available, each node downloads the portion of the updates that concern that node (based on the atom bucket and document bucket assignment to segment nodes). The serving nodes download the updates and also transform them by reassigning document Ids to facilitate efficient index merge.

Periodically the serving nodes are instructed to merge the updates accumulated into the index served by the node. For document level consistency the merge is constrained to include only the set of index build updates that are present on all the nodes in that segment. Once the set of updates for a round of update merge has been established, the index update reduces to an n way merge of the served index files with the update files.

Listed below is an outline of the update merge process.

1) Merge URL → Document Id map in the served index with updates to the Map that were computed as a part of the transformation process and build a bit vector (D) of documents deleted from the index. This reduces to a simple n-way merge of the map files with conflict resolution handled as follows
    a. If there are multiple entries for a URL then the highest document id wins and the bits for other document ids for the document are set in the deleted documents bit vector (D).
2) Inverted Index Merge is an n-way Merge of the posting lists from the base index and the inverted index update files. The postings for document ids that have bits set in deleted document bit vector (D) are dropped from the merged index.
3) Forward index is also an n-way merge of the served index file with forward index update files. The per document records for document ids that have bits set in deleted document bit vector (D) are dropped from the merged index.

3.9 Index Growth

The number of documents indexed by a Maguro machine is determined by local HDD capacity. The number of machines (N) in a Maguro segment is determined by the QPS and serving latency SLA (Service Level Agreement) requirements as these dictate the HDD IOPS and network bandwidth that the segment must support. Consequently, index growth is achieved by adding more segments to the system architecture rather than adding more machines to a segment. Adding more machines to a segment while keeping the number of documents indexed per machine constant will increase serving latency as more postings must be examined to return relevant results. The downside of adding entire segments rather than increasing the size of a segment is that index growth in not very granular, but this is not a significant concern for the tail.

3.10 Discussion

Maguro achieves its cost-efficiency goals for serving a large tail document corpus through a well-designed and synergistic combination of techniques that exploit low HDD costs along with availability of SSD and high speed commodity networks. The use of HDD allows each machine to index and serve a significantly larger amount of documents. This also forces the index to be partitioned across machines by atoms rather than documents due to HDD IOPS considerations as described earlier. Since atoms are partitioned across machines, multi-word queries require postings lists to be transferred across the network and intersected and benefit from a high-speed network. The use of HDD also permits indexing n-grams, tuples, and phrases in addition to unigrams and allows query planning to leverage this to reduce the number of remote posting lists that need to be transferred over the network for a multi-term query. Posting lists contain pre-computed ranking scores and this enables tiering posting lists based on these scores. This use of tiering for posting lists cuts down on the average quantity of remote postings that need to be transferred over the network. Pre-computing and storing ranking scores in the inverted index trades off experimental agility for execution efficiency and is an appropriate design point for indexing the web's long tail of content. Finally, separating the index data used for final L2 ranking and placing this on SSD frees this ranking from HDD IOPS constraints and increases the number of documents that can be ranked.

4. EXPERIMENTAL EVALUATION

Maguro indexes tail documents and is part of the serving stack in Bing. In this section we evaluate the serving efficiency and scaling characteristics of Maguro by comparing it against the baseline serving system, which is a conventional document partitioned, RAM-based architecture, that indexes and serves head documents.

4.1 Methodology and Metrics

Search is a large-scale online distributed system and both query latency, and throughput, measured in queries per second (QPS), are key performance metrics. Query latency has strict SLA requirements (average latency, 95% latency, etc.) that must be satisfied both for good user experience and to meet contractual obligations. Hence the performance objective is to maximize the system throughput in terms of QPS while successfully meeting all query latency SLAs. However, this QPS metric and overall system cost is highly sensitive to the configuration of the search engine in terms of how many million documents are indexed by a single machine. To account for this, we use *DQ*, which is the product of QPS and millions of documents indexed per machine, as our search efficiency metric. Computing *DQ* for a document partitioned architecture is trivial as queries are sent to all machines in parallel. However, for an atom partitioned architecture only a subset of machines participate in each query so the effective *DQ* of a machine in an atom partitioned segment is computed as ((*Documents indexed by the segment*) x (*QPS of the segment*))/(*Number of machines in the segment*).

Search relevance as measured by normalized discounted cumulative gain (*NDCG*) is another key search engine metric [11]. For relevance measurements, Maguro is queried in parallel with the baseline system serving head documents, results from both tiers are aggregated, and the top scoring results across these tiers are surfaced. All measurement reported here are for Maguro configurations where the *NDCG* as measured on multiple collections of search queries used by the Bing relevance team is either at parity or better than the baseline system when Maguro results are not surfaced.

We perform all measurements using a custom capacity and latency testing tool to send several millions of user queries taken from query logs to production beds serving the baseline index and the tail index served by Maguro, that were temporarily removed from the active serving rotation.

4.2 Comparative search efficiency

We compare the search efficiency of Maguro measured in DQ against the baseline system that indexes and serves head documents. We note that the comparison is likely biased against the baseline system due to availability and usage of many more signals for head documents as compared to tail documents that must be taken into consideration while matching and ranking documents, though the magnitude of improvement suggests that this is a second order effect.

The first set of comparisons measure the performance of the Maguro search engine running on identical hardware as the baseline system. Next, we measure the efficiency of the Maguro system running on machines with a fast network interconnect. In addition, for both sets of tests we also evaluate a Maguro configuration where use of n-grams and tuples in query formulation is disabled. Figure 5 shows the results of these measurements. The results indicate that Maguro shows over 12x efficiency gains over the baseline system running on identical hardware. Using n-grams and tuples in query formulation contributes a little bit less than 3x to this overall efficiency gain. On hardware with a fast interconnect, Maguro's efficiency improvements dramatically increase to over 40x the baseline system, with usage of n-grams and tuples in query formulation again contributing a bit less than 3x to the overall efficiency gain. The faster network interconnect permits increasing the QPS the system can sustain while still meeting its latency SLA.

Maguro's efficiency arises from using hard disks to significantly increase the number of documents that can be indexed and served per machine and the atom partitioned serving architecture reduces the number of machines that need to participate in every query. Maguro's phrase-based indexing and query formulation further reduces both the number of machines that must participate in each query as well as the computation needed to answer the query.

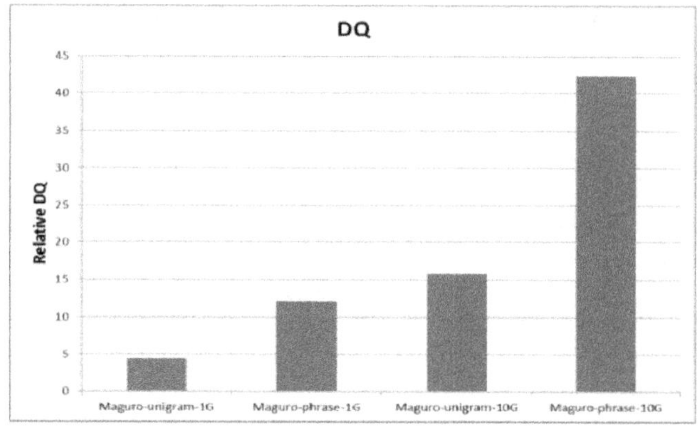

Figure 5: Maguro performance characteristics

Figure 6 shows the index size comparison at different scales between Maguro's phrase based index and a unigram index for the same set of documents. Maguro is selective about indexing n-grams and tuples as described in section 3 but despite this the index size is over 20x larger. This index size increase is possible because Maguro stores its index on hard disk (several terabytes per machine), and is justified because the use of n-grams and tuples provides almost a 3x improvement in serving efficiency.

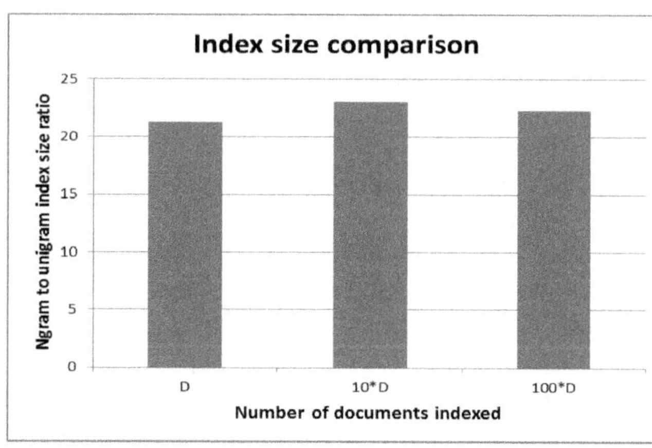

Figure 6: Maguro index size

4.3 Serving latency characteristics

Search is an online distributed system and users expect quick responses to their queries. In addition, the user experience is not just influenced by the average query response latency but it is also sensitive to higher percentile latencies, such as the 95% latency. Providing low latency response even at the 95% is extremely challenging for large distributed systems where many machines must participate in computing the response. In addition, for a consistent user experience the gap between the average latency and 95% latency should not be too large.

Figure 7 shows the 95% latency comparison between the baseline search engine and Maguro at three different scale points. Each scale point corresponds to system configurations that index the same number of documents. The first data point corresponds to a single machine configuration for the baseline system indexing several million documents. Since the smallest Maguro configuration is an atom-sharded segment that involves many more machines, the 95% latency is around 70% higher than the baseline single machine system. The next data point corresponds to the baseline system indexing all the head documents. Maguro uses an identical number of machines (as the first configuration) to index these amount of documents and as a result its 95% latency is comparable to the first configuration. However, since the baseline system now has to send the query to many more machines, its 95% latency is now three times higher than the first configuration and also much higher than the Maguro system indexing the same number of documents. Finally, the third data point corresponds to the full Maguro system indexing all the tail documents. The increase in 95% latency for Maguro is modest even at this scale and still lower than the 95% latency of the baseline system in the second configuration where the number of documents indexed is significantly smaller. The baseline system does not have sufficient machine capacity to index and serve this amount of documents. But even if it were capable, the 95% latency would be much higher due to the large number of machines required.

Maguro's 95% latency is lower than the baseline system primarily because a smaller number of machines are involved in responding to individual user queries. This reduction in machine fan-out arises from indexing a larger number of documents per machine by leveraging hard disk and from Maguro's phrase-based atom partitioned architecture where only machines than contain query atoms participate in computing the query response. This low machine fan out also enables Maguro to scale out and index a large number of documents without significantly impacting the 95% latency.

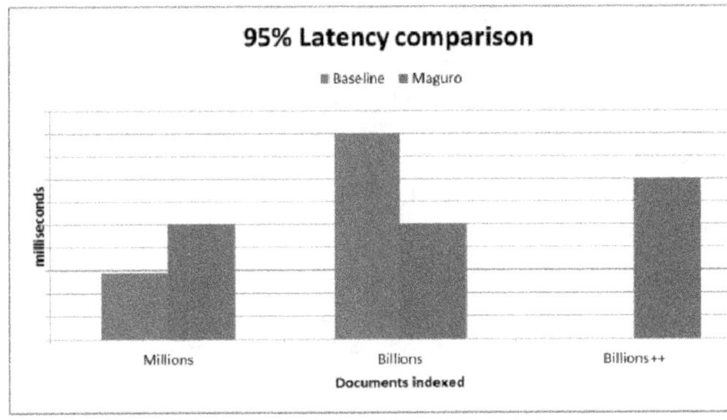

Figure 7: 95% Latency scaling

Figure 8 indicates the ratio of 95% latency to average latency as the load on the system is increased for system configurations corresponding to the second data point in Figure 7. Maguro, despite being a hard disk based index, has a reasonable 95% to average latency ratio. In addition, due to its comparatively lower machine fan-out, Maguro has stable 95% latencies that increase at a lower rate than the average latency. As a result, the ratio of 95% to average latency decreases as the load on the system is increased. By contrast, the baseline index serving system shows more conventional behavior where the ratio of 95% to average latency grows with increasing load.

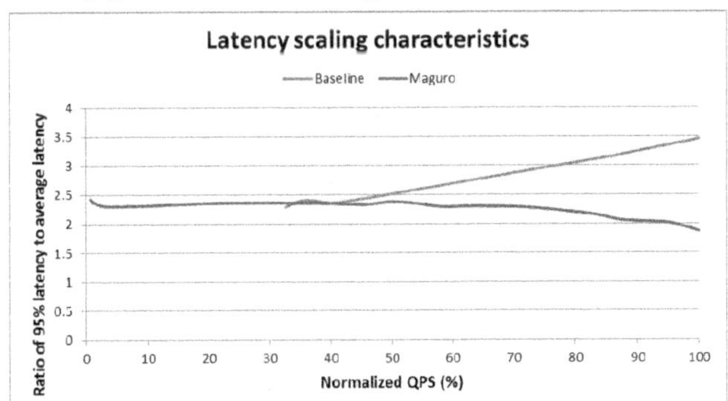

Figure 8: Latency scaling with increasing load

5. RELATED WORK

Discussions around methods for distribution of inverted posting lists have been studied for many years. Conclusions vary quite a bit, there are several papers that conclude on that term-sharded models are superior on performance [18]. Though, the commercial scale of search engines and the impact on commodity hardware usage and datacenter network models makes it hard to rely too much on these results.

The overall aspects of a search engine architecture is described in several keynote talks, and also described in [3].

6. CONCLUSIONS

Maguro is designed for efficiently searching very large collections of text content of up to 1 trillion documents at low cost. It achieves this by using hard disks to significantly increase the number of documents that can be indexed and served per machine. In addition, it employs an atom partitioned serving architecture to reduce the number of machines that need to participate in every query. Finally, Maguro's phrase-based indexing and query formulation uses a large selection of n-grams and tuples to additionally reduce both the number of machines that must participate in each query as well as the computation needed to answer the query.

Maguro achieves 12x cost efficiency improvement over Bing's baseline search engine that serves head content on the same hardware, and over 40x improvement, when run on hardware with a faster network interconnect. By reducing the number of machines that participate in computing the query results, Maguro is able to demonstrate better latency scaling characteristics and enables providing fast and consistent query response even when indexing and serving a large collection of tail documents. Maguro is part of the serving stack in Bing and allows us to scale the index significantly better.

7. ACKNOWLEDGEMENTS

Special thanks to Daniel Yuan, Madan Musuvathi, Reddy Duggempudi, Vishesh Parikh, Tanj Bennett, Richard Kasperski, Dexin Zhu, Lin Song, Nan Zhang, Jinru He and Bing Shi who made several contributions to the Maguro system. In addition, we would like to thank Qi Lu, Harry Shum, and Chad Walters for their support throughout the project.

8. REFERENCES

[1] Badue C., Baeza-Yates R., Ribeiro-Neto B., and Ziviani N. 2001. Distributed query processing using partitioned inverted files. In G. Navarro, editor, *Proc. String Processing and Information Retrieval Symp.*, IEEE Computer Society, Laguna de San Rafael, Chile, 10–20.

[2] Baeza-Yates, R., Ribeiro-Neto, B. 1999. *Modern information retrieval.* ACM Press, New York, NY.

[3] Barroso, L. A., Dean, J., & Holzle, U. 2003. Web search for a planet: The Google cluster architecture. *IEEE Micro, 23, 2*, 22–28.

[4] Bing L. 2011. *Web Data Mining: Exploring Hyperlinks, Contents, and Usage Data*, Springer Berlin Heidelberg.

[5] Broder, A., Carmel, D., Herscovici, M., Soffer, A., Zien, J. Efficient query evaluation using a two-level retrieval process. In *Proceedings of the CIKM,* 2003.

[6] Chaiken, R., Jenkins, B., Larson P., Ramsey, B., Shakib, D., Weaver, S., Zhou J. SCOPE: Easy and efficient parallel processing of massive data sets. *Proc. VLDB Endow. 1, 2.* August 2008.

[7] Greenberg, A., Hamilton, J., Jain N., Kandula, S., Kim, C., Lahri, P., Maltz, D., Patel, P., Sengupta, S. VL2: A scalable and flexible data center network. *Communications of the ACM,* March 2008.

[8] Greenberg, A., Lahri, P., Maltz, D., Patel, P., Sengupta S. Towards a next generation data center architecture: scalability and commoditization. *Proc. ACM workshop on Programmable routers for extensible services of tomorrow.,* 2008.

[9] Isard, M., Mihai, B., Yuan, Y., Birell, A., Fetterly, D. Dryad: Distributed Data-parallel Programs from Sequential Building Blocks. *Proc. Of ACM Eurosys,* 2007.

[10] Isard, M. 2007. Autopilot: Automatic Data Center Management, in *Operating Systems Review*, 41, 2 (April 2007), 60-67.

[11] Jarvelin, K., Kekalainen, J. Cumulated gain-based evaluation of IR techniques. In *ACM Transactions on Information Systems 20(4).* 2002.

[12] Lorch J. R., Adya A., Bolosky W. J., Chaiken R., Douceur J. R., Howell J. 2006. The smart way to migrate replicated stateful services, In *Proceedings of ACM Eurosys.*

[13] Manning C. D., Raghavan P., Schutze H. 2008. *Introduction to Information Retrieval*, Cambridge University Press.

[14] Marin, M., Gomez, C., Gonzalez, S., Costa, G.V. 2008. Scheduling Intersection Queries in Term Partitioned Inverted Files, 14th European Conference on Parallel and Distributed Computing (EuroPar 2008), LNCS, Springer (Aug. 26-29), Spain.

[15] Melink, S., Raghavan, S., Yang, B., Garcia-Molina, H. 2001. Building a distributed full-text index for the web. *ACM Trans. Inf. Syst.* 19, 3, 217–241.

[16] Moffat, A., Webber, W., Zobel, J. 2006. Load balancing for term-distributed parallel retrieval. In *Proceeding of SIGIR 2006: 29th annual international ACM SIGIR conference on Research and development in information retrieval*, 348–355.

[17] Moffat, A., Webber, W., Zobel, J., Baeza-Yates, R. 2007. A pipelined architecture for distributed text query evaluation. *Information Retrieval*, 10, 3, 205-231.

[18] Ribeiro-Neto, B., Barbosa, R. Query performance for tightly coupled distributed digital libraries. *In Proc. ACM Digital Libraries*, June 1998.

[19] Tomasic, A., H. Garcia-Molina, H. 1996. Performance issues in distributed shared-nothing information-retrieval systems. *Information Processing & Management*, 32, 6, 647–665.

Sponsored Search Auctions

Riccardo Colini-Baldeschi
Sapienza, University of Rome
Via Ariosto 25, 00185
Rome, Italy
colini@dis.uniroma1.it

ABSTRACT

Sponsored search auctions are used to allocate ad slots to advertisers. The standard mechanism for sponsored search auctions is the Generalized-Second-Price (GSP) auction.

Even if GSP seems to be established, a lot of open problems remain in the area and many significant researches have been done in the recent years. My research proposal is focusing in some specific aspects of the sponsored search auctions like revenue maximization and the design of mechanisms that obtain some form of social efficiency. In this paper we start from a brief history of the sponsored search auctions and then we present the formal model. In the last two sections I will introduce the obtained results and some open problems.

Categories and Subject Descriptors

H.7.2 [**Theory and algorithms for application domains**]: Algorithmic game theory and mechanism design—*Algorithmic mechanism design*

Keywords

Mechanism Design; Algorithmic Game Theory; Auctions

1. INTRODUCTION

Advertisement has a foundamental role in the web since the first GUI browser was released in 1994. At that time ads were sold on a per-impression basis and the advertisers were charged by a flat fee usually for a big stock of ads' impressions. So, the market was not so flexible and only the big companies that could afford such a big payments for their advertisement campaigns could partecipate in the market.

Later in 1997 Overture introduced a new way to deal with the online advertisement campaigns that made the market more flexible and gave to everyone the opportunity to partecipate. In the Overture auction design every advertiser submits a bid that represents how much he wants to pay for a click on his ads and the keywords of interest for his campaign. Then the mechanism computes a ranking for the bidders and allocates to every winner a slot in the page of interest, higher is the bid better is the obtained slot. The auction from Overture is known as General-First-Price (GFP) auction. In this case a bidder is charged by an amount equal to the submitted bid. Unfortunately this mechanism is not stable. The bidder's payment depends directly from the submitted bid and since everyone wants to pay as less as possible, the bidders' strategy is to submit lower bids to obtain the desired slot at the lowest possible price.

This kind of behaviour introduce a main problem to the auctioneer: the bidders want to submit bids that are lower than the real valuations, so the exctracted revenue can be lower than the expected one.

Now, the standard mechanism for sponsored search auctions is the Generalized-second-price (GSP) auction[13]. The mechanism is named second price because every winning bidder pays the next highest bid. The GSP auction has some limits. It has not an equilibrium in dominant strategy and truthtelling may be not an equilibrium.

My research proposal is focusing on the investigation of different settings for sponsored search auctions. First step was to consider a world with budget constraints. Budgets are an important element of the mechanism in sponsored search auctions because they address a real need for the users. As is pointed out in [11] budgets are used in many different ways from users and not only as a limit on liquidity.

Next step is about Bayesian setting. After a deep understanding of the classical and recent literature, there are a lot of open problems in settings like prior-independent and prior-free auctions that can be investigated.

The structure of the paper is the follow. In Section 2 the setting is defined, in Section 3 the state of the art is presented and in Section 4 and Section 5 the obtained results, the open problems and the future directions are described.

2. THE MODEL

In sponsored search (or adword) auctions advertisers bid on keywords. We have:

- A set $I = \{1, \ldots, n\}$ of n bidders,
- a set $K = \{1, \ldots, t\}$ of t keywords,
- a set $J = \{1, \ldots, m\}$ of m slots for each keyword,
- each keyword has m slots and each slot j has a quality α_j with $1 \leq j \leq m$ and $\alpha_j \geq \alpha_{j+1}$ $\forall j, j+1 \in J$,

WSDM'13, February 4–8, 2013, Rome, Italy.

- each bidder i has a valuation $v_i \in \mathbb{R}^+$ and a budget $b_i \in \mathbb{R}^+$.

The valuation of the bidders is private knowledge. To each bidder is assigned at most one slot in a keyword and his valuation for a slot is assumed to depend linearly on the click-through-rates (CTR). Moreover, valuations are assumed to be additive, i.e., the total valuation of a bidder is equal to the sum of his valuations for all the slots that are assigned to him. A further key ingredient of an adword auction is that bidders specify a budget on the payment charged for the ads, linking the different rounds. Budgets are public information in the auction, otherwise we cannot achieve any positive result (see [11]).

With these parameters the mechanism has to compute an allocation of the resources to the bidders. An allocation (X, p) is a three-dimensional matrix $X = (x_{i,j,k})_{(i,j,k) \in I \times J \times K}$ with $x_{i,j,k} \in [0, 1]$, that represents the probability that bidder i allocates slot j in keyword k, and a payment vector $\mathbf{p} = \{p_1, \ldots, p_n\}$ that define the payment of each bidder. As above, $\sum_{j=1}^{m} x_{i,j,k} \leq 1 \ \forall i \in I, \forall k \in K$. Now, a valuation is how much a bidder wants to pay for the top slot of every keyword. So we need to weight the valuation with the quality of the allocated slots. The weighted capacity $c_i = (\sum_{j \in J} \sum_{k \in K} \alpha_j x_{i,j,k})$ represents the total weight for the valuation of each bidder $i \in I$.

The utility of bidder i for an allocation (X, p) is defined by

$$u_i := \begin{cases} c_i v_i - p_i, & \text{if } b_i \geq p_i \\ -\infty, & \text{otherwise} \end{cases}$$

.

This setting is non-quasi-linear for the presence of the budgets.

The allocation must obey the following conditions:

- Bidder rationality: $u_i \geq 0$ for all bidders $i \in I$. Every bidder i wants to partecipate in the auction,
- Auctioneer rationality: the utility of the auctioneer fulfills $\sum_{i \in I} p_i \geq 0$. The auctioneer has incentives to sell his goods. And
- No positive transfer: $p_i \geq 0$ for all bidders $i \in I$. The auctioneer does not pay anything to the bidders.

A natural question arises when we have to deal with budgets. What is the correct concept of social efficiency? The standard objective of social welfare maximization is no more valid. A different property in terms of social efficiency is Pareto-optimality. An allocation (X, p) is Pareto optimal if and only if there is no other allocation (X', p') such that

- the utility of every bidder in (X', p') is not less than his utility in (X, p), $u'_i \geq u_i \ \forall i \in I$,
- the utility of the auctioneer in (X', p') is not less than his utility in (X, p), $\sum_{i \in I} p'_i \geq \sum_{i \in I} p_i$, and
- at least one bidder or the auctioneer strictly increases his utility in (X', p') compared with (X, p).

Note that in quasi-linear setting Pareto-optimal allocations maximize the social welfare.

A different notion of social efficiency is represented by the envy-freeness. We can define an allocation to be envy-free bundle pricing if for every pair of bidders $i, j \in I$, it holds that $u_i(S_i) \geq u_i(S_j)$, where S_i is the bundle of slots assigned to bidder i and S_j is the bundle of slots assigned to bidder j. In other words, no bidder wants to change his allocation with the allocation of another bidder.

3. STATE OF THE ART

The deterministic Vickrey auction [22] was designed to maximize social welfare in settings where all items are different and bidders have arbitrary valuation functions. However, deterministic and incentive compatible auctions that maximize social welfare do not exist for the multi-unit case for general valuations if there are private budget constraints. This was shown in the seminal paper by Dobzinski, Lavi, and Nisan [11]. They considered the multi-unit case with additive valuations, which in the sponsored search setting corresponds to slots with identical CTR, each round with only one slot for sale. They gave an incentive compatible auction based on Ausubel's ascending clinching auction [4] that produces a Pareto optimal allocation if budgets are public. They also showed that this assumption is strictly needed, i.e., that no deterministic mechanism for private budgets exists if we insist on incentive compatibility and on obtaining an allocation that achieves some form of efficiency. Pareto optimality is a basic notion for the efficiency of an allocation. It seems to be the least one should aim for. If an allocation was not Pareto optimal then bidders could trade amongst themselves and improve their utilities, thus increasing efficiency.

Ascending clinching auctions are used in the FCC spectrum auctions, see [20, 4]. For a motivation of adword auctions see [2] on Google's auction for TV ads. Fiat et al. [15] studied an extension of the multi-unit case of [11] to a combinatorial setting where items are distinct and different bidders may be interested in different items. The auction presented in [15] is incentive compatible and Pareto optimal for additive valuations and single-valued bidders (i.e., every bidder does not distinguish between the keywords in his interest set). This result is possible only if the sets of interest are public. Bhattacharya et al. [6] showed that for one infinitely divisible item, a bidder cannot improve his utility by underreporting his budget. This leads to a randomized incentive compatible in expectation algorithm for one infinitely divisible item with both private valuations and budgets. Aggarwal et al. [1] and Ashlagi et al. [3] studied envy-free outcomes that are bidder optimal, respectively Pareto optimal in an one-round adword auction. In this setting they give (under certain conditions in [1]) an incentive compatible auction with both private valuations and budgets. Recently, Lavi and May [19] and Dutting et al. [12] showed impossibility results for public budgets in various settings with heterogeneous items.

About the envy-free literature on revenue maximization. Item pricing is the context of many recent papers on envy-free allocation [18, 10, 5]. In the literature there are many inapproximability results and a lot of approximation algorithm to determine a pricing scheme for revenue optimal item prices envy-free allocation in combinatorial settings. It is showed that in some particular settings revenue optimal bundle priced envy free allocation can be computed in polynomial time (see [16]). Many times it is possible to distinguish between the unlimited supply case [18, 10, 5] and the limited supply case [18]. In [14] is considered the limited supply setting. The combination of envyfreeness and incentive-compatibility is studied also in the setting of capacitated agents [8].

4. RESEARCH AREA

My research is focusing on the investigation of various models that we can use to define the sponsored search auctions' scenarios.

The models can be different in many aspects. Here are highlighted those that are relevant in my research proposal.

The valuation function can be:

- diminishing valuation function: is a function $v_i : \{1, \dots, |K|\} \to \mathbb{R}^+$ such that if an agent i allocates x keywords, with $0 \leq x \leq t$, then his valuation for the keyword $x+1$ cannot be greater than his valuation for keyword x, $v_i(x+1) \leq v_i(x)$.
- per item valuation function: is a function $v_i : k \to \mathbb{R}^+$. Agent i has a (possible) distinct valuation for each keyword.
- additive valuation: an agent i declares a value $v_i \in \mathbb{R}^+$ and his valuation for any bundle of $X \subseteq K$ keywords assigned to him is $v_i \cdot |X|$.

How agents consider keywords:

- identical keywords: all agents are interested in all keywords.
- different keywords: each agent i is interested only in a subset of keywords, $S_i \subseteq K$ and every keyword $k \notin S_i$ that is not desired from agent i has $v_i(k) = 0$.

The slots:

- no slots: each keyword has only one slot, $|J| = 1$.
- identical slots: each keyword has m slots but all slots have the same CTR, $\alpha_j = \alpha_{j+1}\ \forall j, j+1 \in J$.
- different slots: each keyword has m slots and all slots have CTRs such that $\alpha_j \geq \alpha_{j+1}\ \forall j, j+1 \in J$.

The first problem investigated during my Master Thesis is the single-valued combinatorial auction. In [15] is provided an auction that is Pareto-optimal, individually rational and makes no-positive-transfers.

Their techniques are extended in the Master Thesis to the identical multi-slot per keyword setting. In the identical multi-slots setting we need to redefine the concept of trading path introduced in [15].

In [15] the notion of trading path is described over a B-matching graph with agents and keywords on different sides. The agents have capacities equals to the agents' demands and keywords have capacities equal to 1. Now we have capacities equal to m on the keywords' side.

This introduces the possibility of having cycles along the trading paths. So, a characterization of Pareto-optimality that deals also with no-simple-paths (paths with one or more cycles) is provided. Through this new characterization it is designed a Pareto-optimal, individually rational and no-positive-transfer auction for the identical multi-slots setting.

Moreover in my Master Thesis it is showed that when the agents have private diminishing valuation functions there are no incentive compatible, Pareto-optimal, individually rational auction. The intuition is that an agent can have incentive to lie in valuation that he will not use to buy anything, declaring higher values. In this way he can maintain his demand a little bit higher during the auction and obtain that other agents pay their keywords a little bit more. This produce a negative impact on the budget of the other agents, so their demands will decrease earlier and the lier agent can buy his keywords at a lower price.

These results are extended in a joint work with Monika Henzinger, Stefano Leonardi and Martin Starnberger [9] during the first year of my PhD. In this work we studied the multi-unit auction with many different slots per item and bidders with flat valuations and budgets. The clinching auction of [11] repeatedly increases the price for an item and checks whether the demand still allows to sell all the remaining unsold items. We extend this to with divisible slots as follows: We define a price per capacity and give different weights to different slots depending on their CTRs. To perform the check whether all remaining unsold items can still be sold we solve suitable linear programs. To show the Pareto optimality of the modified auction we give a novel characterization of Pareto optimality for adword auctions. We then show that if the outcome of the auction did not fulfill this new characterization then one of the linear programs solved by the auction would not have computed an optimal solution. Since this is not possible, it follows that the outcome is Pareto optimal. After solving the divisible case we round the outcome for the divisible case to the indivisible case. This requires a novel swapping algorithm that guarantees that each bidder receives at most one slot of each round.

An independent work by Goel et al [17] also provides an incentive compatible, individually rational and Pareto-optimal auction for sponsored search.

5. OPEN PROBLEMS

A particoular area of interest inside sponsored search auction is about revenue maximization. A nice point of view is highlighted in [14] where arise the concept of unfair pricing scheme. A price scheme is unfair if two identical items can be sold to different bidders at different prices. Unfortunately, many auctions that are in use produce unfair prices. Moreover, if we insist on incentive compatible multi-unit auctions (with respect to valuation), the unfair [11] auction is the only possibility. The goal is to find an algorithm that apply a fair pricing schema and maximize the revenue. In [14] is shown that an item pricing schema (same price for every item) obtain a revenue that is at least an half of the revenue extracted with a bundle price schema (different price for different bundles of items).

So, we drop the incentive-compatible constraint and we focus on the envy-free auction. Here we have a couple of questions that can be immediately discussed.

- Does the revenue-maximization envy-free pricing problem admit a polynomial time approximation scheme?

The problem of maximizing the revenue from an envy-free bundle pricing scheme is demonstrated to be NP-Hard[14] because it is equivalent to the k-subset sum problem. So we wanto to find an algorithm to compute an ϵ approximation to the optimal revenue in a polinomyal time.

- Can we find some similar results in the challenging setting of combinatorial auctions?

The main problem of the combinatorial auctions with respect to the multi unit auction is that in the latter the items are considered only in the "quantitative" way, i.e. we are interested only in how many items go to each bidder and not in "name" of the assigned items. To introduce this changing we have to change some key steps in the auction. If we think how can we extend the setting of [14] in a single-valued combinatorial way we can notice two main problems in the auction described. In [14] the authors computed the total demand of the bidders using a sum over the demand of the bidders. This cannot be apply to the combinatorial setting because now we are interested in how many items each bidder requests and also in which items each bidder requests. So we have to replace the sum with some other techinques like flow network or weighted matching graph. A second problem is the market. For the structure of the combinatorial setting if we have preference sets that create a partition into the market we cannot achieve the same bound with an item-price schema.

Another important setting is when agents have valuations that are drawn from probability distribution. A major result in this setting is given by Myerson in [21] where is defined the optimal auction for revenue maximization. A lot of work has been done in recent years in this setting. A full understanding of the classical and new results on approximation on mechanism design, multidimensional mechanism design, correlated distribution in Bayesian setting and budgeted case could be a nice starting point to begin an active exploration of the area.

6. REFERENCES

[1] G. Aggarwal, S. Muthukrishnan, D. Pál, and M. Pál. General auction mechanism for search advertising. In *WWW '09: Proceedings of the 18th international conference on World wide web*, pages 241–250. ACM, 2009.

[2] S. Albers, A. Marchetti-Spaccamela, Y. Matias, S. E. Nikoletseas, and W. Thomas, editors. *Automata, Languages and Programming, 36th Internatilonal Collogquium, ICALP 2009, Rhodes, greece, July 5-12, 2009, Proceedings, Part II*, volume 5556 of *Lecture Notes in Computer Science*. Springer, 2009.

[3] I. Ashlagi, M. Braverman, A. Hassidim, R. Lavi, and M. Tennenholtz. Position auctions with budgets: Existence and uniqueness. *The B.E. Journal of Theoretical Economics*, 10(1), 2010.

[4] L. M. Ausubel. An efficient ascending-bid auction for multiple objects. *American Economic Review*, 94(5):1452–1475, 2004.

[5] M.-F. Balcan, A. Blum, and Y. Mansour, editors. *Item pricing for revenue maximization*. ACM, 2008.

[6] S. Bhattacharya, V. Conitzer, K. Munagala, and L. Xia. Incentive compatible budget elicitation in multi-unit auctions. *CoRR*, abs/0904.3501, 2009.

[7] N. Chen, E. Elkind, and E. Koutsoupias, editors. *Internet and Network Economics - 7th International Workshop, WINE 2011, Singapore, December 11-14, 2011. Proceedings*, volume 7090 of *Lecture Notes in Computer Science*. Springer, 2011.

[8] E. Cohen, M. Feldman, A. Fiat, H. Kaplan, and S. Olonetsky. Truth, envy, and truthful market clearing bundle pricing. In Chen et al. [7], pages 97–108.

[9] R. Colini-Baldeschi, M. Henzinger, S. Leonardi, and M. Starnberger. On multiple keyword sponsored search auctions with budgets. In A. Czumaj, K. Mehlhorn, A. M. Pitts, and R. Wattenhofer, editors, *ICALP (2)*, volume 7392 of *Lecture Notes in Computer Science*, pages 1–12. Springer, 2012.

[10] E. D. Demaine, M. T. Hajiaghayi, U. Feige, and M. R. Salavatipour. Combination can be hard: approximability of the unique coverage problem. In *SODA*, pages 162–171. ACM Press, 2006.

[11] S. Dobzinski, R. Lavi, and N. Nisan. Multi-unit auctions with budget limits. In *FOCS*, pages 260–269. IEEE Computer Society, 2008.

[12] P. Dütting, M. Henzinger, and M. Starnberger. Auctions with heterogeneous items and budget limits. 2012.

[13] B. Edelman, M. Ostrovsky, and M. Schwarz. Internet advertising and the generalized second price auction: Selling billions of dollars worth of keywords. *American Economic Review*, 97(1):242–259, 2005.

[14] M. Feldman, A. Fiat, S. Leonardi, and P. Sankowski. Revenue maximizing envy-free multi-unit auctions with budgets. In B. Faltings, K. Leyton-Brown, and P. Ipeirotis, editors, *ACM Conference on Electronic Commerce*, pages 532–549. ACM, 2012.

[15] A. Fiat, S. Leonardi, J. Saia, and P. Sankowski. Single valued combinatorial auctions with budgets. In Y. Shoham, Y. Chen, and T. Roughgarden, editors, *ACM Conference on Electronic Commerce*, pages 223–232. ACM, 2011.

[16] A. Fiat and A. Wingarten. Envy, multi envy, and revenue maximization. In S. Leonardi, editor, *WINE*, volume 5929 of *Lecture Notes in Computer Science*, pages 498–504. Springer, 2009.

[17] G. Goel, V. S. Mirrokni, and R. P. Leme. Polyhedral clinching auctions and the adwords polytope. *CoRR*, abs/1201.0404, 2012. To appear in 44th ACM Symposium on Theory of Computing (STOC 2012), New York, May 2012.

[18] V. Guruswami, J. D. Hartline, A. R. Karlin, D. Kempe, C. Kenyon, and F. McSherry. On profit-maximizing envy-free pricing. In *SODA*, pages 1164–1173. SIAM, 2005.

[19] R. Lavi and M. May. A note on the incompatibility of strategy-proofness and pareto-optimality in quasi-linear settings with public budgets - working paper. In Chen et al. [7], page 417.

[20] P. Milgrom. Putting auction theory to work: The simulteneous ascending auction. *Journal of Political Economy*, 108(2):pp. 245–272, 2000.

[21] R. Myerson. Optimal auction design. *Mathematics of Operations Research*, 6(1):58–73, 1981.

[22] W. Vickrey. Counterspeculation, auctions, and competitive sealed tenders. *The Journal of Finance*, 16(1):8–37, 1961.

On the Prediction of Popularity of Trends and Hits for User Generated Videos

Flavio Figueiredo
Computer Science Department
Universidade Federal de Minas Gerais
flaviov@dcc.ufmg.br

ABSTRACT

User generated content (UGC) has emerged as the predominant form of media publishing on the Web 2.0. Motivated by the large adoption of video sharing on the Web 2.0, the objective of our work is to understand and predict popularity trends (e.g, will a video be viral?) and hits (e.g, how may views will a video receive?) of user generated videos. Such knowledge is paramount to the effective design of various services including content distribution and advertising. Thus, in this paper we formalize the problem of predicting trends and hits in user generated videos. Also, we describe our research methodology on approaching this problem. To the best of knowledge, our work is novel in focusing on the problem of predicting popularity trends complementary to hits. Moreover, we intend on evaluating efficacy of our results not only based on common statistical error metrics, but also on the possible online advertising revenues our predictions can generate. After describing our proposal, we here summarize our latest findings regarding (1) uncovering common popularity trends; (2) measuring associations between UGC features and popularity trends; and (3) assessing the effectiveness of models for predicting popularity trends.

Categories and Subject Descriptors

C.4 [**Computer Systems Organization**]: Performance of Systems—*Measurement techniques*; H.3.5 [**Information Storage and Retrieval**]: Online Information Services—*Web-based services*

Keywords

UGC; video; popularity; trends

General Terms

Human Factors; Design; Measurement

1. INTRODUCTION

On the Web 2.0, user generated content (UGC) has become the de-facto form of media publishing on some of the most popular Internet applications nowadays [6]. Focusing on video content, websites such as YouTube [1] receive over 800 million unique users monthly, attracting over 1 million different advertisers [23]. Even niche applications, such as Vimeo [2], which focuses on independent filmmakers, manage to attract over 70 million unique users monthly [19].

Given the success of such applications and the current large volume of videos consumed daily, understanding how users find such content and how content popularity evolves provide valuable insights for content generators, online advertisers and Internet service providers (ISPs), amongst others. For instance, from a systems perspective, understanding these properties may drive the design of better analytic tools, a major market segment nowadays. Online advertisers may also benefit from this information to better place contextual advertisements, while ISPs could exploit it to develop more cost-effective content delivery platforms and caching systems. From a social perspective, understanding the properties of video popularity trends could be used to better comprehend the human dynamics of consumption processes [7]. Also, content producers could use insights on how user collaboration and collaborative social activities on Web 2.0 applications may impact content popularity, providing information on aspects related to their own fame on video sharing applications.

Most previous efforts, which are focused on predicting the popularity of a piece of content measured at a specific future date [16–18, 22], are still preliminary, as they provide limited knowledge on which features and system mechanisms (e.g., search, related videos, etc) contribute the most to popularity growth. Analyzing the importance of such features to popularity growth is key to provide scalable alternatives to service design, as solutions based on content analysis are less scalable in (user generated) videos. Moreover, there is little effort towards predicting popularity evolution (or trends), which may also provide valuable knowledge. For instance, online advertisers and content delivery systems could benefit more from predicting not only a final popularity measure for UGC, but also whether its popularity trend is increasing and how stable it is likely to be over time.

In sum, our proposed research aims at understanding the importance and utility of various features, particularly referrers (i.e, incoming links to videos), on the popularity evolution of individual user generated videos and exploiting them to develop methods to predict future popularity measures and trends of those videos.

The rest of this paper is organized as follows. Section 2 describes our problem statement and research goals. We describe our current methodology on addressing our goals on Section 3. The current state of our research is described in Section 4 while our related work is addressed in Section 5. Section 6 concludes this paper.

WSDM'13, February 4–8, 2013, Rome, Italy.

[1] `http://youtube.com`
[2] `http://vimeo.com`

2. PROBLEM STATEMENT AND RESEARCH GOALS

In general terms, the problem we intend to address is defined as follows. Given a collection V of user generated videos, we define for each video $\mathbf{v} \in V$ a set of referrer, popularity, content and social features related to $\mathbf{v}$. We are interested in understanding the importance of each of these features when applied to the task of predicting how the popularity of individual videos will evolve from a reference time t to a target time $t + \delta$, considering that the information related to each of these features is available only up to the reference time t and δ is a time interval. For example, referrer features of a video only account for the views a video received via some incoming links up to time t. Moreover, we intend to develop methods to predict future popularity measures and popularity trends of individual videos. Thus, for each video we also define $\mathbf{s}_v$ as a vector of views received by the video at different dates (e.g, each week). As stated, referrer features capture information on incoming links to videos. We are particularly interested in these features since they provide valuable information on how users reach UGC content on the Web 2.0. As a basis for comparison, we also plan to study: (1) popularity features, which are related to temporal data about the evolution of popularity of individual videos; (2) content features, such as the category and tags of video; and (3) social features, which capture information about the user who created and uploaded the video (e.g., number of followers or user-rank) [20].

More specifically, our research goals (RGs) are the following:

RG1 - Understanding Referrer Importance: Our first research goal focuses on characterizing and modeling: (1) how video popularity evolves over time; and, (2) how video popularity evolution correlates with the referrers that lead users to videos (as well as with other content, social and popularity features). We note that, unlike previous work, which correlated different features of YouTube with final popularity [2,20], here we are concerned with measuring the impact of referrers on how the popularity of each video evolves over time [9,20].

RG2 - Predicting Video Popularity: After data characterization and modeling, we intend to exploit the available data to answer the following question: Is it possible to predict how the popularity of individual videos evolves over time? In other words, we want to know if it is possible to model the popularity curve (or trend) of each video. Although previous studies point out that modeling the popularity trend of individual videos is intractable [1], some recent results we obtained suggest that this might be possible. We shall detail more of this in Section 3. We also intend to investigate whether more effective methods to predict the popularity measure of a video at a target date can be devised by exploiting the developed popularity trend prediction models (e.g., by building specialized models to pre-defined popularity trends).

RG3 - Applications for Popularity Prediction: As an applied step of our research, we intend to investigate whether our popularity prediction methods could be exploited for generating revenue in advertising campaigns. Online advertisement is a multi-billion dollar industry [15] and in UGC applications, traditional keyword-targeted or content-targeted advertising may not be suitable since viral content attracts millions of views at small time windows [4]. Thus, popularity prediction might be useful to supplement traditional tools and provide advertisers with more information to determine how much they are willing to pay per click per content. As far as we know, this has not been investigated before since research on UGC popularity prediction is still at its infancy. Thus, it is a good research opportunity and a means to validate the effectiveness of our prediction methods.

3. METHODOLOGY

The initial step in studying the challenges described above is data collection. In order to understand popularity growth of videos we can collect data from applications like YouTube or Vimeo. Both provide on their websites time series of popularity of different videos. They also provide data on the top 10 referrers that led users to videos. Moreover, some notion of popularity can be inferred from the timestamps of user comments, a piece of temporal information largely available in many Web 2.0 applications. Although availability of only the top 10 referrers per video poses as a limit, we note that these referrers account for a non-negligible amount of video views (in the order of billions) [9], which can be made useful for popularity time series prediction tasks. Most of the work we have done so far is based on data collected in this fashion. That is, we already have a dataset containing the popularity curves and top 10 referrers related to more than a billion views for YouTube videos. We note that we also intend to investigate the possibility of monitoring and collecting traffic from a large local network, specifically our university campus network (as in [14]).

After data collection, we will characterize the importance of referrer features, as well as other popularity, content and social features, for the evolution of popularity of videos. We plan to proceed as follows. Initially we will determine classes of popularity trends based on a recent time series- clustering algorithm [21]. We then plan to correlate these classes and popularity measures at specific target times with the selected features (RG1). For prediction (RG2), traditional machine learning techniques (e.g., classification and regression models) will be used to infer not only the final popularity measure at a target time but also the popularity trend (i.e., class) of individual videos, using, as input, feature values collected up to a reference time. For example, we plan to use these classes to train supervised classifiers to predict the trends of individual videos. Class specific regression tasks [17, 18] can then be used, after classification, to build specialized models that predict popularity measures for videos with specific popularity trends. Indeed, we have some preliminary results that show that some accuracy can be achieve in both the classification and regression tasks. One particular aspect to consider in our evaluation of the prediction methods is whether accurate predictions can be made using only feature values collected prior to the video's popularity peak. This is particularly important as many videos exhibit a popularity distribution with a clear single peak [7,9]. Thus, it is desirable to produce accurate predictions before the interest in the content starts diminishing.

Most previous studies of popularity prediction [16,18,22] are focused only on prediction accuracy metrics such as coefficient of determination or squared errors. We here intend to not only use these traditional metrics but also assess if advertising markets [8, 13, 15] can benefit from our popularity prediction models (RG3). For example, we aim at understanding if, even with errors, our predictions generate revenue. In traditional keyword-targeted (see Chapter 15 of [8]) or content-targeted [15] advertising, the popularity evolution of query terms and web pages can be ignored since such content is expected to remain popular for a large period of time. In the context of user generated videos, this is not the case [4, 7, 9]. Viral videos can garner millions of views at small time windows [4] and even those videos that are not viral may exhibit single-peaked based popularity distributions. The question we raise here is: How can advertisement-campaigns make use of content popularity pre-

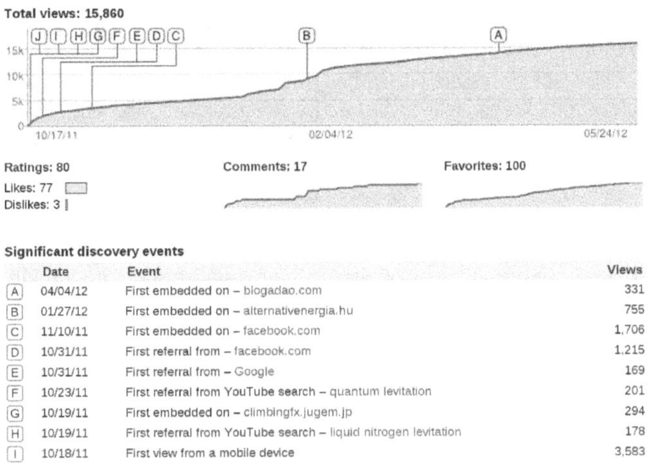

Figure 1: Example of Video Features

dictions in user generated video applications? We note that this is different from the task of assigning relevant-ads to content [15]. In user generated video applications, textual information such as tags or comments [10, 11] can be explored for this task.

A common setting in online advertising is the pay-per-click approach. In this setting, advertisers pay content providers per click which generates traffic to their website [15]. Here, we plan to study if the prediction of popularity measures (i.e., hits) and trends (evolution) can be used in conjunction with simple models of revenue estimation [13]. In simple terms, we want to verify if, in the case where click prices is determined by popularity predictions, these predictions are good enough in order to generate revenue. To this end, we plan to compare if our predictions generate revenues as good as the ones expected from the actual popularity evolution of each video. We intend to use revenue estimation models that assume fixed revenue per click for all videos, fixed revenue per click for each video (i.e., the revenue per click varies with the video's popularity) as well as models that assume revenue per click evolving based on temporal and popularity information [13]. Our evaluation will be performed in several synthetic (but relevant) scenarios, built from the model parameters [13].

4. CURRENT RESULTS

We now discuss some current results focused on research goals RG1 and RG2. We refer the reader to our published work [9] for a in-depth characterization of our datasets.

Our work analyzes features that are public available at YouTube. An example of such data is provided in Figure 1: for each video, YouTube provides the cumulative popularity time series as well as what they call *Significant Discovery Events*, which represent the the top 10 referrers (i.e., incoming links) that attracted more views to the video. Along with the number of views each referrer was responsible for, YouTube also provides the date of the first event triggered by that referrer. Moreover, the application also provides the cumulative time series related to other video features, such as the number of comments and the number of times the video was marked as favorite. Using HTML scrapping or the YouTube's API[3], it is also possible to collect other pieces of information, such as the category to which the video belongs (e.g., music, comedy, pets, autos etc.).

Due to space constraints, we shall discuss our results in only one

[3]`https://developers.google.com/youtube/`

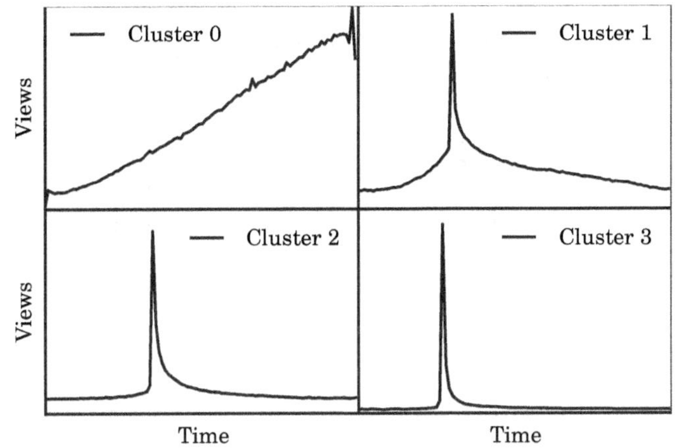

Figure 2: Discovered Trends by the KSC Algorithm.

Table 1: Summary of Popularity Trends

	$C0$	$C1$	$C2$	$C3$
# of Videos	4,023	6,718	5,031	3,790
Avg. # of Views	305,130	108,844	64,274	127,768
Avg. Change Rate #Views	47	7	4	4
Avg. Peak Fraction	0.03	0.03	0.08	0.28

of our three distinct video datasets [9]. This dataset is composed of 24,482 videos collected as results of random queries submitted to YouTube's search API. For each video, the datasets contain the video category and the statistics depicted in Figure 1, namely: the time series of the number of views, comments and favorites as well as the top-10 referrers, along with the total number of views each referrer was responsible for and the date of the first access from it.

4.1 Trend Discovery

The initial step of our study is the extraction of temporal patterns of popularity evolution. For this task we implemented a recently proposed time series clustering algorithm, called K-Spectral Clustering (KSC)[4], which was shown to be effective in detecting popularity patterns of other types of UGC content [21]. We selected this time series clustering algorithm, as opposed to alternative methods (e.g., Dynamic Time Warping or analytical modeling [7]) because the clustering is performed independently of shifts (i.e., dates) and scale (i.e., volume), focusing rather on the overall shape of the time series. The algorithm make's use of video's popularity time series $\mathbf{s_v}$ as input. The number of clusters was defined based on common cluster quality measures [21].

Figure 2 shows the discovered trends which govern popularity evolution on YouTube videos. Each graph shows the number of views as function of time. Moreover, Table 1 presents, for each cluster, the number of videos that belong to it as well as the average number of views, the average change rate in the number of views, and the fraction of views at the peak time window of these videos. The average change rate in the number of views of a given video v is computed as the average difference between two (non-cumulative) measures taken in successive time windows. Thus, it captures the trend in the number of views of the video: a positive (negative) change rate indicates that the number of views measured during each time window is increasing (decreasing) with time, whereas a change rate equal to 0 indicates stability. Table 1

[4]We have implemented a parallel version of the KSC algorithm which is available at `http://goo.gl/0dmHc`

Table 2: Summary of Features

Feature Class	Feature Name	Type
Content	Video category	Categorical
	Upload date	Numerical
	Video age	Numerical
	Time window size (w)	Numerical
Link	Referrer first date	Numerical
	Referrer number of views	Numerical
Popularity	# of views	Numerical
	# of comments	Numerical
	# of favorites	Numerical
	Avg. change rate in # of views	Numerical
	Avg. change rate in # of comments	Numerical
	Avg. change rate in # of favorites	Numerical
	Peak fraction	Numerical

shows the average change rate computed over the total duration of the video's lifespan. The peak fraction, also shown in Table 1, is the ratio of the maximum in $\mathbf{s}_v$ divided by the total of views of the video (i.e., the sum of all elements in $\mathbf{s}_v$).

As shown in the figure, Cluster 0 consists of videos that remain popular over time, even attracting a larger number of views during each time window as time passes, as indicated by the large positive change rates shown in Table 1. The videos in cluster 0 have also no significant peaks, as the average fractions of views in the peak windows, shown in Table 1, are very small. The other three clusters are predominantly defined by a single peak in popularity followed by a steady decline. The main difference is the rate of decline, which is much slower in Cluster 1, somewhat faster in Cluster 2, and very sharp in Cluster 3. This difference is more clear if we analyze the peak fractions and the average change rates in Table 1. We note that these three clusters were previously uncovered in other YouTube datasets [7,9], being referred to as *Viral, Quality and Junk* respectively. However, unlike these previous efforts, which relied mostly on peak popularity analyzes, we here use an unsupervised learning algorithm which makes our task of discovering popularity trends more general and robust. For example, the thresholds in peak volume which define Clusters 1, 2 and 3 in these previous studies are not clearly defined. In contrast, such peaks emerge clearly in our clusters (as shown in Table 2). Moreover, no previous study that analyzed video popularity time series or other UGC time series has identified a trend similar to Cluster 0, possibly because of the models adopted, which focus on power-law like behavior [7,9].

4.2 Predicting Trends

We now focus on the task predicting popularity trends, as it complements various recent efforts towards predicting final popularity measures of UGC [16,18,22]. Our prediction model is based on extremely randomized ensemble trees [12]. We choose this technique because it has been shown to be effective on different datasets, requiring little or no preprocessing. Moreover, the learned models can be more easily interpreted, in comparison with other techniques such as Support Vector Machines

For classification, we make use of the feature vector $\mathbf{v}$. The analyzed features analyzed, which can be derived from our datasets, are grouped into three classes, namely, content features, link features, and popularity features, as shown in Table 2.

The popularity features, measured during a defined monitoring period, capture not only the total number of views, comments and times the video was marked as favorite during that period but also the trend in these measures captured by the average change rates. We also include the peak fraction as a popularity feature. Jointly, this set of features tries to capture properties of the popularity curve (during the monitoring period).

The prediction model is learned from a training set of pre-labeled videos, i.e., videos whose popularity trends are known. The effectiveness of the model is then evaluated in a different set of videos (test set). For each video $\mathbf{v}$ in the test set, the prediction is performed based on features associated with $\mathbf{v}$ collected during a given monitoring period, starting at video's upload. We then assess the effectiveness of the classifier as function of the monitoring period. We evaluate the accuracy of our prediction model using the $F1$ and Macro-$F1$ metrics using a 5-fold cross validation.

Table 3: Per-trend and Macro F1 Scores with 95% Confidence Intervals

	Monitoring Period			
Trend	1% of Lifespan	20%	50%	100%
C0	0.35±0.01	0.34±0.02	0.47±0.02	0.64±0.02
C1	0.52±0.01	0.60±0.01	0.67±0.02	0.75±0.01
C2	0.30±0.01	0.51±0.01	0.68±0.02	0.78±0.03
C3	0.43±0.02	0.75±0.01	0.86±0.01	0.91±0.03
Macro	0.40±0.01	0.55±0.01	0.67±0.01	0.77±0.02

Table 3 shows average $F1$ results for each class (i.e., popularity trend) as well as the overall Macro $F1$, along with corresponding 95% confidence intervals, for different monitoring periods, for each dataset. We start by noting that, even if the monitoring period is limited to a single window (1% of the video's lifespan), which corresponds to roughly a week, Macro $F1$ results are of 0.4. These results are much better than randomly choosing the popularity trend of a given video, which results in a Macro F1 of 0.25 for our four classes. Moreover, as the monitoring period increases, prediction accuracy also increases. For instance, if 20% of the video's lifespan is monitored, Macro F1 reaches from 0.55. Delving into the model accuracy for each class, we find that $C0$ is the hardest one to predict (lower F1 results) while $C3$ is usually the easiest one, in all three datasets.

5. RELATED WORK

Cha et al. [5] and Gill et al. [14] performed two of the earliest analyses of YouTube. While the first focused on data crawled from YouTube, the latter was based on traffic going to YouTube from an university campus. More recently, Wattenhofer et al. [20] analyzed the correlation between YouTube video popularity and properties of various online social networks (OSN) created among users of the system. These studies focused on single snapshots of data, thus they did not account for temporal data, thus failing to analyze the long-term popularity evolution. Broxton et al. [4] defined a mechanism to determine if a video will be viral based on the fraction of viral referrers (direct links or OSN referrers) it attracts on short periods of time. Very popular videos with a large fraction of such referrers are likely to be viral. Brodersen et al. [3] made use of the same model to determine, amongst other things, if viral videos receive most views from the same geographic region. Moreover, Borghol et al. [2] assessed the importance of referrer and content features to the final popularity of videos.

These previous studies provide some insights into which factors impact popularity growth of individual videos. However, there is still little knowledge about which video features (e.g., content, referrer and popularity features) and system mechanisms (e.g., search) contribute the most to the evolution of popularity of individual videos. That is, unlike most previous work, we here intend to correlate these features with popularity evolution trends of individual videos. In [9], we performed a preliminary characterization of popularity evolution patterns of YouTube videos and the impact of various features on such patterns. Our intention is to extend this characterization by applying a recently proposed method to identify such trends [21] as well as to exploit the knowledge obtained in more cost-effective popularity prediction methods.

Considering the task of popularity prediction, Yin et al. [22] proposed a model to predict the ranking of popular items. For this task, the authors took into account user personalities when casting votes, and developed a Bayesian model for ranking prediction. They tested their model in a popular smart phone application, JokeBox [5]. A similar effort was pursued by Lerman and Hogg [16]. The authors also made use of voting models to perform content popularity prediction, applying their model to the news sharing applications Digg [6]. The efficacy of these models on video sharing applications is debatable. Firstly, JokeBox and Digg are websites focused on user voting. Although this feature is available on video sharing applications such as YouTube, it is not one of the primary use cases of the applications. Thus, models based on this kind of data would have to deal with sparsity problems. Moreover, these methods require sensitive user data, which, due to scale or privacy issues, is not publicly available in most video sharing applications.

The studies performed by Szabo and Hubberman [18] and Pinto et al. [17] are much close to ours. Both works analyzed YouTube videos and noted that long term popularity values are related to early popularity observations at a logarithmic scale. A similar result was also reported by Borghol et al. [2]. Based on such observation, the authors proposed a simple popularity prediction model based on linear regression. Both models were based on only one kind factor, i.e., early popularity views at a specific reference date. Although very simple, these models achieve somewhat accurate predictions of popularity measures for YouTube videos. We plan to extend these models to predict not only popularity measures at specific target dates but also the popularity evolution trend (or curve) of individual videos. To our knowledge, our work is the first to address this task in user generated videos. Moreover, unlike all previous efforts which focus only on statistical error metrics (e.g. coefficient of determination-R^2 or mean squared errors-MSE), we intend to validate the effectiveness of our prediction models in real world applications, i.e., advertising [13, 15].

6. SUMMARY

Nowadays, an enormous amount of user generated content is uploaded to Web 2.0 applications on a daily basis. Given the importance and volume of this type of content, understanding how trends in UGC popularity evolves over time provides substantial knowledge about how users find and consume collaborative content on the Internet. In this work presented a methodology and some initial results on the task of predicting trends and hits in user generated videos. We believe that this research has the potential to expand the knowledge on Web 2.0 applications and user generated content, providing valuable insights and techniques for content producers, online advertisers, and ISPs, as discussed in Section 1.

As a final note we point out that although focused on YouTube videos, the knowledge we here produce could be extended to other kinds of content such as images or text. It would be interesting to see if similar referrers are responsible for the popularity of different types of content. Moreover, comparing how popularity evolves across media and identifying the factors that are responsible for this evolution can be used by content producers and viral marketeers to decide on which application they should focus their products on.

[5]JokeBox is a smart phone application in which user share and up/down vote jokes.

[6]`http://www.digg.com`

ACKNOWLEDGEMENTS

This research is partially funded by the Brazilian National Institute of Science and Technology for Web Research (MCT/CNPq/INCT Web Grant Number 573871/2008-6).

7. REFERENCES

[1] Y. Borghol, S. Mitra, S. Ardon, N. Carlsson, D. Eager, and A. Mahanti. Characterizing and modelling popularity of user-generated videos. *Performance Evaluation*, 68(11):1037–1055, Nov. 2011.

[2] Y. Borghol, N. S. Wales, S. Ardon, and D. Eager. The Untold Story of the Clones: Content-agnostic Factors that Impact YouTube Video Popularity. In *Proc. KDD*, 2012.

[3] A. Brodersen, S. Scellato, and M. Wattenhofer. YouTube around the world. In *Proc. WWW*, Apr. 2012.

[4] T. Broxton, Y. Interian, J. Vaver, and M. Wattenhofer. Catching a viral video. *Journal of Intelligent Information Systems*, pages 1–19, Dec. 2011.

[5] M. Cha, H. Kwak, P. Rodriguez, Y.-Y. Ahn, and S. Moon. Analyzing the Video Popularity Characteristics of Large-Scale User Generated Content Systems. *IEEE/ACM Transactions on Networking*, 17(5):1357–1370, Oct. 2009.

[6] G. Cormode and B. Krishnamurthy. Key Differences between Web1.0 and Web2.0. *First Monday*, 13(6), 2008.

[7] R. Crane and D. Sornette. Robust dynamic classes revealed by measuring the response function of a social system. *Proceedings of the National Academy of Sciences (PNAS)*, 105(41):15649–53, Oct. 2008.

[8] D. Easley and J. Kleinberg. *Networks, Crowds, and Markets: Reasoning About a Highly Connected World*. Cambridge University Press, 1 edition, July 2010.

[9] F. Figueiredo, F. Benevenuto, and J. Almeida. The tube over time: characterizing popularity growth of youtube videos. In *Proc. WSDM*, 2011.

[10] F. Figueiredo, H. Pinto, F. Belém, J. Almeida, M. Gonçalves, D. Fernandes, and E. Moura. Assessing the quality of textual features in social media. *Information Processing & Management*, Apr. 2012.

[11] K. Filippova and K. B. Hall. Improved video categorization from text metadata and user comments. In *Proc. SIGIR*, 2011.

[12] P. Geurts, D. Ernst, and L. Wehenkel. Extremely Randomized Trees. *Machine Learning*, 63(1):3–42, 2006.

[13] A. Ghose and S. Yang. An Empirical Analysis of Search Engine Advertising: Sponsored Search in Electronic Markets. *INFORMS: Management Science*, 2010.

[14] P. Gill, M. Arlitt, Z. Li, and A. Mahanti. Youtube traffic characterization: a view from the edge. In *Proc. IMC*, Oct. 2007.

[15] A. Lacerda, M. Cristo, M. A. Gonçalves, W. Fan, N. Ziviani, and B. Ribeiro-Neto. Learning to advertise. In *Proc. SIGIR*, 2006.

[16] K. Lerman and T. Hogg. Using a model of social dynamics to predict popularity of news. In *Proc. WWW*, Apr. 2010.

[17] H. Pinto, J. Almeida, and M. Gonçalves. Using early view patterns to predict the popularity of YouTube videos. In *Proc. WSDM*, 2013.

[18] G. Szabo and B. A. Huberman. Predicting the Popularity of Online Content. *Communications of the ACM*, 53(8):80–88, 2010.

[19] Vimeo. Advertise on Vimeo. http://vimeo.com/about/advertisers, 2012.

[20] M. Wattenhofer, R. Wattenhofer, and Z. Zhu. The YouTube Social Network. In *Proc. ICWSM*, 2012.

[21] J. Yang and J. Leskovec. Patterns of temporal variation in online media. In *Proc. WSDM*. ACM Press, Feb. 2011.

[22] P. Yin, P. Luo, M. Wang, and W.-C. Lee. A straw shows which way the wind blows: Ranking Potentially Popular Items from Early Votes. In *Proc. WSDM*, Feb. 2012.

[23] Youtube. YouTube Press Statistics. http://www.youtube.com/t/press_statistics, 2012.

On the Quest of Discovering Cultural Trails in Social Media

Ruth Garcia
Web Research Group
Universitat Pompeu Fabra
Yahoo! Research Barcelona
Barcelona, Spain
ruth.garcia@upf.edu

ABSTRACT

With the constant increasing reach of the Web and in particular of Social Media, people create and share content that harbors information about habits, norms, preferences and values. Consequently, studying how *culture* influences users in online social media has increased the interest of several sectors such as the advertising industry, search engines and corporations. As a consequence, anthropological and computational models need to interact and complement each other to better target these new demands. Recently, several studies have analyzed culture from large-scale data but not many took into consideration the cultural models proposed by anthropological theory. By carrying out several experiments on large scale data from the Web, we propose to combine theoretical concepts of culture with information technology techniques to process, analyze, model and interpret data from the Web. We plan to discover synergies between traditional social studies of culture and those derived from our experiments.

Categories and Subject Descriptors

H.2.8 [**Database Application**]: Data Mining; H.4 [**Information Systems Applications**]: Miscellaneous

General Terms

Experimentation, Measurement

Keywords

Cross-cultural Differences, Social Media, Social Networks, Sentiment Analysis

1. INTRODUCTION

Defining the term *culture* is not a simple task and it can lead to several disagreements even for people who deeply study it. In fact, the most accepted cultural models lack homogeneity. Furthermore, the way culture is defined, studied and shaped can also vary according to its context, purpose or function. A popular definition of culture comes from Hofstede: "culture is the collective programming of the mind that distinguishes the member of one group or category of people from others" [11, 13].

Due to the globalization and emergence of the Web 2.0, measuring and interpreting *culture* is imperative in several areas such as global information management, the internet advertising industry and web business applications [1, 26] as well as search engines that are attempting to provide more personalized search results. In fact, the now massive User Generated Content (UGC) in microblogs, social networks and other online spaces has given space to a huge repository of great cultural value. Although cultural information in UGC is inherently noisy, it can be extracted automatically and is plentiful. Moreover, the modern large scale analytic algorithms and tools available make its analysis and processing possible.

For all these reasons, the study of culture can be beneficial in several aspects. First, it can help identify synergies between cultural social studies manually generated and those automatically generated from "big data" on the Web. Second, understanding how culture affects user behavior online can give insights to user interface design and business strategy like e-commerce applications. In fact, previous studies showed that underestimating the impact of culture in user behavior has led some multinational corporations to fail when attempting to enter the market of new countries [23]. Third, modeling differences and similarities between cultures and how they change or remain the same in time can lead to the discovery of unexpected data (serendipity).

This PhD proposal focuses on exploring, analyzing and interpreting the role of culture in large scale UGC. Our methodology is to use Hofstede's theoretical basis for describing cultural characteristics. In order to extract, process and analyze features, we will use techniques from *data mining*, *sentiment analysis* and *network analysis*. Finally, quantitative user studies are also planned to be executed on groups of people from different backgrounds and cultures to observe and measure how culture affects online behavior.

2. BACKGROUND

2.1 Classification of Culture

One of the most influential works on modeling and defining culture comes from Dr. Geert Hofstede [10, 13]. He focused on how countries can be compared and contrasted in terms of only few values. He defended that culture is

WSDM'13, February 4–8, 2013, Rome, Italy.

a collective phenomenon but with varying individuals distributed as in a bell curve: "the variation between cultures is the shift of the bell curve when one moves from one society to the other"[11]. The values to compare cultures are called *cultural dimensions.* These dimensions were proposed as definition and they have a meaning *only* when making comparisons. Up to now, Hofstede built a cultural dimension model (CDM) made of six categories [11]. These dimensions are based on a broad empirical survey made in more than 70 countries. Relative scores are assigned to compare countries based on these dimensions and these scores only have a meaning if compared to other countries[1]. These dimensions are related to 1) the level of acceptance of unequal distribution of power, 2) individualism and collectivism, 3) masculinity and femininity, 4) the stress involved when dealing with uncertainty, 5) importance of tradition and 6) indulgence vs. restraint. These dimensions are seen more deeply in section 4.

In contrast to Hofstede's classification of culture at the national level, in the famous" The Clash of Civilizations?" [14], Huntington classified culture in a broader sense. He grouped cultures as civilizations, that is, the "highest cultural grouping of people and the broader level of cultural identity people have". He made an interesting point in identifying eight major civilizations based on their cultural differences: Western, Confucian, Japanese, Islamic, Hindu, Slavic-Orthodox, Latin American and possibly African civilizations.

2.2 Applications of Hofstede's work

There is not a clear and unified method to associate empirical data in different scenarios with Hofstede's dimensional cultures. Several methods have been adapted to specific situations. For example, Lipi et al. [18] measured how culture affects non-verbal expressions in conversations. They proposed a parameter based model employing Bayesian network techniques where culture is connected to Hofstede dimensions which are also connected with nonverbal expressions. For each node in the Bayesian network, probabilities are assigned according to Hofstede's CDM and to results obtained from experiments. Basically, when a country is chosen, the model outputs the estimated probability of behavior expressive parameters (Rigidness, Mirroring, etc). This approach forces the results to be probabilistically dependent of CDM.

Oh et al. [20, 19] also presented a model that integrates CDM and empirical data based on phone applications. First, they collected information about mobile-phone applications downloaded in several countries and classified each application according to its content (Finance, Entertainment, etc). Second, they defined a group of dimensions inspired in Hofstede and Schwartz as a basic framework for analysis. Then they used a Delphi Survey with 5-point Likert scales to assign values to each application according to the framework established by them. Next, for each phone application they calculated a *Cultural Dimensions Score of Content* (CSC) [19] based on the Delphi survey as to assign a CSC value to each application. Finally, they used this CSC score to calculate a *Cultural Index Score for Country*(CSIC) [20] which represents the country's inclination to a given cultural dimension.

Several techniques are used to present similarities and differences of CISC values at the national level. Probably due to limited access to free downloaded phone applications, their results showed different characteristics from what Hofstede's and Schwartz have reported.

Other studies provided theoretical insights such as Chau et al. [4] who argued that individualism and collectivism are particularly relevant in studying the use of services built around Web 2.0, including OSN. Likewise, Ford et al. [7] discussed how to accommodate one of the five cultural dimensions in user interfaces to increase usability.

2.3 Cultural studies in OSN

Several studies reporting culture analysis of large-scale data from the Web have not followed a formal framework of cultural classification; however, the cultural insights reported have been interesting. For example, Poblete et al. [21] and Garcia et al. [8] carried out a study on understanding differences between the 10 most active countries in Twitter in the way they use social media, express emotions and interact with others. They identified correlations between language dependent and independent features. Yanai et al. [28], followed several algorithms to detect representative pictures from Flickr per region in the world. Furthermore, they categorized pictures and compare how photos of the same topic vary according to the country. Kling et al. [15] identified cultural relatedness of countries by assigning travel profiles to users in Flickr. They compared travel patterns of countries by identifying the home country of users and the countries where users have traveled. Hochman et al. [9] used around 550,000 images of Instagram from NY and Tokyo. They offered a comparative visualization research that indicates differences in color preferences, production, and varied hue's intensities which all shape a unique, local, "Visual Rhythm." Wang et al. [27] made an interesting cross-cultural comparison of the work load of scientists in America, China and Germany. They analyzed the day and time technical papers are downloaded from a popular scientific publisher's website. They concluded that there are some interesting differences but the common ground is that scientists are workaholics.

Table 1 summarizes the acronyms that will be used in this proposal:

Acronym	Meaning
UGC	User Generated Content
OSN	Online Social Network
CDM	Cultural Dimension Model
CSC	Cultural Score of Content
CISC	Cultural Index Score for Country
ANEW	Affective Norms for English Words

Table 1: Acronyms used

2.4 Hofstede in the Social Web

Our work differs from existing cultural research in multiple aspects: a) We plan to propose a model to represent cultural dimensions from UGC, user's interactions and network structure of *Online Social Networks.* b) we plan to use different time granularities to analyze culture and c) the context of our research is strictly based on large scale data from the Web which differs significantly from many of the previous cultural studies. To the best of our knowledge, there are not enough studies that associate Hofstede's model and cultural aspects of large-scale data.

[1]Comparisons of countries based on cultural dimensions can be dynamically obtained from Hofstede web page http://geert-hofstede.com/.

3. RESEARCH QUESTIONS

We propose to mine, process and analyze massive data likely to contain cultural information. We are not interested in comparing "specific nations/societies" but more interested in the process of modeling data to discover cultural differences so that the same process can be applied to any society/nation. We are also interested in reporting serendipity, that is, the non expected information discovery from our studies. In this regard, during the PhD, we will address the following questions in order:

- **How to model data from online social websites as to best represent Hofstede cultural dimensions?**
- **Can we find synergies between cultural data from online social websites and cultural findings from Hofstede?**

4. METHODOLOGY

In this study, we use Hofstede's six cultural dimensions as our basic framework for analysis. Some of the datasets we plan to use during the PhD can be extracted from public APIs while others can be provided by the laboratory where this PhD will be pursued. *We focus only on datasets with users' geo-location information(discovered by ips, locations reported by users, etc)* and profile description. Tentative datasets to be explored are 1) Twitter public API and other microblogs such as Sina Weibo, 2) Yahoo search/e-mail logs, 3) Yahoo! Answers and 4) Flickr. Whether to use all the listed datasets or all of them is something to be decided during the PhD [2]. Moreover, we plan to use Hadoop and Pig Latin to analyze data and other tools or dictionaries for language and geo-location detection.

For the analysis of cultural dimensions in large-scale data, it is important first to classify data based on the type of the analysis intended to be done. We propose two main types:

1. Language dependent: features specially related to sentiment analysis. In order to target sentiment analysis in different languages we propose to use the Affective Norms for English Words [2] and its adaptation to different languages [16, 22]. These dictionaries provide scores to the psychological reaction to which humans have to a specific word, according to a scale which ranges from pleasant to unpleasant. On the other hand, the Linguistic Inquiry and Word Count (LIWC) program is also used to calculate the degree to which people use different categories of words across a wide array of texts, and determine the degree any text uses positive or negative emotions, self-references, causal words, and 70 other language dimensions [25].
2. Language independent: features related to social network structure analysis, analysis of activity and interactions among users such as counting the number of conversational posts (i.e in Twitter it is possible to address a particular user with the symbol @ before the user name @username) .

Furthermore, we also propose to classify data on a temporal basis: per day, week, month or year. Temporal analysis is specially interesting in event coverage(protests, elections, holidays, etc) and evolution of user behavior.

[2]Currently, the research done so far has been made on Twitter

After making a distinction of the type of data to be studied and the temporal constrains to consider, we are now ready to address two main problems:

1. How to associate human behavior manifested online to Hofstede's cultural dimensions? This question arises when cultural behavior is identified and available in data and there is lack of consensus to associate findings to a particular cultural dimension.
2. How large-scale online social data can be modeled as to represent one or more cultural dimensions? We target this question when there is the hypothesis that data related to a particular cultural dimension can be found in online social activity such as in the affect of text, interaction with friends, network structure, etc. We attempt to explain cultural findings based on cultural dimensions.

In order to associate data to CDM we propose to follow an adaptation of the work done by Oh et al. [20, 19] and mentioned in section 2.2) use Delphi survey to determine the association of each CDM to the cultural characteristic/feature to be considered and 2) calculate a cultural index score per country for each specific dimension. The model will be adapted to web content, user interactions and social network characteristics. The following equations define each score (refer to [20, 19] for more information) :

$$CSC = \frac{\left(\sum_{i=1}^{j} *n_i\right)}{N} \tag{1}$$

$$CISC = \sum_{a=1}^{z} A\left(CSC * \left(\frac{dm_a}{DM} - \left(\frac{\sum_{a=1}^{z} \frac{dm_a}{DM}}{N}\right)\right)\right) \tag{2}$$

where A is a constant, a is the dimension based on CDM, dm_a is the total number of users at the national level with dimension a, DM is total amount of users with all dimensions and N is the total amount of target countries for the analysis.

We believe that the Delphi method is well suited to target lack on consensus when mapping data to cultural dimensions. The Delphi method is an iterative process that collect and distill the judgments of experts using a series of questionnaires. Each subsequent questionnaire is developed based on the results of the previous questionnaire. The process stops when consensus is reached or when sufficient information has been exchanged. Delphi surveys can be applied to problems that benefit from the subjective judgments of individuals on a collective basis [24]. This is the most appropriate solution we have found to map cultural data to CDM.

On the other hand, to target the second problem of modeling data to CDM, we have to give a closer look to Hofstede's cultural dimensions. With each definition, we present an example of how large-scale data can be related with CDM. It is still to be decided the definite data to be used.

- Power Distance (PD)- high vs. low: the extent to which the less powerful members of institutions and organizations within a country expect and accept that power is distributed unequally. In a country classified as small-power-distance country, people would tend to easily approach and contradict their bosses. On the contrary, people from high-power-distance countries will unlikely approach and contradict their bosses directly. For example, several studies have been made on the popularity of users in social media such as Cha et al. [3], one could explore the level of communication between users with high, average and low popularity for certain countries and relate these findings with PD scores.

- Individualism (IDV)- high vs. low: the level of integration into a group. Individualist societies (high IDV) represent loose ties between individuals where everyone is expected to look after him or herself and his or her immediate family. Collective (low IDV) societies represent individuals integrated into strong, cohesive groups where they protect each other in exchange of loyalty. For example, we can explore this dimensions in Twitter by measuring the amount of conversation exchanged with others as well as comparing the *unfollow* [17] dynamics of users.
- Gender (Gn) -masculinity vs. femininity: the description of roles between genders in a society. Feminine represents societies where emotional gender roles overlap: both men and women are supposed to be modest, tender, and concerned with the quality of life.Masculinity represents societies where emotional gender roles are clearly distinct: men are supposed to be assertive, tough, and focused on material success, whereas women are supposed to be more modest, tender, and concerned with the quality of life. For example, this dimension could be explored in social media by studying the use of adjectives and superlatives between women and men per country.
- Uncertainty avoidance (UA)- high vs. low: the extent to which members of a society feel threatened or uncomfortable in novel, surprising or unknown situations.This dimension can be measured by nervous stress , anxiety and the need for written or unwritten rules [12]. For example, measuring words expressing anxiety in social media can be an alternative to explore this dimension.
- Time orientation (LTO)- short vs. long: in essence, short-term oriented societies stand for the fostering of virtues related to the past and present (tradition, saving one's face, fulfilling social obligations) while long-term societies are more concerned with virtues oriented toward future rewards (perseverance and thrift). For example, this dimension could be studied in social media by identifying affiliations of users to certain groups. Many social sites are not only made of users but also groups representing ideologies, beliefs, etc.
- Indulgence versus Restraint (IVR): Indulgence is related to societies allowing free gratification where there is a high correlation between happiness, life control and importance of leisure as personal value. On the other hand, restraint refer to societies that control more gratification by means of strict social norms. In social media, we can combine studies made on happiness in blogs and microblogs such as in the work of Dodds et al. [5, 6] with this dimension.

5. RESEARCH TO DATE

We want to divide the years of research into the following stages: a) the first year to the analysis phase, b) the second year to the distillation of data into Hofstede's dimensions of cultures, c) the third year into using models to represent large-scale data into the form of Hofstede's cultural dimensions using one or more metrics and 4) the fourth year to report synergies and to replicate models into different datasets. During the first stage of our proposal, two experiments have been carried out to explore culture in microblogs. These experiments inspired the search of finding a model of culture than can be use in large-scale data. A summary of our finding are described in section 5.1.

5.1 Culture on the Use of Social Media

We conducted a large scale analysis of the behavior of millions of users in Twitter to observe significant differences among countries and the way they use social media during one whole year. More details about this work can be found in Garcia et al. [8] and Poblete et al. [21]. We covered the following categories: a) level of activity and languages used in the 10 countries that tweet the most, b) temporal happiness levels of tweets in two different languages for all active countries, c) the content of tweets in terms of mentions, hashtags, urls and re-tweets and d) the network structure: reciprocity, ties and social network.

Language independent findings are shown in the two right images in Figure 1. We can appreciate for instance that Australia differs notably from Indonesia's network. Indonesia has lower density and a larger core component which increases path lengths between nodes.

On the other hand, language dependent analysis is shown in he two right graphs in Figure 1. The graphs show the weighted happiness level per month when analyzing English and Spanish tweets. Note that the Spanish sentiment analysis is based on the ANEW list adapted to Spanish language by Redondo et al. [22]. We plan to carry out future studies using the Portuguese adapted dictionary of ANEW by Kristensen et al. [16] as well. In order to compute the "weighted average happiness level", we used the algorithm proposed by Dodds et al. [6, 5]:

$$h_{avg}(T) = \frac{\sum_{i=1}^{N} h_{avg}(w_i) f_i}{\sum_{i=1}^{N} f_i} = \sum_{i=1}^{N} h_{avg}(w_i) p_i \quad (3)$$

where T represents all of the tweets per country for a particular time period and for a specific language (Spanish or English). Moreover, f_i is the frequency of the ith of N distinct words for which there is an estimate of average happiness (i.e., from the ANEW list [2]).

On the other hand, we studied the content and frequency of tweets and observed that the ratio tweet/user in Indonesia is the highest if compared to other active countries. Moreover, Indonesia also mentions other users in almost 60% of their tweets (highest value of all active countries). These insights suggest the collective nature of Indonesia. More research is needed to make comparisons using Hofstede's CDM.

6. ACKNOWLEDGMENTS

This PhD. is carried out under the supervision of Dr. Ricardo Baeza-Yates and Dr. Alejandro Jaimes.

7. REFERENCES

[1] F. Bonchi, C. Castillo, A. Gionis, and A. Jaimes. Social network analysis and mining for business

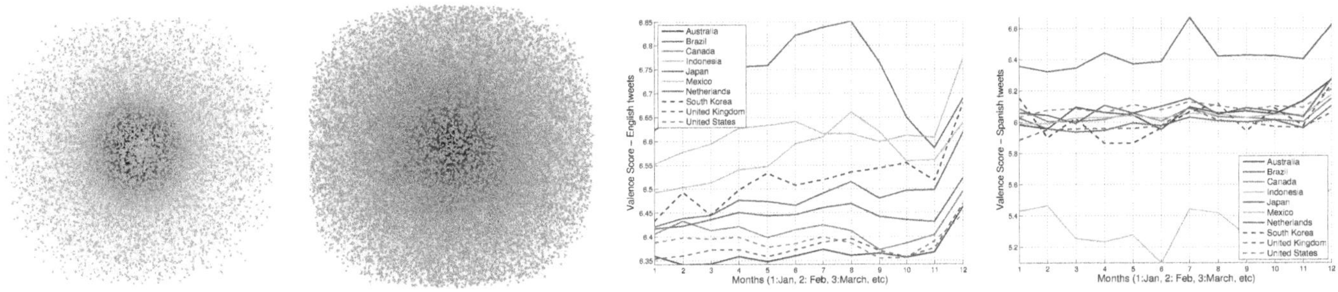

Figure 1: Network snapshot of Australia and Indonesia keeping edges of the same countries (left) and average happiness level for English Tweets per month for each country (right).

applications. *ACM Trans. Intell. Syst. Technol.*, 2:22:1–22:37, May 2011.

[2] M. M. Bradley and P. J. Lang. Affective norms for english words (ANEW): Stimuli, instruction manual, and affective ratings. In *In Technical Report C-1, The Center for Research in Psychophysiology*, Gainesville, Florida, 1999.

[3] M. Cha, H. Haddadi, F. Benevenuto, and K. P. Gummadi. Measuring user influence in twitter: The million follower fallacy. In *in ICWSM '10*, 2010.

[4] P. Y. Chau. Cultural differences in diffusion, adoption, and infusion of web 2.0. *Journal of Global Information Management*, 16(1):i–iii, 2008.

[5] P. Dodds and C. Danforth. Measuring the happiness of large-scale written expression: Songs, blogs, and presidents. *Journal of Happiness Studies*, 11(4):441–456, August 2010.

[6] P. S. Dodds, K. D. Harris, I. M. Kloumann, C. A. Bliss, and C. M. Danforth. Temporal patterns of happiness and information in a global social network: Hedonometrics and Twitter. *Computing Research Repository abs/1101.5120v3[physics.soc-ph]*, Feb. 2011.

[7] G. Ford and P. Kotzé. Designing usable interfaces with cultural dimensions, 2005.

[8] R. Garcia, M. Medoza, B. Poblete, and A. Jaimes. Microblogging without borders: Differences and similarities. In *ACM WEBSCI'11, Koblenz-Germany*, June, 2011.

[9] N. Hochman and R. Schwarts. Visualizing instagram: Tracing cultural visual rhythms. Association for the Advancement of Artificial Intelligence, 2012.

[10] G. Hofstede. *Culture's Consequences, International Differences in Work-Related Values.* Sage Publications, Inc, CA, 1980.

[11] G. Hofstede. Dimensionalizing cultures: The hofstede model in context. *Online Readings in Psychology and Culture*, 2(1), 2011.

[12] G. Hofstede, G. J. Hofstede, and G. Hofstede. *Cultures and Organizations: Software of the Mind.* McGraw-Hill, 2 edition, June 2004.

[13] G. H. Hofstede. *Culture's consequences : comparing values, behaviors, institutions, and organizations across nations.* Sage Publications, Thousand Oaks, California, 2nd ed edition, 2001.

[14] S. P. Huntington. The clash of civilizations. *Foreign Affairs*, 72:22, 1992.

[15] C. C. Kling and T. Gottron. Detecting culture in coordinates: cultural areas in social media. DETECT '11, pages 11–16, New York, NY, USA, 2011. ACM.

[16] C. H. Kristensen, C. F. A. d. A. Gomes, A. R. Justo, and K. Vieira. Normas brasileiras para o Affective Norms for English Words. *Trends in Psychiatry and Psychotherapy*, 33:135 – 146, 00 2011.

[17] H. Kwak, H. Chun, and S. Moon. Fragile online relationship: a first look at unfollow dynamics in twitter. In *CHI 2011*, CHI '11, pages 1091–1100, New York, NY, USA, 2011. ACM.

[18] A. A. Lipi, Y. Nakano, and M. Rehm. A parameter-based model for generating culturally adaptive nonverbal behaviors in embodied conversational agents, 2009.

[19] J.-M. Oh and N. Moon. A cultural dimensions model based on smart phone applications. *JIPS*, pages 209–220, 2011.

[20] J.-M. Oh and N. Moon. Towards a cultural user interface generation principles. *Multimedia Tools and Applications*, pages 1–22, 2012.

[21] B. Poblete, R. Garcia, M. Mendoza, and A. Jaimes. Do All Birds Tweet the Same? Characterizing Twitter Around the World. In *CIKM 2011*, Glasgow,UK, October 2011.

[22] J. Redondo, I. Fraga, I. Padrn, and M. Comesaa. The spanish adaptation of anew (affective norms for english words). In *Volumne 39*, number 3, pages 600–605. Psychonomic Society Publications, 2007.

[23] D. Ricks. *Blunders in International Business.* Wiley, 2009.

[24] G. J. Skulmoski, F. T. Hartman, and J. Krahn. The delphi method for graduate research. *JITE*, pages 1–21, 2007.

[25] Y. R. Tausczik and J. W. Pennebaker. The psychological meaning of words: Liwc and computerized text analysis methods. 2010.

[26] E. Vitkauskaite. Cultural adaptation issues in social networking sites. *Economics and Management: 2011.16 ISSN 1822-6515*, 2011.

[27] X. Wang, S. Xu, L. Peng, Z. Wang, C. Wang, C. Zhang, and X. Wang. Exploring scientists' working timetable: Do scientists often work overtime? *Journal of Informetrics*, 6(4):655–660, 2012.

[28] K. Yanai, K. Yaegashi, and B. Qiu. Detecting cultural differences using consumer-generated geotagged photos. LOCWEB '09, pages 12:1–12:4, New York, NY, USA, 2009. ACM.

Towards Web-Scale Structured Web Data Extraction

Tomas Grigalis
Vilnius Gediminas Technical University
Sauletekio av. 11,
LT-10223 Vilnius, Lithuania
tomas.grigalis@vgtu.lt

ABSTRACT

In this paper we present an ongoing PhD research on unsupervised and domain-independent structured data extraction from the Web. We propose a novel method to extract structured data records from template-generated Web pages. The method is based on clustering visually similar Web page elements by exploiting their visual formatting and HTML structural features. Tag paths of clustered Web page elements are then employed to derive extraction rules. These rules, called wrappers, can be later reused on thousands of same template-generated Web pages. This opens the possibility for the proposed method to be deployed in Web-Scale structured data extraction systems.

Categories and Subject Descriptors

H.0 [**Information Systems**]: General; H.3.3 [**Information Systems**]: Information Search and Retrieval

General Terms

Design, Experimentation, Performance

Keywords

web data extraction, structured data, wrapper induction

1. INTRODUCTION

Many template-generated Web sites contain structured data. Upon a page request, this data is retrieved from underlying database and inserted into a Web page template. The resulting structural similarity of template-generated Web pages is an important feature for data extraction. For example, it is possible to write simple data extraction rules, also known as wrappers, for each kind of template, and later reuse these rules on all Web pages of the same template. This enables extracting data from many Web pages using only one wrapper. Consider, for example, such sites as imdb.com or ebay.com that contain thousands or even millions of Web pages generated using one of their templates. So using only one wrapper for each individual template it is possible to extract structured data from thousands of Web pages.

Data on the Web is about everything. An ability to find, extract and integrate that data can bring huge benefits. Indeed, it can fundamentally shift the search to allow a more semantic view of content [11]. Currently search engines see the Web as hyper-linked pages, each containing a bag of words. A user searching the Web is presented with list of links to the Websites. However, the true value of the Web lies in the wealth of information provided by those pages [11]. So instead of following the links, search engine users could instantly see the exact information they were looking for: let it be list of movies, books, flights, real estate listings or any other entities [30]. Furthermore, Web scale data extraction could enable and speed up data integration from multiple Web sources [6]. This would lead to building enormous size knowledge bases. A long standing goal for the Web search, that is - to return answers in the form of facts, would be much more tangible [6]. So a Web-scale structured data extraction could fundamentally change the way we see and browse the Web today.

One of the biggest challenges in information extraction research field is to develop effective techniques for Web-Scale data extraction [13]. We believe that the ability to automatically generate wrappers for any template-generated Web site is be a big step in tackling the grand challenge. The idea of automatically inferring wrappers and then extracting data is not new and has received a lot of extensive research [9, 12, 33, 34]. However, state-of-the-art solutions are not yet suitable for truly domain-independent and automatic Web-scale structured data extraction. Web-scale extraction, at the level of precision and recall high enough to power real applications, has remained an open challenge [5].

In this paper we present an ongoing PhD research on unsupervised and domain-independent Web-scale structured data extraction. We have developed a prototype system, called ClustVX [18], which generates data extracting wrappers for any given Web page. For our system to run correctly, the Web page must be template-generated, contain a list of structured data in any format, and there should be more than two data records. Data extraction process begins when ClustVX clusters visually similar Web page elements by exploiting their visual formatting and structural similarity. In other words, for each Web page element we encode structural and visual features into one string, which we call Xstring. We cluster Xstrings. Resulting clusters are then used to derive data extracting Xpath wrappers.

WSDM'13, February 4–8, 2013, Rome, Italy.

The main contributions of our research are the following (we also believe these are key, but not least, requirements for unsupervised Web-scale structured Web data extraction system):

1. Our prototype system can extract structured data from any visual representation in a Web page. We are not limited to simple tables or lists like some approaches [7, 14, 29].
2. We have developed a fully domain independent system. Data on the Web is about everything [6] and that data is presented in very heterogeneous forms. However, humans understand the structure of any data easily by analyzing repeating visual patterns on a given Web page [25]. This observation, together with structural similarity of data records in template-generated Web pages, let us to build truly domain independent structured data extraction system. Of course, extracted data does not have any semantics attached to it, however we believe that this is another field of research. Semantic analysis of extracted data can be made in the later stages.
3. Our system is unsupervised. Unlike other approaches [3, 19] we do not need any manual human effort to induce wrappers and extract structured data. We believe that manual human efforts do not scale to the Web.
4. We automatically generate easily reusable Xpath wrappers. Data extraction involves some computation runtime depending on the algorithm. In some cases [17, 24] (as also in our), where visual features of Web page elements are used, even more runtime is needed for visually rendering a Web page. All those time consuming tasks add up, and when we approach Web-Scale data extraction, runtime becomes a bottleneck. However, if we can generate wrappers, we need more time only once per new template. On all other pages of the same template we can use generated Xpath wrappers. Xpath as a language for data extraction has been proved to be very effective [3, 12, 17, 19, 26].
5. We can handle sophisticated Web pages with asynchronous JavaScript requests that load structured data on-the-fly. In case we need it, and always during wrapper generation, we load Web pages in contemporary Web browser. The browser engine handles all embedded JavaScripts, Cascading Style Sheets, and etc.

Finally, we demonstrate the effectiveness of our approach to extracting structured web data. We experimentally test ClustVX on three publicly available benchmark data sets containing in total of 7098 data records from 353 different template-generated Web pages. ClustVX consistently achieves very high quality in terms of precision and recall and outperforms other similar approaches.

2. RELATED WORK

A lot of research addresses the problem of Web data extraction. We categorize proposed approaches according to these aspects: the level of automation (supervised versus unsupervised), the object of extraction (structured data versus entities from regular text), wrapper induction (are wrappers generated or do we need to run full extraction algorithm on every new page), and dependence on a domain (domain independent versus domain dependent/centric). In this section we review all of those categories and name some examples.

The level of automation in Web data extraction systems determines how much manual effort is required to extract data from Web pages or to generate data extracting rules. Supervised learning approaches [3, 8, 19, 20] need manual effort to learn data extracting rules. The main two disadvantages of supervised learning approaches are time consuming manual labeling process and matching already generated wrappers to constant changes of Web page structure. For example, every time a structure of a Web page changes a data extracting wrapper can no longer work correctly. To update the broken wrapper a Web page must be relabeled. This is very time consuming task. Although supervised learning approaches work pretty well on a small number of labeled Websites and can, indeed, extract millions of data records [19], they are not suitable for general Web-scale data extraction.

There are systems [15, 28] that extract data from regular text. Usually these approaches employ various natural language processing techniques and search text for facts. A fact is represented as a tuple consisting of an entities (real world objects) and their relationship. For instance, given the sentence, "McCain fought hard against Obama, but finally lost the election," a data extraction system of this kind should extract two tuples, (McCain, fought against, Obama), and (McCain, lost, the election) [16]. This way millions of facts are extracted from Web-scale text corpus and put into knowledge bases. However, these systems are not yet applicable to extract structured data, where structure is defined at a database level.

Many automatic structured web data extraction systems search for repeating patterns in a Web page. There exist several approaches to this problem:

1. To look at Web pages as sequence of characters or set of HTML tree paths and to search for repeating patterns in them [2, 9, 25].
2. To consider Web pages as HTML trees, that are built by parsing HTML markup code, and then find similarities by comparing branches of those trees one against another [22, 23].
3. To analyze rendered visual appearance of a Web page and to look for repeating visual patterns [24].
4. To use hybrid approach, where visual and structural repeating patterns are combined together to better locate data records in a Web page [32, 33]. In this paper presented ClustVX system belongs to this category. However, contrary to the referred approaches, it employs tag path with embedded visual features clustering technique, instead of HTML tree or string matching.

Although the reported precision and recall of those systems is very high, there is lack of information about deployment of those methods in a real world setting with thousands of Websites. Furthermore many approaches from this category lack easily reusable and maintained wrappers. For example, none of those systems generates Xpath wrappers, that have been shown in recent works [3, 12, 17, 19, 26] to be very efficient in Web data extraction.

Domain dependent approaches [17, 27] use some basic knowledge about the specific domain that is targeted for data extraction. That knowledge about a domain may be a list of words that should be located, regular expressions to be matched, ontology or visual features to be recognized, and etc. Related to this category are systems [7, 14, 29], that extract data from a limited set of HTML tag names. Although shown to be capable in unsupervised and domain-independent way to extract structured data from millions of Web sources, those methods are limited to extracting data from simple Web tables and lists. And as we know, structured data on the Web is presented in many different forms, often outside the scope of simple tables and lists. Thus these systems miss a lot of structured data.

3. THE PROPOSED APPROACH

Proposed approach, called ClustVX, is based on two fundamental observations. First, vast amount of information on the Web is presented using fixed templates that are filled with data from underlying databases. For example, Fig. 1(a) shows three data records representing information about three digital cameras in an online store. The three data records are listed according to some unknown style template and the embedded information comes from a database. This also means, that each data record has almost the same Xpath (tag path from a root node in HTML tree to the particular Web page element), where only a few node index numbers differ. Second, although the templates and underlying data differ from site to site, humans understand them easily by analyzing repeating visual patterns on a given Web page [25]. We hypothesize, that the data which has the same semantic meaning is visualized using the same style. For example in Fig. 1(a) prices have biggest font size and are bold, title is grey, each data record has a picture. ClustVX exploits both of these two observations by representing each Web page element with a combination of its tag path (in HTML tree) and visual features (from rendered view), such as font, color and etc. For each visible, text containing, and child nodes absent Web page element we encode this combination into the string called Xstring. Clustering Xstrings allows us to identify visually similar elements, which are located in the same region of a Web page and in turn have the same semantic meaning. See Fig. 1(b) where price elements are clustered together according to their Xstring. Subsequent data extraction, using inferred wrappers, leads to a machine readable structured data that is shown in Fig. 1(c).

(a) An example of three digital cameras (data records) in a Web page

Cluster	Xpath	Font	Color
£119.99 **£129.99** **£111.99**	/html/body/div[1]/div[3]/a /html/body/div[2]/div[3]/a /html/body/div[3]/div[3]/a	Arial Arial Arial	Grey Grey Grey
Xstring	htmlbodydivdiva-Arial,Grey		
Wrapper	/html/body/div[*]/div[3]/a		

(b) A cluster with visually similar price elements

Image 1	Fuji FinePix...	562/6283	£119.99
Image 2	Fujifilm XP30...	559/5101	£129.99
Image 3	Samsung ST200F...	559/7635	£111.99

(c) Desired extraction results

Figure 1: An example of structured Web data extraction using ClustVX.

3.1 Web Page Preprocessing

First of all a Web page is retrieved and rendered in a contemporary Web browser. This is very important step, since Web browser handles all Web 2.0 features, such as client-side scripting, AJAX request and etc. All visual styling information from HTML source code and CSS files are also processed by the browser. Currently we are using Mozilla Web browser. All HTML text formatting tags, such as < `b` >, < `em` >, are removed from a Web page. Otherwise, one text segment may be split among many text tokens and each token will have unique Xpath. This may lead to incorrectly clustering these text tokens into different clusters, while whole text segment must be place into one cluster.

3.2 Clustering

An Xstring representation is generated for each visible Web page text element. As we see in Fig. 1(b) Xstring consists of a) tag names from Xpath b) visual features of that element (font style, color, weight, etc.). Structural feature (string of tag names) identifies the position in an HTML document. Visual features, which are obtained by calling API of Web browser, enhance an understanding of semantic similarity between Web page elements. This helps to correctly cluster web page elements: if an element has the same visual properties as other elements in a cluster, we put that element there. In other words, if two elements have same Xstrings, they are put into the single cluster. So all visible Web page elements are clustered according to their Xstring. Resulting clusters contain only semantically similar Web page elements. In Fig. 1(b) we see a cluster of price elements that all have the exactly same Xstring and therefore belong to the same cluster. Other clusters would contain titles, pictures, model numbers, and so on. Currently ClustVX system does not semantically annotate any cluster and we see each cluster just as a bag of text strings.

3.3 Data Area Identification

Each clustered web page element has an unique Xpath string, which points to the exact location of that element in the HTML tree. Using this information it is easy to identify in a Web page data areas that contain data records. By calculating longest common tag path prefix of Xpath from particular cluster, we find the tag path of a data region. The same prefix tag path of the same data region will appear in each cluster that contains elements from one particular data region.

3.4 Record Segmentation and Extraction

Data record segmentation and extraction process is based on two observations about data record representation in a Web page. First, a group of data records is usually rendered in a contiguous region of a Web page [32] and contains visual regularity. Second, a group of data records is formed by some child subtrees and at some level each data record has same parent node [32]. Thus, by calculating longest common prefix of Xpaths from each cluster, we can find the exact locations of data record groups (data regions) in a page. For a simple example, consider the Fig. 1(b), where Xpaths of clustered price elements are located. First, we find

Table 1: Experimental evaluation results of ClustVX system compared to other state-of-the-art methods [18]

Data Set	TBDW				VINTS-2			Alvarez	
System	ClustVX	G-STM	DEPTA	FiVaTech	ClustVX	G-STM	DEPTA	ClustVX	Alvarez
Precision	**99.81%**	99.80%	99.50%	97.00%	**98.57%**	98.50%	95.10%	**98.20%**	97.90%
Recall	**99.52%**	96.60%	85.30%	97.40%	**98.51%**	96.70%	83.90%	**99.69%**	98.30%

Table 2: Benchmark data sets used for evaluation

Data Set	TBDW	ViNTs-2	Alvarez
Templates (sites)	51	102	200
Pages per site	5	11	1
AVG records	21	24	18
Total records	1052	2489	3557

the longest common prefix (/html/body) of these clustered Xpaths. The prefix leads us to the particular region of a Web page, where these data records are located. Then, the longest common suffix (/div[3]/a) is the price path in the data record. The Xpath substring between prefix and suffix (/div[*]) is used to segment data region into data records. All clusters that have the same longest common Xpath prefix represent one particular data region. There may exist many data regions in one page and ClustVX locates them all. So derived Xpaths are used to segment data records and extract data.

4. EXPERIMENTAL EVALUATION

We evaluate ClustVX using the three publicly available benchmark data sets containing in total of 7098 data records from 353 different template-generated Web sites:

1. TBDW Ver. 1.02 [31] (51 web sites, 1052 data records)
2. ViNTs dataset 2 [33] (102 web sites, 2489 data records)
3. M. Alvarez et al. [2] (200 web sites, 3557 data records)

See Tab. 2 for details. These data sets contain Web pages retrieved from different template Web sites. Each Web page contains data records, which should be extracted. To evaluate ClustVX we take and count only one Web page per site, because all pages in one site use the same template.

We compare the evaluation results of ClustVX system to these state-of-the-art automatic structured data extraction systems: M. Alvarez et. al. [2], G-STM [22], FiVaTech [23] and DEPTA [32]. Since none of these systems are available to download, we use the evaluation results reported in corresponding publications. As shown in Tab. 1, where best results are marked in bold, ClustVX consistently outperforms other approaches.

5. DEMO

For demonstration purposes the proposed ClustVX system has been implemented using PERL scripting language. The online demo is available at http://clustvx.no-ip.org

6. DISCUSSION AND FUTURE WORK

We have introduced an ongoing PhD research on unsupervised and domain-independent structured data extraction. Until recently our work has been concentrated on pursuing two main research questions: how is structured data embedded in Web pages and how can we efficiently extract it. We have demonstrated that visual cues of a rendered Web page together with structural similarity of data records can be successfully exploited to identify and extract lists of structured data. A prototype system, named ClustVX, has been implemented to support our claims. The experimental evaluation results of ClustVX system on three public benchmark datasets demonstrate a high effectiveness. However, experiments validating our approach have been conducted with relatively small amount of different template Websites that are also outdated. Thus we cannot yet claim truly "web scale" data extraction, however, we are pursuing this goal. Furthermore we need to further crystalize our measurement and methodology and identify the most appropriate statistical tests.

During experimental evaluation we ran into the problem of obtaining a Web-scale data set that could be used in our experiments. We need a data set containing thousands or even millions of web pages. As a possible solution, we bring up for discussion the possibility of employing the power of crowdsourcing by the help of Amazon Mechanical Turk service [1] to build a proper data set. The Amazon service lets to present simple human intelligence requiring tasks, such as labeling data or telling if extraction was successful, to thousands of voluntary workers, which are paid on per hour or per task basis. For example, we could ask thousands of such volunteers to find a web page with structured data, label it, and include the page into a data set.

Currently we are able to generate wrappers and extract data from lists of structure data, where at least two data records are present in a page. However, structured data on the Web is also present in other forms, such as in product detail pages, where there is only one data record describing one particular product. We are going to address this kind of structured data extraction problem in our further research.

There also remains an open question of technical contribution leading this PhD research. Is simple wrapper generating demo enough? Or should we implement a more complete end-to-end structured data extraction system? Of course, this goal would require dealing with such problems as Web page clustering [4], intelligent crawling [21], wrapper maintenance [10], adding visual feedback for correcting errors, and etc. However, these research problems may be way out of scope of our main research questions.

7. ACKNOWLEDGEMENT

This PhD is under supervision of prof. Antanas Cenys.

8. REFERENCES

[1] O. Alonso, D. Rose, and B. Stewart. Crowdsourcing for relevance evaluation. In *ACM SIGIR Forum*, volume 42, pages 9–15. ACM, 2008.

[2] M. Álvarez, A. Pan, and e. a. Raposo. Extracting lists of data records from semi-structured web pages. *Data & Know. Engineering*, 64(2):491–509, 2008.

[3] R. Baumgartner, S. Flesca, and G. Gottlob. Visual web information extraction with lixto. In *Proc. VLDB*, pages 119–128, 2001.

[4] L. Blanco, N. Dalvi, and A. Machanavajjhala. Highly efficient algorithms for structural clustering of large websites. In *Proc. WWW*, pages 437–446. ACM, 2011.

[5] P. Bohannon, N. Dalvi, Y. Filmus, N. Jacoby, S. Keerthi, and A. Kirpal. Automatic web-scale information extraction. In *Proceedings of the 2012 international conference on Management of Data*, pages 609–612. ACM, 2012.

[6] M. Cafarella, A. Halevy, and J. Madhavan. Structured data on the web. *Communications of the ACM*, 54(2):72–79, 2011.

[7] M. Cafarella, A. Halevy, D. Wang, E. Wu, and Y. Zhang. Webtables: exploring the power of tables on the web. *Proceedings of the VLDB Endowment*, 1(1):538–549, 2008.

[8] C. Chang and S. Lui. Iepad: information extraction based on pattern discovery. In *Proc. WWW*, pages 681–688. ACM, 2001.

[9] V. Crescenzi, G. Mecca, P. Merialdo, et al. Roadrunner: Towards automatic data extraction from large web sites. In *Proc. of the Int. Conf. on VLDB*, pages 109–118, 2001.

[10] N. Dalvi, P. Bohannon, and F. Sha. Robust web extraction: an approach based on a probabilistic tree-edit model. In *Proceedings of the 35th SIGMOD international conference on Management of data*, pages 335–348. ACM, 2009.

[11] N. Dalvi, R. Kumar, B. Pang, R. Ramakrishnan, A. Tomkins, P. Bohannon, S. Keerthi, and S. Merugu. A web of concepts. In *Proceedings of the twenty-eighth ACM SIGMOD-SIGACT-SIGART symposium on Principles of database systems*, pages 1–12. ACM, 2009.

[12] N. Dalvi, R. Kumar, and M. Soliman. Automatic wrappers for large scale web extraction. *Proceedings of the VLDB Endowment*, 4(4):219–230, 2011.

[13] N. Dalvi, A. Machanavajjhala, and B. Pang. An analysis of structured data on the web. *Proceedings of the VLDB Endowment*, 5(7):680–691, 2012.

[14] H. Elmeleegy, J. Madhavan, and A. Halevy. Harvesting relational tables from lists on the web. *Proceedings of the VLDB Endowment*, 2(1):1078–1089, 2009.

[15] O. Etzioni, M. Banko, S. Soderland, and D. Weld. Open information extraction from the web. *Communications of the ACM*, 51(12):68–74, 2008.

[16] O. Etzioni, A. Fader, J. Christensen, S. Soderland, and M. Center. Open information extraction: The second generation. In *Twenty-Second International Joint Conference on Artificial Intelligence*, 2011.

[17] T. Furche, G. Gottlob, G. Grasso, Ö. Gunes, X. Guo, A. Kravchenko, G. Orsi, C. Schallhart, A. Sellers, and C. Wang. Diadem: Domain-centric, intelligent, automated data extraction methodology. 2012.

[18] T. Grigalis, L. Radvilavičius, A. Čenys, and J. Gordevičius. Clustering visually similar web page elements for structured web data extraction. *Web Engineering*, pages 435–438, 2012.

[19] P. Gulhane, A. Madaan, R. Mehta, J. Ramamirtham, R. Rastogi, S. Satpal, S. Sengamedu, A. Tengli, and C. Tiwari. Web-scale information extraction with vertex. In *Data Engineering (ICDE), 2011 IEEE 27th International Conference on*, pages 1209–1220. IEEE, 2011.

[20] C. Hsu and M. Dung. Generating finite-state transducers for semi-structured data extraction from the web. *Information systems*, 23(8):521–538, 1998.

[21] J. Jiang, X. Song, N. Yu, and C. Lin. Focus: learning to crawl web forums. *IEEE Transactions on Knowledge and Data Engineering*, 2012.

[22] N. Jindal and B. Liu. A generalized tree matching algorithm considering nested lists for web data extraction. In *The SIAM Int. Conf. on Data Mining*, pages 930–941, 2010.

[23] M. Kayed and C. Chang. Fivatech: Page-level web data extraction from template pages. *IEEE Trans. on Know. & Data Engineering*, 22(2):249–263, 2010.

[24] W. Liu, X. Meng, and W. Meng. Vide: A vision-based approach for deep web data extraction. *Knowledge and Data Engineering, IEEE Transactions on*, 22(3):447–460, 2010.

[25] G. Miao, J. Tatemura, W. Hsiung, A. Sawires, and L. Moser. Extracting data records from the web using tag path clustering. In *Proc. WWW*, pages 981–990. ACM, 2009.

[26] J. Myllymaki and J. Jackson. Robust web data extraction with xml path expressions. *IBM Research Report*, 23, 2002.

[27] W. Su, J. Wang, and F. Lochovsky. Ode: Ontology-assisted data extraction. *ACM Transactions on Database Systems (TODS)*, 34(2):12, 2009.

[28] F. Suchanek, G. Kasneci, and G. Weikum. Yago: a core of semantic knowledge. In *Proc. WWW*, pages 697–706. ACM, 2007.

[29] J. Wang, B. Shao, H. Wang, and K. Zhu. Understanding tables on the web. *Technique report. Microsoft Research Asia*, 2011.

[30] G. Weikum and M. Theobald. From information to knowledge: harvesting entities and relationships from web sources. In *Proceedings of the twenty-ninth ACM SIGMOD-SIGACT-SIGART symposium on Principles of database systems*, pages 65–76. ACM, 2010.

[31] Y. Yamada, N. Craswell, T. Nakatoh, and S. Hirokawa. Testbed for information extraction from deep web. In *Proc. WWW*, pages 346–347. ACM, 2004.

[32] Y. Zhai and B. Liu. Web data extraction based on partial tree alignment. In *Proc. WWW*, pages 76–85. ACM, 2005.

[33] H. Zhao, W. Meng, Z. Wu, V. Raghavan, and C. Yu. Fully automatic wrapper generation for search engines. In *Proc. WWW*, pages 66–75. ACM, 2005.

[34] S. Zheng, R. Song, J. Wen, and C. Giles. Efficient record-level wrapper induction. In *Proceedings of the 18th ACM conference on Information and knowledge management*, pages 47–56. ACM, 2009.

Building User Profiles to Improve User Experience in Recommender Systems

Anisio Lacerda
Univ. Federal de Minas Gerais, Brazil
and Zunnit Technologies, Brazil
anisio@dcc.ufmg.br

Advisor: Nivio Ziviani
Univ. Federal de Minas Gerais, Brazil
nivio@dcc.ufmg.br

ABSTRACT

Recommender systems are quickly becoming ubiquitous in many Web applications, including e-commerce, social media channels, content providers, among others. These systems act as an enabling mechanism designed to overcome the information overload problem by improving browsing and consumption experience. Crucial to the performance of a recommender system is the accuracy of the user profiles used to represent the interests of the users. In this proposal, we analyze three different aspects of user profiling: (i) selecting the most informative events from the interaction between users and the system, (ii) combining different recommendation algorithms to (iii) including trust-aware information in user profiles to improve the accuracy of recommender systems.

General Terms

Algorithm, Performance, Experimentation, Economics

Keywords

Recommender Systems, Novelty, Diversity

1. INTRODUCTION

Recommender systems are mechanisms devoted to overcoming problems that are inherent to information overload, providing intelligent information access and delivery, potentially improving browsing and consumption experience [10]. Recommender systems benefit from a detailed representation of the users' interests to personalize the results and improve experience. In order to understand the preferences of users, recommender systems require a proper *representation* of their interests and intents.

In this work we focus on generating compact and effective user profiles from user past behavior in recommender systems scenarios. The task of building the right profile can be divided in two phases: (i) finding the appropriate descriptive features and (ii) designing models to explore these features to achieve the systems goal. We model the input data for recommender systems as interactions between entities. The generated data are pairs of elements coming from two sets of objects called dyads [5]. Formally, the data consists of dyads $\{(r_i, c_i)\}_{i=1}^{n}$ (i.e., pairs of objects) with associated labels $\{y_i\}_{i=1}^{n}$.

WSDM'13, February 4–8, 2013, Rome, Italy.

The dyadic prediction task consists in determine labels for unobserved dyads, that is for pairs (r', c'). Given that we are interested on the interaction between users and items in recommender systems, the dyads are composed of pairs (users, items). A side-information is additional evidence for each member of a dyad. Thus, when considering a movie recommender system, age and gender are examples of side-information about users; when considering items, title and category of the movie are examples of side-information about items. For the same movie recommender system, the set of ratings for a movie is an example of labels.

An important problem related to the absence of side-information is known as cold-start problem, where the test set contains a dyad (r', c') where at least one of r' or c' is not present in any training set dyad. In recommender systems, it occurs when the system needs to predict how a user will rate a movie that is yet to be released, and thus has no existing ratings. In the following sections, we present some initial results on using the category of items to alleviate this problem.

Normally, Web dyadic data shares the following aspects [5]:

- High-dimensional: The two involved sets are often very large, e.g., the set of distinct users and all movies for (user, movie) dyadic data.
- Sparse: Measurements are sparse relative to all possible dyads, e.g., a user does not rate all movies.
- Dynamic: Web dyadic data keeps growing every single second in terms of both the observed dyads and the dimensionality, e.g., new users join movie recommender systems and rate movies they are interested all the time.

In order to alleviate these issues, we divided the task of building the user profile into two phases: (i) weighting accordingly the most descriptive dyads and (ii) designing models to explore these dyads to achieve the systems goal. We will also consider the list of items returned when extracting user preferences.

We will consider a simple method for user profile updating based on their age in the system, as we know this feature has a great influence in the user behaviour. According to [7], in recommender systems, new users have different needs from experienced users. New users may benefit from methods that generates highly ratable items, as they need to establish trust and rapport with a recommender before taking advantage of the recommendations it offers. Hence, the system needs to be able to evolve user profiles according to their needs as they age in the system.

2. OBJECTIVES

There are several tasks and challenges associated with modern recommender systems. A typical task can be stated as follows: given a set of items that are known in advance to be associated with a user (i.e., past preference data), the system must return a ranked list of suggested items, so that more interesting items appear in the top of the rank [10].

The notion of interestingness, however, may be subjective, encompassing a broad repertoire of measures, including: (i) accuracy (how well the suggested items meet the user's information need), (ii) novelty (how well the system promotes unknown items to the users), and (iii) diversity (how different the suggested items are with respect to each other). In order to find a proper balance between these metrics, we intent to: (i) select the most informativeness dyads to build the user profile, and (ii) use a linear combination of the relevance estimated by n different existing recommendation algorithms.

Recommender Systems based only on dyadic data (Collaborative Filtering – CF) rely on a simple intuition: items appreciated by people similar to someone will also be appreciated by that user. The process of comparing two users involves comparing the preferences they provided to items, which can be compromised by high-dimensional and sparse properties of the dyadic data. Our intent is to search for similar users as CF does but to search for trustable users by exploiting the social graph and incorporated this information on user profiles.

Following we summarize our research questions:

1. How can we select the most informative events to build an descriptive user profile?
2. How can we combine different algorithms to balance accuracy, novelty, and diversity?
3. How can we incorporate trust-aware network metrics in user profiles?

3. METHODOLOGY

In Table 1, we present the properties of the datasets that we will use in this research. For movie recommendation, we will use the MovieLens dataset [8]. As representative of trust-aware recommender systems we will use the Epinions dataset [6] and the Flixster dataset [13]. For music recommendation, we will use the Lastfm with an implicit preference dataset from [2].

The testing methodology we adopted in this paper is similar to the one described in [3], which is appropriate for the top-N recommendation task. For the measures of precision, recall and F1 we will use the definitions presented in [1]. In the case of implicit feedback (i.e., Last.fm), we normalized the observed item access frequencies of each user to a common rating scale [0,5], as used in [11].

In order to measure the novelty of the recommendations, we will use a popularity-based item novelty model proposed in [11], so that the probability of an item i being seen is estimated as:

$$P(seen|i_k) = \frac{|u \in U|r(u,i) \neq \emptyset|}{|U|} \quad (1)$$

where U denotes the set of users. Since the testing methodology supposes that most of the 1,000 additional unrated items are not relevant, we used the metrics in the framework proposed in [11] without relevance awareness. The novelty of a top-N recommendation list from R presented to user u is therefore given by:

$$nov(R(N)) = EPC(N) = C \sum_{i_k \in R}^{i_N} rd(k)(1 - p(seen|i_k)) \quad (2)$$

where $rd(k)$ is a rank discount given by $rd(k) = 0.85^{k-1}$[11] and C is a normalizing constant given by $1/\sum_{i_k \in R}^{i_N} rd(k)$. Therefore, this metric is rank-sensitive (i.e. the novelty of the top-rated items counts more than the novelty of other items). As is the case with precision and recall, we average the EPC@N value of the top-N recommendation lists over the test set.

We used a distance based model in order to measure the diversity of the recommendation lists. Once again, we used the metrics from [11] without relevance-awareness. The recommendation diversity, therefore, is given by:

$$div(R(N)) = EILD(N) = \sum_{\substack{i_k \in R \\ i_l \in R \\ l \neq k}}^{i_N, l_N} C_k rd(k) rd(l|k) d(i_k, i_l) \quad (3)$$

where $rd(l|k) = rd(max(1, l-k))$ reflects a relative rank discount between l and k, and $d(i_k, i_l)$ is the cosine similarity between two items, given by:

$$d(i,j) = \frac{|\mathbf{U_i} \cap \mathbf{U_j}|}{\sqrt{|\mathbf{U_i}|}\sqrt{|\mathbf{U_j}|}} \quad (4)$$

such that $\mathbf{U_i}$ denotes the users that liked item i, and $\mathbf{U_j}$ denotes the users that liked item j.

4. ANSWERING THE RESEARCH QUESTIONS

In Figure 1, we present an overview of the user profiling process, which is divided into three different steps. First, we investigate approaches to select the most informative instances to build the user profile. Second, we are interested on strategies to combine the informative selected instances and other evidence to match the most relevant items to users. Third, given that the user preferences changes over time, we investigate methods to reflect these changes.

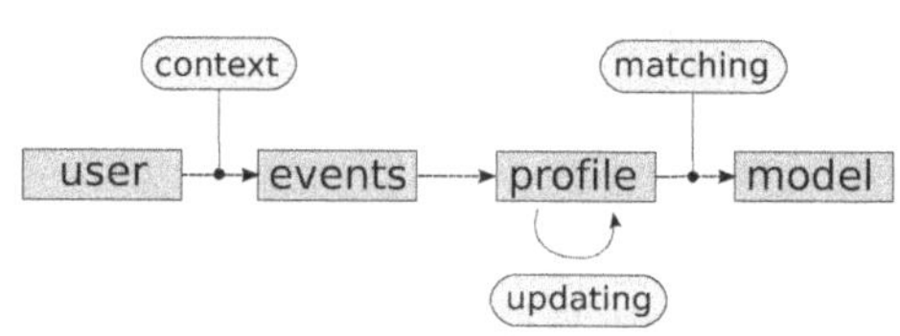

Figure 1: Overview of the user profiling process

4.1 Using Context to Select the Most Informative Events

In this section, we investigate the user context to select the most informative training instances. We start by discussing how different ranked lists are produced for each user, so that each one is particularly effective with respect to a specific interestingness measure (i.e., accuracy, diversity, or novelty). Then, we discuss a future direction to aggregate the multiple ranked lists that were produced, resulting in a final ranked list.

4.1.1 Related Work

In [2], the authors introduced the notion of "topic diversification", which ensures diversity by balancing suggestions across different topics. In terms of novelty, we adopt a metric that is closer to the metric proposed in [3], which assumes that less popular items are less likely to be widely known by users, and thus a penalty is imposed depending on the frequency or popularity of the suggested items.

Table 1: Statistics of Datasets.

	Datasets			
	Movielens	Epinions	Flixster	Lastfm
# users	6,040	49,290	1,000,000	992
# items	3,883	139,738	49,000	1,300,000
# preferences	1,000,209	664,824	8,200,000	19,150,868
Trust statements	–	487,181	26,700,000	–
Rating range	1 - 5	1 - 5	0.5 - 5.0	–
Feedback	Explicit	Explicit	Explicit	Implicit

4.1.2 Learning Optimal Ranked Lists for Multi-Objective Recommender Systems

The first step of our approach consists in performing consecutive queries over a large set of events E, where each event $x \in E$ consists of a set of (user, item) dyads and the respective labels. Each query selects an event in E exhibiting a property P which is related to a specific interestingness measure M. The selected event is appended into the training-set D, which represents the user profile, and a classifier is updated accordingly. This querying procedure iterates selecting examples that exhibit the desired property and updating the classifier, until a desired level of performance is achieved.

We used three different query strategies to select examples from E: (i) *accuracy-oriented*: the event selected is the one that the classifier is more uncertainty about, *diversity-oriented*: selects examples from E that are not redundant with respect to events already included into D, and *novelty-oriented*: selects events from E for which the corresponding topk items are less popular.

The baselines used were a naive recommendation approach ("most popular") as a lower bound, and we expect that all proposed approaches outperform this naive approach in all evaluation metrics considered. Further, we also employ a strong baseline, WRMF [4], which is a state-of-the-art weighted matrix factorization approach. We conducted five-fold cross validation, and the results reported for each evaluated recommendation approach correspond to the av- erage of the five trials. Statistical significance tests were performed using a 2–sided paired t–test with p–value < 0.05.

In Table 2 we show the results obtained by each evaluated recommendation approach in the MovieLens subsets. As expected, suggesting only the most popular items leads to poor recommendation performance in all evaluation metrics. In contrast, WRMF was the best performer in terms of precision. It outperformed our accuracy-oriented approach, with differences that are up to 7.6%. Closer recommendation performance was obtained only at p@10 and for subsets composed of moderate and large number of tags per object.

On the other hand, WRMF performed extremely poor in terms of diversity and novelty. This trend holds for all three subsets. As expected, our diversity-oriented approach was the best performer in terms of diversity, and our novelty-oriented approach was the best performer in terms of novelty. Also, the precision achieved by our diversity- and novelty-oriented approaches was much higher than the precision achieved by the naive ("most popular") approach.

4.2 Combining Different Algorithms to Balance Accuracy, Novelty, and Diversity

In this section, we investigate the hypothesize that it is possible to properly aggregate different recommendation algorithms, so that the resulting hybrids balances the level of accuracy, diversity and novelty in its suggestions.

4.2.1 Related Work

Historically, the typical goal of a recommender system is to maximize accuracy as much as possible in predicting and matching user information needs, often by considering individual delivered items in isolation [10]. More recently, however, it has become a consensus that the success of a recommender system depends on other dimensions of information utility, notably the diversity and novelty of the suggestions performed by the system [10]. More specifically, even being accurate, obvious and monotonous recommendations are generally of little use, since they do not expose users to unprecedent experiences. In the rest of this section we present previous related work, detail the current state of our work[1], and finally discuss the ongoing research.

4.2.2 Pareto-Eficient Hybrid Algorithm to Combine Recommender Systems

In order to provide suggestions that accounts for accuracy, diversity, and novelty, we investigate a hybrid recommendation approach that combines well-established recommendation algorithms (e.g., simple algorithms as well as representative of the state-of-the-art). Our proposed hybridization approach consists in finding appropriate weights for the constituent algorithms. By considering each dimension (i.e., accuracy, novelty and diversity) as a separate objective, we reduce the hybridization task to a multi-objective optimization problem, in which we search for the optimal combination of weights that maximizes accuracy, diversity and novelty.

Since the considered objectives are potentially conflicting, we employ an evolutionary search for optimal hybrids. Evolutionary algorithms denote a class of optimization methods that are characterized by a set of candidate solutions (aka individuals) called a population, which is maintained during the entire optimization process. The population of individuals evolves towards better (and potentially optimal) solutions by employing genetic operators, such as reproduction, mutation and crossover. In our context, each individual represents a possible combination of weights (i.e., a possible hybrid).

Optimal hybrids lie in the so-called Pareto frontier [15], and are optimal in the sense that no hybrid in the frontier can be improved upon without hurting at least one of its objectives. Therefore, the evolutionary algorithm evolves the population towards producing hybrids that are located closer to the Pareto frontier, and then a linear search returns

[1]A detailed version of the current state is presented in [9].

Table 2: Recommendation effectiveness for different subsets of the MovieLens dataset.

Approach	Precision			Diversity			Novelty		
	p@3	p@5	p@10	d@3	d@5	d@10	n@3	n@5	n@10
most popular	.244	.212	.169	.350	.365	.391	.026	.071	.232
WRMF	.352	.319	.241	.377	.392	.413	.290	.391	.545
accuracy-oriented	.332	.307	.226	.418	.434	.451	.332	.449	.607
diversity-oriented	.319	.304	.217	.442	.455	.475	.340	.455	.614
novelty-oriented	.274	.238	.196	.422	.451	.473	.358	.469	.629

the most dominant hybrid [15], which is likely to balance accuracy, novelty and diversity.

We conducted a systematic evaluation involving different recommendation scenarios, with explicit user feedback (i.e., movies from the MovieLens dataset). We selected eight recommendation algorithms to provide the base for our hybrids. To represent latent factor models, we selected PureSVD with 50 and 150 factors (PureSVD50 and PureSVD150) [3]. As a baseline for constituent method we used "MostPopular". As hybrid baseline, we used a voting-based hybrid based on Borda-Count (BC) and STREAM as baseline, a stacking-based approach with additional meta-features.

In Table 3 we show the accuracy results (recall and precision) over different values of N. Since both EPC(novelty) and EILD(diversity) are rank-sensitive metrics, we only presented their values for N = 20. There is a clear compromise between accuracy, novelty and diversity of these algorithms. The constituent algorithm that provides the most accurate recommendations is PureSVD50. TopPop provided the most diverse recommendations, although it performs significantly worse in accuracy and novelty. Regarding the performance of the baselines in the MovieLens dataset, STREAM performs worse then PureSVD50 on accuracy, maintaining the same level of novelty and performing better in terms of diversity. Borda Count performed poorly on accuracy and reasonably well in terms of novelty and diversity.

We compared PO-acc (Pareto-Optimal Accuracy) with PureSVD50, which is the stand-alone algorithm with the most accurate recommendations. PO-acc performs much better on diversity (and equally well on novelty). We compared PO-nov (Pareto-Optimal Novelty) with Pure-SVD150, which presented the most novel recommendations to the users, with reasonable accuracy. PO-nov performs slightly better on novelty than PureSVD150, but performs much better in terms of accuracy, and slightly on diversity. Finally, we compared PO-div (Pareto-Optimal Diversity) with MostPopular, the algorithm with the most diverse recommendations. PO-div loses very slightly on diversity, while improving on accuracy and novelty.

Hybrids in the Pareto frontier can be selected according to a certain need, allowing the recommender system to adjust the compromise between accuracy, novelty and diversity, so that the recommendation emphasis can be adapted dynamically according to the needs of each user (i.e., new users may benefit more from more accurate suggestions, whereas older users may require more novel and diversified suggestions). The ongoing research on these topic is to determine the exact moment during the user life-time usage of recommender system that is more appropriate to provide more diversified or novel items. In other words, we are interested on precisely identify the moment that users are more open to receive diversified results.

4.3 Incorporating Trust-Aware Metrics in User Profiles

In this section we present our proposal for enhancing Recommender Systems by use of trust information in the Slope One algorithm. In Section 1, we mentioned that web dyadic data shares some important aspects, high-dimensionality, sparsity, and dynamics. In other words, in popular domains such as movies, the number of items is very large while the number of items rated by every single user is in general small. This means that it is very unlikely two random users have rated any items in common and hence they are not comparable. In order to alleviate this problem we investigate a method to incorporate trust information into the user profiles. The rest of this section is organized as follows, first we briefly present the Slope One Algorithm and an extension known as Weighted Slope One. Then we show the current state of our research and discuss the results. Finally, we present the ongoing research path that we intent to follow.

4.3.1 Related Work

There are also other variants of the Slope One algorithm in the literature. For example, in [12], the authors propose an algorithm based on Slope One and user-based collaborative filtering to improve the recommendation performance of the second one. This approach addresses the issue by using the Slope One to fill the missing ratings and then using the user-based collaborative filtering to produce recommendations. Zhang [14] applies the Slope One algorithm in the same way as[12]. The difference between both approaches is that the first one uses an item-based collaborative algorithm to perform the recommendations.

4.3.2 A Collaborative Filtering Method Using User Trust-Aware Evidences in Slope One Algorithm

In order to incorporate trust information in the user profiles, we investigate an appropriate method to extend the Slope One, which is a family of algorithms for collaborative filtering, introduced in [12]. The Slope One basic principle is of "popularity differencial" between users and items. In a pairwise fashion, it determines how much better one item is liked than another. In order to measure this differential it subtracts the average rating of the two items. In turn, this difference can be used to predict another userâĂŹs rating of one of those items, given their rating of the other. We choose the Slope One algorithm because it is easy to extend and provide competitive suggestions.

One of the drawbacks of Slope One is that the number of ratings observed is not taken into consideration. Thus, we proposes variants of the Weighted Slope One, which performs predictions based on the items already rated by the user and these items are always equally considered. Specifically, we investigate the use of a measure of personalized item prediction efficiency for users, which is named as item

Table 3: Results for Recommendation Algorithms on the MovieLens dataset, with the three objectives (i.e., accuracy, novelty, and diversity). The recommender methods variants are grouped into: (i) constituent algorithms, (ii) hybrid baselines, and (iii) our proposed hybrids. We used the symbols: †, •, ⋄ to point out our method and the respective baseline. For instance, PSVD150 is the baseline with respect to the selected PO-nov individual. For each group, the best results for each metric are in bold. Underlined values means that the selected individual and the respective baseline are statistically different (95%).

		Accuracy								Novelty	Diversity
	Algorithm	R@1	R@5	R@10	R@20	P@1	P@5	P@10	P@20	EPC@20	EILD@20
Consts.	PSVD50 †	**0.1900**	**0.4155**	**0.5402**	**0.6643**	**0.1900**	**0.0831**	**0.0540**	**0.0332**	0.8070	0.1667
	PSVD150 •	0.1237	0.3203	0.4450	0.5658	0.1237	0.0641	0.0445	0.0283	0.8519	0.1375
	TopPop ⋄	0.0722	0.2061	0.2895	0.3994	0.0722	0.0412	0.0289	0.0200	0.7079	**0.2598**
Baselines	STREAM	**0.1792**	**0.3961**	**0.5169**	**0.6426**	**0.1792**	**0.0792**	**0.0517**	**0.0321**	0.8078	0.1914
	BC	0.0473	0.1657	0.2639	0.4352	0.0473	0.0331	0.0264	0.0218	**0.8210**	0.1609
	EW	0.1562	0.3574	0.4752	0.5980	0.1562	0.0715	0.0475	0.0299	0.7441	**0.2284**
Our Hybs	PO-acc †	**0.1999**	**0.4227**	**0.5432**	**0.6705**	**0.1999**	**0.0845**	**0.0543**	**0.0335**	0.7977	0.1897
	PO-nov •	0.1513	0.3725	0.4854	0.6111	0.1513	0.0745	0.0485	0.0306	**0.8597**	0.1411
	PO-div ⋄	0.0820	0.2271	0.3269	0.4470	0.0820	0.0454	0.0327	0.0223	0.7138	**0.2563**

usefulness, as a component of the weighting system of the Weighted Slope One algorithm. We propose to use the concept of web of trust to compute the weights [6].

We compare the Weighted Slope One (WSO) with our four proposed strategies: (i) Input Degree Based Slope One (IDSO), relies on the number of users that trusts on the active user; (ii) Linear Item Usefulness Slope One algorithm (LIUSO), relies on the linear difference between the maximum mean average error (MAE) and the MAE of the current item; (iii) Exponential Item Usefulness Slope One algorithm (EIUSO), relies on the exponential value of the previous difference; (iv) Mixed Slope One (MSO), is a linear combination of the previous strategies.

Table 4: Results for Flixster dataset

Threshold	Metric	WSO	IDSO	LIUSO	EIUSO
4	MAE	.741	1.954	.734	.714
	RMSE	1.059	2.499	1.056	1.058
	Precision	81.2%	59.8%	80.7%	79.2%
	Recall	42.0%	33.3%	44.2%	50.2%
	F1	55.4%	42.7%	54.8%	61.5%
	Gain (F1)	–	−12.7%	−0.6%	6.1%
Mean	MAE	.741	1.954	.747	0.714
	RMSE	1.059	2.499	1.068	1.058
	Precision	60.4%	52.1%	59.2%	61.2%
	Recall	53.8%	37.6%	52.5%	69.2%
	F1	56.9%	43.7%	55.6%	64.9%
	Gain (F1)	–	−13.2%	−1.3%	8.0%

In Table [4], we show the results obtained by each method in the Flixster dataset. Note that we split the experiment into two subsets by considering only ratings greater than 4 and ratings greater than the mean of all ratings. All results are statistically significant. The IDBSO method was poor in all thresholds considered. On the other hand, the IDBSO, EIUSO, and MSO methods perform better than baseline from 2.2% to 6.%.

5. CONTRIBUTIONS

By addressing the research topics, this work foresees the following contributions:

- A set of new performance-oriented approaches that produce ranked lists of suggested items that are either accurate, diverse and novel.
- A hybridization technique for combining different recommendation algorithms, following the Strength Pareto approach.
- A set of methods to incorporate trust information in Collaborative Filtering systems.

6. REFERENCES

[1] R. Baeza-Yates and B. Ribeiro-Neto. *Modern Information Retrieval (Second edition)*. Pearson, 2011.

[2] O. Celma and P. Herrera. A new approach to evaluating novel recommendations. In *ACM RecSys*, pages 179–186, 2008.

[3] P. Cremonesi, Y. Koren, and R. Turrin. Performance of recommender algorithms on top-n recommendation tasks. In *RecSys*, pages 39–46, 2010.

[4] Y. Hu, Y. Koren, and C. Volinsky. Collaborative filtering for implicit feedback datasets. In *Proceedings of the 8th IEEE International Conference on Data Mining*, pages 263–272, 2008.

[5] D. Kenny, D. Kashy, william Cook, and J. Simpson. *Dyadic Data Analysis*. The Guilford Press, 2006.

[6] P. Massa and P. Avesani. Trust-aware bootstrapping of recommender systems. In *ECAI Workshop on Recommender Systems*, pages 29–33, 2006.

[7] S. McNee, J. Riedl, and J. Konstan. Being accurate is not enough: how accuracy metrics have hurt recommender systems. In *CHI Extended Abstract*, pages 1097–1101, 2006.

[8] B. N. Miller, I. Albert, S. K. Lam, J. A. Konstan, and J. Riedl. Movielens unplugged: experiences with an occasionally connected recommender system. In *IUI*, pages 263–266, 2003.

[9] M. T. Ribeiro, A. Lacerda, A. Veloso, and Z. Nivio. Pareto-efficient hybridization for multi-objective recommender systems. In *ACM RecSys*, pages 9–16, 2012.

[10] F. Ricci, L. Rokach, B. Shapira, and P. B. Kantor, editors. *Recommender Systems Handbook*. Springer, 2011.

[11] S. Vargas and P. Castells. Rank and relevance in novelty and diversity metrics for recommender systems. In *ACM RecSys*, pages 109–116, 2011.

[12] P. Wang and H. Ye. A personalized recommendation algorithm combining slope one scheme and user based collaborative filtering. In *ISECS*, pages 152–154, 2009.

[13] R. Zafarani and H. Liu. Social computing data repository at ASU, 2009.

[14] D. Zhang. An item-based collaborative filtering recommendation algorithm using slope one scheme smoothing. In *ISECS*, pages 215–217, 2009.

[15] E. Zitzler and L. Thiele. Multi-objective evolutionary algorithms: a comparative case study and the strength pareto approach. *IEEE Trans. on Evolutionary Computation*, 3(4):257–271, 1999.

Web Usage Mining for Enhancing Search-Result Delivery and Helping Users to Find Interesting Web Content

Ida Mele
Sapienza, University of Rome
Rome, Italy
mele@dis.uniroma1.it

ABSTRACT

Web usage mining is the application of data mining techniques to the data generated by the interactions of users with web servers. This kind of data, stored in server logs, represents a valuable source of information, which can be exploited to optimize the document-retrieval task, or to better understand, and thus, satisfy user needs.

Our research focuses on two important issues: improving search-engine performance through static caching of search results, and helping users to find interesting web pages by recommending news articles and blog posts.

Concerning the static caching of search results, we present the *query covering* approach. The general idea is to populate the cache with those documents that contribute to the result pages of a large number of queries, as opposed to caching the top documents of most frequent queries.

For the recommendation of web pages, we present a graph-based approach, which leverages the user-browsing logs to identify *early adopters*. These users discover interesting content before others, and monitoring their activity we can find web pages to recommend.

Categories and Subject Descriptors

H.3.3 [**Information Search and Retrieval**]: [Information filtering][Search process]; H.2.8 [**Database Applications**]: [Data mining]

General Terms

Algorithms; Experimentation.

Keywords

Web usage mining; Caching; Recommendation.

1. MOTIVATIONS FOR THE RESEARCH

The World Wide Web gives an abundance of information to the users, and this makes the identification of relevant content difficult. Web mining tries to address this problem. It consists in the application of machine learning and data mining techniques, which allow the automatic extraction of meaningful patterns and relationships from large collections of web data. Web mining can be divided into three main subareas: (*i*) *web content mining*, which infers knowledge from the content (i.e. text and graphics) of web pages, (*ii*) *web structure mining*, which extracts information from data describing the organization of web content, and (*iii*) *web usage mining*, which captures usage patterns by analyzing data generated from the interactions of the users with the Web. There is not a clear-cut distinction among these categories, and all three mining tasks can be combined.

Our research work is strongly related to the field of web usage mining. In particular, we exploit the implicit information given by users, that are stored in query and browsing-activity logs, in order to help web users to find information easily and quickly. The contributions we propose are twofold: First, we face the problem of improving search-engine performance. Second, we tackle the problem of page recommendation.

Improving search-engine performance. Optimization of search-engine performance is obviously of paramount importance, given that a typical search engine receives a huge number of queries every second, and users expect very low response times. To this end, search engines employ a variety of caching techniques as a means to provide results timely and with minimal reduction in quality. Several works suggest using a static cache of documents. This cache stores results that are relevant to the most frequent queries [23, 12]. Although this approach is very simple, it may require a lot of cache space. In our research work, we propose strategies for optimizing the space utilization of the static cache.

Web-page recommendation. Search engines help people to search for information on the Internet, but the web search is effective only when the users have a clear idea of what they want. Often, people have no specific information need, for example they surf the Web to read news, interesting blog posts, etc. Recommender systems produce suggestions, and they are effective in static and relatively noise-free environments. The design of recommender systems for web content poses significant challenges due to the dynamic nature of web pages, and the high level of noise introduced by the analysis of the user-browsing data. We handle these problems by proposing a graph-based approach, which allows to find interesting news articles soon in order to recommend them to the web users.

WSDM'13, February 4–8, 2013, Rome, Italy.

2. RELATED WORK

In this Section, we present the state of the art for the main topics of our research.

Web usage mining. Web usage mining aims to capture, model, and analyze the behavioral patterns and profiles of users interacting with the Web. Data stored in usage logs can be used for solving navigational problem [24], improving web search [3], recommending queries [5], suggesting authoritative web sites [22], and enhancing performance of search engines [23]. A good survey of web usage mining can be found in [21].

Query-log analysis. Several studies have analyzed query-log data to understand the behavior of search-engine users. In [20], Spink et al. point out that users tend to submit short queries and look at few pages of results. They prefer to refine queries rather than to navigate answer pages deeper, and they do not exploit advanced search features.

Another important finding is that the frequency of queries is power-law distributed: a lot of queries are submitted once or twice, while a few queries are submitted many times [19]. These queries are also popular, so they are shared by different users reflecting a *spatial locality* in the query stream [23]. Further studies emphasize a *temporal locality* in query stream: repeated submissions of queries on the same topic are separated by a small number of other queries [15, 12].

Caching of query results. The locality properties, observed in the query stream, suggest caching pre-computed answers or partial data used in the computation of new answers. The work [17] exploits frequent queries to enhance the retrieval process. However, the simple popularity-based cache may poorly address the issue of temporal locality [15]. In [12], the authors present a *Static-Dynamic Cache (SDC)*, where the static portion has fixed entries to store results of most frequent queries, and the dynamic portion is managed by a replacement policy to intercept the variations in the query stream. In [4], the authors study the impact of the tail of the query distribution on caches of search engines.

Diversification of search results. Result diversification is of use for *ambiguous queries* (e.g., "python") and *broad queries* with many potential user intents (e.g., "java programming language"). Some diversification strategies are based on removing documents that are similar in order to avoid the redundancy of information [6, 8]. Others make explicit use of the knowledge about the different topics covered by queries and documents [1, 7].

Web-page recommendation. Recommender systems allow to learn user preferences and to make recommendations. They can be employed to recommend products (e.g., books, movies, music, etc.) and web content (e.g., news, photos, etc.). Recommender systems can be: (*i*) *content based*, the system recommends items similar to the ones the user preferred in the past, (*ii*) *collaborative-filtering based*, the system recommends items that people with similar tastes liked in the past, and (*iii*) *hybrid*, the system combines content and collaborative-filtering based methods.

In the last years, a lot of attention has been devoted to the recommendation of web news. In [18], the authors present a recommender system based on human judgments. In [11], Das et al. identify clusters of users with similar interests by exploiting the user-click data.

3. PROPOSED RESEARCH

In this Section, we describe the research issues which we want to focus on. Then, we present our approaches to address these issues, and we show some preliminary results, which corroborate our proposals.

3.1 Improving search-engine performance

Every day millions of users submit queries to search engines and the amount of data involved in processing a query is huge. The users desire to receive a list of relevant and authoritative results rapidly, therefore the search engines employ caching techniques to provide high quality results in short time.

Modern search engines cache posting lists of most frequent query terms or the results of the queries. In the second case, depending on the available space, the cache can store the entire page of results or single documents. A drawback of the latter approach with respect to the former is that query response times will be higher, since result pages must be constructed by using the documents in cache. On the other hand, this approach presents the advantage that the same document can be used to serve multiple queries, so that the cache space is used efficiently. The search-result cache can be *static* or *dynamic*, and a combination of both techniques can be employed [12]. The static cache is subject to periodical updates and the documents to cache are precomputed using historical information. The dynamic cache stores results according to the query sequence.

For our research work, we consider the scenario of the static caching of query results, where the cache stores single documents (snippet and satellite information returned to users in response to their queries). We propose *query covering* as a strategy for effectively and efficiently caching results of queries. The idea is to use statistical information about the user-querying behavior, so as to populate the cache with a set of documents that in the average will maximize the number of queries that are entirely served by the cache. We examine the problem of query covering under a simple information retrieval model, in which each document is either relevant or irrelevant to a query [2]. Then, we improve this approach by proposing a weighted version of query covering, where weights capture the degree of relevance of the documents to the queries. The weighted approach selects high-ranked documents, which appear in the result lists of several queries. This allows to optimize the cache space, ensuring the quality of the results. Finally, we prove that the weighted approach can be used for different purposes, such as the diversification of cached documents.

3.1.1 Approach

We consider a simple framework in which users submit queries to a document retrieval system over time. The document retrieval system hosts a document collection. In addition, to improve response time, the system uses a document cache. Whenever a query is submitted, the system checks the cache, if all requested documents are stored in the cache, the system builds the final page of results, otherwise it incurs a *cache miss*, that is, a penalty reflecting that the system has to carry out a time-expensive operation, such as the retrieval of documents from the document collection.

We assume that we have full knowledge of the document set, and in particular we know what documents are relevant to what queries. Furthermore, we assume to have no knowledge about queries that will be submitted in the future, but we have a relatively good estimate of their distribution. We want to create a universal map from each query to a set of relevant documents for the query, so that, when a query is issued, the system can fetch the documents from the cache and use them to serve the current query as well as possibly future ones.

The problem can be seen as a *stochastic* generalization of the *set cover problem* [14], in which elements correspond to queries and documents correspond to sets. We need to define a fixed mapping from elements to covering sets without knowledge of the elements to cover, since we have no a priori knowledge of the future queries.

Our theoretical finding is that knowing the query distribution suffices to provide algorithms with logarithmic approximations of the optimal solution. In [2], we prove that there exists a set of documents that covers a large fraction of the queries and a simple greedy approach is able to find it. Moreover, we present a greedy algorithm, which selects the most cost-effective documents, namely, the documents appearing in the result lists of a large number of uncovered queries. This greedy algorithm ignores the degree of relevance of the document to the query. Hence, we propose to overcome this limitation by using a new approach, which associates weights to query-document pairs.

The weighted version of the greedy algorithm gives preference to the documents that cover the largest *total weight* among the uncovered queries. We believe that the weighted approach is general and versatile, and it may be used for different optimization criteria by suitably defining weights. In particular, we propose two definitions of weights:

- **Document relevance.** The weights reflect the degree of relevance of the document to the query. The weight of the document d for the query q decreases as the position of d in the result list of q increases.
- **Document diversification.** We want to cache documents maximizing the coverage of all possible intents behind user queries. Hence, the weight of a document depends on the position of the document within the result list and on the extent to which the document covers different intents for the query. Following Capannini et al. [7], we interpret the specializations of a given query as possible subtopics (intents) of that query. The weight of the document d for the query q is computed as the sum of the values of its *utility score* for every specialization q' of q, each weighted by the probability of that transition between q and q'. The utility score captures the similarity between the document, that is a result of the query, and each document appearing in the result list of the query specializations.

3.1.2 Experiments

For the experiments, we use a real-world query log dataset. We split the dataset into time periods (e.g., one day or one week). Queries submitted in the ith time period form the *training set*, and they are used to learn the query distribution and to select a static collection of documents for the cache. Queries of the $(i+1)$th time period, constitute the *test set*, and they are exploited to assess the performance of the query covering approach.

To evaluate the performance we use: (*i*) `recall`, the percentage of queries from test set covered by cached documents, (*ii*) `num_doc`, the number of cached documents, and (*iii*) `p@n` (precision-at-n), given a query in the test set, it is the proportion of the top-n results that are found in the cache. Then, we compute the average over all covered queries from test set.

We denote with `Unweighted`, the implementation of the greedy algorithm presented in [2]. For the weighted approach, we propose to design two different implementations which correspond to different definitions of covering: the query is covered if the overall weight of its results is at least a given threshold W (`Threshold` algorithm), or if the number of results is at least a given cardinality k (`Cardinality` algorithm). We compare the performance of our approaches against Top$k$ performance. Top$k$ selects first k results for most frequent queries. This approach is naïve, but it gives us an upper bound of the coverage that can be achieved with a given collection of documents.

The preliminary results of `recall` and `num_doc` for $k = 10$, and $W = 10.0$, varying the percentage of queries from training set we desire to cover, are shown in Figure 1(a) and (b). As expected Top$k$ has the best recall, however greedy approaches are following closely. Moreover, if we observe the dimension of the cache, for Top$k$ the required space grows linearly with the number of queries in the training set that are covered, while the `num_doc` is optimized with covering approaches, for which we observe a steep increase after 40% of covered queries. This leads us to an important observation: we can just cover a smaller fraction of queries from training set, for example 30% or 40%, to have a good recall and at the same time a limited utilization of cache space.

The precision (`p@n`) is the proportion of the top-n results found in the cache. In Figure 1(c) is reported the `p@n`, for $n = 5, 10$, of the covered queries from the test set. As expected, good precisions are achieved with Top$k$, `Threshold` and `Cardinality`, while `Unweighted` performs worse.

The performance of the diversification approach are evaluated following the guidelines of the *TREC* Diversity Task [9]. We consider two intent-aware metrics: α-NDCG [10] with $\alpha = 0.5$ and IA-P [1]. The greedy approach allows to achieve good values of intent-aware metrics, and at the same time it saves a lot of cache space. In particular, the cache usage is approximately one order of magnitude less than the naïve heuristic.

3.2 Web-page recommendation

The systems for web-page recommendation are based on collaborative-filtering approaches. The underlying idea is to exploit the user-browsing logs (e.g. the click information), in order to identify users with similar interests and tastes [11]. These recommender systems deal with very high levels of noise, since visiting a web page is not a clear indication of interest as renting a DVD or buying a book. Further, the web pages to recommend are not an input of the recommendation algorithm, and the systems have to discover the interesting pages to recommend. We address these issues by leveraging not only the user similarity, but also the *latent temporal patterns* of user visits to web pages. In [16], we present a graph-based approach called *early-adopter graph*. We propose to use this graph to identify those users who discover interesting pages before others. These users are called *early adopters*, a term we borrow from social sciences,

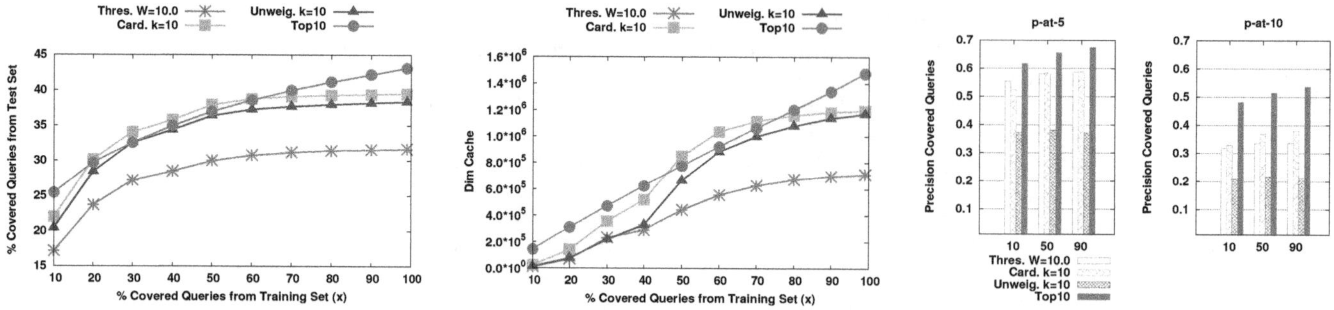

(a) Recall (b) Dim. Cache (c) Precision

Figure 1: Recall, dimension of the cache, and precision-at-n vs. % of covered queries of training set.

economics, and marketing research, in which early adopters are people who embrace new technologies before others, buy new products soon after their release, and play an important role in influencing others to adopt innovations. By tracking the browsing activity of early adopters we can identify new interesting pages early, and recommend these pages to users who share interests with the early adopters. In particular, we consider news and blog pages, as these pages are more dynamic and more appropriate for recommendation tasks.

3.2.1 Approach

The early-adopter graph G is an attributed, directed and weighted graph, where nodes correspond to users and an edge between two users, u and v, expresses the fact that the two users visited the same page and that the *temporal* rule "*u visited the page before v*" holds. We build the graph by extracting from a toolbar log the triples (u, p, t), where: (i) u is the anonymous identifier of the user, (ii) p is the url of the visited page, and (iii) t is the timestamp of the visit of u at p. Given a page p_j, we organize the visits that p_j received by all users in a chronologically-sorted access list $A(p_j) : \langle(u_1, t_{1j}), (u_2, t_{2j}), \ldots, (u_n, t_{nj})\rangle$, where t_{ij} is the timestamp of the first visit of user i to the page j. Obviously, the early adopters tend to appear at the beginning of the access list. We propose different measures of the early adoption. More in detail, the early-adopter score $\sigma(u)$ is computed by considering the position of the user in the access list (*relative position*), or the timestamp of the visit (*time distance*). In both cases, the more a user u exhibits an early-adopter behavior, the higher is the value of $\sigma(u)$. Furthermore, we model each user u by a topic distribution $\vec{\theta}_u$: given a set of topics T, the z-th coordinate θ_{uz} denotes the interest of the user u in the topic $z \in T$, and it is computed using the empirical frequency that a user visits the pages whose topic is z.

The edge weight $w(u, v)$ represents the likelihood that a page visited by u is then visited by v. We propose and evaluate different edge-weighting schemes to compute the strength of the connections. The definitions of the edge weights are inspired by the *Bernoulli* and *Jaccard* measures described in [13]. The Bernoulli measure interprets each visit of u to a page as a hypothetical attempt of u to influence v in visiting the same page. The Jaccard measure considers also the pages visited by v and not by u, and it captures whether v follows *mostly* the actions of u and not many more.

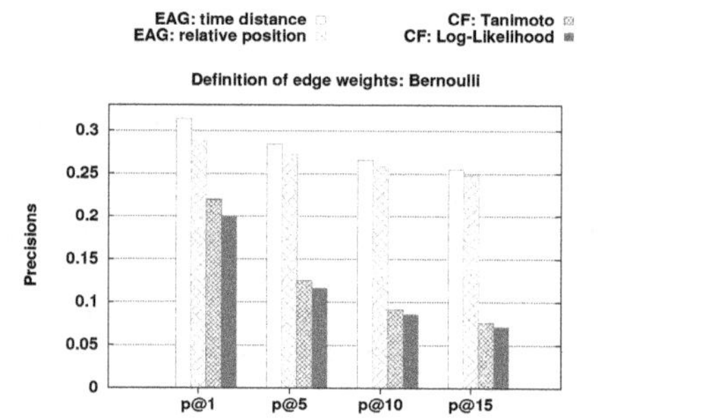

Figure 2: Precision of recommendations: early-adopter graph (EAG) vs. collaborative-filtering approaches (CF).

Our recommendation approach leverages the information found in the early-adopter graph G. Given an arc (u, v) we consider suggesting to user v pages that have been visited by the user u. To improve the relevance of our recommendations, we rank recommendations by using the early-adopter score $\sigma(u)$ of the user u from whom the recommendation originates, as well as the edge weight $w(u, v)$. Additionally, we use page topics to boost scores of pages whose topics match the interests of the user v. When a page p is suggested to v by different early adopters, the final *recommendation score* $s(v, p)$ is the sum of the contributions of the early adopters for the user v.

3.2.2 Experiments

We evaluate our recommendation algorithm using *Yahoo! Toolbar* dataset. We split our dataset, at the level of pages, in two portions: *training* and *test* sets. The training subset is used to build the early-adopter graph, learn the early-adopter scores, and the topics of interests of the users.

Given a user v and the set of v's early-adopters, namely, the in-neighborhood of v $(N^-(v))$, the algorithm recommends to v the pages visited by $u \in N^-(v)$. Then, it ranks the pages by the recommendation scores.

The recommendations are evaluated with `precision-at-k` (`p@k`) for $k = 1, 5, 10, 15$, which gives an indication of the percentage of recommended pages that are actually visited by v. As we can see from Figure 2, the resulting system outperforms other out-of-the-shelf recommendation systems based on collaborative filtering, and where the user similarity is given by *Tanimoto* or *Log-Likelihood* coefficients.

4. OPEN RESEARCH ISSUES

Open problems are related to the optimization of search-engine performance. First, it would be interesting to design and analyze a dynamic caching policy able to cope with *spikes* in the query distribution. These spikes could be due to sudden events. Second, we propose to create a two-level static cache, where a first-level cache stores documents relevant to most frequent queries, while a second-level cache stores documents chosen by the weighted greedy approach.

For the diversification purpose, we aspire to find a dynamic approach which decrements the weights of documents that satisfy topics already covered, in order to favor those documents that are relevant to uncovered topics.

Moreover, we propose to investigate the application of covering approaches to the optimization of other aspects of the web search. For example, an important search functionality is represented by the *phrase queries*. Such queries are characterized by quotation marks, and can be issued to the search engine in order to find documents that contain an exact sequence of words. The standard way to process a phrase query is using an index with positional information. However, processing phrase queries is complex and rather expensive, especially if the phrase presents *stop words*, which cannot be ignored. There are different techniques to optimize the phrase-query processing, and one of them is using a *phrase index*. For large collection of documents, indexing all possible phrases is prohibitive, and a challenging task consists in identifying the set of phrases to index. We believe that the covering strategies can help to take this decision: given a set of possible queries, we extract phrases from them, and then we can use a greedy approach to identify those phrases which cover as many queries as possible. These phrases represent good candidates to be indexed.

Concerning the early-adopter graph, we plan to use different influence models to learn the edge weights. Then, we would like to investigate the application of the early-adopter model to other domains.

5. REFERENCES

[1] R. Agrawal, S. Gollapudi, A. Halverson, and S. Ieong. Diversifying search results. In *WSDM*, 2009.

[2] A. Anagnostopoulos, L. Becchetti, S. Leonardi, I. Mele, and P. Sankowski. Stochastic query covering. In *WSDM*, 2011.

[3] R. Baeza-Yates, C. Hurtado, and M. Mendoza. Improving search engines by query clustering. *J. Am. Soc. Inf. Sci. Technol.*, 58(12):1793–1804, 2007.

[4] R. Baeza-Yates, F. Junqueira, V. Plachouras, and H. F. Witschel. Admission policies for caches of search engine results. In *SPIRE*, 2007.

[5] P. Boldi, F. Bonchi, C. Castillo, D. Donato, A. Gionis, and S. Vigna. The query-flow graph: model and applications. In *CIKM*, 2008.

[6] A. Bookstein. Information retrieval: A sequential learning process. *Journal of the American Society for Information Science*, 34(5):331–342, 1983.

[7] G. Capannini, F. M. Nardini, R. Perego, and F. Silvestri. Efficient diversification of web search results. *Proc. VLDB Endow.*, 4:451–459, 2011.

[8] J. Carbonell and J. Goldstein. The use of MMR, diversity-based reranking for reordering documents and producing summaries. In *SIGIR*, 1998.

[9] C. L. Clarke, N. Craswell, and I. Soboroff. Overview of the TREC 2009 Web Track. In *TREC*, 2009.

[10] C. L. Clarke, M. Kolla, G. V. Cormack, O. Vechtomova, A. Ashkan, S. Büttcher, and I. MacKinnon. Novelty and diversity in information retrieval evaluation. In *SIGIR*, 2008.

[11] A. Das, M. Datar, A. Garg, and S. Rajaram. Google news personalization: scalable online collaborative filtering. In *WWW*, 2007.

[12] T. Fagni, R. Perego, F. Silvestri, and S. Orlando. Boosting the performance of web search engines: Caching and prefetching query results by exploiting historical usage data. *ACM Trans. Inf. Syst.*, 24(1):51–78, 2006.

[13] A. Goyal, F. Bonchi, and L. V. S. Lakshmanan. Learning influence probabilities in social networks. In *WSDM*, 2010.

[14] F. Grandoni, A. Gupta, S. Leonardi, P. Miettinen, P. Sankowski, and M. Singh. Set covering with our eyes closed. In *FOCS '08*, pages 347–356. IEEE Computer Society, 2008.

[15] E. P. Markatos. On caching search engine query results. *Computer Communications*, 24(2):137–143, 2001.

[16] I. Mele, F. Bonchi, and A. Gionis. The early-adopter graph and its application to web-page recommendation. In *CIKM*, 2012.

[17] V. V. Raghavan and H. Sever. On the reuse of past optimal queries. In *SIGIR*, 1995.

[18] P. Resnick, N. Iacovou, M. Suchak, P. Bergstrom, and J. Riedl. Grouplens: an open architecture for collaborative filtering of netnews. In *CSCW*, 1994.

[19] C. Silverstein, M. Henzinger, H. Marais, and M. Moricz. Analysis of a very large web search engine query log. In *ACM SIGIR Forum*, pages 6–12, 1999.

[20] A. Spink, D. Wolfram, M. B. J. Jansen, and T. Saracevic. Searching the web: the public and their queries. *J. Amer. Soc. Inform. Sci. Tech.*, 52(3):226–234, 2001.

[21] J. Srivastava, R. Cooley, M. Deshpande, and P.-N. Tan. Web usage mining: discovery and applications of usage patterns from Web data. *SIGKDD Explor. Newsl.*, 1(2):12–23, 2000.

[22] R. W. White, M. Bilenko, and S. Cucerzan. Studying the use of popular destinations to enhance web search interaction. In *SIGIR*, 2007.

[23] Y. Xie and D. O'Hallaron. Locality in search engine queries and its implications for caching. In *IEEE Infocom 2002*, pages 1238–1247, 2002.

[24] J. Zhu, J. Hong, and J. G. Hughes. Pagecluster: Mining conceptual link hierarchies from web log files for adaptive web site navigation. *ACM Trans. Internet Technol.*, 4(2), 2004.

Advanced Graph Mining for Community Evaluation in Social Networks and the Web

Christos Giatsidis
École Polytechnique, France
giatsidis@lix.polytechnique.fr

Fragkiskos D. Malliaros
École Polytechnique, France
fmalliaros@lix.polytechnique.fr

Michalis Vazirgiannis
AUEB, Greece and
École Polytechnique, France
mvazirg@lix.polytechnique.fr

ABSTRACT

Graphs constitute a dominant data structure and appear essentially in all forms of information. Examples are the Web graph, numerous social networks, protein interaction networks, terms dependency graphs and network topologies. The main features of these graphs are their huge volume and rate of change. Presumably, there is important hidden knowledge in the macroscopic topology and features of these graphs. A cornerstone issue here is the detection and evaluation of communities – bearing multiple and diverse semantics.

The tutorial reports the basic models of graph structures for undirected, directed and signed graphs and their properties. Next we offer a thorough review of fundamental methods for graph clustering and community detection, on both undirected and directed graphs. Then we survey community evaluation measures, including both the individual node based ones as well as those that take into account aggregate properties of communities. A special mention is made on approaches that capitalize on the concept of degeneracy (k-cores and extensions), as a novel means of community detection and evaluation. We justify the above foundational framework with applications on citation graphs, trust networks and protein graphs.

Categories and Subject Descriptors

H.4 [**Database Management**]: Database applications—*Data mining*

General Terms

Algorithms; Measurement

Keywords

Community structure; Community detection; Social network analysis; Graph mining

1. INTRODUCTION

Graphs (or networks) appear in several diverse domains, including sociology, biology, neuroscience and information management. An interesting feature of real networks is the clustering or community structure property, i.e., the structure is based into a modular organization; nodes within the same module (cluster or community) tend to be highly similar sharing common features, while on the other hand, nodes of different modules show low similarity. Typically, the communities correspond to densely connected groups of nodes, where the number of edges within a community is much higher than the number of edges across different communities.

Detecting and evaluating the community structure of real-world graphs constitutes an essential task in the area of graph mining and social network analysis. For example, in the link structure of the Web, communities correspond to groups of web pages that share common topics, and therefore, revealing the underlying community structure is a crucial application from a web search engine perspective. Similarly, communities in a social network (e.g., Facebook, Twitter) correspond to individuals with increased social ties (e.g., friendship relationships, common interests). Broadly speaking, community discovery and evaluation can contribute in our understanding of a social system, summarizing the interactions within the system in a concise manner.

The aim of this tutorial is to review basic methods and tools for the task of community detection and evaluation in real graphs. Since a plethora of diverse approaches have been presented in the area, we focus on the fundamental ones, demonstrating their basic methodological principles.

2. BRIEF OUTLINE

The goal of the tutorial is to present community detection and evaluation techniques as mining tools for social networks and the Web. More precisely, the following key topics are covered by the tutorial: (i) Introduction and preliminaries on graphs and graph mining - social network analysis; (ii) topics in graph clustering and community detection; (iii) clustering and community detection in directed graphs; (iv) degeneracy-based community evaluation.

The tutorial commences by presenting fundamental graph concepts and models for undirected, directed and signed graphs along with their properties. It continues with a thorough review of graph clustering and community detection techniques. Then, we present how the graph clustering task can be treated in directed graphs, where the presence of directed edges conveys essential semantics. Next, some topics on community evaluation measures are presented for both individual nodes, as well as aggregate metrics. Special mention is made to the degeneracy (k-cores and extensions) approach for community evaluation in directed and signed graphs, presenting also several case studies on real-world

WSDM'13, February 4–8, 2013, Rome, Italy.
ACM 978-1-4503-1869-3/13/02.

networks, such as co-authorship networks, citation networks, trust networks and the Web graph.

Next, we outline the basic points that will be covered in the tutorial.

- Graph fundamentals
  - i. The Erdős-Rényi model
  - ii. Basic graph concepts including clustering, density, locality, connectivity, coherency
- Fundamental techniques of graph clustering and community detection
  - i. A taxonomy of graph clustering algorithms
- Graph partitioning
- Hierarchical graph clustering algorithms
- Partitional clustering
- Spectral graph clustering
- Modularity-based methods
- Modularity optimization
  - i. Greedy techniques
  - ii. Simulated annealing
  - iii. Extremal optimization
  - iv. Spectral optimization
- Dynamic algorithms
- Clustering and community detection in directed graphs
  - i. A taxonomy of clustering algorithms in directed graphs
  - ii. Graph transformations maintaining edge directionality
  - iii. Extending objective functions to directed graphs
  - iv. Alternative approaches: information theoretic based methods, probabilistic models and statistical inference
- Community evaluation measures
  - i. Individual node metrics
  - ii. Aggregate metrics
- Degeneracy based community evaluation
  - i. Degeneracy concept
  - ii. Degeneracy for undirected/directed/signed graphs
  - iii. Case studies: DBLP and arXiv citation graphs; Wikipedia graph; Epinions signed graph
- New directions for research in the area of graph mining for community evaluation

More details about the tutorial can be found in the following url: `http://www.lix.polytechnique.fr/~mvazirg/WSDM2013_tutorial/`.

Acknowledgements

The authors are partially supported by the DIGITEO Chair grant LEVETONE in France. Fragkiskos D. Malliaros is a recipient of the Google Europe Fellowship in Graph Mining, and this research is supported in part by this Google Fellowship.

3. REFERENCES

[1] D. Chakrabarti and C. Faloutsos. Graph mining: Laws, generators, and algorithms. *ACM Comput. Surv.*, 38(1), 2006.

[2] A. Clauset, M. E. J. Newman, and C. Moore. Finding community structure in very large networks. *Physical Review E*, 70(6):066111+, 2004.

[3] M. Coscia, F. Giannotti, and D. Pedreschi. A classification for community discovery methods in complex networks. *Statistical Analysis and Data Mining*, 4(5):512–546, 2011.

[4] L. Danon, A. D. Guilera, J. Duch, and A. Arenas. Comparing community structure identification. *Journal of Statistical Mechanics: Theory and Experiment*, 2005(9):P09008–09008, 2005.

[5] P. Erdős and A. Rényi. On the evolution of random graphs. *Publ. Math. Inst. Hung. Acad. Sci*, 5:17–61, 1960.

[6] S. Fortunato. Community detection in graphs. *Physics Reports*, 486(3-5):75 – 174, 2010.

[7] C. Giatsidis, D. M. Thilikos, and M. Vazirgiannis. D-cores: Measuring collaboration of directed graphs based on degeneracy. In *ICDM*, pages 201–210, 2011.

[8] C. Giatsidis, D. M. Thilikos, and M. Vazirgiannis. Evaluating cooperation in communities with the k-core structure. In *ASONAM*, pages 87–93, 2011.

[9] M. Girvan and M. E. J. Newman. Community structure in social and biological networks. *Proceedings of the National Academy of Sciences*, 99(12):7821–7826, 2002.

[10] J. Leskovec, K. J. Lang, A. Dasgupta, and M. W. Mahoney. Community structure in large networks: Natural cluster sizes and the absence of large well-defined clusters. *Internet Mathematics*, 6(1):29–123, 2009.

[11] M. E. J. Newman. Modularity and community structure in networks. *Proceedings of the National Academy of Sciences*, 103(23):8577–8582, 2006.

[12] M. E. J. Newman and M. Girvan. Finding and evaluating community structure in networks. *Physical Review E*, 69(2):026113+, 2003.

[13] M. Rosvall and C. T. Bergstrom. Maps of random walks on complex networks reveal community structure. *Proceedings of the National Academy of Sciences*, 105(4):1118–1123, 2008.

[14] V. Satuluri and S. Parthasarathy. Symmetrizations for clustering directed graphs. In *EDBT*, pages 343–354, 2011.

[15] S. Schaeffer. Graph clustering. *Computer Science Review*, 1(1):27–64, 2007.

[16] U. von Luxburg. A tutorial on spectral clustering. *Statistics and Computing*, 17(4):395–416, 2007.

Anomaly, Event, and Fraud Detection in Large Network Datasets

Leman Akoglu
Stony Brook University
Dept. of Computer Science
leman@cs.stonybrook.edu

Christos Faloutsos
Carnegie Mellon University
School of Computer Science
christos@cs.cmu.edu

ABSTRACT

Detecting anomalies and events in data is a vital task, with numerous applications in security, finance, health care, law enforcement, and many others. While many techniques have been developed in past years for spotting outliers and anomalies in unstructured collections of multi-dimensional points, with graph data becoming ubiquitous, techniques for structured *graph* data have been of focus recently. As objects in graphs have long-range correlations, novel technology has been developed for abnormality detection in graph data.

The goal of this tutorial is to provide a general, comprehensive overview of the state-of-the-art methods for anomaly, event, and fraud detection in data represented as graphs. As a key contribution, we provide a thorough exploration of both data mining and machine learning algorithms for these detection tasks. We give a general framework for the algorithms, categorized under various settings: unsupervised vs. (semi-)supervised, for static vs. dynamic data. We focus on the scalability and effectiveness aspects of the methods, and highlight results on crucial real-world applications, including accounting fraud and opinion spam detection.

Categories and Subject Descriptors

H.2.8 [**Database Applications**]: Data mining; E.1 [**Data Structures**]: Graphs and networks

Keywords

graph mining, anomaly detection, event detection, fraud

1. MOTIVATION AND OVERVIEW

When analyzing data, knowing what stands out in the data is often at least, or even more important and interesting than learning about its general structure. The branch of data mining concerned with discovering rare occurrences in datasets is called abnormality detection. This problem domain has numerous applications in security, finance, health care, law enforcement, and many others. In addition to revealing suspicious behavior, anomaly detection is vital for spotting rare events, such as rare diseases or side effects in medical domain.

To tackle the abnormality detection problem, many techniques have been developed in past years, especially for spotting outliers and anomalies in unstructured collections of multi-dimensional data points. On the other hand, graphs provide a powerful machinery for representing a wide range of data types in physical, biological, social, and information systems. As such, graph data (a.k.a. network, relational data) have become ubiquitous in the last decade. As a result, researchers have recently intensified their study of methods for anomaly detection in structured *graph* data.

Graph representation of datasets inherently impose long-range correlations among the data objects. For example in a reviewer-product review graph data, the extent a reviewer is fraudulent depends on what ratings s/he gave to which products, as well as how other reviewers rated the same products to an extent how trustful their ratings are, which in turn again depends on what other products they rated, and so on. As can be seen, due to this long-range correlations in graph datasets, detecting abnormalities in graph data is a significantly different task than that for points lying in a multi-dimensional feature space. In addition, the problem is challenging due to the large scale and dynamic nature of real-world graphs.

The main highlights of this tutorial are the following.

- We give a comprehensive overview of abnormality detection techniques for graph data for the *first* time
- We thoroughly explore techniques from both data mining (unsupervised, exploiting graph structure) and machine learning (semi-/supervised methods, employing relational learning).
- We put the abnormality (anomaly, event, fraud) detection methods under a unified lens, point out their connections and applications on diverse real-world tasks, e.g. accounting fraud, opinion spam, auction fraud.

2. TARGET AUDIENCE AND LEARNING OBJECTIVES

The target audience of this tutorial are researchers and practitioners who wish to know the most important techniques for outlier, anomaly, fraud, and event detection, with a focus on graph data. The tutorial would be of interest both to the data mining and machine learning community.

The audience is not expected to be familiar with the area, however the attendees should have basic knowledge on graph mining and machine learning. Through this tutorial, the participants will learn important techniques to attack the anomaly detection problem in data represented as graphs. The techniques are presented under changing settings; with or without ground truth data as well as for static or dynamically changing data.

WSDM'13, February 4–8, 2013, Rome, Italy.
ACM 978-1-4503-1869-3/13/02.

Part 0: **Introduction**
Part I: **Anomaly detection in static data**

(a) Overview: Outlier detection in clouds of data points
(b) Anomaly detection in *graph* data
  i. Anomalies in unlabeled graphs [3, 13]
  ii. Anomalies in node-/edge-labeled graphs [4, 8]

Part II: **Event detection in dynamic data**

(a) Overview: Event detection in time series of data
(b) Event detection in time series of *graph* data
  i. Graph-distance based methods [10]
  ii. Phase-transition based methods [2, 12]

Part III: ***Graph*-based fraud detection**

(a) Theory and Algorithms: Introduction to relational learning [5, 11, 14],
(b) App.s: Relational learning for fraud detection
  i. Online auction fraud [9], opinion spam [1]
  ii. Accounting fraud risk [7], Web spam [6]

Table 1: Tutorial outline

3. TUTORIAL OUTLINE

The tutorial has 3 major parts, each of which is also organized into 2 main sections.

The first part focuses on anomaly detection methods for (a) collections of multi-dimensional data points, and (b) static graph data. The former is presented both for numerical and categorical data. Anomaly detection in graph data is covered for both unlabeled and labeled graphs, where each node and edge contains a label to identify its type.

The second part focuses on change detection approaches for (a) temporal data sequences, and (b) time-varying graph data. The former is categorized into instantaneous versus drifting change, after which specialized approaches for graphs based on edit distances and connectivity structure are presented.

The third part focuses on fraud detection using graph-based approaches. Firstly in (a), we give background on the theory and algorithms for relational learning. Later in (b) we demonstrate these algorithms in action, for diverse real-world fraud detection applications.

4. RELATION TO WSDM 2013 AREAS

Given the long list of applications and challenges they pose, abnormality detection is a very popular research topic. Not only the problems are mathematically interesting from a scientific point of view but, with their many applications in diverse fields, are also appealing from practitioners' point of view. As a result, the abnormality detection draws attention from many researchers in both industry and academia.

On the other hand, given the popularity of the topic, it is increasingly hard to keep up with the information overload arising from new approaches developed worldwide. To make the matter worse, the new contributions are dispersed into, although strongly related, fragments. That is, methods in this topic are grouped into outlier, anomaly, fraud, event, change, drift, fault detection separately. Our tutorial brings these concepts in one place and highlights their connections.

5. TUTORS' BIO AND EXPERTISE

LEMAN AKOGLU is an Assistant Professor at Stony Brook University, and received her Ph.D. from Carnegie Mellon University in 2012. She has won 2 "Best Paper" awards, published 15 refereed articles in major data mining venues, and is one of the inventors of 3 U.S. patents, filed by IBM T. J. Watson Research. Her research interests are in data mining, machine learning, and applied statistics with a focus on pattern mining, and anomaly and event detection in large dynamic data using graph mining and compression.

CHRISTOS FALOUTSOS is a Professor at Carnegie Mellon University. He has received the Research Contributions Award in ICDM 2006, the Innovations award in KDD 2010, 18 "best paper" awards, and several teaching awards. He has given over 30 tutorials and over 10 invited distinguished lectures. His research interests include data mining for graphs and streams, fractals, and database performance.

6. REFERENCES

[1] L. Akoglu, R. Chandy, and C. Faloutsos. Opinion fraud detection in review networks. In *Technical Report CMU-CS-12-130*, 2012.

[2] L. Akoglu and C. Faloutsos. Event detection in time series of mobile communication graphs. In *Army Science Conference*, 2010.

[3] L. Akoglu, M. McGlohon, and C. Faloutsos. OddBall: Spotting anomalies in weighted graphs. In *PAKDD*, 2010.

[4] W. Eberle and L. B. Holder. Anomaly detection in data represented as graphs. *Intell. Data Anal.*, 11(6):663–689, 2007.

[5] L. Getoor, N. Friedman, D. Koller, A. Pfeffer, and B. Taskar. Probabilistic relational models. In *Intro. to Stat. Relational Learning*. MIT Press, 2007.

[6] Z. Gyogyi, H. Garcia-Molina, and J. Pedersen. Combating web spam with TrustRank. In *Proc. VLDB*, 2004.

[7] M. McGlohon, S. Bay, M. G. Anderle, D. M. Steier, and C. Faloutsos. Snare: a link analytic system for graph labeling and risk detection. In *KDD*, pages 1265–1274, 2009.

[8] C. C. Noble and D. J. Cook. Graph-based anomaly detection. In *KDD*, pages 631–636, 2003.

[9] S. Pandit, D. H. Chau, S. Wang, and C. Faloutsos. Netprobe: a fast and scalable system for fraud detection in online auction networks. In *WWW*, 2007.

[10] B. Pincombe. Anomaly detection in time series of graphs using arma processes. *ASOR Bulletin.*, 24(4):2–10, 2005.

[11] P. Sen, G. Namata, M. Bilgic, L. Getoor, B. Gallagher, and T. Eliassi-Rad. Collective classification in network data. *AI Magazine*, 29(3):93–106, 2008.

[12] J. Sun, C. Faloutsos, S. Papadimitriou, and P. S. Yu. Graphscope: parameter-free mining of large time-evolving graphs. In *KDD*, pages 687–696, 2007.

[13] J. Sun, H. Qu, D. Chakrabarti, and C. Faloutsos. Neighborhood formation and anomaly detection in bipartite graphs. In *ICDM*, pages 418–425, 2005.

[14] B. Taskar, P. Abbeel, and D. Koller. Discriminative probabilistic models for relational data. In *UAI*, pages 485–492, 2002.

Models and Algorithms for Social Influence Analysis

Jimeng Sun[†] and Jie Tang[‡]
[†]IBM TJ Watson Research Center, USA
[‡]Department of Computer Science and Technology, Tsinghua University, China
jimeng@us.ibm.com, jietang@tsinghua.edu.cn

ABSTRACT

Social influence is the behavioral change of a person because of the perceived relationship with other people, organizations and society in general. Social influence has been a widely accepted phenomenon in social networks for decades. Many applications have been built based around the implicit notation of social influence between people, such as marketing, advertisement and recommendations. With the exponential growth of online social network services such as Facebook and Twitter, social influence can for the first time be measured over a large population. In this tutorial, we survey the research on social influence analysis with a focus on the computational aspects. First, we introduce how to verify the existence of social influence in various social networks. Second, we present computational models for quantifying social influence. Third, we describe how social influence can help real applications. In particular, we will focus on opinion leader finding and influence maximization for viral marketing. Finally, we apply the selected algorithms of social influence analysis on different social network data, such as twitter, arnetminer data, weibo, and slashdot forum.

Categories and Subject Descriptors

J.4 [**Computer Applications**]: Social Behavioral Sciences; H.1 [**Information Systems**]: Models and Principles

General Terms

Algorithms, Experimentation, Measurement

Keywords

Social influence, Social network, Influence Maximization

1. OUTLINE

As social networks have become popular in many domains, more and more people make decisions based on their interactions from social networks. For example, people often pick what restaurants to go to based on recommendations and reviews from Yelp. As the growth of social networks in all domains, such behaviors of social influence become more and more prevalent. More and more people make decisions and changes influenced by their social networks.

In this tutorial, we survey the theories, algorithms and applications on social influence analysis.

First, we give the definition of social influence and introduce related concepts such as homophily, conformity, and selection.

WSDM'13, February 4–8, 2013, Rome, Italy.
ACM 978-1-4503-1869-3/13/02.

Second, we describe methodologies for verifying the existence of influence in various social networks. The methods include shuffle test and randomization test. We will give real world examples to demonstrate how the social influence behaves in different social networks.

Third, we present models and algorithms for quantitative analysis of social influence, which goes beyond macro-level analysis. Employing several large social networks (including Twitter and Weibo) as the examples in our study, we introduce how social influence affect individual behaviors and change the network structure.

Finally, we survey applications of social influence. In particular, we introduce opinion leader finding and influence maximization for viral marketing, which have many important applications in the real world. In particular, we focus on node-specific statistics for opinion leader finding. Then we describe structural effects of both edges and nodes for influence maximization. In addition, we will present methods for predicting customer behavior and online advertising through viral marketing.

To conclude, the tutorial has the following outline.

- Preliminaries
  - Definition of social influence
  - Homophily
  - Influence and Selection
  - Other related concepts
- Existential Test for Social Influence
- Computational models for Social Influence
  - Learning influence probability
  - Influence and action dynamics
  - Influence and interaction
  - Influence maximization models
- Influence Applications
  - Opinion leader finding
  - Influence maximization for viral marketing

2. BIOGRAPHY

Jimeng Sun is a research staff member at Healthcare Transformation group, IBM T. J. Watson lab. He received a Bachelor and MPhil in Computer Science from Hong Kong University of Science and Technology in 2002 and 2003. After that, he obtained a MS and PhD degree in Computer Science from Carnegie Mellon University in 2006 and 2007. His research interests include data mining for streams and networks, databases and healthcare analytics. He has received the best research paper award in ICDM 2008, the best research paper award in SDM 2007. He has published over 40 refereed articles and two book chapters. He filed four patents and has given five tutorials. He has served as a program committee member of KDD, ICDM, SDM, CIKM, and SIGMOD, senior committee member for SDM 2010-2011, 2013, for KDD 2013.

Jie Tang is an associate professor at the Department of Computer Science and Technology, Tsinghua University. He serves as the director of Scientific Office of the Department of Computer Science. His main research interests include social network analysis and data mining. He has been a visiting scholar at Cornell University, Chinese University of Hong Kong, Hong Kong University of Science and Technology, and Leuven University. He has published over 100 research papers in major international journals and conferences including: KDD, IJCAI, WWW, SIGMOD, ACL, Machine Learning Journal, TKDD, and TKDE. He serves as Local Chair of SIGKDD'12, Publications Co-Chairs of SIGKDD'11, Program Chair of ADMA'11, Program Chair of SocInfo'12, and also serves as the PC member of more than 50 international conferences.

Acknowledgements
Jie Tang is supported by the Natural Science Foundation of China (No. 61222212, No. 61073073, No. 61170061), Chinese National Key Foundation Research (No. 60933013, No.61035004), a special fund for Fast Sharing of Science Paper in Net Era by CSTD, and National Basic Research Program of China (No. 2011CB302302).

3. REFERENCES

[1] N. Agarwal, H. Liu, L. Tang, and P. S. Yu. Identifying the influential bloggers in a community. In *Proceedings of the 1st ACM International Conference on Web Search and Data Mining (WSDM'08)*, pages 207–217, 2008.

[2] A. Anagnostopoulos, R. Kumar, and M. Mahdian. Influence and correlation in social networks. In *Proceeding of the 14th ACM SIGKDD international conference on Knowledge discovery and data mining (KDD'08)*, pages 7–15, 2008.

[3] S. Aral, L. Muchnika, and A. Sundararajan. Distinguishing influence-based contagion from homophily-driven diffusion in dynamic networks. *Proceedings of the National Academy of Sciences*, 106(51):21544–21549, 2009.

[4] E. Bakshy, B. Karrer, and L. A. Adamic. Social influence and the diffusion of user-created content. In *EC '09: Proceedings of the tenth ACM conference on Electronic commerce*, pages 325–334, New York, NY, USA, 2009. ACM.

[5] P. Bonacich. Power and centrality: a family of measures. *American Journal of Sociology*, 92:1170–1182, 1987.

[6] R. M. Bond, C. J. Fariss, J. J. Jones, A. D. I. Kramer, C. Marlow, J. E. Settle, and J. H. Fowler. A 61-million-person experiment in social influence and political mobilization. *Nature*, 489:295–298, 2012.

[7] W. Chen, Y. Wang, and S. Yang. Efficient influence maximization in social networks. In *Proceedings of the 15th ACM SIGKDD International Conference on Knowledge Discovery and Data Mining (SIGKDD'09)*, pages 199–207, 2009.

[8] R. B. Cialdini and N. J. Goldstein. Social influence: compliance and conformity. *Annu Rev Psychol*, 55:591–621, 2004.

[9] D. Crandall, D. Cosley, D. Huttenlocher, J. Kleinberg, and S. Suri. Feedback effects between similarity and social influence in online communities. In *Proceeding of the 14th ACM SIGKDD international conference on Knowledge discovery and data mining (KDD'08)*, pages 160–168, 2008.

[10] P. W. Eastwick and W. L. Gardner. Is it a game? evidence for social influence in the virtual world. *Social Influence*, 4(1):18–32, 2009.

[11] S. M. Elias and A. R. Pratkanis. Teaching social influence: Demonstrations and exercises from the discipline of social psychology. *Social Influence*, 1(2):147–162, 2006.

[12] T. L. Fond and J. Neville. Randomization tests for distinguishing social influence and homophily effects. In *Proceeding of the 19th international conference on World Wide Web (WWW'10)*, 2010.

[13] M. Gomez-Rodriguez, J. Leskovec, and A. Krause. Inferring Networks of Diffusion and Influence. In *Proceedings of the 16th ACM SIGKDD International Conference on Knowledge Discovery and Data Mining (SIGKDD'10)*, pages 1019–1028, 2010.

[14] A. Goyal, F. Bonchi, and L. V. Lakshmanan. Learning influence probabilities in social networks. In *Proceedings of the 3st ACM International Conference on Web Search and Data Mining (WSDM'10)*, pages 207–217, 2010.

[15] D. Kempe, J. Kleinberg, and E. Tardos. Maximizing the spread of influence through a social network. In *Proceedings of the ninth ACM SIGKDD international conference on Knowledge discovery and data mining (KDD'03)*, pages 137–146, 2003.

[16] L. Liu, J. Tang, J. Han, M. Jiang, and S. Yang. Mining Topic-Level Influence in Heterogeneous Networks. In *Proceedings of the Nineteenth Conference on Information and Knowledge Management (CIKM'2010)*, pages 199-208, 2010.

[17] L. Liu, J. Tang, J. Han, and S. Yang. Learning Influence from Heterogeneous Social Networks. In *Data Mining and Knowledge Discovery (DMKD)*, 25(3):511–544, 2012.

[18] M. E. J. Newman. A measure of betweenness centrality based on random walks. *Social Networks*, 2005.

[19] J. Sun and J. Tang. A Survey of Models and Algorithms for Social Influence Analysis. *Social Network Data Analytics, Aggarwal, C. C. (Ed.), Kluwer Academic Publishers*, pages 177–214, 2011.

[20] C. Tan, J. Tang, J. Sun, Q. Lin, and F. Wang. Social action tracking via noise tolerant time-varying factor graphs. In *Proceedings of the 16th ACM SIGKDD International Conference on Knowledge Discovery and Data Mining (SIGKDD'10)*, pages 807–816, 2010.

[21] C. Tan, L. Lee, J. Tang, L. Jiang, M. Zhou, and P. Li. User-level sentiment analysis incorporating social networks. In *Proceedings of the 17th ACM SIGKDD International Conference on Knowledge Discovery and Data Mining (SIGKDD'11)*, pages 1397–1405, 2011.

[22] J. Tang, J. Sun, C. Wang, and Z. Yang. Social influence analysis in large-scale networks. In *Proceedings of the 15th ACM SIGKDD International Conference on Knowledge Discovery and Data Mining (SIGKDD'09)*, pages 807–816, 2009.

[23] D. J. Watts and S. H. Strogatz. Collective dynamics of 'small-world' networks. *Nature*, pages 440–442, Jun 1998.

Data-Driven Political Science

Ingmar Weber
Qatar Computing Research Institute
Doha, Qatar
ingmarweber@acm.org

Ana-Maria Popescu
Pinfluencer
San Francisco, California
anamaria.popescug@gmail.com

Marco Pennacchiotti
eBay Inc.
San Francisco, California
mpennacchiotti@ebay.com

ABSTRACT

The tutorial will summarize the state-of-the art in the growing area of computational political science. Like many others, this research domain is being revolutionized by the availability of open, big data and the increasing reach and importance of social media. The surging interest on the part of the academic community is matched by intense efforts on the part of political campaigns to use online data in order to learn how to best disseminate information and reach the right potential donors or voters. In this context, a tutorial can summarize existing methods in a fascinating, high-interest area and allow participants with diverse backgrounds to get inspiration from the methods and problems studied. The tutorial will feature seminal research concerning (i) political polarization, (ii) election prediction and polling, and (iii) political campaigning and influence propagation. The goal is not only to familiarize attendees with ideas from related conferences such as WWW, ICWSM or CIKM, but also to present ideas and quantitative methods closer to political science such as Poole's and Rosenthal's NOMINATE score for a politician's political orientation.

Categories and Subject Descriptors

J.4 [**Social and Behavioral Sciences**]: Sociology; H.3.5. [**Online Information Services**]: Web-based services

General Terms

Experimentation, Human Factors, Theory

Keywords

political science, big data, election prediction

1. TARGET AUDIENCE AND OBJECTIVE

This half-day tutorial targets researchers from the growing area of computational social science as well as, more generally, researchers with interests in web and data mining or its applications to political science. Attendees will be familiarized with the problems studied, the methods applied and the datasets used in a range of research work in computational political science both before but mostly after the start of the Web era. After the tutorial, participants will have an in-depth knowledge of the current state-of-the-art concerning (i) quantifying political polarization, (ii) election predictions and (iii) quantitative analysis of political campaigning.

WSDM'13, February 4–8, 2013, Rome, Italy.
ACM 978-1-4503-1869-3/13/02.

2. OUTLINE

The tutorial will cover seminal and important academic papers and techniques in the area of Data-Driven Political Science [1]. It will be organized in three topically coherent parts with a focus on (i) political polarization, (ii) election predictions and polling, and (iii) political campaigning and influence propagation. Each part will roughly last 1 hour.

2.1 Political polarization:

We will discuss studies and measures of political polarization where the object of polarization can be a politician, a social media user, a web site, a web search query, or text such as a political speech. Focus will be given to (i) how to define and validate political polarization and political orientation, (ii) how to compute it algorithmically, and (iii) the datasets being used in studies. The methods presented will include some well-known in political science, but not traditionally used in computer science, such as the NOMINATE score and its variants. While we will focus on the U.S. political system due to its simple left/right structure, we will discuss ways to generalize existing methods to multi-dimensional political systems [2,3,4,5,6,7,8,9,10,11,12,13].

2.2 Election predictions and polling:

Recently, many new approaches to using social media for election predictions have been presented. Some studies claim good results even using mere per-party tweet counting but others have cast serious doubts on those results and the methodology. We will give a survey of these different approaches and their results. We will also feature prediction market-based approaches and other novel methods to political forecasting and polling [14,15,16,17,18,19,20,21].

2.3 Political campaigning and influence propagation

Social media and the Web in general can be used to observe political activity but also to shape politics, in particular through political campaigning and attempts to start grassroot movements among enthusiastic political followers. We will describe studies covering either centralized political campaigning or the effects of "viral" propagation on political opinions. The focus here will be on methods that quantify the effects of such campaigns [22,23,24,25,26,27,28].

3. ORGANIZERS' BIOS

Ingmar Weber is a senior scientist at the Qatar Computing Research Institute. His research covers a wide subject area from classical information retrieval, to sponsored search, to interdisciplinary studies in web science. While at Yahoo! Research Barcelona, he led the development of the Political Search Trends and Political Hashtag Trends demos which assign political leanings to search queries and Twitter hashtags respectively. In August 2012 he taught the course "An

Introduction to Web Science" at the RuSSIR summer school, featuring elements from computational political science. Together with Ana-Maria and Marco he organized the PLEAD (Politics, Elections and Data) workshop at CIKM 2012.

Ana-Maria Popescu is a research scientist working with early stage social startups. Previously, she was a text mining scientist at Yahoo! Labs where she most recently worked on social media mining and user modeling. While at Yahoo!, she co-led the Twitter analytics effort for the Yahoo! News Election 2012 coverage. Ana obtained her Ph.D. in 2007 from University of Washington with a thesis in information extraction from the Web.

Marco Pennacchiotti is an applied scientist and principal engineer at eBay, where he leads the science on social media. Before joining eBay in June 2012, he was a research scientist at Yahoo! Labs, focusing on text mining, information extraction applied to big data and social media. At Yahoo!, he wrote papers focusing on user-profiling also applied to the political domain. Marco obtained a Ph.D. in natural language processing and information extraction in 2007 from the University of Rome, Italy.

4. REFERENCES

[1] Weber, I., Popescu, A.-M., and Pennacchiotti, M. 2012. PLEAD 2012: politics, elections and data. In *CIKM'12.*

[2] Pennacchiotti, M., and Popescu, A.-M. 2011. Democrats, republicans and Starbucks afficionados: user classification in twitter. In *KDD'11.*

[3] Weber, I., Garimella, V. R. K., and Borra, E. 2012. Political Search Trends. In *SIGIR'12.*

[4] Zhou, D. X., Resnick, P., and Mei, Q. 2011. Classifying the political leaning of news articles and users from user votes. In *ICWSM'11.*

[5] Borra, E., and Weber, I. 2012. Political Insights: Exploring partisanship in Web search queries. *First Monday* 17, 7.

[6] Laver, M., Benoit, K., and Garry, J. 2003. Extracting policy positions from political texts using words as data. *APSR*, 97, 2.

[7] Weber, I., Garimella, V. R. K., and Borra, E. 2012. Mining Web Query Logs to Analyze Political Issues. In *WebSci'12.*

[8] Weber, I., Garimella, V. R. K., and Teka, A. 2013. Political Hashtag Trends. In *ECIR'13.*

[9] Malouf, R., and Mullen, T. 2008. Taking sides: user classification for informal online political discourse. *Internet Research*, 18.

[10] Conover, M., Ratkiewicz, J., Francisco, M., Goncalves, B., Flammini, A., and Menczer. F. 2011. Political polarization on twitter. In *ICWSM'11.*

[11] Efron. M. 2004. The liberal media and right-wing conspiracies. In *CIKM'04.*

[12] Slapin, J., and Proksch. S. 2008. A scaling model for estimating time-series party positions from texts. *AJPS*, 52, 3.

[13] Poole, K. T., and Rosenthal, H. 1985. A spatial model for legislative roll call analysis. *AJPS*, 29, 2.

[14] Jungherr, A., Jürgens, P., and Schoen. H. 2012. Why the pirate party won the German election of 2009 or the trouble with predictions. *SSCR*, 30, 2.

[15] Tumasjan, A., Sprenger, T., Sandner, P., and Welpe, I. 2010. Predicting elections with twitter: What 140 characters reveal about political sentiment. In *ICWSM'10.*

[16] Rothschild, D. 2009. Forecasting Elections Comparing Prediction Markets, Polls, and Their Biases. *Public Opinion Quarterly*, 73, 5.

[17] Gayo-Avello, D., Metaxas, P. T., and Mustafaraj. E. 2011. Limits of electoral predictions using twitter. In *ICWSM'11.*

[18] Metaxas, P., Mustafaraj, E., and Gayo-Avello, D. 2011. How (not) to predict elections. In *PASSAT'11.*

[19] Lui, C., Metaxas, P. T., and Mustafaraj, E. 2011. On the predictability of the US elections through search volume activity. In *IADIS'11.*

[20] Jin, X., Gallagher, A. C., Cao, L., Luo, J., and Jiawei, H. 2010. The wisdom of social multimedia: using Flickr for prediction and forecast. In *MM'10.*

[21] Hummel, P., and Rothschild, D. 2013. Fundamental Models for Forecasting Elections. In *AEA'13.*

[22] Cogburn, D. L., and Espinoza-Vasquez, F. K. 2011. From networked nominee to networked nation: Examining the impact of Web 2.0 and social media on political participation and civic engagement in the 2008 Obama campaign. *Journal of Political Marketing*, 10, 1-2.

[23] Small, T. 2008. The facebook effect? On-line campaigning in the 2008 Canadian and U.S. elections. *Policy Options*, November.

[24] Smith, A. 2009. The internet's role in campaign 2008. *Pew Internet & American Life Project*, 15.

[25] Kushin, M. J., and Yamamoto, M. 2010. Did social media really matter? College students' use of online media and political decision making in the 2008 election. *Mass Communication and Society*, 13, 5.

[26] Dimitrova, D., Shehata, A., Strömbäck, J., and Nord, L. W. 2011. The effects of digital media on political knowledge and participation in election campaigns: Evidence from panel data. *Communication Research*, November.

[27] Hong, S., and Nadler. D. 2012. Which candidates do the public discuss online in an election campaign? The use of social media by 2012 presidential candidates and its impact on candidate salience. *Government Information Quarterly*, 29, 4.

[28] Vitak, J., Zube, P., Smock, A., Carr, C. T., Ellison, N, and Lampe, C. 2011. It's complicated: Facebook users' political participation in the 2008 election. *CyberPsychology, behavior, and social networking*, 14, 3.

Exploring Structure and Content on the Web: Extraction and Integration of the Semi-Structured Web

Tim Weninger Jiawei Han
University of Illinois at Urbana-Champaign
Urbana, IL 61801
{weninge1, hanj}@illinois.edu

ABSTRACT

In this tutorial we view the World Wide Web as a type of massive, decentralized database. At present, this "Web database" is presented in a manner largely devoid of any consistent meaning or schema. That is not to say that Web-data lacks an underlying organization; in fact, most Web content is generated from an underlying schema-bound, or otherwise structured database. Information extraction is generally concerned with the reconciliation of unstructured or semi-structured Web content with the neatly structured database paradigm. With this Web-database in hand, researchers and practitioners have recently begun developing mechanisms which return structured results in response to an unstructured query. These new developments are a product of (1) record, list and table extraction from large numbers of semi-structured Web pages, (2) integration of these disparate extraction results into a consistent form, and (3) analysis of the newly extracted and integrated Web data.

Among the many fruits of this line of work is the ability for semi-structured Web data to enhance the search capabilities of a schema-bound database. Alternatively, structured database records have also been used to augment Web page collections typically used by Web search engines. We will cover several key technologies, and principles explored so far in the area of Web information extraction, search and exploration.

Categories and Subject Descriptors

I.2.6 [**Artificial Intelligence**]: Learning; G.3 [**Probability and Statistics**]: Probabilistic algorithms, Nonparametric statistics

General Terms

Management, Design, Algorithms

Keywords

information extraction, information integration, semi-structured data

1. INTRODUCTION

Extraction, Search and Exploration of Semi–Structured Web pages is an increasingly popular task because of its potential impact on the way information is managed and retrieved. For example, a bibliographic database of computer science research publications (*e.g.*, DBLP) could be integrated with information from the authorsŠ homepages. This integration would allow for a free-text query to return structured, (database-style), results. Alternatively, a structured (SQL-style) query could be used to return Web results. Furthermore, the unstructured and structured information could be used to mutually enhance one another providing more informative search results.

The general process of this effort is to take semi-structured, HTML-style Web data transform it into relatively structured, manipulable information. This process becomes especially challenging when working with a data source as vast and varied as the World Wide Web. Researchers have found that most Web sites, especially large sites, contain informative structures. This observation has led to the development of several approaches that leverage the structural similarities of Web pages (from a common Web site) to learn Web wrappers [3, 1] that extract content [12], data records [8, 14], lists [5, 10], and tables [2]. The extracted content is often put into a database for later retrieval, however, it is usually not sufficient to extract content from only a single site. Instead, information from many sites are gathered in order to enhance the information en masse [6, 4]. In these cases, content extraction is only part of the story; we may also choose to integrate the data into a consistent database with a single schema [9], or link data records with Web pages [13]. These efforts usually rely on heuristic assumptions of Web page presentation, the final section of this tutorial explores recent efforts to develop more principled approaches with the same goal [11].

2. TUTORIAL OUTLINE

This half-day tutorial will review many of the recent contributions to Web extraction, search and exploration. Each topical section will cover techniques and features common to many of the related systems. We will also discuss technical challenges with these systems and analyze several domains in need of further research.

1. The Web as a database: from the World Wide Web to the database
    (a) What is the Semi-Structured Web?
    (b) How is the Web like a database? How is the Web *not* like a database?
    (c) Exploring the power of links within the Web Database
2. Preliminaries of Web Data Analysis
    (a) HTML, XML, the DOM and their relationship
    (b) The Web as an information network
        i. Measuring information networks: Density, connectivity, centrality, reachability analysis
        ii. General statistical behavior of the Web: The small world phenomenon, the power-law distribution, and scale free networks
3. Information Extraction from Web Data

WSDM'13, February 4–8, 2013, Rome, Italy
ACM 978-1-4503-1869-3/13/02.

(a) Content Extraction: supervised methods, heuristic and unsupervised content extraction
(b) Domain dependent record extraction: wrapper generation, XPaths
(c) Domain independent record extraction
    i. DOM-only methods: MDR, DEPTA, WebTables, WWWT, Google Sets
    ii. Visual-only methods: VIPS, SRQ, ViDE
    iii. Hybrid methods: HyLiEn, VENTex
(d) Wrangling data records: from data records to tabular data
(e) Annotating schema-less tabular data: applying labels to schema free structured data
(f) Remaining challenges of record extraction: forums, reviews, threaded discussions

4. Web Information Network Analysis

    (a) Parallel Paths through the Web: entity-pages, link paths
    (b) Relational databases across the Web: hyperlinks as foreign keys
    (c) Propagating and appending extracted records and tables
    (d) Augmenting existing databases with Web data: Case study with DBLP and IMDB
    (e) The hierarchical web
    (f) New and remaining challenges: integration, scale, veracity analysis

3. RELATED WORK

Semi-structured information extraction, integration and analysis is a core topic in the general context of Web Search and Data Mining. As such, we expect this tutorial to have a broad appeal to both academics and industry practitioners. Furthermore, many of the works explored in this tutorial include cross-cutting technologies from the database and information retrieval fields.

This is the first tutorial proposal on this topic, and had not heard of any similar tutorials from recent, related venues. Cafarella and Halevy, two of the organizers of the WebTables project, gave a tutorial on Web Data Management at SIGMOD 2011 that explored some of the Web information extraction topics that we plan to cover, however their coverage was from a data management perspective.

Finally, some of the UIUC-based publications encompassed by this proposal have appeared in keynote addresses given by the co-presenter at recent conferences [7]. However, we plan for this tutorial to cover a broad set of techniques from several researchers, not just our own work.

4. ABOUT THE PRESENTERS

Tim Weninger is a Ph.D Candidate in the Department of Computer Science at the University of Illinois Urbana-Champaign. His research interests are in Web mining, Web search and information networks, as well as topic models, data mining, and social media; he has also taught the database foundations class at UIUC. Tim is a recipient of the National Defense Science and Engineering Graduate Fellowship (NDSEG) and the National Science Foundation Graduate Research Fellowship (NSF GRFP). He has served as a reviewer for TKDD, KDE, KAIS and DMKD journals as well as an external reviewer or PC member for dozens of international conferences and workshops.
URL: `http://www.cs.illinois.edu/homes/weninge1/`

Jiawei Han is a full Professor in the Department of Computer Science at the University of Illinois at Urbana-Champaign. He has been working on research into data mining, data warehousing, database systems, data mining from spatiotemporal data, multimedia data, stream and RFID data, social network data, and biological data, with over 350 journal and conference publications. He has chaired or served in over 100 program committees of international conferences and workshops, and serves as the founding Editor-In-Chief of ACM Transactions on Knowledge Discovery from Data. He is an ACM Fellow and has received 2004 ACM SIGKDD Innovations Award and 2005 IEEE Computer Society Technical Achievement Award. His book "Data Mining: Concepts and Techniques" (2nd ed., Morgan Kaufmann, 2006) has been popularly used as a textbook worldwide.
URL: `http://www.cs.uiuc.edu/~hanj/`

5. REFERENCES

[1] L. Blanco, V. Crescenzi, P. Merialdo, and P. Papotti. Flint: Google-basing the Web. In *EDBT*, pages 720–724. ACM Press, Mar. 2008.

[2] M. J. Cafarella, A. Halevy, D. Z. Wang, E. Wu, and Y. Zhang. WebTables: exploring the power of tables on the web. *VLDB*, 1(1):538–549, Aug. 2008.

[3] V. Crescenzi, G. Mecca, and P. Merialdo. RoadRunner: Towards Automatic Data Extraction from Large Web Sites. *VLDB*, pages 109–118, Sept. 2001.

[4] H. Elmeleegy, J. Madhavan, and A. Halevy. Harvesting relational tables from lists on the web. *The VLDB Journal*, 20(2):209–226, Mar. 2011.

[5] F. Fumarola, T. Weninger, R. Barber, D. Malerba, and J. Han. HyLiEn: A Hybrid Approach to General List Extraction on the Web. In *WWW*, page 35. ACM Press, 2011.

[6] R. Gupta and S. Sarawagi. Answering Table Augmentation Queries from Unstructured Lists on the Web. *PVLDB*, 2(1):289–300, 2009.

[7] J. Han. Construction of Web-Based, Service-Oriented Information Networks: A Data Mining Perspective. In H. Gao, L. Lim, W. Wang, C. Li, and L. Chen, editors, *WAIM*, volume 7418 of *Lecture Notes in Computer Science*, page 6, Berlin, Heidelberg, 2012. Springer Berlin Heidelberg.

[8] B. Liu, R. Grossman, and Y. Zhai. Mining data records in Web pages. In *SIGKDD*, page 601. ACM Press, Aug. 2003.

[9] I. Mansuri and S. Sarawagi. Integrating Unstructured Data into Relational Databases. In *ICDE*, page 29. IEEE, Apr. 2006.

[10] S. Tong and J. Dean. System and methods for automatically creating lists., 2008.

[11] T. Weninger, Y. Bisk, and J. Han. Document Topic Hierarchies from Document Graphs. In *CIKM*, Maui, Hawaii, 2012.

[12] T. Weninger, W. H. Hsu, and J. Han. CETR. In *WWW*, page 971. ACM Press, Apr. 2010.

[13] T. Weninger, C. Zhai, and J. Han. Building enriched web page representations using link paths. In *HT*, page 53. ACM Press, June 2012.

[14] Y. Zhai and B. Liu. Structured Data Extraction from the Web Based on Partial Tree Alignment. *IEEE Transactions on Knowledge and Data Engineering*, 18(12):1614–1628, Dec. 2006.

Temporal Web Dynamics and its Application to Information Retrieval

Kira Radinsky*
Technion, Israel Institute of Technology
kirar@cs.technion.ac.il

Fernando Diaz,
Susan Dumais, Milad Shokouhi
Microsoft Research
{fdiaz,sdumais,milads}
@microsoft.com

Anlei Dong and Yi Chang
Yahoo! Labs
{anlei, yichang}
@yahoo-inc.com

ABSTRACT

The World Wide Web is highly dynamic and is constantly evolving to cover the latest information about the physical and social updates in the world. At the same time, the changes in web contents are entangled with new information needs and time-sensitive user interactions with information sources. To address these temporal information needs effectively, it is essential for the search engines to model web dynamics and understand the changes in user behavior over time that are caused by them.

In this *full-day* tutorial, we focus on modeling time-sensitive content on the web, and discuss the state-of-the-art approaches for integrating temporal signals in web search. We address many of the related research topics including those associated with searching dynamic collections, defining time-sensitive relevance, understanding user query behavior over time, and investigating the main reasons behind content changes. We also cover algorithms, evaluation methodologies and metrics for time-aware search, and discuss the latest breakthroughs and open challenges.

Categories and Subject Descriptors

H.3.3 [**Information Storage and Retrieval**]: Search process; H.3.3 [**Information Storage and Retrieval**]: Information filtering; H.3.3 [**Information Storage and Retrieval**]: Retrieval models

Keywords

Web Dynamics

1. TARGET AUDIENCE AND RELATION TO WSDM AREAS

Addressing time-sensitive intents is a core problem for retrieval systems and involves several challenges in terms of intent classification, ranker training and result evaluation. The intended audience for this tutorial includes students, researchers and engineers from academia and industry interested in any temporal aspect of search.

Given the broad range, cross-media, (and cross-device) nature of time-sensitive information access and retrieval, we believe that the techniques covered in the tutorial will be found relevant to a large group of WSDM participants.

*primary contact

WSDM'13, February 4–8, 2013, Rome, Italy.
ACM 978-1-4503-1869-3/13/02.

2. AIMS/LEARNING OBJECTIVES AND RELATED TUTORIALS

The goals of this tutorial are:

1. To synthesize and present experimental techniques in analyzing temporal patterns in information sources
2. To describe the related time-aware models for improving information access and retrieval. Participants will receive a background on the problems, algorithmic solutions and evaluation methods concerning systems with temporal dynamics in information access and retrieval. The authors are not aware of any related tutorials, nor has this tutorial been given before

3. FORMAT AND OUTLINE

We will present this full-day tutorial primarily as a set of lectures by researchers experienced with temporal web data. While the tutorial will be in the form of a presentation, attendees will be encouraged to ask questions throughout. We do expect to have engaging and fruitful discussions given the broad range of topics that will be covered.

1. Modeling Dynamics
   (a) Web Content Dynamics
      i. Modeling change in real-time content creation: Modeling online and social media dynamics [3, 16, 11];Modeling document bursts [13];
      ii. Modeling change in static content: Modeling document changes [1, 5]; Modeling document topic dynamics over time [4, 23].
      iii. Modeling Web graph dynamics: Modeling web graph evolution over time [17];Modeling information flow in the web graph [15]
   (b) Web User Behavior Dynamics
      i. Dynamics of individual users
         - Dynamics of information seeking behavior within a session (e.g. reformulation, frustration, switching, success) [10, 12]
         - Dynamics of information seeking behavior across sessions (e.g. stages of a 'wedding task')
      ii. Dynamics of groups of users
         - Modeling users behavior over time [21]
         - Detecting trends in user queries and interests [6, 14]
         - Temporal dynamics in microblogs/social media

(c) Multidimensional dynamics (e.g. spatio-temporal analysis) [24, 25].
(d) Methods for Evaluating Web Dynamics

2. Applications to Information Retrieval

(a) Applications for Natural Language Processing : Utilizing Wikipedia dynamics [2]; Utilizing Web Content dynamics [18]
(b) Applications for News events prediction [19, 20]
(c) Applications for time-sensitive web search: discovering fresh content [9]; time-sensitive relevance: freshness and relevance [8]; time-sensitive ranking [8, 9]; time-sensitive query suggestion [22]; federated search [6, 14]; supporting users in understanding time [1];
(d) Recommendation: how to recommend the most relevant and buzzy queries to users [7]? How to recommend relevant content?

4. REFERENCES

[1] E. Adar, J. Teevan, S. D., and J. Elsas. The web changes everything: understanding the dynamics of web content. In *Proc. of WSDM*, 2009.

[2] A. Aji, Y. Wang, E. Agichtein, and E. Gabrilovich. Using the past to score the present: extending term weighting models through revision history analysis. In *Proc. of CIKM*, 2010.

[3] J. Allan, editor. *Topic Detection and Tracking: Event-based Information Organization*, volume 12. Springer, 2002.

[4] D. M. Blei and J. D. Lafferty. Dynamic topic models. In *ICML*, 2006.

[5] J. Cho and H. García-Molina. Estimating frequency of change. *TOIT*, 3(3):256–290, 2003.

[6] F. Diaz. Integration of news content into web results. In *Proc. of WSDM*, 2009.

[7] A. Dong, J. Bian, X. He, S. Reddy, and Y. Chang. User action interpretation for personalized content optimization in recommender systems. In *Proc. of CIKM*, 2011.

[8] A. Dong, Y. Chang, Z. Zheng, G. Mishne, J. Bai, R. Zhang, K. Buchner, C. Liao, and F. Diaz. Towards recency ranking in web search. In *Proc. of WSDM*, 2010.

[9] A. Dong, R. Zhang, P. Kolari, J. Bai, F. Diaz, Y. Chang, Z. Zheng, and H. Zha. Time is of the essence: improving recency ranking using twitter data. In *Proc. of WWW*, 2010.

[10] S. Fox, K. Karnawat, M. Mydland, S. Dumais, and T. White. Evaluating implicit measures to improve web search. *ACM Trans. Inf. Syst.*, 23(2):147–168, 2005.

[11] M. Goetz, J. Leskovec, M. McGlohon, and C. Faloutsos. Modeling blog dynamics. In *ICWSM*, 2009.

[12] A. Hassan, Y. Song, and L.-w. He. A task level metric for measuring web search satisfaction and its application on improving relevance estimation. In *Proc. of CIKM*, 2011.

[13] J. Kleinberg. Bursty and hierarchical structure in streams. *Data Mining and Knowledge Discovery*, 7:373–397, 2003.

[14] A. C. König, M. Gamon, and Q. Wu. Click-through prediction for news queries. In *Proc. of SIGIR*, 2009.

[15] J. Leskovec. Social media analytics: tracking, modeling and predicting the flow of information through networks, 2011.

[16] J. Leskovec, L. Backstrom, and J. Kleinberg. Meme-tracking and the dynamics of the news cycle. In *Proc. of KDD*, 2009.

[17] J. Leskovec, J. Kleinberg, and C. Faloutsos. Graphs over time: densification laws, shrinking diameters and possible explanations. In *Proc. of KDD*, pages 177–187, 2005.

[18] K. Radinsky, E. Agichtein, E. Gabrilovich, and S. Markovitch. A word at a time: Computing word relatedness using temporal semantic analysis. In *Proc. of WWW*, 2011.

[19] K. Radinsky, S. Davidovich, and S. Markovitch. Predicting the news of tomorrow using patterns in web search queries. In *Proc. of the WI*, 2008.

[20] K. Radinsky, S. Davidovich, and S. Markovitch. Learning causality for news events prediction. In *Proc. of WWW*, 2012.

[21] K. Radinsky, K. Svore, S. Dumais, J. Teevan, A. Bocharov, and E. Horvitz. Modeling and predicting behavioral dynamics on the web. In *Proc. of WWW*, 2012.

[22] M. Shokouhi and K. Radinsky. Time-sensitive query auto-completion. In *Proc. of SIGIR*, 2012.

[23] C. Wang, D. M. Blei, and D. Heckerman. Continuous time dynamic topic models. In *UAI*, 2008.

[24] E. Yom-Tov and F. Diaz. Location and timeliness of information sources during news events. In *Proc. of SIGIR*, 2011.

[25] E. Yom-Tov and F. Diaz. Out of sight, not out of mind: on the effect of social and physical detachment on information need. In *Proc. of SIGIR*, 2011.

WSDM 2013 Tutorial

(Big) Usage Data in Web Search

Ricardo Baeza-Yates
Yahoo! Labs, Barcelona, Spain
rbaeza@acm.org

Yoelle Maarek
Yahoo! Labs, Haifa, Israel
yoelle@ymail.com

Categories and Subject Descriptors
H.3.3 [Information Search and Retrieval]

General Terms
Algorithms, Human Factors

Keywords
Web Retrieval, User Interaction

EXTENDED ABSTRACT
Web Search, which takes its root in the mature field of information retrieval, evolved tremendously over the last 15 years. The field encountered its first revolution when it started to deal with huge amounts of Web pages. Then, a major step was accomplished when engines started to consider the structure of the Web graph and leveraged link analysis in both crawling and ranking. Finally, a more discrete, but no less critical step, was made when search engines started to monitor and exploit the numerous (mostly implicit) signals provided by users while interacting with the search engine. In this tutorial we focus on this "revolution" of large scale usage data.

In the first part of this tutorial, we focus on usage data, which typically refers to any type of information provided by the user while interacting with the search engine. It comes first under its raw form as a set of individual signals, but is typically mined after multiple signals have been aggregated and linked to the same interaction event. The two major types of such data are (1) *query streams*, which include the query string that the user issued, together with the time-stamp of the query, a user identifier, possibly the IP of the machine on which the browser runs, and (2) *click data*, which include the reference to the element the user clicked on the page together with the timestamp, user identifier, possibly IP, the rank of the link if it is a result, etc.

Exploiting usage data under its multiple forms brought an unprecedented wealth of implicit information to Web Search. We discuss in the second part of this tutorial some of the key Web search applications that it made possible. One such example is the query spelling correction feature embodied now in all search engines. In fact, after years of very sophisticated spell checking research, simply counting similar queries at a small edit distance would in most cases surface the most popular spelling as the correct one, a beautiful and simple demonstration of the wisdom of crowds principle.

In practice, such a feature clearly uses more sophisticated techniques than direct counting, but this simple example illustrates how even trivial "data crunching" over big *real* data brings more value than sophisticated techniques on small datasets. Query logs have also revolutionized query assistance tools such as related queries (recommended queries after the search was issued) or query completions (suggested queries as the query is being typed). While, in the past, query assistance tools would analyze the document corpus in order to identify phrases that could serve as alternate queries, the tremendous growth in Web search engine traffic allowed these tools to mostly rely on real user-issued queries. Using query logs as the source corpus significantly improved the quality of suggestions, at least as perceived by the user. In practice, query assistance tools are now deployed on all major Web search engines, and their quality improves as query logs grow. An additional revolutionary benefit of usage data is to consider clicks as a measure of satisfaction or at least of interest from the user, as if the user, by clicking, had actually voted in favor of the clicked element. One major reason of the quick pace of innovation in Web search can be credited to these "pseudo-votes". Instead of testing a new feature, or any sort of change, on a small sample of beta-users in a controlled environment, search engines now use real users on a much larger scale. Various metrics are used to verify whether users react positively or not to the change, thus helping search engines to decide whether to deploy the change to all users. After deployment, user behavior is constantly monitored, not only at pre-launch time, and features for which clicks or other metrics are decreasing might be discontinued or retired as it often happens.

In spite of its multiple benefits, adequately leveraging usage data is not always straightforward. We discuss, in the third part of this tutorial, the effects of three major factors that often pull in opposite directions:

- **Size of the data**: Large-scale or big usage data is a key pre-requisite to inferring new insights. As a consequence, the needs of the crowd dominate long-tail needs, which are expressed by definition by very few individuals. Averaging on the more popular needs can dominate so much, in some cases, that it conflicts with some specific needs that personalization should address. More data also brings algorithmic challenges as we need faster and faster algorithms. Hence, we can have a trade-off between the quality of the output and the performance to obtain it.
- **Personalization**: In order for search engines to personalize their services for a specific user, threy obviously need enough data to know more about the persona behind the individual, at the risk of exposing some private aspects. Hence, personalization in many cases might conflict with the user's privacy.

WSDM'13, February 4-8, 2013, Rome, Italy.
ACM 978-1-4503-187=69-3/13/02.

Econometric Analysis and Digital Marketing: How to Measure the Effectiveness of an Ad

Ayman Farahat
Adobe Inc.
farahat@adobe.com

James G. Shanahan
Independent Consultant
James.Shanahan@gmail.com

ABSTRACT

Over the past 18 years online advertising has grown to a \$70 billion industry worldwide annually. Despite this impressive growth, online advertising faces many (and some would say traditional) challenges including how to measure the efficiency or the potential loss of sales caused by the inefficient use of advertising dollars. Consequently, it is vital to measure, maximize, and benchmark the efficiency of advertising media expenditures. This tutorial introduces the field of econometrics as a means of measuring the effectiveness of digital marketing. Econometrics is a field that extends and applies statistical methods to the analysis of economic phenomena. In that vein, econometrics goes beyond traditional statistics and explicitly recognizes the complexities of human behavior. Consider for example the impact of deep discounts on survival of restaurants. Struggling businesses are more likely to offer these deep discounts and eventually fail. A naive application of statistical techniques will overestimate the impact of deep discounts on business survival. In this case, the discounts are an endogenous variable as compared to an exogenous variable. This type of specification error highlights why we need a deeper look at the variables that go into statistical models. Econometrics addresses these and other issues in a formal and rigorous manner.

Categories and Subject Descriptors

J.4 [**SOCIAL AND BEHAVIORAL SCIENCES**]: Economics

General Terms

Economics,Measurement

Keywords

Econometrics, Marketing Mix Models,Treatment effect

1. LEARNING OBJECTIVES

In this tutorial, we will give an overview of modern econometric techniques and show how they can be applied at scale. In particular, we highlight the difference between exogenous and endogenous variables and how the latter can lead to biased estimates of treatment effects. In addition, we will present best practices and case studies in testing the efficiency of the advertising across a variety of media types and channels: print, broadcast, and the Internet, social media etc., highlighting how econometrics can be used to accurately evaluate the causal impact of various marketing efforts. We also describe when the casual impact cannot be estimated. While, there have been a few studies that attempted to quantify the impact of these technologies, they have been plagued with selection bias and have often blurred the distinction between causation and correlation; these will also be covered in detail. In addition, this tutorial will overview the ever evolving field of digital advertising detailing the key business models and technologies that drive field. This half-day tutorial (3-4 hours) focuses on helping researchers and developers attending WSDM develop new skills in econometrics as well providing an account of the latest developments in this diverse discipline of online advertising. In doing so it will provide a clear and detailed overview of the math, the science, and business models that are transforming the field of (online) advertising along the following themes: selection bias, vector autoregression (VAR), impulse response functions, seemingly unrelated regression (SURE), Marketing mix models, sponsored search, display advertising, business models; market size and scope; economic models; new directions such as social advertising, behavioral targeting, new market places such as ad exchanges; challenges and open issues that face online advertising from a econometric perspective. Above all, we will emphasis why human and social systems differ from mechanical and physical systems and why techniques from the latter often ignore the subtitles of the former.

1.1 Case Studies

Participants will learn how math and science of measuring the effectiveness of digital advertising and marketing has been successfully applied to a number of application including

- Marketing mix models
- Advertising effectiveness - daily deals
- How much is star worth in recommender systems?
- Advertising effectiveness online versus online offline
- Attribution models
- Impact of social network structure on content propagation
- Does Retail Advertising Work? Measuring the Effects of Advertising on Sales

WSDM'13, February 4–8, 2013, Rome, Italy.
ACM 978-1-4503-1869-3/13/02.

WSCD2013: Workshop on Web Search Click Data 2013

Pavel Serdyukov
Yandex
Leo Tolstoy 16
Moscow, Russia
pavser@yandex-team.ru

Georges Dupret
Yahoo! Labs
701 First Avenue
Sunnyvale, USA
gdupret@yahoo-inc.com

Nick Craswell
Microsoft Corporation
One Microsoft Way
Redmond, USA
nickcr@microsoft.com

ABSTRACT

WSCD 2013[1] is the third workshop on Web Search Click Data, following WSCD 2009 and WSCD 2012. It is a forum for new research relating to Web search usage logs and for discussing desirable properties of publicly released search log datasets. Research relating to search logs has been hampered by the limited availability of click datasets. This workshop comes with a new dataset based on logged user search behaviour and an accompanying challenge to predict switches between search engines within a given search session.

Categories and Subject Descriptions: H.3.3 [Information Storage and Retrieval]: Information Search and Retrieval

General Terms: Metrics, Experimentation, Performance

Keywords: information retrieval measures, evaluation

1. INTRODUCTION

Web search click data has caught the interest of a growing community of professional during the last decade. It provides a snapshot of the typical information access patterns of the user population, unlike a group of relevance judges or the tags provided on collaborative sites. Issued queries and clicked document records have the potential to give an accurate view of millions of people's daily interests, how these interests evolve, how they are related, etc.

Of particular interest is the relation between log data and the user decision process that generated it. A user interacting with a search engine might at any point decide to click on a new link, request a new page of results, reformulate his query, switch search engine or end the session. Understanding how a sequence of actions relates to the user satisfaction is key to improve the experience and the popularity of the search engine. This applies to web search in general but also to most verticals like "local search" and to newer research areas like "diversity" where the question is how to introduce diversity in document ranking or "personalization" where the goal is to adapt the search results to take into account what is known from the user who issued the query.

In this workshop, we attempt to address these issues but also explore novel applications and use of such data for enhancing the user search experience.

2. SWITCHING DETECTION CHALLENGE

Research on the incorporation of click data into information retrieval systems, and for understanding user search, has been hampered by a lack of shared datasets. This workshop provides a common click dataset and a forum for presenting new results and analysis in the area. The dataset includes user sessions extracted from Yandex[2] logs, with queries, URL rankings, clicks and also search engine switching actions. To allay privacy concerns the user data is fully anonymized. So, only meaningless numeric IDs of users, queries, sessions, and URLs are released. In connection to the sharing the dataset, the workshop is running a challenge, named The Switching Detection Challenge[3]. The evaluation of systems participating in the Challenge is purely data-driven and focused on predicting user search engines switches for a sample of held-out sessions. Our motivation for running this challenge is the following.

Users often use more than one search engine to satisfy their information needs. When a user deliberately switches from one engine to another in order to continue their search, this means they require additional information and perspectives. This may be because their information need requires more than one engine can provide, or because the first engine has failed. For some search sessions, the fact of switching can be easily monitored. For instance, users might click a search engine URL on the search engine result page (Yandex has always had links to all major search engines at the bottom of its results) or the fact of switching might be monitored via the browser toolbar. However, the same users might switch in a way, which cannot be monitored. For instance, they might use their browser bookmarks to switch the engines, or they might use another browser (without the toolbar installed).

Detecting the fact of switching, when switching events cannot be monitored directly is difficult, and is not yet a solved problem. It is important for understanding of users' satisfaction with the search engine and the complexity of search. This Challenge and the shared dataset aims to enable a whole new set of researchers to study the problem of search engine switching detection.

The Challenge runs from 22nd October 2012 till 22nd De-

[1]http://research.microsoft.com/en-us/um/people/nickcr/wscd2013/

[2]http://yandex.com

[3]http://switchdetect.yandex.ru/en

WSDM'13, February 4–8, 2013, Rome, Italy.
ACM 978-1-4503-1869-3/13/02.

cember 2012. At the time of publication of this abstract (3rd December 2012), 71 teams were actively participating in the Challenge (i.e. submitted at least one result).

3. PREVIOUS WSCD WORKSHOPS

The first WSCD 2009 workshop used Microsoft click logs. The previous WSCD 2012 workshop used Yandex click log dataset. This dataset included user sessions, with queries, rankings and clicks. Unlike previously published click datasets, it also included relevance judgments for the ranked URLs, for the purposes of training relevance prediction models. To allay privacy concerns the user data was fully anonymized. So, only numeric IDs of queries, sessions, and URLs were released. The queries were grouped only by sessions and no user IDs were provided. Using that dataset, the Relevance Prediction Challenge was organized[4], which took place from October 15 to December 22, 2011. The primary goal for participants was ranking of URLs according to their relevance mined solely from the query log. As a result, 483 teams had registered and downloaded the data and around 100 of them submitted their results (around 1400 submissions). Prizes from $5000 to $1000 were awarded to the best academic participants. The workshop featured 5 talks by the best industrial and academic participants[5].

4. ADDITIONAL ORGANIZERS

The Challenge is also co-organized by Eugene Kharitonov and Alexey Gorodilov from Yandex, who have done the most work on data preprocessing and maintaining the submission system.

[4]http://imat-relpred.yandex.ru/en

[5]http://research.microsoft.com/en-us/um/people/nickcr/wscd2012/schedule.htm

3rd Workshop on Context-awareness in Retrieval and Recommendation

Matthias Böhmer
DFKI GmbH
Saarbrücken, Germany
matthias.boehmer@dfki.de

Ernesto W. De Luca
University of Applied Science Potsdam
Potsdam, Germany
deluca@fh-potsdam.de

Alan Said
Technische Universität Berlin
Berlin, Germany
alan@dai-lab.de

Jaime Teevan
Microsoft Research
Redmond, WA, USA
teevan@microsoft.com

ABSTRACT

Context-aware information is widely available in various ways and is becoming more and more important for enhancing retrieval performance and recommendation results. The current main issue to cope with is not only recommending or retrieving the most relevant items and content, but defining them ad hoc. Other relevant issues include personalizing and adapting the information and the way it is displayed to the user's current situation and interests. Ubiquitous computing further provides new means for capturing user feedback on items and providing information.

Keywords

Context-awareness, information retrieval, recommender systems.

Categories and Subject Descriptors

H.3.4 [**Information Technology and Systems Applications**]: Decision support; H.3.3 [**Information Storage and Retrieval**]: Information Filtering, Relevance feedback, Retrieval models, Search process, Selection process

General Terms

Algorithms, Design, Experimentation, Human Factors.

1. CONTENTS AND MAIN GOALS

The first installment of the CaRR Workshop [4] received enthusiastic feedback from the context-awareness community with a total of 15 submitted papers and more than 30 attendees at IUI 2011 in Palo Alto. A total of 9 papers were accepted for presentation at the workshop and publication in the proceedings [1]. An indication that *context-awareness in retrieval and recommendation* is a very interesting and timely topic. Among the issues discussed at the workshop were: how context-awareness has changed the goal of retrieval and recommendation, e.g. drifting from recommendations that fit to the general user interest to ad-hoc recommendations that fit to the user's context. Additional topics covered were new emerging areas where the role of retrieval and recommendation increases, e.g. recommending places to go, activities to take, or apps to use. The second installment of the CaRR Workshop [2, 3] took place at IUI 2012 in Lisbon, Portugal on February 14, 2012. It received very positive feedback from the context-awareness community with a total of 10 submitted papers and more than 30 attendees. The topics covered in the workshop were discussing the roles of context in information retrieval and recommendations a choice and decision making perspective. Different work was presenting the use of context with techniques for personalization and recommendation of items. The use of context in music retrieval and user modeling was also discussed.

The third edition of the CaRR Workshop[1] took place in Rome, Italy on February 5, 2013 and continued focusing on the integration of context for retrieval and recommendation. The contexts focused on were a general content context and a user-centric content context. The general content context is a common case defined by time, weather, location and many similar other aspects whereas the user-centric content context is given by user profiles, e.g. language, interests, devices used for interaction, etc.

Other important issues addressed included the importance of developing context-aware systems that can generate and present situation-specific information. The need of personalizing and adapting information is accentuated when we consider this kind of device- and interaction-based context.

The aim of the CaRR Workshop was to invite the community to a discussion in which we tried to find new creative ways to handle context-awareness. Furthermore, the workshop aimed at exchanging new ideas between different communities involved in research, such as HCI, machine learning, Web mining, information retrieval and recommender systems.

2. RESEARCH QUESTIONS

The workshop was especially intended for researchers working on multidisciplinary tasks, to discuss problems and synergies. Ideas on creative and collaborative approaches for

WSDM'13, February 4–8, 2013, Rome, Italy.
ACM 978-1-4503-1869-3/13/02.

[1] `http://carr-workshop.org`

context-aware retrieval and recommendation were of special interest.

The participants were encouraged to address the following questions:

- What is context?
- Which benefits come from context-aware systems?
- In what ways can context improve the Web experience?
- How can we combine general- and user-centric context-aware technologies?
- How should context affect the way information is presented?

3. TOPICS

The topics of interest included, but were not limited to:

- Context-aware data mining and information retrieval
- Context-aware profiling, clustering and collaborative filtering
- Use of context-aware technologies in Web search
- Ubiquitous and context-aware computing
- Use of context-aware technologies in UI/HCI
- Context-aware advertising
- Recommendations for mobile users
- Context-awareness in portable devices
- Mobile and social search

4. WORKSHOP ORGANIZERS

Matthias Böhmer is a researcher at the Innovative Retail Laboratory of the German Research Center for Artificial Intelligence (DFKI) in Saarbrücken, Germany. His main research focus is understanding and supporting mobile application usage, in particular on context-aware recommender systems that suggest mobile applications. He is interested in deducing the contextual relevance of particular apps from a user's device interaction, e.g. usage patterns or icon arrangement.

Ernesto William De Luca is professor for information science at the University of Applied Science Potsdam. He is the author of more than 70 papers on national and international conferences and journals in the fields of Computational Linguistics, Information Retrieval, Adaptive Systems and other related areas. He has chaired a number of workshops on semantic personalization, context-awareness in recommender systems and related topics.

Alan Said is a research associate at the Competence Center for Information Retrieval and Machine Learning at the DAI Lab, Technische Universität Berlin. He has authored papers on national and international conferences in the fields of recommender systems, evaluation, social networks, context-awareness and other related areas. He has chaired workshops and conferences on recommender systems and related topics.

Jaime Teevan is a Senior Researcher in the Context, Learning, and User Experience for Search Group at Microsoft Research, and an Affiliate Assistant Professor in the Information School at the University of Washington. She studies how people use digital information, particularly as related to their social and temporal context, and builds tools to help better support these information interactions. She has published numerous technical papers, including several best papers, and was Chair of the WSDM 2012 conference.

5. PROGRAM COMMITTEE MEMBERS

- Omar Alonso - Microsoft, USA
- Hideki Asoh - AIST, Japan
- Linas Baltrunas - Telefonica Research, Spain
- Shlomo Berkovsky - NICTA, Australia
- Toine Bogers - RSLIS, Denmark
- Robin Burke - DePaul University, USA
- Li Chen - Hong Kong Baptist University, China
- Paolo Cremonesi - Politecnico di Milano, Italy
- Carsten Eickhoff - TU Delft, The Netherlands
- Ido Guy - IBM, Israel
- Frank Hopfgartner - TU Berlin, Germany
- Brijnesh J. Jain - TU Berlin, Germany
- Anthony Jameson - DFKI, Germany
- Alexandros Karatzoglou - Telefonica Research, Spain
- Alfred Kobsa - University of California, Irvine, USA
- Antonio Krüger - DFKI, Saarbrücken, Germany
- Petteri Nurmi - HIIT, Finland
- Till Plumbaum - TU Berlin, Germany
- Karthik Raman - Cornell, USA
- Francesco Ricci - Free University of Bozen-Bolzano, Italy
- Markus Schedl - Johannes Kepler University, Austria
- Yue Shi - TU Delft, The Netherlands
- Domonkos Tikk - Gravity R&D, Hungary
- Yong Zheng - DePaul University, USA

6. ACKNOWLEDGEMENTS

The organizers would like to thank all the authors for contributing to CaRR 2013 and all the members of the program committee for ascertaining the scientific quality of the workshop.

7. REFERENCES

[1] *CaRR '11: Proceedings of the 2011 Workshop on Context-awareness in Retrieval and Recommendation*, New York, NY, USA, 2011. ACM.

[2] *CaRR '12: Proceedings of the 2nd Workshop on Context-awareness in Retrieval and Recommendation*, New York, NY, USA, 2012. ACM.

[3] E. W. De Luca, M. Böhmer, A. Said, and E. Chi. 2nd workshop on context-awareness in retrieval and recommendation: (carr 2012). In *Proceedings of the 2012 ACM international conference on Intelligent User Interfaces*, IUI '12, pages 409–412, New York, NY, USA, 2012. ACM.

[4] E. W. De Luca, A. Said, M. Böhmer, and F. Michahelles. Workshop on context-awareness in retrieval and recommendation. In *Proceedings of the 16th international conference on Intelligent user interfaces*, IUI '11, pages 471–472, New York, NY, USA, 2011. ACM.

Workshop on Large-Scale and Distributed Systems for Information Retrieval (LSDS-IR 2013)

Ismail Sengor Altingovde
L3S Research Center
30167 Hannover, Germany
altingovde@l3s.de

Craig Macdonald
University of Glasgow
Glasgow, G12 8QQ, UK
craigm@dcs.gla.ac.uk

Nicola Tonellotto
National Research Council
56124 Pisa, Italy
nicola.tonellotto@isti.cnr.it

ABSTRACT

The LSDS-IR'13 workshop aims to bring together both information retrieval practitioners from industry, as well as academic researchers concerned with efficient and distributed IR systems. The workshop also welcomes contributions that propose different ways of leveraging diversity and multiplicity of resources available in distributed systems. The main goal of the workshop is to attract people from industry and academia to present and discuss ideas, problems and results in efficiency of large scale and distributed information retrieval systems, and to foster their participation to the WSDM conference.

Categories and Subject Descriptors: H.3.3 [Information Storage & Retrieval]: Information Search & Retrieval

Keywords: Distributed search, large-scale systems, scalability, efficiency

1. OVERVIEW

The growth of the Web and user bases lead to important performance problems for large-scale distributed information retrieval (IR) systems. Scalability and efficiency of these systems also have an impact on their effectiveness. Consequently, scalability and efficiency in the context of retrieval systems continue to be an important topic in IR research. Even within research laboratory settings, the size of the standard datasets have becoming exceedingly large (e.g. ClueWeb09: 1 billion documents, 25Tb uncompressed), requiring efficient and often distributed architectures to facilitate large-scale experimentation. Traditionally, Web-scale search engines employ large and highly replicated systems, operating on computer clusters in one or few data centers. Coping with the increasing number of user requests and indexable pages requires adding more resources. However, data centers cannot grow indefinitely. Scalability problems in information retrieval have to be addressed in the near future, and new distributed applications are likely to drive the way in which people use the Web. Distributed IR is the point in which these two directions converge. This workshop provides space for researchers to discuss these problems and to define new directions for the work on distributed information retrieval.

WSDM'13, February 4–8, 2013, Rome, Italy.
ACM 978-1-4503-1869-3/13/02.

2. TOPICS OF INTEREST

In terms of author audience, we solicited technical and position paper submissions with the following (but not limited to) research topics:

- Novel distributed IR applications
- Web search in the cloud: applications of cloud computing to IR
- Energy-aware processing techniques for web search
- IR algorithms on novel computing architectures
- Efficiency for feature-based models
- Efficiency and scalability in distributed query processing
- Query forwarding algorithms for multi-site search engines
- Inverted index partitioning and replication models
- Lossy and lossless inverted index compression
- Collection selection and result merging in federated IR
- Distributed web crawling
- Distributed indexing and retrieval of dynamic information sources
- Caching for search engines
- Heterogeneous distributed data integration and organization
- Retrieval models for distributed IR
- Standards and benchmarks for distributed IR
- Evaluation of the impact of search efficiency on user satisfaction

Workshop on Semantic Personalized Information Management (SPIM'13)

Till Plumbaum
Technische Universität Berlin
Berlin, Germany
till@dai-lab.de

Ernesto William De Luca
University of Applied Science Potsdam
Potsdam, Germany
deluca@fh-potsdam.de

Aldo Gangemi
University of Rome "La Sapienza",
Rome, Italy
gangemi@loa-cnr.it

Michael Hausenblas
National University of Ireland
Galway, Ireland
michael.hausenblas@deri.org

ABSTRACT

The SPIM workshop focuses especially on people that are working on the social or semantic Web, machine learning, user modeling, recommender systems, information retrieval, semantic interaction, or their combination. The goal is to bring together researchers and practitioners to initiating discussions on the different requirements and challenges coming with the social and semantic Web for personalized information retrieval systems. The workshop aims at improving the exchange of ideas between the different research communities and practitioners involved in the research on semantic personalized information management.

Categories and Subject Descriptors

H.3.4 Information Technology and Systems Applications: Decision support; H.3.3 Information Storage and Retrieval: Information Filtering, Relevance feedback, Retrieval models, Search process, Selection process

General Terms

Algorithms, Human Factors, Standardization

Keywords

Personalization, Semantic Web, Information Retrieval, Ontology, Information Management

WSDM'13, February 4–8, 2013, Rome, Italy.
ACM 978-1-4503-1869-3/13/02.

1. INTRODUCTION

Finding and managing information on the Web is a crucial task in our everyday life. Therefore, web information systems (WIS) like search engines or question-answering systems have become an essential tool for the majority of users for finding information on the Web. While today's WIS are adequate for most simple, keyword-based retrieval tasks, they still struggle to understand a users intention behind a query and to deliver information in a personalized way. With the rise of the Social and Semantic Web, new opportunities emerge for semantic web information systems to better match user needs.

Of special interest are practical approaches and ideas that aggregate social data from different applications or combine data from social platforms like Facebook with Semantic Web and Linked Open Data[1] sources to enhance the performance of WIS. While there is already research done in the area, no standards or commonly agreed techniques are available. This workshop can prepare the ground for standardized techniques allowing data and knowledge exchange between IR systems.

1.1 Objectives

The workshop aims at improving the exchange of ideas between the different research communities and practitioners involved in the research on semantic personalized information management. Our goal is to bring together researchers and practitioners to initiating discussions on the different requirements and challenges coming with the Social and Semantic Web for personalized information retrieval systems.

The topics of interest include, but are not limited, to the following aspects:

- Knowledge Modeling and Engineering
  - Ontology-based user modeling and user model aggregation
  - Exploiting Linked Open Data for PIM
- Applications for SPIM
  - Systems that create, exploit, and evaluate semantic technologies for improving PIM
  - Semantic search: information retrieval, extraction and filtering

[1] http://linkeddata.org/

- Personalized search: ranking integration, privacy issues, novelty and serendipity
- Semantic and context aware recommendation systems

- Social Networks and their analysis
- Opining mining and Social Web
- Personalized interaction in mobile, ubiquitous and context-aware computing
- Use of semantic technologies in HCI
- Hybridizing Semantic Web and Machine Learning techniques for PIM
- New personalization algorithms for large semantic data sets

2. WORKSHOP ORGANIZERS

Ernesto William De Luca is substitute Professor for Information Science at the University of Applied Sciences Potsdam. He is author of more than 70 papers on national and international conferences and journals in the fields of Information Retrieval, Machine Learning, Adaptive Systems and other related areas. He has chaired a number of workshops on semantic personalization, context-awareness in recommender systems and related topics.

Till Plumbaum is Co-director of the Competence Center of Information Retrieval at DAI Lab. He has published over 35 papers on national and international conferences and journals in the fields of user modeling, information retrieval, semantic technologies, adaptive systems and other related areas. He has chaired a number of workshops on semantic personalization, social and Semantic Web and related topics.

Aldo Gangemi is Senior Researcher at CNR-ISTC Rome where he coordinates the Semantic Technology Lab. He focuses on ontology design, semantic social networks, hybridation of NLP, lexical and semantic resources, and semantic interoperability for organizational data. Aldo has published more than 100 refereed articles in proceedings of international conferences, journals, and books. He has experience with organizing conferences and workshops on semantic technologies and ontology

Michael Hausenblas is Research Fellow at DERI, NUI Galway where he is coordinating the Linked Data Research Centre. He focuses on Linked Data discovery and Dataset Dynamics as well as the write-enabled Linked Data Web, on the one hand and application domains - including Linked Government Data and streamed Linked Data - on the other hand. He has published over 45 papers at conferences, workshops and in journals and served on over 40 Program Committees He has experience with organizing workshops on Linked Data, semantic technologies and privacy on the social and Semantic Web.

3. PROGRAM COMITTEE

- Federica Cena, Universita' degli Studi di Torino, Italy
- Richard Cyganiak, DERI, Ireland
- Ernesto William De Luca, FH Potsdam, Istanbul
- Fabien Gandon, INRIA, France
- Aldo Gangemi, University of Rome "La Sapienza", Italy
- Ana Garcia-Serrano, Spanish Open University, Spain
- Michael Hausenblas, National University of Ireland, Ireland
- Jérôme Kunegis, University Koblenz-Landau, Germany
- Pasquale Lops, University of Bari "Aldo Moro", Italy
- Andreas Lommatzsch, TU Berlin, Germany
- Till Plumbaum, TU Berlin, Germany
- Georg Ruß, TecData AG, Swiss
- Alan Said, TU Berlin, Germany
- Rafael Schirru, DFKI, Germany
- Armando Stellato, University of Rome "Tor Vergata", Italy
- Jierui Xie, Rensselaer Polytechnic Institute, USA
- Zheng Yong, DePaul University, USA

4. ACKNOWLEDGMENTS

The organizers would like to thank all the authors for contributing to SPIM and all the members of the program committee for ascertaining the scientific quality of the workshop.

Search and Exploration of X-Rated Information (SEXI 2013)

Vanessa Murdock
vanessa.murdock@yahoo.com

Charles L.A. Clarke
University of Waterloo
claclarke@plg.waterloo.edu

Jaap Kamps
University of Amsterdam
kamps@uva.nl

Jussi Karlgren
Gavagai Stockholm
jussi@gavagai.se

ABSTRACT

Adult content is pervasive on the Web, has been a driving factor in the adoption of the Internet medium. It is responsible for a significant fraction of traffic and revenues, yet rarely attracts attention in research. We propose that the research questions surrounding adult content access behaviors are unique, and we believe interesting and valuable research in this area can be done ethically. The workshop on *Search and Exploration of X-Rated Information* (SEXI) addresses these issues for information access tasks related to adult content.

Categories and Subject Descriptors

H.3.3 [**Information Search and Retrieval**]: Clustering, Information filtering, Search process

General Terms

Algorithms, Measurement, Experimentation, Human Factors

Keywords

Adult content, user generated content

1. INTRODUCTION

Adult content is pervasive on the Web, has been a driving factor in the adoption of the Internet medium. It is responsible for a significant fraction of traffic and revenues, yet rarely attracts attention in research [1,5]. The scientific community has spent considerable energy studying user-generated content and information access on the Web, to the exclusion of adult content. This is understandable, as the topic is distasteful to some, and requires special legal and ethical considerations when asking employees, contractors and students to analyze and process the data. Furthermore, the methods that work for other types of information access behavior are assumed to work for all types of content, including adult content.

WSDM'13, February 4–8, 2013, Rome, Italy.
ACM 978-1-4503-1869-3/13/02.

We propose that this is an incorrect assumption. In fact, even core concepts such as relevance and diversity, which are fundamental to any application involving information seeking and access, are defined differently for adult content. Adult queries frequently fall outside of the taxonomy of queries (informational, transactional, navigational) that applies to standard Web queries. Users searching for adult content frequently have an entertainment need, rather than an information need. Thus, because of the nature of the content, the user may be more satisfied with multiple similar images, than with a set of search results that capture different meanings of the query terms. Furthermore, understanding that a user is searching for a term in an adult context often disambiguates the term.

For example, consider the query ``bikini". In a non-adult context, the user might be querying about a ham and cheese sandwich, or may be interested in viewing catalog photos of bikinis to purchase, or perhaps would like images of the Bikini Islands. Since the search engine cannot be sure, one strategy is to represent multiple senses of the query in the results presented to the user. In an adult context, catalog photos, or images of sandwiches and islands will be more than an annoyance. Images of people wearing bikinis, although repetitive and not representing a diverse sense of the query term, is what the user is expecting.

Equal in importance to serving adult content in the best possible way, is the issue of avoiding serving adult content to those who are not looking for it. Many innocuous terms (such as ``snake," ``cougar," ``swimsuit") have adult connotations. Understanding when a person is uploading adult content is important. Often the only information available to determine the adultness of an image or video are the vague tags the user applies. Complicating the interpretation of the tags is that adult content may be described euphemistically with ordinary nouns that reflect a particular visual imagery. Similarly, when a person issues a query, it is not always clear whether they are searching for adult content, and it is extremely important for the search engine to understand this before serving adult content to a person who is not expecting it.

2. OPEN QUESTIONS

We seek a greater understanding of the particular issues in accessing adult content, especially user-generated adult content on the Web. The focus of the workshop will be to put this area of research on the agenda, and explore the basic research questions that should be addressed in the field, the types of data needed for research, and the barriers to doing research this area. Due to the lack of attention to this area of research there are many open questions.

Classification Even researchers and search applications not interested in adult content will have to deal with it in order to avoid it---presenting adult content to innocuous searchers is clearly a massive failure both for the individual searcher as well as for the reputation of the service. What are automatic methods for identifying adult content, in particular adult user-generated content? How can we identify adult content in video, images, and text? What is the best way to identify adult query intent, and deal with ambiguous requests? What are the appropriate ad placement strategies in adult content?

Access Access to adult content seems to require a different approach than the ubiquitous navigation search---with searchers exhibiting an exploratory information seeking behavior, characterized by a diverse set of relevance criteria. How should adult content be ranked? How should search, exploration, and recommendation be balanced? How does searching adult content relate to search on adult chat sites and social networks? Is there a benefit to personalizing adult content?

Evaluation Given the distinct nature of adult content and the diverse relevance criteria, appropriate evaluation is crucial. What is a relevant result, and what are suitable metrics for relevance? Is adult content a recall-oriented, or precision-oriented task? What is the right level of evaluation---individual requests or whole search sessions? What is similarity and diversity in adult content? How important is the avoidance of failure, relative to success? Are searchers for adult content more tolerant of non-relevant results?

Ethics What are the ethical issues in working with adult content in an academic environment? What are the ethical implications for the search industry, given that it partly facilitates the online adult industry? How can adult material be made available so as to promote responsible behavior through the whole chain from production to consumption? Is adult user-generated content more ethical than professionally produced media?

The outcome will be to define a set of research areas, to elucidate the special issues surrounding the access of user-generated adult content. We discuss a set of best practices for working with this data in an academic environment, and propose a research agenda for the near future.

3. RELEVANCE

The adult entertainment industry is in decline. Because of an increasing amount of amateur adult content that is uploaded to the Web every day, it is difficult for the professional industry to remain competitive [2,3,4,6]. Although the industry is in decline, the demand for online porn, in particular free online porn, remains constant. This transition moves adult content to the center of the search industry.

Searches for adult content represent a significant portion of search engine query logs. The industry generates billions of dollars in revenue, from paid sites as well as contextual advertising. On the other side of the coin, porn sites have a high volume of traffic, but are also one of the primary mechanisms for spreading malware. For these reasons, the workshop is relevant and important to improve information access for every user, and not just users searching for porn.

As stated in the Introduction, user-generated adult content is quickly becoming the predominant adult content on the web. Although it lacks high quality production values, it is sought by users because it is frequently free, and represents a reality and a diversity of human behavior that may be lacking in professionally produced content. According to an article in the Los Angeles Times [4]: "Sites like Pornhub, YouPorn and RedTube attract more users than TMZ and the Huffington Post. The porn sites are even bigger than Pirate Bay, the top portal for illegal downloads of movies, TV shows and music...." As these are sites that allow regular users to upload their own adult content, this represent a paradigm shift in the porn industry. In fact, it is putting the professional porn industry out of business. From the same article, "Reliable revenue and employment figures for the adult industry don't exist, since no analysts or economists track it. Adult Video News estimated in 2006 that it was worth $13 billion, but Paul Fishbein, editor of the trade publication, said the number was `an educated guess.'"

In short, this topic is central to the Web in all aspects, ranging from Web search to data mining and classification of web data. It is the topic that everyone knows about, but no-one speaks about. This workshop is the first of its kind in the information retrieval research community.

4. REFERENCES

[1] Azzopardi, L. Searching for unlawful carnal knowledge. In Belkin, N.J. et al. (eds.). *Proceedings of the SIGIR'11 Workshop on "entertain me": Supporting Complex Search Tasks*, pp 17-18. ACM Press, 2011.

[2] Economist. Hard times: A big industry in northern los angeles is among the worst hit by the recession. *The Economist*, September 10, 2009. http://www.economist.com/node/14416740 .

[3] Friess, S. Porn industry seats recession, piracy. *AOL News*. January 9, 2011. http://www.aolnews.com/2011/01/09/porn-industry-facing-hard-times-in-struggling-economy

[4] Fritz. B. Tough times in the porn industry. *The Los Angeles Times*. August 10, 2009. http://www.latimes.com/news/local/la-fi-ct-porn10-2009aug10,0,3867866,full.story .

[5] Halavais, A. C. Small pornographies. *SIGGROUP Bulletin*, 25(2):19-22, 2005. http://doi.acm.org/10.1145/1067721 .

[6] Theroux, L. Louis Theroux on porn: The decline of an industry. *BBC News Magazine*, June 8, 2012. http://www.bbc.co.uk/news/magazine-18352421.

Author Index

www.ingramcontent.com/pod-product-compliance
Lightning Source LLC
LaVergne TN
LVHW080103011026
849160LV00013B/1022